China

Damian Harper

Andrew Burke, Julie Grundvig, Carolyn B Heller, Thomas Huhti,
Bradley Mayhew, Min Dai, Christopher Pitts, Eilís Quinn

RUSSIA

KAZAKHSTAN

Irtysh River

Balkhash Lake

Jímúnãi
Tãchéng   Bù'ĕrjìn

MONGOLIA

ALMATY
Korgas   Yíníng
BISHKEK
KYRGYZSTAN   Ürümqi

Torugart
Pass (3752m)   Turpan
Irkeshtam
Pass   Kashgar (Kāshí)

SILK ROAD (p839)
Follow in the footsteps
of Central Asian traders
along the southern Silk Road   GÃNSÙ

XÏNJIÃNG   Dünhuáng   Jiāyùguān

Khunjerab   Zhāngyè
Pass (4800m)
315   Wŭwèi

Xïníng

Under
admistration   Gólmud   Qïnghǎi Hú
of China   109   QÏNGHǍI
                                                    Xiàhé

LHASA (p917)
Ride the world's
highest train to the   214
Rooftop of the World

TIBET   SÏCHUÃN

NEW DEHLI   219   318

NEPAL   Shigatse
Tíngri   Sakya   Lhasa   Shangri-la
Zhāngmù   Gyantse
Agra   KATHMANDU   Mt Everest   Lìjiāng
Kanpur   (8848m) THIMPHU   Xiàguān
Lucknow   BHUTAN   (Dàlí City)
Allahabad   Varanasi   **LÌJIÃNG (p709)**
Patna   River   Künmíng   Yúnnán's must-see
INDIA   INDIA   traveller mecca

BANGLADESH   Rùilì Wāndïng
DHAKA   YÚNNÁN
Calcutta   Gèjiù
MYANMAR
Símáo

Mandalay

—20°N

Bay of Bengal   LAOS

90°E   THAILAND   VIENTIANE

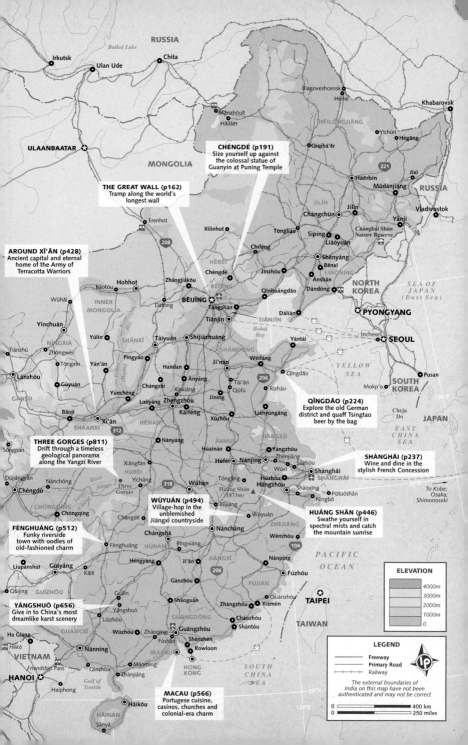

CHÉNGDÉ (p191)
Size yourself up against the colossal statue of Guanyin at Puning Temple

THE GREAT WALL (p162)
Tramp along the world's longest wall

AROUND XĪ'ĀN (p428)
Ancient capital and eternal home of the Army of Terracotta Warriors

QĪNGDĂO (p224)
Explore the old German district and quaff Tsingtao beer by the bag

SHÀNGHĂI (p237)
Wine and dine in the stylish French Concession

THREE GORGES (p811)
Drift through a timeless geological panorama along the Yangzi River

WŪYUÁN (p494)
Village-hop in the unblemished Jiāngxī countryside

HUÁNG SHĀN (p446)
Swathe yourself in spectral mists and catch the mountain sunrise

FÈNGHUÁNG (p512)
Funky riverside town with oodles of old-fashioned charm

YÁNGSHUÒ (p656)
Give in to China's most dreamlike karst scenery

MACAU (p566)
Portugese cuisine, casinos, churches and colonial-era charm

ELEVATION

	4000m
	3000m
	2000m
	1000m
	0

LEGEND

Freeway
Primary Road
Railway

The external boundaries of India on this map have not been authenticated and may not be correct

0 ————— 400 km
0 ————— 250 miles

Destination China

Eagerly assuming its place among the world's top travel destinations, China is an epic adventure whichever way you take it. From the wide open and empty panoramas of Tibet to the push and shove of Shànghǎi, from the volcanic dishes of Sìchuān to beer by the bag in seaside Qīngdǎo, a journey through this colossus of a country is a mesmerising encounter with the most populous and perhaps most culturally idiosyncratic nation on earth.

Curator of the world's oldest continuous civilisation, China will have you bumping into history at every turn. But it's not just a museum of imperial relics, for the frisson of development that has left China's coastline glittering with some of the world's most up-to-the-minute cities propels the land on with a forward-thinking dynamism.

The sheer diversity of China's terrain takes you from noisy cities fizzing with energy to isolated mountain-top Ming-dynasty villages where you can hear a pin drop. Pǔdōng's ambitious skyline is a triumphant statement, but it couldn't be further from the worldly renunciation acted out in Tibet's distant monasteries.

And it's the people – unavoidable in their immense numbers – who provide the ceaseless drama and entertainment. Loud, garrulous and quick thinking, you'll see the Chinese squeezing onto dangerous-looking buses, walking in pyjamas around Shànghǎi or inviting each other to sit down to some of the most varied cuisine in the world. Animated by a palpable sense of pride, and with the Běijīng Olympics on the cusp of arrival, the Chinese are revelling in their country's ascendency. Everyone is talking about China, so why not find out what all the fuss is about.

Dynastic China

Take a sunset stroll along the Great Wall at Jīnshānlǐng (p173), outside Běijīng

BILL BACHMANN

KEREN SU

Greet the laughing Buddha of Lingyin Temple (p319) in Hángzhōu

Explore the intriguing Ten Thousand Buddha Cave in Longmen Caves (p465), a World Heritage site, in Hénán

KRZYSZTOF DYDYNSK

Excavated terracotta warriors (p428) stand guard over the tomb of Qin Shi Huang, outside Xī'ān

JULIET COOMB

Admire the vivid colours of Nine Dragon Screen (p134) in Beihai Park, Běijīng

KRZYSZTOF DYDYNSKI

Marvel at the intricate ceiling decoration of the Imperial Vault of Heaven (p131) in the Temple of Heaven, Běijīng

KRZYSZTOF DYDYNSKI

BILL WASSMAN

Visit the stately Big Goose Pagoda (p424) in Xī'ān, Shaanxi

Ancient Villages

Wander among the historic buildings on Nan Dajie in Píngyáo (p407), Shānxī

Experience local life in Lǐkēng (p495), Jiāngxī

Delight in the picturesque cliff-top village of Guōliàngcūn (p467) in Hénán

Unwind in rural Luótiáncūn (p491), Jiāngxī

Explore the fascinating *tǔlóu* (earth buildings) of Yǒngdìng (p350) in Fújiàn

KEREN SU

Browse the alleys of Fènghuáng (p512) in Húnán

DAMIAN HARPER

Be charmed by riverside Wanming Pagoda (p514) in Fènghuáng, Húnán

DAMIAN HARPER

10

Minority Cultures

A Bai woman carries a basket of batik fabric in Dàlǐ (p703), Yúnnán

KEREN SU

Enjoy a Naxi Orchestra performance (p714) in Lìjiāng, Yúnnán

KRAIG L

KEREN SU

Detail of a necklace worn by Miao people,
Kǎilǐ (p681), Guìzhōu

An Uighur girl makes carpet in Kashgar
(p832), Xīnjiāng

KEREN SU

BILL WASSMAN

Woman adorned in colourful jewellery, Tibet (p912)

Great Escapes

Hitch a ride on a camel train through the Taklamakan Desert (p835) in Xīnjiāng

A local scales the rugged slopes of Tiger Leaping Gorge (p718), Yúnnán

Catch a breathtaking view of Nam-tso lake (p927) in Tibet

Stand in awe of the Pamir Plateau on the Karakoram Hwy (p838), Xīnjiāng

Contents

Regional Map Contents

The Authors

DAMIAN HARPER
Coordinating author, Ānhuī, Shànghǎi, Jiāngxī, Húnán & Cruising the Yangzi

A growing penchant for taichi and a meandering career in bookselling (London, Dublin, Paris) persuaded Damian to opt for a four-year degree in Chinese at London's School of Oriental and African Studies. A year of study in Běijīng and employment in Hong Kong further honed his irrepressible tendencies for wandering, inclinations that have led Damian to contribute to over a dozen guidebooks for Lonely Planet, including *Shanghai, Beijing, Hong Kong, China* and *Malaysia, Singapore & Brunei*. Married with two children, Damian and his family divide their time between China and Honor Oak Park in southeast London.

The Coordinating Author's Favourite Trip

After spending a week in autumnal Běijīng (p110), I'll get seaside Qingdǎo (p224) on my itinerary but squeeze in a night in Zhūjiāyù (p210) for its earthy charms. Heading to Hénán, I'll rustle up transport to the mountain-top village of Guōliàngcūn (p467) for a night, before taking the train to Shànghǎi (p237) from Zhèngzhōu (p457) for a complete contrast. From Shànghǎi, I'll ride hard sleeper on an overnight train to Túnxī (p441) for its surrounding villages and mountains and the magnificence of Huáng Shān (p446). From Túnxī I'll take a bus across the border to Wùyuán (p494) for its idyllic countryside and traditional village panoramas, from where I'll make my way to Macau (p518) and Hong Kong (p518) to be tempted into flying to Kūnmíng (p688) for an exploration of Yúnnán province.

ANDREW BURKE
Hong Kong, Macau & Hǎinán

Andrew's relationship with Hong Kong began when he moved there in 2001. Since then he has experienced first-hand the ongoing evolution of this city that never sleeps, and its increasingly less sleepy neighbour, Macau. He worked at the *South China Morning Post* newspaper during the dark days of SARS, marched in Hong Kong's 500,000-strong protest of 1 July 2003, and developed an abiding affection for the region, despite the pollution. Today Andrew calls Bangkok home but gets back to Hong Kong at least once a year, working as a journalist and photographer. This is his 10th book for Lonely Planet, a list that includes Lonely Planet's *Hong Kong Citiescape*.

LONELY PLANET AUTHORS

Why is our travel information the best in the world? It's simple: our authors are independent, dedicated travellers. They don't research using just the internet or phone, and they don't take freebies in exchange for positive coverage. They travel widely, to all the popular spots and off the beaten track. They personally visit thousands of hotels, restaurants, cafés, bars, galleries, palaces, museums and more – and they take pride in getting all the details right, and telling it how it is. For more, see the authors section on www.lonelyplanet.com.

JULIE GRUNDVIG   The Culture, Food & Drink, Jiāngsū, Zhèjiāng, Fújiàn & Guǎngdōng

Julie first travelled to mainland China in the early 1990s where she hitchhiked her way from Yúnnán to Xīnjiāng, before finally settling in Xī'ān to study Chinese art and literature. Later came an MA in classical Chinese and a stint in Běijīng teaching English and working in an art gallery. She is currently associate editor for the journal *Yishu: Journal of Contemporary Chinese Art* and coauthor/contributor of several Lonely Planet titles, including *Taiwan* and *China*. She currently lives in Vancouver, BC, Canada.

CAROLYN B HELLER   Liáoníng, Jílín, Hēilóngjiāng & Inner Mongolia

Carolyn has been fascinated with China since she first discovered egg rolls at the Dragon Inn in her hometown of Bloomington, Indiana. She's an avid traveller and passionate food-lover who has eaten on the streets, in fine restaurants, and everywhere in-between in nearly 40 countries. She has written for publications ranging from the *Boston Globe*, the *Zagat Survey* and the *Los Angeles Times* to *FamilyFun* magazine and *Travelers' Tales Paris*. She lives with her husband and daughters in Vancouver, British Columbia, where she studies Mandarin and eats Chinese food whenever she can. This is her third book for Lonely Planet.

THOMAS HUHTI   Sìchuān, Tibet & Xīnjiāng

Thomas hails from Wisconsin in the US and still calls it home when not lugging his pack around the world. A linguistics major in university, he chanced upon Mandarin while fleeing the pesky grammar of Indo-European. A semester abroad was followed by a two-year language and research stint in Taiwan and the People's Republic of China. He spent five years bumming the planet as a freelance writer before joining Lonely Planet. Among other books, this is his fifth tour of duty on *China;* he also coauthored the first edition of *Southwest China*. He would always rather be playing ice hockey or tromping through forests with his yellow lab Bighead Bobo.

BRADLEY MAYHEW   Gānsù, Níngxià & Qīnghǎi

Bradley started travelling in China almost 20 years ago while studying Chinese (Oriental Studies) at Oxford University. He's since been back over 20 times and has made it to almost every remote corner of western and southwestern China. At various times he's led adventure tours along the Silk Road and even worked for a while in Běijīng for a company trying to import *Sesame Street*. More recently he wrote the first two editions of Lonely Planet's *Shanghai* and *Southwest China* guides. These days he lives in Yellowstone County, Montana, where he tries in vain to get a decent flight connection to Asia. He is the coauthor of Lonely Planet guides to *Bhutan*, *Tibet*, *Nepal* and *Central Asia*.

MIN DAI
Běijīng, Tiānjīn, Shāndōng, Hénán & Húběi

Originally hailing from Shāndōng province in north China, Min Dai has spent much of her working life with deadlines breathing down her neck, from submitting news online for the BBC World Service to knocking hefty translation projects into shape and researching and writing for Lonely Planet, while keeping her two children amused and entertained. A student for four years in Běijīng, Min Dai currently lives in Shànghǎi, nursing plans to eventually return to north China via Honor Oak Park in south London, her other home.

CHRISTOPHER PITTS
Héběi, Shānxī & Shaanxi

Born in the year of the Tiger, Chris' first expedition to China ended in failure when he tried to dig there from Pennsylvania at the age of six. Hardened by reality but still infinitely curious about the other side of the world, he went on to study Chinese literature in Colorado, Kūnmíng and Táinán, offsetting his years abroad by working in a Chinese bookstore in San Francisco and as an editor in Berkeley. A chance meeting in a Taiwanese elevator wound up letting him off in Paris, where he currently lives with his family, Perrine, Elliot and Céleste. He is also the coauthor of Lonely Planet's *Shanghai*.

EILÍS QUINN
Guǎngxī, Guìzhōu, Yúnnán & Chóngqìng

Eilís grew up in Vancouver, Canada, where visits to the city's mammoth Chinatown sowed a fascination with China and foreign languages. A degree in East Asian Studies finally took her to the Middle Kingdom for real, where she landed at university in southwest China. Back in Canada, with degrees in Chinese, Russian and German, she resisted the pull of yet another language BA and opted for journalism instead. She went on to toil in the newsrooms of the Canadian Press news wire service, the *New York Daily News*, the *Toronto Star* and the *Montreal Gazette*. She previously worked on Lonely Planet's *Best of Beijing* and now lives in Montreal.

CONTRIBUTING AUTHORS

David Andrew wrote the Environment chapter. David's passion for wildlife has led him to study and write about the subject in all corners of the globe. As a biologist he has studied giant pandas in southwest China and seabirds in Antarctica, and as an author he has written or cowritten all five of Lonely Planet's *Watching Wildlife* series. He was the founding editor of Birds Australia's *Wingspan* magazine and a former editor of *Wildlife Australia*; and has travelled to and written about wildlife and ecotourism in places as diverse as Madagascar, the Galápagos Islands, Borneo and New Guinea.

Dr Trish Batchelor wrote the Health chapter and has specialised in travel medicine for over 15 years. She has travelled extensively in Asia, Africa and South America and has worked for extended periods in India and Nepal. She has a particular passion for high-altitude trekking and a special interest in the impact of tourism on host countries. She is currently medical director of The Travel Doctor clinic in Canberra, Australia, medical advisor to The Travel Doctor group in New Zealand, and is a committee chairperson in the International Society of Travel Medicine.

Lin Gu wrote the Coming Home boxed text in the History chapter. He recently left a position as Beijing-based writer for *China Features* and joined the Graduate School of Journalism at UC Berkeley as a visiting scholar. In eight years covering China, he has reported on a number of issues, including social migration and environmental protection. Lin was a regular contributor to the radio talk programmes which replaced Alistair Cooke's 'Letter from America' on Alistair's death. He has also written and presented on current affairs in China for the BBC. Lin has a master's degree in social anthropology from Cambridge University and was the two-time recipient of the Developing Asia Journalism Award for his coverage of the AIDS crisis in China and controversy over genetically modified rice in the country.

Getting Started

From low-cost independent exploration to luxury tours and every shade in between, China offers a sometimes bewildering choice of travel options. With China being so vast and travel experiences so varied, visitors need to take a long and hard look at the map, to determine exactly what it is that they want their China experience to be. The Itineraries chapter (p26) aims to provide you with options for your visit. The only part of China you will need to carefully plan is travel to Tibet, as bureaucratic obstacles, travel restrictions and health issues will require your consideration and attention.

WHEN TO GO

See Climate Charts (p938) for more information.

Travel to China is possible year-round, as long as you're prepared for what the season can throw at you. Spring (March to May) and autumn (September to early November) can be the best time to be on the road, as you avoid the blistering heat of summer (June to August) and stinging chill of winter (November to February/March). Autumn in Běijīng, for example, is particularly pleasant, as are early spring and autumn in Hong Kong. Summer is the busiest tourist season, and getting around and finding accommodation during the peak summer crush can be draining.

North China is hot and largely dry in summer, especially in the baking northwest (but Běijīng is also uncomfortable). The Yangzi River (Cháng Jiāng) region is very hot and humid, and southern China, with a coastline harassed by typhoons, also swelters. Rainfall rarely falls in quantities that can disrupt travel plans, except on the southern coastline during the typhoon season.

Winter is the low season (except for Hǎinán) and can be the quietest time of year, but while Hong Kong in winter is comfortably nippy, north China is a frozen expanse, especially in the northeast, northwest and Inner Mongolia. Wintering in clement central and southern Yúnnán province is enjoyable, but the higher altitude north of the province is frigid. Winter is inadvisable for travel to high-altitude areas in China, although summer visits to high-lying areas such as Qīnghǎi and parts of Tibet can be recommended.

Major public holidays can make travel difficult, and sights can be crammed with vacating Chinese. Manoeuvring around China with 1.3 billion others at Chinese New Year (p944) can be daunting, but you also get to see the country at its most colourful and entertaining. Hotel rates (see the boxed text, opposite) become very expensive during the May Day holiday (now a week long from 1 May) and National Day on 1 October (likewise a week long), and train tickets can be difficult to procure.

DON'T LEAVE HOME WITHOUT...

- Checking the visa situation (p953)
- Checking travel advisory bureaus
- Checking on your recommended vaccinations (p977)
- A copy of your travel insurance policy details (p946)
- Good deodorant – hard to find in China
- Reading matter for those endless train trips
- A sense of adventure

HOTEL ROOMS

Rack rates are quoted for hotels in this book, although generally the only time you will pay the full rate is during the major holiday periods, namely the first week of May, the first week of October and Chinese New Year. At other times, you can expect to receive discounts ranging between 10% and 50%. This does not apply to youth hostels or budget guesthouses, which tend to have set rates.

COSTS & MONEY

Once cheap, China has long become increasingly expensive. However, simply knowing where and how to travel according to your budget allows you to live well within your means.

The most expensive destinations are Hong Kong, Macau, Běijīng, Shànghǎi, Guǎngzhōu, the eastern coastal provinces and Special Economic Zones (SEZ). Běijīng and Shànghǎi especially can be intolerably dear. Look around, get savvy and acquire a sense of where locals shop. Quickly try to get a sense of proportion; be sensible and cautious about where you shop, and what you buy. Learn to haggle. Since you're using a new currency, take your time to accurately convert prices. Even Běijīng and Shànghǎi can be cheap if you're shrewd and careful.

Staying in dormitories – now an increasingly widespread option – travelling by bus or bicycle rather than taxi, eating from street stalls or small restaurants, refraining from buying anything and resisting the urge to splurge means it is possible to live on around US$25 (Y200) per day. Accommodation will take the largest chunk, but in cities where dormitory accommodation is unavailable you will have to settle for accommodation with rates from US$20 (Y160) for a double (singles are rarely available).

Western China and the interior remain relatively inexpensive. Popular backpacker getaways, such as Yúnnán, Sìchuān, Guǎngxī, Gānsù, Xīnjiāng, Qīnghǎi and Tibet, abound in budget accommodation and cheap eats.

Food costs remain reasonable throughout China, and the frugal can eat for as little as US$5 (Y40) a day. Transport costs can be kept to a minimum by travelling by bus or hard-seat on the train. Train travel is reasonable, and is generally about half the price of air travel. Flying in China is expensive, but discounting is the norm and those with less time will find it indispensable for covering vast distances.

Midrange hotel doubles start at around US$30 (Y240) and you can eat in midrange restaurants from around US$5 (Y40). Midrange comfort can be bought in China for around US$60 (Y480) a day, making it neither a very cheap nor an exorbitant way to see the land.

Top-end travel in China? Five-star hotel rooms can reach US$300 (Y2400) a night in the big cities and you can expect to pay upwards of US$100 (Y800) for a meal at one of the country's swishest restaurants. You'll find yourself well catered for, unless you venture too far from the big cities.

TRAVEL LITERATURE

Fried Eggs with Chopsticks (2005) by Polly Evans, an occasionally hilarious account of travel around this huge country, is perhaps the perfect partner to pack for those long bus journeys.

Author Sun Shuyun follows in the footsteps of 7th-century Buddhist monk Xuanzang (who trekked to India from China to return with bundles of *sutras*), setting off along the Silk Road from Xī'ān in her absorbing *Ten Thousand Miles Without a Cloud* (2003). Ideal reading matter for travellers doing the northwest.

HOW MUCH?

Cigarettes: from Y3.5

International Herald Tribune from a five-star hotel: Y23

City bus ticket: Y1

Hour in an internet café: Y1.5-Y3

City map: Y3-5

TOP TENS

Top Ten Movies

Some cinematic homework is a sure way to hit the ground running in China. The country's film genres sprawl from energetic Hong Kong *wǔdǎpiàn* (kung fu), violence and slapstick, through the decadent excesses of the mainland fifth generation to the sombre palate of the sixth generation and beyond.

- *Raise the Red Lantern* (1991) Director: Zhang Yimou
- *Judou* (1989) Director: Zhang Yimou
- *Chungking Express* (1994) Director: Wong Kar Wai
- *City on Fire* (1987) Director: Ringo Lam
- *In the Mood for Love* (2000) Director: Wong Kar Wai
- *Drunken Master 2* (1994) Directors: Lau Karleung & Jackie Chan
- *Infernal Affairs* (2002) Directors: Lau Waikeung & Mak Siufai
- *Beijing Bicycle* (2001) Director: Wang Xiaoshuai
- *The Gate of Heavenly Peace* (1995) Directors: Richard Gordon & Carma Hinton
- *Farewell My Concubine* (1993) Director: Chen Kaige

Top Ten Reads

Getting some paperwork can also gear you up for your China trip, so try some of the following penned by Chinese and non-Chinese authors.

- *The China Dream: The Elusive Quest for the Greatest Untapped Market on Earth* (2002) Joe Studwell
- *Mao: The Unknown Story* (2005) Jung Chang & Jon Halliday
- *Foreign Devils on the Silk Road* (1984) Peter Hopkirk
- *The Chinese* (2001) Jasper Becker
- *The Tiananmen Papers* (2001) Compiled by Zhang Liang; edited by Andrew Nathan and Perry Link
- *God's Chinese Son* (1997) Jonathan Spence
- *The Search for Modern China* (1991) Jonathan Spence
- *Soul Mountain* (2000) Gao Xingjian
- *The Rape of Nanking* (1998) Iris Chang
- *The Republic of Wine* (2001) Mo Yan

Top Ten Temples

China's far-flung temple brood can have your compass spinning as fast as your head, but ease the way and pick from this definitive list of top shrines.

- Lama Temple, Běijīng (p134)
- Temple of Heaven, Běijīng (p130)
- Puning Temple, Chéngdé (p193)
- Tashilhunpo Monastery, Shigatse, Tibet (p930)
- Labrang Monastery, Gānsù (p856)

- Jokhang Temple, Lhasa (p920)
- Confucius Temple, Qūfù (p220)
- Tǎ'ěr Sì, Around Xīníng, Qīnghǎi (p903)
- Dai Temple, Tài'ān (p211)
- Dafo Temple, Zhèngdìng (p189)

A vivid and gritty account of his penniless three-year meandering around China in the 1980s, *Red Dust* (2001) by Ma Jian traces the author's flight from the authorities in Běijīng to the remotest corners of the land.

River Town: Two Years on the Yangtze (2001) by Peter Hessler is full of poignant and telling episodes during the author's posting as an English teacher in the town of Fúlíng on the Yangzi River. Hessler perfectly captures the experience of being a foreigner in today's China in his observations of the local people.

Revolving around the same waterway, *The River at the Centre of the World* (1998) by Simon Winchester follows the author on his journey along the river from the mouth of the Yangzi River north of Shànghǎi to its source high up on the Tibet–Qinghai plateau.

First published in hardback in 1936, *News from Tartary: A Journey from Peking to Kashmir* by Peter Fleming is a classic account of the author's journey from China to India during a chaotic chapter in China's history.

INTERNET RESOURCES

China Minority Travel (www.china-travel.nl) Offers tailor-made trips to south China and Tibet.

China.org.cn (www.china.org.cn) Sanitised info on all aspects of China and up-to-the-minute news in 10 languages, including Esperanto.

China Today (www.chinatoday.com) Reams of info on China.

Lonely Planet (www.lonelyplanet.com) Useful summaries on travelling through China and travel tips from travellers on the Thorn Tree Travel Forum.

WildChina (www.wildchina.com) Far-flung treks around China, organised within China. Monthly email newsletter.

Zhongwen: Chinese Characters and Culture (www.zhongwen.com) Includes a pinyin chat room and an online dictionary of Chinese characters.

Itineraries
CLASSIC ROUTES

SOUTHWEST TOUR
Two to Four Weeks/Hong Kong to Yúnnán

Four days in **Hong Kong** (p518) and **Macau** (p566) will prime you for deeper forays into China proper, with a night or two in **Guǎngzhōu** (p587) for the city and its surrounding sights before jumping on a sleeper (train or bus) to **Guìlín** (p650) for classic views and a boat trip to famed **Yángshuò** (p656). Some travellers are seduced by Yángshuò's otherworldly landscapes into long sojourns, so prepare to overstay. Backtrack to Guìlín and hop on a bus to **Lóngshèng** (p663) and **Sānjiāng** (p664), not far from the Guǎngxī–Guìzhōu border, for its spectacular blend of scenery and minority villages. If you have time, incursions over the border into minority-rich **Guìzhōu** (p666) are tempting diversions. Onward travel from Guìlín to **Kūnmíng** (p688) by train or plane allows you to spend a few days there before flying or taking the bus northwest to **Dàlǐ** (p703) and from there on to **Lìjiāng** (p709). Alternatively, fly or take the bus to the fertile **Xīshuāngbǎnnà region** (p730) south of Kūnmíng, where an abundance of hiking opportunities around China's southwest borders rounds off your tour.

You'll be journeying to some of China's most alluring destinations on this 2000km tour, taking in key landscape panoramas and ethnic minority areas. The journey can be done in a whistle-stop few weeks or less, but a month will give you time to savour the region.

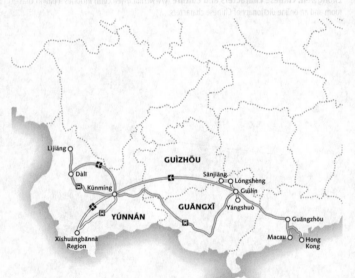

THE HISTORY TOUR: BĔIJĪNG TO THE SILK ROAD

Three to Four Weeks/Bĕijīng to Xī'ān & Dūnhuáng

Four days in **Bĕijīng** (p110) should be ample for its sights, from the **Great Wall** (p162) to the **Forbidden City** (p133) and the **Summer Palace** (p139). Take the bus or train to **Dàtóng** (p413) in Shānxī to gawp at the Buddhist magnificence of the **Yungang Caves** (p416) outside town. Hop on a bus from Dàtóng to the Buddhist mountain of **Wǔtái Shān** (p411) for several days before bussing it to **Tàiyuán** (p404) en route to the old walled town of **Píngyáo** (p407). A detour east by train from Tàiyuán to **Shíjiāzhuāng** (p186) and the charming temple town of **Zhèngdìng** (p189) north of the city is eminently feasible. From Tàiyuán take the train south to explore the historic walled city of **Kāifēng** (p468), traditional home of China's Jews, before heading west by train to the former dynastic capital of **Luòyáng** (p462) and the magnificent Buddhist spectacle of the **Longmen Caves** (p465). Take the train west again from Luòyáng to **Xī'ān** (p420) for four days of sightseeing in the former capital of the Tang dynasty, visiting the **Army of Terracotta Warriors** (p428) and clambering up the Buddhist mountain of **Huá Shān** (p433). Xī'ān traditionally marked the start of the Silk Road and the **Mogao Caves** (p866) outside **Dūnhuáng** (p864) – reachable by plane from Xī'ān – is one of the trade route's most spectacular marvels. Return to Bĕijīng by plane from either Xī'ān or Dūnhuáng.

For many travellers, this tour is what coming to China is all about. Spanning around 2500km from Bĕijīng to Dūnhuáng, you will be visiting the major imperial monuments – including the Great Wall and the Terracotta Army – and religious sites of North China. Manageable in three weeks, a month-long tour would allow for a more relaxed expedition.

COASTAL HIGHLIGHTS & TREATY PORTS TOUR   Three to Four Weeks/
Běijīng to Hong Kong & Macau

Having toured **Běijīng** (p110), take the train to **Tiānjīn** (p177) and spend a day wandering around its historic collection of European-style buildings. From Tiānjīn jump on the train for two days at least to breezy **Qīngdǎo** (p224), the port city in Shāndōng province graced with impressive early-20th-century German architecture. From Qīngdǎo take the overnight train to **Jǐ'nán** (p206) and seek out the earthy charms of the Ming and Qing dynasty village of **Zhūjiāyù** (p210). From Jǐ'nán, continue by train to booming **Shànghǎi** (p237) – stopping off in **Tài'ān** (p211) to climb **Tài Shān** (p214) if you have slack in your itinerary. Spend three days touring Shànghǎi's intoxicating mix of old European-style buildings and dashing modern architecture before doing day trips to the gardens and temples of **Sūzhōu** (p302) and the canal scenes of **Tónglǐ** (p310). From Shànghǎi take the train to famed **Hángzhōu** (p315) for several days in the historic capital of Zhèjiāng. Then board the overnight sleeper to coastal **Xiàmén** (p344) for two days exploring the pleasant port city and admiring the gorgeous, historic European architecture and charm of sleepy **Gǔlàng Yǔ** (p348). An inevitable conclusion to this loop along the coast comes with three days in **Hong Kong** (p518), perched on the south of Guǎngdōng, with the Chinese-Portuguese heritage of **Macau** (p566) a short boat trip away.

Voyaging down the eastern flank of China from Běijīng to Hong Kong, this tour covers over 3000km, taking in the major highlights and historic maritime towns along the coast. One of China's most fascinating journeys, this three- to four-week trip passes through some of the must-see sights of Qīngdǎo, Sūzhōu, Shànghǎi and Hángzhōu.

ROADS LESS TRAVELLED

QĪNGHǍI TO SÌCHUĀN   One Week/Xīníng to Chéngdū

Skirt the flanks of Tibet on your way from **Xīníng** (p901) to **Chéngdū** (p754) in
Sìchuān. The scenery en route is magnificent and perfect for a more offbeat
China experience – but do this trip only in summer (it can be dangerously
cold even in spring) and take lots of food with you (you won't be able to
change money or cash travellers cheques). Be prepared for wild dogs, bus
breakdowns, irregular transport connections and basic accommodation. You
can jump on a sleeper bus or plane (if Yùshù's airport is open, ask in Xīníng)
from Xīníng to the trading town of **Yùshù** (Jyekundo; p908) in the south of
Qīnghǎi, which stages a marvellous annual horse festival on 25 July. Spend
several days visiting the surrounding monasteries and exploring the deeply
Tibetan disposition of the region and its valleys. Trips south into Tibet are
feasible but check first (p911). Hop on a minibus to **Xiēwú** (Zhiwu; p910) and
continue east to **Sêrshu Dzong** (Shíqú; p788) in northwest Sìchuān and on to
Sêrshu (Shíqú Xiàn; p788), where bus connections run through some stunning scenery all the way to **Kāngdìng** (Dardo; p778), via **Manigango** (Yùlóng;
p786) and **Gānzī** (Ganze; p785). Continue along the Sìchuān–Tibet Hwy by
bus to Kāngdìng and then on to Chéngdū.

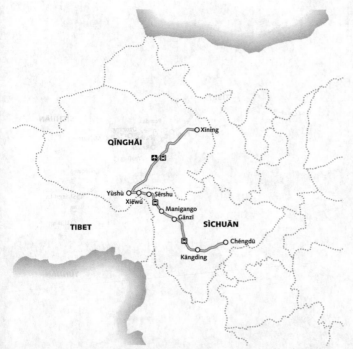

Traversing the
wilds of western
China, this spec-
tacular overland
1000km+ tour
takes you into
Sìchuān through
the mountainous
back door from
Qīnghǎi. Manage-
able in one week,
allow more time
for unforeseen
complications and
prepare for rough,
no-frills travel.

YÚNNÁN INTO TIBET
Eight Days/Lìjiāng to Lhasa

Kick off this trip walking **Tiger Leaping Gorge** (p718), north of gorgeous **Lìjiāng** (p709), before taking the bus to **Shangri-la** (Zhōngdiàn; **p724**), where your adventure proper begins. This epic, once-in-a-lifetime journey takes you from Shangri-la (Tibetan name: Gyalthang) through a breathtaking landscape of valleys, mountains and Tibetan villages to **Lhasa** (p917) in Tibet. You'll need a minimum of eight days for the trip, and the optimum months for travel are late spring (April and May) and autumn (September and October); winter is definitely out as the route crosses half a dozen passes over 4500m. Embark on this journey only if you are in good health (medical facilities en route are basic) and ensure you read the Health chapter for information on acute mountain sickness (p982). Joining a tour (which can arrange all the necessary permits, vehicle, driver and guide for you) is the best and safest way as individual travel through Tibet is not permitted, but increasing numbers of travellers are hitching through reportedly with little hassle. Several outfits (p726) in Shangri-la can make all the necessary arrangements. Your first stop after Shangri-la is **Déqìn** (Dechen; p727) before reaching the town of **Yánjīng** (Yandin) in southeastern Tibet's Chamdo Prefecture. Continue your journey by road to **Markam** (Mángkāng), then west to **Dzogang** (Zuǒgòng) and on to **Pasho** (Bāsù) via **Pomda** (Bāngdá; Bamda). The journey then continues to **Rawok** (Ranwu) and the gorgeous alpine lake of **Rawok-tso**, and on to Lhasa via **Pomi** and **Bayi**. From Lhasa, you then have the option of taking the train into China proper, to Běijīng, Shànghǎi or virtually any other part of the land.

This enticing 1000km+ overland adventure takes you from southwest China into Tibet through some of China's most visually spectacular scenery. Concluding in Lhasa, the tour will involve considerable preparatory work (and flexibility time-wise), but it's second to none for those seeking a more exploratory taste of China.

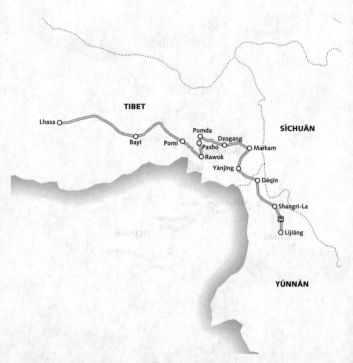

TAILORED TRIPS

CHINA'S TRADITIONAL VILLAGES

For barrel loads of rusticity, start this bucolic tour with a visit to **Chuāndǐxià** (p176) outside Běijīng before journeying to the ancient authentically unspoiled village of **Zhūjiāyù** (p210) in Shāndōng. From Jǐ'nán voyage west to the ancient stony hamlet of **Yújiācūn** (p190) in Héběi before popping down south to the high-altitude, tranquil village of **Guōliàngcūn** (p467) in Hénán, but pack a torch for power cuts and an easel and canvas for the views. You're literally spoiled for choice in southern Ānhuī, where a cluster of irresistible villages – **Hóngcūn** (p444), **Xīdì** (p443), **Nánpíng** (p444), **Guānlù** (p444) and **Yúliáng** (p445) – vie for your attention. Just across the border in northeastern Jiāngxī, the villages surrounding **Wùyuán** (p494), including **Lǐkēng** (p495), **Xiǎoqí** (p496) and **Qīnghuá** (p495), lie embedded in some of China's most idyllic scenery. Also in Jiāngxī, the trinity of small villages around **Luótiáncūn** (p491) makes a great escape from drab Nánchāng. To the west, Húnán abounds with minority villages and towns, from **Déhāng** (p511) to riverine **Fènghuáng** (p512), and intrepid explorers could even make the long trip to the isolated Tujia village of **Yúmùzhài** (p486) in the far-off southwestern corner of Húběi. Continue west to the ancient town of **Lǎngzhōng** (p768) in Sìchuān before rounding off your trip by seeking out the 600-year-old village of **Dǎngjiācūn** (p435) outside Hánchéng in Shaanxi.

CHINA'S SACRED SITES

Follow the temple trail around **Běijīng** (p110) and journey to **Chéngdé** (p191) to stand in amazement before the divine statue of Guanyin (p196) in **Puning Temple** (p193). Travel southwest to the Buddhist mountain of **Wǔtái Shān** (p411) for its constellation of Buddhist shrines, before voyaging southeast to **Zhèngdìng** (p189) for a lazy stroll around its charming legacy of pagodas and temples. East in Shāndōng rises massive **Tài Shān** (p214), China's most sacred Taoist peak, overlooking the magnificent **Dai Temple** (p211). The Buddhist Goddess of Compassion (p196) dwells on **Pǔtuóshān** (p332), off the Zhèjiāng coast. Rising up from Hénán province, Sōng Shān is home to the renowned **Shaolin Temple** (p460) and its legendary band of warrior monks. Outside **Luòyáng** (p462), the Buddhist **Longmen Caves** (p465) draw both the devout and sightseers, while west again in Shaanxi, **Xī'ān** (p420), famed for its Tang dynasty pagodas, is the gateway to Taoist **Huá Shān** (p433). Martial arts students can immerse themselves in the Taoist mysteries of **Wǔdāng Shān** (p481) to the southeast, while **Éméi Shān** (p769), in Sìchuān to the southwest, is one of China's most celebrated Buddhist peaks. The world's largest Buddha sits at nearby **Lèshān** (p774). In the far west rises Tibet, with its unique and idiosyncratic Buddhist traditions, exemplified by **Jokhang Temple** (p920), **Barkhor** (p919), **Potala Palace** (p920), **Samye Monastery** (p927) and **Tashilhunpo Monastery** (p930) in **Shigatse** (p929).

THE SUPERLATIVE TOUR

China abounds with superlatives, from the world's highest lake to the planet's largest statue of Buddha. Kick off your trip in **Hong Kong** (p518), where you can take a ride on the **Mid-Levels Escalator** (p523), the world's longest escalator. East along the coast, **Shànghǎi** (p237) inevitably has a crop of superlatives: the stunning **Jinmao Tower** (p256) – the tallest building in China – contains the world's longest laundry chute and the world's tallest atrium, both in the **Grand Hyatt** (p262), the world's highest hotel above ground level. A journey by boat (p811) from **Chóngqìng** (p799) – by some estimates the world's largest city – through the **Three Gorges** (p811) gets you up close to the biggest **dam** (p484) in the world, while a trip to **Běijīng** (p110) brings you to the world's largest public square – **Tiananmen Square** (p124) – and the world's longest fortification, the **Great Wall** (p162).

Head to **Chéngdé** (p191) to gaze at the world's largest wooden statue (Guanyin) in Puning Temple and size up the world's largest Buddha at **Lèshān** (p774). If you get as far to **Ürümqi** (p821), make a note that you're in the world's furthest city from the sea. Naturally **Tibet** (p912) has a few choice superlatives, including the **world's highest railway above sea level** (p924), **Nam-tso Lake** (p927), the highest lake in the world, and **Mt Everest** (p932), the world's highest mountain. While taking the superlative tour, look around you at the Chinese, the most populous population on earth.

WORLD HERITAGE SITES

China has over 30 Unesco World Heritage Sites; **Běijīng** (p110) alone has the **Forbidden City** (p133) at the heart of the capital, the **Summer Palace** (p139) and the **Temple of Heaven** (p130), and outside the city, the **Great Wall** (p162), the **Ming Tombs** (p174) and **Eastern Qing Tombs** (p175). En route to the Manchu **Imperial Palace** (p359) in **Shěnyáng** (p358), stop off in **Chéngdé** (p191) to admire the **Bìshǔ Shānzhuāng** (p192) and the **Eight Outer Temples** (p193). The quaint town of **Píngyáo** (p407) is a charming snapshot of old China. Also in Shānxī, the **Yungang Caves** (p416) have – like the **Mogao Caves** (p866), **Longmen Caves** (p465) and the **Dàzú County grotto art** (p809) – the most important array of Buddhist carvings in China. In Shāndōng the Taoist mountain of **Tài Shān** (p214) and the hometown of Confucius, **Qūfù** (p218), are places of national veneration. China's most pictur-

esque peak is surely **Huáng Shān** (p446), but there are other mountains, including **Éméi Shān** (p769) and **Qīngchéng Shān** (p766), and the European charms of **Lúshān** (p497). The classic gardens of **Sūzhōu** (p302) are a picturesque tableau, but if you want rugged and scenic getaways, explore **Jiǔzhàigōu** (p795), **Wǔlíngyuán** (p515), **Huánglóng** (p794) or **Wǔyí Shān** (p353), although expect tourist hordes to accompany you. The **Historic Centre of Macau** (p566) brings a charming Portuguese flavour to your China trip, **Hóngcūn** (p444) and **Xīdì** (p443) are both beautiful villages in south Ānhuī, while **Lìjiāng** (p709) remains lovely. The whole of Tibet to the northwest deserves to be a World Heritage Site; for now only the **Potala Palace** (p920) in Lhasa gets on the list.

Snapshot

A land curiously both in the throes of dramatic transition yet somehow eternally the same, China is certainly going places. A railway – a contraption once abhorred for its negative effects on feng shui and ruinous interference with ancestral graves – now links dusty Běijīng in the arid north of China with Lhasa in far-off Tibet, lashing this last region by rail to the Chinese heartland. The train's engines will be fed oxygen in the thin air, and so will the passengers, who will no doubt savour the pure gas after enduring Běijīng's notoriously foggy haze (see The Great Pall of China boxed text, p113).

The monumental Three Gorges Dam, cloaked in as much controversy as the banks of mist that roll along the Yangzi River (Cháng Jiāng), was completed in 2006, three years ahead of schedule. China lifted man into space for the first time in 2003, a feat it repeated in 2005, and you can rocket from Shànghǎi's Pudong airport into town at a blinding 430km/h on China's first Maglev train (although your hair can turn grey waiting for your rush-hour bus to move on Běijīng's congested streets).

China reportedly sucks up half the world's concrete and a third of its steel, and nearly half of all tropical hardwood logs are destined for China's growing square kilometres of wood strip flooring. Sex-toy shops are ubiquitous in China from Ānyáng to Jǐngdézhèn, a fact underscored by a piece of trivia that would have Mao Zedong gyrating in his mausoleum: 70% of the world's sex toys are 'Made in China'. The local instinct for capitalist opportunism sharpened further when touts started buying up queue tickets at China's notoriously slow-moving banks and selling them off to the highest bidder as the numbers drew near.

The country is facing a shortage of pilots to fly its growing fleet of commercial airplanes and industry insiders suggest that over 100 foreign pilots are now in the skies above China, in defiance of government regulations. Gazing into the future, if three out of four Chinese people own a car, a fleet of 1.1 billion cars will be competing for parking spaces. Little wonder car manufacturers are sick with excitement.

The thrill and trauma of change is everywhere. In its mad dash to turn itself into a modern citadel, Běijīng has irretrievably obliterated much of its precious history. As the Chinese-American architect IM Pei has observed, city planners should have kept the magnificent city walls and built the skyscrapers outside. To ease its conscience, Běijīng paradoxically rebuilt the magnificent Yongding Gate (although the facsimile fails to match the original) after felling it in the 1950s.

If high-rises float your boat, go to Shànghǎi, which now has nearly double the number of skyscrapers as New York. The only way is up, one might say, and Shànghǎi's streets change appearance almost overnight, but the city still has to deal with its yellow tap water, overpowering pollution and traffic congestion that is rivalling Běijīng's epic gridlock.

Famed for their exotic tastes, Chinese diners, who get through 45 billion pairs of chopsticks annually, were recently treated to China's first restaurant specialising in yak, donkey and seal penises, which opened in Běijīng. If that's not your cup of *cha*, the latest fad is delicious Chinese Tujia pizza, a savoury and aromatic disc of bread sprinkled with crumbs of meat that should set you back a mere Y2.

Pollution continues to have a ruinous effect on the land. In 2005 a senior environmental official warned that pollution levels could quadruple within

FAST FACTS: CHINA

Population: 1.3 billion

Life expectancy male/female: 70.4/73.7 years

GDP growth: 9.6%

GDP per capita: US$6800

Adult literacy: 86%

Internet users: 134 million

Major exports: textiles, clothing, footwear, toys and machinery

Religions: Buddhism, Taoism, Islam, Christianity

Number of Chinese characters: over 56,000

15 years, unless serious efforts were made to make the country more energy efficient.

Bird flu, the source of so much global panic in 2005–06, infected large numbers of birds in China, but fortunately has so far failed to mutate into a form transmissible from person to person. Even so, a run on Tamiflu saw Shànghǎi chemists rapidly running out of the drug, which then resurfaced on the black market with a hefty mark-up.

North China's drought shows little sign of abating. Tiānjīn now reportedly has per capita water supplies lower than Saudi Arabia's, and China has the world's most developed rain-seeding program. The US$64 billion north-south water diversion project aims to suck water from the Yangzi River to slake the thirst of the increasingly parched north.

China's awkward tango with the internet took a further stumble when a fire in 2002 in an internet café left many dead. The authorities responded by closing thousands of internet cafés throughout the nation. Běijīng's population of internet cafés is well down on just a few years ago, but employment is assured for a reputed 30,000 cyberspace police who strictly monitor content and weed out foreign pollutants, such as the BBC News website and Wikipedia.

All is not well down on the farm, as countryside unrest grows in both frequency and severity. Official Chinese figures report 74,000 incidents (riots or illegal demonstrations), many of them rural, in 2004.

History Korina Miller & Damian Harper

Littered with sieges, cults, kidnappings, indolent emperors, magnificent inventions, works of genius and grand gestures like the Terracotta Warriors of the Qin dynasty and the communists' Long March, Chinese history twists its way through nearly 6000 years. Often touted as the world's oldest surviving civilisation, China has seen as many changes as the Great Wall has bricks. The territorial reach of the state, the origin of its rulers, how people speak and dress, and even what they eat, have all changed beyond recognition more than once. Together, the history of the many societies that have flourished on this country's soil form the tale the Chinese tell about their origins.

LEGENDS OF YORE

While China's earliest history is made up of the stuff of legends and has no contemporary written record, archaeology confirms that societies have been putting down roots in China since antiquity. Excavations at Bànpō (p430), not far from present-day Xī'ān, show that a sedentary agricultural community flourished nearly 6000 years ago. A second early culture was discovered in present-day Shāndōng. Known as Longshan culture, it shows the beginning of metallurgy and appears to have been the driving force behind the Bronze Age Shang dynasty.

TELLTALE SIGNS: THE SHANG

In 1899 peasants working near present-day Ānyáng unearthed pieces of polished bone and turtle shells. These relics were inscribed with characters and dated back to around 1500 BC, the time of the Shang dynasty. Housed in Ānyáng's museum (p467), these are the earliest examples of the elaborate writing system still used in China today.

Shang culture spread throughout much of north China, stretching from Shāndōng to Shaanxi and Héběi to Hénán. It was headed by a sacred kingship, who was supported by officials, armies and a peasantry that supplied labour for the building of city walls and other public works. There was also a skilled artisanry, which produced the magnificent bronzeware for which this dynasty is known; visit the Henan Provincial Museum for fabulous examples (p457).

ENTER CONFUCIUS: THE ZHOU

Around three millennia ago the last Shang sovereign was defeated by the forces of Zhou, who hailed from present-day Shaanxi province. The Zhou went on to rule over an increasingly large territory, reaching up to Běijīng in

> Bones found near Ānyáng in 1899 were Shang dynasty oracle bones. The bones were inscribed and heated, and the resulting cracks were interpreted as responses from deceased ancestors.

PEKING MAN

In the 1920s and 1930s Chinese archaeologists unearthed *homo erectus* skulls, stone tools and animal bones believed to be between 500,000 and 230,000 years old. Was this the birthplace of Chinese civilisation? Unfortunately, we're unlikely to ever know. Research was never carried out on Peking Man's bones because, on the eve of the Japanese invasion, the remains mysteriously disappeared – some fear to the bottom of the sea.

TIMELINE **c 4000 BC**

Dynastic rule commences with the Xia; early settlements set up home in modern-day Shaanxi and Hénán

c 3000 BC

Emperor Fuxi (part man, part dragon) ushers in the legendary period of 'Three Emperors and Five Sovereigns'

CHINESE DYNASTIES

Dynasty	Period	Site of capital
Xia	2200–1700 BC	
Shang	1700–1100 BC	Ānyáng
Zhou	1100–221 BC	
Western Zhou	1100–771 BC	Hào (near Xī'ān)
Eastern Zhou	770–221 BC	Luòyáng
Qin	221–207 BC	Xiányáng
Han	206 BC–AD 220	
Western Han	206 BC–AD 9	Xī'ān
Xin	AD 9–23	Xī'ān
Eastern Han	AD 25–220	Luòyáng
Three Kingdoms	AD 220–80	
Wei	AD 220–65	Luòyáng
Shu (Shu Han)	AD 221–63	Chéngdū
Wu	AD 229–80	Nánjīng
Jin	AD 265–20	
Western Jin	AD 265–317	Luòyáng
Eastern Jin	AD 317–420	Nánjīng
Southern & Northern Dynasties	AD 420–589	
Southern Dynasties		
Song	AD 420–79	Nánjīng
Qi	AD 479–502	Nánjīng
Liang	AD 502–57	Nánjīng
Chen	AD 557–89	Nánjīng
Northern Dynasties		
Northern Wei	AD 386–534	Dàtóng, Luòyáng
Eastern Wei	AD 534–50	Linzhang
Northern Qi	AD 550–77	Linzhang
Western Wei	AD 535–56	Xī'ān
Northern Zhou	AD 557–81	Xī'ān
Sui	AD 581–618	Xī'ān
Tang	AD 618–907	Xī'ān
Five Dynasties & Ten Kingdoms	AD 907–60	
Later Liang	AD 907–23	Kāifēng
Later Tang	AD 923–36	Luòyáng
Later Jin	AD 936–47	Kāifēng
Later Han	AD 947–50	Kāifēng
Later Zhou	AD 951–60	Kāifēng
Liao	AD 907–1125	
Song	AD 960–1279	
Northern Song	AD 960–1127	Kāifēng
Southern Song	AD 1127–1279	Hángzhōu
Jin	AD 1115–1234	Kāifēng, Běijīng
Yuan	AD 1206–1368	Běijīng
Ming	AD 1368–1644	Nánjīng, Běijīng
Qing	AD 1644–1911	Běijīng
Republic of China	AD 1911–49	Běijīng, Chóngqìng, Nánjīng
People's Republic of China (PRC)	AD 1949–	Běijīng

c 1700 BC	604 BC
Members of the Shang dynasty master bronze-ware production	Laotzu, the founder of Taoism, is reputedly born

the north and down to the lower Yangzi River (Cháng Jiāng) valley in the south. To overcome the difficulties of ruling such a vast area, the Zhou established a feudal system whereby landlords governed over principalities that were contained within walled cities.

In 771 BC the Zhou capital moved from a site near Xī'ān to one further east, leading present-day historians to divide this period into Western and Eastern Zhou. During the period of Eastern Zhou law codes were written down, iron was discovered and the fortunes of the landed aristocracy waned, while self-made men achieved places at court and merchants grew wealthy.

The Zhou's control over the principalities began to fade as landlords began to fight among themselves. The Eastern Zhou was a time riddled with strife, prompting reflection and philosophising on the part of one Master Kong (Kong Fuzi), better known in the West as Confucius.

Confucius (551–479 BC) grew up in the old state of Lu, at the present-day site of Qūfù (p218) in Shāndōng province. The descendant of a minor noble family, he set off at an early age in search of an able and righteous ruler who might lead the world back to virtuous paths. In this mission he was doomed to disappointment, and his death in 479 BC was to be followed by an ever keener struggle among the states for power.

Confucius did achieve enormous success as a teacher and moral exemplar, and the structure of Chinese society today remains very much rooted in his teachings. He gave voice to many of the sentiments of his age, and his contemporaries included luminaries such as Laotze (Laozi), the founder of philosophical Taoism, and Mozi (born nine years after Confucius' death), who preached a creed of universal love. For more on Confucian beliefs, see p64 and the boxed text on p221, or head to Qūfù for a good dose of hands-on history.

CROSSING SWORDS: THE QIN

The principalities had been fighting with one another for more than 250 years, during what became known as the Warring States period. This dark era finally came to an end in 221 BC when the western state of Qin, having conquered the Zhou 35 years earlier, succeeded in subduing the remaining states to establish centralised rule.

'The First Emperor of Qin' (Qin Shi Huang) won and reigned by the sword. His ruling philosophy focused on law and punishment, and dealt a blow to Confucius' teachings of rights and morality. His martial fanaticism was none too subtle; check out his tomb near Xī'ān, which is protected by the extraordinary Army of Terracotta Warriors (p428).

Qin Shi Huang pursued campaigns as far north as Korea and south down to Vietnam while, at home, he began linking existing city walls to create the beginnings of the Great Wall. The 'First Emperor' also laid the foundations for a unified, integrated empire. He introduced a uniform currency, standardised the script and developed infrastructure through a network of roads and canals.

Qin Shi Huang's heir to the imperial throne proved ineffectual and, shaken by rebellion, the Qin capital fell after only 15 years to an army led by the commoner Liu Bang. Liu lost no time in taking the title of emperor and establishing the Han dynasty.

The conquering Zhou beheaded the Shang leader, but granted his son a state to rule, thereby hoping to diminish the wrath of the Shang ancestors.

The First Emperor of Qin burned thousands of books and killed countless scholars to eliminate potential challenges to his rule.

The Emperor and the Assassin (1999) is the epic tale of the First Emperor of Qin and his lust for power. Woven with murder, love and political intrigue, this film is beautifully shot and a must see whether you're a history buff or not.

551 BC	221 BC
Confucius is born	The First Emperor of Qin conquers the surrounding states to create the first unified China

WIDENING THE NET: THE HAN

The Han dynasty brought further unification of the empire as vassal states that had lingered on the outskirts were swept up under its reign. Emperor Wu, who reigned from 140 BC to 87 BC, established supremacy over neighbouring societies to the north and west, recruited able men to serve the dynasty as officials, and promoted Confucian education. An examination system was introduced and would go on to become a hallmark of government in the late imperial era; visit the Imperial College (p134) in Běijīng to learn more.

After more than a century the Han gave way to the Xin dynasty (AD 9–23), led by the radical reformer Wang Mang. This 14-year blip divides the dynasty into Former (Western) and Later (Eastern) Han periods.

Venturing Down the Silk Road

Pick up a copy of *Shi Ji* or *Records of the Grand Historian* by Sima Qian, translated by Burton Watson. Written during the Han dynasty, Sima chronicles history from antiquity to his own time, based on court records and conversations with courtiers and generals.

The expansion of the Han brought the Chinese into contact with the 'barbarians' that encircled their world. As a matter of course, this contact brought both military conflict and commercial gains.

To the north, the Xiongnu (a name given to various nomadic tribes of central Asia) posed the greatest threat to China. Military expeditions were sent against these tribes, initially with much success. This in turn provided the Chinese with access to Central Asia, opening up the routes that carried Chinese silk as far afield as Rome.

Diplomatic links were also formed with central Asian tribes, and the great Chinese explorer Zhang Qian provided the authorities with information on the possibilities of trade and alliances in northern India. During the same period, Chinese influence percolated into areas that were later to become known as Vietnam and Korea.

UNITY & DIVISION

They say the momentum of history was ever thus: the empire, long divided, must unite; long united, must divide.

Luo Guanzhong

With these words, the storyteller of *Romance of the Three Kingdoms* (14th century) sums up the seemingly endless warring and reconstruction that followed the Han dynasty. Between the early 3rd and late 6th centuries AD north China saw a succession of rival kingdoms struggling for power. During this time of disunity a strong division formed between north and south China. The north was controlled by non-Chinese rulers and torn by warfare. Many people from the north consequently fled, carrying Chinese culture into previously non-Chinese territories. Meanwhile, the south experienced significant economic growth as Jiankang, later to become Nánjīng, served as capital for a succession of dynasties.

Culture Vultures

The most successful northern regime during this period was the Northern Wei dynasty (386–534), founded by the Tuoba, a people from the north. The Tuoba embraced Buddhism wholeheartedly and left behind some of China's top Buddhist art. Visit the cave temples near Dūnhuáng (p866) and outside Dàtóng (p416) for a glimpse. The Wei reallocation of lands to peasants and the division of the capital city into wards also outlasted the dynasty.

214 BC	c 100 BC
Emperor Qin indentures thousands of labourers to link existing city walls into one Great Wall	Chinese traders and explorers follow the Silk Road all the way to Rome

BRIDGING THE GAP: THE SUI

The Wei dynasty fell in 534. It was succeeded by a series of rival regimes until nobleman Yang Jian (d 604) seized all before him to establish the Sui dynasty (581–618). While the Sui was a short-lived dynasty, its accomplishments were many. Yang Jian's great achievement was to bring the south back within the pale of a northern-based empire.

Yang Jian's son, Sui Yangdi, has gone down in history as an unsavoury character who had more time for wine and women than for politics; the dynasty went into rapid decline under his rule. Nevertheless, he did contribute greatly to the unification of south and north through the construction of the Grand Canal. The canal combined earlier canals and linked the lower Yangzi River valley to Chāng'ān via the Yellow River (Huáng Hé). When Běijīng became capital of the Yuan dynasty, it was rerouted and extended northward, and remained the empire's most important communication route between south and north until the late 19th century.

After instigating three unsuccessful incursions onto Korean soil, resulting in disastrous military setbacks, Yangdi faced revolt on the streets and was assassinated in 618 by one of his high officials.

THE GOLDEN ERA: THE TANG

The reams of literature produced during the Tang dynasty has prompted historians to think of it as the Golden Age. The *Three Hundred Tang Poems*, compiled from over 48,000 poems preserved from this time, provides Chinese conversation with quotable quotes, much as Shakespeare does in English.

Sui Yangdi was succeeded as emperor by his own leading general, Li Yuan, who seized the capital, declared the founding of the Tang dynasty and within 10 years had eliminated the last rival claimant to the throne. To discourage the development of regional power bases, the empire was subsequently divided into 300 prefectures *(zhōu)* and 1500 counties *(xiàn)*, establishing a pattern of territorial jurisdiction that persists, with some modifications, to this day.

Li Yuan's achievements were consolidated by his son, the much admired Taizong (626–49). The relationship between Taizong, the able ruler, and his wise minister Wei Zheng (580–645) was regarded as a model one by later Confucianists. On the other hand, Taizong's concubine, Wu Zhao, was seen as a good example of what should be avoided in government.

All that Glitters...

Following Taizong's death, Wu (625–705) wielded increasing influence over the court. In 690 she managed to declare a new dynasty, the Zhou, with herself as emperor – the only woman in Chinese history to ever officially hold this position. Wu was regarded as infinitely cruel (some claim she even murdered her own son); however, it was under her leadership that the empire reached its greatest extent, spreading well north of the Great Wall and far west into inner Asia. The rich repository of texts and paintings at Dūnhuáng (p864) in Gānsù testifies to the Zhou's intense use of the Silk Road to India, Persia and on to the Mediterranean. During the 7th and 8th centuries major cities, like the capital Chāng'ān, the Yangzi port of Yángzhōu and the coastal port Guǎngzhōu, were crowded with foreign merchants. Wu later moved the capital to the more easily supplied Luòyáng.

The website http://etext .lib.virginia.edu/chinese /frame.htm gives you the opportunity to view the Golden Era from the eyes of its poets. This site has all 300 Tang Poems online along with English translations.

Made in AD 868, a Chinese Tang dynasty copy of the *Diamond Sutra* is the world's oldest entire printed book.

c 50 BC	c AD 600
One of the first documented accounts of tea-drinking in China	The Grand Canal is constructed

Wu also replaced many aristocratic officials with scholars chosen through examinations. Her strong promotion of Buddhism, however, alienated her from these Confucian officials and in 705 she was forced to abdicate to Xuan Zong.

The Anti-Midas Touch

Emperor Xuan Zong took the reigns of power and moved the capital back to Chāng'ān. He re-established permanent armies, appointing minorities from the frontiers as generals, in the belief that they were so far removed from the political system and society that ideas of rebellion and coups would not enter their minds. Nevertheless, it was An Lushan, a general of Sogdian-Turkic parentage, who took advantage of his command in north China to make a bid for imperial power. The fighting, which dragged on for around eight years, overran the capital and caused massive dislocations of people and millions of deaths.

Following the failed rebellion, the aristocracy declined and a mercenary army was hired to support the imperial house. The dynasty grew increasingly dependent on the south, and began to close the door to inner and western Asia. Ideas and beliefs of the past were revived, paving the way for a comeback of Confucianism during the Song dynasty. Buddhism, on the other hand, was outlawed by Emperor Wuzong from 842 to 845. Although the ban was later modified, Buddhism never regained the power and prestige in China that it had enjoyed up until that time.

Tang power gradually weakened during the 8th and 9th centuries. In the northwest, Tibetan warriors overran Tang garrisons, while to the south the Nanzhao kingdom of Dàlǐ, Yúnnán, posed a serious threat to Sìchuān. Meanwhile, in the Chinese heartland of the Yangzi River region and Zhèjiāng, heavy taxes and a series of calamities engendered wide-ranging discontent that culminated in the Huang Chao rebellion (874–84). This reduced the empire to chaos and resulted in the fall of the capital in 907.

The superb www.con fucius.org offers a look at the philosophy that changed the course of China. The grand sage's *Lun Yu* (Classic Sayings) is available in 21 languages, along with photos of his calligraphy, speeches and a biography.

GOING SOUTH: THE SONG

Another period of disunity followed the fall of the Tang until the Northern Song dynasty (960–1127) was established. The Northern Song was a rather small empire coexisting with the non-Chinese Liao dynasty (which controlled a belt of Chinese territory south of the Great Wall) and rather less happily with the Western Xia, another non-Chinese power that pressed hard on the northwestern provinces. In 1126 the Song lost its capital, Kāifēng, to a third non-Chinese people, the Jurchen, who had previously been their allies against the Liao. The Song was driven to its southern capital of Hángzhōu for the period of the Southern Song (1127–1279).

The Jurchen, forebears of the Manchu, established the Jin dynasty with a capital near Běijīng. A treaty was drawn up with the Southern Song that divided the empire along the boundary of Huái Hé. The Jin dynasty pulled rank over the Southern Song, demanding the payment of tribute in the form of silk, tea and silver.

Nevertheless, the Song dynasty, North and South, was a time of enormous economic and cultural vitality. Considerable advances were made in archaeology, mathematics, astronomy, geography and medicine. Philosophy, poetry, painting and calligraphy flourished. Agricultural productivity was booming,

Buddhist pilgrim Xuan Zhuang sets out for India, returning 16 years later with countless holy texts	Wu Zhao is the first and only woman to become emperor

brought on by the spread of rice cultivation since the 8th century, and this left a surplus of labour that was used to develop secondary industries, like mining, ceramics and silk manufacture. The tea-bush and lacquer trees were cultivated, and gunpowder and moveable type were invented. Paper making and print technology experienced significant advances, and a busy trade with Southeast Asia and Japan sent Song copper currency far afield.

All of these developments nurtured urbanisation and commercial classes. Kāifēng (p468) emerged as the great centre of Northern Song politics, culture and commerce. Merchants flourished, while the aristocracy more or less disappeared. Many Tang restrictions on society were abolished as the urban population became more liberated; the removal of the curfew led to a thriving nightlife. Hángzhōu (p315) prospered as capital of the Southern Song, and to this day retains its reputation as one of the most beautiful and cultured cities in the empire.

An educated class of high social standing became a distinguishing feature of Chinese society as Confucianism achieved a dominance it was to retain until the 19th century. The Song refined and expanded the examination system, selecting officials from the successful candidates.

The Wrath of Khan

While the Song literati were busy studying moral codes, Genghis Khan (1167–1227) was beginning to flex his muscles in Mongolia. The son of a chieftain, Genghis commenced his awesome rise to power by avenging his father's murder. By 1206 he was recognised as supreme ruler of the Mongols. The Mongols, despised for what was considered their ignorance and poverty, had occasionally gone to war with the Chinese but had always lost. In 1211 Genghis Khan turned his sights on China, penetrated the Great Wall two years later and took Běijīng in 1215. He fought the Jin in the east, destroyed the Western Xia in the west and advanced on Russia. Under his descendants, a great Mongol empire was formed, stretching from the Ukraine and Persia to Korea and the northern limits of Vietnam.

The Jin fell in 1234. Hángzhōu, the Southern Song capital, was taken in 1276. The court fled and Southern Song resistance ended in 1279.

GRAND OPENING: THE YUAN

Kublai Khan, grandson of Genghis, now reigned over all of China as emperor of the Yuan dynasty. He had inherited the largest empire the world had ever known. Foreigners were easily incorporated into this ethnically complex empire as land routes were reopened. European missionaries and traders, such as Marco Polo, went to and fro across the Eurasian continent. The Khan's capital, Khanbalig, was on the site of present-day Běijīng; today all that's left of his palace is a giant jade urn in Beihai Park (p134).

The site www.eyewitness tohistory.com/khan.htm has Marco Polo's eyewitness account of Kublai Khan's battle of 1287, as well as a brief history of the battle.

Under Khan, the entire population was divided into categories of Han, Mongol and foreigner, with the top administrative posts reserved for Mongols. The examination system was revived in 1315, but the Mongols and their non-Chinese allies were still strongly favoured, causing resentment among the Chinese literati.

Although they were a mighty military power, the Mongols were not masterminds at politics or economics and were soon faced with insurmountable opposition. The Mongols controlled China for less than a century; by

The major inventions of the premodern world – paper, printing, gunpowder and the compass – are all commonly used in China

Genghis Khan conquers Běijīng

the middle of the 14th century rebellions raged through central and north China.

Chief among the rebel groups were the Red Turbans who followed a whole gamut of religions – from Buddhism to Manichaeism, Taoism and Confucianism. By 1367 Zhu Yuanzhang, originally an orphan and Buddhist novice, had climbed to the top of the rebel leadership and in 1368 he established the Ming dynasty, restoring Chinese rule.

FORTRESS MENTALITY: THE MING

A man of no great education, Zhu Yuanzhang was a born leader and a strong if harsh ruler. Remembered for his tyranny (he had some 10,000 scholars and their families put to death in two paranoid purges of his administration), he also did much to set China back on its feet in the aftermath of the Yuan collapse.

Yuanzhang established his capital in Nánjīng, but by the early 15th century the court had begun to move back to Běijīng. A massive reconstruction project was commenced under Emperor Yongle, who reigned from 1403 to 1424, establishing the Forbidden City (p133) much as it remains today. A burgeoning commercial and residential suburbia grew up south of the walled city, and was itself enclosed by a wall in 1522. In this form the city survived through to the 1950s.

In the early Ming, relations with inner Asia were at an all-time low. Yongle had usurped power from his nephew and the civil war that this provoked left him looking overseas to establish his credentials as ruler. In 1405 he launched the first of seven great maritime expeditions. Led by the eunuch general Zheng He (1371–1433), the fleet consisted of more than 60 large vessels and 255 smaller ones, carrying nearly 28,000 men. The fourth and fifth expeditions departed in 1413 and 1417, and travelled as far as Aden, on the present Suez Canal. The great achievement of these voyages was to bring tribute missions to the capital, including two embassies from Egypt.

In his book, *1421: The Year China Discovered America*, author Gavin Menzies argues that a huge fleet of Chinese junks reached the New World over 70 years before Columbus.

Retreat!

In 1439 a dramatic invasion by the Mongols resulted in the capture and year-long imprisonment of the then-emperor. The Ming reaction was to retreat into itself. The Great Wall was lengthened by 600 miles in the second half of the century, turning it into one of the great building feats of history. The coast, however, was more difficult to defend. In the middle of the 16th century the coastal provinces were harassed by pirate ships and their suppression took great effort.

Around this time, ships also arrived from Europe. The Ming allowed these foreigners to enter their domain, and in 1557 the Portuguese gained the right to establish a permanent trade base in Macau. Traders were quickly followed by missionaries and the Jesuits, led by the formidable Matteo Ricci, made their way inland and established a presence at court. There they made a great impression with their skills in astronomy and in casting canons.

The Portuguese presence linked China directly to trade with the New World. New crops, such as potatoes and maize, were introduced and New World silver was used to pay for Chinese exports such as tea, porcelain and ceramics. Commerce via merchant banks became important, absentee landlordism and tenant farming became common, and urbanisation intensified.

1279–1368	1286
Kublai Khan's vast Mongol empire includes all of China	The Grand Canal is extended to Běijīng, assuming its familiar form

A House of Cards

The Ming Government was undermined by the power eunuchs wielded at court and by struggles between officials. Strong emperors were needed to maintain order, but were few and far between. Zhu Houchao, ruler from 1505 to 1521, handed over matters of state to his chief eunuch so that he could devote his attention to his concubines. This was soon followed by the Tianqi reign (1621–28), a government dominated by the eunuch Wei Zhongxian (1568–1627), who purged officials and built temples in honour of himself.

Such poor leadership could not have happened at a worse time. North of the border, the Jurchen people were consolidated into a militarised state, and by the 1620s they were carrying out periodic raids, sometimes deep into Chinese territory. At the same time floods and drought devastated large areas of north China, encouraging banditry that swelled into rebellions.

The Manchu to the north had long been growing in power and looked with keen interest to the convulsions of rebellion in their huge neighbour. Taking advantage of the turmoil they saw, they launched an invasion, but were initially held back by the Great Wall. Eventually a Ming general let them pass, believing that an alliance with the Manchu was the only hope for defeating the peasant rebel armies that now threatened Běijīng itself.

In 1644 Běijīng fell, not to the Manchu but to the peasant rebel Li Zicheng, who sat on the throne for one day before fleeing from the Chinese troops who helped put a Manchu emperor in his place.

Emperor Jiajiang (r 1521–67) of the Ming dynasty kept over 1000 concubines. His treatment of them was notoriously cruel; over 200 died of abuse.

HEAVY-HANDED: THE QING

The Manchu proclaimed their new dynasty the Qing (1644–1911), although it took them four decades to stamp out Ming loyalists in the south and pacify the entire country. This victory for the Qing came at great cost to the population, with acts of severe brutality and massacres.

The Qing neutralised threats from inner Asia by incorporating their homeland of Manchuria into the empire as well as that of the Mongols, whom they had subordinated. Their cultural policy involved a careful balance of attention to the Chinese, Manchu, Mongols and Tibetans. They courted the literati via the examination system and great literary projects. Their own people were appointed to key positions in the bureaucracy, but matching positions were created for Chinese officials.

As an alien dynasty, the Qing remained keen to establish its own legitimacy. Chinese men were forced to wear their hair in the Manchu style (the front shaved and the back braided into a long tail), a look you'll quickly recognise as a sign of 'Chineseness' used in countless Western cartoons. Harsh censorship was practised during the 18th century, with a literary inquisition begun in the 1770s and cruel punishments inflicted on authors of works containing anti-Manchu sentiments. Despite such ideological control, scholarship flourished.

Women's Cultural Battleground

Women became a site of Chinese cultural resistance to Manchu rule. Chinese women continued to wear Chinese-style dress, with skirts worn over loose jackets and trousers, as opposed to the one-piece robe worn by Manchu women. Foot binding, in force from perhaps the 10th or 11th centuries, persisted despite Qing prohibitions. Chinese women remained devout to

1368

Chinese rule is restored with the Ming dynasty

1406

Ming Emperor Yongle begins construction of the 800 buildings of the Forbidden City

Chinese men, continuing to honour them through the practice of widow suicide. The Manchu showed considerable political skill in moving from opposition to endorsement of widow suicide, awarding honours to women who followed their husbands to the grave.

Tackling the Neighbours

Tibet was made a Chinese colony in 1751 and granted regional autonomy under the watchful eye of a Qing resident. Before this date it had many encounters with Běijīng; visit Lama Temple (p134) in Běijīng to learn more about this lopsided relationship. Although never fully integrated into the Chinese administrative system, the strategically important high plateau of Tibet was a cornerstone of Qing geopolitical strategy, particularly in the face of threats from the British and Russians.

> 'A great rebellion broke out in the 1860s, and was defeated in 1877 only at enormous expense and cost to life'

Xīnjiāng, home to the Muslim Uighur, was also under special administrative control throughout much of the Qing dynasty. A great rebellion broke out in the 1860s, and was defeated in 1877 only at enormous expense and cost to life on both sides. Regular provincial administration was established and Chinese people were settled within the Xīnjiāng borders.

Taiwan, home to a number of Austronesian peoples, had been colonised by the Dutch in the early 17th century and then occupied by the Ming loyalist Zheng Chenggong (Koxinga; 1624–62), who defeated the Dutch to make the island his base of resistance against the Manchu. The Manchu conquered Taiwan in 1683, and incorporated it into Fújiàn province. Garrison towns were constructed, evolving into walled cities that housed the Chinese officials dispatched to administer the territory. In 1872, after the island was briefly occupied by the Japanese, the Manchu made it into an independent province. In 1895 it was ceded to the Japanese as part of the settlement following the Sino-Japanese War of 1894. Nevertheless, the issue of its relationship with the mainland remains a lasting point of contention.

The population of the Qing more than doubled from the middle of the 17th century to reach around 350 million at the end of the 18th century. This may have been due to the introduction of New World crops, which could be grown in relatively harsh conditions, as well as increasingly efficient famine relief and flood control. A surge in population unsurprisingly led to increased pressure on resources, and land-hungry Han migrants headed west and south into lands of aboriginal peoples. With them went the Qing administration, which soon had ethnic conflict on its hands and, ultimately, rebellions. Suppressing these placed an enormous strain on the imperial treasury, contributing to the dynasty's downward spiral in the 19th century.

The Opium War & British Hong Kong

The early Qing emperors had shown a relatively open attitude towards Europeans in China, but this changed in the 18th century. Qianlong, ruler from 1736 to 1795, imposed strict controls on maritime trade, which from 1757 was limited to the single port of Guǎngzhōu.

Chinese exports well exceeded imports at Guǎngzhōu until Westerners hit upon the opium trade. Opium had long been a popular drug in China, but had been outlawed since the early 18th century. The Portuguese first discovered that there was profit to be made through opium, and began trading it between India and China. The British soon joined in. Stronger Chinese

1557	c 1640
The Portuguese establish a permanent trade base in Macau	The traditional *qipao* becomes a fashionable frock for women

prohibitions against the use and sale of the drug followed, but were far from effective as many officials were opium addicts and therefore assisted in smuggling it into China. By the early 19th century the opium trade had grown to the point of shifting the balance in trade in favour of the Westerners.

In March 1839 Lin Zexiu, an official of great personal integrity, was dispatched to Guǎngzhōu to put a stop to the illegal traffic once and for all. He acted promptly, demanding and eventually getting some 20,000 chests of opium stored by the British in Guǎngzhōu. The British believed they were due compensation and, without it, had the pretext for military action. In 1840 a British naval force assembled in Macau and moved up the coast to Běi He, not far from Běijīng. The Opium War was on.

The emperor watched with mild distress and authorised a negotiation that managed to fob off the first British force with a treaty that neither side ended up recognising. This increased British frustration, leading to an attack on Chinese positions close to Guǎngzhōu.

A second treaty was drawn up, ceding Hong Kong to the British, and calling for indemnities of Y6,000,000 and the full resumption of trade. The furious Qing emperor refused to recognise the treaty, and in 1841 British forces once again headed up the coast, taking Fújiàn and eastern Zhèjiāng. In the spring of 1842 an army inflated with reinforcements moved up the Yangzi River. With British guns trained on Nánjīng, the Qing fighting spirit evaporated and they reluctantly signed the humiliating Treaty of Nanking (Nanjing). This left Hong Kong in the hands of the British 'in perpetuity'.

In 1898 the New Territories adjoining Kowloon were 'leased' to the British for 99 years; the British later agreed to hand the entire colony back to China when the lease on the New Territories expired. For more details on the handover, see p519.

'The Taipings forbade gambling, opium, tobacco and alcohol, and outlawed foot binding for women, prostitution and slavery'

Christ's Kid Brother?

By the 19th century the increased presence of missionaries had fuelled hatred against 'foreign devils', leading to further rebellion throughout the provinces (see the boxed text, below).

Also at this time, the Taiping Rebellion erupted in 1850 in the southern province of Guǎngxī, and commanded forces of 600,000 men and 500,000 women as it raged through central and eastern China. The Taipings owed much of their ideology to Christianity. Its leader was Hong Xiuquan, a failed examination candidate from Guǎngdōng province whose encounters with Western missionaries had led him to believe he was the younger brother of Jesus Christ. The Taipings forbade gambling, opium, tobacco and alcohol,

---

BOXED UP

Culled from secret societies, the Boxers were a xenophobic group who erupted in rebellion at the end of the 19th century with violent attacks on missionaries and their families. Tired of the foreigners themselves, the Qing Court decided to support the Boxers. Armed with this backing and with charms and martial-arts techniques that they believed made them impervious to Western bullets, the Boxers began massacring foreigners at random and the famous 50-day siege of Běijīng's Foreign Legations began. It wasn't long before Western allies landed, handed the Qing Court a crippling foreign debt and knocked the Boxers down for the count.

1644	1751
Conquerors from Manchuria establish the Qing dynasty	Tibet becomes a Chinese colony

DRAGON WOMAN

Like many other Qing-dynasty teenagers, at the age of 15, Cixi (1835–1908) gave up her true love to become one of Emperor Xianfeng's concubines. Her cunningness and intelligence soon made her a favourite of the emperor, particularly after she gave birth to his only son in 1856. Cixi's subsequent rise to power was largely due to the convenient deaths of her adversaries. Xianfeng died at the age of 30 and his empress followed suit a few years later. This made Cixi's five-year-old son, Tongzhi, the new emperor, and Cixi herself the ruling Dowager Empress.

Cixi held on to the government reins for over 40 years in total, galloping over anyone who got in her way – including her own son and, on his death, Emperor Guangxu, whom she positioned to replace her son. Other opponents were slowly starved, thrown down wells or locked away. She spent her reign focusing on her own position rather than the country's; at the end of her life she left nine storerooms of personal treasures, a refurbished Summer Palace and the Qing dynasty in an irreparable state of decline. To see one of her more ridiculous 'achievements', take a gander at the marble boat in Běijīng's Summer Palace (p139).

advocated agricultural reform, and outlawed foot binding for women, prostitution and slavery. The rebellion took tens of millions of lives before being suppressed in 1864 by a coalition of Qing and Western forces – the Europeans preferring to deal with a corrupt and weak Qing government rather than a powerful, united China governed by the Taipings.

The Second Opium War

With Hong Kong in the hands of the British following the first Opium War, official trade was diverted to Shànghǎi. This left Hong Kong's economy in dire straits. With the attention of the Qing court focused on the Taiping Rebellion, the foreign powers struck again. The Anglo-French expedition of 1856 to 1860, sometimes called the Second Opium War, ended with the occupation of Běijīng and the flight of the court to Jehol (Chéngdé; p191). The final outcome was the Treaty of Tianjin, which opened further Treaty ports and established a regular diplomatic corps in Běijīng. At the same time, further massive rebellions were brewing: the Nian in central north China, the Panthay in Yúnnán and the Donggan in the northwest.

'The unique architecture and atmosphere of the old French Concession makes it worth a wander even today'

Bringing Home the Enemy

In the second half of the 19th century China sent embassies and students to the West. The goal was to pick up pointers from the enemy on how to strengthen Chinese military technology and industrial development. The Treaty-port cities, especially Shànghǎi, became the face of modernisation in China. Factories, banks, newspapers, new-style schools, bicycles, trains, and eventually motor cars, trade unions, chambers of commerce and political parties all made their appearance. In Shànghǎi, land conceded to Western nations quickly outgrew the old city. The unique architecture and atmosphere of the old French Concession makes it worth a wander even today (p253).

In the late 1890s China was in danger of being 'cut up like a melon, divided like a bean', as further leases of land and spheres of influence were ceded to the foreign powers. The Western powers were soon joined by the Japanese who, after a small scrap on Korean soil with Chinese forces, were ceded Taiwan in 1895. The same treaty granted the Japanese (and thereby other

1839	1842
The British hand over 20,000 chests of opium to Chinese officials, the pretext for the Opium Wars	Hong Kong is ceded to the British in perpetuity

100 DAYS REFORMS

A visionary reformer, Kang Youwei (1858–1927) became a key adviser to the Qing emperor following China's disastrous war with Japan. The result was the famous '100 Days Reforms' of 1898, which were expected to set China on the modernising path already taken by Japan. Reforms to the bureaucracy and examination system were proposed, as well as social reforms like the abolition of foot binding. Sadly, '100 Days' ended with a palace coup staged by the supposedly retired Dowager Empress Cixi, the house arrest of the Emperor Guangxu, the execution of some reformist activists and the flight of others, including Kang.

foreign powers) the right to construct their own factories in Shànghǎi. In 1898 Germany gained a lease in Qīngdǎo after Lutheran missionaries were murdered inland. They commenced building a railway that became the focus of protests by local people upset at the disturbance of feng shui. You'll still find a strong 'Germanness' in the air when you visit Qīngdǎo, in its brewery (p226) and old town architecture.

The Fall of the Qing

In 1908 the Dowager Empress died and two-year-old Emperor Puyi ascended to the throne. The Qing was now rudderless and teetered on the brink of collapse.

As an increasing number of new railways were financed and built by foreigners, public anger grew and gave birth to the Railway Protection Movement that spread and took on an anti-Qing nature. The movement turned increasingly violent, especially in Sìchuān, and troops were taken from Wǔhàn to quell the disturbances.

As it happened, republican revolutionaries in Wǔhàn were already planning an uprising. With troops dispensed to Sìchuān, they seized the opportunity and were able to not only take control of Wǔhàn, but to ride on the back of the large-scale Railway Protection uprisings to victory all over China.

On 29 December 1911, representatives from 17 provinces throughout China gathered to establish the Provisional Republican Government of China. China's long dynastic cycle had come to an end.

EARLY DAYS OF THE REPUBLIC

On the same day that the Provisional Republican Government of China was established, Sun Yatsen (1866–1925) was elected as its provisional president. Educated in Hawaii and Hong Kong, a Christian and trained medical practitioner, Sun developed a political programme based on the 'Three Principles of the People': nationalism, popular sovereignty and livelihood. In 1895 his 'Revive China Society' initiated one of the country's first republican uprisings, after which Sun fled to Japan and on to Europe. Determined to arrest and execute him, Qing authorities hunted Sun down in London, where they kidnapped him and held him in the Chinese embassy. Sun managed to sneak out a message to one of his teachers who, in turn, alerted the British Government. The Chinese embassy was forced to release their prisoner.

Sun went on to build backing for the revolution he dreamt of for China. Supporters from Chinese communities abroad, as well as among disaffected members of the Qing army, grew in number. When his revolutionist followers

A modern classic, *The Last Emperor* (1988) is the tragic story of Puyi, China's final emperor who ascended the throne at age two. Although it's rather slow-paced, this film boasts great cinematography and is well worth it if you have a few hours to spare.

1850	1908
The anti-Qing Taiping Rebellion erupts but ultimately fails to establish its Christian ideology throughout China	Two-year-old Puyi ascends the throne as China's last emperor

began their campaign for victory in Wǔhàn, Sun watched from abroad. It wasn't until the meeting in Nánjīng in December 1911 and the establishment of the Provisional Republic of China that Sun returned to his homeland to be named president.

Lacking the power to force a Manchu abdication, Sun had no choice but to call on the assistance of Yuan Shikai, the head of the imperial army, and the same man that the Manchu had called on to put down the republican uprisings. The republicans promised Yuan Shikai the presidency if he could negotiate the abdication of the emperor, which he achieved. The favour cost the republicans dearly. Yuan Shikai placed himself at the head of the republican movement and forced Sun Yatsen to stand down.

Yuan lost no time in dissolving the Provisional Republican Government and amending the constitution to make himself president for life. When this met with regional opposition, he took the natural next step in 1915 of pronouncing himself China's latest emperor. Yúnnán seceded, taking Guǎngxī, Guìzhōu and much of the rest of the south with it. Forces were sent to bring the breakaway provinces back into the imperial ambit, and in the midst of it all, Yuan died.

Between 1916 and 1927 the government in Běijīng lost power over the far-flung provinces and China was effectively fragmented into semi-autonomous regions governed by warlords. Nevertheless, Sun's labour had not been in vain. On 4 May 1919 large demonstrations took place outside the Gate of Heavenly Peace (p126) in Běijīng following the decision of the WWI Allies to pass defeated Germany's rights in Shāndōng over to Japan. This surge of nationalist sentiment in China began a movement that was rooted in Sun's earlier revolution and paved the way for the changes that were to come.

Wild Swans by Jung Chang offers a backdoor view into Chinese history, following three generations of women from the final days of Imperialism to post–Cultural Revolution China. She followed this epic tale in 2005 with her collaborative warts-and-all portrait of Mao Zedong, *Mao: The Unknown Story,* cowritten by Jon Halliday.

KUOMINTANG & COMMUNISTS

By 1920 the Kuomintang (KMT; Nationalist Party) had emerged as the dominant political force in eastern and southern China. The other main contender was the Chinese Communist Party (CCP), composed of Marxist groups who had banded together in the same year. While each group had differing visions for a modern China, enough common ground existed for the establishment of a united front (partly prompted by Sun Yatsen's need for military assistance from the Soviet Union) between the CCP and the Kuomintang.

The union was short-lived. After Sun Yatsen's death in 1925 a power struggle emerged in the Kuomintang between those sympathetic to the communists and those who favoured a capitalist state supported by a military dictatorship. The latter group was headed by Chiang Kaishek (1887–1975).

In 1926 Chiang Kaishek attempted to grind the growing influence of communists to a halt by expanding his own power base. He attempted this first through a Northern Expedition that set out to wring power from the remaining warlords. The following year he took more direct action, ordering the massacre of thousands of Shànghǎi communists and trade union representatives.

By the middle of 1928 the Northern Expedition had reached Běijīng, and a national government was established with Chiang holding both military and political leadership. Nevertheless, only about half of the country was

1911–16	1927
Dynastic rule comes to an end with Sun Yatsen's Republican Government	Chiang Kaishek's Kuomintang massacres over 5000 communists in Shànghǎi

under the direct control of the Kuomintang; the rest was still ruled by local warlords.

At this time China was heavily laden with social problems: child slave labour in factories; domestic slavery and prostitution; the destitute starving in the streets; and strikes ruthlessly suppressed by foreign and Chinese factory owners. The communists proposed solutions to these problems, namely the removal of the Kuomintang. Not surprisingly, Chiang became obsessed with stamping out the influence of the communists.

Grassroots Rebellion

After the massacre of 1927, the communists became divided in their views of where to base their rebellion – on large urban centres or in the country-side. After costly defeats in Nánchāng and Chángshā, the tide of opinion started to shift towards Mao Zedong (1893–1976; p506), who advocated rural-based revolt.

Communist-led uprisings in other parts of the country met with some success; however, the communist armies remained small and hampered by limited resources. It wasn't until 1930 that the ragged communist forces had turned into an army of perhaps 40,000, which presented such a serious challenge to the Kuomintang that Chiang waged extermination campaigns against them. He was defeated each time, and the communist army continued to expand its territory.

The Long March(es)

Chiang's fifth extermination campaign began in October 1933. Many of the communist troupes had begun disregarding Mao's authority and instead took the advice of those who advocated meeting Chiang's troops in pitched battles. This strategy proved disastrous. By October 1934 the communists had suffered heavy losses and were hemmed into a small area in Jiāngxī. On the brink of defeat, the communists decided to retreat from Jiāngxī and march north to Shaanxi to join up with other communist armies in Shaanxi, Gānsù and Níngxià.

Rather than one long march, there were several, as various communist armies in the south made their way to Shaanxi. The most famous (and commonly referred to as *the* Long March) was from Jiāngxī province. Beginning in October 1934, it took a year to complete and covered 8000km over some of the world's most inhospitable terrain. On the way the communists confiscated the property of officials, landlords and tax-collectors, and redistributed land to the peasants whom they armed by the thousands with weapons captured from the Kuomintang. Soldiers were left behind to organise guerrilla groups to harass the enemy. Of the 90,000 people who started out in Jiāngxī, only 20,000 made it to Shaanxi. Fatigue, sickness, exposure, enemy attacks and desertion all took their toll.

The march brought together many people who held top positions after 1949, including Mao Zedong, Zhou Enlai, Zhu De, Lin Biao, Deng Xiaoping and Liu Shaoqi. It also established Mao as the paramount leader of the Chinese communist movement. En route, the posse took a breather in Zūnyì (p673), Guìzhōu; if you're in the neighbourhood, you can take in some of the sights. Serious Long March history buffs might also check out Lúdìng (p781) in Sìchuān.

Red Star Over China, by Edgar Snow, is a journalist's first-hand perspective of China in the early days of the Communist Revolution. His portrayal of Mao may seem overly sympathetic, if not partisan, but Snow considers the situation from several perspectives.

1935	1937
Mao Zedong is recognised as head of the Chinese Communist Party in a meeting at Zūnyì	Japan invades China

Japanese Invasion

All the internal upheaval going on in China gave the Japanese the moment they'd been waiting for. In September 1931 they invaded and occupied Manchuria, setting up a puppet state with Puyi, the last Manchu emperor. (Check out his digs and one of the settings for Bertolucci's film *The Last Emperor* in Chángchūn, p375.) Chiang, still obsessed with the threat of the communists, did nothing to resist Japan's invasion and instead focused on his fifth extermination drive. The Kuomintang was bitterly criticised for not defending against the Japanese.

In particular, Manchurian General Zhang Xueliang (1898–2001) was not impressed. In 1936 he kidnapped President Chiang Kaishek and forced him to agree to a Second United Front with the CCP to resist Japan. Zhang, hero of the hour, later surrendered to the Kuomintang and spent the next half-century under house arrest in China and then in Taiwan. He was eventually released after Chiang Kaishek's death in 1975.

The site www.china knowledge.de/History /history.htm has in-depth coverage of China's dynasties and eras, with links to more specific information on everything from the religion to the technology to the economy of each period.

The rest of China was invaded by Japan in the middle of 1937. The Nánjīng massacre of 1937 (see the boxed text, p287), human experiments in biological warfare factories in Hāěrbīn (p392) and 'burn all, loot all, kill all' campaigns quickly made it one of the most brutal occupations of the 20th century. China experienced massive internal migrations, and was subjected to a process of divide and rule through the establishment of puppet governments.

The Kuomintang was forced into retreat by the Japanese occupation. Its wartime capital was Chóngqìng (p799), a higgledy-piggledy town piled up on mountains in the upper reaches of the Yangzi River. The city was subjected to heavy Japanese bombardments, but logistical difficulties prevented it from being approached by land.

Civil War

Following Japan's defeat and the end of WWII, the USA attempted unsuccessfully to negotiate a settlement between the CCP and the Kuomintang. The CCP had expanded enormously during the war years, filling a vacuum in local government in vast areas behind and beyond Japanese lines, and creating a base from which it would successfully challenge the Kuomintang's claims to legitimacy.

Civil war broke out in 1946. While their base at Yán'ān (p436) was destroyed by the Nationalists, communist forces managed to outmanoeuvre the Kuomintang on the battle ground of Manchuria. Three great battles were fought in 1948 and 1949 in which the Kuomintang were not only defeated, but thousands of Kuomintang troops defected to the communists. The USA, which had lost its wartime hero status and become an object of popular vilification in China, was dismayed by the failure of the Kuomintang and refused it further support. Meanwhile, the Soviet Union played a two-faced game of alliances in the early postwar period, recognising the Nationalist government, but eventually facilitating CCP ambitions.

In Běijīng on 1 October 1949 Mao Zedong proclaimed the foundation of the People's Republic of China (PRC, Zhōnghuá Rénmín Gònghéguó). Chiang Kaishek fled to the island of Formosa (Taiwan), taking with him the entire gold reserves of the country, and what was left of his air force and navy. To prevent an attack from the mainland, President Truman ordered a protective US naval blockade.

1946	1949
Civil war breaks out	The PRC is established

THE PEOPLE'S REPUBLIC OF CHINA

The PRC began its days as a bankrupt nation. Unbridled inflation and a Kuomintang legacy of economic mismanagement left the economy in chaos. The country had just 19,200km of railways and 76,800km of useable roads – all in bad condition. Irrigation works had broken down, and livestock and animal populations were dwindling. Agricultural output plummeted and industrial production was half that of the prewar period.

With the communist takeover, China seemed to become a different country. Unified by the elation of victory and the immensity of the task before them, and further bonded by the Korean War and the necessity to defend the new regime from possible US invasion, the communists made the 1950s a dynamic period. They embarked upon land reform, recognised the role of women and attempted to restore the economy.

By 1953 inflation had been halted, industrial production was back to prewar levels, and land had been confiscated from landlords and redistributed to the peasants. On the basis of earlier Soviet models, the Chinese embarked on a massive five-year plan that was fairly successful in lifting production.

At the same time the CCP increased its social control by organising the people according to their work units *(dānwèi)*, and dividing the country into 21 provinces, five autonomous regions and two municipalities (Běijīng and Shànghǎi). Around 2200 county governments held jurisdiction over nearly one million party sub-branches.

A Hundred Flowers

Behind the PRC's rapid economic development lingered immense social problems. Many Kuomintang intellectuals had stayed rather than flee to Taiwan, and still more overseas Chinese, many of them highly qualified, returned to China after its 'liberation' to help in the huge task of reconstruction. Returning Chinese and those of suspect backgrounds were given extensive re-education courses in special universities. Meanwhile, writers, artists and film-makers were subject to strict ideological controls guided by Mao's writings on art.

In the upper levels of the party, opinions were divided as to how to deal with these intellectuals and artists. Mao proposed 'letting a hundred flowers bloom' in the arts and 'a hundred schools of thought contend' in the sciences by welcoming open criticism. In 1957 intellectuals around the country responded with glee. Complaints poured in on everything from party corruption to control of artistic expression, from the unavailability of foreign literature to low standards of living; but most of all, criticisms focused on the CCP monopoly on power and the abuses that went with it.

Either the party had second thoughts about the critique or, as many now believe, the campaign was a trap to 'weed out' rightists. An anti-rightist campaign was launched and within six months 300,000 intellectuals had been branded rightists, removed from their jobs and, in many cases, incarcerated or sent to labour camps for thought reform. Some would stay in these camps for up to 20 years.

To Live (1994) follows one family through the Communist Revolution, the Great Leap Forward and the Cultural Revolution, depicting how these monumental upheavals affected the average Chinese citizen. Made in China, but later banned, this film is interesting for its Chinese perspective on historical events.

The Great Leap Forward

China's agricultural output continued to lag and, as urban populations burgeoned around industrialised areas, the question of how to feed the people grew increasingly urgent.

1957	1958–60
Mao weeds out 'rightist' intellectuals through the Hundred Flowers campaign	The Great Leap Forward causes mass starvation

China embarked on the Great Leap Forward (1958–60), one of the greatest failed economic experiments in human history. A radical programme was initiated to create massive agricultural communes, drawing large numbers of people from the country and urban areas into enormous water control and irrigation projects. In Mao's view, revolutionary zeal and mass cooperative effort could overcome any obstacle and transform the Chinese landscape into a productive paradise.

The communists tried to abolish money and all private property, and told everyone to build backyard blast furnaces to increase steel production. Lacking iron ore, peasants had to melt down farm tools, pots and doorknobs to meet their quota of steel 'production'. The villages later discovered that the steel produced was basically worthless.

Despite the enthusiastic forecasts for agricultural production, there remained little incentive to work in the fields. Large numbers of rural workers engaged in the worthless blast furnace projects, resulting in a massive slump in grain output. Bad weather in 1959 and the withdrawal of Soviet aid in 1960 made matters worse.

All effort was made to cover up the ensuing disaster and so no foreign assistance was sought. China plunged into a famine of staggering proportions – an estimated 30 million Chinese starved to death (some put the figure at 60 million). The enormous failure of the Great Leap Forward led Mao to resign as head of state, although he remained Chairman of the Communist Party.

Sino-Soviet Split

Mao watched in horror as the USSR developed a policy of peaceful coexistence with the USA. Khrushchev's de-Stalinisation speech and what Mao saw as growing moderation in the Soviet leadership did nothing to mend Mao's increasingly frosty view of his neighbours. When Khrushchev refused to provide China with the promised prototype atomic bomb and sided with the Indians in a Sino-Indian border dispute, Sino-Soviet relations hit a low. In 1960 the Soviets brought their foreign experts home from China.

The Cultural Revolution

Mao's extreme views, his recent disastrous policy decisions and his opposition to bureaucratisation led to his increasing isolation within the party. To get back into the limelight of leadership, he set about cultivating a personality cult. His right-hand man was Lin Biao, the minister of defence and head of the People's Liberation Army (PLA). He was also supported by Yao Wenyuan, Zhang Chunqiao and Jiang Qing (Mao's wife), a group that – along with Wang Hongwen – later became known as 'the Gang of Four'.

In the early 1960s Lin compiled a collection of Mao's selected thoughts into the 'little red book'. Studied by PLA troops and introduced into the general education system, this was to become one of the symbols of the era; you can still find well-used copies for sale in markets throughout the country.

In the early 1960s a play was released that criticised Mao. A campaign against the play began towards the end of 1966; the purge of the arts that followed was the springboard for the Cultural Revolution (Wénhuà Dàgémìng; 1966–76). Sanctioned by Mao, wall posters went up at Beijing University attacking the university administration and criticising Mao's opposition within the CCP. Before long students were being issued red armbands and taking to

In the 1960s and 1970s, labyrinthine tunnels were built beneath Běijīng in the event of nuclear war with Russia; they can still be seen at the Beijing Underground City (see the boxed text, p130).

1966	1971
The birth of the Red Guards and the Cultural Revolution	The US national table-tennis team becomes the first American delegation to set foot in China in 49 years; Nixon soon follows

the streets. The Red Guards (Hóngwèibīng) had been born. By August 1966 Mao was reviewing mass parades of the Red Guards in Tiananmen Square, chanting and waving copies of his little red book.

Nothing was sacred in the brutal onslaught of the Red Guards as they rampaged through the country. Schools were shut down; intellectuals, writers and artists were dismissed, killed, persecuted or sent to labour in the countryside; scientific, artistic, literary and cultural publications ceased; and temples were ransacked and monasteries disbanded. Physical reminders of China's 'feudal', 'exploitative' or 'capitalist' past – everything from monuments to musical instruments – were destroyed.

Sometimes for fear of being accused themselves, neighbours and even family members began to turn on one another in the search for 'capitalist roaders'. Millions of people are estimated to have died in these years through beatings, executions, suicide or denial of medical care. Violence, social disorder and economic upheaval were rife. The 'four olds' – old customs, old habits, old culture and old thinking – were all to be eliminated. Gender equality was promoted, but there was little room for personal life. Families were split up; sex and romance were frowned upon. Dress codes were as strict as under the most rigid religious regime with the blue 'Mao suit'.

For Mao, the Cultural Revolution succeeded in establishing his power and in supplanting President Liu Shaoqi and party Secretary-General Deng Xiaoping. Liu Shaoqi died in prison in 1969, a fact concealed from the public till 1980. According to the official version of events, Lin Biao plotted a coup in 1971, was exposed, and died in a mysterious plane crash over Mongolia.

Some measure of political stability returned during the closing years of the Cultural Revolution. Zhou Enlai, who had supported Mao from the sidelines, exercised the most influence in the day-to-day governing of China. Among other things, he worked towards restoring China's trade and diplomatic contacts with the outside world. In the 1970s China was admitted into the UN, re-establishing formal diplomatic relations with the USA in 1979.

In 1973 Deng Xiaoping, vilified as China's 'No 2 Capitalist Roader' during the Cultural Revolution, returned to power as Deputy Premier. Nevertheless, Běijīng politics remained factional and divided. On the one side was Zhou, Deng and a faction of 'moderates' or 'pragmatists', and on the other were the 'radicals', 'leftists' or 'Maoists' led by Jiang Qing. As Zhou's health declined, the radicals gradually gained the upper hand.

During this period Mao was watching from the wings. He'd been sick for many years and was diagnosed with Lou Gehrig's disease, an extremely rare motor-neuron disorder that left him dead by September 1976. The official line soon surfaced that Mao was 70% right and just 30% wrong in his leadership of the country.

Premier Zhou Enlai died in January 1976, and in April a crowd of mourners in Tiananmen Square erupted into a demonstration that was violently suppressed. Deng fell under attack again from Madame Mao and disappeared from public view as Hua Guofeng, Mao's chosen and groomed protégé, was made acting premier. When the Gang of Four opposed Hua, he had them arrested. Celebrations took place throughout China. When the Gang finally came to trial in 1980, the blame for the entire Cultural Revolution fell on

The Private Life of Chairman Mao, by Li Zhisui, is a fascinating and intimate (if somewhat disturbing) look into the world of this historical giant. Li was Mao's personal physician for 22 years and tells us everything from Mao's sexual habits to his political views.

1973	1976
Deng Xiaoping returns to power as Deputy Premier	Mao Zedong dies, aged 83

their shoulders. Jiang Qing and Zhang Chunqiao were sentenced to death, with a two-year reprieve. Neither was ever actually executed. Jiang Qing's death sentence was commuted and she lived under house arrest until 1991, when she committed suicide by hanging.

Most of China's middle-aged and elderly population are survivors of the Cultural Revolution; be mindful if discussing this period of history with them as few went untouched by the horrors of the time.

POST-MAO CHINA

The final two decades of the 20th century saw a grand reversal of the traditional knee-jerk obeisance to Marxist-Leninist ideology. With Mao Zedong gone, the celebrated Deng Xiaoping era commenced as he returned to power for the third time as vice-premier, vice-chairman of the party and chief of staff. The event marked his emergence as paramount leader of the nation, a position he rapidly consolidated, calling for wide-ranging reforms.

Aiming to undo the damage inflicted on China by the Cultural Revolution and decades of post-revolutionary economic mismanagement, Deng Xiaoping unveiled his programme of the 'Four Modernisations' (agriculture, industry, science and technology, and defence). In the process, China increased contact with the capitalist economies of the West and opened its doors to foreign visitors.

Special Economic Zones were established along China's coast, while in rural China the 'Responsibility System' allowed people to sell their agricultural surpluses on the open market. In 1993 Deng Xiaoping famously proclaimed that 'to get rich is glorious' as the government began to trim down capital-squandering state-owned industries. The new 'ideology' was declared 'socialism with Chinese characteristics', although it was clearly an overdue attempt to pull the land out of its potentially disastrous economic and social tailspin.

Deng Xiaoping was hardly an economic guru, but his tinkering unleashed the long-repressed capitalist instincts of the Chinese. Yet despite its very real successes, one of the lasting failures of the Deng Xiaoping reform era was its dearth of political evolution. The era directly paved the way to the China of today, with all of its massive impetus and glaring social and political contradictions.

Those contradictions are still best exemplified by the events of and leading up to 4 June 1989. Since 1978 demands had been heard for a 'fifth modernisation': democracy. The mass memorial that followed the death of reform-minded Party Secretary-General Hu Yaobang in 1989 turned into a popular, peaceful rebellion. Workers and hundreds of thousands of students gathered in Běijīng's Tiananmen Square (p124) to press ever-escalating demands for political reform on the beleaguered party leadership. After imposing martial law on the capital, Deng Xiaoping sanctioned the forcible dispersal of the demonstrators. Hundreds were killed in the surrounding streets as the army cleared the squares late on 3 June and in the early hours of 4 June.

The era also saw the arrival of population control, first introduced in 1980. The strict measures certainly slowed China's growing population, but at the cost of intervening in one of the most basic of human rights, that of reproduction. Unforseen further costs include a rapidly ageing society, the psychological harm inflicted on children growing up without siblings and the 'bachelor bomb': a massive body of young men (23 million-strong) who will never find a Chinese wife, a consequence of the practice of female-specific abortions.

1980	1987
The one-child policy is enforced	*The Last Emperor*, filmed in the Forbidden City, collects an Oscar for Best Picture

THE 21ST CENTURY

As China grew in stature at the dawn of the 21st century, Deng Xiaoping's successor, Jiang Zemin, claimed popular success in playing the world stage. During his tenure, Hong Kong and Macau returned to China, Běijīng was successful in its Olympics bid for 2008 and China was steered into the World Trade Organization (WTO). Nevertheless, China's economic picture remained at best hazy as Jiang pinned all of his hopes on the WTO, while the lumbering state sector remained an unresolved burden on the economy.

Groomed to take the seat of power since the early 1990s, Hu Jintao – who became president in 2003 – is China's first modern leader to come into the communist fold post-1949. Hopes that Hu was a reformer were quietly suffocated, however, as the president committed himself to unbending controls over political opposition and a tightening of the management of information.

In Hu's bid to purge society of 'liberal elements', policing of the internet was even more rigorously enforced and publications (including the notable closure of the high-profile *Freezing Point*, a popular weekly supplement of the *China Youth Daily*) were shut down. Nicknamed the 'Great Firewall of China', Běijīng has installed a highly effective system for filtering the internet, with around 10% of websites blocked. The official line is that the state remains opposed to the 'spreading of news with content that is against national security and public interest'.

Aware that it is in a struggle for its own survival, the Communist Party has increasingly relaxed controls preventing the creation of private wealth. The result is a land of opportunity pumped up by astonishing growth in GDP. It is also a land riven by a growing divide between the haves and have-nots, a spectacular trouncing of the most basic axiom of Marxist and CCP orthodoxy. The supreme irony has been that the very force that communism arose to overturn (capitalism) gave the CCP a new lease of life.

The principal fault-line lies between the flourishing south and east-coast provinces and the more backward inland provinces, especially the land-locked west. To redress the imbalance, the government has launched an ambitious Develop the West campaign to lure businesses, investment and graduates to China's poorer western regions.

Rural protests have increased in frequency in recent years, sparked by land confiscations, environmental pollution and high taxes, levied by corrupt officials. According to Chinese government figures, 74,000 riots or demonstrations took place during 2004, up from 58,000 the previous year. With increasing concern at the threat posed by protest and revolt, Běijīng has plans to install special police units in 36 Chinese cities, specifically targeted at quelling riots and disturbances.

China has also made some astonishing achievements in recent years, putting its first man in space in 2003 (a feat it repeated in 2005), completing the Three Gorges Dam in 2006 – ahead of schedule – and, in the same year, putting finishing touches to a railway to Lhasa in Tibet, a technically challenging feat that some said was impossible. Also in the pipeline were plans for a further 48 airports to meet the massive surge in air travel.

China's economic advances over recent years have continued to dazzle (see p61). In 2004 China's GDP grew by a flabbergasting 9.6%. China now accounts for almost 30% of global steel production and a whopping 46%

'In Hu's bid to purge society of "liberal elements", policing of the internet was even more rigorously enforced and publications were shut down'

1989	1997
Hundreds of civilians are killed by Chinese troops in the streets around Tiananmen Square	Britain returns Hong Kong to the PRC

COMING HOME *Lin Gu*

Wang Ruihai will never eat instant noodles again. He survived on the cheap noodles in the winter of 2003, when he couldn't find himself a job in Běijīng. Rather than being unemployed, the 25-year-old enrolled in a two-month computer-hardware maintenance course, believing that ignorance of a computer is even worse than illiteracy. All he had left after tuition and rent of the room with a broken window and no heating he shared with three other trainees was Y200 (about US$25).

Wang first came to Běijīng in the winter of 1999. 'Do you want to find something to do in Běijīng?' his father had asked him one day when they were toiling in the fields. Like most of his former schoolmates who were dashing off to the Chinese capital for work or college, the answer was obvious.

Together with his uncle, Wang left his family and headed for the big city, more than six hours from his village in Héběi province. They landed at a briquette factory, where Wang's job was to transport the honeycomb-shaped fire starters on a flat-board tricycle into factory storage. He earned Y700 (about US$88) a month, and life there was harsh. He almost lost a thumb to an assembly line. Less than three months passed before spring festival and the traditional time for family reunion, so Wang happily went home to the countryside.

Yet Běijīng kept calling to him. In 2001 Wang returned and worked for a cleaning company in a new apartment compound of 14 buildings in the northwest of the city, where the bulk of the residents were college teachers, foreign students and IT professionals. Every morning he got up at 3am, collected garbage from three apartment buildings by 5am and transported it to the processing station by 8am. His work clothes were often stained with sewage. Once, when Wang was about to share an elevator with a resident, the tenant frowned and covered her nose; at other times, they simply waited for the next elevator.

Wang doesn't blame them. 'The key to solving the problem of discrimination is in our own hands, as long as we try to make the best of ourselves.' All of Wang's workmates were rural migrants like himself, for no city resident had the least interest in this line of work. As everyone knows, all the dirty jobs in Běijīng are done by rural migrants.

Běijīng became a ghost city in spring 2003 when SARS evacuated the capital. Few dared to linger in a public space, but there were some exceptions: a team of volunteers came to Wang's workplace, distributing thermometers and gauze masks as preventive measures against SARS.

of world concrete production, while 40% of the world's television sets are made in China. The figures continue to astound, while perennial concerns that China's economy is overheating or facing meltdown have so far failed to shake overall confidence in foreign investment. Nay-sayers regularly point to the country's debt-ridden banking sector as a source of impending economic collapse, but the phenomenon of China's economic miracle has continued to surge ahead. Even property prices, which reached almost unsustainable levels in 2005, could only be marginally controlled by painful taxes imposed on vendors, in a bid to stifle speculation.

Modern China has few true intellectuals (out of fashion since the Hundred Flowers and the Cultural Revolution) or true ideologues, and the Communist Party has increasingly relied on nationalism to fill the ideological emptiness at the heart of society and to further shore up its standing and legitimacy. Meanwhile, a flowering of creeds and a growing interest in Christianity has similarly rushed to fill the spiritual vacuum. The ongoing crackdown on Falun Gong that began in 1999 is a measure of Běijīng's continual fear of

1999	2001
Falun Gong protest silently in Běijīng, prompting a crackdown	China joins the World Trade Organization

Later, they organised a party for lonely workers, and told Wang about a newly established cultural centre that tailored to rural migrants just like him.

The city's four million rural migrants have five nongovernment organisations that manage such gathering places. Out of 1.3 billion Chinese, around 150 million are migrating, mostly from the countryside to the city.

What motivates this giant mobile camp is the widening gap between rural and urban, poor and wealthy. There has long been an outcry for equal treatment towards rural migrants in terms of rights to work, medical care and education, with reports of injustices often occupying mainland newspaper headlines. For millions of hardworking women and men like Wang, their lot seems unlikely to change fast anytime soon. But small, incremental improvements are always possible.

Wang's most recent migration was in March 2005, when he became a photography assistant at a Taiwanese-owned wedding photo studio in downtown Běijīng, based on his one year as a trainee photographer in a small city in Héběi. The normal pay is about Y1000 (about US$125) per month, but it can rise up to Y1700 (about US$213) at peak season. It's the first step on the ladder.

Wang's boss, a young photographer surnamed Zhang, was impressed by Wang as being 'both attentive and reliable'. 'Glamorous as it may appear, this is a place where people with a lower-class background can possibly grab a chance,' Zhang says. 'You may speak Mandarin with an accent, but so what? As long as you have guts!'

Wang now finds his feelings for Běijīng are changing. Today, it's more than just a paying gig. He witnesses constant injustice against migrant workers, and yearns to do something about it. He joins other volunteers in visiting hospitalised migrants, and performs skits in schools for migrant children and at construction sites. He's also organised a photography team, where fellow migrants may exchange their ideas about photography while improving their photographic skills.

'Taking photos isn't just for fun. It's a way of documenting our lives,' he says. On a day off work, Wang likes to ride across the city on his bicycle, camera at his side. The remnants of an ancient courtyard being demolished by bulldozers, a gang of construction workers at lunch break taking in the shade – these are the typical targets of his lens.

A little timid and at 1.7m none too tall, Wang Ruihai is above all a good listener. He smiles as others exchange gossip at the cultural centre. The best moment for him, he says, is when they all sit down to eat together.

'It's like coming home.'

losing ground to noncommunist doctrines. The fate of Falun Gong prisoners in China is among the many human-rights issues regularly raised by international rights organisations.

Environmental issues also make for rather worrying reading. China's appetite for energy is growing daily: currently the nation accounts for 12% of world energy usage, but consumption is growing at four times the world average. In 2004, China overtook Japan as the world's second-largest importer of oil, after the USA. China is the world's largest miner of coal (about one-third of global production), and its coal mines are responsible for chronic pollution and a shocking level of industrial accidents (6000 deaths in 2005). Around 25 million trees are felled annually to feed the nation's appetite for disposable chopsticks. Many observers noted that the 2005 toxic chemical spill into the Songhua River that polluted Hāěrbīn's water supplies was an accident waiting to happen. The world also woke up to the knowledge that there are inadequate global resources to feed and supply a China aiming for the same living standards as the USA.

2003	2006
China sends its first astronaut into space	The Three Gorges Dam is completed

China is currently undergoing the largest rural–urban migration ever seen, with millions moving to the cities in search of work and bringing increasing pressure to bear on the environment. Amazingly, China has also become the world's third-largest food donor, despite becoming a net importer of food.

As China grows in self-belief, it is also making its presence felt in the international realm. China is investing heavily in Africa, part of a policy of diversifying its sources of oil in order to quench a growing thirst for fossil fuels, at a time when the Middle East is increasingly in turmoil.

However, China's growing international profile sits uneasily with its non-interventionist policies. Pragmatically business-minded, Běijīng takes little interest in human-rights abuses in countries it does or does not do business with. A case in point: China's lucrative oil deals with Khartoum encouraged it to oppose efforts to impose UN sanctions on Sudan for the massacres in Darfur. China has also befriended nations such as North Korea, Myanmar and Zimbabwe, states widely shunned by the rest of the international community. Long-standing ally North Korea is particularly dependent on Chinese goodwill (especially in the form of food and economic aid), but tested that friendship with its widely condemned nuclear weapons test in October 2006. Critics argue that for China to take a leading role in international affairs, it will need to be seen as more than a purely opportunistic player.

Sino-US relations continue to be of primary strategic importance, especially as China grows in regional and global importance. Optimists point to the growing interdependency of Chinese and American economic ties, and the more cordial atmosphere of cooperation since the Al-Qaeda attacks of 9/11. Pessimists see Taiwan as a potential flashpoint (the US has pledged to militarily support the island in the event of a Chinese invasion) between the two powers.

Běijīng's primary concerns remain domestic and close to home. Beset with concerns about Taiwan, Běijīng is increasingly frustrated at its rebuffed efforts at wooing the 'renegade province' back into the fold. Perhaps ironically, in 2006 Běijīng was pinning its hopes on the restoration of a Kuomintang government on the island, to banish fears of a declaration of Taiwanese independence from President Chen Shuibian.

Also hogging the headlines in China is Japan, a nation that China eyes with undiminished suspicion. Japan's failure to fully apologise for its invasion of China in the 1930s and the subsequent atrocities (see the boxed text, p287), along with the regular appearance of Japanese Prime Minister Junichiro Koizumi at the Yasukuni Shrine (where Japanese war criminals are honoured, among other war dead), enrages the Chinese. At the time of writing it was uncertain whether Koizumi's successor as prime minister, Shinzo Abe, would continue the controversial visits. Anti-Japanese sentiment is commonly heard, especially – and perhaps surprisingly – among the young. This, and Běijīng's continuing policy of promoting a spirit of nationalism among the Chinese, prompted the anti-Japanese riots of 2005.

The turbulent story of China continues unabated…

China's modern-day Triads (gangs associated with criminal activity, like drug trafficking) are believed to be the descendants of secret societies originally set up to resist the Manchus.

2006	2008
The railway to Lhasa in Tibet begins operation	Běijīng to host the 2008 Summer Olympic Games

The Culture Julie Grundvig

THE NATIONAL PSYCHE

China today is bursting with commercial and creative energy; everywhere you travel you'll see the vibrancy and strength of a people in the thrust of modernisation, while still trying to make peace with the past. As China leaps headfirst into the 21st century, it's seeking to find its place in the international community without compromising its rich cultural heritage.

China's humiliation at the hands of the West and Japan in the 19th and early 20th centuries still exerts a powerful influence on the Chinese psyche, creating for many a conflicting mix of emotions. The Chinese proudly extol their country's inventions of gunpowder, printing and paper currency, while simultaneously embracing Western business ideas and spending hours at late-night English classes. There's worry that Western values may destroy the heart of traditional Chinese culture, but there's also a strong drive to transform the insularity that has defined China for hundreds of years. More Chinese citizens want to be seen as participants in a global world, progressive and open to new ideas.

Modernisation has brought its share of headaches – pollution, rising crime, and unemployment, to name a few. The surge of new wealth in China has left millions behind. It's estimated that one out of eight Chinese live in absolute poverty and factory shutdowns have left millions unemployed. Mass migration of peasants to urban centres has put a huge toll on cities, causing water shortages, lack of housing and environmental pressure. The government has incentives in place to deal with these issues, but progress is very slow.

Even with so many changes taking place, traditional values persist. Many beliefs derive largely from the pervasive influence of Confucian philosophy on Chinese culture, which forms the very core of Chinese identity. The Chinese value the importance of the family, the cultivation of morality and self-restraint, and the emphasis on hard work and achievement. It's assumed that the family as a whole will thrive and prosper if harmony prevails at home. Strong family connections and community ties are what keep the Chinese going, even in times of difficulty.

Disillusionment with Communist party policies has resulted in more people speaking out and demanding changes. Private action groups are springing up all over the country, seeking to address social needs that are ignored or neglected by the government, including care of the disabled, equal rights for gays and lesbians, AIDS prevention, environmental protection and help for battered women. Artists and writers are freeing themselves from earlier political restraints, contributing to a burgeoning music, literary and art scene that has been stifled for many years. Censorship is still very common, though what defines something as 'taboo' or 'off limits' can be arbitrary.

With an increasingly open society, and with more exposure to the outside world, the Chinese have great hopes that their country will progress as a modern, equitable nation and be accepted as a strong player in the international community.

Big Breasts and Wide Hips by Mo Yan and translated by Howard Goldblatt (Arcade Publishing, 2004) traces the rise and decline of a Chinese family during the tumultuous 20th century.

LIFESTYLE

Chinese culture has always revolved around the family, considered the bedrock of a stable and harmonious society. There's a traditional belief that the more family members living under the same roof, the more prosperous the household. With most urban Chinese living in tiny apartments, the traditional family structure of many generations living together is changing, with younger generations moving out to pursue new career and educational opportunities. Parents enjoy a very tight bond with their children and extended family remains important, with grandparents commonly acting as caretakers for grandchildren while adult children work and financially support their ageing parents.

The Diary of Ma Yan (Harper Collins, 2004) is a translation of the diary of a teenage girl from rural Níngxià province who writes movingly of her family's struggle to pay for her education.

The rapid development of the past three decades has raised the standard of living for many Chinese, especially for those along the wealthy east coast. 'You are what you have' has become the motto for China's new yuppies, who see a car and a large apartment as the symbols of success. Also at the forefront of a changing China is the computer-savvy younger generation, who are not only downloading the latest pop songs, games and movies, but engaging in heated debates on everything from education to premarital sex on blogs and internet chat sites. The 2005 'Supergirl' phenomenon, an *American Idol*–type singing contest, selected its winner from more than 3.5 million text messages sent in by viewers. Out of all this techno-blitz, new voices are emerging to challenge the way China sees itself in the 21st century.

China has more than 100 million internet users.

Perhaps the biggest changes in China are attitudes towards sex and marriage. Many of China's younger generation are putting off marriage until they've completed university, settled into a good job and have acquired enough money to cover all the basics before settling down to raise a family. Divorce, traditionally looked down upon in Chinese society, is on the rise, and more young people are living together before tying the knot. These laid-back attitudes have raised fear in some who see the disintegration of traditional Chinese values.

The World (2004) by Jia Zhangke is an excellent look at the effects of globalisation in China, as seen through the eyes of young workers at a Běijīng theme park.

The most difficult social problem in China is the growing gap between rich and poor. City dwellers earn more than those in rural areas, who eke out a meagre living on diminishing plots of land, while trying to pay for rising costs in education and healthcare. Government incentives, such as cutting land tax and providing partial education benefits, have done little to stem the tide of rural migrants flooding into cities. Peasant unrest is on the rise and the government knows it must act quickly to prevent further dissent.

China is an enormous country with many regional differences and you'll find that the behaviour of the Chinese may differ from place to place, according to custom and exposure to the outside world. This is especially true in the countryside, which can offer a remarkably different view of China than what can be seen in cities. You'll come away amazed at the diversity of the people and places you've encountered.

ETIQUETTE DOS & DON'TS

- When beckoning to someone, wave them over to you with your palm down, motioning to yourself.
- If someone gives you a gift, put it aside to open later to avoid appearing greedy.
- Never write anything in red ink unless you're correcting an exam. Red ink is used for letters of protest.
- Don't give clocks as gifts. The phrase 'to give a clock' in Mandarin sounds too much like 'attend a funeral'.
- Always take your shoes off when entering a Chinese home.
- When meeting a Chinese family, greet the eldest person first as a sign of respect.
- Always present things to people with both hands, showing that what you are offering is the fullest extent of yourself.

VISITING THE HAN, SOLO

China has done its best to degrade its historical sites through war, revolution and that latest bane: real-estate development and road widening. What's left is frequently hung with ticket prices that rise in arbitrary, massive increments. Leave the tour coaches behind, escape the big cities and go in search of the Han Chinese in their homely heartland, the traditional village, which tends to have more independent economies, and stunning surrounding countryside to boot. Money goes to generating the villages and provides locals with a source of income other than agriculture. Furthermore, trips to small villages, such as **Guóliàngcūn** (p467), **Zhūjiāyù** (p210) and **Lǐkēng** (p495), can be very cheap as you can stay in local family hostels, rather than in white-tiled, midrange Chinese hotels with cheap marble foyers, scowling staff and 3am wake-up calls from xiǎojie (young, often unmarried women) eager to give you a massage. See China's Traditional Villages tour (p31) in the Itineraries chapter for suggested escapes. You may never want to come back.

ECONOMY

Under Mao, China's economy was a prisoner to ideology and incompetence. Deng Xiaoping's tenure (essentially 1977–97) was a period of reform, continued in perhaps less dramatic fashion by Jiang Zemin (1989–2002) and currently Hu Jintao. Deng chose a pragmatic approach to achieving the so-called 'Four Modernisations': namely, modernisation of China's industry, agriculture, defence, and science and technology.

Today China has one of the fastest growing economies in the world. Previously a state-controlled economy, the Chinese government introduced market-oriented economic reforms in the early 1980s. Now only a third of its economy is directly controlled by the state. China is strong in manufacturing and agriculture, but its service sector is slowly catching up, accounting for 32.5% of the economy. China's cheap labour costs have turned the country into 'the world's factory', manufacturing most of the world's clothing, electronics and household items. In 2005 China's global trade surplus was at US$102 billion. China is also one of the largest importers in the world, buying cars, high-tech products, raw minerals, machineries and equipment, chemicals and petroleum. However, China's shrinking agricultural sector still employs over 40% of its workforce and keeps China as the largest agricultural country in the world.

China's GDP per capita is US$6800, making China the second largest economy after the US. China's recent gain in trades has upset many trade protectionists, particularly in the US and Europe, who have been pressing China to revalue the yuán to soften China's competitive pricing edge on its exports. In 2005 they achieved a moderate success when China unpegged the yuán to the dollar, driving it up around 2% against the greenback.

China is the world's second biggest oil user after the US.

A slightly more expensive yuán doesn't mean bad news for visitors. China's continuing economic reforms are bringing in more competition in virtually every sector, resulting in lowered prices and better services. The increase of living standards in China also means better infrastructure, improved transportation systems, better healthcare and environmental protection, all of which are good news if you're travelling in China.

POPULATION

China is home to 56 ethnic groups, with Han Chinese making up 92% of the population. Because Han Chinese are the majority, China's other ethnic groups are usually referred to as shaoshu minzu (minority nationals). Han live throughout the country but are mainly concentrated along the Yellow River, Yangzi River and Pearl River basins.

China's minority groups are also found throughout the country, but their main distributions are along the border regions of northwest and southwest China and from the north to the northeast. Yúnnán is home to more than 20 ethnic groups and is one of the most ethnically diverse provinces in the country. The largest minority groups in China include the Zhuang, Manchu, Miao, Uighur, Yi, Tujia, Tibetan, Mongolian, Buoyi, Dong, Yao, Korean, Bai, Hani, Li, Kazak and Dai.

Red Poppies: A Novel of Tibet by Alai, and translated by Howard Goldblatt and Sylvia Li-chun Lin (Houghton Miflin, 2002), is a powerful novel about opium production in Tibet during late imperial China.

Maintaining amicable relations with the minorities has been a continuous problem for the Han Chinese. Tibet and Xīnjiāng are heavily garrisoned by Chinese troops, partly to protect China's borders and partly to prevent rebellion among the local population. The Chinese government has also set up special training centres, such as the Nationalities University in Běijīng, to train minority cadres for these regions.

China faces enormous population pressures, despite comprehensive programs to curb its growth. Over one-third of China's 1.3 billion live in urban centres, putting great pressure on land and water resources. It's estimated that China's total population will continue to grow at a speed of 10 million each year, even with population programs such as the one-child policy.

The one-child policy was railroaded into effect in 1979 without a careful analysis of its logic or feasibility. The original goal was to keep China's population to one billion by the year 2000 and then massaged down to an ideal of 700 million by 2050. The policy was originally harshly implemented but rural revolt led to a softer stance; nonetheless, it has generated much bad feeling between local officials and the rural population. All non-Han minorities are exempt from the one-child policy.

Rural families are now allowed to have two children if the first child is a girl, but some have upwards of three or four kids. Additional children often result in fines and families having to shoulder the cost of education themselves, without government assistance. Official stated policy opposes forced abortion or sterilisation, but allegations of coercion continue as local officials strive to meet population targets. The government is taking steps to punish officials who force women to undergo inhumane sterilisation procedures. Families who do abide by the one-child policy will often go to great lengths to make sure their child is male. In parts of China, this is creating a serious imbalance of the sexes – in 2005, 119 boys were born for every 100 girls. That could mean that by 2020, over 40 million men may be unable to find spouses.

Experts claim that China needs at least 30 more years to achieve zero population growth. However, a sharp drop in the birth rate may lead to problems as young workers become fewer and the number of senior citizens grows larger. In 2006 over 14% of China's population was over 60. This is expected to increase to 15.6% by 2020. How to support such a large aging population has yet to be addressed.

Kung Fu Hustle (2005) is an entertaining comedy of wannabe gangsters in 1930s Shànghǎi that's a throwback to early martial art films. It's directed by Stephen Chow, who also made *Shaolin Soccer*.

SPORT

The Chinese have a very long, rich sports history. Archaeological evidence shows that people in China over 4000 years ago were combining physical movements with breathing exercises to increase longevity – what we now know as taichi *(tàijíquán;* see the boxed text, opposite). Early murals and pottery from as far back as the Western Zhou dynasty (1066–771 BC) show people playing games resembling modern-day archery, acrobatics, martial arts, wrestling and various types of ball games. Most of these games were enjoyed by the well-to-do, who had time to invest in recreational activities.

During the Tang dynasty equestrian polo was at the height of fashion for aristocrats and officials. There are numerous paintings, ceramics and mirrors

CHINESE MARTIAL ARTS

Many martial arts of the East have their foundations deeply entwined with the philosophies, doctrines, concepts and religious beliefs of Confucianism, Buddhism and Taoism. It is certainly true that most of the martial art systems in existence today owe their development and ultimate dissemination to the monks and priests who taught and transferred such knowledge over much of Asia throughout history.

In China today the existing various martial art styles number into the hundreds; many still not known to the Western world, and each style reflecting its own fighting philosophy and spirit. The following is a thumbnail sketch of two of the arts that you may see while travelling in China.

Shàolín Boxing

Shàolín boxing is one of the major branches of Chinese martial arts. The art is said to have originated at Shaolin Temple (p460) on Sōng Shān in Hénán province. Shàolín monk fighters were trained to help protect the temple's assets. The martial art routines of Shaolin Temple were not organised into a complete system until some 30 to 40 years later when Indian monk Bodhidharma visited the site.

Bodhidharma taught the monks various kinds of physical exercises to limber up the joints and build a good physique. These movements were expanded over time and a complicated series of Chinese boxing (or forms) evolved. By the Sui and Tang dynasties, Shaolin boxing was widely known.

The fighting styles originating from Shaolin Temple are based on five animals: dragon, snake, tiger, leopard and crane. Each animal represents a different style, each of which is used to develop different skills.

The temple's famous forms have had a profound influence on many of today's martial arts, and the temple is still being utilised today.

Taichi (Shadow Boxing)

Taichi or tàijíquán is a centuries-old Chinese discipline promoting flexibility, circulation, strength, balance, relaxation and meditation. While the art is seen by many outside China as a slow-motion form of gentle exercise, it is traditionally practised as a form of self-defence. Taichi aims to dispel the opponent without the use of force and with minimal effort. It is based on the Taoist idea that the principle of softness will ultimately overcome hardness. According to legend, it is derived from the movements of animals.

A major part of studying taichi is the development of chi (qì), or life energy that can be directed to all parts of the body with the help of mental training. Chi must flow and circulate freely in the body.

It is traditionally accepted that Zhang San Feng (see the boxed text, p482) is the founder of tàijíquán. Due to different needs and environments, various styles of taichi evolved. The most popular form of taichi is the Yang style, which is not too difficult to learn in its simplified form (though the full form has 108 postures) and is not strenuous. Other styles, such as the Chen style, call for a wider array of skills as the postures are painfully low and the kicks high, so endurance and flexibility are important. Chen style is popular with younger exponents and clearly has its roots in Shaolin, mixing slow movements with fast, snappy punches. Other styles include the Sun and Wu styles.

from this period that depict men and women engaging in the sport. Board games also became popular around this time and people enjoyed playing a game similar to contemporary mah jong. Long-distance running and hunting were popular sports for soldiers and the nobility.

During the Song dynasty one of the most well-liked sports was kicking around a leather ball stuffed with hair. This sport, similar to football (soccer), was enjoyed by both officials and ordinary people. In 2003 the international football association FIFA officially recognised China as the birthplace of football, which is believed to have originated in present-day Shāndōng province. Golf is another sport with a long history – as far back as the Yuan dynasty the Chinese were hitting balls into holes in the ground with sticks.

It was during the Qing dynasty that modern sports, such as basketball, gymnastics, volleyball and swimming, came to China and Chinese athletes began participating in international sports events, such as the Olympics and the Asian Games. Some Chinese athletes have achieved worldwide recognition, such as the basketball player Yao Ming, who now plays for the Houston Rockets.

Did you know that in 2004 the All China Sports Federation recognised video games as a legitimate sport?

Some sports China excels in today are table tennis, volleyball, gymnastics and women's wrestling, with many athletes bringing home international awards for their efforts. China's latest addition to its sports repertoire is cricket, with a five-year plan to introduce the sport to schools and universities with the eventual hope of qualifying for the 2019 World Cup.

The first Chinese to win an Olympic gold medal was pistol-shooting champion Xu Haifeng at the 1984 Olympic Games. Deng Yaping is China's most celebrated table-tennis player, winning four gold medals in the 1992 and 1996 Olympic Games. In 1996, Wang Junxia became the first Chinese gold medallist in track and field, winning the 5000m. In the 2004 Olympic Games held in Athens, Greece, the Chinese took home 32 gold medals, 17 silver and 14 bronze, ranking second after the USA. In 2005, 18-year-old Ding Junhui won the UK snooker title.

With China set to host the 2008 summer Olympics in Běijīng, Chinese athletes are already being primed for the spotlight. The government is pouring money into the building of ultramodern sporting facilities in an effort to show off Běijīng as a world-class city on par with Olympic host cities of the past. Other participating Chinese cities include Qīngdǎo (sailing), Hong Kong (equestrian), Tiānjīn and Shànghǎi (football).

RELIGION

Chinese religion has been influenced by three streams of human thought: Taoism, Confucianism and Buddhism. All three have been inextricably entwined in popular Chinese religion along with ancient animist beliefs. The founders of Taoism, Confucianism and Buddhism have been deified. The Chinese worship them and their disciples as fervently as they worship their own ancestors and a pantheon of gods and spirits.

Muslims are believed to be one of the largest identifiable religious group still active in China today, numbering perhaps 3% to 5% of the nation's population. Christians make up a similar percentage. The government has not published official figures for the number of Buddhists. It's impossible to determine the number of Taoists, but the number of Taoist priests is very small.

Confucianism

Although more a philosophy than a religion, Confucianism (Rújiā Sīxiǎng) has become intertwined with Chinese religious beliefs (see p221).

Confucius was born of a poor family around 551 BC in the state of Lu in modern-day Shāndōng. His ambition was to hold a high government office and to reorder society through the administrative apparatus. At most he seems to have had several insignificant government posts, a few followers and a permanently blocked career.

At the age of 50 he perceived his divine mission, and for the next 13 years tramped from state to state offering unsolicited advice to rulers on how to improve their governing, while looking for an opportunity to put his own ideas into practice. That opportunity never came, and he returned to his own state to spend the last five years of his life teaching and editing classical literature. He died in 479 BC, aged 72.

The glorification of Confucius began after his death. Mencius (372–289 BC), or Mengzi, helped raise Confucian ideals into the national consciousness with the publication of *The Book of Mencius*.

The central theme of Confucianism is the conduct of human relationships for the attainment of harmony and overall good. Society was an ordinance of heaven and the five relationships: ruler and subject, husband and wife, father and son, elder and younger, and friends. Respect flows upwards, from young to old, from subject to ruler. Confucian texts, such as the *Classics of Rituals (Liji)*, were used as part of the imperial examinations to educate aspiring officials on proper conduct. Drawing from the texts, emperors sought to establish a common set of moral values to create a unified empire. Virtues like filial piety, honesty and loyalty formed the basics for all schooling and were the common moral ideal for the elite.

In its early years Confucianism was regarded as a radical philosophy, but over the centuries it has come to be seen as conservative and reactionary. Confucius was strongly denounced by the communists as yet another incorrigible link to the bourgeois past. During the Cultural Revolution Confucian temples, statues and Confucianists themselves took quite a beating at the hands of rampaging Red Guards. Confucian temples, particularly the ones at Qūfù (p218) in Shāndōng province, have been restored.

'In its early years Confucianism was regarded as a radical philosophy'

Taoism

It is said that Taoism (Dàojiào) is the only true 'home-grown' Chinese religion – Buddhism was imported from India and Confucianism is mainly a philosophy. According to tradition, the founder of Taoism was a man known as Laotzu, variously spelled in Western literature as 'Laotse', 'Laotze' and the pinyin variant 'Laozi'. He is said to have been born around 604 BC, but there is some doubt that he ever lived at all. Almost nothing is known about him, not even his real name.

At the end of his life Laotzu is said to have climbed on a water buffalo and ridden west towards what is now Tibet, in search of solitude for his last few years. On the way he was asked by a gatekeeper to leave behind a record of his beliefs. The product was a slim volume of only 5000 characters: the

ANCESTORS, GHOSTS AND GHOULS

Beliefs about ancestor worship permeate almost every aspect of Chinese philosophy. Most homes have their own altar, where family members pay their respects to deceased relatives by burning paper money and providing offerings. It's believed that a person possesses two 'souls' – a *guǐ*, which is Yin and represents everything dark, damp and earthy, and a *shén*, which is Yang, and represents light, goodness and strength. When a person dies, the two souls go in separate directions. The *shén* heads upwards to heaven and the *guǐ* descends to the underworld. If a person has suffered a tragic death like murder or suicide, dies too young or is neglected after death, the *guǐ* lingers on earth, often seeking revenge. Chinese literature is full of tales of ghosts that come back and play havoc in people's lives until their grievances are satisfied and they get a proper burial. Evil spirits can be anywhere, lurking on lonely roads, in abandoned houses and even in toilets. They commonly haunt at night when Yin is strongest. Most popular in stories and movies are tales of young women, often in the guise of foxes, who bewitch young men and lure them to their death.

Nowadays, while ancestors are still revered, most Chinese scoff at the belief that ghosts can come back from the dead to punish the living, though traditional beliefs still persist in the countryside.

THE CHINESE ZODIAC

Astrology has a long history in China and is integrated with religious beliefs. If you want to know your sign in the Chinese zodiac, look up your year of birth in the chart, but remember that Chinese astrology goes by the lunar calendar. The Chinese Lunar New Year usually falls in late January or early February, so the first month will be included in the year before. Future years are included here so you'll know what's coming:

- Rat: generous, social, insecure, prone to laziness; 1936, 1948, 1960, 1972, 1984, 1996, 2008, 2020
- Ox/Cow: stubborn, conservative, patient; 1937, 1949, 1961, 1973, 1985, 1997, 2009
- Tiger: creative, brave, overbearing; 1938, 1950, 1962, 1974, 1986, 1998, 2010
- Rabbit: timid, amicable, affectionate; 1939, 1951, 1963, 1975, 1987, 1999, 2011
- Dragon: egotistical, strong, intelligent; 1940, 1952, 1964, 1976, 1988, 2000, 2012
- Snake: luxury seeking, secretive, friendly; 1941, 1953, 1965, 1977, 1989, 2001, 2013
- Horse: emotional, clever, quick thinker; 1942, 1954, 1966, 1978, 1990, 2002, 2014
- Goat: charming, good with money, indecisive; 1943, 1955, 1967, 1979, 1991, 2003, 2015
- Monkey: confident, humorous, fickle; 1944, 1956, 1968, 1980, 1992, 2004, 2016
- Rooster: diligent, imaginative, needs attention; 1945, 1957, 1969, 1981, 1993, 2005, 2017
- Dog: humble, responsible, patient; 1946, 1958, 1970, 1982, 1994, 2006, 2018
- Pig: materialistic, loyal, honest; 1947, 1959, 1971, 1983, 1995, 2007, 2019

Tao Te Ching (Dào Dé Jīng) or *The Book of the Way*. He then rode off on his buffalo. It's doubtful that Laotzu ever intended his philosophy to become a religion.

Zhuangzi (399–295 BC) picked up where Laotzu left off. Zhuangzi (also called Chuangtzu) is regarded as the greatest of all Taoist writers and his collection of stories, *The Book of Zhuangzi*, is still required reading for anyone trying to make sense of Taoism. However, like Laotzu, Zhuangzi was a philosopher and was not actually trying to establish a religion.

At the centre of Taoism is the concept of Tao *(dào)*. Tao cannot be perceived because it exceeds senses, thoughts and imagination; it can be known only through mystical insight and cannot be expressed with words. The opening lines of Laotzu's *The Book of the Way* advise that the Tao that can be expressed is not the real Tao. Tao is the way of the universe, the driving power in nature, the order behind all life and the spirit that cannot be exhausted. Tao is the way people should order their lives to keep in harmony with the natural order of the universe.

The philosophy of Taoism is based on *The Book of the Way*. An amalgamation of folk beliefs and ritual, Taoism placed an emphasis on individual freedom, laissez-faire government and harmony with nature. The Tao, or way, according to Laotzu, is the essence of all things in the universe but ultimately cannot be defined. A central facet of Taoism is the concept of *wuwei* or 'nonaction', meaning to live in harmony with the universe without forcing things to your will.

In time Taoism split into two branches – religious Taoism and philosophical Taoism, each taking very different approaches to Laotzu's teachings. Religious Taoism, borrowing concepts from Buddhism and folk religion, became ultimately concerned with the afterlife and achieving immortality. Taoist magicians banished demons through exorcisms and won over the public with demonstrations of their supernatural powers. China lost several

Did you know that in early China Taoist magicians used chicken blood to ward off spectres?

emperors who died after drinking elixirs given to them by Taoists promising eternal life. Philosophical Taoism remained a way of life for hermits and sages, those who withdrew from the public life.

Taoism today has been much embraced in the West by many who offer their own various interpretations of what Laotzu and Zhuangzi were really trying to tell us.

Buddhism

Buddhism (Fó Jiào) was founded in India by Siddhartha Gautama (563–483 BC), a prince brought up in luxury who became disillusioned by the world around him. At the age of 30 he sought 'enlightenment' by following various yogic disciplines. After several failed attempts he devoted the final phase of his search to intensive contemplation. One evening he slipped into deep meditation and emerged having achieved enlightenment. His title 'Buddha' means 'the awakened' or 'the enlightened one'.

The cornerstone of Buddhist philosophy is the view that all life is suffering. Everyone is subject to the traumas of birth, sickness, decrepitude and death, and to separation from what they love.

The cause of suffering is desire – specifically the desires of the body and the desire for personal fulfilment. Happiness can only be achieved if these desires are overcome, and this requires following the 'eightfold path'. By following this path the Buddhist aims to attain nirvana: a state of complete freedom from greed, anger, ignorance and the various other fetters of existence.

When Buddhism entered China from India, its exotic nature, with chanting, strange coloured robes, incense and foreign images, was an attraction for many Chinese disillusioned with the uptight formalism of Confucianism. Buddhism offered answers to the afterlife that neither Taoism nor Confucianism could address, with its elaborate explanations of karma and how to find relief from suffering.

Slowly, the religion drew more followers, gathering firm support in northern China and gradually moving south. However, Buddhism had its share of critics, and many Chinese were afraid that the foreign religion was a threat to the Chinese identity, which was firmly grounded in Confucianism. The growth of Buddhism was slowed by persecutions and outright abolishment by various emperors.

The Buddhist writings that have come down to us date from about 150 years after the Buddha's death. By the time these texts came out, divisions had already appeared within Buddhism. Some writers tried to emphasise the Buddha's break with Hinduism, while others tried to minimise it. At some stage Buddhism split into two major schools: Theravada and Mahayana.

The Theravada or 'doctrine of the elders' school (also called Hinayana or 'little vehicle' by non-Theravadins) holds that the path to nirvana is an individual pursuit. It centres on monks and nuns who make the search for nirvana a full-time profession. This school maintains that people are alone in the world and must tread the path to nirvana on their own; buddhas can only show the way. Theravada is the main school of Buddhism in Sri Lanka, Myanmar, Thailand, Laos and Cambodia.

The Mahayana, or 'big vehicle', school holds that since all existence is one, the fate of the individual is linked to the fate of others. The Buddha did not just point the way and float off into his own nirvana, but continues to offer spiritual help to others seeking nirvana. Mahayana is the main school of Buddhism in Vietnam, Japan, Tibet, Korea, Mongolia and China.

Mahayana Buddhism is replete with innumerable heavens, hells and descriptions of nirvana. Prayers are addressed to the Buddha and combined with elaborate ritual. There are deities and bodhisattvas – a rank of

'Mahayana Buddhism is replete with innumerable heavens, hells and descriptions of nirvana'

supernatural beings in their last incarnation before nirvana. Temples are filled with images such as the future buddha, Maitreya (often portrayed as fat and happy over his coming promotion), and Amitabha (a saviour who rewards the faithful with admission to a Christian-like paradise). The ritual, tradition and superstition that Buddha rejected came tumbling back in with a vengeance.

In Tibet and areas of Gānsù, Sìchuān and Yúnnán, a unique form of the Mahayana school is practised: Tantric or Lamaist Buddhism (Lǎma Jiào). Tantric Buddhism, often called Vajrayana or 'thunderbolt vehicle' by its followers, has been practised since the early 7th century AD and is heavily influenced by Tibet's pre-Buddhist Bon religion, which relied on priests or shamans to placate spirits, gods and demons.

Generally speaking, it is much more mystical than other forms of Buddhism, relying heavily on *mudras* (ritual postures), mantras (sacred speech), *yantras* (sacred art) and secret initiation rites. Priests called lamas are believed to be reincarnations of highly evolved beings; the Dalai Lama is the supreme patriarch of Tibetan Buddhism.

'Although the Arabs were eventually supplanted by the Turks, the strength of Islam has continued to the present day'

Islam

The founder of Islam (Yīsīlán Jiào) was the Arab prophet Mohammed. Strictly speaking, Muslims believe it was not Mohammed who shaped the religion but God, and Mohammed merely transmitted it from God to his people. The proper name of the religion is Islam, derived from the word *salam,* which primarily means 'peace', and in a secondary sense 'surrender' or 'submission'. The full connotation is something like 'the peace that comes by surrendering to God'. The corresponding adjective is 'Muslim'.

The Prophet was born around AD 570 and came to be called Mohammed, meaning 'highly praised'. His ancestry is traditionally traced back to Abraham, who had two wives, Hagar and Sarah. Hagar gave birth to Ishmael, and Sarah had a son named Isaac. Sarah demanded that Hagar and Ishmael be banished. According to Islam's holy book, the Koran, Ishmael went to Mecca, where his line of descendants can be traced down to Mohammed. There have been other true prophets before Mohammed, but he is regarded as the culmination of them and the last.

Mohammed said that there is only one God, Allah. The name derives from joining al, which means 'the', with Llah, which means 'God'. His uncompromising monotheism conflicted with the pantheism and idolatry of the Arabs. His moral teachings and vision of a universal brotherhood conflicted with what he believed was a corrupt social order based on class divisions.

The initial reaction to his teachings was hostile. He and his followers were forced to flee from Mecca to Medina in 622, where Mohammed built a political base and an army that eventually defeated Mecca and brought all of Arabia under his control. He died in 632, two years after taking Mecca. By the time a century had passed the Arab Muslims had built a huge empire that stretched all the way from Persia to Spain. Although the Arabs were eventually supplanted by the Turks, the strength of Islam has continued to the present day.

Islam was brought to China peacefully. Arab traders who landed on the southern coast of China established their mosques in great maritime cities like Guǎngzhōu and Quánzhōu, and Muslim merchants travelling the Silk Road to China won converts among the Han Chinese in the north of the country. There are also large populations of Muslim Uighur people (of Turkic descent), whose ancestors first moved into China's Xīnjiāng region during the Tang dynasty.

RELIGION & COMMUNISM IN TODAY'S CHINA

Today the Chinese communist government professes atheism. It considers religion to be super-stition, a remnant of old China used by the ruling classes to keep power. This is in line with the Marxist belief that religion is the 'opiate of the people'.

Nevertheless, in an effort to improve relations with the Muslim, Buddhist and Lamaist minorities, in 1982 the Chinese government amended its constitution to allow freedom of religion. However, only atheists are permitted to be members of the Chinese Communist Party (CCP). Since almost all of China's 55 minority groups adhere to one religion or another, this rule precludes most of them from becoming party members.

Traditional Chinese religious beliefs took a battering during the Cultural Revolution when monasteries were disbanded, temples were destroyed, and the monks were sometimes killed or sent to the fields to labour. While traditional Chinese religion is strong in places like Macau, Hong Kong and Taiwan, in mainland China the temples and monasteries are pale shadows of their former selves.

Since the death of Mao, the Chinese government allowed many temples (sometimes with their own contingent of monks and novices) to reopen as active places of worship. All religious activity is firmly under state control and many of the monks are caretakers within renovated shells of monasteries, which serve principally as tourist attractions.

Of all the people in China, the Tibetan Buddhists felt the brunt of Mao's Cultural Revolution (1966–76). The Dalai Lama and his entourage fled to India in 1959 when the Tibetan rebellion was put down by Chinese troops, and the theocracy, which had governed Tibet for centuries, was abolished during the ensuing democratic reform. During the Cultural Revolution the monasteries were disbanded (some were levelled to the ground). Some Tibetan temples and monasteries have been reopened, and the Tibetan religion is still a very powerful force among the people.

In spring 1999 the CCP was caught off-guard by a congregation of thousands of practition-ers of a quasi-Buddhist health system, Falun Gong (Art of the Wheel of the Law), outside the political headquarters of Zhongnanhai in Běijīng. Falun Gong was branded a cult *(xiéjiào)* and outlawed.

The tussle between the party and Falun Gong quickly relocated to Tiananmen Square, where followers routinely appeared with banners, only to be pounced upon by patrolling plain-clothes police. Thousands of Falun Gong believers have been sent to prison where human-rights watch-dogs say many are badly treated or killed.

Christianity

The earliest record of Christianity (Jīdū Jiào) in China dates back to the Nesto-rians, a Syrian Christian sect. They first appeared in China in the 7th century when a Syrian named Raban presented Christian scriptures to the imperial court at Chāng'ān (present-day Xī'ān). This event and the construction of a Nestorian monastery in Chāng'ān are recorded on a large stone stele made in AD 781, now displayed in the Shaanxi History Museum (p424) in Xī'ān.

The next major Christian group to arrive in China were the Jesuits. The priests Matteo Ricci and Michael Ruggieri were permitted to set up base at Zhàoqìng in Guǎngdōng in the 1580s, and eventually made it to the imperial court in Běijīng. Large numbers of Catholic and Protestant missionaries established themselves in China following the intrusion into China by the Western powers in the 19th century but left soon after the communists took over in 1949. Now Christians are estimated to comprise about 3% to 5% of China's population.

Judaism

Kāifēng (p468) in Hénán province has been the home of the largest com-munity of Chinese Jews. Their religious beliefs of Judaism (Yóutài Jiào) and almost all the customs associated with them have died out, yet the descend-ants of the original Jews still consider themselves Jewish. Just how the Jews got to China is unknown. They may have come as traders and merchants along the Silk Road when Kāifēng was the capital of China, or they may have emigrated from India.

WOMEN IN CHINA

In traditional China, an ideal woman's behaviour was governed by the 'three obediences and four virtues' of Confucian thought. The three obediences were submission to the father before marriage, husband after marriage and sons in the case of widows. The four virtues were propriety in behaviour, demeanour, speech and employment. The Communist party after 1949 tried to outlaw old customs and put women on equal footing with men. They abolished arranged marriages and encouraged women to get an education and join the workforce. Pictures from this time show sturdy, ruddy-cheeked women with short cropped hair and overalls, a far cry from the pale, willowy beauties of Chinese poetry and traditional paintings.

Today Chinese women officially share complete equality with men, though in reality there's still a long way to go. Chinese women suffer from low political representation, strict family policies and a lack of career opportunities. Despite these negatives, the women's movement has made considerable progress. The Marriage Law of 1980, amended in 2001, gives victims of spousal abuse official protection and orders that abusers be punished to the fullest extent of the law. Victims can also sue for damages. In education, women make up 44% of students in colleges and universities, and their average life expectancy is 73, three years more than men.

Women's improved social status has meant that more women are putting off marriage until their late twenties, instead choosing to focus on education and career opportunities. Equipped with a good education and a high salary, they have high expectations of their future husbands. Premarital sex and cohabitation before marriage are increasingly common in larger cities and lack the stigma they had several years ago.

Did you know that women make up 20% of China's entrepreneurs?

ARTS

With such a long, unbroken history and culture, China has made one of the greatest artistic contributions to mankind. Sadly, much of China's ancient art treasures have been destroyed in times of civil war or dispersed by invasion or natural calamity. Many of China's remaining great paintings, ceramics, jade and other works of art were rescued by exile beyond the mainland – in Taiwan, Singapore, Hong Kong and elsewhere.

The West has also been guilty of ransacking China's heritage, making off with religious art and scriptures from such grottoes as Dūnhuáng (p864; see also the boxed text on p867). Fortunately since the early 1970s a great deal of work has been done to restore what was destroyed in the Cultural Revolution.

China today has a flourishing contemporary art scene, with private galleries competing with government-run museums and exhibition halls. Chinese artists are increasingly catching the attention of the international art world and joint exhibitions with European or American artists are now common. Two of the more prestigious exhibitions are the Shanghai Biennale and the Guangzhou Triennale, which showcase artworks from China's leading contemporary artists.

Visual Arts

CALLIGRAPHY

Calligraphy has been traditionally regarded in China as the highest form of artistic expression. The basic tools, commonly referred to as 'the four

---

THE BEST PLACES TO SEE CONTEMPORARY ART IN CHINA

- The Courtyard, Běijīng (p151)
- Factory 798, Běijīng (p138)
- Red Gate Gallery, Běijīng (p130)
- Shanghai Gallery of Art, Shànghǎi (p255)
- Shanghai Duolun Museum of Modern Art, Shànghǎi (p256)
- 50 Moganshan Road Art Centre, Shànghǎi (p255)

---

treasures of the scholar's study', are paper, ink, ink-stone (on which the ink is mixed) and brush. These materials, which are shared by Chinese painters, reflect the close relationship between Chinese painting and calligraphy.

Calligraphy is still an extremely popular pastime in China and a major area of study. It can be seen all over China – on documents, artworks, in temples, adorning the walls of caves, and on the sides of mountains and monuments. There is an annual calligraphy festival (p328) held every year outside Shàoxīng in Zhèjiāng province.

For indepth articles and reviews on contemporary Chinese art and artists head to www.new chineseart.com run by the Shànghǎi-based gallery Art Scene China.

PAINTING

Chinese painting is the art of brush and ink applied onto *xuān* (paper) or silk. The basic tools are those of calligraphy, which has influenced painting in both its style and theory. The brush line, which varies in thickness and tone, is the important feature of a Chinese painting, along with calligraphy itself, which is usually incorporated in the form of an inscription or poem along with the artist's seal. Shading and colour play only a minor symbolic and decorative role.

From the Han dynasty until the end of the Tang dynasty, the human figure occupied the dominant position in Chinese painting. The practice of seeking places of natural beauty and communing with nature first became popular among Taoist poets and painters, and landscape painting for its own sake started in the 4th and 5th centuries.

From the 11th century onwards landscape was to dominate Chinese painting. Towards the end of the Ming dynasty a group of painters known as the Individualists diverged from traditional techniques with unusual compositions and brushwork; however, it was not until the 20th century that there was any real departure from native traditions.

When the communists came to power, much of the country's artistic talent was turned to glorifying the revolution and bombarding the masses with political slogans. Colourful billboards of Mao waving to cheering crowds holding up the little red book were popular, as were giant Mao statues standing above smaller statues of enthusiastic workers and soldiers.

Since the late 1970s the Chinese art scene has gradually recovered. The work of traditionally influenced painters can be seen for sale in shops and galleries all over China, while in the major cities a flourishing avant-garde scene has emerged. The work of Chinese painters has been arguably more innovative and dissident than that of writers, possibly because the political implications are harder to interpret by the authorities.

CERAMICS

The Chinese began making pottery over 8000 years ago. The first vessels were handcrafted earthenware, primarily used for religious purposes. The invention of the pottery wheel during the late Neolithic period led to the

CONTEMPORARY CHINESE ART ON THE EDGE

With its many private galleries and an escalating art market, China's contemporary art scene is booming. After Mao's death in 1976 China underwent a creative renaissance that continues to this day. It was in the 1970s and 1980s that artists began challenging traditional Chinese aesthetics, creating bold political works that challenged government authority. The Chinese avant garde was born during this time, heavily influenced by Western techniques. After the events of 4 June 1989 contemporary art took a critical turn. Disillusioned with the current political system and the rampant consumerism sweeping the country, artists began to create works permeated with feelings of loss, loneliness and social isolation, a far cry from the idealism of earlier years. Artists Feng Lijun and Yue Mingjun created grotesque portraits of themselves that conveyed a sense of boredom and mock joviality, an apt portrayal of the mood during this period.

The explosive development of the past two decades has had artists grappling with issues such as environmentalism, materialism, and the widening gap between rich and poor. The Běijīng-based artist Yin Xiuzhen has become known internationally for her commentaries on urban waste and the destruction of China's traditional architecture. While the Chinese authorities view Chinese art as a valuable, exploitable commodity, they keep a close eye on artists deemed too reactionary. One of the best places to see cutting-edge art that won't be shown in any state-run museums is at Factory 798 (p138) on the outskirts of Běijīng. The area is home to a vibrant community of Chinese and international artists, and hosts many worthwhile exhibitions. Shànghǎi and Guǎngzhōu are also home to a thriving art culture and dozens of lively, enigmatic galleries.

establishment of foundries and workshops and the eventual development of a ceramics industry.

Over the centuries Chinese potters perfected their craft, introducing many new exciting styles and techniques. Art thrived under the Tang dynasty and the ceramic arts were no exception. One of the most famous styles from this period is 'three-coloured ware', named because of the liberal use of bright yellow, green and white glaze. Blue-green celadons were another popular item, and demand for them grew in countries as far away as Egypt and Persia.

The Yuan dynasty saw the first production of China's most famous type of porcelain, often referred to simply as 'blue-and-white'. Cobalt blue paint, obtained from Persia, was applied as an underglaze directly to white porcelain with a brush, and then the vessel was covered with another transparent glaze and fired. This technique was perfected under the Ming dynasty and ceramics made in this style became hugely popular all over the world, eventually acquiring the name 'Chinaware', whether produced in China or not. Jǐngdézhèn (p492) in Jiāngxī province was established during the Yuan dynasty as the centre of the ceramics industry and still retains that importance today.

During the Qing dynasty porcelain techniques were further refined and developed, showing superb craftsmanship and ingenuity. British and European consumers dominated the export market, having an insatiable appetite for Chinese vases and bowls decorated with flowers and landscapes. The Qing is also known for its stunning monochromatic ware, especially the ox-blood vases, and enamel decorated porcelain.

'Art thrived under the Tang dynasty and the ceramic arts were no exception'

Jǐngdézhèn remains an excellent place to visit ceramic workshops and purchase various types of ceramic wares, from Mao statues to traditional glazed urns. Another place to pick up pottery is at Dīngshān (p302) in Jiāngsū province, which is famous for ceramic teapots. The Shanghai Museum (p252) also boasts an impressive collection of ceramics.

SCULPTURE

Chinese sculpture dates back to the Zhou and Shang dynasties, when small clay and wooden figures were commonly placed in tombs to protect the dead and guide them on their way to heaven. Often these figures were in the shape of animals – dragons, lions and chimeras, all creatures with magical powers that could quell lurking evil spirits. Sculptures of humans became more common in succeeding dynasties – perhaps the best example is the amazing army of Terracotta Warriors (p428) found in the tomb of Qin Shi Huang outside present-day Xī'ān.

It wasn't until the introduction of Buddhism in China that sculpture moved beyond tomb figurines to other realms of figurative art. The Buddhist caves of Dàtóng (p416) in Shānxī province date back to the 4th century and are an excellent example of the type of art that was introduced to China from India. The enormous figures of the Buddhas, carved directly into the rock, are stiff and formal, their garments embellished with Indian patterns and flourishes. The 4th-century Longmen Caves (p465) in Hénán province are similar in style to those at Dàtóng, with great profusions of sculptures and Indian iconography. The later cave sculptures at Lóngmén, primarily those completed during the Tang dynasty, take on a more Chinese feel, with elongated features and less stiffness in form.

The best place to see early Buddhist sculpture is at the marvellous Mogao Caves of Dūnhuáng (p866) in Gānsù province. Here, Indian- and central Asian–style sculptures, particularly of the Tang dynasty, carry overtly Chinese characteristics – many statues feature long, fluid bodies and have warmer, more refined facial features. It's also common to see traditional Chinese dragons and lions mingling with the demons and gods of Indian iconography.

The caves in Dàzú County (p809), built during the Song dynasty, are another fascinating place to see cave art. The caves feature a wild assortment of sculpture, including Buddhist statues, animals and people. Many of the sculptures are more colourful and lively than those of Dūnhuáng and remarkably well preserved.

BRONZE VESSELS

Bronze is an alloy whose chief elements are copper, tin and lead. Tradition ascribes the first casting of bronze to the legendary Xia dynasty of 5000 years ago.

Shang-dynasty bronzes are marvellous specimens, often fabulously patterned with *tāotiè*, a type of fierce animal design. Zhou-dynasty bronze vessels tend to have long messages in ideographic characters; they describe wars, rewards, ceremonial events and the appointment of officials.

Bronze mirrors had already developed into an artistic form by the Warring States period. Ceramics gradually replaced bronze utensils by Han times, but bronze mirrors were not displaced by glass mirrors until the Qing dynasty. The backs of bronze mirrors were inscribed with wishes for good fortune and protection from evil influence.

JADE

The jade stone has been revered in China since Neolithic times. Jade (*yù*) was firstly utilised for tools because of its hardness and strength, but later appeared on ornaments and ceremonial vessels for its decorative value. During the Qin and Han dynasties it was believed that jade was empowered with magical and life-giving properties, and the dead were buried with jadeware. Opulent jade suits, meant to prevent decomposition, have been found in Han tombs, while Taoist alchemists, striving for immortality, ate elixirs of powdered jade.

Jade's value lies not just in its scarcity, but depends also on its colour, hardness and the skill with which it has been carved. While the pure white form is the most highly valued, the stone varies in translucency and colour,

'During the Qin and Han dynasties it was believed that jade was empowered with magical and life-giving properties'

including many shades of green, brown and black. China's most famous jade comes from Hotan (p840) in Xīnjiāng province; much of what is sold in Hong Kong is fake.

FUNERARY OBJECTS

As early as Neolithic times (9000–6000 BC), offerings of pottery vessels and stone tools or weapons were placed in graves to accompany the departed.

During the Shang dynasty precious objects, such as bronze ritual vessels, weapons and jade, were buried with the dead. Dogs, horses and even human beings were sacrificed for burial in the tombs of great rulers, later replaced by replicas (usually in pottery).

The cosmopolitan life of Tang China was illustrated by its funerary wares; western and central Asians flocked to the capital at Chāng'ān, and were portrayed in figurines of merchants, attendants, warriors, grooms, musicians and dancers.

Guardian spirits are some of the strangest funerary objects. A common one has bird wings, elephant ears, a human face, the body of a lion, and the legs and hooves of a deer or horse, all rolled into one.

Literature

China has a very long, fascinating literary tradition. Unfortunately, unless you can read Chinese, it remains out of reach. Many of the translations of the past decade have produced rather stilted, bland versions of Chinese classics, modern short stories and poetry. In recent years publishing houses have been putting more effort into their translations, though the selection remains limited.

PREMODERN LITERATURE

Prior to the 20th century there were two literary traditions in China: the classical and the vernacular. The classical canon, largely Confucian in nature, consisted of a core of texts written in ancient Chinese that had to be mastered thoroughly by all aspirants to the Chinese civil service, and was the backbone of the Chinese education system – it was nearly indecipherable to the masses.

The vernacular tradition arose in the Ming dynasty and consisted largely of prose epics written for entertainment. For Western readers it is the vernacular texts, precursors of the contemporary Chinese novel, that are probably of more interest. Most of them are available in translation and provide a fascinating insight into life in China centuries past.

For a comprehensive website that discusses the philosophy and practice of the *I Ching* check out www.taopage .org/iching. It's possible to download the *I Ching* to your phone.

Classical

I Ching (Yìjīng), or *Book of Changes*, is the oldest Chinese classical text and dates back to antiquity. Stemming from an ancient system of cosmology, it expresses the wisdom and philosophy of early China. The *I Ching* uses 64 hexagrams, composed of broken and continuous lines, to represent a balance of opposites (Yin and Yang), the inevitability of change and the evolution of events. If interpreted correctly, the hexagrams can advise on moral conduct and foretell the future.

Analects (Lúnyǔ) is a collection of sayings attributed to Confucius that were remembered by his followers and compiled over a period of years. The Analects contain all the essential tenets of Confucianism, including filial piety, respect to ancestors and adherence to ritual. Many still consider Arthur Waley's 1938 translation to be the best.

Tao Te Ching (Dào Dé Jīng) or *The Book of the Way* is (tentatively) attributed to Laotzu, a sixth-century philosopher. According to the *Tao Te*

Ching, the Tao, often translated in the West as 'the way', is the highest form of truth and can never be defined (see Taoism, p65). The *Tao Te Ching* forms the central canon of Taoist philosophy. Moss Roberts' *Dao De Jing: The Book of the Way* (University of California Press, 2001 and 2004) is the most complete translation.

Vernacular

Water Margin/Outlaws of the Marsh (Shuǐhǔ Zhuàn) by Shi Nai'an and Luo Guanzhong is a rollicking tale of a group of outlaws (with good hearts) who fight against corruption and evil during the Northern Song dynasty. This book is considered one of the great historical epics of China, along with *Romance of the Three Kingdoms*.

Romance of the Three Kingdoms (San Guo Zhì Yǎnyì) by Luo Guanzhong is a swashbuckling historical novel about the legendary battles that took place during the latter half of the Han dynasty, when the country was divided into three kingdoms. The novel remains as popular today in China as it was when it first appeared in the Ming dynasty. The best translation is by Moss Roberts (University of California Press, 1999), whose English version of the novel is highly readable and entertaining.

Dream of the Red Chamber (Hónglóu Mèng) by Cao Xueqin, also translated as *The Dream of Red Mansions* and *The Story of the Stone*, is a novel of manners about the decline of a genteel family in 18th-century China. The preferred translation is by David Hawkes (Penguin, 1973), who provides a captivating rendition of the original.

Journey to the West (Xīyóu Jì) by Wu Cheng'en is a delightful novel about the Buddhist monk Xuanzhang's pilgrimage to India, accompanied by the rebellious 'Monkey King' Sun Wukong. The monkey's rebellious nature causes a wild assortment of misadventures. Two of the best translations of *Journey to the West* are by Arthur Waley (John Day, 1943) and Anthony Yu (University of Chicago Press, 1990).

CHINESE POETRY

The earliest collection of Chinese poetry is the *Book of Songs (Shījīng)*, which includes over 300 poems dating back to the sixth century BC. The poems were gathered by royal musicians who lived in the many feudal states clustered on the banks of the Yellow River during the Zhou dynasty. The poems were originally meant to be sung, and centre on love, marriage, war, hunting and sacrifice.

China's greatest early poet is Qu Yuan, who lived during the Warring States period (475–221 BC) and is known for his romantic, lyric poetry. After being sent into exile by the King of Chu, Qu Yuan wrote an autobiographic poem 'Sorrow After Departure', depicting his grief at being sent from his home. On the fifth day of the fifth lunar month, Qu Yuan drowned himself in the Milo River. The Dragon Boat Festival is now celebrated in his memory.

The Tang dynasty is considered the 'golden age' of Chinese poetry. It was during this time that two of China's greatest poets, Li Bai and Du Fu, lived. During the Song dynasty lyric poetry called *ci* emerged, which expressed feelings of passion and desire. Su Shi (Su Dongpo) is the most famous poet during this period. After the Tang and Song dynasties poetry lost favour for more narrative prose and interest did not rise again until the Qing dynasty.

Stone Turtle by Mai Mang (Godavaya, 2005) is a bilingual collection of contemporary Chinese poetry that delves into the poet's elusive search for identity in America after leaving China in 1993.

MODERN & CONTEMPORARY LITERATURE

By the early 20th century Western novels had begun to appear in Chinese translations in increasing numbers. Chinese intellectuals began to look at their own literary traditions more critically, in particular the classical one, which was markedly different in form from the Chinese that was spoken by modern Chinese.

After China came under the control of the communists, most writing in 20th-century China tended to echo the CCP line, with formulaic language and predictable plotlines. Writing was rigid and unimaginative, with little allowance for creative embellishment.

Things changed after Mao's death in 1976, when Chinese artists and writers were finally able to throw off political constraints and write more freely. Writers for the first time dared to explore the traumatic events of the 20th century that had reshaped the Chinese landscape. China's economic progress has spawned a new generation of authors, many of whom remember little about the Cultural Revolution and instead are most affected by the day-to-day realities of living in the city. Growing up without war or poverty, young writers are instead writing about the loneliness and decadence of urban life.

The True Story of Ah Q by Lu Xun (Chinese University Press, 2002), and translated by Gladys Yang and Yang Xianyi, was first published in 1921 by an author who is regarded by many as the father of modern Chinese literature. Lu Xun was the first of the major Chinese writers to write in colloquial Chinese. *Ah Q* is a moving tale of a simple-minded man caught up in the turmoil of the 1911 revolution.

Blades of Grass: The Stories of Lao She (University of Hawaii Press, 1999), translated by William Lyell, is a collection of 14 stories by Lao She, one of China's most famous 20th-century writers. The stories contain poignant descriptions of people living through times of political upheaval and uncertainty. Lao She faced severe persecution during the Cultural Revolution and committed suicide.

Family by Ba Jin (Anchor Books, 1972) is the first in a trilogy that also includes *Autumn* and *Spring*. Influenced by the May 4th Movement, the novel offers a scathing view of Chinese feudalism.

Wild Swans by Jung Chang (Touchstone Books, 2003) is a gripping saga about three generations of Chinese women struggling to survive the tumultuous events of 20th-century China. This book has been banned in China for its frank depictions of modern Chinese life.

Half of Man Is Woman by Zhang Xianliang (WW Norton & Co, 1998), translated by Martha Avery, is a candid exploration of sexuality and marriage in contemporary China, and considered one of the most controversial novels to appear in the 1980s.

Please Don't Call Me Human by Wang Shuo (Hyperion East, 2000), translated by Howard Goldblatt, is a mocking look at the failures of China's state security system. Wang Shuo has been dubbed China's 'hooligan author' for his criticism of government policies. Wang's works appeal to a broad spectrum of Chinese society, despite being banned.

The Book and the Sword: Gratitude and Revenge by Jin Yong (Oxford University Press, 2004), translated by Graham Earnshaw, is the first feature-length novel written by China's most well-known martial arts novelist. The story revolves around the Red Flower Society, in a battle to overthrow the Manchu dynasty. Taut and suspenseful, the story has wowed Chinese audiences since its initial publication in 1955.

War Trash by Ha Jin (New York, Pantheon Books, 2004) tells the haunting story of a young Chinese soldier taken prisoner by the Americans during the Korean War. Winner of the 2005 Pen/Faulkner Prize for fiction, the historical novel is made more timely and profound by the events of today. Ha Jin won the PEN/Faulkner Award, in addition to a National Book Award, for his 2000 novel *Waiting*.

Figments of the Supernatural by China's most acclaimed young writer, Chi Zijian, and translated by Simon Patton (James Joyce Press, 2004) is a poignant collection of short stories about rural life in China.

Cinema

Cinema in China can be traced back to 1896, when a Spanish entrepreneur by the name of Galen Bocca showed a series of one-reel films to astonished crowds at an entertainment plaza in Shànghǎi. Bocca's films drew large audiences, who packed the plaza nightly to witness the marvellous new medium. Soon after permanent film-only theatres were being built in Běijīng and Shànghǎi, and the Chinese film craze had officially begun.

The first films shown in China were largely Western, with shots of European cities and frolicking Westerners. As film took hold in China, there grew a demand for films that echoed Chinese tastes. By the 1920s three of the most important genres in Chinese cinema were established: historical dramas, costume dramas set in classical China and most importantly, 'swordsmen films', which would evolve into the modern martial arts film.

For an extensive list of links to Chinese film reviews go to www.chinesecinemas.org.

In 1931 the Nationalist Party in Nánjīng placed restrictions on films that were seen as promoting dissent or immorality. The Lianhua Film Company had close connections with the Nationalist Party, and with funding and government support created some of the most important films and film stars in what has been dubbed China's 'Golden Age of Cinema'. This age came to a standstill with the invasion of Shànghǎi by Japan in 1937, when many filmmakers fled to Hong Kong or went into hiding.

Civil war and the establishment of the People's Republic of China in 1949 was a setback for the film industry, which was forced to follow rigid political guidelines. Heroic tales of the revolutionary struggle (gémìng piàn) made filmmaking into a kind of communist comic strip of beatific peasants and peerless harvests. The Cultural Revolution added its own extremist vision to this surreal cinematography.

After the death of Mao Chinese filmmakers began to break free from years of political repression. The major turning point took place with the graduation of the first intake of students since the end of the Cultural Revolution from the Beijing Film Academy in 1982. This group of directors, the best known being Zhang Yimou, Chen Kaige and Tian Zhuangzhuang, became known collectively as the 'Fifth Generation'.

The first film to create an international stir was Chen Kaige's *Yellow Earth* (1984), a beautifully shot film about a communist cadre who visits a remote village to collect folk songs and inspires a young woman to flee the village and join the communists. The film held little interest for Chinese audiences and the government disparaged the film as too pessimistic. However, Western audiences loved the film and it spurred a taste in the West for Chinese cinema. Chen's later film *Farewell My Concubine* (1993) also received critical acclaim in Western countries.

Zhang Yimou followed Chen's success with *Red Sorghum* (1987), set in a northern Chinese village during the Japanese invasion. *Red Sorghum* won the Golden Bear at the Berlin Film Festival and also introduced to the Western world the actress Gong Li, who became the poster girl of Chinese cinema in the 1990s. She also appeared in Zhang Yimou's *Ju Dou* (1990), *The Story of Qiu Ju* (1991), *Raise the Red Lantern* (1991), *To Live* (1994) and *Shanghai Triad* (1995), all popular in the West. These films generated a great deal of criticism in China, particularly for their candid approach to politically sensitive issues. Tian Zhuangzhuang's *The Blue Kite* (1993), a brilliant but heartbreaking movie that chronicles the events of the Cultural Revolution, was considered so controversial the filmmaker was banned from moviemaking for years.

In 2002, Zhang Yimou released *Hero*, with big names Maggie Cheung, Jet Li, Zhang Zhiyi and Tony Leung. It proved to be a hit with Chinese and

Westerners alike. This was followed by other big-budget flicks like *House of Flying Daggers* (2004) and *The Promise* (2005).

In the 1990s China's 'Sixth Generation' of Chinese filmmakers began to create films that were a reaction against the Fifth Generation's need to please Western audiences. In 1990 Beijing Film Academy graduate Zhang Yuan created *Mama,* a beautiful but disturbing film about a mother and her autistic child. This small film, created without government sponsorship, started a trend in independent films that continues today. Some of these indie filmmakers include Wang Xiaoshuai, *Beijing Bicycle* (2000), Jia Zhangke, *Unknown Pleasure* (2002), Jiang Wen, *Devils on the Doorstep* (1999) and Lu Xuechang, *The Making of Steel* (1996). Their films are far grittier, more urban observations than their Fifth Generation precursors. As a result, many Sixth Generation directors are blacklisted by the authorities and are not allowed to travel outside of China to attend film festivals.

Except for a few directors who are able to attract domestic and overseas investments, such as Chen Kaige and Zhang Yimou, filmmakers are continually dealing with a shortage of funds, small audiences and high ticket prices. Many Chinese prefer Hollywood blockbusters to local movies, with the exception of Hong Kong martial arts movies. In 2005 *Harry Potter and the Goblet of Fire* was one of China's most popular films. However, rising ticket prices put many movies out of reach for the average Chinese and contribute to dwindling audiences. Still, the movie industry carries on, producing often surprisingly high-quality movies on tiny budgets that few Westerners, or even Chinese, get to see.

In 2006 the *Da Vinci Code* was set to be the biggest foreign money-maker in China but was pulled suddenly from cinemas. It's uncertain whether it was banned because of its religious content or because officials wanted to give more attention to local Chinese films.

The first American movie to be shown in China was *The Fugitive* starring Harrison Ford in 1994.

HONG KONG & BEYOND

Hong Kong cinema has always been uniquely Chinese – a ramshackle, violent, slapstick, chaotic, vivid and superstitious world. Money, vendettas, ghosts, gambling and romance are endlessly recycled themes.

You can't discuss Hong Kong cinema without mentioning Jackie Chan, the stunt-icon martial artist who has thrilled both Western and Chinese audiences with his gravity-defying, body-bruising feats of madness. Hong Kong action woman Michelle Yeoh has also performed her own share of amazing feats – she even broke her neck when she fell 6m from a highway overpass while filming Ann Hui's *The Stuntwoman* (1996).

John Woo's gun-toting films are probably the most celebrated of the action films *(dòngzuò piān)*. The master of slow motion and ultraviolence *(Hard Boiled; City On Fire)* has been seduced by Hollywood and now works on gargantuan budget spectaculars *(Face/Off; Mission Impossible 2)*.

Another iconic director and screenwriter of Hong Kong cinema is Wong Kar Wai, famous for his edgy camera work and inventive, atmospheric storytelling. Wong's first film, *As Tears Go By* (1988), starring megapop stars Andy Lau and Jack Cheung, became an instant classic with its Canto-pop soundtrack and gritty urban landscape. *Chungking Express* (1994) made Wong a household name and is considered a remarkable portrayal of Hong Kong urban life. In 1997 Wong became the first Chinese to win the best director award at Cannes for *Happy Together* (1997), a film about a gay couple living in Buenos Aires. Wong's recent creations, *In the Mood for Love* (2000) and *2046* (2004) are mood-saturated pieces about almost-lovers caught in a web of isolation and longing. The slow-motion sequences and stylised camera work cemented Wong's place as one of Hong Kong's most celebrated directors.

In 2000 Taiwan director Ang Lee's Oscar-winning epic tale *Crouching Tiger, Hidden Dragon* caused quite a stir among Western audiences, but the Chinese, a public with loftier expectations of cinematic kung fu and death-defying stunts, panned it. Regardless, for many Westerners it was their first taste of Chinese cinema and it left them wanting more. The movie also launched the career of actress Zhang Ziyi, who replaced Gong Li as the new female icon of Chinese cinema.

Music
TRADITIONAL MUSIC
Musical instruments have been unearthed from tombs dating back to the Shang dynasty and Chinese folk songs can be traced back at least this far. Traditional Chinese instruments are often based on ancient Chinese poetry, making them very symbolic in form. Two books of the Confucian canon, the *Book of Songs* (p75) and the *Book of Rites* both dwell on music, the first actually being a collection of songs and poems, formerly set to music.

The traditional Chinese music scale differs from its Western equivalent. Unlike Western music, tone is considered more important than melody. Music to the Chinese was once believed to have cosmological significance and in early times, if a musician played in the wrong tone, it could indicate the fall of a dynasty.

Traditional Chinese musical instruments include the two-stringed fiddle (*èrhú*), four-stringed banjo (*yuè qín*), two-stringed viola (*húqín*), vertical flute (*dòngxiāo*), horizontal flute (*dízi*), piccolo (*bāngdí*), four-stringed lute (*pípa*), zither (*gǔzhēng*) and ceremonial trumpet (*suǒnà*). Traditional music places a lot of emphasis on percussion, which is what you'll most likely hear at funerals, temples and weddings.

China's ethnic minorities have preserved their own folk song traditions; a trip to Lìjiāng in Yúnnán gives you the chance to appreciate the ancient sounds of the local Naxi orchestra (p714). The communist anthem 'The East is Red' developed from a folk song popular in northern China and later became a defining element of the Cultural Revolution. Chen Kaige's *Yellow Earth* (p77) contains many beautiful folk songs of this region.

Many department stores in China sell traditional Chinese instruments like flutes and piccolos, and most music stores sell recordings of opera and instrumental music.

The Conservatory of Music (p271) in Shanghai offers short and long-term programs for serious students of traditional or contemporary Chinese music.

Chinese Opera
Chinese opera has been formally in existence since the northern Song dynasty, developing out of China's long balladic tradition. Performances were put on by travelling entertainers, often families, in teahouses frequented by China's working classes. Performances were drawn from popular legends and folklore. Beijing opera evolved in the 19th century as a popular form of entertainment for both the imperial family and the general populace.

There are over three hundred types of opera in China, Běijīng opera being the most familiar to Westerners. Other types include Yue opera and Kunqu opera, among others. Yue opera is commonly performed in Guǎngdōng, Hong Kong and Macau. Its singing and dialogue are all in Cantonese dialect. In addition to Chinese traditional instruments, Western instruments such as the violin, saxophone, cello and double bass are also used. Kunqu opera, originating in Jiāngsū, is notable for its soft melodies and the use of the flute.

'There are over three hundred types of opera in China, Běijīng opera being the most familiar to Westerners'

Chinese opera is fascinating for its use of makeup, acrobatics and elaborate costumes. Face painting derives from the early use of masks worn by players, and each colour suggests the personality and attributes that define a character. Chinese audiences can tell instantly the personality of characters by their painted faces. In addition, the status of a character is suggested by the size of headdress worn – the more elaborate, the more significant the character. The four major roles in Chinese opera are the female role, the male role, the 'painted-face' role (for gods and warriors) and the clown.

POPULAR MUSIC

China's thriving music industry came about in the 1980s, a time when many younger Chinese were becoming more exposed to international music trends. The energetic Hong Kong song industry had for years been popular in China, with its twinkle-eyed and pretty emissaries (Aaron Kwok, Faye Wong, Andy Lau, Kelly Chen, Jackie Cheung et al) warbling their catchy, saccharine melodies. Further north, however, their harmless songs of love and loss impacted with a growing rock scene. Cui Jian, the singer and guitarist whose politically subversive lyrics provoked authorities, led the way for a slew of gritty bands who hacked away at the edifice of rock and metal (Tang dynasty) and punk (Underground Baby, Brain Failure). Today major cities such as Běijīng and Shànghǎi have a thriving underground music scene and plenty of places to hear live music. The Midi Music School in Běijīng hosts the annual Midi Modern Music Festival between September and November, with local and international bands playing everything from heavy metal to New Wave.

For insight into China's contemporary rock scene and information on the latest bands go to www.rockinchina.com.

Architecture

China's architectural history stretches back more than 3000 years, making it one of the longest of any civilisation. Many different materials and finishes can be seen throughout Chinese architecture – wood, rammed earth, masonry, stone, thatch, tiles, plaster and paint. Its use depended on function, cost, availability and aesthetics.

HISTORY

Few structures survive from before the 8th century AD. Many early buildings were constructed in wood, which have long since disappeared, with more durable buildings often destroyed by war. Much of what is known has been gathered from references to building in literature, song and artwork.

Until Qin Shi Huang became the first emperor around 220 BC and unified China under a centralised system, there was no such thing as a Chinese national architecture. Under Qin Shi Huang's rule large and impressively decorated structures were built. This period saw the beginnings of what would later become the Great Wall.

It is from the Tang and Song dynasties that the first surviving structures appear. Buildings were painted in bright colours, with great attention to detail. When the Mongols ousted the Song in the late 13th century they contributed little of their own culture to architecture, instead choosing to imitate and rebuild the style of the Chinese.

Běijīng was the long-standing capital during the Ming and Qing dynasties. The Forbidden City (p133) showcases the architecture of the time. In it we can see the epitome of traditional Chinese architectural ideas of monumentality and symmetry, with strong use of colour and decoration.

WESTERN INFLUENCE & MODERN ARCHITECTURE

China had early contact with foreign traders along the Silk Road, but it was not until the establishment of Western trading headquarters and banks in the late 18th century that a colonial influence in architecture made its presence felt. The Portuguese, Germans, British, Dutch, Spanish and Russians, among others, established communities and constructed buildings using foreign architects and Chinese craftsmen.

It was not until the 20th century that Chinese architects designed Western-style buildings themselves. Buildings with sleek, clean lines, flat roofs and materials such as steel and glass had appeared in Shànghǎi by the 1940s. There was for some time a push to revive the traditional Chinese style, but this proved uneconomical and was eventually abandoned.

The 1990s especially saw China drawing up an increasingly ambitious building agenda. Běijīng, in particular, is being transformed for the 2008 Olympics and losing much of its traditional architecture. With so many construction projects currently under way, it's uncertain what China will look like in the not so distant future. Some towns and villages, such as Lìjiāng (p709), Hóngcūn (p444) and Xīdì (p443), have been designated Unesco World Heritage sites and are good places to see China's few remaining traditional buildings. Away from the wealthy eastern seaboard, it's still possible to see traditional-style houses in the countryside and less-developed cities.

RELIGIOUS ARCHITECTURE

All Buddhist, Taoist and Confucian temples are built on a north–south axis, with the main door of each hall facing south. Běijīng's *hútòng* courtyards were traditionally also constructed on this axis. Most temples tend to follow a strict schematic pattern, depending on the faith. The shape of the roof, the placement of the beams and columns, and the location of deities are all carefully placed following the use of feng shui (meaning wind and water), a complex cosmological system designed to create harmonious surroundings in accordance with the natural laws of the universe.

The exteriors of many temples in China look similar. However, Taoist, Buddhist and Confucian temples are all fairly easy to distinguish once you know what to look for. Buddhist temples have fewer images, except for statues of the Buddha, seated in the middle of the temple on an altar. Guanyin is the next most common deity you'll see, sometimes accompanied by other bodhisattvas. Pagodas are common features of Buddhist temples, built to house Sanskrit sutras, religious artefacts and documents, or to store the ashes of the deceased. A number of pagodas stand alone in China, their adjacent temples gone.

Taoist and folk temples are much gaudier inside, with brightly painted statues of deities and colourful murals of scenes from Chinese mythology. On the main altar is the principle deity of the temple, often flanked by some lesser-ranked gods. Fierce-looking temple guardians are often painted on the doors to the entrance of the temple to scare away evil spirits. Large furnaces also stand in the courtyard; these are for burning 'ghost money', paper money meant to keep the ancestors happy in heaven.

Wǔtái Shān (p411), Tài Shān (p214), Qīngchéng Shān (p766), Wǔdāng Shān (p481) and Pǔtuóshān (p332) are some of China's famous sacred mountains, and are excellent places to visit Buddhist and Taoist temples.

Confucian temples are the most sedate and lack the colour and noise of Taoist or Buddhist temples. Not nearly as active or as colourful as their Taoist or Buddhist cousins, they often have a faded and musty feel. Their courtyards are a forest of stelae celebrating local scholars, some supported on the backs of *bìxì* (mythical tortoise-like animals). The Confucius temples in Qūfù (p220), Shāndōng province, and Běijīng (p134) are very famous. You can also see Confucian temples in many other Chinese towns, though they're often outnumbered by their Taoist counterparts.

'With so many construction projects currently under way, it's uncertain what China will look like in the not so distant future'

In addition to Buddhist, Taoist and Confucian buildings, Islamic architecture may also be found across China, most of it dating after the 14th century, and influenced by central Asian styles and often combined with local Chinese style.

Gardens

Chinese garden design reached its fullest development during the late Ming dynasty, when gardens were commonly found in homes of the elite. Gardens were particularly prevalent in southeastern China south of the Yangzi River, especially in Hángzhōu (p315), Yángzhōu (p294) and Sūzhōu (p302).

For a terrific resource on Chinese gardens and architecture with information on their origin, aesthetics and design go to http://depts .washington.edu /chinaciv/home /3garintr.htm.

Rather than lawn and flowers, the three principle elements of Chinese gardens are rock, water and stone, arranged in formations that mimic well-known mountains or paintings. Gardening was considered an intellectual pursuit, and calligraphy, poetic names, references to literary classics and other complementary art forms are featured in many Chinese gardens.

Although many are parklike in scale, historically Chinese gardens were nothing like the public parks of today. They were compounds to which only a tiny portion of the population ever had access. The larger and grander of these were imperial, existing to please and entertain the emperor. In prosperous regions, private gardens also proliferated in certain periods. At its peak Sūzhōu had hundreds of gardens, and the city was registered as a Unesco World Heritage site in 1997 in recognition of those that remain. The numerous pavilions dotted around the gardens were used for everything from meditating and playing chess to musical performances and banqueting.

Environment David Andrew

Covering a massive area of 9.5 million sq km, China straddles natural environments as diverse as subarctic tundra in the north and tropical rainforests in the south. It stretches from the world's highest mountain range and one of its hottest deserts in the west to the typhoon-lashed coastline of the China Sea. Dissecting this vast landscape are countless waterways, including one of the world's great waterways – the mighty Yangzi River (Cháng Jiāng).

Not surprisingly, this vast area hosts an incredible variety of landscapes and biodiversity, but as a traveller it's often hard to envisage a world beyond the choking fumes of a Chinese city. Two-thirds of China may be mountain, desert or otherwise unfit for cultivation, but boy do they pack 'em into the remaining third. There is seemingly no respite from humanity anywhere on the beaten path, and you'll be sharing some of the better-known natural areas with hordes of Chinese tourists trying to get away from it all. But with a little effort (actually, quite a bit of effort in some cases) it is possible to visit and enjoy some of China's wild places, a world far different from the relentless materialism of modern cities. Infrastructure is often lacking and the experience won't always match the expectations of those who have been on, say, an African safari. It's early days for the country's ecotourism industry, however, and the situation can only improve (see the boxed text, p84).

Spelunkers will be awed by Guìzhōu's Zhijin Cave (p678), one of the world's largest underground labyrinths. Geologists will be astounded by Guǎngxī's bizarre karst landscape at Guìlín (p650). Hikers after a challenge with views will find it at the holy Éméi Shān (p769), and photographers (and everyone else) will be gobsmacked by the gorgeous alpine scenery of Jiǔzhàigōu (p795).

Unfortunately, China also faces some serious environmental problems. Breakneck economic growth has meant untrammelled industrial development, which goes hand-in-hand with environmental toxins and pollution. Environmental laws are often unpoliced, and until recently China lacked an environmental voice among the people. Things are improving in some areas, but be prepared to encounter heavy pollution, piles of litter and dirty waterways.

'Spelunkers will be awed by Guìzhōu's Zhijin Cave (p678), one of the world's largest underground labyrinths'

THE LAND

Broadly speaking, China is made up of three major physical regions. The first and highest of these is the Tibetan plateau, encompassing the regions of Qīnghǎi and Tibet, which averages 4500m above sea level. Peaks of the towering Himalayan mountain range at its southern rim average about 6000m above sea level, and 40 peaks rise to 7000m or more. Mt Everest (p932), known to the Chinese as Zhūmǔlángmǎfēng, lies on the Tibet–Nepal border. This region features low temperatures, high winds and intense solar radiation. Snowmelt in these mountains feeds the headwaters for many of the country's largest rivers, including the Yellow (Huáng Hé), Mekong (Láncāng Jiāng), Salween (Nù Jiāng) Rivers and, of course, the mighty Yangzi (Cháng Jiāng).

The second major region is a vast, arid area in northwestern China that features inhospitable sandy and rocky deserts. North from the plateaus of Tibet and Qīnghǎi lies Xīnjiāng's Tarim Basin, the largest inland basin in the world. Here you'll find the Taklamakan Desert (p839), China's largest, as well as the country's biggest shifting salt lake, Lop Nur in Xīnjiāng. (Lop Nur was also the site of China's nuclear-bomb testing.) The Tarim Basin

SUSTAINABLE TRAVEL

Not so long ago, the enjoyment of wildlife-watching for its own sake would have been anathema to communist ideology, but with typical pragmatism Chinese entrepreneurs have begun to realise the potential of domestic and foreign ecotourism. And while China's ecotourism industry is in its infancy, rest assured it will catch on fast – probably faster than the bureaucracy can implement and enforce sensible guidelines.

Westerners are sometimes shocked at the way animals are treated in China. Many traditional medicines and dishes contain wild animal parts and, as in many areas of the world, a few ruthless operators may flaunt wildlife protection laws to enable visitors to enjoy themselves. It's not all bad, of course, and attitudes are definitely changing, but travellers can make informed choices when choosing tour operators, opting for environment-friendly operators whenever possible, and when buying souvenirs.

The language barrier can be a problem in many parts of China, but when choosing a tour operator try to find out whether they:

- employ local people, and use local products and services
- make contributions to the parks and places they visit
- sponsor local environmental projects
- keep tour groups small to reduce the impact on the environment
- aid environmental and wildlife researchers
- educate travellers about wildlife, the environment and local cultures.

Bear in mind that this isn't Africa or Central America, and 'ecotour' operators are still finding their feet, so don't expect a 'yes' to every question. But if you get a 'no' to all of them, try to ascertain how the company *does* contribute to sustainable tourism and if the answer doesn't ring true, consider looking elsewhere.

Travellers have reported seeing parts of endangered animals for sale in remote (and even not-so-remote) areas. Before buying souvenirs, check that they have not been made with parts of protected and/or endangered animals. And check with your country's importation laws before you waste your money – items manufactured from protected wildlife may be confiscated at customs when you return home anyway.

Poachers trading in protected species can find themselves behind bars for up to 15 years, while those found smuggling the internationally revered giant panda face death. Even consumers can be punished, a law that has been around for some time but only recently enforced. So before you swallow that time-honoured remedy, ask for the ingredients. Despite laws banning their capture, protected and endangered animals continue to be led to the chemist counters of China. Ingredients to watch for include bear bile, rhinoceros horns, dried seahorse, musk deer, antelope horns, leopard bones, sea lions, macaques, alligators, anteaters, pangolins, green sea turtles, freshwater turtles, rat snakes and giant clams.

As traditional Chinese medicine (TCM) makes it big globally, international laws prohibiting the trade of many species have forced practitioners to seek out alternative ingredients. Tiger bones, for instance, are being replaced with the bones of rodents. The difficulty lies in persuading Chinese consumers to accept such alternatives – rodent bones just don't come close to tiger bones in prestige.

And don't forget to offer encouragement to locals who have provided a valuable service. Try to avoid the vulgar habit of tipping – the official line usually discourages this anyway. Instead, consider donating something that park staff, or your tour guide or driver, would appreciate, especially if you feel they have a natural interest or talent. (For example, if you're about to leave the country you could leave behind your well-thumbed bird book.) Such gifts are way beyond the procurement power of most tour guides and will help further their interest in providing a sustainable tour experience.

is bordered to the north by the lofty Tiān Shān (p827) mountains. Also in Xīnjiāng is China's hot spot, the low-lying Turpan Basin (p827), known as the 'Oasis of Fire'. China's best-known desert is of course the Gobi, although most of it lies outside the country's borders.

The third major region comprises about 45% of the country and contains 95% of the population. This densely populated part of China descends like a staircase from west to east, from the inhospitable high plateaus of Tibet and Qīnghǎi to the fertile but largely featureless plains and basins of the great rivers that drain the high ranges. These plains are the most important agricultural areas of the country and the most heavily populated. It's hard to imagine, but the plains have largely been laid down by siltation by the Yangzi and other great rivers over many millennia. The process continues: the Yangzi alone deposits millions of tonnes of silt annually and land at the river mouth is growing at the rate of 100m a year. Hardly any significant stands of natural vegetation remain in this area, although several mountain ranges are still forested and provide oases for wildlife and native plants.

The Yellow River, about 5460km long and the second-longest river in China, is often touted as the birthplace of Chinese civilisation. China's longest river, the Yangzi, is one of the longest rivers in the world. Its watershed of almost 2 million sq km – 20% of China's land mass – supports 400 million people. Dropping from its source high on the Tibetan plateau, it runs for 6300km to the sea, of which the last few hundred kilometres is across virtually flat alluvial plains. The Yangzi has been an important thoroughfare for humans for centuries, used throughout China's history for trade and transport; it even has its own unique wildlife, but all this has been threatened by the controversial Three Gorges Dam Project (see the boxed text, p814). The dam will generate power and is supposed to thwart the Yangzi's propensity to flood – floodwaters periodically inundate millions of hectares and destroy hundreds of thousands of lives.

'The Yellow River, about 5460km long, is often touted as the birthplace of Chinese civilisation'

The remote Spratly Islands (Nánshā) in the South China Sea are claimed by China and other countries, including the Philippines, Vietnam, Taiwan, Brunei and Malaysia. In 1989 the Chinese forcefully took the Paracel Islands (Xīshā) from Vietnam. China and Vietnam have had a long history of conflict, which led to fighting as recently as 1979, when 120,000 Chinese troops invaded and captured several Vietnamese towns before withdrawing. China fought and won a border war with India in the 1960s, but the boundary issue remains unresolved and a potential source of further conflict between these two nuclear states.

WILDLIFE

China's varied topography sets the stage for an incredible variety of habitats, ranging from tropical rainforests in the south to subarctic wilderness in the north, barren cold and hot deserts, and high mountains. China's wild animals include nearly 400 species of mammal – including some of the world's rarest and most charismatic species: more than 1300 bird species, 424 of reptile and more than 300 species of amphibian. Unfortunately, the country's enormous human population and rapidly expanding economy have had a considerable impact on this rich natural heritage; many of these same species are now rare or critically endangered. Many animals are officially protected, though illegal hunting and trapping continue. The biggest challenges to wildlife conservation are habitat destruction and deforestation to feed encroaching agriculture and urbanisation, although slow improvements are being made in some areas.

Watching China's wildlife in its natural habitat still requires a great deal of time, patience and luck – for example, without specialist knowledge your chances of seeing large animals in the wild are virtually nil – but almost pristine reserves are within a relatively easy distance of travellers' destinations such as Chéngdū and Xī'ān. More and more visitors are including visits to protected areas as part of their itinerary for a look at China's elusive wildlife residents – outside of zoos.

Plants

China is home to more than 32,000 species of seed plant and 2500 species of forest tree, plus an extraordinary plant diversity that includes some famous 'living fossils' – a diversity so great that a comparison between the vegetation of Jílín province in the semifrigid north and Hǎinán province in the tropical south would find few plant species shared by the two provinces. Major habitats include: coniferous forests, dominated by fir, spruce and hemlock, sometimes mixed with bamboo thickets; deciduous broadleaf forests, similar to but richer in species than equivalent forests in Europe and North America; tropical and subtropical rainforests, which grow chiefly in the southeast and southwest, and are particularly rich in both plant and animal species; and floristically less well endowed habitats such as wetlands, deserts and alpine meadows. There are still many reserves where intact vegetation ecosystems can be seen at first-hand, but few parts of the country have escaped human impact. Deforestation continues apace in many regions and vast areas are under cultivation with monocultures such as rice.

Many plants commonly cultivated in Western gardens today originated in China, and among them is the ginkgo tree, a famous 'living fossil' whose unmistakeable imprint has been found in rocks 270 million years old. The ginkgo has both male and female plants, and has been cultivated as an ornamental tree both in and outside China for centuries. Until recently it was thought to be extinct in the wild, but two small populations are now protected in Zhèjiāng province's Tian Mu Shan Reserve. Scientists were somewhat astonished to find specimens of *Metasequoia*, a 200-million-year-old conifer long thought extinct, growing in an isolated valley in Sìchuān. This ancient pine is related to the huge redwoods of West Coast USA and is the only such example that grows outside of the western hemisphere. The unique dove tree or paper tree, whose greatly enlarged white bracts look like a flock of doves, grows only in the deciduous forests of the southwest and is becoming increasingly rare.

Apart from rice, the plant probably most often associated with China and Chinese culture is bamboo, of which China boasts some 300 species. Bamboos grow in many parts of China, but bamboo forests were once so extensive that they enabled the evolution of the giant panda, which eats virtually nothing else, and a suite of small mammals, birds and insects that live in bamboo thickets. Some bamboo species have long been cultivated by people for building material, tools and food. Most of these useful species are found in the subtropical areas south of the Yangzi, and the best surviving thickets are in southwestern provinces such as Sìchuān.

Deciduous forests cover mid-altitudes in the mountains, and are characterised by oaks, hemlocks and aspens, with a leafy understorey that springs to life after the winter snows have melted. Among the more famous blooms of the understorey are rhododendrons and azaleas, and many species of each grow naturally in China's mountain ranges. They are best viewed in spring, although some species flower right through summer; one of the best places to see them is at Sìchuān's Wolong Nature Reserve (p767), where rare azaleas bring tourists in summer. Both rhododendrons and azaleas grow in distinct bands at various heights on the mountainsides, which are recognisable as you drive through the reserve to the high mountain passes. At the very highest

Bamboo comprises 99% of the giant panda's diet, and it spends up to 16 hours a day feeding, during which time it may eat up to 20kg of bamboo shoots, stems and leaves.

elevations, the alpine meadows grazed by yaks are often dotted with showy and colourful blooms.

For a good look at plants from China's north, visit Běijīng's Botanic Gardens (p141).

Mammals

Hardly a day goes by without China's favourite animal, the giant panda, hitting the news either at home or around the world. After several Western nations, including Australia, protested against China's rather profligate use of pandas as 'good-will ambassadors' (read: cash cows), the government now seems genuine about panda conservation, as it is about the conservation of many other species. Nonetheless, a pair of pandas was recently offered to Taiwan, so panda diplomacy looks set to continue.

The giant panda is the most famous denizen of western Sìchuān, although you have zip chance of seeing them on the steep, bamboo-covered slopes of the Himalayan foothills. It really is an amazing animal (see the boxed text, p758), as well as being universally appealing, and a recent census has revised the world population upwards after an estimated 39 pandas were located in Wanglang Nature Reserve, Sìchuān. Another positive development has been the 'bamboo tunnel', an area of reforestation designed to act as a corridor for the pandas to move between two fragmented patches of forest.

The Last Panda by George Schaller is an evocative book describing his ground-breaking field research on the giant panda with a Chinese team during the 1980s in the forests of Sìchuān's Wolong Nature Reserve.

China's high mountain ranges form natural refuges for wildlife, many of which are now protected in parks and reserves that have escaped the depredations of loggers and dam-builders. The barren high plains of the Tibetan plateau are home to several large animals, such as the *chiru* or Tibetan antelope, Tibetan wild ass, wild sheep and goats, and wolves. In theory, many of these animals are protected but in practice poaching and hunting still pose a threat to their survival. One animal you won't see outside of zoos is the beautiful snow leopard, which normally inhabits the highest parts of the most remote mountain ranges and is rarely encountered even by researchers. This small, retiring leopard has a luxuriant coat of fur that insulates it against the cold. It preys on mammals as large as mountain goats, but unfortunately it is persecuted for allegedly preying on livestock.

The Himalayan foothills of western Sìchuān – still big hills by anyone's standards – support the biggest diversity of mammals in China. Aside from giant pandas, other mammals found in this region include the panda's small cousin, the raccoon-like red panda, as well as Asiatic black bears and leopards. Among the grazers are golden takin, a large goatlike antelope with a yellowish coat and a reputation for being cantankerous, argali sheep and various deer species including the diminutive mouse deer. You have virtually no chance of seeing any of these animals in the wild (we know of only one person who has seen a wild red panda in years of leading tours to China – and it's not even endangered), but you may be lucky enough to see small mammals, such as squirrels, badgers and martens if you can get far enough away from people and their dogs.

The sparsely inhabited northeastern provinces abutting Siberia are inhabited by reindeer, moose, musk deer, bears, sables and Manchurian tigers. The world's largest tiger, the Manchurian Tiger (Dongbeihu) – also known as the Siberian Tiger – only numbers a few hundred in the world, its remote habitat being one of its principal saviours. Overall, China is unusually well endowed with big and small cats. Apart from tigers, it also supports three species of leopard, including the beautiful clouded leopard of tropical rainforests, plus several species of small cat, such as the Asiatic golden cat and a rare endemic species, the Chinese mountain cat.

Rainforests are famous for their diversity of wildlife, and the tropical south of Yúnnán province, particularly the area around Xīshuāngbǎnnà (p730), is one of the richest in China. These forests support herds of Asiatic elephants and Indochinese tigers, although most of your wildlife encounters here will be of the feathered kind.

The Yangzi floodway was big enough to favour the evolution of distinct large animals, including the Yangzi dolphin *(baiji)* and Chinese alligator, both now desperately endangered (see p90). The Yangzi dolphin is one of just a few freshwater dolphin species in the world (others occur in the Ganges and Amazon river systems) and is by far the rarest. Once common, it has succumbed to drowning in fishing nets and lethal injuries from ship's propellers, now ubiquitous in a river that for centuries was trafficked by sailing vessels.

One famous victim of China's many wars was the *milu*, known to the West as Père David's deer, which became extinct during the Boxer Rebellion. Fortunately, a herd had been translocated to a private location in England, where they thrived, and late in the 20th century a number were used to set up breeding herds in China once again. There are now some 2000 *milu* in special reserves in the Yangzi basin.

The wild mammals you are most likely to see are several species of monkey. The large and precocious Père David's macaque is common at Éméi Shān (p769), in Sìchuān, where bands often intimidate people into handing over their picnics; macaques can also be seen on Hǎinán's Monkey Island (p629). Several other monkey species are rare and endangered, including the beautiful golden monkey of the southwestern mountains and the snub-nosed monkey of the Yúnnán rainforests. But by far the most endangered is the Hainan gibbon, which thanks to massive forest clearance is down to just a few dozen individuals on the island of Hǎinán.

Birds

Most of the wildlife you'll see will be birds, and with more than 1300 species recorded, including about 100 endemic or near-endemic species, China offers some great bird-watching opportunities. Spring is usually the best time to see them, when deciduous foliage buds, migrants return from their wintering grounds and nesting gets into full swing. Even city parks and gardens in all but the most polluted cities will support a few species at this time of year. **BirdLife International** (www.birdlife.org/regional/asia/), the worldwide bird conservation organisation, recognises 12 Endemic Bird Areas (EBAs) in China, nine of which are wholly within the country and three are shared with neighbouring countries.

Although the range of birds is huge, China is a centre of endemicity for several species and these are usually the ones that visiting birders will seek out. Most famous are the pheasant family, of which China can boast 62 species, including many endemic or near-endemic species. Most male pheasants are large showy birds, but among the more spectacular examples are Lady Amherst's pheasant, the gorgeous golden pheasant, Reeves' pheasant (which has a tail up to 1.5m in length), and the iridescent Chinese monal.

Other families well represented in China include the laughing thrushes, with 36 species; parrotbills, which are almost confined to China and its near neighbours; and many members of the jay family. The crested ibis is a pinkish bird that feeds in the rice paddies on invertebrates, and was once found from central China to Japan. It is now extinct in the wild in Japan, but a captive breeding and release programme has seen its numbers climb to over 400 in Shaanxi and adjoining provinces.

Keen bird-watchers should carry *The Field Guide to the Birds of China* by J MacKinnon, which illustrates and describes all 1300 species that have been recorded in China and gives valuable background on their ecology and conservation.

Among China's more famous large birds are cranes, and nine of the world's 14 species have been recorded here. In Jiāngxī province, on the lower Yangzi, a vast series of shallow lakes and lagoons was formed by stranded overflow from Yangzi flooding. The largest of these is Lake Poyang, although it is only a few metres deep and drains during winter. Vast numbers of waterfowl and other birds inhabit these swamps year-round, including ducks, geese, herons and egrets. Although it is difficult to get to, birders are increasingly drawn to the area in winter, when many of the lakes dry up and attract flocks of up to five crane species, including the endangered, pure white Siberian crane. The number of waterfowl swells with migratory ducks and geese escaping the harsh winter of the far north. It is not known how the Three Gorges Dam will affect this valuable wintering ground.

Parts of China are now established on the itineraries of global ecotour companies, although the country is so vast that few visitors manage more than one or two sites per trip. Check websites such as www.eurobirding.com for birders' trip reports and more information on bird-watching in China. Recommended destinations in which you should see a good variety of interesting species, plus several of the endemic birds, include Zhalong Nature Reserve (p398), one of several vast wetlands in Hēilóngjiāng province. Visit in summer to see breeding storks, cranes and flocks of wildfowl before they fly south for the winter. Běidàihé, on the coast of the China Sea, is well known for migratory birds on passage. Běidàihé is within easy reach of Běijīng, and bird-watching tours go there in spring and autumn to check out the migrants.

Not many birders make it to the Tibetan plateau, but Qīnghǎi Hú (p904) is a breeding ground for cranes, wild geese, sandpipers and countless other birds, including a couple that are endemic to this inhospitable region. In 2005 some 6300 birds, mainly wild geese, were found dead in the area. Some tested positive to the H5N1 virus (bird flu), although the source of the infection remains unclear and could have been local poultry farms.

Caohai Lake (p679), in northwestern Guìzhōu province, is the most important wetland in this part of the country and supports overwintering black-necked cranes, as well as other cranes, storks and waterfowl.

Jiǔzhàigōu (p795) is not just an amazing scenic spot – it is home to some rare and endemic Chinese birds, such as the Sichuan owl, although you will have to work hard to escape the crowds of noisy, camera-toting Chinese tourists.

Even a short stopover in Hong Kong can be rewarding, especially in winter when Mai Po Marsh (p536) is thronged with migratory wildfowl and waders, including the rare spoon-billed sandpiper. The **Hong Kong Bird Watching Society** (www.hkbws.org.hk) organises regular outings and publishes a newsletter in English.

Most bird-watchers and bird tours head straight for Sìchuān, which offers superb birding in sites such as Wolong (p767). Here, several spectacular pheasants, including golden, blood and kalij pheasants, live on the steep forested hillsides surrounding the main road. As the road climbs towards Beilanshan Pass, higher altitude species such as eared pheasants and the spectacular Chinese monal may be seen. Alpine meadows host smaller birds, and the rocky scree slopes at the pass hold partridges, the beautiful grandala and the mighty lammergeier or bearded vulture, with a 2m wingspan.

Reptiles & Amphibians

The Chinese alligator – known as the 'muddy dragon' – is one of the smallest of the world's crocodilians, measuring only 2m in length, and is harmless to humans. But owing to habitat clearance and intense pressure

At www.cnbirds.com China Birding can fill you in on overwintering sites, migration routes and the geographical distribution of your feathered friends in China. It also has lots of excellent photos.

to turn its wetlands to agriculture along the lower Yangzi, fewer than 130 of these crocs still exist in the wild. A captive breeding programme has been successful, but as yet there are few options for releasing this rare reptile back into the wild.

The cold, rushing rivers of the southwestern mountains are home to the world's largest amphibian, the giant salamander. This enormous amphibian can reach 1m in length and feeds on small aquatic animals. Unfortunately, it is now critically endangered in the wild and, like so many other animals, hunted for food. More than 300 other species of frog and salamander occur in China's waterways and wetlands, and preying on them is a variety of snakes, including cobras and vipers. One of China's more unusual national parks is Snake Island, near Dàlián in Liáoníng province. This 800-hectare dot in the China Sea is uninhabited by people, but supports an estimated 130,000 Pallas' pit vipers, an extraordinary concentration of snakes that prey on migrating birds that land on the island every spring and autumn in huge numbers. By eating several birds each season, the snakes can subsist on lizards and invertebrates for the rest of the year until migration time comes round again.

Endangered Species

It is sometimes said that the people of southern China will eat anything with four legs except a table. While this is not *entirely* true, the list of animals that are served up at dinner or bottled for traditional remedies is depressingly long. Just about every large mammal you can think of is on China's list of endangered species, as are many of the so-called 'lower' animals and plants. **Earth Trends** (http://earthtrends.wri.org) lists 168 threatened species of higher plant, 79 of mammal, 74 of bird, 31 of reptile and one amphibian.

Threats facing native animals include the usual suspects: deforestation, pollution, hunting and trapping for fur, body parts and sport. The Convention on International Trade in Threatened and Endangered Species (CITES) records legal trade in live reptiles and parrots, and astonishingly high numbers of reptile and wild cat skins. One can only guess at the number of such products being collected or sold unofficially.

In spite of the unequal odds against them, a number of rare animals continue to survive in the wild in small and remote areas. Notable among them are the Chinese alligator in Ānhuī, the giant salamander in the fast-running waters of the Yangzi and Yellow Rivers, the Yangzi River dolphin in the lower and middle reaches of the river, and the pink dolphin of the Hong Kong islands of Sha Chau and Lung Kwu Chau (these animals may be seen on dolphin-spotting trips in Hong Kong Harbour). The famed giant panda is confined to the fauna-rich valleys and ranges of Sìchuān, but your best chances for sighting one is in Chéngdū's Giant Panda Breeding Research Base (p757). For more on these charismatic creatures, see the boxed text, opposite. You may be lucky enough to chance upon a golden monkey in the mountains of Sìchuān, Yúnnán and Guìzhōu. Other animals to make the endangered list include the snow leopard, Indochinese tiger, chiru antelope, crested ibis, Asiatic elephant, red-crowned crane and black-crowned crane.

Snakes feature prominently on China's menus – more than 10,000 tonnes of serpents are dished up every year to diners – and in traditional Chinese medicine, because snake parts are said to restore health and improve sexual prowess. The venom of dangerous species such as vipers is particularly sought for medicine. The situation is so dire that no fewer than 43 of China's 200 snake species are said to be endangered. Fortunately, nature has a way of

The www.wwfchina .org website has details of the Worldwide Fund for Nature's (WWF) projects for endangered and protected animals in China. You'll also find a kids' page for the budding biologists in the family.

SEARCHING FOR THE ELUSIVE GIANT PANDA David Andrew

The giant panda's solitary nature makes it extremely hard to observe in the wild, and even today, after decades of intensive research and total protection in dedicated reserves, sightings are rare. A few years ago the thought of travelling to China to track giant pandas seemed an impossible dream, but in 2005 I was lucky enough to be involved in field research on the animals in Changqing Nature Reserve, Shaanxi province.

Changqing Nature Reserve boasts a comparatively high density of pandas, and trained local guides monitor the bears' movements year-round. But even so, the pandas are still mighty hard to find: the terrain is ruggedly mountainous and we spent days clambering up steep hillsides only to lose the trail among the dense bamboo thickets. The guides assured us the weather was to blame, as it had been unseasonably hot and the pandas had sought the comparative coolness of the mountain tops.

We didn't manage to see any pandas on the first field trip of the study, but we vowed to return in the dead of winter when, the guides assured us, pandas were easier to track in the snow. Fortunately, giant pandas leave abundant traces of their passage, so to speak, and their droppings gave us enough clues to their life histories, population dynamics and feeding habits to make the study a success.

Changqing Nature Reserve is open to visitors and is well worth a visit for its relatively unspoilt montane forest and the chance to see giant pandas in the wild. Find out more at www.cqpanda.com.

fighting back and the depletion of snake numbers leads pretty quickly to an increase in rodent numbers, with resulting crop destruction.

Intensive farmland cultivation, the reclaiming of wetlands, river damming, industrial and rural waste, and desertification are reducing unprotected forest areas and making the survival of many of these species increasingly precarious. Although there are laws against killing or capturing rare wildlife, their struggle for survival is further complicated as many remain on the most-wanted lists for traditional Chinese medicine and dinner delicacies.

PROTECTED AREAS

Since the first nature reserve was established in 1956, around 2000 more protected areas have joined the ranks, protecting about 14% of China's land area (see the map on p92). Various categories of reserve are recognised, ranging from nature reserves, wilderness areas and national parks to areas managed for sustainable use. Together they offer the traveller the chance to enjoy an incredible variety of landscapes, although infrastructure is often lacking and access may be well off the beaten track. Although China has many World Heritage-listed sites, most of these are for cultural reasons, rather than natural attributes; and some areas in need of protection, such as marine ecosystems, are notably lacking.

While many of the parks are intended for the preservation of endangered plants and animals, don't expect to see any wild animals except for some precocious monkeys at various sacred mountains (although birders will usually find something to look at). And before you pack your hiking gear and binoculars, be prepared to share many of the more popular reserves with expanding commercial development. Tourism is generally welcomed into these reserves with open arms, meaning pricey hotels, more roads, gondolas, hawkers and busloads of tourists. With a little effort, you can often find a less beaten path to escape down, but don't expect utter tranquillity. It's better to take it in your stride and remember that most Chinese visitors won't be up at dawn to see wildlife, so get an early start.

'With a little effort, you can often find a less beaten path to escape down, but don't expect utter tranquillity'

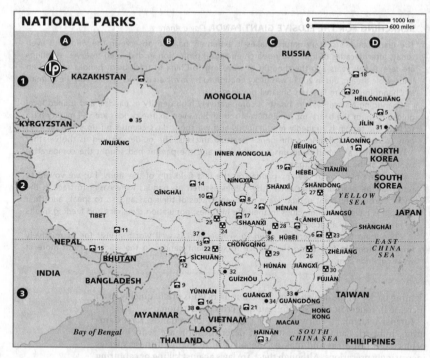

NATIONAL PARKS

ENVIRONMENTAL ISSUES

As a developing country with rapid industrialisation, it's not surprising that China has some hefty environmental issues to contend with. Unfortunately, China's huge population makes its environmental plights infinitely bigger than those of most other nations. Sometimes astounding levels of industrial pollution render whole cities barely habitable by Western standards, and air pollution, deforestation, endangered species, and rural and industrial waste are all taking their toll.

With the 2008 Olympics and the country's entry into the World Trade Organization (WTO), China seems to have changed its policy of 'industrial catch-up first, environmental clean-up later' to one of tidying up its environmental act now. Nevertheless, analysts continue to point to an impending environmental catastrophe, fearing that the efforts could well be too little, too late.

The impact of China's environmental problems doesn't stop at the country's borders – acid rain, desert sandstorms, and silted and polluted rivers are all too familiar to China's neighbours. Across the north of China, rampaging natural fires are believed to consume more than 200 million tonnes of coal a year, further exacerbating China's contribution to global warming.

China's authoritarian system does yield occasional advantages, however. When the penny finally drops, action can be taken quickly and sometimes effectively to slow or halt environmental degradation, despite having to overcome years of bureaucratic foot-dragging and inertia. In this way the clear-felling of mountain ranges was quickly stopped when it was realised that it led to catastrophic flooding and huge loss of life. Likewise, top-down management can enforce wildlife protection in a way that is lacking at a grass-roots level in rural China.

'China's huge population makes its environmental plights infinitely bigger than those of most other nations'

Energy Use & Air Pollution

Seven of the world's 10 most polluted cities are in China, and some make American cities like Los Angeles look clean in comparison. The problem is worst in winter, when temperature inversion smothers most of the country's major cities under a great canopy of smog. The incredible rise in automobile use and ownership has been partly to blame, but the biggest source of air pollution is coal. It provides some 70% of China's energy needs and around 900 million tonnes of it goes up in smoke yearly. The result is immense damage to air and water quality, agriculture and human health, with acid rain falling on about 30% of the country. Neighbouring Korea and Japan complain about damage to their forests from acid rain that is believed to have come from China, and indeed satellites have detected black, sulphurous clouds drifting out to sea from China and over the Pacific Ocean. As demand quickly outstrips domestic resources of coal, the government has made some efforts to seek out alternative sources of energy. Plans to construct natural gas pipelines are under way and taxes have been introduced on high-sulphur coals.

Desertification

Deforestation and overgrazing have accelerated the desertification of vast areas of China, particularly in the western provinces. Deserts now cover almost one-fifth of the country and China's dustbowl is the largest in the world. The Ministry of Land and Resources says the total area under the threat of desertification may amount to more than a quarter of China's land area. Běijīng itself is threatened by a rolling tide of sand advancing on the capital from the Gobi Desert that is responsible for massive dust storms every spring (see the boxed text, p95). As usual, people are the problem: agricultural reforms which deregulated stocking levels have prompted the overstocking of grazing land with livestock and the resulting unsustainable stripping of vegetation. The government has imposed selective bans on stock levels but, once again, unless these are enforced it may be too little, too late. United Nations experts estimate the annual direct damage to China's economy through desertification at US$6.5 billion, and the livelihood of some 400 million people is threatened by the encroaching sands of the Gobi, Taklamakan and Kumtag Deserts.

Water & Wetlands

The Grand Canal, once billed as China's third great waterway (after the Yangzi and Yellow Rivers), is the longest artificial canal in the world. It once stretched for 1800km from Hángzhōu in south China to Běijīng in the north. Today, however, most of the Grand Canal is silted over and no longer navigable. Siltation due to deforestation and increased runoff is just one of several problems affecting China's waterways. It is estimated that China annually

'Deforestation and overgrazing have accelerated the desertification of vast areas of China'

TOP NATIONAL PARKS

Reserves	Features	Activities	When to visit	Page
Chángbái Shān	China's largest reserve: cranes, deer, tigers and some 300 medicinal plants	hiking	Jun–early Sep	p380
Éméi Shān	luxuriant scenery along a steep, ancient pilgrim route; monkeys; Buddhist sights	hiking, monastery stays	May–Oct	p769
Jiǔzhàigōu	stunning alpine scenery and gem-coloured lakes; takins, golden monkeys	hiking, Tibetan village stays	Jun–Oct	p795
Tài Shān	holy mountain with gobsmacking views; Taoist sights	hiking	May–Oct	p214
Wǔlíngyuán Scenic Area	craggy peaks, waterfalls, caves, subtropical forest	rafting, hiking	Jun–Oct	p515

dumps three billion tonnes of untreated water into the ocean via its rivers, a statement that won't likely shock you if you take a look at some of the water flowing under the bridges as you journey across the country.

China's rivers and wetlands face great pressure from draining and reclamation, as well as pollution from untreated industrial and domestic waste. This poor-quality water, coupled with often acute water shortages, is creating significant environmental health hazards. Some reports suggest that half the population is supplied with polluted water.

Another of China's biggest water problems is that the resource is too cheap and overused by farmers, industry and the general public, but the government is fearful of raising the price. Drought often hits north and west China while northeast and central China are flooded: waste, silting up of riverbeds, overextraction of water and the general abuse of the environment worsen the situation. The communists' cure-all to China's water problems is the damming of the Yangzi River. For more on this monumental project, see p814.

TRAVEL WIDELY, TREAD LIGHTLY, GIVE SUSTAINABLY – THE LONELY PLANET FOUNDATION

The Lonely Planet Foundation proudly supports nimble nonprofit institutions working for change in the world. Each year the foundation donates 5% of Lonely Planet company profits to projects selected by staff and authors. Our partners range from Kabissa, which provides small nonprofits across Africa with access to technology, to the Foundation for Developing Cambodian Orphans, which supports girls at risk of falling victim to sex traffickers.

Our nonprofit partners are linked by a grass-roots approach to the areas of health, education or sustainable tourism. Many – such as Louis Sarno who works with BaAka (Pygmy) children in the forested areas of Central African Republic – choose to focus on women and children as one of the most effective ways to support the whole community. Louis is determined to give options to children who are discriminated against by the majority Bantu population.

Sometimes foundation assistance is as simple as restoring a local ruin like the Minaret of Jam in Afghanistan; this incredible monument now draws intrepid tourists to the area and its restoration has greatly improved options for local people.

Just as travel is often about learning to see with new eyes, so many of the groups we work with aim to change the way people see themselves and the future for their children and communities.

THE GREEN WALL OF CHINA

If you visit Běijīng in spring and experience the sand storms that send residents rushing around with plastic bags over their heads, you may not be so surprised to hear that the city may one day be swallowed up by the Gobi Desert. Only 150km away, the winds are blowing the sands towards the capital at a rate of 2km a year, with 30m dunes closing in. In their wake, these massive dust storms have left entire towns abandoned and environmental refugees numbering in the millions. They've also brought about bizarre weather effects, such as 'black winds' and 'mud rains', even finding their way across the Pacific to drop grit on Vancouver and bring unreal sunsets to San Francisco.

The problem is overgrazing and deforestation, for every month 200 sq km of arable land in China becomes a desert. China's government has pledged US$6.8 billion to plant a 'green wall' of millions of trees between Běijīng and the sands; at 5700km long, it will be longer than the Great Wall of China. Under the scheme, the government pays farmers to plant trees and is claiming a partial victory despite ongoing problems, such as trees dying, over-irrigation, erosion and corruption. China's State Forestry Administration states that desertification has slowed from more than 10,400 sq km annually at the end of the last century to about 3000 sq km since 2001. But while the frequency of sandstorms has apparently decreased since the 1990s, their intensity has increased: one storm in 2006 dumped an estimated 330,000 tonnes of dust on the capital. In 2006 China agreed to work with neighbouring countries to combat desertification in northeast Asia.

Environmental Awareness

China has a long tradition of celebrating nature, from landscape paintings to poems dwelling on the beauty of mountain peaks shrouded in mist. However, today, as in times gone by, the luxury of soliloquising over bounteous nature is afforded to only a few: the vast majority of people are too busy just trying to survive. And as in many nations of the world, the unfortunate corollary of this is that overexploitation of resources by a massive (and growing) population simultaneously destroys the land and environment it needs to survive.

Compelling economic pressure to exploit the environment has been exacerbated by a lack of knowledge on the part of China's citizens who have been given no education or information on ecology. Waking up to this, the government now bombards viewers with green directives on TV, from saving water to planting trees and litter disposal. In the dour 1970s, such environmental concerns were more likely to be dismissed as a bourgeois conspiracy. These days a growing middle class finds itself wooed by advertisements for environmentally friendly washing powders and detergents.

There is legislation to curb the worst excesses of industry, but these laws are rarely enforced. Corrupt officials are partly to blame, but the drag on economic expansion is also cited as a factor. There has been an increase in the severity of penalties for violating China's conservation laws, with the death penalty and life sentences not uncommon. However, there remains little room for robust debate of the issues in the media.

More than 2000 environmental groups have sprung up since the advent of the first environmental NGO (nongovernmental organisation) in China, Friends of Nature, in the mid-1990s. Hundreds of thousands of Chinese now participate in activities ranging from politically 'safe' issues, such as biodiversity protection and environmental education, to cutting-edge environmental activism such as dam protests, energy conservation and the prosecution of polluters through the court system. The government in general tolerates these activities, as it realises that environmental NGOs can fill gaps in official efforts to protect the environment. Although many NGOs are politically savvy, to a great extent they still rely on international funding and may thus attract criticism for being 'directed' by outside agencies.

Roadside billboards proclaiming that 'Wildlife is not food' in English and Chinese are an encouraging sign that attitudes to wildlife conservation are starting to change.

Food & Drink Julie Grundvig

To the Chinese, food is life, health and good fortune. The Chinese live to eat and China's cuisine is as varied as its geography and peoples. Wherever you travel, you'll come across a panoply of different cooking styles and dishes, all making good use of fresh, local ingredients and spices. There's something for everybody, from the peppery flavours of Sìchuān to the delicate seasonings of Guǎngdōng. Bring your appetite because when it comes to eating, China will not let you down.

There's a common Chinese saying that goes 'For the people food is their heaven'. This passion for food has shaped Chinese culture, with cooks developing and perfecting their art even in the harshest of living conditions. To save cooking fuel, meat and vegetables were chopped into tiny pieces to ensure faster cooking and dishes were served communally to make sure everyone got something to eat. What has resulted is a triumphant blending of inventiveness, flavour and economy.

In a traditional Chinese meal, grains are always the centrepiece, served with vegetables and soybean products and, if affordable, meat or fish. The Chinese commonly greet each other with the question 'Nǐ chī fàn le ma?' ('Have you eaten yet?'). Fàn may be loosely translated as 'grain' – as opposed to cài, which literally means 'vegetable' and, by extension, any accompaniment to grain in a meal. The principle that a proper meal is based around a staple grain dates back at least to the Shang dynasty (1700–1100 BC) and remains fundamental to Chinese cuisine wherever it is found.

A well-prepared Chinese dish is expected to appeal to the senses: smell, sight, taste and touch. There's always a blending of Yin and Yang, the principles of balance and harmony – bland dishes paired with strong, crisp dishes paired with soft. The dichotomy between fàn and cài also shows how Yin and Yang are applied in everyday life. To be more specific, most vegetables and fruits are Yin foods, generally moist or soft, and are meant to have a cooling effect, nurturing the feminine aspect of our nature. Yang foods – fried, spicy or with red meat – are warming and nourish the masculine side of our nature.

China's geographical and climatic differences, together with local cooking styles, have created many different schools of cuisine. Generally, cooking in China is divided into four broad schools, the Northern, Eastern, Western and Southern schools, which can be further subdivided into smaller categories. The Chinese sum up their cooking as 'south is sweet, north is salty; east is spicy and west is sour.' It wasn't until China was overrun by the Mongols in the 12th century, when the Song court fled south of the Yangzi River, that these regional schools were codified and developed. Widespread urbanisation, made possible by the commercialisation of agriculture and food distribution, gave rise to the restaurant industry, which in turn facilitated the development of the regional cuisines. Improved communications, notably the building of the Grand Canal to link many of China's innumerable waterways, allowed food to be brought from and supplied to any part of the kingdom.

The most significant development in Chinese cuisine took place in the Qing dynasty (1644–1911), when crops were introduced from the New World. Maize, sweet potatoes and peanuts – which flourished in climates where rice, wheat and millet wouldn't grow – made life possible in formerly uninhabitable areas. The other significant import from the New World was red chillies, which are not only a spice, but also a concentrated source of vitamins A and C.

Did you know that chilli peppers came to China from Peru and Mexico in the Ming dynasty?

TRAVEL YOUR TASTEBUDS

Eating in China can be an overwhelming experience, especially with the variety of delicious foods to try. With so many regional delicacies, it's truly a gourmand's paradise. In the north, fill up on a tasty dish of wontons (*húntún*) stuffed with juicy leeks and minced pork, or Mongolian hotpot (*ménggǔ huǒguō*), a hearty brew of mutton, onions and cabbage.

When travelling through China's arid northwest, consider trying a bowl of noodles topped with sliced donkey meat (*lǘròu huáng miàn*) or sizzling lamb kebobs (*kǎo yángròu*). Make sure to stop in Xī'ān for a warming bowl of mutton broth and shredded flat bread (*yángròu pàomó*). The hand-pulled noodles (*lāmiàn*) of Lánzhōu are also a non-miss.

If you're in the mood for something sweet and savoury, head to Shànghǎi for delicious honey-smoked carp (*mìzhī xūnyú*) or a tongue-tingling plate of hot and sour squid (*suānlà yóuyú*). Cleanse your palate with a glass of heady Shàoxīng yellow wine (*Shàoxīng huángjiǔ*) or the more delicate flavours of Dragonwell tea (*lóngjǐng chá*). About to climb the misty peaks of Huángshān? Gear up for your ascent with a dish of Huángshān braised pigeon (*Huángshān zhēnggē*).

For those who like it hot, nothing is better than the fiery flavours of Sìchuān. You can start with mouth-numbing tofu (*mápó dòufu*), followed up with spicy chicken with peanuts (*gōngbào jīdīng*). If the smoke still isn't coming out of your ears, we dare you to order boiled fish smothered in chilli (*shuǐzhǔ yú*). That'll really get you breathing fire.

In the south, enjoy morning dim sum in Guǎngzhōu or a bowl of Cantonese snake soup (*shé gēng*) in one of the city's boisterous night markets. While in Macau, taste the Macanese dish *porco à alentejana*, a mouthwatering casserole of pork and clams.

And don't forget delectable stinky tofu (*chòu dòufu*) – some say it's the equivalent to European stinky cheese.

STAPLES & SPECIALITIES

For breakfast, the Chinese generally eat very light. They may have a bowl of rice porridge (*zhōu* or *congee*) often accompanied by pickles and *yóutiáo* (deep-fried dough sticks), along with steamed buns, served plain or with fillings. This is usually washed down with hot soybean milk, sweetened or plain. Other dishes can include rice-noodle soups, boiled eggs, fried peanuts and dumplings.

The Chinese eat lunch between 11.30am and 2pm, many taking their midday meal from any number of small eateries on the streets. For Chinese on the run, lunch and dinner generally consist of rice or noodles, topped with a vegetable and/or some meat. For more formal affairs with family and friends, lunch and dinner usually consist of several meat and vegetable dishes and a soup. Banquets can be overwhelming affairs, with 20- to 30-course dinners being common.

Rice

To the Chinese, rice is a symbol of life itself. There's a saying in Chinese that 'precious things are not pearls or jade but the five grains'. An old legend about the origin of rice claims that rice is actually a gift from the animals. Many centuries ago, China was swept by floods that destroyed all the crops and caused massive starvation. One day, some villagers saw a dog running towards them. On the dog's tail were bunches of long yellow seeds. When the villagers planted the seeds, the rice grew and hunger disappeared.

The Chinese revere rice not only as their staff of life but also for its aesthetic value. Its mellow aroma is not unlike bread. Its texture when properly done – soft yet offering some resistance, the grains detached – sets off the textures of the foods that surround it. Flavours are brought into better focus by its simplicity. Rice is the unifier of the table, bringing all the dishes into harmony. Rice isn't just steamed: it's boiled, stir-fried, roasted and used in everything from noodles to desserts.

A terrific blog dedicated to everything related to Chinese food is at www .eatingchina.com. There's great background on Chinese recipes, tea and holiday foods.

Noodles

Noodles are a staple in the north and eaten there more than rice, which is more commonly eaten in southern China. It's believed that the Chinese have been feasting on noodles for approximately 4000 years. Legend credits Marco Polo with introducing pasta to Italy in 1295.

Noodles can be made by hand or by machine, but many people agree that hand-pulled noodles (lāmiàn) are the tastiest. Watching the noodles being made is almost as much of a treat as eating them. First the cook stretches the dough by hand, then shakes it gently up and down and swings it so the dough twists around itself many times until it becomes firm. The dough is pulled and stretched until it becomes very fine.

Regional Cuisines

NORTHERN SCHOOL

In 2005 the remains of a 4000-year-old noodle dish were discovered in an upturned pot next to China's Yellow River.

In the north, wheat or millet traditionally are eaten rather than rice. The most famous Chinese dish of all, Peking duck, is served with typical northern ingredients: wheat pancakes, spring onions and fermented bean paste. There is a heavy reliance on freshwater fish and chicken in the north; cabbage is ubiquitous and seems to fill any available space on trains, buses and lorries in the winter.

Not surprisingly, the influence of the Mongols is felt most strongly in the north, and two of the region's most famous culinary exports – Mongolian barbecue and Mongolian hotpot – are adaptations from Mongol field kitchens. Animals that were hunted on horseback could be dismembered and cooked with wild vegetables and onions using soldiers' iron shields on top of hot coals as primitive barbecues.

Alternatively, soldiers could use their helmet as a pot, filling it with water, meat, condiments and vegetables to taste. Mutton is now the main ingredient used in Mongolian hotpot.

Roasting was once considered rather barbaric in other parts of China and is still more common in the north. The main methods of cooking in the northern style, though, are steaming, baking and 'explode-frying' (dropping items into a wok of hot oil and having them sizzle or 'explode', like deep-frying). This way, the food cooks very quickly. The last of these is the most common, historically because of the scarcity of fuel and, more recently, due to the introduction of the peanut, which thrives in the north and produces an abundance of oil. Although northern-style food has a reputation for being unsophisticated and bland, it has the benefit of being filling and therefore well suited to the cold climate.

EASTERN SCHOOL

The eastern region – blessed with the bounty of the Yangzi River and its tributaries, a subtropical climate, fertile soil and a coastline – has long been a mecca for gastronomes. The Southern Song capital of Hángzhōu, on the banks of West Lake with abundant fish including the highly esteemed silver carp, is the birthplace of the restaurant industry. At least one restaurant, the Louwailou Restaurant (p321), has been around since 1848. Sūzhōu (p302) is equally famous for its cuisine, which has been eulogised by generations of poets.

A vast variety of ingredients and condiments is available, which has led to a wide diversity of cuisine within the region. Explode-frying is used here, too, but not as much as the form of frying known throughout the world as archetypically Chinese: stir-frying in a wok. Another eastern style of cooking that has been exported to the rest of the world (from Fújiàn via Taiwan) is the red-stew, in which meat is simmered slowly in dark soy sauce, sugar and spices. Indeed, many Fújiàn dishes rely on a heavy, meaty stock for their distinctive flavour. Nonetheless, it is in this region that Chinese vegetarian cuisine reached its apex, partly thanks to the availability of fresh ingredients and partly to the specialisation of generations of chefs. As might be expected, seasoning is light to allow the natural flavours of the fresh ingredients to be fully appreciated.

WESTERN SCHOOL

The Western school is renowned most for its use of the red chilli, introduced by Spanish traders in the early Qing dynasty. While northern foods evolved to provide lasting satisfaction in a cold climate, Sìchuān dishes tend to dry out the body through perspiration, which helps it adjust to the intense humidity.

Pork, poultry, legumes and soya beans are the most commonly used items, supplemented by a variety of wild condiments and mountain products, such as mushrooms and other fungi, as well as bamboo shoots. Seasonings are heavy: the red chilli is often used in conjunction with Sìchuān peppercorns, garlic, ginger and onions. Meat, particularly in Húnán, is marinated, pickled or otherwise processed before cooking, which is generally by stir- or explode-frying.

The cuisine of the Western school has a reputation of being down-to-earth, rather like the inhabitants of the region. Mao Zedong hailed from Húnán and remained fond of the hot foods from his native province throughout his life. However, it was due to the Nationalists in the civil war that Sìchuān cuisine gained international recognition. Fleeing the Japanese in 1937, the Nationalist government took refuge in Chóngqìng until the end of the war in Asia. On its return to Nánjīng and Shànghǎi, thousands of Sìchuān chefs were brought along. Most of them continued on to Taiwan when the Nationalist government was forced to flee once more, and from there spread out across the globe.

SOUTHERN SCHOOL

The food from this region is easily the most common form of Chinese food found in the Western world since most overseas Chinese have their roots in the Guǎngdōng region. The humid climate and heavy rainfall mean that rice has been a staple here since the Chinese first came to the region in the Han era (206 BC–AD 220). The Southern school also benefits from a cornucopia of ingredients to choose from, although the choice is even more exotic than that of the Eastern school. Stir-frying is by far the most favoured method of cooking, closely followed by steaming. Dim sum, now a worldwide Sunday institution, originated in this region; to go *yum cha* (Cantonese for 'drink tea') still provides most overseas Chinese communities with the opportunity to get together at the weekend.

Not only are the ingredients more varied than elsewhere in China, methods of preparation also reach their peak of sophistication in the south, where the appearance and texture of foods are prized alongside their freshness. Such refinement is a far cry from the austere cuisine of the north and the earthy fare of the west. Consequently, the southerners' gourmandising and exotic tastes – for dogs, cats, raccoons, monkeys, lizards and rats – have earned them a long-established reputation around China.

> At http://www.china vista.com/culture /cuisine/recipes.html there is a great collection of Chinese recipes divided by province. If you want to make your own Peking duck, come here!

DRINKS
Nonalcoholic Drinks

Tea is *the* national drink in China and when visiting a restaurant the first thing you'll be asked is *'hé shénme chá?'* ('what kind of tea do you want?'). In cheaper

---

A NICE CUP OF TEA

Tea is a fundamental part of Chinese life. In fact, an old Chinese saying identifies tea as one of the seven basic necessities of life, along with fuel, oil, rice, salt, soy sauce and vinegar. The Chinese were the first to cultivate tea, and the art of brewing and drinking tea has been popular since the Tang dynasty (AD 618–907).

China has three main types of tea: green tea *(lǜ chá)*, black tea *(hóng chá)* and *wūlóng* (a semifermented tea, halfway between black and green tea). In addition, there are other variations, including jasmine *(mòlìhuāchá)* and chrysanthemum *(júhuā chá)*. Some famous regional teas of China are Fújiàn's *tiě guānyīn*, *pú'ěr* from Yúnnán and Zhèjiāng's *lóngjǐng* tea. Eight-treasure tea *(bābǎo chá)* consists of rock sugar, dates, nuts and tea combined in a cup and makes a delicious treat. Tea is to the Chinese what fine wine is to the French, a beloved beverage savoured for its fine aroma, distinctive flavour and pleasing aftertaste.

---

restaurants you'll be served on-the-house pots of weak jasmine or green tea but in more expensive places you have a choice of higher-quality (and higher priced) brands. You can also buy tea in tea shops or in supermarkets.

Traditionally, Chinese would never put milk or sugar in their tea but things are changing. Now 'milk tea' *(nǎi chá)* is available everywhere in China, often served as a sweet treat. There's also what some call 'Hong Kong' tea, which is (believe it or not) coffee brewed with a heart-stopping amount of sugar, tea and milk. Modern, trendy teahouses are springing up all over China and are a popular place for young urbanites to socialise.

> Did you know that tea was once used as a form of currency in China?

Coffee house chic has hit China in a big way and Western-style coffee houses can be found everywhere. The coffee chain Starbucks has become fashionable for trendy youth with money to burn. There are also local chains that can brew up a cup of semi-decent coffee for about Y10 to Y20, depending upon the establishment.

Soft drinks such as Sprite and Coca-Cola are easily found, along with ice teas and fruit drinks. Bottled water is on sale all over the place but check the cap before buying to see if it's sealed.

Milk is available fresh or powdered from supermarkets and convenience stores. Popular are sweet yogurt drinks in bottles sold in stores or fresh yogurt sold at some street stalls.

Alcoholic Drinks

If tea is the most popular drink in China, then beer must be number two. By any standards the top brands are good. The best known is Tsingtao, made with a mineral water that gives it a sparkling quality. It's essentially a German beer since the town of Qīngdǎo (formerly spelled 'Tsingtao'), where it's made, was once a German concession and the Chinese inherited the brewery (p226). Experts claim that draft Tsingtao tastes much better than the bottled stuff. A bottle will normally cost Y1.50 to Y2 in street shops, around Y15 to Y20 in a bar.

China has cultivated vines and produced wine for an estimated 4000 years. The word 'wine' gets rather loosely translated – many Chinese 'wines' are in fact spirits. Rice wine is intended mainly for cooking rather than drinking. Chinese wine-producing techniques differ from those of the West. Western producers try to prevent oxidation in their wines, but oxidation produces a flavour that Chinese tipplers find desirable and go to great lengths to achieve. Chinese diners are also keen on wines with different herbs and other materials soaked in them, which they drink for their health and for restorative or aphrodisiac qualities.

Wine with dead bees, pickled snakes or lizards is desirable for its alleged tonic properties – in general, the more poisonous the creature, the more potent the tonic's effects. *Maotai*, a favourite of Chinese drinkers, is a spirit made from sorghum (a type of millet) and used for toasts at banquets.

CELEBRATIONS
Holidays
Food plays a major role in Chinese holidays. For many Chinese, the appearance of a food is symbolic. Chinese like to eat noodles on birthdays and on the New Year (p944) because their long thin shape symbolises longevity. That's why it's bad luck to break the noodles before cooking them. During the Chinese New Year, it's common to serve a whole chicken because it resembles family unity. Clams and spring rolls are also served during New Year festivities because their shapes represent wealth: clams resemble bullion and spring rolls are shaped like bars of gold.

Fish also plays an important role during New Year celebrations. The word for fish, *yú*, sounds similar to the word for abundance. It's customary to serve a fish at the end of the evening meal, symbolising a wish for prosperity in the coming year.

Certain holiday foods stem from legends. For example, the tradition of eating moon cakes (*yuè bǐng*), a sweet cake filled with sesame seeds, lotus seeds, dates and other fillings during China's Mid-Autumn Festival (p945), is based on a story from the 14th century. Supposedly, when China was battling the Mongol invasions, a certain general had a plan to take back Mongol-held territory. He dressed up as a Taoist priest, entered the city and distributed moon cakes to the populace. Hidden within the cakes were notes instructing the people to revolt and overthrow the Mongols to retake their city. The people did as instructed and threw the Mongols out.

Zòngzi (dumplings made of glutinous rice wrapped in bamboo or reed leaves) are eaten during the Dragon Boat Festival (p945) and have a very long history in China. According to legend, such dumplings were thrown into the river as fish food to keep them from eating the body of Qu Yuan (p75), a poet who committed suicide during the Warring States period (475–221 BC). Now the dumplings are eaten throughout China as well as Southeast Asia.

The delightful children's book *Moonbeams, Dumplings & Dragon Boats* by Nina Simonds and Leslie Swartz (Harcourt, 2002) is filled with recipes from Chinese holidays, including how to make your own moon cakes and dumplings.

Banquets
The banquet is the apex of the Chinese dining experience. Virtually all significant business deals in China are clinched at the banquet table.

Dishes are served in sequence, beginning with cold appetisers and continuing through 10 or more courses. Soup, usually a thin broth to aid digestion, is generally served after the main course.

The idea is to serve or order far more than everyone can eat. Empty bowls imply a stingy host. Rice is considered a cheap filler and rarely appears at a banquet – don't ask for it, as this would imply that the snacks and main courses are insufficient, causing embarrassment to the host.

It's best to wait for some signal from the host before digging in. You will most likely be invited to take the first taste. Often your host will serve it to you, placing a piece of meat, chicken or fish in your bowl. If a whole fish is served, you might be offered the head, the cheeks of which are considered to be the tastiest part. Try to take at least a taste of what is given to you.

Never drink alone. Imbibing is conducted via toasts, which will usually commence with a general toast by the host, followed by the main guest reply toast, and then settle down to frequent toasts to individuals. A toast is conducted by raising your glass in both hands in the direction of the toastee and crying out '*gānbēi*', literally 'dry the glass'. Chinese do not clink glasses. Drain your glass in one hit. It is not unusual for everyone to end up very drunk, though at very formal banquets this is frowned upon.

Don't be late for a formal banquet; it's considered extremely rude. The banquet ends when the food and toasts end – the Chinese don't linger after the meal. You may find yourself being applauded when you enter a large banquet. It is polite to applaud back.

WHERE TO EAT & DRINK

It's hard to go hungry in China as just about everywhere you go there will be myriad food options to suit most budgets. The word *fàndiàn* usually refers to a large-scale restaurant that may or may not offer lodging. A *cānguǎn* is generally a smaller restaurant that specialises in one particular type of food. The most informal type of restaurant is the *cāntīng*, which has low-end prices, though the quality of the food can be quite high.

Breakfast is served early in China, mainly between 6am and 9am. In larger cities many restaurants serving lunch and dinner open from 11am to 2pm, reopen around 5pm and close at 9pm. In smaller cities, restaurants may close as early as 8pm. Some street stalls stay open 24 hours.

Tourist-friendly restaurants can be found around tourist sights and often have English signs and menus. Sometimes food can be quite overpriced and geared towards foreign tastes. It's easy to find restaurants that cater to Chinese clientele – just look for noisy, crowded places, the noisier the better. These restaurants may not have English menus but it's OK to look at what other people are having and indicate to the wait staff what you want by pointing. You can also use the Menu Decoder (p106).

Eating solo in China can be a lonely experience, since Chinese food is meant to be shared by groups of people. Larger restaurants cater to groups of people and portions may be too large for someone dining solo. Smaller restaurants off the main streets are more welcoming, though the menus can be repetitious. For variety, solo travellers can try eating at any of the growing number of cafés and family-style restaurants that offer set meals, usually a main course served with salad and soup, at very reasonable prices. Self-serve cafeterias (*zìzhù cān*) are another option and offer plenty of meat and vegetable dishes to choose from.

Hotels in larger cities often serve high-end regional dishes and international food, everything from Indian to French cuisine.

Quick Eats

Eating in China's bustling night markets is an experience not to be missed. Some of the country's best treats can be sampled in the markets, making them a gourmet's paradise. Hygiene is always a question, so make sure to eat only at the busiest of places to avoid getting sick.

Dumplings (*jiǎozi*) are a popular snack item in China and a delicious, inexpensive way to fill up. They're best described as Chinese ravioli, stuffed with meat, spring onion and greens. They are sometimes served by the bowl in a soup, sometimes dry by weight (250g or half a *jīn* is normally enough). Locals mix chilli (*làjiāo*), vinegar (*cù*) and soy sauce (*jiàngyóu*) in a little bowl according to taste and dip the dumpling in. Dumplings are often created by family minifactories – one stretches the pastry, another makes the filling and a third spoons the filling into the pastry, finishing with a little twist.

Other street snacks include fried tofu, tea eggs (soaked in soy sauce) and baked sweet potatoes, which can be bought by weight.

In addition to the markets, there are innumerable snack stalls set up around markets, train stations and bus stations. These are the places to grab something on the run, including *bāozi*, steamed buns stuffed with meat or vegetables, as well as grilled corn, mutton kebabs, noodles and plenty of regional specialities.

The fast food industry in China is increasing by 20% annually.

DUMPLINGS, UNWRAPPED

There's an old saying that 'Nothing tastes better than dumplings'. In fact, the Chinese have been eating this tasty home-style food since the Han dynasty! Dumplings have traditionally been eaten during Chinese New Year, their half-moon shape thought to resemble ancient gold ingots and bring good luck. The word *jiǎozi* (dumpling) can be translated as 'saying goodbye to the past and welcoming the new'. Nowadays, you can get them at any time of year but they're most popular in the north. Try this recipe for your own version of this tasty dish.

Chinese Dumplings
(makes 35-40 dumplings)

1 pack dumpling wrappers
300g (10oz) ground pork
150g (5oz) minced Napa cabbage
2 bunches minced coriander
1 bunch minced green onions
100g (3½oz) chopped ginger
2 cloves finely chopped garlic
20ml (1 tbsp) dark soy sauce
20ml (1 tbsp) sesame oil

Sauce
80ml (4 tbsp) light soy sauce
20ml (1 tbsp) sesame oil
20ml (1 tbsp) vinegar
Chilli oil to taste
2 cloves chopped garlic

- Combine the ingredients for the filling.
- Moisten the edges of a dumpling wrap and put a small amount of filling in the centre.
- Fold the wrap over and pinch together in a crescent shape, making a tight seal.
- Place the dumplings one at a time into a large pot of boiling water. When the water comes to a hard boil, pour in one cup of cold water. Wait for the water to come to a boil again and repeat with the cold water. Do this one more time. When the dumplings rise to the top, drain and transfer to a large plate. Don't overcook or the dumplings will fall apart.
- Mix all the ingredients together for the sauce and serve in small, individual bowls.

VEGETARIANS & VEGANS

Vegetarianism in China can be traced back over 1000 years. The Tang dynasty physician Sun Simiao extolled the virtues of vegetarianism in his 60-volume classic, *Prescriptions Worth More Than Gold*. Legend has it that Sun lived to the ripe old age of 101.

Because of China's history of poverty and famine, eating meat is a status symbol, symbolic of health and wealth. Many Chinese remember all too well the famines of the 1950s and 1960s when having anything to eat at all was a luxury. Eating meat (as well as milk and eggs) is a sign of progress and material abundance. Even vegetables are often fried in animal-based oils, and soups are most commonly made with chicken or beef stock.

In larger cities such as Běijīng, Shànghǎi, Guǎngzhōu and Hong Kong, vegetarianism is slowly catching on and there are new chic vegetarian eateries appearing in fashionable restaurant districts. These are often pricey establishments and you pay for ambience as well as the food.

Chinese vegetarian food often consists of 'mock meat' dishes, which are made from tofu, wheat gluten and vegetables. Some of the dishes are quite fantastic to look at, with vegetarian ingredients sculpted to look like spare ribs or fried chicken. Sometimes the chefs go to great lengths to even create 'bones' from carrots and lotus roots. Some of the more famous vegetarian dishes include vegetarian 'ham', braised vegetarian 'shrimp' and sweet-and-sour 'fish'.

Buddhist temples often have their own vegetarian restaurants where you can fill up on a delicious vegetarian meal quite cheaply.

EATING WITH KIDS

Eating out with children in China can be a challenge. Budget eateries won't have special menus for children nor will they supply booster seats. Higher-end restaurants may be able to offer these things but it's best to check in advance. On the up side, in larger cities there are now more family-style restaurants that offer set meals and cater to families. Some of these places have special meals for children, usually consisting of fried chicken or fish. Fast-food restaurants are another option that offer a kid-friendly atmosphere.

Supermarkets in China sell Western baby formula and baby foods, as well as infant cereals. For more information on children see p937.

HABITS & CUSTOMS

Chinese dining habits reflect traditional Chinese values that cherish close family ties and friendships. Eating communally is a way to celebrate togetherness and create an atmosphere of warmth and congeniality.

Restaurants in China are noisy, crowded places, where people come to relax and get away from the pressures of work and school. While friends in the West go out for a beer, the Chinese will opt for a 'hot and noisy' meal, which is sometimes punctuated with increasingly vociferous shots of spirits.

Daughter of Heaven, A Memoir with Earthly Recipes by Leslie Li (Time Warner, 2005) is the story of a Chinese-American woman and her grandmother, whose cooking shapes the most significant events in her childhood.

Typically, the Chinese sit at a round table and order dishes from which everyone partakes; ordering a dish just for yourself would be unthinkable. It's not unusual for one person at the table to order on everyone's behalf. Usually among friends only several dishes will be ordered but if guests are present, the host will order at least one dish per person, possibly more. At formal dinners, be prepared for a staggering amount of food, far more than anyone could eat.

Epicureans will tell you that the key to ordering is to get a balance of textures, tastes, smells, colours and even temperatures. Most Chinese meals start with some snacks, perhaps some peanuts or pickles. Following the little titbits are the main courses, usually some meat and vegetable dishes. Soup is often served at the end of the meal (except in Guǎngdōng where it's served first) as well as noodles or rice.

Traditionally, the Chinese had a number of taboos regarding table etiquette. Nowadays, these rules are much more relaxed and foreigners are given special allowances for social gaffes. However, there are some basic rules to follow when eating with Chinese friends or colleagues that will make things at the table go more smoothly.

Everyone gets an individual bowl and a small plate and tea cup. It's quite acceptable to hold the bowl close to your lips and shovel the contents into your mouth with chopsticks. If the food contains bones or seeds, just put them out on the tablecloth or in a dish reserved for this purpose. Restaurants are prepared for the mess and staff change the tablecloth after each customer leaves.

EATING DOS & DON'TS

◾ Don't wave your chopsticks around or point them at people. This is considered rude.

◾ Don't drum your chopsticks on the sides of your bowl – only beggars do this.

◾ Never commit the terrible faux pas of sticking your chopsticks into your rice. Two chopsticks stuck vertically into a rice bowl resemble incense sticks in a bowl of ashes, which is considered an omen of death.

◾ Don't discuss business or unpleasant topics at dinner.

◾ Don't let the spout of a teapot face towards anyone. Make sure it is directed outward from the table or to where nobody is sitting.

◾ Never flip a fish over to get to the flesh underneath. If you do so, the next boat you pass will capsize.

Chopstick skills are a necessary means of survival when eating out in China. Don't despair if at first much of the food lands on the table or in your lap and not in your bowl. Eating this way takes practice and most Chinese are pretty understanding when it comes to foreigners and chopstick problems.

When eating from communal dishes, don't use your chopsticks to root around in a dish for a piece of food. Find a piece by sight and go directly for it without touching anything else. And remember that while dropping food is OK, be sure to never drop your chopsticks as this is considered bad luck.

Most Chinese think little of sticking their own chopsticks into a communal dish, though this attitude is changing because of SARS. Most high-end restaurants now provide separate serving spoons or chopsticks to be used with communal dishes. If these are provided, make sure to use them. You should never use a personal spoon to serve from a communal plate or bowl.

Don't be surprised if your Chinese host uses their chopsticks to place food in your bowl or plate. This is a sign of friendship and the polite thing to do is to smile and eat whatever has been given you. If for some reason you can't eat it, leave it in your bowl or hide it with rice.

Remember to fill your neighbours' tea cups when they are empty, as yours will be filled by them. You can thank the pourer by tapping two fingers on the table gently. On no account serve yourself tea without serving others first. When your teapot needs a refill, signal this to the waiter by taking the lid off the pot.

Probably the most important piece of etiquette comes with the bill: the person who extended the dinner invitation is presumed to pay, though everyone at the table will put up a fight. Don't argue too hard; it's expected that at a certain point in the future the meal will be reciprocated. Tipping is not the norm in China.

Some Chinese believe eating pigs' feet regularly will slow down the aging process.

COOKING COURSES

Some Western tour operators offer 'culinary tours' of China that give visitors the opportunity to try their hand at Chinese cooking. Travellers have recommended the tour 'China Gourmet Traveller' offered by Intrepid Tours. The 15-day journey takes you through Shànghǎi, Xī'ān, Běijīng, Hong Kong and Yángshuò where you can try a variety of regional dishes as well as participate in cooking classes. Check out Intrepid's website at www.intrepidtravel.com.

EAT YOUR WORDS

See the Language chapter (p985) for pronunciation guidelines.

Useful Words & Phrases

I'm vegetarian.	Wǒ chī sù.	我吃素
I don't want MSG.	Wǒ bú yào wèijīng.	我不要味精
Let's eat!	Chī fàn!	吃饭
Not too spicy.	Bù yào tài là.	不要太辣
Cheers!	Gānbēi!	干杯
chopsticks	kuàizi	筷子
fork	chāzi	叉子
hot	rède	热的
ice cold	bīngde	冰的
knife	dàozi	刀子
menu	càidān	菜单
set meal (no menu)	tàocān	套餐
spoon	tiáogēng/tāngchí/sháozi	调羹/汤匙/勺子
bill (check)	mǎidān/jiézhàng	买单/结帐

Menu Decoder

NORTHERN SCHOOL

Běijīng kǎoyā	北京烤鸭	Peking duck
jiāo zhá yángròu	焦炸羊肉	deep-fried mutton
jiǔ zhuǎn dàcháng	九转大肠	spicy braised pig's intestine
qīng xiāng shāo jī	清香烧鸡	chicken wrapped in lotus leaf
sān měi dòufu	三美豆腐	sliced bean curd with Chinese cabbage
shuàn yángròu	涮羊肉	lamb hotpot
sì xǐ wánzi	四喜丸子	steamed and fried pork, shrimp and bamboo shoot balls
yuán bào lǐ jí	芫爆里脊	stir-fried pork tenderloin with coriander
zào liū sān bái	糟溜三白	stir-fried chicken, fish and bamboo shoots

EASTERN SCHOOL

jiāng cōng chǎo xiè	姜葱炒蟹	stir-fried crab with ginger and scallions
mìzhī xūnyú	蜜汁熏鱼	honey-smoked carp
níng shì shànyú	宁式鳝鱼	stir-fried eel with onion
qiézhī yúkuài	茄汁鱼块	fish fillet in tomato sauce
qīng zhēng guìyú	清蒸鳜鱼	steamed Mandarin fish
sōngzǐ guìyú	松子鳜鱼	Mandarin fish with pine nuts
suānlà yóuyú	酸辣鱿鱼	hot-and-sour squid
yóubào xiārén	油爆虾仁	fried shrimp
zhá hēi lǐyú	炸黑鲤鱼	fried black carp
zhá yúwán	炸鱼丸	fish balls

WESTERN SCHOOL

bàngbàng jī	棒棒鸡	shredded chicken in a hot pepper and sesame sauce
dàsuàn shàn duàn	大蒜鳝段	stewed eel with garlic
gānshāo yán lǐ	干烧岩鲤	stewed carp with ham and hot-and-sweet sauce
gōngbào jīdīng	宫爆鸡丁	spicy chicken with peanuts

huíguō ròu	回锅肉	boiled and stir-fried pork with salty and hot sauce
málà dòufu	麻辣豆腐	spicy tofu
shuǐ zhǔ niúròu	水煮牛肉	fried and boiled beef, garlic sprouts and celery
yúxiāng ròusī	鱼香肉丝	'fish-resembling' meat
zhàcài ròusī	榨菜肉丝	stir-fried pork or beef tenderloin with tuber mustard
zhāngchá yā	樟茶鸭	camphor tea duck

SOUTHERN SCHOOL

bái zhuó xiā	白灼虾	blanched prawns with shredded scallions
dōngjiāng yánjú jī	东江盐焗鸡	salt-baked chicken
gālí jī	咖喱鸡	curried chicken
háoyóu niúròu	蚝油牛肉	beef with oyster sauce
kǎo rǔzhū	烤乳猪	crispy suckling pig
mì zhī chāshāo	密汁叉烧	roast pork with honey
shé ròu	蛇肉	snake
tángcù lǐjí/gǔlǎo ròu	糖醋里脊/咕老肉	sweet-and-sour pork fillets
tángcù páigǔ	糖醋排骨	sweet-and-sour spare ribs

Food Glossary
COOKING TERMS

chǎo	炒	fry
hóngshāo	红烧	red-cooked (stewed in soy sauce)
kǎo	烤	roast
yóujiān	油煎	deep-fry
zhēng	蒸	steam
zhǔ	煮	boil

RICE DISHES

jīchǎofàn	鸡炒饭	fried rice with chicken
jīdàn chǎofàn	鸡蛋炒饭	fried rice with egg
jīdàn mǐfàn	米饭	steamed white rice
shūcài chǎofàn	蔬菜炒饭	fried rice with vegetables
xīfàn; zhōu	稀饭; 粥	watery rice porridge (congee)

NOODLE DISHES

húntún miàn	馄饨面	wontons and noodles
jīsī chǎomiàn	鸡丝炒面	fried noodles with chicken
jīsī tāngmiàn	鸡丝汤面	soupy noodles with chicken
májiàng miàn	麻酱面	sesame paste noodles
niúròu chǎomiàn	牛肉炒面	fried noodles with beef
niúròu miàn	牛肉汤面	soupy beef noodles
ròusī chǎomiàn	肉丝炒面	fried noodles with pork
shūcài chǎomiàn	蔬菜炒面	fried noodles with vegetables
tāngmiàn	汤面	noodles in soup
xiārén chǎomiàn	虾仁炒面	fried noodles with shrimp
zhájiàng miàn	炸酱面	bean and meat noodles

BREAD, BUNS & DUMPLINGS

cōngyóu bǐng	葱油饼	spring onion pancakes
guōtiē	锅贴	pot stickers/pan-grilled dumplings
mántou	馒头	steamed buns

ròu bāozi	肉包子	steamed meat buns
shāo bǐng	烧饼	clay-oven rolls
shuǐjiān bāo	水煎包	pan-grilled buns
shuǐjiǎo	水饺	boiled dumplings
sùcài bāozi	素菜包子	steamed vegetable buns

SOUP

húntún tāng	馄饨汤	wonton soup
sān xiān tāng	三鲜汤	three kinds of seafood soup
suānlà tāng	酸辣汤	hot-and-sour soup

BEEF DISHES

gānbiān niúròu sī	干煸牛肉丝	stir-fried beef and chilli
háoyóu niúròu	蚝油牛肉	beef with oyster sauce
hóngshāo niúròu	红烧牛肉	beef braised in soy sauce
niúròu fàn	牛肉饭	beef with rice
tiěbǎn niúròu	铁板牛肉	sizzling beef platter

CHICKEN & DUCK DISHES

háoyóu jīkuài	蚝油鸡块	diced chicken in oyster sauce
hóngshāo jīkuài	红烧鸡块	chicken braised in soy sauce
jītuǐ fàn	鸡腿饭	chicken leg with rice
níngméng jī	柠檬鸡	lemon chicken
tángcù jīdīng	糖醋鸡丁	sweet-and-sour chicken
yāoguǒ jīdīng	腰果鸡丁	chicken and cashews
yāròu fàn	鸭肉饭	duck with rice

PORK DISHES

biǎndòu ròusī	扁豆肉丝	shredded pork and green beans
gūlū ròu	咕噜肉	sweet-and-sour pork
guōbā ròupiàn	锅巴肉片	pork and sizzling rice crust
háoyóu ròusī	蚝油肉丝	pork with oyster sauce
jiàngbào ròudīng	酱爆肉丁	diced pork with soy sauce
jīngjiàng ròusī	京酱肉丝	pork cooked with soy sauce
mùěr ròu	木耳肉	wood-ear mushrooms and pork
páigǔ fàn	排骨饭	pork chop with rice
qīngjiāo ròu piàn	青椒肉片	pork and green peppers
yángcōng chǎo ròupiàn	洋葱炒肉片	pork and fried onions

SEAFOOD DISHES

gélì	蛤蜊	clams
gōngbào xiārén	宫爆虾仁	diced shrimp with peanuts
háo	蚝	oysters
hóngshāo yú	红烧鱼	fish braised in soy sauce
lóngxiā	龙虾	lobster
pángxiè	螃蟹	crab
yóuyú	鱿鱼	squid
zhāngyú	章鱼	octopus

VEGETABLE & BEAN CURD DISHES

báicài xiān shuānggū	白菜鲜双菇	bok choy and mushrooms
cuìpí dòufu	脆皮豆腐	crispy skin bean curd
hēimù'ěr mèn dòufu	黑木耳焖豆腐	bean curd with wood-ear mushrooms
hóngshāo qiézi	红烧茄子	red-cooked aubergine

jiācháng dòufu	家常豆腐	'home-style' tofu
jiāngzhī qīngdòu	姜汁青豆	string beans with ginger
lúshuǐ dòufu	卤水豆腐	smoked bean curd
shāguō dòufu	砂锅豆腐	clay pot bean curd
sùchǎo biǎndòu	素炒扁豆	garlic beans
sùchǎo sùcài	素炒素菜	fried vegetables
tángcù ǒubǐng	糖醋藕饼	sweet-and-sour lotus root cakes
yúxiāng qiézi	鱼香茄子	'fish-resembling' aubergine

FRUIT

bālè	芭乐	guava
fènglí	凤梨	pineapple
gānzhè	甘蔗	sugar cane
lí	梨	pear
lìzhī	荔枝	lychee
lóngyǎn	龙眼	'dragon eyes'
mángguǒ	芒果	mango
píngguǒ	苹果	apple
pútáo	葡萄	grape
xiāngjiāo	香蕉	banana
xīguā	西瓜	watermelon

DRINKS

bái pútáo jiǔ	白葡萄酒	white wine
báijiǔ	白酒	Chinese spirits
chá	茶	tea
dòujiāng	豆浆	soya bean milk
hóng pútáo jiǔ	红葡萄酒	red wine
kāfēi	咖啡	coffee
kāi shuǐ	开水	water (boiled)
kěkǒu kělè	可口可乐	Coca-Cola
kuàngquán shuǐ	矿泉水	mineral water
mǐjiǔ	米酒	rice wine
nǎijīng	奶精	coffee creamer
niúnǎi	牛奶	milk
píjiǔ	啤酒	beer
qìshuǐ	汽水	soft drink (soda)
suānnǎi	酸奶	yogurt
yézi zhī	椰子汁	coconut juice

Běijīng 北京

Seesawing wildly between burning summers and frostbitten winters while scoured by spring sandstorms, arid Běijīng is host city to the 2008 Olympics and emblematic of a nation undergoing a gut-wrenching transformation.

A city of neatly ordered design accentuated by sporadic authoritarian statements (Tiananmen Sq, the Great Hall of the People), Běijīng still stumps first-time visitors who arrive expecting a ragged tableau of communist China, only to be bowled over by its modernity and immensity and struck by Běijīng's optimistic verve and sheer commercial vibrancy.

The colossal flyovers and multilane boulevards heave with two million cars as the must-have commodity – once a TV or washing machine – is now a VW Passat or a Buick. Yet ample pockets of historical charm survive, especially along Běijīng's characteristic *hútòng*, the maze of narrow alleys that shelters the city's delightful courtyard architecture. The city has also managed to sustain an epic grandeur from its Imperial days, laying claim to some of China's superlative sights, including the Great Wall, the Forbidden City, Temple of Heaven Park and the Summer Palace.

Winers and diners are spoiled for choice in Běijīng's inventive bar and restaurant world. Peking duck – an oft-copied national institution – is really only true to form in the capital.

Frank and uncomplicated, Běijīng's denizens chat in Běijīnghuà – the gold standard of Mandarin – and marvel at their good fortune for occupying the centre of the known world. And for all its diligence and gusto, Běijīng dispenses with the persistent pace of Shànghǎi or Hong Kong, and locals instead find time to sit out front, play chess and watch the world go by.

HIGHLIGHTS

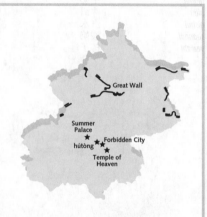

- Follow in the footsteps of eunuchs and emperors roaming the **Forbidden City** (p133)

- Hire a bike and whizz through Běijīng's **hútòng** (p136), the city's delightful alleyways

- Walk along the **Great Wall** (p162), the dividing line between China and the barbarian hordes

- Put aside a day to amble around the huge **Summer Palace** (p139)

- Fathom the cosmic harmonies of the **Temple of Heaven** (p130)

Great Wall

Summer Palace

Forbidden City

hútòng

Temple of Heaven

■ AREA CODE: ☎010 | ■ POPULATION: 15.2 MILLION | ■ www.beijingpage.com

BEIJING MUNICIPALITY 北京市

0 — 40 km
0 — 20 miles

HÉBĚI

To Chéngdé
(24km)

Jinshanling
Great Wall

Gùběikǒu

Tianxian
Falls

Jingdudiyá
Falls &
Heilóng Pool

Simatái
Great Wall

Bai River

Mùtiányù
Great Wall

Mt Wuling
(2116m)

HÉBĚI

Songshan
Nature
Reserve

Haituo
Mountain
(2241m)

Longqing
Gorge

Huanghua
Great Wall

Miyun
Reservoir

Bailong
Pool

To Zhāngjiākǒu
(73km)

Kāngxī
Grasslands

Duijiu
Valley

Mùtiányù

Hongluo
Temple

Miyún

To Zūnhuà
(45km)

Eastern
Qing
Tombs

Guanting
Reservoir

Badaling
Great Wall

Jūyōngguān

Ming
Tombs

Huáiróu
Reservoir

Huáiróu

Hǔdòngshuǐ

Pan
Mountains

Chāngpíng

Shùnyì

Haizi
Reservoir

Yuqiao
Reservoir

Mt Ling
(2303m)

Chuāndǐxià

Zhǎitáng

Tanzhe
Temple

Capital
Airport

See Běijīng Map
(pp116–17)

BĚIJĪNG

Tóngzhōu

**DACHANG
(Autonomous
Muslim County)**

Bǎodǐ

To Qínhuángdǎo
(200km)

Jietai
Temple

Dàxīng

Shídù

Yúnjú
Temple

Fángshān

Yongding River

Langfáng

TIĀNJĪN

HÉBĚI

Wǔqīng (Yàngcūn)

To Shíjiāzhuāng
(200km)

To Tiānjīn
(23km)

HISTORY

Běijīng – affectionately called Peking by diplomats, nostalgic journalists and wistful academics – seems to have presided over China since time immemorial. In fact, Běijīng (Northern Capital) – positioned outside the central heartland of Chinese civilisation – emerged as a cultural and political force that would shape the destiny of China only with the 13th-century Mongol occupation of China.

Located on a vast plain that extends south as far as the distant Yellow River (Huáng Hé), Běijīng benefits from neither proximity to a major river nor the sea. Without its strategic location on the edge of the North China Plain, it would hardly be an ideal place

to locate a major city, let alone a national capital.

The area southwest of Běijīng was inhabited by early humans some 500,000 years ago. Ancient Chinese chronicles refer to a state called Yōuzhōu (Secluded State) existing during the reign of the mythical Yellow Emperor, one of nine states that existed at the time, although the earliest recorded settlements in Chinese historical sources date from 1045 BC.

In later centuries, Běijīng was successively occupied by foreign forces, promoting its development as a major political centre. Before the Mongol invasion, the city was established as an auxiliary capital under the Khitan Liao and later as the capital under the Jurchen Jin, when it underwent significant transformation

BĔIJĪNG

into a key political and military city. The city was enclosed within fortified walls for the first time, accessed by eight gates.

In AD 1215 the great Mongol warrior Genghis Khan and his formidable army razed Bĕijīng, an event that was paradoxically to mark Bĕijīng's transformation into a powerful national capital; a status it enjoys to the present day, bar the first 53 years of the Ming dynasty and 21 years of Nationalist rule in the 20th century.

The city came to be called Dàdū (Great Capital), also assuming the Mongol name Khanbalik (the Khan's town). By 1279 Kublai Khan, grandson of Genghis Khan, had made himself ruler of the largest empire the world has ever known, with Dàdū its capital. Surrounded by a vast rectangular wall punctured by three gates on each of its sides, the city was centred on the Drum and Bell Towers (p135; located near to their surviving Ming dynasty counterparts), its regular layout a paragon of urban design.

After seizing Bĕijīng, the first Ming emperor Hongwu (r 1368–98) renamed the city Bĕipíng (Northern Peace) and established his capital in Nánjīng in present-day Jiāngsū province to the south. It wasn't until the reign of Emperor Yongle (r 1403–24) that the court moved back to Bĕijīng. Seeking to rid the city of all traces of 'Yuán Qi' (literally 'breath of the Yuan dynasty'), the Ming levelled the fabulous palaces of the Mongols along with the Imperial City, while preserving much of the regular plan of the Mongol capital. The Ming was the only pure Chinese dynasty to rule from Bĕijīng (bar today's government).

During Ming rule, the huge city walls were repaired and redesigned. Yongle is credited with being the true architect of the modern city, and much of Bĕijīng's hallmark architecture, such as the Forbidden City and the Temple of Heaven, date from his reign. The countenance of Ming dynasty Bĕijīng was flat and low-lying – a feature that would remain until the 20th century – as law forbade the construction of any building higher than the Forbidden City's Hall of Supreme Harmony. The basic grid of present-day Bĕijīng had been laid and the city had adopted a guise that would survive until today.

The Manchus, who invaded China in the 17th century and established the Qing dynasty, essentially preserved Bĕijīng's form. In the last 120 years of the Qing dynasty, Bĕijīng,

and subsequently China, was subjected to power struggles and invasions and the ensuing chaos. The list is long: the Anglo-French troops who in 1860 burnt the Old Summer Palace to the ground; the corrupt regime of Empress Dowager Cixi; the catastrophic Boxer Rebellion; General Yuan Shikai; the warlords; the Japanese occupation of 1937; and the Kuomintang. Each and every period left its undeniable mark, although the shape and symmetry of Bĕijīng was maintained.

Modern Bĕijīng came of age when, in January 1949, the People's Liberation Army (PLA) entered the city. On 1 October of that year Mao Zedong proclaimed a 'People's Republic' to an audience of some 500,000 citizens in Tiananmen Sq.

Like the emperors before them, the communists significantly altered the face of Bĕijīng to suit their own image. The *páilou* (decorative archways) were brought down, as whole city blocks were pulverised to widen major boulevards. From 1950 to 1952, the city's magnificent outer walls were levelled in the interests of traffic circulation. Soviet experts and technicians poured in, leaving their own Stalinesque touches.

The past quarter of a century has transformed Bĕijīng into a modern city, with skyscrapers, slick shopping malls and heaving flyovers. The once flat skyline is now crenellated with vast apartment blocks and office buildings. Recent years have also seen a convincing beautification of Bĕijīng: from a toneless and unkempt city to a greener, cleaner and more pleasant place.

The mood in today's Bĕijīng is far removed from the Tiananmen Sq demonstrations of spring 1989. With the lion's share of China's wealth in the hands of city dwellers, Bĕijīng has embraced modernity without evolving politically. There's a conspicuous absence of protest in today's Bĕijīng and you won't see subversive graffiti or wall posters. With the Communist Party unwilling to share power, political reform creeps forward in glacial increments. An astonishing degree of public political apathy exists, at least partially explained by in-built inclinations to bow to authority and a suppression of democratic instincts among the middle classes, who are doing so well out of the CCP's economic successes. Political dissent has been forced into the shadows or fizzes about fitfully in cyberspace, pursued by internet police ironing out any wrinkles that may impede construction of a 'harmonious society'.

Some of Běijīng's greatest problems could be environmental rather than political, although the two interweave. The need for speedy economic expansion, magnified by preparations for the 2008 Olympics, has put extra pressure on an already degraded environment. Water and land resources are rapidly depleting, the desert sands are crawling inexorably closer and the city's air quality has become increasingly toxic (see the boxed text, right).

As the burgeoning middle classes transform Běijīng into an increasingly pet-ridden city, that scourge of dog-owning societies – dog poo – is building up, so watch your step (although it's nothing compared with Brussels quite yet).

CLIMATE

Autumn (September to early November) is the optimal season to visit Běijīng as the weather is gorgeous and fewer tourists are in town. Local Běijīngers describe this short season of clear skies and breezy days as *tiāngāo qìshuǎng* (literally 'the sky is high and the air is fresh'). In winter, it's glacial outside (dipping as low as -20°C) and the northern winds cut like a knife through bean curd. Arid spring is OK, apart from the awesome sand clouds that sweep in from Inner Mongolia and the static electricity that discharges everywhere. Spring also sees the snowlike *liǔxù* (willow catkins) wafting through the air and collecting in drifts. From May onwards the mercury can surge well over 30°C. Běijīng simmers under a scorching sun in summer (reaching over 40°C), which also sees heavy rainstorms late in the season. Maybe surprisingly, this is also considered the peak season, when hotels typically raise their rates and the Great Wall nearly collapses under the weight of marching tourists. Air pollution can be intolerable in both summer and winter (see the boxed text, right).

ORIENTATION

With a total area of 16,800 sq km, Běijīng municipality is roughly the size of Belgium.

The city itself may appear unforgivingly huge, but Běijīng is a city of very orderly design. Think of the city as one giant grid, with the Forbidden City at its centre. Street names can be confusing. Jianguomenwai Dajie (建国

THE GREAT PALL OF CHINA

With an estimated three million cars expected to be congesting Běijīng's streets by 2008, the city is having an uphill struggle keeping its air clean. In 2005 Běijīng was identified by the European Space Agency as having the world's highest levels of nitrogen dioxide, a pollutant that contributes to the city's awful air. If being a chain-smoker has ever been an ambition, now is your chance: health experts warn that breathing the Běijīng air could be the equivalent of smoking 70 cigarettes a day. Coal is still liberally burnt in the capital, and spent cylindrical honeycomb briquettes of *fēngwōméi* (coal) lie heaped along *hútòng* (narrow alleys) in wintertime. On bad days, visibility is much reduced as a curtain of thick haze descends over town.

门外大街) means 'the avenue (大街; dajie) outside (外; wai) Jianguo Gate (建国门; Jianguomen)' – that is, outside the old wall – whereas Jianguomennei Dajie (建国门内大街) means 'the avenue inside Jianguo Gate'. The gate in question no longer exists, so it survives in name alone.

A major boulevard can change names six or even seven times along its length. Streets and avenues can also be split along compass points: Dong Dajie (东大街; East Ave), Xi Dajie (西大街; West Ave), Bei Dajie (北大街; North Ave) and Nan Dajie (南大街; South Ave). All these streets head off from an intersection, usually where a gate once stood. Unlike countless other Chinese cities, Běijīng is one place where you won't find a Jiefang Lu (Liberation Rd), Renmin Lu (People's Rd), Zhongshan Lu (Zhongshan Rd) or a Beijing Lu (Beijing Rd). Five ring roads circle the city centre in concentric rings.

Bus and taxi are the main methods of transport to the centre from Běijīng's Capital Airport, 27km away. See p160 for more info.

Maps

A map of Běijīng is essential to navigation around this massive, bustling metropolis. English-language maps of Běijīng can be picked up for free at most big hotels and branches of the Běijīng Tourist Information Center (p124). They are also available at the Foreign Languages Bookstore (p114) and other

BEIJING

BĚIJĪNG IN...

Two Days

Běijīng's top sight is undeniably the **Forbidden City** (p133); you will need at least a morning to cover the palace and some of the nearby sights of **Tiananmen Square** (p124). Take the subway from Tiananmen Xi to Wangfujing and lunch at **Qianmen Quanjude Roast Duck Restaurant** (p149) or **Wangfujing Snack Street** (p148). Jump in a taxi to the **Temple of Heaven** (p130) or spend the afternoon on our **bicycle tour** (p142).

Rise early the next day for a trip to the **Great Wall** (p162) and the **Ming Tombs** (p174), and spend the evening enjoying a performance of **Chinese acrobatics** (p154) before rounding off the day wining and dining in **Sanlitun** (p152).

Three Days

Follow the two-day itinerary, and on your third day make an early morning visit to the **Lama Temple** (p134) before browsing among the stalls and bric-a-brac shops of **Liulichang** (p156). In the afternoon, walk along the restored **Ming City Wall** (p130) from Chongwenmen to the South-east Corner Watchtower or make an expedition to the **Summer Palace** (p139). In the evening, dine at **Xiao Wang's Home Restaurant** (p151) or the **Courtyard** (p151), snack at **Donghuamen Night Market** (p150) or spend the evening enjoying **Beijing opera** (p153) at one of the city's numerous theatres.

bookshops with English-language titles. Pushy street vendors hawk cheap Chinese character maps near subway stations around Tiananmen Sq and Wangfujing Dajie; check they have English labelling before you purchase. Look out for the Beijing Tourist Map (Y8), labelled in both English and Chinese.

INFORMATION
Bookshops & Libraries

Bookworm Café (Shūchóng; Map p122; ☎ 6586 9507; www.beijingbookworm.com; Bldg 4, Nan Sanlitun Lu; half-/1-year library membership Y200/300) Growing section of new and almost new books for sale. Library members can borrow a maximum of two books at a time.

China Cultural Heritage Bookshop (Cathay Bookshop; Wénhuà Yíchǎn Shūdiàn; Map pp118–19; ☎ 6303 1602; 57 Liulichang Xijie; ⏰ 9am-6pm) On the northern side of Liulichang Xijie, this branch of the Cathay Bookshop has absorbing ground-floor exhibits of old literature and maps in Chinese relating to Běijīng.

Foreign Languages Bookstore (Wàiwén Shūdiàn; Map p123; ☎ 6512 6911; 235 Wangfujing Dajie) The 3rd floor is where you want to be: strong children's, fiction and nonfiction sections plus a smattering of travel guides and seats for tired legs.

Le Petit Gourmand (Xiǎo Měishíjiā; Map p122; ☎ 6417 6095; www.lepetitgourmand.com.cn; Tongli Studio, Sanlitun Beilu; ⏰ 10am-1am) There's an excellent and lovingly looked after selection of over 10,000 books at this restaurant-cum-library. Take to the outside terrace in summer. Maximum two books per loan (two weeks max period); membership provided upon donation of five books.

National Library (Guójiā Túshūguǎn; Map pp118–19; ☎ 8854 4114; 39 Baishiqiao Lu; ⏰ 9am-5pm)

Xidan Bookshop (Xīdān Túshū Dàshà; Map pp118–19; ☎ 6607 8477; 17 Xichang'an Jie) Iffy English-language section (Agatha Christie in the Best Sellers section) in basement.

Yansha Bookstore (Túshū Tiāndì; Map pp118–19; ☎ 6465 1188; 4th fl, Lufthansa Center Youyi Shopping City, 50 Liangmaqiao Lu) OK bookshop with a modest selection of English-language travel guides and novels amid immobile slabs of art and design titles.

Internet Access 网吧

Defying global trends, internet cafés have become increasingly scarce over the past five years. With the 2008 Olympics looming, Běijīng is stranded on the hard shoulder as other nations cruise the information superhighway, with internet café numbers dwindling and websites increasingly blocked (10% of all sites are inaccessible). Information is neutralised by an army of Chinese censors who are assigned to repel unpalatable opinion.

Typical internet café rates are Y3 per hour, although some best-avoided tourist cafés charge upwards of Y20. Many cheaper hotels and youth hostels provide internet access at around Y10 per hour.

Beijing Huohu Shiji Internet Cafe (Běijīng Huǒhú Shíjì Wǎngbā; Map p122; Chunxiu Lu; per hr Y3; ⏰ 8am-midnight) North of intersection with Xingfucun Zhonglu on Chunxiu Lu, south of Red House.

Chengse 520 Internet Café (Chéngsè 520 Wǎngbā; Map pp118-19; 3rd fl, 7 Dazhalan Jie; per hr Y4; ☎ 8am-3am) Through clothing market and up the stairs in Dashilar.

Dayusu Internet Café (Dàyǔsù Wǎngbā; Map pp118-19; 2 Hufang Lu; per hr Y3; ☺ 8am-midnight) No English sign, but it's around three shops north of Bank of China on Hufang Lu.

Hulindao Internet Café (Húlíndào Wǎngbā; Map pp118-19; 2nd fl, cnr Dianmenwai Dajie & Yandai Xiejie; per hr Y3; ☺ 8am-midnight) Look for the characters '上网'.

Internet Café (Wǎngbā; Map pp116-17; Shop 2601, 2nd fl, Soho New Town, off Jianguo Lu; per hr Y3; ☺ 24hr) It's next to exit B of Dawanglu subway station.

Internet Café (Wǎngbā; 2nd fl, 1 Beijingzhan Qianjie; per hr Y5; ☺ 24hr) Very new. Above the Beijing City Central Youth Hostel.

Moko Coffee Bar (Mòkè Wǎngbā; Map p123; ☎ 6525 3712, 6559 8464; 57 Dongsi Nandajie; per hr upstairs/downstairs Y4/15; ☺ 24hr) No English sign, but it's next to a chemist. Downstairs rates include a drink.

Qian Yi Internet Café (Qiányì Wǎngluò Kāfēiwū; Map pp118-19; ☎ 6705 1722; 3rd fl, Old Station Bldg, Qianmen Dongdajie; per hr Y20; ☺ 9am-midnight) Outrageously expensive. A much cheaper internet café (Y4 per hour) exists on the same floor, but foreigners may not be admitted.

Medical Services

Běijīng has some of the best medical facilities and services in China, bar Hong Kong. Ask your embassy for a list of English-speaking doctors and dentists, and hospitals that accept foreigners.

Beijing Union Medical Hospital (Běijīng Xiéhé Yīyuàn; Map p123; ☎ 6529 6114, emergencies 6529 5284; 53 Dongdan Beidajie; ☺ 24hr) Foreigners' and VIP wing in the back building.

Hong Kong International Medical Clinic (Běijīng Xiānggǎng Guójì Yìwù Zhěnsuǒ; Map p122; ☎ 6553 2288; www.hkclinic.com; 9th fl, Office Tower, Hong Kong Macau Center, Swissôtel, 2 Chaoyangmen Beidajie; ☺ 9am-9pm) Medical and dental clinic.

International SOS (Běijīng Yàzhōu Guójì Jǐnjí Jiùyuán Yīliáo Zhōngxīn; Map p122; ☎ clinic appointments 6462 9112, dental appointments 6462 0333, emergencies 6462 9100; www.internationalsos.com; Bldg C, BITIC Ying Yi Bldg, 1 Xingfu Sancun Beijie; ☺ 9am-6pm Mon-Fri) Expensive, high-quality clinic with English-speaking staff.

PHARMACIES

Pharmacies selling Chinese (zhōngyào) and Western medicine (xīyào) are widespread and are identified by green crosses. You do not necessarily need a prescription for drugs, so ask at the pharmacy first. Some pharmacies offer 24-hour service; typically this means that you can get your medicine through a window during the night, after the pharmacy itself is officially shut.

Quanxin Pharmacy (Quánxīn Dàyàofáng; Map pp118-19; 153 Wangfujing Dajie; ☺ 8.30am-10pm) Large pharmacy opposite St Joseph's Church.

Wangfujing Medicine Shop (Wángfǔjīng Yīyào Shāngdiàn; Map p123; ☎ 6524 0122; 267 Wangfujing Dajie; ☺ 8.30am-9pm) Large range of both Western and Chinese drugs.

Watson's (Qūchénshì) Chaoyangmenwai Dajie (Map pp118-19; 1st fl, Full Link Plaza, 19 Chaoyangmenwai Dajie); Dongchan'an Jie (Map p123; Oriental Plaza, 1 Dongchan'an Jie) Branches purvey some medicines, but are more geared towards selling cosmetics, sunscreens and the like.

Money

Foreign currency and travellers cheques can be changed at large branches of the Bank of China, CITIC Industrial Bank (Map pp118-19), the airport and hotel moneychanging counters, and at several department stores (including the Friendship Store), as long as you have your passport. Hotels give the official rate, but some will add a small commission. Useful branches of the Bank of China with foreign-exchange counters include a branch next to Oriental Plaza on Wangfujing Dajie, in the Lufthansa Center Youyi Shopping City, and in the China World Trade Center. For international money transfer, branches of Western Union can be found in the International Post Office (p124) and at the post office at No 3 Gongrentiyuchang Beilu (☎ 6416 7686; Map pp118-19).

If you have an Amex card, you can also cash personal cheques at CITIC Industrial Bank and large branches of the Bank of China.

ATMs that accept foreign credit cards and are linked to international bank settlement systems such as Cirrus and Plus can be found in increasing numbers. The best places to look are in and around the main shopping areas (such as Wangfujing Dajie) and international hotels and their associated shopping arcades; some large department stores also have useful ATMs. There's a Bank of China ATM in the

(Continued on page 124)

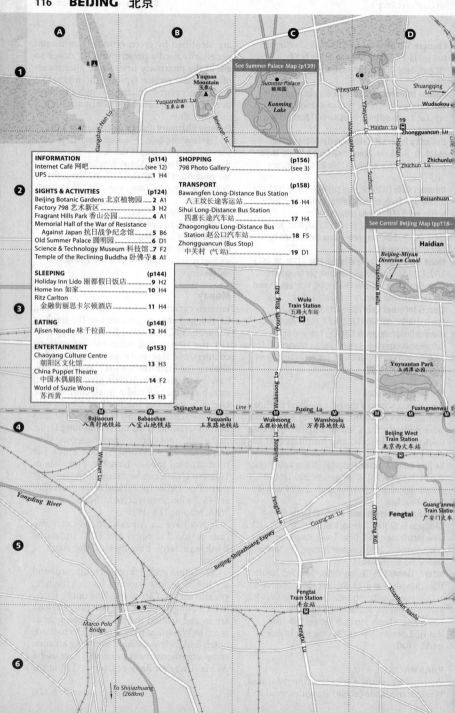

INFORMATION (p114)
Internet Café 网吧 .... (see 12)
UPS **1** H4

SIGHTS & ACTIVITIES (p124)
Beijing Botanic Gardens 北京植物园 **2** A1
Factory 798 艺术新区 **3** H2
Fragrant Hills Park 香山公园 **4** A1
Memorial Hall of the War of Resistance
  Against Japan 抗日战争纪念馆....**5** B6
Old Summer Palace 圆明园..................**6** D1
Science & Technology Museum 科技馆 ..**7** F2
Temple of the Reclining Buddha 卧佛寺 **8** A1

SLEEPING (p144)
Holiday Inn Lido 丽都假日饭店 **9** H2
Home Inn 如家 **10** H4
Ritz Carlton
  金融街丽思卡尔顿酒店 **11** H4

EATING (p148)
Ajisen Noodle 味千拉面 **12** H4

ENTERTAINMENT (p153)
Chaoyang Culture Centre
  朝阳区文化馆........................**13** H3
China Puppet Theatre
  中国木偶剧院......................**14** F2
World of Suzie Wong
  苏西黄................................**15** H3

SHOPPING (p156)
798 Photo Gallery......................... (see 3)

TRANSPORT (p158)
Bawangfen Long-Distance Bus Station
  八王坟长途客运站 **16** H4
Sihui Long-Distance Bus Station
  四惠长途汽车站 **17** H4
Zhaogongkou Long-Distance Bus
  Station 赵公口汽车站..................**18** F5
Zhongguancun (Bus Stop)
  中关村 (气站)..............................**19** D1

See Summer Palace Map (p139)

Yuquan Mountain 玉泉山 ▲

Summer Palace 颐和园

Kunming Lake

See Central Beijing Map (pp118–

Haidian

Beijing-Miyun Diversion Canal

Xisanhuan Beilu

Yuyuantan Park 玉渊潭公园

Wulu Train Station 五路火车站

Shijingshan Lu   Fuxing Lu   Fuxingmenwai

Ⓜ Baijiaocun 八角村地铁站   Ⓜ Babaoshan 八宝山地铁站   Ⓜ Yuquanlu 玉泉路地铁站   Ⓜ Wukesong 五棵松地铁站   Ⓜ Wanshoulu 万寿路地铁站   Ⓜ   Ⓜ

Line 1

Beijing West Train Station 北京西火车站

Yongding River

Guang'anmen Train Station 广安门火车

Fengtai

Beijing-Shijiazhuang Expwy

Guang'an Lu

Fengtai Train Station 丰台站

Marco Polo Bridge

To Shijiazhuang (268km)

Kangxian Man Lu

Yuquanshan Lu

Beiwazih Lu

Yiheyuan Lu

Wanquanhe Lu

Haidian Lu

Suzhou Lu

Zhichun Lu

Shuangqing Lu

Wudaokou

Zhongguancun Lu

Zhichunlu

Beisanhuan

Fourth Ring Rd

Wukesong Lu

Fengtai Lu

Wuhan Lu

Third Ring Rd

Xisanhuan Nanlu

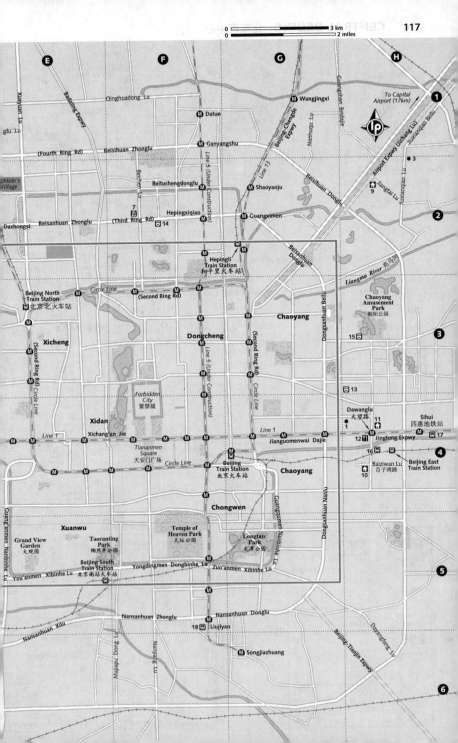

CENTR

0 |———| 3 km
0 |———| 2 miles

E **F** **G** **H**

1

To Capital
Airport (17km)

Xueyuan Lu

Baoding Expwy

Qinghuadong Lu

gfu Lu

Datun

Wangjingxi

Guanghan Bridge

Beijing-Chengde Expwy

Nanhuqu Lu

Beihuan Donglu

Airport Expwy (Jichang Lu)

Jiuxianqiao Beilu

Jiuxianqiao Lu

Jiangtai Lu

3

(Fourth Ring Rd)
Beisihuan Zhonglu

Ganyangshu

Line 13

9

2

Beichen Lu

Beituchengdonglu

Shaoyaoju

thlete's
village

Hepingxiqiao

(Third Ring Rd)

7

14

Guangximen

Beisanhuan
Donglu

Dazhongsi

Beisanhuan Zhonglu

Line 5 (Under Construction)

Liangma River 亮马河

Chaoyang
Amusement
Park
朝阳公园

Beijing North
Train Station
北京北火车站

Circle Line

Hepingli
Train Station
和平里火车站

(Second Ring Rd)

Chaoyang

Dongsanhuan Beilu

15

3

Xicheng

Dongcheng

(Second Ring Rd)

Circle Line

13

(Second Ring Rd) Circle Line

Forbidden
City
紫禁城

Line 5 (Under Construction)

Dawanglu
大望路

11

Sihui
四惠地铁站

1

Xidan

Line 1

Line 1

Xichang'an Jie

Jianguomenwai Dajie

12

Jingtong Expwy

17

16

Baiziwan Lu
百子湾路

Beijing East
Train Station

Tiananmen
Square
天安门广场

Circle Line

Beijing
Train Station
北京火车站

Chaoyang

10

Guangqumen Nanbinhe Lu

Chongwen

Guang'anmen Nanbinhe Lu

Xuanwu

Grand View
Garden
大观园

Taoranting
Park
陶然亭公园

Temple of
Heaven Park
天坛公园

Longtan
Park
龙潭公园

Dongsanhuan Nanlu

Beijing South
Train Station
北京南站火车站

Yongdingmen Dongbinhe Lu

Zuo'anmen Xibinhe Lu

You'anmen Xibinhe Lu

5

Nansanhuan Xilu

Maliandao Lu

Nanwei Lu

Nansanhuan Zhonglu

Nansanhuan Donglu

Beijing-Tianjin Expwy

Dajingchang Lu

18

Liujiyao

Songjiazhuang

6

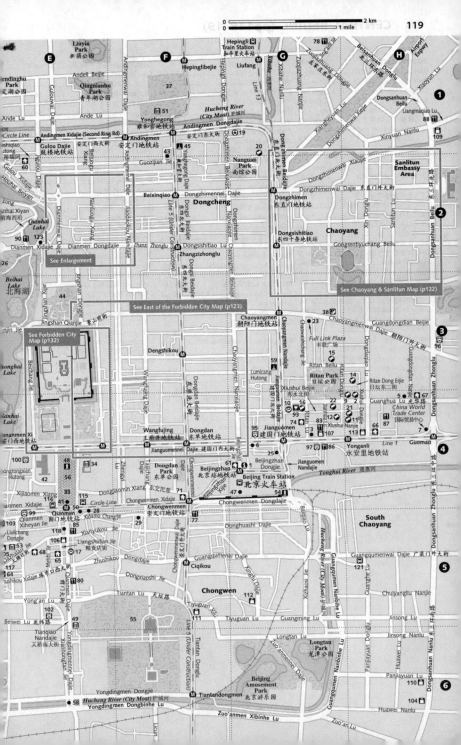

0 ____ 2 km
0 ____ 1 mile

E

Liuyin Park 柳荫公园

dendinghu Park 定湖公园

Qingnianhu Park 青年湖公园

Ande Lu

Ande Lu

Circle Line

Andingmen Xidajie (Second Ring Rd)

Gulou Dajie 鼓楼地铁站

shiqiao tong tong 杨梅竹斜街

Gulou Xidajie

60

Qianhai Lake 前海湖

90 123

Dianmen Xidajie 地安门西大街

26

See Enlargement

Beihai Lake 北海湖

44

Jingshan Qianjie 景山前街

njin Lu

anghai Lake

anghai Lake

anmen Xi 安门西地铁站

100

Xijiaomin Xiang

ongrongxian Hutong

42

116 41

99 Qianmen 前门地铁站

103 Qianmen Xiheyan Jie

118 85

Liuliduchang Dongjie

106

53 68 17

112 64

ushikou Xidajie 珠市口西大街 80

Yong'an Lu

102

49

Beiwei Lu 北纬路

Tianqiao Nandajie 天桥南大街

55

58 Hucheng River (City Moat) 护城河
Yongdingmen Dongbinhe Lu

F

Hepinglibeijie

Hepingli Train Station 和平里火车站

Liufang

37

Yonghegong 雍和宫地铁站

51

Andingmen Dongdajie

Hucheng River (City Moat) 护城河

安定门东大街 19

45

Guozijian Jie

43

Beixinqiao

Dongzhimennei Dajie

Zhanzi Zhonglu

Dongsishitiao Lu

Zhangzizhonglu

See East of the Forbidden City Map (p123)

Chaoyangmen 朝阳门地铁站

See Forbidden City Map (p132)

Dengshikou

59

Lumicang Hutong

Wangfujing 王府井地铁站

Dongdan 东单地铁站

Jianguomennei Dajie 建国门内大街

Jianguomen 建国门地铁站

Dongdan Park 东单公园

48

34

56

33

115

50

Xdamo Changje

29

Xianyukou Jie

Liangshidian Jie 粮食店街

Zhushikou Dongdajie

Dongxiaoshi Jie

Tiantan Lu 天坛路

Ciqikou

Guangqumennei Dajie

Chongwen

112

111

Tiyuguan Xilu

Tiyuguan Lu

Guangming Lu

Beijing Amusement Park 北京游乐园

Tiantandongmen 天坛东门地铁站

Zuo'anmen Xibinhe Lu

G

78

Xidahe Nanlu

Xiaojie

Dong zhimen Beidajie 东直门北大街

Dongzhimen 东直门地铁站

东直门地铁站

Dongzhimennei Dajie 东直门内大街

Dongzhimenwai Dajie 东直门外大街

23

38

Chaoyangmenwai Dajie 朝阳门外大街

Full Link Plaza 丰联广场

15

Ritan Beilu

Ritan Park 日坛公园

Xiushui Beijie 秀水北街

10 16

93

74

3

95

Jianguomen

25

Beijingzhan Xijie 北京站西街

61

Beijing Train Station 北京火车站

47

54

Donghuashi Dajie

Guangqumennei Dajie

Xingfu Dajie

Xinhua Jie

H

Beisanhuan Donglu 北三环东路

Airport Expwy

Xiaoyun Lu

Dongsanhuan Beilu 东三环北路

Liangmaqiao Lu

88

109

1

Xinyuan Nanlu

Zuojiazhuang Dongli

Sanlitun Embassy Area

Dongsanhuan Beilu 东三环北路

Chaoyang

Gongrentiyuchang Beilu 工人体育场北路

See Chaoyang & Sanlitun Map (p122)

2

Guangdongdian Beijie 光东店北街

96

3

14

67

9

Guanghua Lu 光华路

China World Trade Center 国际贸易中心

66 87

Yonganli 永安里地铁站

86

Guomao 国贸

4

Line 1

Jianguomen Dongjie

Jianguomen Nandajie

Tonghui River 通惠河

South Chaoyang

Guangqumenwai Dajie 广渠门外大街

121

5

Chulyanglu Nanjie

Jinsong Lu

Jinsong Nanlu

Huawei Lu

Panjiayuan Lu

110

104

6

Dongsanhuan Zhonglu 东三环中路

Dongsanhuan Nanlu 东三环南路

Huawei Nanlu

0 ___ 500 m
0 ___ 0.3 miles

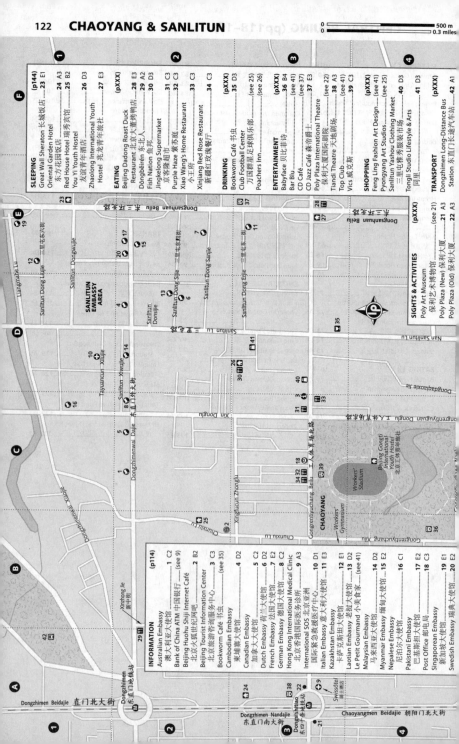

0 — 500 m
0 — 0.3 miles

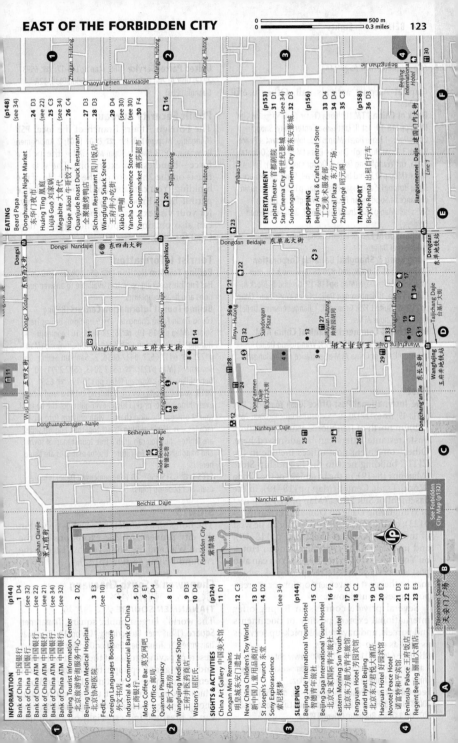

Zhuan'r Hutong

Chaoyangmen Nanxiaojie

Dafangjia Hutong

Lumicang Hutong

Beijing International Hotel

Jingshan Qianjie

景山前街

Jingshan Houjie

景山后街

Shijia Hutong

Dongsi Nandajie 东四南大街

Dongdan Beidajie 东单北大街

Dongsi

Dongsi Xidajie 东四西大街

Dengshikou

Ganmian Hutong

Neiwu Jie

Jinbao Lu

Dengshikou Dajie

Wangfujing Dajie 王府井大街

Jinyu Hutong

Sundongan Plaza

Shuifuyuan Hutong 帅府园胡同

Dongdan Ertiao

Dongdan

东单地铁站

Wangfujing Dajie 王府井大街

Wangfujing 王府井地铁站

Taijichang Dajie 台基厂大街

Wangfujing Dajie

Dengshikou Xije

Donghuangchenggen Nanjie

Beihenan Dajie

Zhide Huang 智德北巷

Nanhenan Dajie

Dong'anmen Dajie 东安门大街

Dongchang'an Jie 东长安街

Beichizi Dajie

Nanchizi Dajie

Forbidden City 紫禁城

See Forbidden City Map (p132)

Jianguomennei Dajie 建国门内大街

Line 1

Tiananmen Square 天安门广场

天安门广场

(Continued from page 115)

Capital Airport arrivals hall. Other useful ATMs:

Bank of China ATM Lufthansa Center Youyi Shopping City (Map pp118-19; 1st fl; Lufthansa Center Youyi Shopping City); Novotel Peace Hotel (Map p123; foyer, Novotel Peace Hotel, 3 Jinyu Hutong); Oriental Plaza (Map p123; Oriental Plaza, cnr Wangfujing Dajie & Dongchang'an Jie); Peninsula Palace (Map p123; 2nd basement level, Peninsula Palace, 8 Jinyu Hutong); Sundongan Plaza (Map p123; next to main entrance of Sundongan Plaza on Wangfujing Dajie); Swissôtel (Map p122; 2nd fl, Swissôtel, 2 Chaoyangmen Beidajie)

Citibank ATM East of International Hotel on Jianguomennei Dajie.

Hong Kong & Shanghai Banking Corporation (HSBC; ☎ 6526 0668, 800-820 8878; www.hsbc.com .cn) Jianguomen Dajie (Map pp118-19; Ground fl, Block A, COFCO Plaza, 8 Jianguomen Dajie); China World Hotel (Map pp118-19; Suite L129, Ground fl, 1 Jianguomenwai Dajie) All have 24-hour ATMs.

Industrial & Commercial Bank of China ATM (Gōngshāng Yínháng; Map p123; Wangfujing Dajie) Opposite Bank of China ATM at entrance to Sundongan Plaza.

Post

The **International Post Office** (Guójì Yóudiànjú; Map pp118-19; ☎ 6512 8120; Jianguomen Beidajie; ☷ 8am-7pm) is 200m north of Jianguomen subway station; poste restante letters can be addressed here. Other convenient post offices include in the CITIC building next to the Friendship Store (Map pp118–19); in the basement of the China World Trade Center (Map pp118–19); in the basement of Silk Street (Map pp118–19); east of Wangfujing Dajie on Dongdan Ertiao (Map p123); on the south side of Xichang'an Jie west of the Beijing Concert Hall (Map pp118–19); and just east of the Qianmen Jianguo Hotel, on Yong'an Lu (Map pp118–19). You can also post letters via your hotel reception desk, which may be the most convenient option, or at green post boxes around town.

Several private couriers in Běijīng offer international express posting of documents and parcels, and have reliable pick-up services as well as drop-off centres.

DHL (☎ 6466 2211, 800-810 8000; www.dhl.com; 45 Xinyuan Jie) Further branches in the Kempinski Hotel, the China World Trade Center and COFCO Plaza.

Federal Express (FedEx; Map pp118-19; ☎ 6561 2003, 800-810 2338; Hanwei Bldg, 7 Guanghua Lu) Also in Room 107, No 1 Office Building, Oriental Plaza.

United Parcel Service (UPS; Map pp116-17; ☎ 6593 2932; Unit A, 2nd fl, Tower B, Beijing Kelun Bldg, 12A Guanghua Lu)

Public Security Bureau

The Foreign Affairs Branch of the local **PSB** (Gōngānjú; Map pp118-19; ☎ 8402 0101; 2 Andingmen Dongdajie; ☷ 8.30am-4.30pm Mon-Sat) – the police force – handles visa extensions. The visa office is on the 2nd floor on the east side of the building. You can also apply for a residence permit here. Expect to wait up to five days for your visa extension to be processed. You can also obtain passport photographs here (Y30 for five).

Tourist Information

Beijing Tourism Hotline (☎ 6513 0828; ☷ 24hr) Has English-speaking operators available to answer questions and hear complaints.

Beijing Tourist Information Centers (Běijīng Lǚyóu Zīxún Fúwù Zhōngxīn; ☷ 9am-5pm) Beijing Train Station (Map pp118-19; ☎ 6528 4848; 16 Laoqianju Hutong); Capital Airport (☎ 6459 8148); Chaoyang (Map p122; ☎ 6417 6627, 6417 6656; 27 Sanlitun Beilu); Dongcheng (Map p123; ☎ 6512 3043, 6512 2991; 10 Dengshikou Xijie); Xuanwu (Map pp118-19; ☎ 6351 0018; xuanwu@bjta.gov.cn; 3 Hufang Lu) In a land where everything has its price, China never quite got the hang of tourist offices. The local chain – with uniform turquoise façades – is slowly getting its act together. English skills are limited, but you can grab a free tourist map of town and handfuls of free literature. Useful branches are listed here.

CITS (☎ 6515 8587; 28 Jianguomenwai Dajie) Is more useful for booking tours.

SIGHTS

The lion's share of Běijīng's sights lie within the city proper. Notable exceptions are the Great Wall and the Ming Tombs, listed in the Around Běijīng section (p162).

Chongwen & South Chaoyang
崇文区、朝阳南区

TIANANMEN SQUARE 天安门广场
The world's largest public square, **Tiananmen Square** (Tiānānmén Guǎngchǎng; Map pp118-19; subway Tiananmen Xi, Tiananmen Dong or Qianmen) is a vast desert of paving stones at the heart of Běijīng and a poignant epitaph to China's hapless democracy movement. It may be a grandiose, Maoist tourist trap, but there's more than enough space to stretch your legs and the view can be breathtaking, especially on a clear day

BĚIJĪNG OLYMPICS

The first Olympics to be held in a developing country in two decades, the 2008 Olympics is a high-tide mark in Běijīng's ambitions to project itself onto the world stage. Craving global attention and receiving it, Běijīng aims to secure a standing ovation for its XXIX Olympiad. It seems only appropriate that a country casting itself as an economic powerhouse and emerging superpower should host the world's most prestigious sports event. The event is also an opportunity to showcase athletic talent in China and unseating the USA at the top of the medals tables would be a further fillip for this country that frets about its international profile.

Wrestling with the surging growth in car ownership and a vastly more mobile population, Běijīng seized the opportunity to reshape the transport infrastructure of the city. To this end, Běijīng has hurled billions of dollars into an Olympian makeover for the capital, which will include the world's largest airport terminal and a hugely extended underground system.

Among achievements that have been lauded worldwide is a frenzied construction schedule that has been the equivalent of the 100m dash – completed ahead of target and generating employment for almost two million people. Much history – an irretrievable commodity – has been levelled in the process, although some has been re-created, such as the gate at Yongding Men (see the boxed text, p128). Many of the city's delightful *hútòng* (see p136) have either been obliterated or drastically clipped by road-widening schemes. Even the historic areas around Qianmen and Dashilan have seen whole areas demolished by real-estate developers.

And as taxi drivers grapple with basic English idiom in preparation for the deluge of foreigners, up to 50% of car owners may have their vehicles forced off the roads as Běijīng contemplates drastic measures to clean up the city's noxious air. Officials proudly trumpet a 'Green Olympics', but this may be setting the bar too high for Běijīng's trailing foot – the haze that frequently settles over town (see the boxed text, p113). As Běijīng is one of the world's most polluted cities, further drastic measures could include the temporary closure of factories and construction sites in the run-up to the sporting event.

Most of the games will be held in Běijīng, but other events will be staged in five other Chinese cities, including Tiānjīn, Shěnyáng, Qínhuángdǎo and Shànghǎi, with the sailing events held in the lovely seaside town of Qīngdǎo.

Once again, the Olympic Games have become politically charged. Běijīng is anxious to portray itself as something more than a crony-Communist regime with a questionable human-rights record. But the approval rating for the Olympics among Běijīng residents – who find it far simpler to separate sport and politics – is overwhelmingly massive, despite the run-up to the games being hobbled by accusations of corruption.

Domestic reporting on the Olympic Games is upbeat, as is the official website of the games (www.en.beijing2008.com). Běijīng may not be winning any medals for access to information, with endless websites (the BBC News and Wikipedia are but a few) blocked to the Chinese, but it has pledged that reporters will be able to report freely and as such it will have to endure levels of journalistic scrutiny never before experienced by a Chinese city outside of Hong Kong.

Let the games commence!

and at nightfall. Kites flit through the sky, children stamp around on the paving slabs and Chinese out-of-towners huddle together for the obligatory photo opportunity with the great helmsman's portrait.

The square is laid out on a north–south axis. Threading through Front Gate (p127) to the south, the square's meridian line is straddled by the Chairman Mao Memorial Hall (p127), cuts through the Gate of Heavenly Peace (p126) to the north and cleaves through the Forbidden City (p133) behind.

In the square, you stand in the symbolic centre of the Chinese universe. The rectangular arrangement, flanked by halls to the east and west, to an extent echoes the layout of the Forbidden City. As such, the square employs a conventional plan that pays obeisance to traditional Chinese culture, while its ornaments and buildings are largely Soviet inspired.

Mao conceived the square to project the enormity of the Communist Party, so it's all a bit Kim Il Sung-ish. During the Cultural Revolution the chairman, wearing a Red

---

THE SQUARE OF THE GATE OF HEAVENLY PEACE

It may be named after the Ming dynasty gate crowning its northern perimeter, but Tiananmen Sq as we see it today is very much a modern creation. During Ming and Qing times, part of the Imperial City Wall (Huáng Chéng) called the Thousand Foot Corridor (Qiānbù Láng) poked deep into the space today occupied by the square, enclosing a section of the imperial domain. The wall took the shape of a 'T', emerging from the two huge, and now absent, gates – Cháng'ān Zuǒ Mén and Cháng'ān Yòu Mén – that rose up south of the Gate of Heavenly Peace before running south to Daming Gate (Dàmíng Mén). Called Daqing Gate (Dàqīng Mén) during Manchu times, the gate was renamed Zhonghua Gate (Zhōnghuá Mén) during the short-lived republic, before being felled to make way for Chairman Mao's memorial hall. East and west of the Thousand Foot Corridor stood official departments and temples, including the Ministry of Rites, the Ministry of Revenue, Honglu Temple and Taichang Temple, sites now occupied by the Great Hall of the People (opposite) and the China National Museum (p128).

Guard armband, reviewed parades of up to a million people here. In 1976 another million people jammed the square to pay their last respects to Mao. In 1989 army tanks and soldiers forced pro-democracy demonstrators out of the square. Although it seems likely that no-one was actually killed within the square itself, a well-documented slaughter occurred at Muxidi, to the west. Despite being a public place, the square remains more in the hands of the government than the people; it is monitored by closed-circuit TV cameras, and plain-clothes police are primed to paralyse the first twitch of dissent.

West of the monolithic Great Hall of the People (opposite), the bulbous, titanium-and-glass **National Grand Theatre** could be mistaken for an alien mother ship that has landed to refuel. Still waiting to open at the time of writing, the project has undergone delays, while critics have questioned both its incongruous styling and the wisdom of erecting such a shimmering building in Běijīng's notoriously dust-laden air.

If you get up early you can watch the flag-raising ceremony at sunrise, performed by a troop of PLA soldiers drilled to march at precisely 108 paces per minute, 75cm per pace. The same ceremony in reverse is performed at sunset, but you can hardly see the soldiers for the throngs gathered to watch. The square is illuminated at night.

Bicycles cannot be ridden across Tiananmen Sq – apparently tanks are OK – but you can walk your bike.

GATE OF HEAVENLY PEACE 天安门

Hung with a vast likeness of Mao, the **Gate of Heavenly Peace** (Tiānānmén; Map p132; ☎ 6309 9386; admission Y15, bag storage Y1-6; ✆ 8.30am-4.30pm; subway Tiananmen Xi or Tiananmen Dong) is a potent national symbol. Built in the 15th century and restored in the 17th century, the double-eaved gate was formerly the largest of the four gates of the Imperial Wall that enveloped the imperial grounds.

Of the pair guarding the gate, folklore attests that the westerly stone lion blocked Li Chuangwang when he invaded Běijīng at the end of the Ming dynasty. Li fended the lion off by stabbing its belly with his spear while on horseback, leaving a mark that remains. Other locals insist that it is a bullet hole – the work of allied-force guns after troops entered Běijīng to quell the Boxer Rebellion in 1900. For more on the Boxer Rebellion see the boxed text, p45.

The gate is divided into five doors and reached via seven bridges spanning a stream. Each of these bridges was restricted in its use and only the emperor could use the central door and bridge.

Today's political coterie review mass troop parades from here and it was from this gate that Mao proclaimed the People's Republic on 1 October 1949. The dominating feature is the gigantic portrait of the ex-chairman, to the left of which runs the poetic slogan 'Long Live the People's Republic of China' and to the right 'Long Live the Unity of the Peoples of the World'. The portrait was famously pelted with paint-filled eggs during the 1989 demonstrations in the square; the iconoclasts were workers from Mao's home province of Húnán. A number of spares of the portrait exist and a fresh one was speedily requisitioned.

Climb up to great views of Tiananmen Sq and peek inside at the impressive beams and overdone paintwork. Other diversions include video presentations and paintings of the flag-raising ceremony, featuring jubilant representatives of China's ethnic minorities.

There is no fee for walking through the gate, but if you climb it you will have to buy an admission ticket. Security is intense with metal detectors and frisking awaiting visitors.

DUAN GATE 端门

Sandwiched between the Gate of Heavenly Peace and Meridian Gate, **Duan Gate** (Duān Mén; Map p132; admission Y10; 8.30am-4.30pm) was stripped of its treasures by foreign forces quelling the Boxer Rebellion. The hall today is hung with photos of old Běijīng but steer your eyes to the ceiling, wonderfully painted in its original colours and free of the cosmetic improvements so casually inflicted on so many of China's other historic monuments.

FRONT GATE 前门

The **Front Gate** (Qián Mén; Map pp118-19; admission Y10; 8.30am-4pm; subway Qianmen) actually consists of two gates. The northerly gate, 40m-high Zhèngyáng Mén, dates from the Ming dynasty and was the largest of the nine impressive gates of the inner city wall separating the Inner or Tartar (Manchu) City from the Outer or Chinese City. Partially destroyed during the Boxer Rebellion of 1900, the gate was once flanked by two temples that have vanished. With the disappearance of the city walls, the gate sits out of context, and was undergoing extensive repairs at the time of writing. Similarly torched during the Boxer Rebellion, the Arrow Tower (Jiàn Lóu) to the south also dates from Ming times and was originally connected to Zhèngyáng Mén by a semicircular enceinte, which was swept aside in the early 20th century. To the east is the former British-built **Old Station Building** (Lǎo Chēzhàn; Qian Men Railway Station), now housing shops and restaurants.

GREAT HALL OF THE PEOPLE 人民大会堂

On a site previously occupied by Taichang Temple, the Jinyiwei (the Ming dynasty secret service) and the Ministry of Justice, the **Great Hall of the People** (Rénmín Dàhuìtáng; Map pp118-19; 6309 6668; admission Y20, bag storage Y2; 9am-3pm; subway Tiananmen Xi), on the western side of Tiananmen Sq, is where the National People's Congress convenes. The 1959 architecture is

monolithic and intimidating; the tour parades visitors past a choice of 29 of its lifeless rooms, named after the provinces that make up the Chinese universe. Also on the billing is the 5000-seat banquet room where US President Richard Nixon dined in 1972, and the 10,000-seat auditorium with the familiar red star embedded in a galaxy of lights in the ceiling. The Great Hall is closed to the public when the People's Congress is in session.

CHAIRMAN MAO MEMORIAL HALL 毛主席纪念堂

Chairman Mao died in September 1976 and his **Memorial Hall** (Máo Zhǔxí Jìniàntáng; Map pp118-19; admission free, camera storage Y2-5, bag storage Y2-10; 8.30-11.30am Tue-Sun, 2-4pm Tue & Thu, not open pm in Jul & Aug; subway Tiananmen Xi, Tiananmen Dong or Qianmen), on the southern side of Tiananmen Sq, was constructed shortly thereafter on the former site of Zhonghua Gate (see the boxed text, opposite).

Easy as it now is to vilify his excesses, many Chinese show deep respect when confronted with the physical presence of Mao. You will be reminded to remove your hat and you can fork out Y3 for a flower to deposit at the foot of a statue of the erstwhile despot in the entrance hall if you wish. The Great Helmsman's mummified corpse lies in a crystal cabinet, draped in an anachronistic red flag emblazoned with hammer and sickle, while impatient guards in white gloves brusquely wave the hoi polloi on towards further rooms, where a riot of Mao kitsch – lighters, bracelets, statues, key rings, bottle openers, you name it – ensues. Don't expect to stumble upon Jung Chang signing copies of her *Mao, the Unknown Story*. At certain times of the year

THE REBUILDING OF BĚIJĪNG

Steered onto the subject, every other Běijīng cabbie will bemoan the demolition of the capital's city walls. Felled in the interests of traffic circulation, perhaps, but just how many cars were there in 1950s Běijīng? Had they pulled through, the vast city walls and their magnificent gates would undoubtedly be major tourist money-spinners if not Unesco World Heritage sites.

Běijīng has belatedly begun to pick up the pieces: you can mull over the sad remains of Dongan Men (Map p123), wander alongside vestiges of the city wall at Chongwen Men or size up the reconstructed gate of Yongding Men. The most stalwart survivors are the city gates and towers that – apart from the Southeast Corner Watchtower and Deshengmen – lie along the north–south meridian line that essentially cleaves Běijīng in two.

Yongding Men, the largest gate complex in the Outer City and the southernmost point on the axis, was rebuilt in 2004. In reality, the former bastion consisted of a gate and arrow tower (similar to the Front Gate) linked by a semicircular enceinte, so today's copy only hints at the grandeur of the original. Yongding Men was demolished in 1957, making way for the bridged road that has now been severed to accommodate the rebuilt gate, making its demolition and recent substitution a questionable exercise.

With swathes of *hútòng* falling to the wrecking ball, fake *hútòng*-style brick cladding has become customary. Recently widened Jiugulou Dajie has been flanked by cheap *hútòng* brickwork while Chaoyangmen Nanxiaojie, once a delightfully battered road lined with small shops and *hútòng* openings, has been broadened into a vast thoroughfare, topping and tailing the alleyways along its length and thoroughly deleting its personality.

the body requires maintenance and is not on view. Bags need to be deposited at the building east of the memorial hall across the road from Tiananmen Sq (if you leave your camera in your bag you will be charged for it).

MONUMENT TO THE PEOPLE'S HEROES
人民英雄纪念碑

North of Mao's mausoleum, the **Monument to the People's Heroes** (Rénmín Yīngxióng Jìniànbēi; Map pp118-19; subway Tiananmen Xi, Tiananmen Dong or Qianmen) was completed in 1958. The 37.9m-high obelisk, made of Qīngdǎo granite, bears bas-relief carvings of key patriotic and revolutionary events (such as Lin Zexu destroying opium at Hǔmén in the 19th century, and Tàipíng rebels), as well as appropriate calligraphy from communist bigwigs Mao Zedong and Zhou Enlai (p52). Mao's eight-character flourish proclaims 'Eternal Glory to the People's Heroes'.

CHINA NATIONAL MUSEUM
中国国家博物馆

Housed in a sombre 1950s edifice in bad need of a total revamp, this **museum** (Zhōngguó Guójiā Bówùguǎn; Map pp118-19; admission Y30; audio tour Y30; 8.30am-4.30pm; subway Tiananmen Dong), on the eastern side of Tiananmen Sq, suffers from bad lighting, a cheap and tawdry layout and sporadic English captions. At the time of

writing only three halls were open, the most absorbing of which exhibit gorgeous bronzes and ceramics (look out for the bronze, rhino-shaped *Zun* inlaid with gold and silver designs from the Western Han).

ZHONGSHAN PARK 中山公园

This lovely little **park** (Zhōngshān Gōngyuán; Map p132; admission Y3; 6am-9pm; subway Tiananmen Xi), west of the Gate of Heavenly Peace, has a section hedging up against the Forbidden City moat. Formerly the sacred Ming-style Altar to the God of the Land and the God of Grain (Shèjìtán) where the emperor offered sacrifices, this park is clean, tranquil and tidy, and a refreshing prologue or conclusion to the magnificence of the adjacent imperial residence.

WORKERS CULTURAL PALACE
劳动人民文化宫

On the Forbidden City's southeastern flank, the **Workers Cultural Palace** (Láodòng Rénmín Wénhuà Gōng; Map p132; admission Y2; 6.30am-7.30pm; subway Tiananmen Dong), east of the Gate of Heavenly Peace, was the site of the emperor's premier place of worship, the Supreme Temple (太庙; Tài Miào). The huge halls of the temple remain, their roofs enveloped in imperial yellow tiles. The effect is not unlike the Forbidden City, without the crowds. Take the northwestern exit from the grounds of the palace and find yourself just by the Forbidden City's Meridian Gate and point of entry to the palace.

IMPERIAL CITY MUSEUM 皇城艺术馆
This **museum** (Huáng Chéng Yishùguǎn; Map p132; ☎ 8511 5104/114; 9 Changpu Heyan; adult/student Y20/10, audio tour Y50; ⏰ 9am-4.30pm; subway Tiananmen Dong) is devoted to the Imperial City Wall (Huáng Chéng), which – apart from a few brief stretches – no longer exists. The museum is the centrepiece of a surviving section of the Imperial City wall, southeast of the Forbidden City, that has been dolled up and converted into a park (residents were moved on). The park is decorated with a graceful marble bridge, rock features, paths, a stream, willows, magnolias, scholar trees and walnut trees.

Within the museum, a diorama reveals the full extent of the yellow-tiled wall, which encompassed a vast chunk of Běijīng virtually seven times the size of the Forbidden City. In its heyday, 28 large temples could be found in the Imperial City alone, along with many smaller shrines. Further galleries have exhibits of imperial ornaments such as *ruyi* (sceptres), porcelain and enamelware and the weapons and armour of the guards who defended the Imperial City.

IMPERIAL ARCHIVES 皇史宬
Tucked away retiringly east of the Forbidden City, the tranquil **Imperial Archives** (Huángshǐ Chéng; Map p132; 136 Nanchizi Dajie; admission free; ⏰ 9am-7pm; subway Tiananmen Dong) were the former repository of the imperial records, decrees, the 'Jade Book' (the imperial genealogical record) and vast encyclopaedic works, including the *Yongle Dadian* and the *Daqing Huidian*. With strong echoes of the imperial palace, the courtyard contains well-preserved halls, the **Wan Fung Art Gallery** (Yúnfēng Huàyuàn; Map p132; www .wanfung.com.cn; ⏰ noon-6pm Mon, 10am-6pm Tue-Sun) and further art galleries.

ANCIENT OBSERVATORY 古观象台
Běijīng's ancient **observatory** (Gǔ Guānxiàngtái; Map pp118-19; admission Y10; ⏰ 9-11.30am & 1-4.30pm Tue-Sun; subway Jianguomen) forlornly overlooks the shuddering flyovers of the Second Ring Rd.

The original observatory dated back to Kublai Khan's days, when it lay north of the present site.

Climb to the roof for its magnificent array of Jesuit-designed astronomical instruments. The

MAOSOLEUM
On 9 September 1976 the ruling Politburo had an important decision to make. Mao Zedong had passed away and something had to be done with his body. While pickling doesn't immediately come to mind, China's leaders looked to Russia and Vietnam where Lenin and Ho Chi Minh's bodies laid well preserved. Mao's personal doctor, Li Zhisui, was somewhat anxious with his task at hand. Unsure as to how well his first attempt at 'preservation in perpetuity' would go, he had a wax replica of Mao constructed as backup.

Mao in all of his formaldehyde glory went on display in Tiananmen Sq one year later. His mausoleum (p127) was built by workers and with supplies from each of the provinces, a symbolic show of the spread of Mao's supremacy throughout the country. Inside, Mao's glass-topped casket lies upon a black stone from Tài Shān as a reminder of an infamous Chinese quote from Sima Qian: 'One's life can be weightier than Mt Tai or lighter than a goose feather'. Each evening the casket is lowered into a refrigerator where it rests alongside the wax version, leaving many visitors to wonder which Mao they are actually viewing.

In February 2004, six Chinese scholars drafted a proposal asking authorities to remove the corpse from display and bury it in Mao's hometown of Sháoshān in Húnán. They claimed that to worship the corpse of a ruler is a display of a 'slave-based society' and that a body returning to dust in the ground is part of Chinese tradition. Their main concern, however, seems to be the world gaze that will be falling upon Běijīng with the 2008 Olympics. They want the ghoulish exhibition gone in order for the city to appear 'civilised' and 'worthy of hosting the games'. Others claim that the mausoleum ruins the feng shui of Tiananmen Sq.

Mao himself wanted to be cremated. But whether the wishes of the Chairman himself will be honoured or whether he'll retain his symbolic place of reverence is in the hands of the Politburo.

GOING UNDERGROUND

By 1969, as the USA landed men on the moon, Mao had decided the future for Běijīng's people lay underground. Alarmist predictions of nuclear war with Russia dispatched an army of Chinese beneath the streets of Běijīng to burrow a huge warren of bombproof tunnels. The task was completed Cultural Revolution–style – by hand – and was finished in 1979, just as Russia decided to bog down in Afghanistan instead.

A section of tunnels enticingly known as the **Beijing Underground City** (Běijīng Dìxiàchéng; Map pp118-19; 62 Xidamo Changjie; admission Y20; ⏰ 8.30am-6pm; subway Chongwenmen) can be explored. English-language tours guide you along parts of this mouldering warren, past rooms designated as battlefield hospitals, a cinema, arsenals, other anonymous vaults and portraits of Mao Zedong. There's even a rudimentary elevator, floodproof doors and a ventilation system to expel poisonous gasses. Most of the tunnels are around 8m below ground, so it's cold and very damp, with the humidity increasing the deeper you go (sections at greater depths are flooded). Clad in combat gear, the guide waves down dark and uninviting tunnels, announcing their destination: one leads to the Hall of Preserving Harmony in the Forbidden City, another winds to the Summer Palace, while yet another reaches Tiānjīn (a mere 130km away), or so the guide insists. A tiresome detour to an underground silk factory concludes the trip – pass on the pricey duvet covers and pillow cases and make for the door. Emerging from the exit, head east and take a peek down the first alley on your right – Tongle Hutong – one of Běijīng's narrowest.

Jesuits, scholars as well as proselytizers, arrived in 1601 when Matteo Ricci and his associates were permitted to work with Chinese scientists. Outdoing the resident Muslim calendar-setters, they were given control of the observatory, becoming the Chinese court's official advisers.

Of the eight bronze instruments on display, six were designed and constructed under the supervision of the Belgian priest Ferdinand Verbiest, who came to China in 1659 as a special employee of the Qing court.

During the Boxer Rebellion, the instruments disappeared into the hands of the French and Germans. Some were returned in 1902 and others were returned after WWI, under the provisions of the Treaty of Versailles (1919).

MING CITY WALL RUINS PARK
明城墙遗址公园

Running the entire length of the northern flank of Chongwenmen Dongdajie is this slender **park** (Míng Chéngqiáng Yízhǐ Gōngyuán; Map pp118-19; Chongwenmen Dongdajie; admission free; ⏰ 24hr; subway Chongwenmen) alongside a section of the Ming inner city wall.

The restored wall runs for around 2km, rising up to a height of around 15m and interrupted every 80m with buttresses (dūn tái), which extend south from the wall to a maximum depth of 39m.

The park extends from the former site of Chongwen Men (one of the nine gates of the inner city wall), to the **Southeast Corner Watchtower** (Dōngnán Jiǎolóu; Dongbianmen; Map pp118-19; ☎ 8512 1554; admission Y10; ⏰ 9am-5pm; subway Jianguomen or Chongwenmen). Its green-tiled, twin-eaved roof rising up imperiously, this splendid Ming dynasty fortification is punctured with 144 archer's windows. The highly impressive interior has some staggering carpentry: huge red pillars surge upwards, topped with solid beams. The 1st floor is the site of the **Red Gate Gallery** (Hóngmén Huàláng; ☎ 6525 1005; www.redgate gallery.com; admission free; ⏰ 10am-5pm). You can hunt down a further section of original, collapsing Ming wall if you follow Jianguomen Nandajie around to the north.

TEMPLE OF HEAVEN PARK 天坛公园
A paragon of Ming design, the main hall of the **Temple of Heaven** (Tiāntán Gōngyuán; Map pp118-19; Tiantan Donglu; admission park/through ticket low season Y10/30, high season Y15/35, audio tour available at each gate Y40; ⏰ park 6am-9pm, sights 8am-6pm; subway Chongwenmen or Qianmen) has come to symbolise Běijīng. Set in a walled 267-hectare park with a gate at each compass point, the temple originally served as a vast stage for solemn rites performed by the Son of Heaven, who prayed here for good harvests, and sought divine clearance and atonement for the sins of the people.

Seen from above, the temple halls are round and the bases square, shapes respectively symbolising heaven and the earth. Further observe that the northern rim of the park is semicircular, while its southern end is square. The traditional approach to the temple was from the south, via **Zhaoheng Gate** (昭亨门; Zhāohēng Mén); the north gate is an architectural afterthought.

The 5m-high **Round Altar** (圜丘; Yuánqiū; admission Y20) was constructed in 1530 and rebuilt in 1740. Consisting of white marble arrayed in three tiers, its geometry revolves around the imperial number nine. Odd numbers possess heavenly significance, with nine the largest single-digit odd number. Symbolising heaven, the top tier is a huge mosaic of nine rings, each composed of multiples of nine stones, so that the ninth ring equals 81 stones. The stairs and balustrades are similarly presented in multiples of nine. Sounds generated from the centre of the upper terrace undergo amplification from the marble balustrades (the acoustics can get noisy when crowds join in).

The octagonal **Imperial Vault of Heaven** (皇穹宇; Huáng Qióngyǔ) was erected at the same time as the Round Altar, its shape echoing the lines of the Hall of Prayer for Good Harvests. The hall contained tablets of the emperor's ancestors, employed during winter solstice ceremonies.

Wrapped around the Imperial Vault of Heaven just north of the altar is the **Echo Wall** (回音壁; Huíyìnbì; admission Y20). A whisper can travel clearly from one end to your friend's ear at the other – unless there's a bellowing tour group in the middle (get here early for this one).

The dominant feature of the whole complex is the standout **Hall of Prayer for Good Harvests** (祈年殿; Qínián Diàn; admission Y20), an astonishing structure with a triple-eaved umbrella roof mounted on a three-tiered marble terrace. The wooden pillars support the ceiling without nails or cement – for a building 38m high and 30m in diameter, that's quite an accomplishment. Built in 1420, the hall was hit by a lightning bolt during the reign of Guangxu in 1889 and a faithful reproduction based on Ming architectural methods was erected the following year. At the time of writing, the hall was being restored.

NATURAL HISTORY MUSEUM 自然博物馆
The main entrance hall to the overblown, creeper-laden **Natural History Museum** (Zìrán Bówùguǎn; Map pp118-19; 126 Tiānqiáo Nándàjiē; admission Y30; 8.30am-5pm, no tickets sold after 4pm; subway Qianmen) is hung with portraits of the great natural

historians, including Darwin and Linnaeus (here spelt Linnacus). Escort kiddies to the revamped dinosaur hall facing you as you enter, which presents itself with an overarching skellybone of a *Mamenchisaurus jingyanensis* – a vast sauropod that once roamed China – and a much smaller *protoceratops*. Creepy crawlies are consigned to the 2nd floor, and there's an aquarium with Nemo-esque clown fish and an exhibition on the origins of life on earth, but the lack of English captions is baffling.

Some of the exhibits, such as the spliced human cadavers and genitalia in the notorious Hall of Human Bodies are best reserved for those with strong constitutions, while visiting with munchkins could subject them to months of vivid nightmares. Visiting exhibitions are occasionally staged, again without English explanations. Some halls were being revamped at the time of writing.

BEIJING PLANNING EXHIBITION HALL
北京市规划展览馆
This overpriced and little-visited **exhibition hall** (Běijīng Shì Guīhuà Zhǎnlǎnguǎn; Map pp118-19; 6701 7074; 20 Qianmen Dongdajie; admission Y30; 9am-5pm Tue-Sun) takes particular pains to present Běijīng's gut-wrenching, *hútòng*-felling metamorphosis in the best possible light. English labelling is scarce; the only exhibits of note are a detailed bronze map of town in 1949 – ironically the very year that sealed the fate of old Peking – and a huge, detailed diorama of the modern metropolis. The rest of the exhibition is a paean to modern city planning and the unstoppable advance of the concrete mixer, while 3-D films praise 'The New Beijing'. The all-white 'Future Home' on the 4th floor serves only to emphasise how wide off the mark things are: anyone living here for more than five minutes would be foaming at the mouth.

SONGTANGZHAI MUSEUM
松堂斋民间雕刻博物馆
This small **museum** (Sōngtángzhāi Mínjiān Diāokè Bówùguǎn; Map pp118-19; 14 Liulichang Dongjie; admission by donation; 9am-6pm Tue-Sun) has few English captions, but it's one of the few places you can get to see traditional Chinese carvings assembled together. Well worth popping into if wandering Liulichang (p156), here you can seek out the gateway from Jiāngxī with its elaborate architraving, and examine old drum stones, Buddhist effigies, ancient pillar bases and carved stone lions.

BĚIJĪNG

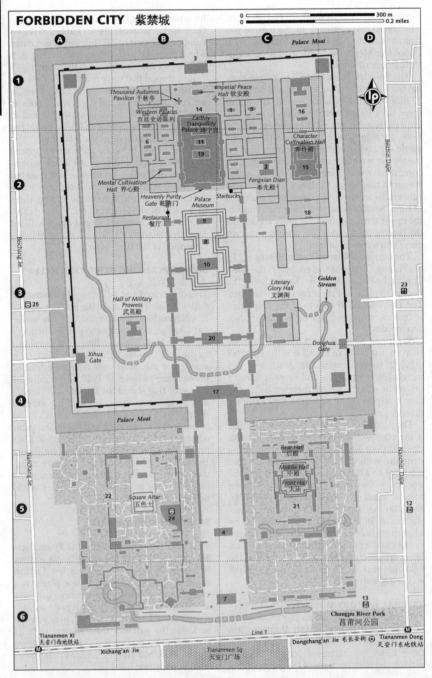

FORBIDDEN CITY 紫禁城

0   300 m
0   0.2 miles

Palace Moat

Thousand Autumns Pavilion 千秋亭

Imperial Peace Hall 钦安殿

Western Palaces 宫廷史迹陈列

Earthly Tranquillity Palace 坤宁宫

14

5

16

11

19

Character Cultivation Hall 养性殿

15

6

Mental Cultivation Hall 养心殿

2

Fengxian Dian 奉先殿

Heavenly Purity Gate 乾清门

Palace Museum

Starbucks

18

Restaurant 餐厅

9

8

10

Hall of Military Prowess 武英殿

Literary Glory Hall 文渊阁

Golden Stream

Xihua Gate

20

Donghua Gate

17

Palace Moat

Rear Hall 后殿

Middle Hall 中殿

Front Hall 太庙

Square Altar 五色土

22

24

21

4

7

13

Changpu River Park 菖蒲河公园

Tiananmen Xi 天安门西地铁站

Line 1

Dongchang'an Jie 东长安街 | Tiananmen Dong 天安门东地铁站

Xichang'an Jie

Tiananmen Sq 天安门广场

Běichízi Dàjiē

Běicháng Jiē

Nánchāng Jiē

Nánchízi Dàjiē

3

25

23

12

Dongcheng 东城

FORBIDDEN CITY 紫禁城

So called because it was off limits for 500 years, the **Forbidden City** (Zǐjìn Chéng; Map p132; ☎ 6513 2255; admission Y40, for all halls Y60; ⌚ 8.30am-4pm May-Sep, to 3.30pm Oct-Apr; subway Tiananmen Xi or Tiananmen Dong) is the largest and best-preserved cluster of ancient buildings in China. It was home to two dynasties of emperors, the Ming and the Qing, who didn't stray from this pleasure dome unless they absolutely had to.

The admission price is value for money, considering rampant ticket-price inflation elsewhere in China. Allow yourself a full day for exploration, or perhaps several separate trips if you're an enthusiast. The palace's ceremonial buildings lie on the north–south axis of the Forbidden City, from the **Meridian Gate** (Wǔ Mén; Map p132) in the south to the **Divine Military Genius Gate** (Shénwǔ Mén; Map p132) to the north.

Restored in the 17th century, Meridian Gate is a massive portal that in former times was reserved for the use of the emperor. Across the Golden Stream, which is shaped to resemble a Tartar bow and is spanned by five marble bridges, is **Supreme Harmony Gate** (Tàihé Mén; Map p132), overlooking a massive courtyard that could hold imperial audiences of up to 100,000 people.

Raised on a marble terrace with balustrades are the Three Great Halls (Sān Dàdiàn), the heart of the Forbidden City. The **Hall of Supreme Harmony** (Tàihé Diàn; Map p132) is the most important and the largest structure in the Forbidden City. Built in the 15th century, and restored in the 17th century, it was used for ceremonial occasions, such as the emperor's birthday, the nomination of military leaders and coronations.

Inside the Hall of Supreme Harmony is a richly decorated Dragon Throne (Lóngyǐ) where the emperor would preside (decisions final, no correspondence entered into) over his trembling officials.

Behind the Hall of Supreme Harmony is the smaller **Hall of Middle Harmony** (Zhōnghé Diàn; Map p132) that served as a transit lounge for the emperor. Here he would make last-minute preparations, rehearse speeches and receive close ministers.

The third hall, which has no support pillars, is the **Hall of Preserving Harmony** (Bǎohé Diàn; Map p132), used for banquets and later for imperial examinations. To the rear is a 250-tonne marble imperial carriageway carved with dragons and clouds, which was moved into Běijīng on an ice path. The emperor was conveyed over the carriageway in his sedan chair as he ascended or descended the terrace.

The basic configuration of the Three Great Halls is echoed by the next group of buildings, smaller in scale but more important in terms of real power, which in China traditionally lies in the northernmost part.

The first structure is the **Palace of Heavenly Purity** (Qiánqīng Gōng; Map p132), a residence of Ming and early Qing emperors, and later an audience hall for receiving foreign envoys and high officials.

Immediately behind rises the **Hall of Union** (Jiāotài Diàn; Map p132) and at the northern end of the Forbidden City is the 7000-sq-metre **Imperial Garden** (Yùhuā Yuán; Map p132), a classical Chinese garden of fine landscaping, with rockeries, walkways and pavilions.

The western and eastern sides of the Forbidden City are the palatial former living quarters, once containing libraries, temples, theatres, gardens and even the tennis court of the last emperor. These buildings now function as museums requiring extra admission fees.

The **Clock Exhibition Hall** (Zhōngbiǎo Guǎn; Map p132) is one of the unmissable highlights of the Forbidden City. Located at the time of writing in the Fengxian Hall (Fèngxiàn Diàn), the exhibition contains a fascinating array of elaborate timepieces, many gifts to the Qing emperors from overseas. Many of the 18th-century examples are imported through Guǎngdōng from England; others are from Switzerland, America and Japan. Exquisitely wrought, fashioned with magnificently designed elephants and other creatures, they all display an astonishing artfulness and attention to detail. Standout clocks include the 'Gilt Copper Astronomy Clock' equipped with a working model of the solar system and the automaton-equipped 'Gilt Copper Clock with a robot writing Chinese characters with a brush'. The Qing court must surely have been amazed by their ingenuity. Time your arrival with 11am or 2pm and treat yourself to the clock performance in which choice timepieces strike the hour and give a display to wide-eyed children and adults.

Other exhibits in further palace halls include the excellent Jewellery Exhibition, the Enamels Exhibition and the Jadeware Exhibition. To the horror of many, a Starbucks has wormed its way onto the palace grounds.

BEIHAI PARK 北海公园
Entered via four gates, **Beihai Park** (Běihǎi Gōngyuán; Map pp118-19; ☎ 6407 1415; admission Y5, Jade Islet Y10; ⏰ 6.30am-8pm, buildings open to 4pm; subway Tiananmen Xi, then bus 5), northwest of the Forbidden City, is largely lake.

The site is associated with Kublai Khan's palace, the navel of Běijīng before the creation of the Forbidden City. All that remains of the Khan's court is a large jar made of green jade in the **Round City** (团城; Tuánchéng), near the southern entrance.

Dominating **Jade Islet** (琼岛; Qióngdǎo) on the lake, the 36m-high **White Dagoba** (白塔; Báitǎ) was originally built in 1651 for a visit by the Dalai Lama, and was rebuilt in 1741. You can reach the dagoba through the **Yong'an Temple** (永安寺; Yǒngān Sì), included in the Beihai Park Y10 ticket.

Xītiān Fànjìng (西天梵境; Western Paradise), situated on the northern shore of the lake, is an excellent temple (admission included in park ticket). The first hall, the Hall of the Heavenly Kings, takes you past Milefo, Weituo and the four Heavenly Kings. The

Dacizhenru Hall dates to the Ming dynasty and contains three huge statues of Sakyamuni, the Amithaba Buddha and Yaoshi Fo (Medicine Buddha).

The nearby **Nine Dragon Screen** (九龙壁; Jiǔlóng Bì), a 5m-high and 27m-long spirit wall, is a glimmering stretch of coloured glazed tiles.

Beihai Park is a relaxing place to stroll around, grab a snack, sip a beer, rent a rowing boat, and watch calligraphers practising characters on the paving slabs with brush and water, and couples cuddling on a bench in the evening.

LAMA TEMPLE 雍和宫
The **Lama Temple** (Yōnghé Gōng; Map pp118-19; ☎ 6404 4499, ext 252; 28 Yonghegong Dajie; admission Y25, English audio guide Y20; ⏰ 9am-4pm; subway Yonghegong) is Běijīng's most magnificent Buddhist temple: beautiful rooftops, stunning frescoes, magnificent decorative arches, tapestries, incredible carpentry and a great pair of Chinese lions.

The most renowned Tibetan Buddhist temple outside Tibet, the Lama Temple was converted to a lamasery in 1744 after serving as the former residence of Emperor Yong Zheng.

The temple's most prized possession is its 17m-high sandalwood statue of the Maitreya Buddha in the Wanfu Pavilion. An absorbing exhibition at the rear displays numerous Tibetan items and chronicles the lineage of the Dalai Lamas.

CONFUCIUS TEMPLE & IMPERIAL COLLEGE 孔庙、国子监
Long neglected like a discarded piece of unloved bric-a-brac, the arid **Confucius Temple** (Kǒng Miào; Map pp118-19; 13 Guozijian Jie; admission Y10; ⏰ 8.30am-5pm; subway Yonghegong) is a quiet sanctuary from Běijīng's congested, smoggy streets and snarling traffic. In an Olympic makeover, China's second-largest Confucian temple was having its main hall – housing a statue of Kongzi (Confucius) – restored at the time of writing. Some of Běijīng's last remaining *páilou* bravely survive in the *hútòng* outside (Guozijian Jie). At the rear is a forest of 190 stelae (stones or slabs decorated with figures or inscriptions) recording the 13 Confucian classics, consisting of 630,000 Chinese characters.

Like everywhere in town, there are skeletons in the temple cupboard and an unpleasant footnote lurks unrecorded behind the tourist blurb. Běijīng writer Lao She was dragged here in August 1966, forced to his knees in front of a bonfire of Beijing opera costumes to confess his antirevolutionary crimes, and beaten. The much-loved writer drowned himself the next day in Taiping Lake.

West of the Confucius Temple is the **Imperial College** (Guózǐjiān; Map pp118–19), where the emperor expounded the Confucian classics to an audience of thousands of kneeling students, professors and court officials – an annual rite. Built by the grandson of Kublai Khan in 1306, the former college was the supreme academy during the Yuan, Ming and Qing dynasties. On the site is a marvellous glazed, three-gate, single-eaved decorative archway, called a *liúlí páifāng* (glazed archway). The Biyong Hall beyond is a twin-roofed structure with yellow tiles surrounded by a moat and topped with a gold knob.

DITAN PARK 地坛公园
Cosmologically juxtaposed with the Temple of Heaven and Běijīng's other altars, **Ditan Park** (Dìtán Gōngyuán; Map pp118–19; admission Y2, admission to the altar Y5; 6am-9pm), east of Andingmenwai Dajie, is the Temple of the Earth. The park's large **altar** (方泽坛; *fāngzé tán*) is square in shape, symbolising the earth. At the Chinese New Year, a temple fair is staged in the park. Within the park, the art gallery **One Moon** (Yìyuè Dāngdài Yìshù; Map pp118–19; 6427 7748; www.onemoon art.com; 11am-7pm Tue-Sun) displays thoughtful contemporary Chinese art from a 16th-century dynasty temple hall, a funky meeting of the Ming and the modern. If visiting the art gallery alone, the entrance fee to the park should be waived.

JINGSHAN PARK 景山公园
With its priceless views, **Jingshan Park** (Jǐngshān Gōngyuán; Map pp118–19; 6403 3225; admission Y2; 6am-9.30pm; subway Tiananmen Xi, then bus 5), north of the Forbidden City, was shaped from the earth excavated to create the palace moat. The hill supposedly protects the palace from the evil spirits – or dust storms – from the north (the billowing dust clouds in the spring have to be seen to be believed).

Clamber to the top for a magnificent panorama of the capital and an unparalleled overview of the russet roofing of the Forbidden City. On the eastern side of the park a locust tree stands in the place where the last of the

Ming emperors, Chongzhen, hung himself as rebels swarmed at the city walls.

ST JOSEPH'S CHURCH 东堂
One of the four principal churches in Běijīng, **St Joseph's Church** (Dōng Táng; Map p123; 74 Wangfujing Dajie; 6.30-7am Mon-Sat, to 8am Sun; subway Wangfujing) is also called the East Cathedral. Originally built in 1655, it was damaged by an earthquake in 1720 and rebuilt. The luckless church also caught fire in 1807, was destroyed again in 1900 during the Boxer Rebellion, and restored in 1904, only to be shut in 1966. It has been fully repaired and is now a more sublime feature of Wangfujing's commercial face-lift. A large square in front swarms with children playing and Chinese models in bridal outfits pose for magazine covers.

DRUM TOWER & BELL TOWER 鼓楼、钟楼
Repeatedly destroyed and restored, the **Drum Tower** (Gǔlóu; Map pp118–19; 6401 2674; Gulou Dongda-jie; admission Y20; 9am-4.30pm) originally marked the centre of the old Mongol capital. The drums of this later Ming dynasty version were beaten to mark the hours of the day. Stagger up the incredibly steep steps for impressive views over Běijīng's *hútòng* rooftops. Among the drums is the large and dilapidated **Night Watchman's Drum** (*gēnggǔ; gēng* being one of the five two-hour divisions of the night) and an array of reproduction drums.

Fronted by a Qing dynasty stele, the **Bell Tower** (Zhōnglóu; Map pp118–19; 6401 2674; Zhonglou-wan Hutong; admission Y15; 9am-4.30pm) originally dates from Ming times. The Ming structure went up in a sheet of flame and the present structure is a Qing edifice dating from the 18th century. Augment visits with drinks at the Drum & Bell Bar (p153).

Both the Drum and Bell Towers can be reached on bus 5, 58 or 107; get off at the namesake Gulou stop.

CHINA ART GALLERY 中国美术馆
The **China Art Gallery** (Zhōngguó Měishùguǎn; Map p123; 6400 6326; 1 Wusi Dajie; admission Y5; 9am-5pm, last entry 4pm) has a range of modern paintings and hosts occasional photographic exhibitions. The art on display is often typical of mainstream Chinese aesthetics (predominantly dark colours and safe subject matter) so it can be rather undemanding and anyone expecting testing artwork may be disappointed, but works from overseas collections are far more

BĚIJĪNG'S HÚTÒNG

If you want to plumb Běijīng's homely interior, and move beyond the must-see tourist sights and the shopping-mall glitz of town, voyage into the city's *hútòng* (胡同; narrow alleyways). Many of these charming alleyways have survived, crisscrossing east–west across the city and linking to create a huge, enchanting warren of one-storey, ramshackle dwellings and historic courtyard homes.

Hútòng may still be the stamping ground of a quarter of Běijīng's residents, but many are sadly being swept aside in Běijīng's race to manufacture a modern city of white tile high-rises. Marked with white plaques, historic homes are protected, but for many others a way of life hangs precariously in balance.

History

After Genghis Khan's army reduced the city of Běijīng to rubble, the city was redesigned with *hútòng*. By the Qing dynasty there were over 2000 such passageways riddling the city, leaping to around 6000 by the 1950s; now the figure has dwindled again to around 2000.

Hútòng land is a hotchpotch of the old and the new, with Qing dynasty courtyards riddled with modern brick outhouses and socialist-era conversions, and cruelly overlooked by grim apartment blocks.

Sìhéyuàn

Old walled courtyards (*sìhéyuàn*) are the building blocks of this delightful world. Many are still lived in and hum with activity. From spring to autumn, men collect outside their gates, drinking beer, playing chess, smoking and chewing the fat. Inside, trees soar aloft, providing shade and a nesting ground for birds.

More venerable courtyards are fronted by large, thick, red doors, outside of which perch either a pair of Chinese lions or drum stones (*bǎogǔshí*; two circular stones resembling drums, each on a small plinth and occasionally topped by a miniature lion or a small dragon head).

Foreigners long ago cottoned on to the charm of courtyards and breached this very conservative bastion; however, many have been repelled by poor heating, no hot water, no cable TV, dodgy sanitation and no place to park the SUV. Many *hútòng* homes still lack toilets, which explains the multitude of malodorous public loos strung out along the alleyways. Other homes

compelling. The absence of a permanent collection means that all exhibits are temporary. There are no English captions, but it's still a first-rate place to see modern Chinese art and, maybe just as importantly, to watch the Chinese looking at art. Take trolley buses 103, 104, 106 or 108 to Meishu Guan bus stop (on Wusi Dajie).

ZHIHUA TEMPLE 智化寺

Běijīng's surviving temple brood has endured slapdash renewal that regularly buries authenticity beneath casual restoration work. This rickety **shrine** (Zhìhuà Sì; Map pp118-19; 5 Lumicang Hutong; admission Y20; ☯ 8.30am-4.30pm; subway Jianguomen/Chaoyangmen) is thick with the flavours of old Peking, having eluded the Dulux treatment that invariably precedes entrance-fee inflation and stomping tour groups. You won't find the coffered ceiling of the third hall (it's in

the USA) and the Four Heavenly Kings have vanished from **Zhihua Gate** (智化门; Zhìhuà Mén), but the **Scriptures Hall** encases a venerable Ming dynasty revolving wooden library, and the highlight **Ten Thousand Buddhas Hall** (万佛殿; Wànfó Diàn) is an enticing two floors of miniature niche-borne Buddhist effigies and cabinets for the storage of sutras. Creep up the steep wooden staircase at the back of the hall to visit the sympathetic effigy of the Vairocana (毗卢) Buddha seated upon a multipetalled lotus flower in the upper chamber, before wondering the fate of the 1000-Armed Guanyin that once presided over the **Great Mercy Hall** at the temple rear.

SCIENCE & TECHNOLOGY MUSEUM 科技馆

Some exhibits at this **museum** (Kējìguǎn; Map pp116-17; 1 Beisanhuan Zhonglu; Hall A/B/C Y30/30/20, through ticket Y50; ☯ 9am-4.30pm Tue-Sun; subway Gulou Dajie) are showing

have been thoroughly modernised and sport varnished wood floors, fully fitted kitchens, a Jacuzzi and air-con.

Wind-Water Lanes

Hútòng nearly all run east–west to ensure that the main gate faces south, satisfying feng shui requirements. This south-facing aspect guarantees a lot of sunshine and protection from more negative forces from the north. This positioning also mirrors the layout of all Chinese temples, nourishing the Yang (the male and light aspect), while checking the Yin (the female and dark aspect).

Little connecting alleyways that run north–south link the main alleys. The resulting rectangular waffle-grid pattern stamps the points of the compass on the Běijīng psyche. You may hear a local saying, for example, '*wǒ gāoxìng de wǒ bù zhī běi le*', meaning 'I was so happy, I didn't know which way was north' (an extremely disorientating state of joy).

Names

Some *hútòng* are christened after families, such as Zhaotangzi Hutong (Alley of the Zhao Family). Others simply take their name from historical figures or features, while some have more mysterious associations, such as Dragon Whiskers Ditch Alley. Others reflect the merchandise plied at local markets, such as Ganmian Hutong (Dry Flour Alley) or Chrysanthemum Lane.

Hútòng Tour

The best way to see the *hútòng* is just to wander around the centre of Běijīng as the alleyways riddle the town within the Second Ring Rd. Otherwise, limit yourself to historic areas, such as around the Drum Tower (p135) or the area around the Lusongyuan Hotel (p146). Alternatively, jump on a bike (see the Bicycle Tour, p142), or do the pedicab tourist trip with the **Beijing Hutong Tour Co Ltd** (☎ 6615 9097, 6400 2787; ☯ day tours 8.50am & 1.50pm, evening tours 6.50pm May-Oct) or the **Chinese Culture Club** (☎ 6432 9341, ext 18; www.chinesecultureclub.org; 29 Liangmaqiao Lu). Small two-carriage open-air coaches leave from Wangfujing Dajie opposite Wangfujing Snack St (p148) on the south side of Wangfujing Dajie for 40-minute rides among the *hútòng* (Y15). Any number of other pedicab tours infest the roads around the Shichahai Lakes – they will circle you like hyenas, baying '*hútòng, hútòng*'.

their age, but kids can run riot among the main hall's three floors of hands-on displays. Watch **industrial robots** perform a flawless taichi sword routine, try chatting with the **speech robot** who only seems able to say '对不起 我没有听懂你的话' ('Sorry, I didn't catch you'), follow a **maglev train** gliding along a stretch of track or test out a **bulletproof vest** with a sharp pointy thing. You could spend half the day working through the imaginative and educational displays in the main hall, but if you want to make a real go of it, Hall B (astrovision theatre) and Hall C (Children's Scientific Entertainment Hall) offer extra diversions for boffins, young and old. English captions throughout.

Chaoyang 朝阳区

DONGYUE TEMPLE 东岳庙
Dedicated to the Eastern Peak (Tài Shān, p214) of China's five Taoist mountains, the **Dongyue Temple** (Dōngyuè Miào; Map pp118-19; ☎ 6553 2184; 141 Chaoyangmenwai Dajie; admission Y10; ☯ 9am-4.30pm Tue-Sun; subway Chaoyangmen) is an unsettling and fascinating experience. The temple is actively minded by Taoist monks attending to a world entirely detached from the surrounding highrises and commercial mayhem. The temple's substantial *páifāng* (memorial archway) lies to the south, divorced from its shrine by the intervention of Chaoyangmenwai Dajie.

Stepping through the entrance pops you into a Taoist Hades, where tormented spirits reflect on their wrongdoing and atonement beyond reach. Take your pick: you can muse on life's finalities in the **Life and Death Department** or the **Final Indictment Department**. Otherwise, get spooked at the **Department for Wandering Ghosts** or the **Department for Implementing 15 Kinds of Violent Death**. English explanations detail each department's function.

The huge **Daiyue Hall** (Dàiyuè Diàn) is con-secrated to the God of Tài Shān, who manages the 18 layers of hell. Visiting during festival time, especially during the Chinese New Year and the Mid-Autumn festival, sees the temple at its most colourful; see p944 for more about festivals.

POLY ART MUSEUM 保利艺术博物馆
This excellent new-generation **museum** (Bǎolì Yìshù Bówùguǎn; Map p122; ☎ 6500 8117; new Poly Plaza; admission Y50; ☻ 9.30am-4.30pm Tue, Thu & Sat, group reservations Mon, Wed & Fri; subway Dongsishitiao) has well-presented exhibits of Shang and Zhou dynasty bronzes as well as carved stone Buddhist effigies sculpted between the North-ern Wei and Tang dynasties. It is a sublime display, but be sure to take note of the often unaccommodating opening hours for individuals.

FACTORY 798 艺术新区
This disused and sprawling electronics **fac-tory** (Map pp116-17; cnr Jiuxianqiao Lu & Jiuxianqiao Beilu; admission free) found a new lease of life several years ago as the focus for Běijīng's feisty art community. Wander the former factory work-shops and peruse the artwork on view at its highlight galleries, **White Space at 798** (☎ 8456 2054; 2 Jiuxianqiao Lu; ☻ noon-6pm Tue-Sun) and **Beijing Tokyo Art Projects** (☎ 8457 3245; ☻ 10am-6.30pm) or admire the photographic stills at **798 Photo Gal-lery** (Bǎinián Yìnxiàng; ☎ 6438 1784; www.798photogallery .cn; 4 Jiuxianqiao Lu).

Fengtai & Xuanwu 丰台区、宣武区
WHITE CLOUD TEMPLE 白云观
Founded in AD 739, **White Cloud Temple** (Báiyún Guàn; Map pp118-19; ☎ 6346 3531; Baiyun Lu; admission Y10; ☻ 8.30am-4.30pm May-Sep, to 4pm Oct-Apr) is a lively, huge and fascinating temple complex of numerous shrines and courtyards, tended by distinctive Taoist monks with their hair twisted into topknots. As with many of Chi-na's temples, the White Cloud Temple has been repeatedly destroyed and today's temple halls principally date from Ming and Qing times.

Drop by White Cloud Temple during Chi-nese New Year and be rewarded with the spec-tacle of a magnificent temple fair (miàohuì). Worshippers funnel into the streets around the temple in their thousands, lured by arti-sans, street performers, wǔshù (martial arts) acts, craftsmen, traders and a swarm of snack

merchants. Near the temple entrance, a vast queue snakes slowly through the gate for a chance to rub a polished stone carving for good fortune.

Beyond, throngs of worshippers further fortify their luck by tossing metal discs (Y10 for 50) at bell-adorned outsize coins sus-pended from a bridge.

To find the temple, walk south on Baiyun Lu and cross the moat. Continue south along Baiyun Lu and turn into a curving street on the left; follow it for 250m to the temple entrance.

COW STREET MOSQUE 牛街礼拜寺
Dating back to the 10th century, this **mosque** (Niújiē Lǐbài Sì; Map pp118-19; ☎ 6353 2564; 88 Niu Jie; admission Y10, free for Muslims; ☻ 8am-sunset) was de-signed in a Chinese-temple style, is the largest in town and was the burial site for several Islamic clerics. The temple is given over to a profusion of greenery as well as flourishes of Arabic. There is a main prayer hall (which you can enter only if you are Muslim), women's quarters and the Building for Observing the Moon (望月楼; Wàngyuèlóu), from where the lunar calendar was calculated. Dress ap-propriately (no shorts or short skirts). To get here take bus 6 to Niu Jie or bus 10 to the Libaisi stop.

FAYUAN TEMPLE 法源寺
In a lane just east of Cow St Mosque is this bustling **temple** (Fǎyuán Sì; Map pp118-19; ☎ 6353 3966/4171; 7 Fayuansi Qianjie; admission Y5; ☻ 8.30-11.30am & 1.30-3.30pm Thu-Tue), originally constructed in the 7th century and still a hive of activity. Now the China Buddhism College, the temple was originally built to honour Tang soldiers who had fallen during combat against the northern tribes. From the entrance of Cow St Mosque, walk left 100m then turn left into the first hútòng. Follow the hútòng for about 10 minutes and you'll arrive at Fayuan Temple.

CAPITAL MUSEUM 中国首都博物馆
This new **museum** (Zhōngguó Shǒudū Bówùguǎn; Map pp118-19; ☎ 6337 0491; www.capitalmuseum.org.cn; 16 Fuxingmenwai Dajie; admission Y20; ☎ 9am-5pm) staged a headline-grabbing exhibition in 2006 from the collection of the British Museum. Per-manent collections include ancient bronzes, Buddhist statues, jade, calligraphy, paintings and ceramics.

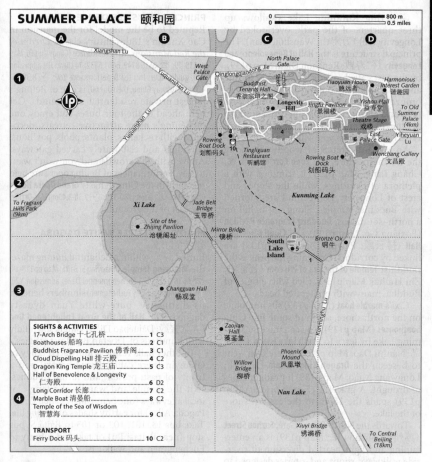

SUMMER PALACE 颐和园

SIGHTS & ACTIVITIES
17-Arch Bridge 十七孔桥 1 C3
Boathouses 船坞 2 C1
Buddhist Fragrance Pavilion 佛香阁 3 C1
Cloud Dispelling Hall 排云殿 4 C2
Dragon King Temple 龙王庙 5 C3
Hall of Benevolence & Longevity
  仁寿殿 6 D2
Long Corridor 长廊 7 C2
Marble Boat 清晏船 8 C2
Temple of the Sea of Wisdom
  智慧海 9 C1

TRANSPORT
Ferry Dock 码头 10 C2

Haidian & Xicheng 海淀区、西城区
SUMMER PALACE 颐和园

One of Běijīng's most visited sights, the immense park of the **Summer Palace** (Yíhé Yuán; Map p139; ☎ 6288 1144; 19 Xinjian Gongmen; admission Y30, through ticket Y50, audio guides Y30; ⏰ 8:30am-5pm) requires at least half a day of your time.

Teeming with tour groups from all over China and beyond, this opulent dominion of palace temples, gardens, pavilions, lakes and corridors was once a playground for the imperial court. Royalty took refuge here from the insufferable summer heat that roasted the Forbidden City. The site had long been a royal garden and was considerably enlarged and embellished by Emperor Qianlong in the 18th century. He marshalled 100,000 labour-

ers to deepen and expand **Kunming Lake** (昆明湖; Kūnmíng Hú; Map p139), and reputedly surveyed imperial navy drills from a hill-top perch.

Anglo-French troops left their mark, damaging the buildings during the Second Opium War (1856–60). Empress Dowager Cixi commenced a refit in 1888 with money earmarked for a modern navy; the marble boat at the northern edge of the lake was her only nautical – albeit unsinkable – concession.

Foreign troops, incensed by the Boxer Rebellion, had another go at roasting the Summer Palace in 1900, prompting further restoration work. By 1949 the palace had once more fallen into disrepair, eliciting a major overhaul.

Glittering Kunming Lake swallows up three-quarters of the park, overlooked by Longevity Hill (万寿山; Wànshòu Shān). The principal structure is the **Hall of Benevolence and Longevity** (仁寿殿; Rénshòu Diàn; Map p139), by the east gate, housing a hardwood throne and attached to a courtyard decorated with bronze animals, including the mythical *qílín* (a hybrid animal that only appeared on earth at times of harmony). Unfortunately, the hall is barricaded off so you will have to peer in.

An elegant stretch of woodwork along the northern shore, the **Long Corridor** (长廊; Cháng Láng; Map p139) is trimmed with a plethora of paintings, while the slopes and crest of Longevity Hill behind are adorned with Buddhist temples. Slung out uphill on a north–south axis, **Buddhist Fragrance Pavilion** (佛香阁; Fóxiāng Gé; Map p139) and **Cloud Dispelling Hall** (排云殿; Páiyún Diàn; Map p139) are linked by corridors. Crowning the peak is the Buddhist **Temple of the Sea of Wisdom** (智慧海; Zhì Huìhǎi; Map p139), tiled with effigies of Buddha, many with obliterated heads.

Cixi's **marble boat** (Map p139) sits immobile on the north shore, south of some fine Qing **boathouses** (Map p139). You can traverse Kunming Lake by ferry to **South Lake Island** (南湖岛; Nánhú Dǎo; Map p139), where Cixi went to beseech the **Dragon King Temple** (龙王庙; Lóngwáng Miào; Map p139) for rain in times of drought. A graceful 17-arch bridge (Map p139) spans the 150m to the eastern shore of the lake.

Towards the North Palace Gate, **Suzhou Street** (苏州街; Sūzhōu Jiē; Map p139) is an entertaining and light-hearted diversion of riverside walkways, shops and eateries designed to mimic the famous Jiāngsū canal town.

The Summer Palace is about 12km northwest of the centre of Běijīng. Take the subway to Xīzhímén station (close to the zoo), then a minibus or bus 375; the nearest light rail station is Wudaokou (then take bus 331). Other useful buses here include 331 and 801 (both from the Old Summer Palace) and 808 from the Qianmen area. You can also get here by bicycle; it takes about 1½ to two hours from the centre of town. Cycling along the road following the Beijing-Miyun Diversion Canal is pleasant, and in summer there's the option of taking a **boat** (☎ 8836 3576; Houhu Pier; one way/return incl Summer Palace admission Y70/100) from behind the Beijing Exhibition Center near the zoo; the boat voyages via locks along the canal.

PRINCE GONG'S RESIDENCE 恭王府

Reputed to be the model for the mansion in Cao Xueqin's 18th-century classic *Dream of the Red Mansions*, this **residence** (Gōngwáng Fǔ; Map pp118-19; ☎ 6616 8149, 6601 6132; 14 Liuyin Jie; admission Y20, guided tours incl tea & performance Y60; ☷ 8.30am-4.30pm; subway Gulou, then bus 60) is one of Běijīng's largest private residential compounds. Get here ahead of the tour buses and enjoy one of Běijīng's more attractive retreats, decorated with rockeries, plants, pools, pavilions, corridors and elaborately carved gateways. Arrive with the crowds and you won't want to stay. Performances of Beijing opera are held regularly in the Qing dynasty **Grand Opera House** (☎ 6618 6628; tickets Y80-120; ☷ 7.30-8.40pm Mar-Oct) in the east of the grounds.

MIAOYING TEMPLE WHITE DAGOBA 妙应寺白塔

Buried away within a delightful *hútòng* maze, the **Miaoying Temple** (Miàoyīng Sì Báitǎ; Map pp118-19; ☎ 6616 0211; 171 Fuchengmennei Dajie; admission Y20; ☷ 9am-4pm; subway Fuchengmen) slumbers beneath its distinctive, pure-white Yuan dynasty dagoba. The **Hall of the Great Enlightened One** (大觉宝殿; Dàjuébǎo Diàn) glitters splendidly with hundreds of Tibetan Buddhist effigies.

In other halls reside a four-faced effigy of Guanyin (here called Parnashavari) and a trinity of past, present and future Buddhas. Exit the temple and wander the tangle of local alleyways (one bemusingly called Green Pagoda Alley) for earthy shades of *hútòng* life. Take bus 13, 101, 102 or 103 to Báitǎ Sì bus stop (near Baitasi Lu) or take the subway to Fuchengmen and walk east.

BEIJING ZOO 北京动物园

The inhabitants of **Beijing Zoo** (Běijīng Dòngwùyuán; Map pp118-19; ☎ 6831 4411; 137 Xizhimenwai Dajie; admission Y15, pandas extra Y5; ☷ 7.30am-6pm) are saddled with grimly dated design features – concrete and glass cells – but the crowd-pulling pandas have plusher living quarters for good behaviour. The polar bears pin all their hopes on graduating from their concrete hell to the more impressive **Beijing Aquarium** (Map pp118-19; ☎ 6217 6655; adult/child Y100/50; ☷ 9am-6pm low season, to 10pm high season) in the northeastern corner of the zoo. In other respects, however, the zoo serves as a pleasant park and an excellent place for a stroll among the trees and ponds.

Getting to the zoo is easy enough; take the subway to Xīzhímén station. From here, it's a

15-minute walk heading west or a short ride on any of the trolley buses.

OLD SUMMER PALACE 圆明园

Located northwest of the city centre, the original **Summer Palace** (Yuánmíng Yuán; Map pp116-17; ☎ 6262 8501; admission Y10, palace ruins Y15; ◷ 7am-7pm), northeast of the Summer Palace, was laid out in the 12th century. Resourceful Jesuits were later employed by Emperor Qianlong to fashion European-style palaces for the gardens, incorporating elaborate fountains and baroque statuary. During the Second Opium War, British and French troops destroyed the palace and sent the booty abroad. Much went up in flames, but a melancholic array of broken columns and marble chunks remain.

Trot through the southern stretch of hawkers and arcade games to the more subdued ruins of the European Palace in the **Eternal Spring Garden** (长春园; Chángchūn Yuán) to the northeast. Alternatively, enter by the east gate, which leads to the palace vestiges. The mournful composition of tumbledown palace remains lies strewn in a long strip; alongside are black-and-white photos displaying before and after images of the residence. It's here that the **Great Fountain Ruins** (大水法遗址; Dàshuǐfǎ Yízhǐ), considered the best-preserved relic, can be found.

West of the ruins you can lose your way in an artful reproduction of a former maze called the **Garden of Yellow Flowers** (迷宫; Mígōng).

The gardens cover a huge area – some 2.5km from east to west – so be prepared to do some walking. Besides the ruins, there's the western section, the **Perfection and Brightness Garden** (圆明园; Yuánmíng Yuán) and the southern compound, the **10,000 Spring Garden** (万春园; Wànchūn Yuán).

To get to the Old Summer Palace, take minibus 375 from the Xīzhímén subway station, or get off at the Wudaokou subway station. Minibuses also connect the new Summer Palace with the old one, or a taxi will take you for Y10.

FRAGRANT HILLS PARK 香山公园

Easily within striking distance of the Summer Palace is the Western Hills (Xī Shān), another former villa-resort of the emperors. The part of the Western Hills closest to Běijīng is known as **Fragrant Hills Park** (Xiāngshān Gōngyuán; Map pp116-17; admission Y10; ◷ 7am-6pm).

You can either scramble up the slopes to the top of **Incense-Burner Peak** (香炉峰; Xiānglú Fēng) or take the **chairlift** (one way/return Y30/50; ◷ 9am-4pm). Běijīngers love to flock here in autumn when the maple leaves saturate the hillsides in great splashes of red.

Near the north gate of Fragrant Hills Park is **Azure Clouds Temple** (碧云寺; Bìyún Sì; admission Y10; ◷ 8am-5pm), which dates back to the Yuan dynasty. The Mountain Gate Hall contains two vast protective deities: 'Heng' and 'Ha'. Next is a small courtyard containing the drum and bell towers, leading to a hall with a wonderful statue of Milefo: it's bronze, but coal black with age. Only his big toe shines from numerous inquisitive fingers.

The next hall contains statues of Sakyamuni and Bodhisattvas Manjushri, Samantabhadra and Avalokiteshvara (Guanyin), plus 18 *luóhàn* (Buddhists, especially a monk who has achieved enlightenment and passes to nirvana at death); a marvellous golden carved dragon soars above Sakyamuni. The Sun Yat-sen Memorial Hall behind contains a statue and a glass coffin donated by the USSR on the death of Mr Sun (see p47).

At the very back is the marble Vajra Throne Pagoda where Sun Yatsen was interred after he died, before his body was moved to its final resting place in Nánjīng. The Hall of Arhats contains 500 *luóhàn* statues.

To reach Fragrant Hills Park by public transport, take bus 360 from the zoo or bus 318 from Pingguoyuan underground station.

BEIJING BOTANIC GARDENS 北京植物园

Located 2km east of Fragrant Hills Park, the well-tended **Botanic Gardens** (Běijīng Zhíwùyuán; Map pp116-17; admission Y5; ◷ 6am-8pm), set against the backdrop of the Western Hills, make for a pleasant outing among bamboo fronds, pines and lilacs. The **Běijīng Botanic Gardens Conservatory** (admission Y40) contains 3000 different types of plants and a rainforest house.

Located about a 15-minute walk north from the front gate (follow the signs) near the Magnolia Garden is the **Temple of the Reclining Buddha** (Wòfó Sì; Map pp116-17; admission Y5; ◷ 8am-5pm). First built in the Tang dynasty, the temple's centrepiece is a huge reclining effigy of Sakyamuni weighing in at 54 tonnes, which 'enslaved 7000 people' in its casting. On each side of Buddha are sets of gargantuan shoes, gifts to Sakyamuni from various emperors in case he went for a stroll.

To get here take the subway to Pingguoyuan then bus 318, bus 333 from the Summer Palace or bus 360 from Beijing Zoo.

BICYCLE TOUR

Běijīng's sprawling distances and scattered sights can make for blistering sightseeing on foot, but whizzing around the city's streets and alleyways by bike allows you to take it all in at just the right speed. Hop on a pair of wheels, get that bell jangling and join us on this eye-opening tour past some of the city's finest monuments and through Běijīng's gritty and crumbling *hútòng*.

Our tour starts on Dongchang'an Jie, northeast of Tiananmen Sq. Cycle through the purple-red archway of Nanchizi Dajie (南池子大街) and north along the tree-lined street; you'll pass the **Imperial Archives** (1; p129) to your right, a quiet courtyard with echoes of the Forbidden City. Further up to your left you'll see the eastern entrance to the **Workers Cultural Palace** (2; p128), from where you can glimpse the imperial yellow roof of the Supreme Temple (太庙; Tài Miào).

Further along Nanchizi Dajie, the halls and towers of the Forbidden City become visible to the west; hang a left at the intersection with Donghuamen Dajie (东华门大街), pass the Courtyard restaurant (p151; and downstairs art gallery) to your right, then head left again and follow the road sandwiched between the moat and the palace walls.

Note in particular the southeast corner tower of the wall of the **Forbidden City** (3; p133). The walls around the palace, 10m high and containing 12 million bricks, are adorned at each corner with one such tower (角楼; *jiǎolóu*). Each tower is of highly elaborate construction with exceptional roof arrangements, supporting three eaves.

The trip around the moat is a spectacular route with unique views of historic Běijīng. Cycle through the large gate of Quezuo Men (阙左门) and past the face of the Meridian Gate (午门), imposing entrance to the Forbidden City. Sweep through the gate of Queyou Men (阙右门) opposite, south of which is **Zhongshan Park** (4; p128), to continue around the moat. To the west lie the eastern gates of Zhōngnánhǎi (中南海), which is the out-of-bounds nerve centre of political power in Běijīng.

Head north onto Beichang Jie (北长街), west of the Forbidden City, and note the bright red doors and brass knockers of several

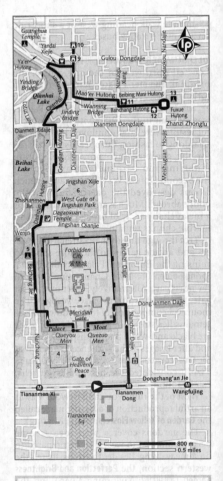

sìhéyuàn (courtyard homes) strung out along the road. You'll pass Fuyou Temple (福佑寺; Fúyòu Sì) to your right – sadly locked away behind closed gates and the palace wall.

On your left are the remains of **Wanshouxinglong Temple** (5; 万寿兴隆寺; Wànshòuxīnglóng Sì; 39 Beichang Jie), its band of monks long replaced by lay residents. The temple once housed

TOUR FACTS

Start Dongchang'an Jie, northeast of Tiananmen Sq
Finish Wen Tianxiang Temple
Distance 7km
Duration 1½ hours

surviving imperial eunuchs after the fall of the Qing dynasty.

Reaching the T-junction with Jingshan Qianjie (景山前街) and Wenjin Jie (文津街), follow the road right onto Jingshan Qianjie, but disembark at the bend in the road and wheel your bike across the street to continue up the first *hútòng* – Dashizuo Hutong (大石作胡同) – heading north on the other side of the road (the *hútòng* opening is in line with the west bank of the palace moat). Just east of here is the vast and sadly inaccessible Taoist Dagaoxuan Temple (大高玄殿; Dàgāoxuán Diàn; 23 Jingshan Xijie), its eastern wall hedging up against Jingshan Xijie, its halls visible through the archway opening onto Jingshan Qianjie.

Wiggling north, Dashizuo Hutong is where the stone for the Forbidden City was carved. Like many alleys in modern Běijīng, it's a mix of tumbledown dwellings and charmless modern blocks. Follow the alley to its conclusion, and exit opposite the west gate of **Jingshan Park** (**6**; p135); directly west along Zhishanmen Jie (陟山门街) is the east gate of Beihai Park.

Cycle north along Jingshan Xijie (景山西街) and at the northern tip of the street head up Gongjian Hutong (恭俭胡同); its entrance lies virtually straight ahead but slightly to the west. Exit the alley on Dianmen Xidajie (地安门西大街); if you want to visit **Beihai Park** (**7**; p134) to your west, push your bike along the southern side of Dianmen Xidajie and you'll soon arrive at the park's north gate.

Continuing north, push your bike over the pedestrian crossing then cycle along Qianhai Nanyan (前海南沿), running along the eastern shore of Qianhai Lake. On the western side of the lake is Lotus Lane, a strip of cafés and restaurants. You will see the small, restored white marble Jinding Bridge (金锭桥; Jīndìng Qiáo) and to its east, Wanning Bridge (万宁桥; Wànníng Qiáo), much of which dates from the Yuan dynasty. Look over the sides of Wanning Bridge and note the timeworn statues of water dragons on either bank.

Continue north along to Yinding Bridge (银锭桥; Yíndìng Qiáo) and trundle east along Yandai Xiejie (烟袋斜街) with its shops, bars and cafés, which have dislodged the dilapidated businesses that operated here. The ancient Guangfuguan Taoist Temple is now a café called the **Guangfuguan Greenhouse** (**8**; p153). For a short diversion, from Yinding Bridge cycle northwest along Yaer Hutong (鸦儿胡同) to the Buddhist Guanghua Temple (广化寺) at No 31, where admission is free.

Exiting Yandai Xiejie onto bustling Dianmenwai Dajie (地安门外大街), you will see the **Drum Tower** (**9**; p135) rising massively ahead and obscuring the **Bell Tower** (**10**; p135) to the north; both are worth a visit, perhaps tied in with a cup of coffee at the Drum & Bell Bar (p153). Head south and turn east onto Mao'er Hutong (帽儿胡同), which, despite being quite modern in its earlier section, gradually emerges into something more traditional.

At the first main junction along Mao'er Hutong, the alley changes its name to Beibing Masi Hutong (北兵马司胡同), the two alleys divided by the north–south-running Nanluogu Xiang (南锣鼓巷), which is one of Běijīng's most famous alleyways. Cycle down Nanluogu Xiang and if you want to rest, take in a coffee of the relaxed, snug courtyard surrounds of the **Passby Bar** (**11**; Guòkè; ☎ 8403 8004; 108 Nanluogu Xiang; 🕐 7pm-2am) on the corner of the second *hútòng* turning on your left as you cycle south.

Take the first turning on your left just beyond the Passby Bar at the street sign that says 'Police Station'. You are now cycling down Banchang Hutong (板厂胡同), a charming stretch of old *sìhéyuàn*, a number of which are adorned with plaques attesting to their historic significance. You'll pass the old **Lusongyuan Hotel** (**12**; p146) on the right-hand side of the road at No 22, an old courtyard house now serving as a hotel. As Banchang Hutong meets Jiaodaokou Nandajie, cycle into the first *hútòng* entrance on your right – Fuxue Hutong (府学胡同). A very short way along the alley on the left-hand side is the **Wen Tianxiang Temple** (**13**; 文天祥祠; 63 Fuxue Hutong; adult Y10; 🕐 9am-5pm Tue-Sun), a shrine fronted by a huge *páilou* (decorated archway).

COURSES

Whether it's learning Chinese, making Chinese kites or delving into the mysteries of taichi, the recommended **Chinese Culture Club** (☎ 6432 9341, ext 18; www.chinesecultureclub .org; 29 Liangmaqiao Lu) offers a range of cultural programmes, taught in English and aimed squarely at foreign visitors and expats. The club also conducts popular tours around

Běijīng and expeditions to other – including off-the-beaten-track – parts of China and presents lectures on a variety of subjects including art, philosophy and film.

BĚIJĪNG FOR CHILDREN

Baby food and milk powder are widely available in supermarkets, as are basics like nappies, baby wipes, bottles, creams, medicine, clothing, dummies (pacifiers) and other paraphernalia. Virtually no cheap restaurants, however, have high chairs and finding baby-changing rooms is next to impossible.

Current and forthcoming events (from plays to arts and crafts events and seasonal parties) for children in Běijīng are listed in the monthly English language–culture magazine **That's Beijing** (www.thatsbeijing.com). Note that many museums and attractions have a cheaper rate for children, usually applying to children under 1.3m, so ask.

Many kids will dig their heels in when confronted with the measureless museum-style torpor of the Forbidden City and the Ming Tombs. Thanks to China's one-child policy, however, Běijīng's poor siblingless tykes are spoiled rotten by their parents and the city is bursting with activities to keep all those demanding little egos occupied.

Beijing Aquarium (p140) has piranha, sharks, whales and dolphins. In the evenings, China Puppet Theatre (p156) regularly casts a spell over its audience of little (and not-so-little) ones. Some displays at the Science & Technology Museum (p136) need some servicing, but what is left is hugely entertaining and educational, and enough to fill half a day.

Le Cool Ice Rink (Map pp118-19; ☎ 6505 5776; Basement 2, China World Trade Center, 1 Jianguomenwai Dajie; per 90min Y30-50; ⏰ 10am-10pm) This is probably the best and most accessible indoor ice rink in town. It's easy to reach, surrounded by the shops of the China World Trade Center. Charges vary depending on the time of day you skate; skate hire is extra.

New China Children's Toy World (Xīn Zhōngguó Értóng Yòngpǐn Shāngdiàn; Map p123; Wangfujing Dajie) If your children are fed up with window-shopping, take them to this huge toy emporium.

Sony ExploraScience (Suǒní Tànmèng; Map p123; ☎ 8518 6380; A201, Oriental Plaza, 1 Dongchang'an Jie; adult/child Y30/20; ⏰ 9.30am-5.30pm Mon-Fri, 10am-7pm Sat & Sun, closed second Mon & Tue every month) A hands-on foray into the world of science. Full of gadgets, it's perfect for inquisitive children and little Einsteins.

FESTIVALS & EVENTS

Usually held in late January or February, the Spring Festival, or Chinese New Year (p944) sees Běijīng in full party mood as it's the top festival on the calendar – the equivalent of Christmas. A week-long holiday commencing on the New Year itself, this can be a great time to see Běijīng at its most colourful and to catch temple fairs (eg at the White Cloud Temple), although remember everyone is on holiday with you and avoid travelling around China at this time as train, bus and air tickets can be scarce. The two other big week-long holiday periods are the 1 May and 1 October holidays, when hotel prices rise to their maximum and tourist sights are swamped with visitors.

SLEEPING

Běijīng has a wide range of accommodation options, from hostels to two- and three-star midrange options and four- and five-star hotels. Fierce competition in the run-up to the 2008 Olympics is rapidly developing all sectors of the accommodation market. Downtown hotels located near Wangfujing Dajie, the Forbidden City and Tiananmen Sq are easy to find in all budget groups. Prices quoted here are rack rates. While these are the rates you can expect to pay in the budget bracket, always ask what discounted rates (折扣; *zhékòu*) are at midrange and top-end hotels, as promotional offers are typically in force, except during the holiday season (see Festivals & Events above).

Chongwen & South Chaoyang
BUDGET

Leo Hostel (Guǎngjùyuán Fàndiàn; Map pp118-19; ☎ 6303 1595; www.leohostel.com; 52 Dazhalan Xijie; 大栅栏西街52号; 12-bed/4-bed dm Y45/70, d with toilet Y200-240, without Y140-160; ✕ 🖳) Popular and crowded, it's best to phone ahead to book a room at this bargain hostel tucked away down Dazhalan Xijie. It has an attractive interior courtyard decked out with plastic plants, OK dorm rooms (pricier dorms with toilet), simple but passable doubles, a small but busy bar and a great location. Staff at reception make solid efforts at wooing international backpackers.

our pick **Far East International Youth Hostel** (Yuǎndōng Guójì Qīngnián Lǚshè; Map pp118-19; ☎ 6301 8811, ext 3118; courtyard@elong.com; 113 Tieshuxie Jie; 铁树斜街113号; dm low/high season incl breakfast Y45/60; ✕ 🖳) This hostel is in a pretty old courtyard opposite the hotel of the same name. There's bike rental (Y20 per day, Y200 deposit), kitchen, washing facilities, café-bar and a tourist desk. Rooms come without TV, phone or shower. The free breakfast includes bread, butter, jam, fruit and a glass of orange juice; alternatively fork out Y19 for a full Western-style breakfast. Thirty minutes of free internet access is included in the price.

Beijing City Central Youth Hostel (Běijīng Chéngshì Guójì Qīngnián Lǚshè; Map pp118-19; ☎ 6525 8866, 8511 5050; www .centralhostel.com; 1 Beijingzhan Qianjie; 北京站前街 1号; 4-8 bed dm Y60, s with/without shower Y160/120, d Y298; ☒) Across the road from Beijing Train Station and right by the underground, this newly opened hostel compensates for lack of character with a definitive location. Notice board, info desk, TV and video room, kitchen and a handy internet café (Y5 per hour) on the 2nd floor.

Eastern Morning Sun Youth Hostel (Běijīng Dōngfāng Chénguāng Qīngnián Lǚguǎn; Map p123; ☎ 6528 4347; fl B4, Oriental Plaza, 8-16 Dongdansantiao; 东单三条8-16号 东方广场B4楼; s/d/tr Y80/120/180; ☒ 🖵) Buried four floors below ground, this hostel's strong points are its extravagant location just off Wangfujing Dajie and cheapish rooms.

MIDRANGE
Home Inn (Rújiā; Map pp118-19; ☎ 6317 3366; www .homeinns.com; 61 Liangshidian Jie, Dashilar; 大栅栏粮 食店街61号; d Y178-218; ☒ 🖵) One of the most central of the branches in this snappy new chain, aimed at the budget end of midrange. Double rooms are small but clean, with modern fittings and bright furnishings. Parallel to Qianmen Dajie, the road outside is gritty and a bit sordid, but Tiananmen Sq is a mere 10-minute trot north. There's internet access (Y10 per hour) and a restaurant. Another branch is at 20 Baizivan Lu (Map pp116–17; ☎ 8777 1155; 百子湾路20号; d Y239).

Far East Hotel (Map pp118-19; s/d/tr Y238/398/378, q per bed Y75) Opposite Far East International Youth Hostel, this is an unremarkable two-star hotel with clean rooms.

Novotel Xinqiao (Běijīng Xīnqiáo Nuòfùtè Fàndiàn; Map pp118-19; ☎ 6513 3366; www.accorhotels.com/asia; 2 Dongjiaomin Xiang; 东交民巷2号; standard & superior d Y1500-1830; ☒ 🖵) The location isn't as tempting as the Wangfujing branch, but the nearby Chongwenmen underground station is handy. Staff is a bit harried, although rooms are modern, if rather unremarkable and thin on home comforts. There's a big choice of restaurants and bars and a handy post office (open 8am to 6pm) on the ground floor, an outdoor tennis court and efficient wheelchair access.

TOP END
Kerry Center Hotel (Jiālǐ Zhōngxīn Fàndiàn; Map pp118-19; ☎ 6561 8833; hbkc@shangri-la.com; 1 Guanghua Lu; 光华 路1号; d US$240-320, ste US$360-2000; ☒) Another efficient link in the Shangri-La chain, this modern and stylish hotel aims squarely at the business-traveller market. Rooms are spacious and neat, with broadband internet connection, minibar, shower and bath, iron and ironing board. There may not be much character, but an uncluttered feel pervades and you can chill out to smooth sounds at Centro (p152) and shop at the adjacent Kerry Mall.

our pick St Regis (Běijīng Guójì Jùlèbù Fàndiàn; Map pp118-19; ☎ 6460 6688; fax 6460 3299; 21 Jianguomenwai Dajie; 建国门外大街21号; d US$340, ste US$500-5300; ☒) First-rate, top-notch elegance complemented by professionalism and a superb location, the St Regis is probably Běijīng's best hotel. The splendid foyer and an enticing complement of restaurants compound this hotel's undeniable allure. In the Club Wing you can find a bowling centre, squash courts, cigar and wine lounges and the Astor Grill.

China World Hotel (Zhōngguó Dàfàndiàn; Map pp118-19; ☎ 6505 2266; www.shangri-la.com.cn; 1 Jianguomenwai Dajie; 建国门外大街1号; d US$340, ste US$620-3800; ☒ 🖵) The gorgeous five-star China World delivers an outstanding level of service to its well-dressed complement of largely executive travellers. The sumptuous foyer is a masterpiece of Chinese motifs, glittering chandeliers, robust columns and smooth acres of marble. Rooms are modern and amenities extensive, while shopping needs are all met at the China World Trade Center.

Grand Hyatt Beijing (Běijīng Dōngfāng Jūnyuè Dàjiǔdiàn; Map p123; ☎ 8518 1234; www.beijing.grand.hyatt.com; 1 Dongchang'an Jie; 东长安街1号; d US$443; ☒ 🖾) A stunning hotel crowning Oriental Plaza right in the heart of town, the Hyatt matches its top-notch design and splendid interior with exemplary service. Rooms are modern and comfortable and the oasislike swimming pool is way, way overboard. For dining, four impressive restaurants compete for your attention.

Dongcheng
BUDGET
Peking Downtown Backpackers Accommodation (Dōngtáng Kèzhàn; Map pp118-19; ☎ 8400 2429; www .backpackingchina.com; 85 Nanluogu Xiang; 南锣鼓巷 85号; 8-/4-/3-bed dm Y50/60/70, windowless d per bed Y60, d per bed Y80; ☒ 🖵) For backpacker arrivals

in Běijīng, the central *hútòng* location is hard to beat. Doubles are tidy (but no TV), with plastic wood floors and clean shower rooms. Free breakfast and free pickup from Capital Airport – you pay the toll (Y20) and the parking fee (if the driver has to wait more than half an hour). There's bike rental (Y20 per day, Y300 deposit), internet access (Y6 per hour) and an adjacent backpacker restaurant.

Beijing Saga International Youth Hostel (Běijīng Shíjiā Guójì Qīngnián Lǚshè; Map p123; ☎ 6527 2773; www .sagahostel.com; 9 Shijia Hutong; 史家胡同9号; dm/tr Y50/240, d member/nonmember Y180/198; 🗙 🖵) Enjoying a top location on the historic Shijia Hutong, this popular hostel has clean, well-kept rooms, a spacious seating area in the main lobby, table football, a refectory and bar and internet access (Y10 per hour).

Beijing Jade International Youth Hostel (Zhìdé Qīngnián Lǚshè; Map p123; ☎ 6525 9966; www.xihua hotel.com; 5 Zhide Beixiang; 智德北巷5号; dm member/ nonmember Y50/60, tw Y280/380; 🗙 🖵) This hostel offers clean dorm rooms and good-value twins, although the atmosphere seems less like a hostel than a mainstream Chinese hotel. The Forbidden City is visible from the upper floors and gorgeous courtyard houses are slung out on either side, including the historic Meng Gongfu residence at No 3. There's internet access (Y10 per hour) and bike rental (Y20).

MIDRANGE

Lusongyuan Hotel (Lǚsōngyuán Bīnguǎn; Map pp118-19; ☎ 6404 0436; 1syhotel@263.net; 22 Banchang Hutong; 板厂胡同22号; dm/s/d/ste US$10/35/60/110; 🗙 🖵) Built by a Mongolian general during the Qing dynasty, this courtyard hotel enjoys an ideal *hútòng* location. Pocket-sized singles come with pea-sized baths (albeit quite cute); dorms have three beds (with TV, no windows, common shower) and there is just one suite. Rooms facing onto the courtyard are slightly more expensive. There's also bike rental (half/ full day Y15/30) and an email centre (open 7.30am to 10pm; Y5 for 10 minutes).

Fangyuan Hotel (Fāngyuán Bīnguǎn; Map p123; ☎ 6525 6331; www.cbw.com/hotel/fangyuan; 36 Dengshikou Xijie; 灯市口西街36号; d incl breakfast from Y298; 🗙 🖵) Its front door guarded by a pair of stone felines, rooms at the optimally located two-star Fangyuan have undergone a minor refit. Staff is used to dealing with foreign travellers, so mercifully there are few of the typical two-star blank expressions at reception. Breakfast is free, but it's of the boiled egg and congee

variety. Internet access is Y10 per hour, bike rental Y20 per day.

Bamboo Garden Hotel (Zhúyuán Bīnguǎn; Map pp118-19; ☎ 6403 2229; fax 6401 2633; 24 Xiaoshiqiao Hutong; 小石桥胡同24号; s Y380, d Y680-880, ste Y760; 🗙 🖵) Cosy and tranquil, this courtyard hotel gets good reviews, but staff lacks motivation. Rooms are tastefully decorated with reproduction Ming furniture and the abundant foliage is pleasant, although the *hútòng* setting is let down by the modern block opposite.

ourpick Haoyuan Hotel (Hǎoyuán Bīnguǎn; Map pp118-19; ☎ 6512 5557; www.haoyuanhotel.com; 53 Shijia Hutong; 史家胡同53号; d standard/deluxe Y585/715, suite Y780-1040; 🗙 🖵) Treat yourself to the Haoyuan's lovely and spacious brand of standard double rooms, delightfully arranged with classical Chinese furniture, and let the red lantern-hung courtyard feng shui weave its magical charms. If you get carried away, hang your hat in one of the suites in the rear tree-dotted courtyard, one with its own sauna, the other a Jacuzzi. Internet is Y10 per hour. Reception is on the left as you enter; pursue discounts during the slack season.

Novotel Peace Hotel (Běijīng Nuòfùtè Hépíng Bīnguǎn; Map p123; ☎ 6512 8833; www.accorhotels.com/asia; 3 Jinyu Hutong; 金鱼胡同3号; d West/East Wing Y1494/1826; 🗙 🖵) This efficient, refurbished four-star hotel has a fresh and cosmopolitan character. Eschewing the gaudiness of some top-league hotels, there's an uncomplicated elegance, a useful travel service and bookshop (for newspapers) and the location, with Wangfujing Dajie just around the corner, is spot on. The cheaper rooms – not huge but perfectly serviceable – are in the older and more scuffed West Wing.

TOP END

Among soon-to-open, high-profile luxury hotels are the 320-room Ritz-Carlton (Map pp116–17), slated for an early 2007 opening, and the Regent Beijing (Map p123), which should be open by the time you read this.

Peninsula Palace (Wángfǔ Fàndiàn; Map pp118-19; ☎ 6559 2888; www.peninsula.com; 8 Jinyu Hutong; 金鱼胡同8号; d/ste US$350/460; 🗙 🖵) Owned by the Peninsula Group, this lavish hotel remains at the cutting edge of the glittering five-star hotel market. It boasts two excellent restaurants, including the elegant Huáng Tíng (p151), and a multitiered, hyper-exclusive basement shopping mall. Promotional prices frequently take the sting out of the whopping tariff, so ask.

Chaoyang

BUDGET

Beijing Gongti International Youth Hostel (Běijīng Gōngtǐ Qīngnián Lǚshè; Map p122; ☎ 6552 4800; bih -yh@sohu.com, gongti@hotmail.com; East Gate, Workers' Stadium; 工人体育场东门; 4-/2-bed dm Y50/70, s Y100; 🖳) This clean hostel offers both value and good positioning. Dorm rooms (Y10 extra for nonmembers) are bright, clean and spacious, and come with phone (incoming only), TV and radiator. Communal showers are clean, and internet access costs Y10 per hour. Non HI-members pay an extra Y20 for single rooms. There's no lift.

Zhaolong International Youth Hostel (Zhàolóng Qīngnián Lǚshè; Map p122; ☎ 6597 2299; www.zhao longhotel.com.cn; 2 Gongrentiyuchang Beilu; 工人体育场 北路2号; 6-/4-/2-bed dm Y50/60/70; 🖳 🖳) This is a six-floor block behind the Zhaolong Hotel off Dongsanhuan Beilu that offers clean rooms, laundry (Y10/20 per small/big load), kitchen, reading room, safe, bike rental (Y30 per day) and internet access (Y10 per hour). Non-members pay an extra Y10 for all room types. Breakfast is an additional Y10 (served 7am to 10am). Book rooms in youth hostels nation-wide for a Y10 deposit.

You Yi Youth Hostel (Yǒuyì Qīngnián Jiǔdiàn; Map p122; ☎ 6417 2632; fax 6415 6866; 43 Beisanlitun Lu; 北三里屯 路43号; dm/tw incl breakfast Y70/180; 🖳 🖳) Located right behind Poachers Inn, this hostel offers bright and spacious twins (with phone, TV, air-con and radiator). There are a few dorms and there's free laundry service (dump your dirty rags in the cart for washing and drying), which is a hospitable gesture. Internet service is Y10 per hour. Breakfast is between 7.30am and 9am and includes toast, coffee, eggs and sausages.

MIDRANGE

Red House Hotel (Ruìxiù Bīnguǎn; Map p122; ☎ 6416 7500; www.redhouse.com.cn; 10 Chunxiu Lu; 春秀路10号; s/tw/ste incl breakfast Y350/400/600; 🖳 🖳) Putting you within orbit of the Sanlitun bar scene, rooms at Red House Hotel are clean and tidy, with wood-strip flooring, traditional-style furniture and good shower rooms. There's bike rental (Y30 per day), a handy on-site pub with essential English Premier League football action (see Club Football Centre, p152), free laundry and local calls are on the house.

Oriental Garden Hotel (Dōngfāng Huāyuán Fàndiàn; Map p122; ☎ 6416 8866; fax 6415 0638; 6 Dongzhimen Nandajie; 东直门南大街6号; s/d/ste US$120/186/226;

🖳 🖳) This four-star Chinese-run business hotel has comfortable and attractive guest rooms, Cantonese and Shànghǎinese restaurants and a coffee shop.

Fengtai & Xuanwu

BUDGET

Beijing Feiying International Youth Hostel (Běijīng Fēiyīng Qīngnián Lǚshè; Map pp118–19; ☎ 6315 1165; iyhfy@yahoo.com.cn; No 10 Bldg, Changchun Jie Hou Jie, Xuan-wumen Xidajie; 长椿街后街宣武门西大街10号楼; 10-/5-bed dm Y30/50, d 180; 🖳 🖳) Rather away from it all as youth hostels go. Take the subway to Changchunjie, then take exit C and head east past the McDonalds for around 200m. Bicycle hire, washing machine, kitchen, tourist info plus internet access (Y10 per hour); no lift.

MIDRANGE

Qianmen Jianguo Hotel (Qiánmén Jiànguó Fàndiàn; Map pp118–19; ☎ 6301 6688; fax 6301 3883; 175 Yong'an Lu; 永 安路175号; s/d/tr/ste incl breakfast Y620/760/910/1100; 🖳 🖳) Extremely popular with tour groups lured by its combination of excellent location and value, this place makes considerable efforts to ward off that great leveller: the generic three-star Chinese hotel feel. The interior verges on elegance and business is brisk so staff is on its toes, even if sometimes a bit reluctant. Rooms are spacious, clean and attractively carpeted and come with satellite TV and phones in bathrooms. The Liyuan Theatre (p154) is at the rear of the lobby.

TOP END

Marco Polo (Běijīng Mǎgē Bóluó Jiǔdiàn; Map pp118–19; ☎ 6603 6688; www.marcopolohotels.com; 6 Xuanwumennei Dajie; 宣武门内大街6号; d/ste US$170/280; 🖳 🖳) This unfussy four-star hotel has eschewed the gaudy top-end route, but it may have lost some crispness. A length in the hotel pool may only take a few strokes, but the basement Clark Hatch Fitness Centre is well equipped, and it's still the best in this part of town with underground stations nearby.

Haidian & Xicheng

TOP END

Shangri-La Hotel (Xiānggé Lǐlā Fàndiàn; Map pp118–19; ☎ 6841 2211; slb@shangri-la.com; 29 Zizhuyuan Lu; 紫竹 院路29号; d US$180; 🖳) Located in west Běijīng and well positioned for trips to the Summer Palace, the Shangri-La has a top-notch selection of restaurants, bars and shops as well as a fine spread of rooms.

BĚIJĪNG

Beijing Marriott West (Běijīng Jīnyù Wànháo Jiǔdiàn; Map pp118-19; ☎ 6872 6699; www.marriotthotels.com; 98 Xisanhuan Beilu; 西三环北路98号; d US$350; 🅿 🖥) The Marriott is a fine hotel, with vast, fully equipped and very comfortable rooms, but the location, near the intersection of Fucheng Lu and the Third Ring Rd, is a big drawback. Amenities include tennis courts, a bowling centre and a health club. Seek discounts.

Further Afield
Holiday Inn Lido (Lìdū Jiàrì Fàndiàn; Map pp116-17; ☎ 6437 6688; fax 6437 6237; cnr Jichang Lu & Jiangtai Lu; 近机场路将台路; d US$150; 🅿) This hotel is a bit stranded on the road to the airport, but it's a highly popular and first-rate establishment with excellent amenities and a resourceful shopping mall.

EATING
Běijīng cuisine (京菜; jīngcài) is one of the four major Chinese styles of cooking, so trying home-town specialities should be obligatory for each and every foodie. And just about any fickle fancy meets its match, so plunge in and start twiddling those chopsticks – some of your best Běijīng memories could well be table-top ones. Běijīng's contemporary culinary frenzy has cobbled together everything from (it was just a matter of time) Hutong pizza to fast-food style hotpot (see the boxed text, p150) and fish and chips.

This may be Běijīng, but eating out doesn't necessary require excessive capital: listed here are restaurants that offer the best food and value within a range of budgets. The cheapest of meals come in at under Y30 to Y40, midrange dining costs between Y40 and Y100, while top-end choices cost over Y100.

Chongwen & South Chaoyang
BUDGET
For convenient dining and a Pan-Asian selection under one roof, try one of the ubiquitous food courts that can be found in shopping malls throughout the city.

Wangfujing Snack Street (Wángfǔjǐng Xiǎochījiē; Map p123; kebabs from Y3, dishes from Y5; 🕑 lunch & dinner) West off Wangfujing Dajie, and fronted by an ornate archway, this bustling and cheery corner of restaurants and stalls is overhung with colourful banners and bursting with flavour. It's a great place to hoover up Xīnjiāng or Muslim Uighur staples such as lamb kebabs and flat bread. Sit down with steaming bowls

of spicy *málà tàng* (麻辣烫; spicy noodle soup), *zhájiàngmiàn* (炸酱面; noodles in fried bean sauce), *Lánzhōu lāmiàn* (兰州拉面; Lánzhōu noodles), *Shāndōng jiānbǐng* (山东煎饼; Shāndōng pancake), *Yúnnán guòqiáo mixiàn* (云南过桥米线; Yúnnán across-the-bridge noodles) and oodles of spicy Sìchuān food (川菜; *chuāncài*).

Beard Papa (Map p123; CC09, basement, Oriental Plaza, 1 Dongchang'an Jie; cream puffs Y6) Astonishingly scrummy, high-cholesterol takeaway cream puffs – out of this world and ultramoreish.

Megabite (Dàshídài; Map p123; basement Oriental Plaza, 1 Dongchang'an Jie; dishes from Y10) Perfect for on-the-spot dining, this huge food court has point-and-serve Chinese and other Asian dining options all under one roof. Purchase a card at the kiosk at the entrance, load up with credits (Y30 to Y500) and browse among the canteen-style outlets for whatever takes your fancy, then continue shopping.

Niúgē Jiǎozi (Map p123; ☎ 6525 7472; 85 Nanheyan Dajie; meals Y20; 🕑 7am-10pm) Swat aside the proffered English tourist menu at this busy little *jiǎozi* (饺子) outfit or you could be stung, and stick to what this place does best – servings of steaming, plump dumplings. *Jiǎozi* arrive per *liǎng* (两; one *liǎng*: five morsels); aim for the lamb and onion (羊肉大葱; Y5 per *liǎng*), beef and celery (牛肉芹菜; Y4 per *liǎng*) or the chive and egg (韭菜鸡蛋; Y4 per *liǎng*). Alternatively, maintain your composure and dive into the Chinese menu with a dictionary. The restaurant has no English sign, but it is opposite the building with the sign on the roof saying 'Hualong Street'.

Gongdelin Vegetarian Restaurant (Gōngdélín Sùcàiguǎn; Map pp118-19; ☎ 6511 2542; 158 Qianmen Dajie; meals Y40-50; 🕑 lunch & dinner) This veteran veggie diner still ranks as one of Běijīng's premier bloodless dining experiences despite begging for a revamp like its Shànghǎi sibling. Restore your karma with dishes of mock meat and fake fowl; pass on the roasted hedgehog if you want but do consider the deep-fried fresh fish (Y30). Service can be pedestrian and the downstairs décor utilitarian, but the well-thumbed English menu is handy and herbivores needing more style can always head upstairs.

MIDRANGE
Makye Ame (Mǎjí Āmǐ; Map pp118-19; ☎ 6506 9616; 2nd fl, A11 Xiushui Nanjie; dishes from Y20; 🕑 lunch & dinner) Tucked away behind the Friendship Store,

STREET FOOD BĚIJĪNG STYLE

Off the main roads and in Běijīng's alleys is a world teeming with steaming food stalls and eateries buzzing with activity. Be adventurous and eat this way, and you dine as most Běijīngers do.

Breakfast can be easily catered for with a *yóutiáo* (油条; deep-fried dough stick), a sip of *dòuzhī* (豆汁; bean curd drink) or a bowl of *zhōu* (粥; porridge). Other snacks include the crunchy, pancakelike and filling *jiānbǐng* (煎饼); *jiānbǐng* vendors are easily spotted as they cook from tricycle-mounted, white-painted wooden stalls where pancakes are fried on a large circular griddle. The heavy, meat-filled *ròubǐng* (肉饼; cooked bread filled with finely chopped pork) are life-savers and very cheap. A handy vegetarian option is *jiǔcài bǐng* (韭菜饼; bread stuffed with cabbage, chives, leek or fennel and egg). *Dàbǐng* (大饼; a chunk of round, unleavened bread sprinkled with sesame seeds) can be found everywhere and of course there's *mántou* (馒头; steamed bread).

Málà tàng (麻辣烫) is a spicy noodle soup (very warming in winter) in which bob chunks of *dòufu* (豆腐; tofu), cabbage and other veggies; choose your own ingredients from the trays. Also look out for *ròu jiāmò* (肉夹馍), a scrumptious open-your-mouth-wide bun filled with diced lamb, chilli and garlic shoots. Another must are *kǎo yángròu chuàn* (烤羊肉串; lamb kebabs), which make for a scrumptious and cheap snack or meal. You can find kebab outlets in several places around town; try the more expensive Donghuamen Night Market (p150), Wangfujing Snack St (opposite) or cheaper options that are hidden away down *hútòng* (look for the billowing plumes of smoke), where skewers go for around Y0.50. If you want your kebabs spicy ask for *là* (辣); if you don't, ask for *búlà* (不辣). Vendors usually belong to either the Muslim Hui or Uighur minority.

Hóngshǔ (红薯; baked sweet potatoes) are cheap filling snacks (around Y2) sold at street stalls throughout the city during winter. Vendors attach oil drums to their bikes, which have been converted into mobile ovens. Choose a nice soft sweet potato and the vendor will weigh it and tell you how much it costs.

this is one of two branches of this successful Tibetan dining experience. There's a comfy upper room decked out with Tibetan ornaments and a suitably exotic menu ranging from lamb ribs (Y40), through boiled yak with chilli (Y40), to *tsampa* (roasted barley meal), yoghurt, butter tea and cooling salads (from Y20).

Biànyìfāng Kǎoyādiàn (Map pp118-19; ☎ 6712 0505; 2a Chongwenmenwai Dajie; economy/standard half duck Y44/69; ☼ lunch & dinner) Dating back to the reign of the Qing emperor Xianfeng, Biànyìfāng offers midrange comfort reminiscent of a faded Chinese three-star hotel. The duck is nonetheless excellent, roasted in the *menlu* style, but be on your guard if waiting staff immediately steer you towards the pricier Huaxiangsu-style fowl (half/whole Y84/168). It's next to the Hademen Hotel.

Qianmen Quanjude Roast Duck Restaurant (Qián-mén Quánjúdé Kǎoyādiàn; Map pp118-19; ☎ 6511 2418; 32 Qianmen Dajie; half duck Y58, scallions & sauce Y2; ☼ lunch & dinner) As fundamental to a Běijīng trip as a Great Wall hike, to miss out on Peking duck (烤鸭; *kǎoyā*) you'd have to be completely quackers. This place is geared mainly to the tourists, with photos of George Bush poking a duck with his finger and Fidel Castro sizing up an imaginary duck with his hands. Another branch (☎ 6301 8833; 14 Qianmen Xidajie) is nearby and there's also one off Wangfujing Dajie (see Quanjude Roast Duck Restaurant below).

Kǎoròujì (Map pp118-19; ☎ 6404 2554; 14 Qianhai Dongyuan; meals Y60) Bright, brash perhaps and not ideal if you're angling for a candelit soiree, but this old-timer's credentials date back to Qing times. A lakeside culinary landmark, it's been dolled up for diners who insist on revisiting its wholesome Muslim menu. The roast lamb with cumin (Y58) is a surefire suggestion, followed by a slow meander round the edges of Houhai Lake.

Liújiā Guō (Map p123; ☎ 6524 1487; 19 Nanheyan Dajie; meals Y80; ☼ lunch & dinner) Eye-poppingly hot Húnán (湘菜; Xiāngcài) cuisine is a cauldron of flaming flavour, marked by the wanton use of chilli and spices. Liújiā Guō, however, goes easy on the seasoning, serving up medium-hot dishes that won't have you gagging. The grilled beef (Y28) is sizzlingly excellent and the 'Mao family fashion braised pork' (Y28) is fantastic: rich chunks of fatty pork steeped in a strong sauce.

Quanjude Roast Duck Restaurant (Quánjúdé Kǎoyādiàn; Map p123; ☎ 6525 3310; 9 Shuaifuyuan Hutong;

HOT SPOT

Hotpot dining is an addictive activity and that's not just because some Chinese chefs took to lacing pots with opium seeds back in the heady 1990s. The steaming hub of a good night out with friends, huǒguō (火锅; hotpot) is a particularly moreish way of filling up on both excellent nosh and chitchat while blasting away the piercing cold of winter. But what if you just want a solo hotpot without the jaw-jaw? Perched alone over a sweltering hotpot in a swanky restaurant can be both pricey and impractical. Go elbow to elbow instead with diners at **Yíngjiā Huǒguō** (Yingjia Hotpot; Map pp118-19; basement level 1, 77th Street Plaza, Xidan Culture Square; meal Y20), the equivalent of hotpot fast-food style. You get your own small pot and snappy service.

Choose a soup base, málà (麻辣; spicy) or qīngtāng (清汤; mild/clear), and select from the (Chinese only) menu: yángròupiàn (羊肉片; lamb slices; Y10), dàbáicài (大白菜; cabbage; Y4), dòufu (豆腐; tofu; Y4), tǔdòu (土豆; potato; Y4) and more. Note to those with delicate constitutions: the spicy version is like a shot of Tabasco up each nostril. Hard veggies need time softening up in the boiling broth, but just scald the colour from the lamb slices before chomping, and don't forget to dunk everything from the pot in májiàng (麻酱; sesame paste; free) before devouring. If it all gets a bit heated, douse your scorched tongue with draught beer for a mere Y5. If you can't get a seat, another fast-food hotpot chain bringing solo diners out in a sweat is **Xiābǔ** (Map p123; ☎ 6025 9312; 2nd fl, Henderson Centre, Jianguomennei Dajie; meal Y25).

set menu incl duck, pancakes, scallions & sauce Y168; ⏰ lunch & dinner) Less touristy than its Qianmen sibling, this branch of the celebrated chain has a handy location off Wangfujing Dajie for shopping-laden diners. The roast duck (half duck Y54, minus pancakes, scallions and sauce) is flavoursome and a key ingredient to a Běijīng sojourn.

Dongcheng

BUDGET

Donghuamen Night Market (Dōnghuāmén Yèshì; Map p123; Dong'anmen Dajie; ⏰ 3-10pm, closed Chinese New Year) A sight in itself, the bustling night market near Wangfujing Dajie is a food zoo: lamb kebabs, beef and chicken skewers, corn on the cob, chòu dòufu (臭豆腐; smelly tofu), cicadas, grasshoppers, kidneys, quails' eggs, squid, fruit, porridge, fried pancakes, strawberry kebabs, bananas, Inner Mongolian cheese, stuffed aubergines, chicken hearts, pitta bread stuffed with meat, shrimps and more. Zero in on the dragon-spouted copper kettles of xìngrén chá (杏仁茶) vendors: a bowl of the sugary almond-flavoured paste, seeded with peanuts, berries and sesame seeds, will leave the sweet-toothed doing cartwheels. It's for tourists, not locals, so expect to pay rather inflated prices.

Bāguó Bùyī (Map pp118-19; ☎ 6400 8888; 89-3 Dianmen Dongdajie; dishes from Y8; ⏰ lunch & dinner) This popular Sìchuān restaurant has a marvellous Chinese inn–style restaurant setting with balconies and a central stairway, and dolled-up

waiting staff in attendance. The ambience bursts with both character and theatre, and there's a range of good-value dishes.

Here Café (Zhèlǐ Kāfēiguǎn; Map pp118-19; 97 Nanluogu Xiang; meals Y30; ⏰ 10am-1am) Over recent years the backwater hútòng charms of Nanluogu Xiang have been transformed into a torrent of flung-together cafés, gift shops and backpacker accommodation. This funky, laid-back hole offers middling, cheap Western traveller food but the mood – with misshapen armchairs, books flung about, wobbly tables, grizzly Tom Waits on the stereo – tends towards a charming, arty disarray.

Fish Nation (Yúbāng; Map pp118-19; ☎ 6401 3249; www .fishnation.cn; 31 Nanluogu Xiang; meals Y30; ⏰ 11.30am-2am Mon-Thu, to 4am Fri & Sat) Someone knows what they are doing in this English chippie: fat, slightly soggy chips, chunky, battered fish, lemon slices, malt vinegar fumes and splodges of ketchup. They'll be wrapping takeaways in pages from People's Daily next. There's hardly enough room to swing a catfish in the phonebox sized Sanlitun outlet (Map p122; ☎ 6415 0119; ⏰ 11.30am-2am Mon-Thu, to 4am Fri & Sat), round the corner from Poachers Inn, but the roomy main branch comes with a terrace.

MIDRANGE

Sichuan Restaurant (Sìchuān Fàndiàn; Map p123; ☎ 6513 7591/3; 37a Dong'anmen Dajie; meals Y50; ⏰ lunch & dinner) This spacious restaurant is rather worn and the manager's office is still forlornly hung with a portrait of Mao, but the dishes are well worth your time and portions are generous. Try the filling crispy *zhǐbāo yángròu* (纸包羊肉; tinfoil-wrapped mutton), while the *yúxiāng qiézi* (鱼香茄子; deep-fried eggplant with garlic and chilli sauce) is tender and swimming in a sea of hot red chilli oil.

Ottos Restaurant (Rìchāng Cānguǎn; Map pp118-19; ☎ 6405 8205; Dianmen Xidajie; meals Y60; ☼ 24hr) Loud and cavernous with a bright menu, harried staff and constant waves of diners piling in for its flavoursome Hong Kong dishes, Ottos offers no-nonsense and tasty food in decent helpings. The fiery *hēijiāo zhūpái* (黑椒猪排; pork in black pepper sauce) hits the spot. It's east of the north gate of Beihai Park. Further branch in Dongdan.

Xiao Wang's Home Restaurant (Xiǎowáng Fǔ; Map pp118-19; ☎ 6594 3602, 6591 3255; 2 Guanghua Dongli; meals Y70; ☼ lunch & dinner) Treat yourself to home-style Běijīng cuisine from this excellent restaurant and go for one of Xiao Wang's specials. The *piāoxiāng páigǔ* (deep-fried spareribs with pepper salt; Y38) are gorgeous: dry, fleshy, crispy chops with a small pile of fiery pepper salt. Xiao Wang's fried hot and spicy Xīnjiāng-style *zīran jīchì* (chicken wings; Y35) is deservedly famous and the Peking duck is crispy and lean (Y88 per duck, Y5 for sauce, scallions and pancakes). There's outside seating and a further, more sedate, branch can be found in the Sanlitun area (Map p122; ☎ 6594 3602, 6591 3255; 4 Gongrentiyuchang Beilu; meals Y70; open lunch and dinner).

Yuèlù Shānwū (Map pp118-19; ☎ 6617 2696; 19a Qianhai Xiyan; ☼ lunch & dinner) With luxurious views over Qianhai Lake from Lotus Lane – a lakeside strip of cafés, restaurants and shops – this neat Húnán restaurant has a tasty and celebrated menu from the province of fierce flavours.

Sānshēng Wànwù (Map pp118-19; ☎ 6404 2778; 37 Yandai Xiejie; set meals from Y120; ☼ noon-midnight) In the alley alongside Guangfuguan Greenhouse (p153), Sānshēng Wànwù serves Taoist meals within one of the temple halls (phone or visit ahead as the food and restaurant need to be prepared in advance).

TOP END

Huáng Tíng (Map p123; ☎ 8516 2888, ext 6707; Peninsula Palace, 8 Jinyu Hutong; meals Y150; ☼ lunch & dinner) Faux old Peking is taken to an extreme in the courtyard setting of Huáng Tíng. Despite its artificiality and location (in a five-star hotel), the ambience is impressive. Local dishes include whole Peking duck (Y220), roast suckling pig (Y100), braised spareribs in tangy brown sauce (Y70) and braised Běijīng-style meatball with cabbage (Y40).

Courtyard (Sihéyuàn; Map p132; ☎ 6526 8883; cyrest@95777.com; 95 Donghuamen Dajie; meals from Y200; ☼ lunch & dinner) The Courtyard enjoys an excellent location by the east gate of the Forbidden City. The minimalist art gallery (☎ 6526 8882) in the basement provides cerebral nutrition and the cigar divan upstairs is the perfect conclusion to a meal, but it's the view and international menu that hog the limelight. Sunday lunch is an affordable option at Y150 per person.

Chaoyang
MIDRANGE

Dōngběirén (Map p122; ☎ 6415 2855; 1a Xinzhong Jie; meals Y50) The hearty northeastern bandwagon has made it to town, its smiling gaggle of rouge-cheeked and pig-tailed *xiǎojie* (waitresses) in tow, bringing its excellent nosh, garrulous atmosphere (with periodic singing from the waitresses) and trademark festive spirit with it.

Xinjiang Red Rose Restaurant (Map p122; ☎ 6415 5741; Xingfuyicun Qixiang; meals Y50; ☼ lunch & dinner) Unsubtle perhaps, but its maelstrom of table-top dancing, live Uighur music (7.30pm to 9pm) and belly dancers is excellent entertainment with a beer or two. Pass on the whole roast lamb (Y800) unless you haven't eaten for a week, but the roast leg of lamb (Y30 per *jīn*) and chunky lamb kebabs (Y5 each) are filling enough. It's opposite Workers' Stadium north gate.

Beijing Dadong Roast Duck Restaurant (Běijīng Dàdǒng Kǎoyā Diàn; Map p122; ☎ 6582 2892/4003; 3 Tuanjiehu Beikou; duck Y98; ☼ lunch & dinner) A long-term favourite of the Peking duck scene, this restaurant has a tempting variety of fowl. The hallmark bird is a crispy, lean duck without the usual high fat content (trimmed down from 42.38% to 15.22% for its 'Superneat' roast duck, the brochure says), plus plum (or garlic) sauce, scallions and pancakes. Also carved up is the skin of the duck with sugar, an imperial predilection.

Purple Haze (Zǐsūtíng; Map p122; ☎ 6413 0899) A chilled-out, smooth and snappy finish, Thursday-night jam sessions, a small library of foreign literature and an enticing bar area for apéritif-sinking makes this a stylish foray into the world of Thai cooking. It's opposite Workers' Stadium north gate.

SELF-CATERING

Supermarkets are plentiful and most visitors will find what they need, but delis stock wider selections of foreign cheeses, cured meats and wines.

The enormous Lufthansa Center Youyi Shopping City, a multistorey shopping mall in the northeast of town has a branch of the **Yansha Supermarket** (Map pp118–19) in the basement, chock-a-block with imported goods. **Carrefour** (Jiālèfú; ☑ 8am-9.30pm) Chaoyang (Map pp118-19; ☎ 8460 1030; 6b Beisanhuan Donglu); Fengtai (☎ 6760 9911; 15 No 2 district Fangchengyuan Fangzhuang); Haidian (☎ 8836 2729; 54a Zhongguancun Nandajie); Xuanwu (☎ 8636 2155; 11 Malian Dao) stocks virtually everything you may need, takes credit cards and provides ATMs and a home-delivery service. There is also a branch in Zhongguancun.

There's a well-stocked supermarket (Map pp118–19) in the basement of Scitech Plaza, a department store on the southern side of Jianguomenwai Dajie, where you can find an extensive range of coffee.

Other useful supermarkets:

Jingkelong Supermarket (Map p122; Sanlitun)

Park N Shop (Map pp118-19; basement, Full Link Plaza, 18 Chaoyangmenwai Dajie)

Further Afield

Ajisen Noodle (Wèiqiān Lāmiàn; Map pp116-17; ☎ 8589 1475; 3201 block S, Soho New Town, off Jianguo Lu; meals Y25; subway Dawanglu) Ajisen's flavoursome noodles – delivered in steaming bowls by fleet-foot black-clad staff – will have your ears tingling and your tummy quivering. Dishes are miraculously as tasty as they appear on the photo menu and tea comes free with cups punctiliously refilled. Queues often form here, so prepare to wait in line and pay up front. Further branches around town and nationwide.

DRINKING

Běijīng has a glut of drinking options and a judicious appraisal is recommended before diving in willy-nilly. New bars trip over themselves to cash in on the latest fad, swinging open doors onto samey interiors where a palpable sense of bankruptcy hangs in the air. After folding, a month passes and the bar reopens under new management, to repeat the process. The bandwagon may roll on, but after the dust settles, enough spots with a dose of character and a shot of style find themselves occupying a profitable niche in the fickle and easily bored expat scene.

The bars infesting Sanlitun in the Chaoyang district have long formed one major hub of the expat drinking life. Standout bars remain buried away from the main drag, itself called Sanlitun Lu, where largely mediocre watering holes are manned by pushy types at the door. The much superior Sanlitun Nanlu to the south has been flattened, prompting a mass exodus of bars. The Sanlitun formula

has been transplanted to the lakeside streets running along the northern and southern shores of Houhai Lake (Houhai Nanyan and Houhai Beiyan), which now heave with bars offering an unvarying concoction of wooden doors, wind chimes, Southeast Asian masks, batik lampshades and cushion-strewn sofas. Nearby Yandai Xiejie – a small street just east of Silver Ingot Bridge – has recruited a flourishing population of cafés, bars and souvenir shops, while a further band of bars has opened along Nanluogu Xiang, southeast of the Drum Tower, and other outfits are doing their own thing, in their own part of town.

Poachers Inn (Map p122; ☎ 6417 2632; 43 Beisanlitun Lu; ☑ 8pm-late) Cavernous Poachers literally heaves with exuberant throngs and a thumping, hammering bass at the weekend, when it's party central and the volume reaches unusual levels.

Centro (Xuànkù; Map pp118-19; ☎ 6561 8833, ext 6388; Kerry Center Hotel, 1 Guanghua Lu; ☑ 24hr) Swish and stylish, Centro is a seductive lounge bar with low mood lighting, illuminated table tops, a black glossy bar and discreet, quiet corners caressed by relaxing chill-out tunes and ambient sounds. A cushy refuge at the end of a hectic day, here you can be granted respite from the frantic clutter of contemporary Běijīng. There's live music (including jazz) at night and a DJ spins sounds at weekends.

Club Football Center (Map p122; ☎ 6417 0497; Red House Hotel, 10b Chunxiu Lu; ☑ 11am-2am) Běijīng's most genuine British pub, with wall-to-wall football trophies, scarves, premiership memorabilia, live big-screen action and English-speaking staff all professionally dedicated to adoration of the beautiful game. Sign up and get email alerts for forthcoming matches.

Guangfuguan Greenhouse (Guǎngfúguàn De Wēnshì; Map pp118-19; ☎ 6400 3234; 36 Yandai Xiejie) This laid-back place on the bar-cluttered Yandai Xiejie gets full marks for novelty. Formerly the Guangfu Taoist Temple, the shrine has been requisitioned for the city's exploding bar scene and simply decked out with art posters, including one of a cavorting Allen Ginsberg. For Taoist dining, take the alley alongside to Sānshēng Wànwù (p151).

Huxley's (Bĕijīng Débǐ Jiǔbā; Map pp118-19; 16 Yandai Xiejie) Its 'shut up just drink' slogan a no-nonsense catchphrase for boozers Bĕijīng-wide, specials here include 12 shots of absinthe for Y100, half-price shooters on Monday, all you can drink on Thursdays (Y50) and microbrewery ale for Y25 a go.

John Bull Pub (Zūnbó Yīngshì Jiǔbā; Map pp118-19; ☎ 6532 5905; 44 Guanghua Lu) Sinking pints of bitter, noshing steak-and-kidney pie, staggering to the ockie for a round of darts while moaning about the weather or the NHS (National Health Service), the portly British expat set gravitates here for its snug weeknight atmosphere (often as quiet as a library), comfy furniture and bar staff trotting out excellent English.

Bookworm Café (Shūchóng; Map p122; ☎ 6586 9507; www.beijingbookworm.com; Bldg 4, Nan Sanlitun Lu; ☾ 8am-1am) Deftly bridging the crevasse separating hungry expat minds from Bĕijīng's inept book trade, the Bookworm has emerged as one of the city's foremost cultural enclaves. Join the bibliophiles swooning over the massive English-language book collection (14,000 plus) and jot this place down as a first-rate spot for a get-together, a solo coffee or a major reading binge.

Eje Bar (Zhóuba; Map pp118-19; ☎ 8404 4424; www.ejebar.com; 20 Guoxue Hutong; ☾ 2pm-late) The self-styled (and probably accurate) 'hardest-to-find bar in Bĕijīng' is well worth the effort, but pack a compass. Tucked away behind the rear wall of the Confucius Temple, this cultured courtyard bar is sedately arranged with sofas and set to the chirruping of grasshoppers. Away from even the remotest action, it's well worth a detour. Arriving at night is like reaching the light at the end of a tunnel: from Yonghegong Dajie follow Guanshuyuan Hutong (官书院胡同) round the corner, take the first right and you will see the Confucius Temple ahead on your

left. Follow the road round to your right, take the first left and it's opposite the temple's rear wall (check the bar website for a map).

Drum & Bell Bar (Map pp118-19; ☎ 8403 3600; 41 Zhonglouwan Hutong) Clamber to the roof terrace of this bar romantically slung between its namesake towers, duck under the thicket of branches and seat yourself down amid an idyllic panorama of low-rise Bĕijīng rooftops. Rickety, a bit slapdash perhaps, but supreme – and it serves crinkle-cut chips (Y20).

ENTERTAINMENT

Today's Bĕijīng has seen a revolution in leisure, and the entertainment industry is in full throttle. Beijing opera, acrobatics and kung fu are solid fixtures on the tourist circuit, drawing regular crowds. Classical music concerts and modern theatre reach out to a growing audience of sophisticates, while night owls will find something to hoot about in the live-music and nightclub scene.

Beijing Opera & Traditional Chinese Music

There are many types of Chinese opera, but Beijing opera (京剧; Jīngjù) is by far the best known. The form was popularised in the West by the actor Mei Lanfang (1894–1961), who is said to have influenced Charlie Chaplin.

The operatic form bears little resemblance to its European counterpart. Its colourful blend of singing, dancing, speaking, swordsmanship, mime, acrobatics and dancing can swallow up an epic six hours, but two hours is more usual.

There are four types of actors' roles: the *shēng*, *dàn*, *jìng* and *chǒu*. The *shēng* are the leading male actors and they play scholars, officials, warriors and the like. The *dàn* are the female roles, but are usually played by men (Mei Lanfang always played a *dàn* role). The *jìng* are the painted-face roles, and they represent warriors, heroes, statesmen, adventurers and demons. The *chǒu* is basically the clown.

Language is typically archaic Chinese and the screeching music may not have you tapping your foot, but visually it's a treat, with elaborate costumes and bright, magnificent make-up. Western viewers find the energetic battle sequences riveting, as acrobats leap, twirl, twist and somersault into attack – it's not unlike boarding a Bĕijīng bus during rush hour.

At most well-known Beijing opera venues, shows last around 90 minutes and are generally performed by major opera troupes. Westerners tend to see versions that are noisy and strong on acrobatics and *wǔshù* (martial) routines, rather than the more sedate traditional style.

Zhengyici Theatre (Zhèngyìcí Jùchǎng; Map pp118-19; ☎ 8315 1649; 220 Qianmen Xiheyan Jie; tickets from Y50; ⏰ performances 7.30-9pm) Formerly an ancient temple, this ornately decorated building is the country's oldest wooden theatre and the best place in town for Beijing opera and other operatic schools like Kunqu (昆曲).

Huguang Guild Hall (Húguǎng Huiguǎn; Map pp118-19; ☎ 6351 8284; 3 Hufang Lu; tickets from Y150; ⏰ performances 7.30-8.45pm) Decorated in similar fashion to the Zhengyici Theatre, with balconies surrounding the canopied stage, this theatre dates back to 1807. The interior is magnificent, coloured in red, green and gold. There's also a small opera museum (admission Y10; open 9am to 11am and 3pm to 7.30pm) opposite the theatre, displaying scores, old catalogues and operatic paraphernalia, including colour illustrations of the *liànpǔ* (脸谱; the different types of Beijing opera facial make-up).

Chang'an Grand Theatre (Cháng'ān Dàjùchǎng; Map pp118-19; ☎ 6510 1309; Chang'an Bldg, 7 Jianguomennei Dajie; tickets Y40-150; ⏰ performances 7.15pm) This theatre offers a genuine experience of Beijing opera, with an erudite audience chattering knowledgably among themselves during weekend matinée classics and evening performances.

Lao She Teahouse (Lǎo Shě Cháguǎn; Map pp118-19; ☎ 6303 6830, 6302 1717; www.laosheteahouse.com; 3rd fl, 3 Qianmen Xidajie; evening tickets Y60-130; ⏰ performances 7.30pm) This popular teahouse has nightly shows of Beijing opera, crosstalk and acrobatics. Walk in past a statue of former US president George Bush on your right and head upstairs for performances of folk music (2.30pm to 5pm Monday to Friday), folk music and tea ceremonies (3pm to 4.30pm Friday), theatre (2pm to 4.30pm Wednesday and Friday), and matinée Beijing opera shows (3pm to 4.30pm Sunday). Evening performances of Beijing opera, folk art, music, acrobatics and magic are the most popular. Phone ahead or check online for the schedule.

Sanwei Bookstore (Sānwèi Shūwū; Map pp118-19; ☎ 6601 3204; 60 Fuxingmennei Dajie; cover charge Y50; ⏰ performances 8.30-10.30pm Sat) Opposite the Minzu Hotel, this place has a small bookshop on the ground floor and a teahouse on the second. It features music with traditional Chinese instruments on Saturday night.

Liyuan Theatre (Líyuán Jùchǎng; Map pp118-19; ☎ 8315 7297; Qianmen Jianguo Hotel, 175 Yong'an Lu; tickets downstairs Y80, VIP sections Y150-280; ⏰ performances 7.30-8.40pm) Regular opera performances are held for Beijing opera greenhorns at this tourist-oriented theatre in the Qianmen Jianguo Hotel (p147). Have a chummy photo (Y10) taken with the cast or watch make-up application.

You can also enjoy Beijing opera within the Qing dynasty Grand Opera House in the setting of Prince Gong's Residence (p140), one of Běijīng's landmark historic courtyards. Phone ahead (☎ 6618 6628) to check on performance times (note that performances are only held March to October).

Acrobatics & Martial Arts

Two thousand years old, Chinese acrobatics is one of the best deals in town. Matinée Shaolin performances are held at the Liyuan Theatre (above).

Chaoyang Culture Center (Cháoyáng Qū Wénhuàguǎn; Map pp116-17; ☎ 8062 7388; 17 Jintaili; tickets Y180-380; ⏰ performances 7.20-8.30pm) Shaolin Warriors perform their punishing stage show here; watch carefully and pick up some tips for queuing for tickets during rush hour in the Běijīng underground.

Chaoyang Theatre (Cháoyáng Jùchǎng; Map pp118-19; ☎ 6507 2421; 36 Dongsanhuan Beilu; tickets from Y80; ⏰ performances 7.30pm) Probably the most accessible place for foreign visitors and often bookable through your hotel, this theatre is the venue for visiting acrobatic troupes filling the stage with plate-spinning and hoop-jumping.

Tiandi Theatre (Tiāndì Jùchǎng; Map p122; ☎ 6416 0757/9893; 10 Dongzhimen Nandajie; tickets Y100-300; ⏰ performances 7.15pm) Around 100m north of the old Poly Plaza, here young performers from the China National Acrobatic Troupe knot themselves into mind-bending and joint-popping shapes. It's a favourite with tour groups, so book ahead. You can also visit the circus school to see the performers training (☎ 6502 3984). Look for the white tower resembling something from an airport – that's where you buy your tickets (credit cards not accepted).

Tianqiao Acrobatics Theatre (Tiānqiáo Zájì Jùchǎng; Map pp118-19; ☎ 6303 7449, English 139 100 018 60;

Tianqiao; tickets Y100-200; ☽ performances 7.15-8.45pm) West of the Temple of Heaven, this is one of Běijīng's most popular venues. The entrance is down the eastern side of the building.

Red Theatre (Hóng Jùchǎng; ☎ 6714 2473; 44 Xingfu Dajie; tickets Y180-680; ☽ performances 7.30-8.50pm) Nightly kung fu shows aimed squarely at tourist groups are performed here.

Nightclubs

Běijīng's discos may not be cutting edge, but they pack in loyal, sweaty patrons and should wow Westerners who thought the city was still stuck in the past. Most budgets meet their match, from student dives to sharper venues and top-end clubs. See also Poachers Inn, p152.

Bar Blu (Map p122; ☎ 6417 4124; Tongli Studio, San-litun Beilu; ☽ 4.30am Fri & Sat) Its floor glowing with namesake blue underfloor lighting, this funky Tongli Studio wi-fi bar above Le Petit Gourmand has a nightly DJ, upstairs terrace and doses of nostalgia every Thursday with its '70s, '80s and '90s night.

Top Club (Map p122; ☎ 6413 1019; 4th fl, Tongli Studio, Sanlitun Beilu) On the floor above Bar Blu, this club has a humungous rooftop terrace.

Babyface (Map p122; ☎ 6551 9081; 6 Gongti Xilu; ☽ 8pm-4am) At the south gate of the Workers' Stadium, the nationwide Babyface chain has upped the stakes in the 'Běijīng's coolest club contest' with this slick outfit.

Vics (Wēikèsī; Map p122; ☎ 6593 6215; Workers' Stadium north gate; tickets Fri/Sat Y35/50; ☽ 7pm-late) South of the Outback Steakhouse, Vics is decked out with couches, a pool table and a sweaty dance floor. This is perhaps Běijīng's most popular place, with a selection of hip-hop, R&B, pop and soul attracting solid crowds. Wednesday is ladies night, and Friday and Saturday nights see things thumping and jumping till 7am.

World of Suzie Wong (Sūxi Huáng; Map pp116-17; ☎ 6593 7889; 1a Nongzhanguan Lu, Chaoyang Amusement Park west gate, through Q bar entrance; beers from Y15; ☽ 7pm-3.30am) This elegant lounge bar attracts glamorous types who recline on traditional wooden beds piled up with silk cushions and sip daiquiris. There's attentive service, fine cocktails and beer, and the music is varied, from House, through chill-out, to techno, pop and rock.

Club Banana (Bānànà; Map pp118-19; ☎ 6526 3939; Scitech Hotel, 22 Jianguomenwai Dajie; tickets Y20-50; ☽ 8.30pm-4am Sun-Thu, to 5am Fri & Sat) Mainstay of Běijīng club land, Banana is loud and to the

point. Select from the techno, acid jazz and chill-out sections according to your energy levels or the waning of the night.

Contemporary Music

The instinct for syrupy Chinese pop is deeply ingrained in the mainland psyche, but some of Běijīng's residents have grittier tastes that require more bite. Nodding its head to a growing medley of sounds, China's increasingly brazen capital has found an exciting language with which to articulate the new *Zeitgeist*. On the downside, international pop and rock acts of any worth rarely make it to Běijīng, but there are several places around town where you can take in Běijīng's home-grown music scene. Taking up the rear are Filipino cover bands, who perform at American-style burger bars.

CD Jazz Café (CD Juéshì Jùlèbù; Map p122; ☎ 6506 8288; C16 Dongsanhuan Beilu; ☽ 5pm-12.30am) This is a popular club with live jazz and jazz-funk performances from Thursday to Saturday and a swing night on Monday. It's tucked away south of the Agricultural Exhibition Center behind an overhead walkway vaulting over Dongsanhuan Beilu and next to CD Café, which serves Italian food.

What Bar? (Map p132; ☎ 133 411 227 57; 72 Beichang Jie; entrance on live music nights incl 1 beer Y20; ☽ 3pm to late, live music from 9pm Fri & Sat) Microsized and slightly deranged, this cubbyhole of a bar stages regular rotating, grittily named bands (Three Bitches, The Gamblers etc). It's north of the west gate of Forbidden City.

Classical Music

As China's capital and the nation's cultural hub, Běijīng has several venues where classical music finds an appreciative audience. The annual 30-day **Beijing Music Festival** (www .bmf.org.cn) is staged between October and November, bringing with it international and home-grown classical music performances. Under construction since 2001, the US$324 million, 6,000-seat, titanium-and-glass National Grand Theatre (Map pp118-19), to the west of Tiananmen Sq, has suffered delays and was still waiting for its unveiling at the time of research.

Beijing Concert Hall (Běijīng Yīnyuè Tīng; Map pp118-19; ☎ 6605 7006; 1 Beixinhua Jie; tickets Y50-500; ☽ performances 7.30pm) The 2000-seat Beijing Concert Hall showcases evening performances of classical Chinese music as well as international repertoires of Western classical music.

Forbidden City Concert Hall (Zhōngshān Gōngyuán Yīnyuè Táng; Map p132; ☎ 6559 8285; Zhongshan Park; tickets Y50-500; ☺ performances 7.30pm) Located on the eastern side of Zhongshan Park, this is the venue for performances of classical and traditional Chinese music.

Poly Plaza International Theatre (Bǎolì Dàshà Guójì Jùyuàn; Map p122; ☎ 6506 5345; old Poly Plaza, 14 Dongzhimen Nandajie; tickets Y100-1280; ☺ performances usually at 7.30pm) Situated in the old Poly Plaza right by Dongsishitiao subway station, this venue hosts a wide range of performances, including classical music, ballet, traditional Chinese folk music and operatic works.

Theatre

Only emerging in China in the 20th century, *huàjù* (话剧; spoken drama) never commanded a large following in China. As an art, creative drama is still unable to fully express itself and remains sadly gagged and sidelined. But if you want to know what's walking the floorboards in Běijīng, try some of the following.

Capital Theatre (Shǒudū Jùyuàn; Map p123; ☎ 6524 9847; 22 Wangfujing Dajie; ☺ performances 7pm Tue-Sun) Situated right in the heart of the city on Wangfujing Dajie, this central theatre has regular performances of contemporary Chinese productions from several theatre companies.

China Puppet Theatre (Zhōngguó Mùòu Jùyuàn; Map pp116-17; ☎ 6422 9487; 1a Anhua Xili, Beisanhuan Lu; tickets Y30-100) This popular theatre has regular events, including shadow play, puppetry, music and dance.

The huge Chang'an Grand Theatre (p154) largely stages productions of Beijing opera with occasional classical Chinese theatre productions.

Cinemas

The following are two of Běijīng's most central multiscreen cinemas.

Star Cinema City (Xinshìjì Yǐngchéng; Map p123; ☎ 8518 5399; shop BB65, basement, Oriental Plaza, 1 Dongchang'an Jie; tickets Wed-Mon Y50, Tue Y35) This six-screen cinema is centrally located and plush (with leather reclining sofa chairs).

Sundongan Cinema City (Xīndōngān Yǐngchéng; Map p123; ☎ 6528 1988; 5th fl, Sundongan Plaza, Wangfujing Dajie; tickets Y40) Don't expect a huge selection, but you can usually find a Hollywood feature plus other English-language movies here.

SHOPPING

There are several notable Chinese shopping districts offering abundant goods and reasonable prices: **Wangfujing Dajie** (王府井大街), **Xidan** (西单) and **Qianmen** (前门), including Dashilar. The *hútòng* of **Dashilar** (大栅栏; Map pp118–19) runs southwest from the northern end of Qianmen Dajie, south of Tiananmen Sq. It's a great jumble of silk shops, old stores, theatres, herbal medicine shops, and food and clothing specialists.

More luxurious shopping areas can be found in the embassy areas of Jianguomenwai (建国门外) and Sanlitun (三里屯); also check out five-star hotel shopping malls. Shopping at open-air markets is an experience not to be missed. Běijīng's most popular markets are the Silk Street, the Sanlitun Yashou Clothing Market, Panjiayuan and the Pearl Market. There are also specialised shopping districts such as Liulichang.

Běijīng's premier antique street, **Liulichang** (琉璃厂; Map pp118–19) is not far west of Dashilar. Worth delving along for its quaint, albeit dressed up, age-old village atmosphere, Liulichang's shops trade in (largely fake) antiques. Alongside ersatz Qing monochrome bowls and Cultural Revolution kitsch, you can also rummage through old Chinese books, paintings, brushes, ink and paper. Prepare yourself for pushy sales staff and stratospheric prices; wander round and compare price tags. If you want a chop (carved seal) made, you can do it here. At the western end of Liulichang Xijie, a collection of ramshackle stalls flogs bric-a-brac, Buddhist statuary, Cultural Revolution pamphlets and posters, fake Tang dynasty *sāncǎi* (three-colour porcelain), shoes for bound feet, silks, handicrafts, Chinese kites, swords, walking sticks, door knockers etc.

Arts & Crafts

Pyongyang Art Studios (Map p122; ☎ 6416 7544; Red House Hotel, 10 Chunxiu Lu) Unsurpassed communist kitsch is delivered straight to your hands here from the axis of evil. Finger maps of Pyongyang and turn over edifying literature (*Towards the Eminence of Socialism*), North Korean ciggies (Y20 per pack), liquor, T-shirts (Y80), posters villifying America, DPRK flags (Y150), postcards (Y80) and badges (Y30) or grab a second impression of *The US Imperialists started the Korean War* (Y100) – while stocks last.

Tongli Studio Lifestyle & Arts (Tónglǐ; Map p122; Sanlitun Beilu; 11am-9pm) This trendy lifestyle and arts shopping market in Sanlitun has four floors of small shops (selling ceramics, clothing, jewellery, jade, and arts and crafts, among other decorative quality items), cafés, bars and clubs.

Beijing Curio City (Běijīng Gǔwán Chéng; Map pp118-19; ☎ 6774 7711; 21 Dongsanhuan Nanlu; 9.30am-6.30pm) South of Panjiayuan, Curio City is four floors of gifts, scrolls, ceramics, carpets, duty-free shopping and furniture. It's an excellent place to turn up knick-knacks and souvenirs, especially on Sundays.

Beijing Arts & Crafts Central Store (Gōngyì Měishù Fúwùbù; Map p123; ☎ 6523 8747; 200 Wangfujing Dajie) This centrally located store (with a sign outside saying Artistic Mansion) is well known for its good selection of jade (plus certificates of authenticity), jewellery, pearls, jadeite, cloisonné vases, silks, carpets and other Chinese arts and crafts.

798 Photo Gallery (Bǎinián Yīnxiàng; Map pp116-17; ☎ 6438 1784; www.798photogallery.cn; 4 Jiuxianqiao Lu) A trendy component of Factory 798 (p138), the huge, active industrial art park in northwest Běijīng, this photographic gallery has a collection of intriguing prints for sale from the Cultural Revolution, including black-and-white photos (Y3000) of Mao Zedong signed by the photographer, Houbo.

Cuì Wén Gé (Map pp118-19; ☎ 8316 5899; 58 Liulichang Dongjie) Don't expect any bargains, but there's a riveting array of temple ornaments, ceramics, traditional roof figures, antique fans, bronzes, ceramics, antique ivory Bodhisattvas and more at this Liulichang antiques specialist; don't miss the collection of *thangka* (Tibetan sacred art) upstairs.

Carpets

Torana Carpets (Kāngchén; Map pp118-19; ☎ 6465 3388, ext 5542; www.toranahouse.com; Shop 8, Kempinski Hotel, 50 Liangmaqiao Lu; 10am-10pm) You may pay more for your carpets here (ranging from around Y2000 to Y16,000), but you can be assured that what you are buying are genuine, handmade carpets from Tibet. The company also sells antique Tibetan carpets and furniture, with a further branch in Shànghǎi.

Qianmen Carpet Company (Qiánmén Dìtǎnchǎng; Map pp118-19; ☎ 6715 1687; 59 Xingfu Dajie) This carpet store, just north of the Tiantan Hotel, stocks a good selection of handmade carpets and prayer rugs with natural dyes from Tibet,

Xīnjiāng and Mongolia. Prices start at around Y2000.

Clothing

Silk Street (Xiùshuǐ Jiē; Map pp118-19; cnr Jianguomenwai Dajie & Dongdaqiao Lu; 9am-9pm; underground Yonganli) Seething with shoppers and polyglot vendors who try their luck with the contents of your wallet in several tongues, Silk Street is where the Silk Market has repositioned itself. Long notorious as a bedlam of fake knockoffs, the pirated designer labels remain, although at the time of writing a consortium of big names (North Face, Gucci, Boss, Dunhill et al) had successfully driven their brands from the shelves. The market sprawls riotously from floor to floor, shoving piles of rucksacks, shoes, clothing, silk, cashmere, tailor-made cheongsam, rugs, jade, pearls and trashy Rolexes into the open mits of travellers and expats. Haggle like hell and dispatch your postcards from the basement post office (open 9am to 5pm), next to the food court.

Sanlitun Yashou Clothing Market (Sānlǐtún Yǎxiù Fúzhuāng Shìchǎng; Map p122; 58 Gongrentiyuchang Beilu) After slogging through this hopping, five-floor bedlam of shoes, boots, handbags, suitcases, jackets, silk, carpets, batik, lace, jade, pearls, toys, army surplus and souvenirs, ease the pressure on your bunions with a foot massage (Y50 per hour) or pedicure (Y40) on the 4th floor and restore calories in the 5th-floor food court.

Feng Ling Fashion Art Design (Map p122; ☎ 6417 7715; 302, Tongli Studio, Sanlitun Beilu) Eye-catching designs and stylish takes on Mao suits, *qípáo* (cheongsam) and evening dresses.

Department Stores & Malls

Oriental Plaza (Dōngfāng Guǎngchǎng; Map p123; www.orientalplaza.com; 1 Dongchang'an Jie; 9.30am-9.30pm) You could spend a day in this staggeringly large shopping mega-complex at the foot of Wangfujing Dajie. Prices may not be cheap, but window-shoppers will be overjoyed. There's a great range of shops and restaurants, an excellent basement food court and it's kid-friendly, with nappy-changing rooms, a play room downstairs and Sony Explora Science (p144).

Lufthansa Center Youyi Shopping City (Yànshā Yǒuyì Shāngchǎng; Map pp118-19; 50 Liangmaqiao Lu) The gigantic Lufthansa Center is a well-stocked and long-established multilevel shopping mall. You can find most of what you need here, including several restaurants, kids' toys on the 6th floor and international-access ATMs on the ground floor.

Friendship Store (Yǒuyì Shāngdiàn; Map pp118-19; ☎ 6500 3311; 17 Jianguomenwai Dajie) This place could be worth a perusal for its upstairs touristy junk, supermarket and deli.

Kites

Zhāoyuángé (Map p123; ☎ 6512 1937; 41 Nanheyan Dajie) If you love Chinese kites, you will love this minute shop on the western side of Nanheyan Dajie, south of the Liújiā Guō restaurant. Chinese paper kites range from Y10 for a simple kite, up to around Y300 for a dragon; you can also browse Beijing opera masks, chopsticks, Mao badges and *zǐshā* teapots. The owner does not speak much English, but you can look around and make a selection.

Markets

Pānjiāyuán (Map pp118-19; ☼ dawn-around 3pm Sat & Sun) Hands down the best place to shop for *yìshù* (arts), *gōngyì* (crafts) and *gǔwán* (antiques) in Běijīng is Pānjiāyuán (aka the Dirt Market or the Sunday Market). The market only takes place on weekends and has everything from calligraphy, Cultural Revolution memorabilia and cigarette-ad posters to Buddha heads, ceramics and Tibetan carpets.

The market sees up to 50,000 visitors daily scoping for treasures. If you want to join them, early Sunday morning is the best time. You may not find that rare Qianlong *dǒucǎi* stem cup or late-Yuan-dynasty *qīnghuā* vase that will ease you into early retirement, but what's on view is no less than a compendium of Chinese curios and an A–Z of Middle Kingdom knick-knacks. Bear in mind that this market is chaos, especially if you find crowds

or hard bargaining intimidating. Also, ignore the 'don't pay more than half' rule here – some vendors may start at 10 times the real price. Make a few rounds at Pānjiāyuán before forking out for anything, to compare prices and weigh it all up. It's off Dongsanhuan Nanlu (Third Ring Rd); take the subway to Guomao, then bus 28.

Pearl Market (Hóngqiáo Shìchǎng; Map pp118-19; ☎ 6711 7429; Tiantan Donglu; ☼ 8.30am-7pm) The cosmos of clutter across from the east gate of Temple of Heaven Park ranges from shoes, leather bags, jackets, jeans, silk by the yard, electronics, Chinese arts, crafts and antiques to a galaxy of pearls (freshwater and seawater, white and black), on the 3rd floor. Prices for the latter vary incredibly with quality. Pop down to the basement for a selection of scorpions, snake meat, snails and more and if you have kids in tow, don't miss the Kids Toys market (Hóngqiáo Tiānlè Wánjù Shìchǎng; open 8.30am to 7pm) in the building behind, stuffed to the gills with soft toys, cars, kits, electronic games, film tie-ins, models and more. Pearl Market is across from the east gate of the Temple of Heaven Park.

GETTING THERE & AWAY

As the nation's capital, getting to Běijīng is straightforward. Rail and air connections link the capital to virtually every point in China, and fleets of buses head to abundant destinations from Běijīng. Using Běijīng as a starting point to explore the rest of the land makes perfect sense.

Air

Běijīng has direct air connections to most major cities in the world. For more information about international flights to Běijīng, see p956.

DOMESTIC AIR FARES FROM BĚIJĪNG

Domestic flights from Běijīng include the following destinations (fares are for one-way flights): Chángchūn (Y960, 80 minutes), Chéngdū (Y1440, two hours, 20 minutes), Dàlián (Y710, 70 minutes), Fúzhōu (Y1530, 2½ hours), Guǎngzhōu (Y1700, two hours, 50 minutes), Guìlín (Y1590, 4½ hours), Hāěrbīn (Y1000, 1½ hours), Hǎikǒu (Y2190, three hours, 40 minutes), Hángzhōu (Y1050, 50 minutes), Héféi (Y990, one hour, 40 minutes), Hohhot (Y500, one hour), Hong Kong (Y2800, three hours), Jílín (Y960, 80 minutes), Kūnmíng (Y1810, four hours), Lánzhōu (Y1100, two hours), Lhasa (Y2040, 4½ hours), Nánjīng (Y930, one hour, 35 minutes), Nánníng (Y1870, three hours, 25 minutes), Qīngdǎo (Y660, 50 minutes), Shànghǎi (Y1030, two hours), Tàiyuán (Y510, 50 minutes), Ūrūmqi (Y2410, 3½ hours), Wǔhàn (Y990, two hours), Xī'ān (Y1050, 1½ hours), Xīníng (Y1450, two hours) and Zhèngzhōu (Y690, 70 minutes).

Purchase tickets for Chinese carriers flying from Běijīng at CAAC in the **Aviation Building** (Mínháng Yíngyè Dàshà; Map pp118-19; ☎ 6656 9118, domestic 6601 3336, international 6601 6667; 15 Chang'an Jie; ☯ 7am-midnight) or from one of the numerous other ticket outlets and service counters around Běijīng, and through most midrange and above hotels. Discounts are generally available, so it is important to ask.

A downtown check-in service desk is situated just inside the door, available for passengers with carry-on luggage only (open 8am to 5pm; domestic flights only); you must check in at least three hours prior to departure.

You can make inquiries for all airlines at Běijīng's **Capital Airport** (Map p111; ☎ from Běijīng only 962 580). Call ☎ 6454 1100 for information on international and domestic arrivals and departures.

Daily flights connect Běijīng to every major city in China. There should be at least one flight a week to smaller cities throughout China. The prices listed in this book are approximate only and represent the nondiscounted air fare.

Bus

No international buses serve Běijīng, but there are plenty of long-distance domestic routes served by national highways radiating from Běijīng.

Běijīng has numerous long-distance bus stations (长途汽车站; *chángtú qìchēzhàn*), positioned roughly on the city perimeter in the direction you want to go.

Buses from **Bawangfen long-distance bus station** (Bāwángfén Chángtú Kèyùnzhàn; Map pp116-17) in the east of town serve Tiānjīn (Y31, regular), Bāotóu (Y131, once daily) and Qínhuángdǎo (Y61), plus destinations in the northeast including Chángchūn (Y221, four daily), Shěnyáng (Y151, regular), Dàlián (Y219, three daily) and Hāěrbīn (280, twice daily). The nearby **Sihui long-distance bus station** (Sìhuì Chángtú Qìchēzhàn; Map pp116-17) has departures to Tiānjīn (Y23, hourly) Chéngdé (Y46, regular), Chángchūn (Y240, one daily), Dàlián (Y280, one daily), Dāndōng (Y224, one daily) and Jílín (Y248, one daily).

Liuliqiao long-distance bus station (Liùlíqiáo Chángtúzhàn; Map pp118-19; ☎ 8383 1717), southwest of Beijing West Train station, has buses north, south and west of town including Dàtóng (Y81, regular), Bāotóu (Y121, five

daily), Shíjiāzhuāng (Y73, regular), Chéngdé (Y46, regular), Luòyáng (Y149, four daily), Zhèngzhōu (Y129, three daily), Xī'ān (Y180), Héféi (Y180), Yínchuān (Y237) and even Xiàmén (Y480).

The nearby **Lianhuachi long-distance bus station** (Liánhuāchí Chángtú Qìchēzhàn; Map pp118-19) has buses south to Shíjiāzhuāng (Y50, regular), Luòyáng (Y165, once daily), Ānyáng (Y105, twice daily), Jǐ'nán (Y100, once daily) and Yán'ān (Y245, once daily).

Another important station is at **Zhaogongkou** (Map pp116-17; ☎ 6722 9491, 6723 7328) in the south (useful for buses to Tiānjīn).

Train

Travellers arrive and depart by train at **Beijing Train Station** (Běijīng Huǒchēzhàn; Map pp118-19; ☎ 5101 9999), southeast of the Forbidden City, or the colossal **Beijing West Train Station** (Běijīng Xīzhàn; Map pp118-19; ☎ 5182 6273) in the southwest. Beijing Train Station is served by its own underground station, making access simple. International trains to Moscow, Pyongyang (North Korea) and Ulan Bator (Mongolia) arrive at and leave Beijing Train Station; trains for Hong Kong and Vietnam leave from Beijing West Train Station. Buses 122 and 721 connect Beijing Train Station with Beijing West Train Station. For information on the train to Lhasa, see p924.

The Běijīng–Shànghǎi maglev idea may have been quietly put to sleep, but new overnight soft-sleeper express (直特; *zhítè*) trains do the trip in 12 hours, with several trains (Z1, Z5, Z7, Z13 and Z21; 7.35pm, 7.14pm, 7.21pm, 7.07pm and 7pm respectively, lower/upper bunk Y499/478) departing nightly. Other fast express trains from Beijing Train Station include Sūzhōu (Z85, 7.28pm, hard sleeper Y309, 11 hours, 20 minutes) and Hángzhōu (Z9, 6.53pm, soft sleeper only Y554, 13½ hours).

Typical train fares and approximate travel times for hard-sleeper tickets to destinations from Beijing Train Station include: Chángchūn (Y239, 9½ hours), Dàlián (Y257, 12 hours), Dàtóng (Y70, 5½ hours), Hángzhōu (Y363, 15 hours), Hāěrbīn (Y281, 11½ hours), Jǐ'nán (Y137, 4½ hours), Jílín (Y263, 12 hours), Nánjīng (Y274, 11 hours), Qīngdǎo (Y215, nine hours), Shànghǎi (Y327, 13½ hours; soft-sleeper express 12 hours), Sūzhōu (Y309, 11 hours), Tiānjīn (Y30, 80 minutes, hard seat) and Ürümqi (Y652, 44 hours).

The fast soft sleeper Z19 express train departs daily from Beijing West Train Station for Xī'ān (Y417, 11½ hours) at 8.28pm. Other typical train fares and approximate travel times for hard-sleeper tickets to destinations from Beijing West Train Station include: Chángshā (Y345, 14 hours), Chéngdū (Y418, 26 hours), Chóngqìng (Y430, 25 hours), Guǎngzhōu (Y458, 22 hours), Guìyáng (Y490, 29 hours), Hànkǒu (Y281, 10 hours, 20 minutes), Kūnmíng (Y578, 40 hours), Lánzhōu (Y390, 20½ hours), Shēnzhèn (Y467, 23½ hours), Shíjiāzhuāng (Y50, hard seat, two hours, 45 minutes), Kowloon (Y480, 24 hours, 23 minutes), Ürümqi (Y652, 44 hours), Yínchuān (Y262, 19 hours), Xī'ān (Y274, 12 hours), Yíchāng (Y319) and Xīníng (Y430, 24½ hours).

Beijing South Train Station (Yǒngdìngmén Huǒchēzhàn; Map pp118–19; ☎ 5183 7262) serves a limited number of destinations in Héběi, Hénán, Shǎnxī and Inner Mongolia; Inner Mongolia is also served by trains from **Beijing North Train Station** (Běijīng Běizhàn; Map pp118–19; ☎ 5186 6223). Bus 20 connects Beijing Train Station and Beijing South Train Station.

The queues at Beijing Train Station can be overwhelming. At the time of writing, the ticketing office for foreigners attached to the soft-seat waiting room (guìbīn hòuchēshì) on the 1st floor was no longer open, although an English-speaking service was available at ticket window No 26. Information is available at ticket window No 29. A **foreigners ticketing office** (☺ 24hr) can be found on the 2nd floor of Beijing West Train Station.

GETTING AROUND
To/From the Airport
Běijīng's Capital Airport is 27km from the centre of town or about 30 minutes to one hour by car depending on traffic.

Numerous buses run to and from the airport. Almost any bus that gets you into town will probably do; then you can hop in a taxi and speed to a hotel or link up with the underground system.

Express bus routes run into town every 30 minutes between 5.30am and 7pm daily, although some run longer hours. The most popular bus is Route A (Y16), which runs 24 hours (with less frequent services between 10pm and 5.30am) from the airport to Sanyuanqiao, Dongzhimen (underground station), Dongsishitiao (underground station) and the International Hotel (Guójì Fàndiàn; just north

of Beijing Train Station). Route B (Y16) runs along the north Third Ring Rd and then south past the Friendship Hotel to the metro stop at Gongzhufen. From the city to the airport, the most useful place to catch the bus is at the west door of the International Hotel, where buses leave every half-hour between 6am and 7.30pm (Y16). You can also take buses (☎ 6459 4375/4376; Y16; one hour) from the eastern end of the Aviation Building (Map pp118–19) on Xichang'an Jie in Xidan District; departures are every 30 minutes between 5.45am and 7.30pm.

Many top-end hotels runs shuttle buses from the airport to their hotels.

A light-rail link from Capital Airport to Běijīng is under construction, but is not due for completion until June 2008.

A taxi (using its meter) should cost about Y85 from the airport to the centre, including the Y15 airport expressway toll. A well-established illegal taxi operation at the airport attempts to lure weary travellers into a Y300-plus ride to the city, so be on your guard. If anyone approaches you offering a taxi ride, ignore them and insist on joining the queue for a taxi outside. When you get into the taxi, make sure the driver uses the meter. It is also useful to have the name of your hotel written down in Chinese to show the driver.

Bicycle
It's tempting to take to two wheels around Běijīng: the city is as flat as a chessboard, there are ample bicycle lanes and other vehicular traffic is often at a standstill. The increase in traffic in recent years has made biking along major thoroughfares more dangerous and nerve-racking, however. Cycling through Běijīng's hútòng is far safer and an experience not to be missed (see the Bicycle Tour, p142).

Budget hotels often hire out bicycles, which cost around Y20 per day (plus a deposit); rental at upmarket hotels is far more expensive. Rental outfits are increasingly common, including a centrally located streetside operation on Jinyu Hutong (☎ 6313 1010; standard bike per hr/day Y10/50, mountain bike Y20/80), just west of the Novotel Peace Hotel. There's also the expensive **Universal Bicycle Rental Outlet** (Map pp118–19; s/tandem bike per hr Y10/20, deposit Y500; ☺ 1–10pm Mon-Fri, 10am–10pm Sat & Sun), with an outlet on the east shore of Qianhai Lake, **Bird of Freedom** (Zìxíngchē Chūzū Fúwùzhàn; Map pp118–19; ☎ 6313 1010; 47 Qianmen Dajie; per hr

Y15-20, per day Y50-60, deposit Y300-600; ☺ 7am-8pm), opposite Qianmen Quanjude Roast Duck Restaurant, and bike rental from the shop at 77 Tieshu Xiejie (Y20 from 7am-11pm; deposit Y200).

Car

At the time of writing, foreign visitors were effectively barred from driving in Běijīng, host city of the 2008 Olympics. Only residents who have lived in Běijīng for one year can apply and licence application procedures take a month to process. Check with **Hertz** (☎ 800-810 8833; 5 Jianguomenwai Dajie; ☺ 9am-5pm) at the Jianguo Hotel for the latest news. Taxis are cheap and hiring a driver is a proposition, which can be arranged through Hertz (from Y520 per day), at major hotels, **CITS** (☎ 6515 8587) or other travel agencies.

Public Transport

BUS

Relying on buses (公共汽车; *gōnggòng qìchē*) can be knuckle-gnawingly frustrating unless it's a short hop; thick congestion often slows things to an infuriating crawl (average speed below 10km/h) where Běijīng creeps by in slow motion. The growth in bus lanes (target: 400km of bus lanes in town by 2008) should speed things up. Getting a seat can verge on the physical, especially at rush hour. Běijīng's Chinese-only bus routes on bus signs are fiendishly foreigner-unfriendly, although the name of the stop appears in pinyin.

Fares are typically Y1 or under depending on distance, although plusher, air-conditioned buses are more expensive. You generally pay the conductor once aboard the bus, rather than the driver.

Buses run 5am to 11pm daily or thereabouts, and stops are few and far between. It's important to work out how many stops you need to go before boarding. If you can read Chinese, a useful publication (Y5) listing all the Běijīng bus lines is available from kiosks; alternatively, tourist maps of Běijīng illustrate some of the bus routes. If you work out how to combine bus and subway connections, the subway will speed up much of the trip.

Buses 1 to 124 cover the city core; 200-series are night buses (*yèbān gōnggòng qìchē*), while buses 300 to 501 are suburban lines.

Useful standard bus routes:

1 Runs along Chang'an Jie, Jianguomenwai Dajie and Jianguomennei Dajie, passing Sihuizhan, Bawangfen, Yonganli, Dongdan, Xidan, Muxidi, Junshi Bowuguan, Gongzhufen and Maguanying along the way.

4 Runs along Chang'an Jie, Jianguomenwai Dajie and Jianguomennei Dajie: Gongzhufen, Junshi Bowuguan, Muxidi, Xidan, Tiananmen, Dongdan, Yonganli, Bawangfen and Sihuizhan.

5 Deshengmen, Dianmen, Beihai Park, Xihuamen, Zhongshan Park and Qianmen.

15 Beijing Zoo, Fuxingmen, Xidan, Hepingmen, Liulichang and Tianqiao.

20 Beijing South Train Station, Tianqiao, Qianmen, Wangfujing, Dongdan and Beijing Train Station.

44 (outer ring) Xinjiekou, Xizhimen Train Station, Fuchengmen, Fuxingmen, Changchunjie, Xuanwumen, Qianmen, Taijichang, Chongwenmen, Dongbianmen, Chaoyangmen, Dongzhimen, Andingmen, Deshengmen and Xinjiekou.

54 Beijing Train Station, Dongbianmen, Chongwenmen, Zhengyi Lu, Qianmen, Dashilar, Temple of Heaven, Yongdimen and Haihutun.

103 Beijing Train Station, Dengshikou, China Art Gallery, Forbidden City (north entrance), Beihai Park, Fuchengmen and Beijing Zoo.

332 Beijing Zoo, Weigongcun, Renmin Daxue, Zhongguancun, Haidian, Beijing University and Summer Palace.

Special double-decker buses 1 to 8 run in a circle around the city centre and are slightly more expensive but spare you the traumas of normal public buses and you should get a seat.

SUBWAY & LIGHT RAILWAY

The subway (地铁; *dìtiě*) is both reliable and fast, although it's modest and much older than Shànghǎi's slicker system. Trains are showing their age, platforms are dated and paper tickets remain the norm (to be replaced before the 2008 Olympics), but five new subway lines are under construction. Four lines exist: the Circle Line (Huánxiàn; also called Line 2), Line 1 (Yīxiàn; running east–west), Line 13 and the Batong line (Bātōngxiàn). The fare is a flat Y3 on all lines, regardless of distance (Y5 if you swap between Line 13 and the rest of the subway system).

Trains run at a frequency of one every few minutes during peak times and operate from 5am to 11pm daily. Banisters up the platform stairs to the exit are marked with Braille (disabled passengers note that escalators often only go up). Only a few platforms have seats, and none have toilets. Stops are announced in English and Chinese. Subway stations (地铁站; *dì tiě zhàn*) are identified by subway symbols, a blue, encircled English capital 'D'.

BĚIJĪNG

Lines currently under construction are lines 4, 5, 8, 9, 10 and the airport line. Line 4 is due to open in 2009, linking northwest Běijīng with the south of the city. Line 5, due to open in mid 2007, will run north–south, intersecting with the Circle Line at Yonghegong and Chongwenmen, and intersecting with Line 1 at Dongdan. Line 8 (the Olympic Branch Line) will connect with the Olympic Park and is due for completion in 2008. Line 10 will run from Jingsong in the southeast through Guomao and onto Wanliu in the northwest of town; it is due for completion in 2008.

Line 1

This line has 23 stations and runs from Sihuidong to Pingguoyuan, a western suburb of Běijīng. For station names, see the Beijing Transport Network map (p170).

Line 2 (Circle Line)

This 16km line has 18 stations. For station names, see the Beijing Transport Network map (p170). The Circle Line intersects with Line 1 at Fuxingmen and Jianguomen. Trains take an average of two minutes between stations with a complete loop taking around 40 minutes.

Line 13

Classified as part of the subway system but actually a light-rail link (operating between 6am and 9pm), Line 13 runs in a northern loop from Xizhimen to Dongzhimen, stopping at 14 stations (approximately three minutes per station) in between. As with the subway, tickets to anywhere on Line 13 are Y3, while Y5 gets you a ticket to any station on the other lines of the underground system. The line is not of great use for tourist sights, apart from the Wudaokou stop for the Old Summer Palace and Summer Palace. An extension to the line is currently being built that will link Dongzhimen to Běijīng's Capital Airport (due for completion in 2008).

Batong Line

The Batong Line links Sihui on Line 1 with Tuqiao in the southeastern suburbs.

Taxi

Běijīng taxis come in different classes, with red stickers on the side rear window declaring the rate per kilometre. Y2 taxis (Y10 for the first 3km; Y2 per kilometre thereafter)

include a new fleet of Hyundai cars, which are spacious and have air-con and rear seatbelts. The most expensive taxis are Y12 for the first 3km and Y2 per kilometre thereafter. Taxis are required to switch on the meter for all journeys (unless you negotiate a fee for a long journey out of town). Between 11pm and 6am there is a 20% surcharge added to the flag-fall metered fare. The cheap *xiali* bone-rattler taxis have been phased out.

Běijīng taxi drivers speak little, if any English, despite encouragement to learn 100 basic phrases in the run up to 2008. If you don't speak Chinese, bring a map or have your destination written down in characters. It helps if you know the way to your destination; sit in the front (where the seatbelt works) with a map.

Cabs can be hired for distance, by the hour, or by the day (a minimum of Y350 for the day). Taxis can be hailed in the street, summoned by phone or you can wait at one of the designated taxi zones or outside hotels. Call ☎ 6835 1150 to register a complaint. Remember to collect a receipt (ask the driver to *fāpiào*); if you accidentally leave anything in the taxi, the driver's number appears on the receipt so he or she can be located.

AROUND BĚIJĪNG

THE GREAT WALL 长城

He who has not climbed the Great Wall is not a true man.

Mao Zedong

China's mandatory, must-see sight, the Great Wall (Chángchéng) wriggles fitfully from its scattered remains in Liáoníng province to Jiāyùguān in the Gobi Desert.

The 'original' wall was begun over 2000 years ago during the Qin dynasty (221–207 BC), when China was unified under Emperor Qin Shi Huang. Separate walls that had been constructed by independent kingdoms to keep out marauding nomads were linked together. The effort required hundreds of thousands of workers – many of whom were political prisoners – and 10 years of hard labour under General Meng Tian. An estimated 180 million cubic metres of rammed earth was used to form the core of the original wall, and legend has it that one of the building materials used was the bones of deceased workers.

The wall never really did perform its function as an impenetrable line of defence. As Genghis Khan supposedly said, 'The strength of a wall depends on the courage of those who defend it'. Sentries could be bribed. However, it did work very well as a kind of elevated highway, transporting people and equipment across mountainous terrain. Its beacon tower system, using smoke signals generated by burning wolves' dung, quickly transmitted news of enemy movements back to the capital. To the west was Jiāyùguān, an important link on the Silk Road, where there was a customs post of sorts and where unwanted Chinese were ejected through the gates to face the terrifying wild west.

During the Ming dynasty a determined effort was made to rehash the bastion, this time facing it with some 60 million cubic metres of bricks and stone slabs. This project took over 100 years, and the costs in human effort and resources were phenomenal. The investment failed to curb the Manchu armies from storming the Middle Kingdom and imposing over two and a half centuries of foreign rule on China.

The wall was largely forgotten after that. Lengthy sections of it have returned to dust and the wall might have disappeared totally had it not been rescued by the tourist industry. Several important sections have been rebuilt, kitted out with souvenir shops, restaurants and amusement-park rides, and formally opened to the public.

The most touristed area of the Great Wall is at Bādáling. Also renovated but less touristed are Sīmǎtái and Jīnshānling. Not impressed with the tourist-oriented sections, explorative travellers have long sought out unrestored sections of the wall (such as at Huánghuā) for their more genuine appeal. The Chinese government periodically isolates such sections or slaps fines on visitors. The authorities argue that they are seeking to prevent damage to the unrestored wall by traipsing visitors, but they are also keen to direct tourist revenue towards restored sections.

The wall has suffered more from farmers pillaging its earthen core for use on the fields, and for its bountiful supply of shaped stone, stripped from the ramparts for use in road and building construction. A recent outcry over drunken summer raves and 'orgies' at

---

A TALL STORY

The myth that the Great Wall is visible with the naked eye from the moon was finally buried in 2003, when China's first astronaut Yang Liwei failed to spot the barrier from space. The wall can be seen from a low earth orbit, but so can many other objects of human construction, such as motorways and railways. Looked at from above, the relative width and uniform colour of large roads renders them more distinct than the Great Wall, a structure even less visible from the moon, where even individual continents are barely perceptible. The myth has been edited from Chinese textbooks, where it has cast its spell over generations of Chinese.

Jīnshānling has upped public concern over the fortification's sad decline.

When choosing a tour, it is essential to check that the tour goes to where you want to go. Great Wall tours are often combined with trips to the Ming Tombs (p174), so ask beforehand; if you don't want to visit the Ming Tombs, choose another tour.

Far more worrying, some tours make painful and expensive diversions to jade factories, gem exhibition halls and Chinese medicine centres. At the latter, tourists are herded off the bus and analysed by white-coated doctors, who diagnose ailments that can only be cured with high-priced Chinese remedies (supplied there and then). The tour organisers receive a commission from the jade showroom/medicine centre for every person they manage to funnel through, so you are simply lining other people's pockets. When booking a tour, check such scams and unnecessary diversions are not on the itinerary. As with most popular destinations in China, try to avoid going on the weekend.

Bādáling 八达岭

Most visitors encounter the Great Wall at **Bādáling** (Bādáling Chángchéng; Map p111; ☎ 6912 1338/1423/1520; admission Y45; ⏰ 6am-10pm summer, 7am-6pm winter), its most-photographed manifestation, 70km northwest of Běijīng. The scenery is raw and yields choice views of the wall snaking archetypally into the distance over undulating hills. Unless you visit during the bitterly cold days of winter, however, don't anticipate a one-to-one with the wall, and prepare for guard rails, a carnival of souvenir stalls and squads of tourists surging over the ramparts. A summer weekend trip reminds visitors that China has the world's largest population, so opt for a weekday excursion.

Two sections of wall trail off in opposite directions from the main entrance. The restored wall crawls for a distance before nobly disintegrating into ruins; unfortunately you cannot realistically explore these more authentic fragments. Cable cars exist for the weary (Y60 round trip).

The section of masonry at Bādálǐng was first built during the Ming dynasty (1368–1644), and was heavily restored in both the 1950s and the 1980s. Punctuated with *dílóu* (watchtowers), the 6m-wide wall is clad in brick, typical of the stonework employed by the Ming when they restored and expanded the fortification.

The admission fee also includes a 15-minute film about the Great Wall at the **Great Wall Circle Vision Theatre** (☼ 9am-5.45pm), a 360-degree amphitheatre, and the **China Great Wall Museum** (☼ 9am-4pm).

GETTING THERE & AWAY

Bus 919 (slow/fast Y5/10) leaves regularly (every 10 minutes) for Bādálǐng from the old gate of Deshengmen, about 500m east of the Jishuitan subway stop. The last bus leaves Bādálǐng for Běijīng at 6.30pm.

Convenient tour buses leave from the twin depots of the **Beijing Sightseeing Bus Centre** (Běijīng Lǚyóu Jísàn Zhōngxīn; Map pp118-19; ☎ 8353 1111) northeast and northwest of Qianmen alongside Tiananmen Sq. The main depot is the western station. Line C (Y80 return including entry to Great Wall; departures 6.30am to 10am) runs to Bādálǐng; Line A runs to Bādálǐng and the Ming Tombs (Y140 including all entrance tickets and meals; departures 6.30am to 10am).

Everyone else and his dog does trips to Bādálǐng, including **CITS** (☎ 6512 3075; www.cits .com.cn; 57 Dengshikou Dajie), the Beijing Tourist Information Center (p124) and hotels. Hotel tours can be convenient (and should avoid rip-off diversions), but avoid high-price excursions (up to Y300 per person). A taxi to the wall and back will cost a minimum of Y400 for an eight-hour hire with a maximum of four passengers.

Mùtiányù 慕田峪

Renowned for its Ming dynasty guard towers and stirring views, the 2250m-long granite section of wall at **Mùtiányù** (Map p111; admission Y35; ☼ 6.30am-6pm), 90km northeast of Běijīng in Huáiróu County, dates from Ming dynasty remains, built upon an earlier Northern Qi dynasty conception. It was developed as an alternative to Bādálǐng and is, in the balance, a less commercial experience despite motivated hawking and tourist clutter. The wall here similarly comes replete with a **cable car** (round trip Y50; ☼ 8.30am-4.30pm). October is the best month to visit, with the countryside drenched in autumn hues.

GETTING THERE & AWAY

From **Dongzhimen long-distance bus station** (Dōngzhímén Chángtú Qìchēzhàn; Map p122; ☎ 6467 4995) take either bus 916 or 980 (both Y8, one hour 40 minutes) to Huáiróu (怀柔), then change for a minbus to Mùtiányù (Y25).

The weekend Line A bus to Mùtiányù and Hongluo Temple (Hóngluó Sì) runs on Sundays and public holidays (Y110; price includes entrance ticket and return fare) between 6.30am and 8.30am from the **Beijing Sightseeing Bus Centre** (Běijīng Lǚyóu Jísàn Zhōngxīn; Map pp118-19; ☎ 8353 1111), northeast and northwest of Qianmen alongside Tiananmen Sq and also from outside the South Cathedral at Xuanwumen.

Jūyōngguān 居庸关

Rebuilt by the industrious Ming on its 5th-century remains, the wall at **Jūyōngguān** (Juyong Pass; Map p111; admission Y40; ☼ 6am-4pm) is the closest section of the Great Wall to town. Fifty kilometres northwest of Běijīng, the wall's authenticity has been restored out, but it's typically quiet and you can undertake the steep and somewhat strenuous circuit in under two hours.

GETTING THERE & AWAY

Jūyōngguān is on the road to Bādálǐng, so the public buses and numbered tour buses for Bādálǐng listed opposite will get you there. From the two depots of **Beijing Sightseeing Bus Centre** (Běijīng Lǚyóu Jísàn Zhōngxīn; Map pp118-19; ☎ 8353 1111), northeast and northwest of Qianmen alongside Tiananmen Sq, Line B buses take in both Jūyōngguān and Dìng Líng at the Ming Tombs (Y125 including entrance tickets; departures 6.30am to 10am).

(Continued on page 173)

JONATHAN SMITH

Summer Palace (p139), with Kunming Lake in the foreground, Běijīng

Forbidden City (p133), Běijīng

Guard near Mao Zedong portrait, Tiananmen Square (p124), Běijīng

GLENN BEANLAND

ANTONY GIBLIN

National Grand Theatre (p126), Běijīng

DENNIS COX / ALAMY

GREG ELMS

Peak Tram (p523) ascending Victoria Peak, Hong Kong

Star Ferry (p563) docking at Tsim Sha Tsui, Hong Kong

ANDREW BURKE

GRE

View of Central (p523) from Victoria Peak, Hong Kong

Incense coils at Man Mo Temple (p523), Hong Kong

GRE

Nanjing Rd (p251), Shànghǎi

GREG ELMS

The Bund (p251), Shànghǎi

GREG ELMS

Cafés and bicycles line Huaihai Rd in the former French Concession (p253), Shànghǎi

CHRIS MELLOR

Cargo ships on Huangpu River, Pudong New Area (p256), Shànghǎi

GREG ELMS

JULIET COOMBE

Woman selling potato cakes, Xī'ān (p420), Shaanxi

GREG ELMS

Head of a general, Army of Terracotta Warriors (p428), Shaanxi

Buddhist images in Da Ci'en Temple (p424), Xī'ān, Shaanxi

KRZYSZTOF DYDYNSKI

Miao worker, Déhāng (p511), Húnán

River scene, Déhāng (p511), Húnán

Riverside, Fènghuáng (p512), Húnán

Legend

- Line 1
- Line 2
- Line 13
- Batong Line
- Lines Under Construction
- Railway Line

Stations:

Capital Airport

Taipingzhuangbei, Taipingzhuang, Beiyuan, Wangjingxi, Guangximen, Liufang, Dongzhimen, Dongsishitiao, Chaoyangmen

Sihuidong, Sihui, Dawanglu, Guomao, Yonganli, Beijingzhan

Gaobeidian, Guangboxueyuan, Shuangqiao, Guanzhuang, Baliqiao, Tongzhoubeiyuan, Guoyuan, Jiukeshu, Liyuan, Linheli

Lishuiqiao, Lishuiqiaobei, Lishuiqiao, Dayangfang, Datun, Ganyangshu, Beituchengdonglu, Hepingxiqiao, Hepinglibei, Yonghegong, Beixinqiao, Zhangzizhonglu, Dongsi, Dengshikou, Dongdan, Jianguomen, Beijing Train Station, Ciqikou, Tiantandongmen, Puhuangyu, Liujiayao, Songjiazhuang

Lishuiqiao, Huoying, Huilongguan, Longze, Xierqi, Shangdi, Wudaokou, Zhichunlu, Dazhongsi

Olympic Area

Andingmen, Gulou Dajie, Jishuitan, Xizhimen

Tiananmen Xi, Tiananmen Dong, Wangfujing, Qianmen, Hepingmen, Xuanwumen, Majialou

Chang'anjie, Xidan, Fuxingmen, Chegongzhuang, Fuchengmen, Nanlishilu, Muxidi

Lunshouwuguan, Gongzhufen, Wansoulu, Wukesong, Yuquanlu, Babaoshan, Bajiaocun, Bajiaoyouleyuan, Pingguoyuan

Beijing North Train Station, Beijing West Train Station, Beijing Train Station, Hepingli Train Station, Wulu Train Station

Beishihe, Wanliu, Beigongmen

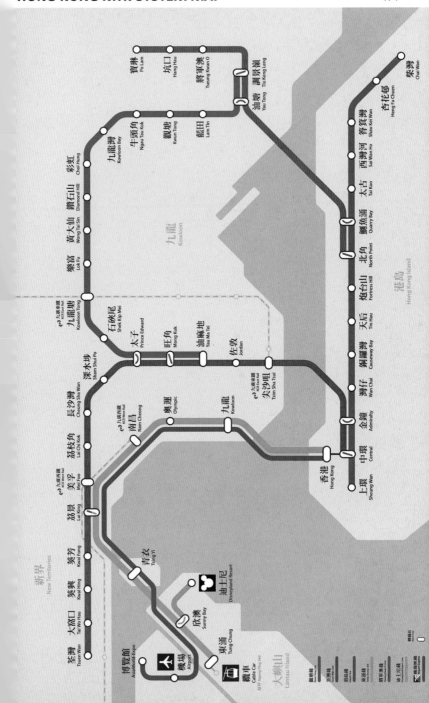

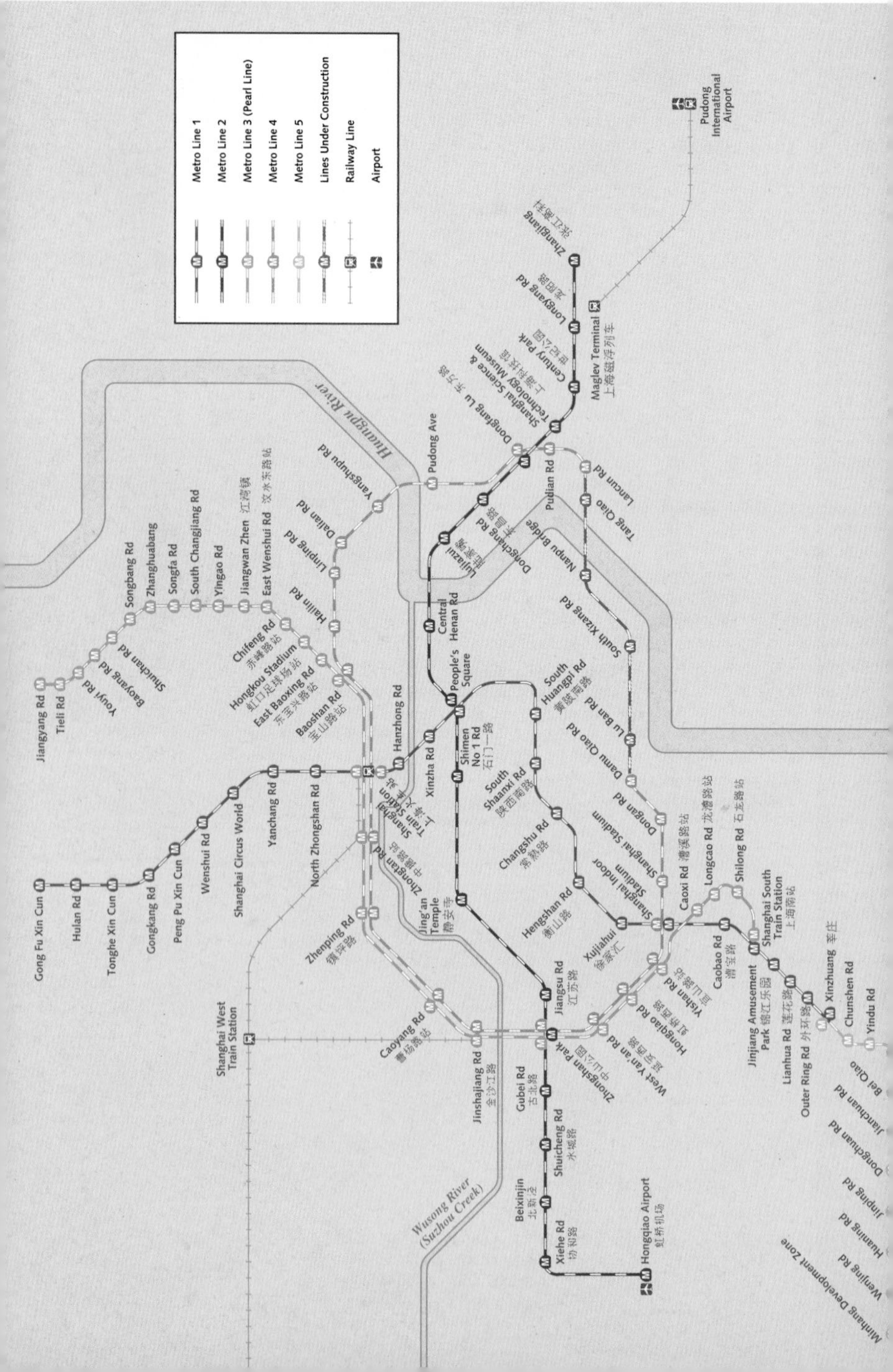

Metro Line 1
Metro Line 2
Metro Line 3 (Pearl Line)
Metro Line 4
Metro Line 5
Lines Under Construction
Railway Line
Airport
Pudong International Airport
Zhangjiang 张江高科
Longyang Rd 龙阳路
Maglev Terminal 上海磁浮列车
Century Park 世纪公园
Shanghai Science & Technology Museum 上海科技馆
Dongfang Lu 东方路
Huangpu River
Pudong Ave
Yangshupu Rd
Dalian Rd
Linping Rd
Hailin Rd
Lujiazui 陆家嘴
Dongchang Rd 东昌路
Pudian Rd
Lancun Rd
Tang Qiao
Nanpu Bridge
South Xizang Rd
Lu Ban Rd
Damu Qiao Rd
Dongan Rd
Shanghai Stadium 漕溪路站
Shanghai Indoor Stadium
Caoxi Rd 漕溪路站
Longcao Rd 龙漕路站
Shilong Rd 石龙路站
Shanghai South Train Station 上海南站
Caobao Rd 漕宝路
Jinjiang Amusement Park 锦江乐园
Lianhua Rd 莲花路
Outer Ring Rd 外环路
Xinzhuang 莘庄
Chunshen Rd
Yindu Rd
Bei Qiao
Jianchuan Rd
Dongchuan Rd
Jinping Rd
Huaning Rd
Wenjing Rd
Minhang Development Zone
Jiangyang Rd
Tieli Rd
Youyi Rd
Baoyang Rd
Shuichan Rd
Songbang Rd
Zhanghuabang
Songfa Rd
South Changjiang Rd
Yingao Rd
Jiangwan Zhen 江湾镇
East Wenshui Rd 汶水东路站
Chifeng Rd 赤峰路站
Hongkou Stadium 虹口足球场站
East Baoxing Rd 东宝兴路站
Baoshan Rd 宝山路站
Hanzhong Rd
Central Henan Rd
People's Square
Xinzha Rd
Shimen No 1 Rd 石门一路
South Huangpi Rd 黄陂南路
South Shaanxi Rd 陕西南路
Changshu Rd 常熟路
Hengshan Rd 衡山路
Xujiahui 徐家汇
Shanghai Train Station 上海火车站
Zhongshan Rd 中潭路站
Jing'an Temple 静安寺
Gong Fu Xin Cun
Hulan Rd
Tonghe Xin Cun
Gongkang Rd
Peng Pu Xin Cun
Wenshui Rd
Shanghai Circus World
Yanchang Rd
North Zhongshan Rd
Zhenping Rd 镇坪路
Caoyang Rd 曹杨路站
Shanghai West Train Station
Jinshajiang Rd 金沙江路
Jiangsu Rd 江苏路
Zhongshan Park 中山公园
West Yan'an Rd 延安西路
Hongqiao Rd 虹桥路
Yishan Rd 宜山路站
Gubei Rd 古北路
Shuicheng Rd 水城路
Beixinjin 北新泾
Xiehe Rd 协和路
Hongqiao Airport 虹桥机场
Wusong River (Suzhou Creek)

(Continued from page 164)

Sīmǎtái 司马台

In Mìyún County 110km northeast of Běijīng, the stirring remains at **Sīmǎtái** (Map p111; admission Y30; ✪ 8am-5pm) make for a more exhilarating Great Wall experience. Built during the reign of Ming dynasty emperor Hongwu, the 19km section is an invigorating stretch of watchtowers, precarious plunges and scrambling ascents.

This rugged section of wall can be heart-thumpingly steep and the scenery exhilarating, although the masonry has been scheduled for a makeover, which could pacify its wilder moments. The eastern section of wall at Sīmǎtái is the most treacherous, sporting 16 watchtowers and dizzyingly steep ascents that require free hands. Deemed too dangerous, the section beyond the 12th watchtower is currently inaccessible.

Sīmǎtái has some unusual features, such as 'obstacle-walls'. These are walls-within-walls used for defending against enemies who had already scaled the Great Wall. The cable car (round trip Y50) saves valuable time and is an alternative to a sprained ankle. Take strong shoes with a good grip. Unfazed by the dizzying terrain, hawkers make an unavoidable appearance.

GETTING THERE & AWAY
Take a minibus (Y10, 1¼ hours) to Mìyún (密云) or bus 980 (Y10) from **Dongzhimen long-distance bus station** (Dōngzhímén Chángtú Qìchēzhàn; Map p122; ✆ 6467 4995) and change to a minibus to Sīmǎtái or a taxi (round trip Y120).

The weekend Line D tour bus (Y95; price includes entrance ticket) runs to Sīmǎtái from the **Beijing Sightseeing Bus Centre** (Běijīng Lǚyóu Jísàn Zhōngxīn; Map pp118-19; ✆ 8353 1111), northeast and northwest of Qianmen alongside Tiananmen Sq and also from outside the South Cathedral at Xuanwumen. Buses depart on Fridays and Saturdays and public holidays between 6.30am and 8.30am.

Backpacker hotels often run morning minibus trips (Y60 to Y80, not including ticket). A taxi from Běijīng for the day costs about Y400.

Jīnshānlǐng 金山岭

The Great Wall at **Jīnshānlǐng** (Jīnshānlǐng Chángchéng; Map p111; admission Y40), near the town of Gǔběikǒu, has 24 watchtowers and remains relatively undeveloped. More significantly, it marks the starting point of a 10km hike to Sīmǎtái. The journey takes around four hours as the trail is steep and stony and parts of the wall have collapsed and are in a state of ruin, but it can be traversed without too much difficulty. Arriving at Sīmǎtái, however, you may have to buy another ticket.

You can do the walk in the opposite direction, but getting a ride back to Běijīng from Sīmǎtái is easier than from Jīnshānlǐng. Of course, getting a ride should be no problem if you've made arrangements with your driver to pick you up (and didn't pay in advance).

GETTING THERE & AWAY
From **Dongzhimen long-distance bus station** (Dōngzhímén Chángtú Qìchēzhàn; Map p122; ✆ 6467 4995), take a minibus (Y10, 1¼ hours) or bus 980 (Y10) to Mìyún (密云), change to a minibus to Gǔběikǒu (古北口), and get off at Bākèshíyíng (巴克什营; Y7). If you are heading to Chéngdé (in Héběi province), you will pass Jīnshānlǐng en route.

Huánghuā 黄花

A wilder wall experience close to Běijīng can be unearthed at **Huánghuā** (Huánghuā Chángchéng; Yellow Flower Fortress; Map p111), where the Great Wall clings in two sections to hillsides adjacent to a reservoir. Around 60km north of Běijīng, Huánghuā is a classic and well-preserved example of Ming defence, with high and wide ramparts, intact parapets and sturdy beacon towers. The wall here has been partially restored, but much original and overgrown brickwork – and rubble – remains. Note that the wall rears up into steep inclines in parts and sturdy hiking boots are recommended to cope with often hazardous surfaces.

It is said that Lord Cai masterminded this section, employing meticulous quality control. Each *cùn* (inch) of the masonry represented one labourer's whole day's work. When the Ministry of War got wind of the extravagance, Cai was beheaded for his efforts. In spite of the trauma, his decapitated body stood erect for three days before toppling. Years later, a general judged Lord Cai's wall to be exemplary and he was posthumously rehabilitated.

Accessed across the dam, the eastern section rises abruptly from a solitary watchtower. It's possible to make it all the way to the Mùtiányù section of the wall, but it'll take you a few days and some hard clambering (pack a sleeping bag). Locals may make occasional appearances to levy ticket fees of one or two *kuài* to traverse sections of wall; these are unofficial ticket charges and some travellers have reported being threatened after refusing to pay.

The section immediately to the west rises over the hill in a trail of rubble so you'll have to clamber up the hillside from the south. Alternatively, walk south and take the first turning (about 500m down) on the right, walk through the village, keep going until the river bends to the right and take the right fork following the river. Keep bearing right all the way (you'll pass fading Cultural Revolution Chinese characters on a corner that proclaim 'Long Live Chairman Mao' and just around the corner 'The Red Heart Faces the Communist Party'). Soon you'll see a watchtower ahead – the path leads up to it. The whole jaunt should take 45 minutes, and you can continue along the wall. Be warned that the wall here is narrow and crumbling, so don't carry on unless you feel confident.

Several places have sprung up offering beds. The shack at the entrance to the eastern section of the wall, **Xiaohong's Shop** (☎ 6165 1393/2350; damatthewall@hotmail.com) can get you a simple bed for as little as Y10 and you can get something to eat here as well. **Jīntáng Shānzhuāng** (☎ 6165 1134; d Y348) is a more upmarket, resort-style establishment overlooking the reservoir, north of Xiaohong's Shop.

GETTING THERE & AWAY
From the **Dongzhimen long-distance bus station** (Dōngzhímén Chángtú Qìchēzhàn; Map p122; ☎ 6467 4995) take bus 961 (Y8, two hours, two morning and afternoon departures) to Huánghuā. The last bus back to Běijīng is at 2.30pm. Ask for Huánghuāchéng (黄花城) and don't get off at the smaller Huánghuāzhèn by mistake. Buses 916 (Y8, one hour; air-con) and 936 (Y6, one hour) also run from Dōngzhímén long-distance bus station to Huáiróu (怀柔), departing frequently between 5.30am and 6.30pm. From Huáiróu you can take a minibus directly to Huánghuā (Y4, 40 minutes) or hire a minicab from Huáiróu to Huánghuā (Y60 round trip).

MING TOMBS 十三陵
The **Ming Tombs** (Shísān Líng; Map p111; admission per tomb; ⏰ 8am-5.30pm), about 50km northwest of Běijīng, are the final resting place of 13 of the 16 Ming emperors. The Confucian layout and design may intoxicate more erudite visitors, but some find the necropolis lifeless and ho-hum. Imperial shrines lack the vibrancy and

colour of Buddhist or Taoist temples, and their motifs can be bewilderingly inscrutable.

The Ming Tombs follow a standard layout for imperial tomb design. The plan typically consists of a main gate *(líng mén)* leading to the first of a series of courtyards and the main hall, the **Hall of Eminent Favours** (灵恩殿; Líng'ēn Diàn). Beyond lie further gates or archways, leading to the **Soul Tower** (明楼; Míng Lóu), behind which rises the burial mound.

Three tombs (open 8am to 5pm) have been opened up to the public: Cháng Líng, Dìng Líng and Zhāo Líng.

Cháng Líng (长陵; admission Y45), burial place of the emperor Yongle, is the most impressive, with its series of magnificent halls lying beyond its yellow-tiled gate. Seated upon a three-tiered marble terrace, the most notable structure is the Hall of Eminent Favours, containing a recent statue of Yongle and a breathtaking interior with vast *nanmu* (cedarwood) columns. The pine-covered burial mound at the rear of the complex is yet to be excavated and is not open to the public.

Dìng Líng (定陵; admission incl museum Y60), the burial place of the emperor Wanli, contains a series of subterranean interlocking vaults and the remains of the various gates and halls of the complex. Excavated in the late 1950s, this tomb is of more interest to some visitors as you are allowed to descend into the underground vault. Accessing the vault down the steps, visitors are confronted by the simply vast marble self-locking doors that sealed the chamber after it was vacated. The tomb is also the site of the absorbing **Ming Tombs Museum** (Shísān Líng Bówùguǎn; admission Y20).

Zhāo Líng (昭陵; admission Y30), the resting place of the 13th Ming emperor Longqing, follows an orthodox layout and is a tranquil alternative if you find the other tombs too busy.

The road leading up to the tombs is the 7km **Spirit Way** (神道; Shéndào; admission Y20; ⏰ 7am-8pm). Commencing with a triumphal arch, the path enters the Great Palace Gate, where officials once had to dismount, and passes a giant *bìxì* (a mythical tortoise-dragon-like animal), which bears the largest stele in China. A magnificent guard of 12 sets of stone animals and officials ensues.

Getting There & Away
Tour buses usually combine visits to one of the Ming Tombs with trips to the Great Wall at Bādálǐng (see p164 for information about

buses to and from Bādálǐng). Also see the Jūyōngguān (p164) entry for details of tour buses that include visits to Dìng Líng.

To go independently, take bus 345 (branch line, 支线; zhīxiàn) from Deshengmen (500m east of Jishuitan subway station) to Chāngpíng (昌平; Y6, one hour). Get off at the Chāngpíng Dōngguān stop and change to bus 314 for the tombs. Alternatively, take the standard bus 345 to Chāngpíng and then take a taxi (Y20, 10 minutes) to the tombs.

EASTERN QING TOMBS 清东陵

The area of the **Eastern Qing Tombs** (Qīng Dōng Líng; Map p111; admission Y55; ☼ 8am-5pm), 125km northeast of Běijīng, could be called Death Valley, housing as it does five emperors, 14 empresses and 136 imperial consorts. In the mountains ringing the valley are buried princes, dukes, imperial nurses and others.

A spirit way is a principle feature here, as at the Ming tombs. The emperors buried here are: Qianlong (裕陵; Yù Líng), Kangxi (景陵; Jǐng Líng), Shunzhi (孝陵; Xiào Líng), Xianfeng (定陵; Dìng Líng) and Tongzhi (惠陵; Huì Líng). Emperor Qianlong (1711–99) started preparations when he was 30, and by the time he was 88 he had used up 90 tonnes of his silver. His resting place covers half a square kilometre. Some of the beamless stone chambers are decorated with Tibetan and Sanskrit sutras, and the doors bear bas-relief Bodhisattvas. All the emperors' tombs are open to visitors apart from Huì Líng's.

Empress Dowager Cixi also got a head start. Her tomb, Dìng Dōng Líng (定东陵), was completed some three decades before her death and also underwent considerable restoration before she was finally laid to rest. It lies alongside the tomb of Empress Cian. The phoenix (symbol of the empress) appears above that of the dragon (the emperor's symbol) in the artwork at the front of Cixi's tomb – not side by side as on other tombs. Cixi's and Qianlong's tombs were plundered in the 1920s.

Getting There & Away

The easiest way to reach the Eastern Qing Tombs is on the weekend Line E tour bus (Y145; price includes entrance ticket), which runs on Saturdays and public holidays between 6.30am and 8.30am from the **Beijing Sightseeing Bus Centre** (Běijīng Lǚyóu Jísàn Zhōngxīn; Map pp118-19; ☎ 8353 1111), northeast and northwest of Qianmen alongside Tiananmen Sq

and also from outside the South Cathedral at Xuanwumen. Pedicabs are available at the tombs (Y15).

A taxi from Běijīng should cost around Y350 for the day trip to the tombs.

TANZHE TEMPLE 潭柘寺

Forty-five kilometres west of Běijīng, **Tanzhe Temple** (Tánzhè Sì; Map p111; admission Y35; ☼ 8.30am-6pm) is the largest of all of Běijīng's temples. Delightfully climbing the hills amid trees, the temple has a history that extends way back to the 3rd century, although most of what you see is of far more recent construction. The temple grounds are overhung with towering cypress and pine trees; many are so old that their gangly limbs are supported by metal props.

The highlight of a trip to the temple is the small **Talin Temple** (Tǎlín Sì), by the forecourt where you disembark the bus, with its collection of stupas (reliquaries for the cremated remains of important monks) reminiscent of the Shaolin Temple. You can tour them while waiting for the return bus. An excellent time to visit Tanzhe Temple is around mid-April, when the magnolias are in bloom.

Getting There & Away

You can take the weekend Line L tour bus (Y115), which runs on Saturdays and public holidays between 6.30am and 8.30am from the **Beijing Sightseeing Bus Centre** (Běijīng Lǚyóu Jísàn Zhōngxīn; Map pp118-19; ☎ 8353 1111), northeast and northwest of Qianmen alongside Tiananmen Sq and also from outside the South Cathedral at Xuanwumen.

Alternatively, you can take the subway to the Pingguoyuan stop and take bus 931 (Y3) to the last stop for Tanzhe Temple (don't take the bus 931 branch line – 支线, zhīxiàn – however).

JIETAI TEMPLE 戒台寺

About 10km southeast of Tanzhe Temple is this smaller, but more engaging **temple** (Jiètái Sì; Map p111; admission Y35; ☼ 8am-6pm). Jietai (Ordination Terrace) Temple was built around AD 622 during the Tang dynasty, with major modifications made during the Ming dynasty.

The main complex is dotted with ancient pine trees; the **Nine Dragon Pine** is claimed to be over 1300 years old, while the **Embracing Pagoda Pine** does just what it says.

Getting There & Away

Take the weekend Line L tour bus (Y115), which runs on Saturdays and public holidays between 6.30am and 8.30am from the **Beijing Sightseeing Bus Centre** (Běijīng Lǚyóu Jísàn Zhōngxīn; Map pp118-19; ☎ 8353 1111), northeast and northwest of Qianmen alongside Tiananmen Sq and also from outside the South Cathedral at Xuanwumen. Alternatively, take the subway to the Pingguoyuan stop and take bus 931 (Y3). This bus stops near Jietai Temple, which is a 10-minute walk uphill from the bus stop.

MARCO POLO BRIDGE 卢沟桥

Described by the great traveller himself, this 266m-long grey marble **bridge** (Lúgōu Qiáo; Map pp116-17; ☎ 8389 3919; 88 Lugouqiaochengnei Xijie; admission Y15; ⊗ 8am-5pm) is host to 485 carved stone lions. Each animal is different, with the smallest only a few centimetres high, and legend maintains that they move around during the night.

Dating from 1189, the stone bridge is Běijīng's oldest (but is a composite of different eras; it was widened in 1969), and spans the Yongding River (永定河) near the small walled town of Wǎnpíng (宛平城), just southwest of Běijīng.

Despite the praises of Marco Polo and Emperor Qianlong, the bridge wouldn't have rated more than a footnote in Chinese history were it not for the famed Marco Polo Bridge Incident, which ignited a full-scale war with Japan. On 7 July 1937, Japanese troops illegally occupied a railway junction outside Wǎnpíng. Japanese and Chinese soldiers started shooting, and that gave Japan enough of an excuse to attack and occupy Běijīng.

The **Memorial Hall of the War of Resistance Against Japan** (Map pp116–17) is a gory look back at Japan's occupation of China, but the lack of English captions renders much of its information meaningless. Also on the site

are the Wanping Castle, Daiwang Temple and a hotel.

Getting There & Away

Take bus 6 from the north gate of Temple of Heaven Park to the last stop at Liuli Bridge (六里桥; Liúlí Qiáo) and then either bus 339 or 309 to Lúgōu Xīnqiáo (卢沟新桥); the bridge is just ahead.

CHUĀNDĪXIÀ 川底下

Nestled in a valley 90km west of Běijīng and overlooked by towering peaks is **Chuāndīxià** (Map p111; admission Y20), a gorgeous cluster of historic courtyard homes and old-world charm. The backdrop is lovely: terraced orchards and fields, with ancient houses and alleyways rising up the hillside.

Chuāndīxià is also a museum of **Maoist graffiti and slogans**, especially up the incline among the better-preserved houses. Despite their impressive revolutionary credentials, Chuāndīxià's residents have sensed the unmistakable whiff of the tourist dollar on the north-China breeze, and T-shirt vendors have appeared.

Two hours is more than enough to wander around the village as it's not big. A number of houses also sell local produce, including *fēngmì* (honey) and *hétao* (walnuts).

Getting There & Away

If travelling by public transport, bank on taking well over three hours from central Běijīng. Take bus 929 (make sure it's the branch line, or *zhīxiàn* 支线, not the regular bus) from the bus stop at the right of Pingguoyuan subway station to Zhāitáng (斋堂; Y7, two hours), then hire a taxi van (Y10). If going in the off season, arrange with the taxi van to return to pick you up. The last bus returns from Zhāitáng to Pingguoyuan at 4.20pm. If you miss the last bus, a taxi will cost around Y80 to Pingguoyuan.

Tiānjīn 天津

Like Běijīng, Shànghǎi and Chóngqìng, Tiānjīn belongs to no province – it's a special municipality, with considerable autonomy. Its history as a foreign concession, large port and European architecture suggest muted echoes of Shànghǎi, but Tiānjīn is often overlooked by travellers charging to Běijīng.

Tiānjīn is proud of its impressive concession-era architecture, which lends the city a kind of shabby nobility. In the run-up to the 2008 Olympics, the city is sprucing itself up and many notable buildings have plaques detailing their histories.

Not to be upstaged by big brother Běijīng, Tiānjīn has joined in the frenzied sport of demolition and road-widening, levelling huge swathes of the city. Its modest subway system has been modernised and extended; dramatic new bridges span the Hai River; and modern architecture pokes into the stark skies. But the city still exemplifies the disparities of modern China, with smart office complexes overlooking dilapidated courtyards from which spill chickens and geese.

This coincides with a drought that surpasses even Běijīng's famed thirst; Tiānjīn's per capita water supplies are reportedly worse than Saudi Arabia's. As a result, dust invades every nook and cranny and shiny new buildings are rapidly coated in a sprinkling of dirt.

Tiānjīn remains a long way from cosmopolitanism: clutching throngs of taxi drivers mill around the train station exit and locals sit around, waiting for something to happen. Accommodation tends to be expensive, but you can travel down from Běijīng in less than 1½ hours so a day-trip could suffice.

HIGHLIGHTS

- Take stock of central Tiānjīn's grand **treaty port architecture** (p179)
- Explore **Ancient Culture Street** (p181) and delve into the Tianhou Temple
- Rummage for knick-knacks in Tiānjīn's **Antique Market** (p181)
- Join worshippers seeking guidance at the **Monastery of Deep Compassion** (p181), Tiānjīn's leading Buddhist shrine
- Trek out of town to the historic **Shi Family Courtyard** (p184)

Shi Family Courtyard ★   ★ Tiānjīn

■ AREA CODE: ☎022 | ■ POPULATION: 42.1 MILLION

HISTORY

Historically, Tiānjīn's fortunes have always been linked to those of Běijīng. When the Mongols established Běijīng as the capital in the 13th century, Tiānjīn rose to prominence as a grain-storage point. With the Grand Canal fully functional as far as Běijīng, Tiānjīn was at the intersection of both inland and port navigation routes. By the 15th century, the town had become a walled garrison.

The British and French settled in, and were joined by the Japanese, Germans, Austro-Hungarians, Italians and Belgians between 1895 and 1900. Each concession was a self-contained world with its own prison, school, barracks and hospital.

This life was disrupted only in 1870 when locals attacked a French-run orphanage and killed, among others, 10 nuns – the Chinese thought the children were being kidnapped to be eaten (confusion over the meaning of the sacrament and the consumption of the body and blood of Christ). Thirty years later, during the Boxer Rebellion, the foreign powers levelled the walls of the old Chinese city.

The notorious Tángshān earthquake of 28 July 1976 registered 8.2 on the Richter scale and killed nearly 24,000 people in the Tiānjīn area in the same year that Mao also shook China by dying (a synchronicity of events hardly lost on the Chinese). The city was badly rocked, but escaped the devastation

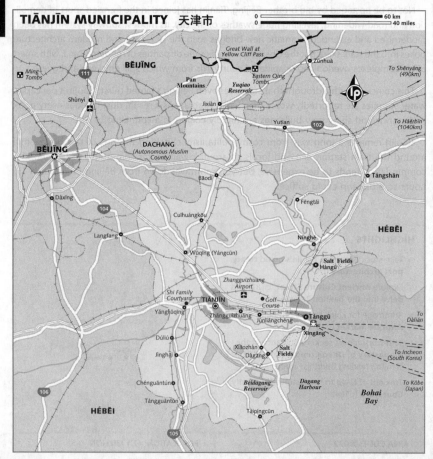

that virtually obliterated nearby Tángshān, where an estimated 240,000 residents died.

ORIENTATION
Tiānjīn is a large municipality, most of which is rural. Sights and hotels are largely dispersed around Tiānjīn, making navigation tiring, although the central district is compact. The main train station is north of the Hai River, which divides central Tiānjīn into two. South of the station were the foreign concessions, across Jiefang Bridge, and on and around Jiefang Lu.

Maps
Maps of Tiānjīn can be bought from map sellers around the train station.

INFORMATION
Bookshops
Xinhua Bookshop (127 Binjiang Dao)

Internet Access 网吧
Internet cafés in Tiānjīn operate inconveniently on the fringes of society.
Yadu Internet Café (Yàdū Wǎngbā; Yanhe Lu; per hr Y2; ☼ 24hr) Thirty metres north of the Rainbow Bar, over the river just east off Zijinshan Lu.

Medical Services
Zhongxin Pharmacy (Zhōngxīn Yàoyè; 181 Binjiang Dao; ☼ 24hr)

Money
ATMs (accepting Cirrus, Visa, MasterCard and Plus) can be found in the New World Astor Hotel, Tianjin Holiday Inn, Sheraton Hotel and around town.
Bank of China (Zhōngguó Yínháng; 80-82 Jiefang Beilu) ATM accepting MasterCard, Visa, Cirrus and Plus.
HSBC (Huìfēng Yínháng; Ocean Hotel, 5 Yuanyang Guangchang)
International Building (Guójì Dàshà; 75 Nanjing Lu) ATM accepting Cirrus, Plus, MasterCard and Visa cards on the ground floor.

Post
Dongzhan post office (Dōngzhàn yóujú; ☼ 8.30am-6.30pm) Has Express Mail Service and poste restante; next to the main train station.
Post office (yóujú; 153 Jiefang Beilu)

Public Security Bureau
PSB/Exit-Entry Administration Bureau (Gōngānjú/Chūrùjìng Guǎnlǐjú; ☎ 2445 8825; 19 Shouan Jie)

Tourist Information & Travel Agencies
China International Travel Service (CITS; Zhōngguó Guójì Lǚxíngshè; ☎ 2810 9988; www.tj-cits.com; 22 Youyi Lu; ☼ 8.30am-5pm Mon-Fri)
Tianjin Tourism Bureau (☎ 2835 4860; fax 2835 2324; 22 Youyi Lu; ☼ 8.30am-5pm) Next door to CITS.

SIGHTS
Treaty Port Architecture
公约港建筑
Central Tiānjīn is a museum of European architecture from the turn of the 20th century, stuffed with concession-era details: stately banks, churches, old warehouses and buildings with lobbies revealing old wooden staircases leading up into dark European interiors.

Walking north along **Jiefang Beilu**, at No 108 is the decaying nobility and wrought-iron balconies of the former **Kincheng Bank** (Jīnchéng Yínháng; built in 1937). Standing a little bit further north on the corner is the old former site of the **Huabi Bank**, dating from the 1920s. On the other side of Jiefang Beilu, at No 157, is the former address of **Jardine Matheson & Co** (Yíhé Yángháng), decorated with huge pillars. North on the next corner at No 153 is the former **Chartered Bank of India, Australia and China** (Màijiālì Yínháng), a colossal and overblown edifice with vast pillars, now serving as a post office. The grandiose and huge former **Citibank Building** (First National City Bank of New York; Huāqí Yínháng) across the road at No 90 dates from 1918; now it's the Agricultural Bank of China. Pop in and have a peek at the interior during banking hours. The former **Hong Kong & Shanghai Bank Building** (Huìfēng Yínháng), a pompous creation further along at No 82 now houses the Bank of China, opposite the old address of the **Sino-Russian Bank** (Huàè Dàoshèng Yínháng) dating from 1895. Next door to No 82 is the former **Yokohama Specie Bank Ltd** (Héngbīn Zhèngjīn Yínháng) dating from 1926 and now also a Bank of China. Across the way on the corner is the old address of the monumental **Sino-French Industrial and Commercial Bank** (Zhōngfǎ Gōngshāng Yínháng), dating from 1932. The **Former Tientsin (Tianjin) Post Office** can be found across the way, while around the corner on Chengde Dao is the former **French Municipal Administration Council Building** (built in 1924), now a library.

Erected by the French in 1917, the **Catholic church** (Xīkāi Tiānzhǔ Jiàotáng; Binjiang Dao; ☼ 5.30am-4.30pm) is the largest church in Tiānjīn.

lonelyplanet.com

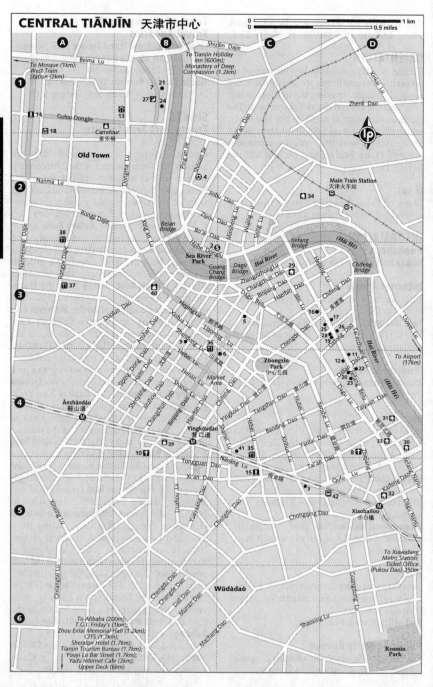

CENTRAL TIĀNJĪN 天津市中心

The area called **Wǔdàdaò** (五大道; Five Large Roads) is rich in European-style villas and the former residences of the well-to-do of the early 20th century. Consisting of five roads in the south of the city – Machang Dao, Changde Dao, Munan Dao, Dali Dao and Chengdu Dao – the streetscapes are European, lined with charming houses dating from the 1930s.

Antique Market 古玩市场

Vendors sprawl in every direction along the *hútòng* (narrow alleyways) of the **Antique Market** (Gǔwán Shìchǎng; cnr Jinzhou Dao & Shandong Lu; 🕙 7.30am-3pm Sat & Sun). Sift through its stamps, silverware, porcelain, clocks, Mao iconography and Cultural Revolution memorabilia. The market is best on Sundays, but die-hard vendors set up shop during the week.

Ancient Culture Street 古文化街

Recently expanded, spruced up and its stall-holders housed inside reconstructed, faux *ye olde* Tiānjīn buildings, **Ancient Culture Street** (Gǔwénhuà Jiē) is stuffed with vendors flogging Chinese calligraphy, paintings, tea sets, paper cuts, clay figurines and chops. It's now a full-on commercial tourist bonanza with fake *hútòng* styling and goods from all over China. A **tourist centre** (shut at the time of writing) can be found in the old **theatre** (戏楼; *xìlóu*).

On the western side of the street is the fascinating **Tianhou Temple** (Tiānhòu Gōng; admission Y3; 🕙 8.30am-4.30pm). Tianhou (Heaven Queen), goddess of the sea, is also known as Mazu and Niangniang. The main hall is the Niangniang Palace, with its effigy of Tianhou in a glass case, flanked by ferocious-looking weapons and attendant monsters. Also incorporated into the street is the **Jade Emperor Pavilion** (玉皇阁; Yùhuáng Gé), an ancient solitary twin-eaved hall.

Monastery of Deep Compassion 大悲禅院

The **Monastery of Deep Compassion** (Dàbēichán Yuàn; ☎ 2626 1769; 40 Tianwei Lu; admission Y4; 🕙 9am-4.30pm) is Tiānjīn's most important Buddhist temple. Worshippers congregate outside the **Shijiabao Hall** (Shìjiābǎo Diàn), which houses a large, central statue of Sakyamuni (Buddha) flanked by 18 *luóhàn* (Buddhist monks). The next large hall contains a huge and golden multi-armed statue of Guanyin, whose eyes follow you around the hall. The road leading up to the temple is an extraordinary market of religious paraphernalia, including prayer mats, books, Buddhist rosaries, talismans, statues, incense and gifts for Buddha.

Old Town 老城区

Originally enclosed by a wall, the old town is easily identified as a rectangle whose

TIĀNJĪN

boundaries are roughly Beima Lu (North Horse), Nanma Lu (South Horse), Xima Lu (West Horse) and Dongma Lu (East Horse). At the old town's centre rises the restored **Drum Tower** (Gǔ Lóu; Chengxiang Zhonglu; admission Y10; ☽ 9am-4.30pm). Decorated with *páilou* (decorative archways), the pedestrianised shopping street north of the Drum Tower is excellent for calligraphy brushes, snuff bottles, fans, silk, ceramics, jade, taichi swords, chops and jewellery. Near the Drum Tower is the **Guangdong Guild Hall** (Guǎngdōng Huì Guǎn; ☎ 2727 3443; 31 Nanmenli Dajie; ☽ 9am-4pm Tue-Sun), built in 1907 and also known as the Museum of Opera. A Ming dynasty relic, it's worth poking around the **Confucius Temple** (Wén Miào; ☎ 2727 2812; 1 Dongmennei Dajie; admission Y8; ☽ 9am-4.30pm Tue-Sun) for its daily antiques market (Wénmiào Gǔwán Chéng) selling piles of books, propaganda posters and pamphlets from the Cultural Revolution (genuine posters cost between Y30 and Y100) – weekends are busiest.

Mosque 清真寺

Chinese in style, this large **mosque** (Qīngzhēnsì; 6 Dasi Qian) is an active place of worship. Not officially open to the public unless you're Muslim, you may not be allowed in (although ensure you're suitably attired). The area surrounding the mosque is an intriguing maze of *hútòng*.

Zhou Enlai Memorial Hall
周恩来纪念馆

Former Chinese premier Zhou Enlai grew up in Shàoxīng (p325), Zhèjiāng province, but attended school in Tiānjīn, so his classroom desk and schoolbooks are enshrined at this **memorial hall** (Zhōu Ēnlái Jìniànguǎn; ☎ 2352 9257; 1 Shuishang Gongyuan Beilu; admission Y10; ☽ 8.30am-5pm) near Shuishang Park (Shuǐshàng Gōngyuán).

SLEEPING

A largely unappealing choice of accommodation heightens temptations to make Tiānjīn a day trip from Běijīng. Expect discounts in all but the cheapest hotels, but prepare for an additional 15% service charge for hotels in the midrange and up bracket.

Budget

Xinlong Hotel (Xīnlóng Jiǔdiàn; ☎ 6053 2888; fax 6053 2999; Longmen Dasha, Tianjin Zhan; 天津站龙门大厦内; d Y168-198; ☒) Rooms at this hotel right by the train station are pleasantly decorated, comfort-

able and commodious, with kettle, mini-bar and an overall sense of being well-tended.

Home Inn (Rújiā; ☎ 5899 6888; 32 Binjiang Dao; 滨江道32号; d Y179-199; ☒) Friendly staff and a modern attitude make this new hotel a great choice on the south side of Jiefang Bridge. Rooms are decked out with plastic wood flooring, water cooler, generic artwork and sharp colours, and have bright, well-scrubbed shower rooms. Free broadband; ground floor restaurant.

Midrange

Tianjin First Hotel (Tiānjīn Dìyī Fàndiàn; ☎ 2330 9988; fax 2312 3000; 158 Jiefang Beilu; 解放北路158号; r/ste Y664/913; ☒) There's more than a whiff of under-investment about this historic place and the noisy water feature and loud pine-wood panelling in the lobby jar with its attempts at Old-World charm. Good discounts.

Top End

Renaissance Tianjin Hotel (Bīnjiāng Wànlì Jiǔdiàn; ☎ 2302 6888; www.renaissancehotels.com; 105 Jianshe Lu; 建设路105号; d Y805; ☒ ☒) Despite the weird-looking portico with overblown white pillars, this is an elegant hotel with smartly furnished, broadband-equipped and fresh rooms (with smallish bathrooms), 24-hour pool plus an excellent and crisp fitness centre.

Hyatt Regency (Kǎiyuè Fàndiàn; ☎ 2330 1234; www .hyatt.com; 219 Jiefang Beilu; 解放北路219号; d Y980; ☒) The four-star Hyatt is a relaxed and smart hotel with substantial gloss and a great location. Lift attendants are dapper, staff is polite, but standard rooms have rather scuffed furniture and bathtubs are cramped.

Sheraton Hotel (Xǐláidēng Dàjiǔdiàn; ☎ 2334 3388; www.sheraton.com; Zijinshan Lu; 紫金山路; d incl breakfast Y1298; ☒) An excellent hotel with monthly promotions that make a stay here affordable even to those on a modest budget.

EATING

Gǒubùlǐ (☎ 2730 2540; 77 Shandong Lu; set menu Y13-18) Located between Changchun Dao and Binjiang Dao, this is the king of dumpling shops with a century-old history. The house speciality is *bāozi* (steamed dough bun), filled with high-grade pork, spices and gravy. There are numerous branches around town.

Little Sheep (Xiǎo Féiyáng; ☎ 2730 8318; Rongye Dajie; meals Y50) Perfect for expelling the miserable cold of a Tiānjīn winter and bringing colour to your cheeks, herd around a steaming Sìchuān or Mongolian hotpot and order up hearty plates of lamb (羊肉片; *yángròupiàn*), slabs of chilly bean curd (豆腐; *dòufu*), crispy clumps of bean shoots (豆苗; *dòumiáo*), Chinese cabbage (白菜; *báicài*) and lashings of beer. Four branches in town.

T.G.I. Friday's (Xīngyīwǔ Cāntīng; ☎ 2300 5555/5656; Tàidá Guójì Huìguǎn Bldg, 7 Fukang Lu; meals from Y100) With all the usual props, salads, burgers, pasta, steaks, chicken and seafood dishes, T.G.I.'s is a handy expat bolthole.

ENTERTAINMENT

Besides the following recommendations, try to score a copy of the magazine *Jin*, which has listings of restaurants, bars and cultural events in town. A useful expat community website is www.tianjinexpats.net.

Alibaba (Ālǐbābā; ☎ 2351 3976; Tongan Dao, Weihuali Xiaoqu, 4 Tongan Nanli; bottle of Qingdao Y8; 🕙 11am-1pm) A loyal student crowd packs onto the sofas of easy-going and scruffy Alibaba's, tucked away behind an anonymous wooden door south off Tongan Dao. Walk down Tongan Nanli (同安南里) and it's around four buildings down on the right.

Upper Deck (Èrlóu Jiǔbā; ☎ 8836 9177; 107 Meijiang Dao; draught beer Y25, brunch adult/child Y65/35; 🕙 11am-11pm) Loud, brash and popular with the American expat crowd hungry for burgers and draught *píjiǔ*, this hospitable sports bar runs enthusiastically to table-football, a kiddies' play area, a pool, a library, good Sunday brunches, jam nights and live blues, jazz and rock.

Making a neon splash in the centre of town, the Youyilu Bar Street (友谊路风情酒吧街; Yǒuyìlù Fēngqíng Jiǔbājiē) is dotted with karaoke parlours and bars, including **Western Heaven** (Xībù Tiāntáng; ☎ 2837 1533; 🕙 7pm-2am), where you can hide away in the dark corners of its all-wood interior, play darts or nod off to tame sounds from live music acts.

GETTING THERE & AWAY
Air

Tiānjīn's Binhai International Airport (Tiānjīn Bīnhǎi Guójì Jīchǎng; ☎ 2490 2950) is 15km east of the city centre.

Tickets can be bought from CITS and at the following.

All Nippon Airways (Quánrì Kōng; ☎ 2339 6688; 1st fl, Hyatt Regency, 219 Jiefang Beilu)
CAAC (☎ 2330 1543, 8331 1666; 103 Nanjing Lu)
JAL (☎ 2313 9766; International Bldg, 75 Nanjing Lu)
Korean Air (Dàhán Hángkōng; ☎ 2399 0088; International Bldg, 75 Nanjing Lu)

Tianjin Air-Sales Agency (☎ 2330 3480; Room 101, International Bldg, 75 Nanjing Lu) Can book flights on most airlines.

Boat

Tiānjīn's harbour is Tánggū, 50km (30 minutes by train or one hour by bus) from Tiānjīn. See p184 for details of arriving and departing by boat.

Bus

Convenient express buses to Běijīng (Y20, 1½ hours, 6am to 6pm) depart hourly from Tiānjīn's main train station. Scads of other buses depart from here to other destinations around China, including Dàlián (Y150, sleeper) and Qīngdǎo (Y150). A shared taxi to Běijīng from the main train station will cost around Y50 per person. Regular buses to Zhaogongkou bus station in Běijīng (p159; Y30, 6.30am to 6.30pm) also run from the **Liuyisan Lu bus station** (☎ 2311 2278; Liùyīsān Lù Qìchēzhàn) off Nanjing Lu. In Běijīng, Tiānjīn-bound buses (Y30, 1½ hours, every 30 minutes) run from the Zhaogongkou bus station (p159), the Sihui bus station (p159; Y23, every hour) or the Bawangfen bus station (p159; Y31, regularly).

Train

Tiānjīn has three train stations: main, north and west. Most trains leave from the **main train station** (Tiānjīn Zhàn; ☎ 6053 6053). If you have to alight at the **west train station** (☎ 2618 2662), bus 24, which runs 24 hours, will take you to the main train station.

A major north–south train junction, Tiānjīn has frequent trains to Běijīng (Y25 to Y35), extensive links with the northeastern provinces, and lines southwards to Ānyáng (hard seat/sleeper Y92/170), Jǐ'nán (hard seat/sleeper Y40/Y88), Nánjīng (hard seat/sleeper Y137/249), Qīngdǎo (hard seat/sleeper Y78/156), Shànghǎi (hard sleeper Y301), Shíjiāzhuāng (hard seat/sleeper Y55/139), Zhèngzhōu (hard seat/sleeper Y98/184) and other cities.

GETTING AROUND
To/From the Airport

Taxis ask for Y40 to Y50 to the airport from the city centre. Minibuses for Běijīng's Capital Airport leave from the CAAC ticket office every 30 minutes from 4am to 5.30pm (Y70, 2½ hours); from Běijīng Capital Airport to Tiānjīn, buses run from 7am to 10.30pm.

TIĀNJĪN

Bus

Key local transport junctions are the areas around the three train stations. Bus 24 runs between the main and west stations 24 hours a day. Bus 8 starts at the main train station then zigzags down to the southwest of town. With the exception of bus 24, buses run from 5am to 11pm.

Subway

After extensions and upgrades, including an extension of Line 1, the subway (*dìtiě*) has reopened. There are several other lines in the planning stages, with an ambitious plan to have seven lines in operation by 2010. A light rail (Metro Line 9) connects Tiānjīn with the port of Tánggū (right).

Taxi

A pestilence of *xiali* taxis and *sānlúnchē* (motor tricycles) swarms along Tiānjīn's streets. For standard taxis, flag fall is Y8 for the first 3km, then Y1.50 per kilometre thereafter.

AROUND TIĀNJĪN

SHI FAMILY COURTYARD
石家大院

In Yángliǔqīng in the western suburbs of Tiānjīn is the marvellous **Shi Family residence** (Shí Jiā Dàyuàn; admission Y20; 9am-4.30pm), composed of several courtyards. Belonging to a prosperous merchant family, the residence contains a theatre and 278 rooms, some of which are furnished. From Tiānjīn, take bus 153 from the west train station or bus 672 from the Tianjin Department Store to Yángliǔqīng. A taxi will cost Y70 return.

TÁNGGŪ 塘沽

About 50km from Tiānjīn, Tánggū is one of China's major international seaports. There's little of interest in Tánggū and most travellers visit to catch ferries to Dàlián (northeast China), Kōbe (Japan) or Incheon (South Korea).

Dagu Fort (大沽炮台; Dàgū Pàotái; Paotai Lu; admission Y10; 8am-6pm) This fort on the southern bank of the Hai River dates from the 16th century. There is a small museum chronicling the various invasions by foreign imperialists and a collection of large iron cannons. Bus 110 from Tánggū train station drops you at the end of the road; from there it's a five- or 10-minute walk to the fort.

Getting There & Away

Frequent minibuses and buses to Tánggū (Y5) leave from the main train station, including bus 835 (Y4). In Tánggū, minibuses to Tiānjīn run from outside the train station. A light rail system runs between Zhongshanmen station in southeast Tiānjīn and Donghailu station in Tánggū (50 minutes, roughly every 15 minutes, first/last train 7am/7pm).

If travelling by sea, there are daily boats to Dàlián (Y167 to Y697, 13 to 16 hours), and a weekly ferry to Kōbe (from Y1875, 48 hours) and Incheon (Y888 to Y1590, 28 hours). Check in two hours before departure for international sailings.

Tickets can be purchased at the **Passenger Ferry Terminal** (Tiānjīngǎng Kèyùnzhàn; 2570 6728), but if you are in Tiānjīn buy in advance from the **ticket office** (shòupiàochù; 2339 2455; 1 Pukou Dao); for tickets to Incheon, go to **Tianjin-Inchon International Passenger Co** (2311 2843; 56 Changde Dao; 8.30am-5.30pm).

Héběi 河北

Héběi is Běijīng's forgotten cousin from the countryside: she's got less money, wears last year's fashions and can catch a chicken faster than a taxi, but hey, she's still family. But while cuisine, language and favourite opera songs may overlap, the similarities end there. The capital is slick, modern and cosmopolitan; the province has more of a rough-edged charm comprised of grazing sheep, brown earth and fields of corn and wheat.

Don't let those tattered edges put you off though; Héběi is more than just one big stretch of farmland. It first put itself on the world map in the 1920s, when dragon bones uncovered in Zhōukǒudiàn (southwest of Běijīng) turned out not to belong to some mythical creature, but instead to *Homo erectus,* the precursor to modern humans. At the time, the remains – which may date back as far as 500,000 years – gave rise to a short-lived theory that humankind originated in Asia. (This has since been refuted.)

And even if it's not the cradle of civilisation, Héběi is hardly disappointing – especially as there are a number of sights that can be done as a weekend getaway from the capital. Chief among them is Chéngdé, the majestic 18th-century summer retreat of the Qing emperors. Twentieth-century rulers preferred seaside Běidàihé, but much more impressive is the Great Wall, whose serpentine roller-coaster ride begins nearby at the sea's edge and continues across the province's rugged northern Yanshan Mountains. What you may remember most though are trips to low-key towns like Yújiācūn and Jīmíngyì, where you'll be rewarded with overwhelming hospitality and a glimpse into the hard-working lives of China's many farmers.

HÉBĚI

HIGHLIGHTS

■ Escape the capital for some downtime at the rustic imperial retreat at **Chéngdé** (p192)

■ Scramble up **Jiǎo Shān** (p200) at Shānhǎiguān for sparkling ocean vistas and a little Great Wall adventure

■ Check out one of China's more unusual rock collections – the village of **Yújiācūn** (p190)

■ Strike off for **Jīmíngyì** (p198), a 13th-century stop on the pony express

■ Count temples and compare pagoda styles at the ancient walled town of **Zhèngdìng** (p189)

Chéngdé ★
Jīmíngyì ★
Jiǎo Shān ★
★ Zhèngdìng
★ Yújiācūn

■ POPULATION: 68.5 MILLION   ■ www.hebei.com.cn/node2/english

HÉBĚI 河北

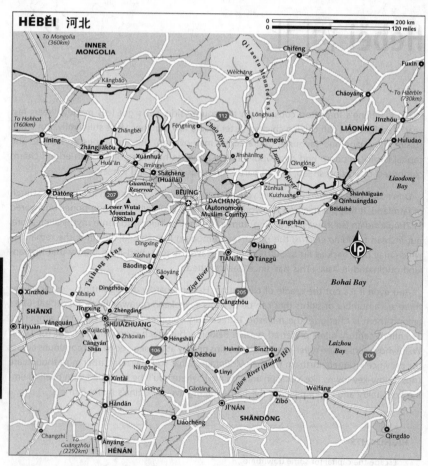

Climate

Considerable temperature differences exist between the mountainous north and the south of the province, as well as between coastal and inland regions, but generally speaking Héběi gets very hot in summer (with an average temperature of 20°C to 27°C in July) and freezing cold in winter (average temperature in January -3°C) with dust fallout in spring and heavy rains in July and August. Autumn (September to November) is the best season to visit.

Getting There & Away

Běijīng and Tiānjīn are the most convenient bases for exploring the province. Héběi is also linked to numerous other domestic destinations by both bus and rail.

Getting Around

The provincial rail hub is at Shíjiāzhuāng, with rail links to all major towns and cities in Héběi. Travel to Chéngdé, Jīmíngyì and Shānhǎiguān is best done from Běijīng or Tiānjīn. Bus connections cover the entire province.

SHÍJIĀZHUĀNG 石家庄

☎ 0311 / pop 2.1 million

Thoroughly eclipsed by the larger cities of Běijīng and Tiānjīn, Shíjiāzhuāng is a definitive provincial capital: it's a bustling, modern sprawl with little on offer culturally apart from a museum. It is a good departure point for exploring southern Héběi though, and the sights nearby – including historic Zhèngdìng (p189) and rural Yújiācūn (p190) – are interesting enough to warrant the short trip down from Běijīng.

Orientation
Most of the city's hotels and sights can be found along the east–west running Zhongshan Lu, which divides into Zhongshan Xilu and Zhongshan Donglu, and the area around the train station.

Information
Bank of China (Zhōngguó Yínháng; Jinqiao Beidajie) Through the west door of Dongfang City Plaza Shopping Center.

Bank of China ATM (Qŭkuănjī; 97 Zhongshan Xilu) Outside on the southwest corner of Dongfang City Plaza Shopping Center.

Hualian Jingyi Internet Bar (Huálián Jīngyì Wăngbā; 2nd fl, Zhanqian Jie; per hr Y2; ⏰ 8am-midnight) Through the south entrance of the big department store opposite the train station – look for 'Sushi Beef Noodle' (but don't eat there).

Post office (Yóujú; cnr Gongli Jie & Zhongshan Xilu; ⏰ 24hr)

Public Security Bureau (PSB; Gōngānjú; 83 Minzu Lu)

Visa office (☎ 8702 4274; 8 Liming Jie; ⏰ 8am-noon & 1-5pm) Around the corner from the PSB.

Sights
HEBEI PROVINCIAL MUSEUM
河北省博物馆
Hébĕi's ageing **museum** (Hébĕi Shěng Bówùguǎn; ☎ 8604 5642; Zhongshan Donglu; admission Y10; ⏰ 9am-5pm May-Oct, 8.30-11.30am & 2-5.30pm Nov-Apr, closed Mon) is in desperate need of a face-lift (or even a whole new face), but looks aside, the old gal still has some worthwhile stories to tell. Skip 'Hebei Today' downstairs and head for the 2nd floor where you'll find exhibitions ranging from prehistoric pottery to later artefacts, including imaginative bronzes, Buddhist statuary and a constellation of pottery figures from the Northern Qi. The central hall is devoted to a photo exhibit of the Great Wall, while a separate hall at the rear displays excavations from the Mancheng Western Han tombs, including two jade Han burial suits, one of which is sewn with 1.1kg of gold thread.

REVOLUTIONARY MARTYRS' MAUSOLEUM
烈士陵园
This **mausoleum** (Lièshì Língyuán; ☎ 8702 2904; 343 Zhongshan Xilu; admission Y3; ⏰ 7.30am-6pm) is located in a pleasant tree-shaded park. Among the shrines to communist martyrs is the tomb of the Canadian guerrilla doctor Norman Bethune (1890–1939). Bethune served as a surgeon with the Eighth Route Army in the war against Japan, and is eulogised in Mao Zedong Thought – 'We must all learn the spirit of absolute selflessness from Dr Norman Bethune'.

Sleeping
BUDGET
Jīnghuá Fàndiàn (☎ 8702 5068; 14 Zhanqian Jie; 站前街14号; tw Y70-160, tr Y86-280; ✷) The Jīnghuá has 12 storeys of wall-to-wall carpeting and marvellous views of Shíjiāzhuāng's smokestacks. Directly across from the bus station.

Yínquán Jiŭjiā (☎ 8598 5999; 12 Zhanqian Jie; 站前街12号; tw Y118-198; ✷) The linoleum flooring in the economy rooms here offsets the spartan touches (no soap or towels), making it more enticing than the Jīnghuá. The more expensive rooms are inexplicably less attractive.

MIDRANGE
Bailin Hotel (Bǎilín Dàshà; ☎ 8598 5688; fax 8598 5588; 24 Zhanqian Jie; 站前街24号; s Y220, tw Y280-320, tr Y560; ✷) The singles have huge beds and the pricier twins at this three-star hotel should guarantee a good night's sleep. The TV video channel shows films of varying quality, but the staff is generally courteous and the location opposite the train station is excellent. Try the Huìwén Dàjiŭdiàn next door if it's full.

TOP END
World Trade Plaza Hotel (Shìmào Guǎngchǎng Jiŭdiàn; ☎ 8667 8888; www.wtphotels.com; 303 Zhongshan Donglu; 中山东路303号; d/studios/ste Y818/988/1318; ✷) This is the city's finest and most elegant hotel, a splendid five-star affair with huge and luxurious rooms that come with broadband internet access, drinking water on tap and satellite TV. There's a deli, Chinese restaurant, Brazilian barbecue, café and bar.

Eating
Tudari (Tŭdàlì; Jinqiao Beidajie; meals from Y15) You may need to wait for a seat at this Korean barbecue chain, but that'll give you time to decipher the menu (hint: 'kraut' is *kimchi*). In addition to a tantalising selection of kebabs, there are also noodles (Y8 to Y15) and personal hotpots (Y18 to Y28). It's opposite the Dongfang City Plaza Shopping Center.

Qiánqīnggé Zhōupù (18 Zhanqian Jie; meals from Y20) As well as dozens of different types of *zhōu*

HÉBĚI

(porridge) in steaming buckets, this highly popular and busy restaurant serves up exceedingly tasty Chinese staples such as the crispy *hóngshāo páigǔ* (红烧排骨; braised spareribs; Y18). Filling porridge comes in all flavours, including *bābǎo* (八宝; a sweet concoction including berries and nuts; Y2) and *dìguā* (地瓜; sweet potato; Y2).

Shopping
Dongfang City Plaza Shopping Center (Dōngfāng Dàshà; 97 Zhongshan Xilu; ⊙ 9am-9pm) This shopping centre is located west of the train station.

Getting There & Away
AIR
Shíjiāzhuāng is connected by air to most major cities in China.

BUS
From the long-distance bus station (*chángtú qìchēzhàn*) there are frequent buses to Běijīng

(Y50 to Y74, 3½ hours), Jǐ'nán (Y82, four hours), Tiānjīn (Y45 to Y90, four hours) and Zhèngzhōu (Y107, six hours). All of these buses run roughly from 7am to 6pm.

Other destinations include Qínhuángdǎo (Y130, 6½ hours, departure 11am) and Qīngdǎo (Y150, seven hours, departure 11am). For luxury buses go to the left-hand ticket windows (almost all buses); for old-school clunkers go to the right-hand side windows.

TRAIN
Shíjiāzhuāng is a major rail hub with comprehensive connections, including regular trains to/from Beijing West (express Y50, 2½ hours). Other destinations include Chéngdé (Y88, 10½ hours), Qínhuángdǎo (Y160, 8½ hours), Dàtóng (Y148, 11½ hours), Chángchūn (Y240, 16 hours), Jǐ'nán (hard seat Y24, five hours), Guǎngzhōu (Y409, 20½ hours), Nánjīng (Y246, 13½ hours) and Shànghǎi (Y320, 18½ hours).

Getting Around

Shíjiāzhuāng's airport is 40km northeast of town. **Civil Aviation Administration of China buses** (CAAC; 中国民航; Zhōngguó Mínháng; ☎ 8505 4084; Y15) to the airport depart from the CAAC office at 471 Zhongshan Donglu; the office can be reached on bus 5. There are two or three buses per day, with the first leaving at around 5.40am and the last leaving at around 5pm. A taxi to the airport will take about an hour and costs Y130. Taxis are Y5 at flag fall.

AROUND SHÍJIĀZHUĀNG
Zhèngdìng 正定
☎ 0311 / pop 130,280

From atop Zhèngdìng's South Gate, you can see the silhouettes of four distinct pagodas jutting prominently above the sleepy town. Remnants of a traditional skyline in China are an unusual sight, and these are an excellent example of the country's former architectural ingenuity. Nicknamed the town of 'nine towers, four pagodas, eight great temples and 24 golden archways', Zhèngdìng seems to have misplaced (or miscounted) a number of the original 45 monuments, but it nevertheless retained the magnificent Dafo Temple, which is enough to make up for having lost all nine towers.

The through ticket (*tōngpiào*; Y60) gets you access to all sights except Linji Temple. Opening hours are from 8am to 6pm.

ORIENTATION

All of the attractions are either off the east–west Zhongshan Lu or the north–south Yanzhao Nandajie. Beginning with Dafo Temple, you can see almost everything by walking west until reaching Yanzhao Nandajie, and then continuing south until the city gate. There's a small map (in Chinese) on the back of the through ticket.

SIGHTS

Of Zhèngdìng's many monasteries, the most famous is Longxing Temple (隆兴寺), more popularly known as **Dafo Temple** (大佛寺; Dàfó Sì; ☎ 878 6560; Zhongshan Donglu; admission Y40), or Big Buddha Temple, located in the east of town.

Dating from AD 586, much of the temple has since been restored. You are met in the first hall by the corpulent Milefo, apparently chubby enough that the caretakers decided to pluralize him – he's now dubbed the 'Monks

with a Bag'. The four Heavenly Kings flanking him in pairs are typically vast and disconcerting.

Beyond is the Manichaean Hall, with a huge gilded statue of Sakyamuni and some magnificent faded wall frescoes. At the rear of the hall is a distinctly male statue of the goddess **Guanyin** (see the boxed text, p196), seated in a lithe pose with one foot resting on her/his thigh (a posture known as *lalitásana*) and surrounded by *luóhàn* (those freed from the cycle of rebirth).

The **Buddhist Altar** behind houses an unusual bronze two-faced Buddha that was cast during the Ming dynasty, gazing north and south. There are two halls behind the Buddhist Altar. On the left is the Zhuanlunzang Pavilion, which contains a remarkable revolving octagonal wooden bookcase. The hall to the right holds a magnificent painted and gilded Buddha.

Beyond these halls lie two stele pavilions that you pass on the way to the vast **Pavilion of Great Mercy** (大悲阁; Dàbēi Gé), which houses a bronze colossus of Guanyin, the Goddess of Mercy. At 21.3m high, cast in AD 971 and sporting a third eye, the effigy may lack the beauty and artistry of her sibling in Chéngdé's Puning Temple (p193), but she is still impressive. You can climb all the way up into the galleries surrounding Guanyin for free. The wooden hall in which the goddess is housed was rebuilt in 1999 after consulting Song-dynasty architecture manuals.

Within the hall at the rear is a four-faced Buddha (the Buddha of four directions), crowned with another four-faced Buddha, upon which is supported a further set.

About five minutes west (right as you exit) of Dafo Temple is **Tianning Temple** (天宁寺; Tiānníng Sì; admission Y5). Enter off an alleyway leading north, and cross the remains of a now vanished temple hall. The 41m-high Tang-dynasty **Lofty Pagoda** (凌霄塔; Língxiāo Tǎ) – also called Mùtǎ or Wooden Pagoda – originally dates from AD 779; it was later restored in AD 1045. The octagonal, nine-eaved and spire-topped pagoda is in fine condition and typical of Tang brickwork pagodas. If you wish to clamber up inside, torches are provided, but mind your head and the steep stairs. The views from the top are not great as the windows are small.

Further west on Zhongshan Xilu, past the intersection with Yanzhao Nandajie, is the

Confucius Temple (文庙; Wén Miào; admission Y5); however, there is little to see here.

Heading south on Yanzhao Nandajie brings you to **Kaiyuan Temple** (开元寺; Kāiyuán Sì; admission Y10), which originally dates from AD 540. Destroyed in 1966, little remains of the temple itself aside from some leftover good vibes (it's a popular spot for qi gong and taichi practitioners). The **Bell Tower** has survived, but the drawcard is the dirt-brown **Xumi Pagoda**, a well-preserved and unfussy early-Tang-dynasty brickwork, nine-eaved structure, topped with a spire. Its round, arched doors are particularly attractive, as are the carved figures on the base.

Also displayed is a colossal stone *bìxì* (mythical, tortoise-like dragon) near the entrance with a vast chunk of its left flank missing and its head propped up on a plinth. Dating from the late Tang era, the creature was excavated in 2000 from a street in Zhèngdìng.

About 200m south of Kaiyuan Temple on the other side of the road is the **Liang Family Ancestral Temple** (梁氏宗祠; Liángshì Zōngcí; admission Y5; often closed), a Ming-dynasty, five-bay wide single hall topped with dark tiles.

The active monastery of **Linji Temple** (临济寺; Línjì Sì; Linji Lu; admission Y8), around 700m southeast of Kaiyuan Temple, is notable for its tall, elegant, carved brick **Chengling Pagoda** (topped with an elaborate lotus plinth plus ball and spire) and the main hall behind, with a large gilt effigy of Sakyamuni and 18 golden *luóhàn*. At the rear of the hall is Puxian astride an elephant, Wenshu on a lion and a figure of Guanyin. In the Tang dynasty, the temple was home to one of Chan (Zen) Buddhism's most eccentric and important teachers, Linji Yixuan, who penned the now famous words, 'If you meet the Buddha on the road, kill him!'

Nothing remains of **Guanghui Temple** (广惠寺; Guǎnghuì Sì; admission Y10) further south, except its unusual Indian-style pagoda decorated with lions, elephants, sea creatures, *púsa* (Bodhisattvas) and other figures (some missing). With a brick base and four doors, the pagoda has stone-carved upper storeys and a brickwork cap. You can climb to the top.

Part of Zhèngdìng's main street (Yanzhao Dajie) has been restored and is now a pleasant stretch of traditional Chinese roofing and brickwork called the **Zhengding Historical Culture Street** (正定历史文化街; Zhèngdìng Lìshǐ Wénhuà Jiē). At the southern end of the street is **Changle Gate** (长乐门; Chánglè Mén; admission Y10; 8am-6pm), also known as Nanchengmen or South Gate. The original wall (which dates back to the Northern Zhou) was made up of an outer wall *(yuèchéng)* and an inner wall *(nèichéng)*, with enceintes *(wèngchéng)*, and had a total length of 24km. You can climb onto Changle Gate where there is a small exhibition. Extending away from the gate to the east and west are the dilapidated remains of the wall, sprouting grass and trees.

GETTING THERE & AWAY

From Shíjiāzhuāng, minibus 201 (Y3, 45 minutes) runs regularly to Zhèngdìng from Daocha Jie, slightly south of the main bus stop in the train station square. The minibus goes to Zhèngdìng bus station, from where you can take minibus 1 to Dafo Temple (Y1). Regular train services also run through Zhèngdìng from Shíjiāzhuāng.

GETTING AROUND

Zhèngdìng is not huge and walking is relatively easy as the sights are largely clustered together. Taxis within Zhèngdìng are around Y10; three-wheel motorcycles cost Y4 for anywhere in town. Bus 1 runs from the local bus station to Dafo Temple and bus 3 runs to the train station.

Yújiācūn 于家村

pop approximately 1600

Hidden away in the hills near the Héběi–Shānxī border is the unusual little village of **Yújiācūn** (admission Y20), where nearly everything, from the houses to the furniture inside them, was originally made of stone. As such, Yújiācūn today is remarkably well preserved: the cobbled streets lead past traditional Ming- and Qing-dynasty courtyard homes, old opera stages and tiny temples. Actually, 'traditional' doesn't quite describe it: this is a model Chinese clan-village, where 95% of the inhabitants all share the same surname, Yu. One of the more unusual sights is inside the **Yu Ancestral Hall** (于氏宗祠; Yúshì Zōngcí), where you'll find the 24-generation family tree. There are five tapestries, one for the descendants of each of the original Yu sons who founded the village.

Another peculiarity is the three-storey **Qingliang Pavilion** (清凉阁; Qīngliáng Gé), completed in 1581. Supposedly the work of one thoroughly crazed individual (Yu Xi-chun, who wanted to be able to see Běijīng from the top), it was, according to legend, built entirely at night, over a 25-year period, without the help of any other villagers. It was certainly built by an amateur architect: there's no foundation, and the building stones (in addition to not being sealed by mortar) are of wildly different sizes, giving it an asymmetrical look that's quite uncommon in Chinese architecture.

It's definitely worth spending the night here. As the sun sets, the sounds of village life – farmers chatting after a day in the fields, clucking hens, kids at play – are miles away from the raging pace of modern Chinese cities. Villagers rent out rooms for Y10 per person; home-cooked meals are another Y10 each.

GETTING THERE & AWAY

All roads to Yújiācūn pass through Jǐngxíng (井陉), about 35km west of Shíjiāzhuāng. The two fastest trains to Jǐngxíng (Y8, 50 minutes) depart at 6.30am and 1.35pm; trains back to Shíjiāzhuāng depart at 5pm, 6.06pm (two hours) and 8pm. Otherwise, there are regular buses (Y6, one hour) running throughout the day between Shíjiāzhuāng's Xiwang Station (洗王站, Xǐwáng Zhàn) and Jǐngxíng. Take bus 9 to get to Xiwang from the Shíjiāzhuāng train station.

From Jǐngxíng you can catch buses to Yújiācūn (Y4, one hour, departures 7am to 6.30pm) and Cāngyán Shān (Y5, one hour, departures 9am to 1pm, returns noon to 5pm). Buses arrive at and depart from various intersections in town; you can walk or take a taxi for Y5. Alternatively, hire a taxi for one destination (Y80 return) or for the day (Y200).

Cāngyán Shān 苍岩山

Cāngyán Shān (admission Y50) is the site of the transcendent cliff-spanning Hanging Palace, a Sui-dynasty construction perched halfway up a precipitous gorge. Given the dramatic location, it must have been at one time an impressive temple complex, though these days the best views after the main hall are of the surrounding canyons (thankfully the chairlift doesn't mar too many photos). It's a quick, steep jaunt up to the palace, and then another 45 minutes past scattered pagodas and shrines to the new temple at the summit. The standard lunar festivals see a lot of worshippers and are a good time to visit if you don't mind crowds.

In theory, morning buses (Y25, two hours) for Cāngyán Shān leave from Shíjiāzhuāng in summer, returning in the late afternoon. In reality, it's best to combine it with a trip to Yújiācūn and catch more reliable transport to Jǐngxíng (see left).

Zhaozhou Bridge 赵州桥

This **bridge** (Zhàozhōu Qiáo; admission Y30) in Zhàoxiàn County, about 40km southeast of Shíjiāzhuāng and 2km south of Zhàoxiàn town, has spanned Jiao River (Jiǎo Hé) for 1400 years and is China's oldest-standing bridge. The world's first segmental bridge (ie its arch is a segment of a circle, as opposed to a complete semicircle), it predates other bridges of this kind throughout the world by 800 years. In fine condition, it is 50m long and 9.6m wide, with a span of 37m. Twenty-two stone posts are topped with carvings of dragons and mythical creatures, with the centre slab featuring a magnificent *tāotiè* (an offspring of a dragon).

To get to the bridge from Shíjiāzhuāng's long-distance bus station, take bus 30 to the south bus station (南焦客运站; *nánjiāo kèyùnzhàn*). Then take a minibus to Zhàoxiàn town (Y6, one hour). There are no public buses from Zhàoxiàn to the bridge, but you can hop on a *sānlúnchē* (three-wheeled motor scooter) for Y3.

CHÉNGDÉ 承德

☎ 0314 / pop 700,000

Originally known as Rèhé (and as 'Jehol' in Europe), Chéngdé evolved during the first half of the Qing dynasty from hunting grounds to full-scale summer resort and China's centre of foreign affairs. The Manchu emperors, beginning with Kangxi, came here to escape the stifling summer heat of Běijīng and get back to their northern roots, primarily by hunting, fishing and watching archery competitions. The court also took advantage of Chéngdé's strategic location between the northern steppes and the Chinese heartland to hold talks with the border groups – undoubtedly more at ease here than in Běijīng – who posed the greatest threats to the Qing frontiers: the Mongols, Tibetans, Uighurs and, eventually, the Europeans.

What remains today is the elegantly simple Bìshǔ Shānzhuāng (Fleeing-the-Heat Mountain Villa), not nearly as ornate as the Forbidden City, but no less grand. The walled enclosure behind the palace is the site of China's largest regal gardens, and surrounding the grounds is a remarkable collection of politically inspired temples, built to host dignitaries such as the sixth Panchen Lama. Grab a bike, pedal through the enchanting countryside and make sure you take in the jaw-dropping statue of Guanyin at Puning Temple – one of Buddhist China's most incredible accomplishments.

History

Although the Qing emperors were already firmly entrenched in the Chinese bureaucracy by the beginning of the 18th century, they nevertheless strove to maintain a separate Manchu identity. In addition to preserving their own language and dress, the court would embark on long hunting expeditions, heading north towards the Manchu homeland. In 1703 one expedition passed through the Chéngdé valley, where Emperor Kangxi became so enamoured with the surroundings that he decided to build a hunting lodge, which gradually grew into the summer resort.

Rèhé (Warm River; named after a hot spring here), as Chéngdé was then known, grew in importance and the court began to spend increasingly more time here – sometimes up to several months a year. To get a sense of the former imperial grandeur, imagine the procession as it set out from Běijīng: some 10,000 people accompanied the emperor on the seven-day journey.

The resort reached its peak under Emperor Qianlong (r 1735–96), who commissioned many of the 12 outlying temples (only eight remain) in an attempt to simultaneously welcome and awe ethnic groups from Mongolia, Tibet and Xīnjiāng.

In 1793 British emissary Lord Macartney arrived and sought to open trade with China. The well-known story of Macartney refusing to kowtow before Qianlong probably wasn't the definitive factor in his inevitable dismissal (though it certainly made quite an impression on the court) – in any case, China, it was explained, possessed all things and had no need for trade.

The palace was eventually abandoned after Emperor Jiaqing died there in 1820. He was purportedly struck by lightning – fact or fiction, it was nonetheless interpreted to be an especially ominous sign.

Orientation

Set in a pleasant river valley bordered by hills, the modern town spreads out south of the Bìshǔ Shānzhuāng and the Eight Outer Temples. The train station is in the southeast of town on the east side of the Wulie River (Wǔliè Hé), with most hotels and restaurants of note on the west side of the river.

Information

There is a handful of internet cafés (Y2 per hour) off Shaanxiying Jie.

Bank of China (Zhōngguó Yínháng; 4 Dong Dajie) Central branch with ATM access; there's a smaller branch at 19 Lizhengmen Dajie, also with an ATM.

China International Travel Service (CITS; Zhōngguó Guójì Lǚxíngshè; ☎ 202 4816; 2nd fl, 3 Wulie Lu) In the government compound on the right-hand side. The staff speaks some English, but otherwise the office is of little help.

Post office (Yóujú; cnr Lizhengmen Dajie & Dong Dajie; ☯ 8am-6pm)

PSB (Gōngānjú; ☎ 202 2352; ☯ 8.30am-5pm Mon-Fri) At the rear of a compound off Wulie Lu.

Xiandai Internet Café (Xiàndài Wǎngbā; Chezhan Lu; per hr Y2; ☯ 24hr) West of the train station.

Sights

Winter admission and hours are applicable from 16 October to 14 April.

BÌSHǓ SHĀNZHUĀNG 避暑山庄

The Qing emperors lived, worked and played in this **summer resort** (admission Y90, winter Y50, audio guide Y10 plus Y1000 deposit; ☯ palace 7am-5pm, park 5.30am-6.30pm), composed of a main palace complex and enormous park-like gardens, all of which is enclosed by a 10km-long wall.

Entering through Lizheng Gate (Lìzhèng Mén), you arrive at the **Main Palace** (Zhèng Gōng), a series of nine courtyards containing five elegant, unpainted halls whose rusticity is complemented by the towering pine trees growing throughout the complex. Note that the wings in each courtyard have various exhibitions (porcelain, clothing, weaponry) on display, and most of the halls have period furnishings.

The first hall is the refreshingly cool Hall of Simplicity and Sincerity, built of an aromatic cedar called *nánmù*, and displaying a carved throne draped in yellow silk. Other prominent halls include the emperor's study (Study of Four Knowledges) and living quarters (Hall of Refreshing Mists and Waves). On the left-hand side of the latter is the imperial bedroom. The lucky bed partner for the night was ushered in through the door with no exterior handle (to ensure privacy and security for the emperor) after being stripped and searched by eunuchs. Two residential areas branch out from here: the empress dowager's **Pine Crane Palace** (松鹤斋; Sōnghè Zhài), to the east, and the smaller Western Apartments, where the concubines (including a young Cixi) resided.

Exiting the Main Palace brings you to the gardens and forested hunting grounds, whose landscapes were borrowed from famous southern scenic areas in Hángzhōu, Sūzhōu and Jiāxīng, as well as the Mongolian grasslands. The 20th century took its toll on the park, but you can still get a feel for the original scheme of things.

The double-storey **Misty Rain Tower** (Yānyǔ Lóu), on the northwestern side of the main lake, was an imperial study. Further north is the **Wenjin Pavilion** (Wénjīn Gé), built in 1773 to house a copy of the *Siku Quanshu*, a major anthology of classics, history, philosophy and literature commissioned by Qianlong. The anthology took 10 years to put together, and totalled an astounding 36,500 chapters. Four copies were made, only one of which has survived (now in Běijīng). In the east, tall **Yongyousi Pagoda** (Yǒngyòusì Tǎ) soars above the fragments of its vanished temple.

About 90% of the compound is taken up by lakes, hills, forests and plains (where visitors now play football), with the odd vantage-point pavilion. At the northern part of the park the emperors reviewed displays of archery, equestrian skills and fireworks. Horses were also chosen and tested here before hunting sorties.

Just beyond the Main Palace are electric carts that whiz around the grounds (Y40); further on is a boat-rental area (Y10 to Y50 per hour). Almost all of the forested section is closed from November through May because of fire hazard, but fear not, you can still turn your legs to jelly wandering around the rest of the park.

GUANDI TEMPLE 关帝庙

Requisitioned years ago by the local government to house generations of Chéngdé residents, the restored **Guandi Temple** (Guāndì Miào; admission Y20), west of the main gate, is a welcome addition to Chéngdé's temple population. Also called the Wumiao, the Guandi Temple is a Taoist temple dedicated to Guān

Yǔ, first built during the reign of Yongzheng, in 1732. Enter the temple past the protective guardians of the Green Dragon (also called the Blue Dragon) on your right and the White Tiger (also called the White Lion) on your left in the **Shanmen Hall**. The **Chongwen Hall** on the right contains modern frescoes of Confucius while in the **Shengmu Hall** on the left is a statue of the Princess of Azure Clouds, the patron deity of Tài Shān (a mountain in Shāndōng), holding a baby. The hall ahead contains a statue of Guandi himself (see the boxed text on p410), the Taoist God of War and patron guardian of business. In the courtyard at the rear are two **stelae**, supported on the backs of a pair of disintegrating *bìxì*. The right-hand hall here is dedicated to the God of Wealth (Cáishén), the left-hand hall to the God of Medicine and his co-practitioners. The **Hall of the Three Clear Ones** (三清殿) stands at the rear to the left, while the central rear hall contains a further statue of Guandi. The former inhabitants of the temple grounds (the citizens of Chéngdé) have been moved on and the temple is now home to a band of Taoist monks, garbed in distinctive jackets and trousers, their long hair twisted into topknots.

EIGHT OUTER TEMPLES 外八庙

Skirting the northern and eastern walls of the Bìshǔ Shānzhuāng are eight impressive temples *(wài bā miào)*, unusual in that they were built primarily for diplomatic rather than spiritual reasons. Some were based on actual Tibetan Buddhist monasteries (and one on the Potala Palace), though in keeping with the political inspiration, the emphasis was, of course, primarily on appearance. Smaller temple buildings are sometimes solid, and the Tibetan façades (with painted windows) are often fronts for traditional Chinese temple interiors. The surviving temples and monasteries were all built between 1713 and 1780; the prominence of Tibetan Buddhism was as much because of the Mongols (fervent Lamaists) as it was for visiting Tibetan leaders.

Bus 6 taken to the northeastern corner will drop you in the vicinity, though pedalling the 12km (round trip) by bike is an excellent idea. You can also rent a cab for four hours (Y70).

Puning Temple 普宁寺
Chéngdé's only active temple, **Puning Temple** (Pǔníng Sì; Puningsi Lu; admission Y50, winter Y40; ⏰ 7.30am-6pm, winter 8am-5pm) was built in 1755

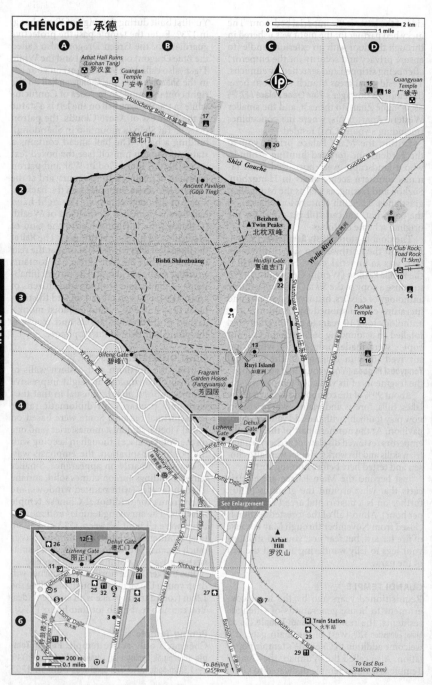

CHÉNGDÉ 承德

Arhat Hall Ruins
(Luóhàn Táng)
罗汉堂

Guangan
Temple
广安寺

Huancheng Beilu 环城北路

Xibei Gate
西北门

Shizi Gouche

Ancient Pavilion
(Gǔjù Tíng)

Beizhen
Twin Peaks
北枕双峰

Bìshǔ Shānzhuāng

Huidiji Gate
惠迪吉门

Bifeng Gate
碧峰门

Fragrant
Garden House
(Fāngyuánjū)
芳园居

Lizheng
Gate

Dehul
Gate

Lizhengmen Dajie

Dong Dajie

Wulie Lu 武烈路

Shangyingzi Jie

Nanyingzi Dajie

Zhongxing Lu

See Enlargement

Guangyuan
Temple
广缘寺

Puning Lu 普宁路

Guodao 国道

Wulie River

To Club Rock;
Toad Rock
(1.5km)

Pushan
Temple

Shanzhuang Donglu 山庄东路

Huancheng Donglu 环城东路

Ruyi Island
如意洲

Arhat
Hill
罗汉山

Xinhua Lu

Cuiqiao Lu

Baodishan Lu 宝地山路

Train Station
火车站

Chezhan Lu 车站路

To Beijing
(255km)

To East Bus
Station (2km)

Lizheng Gate
丽正门

Dehul Gate
德汇门

Lizhengmen Dajie 丽正门大街

Dong Dajie 东大街

Nanyingzi Dajie

Zhongzhou Dajie

Wulie Lu 武烈路

HÉBĚI

in anticipation of Qianlong's victory over the western Mongol tribes in Xīnjiāng. It was supposed to be modelled on the earliest Tibetan Buddhist monastery (Samye), although the first half of the temple is distinctly Chinese; the Tibetan buildings are at the rear.

Enter the temple grounds to a stele pavilion with inscriptions by the Qianlong emperor in Chinese, Manchu, Mongol and Tibetan. Behind are arranged halls in a typical Buddhist temple layout, with the **Hall of Heavenly Kings** (天王殿; Tiānwáng Diàn) and beyond, the **Mahavira Hall** (大雄宝殿; Dàxióngbǎo Diàn). The hall contains three images of the Buddhas of the three generations. Behind lie some very steep steps (the temple is arranged on a mountainside) leading to a gate tower, which you can climb.

On the terrace at the top of the steps is the huge **Mahayana Hall**. To the right and left are stupas and square, block-like Tibetan-style buildings, decorated with attractive water spouts. Some buildings on the terrace have been converted to shops, while others are solid, serving a purely decorative purpose.

The highlight of any trip here is the heart-arresting golden statue of **Guanyin** (the Buddhist Goddess of Mercy) in the Mahayana Hall; see the boxed text, p196. The effigy is astounding: over 22m high, it's the highest of its kind in the world and radiates a powerful sense of divinity. Mesmerising in its scale, this labour of love is hewn from five different kinds of wood (pine, cypress, fir, elm and linden). Guanyin has 42 arms, with each palm bearing an eye, and each hand holding instruments, skulls, lotuses and other Buddhist devices. Tibetan features include the pair of hands in front of the goddess, below the two clasped in prayer, the right one of which holds a sceptre-like *dorje* (*vajra* in Sanskrit), a

masculine symbol, and the left a *dril bu* (bell), a female symbol. On Guanyin's head sits the Teacher Longevity Buddha (Shizunwuliangshoufo). To her right stands a colossal male guardian and disciple called Shancai, opposite his female equivalent, Longnü (Dragon Girl). Unlike Guanyin, they are both painted, although their paintwork is in poor condition. On the wall on either side are hundreds of small effigies of Buddha.

You can clamber up to the first gallery (Y10) for a closer inspection of Guanyin; torches are provided to cut through the gloom so you can pick out the uneven stairs (take care). Sadly, the higher galleries are often out of bounds, so an eye-to-eye with the goddess may be impossible. If you want to climb the gallery, try to come in the morning, as it is often impossible to get a ticket in the afternoon.

Puning Temple has a number of friendly Lamas who manage their domain, so be quiet and respectful at all times. You can catch bus 6 from in front of the Mountain Villa Hotel to Puning Temple.

Putuozongcheng Temple 普陀宗乘之庙

The largest of the Chéngdé temples, **Putuozongcheng Temple** (Pǔtuózōngchéng Zhīmiào; Shizigou Lu; admission Y40, winter Y30; ◷ 8am-6pm, winter 8.30am-5pm) is a minifacsimile of Lhasa's Potala Palace and houses the nebulous presence of Avalokiteshvara (Guanyin); see the boxed text, p196. The temple is a marvellous sight on a clear day, its red walls standing out against its mountain backdrop. Enter to a huge stele pavilion, followed by a large triple archway topped with five small stupas in red, green, yellow, white and black. In between the two gates are two large stone elephants whose knees bend impossibly. The scale of the place comes into relief when you reach the Red Palace and look up – it's an astonishing sight, especially when framed against a blue sky.

Fronted by a collection of prayer wheels and flags, the **Red Palace** (also called the Great Red Platform) contains most of the main shrines and halls. Continue up past an exhibition of *thangka* (sacred Tibetan paintings) in a restored courtyard and look out for the marvellous sandalwood pagodas in the front hall. Both are 19m tall and contain 2160 effigies of the Amitabha Buddha. Among the many exhibits on view are displays of Tibetan Buddhist objects and instruments, including a *kapala* bowl, made from the skull of a young girl. The main hall is located at the very top, surrounded by several small pavilions; the climb to the top is worth it for the views. In the uppermost hexagonal pavilion in the northwest part of the roof is a small statue of Guanyin. The temple's sacred aura is sadly spoiled by the numerous souvenir stalls, but the faithful can buy a bust of Chairman Mao from the Buddhist Statue Shop.

Other Temples & Sights

The **Temple of Sumeru, Happiness and Longevity** (Xūmífúshòu Zhīmiào; Shizigou Lu; admission Y30, winter Y20; 8am-5.30pm, winter 8.30am-5pm) is another huge temple, around 1km to the east of the Putuozongcheng Temple. It was built in honour of the sixth Panchen Lama, who stayed here in 1781, and it incorporates elements of Tibetan and Chinese architecture, being an imitation of a temple in Shigatse, Tibet. Note the eight huge, glinting dragons (each said to weigh over 1000kg) that adorn the roof of the main hall.

The peaceful **Pule Temple** (Pǔlè Sì; admission Y30, winter Y20; 8am-6pm, 8.30am-5pm winter) was built in 1776 for the visits of minority envoys (Kazakhs among them). At the rear of the temple is the unusual Round Pavilion, reminiscent of the Hall of Prayer for Good Harvests at Běijīng's Temple of Heaven (p131). Inside is an enormous wooden mandala (a geometric representation of the universe).

It's a 30-minute walk to **Club Rock** (棒槌峰; Bàngchuí Fēng) from Pule Temple – the rock is said to resemble a club used for beating laundry dry. Nearby is **Toad Rock** (蛤蟆峰; Hámá Shí). There is pleasant hiking, good scenery and commanding views of the area. You can save yourself a steep climb to the base of Club Rock (admission Y20) and Toad Rock by taking the chairlift (Y45 return), but it's more fun to walk if you're reasonably fit. Bus 10 will take you to Pule Temple. East of

---

GUANYIN

The boundlessly compassionate countenance of Guanyin, the Buddhist Goddess of Mercy, can be encountered in temples all over China. The goddess (more strictly a Bodhisattva or a Buddha-to-be) goes under a variety of aliases: Guanshiyin (literally meaning 'Observing the Cries of the World') is her formal name, but she is also called Guanzizai, Guanyin Dashi and Guanyin Pusa or, in Sanskrit, Avalokiteshvara. In Japan she is known as Kannon and in Cantonese as Guanyam. Guanyin shoulders the grief of the world and dispenses mercy and compassion. Christians will note a semblance to the Virgin Mary in the aura surrounding the goddess.

In Tibetan Buddhism, her earthly presence manifests itself in the Dalai Lama, and her home is the Potala Palace (p920) in Lhasa. In China, her abode is the island of Pǔtuóshān (p332) in Zhèjiāng province, whose first two syllables derive from the name of her palace in Lhasa.

In temples throughout China, Guanyin is often found at the very rear of the main hall, facing north (most of the other divinities, apart from Weituo, face south). She typically has her own little shrine and stands on the head of a big fish, holding a lotus in her hand. On other occasions, she has her own hall, which is generally towards the rear of the temple.

The goddess (who in earlier dynasties appears to be male rather than female) is often surrounded by little effigies of the *luóhàn* (or *arhat*, those freed from the cycle of rebirth), who scamper about; the Guanyin Pavilion outside Dàlǐ (p709) is a good example of this. Guanyin also appears in a variety of forms, often with just two arms, but sometimes also in a multi-armed form (as at the Puning Temple here in Chéngdé). The 11-faced Guanyin, the horse head Guanyin, the Songzi Guanyin (literally 'Offering Son Guanyin') and the Dripping Water Guanyin are just some of her myriad manifestations. She was also a favourite subject for *déhuà* (white-glazed porcelain) figures, which are typically very elegant.

Puning Temple is **Puyou Temple** (Pǔyòu Sì; admission Y20; ☽ 8am-6pm). While dilapidated, there is a plentiful contingent of merry gilded *luóhàn* in the side wings.

Anyuan Temple (Ānyuàn Miào; admission Y10; ☽ 8am-5.30pm summer only) is a copy of the Gurza Temple in Xīnjiāng. Only the main hall remains, which contains deteriorating Buddhist frescoes. **Puren Temple** (Pǔrén Sì), built in 1713, is the earliest temple in Chéngdé, but is not open to the public. Surrounded by a low red wall, **Shuxiang Temple** (Shūxiàng Sì) also appears to be closed. You can try your luck, or at least look at the pair of huge stone lions sitting outside. Just to the west of Shuxiang Temple is a military-sensitive zone where foreigners are not allowed access, so don't go wandering around.

Tours

The only practical way to see all sights in one day is to take a tour by minibus, most of which start out at 8am. Most hotels run group tours from around Y50 per day (excluding admission prices).

Sleeping

For such an important tourist destination, Chéngdé has a particularly unremarkable range of accommodation. No budget hotels were accepting foreigners at the time of writing.

MIDRANGE

Mountain Villa Hotel (Shānzhuāng Bīnguǎn; ☎ 209 1188; www.hemvhotel.com; 11 Lizhengmen Lu; 丽正门路11号; tw Y280-480, tr Y210; 🈂️) The Mountain Villa has a plethora of rooms and offers pole positioning for a trip inside the Bìshǔ Shānzhuāng, making it one of the best choices in town. One wing or another is always being renovated, so try to find the newest rooms if you're not big on the smell of stale smoke. Take bus 7 from the train station and from there it's a short walk. All major credit cards are accepted.

Jingcheng Hotel (Jīngchéng Fàndiàn; ☎ 208 2027; train station square; 火车站广场; tw Y260, tr Y240; 🈂️) Although the train station location isn't great, you can often find discounts of over 50% through April. Overall, it's kept in good condition; the 2nd floor has the best rooms.

Míngzhū Dàjiǔdiàn (☎ 202 1188; Xiaonanmen Dongce; 小南门东侧; tw Y380; 🈂️) Definitely a last-minute backup (unless you get the 75% discount); the only thing that's been refur-

bished here since the turn of the century is the staff, who are full of youthful enthusiasm. Most rooms feature ragged carpeting and dim fluorescent lights.

TOP END

Qǐwànglóu Bīnguǎn (☎ 202 2196; 1 Bifengmen Donglu; 碧峰门东路北1号; tw Y500-600, ste Y1500; 🈂️) Qǐwànglóu boasts a serene setting alongside the Summer Villa's walls, accentuated by the hotel's courtyard gardens. Don't come with expectations of Qianlong-style opulence, however – the rooms aren't quite as nice as at the Yunshan Hotel. Stay in the new back building.

Yunshan Hotel (Yúnshān Dàjiǔdiàn; ☎ 205 5888; 2 Banbishan Lu; 半壁山路2号; d/ste Y680/1600; 🈂️ 💻) Despite the ghastly exterior (white tiles, office block-style), the rooms at this four-star hotel are clean, elegant and spacious, and benefit from regular redecoration. They have minibars, bathrooms and internet access, and on-request DVDs. The hotel has a business centre, a western restaurant, a sauna and lobby bar.

Eating

Chéngdé is famous for wild game (notably venison, *lùròu*, and pheasant, *shānjī*), but don't expect to see too much on the menus these days. One delicious local speciality that's easy enough to find is almond milk (杏仁露; *xìngrén lù*). There's also no shortage of street food; head for Shaanxiying Jie (northern end of Nanyingzi Dajie) for a good choice of barbecue (*shāokǎo*) and Muslim noodle restaurants.

Zhōudǐngjì (11-18 Lizhengmen Dajie; meals Y5-15) There are all sorts of cheap snacks here, from steamed buns and porridge for breakfast to noodles and dumplings for lunch and dinner. Look for the red and gold façade.

Dongpo Restaurant (Dōngpō Fànzhuāng; ☎ 210 6315; Shanzhuang Donglu; dishes Y6-48) With red lanterns outside and steaming *shāguō* (砂锅; claypot) at the door, this lively restaurant has a fantastic array of Sìchuān dishes. Classics like the warming *huíguōròu* (回锅肉; crispy pork steeped in hot sauce; Y17) are excellent, but the best choices are invariably on the seasonal and house specials menus. Both have photos, some English and a chilli index. There's another branch across from the train station.

Xīláishùn Fànzhuāng (6 Zhonggulou Dajie; dishes Y10-40) The gathering place for local Muslims, this

HÉBĚI

unassuming restaurant is a great choice for those undaunted by Chinese-only picture menus. Excellent choices include beef fried with coriander (烤牛肉; *kǎo niúròu*; Y24) and sesame duck kebabs (芝麻鸭串; *zhīma yāchuàn*; Y25). You can also find local specialities such as venison (铁板鹿肉; *tiěbǎn lùròu*; Y40) and spicy pheasant with peanuts (宫爆山鸡; *gōngbào shānjī*; Y40). Look for the mosque-style entrance.

Beijing Roast Duck Restaurant (Běijīng Kǎoyādiàn; ☎ 202 2979; 22 Wumiao Lu; duck Y50) If you just can't get enough *kǎoyā*, this central restaurant across the way from the Guandi Temple offers tasty duck roasted over fruit-tree wood.

Getting There & Away

Buses for Chéngdé leave Běijīng hourly (Y46, four hours) from both the Liuliqiao and Sihui long-distance bus stations. Upon arrival, it's preferable to get off at the train station if given the choice. Minibuses from Chéngdé leave every 20 minutes for Běijīng from the train station parking lot, also stopping in front of the Yunshan Hotel. The Jingcheng Expressway (Běijīng–Chéngdé) should be completed by 2007, which will shorten the voyage to 2½ hours. The downside is that it may no longer be possible to hop off at the Great Wall at Jīnshānlǐng (p173), but ask anyway.

The east bus station (*dōng zhàn*) is 2km south of the train station, with morning buses to Qínhuángdǎo (Y66, five hours, close to Shānhǎiguān) and Tiānjīn (Y67, six hours).

Regular trains run between Běijīng and Chéngdé, with the first and most convenient departing Běijīng at 7.16am and returning at 2.40pm. The fastest trains take four hours (Y41 hard seat, Y61 soft seat); slower trains take around seven hours. There are also connections to Shěnyáng (Y97, 13 hours, 6.55am), Dāndōng (Y126, 17 hours, 6.39pm) and Tiānjīn (Y65, nine hours, 9.53pm).

Getting Around

Taxis are Y5 at flag fall, which should get you to most destinations in town. There are several minibus lines (Y1), including minibus 5 from the train station to Lizhengmen Dajie, 1 from the train station to the east bus station and 6 to the Eight Outer Temples, grouped at the northeastern end of town. Biking around town is an excellent way to go; however, at last check the only place renting bikes was the Mountain Villa Hotel (Y50 per day).

JĪMÍNGYÌ 鸡鸣驿
pop approximately 1000

As ragged and forlorn as a cast-off shoe, tiny Jīmíngyì is a characteristic snapshot of the Héběi countryside: disintegrating town walls rise above fields of millet and corn, while the occasional flock of sheep *baa*s its way through one of the main gates in the early morning. The oldest remaining post station in China, Jīmíngyì is a long way off from the gleaming capital – much further than the 140km distance would indicate. The rural pace of life and unrestored charm are what make the place attractive, though at its height during the Ming and Qing dynasties it was a town of considerably more bustle, as evidenced in the numerous surviving temples.

History

Imperial China had a vast network of postal routes used for transporting official correspondence throughout the country for well over 2000 years. The post stations, where couriers would change horses or stay the night, were often fortified garrison towns that also housed travelling soldiers, merchants and officials. Marco Polo estimated some 10,000 post stations and 300,000 postal-service horses in 13th-century China – while Marco clearly understood that a little embellishment is what makes a good story, there is little doubt the system was well developed by the Yuan dynasty (AD 1206–1368). Jīmíngyì was established at this time under Kublai Khan as a stop on the Běijīng–Mongolia route. In the Ming dynasty, the town expanded in size as fortifying the frontiers with Chinese soldiers became increasingly important.

Sights

Wandering along the peeling adobe walls of Jīmíngyì's courtyard houses takes you past scattered temples, including the simple **Confucius Temple** (孔庙; Kǒng Miào; admission Y5), which, like many Confucius temples, also doubled as a school. Not far from here is the larger **Taishan Temple** (泰山庙; Tàishān Miào; admission Y5), whose Qing murals depicting popular myths (with the usual mix of Buddhist, Taoist and Confucian figures) were whitewashed – some say for protection – during the Cultural Revolution. A professor from Qinghua University helped to uncover them; you can still see streaks of white in places. Other small temples that can be visited include the **Temple of the God of Wealth** (财神庙; Cáishén Miào; admission Y5) and the **Temple of the Dragon King** (龙神庙; Lóngshén Miào; admission Y5).

Jīmíngyì's walls are still standing; ascend the **East Gate** (东门; Dōng Mén) for fine views of the town, surrounding fields and Jiming Mountain to the north. Across town is the West Gate; the **Temple of the Town Gods** (城隍庙; Chénghuáng Miào), overgrown with weeds and in ruins, stands beneath it. There are a few intriguing Qing caricatures of Yuan-dynasty crime fighters remaining on the chipped walls. The largest and oldest temple in the area is the **Temple of Eternal Tranquillity** (永宁寺; Yǒngníng Sì), located 12km away on Jiming Mountain.

The infamous Empress Dowager Cixi passed through here on her flight from Běijīng; for Y5 you can see the room she slept in, but it's decidedly unimpressive.

Sleeping & Eating

Most people visit Jīmíngyì as a day trip, but spending the night is a great way to experience village life once others have returned to Běijīng's luxuries. You can arrange to stay with one of the villagers for Y10 to Y15; a home-cooked meal will cost the same. There are a few noodle shops outside the north wall.

Getting There & Away

Jīmíngyì is only accessible from the larger town of Shāchéng (沙城), from where buses leave (Y3, 30 minutes, 8.30am to 5pm) as they fill up. You'll be dropped off along the north wall.

Getting to Shāchéng from the capital is straightforward. There are frequent buses from Běijīng's Liuliqiao Station (Y26 to Y30, two hours) between 6.40am and 7.20pm. There are also trains from Beijing West (hard seat Y9 to Y16, 2½ to three hours) leaving at 9.12am, 1.05pm, 1.40pm and 7.30pm; one train from Běijīng's main station departs at 11.40pm. Buses back to Běijīng run from 8.30am to 4pm. There are trains at all hours, but the terminus varies between the main, west, south and north train stations. You can also catch a train on to Dàtóng (Y35, 3½ hours) at 6.40am, 11.40am, 2pm and 4pm.

You'll need to take a taxi (Y5) or motor tricycle between Shāchéng's train and bus stations. You can store luggage at the bus station (Y1).

SHĀNHǍIGUĀN 山海关
☎ 0335 / pop 19,500

The walled town of Shānhǎiguān guards the narrow plain that leads to northeastern China, and is the renowned site where the Great Wall snakes out of the hills to meet the sea. In the rush to keep up with Běijīng and Shànghǎi, Shānhǎiguān began demolition of much of the historic part of town in 2006. While renovation of the poor, run-down buildings was necessary, the current plan is simply to rebuild the entire town from the ground up (in the 'original style') – all in the course of a single year. It may sound like a tall order, but hey, that's China for you.

Given that our crystal ball was thoroughly obscured by construction dust, it's hard to say what exactly the future has in store. The town walls and monuments should be left untouched, meaning that there's still reason to visit, particularly for Great Wall aficionados. Unfortunately, though, much of the historic charm may be gone for good.

History

It makes some sense that the Ming dynasty (AD 1368–1644), following hard on the heels of the traumatic Yuan dynasty (when China was ruled by the Mongols), was characterised by a period of conservative, xenophobic rule. Shānhǎiguān is a perfect example of the Ming mentality. The garrison town and wall here were developed in order to seal off the country from the Manchus, whose ancestors previously ruled northern China during the Jin dynasty (AD 1115–1234). This strategy worked, for a while anyway, but as the Ming grew weaker, the wall's fatal flaw was exposed.

In 1644, after Chinese rebels seized Běijīng, General Wu Sangui decided to invite the Manchu army through the impregnable pass to help suppress the uprising. The plan worked so well that the Manchus went on to take over the entire country and establish their own Qing dynasty.

An ironic footnote: in 1681 Qing rulers finished building their own Great Wall, known as the Willow Palisade (a large ditch fronted by willow trees), which stretched several hundred miles from Shānhǎiguān to Jílín, with another branch forking south to Dāndōng from Kāiyuán. The purpose, of course, was to keep the Han Chinese and Mongols out of Manchuria.

SHĀNHǍIGUĀN 山海关

Information
Bank of China (Zhōngguó Yínháng; ☺ 8.30am-noon & 1.30-5.30pm) South of the Great Wall Museum on Diyiguan Lu; there's no international ATM.

Post office (Yóujú; ☺ 8am-5.30pm) On the east side of Nan Dajie.

PSB (Gōngānjú; ☎ 505 1163) Opposite the entrance to First Pass Under Heaven on the corner of a small alleyway.

Yimei Internet Café (Yīmèi Wǎngbā; Xinglong Jie; per hr Y2; ☺ 7am-midnight) South of the South Gate.

Sights
FIRST PASS UNDER HEAVEN 天下第一关
The **First Pass Under Heaven** (Tiānxià Dìyi Guān; cnr Dong Dajie & Diyiguan Lu; admission Y40; ☺ 7.30am-6.30pm, to 5.30pm Oct-Apr) is also known as East Gate (Dōng Mén). Shredded by the wind, tattered flags flap along a restored section of wall, itself studded with watchtowers, dummy soldiers and tourist paraphernalia. Long views of factories stretch off to the east as decayed sections of battlements trail off into the hills. The wall here is 12m high and the principal watchtower – two storeys with double eaves and 68 arrow-slit windows – is a towering 13.7m high.

The calligraphy at the top (attributed to the scholar Xiao Xian) reads 'First Pass Under Heaven'. Several other watchtowers can also be seen and there's a *wèngchéng* (enceinte) extending out east from the wall. Along the west edge of the wall south of the entrance is a pleasant grassy park where you can stretch your legs.

If you purchase the Y50 admission ticket you can visit the vaguely interesting 18th-century **Wang Family Courtyard House** (Wángjiā Dàyuán; 3 Dongsantiao Hutong; ☺ 7.30am-6pm), which is a large residence with an amateur display of period furnishings.

GREAT WALL MUSEUM 长城博物馆
Down the street, this **museum** (Chángchéng Bówùguǎn; Diyiguan Lu; admission Y10; ☺ 7.30am-6.30pm, 8am-5.30pm Oct-Apr) is housed in a pleasant, one-storey traditional Chinese building with up-turned eaves. This is an interesting way to explore the history of the wall, thanks to its collection of photographs and memorabilia. There are no captions in English. Admission is included in First Pass Under Heaven tickets.

JIĀO SHĀN 角山
Shānhǎiguān's most exciting activity is a hike up the Great Wall's first high peak, **Jiǎo Shān** (admission Y15; ☺ 7am-sunset). From here you'll have a telling vantage point over the narrow tongue of land below and one-time invasion route for northern armies. (The horizon's sparkling expanse of water should also inspire those unmoved by military strategy.) For something more adventurous, you can follow the wall's unrestored section indefinitely past the watchtowers or hike over to the secluded **Qixian Monastery** (栖贤寺; Qīxián Sì; admission Y5).

It's a steep 20-minute clamber from the base, or a cable car can yank you up for Y20. Jiǎo Shān is a 4km bike ride north of town; otherwise take a taxi (Y10).

OLD DRAGON HEAD 老龙头
Old Dragon Head (Lǎolóngtóu; admission Y50; ☺ 7.30am-5.30pm) is the mythic origin/conclusion of the

Great Wall at the sea's edge, 4km south of Shānhǎiguān. What you see now was reconstructed in the late 1980s – the original wall crumbled away long ago. The name derives from the legendary carved dragon head that once faced the waves.

As attractions go, it's essentially a lot more hype than history. Avoid buying the extortionate ticket and take the left-hand road to the sea (just past the bus stop) where you can walk along the beach to the base of the Great Wall. The salt breeze and glittering ocean make for a great picnic site, and you can join the periwinkle-pickers and cockle-hunters on the rocks. Bus 25 (Y1) goes to Old Dragon Head from Shānhǎiguān's South Gate. Watch out for the touts who will do anything to pull you into a peripheral attraction of no interest.

MENGJIANGNU TEMPLE 孟姜女庙
Mengjiangnu Temple (Mèngjiāngnǚ Miào; admission Y30; 7am-5.30pm) is a Song–Ming reconstruction 6km east of Shānhǎiguān. It has coloured sculptures of Lady Meng and her maids and calligraphy of a famous Chinese story, 'Looking for Husband Rock'. In the tale, Meng Jiang's husband was press-ganged into wall-building because his views conflicted with those of Emperor Qin Shi Huang. When winter came Meng set off to take her husband Wan warm clothing, only to discover that he had died from the hard labour. Meng wandered the Great Wall, thinking only of finding Wan's bones to give him a decent burial. The wall, a sensitive soul, was so upset that it collapsed, revealing the skeleton entombed within. Overcome with grief, Meng hurled herself into the sea from a boulder. A taxi here should cost around Y12.

Sleeping
Shānhǎiguān does not have many hotels, though they are cheaper than in Běidàihé.

BUDGET
Lida Restaurant (Lìdá Hǎixiān Jiǔlóu; 505 1476; Dong Dajie; 东大街; tw/q Y30/40; May-Sep) Very simple lodgings are on offer at the rear of the Lida Restaurant (right). Unfortunately, the owners were unsure as to the fate of their building. Call ahead.

Jiguan Guesthouse (Jīguān Zhāodàisuǒ; 505 1938; 17 Dongsitiao Hutong; 东四条胡同17号; tw/tr Y180/260;) One of the few original sìhéyuàn (traditional courtyard houses) slated to

survive demolition, this is a pleasant place with rooms off two courtyards. The twins have clean, tiled floors and TV; one room has no bathroom (Y80). It's about 50m down Dongsitiao Hutong on the north side; there's no English sign.

MIDRANGE
Friendly Cooperate Hotel (Yíhé Jiǔdiàn; 593 9069; 4 Nanhai Xilu; 南海西路4号; tw/tr/q Y288/388/400;) This well-maintained two-star hotel just south of the Xinghua Market has large, clean and smart double rooms with water cooler, TV, phone and bathroom. Staff are pleasant and there's a restaurant next door.

Shānhǎiguān Dàjiǔdiàn (506 4488; 107 Guancheng Nanlu; 关城南路107号; tw/tr Y288/430;) Overlooking a park, this is a good choice if the Friendly Cooperate is full or you're arriving late at night by train.

Eating
Due to impending construction, restaurants in the old town were virtually nonexistent at the time of writing. Small eateries and kebab sellers used to line Nan Dajie, though only time will tell if they're gone for good. Currently, the best food options are the larger restaurants south of the walls along Nanguan Dajie.

Lida Restaurant (Lìdá Hǎixiān Jiǔlóu; 505 1476; Dong Dajie; meals Y35) This cheerful place serves/served local, northeastern and Sìchuānese fare. Because of its choice location inside the walls, it may be gone by the time you read this. If not, celebrate with a plate of huíguōròu (Y25), a bowl of tasty hēimǐ (black rice; Y2) or some steaming jiǎozi (dumplings; Y5). The owner speaks a little English and has cheap beds out the back (see left).

Getting There & Around
See p203 for information on getting to Shānhǎiguān.

Cheap taxis are Y5 flag fall and Y1.4 per kilometre after that. Motor tricycles cost Y2 to go anywhere in Shānhǎiguān. Bike rental costs Y30 per day, though you'll have to scout out for new stalls.

BĚIDÀIHÉ 北戴河
0335 / pop 61,000
The summer seaside resort of breezy Běidàihé was first cobbled together when English railway engineers stumbled across the beach in the 1890s. Diplomats, missionaries and business

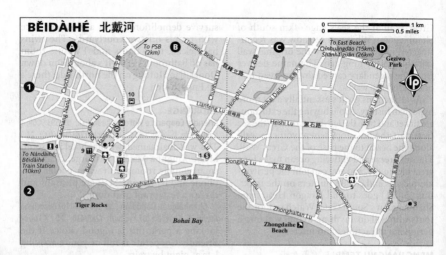

BĚIDÀIHÉ 北戴河

people from the Tiānjīn concessions and the Běijīng legations hastily built villas and cottages in order to indulge in the new bathing fad.

Some time after Liberation, the cream of China's leaders began congregating here each July for a summer retreat. But President Hu, apparently not much of a swimmer, has since ended the tradition, abandoning the resort to the middle class and nostalgic cadres. In addition to inspiring Mao to poetry, Běidàihé has starred tragic personalities such as Jiang Qing and Lin Biao. Lin reputedly plotted his frantic escape from Běidàihé in 1971 after a failed coup; the official line is that he died when his jet crashed hours later in Mongolia. (A much better urban legend claims that Zhou Enlai strangled him in his Běidàihé villa.)

During the summer high season (May to October) Běidàihé comes alive with vacationers who crowd the beaches and eat at the numerous outdoor seafood restaurants. During the low season, the town is dead.

Information

Bank of China (Zhōngguó Yínháng; near cnr of Dongjing Lu & Binhai Dadao; ☼ 8.30am–noon & 1.30–5.30pm) Has foreign currency exchange but no ATM.

Post office (Yóujú; Haining Lu)

Public Security Bureau (PSB; Gōngānjú; ☎ 404 1032; Lianfeng Beilu) Located in a new government compound 2km from town; a taxi here will run to around Y15.

Sights & Activities

Wandering the streets and seafront of Běidàihé in summer is enjoyable, as is hiring a bike or tandem (shuāngzuò zìxíngchē) and whizzing around the beachfront roads. Otherwise, fork out for a rubber ring, inner tube and swimming trunks from one of the street vendors and plunge into the sea (after elbowing through the crowds).

Always be on the lookout for Běidàihé's peculiar revolutionary emblems and seaside kitsch, including a statue of **Gorky** (Gāoěrjī) surrounded by outsized seashells. For those in pursuit of bad taste, Běidàihé comes up trumps with its **Biluó Tǎ** (Emerald Shell Tower) – it's quite ghastly.

Sleeping

Many foreign travellers stay in Shānhǎiguān (p201), as accommodation is expensive and limited in town. The resort is only fully open during the summer season (May to October); many hotels shut up shop in the low season.

Yuehua Hotel (Yuèhuá Bīnguǎn; ☎ 404 1575; 90 Dongjing Lu; 东经路90号; s/tw/tr Y400/400/400; ☼ Apr–Oct; 🞰) Smack in the centre of town, this three-star hotel has a spacious lobby and ponderous cladding on the exterior. Good discounts apply during slack periods.

Beidaihe Friendship Hotel (Běidàihé Yǒuyì Bīnguǎn; ☎ 404 8558; fax 404 1965; 1 Yingjiao Lu; 鹰角路1号; d Y480–680; ☼ Apr–Oct; 🞰) Set in huge, grassy green grounds in the east of town, this hotel is a good deal with tidy doubles and singles. The cheaper doubles (also clean) are at the rear in stone terraced houses. You can exit the rear entrance, mosey down the road and get straight onto the beach.

INFORMATION	SLEEPING	Youyi Restaurant
Bank of China	Beidaihe Friendship Hotel	友谊酒店.................................**9** A2
中国银行.................................**1** B2	北戴河友谊宾馆.................**5** D2	
Post Office 邮局.................**2** A1	Guesthouse for Diplomatic	TRANSPORT
	Missions 外交人员宾馆.........**6** A2	Bus Station
SIGHTS & ACTIVITIES	Yuehua Hotel 悦华宾馆.........**7** A2	海滨汽车站.................................**10** B1
Biluó Tǎ		Buses to Běijīng
碧螺塔.................................**3** D2	EATING	到北京的班车.................**11** A1
Statue of Gorky	Kiessling's Restaurant	Train Ticket Office
高尔基像.................................**4** A2	起士林餐厅.................**8** A2	火车票售票处.................**12** A2

Guesthouse for Diplomatic Missions (Wàijiāo Rényuán Bīnguǎn; ☎ 404 1287; fax 404 1807; 1 Bao Sanlu; 保三路1号; tw Y650-780, tr 480; ☺ Apr-Oct; ⚂) This guesthouse remains an appealing place to stay and has outdoor porches, so relax in the breeze and enjoy the hotel's beach. There's also tennis and weekend barbecues.

Eating

A whole string of seafood restaurants (hǎixiāndiàn) is strung out along Bao Erlu, near the beach; you can't miss them or their vocal owners. Choose your meal from the slippery knots of mysterious sea creatures kept alive in buckets on the pavement. Also look out for one of the ubiquitous fruit sellers wheeling their harvest around on bicycles, selling grapes, peaches, bananas, peanuts etc. Several small supermarkets can be found near the junction of Dongjing Lu and Haining Lu.

Youyi Restaurant (Yǒuyì Jiǔdiàn; ☎ 404 1613; Bao Erlu; meals Y30, seafood Y60) This popular seafood restaurant stays open off-season – choose from the bowls, buckets and pots of fresh aquatic life. Dishes include tomato and shrimps (Y38), drunken prawns (price depends on season), suāncàiyú (酸菜鱼; fish slices with pickled cabbage; Y35) and staple Sìchuān standards.

Kiessling's Restaurant (Qǐshílín Cāntīng; ☎ 404 1043; Dongjing Lu; ☺ Jun-Aug) A relative of the Tiānjīn branch, this place serves both Chinese and international food, and has pleasant outdoor seating.

Getting There & Away

Getting to Běidàihé or Shānhǎiguān is best done via Qínhuángdǎo, the largest city in the area. There are four express trains from Běijīng to Qínhuángdǎo (soft seat Y75, three hours), leaving at 7.30am, 8.30am, 2pm and 7.47pm. The earliest stops at Běidàihé (2½ hours); the 2pm stops at Shānhǎiguān (3½

hours). From Qínhuángdǎo, you can catch bus 33 to Shānhǎiguān (Y2, 30 minutes) or bus 34 to Běidàihé (Y2, 30 minutes) from in front of the train station on Yingbin Lu. There are plenty of other trains that pass through one of the three stations, though these can take up to six hours and may arrive at an inconvenient time.

There are express trains from Qínhuángdǎo back to Běijīng at 7.14am, 8.47am, 1.37pm and 4.19pm. It can be difficult to get tickets to Běijīng from the other two stations. Other destinations from Qínhuángdǎo include Tiānjīn (Y44, 3½ hours), Shíjiāzhuāng (Y160, 8½ hours), Shěnyáng (Y63 hard seat, five hours) and Hāěrbīn (Y230, 12 hours).

Comfortable buses leave for Běijīng's Bawangfen Station from Qínhuángdǎo (Y62 to Y66, 3½ hours) between 7am and 7pm. There are also direct buses from Qínhuángdǎo to Chéngdé (Y61, 5½ hours), departing hourly from 7am to 11am, and at 5pm. A convenient place to pick up a bus to Běijīng in Běidàihé is from the east side of Haining Lu, just north of the post office (Y66, three hours, departures at 6am, 12.30pm and 4pm).

Near Shānhǎiguān, Qínhuángdǎo's little airport has flights from Dàlián, Shànghǎi, Tàiyuán, Hāěrbīn and Chángchūn.

Getting Around

Buses 5 and 22 (via Nándàihé) connect Běidàihé train station to the bus station (Y4) or you can take a taxi (Y15). Buses connect all three towns, generally departing every 30 minutes from 6am to 6.30pm.

Cheap taxis in Běidàihé and Qínhuángdǎo are Y5 flag fall and Y1.4 per kilometre after that.

Bikes and tandems are available along Zhonghaitan Lu, east of Bao Erlu (Y10 per hour).

HÉBĚI

Shāndōng 山东

In today's China of dolled-up attractions and hyped-up travel fads, the decidedly northern province of Shāndōng – its name means 'East of the Mountains' – manages to maintain an alluring authenticity, despite being one of the nation's most visited regions.

Shāndōng's glittering CV makes for an impressive roll call. Native son Confucius, philosopher/social theorist *extraordinaire*, lived here as did that iconic champion of Confucian thought, Mencius. Wang Xizhi, China's most famous calligrapher, and Zhuge Liang, the supreme military strategist of the Three Kingdoms period, hail from these parts, and film icon Gong Li, who set new benchmarks for Chinese beauty, grew up in Jǐ'nán.

The Yellow River (Huáng Hé), the massive and muddy waterway that enjoys an almost mythical status among Chinese, reaches the sea in Shāndōng after its serpentine journey from the Tibet-Qīnghǎi plateau. Tài Shān, the holiest of China's five sacred peaks, is by far China's most climbed mountain. Qīngdǎo is a breath of fresh air on the Shāndōng peninsula, with its remarkable German heritage intact and a slot secured for the sailing events of the 2008 Olympics. Its eastern seaboard location also guarantees that Shāndōng is one of China's wealthiest provinces.

Yet neither fame nor fortune has gone to its head. Shāndōng folk are celebrated China-wide for their honesty and forthrightness. No-nonsense Shāndōng food is to the point: wholesome, salty and devoid of fancy trimmings. The peculiarities of the local Putonghua are not enough to confound most speakers of Mandarin, and for those anxious to eke out the province's bucolic side, the earthy textures of the ancient village of Zhūjiāyù are ideal.

SHĀNDŌNG

HIGHLIGHTS

- Tackle high-altitude **Tài Shān** (p214), China's most famous Taoist peak
- Explore the ancient walled town of **Qūfù** (p218), the centre of the Confucian universe
- Sink a glass or two of Tsingtao beer in seaside **Qīngdǎo** (p224)
- Meander round the Ming dynasty village of **Zhūjiāyù** (p210), outside Jǐ'nán
- Weave your way around **Yantai Hill Park** (p232) in Yāntái for flavours of yesteryear Europe

★ Yantai Hill Park
★ Zhūjiāyù
★ Tài Shān
★ Qīngdǎo
★ Qūfù

- POPULATION: 93.4 MILLION
- www.china-sd.net/eng/

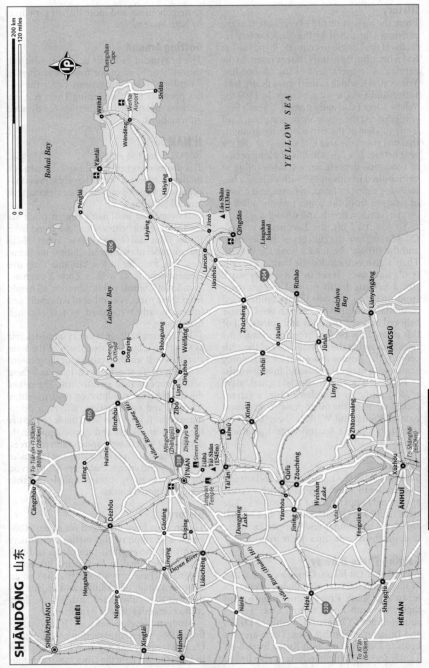

SHĀNDŌNG 山东

History

From the earliest record of civilisation in the province (furnished by the black pottery remains of the Lóngshān culture), Shāndōng has had a tumultuous history. It was victim to the capricious temperament of the oft-flooding Yellow River, which caused mass death, starvation and a shattered economy. In 1899 the Yellow River (also aptly named 'China's Sorrow') flooded the entire Shāndōng plain; a sad irony in view of the two scorching droughts that had swept the area that same year and the year before. The flood followed a long period of economic depression, a sudden influx of demobilised troops in 1895 after China's humiliating defeat by Japan in Korea, and droves of refugees from the south moving north to escape famines, floods and drought.

To top it all off, the Europeans arrived; Qīngdǎo fell into the clutches of the Germans, and the British obtained a lease for Wēihǎi. Their activities included the building of railroads and some feverish missionary work (for a historic Jesuit map of the province from 1655, go to www.library.csuhayward.edu/atlas/xantung.htm), which the Chinese believed angered the gods and spirits. All of this created the perfect breeding ground for rebellion, and in the closing years of the 19th century the Boxers arose out of Shāndōng, armed with magical spells and broadswords.

Today Jǐ'nán, the provincial capital, plays second fiddle to Qīngdǎo's tune, a refrain picked up on by the other prospering coastal cities of Yāntái and Wēihǎi. Shengli Oilfield, inland, is China's second-largest producer of oil.

Climate

Summers (May to August) are hot and winters (November to March) are cold, with an average annual temperature of 11°C to 14°C. The coastal cities of Qīngdǎo, Yāntái and Wēihǎi are cooler in summer and warmer in winter than the towns and cities of the interior.

Getting There & Away

Airports exist at Jǐ'nán, Qīngdǎo, Yāntái and Wēihǎi, with international flights to cities in Japan and South Korea from Qīngdǎo and flights to South Korea from Yāntái. Ferries run from both Yāntái and Wēihǎi to Dàlián and Incheon in South Korea. There are also boats to Dàlián and South Korea from both Yāntái and Wēihǎi. Shāndōng is also linked to neighbouring and more distant provinces by both bus and rail.

Getting Around

The provincial rail hub is Jǐ'nán, with rail connections to all major towns and cities in Shāndōng. Bus connections cover the entire province (see the Getting There & Away sections under each destination for detailed information).

JǏ'NÁN 济南

☎ 0531 / pop 1.96 million

The prosperous provincial capital Jǐ'nán is a modern Chinese city that largely serves travellers as a transit point to other destinations around Shāndōng.

Downplayed in Jǐ'nán's tourist pitch are the Chinese celebrities who have come from Jǐ'nán. Film idol Gong Li grew up here. Bian Que, founder of traditional Chinese medicine, Zou Yan, founder of the Yin and Yang five element school, as well as Zhou Yongnian, founder of Chinese public libraries, all herald from these parts. A number of nationally and internationally recognised writers also hail from Jǐ'nán.

Its German heritage is not as unmistakable as Qīngdǎo's, but the area south of the train station is well worth a wander for the pleasant ordering of its streets, lined here and there with European-style architecture. The rest of the city is being resculpted by road-widening schemes and construction, although determined efforts have also been made to prettify the city with plants and grass. Appealingly decked out with flowers and ornamental trees, the commercial street of Quancheng Lu exudes a vibrancy and energy that keeps shoppers on the go, restored by shots of bubble tea from regularly spaced kiosks.

History

The area has been inhabited for at least 4000 years, and some of the earliest reminders of this are the eggshell-thin pieces of black pottery unearthed in Lóngshān, 30km east of Jǐ'nán. These provide the first link in an unbroken chain of tradition and artistic endeavour that culminated in the beautifully crafted ceramics of later dynasties.

Modern development in Jǐ'nán stems from 1899, when construction of the Jǐ'nán–Qīngdǎo railway line began. When completed in 1904, the line gave the city a major communications role. The Germans had a concession near the train station after Jǐ'nán was opened to foreign trade in 1906, and crumbling residences from the era survive. The fine, huge German building on Jing Yilu across the way from the Shandong Hotel is the Jǐ'nán railway department; it's made of the same stone, and in the same style, as much of the architecture in Qīngdǎo.

Orientation

Jǐ'nán is a sprawling city, making navigation arduous for first timers. The main train station is in the west of town, south of which lies a grid of roads where some history and charm survive. The east–west roads in this grid are called Jing Yilu (Longitude One Rd), Jing Erlu (Longitude Two Rd) and so on, while the north–south roads are named Weiyi Lu (Latitude One Rd), Wei Erlu (Latitude Two Rd) and so forth. The major landmark in the east of town is Daming Lake (Dàmíng Hú), south of which can be found the major shopping zone of Quancheng Lu and Quancheng Sq.

Information

Bank of China (Zhōngguó Yínháng; 22 Luoyuan Dajie; ⏰ 9am-5pm Mon-Fri) Foreign exchange and ATMs that take international cards.

Fast Lane Internet Café (Kuàichēdào Wǎngbā; 24 Xiaowei Liulu; per hr Y2; ⏰ 7am-midnight)

Internet Café (Wǎngbā; per hr Y2.50; ⏰ 24hr) Beneath Tianlong Hotel opposite train station.

Post office (yóujú; 162 Jing Erlu, cnr Wei Erlu; ⏰ 8am-6.30pm) A red-brick building with pillars, capped with a turret.

Public Security Bureau (PSB; Gōngānjú; ☎ 8691 5454, visa enquiries ext 2459; 145 Jing Sanlu, cnr Wei Wulu; ⏰ 8am-noon & 2-5.45pm Mon-Fri)

Shandong Travel Service (Shāndōng Lǚxíngshè; ☎ 8260 0660/9; fax 8260 0226; 86 Jing Shilu; ⏰ 8.30am-5.30pm) South on Lishan Lu.

Shengli Hospital (Shènglí Yīyuàn; ☎ 8793 8911; 324 Jing Wulu)

Shengwang Internet Café (Shèngwàng Wǎngbā; 301 Jing Erlu; per hr Y1; ⏰ 24hr)

Xinhua Bookstore (Xīnhuá Shūdiàn; Luoyuan Dajie; ⏰ 9am-9pm) Opposite the Sofitel Silver Plaza Hotel.

Sights

The city's much-vaunted springs are over-promoted in the tourist blurb, being of limited interest, although strolling around their adjacent parks can be a pleasant escape from Jǐ'nán's foot-numbing distances. Tucked away down some steps just west of **Five Dragon Pool Park** (admission Y5) survives a small **Guandi Temple** (Guāndì Miào; admission free) where the red-faced God of War (p410) strokes his beard and glares out over a row of candles in the main shrine. The magnificent **Hong Lou Church** (洪楼教堂; Hónglóu Jiàotáng), northeast of the centre, is a well-preserved relic from the days of the German concession.

MOSQUE 清真寺

Fronted by a spirit wall and an impressive gate tower and laid out with pines, greenery and several stelae commemorating its periodic restoration, this lovely Chinese-style **mosque** (Qīngzhēn Sì; 47 Yongchang Jie; admission free) dates from the late 13th century. The long rooftops of the mosque are clearly visible running along Luoyuan Dajie. Walk in and look around, be quiet and respectful at all times, and dress modestly (no shorts or skirts); the 50m-long prayer hall is inaccessible to non-Muslims. The entrance is to the right of the main gate. The mosque is located on the left-hand side of Yongchang Jie, a street leading into the Hui (Muslim Chinese) quadrant of Jǐ'nán, where you can find stalls and restaurants cooking up Muslim food (see p208).

THOUSAND BUDDHA MOUNTAIN & JINAN MUSEUM 千佛山、济南博物馆

Adding some Buddhist mystery to Jǐ'nán are the statues in this **park** (Qiānfó Shān; 18 Jingshi Yilu; admission Y15; ⏰ 6am-7pm) to the southeast of the city centre. A cable car (one way Y15, return Y25) runs up the mountain. Buses 2 and K51 go to the park from the train station. **Jinan Museum** (Jǐ'nán Bówùguǎn; admission Y3; ⏰ 8.30am-4.30pm Tue-Sun) is a short walk west of the Thousand Buddha Mountain entrance on Jingshi Yilu, with galleries devoted to painting, calligraphy and ceramics, sadly headless statues of Buddhist figures from the Tang dynasty and a delightful miniature boat carved from a walnut shell. There are no English captions.

Sleeping

Shandong Hotel (Shāndōng Bīnguǎn; ☎ 8605 5286/7881; 92 Jing Yilu; 经一路92号; s Y130, d Y160-180, tr Y240; 🖳) On the corner of Jing Yilu and Wei Sanlu, this old-timer is well-used to dealing with budget travellers, and the acceptable although slightly ravaged rooms with large shower rooms still make it one of the cheapest and

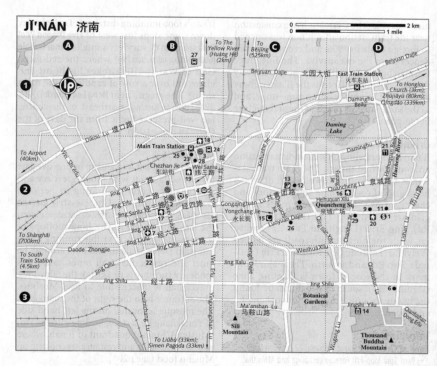

most convenient in town. Modest discounts are available.

Jinan Railway Hotel (Jǐ'nán Tiědào Dàjiǔdiàn; ☎ 8601 2118; fax 8601 2188; s/d/tr/ste Y300/368/468/800; ☒) Next to the main train station, this three-star hotel has polite staff, a heavily inlaid revolving door and an impressive lobby hung with a huge and glistening chandelier. Rooms are a bit more faded and bathrooms may need an overhaul, but discounts can chop 50% off room prices (you may get a single for Y140) and there's a useful 24-hour restaurant next door.

Jinan (Tsinan) Hotel (Jǐ'nán Fàndiàn; ☎ 8793 8981; fax 8793 2906; 240 Jing Sanlu; 经三路240号; d Bldg No 1/2/3 80/160/220, Mao Zedong Presidential ste Y1880; ☒) The setting here, within a small wooded garden, is a blessing for those suffering from a concrete overdose, although rooms at this two-star hotel were undergoing refurbishment at the time of writing. Reception is in Building No 4, and there is a north and south gate.

Sofitel Silver Plaza Jinan (Sùfēitè Yínzuò Dàfàndiàn; ☎ 8606 8888; www.accorhotels.com/asia; 66 Luoyuan Dajie; 泺源大街66号; d Y1245; ☒) A colossal five-star tower in the heart of the commercial district, the Sofitel's standard rooms – spacious

with light-wood furniture and quite ornate bathrooms – are perhaps in need of refurbishment, but the rest of the hotel retains an overall crispness. Facilities include a small deli (selling fresh bread), a swimming pool, and European, Japanese and Chinese restaurants. The hotel has an ATM that takes international cards. Ask for discounts or promotional rates.

Crowne Plaza Jinan (Jǐ'nán Guìhé Huángguān Jiàrì Jiǔdiàn; ☎ 8602 9999; www.crowneplaza.com; 3 Tianditan Jie; 天地坛街3号; d 1250; ☒) The very elegant Crowne Plaza runs from a stylish lobby with Art Deco touches (including illuminated pillars) to excellent rooms. Facilities include a deli off the lobby selling cakes and bread, an elegant indoor swimming pool, a bowling alley, a basement car park and fine international restaurants.

Eating

The area around the main train station is good for cheap eats. The alley off Jing Wulu, between Wei Erlu and Wei Sanlu, is a good place to go. Marked by a *páilou* (decorative arch), Furong Jie north of Quancheng Lu welcomes

INFORMATION			
Bank of China 中国银行	1 D2		
Fast Lane Internet Café			
快车道internet吧	2 B2		
Internet Café 网吧	3 B2		
Post Office 邮局	4 B2		
PSB 公安局外事科	5 B2		
Shandong Travel Service			
山东旅行社	6 D3		
Shengli Hospital			
省立医院	7 B2		
Shengwang Intenet Café			
盛旺网吧	8 B2		
Xinhua Bookstore			
新华书店	9 D2		

SIGHTS & ACTIVITIES			
Baotu Spring Park 趵突泉	10 C2		
Black Tiger Spring 黑虎泉	11 D2		

Five Dragon Pool Park			
五龙潭公园	12 C2		
Guandi Temple			
关帝庙	13 C2		
Jinan Museum			
济南博物馆	14 D3		
Mosque 清真寺	15 C2		

SLEEPING			
Crowne Plaza Jinan			
济南贵和皇冠假日酒店	16 D2		
Jinan (Tsinan) Hotel			
济南饭店	17 B2		
Jinan Railway Hotel			
济南铁道大酒店	18 B2		
Shandong Hotel			
山东宾馆	19 B2		
Sofitel Silver Plaza Hotel			
索菲特银座大饭店	20 D2		

EATING			
Quanjude Roast Duck Restaurant			
全聚德烤鸭店	21 D2		
Yuèdū Jiǔlóu 粤都酒楼	22 B3		

TRANSPORT			
Air Ticket Office 航空售票	23 B2		
Bus Station 汽车站	24 B2		
China Eastern Airlines			
东方航空公司	25 B2		
Jinan International Airport Ticket			
Office 济南国际机场售票处	26 C2		
Long-Distance Bus Station			
长途汽车站	27 B1		
Shandong China Railway			
International Travel Service			
山东中铁国路公	28 B2		
Yuquan Simpson Hotel			
玉泉森信大酒店	29 D2		

with a cavalcade of aromas, from Sìchuān cuisine to zhōu (粥; porridge), lamb kebabs, noodles, tiěbǎn (铁板; hot plate), squid on a stick and oodles of other snacks.

If you are looking for grilled meats (烧烤; shāokǎo), lamb kebabs and vendors of wuxiang peanuts (五香花生米; wǔxiāng huāshēngmǐ), then go no further than Yinhuchi Jie (饮虎池街) in the Muslim Hui minority district (回民小区; Huímín Xiǎoqū) that heads north from Luoyuan Dajie east of the mosque (p207). Lit up in a blaze of neon at night, here you can take your choice from any of the roadside restaurants and kebab vendors filling the air with the aromas of roast lamb.

Yuèdū Jiǔlóu (☎ 8708 8567; 588 Jing Qilu; meals Y30) Trendily fitted out with stylish furniture and dishes (prepared but uncooked) helpfully arranged on chilled shelves, this popular restaurant has been serving up Cantonese fare to loyal Jǐ'nán patrons for years. Peruse the enormous selection or take a look at the huge choice of seafood in fish tanks.

Quanjude Roast Duck Restaurant (Quánjùdé Kǎoyādiàn; ☎ 8642 8888; 61 Heihuquan Beilu; half/whole duck Y28/56) This is a large and spacious branch of the famous Běijīng roast duck restaurant (p149). There are Shāndōng, Běijīng and Sìchuān dishes, including jiācháng shāo dòufu (family-style cooked tofu, Y12) and tiěbǎn yángtuǐ (lamb leg hot plate, Y30), but most people come for the duck. The zhá mógu (fried mushrooms, Y15) are tasty, but a bit dry. Wash it all down with a bottle of Maotai (Y580), Wuliangye (Y580) or a small bottle of Erguotou (Y6). You can get here on bus 83 from the main train station.

Getting There & Away

AIR

Jǐ'nán is connected to most major cities, with daily flights to Běijīng (Y640, one hour), Dàlián (Y910, one hour), Guǎngzhōu (Y1550, 2½ hours), Hāěrbīn (Y1130, 1¾ hours), Kūnmíng (Y1710, two hours), Shànghǎi (Y760, one hour), Xī'ān (Y870) and Yāntái (Y210, 45 minutes).

The **Jinan International Airport Ticket Office** (☎ 8611 4750) is at 66 Luoyuan Dajie. A **China Eastern Airlines** (☎ 693 4715/6, 24hr ticketing 693 4715/6; 165-2 Chezhan Jie) office is located just south of the main train station; an **air ticket office** (hángkōng shòupiào; ☎ 8834 2525, 24hr ticketing 8834 2525) is also located directly opposite the train station.

BUS

Jǐ'nán has at least three bus stations. The two most useful for travellers are the long-distance bus station (chángtú qìchē zhàn) in the north of town and the bus station opposite the main train station.

The **bus station** (☎ 8691 0789) opposite the main train station is efficient, with regular minibuses to Tài'ān (Y15, 1½ hours, every 30 minutes) and Qūfù (Y30, 2½ hours, every 30 minutes) until 7.30pm. Other destinations include Běijīng (Y106, nine hours, eight daily), Shànghǎi (Y216, 20 hours, 4.30pm and 7pm) and Tiānjīn (Y85, five daily), and regular departures head to Yāntái (Y110, five hours, every hour) and Qīngdǎo (Y95, 4½ hours, every hour) until 6.30pm.

The **long-distance bus station** (Jǐ'nán Chángtú Qìchē Zǒngzhàn; ☎ 8691 0789) on Jiluo Lu has frequent buses to plentiful destinations including

SHĀNDŌNG

Běijīng (Y106, 6½ hours, every 50 minutes), Qīngdǎo (Y50, 3½ hours, every 30 minutes), Yāntái (Y110, 4½ hours, every hour) and Wēihǎi (Y139, six hours, every hour).

TRAIN

There are two train stations in Jǐ'nán: most trains use the main train station (Jǐ'nán huǒchē zhàn), but a handful arrive and depart from the east train station (huǒchē dōngzhàn).

Jǐ'nán is a major link in the east-China rail system. From here there are direct trains to Běijīng (hard seat Y90, four to seven hours), Shànghǎi (Y136, nine to 14 hours) and Qīngdǎo (Y49, four hours). A night train runs to Zhèngzhōu (Y83, nine hours) and to Xī'ān (Y149, 17 hours).

Tickets are available from the train station and (for a service fee) from the **Shandong China Railway International Travel Service** (Shāndōng Zhōngtiě Guólǔ; ☎ 8242 8315; 16 Chezhan Jie; ☼ 8am-5.30pm), near the train station, or at your hotel.

Getting Around
TO/FROM THE AIRPORT

Jǐ'nán's **Yaoqiang airport** (☎ 8208 6666) is 40km from the city and can be reached in around 40 minutes. Buses (Y20) run to the airport from the Yuquan Simpson Hotel (Yùquán Sēnxin Dàjiǔdiàn) on Luoyuan Dajie every hour between 6am and 6pm. A taxi will cost around Y100.

BUS & TAXI

Bus 33 connects the long-distance bus station with the main train station. Bus K51 runs from the main train station through the city centre and then south past Baotu Spring Park and on to Thousand Buddha Mountain. Taxis start at Y7 for the first 3km, then Y1.2 per kilometre thereafter.

AROUND JǏ'NÁN
Zhūjiāyù 朱家峪
☎ 0531

With its coffee-coloured soil and unspoiled bucolic panoramas, the charming stone **village** (admission Y15) of Zhūjiāyù, 45km east of Jǐ'nán, provides a fascinating foray into one of Shāndōng's oldest intact hamlets. Local claims that a settlement has been here since Shang times (1700–1100 BC) may be a case of 'blowing the cow' (chuīniú) – the Chinese for 'bragging' – but even though most

of Zhūjiāyù's buildings date from the more recent Ming and Qing dynasties, walking its narrow streets is a journey way back in time.

Shielded by hills on three sides, Zhūjiāyù can be fully explored in a morning or afternoon. Pay at the main gate in the restored **wall** enclosing the northern flank of the village that divides the old part of Zhūjiāyù from its uninteresting modern section, and walk along the Ming dynasty **double track old road** (双轨古道; shuānggui gǔdào), which leads to the **Wenchang Pavilion** (文昌阁; Wénchāng Gé), an arched gate topped by a single-roofed hall dating from the Qing dynasty. On your left is the **Shanyin Primary School** (山阴小学; Shānyīn Xiǎoxué), a delightful series of courtyards and halls, several of which now contain exhibitions detailing local agricultural tools and techniques. Unexpectedly, a huge portrait of **Chairman Mao** rears up ahead, painted on a screen and dating from 1966. The colours are slightly faded, but the image is surprisingly vivid.

The rest of the village largely consists of ancestral temples, including the **Zhu Family Ancestral Hall** (朱氏家祠; Zhūshì Jiācí), packed mudbrick homesteads (many of which are deserted and collapsing), small shrines and a delightful crop of arched **stone bridges** (shíqiáo). Note the occasional carved wood lintels over doorways and hunt down the **Lijiao Bridge** (立交桥; Lìjiāo Qiáo), a brace of ancient arched bridges dating from 1671. Zhūjiāyù becomes almost Mediterranean in feel when you reach the end of the village and dry-stone walls rise in layers up the hills. Climb past a statue of Guanyin to the **Kuixing Pavilion** (魁星楼; Kuíxing Lóu ; Y2) crowning the hill above the village for lovely views of the surrounding countryside.

If you want to spend the night in the peace and tranquillity of the village, check into the **Gucun Inn** (古村酒家; Gǔcūn Jiǔjiā; ☎ 8380 8135; d with shower Y60), a lovely old building with a courtyard and a spirit wall decorated with a peacock, 80m from the Lijiao Bridge. For eats, there are a few restaurants in the old village and occasional streetside chefs fry up live scorpions for peckish visitors.

GETTING THERE & AWAY

To reach Zhūjiāyù from Jǐ'nán, take a bus (Y12, 1½ hours, every 15 minutes, 6am to 7.30pm) to Míngshuǐ (明水; also called Zhāngqiū, 章丘) from the south station of the **long-distance bus station** (Jǐ'nán Chángtú Qìchē Zǒngzhàn) on Jiluo Lu. From Míngshuǐ long-distance bus station take a bus (Y3, 35 minutes, every hour, 7am to 6pm) to Zhūjiāyù; if there are not enough travellers going to Zhūjiāyù, you may be dropped off at the bottom of the road, where it's a further 2km to the village. Heading back to Míngshuǐ, buses leave from Zhūjiāyù on the hour (Y3, 35 minutes). Regular minibuses (Y12, 1½ hours, every 15 minutes from 5am to 6pm) return to Jǐ'nán from the Míngshuǐ long-distance bus station.

Simen Pagoda 四门塔

Near the village of Liǔbù (柳埠), 33km southeast of Jǐ'nán, are some of the oldest Buddhist structures in Shāndōng. Shentong Monastery holds **Simen Pagoda** (Sìmén Tǎ; Four Gate Pagoda; admission Y20; 8am-6pm), which dates back to the 6th century and is possibly the oldest stone pagoda in China. The surrounding hills are old burial grounds for the monks of the monastery.

Standing close to the Shentong Monastery and surrounded by stupas, **Longhu Pagoda** (龙虎塔; Lónghǔ Tǎ; Pagoda of the Dragon and the Tiger) dates to the Tang dynasty. Higher up is Thousand Buddha Cliff (千佛崖; Qiānfó Yá), with carved grottoes containing Buddhas.

To reach Simen Pagoda from Jǐ'nán, take bus 67 (Y3, 1½ hours) to the Sìmén Tǎ stop. The Shandong Travel Service (p207) can arrange tours.

TÀI'ĀN 泰安

☎ 0538 / pop 787,375

Gateway town to the mountain of Tài Shān looming above, Tài'ān is much wealthier and more with-it than retiring Qūfù to the south. Tài'ān has several sights of interest and as you will need the better part of a day for the mountain, spending the night here is advised.

Orientation

The most appealing part of town lies in the vicinity of the Dai Temple, Hongmen Lu, and the east–west running Dongyue Dajie and Shengping Jie. This area also contains a range of hotels, internet cafés and restaurants. The train and long-distance bus stations are in the less attractive west part of town. Maps are widely available from street vendors.

Information

Bank of China (Zhōngguó Yínháng; 48 Dongyue Dajie; 8.30am-5pm) Has a 24-hour ATM accepting Visa, MasterCard, Cirrus, JCB and Amex.

Big World Internet (Dàshìjiè Wǎngbā; Hongmen Lu; per hr Y1.50-2; 8am-midnight)

Central Hospital (Zhōngxīn Yīyuàn; ☎ 822 4161; 29 Longtan Lu)

China International Travel Service (CITS; Zhōngguó Guójì Lǚxíngshè; ☎ 820 7797; www.taishan-cits.com; ground fl, Puzhao Hotel, off Puzhaosi Lu)

Kunyu Internet Café (Kūnyǔ Wǎngbā; 18 Hongmen Lu; per hr Y1.50; 24hr)

Post Office (yóujú; 9 Dongyue Dajie; 8am-7pm summer, to 6pm winter)

Public Security Bureau (PSB; Gōngānjú; ☎ 827 5264; cnr Dongyue Dajie & Qingnian Lu; 8.30am-noon & 1-5pm Mon-Fri) The visa office is in the eastern side of this huge, modern building.

Shuyu Pingmin Pharmacy (Shùyù Píngmín Dàyàofáng; Dongyue Dajie) It has 24-hour service.

Tai'an Tourism Information Centre (Tài'ānshì Lǚyóu Zīxún Zhōngxīn; 24hr) In front of the train station.

Wanjing Internet Café (Wànjìng Wǎngbā; 180 Daizong Dajie; per hr Y1.50; 7am-midnight)

Xinhua Bookshop (Xīnhuá Shūdiàn; 80-82 Qingnian Lu; 8.30am-7.30pm summer, to 6pm winter)

Sights

DAI TEMPLE 岱庙

With its eternal-looking trees and commanding location at the hub of Tài'ān, this magnificent **temple complex** (Dài Miào; ☎ 822 3491; Daibeng Lu; admission Y20; 7.40am-6.50pm, last tickets 6.30pm) was a traditional pilgrimage stop on the route to the mountain and the site of sacrifices to the god of Tài Shān. It also forms a delightful portrait of Chinese temple architecture, with birds squawking among the hoary cypresses and ancient stelae looking silently on. Most visitors enter by the north gate at the south end of Hongmen Lu, although entering the complex via the southern gate allows you to follow the traditional passage through the temple.

Just within the north gate two attractive gardens are arranged with potted ornamental trees on either side. The main hall is the colossal twin yellow-eaved, nine-bay wide **Hall of Heavenly Blessing** (天贶殿; Tiānkuàng Diàn), which dates to AD 1009. The dark interior is decorated with a marvellous, flaking, 62m-long Song dynasty fresco depicting Emperor Zhenzong as the god of Tài Shān. Among the cast of characters are elephants, camels and lions, but the gloomy interior makes it hard to discern much. Also in the hall is a statue of the God of Tài Shān, seated in front of a tablet that reads 'Dōngyuè Tàishān zhī Shén' ('God

SHĀNDŌNG

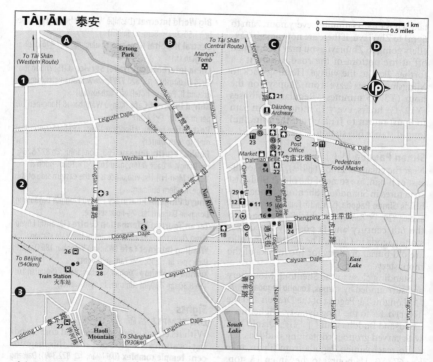

TÀI'ĀN 泰安

of the Eastern Peak Tài Shān'). Photography is not allowed inside.

South of the hall are several stelae supported on the backs of fossilized-looking *bìxì* (mythical tortoiselike dragons). Look out for the scripture pillar, its etched words long lost to the Shāndōng winds and inquisitive hands.

In the Han Bai courtyard stand cypresses supposedly planted by the Han emperor Wudi. Near the entrance to the courtyard is a vast *bìxì* with five-inch fangs.

Try to come in spring, when the trees are in bloom. To the south of the south gate (正阳门; Zhèngyáng Mén) is the splendid Dàimiào Fāng, an ornamental arch (*páifāng*) decorated with four pairs of heavily weathered lions, and dragon and phoenix motifs. Also south of the temple, the **Yaocan Pavilion** (遥参亭; Yáocān Tíng; admission Y1) contains a hall dedicated to effigies of the Old Mother of Taishan (Taishan Laomu), Bixia and a deity (Songzi Niangniang) entreated by women who want children. Further south still, a final memorial arch stands flanked by two iron lions alongside busy Dongyue Dajie.

CHRISTIAN CHURCH 基督教堂

This German-built, possibly early-20th-century **church** (2 Dengyun Jie) lies tucked away in the heart of Tài'ān. Largely hidden behind a wall just west off Qingnian Lu (on a small side street called Dengyun Jie, literally 'Climb the Clouds Street'; 登云街), this sweet little House of the Lord has Gothic arches, stone walls, a small belfry and regular services. The white building at the front is possibly the old church house. Other German relics include the towering old train station building – a solid stone-built structure immediately east of Tàishān train station – emblazoned with the characters 'Tài'ān Zhàn' (Taian Station).

Sleeping

Jixiang Hotel (Jíxiáng Lǚguǎn; ☎ 677 9943; Daimiao Beijie; 岱庙北街; s & d Y40) In the block on the corner of Daimiao Beijie and Hongmen Lu opposite the north gate of Dai Temple, this simple budget hotel is tucked away in the corner of the ground floor courtyard. All 20 basic rooms come with fan (no air-con) and TV, with common loo and shower. No English sign and limited English spoken.

INFORMATION		SIGHTS & ACTIVITIES		Taishan Hotel 泰山宾馆...............21 C1

INFORMATION
Bank of China 中国银行...............1 B2
Big World Internet
　大世界网吧...............2 C2
Central Hospital
　中心医院...............3 A2
CITS 中国国际旅行社...............4 B1
Kunyu Internet Café
　坤宇网吧...............5 C2
Post Office 总邮局...............6 C2
PSB 公安局...............7 C2
Shuyu Pingmin Pharmacy
　漱玉平民大药房...............8 C2
Tai'an Tourism Information Centre
　泰安市旅游咨询中心...............9 A3
Wanjing Internet Café
　万景网吧...............10 C2
Xinhua Bookshop 新华书店...............11 C2

SIGHTS & ACTIVITIES
Christian Church
　基督教堂...............12 C2
Dai Temple 岱庙...............13 C2
North Entrance to Dai Temple
　岱庙北入口处...............14 C2
South Entrance to Dai Temple
　岱庙南入口处...............15 C2
Yaocan Pavilion 遥参亭...............16 C2

SLEEPING
Jixiang Hotel 吉祥旅馆...............17 C2
Overseas Chinese Hotel
　华侨大厦...............18 C2
Roman Holiday
　罗马假日商务酒店...............19 C1
Taishan Grand Hotel
　泰山大酒店...............20 C1

Taishan Hotel 泰山宾馆...............21 C1
Yuzuo Hotel 御座宾馆...............22 C2

EATING 🍴
Ā Dōng de Shuǐjiǎo
　阿东的水饺...............23 C2
Dàoxiāngyuán 稻香园...............24 C2
Shuzhuang Hotpot Restaurant
　蜀庄火锅城...............25 C2

TRANSPORT
Bus 3 (to Tài Shān)
　三路汽车往泰山...............26 A3
Long-Distance Bus Station
　长途汽车站...............27 A3
Tai Shan Bus Station
　泰山汽车站...............28 A3
Ticket Office 航空订票处...............29 C2

Taishan Grand Hotel (Tàishān Dàjiǔdiàn; ☎ 822 7211; fax 822 6162; 210 Daizong Dajie; 岱宗大街210号; d Y280-460, ste Y680; 🖳) One of Tài'ān's old hotels, this hotel has a good location with views of Tài Shān or the Dai Temple and the rooms are – worn but comfy enough – enjoy good discounts.

Yuzuo Hotel (Yùzuò Bīnguǎn; ☎ 826 9999; fax 822 3179; 3 Daimiao Beijie; 岱庙北街3号; d Y280-480, tr Y360, ste Y460-680; 🖳) Pleasantly positioned next to the Dai Temple and attractively trimmed with lights at night, this peaceful hotel is manned by polite staff and ranges among low-rise, two-storey blocks. Pricier 'A' double rooms are smarter than the older-looking 'B' rooms. There's a small pharmacy, supermarket, restaurant (cooking up Taoist dishes) and slow-moving dance hall.

Roman Holiday (Luómǎ Jiàrì Shāngwù Jiǔdiàn; cnr Hongmen Lu & Daizong Dajie; 近红门路, 岱宗大街; s & d Y298) Crisp and neat rooms come with see-through showers, glass sinks and all mod-cons in this modern, packaged business-esque four-storey hotel with an odd name. It's formulaic and there's no character, but it's a notch above much of the local competition in the midrange market.

Taishan Hotel (Tàishān Bīnguǎn; ☎ 822 5678; fax 822 1432; 26 Hongmen Lu; 红门路26号; d incl breakfast Y300-420; 🖳) At the foot of Tài Shān on Hongmen Lu, the tour-group oriented three-star Taishan Hotel has two kinds of doubles: the large, clean 'A' rooms and the darker, older and cheaper 'B' rooms. The five-storey hotel is well staffed, with a shop and ticketing service. The breakfast is buffet style.

Overseas Chinese Hotel (Huáqiáo Dàshà; ☎ 822 0001; fax 822 8171; 15 Dongyue Dajie; 东岳大街15号; d Y400-600, ste Y1000-1980; 🖳) Beyond the huge golden effigy of Milefo (the laughing Buddha) in the lobby and the deserted 'English Inspiration City Club' bar, this four-star hotel has zero charm, but the rooms are fine. Some doubles have computers, while at the other end of the scale, 30% discount brings the cheapest doubles down to around Y280.

Eating

Ā Dōng de Shuǐjiǎo (☎ 827 3644; 178 Daizong Dajie; meals Y25-35) This handily located, clean dumpling restaurant fills you up with jiǎozi (饺子; stuffed dumplings), including yángròu (羊肉; lamb, Y16 per jīn – half a jīn is enough for one), sūsānxiàn (素三线; vegetable, Y10 per jīn) and xiānggūròu (香菇肉; Chinese mushroom and meat, Y14 per jīn). Other staples include soups and hóngshāo qiézi (红烧茄子; braised aubergine, Y8), sweet and laced with garlic. A sister branch (Ā Dōng Jiāchángcài) is around the corner at 25 Hongmen Lu.

Shuzhuang Hotpot Restaurant (Shǔzhuāng Huǒguōchéng; cnr Daizong Dajie & Hushan Lu; meals Y40) If you're a group then order lashings of beer and sweat it out around the hotpot fishing out strips of yángròu (羊肉; New Zealand lamb, Y12), yúwán (鱼丸; fish balls, Y10), xiān xiānggū (鲜香菇; mushrooms, Y8), xiān dòufu (鲜豆腐; fresh tofu, Y4), tǔdòu piàn (土豆片; potato slices, Y4) and báicài (白菜; Chinese cabbage, Y4) from the boiling broth. Singletons don't despair: individual pots are also provided, heated over an alcohol flame.

Dàoxiāngyuán (48 Shengping Jie) This brightly lit bakery runs to several branches in town, with a great choice of fresh, chunky chilled sandwiches (Y3.50 to Y5; tuna, chicken, bacon, ham), tarts, fresh bread, cream puffs (Y2) and cakes.

SHĀNDŌNG

Getting There & Away

AIR

The nearest large airport is at Jǐ'nán. Tickets can be purchased from the **ticket office** (hángkōng dìngpiàochù; ☎ 827 0855; 111 Qingnian Lu; ⏰ 8am-6pm Mon-Sat).

BUS

There are four long-distance bus stations in Tài'ān. Handy buses leave from outside Tàishān train station (Y16, every 30 minutes, 6.30am to 6pm). From the **long-distance bus station** (chángtú qìchēzhàn; ☎ 210 8606; Panhe Lu), south of the train station, are buses to Jǐ'nán (Y20, 1½ hours, every 30 minutes, 6.10am to 6.40pm), Kāifēng (Y63, one daily), Qūfù (Y16, one hour, every 20 minutes), Qīngdǎo (Y95, three to four hours, 6am, 8am and 2.30pm), Yāntái (Y114, four hours, 7am), Wēihǎi (Y129, several per day) and Běijīng (Y129, four hours, 8.30am and 2.30pm). From the **Tai Shan Bus Station** (Tài Shān Qìchēzhàn; Caiyuan Dajie), there are regular buses to Jǐ'nán (Y11.5 to Y16, 1½ hours, every 30 minutes, 6am to 6pm).

TRAIN

Exiting Tàishān station, the first thing you see is a huge white bust of Lei Feng, an iconic soldier of the Mao era. Trains run to Běijīng (hard seat Y79, six hours, five daily), Jǐ'nán (hard seat Y7, one hour, nine daily), Yǎnzhōu (for Qūfù; hard seat Y15), Shànghǎi (Y102, 10 daily) and Qīngdǎo (Y80, five hours).

Getting Around

There are three main bus routes. Bus 3 (Y1) runs from the Tài Shān central route trailhead to the western route trailhead at Tianwai Village (Tiānwài Cūn) via the train station. Buses 1 and 2 also end up near the train station.

Taxis can be found outside the train station; they start at Y5 (then Y1.50 per kilometre thereafter).

TÀI SHĀN 泰山

☎ 0538

Southern Chinese claim 'myriad mountains, rivers and geniuses' while Shāndōng citizens smugly contest they have 'one mountain, one river and one saint', implying they have the last word on each: Tài Shān, the Yellow River and Confucius. Tài Shān is the most revered of China's five sacred Taoist peaks, with imperial sacrifices to heaven and

earth offered from its summit. Only five of China's emperors ever climbed Tài Shān, although Emperor Qianlong of the Qing dynasty scaled it 11 times. From its heights Confucius uttered the dictum 'The world is small'; Mao lumbered up and declared 'The East is Red'. You, too, can climb up and say 'I'm knackered'.

Tài Shān is a unique experience; its supernatural allure (see the boxed text, p217) attracts the Chinese in droves. Bixia, the Princess of the Azure Clouds, a Taoist deity whose presence permeates the temples dotted along the route, is a powerful cult figure for the rural women of Shāndōng and beyond. Tribes of wiry grandmothers – it's said that if you climb Tài Shān you'll live to 100 – trot up the steps with surprising ease, their target the cluster of temples at the summit where they burn money and incense, praying for their progeny. Sun worshippers muster wide-eyed on the peak, straining for the first flickers of dawn. In ancient Chinese tradition, it was believed that the sun began its westward journey from Tài Shān.

Tài Shān is 1545m above sea level, with a climbing distance of 7.5km from base to summit on the central route. The elevation change from Midway Gate to Heaven (Zhōngtiān Mén), halfway up the mountain, to the summit is approximately 600m. The mountain is not a major climb, but with 6660 steps to the summit, it can be gruelling. One wonders how many backs were broken in the building of the temples and stone stairs on Tài Shān – a massive undertaking accomplished without any mechanical aids.

Climate

Bear in mind that weather conditions on the mountain vary considerably compared with Tài'ān (p211). Clouds and mist frequently envelop the mountain, particularly in summer. The best times to visit are in spring and autumn when the humidity is low, although old-timers suggest that the clearest weather is from early October onwards. In winter the weather is often fine, but very cold. The tourist season peaks from May to October.

Due to weather changes, you're advised to carry warm clothing with you, no matter what the season. The summit can be very cold, windy and wet; army overcoats are available there for hire and you can buy waterproof coats from one of the vendors.

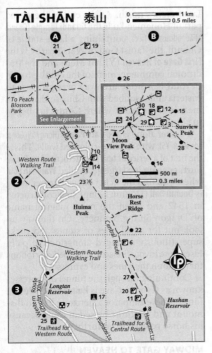

TÀI SHĀN 泰山

Climbing Tài Shān

The town of Tài'ān lies at the foot of Tài Shān and is the gateway to the mountain. Low-season tickets are Y80 (1 December to 31 January), high-season tickets are Y100 (1 February to 30 November); student and senior tickets are half price. Voluntary insurance is available for Y2. Avoid coinciding your climb with the public-holiday periods held in the first weeks of May and October, otherwise you will share the mountain with what the Chinese call '*rén shān rén hǎi*' – literally a 'mountain of people and a sea of persons'.

ON FOOT

It's possible to spend the night at Midway Gate to Heaven (halfway up the mountain) or on the summit. Allow two hours for climbing between each of these points, and a total of eight hours for the round trip (although you can get down to the ticket office from the Midway Gate to Heaven in an hour, at speed). Allowing several more hours would make the climb less strenuous and give you more time to look around.

If you want to see the sunrise, dump your gear at the train station or at a guesthouse in Tài'ān and time your ascent so that you'll reach the summit before sundown. Stay overnight at one of the summit guesthouses and get up early the next morning for the famed sunrise. It's possible to scale the mountain at night and some Chinese do this, timing it so that they arrive before sunrise. The way is lit by lamps, but it is advisable to take a torch, as well as warm clothes, food and water.

There are two main paths up the mountain: the central route and the western route, converging midway at Midway Gate to Heaven. Most people slog up the central route (once the imperial route and littered with cultural relics) and head down (usually by bus) along the western route. Other trails run through orchards and woods.

BY MINIBUS & CABLE CAR

From the roundabout at Tianwai Village (天 外村; Tiānwài Cūn), at the foot of the western route, minibuses (one way Y20) depart every 20 minutes (when full) to Midway Gate to Heaven, halfway up Tài Shān. The minibuses operate 4am to 8pm during high season, less regularly during low season. Bus 3 runs to Tianwai Village from Tài'ān's train station. Frequent buses come down the mountain; however, you may have to wait several buses for a seat.

It's about a five-minute walk from Midway Gate to Heaven to the **cable car** (kōngzhōng suǒdào; adult/child Y45/20; 7am-6pm 16 Apr-15 Oct, 8am-5.30pm 16 Oct-15 Apr). The journey takes around 10 to 15 minutes to travel to **Moon View Peak** (Yuèguān Fēng), near the South Gate to Heaven (Nántiān Mén). Be warned, high season and weekend queues may force you to wait up to two hours for a ride.

The same applies when you want to descend from the summit; fortunately, there is another **cable car** (suǒdào; adult/child Y45/20; 7.30am-5.30pm 16 Apr-15 Oct, 8am-5pm 16 Oct-15 Apr) that only carries six passengers and is as regular as clockwork. It takes you from north of South Gate to Heaven down to **Peach Blossom Park** (桃花源; Táohuā Yuán), a scenic area behind Tài Shān that is also worth exploring. From here you can take a minibus to Tài'ān (Y20, 40 minutes). You can reverse this process by first taking a minibus from Tài'ān train station to Peach Blossom Park and then ascending by cable car.

CENTRAL ROUTE

On this route you'll see a bewildering catalogue of bridges, trees, rivers, gullies, towers, inscriptions, caves, pavilions and temples. Tài Shān functions as an outdoor museum of calligraphic art, with the prize items being the **Rock Valley Scripture** (Jīng Shíyù) along the first section of the walk and the **North Prayer Rock** (Gǒngběi Shí), which commemorates an imperial sacrifice, at the summit. Lost on most foreigners are the literary allusions, word games and analogies spelt out by the calligraphy decorating the journey.

Purists commence their ascents of Tài Shān after a south–north perambulation through the Dai Temple (p211), in imitation of imperial custom. From the Dai Temple, Hongmen Lu stretches north. At the end of the paved part of Hongmen Lu is the **Guandi Temple** (Guāndì Miào; admission free), containing a large statue of Guandi, the Taoist God of War. Nearby is the **First Gate of Heaven** (Yītiān Mén) and the traditional commencement of the climb proper. Beyond is a stone archway overgrown with wisteria and inscribed with Chinese characters meaning 'the place where Confucius began to climb'.

Further along is **Red Gate Palace** (Hóng Mén Gōng; admission Y5), with its wine-coloured walls. This is the first of a series of temples dedicated to Bixia. Further again is a large gate called **Wànxiān Lóu**, where you find the ticket office. Further along is **Doumu Hall** (Dǒumǔ Gōng), first constructed in 1542 and given the more magical name of 'Dragon Spring Nunnery'. On the way up look out for small piles of stones and rocks superstitiously arranged alongside the path. Elsewhere invocations are inscribed on ribbons that festoon the pines and cypresses.

Continuing through the tunnel of cypresses known as Cypress Cave is **Huima Peak** (Huímǎ Ling), where Emperor Zhenzong had to dismount and continue by sedan chair because his horse refused to go further.

MIDWAY GATE TO HEAVEN 中天门

The second celestial gate is where you can rest your legs, allow your pulse to slow and perhaps peruse the small and smoky **God of Wealth Temple** (财神庙; Cáishén Miào). Further ahead is **Five Pine Pavilion** (Wǔsōng Tíng), where, in 219 BC, Emperor Qin Shi Huang was overtaken by a violent storm and was sheltered by the pine trees. He promoted them to the fifth rank of minister.

Ahead is the arduous **Path of Eighteen Bends** (十八盘) that eventually leads to the summit; climbing it is performed in slow motion by all and sundry as legs turn to lead. You'll pass **Opposing Pines Pavilion** (Duìsōng Tíng) and the **Welcoming Pine** (Yíngkè Sōng) – every mountain worth its salt in China has one – with a branch extended as if to shake hands. Beyond is the **Archway to Immortality** (Shēngxiān Fāng). It was believed that those passing through the archway would become celestial beings. From here to the summit, emperors were carried in sedan chairs.

SOUTH GATE TO HEAVEN 南天门

The final stretch takes you to South Gate to Heaven, the third celestial gate. Walk along

TÀI SHĀN

Tài Shān's place in the hearts and minds of the Chinese people is deeply rooted in their most ancient creation myth – the story of Pan Gu. In the beginning when all was chaos, and heaven and earth were swirling together, Pan Gu was born and promptly set about separating the ground and the sky. With each passing day he grew taller, the sky grew higher and the earth grew thicker, until, after 18,000 years, the two were fully separated and Pan Gu died of exhaustion. As his body disintegrated, his eyes became the sun and the moon, his blood transformed into rivers, his sweat fell as rain, and his head and limbs became the five sacred Taoist mountains of China, Tài Shān among them.

Maybe because it sprang from Pan Gu's head, or perhaps because of its location in the dominant east (which signifies birth and spring), Tài Shān is the most revered of the five holy Taoist peaks. The throngs of modern visitors are but recipients of a tradition of pilgrimage and worship that stretches back to earliest historical times.

For nearly 3000 years emperors have paid homage, a few reaching the summit, all contributing to the rich legacy of temples, trees, pavilions and calligraphy. Originally made for sacrifices, these visits soon acquired a political significance: it was thought heaven would never allow an unworthy ruler to ascend, so a successful climb denoted divine approval.

Emperors aside, China's three most prominent schools of thought also hold Tài Shān dear. A second legend has it there once lived a she-fox on Tài Shān, who, by living a strict Taoist existence, transformed into a goddess named Bixia (Princess of the Azure Clouds). There she remained happily until the arrival of Sakyamuni, the founder of Buddhism, who fell in love with the place and asked her to leave. Bixia refused and Sakyamuni was forced to flee when he tried unsuccessfully to trick her into leaving. Today Bixia is venerated as the protector of peasant women and as the bringer of dawn. A Taoist monk named Lang established the first temples on the mountain in 351 BC, and the most influential remain those dedicated to Bixia.

Thus Tài Shān has become a repository of Chinese culture, spanning dynasties and religions, and prompting the modern Chinese writer Guo Moruo to describe the mountain as 'a partial miniature of Chinese culture'. Indeed, it is probably best to bear this analogy in mind when you visit, as modern China is definitely leaving its mark. Even by the Qing dynasty there were several hundred thousand visitors each year, and during the week-long May Day holiday in 2006, a staggering 190,000 people crowded onto the mountain.

Tian Jie to **Azure Clouds Temple** (Bìxiá Cí; admission Y5), with its sublime perch in the clouds, where elders offer money and food to the deities of Bixia, Yanguang Nainai and Taishan Songzi Niangniang (the latter helping women bear children). The iron tiling on the temple buildings is intended to prevent damage by strong winds, and *chīwěn* (ornaments meant to protect against fire) decorate the bronze eaves.

Climbing higher, you will pass the Taoist **Qingdi Palace** (青帝宫; Qīngdì Gōng), before the fog- and cloud-swathed **Jade Emperor Temple** (Yùhuáng Dǐng) comes into view, perched on the highest point (1545m) of the Tài Shān plateau. Within is an effigy of the Jade Emperor, an attendant statue of Taishan Laojun and some frescoes.

In front of the temple is the one piece of calligraphy that you really can appreciate – the **Wordless Monument** (Wúzì Bēi). One story goes that it was set up by Emperor Wu 2100 years ago – he wasn't satisfied with what his scribes came up with, so he left it to the viewer's imagination. Others attribute the monument to Qin Shi Huang (p37). In the courtyard stands a rock inscribed with the elevation of the mountain. Pilgrims toss coins into two urns at the exact peak (Tàishān Jídǐng) below a tablet upon which is written the ancient Taoist character for Tài Shān. Near the Shenqi Hotel (p218) stands a **Confucius Temple** (Wén Miào), where statues of Confucius (Kongzi), Mencius (Mengzi), Zengzi and other Confucian luminaries are venerated.

The main sunrise vantage point is the **North Prayer Rock** (Gǒngběi Shí; see opposite); if you're lucky, visibility extends to over 200km, as far as the coast. The sunset slides over the Yellow River side. At the rear of the mountain is the **Rear Rocky Recess** (Hòu Shíwù), one of the better-known spots for viewing pine trees, where some ruins can be found tangled in the

SHĀNDŌNG

foliage. It's a good place to ramble and lose the crowds for a while.

WESTERN ROUTE

The most popular way to descend the mountain is by bus via the western route. The footpath and road intercept at a number of points, and are often one and the same. Given the amount of traffic, you might prefer to hop on a bus rather than inhale its exhaust. If you do hike down, the trail is not always clearly marked. (Note that buses will not stop for you once they have left Midway Gate to Heaven.)

Either by bus or foot, the western route treats you to considerable variation in scenery, with orchards, pools and flowering plants. The major attraction along this route is **Black Dragon Pool** (Hēilóng Tán), which is just below **Longevity Bridge** (Chángshòu Qiáo) and is fed by a small waterfall. Swimming in the waters are rare carp, which are occasionally cooked and served to visitors. Mythical tales swarm about the pool, said to be the site of underground carp palaces and of magic herbs that turn people into beasts.

An enjoyable conclusion to your descent is a visit to **Puzhao Temple** (Pǔzhào Sì; Pervading Light Temple; admission Y5; ☼ 8am-5.30pm). One of the few strictly Buddhist shrines in the area, this simple temple dates to the Southern and Northern dynasties (AD 420–589). An arrangement of ancient pine trees and small halls rising in levels up the hillside, the temple provides a quiet and restful end to the hike.

Sleeping & Eating

Accommodation prices here don't apply to holiday periods, such as the first week of May and October, when room prices can triple. At other times, ask for discounts.

Xianju Hotel (Xiānjū Fàndiàn; ☎ 823 9984; fax 822 6877; 2 Tian Jie; 天街2号; s/d/tr/q Y420/560/660/980) Situated just before the *páilou* marking Tian Jie beyond the South Gate to Heaven, this two-star hotel has a decent selection of rooms.

Shenqi Hotel (Shénqí Bīnguǎn; ☎ 822 3866; fax 821 5399; s Y580, d Y680-780, ste Y6800-8800; ☒) The only three-star hotel on the summit, this reasonably smart hotel has a restaurant (serving Taoist banquets) and a bar, and is accessed up some steep steps. Rooms are reasonably clean, but nothing special (sun watchers are roused well before sunrise).

There is no food shortage on Tài Shān; the central route is dotted with teahouses, stalls,

vendors and restaurants. Your pockets are likely to feel emptier than your stomach, but keep in mind that all supplies are carried up by foot and that the prices rise as you do.

QŪFÙ 曲阜
☎ 0537 / population 88,000

Of monumental significance to the Chinese is the walled town of Qūfù, birthplace of Confucius, with its traditional harmonies of carved stone, timber and imperial architecture. Inscribed everywhere in Qūfù is Confucius' upbeat dictum: '有朋自远方来不亦乐乎' ('Is it not a joy to have friends come from afar?') Taking the sage's wisdom at face value, name-chop hawkers, pedicab drivers and map-sellers joyfully press their goods and services on out-of-towners and fending it all off can be draining.

Orientation

The old walled core of Qūfù is small and easy to get around, a charming grid of streets built around the Confucius Temple and Confucius Mansions at its heart, with the Confucius Forest north of town. Gulou Jie bisects the town from north to south, and the bus station is in the south of town.

Information
BOOKSHOPS

Xinhua Bookstore (Xīnhuá Shūdiàn; Gulou Nanjie; ☼ 8am-6.30pm summer, to 5.30pm winter) Opposite southeast corner of Drum Tower.

INTERNET ACCESS 网吧

Xiuxian Hotel Internet Café (Xiūxián Bīnguǎn Wǎngbā; 2nd fl, 20 Gulou Nanjie; per hr Y2; ☼ 8am-midnight)

Zhixin Internet Café (Zhīxīn Wǎngbā; per hr Y3; ☼ 8am-midnight) It's located in an alley east off Shendao Lu. Head north up Shendao Lu and take first turn-off on left.

MEDICAL SERVICES

Gulou Pharmacy (Gǔlóu Yàodiàn; 12 Gulou Beijie; ☼ 7.30am-8pm)

People's Hospital (Rénmín Yīyuàn; ☎ 441 2440; Tianguandi Jie)

People's No 2 Hospital (Rénmín Dìèr Yīyuàn; 7 Gulou Beijie)

MONEY

Bank of China (Zhōngguó Yínháng; 96 Dongmen Dajie; ☼ 8am-6pm) Foreign exchange, but no ATM for foreign cards.

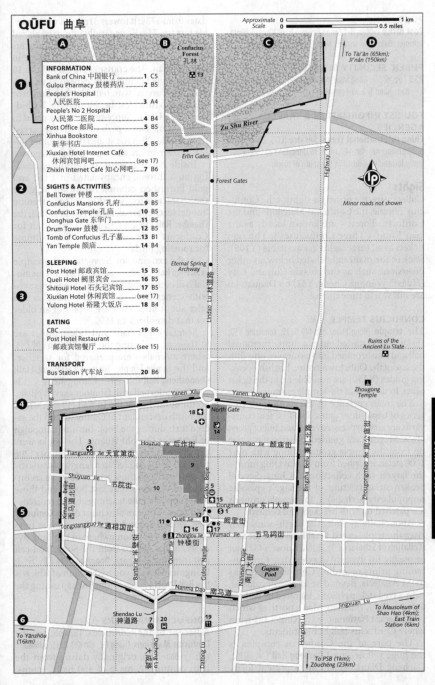

QŪFÙ 曲阜

Approximate Scale
0 — 1 km
0 — 0.5 miles

Confucius Forest 孔林

To Tài'ān (65km); Jǐ'nán (150km)

Zu Shu River

Erlin Gates

Forest Gates

Minor roads not shown

Eternal Spring Archway

Ruins of the Ancient Lu State

Zhougong Temple

Yanen Xilu — Yanen Dōnglu

North Gate

Houzuo Jie 后作街

Yanmiao Jie 颜庙街

Tianguandi Jie 天官第街

Shuyuan Jie 书院街

Dongmen Dajie 东门大街

Queli Jie

Wumaci Jie

五马祠街

Zhonglou Jie 钟楼街

Tongxiangguo Jie 通相国街

Gupan Pool

Nanma Dao 南马道

Jingxuan Lu

To Mausoleum of Shao Hao (4km); East Train Station (6km)

Shendao Lu 神道路

To Yǎnzhōu (16km)

To PSB (1km); Zōuchéng (23km)

SHĀNDŌNG

POST

Post office (yóujú; 8-1 Gulou Beijie; ⏰ 7.30am-6.30pm summer, 8am-6pm winter) North of the Drum Tower.

PUBLIC SECURITY BUREAU

PSB (公安局; Gōngānjú; ☎ 441 1403; 1 Wuyuntan Lu; ⏰ 8am-noon & 2.30-6pm Mon-Fri)

TOURIST INFORMATION & TRAVEL AGENCIES

China International Travel Service (CITS; Zhōngguó Guójì Lǚxíngshè; ☎ 449 1492; 36 Hongdao Lu) Inconveniently located way down in the south of town.

Sights

Collectively, the principle sights – the Confucius Temple, the Confucius Mansions and the Confucius Forest – are known locally as the 'Sān Kǒng' ('Three Confuciuses'). Through tickets to all three sights are available (Y105). Stick to the main sights listed below, as other diversions such as the Huaxia Cultural City (Huáxià Wénhuà Chéng; Y32) on Daquan Lu are not worth the expense.

CONFUCIUS TEMPLE 孔庙

The **temple** (Kǒng Miào; ☎ 449 5235; admission Y52; ⏰ 8am-5.30pm) started out as a simple memorial hall and mushroomed into a complex one-fifth the size of the Qūfù town centre. English-speaking guides (Y150) are available from the ticket office to the east of the temple entrance.

The main entrance in the south leads to a series of triple-door gates. The first few courtyards are airy, cypress-covered and full of green grass. Magnificent gnarled, twisting pines rise up from the temple grounds along with over 1000 stelae, inscribed from Han to Qing times – the largest such collection in China. Several broken stelae (victims of the sage's episodic unpopularity perhaps) in the temple grounds are patched up with brackets and cement.

About halfway along the north–south axis rises the triple-eaved **Great Pavilion of the Constellation of Scholars** (奎文阁; Kuíwén Gé), an imposing Jin dynasty wooden structure containing prints recording Confucius' exploits in the Analects. Beyond lie a series of colossal, twin-eaved stele pavilions, followed by **Dacheng Gate** (大成门; Dàchéng Mén), north of which is the **Apricot Platform** (杏坛; Xìng Tán) from where Confucius taught his students.

The core of the Confucian complex is the huge yellow-eaved **Dacheng Hall** (大成殿; Dàchéng Diàn), which, in its present form,

dates from 1724; it towers 31m on a white marble terrace. The Kong family imported glazed yellow tiling for the halls in the Confucius Temple, and special stones were brought in from Xīshān. The craftspeople carved the 10 dragon-coiled columns so expertly that they had to be covered with red silk when Emperor Qianlong visited lest he felt that the Forbidden City's Hall of Supreme Harmony paled in comparison. The superb stone they're carved from is called 'fish roe stone'; the smoother pillars at the rear are also carved with dragons.

Inside is a huge statue of Confucius residing on a throne, encapsulated in a red and gold burnished cabinet. Above the sage are the characters for 'wànshì shībiǎo', meaning 'model teacher for all ages'. The next hall, the **Chamber Hall** (寝殿; Qǐn Diàn), was built for Confucius' wife and now provides a home for roosting birds.

At the extreme northern end of the temple is **Shengji Hall** (圣迹殿; Shèngjì Diàn), a memorial hall containing a series of stones engraved with scenes from the life of Confucius and tales about him. They are copies of an older set that dates back to 1592.

Several other halls and side temples are at the rear, including the **Holy Kitchen** (神庖), where animals were prepared for sacrifice, and the **Family Temple**. East of Dacheng Hall, **Chongsheng Hall** (崇圣祠; Chóngshèng Cí) is similarly adorned with fabulous carved pillars. South of the hall is the **Lu Wall** (鲁壁), where the ninth descendant of Confucius hid the sacred texts during the book-burning campaign of Emperor Qin Shi Huang. The books were discovered again during the Han dynasty (206 BC–AD 220), and led to a lengthy scholastic dispute between those who followed a reconstructed version of the last books and those who supported the teachings in the rediscovered ones. You can also hunt down **Confucius' Well**. Dotted around are ancient scholar trees (some with roots somewhere in the Tang dynasty) and a gingko from the Song. You can exit from the east gate, **Donghua Gate** (东华门; Dōnghuá Mén), if you wish, south of which is the **Bell Tower** (钟楼; Zhōnglóu), spanning the width of Queli Jie.

CONFUCIUS MANSIONS 孔府

Adjacent to the Confucius Temple are the **Confucius Mansions** (Kǒng Fǔ; ☎ 441 2235; admission Y32; ⏰ 8am-5pm), originally dating from the 16th century. A maze of 450 halls, rooms,

CONFUCIANISM

Qūfù is the birth and death place of the sage Confucius (551–479 BC), whose impact was not felt during his own lifetime. He lived in abject poverty and hardly put pen to paper, but his teachings were recorded by dedicated followers in *The Analects of Confucius*. His descendants, the Kong (孔) family, fared considerably better.

As the original Confucian temple at Qūfù (dating from 478 BC) was enlarged, remodelled, added to, taken away from and rebuilt, the majority of the present buildings date from the Ming dynasty. In 1513 armed bands sacked the temple and the Kong residence, resulting in walls being erected around the town from 1522 to 1567 to fortify it. These walls were recently removed, but vestiges of Ming town planning, such as the extant Drum and Bell Towers (Gǔlóu and Zhōnglóu), remain.

Less a religion than a code that defined hierarchical relationships, Confucianism has had a profound impact on Chinese culture. It teaches that son must respect father, wife must respect husband, commoner must respect official, official must respect ruler and so on. The essence of its teachings are obedience, respect, selflessness and working for the common good.

You would think that this code would have fitted nicely into the new order of communism, yet it was swept aside because of its connections with the past. Confucius was seen as a kind of misguided feudal educator, and clan ties and ancestor worship were viewed as a threat. In 1948 Confucius' direct heir, the first-born son of the 77th generation of the Kong family, fled to Taiwan, breaking a 2500-year tradition of Kong residence in Qūfù.

While the current popularity of the great sage is undeniable, it is debatable as to what extent his teachings are taking fresh root in China. The majority of devotees around Qūfù are middle-aged or elderly, suggesting that the comeback of Confucianism is more likely a re-emergence of beliefs never effectively squashed by the communists. Chinese scholars are making careful statements reaffirming the significance of Confucius' historical role and suggesting that the 'progressive' aspects of his work were even cited in the writings of Mao Zedong. Confucius, too, it seems, can be rehabilitated.

buildings and side passages, getting around requires a compass. Not everything comes with English captions.

The Confucius Mansions were the most sumptuous aristocratic lodgings in China, indicative of the Kong family's former great power. From the Han to the Qing dynasties, the descendants of Confucius were ennobled and granted privileges by the emperors. They lived like kings themselves, with 180-course meals, servants and consorts. Confucius even picked up some posthumous honours.

Qūfù grew around the Confucius Mansions and was an autonomous estate administered by the Kongs, who had powers of taxation and execution. Emperors could drop in to visit; the Ceremonial Gate near the south entrance was opened only for this event. Because of this royal protection, huge quantities of furniture, ceramics, artefacts and customary and personal effects survived, and some may be viewed. The Kong family archives are a rich legacy and also survived.

The Confucius Mansions are built on an 'interrupted' north-to-south axis. Grouped by the south gate are the former administrative offices (taxes, edicts, rites, registration and examination halls).

The **Ceremonial Gate** (重光门; Chóngguāng Mén) leads to the **Great Hall** (大堂; Dà Táng), two further halls and then the **Neizhai Gate** (内宅门; Nèizhái Mén), a gate that seals off the residential quarters (used for weddings, banquets and private functions). The large '*shòu*' character (壽, meaning 'longevity') within the single-eaved **Upper Front Chamber** (前上房; Qián Shàng Fáng) north of Neizhai Gate was a gift from Qing empress Cixi. The **Front Chamber** (前堂楼; Qián Táng Lóu) was where the duke lived and is interestingly laid out on two floors – rare for a hall this size.

East of the Neizhai Gate is the **Tower of Refuge** (避难楼; Bìnán Lóu), where the Kong clan could gather if the peasants turned nasty. It has an iron-lined ceiling on the ground floor, a staircase that could be yanked up into the interior, a trap and provisions for a lengthy retreat. Grouped to the west of the main axis are former recreational facilities (studies, guestrooms, libraries and small temples). To the east is the odd kitchen, ancestral temple and the family branch apartments.

SHĀNDŌNG

One of the best features of the mansions is the garden at the rear, where greenery, foliage, flowers, blossoming trees (in spring), bamboo and a sense of space waits. Take a seat in one of the old pavilions and relax.

CONFUCIUS FOREST 孔林

North of town on Lindao Lu is the serene **Confucius Forest** (Kǒng Lín; admission Y40; ⏰ 7.30am-6pm), the largest artificial park and best preserved cemetery in China.

The pine and cypress forest of over 100,000 trees (it is said that each of Confucius' students planted a tree from his birthplace) covers 200 hectares and is bounded by a wall 10km long. Confucius and his descendants have been buried here over the past 2000 years, and are still being buried here today. Flanking the approach to the **Tomb of Confucius** (Kǒngzi Mù) are pairs of stone panthers, griffins and larger-than-life guardians. The Confucian barrow is a simple grass mound enclosed by a low wall and faced with a Ming dynasty stele. The sage's sons are buried nearby and scattered through the forest are dozens of temples and pavilions. Small minibuses offer tours (Y10).

To reach the forest takes about 30 minutes by foot, 15 minutes by taxi or you can attempt to catch the infrequent bus 1.

YAN TEMPLE 颜庙

This tranquil and little-visited **temple** (Yán Miào; Yanmiao Jie; admission Y10; ⏰ 8am-5pm) northeast of the Confucius Mansions opens to a large grassy courtyard with some vast stele pavilions sheltering dirty stelae and antediluvian bìxì. The main hall, **Fusheng Hall** (复圣殿; Fùshèng Diàn), is 17.5m high, with a hip and gable roof, and a magnificent ceiling decorated with the motif of a dragon head. Outside the hall are four magnificently carved pillars with coiling dragon designs and a further set of 18 octagonal pillars engraved with gorgeous dragon and floral patterns.

MAUSOLEUM OF SHAO HAO 少昊陵

One of the five legendary emperors of Chinese antiquity, Shao Hao's pyramidal Song dynasty **tomb** (Shào Hào Líng; admission Y20; ⏰ 8am-5pm), 4km northeast of Qūfù, is constructed from huge stone blocks, 25m wide at the base and 6m high, topped with a small temple. Today the temple is deserted, but the atmosphere is serene.

Bus 2 from the bus station will drop you 350m south of the tomb, or take a taxi (Y10) or pedicab (Y10).

Festivals & Events

Following tradition, there are two fairs a year in Qūfù – spring and autumn – when the place comes alive with craftspeople, healers, acrobats, peddlers and peasants. It also hosts a big party on 28 September to mark Confucius' birthday.

Sleeping

Accommodation is at its priciest during the high season (1 May to 8 May and 24 September to 8 October), but outside these times push for discounts.

BUDGET

Xiuxian Hotel (Xiūxián Bīnguǎn; ☎ 441 7128; 20 Gulou Nanjie; 鼓楼南街20号; 6-/3-bed dm Y20/60, s/d Y120/120, tr without toilet Y60-80; 🈯 🖳) This small place is cheap and simple with a useful internet café (p218), six- and three-person dorms and good low-season discounts on double and single rooms. Note some rooms are without windows. The owners can arrange ticketing and a bus to Yǎnzhōu (Y30 per person). The hotel has no English sign, but it's near the Drum Tower on the east side of Gulou Nanjie.

Shitouji Hotel (Shítou Jì Bīnguǎn; ☎ day/night 319 1806/319 1808; 16 Gulou Nanjie; 鼓楼南街16号; d Y40-60, tr Y30-80; 🈯) Just round the corner from the Xiuxian Hotel, here there's a range of budget accommodation from cheap and clean triples with plastic wood flooring, common toilet, air-con and TV to good doubles with air-con, TV and (squat) loo/shower.

MIDRANGE

Post Hotel (Yóuzhèng Bīnguǎn; ☎ 448 0874; 8 Gulou Beijie; 鼓楼北街8号; economy room Y160, s/d/tr Y280/260/360; 🈯) This well-placed hotel east of the Confucius Mansions has grotty economy rooms (no windows or air-con); other rooms are an improvement although they can be a bit grubby.

Yulong Hotel (Yùlóng Dàfàndiàn; ☎ 441 3469; fax 441 3209; 1 Gulou Dajie; 鼓楼大街1号; high season s/d Y260/380; 🈯) This pleasant hotel with a traditional roof is attractively positioned just within the wall in the north of town. Rooms are comfortable and discounts are commonly available.

Queli Hotel (Quèlǐ Bīnshè; ☎ 441 2022; 15 Zhonglou Jie; 钟楼街15号; s/d Y298/398; 🈯) Perhaps the best deal in town with a splendid location, the Queli looks very much the part as *the* tourist hotel. The traditional styling is attractive, built of grey brick with tiles, water features and regulation photos of Chinese dignitaries visiting at the entrance.

Eating

Wumaci Jie, east of Gulou Nanjie, turns into a huge night market in the evenings. A string of cheap restaurants can be found on the north side of Jingxuan Lu, opposite the Confucius Mansions Hotel in the south of town. Look out for sellers of *jiānbǐng guǒzi* (煎饼裹子; Y2), a steaming crepe-like parcel of egg, vegetables and chilli sauce. The local variant of KFC is **CBC** (China Best Chicken; cnr Gulou Nanjie & Jingxuan Lu), adjacent to a useful branch of Liánhuá, a well-stocked supermarket.

Post Hotel Restaurant (8 Gulou Beijie) Equipped with an English menu, this clean restaurant has pricey tourist items, such as Kong Family Beancurd (Y28), but go instead for the better-value *mápó dòufu* (麻婆豆腐; Y8) or *jiǎozi* (饺子) available in *zhūròu* (猪肉; pork, Y14 per *jīn*) and *yángròu* (羊肉; lamb, Y16 per *jīn*).

Shopping

Being a major tourist town, Qūfù is overrun with streetside vendors hawking pocket copies of the *Analects* (Lúnyǔ), Confucius biscuits, name chops (done in three minutes), effigies, ornaments, walking sticks, bows, amulets, pipes, fans, swords, and every type of souvenir associated with the great philosopher/sage. You can even get your name in Chinese carved on a grain of rice (Y15). Queli Jie is full with souvenir stalls.

Getting There & Away

BUS

From the **bus station** (☎ 448 1554) in the south of town, buses connect with Tài'ān (Y14, one hour, every 30 minutes), Jǐ'nán (Y35, two hours, every 20 minutes), Yǎnzhōu (Y4, 30 minutes, every 15 minutes), Zōuchéng (Zōuxiàn; Y6, 35 minutes, every six minutes), Qīngdǎo (Y110, five hours, 8.30am and 4.30pm) and Xī'ān (Y150, 10 hours, 2pm). Left luggage is available at the station (Y4).

TRAIN

When a railway project for Qūfù was first tabled, the Kong family petitioned for a change of routes, claiming that the trains would disturb Confucius' tomb. They won and the nearest tracks were routed to Yǎnzhōu, 16km west of Qūfù. Eventually another **train station** (☎ 442 1571) was constructed about 6km east of Qūfù, but only slow trains stop there, so it is more convenient to go to **Yǎnzhōu train station** (☎ 341 5239), on the line from Běijīng to Shànghǎi. Destinations include Běijīng (Y45 to Y81, five daily), Nánjīng (Y36, two daily), Jǐ'nán (Y12 to Y22, two hours, frequent), Qīngdǎo (Y38, 10 daily), Shànghǎi (Y53 to Y94) and Tiānjīn (Y36 to Y64). A taxi from Yǎnzhōu train station to Qūfù costs around Y40.

Getting Around

Minibuses to Yǎnzhōu train station (Y3.5, every 15 minutes, 5.30am to 5.30pm) leave from the bus station in the south of town. In the return direction, minibuses connect Yǎnzhōu bus station (walk straight ahead as you exit the train station, cross the parking lot and turn right; the bus station is after 50m on the left) with Qūfù (Y3.5, every 15 minutes, 5.30am to 5.30pm).

There are only two bus lines and service is not frequent. Probably most useful for travellers is bus 1, which travels along Gulou Beijie and Lindao Lu, connecting the bus station with the Confucian Forest. Bus 2 travels from east to west along Jingxuan Lu.

Pesky pedicabs (Y2 to Y3 to most sights within Qūfù) infest the streets, chasing all and sundry. Decorated tourist horse carts can take you on 30-minute tours (Y20 to the Confucius Forest from Queli Jie).

ZŌUCHÉNG 邹城

☎ 0537 / pop 191,654

Zōuchéng (also called Zōuxiàn, 邹县) is the home town of Mencius (372–289 BC), regarded as the first great Confucian philosopher. Far more relaxed than Qūfù, the town is less a carnival of easily excitable hawkers and bleating pedicab drivers.

A marvellous complex of heritage architecture, the **Mencius Temple** (孟庙; Mèng Miào; Miaoqian Lu; joint ticket with Mencius Mansions Y40; ☼ 8am-6pm) originally dates to the Song dynasty, but has been repeatedly damaged. A colossal complex ossified with age, overgrown with weeds and liberally scratched with the names of visitors, the temple badly needs a shot of restoration.

An otherworldly mood reigns: *bìxì* glare out from ancient pavilions, gnarled, ancient cypresses soar aloft from the desiccated soil, birds squawk from the branches overhead while rows of stelae commemorate forgotten events. The **Hall of the Second Sage** (亚圣殿; Yàshèng Diàn) dates from 1121, a huge twin-roofed hall with external octagonal pillars. Ceremonial spots include the small Pool for Burning Funeral Orations, now scattered with cigarette butts, while a collection of headless statues at the rear testifies to China's often anti-Confucian mood swings.

The layout and buildings of the **Mencius Mansions** (孟府; Mèng Fǔ; Miaoqian Lu) alongside is far less ceremonial, with corridors, living quarters and a small garden of rose bushes adding a more human dimension. The Mansions are also home to the Center of Confucian Studies at Shandong University.

Zōuchéng is 23km south of Qūfù, and can easily be visited as a day trip from Qūfù. Buses run from Qūfù bus station (Y6, every six minutes, 35 minutes), dropping you off at the roundabout on Yishan Beilu (峄山北路) in Zōuchéng, from where you can take a motorised pedicab (Y10) or taxi (Y10) to the Mencius Temple and Mencius Mansions in the south of town. A taxi from Qūfù to Zōuchéng will cost around Y50 to Y60.

QĪNGDǍO 青岛

☎ 0532 / pop 1.6 million

A breath of crisp sea air for anyone emerging from China's polluted urban interior, Qīngdǎo is hardly old-school China – parts of town resemble Bavaria – but its effortless blend of German architecture and modern city planning puts Chinese white-tile towns to shame. Its German legacy more or less intact, Qīngdǎo takes pride in its unique appearance: the Chinese call the town 'China's Switzerland'. The beaches may be overhyped, the local Putonghua carries a thick accent, and a metro system wouldn't go amiss, but the dilapidated charms of the hilly old town are captivating and the port city is hosting the sailing events of the 2008 Olympics, prompting a further investment gale into the prosperous town. Wander at will round cobbled, higgledy-piggledy alleys, poke around stone-clad Teutonic vestiges, quaff the famous local brew (Tsingtao) and ditch the diet: Qīngdǎo has some of the best kebabs and seafood in north China.

History

Before catching the acquisitive eye of Kaiser Wilhelm II, Qīngdǎo was an innocuous fishing village, although its excellent strategic location had not been lost on the Ming, who built a battery here. German forces wrested the port town from the Chinese in 1898 after the murder of two German missionaries, and Qīngdǎo was ceded to Germany for 99 years. Under German rule the famous Tsingtao Brewery opened in 1903, electric lighting was installed, missions and a university were established, the railway to Jǐ'nán was built, the Protestant church was handing out hymnals by 1908, a garrison of 2000 men was deployed, and a naval base established.

In 1914 the Japanese moved into town after the successful joint Anglo-Japanese naval bombardment of the port. Japan's position in Qīngdǎo was strengthened by the Treaty of Versailles, and they held the city until 1922 when it was ceded back to the Kuomintang. The Japanese returned in 1938, after the start of the Sino-Japanese war, and occupied the town until defeated in 1945.

These days, Qīngdǎo is the fourth-largest port in China and the second-largest city in the province of Shāndōng. Booming industry and an entrepreneurial spirit have successfully carried the city into the 21st century, making it a clean, modern and thriving town.

Orientation

Backing onto mountainous terrain to the northeast and hedged in between Jiaozhou Bay, Laoshan Bay and the Yellow Sea, Qīngdǎo is divided into two distinct entities. The ragged old town (老城区; lǎochéng qū) in the east lays claim to Qīngdǎo's antique charms, architectural streetscapes and the historic train station, while trendy bars and restaurants drag the white-collar in-crowd to the eastern business district, where Qīngdǎo's best hotels tower over supermarkets and well-heeled shoppers.

Information

BOOKSHOPS

Xinhua Bookstore (Xīnhuá Shūdiàn; 10 Henan Lu) On the corner of Guangxi Lu and Henan Lu.

INTERNET ACCESS 网吧

Book City (Shū Chéng; 67 Xianggang Zhonglu) At the junction of Xianggang Zhonglu and Yan'erdao Lu.

How Do Internet Café (Hǎodú Wǎngbā; 2 Dagu Lu; per hr Y2; 🕑 6am-9pm)

MEDICAL SERVICES
People's Hospital (Rénmín Yīyuàn; ☎ 8285 2154; 17 Dexian Lu)

MONEY
Bank of China (Zhōngguó Yínháng; 66 & 68 Zhongshan Lu; ☯ 8am-5pm) On the corner of Zhongshan Lu and Feicheng Lu, housed in a building built in 1934, it offers foreign-currency exchange and the external ATM accepts foreign cards.
Bank of China (Yuyuan Dasha, 75 Xianggang Xilu) External 24-hour ATM with international access.
Jusco (☯ 8.30am-10pm) On the ground floor of Jusco shopping centre. ATM accepts MasterCard, Visa, Cirrus, Amex and JCB.
Shangri-La Hotel (Xiānggélǐlā Dàjiǔdiàn; 9 Xianggang Zhonglu) ATM accepts MasterCard, Visa, Cirrus, JCB and Amex.

POST
Post office (yóujú; 51 Zhongshan Lu; ☯ 8.30am-6pm) Opposite the large Parkson building.

PUBLIC SECURITY BUREAU
PSB (Gōngānjú; ☎ 8579 2555, ext 2860; 272 Ningxia Lu; ☯ 9-11.30am & 1.30-4.30pm Mon-Fri) Inconveniently located in the east of town. Bus 301 goes from the train station and stops outside the terracotta-coloured building (stop 14). Another small branch of the PSB is at 1 Qufu Lu.

TOURIST INFORMATION
China International Travel Service (CITS; Zhōngguó Guójì Lǚxíngshè; ☎ 8389 2065/1713; Yuyuan Dasha, 73 Xianggang Xilu; ☯ 8am-5pm) Just west of Bank of China.
Qingdao Tourism Information & Service Station (Qīngdǎo Shì Lǚyóu Zīxún Fúwùzhàn) Small kiosks dotted around town, including at Zhan Bridge. Useful for maps (Y6), if little else.

Sights
Beyond Qīngdǎo's fast-paced beaches and hilly parks, most sights are pleasantly squeezed into the old town, where no excuse is needed to saunter around, losing yourself down side streets and gawping at the astonishing local architectural vernacular. The Qingdao Municipal Government has put up plaques identifying notable historic buildings and sites.

Completed in 1934, the twin-spired **St Michael's Catholic Church** (Tiānzhǔ Jiàotáng; ☎ 8591 1400; 15 Zhejiang Lu; admission Y6; ☯ 8am-5pm Mon-Sat, noon-5pm Sun), up a steep hill off Zhongshan Lu, is an imposing edifice with a cross on each spire. The church was badly damaged during the Cultural Revolution and the crosses were torn off. God-fearing locals rescued them, however, and buried them in the hills. The interior is splendid, with white walls, gold piping, replaced sections of stained glass all around and a marvellously painted apse. The baptismal font and statues have captions in English and Chinese, and there is a large portrait of St Teresa of Lisieux, although it's astonishing that you have to pay to enter a church. Vendors muster outside selling crucifixes and souvenirs and a daily **fish market**, featuring colourful exotica from the depths, sets up on Feicheng Lu, which leads up to the church from Zhongshan Lu. Put aside time to roam the area round here – a lattice of ancient hilly streets where old folk sit on wooden stools in decrepit doorways, playing chess and shooting the breeze. North of the church a slogan from the Cultural Revolution has survived above the doorway of 19 Pingdu Lu; it is very clear and no-one has bothered to paint over it. It says (in Chinese) 'Long live Chairman Mao'.

Zhongshan Lu itself has numerous **dried fish shops** worth browsing around (eg at 39 Zhongshan Lu).

Located on Jiangsu Lu, a street notable for its German architecture, the **Protestant Church** (Jīdū Jiàotáng; 15 Jiangsu Lu; admission Y3; ☯ 8.30am-5pm, weekend services) was designed by Curt Rothkegel and built in 1908. The interior is simple and Lutheran in its sparseness, apart from some delightful carvings on the pillar cornices. You can climb up to inspect the mechanism of the clock (Bockenem 1909) and views out over the bay. It is also well worth wandering along nearby Daxue Lu for a marvellous scenic view of old German Qīngdǎo.

To the east of Xinhaoshan Park remains one of Qīngdǎo's most interesting pieces of German architecture, **Qīngdǎo Yíng Bīnguǎn** (Qingdao Ying Hotel; admission Y15; ☯ 8.30am-5pm), the former German governor's residence and a replica of a German palace (now a museum). Built in 1903, it is said to have cost 2,450,000 taels of silver. When Kaiser Wilhelm II got the bill, he immediately recalled the extravagant governor and sacked him. In 1957 Chairman Mao stayed here with his wife and kids on holiday.

The restored **Tianhou Temple** (Tiānhòu Gōng; 19 Taiping Lu; admission Y8; ☯ 8am-6pm) is a small temple dedicated to Tianhou (Heaven Queen), Goddess of the Sea and protector of sailors, also known as Mazu and Niangniang. The main hall contains a colourful statue of Tianhou, flanked by two figures and a pair of fearsome guardians. Other halls include the Dragon

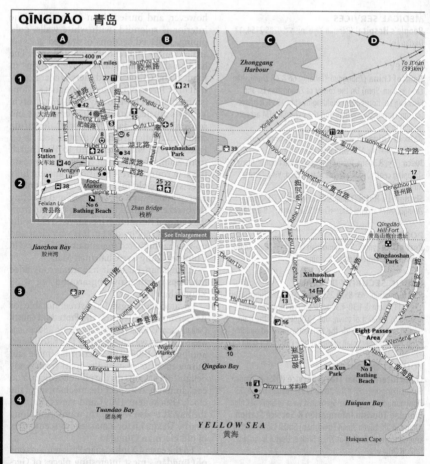

King Hall (龙王殿; Lóngwáng Diàn; where in front of the Dragon King lies a splayed pig) and a shrine to the God of Wealth.

The castle-like villa of **Huàshí Lóu** (Huashi Bldg; 18 Huanghai Lu; admission Y5; 7.30am-7pm) was originally the home of a Russian aristocrat, and later the German governor's retreat for fishing and hunting. The Chinese call it the 'Chiang Kaishek Building' as the generalissimo secretly stayed here in 1947.

Poking like a lollipop into Qingdao Bay south of No 6 Bathing Beach and dominated by its white German-built lighthouse, the **Little Qingdao** (Xiǎo Qīngdǎo; 8286 3944; 8 Qinyu Lu; admission Y15; 7.30am-6.30pm) peninsula is excellent for throwing off the crowds battling it out on the beaches. Despite the name –

'Little Green Island' – it's actually a peninsula, lashed to the shore by a slender sandbar (called Qinyu Lu). Set your alarm to catch early morning vistas of the hazy bay and the town coming to life from the promontory's leafy park.

Established in 1903 by the beer-loving Germans, the **Tsingtao Brewery** (Qīngdǎo Píjiǔchǎng; 8383 3437; 56 Dengzhou Lu; admission Y30; 9am-4.30pm) makes the finest brew in China with the mineral waters of nearby Láo Shān. Phone ahead to book a tour to examine the brewery, its fixtures and props.

BEACHES

Qīngdǎo is famed for its six beaches, which are pleasant enough, but don't go expecting

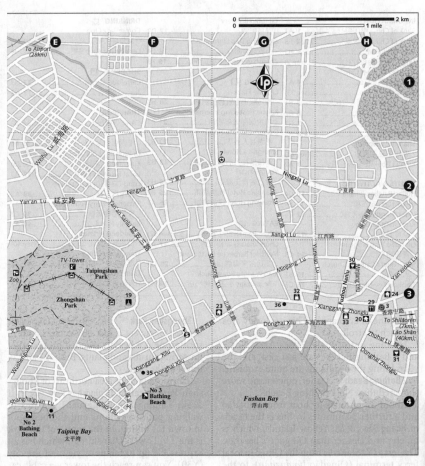

Bondi Beach. Chinese beach culture is low-key and quite tentative, although the main swimming season (June to September) sees hordes of sun seekers fighting for towel space. Shark nets, lifeguards, lifeboat patrols and medical stations are at hand.

It comes as little surprise that Qīngdǎo's best beach is draped along the shore way off in the east of town, far from the shrieking rubber-ring/buckets-and-spade crowd. South of the dramatic mountain bulk of Fushan, **Shílǎorén** (石老人; Donghai Donglu; admission free; ☺ all day) is a gorgeous 2.5km-long strip of clean sand and seawater-smoothed seashells, occasionally engulfed in banks of mist pouring in from offshore. Early morning runs here are divine – and yours may be the only

set of footprints on the sand. To get here, take bus 317 from Taipingjiao (Y2) or hop in a taxi.

Close to the train station is the **No 6 Bathing Beach**, neighbouring **Zhàn Qiáo** (Zhan Bridge), a pier that reaches out into the bay and is tipped with the eight-sided **Huilan Pavilion** (Huílán Gé).

The sand of **No 1 Bathing Beach** is coarse-grained, engulfed in seaweed, and bordered by concrete beach huts and bizarre statues of dolphins. The nearby **Eight Passes Area** (八大关; Bādàguān) is well known for its sanatoriums and exclusive guesthouses. The spas are scattered in lush wooded zones off the coast, and each street is lined with a different tree or flower, including maple, myrtle, peach, snow pine or crab apple. This is a lovely area in which to stroll.

Heading out of Eight Passes Area, Nos 2 and 3 Bathing Beaches are just east, and the villas lining the headlands are quite exquisite. **No 2 Bathing Beach** is cleaner, quieter and more sheltered than No 1 Bathing Beach.

About 30 minutes by boat from Qīngdǎo and a further 30 minutes by bus is the beach of **Huáng Dǎo** (黄岛; Yellow Island), which is quieter and cleaner than Qīngdǎo's beaches. The ferry (Y15) leaves from the Qīngdǎo local ferry terminal (Qīngdǎo lúndùzhàn), to the west of the train station. The first departure is at 6.30am, with the final boat returning at 9pm. Once you reach the island, take bus 1 to its terminus (Y2.50).

PARKS

The charm of small **Guanhaishan Park** (Guānhǎishān Gōngyuán) lies in finding it: the route winds up a small hill through restful lanes; the park is at the top. Although small, the park was used as a golf course by the Germans.

Down the hill and to the east is **Xinhaoshan Park** (信号山公园; Xìnhàoshān Gōngyuán; admission Y15), the summit of which is capped by the carbuncular towers known as the *mógu lóu* (mushroom buildings).

Zhongshan Park (中山公园; Zhōngshān Gōngyuán; admission Y3) covers a vast 80 hectares, and in springtime is a heavily wooded profusion of flowering shrubs and plants. Buses 25 and 26 travel to the park.

The mountainous area northeast of Zhongshan Park is called **Taipingshan Park** (太平山公园; Tàipíngshān Gōngyuán), an area of walking paths, pavilions and the best spot in town for hiking. In the centre of the park is the TV Tower (Diànshì Tǎ), which has an express lift up to fabulous views of the city (Y30). You can reach the tower via cable car (Y20). Also within the park is Qīngdǎo's largest temple, **Zhanshan Temple** (Zhànshān Sì; admission Y5; ⏰ 8.30am-4.30pm). The temple has a number of dramatic sandalwood Buddhas covered in gold foil.

Festivals & Events

The summer months see Qīngdǎo overrun with tourists, particularly in the second and third weeks of July, when the **annual trade fair** and **ocean festival** is held. Another festival to look out for is the **beer festival** in August/September. Gardeners may be interested to note that Qīngdǎo's **radish festival** is in February, the **cherry festival** in May and the **grape festival** in September (Qīngdǎo is a major producer of wine).

Sleeping

BUDGET

All prices quoted are for the high season; bargain during the low season.

Kaiyue Hostelling International (Kǎiyuè Guójì Qīngnián Lǚguǎn; ☎ 8284 5450; 31 Jining Lu; 济宁路 31号; dm from Y35, d Y180) Handily located a short walk from the train station on a road off Zhongshan Lu in the old town.

Youth Hostel (Bēibāokè Qīngnián Lǚguǎn; ☎ 8592 2506; 17 Yan'erdao Lu; 燕尔岛路17号; dm from Y48, d Y130) Located near Jusco and Carrefour and within walking distance of the Minjiang Lu bar street in the commercial east of town. Go through the gate, don't go up the steps; under 26s get Y8 off.

Zhanying Hotel (Zhànyíng Bīnguǎn; ☎ 8296 1980; 11 Mengyin Lu; 蒙阴路11号; d Y80; ⊠) Conveniently located a few minutes' walk from the train station just south of a marvellous old German building (now a PSB office) and at the heart of the old town, this small hotel has simple, good-value rooms that enjoy frequent discounting during the nonsummer slack period. Phoning ahead is advised; push for low season discounts.

MIDRANGE

Railway Hotel (Tiědào Dàshà; ☎ 8606 7888; fax 8286 0497; 2 Tai'an Lu; 泰安路2号; d/q/ste Y280/480/680; ⊠) Located at the train station, the perfectly reasonable high-rise Railway Hotel is well located in the old part of town, with clean rooms, polite service and an external elevator. Discounts are not uncommon, even during summer months – and doubles can be netted for around Y160.

Zhanqiao Hotel (Zhànqiáo Bīnguǎn; ☎ 8288 8666; fax 8287 0936; 31 Taiping Lu; 太平路31号; non-seaview d Y298-498, seaview d Y698; ⊠) A downtown fixture a few minutes' walk west of Qīngdǎo's Tianhou Temple, this seaboard hotel is rather somnolent with slow-moving staff. The hotel hides its cheaper doubles round the side and back, but the pricier rooms facing Qīngdǎo's surf are what staying here is all about. In former times it was the Prince Heinrich Hotel; Sun Yatsen stayed here in 1912 and is commemorated by a bust outside.

TOP END

Oceanwide Elite Hotel (Fànhǎi Míngrén Jiǔdiàn; ☎ 8288 6699; fax 8289 1388; 29 Taiping Lu; 太平路29号; non-seaview d Y960, seaview d Y1160, ste Y2360; ⊠) This five-floor, low-rise, four-star hotel benefits from a superb location overlooking Qingdao Bay (as long as you opt for the pricier seaview rooms) in the old part of town.

Crowne Plaza (Qīngdǎo Yízhōng Huángguān Jiàrì Jiǔdiàn; ☎ 8571 8888; www.sixcontinentshotels.com; 76 Xianggang Zhonglu; 香港中路76号; d/ste Y1162/2324; ⊠) A glittering 38-floor tower rising above Qīngdǎo's crackling commercial district, you won't be bumping into much old-town charm here, but business travellers can content themselves instead with the warm honey-coloured hues of the splendid foyer, the fully equipped rooms, the indoor pool, a choice of five restaurants and professional standards of service. Free, well-produced English maps of Qīngdǎo are provided at the concierge desk.

Shangri-La Hotel (Xiānggélǐlā Dàjiǔdiàn; ☎ 8388 3838; www.shangri-la.com; 9 Xianggang Zhonglu; 香港中路9号; s/d US$175/195, 15% service charge; ⊠) In Qīngdǎo's commercial district in the east of town, the excellent Shangri-La delivers all the high-quality business hallmarks of the chain, with plush rooms and attentive service.

Eating

Qīngdǎo is a cauldron of good food. The waterfront area is brimming with restaurants, from No 6 Bathing Beach almost all the way to No 1 Bathing Beach. For more upmarket and varied dining options, head to the commercial district in the east of town, and especially the bars and restaurants along Yunxiao Lu and Minjiang Lu. The lively street Zhongyuan Meishi Jie is packed with seafood restaurants; the entrance is off Xianggang Zhonglu, east of Carrefour.

Chūnhélóu (Chūnhélóu Fàndiàn; ☎ 8282 4346; 146 Zhongshan Lu; meals from Y20; ⏱ 6am-10pm) Dating back to 1891, this unremarkable-looking restaurant remains very popular. Downstairs is a busy help-yourself-to-as-much-as-you-can-eat type diner, with a smarter option upstairs.

Meida'er Barbecue Restaurant (Měidáér Shāokǎodiàn; ☎ 8382 0368; Taishan Lu; lamb kebab Y1.50, meals Y30; ⏱ 10am-2am) Sooner or later, Qīngdǎo's legendary kebabs will require your undivided attention, and where better to start than on Taishan Lu – the local Barbecue Street. Allow this trusty chain restaurant to thrust a thirst-quenching beer into one hand and scrummy lamb (羊肉串; yángròu chuàn), pork (猪肉串; zhūròu chuàn) or seafood kebabs into the other.

Ajisen Ramen (Wèiqiān Lāmiàn; ☎ 8580 6375; 1st fl, Carrefour, 21 Xianggang Zhonglu; meals Y30; ⏱ 8.30am-11pm)

A chain that has the nation hopping must be doing something right. Ajisen Ramen's noodles – steaming blasts of chilli-infused flavour ferried to the table by black-attired staff – truly hit the spot. Flesh the meal out further with fried dumplings (Y8), potato balls (Y6) or deep-fried shrimp (Y14). Pay as you order.

Xiao Wangfu Roast Duck Restaurant (Xiǎo Wángfǔ Kǎoyādiàn; ☎ 8575 0208; 20 Yan'er Dao; whole roast duck Y68; ☼ 9am-10pm) Excellently located just north of the Crowne Plaza, this small and homely corner eatery is easily spotted for its traditional portico, red lanterns and white tablecloths drying outside. The duck is recommended and there's a range of pre-prepared chilled dishes just inside the door that makes ordering a breeze – just point, take your seat with a bottle of Tsingtao stout (Y20) and wait.

Drinking

Qīngdǎo's bars concentrate within the commercial and business district in the east of town. Check www.myredstar.com for current listings. You can buy Tsingtao beer by the bag from numerous shops, but pouring it requires skill.

Corner Jazz Club (Jiējiǎo Juéshì Bā; ☎ 8575 8560; 153 Minjiang Lu) Its candlelit tables and mezzanine attracting a youngish expat and local crowd, this spacious and atmospheric bar gets Qīngdǎo fingers snapping to motley live sounds every Tuesday (8.30pm to 10.30pm). Staff speak excellent English and manage a well-stocked bar, while the paraphernalia extends to table football and darts.

Lennon Bar (Liènóng Cānbā; ☎ 8589 3899; 20 Zhuhai Lu) Vast two-floor temple to Beatles culture with a loyal following, a good atmosphere and a lived-in feel. There's also table football, a pool table and live music (on Thursday).

Babyface Qingdao (☎ 8596 9898; 71 Xianggang Zhonglu) The coolest and most stylish club in town, with top-flight DJs, extremely loud music and a cross-section of Qīngdǎo's best-dressed pretty young things.

Shopping

In the old town, Zhongshan Lu is dotted with bargain shops, chain stores, clothing retailers, outlets selling dried fish produce and distressed-looking, empty towers (offices worth their salt have all moved east). A sprawl of straw hats, clothes, shoes, bags and jewellery, Liaocheng Road Market is the

spot for bargain local produce. In the superstore category, **Jusco** (Jiāshìkè; ☼ 9am-11pm), near the southeast corner of Fuzhou Nanlu and Xianggang Zhonglu, and **Carrefour** (Jiālèfú; ☼ 8.30am-10pm), on the northwest corner of Nanjing Lu and Xianggang Zhonglu, seethe with shoppers in the commercial eastern district.

Getting There & Away

AIR

There are flights to most large cities in China, including daily services to Běijīng (Y700) and Shànghǎi (Y760) and five flights a week to Hong Kong (Y2400). International flights include daily flights to Seoul, along with flights to Osaka and Fukuoka in Japan. Direct flights to Frankfurt are planned. For flight information call **Liuting International Airport** (☎ 8471 5139).

Tickets can be purchased at the following:

CAAC (Zhōngguó Mínháng) Zhongshan Lu (☎ 8289 5577; 29 Zhongshan Lu); Xianggang Lu (☎ 24hr ticketing 8577 5555; 30 Xianggang Lu)

China Southern (Zhōngguó Náfāng Hángkōng Gōngsī; ☎ 8389 6148; Haitian Hotel, 48 Xianggang Xilu)

Dragonair (Gǎnglóng Hángkōng; ☎ 8577 6110; Hotel Equatorial, 28 Xianggang Zhonglu; ☼ 9am-5pm Mon-Sat)

Korean Air (Dàhán Hángkōng; ☎ 8387 0088; Haitian Hotel, 48 Xianggang Xilu)

Shandong Airlines (Shāndōng Hángkōng; ☎ 8288 9160, 286 5870; train station ticket office) It also sells Yāntái to Dàlián boat tickets.

BOAT

Ferries to other Chinese ports no longer depart from Qīngdǎo. International boats depart from the **passenger ferry terminal** (Qīngdǎogǎng Kèyùnzhàn; ☎ 8282 5001; 6 Xinjiang Lu) for both Incheon (from Y750, 16 hours, Monday, Wednesday and Friday) and Gunsun (Y700, 19 hours, Monday, Wednesday and Saturday) in South Korea and Shimonoseki (Y1200, 36 hours, Monday, Thursday and Saturday) in Japan. To reach Dàlián by boat, you will have to go from Yāntái (opposite) or Wēihǎi (p235), but tickets can be purchased from the Shandong Airlines ticket office.

BUS

Both buses and minibuses depart from the area next to the massive Hualian Building, south of the train station. The **ticket offices** (☎ 8267 6842) are in the small pastel-coloured huts in the bus station.

There are buses departing for Wēihǎi (Y42.50, every 20 minutes, 6am to 6pm), Yāntái (Y31, every 15 minutes, 6.30am to 5.30pm) and Jǐ'nán (Y50, every 50 minutes, 8.50am to 4pm). There are also daily buses to Běijīng (Y219, 13 hours, 7.30pm), Hángzhōu (Y221, 20 hours, 3.50pm), Héféi (Y128, 9am and 3.30pm) and Shànghǎi (Y201, 18 hours, 10.30am and afternoon departures).

TRAIN

All trains from Qīngdǎo go through Jǐ'nán, except the direct Qīngdǎo to Yāntái and Wēihǎi trains. There are two trains a day to Yāntái (hard seat Y22, four hours), several to Wēihǎi (Y12, four to six hours) and regular services to Jǐ'nán (Y55, four to six hours). There are two express trains daily to Běijīng (Y215, 10 hours), and trains to Shànghǎi (Y290, 15 hours, 1.58pm), Tài'ān (hard seat Y34, five hours) and Zhèngzhōu (Y120, 3.05pm).

Apart from at the marvellous ticket office at the train station – German-built with a clock tower, red tiles and practically a sight in itself – train (and air) tickets can be bought for a service charge at several places around town, including a useful **ticket office** (Qīngdǎo Huǒchēzhàn Biànjié Shòupiàochù; Feixian Lu; ⏲ 24hr) on the north side of Feixian Lu, just round the corner from the train station.

Getting Around
TO/FROM THE AIRPORT

Qīngdǎo's sparkling **Liuting International Airport** (☎ 8471 5139) is 30km north of the city. Taxi drivers should ask between Y90 and Y100 to drive into town. Buses leave every 30 minutes from the CAAC office between 6am and 6pm (Y10).

BUS

Most transport needs can be catered for by the bus 6 route, which starts at the northern end of Zhongshan Lu, runs along it to within a few blocks of the train station and then goes east to the area above No 3 Bathing Beach. Bus 26 from the train station runs along the coast and past Zhongshan Park before heading north at the end of No 3 Bathing Beach. Minibuses also follow these routes (Y2).

TAXI

Flag fall is Y7 for the first 3km and then Y1.50 per kilometre thereafter.

LÁO SHĀN 崂山

This **mountain** (admission Y50), 40km east of Qīngdǎo, is a famous Taoist retreat, with temples, waterfalls and secluded walking trails. Covering some 400 sq km, this is where Láo Shān mineral water starts its life. The mountain is associated with Taoist legend and myth, with the central attraction being the Song dynasty **Great Purity Palace** (太清宫; Tàiqīng Gōng; admission Y10). The first Song emperor established the palace as a place to perform Taoist rites to save the souls of the dead. From the Great Purity Palace, there are paths leading to the summit of Láo Shān.

The cable car up the first half of the mountain costs Y30 (Y50 return) and a ride up the second half costs Y20. From Qīngdǎo, bus 304 runs to Láo Shān (Y6.50, one to two hours). Buses can be picked up at the Zhàn Qiáo stop by No 6 Bathing Beach from around 6.30am; get off at the entrance to the first cable car up Láo Shān. Returning, the last bus leaves Láo Shān at 5pm.

Tour buses to Láo Shān (Y25 return) ply the streets of Qīngdǎo from 6am onwards, but visit at least four other 'sights' on the way to the mountain.

YĀNTÁI 烟台
☎ 0535 / pop 652,000

A prosperous ice-free port on the northern coast of the Shāndōng peninsula, Yāntái sees a steady stream of visitors from Qīngdǎo, some destined by ferry to Dàlián (p363), others scampering west along the coastline to the pavilion at Pénglái. Good for a day or two, the town makes for a relaxed sojourn, with a sprinkling of foreign concession architecture, popular beaches, a growing bar scene and a tempting panoply of pleasant restaurants.

History

Starting life as a defence outpost and fishing village, Yāntái's name literally means 'Smoke Terrace'; wolf-dung fires were lit on the headland during the Ming dynasty to warn fishing fleets of approaching pirates. Its anonymity abruptly ended in the late 19th century when the Qing government, reeling from defeat in the Opium War, handed Yāntái to the British who established a treaty port here, calling it Chefoo (Zhifu). Several nations, Japan and the USA among them, had trading establishments here and the town became something of a resort area.

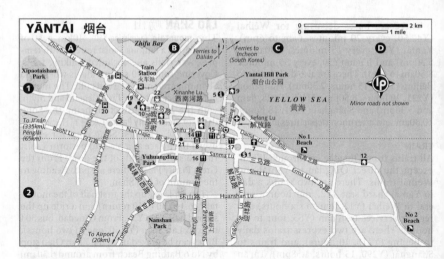

Orientation

The train and bus stations are in the west of town near the harbour, where budget hotels tend to congregate. The beaches are in the east of town, while most of the sights, treaty port buildings and restaurants are in the central districts.

Information

Several internet cafés can be found inside Times Sq (Shídài Guǎngchǎng), west of the International Seaman's Club.

Bank of China (Zhōngguó Yínháng; 166 Jiefang Lu) ATM accepts Visa, MasterCard, JCB and Amex.

Chunhehang Pharmacy (Chūnhèhéng Yàotáng; Beima Lu) Next to the International Seaman's Club.

Post office (yóujú; Diànxìn Dàlóu; cnr Nan Dajie & Dahaiyang Lu)

Public Security Bureau (PSB; Gōngānjú; ☎ 653 5621; 78 Shifu Jie; ☺ 8am-5.30pm Mon-Sat) On the corner of Chaoyang Jie. The office for foreigners is on the 6th floor.

Yantai Tourist Information & Service Center (Yāntáishì Lǚyóu Fúwù Zhōngxīn; ☎ 663 3222; 32 Haian Lu) Next to Yantai Hill Park gate, at north end of Chaoyang Jie.

Yantaishan Hospital (Yāntáishān Yīyuàn; ☎ 622 4411; 91 Jiefang Lu)

Sights

YANTAI HILL PARK 烟台山公园

This absorbing **park** (Yāntáishān Gōngyuán; admission Y20; ☺ 6.30am-7.30pm summer, 7am-5.30pm winter) is a veritable museum of well-preserved Western treaty port architecture. Containing a model ship exhibition, the **Former American Consulate**

Building retains some original interior features. Nearby, the former **Yantai Union Church** dates from 1875, although it was later rebuilt. The **Former British Consulate** building houses a China Fossils Exhibition and the **British Consulate Annexe** looks out onto an attractive English garden. In the north of the park, the **Former Danish Consulate** is a crenellated structure dating from 1890, decorated on the outside with 'brutalism granite', or so the blurb says. Wander in and walk around and up the staircase, perusing the period furniture, the laid-out kitchen and dining room. At the top of the hill is the Ming dynasty **Dragon King Temple**, which once found service as a military headquarters for French troops in 1860 and is now home once again to a statue of the Dragon King himself. The wolf-dung fires were burned from the **smoke terrace** above, dating from the reign of Hongwu; climb up for views (binoculars Y2) out to sea and the island of Zhifu (Chefoo). In the west of the park, the 1930s-built **Japanese Consulate** is a typically austere brick lump, equipped with a 'torture inquisition room'.

YANTAI MUSEUM 烟台博物馆

The **Yantai Museum** (Yāntái Bówùguǎn; 257 Nan Dajie; admission Y10; ☺ 9am-noon & 1-4.30pm) is located within a fabulous guildhall built by merchants and sailors of Fújiàn as a place of worship to Tianhou (Heaven Queen), Goddess of the Sea and protector of sailors.

The main hall of the museum is known as the **Hall of Heavenly Goddess**, designed and finished in Guǎngzhōu, and then shipped to Yāntái for assembly. Beyond the hall, at the centre of the courtyard, is the museum's most spectacular sight: a brightly and intricately decorated gate. Supported by 14 pillars, the portal is a collage of hundreds of carved and painted figures, flowers, beasts, phoenixes and animals. The carvings depict battle scenes and folk stories, including *The Eight Immortals Crossing the Sea*.

At the southern end of the museum is a theatrical stage that was first made in Fújiàn and then shipped to Yāntái. Apparently Tianhou wasn't particularly fond of that stage, as it was lost at sea during transportation and had to be reconstructed in Yāntái. The stage continues to be used for performances to celebrate Tianhou's birthday (see Mazu's Birthday, p945) and anniversary of deification.

OTHER SIGHTS

Of Yāntái's two beaches, **No 1 Beach** (Dìyī Hǎishuǐ Yùchǎng), a long stretch of soft sand along a calm bay area is superior to **No 2 Beach** (Dìèr Hǎishuǐ Yùchǎng), which is less crowded, but more polluted. Both beaches can be reached by bus 17.

On Dama Lu, west of No 1 Beach, is a small, active **Catholic Church** (天主教堂; Tiānzhǔ Jiàotáng) built during treaty port days. The church has a wooden ceiling, pictures of the Stations of the Cross and a gallery.

Sleeping

BUDGET

International Seaman's Super 8 Hotel (Hǎiyuán Sùbā Bīnguǎn; ☎ 669 0909; fax 669 0606; 68 Beima Lu; 北马路68号; s/d/ste Y168/198/380; 🖵) Across from the train station, the able-bodied Seaman has been fed a shot of rum by the Super 8 group, emerging with newly renovated rooms and

new management, although doubles facing the station can be noisy.

Yinpeng Hotel (Yínpéng Bīnguǎn; ☎ 626 0655; fax 626 0755; 59 Beima Lu; 北马路59号; s/tr Y180/260, d Y196-220; 🖵) This two-star hotel next to a UBC Coffee outlet is small but well kept, with clean rooms with tiled floors. There's no lift, so rooms get cheaper the higher you climb; low-season discounts can be easy to obtain.

MIDRANGE

Shandong Pacific Hotel (Shāndōng Tàipíngyáng Dàjiǔdiàn; ☎ 658 8866; fax 621 5204; 74 Shifu Jie; 市府街74号; s & t Y660-880; 🖵) This central four-star hotel (white tile high-rise with an iridescent stainless-steel lobby portico) is an above average choice. Rooms have water coolers, extra large TV sets and particularly clean bathrooms. Rooms to the north have sea views, and there's a choice of Japanese, Korean and Western dining options. Facilities include a swimming pool, bowling and billiards.

Golden Gulf Hotel (Jīnhǎiwān Jiǔdiàn; ☎ 663 6999; fax 663 2699; 34 Haian Lu; 海安路34号; d Y760-960; 🖵) Located near Yantai Hill Park, this six-floor hotel is a clean place offering homy rooms equipped with water cooler, internet access and fridge. The hotel's Golden Gulf Grill serves steaks and meat grills.

TOP END

Yantai Marina Hotel (Yāntái Jiàrì Jiǔdiàn; ☎ 666 9999; marinaht@public.ytptt.sd.cn; 128 Binhai Beilu; 滨海北路128号; non-seaview d/ste Y780/1380, seaview d/ste Y880/1980; 🖵) Rooms at this 25-floor Chinese-style hotel are clean, spacious and recently restored, with excellent views from the seaview rooms. A revolving restaurant is on the 25th floor and there's a 2.8 tonne stone ball and a statue of Milefo in the lobby. Take a trip in the external glass elevator for fantastic views over the bay.

SHĀNDŌNG

234 SHĀNDŌNG •• Pénglái

Eating

In the summer months a night market sets up along Shengli Lu, good for cheap kebabs and beer.

For spicy food, bundle along to Taohua Jie, a street stuffed with Sìchuān restaurants directly north of Yantai Museum.

Cháotiānjiāo (☎ 623 0966; 71 Taohua Jie; meals Y25) This small eatery on Taohua Jie (there are two branches, one on either side of the road) has no English menu, but be sure to try the excellent and filling *suāncài yú* (酸菜鱼; fish and pickled cabbage soup, small Y15, big Y20). The *huíguōròu* (回锅肉; twice cooked pork, Y8) is scrumptious, and the *málàjī* (麻辣鸡; spicy chicken, small Y10, big Y15) hot and tasty.

Háojiāxiāng (☎ 662 7588; 51 Shifu Jie; set meals Y25) This lively and popular restaurant serves excellent steaks, ribs and grills. Sit down in the soft sofa seats and try the tasty *hēijiāo zhūpái* (黑椒猪排; black pepper pork chops, Y30).

Sculpting in Time (Diāokè Shíguāng; ☎ 622 1979; 17-18 Shifu Jie; meals Y30; 🕙 10.30am-midnight) This little bar-restaurant has character, with alcoves and small side rooms with saloon-style swing doors and walls hung with photos of film stars and luminaries. On the menu are pizza and steaks, and there's live music nightly. Tsingtao beer will set you back Y10.

Drinking

The section of Chaoyang Jie north of Beima Lu has a good selection of bars and clubs.

Getting There & Away

AIR

Book tickets at the **CAAC office** (Zhōngguó Mínháng; ☎ 624 5596; 6 Dahaiyang Lu; 🕙 8am-6pm) or at **Shandong Airlines** (Shāndōng Hángkōng; ☎ 658 4143; 236 Nan Dajie; 🕙 8am-6pm).

There are flights to Hong Kong (Y1600, three hours, twice weekly), daily flights to Běijīng (Y770, one hour, four daily) and Shànghǎi (Y900, 1½ hours, three daily), twice-weekly flights to Guǎngzhōu (Y1930, three hours), daily flights to Seoul (Y1465) and twice-weekly flights to Osaka (Y1980).

BOAT

You can purchase tickets for express boats to Dàlián (Y220, 3½ hours, 8.30am, 10am and 1pm) at the **Yantai passenger ferry terminal** (Yāntáigǎng Kèyùn Zhàn; ☎ 674 1774; 155 Beima Lu) or from the numerous ticket offices east of the train station; tickets can only be purchased on the day of travel. There are also numerous slow boats departing daily for Dàlián (seat/bed Y80/90, 2nd class Y220, seven hours) at 9am. Boats to Incheon (from Y960, roughly 16 hours, 5.30pm Monday, Wednesday and Friday) in South Korea also leave from the Yantai terminal.

BUS

Buses depart from outside the train station for Běijīng (sleeper Y150, 15 hours, several daily), Jǐ'nán (Y66, six hours, every 40 minutes), Wēihǎi (Y20, one hour) and other destinations. From the **long-distance bus station** (chángtú qìchēzhàn; Qingnian Lu) there are buses to numerous destinations, including Jǐ'nán (Y98, every 50 minutes), Pénglái (Y15, 1½ hours, every 30 minutes), Qīngdǎo (Y60, every 25 minutes) and Wēihǎi (Y17, every 30 minutes). Sleeper buses also run to destinations further afield, including Shànghǎi (Y193, 16 hours, 7.15am) and Tiānjīn (Y113, 15 hours, twice daily).

Minibuses to Pénglái (Y15, 1½ hours, 5.30am to 6pm) depart every 15 to 20 minutes from the **Beima Lu bus station** (cnr Beima Lu & Qingnian Lu).

TRAIN

Yāntái **train station** (☎ 9510 5175) has trains to Běijīng (Y249, 15 hours, daily), Jǐ'nán (Y38, eight hours, several per day), Qīngdǎo (Y22, four hours, several per day), Shànghǎi (Y190, 20 hours, twice daily) and Xī'ān (Y210, 15 hours, twice daily).

Getting Around

Yantai Airport (☎ 624 1330) is approximately 20km south of town. Airport buses (Y10, 30 minutes) depart from the CAAC office around two hours before flights; a taxi will cost around Y40 to Y50.

Bus 3 does a loop of town, running past the train station, south down Xinanhe Lu and west on Yuhuangding Xilu. Bus 17 runs between the two beaches. Taxi flag fall is Y5, and Y1.30 per kilometre thereafter.

PÉNGLÁI 蓬莱

☎ 0535

About 65km northwest of Yāntái, the 1000-year-old **Penglai Pavilion** (蓬莱阁; Pénglái Gé; ☎ 564 8106; admission Y70; 🕙 7am-6.30pm summer, 8am-5pm winter) is closely entwined in Chinese mythology with the legend of the Eight Immortals

Crossing the Sea. Perched on a cliff top overlooking the waves, the pavilion harbours a fascinating array of temples and looks out onto wonderful views of fishing boat flotillas.

Besides the pavilion, Pénglái draws crowds for its optical illusion that locals claim appears every few decades. On 17 June 1988 a mirage appeared that lasted for over five hours, revealing two islands with roads, trees, buildings, people, bridges and vehicles.

Pénglái is easily visited as a day trip from Yāntái. See opposite for bus details. The last return bus to Yāntái leaves Pénglái at 6pm.

WĒIHǍI 威海

☎ 0631 / pop 136,000

About 60km east of Yāntái, the booming port city of Wēihǎi was the site of China's most humiliating naval defeat, when the entire Qing navy (armed with advanced European warships) was annihilated by a smaller Japanese fleet in 1895.

The British hung onto a concession here until 1930, though little remains to remind you of its colonial heritage.

Today visitors are drawn to Wēihǎi for its golden coastline, Liugong Island and to catch passenger ferries to South Korea.

Information

Bank of China (中国银行; Zhōngguó Yínháng; 38 Xinwei Lu; ☼ 8am-6pm Mon-Fri summer, to 5pm winter) Currency exchange.

China Post (邮局; Yóujú; 40 Xinwei Lu)

CITS (中国国际旅行社; Zhōngguó Guójì Lǚxíngshè; ☎ 581 8616; 3rd fl, 96 Guzhai Dong Lu)

China Travel Service (CTS; 中国旅行社; Zhōngguó Lǚxíngshè; ☎ 520 3477; 46 Haibin Lu)

Public Security Bureau (PSB; 公安局; Gōngānjú; ☎ 521 3620; 111 Chongqing Jie)

Xinhua Bookstore (新华书店; Xīnhuá Shūdiàn; 1 Heping Lu) On the corner with Dongcheng Lu.

Sights

DINGYUAN WARSHIP 定远战舰

Anchored in Weihai Bay off Haibin Park is this lifesize replica of the German-built **Dingyuan** (☎ 520 7806; admission Y50; ☼ 7am-6pm), a Qing dynasty warship dispatched to the bottom of the sea by Japanese torpedo boats during the Sino-Japanese War (1894–95). Board the highly detailed US$6 million warship, an exact facsimile of the original *Dingyuan* (Ting Yuen), and examine it at close quarters along with its exhibits commemorating the clash

between Japan and China that annihilated the Qing fleet.

LIUGONG ISLAND 刘公岛

Liugong Island (Liúgōng Dǎo) lies 2km off the coast in the Wēihǎi Gulf. The island was established as a stronghold during the Ming dynasty to guard against Japanese pirates. Later the Qing government made Liugong Island their naval base, and after their crushing defeat at the hands of the Japanese the island was occupied by Japanese troops for three years.

In 1898 the British wrested control of the area and governed it for 32 years. During this time they built schools, churches and even teahouses, transforming the island into a summer resort for the British Navy. In 1948 Chiang Kaishek and his troops arrived, shortly followed by the communists.

Today the island's main attraction is the well-kept and airy **Museum of the 1894–1895 Sino-Japanese War** (中国甲午战争博物馆; Zhōngguó Jiǎwǔ Zhànzhēng Bówùguǎn; admission Y30; ☼ 7am-5.30pm). The museum is to the west as you exit the ferry terminal, housed in the old offices of the North Sea Fleet commanders. Displays include the anchor of the *Zhenyuan*, a cruiser seized by the Japanese, dioramas of the naval engagement, and shells and fragments of the warship *Jiyuan* (built in Germany), including a high-pressure water desalinisation tank. A Royal Navy torpedo is also displayed and two Krupp cannons.

The island also provides some ideal hiking trails into the hills in the north.

Ferries run every 10 minutes to Liugong Island (Y40 return, 20 minutes, price includes a boat trip around the island) between 7am and 5pm from the **Liugongdao Ferry Terminal** (48 Haibin Lu), south of the passenger ferry terminal. The last ferry returning to Wēihǎi leaves at 6pm. There is no accommodation on the island. Buggies whizz around the island for Y10.

INTERNATIONAL BEACH 国际海水浴场

Wēihǎi's International Beach (Guójì Hǎishuǐ Yùchǎng) draws large crowds for its long stretch of golden sand, comparably clean waters and large swimming area.

Sleeping

Hailin Hotel (海林宾馆; Hǎilín Bīnguǎn; ☎ 522 4931; fax 528 2632; 146 Tongyi Lu; 统一路146号; d/tr/ste Y160/210/480) This simple, unfussy and pleasantly designed two-star hotel, near the corner with Heping Lu, offers good value. Standard rooms come with water cooler, large shower room, TV, phone and clean furniture.

Sunshine Hotel (阳光大厦; Yángguāng Dàshà; ☎ 520 8999; 88 Tongyi Lu; 统一路88号; d/ste Y680/980) Rooms here are pleasant, with wood flooring, matching twin beds and new showers. Suites are particularly spacious and clean, with inset lights, funky shower rooms and a dose of style. Push for discounts outside of the May and October holiday periods.

Eating

Lichao Restaurant (李朝牛汤; Lǐcháo Niútāng; ☎ 523 6796; north Bldg, 73 Haigang Lu; meals Y25; ☻ 8.30am-noon & 1-5pm) Get into the Korean feel at this lively barbecue grill (shāokǎo) restaurant and order up a platter of lamb (yángròu) plus six vegetable dishes (including kimchi, dòufu, carrot, radish, fish and lettuce; Y25). Grill your lamb slices, dip them in làjiāo (chilli), wrap in lettuce and eat. Round it all off with some soothing and sweet zǎochá (jujube tea). Also on the menu are other meats, including beef and pork.

Kāixin Cǎomào (开心草帽; ☎ 521 7978; 88-8 Tongyi Lu) This is a small café-bakery next to Sunshine Hotel, where you can snack up on egg tarts and sink a glass of milk.

Getting There & Around

AIR

Wēihǎi's airport is 80km away. Flights to cities include Běijīng (Y530, one hour), Guǎngzhōu (Y1460, three hours) and Shànghǎi (Y610, 1½ hours). A taxi from the airport to town will cost around Y80.

BOAT

Ferries sail to Incheon (1st/2nd class Y950/810, 15 hours), in South Korea, at 7pm on Tuesday, Thursday and Sunday. Tickets are generally only available on the day of travel from the ticket office on Haibin Lu to the south of the passenger ferry terminal (wēihǎi gǎng kèyùnzhàn).

Boats to Dàlián leave daily at 9.30am and 9pm (2nd class Y280, eight hours). Tickets should be bought from the International building adjacent to the passenger ferry terminal.

BUS

From the **long-distance bus station** (☎ 522 4591) at the southern end of Dongcheng Lu there are comfortable air-con Volvo buses departing hourly to Yāntái (Y21, one hour, 6am to 5.40pm) and Qīngdǎo (Y68, four hours, 6.30am to 5.30pm). There are also five buses to Jǐ'nán (Y139, eight hours), and a bus to Shànghǎi (Y169, 16 hours) and Běijīng (Y142, 13 hours).

Smaller Iveco buses also run hourly to Yāntái (Y17.50), Qīngdǎo (Y42.50) and Jǐ'nán (Y79.50). There is also a direct bus to Pénglái at 8am (Y24, two hours).

TRAIN

Located in the south of town, the train station has poor connections. There are trains to Běijīng (Y205, once daily), Tiānjīn (Y183, once daily) and Jǐ'nán (Y102, twice daily). Buy tickets at the train station or at the **ticket office** (☎ 520 8000; 120-1 Tongyi Lu), near the Sunshine Hotel (it also sells air tickets).

SHĀNDŌNG

Shànghǎi 上海

Whore of the Orient, Paris of the East; city of quick riches, ill-gotten gains and fortunes lost on the tumble of dice; the domain of adventurers, swindlers, gamblers, drugrunners, tycoons, missionaries, gangsters and backstreet pimps; the city that plots insurrection and dances as the revolution shoots its way into town – Shànghǎi was a dark memory during the long years of forgetting that the Communists visited upon their new China.

After decades going to seed, Shànghǎi's spectacular reversal and alchemic transformation has made it the talk of the town. No other city in China has reversed its decline with such acumen. Somehow managing to typify modern China while being quite unlike anywhere else in the country, Shànghǎi has in the process become an oft-quipped byword for excess, style and full-on construction.

A largely modern upstart, Shànghǎi today compensates for its youthful pedigree with a new-found panache and sense of certainty. As such, Shànghǎi is – like Hong Kong – a city best seen as a prologue or epilogue to your China experience. Shànghǎi is real China, but perhaps just not *the* real China you were after.

For visitors, the city can hardly match the epic history of Běijīng or Xī'ān. Yet Shànghǎi has a unique story to tell and no other Chinese city does foreign concession streetscapes in quite the same way. The Bund, French Concession and the Shanghai Museum are incomparable top sights that cannot be missed. And you can at least warm to the growing acres of neon across the Huangpu River in Lùjiāzuǐ, even if setting foot in Pǔdōng can leave you cold.

HIGHLIGHTS

- Feast on Shànghǎi's tastiest views from the **Bund** (p251), the city's most historic chunk of real estate
- Wine and dine your way through the leafy backstreets of the historic former **French Concession** (p253)
- Open the lid to four millennia of Chinese history at the **Shanghai Museum** (p252)
- Reach new altitudes in the **Jinmao Tower** (p256), Pǔdōng's most iconic building and China's tallest skyscraper
- Marvel at the Yuyuan Gardens and other sights of the **Old Town** (p254)

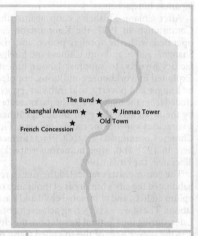

The Bund ★
Shanghai Museum ★ ★ ★ Jinmao Tower
French Concession ★ Old Town

SHÀNGHǍI

| AREA CODE: ☎021 | POPULATION: 15 MILLION | www.cityweekend.com.cn |

HISTORY

As anyone who wanders along the Bund or through the backstreets of the former French Concession can see, Shànghǎi (the name means 'by the sea') is a Western invention. As the gateway to the Yangzi River (Cháng Jiāng), it was an ideal trading port. When the British opened their first concession in 1842, after the first Opium War, it was little more than a small town supported by fishing and weaving. The British changed all that.

The French followed in 1847, an International Settlement was established in 1863 and the Japanese arrived in 1895 – the city was parcelled up into autonomous settlements, immune from Chinese law. By 1853 Shànghǎi had overtaken all other Chinese ports. By the 1930s the city had 60,000 foreign residents and was the busiest international port in Asia.

Built on the trade of opium, silk and tea, the city also lured the world's great houses of finance, which erected grand palaces of plenty. One of the most famous traders was Jardine Matheson & Company. In 1848 Jardine's purchased the first land offered for sale to foreigners in Shànghǎi and grew into one of the great *hongs* (literally a business firm).

Shànghǎi also became a byword for exploitation and vice; its countless opium dens, gambling joints and brothels managed by gangs were at the heart of Shànghǎi life. Guarding it all were the American, French and Italian marines, British Tommies and Japanese bluejackets.

After Chiang Kaishek's coup against the Communists in 1927, the Kuomintang cooperated with the foreign police and the Shànghǎi gangs, and with Chinese and foreign factory owners, to suppress labour unrest. Exploited in workhouse conditions, crippled by hunger and poverty, sold into slavery, excluded from the high life and the parks created by the foreigners, the poor of Shànghǎi had a voracious appetite for radical opinion. The Chinese Communist Party (CCP) was formed here in 1921 and, after numerous setbacks, 'liberated' the city in 1949.

The communists eradicated the slums, rehabilitated the city's hundreds of thousands of opium addicts, and eliminated child and slave labour. These were staggering achievements. Later, during the Cultural Revolution, the city was the power base of the so-called Gang of Four (see p52).

Shànghǎi's long malaise came to an abrupt end in 1990, with the announcement of plans to develop Pǔdōng, on the eastern side of the Huangpu River. Shànghǎi's ambition is to become a major financial centre along with its emerging economic strength. Lùjiāzǔi, the area that faces off the Bund on the Pǔdōng side of the Huangpu, has blossomed as a modern high-rise counterpoint to the austere, old-world structures on the Bund.

Shànghǎi's burgeoning economy, its leadership and its intrinsic self-confidence have put it miles ahead of other cities in China. Nothing would satisfy the central government more than for Shànghǎi to replace Hong Kong as China's frontier on the future, swinging the spotlight of attention from the ex-colony onto a home-grown success story.

Shànghǎi remains shackled to a past it is both suspicious and proud of, and nobody can predict what the city will look like two decades from now. But as the Chinese saying goes, *jiùde bùqù, xīnde bùlái* (if the old doesn't go, the new won't come).

But despite the fanfare, Shànghǎi is hardly an international city (anyone who has been to Kuala Lumpur will immediately spot the difference) and a curious absence of creative energy can make this fast-changing city seem oddly parochial and inward-looking.

CLIMATE

Shànghǎi starts the year shivering in midwinter, when temperatures can drop below freezing, vistas are grey and misty and the damp chill soaks into the bones. April to mid-May is probably one of the best times to visit weatherwise, along with autumn (late September to mid-November). Summer is the peak travel season but the hot and humid weather makes conditions outside uncomfortable, with temperatures sometimes as high as 40°C (104°F) in July and August. Watch out for sudden stingingly hot days at the tail end of summer, affectionately known as the Autumnal Tiger (Qiūlǎohǔ). In short, you'll need silk long johns and down jackets for winter, an ice block for each armpit in summer, and an umbrella wouldn't go astray in either of these seasons.

LANGUAGE

Spoken by 13 million people, the Shanghainese dialect belongs to the Wu dialect, named after the kingdom of Wu in present-day Jiāngsū province. To Mandarin or Cantonese speakers, Shanghainese sounds odd, perhaps because it is a more archaic branch of Chinese. Furthermore, the tonal system of Shànghăihuà differs considerably from Mandarin and Cantonese, displaying closer similarities to African tonal languages. A marked Japanese sound to the Shànghăi dialect can also be heard. Due to the increasing prevalence of Mandarin and the absence of a standard form of Shanghainese, the dialect is constantly changing and is quite different to how it was spoken a few generations ago.

ORIENTATION

Shànghăi municipality covers a huge area, but the city proper is more modest. Broadly, central Shànghăi is divided into two areas: Pŭdōng (east of the Huangpu River) and Pŭxī (west of the Huangpu River). The First Ring Rd does a long elliptical loop around the city centre proper.

The historical attractions belong to Pŭxī, where Shànghăi's personality is also found: the Bund, major sights, the principal shopping streets, the former foreign concessions, and Shànghăi's trendiest clusters of bars, restaurants and nightclubs are all in Pŭxī.

Unlike Běijīng, Shànghăi is not a city of predictable design, so navigation can be exhausting. The area around the Bund is the historical heart of the former International Settlement. From here East Nanjing Rd, China's busiest shopping street, runs west to Renmin (People's) Sq, a centre of gravity of sorts overlooked by the dazzling form of Shànghăi's third tallest building, Tomorrow Square, and home to the Shanghai Museum, Grand Theatre and the frantic Metro Line 1 and Line 2 interchange. West Nanjing Rd continues west from here in a glitzy blur of malls, hotels and well-heeled shoppers.

South of the Bund, the Old Town is a ragged maze of narrow lanes pinched between closely packed houses, laundry hung from overhead windows, and smoky temples. The location of the original town of Shànghăi, this is the oldest part of the city.

South of Yan'an Rd, and west of the Old Town, the former French Concession is a large and leafy quarter of shops, bars and restaurants, popular with expats and white-collar Chinese.

Rearing up east of the Huangpu is the kit-city of Pŭdōng, a special economic zone of maglev trains, mega-malls, banks, glisten-ing skyscrapers, building sites and residential complexes, eventually petering out into farmland. Swish in parts, Pŭdōng has a manufactured feel that can be alienating.

In the central district (around Nanjing Rd) the provincial names run north–south, and city names run east–west. Some roads use compass points, such as South Sichuan Rd and North Sichuan Rd. Encircling Shànghăi proper, Zhongshan Rd is split by sectors, such as East Zhongshan No 2 Rd and East Zhongshan No 1 Rd.

Maps

English maps of Shànghăi are available at the Foreign Languages Bookstore (below), major hotel bookshops and occasionally from street hawkers (most of the latter are Chinese-only).

The bilingual *Shanghai Tourist Map*, produced by the Shanghai Municipal Tourism Administration, is free at hotels and Tourist Information Centres (p241).

INFORMATION
Bookshops

Most hotels, including the Peace Hotel (p262), sell English-language books on Shànghăi. Fuzhou Rd has traditionally been the bookshop street of Shànghăi.

Chaterhouse Booktrader (Map pp244-5; ☎ 6391 8237; Shop B1-E, Shanghai Times Square, 93 Central Huaihai Rd) A great hit with literature-starved expats for its selection of books and mags, but prices can make your head spin.

Foreign Languages Bookstore (Wàiyŭ Shūdiàn; Map pp244-5; ☎ 6322 3200; 390 Fuzhou Rd; ☯ 9.30am-6pm, to 7pm Fri & Sat; metro Middle Henan Rd) The 1st floor has a good range of postcards, maps and English-language books on Shànghăi. The 4th floor (Shanghai Book Traders) has a wide range of imported books and novels, including a strong children's section.

Garden Books (Tāofèn Xīwén Shùjú; Map pp248-9; ☎ 5404 8729; 325 Changle Rd; ☯ 10am-10pm) More style than substance, but loads of literature in French upstairs.

Old China Hand Reading Room (Hànyuán Shūwū; Map pp248-9; ☎ 6473 2526; 27 Shaoxing Rd) Restful bookshop-cum-café with an absorbing range of books on art, architecture and culture.

Shanghai Museum (Shànghăi Bówùguăn; Map pp244-5; 201 Renmin Ave; metro Renmin Sq) There is an excellent range of books on Chinese art, architecture, ceramics and calligraphy, as well as a wide selection of cards and slides.

SHÀNGHĂI

Cultural Centres

Alliance Française (Fǎyǔ Péixùn Zhōngxīn; Map pp244–5; ☎ 6357 5388; www.alliancefrancaise.org.cn; 5th & 6th fl, 297 Wusong Rd) French films every week, musical events, a large French library and the occasional exhibition.

British Council (Yīngguó Wénhuà Jiāoyùchù; Map pp244–5; ☎ 6391 2626; www.britishcouncil.org.cn; Pidemco Tower, 318 Fuzhou Rd; ☼ 8.30am–noon & 1.30–5pm Mon-Fri; metro Middle Henan Rd) Recent British newspapers and music magazines like *Q* and *NME*.

Internet Access 网吧

Internet cafés are all over town, but there's a frequent turnover of locales. You'll need your passport for ID in most places.

China Telecom (Zhōngguó Diànxìn; Map pp244–5; 30 East Nanjing Rd; per min/hr Y0.30/10; ☼ 7am-10.30pm)

Eastday B@r (Dōngfāng Wǎngdiàn; Map pp248–9; 24 Ruijin No 2 Rd; per hr Y3; ☼ 8am-2am)

Highland Internet Café (Gāozhìdiǎn Wǎngbā; Map pp242–3; Dingxi Rd; per hr Y3) Next to KFC.

Shanghai Library (Shànghǎi Túshūguǎn; Map pp248–9; ☎ 6445 5555; 1555 Central Huaihai Rd; ground-fl terminals per hr Y4; ☼ 9am-6pm) Bring your passport for ID; minimum one hour.

Internet Resources

City Weekend (www.cityweekend.com.cn) A good listings website that has a searchable database of articles.

SH (www.8days.sh) This is the latest player on the city scene, brought to you by veterans of *That's Shanghai*.

Shanghai-ed (www.shanghai-ed.com) Everything from what's on to historical essays, though parts are a bit outdated.

Shanghai Expat (www.shanghaiexpat.com) A must-see if you are thinking of relocating to Shànghǎi, though some links don't work.

Shanghai Guide (www.shanghaiguide.com) This is a good guide to living in Shànghǎi, with a strong focus on tourism.

SmartShanghai.com (www.smartshanghai.com) For fashion, food, fun and frolicking.

Tales of Old China (www.talesofoldchina.com) Lots of reading on Old Shànghǎi, with the text of hard-to-find books online.

That's Shanghai (www.thatssh.com) Always on top of what's happening in Shànghǎi entertainment.

www.shanghaiist.com Aimed at expats; ask an expert if you have a specific query.

SHÀNGHĂI IN...

Two Days

Give yourself a couple of hours to stroll the **Bund** (p251), preferably at night or early morning. For a different perspective, enjoy sweeping views of the Bund from the Pǔdōng side (take the tourist tunnel or the metro) and then visit the **Jinmao Tower** (p256). To fully savour the occasion, dine at one of the **restaurants** (p265) on the Bund or at the Grand Hyatt if in Pǔdōng (reservations advised in both instances).

To fill out the first day take the metro to the **Shanghai Museum** (p252), one of China's finest, which deserves the best part of half a day.

The other great attraction of Shànghǎi is the Old Town, incorporating **Yuyuan Gardens** (p254) and the surrounding teahouses and bazaar, so take a taxi here for your second day. If you don't like crowds then give this a miss at the weekends. After a visit to Yuyuan Gardens add on a walk to **Dongtai Rd Antique Market** (p272) for some shopping and then take lunch (or dinner) at one of **Xīntiāndì's** (p253) trendy restaurants.

Try to save time for one big night out in Shànghǎi to experience the modern side of the city. Take in the **acrobats** (p271) or a performance at the **Grand Theatre** (p270), try one of the excellent restaurants and then take your pick of the **bars** (p268) and **clubs** (p270).

Four Days

With more time, savour a slower-paced Shànghǎi and fit in a walk through the faded 1930s architecture of the French Concession backstreets, where Shànghǎi still shows its old magic.

You'll also have time to hop aboard a **boat cruise** (p258) for views of the Bund. From the Bund, stroll along China's most famous shopping street, **East Nanjing Rd** (p251), which links the Bund with the Shanghai Museum.

Finally, if you have time after all the shopping, take a half-day trip out to **Qībǎo** (p257) for its old canal-town flavours, or a day trip to **Mùdú** (p312) or **Tónglǐ** (p310) in neighbouring Jiāngsū province.

Media

The first thing to do is to grab a free copy of the monthly *That's Shanghai* from a top-end hotel, followed swiftly by issues of *City Weekend*, *Shanghai Talk* or the weekly *SH (8 Days)*. These offer an instant plug into what's on in town, from art exhibitions and club nights to restaurant openings.

Foreign newspapers and magazines are available from the larger tourist hotels and some foreign language bookstores (see p239).

The two local government–produced English newspapers are the **Shanghai Daily** (www .shanghaidaily.com; Y2), published Monday to Saturday – not quite a daily – which is OK for international news, and the weekly **Shanghai Star** (www.shanghai-star.com.cn; Y2).

Medical Services

Huashan Hospital (Huáshān Yīyuàn; Map pp248-9; ☎ 6248 9999, ext 2351; 12 Central Wulumuqi Rd) Hospital treatment and out-patient consultations are available at the 15th-floor foreigners' clinic, which has a Hong Kong joint-venture section.

International Medical Care Centre (IMCC)/ Shanghai First People's Hospital (Shànghǎi Shì Dìyī Rénmín Yīyuàn; Map pp244-5; ☎ 6306 9480, 6324 0090, ext 2101; 585 Jiulong Rd, northeast Shanghai)

Shanghai United Family Hospital (Shànghǎi Hémùjiā Yīyuàn; Map pp242-3; ☎ 5133 1900, 24hr emergency 5133 1999; www.unitedfamilyhospitals.com; 1139 Xianxia Rd, Changning District) Complete private hospital, staffed by doctors trained in the West. Medical facilities run to inpatient rooms, operating rooms, an intensive care unit and birthing suites.

World Link (Ruìxīn Guójì Yīliáo Zhōngxīn; Map pp244-5; ☎ 6279 7688; www.worldlink-shanghai.com; Suite 203, Shanghai Centre, 1376 West Nanjing Rd; ☯ 9am-7pm Mon-Fri, to 4pm Sat, to 3pm Sun) Private medical care by expat doctors, dentists and specialists. For nonmembers, expect a doctor's consultation fee of US$70 and an ambulance charge of US$100.

World Link Hongqiao Clinic (Ruìxīn Guójì Yīliáo Zhōngxīn; Map pp242-3; ☎ 6405 5788; fax 6405 3587; Unit 30, Mandarine City, 788 Hongxu Rd; ☯ 9am-7pm Mon-Fri, to 4pm Sat, to 3pm Sun)

Money

Almost every hotel has money-changing counters. Most tourist hotels, restaurants, banks and Friendship Stores accept major credit cards. ATMs at various branches of the Bank of China and the Industrial and Commercial Bank of China (ICBC) accept most major cards.

Bank of China (Zhōngguó Yínháng; Map pp244-5; The Bund; ☯ 9am-noon & 1.30-4.30pm Mon-Fri, 9am-noon Sat) Right next to the Peace Hotel. Tends to get crowded, but is better organised than Chinese banks elsewhere around the country (it's worth a peek for its grand interior). Take a ticket and wait for your number. For credit card advances head to the furthest hall (counter No 2).

Citibank (Huāqí Yínháng; Map pp244-5; The Bund) Useful ATM open 24 hours.

Hong Kong & Shanghai Bank (HSBC; Huìfēng Yínháng) Has ATMs in the Shanghai Centre on West Nanjing Rd (Map pp244-5), at Pudong Airport arrivals hall and at 15 East Zhongshan No 1 Rd on the Bund (Map pp244-5).

Post

Larger tourist hotels have post offices where you can mail letters and small packages, and this is by far the most convenient option.

DHL (☎ 6536 2900, 800-810 8000; www.dhl.com) Kirin Plaza (Map pp242-3; 5th fl, 666 Gubei Rd); Shanghai Centre (Map pp244-5; 1376 West Nanjing Rd)

FedEx (☎ 6275 0808; www.fedex.com; 10th fl, Aetna Building, 107 Zunyi Rd)

International Post Office (Guójì Yóujú; Map pp244-5; 2nd fl, cnr North Sichuan Rd & North Suzhou Rd; ☯ 8.30-11am & 1-4.30pm) The section for international parcels is in the same building around the corner; poste restante is at counter No 7.

UPS (Map pp248-9; ☎ 6391 5555; www.ups.com; room 1318-38, Shanghai Central Plaza, 381 Central Huaihai Rd)

Public Security Bureau

PSB (Gōngānjú; Map pp242-3; ☎ 6854 1199; 1500 Minsheng Rd; ☯ 9am-5pm Mon-Sat) Handles visas and registrations; 30-day visa extensions cost around Y160. Near Jinxiu Rd.

Telephone

IP cards are the cheapest way to call internationally (Y1.80 per minute to the US) but may not work with hotel phones.

China Mobile (Zhōngguó Yídòng Tōngxìn; Map pp244-5; 21 Yuanmingyuan Rd) Head here for queries about cell-phones.

China Telecom (Zhōngguó Diànxìn; Map pp244-5; ☯ 7am-10.30pm) Branch office next to the Peace Hotel on East Nanjing Rd.

Tourist Information

Tourist Information and Service Centres are located near several major tourist sights. The standard of English varies from good to nonexistent and the centres primarily function to

(Continued on page 251)

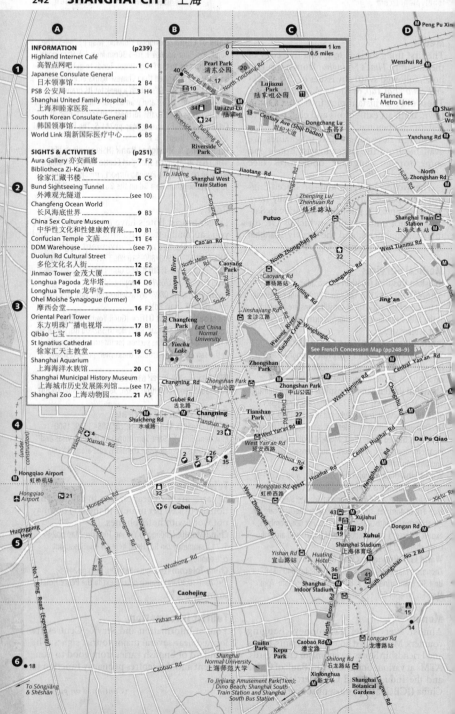

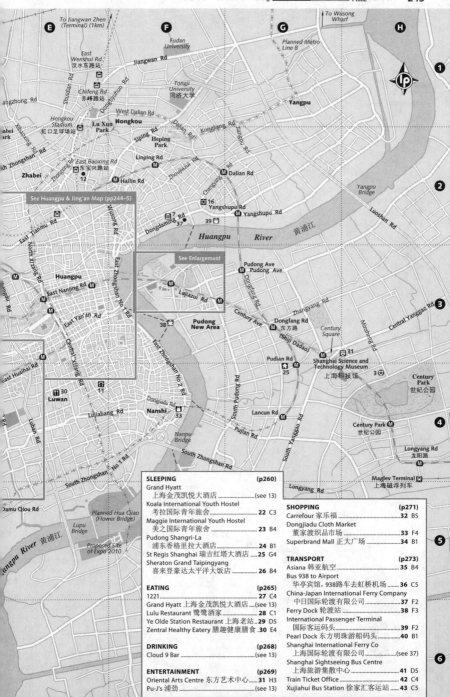

0 ——————— 2 km
0 ——————— 1 mile

E To Jiangwan Zhen (Terminal) (1km)

F Fudan University

G Planned Metro Line 8

H To Wusong Wharf

East Wenshui Rd 汶水东路站

Jiangwan Rd

Chifeng Rd 齐峰路站
赤峰路

Tongji University 同济大学

Yangpu 杨浦

East Dalian Rd

West Dalian Rd

Hongkou Stadium 虹口足球场站
Hongkou 虹口

Lu Xun Park 鲁迅公园

Siping

Heping Park

Kongjiang Rd

Dalian Rd

Zhabei 闸北

East Baoxing Rd 东宝兴路站

Linping Rd

Hailun Rd

Chengjiang

Dalian Rd

Yangpu Bridge 杨浦大桥

Luoshan Rd

Yangpu Bridge

East Tianmu Rd

Wusong Rd

16 Yangshupu Rd

M Yangshupu Rd

Dongdaming Rd

7 37
39

Huangpu River 黄浦江

North Xizang Rd
East Zhongshan No 1 Rd

Huangpu 黄浦

See Huangpu & Jing'an Map (pp244–5)

See Enlargement

Pudong Ave
Pudong Ave 浦东大道

East Nanjing Rd

M Lujiazui Rd

Lujiazui Rd

Dongchang Rd

Zhangyang Rd

East Yan'an Rd

38

Pudong New Area 浦东新区

Century Ave

Dongfang Rd 东方路

Shiji Dadao 世纪大道

Century Square

Minsheng Rd

Central Yanggao Rd

Shanghai Science and Technology Museum 上海科技馆

31

3

Century Park 世纪公园

East Xizang Rd

East Zhongshan No 2 Rd

Pudian Rd
25

South Pudong Rd

30

East Huaihai Rd

11

Luwan 卢湾

Dongjiadu Rd

Nanshi 南市

33

Lancun Rd

South Yanggao Rd

Century Park 世纪公园
Longyang Rd 龙阳路

Lijiabang Rd

Pujian Rd

Nanpu Bridge 南浦大桥

Maglev Terminal 上海磁浮列车

Longyang Rd

Damu Qiou Rd

South Zhongshan Rd

South Zhongshan No 1 Rd

Lupu Bridge

Planned Hua Qiao (Flower Bridge)

Proposed Site of Expo 2010

Libao Rd

Nampu Bridge

Huangpu River 黄浦江

Ⓐ   Ⓑ   Ⓒ   Ⓓ

Panjiawan Rd

1

Zhongxing Rd

Jiatong Rd

● 100

Shanghai Train
Station
上海火车站 Ⓜ

94

Moganshan Rd

Hengfeng Rd 恒丰路

West Gonghe Rd

Yongxing Rd

🏛 18

Aomen Rd

39

● 101

55 🏛   Meiyuan Rd

West Tianmu Rd 天目西路

2

Changshou Rd 常熟路

Suzhou Creek

Yutong Rd

Central Tianmu Rd

Datong Rd

Wuzhen Rd

Changhua Rd

Jiangning Rd

North Shaanxi Rd

Anyuan Rd North Shaanxi Rd

23
22 🏛

江宁路

(Wusong River)

Hanzhong Rd 汉中路
98 🏛 🏛

20 🏛

Changping Rd

3

Datian Rd

新闸路

Xinzha Rd

North Chengdu Rd 成都北路

Shanghaiguan Rd

Huangpu

🏛 40

North Shaanxi Rd

Wuding Rd

Shimen No 2 Rd 石门二路

Haifang Rd

Changping Rd

4

Kangding Rd

Jing'an

Xikang Rd

Xinzha Rd 新闸路

West Beijing Rd 北京西路

Changde Rd

West Nanjing Rd 南京西路

Wuding Rd

Taixing Rd

Shimen No 1 Rd 石门一路
73 Ⓜ
🏛

Shimen No 1 Rd 石门一路

Wujiang Rd

Qinghai Rd

Jian

Xinzha Rd 新闸路

Jiaozhou Rd

West Beijing Rd 北京西路

74 🏛

Nanyang Rd

48 14
🏛 ● 79
58 🏛

91 🏛

North Maoming Rd

South Shaanxi Rd

88 🏛

2 🏛
86 🏛

52 🏛

38 🏛

Weihai Rd

Changde Rd

Tongren Rd

72 🏛

57 🏛

62 🏛

West Nanjing Rd 南京西路

Jing'an
Temple
静安寺

24 ●
17 ℹ

6

Jing'an
Park
静安公园

Central Yan'an Rd 延安中路

Julu Rd

Jinxian Rd

Ruijin No 1 Rd 瑞金一路

Fumin Rd

Changle Rd

0   1 km
0   0.5 miles

E   **F**   **G**   **H**

Coinjang Rd
Huiwen Rd
99
North Jiangxi Rd
Baoshan Rd 宝山路
Jiulong Rd
15
Wusong Rd 吴淞路
Hailing Rd

1

Baoshan Rd 宝山路站
Wujing Rd
Zhapu Rd
Kunshan Rd
North Shanxi Rd

East Tianmu Rd 天目东路
Anqing Rd
Kangce Rd
Huaxing Rd
North Zhejiang Rd
1
68
Wuchang Rd

新疆路
Xinjiang Rd
North Fujian Rd
Tangqu Rd
North Henan Rd
Tiantong Rd
Tiantong Rd

2

Qufu Rd
North Suzhou Rd
11
34 49
Zhapu Rd
Pudong Rd
13 Huangpu Rd
Garden
Bridge
25

Suzhou Creek (Wusong River)
South Suzhou Rd
44
Central Jiangxi Rd
102
Yuanmingyuan Rd
Huangpu
Park 黄浦公园
Bund
Sightseeing
Tunnel
19

inzha Rd 新闸路
Xinzha Rd 新闸西路
East Beijing Rd 北京东路
Ningbo Rd
South Shanxi Rd
Tianjin Rd
6
Dianchi Rd
90
4
7
46
47
64
3
Huangpu River 黄浦江

West Beijing Rd 北京西路
Central Xizang Rd 西藏中路
Central Fujian Rd
Central Zhejiang Rd
Middle
Henan Rd
河南中路
84
M
87
92
56
10
East Zhongshan No 1 Rd

Shanghai Shimao International Plaza
上海世茂国际广场
26
27
36
85
Jiujiang Rd
Hankou Rd
43
70
12
35 60
32
East Yan'an
Road Tunnel

50
93
East Nanjing Rd
南京东路
16
51
Fuzhou Rd 福州路
9
5
89
Guangdong Rd
3
53
97
8 21
96
4

45
Renmin Park
人民公园
75
63
82

Renmin
Square 人民广场
78
East Yan'an Rd 延安东路
41
Renmin Rd 人民路

Renmin Park
人民公园
69
30
Yunan Rd
Youijia Rd
East Ninghai Rd
East Jinling Rd
Fuyou Rd
61 33
Anren Jie
71

42
28
Sanjiao
Park
37
77
29
103
67
54
76
East Huaihai Rd 淮海东路
83
Central Fangbang Rd
Huachang Rd
21
31
5

Wusheng Rd
Central Jinling Rd
East Huaihai Rd 淮海东路
Dajing Rd
Zhoujin Rd

95
80
Shouning Rd
South Henan Rd
Qinglian Jie
Old Town
Waicangqiao Rd
6

Huangpi
Rd 黄陂南路
66
Huaihai
Park 淮海公园
81
Jinjia Fang

Xing'an Rd
Chongde Rd
Dongtai Rd
Taicang Rd
South Huaihai Rd
Madang Rd
Hubin Rd

HUANGPU & JING'AN

A
B
C
D

1

Wanghangdu Rd 万航渡路

West Wuding Rd

West Beijing Rd

Jiaozhou Rd

Changde Rd

Tongren Rd

2

61

Planned
Metro Lines

58

Jing'an
Temple
30 静安寺

Jing'an
Park
静安公园

Central Yan'an Rd 延安中路

Yuyuan Rd 愚园路

M Jiangsu Rd
江苏路

West Nanjing Rd 南京西路

59

35

3

38

37

2

Zhenning Rd

North Wulumuqi Rd 乌鲁木齐北路

57

Huashan Rd 华山路

5

West Yan'an Rd 延安西路

Jiangsu Rd 江苏路

Lixi Rd

Dong Zhuanbang

Changle Rd

Anfu Rd

55

Changshu Rd

Caojiayan Rd

45

Ding Xiang
Garden
丁香花园

Wuyuan Rd 五原路

Changshu Rd 常熟路

3

22

24

33

23

West Fuxing Rd 复兴西路

48

11

6

Baoqing Rd 宝庆路

Huaihai Rd

Pingwu Rd

Huashan Rd 华山路

Xingfu Rd

Xinguo Rd

Wukang Rd

Yongfu Rd

4

29

44

Taojiang Rd

26

Dongping Rd

39

4

10

Niugiao
Bang

8

Panyu Rd

Fahuazhen Rd

Central Huaihai Rd 淮海中路

Wuxing Rd

Hengshan Rd
衡山路 M

South Wulumuqi Rd

Yongjia Rd

5

49

Hengshan Rd

Cao'an Rd

Xinhua Rd

West Huaihai Rd 淮海西路

Kangping Rd

Yuqing Rd

Tianping Rd

Guangyuan Rd

18

6

Jiaotong
University

43

Huashan Rd

Hengshan Rd 衡山路

Ding'an Rd

(Continued from page 241)

book hotel rooms, put you on a tour and sell you souvenirs, but free maps and some information are available. Useful branches include those at Century Square, 561 East Nanjing Rd (Map pp244–5; ☎ 5353 1117); near the Temple of the Town Gods (Map pp244–5; ☎ 6355 5032; 149 Jiujiaochang Rd); and across the road from Jing'an Temple (Map pp244–5; ☎ 6248 3259; 1699 West Nanjing Rd).

The international arrivals hall of Hongqiao Airport has a tourist information booth with staff who give out maps and are helpful. There was no comprehensive tourist information booth at Pudong International Airport at the time of writing but plans were afoot to install one. The useful **Shanghai Information Centre for International Visitors** (☎ 6384 9366; No 2, Alley 123, Xingye Rd, Xintiandi) is at **Xīntiāndì** (p253).

Tourist Hotline (☎ 6252 0000; ☽ 9am-9pm) Has a limited English-language service.

Travel Agencies

See p273 for details on train and ferry ticket agencies and airline offices.

China International Travel Service (CITS; Zhōngguó Guójì Lǚxíngshè; Map pp244–5; ☎ 6323 8770; 5th fl, Guangming Bldg, 2 East Jinling Rd) Can book air and train tickets. The head office is at 1277 West Beijing Rd (☎ 6289 4510/8899).

Shanghai Spring International Travel Service (Chūnqiū Guójì Lǚxíngshè; Map pp244–5; ☎ 6351 6666; www.china-sss.com; 347 Central Xizang (Tibet) Rd) Centrally located, IATA-bonded and good for air tickets.

STA Travel (☎ 6353 2683; www.statravel.com.cn; Suite 305,158 Hanzhong Rd; ☽ 9am-6pm Mon-Fri, 10.30am-3.30pm Sat) Sells train and air tickets, and can issue International Student Identity Cards.

SIGHTS
The Bund & East Nanjing Rd

The area around the Bund is the tourist centre of Shànghăi and the city's most famous mile.

THE BUND 外滩

The Bund (Wàitān) is an Anglo-Indian term for the embankment of a muddy waterfront. The Bund was once situated only a few feet from the Huangpu River (黄浦江; Huángpǔ Jiāng) but in the mid-1990s the road was widened and a 771m-long flood barrier was built (the river now lies above the level of Nanjing Rd due to subsidence).

The Bund is symbolic of Shànghăi and provided – and still provides – a grand façade for those arriving in Shànghăi by river. To Europeans, it was Shànghăi's Wall St, a place of feverish trading, of fortunes made and lost. Constant throngs of Chinese and foreign tourists pad past the porticoes of the Bund's grand edifices with maps in hand and gaze at Pǔdōng from the promenade. The buildings themselves – many in need of a good scrubbing – loom serenely; a vagabond assortment of neoclassical 1930s downtown New York styles and monumental antiquity, some have been converted to accommodate bars, restaurants, galleries and fashion boutiques.

Particularly beautiful at night, the optimum activity on the Bund is to simply stroll, comparing the bones of the past with the geometry of the future in Pǔdōng's skyline. See the walking tour (p258) for a rundown of the buildings on the Bund.

Amble along the elevated riverside promenade beside the Huangpu River for visions of China's tireless tourist boom: vocal hawkers, toy sellers, the endless squawk of 'Huānyíng Guānglín' ('Welcome'), coin-operated telescopes and gaggles of wide-eyed out-of-towners. Take a **boat trip** on the Huangpu River (see p258) or relax at some fabulous restaurants and bars. Trips to Pǔdōng via the mind-warping Bund Sightseeing Tunnel (p256) or by metro from Middle Henan Rd station are further options.

The Bund is undergoing further transformations as the ambitious North Bund Development project revamps the area north of Dianchi Rd to Suzhou Creek (Wusong River).

On the south end of the Bund, **Three on the Bund** (Wàitān Sānhào; Map pp244–5; www.threeonthebund .com) combines Armani and Evian with the Shanghai Gallery of Art (admission free), several top-end bars and restaurants (see the boxed text, p268). In a similar vein is **No 18 the Bund** to the north – the former headquarters of the Chartered Bank of Australia, India and China – where fabulous shopping and dining options and a creative centre attract a stylish clientele.

EAST NANJING RD 南京东路

East Nanjing Rd, from the Peace to the Park Hotels, has long been China's golden mile. Pleasantly pedestrianised from Xizang (Tibet) Rd to Henan Rd, the frantic commercial strip

TOP FIVE BOOKS ON SHÀNGHĂI

- *Shanghai* by Harriet Sergeant. A recommended reconstruction of Shànghǎi's swinging history.

- *Shanghai: The Rise and Fall of a Decadent City* by Stella Dong. Another well-researched history of the good-old bad-old days.

- *In Search of Old Shanghai* by Pan Ling. An easy read into the characters of Shànghǎi's murky past.

- *New Shanghai: The Rocky Rebirth of China's Legendary City* by Pamela Yatsko. Bring yourself up to date with this portrait of the new Shànghǎi.

- *Candy* by Mian Mian. Hip modern novel from a darling of the city's social set, proving that sex, suicide and drug addiction aren't just limited to Shànghǎi's past.

affords excellent nocturnal views and has several historic buildings, including the **No 1 Provisions Store** (Dìyī Shípǐn Shāngdiàn; Map pp244-5; 720 East Nanjing Rd), built as the Sun Sun store in 1926, and **No 1 Department Store** (Dìyī Bǎihuò Shāngdiàn; Map pp244-5; 800 East Nanjing Rd), which opened in 1936 as the Sun Company and was for decades China's largest and most famous department store.

At the east end of Renmin Park, the Park Hotel (Map pp244–5) is notable for its brooding Art Deco design. Built as a bank in 1934, it was the tallest building in the Far East at the time (and Shànghǎi's tallest until the 1980s).

Renmin Square 人民广场

East Nanjing Rd and West Nanjing Rd divide at **Renmin Park** (Rénmín Gōngyuán; Map pp244-5; admission Y2; 6am-6pm). Containing the recently opened, new-fangled and private Museum of Contemporary Art, the park and the adjacent Renmin (People's) Sq were once the site of the Shanghai Racecourse.

Overshadowed by the dramatic, new-fangled form of JW Marriott Tomorrow Square, Renmin Sq today is occupied by the Shanghai Museum, the Shanghai Grand Theatre and the Shanghai Urban Planning Exhibition Hall.

SHANGHAI MUSEUM 上海博物馆

The must-see **Shanghai Museum** (Shànghǎi Bówùguǎn; Map pp244-5; 6372 3500; 2 Renmin Ave; adult/child or student Y20/5; 9am-5pm Sun-Fri with last entry 4pm, to 7pm Sat) has none of the dry exhibits and yawning security guards that plague China's provincial museums. While guiding you through the craft of millennia, the museum simultaneously takes you through the pages of Chinese history. Expect to spend half, if not most of, a day here.

Designed to recall the shape of an ancient Chinese *dǐng* vessel, the architectural landmark is home to one of the most impressive collections in China. Take your pick from the archaic green patinas of the Ancient Chinese Bronze Gallery through to the silent solemnity of the Chinese Sculpture Gallery; from the exquisite beauty of the ceramics in the Zande Lou Gallery to the measured and timeless flourishes captured in the Chinese Calligraphy Gallery. Chinese painting, seals, jade, Ming and Qing furniture, coins and ethnic costumes are also on offer, intelligently displayed in well-lit galleries. Seats are provided outside galleries on each floor when lethargy strikes.

Photos are allowed in some galleries. The audio guide (available in eight languages) is well worth the extra Y40, and don't overlook the excellent museum shop on the ground floor – but be warned of high prices in the teahouse.

The Shanghai Museum, the Shanghai Art Museum and the Grand Theatre (p270) can be visited on a combined ticket (Y50).

SHANGHAI ART MUSEUM 上海美术馆

This **museum** (Shànghǎi Měishùguǎn; Map pp244-5; 6327 2829; 325 West Nanjing Rd; adult/student Y20/10; 9am-5pm, last entry 4pm) is the city's premier art gallery. Refreshingly cool in summer, the interior galleries – arranged over three floors – are perfectly suited to exhibiting art, with well-illuminated alcoves and a voluminous sense of space. Some of the art is hit and miss, but the building (the former Shanghai Racecourse Club) is gorgeous, and delicious meals and views await on the roof at Kathleen's 5 (p265).

SHANGHAI URBAN PLANNING EXHIBITION HALL 上海城市规划展示馆

This **exhibition hall** (Chéngshì Guīhuà Zhǎnshìguǎn; Map pp244-5; 6372 2077; 100 Renmin Ave; adult Y30; 9am-5pm Mon-Thu, to 6pm Fri-Sun, last ticket sold 1hr before closing) paints a bold picture of the future evolution of Shànghǎi. The highlight is the scale plan of future Shànghǎi, but photographs of old Shànghǎi generate the right balance.

French Concession 法国租界

Shànghǎi *sans* the French Concession would be like London minus Kensington and Chelsea. A residential, retail, restaurant and bar district with atmospheric tree-lined streets, the French Concession is a name you won't find appearing on any Chinese maps, but it ranges elegantly from Huangpu District, through the districts of Luwan and Xuhui and slices of Changning and Jingan Districts. The cream of Shànghǎi's old residential buildings and Art Deco apartment blocks, hotels and edifices are preserved here, while commercial Huaihai Rd teems with shoppers. The district naturally tends towards gentrification (eg along Xinhua Rd), but it's also a trendy and happening enclave, excellent for random exploration, on foot or bike, in a slow progression from café to café or by full immersion in Xīntiāndì, a hip and stylish quadrant of restored *shíkūmén* (literally 'stone-framed doorway') houses, signature restaurants and bars.

SITE OF THE 1ST NATIONAL CONGRESS OF THE CCP 中共一大会址

The CCP was founded in July 1921 in this French Concession building, now a **museum** (Zhōnggòng Yīdàhuìzhǐ; Map pp248-9; ☎ 5383 2171; 76 Xingye Rd; admission Y3; ☒ 9am-5pm) with photographs and reconstructions of the historic meeting, with English captions. Whether or not you sympathise with *mǎlièzhǔyì* (Marxist-Leninism), the certainties of that era manage to exude a particular nostalgic appeal in today's China. South across the way is the small and quaint Postal Museum.

NO DOGS OR CHINESE

Famously, a sign at the entrance to Huangpu Park announced 'No Dogs or Chinese Allowed'. Or that's how posterity remembers it. In actual fact the restrictions on Chinese and dogs were listed in separate clauses of a whole bevy of restrictions. The regulation was finally rescinded in 1928 but has since become a powerful symbol of Shànghǎi's semicolonial rule.

XĪNTIĀNDÌ 新天地

The ambitious business, entertainment and cultural complex of **Xīntiāndì** (Map pp248-9; www.xintiandi.com; Taicang Rd & Madang Rd) has quickly become the city's most stylish domain of restaurants, bars and designer shops. The heart of the complex, just off South Huangpi Rd, consists of several blocks of renovated (largely rebuilt) traditional *shíkūmén* houses, low-rise tenement buildings built in the early 1900s, brought bang up to date with a stylish modern twist. A small museum, the **Shikumen Open House Museum** (Map pp248-9; admission Y20; ☒ 10am-10pm) depicts traditional life in a 10-room Shànghǎi *shíkūmén*.

SUN YATSEN'S FORMER RESIDENCE 孙中山故居

China brims with Sun Yatsen memorabilia, and this **former residence** (Sūn Zhōngshān Gùjū; Map pp248-9; ☎ 6437 2954; 7 Xiangshan Rd; admission Y8; ☒ 9am-4.30pm), on the former rue Molière, is where the founder of modern China (Guófū) lived for six years. After Sun's death, his wife, Song Qingling (1893–1981) remained here until 1937, watched by plain-clothes Kuomintang and French police. The two-storey house is decorated with period furnishings, despite looting by the Japanese.

TAIKANG ROAD ART CENTRE 泰康路艺术中心

Shànghǎi is light on artistic focus, which makes this **art centre** (Tàikāng Lù Yìshù Zhōngxīn; Map pp248-9; Lane 210, Taikang Rd) welcome. It's a community of art galleries, cafés and shops hidden down an alley, while an adjacent multistorey warehouse hides a handful of design studios, media companies and home-décor boutiques, many of which front the small alley on the east side of the building.

Highlights here include the **Pottery Workshop** (Lètiān Táoshè; ☎ 6445 0902; www.ceramics.com.hk; 220 Taikang Rd), which exhibits and sells designer pottery and, further down the alley, the **Deke Erh Art Centre** (Ěrdōngqiáng Yìshù Zhōngxīn; Map pp248-9; ☎ 6415 0675; www.han-yuan.com; No 2, Lane 210, Taikang Rd), an impressive warehouse space with ground-floor exhibits and 1st-floor photos. Further along, you can find cafés, trendy handbag and clothes shops and more.

PROPAGANDA POSTER ART CENTRE 宣传画年画艺术中心

If phalanxes of red tractors, bumper harvests, muscled peasants and lantern-jawed proletariat get you going, this small **gallery** (Xuānchuánhuà Niánhuà Yìshù Zhōngxīn; Map pp248-9; ☎ 6211 1845, 139 018 412 46; Room B-0C, President Mansion, 868 Huashan Rd; admission Y20; ☉ 9.30am-4.30pm) in the bowels of a residential block will truly fire you up. With a collection of 3000 original posters from the 1950s, 1960s and 1970s – the golden age of Maoist poster production – here you can go weak-kneed at the cartoonworld of anti-US defiance. Once you find the main entrance, a guard will point you the way.

Old Town 老城市
YUYUAN GARDENS & BAZAAR 豫园
With its shaded alcoves, glittering pools churning with carp, pavilions, pines sprouting wistfully from rockeries, whispering bamboo, jasmine clumps, stony recesses and roving packs of Japanese tourists, these **gardens** (Yùyuán; Map pp244-5; ☎ 6326 0830; 218 Anren Street; adult/child Y30/10; ☉ 8.30am-5.30pm) are one of Shànghăi's premier sights, but weekends can be overpowering.

The Pan family, rich Ming dynasty officials, founded the gardens, which took 18 years (1559-77) to be nurtured into existence before bombardment during the Opium War in 1842. The gardens took another trashing during French reprisals for attacks on their nearby concession by Taiping rebels. Restored, they are a fine example of Ming garden design.

Next to the entrance to the Yuyuan Gardens is the Huxinting Teahouse (p269), once part of the gardens and now one of the most famous teahouses in China.

Enveloping the gardens is a glorified shopping centre, jammed with **antique** and **souvenir shops**, which spills into Central Fangbang Rd. See p266 for details on the surrounding bazaar's justifiably famous and delicious snacks. The nearby **Temple of the Town Gods** (Chénghuáng Miào; Map pp244-5; admission Y5) is also worth investigating.

CONFUCIAN TEMPLE 文庙
This pretty and well-tended **temple** (Wén Miào; Map pp242-3; 215 Wenmiao Rd; admission Y10; ☉ 9am-5pm) to the dictum-coining sage-cum-social theorist is a cultivated acreage of acers, pines, magnolias and birdsong. Originally dating from 1294, the temple was moved to its current site in 1855, at a time when Christian Taiping rebels were sending much of China

skywards in huge sheets of flame. The main hall for worshipping Confucius is the twineaved Dacheng Hall (Dàchéng Diàn), complete with a statue of the sage outside, the Magnolia grandiflora on either side of its main door garlanded with ribbons left by the devout.

West Nanjing Rd & Jing'an 南京西路、静安
Lined with sharp top-end shopping malls, clusters of foreign offices and a dense crop of embassies and consulates, West Nanjing Rd is where Shànghăi's streets are paved with gold, or at least Prada and Gucci.

For views into Shànghăi's past, gaze at the Shanghai Exhibition Centre, where architectural buffs will appreciate its monumentality and unsubtle communist strokes – there was a time when Pŭdōng was set to look like this.

JADE BUDDHA TEMPLE 玉佛寺
One of Shànghăi's few active Buddhist monasteries, this **temple** (Yùfó Sì; Map pp244-5; ☎ 6266 2668; 170 Anyuan Rd; admission Y10; ☉ 8.30am-4.30pm) was built between 1911 and 1918.

The **Hall of Heavenly Kings** (Tiānwáng Diàn) houses a splendid statue of the Laughing Buddha back to back with a fabulous effigy of Weituo, the guardian of Buddhism. Festooned with red lanterns, the first courtyard leads to the twin-eaved **Great Treasure Hall** (Dàxióngbǎo Diàn), where worshippers pray to the past, present and future Buddhas, seated on splendidly carved thrones.

But the centrepiece is the 1.9m-high pale green **Jade Buddha** (Yùfó), seated upstairs in his own hall. It is said that Hui Gen (Wei Ken), a Pŭtuóshān monk, travelled to Myanmar (Burma) via Tibet, lugged five jade Buddhas back to China and then sought alms to build a temple for them. The beautiful effigy of Sakyamuni, clearly Southeast Asian in style, gazes ethereally from a cabinet. An additional charge of Y10 is levied to see the statue (no photographs).

An equally elegant reclining Buddha is downstairs, opposite a much more substantial copy in stone. A large **vegetarian restaurant** (☎ 6266 5596) attaches to the temple at 999 Jiangning Rd.

In February the temple is very busy during the Lunar New Year, when some 20,000 Chinese Buddhists throng to pray for prosperity.

JING'AN TEMPLE 静安寺
This **temple** (Jìng'ān Sì; Map pp244-5; 1686-1688 West Nanjing Rd; admission Y5; 7.30am-5pm) was originally built in AD 247 but was largely destroyed in 1851 and suffered further trauma during the Cultural Revolution.

The temple remains in a state of incomplete renovation. The temple's drum and bell towers have been well restored, but anyone familiar with the layout of Buddhist temples may be shocked at the flight of steel steps in the main courtyard leading to what resembles a WWII German bunker. Further halls have yet to fully mature; for now they sport concrete pillars, modern statues and carvings.

50 MOGANSHAN ROAD ART CENTRE
莫干山路50号
Put aside a morning or afternoon exploring this **complex** (Mògānshānlù Wǔshí Hào; Map pp244-5; 50 Moganshan Rd; admission free) of industrial buildings hedging up against Suzhou Creek in the north of town. Poke around its warren of galleries – hung with challenging and provocative art – and look out over the vessels ploughing along Suzhou Creek.

Paint-speckled artists lounge around smoking while their creations dry and families still resident here are getting used to Western art

hunters stumbling through their courtyards. **ShanghArt** (Xiānggénà Huàláng; Map pp244-5; 6359 3923; www.shanghartgallery.com; Bldg 16 & 18) has a vast exhibition space with invigorating displays of artworks. A cavernous warehouse space, **Eastlink Gallery** (Dōngláng; Map pp244-5; 6276 9932; 5th fl, Bldg 6) has a mixed bag of antiques, artworks and Cultural Revolution–era posters. When your legs finally sag, take a seat at **Bandu Cabin** (Map pp244-5; 6276 8267; www.bandumusic.com; Bldg 11), a small café that sells its own Chinese music and stages traditional Chinese music performances.

Northeast Shànghǎi
The gritty northeast districts of Zhabei and Hongkou are little visited but offer some interesting backstreets and a handful of minor sights.

DUOLUN ROAD CULTURAL STREET
多伦文化名人街
This restored and rather grubby **street** (Duōlún Wénhuà Míngrén Jiē; Map pp242-3) of fine old houses was once home to several of China's most famous writers (as well as Kuomintang generals). Today it is lined with art supply stores, curio shops, galleries, teahouses and cafés, as well as statues of the writers Lu Xun and Guo Moruo.

TOP FIVE SHÀNGHĂI ART GALLERIES

- Located within the 50 Moganshan Road Art Centre (above), **ShanghArt** (Xiānggénà Huàláng; Map pp248-9; 6359 3923; www.shanghartgallery.com; Bldg 16 & 18, 50 Moganshan Rd; Bldg 16 10am-6pm, Bldg 18 noon-6pm) showcases compelling works from path-breaking Chinese artists.

- With contemporary Chinese art from pop to modern in a lovely restored 1930s villa, **Art Scene China** (Yìshùjìng Huàláng; Map pp248-9; 6437 0631; www.artscenechina.com; No 8, Lane 37, West Fuxing Rd) has a gallery, **Art Scene Warehouse** (Map pp244-5; 6277 2499; www.artscene warehouse.com; 2nd fl, Bldg 4, 50 Moganshan Rd; 10.30am-8pm Tue-Sun), at 50 Moganshan Road Art Centre.

- The old warehouse space of **Aura Gallery** (Yìàn Huàláng; Map pp242-3; 6595 0901; www.aura-art.com; 5th fl, 713 Dongdaming Rd; noon-8pm Tue-Sun) houses changing exhibits by young contemporary Chinese artists. While here, check to see what's exhibiting at the 3rd-floor **DDM Warehouse** (3501 3212; www.ddmwarehouse.cn; closed Sun).

- **Creek Art Centre** (Sūhé Xiàndài Yìshùguǎn; Map pp244-5; www.creekart.cn; 11am-7pm Tue-Sun) is a converted old creekside flourmill finding a new lease of life as a gallery promoting emerging talents from Shànghǎi's garret community, with a popular restaurant, café and bar on floors above.

- In keeping with its companion sophisticates at this exclusive Bund address, the spacious **Shanghai Gallery of Art** (Hùshēn Huàláng; Map pp244-5; 6323 4549; www.threeonthebund.com; 3rd fl, Three on the Bund, 3 East Zhongshan No 1 Rd) regularly stages fresh exhibitions in a challenging array of creative media, from experimental music to sculpture and contemporary art.

Resembling a polytechnic physics block, the **Shanghai Duolun Museum of Modern Art** (☎ 6587 6902; www.duolunart.com; 27 Duolun Rd; admission Y10; ◷ 10am-6pm Tue-Sun) has a focus on experimental contemporary art. Further along the street, the standout brick **Hongde Temple** (☎ 5696 1196; 59 Duolun Rd) was built in 1928 in a Chinese style as the Great Virtue Church.

Pick through the galleries and antique shops, including Wang Zaoshi's fabulous collection of 10,000 Mao badges (No 183; Y2) and **Dashanghai** (181 Duolun Rd), a deluge of Mao-era badges and posters, old records, photos, books, typewriters and assorted Shànghăi bric-a-brac from the decadent days.

If you need a break, join film buffs at the **Old Film Café** (☎ 5696 4763; 123 Duolun Rd; Brazilian coffee Y22; ◷ 10am-midnight), next to the 18.15m-high Xishi Bell Tower at the bend in the road. The street ends in the north at the third Kuomintang residence, the Moorish-looking **Kong Residence** (250 Duolun Rd), built in 1924, with its Middle Eastern tiles and windows.

OHEL MOISHE SYNAGOGUE 摩西会堂

This **synagogue** (Móxī Huìtáng; Map pp242-3; ☎ 6541 5008; 62 Changyang Rd; admission Y50; ◷ 9am-4.30pm Mon-Fri) was built by the Russian Ashkenazi Jewish community in 1927. The synagogue lies in the heart of the Jewish ghetto, created in the 1940s when most of Shànghăi's 30,000 Jews were forced into the area by the Japanese after fleeing Nazi Germany.

Pŭdōng New Area 浦东新区

Prior to 1990, the colossal **Pudong New Area** (Pŭdōng Xīnqū; Map pp242-3), stretching off to the East China Sea east of the Huangpu River, constituted 350 sq km of boggy farmland. Since then Pŭdōng has become China's financial heartbeat and the skyscraper-fragmented skyline of Lùjiāzuĭ one of Shànghăi's most photographed panoramas.

Pŭdōng's wide roads, hit-and-miss architecture, inanimate layout and dreary bar scene hardly make it a place for lingering unless you are packing a briefcase. For the visitor, its main attractions include some fine museums, the highlight Jinmao Tower, the views back to the Bund and some of Shànghăi's best hotels.

There are many ways to get across the river to Pŭdōng but the weirdest has to be the **Bund Sightseeing Tunnel** (Wàitān Guānguāng Suìdào; Map pp242-3 & Map pp244-5; ☎ 5888 6000; 300 East Zhongshan No 1 Rd; admission one way/return Y30/50; ◷ 8am-10.30pm Mon-Thu, to 11pm Fri-Sun), where train modules convey speechless passengers through a tunnel of garish lights between the Bund and the opposite shore.

Riverside Park (Bīnjiāng Gōngyuán; Map pp242-3; admission free) offers good river-level views of the Bund, along with several coffee bars and a rare opportunity to sit and rest.

ORIENTAL PEARL TOWER 东方明珠电视塔

Best viewed when illuminated at night, this poured-concrete shocker of a tripod **TV Tower** (Dōngfāng Míngzhū Diànshì Tă; Map pp242-3; ☎ 5879 8888; 1 Century Ave; tickets Y50-180; ◷ 8am-9.30pm) has become a symbol of Pŭdōng and of Shànghăi's surging renaissance.

It's worth exploring, if only for the Shanghai Municipal History Museum and because it's one part of town where you can't see the tower itself, although its vulgar form is matched by an excruciatingly Byzantine ticket system. You can go to the second bauble and outdoor viewing platform (Y50); the second bauble and the Municipal Historical Museum (Y70); or the lower two baubles and the museum (Y85). It's Y100 to visit all three baubles, while Y150 throws in lunch as well.

SHANGHAI MUNICIPAL HISTORY MUSEUM 上海城市历史发展陈列馆

This modern **museum** (Shànghăi Chéngshì Lìshǐ Fāzhǎn Chénlièguǎn; Map pp242-3; ☎ 5879 8888; admission Y35, audio tour Y30; ◷ 8am-9.30pm) in the base of the Oriental Pearl Tower has fun multimedia presentations and imaginative displays that re-create the history of Shànghăi with an emphasis on the pre-1949 era. Find out how the city prospered on the back of the cotton trade and junk transportation, when it was known as 'Little Sūzhōu'. Life-size models of traditional shops are manned by lifelike waxworks and there's a wealth of historical detail, including a boundary stone from the International Settlement and one of the pair of bronze lions that originally guarded the entrance to the Hong Kong and Shanghai Bank on the Bund.

JINMAO TOWER 金茂大厦

The crystalline **Jinmao Tower** (Jīnmào Dàshà; Map pp242-3; ☎ 5047 5101; 88 Shiji Dadao; adult/child Y50/25, audio tour Y15; ◷ 8.30am-10pm) is Pŭdōng's most arresting modern spire. China's tallest building (420.5m), the 53rd to the 87th floors are rented out to the Grand Hyatt. An observation deck on the 88th floor puts you virtually among the cirrus but consider sinking a drink in the Cloud 9 Bar (p269) on the 87th floor instead and time your visit at dusk for both day and night views. The 'No Climbing' signs at the foot of the building recall the French 'Spiderman' Alain Robert's attempt at scaling the tower in 2001. He failed to get authorisation, but glance up the side of the building and you're spoiled for choice for handholds (a shoe salesman from Ānhuī province climbed it on impulse in 2001). Next to the Jinmao is the site of the Shanghai World Finance Building, on the drawing board since the mid-1990s; when finished it will total 90 storeys and 460m.

CHINA SEX CULTURE MUSEUM
中华性文化和性健康教育展
Travellers should find time for this intriguing **exhibition** (Zhōnghuá Xìng Wénhuà hé Xìng Jiànkāng Jiàoyùzhǎn; Map pp242-3; 2789 Riverside Ave; admission Y20; ☉ 8am-10.30pm Mon-Thu, to 10pm Fri-Sun), a fascinating foray into Chinese sexuality and erotica. Among the mating tortoises, copulating beasts and jade phalluses, search out the knife that raised eunuch's voices to the correct register and the special coins once used as quid pro quo in China's brothels of yore.

Southern Shànghǎi
The Xújiāhuì area, known to 1930s expat residents as Ziccawei or Sicawei, once had a sizeable Jesuit settlement. **St Ignatius Cathedral** (Tiānzhǔjiào Táng; Map pp242-3; ☎ 6253 0959; 158 Puxi Rd; ☉ 1-4.30pm Sat-Sun) is a notable survivor, but try to make it to the **Bibliotheca Zi-Ka-Wei** (Map pp242-3; ☎ 6487 4095, ext 208; 80 North Caoxi Rd; admission free; ☉ 9am-5pm Mon-Sat, library tours 2-4pm Sat), the former Jesuit library; the free tour of the main library of antiquarian tomes on Saturdays is a must. English guides are on hand to take you through a truly magnificent collection of antiquarian tomes, arranged in a beautiful historic library laid out on one floor with a gallery above. One of Shànghǎi's top sights, the 15-minute tours are limited to 10 people, so phone ahead.

Southwest of here, **Longhua Temple** (Lónghuá Tǎ; Map pp242-3; ☎ 6457 6327; 2853 Longhua Rd; admission Y10; ☉ 7am-5pm) is across the way from its namesake pagoda and is the oldest and largest monastery in Shànghǎi, said to date from the 10th century.

Take the light rail to Longcao Rd station and head east along North Longshui Rd for about 1km. Bus 44 goes there from Xújiāhuì.

Further south, the **Shanghai Botanical Gardens** (Shànghǎi Zhíwùyuán; Map pp242-3; ☎ 6451 3369; 997 Longwu Rd; admission Y15; ☉ 6am-6pm) are a refreshing escape from Shànghǎi's synthetic cityscape. The exhibition greenhouse offers a chance to get close to tropical flora (admission Y40) and there's an adventure playground, dodgems, bike hire and a bouncing castle for the kids. Electric buggies tour visitors around the grounds.

Hongqiao 虹桥
The western area of Hongqiao is mainly a centre for international commerce and trade exhibitions. Apart from office blocks, there are a few foreign restaurants, hotels, shopping malls and Hongqiao Airport.

SHANGHAI ZOO 上海动物园
This fun **zoo** (Shànghǎi Dòngwùyuán; Map pp242-3; ☎ 6268 7775; 2381 Hongqiao Rd; cnr Hami Rd; admission Y30, elephant show Y20; ☉ 6am-6pm, later in summer) is perfect for a day out. The beasts – from woolly twin-humped Bactrian camels to spindly legged giraffes and giant pandas – are definite crowd-pleasers, but Shànghǎi folk are also here for one of the city's most picturesque and well-tended acreages of green grass. Children flock to the Children's Zoo, where they can shower chubby piglets and billy goats with handfuls of grain, prance about on the bouncing castle (Y10), fish for goldfish (Y2 per minute) or ride ponies (Y5).

QĪBĂO 七宝
This **ancient town** (Map pp242-3; Minhang district; through ticket to numerous sights Y30) dates back to the Northern Song dynasty (AD 960–1127). Easily reached, the ancient settlement prospered during the Ming and Qing dynasties and is littered with traditional, historic architecture, threaded by small, busy alleyways and cut by a picturesque canal. If you can blot out the crowds, Qībǎo brings you some of the flavours of old China.

Worth ferreting out is the Catholic Church, adjacent to a convent off Qibao Nanjie, south of the canal. The single-spire **edifice** (☎ 6479 9317; 50 Nanjie; ☉ dawn to dusk) dates back to 1867; pop inside and admire the bright, whitewashed interior, cooled by overhead fans. Half-hour **boat rides** (per person Y10; ☉ 8.30am-4.30pm) along the picturesque canal slowly ferry passengers from Number One Bridge to Dōngtángtán and back.

Souvenir hunters and diners will be agog at the choice of shops and eateries simply stuffed along the narrow streets. Wander along Bei Dajie north of the canal for a plethora of small shops selling fans, dolls, tea and wooden handicrafts from traditional two-storey dwellings.

Bus 92 (B line) departs for Qībăo from Shanghai Stadium, otherwise a taxi from the centre of town will cost around Y55.

ACTIVITIES

Huangpu River Trip 黄浦江游览船

The Huangpu River offers some stirring views of the Bund and the riverfront activity (Shànghăi is one of the world's largest ports). Most **tour boats** (huángpŭ jiāng yóulănchuán; Map pp244-5; ☎ 6374 4461; 219-239 East Second Zhongshan Rd) depart from the dock (Map pp244–5) on the Bund, near East Jinling Rd; popular 30-minute **cruises** (tickets Y40-70; ⏰ 10am-8pm) also depart hourly from the Pearl Dock in Lùjiāzŭi in Pŭdōng.

The tour boat passes an enormous variety of craft – freighters, bulk carriers, roll-on roll-off ships, sculling sampans, giant cranes and the occasional junk.

The river trip is big business. Eleven different companies and 28 boats offer tours along the Huangpu River – including improvised, creaking old ferries – with new vessels constantly coming on stream. The one-hour cruise (Y25 to Y35) takes in the Yangpu Bridge. There are also 3½-hour cruises (Y70/90 lower/upper deck, other boats Y50 to Y100), a 60km return trip northwards up Huangpu River to Wusongkou, the junction with the Yangzi. More expensive tickets often include refreshments.

Departure times vary, but there are afternoon and evening departures for all three categories during weekdays, with the addition of morning cruises on weekends. For an idea of boats and prices see www.pjrivercruise.com.

WALKING TOUR

This comprehensive, easy-to-manage walk guides you along the Bund, Shànghăi's most memorable mile. The walk can be done either by day or by night; during the evening the buildings are closed but the Bund is spectacularly illuminated and the nocturnal views to Pŭdōng are delicious. The walk can be done

from either the west side of East Zhongshan No 1 Rd (the Bund) or along the elevated promenade on the other side of the road overlooking the river.

At the northern end of the Bund, on the north bank of Suzhou Creek, rises the brick pile of **Broadway Mansions** (1; p261), built in 1934 as an exclusive apartment block. The Foreign Correspondents' Club occupied the 9th floor in the 1930s and used its fine views to report the Japanese bombing of the city in 1937. The building became the headquarters of the Japanese army during WWII.

Just across Huangpu Rd from the **Russian consulate (2)** is the distinguished **Pujiang Hotel** (3; p261). First opened as the Astor House Hotel (a name it is reassuming) in 1846, this was Shànghăi's first hotel, later becoming the Richard Hotel.

Head south over Waibaidu Bridge (also called Garden Bridge), which dates from 1907; before 1856 all crossings had to be made by ferry. The first bridge here was the wooden Wills Bridge where a charge was levied on users. Walk down the west side of the steel bridge and look carefully at the south wall of Suzhou Creek; the row of large Chinese characters that has been partially obliterated is a **political slogan (4)** from the Cultural Revolution (1966–1976) era.

Huangpu Park (Huángpŭ Gōngyuán) – Shànghăi's first park – serves as a receptacle for the numbing Monument to the People's Heroes, beneath which is **Bund Historical Museum** (5; Wàitān Lìshǐ Jìniànguăn; admission free; ⏰ 9am-4.15pm), worth a stop for its great old photos of the Bund. Huangpu Park was the site of the infamous (and legendary) sign that forbade entry to 'dogs or Chinese' (see the boxed text on p253). In fact there never was such a sign, though the spirit of the law certainly existed.

On the other side of the road, pass the 1873 **former British consulate (6**; No 33), the Bund's first building. Further down, at No 27, is the former headquarters of early opium traders **Jardine Matheson (7)**, which became one of Shànghăi's great *hongs*.

The imposing **Bank of China (8**; p241) building, at No 23, was built in 1937 with specific instructions to surpass the adjacent Cathay (Peace) Hotel in height. The building is a perhaps curious architectural mishmash, designed in a New York/Chicago style and later topped with a blue Chinese roof.

The landmark 1926 to 1929 **Peace Hotel (9**; p262) was once the most luxurious hotel

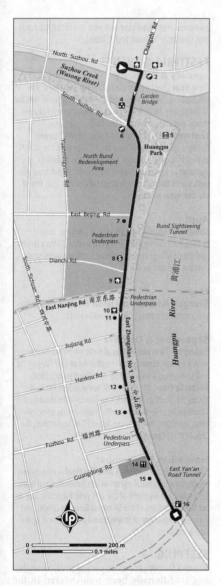

Originally the Chartered Bank of Australia, India and China, **Bund 18 (10)** is the embankment's latest high-profile commercial conversion and place to be seen in. Pop up to Bar Rouge on the 7th floor for sumptuous views.

Next door at No 17 is the former home of the **North China Daily News (11)**. Known as the 'Old Lady of the Bund' the *News* ran from 1864 to 1951 as the main English-language newspaper in China and the mouthpiece of the foreign-run municipality commission. Look above the central windows for the paper's motto. Huge Atlas figures support the roof.

Three buildings down, at No 13, the **Customs House (12)** was built in 1925. The original customs jetty stood across from the building, on the Huangpu River. The building is topped by a clock face and 'Big Ching', a bell that was modelled on Big Ben, replaced during the Cultural Revolution by loudspeakers from which issued revolutionary slogans and songs. The clockworks were restored in 1986 for the visit of Queen Elizabeth II.

Next door to Customs House at No 12 is the grandest building on the Bund, the former **Hong Kong & Shanghai Bank (13**; HSBC). The bank was established in Hong Kong in 1864 and in Shànghăi in 1865 to finance trade, soon becoming one of the richest banks in Shànghăi, arranging the indemnity paid after the Boxer Rebellion. When the current building was constructed in 1923 it was the second-largest bank in the world and reportedly 'the finest building east of Suez'. Today the building is occupied by the Pudong Development Bank. Enter the building and marvel at the beautiful mosaic ceiling (no photographs allowed), featuring the 12 zodiac signs and the world's eight great banking centres.

At No 3 is the impressive restaurant and retail development of **Three on the Bund (14**; p251).

The 1911 **Shanghai Club (15)**, the city's best-known bastion of British snobbery, stood at No 2 on the Bund. The plutocratic club had 20 rooms for residents, but its most famous

in the Far East, when it was known as the Cathay. It remains an Art Deco masterpiece (see the boxed text, p262) with a wonderful lobby (only half its original size), and if you're lucky visit the famous ballroom with its sprung floor. The Gang of Four used the hotel as an operations base during the Cultural Revolution.

accoutrement was the bar, which at 110ft (about 33.6m) was said to be the world's longest. Businessmen would sit here according to rank (no Chinese or women were allowed in the club), with the *taipans* (company bosses) closest to the view of the Bund, sipping chilled champagne and comparing fortunes.

Just across from the overpass you can see the 49m-tall **Meteorological Signal Tower (16)**, originally built in 1908 opposite the French consulate and, in 1993, moved 22m north as part of the revamping of the Bund. Today there is a small collection of old prints of the Bund and a replica 1855 map of the Bund. Admission is free.

By the overpass is East Yan'an Rd, once a canal and later filled in to become Ave Edward VII, the dividing line between the International Settlement and the French Concession.

SHÀNGHǍI FOR CHILDREN

Shànghǎi's parks can be tame for kids, though amusement and water parks are favourites and a blessing in summer when temperatures soar. The zoo and circus are other favourite standbys. There are several kids' stores around town, particularly along East Nanjing Rd.

In general 1.4m is the cut-off height for children's cheaper fares or entry tickets. Children under 0.8m normally get in free.

Shanghai Zoo (p257) has acres of green space and is ideal for family outings.

Changfeng Ocean World (Chángfēng Hǎidǐ Shìjiè; Map pp242-3; ☎ 5281 8888; Gate No 4, 451 Daduhe Rd, Changfeng Park; adult/child over 1m Y110/80) Adults may find this subterranean aquarium dank, dark, dingy and dear, but the little people will adore the clown fish and shark tunnel. Attention parents with strollers – the lift bypassing the slog down the stairs may or *may not* work.

Dino Beach (热带风暴; Rèdài Fēngbào; ☎ 6478 3333; 78 Xinzhen Rd; adult Tue Y30, Mon & Wed-Fri Y60, Sat & Sun Y80, child half price; ☺ 9am-9pm Jun-Sep) Way down south in Minhang District is a popular summer place with a beach, a wave pool, water slides and tube hire to beat the summer heat, but it can be heaving at the weekends.

Jinjiang Amusement Park (锦江乐园; Jǐnjiāng Lèyuán; ☎ 6468 0844; 201 Hongmei Rd; admission Y60) Has roller coasters, rides and a huge Ferris wheel in the southern suburbs, with its own metro stop.

Shanghai Aquarium (Hǎiyáng Shuǐzúguǎn; Map pp242-3; ☎ 5877 9988; 158 North Yincheng Rd; adult/ senior/child Y110/65/70; ☺ 9am-9pm) Education meets entertainment at this slick, impressive Singaporean joint venture. The 155m-long underwater viewing tunnel is awesome. Try to time your visit with one of the fish feedings (currently 10.30am and 3.30pm).

FESTIVALS & EVENTS

January & February

New Year Longhua Temple (p257) has large New Year celebrations, with dragon and lion dances. At New Year the abbot strikes the bell 108 times while the monks beat on gongs and offer prayers for the forthcoming year.

Lantern Festival A colourful time to visit Yuyuan Gardens (p254). People take the time to walk the streets at night carrying coloured paper lanterns and make *yuánxiao or tángyuán* (sweet dumplings of glutinous rice with sweet fillings). The festival falls on the 15th day of the first lunar month.

April

Longhua Temple Fair This fair at Longhua Temple (p257), held during April or May, is eastern China's largest and oldest folk gathering, with all kinds of snacks, stalls, jugglers and stilt walkers.

May

Shanghai International Music Festival Week-long programme of concerts and musical events.

September & October

Shanghai Tourism Festival Kicks off in mid-September with a parade down Central Huaihai Rd or East Nanjing Rd and then offers a wide variety of cultural programmes.

Formula One (☎ 6956 6999; www.icsh.sh.cn; 2000 Yining Rd, Jiading) The slick new Shanghai International Circuit hosts several high-profile motor-racing competitions, including the hotly contested F1 in September, the China Circuit Championship and Moto GP.

November & December

Shanghai International Arts Festival A month-long programme of cultural events in late November and early December and highlight of the arts year. Events include an art fair, exhibitions of the Shanghai Biennale (2008), and a varied programme of international music, dance, opera and acrobatics.

SLEEPING

From a foreign traveller perspective, Shànghǎi has traditionally been well-covered in the midrange bracket (Y400 to Y1000 for a double room) and visitors are dazzled by the choice in the top-end range (Y1000 to Y3000), but the budget market is catching up with a growing band of youth hostels.

Top-end hotels fall into two categories: the fuddy-duddy historic hotels of old Shànghǎi where guests can wrap themselves in nostalgia, and the stylish new breed of modern hotel, bursting with the latest amenities and sparkling with highly polished service.

Rack rates are listed here, but discounts (20% to 30% at least) are standard (outside of holiday periods) in all hotels apart from hostels and the very cheapest. Four- and five-star hotels add on a 10% or 15% service charge but this is again often negotiable. Note that most hotels listed here have air-conditioning and broadband internet access (the latter often overpriced).

The Bund & East Nanjing Rd
BUDGET
Ming Town Hiker Youth Hostel (Míngtáng Shànghǎi Lǚxíngzhě Qīngnián Lǚguǎn; Map pp244-5; ☎ 6329 7889; 450 Central Jiangxi Rd; 江西中路450号; dm from Y50, d Y288; 🖳) A short hike from the Bund, this is a welcome arrival. Rooms include tidy four- and six-bed dorms with pine bunk beds and three good-value luxury doubles, decorated in a Chinese style with huge beds and shower room. There's a bar, free movies, bike rental and internet access (free for guests). IYH members qualify for a Y5 discount.

Captain Hostel (Chuánzhǎng Qīngnián Jiǔdiàn; Map pp244-5; ☎ 6325 5053; www.captainhostel.com.cn; 37 Fuzhou Rd; 福州路37号; dm Y60, d Y400-1200; 🖳) All's shipshape at the able-bodied Captain, where discerning landlubbers stow themselves away in this old turn-of-the-century building off the Bund. There are clean dorms with bunk beds, OK double rooms and a top-floor bar (reached via a crummy lift) for tots of rum, drunken sailors and long views over the Huangpu River. Facilities include a handy notice board, internet access (pricey), free use of a microwave, washing machine, bike hire and lobby café. A YHI card garners a Y5 discount.

Pujiang Hotel/Astor House Hotel (Pújiāng Fàndiàn; Map pp244-5; ☎ 6324 6388; www.pujianghotel.com; 15 Huangpu Rd; 黄浦路15号; dm Y70, d from Y580-1280) Built on the site of the Richards Hotel, the Pujiang was originally called the Astor House Hotel, a name it has nostalgically readopted. For those counting their shekels, it's central, has loads of style and rooms are vast. Management trumpets that Albert Einstein, Bertrand Russell and Charlie Chaplin all stayed here (though presumably not in the dorm rooms and not together). The galleries upstairs look like they belong in a Victorian asylum, there's a nobility about the place and the address is choice.

YMCA Hotel (Qīngniánhuì Bīnguǎn; Map pp244-5; ☎ 6326 1040; www.ymcahotel.com; 123 South Xizang (Tibet) Rd; 西藏南路123号; dm/d Y100/460) Built in 1929, the three-star YMCA's tired four-bed dorms and doubles may not hit the sweet spot, but the location – on the borders of the Old City and just southeast of Renmin Sq – hits the mark.

Jinjiang Inn (Jǐnjiāng Zhīxīng Lǚguǎn; Map pp244-5; ☎ 6326 0505; www.jj-inn.com; 33 South Fujian Rd; 福建南路33号; s/d Y198/238) This central branch of this hotel chain has bright, airy doubles with shower rooms, some with pleasant views over parkland on the noisier Fujian Rd side. Rooms facing inwards are smaller, cheaper and quieter; the higher-floor rooms are generally best.

MIDRANGE
East Asia Hotel (Dōngyà Fàndiàn; Map pp244-5; ☎ 6322 3233; fax 6322 4598; 680 East Nanjing Rd; 南京东路680号; d from Y420) Renovated in 2005, the two-star East Asia Hotel is a popular old-timer and long-standing fixture on the cheap Shànghǎi room circuit. It's very central but some of the rooms don't have windows. Reception is on the 2nd floor through a clothing shop.

Metropole Hotel (Xīnchéng Fàndiàn; Map pp244-5; ☎ 6321 3030; fax 6321 7365; 180 Central Jiangxi Rd; 江西中路180号; d/ste Y650/1200) The gaunt-looking Metropole was one of Shànghǎi's most glamorous hotels in the 1930s. Some Art Deco flourishes suggest the glamour of yore but the interior does little to shake the mood of a standard smoky Chinese hotel.

Park Hotel (Guójì Fàndiàn; Map pp244-5; ☎ 6327 5225; fax 6327 6958; 170 West Nanjing Rd; 南京西路170号; s Y650-810, d Y1215; metro Renmin Park) Erected in 1934, this hotel was the tallest of its day. The Shànghǎi Chinese said that if you looked all the way to the top of the Park, your hat would fall off. The lobby is an extravagant slice of old Art Deco styling and rooms are comfortable, but book ahead for fine views of Nanjing Rd and Renmin Park.

Broadway Mansions (Shànghǎi Dàshà; Map pp244-5; ☎ 6324 6260; www.broadwaymansions.com; 20 North Suzhou Rd; 苏州北路20号; s/d Y780/1070) Looming over Suzhou Creek is this classic 1934 monument, which boasts superb views over the north Bund, the Huangpu River and Pǔdōng. Aim for the pricier Bund-facing doubles (with the best views) on higher floors or one of the tastefully furnished executive guest rooms.

SHÀNGHÃI

TOP END

Peace Hotel (Hépíng Fàndiàn; Map pp244-5; ☎ 6321 6888; www.shanghaipeacehotel.com; 20 East Nanjing Rd; 南京东路 20号; d/ste Y1300/3060) Exploiting a much-coveted market niche as the most definitive chunk of surviving Art Deco in town, the Peace has quality-control issues (so-so rooms, indifferent staff, mustiness) that leave a whopping dent in its crown. The national deluxe suites are elegantly laid out in different national styles: English, American, French, Chinese, Indian and others. Discounts, of up to 40%, are welcome.

Peace Palace Hotel (Map pp244-5; ☎ 6329 1888; peacehtl@public.sta.net.cn; 23 East Nanjing Rd; 南京东 路23号) Across East Nanjing Rd and part of the Peace Hotel, this is an older annexe with similar rates that dip quite low in winter.

Radisson Hotel Shanghai New World (Map pp244-5; ☎ 6359 9999; www.radisson.com/shanghaicn_newworld; 88 West Nanjing Rd; 南京西路88号; d Y1460) The UFO atop this Radisson tower is typically derivative noughties Shànghăi. In this case, the spaceship's B-movie sci-fi lines echo the clock tower of the Pacific Hotel below and the cupolas of the adjacent New World. The eclectic interior design is showy and devoid of panache, although standard rooms (with free broadband) in this new hotel are excellent and views are great.

Other top-end chain hotels near East Nanjing Rd:

Ramada Plaza (Nán Xīnyà Huáměidá Dàjiŭdiàn; Map pp244-5; ☎ 6350 0000; www.ramadainternationalhotel .com; 700 Jiujiang Rd; 九江路700号; d from Y1460)

Westin Shanghai (Wēisītíng Dàfàndiàn; Map pp244-5; ☎ 6335 1888; www.westin.com; 88 Central Henan Rd; 河南中路88号; d from Y2915; 🏊) Luxurious and stylish.

Pŭdōng
TOP END

our pick **Grand Hyatt** (Jīnmào Kăiyuè Dàjiŭdiàn; Map pp242-3; ☎ 5049 1234; www.hyatt.com; 88 Century Ave; 世纪大 道88号; d from Y2590; 🏊) One of the brightest stars in the Shànghăi hotel firmament, the Grand Hyatt is no place for those with vertigo. Commencing on the 54th floor of the Jinmao Building in Pŭdōng, it shoots up another 33 stylish storeys; check out the atrium. Rooms are packed with gadgets (TV internet access, fog-free mirrors, three-jet showers and sensor reading lamps) but keeping the glass basins clean must keep chambermaids cursing. Good discounts are available, but the hotel is often full, so book well ahead.

Pudong Shangri-La (Pŭdōng Xiānggélĭlā Dàjiŭdiàn; Map pp242-3; ☎ 6882 6888; www.shangri-la.com; 33 Fucheng Rd; 富城路33号; s/d Y2590/2753; 🏊) With its muted Chinese motifs and fine views of the Bund, the 28-floor Shangri-La is a solid luxury choice in the heart of Lùjiāzŭi, backed up by a towering V-topped annexe, completed in 2005.

St Regis Shanghai (Ruìjī Hóngtă Dàjiŭdiàn; Map pp242-3; ☎ 5050 4567; www.stregis.com/shanghai; 889 Dongfang Rd; 东方路889号; s/d Y2915/2996; 🏊) The luxurious St Regis mixes hi tech (Bose radios, broadband internet) with old-style service. The 24-hour

---

THE CATHAY HOTEL

The Peace Hotel is a ghostly reminder of the immense wealth of Victor Sassoon. From a Baghdad Jewish family, Sassoon made millions out of the opium trade and then ploughed it back into Shànghăi real estate and horses.

Sassoon's quote of the day was 'There is only one race greater than the Jews, and that's the Derby'. His office-cum-hotel was completed in 1930 and was known as Sassoon House, incorporating the Cathay Hotel from the 4th to 7th floors. From the top floors Sassoon commanded his real estate – he is estimated to have owned 1900 buildings in Shànghăi.

Like the Taj in Bombay, the Stanley Raffles in Singapore and the Peninsula in Hong Kong, the Cathay was *the* place to stay in Shànghăi. The guest list included Charlie Chaplin, George Bernard Shaw and Noel Coward, who wrote *Private Lives* here in four days in 1930 when he had the flu. Sassoon himself resided in a suite on the top floor, with its unsurpassed 360-degree views, just below the green pyramidal tower. He also maintained Sassoon Villa, a Tudor-style villa out near Hongqiao Airport.

After the communists took over the city, the troops were billeted in places like the Cathay and Picardie (now Héngshān Bīnguăn on the outskirts of the city), where they spent hours experimenting with the elevators, used bidets as face-showers and washed rice in the toilets – which was all very well until someone pulled the chain.

In 1953 foreign owners tried to give the Cathay to the Chinese Communist Party in return for exit visas. The government refused at first, but finally accepted after the payment of 'back taxes'.

personal butlers will record your pillow preference for your next visit just before bringing you a coffee and fixing your laptop. Women can check into the ladies-only floors if they want and all guests are welcome in the executive club facilities.

French Concession

BUDGET

Motel 168 (Mòtài Liánsuǒ Lǚdiàn; Map pp248-9; ☎ 5117 7777; www.motel168.com; 1119 West Yan'an Rd; 延安西路1119号; tw Y198-228) The Motel 168 formula is clean and smooth with traces of modern flair, but the presentation is bland and the finish cheap. Standard twins are well designed, with clean and compact shower rooms. Useful branches near both airports include 29 Huaxiang Rd (☎ 5119 6888) and 1148 Wuzhong Rd (☎ 6401 9188) for Hongqiao Airport and 2255 East Huaxia Rd (☎ 5117 2000) for Pudong airport.

MIDRANGE

Jinchen Hotel (Jīnchén Dàjiǔdiàn; Map pp248-9; ☎ 6471 7000; www.jinchenhotel.com; 795-809 Central Huaihai Rd; 淮海中路795-809号; s/d from Y780) Arranged over seven floors, the small, brick Jinchen is excellently located on Central Huaihai Rd, offering clean, tastefully furnished rooms equipped with broadband, although carpets are a bit tatty.

our pick Ruijin Guesthouse (Ruìjīn Bīnguǎn; Map pp248-9; ☎ 6472 5222; www.shedi.net.cn/outedi/ruijin; 118 Ruijin No 2 Rd; 瑞金二路118号; s/d Y800/1200) The Ruijin has elegant grounds and a series of old mansions converted into rooms. Building No 1 was the former Morris (founder of the *North China Daily News*) estate while some of the city's most romantic and stylish restaurants and bars charmingly nestle in the gardens.

Mason Hotel (Měichén Dàjiǔdiàn; Map pp248-9; ☎ 6466 2020; www.masonhotel.com; 935 Central Huaihai Rd; 淮海中路935号; s/d Y900/1080) From its discreet outward appearance to the hotel's small and well-proportioned lobby (with Art Deco-style motifs and casual black leather furniture), this boutique-style hotel is both relaxed and intimate. Reasonably recently restored double rooms (all with broadband) face either onto Huaihai Rd (a bit noisy) or overlook a splendid backdrop of redbrick *longtang* (alleyway) housing to the rear. There's also a rooftop beer garden and a Starbucks on the ground floor.

Hengshan Hotel (Héngshān Bīnguǎn; Map pp248-9; ☎ 6437 7050; fax 6433 5732; 534 Hengshan Rd; 衡山路 534号; d from Y1000) The former 1930s Picardie Apartments still hold a few hints of their original interior Art Deco charm. The quality of hotel has been elevated over recent years, with renovations and investment restoring some crispness and gloss to both the service and presentation, and the location is good.

TOP END

Regent Shanghai (Lìjīng Dàjiǔdiàn; Map pp248-9; ☎ 6115 9988; www.regenthotels.com; 1116 West Yan'an Rd; 延安西路1116号; d Y1550; 🏊) The latest star in Shànghǎi's glittering galaxy of luxury hotels, the 53-storey Regent has gorgeous rooms, equipped with 42-inch plasma TV screens and spacious, deep baths and rainforest showers. Further soak away the stress in the 30m infinity-edged swimming pool.

Radisson Plaza Xingguo Hotel (Xīngguó Bīnguǎn; Map pp248-9; ☎ 6212 9998, toll free reservation in China 800-3333 3333; www.radissonasiapacific.com; 78 Xingguo Rd; 兴国路78号; city view s/d Y1830/1990, garden view s/d Y1990/2160; 🏊) The hotel is luxurious enough, but it is the gorgeous garden setting – ornamented with villas, pines, palms and magnolias – that steals the show. If staying in the main hotel, it's worth paying extra for the garden view. The full range of fitness and exercise facilities is offered, managed by Clark Hatch Gymnasium. The villas are largely rented out to long-term residents although Villa No 1 is open to guests.

Garden Hotel (Huāyuán Fàndiàn; Map pp248-9; ☎ 6415 1111; www.gardenhotelshanghai.com; 58 South Maoming Rd; 茂名南路58号; s/d Y2025/2185; 🏊) The elegant Japanese-run five-star Okura Garden boasts lovely grounds on the site of the old French Club (the Cercle Sportif Français). Rooms in the huge modern tower are a bit tired but refurbishments are underway, while bathrooms are on the smallish side.

Jinjiang Hotel (Jǐnjiāng Fàndiàn; Map pp248-9; ☎ 6258 2582; 59 South Maoming Rd; 茂名南路59号; Cathay Bldg d Y2900, Jin Nan Bldg d Y3300, Grosvenor Villa ste Y8000; 🏊) Stylish and well-located at the swish hub of the elegant French Concession, the Jinjiang consists of the main Georgian-style Cathay Building, the refurbished Jin Nan Building (south building) and the lavish five-star Grosvenor Villa.

West Nanjing Rd

BUDGET

Easy Tour Youth Hostel (Shànghǎi Yìtú Qīngnián Jiǔdiàn; Map pp244-5; ☎ 6327 7766; 57 Jiangyin Rd; 江阴路57号;

dm/s/d Y60/270/330) The setting and location – just west off Renmin Sq in a building with a bit of history overlooked by the rocketing form of JW Marriott Tomorrow Square – are up there with the best, but this place is a bit drab and scuffed and some rooms are damp. The hostel can be tricky to find – it's tucked away in the first corner as you head west along Jiangyin Rd next to a narrow alleyway. Look for the signs.

Home Inn (Rújiā; Map pp244-5; ☎ 6255 3970; www .homeinns.com; Lane 421, Changping Rd; 昌平路421弄; s/d Y199/239) With 14 branches in Pŭxī and Pŭdōng (see website), the Home Inn chain is scattered fitfully about town, this being one of the more central locations. The formula dishes up clean, modern and small rooms largely aimed at lower-rung business travellers; the effect is reliably fresh, if a bit cheap. At the time of writing a handy branch of Home Inn was due to open in the vicinity of Shànghăi train station.

MIDRANGE

Shanghai Haigang Hotel (Hăigăng Bīnguăn; Map pp244-5; ☎ 6255 3553; 89 Taixing Rd; 泰兴路89号; d incl breakfast Y398) This clean and pleasant hotel has some stylish touches and a great location by the metro line and a street of restaurants. The cheapest rooms here have interior facing windows.

TOP END

JW Marriott Tomorrow Square (Míngtiān Guăngchăng JW Wànyí Jiŭdiàn; Map pp244-5; ☎ 5359 4969; www.mar riotthotels.com/shajw; 399 West Nanjing Rd; 南京西路 399号; d Y2590; 🏊) Housed across the upper 24 floors of one of Shànghăi's most dramatic towers, the JW Marriott boasts marvellously appointed rooms with spectacular views and showers with hydraulic massage functions to soak away the stress. Taking a leaf from the Grand Hyatt book, the JW Marriott Tomorrow Square has the highest library in the world above ground level.

Portman Ritz-Carlton (Bōtèmàn Lìjiā Jiŭdiàn; Map pp244-5; ☎ 6279 8888; www.ritzcarlton.com; 1376 West Nanjing Rd; 南京西路1376号; s/d Y2905/3075; 🏊) The Ritz-Carlton remains one of the very best hotels in town, partly due to the attached Shanghai Centre, with its assorted bevy of expat facilities, ranging from a medical clinic to a Starbucks, a popular supermarket, the Long Bar and more. Guest rooms are stylishly designed, with both bathrooms and ward-

robes equipped with swish sliding rosewood doors. Service throughout is excellent.

Other five-star hotels in the neighbourhood include the **Four Seasons** (Sìjì Jiŭdiàn; Map pp244-5; ☎ 6256 8888; www.fourseasons.com; 500 Weihai Rd; 威 海路500号; d from Y3300; 🏊).

Northern Shànghăi

Koala International Youth Hostel (Kǎolā Guójì Qīngnián Lŭshè; Map pp242-3; ☎ 6277 1370; 1447 Xikang Rd; 西康 路1447号; s/tw/family ste Y220/240/380) Don't come here expecting to find dorm beds (there aren't any), but the modern and attractive rooms here are sound, with cable TV, fridge and oven. There's no common area to get on line but a handy internet café next door comes to the rescue.

Zhongya Hotel (Zhōngyà Fàndiàn; Map pp244-5; ☎ 6317 2317; www.zhongyahotel.com; 330 Meiyuan Rd; 梅园路330号; d from Y380) Externally a drab and featureless 25-storey tower, this well-placed value-for-money three-star hotel is handy for rail travellers. Altogether, the Zhongya has more style and character than other midrange (many overpriced) alternatives in the area, but this is a far-from-classy district. Pricier rooms are often a good deal as they are discounted by 50% – but push for discounts on all rooms.

Holiday Inn Downtown (Shànghăi Guăngchăng Chángchéng Jiàrì Jiŭdiàn; Map pp244-5; ☎ 6353 8008; www .holiday-inn.com; 285 West Tianmu Rd & 585 Hengfeng Rd; 天 目西路285号与恒丰路585号; d incl breakfast Y1328) Near the train station, this bizarrely structured hotel consists of two wings in separate buildings. Room rates are the same in both wings and include service charge. The Great Wall wing has the larger fitness centre and the deluxe rooms. Rooms are double-glazed but the area can still be noisy. There's one room adapted for people with disabilities. Discounts of up to 50% available.

Hongqiao

Maggie International Youth Hostel (Měizhī Guójì Qīngnián Lŭshè; Map pp242-3; ☎ 6273 6183; 1825 Tianshan Rd; 天山路1825号; member/nonmember dm Y70/80, d Y180/200) Off in the far west, this place can be useful if arriving at Hongqiao Airport, but it's far from the main sights. Four-bed dorm rooms are clean and come with shower.

Sheraton Grand Taipingyang (Map pp242-3; ☎ 6275 8888; www.sheratongrand-shanghai.com; 5 South Zunyi Rd; 遵义路5号; s/d Y2430/2590) From the fastidiously attired and ever helpful staff (especially the attentive guest relations managers) to the

Chinese ceramics and furniture throughout, this is one of Shànghăi's most elegant and professional hotels. Recently refurbished rooms come with thoughtful touches: teddy bears on the bed at nightly turndown and rubber ducks perched on bathtubs.

EATING

Shànghăi's faddish restaurant scene continues to move up the gears with a determination to impress foodies from all shades of the culinary spectrum. Fashions sweep through the city's kitchens, rewriting cookbooks and consigning yesterday's flavours to the pedal bin. Restaurants open and close with almost seasonal regularity, so expect many more trendy places to have found champions among Shànghăi's diners by the time you read this. Plug into the current trends by reading *That's Shanghai* and its annual *Shanghai Restaurant Guide* (Y50).

While travellers budgeting for extravagant dining will be mesmerised by the sheer variety, those on a tight budget should keep to side streets where small restaurants serve cheap, local food. Other inexpensive food options include the Chinese fast-food chains and food courts in the basement or top floor of almost every department store in town. In pricier restaurants the set lunches offer the best value; dinners are often double the price.

Sample Shànghăi's favourite dumpling, *xiǎolóngbāo* (小笼包), copied everywhere else in China, but only true to form here. For Y5, you can get a steamer with four of these.

The Bund & East Nanjing Rd

A lot's cooking near the Bund: Chinese fast food, bars, coffee shops and a growing troupe of elegant Western and Chinese restaurants, staking out territory along the famous skyline.

For all kinds of cheap eats try the **Zhapu Rd food street** (Map pp244–5) near the Pujiang Hotel or the **Yunnan Rd food street** (Map pp244–5), not far from Renmin Sq.

Megabite (Dàshídài; Map pp244–5; 6th fl, Raffles City; meals Y25) King of the food courts, Megabite offers Chinese and Asian food in abundance for poorly financed and busy diners, with handy branches around town. Prepay, grab a card and head to the stall of your choice for on-the-spot service. Chefs cook it all up in front of you, dispensing with menus. There's also a branch at Carrefour in Gubei.

Ajisen (Wèiqiān Lāmiàn; Map pp244–5; ☎ 6360 7194; 327 East Nanjing Rd; meals Y30) Simply hopping come meal time, this Japanese noodle chain escorts diners to the noodle dish of their choice via easy-to-use photo menus and diligent squads of staff in regulation black T-shirt and jeans. Go for the Kimuchi Dumpling in Hot Pot (Y23) – a steaming, chilli-infused blast of chunky dumplings, spicy cabbage and *jinzhen* mushrooms – guaranteed to bring out a sweat. Oodles of branches in town, including Grand Gateway (Xujiahui).

Number 5 (Map pp244–5; ☎ 6329 4558; www.num berfive.cn; No 5 The Bund, East Zhongshan No 1 Rd; meals Y50) Excellent-value scrummy set lunches (11am to 2pm), comfy furniture and a stylish Bund basement setting make this restaurant-bar ideal for casual and relaxed dining. Come evening, neck a brain haemorrhage, sip a slippery nipple (both Y30), seize a pool cue and tune into late night live jazz sounds. There's also wireless internet access.

Ruzzi (Rúzī; Map pp244–5; ☎ 6360 9031; 528 Fuzhou Rd; meals Y60) With pizzas as crisp and fresh as the layout, this wi-fi-equipped chain is a slick presentation. Park yourself on one of the easy sofas, navigate the user-friendly menu and go for the Huff and Puff Chowder Soup (Y22), the excellent Barbeque Chicken pizza (Y43) and the Classic Banana Split (Y19).

Kathleen's 5 (Map pp244–5; ☎ 6327 2221; www .kathleens5.com.cn; 325 East Nanjing Rd; meal Y250, set lunch Y80-100; ☯ lunch & dinner) The spectacular glassed rooftop of the Shanghai Art Museum (p252) hosts this bright and buzzy restaurant, the Mediterranean menu of which is supplemented by an outside terrace with fine views over Renmin Park.

M on the Bund (Map pp244–5; ☎ 6350 9988; www .m-onthebund.com; 7th fl, 5 The Bund, cnr Guangdong Rd; mains Y100-200, set lunches Y118-138; ☯ closed Mon lunch) Table linen flapping in the breeze alongside exclusive rooftop views to Pǔdōng: the grand dame of the Bund's elegant formula still elicits applause from Shànghăi's gastronomes. Park yourself in a wicker chair, reach for the mismatched bone-handled cutlery and treat yourself to two-/three-course (Y118/138) set lunches or go the whole hog on the crispy suckling pig (Y198). Reservations a must.

Sens & Bund (Map pp244–5; ☎ 6323 9898; 6th fl, Bund 18, 18 East Zhongshan No 1 Rd; meals Y500; ☯ lunch & dinner) The opening of this fine French dining creation from Jacques and Laurent Pourcel – situated deliciously on the Bund – was greeted with euphoria by Shànghǎi's food-lovers, but reserve way ahead if you want a table overlooking the river.

Pǔdōng

Grand Hyatt (Jìnmào Kǎiyuè Dàjiǔdiàn; Map pp242-3; ☎ 5830 3338; Jinmao Tower, 88 Century Ave) If it's a special night out with a view you're after, the steakhouse Grill, Japanese Kobachi, Italian Cucina and Cantonese-style Canton restaurants at the Grand Hyatt really can't be beaten. The breathtaking atrium is a great place to meet. The Grand Café offers stunning views through its glass walls, and a good-value buffet (Y198 to Y228).

Yuyuan Bazaar Area

Nanxiang Steamed Bun Restaurant (Nánxiáng Mántoudiàn; Map pp244-5; ☎ 6355 4206; 85 Yuyuan Rd; meals Y10-20; ☯ 7am-10pm) Take your place in the queue of regulars trailing from this place opposite the Huxinting teahouse and fill yourself up with more than a dozen *xiǎolóngbāo* for a mere Y8. Upstairs offers seating to the scrums.

French Concession

BUDGET

Pamir Restaurant (Pàmiěr Cāntīng; Map pp248-9; 166 Fumin Rd; kebabs Y2, mains Y15) Excellent lamb kebabs, nan bread and Central Asian noodles (try the *suoman* – fried noodle squares with tomatoes and green peppers) offer a refreshing change of tastes at this no-frills Uighur restaurant. Wash it down with a bottle of Xinjiang Black Beer or a pot of *kok chai* (green tea).

Zentral Healthy Eatery (Shànqù Jiànkāng Shànshí; Map pp242-3; ☎ 6374 5815; www.zentral.com.cn; 567 South Huangpi Rd; set meals Y15-18) Clamber out of the MSG sea for affordable lunch sets, crispy and tasty healthy salads, brown rice, sugar-free desserts and sandwiches. Low on oil but high on taste and appeal.

ourpick Dōngběirén (Map pp248-9; ☎ 5228 8288; 2nd fl, 3 South Shaanxi Rd; dishes Y15-50) The *jiǎozi* (饺子; dumplings) at this sprightly outfit are as true to the Chinese northeast as the gaggle of rouge-cheeked, pigtailed Dongbei waiters. Besides tummy-filling lamb, pork and beef dumplings (Y10 to Y16), aim for the tender Sun Island Flaming Dragon Fish (Y48) or the hefty Boneless Pork Knuckle (Y48), but pass on the dry lamb kebabs. Further branch at 46 Panyu Rd (☎ 5230 2230).

Wúyuè Rénjiā (Map pp248-9; ☎ 5306 5410; No 10, Alley 706, Central Huaihai Rd; meals Y20; ☯ lunch & dinner) Stuffed away down an alley off Huaihai Rd, and at a handful of other locations, this pocket-sized noodle house is the best thing since sliced bread. The calming traditional Chinese décor is perfectly complemented by steaming bowls of wholesome noodles. You may have to share your table with a stranger or two, and decoding the cryptic Chinese menu can require patience, but our advice is to go for the *yúxiāng ròusīmiàn* (鱼香肉丝面; fish-flavour pork strips with noodles; Y13) and the fine bite-sized chunks of *cōngyóutāng húntun* (葱油汤馄饨; wonton soup with onion; Y6). The excellent *xiābào shànbèi miàn* comes with shrimp and fried eels in an oniony fish soup (Y16).

ourpick Bǎoluó Jiǔlóu (Map pp248-9; ☎ 5403 7239; 271 Fumin Rd; mains Y20-50) Gather up a boisterous bunch of friends and join Shanghainese night owls queuing down the street all through the night to get into this amazingly busy place. Open till 6am, it's a great place to get a feel for Shànghǎi's famous buzz. Try the excellent *ruìshi niúpái* (瑞士牛排; Swiss steak) or the *bǎoluó kǎomàn* (保罗烤鳗; baked eel; Y55).

Bóduō Xīnjì (Map pp248-9; ☎ 5404 9878; 9 Xinle Rd; meals Y30) Glance through the window of this cramped outpost of Cantonese/Chaozhou cuisine and note the ease with which it takes Shànghǎi's notoriously fickle diners hostage with a much loved, spot-on menu. Three branches in town.

MIDRANGE

Vegetarian Life Style (Zǎozi Shù; Map pp244-5; ☎ 6384 8000; 77 Songshan Rd; mains Y20-38) For light and healthy Chinese organic vegetarian food, with zero and precious little oil, this bright place has excellent dishes, including sweet Wuxi spareribs (Y30) – stuffed with lotus root. No alcohol and no smoking, but there's an English menu.

1221 (Map pp242-3; ☎ 6213 2441; 1221 West Yan'an Rd; meat dishes Y28-38, seafood Y56-76) No-one has a bad thing to say about this stylish expat favourite. The crispy duck (Y48) is excellent, as are the drunken chicken and *yóutiáo niúròu* (油条牛肉; beef with dough strips). The pan-fried sticky rice and sweet bean paste (from the dim sum menu) makes a good dessert. It's also worth ordering the eight-fragrance tea just to watch it served spectacularly out of 60cm-long spouts. The service is excellent.

Dìshuǐdòng (Map pp248-9; ☎ 6253 2689; 2nd fl, 56 South Maoming Rd; mains Y28-45; metro South Shaanxi Rd) Shànghǎi's favourite Hunanese restaurant is surprisingly downhome (with waiters decked out in Hunanese blue cloth) but serves up killer cuisine. Try the *làzi jīdīng* (辣子鸡丁; fried chicken with chilli) or settle for one of the excellent claypot dishes and brace for a chilli onslaught. There's an English menu, though, as ever, the Chinese version offers more range. Booking is advised.

Xìnjíshì Restaurant (Xìnjíshì Cāntīng; Map pp248-9; ☎ 6336 4746; No 9 Xīntiāndì, Lane 181, Taicang Rd; mains Y30-40; 🕑 lunch & dinner) The city is full of excellent Shànghǎi restaurants and this Xīntiāndì choice is among the most popular, and crowded.

Simply Thai (Tiāntài Cāntīng; Map pp248-9; ☎ 6445 9551; 5-C Dongping Rd; mains Y30-60) Everyone raves about this place for its delicious, reasonable dishes and comfortable décor. There's nice outdoor seating and the lunch specials are particularly good value.

Kaveen's Kitchen (Zhènzōng Yìndùcài; Map pp248-9; ☎ 6248 8292; 2nd fl, 231 Huashan Rd; meals Y40; 🕑 lunch & dinner) Above the Old Manhattan Bar, Kaveen's – official caterer for Air India flights out of town – is a well-liked Indian hot spot on Shànghǎi's food map. It's a bit cramped (the owner moved here from Kowloon, so perhaps he doesn't notice) but the menu has room for most tastes, including meat-free. Try the excellent *aloo palak* (spinach and potato) and fill the meal out with a naan.

Azul (Map pp248-9; ☎ 6433 1172; 18 Dongping Rd; tapas Y38-98, set lunch Y48-58, mains Y88-148) This Latin place is popular for its fresh New World cuisine and hip décor. Downstairs is the cool tapas bar and lounging area, while upstairs is Viva, a more formal space with a creative menu.

Kabb (Kǎibó Xīcāntīng; Map pp248-9; ☎ 3307 0798; 5 North Block, Lane 181, Xīntiāndì, 181 Taicang Rd; mains Y65-85) The outside seating and Xīntiāndì location (plus winning bar) bring an extra dimension to the filling menu of whole-hearted American/Mexican and Italian hits: burgers, Tex-Mex, club sandwiches and pasta.

Café Montmartre (Mèngmàntè Xīcānguǎn; Map pp248-9; ☎ 5404 7658; 55 South Xiangyang Rd, set lunch Y55, mains Y65-88) Bumping into a crafty imitation of a Latin Quarter brasserie in the French Concession is like running into an old Parisian friend, wreathed in the aroma of Ricard and Gaulloise fumes. Enter to a round bar and simple café tables below and upstairs seating plus outside

terrace, with French goodies like *croque monsieur* (hot ham and cheese grilled sandwich), crêpes and quiches (Y30 to Y45), as well as the occasional *magret de canard* (duck breast), roasted chicken and set lunches.

Spice Market (Dōngnányà Cāntīng; Map pp244-5; ☎ 6384 6838; 8 Jinan Rd; set lunch/dinner Y68/150) The menu at this attractive restaurant is a Who's Who of Asian dishes, from *pad thai* to *nasi goreng*, along with more interesting fare like the pomelo, chicken and chilli salad (Y35), and grilled whole fish with chilli, dry shrimps and coconut stuffing (Y62).

Brasil Steak House (Bāxī Shāokǎowū; Map pp248-9; ☎ 6437 7288; 1582 Central Huaihai Rd; lunch & dinner Y79; 🕑 11am-11pm) For an artery-clogging carrion feast, carnivores will be doing cartwheels here. Servers rotate with skewered hunks of roasted meat, slicing chunks onto your plate. There's also a buffet salad and dessert bar. It's opposite the Shanghai Library, and there's another branch (Map pp248-9; 1649 West Nanjing Rd; ☎ 6255 9898) next to Jing'an Park.

Mesa (Map pp248-9; ☎ 6289 9108; 748 Julu Rd; mains Y158-228) All space and light, Mesa's impressive Continental menu and weekend brunches work their magic best after aperitifs at its adjacent bar, Manifesto. In warm weather, the voluminous interior further spills out onto the terrace decking above Julu Rd and the play area for kids is a source of joy for overstressed parents.

TOP END

Xīntiāndì has one of the densest concentrations of top-end restaurants, all within a self-contained, smart locale.

Shintori Null II (Xīdūlì; Map pp248-9; ☎ 5404 5252; 803 Julu Rd; mains Y60-100; 🕑 dinner only) The bamboo-lined approach to No 803 Julu Rd does little to prepare diners for the setting of this Japanese restaurant, trendily poised somewhere between a Wehrmacht bunker and a brutalist penal institution. Straight edges, sharp lines, cold concrete, open kitchen: read cerebral dining. The Japanese menu is equally novel; the cold soba noodles arrive in a bowl made of ice.

West Nanjing Rd

Bì Fēng Táng (Map pp244-5; ☎ 6279 0738; 1333 West Nanjing Rd; dishes Y8-25) This is an incredibly popular Cantonese place (five branches around town) dishing up dim sum snacks (shrimp dumplings, honeyed pork, egg tarts et al),

---

SOMETHING SPECIAL

Both of the following restaurants require reservations, preferably several days in advance if you want a plum table with a view.

T8 (Map pp248-9; ☎ 6355 8999; 8 North Block, Xīntiāndì, 181 Taicang Rd; mains Y200, set lunch Mon & Wed-Fri 2/3 courses Y158/198; ☺ dinner to 11.30pm, closed Tue lunch) T8's fame is seemingly unstoppable. Dishes are best described as modern Mediterranean fusion with Asian influences, while the luxurious, seductively dark interior combines with subtle flavours and choice presentation to craft a culinary phenomenon. Dress to impress.

Jean Georges (Map pp244-5; ☎ 6321 7733; jgreservation@on-the-bund.com; 4th fl, Three on the Bund; mains from Y250; ☺ lunch & dinner) The *enfant terrible* of French cooking continues to stake his claim to Shànghãi's top dining experience with this elegant Bund creation. The dark, lush interior was designed by architect Michael Graves and the delectable dishes – the lamb loin with black trumpet mushrooms is outstanding – are matched by attentive, courteous staff. There's a large wine selection, starting at US$50 a bottle.

---

as well as coffee and cheap Budweiser. This branch has an English menu on request and plenty of fine outdoor seating when the weather is good.

Gongdelin Vegetarian Restaurant (Gōngdélín Sùshíchù; Map pp244-5; ☎ 6327 0218; 445 West Nanjing Rd; mains Y15-25) The podgy effigy of Milefo (the laughing Buddha) and the faint aroma of temple incense hint at the Buddhist creed of this elegantly refitted vegetarian restaurant, housed in a red-brick building dating from 1922. The fleshless food – served in a graceful environment of stone flagging and water features – delivers shots of good karma and energizing meat-free calories. The sign says 'Godly Restaurant'.

Lulu Restaurant (Lúlú Jiǔjiā; Map pp244-5; ☎ 6288 1179; 5th fl, Plaza 66, 1266 West Nanjing Rd; dishes Y18-32, seafood Y32-188) The Pǔdōng branch (Map pp242-3) established Lulu's reputation as one of the best bets for decent Shanghainese cuisine but this branch is the epitome of stylish, modern Shànghãi, perfect for a trendy group meal blowout. All your Shanghainese favourites are here, including *xièfěn shízi tóu* (蟹粉狮子头; crab and pork meatballs; Y15 each).

Rendezvous Café (Lǎngdímǔ; Map pp244-5; ☎ 6247 2307; 1486 West Nanjing Rd; meals Y40-50) Far cheaper and better than TGIF's patties, the burgers at no-nonsense Rendezvous put the squeeze on overpriced burger bars citywide. Break your overnight fast with the full-on Y28 American Breakfast – or angle later in the day for the fish and chips (Y48) or seafood spaghetti (Y48). Other branches around town.

Element Fresh (Xīnyuánsù; Map pp244-5; ☎ 6279 8682; Shanghai Centre, 1376 West Nanjing Rd; sandwiches Y35-75, lunch mains Y60-90, dinner Y85-128) The focus at this bright and stylish spot is on fresh, healthy sandwiches and salads; vegetarians can swoon at the roasted eggplant on walnut bread with mozzarella and olives, and revive themselves on fresh juices, imaginative smoothies and excellent coffee. There's an express branch at 279 Wuxing Rd (☎ 5116 9897).

Southern Shanghai

Ye Olde Station Restaurant (Shànghãi Lǎozhàn; Map pp242-3; ☎ 6427 2233; 201 North Caoxi Rd; meals Y40; ☺ lunch & dinner) With dark green shutters and a cream exterior, this is actually the former St Ignatius Convent (1931), facing the Bibliotheca Zi-Ka-Wei (p257). The Shànghãi cuisine is unsurprising, but the setting and period features, from the original tiled floors and upstairs chapel, are unique. Book a table in one of the old train carriages (former passengers include Manchu Empress Cixi and Song Qingling) in the rear garden.

DRINKING
Bars

Shànghãi has several bar strips and no shortage of watering holes, their fortunes cresting and falling with the vagaries of the latest vogue. Drinks are generally expensive, retailing for around Y40 at most popular bars, so squeeze the most out of happy hour. Streets thick with bars include South Maoming Rd, Tongren Rd and Hengshan Rd.

Time Passage (Zuótiān Jīntiān Míngtiān; Map pp248-9; ☎ 6240 2588; 183 Huashan Rd; ☺ 5pm-2am) If you like cheap beer (Y25 a pint) and an undemanding, lived-in ambience, this student-set bar has been charting its chronological passage since 1994. Despite the address, the bar is actually on Caojiayan Rd, smacked by balls from the adjacent tennis court. Live music – often impromptu – takes to the air every Friday and Saturday after 10.30pm, while Tuesday evenings are cut price pints nights.

Barbarossa (Bābālùshā Huìsuǒ; Map pp244-5; ☎ 6318 0220; Renmin Park, 231 West Nanjing Rd; drinks Y40, sheesha Y100; ☺ 10am-2am) Bringing a whiff of Middle Eastern promise to the Pearl of the Orient, this Moroccan-styled theme bar-restaurant sits pondside in Renmin Park like something from a mirage. More than a mere novelty, there's excellent music, fabulous outside seating and remarkable evening views.

O'Malley's Bar (Oūmǎli Cāntīng; Map pp248-9; ☎ 6474 4533; 42 Taojiang Rd; ☺ 11am-2am) The Irish pub theme straddles China from Qīngdǎo to Chéngdū like a gigantic, synthetic Celtic harp, but few come with such enticing lawns or the classy French Concession perch. The fantastic kids' club goes down a real treat with expat families, but the hefty meat breakfast could be a challenge for all but the most unrepentant carnivore.

Malone's American Café (Mǎlóng Měishì Jiǔlóu; Map pp244-5; ☎ 6247 2400; 257 Tongren Rd; ☺ 11am-2am) Love it or hate it, this brisk sports bar has been fruitfully ploughing its own furrow for over a decade. Sitting under the glow of sports TV is a cross-section of expat society, hunched over beers and fish and chips (set lunches Y50), and serenaded by Filipino bands at weekends.

Cloud 9 Bar (Map pp242-3; minimum charge Y100; ☺ from 6pm Mon-Fri, from 11am Sat & Sun) Need a lift at the end of the day? Tired of the low life? Want to reach an absolute high? Viewing the nocturnal lights of town from the 87th floor of the Grand Hyatt through the carbonated fizz of a gin and tonic may hoist you to just the right elevation, although the weary '90s décor needs a shot of adrenaline.

Face Bar (Map pp248-9; ☎ 6466 4328; Bldg 1, Ruijin Guesthouse, 18 Ruijin No 2 Rd; beer Y40-65, cocktails Y50-95) Wonderfully installed on the ground floor of a 1936 mansion, Face exudes a languorous sophistication and a soothing colonial charm. It's elegant, soothing, decorated with chinoiserie and manned by polite waiting staff. Prices aren't cheap but there's nowhere better to take a date or laze in front of the manicured lawn on a summer's afternoon. The excellent but pricey Thai-style Lan Na Thai and Indian-style Hazara restaurants offer top cuisine in the same building.

Tea & Coffee Houses

Boonna Café (Bùnà Kāfēiguǎn; Map pp248-9; ☎ 5404 6676; www.boonnacafe.com; 88 Xinle Rd) The quietly trendy Boonna is set back from the action on leafy Xinle Rd. Shell out a mere Y10 for the house coffee, and leaf through the appetising menu, which runs to banana pancakes (Y20). Patrons get a free 30-minute chunk of internet use.

Coffeelox (Nuòkǎ Kāfēi; Map pp248-9; ☎ 6438 7238; 1988 Huashan Rd) There's no such thing as a free lunch, but the regularly cut-price dishes at this Italian café are the next best thing. Menus rotate, but there's usually a list of cheap offerings, from scrummy pasta bakes (Y18) to tuna spaghetti (Y12), seafood soup (Y6) and pea soup (Y6). With several branches in town, this is one of Shànghǎi's best-value meals, if you forgo the coffee beans.

Kommune (Gōngshè Jiǔbā; Map pp248-9; ☎ 6466 2416; No 7, Lane 210, Taikang Rd) This trendy spot is ideal for a coffee or fruit juice in the Taikang Road Arts Centre (p253), with aluminium furniture as well as full-on Y48 Sunday big breakfasts.

1931 (Map pp248-9; ☎ 6472 5264; 112 South Maoming Rd; dishes Y20-60; ☺ 11am-2am) One of the nicest places is this intimate café-bar outfitted with a 1930s theme and serving coffee, tea, drinks and meals.

Huxinting Teahouse (Húxīntíng Cháguǎn; Map pp244-5; ☎ 6373 6950; Yuyuan Bazaar; pot of tea ground fl Y20-25, upstairs Y40-Y55; ☺ 6am-9.30pm) Next to the Yuyuan Gardens, this ornate spot is one of the best places to sit and look over the mob below and pretend you're part of the scene on a blue willow teacup. Make sure you stay a while, however, as the price is steep for a quick pot of tea, and get here early for one of the prime window seats. Classical Chinese music (no charge) is performed upstairs Friday, Saturday and Sunday at 6.30pm and Monday from 2pm to 5pm.

Bonomi Café (Bōnuòmī Kāfēidiàn; Map pp244-5; ☎ 6329 7506; room 226, 12 East Zhongshan No 1 Rd; coffee Y25-32) This is a lovely little space, hidden away along the prestigious corridors of the landmark HSBC building on the Bund.

ENTERTAINMENT

There's something for most moods in Shànghǎi: opera, rock, hip-hop, techno, salsa and early morning waltzes in Renmin Sq. None of it comes cheap, however (except for the waltzing, which is free). A night on the town in Shànghǎi is comparable to a night out in Hong Kong or Taipei and it's not getting any cheaper.

Venues open and close all the time. Check out the Shànghãi entertainment magazines (see p241) for guidance.

Cinemas

As with the rest of China, only a limited (and generally late) selection of English-language films make it to cinemas and when they do, they are often dubbed in Chinese, so ensure your film is the English version (英文版 yīngwénbǎn). Tickets cost Y40 to Y60, often half price on Tuesdays.

Peace Cinema (Hépíng Yǐngdū; Map pp244-5; ☎ 6361 2898; 290 Central Xizang (Tibet) Rd; Y50) A useful location at Raffles Plaza by Renmin Sq, with an IMAX cinema (Y70).

Studio City (Huányì Diànyǐngchéng; Map pp244-5; ☎ 6218 2173; 10th fl, Westgate Mall, 1038 West Nanjing Rd)

UME International Cineplex (UME; Map pp248-9; ☎ 6384 1122; www.ume.com.cn; 4th fl, No 6, Lane 123, Xingye Rd, Xīntiāndì)

Clubs & Discos

Shànghãi pulls in some top-notch DJs from abroad to its crowd of snappy dance venues. There's a high turnover, so check listings magazines.

Mint (Map pp244-5; ☎ 6247 9666; 2nd fl, 333 Tongren Rd; tickets Y100; ☻ 6pm-2am Mon-Thu, 9pm-7am Fri & Sat) Rattling the windows of the 2nd floor of Hudec's Green House (a pile of 1930s Bauhaus nostalgia in need of a lick of paint), Mint is a languid club for lounging to smooth chill-out sounds, Latin House and funk (happy hour 7pm to 9pm). The entrance price includes a shot of Glenfiddich.

Fabrique (Map pp248-9; ☎ 6415 1600; Bldg 8, 8-10 Central Jianguo Rd; ☻ 9pm-2am Mon-Thu, to 4am Fri-Sat) For the modern and sophisticated set, Fabrique fuses dining, clubbing (House, upbeat dance) and sleek design to bring a sharp, innovative edge to Shànghãi's rapidly evolving and time-sensitive club scene.

Rojam Disco (Map pp248-9; ☎ 6390 7181; 4th fl, Hong Kong Plaza, 283 Central Huaihai Rd; admission Y40-70; ☻ 8.30pm-2am) This is a popular place for techno on the weekends. The cover charge includes one drink.

California Club (Map pp248-9; ☎ 6318 0785; 2 Gaolan Rd; ☻ 6pm-late) Owned by the Lan Kwai Fong group and located in the Park 97 restaurant complex in Fuxing Park, this club is one of the places to be seen. Take a break from the bass in the upstairs Kasbah lounge.

Pu-J's (Map pp242-3; ☎ 5049 1234, ext 8732; Podium 3, Jinmao Tower, 88 Century Avenue; admission Y65-100; ☻ 7pm-2am, closed Sun) The Grand Hyatt's extravagant entertainment multiplex brings you venues to suit your mood: jazz, live music, dance and karaoke.

Gay & Lesbian Venues

Shànghãi has a few places catering to gay patrons, but the locales keep moving around, so check the listings. Men or women, gay or straight, are welcome at the places listed here. For the latest gay venues look for the cryptic comments in local listings magazines.

Eddy's Bar (Jiānóng Kāfēi; Map pp248-9; ☎ 6282 0521; www.eddys-bar.com; 1877 Central Huaihai Rd; ☻ 8pm-2am) A gay-friendly bar-café attracting a slightly more mature Chinese and international gay crowd with inexpensive drinks and neat décor.

Home & Bar (Báilíng Jiǔbā; Map pp248-9; ☎ 5382 0373; 18 Gaolan Rd; ☻ 8pm-2am Wed-Sun) Newly arrived gays from other parts of China and abroad tend to make this their first port of call, Shànghãi's premier and best-known gay bar (admission charge at weekends).

Live Music

Apart from the places listed here, other bars, cafés and restaurants, such as Number 5 (jazz; p265) and Bandu Cabin (traditional Chinese music; p255) stage music performances.

Cotton Club (Map pp248-9; ☎ 6437 7110; 8 West Fuxing Rd; admission free; ☻ 7.30pm-2am Tue-Sun) Decked out in wood and brass with black-and-white stills of jazz greats fixed to the walls, the old-timer Cotton Club snats its fingers nightly to soothing doses of live jazz and blues.

Ark House (Map pp248-9; ☎ 6326 8008; www.ark-lh.com; 15 North Block, Lane 181, Taicang Rd, Xīntiāndì; cover charge Y30-50) This is a rare opportunity to catch underground Chinese bands with an alternative edge. Gigs get going Friday and Saturday from 9.30pm.

Shanghai Grand Theatre (Shànghãi Dà Jùyuàn; Map pp244-5; ☎ 6372 8701; www.shgtheatre.com; 300 Renmin Ave; tickets Y100-680) This state-of-the-art venue is in Renmin Sq and features both national and international opera, dance, music and theatre performances.

Shanghai Concert Hall (Shànghãi Yīnyuè Tīng; Map pp244-5; ☎ 5386 6666; 523 East Yan'an Rd) Equipped with fine acoustics and relocated 66.4m southeast of its former location a few years ago, this 75-year-old building is the venue for regular performances by orchestras including the Shanghai Symphony Orchestra and the Shanghai Broadcasting Symphony Orchestra.

Oriental Arts Centre (Dōngfāng Yìshù Zhōngxīn; Map pp242-3; ☎ 6854 7757; 425 Dingxing Rd; tickets Y80-480) Shànghǎi's latest cultural centre, designed by Paul Andreu, features a 2000-seat philharmonic orchestra hall, a 300-seat chamber music hall and a 100-seat theatre.

Conservatory of Music (Yīnyuè Xuéyuàn; Map pp248-9; ☎ 6431 1792; 20 Fenyang Rd; tickets Y80-380) Classical and traditional Chinese musical performances are held here at 7.15pm (typically on Saturdays and Sundays, but other days as well). Tickets are available from the ticket office just north of the conservatory, amid the musical instrument shops, at 8 Fenyang Rd.

Jinjiang Hotel (Jǐnjiāng Fàndiàn; Map pp248-9; ☎ 6258 2582; 59 South Maoming Rd) This hotel hosts classical music concerts on the first Sunday of the month at 2pm. Tickets cost Y50 and include refreshments.

House of Blues & Jazz (Bùlǔsī Yǔ Juéshì Zhī Wū; Map pp248-9; ☎ 6437 5280; 158 South Maoming Rd; ☉ Tue-Sun 4pm-2am) Serious jazz-lovers should make a beeline to this restaurant and bar where the in-house band (which changes every three months) whips up live music from 10pm to 1am. Sunday night is a free-for-all jam, and Mondays are quiet.

Theatre
Majestic Theatre (Měiqí Dàxìyuàn; Map pp244-5; ☎ 6217 3311/4409; 66 Jiangning Rd; tickets Y20-300) All kinds of performances are held in this former cinema,

---

AND THE BUND PLAYED ON

Chalking up an average age of 76 – older than the Stones – the six-man Peace Hotel Jazz Band at the **Peace Hotel Bar** (Map pp244-5; ☎ 6321 6888; Peace Hotel, 20 East Nanjing Rd; admission Y50; ☉ 8am-1.30am) first started cranking out their septuagenarian jazz classics in 1980. Two of the old-timers – including the band's founder and trumpet player Zhou Wanrong – are former members of China's first all-Chinese band fronted by Jimmy King in the 1940s, which had a regular slot at the Paramount. The veterans' repertoire is a nostalgic, if undemanding, catalogue of 1930s and 1940s numbers.

---

including ballet, local opera and the occasional revolutionary-style opera.

Shanghai Dramatic Arts Centre (Shànghǎi Huàjù Zhōngxīn; Map pp248-9; ☎ 6473 4567; 288 Anfu Rd; tickets Y20-100) Modern plays in Chinese are staged here.

Traditional Performances
Yifu Theatre (Yìfū Wǔtái; Map pp244-5; ☎ 6351 4668; www.tianchan.com; 701 Fuzhou Rd; tickets Y30-150) A block east of Renmin Sq, this is the main opera theatre in town, recognisable by the huge opera mask above the entrance. The theatre stages a variety of regional operatic styles, including Beijing opera (jīngjù), Kunqu opera (kūnqǔ) and Yue opera (yuèjù). A shop in the foyer sells CD recordings of operatic works.

Chinese acrobatic troupes are among the best in the world, and Shànghǎi is a good place to see a performance. If you've never seen a show, it's not to be missed.

Shanghai Centre Theatre (Shànghǎi Shāngchéng Jùyuàn; Map pp244-5; ☎ 6279 8948; 1376 Nanjing West Rd; admission Y100-200) The Shanghai Acrobatics Troupe (Shànghǎi Zájì Tuán) has short but entertaining performances here most nights at 7.30pm.

Lyceum Theatre (Lánxīn Dàxìyuàn; Map pp248-9; ☎ 6256 4832; 57 South Maoming Rd; admission Y30-60) The recently renovated brick Lyceum dates back to 1867, but the theatre moved to the current building – one of Shànghǎi's oldest and most architecturally interesting theatres – in 1931. The theatre stages a variety of performances, including acrobatics, magic shows, ballet and Chinese opera.

SHOPPING
Shànghǎi has long been the most famous shopping city in China and almost all Chinese products and souvenirs find their way here. The traditional shopping streets have always been Nanjing Rd and Huaihai Rd, but now it seems almost every side street is overflowing with boutiques and shops. The Shanghainese live to shop.

Clothing & Shoes
Tall and large people may have difficulty finding their size in Shànghǎi, but it's a shopping paradise for smaller folk.

Try South Maoming Rd (Map pp248–9) and South Shanxi Rd (Map pp244–5) for various boutiques, especially if you're shopping for a *qipao* (Chinese dress, also known as cheongsam). Nanjing Rd (Map pp244–5) and Huaihai Rd (Map pp248–9) have the big-name brands. South Shanxi Rd is packed with small shoe shops with good prices. Xiangyang Market, Shànghǎi's ever popular knock-off clothing market, closed in June 2006.

If you want to make your own clothes or choose your own cloth for a tailor, you won't get stitched up at the **Dongjiadu Cloth Market** (Dōngjiādù Zhīpǐn Shìchǎng; Map pp242–3; cnr Dongjiadu Rd & Zhongshan Dong Erlu), with the cheapest silk (from Y35 per metre), brocade cashmere and other cloth by the metre at a fraction of the cost in the West.

Buses run south from the Bund to the market, or take a taxi.

You can also get slightly pricier silk (Y80 to Y288 per metre) at more convenient locations near the Bund at **Silk King** (Zhēnsī Shāngshà; Map pp244–5; 66 East Nanjing Rd) or **Laokafook Silk & Woollen Store** (Lǎojièfú Sīchóu Níróng Shāngdiàn; Map pp244–5; 257 East Nanjing Rd).

Department Stores

Shànghǎi has some of the best department stores in China, including flashy Western- and Japanese-style outlets that are probably of more interest to residents than to visitors. On the other hand, if you can find your size, there are sometimes good fashion deals in some of the department stores. With competition so fierce, you can even bargain in some department stores, depending on the item.

Hualian Department Store (Húalían Shāngshà; Map pp244–5; ☎ 6322 4466; 635 East Nanjing Rd; ⏰ 9.30am-10pm) Formerly called No 10, and before that the famous Wing On, this place is best for mid- and low-range prices.

Friendship Store (Yǒuyì Shāngdiàn; Map pp244–5; ☎ 6337 3469; 68 East Jinling Rd; ⏰ 9.30am-9.30pm) This is a good place to pick up last-minute souvenirs at fixed prices, and the lack of crowds makes it possible to browse at your leisure. There's an ATM and a money-changing facility here.

West Nanjing Rd has the most glam malls, including **Westgate Mall** (Méilóngzhèn Guǎngchǎng; Map pp244–5; 1038 West Nanjing Rd), with a branch of Isetan and basement supermarket, the exclusive **Plaza 66** (Map pp244–5; 1266 West Nanjing Rd) and **CITIC Square** (Zhōngxīn Tàifù Guǎngchǎng; Map pp244–5; 1168 West Nanjing Rd).

Over in Pǔdōng, across from the Oriental Pearl Tower, the Thai-financed **Superbrand Mall** (Zhèngdà Guǎngchǎng; Map pp242–3; metro Liujiazui) is Shànghǎi's largest.

Photographic Supplies

Major hotels often stock basic photographic supplies. Passport photos are available in most metro stations (Y20).

Guànlóng (Map pp244–5; ☎ 6323 8681; 190 East Nanjing Rd; ⏰ 9am-10pm) You can get slide film, memory sticks and all kinds of camera accessories here at Shànghǎi's foremost photographic supplies shop.

Porcelain

Shanghai Museum (Shànghǎi Bówùguǎn; Map pp244–5; ☎ 6372 3500; 201 Renmin Dadao; ⏰ 9am-5pm) The best place to find decent porcelain is this shop (see p252), which sells imitations of the pieces displayed in the Zande Lou Gallery (within the museum). The imitations are fine specimens and far superior to the mediocre pieces you see in the tourist shops. However, be prepared to pay a hefty whack.

Jingdezhen Porcelain Artware (Jǐngdézhèn Cíqì Diàn; Map pp244–5; ☎ 6253 8865; 1185 West Nanjing Rd; ⏰ 10am-9pm) There's a variety of more prosaic porcelain for sale here and pricey speciality items as well.

Souvenirs, Collectibles & Antiques

Yuyuan Bazaar (Map pp244–5), in the Old Town, is a souvenir-hunter's Mecca. Shops in the bazaar and along nearby Central Fangbang Rd flog calligraphy, pearls from nearby Tài Hú, old banknotes, woodcuts, artwork, blue cloth, teapots and pretty much everything else. Haggle hard as it's all overpriced.

Fuyou Antique Market (Fúyou Gòngyìpǐn Shìchǎng; Map pp244–5; 459 Central Fangbang Rd) There's a permanent antique market here on the 1st and 2nd floors, near the Yuyuan Gardens in the Old Town, but the place really gets humming early on Sunday mornings when local dealers crowd all four floors with ceramics, 'antique' posters, pocket watches, paintings and a host of other collectibles.

Dongtai Rd Antique Market (Dōngtái Lù Gǔshāngpǐn Shìchǎng; Map pp244–5; Dongtai Rd; ⏰ 8.30am-6pm) A short shuffle east of the Old Town perimeter, the Dongtai Rd Antique Market is a magnificent sprawl of curios, knick-knacks and Mao-era nostalgia, though only a fraction of the items really qualify as antique. Haggle hard here. Larger antique shops hide behind the stalls.

Shanghai Antique & Curio Store (Shànghǎi Wénwù Shāngdiàn; Map pp244–5; ☎ 6321 5868; 192-246 Guangdong Rd; ⏰ 9am-5pm) Designated tourist shops like this long-established place are expensive alternatives to the markets. Their range is good, but again, there's a lot of rubbish so you need a shrewd eye.

Yunhong Chopsticks Shop (Yùnhóng Kuàizi Diàn; Map pp244-5; ☎ 6322 0207; 387 East Nanjing Rd) Ideal for souvenir shopping and last-minute panic present purchases, this slender shop on East Nanjing Rd is stuffed with Japanese and Chinese chopsticks of all decorative denominations, from bamboo, through wood to silver, and even gold-plated.

Duolun Rd (p255) is lined with antique shops, art galleries, bookshops and curio stores; dig around and you'll turn up all kinds of stuff, from revolutionary souvenirs to shadow puppets. Duolun Rd is within walking distance of the East Baoxing Rd light rail station.

Supermarkets & Pharmacies
Local supermarkets are in almost every residential area and often stock many Western food items, especially the local chains Hualian and Tops.

City Supermarket (Chéngshì Chāoshì; Map pp244-5; ☎ 6279 8081; Shanghai Centre, 1376 West Nanjing Rd; ☺ 8am-11.30pm) If you crave obscure foods from home or need Western pharmaceutical items in a hurry, this place in the Shanghai Centre is convenient but items are priced to the hilt. There is a free delivery service. Other branches include one in the basement of Times Square, 99 Central Huaihai Rd (Map pp244–5).

Carrefour (Jiālèfú; Map pp242-3; ☎ 6209 8899; 268 South Shuicheng Rd; ☺ 8am-10pm) With eight branches in town, the French hypermarket giant has very reasonable prices for its excellent selection of food, clothes and household items.

Watson's (Qūchénshì) Westgate Mall (Map pp244-5; 1038 West Nanjing Rd); Central Huaihai Rd (Map pp248-9; 787 Central Huaihai Rd) This pharmacy has Western cosmetics, over-the-counter medicines and health products, with many outlets around the city. Prices are similar to those you would pay in Hong Kong.

GETTING THERE & AWAY
Shànghài has rail and air connections to places all over China, ferries travelling up the Yangzi River (Cháng Jiāng), boats along the coast and buses to destinations in adjoining provinces.

Air
Shànghài has international flight connections to most major cities, many operated by China Eastern, which has its base here.

Daily (usually several times) domestic flights connect Shànghài to major cities in China. Prices include Běijīng (Y1150, 1½ hours), Guǎngzhōu (Y1620, two hours), Chéngdū (Y1610, two hours and 20 minutes), Guìlín (Y1310, two hours), Qīngdǎo (Y740, one hour) and Xī'ān (Y1280, two hours), but travel agencies normally offer discounts of up to 40%. Minor cities are less likely to have daily flights, but chances are there will be at least one flight a week, probably more, to Shànghài.

You can buy air tickets almost anywhere, including at major hotels and all travel agencies (see p251). The following airlines have offices in Shànghài.

Aeroflot Russian Airlines (Map pp244-5; ☎ 6279 8033; 203a, Shanghai Centre, 1376 West Nanjing Rd)
Air China (Zhōngguó Mínháng; Map pp248-9; ☎ 5239 7227; www.airchina.com.cn; 600 Huashan Rd)
Air France (Map pp244-5; ☎ 4008 808 808; www.airfrance.com.cn; Room 1301, Novel Plaza, 128 West Nanjing Rd)
Asiana (Hányà Hángkōng; Map pp242-3; ☎ 6219 4000; 2nd fl, Rainbow Hotel, 2000 West Yan'an Rd)
British Airways (Map pp244-5; ☎ 8008 108 012; Room 2609, Westgate Tower, 1038 West Nanjing Rd)
China Eastern Airlines (Zhōngguó Dōngfāng Mínháng; Map pp248-9; ☎ domestic & international 95108; www.ce-air.com; 200 West Yan'an Rd; ☺ 24hr)
Dragonair (Gǎnglóng Hángkōng; Map pp244-5; ☎ 6375 6375; Room 2103-04, Shanghai Plaza, 138 Central Huaihai Rd)
Japan Airlines (JAL; Map pp244-5; ☎ 4008 880 808; Room 435, Plaza 66, 1266 West Nanjing Rd)
KLM (Map pp244-5; ☎ 4008 808 222; www.klm.com; Room 3901b, Ciro Plaza, 388 West Nanjing Rd)
Korean Air (☎ 4006 588 888; www.koreanair.com; 1/F, Yangze New World Hotel, 2099 West Yan'an Rd)
Lufthansa (Map pp248-9; ☎ 5352 4999; www.lufthansa.com.cn; 3rd fl, Bldg One, Corporate Avenue, 222 Hubin Rd)
Malaysia Airlines (Map pp244-5; ☎ 6279 8607; 209, Shanghai Centre, 1376 West Nanjing Rd)
Northwest Airlines (Map pp244-5; ☎ 4008 140 081; www.nwa.com; Suite 207, Shanghai Centre, 1376 West Nanjing Rd)
Qantas (Map pp244-5; ☎ 8008 190 089; Room 3202, Kwah Center, 1010 Middle Huaihai Rd)
Scandinavian Airlines (Map pp248-9; ☎ 5228 5001; www.flysas.com; Room 3901, Nan Zheng Building, 580 West Nanjing Rd)

Singapore Airlines (Map pp248-9; ☎ 6289 1000; www.singaporeair.com; Suite 606-608, Kerry Centre, 1515 West Nanjing Rd)

Thai Airways International (Tàiguó Hángkōng; Map pp248-9; ☎ 5298 5555; www.thaiairways.com; 105 Kerry Centre, 1515 West Nanjing Rd)

United Airlines (Map pp248-9; ☎ 3311 4567; www .cn.united.com; 3301-17 Shanghai Central Plaza, 381 Central Huaihai Rd)

Virgin Atlantic (Wéizhēn Hángkōng; Map pp244-5; ☎ 5353 4600; www.virgin.com; Room 221-23, 12 East Zhongshan First Rd, the Bund)

Boat

Boats are definitely one of the best ways to leave Shànghǎi and they're often also the cheapest, especially for destinations inland along the Yangzi River. Many coastal routes, however, have all but dried up.

Domestic boat tickets can be bought from China International Travel Service (p251) or from the **ferry booking office** (Shànghǎi Gǎng Chuán-piào Dìngshòuchù; Map pp244-5; 1 East Jinling Rd).

Overnight boats (Y99 to Y369, 11 hours) to Pǔtuóshān depart every day at 8pm from the **Wusong Wharf** (吴淞码头; Wúsōng Mǎtou; ☎ 5657 5500; 251 Songbao Rd), almost at the mouth of the Yangzi River; to reach Wusong Wharf, take sightseeing bus 51 from Shanghai Stadium or bus 51.

A high-speed ferry service (Y225, 8am and 2pm) to Pǔtuóshān departs twice daily from the port of Lúcháogǎng south of Shànghǎi. Buses (price included in ferry ticket, two hours) run to Lúcháogǎng from Longyang Rd metro station and Nanpu Bridge (by the bridge). Boats leave Pǔtuóshān daily at 12.30pm and 1.30pm for the return trip to Shànghǎi.

Weekly ferries (every Tuesday) to Osaka and twice-monthly boats to Kōbe in Japan depart from the new **international passenger terminal** (Guójì Kèyùn Mǎtou; Map pp242-3; 100 Yangshupu Rd), by Lintong Rd. Tickets are sold by the two boat operators, **China-Japan International Ferry Co** (中日国际轮渡有限公司; ☎ 6595 7988/ 6888; 18th fl) and **Shanghai International Ferry Co** (上海国际轮渡有限公司; ☎ 6537 5111; www .shanghai-ferry.co.jp; 15th fl), both in the Jin'an Bldg, 908 Dongdaming Rd (Map pp242-3) in the northeast of town. Tickets to either destination (44 hours) range from Y1300 in an eight-bed dorm to Y6500 in a deluxe twin cabin. Reservations are recommended in July and August. Passengers must be at the harbour

three hours before departure to get through immigration. Note that Shanghai International Ferry Co only serves Osaka.

Bus

Shànghǎi has a few long-distance bus stations but the most useful for travellers is probably the **Hengfeng Rd bus station** (Héngfēng Lù Kèyùnzhàn; Map pp244-5; ☎ 6353 7345), not far from Hanzhong Rd metro station. Deluxe buses leave for Běijīng (Y244, 5pm), Sūzhōu (Y30, every 20 minutes, 7.10am to 8pm), Nánjīng (Y88, every 40 minutes, 7.30am to 6.30pm) and Hángzhōu (Y55, every 35 minutes, 7am to 7.20pm).

Buses also leave from the **Xujiahui Bus Station** (Xújiāhuì Kèyùnzhàn; Map pp242-3; ☎ 6469 7325; 211 Hongqiao Rd), departing for Hángzhōu (Y55, 6.30am to 7.20pm) and Níngbō (Y97, 6.40am to 5.40pm). Other destinations include Héféi (Y147), Yángzhōu (Y83), Nánjīng (Y88), Sūzhōu (Y30), Wúxī (Y43) and Wǔhàn (Y307). Buses also depart for Hángzhōu and Sūzhōu from Hongqiao Airport.

The new **South Bus Station** (上海南站汽车站; Shànghǎi Nán Qìchēzhàn) that opened in December 2005 serves several routes to the south, with buses departing for Hángzhōu (Y59, every 20 minutes, 6.40am to 7.20pm), Níngbō (Y99, every 30 minutes, from 6.40am) and Sūzhōu (Y30, every 30 minutes, from 7.20am). Other destinations include Nánjīng (Y88), Héféi (Y149) and Túnxī (Y110).

Buses to Nánjīng (Y88) and Wúxī (Y39) depart daily from the Shanghai Sightseeing Bus Centre (Map pp242-3) at the Shanghai Stadium, where you can also join tours to Sūzhōu (Y148, Saturday and Sunday), Hángzhōu (Y208, Saturday and Sunday), Zhōuzhuāng (Y110, daily), Wūzhèn (Y148, daily), Tónglǐ (Y120), Mùdú (Y110, daily) and other towns in the region. None of the tours have English-speaking guides, but prices include entrance to major attractions.

Train

Shànghǎi is at the junction of the Běijīng–Shànghǎi and Běijīng–Hángzhōu train lines and many parts of the country can be reached by direct train from here.

The easiest option for buying tickets is at the **Longmen Hotel ticket office** (Lóngmén Bīnguǎn huòchēpiào shòupiàochù; Map pp244-5; ☎ 6317 9325; ⏰ 8am-9pm), a short walk west of Shanghai train station. You can book sleepers up to nine days in advance here, with a Y5 service charge. You can also buy tickets at the much more chaotic ticket office to the southeast of the train station (no service charge). The main (24-hour) ticket office is on the other (east) side of the station; ticket office No 10 claims its staff are English-speakers. The main ticket office at Shanghai train station is not in the main train station building, but just to the southeast on the corner of Meiyuan Rd.

Hard-seat and hard-sleeper tickets can also be purchased from the **Train Ticket Office** (230 East Beijing Rd & 1738 West Beijing Rd; ☽ 8am-5pm); soft-seat or soft-sleeper tickets can be bought at another **Train Ticket Office** (Map pp244-5; 121 South Xizang (Tibet) Road; ☽ 8am-10pm) or one of the numerous other small train ticket offices through town, such as on Xinhua Rd (417 Xinhua Rd; open 8am to 8pm). The train ticket booking hotline is ☎ 800 820 7890.

Most trains depart from and arrive at the **Shanghai train station** (Shànghǎi zhàn; Map pp244-5). Replacing the old Meilongzhen Railway Station in the south, Shanghai South train station commenced operation on 1 July 2006, mainly serving destinations such as Chóngqìng, Chéngdū, Chángshā, Nánjīng and Hángzhōu.

Special double-decker 'tourist trains' operate between Shànghǎi and Hángzhōu, and Shànghǎi and Nánjīng (with stops at Wúxī, Sūzhōu, Chángzhōu and Zhènjiāng). A seat to Nánjīng costs Y41 to Y72, depending on the train, and takes three hours.

New, plush overnight express 'Z' class (直特; zhítè) trains do the trip to Běijīng in 12 hours. Trains Z2 (7.19pm), Z6 (7.12pm), Z8 (7.26pm), Z14 (6.58pm) and Z22 (7.05pm) depart daily for Běijīng from Shanghai train station (soft sleeper lower/upper bunk Y499/478). Two different bureaus run the trains; the Shànghǎi and Běijīng. This may seem of little interest, but dinners are thrown in free on Shanghai Railway Bureau trains. Alternatively, fast (特快; tèkuài) train T110 departs Shànghǎi at 8.10pm, arriving in Běijīng at 9.43am the next morning. Fast train K104 departs Shànghǎi at 8.20pm, reaching Běijīng at 9.34am the following morning. Berths go quickly on this popular line so book at least a couple of days in advance.

Train K99 leaves for Hong Kong's Kowloon (Jiǔlóng) district every other day and takes 24 hours. Hard sleepers are Y559 to Y583, though they're more like the soft sleepers on standard Chinese trains. Soft sleepers cost Y910. You can get tickets at the Longmen Hotel ticket office.

Other trains departing from Shànghǎi are: Fúzhōu (Y249, 21 hours), Guǎngzhōu (Y379, 25 hours), Hángzhōu (Y33 hard seat, two hours), Huángshān (Y103, 11½ hours), Kūnmíng (Y519, 46 hours), Chéngdū (Y490, 40 hours), Nánjīng (hard/soft seat Y68/86, three hours), Xī'ān (Y333, 17 hours) and Ürümqi (Y675, 48 hours). All the above fares are hard sleeper unless otherwise noted.

Trains to Lhasa (Tibet) also leave from Shanghai train station; see p925 for details.

GETTING AROUND

Shànghǎi is not a walker's dream. There are some fascinating areas to stroll around, but new road developments, building sites and shocking traffic conditions conspire to make walking an exhausting and often stressful experience.

The buses, too, are hard work; they're not easy to figure out, are difficult to squeeze into and out of and it's hard to know where they are going to stop. The metro system, however, is a dream.

Shànghǎi taxis are reasonably cheap and easy to flag down. Despite the improvements in roadways, Shànghǎi's traffic is returning to gridlock. Whichever mode of transport you use try to avoid rush hours between 8am and 9am, and 4.30pm and 6pm.

To/From the Airport

Hongqiao Airport (Hóngqiáo Fēijīchǎng; Map pp242-3; ☎ 6268 8918) is 18km from the Bund; getting there takes about 30 minutes if you're lucky, or over an hour if you're not. You can take bus 925 from Renmin Sq to the airport. Bus 806 goes from Xújiāhuì and Bus 938 stops in front of the Huating Hotel (Map pp242-3) on West Zhongshan Rd. A CAAC bus (Y5) goes from the northeast corner of Central Yan'an Rd and North Shanxi Rd. All these buses leave the airport from directly in front of the domestic departure hall. Taxis from the centre of town cost from Y50 to Y70, depending on the route taken, traffic conditions and the time of day. Hongqiao Airport is famous for its astonishing taxi queues, and sometimes it takes around an hour to get in a taxi; if you've only been flying for an hour, that's a major bummer. There's a pricier short-stop taxi queue worth contemplating for nearby destinations.

Pudong International Airport (Pǔdōng Guójì Fēijīchǎng; ☎ 3848 4500) handles most international flights and some domestic flights. Always check your ticket to be sure which airport you're arriving at or departing from. **Airport bus 1** (☎ 3848 4500; Y30) runs between Hongqiao and Pudong airports, bus 2 (Y19) runs from Pudong International Airport to the Airport City Terminal (Jīchǎng Chéngshì Hángzhànlóu; Map pp248–9), near Jing'an Temple on West Nanjing Rd, and bus 5 (Y18) goes from Pudong International Airport to Pǔdōng and then the Shanghai train station. Buses run from 7am to 11pm. A taxi to Pudong International Airport from the city centre (one hour) costs around Y140.

The **Maglev train** (☎ 2890 7777; one way/return Y50/80) runs from Pudong airport to its terminal (Map pp242–3) in Pǔdōng in just eight minutes, from where you can transfer to the metro (Longyang Rd station). Trains run every 20 minutes from 8.30am to 5.30pm and hit warp speed at 430km/h; taxis heading in the same direction on the parallel highway look like they are driving backwards. If you have a same-day air ticket, you get 20% off the one-way ticket price.

Major hotels run an airport shuttle to both airports (generally free to Hóngqiáo; Y30 to Pǔdōng).

Bicycle

Captain Hostel (p261) is one of the few places in town offering bike hire (Y10 for four hours, then Y2 per hour).

Bus

Many routes now offer deluxe air-con vehicles (Y2). Some useful bus routes are listed here, though the metro lines may be more convenient. Once on board, keep your valuables tucked away since pickpocketing is easy under such conditions. A tourist bus (Y2) shuttles exhausted shoppers up and down the pedestrian zone of East Nanjing Rd.

11 Travels the Ring Rd around the old Chinese city.

19 Links the Bund area to the Jade Buddha Temple area. Catch it at the intersection of East Beijing Rd and Central Sichuan Rd.

20 Takes you to Renmin Sq from the Bund.

42 Goes from the Bund at Guangdong Rd, passes Renmin Rd close to the Yu Gardens, heads along Huaihai Rd, up Xiangyang Rd then on to Xújiāhuì, terminating at the Shanghai Stadium.

61 Starts from just north of the Broadway Mansions at the intersection of Wusong Rd and Tiantong Rd, and goes past

the PSB (Public Security Bureau) on its way along Siping Rd. Bus 55 from the Bund also goes by the PSB.

64 Gets you to Shanghai train station from near the Bund. Catch it on East Beijing Rd, close to the intersection with Central Sichuan Rd. The ride takes 20 to 30 minutes.

65 Runs from the northeast of Shanghai train station and goes near the long-distance bus station on Gongxing Rd. It passes the Broadway Mansions, crosses Garden Bridge, and then heads directly south along the Bund to the end of Zhongshan Rd.

71 Takes you to the CAAC airport bus stop on Central Yan'an Rd; catch it from East Yan'an Rd close to the Bund.

112 Zigzags north from the southern end of Renmin Sq to West Nanjing Rd, down Shimen No 2 Rd to West Beijing Rd then up Jiangning Rd to Jade Buddha Temple.

911 Leaves from Zhonghua Rd near the intersection with Central Fuxing Rd, close to the Yuyuan Bazaar, and goes up Huaihai Rd, continuing to the zoo and on to Qibao (p257).

Shanghai Sightseeing Buses (see opposite) mostly runs buses to sights outside Shànghǎi, as well as two city bus routes that link up some useful sights:

3 Travels via Renmin Sq to Pǔdōng's Pearl Tower (Y4) and Jinmao Tower (Y4) every 30 minutes from 7am to 5.30pm; pick it up from the stop just south of the Shanghai Museum on East Yan'an Rd.

10 Goes to Central Huaihai Rd, East Nanjing Rd, North Sichuan Rd and Lu Xun Park (Y3) every 15 minutes from 6.30am to 7.30pm.

Ferry

Ferry boats shuttle across the Huangpu every 15 minutes between the southern Bund and the Lùjiāzuǐ district in Pǔdōng (Y0.50, Y2 air-con).

Metro

The Shànghǎi metro system currently runs to five lines and is being ambitiously expanded. The No 1 Line and the No 2 Line are the principle lines that travellers will use; the No 1 Line runs from Xinzhuang station through Renmin Sq to Gong Fu Xin Cun. The No 2 Line runs from Zhongshan Park to Zhangjiang in Pǔdōng, but eventually it will extend to Hongqiao airport and all the way to Pudong airport. The light rail (also called the No 3 Line, or the Pearl Line) runs on the western perimeter of the city from Shanghai South train station to Jiangwan Zhen station in the north of town. The No 4 Line forms an inverted C shape looping from Damu Qiao Rd Station in Pǔxī (following a stretch of the No 3 Line and interconnecting with the No

---

I QUEUE

Unlike a mere 10 years ago, when the tills at McDonald's were besieged by battling scrums of diners, Shànghăi has slowly learned how to queue. Nonetheless, waiting in line still requires a constant alertness. Drop your guard for a second and your hard-won place in the train station ticket queue instantly falls to a granny flapping a handful of cash. Getting a metro ticket remains a free-for-all of lunges, pointy elbows and deft footwork. Ascending the metro is even more extraordinary. No matter how agile you are, how waiflike your physique, a fast-moving blur always slips in ahead of you to fill the seat you had your eyes on. In a bid to educate the public, metro signs exhort passengers to do the decent thing and wait for others to disembark carriages first. In case expats are partly to blame, the exhortation translates as 'After first under on, do riding with civility'. Don't say you weren't warned.

---

1 and No 2 Lines) to Lancun Road station in Pŭdōng. Eventually the No 4 Line will form an entire loop. The No 1 Line has been extended in an elevated section (the No 5 Line) south to the Minhang Development Zone.

Further lines either under construction or in the planning stages include extensions to the east and west of the No 2 Line, a further extension north of the No 3 Line to Jiangyang Rd station, construction of the No 6 Line that will connect north with south Pŭdōng, Line No 8 that will connect northeast and south Shànghăi, and Line No 9 that will eventually connect Sōngjiāng (right) with Chongming Island.

Tickets are between Y3 and Y7 depending on the distance. Stored value tickets are available for Y50 and Y100; they don't offer any savings, but can be used in taxis as well as buses.

Taxi

Flag price is Y11 (for the first 3km) and Y2.10 for each kilometre. From 11pm, there will be a 10% surcharge. Major taxi companies include the following.

Bashi (☎ 96840)
Dazhong (☎ 96822, 82222)
Qiansheng (☎ 6258 0000)

AROUND SHÀNGHĂI

Shànghăi municipality includes the satellite towns of Sōngjiāng, Jiādìng, Jīnshān and Băoshān. The sights listed in this section can be done as day trips.

The most popular day trips from Shànghăi are probably to Mùdú (p312), Tónglĭ (p310), Nánxún (p324) and Wūzhèn (p324), all outside the municipality.

The best way to get to most of the following sights is on one of the punctual and convenient **Shanghai Sightseeing Buses** (Shànghăi Lůyóu Jísàn Zhōngxīn; Map pp242-3; ☎ 6426 5555, Chinese only), based at the eastern end of Shanghai Stadium.

SŌNGJIĀNG 松江

Sōngjiāng County, 30km southwest of Shànghăi, was thriving when Shànghăi was still a dream in an opium trader's eye, though you only get a sense of its antiquity in the timeless backstreets in the west and southwest of town.

The most famous monument is the **Square Pagoda** (方塔; Fāng Tă; admission Y12), located in a park in the southeast of the town. The 48.5m nine-storey tower was built between 1068 and 1077; during reconstruction in 1975 a brick vault containing a bronze Buddha and other relics was discovered under foundations.

Next to the park is the mildly interesting **Songjiang Museum** (松江博物馆; Sōngjiāng Bówùguăn; admission Y8; ☯ 9-11am & 1-4pm Tue-Sun). Other attractions in town include the **Xilin Pagoda**, a 30-minute walk to the west of town, and the **Toroni Sutra Stela**, built in AD 859 and Shànghăi's oldest Buddhist structure. The **Songjiang Mosque** (松江清真寺; Sōngjiāng Qīngzhēnsì; admission Y5), in the west of town, is worth a visit. Built between 1341 and 1367 in the Chinese style, it's one of China's oldest mosques.

Getting There & Away

The best way to get to Sōngjiāng is on sightseeing bus 1A (Y10, 1½ hours), which runs every 30 minutes from Shanghai Stadium. If you don't fancy the walk between sights, cycle rickshaws ferry people around town for a few kuài.

SHANGHAI

SHĒSHĀN 佘山

The resort area of Shēshān, 30km southwest of Shànghǎi, is the only part of Shànghǎi to have anything that even remotely resembles a hill.

Perched magnificently on the top of the West Hill, the Catholic **Sheshan Cathedral** (佘山圣母大殿; Shēshān Shèngmǔ Dàdiàn; admission to hill with/without cable car Y40/30; 🕗 8am-4.30pm) is also called the Basilica of Notre Dame and was completed in 1935.

Next to the church is the **Jesuit observatory** (天文台; Tiānwéntái), built in 1900, with its modern counterpart standing to the west. On the east side of the hill is the 20m, seven-storey **Xiudaozhe Pagoda** (秀道者塔; Xiùdàozhě Tǎ), built between 976 and 984.

Visitors can also journey 8km southwest of Shēshān to Tiānmǎshān (天马山) and the **Huzhu Pagoda** (护珠塔; Hùzhū Tǎ), built in AD 1079 and known as the leaning tower of China. The 19m-high tower started tilting 200 years ago and now has an inclination exceeding the tower at Pisa by 1.5 degrees. There are no buses, so you will need to take a taxi there (Y10).

Getting There & Away

Sightseeing bus 1B (Y10, 1¼ hours) heads to Shēshān every 30 minutes from Shànghǎi, as do private minibuses (Y10). If you want to combine a visit to Shēshān with Sōngjiāng, head to Shēshān first as it's easier to catch a bus on to Sōngjiāng than vice versa. A taxi to/from Shànghǎi costs around Y70 one way.

JIĀDÌNG 嘉定

Jiādìng is a laid-back town surrounded by a canal, located about 20km northwest of

Shànghǎi. Together with Nánxiáng (南翔), the town makes for a pleasant day excursion, especially if you pack a picnic for one of the parks.

Sightseeing bus 6A drops passengers at the **Dragon Meeting Pond** (汇龙潭; Huìlóng Tán; admission Y5), a peaceful garden built in 1588 and named after the five streams that feed into the central pool.

Exit out of the west gate to get to the **Confucius Temple** (文庙; Wén Miào; admission Y10; 🕗 8am-4.30pm), built in 1219. On the way you'll pass 72 carved lions, representing the 72 outstanding disciples of Confucius. The temple houses the **Jiading County Museum**, which exhibits the history of the county as well as some local bamboo carving.

A five-minute walk north of the temple along Nan Dajie takes you to the seven-storey **Fahua Pagoda** (法花塔; Fǎhuā Tǎ) and the interesting cobbled and canalled heart of the town. There are several enticing shops and places to eat around the pagoda.

Five minutes' walk northeast along the canal on Dong Dajie takes you to the enchanting **Garden of Autumn Clouds** (秋霞圃; Qiūxiápǔ; admission Y10), one of the finest gardens around Shànghǎi.

On the way back to Shànghǎi, sightseeing bus 6A passes through the town of Nánxiáng, where (if you are not gardened out) you can stop off at the large **Garden of Ancient Splendour** (古猗园; Gǔyī Yuán), which was built between 1522 and 1566, and then rebuilt in 1746.

Getting There & Away

Sightseeing bus 6A runs to Jiādìng (Y10, one hour) every 20 minutes from Shanghai Stadium via Nánxiáng (Y6, 30 minutes).

Jiāngsū 江苏

Well-to-do Jiāngsū is the envy of its neighbours because of its lush, wet landscape and fertile topography. Because of its abundant agriculture, it's been dubbed the 'land of fish and rice' since ancient times. Situated on the east coast bordering the East China Sea, it's one of China's most densely populated provinces and also one of the most prosperous.

Jiāngsū owes its wealth to the ancient waterways of the Yangzi River and the Grand Canal, which served as the main systems of transport in early times. Jiāngsū made much of its fortune through silk and salt, which was panned off its low-lying marshy coast.

The Grand Canal slices its way from northern Jiāngsū into the lower reaches of the flourishing Yangzi River Delta. The canal, once navigable all the way from Hángzhōu in Zhèjiāng province to Běijīng, has largely silted up but still remains alive in southern Jiāngsū. Some of the province's most historical cities sit by the canal, including the vibrant commercial centres of Sūzhōu and Yángzhōu. The Yangzi River flows through the south of Jiāngsū, serving as an important trading route between the provincial capital of Nánjīng and Shànghǎi.

If you're interested in Chinese history, Jiāngsū has plenty to offer. Cosmopolitan Nánjīng has served as China's capital and has some fascinating museums and historical attractions to explore. Sūzhōu and Yángzhōu are famed for their elegant gardens and fine silk, while the ancient river town of Wúxī serves as a base for scenic Lake Tai. The well-preserved canal towns of Tónglǐ and Mùdú offer close-up views of a China fast disappearing.

HIGHLIGHTS

- Join in an operatic sing-a-long at the fascinating **Kunqu Opera Museum** (p306) in Sūzhōu
- Pay your respects to the 'father of modern China' at the impressive **Sun Yatsen Mausoleum** (p283) in Nánjīng
- Experience the magic of stone and water by taking a ferry ride on beautiful **Lake Tai** (p301)
- Discover the enchanting plants, bamboo and rockery of Sūzhōu's classical **gardens** (p303)
- Liberate your libido at the **Chinese Sex Culture Museum** (p311) in the charming canal town of Tónglǐ

- POPULATION: 74 MILLION
- www.seu.edu.cn/EC/english/js.htm

History

Jiāngsū was a relative backwater until the Song dynasty (960–1279), when it emerged as an important commercial centre because of trading routes opened up by the Grand Canal (see p282). The province particularly flourished in the south, where the towns of Sūzhōu and Yángzhōu played an important role in silk production and began to develop a large mercantile class. While southern Jiāngsū became synonymous for wealth and luxury, the northern parts of Jiāngsū remained undeveloped and destitute.

Prosperity continued through the Ming and Qing dynasties and with the incursion of Westerners into China in the 1840s, southern Jiāngsū opened up to Western influence.

During the Taiping Rebellion (1851–64), the Taipings established Nánjīng as their capital, calling it Tiānjīng or 'Heavenly Capital'.

Jiāngsū was also to play a strong political role in the 20th century, when Nánjīng was established as the capital by the Nationalist Party until taken over by the communists in 1949, who moved the capital to Běijīng.

Today, because of its proximity to Shànghǎi, southern Jiāngsū benefits from a fast-growing economy and rapid development, although northern Jiāngsū still lags behind.

Climate

Jiāngsū is hot and humid in summer (May to August), yet has temperatures requiring coats in winter (from December to February, when

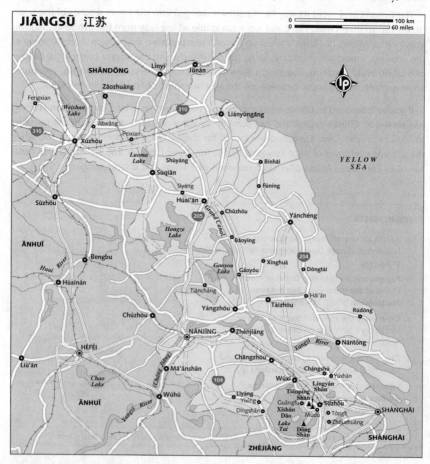

visibility can drop to zero because of fog). Rain or drizzle can be prevalent in winter, adding a misty touch to the land. The natural colours can be brilliant in spring (March and April). Heavy rains fall in spring and summer; autumn (September to November) is the driest time of year, and the best time to visit.

Language

The Wu dialect (Wú yǔ) is the primary language spoken in Jiāngsū and variations of it are heard throughout the province. Mandarin is also spoken, particularly in the northern regions closest to Shāndōng province.

Getting There & Away

Jiāngsū is well connected to all major cities in China. There are numerous flights daily from Nánjīng to points around the country, as well as frequent bus and train connections. In addition, there are ferries between Sūzhōu and Hángzhōu and from Nánjīng to Chóngqìng and Wǔhàn.

Getting Around

Jiāngsū has a comprehensive bus system that allows travellers to get to most destinations within the province without difficulty. Taking the train is also an option and booking tickets has become quite easy as most hotels now operate their own travel agencies.

NÁNJĪNG 南京

☎ 025 / pop 5.29 million

Nánjīng, Jiāngsū's capital, lies in the southwest on the lower stretches of the Yangzi River. It's one of China's more pleasant and prosperous cities, with wide leafy boulevards, chic apartment blocks and mile-high office towers, set among a beautiful landscape of lakes, forested parks and rivers.

The city sports a long historical heritage and has twice served briefly as the nation's capital, first in the early years of the Ming dynasty (1368–1644) and second as the capital of the Republic of China in the early years of the 20th century. Most of Nánjīng's major attractions are reminders of the city's former glory under the Ming.

Today's Nánjīng is a cosmopolitan mix of old and new, where crumbling ruins stand side by side with shopping mega-plazas. Home to several excellent universities and a large foreign student population, the city boasts many international restaurants and a lively nightlife.

History

The Nánjīng area has been inhabited for about 5000 years, and a number of prehistoric sites have been discovered in or around the city. Recorded history, however, begins in the Warring States period (453–221 BC), when Nánjīng emerged as a strategic object of conflict. The arrival of a victorious Qin dynasty (221–207 BC) put an end to this, allowing Nánjīng to prosper as a major administrative centre.

The city's fortunes took a turn for the worse in the 6th century when it was successively rocked by floods, fires, peasant rebellions and military conquest. With the advent of the Sui dynasty (AD 589–618) and the establishment of Xī'ān as imperial capital, Nánjīng was razed and its historical heritage reduced to ruins. Although it enjoyed a period of prosperity under the long-lived Tang dynasty, it gradually slipped into obscurity.

In 1356, a peasant rebellion led by Zhu Yuanzhang against the Mongol Yuan dynasty was successful. The peasants captured Nánjīng and 12 years later claimed the Yuan capital, Běijīng. Zhu Yuanzhang took the name of Hongwu and became the first emperor of the Ming dynasty, with Nánjīng as his capital. A massive palace was built and walls were erected around the city.

Nánjīng's glory as imperial capital was short-lived. In 1420, the third Ming emperor, Yongle, moved the capital back to Běijīng. From then on, Nánjīng's fortunes variously rose and declined as a regional centre, but it wasn't until the 19th and 20th centuries that the city again entered the centre stage of Chinese history.

In the 19th century, the Opium Wars brought the British to Nánjīng and it was here that the first of the 'unequal treaties' were signed, opening several Chinese ports to foreign trade, forcing China to pay a huge war indemnity, and officially ceding the island of Hong Kong to Britain. Just a few years later, Nánjīng became the Taiping capital during the Taiping Rebellion, which succeeded in taking over most of southern China.

In 1864 the combined forces of the Qing army, British army and various European and US mercenaries surrounded the city. They laid siege for seven months, before finally capturing it and slaughtering the Taiping defenders.

JIĀNGSŪ

THE GRAND CANAL 大运河 DÀYÙNHÉ

The world's longest canal, the Grand Canal, once meandered for almost 1800km from Běijīng to Hángzhōu, and is a striking example of China's engineering prowess. Sections of the canal have been silted up for centuries and today perhaps half of it remains seasonally navigable. The government claims that, since liberation, large-scale dredging has increased the navigable length to 1100km. However, with depths of up to 3m, banks that can narrow to less than 9m and with some old stone bridges spanning the route, canal use is restricted to fairly small, flat-bottomed vessels in some places.

The Grand Canal's construction spanned many centuries. The first 85km were completed in 495 BC, but the mammoth task of linking the Yellow River (Huáng Hé) and the Yangzi River (Cháng Jiāng) was undertaken between AD 605 and 609 by a massive conscripted labour force during Sui times. It was developed again during the Yuan dynasty (1271–1368). The canal enabled the government to capitalise on the growing wealth of the Yellow River basin and to ship supplies from south to north.

The canal comes into its own south of the Yellow River, where promoting tourism has ensured year-round navigation. The Jiāngnán section of the canal (Hángzhōu, Sūzhōu, Wúxī and Chángzhōu) is a skein of canals, rivers and branching lakes.

During the 20th century, Nánjīng was the capital of the Republic of China, the site of the worst war atrocity in Japan's assault on China (p287), and the Kuomintang capital from the period of 1928 to 1937 and, again between 1945 and 1949, before the communists 'liberated' the city and made China their own.

Orientation

Nánjīng lies entirely on the southern bank of the Yangzi, bounded in the east by Zijin Mountain. The centre of town is a roundabout called Xinjiekou, a popular shopping district. Nánjīng train station and the main long-distance bus station are in the far north of the city.

The historical sights, including the Sun Yat-sen Mausoleum, Linggu Temple and the Ming Xiaoling Tomb are on Zijin Mountain.

MAPS

Popular Bookmall (Dacun Shuju; Xinjiekou; ☼ 9am-9pm) has English and Chinese maps in its travel section on the 3rd floor. You'll also find versions of local maps at newspaper kiosks and street hawkers around Nánjīng. Some of the upscale hotels give out free English-language maps of the city.

Information

INTERNET ACCESS 网吧

Internet and Coffee Club (Yìjiān Wǎngluò Kāfēiwū; cnr of Shanghai Lu & Huaqiao Lu; ☼ 24hrs) Has internet access for Y2 per hour.

INTERNET RESOURCES

www.mapmagazine.com.cn For current events in Nánjīng.

MEDICAL SERVICES

Jiangsu Provincial Hospital (Jiāngsū Shěng Rénmín Yīyuàn; ☎ 8503 8022; 300 Guangzhou Lu; ☼ 8am-noon, 2-5.30pm) Runs a clinic for expatriates and has English-speaking doctors available.

Nanjing International SOS Clinic (☎ 8480 2842, 24hr alarm centre ☎ 010-6462 9100) On the ground floor of the Grand Metropark Hotel. Staff on duty speak English.

MONEY

Bank of China (Zhōngguó Yínháng; 29 Hongwu Lu; ☼ 8am-5pm Mon-Fri, 8am-12.30pm Sat) Changes major currency and travellers cheques. There's a 24-hour ATM which takes international cards.

POST

Post Office (Yóujú; 2 Zhongshan Lu; ☼ 8am-6.30pm) Postal services and international phone calls.

PUBLIC SECURITY BUREAU

PSB (Gōngānjú) On a small lane called Sanyuan Xiang down a nest of streets west off Zhongshan Nanlu.

TOURIST INFORMATION & TRAVEL AGENCIES

Most hotels have their own travel agencies and can book tickets for a small service charge. They can also arrange tours around town and to neighbouring sights. There are many inexpensive travel agencies along Zhongshan Lu and around the universities.

China International Travel Service (CITS; Zhōngguó Guójì Lǚxíngshè; ☎ 8342 1125; 202 Zhongshan Beilu; 🕒 9am-4pm) Very busy office across from the Nanjing Hotel that arranges tours, and books air and train tickets.

Sights

ZIJIN MOUNTAIN 紫金山

Dominating the eastern fringes of Nánjīng is **Zijin Mountain** (Zǐjīn Shān), or 'Purple-Gold Mountain', a heavily forested area of parks and the site of most of Nánjīng's historical attractions. It's also one of the coolest places to escape from the steamy summers. A half-hour ride on a **cable car** (one-way/return Y15/25) carries you to the top of the 448m hill for a panoramic, if somewhat hazy, view of Nánjīng, or you can walk up the stone path that runs beneath the cable cars. Near the top of the hill is an **observatory** (adult/child Y15/10; 🕒 8.30am-6pm), with a remarkable collection of bronze Ming and Qing astronomical instruments once used by Jesuit missionaries.

Buses 9 or Y1 go from the city centre to the Sun Yatsen Mausoleum at the centre of the mountain. From here, bus 20 runs between all the sites on the mountain from 8am to 5pm, costing Y2 per ride.

SUN YATSEN MAUSOLEUM 中山陵

Smack dab in the middle of the mountain is the **Sun Yatsen Mausoleum** (Zhōngshān Líng; admission Y40; 🕒 7am-6pm). Dr Sun is recognised by the communists and Kuomintang alike as the father of modern China. He died in Běijīng in 1925, leaving behind an unstable Chinese republic. He had wished to be buried in Nánjīng, no doubt with greater simplicity than the Ming-style tomb his successors built for him. Nevertheless, less than a year after his death, construction of this mausoleum began.

The tomb itself lies at the top of an enormous stone stairway – a breathless 392 steps. At the start of the path stands a dignified stone gateway built of Fujian marble, with a roof of blue-glazed tiles. The blue and white of the mausoleum symbolise the white sun on the blue background of the Kuomintang flag.

The crypt is at the top of the steps at the rear of the memorial chamber. A tablet hanging across the threshold is inscribed with the 'Three Principles of the People', as formulated by Dr Sun: nationalism, democracy and people's livelihood. Inside is a statue of Dr Sun seated. The walls are carved with the complete text of the Outline of Principles for the Establishment of the Nation put forward by the Nationalist government. A prostrate marble statue of Dr Sun seals his coffin.

MING XIAOLING TOMB 明孝陵

On the southern slope of Zijin Mountain is the 14th-century **tomb** (Míng Xiàolíng; admission Y60; 🕒 8am-5.30pm) of Emperor Zhu Yuanzhang, the only Ming emperor to be buried outside of Běijīng.

The tomb received the name *xiàolíng* or 'filial tomb' after the death of his wife Empress Ma, also buried here, whose nickname was 'the filial empress'.

The first section of the avenue leading up to the mausoleum takes you along the 'spirit path', lined with stone statues of lions, camels, elephants and horses. There's also a mythical animal called a *xiè zhì* – which has a mane and a single horn on its head – and a *qílín*, which has a scaly body, a cow's tail, deer's hooves and one horn. These stone animals drive away evil spirits and guard the tomb.

As you enter the first courtyard, a paved pathway leads to a pavilion housing several stelae. The next gate leads to a large courtyard with the **Linghun Pagoda** (Línghún Tǎ), a mammoth rectangular stone structure. Behind the tower is a wall, 350m in diameter, surrounding a huge earth mound. Beneath this mound is the tomb vault of Hongwu, which has not been excavated.

The area surrounding the tomb is the **Ming Xiaoling Scenic Area** (Míng Xiàolíng Fēngjǐngqū). A tree-lined, stone pathway winds around pavilions and picnic grounds and ends at scenic **Zixia Lake** (Zǐxiá Hú).

LINGGU TEMPLE 灵谷寺

This large Ming **temple complex** (Línggǔ Sì; admission Y15; 🕒 8am-5.30pm) has one of the most interesting buildings in Nánjīng – the **Beamless Hall** (Wúliáng Diàn), built in 1381 entirely out of brick and stone and containing no beam supports. Buildings during the Ming dynasty were normally constructed of wood, but timber shortages meant that builders had to rely on brick. The structure has an interesting vaulted ceiling and a large stone platform where Buddhist statues once sat. In the 1930s the hall was turned into a memorial to those who died resisting the Japanese. One of the inscriptions on the inside wall is the old Kuomintang national anthem.

JIĀNGSŪ

NÁNJĪNG 南京

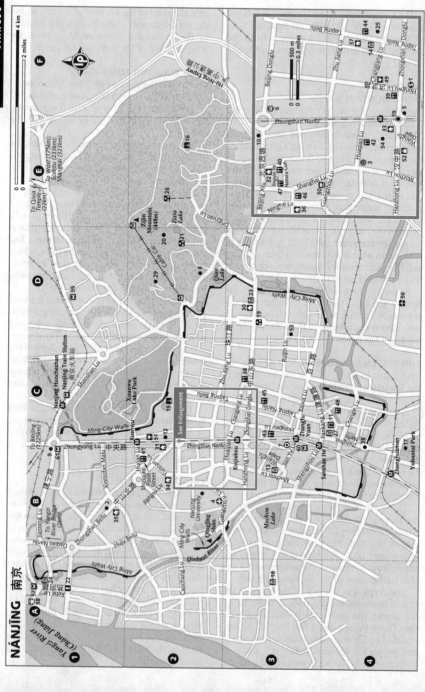

A road runs on both sides of the hall and up two flights of steps to the graceful **Pine Wind Pavilion** (Sōngfēng Gé), originally dedicated to Guanyin as part of Linggu Temple.

The temple itself and a memorial hall to Xuan Zang (the Buddhist monk who travelled to India and brought back the Buddhist scriptures) are close by; after you pass through the Beamless Hall, turn right and then follow the pathway.

Inside the memorial hall is a model of a 13-storey wooden pagoda that contains part of Xuan Zang's skull, a sacrificial table and a portrait of the monk.

Nearby is the colourful **Linggu Pagoda** (Línggǔ Tǎ). This nine-storey, 60m-high, octagonal pagoda was built in 1929 under the direction of a US architect to remember those who died during the revolution.

BOTANIC GARDENS 植物园
This well-manicured labyrinth of **gardens** (Zhíwù Yuán; admission Y15; 8.30am-4.30pm) was established in 1929. Covering over 186 hectares, more than 3000 plant species including roses, medicinal plants and bonsai gardens are on display.

TAIPING HEAVENLY KINGDOM HISTORY MUSEUM 太平天国历史博物馆
Hong Xiuquan, the leader of the Taipings, had a palace built in Nánjīng, but the building was completely destroyed when Nánjīng was taken in 1864.

The **museum** (Tàipíng Tiānguó Lìshǐ Bówùguǎn; 128 Zhanyuan Lu; admission Y10; 8am-6pm) was originally a garden complex, built in the Ming dynasty, which housed some of the Taiping officials before their downfall. There are displays of maps showing the progress of the Taiping army from Guǎngdōng, Hong Xiuquan's seals, Taiping coins, weapons and texts that describe the Taiping laws on agrarian reform, social law and cultural policy. Other texts describe divisions in the Taiping leadership, the attacks by Manchus and foreigners, and the fall of Nánjīng in 1864. Most of the original literature is in Běijīng. The museum will delight Chinese history buffs. Bus Y2 goes to the museum from the Ming Palace Ruins or Taiping Nanlu.

JIĀNGSŪ

NÁNJĪNG MUSEUM 南京博物馆

Just inside the eastern city walls, the giant Nánjīng **museum** (Nánjīng Bówùguǎn; 321 Zhongshan Donglu; admission Y20; ☻9am-5.30pm) houses an array of artefacts from Neolithic times right through to the communist period. The main building was constructed in 1933 in the style of a Ming temple with yellow-glazed tiles, red-lacquered gates and columns.

The museum houses an interesting burial suit made of small rectangles of jade sewn together with silver thread, dating from the Eastern Han dynasty (AD 25–220) and excavated from a tomb discovered in the city of Xúzhōu in northern Jiāngsū. Other exhibits include bricks with the inscriptions of their makers and overseers from the Ming city wall, drawings of old Nánjīng, an early Qing mural of Sūzhōu and relics from the Taiping Rebellion. Everything is labelled in English and well-organised.

NÁNJĪNG TREATY HISTORY MUSEUM 南京条约史料陈列馆

This **museum** (Nánjīng Tiáoyuē Shǐliào Chénlièguǎn; 116 Chao Yue Lou; admission Y6; ☻8.30am-5pm) houses a small collection of photographs, maps and newspaper clippings (no English captions) related to the Nánjīng Treaties. It's all rather yawn-worthy and probably only of interest to those keen on Chinese history. The museum is in **Jinghai Temple** (Jìnghǎi Sì) near the west train station, off Rehe Lu. To get there catch bus 16 from Zhongshan Lu.

MEMORIAL HALL OF THE NÁNJĪNG MASSACRE 南京大屠杀纪念馆

The unsettling exhibits at this **memorial hall** (Nánjīng Dàtúshā Jìniànguǎn; ☎661 2230; 418 Shuiximen Dajie; admission free; ☻8.30am-4.30pm) document the atrocities committed by Japanese soldiers against the civilian population during the occupation of Nánjīng in 1937 (opposite). They include pictures of actual executions – many taken by Japanese army photographers – and a gruesome viewing hall built over a mass grave of massacre victims. Captions are in English, Japanese and Chinese but the photographs, skeletons and displays tell their own haunting stories without words.

The exhibits conclude on a more optimistic note, with a final room dedicated to the post-1945 Sino-Japanese reconciliation. It's in the city's southwestern suburbs; take bus Y4 from Zhonghua Gate or the west train station.

JIĀNGSŪ ART GALLERY 江苏美术馆

This **gallery** (Jiāngsū Měishùguǎn; ☎8664 1962; 266 Changjiang Lu; admission Y10; ☻8-11.30am & 2-5pm) puts on frequently changing exhibits of watercolour and ink paintings by local artists. The artwork is quite interesting but the gallery is very sterile and uninspiring.

MONUMENT TO THE CROSSING OF THE YANGZI RIVER 渡江纪念碑

In the northwest of the city on Zhongshan Beilu, this **monument** (Dùjiāng Jìniànbēi; admission Y20; erected in April 1979, commemorates the crossing of the river on 23 April 1949 and the capture of Nánjīng from the Kuomintang by the communist army. The characters on the monument are in the calligraphy of Deng Xiaoping. To get there catch bus 31 from Taiping Lu.

YANGZI RIVER BRIDGE 南京长江大桥

One of the great achievements of the communists, and one of which they are justifiably proud, is the **Yangzi River Bridge** (Nánjīng Cháng Jiāng Dàqiáo) at Nánjīng. Opened on 23 December 1968, it's one of the longest bridges in China – a double-decker with a 4500m-long road on top and a train line below. There are some wonderful socialist realist sculptures on the approaches.

Apparently the bridge was designed and built entirely by the Chinese after the Russians marched out and took the designs with them in 1960. Given the immensity of the construction it's an impressive engineering feat, before which there was no direct rail link between Běijīng and Shànghǎi. Probably the easiest way to get up on the bridge is to go through the **Bridge Park** (Dàqiáo Gōngyuán; ☎582 2455; adult/child Y12/10; ☻7.30am-6.30pm). Catch bus 67 from Jiangsu Lu, northwest of the Drum Tower, to its terminus opposite the park.

HEAVEN DYNASTY PALACE 朝天宫

This **palace** (Cháotiān Gōng; admission Y30; ☻8am-5pm), off Mochou Lu, was originally established in the Ming dynasty as a school for educating aristocratic children in court etiquette. Most of today's buildings, including the centrepiece of the palace, a Confucian temple, date from 1866 when the whole complex was rebuilt. Today the buildings are used for a range of endeavours, including an artisans' market.

To get here, take bus 4 from the Xinjiekou roundabout; get off two stops to the west.

MING CITY WALLS

Nánjīng enjoyed its golden years under the Ming dynasty and there are numerous remnants of the period. One of the most impressive is the impressive, five-storey Ming city wall, measuring over 33km – the longest city wall ever built in the world. About two-thirds of it still stands. It was built between 1366 and 1386, by more than 200,000 labourers.

The layout of the wall is irregular, an exception to the usual square format of these times; it zigzags around Nánjīng's hills and rivers, accommodating the local landscape. Averaging 12m high and 7m wide at the top, the wall was built of bricks supplied from five Chinese provinces. Each brick had stamped on it the place it came from, the overseer's name and rank, the brick-maker's name and sometimes the date. This was to ensure that the bricks were well made; if they broke they had to be replaced.

MING CITY GATES

Some of the original 13 Ming city gates remain, including the **Centre Gate** (Zhōngyáng Mén) in the north and **Zhonghua Gate** (Zhōnghuá Mén; admission Y8) in the south. The city gates were heavily fortified; Zhonghua Gate has four rows of gates, making it almost impregnable, and could house a garrison of 3000 soldiers in vaults in the front gate building. Today some of these vaults are used as souvenir shops.

MING PALACE RUINS 明故宫

Built by Hongwu, the **Ming Palace Ruins** (Míng Gùgōng; Zhongshan Donglu; admission free; ☺ 6.30am-11pm) is said to have been a magnificent structure after which the Imperial Palace in Běijīng was modelled. Virtually all that remains of it are five marble bridges lying side by side, known as the **Five Dragon Bridges** (Wǔlóng Qiáo), the old ruined **Wu Gate** (Wú Mén) and the enormous column bases of the palace buildings.

The palace suffered two major fires in its first century and was allowed to fall into ruins after the Ming court moved to Běijīng. It was later looted by the Manchus and bombardments by Qing and Western troops finished it off during the Taiping Rebellion.

THE RAPE OF NÁNJĪNG

In 1937, with the Chinese army comparatively weak and underfunded and the Japanese army on the horizon, the invasion into and occupation of Nánjīng by Japan appeared imminent. As it packed up and fled, the Chinese government encouraged the people of Nánjīng to stay, saying: 'All those who have blood and breath in them must feel that they wish to be broken as jade rather than remain whole as tile.' To reinforce this statement, the gates to the city were locked, trapping over half a million citizens inside. Nevertheless, thousands of civilians attempted to follow the retreating government by escaping through Xiaguan Gate, the only gate in the city wall that remained unlocked. Leading up to the gate was a 21m tunnel inside of which reigned panic and mayhem. In the resulting chaos and collisions, thousands of people were suffocated, burned or trampled to death.

What followed in Nánjīng was six weeks of continuous, unfathomable victimisation of civilians to an extent that had yet to be witnessed in modern warfare. During Japan's occupation of Nánjīng, between 300,000 and 400,000 Chinese civilians were killed, either in group massacres or individual murders. Within the first month, at least 20,000 women between the ages of 11 and 76 were brutally raped. Women who attempted to refuse or children who interfered were often bayoneted or shot. It has been reported by those involved that the atrocities committed in Nánjīng were condoned and encouraged by the Japanese officers in command as acceptable and expected military procedure.

The Japanese, however, underestimated the courage and strength of the Chinese people. Instead of breaking the people's will, the invasion only served to fuel a sense of identity and determination. Those who did not die – broken as jade – survived to fight back.

It is hoped that a growing awareness of this horrific event will help to prevent such atrocities from occurring again. As the ancient Chinese proverb says, 'Past experience, if not forgotten, is a guide for the future' (Qián shì bù wàng hòu shì zhī shí).

An excellent book on the subject is the highly acclaimed The Rape of Nanjing by Iris Chang, which details the atrocities suffered by Chinese civilians under the occupation of the Japanese.

You can reach the Ming Palace Ruins by catching bus Y1 from the Nánjīng train station or Zhongyang Lu.

JIMING TEMPLE 鸡鸣寺

Close to the Ming walls and Xuanwu Lake (Xuánwǔ Hú) is the Buddhist **Jiming Temple** (Jīmíng Sì; admission Y5; ☺ 7am-5pm), which was first built in AD 527, during the Three Kingdoms period. It's been rebuilt many times since but has retained the same name (which literally translates as 'rooster crowing') since 1387. This temple is the most active temple in Nánjīng and is packed with worshippers during the Lunar New Year. The area around the temple is quite pretty and worth a look.

FUZI TEMPLE 夫子庙

This ancient Confucian **temple** (Fūzǐ Miào; Gongyuan Jie; admission Y25; ☺ 8am-9pm), in the south of the city in a pedestrian zone, was a centre of Confucian study for more than 1500 years. Fuzi Temple has been damaged and rebuilt repeatedly; what you see here today are newly restored, late-Qing dynasty structures or wholly new buildings reconstructed in traditional style. The main temple is behind the small square in front of the canal.

Across from the temple complex to the east is the **Imperial Examinations History Museum** (Jiāngnán Gòngyuàn Lìshǐ Chénlièguǎn; 1 Jinling Lu; admission Y10; ☺ 8am-6pm). This is a recent reconstruction of the building where scholars once spent months – or years – in tiny cells studying Confucian classics in preparation for civil service examinations.

Today, the area surrounding Fuzi Temple has become Nánjīng's main amusement quarter and is a particularly lively and crowded place on weekends and public holidays, with restaurants and rows upon rows of souvenir shops. The whole area is lit up at night, adding to the kitsch ambience.

Catch bus 1 from Xinjiekou and get off at the last stop.

PRESIDENTIAL PALACE 总统府

After the Taipings took over Nánjīng, they built the Mansion of the Heavenly King (Tiānwáng Fǔ) on the foundations of a former Ming dynasty palace. This magnificent place did not survive the fall of the Taiping but there is a reconstruction and a classical Ming garden, now known as the **Presidential Palace** (Zǒngtǒng Fǔ; 292 Changjiang Lu; admission Y40; ☺ 8am-

5.30pm). Other buildings on the site were used briefly as presidential offices by Sun Yatsen's government in 1912 and by the Kuomintang from 1927 to 1949.

MARTYRS' CEMETERY 烈士墓地

This **cemetery** (Lièshì Mùdì; Yuhuatai Lu; admission Y10; ☺ 7am-10pm) is in the south of the city. Once the Kuomintang's execution grounds, the communists turned it into a garden dedicated to revolutionaries who had lost their lives here. Along with a large monument, there's an English-captioned **museum** (☺ 8am-5.30pm) with a history of the period before 1949 and biographies of revolutionaries.

EARLY REMAINS

Nánjīng has been inhabited since prehistoric times. Remains of a prehistoric culture have been found at the site of the Drum Tower and in surrounding areas. About 200 sites of small clan communities, mainly represented by pottery and bronze artefacts dating back to the late Shang and Zhou dynasties, were found on both sides of the Yangzi.

In AD 212, towards the end of the Eastern Han period, the military commander in charge of the Nánjīng region built a citadel on Qīngjīng Shān (Qingjing Mountain) in the west of Nánjīng. At that time the mountain was referred to as Stone Mountain (Shítou Shān) and so the citadel became known as the Stone City (Shítou Dūshì). The wall measured over 10km in circumference. Today, some of the red sandstone foundations are still visible.

To get here, take bus 75, 21, 91 or 132.

DRUM TOWER 鼓楼

Built in 1382, the **Drum Tower** (Gǔ Lóu; ☎ 442 1495; 6 Zhongyang Lu; admission free; ☺ 8am-midnight) lies roughly in the centre of Nánjīng, on a grassy roundabout. Drums were usually beaten to give directions for the change of the night watches and, in rare instances, to warn the populace of impending danger. Only one large drum remains today.

GREAT BELL PAVILION 大钟亭

East of the Drum Tower, the **Great Bell Pavilion** (Dà Zhōng Tíng; Beijing Donglu; admission free; ☺ 8.30am-5.30pm) houses an enormous bell, cast in 1388 and originally situated in a pavilion on the western side of the Drum Tower. The present tower dates from 1889 and is a small two-storey pavilion with a pointed roof and upturned eaves. A garden and teahouse surround the tower and remain open late into the evening.

Tours

Local tours can be arranged through hotels, the CITS or any of the inexpensive travel agencies on Zhongshan Donglu.

Festivals & Events

The **Nánjīng International Plum Blossom Festival**, held every year from the last Saturday of February to 18 March, draws visitors from around China. The festival takes place on Zijin Mountain near the Ming Xiaoling Tomb when the mountain bursts with pink and white blossoms.

Sleeping

Most Nánjīng accommodation is midrange to top end in price. All rooms have broadband internet, and you can book air and train tickets.

BUDGET

Nanjing Fuzimiao International Youth Hostel (www .Yhananjing.com; 38 Dashiba Jie) This very friendly hostel, located on the edges of Fuzi Temple, has plans to move to a new location in late 2006. It'll still be in Fuzimiao, in a renovated temple near the main entrance.

Nanjing Normal University Nanshan Hotel (Nánjīng Shīfàn Dàxué Nánshān Bīnguǎn; ☎ 8371 6440 ext 6060; 122 Ninghai Lu; 宁海路122号; s/d/tr Y100/198/240) Located on the parklike grounds of Nánjīng University, rooms in this guesthouse feature battle-scarred furniture and dingy carpet. The surrounds, on the other hand, are refreshingly green and quiet. Enter from the university's main gate, turn left and walk up the hill.

Jin's Inn (Jīn Yìcūn; www.jinsinn.com; ☎ 8472 2888; 26 Yunnan Lu; 云南路26号; s/d Y158/198) It's hard to miss this eye-popping orange-and-yellow hotel, standing like a beacon next to its utilitarian grey neighbours. Despite its glowing exterior, rooms are simple, cool and modern. There are four other locations around the city, including one at Fuzimiao.

MIDRANGE

Jingli Hotel (Jìnglì Jiǔdiàn; ☎ 8331 0818; fax 8663 6636; 7 Beijing Xilu; 北京西路7号; s/d Y420/545) This classy hotel on a pretty tree-lined street has upmarket rooms with modern, spotless bathrooms

and amiable service. It's a short walk from here to the Great Bell Pavilion or Nánjīng University.

Zijing Hotel (Zǐjīng Dàjiǔdiàn; ☎ 8444 5999; fax 8664 5129; 37 Taiping Beilu; 太平北路37号; s/d Y480/580) Just a stone's throw from the Presidential Palace and across from Nanjing 1912 (below), this hotel offers spacious rooms and soft beds. Somebody went cuckoo with the décor, though – some rooms have plush orange carpet and pink walls!

Jiangsu Hotel (Jiāngsū Dàjiǔdiàn; ☎ 8332 0888; fax 330 3308; 28 Zhongshan Beilu; 中山北路28号; s/d Y500/600) Not as nice as the Jingli, this hotel is still excellent value for the price, with easy-on-the eyes décor and a convenient location. To compete with the Ramada across the street, rates are slashed as much as 50% on weekdays.

TOP END

Nanjing Hotel (Nánjīng Fàndiàn; ☎ 8341 1888; 259 Zhongshan Beilu; 中山北路259号; s Y608-808, d Y398-808, tr Y838) Set on secluded grounds away from the street, this hotel, built in 1936, offers a selection of nicely furnished, comfortable rooms. The cheaper rooms are in a separate building and discounts of 30% make this place a steal.

Jinling Hotel (Jīnlíng Fàndiàn; ☎ 8471 1888; fax 8471 1666; www.jinlinghotel.com; Xinjiekou; 新街口; d Y1535-1660) In the middle of a busy shopping district, the Jinling has chic four-star rooms with a surfeit of amenities, including a sauna, several restaurants and a gym. Rooms are discounted 30% on weekdays.

Grand Metropark Hotel (Wéijīng Dàjiǔdiàn; ☎ 8480 8888; 319 Zhongshan Donglu; 中山东路319号; s/d US$180/200) This five-star establishment (formerly the Hilton) offers 40 storeys of luxury, including a golf course, bowling alley, swimming pool and state-of-the-art fitness centre. It's in an excellent location next to the Nánjīng Museum and close to Zijin Mountain.

Eating

The two main eating quarters in Nánjīng are at Fuzi Temple and Shiziqiao off Hunan Lu. Both are lively pedestrian areas that come alive at night, packed with people, snack stands and small restaurants. You'll also find a scattering of family-run restaurants in the small lanes around the university district.

Located on the corner of Taipei Beilu and Changjiang Lu, near the Presidential Palace, is a new development called Nanjing 1912, a compound of shiny new bars, clubs, coffee houses and upscale restaurants, most still being built as this book goes to press.

Gold and Silver (Jīnyín Cāntīng; 17-3 Jingyin Jie; mains Y8-25; 🕙 11am-10pm) This is one of many small restaurants around Nánjīng University that cook up inexpensive home-style Chinese dishes. There's an extensive English menu and the owner is very friendly. On the walls are hundreds of pictures of foreigners who've frequented the place over the years.

Great Nanjing Eatery (Nánjīng Dàpáidǎng; 🕿 8330 5777; 2 Shizi Qiao; mains Y10; 🕙 11am-2pm, 5pm-2am) This old-style teahouse is a popular place to try yummy local snacks such as duck-blood soup with rice-noodles (鸭血粉丝汤; *yāxiě fěnsī tāng*) or tofu 'brains' (豆腐脑; *dòufu nǎo*), salty custard-like tofu. There's no English sign so look for the two large stone lions out front.

Skyways Bakery & Deli (Yúnzhōng Shípǐndiàn; 🕿 8663 4834; 3-6 Hankou Xilu; sandwiches Y18; 🕙 9.30am-9.30pm) For fresh-baked bread, sandwiches and coffee, head to this small deli owned by the same people who manage Swede and Kraut. There's a useful bulletin board with notices posting what's happening around town

10,000 Buddhas Vegetarian Restaurant (Wànfózhāi Sùcàiguǎn; 🕿 8451 8531; Pilu Temple; mains Y25-50; 🕙 9am-6pm) Just east of the Presidential Palace on Meiyuan Lu, this temple has a restaurant that offers tasty mock-meat dishes in contemplative surroundings.

Sìchuān Jiǔjiā (171 Taiping Nanlu; 🕿 8460 8801; mains Y25-50; 🕙 11am-11pm) Despite the name, this is also a terrific place to sample local dishes. Here, Nánjīng pressed duck (盐水鸭; *yánshuǐ yā*) is slathered with roasted salt, steeped in clear brine, baked dry and then kept under cover for some time; the finished product should have a creamy-coloured skin and red, tender flesh. The Sìchuān-style dishes are also nice and spicy.

There's no English sign so look for the bright red building and the sign with dancing chilli peppers.

Wǎnqíng Lóu (Dashiba Jie; mains Y30-60; 🕙 9am-10pm) This restaurant is on the opposite side of the river from Fuzi Temple's main square. Here you can try delicious Nánjīng snacks and local specialities in a fun, carnival atmosphere.

If you want to forget all about Chinese food, head over to one of the cluster of restaurants around Nánjīng University catering to adventurous locals and foreign students.

Swede and Kraut (Yúnzhōngcān; 14 Nanxiu Cun; 🕿 8663 8798; meals Y30-80; 🕙 5.30-10pm Tue-Sun) For tasty pasta dishes, pizza and salads, you can't beat this popular university hangout. Portions are large and service is amicable. Booster seats are available for kids here.

Bella Napoli Italian Restaurant (Nàbōlì Yìdàlì Cāntīng; 🕿 8471 8397; 75 Zhongshan Donglu; mains from Y38; 🕙 11am-2pm & 5.30-10.30pm Mon-Fri, 11.30am-11pm Sat & Sun) This place claims to be the most authentic Italian restaurant in town, with a variety of delicious handmade pastas, pizzas and other entrees. Try its delicious ravioli with ricotta and spinach.

Henry's Home Cafe (Hēnglì Zhìjiā; 33 Huaqiao Lu; mains Y40-80; 🕙 11am-9pm) Henry's is a mainstay in Nánjīng, serving up good pasta, pizza, fajitas and steak dishes. Service is competent and it accommodates vegetarians. There's another branch just outside Shízi Qiáo.

Drinking
CAFÉS
The caffeine craze has Nánjīng buzzing and you'll find Western-style coffee shops on almost every city block. What some places call coffee is questionable; for the real stuff head to places around the university area.

Home Sweet Home (Ài Huī Jiā; 🕿 8330 1847; 77-1 Shanghai Lu; coffee from Y18, sandwiches & pastries from Y15; 🕙 10am-10pm) This modest café near the intersection of Guangzhou Lu and Shanghai Lu is a far cry from the ubiquitous coffee house chains sprouting up around the city. Choose from a wide range of coffees, pastries and sandwiches – the ice-mint coffee and brownies are a good afternoon pick-me-up.

BARS
Nánjīng's bar and club scene has exploded over the past few years, though it's still not as vibrant or imaginative as in Shànghǎi. Most clubs and bars are overwhelmingly generic, serving up overpriced drinks and playing the same synthetic music, with few exceptions.

JJ's Lounge Bar (JJ Jiǔbā; 🕿 8469 9557; 89 Zhongshan Nanlu; beer Y25; 🕙 10am-10pm) This is a laid-back haunt with comfy sofas and a wide choice of beer and wine on offer. The place appeals to a wide range of folks – from foreign students to businessmen to trendy urban youth.

Scarlet Bar (Luànshì Jiárén Jiǔbā; 🕿 8440 7656; 29 Gulou Chezhan Dongxiang; beer Y10; 🕙 10am-4am) This small place is on a lane off Zhongyang Lu and is popular with a younger, local crowd. The dancing starts around 10pm.

You'll also find a number of bars in the **Art and Culture Centre** (Nánjīng Wénhuà Yìshù Zhōngxīn; 101 Changjiang Lu) and at Nanjing 1912 near the Presidential Palace.

Entertainment

Jiangsu Kunju Theatre (江苏省昆剧院; Jiāngsū Shěng Kūnjùyuàn; 2 Chaotian Gong; tickets Y30) Excellent *kūnjù* or *kūnqǔ* opera performances are held here. This type of opera is a regional form of classical Chinese opera that developed in the Sūzhōu–Hángzhōu–Nánjīng triangle. It's similar to (but slower than) Beijing opera and is performed with colourful and elaborate costumes. The theatre is next to the eastern entrance of the Heaven Dynasty Palace. Take bus 4 from the Xinjiekou roundabout and get off two stops to the west.

Shopping

There's little you can't buy in Nánjīng – from designer clothing to trinket souvenirs. Hunan Lu has a late-night market and is lined with shops and stalls. It's good for clothes shopping during the day. The area surrounding Fuzi Temple is a pedestrian zone with souvenirs and antiques for sale. Around Hanzhong Lu and Zhongshan Lu you'll find a number of major department stores.

Golden Eagle International Shopping Centre (Jīnyíng Guójì Gòuwù Zhōngxīn; 89 Hanzhong Lu) A little more upmarket, this shopping centre near Xinjiekou is aimed at a younger crowd with more disposable income.

Getting There & Away

AIR

Nánjīng has regular air connections to all major Chinese cities.

The main office for the **Civil Aviation Administration of China** (CAAC; Zhōngguó Mínháng; ☎ 8449 9378; 50 Ruijin Lu) is near the terminus of bus route 37, but you can also buy tickets at most top-end hotels.

Dragonair (Gǎnglóng Hángkōng; ☎ 8471 0181; Room 751-53, World Trade Centre, 2 Hanzhong Lu) has daily flights to Hong Kong.

BOAT

Several ferries depart daily from Yangzi port downriver (eastward) to Shànghǎi (about 10 hours) and upriver (westward) to Wǔhàn (two days); a few boats also go to Chóngqìng

(five days). The passenger dock is in the northwest of the city at No 6 dock (Liù Hào Mǎtóu). Tickets can be booked at the dock in the terminal building. For full details on Yangzi cruises, see p811.

BUS

There are seven long-distance bus stations in Nánjīng and trying to figure out what buses take you where can make your head spin. Before heading out, have your hotel confirm the appropriate bus station. Zhōngyāng Mén is the largest long-distance bus station, located southwest of the wide-bridged intersection with Zhongyang Lu. Buses from here go to Shànghǎi (Y82 to Y88, four hours), Héféi (Y38 to Y54, 2½ hours), Huangshan City (Túnxī; Y76, four hours), Hángzhōu (Y100, four hours) and Sūzhōu (Y64 to Y67, 2½ hours).

Another useful station is the east bus station (qìchē dōngzhàn), where buses go to Zhènjiāng (Y15 to Y24, 1½ hours), Wúxī (Y18 to Y20; 1½ hours) and Yángzhōu (Y27, two hours).

From the train station, take bus 13 north to Zhōngyāng Mén bus station. Bus 2 from Xinjiekou goes to the east bus station.

TRAIN

Nánjīng is a major stop on the Běijīng–Shànghǎi train line, and the station is mayhem. There are several trains a day in both directions. Heading eastward from Nánjīng, the line to Shànghǎi connects with Zhènjiāng, Wúxī and Sūzhōu.

Four daily express trains run between Nánjīng and Shànghǎi (Y47, three hours). Other trains to Shànghǎi take four hours, stopping in Zhènjiāng (Y13, one hour) and Sūzhōu (Y41, 2½ hours). Some of the express trains also stop in Zhènjiāng and Sūzhōu.

There are trains to Hángzhōu (Y73, five hours) and a slow train to Guǎngzhōu (Y387, 32 hours) via Shànghǎi. There's a train from Shànghǎi to Huangshan City (Túnxī) in Ānhuī province that passes through Nánjīng (Y112, seven hours) and also a train to the port of Wúhú on the Yangzi River that continues on to Huangshan City (Túnxī; Y102, seven hours). You can buy train tickets at most hotels for a Y5 to Y10 service charge.

Getting Around

TO/FROM THE AIRPORT

Nánjīng's airport is approximately one hour south of the city. Airport shuttle buses

(Y25) run every half-hour between 6am and 7pm. Buses leave from the Zhongbei station (Zhōngběi kèyùnzhàn) on Zhongshan Nanlu. Most hotels have hourly shuttle buses to and from the airport. A taxi will cost around Y150.

LOCAL TRANSPORT
Nánjīng has a new and efficient metro system that cuts through the centre of the city. There's currently only one line, running from Màigāoqiáo in the north to the Olympic Sports Stadium in the southwest between 6.41am and 10pm. Tickets are Y2 to Y4.

Taxis cruise the streets of Nánjīng – most destinations in the city are Y8, but make sure the meter is switched on.

You can get to Xinjiekou, in the heart of town, by jumping on bus 13 from the train station or the Centre Gate. There are also tourist bus routes that visit many of the sites. Bus Y1 goes from the train and Zhōngyāng Mén bus station through the city to the Sun Yatsen Mausoleum. Bus Y2 starts in the south at the Martyrs' Cemetery, passes Fuzi Temple and terminates halfway up Zijin Mountain.

Many local maps contain bus routes. Normal buses cost Y1 and tourist buses cost Y2.

AROUND NÁNJĪNG
Qixia Temple 栖霞寺
This temple (Qīxiá Sì; admission Y10; ⏰ 7am-5.30pm) on Qixia Mountain, 22km northeast of Nánjīng, was founded by the Buddhist monk Ming Sengshao during the Southern Qi dynasty, and is still an active place of worship. It's long been one of China's most important monasteries, and even today is one of the largest Buddhist seminaries in the country. There are two main temple halls: the Maitreya Hall, with a statue of the Maitreya Buddha sitting cross-legged at the entrance; and, behind this, the Vairocana Hall, housing a 5m-tall statue of the Vairocana Buddha.

Behind the temple is the **Thousand Buddha Cliff** (Qiānfó Yá). Several small caves housing stone statues are carved into the hillside, the earliest of which dates from the Qi dynasty (AD 479–502), although there are others from succeeding dynasties through to the Ming. There is also a small stone pagoda, **Sheli Pagoda** (舍利; Shělì Tǎ), built in AD 601, and rebuilt during the late Tang period. The upper part has engraved sutras and carvings of Buddha;

around the base, each of the pagoda's eight sides depicts Sakyamuni.

You can reach this temple from Nánjīng by a public bus (marked Qīxiá Sì; Y3, one hour) that departs from opposite the train station.

ZHÈNJIĀNG 镇江
☎ 0511 / pop 2.65 million

Just an hour from Nánjīng, Zhènjiāng sits at the crossroads of the Grand Canal and Yangzi River and once served as an important trade centre for silk and, yes, pickles and vinegar. After the Opium Wars, the British and French set up concessions in the northern part of town; the former British consulate is now a museum for visitors. The American writer Pearl S Buck (1892–1973), author of the *Good Earth*, grew up in Zhènjiāng and her former home is now part of a factory complex. Nowadays, apart from a Buddhist temple and several attractive parks, there's little to see and many of the old, interesting parts of the city have been flattened by recent construction.

Orientation & Information
The oldest part of Zhènjiāng is around Daxi Lu, which still has a few old-style lanes to explore with traditional architecture, especially beyond the western end of the street. A new promenade along the shores of the Yangzi is also a pleasant place for a stroll.

Bank of China (Zhōngguó Yínháng; ⏰ 9am-5.30pm) On Zhongshan Lu, just east of the intersection with Jiefang Lu, it has an ATM that takes international cards. There's another branch near the bus station by the train station.

Internet café (per hr Y4) Beside the Shàngyè Dàshà department store on Zhongshan Donglu, near the intersection of Jiefang Lu.

Post and Telephone Office (Zhōngguó Diànxìn) On Dianli Lu, on the corner of Xinma Lu.

Public Security Bureau (PSB; Gōngānjú; 24 Shizheng Lu) Can help in case of emergencies. For visa extensions, it's best to go to Nánjīng.

Sights
JINSHAN PARK 金山公园
This park (Jīnshān Gōngyuán; Gold Hill Park; 62 Jinshan Xilu; admission Y50) otherwise known as 'Gold Mountain', is Zhènjiāng's leading tourist attraction. The park was once an island on the Yangzi, which slowly filled with silt over the years, forming a modest hill and narrow peninsula. Crowds flock to see the expansive Buddhist **Jinshan Temple** (Jīnshān Sì), which sits at the

base of the hill; and to visit the seven-storey, octagonal **Cishou Pagoda** (Císhòu Tǎ; admission Y3), reached by a flight of winding stairs to the top. The pagoda was built over 1400 years ago and restored in 1900 to celebrate the 65th birthday of the Dowager Empress Cixi.

The temple gains its name from a Zen master who is said to have come into copious amounts of gold (*jīn*) after opening the gates at the entrance of the park. There are four caves at the mount; of these **Buddhist Sea** (Fáhǎi) and **White Dragon** (Báilóng) feature in the Chinese legend *The Story of the White Snake*. To get to Jinshan Park take bus 2 to the last stop.

JIAO MOUNTAIN 焦山
Likened to a piece of jade floating in the river, this **island** (Jiāo Shān; admission Y40; 8am-5pm), east of Zhènjiāng, is famous for its lush, mountainous scenery and beautiful views. There's good hiking here with a number of pavilions along the way to the top of the 150m-high mountain, from where **Xijiang Tower** (Xījiāng Lóu) looks out over the Yangzi. At the base of the mountain is **Dinghui Temple** (Dìnghuì Sì), an active Buddhist monastery.

To get to Jiāo Mountain take bus 4 from Zhongshan Xilu or Jiefang Lu to the terminal. From there it's a short walk and a boat ride (included in the ticket), or you can take a cable car (just north of the boat dock) to the top of the hill (Y20).

NORTH HILL PARK 北固山公园
North Hill Park (Běigù Shān Gōngyuán; 3 Dongwu Lu; admission Y20; 7am-7pm) is a green oasis in the middle of a construction zone. It's the site of **Ganlu Temple** (Gānlù Sì), which features an iron pagoda first built in the Tang dynasty. Once 13m high, the pagoda has since suffered damage from fire, lightning and overzealous Red Guards during the Cultural Revolution. Standing gracefully on top of the hill is the scenic **Soaring Clouds Pavilion** (Língyún Tíng), which commands beautiful views of the river and city below. It's on the bus 4 route.

ZHENJIANG MUSEUM 镇江博物馆
Between Jinshan Park and the centre of town is the old British consulate, built in 1890 and now converted into a **museum** (Zhènjiāng Bówùguǎn; 85 Boxian Lu; adult/child Y20/10; 9am-noon & 2-5.30pm). The museum doesn't draw hordes of tourists and it has a great outlook over the black-tiled

roofs in the oldest section of town. It houses a fine collection of pottery, bronzes, gold and silver found in excavations around Zhènjiāng. There are English captions and the building has been nicely restored. To get there catch bus 2 from Zhongshan Lu.

It's well worth taking time to explore the old area surrounding the museum. The staircase to the east leads around to a narrow street known as Boxian Lu. A small stone pagoda, **Zhaoguang Pagoda** (Zhāoguǎng Tǎ), sits above an archway and is said to date from the Yuan dynasty. There are a few antique stores and stalls here, and if you keep following the street all the way up and past the train tracks, you'll hit Changjiang Lu.

Sleeping
Jingkou Hotel (Jīngkǒu Fàndiàn; 522 4866; fax 523 0056; 407 Zhongshan Donglu; 中山东路407号; d Y260-480) The rooms in this central hotel are attractively furnished and some have been recently renovated. Staff seem a bit indifferent to foreign faces and you may have to push hard for a discount.

Zhenjiang Hotel (Zhènjiāng Bīnguǎn; 523 3888; 92 Zhongshan Xilu; 中山西路92号; d Y420-700) Don't be fooled by the glossy lobby in this wannabe up-market hotel – rooms are average, though clean, and somewhat overpriced. However, this hotel is conveniently located near the train station.

International Hotel (Guójì Fàndiàn; 502 1888; fax 502 1777; 218 Jiefang Lu; 解放路218号; d Y660-730) Four-star amenities and sizeable discounts make this sky-high hotel tower a great choice. Rooms are spacious and comfortable. It's also in a handy location near the south bus station.

Eating
You'll find restaurants galore along the side streets off Zhongshan Donglu, west of the intersection with Jiefang Lu.

Zuixiānlóu Jiǔjiā (82 Shanmenkou Jie; mains from Y20; 7am-9pm) This restaurant on a crowded lane off Zhongshan Lu serves tasty noodles and dumplings at reasonable prices. It doesn't have an English menu so you'll need to consult our menu decoder (p106).

Yànchūn Jiǔlóu (87 Jiefang Lu; mains Y25-40; 11am-8pm) One of the most popular spots in town, with very good noodle and rice dishes. Try the steamed crab buns (蟹黄汤包; *xièhuáng tāngbā o*) with ginger and vinegar.

For cheap eats in a lively atmosphere head to the **night market** (yè shìchǎng) parallel and south of Zhongshan Donglu. Things generally get lively around 6pm and last until 2am.

JIĀNGSŪ

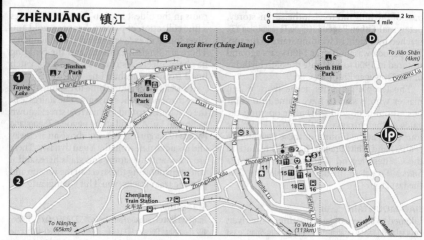

Getting There & Away

BUS

Most buses that depart from the south gate long-distance bus station (nánmén qìchēzhàn) are slow buses. Express buses leave from the express bus station (kuàikè qìchēzhàn) across the street. Buses leave for Nánjīng (Y15, 1½ hours), Shànghǎi (Y64 to Y75, 3½ hours), Wúxī (Y35, two hours) and Sūzhōu (Y51, two hours). Buses for major destinations also leave from the long-distance bus station (chángtōng qìchēzhàn) near the train station. Frequent buses leave here for Yángzhōu (Y11, one hour), which includes a short ferry ride.

TRAIN

Zhènjiāng is on the main Nánjīng–Shànghǎi train line. It's a little over three hours to Shànghǎi (Y52) and an hour to Nánjīng (Y19). Although some of the special express trains don't stop at Zhènjiāng, there's still a choice of schedules.

Most hotels offer a train booking service. The business centre at the International Hotel will book sleepers for a Y30 service charge but it's fairly easy to book sleepers in advance at the train station.

Getting Around

Almost all transport (local buses, pedicabs and motor-tricycles) is close to the train station. Taxis start at Y7.

Bus 2 is a convenient tour bus. It travels east from the train station along Zhongshan Lu to Jiefang Lu. It then swings west to the museums and continues on to the terminus at Jinshan Park. Bus 4, which crosses the bus 2 route in the city centre on Jiefang Lu, runs past North Hill Park and terminates at Jiao Mountain in the east.

YÁNGZHŌU 扬州

☎ 0514 / pop 4.46 million

Yángzhōu, near the junction of the Grand Canal and the Yangzi River, was once an economic and cultural centre of southern China. The city grew rich from the salt trade, attracting merchants and artisans from all over, who set up residences and gardens here.

Like most of China's cities, modern-day Yángzhōu has lost much of its charm to development and many of its once-thriving canals have been paved over. Nevertheless, with its wide leafy streets and beautiful gardens, it's a worthy escape from Jiāngsū's bigger centres, Nánjīng and Sūzhōu. The main tourist sight, Slender West Lake Park, is overrun with tour groups but the other places remain quiet enough. Yángzhōu has enough to keep visitors busy for a couple days or can be visited on a day trip from Nánjīng.

Orientation

Yángzhōu's sights are concentrated around the Grand Canal in the north and northwest parts of the city, and this is where you'll find Slender West Lake and Daming Temple. It's easy to get around by foot in Yángzhōu and walking along the river that winds its way through town is quite pleasant.

INFORMATION	SIGHTS & ACTIVITIES	EATING
Bank of China	Cishou Pagoda ....(see 7)	Night Market 夜市场 13 C2
中国银行 1 C2	Ganlu Temple 甘露寺 6 D1	Yánchūn Jiŭlóu 宴春酒楼 14 C2
Bank of China	Jinshan Temple 金山寺 7 A1	Zuìxiānlóu Jiŭjiā 醉仙楼酒家 15 C2
中国银行 ....(see 17)	Zhaoguang Pagoda 昭光塔 8 B1	
Internet Café 网吧	Zhenjiang Museum 镇江博物馆 ..9 B1	TRANSPORT
.....................................2 C2		Express Bus Station 快客汽车站 16 C2
Post & Telephone Office	SLEEPING	Long-Distance Bus Station
中国电信 3 C2	International Hotel 国际饭店 10 C2	.....................................17 B2
PSB 公安局 4 C2	Jingkou Hotel 京口饭店 11 C2	South Gate Long-Distance Bus
Shangye Dasha (Department Store)	Zhenjiang Hotel 镇江宾馆 12 B2	Station 南门汽车站 18 C2
商业大厦 5 C2		

Information

Bank of China (Zhōngguó Yínháng; 279 Wenchang Zhonglu) Will change travellers cheques and cash. The ATM takes international cards.

No 1 People's Hospital (Yángzhōu Shì Dìyī Rénmín Yīyuàn; 45 Taizhou Lu) Head here if you need medical attention.

Post Office (Yóujú; 162 Wenchang Zhonglu) Conveniently located in the town centre.

Public Security Bureau (PSB; Gōngānjú; 1 Huaihai Lu) Can help with visa extensions.

www.travelchinaguide.com/cityguides/jiangsu/ yangzhou/ Provides facts and history about Yángzhōu.

Yangzhou Tourist Information Service Centre (Yángzhōu Lǚxíngshè; 10 Fengle Shangjie; 9am-5pm) For train and air tickets.

Sights

SLENDER WEST LAKE PARK 瘦西湖公园

Slender West Lake (Shòu Xī Hú; 28 Da Hongqiao Lu; admission Y80 includes He, Ge & Potted Plant Garden; 6.30am-6pm) has been a popular tourist outing since the 3rd century AD and was a favourite vacationing spot of Emperor Qianlong in the 18th century. Stretching noodle-like northwards from Da Hongqiao Lu towards Daming Temple, the lake is similar to its chubbier cousin the West Lake in Hángzhōu, with pretty willow-lined banks dotted with pavilions and gardens. One highlight is the exquisite triple-arched **Five Pavilion Bridge** (Wǔtíng Qiáo), built in 1757, which straddles a lotus pond teeming with fat, happy goldfish.

Another interesting structure is the **24 Bridge** (Èrshísì Qiáo), its back arched high enough to almost form a complete circle, allowing boats easy passage. Near the bridge is Emperor Qianlong's fishing platform – supposedly, local divers used to put fish on the emperor's hook so he'd think the town was lucky and provide them with more funding.

There's an entrance on Da Hongqiao Lu and another entrance at the Five Pavilion Bridge on bus route 5 from Wenhe Lu.

GE GARDEN 个园

This **garden** (Gè Yuán; 10 Yanfu Donglu; 8am-6pm), east of the city centre, is typical of a southern-style garden, with heaps of weirdly shaped rocks, pavilions and lotus ponds. Built in 1883, it was once the home of the painter Shi Tao and was later acquired by an affluent salt merchant.

If you enjoy Chinese gardens, this one will delight, with its crooked pathways, dense bamboo groves and humpback bridges. It's a little out of the way, but worth visiting. Bus 1 from Yanfan Xilu stops nearby on Nantong Donglu.

HE GARDEN 何园

This tiny **garden** (Hé Yuán; 77 Xuningmen Jie; 7.30am-6pm) in the south of town was built by a Qing dynasty salt merchant as his garden residence. It boasts more buildings than actual garden, with airy pavilions and halls surrounded by tree-lined pathways, bamboo and convoluted rockery. There are also some relaxing tea-houses hidden among the shrubs and trees.

YANGZHOU POTTED PLANT GARDEN 扬州盆景园

Don't be put off by the name. This **garden** (Yángzhōu Pénjǐng Yuán; 12 Youyi Lu; 7am-6pm) offers a quiet escape along a small canal dotted with birds and blossoms, archways, bridges, pavilions and a marble boat. There are hundreds of bonsai-style potted plants on display as well as a **bonsai museum**. The entrance fee is steep, but is well worth the price and a must for garden-lovers.

CANALS

Yángzhōu once had 24 stone bridges spanning its network of canals. Although the modern bridges are concrete, they still offer good vantage points to view canal life.

As the Grand Canal actually passes a little to the east of Yángzhōu, you might like to

JIĀNGSŪ

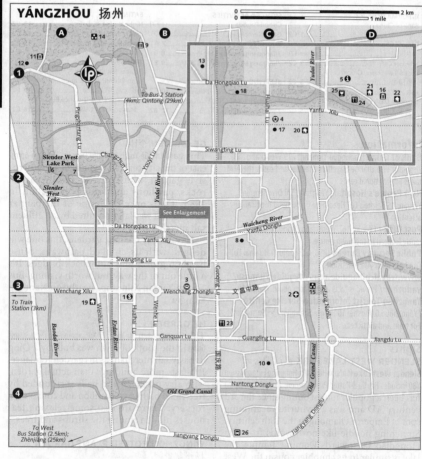

investigate the environs a short way out of town. The bus 2 station in the northeast is a boat dock on the river. Buses 4 and 9 run over a bridge on the canal. There are also two ship locks to the south of Yángzhōu.

DAMING TEMPLE 大明寺

This **temple** (Dàmíng Sì; 1 Pingshantang Lu; admission Y35; ⌚ 7.30am-5pm) is packed with crowds on weekends and holidays. Standing on a hill in the northwest of the city, it's been an important centre for Buddhism since ancient times. Founded more than 1000 years ago, the complex was subsequently destroyed and rebuilt. Then it was destroyed right down to its foundations during the Taiping Rebellion; what you see today is a 1934 reconstruction. The

nine-storey **Qiling Pagoda** (Qílíng Tǎ) nearby was completed in 1996.

The original temple is credited to the Tang dynasty monk Jian Zhen, who was a true jack-of-all-trades, studying sculpture, architecture, fine arts and medicine, as well as Buddhism. In AD 742 two Japanese monks invited him to Japan for missionary work, which turned out to be mission impossible – Jian Zhen made five attempts to get there, failing due to storms. On the fifth attempt he ended up in Hǎinán. On the sixth trip, aged 66, he finally arrived.

Jian Zhen stayed in Japan for 10 years and died there in AD 763. Later, the Japanese made a lacquer statue of him, which was sent to Yángzhōu in 1980.

INFORMATION		Han Dynasty Tomb Museum		SLEEPING	
Bank of China 中国银行 **1** B3		汉墓博物馆 **9** B1		Grand Metropole Hotel	
No. 1 People's Hospital		He Garden 何园 **10** C4		扬州京华大酒店 **19** A3	
扬州市第一人民医院 **2** C3		Martyrs' Shrine 烈士陵园 **11** A1		Lantian Hotel 蓝天大厦 **20** C2	
Post Office 邮电局 **3** B3		Pingshan Hall 平山堂 .... (see 13)		Xiyuan Hotel 西园饭店 **21** D1	
PSB 公安局 **4** C1		Qiling Pagoda 楼灵塔 **12** A1		Yangzhou Hotel 扬州宾馆 ... **22** D1	
Yangzhou Tourist Information		Slender West Lake Entrance			
Service Centre		瘦西湖 **13** B1		EATING	
扬州旅行社 **5** D1		Tang City Wall 唐城遗址 **14** A1		Fuchun Chashe 富春茶社 ... **23** C3	
		Tomb of Puhading		Yěchūn Huáyuán 冶春花园 ... **24** D1	
SIGHTS & ACTIVITIES		普哈丁墓园 **15** C3			
24 Bridge **6** A2		Yangzhou City Museum		DRINKING	
Daming Temple		扬州市博物馆 **16** D1		Cellar Bar 赛乐酒吧 **25** D1	
大明寺 .... (see 12)		Yangzhou Eight Eccentrics Memorial			
Five Pavilion Bridge		扬州八怪纪念馆 **17** C2		TRANSPORT	
五亭桥 **7** A2		Yangzhou Potted Plant Garden		Long-Distance Bus Station	
Ge Garden 个园 **8** C3		扬州盆景园 **18** C1		扬州汽车站 **26** C4	

Near the temple is **Pingshan Hall** (Píngshān Táng), the former residence of the Song dynasty writer and former governor of Yángzhōu, Ouyang Xiu. The building itself dates from the Qing dynasty. A **Martyrs' Shrine** (Lièshì Língyuán) is also nearby.

To the east of Daming Temple you'll find the ruins of the **Tang city wall** (Táng Chéng Yízhǐ; admission Y15), where archaeologists have discovered remnants of bone carvings, ceramics and jade; and the **Han Dynasty Tomb Museum** (Hànmù Bówùguǎn; 16 Xiangbie Lu; admission Y30; 8.30am-4.30pm), which has some interesting exhibits (in Chinese) of artefacts excavated around Yángzhōu.

You can reach Daming Temple by taking bus 5 along Wenhe Lu to the last stop. The temple is a short walk north of here.

TOMB OF PUHADING 普哈丁墓园

This is the **tomb** (Pǔhādīng Mùyuán; 17 Jiefang Nanlu) of the Muslim teacher and scholar Puhading, who died in Yángzhōu in 1275. Believed to be a descendent of the Prophet, Puhading came to China during the Yuan dynasty to spread the Muslim faith. Within the grounds is a mosque but casual visitors are only allowed to enter the grounds from 6am to noon, and you need special permission to visit the tomb. It's on the eastern bank of a canal on the bus 2 route.

YANGZHOU CITY MUSEUM 扬州市博物馆

This excellent **museum** (Yángzhōu Shì Bówùguǎn; 2 Fengle Shanglu; admission free; 8am-5pm) is in a temple originally dedicated to Shi Kefa, a Ming dynasty official who refused to succumb to his new Qing masters and was executed.

On display are several large wooden coffins dating to the Han and Northern Song dynasties, a 1000-year-old wooden boat and a Han dynasty jade funeral suit. Inside the grounds, the museum is surrounded by a curio market.

YANGZHOU EIGHT ECCENTRICS MEMORIAL 扬州八怪纪念馆

This **memorial** (Yángzhōu Bāguài Jìniànguǎn; Huaihai Lu; admission Y15; 8am-6pm) has examples of paintings and calligraphy by Yángzhōu's 'eight eccentrics', a group of Qing painters considered so peculiar by authorities they were excluded from exhibiting in the imperial collection. They were deemed eccentric because of their nonconventional painting techniques and use of bold and uncontrolled brush strokes in their paintings. The eccentrics included the artists Gao Qipei (1672–1734) who painted with his hands and Hua Yan (1682–1786) whose paintings of squirrels now hang in the Palace Museum in Běijīng.

Tours

Tour buses 1 and 5 leave from the West Bus Station and circle all the sights.

Festivals & Events

The **Qintong Boat Festival** is held from 4 to 6 April every year in Qīntóng (溱潼), a small town outside of Yángzhōu. Folk dances are staged on boats from surrounding fishing villages. The boat races attract both Chinese and international tourists.

Sleeping

Yángzhōu's accommodation isn't cheap and there are no true budget hotels. Weekday discounts cut prices in half, though you'll need to remind staff at the front desk.

JIĀNGSŪ

Xiyuan Hotel (Xīyuán Fàndiàn; ☎ 780 7888; fax 723 3870; www.xiyuan-hotel.com; 1 Fengle Shanglu; 丰乐上路1号; s Y488, d Y280-388) This enormous hotel, set back from the canal, was once the site of Emperor Qianlong's imperial villa. Rooms are tastefully designed and pleasing, though don't expect the royal treatment – service is definitely on the chilly side.

Lantian Hotel (Lántiān Dàshà; ☎ 736 0000; fax 731 4101; 159 Wenhe Beilu; 文河北路159号; d Y360-480, tr Y460-560) Very centrally located, this upbeat place offers a choice of decent-quality rooms in a convenient location. It even has its own bowling alley if you happen to get tired of sightseeing.

Yangzhou Hotel (Yángzhōu Bīnguǎn; ☎ 734 2611; fax 734 3599; 5 Fengle Shanglu; 丰乐上路5号; s/d Y480/580) Next door to the Xiyuan and the Yangzhou Museum, this high-rise hotel has friendly management and neat, airy rooms. There are 40% discounts on weekdays.

Grand Metropole Hotel (Yángzhōu Jīnghuá Dàjiǔdiàn; ☎ 732 3888; 1 Wenchang Xilu; 文昌西路1号; d Y700-800) One of the fanciest places in town, this four-star tower has bright, comfortable rooms with good-size bathrooms and attentive staff. It's about a 10-minute walk from the city centre.

Eating

Yángzhōu's most famous culinary export is Yángzhōu fried rice (扬州炒饭; *Yángzhōu chǎofàn*) and, as most travellers who have tried it will confirm, it tastes just like fried rice. Along Da Hongqiao Lu, leading to the entrance to Slender West Lake Park, are a string of small restaurants selling fried rice and other dishes. You should be able to fill up here for under Y20.

Yěchūn Huāyuán (☎ 734 2932; 10 Fengle Xialu; mains Y10-30; ⏱ 7-11.30am & 5-9pm) Close to the Yangzhou Museum, this popular restaurant has excellent dim sum as well as noodle and rice dishes. It's tucked away on a tiny lane next to the canal.

Fùchūn Cháshè (☎ 723 3326; 35 Desheng Qiao; mains Y10-30; ⏱ 8am-9pm) One of Yángzhōu's most famous teahouses, this place is on a lane just off Guoqing Lu, in an older section of town. Try an assorted plate of its famous dumplings for Y30.

Yángzhōu's hotels offer opportunities to try local cuisine in more formal surroundings. The Xiyuan Hotel has a noteworthy restaurant, known for its seafood.

Drinking

Yángzhōu's nightlife is pretty tepid, though there are a few bars strung along the canal near the Yangzhou City Museum that cater to young locals and foreigners

Cellar Bar (Sàilè Jiǔbā; 8 Fengle Shangjie; drinks Y30; ⏱ open late) This mellow place is a favourite with the locals, with cool retro décor, pool tables and lounge seating. It's especially popular on weekends and a great place to wind down.

Shopping

Yangzhou's main shopping drag is on Wenchang Lu, with shopping plazas and international clothing stores. For cheaper items, head to the older section of town near the Fùchūn Cháshè restaurant. There's a line-up of souvenir shops along the canal near the Yangzhou City Museum where you can buy sandalwood fans, reproductions of paintings and ceramics.

Getting There & Away

The nearest airport is located in Nánjīng. Shuttle buses make the trip from larger hotels. There are trains to Guǎngzhōu (Y219, 27 hours) that pass through Nánjīng, and Huángshān. Trains to Shànghǎi (Y97, six hours) pass through Nánjīng, Zhènjiāng, Wúxī and Sūzhōu.

From the Yángzhōu long-distance bus station south of the city centre there are buses to different points in Shànghǎi (Y58 to Y70, 4½ hours) and Hángzhōu (Y75 to Y90, five hours) and Sūzhōu (Y62, three hours). Buses to Nánjīng (Y26, two hours) and Zhènjiāng (Y12, one hour) depart from the west bus station, southwest of the city. Buses cross over the Yangzi by ferry.

Getting Around

Most of the main sights are at the edge of town. Taxis are cheap and start at Y7; the smaller taxis are Y6. The area from the southern entrance of Slender West Lake Park on Da Hongqiao Lu to the City Museum can easily be covered on foot and it's a pleasant walk.

Bus 8 runs from the west bus station to the long-distance bus station, and then makes its way up Guoqing Lu to the north of the city. Bus 5 takes you from the long-distance bus station to Huaihai Lu, Youyi Lu then terminates near Daming Temple.

WÚXĪ 无锡

☎ 0510 / pop 4.3 million

Once prosperous due to its fortuitous position on the Grand Canal, Wúxī has lost much of its former glory and now takes a backseat to more attractive canal towns, such as Sūzhōu and Yángzhōu. Modern-day Wúxī is smoggy and characterless, with little to recommend it. Most people use the city as a base for exploring the more pleasing shores of Lake Tai.

Orientation

The city centre is ringed by Jiefang Lu. The train station and the long-distance bus station are only about a 10-minute walk north of Jiefang Beilu. A network of canals, including the Grand Canal, cuts through the city. Lake Tai is about 5km from the city centre.

Information

Bank of China (Zhōngguó Yínháng; 258 Zhongshan Nanlu; ☽ 9am-5.30pm) Changes travellers cheques and major currency. The ATM here takes international cards.

China Telecom (☽ 7.30am-11.30pm) At the western end of the post office.

Post Office (Yóujú; Renmin Zhonglu) Close to the Bank of China.

Public Security Bureau (PSB; Gōngānjú; ☎ 270 5678 ext 2215; 54 Chongning Lu) Takes care of visa problems.

Wuxi Nanzhan Hospital (Wúxī Nánzhàn Yīyuàn; 97 Tangnan Lu) This hospital has good facilities and is centrally located.

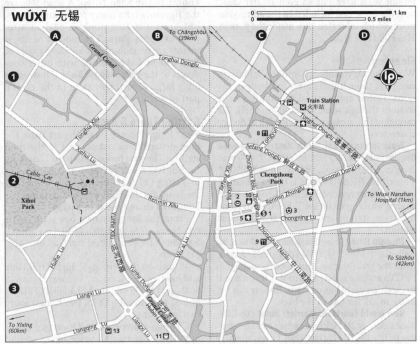

Wuxi Provincial Government (www.wuxi.gov.cn) Information on Wúxī.

Sights

The city of Wúxī has very few tourist attractions, though some of its parks are pleasant enough. The nicest by far is **Xihui Park** (Xīhuì Gōngyuán; Huihe Lu; admission Y45; ☉ 8am-6pm). The highest point in the park is West Hill (Xī Shān), 75m above sea level. If you climb **Longguang Pagoda** (Lóngguāng Tǎ), the seven-storey octagonal structure at the top of the hill, you will be able to take in a panorama of Wúxī and Lake Tai. The brick-and-wood pagoda was built during the Ming dynasty, burned down during the Qing dynasty and rebuilt years later. For an even greater view, take the cable car, included in the admission price, which is located 1km inside the park at Hui Hill (Huì Shān).

Sleeping

Wúxī's hotels mainly fall into the midrange category, though there are a few budget options. Hotels are plentiful around the train station, though some serve as brothels. Be careful in this area at night as it's full of dodgy characters.

Wuxi International Youth Hostel (Wúxī Guójì Qīngnián Lǚshè; ☎ 8275 5990; fax 8273 5427; 49 Renmin Zhonglu; 人民中路49号; s/d/tr per person Y90/55/50) This clean, friendly hostel is the best budget option in overpriced Wúxī. All rooms have shared washing facilities. Take bus K10 from the train station and get off at Dongmen station.

Zhonglu Hotel (Zhōnglǚ Dàjiǔdiàn; ☎ 868 9928; 88 Chezhan Lu; 车站路88号; d Y480-628) Directly across from the train station, this hotel is managed by CTS and is a good place to stay if you need to catch an early bus or train. Rooms can be noisy so ask for one in the back.

New World Courtyard Marriott Hotel (Xīn Shìjiè Wànyí Jiǔdiàn; ☎ 276 2888; www.courtyard.com; 335 Zhongshan Lu; 中山路335号; d Y996-1160) This is the top choice for upmarket rooms right in the centre of things. All rooms include breakfast and are often discounted up to 40%. The hotel also has a helpful ticket office with English-speaking staff.

Eating

It's impossible to go hungry in Wúxī; the best places to find food are around the train station and along Zhongshan Lu.

Lóushànglóu Miànguǎn (61 Tongyun Lu; mains Y5-10; ☉ 24hrs) This large, noisy restaurant has incredibly cheap noodle and rice dishes and is a popular place for lunchtime workers. You'll find more substantial meals on the 2nd floor at higher prices.

Wángxìngjì (221 Zhongshan Nanlu; mains Y10-20; ☉ 7am-8pm) Close to the city centre, this is a long-established Wúxī restaurant that's famous for wonton soup (馄饨; húntun) and delicious steamed dumplings filled with meat or seafood (小笼包; xiǎolóngbāo) for Y8.

Shopping

Silk products and embroidery are good buys. Also look out for the ugly clay figurines known as Huì Shān Nírén. A local folk art, the figurines take many forms and shapes, but are most commonly modelled after famous opera stars. The models of obese infants are symbols of fortune and happiness. You can find these along with other souvenirs at the **Wúxī Shàngyè Dàshà** (343 Zhongshan Lu), a large department store in the central part of town.

Getting There & Away

Most long-distance buses depart from the long-distance bus station next to the train station. The west bus station is on Liangqing Lu but has fewer services. Frequent buses to Yíxīng (Y10, 1½ hours) leave from both the long-distance and west bus stations. For Dīngshān change buses in Yíxīng.

From the long-distance bus station, direct buses go to Shànghǎi (Y40, two hours), Sūzhōu (Y18, 45 minutes) and Nánjīng (Y55, 2½ hours).

Wúxī is on the Běijīng–Shànghǎi train line and has frequent services. There are trains to Sūzhōu (Y12, 30 minutes), Shànghǎi (Y31, 1½ hours) and Nánjīng (Y25, two hours) every two hours or so.

CTS books sleepers for a Y30 service charge but there are numerous ticket agents around the long-distance bus station that book train tickets. There's also a ticket office next to the Zhonglu Hotel.

Overnight passenger boats travel between Wúxī and Hángzhōu on the Grand Canal. Departure is at 5.30pm from the wharf off Hubin Lu. You can book tickets at the wharf. Two-person cabins are Y114 per person and four-person cabins are Y82 per person. The trip takes 13 hours.

Getting Around

It's fairly easy getting around Wúxī by bus. Bus 2 runs from the train station, along Jiefang Lu and across two bridges to Xihui Park. Bus 201 heads from the train station down Zhongshan Lu to the city centre. The Wúxī sightseeing bus is very useful, stopping at all major sights. It has no number, but it's in the first row of buses to the right as you exit the train station. Tickets are Y3 or Y2 depending on the distance.

Taxis start at Y8.

LAKE TAI 太湖

Lake Tai is a freshwater lake dotted with some 90 islands, and features abundant plant and animal life. Surrounded by rolling hills and tea fields, it's been a popular tourist destination for the Chinese since the early 20th century. The lake is also famous for its strangely eroded rocks, a staple of traditional Chinese gardens. The northern part of the lake, which includes Turtle Head Isle, is easily visited from Wúxī, while the southeastern shores include the more rural areas of Dōngshān and Xīshān, both accessible on a day trip from Sūzhōu. On the west side of the lake is Yíxīng County and the pottery centre of Dīngshān.

Sights & Activities

Turtle Head Isle (Yuán Tóuzhǔ; adult/child Y70/35; 6.30am-6pm) is not actually an island, but a peninsula, and is thought to resemble a turtle's head poking up out of the water. The island is quite pretty, though recent construction has taken away some of its allure. The park contains a number of pavilions and teahouses where you can idle away a few hours. Tour buses (included in the admission price), can take you around the lake or you can hop on an electric cart for Y10.

The entrance at the southern end of the park is just north of the **Baojie Bridge** (Bǎojiè Qiáo). This end of the park is peaceful with a lovely narrow road leading up to the **Brightness Pavilion** (Guāngmíng Tíng), the highest point of Turtle Head Isle, offering all-round vistas. The northern end of the park has souvenir stalls and the **Perpetual Spring Bridge** (Chángchūn Qiáo), which leads across a small pond to a rocky vantage point on the lake. Here, there's also a pier with ferries (included in admission) to **Sānshān** (Three Hills Isle), once a bandit's hideaway. Vantage points at the top look back towards Turtle Head Isle, so you can work

out if it really does look like a turtle head. The islands have a number of pavilions and temples as well as three large Buddha statues, the smallest measuring 16m high.

On the southern end of Turtle Head Isle are three amusement parks, **Tang Dynasty World** (Táng Cháo Jǐngqū; admission Y30), **Three Kingdoms World** (Sān Guó Jǐngqū; admission Y35) and **Water Margin World** (Shuǐhǔ Jǐngqū; admission Y35), set up by Wuxi Film Studios. These replica cities were built to film TV dramas based on famous historical novels. A visit to one of these parks offers some tacky fun.

Sleeping

Hotels by Lake Tai offer upmarket rooms in peaceful surroundings.

Taihu Hotel (Tàihú Fàndiàn; ☎ 551 7888; Yonggu Lu; 永固路; d Y498-808) Located on top of a hill overlooking the lake, this five-star hotel has elegantly furnished rooms, some with views. The restaurants and amenities are excellent and worth the price.

Lakeview Park Resort Hotel (Tàihú Huāyuán Dùjiàcùn; ☎ 555 5888; 8 Shanshui Donglu; 山水东路8号;

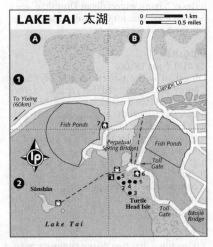

Y700-1000) This hotel has good-quality rooms and friendly management. Surroundings are not as nice as the Taihu Hotel, however, and you're a good distance from the lake on an isolated stretch of road.

Eating

Out by the lake, you have few eating options. There are restaurants at the northern end of the pier and all hotels have restaurants. At the **Clear Ripples Hall** (Chénglán Táng) teahouse, you can enjoy some tea while viewing the lake.

Getting There & Away

Bus 82 goes to Baojie Bridge from the train station in Wúxī. The Wúxī sightseeing bus goes to the northern entrance from the train station.

YÍXĪNG COUNTY 宜兴县

Yíxīng County (Yíxīng Xiàn) is famous for its tea utensils, particularly pots. Delicious tea can be made in an aged Yíxīng teapot simply by adding hot water, or so they say. The potteries of Yíxīng, especially in Dīngshān, are a popular excursion for Chinese tourists but see few foreign visitors.

Dīngshān 丁山

☎ 0510 / pop 100,000

Dīngshān is the pottery centre of Yíxīng County and has enjoyed that reputation since the Qin and Han dynasties; some of the scenes here, especially at the loading dock that leads into Lake Tai, are timeless.

Almost every local family is engaged in the manufacture of ceramics and at least half of the houses are made of the stuff. It's extremely dusty here (and probably not recommended for people with respiratory problems). Everywhere you look vehicles are hauling rocks from the mountains outside of town.

Dīngshān, located about 20km south of Yíxīng town, has two dozen ceramics factories producing more than 2000 varieties of pottery – quite an output for a population of 100,000. Among the products made here are the ceramic tables and garbage bins you'll see around China, jars that are used to store oil and grain, the famed Yíxīng teapots, as well as glazed tiling and ceramic frescoes that are desperately needed as spare parts for tourist attractions – the Forbidden City

in Běijīng is a customer. The ornamental rocks you see in Chinese gardens are also produced here.

Outside of Dīngshān, the **Ceramics Museum** (宜兴陶瓷博物馆; Yíxīng Táocí Bówùguǎn; 150 Dingshan Beilu; admission Y20; ⊗ 7.30am-4.30pm) displays examples of Yíxīng pottery from 6000 years ago to the present day. Nearby workshops have ceramic artisans at work.

SLEEPING

It's easy to visit this area on a day trip from Wúxī but you can also stay overnight.

Yíxīng Guójì Fàndiàn (宜兴国际饭店; ☎ 791 6888; 52 Tongzhenguan Lu; 通贞观路 52号; s Y300-420, d Y360-580) This high-rise hotel has a choice of rooms and prices. Rooms are all varying shades of dull brown but nonetheless clean and spacious. Management can help you arrange trips to Dīngshān.

SHOPPING

If you've taken the trouble to get here, don't leave without buying some pottery. There's a lot of variety, not just the standard Yíxīng style, and it's very cheap. The best place to go is a huge **pottery market** (lóngxī táocí shìchǎng; ⊗ 7.30am-7pm), across the highway from the Ceramics Museum. There are a number of stores and small stalls with literally tonnes of pottery. Mid-size teapots range in price from Y20 to Y300 and make terrific gifts.

GETTING THERE & AWAY

Frequent buses leave from Wúxī's long-distance bus station to Yíxīng (Y15, 1½ hours). From Yíxīng minibuses go back and forth to Dīngshān (Y6, 20 minutes).

SŪZHŌU 苏州

☎ 0512 / pop 5.71 million

Marco Polo once declared that Sūzhōu was one of the most beautiful cities in China (though Hángzhōu was better). While Polo's Sūzhōu was a charming merchant town of whitewashed houses, tree-lined canals and sumptuous gardens, modern Sūzhōu is a bustling city surrounded by factories and high rises. It takes some work to find the charm under the city's glossy veneer, but it's there.

Sūzhōu's main draw is its gardens. There were originally over a hundred but now only a handful exist, some over a thousand years old. The gardens, a symphonic combination of rocks, water, trees and buildings, reflect the Chinese appreciation of balance and harmony. You could easily spend an enjoyable several days exploring the gardens, paying a visit to the excellent Silk Museum and exploring some of Sūzhōu's surviving canals, pagodas and humpbacked bridges.

History

Dating back some 2500 years, Sūzhōu is one of the oldest towns in the Yangzi Basin. With the completion of the Grand Canal during the Sui dynasty, Sūzhōu found itself strategically located on a major trading route, and the city's fortunes and size grew rapidly.

Sūzhōu flourished as a centre of shipping and grain storage, bustling with merchants and artisans. By the 12th century the town had attained its present dimensions. The city walls, a rectangle enclosed by moats, were pierced by six gates (north, south, two in the east and two in the west). Crisscrossing the city were six canals running north to south and 14 canals running east to west. Although the walls have largely disappeared and a fair proportion of the canals have been plugged, central Sūzhōu retains some of its 'Renaissance' character.

By the 14th century, Sūzhōu had established itself as China's leading silk-producing city. Aristocrats, pleasure-seekers, famous scholars, actors and painters were drawn to the place, constructing villas and garden retreats for themselves as they came.

At the height of Sūzhōu's development in the 16th century, the gardens, large and small, numbered more than 100. The town's winning tourist formula – and its image as a 'Garden City' or a 'Venice of the East' – was created out of its medieval mix of woodblock guilds and embroidery societies, whitewashed housing, cobbled streets, tree-lined avenues and canals. Sūzhōu's reputation was boosted by the reputation of its women as the most beautiful in China, largely thanks to the mellifluous local accent, and was sealed with the famous proverb 'In heaven there is paradise, on earth Sūzhōu and Hángzhōu'.

Under the Ming and Qing, the silk industry continued to flourish, with large sheds housing thousands of workers in wretched conditions. Protests were common, with silk workers staging violent strikes as early as the 15th century. In 1860 Taiping troops took the town without a blow and in 1896 Sūzhōu was opened to foreign trade, with Japanese and other international concessions. Since 1949, most parts of the city, including the city walls have been largely demolished, and it's uncertain how much of this once-beautiful city will remain in the future.

Orientation

Besides the numerous small canals, Sūzhōu is surrounded by a large, rectangular outer canal (Waicheng River, or Wàichéng Hé). The main thoroughfare, Renmin Lu, bisects the city into western and eastern halves, while a large canal cuts across the middle. The train and main bus stations are at the northern end of town, on the north side of the outer canal. A large boat dock and another long-distance bus station are at the southern end.

MAPS

The **Xinhua Bookshop** (Xīnhuá Shūdiàn; 164 Guanqian Jie; ☉ 9am-10pm), next to the Temple of Mystery, sells a variety of English- and Chinese-language maps of Sūzhōu.

Information

CITS (Zhōngguó Guójì Lǚxíngshè) has branches next to the train ticket office, beside the Lexiang Hotel and inside the Suzhou Hotel.
Bank of China (Zhōngguó Yínháng; 1450 Renmin Lu) Changes travellers cheques and foreign cash. There are ATMs that take international cards at most larger branches of the Bank of China. Major tourist hotels also have foreign-exchange counters.
Internet cafés Head to Shiquan Jie, where most places charge Y2 to Y3 an hour.
No. 1 Hospital (Sùlìfū Yīyuàn; 96 Shizi Jie) One of many hospitals around town if you need medical assistance.
Post Office (Yóujú) It's on the corner of Renmin Lu and Jingde Lu.
Public Security Bureau (PSB; Gōngānjú; ☎ 6522 5661 ext 20593; 1149 Renmin Lu) Can help with emergencies and visa problems. The visa office is about 200m down a lane called Dashitou Xiang.
www.chinavista.com/suzhou/home.html For general background information on tourist sites in Suzhou.

Sights & Activities

Children under 1.2m get in for half-price to all gardens and into other sights for free. Peak season prices listed are applicable from March to early May, and September to October

GARDEN OF THE MASTER OF THE NETS
网师园

Off Shiquan Jie, this pocket-sized **garden** (Wǎngshī Yuán; off-peak/peak Y20/30; ☉ 8am-5pm), the

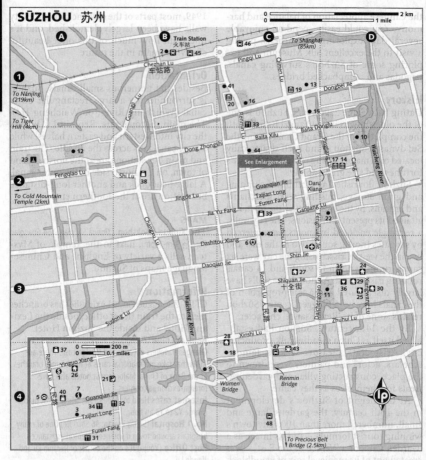

SŪZHŌU 苏州

smallest in Sūzhōu, is considered one of the best preserved gardens in the city. It was laid out in the 12th century, went to seed and later restored in the 18th century as part of the home of a retired official turned fisherman (thus the name). The eastern part of the garden is the residential area – originally with side rooms for sedan-chair lackeys, guest reception and living quarters. The central section is the main garden. The western section is an inner garden where a courtyard contains the **Spring Rear Cottage** (Diànchūn Yì), the master's study. This section, including the study with its Ming-style furniture and palace lanterns, was duplicated and unveiled at the Metropolitan Museum of Art in New York in 1981.

The most striking feature of this garden is its use of space: the labyrinth of courtyards, with windows framing other parts of the garden, is ingeniously designed to give the illusion of a much larger area.

There are two ways to the entry gate, with English signs and souvenir stalls marking the way: you can enter from the alley on Shiquan Jie or an alley off Daichengqiao Lu. Music performances are put on for tourists in the evening (p308).

GARDEN TO LINGER IN 留园
The three-hectare **Garden to Linger In** (Liú Yuán; 79 Liuyuan Lu; admission off-peak/peak Y30/40; ☉ 7.30am-5pm) is one of the largest gardens in Sūzhōu. It was originally built in the Ming dynasty by a doc-

tor who wanted to give his patients a relaxing place to recover from illness.

The winding corridors are inlaid with calligraphy from celebrated masters, their windows and doorways opening onto curiously shaped rockeries, ponds and dense bamboo gardens. Stone tablets hang from the walls with inscriptions written by patients who recorded their impressions of the place. In the northeast section of the garden, there's a gargantuan sculpted rock from Lake Tai; at 6.5m high you couldn't miss it if you tried.

The garden is about 3km west of the city centre. Tourist bus Y2 goes there from the train station or Renmin Lu.

WEST GARDEN TEMPLE 西园寺

This attractive garden was once part of the Garden to Linger In, but was given to a Buddhist temple in the early 17th century. The **temple**, (Xīyuán Sì; Xiyuan Lu; admission Y25; ⏰ 7.30am-5.30pm) with its mustard-yellow walls and gracefully curved eaves, was burnt to the ground during the Taiping Rebellion and rebuilt in the late 19th century. One interesting feature is the Hall of Arhats, with 500 gilded statues of Buddha saints in various expressive poses.

BLUE WAVE PAVILION 沧浪亭

Overgrown and wild, this one-hectare **garden** (Cānglàng Tíng; admission off-peak/peak Y15/20; ⏰ 7.30am-5.30pm) is one of the oldest in Sūzhōu. The buildings date from the 11th century, although they have been rebuilt on numerous occasions since.

Originally the home of a prince, the property passed into the hands of the scholar Su Zimei, who named it after a poem by Qu Yuan (340–278 BC).

Lacking a northern wall, the garden creates the illusion of space by borrowing scenes from the outside – from the pavilions and bridges you can see views of the water and distant hills. **Enlightenment Hall** (Míngdào Táng), the largest building, is said to have been a site for delivery of lectures during the Ming dynasty. Close by, on the other side of Renmin Lu, is the former Confucian Temple.

HUMBLE ADMINISTRATOR'S GARDEN 拙政园

This rambling **garden** (Zhuōzhèng Yuán; 178 Dongbei Jie; admission off-peak/peak Y50/70; ⏰ 7.30am-5.30pm) is the largest of all the gardens and considered by many to be the most impressive. Dating back to the early 1500s, it's a luxuriant five hectares of zigzagging bridges, pavilions, bamboo groves and fragrant lotus ponds; an ideal place for a leisurely stroll. There's also a teahouse and a small museum that explains Chinese landscape gardening concepts.

JIĀNGSŪ

LION'S GROVE GARDEN 狮子林

Near the Humble Administrator's Garden is the **Lion's Grove Garden** (Shīzi Lín; 23 Yuanlin Lu; off-peak/peak Y20/30; ☯ 8.30am-5.30pm) constructed in 1342 by the Buddhist monk Tianru to commemorate his master, who lived on Lion Cliff in Zhèjiāng's Tianmu Mountain. The garden is also associated with the 14th-century artist Ni Zan, who painted a picture of the garden soon after it was completed. The garden is most notable for its large numbers of curiously shaped rocks, meant to resemble lions, protectors of the Buddhist faith.

NORTH TEMPLE PAGODA 北寺塔

This is the tallest **pagoda** (Běisì Tǎ; Renmin Lu; admission Y25; ☯ 7.30am-6pm) south of the Yangzi – at nine storeys it dominates the northern end of Renmin Lu. Climb it for sweeping views of hazy modern-day Suzhōu.

The temple complex goes back 1700 years and was originally a residence; the current reincarnation dates back to the 17th century. Off to the side is **Nanmu Guanyin Hall** (Nánmù Guānyīn Diàn), which was rebuilt in the Ming dynasty with some features imported from elsewhere. There's a teahouse with a small garden out the back.

COUPLE'S GARDEN 耦园

This tranquil **garden** (Ōu Yuán; admission Y15; ☯ 8am-4.30pm) is off the main tourist route and sees few visitors, though the gardens, pond and courtyards are quite lovely. Surrounding the garden are some fine examples of traditional Suzhōu architecture, bridges and canals.

TWIN PAGODAS 双塔

These seven-storey **pagodas** (Shuāng Tǎ; admission Y10; ☯ 7am-4.30pm) were built during the Northern Song dynasty by candidates for the imperial examination who wanted to pay tribute to their teachers. The pagodas stand in the centre of an attractive garden filled with stone sculptures, with a teahouse at the far end.

SUZHŌU MUSEUM 苏州博物馆

The **Suzhou Museum** (Sūzhōu Bówùguǎn; ☎ 754 1534, 204 Dongbei Jie; admission Y10; ☯ 8.15am-4pm) was once the residence of Taiping leader Li Xiucheng. The museum offers some interesting old maps, including those of the Grand Canal, Suzhōu, and heaven and earth. It also houses Qing dynasty stelae forbidding workers' strikes,

and relics such as funerary objects, porcelain bowls and bronze swords unearthed or rescued from various sites around the Suzhōu district. Unfortunately, there are few English captions.

SUZHŌU SILK MUSEUM 丝绸博物馆

A must-see, this **museum** (Sūzhōu Sīchóu Bówùguǎn; 2001 Renmin Lu; admission Y7; ☯ 9am-5pm) houses a number of fascinating exhibitions that detail the history of Suzhōu's 4000-year-old silk industry. Exhibits include a section on silk weaving techniques and a room with live silk worms munching away on mulberry leaves and spinning cocoons. Many of the captions are in English.

KUNQU OPERA MUSEUM 戏曲博物馆

Down a warren of narrow lanes is this small **museum** (Xìqǔ Bówùguǎn; 14 Zhongzhangjia Xiang; admission free; ☯ 8.30am-4pm) dedicated to kūnqǔ, the opera style of the region. The beautiful old theatre houses a stage, old musical instruments, costumes and photos of famous performers. It also puts on occasional performances of kūnqǔ.

PINGTAN MUSEUM 评弹博物馆

West of the Kunqu Opera Museum is the **Pingtan Museum** (Píngtán Bówùguǎn; 3 Zhongzhangjia Xiang; admission Y4), which puts on wonderful performances of píngtán, a singing and storytelling art form sung in the Suzhōu dialect. Shows are at 1.30pm daily.

TEMPLE OF MYSTERY 玄妙观

This Taoist **temple** (Xuánmiào Guàn; Guanqian Jie; admission Y10; ☯ 7.30am-5.30pm) stands in what was once Suzhōu's old bazaar, a rowdy entertainment district with travelling showmen, acrobats and actors. The temple's present surroundings of Guanqian Jie are just as boisterous, but the current showmen are more likely to sell you a fake designer watch than balance plates on their heads.

The temple was founded during the Jin dynasty in the 3rd century AD, and restored many times over its long history. The complex contains several elaborately decorated halls, including **Sānqīng Diàn** (Three Purities Hall), which is supported by 60 pillars and capped by a double roof with upturned eaves. The temple dates from 1181 and is the only surviving example of Song architecture in Suzhōu.

COLD MOUNTAIN TEMPLE 寒山寺

About 2km west of the Garden to Linger In, this **temple** (Hánshān Sì; 24 Hanshansi Long; admission Y20, with Maple Bridge Y45; ☑ 7.30am-5.30pm) was named after the 7th century poet-monk Han Shan. Han Shan has exerted a surprising amount of influence on 20th-century literature, first showing up in the work of Beat writers Gary Snyder and Jack Kerouac, and later in the poetry of Irish Nobel prize–winner Seamus Heaney.

Today, the temple holds little of interest except for a stele by poet Zhang Ji immortalising both the nearby Maple Bridge and the temple bell (since removed to Japan). However, the fine walls and the humpback bridge are worth seeing.

Tourist bus Y3 takes you from the train station to the temple.

PAN GATE 盘门

Straddling the outer moat in the southwest corner of the city, this stretch of the city wall has Suzhōu's only remaining original **coiled gate** (Pán Mén; 1 Dongda Jie; Pan Gate only/with Ruiguang Pagoda Y25/31; ☑ 8am-5pm), which dates from 1355. The exquisite arched Wumen Bridge (Wúmén Qiáo), crosses the canal just to the east. From the gate there are great views of the moat and the crumbling **Ruiguang Pagoda** (Ruìguāng Tǎ), constructed in the 3rd century AD.

To get there, take tourist bus Y5 from the train station or Changxu Lu.

TIGER HILL 虎丘山

In the far northwest of town, **Tiger Hill** (Hǔqiū Shān; Huqiu Lu; admission off-peak/peak Y40/60; ☑ 7.30am-5pm) is extremely popular with local tourists. The hill itself is artificial and is the final resting place of He Lu, founding father of Suzhōu. He Lu died in the 6th century BC and myths have coalesced around him – he is said to have been buried with a collection of 3000 swords and to be guarded by a white tiger.

Built in the 10th century, the leaning **Cloud Rock Pagoda** (Yúnyán Tǎ) stands atop Tiger Hill. The octagonal seven-storey pagoda, also known as Huqiu Pagoda, is built entirely of brick, an innovation in Chinese architecture at the time. The pagoda began tilting over 400 years ago, and today the highest point is displaced more than 2m from its original position.

Tourist buses Y1 and Y2 from the train station go to Tiger Hill.

Tours

Evening boat tours wind their way around the outer canal leaving nightly at 6.30pm (Y35, 80 minutes). The trips are good fun and a great way to experience old Suzhōu. Remember to bring bug repellent as the mosquitos are tenacious. Tickets can be bought at the port near Renmin Bridge, which shares the same quarters with the Grand Canal ticket office.

Festivals & Events

Every September, Suzhōu hosts the **Suzhōu Silk Festival**. There are exhibitions devoted to silk history and production, and silk merchants get to show off their wares to crowds of thousands. If you're interested in purchasing high-quality silk at bargain prices, this is a great festival to attend.

Sleeping

Suzhōu has little to offer in the way of cheap accommodation. Hotels, in general, are terribly overpriced for what you get. On a more positive note, it's often possible to bargain room prices down, so don't be immediately deterred by the posted rates.

BUDGET

Suzhou Youth Hostel (Sūzhōu Guójì Qīngnián Lǚshè; ☎ 6510 9418; www.yha.suzhou.com; 178 Xiangwang Lu; 相王路178号; dm Y40, d Y120-140, tr Y150; ☐) This hostel opened in 2005 and features tidy rooms along with a guest kitchen, laundry and internet access.

Dongwu Hotel (Dōngwú Fàndiàn; ☎ 6519 3681; fax 6519 4590; 24 Wuyachang, Shiquan Jie; 吴衙场24号,市全街; s/d Y80/100, s/d/t with bathroom Y200/280/360) This clean place, off Shiquan Jie, is run by the Suzhou University International Cultural Exchange Institute. Rooms are adequate, if a little threadbare.

Hanting Hotel (Hàntíng Jiǔdiàn; ☎ 6770 1818; fax 6770 1212; 23 Yinguo Xiang; 因国巷23号; s Y218, d Y258-288) Opened in early 2006, this chain hotel features a fresh modern design with laminate floors and sparkling bathrooms. There are free guest-only computers in the lobby. Rooms can be discounted as much as 30%.

MIDRANGE

Gusu Hotel (Gūsū Fàndiàn; ☎ 6520 0566; fax 6519 9727; 5 Xiangwang Lu; 相王路5号; d Y480-620) This tourist staple has good-sized rooms that won't win any prizes in the décor department but are comfortable enough and have decent bathrooms.

Suzhou Hotel (Sūzhōu Fàndiàn; ☎ 6520 4646; fax 6520 5191; 115 Shiquan Jie; 十全街115号; tw/d Y850/1200) This hotel is not as good as its counterparts on Shiquan Jie. Rooms are musty and over-priced but will do in a pinch. Have a look at your room (especially the bathroom) before you commit.

TOP END

Nanlin Hotel (Nánlín Fàndiàn; ☎ 6519 6333; 20 Gunxi-ufang; 滚绣坊20号; s/d Y1080) Set in a large, treed compound off Shiquan Jie and surrounded by gardens, the elegant rooms in this modern hotel are well worth the money. Management is courteous and helpful.

Sheraton Suzhou Hotel & Towers (Sūzhōu Xǐláidēng Dàjiǔdiàn; ☎ 6510 3388; www.sheraton-suzhou.com; 388 Xin-shi Lu; 新市路388号; d Y1660) If you want comfort, this five-star luxury palace makes the grade. Done up pseudo-Ming style, rooms here are luxurious and fitted with all the latest gadgets to make you happy.

Eating

Sūzhōu's restaurants aren't as diverse or so-phisticated as those in Shànghǎi or Nánjīng, but you still won't have any problems finding a place to eat. The Guanqian Jie pedestrian district has a number of restaurants, includ-ing several well-known places that cater to tourist groups. You'll also find here the usual glut of fast-food restaurants and coffee chains. Shiquan Jie, between Daichengqiao Lu and Xiangwang Lu, is lined with bars, restaurants and bakeries.

Some local delicacies to try are sweet-and-sour mandarin fish (松鼠鳜鱼; sōngshǔ guìyú), stewed shredded eel (香油鳝糊; xiāngyóu shànhú) and chicken placed in watermelon rind and steamed (西瓜鸡; xīguā jī).

7&7 (Guanfeng Shangchang; dishes Y4-8; ☑ 24hr) This large, cafeteria-style restaurant near the park in the Guanqian Jie pedestrian area has a line-up of stir-fries, noodle dishes and steamed breads to choose from, all at rock-bottom prices.

Yángyáng Shuǐjiǎoguǎn (144 Shiquan Jie; mains Y5-25; ☑ 7am-3am) In this unassuming eatery you can feast on a dozen tasty boiled dumplings (水饺; shuǐjiǎo) for a mere Y5. The restau-rant also serves inexpensive veggie and meat dishes.

Sōnghé Lóu (☎ 6523 3270; 141 Guanqian Jie; mains from Y20-40; ☑ 11.30am-1.30pm & 5-8.30pm) This 200-year-old restaurant is the most famous in town and supposedly Emperor Qianlong's favourite

when he came to visit. Here you can choose from a variety of Sūzhōu-style dishes, includ-ing the popular mandarin fish. Food is good but expensive and service can be brusque.

Déyuélóu (☎ 6523 8940; 43 Taijian Long; mains Y20-50; ☑ 24hr) Another oldie, this place has been around since the Ming dynasty. The menu features over 300 items, with an emphasis on freshwater fish. It's a popular place for tour groups and the menu is in English.

Mario's Pizza Ristorante Bar Caffe (☎ 6770 4322; 1736 Renmin Lu; mains Y30-50; ☑ 10am-10pm Mon-Fri, to 2.30am Sat & Sun) If you get a hankering for some-thing Italian, head to this simple little place near the North Temple Pagoda. Mario's is by far the best place to eat continental cuisine in Sūzhōu. Try one of its authentic pizzas or pasta dishes – the sauces are all homemade and fabulous.

Drinking

West Street Bar (Xījiē Jiǔláng; 181 Shiquan Jie; drinks Y25-30; ☑ 6pm-late) This three-storey bar is crammed full of Chinese and European antiques. With its homey ambience, eclectic crowd and friendly management, it's a great place to relax with a beer.

Entertainment

Music **shows** (tickets Y70; ☑ 7.30-9.30pm) are per-formed nightly for tourist groups at the Gar-den of the Master of the Nets (p303). Don't expect anything too authentic – better shows are put on at the Pingtan Museum (p306) in the afternoons.

Shopping

Sūzhōu-style embroidery, calligraphy, paint-ings, sandalwood fans, writing brushes and silk underclothes are for sale nearly every-where. For good-quality items at competitive rates, shop along Shiquan Jie, east off Renmin Lu, which is lined with shops and markets selling souvenirs.

Suzhou Antique & Curio Store (Sūzhōu Wénwù Shāngdiàn; 1208 Renmin Lu; ☑ 10am-5.30pm) You can find silk embroidery, ceramics, fans and other traditional crafts in this government-run store. Bargaining isn't an option here.

These items can also be found in the lively **night market** (☑ 6.30-9.30pm) near Shi Lu, which also sells food, clothing and all kinds of trinkets.

The northern part of Renmin Lu has a number of large silk stores.

Dōngwú Sīchóu Shāngdiàn (1546 Renmin Lu; 8am-10pm) It's attached to a silk factory and has clothes, material and bedding for sale. You can find some lovely items here and staff are open to bargaining.

Suzhou Food Centre (Sūzhōu Shípǐn Dàshà; cnr Renmin Lu & Guanqian Jie; 8.30am-9pm) For sweets, cookies, snacks and teas, try this traditional food store at the entrance to Guanqian Jie.

Getting There & Away

AIR

Sūzhōu does not have an airport, but **China Eastern Airlines** (Dōngfāng Hángkōng Gōngsī; 6522 2788; 1138 Renmin Lu) can help with booking flights out of Shànghǎi. For international tickets, you can also try the CITS beside the Lexiang Hotel. Buses leave frequently for Hongqiao Airport in Shànghǎi. Tickets are Y45.

BOAT

Overnight passenger boats travel along the Grand Canal to Hángzhōu and many travellers enjoy this experience. The boat departs at 5.30pm daily and arrives the next morning at 7am. You can purchase tickets at the dock at the southern end of Renmin Lu or at the **Lianhe Ticket Centre** (Liánhé Shòupiàochù; 1606 Renmin Lu; 8am-5pm). Tickets in a four-person cabin cost Y47 to Y88 per person. A two-person cabin costs Y78 to Y130 per person.

For boats leaving from Hángzhōu, see the Hángzhōu section of the Zhèjiāng chapter on p322.

BUS

Sūzhōu has three long-distance bus stations. The main one is at the northern end of Renmin Lu, next to the train station, and a second is at the southern end of Renmin Lu. Both have connections to just about every major place in the region, including Shànghǎi (Y30, 1½ hours), Hángzhōu (Y76, three hours), Wúxī (Y15, 30 minutes), Nánjīng (Y67, 2½ hours) and Zhōuzhuāng (Y15, 1½ hours).

A third station, the Wuxian long-distance bus station (Wúxiàn chēzhàn), further south on Renmin Lu, has similar connections with other buses that are slightly cheaper, but run less frequently than from the other two stations.

Travelling by bus on the Nánjīng–Shànghǎi freeway takes about the same amount of time as the train, but tickets are generally slightly more expensive.

TRAIN

Sūzhōu is on the Nánjīng–Shànghǎi train line. The fastest train to Shànghǎi (Y15) takes about 45 minutes; more frequent trains take one hour. There are also trains to Wúxī (Y12, 30 minutes) and Nánjīng (Y33, 2½ hours). CITS will book sleepers for a Y30 service charge or you can book train tickets on the 2nd floor of the **Lianhe Ticket Centre** (Liánhé Shòupiàochù; 1606 Renmin Lu; 8am-5pm).

If you want to take a day trip from Shànghǎi to Sūzhōu, trains leave Shànghǎi (Y15) every morning at 7.55am and 8.37am, arriving at 8.42am and 9.15am respectively. Express trains depart for Shànghǎi every afternoon at 5.10pm and 6pm and take about one hour. A nightly express train (Y180) runs between Běijīng and Shànghǎi. The trip takes 11½ hours and leaves each city at 7.30pm.

Getting Around

BICYCLE

Riding a bike is the best way to see Sūzhōu, though nutty drivers and increased traffic can be nerve jangling, especially around the train station. Search out the quieter streets and travel along the canals to get the most of what this city has to offer.

There's a bicycle rental shop 100m north of the Silk Museum that charges Y5 a day plus a deposit. Check out the seat and brakes carefully before you pedal off.

BUS

Sūzhōu has some convenient tourist buses that visit all sights and cost Y2. They all pass by the train station. Bus Y5 goes around the western and eastern sides of the city. Bus Y2 travels from Tiger Hill, Coiled Gate and along Shiquan Jie. Buses Y1 and Y4 run the length of Renmin Lu. Buses Y3 and Y4 also pass by Cold Mountain.

TAXI

There are plenty of taxis in Sūzhōu. Fares start at Y10 and drivers generally use their meters. Pedicabs hover around the tourist areas and, like elsewhere in China, can be fairly aggressive. Expect to bargain hard.

GRAND CANAL 大运河

The Grand Canal (Dà Yùnhé) proper cuts to the west and south of Sūzhōu, within a 10km range of the town. Suburban buses 13, 14, 15 and 16 will get you there. In the northwest,

JIÄNGSŪ

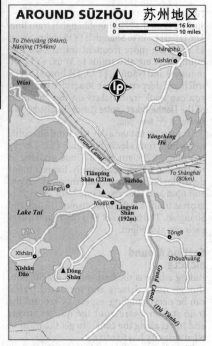

AROUND SUZHŌU 苏州地区

0 — 16 km
0 — 10 miles

To Zhènjiāng (84km);
Nánjīng (154km)

Chángshú

Yúshān

Wúxī

Grand Canal

Yángchéng
Hú

Tiānpíng
Shān (221m)

Guāngfú

Sūzhōu

To Shànghǎi
(80km)

Mùdú

Língyán
Shān
(192m)

Lake Tai

Tónglǐ

Xīshān

Xīshān
Dǎo

Dōng
Shān

Zhōuzhuāng

Grand Canal
(Dà Yùnhé)

bus 11 follows the canal for a fair distance, taking you on a tour of the enchanting countryside. Hop off the bus once you find yourself a nice bridge on which you can perch and watch the world of the canal float by. Parking yourself for too long could make you the main attraction.

Precious Belt Bridge 宝带桥

With 53 arches, this is considered one of China's best bridges (Bǎodài Qiáo). It straddles the Grand Canal and is a popular spot with fisherfolk. The three central humpbacks of the bridge are larger to allow boats through. It recently had some extensive maintenance done and is no longer used for traffic – a modern one has been built alongside it.

Precious Belt Bridge is thought to be a Tang dynasty construction named after Wang Zhongshu, a local prefect who sold his precious belt to pay for the bridge's construction for the benefit of his people.

The bridge is 4km southeast of Sūzhōu. You can get there by taxi (Y15) or a 30-minute bike ride. Head south on Renmin Lu, over the Waicheng River. Turn left on Nanhuan Donglu

after you pass the Wuxian long-distance bus station. Head east until you hit the canal on Dongqing Lu then south to the bridge.

LAKE TAI AREA

The towns surrounding Sūzhōu provide ample opportunity for a visit to Lake Tai and the countryside beyond the lake.

The following destinations can be reached by long-distance bus from Sūzhōu's south long-distance bus station. Tourist bus 4 goes to Língyán Shān and Tiānpíng Shān from the train station.

Scenic **Tiānpíng Shān** (天平山; Lingtian Lu; admission Y10; ⏰ 8am-5.30pm) is a low, forested hill about 13km west of Sūzhōu. It's a wonderful place for hiking or just meandering along one of its many wooded trails. It's also famous for its medicinal spring waters.

Eleven kilometres southwest of Sūzhōu is **Língyán Shān** (灵岩山; Lingtian Lu; admission Y25; ⏰ 6.30am-4.30pm), or 'cliff of the spirits', once the site of a palace where Emperor Qianlong stayed during his inspection tours of the Yangzi River valley. The palace was destroyed during the Taiping Rebellion. Now, the mountain is home to an active Buddhist monastery.

The refreshingly rural island of **Dōng Shān** (东山; admission Y15; ⏰ 7.30am-5pm), 37km southwest of Sūzhōu, connects to Lake Tai by a narrow causeway and is noted for its gardens and the wonderfully secluded **Purple Gold Nunnery** (紫金庵; Zǐjīn'ān). To see eroded Tài Hú rocks 'harvested' for landscaping, visit **Xīshān Dǎo** (西山岛), 33km southwest of Sūzhōu.

TÓNGLǏ 同里

☎ 0512

The canal town of Tónglǐ, only 18km from Sūzhōu, sits near Lake Tai and the Grand Canal and has been around since at least the 9th century. Rich in atmosphere, many of its buildings have kept their traditional façades, with stark whitewashed walls and black-tiled roofs.

Tónglǐ is a popular destination for day trippers from Sūzhōu or Shànghǎi, but it manages to retain a pleasing weather-beaten charm, despite the flocks of tourists on weekends and holidays. With its ancient homes, cobblestone pathways and canals pleasantly shaded with willow trees, it's a great place for a stroll or just whiling away the hours at a waterside teahouse.

5000 YEARS OF EROTICA

Overall, there's not a whole lot distinguishing one canal town from another, and whichever one you choose to visit is ultimately a matter of either convenience or fate (or both). Tónglǐ, however, does have a trump card up its sleeve, though most villagers won't admit it because the card is X-rated. It's the **Chinese Sex Culture Museum** (below). Unfortunately, the name deters most people from even considering a visit, though in reality it is not that racy.

Founded by sociology professors Liu Dalin and Hu Hongxia, the museum's aim is not so much to arouse, but rather to reintroduce an aspect of the country's culture that, ironically, has been forcefully repressed since China was 'liberated' in 1949. The pair have collected several thousand artefacts relating to sex, from the good (erotic landscape paintings, fans and teacups) to the bad (chastity belts and saddles with wooden dildos used to punish 'licentious' women), and the humorous (satirical Buddhist statues) to the unusual (a pot-bellied immortal with a penis growing out of his head topped by a turtle). This is also one of the only places in the country where homosexuality is openly recognised as part of Chinese culture.

Sights

The **Old Town** (☎ 6333 1140; admission Y80, Sex Museum Y20; ⏰ 7.30am-5.30pm) of Tónglǐ is best explored the traditional way, which is to say by wandering aimlessly alongside the canals until you get lost, and then trying to find your way back past the maze of bridges. The whitewashed houses, laundry hanging out to dry and cormorants perched on fishing boats are all so charming that it doesn't really matter where you go, as long as you're fleeing the crowds.

There are three old residences that you'll pass at some point (unless you're really lost), the best of which is **Gēnglè Táng** (耕乐堂), a sprawling Ming dynasty estate with 52 halls spread out over five courtyards in the west of town. The buildings have been elaborately restored and redecorated with paintings, calligraphy and antique furniture to bring back the atmosphere of the original buildings.

In the north of town is the **Pearl Pagoda** (珍珠塔; Zhēnzhū Tǎ), which dates from the Qing dynasty but has recently been restored. Inside, you'll find a large residential compound decorated with Qing-era antiques, an ancestral hall, a garden and even an opera stage where occasional karaoke-style opera performances are held.

In the east is **Tuisi Garden** (退思园; Tuìsī Yuán), Tónglǐ's star attraction. The name of the garden means 'to retire and contemplate', so named because it was a Qing government official's retirement home. The surrounds are quite lovely, with pavilions, sculpted rocks and a pond. In the centre of the garden is a large two-storied hall with intricately tiled floors and terraces looking out over the canal and ancient rooftops. On the 2nd floor were

the living quarters of the unmarried women, who were prevented from co-mingling with guests from outside the family.

Last but not least, you can't miss the **Chinese Sex Culture Museum** (中华性文化博物馆; Zhōnghuá Xìngwénhuá Bówùguǎn; admission Y20), the one place you should make an effort to find. If you thought Confucius was a prude, think again. This progressive museum (see the boxed text, above) was forced out of Shànghǎi in search of a permanent home, though hopefully its present location (in a former girls' school) will last.

Sleeping

Zhèngfú Cǎotáng (正福草堂; ☎ 6333 6358; www.zfct.net; 138 Mingqing Jie; d Y180-480) For a truly unique experience, stay at this traditional residence, beautifully furnished with Qing furniture and antiques. Outside is a courtyard where you can sit and sip tea while the owner plays the *qín* (a seven-stringed plucked instrument) for guests at night. It's down the main tourist street (turn right at the town entrance). You'll have to reserve in advance.

Eating

Along the main canal that bisects the town, practically every building is an outdoor restaurant or tea shop. Most serve basic dishes (Y8 to Y25) and tea (Y5). A plate of fried rice with shrimp (*chǎofàn*) will cost Y20.

Getting There & Away

From Sūzhōu, buses run to Tónglǐ from the bus stop in front of the train station. Buses run every 15 minutes from 6.40am to 5.15pm, and cost Y7. The trip takes about 30 minutes.

A pedicab from the bus station to the Old Town is Y5, or you can walk it in about 10 minutes.

From Shànghǎi, sightseeing buses depart daily from the Shanghai Stadium at 9am, and depart Tónglǐ at 4.30pm; the journey takes up to 1¾ hours depending on traffic. Tickets are Y120 and include admission to the town and all sights, except for the Chinese Sex Culture Museum. You will be dropped off 2km from town at Tónglǐ Lake, from where there's a shuttle (Y4) to the gate. The boat trip on Tónglǐ Lake is free, though of no particular interest.

MÙDÚ 木渎

☎ 0512

Mùdú is another of Jiāngsū's much-touted canal towns, but less touristy than some of its more famous neighbours. Just 20 minutes by bus from Sūzhōu, the town dates back to the Ming dynasty and was once the haunt of wealthy officials, intellectuals and artists. Mùdú's biggest claim to stardom is declared proudly on a sign near the entrance: 'Emperor Qianlong of the Qing Dynasty (1644–1911) visited six times'. Certainly not the biggest or most interesting of the canal towns, it's still an appealing enough place for a day trip from Sūzhōu. Within the old town, several of the traditional canal-side homes have been opened to visitors, giving a glimpse of the opulent lifestyles of the Ming and Qing well-to-do. Mùdú is best-known for its gardens, inspired by the classical gardens of Sūzhōu. Like other water towns, the best way to ditch the crowds is to venture into the warren of narrow streets that branch off of the canals and see what you find.

Sights

Near the entrance to the **Old Town** (☎ 6636 8225; admission Y60; 8am-4.30pm) is the dignified **Bangyan Mansion** (榜眼府第; Bǎngyǎn Fǔdì) of the 19th-century writer and politician Feng Guifen. The mansion is the central focus here, with a rich collection of antique furniture and intricate carvings of stone, wood and brick. The surrounding garden is pretty but fairly typical – lotus ponds, arched bridges, bamboo – and can't compare to the more ornate gardens of Sūzhōu.

By far the most interesting place in Mùdú is the **Hongyin Mountain Villa** (虹饮山房; Hóngyǐn Shānfáng), with its elaborate opera stage, exhibits and even an imperial pier where Emperor Qianlong docked his boat. The stage in the centre hall is really impressive; honoured guests were seated in front and the galleries along the sides of the hall were for women. The emperor was a frequent visitor and you can still see his uncomfortable-looking imperial chair, which faces the stage. Operas are still performed here during the day. Surrounding the stage are some carefully arranged gardens, criss-crossed with dainty arched bridges and walkways. The old residence halls have been wonderfully preserved and have some interesting exhibits, including displays of dusty hats and gowns worn by imperial officers.

In the northwest corner of the old town is the **Yan Family Garden** (严家花园; Yánjiā Huāyuán), which dates back to the Ming and was once the home of a former magistrate. The garden, with its rockeries and a meandering lake, is separated into five sections and divided by walls, with each section meant to invoke a season. Flowers, plants and rocks are arranged to create a 'mood'. If you come over the weekend, the only mood the crowds might invoke is exasperation – it's more inspiring to come on a weekday, when you can enjoy the surroundings in peace. In the garden is a gnarled magnolia tree, supposedly planted by the emperor.

The most pleasurable way to experience Mùdú is by boat. You'll find a collection of traditional skiffs for hire docked outside the Bangyan Mansion. A ride in one of these will take you along the smooth waters of the narrow canals, shaded by ancient bridges and battered stone walls. Boat rides are Y10 per person.

Eating

Along the main street next to the canal is a collection of small restaurants and teahouses selling generic noodle and rice dishes for Y5 to Y10.

Getting There & Away

From Sūzhōu, tourist bus 4 runs from the train station to Mùdú and costs Y2. Make sure to get off at Mùdú Yánjiā Huāyuán Zhàn (木渎严家花园站), which is across from a small road leading to the main entrance. You'll see a big sign and a parking lot full of tour buses. The ride takes about 30 minutes.

From Shànghǎi, deluxe buses run from the Shanghai Stadium directly to Mùdú. They leave at 7.20am and 8.10am and leave Mùdú at 4pm for the return trip. Tickets cost Y110. Alternatively, you can take a bus or train to Sūzhōu and switch to bus 4 at the train station.

Zhèjiāng 浙江

Zhèjiāng may be one of China's smallest provinces but it's hardly insignificant. For centuries it's been a prosperous culture centre, home to some of China's most influential thinkers, politicians and artists. Today Zhèjiāng is a thriving commercial hub, with tourism as its number one draw. Its rich history and natural beauty offer something for every taste, whether you're into biking, ceramic making, or just lounging on the beach.

The province can be divided into two parts: the Yangzi River delta area north of Hángzhōu, a region of green rolling hills, tea plantations and twisting rivers, and the mountainous area to the south that borders the rugged terrain of Fújiàn.

Zhèjiāng's best-known sites are in the north. Hángzhōu, the capital, is home to idyllic West Lake, which Marco Polo once compared to paradise. The city is also famous for its tea and has long been a centre of silk production. Not far from Hángzhōu is the waterside city of Shàoxīng, once the home of such notables as Lu Xun, one of China's most famous 20th-century writers. Further north, along the border of Jiāngsū are the water towns of Wūzhèn and Nánxún, with their arched bridges, winding canals and views of rural life.

Southern Zhèjiāng is a region of wild beauty, with jagged mountain peaks and rocky, unspoiled valleys. The thriving trade city of Wēnzhōu is a perfect place to base yourself for rambles into the countryside. If hiking isn't your thing, perhaps you should head to the tranquil Buddhist island of Pǔtuóshān; with its clean sandy beaches and lively temples it's a wonderful place for some rural respite.

HIGHLIGHTS

- Submit to nature in the spectacular surrounds of **Jīngnìng County** (p337), in Zhèjiāng's deep south
- Fall under the spell of Hángzhōu's enchanting **West Lake** (p317), venerated by poets and emperors alike
- Get down and dirty making your own pottery at the **Southern Song dynasty Guan Kiln** (p320) outside of Hángzhōu
- Travel back in time at the delightful water towns of **Ānchāng** (p329) and **Wūzhèn** (p324)
- Soothe your soul on the peaceful island of **Pǔtuóshān** (p332)

■ POPULATION: 46.4 MILLION   ■ http://english.zjol.com.cn

ZHÈJIĀNG

History

The Yangzi delta was inhabited over 7000 years ago and archaeologists have found the remains of advanced agricultural communities. By the 7th and 8th centuries Hángzhōu, Níngbō and Shàoxīng had become three of the most important trading centres and ports. The Grand Canal (Dà Yùnhé) ends here – Zhèjiāng was part of the great southern granary from which food was shipped to the depleted areas of the north. Their growth was accelerated when, in the 12th century, the Song dynasty moved court to Hángzhōu in the wake of an invasion from the north. Because of intense cultivation, northern Zhèjiāng has lost most of its natural vegetation and is now a flat, featureless plain.

Níngbō was opened up as a treaty port in the 1840s, only to fall under the shadow of its great northern competitor, Shànghǎi. Chiang Kaishek was born near Níngbō, and in the 1920s Zhèjiāng became a centre of power for the Kuomintang.

Climate

Zhèjiāng has a humid, subtropical climate, with hot, sticky summers and chilly winters. Rain hits the province hard in May and June but slows to a drizzle throughout the rest of the year.

The best times to visit are during the spring (late March to early May) when the humidity is lowest and the vegetation turns a brilliant green.

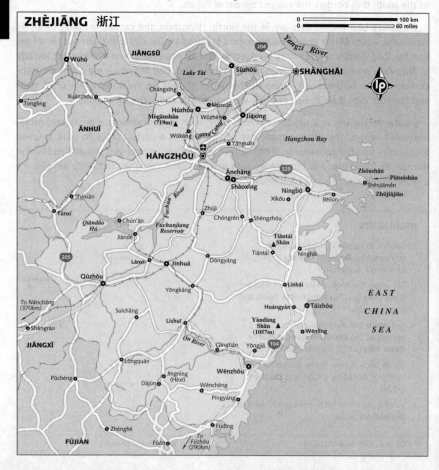

Language

Zhèjiāng residents speak a variation of the Wu dialect (Wú *yǔ*), which is also spoken in Jiāngsū. The dialect is almost unintelligible from city to city and residents rely on standard Mandarin to communicate.

Getting There & Away

Being an important tourist destination, Zhèjiāng is very well connected to the rest of the country by plane, train and bus. Ferries were once the traditional means of getting around the region and are still in use today, though mainly for shuttling hordes of tourists around. Ferries travel from Hángzhōu and Wēnzhōu to Nánjīng, Shànghǎi and Sūzhōu.

Getting Around

As the province is quite small, getting around is easy. For the most part, travelling by bus is safe, fast and convenient. Trains are also an option, though at times more circuitous and slower than buses. Flying is an option, especially for those with cash to spare and limited time.

HÁNGZHŌU 杭州
☎ 571 / pop 6.16 million

Hángzhōu, capital of Zhèjiāng, is one of China's most famous tourist sites. Located at the southern end of the Grand Canal and surrounded by fertile farmlands, the city has been a significant cultural centre for hundreds of years. Current-day Hángzhōu, with its characterless architecture, has little to differentiate it from other modern Chinese cities. The main reason for coming here is to visit the legendary West Lake (Xī Hú), a true beauty in the midst of a concrete jungle.

Praised by emperors and revered by poets, the lake has figured large in the Chinese imagination for centuries. With its willow-lined banks, ancient pagodas and mist-covered hills, being here is like stepping into a classical Chinese watercolour. Despite huge numbers of tourists, West Lake is a delight to explore, either on foot or by bike.

History

Hángzhōu's history goes back to the start of the Qin dynasty (221 BC). When Marco Polo passed through the city in the 13th century he described it as one of the most splendid in the world. Although Hángzhōu prospered greatly after it was linked with the Grand Canal in AD 610, it really came into its own after the Song dynasty was overthrown by the invading Jurchen, predecessors of the Manchus.

The Song capital of Kāifēng, along with the emperor and the leaders of the imperial court, was captured by the Jurchen in 1126. The rest of the Song court fled south, finally settling in Hángzhōu and establishing it as the capital of the Southern Song dynasty.

When the Mongols swept into China they established their court in Běijīng. Hángzhōu, however, retained its status as a prosperous commercial city. In 1861 the Taipings laid siege to the city and captured it, but two years later the imperial armies took it back. These campaigns reduced almost the entire city to ashes, led to the deaths of over half a million of its residents through disease, starvation and warfare, and finally ended Hángzhōu's significance as a commercial and trading centre.

Few monuments survived the devastation, and most of those that did became victims of the Red Guards a century later during the Cultural Revolution. Much of what can be seen in Hángzhōu today is of fairly recent construction.

Orientation

Hángzhōu is bounded to the south by the Qiántáng River and to the west by hills. Between the hills and the urban area is West Lake. The eastern shore of the lake is the developed tourist district; the western shore is quieter.

Information
BOOKSHOPS

Foreign Languages Bookshop (Zhèjiāng Wàiwén Shūdiàn; 446 Fengqi Lu) has a good range of maps and books about Hángzhōu in English and Chinese.

INTERNET ACCESS 网吧

Government crackdowns have made internet cafés difficult to find – many places have closed or changed names and locations frequently. Almost all hotels offer internet facilities, though you'll pay upwards of Y20 per hour to use their services.

Zonline (Zhèjiāng Xiàn; 168 Laodong Lu; ☉ 9am-late) is a large café behind the China Academy of Art. The rate is Y3 an hour, with a Y20 deposit.

INTERNET RESOURCES

www.gotohz.com Current information on events, restaurants and entertainment venues around the city. **www.hangzhou.com.cn** Similar to above site.

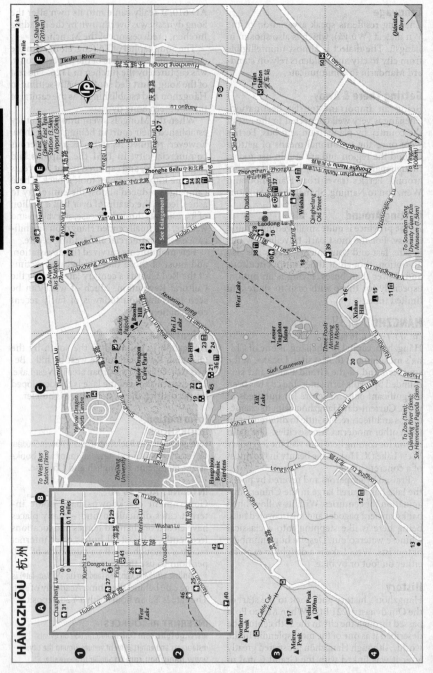

MEDICAL SERVICES

Zhejiang University First Affiliated Hospital
(Zhèjiāng Dàxué Yīxuéyuàn Fùshǔ Dìyī Yīyuàn;
79 Qingchun Lu)

MONEY

It is also possible to change money at high-end hotels (guests only).
Bank of China (Zhōngguó Yínháng; 320 Yan'an Lu;
9am-5pm) This branch of the bank has a secure, well-lit ATM. Travellers cheques can be changed here, as well as at other branches around town.

POST

Post Office (yóujú; Jiefang Lu) This main branch of the post office is at the eastern end of Jiefang Lu. There's also a conveniently located post office on Renhe Lu, close to the West Lake.

PUBLIC SECURITY BUREAU

PSB (Gōngānjú; ☎ 8728 0561; 35 Huaguang Lu;
8.30am-noon & 2.30-5pm) Helps in cases of emergency, in addition to extending visas.

TOURIST INFORMATION & TRAVEL AGENCIES

There's a tourist office immediately to your left as you exit the main train station at the bottom level. It has maps (Y6) in English and Chinese.

Hángzhōu Tourist Centre (Hángzhōu Lǚyóu Jìsǎn Zhōngxīn; ☎ 8796 8560; Yellow Dragon Sports Centre; Wúshān Square; 9am-5pm) Books air and train tickets and can arrange tours. It has friendly, English-speaking staff.

Tourist Complaint Hotline (☎ 8796 9691) Can help with complaints.

Sights & Activities

Hángzhōu grants free admission to all museums and gardens. Sights offer half-price tickets for children between 1m to 1.3m, free for shorties under 1m.

WEST LAKE 西湖

There are 36 lakes in China called **West Lake** (Xī Hú), but this one is by far the most famous. Indeed this is the West Lake from which all others take their name. Originally a lagoon adjoining the Qiántáng River, the lake didn't come into existence until the 8th century, when the governor of Hángzhōu had the marshy expanse dredged. As time passed, the lake's splendour was gradually cultivated: gardens were planted, pagodas built, and causeways and islands were constructed from dredged silt. The poet Su Dongpo famously personified West Lake as a young woman whose beauty was enhanced by her elegant dress.

Su himself had a hand in the lake's development, constructing the **Su Causeway** (Sūdī) during his tenure as local governor in the 11th century. It wasn't an original idea – the poet-governor Bai Juyi had already constructed the **Bai Causeway** (Báidī) some 200 years earlier. Lined by willow, plum and peach trees, today the traffic-free causeways with their half-moon bridges make for excellent outings, particularly on a bike.

Connected to the northern shores by the Bai Causeway is **Gu Hill** (Gū Shān), the largest island in the lake and the location of the **Zhejiang Provincial Museum** (Zhèjiāng Shěng Bówùguǎn; ☎ 8797 1177; 25 Gushan Lu; ☯ 8.30am-4.30pm Tue-Sun; admission free, audioguide Y10), **Zhongshan Park** (Zhōngshān Gōngyuán) and the Louwailou Restaurant (p321). The island's buildings and gardens were once the site of Emperor Qianlong's 18th-century holiday palace and gardens. Also on the island is the intriguing **Seal Engravers' Society** (Xīlíng Yìnshè), dedicated to the ancient art of carving the name seals (chops) that serve as personal signatures. In the northwest is the lovely **Quyuan Garden** (Qūyuàn Fēnghé), a collection of gardens spread out over numerous islets and renowned for its fragrant spring lotus blossoms. Near **Xiling Bridge** (Xīlíng Qiáo) is the tomb of **Su Xiaoxiao** (Sū Xiǎoxiāo Mù), a 5th-century courtesan who died of grief while waiting for her lover to return. It's been said that her ghost haunts the area and the tinkle of the bells on her gown can be heard at night.

The smaller island in the lake is **Lesser Yingzhou Island** (Xiǎo Yíngzhōu) where you can look over at **Three Pools Mirroring the Moon** (Sāntán Yìnyuè), three small towers in the water on the south side of the island; each has five holes that release shafts of candlelight on the night of the mid-autumn festival. From Lesser Yingzhou Island, you can look over to **Red Carp Pond** (Huāgǎng Guānyú), home to a few thousand red carp.

Liulang Wenying Park (Liǔlàng Wènyīng Gōngyuán) was once an imperial garden during the Song dynasty. Nowadays, the park is famous for its willow trees and is the site of the Lunar Festival.

MAUSOLEUM OF GENERAL YUE FEI 岳飞墓

General Yue Fei (1103–42), commander of the southern Song armies, is a fabled figure in literature, opera and movies. During the 12th century, the general led a series of successful battles against Jurchen invaders from the north. Despite his initial successes, he was recalled to the Song court, where he was executed, along with his son, after being deceived by the treacherous prime minister Qin Hui. In 1163, Song emperor Gao Zong exonerated Yue Fei and had his corpse re-buried at the present site.

The **mausoleum** (Yuè Fēi Mù; Beishan Lu; admission Y25; ☯ 7am-5.30pm) is in the compound bounded by a red-brick wall. Inside is a large statue of the general and the words 'return our mountains and rivers', a reference to his patriotism and resistance to the Jurchen. You'll also see over 100 stone stelae, with inscriptions and a poem written by Yue Fei while he was in prison, some paintings depicting the general's life and some interesting statuary.

YELLOW DRAGON CAVE PARK 黄龙洞公园

West of the mausoleum, a path leads upwards above the lake, eventually reaching this secluded mountainside **park** (Huánglóngdòng Gōngyuán; ☯ 7.15am-6pm), tucked deep into the hills and surrounded by bamboo, ponds and teahouses. At the park summit you'll see a small spring with the stone head of a dragon and a stele nearby with an inscription that reads, 'Where there are dragons, there are spirits'.

If you follow the main path eastward, you'll come to the yellow-walled **Baopu Taoist Compound** (Bāopǔ Dàoyuàn; admission Y5; ☯ 7am-5pm), named after the Taoist master Ge Hong (AD 284–364), famous for his longevity elixirs. This is an active place of worship, with chanting in the early morning and evening. Behind the monastery is **Sunrise Terrace** (Chūyáng Tái) with fantastic views of the lake and the sprawling city surrounding it.

If you continue following the path eastwards as it heads down the hill, you'll reach the **Baochu Pagoda** (Bǎochù Tǎ) or 'Precious Stone' pagoda, which looks out over the northeastern shore of the West Lake. Originally built in the 9th century, its current renovation dates to 1933.

LEIFENG PAGODA 雷锋塔

East along the shore is the eye-catching **tower** (Léifēng Tǎ; admission Y40; ☯ 7.30am-11pm) or 'Thunder Peak Pagoda', which you can ascend for fine views of the lake. The original pagoda, built in 975, was a popular spot to watch the sun set over the lake for centuries, until it collapsed in 1924. During its most recent renovation in 2001, Buddhist scriptures written on silk were found in the foundation, along with other treasures. At the bottom of the pagoda is a museum with English captions.

JINGCI TEMPLE 净慈寺
Across the road from the Leifeng Pagoda is this peaceful Chan (Zen) **temple** (Jìngcí Chánsì; admission Y10; ☉ 6am-4.30pm), originally built in AD 954 and now fully restored. Inside the temple is an enormous bronze bell – on the eve of the Lunar New Year, the bell is struck 108 times for prosperity.

LINGYIN TEMPLE 灵隐寺
This **temple** (Língyǐn Sì; Lingyin Lu; admission Y30, Feilai Peak Y35; ☉ 7am-5pm), roughly translated as 'Temple of the Soul's Retreat', is one of Hángzhōu's chief attractions. It was built in AD 326 and, due to war and calamity, has been destroyed and restored no fewer than 16 times.

The walk up to the temple skirts the flanks of **Feilai Peak** (Fēilái Fēng; Peak Flying from Afar), which is supposed to have been magically transported here from India. The real highlights here, though, are the **Buddhist carvings** lining the riverbanks and hillsides – all 470 of them, dating from the 10th to 14th centuries. To get a close-up view of the best carvings, including the famous 'laughing' Maitreya Buddha, follow the paths along the far (east) side of the stream.

The main **temple buildings** are restorations of Qing dynasty structures. The Hall of the Four Heavenly Guardians at the front of the temple is inscribed with the line 'cloud forest Buddhist temple', penned by the Qing emperor Kangxi, who was a frequent visitor to Hángzhōu and was inspired on one occasion by the sight of the temple in the mist and trees. On either side of the entrance are two 1000-year-old stelae.

Behind this hall is the Great Hall, where you'll find the magnificent 20m-high statue of Siddhartha Gautama. This was sculpted from 24 blocks of camphor wood in 1956 and was based on a Tang dynasty original. Behind the giant statue is a startling montage of 150 small figures, which charts the journey of 53 children on the road to buddhahood. During the time of the Five Dynasties (907–60) about 3000 monks lived in the temple.

Bus K7 and tourist bus Y2 (both from the train station), and tourist bus Y1 from the roads circling West Lake, go to the temple. Behind Lingyin Temple is the Northern Peak (Běi Gāofēng), which can be scaled by **cable car** (up/down Y30/40). From the summit there are sweeping views across the lake and city.

QINGHEFANG OLD STREET 清河坊古街
At the south end of Zhongshan Zhonglu is this noisy, bustling pedestrian street (Qīnghéfāng Gǔjiē), with makeshift puppet theatres, teahouses and curio stalls. It's also the home of several traditional medicine shops, including the **Huqing Yutang Chinese Medicine Museum** (Zhōngyào Bówùguǎn; 95 Dajing Gang; admission Y10; ☉ 8am-5.30pm), which is an actual dispensary and clinic. Originally established by the Qing dynasty merchant Hu Xueyan in 1874, the medicine shop and factory retain the typical style of the period.

CHINA ACADEMY OF ART 中国美术学院
Located on the banks of the West Lake, this **art academy** (Zhōngguó Měishù Xuéyuàn; ☎ 8778 8027; 218 Nanshan Lu) was the first of its kind established in China. Founded in 1928, the school teaches painting, design, sculpture and art history to local and international students. There are short-term classes available for those who want to learn traditional Chinese painting. A number of small galleries surround the academy.

SOUTH OF WEST LAKE
The hills south of West Lake are Hángzhōu's most undeveloped area and are a prime spot for walkers, cyclists and green tea connoisseurs. Close to the lake is the **China Silk Museum** (Zhōngguó Sīchóu Bówùguǎn; 73-1 Yuhuangshan Lu; admission free; audio guide deposit Y100; ☉ 9am-4.30pm Tue-Sun). It has good displays of silk samples, and exhibits explain (in English) the history and processes of silk production.

Not far into the hills, you'll begin to see fields of tea bushes planted in undulating rows, the setting for the **China Tea Museum** (Zhōngguó Cháyè Bówùguǎn; Longjing Lu; admission free; ☉ 8.30am-4.30pm) – 3.7 hectares of land dedicated to the art, cultivation and tasting of tea. Further up are several tea-producing villages, all of which harvest China's most famous variety of green tea, *lóngjǐng* (dragon well), named after the spring where the pattern in the water resembles a dragon. You can enjoy

ZHÈJIĀNG

BIKE TOURS

There are numerous possibilities for cycling around Hángzhōu. This circuit loops through the forested hills south of West Lake and takes a half-day minimum; however you could easily stretch it into a longer trip by stopping at the sights along the way. It's by no means the *Tour de Chine*, however it covers approximately 10km and does cross over one pass, so be prepared. Bring plenty of water and a Hángzhōu Travel Guide trail map.

Begin by heading south from the lake on Longjing Lu (龙井路). It's a gradual ascent into the hills, past the **China Tea Museum** (p319) and fields of tea plantations. From here the gradient becomes significantly steeper. When you approach Longjing village, the road forks; put in the extra effort, go left and keep on heading up the mountain on Manjiaolong Lu (满觉陇路) – an easier route is to go right up to Longjing village and over a lower pass down Jiuxi Rd.

Once you've cleared the pass, you'll coast through a small **tea village** (翁家山; Wēngjiāshān). Enjoy the downhill into the forest, but don't go too fast, or you'll miss the turn-off for Yángméilǐng (杨梅岭), a tiny road on your right. This leads down through another village and out onto the forest floor, following a small stream past **Li'an Temple** (里安寺; Lǐān Sì).

Not far after this is **Nine Creeks Park** (九溪烟树; Jiǔxī Yānshù; admission Y2), with a lovely little pool fed by a waterfall (if you came from Lóngjǐng village, this is where you'll end up). From here you'll be wending your way through scenic countryside, until you reach Jiǔxī village (九溪村) at the highway. There are two restaurants and a convenience store in Jiǔxī. Turn left on the highway, and follow Qiántáng River until you reach **Six Harmonies Pagoda** (below). Fork left, go under the bridge, and head north on Hupao Lu, from where it's a reasonably easy ride all the way back to the lake.

one of Hángzhōu's most famous teas at the **Dragon Well Tea Village** (Lóngjǐng Wènchá; admission Y10; 8am-5.30pm), near the first pass. Tourist bus Y3 will take you to the museum and the village.

Three kilometres southwest of the lake, an enormous rail-and-road bridge spans the Qiántáng River. Close by is the 60m-high octagonal **Six Harmonies Pagoda** (Liùhé Tǎ; 16 Zhijiang Lu; admission Y20, Y10 to climb pagoda; 6am-6pm), first built in AD 960. The pagoda also served as a lighthouse, and was supposed to have magical power to halt the 6.5m-high tidal bore which thunders up Qiántáng River every autumn (see p323). Behind the pagoda stretches a charming walk, through terraces dotted with sculptures, bells, shrines and inscriptions.

SOUTHERN SONG DYNASTY GUAN KILN MUSEUM 南宋官窑博物馆
This royal **kiln** (Nánsòng Guānyáo Bówùguǎn; ☎ 8608 3990; 42 Nanfu Lu; admission free; 8.30am-4.30pm Tue-Sun) was once a production site for the famed porcelain and ceramics of the Southern Song dynasty. You can visit the remains of the kiln, where there are some exhibits of ancient kiln tools and equipment. There's also a showroom of Song ceramics and explanations in English that outline the history of ceramic ware in China. You can even try your hand at making

some treasures of your own for a nominal fee (Y20 to Y50). To get here, take tourist bus Y3; the museum is 1.5km from town.

Tours
Just about every midrange and top-end hotel offers tours to West Lake and the surrounding areas. Frequent tours also run from the Hángzhōu Tourist Centre.

Festivals & Events
One of the most important festivals in the region is the International Qiántáng River Tide-Observing Festival, which takes place every autumn in Yánguān, outside Hángzhōu. See p323 for more details.

Sleeping
Hángzhōu's hotels are mainly midrange and top end, with only a few budget options. In the busy summer months and during Chinese New Year, hotels can be booked out, prices soar and finding accommodation can be difficult. Most of the midrange and top-end hotel rooms are equipped with free broadband internet.

BUDGET
Mingtown Youth Hostel (Míngtáng Hángzhōu Guójì Qīngnián Lǚshè; ☎ 8791 8948; 101-11 Nanshan Lu; 南山路

101-11号; dm Y40-50, d Y120-280; 🖳) With its convenient lakeside location and proximity to major tourist sites, this friendly hostel is highly recommended. It offers ticket booking, internet access, and rents bikes and camping gear. The Mingtown also has two other locations: 4 Zhaogong Causeway (赵公堤4号) and 96 Siyiting Siyi Lu (四宜路四宜亭96号) at Wúshǎn. Call ahead to reserve.

Jiexin Century Hotel (International Art Centre Inn; Yìyàn Bīnguǎn; ☎ 8707 0100; 220 Nanshan Lu; 南山路220号; d Y280-498) Affiliated with the China Academy of Art next door, this small guesthouse offers sparsely furnished rooms. The location is terrific, but don't expect the facilities (free bottled water, cable TV) that come with other hotels in this price range. Paintings done by art students hang on the walls.

MIDRANGE & TOP END

Dongpo Hotel (Dōngpō Bīnguǎn; ☎ 8706 9769; 52 Renhe Lu; 仁和路; s Y280, d Y300-420) Located on a small but busy street adjacent to the lake, this hotel provides spotless rooms. Ask for a room in the back to avoid the noise of tourist traffic.

Zhongshan Hotel (Zhōngshān Dàjiǔdiàn; ☎ 8706 8899; fax 8702 2403; 15 Pinghai Lu; 平海路15号; d Y570-680, with lake view Y880-980) A favourite of business travellers, this hotel offers modern, quiet rooms and is about a 10-minute walk to the lake. Rooms are often discounted by as much as 50%.

Overseas Chinese Hotel (Huáqiáo Fàndiàn; ☎ 8707 4401; fax 8707 4978; 15 Hubin Lu; 湖滨路15号; d Y598-663) This hotel was one of the first in Hángzhōu to accept foreigners and is still popular. Rooms are overpriced but in a great location right on the lakefront.

Dahua Hotel (Dàhuá Fàndiàn; ☎ 8718 1888; 171 Nanshan Lu; 南山路171号; d Y780, with lake view Y980) This hotel strives to compete with its lakeside neighbours, though lumpy beds and brusque service keep it at a disadvantage. The hotel's claim to fame is that Mao stayed here.

Wanghu Hotel (Wànghú Bīnguǎn; ☎ 8707 8888; 2 Huancheng Xilu; 环城西路2号; d Y780, ste from Y2580) Good value and in a great location, this hotel has rooms that equal the Sheraton, for much less money. Room choices include the fancily named 'Rivulet Hall', 'Sapphire Hall', or even the 'Olympus Palace' for Y4580. The price includes breakfast.

Shangri-La Hotel (Hángzhōu Xiānggélǐlā Fàndiàn; ☎ 8707 7951; fax 8707 3545; www.shangri-la.com; 78 Beishan Lu; 北山路78号; d Y1000-1150, with lake view Y1450, plus 15% service charge) Situated on the northern shore

of the lake and surrounded by forest, this hotel wins for the most picturesque location. Rooms, however, are ordinary, with plastic décor that is found in most major hotel chains.

Grand Hyatt Regency (Hángzhōu Kǎiyuè Jiǔdiàn; ☎ 8779 1234; www.hangzhou.regency.hyatt.com; 28 Hubin Lu; 湖滨路28号; d Y1700-1850, with lake view Y2050; 🖳) This sprawling megaplaza dominates the eastern lakeshore. In addition to international standard rooms, the hotel offers 5-star luxuries such as a swimming pool, sauna and health club.

Eating

Hángzhōu cuisine emphasises fresh, sweet flavours and makes good use of freshwater fish, especially eel and carp. Dishes to watch for include fatty pork slices flavoured with Shàoxīng wine (东坡肉; *dōngpō ròu*), named after the Song dynasty poet Su Dongpo, and chicken wrapped in lotus leaves and baked in clay, known in English as 'beggar's chicken' (叫化童鸡; *jiàohuàtóng jī*). Bamboo shoots are a local delicacy, especially in the spring when they're most tender.

Some restaurants are institutions in Hángzhōu and do a brisk trade with tourist groups. All have English menus.

Kuiyuan Restaurant (Kuíyuán Guǎn; ☎ 8702 8626; 154 Jiefang Lu; mains Y10; ⏰ 11am-10.30pm) This restaurant is over 100 years old, and has garnered a reputation for its excellent noodle and seafood dishes. Try its delicious fried noodles with eel and shrimp (虾爆鳝面; *xiā bào shàn miàn*).

Tianwaitian Restaurant (Tiānwàitiān Càiguǎn; ☎ 8796 5450; 2 Lingying Tianzhu Lu; mains Y30-90; ⏰ 11am-10pm) Run by the same group who own Louwailou (with a similar menu), this restaurant is near the entrance to Lingyin Temple and is a nice place for lunch.

Louwailou Restaurant (Lóuwàilóu Càiguǎn; 30 Gushan Lu; ☎ 8796 9023; mains Y30-100; ⏰ 9am-10pm) Founded in 1838, this is Hángzhōu's most famous restaurant. The local speciality is sweet and sour carp (西湖醋鱼; *xīhú cùyú*). Service is grumpy but the food is good.

For restaurants that cater mostly to locals, head to Gaoyin Jie, near Wúshǎn Sq, where a lively string of restaurants dish up local specialities.

Lǎo Hángzhōu Fēngwèi (141 Gaoyin Jie; mains Y20; ⏰ 11.30am-9pm) This local watering-hole serves tasty homestyle dishes, including wine-braised bamboo shoots (糟会鞭笋; *zāohuì biānsǔn*) and Dongpo pork. Make sure to try the crispy potato cakes with garlic and chilli (婆婆敲土豆饼; *pópóqiāo tǔdòu bǐng*).

NON-ASIAN

Along Hubin Lu and Nanshan Lu are a glut of Western-style eateries, fast-food joints and bars. On the lakeshore is **Xīhú Tiāndì**, a collection of upscale restaurants and cafés in a leafy garden setting. For picnics, head to **Carrefour Shopping Centre** (Jiālèfú; 135 Yan'an Lu; ⏰ 9am-9pm), which has a good selection of imported foods. On the weekends, shopping here feels like being caught in a stampede.

Drinking

Over the past several years, the bar scene in Hángzhōu has mushroomed. The most popular bar strip is along Nanshan Lu, near the Academy of Art. There are far too many to list; take your pick from those mentioned below or head off and see what you can uncover.

Night and Day (Dénà; ☎ 8777 0275; 240 Nanshan Lu; meals Y56-85, beer Y25; ⏰ 10am-2am) This is a wonderfully atmospheric Chinese bar and restaurant that plays Latin music with dancing after 9pm. The top-floor balcony overlooks West Lake.

Kana's Bar (Kǎnà Jiǔbā; ☎ 8706 3228; 152 Nanshan Lu; beer Y22; ⏰ 6.30pm-3.30am) Owned by a former foreign student, this lively bar attracts an eclectic mix of both locals and tourists. This is the place to be seen on the weekends.

Entertainment

Hángzhōu has several cinemas that screen English-language movies. Close to the lake is the **West Lake Cinema** (Xīhú Diànyǐngyuàn; 95 Pinghai Lu; admission Y30).

Shopping

Hángzhōu is well known for its tea, in particular *longjing* (dragon well) green tea as well as silk, fans and, of all things, scissors. You can find all these things at the **Wúshān Lu night market** (Wúshān Lù Yèshì) in addition to touristy kitsch. Fake ceramics jostle with ancient pewter tobacco pipes, Chairman Mao memorabilia, silk shirts and pirated CDs. Get the gloves off and haggle hard if something catches your eye.

For silk, try the **market** (Sīchóu Shìchǎng; Xinhua Lu; ⏰ 8am-6pm), a couple of blocks east of Zhonghe Beilu. The silk area starts on the north side of Fengqi Lu. Make sure you check that the silk is genuine and not a polyester clone (it should feel smooth and soft between your thumb and finger).

Getting There & Away

AIR

For flights, Hángzhōu is serviced by **Dragonair** (Gǎnglóng Hángkōng Gōngsī; ☎ 8506 8388; 5th fl, Radisson Plaza Hotel, 333 Tiyuchang Lu), with regular connections to all major Chinese cities. There are several flights a day to Běijīng (Y1050), Guǎngzhōu (Y960) and Hong Kong (Y1840).

One place to book air tickets is the **Hángzhōu Xiaoshan International Airport Ticketing Office** (Hángzhōu Xiǎoshān Guójì Jīcháng Shòupiàochù; ☎ 8515 4259; 309 Tiyuchang Lu)

Most hotels will also book flights, generally with a Y20 to Y30 service charge.

BOAT

You can get to Sūzhōu by boat up the Grand Canal from Hángzhōu. There's one boat daily, leaving at 5.30pm. The trip takes about 14 hours. Economy class in a cabin of four people costs Y60 per bed, deluxe cabins for four people are Y88 per bed and two-person cabins cost Y78 to Y130 per bed. Most of the trip is in the dark and you won't get to see much. Buy tickets at the passenger wharf just north of Huancheng Beilu.

BUS

All four bus stations are outside the city centre. The north bus station on Moganshan Lu has buses to Nánjīng (Y120, five hours), Wǔkāng (Y15, 1½ hours) and other points in Jiāngsū. Buses for Qiāndǎo Hú (Y35, four hours) and Huáng Shān (Y60, six hours) leave from the west bus station on Tianmushan Lu.

The east bus station is the most comprehensive, with frequent deluxe buses to Shànghǎi (Y54, 2½ hours), Wūzhèn (Y25; one hour), Shàoxīng (Y22, one hour) and Níngbō (Y42, two hours). Economy buses are cheaper, but slower. Buses to Tiāntái Shān (Y50, six hours) and Hǎiníng (Y24, one hour) also leave from here. The south bus station has buses to Wēnzhōu (Y100, nine hours).

TRAIN

Trains from Hángzhōu's main train station go south to Xiàmén (Y231, 27 hours) and Wēnzhōu (Y112, eight hours) and east to Shàoxīng (Y19, 45 minutes) and Níngbō (Y44, 2½ hours). Most trains heading north have to go to Shànghǎi, but there's a direct train to Běijīng (Y341, 16 hours) from Hángzhōu.

Five express trains run between Hángzhōu and Shànghǎi (Y40, two hours) daily, with some trains continuing through to Sūzhōu. Booking sleepers can be difficult at the Hángzhōu train station, especially to Běijīng. Most hotels can do this for you for a Y20 service charge. You can also buy tickets at the **train ticket booking office** (199 Wulin Lu; ☾ 8am-5pm).

Getting Around
TO/FROM THE AIRPORT
Hángzhōu's airport is 30km from the city centre; taxi drivers ask around Y120 for the trip. Shuttle buses leave from the Marco Polo Hotel.

BICYCLE
Bike hire (Y15 per four hr, Y500 deposit) is available from Mingtown Youth Hostel and from **stalls** (Y8 per hr, Y200 deposit) across from the Yue Fei Mausoleum. Check out the bikes before you take off, especially the brakes.

BOAT
Getting out on the water is one of the best ways to enjoy West Lake. Cruise boats depart from the eastern shore, crossing the lake and visiting the islands en route for Y45. If you want a private ride, you can be paddled around for Y80 per hour. For a romantic evening under the stars, there are night tours of the lake for Y25 per person. If you'd prefer to do the work yourself, there are paddle boats available for Y30 to Y50 an hour.

BUS
Hángzhōu has a clean, efficient bus system and getting around is easy. Bus K7 is very useful – it connects the main train station to the eastern side of the lake. Bus K56 travels from the east bus station to Yan'an Lu and buses 15 and K15 connect the north long-distance bus station to the northwest area of the lake. Tourist bus Y1 circles the lake to Lingyin Temple and bus Y2 goes from the train station, along Beishan Lu and up to Lingyin Temple. Tourist bus Y3 travels around the West Lake to the Silk Museum, China Tea Museum, Dragon Well Tea Village and the Southern Song dynasty Guan Kiln. Tourist bus Y5 will take you out to the Six Harmonies Pagoda. Tickets are Y2 to Y5.

TAXI
Metered taxis are ubiquitous and start at Y10; figure on around Y20 to Y25 from the train station to Hubin Lu.

AROUND HÁNGZHŌU
Qiántáng River Tidal Bore 钱塘江潮
A spectacular natural phenomenon occurs when the highest tides of the lunar cycle cause a wall of water to thunder up the narrow mouth of the Qiántáng River from Hángzhōu Bay (Hángzhōu Wān).

Although the tidal bore can be viewed from the riverbank in Hángzhōu, the best place to witness this amazing phenomenon is on either side of the river at Yánguān, a small town about 38km northeast of Hángzhōu. Among the Chinese, viewing the bore has traditionally been associated with the **Mid-Autumn Festival**, around the 18th day of the eighth month of the lunar calendar. However, you can see it throughout the year when the highest tides occur at the beginning and middle of each lunar month. For tide times, check with the Hángzhōu Tourist Centre (p317).

Hotels and travel agencies offer tours to see the bore during the Mid-Autumn Festival, but you can visit just as easily on your own. Buses to Yánguān leave from Hángzhōu's east bus station for Y20.

Mògānshān 莫干山
☎ 0572
About 60km north of Hángzhōu is the hilltop resort of Mògānshān. Delightfully cool at the height of summer, Mògānshān was developed as a resort for Europeans living in Shànghǎi and Hángzhōu during the colonial era. It's well worth visiting and staying in one of the old villas. There are the obligatory tourist sights, such as old villas that once belonged to Chiang Kaishek and the Shànghǎi gang leader, Du Yuesheng, but the best thing to do in Mògānshān is to lose yourself along the winding forest paths. You can pick up a Chinese map (Y3) at your hotel for some sense of orientation. The main village (Mògānshān Zhèn) is centred around Yinshan Jie (荫山街).

Mògānshān is full of hotels, most of them housed in old villas. Du Yuesheng's old stone villa has been transformed into the **Léidísēn Mògānshān Biéshù** (雷迪森莫干山别墅; ☎ 803 3601; d Y1100-1300), which is now owned by the Radisson group. A cheaper alternative is the pleasant **Jiànquán Shānzhuāng** (剑泉山庄;

ZHÈJIĀNG

☎ 803 3607; 91 Moganshan 莫干山91号; d Y480), which sits below the village. Your only eating options are in the hotels themselves, which all serve palatable food.

Entry to Mògānshān is Y65. The easiest way to get there is from Hángzhōu. Take a minibus from Hángzhōu's north bus station to Wǔkāng (武康; Y13, 40 minutes), which run every half-hour from 6.20am to 7pm. From Wǔkāng you need to hire a taxi (Y35) to reach the top of the mountain.

Buses from Shànghǎi run to Mògānshān in July and August. Three public buses do the Shànghǎi–Wǔkāng trip (four hours; Y42); they leave from a small bus station near Baoshan Rd metro, at 80 Gongxing Rd. Buses depart Shànghǎi at 6.30am, 11.50am and 12.50pm; buses depart Wǔkāng at 6.30am, 7.40am and 1pm.

WŪZHÈN 乌镇
☎ 0573

In the northeast corner of Zhèjiāng, the town of Wūzhèn has been around since the late Tang dynasty, but was only recently painstakingly restored and resurrected as a tourist destination. Like Zhōuzhuāng and other places in southern Jiāngsū, Wūzhèn is a water town whose network of waterways and access to the Grand Canal once made it a prosperous place for its trade and production of silk. The ambitious restoration project recreates what Wūzhèn would have been like in the late Qing dynasty. Most residents still live in the old town, going about their daily lives and have (yet) to be chased out by developers.

Sights

Wūzhèn is tiny and it's possible to see everything in a couple hours. Most people come here on a daytrip from Hángzhōu or Shànghǎi. The main street of the old town, Dongda Jie, is a narrow path paved with stone slabs and flanked by wooden buildings. You pay an entrance fee at the **main gate** (Daqiao Lu; adult/child Y60; ☒ 8am-5pm), which covers entry to all of the exhibits. Some of these are workshops, such as the **Gongsheng Grains Workshop** (三白酒坊; Sānbáijiǔ Fāng), an actual distillery churning out a pungent rice wine ripe for the sampling. Next door, the **Blue Prints Workshop** (蓝印花布作坊; Lán Yìnhuābù Zuòfang) shows the dyeing and printing process for the traditional blue cloth of the Jiāngnán region.

Further down the street and across a small bridge is **Mao Dun's Former Residence** (茅盾故居; Máo Dùn Gùjū). At the time of research it was being renovated – it should be open by the time this book hits the shelves. Revolutionary writer Mao Dun is a contemporary of Lu Xun and the author of *Spring Silkworms* and *Midnight*. Mao Dun's great-grandfather, a successful merchant, bought the house in 1885 and it's a fairly typical example from the late Qing dynasty. There are photographs, writings and other memorabilia of Mao Dun's life, though not much explanation in English.

At the western end of the old town, around the corner on Changfeng Jie, is an interesting exhibit many visitors miss. The **Huiyuan Pawn House** (汇源当铺; Huìyuán Dàngpù) was once a famous pawnshop that eventually expanded to branches in Shànghǎi. It has been left intact and despite the lack of English captions, the spartan décor gives a Dickensian feel to the place.

One of the best reasons to visit Wūzhèn is for the live performances of local Flower Drum opera *(Huāgǔ xì)* held throughout the day in the village square, and shadow puppet shows *(píyǐngxì)* in the small theatre beside the square. The puppet shows in particular are great fun and well worth watching. There are also martial arts performances on the 'boxing boats' in the canal every half hour from 8.30am to 4.30pm. You can hire a boat at the main gate for Y80 a person to take you for a ride down the canal.

Getting There & Away

From Hángzhōu, buses run from the east bus station to Wūzhèn (Y25, one hour), leaving every hour or so from 6.30am to 6.10pm. From Wūzhèn, minibuses make the run to Hángzhōu for Y14.

If you're coming from Shànghǎi, the easiest (but most expensive) way is to take a tour bus from Shanghai Stadium. The Y148 ticket includes the entrance fee to Wūzhèn, return trip to Shànghǎi and a Chinese-speaking guide. Tour buses leave at 8.45am and 9.45am and the trip takes about two hours each way. A cheaper option is to take a bus from the long-distance bus depot behind the train station for Y28.

NÁNXÚN 南浔
☎ 0572

Nestled on the border with Jiāngsū province, about 125km from Hángzhōu, Nánxún is a water town whose contemporary modest appearance belies its once glorious past. Established over 1400 years ago, the town came to prominence during the Southern Song dynasty due to its prospering silk industry. By the time the Ming rolled around, it was one of Zhèjiāng's most important commercial centres. The town shares the typical features of other southern water towns – arched bridges, canals, narrow lanes and old houses – but what sets it apart is its intriguing mix of Chinese and European architecture, introduced by affluent silk merchants who once made their homes here. Nánxún today is a quiet place that remains relatively undisturbed by tourism. Plans are currently in the works, however, to restore or remove some of the old buildings along the canal and give the town a controversial face-lift to increase tourist revenue. Hopefully, even with these new developments, the peace and tranquillity of Nánxún will be preserved.

Sights

Nánxún (☎ 301 5021; admission Y60; ☒ 8am-5pm, winter 8am-4.30pm) isn't large and it won't take more than a couple of hours to see everything. The entrance fee includes all sights. On the back of your ticket is a small map to help you find your way around.

Nánxún's most famous structure is the rambling **100 Room Pavilion** (百间楼; Bǎijiān Lóu) in the northeast corner of town. It was built 400 years ago by a wealthy Ming official to supposedly house his servants. It's a bit creaky but in amazingly good shape for being so old.

Nánxún has some attractive gardens; the loveliest is **Little Lotus Villa** (小莲庄; Xiǎolián Zhuāng), once the private garden of a wealthy Qing official. The villa gets its name from its pristine lotus pond surrounded by ancient camphor trees. Within the garden are some elaborately carved stone gates and a small family shrine.

Close by is the **Jiaye Library** (嘉业堂藏书楼; Jiāyètáng Cángshūlóu), once one of the largest private libraries in southeast China. It was home to over 30,000 books, some dating back to the Tang. Inside is a large woodblock collection and displays of manuscripts. The library is surrounded by a moat – an effective form of fire prevention in the Qing.

The **Zhang Family Compound** (张氏铭旧宅; Zhāngshímíng Jiùzhái) is one of the more interesting old residences in Nánxún. Once

owned by a wealthy silk merchant, it was the largest and most elaborate private residence in southeastern China during the late Qing. The home was constructed with wood, glass, tiles and marble, all imported from France. The buildings are an intriguing combination of European and Chinese architecture surrounded by delicate gardens, fishponds and rockery. Most incongruous is a French-style mansion with red brick walls, wrought iron balconies and louvred shutters. Amazingly there's even a ballroom inside, complete with bandstand. This fondness for Western architecture is also seen in the **Liu Family Compound** (刘氏梯号; Liúshì Tīhào) with its imported stained glass, heavy wooden staircases and red-brick exterior.

It's pleasant after a day of walking to relax at one of the small restaurants facing the canal for a snack or some tea. You'll need to bargain for your meal; don't accept the first price you're told.

Getting There & Away

Nánxún has two bus stations: the Tài'an Lu station (Tài'ān Lù chēzhàn) and another station by the expressway (nánxún qìchēzhàn). Both stations have buses that run to Shànghǎi (Y30, 2½ hours) and Sūzhōu (Y15, one hour) from 5.50am to 5pm. Buses from Shànghǎi leave from the station on Hongjiang Lu from 6am to 7.30pm and from Sūzhōu's south bus station from 7am to 5.50pm.

Buses leave hourly from Hángzhōu's north or east bus station for the town of Húzhōu (湖州; Y25, 1½ hours). From there, you'll need to switch to a Nánxún bus. The 34km trip from Húzhōu to Nánxún costs Y8.

SHÀOXĪNG 绍兴
☎ 0575 / pop 4.3 million

Just 67km southeast of Hángzhōu, Shàoxīng has for years been touted as a charming water town, with winding canals, arched bridges and antiquated residences. Nowadays, the waterways remain but much of Shàoxīng has undergone rampant redevelopment and much of its former romantic image has slipped. However, beneath all the dust and scaffolding, a bit of the old Shàoxīng still remains. There are a few interesting things to see and some excursions out of town that make a stay worthwhile.

History

Shàoxīng has a flourishing administrative and agricultural centre for much of its history. It

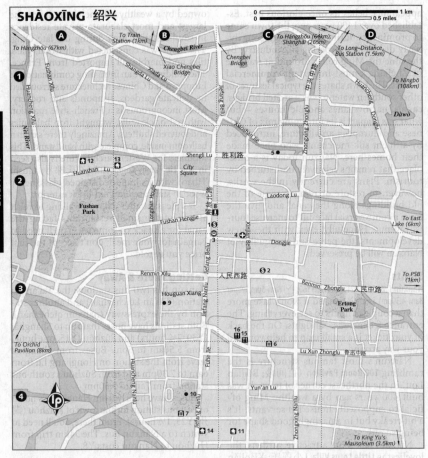

SHÀOXĪNG 绍兴

was capital of the Yue kingdom from 770 to 211 BC.

Shàoxīng was the birthplace of many influential and colourful figures over the centuries, including the mythical 'flood tamer' Yu the Great, the painter and dramatist Xu Wei, the female revolutionary hero Qiu Jin and Lu Xun, the country's first great modern novelist. It's also the home of Shàoxīng wine, which most travellers would agree is definitely an acquired taste.

Orientation

Encircled by bodies of water and rivers, and crossed by canals, Shàoxīng is a pleasant place to explore on foot. The hill in Fushan Park is a good place for shady walks. A large city

square fills up the corner of Shengli Lu and Jiefang Beilu.

Information

Bank of China (Zhōngguó Yínháng; 201 Renmin Zhonglu; 8am-8pm) Changes travellers cheques and major currency. Its ATM accepts international credit cards. There's another branch at 472 Jiefang Beilu.

China Telecom (Zhōngguó Diànxin; per hr Y2; 24hr) There's an office with an internet café on Dongjie near Xinjian Beilu.

Post Office (yóujú; 1 Dongjie; 8am-5pm) Centrally located on the corner of Dongjie and Jiefang Beilu.

Public Security Bureau (PSB; Gōngānjú; ☎ 865 1333 ext 2104) About 2km east of the city centre on Renmin Donglu, near Huiyong Lu.

Shàoxīng Hotel (Shàoxīng Fàndiàn; ☎ 515 5858; fax 515 5565; 9 Huanshan Lu) Can arrange tours and book trips onwards.

Shàoxīng People's Hospital (Shàoxīng Rénmín Yīyuàn; 61 Dongjie)

www.travelchinaguide.com/cityguides/zhejiang /Shaoxing Provides general background information on Shàoxīng.

Xinhua Bookshop (Xīnhuá Shūdiàn; 115 Shengli Lu; ☾ 9am-9pm) Sells English-language maps of the city.

Sights

LU XUN'S FORMER RESIDENCE 鲁迅故居

Lu Xun (1881–1936), one of China's best-known modern writers and author of such stories as *Diary of a Madman* and *Medicine*, was born in Shàoxīng and lived here until he went abroad to study. He later returned to China, teaching in Guǎngzhōu's Zhongshan University in 1927. He was forced to hide out in Shànghǎi's French Concession when the Kuomintang decided his books were too dangerous. His tomb is in Shànghǎi.

There are several sights associated with Lu Xun, grouped together in a cluster of buildings on Lu Xun Zhonglu. A combined ticket to see everything costs Y120. You can visit **Lu Xun's Former Residence** (Lǔ Xùn Gùjū; 393 Lu Xun Zhonglu; ☾ 8am-5.30pm), where his living quarters are faithfully preserved. At the same site is the **Lu Xun Memorial Hall** (Lǔ Xùn Jìniànguǎn; ☾ 8am-5.30pm). You'll see displays of photographs and the novelist's baby clothes, among other things. Opposite is the one-room school he attended as a young boy.

ANCESTRAL HOMES

The **studio** (Qīngténg Shūwū; admission Y2; ☾ 8am-4pm) of the controversial Ming painter, poet and dramatist Xu Wei (1521–93) is off Renmin Lu in a small alley. Born in Shàoxīng, Xu's artistic talents brought him early fame and later he served as a personal assistant to the governor of the southeastern provinces. When the governor was killed for treason, Xu spiralled into madness. Over a period of years, he attempted suicide nine times, once by trying to split his skull with an axe. Later, in a fit of rage he beat his wife to death and was sent to prison. Skilful manoeuvring on the part of his friends got him free.

In his later years, Xu remained in Shàoxīng, living in this study where he spent the remainder of his life painting and writing plays. Some of his dramas are still performed today and his paintings are highly sought after. He's remembered as one of the most innovative artists of the Ming.

The studio, surrounded by a tranquil bamboo garden, is a well-maintained example of 16th-century architecture, with its ivy-covered, whitewashed walls and black-tiled roof. Inside are displays of the artist's paintbrushes, painting and calligraphy.

Another interesting home to visit is **Qiu Jin's Former Residence** (Qiū Jīn Gùjū; 35 Hechang Tang; adult/child Y3/1.50; ☾ 8am-5.30pm), where the pioneering woman revolutionary Qiu Jin was born. Qiu Jin studied in Japan, and was active in women's rights and the revolutionary movement against the Qing government. She was beheaded in 1907 by Qing authorities at the age of 29. There's a memorial **statue of Qiu Jin** on Jiefang Beilu, near Fushan Hengjie.

YINGTIAN PAGODA 应天塔

This **pagoda** (Yìngtiān Tǎ; admission Y2), originally part of a Song dynasty temple, stands gracefully on a hill overlooking modern-day Shàoxīng. Destroyed during the Taiping Rebellion (1850–64) and later rebuilt, the pagoda offers good views from the top.

KING YU'S MAUSOLEUM 大禹陵

According to legend, in 2205 BC Yu the Great became the first emperor of the Xia dynasty, and earned the title 'tamer of floods' after he conquered the dragons that lived underground and caused floods.

A temple and mausoleum complex to honour the 'great-grandfather of China' was first constructed in the 6th century and was added to over the centuries that followed. The **mausoleum** (Dà Yǔ Líng; admission Y50; ☼ 7.30am-5.30pm) is about 4km southeast of the city centre and is composed of several parts: the huge 24m-tall Main Hall, the Memorial Hall and the Meridian Gate (Wǔ Mén). A statue of Yu graces the Main Hall.

Bus 2 will get you to King Yu's Mausoleum from the train station area or from Jiefang Beilu (get off at the last stop).

Festivals & Events

The **Orchid Pavilion Calligraphy Festival** is held each year on the third day of the third lunar month at the Orchid Pavilion (opposite). Calligraphy exhibitions are held as well as calligraphy contests.

Sleeping

Shàoxīng can be done as a day trip from Hángzhōu or used as a stay over if you want to spend some time at the outlying sights.

Jishan Hotel (Jīshān Bīnguǎn; Toulaohekou; 投醪河口; ☎ 806 3838; fax 806 7965; s & d Y188-388) This friendly little hotel behind the Xianheng has reasonably priced rooms, though some smell strongly of cigarettes and beds are very hard. Smell first, pay later.

Longshan Hotel (Lóngshān Bīnguǎn; ☎ 533 6888; fax 515 5308; 500 Shengli Xilu; 胜利西路500号; s Y280, d Y220-480, tr Y300) Rooms are cheap in this popular place but somewhat shabby and bathrooms are outdated. Check the room out before handing over your cash.

Shàoxīng Hotel (Shàoxīng Fàndiàn; ☎ 515 5858; fax 515 5565, 9 Huanshan Lu; 环山路9号; d Y660-1280) One of the nicest places to stay in town, this modern hotel has well-equipped comfortable rooms surrounded by gardens. The restaurant has an excellent reputation.

Xianheng Hotel (Xiánhēng Dàjiǔdiàn; ☎ 806 8688; fax 805 1028; 680 Jiefang Nanlu; 解放南路680号; s & d Y980) Considered to be the poshest place in Shàoxīng, this shiny hotel at the southern edge of town has impeccable rooms coupled with snooty service.

Eating

Take a walk around Shàoxīng and you won't get very far before being struck by an odour so strong it makes you want to plug your nose and run for the hills. What you're smelling is stinky tofu (臭豆腐; *chòu dòufu*), one of Shàoxīng's best-known treats. Believe it or not, the pungent snack actually tastes better than it smells.

Another speciality is yellow rice wine (绍兴黄酒; *Shàoxīng huángjiǔ*), which has been distilled in Shàoxīng for over 2,000 years (see the boxed text, below).

Near the Lu Xun Memorial is **Ā-pó Miànguǎn** (100 Lu Xun Zhonglu; meals Y6-15; ☼ 9am-11pm) with outside seating and good noodle dishes. The signature dish is 'A-Po's noodles with exploding eel'; simply put, it's stir-fried eel with noodles. Across from A-Po's is the very popular **Xiánhēng Jiǔjiā** (44 Lu Xun Lu; meals Y20-30; ☼ 11am-late), which serves traditional Shàoxīng specialities, including Shàoxīng wine, Shàoxīng chicken and stinky tofu.

WARM WINE, HIGH SPIRITS

'Warm a bowl of wine', the dishevelled beggar Kong Yiji pleads in the short story of the same name by Lu Xun, China's celebrated 20th-century writer. Kong Yiji is Lu Xun's most famous literary character, a failed scholar whose only joy comes from the wine he drinks at the local tavern, set in Shàoxīng, Lu Xun's hometown. Kong Yiji's favourite beverage is yellow rice wine (*huáng jiǔ*), a Shàoxīng speciality made from sticky rice, spring water and wheat yeast. The wine is famous for its amber colour and mellow taste, making it a favourite among China's tipplers. It gets its unique taste from a lengthy fermentation process, which includes being aged in an earthen barrel for over five years.

Shàoxīng has been producing yellow wine since around 18 BC. In olden times, a family would bury an elaborately decorated jar of wine at the birth of a daughter and unearth it when the daughter was married. This custom is still practiced in rural counties outside of Shàoxīng.

Traditionally, yellow wine is drunk warm. It's heated in a metal wine pot and half immersed in a bowl of hot water before it's served. The warm wine is thought to be good for the digestion and to build up immunity. The wine also shows up in a variety of Chinese dishes, from chicken to tofu, where its pungent aroma and flavour add quite a punch. Despite its popularity in China, most Westerners find the taste of yellow wine peculiar, likening it to a fine furniture polish.

Getting There & Away

All Hángzhōu–Níngbō trains and buses stop in Shàoxīng. Luxury buses from the long-distance bus station go to Níngbō (Y40, 1½ hours), Hángzhōu (Y22, 45 minutes) and Shànghǎi (Y65 to Y70, three hours)

Getting Around

The bus system in Shàoxīng is fairly straightforward. Bus 1 travels from the train station down Jiefang Beilu and then east to East Lake. Bus 8 travels south down Zhongxing Lu from the long-distance bus station. Taxis are cheap, starting at Y5.

AROUND SHÀOXĪNG
Orchid Pavilion 兰亭

The **Orchid Pavilion** (Lán Tíng; admission Y25; ☼ 8am-5pm) is considered by many Chinese to be one of Shàoxīng's 'must see' spots. The site is where the famous calligrapher Wang Xizhi (AD 321–379) gathered with 41 friends and composed the collection of poetry called the *Orchid Pavilion*. At the pavilion you'll see gardens, Wang's ancestral shrine and stelae with his calligraphy. A calligraphy festival is held yearly in March. The Orchid Pavilion is around 10km southwest of the city and can be reached by bus 3 from Shengli Lu.

ĀNCHĀNG 安昌
☎ 0575

About 40 minutes west of Shàoxīng by bus is the peaceful little water town of **Ānchāng** (admission Y35; ☼ 8am-4.30pm). It sees few visitors, and has yet to be developed into a major tourist attraction. The town has been around since ancient times and was given its present name during the Tang dynasty. Ānchāng has few sites; there's little to do but explore the two main streets along the canal, which are linked by a series of 17 stone bridges. What you'll see is a China that's fast disappearing – the old Ming and Qing style stone houses and shops that line the canal front have seen little restoration and daily life goes on as it has for thousands of years. Townsfolk gather along the canal playing mah jong, cobblers sew cloth shoes and elderly women sit in doorways spinning cotton into yarn.

Some old buildings have opened to the public and are interesting to peruse; the map on the back of your entry ticket has them marked in Chinese. Your best bet is to wander and see what you find. Close to the entrance is a former **bank** (穗康钱庄, *suìkāng qiánzhuāng*), with displays of abacuses and Nationalist-era bank notes in its gloomy, cobwebbed interior. Also interesting and a few minutes' walk from the bank is an old **mansion** (斯干堂, *sīgān táng*) with three large courtyards that have interesting displays of beds, chairs and other Qing-style furnishings.

A real treat is to take a ride in an oilcloth–covered boat down the canal, steered by an elderly boatman who may serenade you with one of the local folksongs. Y10 per person is a reasonable bargaining price.

Bus 118 from Shàoxīng's south bus station will take you on a bumpy roundabout tour of the countryside before dropping you off at Ānchāng's entrance, marked by an arch. The trip costs Y5.

NÍNGBŌ 宁波
☎ 0574 / pop 5.4 million

Although it's some 20km inland on the Yong River, Níngbō rose to prominence during the 7th and 8th centuries as a trading port for tea, ceramics and silk. Ships carrying Zhèjiāng's exports sailed from here to Japan, Korea, the Ryukyu Islands and along the Chinese coast.

By the 16th century, the Portuguese had established a colony in the area north of the Xinjiang Bridge and established themselves as entrepreneurs in the trade between Japan and China, as the Chinese were forbidden to deal directly with the Japanese. During the 18th century, the East India Company also attempted to establish itself in Níngbō, but it wasn't until 1842, after the First Opium War, that the Treaty of Nanking enabled the British to set up a treaty port and British Consulate.

Soon after, Níngbō's once-flourishing trade gradually declined as Shànghǎi boomed. By that time the Níngbō traders had taken their money to Shànghǎi and formed the basis of its wealthy Chinese business community.

Today Níngbō is a thoroughly modern port city that lacks the frenzy of most major urban centres in China. It's a relaxing place to spend the day before heading to the Buddhist island of Pǔtuóshān (p332), one of Zhèjiāng's premier tourist attractions.

Information

Bank of China (Zhōngguó Yínháng; 139 Yaohang Jie; ☼ 8am-5pm) Changes travellers cheques and major currency. There's another smaller branch on Zhongshan Xilu.

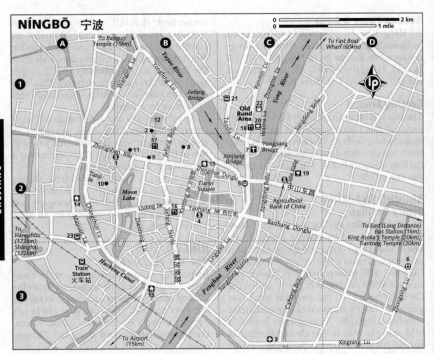

CITS (Zhōngguó Guójì Lǚxíngshè; ☎ 8725 5111; Gongyuan Lu) Behind the Drum Tower on the west side of the pedestrian walkway near Zhongshan Park.

Internet cafés (per 30min around Y2) Look for internet cafés along the pedestrian walkway north of the Drum Tower on Zhongshan Xilu.

Li Huili Hospital (Lǐ Huìlì Yīyuàn; ☎ 8739 2290; 57 Xingning Lu) For medical needs try this hospital on the outskirts of town.

Main post office (yóujú; ☺ 7.30am-8pm) Just south of the Xinjiang Bridge (Xīnjiāng Qiáo).

Public Security Bureau (PSB; Gōngānjú; ☎ 8706 2505; 658 Zhongxing Lu) Handles all visa matters.

www.chinats.com/ningbo For general information on Níngbō.

Sights

Níngbō's most famous attraction is the **Tianyi Pavilion** (Tiānyī Gé; 10 Tianyi Jie; admission Y20; ☺ 8am-5.30pm), which was built during the Ming dynasty and is believed to be the oldest private library in China. Tianyi Pavilion was founded by Fan Qin, head of the Ministry of War during the Ming period. An avid bibliophile, Fan Qin collected scores of rare woodblocks, manuscripts, imperial rosters

of examination candidates and Chinese classics, carefully storing them in this complex of buildings.

Many of the rare documents have been moved to the Zhejiang Provincial Library in Hángzhōu, but some are still on display here for visitors. One of the most whimsical exhibits is a display outlining the history of mah jong in English and Chinese.

The library and outlying buildings, with their black-tiled roofs, are typical of southern architecture. Surrounding the library is a lovely secluded bamboo garden with ponds and rockery. You can reach the library by bus 2, 9, 10 or 14.

Moon Lake (Yuè Hú), near Tianyi Pavilion, is an open park with a wide expanse of green grass and water. This was once the oldest part of town, but recent construction and demolition of old buildings has brought it firmly into the 21st century.

On Zhongshan Xilu, two prominent landmarks have withstood the teeth of modernisation. The stately **Drum Tower** (Gǔ Lóu) marks the entrance to a pedestrian street full of restaurants and internet cafés. Close

INFORMATION		
Bank of China 中国银行	1	B2
CITS (Mirage Hotel)		
中国国际旅行社 (凯州大酒店)	2	B1
Li Huili Hospital 李惠利医院	3	C3
Main Bank of China		
中国银行	4	B2
Main Post Office 邮电居	5	C2
PSB 公安局	6	D3

SIGHTS & ACTIVITIES		
Catholic Church 天主教堂	7	C2
City Hall 市政府	8	B2
Drum Tower 鼓楼	9	B2

Tianyi Pavilion		
天一阁	10	A2
Xiangfeng Pagoda		
咸封塔	11	B2
Zhongshan Park		
中山公园	12	B1

SLEEPING		
Nanyuan Hotel		
南苑饭店	13	B3
Ningbo Hotel		
宁波饭店	14	A2
Ningbo World Hotel		
宁波大酒店	15	B2

EATING		
Food Street 食品街	16	B2
Good Earth Vegetarian		
Restaurant 好地缘	17	B2
Xiāngbàn Yú 香样渔	18	C1

DRINKING		
LBB English Bar 英语酒吧	19	C2
Yihe Teahouse 颐和茶馆	20	C1

TRANSPORT		
North Bus Station 汽车北站	21	C1
Passenger Ferry Terminal		
轮船码头	22	C1
South Bus Station 汽车南站	23	A2

to the tower is the nearby **Xianfeng Pagoda** (Xiánfēng Tǎ).

The once decrepit **bund** (Lǎowàitān) north of the city, across the Xinjiang Bridge, is currently being transformed into a waterfront park. There are few old buildings remaining; most of what you see is quite recent. Close to the passenger ferry terminal is the old Portuguese **Catholic Church** (Tiānzhǔ Jiàotáng; 40 Zhongma Lu; admission free), worth a visit if you're in the area. First built in 1628, it was destroyed and rebuilt in 1872. It's an active church (Mass is held daily at 6am), with a Mediterranean-style whitewashed interior displaying prints of the 14 Stations of the Cross, colourful icons and a vaulted ceiling.

Sleeping

You won't have much luck finding budget accommodation in Níngbō but most hotels offer 30% to 50% discounts. All hotels, unless specified, offer broadband internet.

Ningbo Hotel (Níngbō Fàndiàn; ☎ 8709 7888; 65 Mayuan Lu; 马园路5号; s Y338-358, d Y498-618) This long-established place offers some of the best value in the city, with recently renovated rooms and new bathrooms. It's a quick walk from the south bus station, train station and Tianyi Pavilion.

Ningbo World Hotel (Níngbō Dàjiǔdiàn; ☎ 2788 0088; fax 2788 0788; 145 Zhongshan Donglu; 中山东路145号; d Y768-950) Conveniently located in the centre of town, this hotel has comfortable, good-sized rooms and friendly staff. Sizeable discounts are given on weekdays.

Nanyuan Hotel (Nányuàn Fàndiàn; ☎ 8709 5678; fax 8709 7788; 2 Lingqiao Lu; 灵桥路2号; d Y1020-1780) This elegant five-star establishment offers a wide variety of rooms and is a top choice for business travellers. It's a few minutes walk from here to the train station.

Eating

Seafood is the speciality in Níngbō; check out **'food street'** between Kaiming Jie and Jiefang Lu for the best places to eat.

Tianyi Sq (Tiānyī Guǎngchǎng), between Zhongshan Donglu and Yaohang Jie, has a collection of Chinese and Western fast-food restaurants that serve inexpensive meals. For more formal dining, the old bund area has some good places to eat, including the stylish **Xiāngbàn Yú** (27 Yangshan Lu; ☎ 8735 9677; mains from Y40; ⏲ 11.30am-10pm), which is known for its excellent crab and turtle dishes.

Vegetarians should head to the **Good Earth Vegetarian Restaurant** (Hǎodiyuán; ☎ 8725 5495; 8 Gongyuan Lu; mains from Y8; ⏲ 10.30am-9pm) on the pedestrian street north of the Drum Tower. The red-cooked beancurd with fresh bamboo shoots (红烧豆腐; hóngshāo dòufu) is delicious.

Drinking
TEAHOUSES

Yihe Teahouse (Yíhé Cháguǎn; ☎ 8766 5797; 17 Yangshang Lu; ⏲ 10am-late) Sumptuously decorated with Qing period furnishings, this teahouse offers a variety of teas starting from Y58 per person. With tea comes a free dinner buffet.

BARS

LBB English Bar (14-1 Dahe Xiang; beer Y25; ⏲ 6pm-late) This long-standing place remains popular with locals and foreign teachers. To get here, head down the lane next to the Agricultural Bank of China on Zhongshan Lu.

Getting There & Away
AIR

Níngbō's Lìshè airport has daily flights to Hong Kong (Y1134) and is well-connected to other major Chinese cities. Most hotels will book air tickets for you.

ZHÈJIĀNG

BOAT

There are frequent fast boats to Pǔtuóshān. The trip takes 2½ hours, including a 1½-hour, bone-rattling bus ride from the Níngbō passenger ferry terminal to a fast-boat wharf outside the city. Tickets are Y60, including the bus ride. Buses to the wharf leave from the terminal every half-hour from 5.40am to 3.15pm. The ferries to Shànghǎi are no longer running.

BUS

Long-distance buses to Wēnzhōu (Y119, three hours), Sūzhōu (Y105, 2½ hours) and Tiāntái Shān (Y30, two hours) leave from the orderly long-distance bus station (kèyùn zhōngxīn) on the eastern outskirts of town. From the south bus station (nánzhàn), buses leave frequently for Shànghǎi (Y98, four hours), Hángzhōu (Y42, two hours) and Shàoxīng (Y40, 1½ hours).

TRAIN

Frequent trains run to Hángzhōu (Y44, two hours), Shànghǎi (Y26 to Y84, 3½ hours), Nánjīng (Y84, four hours), Héféi (Y130, 13 hours) and Guǎngzhōu (Y353, 26 hours). Hotels can book tickets for a Y20 surcharge.

Getting Around

Níngbō's airport is a 20-minute drive from town. Free airport shuttle buses leave from most hotels. A taxi to/from the airport should cost around Y50. Taxis around town start at Y8.

AROUND NÍNGBŌ
Baoguo Temple 保国寺

Set in the Lishan Hills 15km northwest of Níngbō is **Baoguo Temple** (Bǎoguó Sì; admission Y12; 8am-4.30pm), one of the oldest wooden buildings south of the Yangzi. Built in 1013, the temple was originally constructed without the use of a single nail, instead relying on a complex system of interlocking beams and brackets. The temple was restored during the Qing (with nails) but it's still possible to see many of the early architectural details. To get here from Níngbō, take bus 332 from the north bus station in the bund area.

King Asoka's Temple 阿育王寺

At the foot of Pushan Mountain, 20km east of Níngbō, is this Chan (Zen) **temple** (Āyùwáng Sì; admission Y5; 7am-4pm) famous for its miniature stupa (15cm) thought to have once belonged

to King Asoka of India, the first major patron of Buddhism. It's believed that the stupa once held the cranium bone of the Buddha, which was supposedly stolen by Red Guards during the Cultural Revolution and never recovered. The easiest way to get to the temple is to hop on one of the frequent minibuses from the east bus station.

Tiantong Temple 天童寺

Situated in the Taibai Mountains close to King Asoka's Temple, this Chan **temple** (Tiāntóng Sì; admission Y5; 6.30am-5.30pm) is one of the largest and most important in China. Founded in AD 300, it's an important pilgrimage site for Chan followers and has attracted some famous visitors over the years, including Dogen (1200–53) who founded the Soto Zen sect in Japan. Bus 332 from Níngbō's east bus station runs to the temple.

PǓTUÓSHĀN 普陀山
☎ 0580

Just south of Shànghǎi and part of the Zhōushān Archipelago, the island of Pǔtuóshān is one of four sacred Buddhist mountains in China. In many ways, it's the China we all dream about – mountain peaks, temples, pagodas, arched bridges, fishing boats, artisans and monks. With its clean beaches and fresh air, it's the perfect island getaway. The best time to visit is midweek, as the island gets very crowded on the weekends.

Orientation

You pay a steep Y110 entrance fee to the island upon arrival, which does not include entry fees to other sights. The central part of town is about 1km north of the ferry terminal and is where most of the hotels are located, as well as Puji Temple. Another way to reach the central square is to take the roads leading west from the ferry terminal; either way takes about 20 minutes. Alternatively, hop on a minibus at the ferry terminal, which will whisk you off to Puji Temple for Y5.

Information

The post office (yóujú) is southwest of Puji Temple and a **Bank of China** (Zhōngguó Yínháng; 8-11am & 1-4.30pm) further west down the road.

Sights

Pǔtuóshān's temples are shrines for Guanyin, the Buddhist Goddess of Mercy, and you will

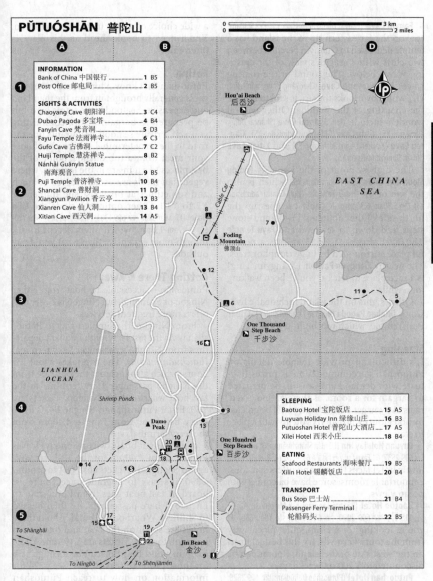

PŬTUÓSHĀN 普陀山

| 0 | 3 km |
| 0 | 2 miles |

INFORMATION
Bank of China 中国银行 1 B5
Post Office 邮电局 2 B5

SIGHTS & ACTIVITIES
Chaoyang Cave 朝阳洞 3 C4
Dubao Pagoda 多宝塔 4 B4
Fanyin Cave 梵音洞 5 D3
Fayu Temple 法雨禅寺 6 C3
Gufo Cave 古佛洞 7 C2
Huiji Temple 慧济禅寺 8 B2
Nánhǎi Guānyīn Statue
  南海观音 9 B5
Puji Temple 普济寺 10 B4
Shancai Cave 善财洞 11 D3
Xiangyun Pavilion 香云亭 12 B3
Xianren Cave 仙人洞 13 B4
Xitian Cave 西天洞 14 A5

SLEEPING
Baotuo Hotel 宝陀饭店 15 A5
Luyuan Holiday Inn 绿缘山庄 16 B3
Putuoshan Hotel 普陀山大酒店 17 A5
Xilei Hotel 西耒小庄 18 B4

EATING
Seafood Restaurants 海味餐厅 19 B5
Xilin Hotel 锡麟饭店 20 B4

TRANSPORT
Bus Stop 巴士站 21 B4
Passenger Ferry Terminal
  轮船码头 22 B5

Hou'ai Beach
后岙沙

EAST CHINA SEA

Cable Car

▲ *Foding Mountain*
佛顶山

One Thousand Step Beach
千步沙

LIANHUA OCEAN

Shrimp Ponds

▲ *Damo Peak*

One Hundred Step Beach
百步沙

To Shànghǎi

To Níngbō

To Shēnjiāmén

Jin Beach
金沙

see her image everywhere. A striking landmark is the **Nánhǎi Guānyīn** (admission Y6), a 33m-high golden statue of Guanyin overlooking the sea at the southernmost tip of the island. It's the first thing you'll see as you approach the island by boat.

Puji Temple (Pǔjì Chánsì; admission free; 5.30am-6pm) stands in the main square of the village and has been around from at least the 17th century. Buses leave from the west side of the temple to various points around the island.

The two large beaches, **One Hundred Step Beach** (Bǎibùshā) and **One Thousand Step Beach** (Qiānbùshā) on the east of the island are attractive and largely unspoilt, although you have to pay for access (Y15).

Fanyin Cave (Fànyīn Dòng; admission Y5; 5.30am-6pm) on the far eastern tip of the island has a temple dedicated to Guanyin perched between two cliffs with a seagull's view of the crashing waves below. The sound of the roaring waves in **Chaoyang Cave** (Cháoyáng Dòng; admission Y12), which overlooks the sea, is said to imitate the chanting of the Buddha. Other natural wonders include the **Shancai Cave** (Shàncái Dòng; admission Y5), **Gufo Cave** (Gǔfó Dòng; admission Y5), **Xianren Cave** (Xiānrén Dòng; admission Y5) and **Xitian Cave** (Xītiān Dòng; admission Y5).

The highest point of the island is **Foding Mountain** (Fódǐng Shān; admission Y5), which is also the site of the **Huiji Temple** (Huìjì Chánsì; admission Y5; 5.30am-6.30pm). A cable car goes up the north side of the mountain (Y40), and stone steps lead down to sea level and **Fayu Temple** (Fǎyǔ Chánsì; admission Y5; 5.30am-6pm), a peaceful place surrounded by huge camphor trees. The nearby **Xiangyun Pavilion** (Xiāngyún Tíng) is a nice place to relax if you've been walking for a while.

Other sights on the island include the five-storey **Duobao Pagoda** (Duōbǎo Tǎ; admission Y15) near Puji Temple, which was built in 1334.

Sleeping

It's difficult to provide reliable details on Pǔtuóshān's accommodation as prices fluctuate with demand and season. Be prepared to bargain for a room, as there are no 'fixed' rates. As you get off the boat, you'll be greeted by hotel touts who can fix you up with a place to stay.

Luyuan Holiday Inn (Lǚyuán Shānzhuāng; 669 0588; fax 609 2537; 61 Fayu Lu; 法雨路61号; d Y458-658) This lovely hotel faces the sea and offers spacious, comfortable rooms; some have balconies with ocean views.

Baotuo Hotel (Bǎotuó Fàndiàn; 118 Meicen Lu; 梅岑路118号; 609 2090; fax 609 1148; s/d Y500/680) If you're looking for a clean, quiet place away from the tourist crowds, try this budget hotel on the west side of the island. Rooms can be discounted to Y200 on weekdays.

Putuoshan Hotel (Pǔtuóshān Dàjiǔdiàn; 609 2828; fax 609 1818; 93 Meicen Lu; 梅岑路93号; d Y450-820) On the road leading west from the ferry terminal, this hotel provides four-star accommodation, with amenities and service to match.

Xilei Hotel (Xīléi Xiāozhuāng; 609 1505; fax 609 2109; 1 Xianghua Jie; 香花街1号; d Y430-1280) Near 100 Step Beach, this tourist favourite offers a wide choice of rooms in varying condition. You'll need to book ahead as this place is often full.

Eating

Pǔtuóshān isn't known for its food; what you get is generally brought in from the mainland and expensive. Seafood is the staple here, but be prepared to bargain before committing yourself. Private seafood restaurants line the road to the ferry terminal, where you choose your meal from a tub outside. Some of the best places to eat in are in the temples, where vegetarian meals are usually served at lunch and sometimes at breakfast and dinner for Y2 to Y10. Other options include the **Xilin Hotel** (Xīlín Fàndiàn; 609 1303; 2 Xianghua Jie; mains Y20-60; 7am-9.30pm), which offers decent meals, though more expensive than what you'd pay outside.

Getting There & Away

Pǔtuóshān is accessible by boat from either Níngbō or Shànghǎi, but Níngbō is closer and offers more frequent services.

From Níngbō, the simplest way to Pǔtuóshān is via the fast ferry, with frequent departures from Níngbō's passenger ferry terminal (lúnchuán mǎtou). The trip takes about 2½ hours, which also includes the bus ride from the Níngbō passenger ferry terminal to the fast boat wharf outside Níngbō. Tickets are Y60. From Pǔtuóshān to Níngbō boats leave every half-hour from 7am to 4.40pm from the ferry terminal.

A daily night boat (two on Sunday) leaves Pǔtuóshān at 4.40pm for the 12-hour voyage to Shànghǎi. Tickets cost Y84 to around Y390; it's easy to upgrade once you're on board. A fast boat goes from Pǔtuóshān to Lúcháo, where passengers are then bussed to Shíliùpù Wharf on the bund. About three hours are spent on the boat and one to two hours on the bus. Tickets are Y195 and Y225. Keep in mind that this can be a rough trip for those prone to seasickness. See p274 for information on how to reach Pǔtuóshān from Shànghǎi.

Getting Around

Walking around Pǔtuóshān is the most relaxing option if you have time. If not, minibuses zip from the ferry terminal to Puji Temple (Y5), where you can transfer to buses going to other sights.

TIĀNTÁI SHĀN 天台山
☎ 0576

Noted for its many Buddhist monasteries, some dating back to the 6th century, **Tiāntái Shān** (Heavenly Terrace Mountain) is the birthplace of the Tiāntái Buddhist sect, which is heavily influenced by Taoism.

From Tiāntái town it's a 3.5km hike to colourful **Guoqing Monastery** (国清寺; Guóqīng Sì; admission Y15; ☺ 7.30am-4pm) at the foot of the mountain. A road leads 25km from the monastery to **Huading Peak** (华顶峰; Huàdǐng Fēng; admission Y25; ☺ 8am-4pm). From here continue by foot for 1km or so to **Baijing Temple** (拜经台寺; Bàijīngtái Sì) on the mountain's summit.

Another sight on the mountain is **Shíliáng Waterfall** (石梁飞瀑; Shíliáng Fēipù; admission Y60; ☺ 8am-4pm). From the waterfall it's a good 5km to 6km walk along a series of small paths to Huading Peak.

Public transport up to the peak and waterfall is sporadic, though you may be able to jump on a motorcycle or hook up with a tour bus. Expect to pay about Y10 to Y20.

There's a **CITS** (中国国际旅行社; Zhōngguó Guójì Lǚxíngshè; ☎ 398 8899) in Tiāntái town at Tiāntái Bīnguǎn that can help arrange tours.

Buses link the mountain with Hángzhōu (Y50, three hours), Shàoxīng (Y27, two hours), Níngbō (Y45, 1½ hours) and Wēnzhōu (Y70, 2½ hours).

WĒNZHŌU 温州
☎ 0577 / pop 7.4 million

Wēnzhōu, a thriving seaport on Zhèjiāng's east coast, is a pivotal player in China's wheeling and dealing free market economy. Strong business ties to Europe and North America have given the city a prosperous air (and a large number of shoe factories). Most travellers find Wēnzhōu rather dull, although there are some scenic places to visit outside the city.

Information

Bank of China (Zhōngguó Yínháng; 113 Chan Jie; ☺ 8-11.30am & 1.15-4.45pm) Changes travellers cheques and major currency. Its ATM accepts international credit cards. There's another branch on Lucheng Lu.

Post Office (yóujú; Xinhe Jie; ☺ 8am-5.30pm) Conveniently located in the city centre.

Public Security Bureau (PSB; Gōngānjú; ☎ 8821 0851) At the end of a small lane called Xigong Jie, north of Guangchang Lu.

Shengyi Internet Bar (Shèngyì Wǎngbā; 201 Renmin Zhonglu; per hr Y4)

Sights

The main scenic site is **Jiangxin Island** (江心岛; Jiāngxīn Dǎo; admission adult/child Y20/15; ☺ 8am-11pm) in the middle of the **Ou River** (Ōu Jiāng). The island park is dotted with pagodas, a lake and footbridges. It's easily reached by ferry, included in the admission, from Jiangxin Pier (Jiāngxīn Mǎtou) on Wangjiang Donglu.

Maguo Temple (Māguǒ Sì; admission Y3) on Songtai Hill next to Renmin Xilu, is a peaceful temple that dates back to the Tang dynasty. It makes an interesting diversion from the concrete and noise of the city.

Sleeping

Wēnzhōu is primarily a business centre and has predominantly midrange hotels, with few budget options. Most hotels have broadband internet.

Wenzhou Hotel (Wēnzhōu Fàndiàn; ☎ 8825 2525; fax 8825 1100; Renmin Zhonglu; 人民中路; s/d Y320/450) Situated on a small side street off Renmin Zhonglu, this unassuming hotel has clean, sizeable rooms with hard-as-board beds. If you need a spine realignment, stay here.

Jinwangjiao Seaview Hotel (Jīnwàngjiǎo Hǎigǎng Dàjiǔdiàn; ☎ 8803 8888; fax 8819 7008; Wangjiang Lu; 望江路; s Y488, d Y498-568) This hotel, with pleasant, airy rooms facing the river, is a good option for those who want to avoid the noise and crowds of the city centre.

Wenzhou International Hotel (Wēnzhōu Guójì Dàjiǔdiàn; ☎ 8825 1111 ext 886; fax 8825 8888; 1 Renmin Donglu; 人民东路1号; www.wzihotel.com; s/d Y530/780) This 26-story hotel is the classiest place in town, with discerningly furnished rooms and friendly English-speaking staff. Rooms are often discounted up to 30%.

Eating

Not surprisingly for a port, Wēnzhōu is known for its seafood, and there are numerous restaurants near the west bus station and the river. For traditional Wēnzhōu specialities such as fish noodles (鱼面, yú miàn) and fish cakes (鱼饼, yú bǐng), head to the 100 year-old **Wēnzhōu Míngdiàn** (195 Jiefang Jie; noodles Y8; ☺ 7am-late). Another good place to look for food is on Wuma Jie, a busy pedestrian street in the middle of town.

For reasonable Western food try **Cafe de Champs-Elysées** (Xiāngxiè Lìshè Xī Cāntīng; cnr Dayiqiao & Jiefang Jie; mains Y20-60, set meals Y38-48; ☺ 10.30am-9.30pm) with set meals and coffee. There's an extensive English menu.

ZHÈJIĀNG

ZHÈJIĀNG

Getting There & Away

AIR
Wēnzhōu's airport has good connections to other Chinese cities. Keep in mind that flights are often delayed or cancelled because of heavy fog. **CAAC** (Zhōngguó Mínháng; ☎ 8833 3197) is in the southeast section of town.

BUS
Wēnzhōu has several bus stations: the west bus station, the Xincheng bus station and the south bus station near the train station. Buses to Fúzhōu (Y227, 10 hours) leave from the south bus station. For long-haul destinations, you're better off taking the train. Frequent buses to Níngbō (Y116, 3½ hours)

and Hángzhōu (Y140, six hours) leave from the Xincheng bus station.

TRAIN
The train line from Wēnzhōu connects the city to Hángzhōu (Y112, eight hours), Shànghǎi (Y94, 9½ hours) and Běijīng (Y405, 30 hours). The train station is south of the city. Take bus 5 or 20 from Renmin Lu. Alternatively, a taxi to the train station will cost around Y20.

There's a **train ticket booking office** near the west bus station.

Getting Around
Wēnzhōu airport is 27km east of the city and taxis charge between Y100 and Y120 for the

trip. A bus goes from the CAAC for Y10. Taxis around the city centre start at Y10.

AROUND WĒNZHŌU
Jǐngnìng County 景宁县
☎ 0578

In southern Zhèjiāng, close to the border of Fújiàn province, Jǐngnìng County (Jǐngnìng Xiàn) is a mountainous, undeveloped region full of rushing rivers and old villages. It's home to the She ethnic group and is the only autonomous national minority district in east China; the She make up about 10% of the Han-dominated population. Despite the large numbers of Chinese tour groups that descend on the area during holidays, the scenery and unspoiled countryside still make it an ideal place to visit.

Hèxī (鹤溪), in Jǐngnìng County, isn't much to get excited about. Get yourself on a minibus (Y3) and head out of town to Dàjūn, 13km away along the river. Here you'll be greeted by elderly women peddling beautiful embroidery;

they may claim it's handmade but don't be fooled (look for a factory tag on the back) and bargain hard.

From Dàjūn you can float back down the river (Xiǎo Xī) on bamboo rafts to the bridge near Hèxī. The trip takes two hours and costs a steep, but negotiable, Y300 per raft. Better yet, take a small boat to the other side of the river and hike around the hills. Chinese maps of the region are available at the Hèxī bus station.

It's possible to stay in Hèxī, though accommodation is basic. One of the better places that deals with foreigners is **Jǐngnìng Bīnguǎn** (景宁宾馆; ☎ 581 0148; 85 Renmin Zhonglu; 人民中路85号; d Y238), which has tolerable rooms with 30% discounts.

To get to Hèxī, take a train from Wēnzhōu (Y34, two hours) or Hángzhōu (Y71, six hours) to the town of Lìshuǐ. Then take bus 3 from the train station to Lìshuǐ's old bus station (lǎo chēzhàn), where you can catch one of the frequent minibuses to Hèxī (Y20, 2½ hours).

Fújiàn 福建

Once home to snake-headed barbarians and elusive immortals, Fújiàn is a region of steep mountains, river valleys and a lush subtropical coastline. While the coastal cities have been engaging in trade for hundreds of years, its mountainous interior remained inaccessible until as late as the 1960s, when the communists built roads through the dense jungle. Rumour has it that the legendary South China tiger still lurks in the most remote mountain regions.

Modern-day Fújiàn's coastline is flourishing, just like it has for centuries. The capital, Fúzhōu, is a 21st-century boomtown, with soaring skyscrapers and never-ending development. The historical port of Xiàmén is much quieter, and unlike Fúzhōu it has managed to keep much of its character over the years. Off its coast, the former foreign enclave of Gǔlàng Yǔ boasts wonderfully preserved colonial buildings and traffic-free streets, making it a refreshing breather from the frenzy of modern China. The enclave is only a stone's throw from the Taiwan-claimed island of Jīnmén (Kinmen), once the site of ferocious battles between mainland communists and the Nationalist party. The old trading centre of Quánzhōu, with its ancient mosque and maritime museum, are potent reminders of the city's once illustrious past, when it was one of the most international ports in the world.

Fújiàn's rugged inland remains relatively unknown, with the exception of the tourist resort of Wǔyí Shān in the northwest and Taimu Mountain near the border of Zhèjiāng province. Both mountains offer fantastic hiking opportunities. Southwest Fújiàn, near Yǒngdìng, is the place to see the unique earthhouses of the Hakka people, one of Fújiàn's many ethnic groups.

HIGHLIGHTS

- Scale one of the last remaining walled cities in China at the ancient city of **Chóngwǔ** (p353)

- Search for immortality among the granite peaks of **Taimu Mountain** (p343), home to Taoist gods and fairies

- See first-hand the junks that once plied the waters off China's coast at the Maritime Museum in **Quánzhōu** (p351)

- Come face to face with ghosts of the past on the sleepy island of **Gǔlàng Yǔ** (p348)

- Kick up some dust at the fascinating Hakka earthhouses of **Yǒngdìng** (p350)

★ Taimu Mountain

Quánzhōu ★   ★ Chóngwǔ
★ Yǒngdìng
★ Gǔlàng Yǔ

■ POPULATION: 35 MILLION   ■ www.amoymagic.com

History

The coastal region of Fújiàn, known in English as Fukien or Hokkien, has been part of the Chinese empire since the Qin dynasty (221–207 BC), when it was known as Min.

Sea trade transformed the region from a frontier into one of the centres of the Chinese world. During the Song and Yuan dynasties the coastal city of Quánzhōu was one of the main ports of call on the maritime silk route, which transported not only silk but other textiles, precious stones, porcelain and a host of other valuables. The city was home to more than 100,000 Arab merchants, missionaries and travellers.

Despite a decline in the province's fortunes after the Ming dynasty restricted maritime commerce in the 15th century, the resourcefulness of the Fújiàn people proved itself in the numbers heading for Taiwan, Singapore, the Philippines, Malaysia and Indonesia. Overseas links were forged that continue today, contributing much to the modern character of the province.

Climate

Fújiàn has a subtropical climate, with hot, humid summers and drizzly cold winters. June through August brings soaring temperatures and humidity, with torrential rains and typhoons common. In the mountainous regions, winters can be fiercely cold. The best time to visit is spring (March–May) and autumn (September–October).

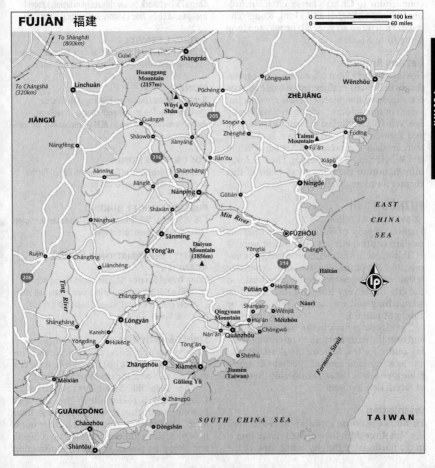

FÚJIÀN 福建

Language

Because of its isolated topography Fújiàn is one of the most linguistically diverse provinces in China. Locals speak variations of the Min dialect, which includes Taiwanese. Min is divided into various subgroups – you can expect to hear Southern Min (Mǐnnán Huà) in Xiàmén and Quánzhōu, and Eastern Min (Dōng Mǐn) in Fúzhōu.

Getting There & Away

Fújiàn is well connected to the neighbouring provinces of Guǎngdōng and Jiāngxī by train and coastal highway. Xiàmén and Fúzhōu have airline connections to most of the country, including Hong Kong, and Taipei and Kaohsiung in Taiwan. Wǔyí Shān has flight connections to China's larger cities, including Běijīng, Shànghǎi and Hong Kong. The coastal freeway also goes all the way to Hong Kong from Xiàmén.

Getting Around

Getting around Fújiàn coastal areas is a breeze, thanks to the well-maintained coastal highway. For exploring the interior, trains are slow but more comfortable and safer than travelling by bus. Wǔyí Shān is linked to Fúzhōu, Quánzhōu and Xiàmén by train. If the train is too slow, there are daily flights between Xiàmén, Fúzhōu and Wǔyí Shān. See the Getting There & Away information in the relevant sections of this chapter for more details.

FÚZHŌU 福州

☎ 591 / pop 6.6 million

Fúzhōu, capital of Fújiàn, is a prosperous modern city that attracts a significant amount of Taiwanese investment, reflected in innumerable shopping centres and expensive restaurants. Unless you're here on business the city holds very little interest, except as a launching pad for visiting Wǔyí Shān or Taimu Mountain.

The city dates back to the 3rd century AD, and over the years became an important trading centre for tea. Marco Polo described the city as a 'veritable marvel', perhaps as applicable then as it is today, considering the scope of recent development.

Orientation

Fúzhōu's city centre sprawls northward from the Min River (Mǐn Jiāng). The train station is in the northeast of the city, while most of the accommodation is on Wusi Lu, sandwiched between Hualin Lu and Dongda Lu. Travellers arriving by bus will be dropped off either at the north long-distance bus station, close to the train station, or the south long-distance bus station at the intersection of Guohuo Xilu and Wuyi Zhonglu. The airport is 50km south of the city.

Information

INTERNET ACCESS 网吧

Look for internet cafés in the alleys running south of Dong Jie near the intersection with Wuyi Beilu. Most places charge Y2 to Y3 an hour.

INTERNET RESOURCES

ChinaTS Network (www.chinats.com/fuzhou) Provides background on Fúzhōu's history and cultural attractions.

MEDICAL SERVICES

Fujian Provincial Hospital (Shěng Èr Rénmín Yīyuàn; 134 Dong Jie) Conveniently located in the city centre.

MONEY

Bank of China (Zhōngguó Yínháng; 136 Wusi Lu; ☺ 8am-6pm) The main branch changes travellers cheques and cash, and has an ATM which handles foreign cards.

POST & TELEPHONE

Post and telephone office (Yóudiàn Dàlóu) On the southeast corner of Dong Jie and Bayiqi Lu.

PUBLIC SECURITY BUREAU

PSB (Gōngānjú; 107 Beihuan Zhonglu) Opposite the Sports Centre in the northern part of town.

TOURIST INFORMATION & TRAVEL AGENCIES

China Travel Service (CTS; Zhōngguó Lǚxíngshè; ☎ 8753 6250; 128 Wusi Lu) Sells airline tickets and offers a number of tours to areas around Fújiàn, but it doesn't book train tickets.

Sights & Activities

Fúzhōu has only a few places of interest for visitors. Most people just pass through the city or use it as a base for sites further afield.

The **Jade Hill Scenic Area** (Yú Shān Fēngjǐngqū), a rocky hill in the centre of Fúzhōu, is attractive enough to spend an hour or so. The hill once overlooked the city but is now dwarfed by the surrounding skyscrapers and shopping plazas. Its principal attraction is the seven-storey **White Pagoda** (Bái Tǎ), built in AD 904. From the top of the pagoda you have peek-a-boo views of the city. Near the pagoda is a small exhibit hall showcasing two silk-wrapped mummies from the Song dynasty. A stern-faced statue of **Mao Zedong** (Máo Zhǔxì Xiàng) salutes the sea of traffic at the foot of Jade Hill.

Near Jade Hill is the granite **Black Pagoda** (Wū Tǎ), which stands on the southern slope of Black Hill (Wū Shān) and dates from the 8th century. It contains some fierce-looking statues of guardian deities. During the Lunar New Year Festival, both the White and Black pagodas are strung with lanterns and look quite festive.

In the northwest of Fúzhōu is **West Lake Park** (Xīhú Gōngyuán; admission Y15; 6am-10pm), with a large artificial lake. It's a popular hang-out for locals on the weekends. The **Fujian Provincial Museum** (Fújiàn Shěng Bówùguǎn; admission Y20; 9am-4pm) in the park is very sci-fi, with lots of columns and spires. Despite its tacky exterior, the exhibits inside are pretty good and include a fascinating 3445-year-old 'boat coffin' unearthed from a cliff in Wǔyíshān.

South of the Min River, across from Jiefang Bridge, is the former **foreign concession area**, now a ramshackle collection of old and new developments. You'll see a few dilapidated colonial buildings, mixed in with more recent construction.

To experience river life along the Min River, consider taking a boat tour from **Taijiang Harbour** (Táijiāng Mǎtou). Boats leave according to demand and prices vary depending upon the number of people who want to take the tour. Most hotels and travel agencies can arrange this trip.

Sleeping

Fúzhōu accommodation falls mainly in the midrange and top-end categories. Many hotels offer discounts, making them affordable even for those on tight budgets. Wusi Lu and Dongda Lu are the best places to look for places to stay. Most hotels are equipped with broadband internet, though you might pay up to Y30 a day for access.

BUDGET & MIDRANGE

Fuzhou Hotel (Fúzhōu Dàjiǔjiā; ☎ 8755 6631; fax 8755 5795; 18 Dongda Lu; 东大路18号; s Y398, d Y358-396, tr Y498) This centrally located hotel has respectable, good-sized rooms with comfortable beds. The

bathrooms are outdated but clean. It's a five-minute walk from here to Jade Hill.

Juchunyuan Hotel (Jùchūnyuán Dàjiǔdiàn; ☎ 8750 2328; fax 8750 2228; 2 Dong Jie; 东街2号; s Y498, d Y438-498, ste Y568) This smart three-star hotel has a monster-size lobby with several restaurants and expensive shopping centres. Rooms are quite large and come with minibars and video on demand. The restaurant of the same name has an excellent reputation for serving some of the best Fújiàn cuisine in town (see below).

Jin Ye Hotel (Jīnyè Dàjiǔdiàn; ☎ 8757 5888; fax 8758 5888; 378 Hualin Lu; 华林路378号; s Y583-638, d Y530-580) The Jin Ye has cosy, tastefully decorated rooms conveniently located near the train station but a bit far from everything else. Ask for a room on the top floor to avoid the noisy street. Half-price discounts are the norm here.

Yushan Hotel (Yúshān Bīnguǎn; ☎ 8335 1668; fax 8335 7694; 10 Yushan Lu; 于山路10号; s Y583-638, d Y539) Located on the grassy park-like grounds of Jade Hill, the Yushan offers fresh, peaceful rooms with upscale amenities. Affable, organised management can help you with air and train tickets.

TOP END

Hot Spring Hotel (Wēnquán Dàfàndiàn; ☎ 8785 1818; fax 8783 5150; 218 Wusi Lu; 五四路218号; d Y1136-1587, ste Y2047-2622) This large hotel has luxurious rooms with excellent facilities, including piped-in hot springs, an on-site bowling alley and several restaurants. It's so nice you may not want to leave.

Eating

Because of its proximity to the Min River and the ocean, Fúzhōu is deservedly famous for both freshwater fish and seafood. The city's most famous dish is the imaginatively named 'Buddha Leaps the Wall' (佛跳墙; Fó Tiào Qiáng), a concoction of 30 different kinds of vegetables, meats and seafood, including abalone, sea slugs, dried scallops, pigeon eggs and mushrooms, stewed for hours in an aged liquor. The story goes that the dish is so delicious, Buddha would leap a wall to get to it.

Juchunyuan Restaurant (Jùchūnyuán Dàjiǔdiàn; ☎ 8753 3604; 2 Dong Jie; Fó Tiào Qiáng Y200; 11.30am-9pm) The most famous restaurant in town is located in the Juchunyuan Hotel (see above) and has built a reputation on Fúzhōu's one-of-a-kind dish.

For cheap noodles and dumplings in a lively nocturnal environment, locals head south to

FÚJIÀN

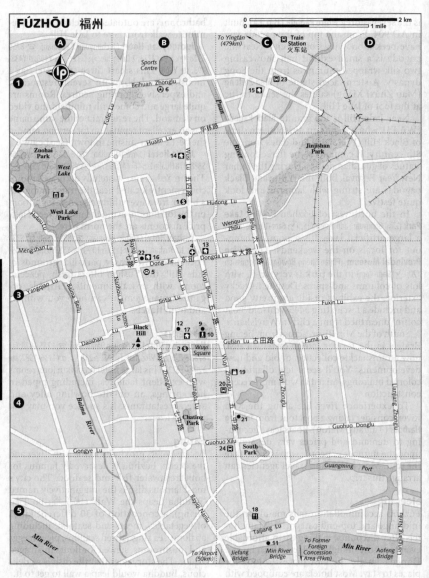

Taijiang Lu – a boisterous, pedestrianised food street *(cài bù xíngjiē)* lined with Ming-dynasty-style wooden buildings and lanterns. Take bus 51 from Wusi Lu to get there.

Shopping

Fúzhōu is famous for its lacquerware, bamboo furniture, and stone and cork carvings. The city is also famous for its 'clay people' *(ní rén)*, which are small clay figurines painted in bright colours.

A good place to look for souvenir items is in the **Huadu Department Store** (Huádū Shāngshà; 49 Wuyi Zhonglu), where you'll find paper parasols, jade combs and other popular Fúzhōu mementos.

INFORMATION		Mao Zedong Statue 毛主席像 10 B3	SHOPPING
Bank of China 中国银行 1 B2		Taijiang Harbour 台江码头 11 C5	Huadu Department Store
Bank of China 中国银行 2 B3		White Pagoda 白塔 12 B3	华都商厦 19 C4
CTS 中国旅行社 3 B2			
Fujian Provincial Hospital		SLEEPING	TRANSPORT
省二人民医院 4 B3		Fuzhou Hotel 福州大酒家 13 B3	Airport Bus, Apollo Hotel
Post & Telephone Office		Hot Spring Hotel 温泉大饭店 14 B2	阿波罗大酒店 20 C4
邮电大楼 5 B3		Jin Ye Hotel 金叶大酒店 15 C1	CAAC
PSB 公安局 6 B1		Juchunyuan Hotel	民航售票处 21 C4
		聚春园大酒店 16 B3	Lida Building (Train Ticket
SIGHTS & ACTIVITIES		Yushan Hotel 于山宾馆 17 B3	Booking Office)
Black Pagoda 乌塔 7 B3			利达大厦 22 B3
Fujian Provincial Museum		EATING	North Long-Distance Bus
省博物馆 8 A2		Juchunyuan Restaurant .... (see 16)	Station 长途汽车北站 23 C1
Jade Hill Scenic Area		Pedestrian Food Street	South Long-Distance Bus
于山风景区 9 B3		菜步行街 18 C5	Station 福州汽车南站 24 C4

Getting There & Away

AIR

The **Civil Aviation Administration of China** (CAAC; Zhōngguó Mínháng; ☎ 8334 5988; Wuyi Zhonglu) has daily flights to major destinations such as Běijīng (Y1550, 2½ hours), Guǎngzhōu (Y830, one hour), Shànghǎi (Y780, 70 minutes), Hong Kong (Y1810, 80 minutes) and Wǔyí Shān (Y490, 30 minutes). Airport buses leave from the **Apollo Hotel** (Ābōluó Dàjiǔdiàn; ☎ 8305 5555; 132 Wuyi Zhonglu) every 25 minutes beginning at 5.50am. The last bus is at 7.15pm. Tickets are Y20 and the 50km trip takes about an hour.

BUS

There are two long-distance bus stations in town: one in the north near the train station, and one at the southern end of town, down from the CAAC office on the corner of Guohuo Xilu and Wuyi Zhonglu. Most services are available from both bus stations.

There are economy bus services departing for Guǎngzhōu (Y180 to Y258, nine hours), Shànghǎi (Y280, 18 hours), Wēnzhōu (Y125 to Y190, 4½ hours), Quánzhōu (Y52 to Y60, two hours) and Xiàmén (Y68 to Y80, three hours). Deluxe buses to Guǎngzhōu (Y258 to Y280, eight hours) and Shēnzhèn (Y260, eight hours) depart from the south bus station. Luxury buses travel to Xiàmén (Y80 to Y99, 2½ hours) from the north bus station. Night buses leave the north bus station for Wǔyí Shān (Y86 to 90, eight hours).

TRAIN

The train line from Fúzhōu heads northwest and joins the main Shànghǎi–Guǎngzhōu line at the Yīngtán junction in Jiāngxī. There are also trains from Fúzhōu to Wǔyí Shān (Y47 to Y72, 5½ hours). There are no trains to Xiàmén.

There are direct trains from Fúzhōu to Běijīng (Y443, 34 hours) and Shànghǎi (Y242, 18½ hours). It's fairly easy to buy tickets at the train station, from a spot about 100m to the left of the main train station building, when you are facing it. Many hotels will book train tickets for a service fee, and there's also a train ticket booking office in the entrance of the **Lida building** (Lidà Dàshà; ⏰ 8am-5pm), opposite the post office.

Getting Around

Fúzhōu is a sprawling city, which makes it difficult to get around by foot. Taxi flag fall is Y10. There's a good bus network, and bus maps are available at the train station or from hotels. Bus 51 travels from the train station along Wusi Lu, and bus 1 goes to West Lake Park from Bayiqi Lu.

TAIMU MOUNTAIN 太姥山

About 2½ hours from Fúzhōu, Taimu Mountain (Tàimǔ Shān) is lesser known than Wǔyí Shān but equally beautiful. Embraced by the views of the sea on three sides, with its jagged limestone peaks perpetually wrapped in mist, the mountain is a magnificent place for hiking. The highest peak in Taimu is only 917m, but with great views of the distant ocean. There's virtually no English spoken and few Western tourists, so unless you arrange a tour from Fúzhōu you're really on your own.

Sights & Activities

Scattered across **Taimu Mountain** (admission Y60; ⏰ 8am-4.30pm) are a number of karst caves, temples that date back to the Tang dynasty, and hoodoos, those curiously shaped rocks that figure so large in the Chinese imagination. Just about every rock on the mountain has been named, from the straightforward ('husband

FÚJIÀN

and wife') to the just plain bizarre ('mouse eating a pig's liver'). Unless you have a guide, they'll probably look like, well, rocks.

There are 36 temples on Taimu, the most notable of them **Guoxing Temple** (国兴寺; Guóxīng Sì), which dates back to the Tang dynasty and still has 360 of its original pillars, an ancient well and a stone pagoda. Another temple on the tourist route is the **One Tile Temple** (一片瓦寺; Yīpiānwǎ Sì), which gets its name from a large stone that protrudes from above and shelters the temple. Come around lunchtime and you'll be served some wonderful vegetarian food. If you have a chance, also try some of the excellent tea, a speciality of the area. Another popular destination is the **Thread of Sky** (一线天; Yīxiàntiān), a narrow crevice over 60m long and 37m high, which tourists squeeze themselves through to the laughs and screams of their companions. For those looking to escape the tourist sites, it's easy to take off on your own, following some of the more unused mountain paths. Travellers have recommended bringing a flashlight (torch; it gets dark early on the mountain) and rain gear for the fickle weather.

Sleeping & Eating

The most scenic area to stay is on the mountain itself. The **Yùhú Bīnguǎn** (玉湖宾馆; ☎ 0593 726 1531; fax 726 3625; d Y400) is near Yuhu Lake and has clean, reasonable accommodation. Rooms are on the frumpy side, but you're not really here for the hotel décor, are you? The hotel restaurant serves good Chinese food and there are several small restaurants near the park entrance that will keep you fed and happy.

Getting There & Away

You'll want to make your ascent from the small town of Qīnyǔ (亲屿), which sits at the base of the mountain. Buses run from Qīnyǔ to the mountain entrance for Y7. Qīnyǔ is 297km by bus from Fúzhōu (Y80, 2½ hours) and 167km from Wēnzhōu (Y35, 1½ hours) in Zhèjiāng province. The bus ride from Fúzhōu takes you along some terrifying mountain roads, with pin-tight curves and steep drops. Close your eyes and hang on tight.

XIÀMÉN 厦门

☎ 0592 / pop 592,372

Xiàmén, also known to the West as Amoy, ranks as the most attractive city in Fújiàn. Many of its old colonial buildings have been

carefully restored and its clean, well-kept streets and lively waterfront district give it a captivating old-world charm rarely seen in Chinese cities.

A visit to Xiàmén isn't complete without a stay on the tiny island of Gǔlàng Yǔ (see p348), once the old colonial home of the Europeans and Japanese. Its breezy seaside gardens and delightful architecture are one of the highlights of visiting Fújiàn.

Xiàmén is unbearably hot and humid in the summer and slightly cooler in the winter. Spring and autumn are when temperatures are at their best, though fickle weather means rain any time of year.

History

Xiàmén was founded around the mid-14th century in the early years of the Ming dynasty. Ming rulers built the city walls and established Xiàmén as a major seaport and commercial centre.

In the 17th century it became a place of refuge for the Ming rulers fleeing the Manchu invaders. Xiàmén and nearby Jīnmén were bases for the Ming armies who, under the command of the pirate-general Koxinga, had as their battle-cry, 'resist the Qing and restore the Ming'.

The Portuguese arrived in the 16th century, followed by the British in the 17th century, and later the French and the Dutch, all of whom attempted rather unsuccessfully to establish Xiàmén as a trade port.

The port was closed to foreigners in the 1750s and it was not until the Opium War that the tide turned. In August 1841 a British naval force of 38 ships carrying artillery and soldiers sailed into Xiàmén harbour, forcing the port to open. Xiàmén then became one of the first treaty ports.

Japanese and Western powers followed soon after, establishing consulates and making the island of Gǔlàng Yǔ a foreign enclave. Xiàmén turned Japanese in 1938 and remained that way until 1945.

Orientation

The town of Xiàmén is on the island of the same name. It's connected to the mainland by a 5km-long causeway bearing a train line, road and footpath. The interesting part of Xiàmén is near the western (waterfront) district, directly opposite the small island of Gǔlàng Yǔ. This is the old area of town, known for its colonial architecture, parks and winding streets.

Information

INTERNET ACCESS 网吧
There are internet cafés scattered around the harbour area. The lanes surrounding Datong Lu are a good place to look. Most cafés charge Y4 per hour.

INTERNET RESOURCES
Amoy Magic (www.amoymagic.com) One of the most comprehensive websites on Xiàmén.

MEDICAL SERVICES
Life Line Medical Clinic (Mìfú Zhěnsuǒ; ☎ 532 3168; 123 Xidi Villa Hubin Beilu; 8am-5pm Mon-Fri, 8am-noon Sat) A clinic for expats, with English-speaking doctors. Telephone operated 24 hours.

MONEY
Bank of China (Zhōngguó Yínháng; 10 Zhongshan Lu) Near the Lujiang Hotel by the waterfront. Has an ATM.
Hong Kong Bank (HSBC; Huìfēng Yínháng; 189 Xiahe Lu) Also changes money and has an ATM.

POST & TELEPHONE
Post and telephone office (Yóudiànjú; cnr Xinhua Lu & Zhongshan Lu)

PUBLIC SECURITY BUREAU
PSB (Gōngānjú; ☎ 226 2203) Opposite the main post and telephone office. The visa section is located in the northeast part of the building, near the entrance on Gongyuan Xilu.

TOURIST INFORMATION & TRAVEL AGENCIES
China International Travel Services (CITS; Zhōngguó Guójì Lǚxíngshè; 335 Hexiang Xilu) There are several offices around town. This branch near Yundang Lake is recommended.
Complaints Hotline (☎ 800 8582, ext 36) For complaints about overpricing, theft, bad taxi drivers etc.

Sights & Activities

NANPUTUO TEMPLE 南普陀寺
On the southern outskirts of Xiàmén city, this modern-looking Buddhist **temple** (Nánpǔtuó Sì; ☎ 208 6490; Siming Nanlu; admission Y3; 8am-5pm) was originally built more than 1000 years ago during the Tang dynasty, and has been destroyed and rebuilt several times over the course of its long history. The most current incarnation dates to the early 20th century. It's an active temple and very busy, with chanting monks and worshippers lighting incense and praying.

Entering the temple through **Heavenly King Hall** (Tiānwáng Diàn) you are met by the tubbellied Milefo (Laughing Buddha), flanked by four heavenly kings. The classical Chinese inscription reads: 'When entering, regard Buddha and afterwards pay your respects to the four kings of heaven'.

Behind Milefo is Wei Tuo, protector of Buddhist monasteries, who safeguards Buddhist doctrine and relics. He holds a stick that points to the ground, indicating that the temple is rich and can provide visiting monks with board and lodging (if the stick is held horizontally it means the temple is poor and is a polite way of saying 'find somewhere else to stay').

In front of the courtyard is the **Great Heroic Treasure Hall** (Dà Xióngbǎo Diàn), a two-storey building containing three Buddhas that represent Buddha in his past, present and future lives.

The **Great Compassion Hall** (Dàbēi Diàn) contains four statues of Guanyin (the Goddess of Mercy). Worshippers cast divining sticks at the feet of the statues to seek heavenly guidance.

The temple has an excellent vegetarian restaurant in a shaded courtyard where you can dine in the company of resident monks.

Take bus 1 from the train station or bus 21 from Zhongshan Lu to reach the temple.

XIAMEN UNIVERSITY 厦门大学
Next to Nanputuo Temple, **Xiamen University** (Xiàmén Dàxué) was established with overseas Chinese funds. Its well-maintained grounds feature an attractive lake and are good for a pleasant, shady stroll. The campus entrance is next to the stop for bus 1. You can walk south to Daxue Lu from the main entrance, where you'll see a nice long stretch of sandy beach.

Not too far from the university is the **Huli Shan Fortress** (Húlǐ Shān Pàotái; admission Y25), a gigantic German gun artillery which was built in 1893 and used to deter foreign imperialists from entering the city. You can rent binoculars here to peer out over the water to Taiwanese-occupied Jīnmén Island, formerly known as Quemoy, claimed by both mainland China and Taiwan. From a small pier next to the fortress you can hire a boat to take you on a one-hour ride around Jīnmén for Y96.

FÚJIÀN

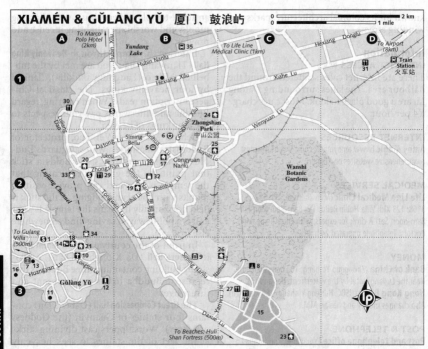

Also close to the university is the **Overseas Chinese Museum** (Huáqiáo Bówùguǎn; 73 Siming Nanlu; admission Y10; ☻ 9am-4.30pm), which has excellent photos and paintings of the history and various activities of Chinese communities abroad.

Tours
CITS (p345) can arrange tours around Xiàmén and Gǔlàng Yǔ. Most hotels can also help with tours.

Festivals & Events
The **Xiamen International Marathon** is held in spring, and draws local and international participants. Runners race around the coastal ring road that circles the island. It's a popular event – in 2006, 20,933 participants from 39 countries participated.

Dragon Boat races are held in Xiàmén every June and are quite a sight.

Sleeping
For ambience, Gǔlàng Yǔ beats Xiàmén hands down as a more memorable and relaxing place to stay. In Xiàmén, hotels are clustered around

the harbour and in the far-eastern section of town near the train station.

Lodging becomes expensive and hard to find around the first week of September, when a large investment fair takes place in the city.

BUDGET
Xiamen International Youth Hostel (Xiamen Guoji Qingnian Lushe; ☎ 208 2345; fax 219 9876; 41 Nanhua Lu; 南华路41号; dm Y50, d Y120-150; ☐) At last a youth hostel comes to Xiàmén! With spick-and-span rooms and smiling staff, this place wins the prize for best budget accommodation in town. It offers internet access, bike rental, kitchen and a ticket-booking office.

Overseas Student Dormitory (Càiqīngjié Lóu; ☎ 208 4528; fax 208 6774; Xiamen University; s/d Y150/180) For plain, spotless rooms check out this modest guesthouse at Xiamen University. It's a great place to meet students and find out what's happening around town. To reach the dormitory walk uphill for about 100m from the university's south gate, then take a left and look out for a purple 10-storey building.

Singapore Hotel (Xīnjiāpō Jiǔdiàn; ☎ 202 6668; fax 202 5950; 113-121 Xian Lu; 西安路121号; s/d Y463) This two-star hotel looks dilapidated on the outside but inside the rooms are adequate enough, though don't expect any mints on your pillow. Check the room out before committing. Rates can be bargained down if you're *really* persistent.

MIDRANGE

Most accommodation in Xiàmén is midrange, shading top end. Many hotels in this range are equipped with broadband internet for an extra Y30 a day if you have your own computer.

Gem Hotel (Jīnhòu Jiŭdiàn; ☎ 399 6666; fax 399 6789; 444 Zhongshan Lu; 中山路444号; s/d Y400, tatami-style r Y680) This hotel has a wildly decorated Las Vegas–style lobby with murals of frolicking cupids and fairies. Thank goodness the rooms are more understated. Make sure you don't get a room above the karaoke hall or it could be a long, agonising night.

Lujiang Hotel (Lùjiāng Bīnguăn; ☎ 202 2922; fax 202 4644; 54 Lujiang Dao; 鹭江道54号; s Y451, d Y400-770, tw Y468) This 1940s-era hotel has one of the best spots in town opposite the Gŭlàng Yŭ ferry terminal. Rooms are pretty good, though aging and rather cramped. The rooms with ocean views feel more spacious. The rooftop restaurant is excellent (see p348).

Xiamen Hotel (Xiàmén Bīnguăn; ☎ 202 2265; fax 202 1765; 16 Huyuan Lu; 虎园路16号; d Y1120-1380) At the high-end of midrange, this well-managed place has spiffy rooms, a glitzy lobby and a great location between two city parks. You might have to fight for a room as it's often booked far in advance by business travellers.

TOP END

There's a wide range of top-end accommodation in Xiàmén, but much of it is badly located in the eastern part of town. Most places offer 50% discounts. Add a 15% service charge to all prices.

Holiday Inn (Jiàrì Huángguān Hăijĭng Dàjiŭdiàn; ☎ 202 3333; fax 203 6666; 128 Zhenhai Lu; 镇海路128号; d US$160-820) The Holiday Inn is in a prime location near the harbour and is one of the more popular spots in town. Rooms are comfortable, if unimaginative (no dancing cupids here), and service is top-notch.

Marco Polo Hotel (Măgē Bōluō Dōngfāng Dàjiŭdiàn; ☎ 509 1888; www.marcopolohotels.com/xiamen; 8 Jianye Lu; 建业路8号; r US$160-225, ste US$295-980) Another one of the big box hotels, this four-star place pulls out all the stops to pamper travellers. Besides elegantly furnished rooms with large bathrooms, there's a nice-sized pool, a bar and several Chinese and Japanese restaurants.

Eating

Being a port city, Xiàmén is known for its fresh fish and seafood, especially oysters and shrimp. You'll find good places to eat around Zhongshan Lu near the harbour. Jukou Jie, near the intersection of Siming Beilu and Zhongshan Lu, has a bunch of Sìchuān and Taiwanese restaurants.

Huang Zehe Peanut Soup Shop (Huángzéhé Huāshēng Tāngdiàn; 20 Zhongshan Lu; snacks Y1-6; ☼ 24hr) This busy restaurant by the harbour is popular for its local snacks, including peanut soup (花生汤; huāshēng tāng), a regional speciality.

FÚJIÀN

Lujiang Hotel Restaurant (☎ 202 2922; 54 Lujiang Dao; meals from Y30; ⏱ 7am-10pm) Overlooking the sea, this rooftop restaurant is one of the nicest places to eat in Xiàmén. Dine al fresco under the stars or inside. In addition to an extensive menu (in English) with Fújiàn specialities, there's also an excellent Cantonese buffet. Reservations for dinner are recommended, especially on the weekends.

World Trade Centre (Shìjiè Màoyì Zhōngxīn; Xiahe Lu) Next to the train station, there is an excellent open-air food court on the 5th floor, with a variety of small fast-food restaurants to choose from.

Near the university, good, cheap, attractive restaurants line Siming Nanlu and Yanwu Jie. Two decent vegetarian restaurants are **Dàfāng Sùcàiguǎn** (412-4 Siming Nanlu; meals Y8; ⏱ 11am-late) and **Gōngdé Sùcàiguǎn** (418-10 Siming Nanlu; meals Y8; ⏱ 10am-9pm). Try the monks' vegetables (罗汉斋; luóhàn zhāi). Nanputuo Temple (see p345) has an excellent vegetarian restaurant with set meals for Y30 to Y80.

Xiàmén also has an assortment of restaurants serving Western-style dishes. One of the more popular places is **Sundance Kid** (252 Lujiang Lu; mains from Y15; ⏱ 10am-late), which dishes up an eclectic assortment of dishes, including pizzas, seafood and roasted mutton with vegetables. There's also free internet and live entertainment on the weekends.

Shopping

Xiàmén has lots of hidden curio and food shops tucked away off the busy streets. There's a crowded night market (yè shìchǎng) on Ding'an Lu, between Zhongshan Lu and Zhenhai Lu.

Getting There & Away

AIR

Xiamen Airlines is the main airline under the CAAC banner in this part of China. There are innumerable ticket offices around town, many of which are in the larger hotels, such as the Holiday Inn.

CAAC has flights to Hong Kong, Kuala Lumpur, Manila, Penang and Singapore. **Silk Air** (☎ 205 3280) flies to Singapore and has an office in the Holiday Inn. **All Nippon Airways** (☎ 573 2888) flies to Osaka, and has ticket agents at the Holiday Inn and Lujiang Hotel. **Dragonair** (☎ 202 5433) is in the Marco Polo Hotel.

Xiàmén airport has flights to all major domestic destinations around China, including

Wǔyí Shān (Y590) four times a week. Airport departure tax is Y90.

BUS

Deluxe and economy buses leave from the long-distance bus station and the ferry terminal. Destinations include Fúzhōu (Y68 to Y99, 2½ to three hours), Wǔyí Shān (Y124 to Y202, nine hours), Quánzhōu (Y27 to Y37, 1½ hours) and Shàntóu (Y100, five hours). There are also express buses to Guǎngzhōu (Y200 to Y300, 12 hours), Shēnzhèn (Y180, nine hours), Hong Kong (Y300 to Y350, 10 hours) and Shànghǎi (Y330 to Y413). Buses also make trips inland to Lóngyán (Y50, three hours) and Yǒngdìng (Y45, five hours).

TRAIN

From Xiàmén there are direct trains to destinations including Hángzhōu (Y231, 26 hours), Shànghǎi (Y281, 27 hours), Běijīng (Y443, 34 hours) and Wǔyí Shān (Y149, 13 hours). Book tickets at the train station or through **CITS** (335 Hexiang Xilu), which will make bookings for a Y35 service fee.

Getting Around

Xiàmén airport is 15km from the waterfront district, about 8km from the eastern district. From the waterfront, taxis cost around Y35. Bus 28 travels from the airport to the ferry terminal via the train station.

Frequent minibuses run between the train station and ferry terminal (Y1). Buses to Xiàmén University go from the train station (bus 1) and from the ferry terminal (bus 2). Taxis start at Y7.

GǓLÀNG YǓ 鼓浪屿

A 10-minute boat trip from Xiàmén, Gǔlàng Yǔ is a relaxing retreat of meandering lanes and shaded backstreets, set in an architectural twilight of colonial villas and crumbling remains. It's well worth spending a few days exploring the place.

The foreign community was well established on Gǔlàng Yǔ by the 1880s, with a daily English newspaper, churches, hospitals, post and telegraph offices, libraries, hotels and consulates. In 1903 the island was officially designated an International Foreign Settlement, and a municipal council with a police force of Sikhs was established to govern it. Today, memories of the settlement linger in the charming colonial buildings that blanket the island and the sound of classical piano wafting from shuttered windows. Many of China's most celebrated musicians have come from Gǔlàng Yǔ.

The best way to enjoy the island is to wander along the streets, peeking into courtyards and down alleys to catch a glimpse of colonial mansions seasoned by local life. Most sights and hotels are just a short walk from the ferry terminal.

Sights

The most interesting attractions on the island are the old colonial residences and consulates, tucked away in the maze of streets leading away from the pier, particularly along Longtou Lu and the back lanes of Huayan Lu. The first site you'll see after stepping off the boat from Xiamen is a tentacle waving statue of an octopus, which marks the entrance to **Xiamen Underwater World** (Xiàmén Hǎidǐ Shìjiè; 2 Longtou Lu; admission Y70; 8am-6pm). Kids (adults too) will enjoy the exhibits of penguins, seals, dolphins and exotic fish. As aquariums go, it's reasonably well maintained, though the tanks are cramped. The immense shark tank is viewed via a tubular passageway.

Southeast of the pier you'll pass the former British consulate, with its whitewashed walls and flower gardens, and the well-preserved **Roman Catholic Church** (Tiānzhǔjiào Táng). If you continue walking south you'll eventually hit **Haoyue Garden** (Hàoyuè Yuán), a rocky outcrop containing an imposing statue of Koxinga in full military dress looking out over the water to Taiwan.

The most prominent attraction on the island is **Sunlight Rock** (Rìguāng Yán), the island's highest point at 93m. On a clear day you can see the island of Jīnmén. At the foot of Sunlight Rock is a large colonial building known as the **Koxinga Memorial Hall** (Zhèngchénggōng Jìniànguǎn; 8-11am & 2-5pm). The hall has an exhibition partly dedicated to the Dutch in Taiwan, and partly to Koxinga's throwing them out. On exhibit are some tattered remains of Koxinga's clothing and his jade belt. Both sights are located in **Sunlight Rock Park** (Rìguāng Yán Gōngyuán; admission Y60; 8am-7pm).

Yingxiong Hill (Yīngxióng Shān) is near the memorial hall and has an open-air aviary (admission Y15) on the top with chattering egrets and parrots.

The waterfront **Shuzhuang Garden** (Shūzhuāng Huāyuán; admission Y30) on the southern end of the island is a lovely place to linger for a few hours. It has a small bonsai *(péncāi)* garden and some delicate-looking pavilions. The garden was built by a Taiwanese businessman who moved here with his family during the Sino-Japanese War (1894–95).

Sleeping & Eating

Gulang Yu International Youth Hostel (Gǔlàng Yǔ Guójì Qīngnián Lǚguǎn; ☎ 106 6066; 18 Lujiao Lu; 鹿礁路18号; 6-bed dm Y45, tw with shared bathroom Y56) This new hostel, in a lovely old brick villa, is bursting with character. Rooms are large, with beamed ceilings and tiled floors, and there's a relaxing garden courtyard. Hot water can be hit or miss (there's only one shower with hot water) and during winter the place is very damp and chilly.

Luzhou Hotel (Lǜzhōu Jiǔdiàn; ☎ 206 5390; fax 206 5843; 1 Longtou Lu; 龙头路1号; s/d Y306) This very modest hotel has few amenities but is conveniently located near the ferry pier in case you're hauling a heavy bag. The more spacious rooms have ocean views with wooden floors.

Gulang Villa (Gǔlàng Yǔ Bièshù; ☎ 206 3280; fax 206 0165; 14 Gusheng Lu; 鼓声路14号; s/d Y428/628) Located on a private beach on the western side of the island, the Gulang is an ideal place to stay if you want an escape from the crowds. The hotel is surrounded by trees and small walking paths, making it a delightful retreat. The in-house restaurant serves very good Fujianese cuisine.

Night Lily Hotel (Xiàmén Bǎihé Bīnguǎn; ☎ 206 0920; 11 Bishan Lu; 笔山路11号; http://nitelily.todayinchina.com; d/tr incl breakfast Y450/500) This secluded 1930s-style bed and breakfast, with its pastel-coloured walls and eclectic mix of Chinese and European antiques, is an unexpected treasure. The large, airy balcony faces the sea, a perfect place for taking some tea in the sun. There are only five rooms so you'll need to book ahead.

Gǔlàng Yǔ is a great place for fish and seafood, especially at the restaurants in the centre of town. You'll find a collection of small eateries in the streets around the ferry terminal, and off Longtou Lu there are many small restaurants and stalls.

Getting There & Away

Ferries to Gǔlàng Yǔ leave from the ferry terminal just west of Xiàmén's Lujiang Hotel. Outbound, it's a free ride on the bottom deck and Y1 for the upper deck. Xiàmén bound it's Y3 on the bottom and Y4 upstairs.

A ROUNDABOUT TOUR OF HAKKA TǓLÓU

Fújiàn's *tǔlóu* (earth buildings) are scattered throughout almost 50 counties in the most remote parts of the province. The most accessible (and set up for tourists) are in the town of **Húkēng** (糊坑; admission Y40), where your ticket grants you admission to four *tǔlóu* and a small cultural museum. By far the best-known *tǔlóu* is **Zhènchéng Lóu** (振城楼), a grandiose structure built in 1912, with two concentric circles and a total of 222 rooms. In the centre of the *tǔlóu* is a large ancestral hall for special ceremonies and greeting guests. Near Zhènchéng Lóu, you'll also see the much older **Kuíjù Lóu** (奎聚楼), which dates back to 1834. It looks less like a traditional *tǔlóu* than its neighbours because of its square (as opposed to round) sides. Also worth visiting is the late-19th-century and (comparatively) pea-sized **Rúshēng Lóu** (如升楼), the smallest of the roundhouses with only one ring and 16 rooms. Your ticket also gets you into the five-storey **Fúyù Lóu** (副裕楼), which boasts some wonderfully carved beams and pillars.

For those of you looking to see some less touristy *tǔlóu*, consider hiring a taxi to take you around the countryside on a *tǔlóu* tour. You'll find taxi drivers in Húkēng and Yǒngdìng who will offer their services for around Y300 a day. Here's a rundown of some lesser-known *tǔlóu* to get you started:

Chéngqǐ Lóu (承启楼) Built in 1709, this granddaddy of *tǔlóu* has more than 400 rooms and once had over 1000 inhabitants. It's in the village of Gāoběi (高北村), about 20km north of Húkēng.

Yíjing Lóu (遗经楼) This massive, crumbling structure, with 281 rooms, two schools and 51 halls, is in the village of Gāobò (高陂村) and was built in 1851.

Huánjí Lóu (环极楼) Peacefully located in the village of Nánxī (南溪村), this spectacular *tǔlóu* dates back to 1693 and is surrounded by rural farmlands and a bubbling creek.

YǑNGDÌNG 永定

☎ 0597 / pop 40,160

Yǒngdìng is a rural area of rolling farmlands and hills in southwestern Fújiàn. Heartland of the Hakka people, it's renowned for its remarkable *tǔlóu* (earth buildings), large, circular edifices resembling fortresses that are scattered throughout the surrounding countryside. Today there are 20,000 of these buildings still in existence, many still inhabited and open to visitors.

The Hakka have inhabited Yǒngdìng and its neighbouring villages for hundreds of years. During the Jin dynasty (AD 265–314) the Hakka peoples of northwest China began a gradual migration south to escape persecution and famine. They eventually settled in Jiāngxī, Fújiàn and Guǎngdōng, where they began to build *tǔlóu* to protect themselves from bandits and wild animals.

These early structures were large enough to house entire clans. The buildings were communal, with interior buildings enclosed by enormous peripheral ones that could hold hundreds of people. Nestled in the mud walls were bedrooms, wells, cooking areas and storehouses, circling a central courtyard. The walls were made of rammed earth and glutinous rice, reinforced with strips of bamboo and wood chips.

Sleeping & Eating

If you've come all this way, why not stay in a *tǔlóu*? Residents will approach you first, eagerly offering their homes as lodging. Make sure to look over the room before you agree to a price. Don't expect accommodation to be anything but basic – you'll get a bed, a thermos of hot water and not much else. You'll also be offered a simple meal cooked over an open fire that may or may not be included in the room price. It's a good idea to bring a flashlight (torch) and bug repellent.

Getting There & Away

To get to Húkēng, first catch a bus from Xiàmén to Lóngyán (Y55, four hours) and then switch to a minibus (Y17, two hours). There are two fast trains daily from Xiàmén to Yǒngdìng (Y30, three hours) that leave at 8.30am and 1.30pm. Yǒngdìng is accessed by bus from Guǎngdōng, Xiàmén (Y45, five hours) or Lóngyán (Y15, one hour). Buses run between Húkēng and Yǒngdìng for about Y10.

QUÁNZHŌU 泉州

☎ 0595 / pop 184,812

Quánzhōu was once a great trading port and an important stop on the maritime silk route. Back in the 13th century, Marco Polo informed his readers that '…it is one of the two ports in the world with the biggest flow of merchandise'. The city reached its zenith as an international port during the Song and Yuan dynasties, drawing merchants from all over the world to its shores. By the Qing, however, it was starting to decline and droves of residents began fleeing to southeast Asia to escape the constant political turmoil.

Today, Quánzhōu is much smaller than Fúzhōu and Xiàmén, and has a small-town feel. Evidence of its Muslim population can still be detected among the city's residents and buildings. It still has a few products of note, including the creamy-white *déhuà* (or 'blanc-de-Chine' as it is known in the West) porcelain figures, and locally crafted puppets.

Orientation

Because Quánzhōu is so small, most of its sights can be reached on foot. The centre of town lies between Zhongshan Nanlu, Zhongshan Zhonglu and Wenling Nanlu. This is where you'll find most of the tourist sights, the bank and the post office. The oldest part of town is to the west, where there are many narrow alleys and lanes to explore that still retain their traditional charm. The Pu River lies to the southwest of the city.

Information

You'll find internet cafés near the PSB on Dong Jie and in the small lanes behind Guandi Temple. Most places charge Y2 to Y3 an hour.

Bank of China (Zhōngguó Yínháng; Jiuyi Jie; ☼ 9am-5pm) This branch also exchanges travellers cheques.

Fuzhou University (www.fzu.edu.cn/fujian/equanz .html) This website has some interesting background on Quánzhōu and other places in Fújiàn.

Post and telephone office (Yóudiànjú; Dong Jie)

Public Security Bureau (PSB; Gōngānjú; ☎ 2218 0323; Dong Jie)

Quanzhou Xiehe Hospital (Quánzhōu Xiéhé Yīyuàn; Tian'an Nanlu) Located in the southern part of town.

Sights

Kaiyuan Temple (Kāiyuán Sì; 176 Xi Jie; admission Y10; ☼ 6am-6pm) is in the northwest of the city and one of the oldest temples in Quánzhōu, dating back to AD 686. Surrounded by trees, it can be distinguished by its pair of two five-storey pagodas. The stone pagodas date from the 13th century and have withstood numerous disasters, the last catastrophe being the Red

Guards who stormed the temple grounds in the 1960s. Inside the pagodas you can see inscriptions from Buddhist folklore. There are good views of Quánzhōu from the top.

Within the grounds of Kaiyuan Temple, behind the eastern pagoda, is a **museum** containing the enormous hull of a Song-dynasty seagoing junk, which was excavated near Quánzhōu in 1974. A ride to the temple by minivan taxi from the long-distance bus station will cost Y6, or take bus 2 from Wenling Nanlu.

The **Qingjing Mosque** (Qīngjìng Sì; 113 Tumen Jie; admission Y2; ☼ 8am-6pm) is one of China's only surviving mosques from the Song dynasty. It was built by Arabs in 1009 and restored in 1309. It looks truly Islamic, without Chinese architectural influence, and is made entirely of stone. Only a few sections of the original building survive, including the walls and columns of the prayer hall.

Behind the mosque is a whimsical **Puppet Museum** (Mù'ǒu Bówùguǎn; 24 Tongzheng Xiang; admission free; ☼ 9am-6pm), with display after display of puppet heads, intricate 30-string marionettes and comical hand puppets. Captions (in English and Chinese) give the history of this unique art form.

Quánzhōu is studded with small temples and can make for an interesting ramble. Another temple worth visiting is **Guandi Temple** (Guāndì Miào; Tumen Jie), located close to the mosque. Dedicated to Guān Yǔ, Three Kingdoms hero and God of War, the temple attracts a steady stream of visitors who come to light incense and pray. Inside the temple are statues of the god and panels along the walls that detail his life. For more on Guān Yǔ, see the boxed text on p410.

The **Mazu Temple** (Tiānhòu Gōng; admission Y5), on the southeastern end of Zhongshan Nanlu, is dedicated to Mazu, Goddess of the Sea, who watches over fishermen. Around the third month of the Lunar New Year (23 March), the temple is packed with worshippers celebrating Mazu's birthday.

The **Maritime Museum** (Quánzhōu Hǎiwài Jiāotōngshǐ Bówùguǎn; Donghu Lu; admission Y10; ☼ 8.30am-5.30pm Tue-Sun) on the northeast side of town explains Quánzhōu's trading history and the development of Chinese shipbuilding. There are wonderfully detailed models of Chinese ships, from junks to pleasure boats, and an intriguing collection of stone carvings, with inscriptions in ancient Syriac.

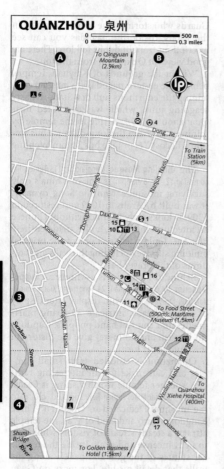

QUÁNZHŌU 泉州

Y515-915) This hotel considers itself one of the most upscale hotels in the city, with a choice of rooms in varying condition. Beds are hard as concrete, though decorations are nicely done.

Eating

Quánzhōu doesn't have a great restaurant scene, so staying here certainly won't be one of your culinary highlights in China. You can find the usual noodle and rice dishes served in the back lanes around Kaiyuan Temple and also along the food street close to Wenling Nanlu.

Overseas Chinese Hotel Restaurant (Huáqiáo Dàshà; Baiyuan Lu; meals Y15; ⏱ 7am-late) The restaurant in this hotel offers reasonably priced Chinese dishes as well as traditional Fújiàn specialities, such as steamed oysters and pounded pork.

Ānjìkèwáng (Wenling Nanlu; meals Y30; ⏱ 11am-9pm) Come to Ānjìkèwáng for traditional Hakka dishes, such as deep-fried chicken and stewed pork.

Qíngqī Shén (teas Y8-70; ⏱ 8am-late) This lovely teahouse with old-time ambience is in a courtyard setting right behind Guandi Temple. You can sit outside with a cup of tea while enjoying a performance of local opera.

Sleeping

Golden Business Hotel (Jīnbǎo Shàngwù Jiǔdiàn; ☎ 2253 0066; fax 2253 8999; Baozhou Zhonglu, Middle Section; 宝洲中路; s & d Y258-399) This hotel is far away from the centre of town but has some of the nicest rooms in Quánzhōu, fitted with pseudo-Qing–style furniture and modern bathrooms. Some rooms have computers.

Overseas Chinese Hotel (Huáqiáo Dàshà; ☎ 2228 2192; fax 2228 4612; Baiyuan Lu; 百源路; tw Y300, s & d Y536-576) This long-standing hotel attempts to stay current, with ongoing renovation to keep its rooms fresh. There's a 'nonsmoking floor', a 'business floor' and even a 'fashionable female' floor to choose from.

Quanzhou Hotel (Quánzhōu Jiǔdiàn; ☎ 2228 9958; fax 2218 2128; 22 Zhuangfu Xiang; 庄府巷22号; s & d

Shopping

Jǐnxiù Zhuàng (101-C Daxi Jie) This is a small shop selling locally made puppets and puppet heads, as well as embroidery and other handicrafts. It's a fun place to browse and the delightful marionettes make great souvenirs.

Another place to find Fújiàn crafts and curios is at the night market (yè shìchǎng) near Qingjing Mosque. It generally gets going around 5pm and lasts until 2am.

Getting There & Around

The long-distance bus station (kèyùn xīn zhàn) is in the southern corner of town on the intersection of Wenling Nanlu and Quanxiu Jie, and serves destinations as far away as Shànghǎi and Guǎngzhōu. Deluxe buses go to Xiàmén (Y19 to Y32, two hours) and Fúzhōu (Y34 to Y41, 3½ hours). Some buses to Fúzhōu leave from the Overseas Chinese Hotel rather than at the bus station. You can buy tickets at the hotel ticket office.

The railway station is in the northeast of town. For Wǔyí Shān (Y149 hard sleeper, 11½ hours) there is an early-morning train that leaves Quánzhōu at 6.30am and gets into Wǔyí Shān at 5pm. There are no overnight trains to Wǔyí Shān.

Quánzhōu's most useful bus is bus 2 (Y1), which goes from the bus station to Kaiyuan Temple. Buses 19 and 23 run from the railway station to the centre of town. Taxi flagfall is Y6.

AROUND QUÁNZHŌU
Chóngwǔ 崇武

About 50km east of Quánzhōu is the ancient 'stone city' of Chóngwǔ, with one of the best-preserved city walls in China. The granite walls date back to 1387 and stretch over 2.5km long and average 7m in height. Scattered around the walls are 1304 battlements and four gates into the city.

The town wall was built by the Ming government as a front-line defence against marauding Japanese pirates, and it has survived the last 600 years remarkably well. Koxinga also took refuge here in his battle against Qing forces. Stone is the traditional building material of this region and the surrounding area is full of stone-carving workshops.

To see the still intact city walls head up Xinhua Jie from the bus station. Along the coast, the **Ancient City Stone Park** (Gǔchéng Fēngjǐngqū; ☎ 2768 3297; admission Y25; ☉ 7am-5pm) consists of over 500 new and ancient statues haphazardly scattered along the cliffs and beach; some of them are eroding attractively into the ocean.

Frequent minibuses depart Quánzhōu's long-distance bus station (Y9, 1½ hours), taking you on a long zigzagging ride through the countryside before finally ending up in Chóngwǔ.

WǓYÍ SHĀN 武夷山
☎ 0599 / pop 22,710

Wǔyí Shān, in the far northwest corner of Fújiàn, has some of the most spectacular, unspoilt scenery in the province. With its plentiful rivers, waterfalls, mountains and protected forests, it's a terrific place for those looking to do some hiking or exploring. It's a popular place for Chinese tourists but if you come midweek or in the off-season (November, March and April) you might have the area to yourself. One word of caution: Wǔyí Shān resort has a notorious reputation for ripping off tourists, so stay alert.

The scenic area lies on the west bank of Chongyang Stream (Chóngyáng Xī), and some accommodation is located along its shore. Most of the hotels are concentrated in the resort district (dù jià qū) on the east side of the river. The main settlement is Wǔyí Shān city, about 10km to the northeast, with the train station and airport roughly halfway between.

Information

Maps of the Wǔyí Shān area are available in bookshops and hotels in the resort district. There are some grubby internet cafés in the back alleys south of Wangfeng Lu (望峰路), charging Y2 to Y4 an hour.

Bank of China (中国银行; Zhōngguó Yínháng; Wujiu Lu; ☉ 9am-5pm) Located in Wǔyí Shān city, this branch will change travellers cheques and has an ATM.

CITS (中国国际旅行社; Zhōngguó Guójì Lǚxíngshè; ☎ 525 0380; 35 Guanjing Lu; ☉ 9am-4pm Mon-Sat) The staff are very helpful, and can arrange train tickets and tours to surrounding ancient cities.

Sights & Activities

The main entrance to Wuyi Shan Scenic Area is at **Wǔyí Gōng** (武夷宫; ☎ 525 2702; admission Y64; ☉ 6am-8pm), about 200m south of the Wuyi Mountain Villa (see p354), near the confluence of the Chóngyáng and Nine Twists Rivers.

Trails within the scenic area connect all the major sites. A couple of nice walks are the 530m **Great King Peak** (大王峰; Dàwáng Fēng), accessed through the main entrance, and the 410m **Heavenly Tour Peak** (天游峰; Tiānyóu Fēng), where an entrance is reached by road up the Nine Twists River. It's a moderate two-hour walk to Great King Peak among bamboo groves and steep-cut rock walls. At the top you'll see some good views of the resort area and the rivers. The trail can be slippery and wet, so bring suitable shoes.

The walk to Heavenly Tour Peak is more scenic, with better views of the river and mountain peaks. The path is also better maintained and less slippery, but it's also the most popular with tour groups so come midweek if you want some peace. At the top, there's a collection of teahouses to refresh yourself as well as pristine views of the river valley.

At the northern end of the scenic area, the **Water Curtain Cave** (水帘洞; Shuǐlián Dòng; admission Y22) is a cleft in the rock about one-third of the way up a 100m cliff face. In winter and autumn, water plunges over the top of the cliff creating a curtain of spray.

One of the highlights for visitors is floating down the Nine Twists River (九曲溪; Jiǔqū Xī) on **bamboo rafts** (zhúpái; Y100; 7am-5pm) fitted with rattan chairs. Departing from Xīng Cūn (星村), a short bus ride west of the resort area, the trip down the river takes over an hour. The boat ride takes you through some magnificent gorge scenery, with sheer rock cliffs and lush green vegetation.

One of the mysteries of Wǔyí Shān is the cavities carved out of the rock faces at great heights that once held boat-shaped coffins. Scientists have dated some of these artefacts back 4000 years. If you're taking a raft down the river, it's possible to see some remnants of these coffins on the west cliff face of the fourth meander or 'twist', also known as **Small Storing Place Peak** (小藏山峰; Xiǎozàngshān Fēng).

Sleeping

Most of the accommodation in Wǔyí Shān is midrange in price and room rates rise and fall according to demand and season. Hotels are mostly concentrated on the east side of the river, though there are a few hotels on the quieter, west side. Discounts are often available midweek.

International Trade Hotel (国贸大酒店; Guómào Dàjiǔdiàn; ☎ 525 2521; fax 525 2521; Wangfeng Lu; 望峰路; d Y240-580) On the eastern side of the resort area, this well-managed hotel gives good discounts midweek for its serviceable, though uninspired, guestrooms.

Wuyishan Tea Hotel (武夷茶苑大酒店; Wǔyí Cháyuàn Dàjiǔdiàn; ☎ 525 6777; d Y480-780) This hotel won't win any accolades for design but it's a good pick for its recently renovated rooms, friendly staff and central location. Try to stay on the upper floors to avoid the ear-splitting wails of karaoke at night.

Bǎodǎo Dàjiǔdiàn (宝岛大酒店; ☎ 523 4567; fax 525 5555; Wangfeng Lu; 望峰路; s/d Y880/780) Situated next to the Bank of China, this centrally located hotel has a curiously furnished lobby decorated with chunky tree-trunk furniture. Rooms are respectable and good-sized with clean bathrooms. It's a popular place for the tour groups so you may need to book ahead.

Wuyi Mountain Villa (武夷山庄; Wǔyí Shānzhuāng; ☎ 525 1888; fax 525 2567; d Y888-988, ste Y1388-2888) This is the most upmarket hotel in Wǔyí Shān and its secluded location on the west side of the river at the foot of Great King Peak makes it (almost) worth the price. Buildings are chalet-style and surrounded by peaceful gardens, a swimming pool and a waterfall. Standoffish service is the only drawback to staying here.

Eating

Frogs, mushrooms and bamboo shoots are the specialities of Wǔyí Shān's cuisine. One of the best places to try these items is at the **Bamboo Palace Restaurant** (大堂竹楼; Dàtáng Zhúlóu; meals Y20-40; 11am-2pm & 5pm-9pm), where you can eat on a patio overlooking the river. The food is excellent and the service good. It's a good idea to bring mosquito repellent, unless you want to be dessert.

Getting There & Away

Wǔyí Shān has air links to Běijīng (Y1350, two hours), Shànghǎi (Y660, one hour), Fúzhōu (Y490, 35 minutes), Xiàmén (Y590, 50 minutes), Guǎngzhōu (Y890, 1½ hours) and Hong Kong (Y1300, two hours).

Frequent buses go to Xiàmén (Y159), Fúzhōu (Y90) and Shàowǔ (Y15, 1½ hours). The other long-distance bus station is in the northwest part of Wǔyí Shān city. Daily buses go south to Fúzhōu (Y86, eight hours), northeast to Wēnzhōu (Y138, 12 hours) and

Nánpíng (Y37, three hours), and north to Shàngráo (Y26, two hours) in Jiāngxī.

Direct trains go to Wǔyí Shān from Quánzhōu (Y149, 11 hours) and Xiàmén (Y149, 14 hours).

Getting Around

The most useful bus is bus 6 which runs between the airport, resort area and train station. Minivans or a public bus (Y2) shuttle between Wǔyí Shān city and the resort dis-trict, and there are minibuses between Wǔyí Shān city and Xīngcūn. The resort area is small enough to walk everywhere, so ignore those pesky trishaw drivers who insist everything is 'too far'.

Expect to pay about Y10 for a motorised trishaw from the resort district to most of the scenic area entrances. A ride from the train station or airport to the resort district will cost Y10 to Y20. Make sure to haggle or you could get scammed.

Liáoníng 辽宁

Beaches, borders and bridges – those are the highlights of a visit to Liáoníng, the gateway to China's northeast, in the region formerly known as Manchuria.

For beaches, head to the seaside city of Dàlián, where stretches of sand lure sun-seekers and restaurants specialise in fresh seafood. Nicknamed 'Hong Kong of the North', fast-growing Dàlián is managing to retain some grand early-20th-century buildings and peaceful parklands even as skyscrapers continue to sprout up. Shopping is a favourite pastime here, with modern malls all around town.

For borders, go east, where Liáoníng meets North Korea. Dāndōng, just across the river from the North Korean city of Sinuiju, draws visitors hoping for a peek at the closed society on the opposite bank. There's not much to look at, but Dāndōng itself offers a mix of Chinese and Korean culture, and just outside the city is the easternmost stretch of the Great Wall, a restored section that still sees comparatively few tourists.

If it's bridges you're after, both Dāndōng and the provincial capital of Shěnyáng oblige. In Dāndōng, a bridge to North Korea ends suddenly mid-river, the result of US bombing in the 1950s. In Shěnyáng, bridges take on a more light-hearted tone, at least if you swing on the hilarious suspended ones in the Shenyang Botanical Garden. Though it's a frenzied modern metropolis, Shěnyáng also lures history buffs with its majestic Imperial Palace; its serene temples, tombs and pagodas; and its intriguing museum about the Japanese occupation of Manchuria in the 1930s.

HIGHLIGHTS

- Sleep on a warship, hang out at the beach or explore the northeast's most modern city in dynamic **Dàlián** (p363)
- Climb the easternmost stretch of the Great Wall, little-touristed **Tiger Mountain Great Wall** (p370), near Dāndōng
- Take a peek at North Korea across the river from bustling bicultural **Dāndōng** (p369)
- Hike among the rocky peaks in the peaceful **Bingyu Valley**, Liáoníng's 'Little Guilin' (p368)
- Swing, balance or teeter across the 50 suspended bridges in the **Shenyang Botanical Garden** (p360)

■ POPULATION: 42.7 MILLION   ■ www.liaoning-gateway.com

History

The region formerly known as Manchuria, including the provinces of Liáoníng, Jílín and Hēilóngjiāng, plus parts of Inner Mongolia, is now called Dōngběi, which simply means 'the northeast'.

The Manchurian warlords of this northern territory established the Qing dynasty, which ruled China from the 1640s until the early 20th century. In the late 1800s and early 1900s, when the Western powers were busy carving up pieces of China for themselves, Manchuria was occupied alternately by the Russians and the Japanese.

These occupations have helped to shape the region's architecture along with its consciousness.

Getting There & Around

Getting around Liáoníng is easy. In addition to the rail lines that crisscross the region, a network of highways between the major cities make bus travel a speedy, comfortable alternative.

Shěnyáng, the province's transport hub, is a convenient starting point for exploring the northeast. Extensive rail connections link Shěnyáng with cities south and north, and you can fly to Shěnyáng from many other Chinese cities, from South Korea or from the Russian Far East.

Alternatively, travel by sea or air to Dàlián, and from there head north by bus or train. Boats connect Dàlián with Shànghǎi, Tiānjīn and several cities in Shāndōng province, while

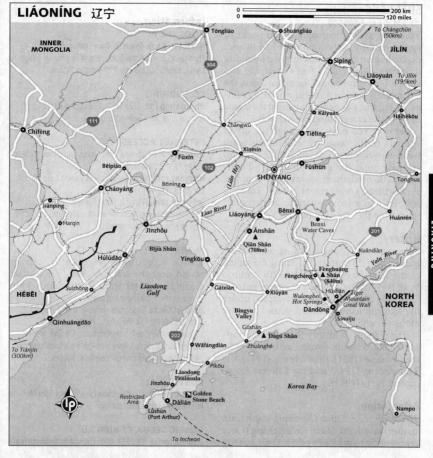

LIÁONÍNG 辽宁

RUSSIA'S INFLUENCE IN LIÁONÍNG

To the outrage of Russia's Tsar Nicholas II, Japan gained control of the Liaodong Peninsula at the southeastern tip of Liáoníng province after defeating the Chinese in the Sino-Japanese War (1894–95). Japan's strength alarmed other foreign powers, and with French and German support, Nicholas II managed not only to get the Japanese to withdraw from Dàlián, but also to gain possession of it as a Russian concession in 1898. The Russians were also permitted to begin building a railway across Manchuria from Vladivostok to Port Arthur (now Lǔshùn), near present-day Dàlián. The Russians moved troops in with the railway, and for the next 10 years effectively controlled northeastern China.

Russia's reign over Liáoníng province was short-lived, however, ending with the Russo-Japanese War (1904–05). Besides the railway network, little visible evidence of this Russian era remains today, except for a touristy 'Russian street' on the north side of Dàlián.

frequent flights link Dàlián with Běijīng and other major cities.

SHĚNYÁNG 沈阳
☎ 024 / pop 6,500,000

Take a sprawling metropolis, add packs of aggressive drivers, throw in some bad air and, depending on the season, crippling humidity or bone-chilling cold – that's Shěnyáng at a glance. To rein in some of the urban chaos, the city recently launched an antijaywalking campaign, but that's done nothing about the manic drivers who career along the walkways!

Yet once you navigate through the urban sprawl, traffic anarchy and challenging weather, well-preserved relics of the Manchu era hide amid the grey socialist-era buildings, as do modern museums that illuminate the northeast's more recent history. Tranquil temples and a large botanical garden offer relief from the city's hubbub.

History
Shěnyáng was a Mongol trading centre as far back as the 11th century, becoming the capital of the Manchu empire in the 17th century. With the Manchu conquest of Běijīng in 1644, Shěnyáng became a secondary capital under the Manchu name of Mukden, and a centre of the ginseng trade.

Throughout its history Shěnyáng has rapidly changed hands, dominated by warlords, the Japanese (1931), the Russians (1945), the Kuomintang (1946) and the Chinese Communist Party (1948).

Orientation
The north train station (běizhàn), south train station (nánzhàn), Shěfú Guǎngchǎng (Government Sq) and Zhōngshān Guǎngchǎng

(Zhongshan Sq) with its towering Mao Zedong statue all serve as transport hubs and landmarks within the city.

Information
BOOKSHOP
Northern Book Town (Běifāng Túshūguǎn; 2nd fl, 43 Zhonghua Lu) Has a small selection of English-language books, mostly classics and 19th-century fiction.

CD BURNING
Photo shop (☎ 2273 3494; 45 Huigong Jie; CDs Y10) Just north of Shifú Guǎngchǎng.

INTERNET ACCESS 网吧
Internet café (Wǎngbā; lower level, north train station; per hr Y3; ☑ 9am-midnight)
Internet café (Wǎngbā; main level, south train station; per hr Y3; ☑ 24hr)
Internet café (Wǎngbā; Shengli Beijie; per hr Y3; ☑ 24hr) One block from the south train station, near the Hépíng Bīnguǎn (Peace Hotel).

MONEY
ATMs accepting foreign cards can be found near the train stations, Zhōngshān Guǎngchǎng and Shìfú Guǎngchǎng. Most large hotels change money.
Bank of China (Zhōngguó Yínháng) Shifú Guǎngchǎng (☎ 2285 6666; 253 Shifu Dalu; ☑ 8am-noon & 1-4pm Mon-Fri); South train station area (96 Zhonghua Lu; ☑ 8am-noon & 1-4pm Mon-Fri) Both branches have 24-hr ATMs and will change travellers cheques.

POST
Post office (Yóujú; 78 Beizhan Lu; ☑ 8am-8pm Mon-Fri) Near the north train station.

PUBLIC SECURITY BUREAU
PSB (Gōngānjú; ☎ 2253 4850; Zhōngshān Guǎngchǎng)

TELEPHONE
China Telecom (Zhōngguó Diànxìn; 185 Shifu Dalu) A short walk west of Shífú Guǎngchǎng.

TOURIST INFORMATION
Liaoning Tourism Bureau (Liáoníng Shěng Lǚyóujú; ☎ 8680 7316; fax 8680 9415; 113 Huanghe Dajie) Near the North Tomb, this office has English-language maps and brochures of the province's attractions.

TRAVEL AGENCY
China International Travel Service (CITS; Zhōngguó Guójì Lǚxíngshè; ☎ 8680 9383; fax 8680 8772; 113 Huanghe Dajie) In the same building as the Liaoning Tourism Bureau.

Sights & Activities
IMPERIAL PALACE 故宫
Shěnyáng's main attraction is this sprawling **palace** (Gùgōng; ☎ 2282 1999; 171 Shenyang Lu; admission Y50; ☼ 8.30am-5.30pm) complex, which resembles a small-scale Forbidden City. Constructed between 1625 and 1636 by Manchu emperor Nurhachi (1559–1626) and his son, Huang Taiji, the palace served as the residence of the Qing-dynasty rulers until 1644.

Don't miss the octagonal **Dazheng Hall** (at the rear of the complex) with its coffered ceiling and elaborate throne, where Nurhachi's grandson, Emperor Shunzhi, was crowned. The central courtyard buildings include ornate ceremonial halls and imperial living quarters, including a royal baby cradle.

The palace is in the oldest section of the city. Take bus 237 from the south train station, or bus 227 from the North Tomb via the east side of the north train station.

THE 'MANCHURIAN INCIDENT'
On 18 September 1931 a bomb damaged a Japanese-controlled railway outside Mukden, the present-day city of Shěnyáng. Although the Japanese blamed Chinese nationalists, historians believe that Japanese troops actually triggered the explosion as an excuse to invade the region. That night, Japanese troops marched into Shěnyáng and occupied the city. By 21 September all of what is now Jílín province was also under Japanese control. The following year, the Japanese established what became known as the puppet state of Manchukuo and ruled Manchuria until the end of WWII.

NORTH TOMB 北陵
Another Shěnyáng highlight is the **North Tomb** (Běi Líng; ☎ 8689 6294; 12 Taishan Lu; admission park/tombs Y6/30; ☼ 6am-6pm) in Beiling Park. This extensive tomb complex, which took eight years to build, is the burial place of Huang Taiji (1592–1643), the founder of the Qing dynasty. The tomb's animal statues lead up to the central mound known as the Luminous Tomb (Zhāo Líng).

Take bus 220 from the south train station or bus 217 from the north train station. Bus 227 from the Imperial Palace via the east side of the north train station also travels to and from the North Tomb.

EAST TOMB 东陵
Also known as Fú Líng, this smaller **tomb** (Dōng Líng; 210 Dongling Jie; admission Y30; ☼ 8am-5pm) is the resting place of Nurhachi and his mistress. It's 15km east of the city centre. Take bus 218 (45 minutes) from the Imperial Palace.

18 SEPTEMBER HISTORY MUSEUM
九一八历史博物馆
This striking modern **museum** (Jiǔ Yī Bā Lìshǐ Bówùguǎn; ☎ 2389 2316; 46 Wanghua Nanjie; admission Y20; ☼ 8.30am-4pm) is named after the date when Shěnyáng was captured by the Japanese in 1931. The exhibits, including more than 800 photographs, explore the Japanese occupation of Manchuria. Gruesome examples of torture on display include a 'rolling cage' (a long metal tube lined with spikes in which prisoners were rolled to death).

Although the exhibits are grim, this is the most comprehensive museum in China dedicated to this period of Chinese history.

Bus 325 from the north train station stops in front of the museum.

LIAONING PROVINCIAL MUSEUM
辽宁省博物馆
Elements of the province's more peaceful history are on view in this art-filled **museum** (Liáoníng Shěng Bówùguǎn; ☎ 2561 3333; Shífú Guǎngchǎng; admission Y20; ☼ 9am-5pm), in a contemporary building facing Government Sq. Liao-dynasty ceramics, ancient Chinese money and carved stone tablets that illustrate the evolution of Chinese calligraphy are among the exhibits.

PAGODA OF BUDDHIST ASHES
无垢净光舍利塔
This 13-storey brick **pagoda** (Wúgòu Jìngguāng Shělì Tǎ; ☎ 8678 1651; 22 Taiwan Jie; admission Y4; ☼ 8.30am-5.30pm)

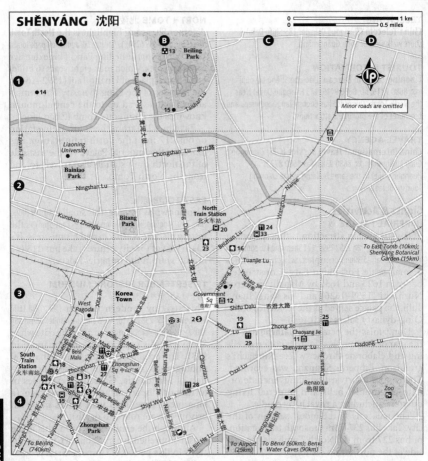

SHĚNYÁNG 沈阳

Minor roads are omitted

To East Tomb (10km);
Shenyang Botanical
Garden (15km)

To Airport   To Běnxī (60km); Benxi
(25km)   Water Caves (90km)

To Běijīng
(740km)

dates back to AD 1044. A small museum on the peaceful grounds includes relics removed from inside the pagoda.

Take bus 205 from the North Tomb or the south train station and get off at the corner of Taiwan Jie and Ningshan Lu. Walk north, cross the bridge and turn right. The pagoda is a three-minute walk north of here. Look for a red gate on the right.

SHENYANG BOTANICAL GARDEN
沈阳植物园

These **gardens** (Shěnyáng Zhíwù Yuán; admission Y50; ☯ 9am-9pm summer, 9am-5pm winter) are filled with plants and flowers native to northeast China. Special exhibitions highlight tulips (May), peonies (June) and chrysanthemums (October).

Even more entertaining than the vegetation are the nearly 50 bridges suspended across a shallow river that visitors try to traverse. There are narrow log bridges – like over-water balance beams – as well as rolling barrels, swinging bridges, floating rafts and more. Cross if you dare; you'll likely end up in the water!

Trains run about once an hour from the north and south stations to the Botanical Garden (Y3, 30 minutes), about 20km east of the city centre.

Sleeping
BUDGET

Méishǎn Bīnguǎn (Main Sun Hotel; ☎ 2273 5538; fax 2272 8048; 48 Xiaoxi Lu; 小西路48号; s Y60-100, d Y120-160) This small hotel is one of Shěnyáng's best-

INFORMATION		
Bank of China 中国银行		**1** A4
Bank of China 中国银行		**2** B3
China Telecom 中国电信		**3** B3
CITS 中国国际旅行社		**4** B1
Internet Café 网吧		**5** A4
Internet Café 网吧		**6** A4
Internet Café 网吧		(see 20)
Japanese Consulate		
日本领事馆		(see 9)
Liaoning Tourism Bureau		
辽宁省旅游局		(see 4)
North Korean Consulate		
北朝鲜领事馆		(see 9)
Northern Book Town		
北方图书城		(see 17)
Photo Shop		**7** C3
Post Office 邮电局		(see 23)
PSB 公安局		**8** A4
Russian Consulate		
俄国领事馆		**9** B4
South Korean Consulate		
韩国领事馆		(see 9)
US Consulate		
美国领事馆		(see 9)

SIGHTS & ACTIVITIES		
18 September History Museum		
九一八历史博物馆		**10** D2
Imperial Palace 故宫		**11** C3
Liaoning Provincial Museum		
辽宁省博物馆		**12** C3
North Tomb 北陵		**13** B1
Pagoda of Buddhist Ashes		
无垢净光舍利塔		**14** A1
Park Entrance 公园门口		**15** B1

SLEEPING		
Fashion Motel 128		
尚姆泰欧宾馆		**16** B3
Golden Triangle Hotel		
金三角饭店		**17** A4
Hépíng Bīnguǎn		
和平宾_和平宾馆		**18** A4
Méishān Bīnguǎn 梅杉宾馆		**19** C3
Shěntiě Dàjiǔdiàn		
沈铁大酒店		**20** B2
Shěntiě Shěnzhàn Bīnguǎn		
沈铁沈站宾馆		**21** A4
Traders Hotel 商贸饭店		**22** A4
Yóuzhèng Dàshà 邮政大厦		**23** B3

EATING		
Carrefour Supermarket 家乐福		**24** C2
Lǎobiān Jiǎoziguǎn 老边饺子馆		**25** D3
Súiyìshāo Kǎoròu Zhuānméndiàn		
随意烧烤肉专门店		**26** A4
Suìyuan Home-Like Restaurant		
随感家常菜馆		**27** A4
View & World Vegetarian		
Restaurant 宽巷子素菜馆		**28** B4
Xiǎo Tǔdòu 小土豆		**29** C3
Zhongxing Shenyang Commercial		
Building		**30** A4

DRINKING		
Jia Music, Food & Drinks 家		(see 17)

SHOPPING		
Night Market		**31** A4

TRANSPORT		
Korean Air		**32** A4
Long-Distance Express		
Bus Station 长途汽车站		**33** C2
S7 Airlines		**34** C4
South Long-Distance		
Bus Station 长途汽车南站		**35** A4

value options. Don't expect lots of space, but most rooms have wooden floors and cosy duvets.

Shěntiě Shěnzhàn Bīnguǎn (Shenyang Railway Station Hotel; ☎ 2358 5888; 2 Shengli Dajie; 胜利大街2号; s Y80, d Y218/60 with/without bathroom; 🕸) Voyeurs will love the standard doubles at this quirky inn next to the south train station – the bathrooms have glass walls! Some of the small rooms without bathrooms have no windows, so look before you book if daylight matters.

Héping Bīnguǎn (Peace Hotel; ☎ 2349 8202; fax 2349 8202; 104 Shengli Beijie; 胜利北街104号; d/q Y100/Y160, s/tr with bathroom Y190/Y280, d with bathroom Y190-380; 🕸) A former budget behemoth, this hotel near the south train station has revamped to be more upscale. There's a range of rooms, from basic to almost chic. The with-bathroom rates include a breakfast buffet.

MIDRANGE
Yóuzhèng Dàshà (Shenyang Post Hotel; ☎ 2259 3333; fax 2259 3077; 78 Beizhan Lu; 北站路78号; d Y120, d with bathroom Y268-328, tr with bathroom Y180; 🕸 🖳) Situated near the north station, this hotel has updated rooms.

Fashion Motel 128 (Shàngmǔ Tái'ōu Bīnguǎn; ☎ 2253 7777; 5 Youhao Jie; 友好街5号; d Y128, d with bathroom Y328-358; 🕸 🖳) If you don't mind the lurid wall colours – peach, lime green, purple – try this quiet low-rise located between the north train station and the long-distance bus station. Discounts put rooms with bathroom under Y200,

including breakfast; they have broadband internet connections too. The hotel entrance is on Beizhan Er Lu, off Youhao Jie.

Shěntiě Dàjiǔdiàn (Railway Hotel; ☎ 6223 1058; fax 6223 2888; 102 Beizhan Lu; 北站路102号; d incl breakfast Y368-386; 🕸 🖳) Bargain for discounts to about Y180 at this surprisingly quiet hotel within the north train station building. Many of the well-kept doubles have modern furnishings and upscale amenities like hair dryers; even older ones (that could use a sprucing-up) are still good value.

Golden Triangle Hotel (Jīnsānjiǎo Fàndiàn; ☎ 2329 2288; fax 2329 2188; 43 Zhonghua Lu; 中华路43号; d incl breakfast Y368-418; 🕸 🖳) The best rooms in this contemporary tower are the salon-sized doubles with modern furnishings and free internet access (including an in-room computer).

TOP END
Traders Hotel (Shāngmào Fàndiàn; ☎ 2341 2288; www .shangri-la.com; 68 Zhonghua Lu; 中华路68号; d Y690-740 plus 15% service charge; 🕸 🕸 🖳) Owned by the Shangri-La chain, this coolly modern hotel delivers top-notch service. The do-anything-for-you staff speak English and there's wireless internet access in the lobby.

Eating
Both the north and south train stations are cheap restaurant zones.

Súiyìshāo Kǎoròu Zhuānméndiàn (As You Please BBQ; ☎ 2383 6974; 24 Beisi Malu; dishes Y5-18; 🕒 lunch

LIÁONÍNG

& dinner) Cook your own pork belly, beef and other meats 'as you please' at this family-run BBQ joint. Sit under the space-age metallic fixtures and ask for *suāncài* (酸菜; pickled cabbage) or sliced potatoes to add to your tabletop grill.

Lǎobiān Jiǎoziguǎn (Lao Bian Dumpling Restaurant; ☎ 2486 5369; 206 Zhong Jie; dumplings Y8-16; ☺ lunch & dinner) Of course, the dumplings are good – this old-favourite has been in business since 1829 – but don't neglect the fresh vegetable dishes and tasty cold plates.

View & World Vegetarian Restaurant (Kuān Xiàngzi Sùcàiguǎn ☎ 2284 8678; 202 Shiyi Wei Lu; dishes Y8-28) Even 'seafood' hotpot and 'lamb' skewers are meat-free at this nearly-vegan paradise, where the artfully presented dishes are decorated with flowers. If you're looking for romance a vegetarian, take a table tucked into a private nook. English menu.

Xiǎo Tǔdòu (Small Potato; ☎ 2291 5040; 37 Xiaoxi Lu; dishes Y10-15; ☺ lunch & dinner) This *dōngběi* (northeastern) eatery is packed with families, couples and groups of all ages who come here for the eponymous potato dish that is anything but small; it's a hearty and delicious stew of spuds and greens in a meaty broth (Y10).

Suíyuán Home-Like Restaurant (Suíyuán Jiācháng Càiguǎn; ☎ 2340 4121; Zhōngshān Guǎngchǎng; dishes Y12-20; ☺ lunch & dinner) Traditional Chinese furnishings and widely spaced tables give this *dōngběi* restaurant a classy feel, but the hearty fare and moderate prices do make it 'home-like' – at least if your mother used to prepare cold meat platters, greens with Sichuan peppercorns and crispy fried breads. The entrance is in the lane behind the Liaoning Hotel.

Inside the **Zhongxing Shenyang Commercial Building** (86 Taiyuan Jie), near the south train station, there's a decent supermarket on the 2nd floor. At the **Carrefour Supermarket** (Jiālèfú; Beizhan Lu), near the long-distance bus station, you can pack a picnic for your travels or grab a quick bite from the food court (dishes Y5 to Y15).

Drinking

Korean restaurants, karaoke bars and coffee shops line the brightly lit (if slightly seedy) Xita Jie. A more upscale choice is **Jia Music, Food & Drinks** (Jiā; ☎ 2387 6655; 43 Zhonghua Lu), a stylish lounge in the same building as the Golden Triangle Hotel.

Shopping

Near the south train station is Taiyuan Jie, one of Shěnyáng's major shopping streets, with a bustling night market. Below Taiyuan Jie is an extensive underground shopping street. Above ground, Taiyuan Jie and nearby Zhonghua Lu are lined with department stores, from Wal-Mart to Parkson's.

Zhong Jie, near the Imperial Palace, is another pedestrian street, where the mix of Japanese architecture and flashy neon makes it an interesting stroll.

Getting There & Away

Large hotels can book airline and train tickets. The travel offices at the **Hépíng Bīnguǎn** (☎ 2340 2066) and the **Traders Hotel** (☎ 2341 2288, ext 6457) are particularly helpful; the latter can usually rustle up an English-speaker to help.

AIR

You can fly from Shěnyáng to a huge number of domestic destinations, including Běijīng (Y710, one hour and 10 minutes), Shànghǎi (Y1300, two hours) and Guǎngzhōu (Y2310, 3¾ hours).

China Southern Airlines (see p957) and **Korean Air** (☎ 2334 1880; www.koreanair.com; 206 Nanjing Beijie) both have daily service to Seoul (Y2900, 1¾ hours). **S7 Airlines** (☎ 2480 8579; www.s7.ru; Yǒnglún Dàjiǔdiàn, 58 Renao Lu) flies to Irkutsk, near Russia's Lake Baikal, on Thursdays and Sundays from May through October (US$210 to US$270, three hours).

BUS

The **long-distance express bus station** (qìchē kuàisù kèyùnzhàn; Huigong Jie) is south of Beizhan Lu, about a five-minute walk from the north train station. See the table on opposite for information.

As you come out of the south train station, cross Shengli Dajie and bear right onto Minzu Lu and you'll be confronted with a line of buses – this is the departure point for the south long-distance bus station. The station itself is further south on Minzu Lu. There are regular departures to Ānshān (鞍山; Y25, 1½ hours), Běnxī (本溪; Y19, one hour) and Huánrén (桓仁; Y54, six hours).

TRAIN

Shěnyáng's major train stations are the north and the south stations. Many trains arrive at one station, stop briefly, then travel to the next.

SHĚNYÁNG BUS TIMETABLES

Destination	Price	Duration	Frequency	Departs
Běijīng	Y190	7½hr	6 daily	8am-10pm
Chángchūn	Y75	3½hr	hourly	7am-6pm
Dāndōng	Y65	3hr	every 30min	6am-7pm
Hāěrbīn	Y140	6½hr	6 daily	8am-3.30pm
Jílín	Y96	4½hr	6 daily	7.30am-4.30pm

However, when departing this isn't always the case, so confirm which station you need. If you're planning to buy sleeper tickets, purchase your ongoing ticket as soon as possible.

The south station has services departing for Hāěrbīn (Y53 to Y76, five to seven hours), Chángchūn (Y28, four to six hours), Dāndōng (Y24, four hours), Běijīng (seat/sleeper Y110/215, eight to 10 hours) and Dàlián (Y55, four to five hours). Express trains from the north train station travel to Běijīng (seat/sleeper Y110/215, eight hours), Guǎngzhōu (seat/sleeper Y305/552, 30 hours) and Shànghǎi (seat/sleeper Y206/373, 27 hours).

Getting Around

A new subway system is under construction in Shěnyáng, scheduled to open in 2008 or '09. Meanwhile, you can get most anywhere in this sprawling city by bus, although you may need to make at least one transfer. Maps of the bus routes (Y5) are sold at the train stations.

Buses 203 and 602 run between the north and south train stations. Bus 227 runs between the North Tomb, the north train station and the Imperial Palace. Bus 207 runs east–west across Government Sq.

Taxis cost Y7 for the first 4km.

The airport is 25km south of the city. Taxis to the airport cost around Y80.

AROUND SHĚNYÁNG
Benxi Water Caves 本溪水洞

Inside the **caves** (Běnxī Shuǐdòng; admission Y85, plus Y5 for tram from ticket office to cave entrance; 8am-5pm), 30km east of Běnxī (which is 60km southeast of Shěnyáng), is a forest of stalactites and stalagmites. You take a boat along the 'Milky Way' (45 minutes), a river that zigzags through caves of differing sizes. Pink, green and blue lights illuminate the formations, making the place feel like a movie set, but the rock shapes are dramatic despite the hokey

lighting. The formations' evocative names – Seal Playing with a Pearl, Tiger's Mouth, Ginseng Baby – are entertaining too.

Coats are provided for the boat journey through the caves, which maintain a constant (chilly) temperature of 10°C.

A direct bus to the caves leaves Shěnyáng's south long-distance bus station at 7.30am and departs the caves at 2.30pm (Y25 each way, 2½ hours).

DÀLIÁN 大连
411 / pop 2,695,000

A recent survey named Dàlián China's 'most liveable city', and if you linger on its beaches, explore its modern museums or stroll through its shopper-thronged pedestrian areas, you'll see why. Perched on the Liaodong Peninsula bordering the Yellow Sea, Dàlián is one of China's most prosperous cities. And even as many flashy towers are being built, this lively, relaxed city retains some early-20th-century architecture and refreshing acres of grass.

Several beaches surround the city, and relaxing by the sea is one of the main reasons travellers visit Dàlián. Dàlián's extremely successful football (soccer) team also lures many fans.

Orientation

The city's hub is Zhōngshān Guǎngchǎng (Zhongshan Sq). Dàlián train station is west of Zhōngshān Guǎngchǎng, facing Shengli Guǎngchǎng (Victory Sq); the ferry terminal is to the northeast. Beaches dot the coast south and west of the centre. Further south, at the end of the peninsula, is Lǚshùn; a military base there is considered a sensitive zone, with much of the area off-limits to foreigners.

Information
BOOKSHOP

Xinhua Bookshop (Xīnhuá Shūdiàn; Map p364; 96 Tongxing Jie) Near Tianjin Jie.

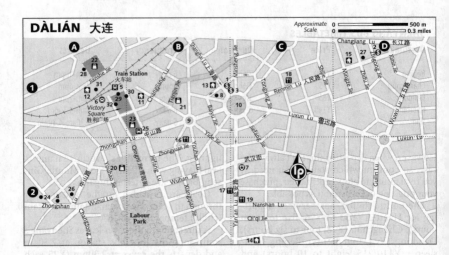

DÀLIÁN 大连

INTERNET ACCESS 网吧
Internet café (Wǎngbā; Map p364; Lower level, train station; per hr Y3) To find this spiffy internet café, exit the train station and turn right. The entrance is on the west side of the building, downstairs.

INTERNET RESOURCES
Daliannews (www.daliannews.com) English-language local news and tourist information.

Shide-global (www.shide-global.com/sports.htm) Background and contact information for the local football (soccer) team.

MONEY
Bank of China (Zhōngguó Yínháng; Map p364; ☎ 8280 5711; 9 Zhōngshān Guǎngchǎng; 🕓 8.30-11.30am & 1-7pm Mon-Fri) Around the corner on Shanghai Lu is a 24-hour ATM.

China Merchants Bank (Map p364; Shengli Guǎngchǎng) ATM; opposite the train station, off Jiefang Lu.

HSBC (Map p364; cnr Renmin Lu & Zhigong Jie) ATM; accepts Cirrus, Plus, MasterCard and Visa cards.

POST
Post office (Yóujú; Map p364; Changjiang Lu, at Shengli Guǎngchǎng; 🕓 8am-6pm) To the right as you exit the train station.

PUBLIC SECURITY BUREAU
PSB (Gōnġānjú; Map p364; ☎ 8363 2718; 16 Yan'an Lu; 🕓 8-11.30am & 1-4.30pm Mon-Fri)

TRAVEL AGENCY
CITS (Zhōngguó Guójì Lǚxíngshè; Map p364; ☎ 8367 8019; www.citsdl.net; 145 Zhongshan Lu; 🕓 8.30am-

5.30pm Mon-Fri) On the 2nd floor of the Central Plaza Hotel (Xiāngzhòu Dàfàndiàn).

Sights & Activities

ZHONGSHAN SQUARE 中山广场
Zhongshan Sq (Zhōngshān Guǎngchǎng; Map p364) is Dàlián's hub: grand buildings, most dating to the early 1900s, encircling a huge roundabout. Dàlián Bīnguǎn, a dignified hotel on the square's south side, appeared in the movie *The Last Emperor*. The square (actually, a circle) is busiest at night, when young people hang out or play hacky sack. An even larger crowd comes to watch the Dàlián Shide football stars on the square's giant TV screen.

FRIENDSHIP SQUARE 友好广场
West of Zhongshan Sq, **Friendship Sq** (Yǒuhǎo Guǎngchǎng; Map p364) is a traffic circle that surrounds a landmark – a vast spheroid that's illuminated like a giant disco ball at night.

LABOUR PARK 劳动公园
In the centre of this hilly **park** (Láodòng Gōngyuán; Map p364; admission Y10; 🕓 7am-7pm) is a giant football, further testimony to the sport's popularity. Take the chairlift (Y40) to the TV Tower (Map p368) for excellent city views and come down via the hilarious 'land slide', a chute that winds down the hill.

DALIAN MODERN MUSEUM
大连现代博物馆
With exhibits like 'Dalian: A City Without Traffic Jams', this gleaming **museum** (Dàlián

INFORMATION		
ATM	**1**	B1
ATM	**2**	D1
Bank of China 中国银行	**3**	C1
China Merchants Bank		
ATM	(see 23)	
CITS 中国国际旅行社	**4**	A2
Internet Bar 网吧	**5**	A1
Post Office 邮局	**6**	A1
PSB 公安局外事科	**7**	C2
Xinhua Bookshop		
新华书店	**8**	B1

SIGHTS & ACTIVITIES		
Friendship Square 友好广场	**9**	B1
Zhongshan Square 中山广场	**10**	C1

SLEEPING		
Bohai Pearl Hotel 渤海明珠酒店	**11**	B1
Broadway Hotel 四方盛世酒店	**12**	A1

Dàlián Fàndiàn		
大连饭店	**13**	B1
Dalian University of Foreign		
Languages Hotel 大外宾馆	**14**	C2
Furama Hotel		
富丽华大酒店	**15**	D1

EATING		
Dàbáicài Gǔtou Guǎn		
大白菜骨头馆	**16**	B2
Tiān Tiān Yú Gǎng		
天天鱼港	**17**	B2
Tiān Tiān Yú Gǎng		
天天鱼港	**18**	C1
Yìxīn Kǎo Ròu		
一心烤肉	**19**	C2

SHOPPING		
New-Mart Shopping Mall	**20**	A2
Night Market	**21**	B1

Triumph Plaza (Kǎixuán		
Shāngchǎng) 凯旋商场	**22**	A1
Underground Shopping		
Centre	**23**	B1

TRANSPORT		
All Nippon Airways 全日空	**24**	A2
Buses to Xinghai Park		
& Fujiazhuang Beach	**25**	B1
CAAC 中国民行	**26**	A2
Dragonair 港龙航空	**27**	D1
JAL	(see 24)	
Light Rail Depot	**28**	A1
Ticket Office for Buses		
to Bingyu Valley	**29**	A1
Ticket Office for Buses		
to Shěnyáng & Běnxī	**30**	B1
Ticket Office for Buses		
to Zhuānghé	**31**	A1
Ticket Offices for Buses		
to Dāndōng & Běijīng	**32**	A1

Xiàndài Bówùguǎn; Map p368; ☎ 8480 1052; 10 Huizhan Jie; admission Y30; ◷ 9am-5pm Apr-Oct, 9am-4.30pm Nov-Mar) resembles a regional public-relations campaign, but it's still a fascinating look at the city's recent (and forthcoming) urban developments.

The museum is near Xinghai Sq, in the southwest of the city. Take bus 23 to the Exhibition Centre stop, about a 20-minute ride from Zhongshan Sq.

BEACHES
Five kilometres southeast of the city centre is **Bàngchuídǎo Jǐngqǔ** (Map p368; admission Y20), a secluded sandy beach on the grounds of Bàngchuídǎo Bīnguǎn, a hotel complex that's a long-time favourite with top-ranking Communist Party members. Unfortunately, there's no bus service to this area; a taxi from town will cost about Y20.

Another good swimming spot is **Fujiazhuang Beach** (Map p368; admission Y5; ◷ 6am-11pm), a deep bay with pebbly sand. Take bus 401 (Y1, 20 to 30 minutes) from the northwest corner of Jiefang Lu and Zhongshan Lu.

Tiger Beach Park (Lǎohǔtān Lèyuán; Map p368) has a massive carved-marble tiger sculpture, a small beach and a honky-tonk amusement park. On either side of the park the coastal road provides excellent views of the ragged cliffs and crashing waves. Buses 30 and 712 from Zhongshan Sq travel to Tiger Beach Park (Y1, 20 to 30 minutes).

Golden Stone Beach (Jīnshítán), 60km north of Dàlián, is an attractive beach with splendid coves and rock formations. There's also a golf course, an amusement park and even a museum of Mao badges! A light-rail line runs to Golden Stone Beach about every 15 minutes from the depot on Triumph Plaza, behind the Dàlián train station (Y8, 50 minutes).

Sleeping
Dalian Sea Rhyme International Youth Hostel (大连海韵国际青年旅舍; Dàlián Hǎiyùn Guójì Qīngnián Lǚshè; Map p368; ☎ 8239 4400; fax 8239 4400; Warship 104, 669 Jiefang Lu; 解放路669号; dm Y45) Dàlián's most unusual accommodation is this warship-turned-hostel docked in the harbour near Tiger Beach. The only windows in the basic two- and four-bed dorms are tiny portholes, and the bathrooms are a little musty, but don't complain – you're on the water! Take bus 712 from Zhongshan Sq to the Polar Aquarium, then walk southwest (with the water on your left) about 10 minutes. To tour the ship without staying here costs Y20.

Broadway Hotel (Sìfāng Shèngshì Jiǔdiàn; Map p364; ☎ 6262 8988; fax 6262 9959; 26-28 Jianshe Jie; 建设街 26-28号; d Y98-198) The best budget choice in the city centre is this new guesthouse behind the train station. The rooms aren't large, but they're neat as a pin. You'll get some street noise when you open the windows though.

Dalian University of Foreign Languages Hotel (Dàwài Bīnguǎn; Map p364; ☎ 8280 1199; fax 8280 1211; 94 Yan'an Lu; 延安路94号; d Y240-300) At this friendly hotel on the University of Foreign Languages campus, rooms are fraying but pleasant. Take bus 23 down Yan'an Lu to its terminus and then, heading west, take the second left on Qilindong Xiang. Go up the hill (past lots of cheap eateries); the hotel is on the right, just before the street curves sharply.

LIÁONÍNG

COMMUNISTS VS KUOMINTANG IN MANCHURIA

The Japanese occupation of Manchuria, which had begun in 1931, ended during WWII. When the 1945 bombings of Hiroshima and Nagasaki forced the Japanese government to surrender, Soviet armies moved into Manchuria. With American assistance, Kuomintang troops moved north to oversee the Japanese retreat and regain control of northern China.

At the same time, however, the communists marched to Manchuria, picking up arms from abandoned Japanese depots en route. Other communist troops headed north by sea from Shāndōng. In November 1945 the Kuomintang attacked the communist fighters.

The communists occupied the Manchurian countryside, and their land-reform policies quickly built up support among the peasants. Soon the 100,000 that had marched into Manchuria had tripled in size, as peasants and ex-soldiers of the Manchurian armies eagerly joined the ranks. Within two years the Red Army had grown to 1.5 million combat troops and four million support personnel.

In 1948, in Manchuria, the communists made their move. Three great battles led by Lin Biao decided the outcome. In the first, in August 1948, the Kuomintang lost 500,000 people. In the second battle, from November 1948 to January 1949, whole Kuomintang divisions went over to the communists. The final battle was fought in and around Běijīng and Tiānjīn. Tiānjīn fell on 23 January and another 500,000 Kuomintang troops switched sides, sealing the Kuomintang's fate and allowing the communists to drive southwards.

Dàlián Fàndiàn (Map p364; ☎ 8263 3171; fax 8280 4197; 6 Shanghai Lu; 上海路6号; s/d Y320/380) This brick building near Zhongshan Sq houses a simple hotel with cosy rooms. Discounts put doubles in the budget range.

Bohai Pearl Hotel (Bóhǎi Míngzhū Jiǔdiàn; Map p364; ☎ 8882 8333; fax 8881 8158; 8 Shengli Guǎngchǎng; 胜利广场8号; d Y758-988, tr Y1080, incl breakfast; ✗ ✗ 🖳) Despite the high posted prices, this 30-storey tower facing the train station is an excellent midrange option, since the staff readily offer discounts of 50% or 60%. The rooms have such upscale amenities as hairdryers and minibars, and an ample buffet breakfast is served in the kitschy revolving restaurant.

Furama Hotel (Fùlihuá Dàjiǔdiàn; Map p364; ☎ 8263 0888; www.furama.com.cn; 60 Renmin Lu; 人民路60号; d Y898 plus 15% service charge; ✗ 🖳) A top international hotel, this glitzy pair of towers has sleek Asian-fusion-style rooms with high-speed internet connections and gracious staff.

Eating & Drinking

You'll find lots of small eateries on the roads leading off Zhongshan Sq and Friendship Sq. The New-Mart Shopping Mall (see opposite) has a huge food court (dishes Y5 to Y8) on the 5th floor and a well-provisioned supermarket on the lower level.

Dàbáicài Gǔtou Guǎn (Map p364; ☎ 8263 6656; 21 Zhongyuan Jie, btwn Youhao Lu & Xiangqian Jie; dishes Y14-28; ☽ lunch & dinner) Friendly, loud and smoky, this informal eatery serves fresh seafood and fiery northern-style fare. Try baby octopus with scallions (Y20) – or point to appealing dishes on display – and cool off with a local beer (Y5 to Y10).

I-55 Coffee Stop & Bakery (爱伍伍美式咖啡站; Àiwǔwǔ Měishì Kāfēizhàn; Map p368; ☎ 8369 5755; 67 Gaoerji Lu; sandwiches & mains Y20-38, coffee Y19-23; ☽ breakfast, lunch & dinner; 🖳) With a library of English-language books, a stack of games, and treats that range from quiche to fresh-squeezed orange juice to oatmeal cookies, this contemporary café is a popular expat hangout. English menu, English-speaking staff and free wireless internet access too.

Yìxīn Kǎo Róu (Yixin Roast Meat Restaurant; Map p364; ☎ 8265 5878; 56 Yan'an Lu; dishes Y16-45; ☽ lunch & dinner) Make like a chef on the tabletop grills at this busy BBQ joint. In spite of the name, you can cook your own shellfish or vegetables (as well as meat).

Tiān Tiān Yú Gǎng (Map p364; ☎ 8280 1111; 41 Yan'an Lu; dishes Y28-80; ☽ lunch & dinner) Choose your meal from the many sea creatures swimming in the tanks at this upscale seafood restaurant. Great veggie dishes too. There's another branch at 10 Renmin Lu (☎ 8280 1118).

The streets around Friendship Sq and the University of Foreign Languages (particularly Qi'qi Jie and Yan'an Lu) are lined with small bars. For a sleazier scene, head for the nightclubs on Changjiang Lu, north of Zhongshan Sq.

Entertainment

Noah's Ark (Nuóyà Fāngzhōu; Map p368; ☎ 8369 2798; 32 Wusi Lu) Local bands play at this long-standing but still cool bar. It's just south of People's Sq, on the western side of the flower market.

Shopping

It seems as if a new mall opens in shopping-crazed Dàlián nearly every week. Qingni Jie, south of Victory Sq, is a pedestrian plaza lined with upscale department stores, including the **New-Mart Shopping Mall** (Map p364; Youhao Jie btwn Zhongshan Lu & Wuhui Lu). Tianjin Jie, a more-pedestrian pedestrian street, has a summer night market. Opposite the train station there's an enormous underground shopping centre below Victory Sq. Another shopping area behind the station is around and below Triumph Plaza (Kǎixuán Shāngchǎng).

Getting There & Away

AIR

Airport shuttles leave from the office of the **Civil Aviation Administration of China** (CAAC; Zhōngguó Mínháng; Map p364; ☎ 8361 2888 domestic reservations, 8361 2222 international reservations; 143 Zhongshan Lu; ☾ 8am-6pm); check with CAAC for times.

Domestic flights include Běijīng (Y710, one hour), Hāěrbīn (Y840, 1½ hours), Shànghǎi (Y1060, 1¾ hours), Guǎngzhōu (Y2050, 3½ hours) and Hong Kong (Y3030, 3½ hours).

Dragonair (Map p364; ☎ 8271 8855; www.dragonair .com; 15th fl, 68 Renmin Lu) has an office near the Furama Hotel. **Japan Airlines** (JAL; Map p364; ☎ 8369 2525; 147 Zhongshan Lu) and **All Nippon Airways** (Map p364; ☎ 8360 6611; 147 Zhongshan Lu) are both in the Senmao Building, near the CAAC. International destinations include Tokyo (Y5250, 2¾ hours), Osaka (Y4480, two hours and 20 minutes) and Seoul (Y2390, one hour).

In summer you can fly from Dàlián to Vladivostok and Khabarovsk (Russia). **Vladivostok Avia** (☎ 8277 9100; fax 8277 9300; www.vladavia .ru) travels to Vladivostok (two hours) several times a week, and **Dal Avia** (www.dalavia.ru) flies to Khabarovsk (2½ hours) on Wednesdays and Saturdays.

BOAT

The Korean-run **Da-In Ferry** (☎ 8270 5082; www .dainferry.co.kr) to Incheon in South Korea departs

from Dàlián on Monday, Wednesday and Friday at 3.30pm (Y920 to Y1850, 18 hours).

Several daily boats go to Yāntái; fast boats make the crossing in under four hours (Y350), while slower boats take six to seven hours (Y50 to 250). Daily boats to Wēihǎi (Y150 to Y720, seven hours) depart at 8.30am, 9am and 9pm. If you really love boat travel, you can go to Tiānjīn (Y172 to Y720, 12 to 15 hours) or Shànghǎi (Y660, 37 hours).

Buy ferry tickets at the passenger ferry terminal in the northeast of Dàlián or from a counter in front of the train station. To the ferry terminal, take bus 13 from the Dàlián train station or bus 708 from Zhongshan Sq.

BUS

Long-distance buses leave from Victory Sq (in front of the train station) and from behind the station (near the light-rail depot). The trick is to find the correct ticket booth for your destination.

Tickets for fast buses to Dāndōng (Y81, 3½ hours) are sold from a booth on the west side of Victory Sq, where eight buses depart daily between 6.20am and 2.40pm. The ticket booth for buses to Běijīng (Y220 to Y280, nine hours, 11am and 9pm) is also on the square's west side.

Buses to Shěnyáng (Y73 to Y81, 4½ hours, hourly) depart from the east side of Victory Sq. The same booth sells tickets to Běnxī (Y60 to Y95, five hours, 9am and 3pm).

Frequent buses to Zhuānghé (Y34, 2½ hours) leave from behind the train station.

TRAIN

Be prepared for chaos at the always jammed Dàlián train station. Try to buy your ticket as early as possible.

Several daily trains run to Shěnyáng (Y55, four hours). Other destinations include Běijīng (seat/sleeper Y140/290, 10 to 12 hours), Hāěrbīn (seat/sleeper Y125/231, 10

WARNING

Before attempting to visit Lǚshùn, at the end of the Liaodong Peninsula, check with Dàlián's PSB (see p364). This area, considered a sensitive military zone, has historically been off limits to foreigners, and the PSB continues to insist that foreign travellers stay away.

AROUND DÀLIÁN 大连地区

hours), Chángchūn (seat/sleeper Y99/171, eight to 9½ hours) and Tōnghuà (seat/sleeper Y71/143, 11 to 12 hours).

At the time of writing, train service to Dāndōng had been discontinued and a new train-ferry link between Dàlián and Yāntái was under construction.

Getting Around

Dàlián's central district is not large and can generally be covered on foot. The airport is 12km northwest of the city centre. Buses 701 and 710 run between Zhongshan Sq and the airport (Y1). A taxi from the city centre will cost about Y30.

Bus 23 runs south down Yan'an Lu. Bus 13 runs from the train station to the passenger ferry terminal. Taxis start at Y8 during the day and Y10 between 11pm and 5am.

AROUND DÀLIÁN

If you can't travel south to Guìlín, get away to 'Little Guilin' – the **Bingyu Valley** (冰峪沟; Bīngyù Gōu; admission Y100; ☼ May-Oct), a riverfront park area about 250km northeast of Dàlián. Boats take you along the river,

where rock formations rise steeply along the banks, and you can hike up or around several of the peaks. While the cliffs may not be as dramatic as their Guìlín counterparts, they're pretty, and a day here makes a relaxing getaway.

On summer weekends there's a direct bus (Y220 return, including park admission) from Dàlián to the Bingyu Valley. It departs at 7am from Victory Sq opposite the train station and returns to Dàlián in the late afternoon. Otherwise, catch the bus to Zhuānghé (Y34, 2½ hours, 15 daily, 6.30am to 4.30pm) behind Dàlián station. From Zhuānghé, minibuses to Bingyu Valley's east gate (Y8, one hour) leave about once an hour.

There are several small guesthouses just outside the east gate. Inside the park, the boxy-looking **Bingyu Furama Hotel** (冰峪富丽华度假村; Bīngyù Fùlìhuá Dùjiàcūn; ☎ 8922 6237; d Y240-300) is nothing like its glitzy counterpart in Dàlián, but it has large rooms overlooking the river. The Furama's restaurant (dishes Y18 to Y38) is quite good; ask for *dàgǔjī* (大骨鸡), a local chicken stew made with several varieties of mushrooms. The boat from the park entrance will bring you to the hotel dock.

Buses from Zhuānghé leave for Dàlián about every 20 minutes until 4pm. To Dāndōng, buses depart Zhuānghé (Y25, three hours) at 6.29am, 7.16am, 8.17am and 1.18pm; leave the park early if you want to catch the last Dāndōng bus.

If you get stuck in Zhuānghé, **Hóngguāng Bīnguǎn** (红光宾馆; ☎ 8981 2684; 369 Xinhua Lu; 新华路369号; d Y100) has clean, simple rooms. Turn right as you exit the bus station; the hotel is one block ahead on the right.

DĀNDŌNG 丹东

☎ 0415 / pop 643,000

Just across the Yalu River (Yālù Jiāng) from North Korea, Dāndōng draws visitors hoping for a brief peek at the Hermit Kingdom. You can't see much, but the contrast between Dāndōng's lively riverfront and the desolate stretch of land along the Korean side is a bit eerie. Outside the city you can visit the easternmost stretch of the Great Wall, which also parallels the border.

Besides its border tourism business, Dāndōng is a hub for trade between China and North Korea. Officially, trucks rumble across the Sino-Korean Friendship Bridge between the two countries, and, unofficially, North Koreans regularly cross the riverfront border to buy food and other supplies. In an effort to reduce this cross-border traffic following North Korea's 2006 underground nuclear test, the Chinese government began erecting a fence between the two countries north of Dāndōng. Whether this fence will be extended along the roughly 1300km frontier that China shares with North Korea – and its effect on trade between the two nations – remains to be seen.

Check with CITS (right) if you want to join a tour to North Korea. You will need to have arranged your visa in advance (most likely at the North Korean embassy in Běijīng). At the time of writing, Israeli and South Korean nationals were not being issued North Korean visas; visas for US citizens have been available on an extremely limited basis for special-event tours.

Orientation

The river is about 500m southeast of the train station. The 'Business and Tourism District' (Shāngmào Lǚyóuqū), lined with riverfront restaurants, is southwest of the Yalu River bridge. The main shopping district is just east of the station.

Information

Bank of China (Zhōngguó Yínháng; ☎ 213 7721; 60 Jinshan Dajie; ⏰ 7.30-11.30am & 1-5pm) There's also a 24-hour ATM in the Business and Tourism District.

CITS (Zhōngguó Guójì Lǚxíngshè; ☎ 213 5854; fax 214 1922; 20 Shiwei Lu at Jiangcheng Dajie; ⏰ 8am-5pm)

Internet café (Wǎngbā; 15 Jiangcheng Dajie; per hr Y2)

Post office (Yóujú; 78 Qiwei Lu; ⏰ 8am-5.30pm)

Public Security Bureau (PSB; Gōngānjú; ☎ 210 3138; 15 Jiangcheng Dajie; ⏰ 8am-12.30pm & 1.30-5.30pm Mon-Fri)

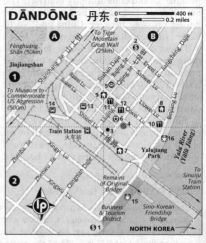

DĀNDŌNG 丹东

Sights & Activities

NORTH KOREAN BORDER 北朝鲜边界

For views of the **border** (Běi Cháoxiǎn Biānjiè), stroll along the riverfront **Yalujiang Park** that faces the North Korean city of Sinuiju.

In 1950, during the Korean War, American troops 'accidentally' strafed the original steel-span bridge between the two countries. The North Koreans dismantled the bridge as far as the midriver boundary line – all that's left on the Korean side is a row of support columns. You can wander along the **remains of the original bridge** (Yālùjiāng Duàn Qiáo; admission Y20; ☺ dawn-dusk), which still shows shrapnel pockmarks and ends abruptly midriver. The Sino-Korean Friendship Bridge, the official border crossing between China and North Korea, runs parallel to the old one.

To get closer to North Korea, take a **boat cruise** (guānguāng chuán) from the tour boat piers on either side of the bridges. The large boats (Y20, 20 minutes) are cheaper than the smaller speedboats (Y35, 10 minutes, from dawn to dusk), but you have to wait for them to fill up with passengers. Either way, you cruise – briefly – along the river right up along the North Korean side. Apart from some locals, a never-moving Ferris wheel and the odd smokestack, there isn't much to see. Nevertheless, if you want to visit North Korea, at least you'll be pretty close.

MUSEUM TO COMMEMORATE US AGGRESSION 抗美援朝纪念馆

With everything from statistics to shrapnel, this **museum** (Kàngměi Yuáncháo Jìniànguǎn; ☎ 387 6322; admission Y30; ☺ 8am-5pm) offers Chinese and North Korean perspectives of the war with the United States (1950–53). Look for the 'last letters home' from American soldiers killed in the conflict. The adjacent North Korean War Memorial Column was built 53m high, symbolising the year the war ended.

Take Bus 3 from just north of the train station and get off at the stadium. Cross the train tracks, walk west towards the Memorial Column and climb the stairs to the museum plaza.

TIGER MOUNTAIN GREAT WALL 虎山长城

About 25km northeast of Dāndōng, this steep, restored stretch of the **Great Wall** (Hǔshān Chángchéng; admission Y30), built during the Ming dynasty, parallels the current North Korean border. Unlike other sections of the wall, this one still sees comparatively few tourists.

ONE STEP ACROSS   *Carolyn B Heller*

The North Korean soldier began sprinting towards us, across the fields to the narrow stream that marked the border between his country and China. His bulky, olive-drab coat flapped behind him, and his rifle, slung over his shoulder, bounced as he ran.

Standing on the China side of the riverbank with my 11-year-old twins and two Chinese students, I cautiously eyed the young soldier as he approached. He ran right up to the edge of the stream, near enough that I could see his smooth cheeks. Instinctively, I put my arms around my daughters' shoulders.

We were just behind the Tiger Mountain Great Wall near Dāndōng, at the point known as Yībùkuà ('one step across') where the Yalu River between the two countries trickles down into a narrow creek. When the soldier reached the shore, he called out something in Mandarin. I didn't catch what he said and looked quizzically at the students.

'Cigarettes,' one of them translated. 'He wants cigarettes.'

We shook our heads, and the students said, *'Méiyǒu.'* Don't have. But one student signalled to the soldier to wait. He jogged over to a vendor selling drinks and snacks, returning with a pack of smokes.

The soldier gestured for the student to follow a path of small rocks that led partway across the stream. The student picked his way across the stones and threw the cigarette pack to the opposite bank. After a furtive glance around, the soldier clambered down and scooped it up. Then he called again.

'Knife?'

'Knife?!' I repeated. Again, we shook our heads.

Then, without another word, the young soldier scooted under a rope hung with tin cans – a makeshift border alarm that clattered as he passed – and made his way back across the fields.

You can hike up the wall, view a short unrestored section and look out over the surrounding countryside. The restored wall ends at a small but worthwhile **museum** (admission Y10). Back near the entrance, a point called Yībùkuà – 'one step across' – marks an extremely narrow part of the river between the two countries.

To return to the entrance, either hike back over the wall or follow the riverfront path. The riverfront trail ends about halfway back, where you have to climb up a short stretch of rocks to a metal walkway, which leads to Yībùkuà. In summer, boatmen often wait near the museum to row you back along the river (Y15, 10 minutes). The river marks the border, so even if it seems unguarded, don't attempt to cross to the other side. A gun-toting soldier may suddenly appear.

Buses to the wall (Y5, 45 minutes) run about every 30 minutes from the Dāndōng long-distance bus station.

Sleeping

Lǚyuàn Bīnguǎn (☎ 212 7777; fax 210 9888; cnr Shiwei Lu & Sanjing Jie; 三经街，十纬路; dm Y35-40, d/ste Y298/400 incl breakfast; ✦) At this friendly guesthouse conveniently located between the train station and the river, rooms range from reasonable three- or four-bed dorms to standard doubles and spacious suites.

Yóudiàn Fàndiàn (Post & Telecommunications Hotel; ☎ 216 6888; fax 216 6888; 78 Qiwei Lu; 七纬路78号; s Y368, d/tr Y298-468, q Y320, all incl breakfast; ✦) Recent renovations have added modern furnishings and new carpets – as well as higher prices – to this old standby. Still, if you can negotiate a room for under Y200, it remains a good deal.

Oriental Cherry Hotel (Yīngtáo Dàjiǔdiàn; ☎ 210 0099; 2 Liuwei Lu; 六纬路2号; d Y318 incl breakfast; ✦ 🖵) Spiffy rooms with contemporary cherry-hued furniture give this tower a touch of class. It's a half-block from the river, and high-floor rooms (especially those on the even-number side) have great river views. High-speed internet connections too.

Eating

For fresh seafood and good Korean fare, explore the riverfront on either side of the bridges.

Ālīláng Xiānzú Fēngwèi (Arirang Korean Restaurant; ☎ 212 2333; Binjiang Lu; dishes Y12-22; ⏰ lunch & dinner) For typical Korean fare, especially seafood, try this popular restaurant opposite Yalujiang

Park. The fish stews, garlicky greens and fiery clams go well with the local Yalu River beer.

Pyongyang North Korean Restaurant (Píngrǎng Gāolì Fàndiàn; ☎ 221 1555; Bawei Lu; dishes Y12-42) The staff seem a bit flustered to see foreigners at this North Korean–run restaurant, but if you ask for grilled beef and local fish you'll dine well. Tables concealed behind screens add to the intrigue.

Zhōnglián Měishíchéng (United Gourmet City; ☎ 253 1888; 13 Wujing Jie; dishes Y18-28; ⏰ lunch & dinner) A mind-boggling array of northeastern dishes, from fresh seafood to hotpot to vegetable stews, are on display in this cavernous restaurant. The woodsy wild mushroom soup is delicious.

Getting There & Away

AIR

Flights to and from Dāndōng are limited; check with CITS (p369) for schedules and bookings. At the time of writing, there were four flights a week to Běijīng (Y960, 1½ hours) and five to Shànghǎi (Y1200, two hours and 20 minutes).

BOAT

The **Dandong International Ferry Co** (☎ 710 0228; www.dandongferry.co.kr) runs a boat to Incheon in South Korea, departing on Tuesday, Thursday and Sunday (Y970 to Y1800, 16 hours). CITS can arrange tickets.

BUS

The **long-distance bus station** (98 Shiwei Lu) is near the train station. See the box on p364 for departure information.

TRAIN

The train station is in the centre of town, north of the river. A lofty Mao statue greets arriving passengers.

Destination	Price	Duration
Běijīng	Y143/254 (seat/sleeper)	14hr
Chángchūn	Y72/136 (seat/sleeper)	9-10hr
Qīngdǎo	Y214 (sleeper)	24hr
Shěnyáng	Y24	4hr

The K27 train from Běijīng to Pyongyang stops at Dāndōng at 7.30am on Monday, Wednesday, Thursday and Saturday (Dāndōng to Pyongyang takes 11 hours). If you have the necessary visas (normally requiring that you travel with a tour group), you can hop aboard.

LIÁONÍNG

DĀNDŌNG BUS TIMETABLES

Destination	Price	Duration	Frequency	Departs
Dàlián	Y81	3½hr	8 daily	6am-2.50pm
Hāěrbīn	Y154	12hr	daily	10am
Huánrén	Y40	5hr	2 daily	8am & 10.10am
Jí'ān	Y43	6½hr	daily	8.30am
Shěnyáng	Y64	3hr	every 30min	5.30am-6.30pm
Tōnghuà	Y46	8hr	2 daily	6.30am & 8.50am

AROUND DĀNDŌNG

Fènghuáng Shān (凤凰山; Phoenix Mountain), about 52km northwest of central Dāndōng near the town of Fèngchéng, is 840m high and dotted with temples, monasteries and pagodas from the Tang, Ming and Qing dynasties. A mountain temple fair in April attracts thousands of people. Buses to Fèngchéng leave from Dāndōng's bus station every 10 minutes between 6am and 5.30pm (Y10, one hour).

Jílín 吉林

China's largest nature reserve is the main attraction for visitors to Jílín province. At Chángbái Shān, the 'Ever-White Mountains,' you can hike along pine-lined paths up to tundra-like moonscapes; the highlight is Heaven Lake, a volcanic crater lake high among the peaks.

In the province's southeast, Unesco have designated the area around the small city of Jí'ān as a World Heritage Site for its relics from the ancient Koguryo kingdom (37 BC to AD 668). This still little-explored region houses pyramids, tombs and other remains from this early civilization, just across the river from present-day North Korea.

Jílín province is home to roughly one million ethnic Koreans, more than 80 percent of whom live in the Korean Autonomous Prefecture in the east of the province. Yánjí, the bilingual capital, makes a convenient base for exploring this region's blend of Korean and Chinese cultures.

Jílín is part of the historic territory of the Manchus, who founded the Qing dynasty (1644–1911). When the Japanese seized Manchuria and shaped it into the puppet state of Manchukuo (1931–45), they established Chángchūn, today's provincial capital, as its head-quarters. In Chángchūn, you can visit the elaborately re-created palace that was home to Puyi, the Qing's so-called Last Emperor.

Summer is the best time to tour Jílín, particularly if you're heading for Chángbái Shān; in winter, heavy snows make the reserve virtually inaccessible. For those who do brave the frigid wintry months, Jílín city stages an Ice Lantern Festival, as well as the spectacle of frost-laden trees along its winding riverbank that sparkle in the winter sun.

HIGHLIGHTS

- Hike to **Heaven Lake** (p381), a volcanic crater lake in stunning Chángbái Shān, China's largest nature reserve
- Visit **Chángbái Shān**'s (p381) waterfalls, hot springs and dense green forests
- Explore Korean-Chinese culture in Yánjí and the **Korean Autonomous Prefecture** (p384)
- Tour the relics of the ancient Koguryo kingdom in **Jí'ān**, on the North Korean border (p385)

★ Yánjí

Heaven Lake
Chángbái Shān ★

★ Jí'ān

- POPULATION: 27.6 MILLION
- www.jl.gov.cn (in Chinese)

JÍLÍN

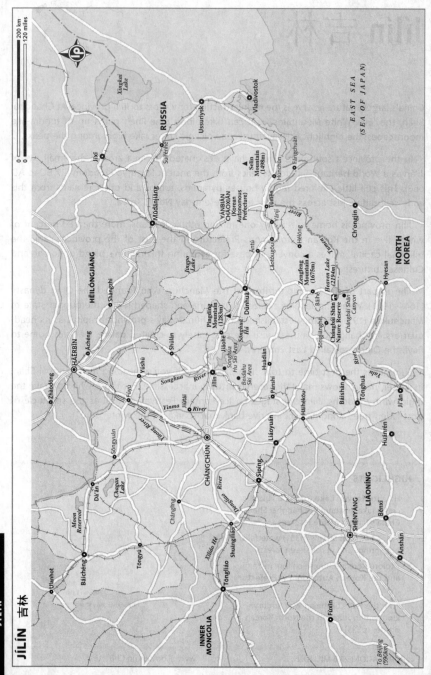

History

When the Japanese occupied Manchuria in the early 1930s, Jílín's capital, Chángchūn, became the centre of Japan's puppet government. In 1932, the Japanese installed Henry Puyi – who had earlier become the 10th (and last) emperor of the Qing dynasty at the tender age of three – as their 'puppet emperor', the executive nominally in charge of the government of the Manchukuo puppet state. Puyi governed the region from a palace in Chángchūn until 1945. After Japan's defeat in WWII, Puyi attempted to flee to Japan. He got as far as Shěnyáng, where Russian troops captured him. In 1950, he was returned to China, where he spent 10 years in a re-education camp. Puyi died in 1967.

Jílín's border with North Korea has dominated the region's more recent history. Since the mid-1990s, thousands of North Koreans have fled into China to escape extreme food shortages. Many try to pass through China, en route to South Korea or to a supportive third country, while others remain in Jílín province, attempting to blend in with the local Korean population, particularly in the Korean Autonomous Prefecture. The Chinese government has not looked favourably on these migrants, refusing to grant them protected refugee status; those captured by Chinese authorities and returned to North Korea face a grim future.

Getting There & Around

The main rail and road routes across Jílín province run north–south through Chángchūn, to Shěnyáng in Liáoníng province and Hāěrbīn in Hēilóngjiāng province. From Chángchūn, eastbound trains and buses go to the city of Jílín; you can reach Jílín city from Shěnyáng or Hāěrbīn as well.

Travel to the province's eastern regions, particularly to the Chángbái Shān Nature Reserve, is more challenging. A regular train chugs east from Chángchūn and Jílín to Yánjí. From Yánjí, buses wind south through the hills toward the small town of Báihé, the main transport centre for Chángbái Shān's northern entrance. Access to Chángbái Shān's western entrance is from the town of Sōngjiānghé, on the train line that runs between Báihé, Tōnghuā and Shěnyáng.

You can reach Jí'ān via Tōnghuā to the north, Shěnyáng to the west or Dāndōng to the south. Between Jí'ān and Chángbái Shān, you can make connections in Tōnghuā.

CHÁNGCHŪN 长春

☎ 0431 / pop 3.04 million

The Japanese capital of Manchukuo between 1933 and 1945, Chángchūn today is an industrial city and a hub of China's booming automobile manufacturing business. Volkswagen has a factory in town, and Toyota has set up a joint venture to build its Prius hybrid cars.

With Soviet assistance, China's first car-manufacturing plant opened here in the 1950s, and that company, now called FAW Group, is China' largest automotive manufacturer. Its stated goal is to 'let every Chinese family own a car' – a scary thought, perhaps, given the traffic that already snarls Chángchūn and other northeast cities.

Orientation

Chángchūn sprawls from north to south. The long-distance bus station and the train station are in the north of the city.

Information

Bank of China (Zhōngguó Yínháng; 1296 Xinmin Dajie; ⌚ 8.30-11.30am & 1-4.30pm) In the Yinmao building, near Nanhu Park (Nánhú Gōngyuán), this branch will change travellers cheques.
China International Travel Service of Jílín Province (CITS; Zhōngguó Guójì Lǚxíngshè; ☎ 566 6541; fax 566 6547; 1448 Xinmin Dajie; ⌚ 8.30am-5pm) In the lobby of the Changbai Shan Hotel (Chángbái Shān Bīnguǎn), this office sells airline tickets and books Chángbái Shān trips.
Foreign Language Bookshop (1660 Tongzhi Jie)
Internet café (wǎngbā; btwn Changbai Lu & Hankou Jie; per hr Y2) In a basement room opposite the train station.
Internet café (wǎngbā; 2522 Tongzhi Jie, 2nd fl; per hr Y2) South of Guilin Lu.
Post office (yóujú; Renmin Dajie; ⌚ 8.30am-5pm) South of the long-distance bus station.
Public Security Bureau (PSB; Gōngānjú; 2627 Renmin Dajie) On the southwestern corner of People's Sq (Rénmín Guǎngchǎng), in a building that dates from the Japanese occupation.

Sights

PUPPET EMPEROR'S PALACE & EXHIBITION HALL 伪皇宫

Chángchūn's main attraction, this restored **palace** (Wěi Huánggōng; 5 Guangfu Lu; admission Y40; ⌚ 8.30am-5pm summer, 8.30am-4.20pm winter, last entry 40 min before closing) is the former residence of Henry Puyi, who was the Qing dynasty's last emperor. His story was the basis for the

CHÁNGCHŪN 长春

Bernardo Bertolucci film of 1987, *The Last Emperor*.

At age three, Puyi became the 10th Qing emperor, though China's 1911 revolution ended his brief reign. Puyi lived in exile until 1932, when the Japanese installed him at this palace as the 'puppet emperor' of Manchukuo.

Puyi's study, bedroom and temple, as well as his wife's quarters, his lover's quarters and his offices, have all been elaborately re-created, right down to his toilet (from where he reportedly approved all government decisions).

From the train station, bus 10 or 18 will drop you within walking distance of the palace.

Sleeping

Elan Fashion Inn (Mǐlán Huāshíshàng Jiǔdiàn; ☎ 564 4988; cnr Tongzhi Jie & Yongchang Hutong; 同志街与永昌胡同交汇处; d without/with bathroom Y68-128, tr without bathroom Y78; ✹) This sparkling budget hotel has cheerful rooms with brightly-hued walls and wood-grain floors. From the train station, take bus 62 or 362 and get off on Tongzhi Jie just south of Jiefang Dalu.

Chūnyì Bīnguǎn (☎ 209 6888; www.chunyihotel.com; 80 Renmin Dajie; 人民大街80号; s/d/tr Y298/320/368 incl breakfast; ✹) From the stained glass to the woodwork, this excellent-value midrange hotel has plenty of old-world charm. It was built in 1909 for senior Japanese and Manchurian officials.

Shangri-La Hotel (Xiānggélǐlā Dàjiǔdiàn; ☎ 898 1818; www.shangri-la.com; 569 Xi'an Dalu; 西安大路569号;

INFORMATION

Bank of China 中国银行	1	A4
CITS 中国国际旅行社	2	A4
Foreign Language Bookshop 外文书店	3	B4
Internet Café 网吧	4	B4
Internet Café 网吧	5	B1
Post Office 邮局	6	B1
PSB 公安局外事科	7	B3

SIGHTS & ACTIVITIES

Puppet Emperor's Palace & Exhibition Hall 伪皇宫	8	C1

SLEEPING 🛏

Chūnyì Bīnguǎn 春谊宾馆	9	B1
Elan Fashion Inn 米兰花时尚酒店	10	B3
Shangri-La Hotel 香格里拉大酒店	11	B2

EATING 🍴

Changchun Mall Food Court	12	B1
French Bakery 红磨坊	13	B4
Sòngjì Zhōupù 宋记粥铺	14	B4

TRANSPORT

CAAC 中国民行	15	C3
Long-Distance Bus Station 长途汽车站	16	B1

d Y1050-1530 plus 15% service charge;) Chángchūn's most upscale hotel is an elegant modern tower off Tongzhi Jie, a main shopping street. The cordial staff speaks English, and there's wireless internet access from the marble and gold lobby.

Eating & Drinking

Inexpensive restaurants serving good *dōngběi* (northeastern) fare are clustered along Guilin Lu and Xikang Lu, between Tongzhi Jie and Renmin Dajie south of People's Sq. In the same area, Longli Lu is lined with bars.

Sòngjì Zhōupù (688 Xikang Lu; dishes Y3-12; 24hr) Head to this inexpensive cafeteria for comfort food *dōngběi* style. Porridge is a speciality, paired with breads and pickled vegetables.

French Bakery (Hóng Mò Fáng; ☎ 562 3994; 745 Guilin Lu; coffees Y15, pastries Y5-10, mains Y10-30; 7.30am-10pm) This long-standing coffee shop satisfies Western-food cravings with croissants, sandwiches and pasta.

For a quick bite near the train station, try the **Changchun Mall Food Court** (162 Liaoning Lu, lower level; dishes Y8-20; lunch & dinner) for noodles, stews, dumplings or hotpot.

Getting There & Away

AIR

Civil Aviation Administration of China (CAAC; Zhōngguó Mínháng; ☎ 879 7777; 480 Jiefang Dalu), with offices in the CAAC Hotel, operates daily flights to most major domestic cities, including Běijīng (Y960, 1½ hours), Shànghǎi (Y1600, 2½ hours), Shēnzhèn (Y2490, five hours) and Dàlián (Y580, one hour).

Asiana Airlines flies daily to Seoul (two hours). China Southern travels to Tokyo on Sundays (two hours and 40 minutes).

BUS

The **long-distance bus station** (kèyùn zhōngxīn; 226 Renmin Dajie) is two blocks south of the train station.

Destination	Price	Duration	Frequency
Běijīng	Y220	7½hr	5 daily
Dàlián	Y147	8hr	several daily
Hāěrbīn	Y85	3½hr	every 30 min
Jílín	Y20	1½hr	every 10-15 min
Shěnyáng	Y85	3½hr	hourly

TRAIN

Regular trains run to Hāěrbīn (Y61, three to four hours), Jílín (Y10, two hours), Shěnyáng (Y28, four to five hours), Běijīng (seat/sleeper Y130/232, nine to 10 hours), Dàlián (seat/sleeper Y99/171, eight to 9½ hours) and Shànghǎi (seat/sleeper Y227/422, 22 to 28 hours).

Getting Around

Chángchūn's airport is 20km east of the city centre, between Chángchūn and Jílín. Airport buses (Y20, 50 minutes) leave from the **CAAC Hotel** (民航宾馆; Mínháng Bīnguǎn; 480 Jiefang Dalu) on the east side of town. A taxi to the airport will cost Y80 to Y100.

Bus 6 follows Renmin Dajie south from the train station. Buses 62 and 362 take a more circuitous route, travelling between the train station and Nanhu Park via the Chongqing Lu and Tongzhi Jie shopping districts.

Taxi fares start at Y5.

JÍLÍN 吉林

☎ 0432 / pop 1.9 million

Industrial Jílín is – surprisingly – noted for its winter scenery, but in any season, you can stroll the pleasant riverfront promenade, or escape the urban hubbub in several large parks.

Information

Bank of China (Zhōngguó Yínháng; 72 Tianjin Jie; 8.30am-4.30pm Mon-Fri, 9am-4pm Sat-Sun) This branch has a 24-hour ATM.

lonelyplanet.com

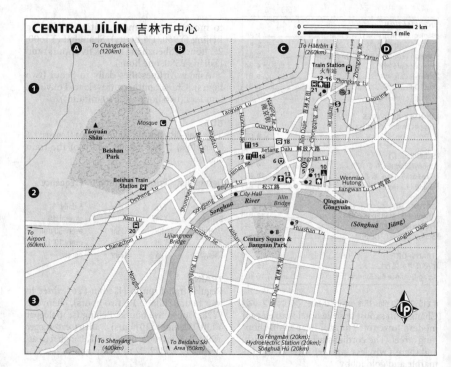

CENTRAL JÍLÍN 吉林市中心

CITS (Zhōngguó Guójì Lǚxíngshè; ☎ 244 1304; fax 245
9204; 1 Chongqing Jie; ☉ 8.30am-6.30pm Mon-Fri,
9am-5.30pm Sat & Sun) Organises skiing trips and tours to
Chángbái Shān.
Internet café (wǎngbā; Nanjing Jie; per hr Y2) Centrally
located in an underground arcade (opposite).
Internet café (wǎngbā; Chongqing Jie; per hr Y2;
☉ 8am-midnight) To the left as you exit the train station.
Photo shop (Zhongxing Jie) Across the park from the
train station, next to the International Hotel.
Post office (yóujú; Jilin Dajie; ☉ 8am-5pm) Just north
of the Jílín Bridge.
Public Security Bureau (PSB; Gōngānjú; ☎ 240 9315;
cnr Beijing Lu & Nanjing Jie)

Sights

ICE-RIMMED TREES 树挂

Jílín is most attractive on January and February mornings when the pine and willow trees
along the Songhua River (Sōnghuā Jiāng) are
covered in spectacular needle-like frost.

The Hydroelectric Station in Fēngmǎn
causes this phenomenon. Water passing
from Sōnghuā Hú (Songhua Lake) through
the power plant becomes a steamy current
that merges with the river and prevents it

from freezing. Vapour rising from the river
overnight meets the −20°C air, causing the
frosty display.

WÉN MIÀO 文庙

Temples dedicated to Confucius were built so
that the great sage would bestow good luck on
hopefuls taking huìkǎo, the notoriously difficult imperial examinations. This temple (Confucius
Temple; Wenmiao Hutong; admission Y15; ☉ 8.30am-4pm)
was originally constructed in 1736, although
the current structures date to 1907.

The buildings include changing exhibits
(with captions in Chinese only) about Confucius and about past and present life in the
region.

The temple entrance is behind Jiāngchéng
Bīnguǎn (hotel). Bus 13 runs near here from
the train station.

CATHOLIC CHURCH 天主教堂

This landmark church (Tiānzhǔ Jiàotáng; 3 Songjiang Lu;
☉ 6.20am-4.30pm Mon-Fri, 8am-4.30pm Sat & Sun), built
in 1917, was completely ransacked during the
Cultural Revolution. In 1980 it reopened and
now holds regular services.

CENTURY SQUARE 世纪广场

South of Songhua River is **Century Sq** (Shìjì Guǎngchǎng), a plaza where in summer locals linger over beer in open-air cafés or whirl around on roller skates. Vendors on the square and across Jilin Dajie rent skates (Y5).

The **Century Boat**, the boxy building in the centre of the square, has an **observation deck** (admission Y10; ⏱ 8.30am-9.30pm summer, 8.30am-4.30pm winter) on the 12th floor.

Buses 3 and 103 come here from the train station.

Festivals & Events

Jílín, like Hāěrbīn, has an **Ice Lantern Festival** (Bīngdēng Jié), at Jiangnan Park (Jiāngnán Gōngyuán) on the southern side of the Songhua River. It runs for about 10 days in January. Contact CITS for exact dates.

Sleeping

Jiāotōng Bīnguǎn (Traffic Hotel; ☎ 255 6859; fax 253 8149; 6 Zhongkang Lu; 中康路6号; s/d/tr Y200-240/240-280/ 280; ✇) A clean, comfortable choice near the train and bus stations, this hotel is nothing fancy, but with discounted prices of Y150 to Y180 it's a good deal.

Tiānshǐ Bīnguǎn (Angel Hotel; ☎ 248 1848; fax 248 0323, 2 Nanjing Jie; 南京街2号; s/d Y228-258, tr Y248 incl breakfast; ✇) This old-fashioned guest-house situated near the river is worn but comfy. The nicest rooms have peek-a-boo river views. Expect discounts to about Y180. To get here, take bus 3 or 103 from the train station.

Jiāngchéng Bīnguǎn (☎ 216 2777; www.jlcta.com. cn; 4 Jiangwan Lu; 江湾路4号; d Y280-330, tr 300 incl breakfast; ✇) Many rooms face the river at this well-maintained older hotel, around the corner from Tiānshǐ Bīnguǎn.

Eating

In summer there's a lively night market on Hunchan Jie, just north of Jiefang Dalu.

Xīnxīngyuán Jiǎoziguǎn (☎ 202 4393; 399 Henan Jie; dishes Y5-10; ⏱ lunch & dinner) Choose from the *dōngběi* cold plates on display – perhaps marinated tofu, pickled greens or wood-ear mushrooms – and pair them with first-rate *jiǎozi* (dumplings). It's on the Henan Jie pedestrian mall.

Xiǎo Tǔdòu (Small Potato; ☎ 131 3441 1505; 6-1 Zhong-kang Lu; dishes Y10-15; ⏱ lunch & dinner) This branch of Shěnyáng's well-known eatery specialising in hearty potato-and-meat stew and other northeastern dishes is near Jílín's long-distance bus station.

Chuānwángfǔ Huǒguō Dà Shìjiè (Chuanwangfu Hotpot World; ☎ 204 0055; 98 Jiefang Dalu; hotpots Y15-30; ⏱ lunch & dinner) At this multistorey hotpot palace, each tasty order comes with several side dishes – pickled garlic, sweet beans, crispy dried shrimp – that you choose from roving carts.

Entertainment

Just east of Henan Jie, there's a huge **underground arcade** (cnr Nanjing Jie & Jiefang Dalu; ⏱ till 10pm Mon-Fri, till midnight Sat & Sun), with video games, a bowling alley, pool tables, internet access and even a small roller-skating rink. The entrance is on the north side of Jiefang Dalu, opposite the plaza.

Getting There & Away

AIR

CAAC (Zhōngguó Mínháng; ☎ 245 4260; Chongqing Jie) is half a block from the CITS office, north of Jilin Bridge. Flights to and from the Jílín area use Chángchūn's airport, about 60km west of Jílín city. Buses to the airport leave the CAAC at 5.30am, 8.30am, noon and 2pm

(Y40, 90 minutes). See p377 for flight schedules and prices.

BUS
Jílín has two long-distance bus stations. The main depot (near the train station) has several daily departures to Hāěrbīn (Y62, five hours) and Shěnyáng (Y96, 4½ hours).

For Chángchūn, buses depart every 15 minutes (Y20, 1½ hours) from Líjiāng bus station (Líjiāng kèyùnzhàn) on Xian Lu, west of the Lijiangmen Bridge. Bus 8 from the train station goes to Líjiāng depot.

TRAIN
Jílín's train station is in the northern part of the city. Frequent trains run to Chángchūn (Y10, two hours). There are daily services to Hāěrbīn (Y25, five hours), Yánjí (seat/sleeper Y45/106, seven hours), Shěnyáng (Y44, six hours) and Dàlián (seat/sleeper Y97/181, 13 hours). Overnight trains go to Běijīng (seat/sleeper Y143/263, 11 to 12 hours), but if you can't nab a sleeper from Jílín, try going from Chángchūn, where there are more frequent Běijīng-bound trains.

Getting Around
Buses 3 and 103 run between the train station and Century Sq. Bus 30 runs up Jilin Dajie. Taxi fares start at Y5.

AROUND JÍLÍN
Ski Resorts
Songhua Hu Ski Area (松花湖滑雪场; Sōnghuā Hú Huáxuě Chǎng; ski season Dec-Feb), 25km southeast of Jílín, attracts beginners and intermediates to its 934m slopes. In milder weather, you can go **boating** (Y40 per hour) or hiking at **Sōnghuā Hú** (admission Y10), the nearby lake. Take bus 9 from Jílín's train station.

Beidahu Ski Area (北大湖滑雪场; Běidàhú Huáxuě Chǎng; ☎ 420 2023; www.beidahuski.com; ski season Dec-Feb) has six lifts and six trails, although the area was expanding as it prepared to host the 2007 Asian Winter Games. The only way to reach Běidàhú, 53km south of Jílín, is by taxi (Y80).

CHÁNGBÁI SHĀN 长白山
☎ 0433 for Báihé and the northern slope
☎ 0439 for Sōngjiānghé and the western slope
China's largest nature reserve, **Chángbái Shān** (Ever White Mountains; admission Y100, transportation fee Y45; ⏱ 7am-6pm northern gate, 6am-4pm western gate) covers

210,000 hectares of dense forest on the eastern edge of Jílín province, straddling the China-North Korea border. Chángbái Shān's main attraction is Heaven Lake, a dramatic volcanic crater lake at the top of a mountain peak.

Chángbái Shān is popular not only with Chinese visitors but also with South Koreans; the area is known as Mt Paekdu, or Paekdusan, in Korean. North Korea claims that Kim Jong Il was born here (although he's actually thought to have been born in Khabarovsk, Russia).

At lower elevations, the forests are filled with white birch and Korean pines; above 2000m the landscape turns treeless and windy. Temperatures, too, can plunge from steamy at the reserve entrance to frigid at the summit. No matter how warm it is in the morning, sudden high winds, rain and dramatic drops in temperature are possible by afternoon.

Chángbái Shān has two separate areas: the busy northern slope (běi pō) and the less-explored western slope (xī pō). Heaven Lake is accessible from both sides of the reserve, but the north and west entrances are separated by 100km by road or rail. The main attraction on the western side is the impressive Chángbái Shān Canyon.

In summer, tour buses bring day-trippers to the northern slope to pose for photos in front of the waterfall, gorge on eggs boiled in the natural hot springs, stampede up to Heaven Lake and rush down again. Since Chángbái Shān is a long haul from anywhere, though, it's worth spending a couple of relaxed days hiking around (just don't hike alone, and bring food and medical supplies if you venture off the beaten tourist trail).

Visiting Chángbái Shān is expensive. Besides the park admission and transportation fees (which pay for shuttle buses inside the park), there are extra charges for the waterfall (including access to the walking path to Heaven Lake) and for a ride in a 4WD vehicle if you prefer not to hike to Heaven Lake. Expect total fees of Y185 to Y225 per day, not including lodging or transport to and from the park.

Orientation
The nearest town to the park's northern entrance is Èrdào Báihé, generally called Báihé (白河), about 20km north of the reserve. From the northern entrance gate (běipō shānmén) to the dàozhànkōu, a parking area where you can board 4WDs for the ride up

to Heaven Lake, it's about 16km. From the *dàozhànkōu* to the *pùbù* (waterfall) is about 3km further.

The town closest to the park's western entrance is Sōngjiānghé (松江河), about 40km northwest of the reserve. From the west gate to Chángbái Shān canyon is about 25km.

Information

Bank of China (中国银行; Zhōngguó Yínháng) There are branches on the main street in Báihé and near the main square in Sōngjiānghé, although neither has an ATM.

Dazheng Travel Agency (大正旅行社; Dàzhèng Lǚxíngshè; ☎ 0439-617 9175; fax 0439-632 5175) In Sōngjiānghé, arranges transportation and tours to the western slope.

Internet café (网吧; wǎngbā; per hr Y2) In Báihé, on the main street, adjacent to the market. On the 3rd floor.

Internet café (网吧; wǎngbā; per hr Y2) In Sōngjiānghé, east of the main square.

Post office (邮局; yóujú; ⊗ 8am-5pm) In Sōngjiānghé, opposite Báitóushān Bīnguǎn.

Sights & Activities

NORTHERN SLOPE 北坡

Heaven Lake 天池

Heaven Lake (Tiān Chí), a deep-blue volcanic crater lake at an elevation of 2194m, is the highlight of Chángbái Shān. The lake, 13km in circumference, is surrounded by jagged rock outcrops and 16 mountainous peaks; the highest is **White Rock Peak** (Báiyán Fēng), which soars to 2749m. Legend has it that the lake is home to a Loch Ness-style 'monster,' but you can see for yourself…

From the *dàozhànkōu*, **4WDs** (Y80 per person) take groups of five passengers up to Heaven Lake. To hike to Heaven Lake (about one hour each way), the path starts at the waterfall; it's not a difficult walk, but you do climb more than 900 steps!

BEWARE OF THE BORDER

The China-North Korea border cuts across Heaven Lake. Unfortunately, the border isn't clearly marked and detailed maps of the area are not available.

Approximately one-third of the lake, the southeastern corner, is on the North Korean side and off-limits. Do not venture east of White Rock Peak or Lakeside Hot Springs at Chángbái Shān's summit. If you think you are nearing the border or are unsure where it exactly lies, do not proceed further!

Waterfall & Hot Springs

The road forks at the *dàozhànkōu*, with one branch climbing steeply to Heaven Lake, and the other leading past several hotels to the **waterfall** (admission Y40) and hot springs. Erdaobai River runs off Heaven Lake, creating this rumbling 68m waterfall that is the source of the Songhua and Tumen Rivers.

On the path to the waterfall, vendors boil eggs in the hot springs, and there's a **bathhouse** where you can soak in the odoriferous waters.

Underground Forest 地下森林

Between the park entrance and the *dàozhànkōu*, about 12km from the north gate, this verdant **forest** (Dìxià Sēnlín) is a pretty hiking spot. Following the trail for about 30 minutes leads to a crater filled in with trees.

WESTERN SLOPE 西坡

Chángbái Shān Canyon 大峡谷

Filled with dramatic rock formations, this **canyon** (Chángbái Shān Dàxiágǔ) measures 70km long, 200m wide and more than 100m deep. There's an easy 40-minute walk along a boardwalk that follows the canyon rim through the forest.

Tours

CITS in Jílín city (p377) runs three-day/two-night trips to Chángbái Shān's northern slope from May to September. Prices start at about Y480, including transportation, lodging and park admission. Other travel agencies in Jílín offer similar packages; ask at any hotel travel desk or at the agencies along Wenmiao Hutong, near the Confucius Temple. Just be aware that a 'three-day' tour from Jílín gives you just one day to explore the reserve – you'll be travelling most of the other two days.

CITS in Yánjí (p383) also organises one-day and multi-day Chángbái Shān tours.

Sleeping & Eating

At the northern slope, there are several hotels inside the park along the road to the waterfall, but they are quite expensive, particularly in July and August. You can save money by staying in Báihé.

At the western slope, several hotels are being constructed just outside the park gate. Until they're completed, stay in Sōngjiānghé, which has plenty of inexpensive and mid-range lodgings.

JÍLÍN

Camping is a possibility, although technically against the rules. Try and find a secluded place and be prepared for changeable weather.

NORTHERN SLOPE
Báihé

Several family-run **guesthouses** (dm Y25-30) surround Báihé's train station. Inexpensive **guesthouses** (d Y60-80) also line the town's main street and adjacent side streets.

Fēnglín Bīnguǎn (枫林宾馆; ☎ 575 1986; d/tr Y60-80/90-120) Inside a pink building opposite the Báihé bus depot is this guesthouse with basic clean rooms. Ask for a room on the quieter north side and make sure the hot water is turned on. Reception is on the second floor.

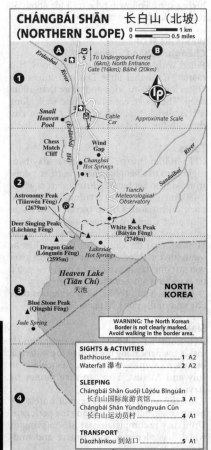

**CHÁNGBÁI SHĀN 长白山 (北坡)
(NORTHERN SLOPE)**

0 — 1 km
0 — 0.5 miles

To Underground Forest (6km); North Entrance Gate (16km); Báihé (20km)

Erdaobai
Erdaobai River
Approximate Scale

Small Heaven Pool
Cable Car
Chess Match Cliff
Wind Gap
Changbai Hot Springs
Tianchi Meteorological Observatory
Astronomy Peak (Tiānwén Fēng) (2679m)
Deer Singing Peak (Lùchàng Fēng)
Dragon Gate (Lóngmén Fēng) (2595m)
White Rock Peak (Báiyán Fēng) (2749m)
Lakeside Hot Springs
Sandaobai River

Heaven Lake (Tiān Chí) 天池

NORTH KOREA

Blue Stone Peak (Qīngshí Fēng)
Jade Spring

WARNING: The North Korean Border is not clearly marked. Avoid walking in the border area.

SIGHTS & ACTIVITIES	
Bathhouse	1 A2
Waterfall 瀑布	2 A2

SLEEPING	
Chángbái Shān Guójì Lǚyóu Bīnguǎn 长白山国际旅游宾馆	3 A1
Chángbái Shān Yùndòngyuán Cūn 长白山运动员村	4 A1

TRANSPORT	
Dàozhànkou 到站口	5 A1

Xīndá Bīnguǎn (信达宾馆; ☎ 5720444;s/dY220/320 incl breakfast; ✗) On Báihé's main drag, at the north end of town, this hotel has pleasant mid-range rooms and a restaurant serving appetising Korean-influenced Chinese fare (dishes from Y8).

Lánjǐng Huāyuán Dùjiàjiǔdiàn (蓝景花园度假酒店; ☎ 575 0222; d Y480, tr 580 incl breakfast; ✗) Báihé's most upscale hotel is opposite Xīndá Bīnguǎn. The spiffy modern doubles are comfortable and the triples are enormous.

Èrdào Shùndá Jiǎozi Chéng (二道顺达饺子城; ☎ 579 7167; dishes Y3-12; ✓ breakfast, lunch & dinner) From early morning till late evening, this family-run eatery is packed with locals. They breakfast on porridge and buns, then return later for handmade dumplings, hearty stews and whatever vegetables are fresh that day. It's two doors east of Fēnglín Bīnguǎn.

One block south of Lánjǐng Huāyuán Dùjiàjiǔdiàn, there's a small market building where you can buy bread, fruit and drinks.

On the Mountain

Chángbái Shān Yùndòngyuán Cūn (Mt Changbai Athletes Village; ☎ 574 6066; fax 574 6055; dm/d Y80/500) This modest place offers some of the least expensive lodging inside the park. It's opposite the dàozhànkōu.

Chángbái Shān Guójì Lǚyóu Bīnguǎn (Mt Changbai International Tourist Hotel; ☎ 574 6001; fax 574 6002; d Y800-900) CITS often books tour groups into this well-appointed hotel, where some rooms have waterfall views.

WESTERN SLOPE

In Sōngjiānghé, there are several cheap (and rather dreary) **guesthouses** (dm Y30-40) near the train station. For something nicer, walk about 10 to 15 minutes towards the town centre.

Báitóushān Bīnguǎn (白头山宾馆; ☎ 631 3716; fax 632 3398; Zhanqian Jie; 站前街; d Y260; ✗) About 1km south of the train station, this standard mid-range hotel has comfortable doubles. Bargain for rooms under Y150.

Lìxīn Bīnguǎn (丽新宾馆; ☎ 633 3619; Zhanqian Jie; 站前街; d & tr Y280; ✗) This brand-new guesthouse has an enthusiastic owner who welcomes guests with cups of tea and helps arrange transport to the reserve. Bargaining should put the cosy rooms under Y150. From Sōngjiānghé station, walk south about 1km; the hotel is on the right.

One block south of Sōngjiānghé's main square is a busy market lane. On the east side of the main square, you'll find small family-run **restaurants** (dishes from Y8).

Getting There & Away
The best time to visit Chángbái Shān is from mid-June to early September, when the roads to the nature reserve aren't iced over.

An airport under construction near Sōngjiānghé is expected to open in 2008. In the meantime, there are two routes to Chángbái Shān: from the south via Tōnghuā (通化), or Shěnyáng or Dāndōng in Liáoníng province; and from the north via Yánjí.

There's one direct train daily from Dāndōng and Shěnyáng to Sōngjiānghé and Báihé. Fares on this line include Báihé to Sōngjiānghé (Y7, two hours), Sōngjiānghé to Shěnyáng (seat/sleeper Y38/86, 11 hours) or Sōngjiānghé to Dāndōng (seat/sleeper Y55/117, 16 hours).

Several daily trains travel between Báihé and Tōnghuā (seat/sleeper Y21/60, six to seven hours), with a stop in Sōngjiānghé. From Tōnghuā, trains leave for Shěnyáng (seat/sleeper Y62/119, six to seven hours), Dàlián (seat/sleeper Y60/117, 13 hours) and Běijīng (seat/sleeper Y132/247, 17 hours).

From Yánjí, between June and September a direct bus to Chángbái Shān leaves at 5.30am and returns at 4pm (one way/return Y55/110). Otherwise, buses depart Yánjí for Báihé (Y33, four hours) daily at 6.30am, 8am, 10.10am, 12.20pm and 2.30pm; several buses return from Báihé to Yánjí between 5.30am and 2pm.

Báihé's train station is north of Měirén Sōng Sēnlín (a forest filled with tall, elegant pine trees), while the rest of town is south of the forest; a taxi from the station into town is Y5. Buses leave from the long-distance bus station off the main street or from in front of the train station.

Sōngjiānghé's train station is at the north end of town, about 2km from the main square. Minicabs take you between the station and the square or nearby hotels for Y2 to Y3.

Getting Around
NORTHERN SLOPE
Minibuses leave for Chángbái Shān's north gate from the Báihé train station and bus depot from 6am to noon, roughly every 40 minutes (Y20 return, 30 minutes). In summer, bus drivers may even find you and arrange to pick you up at your hotel. Unfortunately, buses may not run outside the peak July–

August tourist season, when you may have to hire a taxi (Y120 to Y150 return). If the roads are snow-covered, weigh the risks carefully before you set out.

Both buses and taxis drop you at the north gate, where you change to a park bus. Park buses go to the *dàozhànkōu*, where you can board a 4WD for the final trek to the lake, to the waterfall (where you can hike to the lake) and to the underground forest.

WESTERN SLOPE
From Sōngjiānghé, the only way to get to the mountain is by taxi or with a tour. Expect to pay around Y50 per person or Y200 per car (return) for transportation from town to the west gate (40 minutes).

From the west gate, park buses take you to the starting point for the hike to Heaven Lake or to the canyon rim boardwalk. It's another 40-minute ride from the gate to either of these destinations.

In summer, a **bus** (☎ 617 6359 or 135 0091 9023) runs from the Báihé train station to the western gate. It generally departs daily at 6am, but call to confirm the schedule and price. The cost of the bus ride is covered in the mandatory 'transportation fee' of Y45 that you have to pay along with the Y100 park admission fee. You have to pay these fees when you enter at either the north gate or the west gate

YÁNJÍ 延吉
☎ 0433 / pop 399,000
The capital of China's Korean Autonomous Prefecture, Yánjí feels different from other Chinese cities. Many people are of Korean descent, signs are bilingual (Chinese/Korean) and food is Korean or Korean-influenced. While Yánjí doesn't have many 'sights,' it's an intriguing place to wander around. It's also a transport hub for trips to Chángbái Shān.

Orientation
Buerhatong River (Bùěrhǎtōng Hé) bisects the city. The train and bus stations are south of the river. The commercial district, banks and post office are on the north side.

Information
Bank of China (Zhōngguó Yínháng; ☎ 253 6454; cnr Jiefang Lu & Juzi Jie; ☯ 8.30am-4pm Mon-Fri, 9am-4pm Sat) One block from the post office, just off Renmin Lu, this branch has a 24-hour ATM.

MORE BORDER TALES

Korean-American author Helie Lee has written an absorbing memoir, *In the Absence of Sun*, about her attempts to help her relatives slip across the border from North Korea into China. Her earlier book *Still Life with Rice* recounts how her grandmother and uncle became separated as they tried to leave North Korea for South Korea in the 1950s – events that set the scene for Lee's efforts to reunite her family in China many years later.

CITS (Zhōngguó Guójì Lǚxíngshè; ☎ 272 3500; 558 Yixie Jie, 6th fl) Arranges tours to Chángbái Shān. Take bus 5 from the station to the corner of Yixie Jie and Gongyuan Lu.

Internet café (wǎngbā; Zhanqian Jie; per hr Y2; ☯ 24hr) Two floors of fast computers, north of the train station.

Post & telephone office (Yóujú dàlóu; 78 Renmin Lu; ☯ 8am-4.30pm)

Public Security Bureau (PSB; Gōngānjú; 255 Guangming Jie) Located north of the river.

Sleeping & Eating

For a cheap bed, try one of the **guesthouses** (dm Y25) on the right as you exit the train station.

Dōngběiyà Dàjiǔdiàn (Northeast Asia Hotel; 东北亚大酒店; ☎ 280 8111; fax 282 0970; 109 Changbai Lu; 长白路109号; d Y228-368) Next to the long-distance bus station, this cylindrical tower has cramped doubles with temperamental plumbing. From the train station, head north on Zhanqian Jie and turn right onto Changbai Lu; it's about a 15-minute walk.

Yánbiān Fāyín Bīnguǎn (延边发银宾馆; ☎ 290 8855; 1656 Guanghua Lu; 光华路1656 号; d/tr/ste Y268/298/398 incl breakfast; ▢) The best mid-range choice near the train station, this sleek hotel has contemporary rooms with high-speed internet connections. The breakfast buffet includes a mix of Chinese and Korean dishes. It's about a 10-minute walk from the station; go north on Zhanqian Jie and turn right on Guanghua Lu.

Fēngmào Cānyǐn (丰茂餐饮; ☎ 282 0301; Guanghua Lu; BBQ per person Y15-30; ☯ lunch & dinner) Grill your meat and fish on skewers over tabletop grills at this busy BBQ joint opposite Yánbiān Fāyín Bīnguǎn.

Getting There & Away

AIR

There are daily flights from Yánjí to Běijīng (Y1130, one hour and 40 minutes) and Shěnyáng (Y740, one hour), and four flights a week to Dàlián (Y1100, 2½ hours). Both China Southern and Asiana fly to Seoul (Y2500, 2½ hours). The airport is 5km west of the city centre. CITS books airline tickets.

BUS

Buses to Chángbái Shān and Báihé leave from the long-distance bus station on Changbai Lu. Buses to Jílín, Chángchūn, Hāěrbīn and Mǔdānjiāng depart from in front of the train station.

TRAIN

There are daily trains to Jílín (seat/sleeper Y45/107, seven hours), Chángchūn (seat/sleeper Y51/135, nine hours), Mǔdānjiāng (seat/sleeper Y22/61, seven hours) and Běijīng (seat/sleeper Y168/307, 24 hours).

Getting Around

Bus 5 follows a useful route, looping from the train station north on Yixie Jie, east along Renmin Lu to Guangming Jie and back to the train station.

Taxi fares start at Y5.

AROUND YÁNJÍ

Korean Autonomous Prefecture

延边朝鲜族自治州

The Korean Autonomous Prefecture (Yánbiān Cháoxiǎnzú Zìzhìzhōu) has China's greatest concentration of ethnic Koreans. The majority inhabit the border areas northeast of Báihé, up to the capital Yánjí and the border city of Túmén (图门).

To explore the region, head east from Yánjí to Túmén or even further east to Fángchuān (防川), a sliver of land where China meets North Korea and Russia. To reach Fángchuān, take a bus from Yánjí to Húnchūn (混春), from where you take another bus to the border town.

JÍ'ĀN 集安

☎ 0435/pop 240,000

Across the Yalu River from North Korea, the small city of Jí'ān was once part of the Koguryo (高句丽; Gāogōulì) kingdom, a Korean dynasty that ruled areas of northern China and the Korean peninsula from 37 BC to AD 668. In 2004, Unesco designated the region a World Heritage Site for its extensive Koguryo pyramids, ruins and tombs. Archaeologists have unearthed remains of three cities plus some 40 tombs around Jí'ān and the town of

Huánrén (in Liáoníng province); see below). Many tombs are cairns – essentially heaps of stones piled above burial sites, while others are stone pyramids.

Orientation

Shengli Lu runs east–west through town, with the long-distance bus station at the west end. The main north–south road is Liming Jie, which ends at the river.

Information

Bank of China (中国银行; Zhōngguó Yínháng; 658 Shengli Lu; ☽ 8am-5.30pm Mon-Fri summer, 8am-4.30pm Mon-Fri winter) Three blocks east of the bus station.

Internet bar (网吧; wǎngbā; Dongsheng Jie; per hr Y2) One block north of Shengli Lu.

Post office (邮局; yóujú; 608 Shengli Lu; ☽ 7.30am-5.30pm Mon-Fri summer, 8am-4.30pm Mon-Fri winter)

Public Security Bureau (公安局; PSB; Gōng'ānjú; Liming Jie) Between Shengli Lu and the river.

Yalu River Travel Service (鸭绿江旅行社; Yālǜjiāng Lǚxíngshè; ☎ 622 2266; 888 Shengli Lu, inside Cuìyuán Bīnguǎn) Sells English-language maps of Jí'ān (Y4) and arranges transportation to local sights.

Sights

Most of the **Koguryo sites** (admission Y30 each site; ☽ 8.20am-5.30pm summer, to 4.30pm winter) are outside the city centre.

GENERAL'S TOMB 将军坟

One of the largest pyramid-like structures in the region, this 12m-tall **tomb** (Jiǎngjūnfén) was built during the fourth century for a Koguryo ruler; a smaller tomb nearby is the

resting place of his wife. The site is set among the hills 4km northeast of town.

HAOTAIWANG STELE 好太王碑

Inscribed with 1,775 Chinese characters, the **Haotaiwang Stele** (Hǎotàiwáng Bēi), a 6m-tall stone slab that dates to AD 415, records the accomplishments of Koguryo king Tan De (AD 374–412), known as 'Haotaiwang.' Though the inscriptions are quite faint, a photo exhibit shows a clearer enlarged version; also nearby is Tan De's tomb. The stele is northeast of town, near the General's Tomb.

JÍ'ĀN MUSEUM 集安博物馆

This modern but very small **museum** (Jí'ān Bówùguǎn; 249 Yingbin Lu) displays artefacts from the Koguryo era, including pottery, jewellery, weapons and even coffin nails. It's on the north side of town, a five-minute taxi ride (Y5) from the centre.

Sleeping & Eating

Cuìyuán Bīnguǎn (翠园宾馆; ☎ 622 2123; 888 Shengli Lu; 胜利路888号; dm Y25, d Y220) Two blocks east of the bus station, this run-of-the-mill hotel has basic dorms and tired-looking doubles.

Lùmíng Bīnguǎn (鹿鸣宾馆; ☎ 139 4453 6281; Shengli Lu, between Dongsheng Jie & Liming Jie; 胜利路; d without/with bathroom Y80/160 incl breakfast) With its funky bed frames resembling 1950s Cadillac grills and its exceedingly accommodating staff, this guesthouse with small well-kept rooms is Jí'ān's best inexpensive lodging. It's three blocks east of the bus station on the north side of Shengli Lu.

THE CITY ON THE MOUNTAINTOP

High on Wunu Mountain (五女山; Wǔnǚ Shān; Five Ladies' Mountain; admission Y60) outside the town of Huánrén (桓仁) in the far eastern corner of Liáoníng province, you can visit remains of the ancient Koguryo civilisation, a Korean dynasty that ruled parts of this region from 37 BC to AD 668. The partially-excavated 'Wunu Mountain City' was the first capital of the Koguryo people in northeast China, in the first century BC.

After a steep 45-minute climb (up stairs) to the mountaintop, you can walk through the ruins of the town – the foundation of a building here, the wall of a house there. The individual remains may not be that thrilling, but it's fascinating to contemplate the vast size of the community here, and the views of the surrounding mountains and valleys are worth the hike up.

Buses travel to Huánrén from Dāndōng (Y40, five hours), Shěnyáng (Y56, five hours), Jí'ān (Y20, four hours) and Tōnghuà (Y19, two hours). Taxis from the Huánrén long-distance bus station to Wunu Mountain are Y50-60 (40 minutes). Allow at least three hours at the mountain for the climb up, the circuit through the city remains and the climb down.

See above to learn more about the Koguryo sites in this region.

Xīngǎng Shuǐshàng Cāntīng (新港水上餐厅; New Harbour Floating Restaurant; ☎ 268 5151; Yanjiang Lu, at Liming Jie; dishes Y10-40; ☯ lunch & dinner) Right on the river, this place serves local fish, wild greens and tasty tofu soup. Tables face North Korea, but after sunset the Korean side is eerily dark.

For Korean-Chinese barbecue, follow the meat-scented smoke down the alley near the PSB on the west side of Liming Jie to find several cook-your-own **BBQ joints** (dishes Y8-12).

Other restaurants line the riverfront promenade (Yanjiang Lu), east and west of Liming Jie.

Getting There & Away

The main routes to Jí'ān are via Tōnghuā to the north or from either Shěnyáng or Dāndōng in Liáoníng province. If you're travelling to Chángbái Shān, you can make connections in Tōnghuā.

BUS

The **long-distance bus station** (Shengli Lu) is west of the town centre. There are buses to Tōnghuā (Y20, two hours, 10 daily), Dāndōng (Y36, six hours, 7.30am), Shěnyáng (Y60, eight hours, 6.20am) and Huánrén (Y20, four hours, 6.30am).

TRAIN

The **train station** (Yanjiang Lu) is in the northeast part of town. Two slow trains a day travel from Jí'ān to Tōnghuā (Y10, 2½ to three hours, 6.26am & 12.22pm).

Getting Around

You can easily walk around Jí'ān's small town centre. However, sights are scattered on the outskirts of the city, and you'll need to hire a taxi. Expect to pay Y50 to Y80 for a half-day tour of three to five locations.

Hēilóngjiāng 黑龙江

Blessed – or cursed – with one of the coldest climates in Asia, Hēilóngjiāng (Black Dragon River), surprisingly, promotes its frigid winters as the peak tourist season. And travellers do come – braving the -30°C weather and howling Siberian gales common to the country's northernmost province – primarily to marvel at the elaborate ice sculptures that glitter throughout the city of Hāěrbīn during its famous Ice Lantern Festival.

If you bring warm clothes – and we mean layers of thermals – and restore yourself with hearty stews and the local firewater, you can enjoy this sparkling spectacle. Hēilóngjiāng is also the centre of China's emerging ski industry, offering some of the country's best skiing at Yàbùlì.

In any season, Hāěrbīn is worth visiting for its Russian-influenced architecture and pleasant pedestrian streets, particularly in the Dàolǐqū district near the tree-lined riverfront. When the sun is shining, you can unwind with a walk along the river or on cobblestone-lined Zhongyang Dajie, stopping to sample steamed cornmeal buns or Russian-style sausages.

Other Hāěrbīn attractions include a new museum that illustrates the city's Jewish heritage, a collection of Buddhist and Confucian temples, a park that attempts to protect the rare Siberian tiger and a haunting museum that details grisly wartime experiments by the Japanese.

Between May and September, you can explore the lakes, nature reserves and forests throughout the rest of the province. Things to see include sparkling Jìngpò Hú (Mirror Lake); the Wǔdàlián Chí area, with its volcanic landscapes and mineral springs; the Zhalong Nature Reserve and its rare wild cranes; and the remote regions along the Russian border.

HIGHLIGHTS

- Chill out at Hāěrbīn's **Ice Lantern Festival** (p392), the region's most spectacular winter event
- Explore Hāěrbīn's Russian past and visit a Jewish-heritage museum in the **Dàolǐqū district** (p390)
- Wander the wetlands of **Zhalong Nature Reserve** (p398), a refuge for endangered wild cranes
- Hike through the lava fields of volcanic **Wǔdàlián Chí** (p399)
- Get off the beaten path in the remote **Russian borderlands** (p400)

Hēihé ★

★ Wǔdàlián Chí

★ Zhalong Nature Reserve

★ Hāěrbīn

- POPULATION: 36.8 MILLION
- http://english.northeast.cn

History

Hēilóngjiāng forms the northernmost part of the region formerly known as Manchuria. Like the other provinces in China's Dōngběi (northeast), Hēilóngjiāng's recent history has been influenced by its neighbours, notably Russia, which borders the province to the north and east.

During the mid-1800s Russia annexed parts of Hēilóngjiāng's territory, and in the late 1890s its influence in the region strengthened when Russian workers began the construction of a railway line that linked Vladivostok with Hāěrbīn as well as with Dàlián.

Hēilóngjiāng also saw an influx of Russian refugees following the Russian revolution in 1917. Hāěrbīn still retains Russian-style buildings constructed during this era.

Getting There & Around

Since trains, buses and flights connect Hāěrbīn with other cities throughout China, it's a logical starting point for exploring the far north. From Hāěrbīn, you can travel west to Qíqíhā'ěr, north to Wǔdàlián Chí and the Russian border regions, or travel east to Yàbùlì, Mǔdānjiāng and Jìngpò Hú.

Good highways make bus transport an alternative to the sometimes-slower local trains.

If you're headed for Inner Mongolia, direct trains run from Hāěrbīn to the cities of Hǎilāěr or Mǎnzhōulǐ.

HĀĚRBĪN 哈尔滨
☎ 0451 / pop 4,757,000

If a city of more than four million people can be considered relaxing, Hāěrbīn is so – at least if you join the strollers and shoppers wandering its tree-lined streets and river-front promenade. One of the largest cities in northeastern China, Hāěrbīn is influenced by its relationship with nearby Russia and dotted with architectural gems handed down from the Russian era. Plenty of first-rate snack shops line the streets too, and restaurants serve rib-sticking fare to sustain you as you explore sights ranging from Russian Ortho-dox churches and Buddhist temples to the grim remains of a germ warfare base.

History
In 1896 Russia negotiated a contract to build a railway line from Vladivostok to Hāěrbīn and Dàlián (in Liáoníng province), which brought Russian workers to the region. In the early 1900s large numbers of Russian refugees fled to Hāěrbīn as well. Although the Japanese gained control of the railway after Russia's defeat in the Russo-Japanese War (1904–05), the Russian imprint on Hāěrbīn remained in one way or another until the end of WWII.

Many of the Russian émigrés were Jewish, and by the 1920s Hāěrbīn's Jewish population topped 20,000. The little that remains of this Jewish legacy is on display in a museum of Jewish history and culture housed in a former Hāěrbīn synagogue.

Following the Japanese invasion of Manchu-ria in 1931, the Japanese occupied Hāěrbīn until 1945, when the Soviet army wrested the city back. The following year, as agreed by Chiang Kaishek and Stalin, Kuomintang troops were installed, marking the end of the Russian era.

Hāěrbīn, which derives its name from *alejin* (Manchu for 'honour' or 'fame'), is a sprawling largely industrial city. Russia is once again a major trading partner for this region, and most foreign faces on the streets are Russian.

Orientation
The Dàolǐqū district, just south of the Son-ghua River (Sōnghūa Jiāng), houses most of the historical buildings that give the city its character. North of the river is Sun Island Park (Tàiyángdǎo Gōngyuán); beyond the park, the city is expanding further northward with a number of development projects under way.

The main train station is in the centre of town, opposite the long-distance bus station. Several blocks southeast of the station, along Dongdazhi Jie and nearby Guogeli Dajie, is the main shopping district.

Information
BOOKSHOP
Xinhua Bookshop (Xīnhuá Shūdiàn; 368 Guogeli Dajie) Has a small selection of English-language books, mostly 19th-century novels.

CD BURNING
Photo shop (Zhongyang Dajie; Y15) Near the Flood Control Monument.

INTERNET ACCESS 网吧
Internet bar (wǎngbā; 2nd fl, Hāěrbīn train station; per hr Y3-4) It's even a no-smoking zone!
Yidu Kongjian Wangba (27 Hongzhuan Jie; per hr Y2; ⏱ 24hr) Off Zhongyang Dajie.

MONEY
Most large hotels will also change money.
Bank of China (Zhōngguó Yínháng) Main office (☎ 5363 3518; 19 Hongjun Jie; ⏱ 8.30am-noon & 1-4.30pm) Dàolǐqū (37 Zhaolin Jie; ⏱ 8.30am-4.30pm) Both offices have 24-hour ATMs and will cash travellers cheques.

POST
Post office (yóujú) Dàolǐqū (115 Zhongyang Dajie; ⏱ 8.30am-8pm); train station area (Tielu Jie; ⏱ 8.30am-5pm) The Dàolǐqū branch is between Xi Wu Jie and Xi Liu Jie. The branch in the train station area is to the right as you exit.

PUBLIC SECURITY BUREAU
PSB (Gōngānjú; 26 Duan Jie; ⏱ 8.40am-noon & 1.30-4.30pm Mon-Fri)

TELEPHONE
China Telecom (Zhōngguó Diànxìn; 420 Guogeli Dajie) There's also a telephone office on the 2nd floor of the train station.

TRAVEL AGENCIES
Most midrange and top-end hotels have travel services that book tickets and arrange tours throughout the province.
China International Travel Service (CITS; Zhōngguó Guójì Lǚxíngshè; ☎ 5366 1191; fax 5366 1190; 68 Hongjun Jie)
Harbin Modern Travel Company (☎ 8488 4433; 89 Zhongyang Dajie) This office at Mǎdié'ěr Bīnguǎn offers ski trips to Yàbùlì.

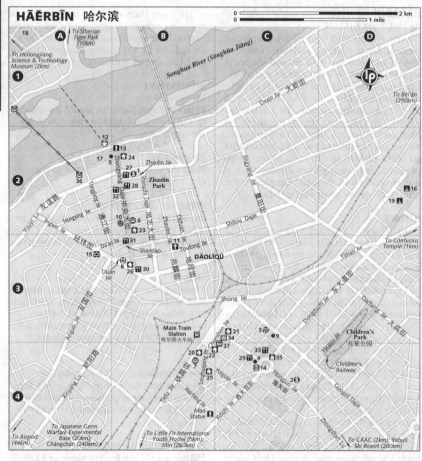

HĀĚRBĪN 哈尔滨

Sights

DÀOLǏQŪ 道里区

Hāěrbīn's Russian legacy lives on in the Dàolǐqū area, along cobblestone-lined Zhongyang Dajie – a pedestrian plaza – and on the surrounding side streets. Though the early-1900s buildings here are now shops, restaurants and hotels, much of the architecture still shows a strong Russian influence, with spires, cupolas and scalloped turrets.

CHURCH OF ST SOPHIA 圣索菲亚教堂

The **Church of St Sophia** (Shèng Suǒfēiyà Jiàotáng; cnr Zhaolin Jie & Toulong Jie; admission Y25; ⏰ 8.30am-5pm), one of Hāěrbīn's most photographed landmarks, is a Russian Orthodox church built in 1907. The church now houses the **Harbin**

Architecture Arts Centre, which displays black-and-white photographs of Hāěrbīn from the early 1900s (captions are in Chinese only).

STALIN PARK 斯大林公园

Locals and visitors alike congregate year-round in **Stalin Park** (Sīdàlín Gōngyuán). The tree-lined promenade, dotted with statues, playgrounds and cafés, is built along a 42km-long embankment that was built to curb the unruly Songhua River. The odd **Flood Control Monument** (Fánghóng Shènglì Jìniàntǎ), built in 1958, commemorates the thousands of people who died in years past when the river overflowed its banks.

In winter, head to the Songhua River for ice-skating, ice hockey, tobogganing and even ice sailing. Equipment for these sports can be hired from vendors along the riverbank. Slightly madder folk astound onlookers by swimming in gaps in the ice.

SUN ISLAND PARK 太阳岛公园

Across the river from Stalin Park is **Sun Island Park** (Tàiyángdǎo Gōngyuán), a 3800-hectare recreational zone offering gardens, forested areas and a 'water world'. In winter it has its own snow-sculpture exhibition. The excellent hands-on **Heilongjiang Science and Technology Museum** (黑龙江省科技馆; Hēilóngjiāngshěng Kējìguǎn; ☎ 8819 0188; admission Y20; 🕑 9am-4.30pm Tue-Sun) is at the west end of the park.

Buy a boat ticket (Y5) from one of the government-run ticket vendors (guóyíng chuánpiào), whose dock is directly north of the Flood Control Monument. Private boat operators, whose touts aggressively seek out customers, charge Y10. You can also take a cable car (one way/return Y30/50) to Sun Island Park from the end of Tongjiang Jie.

SIBERIAN TIGER PARK 东北虎林园

The mission of the **Siberian Tiger Park** (Dōngběi Hǔ Línyuán; ☎ 8808 0098; www.dongbeihu.net.cn in Chinese; 88 Songbei Jie; adult/child Y50/25; 🕑 8am-4.30pm, last tour 4pm) is to study, breed, release and ultimately save the Manchurian tiger from extinction. Though protected by the Chinese government and recognised as an endangered species

worldwide, the tigers' situation remains perilous. Estimates put the remaining number of Siberian tigers living in the wild at fewer than 400, with most in eastern Russia, North Korea and northeastern China.

As you drive safari-like through the fenced-off fields, you get an up-close look at more than 100 of these animals, as well as African lions and a pair of rare white tigers. Although the park reported a baby boom in 2006, with more than 80 tiger cubs born, it's not clear how the park is preparing these animals for the wild, with the minibus drivers encouraging passengers to buy live chickens – or whole cows – to throw to the tigers.

The park is located roughly 15km north of the city. From the northwest corner of Youyi Lu and Zhongyang Dajie in Dàolǐqū, take bus 65 west to its terminus, then walk a block east to get bus 85, heading north on Hayao Lu. The terminus of Bus 85 is about 2km from the park; minicabs take you from there to the entrance (Y15 to Y20 per person, return). Alternatively, a taxi from the city centre is about Y100 return). You can combine the trip with a visit to Sun Island Park. Bus 85 stops at the western end of Sun Island Park en route between the city and the tiger park.

JEWISH MUSEUM 哈尔滨犹太新会堂

In the 1920s the **Hāěrbīn New Synagogue** (Hāěrbīn Yóutài Xīnhuìtáng; 162 Jingwei Jie; admission Y25; 🕑 8.30am-

5pm) was the centre of the city's small but influential Jewish community, most of whom had emigrated east from Russia over the preceding 20 years. The building was converted to a museum in 2004. The 2nd and 3rd floors house interesting exhibits about the history and cultural life of Hāĕrbīn's Jews in the early 20th century; the 1st floor is an (unrelated) architecture exhibition about construction projects under way in the city, including the new Hāĕrbīn subway system.

GERM WARFARE BASE
侵华日军地731部队遗址

In 1939 the Japanese army set up a top-secret germ warfare research centre in Hāĕrbīn, where medical experts performed gruesome experiments on Chinese, Soviet, Korean, Mongolian and British prisoners of war. Over 4000 people were exterminated: some were frozen or infected with bubonic plague, others were injected with syphilis and many were roasted alive in furnaces.

The history of these war horrors is on view at the **Japanese Germ Warfare Experimental Base – 731 Division** (Qīnhuá Rìjūn Dì 731 Bùduì Yízhǐ; ☎ 8680 1556; Xinjiang Dajie; admission Y20; ⏰ 9-11.30am & 1-5pm, last entry 4pm), where grim photos and sculptures illustrate various tortures. In videotaped interviews (with English subtitles), Japanese officers describe what went on at the base with eerie detachment.

The museum is about 20km south of the city, a 45-minute trip on bus 343 from the train station area; board near the post office on Tielu Jie. When you get off the bus, walk in the same direction (west) until you cross the train tracks; the base is on the right.

TEMPLES
To reach these temples, take bus 14 from the train station. Get off when the bus bears right off Dongdazhi Jie onto Yiman Jie. To the Buddhist Pagoda and Temple of Bliss, cross Yiman Jie and walk north to Dongdazhi Jie, which is a pedestrian plaza in front of the temples. To the Confucius Temple, go instead through the arch on the south side of Yiman Jie; it's about a 10-minute walk along Wen Miao Jie.

Seven-Tiered Buddhist Pagoda
七级浮屠塔

Hēilóngjiāng's temple complex, the **Seven-tiered Buddhist Pagoda** (Qījí Fútú Tǎ; 11 Dongdazhi Jie; admission Y10; ⏰ 8.30am-4pm) was built in 1924.

The elegant stone pagoda in the middle of the courtyard makes a great photo op with the Ferris wheel in the adjacent park! The illustrations along the back wall tell classical stories of filial piety. Tickets include admission to the Temple of Bliss next door.

Temple of Bliss 吉乐寺
There's an active Buddhist community in residence at the serene **Temple of Bliss** (Jí Lè Sì; 9 Dongdazhi Jie; ⏰ 8.30am-4pm). The many statues here include Milefo (Maitreya), the Buddha yet-to-come, whose arrival will bring paradise on earth.

Confucius Temple 文庙
This peaceful and seemingly little-visited **temple** (Wén Miào; 25 Wen Miao Jie; admission Y15; ⏰ 8.30am-4pm) claims to be the largest Confucian temple in northeastern China. It was built in 1929.

HEILONGJIANG PROVINCIAL MUSEUM
黑龙江省博物馆

This rather musty **museum** (Hēilóngjiāng Shěng Bówùguǎn; ☎ 5364 4151; 48-50 Hongjun Jie; admission Y10; ⏰ 9am-4pm) may appeal to the archaeologically inclined, with displays showcasing huge dinosaur skeletons and other finds from digs around the province. Also on view is fishskin clothing worn by the Hezhen minority. On the museum's lower level is the **Sea World** aquarium (Y40).

The museum is about a 10-minute walk from the train station; alternatively, take bus 64 from Dàolǐqū.

Festivals & Events
The **Ice Lantern Festival** (Bīngdēng Jié; ☎ 8625 0068; admission to main area Y80, other prices vary), Hāĕrbīn's main winter attraction, is held in Zhaolin Park and along the Songhua River. Fanciful and elaborate ice sculptures in the shapes of animals, plants, buildings or motifs taken from legends sparkle in the frigid air; they've even included a miniature Great Wall and a scaled-down Forbidden City. At night the sculptures are illuminated with coloured lights, turning the area into a temporary fantasy world. Figure-skating shows, hockey tournaments and other winter events round out the calendar. Officially, the festival runs from 5 January to 15 February, although it frequently starts a week earlier and glistens into March. The main entrance is by the Flood Control Monument.

Sleeping

The most convenient places to stay are along Zhongyang Dajie in Dàolǐqū or in one of the many hotels that surround the train station. During the Ice Lantern Festival, expect hotel prices to jump at least 20%.

BUDGET

Little Fir International Youth Hostel (小杉树国际 青年旅馆; Xiǎo Shānshù Guójì Qīngnián Lǚguǎn; ☎ 8300 5008; www.hihostels.com; 83 Xuefu Lu; 学府路83号; dm/d Y25/120; 🖳) Hāěrbīn's Hostelling International affiliate is set in a traditional courtyard house down a lane in the city's university district. The dorm beds are the cheapest in town, and the doubles are a good deal too, so book ahead. Internet access costs Y3 per hr and breakfast is Y3. Though not much English is spoken here, the staff try to make you feel at home.

Take bus 11 or 343 from the train station for about 20 minutes to 'Medical University, 2nd Hospital' (医大二院; Yīdà Èryuàn); continue walking south about three blocks, and turn right at the hostel's sign.

Zhōngdà Dàjiǔdiàn (☎ 8463 8888; fax 8465 2888; 32-40 Zhongyang Dajie; 中央大街32-40号; d Y240-288, tr 388; 🞫) This budget accommodation has spacious rooms and a prime location on Zhongyang Dajie. Discounts bring doubles under Y150, which is dirt cheap for pricy Dàolǐqū, though the whole place (especially the formerly pink carpets) could use a good scrub. Look for the English sign that says 'Big Hotel of Inside'.

MIDRANGE

Tiānzhú Bīnguǎn (☎ 8647 2109; fax 5364 3720; 6 Songhua-jiang Jie; 松花江街6号; s Y248, d Y130, d with bathroom Y208-298, tr Y298; 🞫) This oldie-but-goodie tower has the best-value midrange rooms near the train station; prices include breakfast. Many of the doubles have been nicely updated, and the triples are huge.

Lóngyún Bīnguǎn (☎ 8283 0102; Huochezhan Zhanqian Guangchang; 火车站站前广场; s Y258, d Y268-348, tr Y358; 🞫) Another good choice in the train station area, this 10-storey hotel has well-kept rooms with high-speed internet connections. It's adjacent to the long-distance bus station. Ask for a south-facing room on a high floor if traffic noise bothers you; all rates include breakfast.

Mǎdié'ěr Bīnguǎn (Modern Hotel; ☎ 8461 5846; www .modern.com.cn in Chinese; 89 Zhongyang Dajie; 中央大街 89号; s Y280, d Y348-580; 🞫 🖳) Marble and carved woodwork decorate the common areas of this lovely hotel, built in 1906 by a member of Hāěrbīn's turn-of-the-century Jewish community. Most rooms are large with contemporary furnishings, although a few are older and cheaper (under Y250). The bountiful breakfast buffet is first-rate and is included in the rate.

Lóngmén Dàshà (☎ 8679 1888; 85 Hongjun Jie; 红军 街85号; tower bldg s/d Y480, tr Y870, original bldg d from Y680; 🞫) This hotel is essentially two lodgings in one: the elegant original building, built in 1901 and decked out with marble, gold and elaborate woodwork; and a newer, more prosaic tower. Bargain to get a double for under Y300; rates include breakfast.

TRYING TO GO GREEN?

China's northernmost province has historically been an industrial centre, and it's been plagued with the environmental consequences that heavy industry brings, including the 2005 toxic waste spill in the Songhua River that sent streams of dangerous chemicals coursing through the northeast.

Hēilóngjiāng is also endowed with a wealth of natural resources – more than 40% of the province's territory is forested, and there are more than 6000 lakes and reservoirs. The region is home to the rare Manchurian tiger (p391), and it's a nesting ground for endangered cranes (p398). Some of these resources have fuelled the region's industrial development; the province is a major supplier of wood to companies like furniture giant IKEA.

Yet government officials are beginning to consider the environment, at least as a way to draw tourists to the region's forests, lakes and hills. According to the World Wildlife Fund, Hēilóngjiāng province created 24 new protected forest or wetland areas between 2002 and 2005, and has committed to adding another one million hectares to the protected list by 2010. If that goal is reached, 14% of the province's land area will be under government protection.

Too little too late? Or the dawning of a new era of environmental awareness and developing ecotourism? Only time will tell.

BREAKFAST OF CHAMPIONS

At many midrange hotels throughout northeastern China you can begin your day with a hearty breakfast buffet. Don't expect Western-style bacon and eggs, but you won't go hungry either. The lavish morning spreads typically start with a variety of cold vegetable dishes: perhaps spicy cabbage, wild greens with peanuts or pickled radishes. Hot dishes might include stewed pork, tender eggplant or bean-curd noodles.

Hard-boiled eggs, often bubbling in soy sauce, are a staple, as are puffy steamed breads. And don't forget the congee – plain rice, rice with beans, corn or millet are all cooked into comfortingly soupy hot cereals. If you're lucky, there'll be nut-filled cookies or sugary bean buns to sate the sweet tooth, and you'll be set till supper time.

TOP END

Songhuajiang Gloria Inn (Sōnghuājiāng Kǎilái Shāngwù Jiǔdiàn; ☎ 8463 8855; www.giharbin.com; 257 Zhongyang Dajie; 中央大街257号; d Y588-688; ✕) Half a block from Stalin Park, this inn offers plush rooms in a prime location.

Kūnlún Fàndiàn (☎ 5361 6688; www.hljkunlun.com; 8 Tielu Jie; 铁路街8号; s Y538, d Y538-888, ste Y1188-1388 plus 15% service charge; ✕ ☐) To your right as you exit the train station, this first-class hotel is an oasis of calm with a billiard room, sauna and several restaurants.

Eating

Stroll along Zhongyang Dajie for bakeries, restaurants and bars. Another cool restaurant and bar district is around Guogeli Dajie, near Children's Park.

Dōngfāng Jiǎozi Wáng (Kingdom of Eastern Dumplings; dumplings Y4-8; ✓ lunch & dinner; Dàolǐqū ☎ 8465 3920; 39 Zhongyang Dajie; train station area ☎ 5364 2885; 72 Hongjun Jie) This always-busy dumpling chain serves royal helpings of *jiǎozi* (饺子; dumplings) with a large choice of fillings; try the greens with egg. English menu. The Hongjun Jie branch is a 10-minute walk south of the train station, behind the Overseas Chinese Hotel.

Lǎo Chāng Chūnbǐng (Lao Chang Spring Pancakes; ☎ 8468 5000; lower level, 178 Zhongyang Dajie; dishes Y12-18; ✓ lunch & dinner) A popular local speciality, *chūnbǐng* (春饼) are flat tortilla-like pancakes. Order a variety of fillings to slather on your pancake; then roll it up and eat. One favourite is the spicy-tangy *xiāng là ròu sī* (香辣肉丝), which is pork with coriander and dried hot pepper.

Cafe Russia 1914 (☎ 8456 3207; 57 Xi Toudao Jie; dishes Y18-48, coffees Y18-25, teas Y8-15; ✓ lunch & dinner) This peaceful Russian tearoom just off Zhongyang Dajie looks like grandmother's parlour, filled with old photos and knick-

knacks. Linger over coffee or tea, or dig into hearty home-style dishes like stuffed cabbage and puffy *piroshki*.

Cafe de Eife French Bakery (Āifēi Kāfēidiàn; ☎ 8911 3753; 185 Zhongyang Dajie; pastries Y5-7, coffees Y15-20; ✓ 9am-9pm) Take a break in this tiny corner café stocked with English-language newspapers and international magazines. The Parisian-style pastries go well with espresso.

Outside Mǎdié'ěr Bīnguǎn, a busy snack shop serves kebabs, dumplings and ice cream (Y2 to Y5); nearby, a **food market** (96 Zhongyang Dajie; ✓ 8.30am-8pm) has stalls offering buns, cookies, sausages, fruits and sweets.

About a 15-minute walk from the train station – east of Hongjun Jie and north of Dongdazhi Jie – is a night market, with vendors hawking kebabs, grilled squid and other nibbles.

Entertainment

Běiběi Hànbīng Díshìgāo (Beibei Dry Ice Disco; admission Y20; ✓ 9am-midnight) Underground entertainment takes on a new meaning at this disco/roller-skating rink that is literally underground. It's in the underground shopping centre opposite the train station; take the stairs down from the southwest corner of Hongjun Jie. Admission includes skate hire, but bring your own earplugs.

Shopping

Zhongyang Dajie is lined with department stores, stylish boutiques and souvenir shops, many of which hawk Russian-inspired goods.

Dongdazhi Jie, in the city centre southeast of the train station, is another major shopping street. Below the street, the Hongbo Century Square (Hóngbó Shìjì Guangchang; 红博世纪广场) shopping complex extends for blocks underground.

Getting There & Away

All the large hotels can book airline and train tickets.

AIR

Civil Aviation Administration of China (CAAC; Zhōngguó Mínháng; ☎ 8262 7070; 101 Zhongshan Lu) is in the CAAC Hotel.

Both Air China and **Asiana Airlines** (www .flyasiana.com) fly nonstop to Seoul (Y3200, 2½ hours). China Southern has flights to Khabarovsk (Y1800, 1½ hours) in Siberia and to Vladivostok (1¼ hours). Russian carrier **Vladivostok Avia** (☎ 8228 9471; www.vladavia.ru) flies between Hāěrbīn and Vladivostok (1¼ hours) on Tuesdays and Fridays.

From Hāěrbīn, you can fly to a huge number of domestic destinations, including Běijīng (Y960, one hour and 50 minutes), Shànghǎi (Y1780, two hours and 40 minutes), Shēnzhèn (Y2700, six hours) and Dàlián (Y840, 1½ hours).

BUS

The main long-distance bus station is directly opposite the train station. Buses leave for Mǔdānjiāng at least every 30 minutes (Y60 to Y81, four hours). Other buses run hourly to Qíqíhā'ěr (Y61, 3½ hours) and throughout the day to Jílín (Y61, four hours) and Shěnyáng (Y140, 6½ hours).

At the time of writing, a new international bus service was slated to begin operating between Hāěrbīn and Vladivostok; check at the long-distance bus station for details.

TRAIN

Hāěrbīn is a major rail transport hub with routes throughout the northeast and beyond, including daily service to the following cities:

Destination	Seat/Sleeper Price	Duration
Běijīng	Y154/281	12-13hr
Chángchūn	Y35-41	2½-3hr
Dàlián	Y125/231	9-10hr
Mǔdānjiāng	Y50	4½-5hr
Qíqíhā'ěr	Y50	3-4hr
Shěnyáng	Y76	6hr
Suífēnhé	Y76/143	9hr

To Běijīng, there's also a nightly express train, the Z16 (Y429 soft-sleeper only), which departs at 8.27pm and arrives the next morning at 7.07am.

Trains depart from Hāěrbīn to Vladivostok via Suífēnhé on Wednesdays and Saturdays.

Travellers on the Trans-Siberian Railway to or from Moscow can start or finish in Hāěrbīn (six days). Contact the **Hāěrbīn Railway International Tourist Agency** (哈尔滨铁道国际旅行社; Hāěrbīn Tiědào Guójì Lǚxíngshè; 7th fl, Kūnlún Fàndiàn, 8 Tielu Jie) for information on travelling through to Russia. CITS may also be able to help.

Getting Around

TO/FROM THE AIRPORT

Hāěrbīn's airport is 46km from the city centre. From the airport, shuttle buses (Y20) will drop you at the railway station or the CAAC office. To the airport, shuttles leave regularly from the CAAC office until 6.30pm. A taxi will take 45 minutes to an hour (Y100 to Y125).

BUS

Hāěrbīn's many buses (Y1 to Y2) include buses 101 and 103 which run along Shangzhi Dajie from Stalin Park to the train station. Bus 109 runs from the train station to Children's Park. Bus 64 goes from Dàolǐqū to the Provincial Museum.

At the time of writing, a subway system was under construction, with the first line slated to open in 2007 or 2008.

AROUND HĀĚRBĪN

Yabuli Ski Resort 亚布力滑雪中心

The biggest ski resort in China, Yabuli (Yàbùlì Huáxuě Zhōngxīn), 200km southeast of Hāěrbīn, has 11 runs and nine lifts on Mt Daguokui (Dàguōkuī Shān). Weather permitting; the ski season lasts from December through March.

CITS and other travel agencies in Hāěrbīn (see p389) offer ski packages that include transport, ski passes, equipment rental and accommodation. One-day trips start at around Y400.

If you want to stay overnight, lodging is available at Windmill Village (the resort village) or in several small hotels in nearby Yàbùlì village where beds can often be found for under Y100. Both **Windmill Village** (☎ 0451-5345 5088; fax 0451-5345 5138; www.yabuliski.com; d Y380-780) and the company's Běijīng **sales office** (☎ 010-6463 6126; fax 010-6463 6126) can make bookings for stays in the resort village. In winter, lodging owners in Yàbùlì village will likely find you when you exit the train or bus.

Buses and trains to Yàbùlì depart from Hāěrbīn (Y30 to Y40, three hours) and Mǔdānjiāng (Y14 to Y24, two hours). Minibuses in Yàbùlì village run to the ski resort.

MǓDĀNJIĀNG 牡丹江

☎ 0453 / pop 767,000

A nondescript city of more than half a million people, Mǔdānjiāng's main interest to independent travellers is as a transit point to nearby Jìngpò Hú (Mirror Lake) and the Underground Forest.

Information

Bank of China (中国银行; Zhōngguó Yínháng; ☎ 692 9833; 9 Taiping Lu; ⏰ 8am-4pm Mon-Fri) This office, two blocks south of the train station, will cash travellers cheques. There's a 24-hour ATM one block further south.

China Telecom (中国电信; Zhōngguó Diànxìn; Dongyi Tiaolu) One block east of the post office.

CITS (中国国际旅行社; Zhōngguó Guójì Lǚxíngshè; ☎ 691 1944; 34 Jingfu Jie; ⏰ 8am-5pm) The helpful staff at this office, two blocks east of Taiping Lu, organise day trips to Jingpò Hú. They can also book air and train tickets, and arrange discounted lodging at the lake or in Mǔdānjiāng.

Internet bar (网吧; wǎngbā; per hr Y2) In the lane facing Běilóng Dàjiǔdiàn.

Post office (邮局; yóudiàn; Taiping Lu; ⏰ 8am-5.30pm Mon-Fri) Three blocks south of the bank.

Public Security Bureau (PSB; 公安局; Gōngānjú; Guanghua Jie) Two blocks west of the train station.

Sleeping & Eating

Mǔdānjiāng Fàndiàn (牡丹江饭店; ☎ 692 5833; fax 699 7779; 128 Guanghua Jie; 光花街128号; dm Y20-30, d Y80-140, tr Y168) This budget hotel is convenient if you're just passing through town. When you exit the train station, turn left, walk one block and cross the street to the hotel.

Běilóng Dàjiǔdiàn (北龙大酒店; ☎ 812 8888; 68 Dongyitiao Lu; 东一条路68号; s Y310-360, d Y330-380, ste Y530; 🖳) This midrange tower has standard doubles, as well as a 'garden wing' with rooms in a pseudo-traditional courtyard. Rates include breakfast; check with CITS about discounts. From the station, walk south on Taiping Lu and turn left onto Qixing Jie; the hotel is one block ahead on the right.

Shuānglóng Jiǎozi Wáng (双龙饺子王; Double Dragon Dumpling King; ☎ 691 2111; Qixing Jie; dishes Y8-20; ⏰ lunch & dinner) Good jiǎozi (饺子) and ribsticking northeastern dishes that you choose from a display of ingredients make this eatery popular with local families.

Dongyibuxing Jie, southeast of the train station, is a pedestrian mall with a night market selling kebabs, noodles and other snacks.

Getting There & Away

Mǔdānjiāng has rail and bus connections to Hāěrbīn (Y50, five hours), Suífēnhé (Y30, four to five hours), Yánjí (Y22, seven hours), Túmén (Y20, six hours), Jiāmùsì (Y21, eight hours) and Dōngjīng (Y6, 1¼ hours). Long-distance buses arrive and depart from in front of the train station.

CITS books airline tickets. Flight destinations include Běijīng (Y1190, two hours), Shànghǎi (Y1830, two hours and 20 minutes) and Guǎngzhōu (Y2600, six hours). A taxi to the airport will cost about Y45.

AROUND MǓDĀNJIĀNG

Jìngpò Hú 镜泊湖

The clear reflections of the tree-lined shore and small islands within **Jìngpò Hú** (Mirror Lake; admission Y50) leave no question about why it has been named Mirror Lake. Covering an area of 90 sq km and 45km in length, the lake was formed on the bend of the Mudan River 5000 years ago by the falling lava of five volcanic explosions. Jìngpò Hú is about 100km southwest of Mǔdānjiāng.

Ferries (Y80, two hours) make leisurely tours of the lake, or you can hike along the lakeshore. Near the lake is the **Diaoshuilou Waterfall**, 20m tall and 40m wide; it swells in size during the rainy season but can dry to a trickle at other times of year.

Jìngpò Hú is extremely popular with busloads of Chinese tourists who roll up during the summer months. Visiting during low season, from October to May, is more peaceful, but many hotels and restaurants shut down outside of the summer season.

There's not a lot to do here to occupy more than a day, but if you want to stay over you can choose from more than 50 hotels that encircle the lake. It's worth checking first with CITS in Mǔdānjiāng (see left), since the office can arrange discounted bookings. Expect to pay around Y25 for dorm beds, Y140 for budget doubles and Y280 for midrange doubles.

Many small restaurants at the park entrance and near the lake serve local fish, but ask for prices before you sit down, since fish can run upwards of Y150.

The easiest way to get to Jìngpò Hú is on the direct bus from Mǔdānjiāng that leaves the train station parking lot at 7.30am (one way/return Y20/40, two hours) and departs from the lake at 4.30pm. Outside the summer season the bus may depart and return earlier, so confirm the time.

Regular trains run from Mǔdānjiāng to Dōngjīng (Y6, 1¼ hours). From there it's one hour by minibus (Y10) to the lake, but these buses run only from June to September; at other times you'll have to take a taxi (Y150 to Y200 return).

At Jìngpò Hú, trams take visitors from the park gate to the lake and the waterfall (Y10 per ride).

Underground Forest 地下森林

Although called the **Underground Forest** (Dìxià Sēnlín; admission Y40; June-Sep), the forest has actually grown within the craters of volcanoes that erupted some 10,000 years ago. Hiking around the lush pine forest and several of the 10 craters takes about an hour.

The forest is 50km from Jìngpò Hú. Some of the Mǔdānjiāng–Jìngpò Hú buses add a stop at the forest for an additional Y40; ask before you set out. Otherwise, take a bus or train from Mǔdānjiāng to Dōngjīng and from there change to a minibus for the forest. You can take a taxi from the lake gate to the forest, but drivers charge at least Y200 return.

QÍQÍHĀ'ĚR 齐齐哈尔
☎ 0452 / pop 895,000

Qíqíhā'ěr, a predominantly industrial city 250km northwest of Hāěrbīn, is a gateway to the Zhalong Nature Reserve, a bird-watching area 30km southeast of town. Its quirky name comes from the Daur word for 'borderland'.

Though not really a tourist destination, Qíqíhā'ěr is pleasant enough, with several parks dotting the city; the largest, Longsha Park (龙沙公园; Lóngshā Gōngyuán), houses a small zoo, gardens and lakes. The city also has a mosque and a large Buddhist temple that are worth a look.

Orientation

The train station is east of the city centre. Longhua Lu heads west from the station to the main square, where you'll find the bank, post and telephone offices and shops. Longsha Park is west of the main square.

Information

Bank of China (中国银行; Zhōngguó Yínháng; ☎ 247 5674; 3 Bukui Dajie, off Longhua Lu; 8am-4.30pm Mon-Fri, 8.30am-4.30pm Sat & Sun) An ATM inside the bank accepts cards from several networks. There's a 24-hour ATM at 349 Longhua Lu, near the long-distance bus station.

China Telecom (中国电信; Zhōngguó Diànxìn; 10 Zhonghuan Lu) Next door to the post office on the main square.

CITS (中国国际旅行社; Zhōngguó Guójì Lǚxíngshè; ☎ 240 7538; fax 247 4646)

Internet bar (网吧; wǎngbā; 2nd fl, 342 Longhua Lu; per hr Y2) Opposite the train station, in the pink building between Báihè Bīnguǎn and Tiědào Fàndiàn.

Post office (邮局; yóujú; 6 Zhonghuan Lu; 8am-5pm Mon-Fri) On the main square at the corner of Bukui Dajie.

Public Security Bureau (PSB; 公安局; Gōngānjú; 57 Bukui Dajie; 8-11.30am & 1.30-5pm Mon-Fri) One block north of the Bank of China.

Sights

DACHENG TEMPLE 大乘寺

A towering Buddha greets visitors to this **temple complex** (Dàchéngsì; 449 Minghang Lu, at Zhanqian Dajie; 9am-3pm), set in park-like grounds south

---

WAITING...

If you have a day when Chinese bureaucracy is getting to you, pick up a copy of *Waiting*, the 1999 novel by Liáoníng-born, Hēilóngjiāng-educated author Ha Jin. It tells the story of a doctor in a fictional northeast China city who waits 18 years for the local government to grant him a divorce.

Author Jin, who now lives in the United States, has set many of his works in the Dōngběi region. A recurring theme is the effect of mind-numbing bureaucracy on day-to-day life. *The Crazed* takes place in the northeast around the 1989 Tiananmen Square uprising, while *In the Pond* follows an artist who suffers through a monotonous job in a northeastern fertiliser plant.

Waiting for your visa application to be processed? Stuck in a long line at the train station? Pick up a Ha Jin novel, and remember, it could be worse!

of the train station. Eight buildings are arranged around the main temple, which was constructed in 1939. Take bus 2 south on Zhanqian Jie.

BUKUI MUSLIM TEMPLE 卜奎清真寺
Built in the Chinese style in 1684 (and rebuilt in 1893), this **mosque** (Bǔkuí Qīngzhēnsì; 38 Qingzhen Lu; admission Y6; ☼ 8am-4.30pm) is on the west side of town. Non-Muslims can't enter the prayer hall, but you're free to look around. From the train station, take bus 13 or 101 to Bukui Dajie and walk two blocks west to the mosque.

Sleeping & Eating

Tiědào Fàndiàn (铁道饭店; Railway Hotel; ☎ 212 4579; 336 Longhua Lu; 龙华路336号; dm/s/d incl breakfast Y22/140/200) At this friendly budget hotel one block from Báihè Bīnguǎn, the rooms are aging but clean.

Báihè Bīnguǎn (白鹤宾馆; White Crane Hotel; ☎ 292 1112; fax 212 7639; 85 Zhanqian Dajie; 站前大街85号; dm Y28-50, s Y160-180, d Y170-260, tr Y240; ☒) This tower with helpful staff is to your left as you exit the train station. Rooms range from five-bed dorms to large comfortable doubles, with many options in between. All rates include breakfast.

Hóngfēng Huǒguō (红丰火锅; ☎ 247 7775; Zhonghuan Lu; 中环路; hotpots Y24-30; ☼ lunch & dinner) This bustling restaurant near Longsha Park serves delicious lamb hotpots in individual cook-your-own cauldrons. Solo diners can request half-orders.

The **Fu-Mart Shopping Centre** (132 Longhua Lu), several blocks east of the main square, sells buns, noodles and other prepared foods, as well as fruit, snacks and drinks. Between the main square and Longsha Park, many restaurants line Zhonghuan Lu and the surrounding streets.

Getting There & Around

Frequent trains run between Qíqíhā'ěr and Hāěrbīn; express trains (Y50) make the trip in 2½ hours, local trains (Y37) in 3½ hours. Overnight trains go to Běijīng (seat/sleeper Y182/333, 14½ hours). There are trains north to Běi'ān (北安; Y19) and Hēihé (seat/sleeper Y38/83). A train leaves for Hēihé at 6am, stopping in Běi'ān at 10.30am and arriving in Hēihé at 4.57pm. A second train to Běi'ān leaves at 4.05pm and arrives at 7.43pm.

The long-distance bus station is at 339 Longhua Lu, a five-minute walk west of the train

station. In summer a direct bus to Wǔdàlián Chí leaves at 8.30am (Y40, six hours). Buses north to Hēihé (Y70 to Y80, seven hours) depart daily at 8am and 5.30pm. Buses to Hāěrbīn (Y61, 3½ hours) leave hourly from the parking lot opposite the train station.

There are flights between Qíqíhā'ěr and Běijīng (Y1110, 1¾ hours) on Monday, Thursday and Saturday. A flight to Shànghǎi (Y1850, two hours and 50 minutes) departs on Tuesday and Friday and continues on to Guǎngzhōu (five hours and 50 minutes). An airport bus (Y5, 20 minutes) leaves from the **CAAC office** (☎ 242 4445; 12 Bukui Dajie) in the CAAC Hotel (Mínháng Dàshà) near the main square. There's also an airline ticket office in Báihè Bīnguǎn.

Several buses run along Longhua Lu between the train station and the city centre, including buses 13, 14, 101 and 103. Most buses run from 6am to 7pm.

Taxi fares start at Y6.

ZHALONG NATURE RESERVE
扎龙自然保护区
Bird-lovers flock to this **nature reserve** (Zhālóng Zìrán Bǎohùqū; admission Y20; ☼ 7am-5pm), home to some 260 bird species, including several types of rare cranes. Four of the species that migrate here are on the endangered list: the red-crowned crane, the white-naped crane, the Siberian crane and the hooded crane.

The red-crowned crane (see the boxed text, opposite) is particularly fragile; its numbers worldwide are estimated at only 2400, with roughly half living in northeastern China. The near-extinct bird is, ironically, the ancient symbol of immortality and longevity in Chinese, Korean and Japanese cultures.

One of China's first nature reserves, Zhālóng was set up in 1979. On a bird migration path that extends from the Russian Arctic down into Southeast Asia, the reserve is made up of about 210,000 hectares of wetlands. Hundreds of birds arrive from April to May, rear their young from June to August and depart from September to October. Unfortunately, a significant percentage of the birds visible to visitors live in zoo-like cages.

The best time to visit is in spring. In summer the mosquitoes can be more plentiful than the birds – take repellent!

Zhālóng is 30km from Qíqíhā'ěr. Minibuses travel to the reserve (Y8, one hour) from the corner of Longsha Lu and Zhanqian Dajie

---

CRANE COUNTRY

Northeastern China is home to several nature reserves established to protect endangered species of wild cranes. Zhalong Nature Reserve, near Qíqíhā'ěr in Hēilóngjiāng province is the most accessible and most visited of these sanctuaries, but intrepid bird-lovers may want to seek out the others.

The Xianghai (向海) National Nature Reserve, 310km west of Chángchūn in Jílín province, is on the migration path for Siberian cranes, and the rare red-crowned, white-naped and demoiselle cranes breed here. More than 160 bird species, including several of these cranes, have been identified at the Horqin (科尔沁) National Nature Reserve, which borders Xianghai in Inner Mongolia. North of Xianghai, in Jílín province, the Momoge (莫莫格) National Nature Reserve is also an important wetlands area and bird breeding site.

According to the World Health Organisation, scientists have yet to confirm the role of migratory birds, such as wild cranes, in the spread of avian influenza, although preliminary studies have raised concerns. Birds at the Zhalong Nature Reserve have been immunised against the virus, and at the time of writing, the Xianghai reserve had been closed to visitors, in part due to fears about bird flu and in part because a severe drought was threatening its wetlands areas. Check the status before planning a visit to any of these crane sanctuaries. For more information about China's crane population and these nature reserves, contact the **International Crane Foundation** (www.savingcranes.org).

---

near the Qíqíhā'ěr train station. They leave about once an hour between 6am and noon. The buses return from the reserve parking lot.

Another alternative is to take bus 7 or 9 from the train station and get off at Dàgǎngzi (大岗子); it's only about a five-minute ride. From there, shared vans leave frequently for the Zhǎlóng area and will drop you at the reserve. Locals pay Y5 to Y10, but the driver may ask you for Y20, so it's worth bargaining.

You can also hire a taxi to take you to the reserve. Expect to pay about Y150 return.

If you'd like to stay overnight, the somewhat basic **Zhǎlóng Bīnguǎn** (扎龙宾馆; ☎ 138 3622 7566; d Y168-268) is on the reserve grounds. Call ahead if you're arriving in low season to be sure the hotel is open.

WǓDÀLIÁN CHÍ 五大连池

☎ 0456

Wǔdàlián Chí is a nature reserve about 250km northwest of Hāěrbīn that has been turned into a 'volcano park'. In summer the area's mineral springs draw busloads of tourists, including many Russians, to slurp the allegedly curative waters. The town itself is rather dreary, but the surrounding area has enough exotic-looking lava fields, hot springs and volcanic craters to fill a day or two of exploring.

Don't worry about volcanic eruptions here. The most recent volcanic activity occurred in 1719 and 1720, when lava blocked the nearby

North River (Běi Hé) and formed a series of barrier lakes – the five interconnected lakes that give the area its name.

The best time to visit is between June and October when the weather is mildest. The Daur minority holds a three-day 'water-drinking festival' each year in early June.

The only way to see the sights is by taxi. Expect to pay around Y150 for a day-long loop taking in the lakes, volcanoes and caves.

Sights & Activities

LǍOHĒI SHĀN 老黑山

It's a steep one-hour (return) walk to the summit of **Laohei Mountain** (admission Y60; ⌚ 7.30am-4.30pm), one of the area's 14 volcanoes, but the reward is awesome views from the rim of the crater. Taxis take you to a parking area partway up the volcano where the walking trail begins. From here, it's also a short walk to **Shí Hǎi** (石海; Stone Sea), an expansive lava field that resembles an ocean of lava rocks.

LONGMEN 'STONE VILLAGE' 龙门后塞奇观观光区

At this impressive **lava field** (Lóngmén Hòusài Qíguān Guānguāngqū; admission Y40; ⌚ 9am-4.30pm) on the east side of town, you can stroll amongst the lava rocks on a network of boardwalks.

ICE CAVES

Elaborate ice sculptures lit with funky coloured lights fill both the **Lava Ice Cavern** (熔岩冰洞;

Róngyán Bīngdòng; admission Y30; ⊗ 9am-4.30pm) and the **Lava Snow Cavern** (熔岩雪洞; Róngyán Xuědòng; admission Y30; ⊗ 9am-4.30pm). Sure it's corny, but the sculptures are quite intricate. Rent a warm coat (Y5) if you don't have your own; the caves' temperature is a chilly -10°C year-round.

ZHONGLING TEMPLE 钟灵寺

High on a hill off the road to Lǎohēi Shān, this large **temple** (Zhōnglíng Sì; admission Y10) complex houses several fat golden Buddhas. A tall marble Buddha overlooks the whole place. It's about a 20-minute walk up to the temple from the road.

Sleeping & Eating

The following hotels are all on the main east–west road through the centre of town on either side of the traffic circle. From October to May many lodgings close or reduce their services.

Gōngrén Liáoyǎngyuàn (工人疗养院; Workers Sanatorium; ☎ 722 1569; fax 722 1814; dm/d/tr Y40/180/210; ⊗ May-Nov; 🖳) This complex east of the traffic circle is a popular destination for Russian tourists. The rooms are decent value, and the restaurant serves both Russian and Chinese food (breakfast Y15, dishes Y10 to Y20), including awesome *xī tǔdòu* (西土豆; 'western potatoes', aka French fries).

Dìshuì Wǔdàliánchí Bīnguǎn (地税五大连池宾馆; ☎ 722 3387; d Y140-200) This imposing structure next door to the Workers Sanatorium has airy (if basic) doubles, with run-down bathrooms.

Tiělù Bīnguǎn (铁路宾馆; Railway Guesthouse; ☎ 722 1962; dm Y40-50, d Y240-360) In park-like grounds west of the traffic circle, this red-roofed hotel has huge, light-filled doubles, as well as cheaper standard rooms with and without bathrooms. Make sure the hot water is working though.

One block south of the traffic circle, there's a market street with stalls selling fresh breads, dumplings and fruit.

Getting There & Away

Wǔdàlián Chí has a new bus station on the east side of town. A taxi from the station to most hotels will cost Y5.

In summer, direct buses to Wǔdàlián Chí depart daily from Hāěrbīn's long-distance bus station (Y95, 5½ hours) at 8.30am, 9am, 1.30pm and 4pm. There's also a direct bus daily in summer from Qíqíhā'ěr (Y40, six hours, 8.30am).

Otherwise, you have to travel first to Běi'ān (北安), where you change for a bus to Wǔdàlián Chí. Several trains to Běi'ān run from Hāěrbīn (Y25, 5½ to six hours) or Qíqíhā'ěr (Y27, four hours). Fast buses also travel between Hāěrbīn and Běi'ān (Y52, 4½ hours, six daily). Běi'ān's bus station is one block from the train station.

In Běi'ān buses depart frequently for Wǔdàlián Chí (Y11, 1½ hours). In spring and fall, buses leave Běi'ān at 10.50am, 12.40pm, 3.30pm; in summer there are at least eight buses daily in both directions.

From Běi'ān buses north to Hēihé (Y49, 3½ hours) depart at 8.30am, 11am and 1.30pm; trains to Hēihé are much slower (Y32, six hours).

RUSSIAN BORDERLANDS

Much of the northeastern border between China and Siberia follows the Black Dragon River (Hēilóng Jiāng), known to the Russians as the Amur River. Along the border it's possible to see Siberian forests and dwindling settlements of northern tribes, such as the Daur, Ewenki, Hezhen and Oroqen.

To visit these border regions, you may need permits; check with the PSB in Hāěrbīn (p389). Take a small medical kit, insect repellent and warm clothing.

Major towns in the far north include Mòhé and Hēihé. On the eastern border, Suífēnhé is a gateway to Vladivostok.

Mòhé 漠河

Natural wonders are the attraction in Mòhé, China's northernmost town, dubbed the Arctic of China. In mid-June, the sun is visible for as long as 22 hours. The aurora borealis (northern lights) are another colourful phenomenon here.

Mòhé holds the record for China's lowest plunge of the thermometer: -52.3°C, recorded in 1956. On a normal winter day a temperature of -40°C is common.

An airport is under construction in the Mòhé region, slated to open in 2008. In the meantime, getting to Mòhé requires a train trip north from Qíqíhā'ěr to Jiāgédáqí in Inner Mongolia, then another to Gǔlián, followed by a 34km bus ride.

Hēihé 黑河

Both Chinese tourists and Russian traders are beating a path across the Black Dragon River in Hēihé, a small city across from the Russian river port of Blagoveshchensk. To visit Blagoveshchensk, you need a Russian tourist visa, as well as a re-entry visa for China, both of which must be arranged in Běijīng, so plan ahead.

Boats for Russia, as well as the customs and immigration facilities, are on **Dà Hēihé Dǎo** (Big Black River Island), at the eastern end of Hēihé's waterfront promenade. Also on the island is **International Market City** (Dà Hēihé Guójì Shāngmào Chéng), where Chinese and Russian traders haggle over wholesale shoes and bras. A bridge across the river between the two countries is in the planning stages.

Those without a Russian visa can settle for an hour-long cruise of Black Dragon River (Y10), departing from various points along the riverfront.

If you want to explore minority regions from here, one option is to contact Canada-based **Access China Tours** (☎ 1-800-788-1399; www .accesschinatours.com). It offers group tours of the northeastern provinces, and can also help individuals or small groups arrange a day-trip (or longer) to an Oroqen village 200km from Hēihé.

Two trains a day run to and from Hāěrbīn (seat/sleeper Y92/165, 12 hours). Buses also travel to Hāěrbīn, Běi'ān and Qíqíhā'ěr.

Suífēnhé 绥芬河

Like other borderland outposts, Suífēnhé is seeing an increasing amount of cross-border trade and tourism. To cross the border into Russia from here, you need to have organised a Russian visa in Běijīng.

Suífēnhé is linked by rail to Hāěrbīn (seat/sleeper Y76/143, nine hours) and Mǔdānjiāng (Y30, four to five hours). There is a twice-weekly international passenger train for Vladivostok.

Shānxī 山西

Despite mountainous terrain and a generally inhospitable climate, Shānxī was long a coveted square on the chessboard. Wedged between ancient capitals of the Chinese heartland and the grasslands to the north, the area was a key centre of trade and cultural exchange – as well as bearing witness to centuries of war. But continuous fighting brought more than just destruction; it provided an impetus for Buddhism's philosophy to take root. No other part of China devoted so much early patronage to the religion, and the vestiges, from the Yungang Caves to Tang dynasty temples near Wǔtái Shān, are among the oldest Buddhist sites in China.

One of the major reasons Shānxī has such an impressive collection of rare old buildings and cultural relics is undoubtedly the parched landscape. Left only to farm, Shānxī's inhabitants would have had a dismal time of it, as there is little here that facilitates agriculture. What kept the economy alive over the years was a booming trade in salt, tea, silk, grain and wool, carted back and forth between southern China and Mongolia.

Unfortunately, the province was poorly positioned to take advantage of the 20th century's changes. Isolated by mountain ranges, the region began a long slide back into obscurity, and has found itself having to rely entirely on its enormous resources of coal and ore.

Visiting Shānxī is thus somewhat akin to sitting on a seesaw: the high end rises to see northern China at its traditional best – sacred Buddhist mountains, ancient architecture and the Great Wall – while the other end dips perilously into a future shrouded in coal dust, refinery smoke and all the other environmental ills of the energy-hungry dragon.

HIGHLIGHTS

- Find inspiration – artistic, historic or spiritual – at the Buddhist **Yungang Caves** (p416)
- Pedal a bike through the old-timey streets of **Píngyáo** (p407)
- Ascend sacred peaks and chat with monks at **Wǔtái Shān** (p411)
- Delve into the province's fascinating past at the **Shanxi Museum** (p405) in Tàiyuán
- Set out in search of the fragmented remains of the **Great Wall** (p417)

- POPULATION: 33.3 MILLION

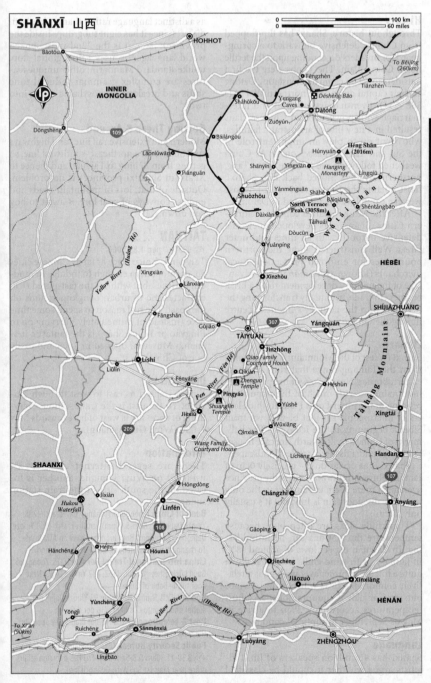

SHĀNXĪ 山西

0   100 km
0   60 miles

HOHHOT

INNER MONGOLIA

To Běijīng (260km)

Bǎotóu

Fēngzhèn

Tiānzhèn

Dōngshèng

109

Shāhūkǒu

Yúngāng Caves

Déshèng Bǎo

Dàtóng

Zuǒyún

Lǎoniúwān

Báilángōu

Húnyuán

Héng Shān ▲ (2016m)

Shānyīn

Yìngxiàn

Hanging Monastery

Línggiū

Piánguān

Shuòzhōu

Yànménguān

Shāhé

Bǎiqiáng

Wǔtái Shān

Shéntángbǎo

Yellow River (Huáng Hé)

Dàixiàn

North Terrace Peak (3058m)

Táihuái ▲

Xingxiàn

Yuánpíng

Dòucūn

Lánxiàn

Dōngyě

HÉBĚI

Fāngshān

Xīnzhōu

SHÍJIĀZHUĀNG

Gǔjiāo

307

TÀIYUÁN

Yángquán

Lìshí

Jìnzhōng

Qiáo Family Courtyard House

Héshùn

Tàiháng Mountains

Liǔlín

Fényáng

Fen River (Fén Hé)

Qíxiàn

Zhèngguó Temple

Píngyáo

Yúshè

Xíngtái

Jièxiū

Shuānglín Temple

Wǔxiāng

209

Wang Family Courtyard House

Qínxiàn

Lìchéng

Handan

107

Jíxiàn

Hóngdòng

Ānzé

Chángzhì

Ānyáng

SHAANXI

Hukou Waterfall

Línfén

Gāopíng

108

Hànchéng

Héjīn

Hóumǎ

Jìnchéng

Xīnxiāng

Yuánqū

Jiāozuò

HÉNÁN

Yùnchéng

Yellow River (Huáng Hé)

Yǒngjì

Xièzhōu

To Xī'ān (90km)

Ruìchéng

Sānménxiá

Luòyáng

ZHÈNGZHŌU

Língbǎo

History

Throughout history, Shānxī has flip-flopped from China's defensive bulwark to a springboard for invaders descending upon the fertile north China plain. The Tuoba were the first outsiders to set up camp here, instating Dàtóng as their capital during the northern Wei (AD 386–534). Eventual assimilation and intermarriage with powerful Han Chinese clans resulted in a new line of aristocratic families, who went on to play an important role in the Sui and Tang dynasty courts. As China weakened following the collapse of the Tang, northern invaders moved back into Shānxī, most notably the Khitan (907–1125), whose western capital was again based in Dàtóng.

After the Ming regained control of northern China, Shānxī was developed anew as a defensive outpost, with an inner and outer Great Wall constructed along the northern boundaries for enforced protection. Local merchants (known as *Jìn shāng*) took advantage of the military development to do a brisk business in trade, eventually transforming the province into the country's financial centre during the Qing dynasty.

Climate

Shānxī ('West of the Mountains') gets its name from the Taihang range that runs along its eastern border. Nearly 70% of the province is mountainous, with much of the population residing in the inner Loess Plateau (thick layers of microscopic silt that blew down from Siberia beginning in the Ice Age). The hallmarks of China's 'yellow earth' are cave houses (*yáodòng*) and a fissured, treeless landscape.

Shānxī is as dry as dust – precisely 0cm of rain in February is normal. All in, the province averages a mere 35cm of rain a year; the only time it really does rain is July, but it's usually only 12cm.

Thankfully skies are often blue, because temperature fluctuations can be intimidating. In Tàiyuán expect lows of around -8°C in January, with wind chills icing that down quite a bit; the summer average high is a relatively comfortable 25°C. Much of the province outside Tàiyuán is mountainous, so adjust temperatures accordingly. Plan to arrive in May or September for optimal conditions.

Language

Shānxī has 45 million speakers of Jin. Linguists argue whether it should be classified as a distinct language rather than a Mandarin dialect (since it has eight subgroups inside the province); if so, it is the 22nd-most spoken world language. Jin uses a final glottal stop, unlike standard Mandarin; other unique features are complex grammar-induced tone shifts and breaking monosyllabic words into two.

Getting There & Around

Modern and extensive rail lines and highways split Shānxī on a northeast–southwest line, so getting from Běijīng to Tàiyuán and thence to Xī'ān (in Shaanxi province) is no problem. Outside of that, lots of mountain roads and endless convoys of coal lorries await to bog you down.

TÀIYUÁN 太原

☎ 0351 / pop 1,830,000

Tàiyuán is a nice place as far as Chinese cities go, cosmopolitan enough to indulge in modern luxuries, but without the fast-paced rush characteristic of urban conglomerations on the coast. The real reason to spend some time here (instead of immediately hurrying on to Píngyáo or Wǔtái Shān) is the fantastic new Shanxi Museum, opened in 2005 and easily one of China's best.

Orientation

Yingze Dajie runs east to west through Tàiyuán. To the east is the train station; everything of necessity is west of here towards May 1st Sq (Wǔyī Guǎngchǎng).

Information

There are several internet cafés (网吧; *wǎngbā*) on Wuyi Dongjie; another is located on the south side of the train station square.

Bank of China (Zhōngguó Yínháng) main branch (288 Yingze Dajie; ❂ 8am-5.30pm); smaller branch (169 Yingze Dajie; ❂ 8am-6pm) Both branches have an ATM inside. To change travellers cheques, go to the main branch.

China International Travel Service (CITS; Zhōngguó Guójì Lǚxíngshè; ☎ 406 3562; 282 Yingze Dajie) Next door to the Bank of China.

Kodak (Jiādá Shùmǎ Zhōngxīn; 93 Yingze Dajie) Burn digital photos onto CDs here; Y10 per disc.

Post & telephone office (yóujú) Diagonally opposite the train station.

Public Security Bureau (PSB; Gōng'ānjú; 9 Houjia Xiang; ❂ 8.30-11.30am & 3-5pm Mon-Fri) Has a foreign affairs office near May 1st Sq (Wǔyī Guǎngchǎng).

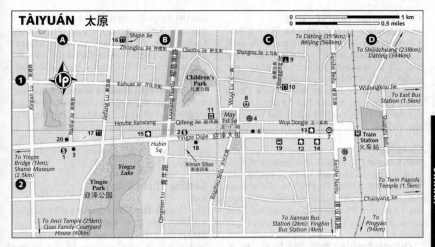

Sights

SHANXI MUSEUM 山西博物院
Shānxī need no longer suffer from an inferiority complex: this new **museum** (Shānxī Bówùguǎn; Binhe Xilu Zhongduan; admission Y20, audio guide Y10 & Y100 deposit; 9am-5pm, last entrance 4pm, closed 15th & 30th each month) leaves all neighbouring provincial museums in the loessial dust. Three floors walk you through all aspects of Shānxī culture, from prehistoric fossils and rare northern dynasty tomb relics to a pantheon of Buddhist statues and detailed local opera and architecture exhibits. All galleries are imaginatively displayed and contain English captions. Highlights include animal-shaped bronze sacrificial vessels (zūn) from the state of Jin (2nd floor), coffin paintings and burial artefacts from the Northern Wei and Qi (3rd floor), a shadow puppet collection (3rd floor) and the architectural exhibit (4th floor).

To get here, take bus 1 across the Yingze Bridge (迎泽大桥), walk back towards the river and then zigzag northeast 15 minutes; look for the inverted pyramid.

CHONGSHAN TEMPLE 崇善寺
The double-eaved wooden hall in this Ming **temple** (Chóngshàn Sì; Dilianggong Jie; admission Y2; 8am-5pm) contains three impressive statues: Samantabhadra (the Bodhisattva of Truth), Guanyin (the Goddess of Mercy with 1000 arms) and Manjusri (the Bodhisattva of Wisdom with 1000 alms bowls). The entrance is down an alleyway off Dilianggong Jie.

SHANXI PROVINCIAL MUSEUM 山西省博物馆
The old provincial museum has two separate locations. The **main museum** (Shānxī Shěng Bówùguǎn; Qifeng Jie; admission Y5; 9am-5pm) is in a temple dedicated to the Taoist immortal Lü Dongbin and contains a ragtag collection of Taoist and Buddhist statues. The **Confucian Temple** (Wén Miào; Dilianggong Jie; admission Y2; 9am-noon & 2.30-6.30pm May-Oct, 9am-5pm Nov-Apr, closed Monday) is located south of Chongshan Temple, and has attractive Ming buildings that hold temporary calligraphy exhibitions and the like.

TWIN PAGODA TEMPLE 双塔寺

This **temple** (Shuāngtǎ Sì; admission Y6; ��8.30am-5.30pm) has two Ming dynasty pagodas, each a 13-storey octagonal structure almost 55m high. It is possible to climb one of the pagodas, but it's only recommended for those who enjoy dark, slippery spiral stairs. Catch a taxi (Y7) here, or take bus 19 or 802 from the train station, both of which get you relatively close.

Sleeping

Tiělù Bīnguǎn (☎ 404 0624; 18 Yingze Dajie; 迎泽大街18号; tw without bathroom Y50-80, tw with bathroom Y98-160, tr Y75, q Y100-120; ☒) The Tiělù does things right: in addition to comfy budget digs, there's a super-friendly staff, a good 2nd-floor restaurant and a blind-massage parlour (per hour Y35).

Chángtài Fàndiàn (☎ 223 0888; fax 403 4931; 60 Yingze Dajie; 迎泽大街60号; s Y180, d & tw Y200-300, tr Y238; ☒) This is a reasonable midrange place to stay. The cheaper rooms are generally better, with newer floors and furnishings. There's a rail ticket office in the lobby.

Huáyuàn Bīnguǎn (☎ 882 8555; fax 404 6980; 9 Yingze Dajie; 迎泽大街9号; s & tw Y288-318; ☒) A decent three-star hotel, with an impressive lobby and unremarkable rooms. English is spoken here.

Yíngzé Bīnguǎn (☎ 882 8888; fax 882 6688; 189 Yingze Dajie; 迎泽大街189号; d from Y1180; ☒ ☒) A plush four-star hotel that might be a horror to look at, but at least it has the trappings of luxury: mahogany furnishings, English-language satellite TV, sauna, gym and medical clinic. You want the west (capitalist) block, not the decaying east (communist) block.

Eating

Shānxī's killer vinegar-noodle combo has garnered fame throughout the world – well, Běijīng's world at least. If you need more than noodles to fuel your stay (gasp!), head to the **food street** (Shípǐn Jiē) northwest of Yingze Dajie, where you'll be able to find restaurants of all flavours.

Tàiyuán Miànshí Diàn (Taiyuan Noodle House; 5 Jiefang Lu; meals from Y20) The 2nd floor here is *the* place to sample Shānxī's bewildering variety of noodles. Classic forms (named after their shape, not ingredients) include cat's ears (猫耳朵; *māo ěrduo*), scissored-wheat noodles (剪子面; *jiǎnzi miàn*), rolled fish (搓鱼; *cuōyú*) and pulled noodles (拉面; *lāmiàn*). Garnishes

consist of pork (肉炸酱; *ròuzhàjiàng*) and mutton (羊肉; *yángròu*), among other things. Spoon it on the noodles, add some vinegar and dig in. There's no English menu – for the best experience, befriend a local and invite them to dinner.

Táiwān Yǒnghé Dòujiāng Dàwáng (Yingze Dajie; from Y1) Stuck for a place to eat near the train station? Try this handy 24-hour chain next to the Tiělù Bīnguǎn, with steamed buns (馒头; *mántou*; Y1), noodles (面条; *miàntiáo*; Y6), set lunches (套餐; *tàocān*; Y18) and other snacks.

Getting There & Away

AIR

The **China Eastern Airlines booking office** (Dōngfāng Hángkōng Gōngsi; ☎ 417 8605; 158 Yingze Dajie; ☒ 8am-8pm) is the main purveyor of tickets in town and is where you hop aboard the airport bus. Useful flights include Běijīng (Y660), Guǎngzhōu (Y1520), Shànghǎi (Y1290) and Xī'ān (Y730).

BUS

Tàiyuán's long-distance bus station (*chángtú qìchēzhàn*) is a five-minute walk west of the train station. Departures include Dàtóng (Y56 to Y86, three hours), Běijīng (Y121, 6½ hours), Zhèngzhōu (Y97 to Y143, 6½ hours), Luòyáng (Y89 to Y94, eight hours) and Xī'ān (sleeper Y139, departures 7pm, 8pm and 10pm).

The Jiannan Bus Station (建南站; Jiànnán Zhàn), 3km south of the train station, serves Píngyáo (Y20, 1½ hours) from 7.30am to 7.30pm; take bus 611 from the train station. Buses to Wǔtái Shān leave from the east bus station (东客站; dōng kèzhàn) and in front of the train station (see p412 for details). Take bus 61 from the train station to get to the east bus station.

TRAIN

It's fairly easy getting sleeper tickets for trains originating from Tàiyuán, but difficult for other trains. For advance purchases go to the **train booking office** (huǒchē shòupiàochù; Yingze Dajie; ☒ 8am-7pm) or the lobby of the Chángtài Fàndiàn. Services leaving from Tàiyuán include trains to Chéngdū (Y296, 28 hours, departure 3.30pm), Dàtóng (Y60, 5½ hours), Luòyáng (Y183, 13 hours, 7.33pm), Zhèngzhōu (Y91, 10 hours, 8.12am) and Shànghǎi (Y310, 22 hours, 6.12pm).

The best trains to Xī'ān (Y99, 10 to 12 hours) leave at 3.30pm and 5.53pm; sleeper berths sell out quickly. The best departures to Běijīng (Y150, eight to 10 hours) leave at noon and 9.30pm.

Getting Around
The useful bus 1 runs the length of Yingze Dajie. Taxi meters start at Y7.

AROUND TÀIYUÁN
Jinci Temple 晋祠寺
Dating from AD 1023, this Buddhist **temple** (Jìncí Sì; admission Y40; ⏰ 8.30am-6pm) is at the source of the Jin River and is a good start for those interested in Shānxī's impressive collection of ancient wooden buildings.

The main building here is the **Hall of the Sacred Mother**, constructed nearly 1000 years ago, with eight wooden dragons twining up the first row of pillars. Inside are 42 Song dynasty clay maidservants of the sacred lady, the mother of Prince Shuyu, who founded the state of Jin (772–403 BC). Adjacent is the **Zhou Cypress**, an unusual tree which has been growing at an angle of about 30 degrees for the last 900 years.

The temple is 25km southwest of Tàiyuán. To get here, take bus 804 from Tàiyuán's train station (Y2, one hour).

PÍNGYÁO 平遥
☎ 0354 / pop 40,000
Possibly the best-preserved ancient walled city in China, Píngyáo has a movie-set charm that makes the hearts of even the most hardened expats skip a beat. But it's not just the superficial beauty of red lanterns swaying against grey-brick walls that makes Píngyáo special; it's the fact that the entire town is still in existence – and unmarred by bathroom tiles. Wander at random through the cobbled, dusty streets and you'll come across government offices, residences and temples, offering rare insight into various aspects of life in imperial China.

It should be no surprise that Píngyáo is mobbed with megaphone-wielding tour groups on weekends and holidays, particularly when the weather is nice. But get beyond the main souvenir strip and it remains very much a real town: the locals are still hanging laundry in courtyards, careening down alleyways on bicycles or sunning themselves in doorways, unchanged even in fame.

QIAO FAMILY COURTYARD HOUSE
乔家大院

This ornately decorated **residence** (Qiáo Jiā Dàyuàn; admission Y40) is where Zhang Yimou's chilling movie *Raise the Red Lantern,* starring Gong Li, was filmed. The complex consists of six courtyards, containing more than 300 rooms, and was built by Qiao Guifa, a small-time tea and bean-curd merchant who rose to riches.

To get to the house from Tàiyuán take any Píngyáo-bound bus. On the right-hand side of the highway you'll see red lanterns and a large gate marking the complex. It's 40km southwest of Tàiyuán. Be forewarned that it's generally packed to the rafters.

History
Píngyáo was a thriving merchant town during the Ming dynasty and centre of a large network of trade that extended from the south of China to Mongolia. Local businessmen had become so successful by the Qing dynasty that they created the country's first banks and cheques, in order to facilitate the transfer of enormous amounts of silver from one place to another. The city fell into poverty in the 20th century, and, without the cash to modernise, Píngyáo's streets have since gone unchanged.

Orientation & Information
The city's main drag is Nan Dajie, also known as Mingqing Jie. Guesthouses, restaurants, museums, temples and souvenir shops are positively ubiquitous on all streets branching from it.

Take cash with you; there's (ironically) no bank. Internet is available at hotels (per hour Y10) or outside the walls on Shuncheng Lu (per hour Y3). The post office is near the corner of Nan Dajie and Xi Dajie. The PSB is in the southwestern part of the old town.

Sights & Activities
Exploring Píngyáo's streets makes for fascinating discovery, leading you past more historic sights than could possibly be covered in this book. There's a one-time admission ticket (Y120, valid for three days) that covers 20 residences, temples and monuments; the ticket office (*gǔchéng shòupiàochù*) is in front of the North Gate. A few of these places stage

SHĀNXĪ

PÍNGYÁO 平遥

INFORMATION
Internet Café 网吧........................1 A2
Post Office 邮电局........................2 C2
PSB 公安局..................................3 B3

SIGHTS & ACTIVITIES
City Tower 市楼.............................4 C2
Confucian Temple 文庙...................5 C3
County Government Offices
县衙署................................(see 12)
Former Residence of Lei Lütai
雷履泰故居..................................6 B3
Rishengchang Financial House
Museum 日升昌............................7 C2
Ticket Office 古城售票处.................8 C1

SLEEPING
Harmony Guesthouse
和义昌客栈..................................9 C3
Pingyao International Financier
Club 国际金融家俱乐部.................10 C2

Tianyuankui Folk Guesthouse
天元奎客栈..................................11 C2
Yamen Youth Hostel
衙门官舍青年旅舍.........................12 C2

EATING
Déjūyuán Bīnguǎn 德居源宾馆....13 C2

TRANSPORT
Bus Station 汽车站........................14 A1
Buses to Xī'ān 去西安的汽车.........15 A1

---

performances, which can cost extra. Opening hours are generally from 8am to 7pm (to 6.30pm in winter).

Among the best sights in town are the **city walls** (chéng qiáng), which date from the early Ming dynasty (1370); notice the stamped bricks beneath your feet. The sloping walls are 10m high, more than 6km in circumference and punctuated by 72 watchtowers, each containing a paragraph from Sun-tzu's *The Art of War*. The main entrance is at the North Gate.

Also not to be missed is the **Rishengchang Financial House Museum** (Rìshēngchāng), the first of many draft banks, or *piàohào*, which operated from the city. It started off as a small dye shop in the late 18th century; as it expanded, a system of cheques and deposits for the remote offices was introduced, which eventually grew into a financial agent for other businesses, individuals and the Qing government, with 57 branches around China. The museum has nearly 100 rooms, including offices, living quarters and a kitchen, as well as several old cheques.

The **Former Residence of Lei Lütai** (Leílǚtái Gùjū), the founder of Rishengchang, offers a tra-

great glimpse at the layout of a lavish courtyard residence. Main rooms are built in the arched *yáodòng* (cave house) style particular to northern China; there are deteriorating frescoes on the walls and heated beds (*kàng*) in each room.

Other sights to check out include the sprawling **county government offices** (xiànyáshǔ), with tax offices, a court, prison and (most importantly) opera stage; and the imposing **Confucian Temple** (Wén Miào), where bureaucrats-to-be came to take the imperial exams. At the centre of everything is the old **City Tower** (Shì Lóu; admission Y5), the tallest building in the city.

Tours

Mr Liu, who runs the Harmony Guesthouse (see opposite), gives reader-approved daylong tours for Y120.

Festivals

A good time to visit Píngyáo is during the Lantern Festival (15 days after Chinese New Year, during the full moon), when a small, country-style parade takes place. Locals flood the streets and vendors sell *yuán xiāo*, a traditional snack made of glutinous rice flour, filled with a sweet sesame and walnut paste and served in soup.

Sleeping & Eating

Harmony Guesthouse (Héyìchāng Kèzhàn; ☎ 568 4952; 165 Nan Dajie; 南大街165号; tw Y100; ✷ ▯) Run by a knowledgeable local couple who speak excellent English, this is a comfortable choice if you don't need antique furnishings.

Yamen Youth Hostel (Yámén Guānshè; ☎ 568 3539; 69 Yamen Jie; 衙门街69号; dm Y40, tw with/without bathroom Y160/120; ✷ ▯) A former Ming residence (the governor's, to be precise), with a beautiful outdoor courtyard, a stylish café and simple but clean rooms.

Tianyuankui Folk Guesthouse (Tiānyuánkuí Kèzhàn; ☎ 568 0069; www.pytyk.com; 73 Nan Dajie; 南大街 73号; tw/tr/ste Y298/270/498; ✷ ▯) One of the more popular and attractive hotels. Traditional courtyard rooms sport *kang*-style beds (ie raised beds heated beneath by a stove), a black-brick interior and obligatory red lanterns; suites are particularly sumptuous.

Pingyao International Financier Club (Guójì Jīnróngjiā Jùlèbù; ☎ 588 8888; www.pibc.cn; 56 Xi Dajie; 西大街56号; d/ste Y1280/1480; ✷) Contemporary high-rollers can live out their Ming fantasies in this gorgeous 18-courtyard compound, replete with carved wooden screens and lacquered furniture.

Píngyáo is a good place to sample Shānxī's infinite variety of wheat and buckwheat noodles, as well as local treats like *túdòu shāo niúròu* (土豆烧牛肉; fried Píngyáo beef and potatoes).

Déjūyuán Bīnguǎn (Xi Dajie; 西大街; dishes Y5-35) Superb Shānxī cuisine served in a traditional courtyard lit by candles and lanterns in the evening.

Getting There & Away

BUS

The Píngyáo bus 'station' is really just the train station parking lot; buses depart for Tàiyuán (Y20, 1½ hours) as they fill. There are theoretically five daily buses to Xī'ān (Y150, six hours; via Yùnchéng, Y100, four hours) leaving from Shuncheng Lu from 8.30am to 4pm, but check when you arrive to verify which ones are definitely running.

TRAIN

Most visitors arrive on a day trip from Tàiyuán, or overnight from Běijīng. There are loads of trains between Tàiyuán and Píngyáo (Y8 to Y22, 1½ to two hours); a good one leaves at 8.35am. From Beijing West there are two trains at 7pm (arrives 5.20am) and 7.43pm (arrives 6.53am); a hard sleeper costs Y140. Although there are also two sleepers back to Běijīng, tickets are extremely limited. You'll have better luck in Tàiyuán.

From Píngyáo to Xī'ān (Y86, 9½ to 11 hours) can be problematic. Guesthouses can sometimes land sleepers (Y40 commission) but don't count on it, especially on weekends in summer or holidays. You may need to pay for a Tàiyuán–Xī'ān ticket (Y99).

Getting Around

Píngyáo can be easily navigated on foot, or you can rent a bike for the day (Y10 to Y20) at your hotel or one of the shops on Xi Dajie. Electric carts whiz around town and to and from the train station for Y5; the city core is closed to motor vehicles.

AROUND PÍNGYÁO

Two notable Buddhist temples within biking distance are **Shuanglin Temple** (双林寺; Shuānglín Sì; admission Y25), 7km south of Píngyáo, and **Zhenguo Temple** (镇国寺; Zhènguó Sì; admission Y20), 12km north. Shuanglin Temple contains rare Song and Yuan painted statues. The interiors of the Sakyamuni Hall and flanking buildings (for the Gods and Goddesses of Hell, Harvests, Protection and Compassion) are particularly exquisite. Zhenguo Temple is less visited, though the restored Hall of Ten Thousand Buddhas supposedly dates back to 926 and contains many 10th-century statues. A taxi to either temple from Píngyáo is Y40 return.

If residential architecture is more your cup of *chá*, both the **Qiao Family Courtyard House** (see the boxed text, p407) and the **Wang Family Courtyard House** (王家大院; Wáng Jiā Dàyuàn; admission Y66) are nearby. The latter is more of a conspicuous castle than cosy home, impressive in grandeur (123 courtyards) but somewhat redundant and lacking in furnishings. Take a bus or train to Jièxiū (介休; Y4, 40 minutes), then switch to the complex-bound bus (Y3, 40 minutes) at the station.

YÙNCHÉNG 运城
☎ 0359 / pop 204,600
If you enjoy exploring obscure parts of rural China, try to stop off at Yùnchéng, near where the Yellow River (Huáng Hé) completes its

SHĀNXĪ

LORD OF THE MAGNIFICENT BEARD

Red-faced, black-whiskered Guān Yǔ is one of the most popular of all Chinese gods. He appears on altars in restaurants and shops, as a character in the opera and video games, and you'll often see him pasted onto front doors. He's known in the West as the God of War, although, like many Chinese deities, he has a confusing assortment of names and roles, also going by Guān Dì, Guān Gōng, Guān Lǎoyè and, best of all, Měirán Gōng (Lord of the Magnificent Beard). His various personas are revered by Taoists, Buddhists, entrepreneurs, the police, secret societies, gangs and the unwell alike. So how did one god come to take on so much?

Like many folk heroes, Guān Yǔ was a real person, born in Xièzhōu sometime during the 2nd or 3rd century AD. He was apparently a formidable general while alive, but it was only after he died that his career really took off. Guān Yǔ's growing popularity as a personage in hand-me-down legends caught the attention of the Buddhists, and in the 6th century they inducted him as Protector of the Dharma. The Taoists were a bit slower on the uptake, although they eventually found a spot for him as a demon-smiting immortal in the celestial palace – after he received a Song emperor's seal of approval, of course.

But it was the 14th-century novel *The Romance of the Three Kingdoms* (三国演义; *Sānguó Yǎnyì*) that gave Guān Yǔ the biggest boost of all. His heroic exploits as a military general were immortalised against a backdrop of action-packed storytelling, and his character traits – loyalty, bravery, righteousness, benevolence (and arrogance) – came to be inseparable from his divinity. He thus symbolises loyalty and honour to secret societies and rebels; honesty and prosperity to businesses; protection and peace for the common folk and the power of healing for those who are ill.

Understandably, China's emperors took no chances with such an omnipotent being. They officially promoted him to the rank of celestial emperor in the late Ming dynasty, tacked on the *nom de guerre* God of War in the early Qing and finally extended his title to a tongue-twisting 24 characters in the 19th century. And who's to say what's to come next?

great sweep through northern China and begins to flow eastwards. Southwestern Shānxī is an unrolling tableau of traditional cave houses, fruit orchards and verdant fields of wheat and rape, though the main attraction is the largest temple in the country dedicated to Guān Yǔ (see the boxed text, above).

This **temple** (关帝庙; Guāndì Miào; admission Y48; ☉ 8am-6.30pm May-Sep, 8.30am-5pm Oct-Apr) is full of unusual imagery, beginning with the sufficiently gory battle murals on the third gate and fierce cavalry decorating the fourth gate. Next is the unusual Bagua Tower (and more carved warriors), followed by Guān Yǔ's terrestrial palace, Chongning Hall, supported by 26 pillars with sinuous dragons in bas relief. You can climb up to the second floor of the **rear building** (Spring and Autumn Tower; admission Y20) for good views of the painted eaves, glazed roof tiles and surrounding landscape.

The temple is in Xièzhōu, 18km south of Yùnchéng. Bus 11 (Y2, 30 minutes) from Yùnchéng's train station terminates here. **Guǎngyuè Bīnguǎn** (广悦宾馆; ☎ 208 0950; 333 Fenghuang Beilu; tw Y50-100; ☒) is a well-run hotel near the Yùnchéng train station.

Getting There & Away

Yùnchéng is on the Tàiyuán–Xī'ān train line; all trains, including daily expresses, stop here. There are direct bus connections from Yùnchéng to Luòyáng in Hénán province (Y47, three hours) and Tàiyuán to the north (Y83 to Y92, 4½ hours). There are also regular and express air-con buses to Xī'ān (Y48 to Y62, three hours) departing half-hourly; these pass by Huá Shān (p433) in neighbouring Shaanxi province. Buses generally run from 6.30am to 6pm.

Buses 1, 2 and 12 run between the bus station and train station.

AROUND YÙNCHÉNG

At Ruìchéng (芮城), located 93km south of Yùnchéng, is the Yuan dynasty **Yongle Taoist Temple** (永乐宫; Yǒnglè Gōng; admission Y30), dedicated to the immortal Lü Dongbin. The valuable 14th-century frescoes inside are unfortunately poorly lit, though the two-hour bus ride from Yùnchéng (Y16) – you can get on or off in Xièzhōu – passes over mountains and through enchanting countryside, making for an unusual detour en route to Xī'ān. In 1959 the temple was moved here brick by brick from a dam site on the Yellow River.

WǓTÁI SHĀN & TÁIHUÁI
五台山、台怀

Wǔtái Shān, or 'the Five Terrace Mountains', is Buddhism's sacred northern range and the earthly abode of Manjusri (Wénshū), the Bodhisattva of Wisdom. Enclosed within a valley formed by five main peaks is the town of Táihuái, the site of some 15 temples and meandering groups of monks and nuns, where countless visitors come to temporarily escape the world of illusion.

The forested slopes outside of town eventually give way to alpine meadows and another 20 temples or so scattered across the hillsides. The windswept summits are located in China's five cardinal directions (north, east, south, west and centre), with the highest being North Terrace Peak (北台顶) at 3058m. Besides temple hopping, Wǔtái Shān offers some great hiking and, with enough persistence, you just might be able to momentarily detach yourself from the world of red dust.

Avoiding high season isn't a bad idea (it's a zoo), but remember that temperatures are often below freezing from October through March, and roads can be impassable. Even in summer the temperature drops rapidly at night.

History
For almost as long as Buddhism has existed in China, Wǔtái Shān has been a place of pilgrimage and study. It's believed that by the 6th century there were already 200 temples in the area, and in the Tang dynasty it was one of the major centres of worship in Asia, attracting tens of thousands of pilgrims from across China, India, Korea and Japan. Almost all temples were destroyed during the official persecution of Buddhism in the 9th century, except for two southwest of Táihuái (see p413). In the Ming dynasty, Wǔtái Shān began attracting large numbers of Tibetan Buddhists (principally from Mongolia) for whom Manjusri holds special significance.

Many temples in Táihuái contain a statue of Manjusri, who is generally depicted riding a lion and holding a sword used to cleave ignorance and illusion. If you have an affinity for either flaw, watch your step.

Information
Take plenty of cash, as there was no place to change money at the time of writing. For internet access, ask the locals where the *wǎngbā* (网吧) is, as it changes location often. If you need to reach the PSB for any reason, talk to the owner of the hotel you're staying at.

Sights
Touring Táihuái will result in temple overdose if you're not careful – and there's no known antidote. It's best to pick a few in town and spend the rest of the time wandering the hillsides, where the crowds thin out and the scenery is at its best. Temple admission prices vary from free of charge to Y8. All travellers – unless you're a card-carrying Tibetan pilgrim – are charged a Y95 entrance fee (Y75 from 15 October to 15 April) for the area.

The distinctive white stupa rising above **Tayuan Temple** (Tǎyuàn Sì) is the most prominent landmark in Wǔtái Shān; almost all pilgrims come through here to spin the prayer wheels at its base. Behind the stupa is the Scripture Hall, whose 9th-century revolving sutra case originally held scriptures in Chinese, Mongolian and Tibetan.

One of the more captivating temples is the enormous **Xiantong Temple** (Xiǎntōng Sì). The whitewashed brick Beamless Hall holds a miniature Yuan dynasty pagoda and remarkable statues of contemplative monks meditating in the alcoves. Further on is the Hall of Manjusri, with a 15-faced, 1000-armed statue of the Bodhisattva. Up the steps from this is the blinding Bronze Hall, 5m high and weighing 50 tonnes. A miniature replica of a Ming pavilion right down to the floral-patterned lattice windows, it was cast in 1606 and is purportedly gilded gold (don sunglasses); ten thousand mini-Buddhas fill the interior. If you continue past Xiantong Temple after exiting, you'll eventually attain **Bodhisattva Peak** (Púsà Dǐng), reached via 108 steps, the number of beads on the Buddhist rosary.

For the best bird's-eye view of Táihuái, you can make the somewhat strenuous trek (or cheat by chairlift, ascent/round trip Y25/48) up to **Dailuo Peak** (Dàiluó Dǐng), on the eastern side of Qingshui River.

About 2.5km south of Táihuái is the isolated and fortress-like **Nanshan Temple** (Nánshān Sì). Beautiful stone carvings adorn many of the archways here. Taoist themes are quite common – you'll see the famous eight immortals

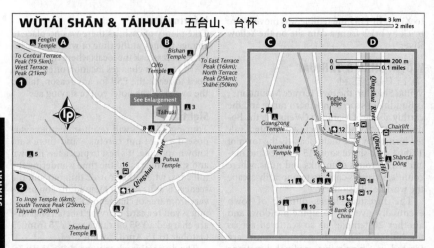

WŪTÁI SHĀN & TÁIHUÁI 五台山、台怀

(above the main entrance) in addition to Lao-tzu. In the upper parts of the temple (also known as Yòuguó Sì; 佑国寺) are carvings of the mythic *Journey to the West*. Enjoy wonderful views of four of the five sacred peaks from the top.

Other temples of note include the **Luohou Temple** (Luóhòu Sì), **Guangren Temple** (Guǎngrén Sì), **Longquan Temple** (Lóngquán Sì) and **Shuxiang Temple** (Shūxiàng Sì). Ten kilometres west of town is the serene **Jinge Temple** (金阁寺; Jīngé Sì), which houses a large 32-armed Guanyin.

In the summer, free Shanxi opera performances are given during the evenings at 7.30pm (and some mornings around 11.30am) at **Wanfo Temple** (Wànfó Gé).

Tours
Privately operated minibuses make half-day and full-day tours (in Chinese; Y40 to Y60) of the outlying temples and peaks, departing from a local minibus tour station on the main road. South Terrace Peak (南台顶; Nántái Dǐng) is said to be the prettiest.

For the two Tang dynasty temples (see opposite), contact **CITS** (☎ 654 3210; Shijuliangcheng Gonglu), located just past the bus station south of town. English-speaking guides are not always available.

Sleeping
There are more hotels in town than there are temples, though most are either very basic or run-down. Guesthouses are in the northern part of town; the standard price per bed ranges from Y20 to Y50. Top-end hotels are south of town and are generally closed out of season. Wherever you stay, make sure to bargain.

Fóguó Bīnguǎn (☎ 654 5962; Zhenjianfang Jie; dm with/without private bathroom Y48/30, d Y100) In a warren of back alleys, this isolated place has a quiet location but so-so rooms. Innumerable similar options surround it.

Number 5 Hotel (Dì Wǔ Zhàodàisuǒ; ☎ 654 5373; Shijuliangcheng Gonglu; tw/tr Y100; 🖳) An old standby that's in better shape than the Fóguó.

Fóyuàn Lóu (☎ 654 2659; Shuxiang Si; tw Y360; 🖳) Showing some wear, this is still one of the best-managed hotels, in an auspicious and secluded location next to Shuxiang Temple.

Qīxiángé Bīnguǎn (☎ 654 2400; fax 654 2183; d & tw from Y380, ste Y898; 🕙 May-Oct; 🖳) With a peaceful setting at the foot of the mountains, this hotel is a top choice. Well-furnished rooms have lovely views of the mountainside.

Eating
Prices are higher here, as nearly all food has to be trucked into the area. Basic but tasty *liángpí* (potato noodles in a spicy soup), fried noodles, fried rice and dumplings are the norm. You'll find a few excellent vegetarian restaurants; most have English menus.

Getting There & Away
Getting to Wǔtái Shān is easiest from Tàiyuán. Buses (Y44 to Y51, four hours) depart from the east bus station from 8am to 1.30pm; two buses also leave from in front of the train sta-

tion at around 9.30am. Alternatively, take the scenic route from Dàtóng (see p415), which is slightly longer. At present, one train from Běijīng (departure 9.15pm) stops 50km away in the town of Shāhé (砂河), but it arrives at a groggy 3.39am. If you take this option, note when buying tickets that the station is called Wǔtái Shān, not Shāhé. Minibuses onwards from Shāhé (Y20, one hour) are infrequent – you may have to catch a taxi (Y70).

There are plenty of buses from Wǔtái Shān to Tàiyuán (Y50, four hours), leaving between 7am and 4pm. Buses to Dàtóng (Y52, five hours) leave three or four times daily from 6am to 1.30pm. In the off-season, there's only one bus at 7.30am; it doesn't run on Sundays. Try cajoling your driver into stopping off at the Hanging Monastery (p417) for 30 minutes en route.

Both buses troll the main strip fishing for passengers. The Wǔtái Shān bus 'station', some 3km south of the village centre, is generally empty.

AROUND WǓTÁI SHĀN

The two oldest wooden buildings in China (clocking in at a wheezing 12 centuries) are located southwest of Táihuái. Both date from the Tang dynasty and, remarkably, see relatively few visitors. Tang buildings were simpler and squatter in appearance, built on raised stone platforms and featured prominent ceiling brackets to hold up the long eaves, which were designed to protect the paper-covered windows from rain falling off the roof.

Near the town of Dòucūn (豆村), 43km from Táihuái, is **Foguang Temple** (佛光寺; Fóguāng Sì; admission Y10), whose elongated main hall was built in 857. It contains three Buddhas surrounded by plump tricolour attendants, all sculpted during the Tang.

A further 45km southwest, near Dōngyě (东冶), is **Nanchan Temple** (南禅寺; Nánchán Sì; admission Y10), which contains a smaller but strikingly beautiful hall built in 782. Both temple complexes contain impressive 12th-century buildings as well.

Most Wǔtái Shān–Tàiyuán buses pass through both towns (make sure to ask your driver), allowing you to hop off and take a taxi the rest of the way. The **CITS** (☎ 654 3210; Shijuliangcheng Gonglu) outside Tàiyuán can also arrange private transport to Foguang (Y100) or both temples (Y200).

DÀTÓNG 大同
☎ 0352 / pop 580,000

Dàtóng isn't going to win any beauty pageants, but who needs good looks when you've got art? Border town extraordinaire, the city has long held a strategic position on the edge of the Mongolian grasslands, first rising to greatness as the capital city of the Tuoba: a federation of Turkic-speaking nomads who united northern China (AD 386–534), converted to Buddhism and, like most other invaders, were eventually assimilated into Chinese culture. The Tuoba's main claim to fame is the Yungang Caves (p416), a collection of sublime 5th-century Buddhist carvings that capture a quiet, timeless beauty that has all but vanished from the modern world.

Despite the area's impressive sights, don't pin too many hopes on finding enlightenment here – Dàtóng is the poster child for all that's environmentally wrong with fossil-fuel addiction. The uplifting remains of times past are balanced out by sulphurous air pollution, contaminated groundwater and suburban slag heaps that grow by 80 million tonnes annually.

Information
ATM (qúkuǎnjī; 19 Xiao Nanjie; ⏰ 24hr) Outside a small branch of the Bank of China.
Bank of China (Zhōngguó Yínháng; Yingbin Xilu) The main branch and only place to cash travellers cheques.
Chain Net Bar (Liánsuǒ Wǎngbā; Xinjian Beilu; per hr Y2) There are several other internet cafés on Huayansi Jie near Huayan Temple.

SHĀNXĪ

CITS train station (☎ 712 4882; ⏲ 6.30am-6.30pm); Yúngāng Bīnguǎn (21 Yingbin Donglu; ☎ 502 1601) The helpful train station office arranges discounted hotels, can purchase train tickets and runs regular tours (in English and French). The main office at the Yúngāng Bīnguǎn wants nothing to do with foreigners.

Post & telephone office (yóudiànjú; cnr Da Xijie & Xinjian Nanlu) South of Red Flag Sq; another post office is near the train station.

Public Security Bureau (PSB; Gōngānjú; Xinjian Beilu; ⏲ 8am-noon & 2-5pm) North of the large Stalinist-style department store.

Sights

Winter hours are applicable from 16 October to 14 April.

HUAYAN TEMPLE 华严寺

Huayan Temple is divided into two separate complexes, one of which is an active monastery (the upper temple), the other being a museum (the lower temple). It was originally built by the Khitan during the Liao dynasty (AD 907–1125), though little survives from that period. Interestingly, the temple faces east, not south; it's said the Khitan were also sun worshippers.

The **upper temple** (Shàng Huáyán Sì; Huayansi Jie; admission Y20; ⏲ 8am-6pm, 8am-5.30pm winter) is immediately recognisable from the Buddhist music blaring out of the shops leading up to the entrance. The main Mahavira Hall dates back to 1140 and is one of the largest Buddhist halls in China. Regular lectures are given here if you want to bone up on the eightfold path (to cease suffering) or hang out with the clergy.

The **lower temple** (Xià Huáyán Sì; Huayansi Jie; admission Y20; ⏲ 8am-6pm, 8am-5.30pm winter) doubles as the city museum and contains assorted relics from the Wei and Liao dynasties. The rear hall, which at one time was a sutra library, was built in 1038 and is the oldest building in Dàtóng. Inside are some remarkable Liao dynasty sculptures.

Both temples are accessed from alleyways leading off the Qing-style Huayansi Jie. Bus 4 from the train station stops nearby.

NINE DRAGON SCREEN 九龙壁

The **Nine Dragon Screen** (Jiǔlóng Bì; Da Dongjie; admission Y20; ⏲ 7am-7pm, 8am-6pm winter) originally served the same function as a temple's spirit wall. Placed in front of an entrance (in this case to a Ming dynasty palace), it inhibited evil spirits

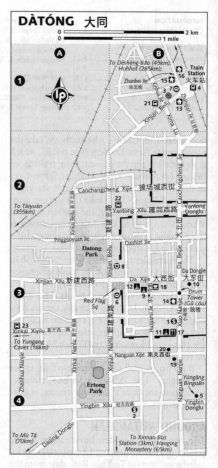

from crossing a threshold and wreaking havoc within. The colourful, glazed-tile wall depicts nine sinuous dragons and is an impressive 8m high, 45m long and 2m thick. Apparently it wasn't enough though, because the palace burnt down long ago.

SHANHUA TEMPLE 善化寺

The grandiose, bracketed wooden halls in this forgotten **temple** (Shànhuà Sì; Nansi Jie; admission Y20; ⏲ 8am-6pm, 8.30am-5.30pm winter) date back nearly 900 years to the 12th century. The rear Hall of Mahavira contains five central Buddhas and expressive statues of celestial generals in the wings. A small dragon screen stands in a western courtyard, moved here from the South Gate.

Tours

The CITS train station office runs tours of the Yungang Caves and Hanging Monastery (see p416) for Y100.

Sleeping

Fēitiān Bīnguǎn (☎ 281 4348; 1 Zhanqian Jie; 站前街 1号; dm/tw/tr Y35/160/210; ❸) The lowest-priced budget and midrange option is this friendly stand-by. Dorm rooms have common bathrooms, but unfortunately access to the showers seems to depend upon the mood of your *fúwùyuán* (floor attendant).

Tóngtiě Bīnguǎn (☎ 713 0758; 5 Zhanbei Jie; 站北 街5号; tw Y158-198, tr Y138, ste Y238-400; ❸) Conveniently located with a quiet setting, the Tóngtiě is really worth it for the reasonably priced plush suites that even come with tea sets.

Hóngqí Dàfàndiàn (☎ 536 6111; fax 536 6666; 11 Zhanqian Jie; 站前街11号; tw Y380; ❸) An excellent midrange choice, this three-star hotel sports psychedelic carpets (shampooed daily!) and bright, welcoming rooms. All credit cards are accepted and some English is spoken.

Garden Hotel (Huāyuán Dàfàndiàn; ☎ 586 5888; www .huayuanhotel.com.cn; 59 Da Nanjie; 大南街59号; d & tw Y720-880; ❸) The only place in northern Shānxī with any semblance of style is the four-star Garden Hotel, which features goose-feather quilts, carved pear-wood bed frames and reproduction antique furnishings. English is limited.

Eating & Drinking

The real treat here is the delicious *shāomài* (烧麦), a steamed pork dumpling with a crinkled top that's dipped in Shānxī vinegar. You can find them everywhere; 20 dumplings (more than enough for one person) should cost about Y10. A good place to take a breather is on Huayansi Jie, where you'll find several teahouses.

Yǒnghé Shífǔ (☎ 204 7999; Xiao Nanjie; dishes Y10-42) Divided into three restaurants, the Yǒnghé is galaxies beyond Dàtóng's other dining options. Take your pick from the main restaurant, which serves fantastic Shānxī, Běijīng and Cantonese specialities (English picture menu provided); the clever personal hotpot bar (keep it simple with the set mutton hotpot, *yángròu tàocān;* 羊肉套餐; Y22); and the perpetually crowded fast-food diner.

Tónghé Dàfàndiàn (☎ 716 6944; 11 Zhanqian Jie; dishes Y12-35) This cavernous palace is easily the nicest choice near the train station. Chefs in the open kitchen whip up fiery Sichuanese and Hunanese fare; there are also less spicy options like fried rice (扬州炒饭; *yángzhōu chǎofàn;* Y10) and steamed veggie buns (素 包子; *sù bāozi;* Y1). It's to the right of the Hóngqí Dàfàndiàn.

Fettle Coffee (Kāfēi Zhuàngtài; 2nd fl, 7 Huayansi Jie; coffee & tea from Y10; ❧ noon-midnight) An intimate 2nd-floor hideout that mixes pebble and slate walkways, a gurgling fountain and blinking strings of Christmas lights. In addition to the caffeinated drinks, there's beer (Y10), fresh fruit juice (Y5), and cards and other games.

Getting There & Away

AIR

Dàtóng's minuscule airport is 20km east of the city, with flights to Běijīng (Y410, daily) and Guǎngzhōu (Y1630, thrice weekly). Tickets are sold at the **Aviation Travel Service** (Hángkōng Shòupiàochù; Nanguan Xijie).

BUS

Dàtóng has three bus stations: the main Xinnan Bus Station (新南站; Xīnnán Zhàn), about 5km south of Red Flag Sq on Xinjian Nanlu; the north station *(qìchē běizhàn)*, near the train station; and the regional station *(chángtú qìchēzhàn)* on Yantong Xilu.

SHĀNXĪ

Buses run hourly between Běijīng's Liuliqiao Station (Y81 to Y92, 4½ hours) and (strangely) Dàtóng's train station. Traffic is sometimes excruciatingly slow on this route, so it's safer to take the train. One bus to Hohhot also leaves from in front of the train station at 7am (Y55, four hours). Express buses to Tàiyuán (Y72 to Y87, three hours) leave the Xinnan Bus Station half-hourly from 7am to 8.30pm.

Getting to Wǔtái Shān is trickier. One local bus leaves the north station at 7am (Y52) year-round, taking anywhere from five to seven hours; it may not run on Sundays. Xinnan Bus Station serves Wǔtái Shān from May through September (Y52, five hours, departure 7.30am); in theory this bus is faster than the north station bus. If you've overslept, Xinnan Bus Station also has regular buses to Shāhé (砂河; Y32, three hours), where you can catch a taxi (Y70) onwards (see p412).

TRAIN

The Běijīng and Inner/Outer Mongolia lines meet in a Y-junction at Dàtóng. It is possible to do Dàtóng as a day trip from Běijīng using night trains coming and going, but you can never be guaranteed of getting a berth back. Trains leave Běijīng's main station at 7.40am (arriving 2.10pm) and 0.46am (arriving 7.03am); tickets are Y105. Other trains depart from Beijing West.

From Dàtóng, there are several trains to Beijing West (Y70 to Y94); the best leave at 8.50am (arriving 2.20pm), 12.27pm (arriving 6.30pm) and 10.20pm (arriving 6.30am). Other destinations include Tàiyuán (hard seat Y30, 5½ hours), Hohhot (hard seat Y40, 4½ hours) and Lánzhōu (Y330, 22 hours). There's also an overnight train to Píngyáo (Y70, nine hours) leaving at 11pm. The shortest queues are at the **advance booking office** (huǒchē shòupiào-chù; cnr Nanguan Nanjie & Nanguan Xijie; ⏰ 8am-6pm), but be aware that sleeper tickets are often booked out. CITS may be able to get you a berth (Y40 commission), but no guarantees.

Getting Around

Flag fall for taxis is Y6. From the train station to Xinnan Bus Station is Y15 (or Y23 on the meter), and from town to the airport is about Y35. Bus 30 (Y1, 30 minutes) runs from the train station to Xinnan Bus Station. Bus 4 goes from the train station through the centre of town, up Da Beijie and turning west on Da Xijie.

AROUND DÀTÓNG
Yungang Caves 云冈石窟

Begun around AD 460, these **grottoes** (Yúngāng Shíkū; admission Y60; ⏰ 8.30am-6pm, 8.30am-5pm winter) are the earliest Buddhist carvings in China. Unlike their contemporaries on the Silk Road, the Mogao Caves in Dūnhuáng (p864) and the Kizil Caves in Kuqa (p832) – both of which feature murals and terracotta sculpture as opposed to stone carvings – the Yungang Caves are quite a distance from the initial influx of Buddhism into China. One reason for this is that the Tuoba were eager to promote an aspect of society that, like themselves, came from beyond the Middle Kingdom.

The mixture of new ideas and artistic styles – from India, Persia and even Greece – resulted in an explosion of youthful creativity, and the figures here emanate an ethereal yet life-like aura. Images surrounding the main statues are equally delicate, and include the omnipresent '1000 Buddha' motif (tiny Buddhas seated in niches), flying apsaras (angels draped in flowing silk), pagodas in bas-relief and obvious Chinese symbols such as dragons and phoenixes. The principal colours – cobalt, turquoise, cinnabar and burnt orange – are reminders of the Central Asian influence. Work went on for over 60 years: by the time the Tuoba had moved their capital to Luòyáng in 494, the majority of the 50,000 statues had already been carved in 252 caves, the numinous legacy extending 1km along the sandstone cliffs of Wǔzhōu Shān.

Today, there are 21 main grottoes, many of which were originally fronted with wooden temples, now gone. To start with the earliest caves, turn left at the main entrance and walk down to Cave 20 (west of here are the smaller Caves 21 to 51, which can also be visited).

Caves 16 to 20 each feature a giant Buddha (representing Wei emperors), the most sublime of which is the seated Sakyamuni in Cave 20, an impressive 14m high and flanked by a standing Bodhisattva. The standing Sakyamuni in Cave 18 was carved with amazing detail, down to the miniature figures in the folds of his robe.

Proceeding from here back towards the entrance are **Caves 5 to 13**, carved between 462 and 495, and containing the finest artwork at Yungang. Caves 9, 10 and 12 are notable for their front pillars and figures bearing musical instruments. The guardians at the entrance to Cave 8 include the Hindu gods Vishnu, seated upon a Chinese peacock or phoenix, and a three-headed, eight-armed Shiva astride a bull. An obviously foreign trident also makes a cameo appearance. Cave 6 contains a central stupa adorned with eight large Buddhas, elephants, musicians, warriors and *apsaras*. The grotto walls are lined with Buddhist parables (the damaged bottom row), each panel a different scene from Siddhartha's life up until enlightenment. Cave 5 is one of the most striking, containing a 17m seated Buddha who radiates a powerful halo of red light and turquoise flames.

Further east are the final **Caves 1 to 4**, whose highlights include intricately chiselled pagodas and, in capacious Cave 3, a seated Buddha flanked by two Bodhisattvas. No guides are available, but decent English descriptions are found in most caves.

The Yungang Caves are located 16km west of Dàtóng, opposite an enormous coal mine. To get here, take bus 3 (Y1.5, 30 minutes) from Dàtóng's Xīnkāilǐ bus station (road work may alter this – check with your hotel). Bus 4 runs to Xīnkāilǐ bus station from the train station through the centre of town. The CITS tour also spends half a day at the caves.

Scattered across the countryside and above the caves are the remains of Ming beacon towers (烽火台; *fēnghuǒtái*), part of the signal system used to protect the pass leading to Mongolia. You can visit a beacon tower and spur of the Great Wall by taking bus 3 from the Yungang Caves one stop back towards town, then walking some 15 minutes up through the mining village, or hiring a motorcycle (Y10) to take you the rest of the way.

Great Wall 长城

Shānxī's section of the **Great Wall** (Chángchéng) is much different from what you see around Běijīng: it's made entirely of earth and there's little tourism or, unfortunately, conservation. With a little advance research, you'll be able to find a smattering of historic forts, scenic ruins and occasional hikes through the countryside – tempting fare for the intrepid.

One possibility is **Déshèng Bǎo** (得胜堡; Achieving Victory Fort), a 16th-century pass 45km due north of Dàtóng. Buses to Fēngzhèn (丰镇) should be able to drop you off here (or close). A taxi (Y100 return), however, will facilitate further exploration.

Hanging Monastery 悬空寺

Built precariously into the side of a cliff, the Buddhist **Hanging Monastery** (Xuánkōng Sì; admission Y60; ☀ 7.30am-6pm) is made all the more stunning by the long support stilts that extend downward from its base, furthering the appearance that there really isn't a whole lot keeping the structure from one day smashing to bits in the riverbed below. The temple was originally lower to the ground and was raised over the centuries to protect it from floods rushing down the Jinlong Canyon. The halls have been built along the contours of the cliff face and are connected by rickety catwalks and corridors. Be forewarned that the place is pretty touristy – if you skip it, you missed some great photos, but it's no cultural heavyweight like the Yungang Caves.

The monastery is located on Taoism's sacred northern mountain (Héng Shān), 5km outside the town of Húnyuán and 65km southeast of Dàtóng. Buses to Húnyuán (Y15, one hour) run from Dàtóng's regional bus station. From Húnyuán you can catch a taxi (Y30 return). The standard CITS tour also runs here.

Another option is the bus from Wǔtái Shān, which goes directly past the monastery and may stop for half an hour (don't count on it).

Mù Tǎ 木塔

The 11th-century **Wooden Pagoda** (admission Y60; ☀ 7.30am-7pm, 8am-5.30pm winter) is one of the planet's oldest wooden buildings. Not a single nail was used in the construction of the nine-storey, 67m-high structure, which has thus far survived seven major earthquakes.

The pagoda is located in Yìngxiàn, 70km south of Dàtóng. It's possible to travel here from the Hanging Monastery, then head to Wǔtái Shān the next morning. Yìngxiàn has a couple of decent hotels.

Tours of the Hanging Monastery sometimes include Mù Tǎ. Otherwise, buses run to Yìngxiàn from Dàtóng's Xinnan Bus Station (Y13, 1½ hours).

Shaanxi (Shǎnxī)
陕西

Shaanxi *is* Chinese history, ancient and modern. Peruse any text on China and the pages for this province are laden with the words 'centre', 'nucleus' and 'heart', not to mention the ubiquitous 'cradle'. Shaanxi's influence may even extend to the most fundamental of Western concepts about the Middle Kingdom – the name 'China' is possibly derived from the Qin dynasty (pronounced 'chin'), whose capital was near Xī'ān.

It may not look much like the centre of Chinese civilisation these days, but in its time the Wei River valley occupied a perfect location. The land was fertile enough to feed a large population, nomadic invaders were close enough to necessitate military strength and it was the crossroads of major trade routes and China's main link with the outside world.

And while emperors and prime ministers were busy plotting the expansion of an empire, another complementary facet of Chinese culture was quietly evolving in the Qinling Mountains to the south. These mountains were the home of many of China's reclusive sages, those who found government service overly corrupt, or simply unfulfilling. Most famous of all was Laotzu, who – according to one legend – was brought to Lóuguāntái by the border pass guard, Yin Xi, to transmit his wisdom: the end result being the terse and mysterious *Tao Te Ching (Dào Dé Jīng)*.

For travellers, what matters most is that Shaanxi is loaded with extraordinary archaeological sights. Yet keep in mind that history didn't stop with the ancient world. In 1935 the Chinese Communist Party (CCP) finally found respite in the loess caves of Yán'ān, and, for the next decade this new haven in the hills became the CCP's broadcast centre for revolutionary thought.

HIGHLIGHTS

- Take stock of China's imperial beginnings at the imposing **Army of Terracotta Warriors** (p428)

- Look down on enthralling excavations at the **Tomb of Emperor Jingdi** (p431)

- Get some perspective while strolling atop Xī'ān's formidable old **city walls** (p424)

- Scale the granite cliffs of Taoism's sacred western peak, **Huá Shān** (p433), for inspiring views of the sunrise and the Qinling Mountains

- Take time out to visit rural China in the village of **Dǎngjiācūn** (p435)

- POPULATION: 37.2 MILLION

SHAANXI (SHĂNXĪ) 陕西

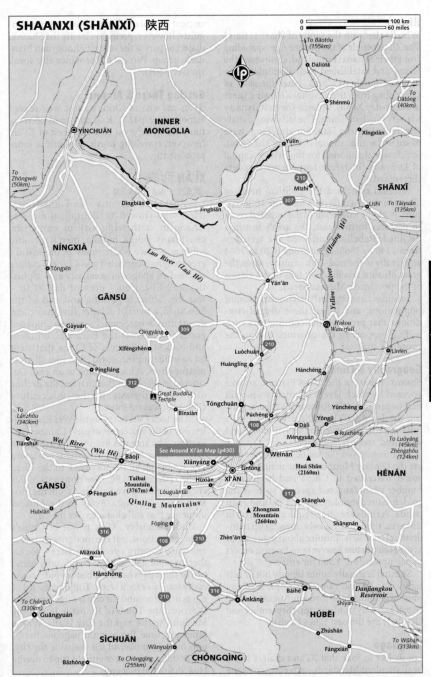

0 ————— 100 km
0 ————— 60 miles

INNER MONGOLIA

YÍNCHUĀN

To Zhōngwèi (50km)

NÍNGXIÀ

Tóngxìn

GĀNSÙ

Gùyuán

Qìngyáng

Xīfēngzhèn

Píngliáng

Luo River (Luò Hé)

Dìngbiān

Jìngbiān

Great Buddha Temple

Bīnxiàn

Tóngchuān

To Lánzhōu (340km)

Tiānshuǐ

Wei River (Wèi Hé)

Bǎojī

GĀNSÙ

Fèngxiàn

Huīxiàn

Taibai Mountain (3767m)

Lóuguāntái

Qinling Mountains

Fóping

Miǎnxiàn

Hànzhōng

To Chéngdū (330km)

Guǎngyuán

Bāzhōng

Wànyuán

To Chóngqìng (255km)

SÌCHUĀN

CHÓNGQÌNG

To Bǎotóu (155km)

Dàliùtǎ

Shénmù

Yúlín

Xīngxiàn

To Dàtóng (40km)

Mǐzhī

210

307

Lìshí

To Tàiyuán (135km)

SHĂNXĪ

Yán'ān

Yellow River (Huáng Hé)

Húkǒu Waterfall

Luòchuān

210

Huánglíng

Línfén

Hánchéng

309

312

108

Pǔchéng

Yùnchéng

Yǒngjì

Ruìchéng

Dàlì

Mèngyuán

Wèinán

To Luòyáng (45km); Zhèngzhōu (124km)

See Around Xī'ān Map (p430)

Xiányáng

Líntóng

XĪ'ĀN

Húxiàn

Huá Shān (2160m)

HÉNÁN

312

Shāngluò

Zhongnan Mountain (2604m)

Zhèn'ān

Shāngnán

108

210

Báihé

Shíyàn

Danjiangkou Reservoir

316

Ānkāng

HÚBĚI

Zhúshān

To Wǔhàn (313km)

Fángxiàn

History
Who lies beneath the sands of Shaanxi time? The Zhou people of the Bronze Age, spreading from their Shaanxi homeland, conquered the Shang and established their dominion over much of northern China. Later the state of Qin, ruling from their capital Xiányáng (near modern-day Xī'ān), became the first dynasty to unify much of China. The following dynasties, including the Han, Sui and Tang, were based in the great capital of Cháng'ān (Xī'ān), which was abandoned for the eastern capital of Luòyáng (in Hénán) whenever invaders threatened.

Shaanxi remained the political heart of China for over a millennia until the 10th century. With the migration of the imperial court to pastures further east, the area's fortunes declined. Rebellions afflicted the territory from 1340 to 1368, again from 1620 to 1644 and finally in the mid-19th century, when the great Muslim rebellion left tens of thousands of the province's Muslims dead.

Famines have regularly decimated peasant populations, and it was these dismal conditions that provided the communists such willing support in the province during the country's civil war.

Geography & Climate
Shaanxi is part of the Loess Plateau, an area covered by thick layers of microscopic silt that began blowing down from Siberia during the Ice Age. The hallmarks of China's 'yellow earth' are cave houses (yáodòng) and a fissured, treeless landscape.

Running across the south of the province are the Qinling Mountains, the major north–south watershed in China and home to a number of endangered species, such as the golden-haired monkey, crested ibis and giant panda. Permits are often required to travel in this area, though it's slowly opening up to individual travellers. Inquire about ecotourism at the **Foping Nature Reserve** (www.fpnr.com); expect to pay upwards of Y500 for entry.

Shaanxi is usually either bloody hot or bitterly cold. Annual rainfall is a sparse 50cm, most of it falling June through August. Spring (April and May) and autumn (September and October) are the best times to visit.

Language
Locals like to joke that Xī'ān's dialect is the 'real' standard Mandarin – after all, it was the ancient capital of China. Those unfunny linguists, however, prefer to classify the Shaanxi dialect as part of the central Zhongyuan Mandarin group. Parts of the province also speak Jin (see p404).

Getting There & Around
Xī'ān has one of China's most well-served airports (see p427). Rail and road connections are quite good east and west of Xī'ān; however, travelling north or south is more problematic.

XĪ'ĀN 西安
☎ 029 / pop 3,256,000
Long before the country – and other countries – kowtowed to Běijīng, there was Cháng'ān: a thriving city of emperors, courtesans, poets, monks, merchants and soldiers; a place where many of the world's great religions coexisted and Chinese culture reached an apogee of creativity and sophistication. Cháng'ān – present-day Xī'ān – was the fabled beginning and end of the Silk Road, a swirl of colours, lute music and desert dust, where camel caravans unloaded goods from across the Eurasian continent and packed up aspects of China that went on to influence the world. But, like all great metropolises, it had to come to an end. Destroyed in rebellions that marked the decline of the Tang dynasty, by the 10th century Cháng'ān was no more.

Xī'ān today sits in the fertile Wei River valley, one of the epicentres of early Chinese civilisation. The area was home to the capitals of several major dynasties (historians can count 11), stretching all the way back to the Zhou in the 11th century BC. The remnants of this ancient world are everywhere – from the First Emperor's Terracotta Army to the Muslim influence that still characterises the city.

Understandably, Xī'ān is one of China's major attractions, but the modern city is also one of the country's great polarisers – you either love it or hate it. Most people only spend two or three days here, but history buffs could easily stay busy for a week. Topping the list of sights in and around the city are the Terracotta Warriors, the Tomb of Emperor Jingdi, the Muslim Quarter and the City Walls. With a little more time, throw in the pagodas, museums or any number of sites outside the city. Better still, arrange an overnight trip to nearby Huá Shān or Hánchéng.

Orientation

Xī'ān retains the same rectangular shape that once characterised Cháng'ān, with streets and avenues forming a neat grid pattern.

The central block of the modern city is bound by the city walls. At the city centre is the enormous Bell Tower, from where Xī'ān's four major streets connect: Bei, Nan, Dong and Xi Dajie. The train station stands at the northeastern edge of the city centre.

Most of the tourist facilities can be found in the vicinity of the Bell Tower. However, some of the city's sights, such as the Shaanxi History Museum, Big Goose Pagoda and Little Goose Pagoda are located south of the city walls.

MAPS

Pick up a copy of the widely available *Xi'an Traffic & Tourist Map* (Y8). This bilingual publication has exhaustive listings and is regularly updated – even the bus routes are correct.

Information

CD BURNING

Burn digital photos onto CDs at the youth hostels (per disc Y25), or at **Kodak** (Jiādá Shùmǎ Zhōngxīn; Nan Dajie; per disc Y30) near the Bell Tower.

INTERNET ACCESS 网吧

All hostels and many hotels offer internet access. There are few internet cafés inside the city walls.
Hàngōng Wǎngbā (per hr Y3) Turn west off Nan Dajie at the KFC and look for the Night Cat disco.

INTERNET RESOURCES

Tour Easy (www.toureasy.net) The online survival guide to Xī'ān.

MEDICAL SERVICES

In the event of an emergency, call ☎ 120.

MONEY

ATM (Qǔkuǎnjī; 24hr) You should have no trouble finding usable ATMs. When in doubt, try the southeast corner of the Bell Tower intersection.
Bank of China (Zhōngguó Yínháng) Juhuayuan Lu (38 Juhuayuan Lu; 8am-8pm); Nan Dajie (29 Nan Dajie; 8am-6pm) You can exchange cash and travellers cheques and use the ATMs at both of these branches.

POST

Post Office (Yóudiàn Dàlóu; Bei Dajie; 8am-8pm)

PUBLIC SECURITY BUREAU

PSB (Gōngānjú; ☎ 1682 1225; 136 Xi Dajie; 8.30am-noon & 2-6pm Mon-Fri) Visa extensions generally take five days.

TRAVEL AGENCIES

China International Travel Service (CITS; Zhōngguó Guójì Lǚxíngshè) Main Office (☎ 8524 1864; fax 5526 1453; 48 Chang'an Beilu); Branch Office (☎ 8760 0227 ext 227; 2nd fl, Bell Tower Hotel, Xi Dajie) The Bell Tower Hotel office is best for organising tours.
Golden Bridge Travel (☎ 8725 7975, fax 8725 8863; Rm 219, 2nd fl, Bell Tower Hotel, Xi Dajie) An alternate choice down the hall from CITS. It gets mixed reviews from readers.

Sights

INSIDE THE CITY WALLS

Bell Tower & Drum Tower 钟楼、鼓楼

The **Bell Tower** (Zhōng Lóu; admission Y20, combined Drum Tower ticket Y30; 8.30am-9.30pm, shorter hr in winter) originally held a large bell that was rung at dawn, while its alter ego, the **Drum Tower** (Gǔ Lóu; Beiyuanmen; admission Y20, combined Bell Tower ticket Y30; 8.30am-9.30pm, shorter hr in winter), marked nightfall. Both date from the 14th century and were later rebuilt in the 1700s (the Bell Tower initially stood two blocks to the west). Musical performances are held inside each from 9am to 11.30am and 2.30pm to 5.30pm. The Bell Tower is entered through the underpass on the north side.

Muslim Quarter

The backstreets leading north from the Drum Tower have been home to the city's Hui community (Chinese Muslims) for centuries. Although Muslims have been here since at least the 7th century, some believe that today's community didn't take root until the Ming dynasty.

The narrow lanes are full of butcher shops, sesame-oil factories, smaller mosques hidden behind enormous wooden doors and proud, stringy-bearded men wearing white skullcaps. Good streets to stroll down are Xiyang Shi, Dapi Yuan and Damaishi Jie, which runs north off Xi Dajie through an interesting Islamic food market.

Great Mosque 清真大寺

One of the largest mosques in China, the **Great Mosque** (Qīngzhēn Dàsì; www.xaqzds.com; Huajue Xiang; admission Y12, free for Muslims; 8am-7pm, 8am-5.30pm Oct-Mar) is a fascinating blend of Chinese and

SHAANXI (SHĂNXĪ)

SHAANXI (SHĂNXĪ)

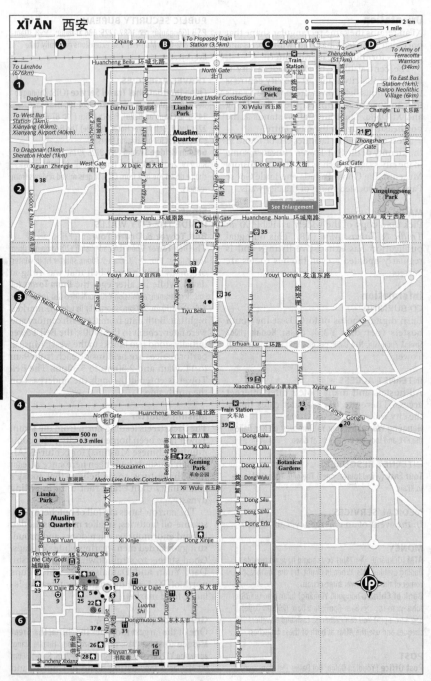

INFORMATION

- ATM 取款机 1 A6
- Bank of China 中国银行 2 B6
- Bank of China 中国银行 3 A6
- CITS 中国国际旅行社 4 B3
- CITS 中国国际旅行社 5 A6
- Golden Bridge Travel .... (see 5)
- Hàngōng Wǎngbā 汉宫网吧 6 A6
- Kodak 佳达数吗中心 7 A6
- Post Office 邮电大楼 8 B6
- PSB 公安局 9 A6

SIGHTS & ACTIVITIES

- 8th Route Army Memorial 八路军西安办事处纪念馆 10 B4
- Bell Tower 钟楼 11 A6
- Bell Tower Square 钟鼓楼广场 12 A6
- Big Goose Pagoda 大雁塔 13 C4
- Drum Tower 鼓楼 14 A6
- Folk House 高家大院 15 A5
- Forest of Stelae Museum 碑林博物馆 16 B6
- Great Mosque 清真大寺 17 A6
- Little Goose Pagoda 小雁塔 18 B3
- Shaanxi History Museum 陕西历史博物馆 19 C4
- Tang Dynasty Arts Museum 唐代艺术博物馆 .... (see 13)
- Tang Paradise Theme Park 大唐芙蓉园 20 D4
- Temple of the Eight Immortals 八仙庵 21 D1

SLEEPING

- Bell Tower Youth Hostel 钟楼青年旅社 .... (see 8)
- City Hotel Xi'an 西安城市酒店 22 A6
- Han Tang Inn 汉唐驿 23 A6
- Howard Johnson Plaza Hotel 金花豪生国际大酒店 24 B2
- Melody Hotel 美伦酒店 25 A6
- Prince Hotel 王子国际酒店 26 A6
- Qixian Youth Hostel 七贤庄 27 B4
- Shuyuan Youth Hostel 书院青年旅舍 28 A6
- Sofitel 索菲特人民大厦 29 B5
- Wényuàn Dàjiǔdiàn 文苑大酒店 30 A6

EATING

- Bell Tower Hotel 钟楼饭店 .... (see 5)
- Dé Fā Cháng 德发长 .... (see 12)
- King Town No 1 秦唐一号中国餐馆 31 B6
- Lǎo Sūn Jiā 老孙家 32 B6
- Máogōng Xiāngcàiguǎn 毛公湘菜馆 33 B3
- Wǔyī Fàndiàn 五一饭店 34 B6

ENTERTAINMENT

- Shaanxi Grand Opera House 陕歌大剧院 35 C2
- Tang Dynasty 唐乐宫 36 C3

TRANSPORT

- Advance Train Ticket Booking Office 代售火车票 37 A6
- Airport Shuttle Bus 民航班车接待处 .... (see 25)
- China Northwest Airlines 西北民航局 38 A2
- Long-Distance Bus Station 汽车省站 39 C4

Islamic architecture. Facing west (towards Mecca) instead of the usual south, the mosque begins with an obvious Chinese temple feature, the spirit wall, designed to keep demons at bay. The gardens, too, with their rocks, pagodas and archways are obviously Chinese, with the exception of the four palm trees at the entrance. Arab influence, meanwhile, extends from the central minaret (cleverly disguised as a pagoda) to the enormous, turquoise-roofed Prayer Hall (not open to visitors) at the back of the complex, as well as the elegant calligraphy gracing most entryways. The present buildings are mostly Ming and Qing, though the mosque is said to have been founded in the 8th century.

To get here, follow Xiyang Shi several minutes west and look for a small alley leading south past a gauntlet of souvenir stands.

Folk House 高家大院

This well-rounded **historic residence** (Gāo Jiā Dàyuán; 144 Beiyuanmen; admission Y15, with tea Y20; 9am-10pm) also serves as an art gallery, entertainment centre and teahouse. Originally the home of the Qing bureaucrat Gao Yuesong, much of the residence has been tastefully restored, and includes reception rooms, bedrooms, servants' quarters, an ancestral temple and a study (now the teahouse).

Tours start with an optional marionette or shadow puppet demonstration (Y10). As the complex currently belongs to the Shaanxi Artists Association, you can also visit artists' studios; if you're interested in traditional Chinese art, this is a great place to consider a purchase. Prices are reasonable (from Y150) and the artwork (paintings, calligraphy, ceramics, photographs and tea ware) is of particularly high quality.

Don't try to find this place looking at the street numbers, as No 144 isn't where it should be.

Forest of Stelae Museum 碑林博物馆

Housed in Xī'ān's Confucius Temple, this **museum** (Bēilín Bówùguǎn; 15 Sanxue Jie; admission Y30; 8am-6.30pm) holds over 1000 stone stelae (inscribed tablets), including the nine Confucian classics and some exemplary calligraphy. Although the main exhibit often leaves foreigners scratching their heads, there are nevertheless a few points of interest. The 2nd gallery holds a Nestorian tablet (AD 781), the earliest recorded account of Christianity in China. (The Nestorians professed that Christ was both human and divine, for which they were booted out of the Church in 431.) The 4th gallery holds a collection of ancient maps and portraits, and is where rubbings (copies) are made, an interesting process to watch.

Worth the admission fee alone is the fantastic sculpture gallery (across from the gift shop), which contains animal guardians, pictorial tomb stones and Buddhist statuary. There are also two temporary exhibits usually on display near the main entrance.

The museum is reached by following Shuyuan Xiang east from the South Gate.

8th Route Army Memorial 八路军西安办事处纪念馆

The Communist Party's austere Xī'ān **headquarters** (Bālùjūn Xī'ān Bànshìchù Jìniànguǎn; Beixin Jie; admission free; 9am-5pm) was located here from 1937 to 1946. The memorial consists primarily of old photos (no English) and one room dedicated to the activist Helen Foster Snow, the wife of journalist Edgar Snow.

OUTSIDE THE CITY WALLS
City Walls 城墙

Xī'ān is one of the few cities in China where the old **City Walls** (Chéngqiáng; admission Y40; 7am-10.30pm, 8am-6pm Oct-Mar) are still standing. Built in 1370 during the Ming dynasty, the walls are 12m high, up to 18m thick at the base and form a rectangle with a perimeter of 14km. The walls are surrounded by a moat, and the park-like strip in between is popular with traditional musicians.

Most sections have been restored or rebuilt, and it is now possible to walk the entirety of the walls in a lazy four hours. You can also cycle from the South Gate (bike hire per half-hour Y15). Access ramps are located inside the major gates with the exception of the South Gate, where the entrance is outside the walls; there's another entrance inside the walls beside the Forest of Stelae Museum.

To get an idea of Xī'ān's former grandeur, consider this: the Tang city walls originally enclosed 83 sq km, an area seven times larger than today's city centre.

Big Goose Pagoda 大雁塔

Xī'ān's most famous landmark, this **pagoda** (Dàyàn Tǎ; 8521 5014; Yanta Nanlu; admission Y25, plus Y20 to climb the pagoda; 8am-6.30pm, 8am-6pm Nov-Apr) was completed in AD 652 to house the Buddhist sutras brought back from India by the monk Xuan Zang. Xuan Zang spent the last 19 years of his life translating scriptures with a crack team of linguist monks; many of these translations are still used today. His travels also inspired one of the most well-known works of Chinese literature, *Journey to the West*.

Surrounding the pagoda is **Da Ci'en Temple**, one of the largest temples in Tang Cháng'ān. The buildings today date from the Qing dynasty.

Bus 610 from the Bell Tower and bus 609 from the South Gate drop you off at the pagoda square; the entrance is on the south side. Of note is the evening fountain show held on the square (see p426).

The **Tang Dynasty Arts Museum** (Tángdài Yìshù Bówùguǎn; admission Y5; 8.30am-5.30pm), on the eastern side of the temple, has a small collection specifically devoted to Tang clothing, architecture and artefacts.

Little Goose Pagoda 小雁塔

This **pagoda** (Xiǎoyàn Tǎ; Youyi Xilu; admission Y18, plus Y10 for 'pagoda mounting'; 8am-6pm) is in the pleasant grounds of Jianfu Temple. The top of the pagoda was shaken off by an earthquake in the middle of the 16th century, but the rest of the 43m-high structure is intact.

Jianfu Temple was originally built in AD 684 to bless the afterlife of the late Emperor Gaozong. The pagoda, a rather delicate building of 15 progressively smaller tiers, was built from AD 707–709 and housed Buddhist scriptures brought back from India by the pilgrim Yi Jing. You can mount the pagoda for a worthy panorama of Xī'ān.

Bus 610 runs here from the Bell Tower; from the South Gate take bus 203.

Shaanxi History Museum 陕西历史博物馆

Shaanxi's **museum** (Shǎnxī Lìshǐ Bówùguǎn; 8525 4727; 90 Xiaozhai Donglu; admission Y35; 8.30am-6pm, 9am-5.30pm Oct-Apr) is often touted as one of China's best, though you may come away feeling there's some unfulfilled potential here. Regardless, what is on display definitely makes for an illuminating stroll through ancient Xī'ān.

The ground floor covers prehistory and the early dynastic period. Particularly impressive are several enormous Shang and Western Zhou dynasty bronze tripods (*dǐng*), Qin burial objects, bronze arrows and crossbows, and four original terracotta warrior statues.

Upstairs, the second section is devoted primarily to Han dynasty relics. The highlights include a collection of about 40 terracotta figurines from the Xianyang Tombs (see p432). There's also an imaginative collection of bronze lamps, Wei figurines and mythological animals.

The third section focuses primarily on Sui and Tang artefacts: expressive tomb guardians; murals depicting a polo match; and a series of painted pottery figurines with elaborate hair styles and dress, including several bearded foreigners, musicians and braying camels.

Most exhibits include labels and explanations in English. Take bus 610 from the Bell Tower or bus 701 from the South Gate.

Temple of the Eight Immortals 八仙庵
This is Xī'ān's largest Taoist **establishment** (Bāxiān Ăn; Yongle Lu; admission Y3; 8am-5pm) and an active place of worship, purportedly built on the site of an ancient wine shop. The temple was constructed to protect against subterranean divine thunder. Scenes from Taoist mythology are painted around the courtyard. On Sunday and Wednesday mornings, there's a popular **antique market** here.

Bus 502 runs close by the temple (eastbound from Xi Xinjie).

Tang Paradise Theme Park 大唐芙蓉园
The city's most popular destination for Chinese tourists is probably this 165-acre Disneyfied **theme park** (Dàtáng Fúróngyuán; Yanyin Gonglu; admission Y50; 9am-10pm), which aims to re-create an entertainment-oriented version of the Tang dynasty.

Sleeping
If you're arriving by air and have not yet booked accommodation, keep in mind that representatives at the shuttle bus drop-off (Melody Hotel) can often get you discounted rooms at a wide selection of hotels.

BUDGET
All hostels in the city offer a similar range of services, including bike hire, internet, laundry, restaurant and travel services. Ask about free pick-up from the train station if you make a reservation.

Qixian Youth Hostel (Qīxián Zhuāng; ☎ 8744 4087; www.hihostels.com; 1 Beixin Jie; 北新街1号; dm Y30-50, tw Y150, s Y280;) This is the most secluded hostel, set in a traditional courtyard house with spacious rooms; the four-bed dorms feature snazzy attached bathrooms. Young communists should make a beeline for this place, as it adjoins the 8th Route Army Memorial (opposite). Take bus 610 from opposite the train station.

Shuyuan Youth Hostel (Shūyuàn Qīngnián Lǚshè; ☎ 8728 7720; www.hostelxian.com; 2 Shuncheng Xixiang; 南门里顺城西巷甲子2号; dm Y30-50; tw/d Y160;) The longest-running and best-equipped hostel, the Shuyuan also has an excellent location next to the South Gate. The laid-back lounge and courtyard areas are great places to hang out with fellow travellers. It's 20m west of the South Gate along the city walls. Take bus 603 from opposite the train station.

Bell Tower Youth Hostel (Zhōnglóu Qīngnián Lǚshè; ☎ 8723 3005; www.xianhostel.cn; 3rd fl, Post Office Bldg, 1 Bei Dajie; 北大街1号; dm Y40-65, tw Y180;) If you're urban at heart, this will probably be your pick, as it's smack in the middle of everything and has a distinct downtown buzz to it. Rooms are more cramped than other places, but some have great views of the Bell Tower, and the staff are exceptionally friendly. Take bus 603 from opposite the train station.

Han Tang Inn (Hàntáng Yǐ; ☎ 8723 1126; www.hostelxian.com; 211 Xi Dajie; 西大街211号; dm/tw/tr Y50/160/210;) West of the Muslim Quarter, the Han Tang has a cosy lounge area with TV and internet access, as well as access to basketball and badminton courts. The entrance is easy to miss; it's just west of Watson's. Take bus 611 from opposite the train station.

MIDRANGE
City Hotel Xi'an (Xī'ān Chéngshì Jiǔdiàn; ☎ 8721 9988; www.cityhotelxian.com; 70 Nan Dajie; 南大街70号; s Y266, tw Y300-600;) One of the better midrange options near the Bell Tower and a reader favourite. The modern rooms are quiet and reasonably priced. The entrance is down an alley 20m west off Nan Dajie. All major credit cards accepted.

Melody Hotel (Meĭlún Jiǔdiàn; ☎ 8728 8888; mlhotel@163.com; 86 Xi Dajie; 西大街86号; s Y328, tw Y400-600;) Overlooking the Drum Tower, the Melody is a reliable midrange choice that sports orange throw cushions in clean but otherwise uninspired rooms. An exercise room, restaurant and bar are on site.

Wényuàn Dàjiǔdiàn (☎ 8310 3000; 45 Xi Dajie; 西大街45号; s Y328, tw Y420-488;) This large but serene three-star hotel claims to be the 'intellectuals homeland'. No-one can explain what exactly this means, but at any rate it's more stylish than its competitors across the road. Ideally located for evening strolls through the Muslim Quarter.

Prince Hotel (Wángzi Guójì Jiǔdiàn; ☎ 8763 2222; fax 8763 2188; 32 Nan Dajie; 南大街32号; s/tw Y680/780;) With a promising location next to Louis Vuitton, the Prince achieves international standards of comfort, though it would certainly benefit from a more daring interior decorator (at least there's cable TV to watch). All major credit cards accepted.

TOP END

There's no shortage of familiar global chains in Xī'ān. Remember to always ask about discounts.

Howard Johnson Plaza Hotel (Jīnhuá Háoshēng Guójì Dàjiŭdiàn; ☎ 8842 1111; www.hojochina.com; 18 Huancheng Nanlu; 环城南路西段18号; d Y1360-1600; ❌ 🔲 🔲 ❌) Located just outside the South Gate, HoJo's new 19-storey tower has great panoramas. The postmodern interior (featuring a white piano encased in a giant glass-and-steel ball) is more Shànghǎi than Xī'ān, but the bottom line is competitively priced five-star chic.

Sofitel (Suǒfēitè Rénmín Dàshà; ☎ 8792 8888; www.sofitel.com; 319 Dong Xinjie; 东新街319号; d Y2000; ❌ 🔲 🔲 ❌) Xī'ān's self-proclaimed 'six-star' hotel is undoubtedly the most luxurious choice in the city. Curved lines and abstract art lend a familiar modernity to the place, although there's unfortunately not much in the way of local character. Reception is in the east wing; discounts out of season exceed 50%.

Eating

Hit the Muslim Quarter for fine eating in Xī'ān. Common dishes here are *mǎjiàng liángpí* (麻酱凉皮; cold noodles in sesame sauce), *fēnzhēngròu* (粉蒸肉; chopped mutton fried in a wok with ground wheat), *ròujiāmó* (肉夹馍; fried pork or beef in pita bread, sometimes with green peppers and cumin), *càijiāmó* (菜夹馍; the vegetarian version) and the ubiquitous *ròuchuàn* (肉串; kebabs).

Best of all is the delicious *yángròu pàomó* (羊肉泡馍), a soup dish that involves crumbling a flat loaf of bread into a bowl and adding noodles, mutton and broth. You can also pick up mouth-watering desserts like *huāshēnggāo* (花生糕; peanut cakes) and *shìbǐng* (柿饼; dried persimmons), which can be found at the market or in Muslim Quarter shops. A good street to wander for a selection of more typically Chinese restaurants is Dongmutou Shi, east of Nan Dajie.

Wǔyī Fàndiàn (Dong Dajie; dishes Y1-10) This cheap ground-floor restaurant is good for staple northern Chinese food, like pork dumplings and hearty bowls of noodles. It's popular with locals and always frenetic and noisy; there's some English on the menu.

King Town No 1 (Qìntáng Yīhào Zhōngguó Cānguǎn; 176 Dongmutou Shi; meals Y10-40) Red tableware and an inviting, modern interior set this place apart from its old-school neighbours. Downstairs serves tempting homestyle dishes (Y4 to Y16; no English); upstairs is a classier Sichuanese-Cantonese restaurant (Y12 to Y40; English menu).

Máogōng Xiāngcàiguǎn (☎ 8782 0555; 99 Youyi Xilu; dishes Y18-38) Dine under the reassuring gaze of the Chairman at one of the most popular and slickest restaurants in town. The Hunanese fare on offer includes smoked pork (Y28; No 2003), super-spicy deep-fried chicken (Y32; No 4012) and all the ribs you can eat. The best branch (锦绣店; jǐnxiùdiàn) is across from the Little Goose Pagoda. There's an English menu.

Lǎo Sūn Jiā (2nd fl, Dong Dajie; dishes Y20-40) The English menu at Xī'ān's most famous restaurant (over a century old) is unfortunately as restricted as an imperial concubine's foot. It doesn't matter, though, because all you need is a fantastic huge bowl of *yángròu pàomó* (Y21).

Dé Fā Cháng (2nd fl, Bell Tower Sq; dumpling banquets from Y60) Dumplings are the speciality here: banquets are a minimum five courses and feature every sort of dumpling shape you could possibly conceive of, from walnuts to flowers to stars and even miniature animals (thankfully these cost extra). Bizarre but delicious.

If you're desperate for Western food, there's no shortage of fast food in town. Otherwise, most top-end hotels serve buffets. The **Bell Tower Hotel** (Xi Dajie; buffet per person Y100) has been recommended by readers.

Entertainment

Xī'ān has enough going on at night to keep most everyone occupied. A number of travellers enjoy the evening **fountain and music show** (🕙 8pm winter, 9pm summer) at the Big Goose Pagoda Sq; it's the largest in Asia. If bars and clubs are more your thing, wander down Nan Dajie, which has the largest concentration of dance spots in the city (look for the lights on the side streets). A more laid-back strip of bars and coffee shops is located near the South Gate on Defu Xiang. Xī'ān also has a number of dinner-dance shows – you either love 'em or find them irrepressibly cheesy.

Tang Dynasty (Táng Yuègōng; ☎ 8782 2222; www.xiantangdynasty.com; 75 Chang'an Beilu; performance only Y200, with dinner Y410) The most famous dinner theatre in the city stages an over-the-top spectacle with Vegas-style costumes, traditional dance, music and singing. It's dubbed into English.

Shaanxi Grand Opera House (Shăngē Dàjùyuán; ☎ 8785 3295; www.tangdynastyshow.com; 165 Wenyi Lu; performance only Y198, with dinner Y278) Less known but no less impressive are the provincial performances by this group.

Shopping

For those who have always dreamed of owning a set of miniature terracotta warriors to serve as bookends or even to protect the backyard from an invasion of barbarian garden gnomes, you're in the right place. You'll be able to find local souvenirs at all the major museums, though these generally cost a small fortune. If your wallet isn't feeling up to the challenge, it's best to hunt down gifts in the Muslim Quarter, where prices can be as much as 20 times cheaper. Make sure that your purchase isn't so cheap that it will crumble in your luggage, though.

Xiyang Shi is a narrow alley running north of the Great Mosque and is probably the best stop for souvenirs. You'll find terracotta warriors, Huxian farmer paintings, shadow puppets, lanterns, tea ware, 'antiques', Mao memorabilia, T-shirts…you name it. Quality varies (almost everything is fake), so check purchases carefully and bargain hard – but don't confuse this with being rude. Smiling always helps. Close by near the Drum Tower is a covered market selling dried fruits and delicious cakes; great for snacks or an ascent of Huá Shān (p433).

Near the South Gate is the Qing-style Shuyuan Xiang, the main street for art supplies, paintings, calligraphy, paper cuts, brushes and fake rubbings from the Forest of Stelae Museum (p423). If you're after high-quality artwork, make sure to visit the Folk House (p423). Serious shoppers should also visit the antique market at the Temple of the Eight Immortals (p425) on Sunday and Wednesday mornings. The Temple of the City Gods (Chénghuáng Miào) also used to have an eclectic market, though at the time of writing it was closed for renovation.

Getting There & Away

AIR

Xī'ān's Xianyang Airport is one of China's best connected – you can fly to almost any major Chinese destination from here, as well as several international ones.

China Northwest Airlines (Xīběi Mínhángjú; ☎ 8870 0000; Laodong Nanlu; ☼ 8am-9pm) runs most flights to and from Xī'ān. It is also somewhat inconveniently located, 1.5km from the West Gate (Xī Mén). Daily flights include Běijīng (Y1050), Chéngdū (Y630), Guăngzhōu (Y1490), Shànghăi (Y1260) and Ürümqi (Y2050).

On the international front, there are four flights weekly to Hong Kong (Y1858) with both China Northwest Airlines and **Dragonair** (港龙航空; Gānglóng Hángkōng; ☎ 8426 0390; Sheraton Hotel, 262 Fenghao Donglu). However, many Hong Kong residents choose to depart from Shēnzhèn (Y1630), which has much better connections. China Northwest Airlines also has flights to Macau, Seoul, Bangkok, Kuala Lumpur, and Nagoya, Fukuoka, Niigata and Hiroshima in Japan.

There are numerous other outlets around town, as well as at most hotels, that sell airline tickets and are more centrally located.

BUS

The most central **long-distance bus station** (qìchē shēngzhàn) is opposite Xī'ān's train station. Note that many more buses run to Huá Shān (10am to 6pm) from in front of the train station.

Other bus stations around town (where you may be dropped off if you arrive by bus) include the **east bus station** (城东客运站; chéngdōng kèyùnzhàn; Changle Lu) and the **west bus station** (城西客运站; chéngxī kèyùnzhàn; Zaoyuan Donglu). Both are located outside the Second Ring Rd; bus 605 travels between the Bell Tower and the east bus station, and bus 103 travels between the train station and the west bus station. A taxi into the city costs Y20 to Y30.

For day trips around Xī'ān, see the relevant sights for transport details.

TRAIN

A new train station (huŏchē zhàn) north of the Second Ring Rd is planned for 2008; until then a temporary station may be set up south of the city, although no-one could confirm this. At the time of writing the old station was still operating as normal.

In any case, buy your onward tickets as soon as you arrive, as sleeper berths are hard to come by. Most hotels and hostels can get you tickets (Y40 commission); there's also an **Advance Train Ticket Booking Office** (Dàishòu Huŏchēpiào; Nan Dajie; ☼ 8.30am-noon & 2-5pm) in the ICBC Bank's south entrance. Otherwise, brave the surging chaos of the main ticket hall.

BUSES FROM XĪ'ĀN'S LONG-DISTANCE BUS STATION

Destination	Price	Duration	Frequency	Departs
Huá Shān	Y25	2hr	3 daily	11am, noon, 2.30pm
Yán'ān	Y78	5½hr	40min	6.40am-4.20pm
Hánchéng	Y47	4hr	half-hourly	7am-4pm
Zhèngzhōu	Y131	6½hr	hourly	7.30am-4.30pm
Luòyáng	Y90	4hr	40min	6.40am-5.50pm
Tàiyuán	Y160	8hr	hourly	8am-4pm
Píngyáo	Y136	7hr	hourly	8am-4pm

Xī'ān is well connected to the rest of the country. Deluxe Z-trains run to/from Beijing West (soft sleeper only Y417, 11½ hours), leaving Xī'ān at 7.23pm and Běijīng at 8.28pm. Several express trains also make the journey (Y274, 12½ hours); departures begin late afternoon.

Other destinations include Chéngdū (Y122, 16½ hours), Chóngqìng (Y113, 14 hours), Guǎngzhōu (Y430, 26 hours), Guìlín (Y334, 27 hours), Jǐ'nán (Y208, 15 to 17 hours), Kūnmíng (Y343, 37 hours), Lánzhōu (Y175, 7½ to nine hours), Luòyáng (Y87, five hours), Píngyáo (Y86, nine to 11 hours), Shànghǎi (Y333, 16 to 21 hours), Tàiyuán (Y99, 10 to 12 hours), Ürümqi (Y287, 31 to 40 hours) and Zhèngzhōu (Y79 to Y133, six to eight hours).

Within Shaanxi, there are two overnight trains to Yúlín (Y160, 12 to 14 hours) via Yán'ān (Y100, eight to 10 hours) departing at 10.10pm and 10.40pm. Buy your tickets in advance. There is also a 7.15am train to Hánchéng (Y24, 4½ hours).

Getting Around

Xī'ān's Xianyang Airport is about 40km northwest of Xī'ān. Shuttle buses run hourly from 6am to 6pm between the airport and the Melody Hotel (Y25, one hour), stopping off at other hotels on the way. Taxis into the city charge over Y100 on the meter.

In the city itself, it's easiest to bike or take taxis, which are relatively cheap with a flag fall of Y6. You can hire bicycles at the youth hostels (average Y10 for four hours).

Of course, seasoned China travellers will no doubt be itching to try out the public buses, which go to all the major sights in and around the city. Bus 610 is a good one: it starts at the train station and passes the Bell Tower, Little Goose Pagoda, Shaanxi History Museum and Big Goose Pagoda. Remember that the packed buses are a pickpocket's paradise, so watch your valuables.

The official word on the city's first metro line is that it will be completed in 2009; many residents, however, say the year 2100 is a better estimate.

AROUND XĪ'ĀN

The plains surrounding Xī'ān are strewn with early imperial tombs, many of which have not yet been excavated. But unless you have a particular fascination for dead bodies and burial sites, you can probably come away satisfied after visiting just one or two sites.

The Army of Terracotta Warriors is obviously the most famous; however, be sure to try and get to the Tomb of Emperor Jingdi as well. Another major attraction is Famen Temple, famous for Buddhist relics – in particular four of the Buddha's fingerbones.

The downside here is that the major sites are in totally different directions. If your time is limited, you'll have to pick and choose. Tourist buses run to almost all of the sites from in front of Xī'ān train station – note, however, that when the current train station closes (p427), the bus routes may change. Ask your hotel for an update.

Sights

EAST OF XĪ'ĀN

Army of Terracotta Warriors 兵马俑

The actual sight of the **Terracotta Army** (Bīngmǎyǒng; www.bmy.com.cn; admission Y90 Mar-Nov, Y65 Dec-Feb; ☯ 8.30am-5.30pm) initially proves to be so boggling that you can't get your head around it. It's hard to imagine, after all, that a subterranean life-size army of thousands has silently stood guard over the soul of China's first unifier for over two millennia. Whether Qin Shi Huang was terrified of the vanquished spirits awaiting him in the afterlife, or, as most archaeologists believe, he expected his rule to continue in death as it had in life – either way, the guardians of his tomb today offer some of the greatest insights we have into the world of ancient China.

The discovery of the Army was, like many major discoveries, entirely serendipitous. In 1974 peasants drilling a well uncovered one of the largest and most important finds of the 20th century: an underground vault that eventually yielded thousands of terracotta soldiers and horses in battle formation. Over the years the site became so famous that many of its unusual attributes are now well known, in particular the fact that no two soldier's faces are alike.

Unfortunately, because you can't get that close to the soldiers *in situ,* some people come away feeling disappointed. To really appreciate a trip here you need background info – if you're not with a guide, the best place to start is with the documentary film in the on-site theatre. The film gives a brief overview of the historical context of the warriors, as well as a primer on how they were sculpted. From here you can then visit the site in reverse, so as to save the most impressive pit for last.

Start with the smallest pit (Pit 3, containing 72 warriors and horses), which is believed to be the army headquarters due to the number of high-ranking officers unearthed here. It's interesting to note that the northern room

would have been used to make sacrificial offerings before battle. Moving on to the next pit (Pit 2, containing around 1300 warriors and horses), you'll have the chance to examine five soldiers up close: a kneeling archer, a standing archer, a cavalryman and horse, a mid-ranking officer and a general. The level of detail is startling: the expressions, hairstyles, armour and even the tread on the footwear are all unique.

The largest pit (Pit 1) is the most imposing. Some 6000 warriors and horses stand here in rectangular battle array, facing east. The vanguard of three rows of archers (both crossbow and longbow) is followed by the main force of soldiers, who originally held spears, swords, dagger-axes and other long-shaft weapons. The infantry were accompanied by 35 chariots, though these, made of wood, have long since disintegrated.

Almost as extraordinary as the soldiers is a pair of bronze chariots and horses unearthed just 20m west of the Tomb of Qin Shi Huang. These are now on display, together with some of the original weaponry, in a small museum to the right of the main entrance.

If you'd like to hire an English-speaking tour guide at the site, you shouldn't have too much trouble. Outside the entrance the price is Y100, while inside you can often talk the guides down to as little as Y50. Keep in mind, however, that the lower you push down their

---

THE MAN BEHIND THE ARMY

History belongs to the winners – or so we often say. But China's history has its own little twist: it wasn't so much dictated by conquerors as it was written by Confucian bureaucrats. Whether or not an emperor got a decent posthumous write-up depended on just how well he treated his staff. No-one better exemplifies this than Qin Shi Huang, who, as the first person to unify China, could have become an unassailable patriarchal figure – if he hadn't eternally ticked off the scholar-official class.

The First Emperor was definitely a chronic overachiever. His accomplishments in 36 years of rule (which began at age 13) are nothing short of amazing. He created an efficient, centralised government that became the model for later dynasties; he standardised measurements, currency and, most importantly, writing (thus getting around the tricky dialect problem); he built over 6400km of new roads and canals; and, of course, he conquered six major kingdoms before turning 40.

But like many classic Type A personalities, Qin Shi Huang struggled with some serious issues: he was a fanatical, paranoid control freak, he enslaved hundreds of thousands of people to work on massive construction projects, he ordered almost all written texts to be burnt and (so legend has it) he took criticism so badly that he buried 460 disapproving scholars alive.

All of that coupled with an adherence to Legalist philosophy (archrivals of the Confucians) did not make the First Emperor popular with later historians. He's essentially remembered as the tyrant he was – but who nevertheless set a precedent for autocratic rule that continues to this day.

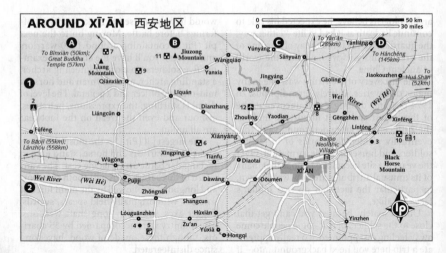

AROUND XĪ'ĀN 西安地区

fee, the faster they'll push you through the site (though you can go back). Expect these prices to be jacked up on peak days.

The Army is easily reached by public bus. From the Xī'ān train station parking lot, take the green Terracotta Warriors minibuses (Y7, one hour) or the less-frequent bus 306 (Y7, one hour), both of which travel via Huaqing Hot Springs. The parking lot for all vehicles is a good 15-minute walk from the site. If you don't feel like walking, electric carts (Y4) zoom back and forth to the ticket office. There's a self-service cafeteria inside (Y38), but the restaurants across from the parking lot are better. If you can, avoid meal times entirely.

Tomb of Qin Shi Huang 秦始皇陵

In its time this **tomb** (Qín Shǐhuáng Líng; admission Y40; 7am-6pm) must have been one of the grandest mausoleums the world had ever seen.

Historical accounts describe it as containing palaces filled with precious stones, underground rivers of flowing mercury and ingenious defences against intruders. The tomb reputedly took 38 years to complete, and required a workforce of 700,000 people. It is said that the artisans who brought it all into being were buried alive within, taking its secrets with them.

Still unexcavated, all there is to see for the time being is a mound (and occasional performances). If you're interested, the tomb is about 1.5km west of the Army of Terracotta Warriors. Take bus 306 from Xī'ān train station.

Huaqing Hot Springs 华清池

The natural hot springs in this **park** (Huáqīng Chí; admission Y70 Dec-Feb, Y40 Mar-Nov; 7am-7pm, 7.30am-6.30pm Nov-Mar) were once the favoured retreat of emperors and concubines during the Tang dynasty. The most famous bather of all was the femme fatale Yang Guifei, a concubine often given the blame for bewitching Emperor Xuanzong and bringing about the devastating An Lushan Rebellion in 756. She's since inspired stinging idioms like, 'hóngyán huòshuǐ – a beautiful face that causes catastrophe' (don't try this on your guide).

There are still public bathhouses here, though you're better off exploring the forested areas of the park, or hiking up to the Taoist temple on Black Horse Mountain (Lí Shān). The temple is dedicated to Nǚwā, who created the human race from clay and also patched up cracks in the sky.

Additionally, there's a small **museum** (Líntóng Bówùguǎn; admission Y24) with an interesting collection of Buddhist artefacts five minutes' walk up the road. Given the exorbitant entrance fee for what's essentially a park, consider skipping it if you're not on a tour. Both the Terracotta Warriors minibuses and bus 306 stop here on the way to and from the Warriors.

Banpo Neolithic Village 半坡博物馆

The **Banpo Neolithic Village** (Bànpō Bówùguǎn; admission Y20; 8am-6.30pm) is of enormous importance for Chinese archaeological studies, though as a tourist site it gets mixed reports. Parts of it were unbearably cheesy (Neolithic matriarchs wearing nylon stockings) before renovation began in 2004. At the time of writing it still hadn't reopened, but hopefully it's been given a touch more class.

Banpo is the earliest example of the Neolithic Yangshao culture. It appears to have been occupied from 4500 BC until around 3750 BC. As less than a quarter of the site has been excavated, little is really known of the early agrarians. However, circumstantial evidence indicates that the culture was possibly matriarchal; also of interest are shamanistic relics that have been unearthed.

The Banpo ruins are divided into three parts: a pottery-manufacturing area, a residential area and a cemetery. These include the remains of 45 houses or other buildings, over 200 storage cellars, six pottery kilns and 250 graves.

The electric trolley 105 from Xī'ān train station and bus 15 from the Bell Tower run past (ask where to get off); it's also generally included on tours. The entrance fee will almost certainly double or triple (or even quadruple) when it reopens.

NORTH & WEST OF XĪ'ĀN
Tomb of Emperor Jingdi 汉阳陵

The **Tomb of Emperor Jingdi** (Hàn Yánglíng; ☎ 371 5373; admission Y45 Mar-Nov, Y30 Dec-Feb; ⏱ 8am-7pm) is easily Xī'ān's most underrated highlight. A Han dynasty emperor influenced by Taoism, Jingdi (188–141 BC) based his rule upon the concept of *wuwei* (non-action or non-interference) and did much to improve the life of his subjects: he lowered taxes greatly, used diplomacy to cut back on unnecessary military expeditions and even reduced the punishment meted out to criminals. The contents of his tomb are particularly interesting, as

they reveal more about daily life than martial preoccupations – a total contrast with the Terracotta Army.

The site has been divided into two sections, the museum and the excavation area. Buy admission tickets at the museum, which holds a large display of numerous terracotta figurines (over 50,000 were buried here), including eunuchs, servants, domesticated animals and even female cavalry on horseback. The figurines originally had movable wooden arms (now gone) and were dressed in colourful silk robes.

However, the tomb itself, which is currently being excavated, is the real reason to make the trip out here. Inside are 21 narrow pits, parts of which have been covered by a glass floor, allowing you to walk over the top of ongoing excavations – it's a must for any amateur archaeologists. It culminates with a giant window through which you can see a large cross-section of one of the pits.

Unfortunately, getting here can be tricky. You can either try to find a Western Tour that visits the site (see p433), hire a taxi (figure on Y200 for a half-day) or take your chances with minibus 3-16, which leaves east of the Xī'ān train station parking lot at the bottom of the entrance ramp. Just make sure that they'll pick you up as well. Alternatively, because the tomb is located about 20km north of Xī'ān on the old airport road, you could potentially stop here if you're taking a taxi to the airport. In any case, take food with you.

A final note: Emperor Jingdi's tomb is also referred to as the Han Jing Mausoleum, Liu Qi Mausoleum and Yangling Mausoleum – if you get confused, consider yourself normal.

Famen Temple 法门寺

Thick with elderly Buddhists, this **temple** (Fǎmén Sì; temple & crypt/museum Y28/32; ⏱ 8.30am-5.30pm) was originally built to house four sacred finger-bones of the Buddha, presented to China by India's King Asoka. In 1981, after torrential rains had weakened the temple's ancient brick structure, the entire western side of its 12-storey pagoda collapsed. The subsequent restoration of the temple produced a sensational discovery. Below the pagoda in a sealed crypt were over 1000 sacrificial objects and royal offerings – all forgotten for over a millennia.

Unless you plan on lining up with the pilgrims in the crypt, it's best to head straight over to the museum (left of the temple entrance), which has four main galleries. The main exhibits are the elaborate gold and silver boxes (stacked on top of one another to form pagodas) and tiny crystal and jade coffins that originally held the four sections of the holy finger. Also on display are ornate incense burners, glass cups and vases (imported from the West along the Silk Road), statues, gold and silver offerings, and an excellent reproduced cross-section of the four-chamber crypt, which symbolised a tantric mandala (a geometric representation of the universe).

Famen Temple is 115km northwest of Xī'ān. Tour bus 2 from Xī'ān train station (Y18, departs 8am) runs to the temple and returns to Xī'ān at 5pm. The temple is also generally included on Western Tours (see opposite).

Xiányáng 咸阳

☎ 0910 / pop 976,200

Over 2000 years ago, Xiányáng was the capital of the Qin dynasty. Its chief attraction today is the **Xianyang City Museum** (咸阳市博物馆; Xiányáng Shì Bówùguǎn; Zhongshan Jie; admission Y20; ☉ 8.30am-5.30pm), which houses a remarkable collection of 3000 50cm-tall terracotta soldiers and horses, excavated from a Han dynasty tomb in 1965. The museum also holds an interesting chronological exhibit of horses in ancient China.

Buses run regularly to Xiányáng from Xī'ān's long-distance bus station (Y7, one hour). From Xiányáng's bus station, you'll see a clock tower ahead on the left-hand side of the road; turn right at this intersection and then left at Xining Jie.

The museum is 20 minutes by foot from the bus station on Zhongshan Jie, a continuation of Xining Jie.

Imperial Tombs 皇陵

A large number of imperial **tombs** (huáng líng) dot the Guānzhōng plain around Xī'ān. They are sometimes included on tours from Xī'ān (see opposite), though none are so remarkable as to be destinations in themselves.

In these tombs are buried the emperors of numerous dynasties, as well as empresses, concubines, government officials and high-ranking military leaders. Admission to the tombs varies from Y15 to Y45; opening hours are 8.30am to 5pm daily (closing later in summer).

The most impressive is the **Qian Tomb** (乾陵; Qián Líng), where China's only female emperor, Wu Zetian (AD 625–705), is buried

together with her husband Emperor Gaozong, whom she succeeded. The long Spirit Way (Yù Dào) here is lined with enormous, lichen-encrusted sculptures of animals and officers of the imperial guard, culminating with 61 (now headless) statues of leaders of ethnic groups in China who attended the emperor's funeral. The two stelae on the ground each stand more than 6m high. The Wordless Stele (Wúzi Bēi) is a blank tablet; one story goes that it symbolises Empress Wu's absolute power, which she considered inexpressible in words. Behind this is a small hill that you can jaunt up for spectacular views of the countryside.

The mausoleum is 85km northwest of Xī'ān; tour bus 3 (Y12, departure 8am) runs here from Xī'ān train station and returns in the early afternoon. The following four tombs are only accessible by taxi or via an organised tour (see Tours, opposite).

Near the Qian Tomb are the tombs of **Princess Yong Tai** (永泰墓; Yǒng Tài Mù) and **Prince Zhang Huai** (章怀墓; Zhāng Huái Mù), both who fell afoul of Empress Wu and were posthumously rehabilitated.

Other tombs include the **Zhao Tomb** (昭陵; Zhāo Líng), which belongs to the second Tang emperor, Taizong, who died in AD 649. This tomb set the custom of building imperial tombs on mountains, thus breaking the tradition of building them on the plains with an artificial hill over them. It's 70km northwest of Xī'ān.

Finally there's the **Mao Tomb** (茂陵; Mào Líng), a cone-shaped mound of rammed earth almost 47m high, and the largest of the Han imperial tombs. It's the resting place of Emperor Wudi (156–87 BC), the most powerful of the Han emperors. It's located 40km northwest of Xī'ān.

Great Buddha Temple 大佛寺

This large **temple** (Dàfó Sì; admission Y8) is quite a distance from Xī'ān, about 115km to the northwest outside Bīnxiàn (彬县). However, it is easy to reach on public transport and, better still, it opens up a route to the Taoist temples of Kōngtóng Shān in Gānsù (see p873). The main Buddha is 30m high and 34m wide; the grotto's exterior is framed by an impressive three-storey fortress tower. Two other caves house nearly 2000 arhat sculptures, shrines and stelae.

Buses to Bīnxiàn (Y32, four hours) leave from Xī'ān's long-distance bus station. From Bīnxiàn it's around 7km north to the temple complex; a motorcycle taxi will cost Y10. From the temple it's easy to flag down buses back (up till about 3.30pm).

Tours

One-day tours allow you to see all the sights around Xĭ'ān more quickly and conveniently than if you arranged one yourself. Itineraries differ somewhat, but there are two basic tours: an Eastern Tour and a Western Tour. Youth hostels have also begun Panda Tours to an endangered animals centre (more zoo than reserve) in the Louguantai National Forest, outside Lóuguāntái.

Most hotels run their own tours, but, as more than one reader has griped, be extremely cautious when booking. Ask what is included (admission fees, lunch, English-speaking guide) and try to get an exact itinerary, unless you don't mind being herded through the Terracotta Warriors faster than you can say 'earthshaking at home and abroad'.

EASTERN TOUR

The Eastern Tour (Dōngxiàn Yóulǎn) is the most popular as it includes the Army of Terracotta Warriors, as well as the Tomb of Qin Shi Huang, Banpo Neolithic Village, Huaqing Hot Springs and possibly the Big Goose Pagoda. Most travel agencies (p421) charge Y300 for an all-day (9am to 5pm), all-in excursion, including admission fees, lunch and guide. The youth hostels also run dependable tours.

It's possible to do a shortened version of this one on your own using the tourist minibuses, which pass by Huaqing Hot Springs, the Terracotta Warriors and the Tomb of Qin Shi Huang. Hiring a taxi for the day (around Y180 for all sights) is another option. It may not save you money, but it will give you more control over your schedule.

WESTERN TOUR

The longer Western Tour (Xīxiàn Yóulǎn) includes the Xianyang City Museum, some of the imperial tombs, and possibly also Famen Temple and (if you insist) the Tomb of Emperor Jingdi. It's far less popular than the Eastern Tour and consequently you may have to wait a couple of days for your agency to organise enough people. Travel agencies charge from Y500 upwards; CITS also hires out private cars (Y980 per day). A taxi for the day will cost anywhere from Y300 to Y600, depending on what you want to visit.

HUÁ SHĀN 华山

One of Taoism's five sacred mountains, the granite domes of Huá Shān were once one of those mythical places where 500-year-old hermits became one with the universe while surviving on an invigorating diet of pine needles and wild herbs. The spectacular scenery is still here: knife-blade ridges, twisted pine trees clinging to ledges, and vast, transcendent panoramas of green mountains and countryside stretching away to the horizon. The Taoists, however, have long been replaced by droves of happy-go-lucky visitors from all walks of life, seemingly loving every minute of the tough climb. So forget about all that New Agey Laotzu stuff – pull on some cloth slippers or high heels and get ready to have some fun!

The Ascent

There are three ways up the mountain to the **North Peak** (Běi Fēng), the first of five summit peaks. Two of these options start from the eastern base of the mountain, at the cable-car terminus. If your legs aren't feeling up to the task, an Austrian-built cable car is the easiest route. It can get you to the North Peak in 10 scenic minutes (one way/return Y60/100; from 7am to 7pm).

The second option is to work your way to the North Peak under the cable-car route. This takes a sweaty two hours, but two sections of 50m or so are quite literally vertical with nothing but a steel chain to grab onto and tiny chinks cut into the rock for footing.

The third option is the most popular and the one that will leave the most memories, both physically and psychologically. A 6km path leads to the North Peak from the village of Huá Shān, at the base of the mountain. It usually takes between three to five hours to reach the North Peak, and another hour or so to get to any one of the others (figure on a minimum eight hours to do the entire circuit, starting from the trailhead). The first 4km up are pretty easy going, but after that it's all steep stairs, and from the North Peak on to the other summits it's also fairly strenuous. Several narrow and almost vertical 'bottleneck' sections can be dangerous when the route is crowded, particularly under wet or icy conditions.

Then again, the scenery is often sublime. Along **Green Dragon Ridge** (Cānglóng Lǐng),

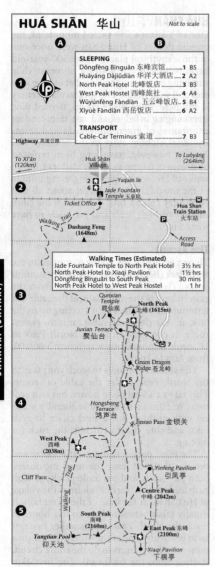

HUÁ SHĀN 华山

Not to scale

SLEEPING
Dōngfēng Bīnguǎn 东峰宾馆	1	B5
Huáyáng Dàjiǔdiàn 华洋大酒店	2	A2
North Peak Hotel 北峰饭店	3	B3
West Peak Hostel 西峰旅社	4	A4
Wǔyúnfēng Fàndiàn 五云峰饭店	5	B4
Xīyuè Fàndiàn 西岳饭店	6	A2

TRANSPORT
Cable-Car Terminus 索道	7	B3

Walking Times (Estimated)
Jade Fountain Temple to North Peak Hotel	3½ hrs
North Peak Hotel to Xiaqi Pavilion	1½ hrs
Dōngfēng Bīnguǎn to South Peak	30 mins
North Peak Hotel to West Peak Hostel	1 hr

which connects the North Peak with the **East Peak** (Dōng Fēng), **South Peak** (Nán Fēng) and **West Peak** (Xī Fēng), the way has been cut along a narrow rock ridge with impressive sheer cliffs on either side.

The South Peak is the highest at 2160m, but all three rear peaks afford great views when the weather cooperates.

There is accommodation on the mountain, most of it quite basic and overpriced, but it does allow you to start climbing in the afternoon, spend the night, and catch the sunrise from either the East Peak or South Peak. Many locals actually make the climb at night, aided by torches (flashlights) and countless tea and refreshment stands. The idea is to start at around 11pm to midnight, which should get you to the East Peak at sunrise. In summer this is certainly a much cooler option, but you do miss the scenery on the way up.

Admission is Y100 (Y50 November to March). To get to the cable car (suǒdào), take a taxi from the village to the parking lot (Y5) and then take a shuttle bus (Y10) the rest of the way.

Sleeping & Eating

You can either spend the night in Huá Shān village or on one of the peaks. Take your own food or eat well before ascending, or you'll be left with instant noodles and processed meat at the top – a proper meal can be eye-poppingly expensive. Don't forget a torch and enough warm clothes.

In the village, look for hotels along Yuquan Jie, the road leading up to the trailhead.

West Peak Hostel (Xīfēng Lǚshè; dm Y30-50; tw Y360) A rustic place atop West Peak that shares the premises with an old Taoist temple.

North Peak Hotel (Běifēng Fàndiàn; dm Y35) This small place is as busy as an anthill, but it is good to know about if you need to stop earlier than planned.

Huáyáng Dàjiǔdiàn (☎ 0913-436 6178; tw Y100, with shared bathroom Y40; ☒) This fairly clean place is 100m from the Huá Shān trailhead. Make sure to bargain.

Wǔyúnfēng Fàndiàn (dm/tw Y50/160) This hotel occupies a strategic location if you're planning on doing a circuit of the rear peaks the next day.

Dōngfēng Bīnguǎn (dm/tw Y80/520) Anything near the East Peak – given the sunrise – is going to cost you. It does have the best location on the mountain, though.

Xīyuè Fàndiàn (☎ 0913-436 4741; fax 436 8213; tw/tr Y200/320; ☒) This hotel is right near the Huá Shān trailhead and has more creature comforts than any other place in the village.

Most mountain accommodation consists of either dorms or private rooms – neither have their own bathrooms and expect nothing remotely luxurious.

Getting There & Away

From Xī'ān to Huá Shān, it's easiest to catch one of the private buses (Y25, two hours) that depart from in front of Xī'ān train station throughout the day. You'll be dropped off on the main street (Yuquan Jie), which is also where buses back to Xī'ān leave, from 7am to about 5.30pm. Coming from the east, try to talk your driver into dropping you at the Huá Shān highway exit if you can't find a direct bus. Don't pay more than Y10 for a taxi into Huá Shān village. There are few buses (if any) going east from Huá Shān. Pretty much everyone catches a taxi to the highway and then flags down buses headed for Yùnchéng, Tàiyuán or Luòyáng. If you can't read Chinese, try to find someone to help you out.

Alternatively, you can try the train. The nearest station is at Mèngyuán, on the Xī'ān–Luòyáng line, about 15km east of Huá Shān. This station is also referred to as Huá Shān, and is served by nearly a dozen trains a day in either direction. Maps of Huá Shān have comprehensive timetables (in Chinese), which will give you a good idea of when the next departure is. Trains to and from Xī'ān take two to three hours (hard seat Y31). Infrequent minibuses run between Huá Shān train station and the village (Y3, 30 minutes); a taxi will cost a minimum Y15.

HÁNCHÉNG 韩城

☎ 0913 / pop 150,000

Hánchéng is best known for being the home-town of Sima Qian (145–90 BC), China's legendary historian and author of the *Shiji* (Records of the Grand Historian). Sima Qian chronicled different aspects of life in the Han dynasty and set about arranging the country's already distant past in its proper (Confucian) order. He was eventually castrated and imprisoned by Emperor Wudi after having defended an unsuccessful general.

Hánchéng makes for a good overnight trip from Xī'ān. It boasts a handful of historic sights, but is far enough away to be off the main tourist circuit. Best of all, you can spend the night and savour homemade noodles in the neighbouring little village of Dǎngjiācūn.

Orientation

Hánchéng is built upon a hill. At the top is the new town (新城; *xīnchéng*), at the bottom is the old town (古城; *gǔchéng*). Hotels, banks and transport are all in the new town.

The train station (火车站; *huǒchē zhàn*) is at the northern end of the new town, the bus station (客运站; *kèyùn zhàn*) is two blocks east on Huanghe Dajie. The street Longmen Dajie (龙门大街) runs from the train station south to the old town.

You can change cash at the **Bank of China** (中国银行; Zhōngguó Yínháng; cnr Renmin Lu & Zhuangyuan Jie; ☼ 8am-6pm).

Sights

CONFUCIUS TEMPLE 文庙

The best sight in Hánchéng's old town is the tranquil **Confucius Temple** (Wén Miào; admission Y15; ☼ 8am-6pm), with dilapidated Yuan, Ming and Qing buildings, a half-moon pool, towering cypress trees and glazed dragon screens. The city museum holds peripheral exhibits in the wings. There are two other temples nearby, which are currently being renovated. A taxi here is Y5.

DǍNGJIĀCŪN 党家村

This 14th-century **village** (admission Y30; ☼ 7.30am-6.30pm) was obviously constructed according to the tenets of feng shui, occupying a sheltered location in a loess valley. Once the home of the Dang clan, successful merchants who ferried timber and other goods across the Yellow River, it's since evolved into a quintessential farming community. There are 125 preserved grey-brick courtyard houses here, remarkable for their carvings and mix of different architectural styles. The elegant six-storey tower is a **Confucian pagoda** (Wénxīng gé).

Dǎngjiācūn is 9km northeast of Hánchéng. To get here, take a minibus (Y2, 20 minutes) from the bus station to the entrance road, from where it's a pleasant 2km walk through fields to the village. Otherwise, you can take a taxi from Hánchéng (Y15).

THE TOMB OF SIMA QIAN 司马迁祠

The **Tomb of Sima Qian** (Sīmǎ Qiān Cí; admission Y35; ☼ 8am-6pm) probably used to be an exquisite place, built atop a hill overlooking fields and the nearby Yellow River. Unfortunately, the scenery has suffered somewhat from an elevated expressway that now dominates the landscape. The circular tomb isn't much to look at, but despite all that, it's quite popular with picnickers.

The tomb is 10km south of town. To get here, take bus 1 from the train station to its terminus at Nánguān and then switch to the green Sīmǎ Miào bus (Y2.5, 20 minutes). You'll have to catch a taxi back (Y15).

Sleeping

The best option is to spend the night in Dǎngjiācūn, where you can find homestays for Y10 (dorm accommodation). The home-cooking here is simple but fantastic.

If you'd prefer to spend the night in town, try the white-tiled **Tiānyuán Bīnguǎn** (天园宾馆; ☎ 529 9388; Longmen Dajie Beiduan; 龙门大街北段; tw/s Y148/228; ✷), across from the train station, or the plush **Yínhé Dàjiǔdiàn** (银河大酒店; ☎ 529 2111; fax 529 2888; Longmen Dajie Nanduan; 龙门大街南段; tw/tr Y300/358; ✷).

Getting There & Away

Hánchéng is really only accessible from Xī'ān, although there is one train that comes down from Běijīng via Tàiyuán.

Half-hourly buses leave Xī'ān's long-distance bus station for Hánchéng (Y47, four hours) from 7am to 4pm daily. Buses back to Xī'ān (Y50) run until 6pm – though these may drop you off at the east bus station. If you're in an exploratory mood, you can also cross over the Yellow River into Shānxī from here.

The best train to Hánchéng (Y24, 4½ hours) leaves Xī'ān at 7.15am. Going back to Xī'ān, you can either catch the 6.28am (6½ hours) or the 1.56pm (4½ hours) train.

Also of note is the 2.53pm local train, which passes through Píngyáo (Y99, arrives 9pm) and Tàiyuán (Y115, arrives 10.47pm) before terminating at Beijing West (Y216, arrives 8.30am). The return train departs from Beijing West at 7.43pm, arriving in Hánchéng at 1pm the next day.

YÁN'ĀN 延安

☎ 0911 / pop 117,200

Depending on whom you believe, Yán'ān was either communism's promised land or the location for the ominous beginnings of Emperor Mao's twisted dystopian rule. Either way, it's irrefutably the place where the Long March finally came to an end in 1935, a beleaguered 9500km away from its start in Jiāngxī province. Yán'ān served as the communists' power base until 1947, and it was from here that they fleshed out the ideologies specific to the Chinese revolution.

As such, Yán'ān is hallowed ground for patriots, and this otherwise nondescript backwater manages to pull in four-million photo-snapping 'red tourists' annually. For most foreign travellers, though, the town does little more than elicit long yawns and drooping eyelids – there's little reason to come here unless you've got a penchant for political history.

Orientation

Yán'ān is intriguingly spread out along a Y-shaped valley formed where the east and west branches of Yan River (Yán Hé) meet. The town centre is clustered around this junction, while the old communist army headquarters is at Yángjiālǐng on the northwestern outskirts of Yán'ān. The train station and south bus station are at the far southern end of Yán'ān, 4.5km from the town centre.

Information

Bank of China (Zhōngguó Yínháng; Beiguan Jie; ✷ 8am-7pm) Inconveniently located, but has an ATM.
Internet café (Wǎngbā; Yan'anshi Dajie; per hr Y2) On the 2nd floor of the post office.
Post and telephone office (Yóudiàn Dàlóu; Yan'anshi Dajie)
PSB (Gōngānjú; Yan'anshi Dajie) There is an office at the Yán'ān Bīnguǎn.

Sights

During their extended stay, the communist leadership moved house quite a bit within Yán'ān. As a result there are numerous former headquarters sites.

One of the most interesting sites is the **Yangjialing Revolution Headquarters Site** (杨家岭革命旧址; Yángjiālǐng Géming Jiùzhǐ; ☎ 211 2671; Zaoyuan Lu; admission Y16; ✷ 7am-7pm summer, 7.30am-6pm winter), 3km northwest of the town centre. Here you can see the assembly hall where the first central committee meetings were held, including the 7th national plenum, which formally confirmed Mao as the leader of the party and the revolution.

Nearby are simple **dugouts** built into the loess earth where Mao, Zhu De, Zhou Enlai and other senior communist leaders lived, worked and wrote. Further uphill are **caves** that used to house the secretariat, propaganda and personnel offices.

Further south is the last site occupied by the communist leadership in Yán'ān, the **Wangjiaping Revolution Headquarters Site** (Wángjiāpíng Géming Jiùzhǐ; ☎ 238 2161; Zaoyuan Lu; admission Y10; ✷ 7am-7pm summer, 8am-5.30pm winter). Of note primarily is the improvement in living standards enjoyed by Mao and top-ranking comrades.

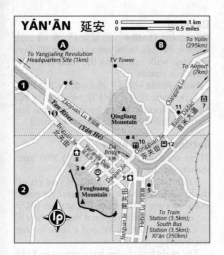

YÁN'ĀN 延安

Both of these sights can be reached by taking bus 1, which runs from the train station along the road east of the river and then heads up Zaoyuan Lu. Bus 3 runs along the other side of the river along Zhongxin Jie; get off when it crosses north over the river. Both of these start at the train station. Bus 8 also passes by all these places and can be caught from Da Bridge.

More accessible from the town is the **Fenghuangshan Revolution Headquarters Site** (Fènghuángshān Gémìng Jiùzhǐ; admission Y9; ⏰ 8am-5.30pm summer, 8am-5pm winter), about 100m north of the post office. This was the first site occupied by the communists after their move to Yán'ān, as reflected by the relatively primitive lodgings of the leading cadres.

In the east of town is the **Yan'an Revolution Museum** (Yán'ān Gémìng Jiǎnshǐ Chénliè; Baimi Dadao; admission Y16; ⏰ 8am-5.30pm), which has a tiny exhibit of farm tools, weaponry and grainy B&W photographs from the good old days. It's located behind the Wénhuà Yìshù Zhōngxīn (文化艺术中心), across from two cooling towers. Take bus 9 here.

Treasure Pagoda (Bǎo Tǎ; admission Y40; ⏰ 6am-9pm), built during the Song dynasty, stands on a prominent hillside southeast of the river junction.

Qingliang Mountain (Qīngliáng Shān; ☎ 211 2236; admission Y10; ⏰ 7am-8pm) is a pleasant hillside park with some nice trails and a few sights, including **Ten Thousand Buddha Cave** (Wànfó Dòng) dug into the sandstone cliff beside the river. The cave has relatively intact Buddhist statues.

Sleeping

Capitalist roaders and counter-revolutionaries take note: sleeping does not come cheaply in Yán'ān.

Yàshèng Dàjiǔdiàn (☎ 213 8336; fax 213 8063; Erdao Jie Zhongduan; 二道街中段; tw Y238-268; dishes Y14-40; ✿) Located in the centre of town, the once-stylish rooms here are clean but less than luxurious. The best food experience in town is found in the rotating restaurant on the top floor of the hotel.

Yán'ān Bīnguǎn (☎ 211 3122; fax 211 4297; 56 Yan'anshi Dajie; 延安市大街56号; s/d from Y480/580; ✿ ✿) It will tout that world leaders lodge here, yet the unimpressive rooms – and indifferent service – aren't really worth the money, unless it offers its usual 20% discount.

Getting There & Away

AIR

There are daily flights to Xī'ān (Y420) and Běijīng (Y960) from the airport (飞机场), 7km northeast of the town.

The airline booking office **Civil Aviation Administration of China** (CAAC; Zhōngguó Mínháng; ☎ 211 1111; ⏰ 8am-noon & 2.30-5.30pm) is located on Baimi Dadao. A bus service (Y5, 8.30am) connects the office with the airport.

BUS

From Xī'ān's long-distance bus station, there are buses to Yán'ān (Y78, 5½ hours) every 40 minutes from 6.30am to 4.20pm. The schedule back to Xī'ān is essentially the same. Buses arrive and depart from the south bus station (汽车南站; *nán zhàn*).

At the east bus station (*dōng zhàn*), there are minibuses to Yúlín (Y51, five hours) every 40 minutes from 5.30am to 5pm. Heading west, there are departures to Yínchuān in Níngxià (Y92 to Y99, eight hours). Buses leave at 8am, 9.30am and 10.30am; sleepers leave at 2.40pm and 4.30pm. You can also get into Shānxī and Hénán.

TRAIN

Heading back to Xī'ān are overnight trains (Y100, eight to 10 hours) leaving at 8.46pm and 10.08pm. Unfortunately, advance tickets in Yán'ān can be hard to come by – consider taking the bus instead. A taxi from the train station into town costs Y10.

YÚLÍN 榆林
☎ 0912 / pop 505,000

A one-time garrison town with a smattering of local character inside its old earthen walls, Yúlín is a rapidly expanding outpost on the fringes of Inner Mongolia's Mu Us Desert. If you happen to be passing through – following the Great Wall, or visiting Genghis Khan's Mausoleum (p894) – this is a good place to break up the trip.

The main north–south pedestrian street in the elongated old town (divided into Běi Dàjiè and Nán Dàjiè) has several restored buildings, including what appears to be an early 20th-century **Bell Tower** (钟楼; Zhōng Lóu). Four kilometres north of Yúlín are some badly eroded 15th-century sections of the Great Wall and a prominent four-storey **beacon tower** (镇北台; zhènběitái; admission Y20; ☉ 8am-6pm).

Sleeping

Chángchéng Fàndiàn (长城饭店; ☎ 328 3109; Yuyang Lu; 榆阳路; tw Y60, without bathroom Y40) Five minutes' walk east along the walls from the main bus station.

Yúxī Dàjiǔdiàn (榆溪大酒店; ☎ 336 3800; Xi Renmin Lu Zhongduan; 西人民路中段; tw/tr Y168/188; 🖳) Decent accommodation by the regional bus station. Staff say the 2nd floor is haunted.

Getting There & Away

There are daily flights to Xī'ān (Y590) from the airport, 10km east of town.

Yúlín has two bus stations. If you get off the bus inside the town walls (near the south gate), you are at the main bus station (汽车站; qìchē zhàn); the regional bus station (客运站; kèyùn zhàn) is located a little further northwest.

The main bus station has sleepers to Xī'ān (Y130, 10 hours) at 5pm, 5.30pm and 6pm. You can also get frequent buses to Yán'ān (Y51, five hours), and morning buses to Tàiyuán (Y89, eight hours) and Yínchuān (Y94, five hours).

The regional bus station has half-hourly buses to Dàliùtǎ (Y7, 1½ hours), from where you can travel by bus or train to Dōngshèng and Bāotóu in Inner Mongolia. Note that the buses to Dōngshèng pass by Genghis Khan's Mausoleum. There are also nonluxury buses going to Xī'ān (Y103, 10 hours) throughout the day.

The train station is 1km west of town. There are three trains to Xī'ān (Y109 to Y144, 12 to 14 hours) via Yán'ān departing at 7.25am, 4.20pm and 6.04pm, but don't count on being able to get sleeper tickets.

Taxis around town and to the train station are Y5.

Ānhuī 安徽

If you only have time for one province, Ānhuī should top your list. It may be poor – supplying the lion's share of the country's *ayi* and *baomu* (domestic helpers) – but its landscape is dramatic and beautiful in equal measure, and Wǎnnán – as the southern part of Ānhuī is called – is home to the lovely Huīzhōu culture that melds over the border with northeastern Jiāngxī. With little of the manic development and breakneck urgency that grips the rest of China, the province is an alluring alternative to the mantle of noise and construction dust cloaking other provinces.

Cut by the Yangzi River (Cháng Jiāng), which occasionally floods the low plains, Ānhuī has conveniently managed to cram all its highlight sights into a small and easily navigable area in the deep provincial south. It is to this well-watered mountainous region, which contrasts spectacularly with the arid northern plains abutting Hénán and Shāndōng, that travellers naturally gravitate.

China's most famous peak – Huáng Shān – has yielded an almost equally high mountain of coffee-table books dedicated to its mist-wreathed panoramas. Famed for its other-worldly fogs and looming granite formations, Huáng Shān's natural beauty is complemented by the sacred mountain aura of nearby Buddhist Jiǔhuá Shān, one of China's holiest places of pilgrimage.

The gorgeous Huīzhōu villages and architecture of Yīxiàn and Shèxiàn fully round out the picture. Visitors basing themselves in Túnxī can use the town as a convenient launching pad for grasping the Taoist secrets of Qíyún Shān and uncovering the charms of Hóngcūn, Xīdì, Shèxiàn and other delightful villages that characterise the region.

HIGHLIGHTS

- Climb into a sea of clouds at **Huáng Shān** (p446), China's most beautiful mountain
- Village hop in **Yīxiàn** (p443) on the trail of some of China's most exquisite villages
- Explore the Huīzhōu architecture of **Shèxiàn** (p445) and the riverine charms of the nearby port village of **Yúliáng** (p445)
- Commune with the Buddhist mysteries of mountainous **Jiǔhuá Shān** (p450)
- Ascend **Qíyún Shān** (p444) in pursuit of its Taoist mystique and fabulous views

★ Jiǔhuá Shān
★ Huáng Shān
Yīxiàn ★
Qíyún Shān ★ ★ Shèxiàn

- POPULATION: 62.3 MILLION

ĀNHUĪ

ĀNHUĪ 安徽

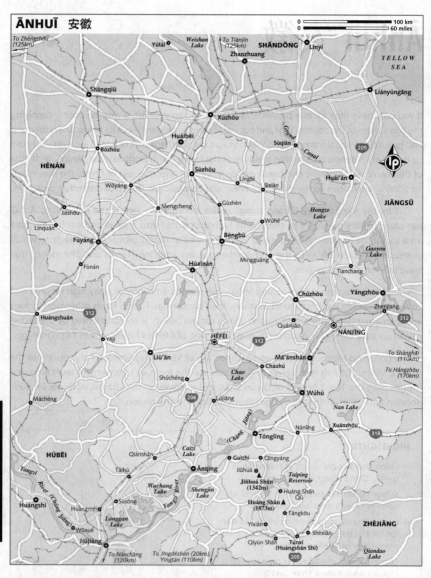

History

The provincial borders of Ānhuī were defined by the Qing government and, except for a few changes to the boundary with Jiāngsū, have remained unchanged. Northern Ānhuī forms part of the North China Plain, where the Han Chinese settled in large numbers during the Han dynasty. The Yangzi River cuts through the southern quarter of Ānhuī, and the area south of the river was not settled until the 7th and 8th centuries.

Climate

Ānhuī has a warm-temperate climate, with heavy rain in spring and summer that brings plenty of flooding. Winters are damp and cold. When travelling through Ānhuī at any time of year, bring rain gear and a warm jacket for the mountain areas.

Language
Ānhuī residents largely speak Mandarin. In the southern parts of the province some people speak the Hui dialect (Huí Yǔ), the language of China's Muslim Hui minority.

Getting There & Away
The historical and tourist sights of Ānhuī are concentrated in the south, and are more accessible from Hángzhōu or Shànghǎi than from the provincial capital, Héféi.

Getting Around
Ānhuī's drawcard sights are easily reached from Túnxī in the south of the province, itself linked by road and rail to other parts of the province and by air to other cities in China.

TÚNXĪ 屯溪
☎ 0559 / pop 1.5 million
The old trading town of Túnxī (Huángshān Shì) is roughly 70km southeast of Huáng Shān. The main springboard for Huáng Shān, Túnxī is also a handy base for exploration of the surrounding Huīzhōu architecture (see the boxed text, p443) at Yīxiàn and Shèxiàn.

Orientation & Information
Túnxī is located at the junction of the Xin'an River (Xīn'ān Jiāng) and Heng River (Héng Jiāng). The older (and most interesting) part of town is in the southwest, around Huang-shan Lu and Xin'an Lu. The newer part of town is in the northeast, near the bus and train stations.

Bank of China (Zhōngguó Yínháng; cnr Xin'an Beilu & Huangshan Xilu; ☾ 8am-5.30pm) Changes travellers cheques and major currencies; 24-hour ATM takes international cards.

CITS (Zhōngguó Guójì Lǚxíngshè; ☎ 252 6184; 3rd fl, 6 Xizhen Jie) Arranges English-speaking guides for tours of Huáng Shān and the surrounding area.

Dawei Internet Café (Dàwèi Wǎngbā; per hr Y2; ☾ 8am-midnight). It's opposite the Bank of China along an alley south of Yuzhong Garden (昱中花园).

Post office (Yóujú; cnr Changgan Lu & Qianyuan Nanlu).

PSB (Gōngānjú; ☎ 231 8768; 108 Changgan Lu; ☾ 8am-noon & 2.30-6pm) Located in the southeastern section of Túnxī. The Exit and Entry Administration Service Center here can arrange travel permits to Yīxiàn (Y50) on the spot.

Sights & Activities
Running a block in from the river, **Lao Jie** (老街; Old St; ☾ 7.30am-10.30pm) is a souvenir street lined with wooden shops and Ming-style Huīzhōu buildings that is open till late at night. On Lao Jie, the **Wancuilou Museum** (Wàncuìlóu Bówùguǎn; ☎ 252 2388; 143 Lao Jie; admission Y36; ☾ 8.30am-9.30pm) provides an in-depth introduction to Huīzhōu architecture, furniture and antiques, elegantly ranging over four floors.

Among Túnxī's heritage buildings, the **Chéngshì Sānzhái** (Dongli Xiang, off Baishu Lu; admission Y20; ☾ 8am-5.30pm) is a splendid example of historic Ming-dynasty Huīzhōu residential architecture, designed with all its trademark ornamentation and emphasis on elegance.

Sleeping & Eating
Huangshan International Youth Hostel (Huángshān Guójì Qīngnián Lǚguǎn; ☎ 211 4522; www.yhahuangshan.com; 58 Beihai Lu; 北海路58号; nonmember dm/s/tw Y35/120/120, member dm/s/tw Y30/100/100; ☒ ☐) Falling apart at the seams, this newish and popular hostel is well located east of the train station along Beihai Lu. Rooms are comfortable enough, but come without TV. There's an internet café (Y5), lobby café, English-speaking staff, washing machine (Y10 per load) and much Chinese graffiti all around.

Longyuan Hotel (Lóngyuán Bīnguǎn; ☎ 212 9777; fax 211 3550; 8-6 Zhanqian Lu; 站前路8-6号; d Y320; ☒) On the eastern flank of the train station concourse, this new, purpose-built seven-storey hotel (no English sign) has a sharp three-star finish and fresh rooms, with frequent discounts bringing double rooms down to around Y200.

Huachen Hotel (Huáchén Jiǔdiàn; ☎ 234 5188; fax 234 5098; 18 Qianyuan Beilu; 前园路18号; d Y360; ☒) The cylindrical steel tower facing you as you exit the train station, this three-star hotel has rooms on several floors that have recently enjoyed refurbishment and good discounts are in effect.

Old Street Hotel (Lǎojiēkǒu Kèzhàn; 253 4466; www.oldstreet-hotel.com.cn; 1 Laojiekou; 老街口1号; s/d/tr incl breakfast Y480/580/680; ☒) At the western end of Lao Jie by Laoda Bridge, this stylish hotel gets guests in the right mood with its Huīzhōu-effect interior, traditionally styled rooms (including wood covers for the air-con, lovely beds, wood-strip flooring and clean, bright showers) and views of the river.

Měishí Rénjiā (1 Lao Jie; dishes Y4-15; ☾ lunch & dinner) At the entrance to Lao Jie, this bustling restaurant – spread over two floors and hung

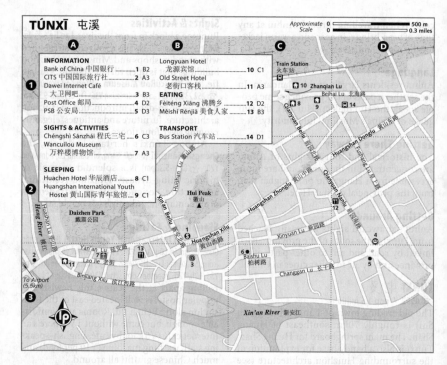

TÚNXĪ 屯溪

Approximate Scale 0 — 500 m / 0 — 0.3 miles

INFORMATION
Bank of China 中国银行 1 B2
CITS 中国国际旅行社 2 A3
Dawei Internet Café
大卫网吧 3 B3
Post Office 邮局 4 D2
PSB 公安局 5 D3

SIGHTS & ACTIVITIES
Chéngshì Sānzhái 程氏三宅 6 C3
Wancuilou Museum
万粹楼博物馆 7 A3

SLEEPING
Huachen Hotel 华辰酒店 8 C1
Huangshan International Youth
  Hostel 黄山国际青年旅馆 9 C1

Longyuan Hotel
龙源宾馆 10 C1
Old Street Hotel
老街口客栈 11 A3

EATING
Fèiténg Xiāng 沸腾乡 12 D2
Měishí Rénjiā 美食人家 13 B3

TRANSPORT
Bus Station 汽车站 14 D1

---

with traditional Chinese *mǎdēng* lanterns – seethes with satisfied customers. Peruse the counter for a range of dishes – *huntun* (won tons; dumpling soup), *jiǎozi* (dumplings), *bāozi* (steamed buns stuffed with meat or vegetables), noodles, claypot and more – on display, have them cooked fresh to order and sink a delicious glass of sweet *zǐmǐlù* (紫米露; Y6), made from purple glutinous rice.

Měishí Jiē (美食街) – literally 'Good Food St' – can be found on Qianyuan Nanlu (前园路) near the junction with Xinyuan Lu (新园路). The street is home to a series of local restaurants specialising in Huīzhōu-style cuisine. Try **Fèiténg Xiāng** (☎ 231 7777; 30 Qianyuan Nanlu; meals Y40-50), which serves a flavoursome *huángshān shuāngdōng* (黄山双冬; bamboo shoots, mushroom and slices of pork; Y26) and a very spicy and sour *xuěcài dòufubāo* (雪菜豆腐煲; pickled cabbage and tofu pot; Y22).

Getting There & Away

AIR

There are flights from **Huangshan City Airport** (黄山市飞机场; Huángshānshì Fēijīchǎng) to Běijīng (Y760, daily, two hours), Guǎngzhōu (Y580, daily, 1½ hours), Shànghǎi (Y290, daily, one hour) and less frequent flights to other cities.

You can buy air tickets at the **Civil Aviation Administration of China** (CAAC; 中国民航; Zhōngguó Mínháng; ☎ 254 1222; 23 Huashan Lu).

BUS

The long-distance **bus station** (☎ 251 5955; Fushang Lu) is 400m east of the train station. Buses run from here to Yìxiàn (Y9, 1½ hours, every 25 minutes), Shèxiàn (Y4.5, 45 minutes, every 10 minutes), Wùyuán (Y30, three hours, twice daily), Qīngyáng (Y35, three hours, twice daily), Jiǔhuá Shān (Y39, four hours, once daily), Héféi (Y78, six hours, every 35 minutes), Shànghǎi (Y98, six hours, once daily), and Wǔhàn (Y170, 11 hours, twice daily).

TRAIN

Trains from Běijīng (Y323 hard sleeper, 21 hours), Shànghǎi (Y169 hard sleeper, 11½ hours) and Nánjīng (Y54, seven hours) stop at Túnxī. Some trains heading south also stop here, such as to Xiàmén (Y217, 32 hours) and Jǐngdézhèn (Y25, 3½ hours). For better connections to southern destinations, first go to Yīngtán (Y51, five hours) in Jiāngxī and change trains there.

Getting Around

Taxis are Y5 at flagfall, with the 5km taxi ride to the airport costing about Y25. Competition among pedicab drivers is fierce, so they are the cheapest way of getting around, costing around Y4 for a trip to Lao Jie from the train station area.

YĪXIÀN 黟县

Easily visited from Túnxī, Yīxiàn is principally famed for the two outstanding historic villages of Xīdì and Hóngcūn, but other settlements are scattered within the region that warrant exploration. Note that foreign visitors to Xīdì, Hóngcūn and other villages in Yīxiàn County require a visitor's permit (Y50), available from the PSB (Gōngānjú) in Tāngkǒu or Túnxī. Visitors are not officially allowed to overnight in Yīxiàn County.

Historic Villages

XĪDÌ 西递

Dating to AD 1047, the village of **Xīdì** (admission Y80) has for centuries been a stronghold of the Hu (胡) clan, descended from the eldest son of the last Tang emperor who fled here in the twilight years of the Tang dynasty. Typical of the elegant Huīzhōu style (see the boxed text, below), Xīdì's 124 surviving buildings reflect the wealth and prestige of the prosperous merchants who settled here.

Xīdì has flirted gaily with its increasing popularity and, as a Unesco World Heritage site, enjoys an increasingly lucrative tourist economy. But the village remains a picturesque tableau of slender lanes, cream-coloured walls topped with horse-head gables, roofs capped with dark tiles, and doorways ornately decorated with carved lintels. The village is a fully functioning community: pans of garlic dry in the sun, families sit within the cool interiors of mouldering homesteads while children's voices resound from the Mingjing School (明经学校; Míngjīng Xuéxiào).

Doorways – frequently capped with upturned eaves and hung with overhead mirrors to ward off bad luck – are fashioned with ancient drum stones (gǔshí) and mirror stones (jìngshí), leading to interiors decorated with elaborate wood carvings on panels, doors and ornamental brackets, all naturally illuminated from above by light wells (tiānjǐng). Wander round the maze of flagstone lanes, examining lintel carvings above doorways decorated with vases, urns, animals, flowers and ornamental motifs, and try to avoid tripping over hordes of high-school artists consigning scenes of stone bridges spanning small streams to canvas.

Xīdì's magnificent three-tiered Ming dynasty decorative arch, the **Húwénguāng Páifāng**, at the entrance to the village is an ostentatious symbol of Xīdì's former standing. Numerous other notable structures are open to inspection, including the **Diji Hall** (迪吉堂; Díjí Táng) and the **Zhuimu Hall** (追慕堂; Zhuīmù Táng), both on Dalu Jie (大路街), and you can clamber up into the 2nd-floor gallery of the grand **Dàfúdì** (admission Y2) on Zhijie (直街).

ĀNHUĪ

HUĪZHŌU STYLE

Huīzhōu architecture is the most distinctive ingredient of the regional personality, representative of the merchant class that held sway in this region of southern Ānhuī (also called Wǎnnán; 皖南) and northeastern Jiāngxī during the Ming and Qing dynasties. Decorative archways (páifāng or páilóu) are ostentatious ornaments that doubled as imposing symbols of prestige and authority. The former merchant houses of Yīxiàn and Shèxiàn are the most typical examples of Huīzhōu architecture; their walls topped on each flank by horse-head gables, originally designed to prevent fire from travelling along a line of houses, and later evolving into decorative motifs.

Strikingly capped with dark tiles, the white walls of Huīzhōu houses are often punctured by high windows, designed to deter burglars. Exterior doorways, often overhung with decorative eaves and carved brick or stone lintels, are sometimes flanked by drum stones (gǔshí) or mirror stones (jìngshí), lead onto interior courtyards delightfully illuminated by light wells (tiānjǐng), rectangular openings in the roof. Many Huīzhōu houses are furnished with intricately carved wood panels and extend to two floors, the upper floor supported on wooden columns.

HÓNGCŪN 宏村

Dating to the southern Song dynasty, the delightful village and Unesco World Heritage site of **Hóngcūn** (admission Y85), 11km northeast of Yīxiàn, has at its heart the crescent-shaped Moon Pond (月沼; Yuè Zhǎo) and is encapsulated by South Lake (南湖; Nán Hú), West Stream (西溪; Xī Xī) and Leigang Mountain (雷岗山; Léigǎng Shān). Famously conceived to resemble an ox, and home to members of the traditionally wealthy Wang (汪) clan, the village is a charming and unhurried portrait of bridges, lakeside views, narrow alleys and traditional halls. Alleyway channels flush water through the village from West Stream to Moon Pond and from there on to South Lake while signs guide visitors on a tour of the principle buildings.

The noble **Chengzhi Hall** (承志堂; Chéngzhì Táng) on Shangshuizhen Lu (上水圳路) dates to 1855 and has a dizzying total of 28 rooms, adorned with fabulous wood carvings, 2nd-floor balconies and light wells. Other notable buildings include the nearby **Deyi Hall** (德义堂; Déyì Táng; admission Y2), the **Hall of the Peach Garden** (桃源居; Táoyuán Jū), with its elaborate carved wood panels, and the **South Lake Academy** (南湖书院; Nánhú Shūyuàn), which enjoys a delicious setting on tranquil South Lake.

Overlooking picturesque Moon Pond is a gathering of further halls, chief among which is the dignified **Lexu Hall** (乐叙堂; Lèxù Táng), a hoary and dilapidated Ming antique from the first years of the 15th century. Turn up bamboo carvings, trinkets and a large selection of tea at the market west of Moon Pond. The pleasant square by Hongji Bridge (宏济桥; Hóngjì Qiáo) on the West Stream is shaded by a vast, ancient Chinese Wingnut tree.

A further foray a kilometre beyond Hóngcūn reveals the village of **Lúcūn** (卢村; admission Y26), famed for the extravagant carved woodwork of its **Mùdiāo Lóu** (木雕楼).

NÁNPÍNG 南屏

With a history of over 1100 years, this intriguing and labyrinthine **village** (admission Y30), 5km to the west of Yīxiàn town, is famed as the setting of Zhang Yimou's 1989 tragedy *Judou*. Numerous ancient ancestral halls, clan shrines and merchant residences survive within Nánpíng's mazelike alleys, including the **Chéngshì Zōngcí** (程氏宗祠) and the **Yèshí Zōngcí** (叶氏宗祠). The **Lǎo Yáng Jiā Rǎnfáng** (老杨家染坊)

residence that served as the principle household of dyer Gongli and her rapacious husband in *Judou* remains cluttered with props, and stills from the film hang from the walls. The entrance price includes the services of a Chinese guide, with limited English skills.

GUĀNLÙ 关麓

Around 8km west of Yīxiàn and further along the road beyond Nánpíng, this small **village's** (admission Y25) drawcard sights are the fabulous households – **Bādàjiā** (八大家) – of eight wealthy brothers. Each Qing dynasty residence shares similar elegant Huīzhōu features, with light wells, interior courtyards, halls, carved wood panels and small gardens. Each an independent entity, the households are interconnected by doors and linked together into a systemic whole. A distinctive aspect of the residences is their elegantly painted ceilings, the patterns and details of which survive. As with Nánpíng, a guide (with iffy English skills) is included in the price.

GETTING THERE & AWAY

Buses (Y9, 1½ hours, every 25 minutes) from the Túnxī long-distance bus station depart between 7am and 5pm for Yīxiàn town, 47km west of Túnxī. Yīxiàn serves as the transport hub for public transport to the surrounding villages. There are buses from Yīxiàn to Guānlù (between 7am and 7pm, Y5). From the Yīxiàn bus station, minibuses depart when full to Xīdì (Y2) and Hóngcūn (Y2), east of Yīxiàn, and they also run infrequently to Nánpíng (Y6). Taxis go to Xīdì (Y10), Hóngcūn (Y20) and Guānlù (Y20) from Yīxiàn. Minibuses sporadically run through Xīdì to Hóngcūn, otherwise return to Yīxiàn for connections to Hóngcūn, or take a taxi from Xīdì to Hóngcūn. The last bus back to Túnxī from Yīxiàn leaves at 5pm. Booking a *miàndì* taxi to take you to all four villages from Yīxiàn can cost as little as Y120 for the day, depending on your bargaining skills.

QÍYÚN SHĀN 齐云山

A 40-minute bus trip west of Túnxī brings you to the lush mountain panoramas of **Qíyún Shān** (admission Y60). Long venerated by Taoists, the reddish sandstone rock provides a mountain home to the temples and the monks who tend to them, while mountain trails lead hikers through some stupendous scenery.

From the bus drop-off, it's a 10-minute walk along the river to the **Deng Feng Bridge**

(登封桥; Dēngfēng Qiáo). Cross the bridge – dwelling on the luxuriant river views – and turn right through the village at the foot of the mountain for a 40-minute clamber up stone steps to the ticket office. Or you can take a cable car (up Y26, down Y14) from the far side of the river up the mountain.

Beyond the ticket office, the **Zhenxian Cave** (真仙洞府; Zhēnxiān Dòngfǔ) houses a complex of Taoist shrines in grottoes and niches gouged from the sandstone cliffs. Seated within the smoky interior of the vast **Tàisù Gōng** (太素宫) further on is an effigy of Zhengwu Dadi, a Taoist deity. A further temple hall, the **Yùxū Gōng** (玉虚宫) is erected beneath the huge brow of a 200m-long sandstone cliff, enclosed around effigies of Zhengwu Dadi and Laotze.

GETTING THERE & AWAY
Take any Yīxiàn-bound bus from Túnxī long-distance bus station and ask the driver to stop at Qíyún Shān (Y6, 45 minutes). Returning to Túnxī, wait at the side of the road for buses coming from Yīxiàn, but note that the last bus from Yīxiàn to Túnxī departs at 5pm.

SHÈXIÀN 歙县
Historic seat of the Huīzhōu region, Shèxiàn is 25km east of Túnxī and can be visited as a day trip from Túnxī. Formerly known as Huīzhōu, the town was the grand centre of the Huīzhōu culture, serving as its capital. Unlike Yīxiàn County, visitor permits are not required for visits to Shèxiàn.

Sights
From the bus station, cross the bridge over the river and go through the modern gate tower and along to **Yánghé Mén** (阳和门), a double-eaved gate tower constructed of wood (admission Y10). Climb it to examine a Ming dynasty stone *xièzhì* (a legendary beast) and elevated views of the magnificent **Xuguo Archway** (许国石坊; Xǔguó Shífāng) below. Fabulously decorated, this is China's sole surviving four-sided decorative archway, with 12 lions (18 in total if you count the cubs) seated on pedestals around it and a profusion of bas-relief carvings of phoenixes, *qilin* (mythical animals), deer, eagles, dragons, leopards, sparrows and mythical creatures.

Continue in the same direction to reach the alleyway to the old residential area of **Doushan Jie** (斗山街古民居; admission Y20, Chinese-speaking guide free), a marvellous street of Huīzhōu houses, with several courtyard residences open to visitors and decorated with exquisitely carved lintels, beautiful interiors and occasional pairs of leaping-on blocks for mounting horses. Look out for the *páifāng* (decorative archway) that has been filled in and incorporated into a wall. The **24 Filial Pictures** (二十四孝行图; Èrshísì Xiàoxíngtú) is a former residence now serving as a kindergarten.

Getting There & Away
Buses from Túnxī long-distance bus station run regularly to Shèxiàn (Y4.5, 45 minutes, every 10 minutes).

AROUND SHÈXIÀN
Yúliáng (渔梁; admission Y30) is a historic riverine port village on the Lian River (Liàn Jiāng). Cobbled Yuliang Jie (渔梁街) is a picturesque alley of buildings and former transfer stations for the wood, salt and tea that plied the Lian River and was shipped to north China; the **tea shop** at No 87 is an example. Note the firewalls separating the houses along the road. Pop into the **Yuanhetang Chinese Medicine Shop** at No 40 to admire the original flooring with the floral design and examine the traditional Huīzhōu arrangement of the **Baweizu Museum** (巴慰祖纪念馆; Bāwèizǔ Jìniànguǎn), also on Yuliang Jie.

The **Lion Bridge** (狮子桥; Shīzi Qiáo) dates to the Tang dynasty, a time when the 138m-long granite **Yuliang dam** (渔梁坝; Yúliáng Bà) across the river was first constructed. Boats can ferry you from the dam for short 15 minutes trips up river (Y15).

If you want to spend the night in Yúliáng, there are rooms with lovely views at the small **inn** (☎ 0559-653 8024; d with/without air-con Y80/50; ✦) facing the entrance to Hundred Steps Ladder (百步阶梯), the alley leading down to the dam. To reach Yúliáng, take a pedicab (Y2) from Shèxiàn's bus station (by the bridge), or jump on bus 1 to Yúliáng (Y1), which runs from Shèxiàn train station.

About 5km west of Shèxiàn, seven decorative arches known as the **Tangyue Decorative Archways** (棠樾牌坊群; Tángyuè Páifāng Qún; admission Y35) stand in a row in a field, erected by a wealthy local family who made their fortune in salt. Take a minibus back to Túnxī and ask the driver to drop you off at the Tángyuè Páifāng Qún, from where it is a further 2km walk to the archways.

ĀNHUĪ

HUÁNG SHĀN 黄山

☎ 0559

When its archetypal granite peaks and twisted pines are wreathed in spectral folds of mist, Huáng Shān's idyllic views easily nudge it into the select company of China's top 10 sights. Legions of poets and painters have drawn inspiration from Huáng Shān's iconic beauty. Yesterday's artists seeking an escape from the hustle and bustle of the temporal world may have been replaced by crowds of tourists, who bring the hustle and bustle with them, but Huáng Shān still rewards visitors with moments of tranquillity, and the unearthly views can be simply breathtaking.

Orientation

Buses from Túnxī (Huángshān Shì) drop you off in Tāngkǒu, the village bisected by a stream at the mountain's foot, or at the terminal near Huang Shan Gate (Huángshān Mén) in upper Tāngkǒu.

The road from Tāngkǒu continues beyond the hot springs area and ends halfway up the mountain at the Cloud Valley Temple Cable Car Station, 890m above sea level, where the eastern steps begin. Another cable car connects the area above the hot springs resort with Jade Screen Peak (Yùpíng Fēng), while a third cable car approaches Huáng Shān from the north.

Maps, raincoats, food, currency exchange, internet access and accommodation are available in Tāngkǒu, which serves as a base for climbers. Lodging is also available in the hot springs area (under redevelopment at the time of writing) and at several points on the mountain, including the summit.

Information

Money can be changed at the **Bank of China** (中国银行; Zhōngguó Yínháng) east of the Tangkou Hotel in the south of Tāngkǒu or at the **Bank of China** (中国银行; Zhōngguó Yínháng; ⏰ 9am-5pm) opposite the Beihai Hotel on the summit (the latter also has an ATM that accepts international cards). Alongside the Bank of China on the summit of Huáng Shān is a **police station** (派出所; pàichūsuǒ; ☎ 558 1388). At the time of writing, the **police station** (公安局; Gōnggānjú; ☎ 556 2311) in Tāngkǒu was about to relocate to offices just east of the river. Travel permits to Yìxiàn can be arranged here.

Internet cafés can be found in Tāngkǒu, including the **Jiaqiaochong Internet Café** (甲壳虫 网吧; Jiǎqiàochóng Wǎngbā; per hr Y3; ⏰ 24hr), with a blue sign on the east side of the river running through Tāngkǒu, and **Lingdian Internet Café** (零点网吧; Língdiǎn Wǎngbā; per hr Y3; ⏰ 8am-midnight), over the bridge on the other side of the river. Several hotels on the mountain have pricier internet access areas for guests and nonguests, with hourly rates of around Y15.

Leave your bags while climbing the mountain either at your hotel in Tāngkǒu or with the English-speaking Mr Hu at **Mr Hu's Restaurant** (☎ 139 562 647 86; Y2). Mr Hu is a useful and ever-present source of local information on Tāngkǒu and Huángshān who can arrange bus tickets and runs a simple restaurant across the way from the Bank of China in Tāngkǒu. Across the other side of the river, Mr Cheng at **Mr Cheng's Restaurant** (☎ 130 855 926 03; Yanxi Dongjie) speaks English with an impressive accent and is similarly a useful source of information (and food).

Routes to the Summit

Regardless of how you ascend Huáng Shān, you'll be stung by a dizzying entrance fee of Y200 (children under 1.1m half price); ticket prices continue to gallop way ahead of inflation. Pay at the eastern steps near the **Cloud Valley Temple Cable Car Station** (云谷寺索道站; Yúngǔsì Suǒdào) or at the **Ciguang Temple** (慈光阁; Cíguāng Gé), where the western steps begin. Minibuses run to both places from Tāngkǒu for Y10.

Three basic routes reach the summit: the short, hard way (eastern steps); the longer, harder way (western steps); and the very short, easy way (cable car). The eastern steps lead up from the Cloud Valley Temple Cable Car Station, and the western steps lead up from the parking lot near Ciguang Temple, about half an hour's walk above the hot springs.

Make sure to pack enough water, food and appropriate clothing before climbing; taking sunscreen is also recommended as the sun can get fierce on clear days from spring onwards. Bottled water and food prices increase the higher you go, so take provisions with you.

As mountain paths are easy to follow and English signs plentiful, guides are unnecessary. The truly indolent can bob up in a sedan chair, bounced along by two porters.

EASTERN STEPS

A medium-fast climb of the 7.5km eastern steps from **Cloud Valley Temple** to **White Goose**

HUÁNG SHĀN 黄山

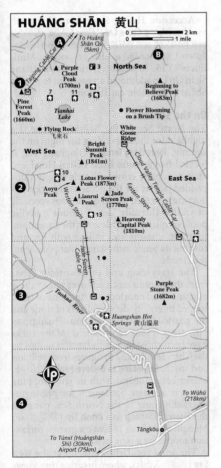

plies the route. While clambering up, note the more ancient flight of steps that makes an occasional appearance alongside the newer set.

Purists can extend the eastern steps climb by several hours by starting at Huang Shan Gate, where a stepped path crosses the road at several points before linking with the main eastern steps trail.

If you have time, the recommended route is a 10-hour circuit hike ascending the eastern steps and coming down via the western steps. Don't underestimate the hardship involved; the steep gradients and granite steps can wreak havoc on your knees, both going up and down.

WESTERN STEPS

The 15km western steps route has some stellar scenery, but it's twice as long and strenuous as the eastern steps, and much easier to enjoy if you're clambering down rather than gasping your way up.

The western steps descent begins at the **Flying Rock** (Fēilái Shí), a boulder perched on an outcrop half an hour from Beihai Hotel, and goes over **Bright Summit Peak** (Guāngmíng Dǐng).

South of **Aoyu Peak** (鳌鱼峰; Áoyú Fēng; 1780m) en route to Lotus Flower Peak, the descent funnels you through a **Gleam of Sky** (一线天; Yīxiàn Tiān), a remarkably narrow chasm – a vertical split in the granite – pinching

Ridge (白鹅峰; Báié Fēng; 1770m) can be done in under two and a half hours. The route is pleasant, but lacks the awesome geological scenery of the western steps (which you can save for your descent).

In spring, azaleas add gorgeous splashes of colour to the greens of the bamboo and pines and wooded slopes of the mountain. Other flowering trees include the Japanese Weigela (*Weigela japonica*), blooming in May and June.

Much of the climb is comfortably shaded and although it can be tiring, it's a doddle compared to the western steps. Slow-moving porters use the eastern steps for ferrying up their massive, swaying loads of food, drink and building materials so considerable traffic

a huge rock suspended above the heads of climbers. Further on, **Lotus Flower Peak** (莲花峰; Liánhuā Fēng; 1873m) marks the highest point, but is occasionally sealed off, preventing ascents. **Lianrui Peak** (莲蕊峰; Liánruǐ Fēng; 1776m) is decorated with rocks whimsically named after animals, but save some kilojoules of energy for the much-coveted and staggering climb – 1321 steps in all – up **Heavenly Capital Peak** (天都峰; Tiāndū Fēng; 1810m) and the stunning views that unfold below. As elsewhere on the mountain, young lovers bring padlocks engraved with their names up here and lash them for eternity to the chain railings. Successful ascents can be commemorated with a gold medal engraved with your name (Y10). Access to Heavenly Capital Peak (and other peaks) is sometimes restricted for maintenance and repair, but the peak was open at the time of writing. The route down the far side of Heavenly Capital Peak descends along a narrow staircase carved with occasionally treacherous steps, so descend slowly.

Further below, the steps lead to the **Banshan Temple** (Bànshān Sì) and below that the Ciguang Temple, where you can pick up a minibus back to Tāngkǒu (Y10) or continue walking to the hot springs area.

Huáng Shān is not one of China's sacred mountains, so little religious activity is evident. The Ciguang Temple at the bottom of the western steps is one of the few temples on the mountain whose temple halls survive, although they have been converted to more secular uses. The first hall now serves as the **Mt Huangshan Visitors Centre** (internet access per hour Y15) where you can pore over a diorama of the mountain range.

CABLE CAR

Minibuses (Y10) ferry visitors from Tāngkǒu to the **Cloud Valley Temple Cable Car** (Yúngǔsì Suǒdào; adult/child peak Y65/35, off-peak Y55/30; 🕐 6.30am-4.30pm). Either arrive very early or late (if you're staying overnight) as queues of more than one hour are the norm. In the peak season (officially 1 March to 30 November), people can wait up to three hours for a ride – you may as well walk.

Minibuses (Y10) also run from Tāngkǒu to the Ciguang Temple, which is linked by the **Jade Screen Cable Car** (Yùpíng Suǒdào; adult/child peak Y65/35, off-peak Y55/30; 🕐 6.30am-5.30pm) to the area just below the Yupinglou Hotel.

Accessing Huáng Shān from the north via the **Taiping Cable Car** (Tàipíng Suǒdào; adult/child peak Y65/35, off-peak Y55/30; 🕐 6.30am-4.30pm Fri & Sat, 7.30am-4.30pm Sun-Thu) is also an option. Minibuses (Y15, 30 minutes) run from Huáng Shān Qū (an additional access point to Huáng Shān) to the cable-car station.

On the Summit

The North Sea (北海; Běihǎi) sunrise is a highlight for those spending the night on the summit. **Refreshing Terrace** (Qīngliáng Tái) is located five minutes from Beihai Hotel and attracts sunrise crowds (hotels supply thick padded jackets for the occasion). Lucky visitors are rewarded with the luminous spectacle of *yúnhǎi* (literally 'sea of clouds'): idyllic pools of mist that settle over the mountain, filling its chasms and valleys with fog and turning its peaks into islands that poke from the clouds.

The staggering and otherworldly views from the summit reach out over huge valleys of granite and enormous formations of rock, topped by gravity-defying slivers of stone and the gnarled forms of ubiquitous Huangshan pine trees *(Pinus taiwanensis)*. Many rocks have been christened with fanciful names by the Chinese, alluding to figures from religion and myth. **Beginning to Believe Peak** (始信峰; Shǐxìn Fēng; 1683m), with its jaw-dropping views, is a major bottleneck for photographers. En route to the North Sea, pause at the **Flower Blooming on a Brush Tip** (梦笔生花; Mèngbǐ Shēnghuā; 1640m), a granite formation topped by a pine tree.

The wind regularly whips up at the **West Sea** (西海; Xīhǎi), where breathtaking views stretch out along a huge gorge and the chains of the observation area are left garlanded with clumps of padlocks by romantic couples.

Clamber up to **Purple Cloud Peak** (丹霞峰; Dānxiá Fēng) for a long survey over the landscape and try to catch the sun as it descends in the west.

Sleeping & Eating

Huáng Shān has five locations where hotels and restaurants can be found. Prices and bed availability vary according to season, and it is a good idea to book ahead.

TĀNGKǑU 汤口

Affordable hotels can be found in Tāngkǒu, a pleasant enough town situated on either side of a small river spanned by several bridges, with a good range of restaurants. Family-run hotel owners may approach you to stay in cheap local rooms, garnering you the best prices.

Tangkou Hotel (汤口宾馆; Tāngkǒu Bīnguǎn; ☎ 556 2400; fax 556 2687; d/tr Y100/120) On the cusp of reopening after renovation at the time of writing, this attractive hotel is set back from the road, and has clean and well-looked-after rooms.

Dazhong Hotel (大众宾馆; Dàzhòng Fàndiàn; d/tr Y100/120; ☎ 556 2453; ✵) A typical example of the simple hotels along the road running through Tāngkǒu, this place has cheap and serviceable rooms, with air-con, TV and phone.

Yuanye Hotel (原野大酒店; Yuányě Dàjiǔdiàn; ☎ 556 3223; fax 556 3533; Yanxi Jie; d Y280, tr Y150-300; ✵) Located overlooking the river on Yanxi Jie, this hotel has clean, bright and frequently discounted rooms. The cheaper triples come with shower and toilet, but no air-con. With no English sign, it's on the right as you head down Yanxi Jie towards the Bank of China. Note that there's no lift.

Restaurants are scattered along Yanxi Jie alongside the river, with several specialising in local Huīzhōu dishes.

Huīzhōu Měishí (徽州美食; ☎ 338 8276; Yanxi Jie; meals Y30) Located on the west bank of the river, this small and friendly family-run restaurant has no English sign, but it's a great spot to sample local Huīzhōu-style cooking, from stewed stone frog (hóngshāo shíjī; 红烧石鸡; Y60) to filling Anhui-style fried noodles (huīshì chǎomiàn; 徽式炒面; Y15) and fried meat slices in Anhui style (huīshì huíguōròu; 徽式回锅肉; Y28).

HOT SPRINGS AREA 温泉区
Undergoing massive redevelopment at the time of writing that may spoil its charms, the hot springs area, 4km further uphill, is a more expensive alternative to staying in Tāngkǒu.

Huangshan Hotel (Huángshān Bīnguǎn; ☎ 558 5808; fax 558 5818; d Y340-420) This place was undergoing redevelopment at the time of writing so prices could well have changed by the time you read this.

Taoyuan Hotel (Táoyuán Bīnguǎn; Peach Blossom Hotel; ☎ 556 2666; fax 556 2666; d Y486-580) This is a pleasant hotel in the hot springs area, with clean, modern rooms, some with views; still open at the time of writing, despite all the construction.

CLOUD VALLEY TEMPLE CABLE CAR STATION 云谷寺索道站
Yungu Hotel (Yúngǔ Shānzhuāng; ☎ 558 6444; s & d Y580) With a lovely setting looking out onto bamboo and forest, this traditionally styled hotel has fine, clean rooms with 20% discounts frequently given. Walk down from the car park in front of the cable-car station.

SUMMIT AREA 山顶
Ideally, Huáng Shān visits include nights on the summit. Note that room prices can rise on Saturdays and Sundays and are astronomical during the week-long 1 May and 1 October holiday periods.

Huángshān Gōngshāngsuǒ (☎ 139 562 681 68; dm off-peak Y80-120, peak Y120-150, tent Y120) Tucked away behind the Bank of China opposite the Beihai Hotel, this cheap and well-positioned spot has rows of dorm rooms rising up the hill (no English sign). Dorms are simple and vary in price and quality, so size them up before deciding. Tents (zhàngpeng; 帐篷) are available for camping at selected points on the summit.

Beihai Hotel (Běihǎi Bīnguǎn; ☎ 558 2555; fax 558 1996; 6-bed dm Y100, tr Y300, s & d Y1280) The four-star Beihai comes with professional service, money exchange, a mobile-phone charging point, café selling hot dogs, a small and unexciting bar and 20% discounts during the week. Larger doubles with bathroom have older fittings than the smaller, better fitted-out doubles (same price). Simple dorms are in the block down the side by the Friendship Store; triples are grotty, but cheap (with common shower/toilet).

Xihai Hotel (Xīhǎi Bīnguǎn; ☎ 558 8888; www.xihaihotel.cn; dm/d/ste Y160/1080/3800) Warm jackets are supplied in rooms for sunrise-watchers, bathrooms are clean, all rooms come with heating and 24-hour hot water, but take a look at the doubles first as some face inwards. Breakfast (Y40), lunch (Y80) and dinner (Y80) buffets are served at the restaurant. The concrete building opposite is **Xīhǎi Shānzhuāng** (☎ 558 8888; d Y1080), with a further selection of doubles with slightly faded shower rooms.

Shilin Hotel (Shílín Fàndiàn; ☎ 558 4040; www.shilin.com; dm/s/d/ste Y200/1080/1280/4880; 🖥) The foyer is rather dark, and cheaper rooms are devoid of views, but the pricier doubles are bright and clean. Nine-bed dorms are also well-kept with bunk beds and shared toilet and shower; the block up the steps from the hotel has good views. The hotel has an internet café (open 24 hours) and a supermarket downstairs.

Huangshan Paiyunlou Hotel (Páiyúnlóu Bīnguǎn; ☎ 558 1558; dm/d/tr Y260/980/1280) Three-star comfort and lovely views can be found at this hotel up from Tiānhǎi Hú (Tianhai Lake), with clean, heated doubles (some with bath, others with shower); rooms on higher floors have superior views. The six-bed dorms are clean and equipped with showers.

The Xihai and Beihai Hotels have bars and restaurants serving international and Chinese food, but it can be difficult to get service outside meal times. The restaurant at the Beihai Hotel is bright and brash but serves a good, spicy and tender *yúxiāng qiézi* (fish-flavour aubergine; 鱼香茄子; Y50) and flavoursome *ròumò dòufu* (tofu and minced meat; 肉末豆腐; Y40). Toast your heady ascent to the summit with a Yúnhǎi (Sea of Clouds; 云海) or a Yíngkèsōng (Welcoming Guest Pine; 迎客松) beer.

WESTERN STEPS 西线台阶

Baiyun Hotel (Báiyún Bīnguǎn; ☎ 556 1708; fax 556 1602; dm/d/tr Y260/1080/1380) Dorms here come with TV and shower, but are a bit old and worn; doubles (with bath) pass muster. No English sign, but the hotel is well sign-posted.

Tianhai Hotel (Tiānhǎi Shānzhuāng; ☎ 558 2626; dm/d Y260/1180) Just before the Baiyun Hotel, this hotel has very clean four-bed dorms with pine bunk beds, kettle, heater, shower and TV.

Yupinglou Hotel (Yùpínglóu Bīnguǎn; ☎ 558 2288; fax 558 2258; dm/d/tr/q Y260/1280/1380/1040; 🖳) Further down the mountain, this four-star hotel is perched on a spectacular 1660m-high lookout just above the Welcoming Guest Pine. Aim for the doubles with the good views at the back as some rooms have small windows with no views. Eight- and six-person dorms all come with shower. A restaurant is attached and there is an internet café (per hour Y15).

Getting There & Away

Buses from Túnxī (aka Huángshān Shì) take around 70 minutes to reach Huáng Shān Gate from the train station entrance (Y10, departures when full) between 6.30am and 8pm. Minibuses back to Túnxī from Tāngkǒu are plentiful, and can flagged down on the road to Túnxī (Y13).

Tāngkǒu has a number of long-distance bus stations, but the most useful for travellers is the **Nanmen long-distance bus station** (Nánmén Chángtú qìchē zhàn; ☎ 557 2602), south of the main Huáng Shān Gate. Buses run to Héféi (Y64, six hours, regular), Jiǔhuá Shān (Y36, three hours, 6.10am), Yīxiàn (Y13, one hour, twice daily), Nánjīng (Y76, six hours, three daily), Hángzhōu (Y59 to Y80, four hours, five daily) and Wǔhàn (Y154 to Y179, nine hours, twice daily). Many buses depart early in the morning.

Getting Around

Minibuses are the easiest and cheapest way to get around Huáng Shān, though they usually don't budge until enough people are on board. In the morning they ferry people to the eastern and western steps (Y10). You can usually find minibuses on Tāngkǒu's streets or on the highway across the bridge. Likewise, minibuses wait at the bottom of mountain routes in the afternoon. Taxis swarm everywhere in Tāngkǒu but require bargaining as they frequently overcharge; a taxi to the Cloud Valley Temple should cost around Y10 per person.

JIǓHUÁ SHĀN 九华山
☎ 0566

One of China's four sacred Buddhist mountains, the 99 peaks of Jiǔhuá Shān form the precipitous domain of the Bodhisattva Dizang (Ksitigarbha), Lord of the Underworld. A significant place of pilgrimage for believers to bless the souls of the recently deceased to ensure them a passage to Buddhist heaven, Jiǔhuá Shān was identified in the 8th century as a worshipping place for Dizang by the Korean Buddhist disciple Kim Kiao Kak (Jīn Qiáojué). Exuding a palpable air of Buddhist mystery and devotion, Jiǔhuá Shān receives throngs of pilgrims for annual festivities held on the anniversary of Kim's death, which falls on the 30th day of the seventh lunar month. The population of monasteries and nunneries has fallen since its Tang dynasty tally of 150, but they can still be found at almost every turn.

Orientation

Six hundred metres above sea level, Jiǔhuájiē village is about halfway up the mountain (or, as locals say, at roughly navel height in a giant Buddha's potbelly). Disembark at the main ticket office, purchase your ticket for the **mountain** (1 Mar-30 Nov Y140, 1 Dec-29 Feb Y110) and proceed to the other side of the terminal for buses on to Jiǔhuájiē village (included in ticket price; every 20 minutes). The bus terminates at the bus station just before the gate (Dàmén) leading to the village, from where the narrow main street heads south up past hotels and restaurants. Chinese-language maps that outline the mountain paths are available.

Information

Bank of China (中国银行; Zhōngguó Yínháng; 65 Huachen Lu) Changes travellers cheques and does foreign exchange; west of main square.

China Post (邮局; Yóujú; 58 Huacheng Lu) Off the main square.

China Travel Service (CTS; 中国旅行社; Zhōngguó Lǚxíngshè; ☎ 501 1588; 3rd fl, 135 Baima Xincun) Located on the far side of a school field.

Huayong Internet Café (华湧网吧; Huáyǒng Wǎngbā; per hr Y3; 🕙 8am-midnight) It's east of the pond on Baima Xincun.

Jiuhuashan Red Cross Hospital (九华山红十字医院; Jiǔhuáshān Hóngshízì Yīyuàn; ☎ 501 1330) West of the pond on Baima Xincun.

Public Security Bureau (PSB; 公安局; Gōngānjú; ☎ 501 1381; 21 Furong Lu)

Sights & Activities

Worshippers hold sticks of incense to their foreheads and face the four directions at the enticingly esoteric yellow **Zhiyuan Temple** (祇园寺; Zhíyuán Sì; admission Y5; 🕙 6.30am-8.30pm) on Furong Lu (芙蓉路) in Jiǔhuájiē, where the colossal twin-eaved **Great Treasure Hall** (Dàxióngbǎo Diàn) rises magnificently beyond the Hall of Heavenly Kings. Up the ancient, misshapen steps overlooking the turtle-filled Fangsheng Pond (Fàngshēng Chí) off the main square, the ancient and venerable **Huacheng Temple** (化成寺; Huàchéng Sì; admission Y8) is replete with pilgrims and foggy with incense smoke.

Hiking up the ridge behind Zhiyuan Temple leads you to the **Bǎisuì Gōng**(百岁宫; admission Y8; 🕙 5am-6pm), an active temple built in 1630 to consecrate the Buddhist monk Wu Xia, whose shrunken, embalmed body is coated in gold and sits shrivelled within an ornate glass cabinet in front of a row of pink lotus candles. The **Five Hundred Luohan Hall** (Wǔbǎi Lúohàn Táng) contains an astonishing gathering of 500 gilded *luohan*, with a four-sided 1000-arm effigy of Guanyin at their centre.

If you don't feel like hiking or facing the monkeys that approach climbers and scavenge for scraps on the way up, take the 'Funicular of Baisuigong' **cable car** (fast up/down Y55/40, ordinary up/down Y40/35; 🕙 7am-5.30pm) to the ridge.

From the top, walk south along the ridge past the Dongya Temple (Dōngyá Chánsì) to the **Huixiang Pavilion** (Huíxiāng Gé), above which towers the recently constructed, seven-storey 10,000 Buddha Pagoda (Wànfó Tǎ), fashioned entirely from bronze; avoid climbing during lightning storms unless you want to light up like a signal flare. A western path leads to town, while the eastern one dips into a pleasant valley and continues past the **Phoenix Pine** (Fènghuáng Sōng) and the cable-car station (up/down Y55/50) to **Tiantai Zheng Peak** (天台正顶; Tiāntái Zhèng Dǐng). The two-hour walk to the summit is tough going, passing small temples and nunneries. Close to the peak pay your respects at the **Tiānrán Guānyīn**, a rock sculpted by the elements and robed in red that miraculously resembles the Buddhist Goddess of Compassion (Guanyin).

Within **Tiantai Temple** (Tiāntái Sì) on Tiantai Zheng Peak (the highest peak is actually Shiwang Peak, 1342m, to the south), a statue of the Dizang Buddha is seated within the **Dizang Hall** (Dìzàng Diàn), while from the magnificent **10,000 Buddha Hall** (Wànfó Lóu) above, a huge enthroned statue of the Dizang Buddha gazes at the breathless masses appearing at his feet. Note the beams above your head that glitter with rows of thousands of Buddhas.

A massive 99m-tall bronze statue of the Bodhisattva Dizang and a vast temple complex is planned for construction near Dajue Qiao off Jiuhuang Gonglu in the south of Jiǔhuá Shān.

Sleeping & Eating

Nanyuan Hotel (南苑旅馆; Nányuàn Lǚguǎn; ☎ 501 1122; 26 Furong Lu; 芙蓉路26号; economy bed Y20, d/tw Y100/120; 🖳) This friendly and family-run two-storey hotel has bright and clean rooms in a tranquil and relaxed location opposite the Tonghui Nunnery (Tōnghuì Ān). Economy rooms sleep five, have common showers and no air-con. Meals are also served. It's up a small trail at the south end of Furong Lu (the main street), beyond the PSB.

Baisuigong Xiayuan Hotel (百岁宫下院; Bǎisùigōng Xiàyuàn; ☎ 501 3118; dm/d/tr Y20/380/480;

ĀNHUĪ

☒) The 10-person dorms are a tad grubby but cheap (common shower) and the hotel is pleasantly arranged around an old temple with a Jade Buddha Hall below and a 1000-arm Guanyin statue in the hall above. Discounts for double are rooms frequently available. It's opposite Zhiyuan Temple, off Furong Lu (芙蓉路).

Ju Long Hotel (聚龙大酒店; Jùlóng Dàjiǔdiàn; ☎ 501 1368; d Y580-680; ☒) Large and rather sprawling three-star hotel just beyond the main gate to the village off Furong Lu and facing the Zhiyuan Temple. Comfy rooms come with clean and well-fitted-out shower rooms, but aim for the east-facing rooms with a view.

Jiǔhuájiē village has plenty of restaurants around the main square and along Furong Lu and Huacheng Lu, which serve variously priced local dishes.

Getting There & Away
Buses from the Jiǔhuáshān Xīnqūzhàn (新区站) – the bus terminus and main Jiǔhuá Shān ticket office 20 minutes by bus north of Jiǔhuájiē village – run to Huángshān (Y40, three hours, twice daily), Qīngyáng (Y5, 30 minutes, every 15 minutes), Tónglíng (Y15, 1½ hours, twice daily), Héféi (Y55, four hours, 18 per day), Wǔhàn (Y115, eight hours, once daily) and Shànghǎi (Y100, eight hours, once daily). One bus a day runs to Jiǔhuá Shān from Tāngkǒu (Y36, three hours, 6.10am). The nearby town of Qīngyáng, from where there are buses to Túnxī (Y35, three hours), Yīxiàn (Y28, four hours), Hángzhōu (Y60, five hours), Héféi (Y45, 3½ hours) and Shànghǎi (Y70, seven hours), has regular buses (Y5, 30 minutes, every 15 minutes) to Jiǔhuá Shān.

Getting Around
Buses (free with entrance ticket, otherwise Y5; 15 minutes) depart every 10 minutes or so from the bus station north of the main gate and drive along Furong Lu, over Furong Bridge (Fúróng Qiáo) and up the road (Dengta Xincun) to the Phoenix Pine (Fènghuáng Sōng) and the cable-car station.

HÉFÉI 合肥
☎ 0551 / pop 1.4 million
The provincial capital, Héféi is a pleasant and friendly city with lively markets, attractive lakes and parks but few scenic attractions.

Orientation
Shengli Lu leads down to Nanfei River then meets up with Shouchun Lu. Changjiang Zhonglu is the main commercial street and cuts east–west through the city. Between Suzhou Lu and Huangcheng Lu, Huaihe Lu has been pedestrianised.

Information
Bank of China (Zhōngguó Yínháng; 155 Changjiang Zhonglu) Changes travellers cheques and major currency. There's an ATM that takes international cards.

China International Travel Service (CITS; Zhōngguó Guójì Lǚxíngshè; ☎ 281 1909; 8 Meishan Lu; ⏲ 8am-5pm) Situated next to Anhui Hotel.

First People's Hospital (Shìyī Yīyuàn; ☎ 265 2893; 322 Huaihe Lu)

Post office (Yóujú; Changjiang Zhonglu) Next to the City Department Store.

Public Security Bureau (PSB; Gōngānjú) Located on the northwest corner of the intersection of Shouchun Lu and Liu'an Lu.

Renzhe Internet Café (Rénzhé Wǎngluò Zhōngxīn; per hr Y2; ⏲ 8am-midnight) It's off Huaihe Lu, about 80m west of Motel 168.

Sights
Small **Mingjiao Temple** (Míngjiào Sì; Huaihe Lu; admission Y5; ⏲ 7am-6pm) sits 5m above ground on the pedestrianised section of Huaihe Lu. Among Héféi's green spaces, **Xiaoyaojin Park** (Xiāoyáojīn Gōngyuán; Shouchun Lu; admission Y5; ⏲ 6am-7pm) and **Baohe Park** (Bāohé Gōngyuán), which contains the splendid **Lord Bao's Tomb** (Bāo Gōng Mùyuán; 58 Wuhu Lu; admission Y15; ⏲ 8am-6pm), are the most pleasant.

Closed for refurbishment at the time of writing, the **Anhui Provincial Museum** (Ānhuī Shěng Bówùguǎn; 268 Anqing Lu; admission Y10; ⏲ 8.30-11.30am & 2.30-5pm Tue-Sun) contains displays of bronzes, Han dynasty tomb rubbings and some fine examples of the wooden architectural style found around Huáng Shān.

Sleeping & Eating
Foreign Experts' Building (专家楼; Zhuānjiālóu; ☎ 360 2881; 96 Jinzhai Lu; 金寨路96路; s Y150, d Y180-240) Comfortable and clean rooms are available in the parklike campus setting of the University of Science and Technology, south of the centre. Reception is in the large building on the north side of the pond.

Motel 168 (Mòtài Liánsuǒ Lǚdiàn; ☎ 216 1111; www .motel168.com; 1 Huaihe Lu; 淮河路1号; s Y168, d Y198-238; ☒) About to open at the time of writing,

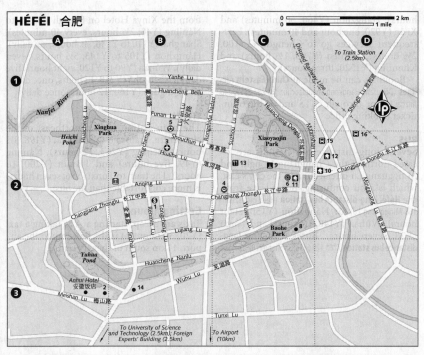

HÉFÉI 合肥

INFORMATION

Bank of China
中国银行 **1** B2
CITS 中国国际旅行社 **2** A3
First Peoples Hospital
市一医院 **3** B2
Post Office 邮局 **4** C2
PSB 公安局 **5** B1
Renzhe Internet Café
仁者网络中心 **6** C2

SIGHTS & ACTIVITIES

Anhui Provincial Museum
安徽省博物馆 **7** B2
Lord Bao's Tomb 包公墓园 **8** C2
Mingjiao Temple 明教寺 **9** C2

SLEEPING 🏠

Holiday Inn 古井假日酒店 **10** D2
Motel 168 莫泰连锁旅店 **11** C2
Xinya Hotel 新亚大酒店 **12** D2

EATING 🍽

Bajiangjun Hotpot 巴将军火锅 **13** C2

TRANSPORT

China Eastern Airlines
东方航空售票处 **14** B3
Héféi Long-Distance Bus Station
省客运站 **15** D2
Long-Distance Bus Station
合肥汽车站 **16** D2

---

this reliable, modern budget/midrange chain hotel was due to offer cheap, clean doubles in a five-floor branch overlooking the bridge on Huancheng Donglu.

Xinya Hotel (Xīnyà Dàjiǔdiàn; ☎ 220 3088; www.xinya hotel.cn; 18 Shengli Lu; 胜利路18号; d/ste incl breakfast Y298/418; ❄) Good discounts bring the comfortable rooms at this business hotel well within range of most budgets. Well located for the bus and train stations, rooms here are spacious and clean and shower rooms come equipped with phones and hairdryers. It has a no-smoking floor.

Holiday Inn (Héféi Gǔjǐng Jiàrì Jiǔdiàn; ☎ 220 6666; www.holiday-inn.com; 1104 Changjiang Donglu; 长江东路1104号; d Y760) This five-star hotel has a well-polished feel and although rooms are a bit tired looking, facilities are good, with swimming pool, health club, wi-fi in pubic areas, nonsmoking rooms, rooms for people with disabilities, a bar on the 4th floor with live music and a good range of restaurants. Substantial discounts are often available.

Bajiangjun Hotpot (Bājiāngjūn Huǒguō; ☎ 261 3777; 118 Suzhou Lu) Popular and centrally located, steaming hotpot restaurant.

Getting There & Away
AIR

Daily flights go to Běijīng (Y900, one hour and 40 minutes), Shànghǎi (Y440, one hour and five minutes), Guǎngzhōu (Y1040, 1½ hours), Hángzhōu (Y460, 50 minutes) and Xī'ān (Y920, one hour and 40 minutes). Less-frequent services go to Chéngdū (Y1100, 2½ hours), Xiàmén (Y790, 1½ hours) and Kūnmíng (Y1520, three hours).

Bookings can be made at **China Eastern Airlines** (Dōngfāng Hángkōng Shòupiàochù; ☎ 282 2357; 246 Jinzhai Lu), or through CITS and at the train-ticket booking office.

BUS
Several long-distance bus stations are located north of the Changjiang Donglu and Mingguang Lu intersection in the city's east, which is a bit confusing. Buses leave from the **Héféi long-distance bus station** (Héféi qìchē zhàn; 168 Mingguang Lu) for Hángzhōu (Y150, eight hours), Wǔhàn (Y140, 10 hours) and Túnxī (Y28, seven hours). Buses from the **long-distance bus station** (☎ 429 6413; 35 Shengli Lu) across

from the Xinya Hotel on Shengli Lu run to Nánjīng (Y40, 2½ hours, every 40 minutes), Shànghǎi (Y110 to Y140, six hours, six daily), Hángzhōu (Y105 to Y143, 5½ hours, seven daily), Wǔhàn (Y90 to Y120, eight hours, five daily), Chángshā (Y218, 12 hours, once daily) and Qīngdǎo (Y160, 12 hours, once daily).

TRAIN
The train station is 4km northeast of the city centre. Trains go to Shànghǎi (Y198, 8½ hours), Běijīng (Y263, 12 hours), Nánjīng (Y49, five hours) and Tiānjīn (Y200, 10 hours). The train to Túnxī (Y96, seven hours) is more comfortable than the bus.

Getting Around
Taxis are cheap, starting at Y5. Taking a taxi (Y20, 30 minutes) is the best way to the airport, 11km south of the city centre.

Hénán 河南

Unassuming and poor, agricultural Hénán lets its western provincial neighbour take credit as the 'cradle' of Chinese civilisation, yet here, Henanese could argue, is where it truly all began.

Neighbouring Shaanxi (Shǎnxī) garners acclaim as the wellspring of Chinese history, yet it is Hénán, smack in the middle of China's nine original regions, that was originally dubbed 'Central Region' – in both a cultural and geographical sense. The land lured settlers – trailing the fickle course of the Yellow River (Huáng Hé) – to take root and populate the fertile plains of its basin. Ancient capitals rose and fell and northern Hénán (particularly time-warped Kāifēng and overlooked Ānyáng) is an east-to-west melange of Chinese dynastic antiquity.

Spirituality blossomed within this dynastic milieu. The province witnessed the initial blooming of Buddhism in China proper; Luòyáng's White Horse Temple is arguably the oldest surviving Buddhist temple in the country. Later, Muslim traders and pilgrims intermarried with Han Chinese and established an Islamic presence. So welcoming were the early emperors that Hénán even found itself the site of China's oldest settlement of Jews.

Hénán today is looked down upon by much of China as a backward, *tǔ* (rural) region where the reform drive has seriously lost steam. But the province plays its history card with assurance and is eager to flaunt its indisputable dynastic credentials.

And it's not all about ancient cities and mouldering ruins: intrepid travellers can eke out some fabulous terrain, including the dizzying high-elevation perch of rural Guōliàngcūn. The province also swarms with pilgrims heading to two of China's drawcard sights, the Shaolin Temple and the stunning Buddhist artistry of the Longmen Caves.

HIGHLIGHTS

- Get a glimpse of nirvana alongside the astonishing Buddhist artistry at the **Longmen Caves** (p465) outside Luòyáng
- Turn over **Kāifēng's** (p468) rich historical heritage before wildly feasting at its night market
- Join Chinese artists decamping to remote, picturesque **Guōliàngcūn** (p467), one of China's most charming traditional villages
- Brush up on your iron-shirt *qìgōng* at the **Shaolin Temple** (p460) before roaming the temple-dotted slopes of **Sōng Shān** (p460)
- Ascend a richly rewarding learning curve at the **Henan Provincial Museum** (p457) in Zhèngzhōu

■ POPULATION: 94 MILLION   ■ www.hnly.com.cn

HÉNÁN

History

It was long thought that tribes who migrated from western Asia founded the Shang dynasty (1700–1100 BC). Shang dynasty settlement excavations in Hénán, however, have shown these towns to be built on the sites of even more ancient – prehistoric even – settlements. The first archaeological evidence of the Shang period was discovered near Ānyáng in northern Hénán. Yet it is now believed that the first Shang capital, perhaps dating back 3800 years, was at Yǎnshī, west of modern-day Zhèngzhōu. Around the mid-14th century BC, the capital is thought to have moved to Zhèngzhōu, where its ancient city walls are still visible.

Hénán again occupied centre stage during the Song dynasty (AD 960–1279), but political power deserted it when the government fled south from its capital at Kāifēng following the 12th-century Juchen invasion from the north. Nevertheless, with a large population on the fertile (although periodically flood-ravaged) plains of the unruly Yellow River, Hénán remained an important agricultural area.

Not until the communist victory was the province able to begin keeping up with its neighbours. Zhèngzhōu, Luòyáng and Kāifēng have sought to bury much of their history under concrete, but exploration yields some tempting glimpses of their ancestry.

Climate

Hénán has a warm-temperate climate: dry, windy and cold (average of -2°C in January)

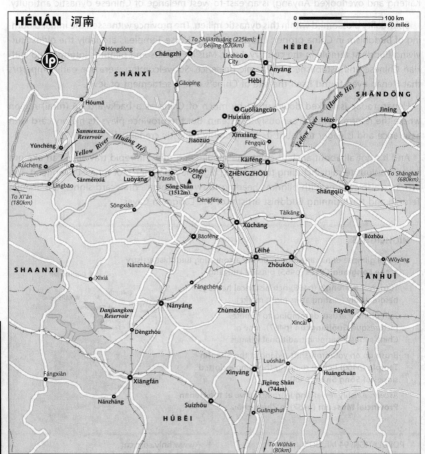

HÉNÁN 河南

in winter, hot (average temperature 28°C) and humid in summer. Rainfall increases from north to south and ranges from 60cm to 120cm annually; most of it falls July to September.

Language
The lion's share of Hénán's 96 million inhabitants speak one of nearly 20 subdialects of Zhōngyuán Huà, itself a dialect of Northern Mandarin. Two of 15 dialects of Jin, a distinct language or a simply a dialect of Mandarin (linguists wrangle), are found in northern Hénán.

Getting There & Around
Hénán is that rarity in China: a province in which travellers can get from point A to point B (inside or outside the province) with relative ease. Zhèngzhōu is a major regional rail hub, and expressways laden with comfy express buses run parallel to rail lines and stretch into southern parts of the province.

Zhèngzhōu is the main hub for flying to/from Hénán (see p459); Luòyáng also has a smaller airport (p464) but it's recommended that you use Zhèngzhōu.

ZHÈNGZHŌU 郑州
☎ 0371 / pop 2 million

The provincial capital of Hénán since 1949, Zhèngzhōu is a sprawling mini-metropolis that, despite its ancient history, retains fewer historical anachronisms than some of its neighbouring cities. The quickly modernising town is not unattractive – with clean, wide boulevards lined with numerous upmarket boutiques and shops branching off around the train station – but its role as a major rail transport junction in the region is the real reason it's the capital city.

Orientation
All places of interest to travellers lie east of the railway line. Northeast of the train station, five roads converge at the prominent modern landmark 7 February Pagoda (Èrqī Tǎ) to form the messy traffic circle 7 February Sq (Èrqī Guǎngchǎng) that marks Zhèngzhōu's not unattractive commercial centre. Erqi Lu runs northward from the traffic circle to intersect with Jinshui Lu near Renmin Park.

Information
Bank of China (Zhōngguó Yínháng; 8 Jinshui Lu; ☉ 9am-5pm)
China International Travel Service (CITS; 中国国际旅行社; Zhōngguó Guójì Lǚxíngshè; ☎ 392 7758;

fax 381 1753; 8th fl, Hǎitōng Dàshà Bldg, 50 Jingqi Lu; ☉ 8.30-noon & 2-6pm Mon-Fri) Inconveniently located in Zhèngzhōu's north. It has also representatives in the pricier Sofitel hotel.

Foreign Languages Bookstore (Wàiwén Shūdiàn; Zhengsan Lu; ☉ 8.30am-6pm) Can put a copy of Anna Karenina or a chunky Trollope in your backpack.

Hanbo Internet (Hànbó Wǎngbā; Shangcheng Lu, per hr Y2; ☉ 8am-midnight) Opposite Chenghuang Temple.

Henan Pharmacy (Hénán Dàyàofáng; ☎ 6623 4256; 19 Renmin Lu; ☉ 24hr)

Internet café (wǎngbā; per hr Y3) Above restaurant at south end of train station concourse.

Little Bear Internet (Xiǎo Xióng Wǎngbā; Jiankang Lu; per hr Y2.50; ☉ 8am-midnight)

Post office (yóujú; ☉ 8am-8pm) South end of train station concourse.

Public Security Bureau Exit-Entry Administrative Office (PSB; Gōngānjú Chūrùjìng Guǎnlǐchù; ☎ 6962 0359; 70 Erqi Lu; ☉ 8.30am-noon & 3-6.30pm summer, 2pm-5.30pm Mon-Fri other seasons) For visa extensions.

Xinhua Bookstore (Xīnhuá Shūdiàn; ☎ 6628 7809; 22 Renmin Lu; ☉ 9am-7.30pm) Small selection of English-language titles

Sights
HENAN PROVINCIAL MUSEUM
河南省博物馆

The emphatically excellent collection of the provincial **museum** (Hénán Shěng Bówùguǎn; 8 Nongye Lu; admission Y20; ☉ 8.30am-6pm) ranges from the awesome artistry of Shang dynasty bronzes (search out the stirring 'Bronze bu with beast mask motif'), oracle bones and further relics from the Yin ruins (so you can bypass Ānyáng, p466) to gorgeous Ming and Qing porcelain specimens. The dioramas of Song dynasty Kāifēng and the magnificent, and now obliterated, Tang dynasty imperial palace at Luòyáng serve to underscore that the bulk of Hénán's glorious past is at one with Nineveh and Tyre. Captions are in Chinese and English; there was no English audio tour at the time of writing.

OTHER SIGHTS
Zhèngzhōu's eastern outskirts are marked by long, high mounds of earth, the remains of the erstwhile **Shang city walls** (Shàngdài Yízhǐ), which can be clambered for walks. The well-restored **Chenghuang Temple** (Chénghuáng Miào; Shangcheng Lu; admission free; ☉ 8am-6pm) bustles with worshippers, while the **Confucius Temple** (Wén Miào; 24 Dong Dajie) was currently undergoing massive restoration at the time of writing.

The **Yellow River** (Huáng Hé; admission Y25; ☉ 6.30am-sunset) is 25km north of town. The road passes near Huāyuánkǒu village, where in April 1938 Kuomintang general Chiang Kaishek blew a dyke to flood Japanese troops. This desperate, ruthless tactic drowned about one million Chinese people and left another 11 million homeless and starving. Bus 16 goes to the river from Erma Lu, north of the train station.

Sleeping

Èrqī Bīnguǎn (Erqi Hotel; ☎ 6661 7688; fax 6696 1268; 168 Jiefang Lu; 解放路168号; d with/without toilet Y216/96, tr Y126; ☒) Net a standard double (pleasant, with a huge bathroom and wood floor) for Y180 after discount at this hotel overlooking the main square. The tiled, frugal Y96 doubles also offer tempting value. The hotel is the semicircular edifice next to the overhead walkway (no English sign).

Golden Sunshine Hotel (Jīnyángguāng Dàjiǔdiàn; ☎ 6696 9999; fax 699 9534; 86 Erma Lu; 二马路86号; d Y110-426; ☒) Beds in the scuffed lower floor cheapies (prices rise with altitude) are like sleeping on planks of wood – good for the spine or so they say. Bonuses include late check out (2pm).

Express by Holiday Inn (Zhōngzhōu Kuàijié Jiàrì Jiǔdiàn; ☎ 6595 6600, 800 830 4088; 115 Jinshui Lu; 金水路115号; s/d Y488/528; ☒ ☒ 🖳) Neat, fresh and snappy new midrange option (linked to the Sofitel by a connecting walkway) with modern rooms. Breakfast included (Y58 for nonguests; open 6am to 10.30am), free broadband in business rooms.

Sofitel (Sùfēitè Guójì Fàndiàn; ☎ 6595 0088; www.accorhotels-asia.com; 289 Chengdong Lu; 城东路289号; d incl breakfast Y1120; ☒ ☒ 🖳 🖳) On balance, the five-star Sofitel may be more goodish four-star, but there are good discounts, useful free English-language maps from the concierge, and the well-designed atrium area bathes the café (with a popular afternoon tea buffet), bar and restaurants below in natural light. There's also wi-fi access.

Eating & Drinking

Guangcai Market (Guāngcǎi Shìchǎng) For street food aplenty, wander this crowded cornucopia of snack stalls in the block northeast of Èrqī Tǎ for *málà tàng* (麻辣烫; spicy soup, with

INFORMATION		SIGHTS & ACTIVITIES		EATING 🍴	
Bank of China 中国银行	1 D2	Chenghuang Temple		Guangcai Market 光彩市场	17 B2
Foreign Languages Bookstore		城隍庙	10 D3	Quánjúdé 全聚德	18 B2
外文书店	2 C2	Confucius Temple 文庙	11 D3		
Hanbo Internet 汉博网吧	3 C3	Shang City Walls		DRINKING 🍷	
Henan Pharmacy		商代城墙遗址	12 D2	Exit 3 Bar	(see 16)
河南大药房	4 C2			Target Pub 目标酒吧	19 C2
Internet Café 网吧	5 B3	SLEEPING 🛏			
Little Bear Internet 小熊网吧	6 B1	Èrqī Bīnguǎn 二七宾馆	13 B3	TRANSPORT	
Post Office 邮政大楼	7 B3	Express by Holiday Inn		Advance Booking Office (Train	
Public Security Bureau Exit-Entry		中州快捷假日酒店	14 D2	Tickets) 火车预售票处	20 B3
Administrative Office		Golden Sunshine Hotel		CAAC 中国民航	21 D2
公安局出入境管理处	8 B2	金阳光大酒店	15 B3	Long-Distance Bus Station	
Xinhua Bookstore 新华书店	9 C2	Sofitel 素菲特国际饭店	16 D2	长途汽车站	22 B3

ingredients chosen from skewered veggies and meat), *bàngzi* (棒子; corn-on-the-cob), *chūn juǎn* (春卷; spring rolls), *miàntiáo* (面条; noodles), *ròuchuán* (肉串; kebabs), *yúwán chuàn* (鱼丸串; fish balls on a stick), *guōtiē* (锅贴; fried dumplings) and more – they are all here among the crowds of diners and rickety tables. At the hub of it all is a small, tiled church.

Quánjúdé (☎ 6623 5108; 108 Erqi Lu; half duck Y38) Escape the noise and fumes at street level for some finger-licking choice Peking duck in a smart upstairs setting. Flick through the photo menu, attended to by polite and efficient staff (who don plastic gloves to roll your pancakes), and observe the chefs firing up the ovens through a glass screen.

Target Pub (Mùbiāo Jiǔbā; ☎ 138 038 570 56; 10 Jingliu Lu; ☉ 7pm-late) A decade in the making, with a lived-in, laid-back vibe, good tunes, mezzanine and an outstanding selection of spirits. Join the expat regulars, seize a chilled beer and let proprietor Lao Wang regale you with his tales of taming the Taklamakan Desert and wheeling it to Paris.

Exit 3 Bar (Kōngjiān; ☎ 6595 0088, ext 8300; 3rd fl, Sofitel, 289 Chengdong Lu; ☉ 8pm-midnight) Formulaic bar with quilted green leather bar stools perhaps, but there's a bona fide snooker table beneath the atrium, plus the sweetener of unlimited Tsingtao beer (Y100).

Getting There & Away
AIR
Civil Aviation Administration of China (CAAC; Zhōngguó Mínháng; ☎ 6599 1111; 3 Jinshui Lu) sells tickets. Airport shuttle buses (Y15, 40 minutes, hourly from 6am to 6.30pm) leave from the CAAC office for the airport, 30km south of the city centre. A taxi to the airport costs around Y100 (40 minutes).

There are daily flights to Běijīng (Y690), Shànghǎi (Y790), Guìlín (Y1130) and Hong Kong (Y2200). Less frequent services fly to Wǔhàn (Y500) and Xī'ān (Y510).

BUS
The most useful long-distance bus station is opposite the train station.

Buses run between approximately 6.30am to 7pm to Luòyáng (Y35, two hours, every 20 minutes), Kāifēng (Y19, one hour, every 25 minutes), Xīnxiāng (Y24, one hour), Dēngfēng (Y19, one hour, every 35 minutes) and Ānyáng (Y50, every 40 minutes). Slow buses to Luòyáng make a stop in Gǒngyì (Y20) or you can take a direct bus.

Buses to the Shaolin Temple (Y21, 1½ to 2½ hours) leave every 20 to 30 minutes between 6am and 11.30pm. Other destinations include Běijīng (Y170 to Y190, eight hours, every 40 minutes) between 8.30am and 10pm.

TRAIN
Zhèngzhōu is a major rail hub with trains to virtually every conceivable destination, including the Běijīng–Kowloon express.

Tickets are easy to buy at the **advance booking office** (☎ 6835 6666; cnr Zhengxing Jie & Fushou Jie; ☉ 8am-noon & 2-5pm).

Hard-seat prices include Ānyáng (Y29, three hours), Běijīng West (Y46 to Y94, seven hours), Hànkǒu (Y36 to Y73, five hours), Kāifēng (Y5.50 to Y13, 1½ hours), Luòyáng (Y10 to Y20, 2½ hours), Shànghǎi (Y64 to Y130, 10 hours), Tàiyuán (Y45, 10 hours) and Xīnxiāng (Y13, 1½ hours).

For Xī'ān take the faster, two-tiered 'tourist train' (Y78 hard seat, 7½ hours) that leaves Zhèngzhōu at 9am and arrives in Xī'ān around 4.30pm.

Getting Around

Bus 2 runs near the Shang City Walls. Bus 39 runs from the train station to the Henan Provincial Museum, and bus 26 runs from the train station past 7 February Sq and along Jinshui Lu to the CAAC office.

Taxis start at Y7, but an additional Y1 fuel charge is levied per trip.

SŌNG SHĀN & DĒNGFĒNG
嵩山，登封
☎ 0371

Three main peaks comprise Sōng Shān, rising to 1512m about 80km west of Zhèngzhōu. In Taoism, Sōng Shān is considered the central mountain, symbolising earth among the five elements. Occupying the axis directly beneath heaven, Taoist Sōng Shān is also famed as the sacred home of the Buddhist Shaolin Temple.

At the foot of 1494m-high **Tàishì Shān** (太室山), a short ride southeast of the Shaolin Temple, sits the squat little town of Dēngfēng. Tatty and squalid in parts, it is used by travellers as a base for trips to surrounding sights or exploratory treks into the hills.

Information

Bank of China (中国银行; Zhōngguó Yínháng; cnr Songshan Lu & Shaolin Dadao; ☺ 8am-5.30pm) ATM.
CITS (中国国际旅行社; Zhōngguó Guójì Lǚxíngshè; ☎ 6288 3442; Beihuan Lu Xiduan) Has helpful, English-speaking staff.
No 2 People's Hospital (第二人民医院; Dìèr Rénmín Yīyuàn; ☎ 6289 9999; 189 Shaolin Dadao) Located on the main road.

Qianshou Internet (牵手网吧; Qiānshǒu Wǎngba; 55 Aimin Lu; per hr Y2; ☺ 7am-midnight)

Sights & Activities
SHAOLIN TEMPLE 少林寺
The overpriced birthplace of *gōngfu*, the **Shaolin Temple** (Shàolín Sì; ☎ 274 9204; admission Y100; ☺ 8am-6.30pm), some 80km southwest of Zhèngzhōu, is a victim of its own success. A frequent target of war, the temple was last torched in 1928, and the surviving halls – many of recent construction – are today besieged by marauding tour groups. Restorations continue with the buzz of chainsaws and the hammering of chisels, occasionally drowned out by blaring music.

Amid the tourist mayhem, communing with the spirit of Shàolín is indeed a tall order. Much *wǔshù* – athletic Chinese martial arts of the performance variety – is in evidence in nearby schools, but there's little true *gōngfu*, which requires not just a tracksuit but years of patient and gruelling physical and mental study.

Enter the temple past stelae of dedication – some from abroad – and make for the signature sights, the **Pilu Pavilion** (毗卢殿; Pílú Diàn), with its famous depressions in the floor apocryphally the work of generations of monks practising their stance work, and the **Guanyin Hall** (观音殿; Guānyīn Diàn), which contains the celebrated frescoes of fighting monks.

Across from the temple entrance, the Arhat Hall within the **Shífāng Chányuàn** (十方禅院) contains legions of crudely fash-

AROUND ZHĒNGZHŌU

MIND & BODY

Legend records that the Shaolin Temple (Shàolín Sì) was founded in the 5th century by an Indian monk. Several decades later another Indian monk named Bodhidharma (Damo) came to the temple, but was refused entrance, so he retired to a nearby cave in which he calmed his mind by resting his brain 'upright'. To do this, Damo sat and prayed toward a cave wall for nine years; temple folklore says his shadow was left on the cave wall. This 'Shadow Stone' is within the Shaolin Temple.

For relief between long periods of meditation, Bodhidharma's disciples imitated the natural motions of birds and animals, movements that evolved over the centuries into physical and spiritual combat routines: Shaolin Boxing (少林拳; Shàolín Quán).

The monks of Shaolin have supposedly intervened continually throughout China's many wars and uprisings – always on the side of righteousness, naturally. Perhaps as a result, their monastery has suffered repeated sackings. The most recent episodes were in 1928, when local warlord Shi Yousan torched almost all the temple's buildings, and in the early 1970s, when Red Guards paid their own disrespects.

---

ioned *luóhàn* (monks who have achieved enlightenment and pass to nirvana at death), while the **Pagoda Forest** (少林塔林; Shàolín Tǎlín), a cemetery of 246 small brick pagodas including the ashes of an eminent monk, is worth visiting if you get here ahead of the crowds. Some of the stupas are in a bad state of neglect while others have entirely collapsed. As you face the Shaolin Temple, paths on your left lead up **Wuru Peak** (五乳峰; Wǔrǔ Fēng). Flee the tourist din by heading into the hills to see the **cave** (达摩洞; Dámó Dòng) where Damo (Bodhidharma) meditated for nine years, or view it through high-powered binoculars (Y2). Note the sign says the cave is 500m away, but it is in fact around 3km. All of the earlier sights are included on the main ticket.

At 1512m above sea level, **Shǎoshì Shān** (少室山) is the area's tallest peak, with a scenic trek beside craggy rock formations along a path that often hugs the cliff. The trek takes about six hours return, covers 15km and takes you to the 782-step **Rope Bridge** (索桥; Suǒ Qiáo). For safety reasons, monks recommend trekking with a friend. The path starts to the east of the Shàolín cable car (Y20), which takes you to part of Shǎoshì Shān. Maps in Chinese are available at souvenir stalls.

To reach the Shaolin Temple, take bus 8 from Dēngfēng (Y1.50, 15 minutes) to the drop off and then a buggy (Y5) to the temple entrance, or walk. Alternatively, take a minibus from either Luòyáng or Zhèngzhōu (Y21, 1½ to 2½ hours). From Shàolín, return buses leave from opposite the Pagoda Forest (last bus leaving at around 8pm).

SONGYANG ACADEMY 嵩阳书院

At the foot of Tàishì Shān (there's a Y10 fee to enter the Tàishì Shān scenic area) sits one of China's oldest academies, **Songyang Academy** (Sōngyáng Shūyuàn; admission Y25; ⏰ 8am-6.30pm). In the courtyard are two cypress trees believed to be around 4500 years old – and still alive! The nearby **Songyue Pagoda** (嵩岳塔; Sōngyuè Tǎ; admission Y25; ⏰ 8am-6.30pm), built in AD 509, is China's oldest brick pagoda.

Take bus 2 (the green one that runs along Zhongyue Dajie) to the last stop and then a motor-rickshaw to the pagoda; the ride should cost Y10 to Y15. A return trip to the academy and pagoda by motor-rickshaw is Y20.

ZHŌNGYUÈ MIÀO 中岳庙

Exuding a more palpable air of reverence than the Shaolin Temple, the ancient and hoary **Zhōngyuè Miào** (admission Y25; ⏰ 6.30am-6.30pm) is a colossal active Taoist monastery complex that originally dates back to the 2nd century BC. Besides attending the main hall dedicated to the Mountain God, walk through the **Huasan Gate** (化三门; Huàsān Mén) and expunge *pengju*, *pengzhi* and *pengjiao* – three pestiential insects that respectively inhabit the brain, tummy and feet. Pay a visit to the **Ministry of Hades** (七十二司; Qīshíer Sī) and drop by the four **Iron Men of Song**, rubbed by visitors to fantastically cure ailments. The temple is 4km east of the city centre. Take the green bus 2 along Zhongyue Dajie.

GUANXING TAI OBSERVATORY 观星台

In the town of Gàochéng, 15km southeast of Dēngfēng, is China's oldest surviving observatory (admission Y10; ⏱ 8am-6.30pm). In 1276 the emperor ordered two astronomers to chart a calendar. After observing from the stone tower, they came back in AD 1280 with a mapping of 365 days, five hours, 49 minutes and 12 seconds, which differs from modern calculations by only 26 seconds. Regular southbound buses from Dēngfēng can take you there; catch them from any large intersection in the southeastern part of town.

Sleeping & Eating

A growing band of four-star hotels charging astronomic rates is making an appearance in Dēngfēng.

Jinan Hotel (金安宾馆; Jīnān Bīnguǎn; ☎ 6285 8299; cnr Zhongyue Dajie & Dongshangbu Jie; 中岳大街与东商埠街交叉口; d with/without shower Y158/238) Regular 50% discounts make rooms here – with crisp linen, serviceable showers and kettle – a bargain (despite grubby carpets).

Shaolin International Hotel (少林国际大酒店; Shàolín Guójì Dàjiǔdiàn; ☎ 286 6188; www.shaolinhotel .com; 16 Shaolin Lu; 少林路16号; s/d from Y338/438; ❄) Increasingly overpriced tourist hotel in the eastern part of Dēngfēng with scads of black Buicks parked outside. Jiang Zemin stayed here, leaving his photo in the lobby and further pumping up prices.

Little Sheep (小肥羊; Xiǎo Féiyáng; ☎ 6286 0122; 131 Zhongyue Dajie; meals Y50) Stomach-warming hotpots from the experts. Shovel plateloads of lamb, lettuce, mushrooms and *dòufu* (tofu) into a scalding broth, extract, dip in sauce and munch.

Also look out for the string of shops along the **Shuyuan River** (书院河; Shūyuàn Hé) specialising in fruit and nuts.

Getting There & Away

The Dēngfēng bus station is on Zhongyue Dajie. Buses to/from Zhèngzhōu (Y20, 1½ hours) and Luòyáng (Y15, two hours) run every 20 to 30 minutes. Four buses a day run to Gǒngyì (Y8, one hour). Hotels in Zhèngzhōu and Luòyáng often arrange day tours (Y40, excluding entrance fees) that include sites along the way.

LUÒYÁNG 洛阳

☎ 0379 / pop 1.4 million

Capital of 13 dynasties until the Northern Song dynasty moved its capital to Kāifēng in the 10th century, Luòyáng is one of China's true ancient dynastic cities. Today it's hard to imagine that Luòyáng was once the centre of the Chinese universe, the Eastern Capital of the great Tang dynasty and home to over 1300 Buddhist temples. The heart of the magnificent Sui dynasty palace complex was centred on the point where today's Zhongzhou Lu and Dingding Lu intersect in a frenzy of honking traffic. Charted on maps of town, the Sui and Tang dynasty walls were arranged in an imposing rectangle north and south of the Luo River.

Luòyáng endured a sacking in the 12th century by Juchen invaders from which it never quite recovered. For centuries the city languished with only memories of greatness, its population dwindling to a mere 20,000 inhabitants by the 1920s. Despite modern overlays, the city remains suspended between eras: travellers may still see ducks wandering the pavements around the train station while sex toy shops and lurid, pink-lit foot-massage parlours infest the north end of Jinguyuan Lu.

Its star long faded, Luòyáng now resembles other fume-laden modern towns in China, with choking air pollution, roaring streets, ample concrete and scant evidence of a once-great citadel.

The surviving signature sight is undoubtedly the splendid Longmen Caves outside town but an annual highlight is the Peony Festival, centred on Wangcheng Park (王城公园; Wángchéng Gōngyuán), held from 15 to 25 April, when the city is flooded with floral aficionados.

Orientation

The bulk of Luòyáng extends across the northern bank of the Luo River (洛河; Luò Hé). The train station and long-distance bus station are located in the north of the city. The chief thoroughfare is Zhongzhou Zhonglu, which meets Jinguyuan Lu leading down from the train station at Wangcheng Sq (王城广场; Wángchéng Guǎngchéng). Few places in town seem to have street numbers, making navigation a headache.

Information

Bank of China (⏱ 8am-4.30pm) The Zhongzhou Xilu office exchanges travellers cheques and has an ATM which accepts MasterCard and Visa, as does the ATM at the Zhōngguó Yínháng office. There's also a branch on the corner of Zhongzhou Lu and Shachang Nanlu that's open until 5.30pm, and another branch just west of the train station has foreign-exchange services.

CITS (Zhōngguó Guójì Lǚxíngshè; ☎ 432 3212, 433 1337; Changjiang Lu) There's also a branch at the Peony Hotel.

Gudu Internet café (Gǔdū Wǎngbā; 111 Jinguyuan Lu; per hr Y2; ☽ 24hr) One of several small 24-hour internet cafés on the east side of Jinguyuan Lu just north of the junction with Tanggong Zhonglu.

Kaixinren Pharmacy (Kāixīnrén Dàyàofáng; ☎ 6392 8315; 483 Zhongzhou Zhonglu; ☽ 24hr)

Luoyang Central Hospital (Luòyáng Shì Zhōngxīn Yīyuàn; ☎ 6389 2222; 288 Zhongzhou Lu) In cooperation with SOS International; it also has a pharmacy.

Post & China Telecom (Yóudiànjú; cnr Zhongzhou Zhonglu & Jinguyuan Lu)

Public Security Bureau (PSB; Gōngānjú; ☎ 393 8397; cnr Kaixuan Lu & Tiyuchang Lu; ☽ 8am-noon & 2-5.30pm Mon-Fri) The Exit-Entry department (出入境大厅; Chūrùjìng Dàtīng) is in the south building.

Western Union (☎ 800 820 8668; Zhongzhou Xilu) Next door to the Bank of China.

Xinhua Bookstore (Xīnhuá Shūdiàn; 3rd-4th fl, 287 Zhongzhou Zhonglu; ☽ 9am-6pm) In the building next to Luoyang Department Store.

Sights & Activities
WHITE HORSE TEMPLE 白马寺
Founded in the 1st century AD, this **temple** (Báimǎ Sì; admission Y35; ☽ 7am-7pm Apr-Oct, hours vary rest of the year) is traditionally considered the first Buddhist temple built on Chinese soil, although the original structures have largely been replaced.

After two Han dynasty court emissaries went in search of Buddhist scriptures, they encountered two Indian monks in Afghanistan who returned together on two white horses to Luòyáng carrying Buddhist sutras and statues. The impressed emperor built the temple to house the monks; it is also their resting place.

In the Hall of the Heavenly Kings, Milefo laughs from within a wonderful old burnished cabinet. Other structures of note include the Big Buddha Hall, the Hall of Mahavira and the Pilu Hall at the very rear, and the standout **Qiyun Pagoda** (齐云塔; Qíyún Tǎ), an ancient 12-tiered brick tower a pleasant five-minutes walk away. It's an active temple, and you may catch the monks hoeing in the fields, or you can hop on an eponymous white horse for a photo-op (Y3).

The temple is located 13km east of Luòyáng, around 40 minutes away on bus 56 from the train station..

LUOYANG MUSEUM 洛阳博物馆
This **museum** (Luòyáng Bówùguǎn; 298 Zhongzhou Zhonglu; admission Y20; ☽ 8am-4.30pm) has a mod-est collection of early pottery figures and fragments. Of more interest is the upstairs diorama of Sui and Tang dynasty Luòyáng: the outer Tang wall was punctured by 18 magnificent gates and embraced the Imperial City with the colossal, five-eaved and circular Tiāntáng (Hall of Heaven) at its heart. To get here, take trolleys 102 or 103, which depart from the train station.

OLD CITY 老城区
The scruffy old city (lǎochéngqū) lies east of rebuilt Lijing Gate (Lìjīng Mén), where a maze of narrow and winding streets rewards exploration, with the **Wen Feng Pagoda** (Wén Fēng Tǎ) serving as a landmark. With a 700-year history, the square, brick pagoda has an inaccessible door on the 2nd storey and a brick shack built onto its south side. Look out for old courtyard houses that survive amid the modern outcrops in this area. The old **Drum Tower** (Gǔ Lóu) rises up at the east end of Dong Dajie (东大街), itself lined with traditional rooftops. A notable historic remnant survives in the two halls of the former **City God Temple** (Chénghuáng Miào; east of cnr Zhongzhou Donglu & Jinye Lu), although it is not open to visitors. Note the intriguing roof ornaments of the green-tiled first hall facing the street.

ZHOU WANGCHENG TIANZI JIALIU MUSEUM 周王城天子驾六博物馆
In 770BC, Zhou dynasty Emperor Ping moved his capital to Luòyì (洛邑) in present-day Luòyáng, which served as dynastic capital for over 500 years and where 25 emperors had their imperial seat. Beyond its collection of bronze ware from Zhou dynasty tombs, the highlight (for archaeologists at least) of this **museum** (Wangcheng Sq; admission Y25; ☽ 8am-10pm) beneath Wangcheng Sq is its excavated horse and chariot pits, also dating from the Zhou.

Sleeping
Mingyuan Hotel (Míngyuán Bīnguǎn; ☎ 6319 1377/0378; lymingyuan@yahoo.com.cn; 20 Jiefang Lu; 解放路20号; dm Y60, s & d/tr Y188/240; ✖ ⬛) This excellent hotel has a convincing CV: affiliation with Hostelling International, spacious, clean rooms with laminated wood flooring, smart furniture, a bowl of apples upon arrival and a tempting location near the train station. Internet access is Y10 per hour. Rates include breakfast.

    Shenjian Hotel (Shénjiàn Bīnguǎn; ☎ 6390 1066; 32 Jiefang Lu; 解放路32号; s/d/tw Y188/198/238; ✖ ⬛)

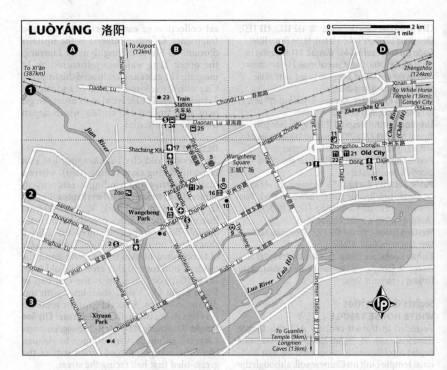

LUÒYÁNG 洛阳

Courteous staff, newly opened, with clean and well-furnished, spacious double rooms, this three-star hotel offers good value for money. It is situated near the train station. Push for discounts (20%). There's no English sign.

Peony Hotel (Mǔdān Dàjiǔdiàn; ☎ 6468 0000; peony smdept@yahoo.com.cn; 15 Zhongzhou Xilu; 中州西路 15号; ✉) Renovated in 2004, standard 'A' doubles are small with midget bathrooms, but are prettily laid out and attractively furnished. A trendy café is on the ground floor.

Eating

Luòyáng's famous Water Banquet resonates along China's culinary grapevine. The main dishes of this 24-course meal are soups and are served up with the speed of 'flowing water' – hence the name.

Night market (Nándàjiē yèshì; cnr Nan Dajie & Zhongzhou Donglu) This lively old city market is a great place for dinner. Barbequed beef and squid, cold dishes and an assortment of bugs can be had for as little as Y2 per dish. Other tasty roadside snacks include *jiǎnpào* (fried pastries filled with chopped herbs and garlic) and

dòushā gāo (豆沙糕; a sweet 'cake' made from yellow peas and Chinese dates).

Zhēn Bù Tóng Fàndiàn (One of a Kind Restaurant; ☎ 399 5787; Zhongzhou Donglu; dishes Y15-45, water banquet from Y60) This is the place to come for a water banquet experience – one half is for the hoi polloi, and one section is upmarket. If 24 courses seem a little excessive, you can opt to pick individual dishes from the menu.

Deheng Roast Duck Restaurant (☎ 6391 2778; 21 Tanggong Xilu; half duck Y30) Snobbish service aside, the duck here is well known in town, and although the restaurant is brightly lit with large tables and mainly geared to group dining, solitary diners can be well fed with half a duck and an extra dish from the menu.

Getting There & Away

AIR

You would do better to fly into or out of Zhèngzhōu. CAAC (Zhōngguó Mínháng; ☎ 6231 0121, 24hr 6539 9366; 196 Chundu Lu) is in an ugly white-tile building north of the railway line, but tickets can be obtained through hotels. Daily flights operate to Běijīng (Y890, one hour), Shànghǎi (Y890, one hour) and other cities.

HÉNÁN

INFORMATION	SIGHTS & ACTIVITIES	EATING
Bank of China 中国银行......1 B1	City God Temple 城隍庙......11 D1	Deheng Roast Duck Restaurant
Bank of China 中国银行......2 A2	Drum Tower 鼓楼......12 D2	德恒烤鸭店......20 B2
Bank of China 中国银行......3 B2	Lijing Gate 丽京门......13 C2	Night Market
CITS 中国国际旅行社......4 A3	Luoyang Museum	南大街夜市......21 D2
CITS 中国国际旅行社......(see 18)	洛阳博物馆......14 B2	Zhēn Bù Tóng Fàndiàn
Gudu Internet Café 古都网吧......5 B2	Weng Feng Pagoda 文峰塔......15 D2	真不同饭店......22 D2
Kaixinren Pharmacy	Zhou Wangcheng Tianzi	
开心人大药房......6 B2	Jialiu Museum	TRANSPORT
Luoyang Central Hospital	周王城天子驾六博物馆......16 B2	CAAC
洛阳市中心医院......7 B2		中国民航......23 B1
Post & China Telecom 邮电局......8 B2	SLEEPING	Jinyuan Bus Station
PSB 公安局......9 C2	Mingyuan Hotel 明苑宾馆......17 B2	锦远汽车站......24 B1
Western Union 全球汇款特快......(see 2)	Peony Hotel 牡丹饭店......18 B2	Long-Distance Bus Station
Xinhua Bookstore 新华书店......10 B2	Shenjian Hotel 神剑宾馆......19 B2	长途汽车站......25 B1

BUS

Regular bus departures from the **Luòyáng long-distance bus station** (Luòyáng chángtú qìchēzhàn; ☎ 6323 3186) include Zhèngzhōu (Y30, 1½ hours, every 20 minutes), Gǒngyì (Y8.50, 40 minutes, every 20 minutes), Kāifēng (Y36, three hours, every 30 minutes) and Xīnxiāng (Y50, 2½ hours). Other destinations include Ānyáng (Y61, four hours), Běijīng (Y173, nine hours), Tàiyuán (Y98.50, eight hours) and Xī'ān (Y71, four hours). The bus station is across from the Luoyang train station.

Buses to similar destinations depart from the **Jinyuan bus station** (Jǐnyuǎn qìchēzhàn) just west of the train station.

Fast buses to Shàolín (Y16, one to 1½ hours) depart every half hour until 4.30pm; slow buses (Y15, two hours) run until 6pm and pass by Dēngfēng. Travel time will speed up when the expressway to Dēngfēng is completed.

TRAIN

Hard-sleeper train-ticket prices include Běijīng West (Y117 to Y185, eight to 10 hours), Dūnhuáng (Y247 to Y401), Shànghǎi (Y153 to Y246, 14 to 15 hours) and Xī'ān (Y67 to Y103, six hours). Regional destinations include Kāifēng (hard seat Y17, three hours) and Zhèngzhōu (hard seat Y11, 1½ hours).

Getting Around

There is no shuttle bus from the CAAC office to the airport, 12km north of the city, but bus 83 runs from opposite the long-distance bus station (30 minutes). A taxi from the train station will cost about Y25.

Buses run until 8pm or 9pm, although bus 5 operates until 11pm. Buses 5 and 41 go to the old city from the train station. Buses 102 and 103 travel from the train station past Wangcheng Park to the Peony Hotel.

The cheapest taxis (xiali) are Y6 at flagfall. Motor-rickshaws are a good way to get around and start at Y2, and motorbike taxis (from Y3) are also ubiquitous.

AROUND LUÒYÁNG
Longmen Caves 龙门石窟

An invaluable Unesco World Heritage site, the ravaged grottoes at Longmen constitute one of China's few surviving masterpieces of Buddhist rock carving. A sutra in stone, the epic achievement of the **Longmen Caves** (Dragon Gate Grottoes; Lóngmén Shíkū; Map p460; admission Y80, English speaking guide Y100; ☑ 6am-8pm summer, 6.30am-7pm winter) was first undertaken by chisellers from the Northern Wei dynasty, after the capital was relocated here from Dàtóng in AD 494. Over the next 200 years or so, more than 100,000 images and statues of Buddha and his disciples emerged from over a kilometre of limestone cliff wall along either bank of the Yi River (Yī Hé), 16km south of the city.

In the early 20th century, many statues were beheaded by unscrupulous collectors or simply extracted whole, many ending up abroad. Also removed were two murals that today hang in the Metropolitan Museum of Art in New York and the Atkinson Museum in Kansas City. Some effigies are slowly returning and heads are being slowly restored to their severed necks, but other statues have had their faces crudely smashed off, deliberate defacement that dates to the dark days of the Cultural Revolution (the Ten Thousand Buddha Cave was particularly damaged during this period).

THREE BINYANG CAVES 宾阳三洞

Construction began on the Three Binyang Caves (Bīnyáng Sān Dòng) during the Northern Wei dynasty. Despite the completion of two of the caves during the Sui and Tang dynasties, statues here all display the benevolent expressions that characterised Northern Wei style.

TEN THOUSAND BUDDHA CAVE 万佛洞
South from Three Binyang Caves, the Tang dynasty Ten Thousand Buddha Cave (Wànfó Dòng) dates from 680. In addition to its namesake galaxy of tiny bas-relief Buddhas there is a fine effigy of the Amitabha Buddha.

LOTUS FLOWER CAVE 莲花洞
The Lotus Flower Cave (Liánhuā Dòng) was carved in 527 during the Northern Wei dynasty and has a large standing Buddha, now faceless. On the cave's ceiling are wispy apsaras (celestial nymphs) drifting around a central lotus flower. An oft-employed symbol in Buddhist art, the lotus flower is a metaphor for purity and serenity.

ANCESTOR WORSHIPPING TEMPLE 奉先寺
Carved in the Tang dynasty between 672 and 675, this temple (Fèngxiān Sì) is the largest structure at Lóngmén and contains the best works of art, despite the evident weathering.

Tang figures tend to be more three-dimensional than the Northern Wei figures. Their expressions and poses also appear more natural and, unlike the other-worldly figures of the Northern Wei, the Tang figures add a fearsome ferocity to their human forms.

The 17m-high seated central Buddha is said to be Losana. Allegedly, the face was modelled on Empress Wu Zetian of the Tang dynasty, who funded the carving of the statue.

MEDICAL PRESCRIPTION CAVE 药方洞
Located south of Ancestor Worshipping Temple is the tiny Medical Prescription Cave (Yàofāng Dòng). The entrance to this cave is filled with 6th-century stone stelae inscribed with remedies for a range of common ailments.

EARLIEST CAVE 古阳洞
Adjacent to the Medical Prescription Cave is the larger Earliest Cave (Gǔyáng Dòng), carved between 495 and 575. It's a narrow, high-roofed cave featuring a Buddha statue and a profusion of sculptures, particularly of flying apsaras.

CARVED CAVE 石窟洞
The Carved Cave (Shíkū Dòng) is the last major cave in the Lóngmén complex and features intricate carvings depicting religious processions of the Northern Wei dynasty.

GETTING THERE & AWAY
The Longmen Caves are 13km south of town and can be reached by taxi (Y30) or bus 81 (Y1) from the east side of Luòyáng's train station.

Guanlin Temple 关林寺
North of the Longmen Caves, this **temple** (Guānlín Sì; admission Y25; ☉ 8am-6pm) is the burial place of the legendary general Guan Yu (see boxed text, p410) of the Three Kingdoms period (220 to 265). The temple buildings were built during the Ming dynasty and Guan Yu was issued the posthumous title 'Lord of War' in the early Qing dynasty. Bus 81 runs past Guanlín Temple from the train station in Luòyáng.

Gongyi City 巩义市
Located between Zhèngzhōu and Luòyáng, Gongyi City (Gǒngyì Shì) is home to a fascinating series of Buddhist caves and tombs built by the Northern Song emperors (c AD 517).

The **Song Tombs** (Sòng Líng; admission Y20), scattered over an area of 30 sq km, are where seven of the nine Northern Song emperors were laid to rest. All that remain of the tombs are ruins, burial mounds and about 700 statues which, amid fields of wheat, line the sacred avenues leading up to the ruins.

Buses running on the old highway (not the freeway) from Luòyáng to Gǒngyì pass by one of these Song Tomb sites. You can get off the bus there and visit the tombs, or you can continue on into Gǒngyì and hire a taxi to visit both the tombs and **Buddhist Caves** (Shíkūsì; admission Y15), where over 7700 Buddhist figures populate 256 shrines. It's possible to do this in half a day; expect to pay about Y80 for the taxi. If you're coming from the direction of Zhèngzhōu, get off at Gǒngyì.

ĀNYÁNG 安阳
☎ 0372 / pop 792,000
Ānyáng, north of the Yellow River near the Hénán–Héběi border, is the site of Yīn, last capital of the antediluvian Shang dynasty.

In the late 19th century, peasants unearthed fragments of polished bone inscribed with an elemental form of Chinese writing. Further etchings on tortoise shells and bronze objects fuelled speculation that this was the site of the Shang capital. Modern Chinese writing derives from these very first pictographs.

Beyond its small scattering of history, modern Ānyáng is a city of limited interest to travellers of a nonarchaeological bent.

Information

CITS (中国国际旅行社; Zhōngguó Guójì Lǚxíngshè; ☎ 592 5650; 1 Youyi Lu; ☼ 8am-noon & 2-6pm Mon-Fri) Has an office located on the 2nd floor of Ānyáng Bīnguǎn (on Youyi Lu).

Dexin Internet Café (德馨网吧; Déxīn Wǎngbā; below UBC Café, Jiefang Dadao; per hr Y2; ☼ 24hr) It's near the intersection with Zhangde Lu.

Post office (yóujú; 1 Yingbin Lu; ☼ 8am-7pm)

Xingkong Internet Café (星空网吧; Xīngkōng Wǎngbā; per hr Y2; ☼ 24hr) Next to Railway Station Hotel as you exit train station.

Sights & Activities

The **Museum of Yin Ruins** (殷墟博物馆; Yīnxū Bówùguǎn; ☎ 393 2171; admission Y50; ☼ 8am-6.30pm) records the achievements of Yin through pottery, oracle bone fragments, jade and bronze artefacts and tomb reconstructions (holding wheeled vehicles with horses and drivers). It's located quite far from town; take bus 1 from the train station to the museum turn-off and walk across the railway tracks, heading along the river for about 10 minutes.

The **Tomb of Yuan Shikai** (袁世凯墓; Yuán Shìkǎi Mù; ☎ 292 2959; Shengli Lu; admission Y30; ☼ 8am-6pm) is a grandiose epitaph to the Qing military official who wrested the presidency from Sun Yatsen and attempted a restoration of the imperial system, crowning himself emperor in 1916. The tomb is 3km east of the Yin museum; take bus 2 from the train station. Get off at the bridge and walk north to the site.

It's worth walking around the town's old quarter, a few blocks east of the train station and south of Jiefang Dadao, where the **Bell Tower** (钟楼; Zhōng Lóu) survives. In the centre of town, the highlight of the **Tianning Temple** (天宁寺; Tiānníng Sì; admission Y10; ☼ 8.30am-6pm) is the five-eaved, climbable **Wenfeng Pagoda** (文峰塔), decorated with splendid Buddhist carvings.

Sleeping & Eating

Sunlight Hotel (阳光宾馆; Yángguāng Bīnguǎn; ☎ 591 0669; 9 Xinxing Jie; 新兴街9号; s & d incl breakfast Y98-168; ☒) The large, spacious and clean doubles with shower, piping-hot water, water cooler and snappy linen and are a bargain. From the train station, walk straight ahead a block to Xinxing Jie and turn right; it's on the left about 50m from the corner (ignore the taxi drivers at the train station).

Anyang Hotel (安阳宾馆; Ānyáng Bīnguǎn; ☎ 592 2219; fax 592 2244; 1 Youyi Lu; 友谊路1号; d Y138-468; ☒) The smarter rooms are in the glitzy main four-star block, with cheaper two-star rooms thrown round the back in building No 3.

Little Sheep (Xiǎoféiyáng; 小肥羊; cnr Jiefang Dadao & Zhangde Lu; meals Y40-50) Quality nationwide chain specialising in steamy lamb hotpot, both spicy Sìchuān (鸳鸯; yuānyāng) and nonspicy Mongolian (内蒙古; nèi měnggǔ). No English menu, but if in doubt, point at the painting of the sheep. The restaurant is next to the Xiangzhou Hotel.

Getting There & Away

BUS

Ānyáng's long-distance bus station, at the end of Yingbin Lu, has regular connections to Zhèngzhōu (Y51, three hours, depart 6.20am to 6.40pm), Luòyáng (Y61, four hours), Xīnxiāng (Y17.50, two hours), Kāifēng (Y38, four hours) and less frequent buses to Tàiyuán (Y91, six hours). To reach the long-distance bus station, turn right after exiting the train station and then take the first left.

TRAIN

Ānyáng is on the main Běijīng–Zhèngzhōu railway line. Regular trains to Zhèngzhōu (Y22, two hours) go through Xīnxiāng (Y14, 1½ hours). Connections to Guǎngzhōu (Y168), Shijiāzhuāng (Y50, three hours) and Běijīng (Y78, six hours) are easy as most express trains stop here.

GUŌLIÀNGCŪN 郭亮村

☎ 0373 / pop 300

Nestled away on its cliff-top perch high up in the Wanxian (Ten Thousand Immortals) Mountains in north Hénán is this delightful high-altitude stone hamlet. For centuries sheltered from the outside world by a combination of sheer inaccessibility and anonymity, Guōliàngcūn shot to fame as the bucolic backdrop to a clutch of Chinese films, which firmly embedded the village in contemporary Chinese mythology.

Today the village attracts legions of artists who journey here to capture the unreal mountain scenery on paper and canvas. New hotels have menacingly sprung up at the village's foot, but the original dwellings – climbing the mountain slope – retain their simple, rustic charms, while long treks through the mind-boggling scenery more than compensate efforts at journeying here.

Approximately 6°C colder than Zhèngzhōu, Guōliàngcūn is cool enough to be devoid of mosquitos year-round (locals say), but pack very warm clothes for winter visits, which can be bone-numbing (hotels are too primitive for central heating). Visiting off season may seem odd advice, but come evening the village can be utterly tranquil, and moonlit nights are intoxicating. Occasional power cuts plunge the village into candlelight, so pack a small torch.

Officially, the entrance charge for Guōliàngcūn is Y35 (admission to the Wanxian Mountains Scenic Area), although your minibus driver may offer you a slightly better price to speed you past the checkpoint.

Sights

All of the delightful **village dwellings**, hung with butter-yellow *bàngzi* (sweet-corn cobs), are hewn from the same local stone that paves the slender alleyways, sculpts the bridges and fashions the picturesque gates of Guōliàngcūn. Walnut-faced old women peek from doorways and children scamper about, but locals are used to the sight of outsiders. There's no need to tiptoe around, but be respectful at all times.

Using the village as a base, set off to explore the gorgeous surrounding landscape. You will have passed by the **Taihang Precipice** (太行绝壁; Tàiháng Juébì) en route to the village, but backtrack down for a closer perspective on these plunging cliffs, with dramatic views from the tunnel carved from the rock face. The **Sky Ladder** (天梯; Tiān Tī) was traditionally the only way in and out of the village. The road beyond the hotel strip out of Guōliàngcūn away from the Sky Ladder does a bracing 5km loop through the mountain valley and past the awe-inspiring curtain of rock above the **Shouting Spring** (喊泉; Hǎn Quán; its flow responding to the loudness of your whoops, so the story goes), the **Old Pool** (老潭; Lǎo Tán) and two caves: the **Red Dragon Cave** (红龙洞; Hónglóng Dòng) and the **White Dragon Cave** (白龙洞; Báilóng Dòng). Vehicles whiz travellers along the route for Y5. Once you've seen the big sights, get off the beaten trail and onto one of the small paths heading into the hills (eg the boulder-strewn brookside trail along the flank of Guōliàngcūn that leads further up into the mountain), but take water.

Sleeping & Eating

Many homesteads in Guōliàngcūn proper have thrown open their doors to wayfarers, offering simple beds for a pittance (Y10 to Y30). Prices can be a bit higher during the summer but can be negotiable off season. The strip of hotels at the foot of the village offers more spacious rooms, some with shower rooms and TVs (from Y30). One of the plushest looking places is the **Guìbīn Yuán** (贵宾园; ☎ 671 0329) toward the end of the hotel strip. There are no restaurants per se, but hoteliers will cook up simple meals on request and a couple of shops sell snacks and essentials.

Getting There & Away

You can reach Guōliàngcūn from Xīnxiāng (新乡), between Ānyáng and Zhèngzhōu. Regular trains run to Xīnxiāng from Ānyáng (Y14, 1½ hours) or Zhèngzhōu (Y13, one hour); buses also link Xīnxiāng with Zhèngzhōu (Y24, one hour, every 25 minutes). Exit the Xīnxiāng train station and take a motortricycle (Y2) to the bus stop 1km away for buses to Huīxiàn (辉县; Y4, 45 minutes, regular). Ask the driver to drop you at the Huīxiàn stop for buses to Guōliàngcūn (Y10, 2½ hours, depart 8am and 1pm). Note that buses from Huīxiàn may have the characters for Guōliàng on the window, but may (depending on passenger number) only stop at Nánpíng (南坪), a village at the base of the road to Guōliàngcūn. From Nánpíng it is a steep 3km walk to Guōliàngcūn up the mountain road, otherwise taxis or local drivers are prone to fleecing (Y40) for the steep haul into the village, especially if travellers are scarce. In the other direction, Huīxiàn-bound minibuses (Y10) depart from the bottom of the mountain road from Guōliàngcūn at 9am, noon and 3pm.

KĀIFĒNG 开封

☎ 0378 / pop 581,000

Of Hénán's ancient capitals, none has more resolutely repelled China's construction offensive than the walled bastion of Kāifēng. You may have to squint a bit here and there, and learn to sift fake overlays from genuine historical sights, but Kāifēng still juggles up a riveting display of age-old charm, magnificent market food, relics from its long-vanished apogee and colourful chrysanthemums (the city flower).

Erstwhile prosperous capital of the Northern Song dynasty (960 to 1126), Kāifēng was established south of the Yellow River, albeit not far enough to escape the river's capricious wrath. After centuries of flooding, the city of the Northern Song largely lies buried 8m to 9m below ground. Between 1194 and 1938 the city was flooded 368 times, an average of once every two years.

HÉNÁN

It's not Píngyáo (p407) – the city is hardly knee-deep in history, and white-tile buildings blight the low skyline – but enough survives above ground level to hint at past glories and reward ambitious exploration. One reason you won't see soaring skyscrapers here is because buildings requiring deep foundations are prohibited, for fear of destroying the city below.

Dynasties aside, Kāifēng was also the first city in China where Jewish merchants settled when they arrived, via India along the Silk Road, during the Song dynasty. A small Christian community also lives in Kāifēng alongside a much larger local Muslim Hui community.

Orientation

The south long-distance bus station and the train station are both about 1km south of the city walls that enclose the larger part of Kāifēng. The city's pivotal point is the Sihou Jie and Madao Jie intersection, where the famed street market really starts hopping at night. Many of the wooden restaurants, shops and houses in this area were constructed during the Qing dynasty in the traditional Chinese style.

Information

Bank of China (Zhōngguó Yínháng) Gulou Jie (64 Gulou Jie); Xi Dajie (cnr Xi Dajie & Zhongshan Lu) Twenty-four hour ATM (MasterCard & Visa) at the Xi Dajie branch.
CITS (Zhōngguó Guójì Lǚxíngshè; ☎ 393 4702; 98 Yingbin Lu; ◷ 9am-5pm) Just north of the Dōngjīng Dàfàndiàn. No maps, little English.
Jidi Internet Café (Jídì Wǎngbā; per hr Y1.50; ◷ 24hr) Off Zhongshan Lu, just south of the PSB.
Kaifeng No 1 People's Hospital (Kāifēng Dìyī Rénmín Yīyuàn; ☎ 567 1288; 85 Hedao Jie)
Post office (yóujú; Ziyou Lu; ◷ 8am-5.30pm) West of Temple of the Chief Minister.
Public Security Bureau (PSB; Gōngānjú; ☎ 532 2242; 86 Zhongshan Lu; ◷ 8.30am-noon & 3-6pm) Gets fairly good reviews on visa renewals.

Sights

TEMPLE OF THE CHIEF MINISTER 大相国寺
First founded in AD 555, this frequently rebuilt **temple** (Dà Xiàngguó Sì; ☎ 566 5982; Ziyou Lu; admission Y30; ◷ 8am-6pm) was destroyed along with the city in the early 1640s when rebels breached the Yellow River's dikes.

Within the **Hall of the Heavenly Kings**, the mission of chubby **Milefo** (the Laughing Buddha) is proclaimed in the attendant Chinese characters

'Big belly can endure all that is hard to endure in the world'. But the temple showstopper is the mesmerising **Four-Faced Thousand Hand Thousand Eye Guanyin** (四面千手千眼观世音), towering within the octagonal **Arhat Hall** (罗汉殿; Luóhàn Diàn) beyond the Great Treasure Hall. Fifty-eight years in the carving, the 7m-tall gilded statue bristles with giant fans of 1048 arms, an eye upon each hand. Note neither photography nor 'fireworks' are allowed. Elsewhere in the temple you can divine your future by drawing straws (chōuqiān) in front of a smaller statue of Guanyin, dine at the on-site vegetarian restaurant or listen to the song of caged birds, one of which squawks 'guì fó' ('kneel down to Buddha').

SHANSHANGAN GUILD HALL 山陕甘会馆
The elaborately styled **guild hall** (Shānshǎn Gān Huìguàn; ☎ 598 5607; 85 Xufu Jie; admission Y15; ◷ 8.30am-6.30pm) was built as a lodging and meeting place during the Qing dynasty by an association of merchants from other provinces. Note the carvings on the roofs, and delve into the exhibition on historic Kāifēng for fascinating dioramas of the old Song city walls and photographs of the city's standout historic monuments.

IRON PAGODA 铁塔
The 55m 11th-century **pagoda** (Tiě Tǎ; ☎ 286 2279; 210 Beimen Dajie; admission Y20; ◷ 7am-7pm) is a slender brick edifice wrapped in glazed rust-coloured tiles. Climb to the top for a further Y10.

Take bus 3 from the train station via Jiefang Lu to the route terminus, not far from the Iron Pagoda; it's a short walk east to the park's entrance from here.

PO PAGODA 繁塔
This stumpy **pagoda** (Pó Tǎ; Pota Xijie; admission Y10; ◷ 8am-6pm) is the oldest Buddhist structure in Kāifēng, dating back to 974. The original was a nine-storey hexagonal building, typical of the Northern Song style. The pagoda is clad in tiles decorated with 108 different Buddha images – note that all the Buddhas on the lower levels have had their faces smashed off. The pagoda is all that survives of Tianqing Temple (天清寺; Tiānqīng Sì), but worshippers still flock here to light incense and pray.

The pagoda is hidden down alleyways east of train station. Cross southward over the railway tracks from Tielubeiyan Jie and take the first alleyway on your left. From here follow the red arrows spray-painted on the walls.

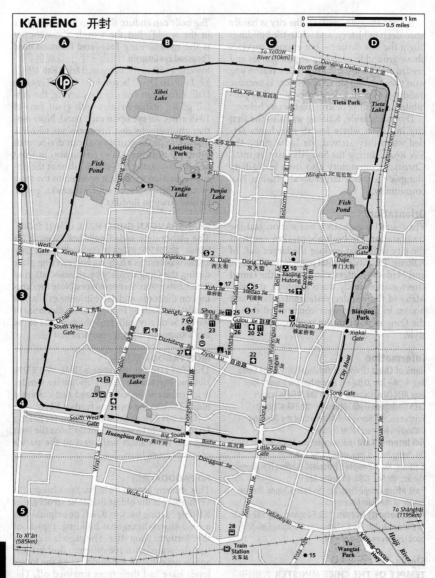

KAIFENG 开封

Bus 15 gets relatively close; ask the driver to let you off at the right stop or grab a taxi.

KAIFENG MUSEUM 开封博物馆

Kāifēng's **museum** (Kāifēng Bówùguǎn; ☎ 393 2178; 26 Yingbin Lu; admission Y10; ❧ 8.30-11.30am & 2-5pm Tue-Sun) is a forlorn place, its lobby decorated with the plundered heads of bronze Bodhisattvas

and other Buddhist deities. A turgid exhibition on revolutionary Kāifēng can be missed, but an extra Y50 allows you to examine two notable Jewish stelae on the 4th floor. The **Kaifeng Institute for Research on the History of Chinese Jews** (☎ 393 2178, ext 8010) has detailed information about the history of the region's Jewish people. Buses 1, 4, 9 and 23 all travel past here.

INFORMATION
Bank of China 中国银行 ... 1 C3
Bank of China 中国银行 ... 2 B3
CITS 中国国际旅行社 ... 3 A4
Jidi Internet Café 基地网吧 ... 4 B3
Kaifeng No 1 People's Hospital 开封第一人民医院 ... 5 C3
Post Office 邮电局 ... 6 B3
PSB 公安局 ... 7 B3

SIGHTS & ACTIVITIES
Dongda Mosque 东大寺 ... 8 C3
Dragon Pavilion 龙亭 ... 9 B2
Former Site of Kaifeng Synagogue 开封犹太教堂遗址 ... 10 C3
Iron Pagoda 铁塔 ... 11 D1
Kaifeng Museum 开封博物馆 ... 12 A4
Kaifeng Riverside Scenic Park Qingming Garden 清明上河园 ... 13 B2
Old Guanyin Temple 古观音堂 ... 14 C3
Po Pagoda 繁塔 ... 15 C5
Sacred Heart of Jesus Church 耶稣圣心堂 ... 16 C3
Shaanshangan Guild Hall 陕山甘会馆 ... 17 C3
Temple of the Chief Minister 大相国寺 ... 18 C4
Yanqing Temple 延庆观 ... 19 B3

SLEEPING
Dajintai Hotel 大金台宾馆 ... 20 C3
Dongjing Hotel 东京大饭店 ... 21 A4
Kaifeng Hotel 开封宾馆 ... 22 C4

EATING
Dìyīlóu Bāozi Guǎn 第一楼包子馆 ... 23 B3
Háoxiǎnglái 豪享来 ... 24 C3
Jiǎozi Guǎn 饺子馆 ... 25 C3
Night Market 鼓楼夜市 ... 26 C3

DRINKING
Xinyue Bar 馨悦酒吧 ... 27 B4

TRANSPORT
Rail Ticket Office 铁路票务中心 ... (see 3)
South Long-Distance Bus Station 长途汽车南站 ... 28 C5
West Long-Distance Bus Station 长途汽车西站 ... 29 A4

CITY WALLS 城墙

Kāifēng is ringed by a relatively intact, much-restored Qing dynasty wall. Encased with grey bricks, the ramparts can be scaled at various points along the perimeter, including the South West Gate. Look out for the sheer rough paths snaking up the incline. Today's bastion was built on the foundations of the Song dynasty **Inner Wall** (内城; Nèichéng). Rising up beyond was the mighty, now-buried **Outer Wall** (外城; Wàichéng), a colossal construction containing 18 gates, which looped south of the Po Pagoda, while the **Imperial Wall** (皇城; Huángchéng) protected the Imperial Palace.

LONGTING PARK 龙亭公园

Site of the former imperial palace, this **park** (Lóngtíng Gōngyuán; ☎ 566 0316; Zhongshan Lu; admission Y35; 🕑 7am-6.30pm) is largely covered by lakes, into which hardy swimmers dive in winter. Climb the **Dragon Pavilion** (Lóng Tíng) for town views.

KAIFENG RIVERSIDE SCENIC PARK QINGMING GARDEN 清明上河园

High on historic kitsch, this overpriced **theme park** (Qīngmíng Shànghéyuán; admission Y60; 🕑 9am-10pm, performances 9am-7.50pm) re-creates the Kāifēng of its heyday, complete with cultural performances, folk art and music demonstrations. There is an entrance and an 'exportation' (exit).

YANQING TEMPLE 延庆观

The modest Taoist **Yanqing Temple** (Yánqìng Guàn; ☎ 393 1800; 53 Guanqian Jie; admission Y15; 🕑 8am-5.30pm) dates to 1233. The intriguingly shaped **Tower of the Jade Emperor**, repeatedly buried during the floods, contains a domed ceiling. At the rear is the **Hall of the Three Clear Ones**, where a trinity of Taoist deities welcomes worshippers.

OTHER SIGHTS

Sadly nothing remains of the **Kāifēng synagogue** (Kāifēng Yóutài Jiàotáng Yízhǐ; 59 Beitu Jie), except a well with an iron lid in the boiler room of the No 4 People's Hospital. The spirit of the synagogue lingers, however, in the name of the brick alley immediately south of the hospital – **Jiaojing Hutong** (Teaching the Scripture Alley; 教经胡同). Delve along the alley until it meets the small Caoshi Jie (草市街), then head south and you will soon see the 43m-high spire of the 1917 **Sacred Heart of Jesus Church** (Yēsū Shèngxīntáng; cnr Caoshi Jie & Lishiting Jie). South is Kāifēng's main Muslim district, whose landmark place of worship is the Chinese-temple–styled **Dongda Mosque** (Dōngdà Sì; 39 Mujiaqiao Jie). Streets here have colourful names, such as Shaoji Hutong (Roast Chicken Alley).

The **Old Guanyin Temple** (Gǔ Guānyīn Táng; Baiyige Jie) just northeast of the No 4 People's Hospital was undergoing a lavish refurbishment at the time of writing. The large temple complex includes a notable hall with a twin-eaved umbrella roof and a sizable effigy of a recumbent Sakyamuni in its Reclining Buddha Hall (卧佛殿; Wòfó Diàn). You can visit the **Yellow River**, about 10km north of the city, although there is little to see as the water level is low these days. Bus 6 runs from near the Iron Pagoda to the Yellow River twice daily. A taxi will cost Y50 to Y60 for the return trip.

Sleeping

Kāifēng's hotel industry is diverse, befitting the town's popularity with travellers. Those on very tight budgets can try their luck at one of the cheap flophouses identified by Chinese signs, otherwise aim for one of the following.

Dajintai Hotel (Dàjīntái Bīnguǎn; ☎ 255 2999; fax 595 9932; 23 Gulou Jie; 鼓楼街23号; dm Y60, junior/senior d Y130/160, tr Y75, all incl breakfast; 🛇) Dating from 1911, this two-star old-timer combines excellent value with a central location on the very fringe of the bustling night market. Try to secure one of the spacious Y160 doubles, with clean furniture, bathroom and water cooler. Winter heating can be sluggish coming on.

Dongjing Hotel (Dōngjīng Dàfàndiàn; ☎ 398 9388; fax 595 6661; 99 Yingbin Lu; 迎宾路99号; bldg 4/3/2 d Y120/200/288; 🛇 🖫) A sprawling, musty and threadbare midrange option dissected into separate buildings and fitfully pepped up by sprinklings of grass and trees.

Kaifeng Hotel (Kāifēng Bīnguǎn; ☎ 595 5589; fax 595 3086; 66 Ziyou Lu; 自由路66号; s Y260, d Y260-360; 🛇) With its harmonies of Chinese roofing and well-tended magnolias, this inviting Russian-built hotel offers a variety of rooms and a central location, although the Dajintai offers better value. Rooms in the pricier Mènghuá Lóu (Building Two) were recently restored.

Eating & Drinking

Night market (cnr Gulou Jie & Madao Jie) This veritable marvel and phenomenon alone justifies trips to Kāifēng, especially at weekends. Join the scrums weaving between stalls busy with hollering Hui Muslim chefs cooking up kebabs and náng bread, red-faced popcorn sellers and vendors of shāo bing (sesame-seed cakes), cured meats, foul-smelling chòu gānzi (臭干子; dry strips of doufu), sweet potatoes, crab kebabs, sugar-coated pears and Thai scented cakes. Pass on the yāxuě tāng (鸭血汤; duck blood soup) if you insist.

Among the flames jetting from ovens and steam rising in clouds prance the vendors of xìngrén chá (杏仁茶; almond tea), a sugary sauce made from boiling water thickened with powdered almond, red berries, peanuts, sesame seeds and crystallised cherries. A bowl costs a mere handful of kuài. Two to three bowls constitute a (very sweet) meal. Xìngrén chá stalls stand out for their unique red pompom-adorned dragon-spouted copper kettles. Also set out to sample ròuhé (肉合; a local snack of fried vegetables and pork, or mutton, stuffed into a 'pocket' of flat bread); there's also a good veggie version. Join the locals at one of the rickety tables. The market slowly peters out into stalls selling clothes, toys and books.

Jiǎozi Guǎn (Gulou Jie; dishes from Y3) On the corner of Shudian Jie and Sihou Jie, this gorgeous three-storey Chinese building has traditional verandas hung with lanterns, excellent dumplings and great views over the night market.

Dìyīlóu Bāozi Guǎn (☎ 565 0780; 8 Sihou Jie; dumplings Y5; ⏰ 7am-10.30pm) The xiǎolóng bāo (small buns filled with pork) served here are so tasty, the restaurant is always packed.

Háoxiǎnglái (☎ 597 5799; 19 Gulou Jie; ⏰ 24hr) Grilled-meat sets kick off from Y25, which gets you a large grilled chop, spaghetti, fried egg, bowl of soup, salad, toast, tea, a desert plus the smallest shot of apéritif imaginable. Kids will love it, there's a handy photo menu and waitresses wheel dim sum and sweet snacks past on carts.

Xinyue Bar (Xīnyuè Jiǔbā; ⏰ 393 6198; first alley south of cnr of Dazhifang Jie & Zhongshan Lu; bottle of Qingdao beer Y10) It's a dark, quiet and cosy bar tucked away west off Zhongshan Lu; look for the green glow of the Heineken sign.

Getting There & Away

AIR

The nearest airport is at Zhèngzhōu (p459).

BUS

Regular buses run to Zhèngzhōu (Y11, every 15 minutes, 6am to 7pm) and Luòyáng (Y35, 8am to 2.30pm) from the west long-distance bus station. Other destinations include Ānyáng (Y24, three hours) and Xīnxiāng (Y18.50, 1½ to two hours). Buses to similar destinations also leave from the south long-distance bus station (opposite the train station).

TRAIN

Kāifēng is on the railway line between Xī'ān and Shànghǎi so trains are frequent, but sleeper tickets can be scarce, so consider leaving from Zhèngzhōu. If time is tight or tickets in short supply, try the **rail ticket office** (tiělù piàowù zhōngxīn; ☎ 396 6888; Yingbin Lu; ⏰ 8am-noon & 2-5pm), next to CITS, for trains from Zhèngzhōu and board the train at Kāifēng (but check the train stops here). Express trains to Zhèngzhōu take about one hour (Y12). Eight trains a day run to Shànghǎi (12 hours). Other destinations include Xī'ān, Héféi, Hángzhōu, Běijīng West and Jǐ'nán.

Getting Around

Buses (Y1) departing from both of Kāifēng's bus stations travel to all the major tourist areas. Gulou Jie, Sihou Jie and Shudian Jie are all good for catching buses. The streets swarm with taxis (flag fall Y5) and pedicabs. Budget hotels may help you rent a bike (Y10 per day).

Húběi 湖北

Lying at China's geographical heart and ringed by five provinces and the municipality of Chóngqìng, Húběi has long been famed for its vital strategic significance. The province is inundated with water and lushly fertile, its landlocked panoramas flushed by the mighty Yangzi River (Cháng Jiāng) and its tributaries, which cleave the province into a mosaic of lakes, waterways and irrigated fields.

The flood-prone Yangzi has delivered periodic devastation but it has also ensured a prosperous trade route, while gouging out the scenic phenomenon of the Three Gorges. Gobsmacked tourists still funnel through Yíchāng for once-in-a-lifetime glimpses of these chasms, now visibly reduced by rising waters amassing behind the Three Gorges Dam. The Yangzi is the powerhouse behind the astonishing hydroelectric potential of the dam – Húběi's most controversial chunk of construction – which could meet a tenth (18,200 megawatts) of China's energy needs. The leviathan river has also increasingly obsessed the parched north of China, which seeks to slake an insatiable thirst by snatching its waters in a gargantuan south-north diversion project.

The bulk – more than 70% – of Húběi undulates aesthetically into hills and mountains, forcing farmers to sculpt the curved landscape into cultivable terraces, and providing slight relief from the summer scorch. The remaining 30% of the province, in the east, is a low-lying plain drained by the Yangzi and Han Rivers. It swivels around the dynamic provincial capital Wǔhàn, a mighty city that simmers feverishly in hothouse temperatures from May to August.

Away from the capital, travellers can put their heads literally into the clouds among the other-worldly Taoist peaks of Wǔdāngshān, explore the scenic landscapes of Shénnóngjià or ferret out the distinctive architecture and ethnic culture of the Tujia minority in Yúmùzhài, in the hilly southwest.

HIGHLIGHTS

- Funnel upstream aboard a cruise through the dwarfing **Three Gorges** (p484) from Yíchāng
- Envelop yourself in the Taoist mysticism, mountain mists and stunning scenery of **Wǔdāng Shān** (p481)
- Ferret through the forests of **Shénnóngjià** (p483), and perhaps stumble across the region's legendary ape-man
- Traipse through Wǔhàn's Hànkǒu district on the trail of its splendid **historical buildings** (p478)
- Journey to sleepy **Yúmùzhài** (p486), a delightfully undisturbed Tujia village in the far-off southwest hills

★ Wǔdāng Shān
★ Shénnóngjià
★ Three Gorges   ★ Wǔhàn
★ Yúmùzhài

- POPULATION: 62.1 MILLION

HÚBĚI

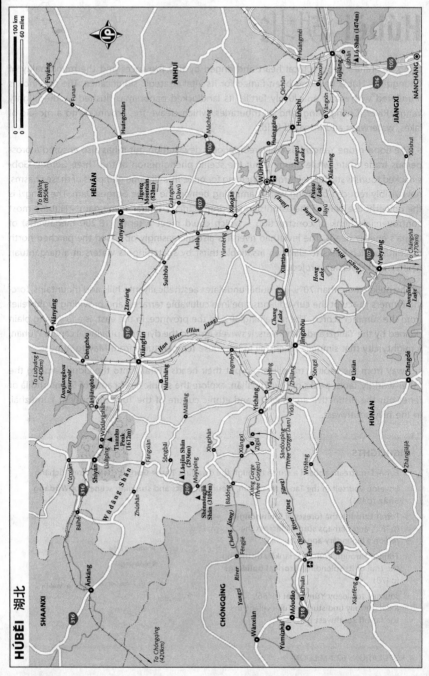

History

Han Chinese settled the plain in 1000 BC. Following the demise of the Eastern Han dynasty in AD 220, warlords skirmished for control from the Yellow River (Huáng Hé) basin all the way through to the southwest regions. Initially weak, the warlords along the Yangzi River finally united and defeated military groups in what is modern-day Húběi. The resultant political manoeuvrings and continued armed struggle ultimately gave rise to the Three Kingdoms Period (AD 220–60). Around the 7th century the region was intensively settled and cultivated, and by the 11th century it was producing a rice surplus, an extraordinary agricultural output that still continues today. In the late 19th century Húběi was the first area in the Chinese interior to undergo significant industrialisation.

Climate

Wǔhàn, the capital, is aptly dubbed one of the four 'Furnaces of China'; in July and August, it's abysmally hot and humid (above 40°C commonly) and no prevailing monsoon winds from the southeast make it this far. The western mountains are far more temperate.

Rainfall is heavy in the southeast (averaging 160cm annually), and decreasing north and west (a mere 80cm per annum average). Expect most of it April through July.

Language

Húběi officially has two dialects of Northern Mandarin – Southwest Mandarin and Lower-Mid Yangzi Mandarin – but these fragment into innumerable local variants. Southeastern Húběi has a number of Gàn (a dialect of Mandarin) speakers.

Getting There & Around

Three Gorges Dam construction has ended Wǔhàn's wonderful reign as a river ferry stop-off, but you can still get to Chóngqìng by ferry. Wǔhàn has one of the best-connected train stations in the country. The east of the province is wonderfully easy to get around, but the rugged west is another matter.

WǓHÀN 武汉

☎ 027 / pop 4,236,000

One of China's most massive and upbeat cities, Wǔhàn is a sprawling and gargantuan alloy of three formerly independent cities: Wǔchāng, Hànkǒu and Hànyáng. Centuries of trade have flooded into Wǔhàn along the irrepressible Yangzi River, and the city's tight clutch of buildings on the waterway pump with levels of money and modernity to rival Shànghǎi. Indeed, the city carries numerous echoes of Shànghǎi: Hànkǒu's Bund and concession-era streetscapes; neon-splashed Jianghan Lu, hopping with shoppers and fizzing with commercial energy; and the towering form of the Minsheng Bank Building (p478).

One of the Yangzi River summer swelter zones, Wǔhàn's feverish temperatures start to climb on a steep and energy-sapping parabola from early summer.

History

Wǔhàn's three mighty chunks trace their capital status back to the Han dynasty, with Wǔchāng and Hànkǒu vying for political and economic sway. The city was prised opened to foreign trade in the 19th century by the Treaty of Nanking. British, German, Russian, French and Japanese enclaves sprang up around Hànkǒu's present-day Zhongshan Dadao, where surrounding streets remain littered with concession-era banks, churches and residential architecture. Wǔhàn is also strongly associated with Sun Zhongshan and the 1911 uprising, which left swathes of the city in ruins and eventually swept away the Qing dynasty. Wǔchāng and Hànyáng were first linked by the enormous 110m-long and 80m-high Wuhan Yangzi River Big Bridge (Wǔhàn Chángjiāng Dàqiáo), completed in 1957. Until then all traffic, including trains, had to be laboriously ferried across the river.

Orientation

Wǔhàn is the only city on the Yangzi that can truly be said to lie on both sides of the river. Wǔchāng on the southeastern bank is faced by Hànkǒu and Hànyáng, themselves divided by the smaller Han River. The city's fragments are stapled together by vast bridges, and ferries cross the Yangzi River throughout the day.

Wǔhàn's centre of gravity is Hànkǒu, focussing around Zhongshan Dadao (and spreading northwest across Jiefang Dadao), where many of the city's famous hotels, historic buildings, department stores, restaurants and street markets are found. The enormous Hànkǒu train station is around 5km northwest of Zhongshan Dadao. The city's main river port is also in Hànkǒu, as was, at the time of writing, Wǔhàn's sole light rail line.

The Tianhe International Airport is about 30km north of Hànkǒu.

On the southeast side of the Yangzi River, Wǔchāng is a modern district of long, wide avenues. Many recreational areas and the

Hubei Provincial Museum are here, as is the city's second train station.

MAPS

Maps can be bought from hawkers that swarm around tourist sights, or from newspaper kiosks around town. Ask at concierge desks at five-star hotels for English-language versions.

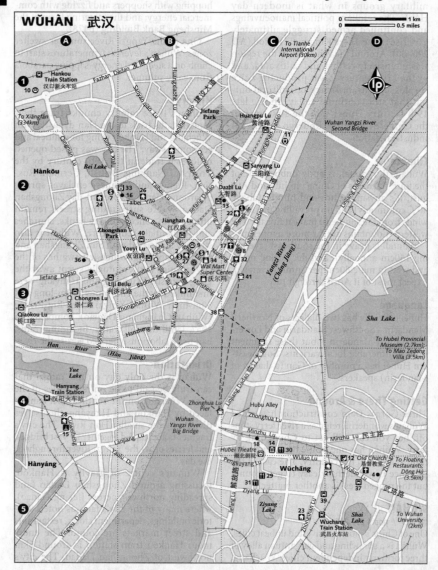

Information

BOOKSHOPS

Foreign Languages Bookstore (Wàiwén Shūdiàn; Zhongnan Lu; 9am-8pm) Good selection of English language novels from Herman Hesse to John Grisham. To left of stairs on 2nd floor.

INTERNET ACCESS 网吧

Green Power Internet Café (Lǜsè Dònglì Wǎngbā; 64 Tianjin Lu; per hr Y2; 24hr)

Guanshengyuan Internet Café (Guānshēngyuán Wǎngbā; 117 Jianghan Lu; per hr Y2; 24hr) On second floor of fleapit hotel of same name.

Net Coffee Internet Café (cnr Tianjin Lu & Dongting Jie; per hr Y2; 24hr)

MEDICAL SERVICES

Pu'an Pharmacy (Pǔ'ān Dàyàofáng; cnr Jianghan Lu & Jianghan Silu; 24hr) Late night service through a hatch.

MONEY

Bank of China (Zhōngguó Yínháng; cnr Zhongshan Dadao & Jianghan Lu) Foreign exchange and credit card advances.

China Construction Bank (Jianghan Erlu, Hànkǒu) Has an ATM.

HSBC (1st fl, New World Department Store, Jianshe Dadao) 24-hour ATM.

POST

Post office (Yóujú; 134 Jianghan Lu) There is another branch outside the Hankou train station.

PUBLIC SECURITY BUREAU

PSB (Gōngānjú; 8271 2355; 306 Shengli Jie; 9-11.30am & 2-5pm) A 20-minute walk northeast of Jianghan Hotel. Visas generally take three days.

TRAVEL AGENCIES

In most cases it is best to ask at your hotel for tourist information.

China International Travel Service (CITS; Zhōngguó Guójì Lǚxíngshè; 5151 5955; cnr Zhongshan Dadao & Yiyuan Lu) Marginally helpful.

Sights

YELLOW CRANE TOWER 黄鹤楼

Once a military observation post, this landmark five-storey **tower** (Huánghè Lóu; 8887 5179; Wuluo Lu; admission Y50; 7.30am-5.30pm, open till later in summer) first rose up during the Warring States period, although this is a Qing dynasty rebuild. The birds immortalised in Li Bai's snappy Tang-dynasty stanzas have long flown and the only cranes visible from here are the steel variety, wheeling slowly over construction sites citywide. **Ming Qing Street**, a brash tourist bazaar just inside the entrance, siphons cash from the swelling crowds dismounting from tour buses. The double-decker bus 64 loops the city and stops near the tower; alternatively, take bus 1, 4 or 10.

HUBEI PROVINCIAL MUSEUM 湖北省博物馆
The highlight of this **museum** (Húbĕi Shĕng Bówùguǎn; ☎ 8679 4127; 1856 Donghu Lu; admission Y30; ☯ 8.30-11.30am & 1.30-4.30pm summer, 11am-4pm rest of year) is its large collection of artefacts from the Zenghouyi Tomb, dating from 433 BC and unearthed in 1978 on the outskirts of the city of Suízhōu. It's well worth a slow exploration.

Of particular interest is the two-tone, seven-note scale produced by 64 bronze bells that are played using hammers and poles. Throughout the day musical performances on duplicate bells are introduced in English.

The museum is located beside the massive Dōng Hú Fēngjǐng Qū (East Lake Scenic Area) in Wǔchāng, well worth exploring for

over a dozen scenic sights, including the hill of Mó Shān, overlooking the lake.

GUIYUAN TEMPLE 归元寺
A huge and rewarding Buddhist monastery complex, this **temple** (20 Cuiweiheng Lu; Y10; ☯ 8am-4.30pm) extends from its front pond – decorated with two huge lotus flowers and swarming with turtles – through numerous halls and courtyards busy with worshippers. Among its relics is a Tang-dynasty tablet carved with an image of Guanyin holding a willow branch; it is housed in the Mahasattva Pavilion (Dàshì Gé). There's also a jade statue of Sakyamuni, Southeast Asian in style and sitting resplendently in the Sutra Collection Pavilion (Cángjīng Gé), together with a large collection of luóhàn (arhat, or Buddhist saint) statues. A vegetarian restaurant can be found within the temple grounds.

Take tourist bus 401; public bus 6 also goes close.

NOTABLE BUILDINGS

Wǔhàn's history of foreign influence has bequeathed a noble crop of heritage architecture dating from the late 19th and early 20th centuries, especially in Hànkǒu. Hànkǒu's concession-era streetscapes hint at Shànghǎi's Bund district, despite the neglected condition of many buildings. Walk down Jianghan Lu (with its echoes of Shànghǎi's Nanjing Lu) and Yanjiang Dadao, where Hànkǒu's Bund is located. The imposing shell of the gutted, French-designed **former Hankou Railway Station**, at the north end of Chezhan Lu, dates from 1900 and remains decorated with green roofing, an eagle over its main door and a plaque that reads 'Hank'eou (Tatchemen)' (in modern pinyin parlance, Hankou Dazhimen). Other treats include the **Bank of China** at the corner of Jianghan Lu and Zhongshan Dadao and the **Russian Orthodox Church** (Dōngzhèng Jiàotáng; 11 Tianjin Lu, cnr Tianjin Lu & Poyang Jie), built in 1881. Newly restored, the church sits alongside a café – its crypt now serving as a nightclub!

Monumental old-world buildings – epitaphs to an increasingly distant age – push up against Yanjiang Dadao; look out for the former **Yokohama Syokin Bank** (dating from 1921) on the corner of Nanjing Lu and the **National City Bank of New York** (142 Yanjiang Dadao).

Near the Yellow Crane Tower in Wǔchāng is the colonial-style red brick **Former Headquarters of the Wuchang Uprising** (Xīnhàigémíng Wǔchāng Qǐyì Jiniànguǎn; also known as Hóng Lóu; admission Y20; ☯ 8.30am-5.30pm), source of the final collapse of the Qing dynasty. Get in the mood by donning a full Republican officer's uniform (Y10) and brandishing a sword for a photo op.

Also in Wǔchāng, **Wuhan University** (Wǔhàn Dàxué), beside Luòjiā Shān in Wǔchāng, was founded in 1913. The university was the site of the 1967 'Wuhan Incident' – a protracted battle during the Cultural Revolution, where machine gun nests were dug on top of the library and supply tunnels were dug through the hill. The old church at 357 Wuluo Lu has been requisitioned by a tae kwon do club.

The **Mao Zedong Villa** (Máo Zédōng Biéshù; Donghu Lu; admission Y10; ☯ 8am-6pm) was one of the Chairman's boltholes and is a tourist fixture for Mao-ophiles.

Though there are scores of reminders of its past, Wǔhàn, like China at large, has at all times one eye – and usually two – firmly fixed on the present. Currently the world's 18th-tallest building, the stunning 331m-high **Minsheng Bank Building** (Xinhua Lu) generated controversy with experts warning that the soft geology of Wǔhàn was unsuited to such a towering edifice.

CHANGCHUN TEMPLE 长春观

This charming Taoist **temple** (Chángchūn Guān; ☎ 8280 1399; admission Y5; ⏰ 7.30am-5pm) in Wǔchāng has roots poking down deep into the Han dynasty. A white-bearded statue of the sagacious Laotzu (also called Taishang Laojun) sits in the Hall of Supreme Purity (Tàiqīng Diàn), assisted in his administrations by an effigy of fellow scribe Zhuangzi. The Jade Emperor is worshipped by faithful in the rear hall, while other believers flock to the God of Wealth, seek guidance from Taoist soothsayers or dine at the ever popular vegetarian restaurant (p480) alongside.

Sleeping

BUDGET

Chufeng Hotel (Chǔfēng Bīnguǎn; ☎ 8586 2561; 23 Qianjin Silu; 前进四路23号; s/d/tr no shower Y48/78/98, s/d Y108/128; ✖) Acceptable rooms here are a bargain at this central Hànkǒu cheapie. There's neither English sign nor English spoken at reception, but sign language, production of passport and opening of wallet should convey the message.

Marine Hotel (Mǎnhǎi Bīnguǎn; ☎ 8804 3396; fax 8807 8717; 460 Zhongshan Lu; 中山路460号; s/d from Y128/138; ✖) Friendly and shipshape, the two-star Marine has welcoming rooms and handy positioning a short walk south across the road from Wǔchāng train station. Rooms are comfy, clean and come with satellite TV. *Fúwùyuán* (attendants) are stationed helpfully on each floor.

MIDRANGE

Yangzi Jiang Hotel (Yángzǐ Jiāng Fàndiàn; ☎ 6884 9388; 16 Cuiweiheng Lu; 翠微横路16号; d Y188; ✖) Bright and tidy rooms with fresh furnishings, plastic wood flooring, clean showers and overall newness, just north of the Guīyuán Temple in Hànyáng. Two meals included per day; further branches around town.

Home Inn (Rújiā; ☎ 8586 1555; 161 Qianjin Yilu; s/d/ste Y159/189/219; ✖) The McDonalds/Volkswagen Santana of the China hotel market, Home Inn is dependable albeit formulaic, aiming squarely at a middle-manager client base. It ensures fresh, bright, colourful (not very spacious) rooms, all with clean shower, plastic wood flooring, a value-for-money price tag, high turnover of guests and a reliable sense of security. Another branch in Wǔchāng.

Dahua Hotel (Dàhuá Fàndiàn; ☎ 8566 3454; fax 8566 5076; 708 Zhongshan Dadao; 中山大道708号; d with shared shower room Y150; s/d 330/380; ✖) A chunk of heritage architecture, the central Dahua has style and substance, with a variety of rooms to suit most budgets. Rooms are quite old, but vary in size with some extending to balconies.

Xuangong Hotel (Xuángōng Fàndiàn; ☎ 6882 2588; www.xuangonghotel.com; 57 Jianghan Yilu; 江汉一路57号; 'B' d Y480, 'A' d Y580, tr Y680; ✖) This heritage building dates from 1931, with an old-world dark style interior and an ace location off the pedestrian shopping street of Jianghan Lu. Rooms come with balcony, drinking water on tap and free internet, but aim for the south-facing and brighter front room (qiánfáng; 前房). Cheaper 'B' rooms are slightly shabbier but fixtures are modern looking and bargaining can secure good discounts all around.

Swiss-belhotel on the Park (Ruìyǎ Guójì Jiǔdiàn; ☎ 6885 1888; www.swiss-belhotel.com; 9 Taibei Yilu; 台北一路9号; s/d from Y595/745, studio/apt Y915/1495-1990; ✖ ✖ 🖥) International four-star boutique hotel offering excellent service, good-value business apartments, family suites and rooms, all with high-speed internet access. Rates include buffet breakfast. Good discounts offered.

TOP END

Jianghan Hotel (Jiāng Hàn Fàndiàn; ☎ 8281 1600; www.jhhotel.com; 245 Shengli Jie; 胜利街245号; d Y782; ✖ ✖) The erstwhile French embassy building, this rather scuffed up four-star hotel has failed to fully capitalise on its history and reputation, with cheap-looking restored wood panelling and flooring, and tacky oils on the walls.

Novotel (Xīnhuá Nuòfùtè Dàfàndiàn; ☎ 8555 1188; 558 Jianshe Dadao; 建设大道558号; s/d/ste Y1168/1248/1743; ✖ 🖥) Near the New World Department Store in Hànkǒu, this five-star hotel offers excellent styling and top-end business comfort, with an excellent range of facilities including tennis courts and a brasserie.

Shangri-La Hotel (Xiānggélǐlā Dàjiǔdiàn; ☎ 8580 6868; www.shangri-la.com; 700 Jianshe Dadao; 建设大道700号; d/ste Y1242/2516; ✖ ✖ 🖥 ✖) The well-equipped Shangri-La maintains its trademark levels of service and facilities, with comfortable rooms aimed at business travellers, although the ground floor Coffee Garden is getting weary, suggesting refit time.

Eating & Drinking

Popular local snacks worth trying include fresh catfish from Dōng Hú in the east of

HÚBĚI

the city, and charcoal-grilled whole pigeons served with a sprinkling of chilli. You can try some of these dishes on the **floating restaurants** at the end of Bayi Lu on the shore of Dōng Hú. To douse the insufferable summer scorch, reach for cups of bubble tea (*nǎichá*; 奶茶; Y2) from roadside vendors and ask for it icy (*bīngde*; 冰的).

Mínyáng Shāobǐng (3 Wulou Lu; Y2) Also known as Chinese-style pizza, this simple hole-in-the-wall outlet serves up delicious, fragrant Tujia (土家) bread pizza (*shāobǐng*; 烧饼; Y2) sprinkled with crumbs of meat and sesame seeds and aromatically seasoned with fried onion and cumin. Filling, cheap and very tasty, with other branches around town.

Night markets (*yèshìchǎng*) spring up east and west of the Jianghan Lu pedestrian zone in Hànkǒu, along Minsheng Lu and on Jiqing Jie (吉庆街), and along Dazhi Lu as it meets Zhongshan Dadao. A boisterous swell of bright, busy *dàpáidàng* (大排档), Jiqing Jie is pungent with the aromas of barbecued live oysters (*shāokǎo shēngháo*; 烧烤生蚝; 15 for Y6), spicy crab hot pot (*xiānglàxiè huǒguō*; 香辣蟹火锅; around Y50), river snails (*fúshòuluó*; 福寿螺; portion Y25), prawn hotpot (*dàxiā huǒguō*; Y38 to Y48) and – at the less appealing end of the spectrum – cow hooves, duck feet, duck hearts and other miscellanea.

Shouyi Garden Snack Street (Shōuyìyuán Xiǎochījiē; Wǔchāng; meals Y20) Innumerable, highly popular food outlets with cuisine from Húnán to Yúnnán and beyond. Purchase cards with credits (minimum Y20, deposit Y5) from the booth and plunge in. It's south off Pengliuyang Lu.

Máojiāwān (☎ 8832 6525; 29 Shouyi Yuan; meal Y30) Elderly Chinese will be horrified, but Wǔhàn's white-collar diners and *lǎowài* (foreigners) have few qualms about being served by corpulent Red Guards scampering to and fro with peppery platters from Mao's home province of Húnán. The overall concept may be in bad taste, but the *Máoshì Hóngshāoròu* (毛氏红烧肉) – a tender pile of plump pork chunks – is succulent, the rice arrives by the steaming bucket load and it's undeniably fun. No English sign.

Changchun Temple Vegetarian Restaurant (145 Wuluo Lu; ☎ 8885 4229; ☺ lunch & dinner; meal Y40) Steer your tummy onto the Taoist way at this celebrated veggie restaurant with Yin-Yang tablecloths and mock-meat dishes (photo menu) and flush down the *chángchūn yú* (长春鱼; Changchun fish; Y38) or *tiěbǎn niúròu* (铁板牛肉; sizzling beef platter; Y18) with a shot of Double Dragon wine (双龙酒宝; Y5 per *liǎng*) from the cabinet of obscure medicinal liquors. Adjacent to the Changchun Temple.

Bordeaux Bar (Bōěrtú; ☎ 8277 8779; 147 Yanjiang Dadao; ☺ 9.30am-2am; bottle of Qingdao Y20) For a smart and relaxing evening sojourn, this soothing spot on Hànkǒu's Bund treats guests to outside seating, a strong-ish wine list and occasional live music ('jazz and punk,' the bartender declares).

Entertainment

Red Passion Club (Jianshe Dadao) This is the most central of many white-hot dance clubs in this zone; just follow the crowds to the others nearby.

Getting There & Away

The best way to get to eastern destinations such as Nánjīng and Shànghǎi is by air, rather than the circuitous rail route.

AIR

Tianhe International Airport (☺ 8581 8888) is 30km northwest of town. The ticket office of the **CAAC** (Civil Aviation Administration of China; Zhōngguó Mínháng; 1089 Jiefang Dadao) is in Hànkǒu, or simply book from the CAAC office in the Swiss-belhotel on the Park (see p479) or **China Southern Airlines** (Zhōngguó Nánfáng Hángkōng Gōngsī; ☎ 8361 1756; 1 Hankong Lu). Major daily flights include Běijīng (Y1080), Guǎngzhōu (Y930), Shànghǎi (Y700) and Xī'ān (Y690). Daily international flights go to Hong Kong (Y1850), and less regular ones to Bangkok, Fukuoka and Macau.

BOAT

There are daily boats to Chóngqìng from the Wuhan Ferry Terminal; boats to other destinations have largely given way to mushrooming air and bus transportation.

BUS

Wǔhàn has several long-distance bus stations. The main **long-distance bus station** (chángtú qìchēzhàn; ☎ 8572 5507; Jiefang Dadao) is in Hànkǒu, between Xinhua Lu and Jianghan Beilu, with regular daily departures to Nánchāng (Y106, seven hours), Yíchāng (Y116, three to four hours), Jiǔjiāng (Y71) and Xiāngfán (Y80 to Y90) and other destinations.

Destinations from **Wuhan Port long-distance bus station** (Wǔhàn Gǎng chángtú qìchēzhàn) include Yíchāng (Y90, three to four hours, regular), Jiǔjiāng (Y55, three daily), Nánjīng (Y192, nine hours, three daily) and Shànghǎi (Y268, 12 hours, four daily).

In Wǔchāng, the **Fujiapo long-distance bus station** (Fùjiāpō qìchē kèyùnzhàn; ☎ 8727 4817) has buses to Yíchāng (Y70 to Y125, three to four hours, every half hour from 6.40am to 8pm), Xiāngfán (Y90, 4½ hours, regular), Wànzhōu (Y180, 18 hours, once daily), Nánjīng (Y192, 9½ hours, once daily), Shànghǎi (Y305, 12 hours, once daily) and Zhāngjiājiè (Y145, 11 hours, once daily). The **Hongji long-distance bus station** (☎ 8807 4048), 200m north of Wuchang train station, has buses going pretty much everywhere, including Shíyàn (Y140, seven hours, regular), Xiāngfán (Y93, regular), Yíchāng (Y71, four hours, regular), Zhāngjiājiè (Y146, 13 hours, once daily), Nánjīng (Y193, nine hours, regular) and Shànghǎi (Y306, 12 hours, once daily).

TRAIN

Wǔhàn is on the main line between Běijīng and Guǎngzhōu; express trains to Kūnmíng, Xī'ān, Hong Kong (Kowloon; 九龙) and Lánzhōu run via the city. Trains to major destinations depart from either the Hànkǒu or Wǔchāng train stations. Trains to Shànghǎi leave from the Wǔchāng station. At Hànkǒu station, hard and soft sleepers must be booked in the small ticket office between the waiting hall and the main ticket office.

There is also a train ticket office in Hànkǒu adjacent to the long-distance bus station.

Tickets for trains originating from Wǔchāng must be purchased at the Wǔchāng station rather than the Hànkǒu station. You can also book tickets at the Wǔchāng bus stations.

Hard sleeper ticket prices include Běijīng (Y248, 12 to 13 hours), Guǎngzhōu (Y257, 15 to 17 hours), Guìlín (Y220, 11 to 12 hours), Shànghǎi (Y262, 17 hours) and Xī'ān (Y215, 15 to 16 hours).

Getting Around

As with all large Chinese cities, Wǔhàn is undergoing a transport crisis as the streets become flooded with cars. The underused light rail is only a partial solution, and even motorbikes take to overhead walkways to get from A to B.

TO/FROM THE AIRPORT

Airport shuttle buses to Tianhe International Airport (Tiānhé Fēijīchǎng, Y15 to Y30, 40 minutes) leave regularly from several locations around town, including the Fujiapo long-distance bus station, Changjiang Guangchang (长江广场) in Hànyáng, and Fanhu (范湖) in Hànkǒu. A taxi to the airport should cost about Y80 and take 30 minutes.

BUS

Wǔhàn is staggeringly huge and although buses crisscross the city, it can be slow-going.

Tourist buses 401 and 402 (each Y5) run to the major attractions in the city, both running along the Hànkǒu riverfront and terminating in the Donghu Lake area.

Other useful buses include 603, passing Jiāng Hàn Fàndiàn to and from the Hànkǒu train station. Bus 9 runs from the train station down Xinhua Lu to the Wǔhàn ferry terminal. Bus 10 connects both train stations.

FERRY

Ferries (Y1.50, every 20 minutes, from 6.30am to 8pm) make swift daily crossings of the Yangzi River between Zhonghua Lu pier in Wǔchāng and the terminal in Hànkǒu.

LIGHT RAIL

Wǔhàn's clean, cheap and efficient light rail (Y1.50 to Y2, every 9 minutes from 6.30am to 9.30pm) whizzes along a modest length of track through 10 stations from Huangpu Lu to Zongguan in Hànkǒu, conveniently collapsing foot-numbing distances and affording a usefully elevated view of the district. The link is to be eventually extended to Hànyáng and Wǔchāng.

TAXI

Flag fall is Y3, then Y1.4 per km thereafter.

WǓDĀNG SHĀN 武当山

☎ 0719

A Unesco World Heritage Site, the gorgeous mountains of **Wǔdāng Shān** (entrance gate ☎ 566 7415; admission peak/off-peak Y110/80, insurance additional Y2; 🕑 6am-10pm) stretch for 400km across northwestern Húběi attracting bands of Taoist worshippers and devotees of Chinese *nèijiā gōngfū* (internal kungfu). There are martial arts schools up here that travellers can join. Wǔdāng Shān may not be one of the five most sacred Taoist mountains in China, but an unmistakable religious aura envelops its temples and crags.

Information

Bank of China (Taihe Dadao) Opposite Laoying Hotel, near the river.

China Post (40 Yongle Lu)

PSB (Gōngānjú; ☎ 566 5541; cnr Wudang Lu & Yuxu Lu)

Wudangshan Hospital (Wǔdāng Shān Yīyuàn; ☎ 566 9120; Taihe Dadao)

Wudangshan Tourist Centre (Nányán) Located at the start of the climb at Nányán; primarily aimed at Chinese tourists.

Xinhua Bookstore (Laoying Lu, off Buxing Jie)

Xinjisu Internet Cafe (Xīnjísù Wǎngbā; Taihe Dadao; per hr Y2; ☯ 24hr) Go through the round arch next to the small post office and climb to the second floor.

Sights & Activities

Although it's tempting to fling oneself onto the first bus up the mountain, Wǔdāng Shān town at the foot of the mountain is worth a wander. The tunnel at the tip of pedestrianised Buxing Jie (步行街) leads to the crumbling **Yuxu Temple** (Yùxū Gōng; 155 Gongyuan Lu; ☯ 8am-5.30pm), a colossal endeavour where two forlorn and roofless stele pavilions housing *bìxì* (mythical tortoise–like creatures) stand in front of an impressive temple hall and a vast courtyard. In the east of town just over the bridge is the **Fire God Temple** (Huǒshén Miào; Taihe Dadao), the roof of one of its small halls jutting out on a level with the pavement. Ming emperors Chengzu and Zhenwu duelled to construct the most temples, most of which survive on the slopes of the mountain.

CLIMBING WǓDĀNG SHĀN

Most travellers climbing Wǔdāng Shān hop aboard minivans (Y10, 45 minutes) from the main gate, around 1km east of town, for the 28km mountain journey to Nányán (南岩) and the start of the most popular trail. When the climb proper starts to turn your legs to jelly, draw strength from those around you: mothers carrying babies, children guiding grandparents, celestial-looking Taoist nuns with knapsacks and the faithful clutching five-foot long sticks of incense. Alternatively, grab a gnarled walking stick (Y5) or even recline into a sedan chair (Y100) and let someone else do the legwork. Otherwise clamber up and ponder some of the mountain's eternal mysteries (such as the signs that proclaim

'Efficaciousness in Wǔdāng Shān will be everywhere in the world').

A 20-minute walk below Nányán on Soaring Flag Peak (Zhǎnqí Fēng) is the splendidly azure-tiled **Purple Cloud Temple** (紫霄宫; Zǐxiāo Gōng; admission Y15; ☯ 7am-6pm), on the other side of an ancient bridge vaulting a belt of green water. Rather than taking the road, take the small stone-stepped path from the temple to return up the hill to Nányán. The **Nanyan Temple** (南岩宫; Nányán Gōng) is near the beginning of the trail.

From Nányán it's a leg-sapping two- to three-hour hike up to the highest summit, the 1612m **Tianzhu Peak** (天柱峰; Heavenly Pillar Peak; Tiānzhù Fēng) or via the brick-red **Three Heavenly Gates**. On the ascent – an ancient stone staircase with zero cushioning – you first encounter the **Langmei Xian Temple** (Langmeixian Gong) where taichi enthusiasts pay homage to founder Zhang San Feng (see boxed text, below). After struggling past the small **Chaotian Temple** (Cháotiān Gōng) and the **Huixian Bridge** (Huìxiān Qiáo), prepare your quadriceps for the shockingly long flight of steps leading to a vanishing point and the **Second Gate of Heaven** (Èrtiān Mén).

Close to the summit, a regal and divine-looking Zhenwu, Ming emperor and Taoist deity, sits within the **Taihe Hall** (Tàihé Gōng), flanked by fearsome attendants. Above is the fortress-like walled bastion called the Forbidden City (Zǐjìnchéng), from where you can stagger to astonishing views from the **Golden Hall** (金殿; Jīn Diàn; admission Y20; ☯ 8.30am-5pm) at

---

THE FOUNDER OF THE FIST OF THE SUPREME ULTIMATE

Zhang San Feng, a Wǔdāng Shān monk in the 13th or 14th century, is reputed to be the founder of the martial art *tàijíquán*, or taichi (p63). A master of Shaolin boxing, Zhang grew dissatisfied with the 'hard' techniques of the Shaolin style and searched for something 'softer'. Sitting on his porch one day, he became inspired by a battle between a huge bird and a snake. The sinuous snake used flowing movements to evade the bird's attacks. The bird, exhausted, eventually gave up and flew away. Taichi is closely linked to Taoism, and virtually all of the Taoist priests on Wǔdāng Shān practise some form of the art.

the pinnacle of Wǔdāng Shān. Constructed entirely of bronze in 1416 and famed for 'the seahorses uttering fog' (according to the blurb), the small two-tiered hall enshrines a bronze statue of Zhenwu, here elevated to the rank of Taoist deity.

Minibuses to Nányán leave from around 6.30am and depart when full, but if you pitch up in late afternoon, you may have to hire an entire minivan (Y40 to Y50), so consider spending the night in Wǔdāng Shān town. In the reverse direction, minivans depart Nányán for the main gate and Wǔdāng Shān town when full (Y10). An alternative is to take a minivan (Y15) to the **cable car** (索道; suǒdào; one way peak/off-peak Y50/45, return peak/off-peak Y80/70; 8.30am-5.30pm Mon-Fri, 8.30am-4pm Sat & Sun) at Qióngtái (琼台) from where it's a 30-minute ride to the summit on a two-person cable car.

The weather on Wǔdāng Shān is notoriously fickle so pack warm layers (snow can fall as late as April) and take something waterproof and an umbrella to keep the mists at bay.

Sleeping

Hotels in town and on the mountain typically offer good discounts of around 50% except during the frantic holiday season (first weeks of May and October).

Taihe Hotel (Tàihé Jiǔlóu; 134 7731 5236; Nányán; d Y40) One of a row of small family hotels down the road in Nányán, simple basement rooms here are without air-con and toilets are shared. A nearby hotel with the same English name but different Chinese name, Tàihé Bīnguǎn, has pricier rooms.

Jinlongdian Hotel (Jīnlóngdiàn Bīnguǎn; 566 8919; cnr Yongle Lu & Taihe Dadao; 近永乐路太和大道; tr without shower Y80, d/tr 160/180) Opposite the Wudangshan Hospital, rooms here (air-con, TV, squat toilet and shower) are OK, and 50% discounts are regularly in force.

Baihui Hotel (Bǎihuì Shānzhuāng; 568 9191; Nányán; d Y280, q no toilet Y160) With some rooms facing the mountain, discounts at this friendly two-star place typically hover at around 50%. It has a Chinese restaurant.

Laoying Hotel (Lǎoyíng Fàndiàn; 566 5347; Taihe Dadao; 太和大道; s/d/tr Y268/268/298) In an unattractive five-storey block set back from the road just west of the bridge over the river, doubles here are functional, with clean carpets, showers and ironing board. The staff are friendly.

Xuanwu Hotel (Xuánwǔ Bīnguǎn; 568 9175; Nányán; d/tr Y428/488) Perhaps because they were renovating, service was rather slack when we visited, but good discounts are generally available.

Many hotels can be found at Nányán on the mountain, including a batch of small family-owned hotels where rooms can be found for as little as Y40. Hotels can also be found in the area of the Qióng Tái cable car station.

Eating

Come evening in Wǔdāng Shān town, lamb kebab vendors set up along Taihe Dadao. On Wenbo Lu (文博路), just off Taihe Dadao, is a small night market where kebab, fish and vegetable chefs cook up dishes on the spot. Although restaurants can be found at Nányán, pack snacks and water for the climb.

Getting There & Away

Wǔdāng Shān town is on the railway line from Wǔhàn to Chóngqìng. Most trains that stop here are slow trains, so you may have to take a minibus to/from either Shíyàn (Y5, one hour) or Liùlǐpíng (one hour). Connections include Běijīng West (Y262, hard sleeper, 20 hours), Chóngqìng (hard seat Y91), Wǔhàn (Wǔchāng, hard seat/sleeper Y64/122, seven hours) and Xiāngfán (Y35, two hours).

The small Wǔdāng Shān bus station is on Taihe Dadao, with regular departures to Shíyàn (Y5 to Y10, one hour) and Xiāngfán (Y30, two to three hours). Slow buses connect with Wǔhàn (Y120, 12 hours) and farther-flung destinations.

SHÉNNÓNGJIÀ 神农架

0719

The Shénnóngjià district in remote northwestern Húběi has the wildest scenery in the province, where old-growth stands of fir and pine flourish among more than 1300 species of medicinal plants. Indeed, the name commemorates a legendary emperor, Shennong, believed to be the founder of herbal medicine and agriculture.

A more modern legend talks of local wild, ape-like creatures – a Chinese equivalent of the yeti or bigfoot. Curiously, the creatures seem to be able to distinguish between peasants and scientists – molesting the former and evading the latter. More real, but just as elusive, are leopards, bears, wild boars and monkeys (including the endangered golden snub-nosed monkey).

Foreign travellers are allowed into the Shénnóngjià district near **Mùyúpíng** (木鱼平), situated 200km northwest of Yíchāng. Two grand peaks, Shénnóngjià Shān (3105m) and Lǎojūn Shān (2936m), dominate. It's an eight-hour bus ride to Mùyúpíng from Yíchāng (Y80), or you can take a boat to Xiāngxī on the Three Gorges (below; five hours) and from there it's a 90km ride to Mùyúpíng. From Mùyúpíng you will have to hire a car to get into the reserve.

CITS (see below) in Yíchāng arranges tours. Other local travel agencies are unaccustomed to travel restrictions for foreigners, leading to adventures with the police.

It may be possible to visit **Sōngbǎi** (松柏), an area in the reserve traditionally off limits to foreigners. Yíchāng CITS reports foreigners were allowed to visit the area when accompanied by tour guides. Check with the PSB in Yíchāng before heading out independently.

YÍCHĀNG 宜昌

☎ 0717 / pop 3.99 million

Slung out east of the Three Gorges Dam, Yíchāng is the gateway to the upper Yangzi and an embarkation point for upstream cruises through the gorges. Opened to foreign trade in 1877 by a treaty between Britain and China, little remains of its foreign concession heritage.

Orientation

Yíchāng spreads along a bend of the Yangzi River. Ferry terminals are located in the west of town and to the east of Yíchāng. Most of city proper is located between Dongshan Dadao to the north and Yanjiang Dadao running alongside the Yangzi River.

Information

Bank of China (Zhōngguó Yínháng; Shengli Silu) Near Longkang Lu.

China International Travel Centre (CITS; Zhōngguó Guójì Lǚxíngshè; Yunji Lu ☎ 625 3088; www.yccits.com; Yunji Lu); Longkang Lu ☎ 622 4388; 18 Longkang Lu) Three Gorges tours.

Post Office (yóujú; cnr Yunji Lu & Yiling Dadao)

PSB Exit/Entry Administration Section (Gōngānjú; 14 Xueyuan Jie; ⏰ 8-11.30am & 2.30-5pm Mon-Fri)

Yinxing Internet Café (Yínxīng Wǎngbā; Erma Lu; per hr Y2; ⏰ 24hr) On Erma Lu, north of the turning with Fusui Lu.

Sights

THREE GORGES DAM 三峡大坝

This vast **dam** (Sānxiá Shuǐlì Shūniǔ Gōngchéng; admission Y90) is a colossal and controversial feat of

engineering (see boxed text, p814). Tours visit the actual site (CITS offers tours for Y120); alternatively take bus 4 (Y1) from Sānmǎtou (三码头) by the Yichang Ferry Terminal to Yèmíngzhū (夜明珠) and change to bus 8 (Y18 return) to the dam from where minibuses (Y20 return) and motorcycle taxis (Y10 return) take you to the top.

Sleeping

Railway Station Hotel (Tiělù Dàjiǔdiàn; ☎ 861 6916; d, tr & q shared toilet & fan Y40, d/tr Y168/210; 🏠) Next to the train station, this is one of few offering cheap, clean beds. Discounts are common, but cheap rooms are often booked out and it's a bit grim.

Yichang Hotel (Yíchāng Fàndiàn; Dongshan Dadao; 东山大道; s/d Y268/288; 🏠) Smart and well-refitted hotel with style and comfort, an elegant foyer and lovely rooms laid out with dark wood furniture and sparkling bathrooms. Discounts are common.

Táohuālíng Fàndiàn (☎ 623 6666; fax 623 8888; 29 Yunji Lu; 云集路29号; d Y548; 🏠 🖥) Pleasant enough four-star hotel with attractive garden, free internet, and rooms on 4th, 5th and 7th floors with their own computers.

Eating & Drinking

Yíchāng's lively bar and club scene is concentrated along Erma Lu and the surrounding alleys located just east of the southern end of Yunji Lu.

Fújì Càiguǎn (☎ 622 2586; 48 Fusui Lu) offers Hunan food in a clean and comfortable setting.

Getting There & Away

AIR

The Three Gorges Airport is 25km southeast of town, with daily flights to Běijīng (Y1300), Shànghǎi (Y1080), Xī'ān (Y840) and other cities. Ticket offices are dotted around near the train station and ferry terminals.

BOAT

Most river stop ferries stop at the **Yichang Ferry Terminal** (Yíchāng Gǎng Kèyùnzhàn; ☎ 622 4354), where tickets are sold. Upstream services include Wànzhōu and Chóngqìng (Y110 to Y770); downstream services are more unreliable and erratic but include Wǔhàn (Hànkǒu; Y46 to Y491, 23 hours), Jiǔjiāng (Y71 to Y703, 31 hours), Nánjīng (from Y104, 50 hours) and Shànghǎi (Y148 to Y1248, 65 hours).

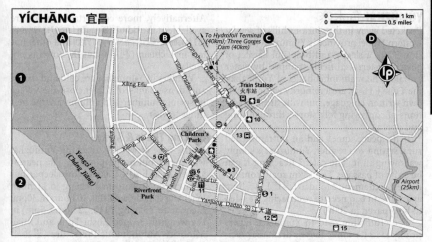

YÍCHĀNG 宜昌

INFORMATION
Bank of China 中国银行 **1** C2
CITS 中国国际旅行社 **2** B2
CITS 中国国际旅行社 **3** C2
Post Office 邮局 **4** C1
PSB / Exit/Entry Administration Section
公安局/出入境管理处 **5** B2
Yinxing Internet Café 银兴网吧 **6** B2

SIGHTS & ACTIVITIES
Yiling Park 夷陵广场 **7** C1

SLEEPING
Railway Station Hotel 铁路大酒店 **8** C1
Táohuālíng Fàndiàn 桃花岭饭店 **9** B2
Yichang Hotel 宜昌饭店 **10** C1

EATING
Fújì Càiguǎn 福记菜馆 **11** B2

TRANSPORT
Dagongqiao Bus & Ferry Terminal
大公桥客运站 **12** C2
Long-Distance Bus Station 长途汽车站 **13** C2
Qingjiang Dasha 清江大厦 **14** B1
Yichang Ferry Terminal 宜昌港 **15** D2

River ferries also stop at the Dàgōngqiáo bus and ferry terminal west of the main ferry terminal.

A speedy hydrofoil service reaches Wànzhōu (six hours) and Chóngqìng (11 hours) from the hydrofoil terminal that is west of town (take bus 3, one hour); boats to Wànzhōu are more frequent as the expressway now links Wànzhōu with Chóngqìng. Tickets can be bought at either of the ferry terminals.

For full details on Yangzi River cruises, see p811.

BUS

Yíchāng's main **long-distance bus station** (chángtú qìchēzhàn; ☎ 644 5314; Dongshan Dadao) is located southeast of the train station. Services run to Wǔhàn (Hànkǒu and Wǔchāng; Y80 to Y115, regular), Lìchuān (Y100, once daily), Xiāngfán (Y60, regular), Nánchāng (Y185, once daily), Chángshā (Y117, once daily) and Shànghǎi (Y350, once daily). Long-distance services also depart from the main ferry terminal; buses include Wǔhàn (Y60, hourly), Zhèngzhōu Y119, once daily) Shànghǎi (Y350, once daily) and the Dàgōngqiáo ferry terminal.

TRAIN

Yíchāng's train station sits atop a punishing flight of steps at the intersection of Dongshan Dadao and Yunji Lu.

Services run to Chángshā (Y194), Hànkǒu (Y94), Xiāngfán (hard seat Y31), Zhāngjiājiè

(Y56), Luòyáng (Y90), Zhèngzhōu (Y145), Xī'ān (Y150), Běijīng West (Y298), Shànghǎi (Y330) and elsewhere.

Getting Around

Six airport shuttle buses (Y20, 30 minutes) depart daily from the Qingjiang Building (清江大厦; Qīngjiāng Dàshà; cnr Dongshan Dadao & Xiling Erlu) between 5.40am and 8.30pm. Taxis to/from the airport cost Y80 to Y100.

YÚMÙZHÀI 鱼木寨

Pocketed away in the glorious hills of south-western Húběi province is Yúmùzhài (admission Y20), a sleepy and beautiful hamlet of glistening terraced fields tramped by water buffalo. The main inhabitants of Yúmùzhài, the Tujia (土家), are a minority without their own written language, but with strong traditions of conveying folk stories through song and opera.

If it's peace, quiet and an untrammelled rural setting you're after, Yúmùzhài is simply wallowing in it. The catch? Reaching it can be a rite of passage. The 18km road from the nearest settlement, Móudào (谋道), is falling apart and in bad need of resurfacing (it's due to be repaved in 2007).

The crumbling road to Yúmùzhài tapers fitfully to its terminus above a dramatic precipice, where totters a magnificent stone **gate-house** – the sole portal to the village. Upon arrival at the gatehouse, simply inscribed with the characters for Yúmùzhài and looked after by a local family, a stone path threads down through the fields, past traditional Tujia buildings and stunning views. It takes several hours to fully explore this region; to wander around the numerous paths and trails, past gorgeous fields, precipitous drops, Tujia stone tablets, old tombs and carvings.

You can stay overnight here, as accommodation is simple but affordable. Beds at peasant homesteads (nóngjiā; 农家) in Yúmùzhài go for around Y20, although you could be directed to a simple bed cushioned with a mattress of straw. Meals are available from households that offer accommodation in the village. If you plan to stay overnight, also factor in the cost of having a driver come to pick you up and return you to Lìchuān or Móudào.

Alternatively, more comfortable rooms are available at the **Lìchuān Bīnguǎn** (☎ 0718 728 2047; 385 Jiefang Lu; 解放路385号; d Y180) and other hotels in Lìchuān (利川), but the town is not pretty.

Winters in Yúmùzhài are cold and damp, and dense banks of fog enclose the village in spring; summer and autumn are the best times to visit.

Getting There & Away

At the time of writing, reaching Yúmùzhài was tricky, but not impossible. The nearest airport is at Ēnshī. Take a slow sleeper bus through the hills from Yíchāng to Lìchuān (Yíchāng to Lìchuān Y100, 10 hours, 6.30pm; Lìchuān to Yíchāng Y110, 12 hours, 5pm) in the weightily named Enshi Tujia and Miao Minority Autonomous Prefecture (恩施土家族苗族自治州; Ēnshī Tǔjiāzú Miáozú Zìzhìzhōu). Buses to Lìchuān also run from Wànzhōu (Y20, two hours) and Fèngjié (Y35, three hours) in Chóngqìng, a direction which allows for a journey through the Three Gorges by hydrofoil from Yíchāng to either Fèngjié or Wànzhōu, for the bus connection to Lìchuān. From Lìchuān you will have to negotiate a taxi or four-wheel drive (around Y150 to Y200 return) to take you to Yúmùzhài, around 60km away from Lìchuān.

Avoid travel to Yúmùzhài during wet weather (eg during spring) as drivers will be loathe to traverse the road if it is muddy and you could be left high and dry. Public buses from Lìchuān only go as far as Móudào (谋道; Y15), but Yúmùzhài is a further 18km away; you could be stuck if unable to find a car from Móudào, so it could be preferable to arrange a car from Lìchuān.

Jiāngxī 江西

Its reputation carved in granite by the fame of Jǐngdézhèn's imperial kilns, and its status immortalised as the starting point of the mythologised Long March, Jiāngxī province is a place where rows of glistening porcelain creations share the spotlight with revolutionary relics.

Which is perhaps to overlook Jiāngxī's stunning swathes of natural beauty. Suspended from the middle and lower reaches of the Yangzi River, Jiāngxī lies in one of China's most crucial watersheds. Home of China's largest freshwater lake – Poyang Lake (Póyáng Hú) – Jiāngxī is the source of much of southeast China and Hong Kong's drinking water. More than 2400 rivers and ecologically crucial lakes spiderweb throughout the province, 60% of which is cloaked in forest. Add to this an undulating landscape of mountains and hills, and Jiāngxī promises some of rural China's most staggeringly beautiful images.

Lúshān and Jǐnggāngshān are celebrated for their scenic mountain views, although prepare to jostle for them with fellow vacationers. It is instead the jaw-dropping scenery around Wùyuán in northeast Jiāngxī, a geographic and cultural extension of gorgeous southern Ānhuī, that truly rewards days and weeks of boggle-eyed exploration. The ancient villages of this region – many cut by sparkling streams and vaulted by charming stone and wood bridges – are some of China's most delightful and picturesque.

Even Nánchāng, the fast-paced provincial capital, has traditional, historic villages within its orbit – including Luótiáncūn – where you can get the ozone out of your hair and pitch yourself into the pastoral panoramas of old China without too much fuss.

HIGHLIGHTS

- Leave modern China behind and explore the picturesque Huīzhōu villages around **Wùyuán** (p494)

- Envelop yourself in the ethereal mists and European charms of **Lúshān** (p497)

- Lose yourself among the traditional alleyways and lanes of **Luótiáncūn, Shuǐnán & Jīngtái** (p491) outside Nánchāng

- Trek lovely **Jǐnggāng Shān** (p499), the 'Cradle of the Chinese Revolution', peppered with more than 100 Red Army historical sites

- Load up with ceramics at **Jǐngdézhèn** (p492), centre of China's porcelain trade

- POPULATION: 41.6 MILLION

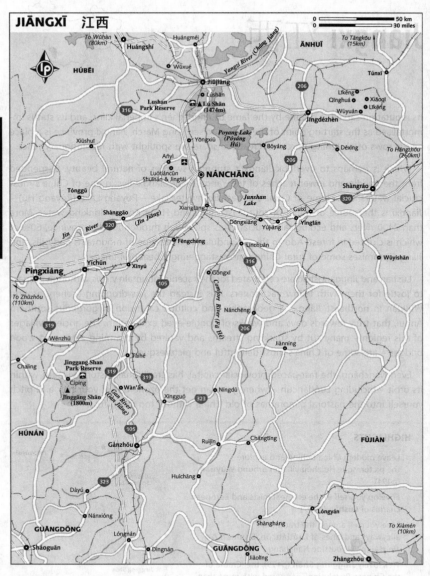

JIĀNGXĪ 江西

History

The Grand Canal (linking major waterways) was built from the 7th century onwards. It opened up the southeastern regions and made Jiāngxī an important point on the trade route from Guǎngdōng. Industries such as silver mining and tea growing later allowed the formation of a wealthy Jiāngxī merchant class.

By the 19th century, however, the province's role as a transport route from Guǎngzhōu was reduced by the opening of coastal ports to foreign ships. Among Jiāngxī's most illustrious native sons is author Mervyn Peake (architect of the gothic fantasy *Gormenghast*), born in Gǔlǐng (Lúshān) to British missionary parents in 1911.

Climate

North-central and central Jiāngxī lie in the Gan River (赣江; Gàn Jiāng) plain and experience a four-season, subtropical climate. Mountains encircle the plain and locals flock to these to escape the summer heat, which averages around 30°C in July. (Temperatures average 3°C to 9°C north to south in January.) Rainfall averages 120cm to 190cm annually and is usually heaviest in the northeast; half falls between April and June.

Language

Most Jiāngxī natives speak one of innumerable local variants of Gàn (赣), a dialect whose name is also used as a shorthand for the province. Cantonese speakers will notice a distinct resemblance to Guǎngdōnghuà (Cantonese), the dialect of Guǎngdōng province, especially in the south of Jiāngxī.

Getting There & Around

All major sites are lashed together via an increasing number of efficient expressways. Nánchāng and Jǐngdézhèn both have airports. Train connections are adequate for most large towns, from where bus connections radiate into the neighbouring provinces of Guǎngdōng, Húnán, Húběi, Ānhuī, Zhèjiāng and beyond.

NÁNCHĀNG 南昌

☎ 0791 / pop 1.9 million

A bustling, busy and booming town, Nánchāng is branded on Chinese consciousness as a revolutionary torchbearer and applauded in China's history books for its role in consolidating the power of the Communist Party. It may come as little surprise therefore that Western travellers, unless otherwise detained, should jump on the first connection out of town to the bucolic charms of Luótiáncūn, Shuǐnán and Jǐngtái outside town, stupendous Wùyuán or the European allure of Lúshān.

Orientation

The city of Nánchāng sprawls along the Gan River (Gàn Jiāng). Zhanqian Lu leads directly west from the train station to the enormous Fushan roundabout, from where Bayi Dadao, the city's most significant north–south artery, radiates northwest.

People's Sq sits at the town's nucleus, from where the pleasant shopping street of Zhongshan Lu heads west.

MAPS

Maps (Y4) are available from the Xinhua Bookshop (Xīnhuá Shūdiàn) on Bayi Dadao across from People's Sq, or from hawkers at the train station.

Information

Bank of China (Zhōngguó Yínháng; Zhanqian Xilu) Foreign exchange, ATM (open office hours only).

Jiangxi International Tour & Aviation Corporation (江西省国际旅游航空服务公司; Jiāngxīshěng Guójì Lǚyóu Hángkōng Fúwù Gōngsī; ☎ 621 5891; 169 Fuzhou Lu)

Nanchang No1 People's Hospital (Shì Dìyī Yīyuàn; 128 Xiangshan Lu)

Post office (yóujú; cnr Bayi Dadao & Ruzi Lu)

Public Security Bureau (PSB; Gōngānjú; Shengli Lu) About 100m north of Minde Lu.

Xintianyou Internet Café (Xīntiānyóu Wǎngbā; per hr Y2; ☀ 24hr) On an alley east off Erqi Nanlu south of Hong Kong Hotel.

Sights

The city's drawcard prerevolutionary monument is the nine-storey **Téngwáng Gé** (Tengwang Pavilion; 7 Yanjiang Beilu; admission Y50; ☀ 8am-4.50pm), first erected during Tang times. The huge **Youmin Temple** (177 Minde Lu; admission Y2; ☀ 8am-5.30pm) has endured considerable reconstruction, but contains some notable statuary.

Nánchāng's grey slabs of communist heritage include **People's Square** (Rénmín Guǎngchǎng), graced with the soulless **Monument to the Martyrs** (Bāyī Jìniàn Tǎ) and flanked to the west by the Stalinist **Exhibition**

BĀYĪ (1 AUGUST)

On 1 August (bāyī in Chinese, now a common street name) 1927, 30,000 troops led by Zhou Enlai and Zhu De seized Nánchāng and held it for several days. The revolt, staged in retribution for a spring massacre of communists by Chiang Kaishek's forces, was largely a fiasco, but the gathering of soldiers marked the beginning of the Chinese communist army. The army retreated south from Nánchāng to Guǎngdōng, but Zhu De led some soldiers and circled back to Jiāngxī to join forces with the ragtag army that Mao Zedong had organised in Húnán. From there, the soldiers sought refuge in Jǐnggāng Shān (Well-Shaped Ridge Mountains).

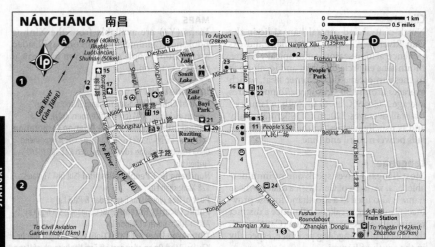

NÁNCHĀNG 南昌

Hall (Zhǎnlǎnguǎn). The **Memorial Hall to the Martyrs of the Revolution** (Gémìng Lièshì Jìniànguǎn; 399 Bayi Dadao; admission Y3; 8.30am-11.30am & 2-5pm) is north of the square, but most of Nánchāng's citizens seem to much prefer **Wal Mart** to the south.

The **Former Headquarters of the Nanchang Uprising** (Bāyī Nánchāng Qǐyì Jìniànguǎn; 380 Zhongshan Lu; admission Y25; 8.30am-5.30pm) is for rainy days (plentiful in spring) and enthusiasts of the Chinese Communist Party.

Sleeping

The train station area is stuffed with hotels, with prices tending toward the midrange.

Lóngmén Lǚguǎn (Longmen Hotel; 713 6035; 199 Rongmen Lu; 榕门路199号; d with/without air-con Y78/30;) There's no English sign at this cheapie near the corner of Rongmen Lu and

Zhangjiang Lu, and language skills are Chinese only. The cheapest rooms are without toilet or air-con, but squat loos are thrown into the pricier Y78 rooms, along with TV and air-con.

Jiāngxī Fàndiàn (Jiangxi Hotel; 885 8888; 356 Bayi Dadao; 八一大道356号; s & d Y120-200, tr Y180;) This reasonable three-star hotel has cosy rooms, a restaurant and a business centre.

Xingqiu Hotel (Xīngqiú Bīnguǎn; 612 6555; Erqi Beilu; 二七北路; d Y238;) In a blue glass tower opposite the train station, this brand-new hotel has fresh and comfortable doubles, cleanly furnished and equipped with spacious shower rooms (complete with exhibitionist glass walls). Discounts are frequently available. No English sign.

Gloria Plaza Hotel (Kǎilái Dàjiǔdiàn; 673 8855, toll free 810 8855; www.gphnanchang.com; 88 Yanjiang

Beilu; 沿江北路88号; d incl breakfast Y980-1050; 🍴 🏊) A quality hotel overlooking the river that has comfortable and tastefully furnished rooms. There's a full range of facilities, including a cheongsam shop, indoor pool, Atrium Café, mobile-phone charging point in the foyer, 24-hour ATM and the Hurricane Karaoke Lounge, if you plan on singing up a storm.

Eating & Drinking

Bāwèitáng (☎ 678 0966; 2nd fl, 65 Shengli Lu; noodle dishes Y4-10; ☎ 9am-10pm) On the corner of Minde Lu and pedestrianised Shengli Lu, this spacious and popular noodle bar has steaming tummy-filling bowls of carbohydrate-rich *miàn* (面; noodles) and *fàn* (饭; rice) dishes. Poke the photo menu, pay at the till, sit down and await your *bāwèitáng lǎoyāmiàn* (八味堂老鸦面; duck and noodles), *luóhàn shàngsùmiàn* (罗汉上素面; vegetables and noodles) or regulation *bāwèitáng dàpáimiàn* (八味堂大排面; pork and noodles). Don't forget to load up on the crispy *cōngyóu xiāngbǐng* (葱油香饼; onion pastries, Y4 for six).

Háoxiānglái (Hǎoxiānglái; ☎ 639 5678; 175 Minde Lu; meals Y25; ☀ 24hr) Handy round-the-clock grills, filling set meals, photo menu and service with a smile. It's by the entrance to Youmin Temple.

Babyface (Bèibǐ Fěishí; ☎ 621 9333; 3rd fl, Beijing Hualian Bldg, Zhongshan Lu; ☀ 7.30pm-3am) Dizzyingly loud, this funky installation from the nationwide chain simply hops with euphoric clubbers and the snappily dressed youth of Nánchāng.

CD Bar (☎ 626 7779; 65 Zhongshan Lu; ☀ 7.30pm-late) Across Zhongshan Lu from Babyface; walk in here past squads of security and straight into a throbbing wall of sound overlooking the lake.

Getting There & Away

AIR

Air tickets can be purchased from the ticket office next to the long-distance bus station, from travel agents in the train station area or at **China Eastern Airlines** (☎ 622 1023, 628 2654; 87 Minde Lu).

Chāngběi airport is 28km north of the city, with flights to Běijīng (Y1310, two hours), Guǎngzhōu (Y730, 1¼ hours), Hong Kong (Y1490, four times weekly, 1½ hours), Shànghǎi (Y790, one hour) and Xī'ān (Y1010, 1¾ hours).

BUS

Regular buses depart from opposite the train station concourse to Jiǔjiāng (Y30, hourly, two hours). Other daily departures from here include Guǎngzhōu (Y160), Nánjīng (Y180) and Shànghǎi (Y220, 6pm); buses to Xiàmén (Y230) leave every other day. From Nánchāng's **long-distance bus station** (kèyùn zhōngxīn; Bayi Dadao), regular buses run to Jiǔjiāng (Y36, two hours), Lúshān (Y40, 1½ hours), Ānyì (Y17, 1½ hours, regular) and Jǐngdézhèn (Y72, four hours), with less frequent buses to Wǔhàn (Y110) and Héféi (Y135). There are also buses to Jǐnggǎng Shān (Y65 to Y90, six to nine hours).

TRAIN

Nánchāng lies off the main Guǎngzhōu–Shànghǎi railway line, but many trains make the detour north via the city. Direct trains operate to Fúzhōu (Y100, 10 to 12 hours), Shànghǎi (Y182, 11½ hours) and Wǔhàn (Y65, 5 hours). Heading west to Chángshā in neighbouring Húnán almost always necessitates a stop in Zhūzhōu. Express trains run daily to Jiǔjiāng (Y22, 2½ hours) and Jǐngdézhèn (Y30, four hours), although the freeway makes it far quicker to do the trip by bus. Buy train tickets in advance at the **Advance Rail Ticket Office** (Tiělù Shòupiàochù; ☎ 160 3009; 393 Bayi Dadao; ☀ 8am-8pm) or at the ticket office next to the long-distance bus station.

Getting Around

Airport buses (Y15, every 30 minutes 6am to 8pm, 40 minutes) leave from the **Civil Aviation Garden Hotel** (民航花园酒店; Mínháng Huāyuán Jiǔdiàn; 587 Hongcheng Lu), south of the town centre. A taxi to the airport costs around Y100.

From the train station, bus 2 goes up Bayi Dadao past the long-distance bus station, and bus 5 heads north along Xiangshan Beilu. Taxis are Y6 at flag fall.

AROUND NÁNCHĀNG
Luótiáncūn, Shuǐnán & Jīngtái
罗田村，水南和京台

Northwest of town and faced on all sides by imposing ornamental gateways (*ménlóu*), the 1120-year-old village of **Luótiáncūn** (☎ 0791-342 1422; admission incl 5 sights Y21), its uneven stone-flagged alleys etched with centuries of wear, makes an ideal day out and rural escape from the urban greys of Nánchāng. A disorientating labyrinth of tight, higgledy-piggledy lanes, disused halls and ancient homesteads assembled from dark stone, Luótiáncūn backs onto a picturesque backdrop of fields and hills that maximise its pastoral charms.

Wander the tight maze of lanes, past hand-worked pumps, ancient wells, stone steps, scattering chickens, lazy cows and conical haystacks, poking your head occasionally through doorways to glimpse wooden interiors softly illuminated by overhead light wells (天井; *tiānjǐng*) and catch snatches of Chinese opera warbling from old radios. There are some lovely buildings here: pick your way along Qianjie (前街; Front Street) and pop over to **Dàshìfūdi** (大世夫第; admission incl in ticket) on Hengjie (横街; Cross Street), an old residence that has marvellous carved wooden panels and is hung with old lanterns called *mǎdēng* (马灯). On the fringes of the village is a fat old camphor tree dating from Tang days; also hunt down the **old well** (古井; *gǔjǐng*), which locals swear is 1000 years old.

From the waterwheel at the foot of Qianjie a flagstone path links Luótiáncūn with its sibling village, **Shuǐnán** (水南). It's only a 500m walk, through field of rapeseed plants. In Shuǐnán, follow the signs to the **Shuinan Folk Museum** (水南民俗馆; Shuǐnán Mínsúguǎn; admission incl in ticket), a further old residence consisting of bedchambers and threadbare exhibits; note how many wooden effigies carved on the interior panels have had their faces smashed off. Toward the edge of the village, the **Guìxiù Lóu** (闺秀楼; admission incl in ticket) is another notable building.

A further 500m down the stone path is the large and pleasant community of **Jǐngtái** (京台), a village with a 1400-year-old history, whose gap-toothed and largely non-*pǔtōnghuà* (Mandarin) speaking denizens are all either surnamed Liu (刘) or Li (李). Again, traipse at will and enjoy the village's hoary barns, stone gateways, musty homesteads, ancestral temple and ancient stage (古戏台; *gǔxìtái*), or wander out into the fields.

Simple peasant family – *nóngjiā* (农家; bed Y15) – accommodation is available in Luótiáncūn, but all three villages can be done as a day trip from Nánchāng.

GETTING THERE & AWAY
Take a bus to Ānyì (Y17, 1½ hours, regular buses from 8am to 4.30pm) from the Nánchāng long-distance bus station. Across from the Ānyì long-distance bus station, buses leave regularly (when full) for Shíbí (石鼻, Y3, 20 to 30 minutes), from where *sānlúnchē* (three-wheeled motorbikes) muster for trips to Luótiáncūn (Y5, 10 minutes). In the return direction, any *sānlúnchē* can return you to Shíbí for the return bus to Ānyì and back to Nánchāng.

JǏNGDÉZHÈN 景德镇
☎ 0798 / pop 312,350
Overlooked by tall brick chimneys and disfigured by swathes of squalor and incessant demolition, Jǐngdézhèn is where China's much-coveted porcelain is fired up, although the imperial kilns that manufactured ceramics for the occupants of the Forbidden City were long ago extinguished. With more china here than the rest of China put together, travellers can rapidly feel glazed: Jǐngdézhèn is hardly an oil painting and is strictly for Chinese porcelain buffs.

Orientation
Lying on the Chang River (Chāng Jiāng), Jǐngdézhèn's main arteries are Zhongshan Lu and Zhushan Lu. The stretch of Ma'anshan Lu towards Zhushan Lu is a flourishing pink light district of massage parlours and 'hairdressers'.

Information
Bank of China (Zhōngguó Yínháng; Ma'anshan Lu) Towards the train station. Travellers cheques are exchanged at the main branch at 448 Cidu Dadao.

China International Travel Service (CITS; Zhōngguó Guójì Lǚxíngshè; ☎ 851 5888; 1 Zhushan Xilu) Next to the Binjiang Hotel just west of the river; offers a one-day porcelain factory tour (Y160).

Jingcheng Internet Café (Jǐngchéng Wǎngbā; Tongzhan Lu; per hr Y2; ⏰ 24hr)

Post office (yóujú; 151 Zhushan Zhonglu) Has maps of town.

Xinhua Bookshop (Xīnhuá Shūdiàn; 3 Yanjiang Donglu)

Youqing Wangluocheng Internet Café (Ma'anshan Lu; per hr Y2; ⏰ 24hr)

Sights & Activities
The tiny older side streets between Zhongshan Lu and the river can be interesting to wander.

The pleasant and absorbing **Jingdezhen Pottery Culture Exhibition Area** (Jǐngdézhèn Táocí Wénhuà Bólǎnqū; ☎ 852 1594; admission Y50; ⏰ 8am-5pm) is situated over the river in the west, and features exhibition galleries, temples, kilns and workshops where craftsmen demonstrate traditional Qing and Ming porcelain-making techniques.

A limited collection of bowls, vases and sculptures are displayed at the modest **Museum of Porcelain** (Táocí Guǎn; ☎ 822 9784; 21 Lianshe Beilu; admission Y15; ⏱ 8-11am & 2.30-5pm), far outclassed by the Shanghai Museum's (p252) collection.

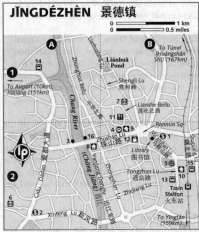

Sleeping & Eating

Jinsheng Hotel (Jīnshèng Bīnguǎn; ☎ 820 7818; 29 Zhushan Lu; 珠山路29号; s/d Y138/168; ✕) This is a reasonable, central hotel with affordable rooms but indifferent service.

Wenyuan Hotel (Wényuàn Dàjiǔdiàn; ☎ 820 8888; 34 Tongzhan Lu; 通站路34号; s/d Y198/218; ✕) A 150m walk north of the train station, this good two-star choice has well-refurbished rooms with good furnishings, new beds, water cooler, clean shower rooms and regular discounts.

Jingdezhen Hotel (Jǐngdézhèn Dàjiǔdiàn; ☎ 851 8888; www.jingdezhenhotel.com; 126-128 Zhushan Zhonglu; 珠山中路126-128号; s & d Y680; ✕ 🖥) Adding a pleasant minty green hue to the grey riverside skyline, the plush four-star Jingdezhen has a vast foyer, acres of marble, lovely computer-equipped rooms, free internet access and neat bathrooms with smallish baths. There's a good Chinese restaurant on the 2nd floor.

Little Sparrow (Xiǎomáquè; ☎ 822 2177; 5 Lianshe Beilu; meals Y20-30; ⏱ 9.30am-9pm) Look out for the seafood restaurant with the twisted brick pillars and white marble steps.

Shopping

Porcelain is ubiquitous in Jǐngdézhèn and you will practically be stumbling over piles on pavements and bumping into heaps on street stalls. The huge and centrally located **Jingdezhen Jinchangli Porcelain Market** (Jǐngdézhèn Jīnchānglǐ Táocí Dàshìchǎng; ☎ 822 8338; 2 Zhushan Lu) on the corner of Zhuhai Lu and Lianshe Nanlu is a good place to start, but smaller shops and markets can be found all over town.

Getting There & Away

AIR

Luójiā airport is 10km northwest of the city. Flights include Shànghǎi (Y500), Shēnzhèn (Y850) and Běijīng (Y1250).

BUS

Buses from the east bus station opposite the train station run to Jiǔjiāng (Y35, 1½ hours, regular), Nánchāng (Y45, 3½ hours, three per day), Shànghǎi (Y182, nine hours, once daily), Nánjīng (Y95, seven hours, once daily) and Hángzhōu (Y118, seven hours, once daily).

The main long-distance bus station is across the river in the northwest of town, with buses to Jiǔjiāng (Y45, 1½ hours, hourly), Nánchāng (Y70, 3½ hours, every 50 minutes), Túnxī (Y40, four hours), Wǔhàn (Y116, five hours, four daily), Shànghǎi (Y180, nine hours, once

CHINA'S CHINA

In 2004, Jǐngdézhèn celebrated its millennium as the country's imperial-decreed ceramics capital, though kilns have been firing up here since the Eastern Han dynasty. During the Jingde period of the Song dynasty, Emperor Zhen Zong decreed that only porcelain from the erstwhile Changnanzhen could grace dynastic tables, a prestigious accolade that lasted through to the Qing dynasty.

Jǐngdézhèn was chosen for its riverine location – facilitating transport to north China – and for its plethora of folk artisans; but its trump card was its proximity to Gāolǐng village's durable (but oddly textured) eponymous clay. The name Gāolǐng has entered the international lexicon as Kaolin (more commonly known as China Clay).

Jǐngdézhèn is home to nine of the 26 Masters of Art and Craft of China, the supreme national honour; the city has the nation's only college of ceramics. Then again, modern mass production may be compromising quality so purchasing good items depends on which factory made the porcelain and how much you want to spend. Growing illegal use of the 'Jǐngdézhèn' trademark at overseas fairs and import shops has made finding real-deal wares somewhat dicey.

daily), Hángzhōu (Y110, seven hours, twice daily), Zhūhǎi (Y230) and other cities.

Buses to Wùyuán (Y19, two hours, first bus 6.30am) and Qīnghuá (Y19, two hours, 8.10am and 1.30pm) leave from the Licun bus station (Lǐcūn zhàn) on Shuguang Lu.

TRAIN

Train connections include Nánchāng (hard seat Y38, 5½ hours), Běijīng (Y360, 24 hours), Shànghǎi (Y117, 17 hours) and Nánjīng (Y86, seven hours) via Túnxī, the gateway to legendary Huáng Shān (Y13, four hours).

Getting Around

A taxi to the airport should cost Y30; no bus runs there. Taxi flagfall starts at Y5.

WÙYUÁN 婺源
☎ 0793

The countryside around Wùyuán in the splendid northeast of Jiāngxī province is home to some of China's most immaculate views. Parcelled away in this fertile and hilly pocket on the fringes of stunning southern Ānhuī and western Zhèjiāng is a scattered cluster of picturesque Huīzhōu (see boxed text, p443) villages where old China remains preserved in enticing panoramas of ancient bridges, glittering rivers, stone-flagged alleyways and the slow, meandering pace of traditional rural life.

Despite lending its name to the entire area, Wùyuán itself – also called Zǐyángzhèn (紫阳镇) – is a far-from-graceful town where the old quarter is perplexingly being felled in mighty sweeps. The **museum** (bówùguǎn; Ruxueshan

Lu; admission Y20; ✆ 8.30am-noon & 2.30-5pm) on the top of a hill above Xingjiang Lu (星江路) in the old area of town is worth a look but most travellers will need no excuses before immersing themselves in the region's tantalising bucolic charms way out beyond the shabby suburbs.

Orientation

Sitting on either bank on a bend in the Xingjiang River (星江河; Xīngjiāng Hé), most of the town's hotels, shops and restaurants are located in the centre and north of town. The main north–south drag is Wengong Lu (文公路), along which cluster hotels and travel agencies, both of which can also be found along the east–west-running Tianyou Lu (天佑路). The north bus station is situated on Wengong Beilu; the west bus station is located in the south on Chengnan Lu (城南路).

Information

Post office (yóujú; cnr Tianyou Donglu & Lianxi Lu)
People's Hospital (Rénmín Yīyuàn; Wengong Nanlu)
Public Security Bureau (PSB; Gōngānjú; 2 Huancheng Beilu; ✆ 8-11.30am & 2.30-5.30pm)
Qitian Internet Cafe (启天网吧; Qǐtiān Wǎngbā; Wengong Nanlu; per hr Y2; ✆ 7am-midnight) Up the stairs on the 2nd floor through the large gateway opposite the Agricultural Development Bank of China.

Sleeping & Eating

It is preferable to stay overnight in one of the villages around town if you want a charming location, but Wùyuán has a larger range of accommodation, with loads of hotels along Wengong Lu.

Xiǎoféiyáng Bīnguǎn (小肥羊宾馆; Xiaofeiyang Hotel; ☎ 748 7899; 68 Wengong Nanlu; 文公南路68号; tw Y60; ✉) Rooms at this hotel above the restaurant of the same name are clean and come with TV and shower. The restaurant below is recommended for its hearty hotpots.

Tianma Hotel (天马大酒店; Tiānmǎ Dàjiǔdiàn; ☎ 736 7666; Wengong Beilu; 文公北路; d Y358; ✉) Handily located across from the north bus station, this smart four-star hotel has decent rooms that are regularly discounted to Y286.

Getting There & Away
From Jǐngdézhèn, buses to Wùyuán (Y19, two hours, regular, first bus 6.30am) and Qīnghuá (Y19, two hours, 8.10am and 1.30pm) leave from the Licun bus station (Lǐcūn zhàn) on Shuguang Lu. From Túnxī in Ānhuī, buses to Wùyuán (Y30, three hours, twice daily) depart from the long-distance bus station.

From Wùyuán **north bus station** (běizhàn; ☎ 734 8585; Wengong Beilu) there are buses to Jǐngdézhèn (Y19, two hours, every hour from 6am to 4.20pm), Túnxī (Y30, three hours, twice daily), Jiǔjiāng (Y69, 3½ hours), Hángzhōu (Y97, six hours, 9.30am), Shànghǎi (Y165, eight hours, 5pm), Wēnzhōu (Y124, six hours, 10am) and other destinations. From Wùyuán west bus station, buses run to similar destinations.

AROUND WÙYUÁN
The area first appeared on the Chinese tourist radar a few years ago, but village life has only fitfully begun to respond to this new economy. For now, washerwomen scrub wads of wet clothing along village riverbanks, plump chickens scamper about, the interiors of ancient halls and traditional homes openly invite inquisitive glances while peasant families offer cheap beds to wayfarers. The languid local tempo has resisted the slippery slide to wholesale repackaging, but that could all change as domestic tourists pour in.

Spring is a delightful time to visit, the fields carpeted in yellow *yóucàihuā* (rapeseed), the trees in flower and the summer crush yet to descend.

In addition to the villages listed here, there are other hamlets worth exploring, including Jiāng Wān (江湾) and Wāngkǒu (汪口).

Qīnghuá 清华
Easily reached by bus (Y5, 30 minutes, regular departures when full) or motorbike (Y20)

from Wùyuán north bus station, the principle asset of retiring Qīnghuá is its 800-year-old Southern Song–dynasty **Caihong Bridge** (彩虹桥; Cǎihóng Qiáo;) with its gorgeous riverine views, but also wander along the old street **Qinghua Laojie** (清华老街), a dilapidated portrait of time-worn stone architecture with carved wood shop fronts, lintels, decorative architraving and old folk stripping bamboo. A memento from early communist days survives along the old street in the bleak form of the old cinema, still emblazoned with full-form, pre-Mao Chinese characters that simply declare 'Qinghua Cinema'.

Wander at will down the small alleys that poke from the main drag and seek out revitalising shots of the local firewater, Qīnghuá Wújiǔ (清华婺酒). For both dinner and sleeping, try the attractively positioned **restaurant** (s/d Y120) next to the waterwheel on the far side of the Caihong Bridge or check into one of the simple *nóngjiā* (农家; literally 'farm households') dotted about Qīnghuá, such as the **Lǎojiē Kèzhàn** (老街客栈; ☎ 0793-724 2359; 355 Qinghua Laojie; 清华老街355号; d Y20), where basic rooms await. Buses also depart from Wùyuán north bus station to the mountain vistas of **Dàzhāng Shān** (大鄣山; Y45, one hour), not far from Qīnghuá.

Lǐkēng 理坑
Two villages named Lǐkēng lie within reach of Wùyuán, and this riverside hamlet of around 300 homesteads is popularly called **Dà Lǐkēng** ('Big Likeng'; admission Y20), as opposed to *Xiǎo* Lǐkēng (Small Likeng) – a different (and more picturesque) settlement northeast of Wùyuán; see p496.

Typical of the local vernacular, many of Lǐkēng's white-painted old houses enclose splendid interior courtyards illuminated from above by light wells (天井; *tiānjǐng*): rectangular openings in the roof that admit both sun and rain. The effect is to bathe interiors in pools of natural light, while rainwater soaks between the stone slabs below to drain away. The cool interiors often rise to two tiers and feature galleries, supported by wooden pillars and brackets, all in their original state.

Wander Lǐkēng's narrow alleyways pinched between towering walls and seek out some of its more impressive structures, such as the **Dàfūdì** (大夫第) – now converted into an antiques shop – and the lovely **Sīmǎdì** (司马第). Sit down on a stone bench alongside the river or cross one of the bridges to the far side and climb the stone-flagged path up the hill into the tea bushes above the village.

As in Qīnghuá, several local households have opened their doors to travellers, with simple beds available from around Y20 per night.

Perhaps the most splendid aspect of visiting Lǐkēng is traversing the hilly countryside from Qīnghuá, a beautiful landscape of fields and valleys cut by shimmering blue rivers and streams of totally unadulterated, pure water. A bus links Qīnghuá and Lǐkēng (around 45 minutes), while motorbikes can shuttle you along the rough road between the two for Y50. Alternatively, take a bus from Wùyuán to Tuóchuān (沱川; Y15) and then a motorbike taxi.

Xiǎoqǐ 晓起
☎ 0793

With a gorgeous riverside perch and enticing village architecture, Xiǎoqǐ (admission Y20), around 36km from Wùyuán, dates back to 787. There are actually two villages sharing the name Xiǎoqǐ: upper Xiǎoqǐ (上晓起) and lower Xiǎoqǐ (下晓起), several kilometres apart. Both are lovely and accommodation is plentiful; try the **Lǎowū Fàndiàn** (老屋饭店; ☎ 729 7402; r with fan Y20), with very simple rooms (shared toilet and shower) upstairs in a marvellous old Qing dynasty building by the river, or the adjacent and similarly styled **Jixutang Hotel** (继序堂饭店; Jìxùtáng Fàndiàn; ☎ 729 7014; r with fan Y15), equipped with a downstairs restaurant. The doorways of both buildings are decorated with richly detailed carved architraving. Buses to Xīkǒu from Wùyuán (Y7, 45 minutes, twice daily) pass through Xiǎoqǐ; a motorbike from Wùyuán to Xiǎoqǐ will cost around Y50 (Y80 return).

Lǐkēng 李坑
☎ 0793

A delightfully picturesque village, Lǐkēng (admission Y30; also known locally as *Xiǎo Lǐkēng*, or 'Small Likeng') enjoys a stupendous riverside setting, hung with lanterns and threaded by tight alleys and tightly bound together by quaint bridges. Come night-time, Lǐkēng is ever more serene, its riverside lanes glowing softly under red lanterns and old-fashioned-style street lamps, while locals navigate darker quarters by torchlight.

Lǐkēng's highly photogenic focal point hinges on the confluence of its two streams,

traversed by the bump of the 300-year-old **Tongji Bridge** (通济桥; Tōngjì Qiáo) and signposted by the **Shenming Pavilion** (申明亭; Shēnmíng Tíng), one of the village's signature sights, its wooden benches polished smooth with age.

Take a lazy boat from the huge old camphor tree near the entrance of the village to Tongji Bridge for Y10. To walk around town, follow the clear signs. Among the *báicài* (Chinese cabbage) draped from bamboo poles and chunks of cured meats hanging out in the air from crumbling, mildewed buildings, notable structures include the **Copper Mansion** (铜录坊; Tónglù Fáng), erected during Qing times by a copper merchant, the rebuilt **old stage** (古戏台; Gǔxìtái), where Chinese opera and performances are still held during festivals, and spirit walls erected on the riverbank to shield residents from the sound of cascading water.

Cross one of the bridges just beyond the old stage and take the stone-flagged path up the hill, past an old camphor tree, past terraced fields, through bamboo and firs and down to the river and the **Li Zhicheng Residence** (李知诚故居), the residence of a military scholar from the Southern Song. Walk in any direction and you will hit the countryside.

Accommodation is easy to find; try the the simple **Qīnglóng Kèzhàn** (青龙客栈; ☎ 726 3053; 25 Wuzheng Jie; 坞正街25号; d with fan no toilet Y40, with air-con & toilet Y100; 🖫), on the far side of Tongji Bridge opposite the old stage, or the clean rooms (with TV and shower) at the **Guāngmíng Chálóu** (光明茶楼; ☎ 726 2039; d with air-con Y40; 🖫), overlooking the river up from the Shenming Pavilion. For snacks, look out for *qīngmíngguǒ* (sweet and salty green dumplings sold by wayside vendors; Y3 for 10). Several notable buildings have been transformed into antiques shops.

Getting Around

Transport throughout the region can be frustrating, as villages are spaced apart and are not always linked by reliable bus connections. Buses depart Wùyuán's north bus station (běizhàn) for many of the villages and sights, including Qīnghuá, Lǐkēng and Dàzhāng Shān, but getting between individual destinations can be trying. Motorbikes (摩的; *módī*) can be hired from Wùyuán for the day (with driver) for around Y130, which should be able to take you to four or five villages (but expect to treat the driver to lunch). Otherwise, sample one-way fares for individual trips by motorbike taxis from Wùyuán are: Qīnghuá (Y20), Xiǎoqǐ (Y50) and Lǐkēng (李坑; Xiǎo Lǐkēng; Y15). From Xiǎoqǐ to Lǐkēng (李坑; Xiǎo Lǐkēng), expect to pay around Y20. Taxis can be hired in Wùyuán, but prices are high (albeit negotiable).

LÚSHĀN 庐山
☎ 0792

With an entrance fee (Y135) almost as steep as its verdant slopes, Lúshān's mountain views and European villa architecture have provided inspiration for legions of visitors while serving as the picturesque backdrop to momentous events from the turgid saga of Chinese communist history. In summer, travellers flock to Lúshān to flee the roaring lowland furnace of the Yangzi River basin while in winter months the peaks lie shrouded in thick banks of preternaturally lovely mists that can chill to the bone.

History

Late-19th-century Westerners established Lúshān, or Kuling as English-speakers called it, as a refreshing summer retreat. Gǔlǐng village was shaped after an English countryside village and its hotchpotch of stone cottages and villas remains today.

In 1959 the Central Committee of the Communist Party held a fateful meeting in Lúshān, which led to Peng Dehuai's dismissal, almost sent Mao into a political wilderness and sowed the seeds for the vicissitudinous rise and fall of Liu Shaoqi and Deng Xiaoping.

In 1970, a meeting of the Politburo in Lúshān – exactly what happened is shrouded in as much mist as the mountains – set the stage for a clash between Lin Biao and Mao. Whatever happened, Lin was dead by the following year.

Orientation & Information

The arrival point is the village of Gǔlǐng, perched 1167m high at the range's northern end and equipped with shops and restaurants, a post office, bank, internet cafés and long-distance bus stations. From Jiǔjiāng, 39km away, return day tours cost from Y180 (including entrance ticket, transportation and guide) and give you about five hours in Lúshān.

Detailed maps showing roads and walking tracks are available from the **Xinhua Bookstore** (Xīnhuá Shūdiàn; 11 Guling Jie), not far from the **Public Security Bureau** (PSB; Gōngānjú; ☎ 828 2452; 20 Guling Jie). You can change money at the **Bank of China** (Zhōngguó Yínháng; 13 Hemian Jie). An **Internet Café** (Wǎngbā; Guling Jie; per hr Y3; ⏲ 8am-midnight) can

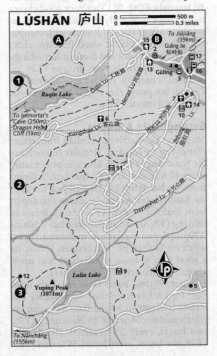

INFORMATION	
Bank of China 中国银行	1 B1
Internet Café 网吧	2 B1
Post Office 邮局	3 B1
PSB 公安局	(see 13)
Xinhua Bookstore 新华书店	4 B1

SIGHTS & ACTIVITIES	
Botanical Gardens 植物园	5 B3
Catholic Church 天主教堂	6 A1
Church 基督教堂	7 B1
Cinema 电影院	8 B1
Lushan Museum 博物馆	9 B3
Meilu Villa 美庐别墅	10 B1
Site of the Lushan Conference 庐山会议旧址	11 B2
Three Ancient Trees 三宝树	12 A3

SLEEPING	
Guling Zhengfu Hotel 牯岭镇政府宾馆	13 B1
Lushan Villa Hotel 庐山别墅村	14 B1
Lushan Yuntian Villa 庐山云天别墅	15 B1

TRANSPORT	
Bus Station	16 B1
Buses to Jiǔjiāng 汽车站售票出	17 B1

be found obliquely opposite the PSB at the bottom of the steps, and a post office can be found in the same area.

Sights & Activities

In addition to Lúshān's tourist attractions, explore the mountain roads and paths on your own.

Once Mao's former residence, the **Lushan Museum** (Lúshān Bówùguǎn; ☎ 828 2341; 1 Lulin Lu; admission free; ⊙ 8am-5.30pm) is littered with paraphernalia detailing the Lúshān communist connection.

Built by Chiang Kaishek in the 1930s, **Meilu Villa** (Měilú Biéshù; 180 Hedong Lu; admission Y15; ⊙ 8am-6pm) is a short walk downhill from Gǔlǐng and consequently crowded with sightseers.

Also called the People's Hall, the **Site of the Lushan Conference** (Lúshān Huìyì Jiùzhǐ; 504 Hexi Lu; admission Y10; ⊙ 8am-5pm) was the venue for the Chinese Communist Party's historic confabs.

At Lúshān's northwestern rim, the land falls away abruptly to spectacular views across Jiāngxī's densely settled plains. A long walking track south around these precipitous slopes passes the **Immortal's Cave** (仙人洞; Xiānrén Dòng) and continues to **Dragon Head Cliff** (龙首崖; Lóngshǒu Yá), a natural rock platform tilted above an eye-popping vertical drop.

The sombre **Three Ancient Trees** (Sānbǎoshù), not far by foot from Lulin Lake (Lúlín Hú), are indeed venerably old: the gingko and two cedar trees were planted five centuries ago by Buddhist monks.

The **Botanical Gardens** (Zhíwù Yuán; ☎ 707 9828; admission Y10; ⊙ 7.30am-5.30pm) are mainly devoted to subalpine tropical plants that thrive in the cooler highland climate. In the open gardens are spreads of rhododendrons, camellias and conifers.

Among Lúshān's old places of worship, the active **Church** (23 Hexi Lu) is a small, Protestant-looking stone building. The **Catholic Church** (12 Xiangshan Lu) is a frugally adorned and well-tended edifice assembled from roughly hewn blocks of stone.

Those with Chinese reading skills can note the largely obliterated political slogans from more tumultuous days above the door of the **building** at 3 Henan Lu, near the corner with Guling Jie. The characters are largely illegible, but the words 'Chairman Mao' are visible.

If so inclined, sit in on screenings of the Chinese classic *Love in Lushan* at the **cinema** (19 Hexi Lu).

Sleeping & Eating

In summer, particularly the stratospherically priced and supercharged weekends and holiday periods, budget travellers should forget about sleeping in Lúshān; do a day trip from the town of Jiǔjiāng instead. Prices here are average in high season; double everything during holidays.

Guling Zhengfu Hotel (Gǔlíngzhèn Zhèngfǔ Bīnguǎn; ☎ 829 6282; 100 Lushan Zhengjie; 庐山正街100号; d Y120) Up the steps above the PSB, this place has OK rooms with shower and good views that can be secured for around Y80 during the low season.

Lushan Yuntian Villa (Lúshān Yúntiān Biéshù; ☎ 829 3555; Guling Jie; 牯岭正街; d Y580-680; 🕸) A move away from Lúshān's typically musty and worn lodging options, this place offers old villa atmosphere with roomy, fresh accommodation and a crisp finish. Angle for discounts.

Lushan Villa Hotel (Lúshān Biéshù Cūn; ☎ 828 2927; fax 828 2927; 182 Zhihong Lu; 脂红路182号; ste Y880-2000) This place has cottages scattered throughout a lovely old pine forest, with discounts of up to 20% available.

Xunyang Hotel (Xúnyáng Bīnguǎn; ☎ 0792-812 3888; 292 Xunyang Lu; d Y268; 🕸) This very good choice in Jiǔjiāng has recently renovated rooms, restored to a high standard, some with computer, glass sinks, plastic wood flooring, clean showers, comfy beds and modern furnishings. During slack periods, rates drop to Y120.

Small, cheapish restaurants abound in Gǔlǐng, but prices rise as you stray from the village and into the hills.

Getting There & Around

Many travellers arrive in Lúshān from either Nánchāng or Jiǔjiāng. Regular buses leave for Nánchāng (Y40, 1½ hours, approximately every 40 minutes, first/last bus 7am/5.30pm) from the **bus station** (☎ 828 1983) just north of the Xiadu Hotel on Hexi Lu. Buses also depart from here for Wǔhàn (Y75, 8am). Buses to Jiǔjiāng (Y8, one hour, first/last bus 7.50am/3.30pm) depart regularly from the small ticket office on Guling Jie. In summer, it may be a good idea to book your return seat upon arrival, particularly for day-trippers.

From Jiǔjiāng, buses leave regularly from 8am for Lúshān from the long-distance bus station (chángtú qìchē zhàn) on Xunyang Lu, which is also connected to Nánchāng (Y36, two hours, every 25 minutes), Jǐngdézhèn (Y35, two hours, every hour), Wùyuán (Y65, three hours, 9.45am), **Shànghǎi** (Y199, 10 hours), **Nánjīng** (Y130, six hours, frequent) and **Wǔhàn** (Y71, 3½ hours). See p491 for details on buses to Lúshān.

Lúshān's myriad footpaths make explorations on foot outstanding, although consider hiring a taxi to visit sights and walking back. Lúshān has copious cable cars and tramways (Y50 to Y60 return).

JǏNGGĀNG SHĀN 井冈山
☎ 0796

With its tree-lined streets and misty mountain ranges, Jǐnggāng Shān (admission Y100, sights extra), near the Húnán–Jiāngxī border, is fêted and mythologised by dewy-eyed party cadres China-wide: in 1927, Mao led 900 men here to be joined by Zhu De's battered forces. It was from these hills that Mao launched the legendary Long March to Shaanxi, guaranteeing Jǐnggāng Shān's conversion from mountain range to revolutionary cradle, communist monument and overrun tourist Mecca. June to October are the optimal travel months.

Orientation & Information
The main township, Cípíng (茨坪; also called Jǐnggāng Shān), is nestled around a small lake in the mountains, 820m above the sea.

Your hotel can possibly help you hire a van for about Y100 to tour major sites, but be careful of overcharging.

Emergency phone numbers, including those of the **PSB** (Gōngānjú; ☎ 655 2360) and **medical help** (☎ 655 2595), are listed on roadside signs. The **Bank of China** (Zhōngguó Yínháng; 6 Nanshan Lu), on the lake's southeastern end, has a 24-hour ATM.

Sights & Activities
Jǐnggāng Shān's natural highland forest is unrivalled, particularly its square-stemmed bamboo and some 26 kinds of alpine azaleas that bloom from late April. Adventurous trekkers can venture into the surrounding mountains for **self-guided walks** on dirt trails.

At **Five Dragon Pools** (五龙潭; Wǔlóng Tán; ☎ 655 6937; admission Y30; ☉ 6am-6pm), about 7km northwest of town, five cascading waterfalls and gorgeous views reward a long but sweatless

trek (with English signs). The total hike can take six hours (three hours each way). Cheat with a cable car (Y50 single).

Magnificent views unfurl from the watching post, **Huángyángjiè** (黄洋界; admission Y7; ☉ 7am-6pm), sitting to the west at more than 1300m above sea level.

Standing 1438m above sea level, **Five Fingers Peak** (五指峰; Wǔzhǐ Fēng; admission Y20; ☉ 7am-6pm) is to the south and is immortalised on the back of the old Y100 banknote.

The **Revolutionary Museum** (革命博物馆; Gémìng Bówùguǎn; ☎ 655 2248; 12 Hongjun Nanlu; admission Y8; ☉ 8am-5.30pm) devotes itself to the Kuomintang and Communists' struggle for control of the Húnán–Jiāngxī area in the late 1920s.

The **Former Revolutionary Quarters** (革命旧居群; Gémìng Jiùzhìqún; Tongmu Linglu; admission Y5; ☉ 8am-6pm) is a reconstruction of the mud-brick building that served as a Communist command centre between 1927 and 1928, and where Mao lived temporarily.

Sleeping
Most hotels in Jǐnggāng Shān unwaveringly cater to the midrange market. Prices coast during weekdays before rocketing on peak weekends.

Túshūguǎn Zhaòdaìsuǒ (图书馆招待所; ☎ 655 2276; 22 Hongjun Beilu; 红军北路; s & tw from Y80) Modest rooms with bathrooms are decent and cheap. It's a 10-minute walk from the bus station, just past the lake. Look for a white sign with red lettering.

Jǐnggǎngshān Bīnguǎn (井冈山宾馆; ☎ 655 2272; fax 655 2551; 10 Hongjun Beilu; tw Y320-680; 🖳) Stay where all PRC chairmen have lain their heads, among a mind-boggling variety of rooms and villas. There's no English sign.

Getting There & Away
Direct buses run from Nánchāng to Jǐnggāng Shān (Y65 to Y90, five hours, three buses daily). Occasional buses also run to Chángshā (Y76, nine hours).

The Jǐnggāng Shān train station is in Tàihé, a minibus ride away (Y25, three hours). An alternative is to take a train to Jí'ān train station and then a bus (Y25, three hours) to Cípíng.

JIĀNGXĪ

Húnán 湖南

Húnán's two most potent exports – its fiery cuisine and the combustible thought of firebrand Mao Zedong – have scorched trails across the Middle Kingdom. *Xiāngcài* restaurants have eyes streaming and foreheads sweating nationwide, and effigies of Mao stand unblinking through the land, monuments to a period of ideological fervour that took China to the brink of ruin.

Communist heritage sites may characterise Chángshā and Shàoshān – revered birthplace of Mao Zedong – and the communist stamp is magnified further by Liu Shaoqi, Peng Dehuai and Hu Yaobang, prominent communist bigwigs and Húnán men. But to exclusively pore over Húnán's revolutionary roll call would be to sell the province way short, for Húnán is blessed with some of China's most stupendous landscapes and fecund scenery.

Spreading east, west and south from the province's Yangzi River basin plain (and Chángshā) are rough, isolated mountain ranges. The splendid Miao hamlet of Déhāng finds itself surrounded by a fanciful panorama of lush terraced fields, waterfalls and the karst peaks that rise in further profusion at the astonishing park of Wǔlíngyuán.

Travellers hunting down classic scenes of China's riverside village life come to rest in Fènghuáng for its unique views and crumbling sense of history. South of Fènghuáng, Hóngjiāng wraps itself around an old quarter riddled with heritage architecture. Travellers eager to commune with sacred China can make a beeline to Héng Shān, where monks pursue a life dedicated to the *dào* – the Way – on the slopes of one of China's holiest Taoist peaks.

HIGHLIGHTS

- Get lost in the gorgeous scenery of **Wǔlíngyuán** (p515) in Húnán's rugged northwest

- Slip the crowds on an early-morning walk along the Yuquanxi Scenic Area outside the Miao village of **Déhāng** (p511)

- Have your camera working overtime in fantastic **Fènghuáng** (p512), Húnán's most captivating historic riverside town

- Marvel at the Han-dynasty mummy at the **Hunan Provincial Museum** (p502) in Chángshā

- Visit Chairman Mao's birthplace and childhood home (and buy a Mao watch) in **Shàoshān** (p506), the obligatory communist-history pilgrimage site

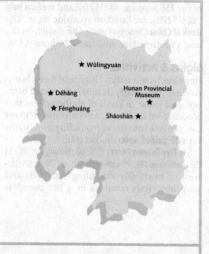

★ Wǔlíngyuán

★ Déhāng   Hunan Provincial Museum ★

★ Fènghuáng

Shàoshān ★

- POPULATION: 64.6 MILLION

History

Between the 8th and 11th centuries the population of Húnán increased fivefold, spurred on by a prosperous agricultural industry along with southerly migration. Under the Ming and Qing dynasties the region was one of the empire's granaries, and vast quantities of rice were shipped over to the depleted north.

By the 19th century, Húnán began to suffer from the pressure of its big population. Land shortage and landlordism caused widespread unrest among Chinese farmers and hill-dwelling minorities. This contributed to the massive Taiping Rebellion (p45) and the communist movement of the 1920s, which later found strong support among Húnán's peasants, establishing a refuge on the mountainous Húnán–Jiāngxī border in 1927.

Climate

Subtropical Húnán has more temperate forested elevations in the east, west and south. The northern half's climate is more fickle, with plunging winter temperatures and snow; the orange-growing south is more bearable. From April to June expect grey skies and most of the province's annual 125cm to 175cm of rain; thereafter, July and August are pressure-cooking months of heat and humidity.

Language

Hunanese (xiāng), the language of Mao, is a Northern Mandarin dialect and has six to

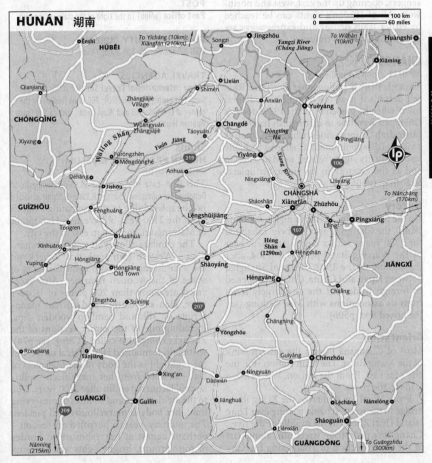

eight 'dialects' of its own. Fewer consonants means confusion – l, n, f and h sounds, for example, are famously pesky. 'Fronting' (eg 'zh' sounds like 'z') is also noticeable.

Gàn, another Northern Mandarin dialect, is spoken in the west and south. Border regions are home to a mosaic of local dialects and minority languages that defy family group classification. Most of Húnán's residents are Han Chinese, but hill-dwelling minorities occupying the border regions include the Miao, Tujia, Dong (a people related to the Thais and Lao) and Yao.

Getting There & Around

The airports at Chángshā, Zhāngjiājiè and Huáihuà are useful points of access for air passengers, opening up the east, west and northwest. All of Húnán's sights can be reached by either train or bus and expressways are tightening up travel times.

CHÁNGSHĀ 长沙

☎ 0731 / pop 2.1 million

Though British philosopher Bertrand Russell described it as resembling 'a mediaeval town' when he passed by in the 1920s, today's Chángshā has little to distinguish itself from other drab Chinese cities, which can come as a visceral disappointment. Chángshā is chiefly known for its sights related to Mao Zedong and as the gateway to his rustic birthplace, Sháoshān (p506).

History

On the fertile plains of the Xiang River (Xiāng Jiāng), the Chángshā area has been inhabited for 3000 years, with a large settlement here by the Warring States period. In 1904, after the signing of the 1903 Treaty of Shanghai between Japan and China, Chángshā opened to foreign trade, but the city largely feeds from its associations with Mao Zedong (see the boxed text, p506).

Orientation

Most of Chángshā lies on the eastern bank of the Xiang River. The train station is in the city's far east. From the station, Wuyi Dadao leads to the river.

From Wuyi Lu, you cross the Xiang River bridge to the western bank, passing over Long Island (Júzi Zhōu) in the middle of the river. Chángshā's pedestrian street runs along part of the south section of Huangxing Lu. City maps are on sale at kiosks around the train station and in hotel shops.

Information

INTERNET ACCESS 网吧

Internet Café (wǎngbā; 1st fl, Xīnxìng Dàshìchǎng, cnr Chezhan Zhonglu; per hr Y3; ⏰ 24hr) Opposite the train station.

Internet Café (wǎngbā; 2nd fl, Sanjiu Chuyun Hotel, 239 Chezhan Zhonglu; per hr Y3) Opposite the train station.

MONEY

Bank of China (Zhōngguó Yínháng; 43 Wuyi Dadao; ⏰ 8.30am–noon & 2.30–5.30pm) The Bank of China ATM at the Huatian Hotel takes international cards, and there's another ATM on Zhongshan Lu.

POST

Post office (yóujú) To the right of the train station exit.

PUBLIC SECURITY BUREAU

PSB (Gōngānjú; ☎ 589 5000; 1 Dianli Lu)

TRAVEL AGENCIES

China International Travel Service (CITS; Zhōngguó Guójì Lǚxíngshè; ☎ 446 8901; 160 Wuyi Dadao) On the corner of Changdao Lu and Wuyi Dadao, just east of Lotus Huatian Hotel.

Sights

HUNAN PROVINCIAL MUSEUM

湖南省博物馆

This first-rate **museum** (Húnán Shěng Bówùguǎn; 50 Dongfeng Lu; admission Y50; ⏰ 8.30am–5.30pm) should not be missed due to its fascinating exhibits from the 2100-year-old Western Han tombs of Mǎwángduī, some 5km east of the city.

The exhibits allow you to get a rare handle on Western Han aesthetics – check out the astonishing expressions on the faces of some of the wooden figurines. Also excavated are more than 700 pieces of lacquer ware, Han silk textiles and ancient manuscripts on silk and bamboo wooden slips, including one of the earlier versions of the Zhōuyì (Yìjīng, also called I Ching: see p74), written in formalised Han clerical script. But the highlight is the body of the Marquess of Dai, extracted from her magnificent multi-layered lacquered coffin after 2100 years. Due to the air-tight seal and 80 litres of preserving fluid, her body is marvellously well pickled. The mummy wears a horrified expression – perhaps aghast at her exposure to hordes of tour groups, bright lights and the surgery she underwent at the hands of modern doctors who removed her internal organs.

A further hall is devoted to marvellous Shang- and Zhou-dynasty bronzes from Húnán; look out for the 'elephant-shaped *zūn*' and the 'cover of square bronze *léi* with inscriptions'.

MAOIST PILGRIMAGE SPOTS

A colossal 1968 statue of Mao – cast out of an aluminium-magnesium alloy in Hēilóng-jiāng – affably greets you at the entrance to the **Changsha City Museum** (Shì Bówùguǎn; 480 Bayi Lu; admission Y10; ☺ 6am-8.30pm). Compare his carriage – right arm raised aloft, heralding a new dawn – with that of his more demure statue in Sháoshān from the 1990s, when the reform drive had long kicked in and Mao was a demigod no more. Head right towards the almost empty **exhibition hall** with the huge red-tiled façade and a huge portrait of a youthful Mao, if only to gawp at its magnificent exterior. Upstairs, visitors are serenaded by a Chinese-language paean to Mao Zedong and his second wife, Yang Kaihui. Also in the museum grounds is the former site of the **Hunan CPC Committee** (Zhōng Gòng Xiānggū Wěiyuánhuì Jiùzhǐ; ☺ 8am-noon & 2-5.30pm), where Mao's living quarters, along with photos and historical items from the 1920s and a wall of Mao's poems are on view.

A small and fun **antiques market** materialises at the museum gate on Friday, Saturday and Sunday.

Hunan No 1 Teachers' Training School (Dìyī Shīfàn Xuéxiào; 324 Shuyuan Lu; admission Y6; ☺ 8am-5.30pm) is where Mao attended classes between 1913 and 1918; he returned as a teacher and principal from 1920 to 1922. A fun self-guided tour takes in Mao's dormitory, some study areas, halls where he held some of his first political meetings and an open-air well where he enjoyed taking cold baths.

YUELU PARK 岳麓公园

This park (Yuèlù gōngyuán), at the bottom of the High Mountain Park, and Hunan University (Húnán Dàxué) are pleasant places to visit on the western bank of Xiang River. The university evolved from the site of the **Yuelu Academy** (Yuèlù Shūyuàn; Lushan Lu; summer Y30, other times Y18; ☺ 7.30am-5.30pm), which was established during the Song dynasty for scholars preparing for civil examinations.

The hike to **Loving Dusk Pavilion** (Àiwǎn Tíng) offers lovely views.

To get to the university, take bus 202 from Wuyi Dado or the train station and get off three stops before the end. Continue downhill and turn right (the bus goes left); walk straight for the Mao statue.

OLD CITY WALLS

The only remaining part of the old city walls is **Tiānxīn Gé** (Heart of Heaven Pavilion; park Y2, pavilion Y5), off Chengnan Xilu, which is an interesting area to explore.

Sleeping

Most hotels able to admit foreigners tend to be quite expensive.

Hunan Normal University Foreign Experts Building (Húnán Shīfàn Dàxué Zhuānjiālóu; ☎ 887 2211; Lushan Lu; 麓山路; d Y30, tw with bathroom Y120-180; ☒) It's in the west, so phone first. Take bus 202 from the train station and disembark at the *shīfàn dàxué* stop. Nearly opposite the stop is a dorm and housing complex with budget rooms. Travellers usually have to slog about 750m uphill to a white building with the rates given here.

Taicheng Hotel (Tàichéng Dàjiǔdiàn; ☎ 217 9999; 309 Chezhan Zhonglu; 车站中路309号; s/d/ste Y238/238/348; ☒) Less busy than other nearby tourist hotels, carpeted rooms here are good and clean and the location near the train station is optimum. Discounts bring doubles down to Y108.

Lotus Huatian Hotel (Fúróng Huátiān Dàjiǔdiàn; ☎ 440 1888; fax 440 1889; 176 Wuyi Dadao; 五一大道176号; s/d Y338-538/Y338-538; ☒) A quite luxurious Chinese-themed four-star hotel offering 30% discounts on rooms, making prices a bargain, especially if you're doing business on a budget.

Dolton Hotel (Tōngchéng Guójì Dàjiǔdiàn; ☎ 416 8888; www.dolton-hotel.com; 149 Shaoshan Beilu; 韶山北路 149号; d Y918; ☒ ☒ ☒) One of the two best hotels in the city (the other being the Huatian Hotel), the rooms and service here rarely fail to impress. An excellent all-round hotel.

Huatian Hotel (Huá Tiān Dàjiǔdiàn; ☎ 444 2888; www.huatian-hotel.com; 380 Jiefang Donglu; 解放东路380号; tw/ste US$88/318 plus 15% service charge; ☒ ☒ ☒ ☒) This much-renovated and reinvigorated five-star hotel has excellent rooms and a much-lauded reputation for good service, backed up by a panoply of select restaurants.

Eating & Drinking

Plenty of street-side stalls pop up at night on Zhaoyang Lu.

Huǒgōngdiàn (☎ 412 0580; 93 Wuyi Dadao) Perhaps famous for its stinky *dòufu* (tofu; as Mao said:

HÚNÁN

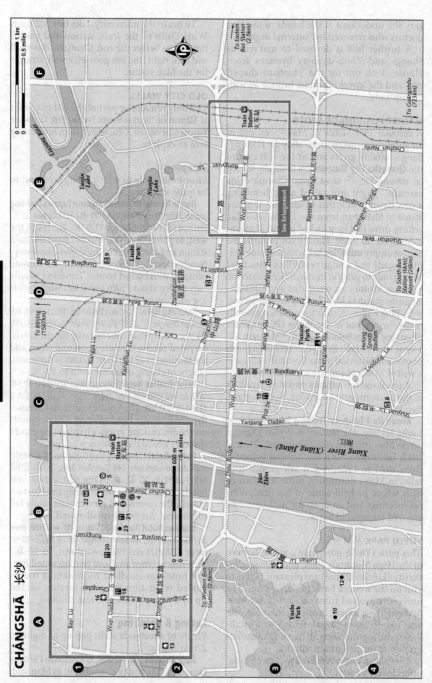

CHÁNGSHĀ 长沙

INFORMATION		
ATM 自动柜员机	**1**	D2
Bank of China 中国银行	**2**	B1
CITS 中国国际旅行社	(see 16)	
Internet Café 网吧	**3**	B1
Internet Café 网吧	**4**	B2
Post Office 邮局	**5**	B1
PSB 公安局	**6**	C3

SIGHTS & ACTIVITIES		
Changsha City Museum		
市博物馆	**7**	D2
Hunan No 1 Teachers' Training		
School 第一师范学校	**8**	C4

Hunan Provincial Museum		
省博物馆	**9**	D1
Loving Dusk Pavilion		
爱晚亭	**10**	A4
Tiānxīn Gé 天心阁	**11**	D3
Yuelu Academy 岳麓书院	**12**	A4

SLEEPING		
Dolton Hotel		
通程国际大酒店	**13**	A2
Huatian Hotel 华天大酒店	**14**	A2
Hunan Normal University Foreign		
Experts Building		
湖南师范大学专家楼	**15**	B3

Lotus Huatian Hotel		
芙蓉华天大酒店	**16**	A1
Taicheng Hotel		
泰成大酒店	**17**	B1

EATING		
Huǒgōngdiàn 火宫殿	**18**	A1
Huǒgōngdiàn 火宫殿	**19**	C3
Xīnhuá Lóu 新华楼	**20**	B1
Xīnhuá Lóu 新华楼	**21**	B1

TRANSPORT		
Bus Station 汽车站	**22**	B1
CAAC 中国民航售票处	**23**	B1

'The stinky *dòufu* at Chángshā's Huǒgōngdiàn smells stinky, but tastes great') but there's much else here, from tasty *dim sum* wheeled round in carts to the excellent *máoshì hóngshāoròu* (毛氏红烧肉; Mao-style braised pork; Y32) and its scrummy pale green vegetable parcels, *xiāngjiān sùcàibāo* (香煎素菜包; Y6 for six). There are three branches in town – another can be found at 78 Pozi Jie (☎ 581 4228).

Xīnhuá Lóu (35 Wuyi Dadao; dishes Y4-25; ⏰ 6.30am-2am) This local institution is a can't-miss option for local dishes; harried staff wheel around trolleys for patrons to pick and choose. Another branch is across the way at 108 Wuyi Dadao (open from 6.30am to 1.30am).

Getting There & Away
AIR
Civil Aviation Administration of China (CAAC; Zhōngguó Mínháng; ☎ 411 2222) is one block west of the train station, next to the Civil Aviation Hotel.

China Southern (☎ office hrs 228 8000, 24hr 950 333; 336 Chezhan Zhonglu; ⏰ 8am-7.30pm) has an office at the train station.

From Chángshā, there are daily flights to major cities such as Běijīng (Y1210), Chéngdū (Y910), Guǎngzhōu (Y690), Shànghǎi (Y890) and Xī'ān (Y890). Flights going to Zhāngjiājiè (Y460) officially (but occasionally optimistically) run daily.

BUS
The **bus station** (61 Chezhan Beilu) across from the train station has limited services.

Buses for Sháoshān (Y20, two hours, every 30 minutes, 8am to 5.30pm), Guìlín (Y166, six hours, three per day), Héng Shān (Y24 to Y32, two to three hours), Hóngjiāng City (Y99, seven hours, 9.50am) and Jīnggǎng Shān (Y77, five hours, 12.30pm) leave from the south bus station (*qìchē nánzhàn*), way down in the south of town. Take bus 107 from the train

station to the south bus station (Y2). From the train station, bus 126 goes to the eastern bus station (*dōngzhàn*), where buses run to Wǔhàn (Y135, four hours) and Yuèyáng (Y55, two hours). Bus 12 followed by bus 315 goes to the western bus station (*xīzhàn*) for buses to Zhāngjiājiè (Y101, seven hours, once daily) and Huáihuà (Y99, 11 hours).

TRAIN
There are two Guǎngzhōu–Chángshā–Běijīng express trains daily in each direction and a daily train to Shànghǎi (Y300, 20 hours) from Chángshā's **train station** (☎ 263 8682). Other routes via Chángshā are Běijīng–Guìlín–Kūnmíng and Guǎngzhōu–Xī'ān–Lánzhōu. Not all trains to Shànghǎi, Kūnmíng and Guìlín stop in Chángshā, so it may be necessary to go to Zhūzhōu first and change there. Trains run to Zhāngjiājiè, but only N375 leaves at a good time (6.30am); the trip takes 12 hours. To Wǔhàn (Y50, three to four hours), it's no problem.

If you're heading to Hong Kong, you can take one of a few overnight Chángshā–Shēnzhèn air-conditioned express trains that get into Shēnzhèn early in the morning. The Běijīng–Kowloon express train also passes through Chángshā. The daily train to Sháoshān (Y11, three hours) leaves at 7.30am, returning at 4.55pm. Counter 7 at the Chángshā train station is supposedly for foreigners.

Getting Around
TO/FROM THE AIRPORT
Huanghua International Airport is 26km from the city centre. CAAC shuttle buses (Y16) depart every 30 minutes between 6.30am and 8.30pm from the Civil Aviation Hotel, next to CAAC on Wuyi Dadao.

TAXI
Taxi fares start at Y3.

SHÀOSHĀN 韶山
☎ 0732

Unassuming Shàoshān, about 130km south-west of Chángshā, looms monumentally as Mao Zedong's birthplace. Three million pilgrims once traipsed here each year (including Mao himself on a return visit in 1959), and a railway line and paved road from Chángshā were laid. Mao's death and Cultural Revolution excesses slowed things, but that didn't stop a statue of the Great Helmsman being erected in Shàoshān in 1993 (the skies ominously darkening when it was unveiled) and huge battalions of tour groups still earmark the village for obligatory obeisance on communist heritage tours.

Orientation & Information
Shàoshān has two distinct parts: the new town clustered around the train and bus stations, and the original Shàoshān village about 5km away.

From the train station, minibuses (Y1.50) and motorcycle taxis head to village sites. Some minibuses will take you to all the key sites and back for Y10.

A branch of CITS (Zhōngguó Guójì Lǔxíngshè) can be found next to Nanan School (see below).

Sights & Activities
The number of Mao-related sights has mushroomed over the years in a lucrative bid to separate tourists from their hard-earned *máo*, but only a handful have a genuine connection with the communist revolutionary.

MAO'S CHILDHOOD HOUSE 毛泽东故居
Standing in front of a pond, this simple mud-brick **house** (Máo Zédōng Gùjū; admission free; ☒ 8am-7pm, closes 5pm outside summer) with a thatched roof and stable is the village's shrine. Mao was born here in 1893 and returned to live here briefly in 1927. Among the paraphernalia are kitchen utensils, original furnishings, bedding, and photos of Mao's parents, with facilities including a small barn and cattle pen. No photography is allowed inside.

NANAN SCHOOL 南岸私塾
This frugal and spartan **school** (Nán'àn Sīshú; admission Y10; ☒ 8am-5.30pm), its interior illuminated

---

THE GREAT HELMSMAN

Mao was born in Shàoshān, not far from Chángshā, in 1893. Once poor, his father served in the military to make money. Ultimately, their new surpluses raised their status to 'rich' peasants.

A famine in Húnán and a subsequent uprising of starving people in Chángshā ended in the execution of the leaders by the Manchu governor, an injustice that deeply affected Mao. At the age of 16 he left Shàoshān to enter middle school in Chángshā. Though not yet antimonarchist, he felt that the country was in desperate need of reform.

In Chángshā, Mao was first exposed to the ideas of revolutionaries active in China, most notably Sun Yatsen's revolutionary secret society. Later that year an army uprising in Wǔhàn quickly spread and the Qing dynasty collapsed. Mao joined the regular army but resigned six months later, thinking the revolution was over when Sun handed the presidency to Yuan Shikai and the war between the north and south of China did not take place.

Voraciously reading newspapers, Mao was introduced to socialism. While at the Hunan No 1 Teachers' Training School (p503), he inserted an advertisement in a Chángshā newspaper 'inviting young men interested in patriotic work to make contact with me…'. Among those who got in touch was Liu Shaoqi, who later became president of the People's Republic of China (PRC); Xiao Chen, who became a founding member of the Chinese Communist Party (CCP); as well as Li Lisan.

Mao graduated in 1918 and went to Běijīng, where he worked as an assistant librarian at Beijing University. In Běijīng he met future co-founders of the Chinese Communist Party: the student leader Zhang Guodao, Professor Chen Duxiu and university librarian Li Dazhao. Chen and Li are regarded as the founders of Chinese communism.

On returning to Chángshā, Mao became increasingly active in communist politics. He became editor of the *Xiang River Review*, a radical Húnán students' newspaper, and began teaching. In 1920 he organised workers and truly felt himself a Marxist. In Shànghǎi in 1921 Mao attended the founding meeting of the CCP and helped organise Húnán's provincial branch. Differing from

by light wells, is where Mao began his education. Climb the stairs to glimpse Mao's place of study, eyeball the teacher's bed downstairs and peer at fading photos of relatives and descendants.

MUSEUM OF COMRADE MAO
毛泽东同志纪念馆

A further paean to Mao, this **museum** (Máo Zédōng Jìniànguǎn; ☎ 568 5347; admission Y30; ☯ 8am-5pm) is without English captions, but the exhibits of his belongings and photos with communist leaders are graphic enough. To the right as you face the museum and opposite the bronze statue of Mao Zedong (decorated with calligraphy from Jiang Zemin) is the **Mao Family Ancestral Hall** (毛氏宗祠; Máo Shì Zōngcí; admission Y10; ☯ 8am-5.30pm) where staff snooze, a precursor to a disentangling of the Mao family genealogy and photos of Chinese leaders paying obligatory visits to Sháoshān.

OTHER SIGHTS

Some 3km up from Sháoshān village is the **Dripping Water Cave** (滴水洞; Dī Shuǐ Dòng; admission

Y32; ☯ 8am-5.30pm). Mao lived in this retreat (no, it's not a cave, but his villa was quite bunker-like) for 11 days in June 1966. The Mao clan are entombed nearby. Buses and motorbikes head here from the car park opposite the Shaoshan Hotel.

Shao Peak (韶峰; Sháo Fēng; admission Y45) is the cone-shaped mountain visible from the village. The summit has a lookout pavilion, and the 'forest of stelae' (毛泽东诗词碑林; Máo Zédōng Shīcí Bēilín; admission Y17) on the lower slopes has stone tablets engraved with Mao's poems.

From Sháoshān village you can take a minibus or motorcycle taxi (Y5) south to the end of the road at the cable-car station. Hiking to the top of the mountain takes about an hour.

Sleeping & Eating

Remember that Sháoshān can be easily done as a day trip from Chángshā, so spending the night can be avoided. In the village itself look out for hotel touts inducing you to stay with a local family or *nóngjiā* (农家); no-one seems to mind.

orthodox Marxists, Mao saw the peasants as the lifeblood of the revolution, and from 1922 to 1925 the CCP organised its first unions of peasants, workers and students. Vengeful warlords impelled Mao's flight to Guǎngzhōu (Canton).

In April 1927, following Chiang Kaishek's massacre of communists, Mao was dispatched to Chángshā to organise what became known as the 'Autumn Harvest Uprising'. Mao's army scaled Jīnggāng Shān's peaks to embark on a guerrilla war – step one towards the 1949 communist takeover.

Mao became the new chairman of the PRC (until his death in 1976) and embarked on radical campaigns to repair his war-ravaged yet jubilant country. In the mid-1950s he became increasingly disillusioned with the Soviets and began to implement peasant-based and decentralised socialist development. The outcome was the ill-fated Great Leap Forward and, later, the chaos of the Cultural Revolution (for details, see p51).

The current regime officially says Mao was 70% correct and 30% wrong. Torturous experiences are remembered – upwards of 70 million Chinese died during his rule – but he is revered as a man who united his people and returned China to the status of world power. 'Great Leader', 'Great Teacher' and 'supremely beloved Chairman' are oft-used monikers; his ubiquitous images reveal a saint who will protect people (or make them rich).

The most controversial dissection of his life and purpose came with the 2005 publication of *Mao: The Unknown Story* by Jung Chang and Jon Halliday, the fruit of 10 years' research. Seeking to balance the hagiographical bias of much Chinese commentary on Mao, Chang and Halliday endeavoured to demolish the myth of the Long March and portray Mao as an unscrupulous schemer whose collusion with communist ideology simply served as a route to total supremacy. Other biographies of Mao Zedong include Ross Terrill's *Mao*, Jerome Ch'en's *Mao and the Chinese Revolution* and Stuart R Schram's *Mao Tse-tung*. The five-volume *Selected Works of Mao Tse-tung* provide abundant insight into his thoughts.

Shàoshān Bīnguǎn (韶山宾馆; ☎ 568 5262; 16 Guyuan Lu; 故园路16号; s/d Y368/398; 🖭) Midrange tourist option tucked away over the road and up the drive behind the statue of Mao Zedong. A variety of buildings offer variously priced rooms including Mao's roost when he paid a return visit to Shàoshān in 1959.

Restaurants are all over the place in the village itself, all typically cooking up Mao's favourite dish, Mao Family Braised Pork (毛氏红烧肉; Máoshì Hóngshāoròu), but expect tourist prices.

Getting There & Away

BUS

Chángshā's southern bus station (qìchē nánzhàn) has several buses a day to Shàoshān (Y20, two hours, every hour) running from 8am onwards. During summertime, travel group kiosks sprout up around the train station. Buses return to Chángshā from Shàoshān's **long-distance bus station** (长途汽车站; chángtú qìchēzhàn; Yingbin Lu), just north of the train station, with the last bus leaving at around 5.30pm.

TRAIN

A daily train (Y11, 3 to 3½ hours) to Shàoshān runs from Chángshā, departing Chángshā at 7.30am and returning from Shàoshān at 4.55pm.

YUÈYÁNG 岳阳

☎ 0730 / pop 529,730

Perched on enormous Dòngtíng Hú (Dongting Lake) and home to a tea so sublime that emperors demanded it as a gift of respect, Yuèyáng has a sprinkling of attractions that can fit into a day trip from Chángshā.

Orientation

Yuèyáng is situated south of the Yangzi on the northeastern shore of Dòngtíng Hú, where the lake flows into the river. Yuèyáng proper is in the southern section of the city, where the train, bus stations, hotels, sights and Buxing Jie (步行街) – the town's pedestrianised street – can be found.

Information

Baihui Internet Café (Bǎihuì Wǎngbā; Buxing Jie; per hr Y2; 🕒 24hr) Upstairs through a clothes store on pedestrianised Buxing Jie.

China Post (yóujú; train station concourse; 🕒 8am-7pm)

CITS (Zhōngguó Guójì Lǚxíngshè; ☎ 823 2010; 25

Yunmeng Lu) This not very helpful office is in the courtyard of the Yunmeng Hotel, on the 2nd floor.

Internet Café (Buxing Jie; per hr Y2; 🕒 24hr) At the western end of Buxing Jie.

Sights & Activities

Yuèyáng's most celebrated landmark, the over-priced **Yueyang Tower** (岳阳楼; Yuèyáng Lóu; Dongting Beilu; admission Y46; 🕒 7.30am-5.45pm) is a historic triple-eaved structure overlooking the lake in the west of town, constructed without a single nail and rising from its namesake park.

Under renovation at the time of writing, the halls of Yuèyáng's impressive **Confucian Temple** (文庙; Wénmiào) are ringed by a long, high brick wall topped with green tiles and cruelly surrounded by the empty shells of deserted apartment blocks. The entire complex exudes substantial nobility, with *Magnolia grandiflora* standing near the entrance and a massive hall at the rear.

Dating back to 1242, the ill-repaired and overgrown **Cishi Pagoda** (慈氏塔; Cí Shì Tǎ; Baota Xiang), off Dongting Nanlu, sprouts a healthy crop of saplings whose roots aim to dislodge as many bricks as possible. Towering from within a courtyard ringed by small family homes and washing hanging out to dry, the pagoda is shrieking out for preservation. There is no access up into the interior of the pagoda itself.

Yuèyáng borders the 3900-sq-km **Dòngtíng Lake** (洞庭湖; Dòngtíng Hú), China's second-largest body of fresh water. Among the several islands in the lake, the most famous is **Junshan Island** (君山岛; Jūnshān Dǎo; admission Y40), where the legendary *yínzhēn chá* (silver needle tea) is grown. Added to hot water, the tea is supposed to remain on the surface, sticking up like tiny needles.

The island is also known for its late-spring or early-summer dragon-boat races, held since ancient times. Trails lined with pavilions cover the island.

Boats (Y40, 45 minutes) leave when full from the Yueyang Tower Ferry Dock (Yuèyáng Lóu Lúnchuán Kèyùnzhàn; ☎ 831 7487), north of the Yueyang Tower, between 8am and 3pm or 4pm. They also operate during similar hours from the dock by the south entrance to the Yueyang Tower.

Sleeping

Xuělián Bīnguǎn (☎ 832 1633; Dongting Beilu; 洞庭北路; s/d/tr Y105/125/135; 🖭) Smart and well looked after, the twins and doubles at this popular and busy hotel near the Yueyang Tower are decent, spacious and clean, and there's a large restaurant attached. From the train station, take bus 22 to the Yueyang Tower.

Yúnmèng Bīnguǎn (☎ 822 1115; fax 822 1115; 25 Yunmeng Lu; 云梦路25号; d Y318; 🔀) Offering good discounts, this three-star hotel has clean and tidy doubles with bathrooms tucked away behind its uninviting exterior. The recommended restaurant serves up a variety of local dishes.

Eating

Yuèyáng cuisine is recognisable for its liberal usage of starch and oil in many dishes. There are good fish and seafood restaurants, particularly on Dongting Beilu, which also has cheap places where you can buy dumplings, noodles and breakfast; food stalls and small restaurants are near Nanyuepo Dock.

Getting There & Away

Yuèyáng is on the main Guǎngzhōu–Běijīng railway line, with trains to Wǔhàn (Y17 to Y33, four hours), Chángshā (Y12 to Y24, 1½ to two hours) and Guǎngzhōu (12 hours). The train station is on Zhanqian Lu, north of Baling Lu.

Buses run to Chángshā (Y36 to Y55, two hours, every 30 minutes from 7am to 6pm), Nánchāng (Y98, nine hours, once daily) and Hànkǒu (Y55, three hours, twice daily) from the Yueyang long-distance bus station (Yuèyáng qìchēzhàn), opposite the humungous Wal Mart on Baling Lu (not far from the train station). Buses to Yíchāng (Y75, seven hours, twice daily) and Zhāngjiājiè (Y115, once daily) leave from the Dongting bus station (Dòngtíng chēzhàn). Buses to Chángshā (Y30) also depart when full from the train station forecourt.

HÉNG SHĀN 衡山
☎ 0734

Around 120km south of Chángshā, **Héng Shān** (☎ 566 2571; admission Y100) is also known as Nányuè (Southern Peak), the name given to the village that marks the start of the climb. The southernmost of China's five Taoist mountains, kings and emperors once came here to hunt and make sacrifices to heaven and earth.

Sights & Activities

Located in Nányuè, the attractive **Nanyue Temple** (南岳大庙; Nányuè Dàmiào; ☎ 566 2353;

admission Y20; ☯ 7am-7pm) dates from the Tang dynasty and was rebuilt during the Qing dynasty. Take note of the column supports, one for each of the mountains in the range, purportedly.

To reach Héng Shān, follow Dengshan Lu north of Nanyue Temple until it curves to your right. Hiking on the paved road or marked paths to **Wishing Harmony Peak** (祝融峰; Zhùróng Fēng), the mountain's highest point, takes four hours and another four hours to descend, although visiting the monasteries, temples, villas and gardens on the mountain takes longer. Minibuses run to the summit for Y12 or there's a cable car (up/down Y30/25) that starts midway on the mountain and goes nearly to the top.

Wishing Harmony Palace (祝融殿; Zhùróng Diàn), built during the Ming dynasty, is the resting place of Zhu Rong, an official 'in charge of fire' during one of China's early periods. Zhu Rong used to hunt on Héng Shān, so Taoists selected the mountain to represent fire, one of the five primordial elements of Chinese philosophy.

Plentiful cheap accommodation can be found along Dengshan Lu and Zhurong Lu. The cheapest option is to find a bed (typically around Y35) above a restaurant along Dengshan Lu. If you want to stay overnight on the mountain, further hotels can be found midway up the mountain as well as on the summit.

Getting There & Away

From the archway on Bei Jie, turn right and the long-distance bus station is a few minutes' walk across the street on your left, where buses run to Chángshā (Y30, two to three hours). Arriving buses may drop you at Dengshan Lu. Trains from Chángshā (Y22, two hours) are an option, but they're slower than buses on the new expressways and require switching to a minibus for a half-hour ride from the railhead.

SHĀN: HILL, MOUNTAIN

This character can be seen either as a mountain range with three peaks or as a mountain in its own right, with its peak in the middle. Either way, it is one of the simplest to remember!

HUÁIHUÀ 怀化

☎ 0745 / pop 127,000

A town built around a railway junction in western Húnán, Huáihuà is useful as a transit point to Fènghuáng (p512) and Hóngjiāng (right), and as a rail conduit to Zhāngjiājiè (p515) or Liǔzhōu.

Information

Bank of China (中国银行; Zhōngguó Yínháng; ☎ 223 4309; 18 Yingfeng Xilu) Near the train station.

China Post (邮局; yóujú; cnr Renmin Nanlu & Hezhou Beilu) Next to KFC.

Internet Café (wǎngbā; either side of the Huaihua Great Hotel on Hezhou Beilu, south of train station; per hr Y2; ⏲ 24hr) There are many other internet cafés just south of the train station.

Sleeping

Huaihua Great Hotel (怀化大酒店; Huáihuà Dàjiǔdiàn; ☎ 226 9888; 18 Hezhou Beilu; 鹤州北路18号; s/d Y168/188; ⚇) A reasonably comfortable three-star hotel with a sparkling foyer, semiprofessional staff and clean, serviceable rooms. Located just south of the train station.

Tianfu Hotel (天副饭店; Tiānfù Fàndiàn; 226 2988; fax 226 4146; 30 Huochezhan Kou; 火车站口30号; s/d/tr Y148/198/248; ⚇) By the train station, this usefully located hotel has neat and recently decorated singles with plastic wood floors and clean shower rooms. There's a variety of rooms so check them over first.

Getting There & Away

Huáihuà's Zhijiang Airport is 35km west of town.

Buses to Fènghuáng (Y26, 2½ hours, every hour from 7.30am to 5.30pm), Jíshǒu (Y33, 3½ hours, three daily) and Guìlín (Y92, 12 hours, once daily) depart from the west bus station (qìchē xīzhàn) on Zhijiang Lu (芷江路). Buses to Hóngjiāng (Y15, 80 minutes, every 40 minutes) depart from the south bus station (qìchē nánzhàn) on Hongxing Nanlu (红星南路), south of town. Bus 19 travels between the train station and the south bus station.

Běijīng–Kūnmíng, Chéngdū–Guǎngzhōu and Shànghǎi–Chóngqìng express trains run via Huáihuà. Ticket prices include Chángshā (Y112, eight hours), Jíshǒu (hard seat Y6 to Y16, two hours), Zhāngjiājiè (hard seat Y15 to Y37, four to 5½ hours) and Yíchāng (hard seat Y31 to Y75). You can also catch a train to Sānjiāng (5½ hours) in northern Guǎngxī.

Taxis start at Y4.

HÓNGJIĀNG OLD TOWN 洪江古商城

☎ 0745

Located 55km south of Huáihuà, Hóngjiāng is a historic town situated at the confluence of the Yuan (沅江) and Wu (Wǔ Shuǐ; 舞水) rivers. Dating back to the Northern Song, much of the city is now modern and developed, but the remarkable Old Town (Hóngjiāng Gǔshāngchéng) recalls the town's Qing-dynasty heyday as a prospering financial centre. The riverine journey by bus to Hóngjiāng alongside the Yuan River is gorgeous; look out for the magnificent white hilltop pagoda sprouting branches that faces you as you cross south over the river.

Sights & Activities

Exploring the **old town** – an activity that can be completed in half a day – is the reason to visit Hóngjiāng. Essentially enclosed within Xinmin Lu (新民路), Yuanjiang Lu (沅江路) and Xiongxi Lu (雄溪路) – the latter becoming Xingfu Lu (幸福路) – the old town undulates in a delightfully higgledy-piggledy and occasionally steep maze of narrow stone flagged alleys and lanes. Its buildings – old banks, merchant businesses and shrines, in the main – have been partially restored, with renovation work continuing. You can poke your head through doorways to admire the interiors, which are often naturally lit up by light wells (天井; tiānjīng), rectangular apertures in the roof that admit both sunshine and rain.

It's easy to get lost in this labyrinth, so meandering in the lanes is inevitable. Notable buildings include the **Taiping Temple** (太平宫; Tàipíng Gōng), built in 1723 and largely destroyed during the Cultural Revolution. Pop in and mourn among the ruins of the main hall and admire the ornamental carvings on the front gate (ménfáng). Other buildings of interest include the sadly decaying **Jífāduizhàn** (吉发堆栈), which dates from 1855, and the **Money God Hall** (财神殿; Cáishén Diàn) on Caishen Lane (财神巷; Caishen Xiang), which dates back to 1683. Occasional slogans from the Cultural Revolution still appear, for example above the door of the old **Newspaper Office** (报馆旧址; Bàoguǎn Jiùzhǐ). Another noteworthy temple is the **Big Buddha Temple** (大佛寺; Dàfó Sì) housing a substantial statue of Sakyamuni and an effigy of a 1000-armed Guanyin.

Sleeping & Eating

A string of restaurants line the riverbank next to Hong Bridge alongside the Wu River selling river food dishes and local dishes.

Qiáotóu Bīnguǎn (桥头宾馆; ☎ 763 4848; 4 Xinmin Lu; 新民路4号; s/d without air-con Y28/48, d with air-con & toilet Y90; ❄) The pricier double rooms are simple and clean with plastic wood floors, shower and squat loo. It's at the base of Xinmin Lu near the Hong Bridge (洪桥; Hóng Qiáo).

Hongjiang Hotel (洪江大酒店; Hóngjiāng Dàjiǔdiàn; ☎ 766 2999; Xinmin Lu; 新民路; s/d Y168/188; ❄) Towering two-star hotel next to the Bank of China on the left-hand side as you walk up Xinmin Lu. Rooms are comfortable enough and you can get into the old town through an alley on the other side of Xinmin Lu. Good discounts.

Getting There & Away

Hóngjiāng old town should not be confused with Hongjiang City (洪江市; Hóngjiāng Shì), the town on the railway to the west. Buses from Huáihuà to Hóngjiāng old town (Y15, 80 minutes, every 40 minutes) depart from Huáihuà's south bus station between 6.50am and 6pm. Buses returning to Huáihuà (Y15, 80 minutes, every hour) leave from the bus station on Yuanjiang Lu, opposite the main entrance to the old town in Hóngjiāng.

JÍSHǑU 吉首

☎ 0743 / pop 103,624

The town of Jíshǒu has little to divert travellers, but it's the gateway to Déhāng (right), a Miao village embedded in picturesque karst scenery to the north of town. It's also a transit point to the historic riverside town of Fènghuáng (p512).

Information

Bank of China (中国银行; Zhōngguó Yínháng; 30 Renmin Beilu) Can change money.

Jinxin Internet Café (金鑫网吧; Jīnxīn Wǎngbā; per hr Y2; ☎ 24hr) On the southeast corner of the train station concourse.

Xiangxi Tourist Service Center (湘西州游客服务中心; Xiāngxī Zhōu Yóukè Fúwù Zhōngxīn; ☎ 823 3333) On the southwest corner of the train station concourse.

Sleeping

Báiyún Bīnguǎn (白云宾馆; ☎ 873 0168; 8 Renmin Beilu; 人民北路8号; d/ste Y188/388; ❄) This four-storey hotel is handily located a short walk

south of the train station. Rooms are smart with wood flooring and clean, bright shower rooms, but there's no lift.

Getting There & Away

Jíshǒu's **train station** (☎ 214 0710) has connections to numerous destinations, including Huáihuà (hard seat Y17), Chángshā (hard seat Y82), Zhāngjiājiè (hard seat Y22), Yíchāng (hard seat Y31) and Xiāngfán (hard seat Y41).

Buses to Déhāng (Y6, 50 minutes, every 20 minutes from 6.40am to 7pm) depart from in front of the train station; buses to Fènghuáng (Y12, one hour, every 20 minutes) leave from the **long-distance bus station** (☎ 137 879 035 58) on Wuling Donglu.

DÉHĀNG 德夯

In a seductive riverine setting overlooked by towering, other-worldly karst peaks, the Miao hamlet of **Déhāng** (admission Y60) to the northwest of Jíshǒu in western Húnán province offers a tantalising spectrum of treks into picturesque countryside. Rising into columns, splinters and huge foreheads of stone, the local karst geology climbs over verdant valleys layered with terraced fields and flushed by clear streams. Side-stepping the bovine traffic and the occasional cowpat could be the only thing distracting your eyes from the gorgeous scenery.

The village itself has been partially dolled up for domestic tourism, but on its fringes the feeling survives of a pleasant riverside minority Miao village where wood-constructed and highly affordable hotels turn Déhāng into an inexpensive and alluring retreat. Avoid the inauthentic, tourist-crowd-oriented Déhāng Miáozhài (德夯苗寨) hub where evening shows are staged, and keep to the narrow lanes and riverside views of the old village leading to the arched **Jielong Bridge** (接龙桥; Jiēlóng Qiáo), where old folk decked out in blue-clothed Miao outfits and bamboo baskets cluster and cows and water buffalo wander quietly around chewing the cud. Occasional Maoist slogans from the Cultural Revolution make an appearance, old men thread together baskets from strips of bamboo and Miao weavers sit hunched over mills, creating colourful cloth for attractive cotton jackets (Y80).

Walks

Surplus to its charming village views, Déhāng is itself located within a huge 164-sq-km

HÚNÁN

geological park where some delightful treks thread into the hills. Try to time your walks for the early morning or late afternoon, when visitor numbers are down. The beautiful **Nine Dragon Stream Scenic Area** (九龙溪景区; Jiǔlóngxī Jǐngqū) winds along a stream out of the village, past Miao peasants labouring in the terraced fields, over a wooden bridge, alongside fields croaking with toads and into an astonishing landscape of peaks blotched with green and valleys carpeted with lush fields. The **Nine Dragon Waterfall** (admission Y10) is so-so, but continue to the end of the trail for the stunning **Liusha Waterfall** (Liusha Pubu; admission free) which descends in fronds of spray onto rocks above a green pool at its foot. The waterfall is particularly impressive after the rain. Climb the steps behind the waterfall for stirring views through the curtains of water. The return walk to the Liusha Waterfall takes about two hours.

Cross the bridge over the river to visit the 2.6km-long **Yuquanxi Scenic Area** (玉泉溪景区; Yùquánxī Jǐngqū), where you follow a path along a valley by the Yuquan Stream, past haystacks (consisting of stout wooden poles sunk into the ground onto which are tossed clumps of hay) and gorgeous belts of layered terraced fields. Walk along the valley for a good 1.5km before the path ducks into a small gorge where you will cross the river at several points and continue on into a thick profusion of green. Cross the **Jade Fountain Gate** (玉泉门; Yùquán Mén) and follow the path to the waterfall which spills down in a single thread of water. If you have the energy, climb the steps up to the **Tianwen Platform** (天问台; Tiānwèn Tái), where fabulous views span out through the gorge above the waterfall and a few simple Miao homesteads find a perch. Note how a whole new series of terraced slopes commence at this altitude.

Another pleasant walk can be made by crossing the river over Jielong Bridge and climbing up the stone-flagged steps through the bamboo for views over the village.

Sleeping & Eating

Several simple inns (客栈; kèzhàn) can be found in the village, overlooking the square, stuffed down alleyways or picturesquely suspended over the river. Travellers aiming for more midrange comfort can stay overnight in Jíshǒu (p511).

Jielongqiao Inn (接龙桥客栈; Jiēlóngqiáo Kèzhàn; ☎ 135 174 309 15; s/tw Y30/40) This small, all-wood inn has a handful of singles and doubles (one of which still reeked of drying varnish) suspended above the river next to the Jielong Bridge. It's inauthentic and sticks out like a sore thumb, but the positioning is excellent and the clean, comfortable rooms come with fan, TV and water bottle. Shower and toilet are communal, down in the damp basement.

Fengyuqiao Inn (风雨桥客栈; Fēngyǔqiáo Kèzhàn; ☎ 135 743 090 26; dm/d Y20/40) Another riverside alternative, over the bridge from the square and at the start of the Yuquanxi Scenic Area trail.

Most inns around the village have small restaurants serving local dishes, and hawkers proffer skewers of grilled fish (táohuāyú; Y1) and crab kebabs (Y10) to travellers from the square and surrounding alleys. Round off snacking with Miao hand-rolled cigars (Y3).

Getting There & Away

The best way to reach Déhāng is to travel via Jíshǒu, a railway town to the south of the village. Regular buses to Déhāng (Y6, 50 minutes) leave from outside Jíshǒu's train station, arriving at and departing (every 20 minutes) from the square/parking lot in Déhāng.

FÈNGHUÁNG 凤凰
☎ 0743
In a round-the-clock siege from Chinese tourists – the Taiping of the modern age – this fascinating riverside town of ancient city walls and gate towers, houses on stilts overlooking the river and hoary temples dotted about the old town can easily fill a couple of days. Home to a lively population of the Miao (苗) and Tujia (土家) minorities, Fènghuáng's architectural legacy shows distressing signs of neglect, so get to see it before it crumbles away under a combined onslaught of disrepair and over-development aimed at luring marauding tour groups.

Orientation

Fènghuáng's old town (凤凰古城; Fènghuáng Gǔchéng) lies on either side of the Tuo River (Tuó Jiāng). The southernmost section of the old town is largely bounded by Jianshe Lu and Nanhua Lu but also extends along Huilong Ge, in the east by the river; the northern part of town is framed by the long curve of Jiang-

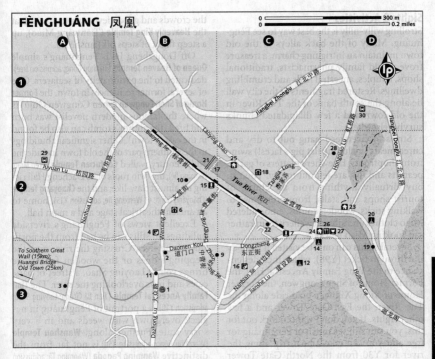

FÈNGHUÁNG 凤凰

SLEEPING (page 513 map)

bei Zhonglu. Both sections are connected by an assortment of bridges: the covered Hong Qiao Bridge, a vehicular bridge, a wooden footbridge and twin rows of stepping stones (跳岩; *tiàoyán*).

Information
Note that no banks can exchange foreign currency in Fènghuáng, so change money

before you arrive. The nearest bank that can exchange money is in Jíshǒu.

Dianxin Internet Café (Diànxīn Wǎngbā; Wenhua Lu; per hr Y2; 8am-midnight) Just south of Fucheng Gate.

Tourism Administrative Bureau of Fenghuang (322 9364; cnr Daomen Kou & Wenxing Jie) It's alongside Culture Square.

Zhongxi Pharmacy (Zhōngxī Yàodiàn; Nanhua Lu, near cnr with Jianshe Lu; 8am-10pm)

Sights & Activities

Strolling willy-nilly is the best way to see Fènghuáng. Many of the back alleys in the old town maintain an intriguing charm, a treasure trove of old family pharmacists, traditional shops, temples, ancestral halls and crumbling dwellings. Restored fragments of the city wall lie along the south bank of the Tuo River in the old town and a few dilapidated chunks survive elsewhere.

Strips of riverweed hang out to dry and cured meats (including flat pig's faces!) swing from shopfronts. Elsewhere platters of garlic, peanuts and fish are left out to dry. You can buy virtually anything from the clutter of tourist shops and stalls, from crossbows to walking sticks, wooden combs, embroidered Miao clothes and silver jewellery from rather sad-looking Miao hawkers.

Several sights can only be visited if you buy the through ticket (Y98), which includes entrance to the Yang Family Ancestral Hall, the Former Home of Shen Congwen, the Former Home of Xiong Xiling, a boat ride along the Tuo River, the East Gate Tower and a few other sights. If you don't want to fork out for this, you can still see much of Fènghuáng for free and you can take a boat trip along the river for Y30 from the North Gate Tower (atmospheric night trips included). Sights are generally all open from 8am to 5.30pm.

Wander along Fènghuáng's restored salmon-coloured **city wall** (chéngqiáng) with its defensive aspect along the southern bank of the Tuo River. Halfway along its length, the **North Gate Tower** (Běimén Chénglóu) is in a tragic state of neglect, scratched with names and downtrodden, but it remains a magnificent structure. While perusing this area, look up at the distinctive roof ridges on buildings above – many adorned with carvings of creatures and fish – which are far better preserved than much at ground level.

Further along the wall you will come to the **Yang Family Ancestral Hall** (Yáng Jiā Cítáng), its exterior still decorated with Maoist slogans from the Cultural Revolution.

To the east is the **East Gate Tower** (Dōngmén Chénglóu), a Qing-dynasty twin-eaved tower dating from 1715. Spanning the river is the magnificent covered **Hong Bridge** (Hóng Qiáo; admission free), from the east of which runs Huilong Ge, a narrow alley of shops, hotels, restaurants and the small Jiangxin Buddhist Temple (江心禅寺; Jiāngxīn Chánsì). A welcome respite from the crowds and good views over town await at the **Heavenly King Temple** (Tiānwáng Miào), up a steep flight of steps off Jianshe Lu.

Off Dongzheng Jie is Fènghuáng's simple **Queen of Heaven Temple** (Tiānhòu Gōng; admission free), dedicated to the parton deity of seafarers. One of several former residences in town, the **Former Home of Shen Congwen** (Shěn Cóngwén Gùjū) is where the famous modern novelist was born and bred (the author's tomb can also be found in the east of town). Other significant buildings in the southern part of the old town include the 18th-century walled **Confucian Temple** (Wén Miào; Wenxing Jie), the twin roofs of its Dacheng Hall rising up almost claw-like; and the **Chaoyang Temple** (Cháoyáng Gōng; 41 Wenxing Jie; admission Y15), home to an ancient theatrical stage and a main hall.

Excellent views of Fènghuáng's riverside buildings on stilts can be had from the north side of the river. Crossing the river over the stepping stones or the wooden footbridge brings you to Laoying Shao, a street of bars, cafés and inns overlooking the river. The **Tian Family Ancestral Temple** (Tián Jiā Cítáng; Laoying Shao; admission Y10) is a portrait of Fènghuáng in neglect: overgrown with weeds and in a very sorry state. Further along, **Wanshou Temple** (Wànshòu Gōng; admission Y50) is not far from the distinctive **Wanming Pagoda** (Wànmíng Tǎ; admission free), erected right on the riverbank.

After sundown, merry tourists gather at the stepping stones across the Tuo River by the North Gate Tower to send flotillas of lighted candles downstream aboard paper flowers. They travel a short distance before either setting fire to their combustible vessels or being doused by the river water.

The **Southern Great Wall** (Nánfāng Chángchéng; admission Y45), a Ming-dynasty construction 13km outside town, can be reached by bus from Fènghuáng, but it doesn't compare with the bastion that fortified north China. Also outside town is **Huangsi Bridge Old Town** (黄丝桥古城; Huángsī Qiáo Gǔchéng; admission Y20), a village similar in character to Fènghuáng.

Sleeping, Eating & Drinking

Inns (客栈; kèzhàn) can be found everywhere in Fènghuáng and provide a cheap and atmospheric means of sampling the village's pleasant nocturnal mien. Note that most inns are quite rudimentary, coming with squat toilets, but are comfortable enough. Prices listed are for the slack season; during the peak holiday season rates can double or even triple.

Fenghuang International Youth Hostel (Fènghuáng Guójì Qīngnián Lǔguǎn; ☎ 326 0546; 11 Shawan; 沙湾 11号; dm/d Y15/50) Well located on the north side of the Tuo River, next to East Pass Gate and not far from the Wanshou Temple, with adequate six- and eight-bed dorm rooms. Air-con is Y20 extra.

Hóngqiáo Biān Kèzhàn (☎ 322 9609; 1 Huilong Ge; 回龙阁1号; d Y60) Clean double rooms (only four rooms in all) with shower and water heater and a romantic position overlooking the river and Hong Bridge. If it's full, try one of the other inns along this road.

Yǒnghóng Kèzhàn (☎ 135 743 064 53; 37 Laoying Shao; 老营哨37号; d Y60) Tidy doubles with balcony and shower, and superb river views; there's a downstairs restaurant.

Lóuwàilóu (☎ 350 2498; 3 Huilong Ge; 回龙阁3号) Alongside the Hóngqiáo Biān Kèzhàn, this restaurant overlooking the river combines fish dishes with great views.

Be on the lookout for street vendors selling a cornucopia of snacks, from crab, fish or potato kebabs and snails to cooling bowls of *liángfěn* (bean-starch jelly); also look for shops selling Miao wines and spirits, and the locally favoured ginger sweets (*jiāngtáng*).

Laoying Shao, a long and narrow street running along the north side of the river, is full of small, rather samey, bars with river views. Other bars can be found along Huilong Ge on the other side of the river, including the **Nomad Bar** (Liúlàngzhě Jiǔbā; ☎ 322 8924; 7 Huilong Ge).

Getting There & Away

Regular buses to and from Jíshǒu (Y12, one hour) depart from and arrive at the **bus station** (qìchē zhàn; Juyuan Lu) in the new part of town. Buses to Huáihuà (Y25, two hours, every 20 minutes) depart from the **Minsuyuan bus station** (Mínsúyuán Tíngchēchǎng; Jiangbei Donglu) in the north of town.

Getting Around

Taxis start at Y2. Bikes (Y20, deposit Y200) can be rented from the shop on Hongqiao Lu and at other outlets, but there is little need to pedal about town.

WŬLÍNGYUÁN & ZHĀNGJIĀJIÈ
武陵源、张家界
☎ 0744

Rising sublimely from the misty subtropical forest of northwest Húnán are 243 peaks surrounded by over 3000 karst upthrusts, a con-

centration not seen elsewhere in the world. The picture is completed by waterfalls, limestone caves (including Asia's largest chamber) and rivers suitable for organised rafting trips. Nearly two dozen rare species of flora and fauna call the region home and botanists delight in the 3000-odd plant species within the park. Even amateur wildlife spotters may get a gander at a clouded leopard or a pangolin.

Known as the **Wulingyuan Scenic Area** (Wǔlíngyuán Fēngjǐngqū; www.zhangjiajie.com.cn), the region encompasses the localities of Zhāngjiājiè, Tiānzǐshān and Suǒxīyù. Zhāngjiājiè is the best known, and many Chinese refer to this area by that name. Recognised by Unesco in 1990 as a World Heritage Site, Wǔlíngyuán is home to three minority peoples: Tujia, Miao and Bai.

Several towns give access to Wǔlíngyuán, but the most popular ones are Zhangjiajie city (Zhāngjiājiè *shì*) and Zhangjiajie village (Zhāngjiājiè *cūn*). The city is near the railway line, while the village is situated nearly 600m above sea level in the Wǔlíng foothills, surrounded by sheer cliffs and vertical rock outcrops.

A staggering fee of Y245 (students Y165), good for two days with extension, plus an insurance fee of Y3, must be paid at the Zhāngjiājiè forest reserve's main entrance just past the village. Admission to other sights within the park can be additional. Chinese maps showing walking trails (only some of them with sites marked in English) are on sale in Zhangjiajie city and village.

Information

Take money with you as the Agricultural Bank of China in Zhangjiajie village does not change money.

Bank of China (中国银行; Zhōngguó Yínháng; 1 Xinmatou Jie, Zhāngjiājiè City) Currency exchange.

Chenlin Internet Cafe (晨琳网吧; Chénlín Wǎngbā; per hr Y2; ☯ 8am-6am) It's 150m north of the Mínsú Shānzhuāng in Zhangjiajie village.

Forest Park First Aid Centre (☎ 571 8819)

Post office (邮局; yóujú) Almost next door to Chenlin Internet Cafe in Zhangjiajie village.

Zhangjiajie CITS (www.zjjtrip.net)

Sights & Activities

The highest area closest to Zhangjiajie village is **Huángshízhài** (黄石寨), and at 1048m it's a two-hour hike up 3878 stone steps (cable car up/down Y52/42).

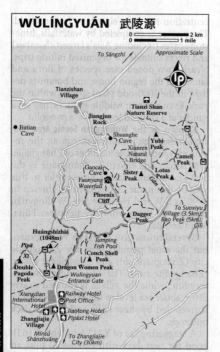

WŬLÍNGYUÁN 武陵源

In the northern section of the reserve, **Tianzi Peak** (天子山; Tiānzǐ Shān) is another popular expedition, also serviced by cable car (up/down Y48/38). As is the custom, every rock, crag and gully has been given a fanciful name.

Organised tours to the park and **Jiutian Cave** (九天洞; Jiŭtiān Dòng; admission Y64) often include a **rafting trip** (piāolǚ), or you can join a tour and just do the rafting trip. While good whitewater rafting trips are possible northwest of Zhāngjiājiè near the Húběi border, you'll have to make special arrangements for the equipment and transport.

Most rivers are pretty tame, so don't expect great thrills, but the scenery is fantastic. The actual rafting usually lasts about two hours, with about the same amount of time taken up in travel to the launch area.

You can join tours or arrange your own through hotels in Zhāngjiājiè or at a travel agency in Zhangjiajie city. The Dongsheng Travel Agency (东升旅行社; Dōngshēng Lǚxíngshè; ☎ 828 6258; 36 Jiefang Lu) offers good rates (Y180 to Y250 per person) for group tours. CITS (中国国际旅行社; Zhōngguó Guójì Lǚxíngshè; ☎ 822

7111; 37 Jiefang Lu) has English speakers and offers rafting tours from Y300 per person.

Sleeping

Try to stay in Zhangjiajie village, where rooms are cheaper and the scenery more pleasant, unless you miss the last bus, in which case you can find a few budget-range places near the bus station.

ZHANGJIAJIE TOWN

Dragon International Hotel (祥龙国际酒店; Xiánglóng Guójì Jiŭdiàn; ☎ 822 6888; fax 822 2935; 46 Jiefang Lu; 解放路46号; tw in older/newer wing Y660/880, plus 15% service charge; ⚂) Self-proclaimed four-star establishment with serviceable rooms.

ZHANGJIAJIE VILLAGE

Most places here accept foreigners; some travellers have also stayed with local families within the park, but don't expect it. For those hiking overnight, there are places to stay inside the park along the popular trail routes. Local visitors often do a two- to three-day circuit hike, going in at Zhangjiajie village and hiking or busing in to villages within the park boundaries such as Tiānzǐshān and Suŏxīyù, which each have a bewildering choice of hotels and hostels. All of the following hotels are on the main road.

Railway Hotel (铁路宾馆; Tiělù Bīnguǎn; ☎ 571 2272; fax 571 2271; d Y150) This place opposite the Zhangjiajie Hotel has OK, simple rooms that can be garnered for Y80 during slack periods.

Mínsú Shānzhuāng (民俗山庄; ☎ 571 9188; fax 571 2516; s/d/tr Y180/288/388; ⚂) Some rooms have balconies at this two-star option but generally things are dirty and tacky with old and worn furnishings and dodgy hygiene. Triples come with bath and doubles with shower.

Jiaotong Hotel (交通宾馆; Jiāotōng Bīnguǎn; ☎ 571 8188; s/d Y258/268) Quietly parked away in a courtyard car park north of the Pipaxi Hotel, this place has cleanish rooms and good discounts that bring singles down to Y120.

Pipaxi Hotel (琵琶溪宾馆; Pípáxī Bīnguǎn; ☎ 571 8888; www.pipaxi-hotel.com; d Y548-648) Well worth it as it's tucked away quietly out of the action. Standard rooms are bright and clean with good bathrooms and balcony; VIP rooms are lovely and large. Redecorated in 2004; 20% discounts are the norm.

Xiangdian International Hotel (湘电国际大酒店; Xiāngdiàn Guójì Jiŭdiàn; ☎ 571 2999; www.xiang

hotel.com; s/d Y680/680) Self-billed as a four star hotel, but in reality we are talking a star lower at this acceptable hotel benefiting from professional service, a pleasing location and pleasant water and rock features, decent rooms, a bowling centre and health centre. There are 30% discounts frequently on offer.

Eating
Simple eating houses are scattered around the village.

Getting There & Away
AIR
Zhangjiajie Airport (☎ 825 3177) is 4km southwest of Zhāngjiājiè city and 40km from the park entrance; a taxi should cost around Y100 to the park. More and more flights link Zhāngjiājiè city with the rest of China, but prepare for frequent cancellations. Daily flights include a growing number of cities, including Běijīng (Y1340), Shànghǎi (Y1330), Guǎngzhōu (Y860), Chóngqìng (Y580), Chángshā (Y580) and Xī'ān (Y690).

BUS & MINIBUS
Minibuses to Zhāngjiājiè village (Y8, 40 minutes) pick up passengers at the car park in front of the train station, but they may not leave till full; otherwise, take bus 2 to the **long-distance bus station** (☎ 822 2417; 回龙路; Huilong Lu), where buses leave every 15 minutes to Zhāngjiājiè village (Y8). Buses to Tiānzǐshān (Y10, every hour) also leave from here, as do buses to Chángshā (Y120, 11 hours, twice daily), Fènghuáng (Y47, four hours, 8.30am and 2.30pm), Jíshǒu (YY44, 2½ hours, every hour), Yuèyáng (Y89, seven hours, 8.20am), Wǔhàn (Y151, 5.30pm), and Shànghǎi (Y435, 20 hours, 10.30am) via Héféi and Nánjīng.

TRAIN
The train station is 8km southeast of the city; buy tickets well in advance of travel. Trains run to Chángshā (hard seat Y71, eight hours, twice daily), Běijīng (Y194, 27 hours, daily) and Guǎngzhōu (Y174, 23 hours, twice daily). Trains also run to Yíchāng, Jíshǒu (hard seat Y22) and Huáihuà (hard seat Y15 to Y37, four to 5½ hours).

HÚNÁN

Hong Kong

If Hong Kong was a person, she'd be a difficult woman to understand. She'd be constantly changing, without losing touch with her heritage. She'd be superstitious, but scientific when she wanted to be. She'd love dim sum, and pizza too. She'd be exotic, but familiar; sexy, but never easy; a gambler, but she'd always know the odds. She'd be immaculately dressed, but she'd know how to let her hair down. She'd be all this, a contradiction and a conundrum, but more than anything she'd be a lot of fun to be around.

Hong Kong's complex personality owes something to its Sino-British past, but it's the decade since that has truly built its character. Surviving a partial reintegration with China, a seven-year economic downturn, avian flu and Severe Acute Respiratory Syndrome (SARS) has given Hong Kong a new self-belief. The city is positively booming and for you, the traveller, it's impossible not to catch the vibe.

Hong Kong is expensive, but it also has something for everyone: shopping malls with bargains galore; romantic vistas across Victoria Harbour to one of the world's most impressive skylines; over 10,000 restaurants and dozens of cuisines; and some of Asia's most rocking nightlife.

There are also surprises. Did you know most of Hong Kong is actually green hills and mountains perfect for hiking? Or that many people still burn 'hell money' for their dead ancestors?

Hong Kong's political and economic systems are still significantly different from those of mainland China. Thus, much of the information elsewhere in this book concerning visas, currency, accommodation, international phone calls and so on does not apply to Hong Kong.

HIGHLIGHTS

- Ride the historic **Peak Tram** (p523), enjoy the view from Victoria Peak and walk back down
- Soak up the glittering skyline from the **Star Ferry** (p563) as it crosses Victoria Harbour
- Haggle like a Hong Konger in the buzzing **Temple St night market** (p535)
- Take a hike across car-free **Lamma Island** (p538) and reward yourself with a seafood lunch
- Feast in **SoHo** (p545) and follow it up with a few drinks in **Lan Kwai Fong** (p557)

- AREA CODE: ☎852   ■ POPULATION: 7 MILLION   ■ www.discoverhongkong.com

HISTORY

Hong Kong was very much a far-flung outpost of the Chinese empire until European traders started importing opium into the country. The British, with a virtually inexhaustible supply from the poppy fields of Bengal, developed the trade aggressively and by the start of the 19th century this 'foreign mud' formed the basis of most of their transactions with China.

China's attempts to stamp out the opium trade, including confiscating and destroying one huge shipment, gave the British the pretext they needed for military action. Two gunboats were sent in and promptly destroyed a Chinese fleet of 29 ships. A British naval landing party hoisted the Union flag on Hong Kong Island in 1841, and the Treaty of Nanking, which brought an end to the so-called First Opium War, ceded the island to the British crown 'in perpetuity'.

At the end of the Second Opium War in 1860, Britain took possession of the Kowloon Peninsula; in July 1898 a 99-year lease was granted for the New Territories.

Through the 20th century Hong Kong grew in fits and starts. Regular political crises in China led to intermittent waves of refugees arriving in Hong Kong. Infrastructure for transport and trade was steadily improved and expats came and went – then like now many were as enamoured with the vibrant colony's social life as much as anything else.

The Japanese army crashed the party in 1941 and by the end of the war Hong Kong's population had fallen from 1.6 million to 610,000. But trouble in China was again to prove instrumental in Hong Kong's development. First, refugees from the communist victory in 1949 swelled the population of Hong Kong to beyond 2 million. Then the Korean War led to a UN trade embargo on China. In response, Hong Kong reinvented itself as one of the world's most dynamic manufacturing and financial services centres.

Hong Kongers proved expert at making money and wise enough to invest some of it in improving the city. Housing improved with the development of high-rise 'New Towns', while the superefficient Mass Transit Railway (MTR, see p564) was built to help get everyone around.

But with so much at stake the 1997 question was worrying Hong Kongers. In 1984 it was agreed China would take over the entire territory from Britain in 1997, but what would become the Special Administrative Region (SAR) of Hong Kong would retain its free-market economy as well as its social and legal systems for 50 years. China called it 'One country, two systems'.

On 1 July 1997, in pouring rain outside the Hong Kong Convention & Exhibition Centre (p534), the British era ended.

In the years that followed, Hong Kong weathered several major storms, from the Asian economic crisis of 1997 to the outbreak of SARS. Add to this a seven-year economic downturn spurred by the sudden puncturing of Hong Kong's property bubble and general mistrust of the government, and by 2003 Hong Kong was almost as low as anyone could remember. Help came from an unlikely source.

Despite a huge protest against the Hong Kong government's attempt to ram through Běijīng-inspired antisubversion legislation, China acted to help Hong Kong's flagging economy by sharply increasing the number of mainland tourists allowed to visit the city. Coinciding with the first signs of a homegrown recovery, mainland tourists arrived and started spending up big.

By early 2006 Hong Kong's stock market was booming, unemployment was low and Sir Donald Tsang was making a better fist of leading the government than his oft-criticised predecessor, Tung Chee Hwa. The downside is the nonprogress towards a directly elected leadership, an issue that looks like being around for some time to come.

CLIMATE

Hong Kong rarely gets especially cold, but it would be worth packing something at least a little bit warm between November and March. Between May and mid-September temperatures in the mid-30s combined with stifling humidity can turn you into a walking sweat machine. This time is also the wettest, accounting for about 80% of the annual rainfall – partly due to regular typhoons.

Ultimately, the best time to visit Hong Kong is between mid-September and February. At any time of the year pollution can be diabolical, most of it pouring across the border from the coal-powered factories of Guǎngdōng, many of them Hong Kong owned.

LANGUAGE

Almost 95% of Hong Kongers are Cantonese-speaking Chinese, though Mandarin is increasingly used. Visitors should have few problems, however, because English is widely spoken and the city's excellent street signs are bilingual. Written Cantonese uses traditional Chinese characters, which not surprisingly are more complicated than the simplified Chinese used on the mainland.

ORIENTATION

Hong Kong's ever-growing 1103 sq km of territory is divided into four main areas: Hong Kong Island, Kowloon, the New Territories and the Outlying Islands.

Hong Kong Island, particularly Central on the northern side, is the economic heart of the colony but comprises only 7% of the total land mass. Kowloon is the densely populated peninsula to the north, the southern tip of which is Tsim Sha Tsui, with lots of hotels, guesthouses and tourist-oriented shops. The New Territories, which officially encompass the 234 outlying islands, occupy more than 88% of Hong Kong's land area.

Hong Kong International Airport, located off Lantau Island about 20km northwest of Central, is easily reached by the Airport Express rail line (p562). The main train station is at Hung Hom, though the KCR East rail line (p564) this services has recently been extended to Tsim Sha Tsui East, making connections much easier. There are several important bus stations, usually located near MTR stations; Central's is situated below the Exchange Sq complex on Connaught Rd.

Maps

Hong Kong is awash with free maps. The *Hong Kong Map*, distributed by the Hong Kong Tourism Board (HKTB), is enough for most travellers. It covers the northern coast of Hong Kong Island from Sheung Wan to Causeway Bay as well as part of the Kowloon Peninsula and has inset maps of Aberdeen, Stanley, Hung Hom, Sha Tin and Tsuen Wan. Lonely Planet also has a *Hong Kong City Map*.

INFORMATION

The **Hong Kong Museums Pass** (7 days $30, 6 months adult/student & senior $50/25, 1yr adult/student & senior $100/50) allows multiple entries to six of Hong Kong's better museums. It's available from HKTB outlets (p522).

Bookshops

Hong Kong is one of the best places to buy books in Asia.

Cosmos Books (Map pp530–1; ☎ 2866 1677; basement & 1st fl, 30 Johnston Rd, Wan Chai; ⊙ 10am-8pm)

Dymocks (Map pp526–7; ☎ 2117 0360; Shop 2007-2011, 2nd fl, IFC Mall, 1 Harbour View St, Central; ⊙ 8.30am-9.30pm Mon-Sat, 9am-9pm Sun)

Page One (Map pp530–1; ☎ 2506 0381; Shop 922, 9th fl, Times Square, 1 Matheson St, Causeway Bay; ⊙ 10.30am-10pm Mon-Thu, to 10.30pm Fri-Sun)

Swindon Books (Map p532; ☎ 2366 8001; www.swindonbooks.com; 13-15 Lock Rd, Tsim Sha Tsui; ⊙ 9am-6.30pm Mon-Thu, 9am-7.30pm Fri & Sat, 12.30-6.30pm Sun)

HONG KONG IN ...

One Day

Catch a tram up to **Victoria Peak** (p523) for a good view of the city and enjoy the views on the walk back down, stopping in **SoHo** (p545) for lunch. Ride up to the **Bank of China Tower's** (43rd fl, 1 Garden Rd, Central; ⊙ 8am-6pm Mon-Fri) observation floor for a free look, before dropping into **Pacific Place** (p558) in Admiralty for some shopping and watching the sun go down from the 7th floor of the **Hong Kong Convention & Exhibition Centre** (p534). After dinner, head in to **Lan Kwai Fong** (p557) for happy-hour drinks and dancing.

Two Days

In addition to the above, you could take the **Star Ferry** (p563) to Tsim Sha Tsui and visit the **Art, Space** or **History Museums** (p535), have dim sum at **Wan Loong Court** (p547) in the Kowloon Hotel, then browse along **Nathan Road** (p535) until you're hungry enough for afternoon tea at the **Peninsula Hong Kong** (p543) hotel. After dark, take a wander up to the **Temple St night market** (p535).

Emergency

In an emergency, call ☎ 999 for fire, police or ambulance services.

Internet Access

Hong Kong is so well wired that dedicated internet cafés can be hard to find. Instead, many travellers get online at their hotel or guesthouse, or log on for free at major MTR stations (eg Central and Tsim Sha Tsui), public libraries and any of the dozens of **Pacific Coffee** (www.pacificcoffee .com) outlets, which also have wi-fi.

Central Library (Map pp530-1; ☎ 2921 0503; www .hkpl.gov.hk; 66 Causeway Rd, Causeway Bay; internet free; ☻ 10am-9pm Thu-Tue, 1-9pm Wed)

City Cyberworks (Map p532; Shop 88b, ground fl, Chungking Mansions, 36-44 Nathan Rd, Tsim Sha Tsui; internet per hr $40; ☻ 9.30am-10pm Mon-Sat, to 7pm Sun)

Cyber Clan (Map p532; ☎ 2723 2821; south basement, Golden Crown Court, 66-70 Nathan Rd, Tsim Sha Tsui; internet per hr midnight-noon Mon-Fri $10, noon-midnight Mon-Fri & all day Sat & Sun $13; ☻ 24hr) Minimum one hour plus $40 deposit.

Pacific Coffee Company (Map pp526-7; ☎ 2868 5100; www.pacificcoffee.com; Shop 1022, 1st fl, IFC Mall, 1 Harbour View St, Central; internet free with coffee; ☻ 7am-11pm) A particularly handy branch.

Media

Hong Kong has two local English-language daily newspapers, the *South China Morning Post* and the *Hong Kong Standard*. Asian editions of *USA Today*, the *International Herald Tribune*, the *Financial Times* and the *Wall Street Journal Asia* are printed in Hong Kong. For lifestyle and entertainment news and listings, the excellent *HK Magazine* and *BC Magazine* are available free in bars and restaurants.

Hong Kong has two English-language terrestrial TV stations: TVB Pearl and ATV World. There's a variety of English-language radio stations, including BBC World Service on AM 675.

Medical Services

Medical care is generally of a high standard in Hong Kong, though private hospital care is quite expensive. The general inquiry number for hospitals is ☎ 2300 6555.

The following are hospitals with 24-hour emergency services:

Matilda International (Map pp524-5; ☎ 2849 0700, 24hr hotline 2849 0111; 41 Mt Kellett Rd, Peak) A rather pricey private hospital atop Victoria Peak – every taxi driver will know it.

Queen Elizabeth (Map p532; ☎ 2958 8888; 30 Gascoigne Rd, Yau Ma Tei) A public hospital.

Money

ATMS

ATMs are almost as common as bum holes in Hong Kong, including at the airport. Most are linked to international money systems, including Cirrus, Maestro, Plus and Visa Electron, as well as Visa and MasterCard credit systems.

CHANGING MONEY

The Hong Kong dollar is pegged to the US dollar at a rate of US$1 to $7.80, though it is allowed to fluctuate a little.

Banks give the best exchange rates, but three of the biggest – HSBC, Standard Chartered and the Hang Seng Bank – levy a $50 commission for each transaction.

Licensed moneychangers are abundant in tourist districts and the ground floor of Chungking Mansions has become a virtual money-changing theme park. Nearby the **Wing Hoi Money Exchange** (Map p532; ☎ 2723 5948; ground fl, Shop No 9b, Mirador Arcade, 58 Nathan Rd, Tsim Sha Tsui; ☻ 8.30am-8.30pm Mon-Sat, to 7pm Sun) has long been reliable and can change most major currencies and travellers cheques. Rates at the airport are poor.

International credit cards are accepted almost everywhere. Some shops may try to add a surcharge to offset the commission charged by credit companies, which can range from 2.5% to 7%. In theory, this is prohibited by the credit companies, but to get around this many shops offer a 5% discount if you pay cash.

COSTS

Hong Kong has become an extremely pricey destination, but if you stay in dormitories and eat budget meals, you can survive – just – on around $250 per day. For anything approaching comfort double that figure.

In general, tipping is not done in Hong Kong; taxi drivers only expect you to round up to the nearest dollar. However, most upmarket restaurants and hotels add a 10% service charge to their bills.

Bargaining is not as common as it once was, though you'll still be surprised how often reputable-looking shops will agree when you ask for a discount.

CURRENCY

The Hong Kong dollar ($) is divided into 100 cents. Bills are issued in denominations of $10, $20, $50, $100, $500 and $1000. Copper coins are worth 50c, 20c and 10c, while the $5, $2 and $1 coins are silver and the $10 coin is nickel and bronze. All prices in this chapter are in HK$.

Post

Hong Kong Post is excellent. For enquiries, call ☎ 2921 2222 or see www.hongkongpost.com. **General post office** (Map pp526-7; 2 Connaught Pl, Central; ☾ 8am-6pm Mon-Sat, 9am-2pm Sun) Pick up poste restante from counter No 29 Monday to Saturday only. **Kowloon post office** (Map p532; ground fl, Hermes House, 10 Middle Rd, Tsim Sha Tsui; ☾ 8am-6pm Mon-Sat, 9am-2pm Sun)

Telephone

Local calls in Hong Kong are free on private phones and cost $1 for five minutes on pay phones. All landline numbers in the territory have eight digits (except ☎ 800 toll-free numbers) and there are no area codes.

Hong Kong's country code is ☎ 852. To call abroad first dial ☎ 001. Phone rates are cheaper from 9pm to 8am weekdays and on the weekend. You can make international direct-dial calls to almost anywhere from public phones with a phonecard. These are available in two forms. Stored-value cards ($100) allow you to call from any phone – public or private – by punching in a PIN code. Hello Smartcards (available in denominations from $50 to $500) work in pay phones. You can buy phonecards at 7-Eleven and Circle K stores, Mannings pharmacies and Wellcome supermarkets.

Connecting to Hong Kong's excellent mobile-phone network is simple. A SIM card with prepaid call time can be as cheap as $90. Mobile phone stores are many, including a cluster on Des Voeux Rd Central (Map pp526-7).

Some handy phone numbers:

Air temperature & time ☎ 18501
International directory assistance ☎ 10013
Local directory assistance ☎ 1081
Reverse charge/collect calls ☎ 10010
Weather ☎ 187 8066

Tourist Information

The enterprising and wonderfully efficient **Hong Kong Tourism Board** (HKTB; ☎ visitor hotline 2508 1234 8am-6pm; www.discoverhongkong.com) maintains

Visitor Information and Service Centres on **Hong Kong Island** (Map pp530-1; Causeway Bay MTR station, near Exit F; ☾ 8am-8pm); in **Kowloon** (Map p532; Star Ferry Concourse, Tsim Sha Tsui; ☾ 8am-6pm); at **Hong Kong International Airport** (Map pp524-5; ☾ 7am-11pm), in Halls A and B on the arrivals level and the E2 transfer area; and at the border to China at **Lo Wu** (2nd fl Arrival Hall, Lo Wu Terminal Bldg; ☾ 8am-6pm). As well as running an immensely useful Visitor Hotline and excellent website, staff are helpful and have reams of free information.

Travel Agencies

China Travel Service (CTS; Map pp526-7; ☎ 2522 0450; ground fl, China Travel Bldg, 77 Queen's Rd, Central; ☾ 9am-6pm Mon-Fri, 9am-5pm Sat, 9.30am-12.30pm & 2.30-5pm Sun)
Phoenix Services Agency (Map p532; ☎ 2722 7378; info@phoenixtrvl.com; room 1404-5, 14th fl, Austin Tower, 22-26a Austin Ave, Tsim Sha Tsui; ☾ 9am-6pm Mon-Fri, to 4pm Sat)
Traveller Services (Map p532; ☎ 2375 2222; www.taketraveller.com; room 1813, Mirimar Tower, 132 Nathan Rd, Tsim Sha Tsui; ☾ 9am-6pm Mon-Fri, to 1pm Sat)

Visas

Most visitors to Hong Kong, including citizens of the EU, Australia, New Zealand, the USA and Canada, can enter and stay for 90 days without a visa. British passport holders get 180 days while South Africans are allowed to stay 30 days without a visa. If you do require a visa, apply at a Chinese embassy or consulate (see p942) before arriving.

For tourist visa extensions, inquire at the **Hong Kong Immigration Department** (Map pp530-1; ☎ 2852 3047; 5th fl, Immigration Tower, 7 Gloucester Rd, Wan Chai; ☾ 9am-4.30pm Mon-Fri, to 11.30am Sat). Extensions ($135) are not readily granted unless there are extenuating circumstances such as illness.

For information on obtaining a China visa in Hong Kong, see p954. Note that if you're planning to visit Hong Kong from China and return there, you'll need a multi-entry Chinese visa.

SIGHTS
Hong Kong Island

The northern and southern sides of Hong Kong Island have totally different characters. The northern side is mostly an urban jungle. Much of the south, on the other hand, remains surprisingly green and relatively undeveloped. The centre of the island is a mountainous, protected area and an easy escape.

SHEUNG WAN, CENTRAL & ADMIRALTY

Central is, as the name suggests, the main business district and it's here you'll see the most eye-popping of Hong Kong's skyscrapers. Just to the west is more traditional Sheung Wan, while Admiralty is to the east.

The gravity-defying **Peak Tram** (Map pp526-7; ☎ 2522 0922; www.thepeak.com.hk; one way/return adult $20/30, child $6/9, senior $7/14; ☼ 7am-midnight) is one of Hong Kong's oldest and most memorable attractions. Rising from the hyperkinetic buzz of Central, the funicular runs every 10 to 15 minutes from the lower terminus on manic Garden Rd up the side of 552m **Victoria Peak** (Map pp526-7) to finish at the newly renovated Peak Tower. It's ultratouristy, sure, but it's quite a trip and on those rare Hong Kong clear days the views from the top are spectacular. If not, going up at night takes the smog out of the equation, and your pictures.

From the upper tram terminus, wander 500m west up Mt Austin Rd, then follow the path to **Victoria Peak Garden** (Map pp526-7) or take the more leisurely stroll around Lugard and Harlech Rds that makes a 3.5km circular **walking trail** around the summit. You can walk down to Central along a track that peels off the circular trail and follows the northern edge of the mountain for a while before zigzagging its way down the hill to Conduit Rd. With more time and more energy, you could tackle the 50km-long **Hong Kong Trail**, which traverses the mountainous spine of the island from the Peak to Big Wave Bay, near delightful Shek O.

The **Hong Kong Zoological & Botanical Gardens** (Map pp526-7; ☎ 2530 0154; Albany Rd, Central; ☼ terrace gardens 6am-10pm, zoo & aviaries 6am-7pm) is a pleasant collection of fountains, sculptures, greenhouses, a playground, a zoo and aviaries. To the east, the **Edward Youde Aviary** (Map pp526-7) in **Hong Kong Park** (Map pp526-7; ☎ 2521 5041; 19 Cotton Tree Dr, Admiralty; ☼ park 6am-11pm, conservatory & aviary 9am-5pm) is home to 90 species of bird. The park also contains the rich **Flagstaff House Museum of Tea Ware** (Map pp526-7; ☎ 2869 0690; 10 Cotton Tree Dr, Admiralty; ☼ 10am-5pm Wed-Mon) in a colonial structure built in 1846. Tea-making classes are held at 4pm and 5pm on Monday and Thursday.

Just north of Hong Kong Park is **St John's Cathedral** (Map pp526-7; ☎ 2523 4157; 4-8 Garden Rd; ☼ 7.15am-6.30pm Mon, Tue, Fri & Sat, 9.30am-5.15pm Wed, 8.30am-1.15pm Thu, 8am-6.30pm Sun), built in 1847 and one of the very few colonial structures extant in Central; enter from Battery Path.

Northwest of the cathedral, linking Des Voeux Rd Central with Queen's Rd Central, **Li Yuen St East** and **Li Yuen St West** (Map pp526-7) are narrow alleys closed to motorised traffic and crammed with shops selling cheap clothing, handbags and jewellery. For exotic produce – from frogs' legs and pigs' heads to durian and mangosteens – and a serious dose of 'how can this be here in the middle of all this high-rise madness', head a few metres uphill to the **Graham St market** (Map pp526-7). The nearby **Mid-Levels Escalator** (Map pp526-7; ☼ down 6-10am, up 10.20am-midnight) is the longest in the world, transporting pedestrians 800m from Queen's Rd Central via SoHo all the way up to Conduit Rd in Mid-Levels in 20 minutes.

To the west of Central is the incense-filled **Man Mo Temple** (Map pp526-7; ☎ 2803 2916; 124-126 Hollywood Rd, Sheung Wan; ☼ 8am-6pm), built in 1847 and one of the oldest in Hong Kong. The temple celebrates the deities Kwan Yu, the righteous, red-cheeked god of war named after a Han dynasty soldier (see the boxed text, p410), and Man Cheung, the civil deity named after a Chinese scholar and statesman of the 3rd century. It's a favourite of both the police and secret societies like the Triads. Early afternoon is good for photos.

Further north is the restored **Western Market** (Map pp526-7; ☎ 2815 3586; 323 Des Voeux Rd Central; ☼ 10am-7pm), built in 1906 and filled with shops selling textiles, knick-knacks and souvenirs, and a dance studio upstairs that's fun to watch.

Hong Kong's art scene has been booming in recent years and many of the more exciting galleries have congregated in the streets of SoHo and NoHo. Among them, **Para/Site Art Space** (Map pp526-7; ☎ 2517 4620; www.para-site.org .hk; 4 Po Yan St, Sheung Wan; ☼ noon-7pm Wed-Sun) is an adventurous, artist-run space that knows no boundaries when it comes to mixing media. **Plum Blossoms** (Map pp526-7; ☎ 2521 2189; www.plumblossoms.com; ground fl, Chinachem Hollywood Centre, 1-19 Hollywood Rd, Central; ☼ 10am-6.30pm Mon-Sat) is one of the most well-established and consistently challenging galleries in Hong Kong.

(Continued on page 534)

INFORMATION (p520)
Hong Kong International Airport
HKTB Centres 香港旅遊發展局
旅客諮詢中心 1 B4
Matilda International
明德國際醫院 2 E5

SIGHTS & ACTIVITIES (p522)
Chi Lin Nunnery 志蓮淨苑........................3 E4
Hong Kong Disneyland
香港廸士尼樂園 4 C4
Hong Kong Heritage Museum
香港文化博物館 5 E3
Kat Hing Wai 吉慶圍..............................6 D2
Kowloon Walled City Park
九龍寨城公園 7 E4
Kwun Yam Shrine 觀音廟......................8 E5
Longevity Bridge 長壽橋 ....(see 8)
Mai Po Marsh Nature Reserve
米埔自然保護區 9 D2
Ngong Ping 360 昂坪360纜車......10 B5
Ocean Park 香港海洋公園 11 E5
Po Lin 寶蓮禪寺...................................12 B5
Shui Tau 水頭 13 D2
Sik Sik Yuen Wong Tai Sin Temple
嗇色園黃大仙祠
....14 E4
Ten Thousand Buddhas Monastery
萬佛寺..15 E3
Tian Tan Buddha Statue
天壇大佛..(see 12)

SLEEPING	(p540)
Ascension House 昇天屋	16 E3
Bali Holiday Resort 優閒渡假屋	(see 18)
Hong Kong Bank Foundation SG Davis Hostel 戴維斯旅舍	17 B5
Man Lai Wah Hotel 文麗華渡假屋	18 D5
Mui Wo Inn 梅窩旅舍	19 C5
Warwick Hotel 華威酒店	20 C5

EATING	(p544)
Bahçe Turkish Restaurant	21 C5
Bookworm Café 南島書蟲	(see 18)
Hong Kee 康記	22 C5
Java Rd Market & Cooked Food Centre 渣華道市場及熟食中心	23 E4
Katiga Street 加太賀	24 E4
Lamma Hilton Shum Kee Seafood Restaurant 森記	25 D5
Stoep Restaurant	26 B5
Top Deck at the Jumbo 珍之寶	27 E5

TRANSPORT	(p560)
Flying Ball Bicycle Co 飛球單車行	28 E4
Friendly Bicycle Shop 老友記單車	(see 21)

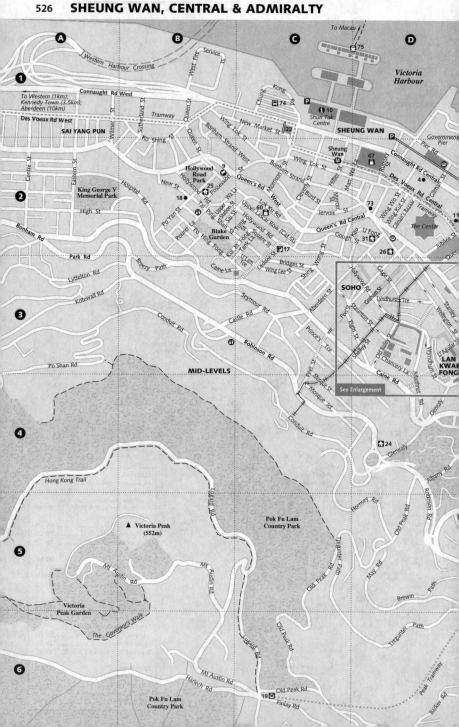

To Macau

A   B   C   D

1

Western Harbour Crossing
West Fire Service

Connaught Rd West
Chung Kong St
74
P
75

To Western (1km);
Kennedy Town (3.5km);
Aberdeen (10km);

Tramway
Des Voeux Rd West
New Market St
Wing Lok St
22
P
10
Shun Tak Centre
SHEUNG WAN

SAI YANG PUN
Ko Shing St
Queen St
Bonham Strand West
Bonham Strand
Wing Lok St
Sheung Wan M
Connaught Rd Central
Government Pier

Victoria
Harbour

2
King George V
Memorial Park

Centre St
Eastern St
Hospital Rd
High St
New St
Hollywood Rd
Hollywood Road Park
Po Yan St
25
9
18
Possession St
Queen's Rd West
Morrison St
Cleverly St
Hillier St
Bonham Strand
67
Des Voeux Rd Central
Mercer St
73
Wing Wo St
Wing Kut St
Cleverly's Bazaar
Tramway
The Center
11

Bonham Rd
Park Rd
Lyttelton Rd
Kotewall Rd
Pound La
Po Hing Fong
Tank La
Upper Station St
Ladder St
Sai St
Square St
Upper Lascar Row (Cat St)
Lok Ku Rd
60
Tung St
Blake Garden
Caine La
Upper Hollywood Rd
17
Gage St
Urtam
Ladder St
Wing Lee St
Bridges St
Shing Wong St
Jervois St
Queen's Rd Central
Gough St
Kau U Fong
31
U Fong
26
Jubilee St
Queen

3
Po Shan Rd
Conduit Rd
Breezy Path
Castle Rd
Seymour Rd
Robinson Rd
Aberdeen St
Prince's Tce
Peel St
Graham St
Staunton St
Elgin St
Shelley St
Old Bailey St
Chancery La
Wyndham St
Aberdeen St
SOHO
Lyndhurst Tce
Wellington St
Stanley St
LAN KWAI FONG
Caine Rd
Glenealy
See Enlargement

MID-LEVELS
Robinson Rd
Mosque St
Mosque Jct
Conduit Rd
24
Glenealy
Albany Rd
Robinson Rd

4
Hong Kong Trail

5
▲ **Victoria Peak**
(552m)
Lugard Rd
Mt Austin Rd
Pok Fu Lam
Country Park
Hornsey Rd
Tregunter Path
Old Peak Rd
Old Peak Rd
May Rd
Brewin
Treanter Path
Peak Tramway
Burkett Rd
Mt Austin Rd

Victoria Peak Garden
The Governor's Walk

6
Mt Austin Rd
Hatlech Rd
19
Old Peak Rd
Finlay Rd
Pok Fu Lam
Country Park
Lugard Rd

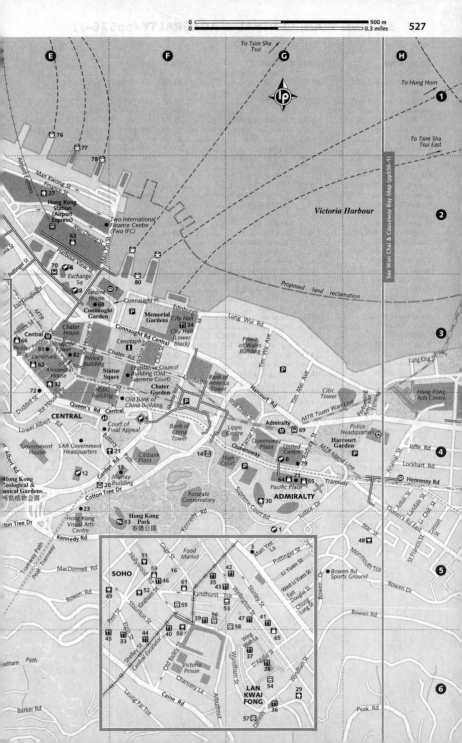

A   B   C   D

1

2

3

4

5

6

To Tsim Sha Tsui

To Hung Hom

Victoria Harbour

See Sheung Wan, Central & Admiralty Map (pp526-7)

MTR Tsuen Wan Line

Proposed Land Reclamation

Lung King St

Expo Dr

Expo Dr East

Expo Dr Central

12

Hong Kong Convention & Exhibition Centre

Atrium

Convention Ave

Expo Dr

Hung Hing Rd

Wan Shing St

34

Marsh Rd

Wan Chai Sports Ground

Fleming Rd

Great Eagle Centre
9

1
Harbour Centre

Harbour Rd

China Resources Building

Causeway Centre

Sun Hung Kai Centre

14

Harbour Rd

Hong Kong Arts Centre

Shui on Centre

Wan Chai Tower

Central Plaza

Exhibition Centre

11

Harbour Dr

Marsh Rd

Jaffe Rd

Lockhart Rd

15

13

Revenue Tower

Immigration Tower

5

7

Tonnochy Rd

Hennessy Rd

MTR Island Line

Tramway

Gloucester Rd

Wan Chai Police Station

Arsenal St

29

30

24

27

Jaffe Rd

Lockhart Rd

Fenwick St

O'Brien Rd

25

Jaffe Rd

Fleming Rd

Lockhart Rd

Stewart Rd

Lockhart Rd Market

10

20

Wan Chai Rd

Morrison Hill Rd

Sharp St West

Bowrington Rd

Anton St

26

Landale St

Li Chit St

Gresson St

Thomson Rd

Lun Fat St

Ship St

Hennessy Rd

Wan Chai

WAN CHAI

MTR Island Line

Southern Playground

3

33

Thomson Rd

Johnston Rd

Mallory St

Heard St

Burrows St

Cross La

Wood Rd

Ol Kwan

Morrison Hill

Queen's Rd East

Sung Tak Rd

4

Queen's Rd East

St Francis St

Tai Wong St East

Swatow St

Amoy St

Lee Tung St

Spring Garden Ln

Stone Nullah Ln

Tai Yuen St

Cross St

Johnston Rd

Tramway

Tai Wo St

Bullock St

Ruttonjee Hospital

Wan Chai Park

Salvation Army St

Wan Chai Rd

Ol Kwan Rd

Morrison Hill

Queen Elizabeth Stadium

Wong Nai Chung Rd

Bowen Dr

Hopewell Centre

Kennedy Rd

Queen's Rd East

Wan Chai Gap Rd

Stone Nullah Ln

Kennedy Rd

MORRISON HILL

Wan Chai Market

Stubbs Rd

Hau Tak La

Muslim Cemetery

St Margaret's College

Catholic Cemetery

Hong Kong Cemetery

To Aberdeen Tunnel (400m); Aberdeen (6km)

Aberdeen Tunnel

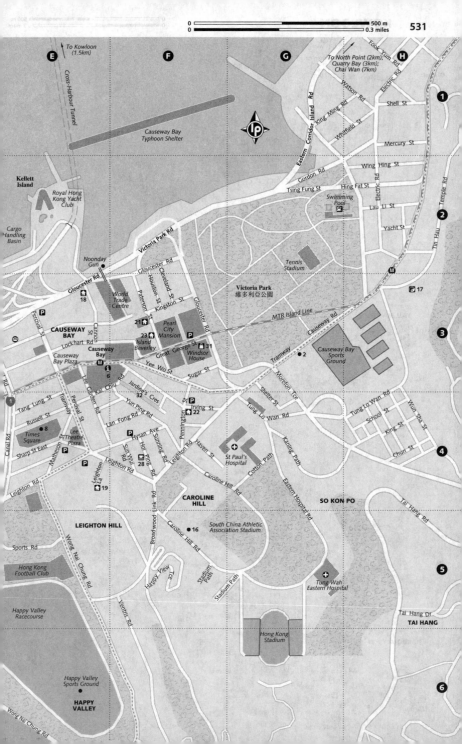

0 — 500 m
0 — 0.3 miles

To Kowloon (1.5km)

E **F** **G** **H**

Fook Yum Rd

To North Point (2km);
Quarry Bay (3km);
Chai Wan (7km)

Watson Rd

Shell St

King's Ming Rd

Eastern Corridor

Electric Rd

Cross-Harbour Tunnel

Whitfield Rd

Mercury St

1

Causeway Bay
Typhoon Shelter

Wing Hing St

Gordon Rd

Tsing Fung St

Hing Fat St

Electric Rd

Tin Hau Temple Rd

Lau Li St

Swimming
Pool

Yacht St

2

Kellett
Island

Royal Hong
Kong Yacht
Club

Victoria Park Rd

Tennis
Stadium

M

Cargo
Handling
Basin

Noonday
Gun

Gloucester Rd

Cleveland St

Houston St

Victoria Park
維多利亞公園

17

Gloucester Rd

18

World
Trade
Centre

Paterson St

Kingston St

Gloucester Rd

MTR Island Line

Causeway Rd

Causeway Bay
Sports
Ground

3

Percival St

**CAUSEWAY
BAY**

Cannon St

21

Pearl
City
Mansion

Tramway

2

Lockhart Rd

23

Island
Beverley

Great George St

P

32

Windsor
House

31

Moreton Tce

Causeway Bay
Plaza

M

Causeway
Bay

6

Yee Wo St

Sugar St

Shelter St

Tung Lo Wan Rd

School St

Wun Sha St

1

Tang Lung St

Kai Chiu Rd

Percival St

Jardine's Cres

P

Irving St

Tung Lo Wan Rd

King St

Chun St

4

Russell St

Yun Ping Rd

22

Pennington St

Leighton Rd

Haven St

Karting Path

Times
Square

8

Lan Fong Rd

Lee
Theatre
Plaza

Matheson St

Hysan Ave

Sun Wui Rd

Hoi Ping Rd

Sunning Rd

St Paul's
Hospital

Cotton Path

Eastern Hospital Rd

Tai Hang Rd

Sharp St East

Canal Rd

P

28

P

Leighton Rd

Leighton La

19

Caroline Hill Rd

Broadwood Link Rd

**CAROLINE
HILL**

South China Athletic
Association Stadium

SO KON PO

5

LEIGHTON HILL

Sports Rd

Wong Nai Chung Rd

16

Caroline Hill Rd

Happy View Tce

Ventris Rd

Tung Wah
Eastern Hospital

Tai Hang Dr

TAI HANG

Hong Kong
Football Club

Stadium Path

Stadium Path

Happy Valley
Racecourse

Hong Kong
Stadium

6

Happy Valley
Sports Ground

**HAPPY
VALLEY**

Wong Nai Chung Rd

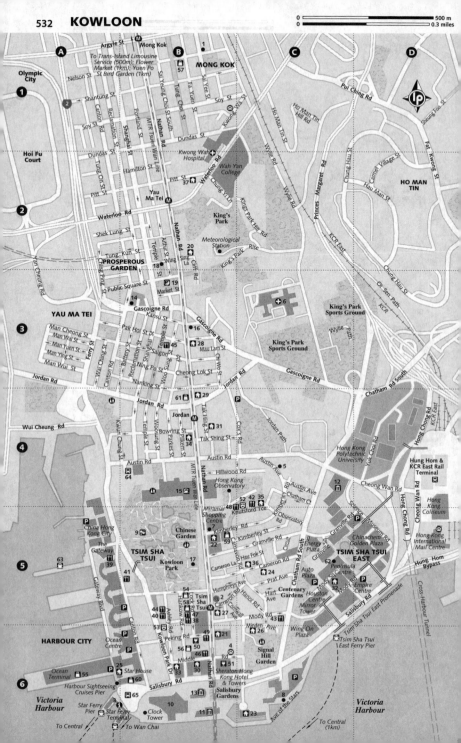

0   500 m
0   0.3 miles

A   B   C   D

1

Olympic City

MONG KOK

Argyle St   Mong Kok

To Trans-Island Limousine Service (500m); Flower Market (1km); Yuen Po St Bird Garden (1km)

57

1

Nelson St

Shantung St

2

Canton Rd

Reclamation St

Portland St

Shanghai St

Sai Yeung Choi St South

Tung Choi St

Fa Yuen St

Sai Yee St

Soy St

Kwong Wa St

Dundas St

Ho Man Tin Hill Rd

Pui Ching Rd

Hoi Fu Court

Soy St

Dundas St

Hamilton St

Pitt St

Kwong Wah Hospital

Wah Yan College

Chung Yi Ln

Wylie Rd

Wylie Rd

Ho Man Tin St

Princes Margaret Rd

Chung Hau

Lomond Village St

HO MAN TIN

2

Waterloo Rd

37

Yau Ma Tei

King's Park

Kings Park Hill Rd

Hau Man St

KCR East

Oi Sin Path

Shek Lung St

Meteorological Station

King's Park Rise

Chung Hau St

KCR

PROSPEROUS GARDEN

Tung Kun St

Temple St

Arthur St

Wing

Sing La

20

18

19

YAU MA TEI

Public Square St

Market St

Gascoigne Rd

Kansu St

14

Pak Hoi St

28

16

Saigon St

45

6

King's Park Sports Ground

King's Park Sports Ground

Wylie Path

3

Man Cheong St

Man Wai St

Man Yuen St

Man Ying St

Man Wui St

Ferry St

Wai Ching St

Battery St

Reclamation St

Shanghai St

Temple St

Woosung St

Ning Po St

Nanking St

Mau Lam St

Cheong Lok St

Saigon St

Jordan Rd

Gascoigne Rd

Chatham Rd South

Jordan Rd

61

29

Jordan

Tak Hing St

Cox's Rd

Jordan Path

4

Wui Cheung Rd

Kwun Chung St

Temple St

Parkes St

Bowring St

34

31

Tak Shing St

Austin Rd

64

Austin Rd

Hillwood Rd

5

Austin Ave

Jordan Path

Hong Kong Polytechnic University

Hong Kong Observatory

12

Cheong Wan Rd

Hung Hom & KCR East Rail Terminal

Yuk Choi Rd

Hong Kong Coliseum

Hong Kong International Mail Centre

15

42 35

52

48

Knutsford Tce

Austin Ave

Chatham Ct

Observatory Rd

Museum Rd

Hong Kong

5

China Hong Kong City

The Gateway

63

39

9

TSIM SHA TSUI

Chinese Garden

Kowloon Park

17

41

Miramar Shopping Centre

22

59

Kimberley Rd

Kimberley Rd

Granville Rd

Granville Circuit

Carnarvon Rd

Hart Rd

Hau Fok St

Chinachem Golden Plaza

TSIM SHA TSUI EAST

62

Peninsula Centre

Energy Plaza

Auto Plaza

Houston Centre

Empire Centre

Hung Hom Bypass

Cameron La

36

24

Cameron Rd

Prat Ave

Mody

32

54

58

Tsim Sha Tsui

47

38

44

40

53

Haiphong Rd

Ashley Rd

Kowloon Park Dr

Peking Rd

2

Cameron Rd

Hankow Rd

27

Humphreys Ave

Hanoi Rd

Hart Ave

Mody Sq

43

Chatham Rd South

Centenary Gardens

Mirror Tower

Minden Ave

Minden Row

Mody Rd

26

Wing On Plaza

Tsim Sha Tsui East Promenade

6

HARBOUR CITY

Ocean Centre

55

25

Star House

60

Ocean Terminal

Harbour Sightseeing Cruises Pier

65

3

21

49

50

46

30

33

56

Middle Rd

Peking Rd

Salisbury Rd

13

51

Signal Hill Garden

4

Sheraton Hong Kong Hotel & Towers

Salisbury Gardens

8

Tsim Sha Tsui East Ferry Pier

Cross-Harbour Tunnel

Star Ferry Pier

Star Ferry Terminal

Clock Tower

10

11

23

Victoria Harbour

To Central

To Wan Chai

Ave of the Stars

To Central (1km)

Victoria Harbour

(Continued from page 523)

WAN CHAI & CAUSEWAY BAY

Just east of Admiralty is Wan Chai, known for its raucous nightlife but by day just an ordinary district of shops and offices. The **Hong Kong Arts Centre** (Map pp530-1; ☎ 2582 0200; www .hkac.org.hk; 2 Harbour Rd, Wan Chai), which contains the **Pao Galleries** (Map pp530-1; ☎ 2824 5330; ☯ 10am-8pm during exhibitions) on the 4th and 5th floors, has regular exhibitions of contemporary art and photography and is a great place to meet hip young Hong Kongers.

The **Hong Kong Convention & Exhibition Centre** (Map pp530-1; ☎ 2582 8888; www.hkcec.com; 1 Expo Dr, Wan Chai) is a colossal building on the harbour boasting the world's largest 'glass curtain' – a window seven storeys high. Ride the escalators to the 7th floor for a superb harbour view. The centre's waterfront wing, with its distinctive 'fly-away' roof, is where the handover to China took place at midnight on 30 June 1997. The **Golden Bauhinia** (Map pp530-1), a 6m-tall statue of the unique flower that became Hong Kong's symbol and flag standard, commemorates the event in all its golden gaudiness.

East of Wan Chai is Causeway Bay, one of Hong Kong Island's top shopping areas. It is dominated by 17-hectare **Victoria Park** (Map pp530-1), which is best visited on weekday mornings when it becomes a slow-motion forest of taichi practitioners. East of the park is Hong Kong's most famous **Tin Hau Temple** (Map pp530-1; 101 Tin Hau Temple Rd, Causeway Bay; ☯ 7am-5pm), a place of worship for at least three centuries. Tin Hau is one of the most popular deities in coastal South China. Known as the Queen of Heaven, her duties include protecting seafarers and there are almost 60 temples dedicated to her in Hong Kong alone. If you visit Macau, you'll notice she is a doppelganger for the goddess A Ma…they're one and the same.

ISLAND SOUTH

The south coast of Hong Kong Island is dotted with decent beaches and other recreational facilities. If you're anxious to reach the beach, hop on bus 6 (or the express 260) to **Stanley** (Map pp524-5) from the Central bus terminus in Exchange Sq. You can rent windsurfing boards and kayaks at **St Stephen's Beach** (Map pp524-5) about 400m south of Stanley Village. Busy **Stanley Market** (Stanley Village Rd; ☯ 10am-6pm) is a covered market filled with cheap clothing and bric-a-brac. It's been a tourist attraction (some

might say 'trap') for years and is best visited during the week. Prepare to bargain.

The same buses also go to picturesque **Repulse Bay** (Map pp524-5); if heading here from Stanley hop on bus 73, which takes you along the coast. At the southeastern end of the bay is the unusual **Kwun Yam shrine** (Map pp524-5), where the surrounding area is filled with an amazing assembly of deities and figures – from goldfish and a monkey god to the more familiar statues of Tin Hau. Crossing **Longevity Bridge** (Map pp524-5) just in front of the shrine is supposed to add three days to your life. There's no word, however, on whether running back and forth all day will add years.

Northwest of Repulse Bay (and accessible on bus 73) is **Deep Water Bay** (Map pp524-5), a quiet inlet with a sandy beach flanked by shade trees, and **Aberdeen** (Map pp524-5). The big attraction at the latter is the busy harbour. Sampans will take you on a half-hour tour for $40 per person (less if there's a group of you). But you can see almost as much on the free 10-minute trip to the harbour's celebrated **floating restaurants** (see the boxed text, p546). From Aberdeen, bus 70 will take you back to Central.

If you're feeling vigorous, the entrance to **Aberdeen Country Park** (Map pp524-5) and **Pok Fu Lam Country Park** (Map pp526-7) is about a 15-minute walk north (and uphill) along Aberdeen Reservoir Rd. From there you can take the long walk up to Victoria Peak and catch the Peak Tram to Central.

To the southeast of Aberdeen, the impressive **Ocean Park** (Map pp524-5; ☎ 2552 0291; www .oceanpark.com.hk; Ocean Park Rd; adult/child $185/93; ☯ 10am-6pm) is a huge amusement and educational theme park complete with roller coasters and other rides, an **atoll reef** and an **aquarium** that was once the largest in the world but was, by the time we asked, 'maybe the largest in East Asia?!'. Whatever, it's quite impressive. Due to competition from the new Hong Kong Disneyland (p537), Ocean Park is getting a face-lift, an operation that's expected to continue until 2010. You can reach Ocean Park on bus 90 from the Central bus terminus; get off at the Aberdeen Tunnel and it's a five-minute walk from there.

Kowloon

Kowloon (locals are more likely to pronounce it Gaolong), the peninsula pointing southward towards Hong Kong Island whose name means 'nine dragons', is a stark blend of locals and tourists, of opulent hotels and crumbling tenements, and of class and sleaze. Many travellers will stay and shop somewhere along its neon-lit main drag, **Nathan Road**, but it's well worth getting into the lively back streets, including the restaurant strip of Ashley Rd, the nightclubs and eateries of Knutsford Tce and the Temple St night market.

The Hong Kong government has grand plans for the reclaimed area west of the Star Ferry Pier known as the West Kowloon Cultural District. Architect Sir Norman Foster has designed an immense, space-age-looking complex of museums, galleries, entertainment venues, a marina and, of course, shops. However, the project has been dogged by controversy and at the time of writing was still not certain to go ahead.

TSIM SHA TSUI
Tsim Sha Tsui sits at the southern tip of Kowloon and is the most touristy part of the city. It's also the logical place from which to start exploring Kowloon. East of the Star Ferry terminal is the Hong Kong Cultural Centre precinct. The **Hong Kong Cultural Centre** (Map p532; ☎ 2734 2009; www.hkculturalcentre.gov .hk; ☾ 9am-11pm), with its curved roof and controversial windowless façade facing one of the most spectacular views in the world, is the first thing you'll see. There are regular performances and exhibitions here; call to find out what's on. Behind the Cultural Centre is the **Hong Kong Museum of Art** (Map p532; ☎ 2721 0116; adult/child, student & senior $10/5, admission free Wed; ☾ 10am-6pm Fri-Wed), with six floors of Chinese antiquities, historical paintings and contemporary art.

Neighbouring **Hong Kong Space Museum & Theatre** (Map p532; ☎ 2721 0226; exhibition halls adult/child & senior $10/5, admission free Wed, planetarium adult $24-32, child & senior $12-16; ☾ 1-9pm Mon & Wed-Fri, 10am-9pm Sat & Sun) has several exhibition halls and a Space Theatre (planetarium), that also shows IMAX films. Children under three aren't welcome at the theatre. To the southeast along Tsim Sha Tsui Promenade, the **Avenue of the Stars** (Map p532) pays homage to the Hong Kong film industry and its stars, with handprints and sculptures, and is a great viewpoint for watching the **Symphony of Light** (☾ 8pm), the world's largest permanent light show projected from atop the buildings of Hong Kong Island.

The lower end of Nathan Rd is known as the **Golden Mile**, a reference to both the price of its real estate and its ability to make money out of tourism. Halfway up the thoroughfare is **Kowloon Park** (Map p532; Nathan & Austin Rds; ☾ 6am-midnight), an oasis of greenery after the hustle and bustle of Tsim Sha Tsui. This is a great place to come to see Hong Kongers enjoying themselves, particularly on Sundays when the place is packed with Filipina, Indonesian and Sri Lankan domestic workers enjoying their day off by singing, dancing and flirting. Sunday is also the day for Kung Fu Corner, a display of traditional Chinese martial arts near the otherwise fairly uninteresting **Sculpture Walk** (Map p532). There's also an **aviary** (Map p532; ☾ 6.30am-6.45pm Mar-Oct, to 5.45pm Nov-Feb), and the **Kowloon Park Swimming Complex** (Map p532; ☎ 2724 3577; adult/child & senior $16/9; ☾ outdoor 6.30am-noon, 1-6pm & 7-10pm Apr-Oct, indoor 6.30am-noon, 1-6pm & 7-9.30pm Nov-Mar).

The **Hong Kong Museum of History** (Map p532; ☎ 2724 9042; 100 Chatham Rd South; adult/child & senior $10/5, admission free Wed; ☾ 10am-6pm Mon & Wed-Sat, to 7pm Sun), in the reclaimed area known as Tsim Sha Tsui East, takes visitors on a fascinating and entertaining wander through Hong Kong's past from prehistoric times to the 1997 handover.

YAU MA TEI & MONG KOK
Just north of Tsim Sha Tsui, in the district known as Yau Ma Tei, the **Jade Market** (Map p532; cnr Kansu & Battery Sts, Yau Ma Tei; ☾ 10am-5pm) is where some 450 stalls sell all varieties and grades of jade. Unless you really know your nephrite from your jadeite, it's wise not to buy expensive pieces here. From here it's a short walk to the incense-filled **Tin Hau Temple** (Map p532; ☎ 2332 9240; cnr Public Square St & Nathan Rd; ☾ 8am-5pm) and to the **Temple St night market** (Map p532; ☾ 4pm-midnight), the liveliest place in town to bargain for cheap clothes, fake name-brand goods and knockoff DVDs.

To the east of the Prince Edward MTR station in Mong Kok is the delightful **Yuen Po St Bird Garden** (☎ 2382 1785; Flower Market Rd, Mong Kok; ☾ 7am-8pm), a place where birds are 'aired', preened, bought, sold and fed bugs with chopsticks by their fussy owners (usually men). Nearby is the fragrant **flower market**, which keeps the same hours but is busiest after 10am, especially on Sunday.

NEW KOWLOON
The southernmost 31 sq km of the New Territories is officially called New Kowloon since

TELLING YOUR FORTUNE

For all Wong Tai Sin's religious significance and supposed medicinal powers, many worshippers come here seeking good health of the hip pocket. In Hong Kong, luck, money and religion are inseparable and Wong Tai Sin Temple is the city's one-stop luck supermarket. But as in any market, you have to pay for the goods. In this case, Hong Kongers consult their choice of dozens of soothsayers. For a fee beginning at about $30 (but do haggle!), these wise ones can divine the future by reading your palm or more exotic mediums, such as the *chim* (fortune sticks) or *sing pei* (aka the Buddha's lips). If the signs are positive, then all is good: you might choose to take the next boat to the casinos of Macau. If not, fear not: Hong Kong is a land of positive fatalism where no fate is beyond change. All that's required is to know what steps to take to change your fate, and for a bit more money the folks at Wong Tai Sin can sort you out.

Boundary St just above Mong Kok technically marks the division between Kowloon and the New Territories. Full of high-rise apartments, the area is less frantic than its neighbours to the south.

Sik Sik Yuen Wong Tai Sin Temple (Map pp524-5; ☎ 2854 4333; Lung Cheung Rd; admission by $2 donation; ☒ 7am-5.30pm) is a large and very active Taoist temple complex built in 1973 and dedicated to the god worshipped by the sick, those trying to avoid illness and others seeking more material fortune. Just below and to the left of the temple is an arcade of fortune tellers (see above), some of whom speak English. It's right next to the Wong Tai Sin MTR station.

Northeast of Wong Tai Sin in the Diamond Hill district is the much more serene **Chi Lin Nunnery** (Map pp524-5; ☎ 2354 1604; 5 Chin Lin Dr; ☒ nunnery 9am-5pm Thu-Tue, garden 6.30am-7pm), a large Buddhist complex with lotus ponds, immaculate bonsai and silent nuns delivering offerings of fruit and rice to Buddha and his disciples. To reach it, take the MTR to Diamond Hill.

Further east, at the edge of the now-abandoned Kai Tak International Airport, is **Kowloon Walled City Park** (Map pp524-5; ☎ 2716 9962; Tung Tau Tsuen, Tung Tsing, Carpenter & Junction Rds; ☒ 6.30am-11pm). The walls that enclose this beautiful park began as the perimeter of a Chinese garrison in the 19th century. Excluded from the 1898 lease of the New Territories, it became a lawless slum that technically remained part of China throughout British rule. The enclave became known for its gangsters, prostitution, gambling and, brace yourself, illegal dentists. The British eventually relocated the 30,000 or so residents, razed the slums and built a park filled with pavilions, ponds and renovated buildings including the Yamen building, which has a scale model of the village in the

mid-19th century. To reach the park, take bus 1 from the Star Ferry bus terminal in Kowloon and alight at Tung Tau Tsuen Rd.

New Territories

Few visitors realise that more than 80% of Hong Kong is unspoilt green hills, mountains and tropical forest. That's a lot of area in which to escape the urban jungle, and most of it is in the New Territories (San Gai in Cantonese). The New Territories are so called because they were leased to Britain in 1898, almost half a century after Hong Kong Island and four decades after Kowloon were ceded to the crown. The area has seen plenty of urbanisation of its own, with high-rise 'New Towns' like Sha Tin going up to create housing. But there remain numerous traditional villages, fabulous mountain walks and sandy beaches with nary a high-rise to be seen, all within an hour or so of Central by public transport.

TAI MO SHAN

Hong Kong's tallest mountain at 957m, Tai Mo Shan (Map pp524–5) rises out of the central New Territories. The climb to the summit isn't too gruelling and the way up is part of the 100km-long **MacLehose Trail** that runs from Tuen Mun in the west to the Sai Kung Peninsula in the east. If you want to hike anywhere along this trail, the 1:25,000 *MacLehose Trail* map, available from the Map Publications Centre (p538) is essential. To get there, take bus 51 from Tsuen Wan MTR station.

KAM TIN & MAI PO MARSH

Yuen Long, which is on both the KCR West Rail and the Light Rail Transit (LRT) rail lines (see p564), is the springboard for Hong Kong's most important grouping of walled villages as well as a world-class nature reserve.

The area around Kam Tin is home to two 16th-century walled villages. Their fortifications serve as reminders of the marauding pirates, bandits and imperial soldiers that Hong Kong's early residents faced. Just off the main road and easily accessible, tiny **Kat Hing Wai** (Map pp524–5) is the more popular of the two. Drop a coin donation in the box at the village's entrance and wander the narrow little lanes. The old Hakka women in traditional clothing will let you take their photograph for the right price (about $10). **Shui Tau** (Map pp524–5), a 17th-century village about a 15-minute walk north of Kam Tin Rd, is famous for its prow-shaped roofs decorated along the ridges with dragons and fish. To reach Kam Tin, take bus 64K, 77K or 54 from Yuen Long.

The 270-hectare **Mai Po Marsh Nature Reserve** (Map pp524–5; ☎ 2526 4473; San Tin, Yuen Long; admission $100 plus $200 deposit; ☒ 9am-5pm), a protected wetland at Deep Bay in the northwestern New Territories, is home to up to 300 species of migratory and resident birds. You can visit on your own (bus 76K from Yuen Long plus a lengthy walk), but most people take the guided visit organised by the **World Wide Fund for Nature Hong Kong** (WWFHK; Map pp526-7; ☎ 2526 4473; www.wwf.org.hk; 1 Tramway Path, Central; ☒ 9am-5pm Mon-Fri); call ahead or register online for a booking. Its three-hour tours ($70) leave the marsh's visitor centre six times between 9am and 3pm on Saturday and Sunday.

SHA TIN
The New Town of Sha Tin is popular not just for its racecourse but also for its **Ten Thousand Buddhas Monastery** (Map pp524–5; ☎ 2691 1067; ☒ 9am-5pm), about 500m northwest of Sha Tin KCR station, which actually has some 12,800 miniature statues lining the walls of its main temple. To reach it, take exit B at Sha Tin KCR station and walk down the ramp, turning left onto Pai Tau St. After a short distance turn right onto Sheung Wo Che St, walk to the end and follow the signs up the 400 steps.

While in Sha Tin do not miss the **Hong Kong Heritage Museum** (Map pp524–5; ☎ 2180 8188; www .heritagemuseum.gov.hk; 1 Man Lam Rd, Tai Wai; adult/student & senior $10/5, admission free Wed; ☒ 10am-6pm Mon & Wed-Sat, to 7pm Sun) in Tai Wai, not far from the new Tai Wai KCR station. Its rich permanent collections (Chinese opera, fine art, ceramics) and extremely innovative temporary exhibits in a dozen different galleries are probably the best in Hong Kong.

SAI KUNG
The Sai Kung Peninsula (Map pp524–5) is the garden spot of the New Territories and is great for outdoor activities, especially hiking, sailing and eating seafood. The New Territories' best beaches are around here and hiring a sampan to deliver you to such a deserted place is both exciting and romantic. To get here from Sha Tin, take bus 299. To explore the eastern side of the Sai Kung Peninsula, take bus 94 from Sai Kung to Wong Shek.

Outlying Islands
In addition to Hong Kong Island, there are 234 islands dotting the waters around Hong Kong but only four have substantial residential communities and easy access by ferry.

LANTAU
Twice the size of Hong Kong Island, Lantau has only about 50,000 residents and you could easily spend a couple of days exploring its hilly walking trails and enjoying its uncrowded beaches.

From **Mui Wo** (Map pp524–5), the main settlement and arrival point for ferries, most visitors board bus 2 to **Ngong Ping** (Map pp524–5), a plateau 500m above sea level in the western part of the island where you'll find **Po Lin** (Map pp524–5; www.plm.com.hk; ☒ 9am-6pm), an enormous monastery and temple complex that contains the **Tian Tan Buddha statue** (Map pp524–5; ☒ 10am-5.30pm), the world's largest outdoor seated bronze Buddha statue, which can be climbed via 260 steps. The new **Ngong Ping 360** (Map pp524–5; www.np360.com.hk; one way/return adult $58/88, child $28/45; ☒ 10am-6pm Mon-Fri, to 6.30pm Sat & Sun) cable car linking Tung Chung and the monastery is being promoted as a major new tourist draw. Apart from what will be a very impressive ride, themed attractions such as theatres and a 'walk with Buddha' will attempt to enlighten you further. Prices rise by about 10% on public holidays.

En route to Ngong Ping you'll pass 3km-long **Cheung Sha Bay** (Map pp524–5; South Lantau Rd), boasting Hong Kong's longest beach. Another place to visit is **Tai O** (Map pp524–5), a picturesque village at the western end of Lantau famous for its pungent shrimp paste, **rope-tow ferry** across a narrow channel of water and temple dedicated to Kwan Yu (aka Kwan Tai).

Lantau's newest but most high-profile attraction is **Hong Kong Disneyland** (Map pp524–5;

HONG KONG

☎ 1830 830; www.hongkongdisneyland.com; adult/child/senior $295/210/170, weekends $350/250/200; ✆ 10am-8pm), which is the expected Disney experience with a few Chinese twists. If one day isn't enough you can stay in one of the two hotels on site. To get there, take the Tung Chung MTR line from Central to Sunny Bay and change for the Disneyland train. A ferry from Central should be running by the time you read this.

LAMMA

With no cars Lamma (Map pp524–5) seems a world away from the hustle and bustle of big city Hong Kong but is only 20 minutes away by ferry. The island boasts decent beaches, excellent walks and a plethora of restaurants in **Yung Shue Wan** (Map pp524–5) and **Sok Kwu Wan** (Map pp524–5), the main settlements to the north and south respectively. A fun day involves taking the ferry to Yung Shue Wan, walking the easy 90-minute trail to Sok Kwu Wan and settling in for lunch at one of the seafood restaurants beside the water. Afterwards, take the ferry from here back to Central.

CHEUNG CHAU & PENG CHAU

Dumbbell-shaped Cheung Chau (Map pp524–5), with a harbour filled with sampans and fishing boats, a windsurfing centre, several fine temples and some lively bars and restaurants makes a fun day out. Not far away is Peng Chau (Map pp524–5), the smallest and most traditionally Chinese of the easily accessible islands.

ACTIVITIES

While tourism authorities can sometimes be responsible for the cheesiest of activities, the HKTB has a few that are interesting, fun and free. From sessions explaining feng shui led by geomancers, through harbour trips on Hong Kong's only remaining sailing junk, the *Duck Ling*, to taichi sessions on the Tsim Sha Tsui waterfront, you really have to pay credit to HKTB for providing a window into Cantonese culture that is often very hard to find by yourself. For a full list of what's on, when and where, go to www.discoverhongkong.com, click on Heritage, then Cultural Kaleidoscope.

Sporting buffs should contact the **South China Athletic Association** (Map pp530–1; ☎ 2577 6932; www.scaa.org.hk in Chinese; 5th fl, Sports Complex, 88 Caroline Hill Rd, Causeway Bay; visitor memberships $50), which has facilities for any number of sports. Another handy website is www.hkoutdoors.com.

Hiking

Hong Kong is an excellent place to hike and there are numerous trails to enjoy on Hong Kong Island, the New Territories and the Outlying Islands. The four main trails are the 100km-long MacLehose Trail (p536); the 78km-long Wilson Trail, which runs on both sides of the harbour; the 70km-long Lantau Trail, a 12-stage footpath that passes over both **Lantau Peak** (934m) and **Sunset Peak** (869m); and the 50km-long Hong Kong Trail (p523).

The **Map Publications Centre** (Map p532; ☎ 2780 0981; 382 Nathan Rd, Yau Ma Tei; ✆ 9am-5pm Mon-Fri, to noon Sat) and the **Government Publications Office** (Map pp526-7; ☎ 2537 1910; Room 402, 4th fl, Murray Bldg, 22 Garden Rd, Central; ✆ 9am-5pm Mon-Fri, to noon Sat) sell maps detailing these hikes.

Running

Good places to run on Hong Kong Island include Harlech and Lugard Rds on the Peak (p523), the running track in Victoria Park (p534) in Causeway Bay, and around Happy Valley Race Course (Map pp530–1).

Taichi

One of the most popular HKTB activities is the **free taichi lessons** (✆ 8-9am Mon & Wed-Fri) along the Ave of the Stars, Tsim Sha Tsui Promenade (see p535).

WALKING TOUR

A one-hour walk through Sheung Wan is a wonderful (and easy) step back into Hong Kong's past. Begin the tour at the Sutherland St stop of the Kennedy Town tram. Have a look at (and sniff of) Des Voeux Rd West's **dried seafood and shrimp paste shops (1)** then turn up Ko Shing St, where there are **herbal medicine wholesalers (2)**. At the end of the street, walk northeast along Des Voeux Rd West and turn right onto New Market St, where you'll find **Western Market (3**; p523) at the corner of Morrison St. Walk south along this street past Bonham Strand, which is lined with **ginseng root sellers (4)**, and turn right on Queen's Rd West. To the right you'll pass **traditional shops (5)** selling bird's nests (for soup) and paper funeral offerings (for the dead).

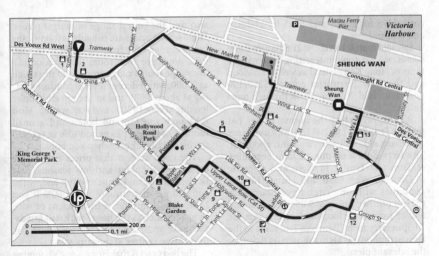

WALK FACTS

Start Kennedy Town tram (Sutherland St stop)

Finish Sheung Wan MTR station

Distance 2km

Duration one hour to 90 minutes, depending on how long you stop in NoHo

Cross Queen's Rd Central and turn left onto **Possession St (6)**, where the British flag was first planted in 1841.

Climbing Pound Lane to where it meets Tai Ping Shan St, look right to spot **Pak Sing Ancestral Hall (7**; ☺ 8am-6pm), originally a storeroom for bodies awaiting burial in China, and left to find two small temples dedicated to **Kwun Yam** (see the boxed text, p196) and **Sui Tsing Pak (8)**.

Descend Upper Station St to the start of Hollywood Rd's many **antique shops (9)**. Continue down Sai St and turn right onto Upper Lascar Row, home of the **Cat St market (10**; ☺ 9am-6pm), with Chinese bric-a-brac, curios and souvenirs. Wander east to the end and climb up Ladder St to the **Man Mo Temple (11**; p523). For a chance to sit down, head back down Ladder St and turn right along the pedestrian way to quiet Gough St, which with its cafés and low-key restaurants is also known as **NoHo (12)**, aka North of Hollywood Rd. Suitably refreshed, take the lane north to Queen's Rd Central, head northeast and turn left (west) on Bonham Strand. From there continue west to

Man Wa Lane (13) where you'll find traditional carved chops (or seals), an excellent gift or memento. The Sheung Wan MTR station is a short distance to the northwest.

HONG KONG FOR CHILDREN

In most respects Hong Kong is a great travel destination for children, although the crowds, traffic and pollution might be off-putting to some parents. In most places (hotels, restaurants and sights) children are well catered for, but if you're pushing a pram the stairs and public transport can be a pain. Sights and activities that are good for children include Hong Kong Disneyland (p537), Hong Kong Space Museum & Theatre (p535), Hong Kong Zoological & Botanical Gardens (p523) and Ocean Park (p534).

Kids also love Hong Kong's more retro forms of transport, including the Star Ferry (p563) and the trams (p565).

Most hotels can recommend babysitters if you've got daytime appointments or want a night out without the kids.

TOURS

Some of the most popular surface tours of the New Territories are offered by the HKTB (p522), including the ever-popular Land Between Tour, which takes in temple complexes, fishing villages, Tai Mo Shan (p536) and the China boundary. For a full-day (6½-hour) tour with lunch it costs $395 for adults and $345 for children under 16 or seniors over 60; a half-day (five-hour) tour without lunch costs $295 for adults and $245 for children and seniors.

Splendid Tours & Travel (☎ 2316 2151; www.splendidtours.com) has some interesting 'orientation' tours of Hong Kong Island as well as Kowloon and the New Territories costing $280/190 per adult/child. You can book through most hotels.

It's cheaper to take the normal ferries, but the **Star Ferry Tour** (☎ 2118 6201; www.starferry.com.hk/harbourtour) is still fair value and good fun. The ferry does a 60-minute loop beginning at Tsim Sha Tsui at 11.05am and stopping at Central, Wan Chai and Hung Hom. It continues with one circuit per hour, with the last one beginning at 9.05pm. Tickets are $40/85 for a single loop day/evening trip; the 7.05pm ferry from Tsim Sha Tsui takes in the 8pm Symphony of Lights show. Get tickets at the relevant piers.

FESTIVALS & EVENTS

Western and Chinese culture combine to create an interesting mix of cultural events and no fewer than 17 official public holidays. However, determining the exact date can be tricky, as some follow the Chinese lunar calendar so the date changes each year. A few key events and their approximate dates are listed here, but for a full schedule with exact dates see www.discoverhongkong.com.

Hong Kong Arts Festival (www.hk.artsfestival.org) February–March.

Man Hong Kong International Literary Festival (www.festival.org.hk) March.

Hong Kong Sevens (www.hksevens.com) Late March or early April.

Hong Kong International Film Festival (www.hkiff.org.hk) April.

International Dragon Boat Races (www.hkdba.com.hk) May–June.

Hungry Ghosts Festival August.

SLEEPING

Hong Kong has the full gamut of accommodation, from cell-like spaces with little more than a bed and fan to palatial suites in some of the world's finest hotels. Compared with other cities in China you'll find rooms relatively expensive, though they can still be cheaper than their US or European counterparts. We have listed the high season rates here.

Most hotels are on Hong Kong Island between Central and Causeway Bay, and either side of Nathan Rd in Kowloon, where you'll also find the largest range of budget places. High-season prices are roughly as follows: the budget range runs from about $150 to $400 for a double or twin room (less in a dorm); midrange rooms range from $400 to as high as $2000, with a decent level of comfort starting at about $800; and in the top end you're looking at about $2000 and way, way up. Most midrange and top-end hotels and a small number of budget places add 13% in taxes to the listed rates; check when you book.

The good news is that prices fall sharply during the shoulder and low seasons, particularly in the midrange and top end, when you can get discounts of up to 60% if you book online, through a travel agent or with an agency such as the **Hong Kong Hotels Association** (HKHA; ☎ 2375 8380; www.hkha.org), which has reservation centres at the airport.

The bad news is that Hong Kong's booming economy means these sort of deals are harder to find than they were. Hong Kong's two high seasons are March to early May (trade fair season) and October to November, though things can also be tight around Chinese New Year (late January or February).

Trade fair season can be crazy, with everywhere from the plush Peninsula to slummy Chungking Mansions booked out or close to it on trade fair days; check their exact dates on www.discoverhongkong.com.

Unless specified otherwise, all rooms listed here have private bathrooms and air-conditioning, and all but the cheapest will have cable TV in English. Many hotels, particularly in the midrange, offer weekly and monthly rates.

Hong Kong Island

Most of Hong Kong Island's top-end hotels are in Central and Admiralty, while Wan Chai caters to the midrange market, though several new midrange places in Central mean there's now more choice. Causeway Bay has quite a few budget guesthouses that are a step up (in both price and quality) from their Tsim Sha Tsui counterparts.

BUDGET

Noble Hostel (Map pp530–1; ☎ 2576 6148; www.noblehostel.com.hk; Flat A3, 17th fl, Great George Bldg, 27 Paterson St, Causeway Bay; s/d/tr $240/340/420) Dapper Mr Lin and his wife have been running this place for more than 20 years. The 26 squeaky-clean rooms are a bit larger than others in this price range, and most have a fridge.

Hong Kong Hostel (Map pp530-1; ☎ 2392 6868, in Japanese 9831 6058; www.hostel.hk; Flat A2, 3rd fl, Paterson Bldg, 47 Paterson St, Causeway Bay; dm $120-150, s/d/tr $340/400/500, without bathroom $250/340/480; 🖳) The hostel formerly known as Wang Fat is a good place to meet other backpackers, with 110 rooms scattered through several floors of a large apartment building. You wouldn't describe the rooms as spacious, but many are newly renovated with phone, TV and fridge. They do vary, however, so look at a few. There are laundry facilities, and there's long-term storage, free internet access and wi-fi. Get a receipt when you pay for your room in advance.

Causeway Bay Guest House (Map pp530-1; ☎ 2895 2013; www.cbgh.net; Flat B, 1st fl, Lai Yee Bldg, 44a-d Leighton Rd, Causeway Bay; s/d/tr $250/350/450) If you want to save on accommodation to spend in the Causeway Bay shoppolopolis, this no-frills but clean seven-room guesthouse might be for you. Enter from Leighton Lane.

Alisan Guest House (Map pp530-1; ☎ 2838 0762; http://home.hkstar.com/~alisangh; Flat A, 5th fl, Hoito Court, 23 Cannon St, Causeway Bay; s/d/tr $350/410/520) Spread through several apartments, the rooms in this small family-run place are clean, the welcome is warm and the advice good; it's a consistent favourite with travellers.

MIDRANGE

Eden (Map pp526-7; ☎ 2851 0303; 148 Wellington St, Central; r $780-1200) So you're out in Lan Kwai Fong, you meet someone you like and things are getting hot. The Eden, marketed as a hotel for 'couples', might be the place for you. In fact, facilitating coupling seems to be the Eden's speciality, with rates for two- and three-hour 'sessions' as well as overnight sessions (check in after 1am). The small but stylish rooms have everything you need: down-filled bedding, DVD players, free wireless broadband, plenty of mirrors and condoms. Service is discreet and we were told it was no problem to leave your bags with reception and check in late (yes, at 1am) to take advantage of the reduced rates (from $420). Rates rise a bit on weekends.

Lan Kwai Fong Hotel (Map pp526-7; ☎ 2850 8899; www.lankwaifonghotel.com.hk; 3 Kau U Fong, Central; r $780-1780; 🖳) Not quite as near to the Lan Kwai Fong nightlife district as you might imagine (it's about a 10-minute walk), this chic new hotel has a modern Chinese flavour in a wonderfully central location near Graham St

market. The service, rooms (the pricier rooms ending in 06 are best) and price are all good.

Central Park Hotel (Map pp526-7; ☎ 2850 0899; www .centralparkhotel.com.hk; 263 Hollywood Rd, Sheung Wan; r $780-1780; 🖳) This new 142-room affair is sleek, modern rooms that, while not tiny, seem bigger than they are through the effective use of mirrors. The location is great, a short walk to SoHo and Central.

Ice House (Map pp526-7; ☎ 2836 7333; www.icehouse .com.hk; 38 Ice House St, Central; r $800-1500) The location, in the heart of Central and staggering distance from Lan Kwai Fong, and the 64 spacious, stylish open-plan 'suites' make the Ice House about the coolest stay in Central and excellent value. Each suite has a kitchenette, work desk, internet access and rain shower.

Bishop Lei International House (Map pp526-7; ☎ 2868 0828; www.bishopleihtl.com.hk; 4 Robinson Rd, Mid-Levels; r $1080-1680, ste from $1880; 🖳 🖳) This 203-room hotel in Mid-Levels is not luxurious but it does have its own swimming pool and some rooms have quite spectacular views. Low season rates are as low as $540.

Garden View International House (Map pp526-7; ☎ 2877 3737; www.ywca.org.hk; 1 MacDonnell Rd, Central; r $1350-1750, ste from $2500) Straddling the border of Central and Mid-Levels, the YWCA-run Garden View has fine views and is one of the better midrange places in Central. Rates are about half in the low season.

Jia (Map pp530-1; ☎ 3196 9000; www.jiahongkong .com; 1-5 Irving St, Causeway Bay; r $1800, ste from $2600; 🖳) Hong Kong's first true boutique hotel is an apartment building conversion inspired by French design guru Philippe Starck. It's chic as hell, from the stunning staff uniforms and postmodern/baroque furnishings to the guests: models in sunglasses loitering in the lobby. Standard rooms (known as studios) are poky, but the restaurants, particularly Opia (p546), are excellent.

Also recommended:

Charterhouse Hotel (Map pp530-1; ☎ 2833 5566; www.charterhouse.com; 209-219 Wan Chai Rd, Wan Chai; r $950-1700, ste from $2000) Book online for big discounts on fairly comfortable rooms.

Wharney Hotel Hong Kong (Map pp530-1; ☎ 2861 1000; www.gdhhotels.com; 57-73 Lockhart Rd, Wan Chai; r $1000-2200, ste from $3600) In the heart of Wan Chai; best value when you get an online deal.

TOP END

Island Shangri-La Hong Kong (Map pp526-7; ☎ 2877 3838; www.shangri-la.com; Supreme Court Rd, Admiralty;

r $2400-3700, ste from $5600; ⬛) The 56-storey Shangri-La boasts some of the best-equipped rooms in Hong Kong, with everything from a four-in-one printer fax thingy to remote-controlled curtains. Check out the 16-storey tall Chinese landscape painting in the upper atrium (from the 39th floor).

Four Seasons Hotel (Map pp526-7; ☎ 3196 8888; www.fourseasons.com; IFC 3, 8 Finance St, Central; r from $3800; ste from $7000; ⬛ ⬛ ⬛) Everything about the Four Seasons is class, from the fine rooms and restaurants to the panoramic harbour views from its location (don't miss the incredible pool at sunset) in the International Financial Centre. But it's the enthusiastic and sophisticated service that is most memorable.

Landmark Mandarin Oriental (Map pp526-7; ☎ 2132 0188; www.mandarinoriental.com; 15 Queen's Rd Central; r $4000-5400, ste from $8800; ⬛) This brand-new boutique five-star hotel in the centre of Central is very nice indeed. Atop the uber-exclusive Landmark shopping complex, the hotel's contemporary design is beautiful throughout the 113 spacious rooms and facilities, and the service top-notch. The drawback: there are no views.

Kowloon

Kowloon has an incredible array of accommodation: from the Peninsula, Hong Kong's poshest hotel, to its infamous neighbour, Chungking Mansions, plus plenty in between.

BUDGET

Chungking Mansions has been synonymous with budget accommodation in Hong Kong for decades. The crumbling block rising out of the prime real estate of Nathan Rd is stacked with dirt-cheap hostels, guesthouses, curry houses, immigrants and all manner of merchants. Rooms are usually miniscule and service is as rudimentary as you'd expect in the cheapest accommodation in town. And while it can seem pretty bleak, you can take comfort in knowing it used to be much worse. In recent years standards have risen (from an admittedly very low base) and when we were there several guesthouses were getting makeovers. Even the lifts have been upgraded, though they're still painfully slow. There are literally dozens of options in Chungking Mansions and the similar Mirador Mansion, just up the street, so shop around.

our pick **Payless Guest House** (Map p532; ☎ 3119 2888; Flat A2, 7th fl, A Block, Chungking Mansions, 36-44 Nathan Rd, Tsim Sha Tsui; s $100-150, d $160-190, tr $220) Jackey Chan, the colourful owner with the familiar name, has transformed this place from just another Chungking dump to the best option in the Mansions. His 30 rooms on two floors have been renovated in sparkling white tiles and the vast majority have windows. All have both air-con and fan, and TVs that actually work.

Park Guesthouse (Map p532; ☎ 2368 1689; fax 2367 7889; Flat A1, 15th fl, A Block, Chungking Mansions, 36-44 Nathan Rd, Tsim Sha Tsui; s/d $140/200, without bathroom $100/150) Small, clean and friendly, the rooms here come with the usual Chungking fare (TV, air-con, phone and a vague curry smell) plus a fridge and some reader recommendations. Room 1504 has the smallest bathtub you'll ever see.

Cosmic Guest House (Map p532; ☎ 2369 6669; www.cosmicguesthouse.com; Flat A1-A2 & F1-F4, 12th fl, Mirador Mansion, 58-62 Nathan Rd, Tsim Sha Tsui; s/tw $150/250) The crystal-clean, quiet, friendly and secure Cosmic is a consistent favourite with travellers. Rooms are relatively bright and some rooms even have rain showers…wedged into 1m-square bathrooms! A good option.

World Wide Guest House (Map p532; ☎ 2311 3550; wwgsthse@biznetvigator.com; Unit E1, 14th fl, Mirador Mansion, 58-62 Nathan Rd, Tsim Sha Tsui; s/d $200/300) This brand-new place has seven comfortable and larger-than-normal rooms, each with a broadband connection ($30 per hour).

Hakkas Guest House (Map p532; ☎ 2771 3656; fax 2770 1470; Flat L, 3rd fl, New Lucky House, 300 Nathan Rd, Yau Ma Tei; s $200-250, d $250-300, tr $300-350) The nine clean rooms here make this the pick of the places in New Lucky House. The owner, affable Kevin Koo, is a keen hiker who sometimes leads country walks on Sunday.

Dadol Hotel (Map p532; ☎ 2369 8882; fax 2311 0250; 1st fl, Champagne Court, 16-20 Kimberley Rd, Tsim Sha Tsui; s/d $350/420) This 41-room hotel tucked away inside a shopping arcade is one of the best deals in Tsim Sha Tsui. There aren't many windows but these rooms are big and very comfortable for the money.

Also recommended:

Travellers Hostel (Map p532; ☎ 2368 7710; www.travellers.com.hk; Flat A1-A4, 16th fl, A Block, Chungking Mansions, 36-44 Nathan Rd, Tsim Sha Tsui; dm $55-60, d $120-140, s/d without bathroom $90/110; ⬛) This aging Chungking landmark is very cheap for a reason.

Man Hing Lung Hotel (Map p532; ☎ 2311 8807; www.manhinglung-hotel.com; Flat F2, 14th fl, Mirador

Mansion, 58-62 Nathan Rd, Tsim Sha Tsui; s $120-150, d $150-200, tr $210-240; 🖵) Clean rooms and a good atmosphere overseen by friendly Mr Chan; free wireless and broadband internet access.

Welcome Guest House (Map p532; ☎ 2721 7793; guesthousehk@hotmail.com; Flat A5, 7th fl, A Block, Chungking Mansions, 36-44 Nathan Rd, Tsim Sha Tsui; s $120-150, d $160-190, s without shower $100) It needs a face-lift but English-speaking owner John Wah makes this place worth a look.

Star Guesthouse (Map p532; ☎ 2723 8951; www .starguesthouse.com; 6th fl, 21 Cameron Rd, Tsim Sha Tsui; s/tw/tr $250/300/350) and its sister property up the road, the **Lee Garden Guest House** (☎ 2367 2284; charliechan@iname.com; 8th fl, D Block, 36 Cameron Rd, Tsim Sha Tsui; s/tw/tr $250/300/350), are owned and run by the charismatic Charlie Chan, who can arrange almost anything. Both have small, clean rooms.

MIDRANGE

Salisbury (Map p532; ☎ 2268 7888; www.ymcahk .org.hk; 41 Salisbury Rd, Tsim Sha Tsui; dm/s $210/$700, d $750-950, ste from $1300) Operated by the YMCA, the rooms here are simple but the facilities and the five-star views are not. Budgeteers who book ahead might get a bed in the four-bed dorms. However, no-one is allowed to stay more than seven consecutive nights and walk-in guests for the dorms aren't accepted if they've been in Hong Kong for more than 10 days.

Rent-A-Room (Map p532; ☎ 2366 3011, 9023 8022; www.rentaroomhk.com; Flat A, 2nd fl, Knight Garden, 7-8 Tak Hing St, Yau Ma Tei; s/d/tr $500/800/$1200; 🖵) Around the corner from Jordan MTR station (take Exit E), this place has 70 compact but immaculate rooms spread across several floors. Each room has shower, safe, TV, telephone (no charge for local calls), internet access and a fridge. These prices are dramatically lower most of the time.

Booth Lodge (Map p532; ☎ 2771 9266; http:// boothlodge.salvation.org.hk; 11 Wing Sing Lane, Yau Ma Tei; s & tw incl breakfast $620-1500) This wedge-shaped, Salvation Army–run place is spartan and clean but fair value in the lower midrange. Standard rooms are about $500 out of season. Reception is on the 7th floor.

Minden (Map p532; ☎ 2739 7777; www.theminden .com; 7 Minden Ave, Tsim Sha Tsui; r $900-1500, ste from $2500) The boutique-ish Minden is a welcome injection of charisma to Hong Kong's midrange hotel gang. Packed with Asian and Western

antiques, curios and furnishings, it's an eclectic mix that works.

our pick Stanford Hillview Hotel (Map p532; ☎ 2722 7822, 2313 7031; www.stanfordhillview.com; 13-17 Observatory Rd, Tsim Sha Tsui; s & d $1000-1680, ste from $2480) At the eastern end of Knutsford Tce, the Stanford is a quality hotel in just about our favourite location in Tsim Sha Tsui, with little traffic noise but seconds from loads of bars and restaurants. Big reductions out of season.

Nathan Hotel (Map p532; ☎ 2388 5141; www .nathanhotel.com; 378 Nathan Rd, Yau Ma Tei; tw & d $1080-1480, ste from $1880) Even the cheapest of the 191 recently renovated rooms here is clean, stylish, spacious and relatively good value, particularly in low season. It's near Temple St; enter from Pak Hoi St.

Also recommended:

YMCA International House (Map p532; ☎ 2771 9111; www.ymcaintlhousehk.org; 23 Waterloo Rd, Yau Ma Tei; dm $330, r $880-1380, ste from $2080) Open to men and women. Dorm rooms (actually cosy singles with share bathroom) are cheap.

Shamrock Hotel (Map p532; ☎ 2735 2271; www .shamrockhotel.com.hk; 223 Nathan Rd, Yau Ma Tei; s $550-1250, d $750-1450, ste from $1500) Good value for the location.

TOP END

Royal Garden Hotel (Map p532; ☎ 2721 5215; www .rghk.com.hk; 69 Mody Rd, Tsim Sha Tsui East; s $2300-3000, d $2450-3150, ste from $4100; 🖵 🏊) This often-overlooked hotel is one of the best-equipped in Kowloon. And with its tasteful rooms, super rooftop recreation facilities (from pool to putting green), fine restaurants and smart service, it's an excellent top-end option.

Marco Polo Hong Kong Hotel (Map p532; ☎ 2113 0088; www.marcopolohotels.com; Harbour City, 3 Canton Rd, Tsim Sha Tsui; s & d $2500-3700, ste from $4900; 🖵 🏊) This is the pick of the three Marco Polo group hotels that each feeds into the vast Harbour City complex. For shoppers or those afraid of HK's pollution, it's heaven – one reader wrote of how pleased they were to be able to shop, eat and sleep without ever going outside!

Peninsula Hong Kong (Map p532; ☎ 2920 2888; www .peninsula.com; Salisbury Rd, Tsim Sha Tsui; r $2900-4200, ste from $4600; 🖵 🏊) Hong Kong's colonial classic is pure elegance with service and up-to-the-minute facilities to match. If you can afford it, the Pen is somewhere everyone should stay at least once.

Hotel Inter-Continental Hong Kong (Map p532; ☎ 2721 1211; www.hongkong-ic.intercontinental.com; 18

Salisbury Rd, Tsim Sha Tsui; r $3300-3900, ste from $5500; 🖥️ 🖥️) It's getting on a bit, but the Intercon still boasts the finest waterfront position in the territory, excellent service and quirky colonial traditions, such as a fleet of Rolls Royces. The view from the Lobby Lounge bar is unbeatable.

New Territories

The New Territories does not offer travellers a tremendous choice in terms of accommodation, but there are both official and independent hostels here, usually in remote areas. The **Country & Marine Parks Authority** (☎ 2420 0529) maintains 28 no-frills camp sites in the New Territories and 11 in the Outlying Islands for hikers and trekkers. They are all free and are clearly labelled on the four trail maps (see p538). To visit the relevant page of the authority's website, go to www.afcd.gov.hk and click on Country & Marine Parks.

Ascension House (Map pp524-5; ☎ 2691 4196; www.achouse.com; 33 Tao Fong Shan Rd, Sha Tin; dm $125) This 11-bed place affiliated with the Lutheran Church is probably the best deal in Hong Kong because the price of a bed includes free laundry service, three meals and 'friendly Scandinavian staff'.

To get there, take the KCR East Rail to Sha Tin station, leave via exit B and walk down the ramp, passing a series of traditional village houses on the left. Between them is a set of steps. Go up these steps, follow the path and when you come to a roundabout, go along the uphill road – Pak Lok Path – to your right. After about 150m you'll see a small staircase on the right; follow the signs from here. The walk should take 15 to 20 minutes. A taxi from Sha Tin station will cost about $20.

Outlying Islands

Lantau, Lamma and Cheung Chau all have accommodation options and are excellent places in which to escape from the hustle and bustle of urban Hong Kong. In fact, we think Lamma is the ideal place to stay if you're on a budget, with excellent-value small hotels and homestays (just pitch up and ask around), a relaxed vibe and only 20 minutes from Central by ferry (though these do stop about midnight). For campers, the Country & Marine Parks Authority (above) maintains nine sites on Lantau. Camping is prohibited on Hong Kong beaches.

Hongkong Bank Foundation SG Davis Hostel (Map pp524-5; ☎ 2985 5610; www.yha.org.hk; Ngong Ping, Lantau; dm under/over 18 yr $35/50, d $150) This is a 10-minute walk from the bus stop near the Tian Tan Buddha statue (see p537) in Ngong Ping; ideal if you want to see sunrise at nearby Lantau Peak. From the bus stop, take the path to your left as you face the Tian Tan Buddha, pass the public toilets on your right and the Lantau Tea Garden on your left and follow the signs to the mazelike steps up to the hostel.

Bali Holiday Resort (Map pp524-5; ☎ 2982 4580; 8 Main St, Lamma; r $250-380, apt $400-500) On Lamma's Main St, this place has newish, well-equipped rooms that, for the money, are much more attractive than the cells in Chungking Mansions. The staff can also find rooms elsewhere on Lamma. Prices double on weekends.

Man Lai Wah Hotel (Map pp524-5; ☎ 2982 0220; hotel@my.netvigator.com; 2 Po Wah Garden, Yung Shue Wan, Lamma; r Mon-Fri $300-350, Sat & Sun $500) This nine-room guesthouse faces you as you get off the ferry and has friendly staff and similarly well-equipped rooms, some with balconies.

Warwick Hotel (Map pp524-5; ☎ 2981 0081; www.warwickhotel.com.hk; Cheung Chau Sports Rd, Tung Wan Beach, Cheung Chau; d with mountain/sea view Mon-Fri $620/690, Sat & Sun $890/990, ste from $1500/1900) This hotel is butt ugly to look at, but you do get a wonderful vista across the sea to Lamma and Hong Kong Island.

There are a couple of hotels near Mui Wo, on Lantau, including the **Mui Wo Inn** (Map pp524-5; ☎ 2984 7225; fax 2984 1916; 14 Tung Wan Tau Rd, Silvermine Bay Beach, Lantau; r incl breakfast Sun-Fri $350, Sat $520), which is the last hotel on Silvermine Bay Beach; look for the ring of faux-classical statues in front. It's not exactly luxurious, but it does have sea views.

EATING

Hong Kong is becoming one of the world's great food cities and especially if you've been on the road in China for a while, you're going to love it. The options are endless, whether it be Cantonese, Chiu Chow (a regional cuisine of southern China), Northern, Shànghǎinese or Sìchuān cuisine from China, or international fare as diverse as Italian and Asian fusion, basic Thai, fiery Indian curries, Malay laksas, scores of Japanese eateries and innovative vegetarian options.

Meals range from cheap and cheerful $25 rice and noodle dishes to well into four figures, though to put it into context you'll find the price of a decent-quality meal will be comparable with similar places in Běijīng or Shànghǎi, and usually cheaper than Sydney, London or New York.

Restaurants are everywhere, but if you can't decide exactly what you fancy it's a good idea to just head to a particular area and choose once you get there.

On Hong Kong Island, SoHo (see below) has easily the biggest range in an attractive setting, while Central, Lan Kwai Fong and Wan Chai are also good bets. In Kowloon, Lock Rd and Ashley Rd in Tsim Sha Tsui have a growing mix of trendy eateries and Knutsford Tce is also worth a look.

While in Hong Kong, you should try dim sum, uniquely Cantonese dishes served for breakfast, brunch or lunch. Dim sum delicacies are normally steamed and you pay by the number of baskets or dishes you order. In larger places these are stacked up on trolleys and wheeled around the dining room; just point at whatever catches your eye as the trolley rolls by. In smaller places you order from a menu card.

In Cantonese restaurants, tea is often served free of charge or at nominal cost and refilled indefinitely. When the teapot is empty and you want a refill, signal the waiter by taking the lid off the pot and resting it on the handle.

Hong Kong Island

The city's best range of food is on Hong Kong Island.

CHINESE

Peking Shui Jiao Wong (Map pp530-1; ☎ 2527 0289; 118 Jaffe Rd, Wan Chai; dishes $25-40; ☻ 7am-11pm Mon-Sat, noon-11pm Sun) The charismatic 'Dumpling King' serves probably the city's best (and cheapest) northern-style dumplings, *guō tiē* (pot stickers) and soup noodles.

Mak's Noodle (Map pp526-7; ☎ 2854 3810; 77 Wellington St, Central; dishes $25-50; ☻ 11am-8pm) The wonton soup noodles (a major hangover cure) and beef brisket noodles have been drawing patrons to this low-key place for decades.

ourpick **Java Rd Market & Cooked Food Centre** (Map pp524-5; 2nd fl, cnr Java Rd & Shuhuk St, North Point; meals $40-100; ☻ 5.30pm-12.30am) It's a little bit out of the way, but this place is a real Hong Kong experience. Located above the Java Rd wet market, it is essentially a giant *dai pai dong* (set of Chinese kitchens) dishing up all manner of cuisine to hundreds in a long hall, all washed down with cheap beer.

Yung Kee (Map pp526-7; ☎ 2522 1624; 32-40 Wellington St, Central; dishes $55-150; ☻ 11am-11.30pm) Operating since 1942, the four-storey Yung Kee is Central's most famous Cantonese restaurant. The roast goose ($100 for one or two people) and dim sum (served 2pm to 5.30pm Monday to Saturday and 11am to 5.30pm Sunday) are the signature dishes, though everything on the phonebook of a menu is pretty good.

Luk Yu Tea House (Map pp526-7; ☎ 2523 5464; 24-26 Stanley St, Central; rice & noodle dishes $65-160, mains $100-350; ☻ 7am-10pm) The Luk Yu is a Hong Kong classic, with distinctive old-style décor and divine dim sum (served between 7am

SOHO

Until 1994, the area now known as SoHo was a decaying neighbourhood of old-style apartments. Then the Central to Mid-Levels Escalator was built, making the steep walk up a nonissue, someone invented the name SoHo (ostensibly meaning South of Hollywood Rd) and everything began to change.

It has been a slow process, but one by one the old rice sellers, butchers, printers and shops selling hell money for the dead have slowly sold up or been priced out by rising rents. Enough remain that it still feels like a Chinese neighbourhood (for now), but these days SoHo is all about food and drink. The range of eateries is enormous and while we have recommended a few individually, it's well worth just lobbing up and wandering the streets until you find somewhere that fits your taste buds and your budget. This is especially pertinent when you consider that places tend to open and close in SoHo faster than brothel doors in Wan Chai.

Most restaurants in SoHo are not cheap, but with so many places and competition so fierce just about everywhere has a lunchtime special from about noon to 2.30pm. These usually involve two or three modestly sized courses for between $75 and $100, which is a big discount from evening prices. Evenings are also good, with happy-hour drinks usually going from about 4pm or 5pm until 8pm or 9pm.

and 5pm) compensating for rather cavalier service.

our pick **City Hall Maxim's Palace** (Map pp526-7; ☎ 2521 1303; 3rd fl, Lower Block, Hong Kong City Hall, 1 Edinburgh Pl; dim sum per person about $100; ⊗ 11am-3pm & 5.30-11.30pm Mon-Sat, 9am-11.30pm Sun) This is the full dim sum experience, in a huge kitschy hall with hundreds of locals, fantastic food and fine harbour views.

SoHo is home to several Chinese restaurants, but two Sìchuān places stand out. **Shui Hu Ju** (Map pp526-7; ☎ 2869 6927; 68 Peel St, Central; meals per person from $250; ⊗ 6pm-midnight) serves delicious, chilli-packed Sìchuān dishes in a delightful Chinese setting that makes you feel like you're dining in one of the neighbouring antiques shops; while **Sìchuān Cuisine Dǎ Píng Huǒ** (Map pp526-7; ☎ 2559 1317, 9051 4496; lower ground fl, 49 Hollywood Rd, Central; meals per person $250; ⊗ 6pm-midnight) serves similarly fiery set meals in sleek surrounds, after which the owner-chef emerges to sing Chinese opera. Book ahead.

OTHER ASIAN

Prawn Noodle Shop (Map pp530-1; ☎ 2520 0268; Shop 4, Rialto Bldg, 2 Landale St, Wan Chai; meals $25-40; ⊗ 11.30am-7.30pm Mon-Sat) One of a string of cheap eateries in little Landale St, this place is famous for its soups, especially the Malay laksa. It's great value for lunch and the tight surrounds make it a good place to meet Hong Kongers.

Koh-i-Noor (Map pp526-7; ☎ 2877 9706; 1st fl, California Entertainment Bldg, 34-36 D'Aguilar St, Lan Kwai Fong; rice & biryani dishes $25-98, mains $44-130; ⊗ noon-3pm & 6-11pm Mon-Sat, 6-11pm Sun) The north Indian cuisine here is as good as you'll find this side of Chungking Mansions and the weekday vegetarian/meat lunch buffet is a bargain at $48/68.

Nha Trang (Map pp526-7; ☎ 2581 9992; 88 Wellington St, Central; mains $30-60; ⊗ noon-11pm) The regular Vietnamese diners in this stylish restaurant are testament to the quality and price of the food.

Lively little Wing Wah Lane, commonly known as Rat Alley, is home to restaurants serving Malay, Thai, Sri Lankan and Indian food. The outdoor eateries, including **Good Luck Thai** (Map pp526-7; ☎ 2877 2971; 13 Wing Wah Lane, Central; dishes $35-120; ⊗ 11am-1am Mon-Sat, 4pm-midnight Sun), are the perfect place to fill up before/while/after sinking a few beers in neighbouring Lan Kwai Fong (p557). It's easy to find; just look for the mega-coiffed touts.

WESTERN & MIDDLE EASTERN

La Kasbah (Map pp526-7; ☎ 2525 9493; Basement, 17 Hollywood Rd; starters from $60, mains $105-155; ⊗ 6.30-11.30pm Mon-Sat) A kind of Frenchified Maghreb caravanserai, La Kasbah serves delightful North African dishes in a wonderfully escapist underground setting.

Peak Cafe Bar (Map pp526-7; ☎ 2140 6877; 9-13 Shelley St; meals $100-180; ⊗ 11am-2am Mon-Fri, 9am-2am Sat, 9am-midnight Sun) The fixtures and fittings of the Peak Cafe, established in 1947, have moved down the hill to this comfy restaurant and bar with excellent nosh, super cocktails and a cinemascope view of passing people on the escalator. The sandwiches ($68 to $98), pizza ($88 to $98) and lunchtime menu are good value.

Top Deck at the Jumbo (Map pp524-5; ☎ 2553 9111; Shum Wan Pier Dr, Wong Chuk Hang, Aberdeen; meals per person from $250; ⊗ 10.30am-11.30pm Mon-Sat, 7.30am-11.30pm Sun) This tourist institution is the larger of two floating restaurants moored in Aberdeen Harbour. But forget the old restaurant and head straight upstairs to Top Deck for fine seafood in a prime indoor/outdoor location. The Sunday unlimited seafood and champagne buffet ($298; 11.30am to 2.30pm) is a great splurge. There's free transport for diners from the pier on Aberdeen Promenade (see p534).

Opia (Map pp530-1; ☎ 3196 9100; Jia Hotel, 1-5 Irving St, Causeway Bay; meals $350-500; ⊗ 6-11pm Mon-Sat) Superstylish Opia and its 'Australian freestyle' cuisine has gobbled up a remarkable number of awards in a short time, which accurately reflects both the food and décor. Not every dish works, but most totally do.

VEGETARIAN

Fragrance Vegetarian Fast Food (Map pp526-7; ☎ 2850 5866; 98 Wellington St, Central; set lunchbox $20; ⊗ 8am-9pm) On the pedestrian way opposite the escalator, the Fragrance does a brisk trade in veggie fast food. It's take away only; sit under the escalator.

Life (Map pp526-7; ☎ 2810 9777; 10 Shelley St, Central; starters & snacks $35-75, mains $60-110; ⊗ 10am-midnight) Life has taken vegetarian Hong Kong by storm, serving vegan food and dishes free of gluten, wheat, onion and garlic over three floors. Recommended – veggie or not.

Fringe Club (Map pp526-7; ☎ 2521 7251; 2nd fl, Dairy Farm Bldg, 2 Lower Albert Rd, Central; set lunches $76-98; ⊗ noon-2pm Mon-Fri) Apart from entertainment, the Fringe serves popular vegetarian lunch-

HONG KONG

time buffets upstairs in its Fotogalerie; there's seating on the roof terrace too.

QUICK EATS & SELF-CATERING

See the boxed text, below, for fast-food options.

city'super (Map pp526-7; ☎ 2234 7128; Shop 1041-1049, 1st fl, IFC Mall, 8 Finance St, Central; ☿ 10.30am-9.30pm) This enormous gourmet supermarket has ready-to-eat food such as sushi and salads, along with lots of fresh but pricey produce. There is another branch in Tsim Sha Tsui (Map p532; ☎ 2375 8222; Shop 3001, 3rd fl, Gateway Arcade, 25-27 Canton Rd, Harbour City; open 10am-10.30pm).

Bagel Factory (Map pp526-7; ☎ 2951 0755; 41-43 Elgin St, Mid-Levels; filled bagels $16-30; ☿ 8am-8.45pm) The innovative filled bagels, good coffee and adjoining bakery make this a great lunch stop.

Kowloon

Kowloon doesn't have the range of Hong Kong Island, but there is still plenty of choice in both cuisine and budget, especially in Tsim Sha Tsui.

CHINESE

Happy Garden Noodle & Congee Kitchen (Map p532; ☎ 2377 2604; 72 Canton Rd, Tsim Sha Tsui; rice & noodle dishes $22-110; ☿ 7am-1am) This top budget option has scores of rice, noodle and *congee* (rice porridge) dishes to choose from, including shrimp wonton noodles ($28).

Wu Kong Shanghai Restaurant (Map p532; ☎ 2366 7244; Basement, Alpha House, 27-33 Nathan Rd, Tsim Sha Tsui; rice & noodle dishes $35-88, mains $60-280; ☿ 11.30am-midnight) This long-running place is known for its cold pigeon in wine sauce and crispy fried eels, but also serves dim sum and a vast array of other dishes.

Spring Deer (Map p532; ☎ 2366 4012; 1st fl, 42 Mody Rd, Tsim Sha Tsui; meals per person from $150; ☿ noon-3pm & 6-11pm) Hong Kong's most famous Peking duck is served here ($280 for the whole bird), but the service can be about as welcoming as a Běijīng winter, c 1967.

Wan Loong Court (Map p532; ☎ 2734 3722; Lower level 2, Kowloon Hotel Hong Kong, 19-21 Nathan Rd, Tsim Sha Tsui; meals per person from $300; ☿ 11am-3pm & 6-11.30pm Mon-Fri, 11am-11pm Sat & Sun) The wonderful modern Cantonese food here is complemented by a famous selection of Chinese desserts.

INDIAN

Gaylord (Map p532; ☎ 2376 1001; 1st fl, Ashley Centre, 23-25 Ashley Rd, Tsim Sha Tsui; mains $56-136, lunch buffets $88; ☿ noon-3pm & 6-11pm) Classy service and live Indian music every night complement the excellent rogan josh, dhal and plenty of vegetarian choices in Hong Kong's oldest Indian restaurant.

Apart from cheap hotels, Chungking Mansions is packed with cheap Indian and Pakistani restaurants (called messes). Lunch or dinner will cost from about $50; for $100 you'll get a blowout, though if you want a drink you'll usually have to BYO. We've listed a few reliable places here, though you could just as happily follow your nose or, better, ask the locals what their favourite is.

Islamabad Club (Map p532; ☎ 2721 5362; Flat C4, 4th fl, C Block, Chungking Mansions, 36-44 Nathan Rd, Tsim Sha Tsui; ☿ noon-3.30pm & 6-10.30pm) This place serves Indian and Pakistani halal food; there's no alcohol.

Swagat Restaurant (Map p532; ☎ 2722 5350; Flat C3-4, 1st fl, C Block, Chungking Mansions, 36-44 Nathan Rd, Tsim Sha Tsui; ☿ noon-10.30pm) The only mess with a liquor licence, Swagat is a bit more expensive but its beer deals (five bottles for $69 when we visited) make it a good place to start an evening.

Taj Mahal Club (Map p532; ☎ 2722 5454; 2nd fl, B Block; ☿ 11am-3pm & 5.30-11.30pm) Like your curry untamed? Try anything Madras.

BUDGET BITES

Hong Kongers love their fast food. And while you can deal with a Mac-attack in one of more than 200 Golden Arches outlets, you can do that anywhere so why not check out one of these (relatively) exotic chains instead. They are all pretty cheap – about $20 to $60 a meal – and branches are everywhere, but especially in large shopping malls and near MTR stations.

Genki Sushi (www.genkisushi.com.sg) Cheap but tasty Japanese fare.

Maxim's (www.maxims.com.hk) A huge range of Canto dishes.

Mix (www.mix-world.com) Excellent smoothies, wraps, salads and free internet.

Olivers (www.olivers-supersandwiches.com) Sandwiches and salads.

Steak Expert (www.steakexpert.com.hk) Cheap meat; watch out for the pepper sauce.

HONG KONG

OTHER ASIAN

our pick **Katiga Street** (Map pp524-5; ☎ 2764 6436; Sung Oi Bldg, 37 Sung Kit St, Hung Hom; meals from $35; ⏱ 11.30am-11.30pm) Known to expats as Japan St, the ground-floor area under the Sung Oi building is home to several lively and cheap Japanese premises all working from the same kitchen. It's a lot of fun, but hard to find. Take a taxi (about $25 from Tsim Sha Tsui) and ask for Bailey St, Hung Hom, then walk down to the Katiga Japanese Food Shop, through that restaurant and take a ticket out the back; they'll take you to the next spare table.

Sushi One (Map p532; ☎ 2155 0633; 23 Ashley Rd, Tsim Sha Tsui; meals $75-200; ⏱ noon-midnight) This is a very trendy new sushi place with a mesmerising fish-tank wall.

WESTERN & MIDDLE EASTERN

Merhaba (Map p532; ☎ 2367 2263; 12 Knutsford Tce; meze & starters $40-70, mains $100-180; ⏱ 4pm-2am Mon-Sat, to 1am Sun) Merhaba is one of the few restaurants on ultracompetitive Knutsford Tce that is consistently busy. The meze is good, and Sunday is happy hour all night.

Wildfire (Map p532; ☎ 3690 1598; 2 Knutsford Tce, Tsim Sha Tsui; pizzas $125, kebabs $168; ⏱ noon-3pm & 6pm-1am) Another safe and popular bet on Knutsford Tce, Wildfire has excellent pizzas and enough skewered meat to satisfy a lion.

VEGETARIAN

Branto Pure Vegetarian Indian Food (Map p532; ☎ 2366 8171; 1st fl, 9 Lock Rd; dishes $30-59; ⏱ 11am-3pm & 6-11pm) This cheap but excellent place serves south Indian dishes; try the *dosa* (crispy crepe from south India) with dipping sauces.

QUICK EATS & SELF-CATERING

See the boxed text, p547, for fast-food options.

Wellcome (Map p532; ☎ 2369 6451; 28 Hankow Rd, Tsim Sha Tsui; ⏱ 8am-10pm) Well-stocked branch of the large supermarket chain.

Big John's Café (Map p532; ☎ 2739 6035; 17 Lock Rd, Tsim Sha Tsui; meals $20-35; ⏱ 8am-7.30pm Mon-Sat) This tiny place is great for a cheap and hearty breakfast or lunch, either Chinese or Western.

Outlying Islands

Eating options are improving on the Outlying Islands. Lamma boasts the biggest range in Yung Shue Wan (cafés, seafood and others) and Sok Kwu Wan (Chinese seafood restaurants). There are also some decent choices on

Lantau, Cheung Chau and, to a lesser extent, Peng Chau. Combined with the journey and the relatively 'rural' settings, these places make fun half-day trips (or vaguely memorable day trips if you begin imbibing at lunchtime).

Bookworm Café (Map pp524-5; ☎ 2982 4838; 79 Main St, Yung Shue Wan, Lamma; breakfasts $25-60, dishes $40-80; ⏱ 10am-9pm Mon-Fri, 9am-10pm Sat, 9am-9pm Sun) This long-running vegetarian café-restaurant serves fantastic fruit juices, organic wine and other fair fare, and doubles as a second-hand bookshop with free wi-fi.

Stoep Restaurant (Map pp524-5; ☎ 2980 2699; 32 Lower Cheung Sha Village, Lantau; mains $45-85; ⏱ 11am-10pm Tue-Sun) Right on quiet Lower Cheung Sha Beach, the Stoep serves up meat, fish and South African *braai* (barbecue; $80 to $150) and a chilled atmosphere.

Hong Kee (Map pp524-5; ☎ 2981 9916; 11a Pak She Praya Rd, Cheung Chau; dishes $45-160; ⏱ 10.30am-10.30pm) The excellent seafood here makes this the top spot on the Cheung Chau waterfront; try the lobster in black bean sauce. From the pier, head left (north) about 150m.

Bahçe Turkish Restaurant (Map pp524-5; ☎ 2984 0222; Shop 19, ground fl, Mui Wo Centre, 3 Ngan Wan Rd, Mui Wo, Lantau; meals from about $70; ⏱ 11.30am-10.30pm Mon-Fri, 10am-10.30pm Sat & Sun) This small Turkish place is recommended for its delicious *sigara böreği* (filo parcels filled with cheese) and *yaparak dolmasi* (stuffed vine leaves).

Lamma Hilton Shum Kee Seafood Restaurant (Map pp524-5; ☎ 2982 8241; 26 First St, Sok Kwu Wan; meals per person $200; ⏱ 10.30am-11.30pm) No hotel rooms here, but there's a huge array of delicious seafood in a village waterside setting. Walk here from Yung Shue Wan and make a day of it.

DRINKING
Cafés & Teahouses

The last few years have seen a miniature explosion of cafés – both local and international – that serve a wide range of coffees. Tea and teahouses (see p99), of course, have been a major component of Chinese culture since time immemorial.

TW Café (Map pp526-7; ☎ 2544 2237; Ground fl, 2-10 Lyndhurst Tce, Central; afternoon tea/coffee $35; ⏱ 8am-8pm) This tiny café offers more than 20 types of coffee and light snacks.

Moon Garden Tea House (Map pp530-1; ☎ 2882 6878; 5 Hoi Ping Rd, Causeway Bay; tea & snacks $120; ⏱ noon-midnight) Choose from many brews here, then

(Continued on page 557)

RICHARD I'ANSON

Neon signs of Casino Lisboa (p582), Macau

Portuguese egg tarts (p581), Macau

OLIVER STREWE

RICHARD I'ANSON

BRUCE YUAN-YUE BI

Boy in tour boat, Tiānyá Hǎijiǎo (p634), Hǎinán

Fountain on Largo do Senado (p572), Macau

KRZYSZTOF DYDYNSKI
Dragon's Backbone Rice Terraces (p663), Guǎngxī

KEREN SU
Dong women from Sānjiāng (p664), Guǎngxī

Chengyang Wind & Rain Bridge (p664), Sānjiāng, Guǎngxī
KRZYSZTOF DYDYNSKI

Fisherman and his cormorants on the Li River, Guìlín (p650), Guǎngxī
KERE

Miao homes, Guìzhōu (p666)

Huangguoshu Falls (p678), Guìzhōu

Traditional embroidery of the Gejia people (p684), Guìzhōu

Miao girls in traditional costume dancing at a festival (p681), Guìzhōu

552

Grand Buddha (p774), Lèshān, Sìchuān

Street in Chéngdū (p754), Sìchuān

JULIET COOMBE

Giant panda cub, Wolong Nature Reserve (p767), Sìchuān

KERE

Dancers, Three Gorges area (p811) of the Yangzi River

Yangzi River cruise boat near the Three Gorges (p811)

Shíbǎozhài (p815), on the Yangzi River

Boatman poling through Little Three Gorges (p816)

Mother and child, Barkhor (p919), Lhasa, Tibet

JANE SWEENEY

Pilgrim, Jokhang Temple (p920), Tibet

ANTHONY PLUMMER

GARRY WEARE

Camp site in the Everest region
(p932), Tibet

Rooftops of Potala Palace (p920), Lhasa, Tibet

JANE SWEENEY

Traditional sand mandala, Lhasa (p917), Tibet

BRADLEY MAYHEW

Prayer flags on a section of the Barkhor *kora* (pilgrim circuit; p919), Lhasa, Tibet

GREG CAIRE

Couple outside yurt, Xīnjiāng (p817)

JANE SWEENEY

Tajik camel driver, Silk Road, Xīnjiāng (p817)

KEREN SU

Uighur man from Kashgar (p832), Xīnjiāng

RICHARD I'AN

Pamir ranges, Xīnjiāng (p817)

BRADLEY MAYHEW

(Continued from page 548)

lose an afternoon perusing tea books, admiring antiques (all for sale) and taking refills from the heated pot beside your table.

Pubs & Bars

Lan Kwai Fong in Central is the best area for bars, attracting everyone from expat and Chinese suits to visiting tourists. There are a stack of bars in the Fong, so just turn up – and don't forget your wallet. Further up the hill, SoHo (p545) has a growing number of bars but more restaurants; it's easily accessed by the Mid-Levels Escalator. In general, pubs and bars in Wan Chai are cheaper and more relaxed; those in Tsim Sha Tsui in Kowloon attract more locals.

It's worth seeking out happy hours, when most pubs, bars and some clubs offer discounts on drinks. Happy hour is usually in the late afternoon or early evening – 4pm to 8pm, say – but times vary from place to place.

HONG KONG ISLAND

1/5 (Map pp526-7; ☎ 2520 2515; 9 Star St, Wan Chai; ☷ 6pm-late Mon-Fri, 8pm-3am Sat) This sophisticated and very stylish lounge bar is a hit with Hong Kong's glamour crowd, which soaks up the latest cocktails from the two-storey-high bar.

Barco (Map pp526-7; ☎ 2857 4478; 42 Staunton St, Central; ☷ 3pm-late) One of our favourite SoHo bars, Barco has great staff, is small enough that it never feels empty and attracts a cool mix of locals and expats. Happy hour is 4pm to 8pm.

Club 71 (Map pp526-7; ☎ 2858 7071; Basement, 67 Hollywood Rd, Central; ☷ 3pm-2am Mon-Sat, 6pm-1am Sun) When Club 64, the counterculture capital of Lan Kwai Fong, was forced to close after rents spiralled, some of the owners relocated to this quiet alley in burgeoning NoHo. Club 71, named after the huge 1 July 2003 protest march, is once again one of the best drinking spots for nonposeurs. It's accessed via a small footpath off either Peel St or Aberdeen St. Happy hour is 3pm to 9pm.

Bohemian Lounge (Map pp526-7; ☎ 2526 6099; 3-5 Old Bailey St, Central; ☷ 4.30pm-late) Suitably Bohemian décor, regular tarot readings and live jazz Thursday to Saturday nights ($120 cover) make this a fun place to hang out.

Also recommended:

Mes Amis (Map pp530-1; ☎ 2527 6680; cnr Lockhart & Luard Rds, Wan Chai; ☷ noon-2am Sun-Thu, to 6am Fri & Sat) One of Wan Chai's busiest bars with nary a bare breast to be seen. Long happy hours.

Nzingha Lounge (Map pp526-7; ☎ 2522 0544; 48 Peel St, Central; ☷ noon-late Mon-Sat) African bar and restaurant with regular events. It's nonsmoking.

KOWLOON

Felix (Map p532; ☎ 2315 3188; 28th fl, Peninsula Hong Kong, Salisbury Rd, Tsim Sha Tsui; ☷ 6pm-2am) Swanky Felix is where to head for amazing views and expensive drinks. Try coming during sunset, then ducking over to Chungking Mansions for a curry for the two-ends-of-the-Hong-Kong-spectrum night out.

Delaney's (Map p532; ☎ 2301 3980; Basement, Mary Bldg, 71-77 Peking Rd, Tsim Sha Tsui; ☷ 8am-3am) This popular Irish pub has the full Irish theme, including good craic most of the time. It's a good choice for watching sports. Happy hour is 5pm to 9pm.

Sky Lounge (Map p532; ☎ 2369 1111; 18th fl, Sheraton Hong Kong Hotel & Towers, 20 Nathan Rd, Tsim Sha Tsui; ☷ 4pm-1am Mon-Fri, 2pm-2am Sat & Sun) It may at first glance look like a departure lounge but, well, the view… Don't take flight: sit down in a scoop chair and sip a drink.

ENTERTAINMENT

To find out what's on, pick up a copy of **HK Magazine** (www.asia-city.com.hk), a comprehensive entertainment listings magazine. It's free, appears on Friday and can be found at restaurants, bars, shops and hotels throughout the territory. Also worth a look is the freebie **bc magazine** (www.bcmagazine.net), which has more complete listings.

Bookings for most cultural events can be made by telephoning **Urbtix** (☎ 2734 9009; www .urbtix.gov.hk; ☷ 10am-8pm). You can also book tickets for many films and concerts and a great variety of cultural events through **Cityline** (☎ 2317 6666; www.cityline.com.hk).

Live Music

Gecko Lounge (Map pp526-7; ☎ 2537 4680; www.gecko .com; Lower ground fl, 15-19 Hollywood Rd; ☷ 4pm-2am Mon-Thu, to 4am Fri & Sat) Entered from narrow Ezra's Lane off Cochrane St or Pottinger St, Gecko is an intimate lounge that attracts a fun crowd, especially for the live jazz sessions Tuesday to Thursday. It also has a great wine list. Happy hour is 4pm to 10pm.

Ned Kelly's Last Stand (Map p532; ☎ 2376 0562; 11a Ashley Rd, Tsim Sha Tsui; ☷ 11.30am-2am) This Aussie pub has jazz nightly 9.30pm till 1am, and food such as meat pies and a mega all-day breakfast ($88). Happy hour is 11.30am to 9pm.

Wanch (Map pp530-1; ☎ 2861 1621; 54 Jaffe Rd; ☻ 4pm-2am) This small venue has live music (mostly rock and folk) seven nights a week from 9pm (10pm on Friday and Saturday), with the occasional solo guitarist thrown in. Happy hour is 4pm to 9pm.

Nightclubs

ourpick Yumla (Map pp526-7; ☎ 2147 2383; www.yumla .com; Lower Basement, 79 Wyndham St, Central; ☻ 5pm-2am Mon-Thu, 5pm-4am Fri & Sat, 7pm-2am Sun) This is probably the hippest and least pretentious club in Hong Kong, with a cool crowd and excellent tunes. Look for the murals and enter from Pottinger St.

Drop (Map pp526-7; ☎ 2543 8856; Basement, On Lok Mansion, 39-43 Hollywood Rd; ☻ 7pm-late Mon-Fri, 10pm-5am Sat) This long-time favourite is not as hip as it has been. Still worth a look, but there's heavy attitude on the door. Happy hour is 7pm to 10pm Monday to Friday.

Dusk till Dawn (Map pp530-1; ☎ 2528 4689; Ground fl, 68-74 Jaffe Rd, Wan Chai; ☻ noon-6am Mon-Sat, 3pm-5am Sun) This fun place is one of Wan Chai's more reliable nightclubs, and even when the dance floor is packed the atmosphere remains friendly rather than sleazy. Happy hour is 5pm to 11pm.

Bahama Mama's Caribbean Bar (Map p532; ☎ 2368 2121; 4-5 Knutsford Tce, Tsim Sha Tsui; ☻ 5pm-late Mon-Sat, 6pm-2am Sun) On the Knutsford Tce strip, Bahama Mama's has an 'island' feel and attracts a youngish crowd. The weekend usually sees DJs playing to a tightly packed dance floor. Happy hour is 5pm to 9pm and midnight to closing Monday to Saturday, all day Sunday.

Club 97 (Map pp526-7; ☎ 2186 1897; Ground fl, Cosmos Bldg, 9-11 Lan Kwai Fong; ☻ 6pm-late Mon-Fri, 8pm-4am Sat & Sun) This schmooze lounge bar has a 'members only' policy to turn away the badly dressed – so make an effort. Happy hour on Friday (6pm to 9pm) is a gay event. On weekends, it kicks after 1am.

Gay & Lesbian Venues
Along with the gay and lesbian clubs and bars listed here, a few straight and mixed clubs, such as Club 97 (above), have gay happy hours or evenings. For the latest G&L news, pick up the free *GMagazine*.

Works (Map pp526-7; ☎ 2868 6102; 1st fl, 30-32 Wyndham St; weekend cover $60-100; ☻ 7pm-2am) Propaganda's sister club, this is a popular starting point for an evening on the town.

Propaganda (Map pp526-7; ☎ 2868 1316; Lower ground fl, 1 Hollywood Rd; weekend cover $100; ☻ 9pm-late Mon-Sat) Most gays make it to Hong Kong's premier gay dance club sooner or later, handing over their dough to legendary door bitch Ricardo. The weekend cover charge gets you into Works on Friday. Enter from Ezra's Lane, which runs between Pottinger and Cochrane Sts.

SHOPPING
Hong Kong is a shopping Mecca where you can find just about anything your heart desires. Finding great deals on computer equipment, cameras and watches (genuine and fake) is not difficult, but for many other items Hong Kong is not the bargain spot it once was.

Central (Map pp526-7) and Causeway Bay (Map pp530-1) are the main shopping districts on Hong Kong Island. Once Hong Kong Island's glitziest shopping mall, the vast **Pacific Place** (Map pp526-7; ☎ 2844 8988; 88 Queensway, Admiralty; ☻ 10.30am-11pm) now battles it out with the ultraschmick **IFC Mall** (Map pp526-7; ☎ 2295 3308; www.ifc.com.hk; 1 Harbour View St) in Central.

Shopping in Kowloon is a bizarre mixture of the down-at-heel and the glamorous; you can find just about anything – especially in Tsim Sha Tsui (Map p532) – and you don't even have to look very hard. If you prefer everything under one roof, head for **Harbour City** (Map p532; ☎ 2118 8666; Canton Rd, Tsim Sha Tsui), an enormous shopping centre with 700 shops in four zones.

The HKTB's (p522) free *Guide to Quality Shops and Restaurants* might be useful if you're looking for a specific item.

Antiques & Curios
For antiques and curios Hollywood Rd (Map pp526-7) should be your first stop, while cheaper Cat St (Map pp526-7) specialises in younger (ie repro) items such as old postcards and Mao paraphernalia.

Arch Angel Antiques (Map pp526-7; ☎ 2851 6848; 53-55 Hollywood Rd, Central; ☻ 9.30am-6.30pm) This well-respected shop has knowledgeable staff and a wide selection of antiques and curios, including many at affordable prices. Everything is authenticated.

Curio Alley (Map p532; Tsim Sha Tsui; ☻ 10am-7pm) This alley between Lock and Hankow Rds is full of carvings, fans, chops (stamps) and other Chinese bric-a-brac that's good for cheap gifts.

Clothing

For boutique brands Hong Kong's malls are the go. But far from being the sole preserve of millionaires, malls such as Pacific Place, IFC Mall and Harbour City also have a good range of mid-priced shops where you should be able to find clothes you'll enjoy wearing, for less than you'd pay at home.

For cheaper attire, Jardine's Bazaar (Map pp530–1) in Causeway Bay isn't bad, while several sample shops and places to pick up cheap jeans are in nearby Lee Garden Rd (Map pp530–1), three streets west. Johnston Rd (Map pp530–1) in Wan Chai also has plenty of midpriced and budget clothing outlets.

In Kowloon, the Temple St night market (p535) has the cheapest clothes. For midpriced items, check out the eastern end of Granville Rd, Austin Ave and Chatham Rd South (Map p532), in Tsim Sha Tsui.

Pacific Custom Tailors (Map pp526–7; ☎ 2845 5377; Shop 110, 1st fl, Pacific Place, 88 Queensway, Admiralty; ☉ 9.30am-8pm Mon-Sat) One of the best choices for bespoke clothing.

Shanghai Tang (Map pp526–7; ☎ 2525 7333; 12 Pedder St, Central; ☉ 10am-8pm Mon-Sat, 11am-7pm Sun) If you fancy a very sexy cheongsam, this is the place. It's also great for gifts and accessories.

Computer Equipment

Hong Kong has some of the lowest prices on earth for laptops, desktops, external drives and absolutely everything else tech-related you can imagine. Just head to one of these four centres and let your head start spinning.

In Square (Map pp530–1; 10th-12th fl, Windsor House, 311 Gloucester Rd, Causeway Bay; ☉ 11am-9pm) This is Causeway Bay's best choice.

Mong Kok Computer Centre (8-8a Nelson St, Mong Kok; ☉ 1-10pm) This place is the cheapest of the lot, but language can be difficult.

Star Computer City (Map p532; 2nd fl, Star House, 3 Salisbury Rd, Tsim Sha Tsui; ☉ 10am-8pm) It's conveniently near to the Star Ferry Pier in Tsim Sha Tsui, but it *only* has two dozen shops!

Wan Chai Computer Centre (Map pp530–1; 1st fl, Southorn Centre, 130-138 Hennessy Rd, Wan Chai; ☉ 10am-8pm Mon-Sat) A warren of dozens of shops just outside Wan Chai MTR; try here first.

Department Stores & Emporiums

Hong Kong's department stores are not the cheapest places to shop, but they're handy if you're in a hurry.

Lane Crawford (Map pp526–7; ☎ 2118 3388; Level 3, IFC Mall, 8 Finance St, Central; ☉ 10am-9pm) This newly opened HQ of Hong Kong's original Western-style department store is very posh.

Wing On (Map pp526–7; ☎ 2852 1888; 211 Des Voeux Rd Central, Sheung Wan; ☉ 10am-7.30pm) 'Forever Peaceful' has a big range of midprice goods and brands.

Yue Hwa Chinese Products Emporium (Map p532; ☎ 2384 0084; 301-309 Nathan Rd, Yau Ma Tei; ☉ 10am-10pm) This enormous place has seven floors of ceramics, furniture, souvenirs, clothing and traditional medicines.

Music

At the Temple St night market (p535) pirate CDs and DVDs are a 'steal'. For the genuine article, try the following:

HMV (Map pp526–7; ☎ 2739 0268; 1st fl, Central Bldg, 1-3 Pedder St, Central; ☉ 9am-10pm) Offers Hong Kong's largest choice of (legitimate) CDs and DVDs.

Hong Kong Records (Map pp526–7; ☎ 2845 7088; Shop 253, 2nd fl, Pacific Place, 88 Queensway, Admiralty; ☉ 10am-8.30pm Mon-Thu, to 9pm Fri-Sun) The hipsters hanging out here will tell you this place stocks some cool sounds among its wide selection of music, including Chinese traditional, jazz and classical.

Photographic Equipment

There are some fantastic camera stores in Hong Kong, but most are not on Nathan Rd. You might pay a bit more at the places listed here, but unlike at 99% of the stores in Tsim Sha Tsui you won't get ripped off.

Photo Scientific (Map pp526–7; ☎ 2525 0550; 6 Stanley St, Central; ☉ 9am-7pm Mon-Sat) Professional photographers come here to shop and we have enjoyed years of good service and fair prices. There is a full range of digital and nondigital cameras and film, all with fixed prices.

Hing Lee Camera Company (Map pp526–7; ☎ 2544 7593; 25 Lyndhurst Tce, Central; ☉ 9.30am-7pm Mon-Sat, 11am-5pm Sun) Hing Lee has a wide range of new and second-hand SLR and 35mm camera bodies and lenses, and they do trade-ins.

Onestop Photo Company (Map p532; ☎ 2723 4668; Shop 2, ground fl, Champagne Ct, 18 Kimberley Rd, Tsim Sha Tsui; ☉ 10.30am-8.30pm) Unusually for Tsim Sha Tsui, this camera shop has prices marked, but bargain anyway.

Sporting Goods

Giga Sports (Map pp526–7; ☎ 2524 6992; Shop 220, 2nd fl, Pacific Place, 88 Queensway, Admiralty; ☉ 10.30am-9.30pm)

This gigantic store has a wide range of sports equipment, clothing and footwear.

KS Ahluwalia & Sons (Map p532; ☎ 2368 8334; 8c Hankow Rd, Tsim Sha Tsui; ◷ 10am-7.45pm Mon-Sat, to 5pm Sun) This long-established store is full of golf, cricket and tennis gear. No prices are marked, so haggle away. Cash only.

Ocean Sky Divers (Map p532; ☎ 2366 3738; www .oceanskydiver.com; 1st fl, 17-19 Lock Rd, Tsim Sha Tsui; ◷ 10.30am-9pm) No parachutes here, but there's a full range of diving and snorkelling gear.

GETTING THERE & AWAY
Air
More than 60 airlines operate between Hong Kong International Airport and about 140 destinations worldwide. Competition keeps fares relatively low, and Hong Kong is a great place to find discounted tickets. For an idea of what fares are available when you're there, look at the classified section of the *South China Morning Post*. To see which airlines fly to Hong Kong and everything you could want to know about Hong Kong International Airport, check out www.hongkongairport.com.

There are few bargain airfares between Hong Kong and China as the government regulates the prices. Depending on the season, seats can be hard to book due to the enormous volume of business travellers and Chinese tourists, so book well in advance. Some normal return fares valid for a year from Hong Kong are: Běijīng $2300; Chéngdū $2500; Guǎngzhōu $600; Kūnmíng $2200; and Shànghǎi $1900. One-way fares are about half the return price.

You should be able to do better than that, however, on both scheduled flights and charters, especially in summer. To Běijīng, China Southern Airlines has a fixed return ticket for as low as $1600. An open ticket valid for 30 days on the same airline is $2200.

However, if you're prepared to travel a couple of hours to Guǎngzhōu or Shēnzhèn, in nearby Guǎngdōng province, then you can find flights for less than half the prices from Hong Kong. Shēnzhèn airport (see p614), in particular, is easily and cheaply reached by bus from Hong Kong and has flights to just about everywhere in China. For an idea of price, check out www.elong.net.

AIRLINES
Airline offices in Hong Kong:
British Airways (BA; Map pp526-7; ☎ 2822 9000; 24th fl, Jardine House, 1 Connaught Place, Central)

Cathay Pacific (CX; Map p532; ☎ 2747 1888; 10th fl, Peninsula Office Tower, 18 Middle Rd, Tsim Sha Tsui)
China Airlines (CI; Map pp526-7; ☎ 2868 2299; Suite 901-907, 9th fl, One Pacific Pl, 88 Queensway, Admiralty)
China Southern/China Eastern Airlines (CZ/MU; Map pp526-7; ☎ 2861 0322; 4th fl, CNAC Group Bldg, 10 Queen's Rd Central)
Dragonair (KA; Map pp526-7; ☎ 3193 3888; 46th fl, Cosco Tower, 183 Queen's Rd Central)
Northwest Airlines (NW; Map pp526-7; ☎ 2810 4288; 19th fl, Cosco Tower, 183 Queen's Rd Central)
Qantas Airways (QF; Map pp526-7; ☎ 2822 9000; 24th fl, Jardine House, 1 Connaught Pl, Central)
Singapore Airlines (SQ; Map pp526-7; ☎ 2520 2233; 17th fl, United Centre, 95 Queensway, Admiralty)
United Airlines (UA; Map pp526-7; ☎ 2810 4888; 29th fl, Gloucester Tower, the Landmark, 11 Pedder St, Central)
Virgin Atlantic Airways (VS; Map pp526-7; ☎ 2532 3030; 8th fl, Alexandra House, 16-20 Chater Rd, Central)

DEPARTURE TAX
Hong Kong's airport departure tax – $120 for everyone over the age of 12 – is always included in the price of the ticket. Those travelling to Macau by helicopter (see p583) must pay the same amount.

However, if you arrive and depart the same day you can get a refund. Once you've checked in at the airport but before passing immigration, take your ticket/receipt and departing boarding pass to the Civil Aviation Department counter on level 7, Departure Hall, Aisle D and make your claim.

Boat
Regularly scheduled ferries link the **China ferry terminal** (Map p532; Canton Rd, Tsim Sha Tsui) in Kowloon and/or the **Macau ferry pier** (Map pp526-7; 200 Connaught Rd, Sheung Wan) on Hong Kong Island with a string of towns and cities located on the Pearl River delta – but not central Guǎngzhōu or Shēnzhèn. For sea-transport information to and from Macau, see p583.

High-speed ferries run by **TurboJet** (☎ 2921 6688; www.turbojet.com.hk) leave the China ferry terminal for Fúyǒng ferry terminal (Shēnzhèn airport) six to eight times a day between 7.30am and 5.30pm ($189, 40 minutes). There are five or six return sailings from Fúyǒng ($171) starting at 9am with the last at 5pm. One boat a day leaves the Macau ferry pier at 8am. Return sailings are at 5.50pm, 7pm and 8.30pm.

HONG KONG

HKIA TO CHINA THE FAST WAY

With domestic airfares much cheaper from airports elsewhere in the Pearl River Delta, a growing number of travellers are heading straight from Hong Kong International Airport (HKIA) to airports in Macau, Shēnzhèn and Guǎngzhōu.

The new **TurboJet Sea Express** (☎ 2859 3333; www.turbojetseaexpress.com.hk) links HKIA to Shēnzhèn airport ($230, 40 minutes) seven or eight times daily between 10am and 9.15pm. It also runs to Macau (see p583). In addition, buses run by **CTS Express Coach** (☎ 2261 2472), **Eternal East Cross Border Coach** (☎ 2261 0176) and **Gogobus** (☎ 2261 0886; www.gogobus.com) link HKIA with many points in southern China, including Dōngguǎn ($100), Fóshān ($130 to $150), Guǎngzhōu ($100) and Shēnzhèn ($100).

CMSE Passenger Transport (☎ 2858 0909; day/night sailing $110/130) has 13 services daily between Hong Kong and Shékǒu (one hour), 20km west of Shēnzhèn and efficiently linked to the town centre. Seven of these leave from the China ferry terminal (between 7.45am and 7pm), while the rest go from the Macau ferry pier (9am to 9pm). Sailings from Shékǒu are between 7.45am and 9.30pm.

Zhūhǎi can also be reached from Hong Kong on seven ferries a day from the China ferry terminal ($177, 70 minutes, from 7.30am to 5.30pm) and eight from the Macau ferry pier (8.40am to 9.30pm) on ferries operated by the **Chu Kong Passenger Transportation Co** (☎ 2858 3876; www.cksp.com.hk). The 14 return sailings from Zhūhǎi run between 8am and 9.30pm.

Chu Kong also has ferries from the China ferry terminal to a number of other ports in southern Guǎngdōng province, including: Hǔmén (Tàipíng; $167, 90 minutes, 9am, 1.45pm and 5.30pm); Kāipíng ($192, four hours, 8.30am); Shùndé ($175, 110 minutes, six sailings between 7.30am and 6pm); Zhōngshān ($196, 90 minutes, nine sailings from 8am to 8pm); and Zhàoqìng ($205, 3¾ hours, 8.15am).

Hong Kong levies a $19 departure tax that is normally included in the ticket price. Trips from China are usually $19 cheaper.

Bus

You can reach virtually any major destination in Guǎngdōng province by bus from Hong Kong. With KCR East Rail services so fast and cheap, however, few buses call on Shēnzhèn proper, though most of the big hotels run minivans to and from that destination for $100 one way. One-way fares from Hong Kong include: Chángshā ($280); Dōngguǎn ($70 to $100); Fóshān ($100); Guǎngzhōu

($80 to $100); Shàntóu ($180); Shēnzhèn airport ($110); Xiàmén ($350); and Zhōngshān ($100 to $130).

Buses are run by a multitude of companies and depart from locations around the territory; the following is only a sampling. Schedules vary enormously according to carrier and place, but buses leave frequently throughout the day. For buses from the airport to China, see above.

CTS Express Coach (☎ 2365 0118; http://ctsbus.hkcts .com) buses depart from locations throughout Hong Kong, including the China Travel Service **main branch** (Map pp526-7; ☎ 2853 3888; 78-83 Connaught Rd Central) and the CTS **Wan Chai branch** (Map pp530-1; ☎ 2832 3888; Southorn Centre, 130-138 Hennessy Rd) on Hong Kong Island and from just south of the **CTS Mong Kok branch** (Map p532; ☎ 2789 5888; 62-72 Sai Yee St) in Kowloon.

Motor Transport Company of Guangdong & Hong Kong (GDHK; ☎ 2317 7900; www.gdhkmtc.com) buses bound for destinations throughout Guǎngdōng leave from the **Cross-Border Coach Terminus** (Map p532; ☎ 2317 7900; Ground fl, Hong Kong Scout Centre, 8 Austin Rd, Tsim Sha Tsui; ⏰ 6.30am-7pm), which is entered from Scout Path.

Trans-Island Limousine Service (☎ 3193 9333; www.trans-island.com.hk) cars and vans leave from Portland St opposite the Hotel Concourse Hong Kong, north of Mong Kok.

Train

Reaching Shēnzhèn by train is a breeze. Board the KCR East Rail train at Hung Hom in Kowloon ($66/33 in 1st/2nd class, 35 minutes) or any KCR East Rail station along the way, and ride it to the China border crossing at Lo Wu. From Shēnzhèn you can take a local train or bus to Guǎngzhōu and beyond.

The most comfortable way to reach Guǎngzhōu is via the Kowloon–Guǎngzhōu express train, which covers the 182km route in approximately 1¾ hours. Trains leave Hung Hom station for Guǎngzhōu East 12 times a day between 7.30am and 7.15pm, returning between 8.35am and 9.23pm. One-way tickets cost $230/190 in 1st/2nd class for adults and $115/95 for children under nine.

There are also direct rail links between Hung Hom and both Shànghǎi and Běijīng. Trains to Běijīng (hard/soft sleeper $574/934, 24 hours) depart on alternate days at 3pm and travel via Guǎngzhōu East, Chángshā and Wǔhàn, arriving at 3.18pm the next day. Trains to Shànghǎi (hard/soft sleeper $508/825, 25 hours) also depart on alternate days at 3pm and pass through Guǎngzhōu East and Hángzhōu East stations, arriving at 4.38pm the next day.

There is one daily departure to Zhàoqìng (adult/child $235/117.50) via Dōngguǎn, Guǎngzhōu East and Fóshān at 2.20pm, arriving in Zhàoqìng at 6.30pm. The train departs Zhàoqìng at 9.37am, reaching Hung Hom at 1.38pm.

Immigration formalities at Hung Hom are completed before boarding; you won't get on the train without a visa for China. Passengers are required to arrive at the station 45 minutes before departure. One-way and return tickets can be booked in advance at CTS (p522) and KCR East Rail stations in Hung Hom, Mong Kok, Kowloon Tong and Sha Tin. Tickets booked with a credit card by phone (☎ 2947 7888) must be collected at least one hour before departure. Get the latest prices and schedules from the KCRC's excellent website www.kcrc.com.

GETTING AROUND

Hong Kong's public transport system is the envy of cities the world over. Fast, easy to navigate, relatively inexpensive and ridiculously easy with the Octopus card payment system. From the moment you arrive you'll be wondering why more cities can't do PT like Hong Kong.

To/From the Airport

The Airport Express line of the MTR is the fastest, easiest and consequently the most expensive public route to/from **Hong Kong International Airport** (HKIA; ☎ 2181 0000; www.hkairport .com) at Chek Lap Kok off the northern coast of Lantau. A gaggle of much cheaper buses connects it with Lantau, the New Territories, Kowloon and even Hong Kong Island.

However, the **Airport Express** (☎ 2881 8888; www.mtr.com.hk) is so easy it's hard to resist. Trains stop literally inside the departures level of the airport, and most airlines allow Airport Express passengers to check in at the Central or Kowloon stations (offices open 5.30am to 12.30am) many hours ahead of departure. Boarding passes are issued, meaning you can forget your luggage, spend the day sightseeing and head straight to immigration once you get to the airport. Trains depart from Hong Kong station (Map pp526–7) in Central every 12 minutes from 5.54am to 1.15am daily, calling at Kowloon station in Jordan and Tsing Yi Island en route. The journey from Central/ Kowloon/Tsing Yi takes 23/20/12 minutes and costs $100/90/60, with children three to 11 and seniors over 65 half price. Adult return fares, valid for a month, are $180/160/110. A same-day return is equivalent to a one-way fare.

Even if you're travelling solo, it's worth hooking up with someone (or more) to take advantage of sizable discounts for groups. Fares to Central are $160/$220/$250 for two/ three/four passengers. When you get off, free Airport Express shuttle buses link Kowloon and Central to largish hotels (check the list at the airport).

Most areas of Hong Kong are linked to the airport by bus, of which there is an enormous choice. The most useful for travellers are the A11 ($40) and A12 ($45), which go past major hotel and guesthouse areas on Hong Kong Island, and the A21 ($33), which serves similar areas in Kowloon. These buses run from about 6am to midnight; the 'N' series of buses follows the same route after midnight. Note that an A11 round-trip ticket is cheaper and can be used for three months.

Cheaper buses from the airport include the E11 ($21) to Hong Kong Island or the S1 ($3.50) to Tung Chung and then the MTR to Kowloon or Central. A taxi from the airport to Central will cost about $335.

For information on ferries from HKIA to Shēnzhèn airport, see p561.

Bicycle

Cycling in built-up Kowloon or Central would be suicidal, but in quiet areas of the Outlying Islands or New Territories a bike can be a lovely way of getting around.

At Silvermine Bay (aka Mui Wo) on Lantau Island, bicycles are available for hire ($10 per hour, $25/35 weekdays/weekend and over-night) from the **Friendly Bicycle Shop** (Map pp524-5; ☎ 2984 2278; Shop 12, Mui Wo Centre, 1 Ngan Wan Rd; ⊗ 10am-8pm Wed-Mon), opposite Wellcome supermarket. Get in early on sunny weekends.

Flying Ball Bicycle Co (Map pp524-5; ☎ 2381 3661; www.flyingball.com; 478 Castle Peak Rd, Cheung Sha Wan; ⊗ 11am-8pm Mon-Sat, to 5pm Sun) is Hong Kong's premier shop for bicycles and cycling accessories. To get there, take the MTR to Cheung Sha Wan and turn right out of Exit C2, take your first right, then first left on Fuk Wing St – it's at the far end.

Boat

Commuting by ferry is the most enjoyable (and surprisingly the cheapest) way of getting around Victoria Harbour.

CROSS-HARBOUR FERRIES

First launched in 1888 (see the boxed text, below), the **Star Ferry** (☎ 2367 7065; www.starferry .com.hk) is as much a tourist attraction as a mode of transport. It operates on four routes, but the most popular one by far is the seven-minute (soon to be less when the new pier opens) run between Tsim Sha Tsui and Central. Seniors travel free on all Star ferries.

Central–Hung Hom Adult/child $5.30/2.70, 15 minutes, from Star Ferry Pier every 15 to 20 minutes 7.20am to 7.20pm Monday to Friday, every 20 minutes 7am to 7pm Saturday and Sunday.

Central–Tsim Sha Tsui $1.70/2.20 lower/upper deck, seven minutes, from Star Ferry Pier every six to 12 minutes 6.30am to 11.30pm.

Wan Chai–Hung Hom Adult/child $5.30/2.70, 10 minutes, from Wan Chai Ferry Pier every 15 to 20 minutes 7.08am to 7.17pm Monday to Friday, every 20 to 22 minutes 7.08am to 7.10pm Saturday and Sunday.

Wan Chai–Tsim Sha Tsui Adult/child $2.20/1.30, eight minutes, from Wan Chai Ferry Pier every eight to 20 minutes 7.30am to 11pm Monday to Saturday, every 12 to 20 minutes 7.40am to 11pm Sunday.

Of the other cross-harbour ferries the route of most interest to travellers is from Queen's Pier (Map pp526–7) in Central to Tsim Sha Tsui East, which runs every 20 minutes from 7.40am (from 8am Sunday) to 8.20pm and costs $4.50 for adults and $2.30 for children and seniors. It is run by the **Discovery Bay Transportation Service** (☎ 2987 7351; www.hkri.com).

Controversy notwithstanding, expect both the Star Ferry Pier and Queen's Pier to have moved a little closer to Kowloon by the time you arrive. Both will be victims of a huge land-reclamation project that is planned to turn the harbour front into an urban recreation zone.

OUTLYING ISLANDS FERRIES

The main companies serving the islands are **New World First Ferry** (NWFF; ☎ 2131 8181; www.nwff .com.hk), which runs services to Lantau, Cheung Chau and Peng Chau, and the **Hong Kong & Kowloon Ferry Co** (☎ 2815 6063; www.hkkf.com.hk), which serves Lamma. Schedules are posted at all ferry piers and the ferry companies' websites, or ask for a pocket-sized timetable. Fares are higher on so-called fast ferries and on Sundays and public holidays. Most ferries depart from the Outlying Islands ferry piers just west of the Star Ferry Pier in Central, though some weekend services to Lantau and Cheung Chau leave from the Star Ferry Pier in Tsim Sha Tsui. NWFF also runs a handy inter-island service connecting Peng Chau, Mui Wo (Lantau Island) and Cheung Chau.

A STAR IS BORN

The Star Ferry service between Pedder's Wharf (now reclaimed land) and Tsim Sha Tsui began in 1888 when boats sailed 'every 40 minutes to one hour during all hours of the day' except on Monday and Friday, when they were seconded for coal delivery. Service has continued ever since, with the only major suspension occurring during WWII.

The old workhorse has figured prominently during several periods of history. During the Japanese invasion in 1941, boats were used to evacuate refugees and Allied troops from the Kowloon Peninsula. And in 1966, when communist China was locked in the grip of the so-called Cultural Revolution, agitators used the ferry company's proposed fare increase of 5c as a pretext for fomenting violent demonstrations.

Until the Cross-Harbour Tunnel opened in 1978 and the first line of the MTR two years later, the Star Ferry was the only way to cross the harbour by public transport. Today it's by far the most enchanting.

Car & Motorcycle

For the uninitiated, driving on Hong Kong's maze of one-way streets and dizzying expressways probably isn't a good idea. But if you're hellbent on ruining your holiday, **Avis** (Map p532; ☎ 2890 6988; Shop 46, ground fl, Peninsula Centre, 67 Mody Rd, Tsim Sha Tsui; ✆ 8am-6pm Mon, 9am-6pm Tue-Fri, 9am-4pm Sat & Sun) will rent you a Toyota Corolla from 2pm on Friday to 10am Monday for $1500; or for $720/3200 a day/week with unlimited kilometres.

Public Transport

TRAVEL & TRANSPORT PASSES

The **Octopus card** (☎ 2266 2222; www.octopuscards .com) is a reusable, prepaid 'smart card' valid on most forms of public transport in Hong Kong and good for purchases in a fast-growing number of stores. It costs $150/100/70 for adults/students aged 12 to 25/children aged three to 11 and seniors over 65, including a refundable deposit of $50. To add more money to your card, just go to one of the add-value machines or the ticket offices located at every MTR station. Octopus fares are between 5% and 10% cheaper than ordinary fares on the MTR, KCR, LRT and certain green minibuses.

The Airport Express Tourist Octopus card costs $220 (including $50 deposit) and allows one trip on the Airport Express, three days' unlimited travel on the MTR and $20 usable on other forms of transport, though you'll want to be travelling a fair bit to make it worthwhile. For $300 you get two trips on the Airport Express and the same benefits. For shorter stays there's the new Tourist MTR 1-Day Pass ($50), valid only on the MTR for 24 hours.

BUS

Hong Kong's extensive bus system will take you just about anywhere. The HKTB (p522) has useful leaflets on the major bus routes or try the Yellow Pages Map website (www. ypmap.com). Most buses run from about 5.30am or 6am until midnight or 12.30am, though there are a handful of night buses including the N121 (running from the Macau ferry pier bus terminus – Map pp526–7 – on Hong Kong Island to Chatham Rd in Tsim Sha Tsui East and on to eastern Kowloon), the N122 (running from North Point on Hong Kong Island to Nathan Rd and on to Lai Chi Kok in Kowloon) and the N112 (running from

Percival St in Causeway Bay to the Prince Edward MTR station in Kowloon).

Fares range from $1.20 to $45, depending on the destination, with night buses costing from $12.80 to $23. You need to have exact change.

There are myriad bus stops and stations, but if you stick with these few you should be right. On Hong Kong Island, the terminuses below Exchange Sq in Central (Map pp526–7) and above Admiralty MTR (Map pp526–7) will get you to Aberdeen, Repulse Bay and Stanley on the southern side of the island. In Kowloon the terminal at the Star Ferry Pier has buses to Hung Hom station and points in eastern and western Kowloon.

KOWLOON-CANTON RAILWAY (KCR)

The **Kowloon-Canton Railway** (KCR; ☎ 2602 7799; www.kcrc.com) consists of two main lines and two smaller lines. KCR East Rail runs from Tsim Sha Tsui East station in Kowloon to Lo Wu, gateway to Shēnzhèn and the mainland. A spur runs from Tai Wai to Wa Kai Sha. KCR West Rail, which opened in late 2003, links Nam Cheong station in Sham Shui Po with Tuen Mun via Yuen Long. Eventually it will be linked to Tsim Sha Tsui East via an extension of the KCR East Rail. The KCR offers excellent transport to the New Territories and some nice vistas.

Trains run every five to eight minutes or every three minutes during rush hour, and fares are cheap, starting at $4.50. A half-hour ride from Tsim Sha Tsui to Sheung Shui/Tuen Mun costs just $12.

LIGHT RAIL TRANSIT (LRT)

The **Light Rail Transit** (LRT; ☎ 2929 3399; www.kcrc .com) operates on eight routes in the western part of the New Territories between Tuen Mun and Yuen Long and feeds the KCR West Rail. Fares are $4 to $5.80.

MASS TRANSIT RAILWAY (MTR)

The **Mass Transit Railway** (MTR; ☎ 2881 8888; www .mtr.com.hk) is arguably the best underground railway on earth. Fast, incredibly efficient and convenient and always on time, it operates on seven lines, including the Airport Express and the new Disneyland spur. You can buy individual tickets or use an Octopus card. Prices range from $4 to $26 ($3.80 and $23.10 with an Octopus card). Short trips, such as crossing from Central to Tsim Sha Tsui, aren't great value, being almost four times more than the ferry. But longer trips are much faster than buses for about the same price. Once you go past the turnstile, you must complete the journey within 90 minutes. The MTR operates from 6am to between 12.30am and 1am. See the route map on p171.

PUBLIC LIGHT BUSES

'Public light buses' (an official term that no-one ever uses) have no more than 16 seats and come in two varieties. Most are painted a cream colour, with either a red or green roof (or sometimes a stripe). Red 'minibuses' supplement the regular bus services and cost $2 to $20. They generally don't run regular routes, but you can get on or off almost anywhere – just yell *ni do, m gói* (here, please). Pay either with an Octopus Card or coins as you exit.

Green-topped minibuses operate on more than 350 set routes and make designated stops. Two popular routes are bus 6 from Hankow Rd in Tsim Sha Tsui to Tsim Sha Tsui East and Hung Hom KCR station, and bus 1 from east of the Star Ferry Pier in Central for Victoria Peak on Hong Kong Island.

TRAM

Hong Kong's century-old trams, operated by **Hongkong Tramways Ltd** (☎ 2548 7102; www .hktramways.com), are the only all double-deck wooden-sided tram fleet in the world. They operate on six overlapping routes, on 16km of track running east–west along the north side of Hong Kong Island. The tram is fun and a bargain at $2 for any trip; pay as you get off.

Taxi

On Hong Kong Island and Kowloon (red taxis), the flag fall is $15 for the first 2km then $1.40 for every additional 200m. In the New Territories (green taxis), flag fall is $12.50 and $1.20 for every subsequent 200m. On Lantau (blue taxis) the equivalent charges are $12 and $1.20. There is a luggage fee of $5 per bag but it's usually only charged for bags you put in the boot. It costs an extra $5 to book a taxi by telephone.

If you go through the Cross-Harbour Tunnel ($10), or the Eastern ($20) or Western Harbour Crossing ($25), you'll be charged double the toll unless you manage to find a cab heading back to its base.

Macau

Macau is a city with two faces. On the one hand, the fortresses, churches and food of its former colonial master Portugal speak to a uniquely Mediterranean style on the China coast. On the other, Macau is the self-styled Las Vegas of the East.

And while that comparison might sound overblown, it's not. During the past few years charismatic-but-sleepy little Macau has experienced the sort of boom usually associated with cities like Shànghǎi. But rather than skyscrapers and office towers, the construction here is all about Vegas-style mega-casinos and hotels. The reason, of course, is that casinos are legal in Macau, while in China and nearby Hong Kong they're not. It's a big market…

There is, however, much more to Macau than gambling. The peninsula and the islands of Coloane and Taipa constitute a colourful palette of pastels and ordered greenery. The Portuguese influence is everywhere: cobbled back streets, baroque churches, stone fortresses, Art Deco buildings and restful parks and gardens. It's a unique fusion of East and West that has been recognised by Unesco, which in 2005 named 30 buildings and squares collectively as the Historic Centre of Macau World Heritage Site. There are also several world-class museums.

Especially if you've been in China for a while you'll also find there is a distinctly different feel to Macau. While about 95% of residents are Chinese, the remainder is mostly made up of Portuguese and Macanese (people with mixed Portuguese, Chinese and/or African blood). It's this fusion of Mediterranean and Asian peoples, lifestyles, temperaments and food – oh, the food – that makes Macau so much fun.

HIGHLIGHTS

- Visit the outstanding **Macau Museum** (p572) at Monte Forte, a fascinating introduction to the territory
- Climb the hauntingly beautiful ruins of the **Church of St Paul** (p572), the very symbol of Macau
- Compare the old-style kitsch of the **Casino Lisboa** (p582) with the Vegas-style cash at the **Sands** (p582)
- Tuck into Portuguese and Macanese soul food at **Litoral, A Lorcha** or **Restaurante Fernando** (p579)
- Wander the narrow streets and lanes of the **Inner Harbour area** (p569) for a peek at Macau's unique personality

Inner Harbour Area ★
Church of ★ ★ Macau
St Paul   Museum
Litoral &   ★ Sands
A Lorcha ★   Casino Lisboa

Restaurante ★
Fernando

| ■ AREA CODE: ☎853 | ■ POPULATION: 482,000 | ■ www.macautourism.gov.mo |

HISTORY

Portuguese galleons first visited Macau to trade in the early 16th century and in 1557, as a reward for clearing out pirates endemic to the area, they were allowed to establish a tiny enclave here. As trade with China grew so did Macau, which became the principal meeting point between China and the West. However, after the Opium War between the Chinese and the British and the subsequent establishment of Hong Kong, Macau went into a long decline.

China's Cultural Revolution spilled over into the territory in 1966–67. The government reportedly proposed that Portugal should leave Macau forever but, fearing the loss of foreign trade, the Chinese refused the offer.

In 1999, under the Sino-Portuguese Pact, Macau was returned to China and designated a Special Administrative Region (SAR). Like Hong Kong, the pact ensures Macau a 'high degree of autonomy' in all matters except defence and foreign affairs for 50 years.

LANGUAGE

Cantonese and Portuguese are the official languages of Macau, though very few people speak Portuguese. English is harder to find here than in Hong Kong, but in most mid-range and top-end hotels, casinos, restaurants and tourist zones you should be able to get by. Mandarin is reasonably well understood, though note that most written Chinese is in traditional characters, not the simplified forms found in Mainland China.

ORIENTATION

Lying 65km west of Hong Kong, on the opposite side of the mouth of the Pearl River, tiny-but-growing Macau measures just 28

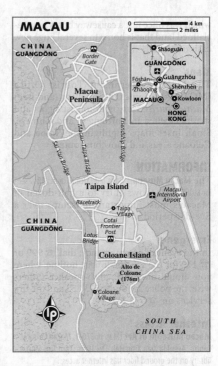

sq km in area. Most of the sights are on the peninsula jutting down from Zhūhǎi on the mainland. Avenida de Almeida Ribeiro (San Ma Lo, or 'New St', in Cantonese), running from Avenida da Praia Grande to the Inner Harbour, is Macau's main street. Its extension, Avenida do Infante Dom Henrique, runs south to the Outer Harbour.

Three bridges lead south to Taipa Island, which in turn is connected to the much quieter Coloane Island by the Cotai Strip,

---

WHAT'S IN A NAME?

The name 'Macau' is derived from the name of the goddess A-Ma, also known as Tin Hau. At the southwestern tip of Macau Peninsula stands the A-Ma Temple; many people believe that when the Portuguese first arrived on this spot and asked the name of the place, they were told 'A-Ma Gau' (bay of A-Ma).

According to legend, A-Ma, a poor girl looking for passage to Canton (now Guǎngzhōu), was turned away by wealthy junk owners. Instead, a poor fisherman took her on board; shortly afterwards a storm blew up, wrecking all the junks but leaving the fishing boat unscathed. When it returned to the Inner Harbour, A-Ma walked to the top of nearby Barra Hill and, in a glowing aura of light, ascended to heaven. In her honour, the fisherman built a temple on the spot where they had landed.

In modern Cantonese, 'Macau' is Ou Mun, meaning 'gateway of the bay'.

MACAU

which was once just a causeway but is now reclaimed land that is home to several huge new casino resorts.

Maps

The Macau Government Tourist Office (MGTO) distributes the excellent (and free) *Macau Tourist Map*, with tourist sights and streets labelled in Portuguese and Chinese. Small inset maps highlight the Taipa and Coloane areas and show bus routes.

INFORMATION

The **Macau Museums Pass** (adult/child under 18 & senior MOP$25/12) allows entry to a half-dozen of Macau's most important museums over a five-day period.

Emergency

In the event of an emergency, dial ☎ 999 or ☎ 112 for the specific tourist hotline, where you should find an English-speaker. Otherwise, the police are on ☎ 573 333 and the fire services on ☎ 572 222.

Internet Access

Macau Museum of Art (Map pp570-1; Macau Cultural Centre, Avenida Xian Xing Hai; ☽ 10am-7pm Tue-Sun) A library on the ground floor has internet access.
Trendway Computer & Cyber (Map p573; ☎ 921 847; 27 Rua de Madeira; per hr MOP$5; ☽ 24hr) Burns CDs, scans, Skype etc.
Unesco Internet Café (Map pp570-1; ☎ 727 066; Alameda Doutor Carlos d'Assumpção; per 30/60min MOP$5/10; ☽ noon-8pm Wed-Mon)

Internet Resources

Useful Macau websites:
Cityguide (www.cityguide.gov.mo) Strong practical information such as transport.

GoMacau (www.gomacau.com) Up-to-date information on hotels, flights, sights, entertainment and activities.
Macau Cultural Institute (www.icm.gov.mo) Macau's cultural offerings month by month.
Macau Government Tourist Office (www.macau tourism.gov.mo) The best source of information for visiting Macau.
Macau Yellow Pages (www.yp.com.mo) Telephone directory, with maps.

Medical Services

Macau's two hospitals both have 24-hour emergency services.
Centro Hospitalar Conde São Januário (Map pp570-1; ☎ 313 731; Estrada do Visconde de São Januário) Southwest of Guia Fort.
Hospital Kiang Wu (Map pp570-1; ☎ 371 333; Rua de Coelho do Amaral) Northeast of the ruins of the Church of St Paul.

Money

ATMS

ATMs are everywhere, especially just outside the Hotel Lisboa, where you'll find half a dozen. Most allow you to choose between patacas and Hong Kong dollars.

CHANGING MONEY

The pataca is pegged to the Hong Kong dollar (see p521) at a rate of MOP$103.20 to HK$100. In effect, the two currencies are interchangeable and Hong Kong dollars, including coins, are accepted here. Chinese renminbi is also accepted in many places at one-to-one, though you can't spend patacas anywhere else, so use them before you leave.

You can change cash and travellers cheques at the banks lining Avenida da Praia Grande and Avenida de Almeida Ribeiro. Major credit cards are accepted by many businesses.

MACAU IN A DAY

Start in the **Largo do Senado** (p572), pick up the pamphlets from the **Macau Government Tourist Office** (above) and wander slowly up to the **Ruins of the Church of St Paul** (p572). Spend an hour or so in the **Macau Museum** (p572) to give it all some context, before getting a feel for Macau's living history as you wander back through the tiny streets towards the Inner Harbour Port and lunch at **Litoral** (p579). After lunch take a look around the **A-Ma Temple** (p574) before jumping on a bus to sleepy **Coloane Village** (p577). Take an easy stroll around here, pick up an egg tart at **Lord Stow's Cafe** (p581) and settle in for some beer, people-watching and eventually dinner at the cheap **Café Nga Tim** (p580). Recharged (or just charged?), head in to the **Casino Lisboa** (p581) for a taste of what this city is all about before enjoying a couple more drinks and a band at **Fisherman's Wharf** (p580). Round out the night at the **Basement** (p581), Macau's coolest bar.

COSTS

Macau is generally much cheaper than Hong Kong, though prices do rise on weekends, and in the case of hotels the rise can be sharp.

As in China, tipping is not expected, though a gratuity offered will not be refused. Top-end hotels add a 10% service charge and a 5% tourism tax to their room rates. Most stores have fixed prices, but most street markets are prepared to bargain a little.

CURRENCY

Macau's currency is the pataca (MOP$), which is divided into 100 avos. Bills are issued in denominations of MOP$10, MOP$20, MOP$50, MOP$100, MOP$500 and MOP$1000. There are copper coins worth 10, 20 and 50 avos and silver-coloured MOP$1, MOP$2, MOP$5 and MOP$10.

Post

Main post office (Map p573; ☎ 323 666; Avenida de Almeida Ribeiro; ☼ 9am-6pm Mon-Fri, to 1pm Sat); ferry terminal branch (Map pp570-1; ☎ 396 8526; ☼ 10am-7pm Mon-Sat) Little red vending machines dispense stamps throughout Macau. Poste restante service is available at counters No 1 and 2 of the main post office.

Telephone

Companhia de Telecomunicações de Macau (CTM; Map p573; ☎ inquiry hotline 601 1000; www.ctm.net; Kam Loi Bldg, 22 Rua do Doutor Pedro José Lobo; ☼ 10.30am-7.30pm) is Macau's main telephone company.

Local calls are free from private phones and most hotel telephones, while public payphones cost MOP$1 for five minutes. All payphones permit International Direct Dialling (IDD) using a phonecard available from CTM for between MOP$50 and MOP$200. Rates are cheaper from 9pm to 8am during the week and all day on weekends.

SIM cards are cheap and widely available. CTM prepaid cards cost from MOP$50 and are good to use in GSM900, 1800 or 1900 mobile phones. Buy them at the ferry terminal.

The international access code is ☎ 00. For Hong Kong, dial ☎ 01 then the number; you do not have to dial Hong Kong's country code (☎ 852). To call Macau from abroad – including from Hong Kong – the country code is ☎ 853.

Some useful numbers:

International directory assistance ☎ 101
Local directory assistance ☎ 181
Weather ☎ 1311

Tourist Information

The well-organised and helpful **Macau Government Tourist Office** (MGTO; ☎ 315 566, hotline 333 000; www.macautourism.gov.mo) has outlets at the **Largo do Senado** (Map p573; ☎ 397 1120; ☼ 9am-6pm), the **Guia Lighthouse** (Map pp570-1; ☎ 569 808; ☼ 9am-1pm & 2.15-5.30pm), the **ruins of the Church of St Paul** (Map p573; ☎ 358 444; ☼ 9.15am-1pm & 2.30-6pm), and the **Macau ferry terminal** (Map pp570-1; ☎ 726 416; ☼ 9am-10pm). Do pick up its themed leaflets (see below for details) on Macau's sights and bilingual maps.

The MGTO also maintains tourist offices in **Hong Kong** (Map pp526-7; ☎ 2857 2287; Room 336-337, Shun Tak Centre, 200 Connaught Rd, Sheung Wan; ☼ 9am-1pm & 2.15-5.30pm) as well as several other countries.

Travel Agencies

China Travel Service (CTS; Map pp570-1; ☎ 700 888; cts@cts.com.mo; 10th fl, Xin Hua Bldg, 35 Rua de Nagasaki; ☼ 9am-5pm) China visas (MOP$150 plus photos) are available to most passport-holders in one day.

Visas

Most travellers, including citizens of the EU, Australia, New Zealand, the USA, Canada and South Africa, can enter Macau with just their passports for between 30 and 90 days. Most others can get a 30-day visa on arrival. They cost MOP$100/50/200 per adult/child under 12/family.

If you're visiting Macau from China and plan to re-enter China you will need to be on a multiple-entry visa. If your visa expires you can obtain a single one-month extension from the **Macau Immigration Department** (Map pp570-1; ☎ 725 488; ground fl, Travessa da Amizade; ☼ 9am-12.30pm & 2.30-5pm Mon-Fri).

SIGHTS & ACTIVITIES

For a city so small, Macau is packed with important cultural and historical sights, including eight squares and 22 historic buildings that have collectively been named the Historic Centre of Macau World Heritage Site by Unesco. Wandering through the squares, *avenida*s and narrow alleys is easily the best way to see the sights and get a feel for what makes Macau unique.

Here we've listed the main sights and a brief description of each. If you're after more detailed descriptions pick up the excellent series of pamphlets by the MGTO before you set off. These include guides to churches,

MACAU

MACAU

MACAU PENINSULA

Grand Prix Circuit

500 m
0.3 miles

GUĂNGDŌNG

Ponte da Amizad

Avenida da Ponte da Amizade

Reservoir

Jetfoil
Pier

Rotunda da
Amizade

Rua Central da Areia Preta

Avenida de Maio

Canal Novo

Avenida do Noroeste

Rua de Muro

Avenida da Ponte da Amizade

Estrada Marginal da Areia Preta

Rua Novo da Areia Preta

Avenida Leste do Hipódromo

Rua Direita
do Hipódromo

Estrada Marginal
do Hipódromo

Rua Dois

Rua Um (Bairro Iao Hon)

Justino Ferreira do Amaral

Avenida de Artur
Tamagnini Barbosa

E do Arco

Estrada da Areia Preta

Avenida de Venceslau de Morais

Montanha
Ilusoa Garden

Estrada de
Ferreira do Amaral

Guia Hill

Guia Tunnel

Rua de Malaca

Rua de Ferreira da Amizade

Rua de Francisco Xavier Pereira

Rua de Mong Há

Mong Há
Hill

Avenida do Coronel Mesquita

Avenida do Almirante Costa Cabral

Avenida de Silva Mendes

Avenida do Conselheiro Ferreira de Almeida

Avenida de Almeida Ribeiro

Rua de Pedro Nolasco da Silva

Rua do Campo

Calçada do Gaio

Vasco da
Gama Garden

Estrada da Vitória

Estrada da Vitória

Estrada de
Cacilhas

Colonial
Buildings

Avenida do Conselheiro Borja

Avenida do Conselheiro

Avenida do General
Castelo Branco

Canidrome

Ilha Verde

Canal dos Patos

Inner Harbour

Rua da Ribeira do Patane

Avenida de Horta e Costa

Estrada do Repouso

Rua de Tomás Vieira

Rua de Coelho do Amaral

Rua de D. Belchior Carneiro

Rua de Tomás Vieira

Rua de São Paulo

Rua do Tarrafeiro

Rua de São Domingos

Avenida de

Lorchas

See Central Macau Map (p573)

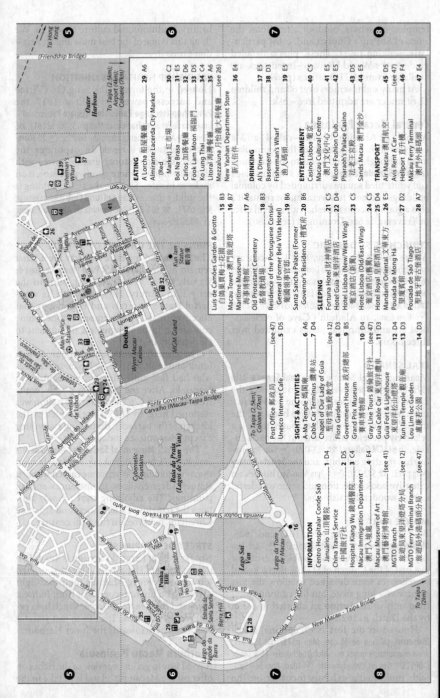

INFORMATION

Centro Hospitalar Conde Saõ	
Januário 山頂醫院	1 D4
China Travel Service	
中國旅行社	2 D5
Hospital Kiang Wu 鏡湖醫院	3 C4
Macau Immigration Department	
澳門入境處	4 E4
MGTO Branch	(see 41)
MGTO Branch	(see 12)
MGTO Ferry Terminal Branch	
旅遊局外港碼頭分局	(see 47)

SIGHTS & ACTIVITIES

A-Ma Temple 媽閣廟	6 A6
Cable Car Terminus 纜車站	7 D4
Chapel of Our Lady of Guia	
聖母雪地殿教堂	(see 12)
Flora Garden	8 D3
Government House 澳門政府總部	9 B5
Grand Prix Museum	
賽車博物館	10 D4
Gray Line Tours 錦倫旅行社	(see 47)
Guia Cable Car 東望洋纜車	11 D3
Guia Fort & Lighthouse	
東望洋松山炮臺	12 D4
Lou Lim Ioc Garden	
盧廉若公園	13 D3
Macau Museum of Art	
澳門藝術博物館	14 D3
Post Office 郵政局	(see 47)
Unesco Internet Cafe	5 D5

Luis de Camões Garden & Grotto	
白鴿巢賈梅士花園	15 B3
Macau Tower 澳門旅遊塔	16 B7
Maritime Museum	
海事博物館	17 A6
Old Protestant Cemetery	
基督教墳場	18 B3
Residence of the Portuguese Consul-	
General (Former Bela Vista Hotel)	
葡國領事官邸	19 B6
Santa Sancha Palace (Former	
Governor's Residence) 禮賓府	20 B6

SLEEPING

Fortuna Hotel 財神酒店	21 C5
Hotel Guia 東望洋酒店	22 D4
Hotel Lisboa (New/West Wing)	
葡京酒店 (新翼)	23 C5
Hotel Lisboa (Old/East Wing)	
葡京酒店 (舊翼)	24 C5
Hotel Royal 皇都酒店	25 D4
Mandarin Oriental 文華東方	26 E5
Pousada de Mong Há	
望廈賓館	27 D2
Pousada de Saõ Tiago	
聖地牙哥古堡酒店	28 A7

EATING

A Lorcha 船屋餐廳	29 A6
Almirante Lacerda City Market	
(Red Market) 紅市場	30 C2
Boi Na Brasa	31 E5
Carlos 加爾餐廳	32 D6
Fook Lam Moon 福臨門	33 D5
Ko Lung Thai	34 C4
Litoral 海灣餐廳	35 A6
Mezzaluna 月怡義大利餐廳	(see 26)
New Yaohan Department Store	
新八佰伴	36 E4

DRINKING

Al's Diner	37 E5
Basement	38 D3
Fisherman's Wharf	
漁人碼頭	39 E5

ENTERTAINMENT

Casino Lisboa 葡京	40 C5
Macau Cultural Centre	
澳門文化中心	41 E5
Nicole Fashion Club	42 D4
Pharaoh's Palace Casino	
法老王宮殿	43 D5
Sands Macau 澳門金沙	44 E5

TRANSPORT

Air Macau 澳門航空	45 D5
Avis Rent A Car	46 F4
Heliport 直升機場	(see 47)
Macau Ferry Terminal	
澳門外港碼頭	47 E4

temples, museums, outdoor attractions, the ruins of St Paul's Church and, most particularly, walking tours. These, plus a detailed guide to the World Heritage–listed sites, are available from MGTO offices (p569).

At many sights seniors over 60 and children 11 or under are admitted free – ask.

Central Macau Peninsula

Avenida de Almeida Ribeiro – called San Ma Lo (New St) in Cantonese – is the peninsula's main thoroughfare and home to the charming **Largo do Senado** (Map p573), a swirling black and white tiled square surrounded by colonial buildings and near to several major sights. It's also a good place to refresh, with several cafés in Travessa de São Domingos (see p580).

CHURCH OF ST DOMINIC

At the end of the square, this 17th-century baroque **church** (Igreja de São Domingos; Map p573; Largo de São Domingos; ☾ 8am-5pm) is arguably the most beautiful in Macau. It contains the **Treasury of Sacred Art** (Tesouro de Arte Sacra; Map p573; ☎ 367 706; ☾ 10am-6pm), an Aladdin's Cave of ecclesiastical art and liturgical plates exhibited over three floors.

LEAL SENADO

Meaning 'Loyal Senate', the **Leal Senado** (Map p573; 163 Avenida de Almeida Ribeiro) looks over the Largo do Senado and is home to Macau's main municipal administrative body and the mayor's office. If you walk through, there is a relatively peaceful courtyard out the back. Inside, the **IACM Gallery** (☎ 988 4180; ☾ 9am-9pm Tue-Sun) has rotating exhibits, and the **Senate Library** (Map p573; ☎ 572 233; ☾ 1-7pm Mon-Sat) houses an extensive book collection and some wonderful carved wooden furnishings.

MONTE FORT

Built by the Jesuits between 1617 and 1626, **Monte Fort** (Fortaleza do Monte; Map p573; ☾ 6am-7pm May-Sep, 7am-6pm Oct-Apr) is accessible by escalator just east of the Church of St Paul. Barracks and storehouses were designed to allow the fort to survive a long siege, but the cannons were fired only once: during an aborted invasion by the Dutch in 1622.

Housed in the fort is exceptional **Macau Museum** (Museu de Macau; Map p573; ☎ 357 911; www.macaumuseum.gov.mo; adult/child under 11 & senior MOP$15/8, free on 15th of month; ☾ 10am-6pm Tue-Sun), with multimedia exhibits focusing on the history, traditions and culture of Macau. We think this is one of the best museums in Asia – don't miss it.

PAWNSHOP HERITAGE EXHIBITION

Housed in the former Tak Seng On (Virtue and Success) pawnshop built in 1917, the **Pawnshop Heritage Exhibition** (Espaço Patrimonial – Uma Casa de Penhores Tradicional; Map p573; ☎ 921 811; 396 Avenida de Almeida Ribeiro; admission MOP$5; ☾ 10.30am-7pm, closed 1st Mon of month) incorporates the fortresslike eight-storey granite tower with slotted windows where goods were stored on racks or in safes. Sharing the same building is the mildly interesting **Cultural Club** (Clube Cultural; Map p573; ☎ 921 811; 390 Avenida de Almeida Ribeiro; ☾ 10.30am-8pm).

RUINS OF THE CHURCH OF ST PAUL

The façade and majestic stairway are all that remain of the **Church of St Paul** (Ruinas de Igreja de São Paulo; Map p573; Rua de São Paulo), built in the early 17th century. However, with its wonderful statues, portals and engravings that effectively make up a 'sermon in stone', some consider it to be the greatest monument to Christianity in Asia.

The church was designed by an Italian Jesuit and built in 1602 by Japanese refugees who had fled anti-Christian persecution in Nagasaki. After the expulsion of the Jesuits from Macau in 1762, a military battalion was stationed here. In 1835 a fire erupted in the kitchen of the barracks, destroying everything except what you see today.

The small **Museum of Sacred Art** (Museu de Arte Sacra; Map p573; Rua de São Paulo; ☾ 9am-6pm) behind the ruins contains polychrome carved wooden statues, silver chalices, monstrances and oil paintings. The adjoining **crypt** (cripta) contains the remains of Vietnamese and Japanese Christians martyred in the 17th century.

STREET OF HAPPINESS

Not far west of Largo do Senado is **Rua da Felicidade** (Street of Happiness). Its red-shuttered terraces were once Macau's main red-light district. You might recognise it from Indiana Jones and the Temple of Doom, which has several scenes shot here. It's fun to just wander west from here towards the Inner Harbour.

Southern Macau Peninsula

A good way to get an overview of the riches on offer on the Macau mainland is to take in the

CENTRAL MACAU

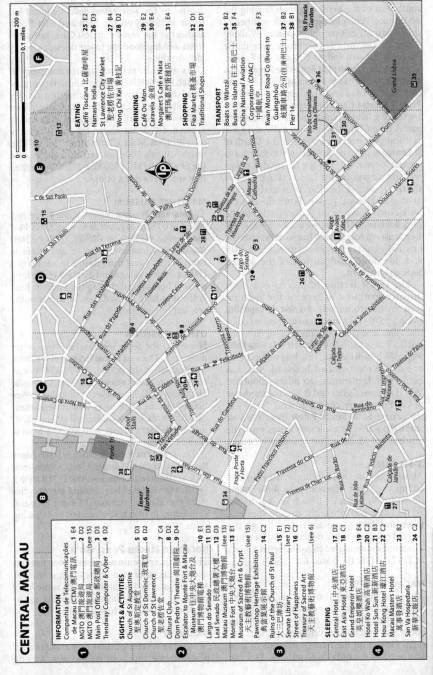

Inner Harbour

St Francis Garden

Grand Lisboa

C de São Paolo

Food Stalls

south part of the peninsula by following the 90-minute 'Penha Peninsula' walk outlined in the tourist office's pamphlet *Macau Walking Tours by Day and Night.* From Avenida de Almeida Ribeiro follow Calçada do Tronco Velho to the **Church of St Augustine** (Igreja de Santo Agostinho; Map p573; Largo de Santo Agostinho; 10am-6pm) built in 1814 and, just opposite, the **Dom Pedro V Theatre** (Teatro Dom Pedro; Map p573; ☎ 939 646; Calçada do Teatro), a colonnaded, 19th-century pastel green building occasionally used for cultural performances. Next is the **Church of St Lawrence** (Igreja de São Lourenço; Map p573; Rua da Imprensa Nacional; 10am-6pm Tue-Sun, 1-2pm Mon) with its magnificent painted ceiling. One of the two towers of the church formerly served as an ecclesiastical prison. From the church, walk down Travessa do Padre Narciso to the pink **Government House** (Sede do Goberno; Map pp570-1; cnr Avenida da Praia Grande & Travessa do Padré Narciso), originally built for a Portuguese noble in 1849 and, for now, headquarters of the Macau SAR government.

The oldest section of Macau is a short distance southwest of here via the beautiful waterfront promenade **Avenida da República** (Map pp570-1). Along here are several colonial villas and civic buildings not open to the public. These include the **former Bela Vista Hotel** (Map pp570-1; Rua de Boa Vista), which as well as being one of the most-storied hotels in Asia, has been a private mansion, secondary school and WWII refugee shelter and is now the residence of the Portuguese consul general. Nearby is the ornate **Santa Sancha Palace** (Palacete de Santa Sancha; Map pp570-1; Estrada de Santa Sancha), once the residence of Macau's Portuguese governors.

A-MA TEMPLE
Almost opposite the Maritime Museum and facing the Inner Harbour, the **A-Ma Temple** (Templo de A-Ma; Map pp570-1; Rue de São Tiago da Barra; 10am-6pm) was probably already standing when the Portuguese arrived, although the present one may only date to the 16th century. The temple is dedicated to A-Ma, better known as Tin Hau (see the boxed text, p567).

MACAU TOWER
At 338m, this **tower** (Torre de Macau; Map pp570-1; ☎ 933 339; www.macautower.com.mo; Largo da Torre de Macau; 10am-9pm Mon-Fri, 9am-9pm Sat & Sun) rises above the Macau Convention & Entertainment Centre on the narrow isthmus of land southeast of Avenida da República. You can

ascend to the **observation decks** (adult/child 3-12 & senior MOP$70/35) on the 58th and 61st floors and eat at the revolving 360 Cafe, but apart from looking good the tower doesn't actually 'do' anything.

As a result, extreme-sports company **AJ Hackett** (☎ 988 8656) has been allowed to organise adventure activities including the relatively tame Skywalk (MOP$198) around an outdoor walkway – no rail, but you are attached to a lanyard – 233m above ground; the more adventurous Mast Climb (from MOP$700) up the mast's 100m of vertical ladders; and the Sky Jump (MOP$588), a 233m 'controlled descent' that's not a bungee.

MARITIME MUSEUM
The **Maritime Museum** (Museu Marítimo; Map pp570-1; ☎ 595 481; 1 Largo do Pagode da Barra; adult/child 10-17 Mon & Wed-Sat MOP$10/5, Sun MOP$5/3; 10am-5.30pm Wed-Mon) has interesting boats and artefacts from Macau's seafaring past, a mock-up of a Hakka fishing village and displays of the long narrow boats raced during the Dragon Boat Festival in June. It used to have access to the sea, but not anymore.

OTHER MUSEUMS
Nearer to the ferry terminal are two other museums. The vast **Macau Museum of Art** (Museu de Arte de Macau; Map pp570-1; ☎ 791 9814; www.artmuseum.gov.mo; Macau Cultural Centre, Avenida Xian Xing Hai; adult/student MOP$5/3, free on Sun; 10am-7pm Tue-Sun) houses visiting exhibits as well as permanent collections of Chinese traditional art and paintings by Western artists who lived in Macau, such as George Chinnery (see opposite).

The **Grand Prix Museum** (Museu do Grande Prémio; Map pp570-1; ☎ 798 4108; basement, Tourist Activities Centre, 431 Rua de Luís Gonzaga Gomes; adult/child 11-19 MOP$10/5; 10am-6pm Wed-Mon) has cars and motorcycles from the Macau Formula 3 Grand Prix and simulators in which you can test your racing skills.

Northern Macau Pensinsula
The northern peninsula sees fewer tourists and is thus quite a good area to just wander around, get lost and find yourself some *hung yan bang* (almond-flavoured biscuits sprinkled with powdery white sugar).

GARDENS
Macau has several gardens that make perfect places to interrupt your wanderings. Among

the best is cool and shady **Lou Lim Ioc Garden** (Jardim Lou Lim Ioc; Map pp570-1; 10 Estrada de Adolfo de Loureiro; ⊙ 6am-9pm), with huge shade trees, lotus ponds, bamboo groves, grottoes and a bridge with nine turns (to escape from evil spirits who can only move in straight lines). Local people use the park to practise taichi or play traditional Chinese musical instruments.

Luís de Camões Grotto & Gardens (Jardim e Gruta de Luís de Camões; Map pp570-1; ⊙ 6am-9pm) is dedicated to the one-eyed poet Luís de Camões (1524–80), who is said to have written part of his epic *Os Lusiadas* in Macau, though there is little evidence that he ever reached the city.

GUIA FORT

As the highest point on the Macau Peninsula, this **fort** (Fortaleza de Guia; Map pp570–1) affords panoramic views of the city and, when the air is clear, across to the islands and China. At the top you'll find a 15m-tall **lighthouse**, built in 1865 and the oldest on the China coast, and the quaint **Chapel of Our Lady of Guia** (Capela de Nossa Señora da Guia; Map pp570-1; ⊙ 9am-5.30pm Tue-Sun), built in 1622.

You could walk up, but it's easier to take the **Guia Cable Car** (Teleférico da Guia; Map pp570-1; one way/return MOP$2/3; ⊙ 8am-6pm Tue-Sun) that runs from the entrance to **Flora Gardens** (Jardim da Flora; Map pp570-1; Travessa do Túnel; ⊙ 6am-7pm), Macau's largest public park.

KUN IAM TEMPLE

Dating back four centuries, **Kun Iam Temple** (Templo de Kun Iam; Map pp570-1; Avenida do Coronel Mesquita; ⊙ 10am-6pm) is Macau's oldest and most interesting temple. The likeness of Kun Iam, the goddess of mercy (see the boxed text, p196), is in the main hall; to the left of the altar and behind glass is a bearded statue believed to represent Marco Polo. The first treaty of trade and friendship between the USA and China was signed in the temple's terraced gardens in 1844.

OLD PROTESTANT CEMETERY

As church law forbade the burial of non-Catholics on hallowed ground, this **cemetery** (Antigo Cemitério Protestante; Map pp570-1; 15 Praça de Luís de Camões; ⊙ 8.30am-5.30pm) was established in 1821 as the last resting place of (mostly Anglophone) Protestants. Among those interred here are Irish-born artist George Chinnery (1774–1852), who spent most of his adult life in Macau painting, and Robert Morrison (1782–1834), the first Protestant missionary to China and author of the first Chinese-English dictionary.

The Islands

Connected to the Macau mainland by three bridges and joined together by an ever-growing area of reclaimed land called Cotai, Coloane and, to a lesser extent, Taipa are oases of calm and greenery, with striking, pastel-coloured colonial villas, quiet lanes, decent beaches and fine Portuguese and Macanese restaurants.

By contrast, the Cotai Strip is development central, with several new mega-casinos sprouting up.

TAIPA

Traditionally an island of duck farms and boat yards, Taipa (Tam Chai in Cantonese) is rapidly becoming urbanised and now boasts major hotels, a university, a racecourse and stadium, high-rise apartments and an airport. But a parade of baroque churches and buildings, temples, overgrown esplanades and lethargic settlements mean it's still possible to experience the traditional charms of the island.

Taipa Village (Map p576), in the south-central part of the island, is a window to the island's past. Here you'll find the stately **Taipa House Museum** (Casa Museum da Taipa; Map p576; ☎ 827 103; Avenida da Praia; adult/student MOP$5/3, free on Sun; ⊙ 10am-6pm Tue-Sun), housed in five waterfront villas that give a sense of how the Macanese middle class lived in the early 20th century. Also in the village is the **Church of Our Lady of Carmel** (Igreja de Nossa Senhora de Carmo; Map p576; Rue da Restauração) built in 1885, and temples including **Pak Tai Temple** (Templo Pak Tai; Map p576; Rua do Regedor). The village **market** is at the end of Rua do Regedor.

You can rent bicycles in Taipa Village from **Mercearia Bicileta Aluguer** (Map p576; ☎ 827 975; 36 Largo Governador Tamagini Barbosa; per hr MOP$18); there's no English but it's next to the Don Quixote restaurant.

COLOANE

A haven for pirates until the start of the 20th century, Coloane (Lo Wan in Cantonese) is now attractive for its sleepy main fishing village, sandy coastline and atmospheric cafés and restaurants. It's also the only part of Macau that doesn't seem to be changing at a head-spinning rate, which can be a relief.

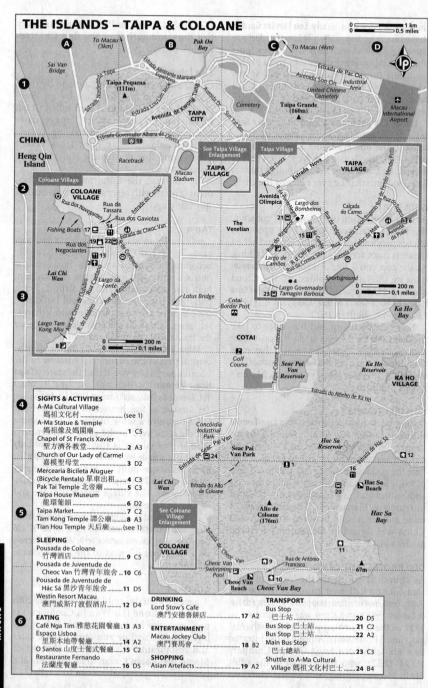

In **Coloane Village** (Map p576) the main attraction is the **Chapel of St Francis Xavier** (Capela de São Francisco Xavier; Map p576; Avenida de Cinco de Outubro; ☾ 10am-8pm), built in 1928, and the delightful square in front. The square is home to a monument commemorating the final routing of pirates in 1910, and a couple of relaxed restaurants. The village has some interesting temples, including the **Tam Kong Temple** (Templo Tam Kong; Map p576; Largo Tam Kong Miu) dedicated to the Taoist god of seafarers.

About 1.5km southeast of Coloane Village is **Cheoc Van Beach** (Bamboo Bay; Map p576), where you can swim in the ocean or in the outdoor pool. Larger and more popular is **Hac Sa Beach** (Black Sand Beach; Map p576) to the northeast.

Atop Alto de Coloane (176m), the 20m-high **A-Ma Statue** (Estátua da Deusa A-Ma; Map p576; Estrada do Alto de Coloane) represents the goddess who gave Macau its name (see the boxed text, p567). Hewn from white jade quarried near Běijīng, it stands beside the enormous **Tian Hou Temple** (Map p576; ☾ 8am-7.30pm) that forms the core of **A-Ma Cultural Village** (Map p576), a religious complex that includes a vegetarian restaurant. A free shuttle runs from the ornamental gate on Estrada de Seac Pai Van every half-hour from 8am to 6pm.

TOURS
Quality Tours, coach trips organised by the MGTO and tendered to such agents as **Gray Line** (Map pp570-1; ☎ 725 813; Room 1015, ground fl, Macau ferry terminal; adult/child 2-9 & senior MOP$98/88) take about five hours. Ask for an English tour.

FESTIVALS & EVENTS
The mixing of two very different cultures and religious traditions for over 400 years has left Macau with a unique collection of holidays, festivals and cultural events. For exact dates, check www.macautourism.gov.mo or the individual event's website (listed below).

Key annual events include the **Macau Arts Festival** (www.icm.gov.mo) in March, the colourful **International Fireworks Display Contest** in September, the **International Music Festival** (www.icm.gov.mo) in October and November and the **Macau International Marathon** (www.sport.gov.mo) on the first Sunday of December. But the biggest event of the year is the **Macau Formula 3 Grand Prix** (www.macau.grandprix.gov.mo), on the third weekend in November, when the city's streets become a racetrack.

Chinese and Portuguese religious festivals and holidays:

Lunar New Year As elsewhere in China, the lunar New Year (or Spring Festival) is a three-day public holiday in late January or early February.

Procession of the Passion of Our Lord (9 February 2008) A colourful procession in February bears a statue of Jesus Christ from the Church of St Augustine through the streets to Macau Cathedral.

A-Ma Festival (29 April 2007, 28 April 2008) Festival honouring the very popular A-Ma (aka Tin Hau), the patron of fisherfolk.

Feast of the Drunken Dragon (24 May 2007; 12 May 2008) People who make their living by fishing close up shop and take a break to enjoy three days of drinking and feasting. Watch for dancing dragons in the streets.

Dragon Boat Festival (19 June 2007; 8 June 2008) As in Hong Kong, this is a major public holiday in June.

SLEEPING
We can't emphasise enough how smart it is to stay in Macau on any night except Saturday. During the week you can find some incredible deals on accommodation, especially but not exclusively in the three- to five-star bracket. On Saturdays rates as much as treble.

These big discounts can be found at travel agencies, hotel websites and specialist sites such as www.gomacau.com and www.macaulastminute.com. The **Shun Tak Centre** (200 Connaught Rd, Sheung Wan) in Hong Kong, from where the ferries to Macau depart, is also good, as are the booths in the arrivals hall of the Macau ferry terminal.

All rooms have air-conditioning and bathroom unless stated. Most midrange and top-end hotels have shuttle buses from the ferry terminal.

Macau Peninsula
Hotels on the mainland are generally split geographically into price constituencies, with many cheap guesthouses and hotels occupying central Macau, around Rua das Lorchas and Avenida de Almeida Ribeiro and the top-end casino-hotels generally in the southeast and centre of town.

BUDGET
San Va Hospedaria (Map p573; ☎ 573 701; www.sanva hotel.com; 67 Rua de Felicidade; s MOP$70, d MOP$80-130) On the 'Street of Happiness' that was once the hub of the red-light district, the San Va is about the cheapest and most charismatic lodging in town. But it's also very basic, with

tiny rooms (room 205 is best), paper-thin walls, no air-con and some rooms without bathrooms.

Central Hotel (Map p573; ☎ 373 888; fax 332 275; 264 Avenida de Almeida Ribeiro; s Sun-Fri MOP$150-188, Sat MOP$173-210, d Sun-Fri MOP$160-198, Sat MOP$210-232) It's cheap. It's central. That's it.

Hotel Ko Wah (Hotel Kou Va; Map p573; ☎ 375 599; 3rd fl, 71 Rua da Felicidade; s/d from MOP$150/180) This welcoming little place is popular with backpackers. It's far from luxurious, but the central location, the price and smiling Miss Shirley make up for that.

Hou Kong Hotel (Map p573; ☎ 937 555; fax 338 884; Travessa das Virtudes; s MOP$309, tw MOP$366-389, tr MOP$550) In the historic Porto Interior area, the newly refurbished Hou Kong retains its wonderful old façade but now offers surprisingly modern rooms for the money. Check a few – some don't have windows.

Macau Masters Hotel (Map p573; ☎ 937 572; www.mastershotel-macau.com; 162 Rua das Lorchas; s/d from MOP$350/400; ✗) A shabby exterior hides a smartly maintained hotel with small but well-equipped rooms.

East Asia Hotel (Map p573; ☎ 922 433; fax 922 431; 1a Rua da Madeira; d MOP$400-450, tr MOP$500, ste MOP$720) The 98-room East Asia, in a quiet street five minutes' walk from Largo do Senado, is one of Macau's better budget options. The rooms aren't inspirational, but they are unusually large and perfectly adequate. Floors six to eight are best.

MIDRANGE

ourpick Pousada de Mong Há (Map pp570-1; ☎ 515 222; www.ift.edu.mo/pousada; Rua de Mong Há; s/d/ste Mon-Fri MOP$400/500/900, s/d/ste Sat & Sun MOP$500/600/1000) This traditional-style and rather attractive little Portuguese inn is run by tourism students. Rates include breakfast and are among the best in the city.

Hotel Guia (Map pp570-1; ☎ 513 888; www.hotelguia -macau.com; 1-5 Estrada do Engenheiro Trigo; r MOP$550-780, ste MOP$1000-2000) At the foot of Guia Hill, this 90-room place is compact but comfortable and pretty good value. It's still within walking distance of most places.

Hotel Sun Sun (Map p573; ☎ 939 393; www.best western.com; 14-16 Praça Ponte e Horta; r MOP$600-980) The Sun Sun is a solid midrange option in one of Macau's more interesting neighbourhoods. The service is reliable and the 178 rooms are comfortable if uninspiring. Ask for an upper floor.

Fortuna Hotel (Map pp570-1; ☎ 786 333; www .hotelfortuna.com.mo; 63 Rua da Cantão; r MOP$980-1120, ste from MOP$1888) In the thick of the casino district, the Fortuna offers decent rooms and attractive midweek rates.

Hotel Royal (Map pp570-1; ☎ 552 222; www.hotel royal.com.mo; 2-4 Estrada da Vitória; r from MOP$1280, ste from MOP$3380) Some people love the Royal, some hate it…it depends on which room you get. Renovated rooms are very nice and the promotional rates, especially those with breakfast, are excellent.

TOP END

Pousada de São Tiago (Map pp570-1; ☎ 378 111; www .saotiago.com.mo; Fortaleza de São Tiago da Barra, Avenida de República; s & d MOP$1620-1960, ste from MOP$2300) The 'St James Inn', built into the ruins of a 17th-century fort, commands a splendid view of the harbour. Rooms were set for an overhaul when we visited.

Hotel Lisboa (Map pp570-1; ☎ 377 666; www .hotelisboa.com; 2-4 Avenida de Lisboa; r from MOP$1650; ✗ 🖳 🏧) After a long-overdue overhaul, Macau's most famous hotel has luxurious rooms to match the reputation. But if you're seeking serenity, this sprawling complex of gaming rooms, restaurants and dancing girls is not for you.

Grand Emperor Hotel (Map p573; ☎ 889 988; www .grandemperor.com; 288 Avenida Comercial de Macau; d from MOP$1800; ✗ 🖳) From the 'Beefeaters' out front to the gold bars under the floor and lifesize portrait of Queen Elizabeth II, this casino-hotel is a festival of royal kitsch that's worth visiting even if you're not staying. If you are, the standard rooms are luxurious, but why not splash out on the 700-sq-m Emperor Suite, with separate rooms for your bodyguards and personal servants…of course.

Mandarin Oriental (Map pp570-1; ☎ 567 888; www .mandarinoriental.com/macau; 956-1110 Avenida da Amizade; r MOP$2000-3900, ste from MOP$5300; ✗ 🖳 🏧) While the Sands Casino has robbed the Mandarin Oriental of its waterfront location, the rooms, excellent restaurants (particularly the Italian food at Mezzaluna, p580) and whole experience here are hard to top.

The Islands

Taipa and Coloane have several midrange hotels and one very nice resort. Macau's two Hostelling International–affiliated hostels are both on Coloane Island. These will soon be joined by several huge hotels on the Cotai Strip.

BUDGET

The very clean **Pousada de Juventude de Cheoc Van** (Map p576; ☎ 882 024; Rua de António Francisco, Coloane; dm/d Sun-Fri MOP$40/70, Sat MOP$50/100) hostel is on the eastern side of Cheoc Van Bay, below the Pousada de Coloane. It has a small kitchen and garden. Book through the **Education & Youth Services Department** (☎ 555 533; www.dsej.gov .mo). You must have a HI card or equivalent; men and women are separated. Ditto for the **Pousada de Juventude de Hác Sá** (Map p576; ☎ 882 701; Rua de Hác Sá Long Chao Kok, Coloane; dm/d/q Sun-Fri MOP$40/50/70, Sat MOP$50/70/100) at the southern end of Hac Sa Beach.

MIDRANGE

our pick **Pousada de Coloane** (Map p576; ☎ 882 143; www .hotelpcoloane.com.mo; Estrada de Cheoc Van, Coloane; r from MOP$750; 🛋) Run by a Portuguese family, this 30-room hotel and its newly renovated, Portuguese-style rooms is wonderfully romantic and excellent value. And the location above Cheoc Van Beach is about as chilled as you'll find. The Portuguese restaurant (open 8am to 10pm) is great.

TOP END

Westin Resort Macau (Map p576; ☎ 871 111; www .westin.com/macau; 1918 Estrada de Hac Sa, Coloane; r/ste from MOP$2200/5000; 🏊 🖥 🛋) On the eastern side of Hac Sa Beach, the five-star Westin is Macau's only top-end hotel that doesn't have a casino. Instead, it offers a chilled beachside experience, with smooth service and plush rooms, each with a large terrace. The golf course on the roof is very cool.

EATING

While Macau is renowned for its Chinese cuisine (especially dim sum), most people come here to sample Portuguese and Macanese food

(see below). For cheap food, the cafés and no-frills Chinese places around Largo do Senado are a good bet.

Portuguese & Macanese

Rua Do Almirante Sérgio, just north of the A-Ma Temple (p574) on Macau Peninsula, is a great place to experience some of Macau's finest Portuguese and Macanese food. **Litoral** (Map pp570-1; ☎ 967 878; 261a Rua do Almirante Sérgio; starters MOP$30-50, mains MOP$60-120; 🕙 noon-3pm & 6-10.30pm) serves delightful Macanese fare, with excellent duck, baked rice and spicy prawn dishes. Nearby **A Lorcha** (Map pp570-1; ☎ 313 193; 289a Rua do Almirante Sérgio; starters MOP$28-46, mains MOP$58-130; 🕙 12.30-3pm & 6.30-11pm Wed-Mon) has a more Portuguese bent; try the chicken with onion and tomato; feijoada; raw codfish salad; or pork ear salad (MOP$26).

Restaurante Fernando (Map p576; ☎ 882 531; 9 Praia de Hac Sa, Coloane; soups MOP$22-26, mains MOP$50-148, rice dishes MOP$60-66; 🕙 noon-9.30pm) Fernando is famed for seafood and is the perfect place for a protracted, boozy lunch by the sea. The bar stays open till midnight.

Espaço Lisboa (Map p576; ☎ 882 226; 8 Rua dos Gaivotas, Coloane; soups MOP$28-65, starters MOP$45-150, mains MOP$88-240; 🕙 noon-3pm & 6.30-10pm Tue-Fri, noon-10.30pm Sat & Sun) Carefully prepared Portuguese fare is served in this charming renovated village house.

Carlos (Map pp570-1; ☎ 751 838; Ground fl, Vista Magnífica Bldg, Rua Cidade de Braga; mains MOP$50-80; 🕙 noon-3pm & 6-11pm Tue-Sun) Forget the menu, just ask Senhor Carlos what he'd like to cook today – you won't be disappointed. Otherwise, try the Macanese minchi (spicy mince with rice and egg on top) or any of the delicious Portuguese dishes.

O Santos (Map p576; ☎ 827 508; 20 Rua da Cunha, Taipa; mains MOP$62-120; 🕙 noon-3pm & 6.30-10.30pm)

PORTUGUESE & MACANESE FOOD

Portuguese cuisine is meat-based and uses a lot of olive oil, garlic and bacalhau (dried salted cod). Popular dishes include caldo verde (a soup of green cabbage or kale thickened with potatoes), pasteis de bacalhau (codfish croquettes), sardinhas grelhadas (grilled sardines) and feijoada (a casserole of beans, pork, spicy sausages, potatoes and cabbage that is actually Brazilian in origin).

Macanese food borrows from Chinese and other Asian cuisines, as well as from those of former Portuguese colonies in Africa and India. It's redolent of coconut, tamarind, chilli, jaggery (palm sugar) and shrimp paste. The most famous Macanese speciality is galinha africana (African chicken) made with coconut, garlic and chillies. Apart from cod, there's plenty of other fish and seafood: shrimp, crab, squid and white fish. Sole is a Macanese delicacy. The former Portuguese enclave of Goa contributes delicious spicy prawns.

This tiny place is famous for its stuffed pork loin and its codfish dishes, especially *bacalhau à zé do pipo* (dried cod baked with mashed potatoes; MOP$72).

Chinese & Other Asian

Wong Chi Kei (Map p573; ☎ 331 313; 17 Largo do Senado; noodle & rice dishes MOP$15-35; ⏱ 8am-midnight) This little Chinese place has been serving cheap noodles and other dishes since 1946.

Ko Lung Thai (Map pp570-1; ☎ 334 067; 23 Rua de Ferreira do Amaral; dishes MOP$25-90; ⏱ 11am-7am) This place that almost never sleeps is one of the most authentic Thai restaurants north of Bangkok.

Café Nga Tim (Map p576; ☎ 882 086; 1 Rua Caetano, Coloane; mains MOP$30-60; ⏱ noon-1am) We love the Sino-Portuguese food, laid-back atmosphere, location (opposite the Chapel of St Francis Xavier) and price at this place.

Namaste India (Map p573; ☎ 372 750; 8 Rua Central; curries MOP$30-60; ⏱ 11am-3pm & 6-11pm) The food in this simple, central Indian place is better than the exterior might suggest.

Fook Lam Mun (Map pp570-1; ☎ 786 622; 259 Avenida da Amizade; meals from MOP$200; ⏱ 11am-3pm & 5.30-11pm Mon-Fri, 8.30am-3pm & 5.30-11pm Sat & Sun) Here it's more about classic Cantonese food (especially the seafood) than the atmosphere.

Western

Caffè Toscana (Map p573; ☎ 370 354; 11 Travessa de São Domingos; meals about MOP$25-50; ⏱ noon-9.30pm Wed-Mon) You can enjoy a full-blown Italian meal at this welcoming café-restaurant, but it's especially recommended for its focaccia (MOP$18 to MOP$27).

Mezzaluna (Map pp570-1; ☎ 567 888; 2nd fl, Mandarin Oriental, 956-1110 Avenida da Amizade; starters MOP$65-100, pizza & pasta MOP$80-125, mains MOP$150-245; ⏱ 12.30-2.30pm & 6.30-11pm Tue-Sun) Mezzaluna serves superb Italian cuisine in classy surrounds. The lunch buffet (two/three courses MOP$150/180) is great value.

Boi Na Brasa (Map pp570-1; ☎ 753 021; 188 Rua de Paris; buffet MOP$98-150; ⏱ 12.30-3pm & 7-11pm Tue-Sun) Forget the menu, just sit down and let the chef carve all manner of meat onto your plate. It does have some salads, but it's mainly a meat-fest.

Markets & Self-Catering

Peninsular Macau's food stalls sell excellent stir-fried dishes; try the *dai pai dong* along Rua do Almirante Sérgio near the Inner Harbour.

Yuk gon (dried sweet strips of pork and other meats) are a Macau speciality, as are *hung yan bang*. You'll see both scattered about older parts of the city, particularly near Rua da Caldeira and Travessa do Matadouro at the northern end of Avenida de Almeida Ribeiro.

Two of the largest markets are the **Almirante Lacerda City Market** (Mercado Municipal Almirante Lacerda; Map pp570-1; 130 Avenida do Almirante Lacerda; ⏱ 6am-8pm), also called the Red Market, in northern Macau, and the **St Lawrence City Market** (Mercado Municipal de São Lourenço; Map p573; Rua de João Lecaros; ⏱ 6am-8pm) in the south.

Opposite the Macau ferry terminal, **New Yaohan Department Store** (Map pp570-1; ☎ 725 338; Avenida da Amizade; ⏱ 11am-10.30pm) has a large supermarket on the 2nd floor.

DRINKING

Despite its reputation as a city of sin, Macau's nightlife has until recently been dominated by dancing girls and casinos. But it's beginning to change. As contrived as **Fisherman's Wharf** (Map pp570–1) might seem, there are a few decent bars and restaurants there and the atmosphere is generally pretty good. The rise of Fisherman's Wharf hasn't been so good for the bar strip in the Dochas area on Avenida Doutor Sun Yat Sen. The bars here are starting to look pretty tired, though they might get a new lease of life when the nearby mega casinos open. For now, don't arrive before about midnight.

Elsewhere, there's a fine line between cafés, most of which serve food as well, and bars. Here we've listed our favourite places for a warm beverage under 'Cafés' and those where we seek something colder (and stronger) under 'Bars'.

Cafés

Macau's many little cafés are great for a coffee break and also for cheap and tasty lunches. If you're anywhere near Largo do Senado, Travessa de São Domingos has plenty of options, including the **Café Ou Mon** (Map p573; ☎ 372 207; 12 Travessa de São Domingos; ⏱ 8am-8pm Tue-Sun) with its great coffee, Ou Mon cake (MOP$9) and Portuguese clientele. It also serves sandwiches (MOP$12 to MOP$25) and other dishes (MOP$50).

Caravela (Map p573; ☎ 712 080; ground fl, Kam Loi Bldg, 7 Pátio do Comandante Mata e Oliveira; ⏱ 8am-10.30pm) This wonderful *pastelaria* (pastry shop) just north of Avenida de Dom João IV serves excellent coffee, delectable pastries (cakes MOP$10 to MOP$25) and good sandwiches.

Margaret's Café e Nata (Map p573; ☎ 710 032; Rua Alm Costa Cabral St; ☒ 6.30am-8pm Mon-Sat, 9am-7pm Sun) This busy little café is famous for its egg tarts and cheap sandwiches.

Lord Stow's Cafe (Map p576; ☎ 882 174; 1 Rua da Tassara; ☒ 7am-10pm Thu-Tue, to 7pm Wed) This place serves baked goodies from the famous bakery around the corner, including its celebrated *pastéis de nata*, a warm egg-custard tart (MOP$6).

Bars

our pick **Basement** (Map pp570-1; ☎ 667 3445; 69 Avenida de Sidónio Pais; ☒ 9am-4am Tue-Sun) The coolest lounge bar in town playing some of the best tunes, this place has a great vibe, particularly on weekends. It's hard to find: take a taxi (MOP$10 to MOP$15 from the Lisboa) and ask for Hoi Fu (hoy foo); it's located downstairs through a small arcade, next to the BCM Bank.

Al's Diner (Map pp570-1; Fisherman's Wharf) This garden-style place on the waterfront serves up cheap beer and more than passable Filipino bands.

ENTERTAINMENT

Not surprisingly, entertainment in Macau is dominated by the casinos. Whether it's an assignation with Lady Luck you seek, or the free shows and events the casinos host, there is plenty to choose from. Even the Cirque de Soleil is coming, scheduled to open in 2008.

But there is more. Cultural performances such as opera are becoming increasingly regular; consult the territory's premier venue, the **Macau Cultural Centre** (Centro Cultural de Macau; Map pp570-1; ☎ 797 7215; www.ccm.gov.mo; Avenida Xian Xing Hai) for details.

Casinos

Casinos and the endless dollars they suck into the city are the lifeblood of Macau (see the boxed text, below). All of them operate 24 hours a day and punters must be at least 18 years old and properly dressed. Standards are rising as competition increases, and even if you don't fancy playing the tables (in many the minimum bet is MOP$100 or more), it's worth taking a look around, enjoying the free shows and just watching the way these temples to Mammon operate.

LAS VEGAS OF THE EAST *Andrew Burke*

A few years ago I was in Macau staying at the Hotel Lisboa. One of the city's most distinctive landmarks, the Lisboa and the casino below had been turning a fat profit since the 1960s. A few other modest casino-hotels were also operating, and the occasional overexcited journalist would describe Macau as the 'Las Vegas of the East'.

But wading through the thick fug of smoke and cacophony of noise in the gaming rooms, sleeping in a room that stank of cigarette smoke, patiently liberating toilet paper one sheet at a time in the casino's bathrooms (a system to prevent mainland punters overusing it) and, heaven forbid, paying for drinks in the casino, the claim sounded like nothing more than marketing puffery.

Then things started to change. Casino mogul Stanley Ho's monopoly was broken and in 2002 Las Vegas operators were invited to set up in competition. With a billion frustrated gamblers on the doorstep, they didn't need to be asked twice. The results are astounding and, on this research trip, I finally started to buy it: Macau is very definitely the Las Vegas of the East.

If you don't believe me, consider this. The tiny territory, just one 40th the size of Hong Kong, will be home to almost 30 casinos by 2008. Those being built on the Cotai Strip are straight out of Las Vegas – the gargantuan Venetian is actually a direct copy, complete with canals and gondolas. Macau's total number of hotel rooms is forecast to grow from about 12,000 in 2006 to more than 50,000 in 10 years time; with them will come huge entertainment venues designed to attract the world's biggest music acts, and the world's biggest spenders. If you still don't believe, then this figure is the killer – Macau is already turning over more money than Las Vegas, with each gaming table 10 times more profitable than its Vegas counterpart.

Whatever you feel about casinos, it's hard to escape the fact that Macau is dominated by them as much as any other place on earth. And with the stated objective to make the Cotai Strip 'an entertainment destination, the likes of which no one has ever seen before in North Asia', you're going to be hearing much more about it in future.

Most of Macau's casinos are located in big hotels. The following is a small selection on Macau Peninsula.

Casino Lisboa (Map pp570-1; ☎ 375 111; 2-4 Avenida de Lisboa) With its garish 1960s exterior and decades of experience catering to Asia's gamblers – both high- and low-rollers – the Lisboa is the best-known casino in Asia. That doesn't mean, however, it's the best. Despite a recent makeover it retains much of its old raunchy personality, with the Crazy Paris Show still sending out the dancing girls, and punters still cramming into smoke-filled gaming rooms. It's a charismatic contrast with the vast new casinos.

Pharaoh's Palace Casino (Map pp570-1; ☎ 788 111; 3rd fl, Landmark Macau, Avenida da Amizade) The kitschy themed gambling areas are another style of casino popular in Macau. Pharaoh's is a sort of midway point between the Lisboa and the Vegas-style places.

Sands Macao (Map pp570-1; ☎ 883 388; Avenida de Amizade) Here you'll find hundreds of machines and more than 300 gaming tables, free drinks to gamblers and constant live entertainment, all in a vast space several stories high. Welcome to Macau's casino future.

Others opening imminently include the Vegas-style Wynn Macau, MGM Grand and Venetian, and the new Grand Lisboa, opposite the Lisboa.

Nightclubs

Nicole Fashion Club (Map pp570-1; Fisherman's Wharf; ☺ 7pm-late) It might sound like it's full of wankers, but when we visited this place was playing a good mix of tunes and had a fun vibe. The indoor-outdoor combo is perfect, and makes it the best place on the Wharf.

Horse Racing

Macau Jockey Club (Map p576; ☎ 821 188, information hotline 820 868; www.macauhorse.com; Estrada Governador Albano de Oliveira, Taipa; admission MOP$20) This has been the venue for horse racing since 1991. You can watch races from the five-storey, air-con grandstands on Saturday from 2pm and Tuesday from 7.30pm (in summer on Wednesday and Saturday from 7.30pm).

SHOPPING

While there is a growing number of luxury outlets and high-fashion boutiques in Macau, few people come here specifically to shop. However, browsing through the traditional antique, ceramic and bric-a-brac shops (Map p573) on or near to Rua de São Paulo, Rua das Estalagens and Rua de São António has been known to turn up once-in-a-lifetime finds. Apart from these, **Asian Artefacts** (Map p576; ☎ 881 022; 9 Rua dos Negociantes; ☺ 10am-7pm) in Coloane Village, with its before and after photos of restored pieces, is recommended.

Around Macau's back lanes, you'll stumble across bustling markets and Chinese shops selling birdcages, dried herbs, medicines and mah jong sets. Try Rua de Madeira or Rua dos Mercadores, which lead up to Rua da Tercena and its flea market (Map p573).

The MGTO distributes a useful pamphlet called *Shopping in Macau*, which highlights neighbourhoods and their specific wares. If you're heading to Hong Kong it's worth buying alcohol, which is stupidly expensive there.

GETTING THERE & AWAY
Air

One and possibly two new low-cost airlines based in Macau are set to make the ultramodern **Macau International Airport** (Map p576; ☎ 861 111; www.macau-airport.gov.mo), on the east coast of Taipa, much busier. For the details of who's flying where check the airport's comprehensive website.

For now, **Air Macau** (NX; Map pp570-1; ☎ 396 5555; www.airmacau.com.mo; Ground fl, 398 Alameda Doutor Carlos d'Assumpção) has the lion's share of that traffic. International destinations include Bangkok, Busan, Manila, Seoul and dozens of flights a week to Taipei and Kaohsiung in Taiwan. Together with Shanghai Airlines and Xiamen Airlines, both found at the **China National Aviation Corporation** (CNAC; Map p573; ☎ 788 034; fax 788 036; lat Teng Hou Bldg, Avenida de Dom João IV) office, Air Macau has at least one flight a day to mainland cities including Běijīng, Fúzhōu, Guìlín, Hángzhōu, Kūnmíng, Nánjīng, Shànghǎi, Shēnzhèn and Xiàmén.

New long-haul budget airline **Viva Macau** (www.vivamacau.com) started operating in September 2006 and is expected to service destinations including Milan, Moscow, Mumbai, Delhi, Jakarta, Manila and Abu Dhabi by late 2007. The website www.gomacau.com is a good place to look for cheap fares.

Other airlines with flights from Macau to destinations in the region:

AirAsia (FD; ☎ in Hong Kong 3167 2299; www.airasia.com)
EVA Airways (BR; ☎ 726 848; www.evaair.com)

Tiger Airways (TR; www.tigerairways.com)
Trans Asia Airways (GE; ☎ 701 556; www.tna.com.tw)

East Asia Airlines/Heli Hong Kong (☎ 727 288, in Hong Kong 2108 9898; www.helihongkong.com) runs a 16-minute helicopter shuttle between Macau and Hong Kong (HK$1700 Monday to Thursday, HK$1800 Friday to Sunday) up to 27 times a day from 9am to 10.30pm (9.30am to 11pm from Hong Kong).

Boat

CHINA

A daily ferry run by the **Yuet Tung Shipping Co** (☎ 574 478; adult/child MOP$124/70) connects Macau with the port of Shékǒu in Shēnzhèn. The boat leaves at 10am, 2pm and 6.30pm and takes 80 minutes; it returns from Shékǒu at 8.15am, 11.45am and 4.45pm. Tickets can be bought up to three days in advance from the point of departure, which is pier 14 (Map p573), just off Rua das Lorchas and 100m southwest of the end of Avenida de Almeida Ribeiro.

Sampans and ferries sail across the Inner Harbour to Wānzái (MOP$12.50) on the mainland from a small pier near where Rua das Lorchas meets Rua do Dr Lourenço Pereira Marques. They depart hourly between 8am and 4pm, returning a half-hour later. A departure tax of MOP$20 is charged.

HONG KONG

Two ferry companies operate services to/from Hong Kong virtually 24 hours a day.

TurboJet (☎ 790 7039, in Hong Kong 2859 3333 information, 2921 6688 bookings; www.turbojet.com.hk; economy/ superclass Mon-Fri MOP$142/244, Sat & Sun MOP$154/260, night crossing MOP$176/275) runs three types of vessels that take between 55 and 65 minutes. From Hong Kong Island, departures are from the Macau ferry pier at the **Shun Tak Centre** (☎ 2859 3359; 200 Connaught Rd, Sheung Wan), and in Macau from the **Macau ferry terminal** (Map pp570-1; ☎ 790 7240).

New World First Ferry (☎ 727 676, in Hong Kong 2131 8181; www.nwff.com.hk) operates high-speed catamarans from the Macau ferry terminal every half-hour or so between 7am and 8.30pm. In Hong Kong they leave the China ferry terminal (Canton Rd, Tsim Sha Tsui) on the half-hour from 7am to 9pm or 10pm. The trip takes 60 to 75 minutes and tickets cost HK$140/175 on weekdays/nights (ie from 6pm to 9pm or 10pm from Hong Kong and 6.30pm to 8.30pm from Macau), and

HK$155/175 on weekends and public holidays. Deluxe class is HK$245/275 on weekdays/nights and HK$260/275 on weekends and public holidays.

Macau is also linked directly to Hong Kong International Airport (p560) by the new **Turbo-Jet Sea Express** (☎ in Hong Kong 2859 3333; www.turbo jetseaexpress.com.hk), leaving at 9.45am, 1pm, 3pm, 4.30pm and 8pm. It costs MOP$200/155/110 per adult/child/infant and takes 45 minutes.

A pier at Macau International Airport is due for completion by the time you read this and will probably be serviced by TurboJet. Apart from direct trips between the airport and Hong Kong, Hong Kong International Airport (HKIA) and some cities in China, passengers should be able to transit straight through to Hong Kong without passing immigration in Macau.

Tickets can be booked up to 28 days in advance and are available at ferry terminals, CTS branches and travel agents. There is also a stand-by queue before each sailing. On weekends and public holidays, book your return ticket in advance.

Bus

Macau is an easy gateway into China. Simply take bus 3, 5 or 9 to the **Border Gate** (Portas de Cerco; Map p567; ☼ 7am-midnight) and walk across. A second, less busy crossing is the **Cotai Frontier Post** (Map p567; ☼ 9am to 8pm), on the causeway linking Taipa and Coloane, which allows visitors to cross over the Lotus Bridge by shuttle bus (HK$4) to the Zhūhǎi Special Economic Zone. Buses 15, 21 and 26 will drop you off at the crossing.

For buses further afield, the **Kee Kwan Motor Road Co** (Map p573; ☎ 933 888) operates from the modest bus station on Rua das Lorchas, 100m southwest of the end of Avenida de Almeida Ribeiro. Buses for Guǎngzhōu (MOP$70, four hours) depart every half-hour and for Zhōngshān (MOP$25, 70 minutes) every 20 minutes between about 8am and 6.30pm. There are buses to Guǎngzhōu (MOP$75) and Dōngguǎn (MOP$80) from Macau International Airport.

GETTING AROUND
To/From the Airport

Airport bus AP1 (MOP$3.30) leaves the airport and zips around Taipa before heading to the Macau ferry terminal and the Border Gate. The bus stops at a number of major hotels en route and departs every 15 minutes from 6.30am to 12.10am. There's an additional charge of MOP$3 for each large piece of luggage. Other services run to Coloane (bus 21 and 26) and the A-Ma Temple (bus 21).

A taxi from the airport to the centre of town is about MOP$40.

Bicycle

Bikes can be rented in Taipa Village (see p575). You are not allowed to cross the Macau–Taipa bridges on a bicycle.

Car

The brightly coloured, open-sided Mokes that have so long been the mainstay of Macau's humble car-hire industry might be on their last lap. Laws forbidding vehicles older than 10 years being hired mean the rental companies are being pressured to retire their fleets in 2007. It's not, however, a *fait accompli*, so ask around when you get there.

Avis Rent A Car (Map pp570-1; ☎ 726 571; www.avis .com.mo; Ground fl, Macau ferry terminal) hires out cheap Suzuki Vitaras for MOP$550 a day during the week and MOP$700 at the weekend.

Public Transport

Public buses and minibuses run on 40 routes from 6.45am till just after midnight, with destinations displayed in Portuguese and Chinese. Fares – MOP$2.50 on the peninsula, MOP$3.30 to Taipa, MOP$4 to Coloane Village and MOP$5 to Hac Sa Beach – must be paid into a box; there's no change.

The *Macau Tourist Map* (p568) has a full list of both bus companies' routes, and a pamphlet listing all bus routes is worth picking up from MGTO outlets. Useful services on the peninsula include buses 3 and 3A, which run between the ferry terminal and the city centre. Bus 3 continues up to the border gate, as does bus 5. From the ferry terminal, bus 12 runs past the Hotel Lisboa and then goes up to the Lou Lim Ioc Garden and Kun Iam Temple.

Buses 21, 21A, 25 and 26A run to Taipa and Coloane.

Taxi

The taxi flag fall is MOP$10 for the first 1.5km and MOP$1 for each additional 200m. There is a MOP$5 surcharge to go to Coloane; travelling between Taipa and Coloane will cost MOP$2 extra.

Journeys starting from the airport cost an extra MOP$5, and large bags an extra MOP$3. For a yellow radio taxi call ☎ 519 519 or ☎ 939 939.

Guǎngdōng 广东

Feisty, rebellious Guǎngdōng is China's fastest-developing province and also one of the richest. For centuries it was isolated from the rest of China by its mountainous topography, forcing the Cantonese to rely on their own pragmatism and innovation for survival.

Situated in the fertile Pearl River Delta on the South China Sea, the Cantonese have always looked outward to the sea for their livelihood. It was along Guǎngdōng's 800km coastline that foreign merchants first made contact with China and the ancient Maritime Silk Road had its beginnings. Guǎngdōng's exposure to the outside world and the independent nature of the Cantonese has often been a thorn in the side of the authorities. In early times, Guǎngdōng was thought to be inhabited by barbarians; it was where disgraced officials from the north were sent into exile.

Guǎngdōng was an economic backwater until Deng Xiaoping's 'open door policy' opened up the province to development. With the establishment of the three Special Economic Zones (see p587) and trading links to Hong Kong, economic activity in the province took off like wildfire and hasn't slowed down yet. The once subtropical landscape is now hidden under a sprawl of smoke-spewing factories. Here you'll witness the future of modern China close up, warts and all.

Even with all the development, there are still some worthwhile places to visit. Guǎngzhōu, the capital, may be chaotic and polluted but it's also world-renowned for its Cantonese cuisine. Close to Guǎngzhōu is Kāipíng, famous for its unique watchtowers, and a journey downriver from Qīngyuǎn to see the ancient temples of Fēilái and Fēixiá is truly a one-of-a-kind experience.

HIGHLIGHTS

- Indulge yourself in the legendary Cantonese cuisine of **Guǎngzhōu** (p587)
- Sail downriver to the secluded temples of **Fēilái and Fēixiá** (p602)
- Explore the surreal fairy-tale watchtowers of **Kāipíng** (p601)
- Create your own ceramic masterpieces at the **Nanfeng Ancient Kiln** (p604) at Fóshān

★ Fēilái & Fēixiá

Nanfeng
Ancient Kiln ★ Guǎngzhōu
★

Kāipíng ★

- POPULATION: 75.9 MILLION

GUĂNGDŌNG

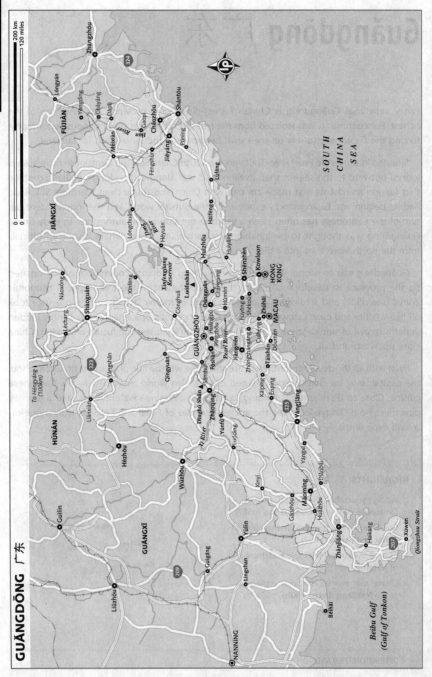

GUĂNGDŌNG 广东

FUJIÀN

JIĀNGXĪ

HÚNÁN

GUĂNGXĪ

SOUTH CHINA SEA

Zhāngzhōu

Lóngyán

Yǒngdìng

Chàyáng

Dàpǔ

Gāopí

Méixiàn

Fèngshùn

Chāozhōu

Pǔníng

Jiēyáng

Shàntóu

Lǐfēng

Hǎifēng

Húyáng

Huìzhōu

Shēnzhèn

Kowloon

HONG KONG

Lóngchuān

Héyuán

Xīnfēng

Xīnfēngjiāng Reservoir

Luófúshān

Chángpíng

Húmén

Shékǒu

Zhūhǎi

MACAU

Nàoxóng

Shàoguān

Lèchāng

Lián xiàn

Yángshān

Qīngyuǎn

Conghuà

Dīnghú Shān

GUĂNGZHŌU

Sānshuǐ

Fóshān

Dōngguǎn

Fúyǒng

Cuìhēng

Zhōngshān

Táishān

Dòumén

Kāipíng

Ēnpíng

Jiāngmén

Yángjiāng

Yángchūn

Héngyáng (100km)

Hézhōu

Wúzhōu

Yúnfú

Luódìng

Xìnyí

Lingshān

Máomíng

Gāozhōu

Huàzhōu

Zhànjiāng

Hǎikāng

Xúwén

Guìlín

Guìgǎng

Yùlín

Guìgǎng

Líuzhōu

Běihǎi

NÁNNÍNG

Beibu Gulf (Gulf of Tonkon)

Qiongzhou Strait

Hàn River

Dōng River

Běi River

Pearl River

Xī River

History

As China's southern gateway, Guăngdōng has had contact with the outside world for over a millennium. Among the first outsiders to make their way here were the Romans, who appeared as early as the 2nd century AD. By the Tang dynasty (618–907 AD), Arab merchants were visiting regularly and a sizeable trade with the Middle East and Southeast Asia had developed.

The first Europeans to settle here were the Portuguese in 1557, who set up base downriver at Macau. They were followed by the Jesuits in 1582, who established themselves at Zhàoqìng, west of Guăngzhōu. The British came along in the 17th century and by 1685 merchant ships from the East India Company were calling at Guăngzhōu. In 1757 an imperial edict gave the *cohong*, a local merchants' guild, a monopoly on China's trade with foreigners, who were restricted to Shamian Island. Trade remained in China's favour until 1773 when the British shifted the balance by unloading 1000 chests of Bengal opium at Guăngzhōu. Addiction swept China like wildfire, eventually leading to the Opium War (see boxed text p611).

Guăngdōng was a hotbed of revolt in the 19th century. The Taiping Rebellion (1848–64), led by the enigmatic Hong Xiuquan, who claimed to be the younger brother of Jesus Christ, tried to establish his own 'Kingdom of Heavenly Peace' and recruit members to overthrow the dynasty. The rebellion was crushed with the help of foreign powers.

Twentieth-century Guăngdōng saw its share of hardships and successes, being the headquarters of both the Nationalist and Communist parties and enduring untold suffering during the Cultural Revolution. After 1978, with the rise of Deng Xiaoping and the decision to adopt an 'open door' economic policy, Guăngdōng became the first province to experience firsthand the effects of economic reforms, with Shēnzhèn, Zhūhăi and Shàntóu set up as Special Economic Zones. Guăngdōng's continued economic success has made it a leading export centre for computers, clothing and household items.

Climate

Guăngdōng's moody subtropical climate means chilly, wet winters and long, humid summers. The rainy season generally lasts from April/May to September and typhoons can be frequent from July/August to October. The best times to visit are in late autumn (October–November) and early spring (March–April).

Language

The vast majority of the people of Guăngdōng speak Cantonese, a dialect distinct from Mandarin. Though it enjoys much less exalted status than the so-called national language, Cantonese is in fact older than Mandarin and classical poetry sounds much better when read using that dialect's pronunciation.

Getting There & Away

Guăngdōng is well connected to the rest of China by bus, plane and train. The easiest entry/exit point to/from the province is Hong Kong via the KCR East Rail line (p561).

Getting Around

Guăngdōng is crisscrossed with a vast network of rail and road lines, making travelling around the province very easy. Trains run north through Shàoguăn and onwards to Húnán province, east to Méizhōu, Shàntóu and Fújiàn province, and west through Zhàoqìng to Guăngxī province. Hydrofoils also run between the Pearl River Delta region and Hong Kong. Frequent buses run to all these locations and more, though they are less comfortable than trains. If you really need to get somewhere fast, there are flights between all major cities in the region.

GUĂNGZHŌU 广州

☎ 20 / pop 3.24 million

Known to many in the West as 'Canton', Guăngzhōu is the first city most travellers to mainland China visit. Wrapped in a perpetual haze of pink smog and flashing neon lights, the city overwhelms with its energy, colour, and sheer size. Influenced by neighbouring Hong Kong, consumerism has swept up the city in a head-spinning frenzy, but scratch away Guăngzhōu's glittery surface and you'll find a place quite special among China's major urban centres. It just takes some time to grow on you.

It wasn't long ago that Guăngzhōu exemplified the worst of rampant urbanisation: never-ending flyovers, ugly architecture and traffic-clogged streets. In recent years, the city has been given a makeover and its scrubbed-up appearance has given it a cosmopolitan edge. Stodgy concrete apartment blocks are giving way to shiny high rises and shopping plazas. Efforts to relieve traffic congestion have resulted in a clean, modern metro system and tougher traffic laws. Trees and flowers have been planted on roadsides and well-kept gardens and parks add splashes of colour to the contemporary grey landscape.

The city remains as chaotic as ever, but underneath all the glitz and noise there are pockets that still retain their character from earlier years. Many of the elegant churches, villas and mansions on the former foreign enclave of Shamian Island have been restored, and you'll find hidden among Guăngzhōu's back lanes some lovely old residences, temples and gardens that haven't been touched in generations.

Of course, you can't talk about Guăngzhōu without mentioning the food. It's here that you'll try Cantonese cuisine cooked at its very best. The city boasts the largest number of restaurants per capita in China; the Cantonese will make certain you won't leave their city hungry.

History

Legend has it that Guăngzhōu was founded by five immortals who descended from the sky on rams and saved the city from starvation. Thus the city earned the nickname 'Goat City' (Yáng Chéng). Goats or no goats, the first settlement on the site of the present-day city dates back to 214 BC, when the so-called First Emperor of Qin sent his troops south to gain control of the sea.

Because of its fortuitous location on the northern end of the Pearl River, Guăngzhōu from early times was China's most important southern port. It was the starting point for the Silk Road of the Sea during the Tang dynasty (AD 618–907), an important maritime route for shipping silk and other goods to the West. It was a trading post for the Portuguese in the 16th century, and for the British in the 17th.

The city was a stronghold of the republican forces after the fall of the Qing dynasty in 1911. Sun Yatsen (1866–1925), the first president of the Republic of China, was born in Cuìhēng village (see p610), and in the early 1920s he led the Kuomintang (KMT; Nationalist Party) in Guăngzhōu, from where the republicans mounted their campaigns against the northern warlords. Guăngzhōu was also a centre of activities for the fledgling Communist Party, and Mao Zedong and other prominent Communist leaders were based here in 1925/26.

Since liberation, Guăngzhōu (Broad Region) has put all its energies into the business of making money. Even when China had effectively cut itself off from most of the rest of the world, what was then called the Canton Trade Fair was the only forum in which the Middle Kingdom did business with the West. Today, it remains a vital import-export centre.

Orientation

Central Guăngzhōu is bounded by semicircular Huanshi Lu, literally 'circle-city road', to the north and Pearl River (Zhū Jiāng) to the south. A larger ring road – the Huancheng Expressway – defines the roughly oval-shaped greater metropolitan area.

MAPS

Good maps of Guăngzhōu in both English and Chinese can be found at newsstands and in the bus and train stations. Bookshops (below) also have a variety of maps for sale.

Information

BOOKSHOPS

Foreign Languages Bookshop (Wàiwén Shūdiàn; ☎ 8333 5185; 2nd fl, 326-328 Beijing Lu; ☂ 9am-6pm Mon-Sat, 10am-6pm Sun) You'll find a few English classics here, though the store is mainly for Chinese students learning English.

Tangning Bookstore (Tángníng Shūdiàn; ☎ 8385 5749; 37 Huale Lu; ☂ 10am-11pm) Has a small selection of contemporary novels written in English.

INTERNET ACCESS 网吧

Internet bars come and go in Guăngzhōu, depending upon the mood of the authorities. The small lanes running off Yanjiang Xilu have some hole-in-the wall cafes, most charging Y2–3 an hour. Coffee shops (p597) are also a good place to look for computers. Hotel business centres offer a wide range of Internet services but can be expensive.

Henan Webmail (Hénán Wăngluò; ☎ 8121 6061; Shamian Sanjie; ☂ 9am-11pm) This tiny café on Shamian charges a stiff but negotiable Y20 an hour.

MEDICAL SERVICES

Can-Am International Medical Centre (Jiāměi Guójì Yīliáo Zhōngxīn; ☎ 8387 9057; 5th fl, Garden Tower, Garden Hotel, 368 Huanshi Donglu) Has English-speaking doctors on staff but it's necessary to call first.

Guăngzhōu No 1 People's Hospital (Dìyī Rénmín Yīyuàn, 1 Panfu Lu) Has a medical clinic for foreigners on the first floor of the complex.
Guăngzhōu Hospital of Traditional Chinese Medicine (Zhōngyī Yīyuàn; ☎ 8188 6504; 16 Zhuji Lu) Offers acupuncture, herbal medicine and other traditional Chinese remedies.

MONEY
Bank of China (Zhōngguó Yínháng; ☎ 8334 0998; 698 Renmin Beilu; 🕑 9am-6pm Mon-Fri, 9am-4pm Sat & Sun) Most branches change travellers cheques and have ATMs that take international cards. There's another branch at Guangdong International Hotel (ground fl, Main Tower, 339 Huanshi Donglu) next to the Friendship Hotel, and also opposite the Furama Hotel (316 Changdi Nanlu).
American Express Guăngzhōu (Měiguó Yùntōng Guăngzhōu; ☎ 8331 1611; fax 8331 1616; room 806, 8th fl, Main Tower, Guangdong International Hotel, 339 Huanshi Donglu; 🕑 9am-5.30pm Mon-Fri) Can cash and sell Amex travellers cheques.

POST & TELEPHONE
China Telecom (Zhōngguó Diànxìn; ☎ 1000; 196 Huanshi Xilu; 🕑 8am-6pm) The main branch is opposite the train station on the eastern side of Renmin Beilu.
Post Office (yóujú; Huanshi Xilu; 🕑 8am-8pm) Conveniently located next to the train station.

PUBLIC SECURITY BUREAU
PSB (Gōngānjú; ☎ 8311 5800/5808; 155 Jean Annul; 🕑 8-11.30am & 2.30-5pm) Helps with all 'aliens' needs. Between Dade Lu and Darin Lu.

TOURIST INFORMATION & TRAVEL AGENCIES
Most hotels offer travel services that, for a small charge, can help you book tickets and tours.
China International Travel Service (CITS; Zhōngguó Guójì Lǚxíngshè; ☎ 8666 6889; 179 Huanshi Xilu; 🕑 9am-6pm) Near the main train station. This office is experienced in helping foreigners book tickets and tours.
China Travel Service (CTS; Zhōngguó Lǚxíngshè; ☎ 8333 6888; 10 Qiaoguang Lu; 🕑 8.30am-6pm Mon-Fri, 9am-5pm Sat & Sun) Offers various tours and books tickets.

Sights & Activities
YUEXIU PARK 越秀公园
A bright swathe of green plunked down in the middle of Guăngzhōu, this vast urban **park** (Yuèxiù Gōngyuán; 13 Jiefang Beilu; admission Y5; 🕑 6am-9pm) encompasses over 93 hectares of gardens, shaded wood paths, historical monuments and museums. Within it, you'll find Guăngzhōu's **Five Rams Statue** (Wǔyáng Shíxiang), a statue of the five immortals attributed to Guăngzhōu's founding. On top of a hill in the centre of the park is the five-story **Zhenhai Tower** (Zhènhăi Lóu), built in 1380. Later incorporated into Guăngzhōu's city wall, it was used as a watchtower to keep out the pirates that once pillaged China's coastal cities. Now the red-walled tower stands alone, the city walls long since removed. During the First Opium War, British troops occupied the tower, and the grounds around the tower hold some of the cannons used by the British during that time. There are sweeping views of Guăngzhōu from the top storey.

In 1928 the tower was rebuilt to house the **Guangzhou City Museum** (Guăngzhōushì Bówùguăn; ☎ 8355 0627; admission Y10; 🕑 9am-5.30pm), which has an excellent collection of exhibits that trace the history of Guăngzhōu all the way back to the Neolithic period. There are also displays that outline Guăngzhōu's trading history with the West, including an exhibit devoted to foreign repression. On the east side of the tower is the **Guangzhou Art Gallery** (Guăngzhōu Měishùguăn), currently under renovation.

Take metro line 2, Yuèxiù Gōngyuán station, or bus 5, 10, 33, 63, 122 or 244.

ORCHID GARDEN 兰园
Across from Yuexiu Park on Jiefang Beilu is this charming **garden** (Lán Yuán; admission Y8; 🕑 8am-5pm) famous for its blossoming orchids. With its winding paths, arched stone bridges and willow-fringed ponds, you may forget you're even in Guăngzhōu. Each admission ticket includes a pot of tea at one of the many teahouses, and if you pay Y20, you can see a traditional tea ceremony. The western edge of the park sits on the site an old Muslim cemetery, supposedly the burial site of Abu Waqas, the uncle of the Prophet, who is credited with bringing Islam to China. His tomb is in a plain stone building oriented towards Mecca. The cemetery is currently closed to non-Muslims.

MAUSOLEUM OF THE NANYUE KING 南越王墓
Just opposite the main entrance to Yuexiu Park, this superb **mausoleum** (Nányuèwáng Mù; ☎ 8666 4920; 867 Jiefang Beilu; admission Y12, audioguide Y10; 🕑 9am-5.30pm) sits on the site of the 2000-year-old Nanyue Kingdom, discovered in 1983 when surprised workers found an ancient

GUĂNGDŌNG

GUĂNGZHŌU 广州

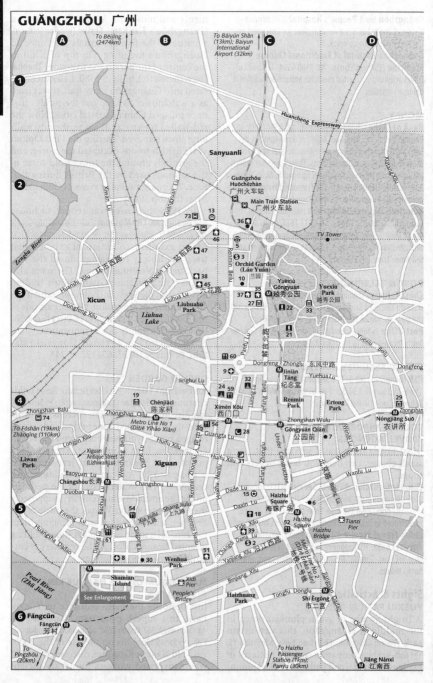

To Běijīng (2474km)

To Báiyún Shān (13km); Baiyun International Airport (32km)

Huancheng Expressway

Sanyuanli

Guăngzhōu Huŏchēzhàn 广州火车站
Main Train Station 广州火车站

TV Tower

Zengbu River

Xiwan Lu

Guāngyuán Lu

Zhannan Lu 站前路

73
13
75
36
4
46
47
5
3
Orchid Garden (Lán Yuán) 兰园
10

Huanshi Xilu
环市西路

Huánshi Xilu

Xicun

Dongfeng Xilu

38
45
Liuhua Lu
天花路
Liuhuahu Park

Liuhua Lake

35
37
27
22
21
Yuèxiù Gōngyuán

Yuexiu Park 越秀公园

Renmin Beilu

Panfu Lu 盘福正路

33

60

Yuexiu
Beilu

Dongfeng
Zhonglu 东风中路

Dongfeng

9
24
59
32
Ximén Kŏu 西门口

Jinian Táng 纪念堂

Yuèhuá Lu

Jinghui Lu

Jiefang Beilu

Renmin
Park

Ertong
Park

29
Zhongshan

19
Chénjiācí 陈家祠
74

Zhongshan Balu

To Fóshān (19km); Zhàoqìng (110km)

Zhongshan Qilu

Metro Line No 1 (Dìtiě Yīhào Xiàn)

Longjin Xilu

Renmin Zhonglu

56
Guangta Lu
28
31
Hùifu Xilu

Zhongshan Wulu

Gōngyuán Qián 公园前

7

Nóngjiăng Suŏ 农讲所

Hùifu Xilu

Xiguan Antique Street (Lizhiwan Lu)

Liwan
Park

Xiguan

Wenming Lu

Wanfu Lu

Baoyuan Lu

Chángshòu 长寿

Changshou Lu

Duobao Lu

Dàde Lu

Daxin Lu

15
18
Haizhu Square 海珠广场

52
6
Haizhu
Bridge

Tianzi
Pier

Ēnning Lu

Longtu Xilu

Dìshípu Lu

54

Shang Jiulu 上九路

Renmin Nanlu

Yide Xilu
39

Datong Lu

61

8
30

Wenhua
Park

51

Pearl River (Zhū Jiāng)

Shamian Island

See Enlargement

Xidi
Pier

People's
Bridge

Changdi Dàmà Lu

Yanjiang Xilu 沿江西路

Binjiang Xilu

Haizhuang
Park

Tongfu Donglu

Shi Ěrgōng 市二宫

6 Fāngcūn

Fāngcūn 芳村

63

To
Pingzhōu (20km)

To Haizhu Passenger Station (1km); Panyu (30km)

Jiāng Nánxī 江南西

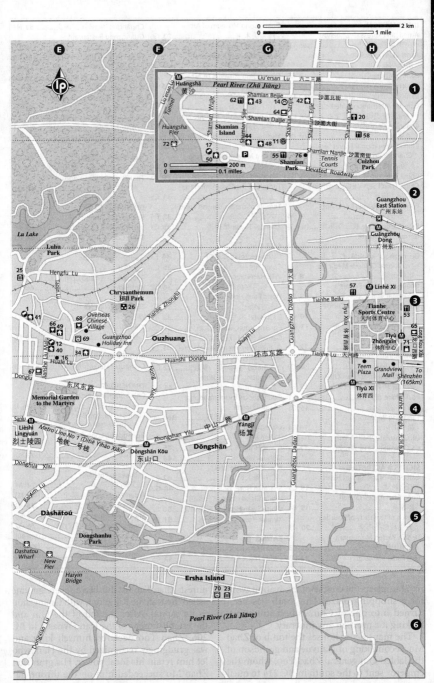

royal tomb in the course of excavation work for a shopping plaza. The tomb has been turned into one of China's best museums, making it a must on any itinerary.

The mausoleum houses the tomb of Zhao Mo, second king of Nanyue and grandson of the fabled Qin general Zhao Tuo, whom the emperor sent to the south in BC 214 to quell

unrest. Zhao Tuo established a sovereign state called the Nanyue Kingdom, with Guăngzhōu as its capital. After the fall of the Qin and the establishment of the Han Dynasty in BC 206, Zhao Tuo declared himself king and was grudgingly recognized by the Han, who let him retain his local power. His grandson Zhao Mo succeeded him on the throne but ruled unsuccessfully. Shortly after Zhao Mo's death, the Han plundered the kingdom in BC 111, claiming the territory as their own.

On display in the museum are Zhao Mo's burial suit, made of thousands of tiny jade tiles – jade was thought to preserve the body and make one immortal – gold jewellery and trinkets, as well as other beautiful artefacts found at the tomb site. Some say that the Nanyue tomb rivals the Ming tombs in Běijīng. Everything in the museum is expertly displayed and the English audio guide is recommended.

TEMPLE OF THE SIX BANYAN TREES 六榕寺

This Buddhist **temple** (Liùróng Sì; 87-89 Liurong Lu; admission Y15; ⏰ 8am-5pm) was built in AD 537 to enshrine Buddhist relics brought over from India. The relics were placed in the octagonal **Decorated Pagoda** (Huā Tǎ), a 57m pagoda which appears from the outside to contain only nine storeys but actually contains 17. The temple was given its current name by the exiled poet Su Dongpo in 1099, who commemorated the banyan trees in the courtyard with a poem. The banyan trees are long gone but you can see the characters (*liùróng*) he wrote hanging above the temple's gateway.

To get here, take bus 56.

GUANGXIAO TEMPLE 光孝禅寺

The **'Bright Filial Piety Temple'** (Guāng Xiào Chán Sì; 109 Jinghui Lu; admission Y5; ⏰ 6am-5pm), about 400m west of the Temple of the Six Banyan Trees, is the oldest temple in Guǎngzhōu and dates back to the 4th century. By the Tang dynasty, it was well established as a centre of Buddhist learning in southern China. Many prominent monks came to teach here, including Bodhidarma, the founder of Chan (Zen) Buddhism.

The temple complex originally contained over 19 halls and several restorations later still feels elegant and spacious. Most of the current buildings date from the 19th century. The most impressive building is the main hall, with its double eaves. Inside is a 10m-high statue of the Buddha. At the back of the hall sits an impressive statue of Guanyin, Goddess of Mercy.

Take metro line 1 to Xīmén Kǒu station.

MOSQUE DEDICATED TO THE PROPHET 怀圣寺

The original building on the site of this **mosque** (Huáishèng Sì; ☎ 8333 3593; 56 Guangta Lu) is thought to have been established in AD 627 by Abu Waqas, one of the Prophet Mohammed's uncles, making it the first of its kind in China. The present mosque dates from the Qing dynasty. The minaret is called 'Smooth Minaret' (Guāng Tǎ) because of its smooth, unadorned appearance. The mosque is closed to non-Muslims and surrounded by heavy security.

Take metro line 1 to Xīmén Kǒu station, or bus 5.

TEMPLE OF THE FIVE IMMORTALS 五仙观

Not far from the mosque is this Taoist **temple** (Wǔxiān Guàn; ☎ 8333 6853; Huifu Xilu; admission Y5; ⏰ 9am-5pm). It dates back to 1377 and is named after the mythical founders of Guǎngzhōu. A statue of the immortal five depicts three men and two women riding their legendary rams through the clouds. The temple includes a main hall, built in typical Ming fashion. To the east of the hall is a small pond with a foot-shaped depression, said to be the footprint of one of the immortals.

CHEN CLAN ANCESTRAL HALL 陈家祠

This enormous **compound** (Chénjiā Cí; ☎ 8181 4559; 34 Enlongji Lu; admission Y10; ⏰ 8.30am-5.30pm), part of the Guangdong Museum of Folk Art (Guǎngdōng Mínjiān Gōngyì Bówùguǎn), is both ancestral shrine and Confucian school. It was built in 1894 by the residents of 72 villages in Guǎngdōng, where the Chen lineage is the predominant family. The complex encompasses 19 buildings of the traditional Lingnan style (combining traditional Chinese, Japanese and Western traditions). All buildings contain exquisite carvings, statuary and paintings and are decorated with ornate scrollwork on the roof tiles, walls, stairs and woodwork of the window frames and doors. The scenes depict stories from Chinese literature and folklore and include real and mythical animals.

Take metro line 1 to Chénjiācí station, or bus 85 or 104.

CATHEDRAL OF THE SACRED HEART 石室教堂

The impressive twin-spired Roman Catholic **cathedral** (Shí Shì Jiàotáng; Yide Xilu; ⏰ 8am-6pm), built between 1863 and 1888, was designed by a French architect in the neo-Gothic style and built entirely of granite. The massive towers reach an impressive height of 48m. The four bronze bells were made in France, as was the original stained glass, most of which has now disappeared. Take bus 8, 82 or 86.

QINGPING MARKET 清平市场

Just north of Shamian Island, what is bizarrely translated as **Peaceful Market** (Qingpíng Shìchǎng; Qingping Lu; 8am-6pm) has vast displays of medicinal herbs, dried mushrooms and other plants, live birds, and tubs of squirming turtles, fish and frogs. Much harder to stomach, though, are its cages of live animals, including kittens and puppies, and more exotic creatures such as bats, owls and monkeys – all put out for human consumption, and some in the most pitiful distress. It is one of the most notorious markets in China, and though it has cleaned up its act in the past several years it remains a disturbing place and is *not* recommended.

SHAMIAN ISLAND 沙面岛

For an instant immersion in Guǎngzhōu's colonial history, head for the leafy oasis of **Shamian Island** (Shāmiàn Dǎo), which was acquired as a foreign concession in 1859 after the two Opium Wars. Shamian ('Sand Surface Island') was little more than a sandbank when early foreign inhabitants – mainly British and French – were granted permission to set up their warehouses here. The French and British established themselves at separate ends of the island; the French took the east and the British the west. The tear-shaped sandbank was connected to the mainland by several bridges, with staunch iron gates that prohibited any Chinese from entering the island.

Major renovation has restored some of the buildings to their original appearance, transforming them into chic restaurants, cafés and hotels. Traffic is restricted on Shamian, making it a peaceful respite from the city. The best way to experience the island is to wander around and look at some of the restored buildings, each bearing a plaque with a brief history.

Shamian Dajie, the main boulevard, is a gentle stretch of gardens, trees, and old men playing Chinese checkers. The Roman Catholic **Church of Our Lady of Lourdes** (Tiānzhǔjiào Lòushèngmǔ Táng; Shamian Dajie; 8am-6pm), built by the French in 1892, is on the eastern end of the thoroughfare.

Take metro line 1 to Huángshā station.

ART MUSEUMS & GALLERIES

The **Guǎngzhōu Museum of Art** (广州艺术博物馆; Guǎngzhōu Yìshù Bówùguǎn; 8365 9337; 3 Luhu Lu; admission Y20; 9am-5pm Tue-Fri, 9.30am-4.30pm Sat & Sun), which opened in 2000, has an extensive collection of works, ranging from ancient

to contemporary Chinese art and sculpture, including works by artists such as Guan Shanyue, Li Xiongcai and Lai Shaoqi. Other interesting exhibits include a fantastic room on the top floor with displays of rare Tibetan tapestries. Another highlight is the room devoted to Liao Bingxiong, a political cartoonist of the 20th century. Take bus 10 or 63.

Guangdong Museum of Art (广东美术馆; Guǎngdōng Měishùguǎn; 8735 1468; www.gdmoa.org; 38 Yanyu Lu; admission Y15; 9am-5pm Tue-Sun) is at the eastern end of Ersha Island (Èrshā Dǎo). Founded in 1997, the museum often shows exhibits of contemporary Chinese artists and has been the site of the Guangzhou Triennale, first held in 2003. Take bus 12, 18 or 89.

REVOLUTIONARY SIGHTS

Sun Yatsen Memorial Hall (Zhōngshān Jìniàn Táng; admission Y5 for the grounds & Y10 for the memorial; 8am-5pm) was built between 1929 and 1931 to commemorate the man whom both the Kuomintang and the Communist Party consider the father of modern China. The stately hall was modelled after the Temple of Heaven in Běijīng. Inside is an auditorium, used now for cultural events, and photos depicting Sun's life. The hall is rather dull and there are no English captions.

The **Peasant Movement Institute** (Nóngmín Yùndòng Jiǎngxísuǒ; 8333 3936; 42 Zhongshan Silu; admission Y5; 9am-4.30pm) was established in 1924 by the Communist Party at the site of a former Confucian temple. Mao Zedong and Zhou Enlai both taught here, before the school closed in 1926. The Institute is subdivided into various departments, such as the main lecture hall, students' dormitories, cafeteria building and leadership quarters. You can see Mao Zedong's re-created personal quarters and even his bed. Take metro line 1 to Nóngjiǎng Suǒ station.

South of the Institute on Zhongshan Sanlu is the **Memorial Garden to the Martyrs** (Lièshì Língyuán; admission Y3; 8am-7pm), dedicated to those killed on 13 December, 1927 under the orders of Chiang Kaishek. The massacre occurred when a small group of workers, led by the Communist Party, were gunned down by Kuomintang forces. In total, over 5,000 lives were lost.

PEARL RIVER CRUISES 珠江游览船

The northern bank of Pearl River is one of the most interesting areas of Guǎngzhōu – filled with people, markets and dilapidated buildings, and a wonderful place to stroll on a warm summer's evening.

The **Guangzhou Passenger Ship Company** (☎ 8333 0397) has up to five evening cruises on the Pearl River (from Y38, 1½ hours) between 7pm and 9pm, and 9.30pm to midnight. Boats leave from the **Tianzi Pier** (Tiānzǐ Mǎtou; Beijing Lu), just east of Haizhu Bridge (Hǎizhū Qiáo; catch metro line 2 from Hǎizhū Guǎngchǎng station), and head down the river as far as Ersha Island (Èrshā Dǎo) before turning back.

Festival & Events

The invitation-only, 10-day **Guǎngzhōu Trade Fair** (Zhōngguó Chūkǒu Shāngpǐn Jiāoyì Huì; ☎ 2608 8888; www.cantonfair.org.cn), also known as the Chinese Export Commodities Fair, has been held twice yearly, usually in April and October, since 1957. Apart from the Spring Festival (Chinese New Year) in late January/early February, this is the biggest event in Guǎngzhōu. The fair is held in complexes on Liuhua Lu opposite the Dong Fang and China Hotels and south of the river in the Pázhōu district.

Sleeping

Guǎngzhōu hotels are expensive. Prices rise even higher during the Guǎngzhōu Trade Fair (above) in the spring and autumn. Despite the horror of posted rates, most hotels offer 50% discounts, depending on the season. Top end (and some midrange) places add 15% service charge to the quoted room rate. Most hotels offer in-room broadband internet access.

Accommodation of all types is centred in three principal areas: around the main train station in the north; along Huanshi Donglu in the northeast; and on Shamian Island and along the river in the south.

TRAIN STATION AREA
Budget
Guǎngzhōu City International Youth Hostel (Guǎngzhōu Guójì Qīngnián Lǚguǎndiàn; dm Y60, s Y80-118, d Y148-178; 🖳) For a rock-bottom cheapie stay at this Hostelling International–affiliated property inside the CITS Hotel. Rooms are grubby but the location near the train station is convenient.

CITS Hotel Guangdong (Guǎngdōng Guólǚ Jiǔdiàn; ☎ 8666 6889, ext 3812; fax 8667 9787; 179 Huanshi Xilu; 环市西路179号; s Y120-430, d Y170-600, tr Y210-750; 🖳 🖳) You've got a choice of rooms (and prices) in this busy hotel right next to the train station. The location is noisy and staff indifferent – only stay here if you have an early train to catch. Bring earplugs.

Home Hotel (Jiāyuán Bīnguǎn; ☎ 6115 6688; fax 6115 6689; 6 Zhanqian Heng Lu; 站前横路6号; s Y298, d Y260-328, tr Y320; 🖳 🖳) Fresh, tidy accommodation can be had at this newish hotel near the train station. Bathrooms are spiffy with modern showers (no tubs). Rooms can be discounted up to 50%.

New Mainland Hotel (Guǎngzhōu Xīn Dàdì Bīnguǎn; ☎ 8622 1638; 108 Zhanqian Lu; 站前路108号; d Y380; 🖳 🖳) Situated in the heart of the wholesale clothing district and very near the train station, this plain-looking hotel offers nondescript rooms with 30% discounts. The bathrooms are modern and clean.

Midrange
Elan Hotel (☎ Mǐlán Huā Jiǔdiàn; ☎ 8622 1788; www .hotel-kopak.com; 32 Zhanqian Heng Lu; 站前横路32号; d Y288-588; 🖳 🖳) Immaculate contemporary-style rooms with a European ambience. There's a computer for guest use in the lobby and all suites contain wi-fi. Rooms can be discounted up to 40%. Staff speak English.

Liuhua Hotel (Liúhuā Bīnguǎn; ☎ 8666 8800; www .lh.com.cn; 194 Huanshi Xilu; 环市西路194号; s&d Y638-788, ste from Y1680; 🖳 🖳) This large, generic-looking hotel sits across from the train station and offers a choice of rooms, some good quality and others a bit tatty. Check the room before handing over your deposit. Discounts of up to 60% are available.

Top End
Dong Fang Hotel (Dōngfāng Bīnguǎn; ☎ 8666 9900; www .dongfanghotel-gz.com; 120 Liuhua Lu; 流花路120号; r from Y800; 🖳 🖳) This five-star luxury hotel, close to the Guǎngzhōu Trade Fair, has everything it takes to make guests happy. There are more than 880 rooms and five restaurants to choose from, and discounts of up to 60% are available.

China Hotel (Zhōngguó Dàjiǔdiàn; ☎ 8666 6888; www .marriothotels.com/canmc; Liuhua Lu; 流花路; s & d US$98-168, ste from US$148; 🖳 🖳 🖳) The rooms in this gigantic hotel are decent value, though not worthy of the hefty rates. Within the hotel are various restaurants, shopping plazas and bars. In fact, the place is so huge you don't even need to go outside. There are discounts of up to 30%.

NORTHEAST AREA
The northeastern part of the city has the highest concentration of top-end hotels and is probably the best area for business travellers.

Midrange

White Cloud Hotel (Báiyún Bīnguǎn; ☎ 8333 3998; www
.baiyun-hotel.com; 367 Huanshi Donglu; 环市东路367号;
s & d Y938; 🗶 🖳) Rooms at this hotel are decent,
though nothing to jump for joy about. With
over a dozen restaurants, you certainly won't
go hungry.

Cathay Hotel (Guótài Bīnguǎn; ☎ 8386 2888; fax
8384 2606; 376 Huanshi Donglu; 环市东路376号; s & d
Y500-680, ste from Y1080; 🗶 🖳) This Hong Kong–
owned hotel is a little creepy, with dark,
gloomy corridors, heavy wood panelling and
eclectic décor. There's an Internet café on the
3rd floor and rooms come with broadband
internet for Y50 a day. Discounts of up to 60%
may be available.

Top End

Garden Hotel (Huāyuán Jiǔdiàn; ☎ 8333 8989; www.the
gardenhotel.com.cn; 368 Huanshi Donglu; 环市东路368号;
s & d US$160-260, ste from US$450; 🗶 🖳 🖳) This
lavish five-star hotel claims to have the largest and grandest lobby in all of Asia – it even
has its own waterfall (though the waterfall at
the White Swan (right) is better). Rooms are
elegant and the service is impeccable.

SHAMIAN ISLAND & RIVERFRONT
Shamian Island is by far the quietest and most
attractive area to stay in Guǎngzhōu; you are
much more likely to meet other travellers
here and the nightlife options are decent.
The riverfront area, with its busy streets and
overpasses, is noisier but less expensive.

Budget

Guangzhou Youth Hostel (Shèngwàibàn Zhāodàisuǒ;
☎ 8121 8606; fax 8121 8298; 2 Shamian Sijie; 沙面四街
2号; dm Y50, s/d/t Y150/200/240; 🖳) For the cheapest beds in Guǎngzhōu, head to this affable
hostel on Shamian Island. This place won't
win any awards for décor, but rooms are clean
and serviceable. There's a useful travel desk
for booking train and plane tickets.

Midrange

Guangdong Victory Hotel (Shènglì Bīnguǎn; ☎ 8121
6688; www.vhotel.com; 53 & 54 Shamian Beijie; 沙面北
街53&54号; 🗶 🖳) There are two branches
of the Victory Hotel on Shamian Island, an
older one at 54 Shamian Beijie (enter from
10 Shamian Sijie) with adequate rooms between Y280 and Y360, and a newer wing at
53 Shamian Beijie with better value doubles
between Y380 and Y660.

Shamian Hotel (Shāmiàn Bīnguǎn; ☎ 8121 8288; www
.gdshamianhotel.com; 52 Shamian Nanjie; 沙面南街52号;
s & d Y238-345, tr Y298; 🗶 🖳) This appealing hotel
is one of the most popular hotels on Shamian.
It was getting a facelift at the time of writing.
Some rooms have a waterfront view.

Xinhua Hotel (Xīnhuá Dàjiǔdiàn; ☎ 8188 9788; fax
8186 8809; 2-6 Renmin Nanlu; 人民南路2-6号; s/d
Y280/320; 🗶 🖳) The best of all the riverfront
hotels, this reasonably priced hotel has spotless rooms and friendly staff. Some rooms
have river views and come with computers.
Discounts of up to 50% are available.

Furama Hotel (Fùlìhuá Dàjiǔdiàn; ☎ 8132 3288; www
.furama.com; 316 Changdi Dama Lu; 长堤大马路316号;
s & d Y450, ste from 900; 🗶 🖳) Rooms in this hotel
are musty and old, though good value when
discounts of 50% are given. Some have sweeping views of the river and are outfitted with
computers.

Top End

White Swan Hotel (Báitiān'é Bīnguǎn; ☎ 8188 6968; www
.whiteswanhotel.com; 1 Shamian Nanjie; 沙面南街1号;
s & d Y1300-1500, ste from Y3100; 🗶 🖳 🖳) This
843-room property is considered the most
prestigious of Guǎngzhōu's hotels, complete
with a waterfall in the lobby and fish ponds.
It has an excellent range of rooms and outlets
(a dozen restaurants and bars), all business
facilities and a shopping arcade.

Eating
Guǎngzhōu's cuisine is justifiably legendary.
Guǎngzhōu is especially famous for its dim
sum, or *yum cha* as it's called in these parts.
You'll find *yum cha* served in restaurants
around the city, especially in some of the
older, more established restaurants. In addition to Cantonese cuisine, Guǎngzhōu has
plenty of other restaurants serving a variety of
regional Chinese dishes. A large expat population means that there are also many other types
of Asian restaurants, and a fair share of good
European restaurants. Outside the restaurants,
cheap food stalls abound, especially in the small
lanes around major shopping areas. Here you
can sample local snacks and delicacies *al fresco*,
while bumping elbows with the locals.

CHINESE
Guangzhou Restaurant (Guǎngzhōu Jiǔjiā; ☎ 8138 0388;
2 Wenchang Nanlu; dishes Y35-80; ⏱ 7am-3pm, 5.30-10pm)
This popular place has been around since
1939 and still draws the crowds. Spread across

three floors, there are a variety of dining rooms and menus. One of the restaurant's most notable dishes is *wenchang* chicken (文昌鸡; *wénchāng jī*), chicken slow-cooked in an aromatic broth and later steamed with vegetables and a light sauce.

Tao Tao Ju Restaurant (Táotáojū Jiǔjiā; ☎ 8139 6111; 20 Dishipu Lu; dishes from Y35; ❤ 6.45am-midnight) The *yum cha* at this restaurant, housed in an academy dating back to the 17th century, is particularly famous. The menu is extensive – over 200 items! Specialities include their trademark ginger and onion chicken (陶陶姜葱鸡; *táotáo jiāngcōng jī*).

Tao Heung Seafood Hotpot Restaurant (Dàoxiāng Hǎixiān Huǒguō Jiǔjiā; ☎ 8331 8888; 197 Dongfeng Xilu; ❤ 6.30-1am) This busy restaurant is famous for its *yum cha* and pastries, especially the steamed egg custard buns (奶皇包; *nǎihuáng bāo*). There are several branches around Guǎngzhōu – try the branch on the 2nd floor of the Guangzhou International Financial Building.

Moslem Restaurant (Huímín Fàndiàn; ☎ 8130 3991; 325 Zhongshan Liulu; dishes from Y25; ❤ 6.30am-midnight) This large restaurant with the imaginative name serves excellent Huí (Chinese Muslim) cuisine. Try the boiled sliced mutton (涮羊肉; *shuàn yángròu*) or the crispy goose (脆皮火鹅; *cuìpí huóé*).

Shanghai and Suzhou Restaurant (Jiáo Jiāngnán; ☎ 8121 5201; 37 Shamian Beijie; dishes from Y20; ❤ 11.30am-2pm, 5pm-late) The sweet and savoury flavours of the Jiāngnán region are the specialty in this stylish yet unpretentious restaurant on Shamian Island. Some good dishes are the shrimp with tomatoes (虾仁番茄; *xiārèn fānqié*) or the Shanghai steamed buns (小笼包; *xiǎo lóngbāo*).

Chuānguó Yǎnyì (☎ 3887 9878; 140-148 Tiyu Donglu, Nanfang Securities Bldg; dishes from Y20; ❤ 10am-2pm, 5-9pm) If you like your food hot, this restaurant will fry your tastebuds with its authentic Sìchuān cuisine, served up with plenty of chillies and hot peppers. The fiery Sìchuān hot pot is the best in Guǎngzhōu.

OTHER ASIAN

Thai Zhen Cow & Bridge (Tàizhēn Niú Qiáo; ☎ 8121 9988; 54 Shamian Beijie; starters & salads Y25-35, mains Y58-78; ❤ 11am-11pm) Though bizarrely named, this upscale restaurant has some of the best Thai food in Guǎngzhōu. The red and green curries are superb. The atmosphere is quite elegant, so put on a clean shirt.

Roku Roku (Liù Lù ☎ 2223 3066; 175-181 Tianhe Beilu 1F; dishes from Y30; ❤ 11am-8pm) Fresh, delicious Japanese noodles, *teppanyaki*, sushi and sashimi are made to order in this friendly Japanese restaurant. Prices are at the high end but worth it for the quality of the food.

VEGETARIAN

Shuǐyúntiān (☎ 8107 2463; 42 Jinghui Lu; dishes from Y10; ❤ 10am-10pm) Mock-meat specialities and other vegetarian fare are served in this Buddhist vegetarian restaurant. There's an excellent lunch buffet for Y22 a person. The English menu is good for a giggle – anyone for 'vegetarian shrimp in bamboo underwear'?

WESTERN

1920 Restaurant & Bar (Kāfēitíng; ☎ 8333 6156; 183 Yanjiang Xilu; mains from Y30, beer from Y28; ❤ 11am-2am) This German restaurant on the riverfront is well-liked by both foreigners and locals. The patio is a nice place to enjoy an imported beer. The menu includes sausages, meatballs and even stuffed goose, if you're really hungry.

La Seine (Sàinàhé Fǎguó Cāntīng; ☎ 8735 2531; 33 Qingbo Lu; soups Y40-68, starters Y48-138, fish & grills Y68-218; ❤ 11am-2.30pm, 5.30pm-midnight) It doesn't get any more French than this in Guǎngzhōu. For authentic *nouvelle* cuisine try this smart restaurant on the first floor of the Xinghai Concert Hall. The weekend brunch (Y78) attracts the well-heeled set.

Lucy's (Lùsī Jiǔbā Cāntīng; ☎ 8121 5106; 3 Shamian Nanjie; Y28-40; ❤ 11am-2am) For comfort food, head to this favourite on Shamian Island. Enjoy decent burgers, buffalo wings, pizza, and beer for Y16 a pint (happy hour is 4pm to 6pm daily). Service is especially welcoming.

Drinking
CAFÉS

Blenz Coffee (Bǎiyí Kāfēi; ☎ 8121 5052; 46 Shamian Dajie; ❤ 7.30am-11.30pm) You'll find this Canadian coffee chain on Shamian Island has palatable coffee and a choice of desserts. Even better than the coffee is the free computer with internet access on the first floor.

People's Cakes and Coffee (☎ 8376 6677; 17 Jianshe Liu Ma Lu; coffee from Y10, sandwiches Y20, pastries from Y9; ❤ 8am-midnight Mon-Fri, ❤ 11am-11pm Sat & Sun) Managed by two Korean sisters, this tiny café is well-recommended. The coffee is good and reasonably priced, especially compared to other establishments around town. Best are the homemade pastries and tasty sandwiches.

Coffee Beanery (Bīnlè Kāfēi; ☎ 8754 0215; 1F, Hilton Sunshine Building, 313 Long Kou Xilu; coffee Y12-68; ☙ 7am-2am) This comfortable coffee shop in the Tianhe area offers a huge range of coffees – from simple house blends to fancy espresso concoctions. For customers, internet access is available from the in-house PCs.

BARS
Guăngzhōu has a number of international-style bars where, in addition to sinking chilled Tsingtao and imported beers, you can you can scoff pizza or burgers, rice or noodles.

Windflower (☎ 8358 2446; 387 Huanshi Donglu; ☙ 6pm-2am) Big comfy couches and a moody atmosphere. The music is contemporary and hip. There isn't a huge range of drinks to choose from, though that doesn't stop the place from being packed on the weekends.

Elephant and Castle (Dàxiàngbăo Jiŭbā; ☎ 8359 3309; 363 Huanshi Donglu; ☙ 5pm-3am) Long frequented by Guăngzhōu's expat crowd, this popular sports bar still pulls in the crowds. Happy hour is from 5pm to 8pm daily.

Located along the Pearl River, across from the White Swan Hotel (p596) is **Baietan Bar Street** (Báiétán Jiŭbā; ☙ 7pm-2.30am), which is cut off from traffic. There are a number of outdoor Chinese restaurants here and it's a great place to eat. The **Overseas Chinese Village** on Heping Lu and nearby Huanshi Donglu has a string of bars catering to foreigners and trendy locals. The names of these places all change frequently so check *That's Guangzhou* (below) for the latest venues. Take metro line 1 to Fāngcūn station.

Entertainment
The free monthly entertainment guide *That's Guangzhou* (www.thatsguangzhou.com) is an invaluable source of information for what's on around town. It's available at most of the major hotels and international-style bars and restaurants.

Xinghai Concert Hall (Xīnghăi Yīnyuè Tīng; ☎ 8735 2766; 33 Qingbo Lu) Home to the Guangzhou Symphony Orchestra (GSO), this is the city's premier venue for classical music. It's on Ersha Island and has two concert halls that are said to have perfect acoustics.

NIGHTCLUBS
The nightlife in Guăngzhōu is growing fast, with new clubs and karaoke joints springing up everywhere. Venues change fast so check *That's Guangzhou* (above) for the latest info.

Wave Bar (Pòcuì Jiŭbā; ☎ 8349 4568; 6 Heping Lu, Overseas Chinese Village; beer Y30, cocktails Y35; ☙ 7pm-2am) This is a popular nightspot for expats to dance and drink. With a full range of tunes to suit everybody, it's one of the best bets for a good night out.

Shopping
Guăngzhōu is a terrific place for shopping, as long as you know where to look. Outside the major department stores, prices are reasonably cheap (especially compared to Hong Kong) and with the overwhelming variety of goods on the market, you can unearth some real treasures.

Haizhu Square (Hăizhū Guăngchăng) has always been a popular spot for discounted clothing and other merchandise. Nearby is one of Guăngzhōu's favourite shopping spots, **Beijing Lu**, a 300m pedestrian street crammed full of shops big and small selling virtually everything imaginable. It's easily reachable from the Gongyuan Qian metro stop. It gets really crowded on the weekends, but that's part of the fun.

A pedestrian shopping street with a bit more character is **Xia Jiulu/Shang Jiulu** ('Up Down Nine Street'). It's in one of the oldest parts of the city, where the buildings retain elements of both Western and Chinese architecture. It's a good place to look for discounted clothing. Also for clothing, try the trendy boutiques on **Huale Lu** behind the Garden Hotel (p596).

If it's antiques you're after, there's no better place to head than **Xiguan Antique Street** (Xīguān Gŭwán Chéng; Lizhiwan Lu) in the Xiguan area, with shops selling everything from ceramic teapots to Tibetan rugs. Even if you're not interested in loading up your pack with ceramic vases, it's still a wonderful place to wander and browse.

Those with more modern desires might want to head to the Tianhe area, with its fashionable shopping plazas. **Teem Plaza** (Tiānhé Chéng Guăngchăng; 208 Tianhe Lu) and **Grandview Shopping Mall** (Zhèngjiā Guăngchăng; 228 Tianhe Lu) – the largest in Asia – are two of Guăngzhōu's newest shopping malls. If you're interested in electronics, make sure to investigate the computer markets at the east end of Tianhe Lu.

Getting There & Away
AIR
China National Aviation Corporation (CNAC; Zhōngguó Mínháng) is represented by **China**

Southern Airlines (Zhōngguó Nánfāng Hánglóng; CZ; ☎ 800-820 6666, 8612 0330; www.cs-air.com; 181 Huanshi Lu; ☺ 9am-6pm), arguably China's best-run airline. The office is southeast of the main train station. The ticketing office on the 2nd floor is open round the clock. For general flight information ring ☎ 96060.

China Southern has six daily flights to Hong Kong (Y1219 one way, 35 minutes). There are also flights to Shànghǎi (Y1390) and Běijīng (Y1810). The domestic airport tax is Y50.

International destinations served by China Southern include Amsterdam, Bangkok, Ho Chi Minh City, Jakarta, Kuala Lumpur, Los Angeles, Melbourne, Osaka, Paris, Penang, Singapore and Sydney. The international airport tax is Y80.

Some foreign airlines with offices in Guǎngzhōu:

Japan Air Lines (☎ 3877 3868; fax 3877 3967; room 4601, Citic Plaza, 233 Tianhe Beilu)

Malaysia Airlines (☎ 8335 8828; fax 8335 8838; shop M04-05, Garden Hotel, 368 Huanshi Donglu)

Singapore Airlines (☎ 2807 2808; fax 8732 0598; Dongshan Plaza, 69 Xianlie Lu)

Thai International (☎ 8365 2333; fax 8365 2488; G3, Garden Hotel, 368 Huanshi Donglu)

United Airlines (☎ 8333 8989, ext 3165; G05, Garden Hotel, 368 Huanshi Donglu)

Vietnam Airlines (☎ 8386 7093, ext 10; M04, Attic, Garden Hotel, 368 Huanshi Donglu)

BOAT

Guǎngzhōu is a major port on China's southern coast but most ferry and catamaran services have been discontinued, victims of improved land transportation. However, there are still services within the greater Guǎngzhōu metropolitan area to/from Hong Kong and far-flung Hǎinán. Tickets are available from CTS Guǎngzhōu (p589) and the travel desks at most top end hotels.

High-speed catamarans, run by the **Nanhai Pinggang Passenger Transport Co** (☎ 8444 8218), make two trips a day from the port of Nánhǎi in Píngzhōu, located about 23km southwest of Guǎngzhōu, to Hong Kong. Boats depart from Nánhǎi at 9.15am and 4pm and from Hong Kong at 8.05am and 2pm. The trip takes 2½ hours and costs Y180/170 in 1st/ 2nd class. Shuttles to Nánhǎi run from the Garden Hotel.

Ferries for Hǎikǒu on Hainan Island (Hǎinán Dǎo) depart from the pier at **Huángpǔ** (☎ 8227 9839), located some 32km southeast of

Guǎngzhōu, at 3.00pm on Tuesday, Thursday and Saturday. The trip takes 18 hours and the prices range from Y180 in 5th class to Y450 in 1st class. In the opposite direction, ferries leave Haikou's **Xiuying Harbour** (☎ 0898 6865 3315) on Monday, Wednesday and Friday at 4pm.

BUS

Guǎngzhōu has several long-distance bus stations with services to all parts of Guǎngdōng, southern Fújiàn, eastern Guǎngxī and even further afield. There are three useful stations clustered around the main train station. These are the Liuhua bus station (Liúhuā Chēzhàn) across Huanshi Xilu in front of the train station, the **Guǎngdōng long-distance bus station** (Guǎngdōng shěng qìchē kèyùn zhàn; Huanshi Xilu) to the right and another long-distance bus station (shì qìchē kèyùn zhàn) over the footbridge leading from the train station. All of these stations have buses to Shēnzhèn (Y60, two hours, every 12 minutes 6am to 11pm), Zhūhǎi (Y72, 2½ hours, every 15 minutes 7am to 9pm), and Kāipíng (Y45, 2 hours, every forty minutes).

Buses for other destinations leaving mostly from the long-distance bus stations include: Fóshān (Y12 to Y14, 45 minutes); Guìlín (sleeper Y150 to Y180, 13 hours); Hǎikǒu (sleeper Y180 to Y280, 16 hours); Nánníng (sleeper Y150 to Y180, 15 hours); Shàntóu (Y90 to Y180, six hours); Zhàoqìng (Y30, 1½ hours); and Zhōngshān (Y30 to Y35, two hours).

If the train station area is too anarchic for you, head to the clean and orderly **Haizhu Passenger Station** (Hǎizhū Kèyùn Zhàn; 182 Nanzhou Lu) in the southern Hǎizhū district. You'll find buses to the same destinations listed above as well as buses to Qīngyuǎn (Y20, 1½ hours) and Méizhōu (Y100, six hours). There are also buses to Yǒngdìng (Y130, sleeper, 11 hours) and Fúzhōu (Y240, sleeper, 15 hours) in Fújiàn. Express buses drop passengers off at the Luó Hú border checkpoint at Shēnzhèn (Y60, one hour, 6.50am to 8.20pm).

The easiest way to get to Hong Kong is by the deluxe buses that ply the Guǎngzhōu-Shēnzhèn freeway in 2½ hours. Most of the top end hotels (see p595), including the Dong Fang, China and Guangdong International Hotels, have tickets and they cost around Y100 (Y250 to Hong Kong International Airport). Direct buses through Zhūhǎi to Macau (Y60, 2½ hours) leave from the China and Garden Hotels.

TRAIN

Guăngzhōu's main train station, which is useful for short-distance destinations such as Zhàoqìng (Y24, 2½ hours), is a chaotic and seething mass of humanity. To get there, catch metro line 2 from Guăngzhōu Huŏchēzhàn station; note that the train station will be moved to outlying Panyu in 2008. The Guăngzhōu east train station, on the other hand, which serves more far-flung destinations, is a model of efficiency. To get there, take metro line 1 Guăngzhōu Dōng Zhàn station. Bus 272 (Y2) links the two stations while bus 271 (Y2) goes between the Liuhua bus station and the Guăngzhōu east train station. Metro line 1 runs to the east train station and line 3 should be linked by the time this book goes to press.

Travellers will find ticketing at the east station a fairly straightforward affair, with separate **ticketing booths** (🕐 7.30am-9pm) for Hung Hom, in Hong Kong's Kowloon (Y186-196, HK$180-190, 1¾ hours), and a dozen fast trains a day between 8.35am and 9.23pm. There are four high-speed through trains per day to Shēnzhèn (Y80, 55 minutes), on the border with Hong Kong. Signs are in English. There are local trains to Shēnzhèn (Y76, two hours) departing every half-hour from about 6.30am to 10.20pm.

Trains also head north from here to Shànghăi (Y427, 21 hours) and Bĕijīng (Y458, 22 hours), as well as destinations all over the country. For details on trains to Lhasa, see p924.

Despite all the hassles at the main Guăngzhōu train station, booking train tickets here is a lot easier than it used to be. There are two separate places to buy them at the station itself. A 24-hour ticketing office is in the hall to the left of the large clock as you face the station. Current, next-day and two-day advance tickets are sold in the white and silver building just east of the station, open daily from 5.30am to 10.30pm.

CITS Guăngzhōu (p589) near the main train station will book train tickets up to five days in advance for a service charge of about Y20.

Getting Around

Greater Guăngzhōu, as defined by the Huancheng Expressway, extends some 20km east to west and more than 10km north to south. Since most of the interesting sights are scattered throughout the city, seeing the place on foot is not exactly practical. The metro (see right) is the speediest and cleanest way to get around.

TO/FROM THE AIRPORT

Guăngzhōu's new Baiyun International Airport (Báiyún Guójì Fēijīchăng), which opened in June 2004, is 34km north of the city. There is an airport shuttle bus (Y13 to Y32, one hour, every 15 to 30 minutes, 7am to 10pm) that leaves from a half-dozen locations around Guăngzhōu, including the China Southern Airlines main office (p598) near the train station. A taxi to/from the airport will cost about Y140.

BICYCLE

Rental bikes are usually available somewhere on Shamian Island; ask at your hotel for details. At the time of research there was a stall on Shamian Erjie in the northeast corner of Shamian Park (Shāmiàn Gōngyuán) with bicycles for rent for Y15 per hour (plus Y400 deposit).

BUS

Guăngzhōu has a large network of motor buses and electric trolley-buses (Y2 to Y5). Unfortunately the network is overstretched and the buses are usually very crowded and slow.

METRO

At the time of writing, Guăngzhōu had only two metro lines. Line 1 runs for 18.5km from Guăngzhōu east train station in the northeast and across Pearl River in the southwest. It goes by many of the city's major sights along Zhongshan Lu, and is also a convenient way to get to Shamian Island. Line 2 goes essentially north-south for 23km from Pázhōu station in the south to Sānyuán Lĭ station in the northeast. It is good for the main train station, many of the sights around Yuexiu Park, and the riverfront hotels. The two lines intersect at one station: Gōngyuán Qián.

More lines are in the works: line 3 was being tested in 2006 and line 4 should be finished by the time this book goes to press.

Depending on the line, the metro runs from about 6.20am to just before 11pm. Fares are Y2 to Y7, depending on the number of stops you travel (eg Y5 for the 10 stops between the two train stations). A better deal for getting around is to buy a transit pass (Yáng chéng tōng; 羊城通), which can be bought from kiosks inside the metro stations and post offices. Passes start at Y50 and require a Y30 deposit, which can be refunded if you keep your receipt. The pass can be used for all public transport including taxis.

TAXI

Taxis are abundant on the streets of Guăngzhōu but demand is great, particularly during the peak hours: from 8am to 9am, and at lunch and dinner.

Taxis are equipped with meters, which are always used, and flagfall is Y7. There is an additional Y1 added on for a fuel surcharge. A trip from the main train station to Shamian Island should cost between Y15 and Y20; from Guăngzhōu east train station to the island is Y40 to Y45.

AROUND GUĂNGZHŌU
White Cloud Hills 白云山

These **hills** (Báiyún Shān; admission Y5), in the northern suburbs of Guăngzhōu, are an adjunct to the **Dayu Range** (大庾岭; Dàyù Lǐng), the chief group of mountains in Guăngdōng. In total there are more than 30 peaks, which were once dotted with temples and monasteries. It's a good hike up to the top – or a leisurely walk down if you take the **cable car** (Y25) – and a refreshing escape from the polluted city below.

Star Touching Peak (摩星岭; Móxīng Lǐng), at 382m, is the highest point in the hills. Local people rate the vista from a precipice called **White Cloud Evening View** (白云晚望; Báiyún Wǎnwàng) as one of the eight great sights of Guăngzhōu.

Famous as a resort since the Tang and Song dynasties, the hills have been thematically restored to attract tourists and now boast a number of attractions, including the **Mingchun Valley Aviary** (鸣春谷鸟园; Míngchūngǔ Niǎoyuán; ☎ 3722 9528; admission Y25; ◷ 8.30am-5pm), which features a wide variety of bird species.

GETTING THERE & AWAY

The hills are about 15km from Guăngzhōu. Bus 24 can take you from Dongfeng Zhonglu, just north of Rénmín Gōngyuán, to the cable car at the bottom of the hill near Luhu Park (Lùhú Gōngyuán). The trip takes between half an hour and one hour, depending on traffic. The bus stops at the park entrance.

KĀIPÍNG 开平
☎ 0750

Scattered throughout the countryside about 140km southwest of Guăngzhōu are a collection of remarkable watchtowers called *diāolóu*. These towers, which display an eclectic mix of European architectural styles from Roman to rococo, were built in the 19th and early 20th

centuries by Chinese returning from overseas. Because of political instability, many of the towers were built as fortresses, meant to keep out bandits and later protect residents from Japanese troops. Each was built with sturdy walls, iron gates, and ports for defence and observation. Out of the 3,000 original *diāolóu*, only 1,833 remain. They are slowly being developed for tourism. The towers are unique to Guăngdōng and can only be seen in the counties surrounding the town of Kāipíng.

The best way to see the *diāolóu* is to head to Kāipíng and from there rent a taxi or take public transport out to the countryside. The largest collection of *diāolóu* are in the quiet village of **Zili** (自立; Zìlì Cūn), about 20 minutes from Kāipíng. Here, 15 crumbling towers, some tilting precariously, rise ominously above a cluster of ancient homes. If you walk to the rear of the village, you'll see **Míngshí Lóu** (铭石楼), the tallest tower, which is open to the public. This was once the most prosperous home in the village. On the top of the building are four towers known as 'swallow nests', each with embrasures, cobblestones and a water sprayer, which was used against bandits. From the windows you'll see a stretch of unspoiled countryside dotted with rice paddies, fish ponds and the jagged outlines of *diāolóu* in the distance.

Another collection of *diāolóu* worth visiting is at **Li Garden** (立园; Lì Yuán; admission Y40; ◷ 8am-5pm) in Tángkǒu county, about a 15-minute taxi ride from Kāipíng. The *diāolóu* here were constructed in 1936 by Mr Xie Weili, a Chinese emigrant to the United States. Authorities have transformed this area into a park for tourists, and though admission is steep, it's a convenient way to see some *diāolóu* in an organized setting. Most of the towers are open to the public and have explanations of their history in English. Some have been left in their original condition to chilling effect, abandoned after residents fled from invading Japanese troops. Left behind are the remnants of smashed-up furniture and quilts torn to shreds by bayonets, among other things.

Other noteworthy *diāolóu* include **Déng Lóu** (灯楼), a five-storey tower built in 1920 called 'Light Tower' because of its powerful searchlight. There's also Nánxìng Xié Lóu, or 'The Leaning Tower' of Nanxing Village, which tilts severely to one side, with its central axis over 2m off centre. Built in 1903, the seven-storey tower has survived numerous typhoons and earthquakes, but may still topple any day.

Also worth a visit is **Ruìshí Lóu** (瑞石楼) located behind Jinjiangli Village, about an hour from Kāipíng. One of the most marvellous of the towers, it has nine stories with a Byzantine-style roof and Roman dome supported by elaborately decorated walls and pillars.

Sleeping

Most people see the *diāolóu* on a day trip from Guǎngzhōu but it's possible to stay overnight in Kāipíng. For reasonable rooms by the river and provincial bus station try the **Overseas Chinese Hotel** (华侨大厦; Huáqiáo Dàshà; ☎ 221 2572; Changsha Xibu Lu; 长沙西郊路; d Y200; ☒ ▣).

Getting There & Away

There are about fifty buses daily to Kāipíng from Guǎngzhōu (Y45, two hours), leaving from the long distance bus stations near the main train station. There are also buses from Zhūhǎi (Y60, 2½ hours) and Shēnzhèn (Y65, 2½ hrs). Buses will drop you off at one of two bus stations, the central Kāipíng bus station (Kāipíng zhōngzhàn) or the provincial station (shì qìchē zhàn), where you can switch to a local bus (Y4–5) that will take you out to the *diāolóu*. Because the *diāolóu* are scattered throughout several counties, most people find it easier to rent a taxi to take them around to the various sites. A taxi to Zìlì from Kāipíng should cost between Y70 and Y80, with an hour's wait included. A taxi from Kāipíng to Li Garden costs around Y22 each way. If you want to see all the towers, your best bet would be to charter a taxi for the day. You'll find taxi drivers waiting in front of the bus stations to take you around. A half day will cost around Y200 and a full day Y400, but you can negotiate these rates.

QĪNGYUǍN 清远

☎ 0763

The industrial town of Qīngyuǎn, about 70km northwest of Guǎngzhōu, sits on the northern banks of the Beijiang River and serves as an important transit point for those heading up to northern Guǎngdōng. Qīngyuǎn itself, a jumble of warehouses and factories, holds little interest. The main attractions lie in the surrounding river valley, a peaceful refuge of pine forests, mountains and deeply eroded canyons. Tucked in the hills about 20km upstream from Qīngyuǎn are the secluded temples of Fēilái (飞来) and Fēixiá (飞霞), both accessible to visitors and well worth visiting.

Ferries to the temples run from Qīngyuǎn's **Bei River dock** (水陆客运站; Shuǐlù kèyùn zhàn), east of Nanmen Jie in the southwest part of town. The ferry costs Y50 per person, though boats don't leave until they're full. To rent a whole boat costs about Y350. The boat schedule varies – it's a good idea to arrive at the dock before 8am to see when boats are leaving that day. The entire trip, from Fēilái onwards to Fēixiá and the return takes about four hours. If the ferry is not available, it's possible to take a bus to Fēixiá (see below).

The first part of the trip takes you along the river past some mountain villages and ancient pagodas to the stately Buddhist temple of **Fēilái** (admission Y18), nestled at the foot of a steep mountain. Though Fēilái has been around for over 1400 years, the current structure dates from the Ming dynasty. The temple is serenely located in a pine forest; follow the narrow path through the forest to the mountain-top pavilion that offers terrific views of the river gorge below. You'll be given about an hour to look around before your boat heads further upstream to the more modern Taoist temple of Fēixiá.

When your boat arrives at **Fēixiá** (admission Y45), about 4km upstream, you'll be dropped off at stairs that lead upwards from the riverbank and onwards to the temple. To get to the temple, follow the stairs from the riverbank through the woods for about 20 minutes. Founded in the late 18th century, it's actually a complex of different halls, courtyards and pavilions connected by tree-lined paths. The entire place, with its imposing walls, low ceilings and mazes of dark corridors feels more like Dracula's castle than a place of refuge. For those who love spooky things, this place will delight.

Sleeping & Eating

Near the Bei River dock in Qīngyuǎn you'll find the **Overseas Chinese Hotel** (华侨大厦; Huáqiáo Dàshà; ☎ 333 7118; 70 Nanmen Jie; 南门街70号; d Y200-250; ☒ ▣), which has adequate rooms in a convenient location.

You'll find restaurants along Nanmen Jie that serve up decent meals. You can also try any number of boats docked along the Bei River that transform into lively restaurants at night. Dinner for two, which includes fresh-caught fish and wild vegetables, will cost about Y100.

Getting There & Away

Buses run about every 15 minutes from Guǎngzhōu's long-distance bus stations near the main train station (Y30, 1½ hours) from 6.30am to 7.30pm. There are also buses from Fóshān (Y45, two hours) and Shēnzhèn (Y60, three hours). Qīngyuǎn's main bus station is about 4km south of the Bei River. Bus 6 travels between the bus station and the town centre. Alternatively, a taxi from the bus station to Nanmen Jie will cost about Y6.

Six buses run daily from Qīngyuǎn's old bus station (jiù qìchēzhàn) to Fēixiá (Y8, 1½ hour). To Fēixiá buses run between 7.30am and 4.30pm and from Fēixiá 9am to 5.30pm. Buses that run between Qīngyuǎn and Yīngdé (Y10, two hours) can drop passengers off at Fēilái.

FÓSHĀN 佛山
☎ 0757 / pop 960,000

Fóshān, 19km southwest of Guǎngzhōu, is one of China's oldest pottery towns. Dating back to the Han dynasty, the city, along with its neighbour Shíwān, is renowned for its ceramics, metal working and wood carving. In addition to its reputation for handicrafts, Fóshān is famous for its magnificent ancestral temple. The city's name, 'Buddha Hill', is derived from three statues of the Lord Gautama that stood on a nearby hill under the Tang (AD 618–907), when Fóshān was an important religious centre.

Information

Bank of China (Zhōngguó Yínháng; cnr Renmin & Zumiao Lu; ☑ 8.30am-5pm Mon-Fri, 9am-4pm Sat) Conveniently located by Zǔ Miào.

China International Travel Service (CITS; Zhōngguó Guójì Lǚxíngshè; ☎ 8363 6888; 75 Fenjiang Zhonglu; ☑ 8am-6pm) Very helpful branch in the Foshan Hotel.

Municipal government website (www.foshan.gov .cn) Excellent website on Fóshān.

Post Office (yóujú; Qinren Lu; ☑ 8.30am-9.30pm) Mail your pottery home here.

Sights
ZǓ MIÀO 祖庙

This ancestral **temple complex** (☎ 8229 3723; 21 Zu-miao Lu; admission Y20; ☑ 8.30am-6.30pm) was founded during the late 11th century and is a marvellous example of southern Chinese architecture. The temple is dedicated to Běidì, Taoist God of the North, commonly represented by a turtle and a snake. You'll see an imposing statue of Běidì in the main hall, along with some extraordinary carved wooden screens. Some of the buildings here have the 'wok-handle' roofs distinctive to the region, as well as ridge

tiles covered with delightful ceramic figures taken from folklore. The compound is part of the **Foshan Museum** (Fóshān Bówùguǎn) and contains some excellent collections, including an extensive display on Cantonese opera and martial arts.

FÓSHĀN 佛山

A short walk north of the ancestral temple is the Buddhist **Renshou Temple** (Rénshòu Sì; ☎ 8225 3053; 9 Zumiao Lu; admission free; ☾ 8am-5pm), a former Ming monastery which remains an active place of worship today. Inside, you'll find a seven-storey pagoda built in 1656 as well as the **Foshan Folk Arts Studio**, famous for its intricately beautiful papercuts.

Still further north, **Liang's Garden** (Liáng Yuán; ☎ 8224 1279; Songfeng Lu; admission Y10; ☾ 8.30am-5.30pm) is an attractive garden complex that dates from the early 19th century. Within is a tranquil lotus pond, willow-lined pathways and carefully arranged rock formations. The residences of the family have all been elegantly restored and are a delight to explore.

Fóshān is small enough to get around on foot and there are some places off of the main arteries that are worth investigation. Most interesting and historical is **Donghua Lane** (Dōnghuá Lì), between Renmin Lu and Jianxin Lu, where the homes, with their distinctive southern-style roofs and doorways, look like they've hardly changed since the Qing dynasty.

SHÍWĀN 石湾

A visit to Fóshān must include a trip to neighbouring Shíwān, one of China's most important ceramics production centres. Streets are lined with pottery shops and you can find all kinds of earthenware here, from porcelain Buddhas to the finest tableware. The highlight is a visit to the **Nanfeng Ancient Kiln** (Nánfēng Gūzào; ☎ 8271 1798; 6 Gaomiao Lu; admission Y15; ☾ 8am-6pm), which contains two 'dragon kilns' from the early Ming that are more than 30m long and have never gone out since the day they fired up. Signs (in English) explain the four-day process from clay to glazed pot. You can visit the workshop, and there's a shop selling exquisite bowls and figurines. You can even try your own hand at making pottery. One-on-one **instruction** (Y35) is with a resident artist (some speak English), and you get to take your masterpiece home.

Sleeping & Eating

Pearl River Hotel (Zhūjiāng Dàjiŭdiàn;1 Qinren Lu; 亲仁路1号; ☎ 8228 87512; d Y260-298, tr Y380; ✸ ▯) Unfortunately, the youth hostel wing of the hotel has been closed down, though with 40% discounts Pearl River remains a good budget option. Rooms are big and spartan.

Carrianna Hotel (Jiānníngnà Dàjiŭdiàn; ☎ 8222 3828; www.fshq-hotel.com; 14 Zumiao Lu; 祖庙路14号;s Y478-648, d Y528-648, ste Y1288; ✸ ▯) This four-star property has friendly staff and bright, spacious rooms. The price includes breakfast. Expect 20% discounts.

In terms of eating options, the hotels mentioned above have reasonably good restaurants. There are some fast food joints and cheap noodle houses along Zumiao Lu and scattered throughout the city centre. For healthier fare, there's a very good **vegetarian restaurant** (dishes from Y10; ☾ 11am-2.30pm & 5-8.30pm) on the third floor of the Renshou Temple.

Getting There & Away

Frequent buses (Y8 to Y14, 45 minutes) link Fóshān's **Zumiao bus station** (Zūmiào chēzhàn; Chengmentou Lu) with the main bus stations in Guăngzhōu. Buses leave every 15 minutes between 6.40am and 11pm. Minibuses (Y10) also go to Guăngzhōu's **Guangfo Bus Station** (Guăngfó Qìchē Zhàn; Zhongshan Balu).

Destinations served from Fóshān's **long-distance bus station** (Fóshān shěng qìchēzhàn; Fenjiang Beilu) include Shēnzhèn (Y80 to Y103) and Zhūhǎi (Y45 to Y60). To get to Hong Kong (Y160, three hours) the Carrianna and Foshan Hotels have daily buses, but you'll need to inquire about the schedule as it often changes.

Trains between Fóshān and Guăngzhōu (Y7 to Y10, 30 minutes) are faster than buses, but there are fewer daily departures. There are several trains daily between Shēnzhèn and Fóshān (Y40, 2½ hours), some dropping passengers off at the Hong Kong border. There is also a direct express train to Hung Hom in Hong Kong (Y240, three hours), with a daily departure at 11.02am (2.20pm from Kowloon).

CITS Foshan in the Foshan Hotel provides a free shuttle to/from the port of Nánhǎi in Píngzhōu, from where high-speed catamarans depart for Hong Kong. There are two buses daily at 8.25am and 2.55pm. From Nánhǎi buses leave for the Foshan Hotel at 11am and 3.10pm.

There's no word on when the metro line between Guăngzhōu and Fóshān will be completed, though they were running a test line in 2006.

A taxi between Guăngzhōu and Fóshān costs about Y80.

Getting Around

Bus 1 (Y2) links the train station with Zǔ Miào. Bus 1 is also good for Shíwān, as is bus 9. Taxis start at Y7; a taxi to Shíwān will cost around Y10.

ZHÀOQÌNG 肇庆

☎ 0758 / pop 3.9 million

Zhàoqìng, lying on the Xī Jiāng some 110km west of Guǎngzhōu, is bordered to the north by lakes and a series of limestone forma-tions that together make up the Seven Star Crags (Qīxīng Yán). The Dǐnghú Shān (Mt Dinghu) protected area to the northeast is one of the most attractive scenic spots in Guǎngdōng.

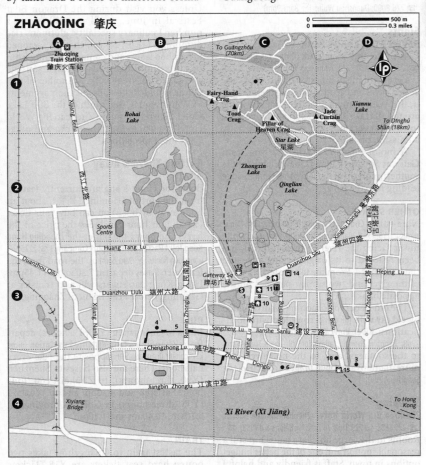

INFORMATION
Bank of China 中国银行.....................**1** C3
China Travel Service
 肇庆中国旅行社........................(see 1)
Post Office 邮局..................................**2** C3

SIGHTS & ACTIVITIES
Chongxi Pagoda 崇禧塔.................**3** D4
Cloud Draped Tower
 披云楼..**4** B3
Old City Walls 古城.........................**5** B3
River View Tower 阅江楼.................**6** C4

Seven Star Crags Park
 七星岩公园.....................................**7** C1

SLEEPING
Hubin Hotel 湖滨大酒店..................**8** C3
Star Lake Hotel 星湖大酒店............**9** C3
Zhenbao Big World Hotel
 珍宝大世界酒店............................**10** C3

EATING
Restaurants & Food Stalls
 餐馆与小吃....................................**11** C3

TRANSPORT
Boats to Seven Star Crags Park
 到七星岩公园的码头.................**12** C3
Local Bus Station (Buses to
 Dǐnghú Shān)
 公共汽车站 (往鼎湖山)............**13** C3
Long-Distance Bus Station
 长途汽车站...................................**14** C3
Zhaoqing Ferry Pier
 (Boats to Hong Kong)
 肇庆码头 (去香港)......................**15** D4

Information

Bank of China (Zhōngguó Yínháng; Duanshou Wulu; ⏱ 8.30am-5.30pm Mon-Fri, 9am-5pm Sat & Sun)

Post Office (yóujú; Jianshe Sanlu; ⏱ 8am-8pm)

China Travel Service (CTS; Zhōngguó Lǚxíngshè; ☎ 226 8090; Duanshou Wulu; ⏱ 8am-9pm)

Sights

SEVEN STAR CRAGS PARK 七星岩公园

Central to this **island park** (Qīxīng Yán Gōngyuán; ☎ 227 7724, 238 7218; admission Y50; ⏱ 8am-5.30pm) is a group of misty limestone hills, with concealed caves and grottoes among their craggy peaks. Willow and kapok trees line the paths around **Star Lake** (Xīng Hú). It's an attractive place to visit but certainly not worthy of the hefty admission price.

A motor boat (Y25) will take you from Gateway Square (Páifáng Guǎngchǎng) at the southernmost tip of the lakes to a small bridge leading into the park.

OTHER SIGHTS

Nine-storey **Chongxi Pagoda** (Chóngxī Tǎ; Guta Nanlu; admission Y5; ⏱ 8.30am-5pm), a red, green and white tower facing the river in the southeast, has been restored to its original Song style and can be climbed. From the top are terrific views of the river and two similar pagodas on the opposite bank.

The oldest part of Zhàoqìng is surrounded by **old city walls** (gǔ chéng) complete with fortifications: **River View Tower** (Yuèjiāng Lóu; ☎ 223 2968; Jiangbin Zhonglu; admission Y8; ⏱ 8.30am-5pm) to the southeast and, to the northwest, the more flamboyant **Cloud Draped Tower** (Pīyú Lóu; Songcheng Xilu).

Sleeping

Zhenbao Big World Hotel (Zhēnbǎo Dàshìjiè Jiǔdiàn; ☎ 229 1888; fax 229 0168; 76 Tianning Beilu; s & d Y138; 🅿) Rooms in this large hotel are faded but still a reasonable option and one of the better budget options in town. Staff is friendly and helpful and the restaurant inside has good food.

Hubin Hotel (Húbīn Dàjiǔdiàn; ☎ 223 2921; fax 227 2248; 82 Tianning Beilu; 天宁北路82号; s & d Y298, tr Y388; 🅿 🖵) Just a stone's throw from the lake, this hotel has excellent well-managed rooms with up to 30% discounts. The triple rooms have broadband Internet.

Star Lake Hotel (Xīnghú Dàjiǔdiàn; ☎ 616 8888; fax 619 3333; 37 Duanzhou Silu; 端州四路37号; s & d 500-600, ste from Y880; 🅿) This 31-storey hotel towers over the lake and central Zhàoqìng. Rooms have

great views, though are somewhat overpriced. For some dizzy fun, take the external glass elevator all the way to the top.

Eating

Unless you visit during the Dragon Boat Festival in June, you'll miss Zhàoqìng's number 1 culinary speciality: glutinous rice dumplings (粽子; zòngzi) that are wrapped in bamboo leaves and contain anything from peanuts and lotus seeds to dried sausage and salted duck-egg yolk. A number of restaurants and food stalls fill the pavements of Wenming Lu, due south of the Star Lake Hotel. The restaurant in Zhenbao Big World Hotel is notable for its *yum cha* and other Cantonese specialities.

Getting There & Away

BOAT

Boats for Hong Kong are currently leaving from the port of Gāomíng (高明), about an hour away by bus. You can buy your ticket (Y150, four hours, includes the price of the ferry) and board the bus at the **Zhaoqing Hong Kong Joint Passenger Transport Company** (☎ 222 5736; Gongnong Nanlu; ⏱ 9am-6pm) up the road from the ferry pier. Buses depart at 7.30am and 1.45pm. Hong Kong passengers will also transfer at Gāomíng, before heading on to Zhàoqìng.

BUS

Buses to Guǎngzhōu (Y30, 1½ hours) depart from Zhàoqìng's **long-distance bus station** (qìchē kèyùnzhàn; Duanzhou Silu) opposite the lake every half hour. There are also buses to Shēnzhèn (Y90, three hours), to Zhūhǎi (Y60, four hours) at 2pm and 4.30pm and to Wúzhōu (Y35, three hours) in Guǎngxī province at 9.10am, 10.40am and 1.20pm.

TRAIN

The fastest train to Guǎngzhōu takes two hours; hard seat tickets are Y18. Tickets booked at CTS or major hotels include a Y10 service charge.

There is a direct express train to Hong Kong (Y240, 4½ hours), with a daily departure at 9.37am (2.20pm from Kowloon).

Getting Around

The **local bus station** (Duanzhou Silu) faces the lake just opposite Gateway Square. Bus 12 links the train and long-distance bus stations with the ferry pier via the centre of town. A taxi to the train station from the centre will cost about Y15.

AROUND ZHÀOQÌNG
Dǐnghú Shān 鼎湖山

This 11.3 sq km protected **reserve** (Mt Dingu; ☎ 262 2510, 222 6386; 21 Paifang Lu; admission Y50), 18km northeast of Zhàoqìng, offers excellent walks among lush vegetation, temples, springs, waterfalls and pools, including one where Sun Yatsen took the waters in the 1920s. As is the custom, every geographical feature has been given a fanciful appellation: Leaping Dragon Pool (Yuèlóng Tán), Immortal Riding a Crane (Xiānrén Qíhè) and so on.

Baoding Garden (Bǎodǐng Yuán), at the reserve's northern edge, contains **Nine Dragon Vessel** (Jiǔlóng Bǎodǐng), the world's largest *ding*, a ceremonial Chinese pot with two handles and three or four legs, unveiled for the millennium. A short distance to the southwest a small boat (Y15) will ferry you to the tiny wooded island in **Ding Lake** (Dǐng Hú), where there is a butterfly preserve. **Qingyun Temple** (Qìngyún Sì), an enormous Buddhist complex of over 100 buildings, was originally built during the Ming dynasty. Don't miss the gilded statues of 500 Buddhist *arhats* (saints), the rice pot capable of feeding 1000 people and the camellia planted in the central courtyard in 1685.

About 1km up from the main gate there's a reserve office where, for a fee of Y30 and presentation of your passport, you can go **hiking** up the trail that follows the river's western bank. The hike takes about four hours and eventually ends up at Qingyun Temple.

INFORMATION
Dǐnghú Shān Reserve Office 鼎湖山树木园...............1 C3

SIGHTS & ACTIVITIES
Baoding Garden 宝鼎园...2 B1
Ding Lake 鼎湖..3 B1
Main Gate 山门...4 D3
Qingyun Temple 庆云寺...5 C2

SLEEPING ⌂
Dinghu Summer Resort 鼎湖山森林建养俱乐部.......6 C2
Mt Dinghu International Youth Hostel
鼎湖山国际青年旅馆...7 C2

TRANSPORT
Bus Stop (Buses to Zhàoqìng) 车站往肇庆...............8 D3

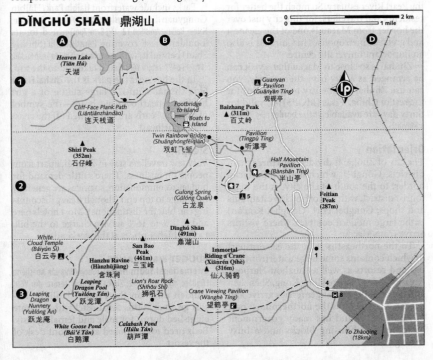

DǏNGHÚ SHĀN 鼎湖山

Mt Dinghu International Youth Hostel (Dǐnghú Shān Guójì Qīngnián Lǚguǎn; dm Y38, s & d Y138-208) Within the Dinghu Summer Resort is this well-maintained hostel with clean, basic rooms not far from the temple. Rooms can be buggy so bring insect spray.

Dinghu Summer Resort (Dǐnghú Sēnlín Jiànyǎng Jùlèbù; ☎ 262 1688; fax 262 1665; s & d Y288-368; 🍴 💻) The scenic location and quiet setting make this place ideal if you want to get away from the city. Rooms are decent, though nothing special. It's the location that counts.

Bus 21 (Y3.50) goes to Dǐnghú Shān from the local bus station in Zhàoqìng. From the reserve's main entrance you can follow the main road north on foot or you can catch one of the electric carts (Y20) that make a loop around the reserve. A taxi from Zhàoqìng to the reserve will cost about Y60.

ZHŪHĂI 珠海
☎ 0756 / pop 1.3 million

Like Shēnzhèn to the northeast, Zhūhăi is a Special Economic Zone (SEZ). But 'Pearl Sea' has never reached the level of success – or excess – of its well-heeled step-sister across the Pearl River estuary. So much the better for residents and travellers, for this city just over the border from Macau is one of the cleanest and greenest metropolises in China. It is also an important university centre.

Zhūhăi is so close to Macau that a visit can be arranged as a day trip; alternatively, you can use Zhūhăi as an entry or exit point for the rest of China. Visas (MOP$100) valid for thirty days are available at the **border** (🕑 7.30am-midnight).

Orientation

The city of Zhūhăi is divided into three main districts. Gǒngběi, which abuts the Macau border, to the south of the city, is the main tourist district, with lots of hotels, restaurants and shops; Gongbei Port (Gǒngběi Kǒu'àn) is the large modern complex where visitors arrive from Macau.

To the northeast is Jídà, the eastern part of which contains some large waterfront hotels and resorts as well as Jiuzhou Harbour (Jiǔzhōu Gǎng), where Hong Kong, Shēnzhèn and Guǎngdōng passenger ferries arrive and depart. Xiāngzhōu is the northernmost part of Zhūhăi City and has many government buildings and housing blocks and a busy fishing port.

Information

Bank of China (Zhōngguó Yínháng) Gongbei (cnr Yingbin Dadao & Yuehai Donglu; 🕑 8.30am-5pm Mon-Fri, 10am-4pm Sat & Sun); Gongbei Port (🕑 8.30am-5pm Mon-Fri, 10am-4pm Sat & Sun) The first office listed is just after customs and immigration coming from Macau.

China Travel Service (Zhōngguó Lǚxíngshè; CTS; ☎ 888 5777; 33 Yingbin Dadao; 🕑 8.30am-5pm Mon-Fri, 10am-4pm Sat & Sun) Next door to the Zhuhai Overseas Chinese Hotel.

Post Office (yóujú; 1041-1043 Yuehai Donglu; 🕑 8am-8pm)

Public Security Bureau (PSB; Gōngānjú; ☎ 864 2114; Guihua Nanlu, Gongbei)

Sights

Apart from a museum and several parks, attractions in Zhūhăi are few. In Jídà, the **Zhuhai City Museum** (Zhūhăishì Bówùguǎn; ☎ 332 4116; 191 Jingshan Lu; admission Y10; 🕑 9am-5pm) is housed on two floors of a large building done up like a Ming-dynasty compound. It contains a small but interesting collection of Tibetan art and artefacts, including gilded cups formed from human skulls; and scroll paintings and calligraphy. Bus 2, 20 and 26 run to the museum.

Parks include waterfront **Haibin Park** (Hǎibīn Gōngyuán), and **Jingshan Park** (Jǐngshān Gōngyuán; Haibin Beilu; admission Y2; 🕑 8am-7pm) noted for its 'boulder forest' covering **Paradise Hill** (Shíjìng Shān) behind it, with a **cable car** (Shíjìng Shān Sùdào; ☎ 213 6477; return Y60) that'll take you to the top.

In the bay near the park is the **Zhuhai Fisher Girl** (Zhūhăi Yúnǚ), a large statue of a girl holding a pearl over her head – the symbol of the city. Pearls are still farmed off the coast to the northeast.

Sleeping

Very few travellers stay in Zhūhăi, apart from people on business. There's little demand for budget accommodation, so prices are generally midrange to top end (though heavy discounting can blur the distinctions). Most hotels here add a 10% to 15% service charge to the bill. Expect higher prices at the weekend.

BUDGET & MIDRANGE

International Youth Hostel (Guójì Qīngnián Xuéshēng Lǚguǎn; ☎ 7711 7712; Zhuhai Holiday Resort; dm Y60) Hidden away on the Zhuhai Holiday Resort grounds is this tiny hostel with separate eight-bed dorms for male and female guests. Beds need to be booked at the front desk of the resort.

Friendship Hotel (Yóuyì Jiǔdiàn; ☎ 813 1818; fax 813 5505; 2 Youyi Lu; 友谊路2号; s Y368-418, d & tw Y388-418, ste from Y568; 🖳) This conveniently located hotel, opposite the border crossing, offers 50% discounts on its tidy but dated (peeling wallpaper, faded carpet) rooms.

Gongbei Palace Hotel (Gōngběi Bīnguǎn; ☎ 888 6833; fax 888 1900; 21 Shuiwan Lu; 水湾路21号; s Y280, d & tw

Y280-380, tr 450, ste from Y680; 🖳 🖳) Its advertised rates notwithstanding, this over-the-top kitsch palace by the waterfront has deep discounts on singles and doubles (as low as Y238).

TOP END
Yindo Hotel (Yíndū Jiǔdiàn; ☎ 888 3388; fax 888 3311; cnr Yingbin Dadao & Yuehai Zhonglu; 迎宾达道与粤海中

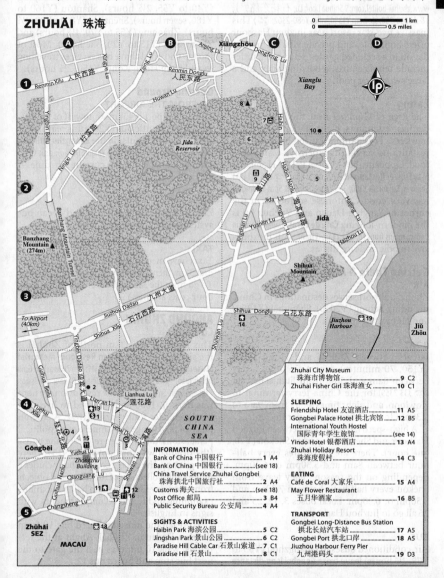

ZHŪHǍI 珠海

INFORMATION
Bank of China 中国银行 **1** A4
Bank of China 中国银行 ....(see 18)
China Travel Service Zhuhai Gongbei
珠海拱北中国旅行社 **2** A4
Customs 海关 ....(see 18)
Post Office 邮局 **3** B4
Public Security Bureau 公安局 **4** A4

SIGHTS & ACTIVITIES
Haibin Park 海滨公园 **5** C2
Jingshan Park 景山公园 **6** C1
Paradise Hill Cable Car 石景山索道 ... **7** C1
Paradise Hill 石景山 **8** C1

Zhuhai City Museum
珠海市博物馆 **9** C2
Zhuhai Fisher Girl 珠海渔女 **10** C1

SLEEPING
Friendship Hotel 友谊酒店 **11** A5
Gongbei Palace Hotel 拱北宾馆 **12** B5
International Youth Hostel
国际青年学生旅馆 ....(see 14)
Yindo Hotel 银都酒店 **13** A4
Zhuhai Holiday Resort
珠海度假村 **14** C3

EATING
Café de Coral 大家乐 **15** A4
May Flower Restaurant
五月华酒家 **16** B5

TRANSPORT
Gongbei Long-Distance Bus Station
拱北长途汽车站 **17** A5
Gongbei Port 拱北口岸 **18** A5
Jiuzhou Harbour Ferry Pier
九州港码头 **19** D3

路交界; s & d Y860-1240, ste from Y1360; [X]) This 310-room hotel next to the main Bank of China is within striking distance of the border and popular with business travellers. Outlets include the Tea Palace (Chá Huángdiàn), which serves traditional Chinese brews and snacks from 8am to 5pm (from Y60 per person).

   Zhuhai Holiday Resort (Zhūhǎi Dùjiācūn; ☎ 333 3838; www.zhuhai-holitel.com; 9 Shihua Dong Lu; 石花东路9号; s & d Y880-980, ste from Y1380, villas Y680-2362; [X]) This massive five-star resort near Jiuzhou Harbour offers both hotel and private villa accommodation in a secluded garden setting. Facilities include tennis courts, a bowling alley and a large swimming pool.

Eating

The area of Gǒngběi near the Macau border has restaurants, night markets and street hawkers. Try Lianhua Lu for bakeries and restaurants serving inexpensive Cantonese food. Opposite the Gongbei Palace Hotel, the **May Flower Restaurant** (Wǔyuèhuā Jiǔjiā; ☎ 818 1111; 31 Shuiwan Lu; meals Y100; ⏱ 7am-2.30pm & 5pm-midnight) has very good Cantonese seafood. On the corner of Yangbin Dadao and Yuehua Lu is the modern-looking **Café de Coral** (Dàjiālè; Yangbin Dadao; mains from Y8; ⏱ 11am-11pm) with inexpensive noodle and rice dishes.

Getting There & Away
AIR

Zhūhǎi's airport serves destinations in China, including Běijīng (Y2050), Shànghǎi (Y1380) and Hángzhōu (Y1230).

BOAT

Jetcats between Zhūhǎi and Hong Kong (Y150, 70 minutes) depart six times a day between 8am and 5pm from **Jiuzhou Harbour** (☎ 333 3359) for the China ferry terminal in Kowloon, and eight times a day from 9am to 9.30pm for the Macau ferry pier in Central.

   A high-speed ferry operates between Jiuzhou Harbour and Shēnzhèn's port of Shékǒu (Y70, one hour). There are departures every half-hour between 8am and 5.30pm or 6.30pm, depending on the season. They leave from Shékǒu every half hour between 7.30am and 5.30pm or 6.30pm. Local buses 3, 12, 25 and 26 all go to Jiuzhou Harbour.

BUS

Air-conditioned buses to Guǎngzhōu (Y55 to Y75, 2½ hours) leave from **Gongbei long-distance**

bus station (Gǒngběi qìchē zhàn; Youyi Lu), departing every 20 minutes between 6am and 9pm. Buses to other points in China depart from either this station or the Kee Kwan bus station below the shopping centre at Gongbei Port. Destinations include Dōngguǎn (Y60 to Y70, 2½ hours), Fóshān (Y60 to Y70, three hours), Hǔmén (Y50 to Y65, two hours), Kāipíng (Y40 to Y55, 2½ hours), Shàntóu (Y160 to Y180, seven hours), Shēnzhèn (Y80 to Y90, 2½ hours), Zhàoqìng (Y55 to Y70, 4½ hours) and Zhōngshān (Y15 to Y20, one hour). Most of the top end hotels have bus services travelling to and from Hong Kong (Y150, 2½ hours).

Getting Around
TO/FROM THE AIRPORT

Zhūhǎi's airport is 43km southwest of the city. An airport shuttle bus (Y20) runs reasonably frequently from outside the **Zhongzhu building** (Zhōngzhū Dàshà; cnr Yuehua Lu & Yingbin Dadao); ask CTS Zhuhai Gongbei for the current schedule. A taxi will cost about Y130.

BUS

Zhūhǎi has a clean, efficient and cheap bus system, with fares pegged at Y2.

TAXI

Taxis have meters and the cost is Y10 for the first 3km, then Y0.60 for each additional 250m. To go from the Macau border to Jiuzhou Harbour costs around Y20.

AROUND ZHŪHǍI
Cuìhēng 翠亨

This small village 33km north of Zhūhǎi is the site of the **Dr Sun Yatsen Residence Memorial Museum** (孙中山故居纪念馆; Sūn Zhōngshān Gùjū Jìniànguǎn; ☎ 0760-550 1691; Cuiheng Dadao; admission Y10; ⏱ 9am-5pm), where the revolutionary hero was born in 1866 and returned to live with his parents for four years in 1892. A solemn place of pilgrimage for Chinese of all political persuasions, the museum re-creates the house (the original was torn down in 1913) where Sun grew up; the village compound includes a remarkable collection of furniture and objects from everyday life. The main hall has exhibits examining his life and accomplishments, with signs in English.

   To reach the museum board bus 10 from Yingbin Dadao in Zhūhǎi. Alight at the terminus, walk 10 minutes past the gate to the next bus stop and board bus 12.

HǓMÉN 虎门
☎ 0769 / pop 197,000

Also known as Tàipíng (太平), 'Tiger Gate' is a small city on the Pearl River whose impact on China's – and the West's – history has been far greater than its present size would suggest. It was here that Commissioner Lin Zexu declared war on the opium trade in China (see boxed text below) by publicly burning shipments of the narcotic in two pits in what is now **Lin Zexu Park** (林则徐公园; Lín Zéxú Gōngyuán; Jiefang Lu; admission Y12; ☼ 8am-5.30pm). The park's **Opium War Museum** (鸦片战争博物馆; Yāpiàn Zhànzhēng Bówùguǎn; ☎ 551 2065; admission Y10; ☼ 8am-5.30pm), commemorating this heroic man's deeds and tracing the history of opium in China, is full of dusty (and rusty) objects and not unreasonable diatribes against the West.

To the north and northwest of the town centre are three batteries that figured prominently in the First Opium War, including the Bogue Fort (沙角炮台; Shājiǎo Pàotái), now part of a closed military base. Just south of **Weiyuan Fort** (威远炮台; Wēiyuǎn Pàotái) on Weiyuan Island (威远岛; Wēiyuǎn Dǎo) is the superb **Sea Battle Museum** (海战博物馆; Hǎizhàn Bówùguǎn; ☎ 550 0322; admission Y20; ☼ 8am-5.30pm), which examines the naval battle of the First Opium War through scale models, dioramas, simulated battle scenes and massive artwork, most with explanatory notes in English. There are numerous other exhibits scattered through four large halls, including large artillery pieces and other relics, as well as an enlightening exhibition on drug addiction in China today.

Buses link Hǔmén's long-distance bus station on Yong'an Lu with Dōngguǎn (Y5, 30 minutes), Guǎngzhōu (Y30 to Y45, 1½ hours), Shēnzhèn (Y35 to Y45, 1½ hours) and Zhūhǎi (Y50 to Y65, two hours). Minibuses (Y10) also go directly from the bus station in Dōngguǎn to the Sea Battle Museum.

You can get to Hong Kong (Y120 to Y170, 1½ hours) from Hǔmén by boat, with three departures a day from the **Taiping Port Pier** (太平港码头; Tàipínggǎng Mǎtou; ☎ 519 0888) southwest of the park at 9.30am, 3.30pm and 5.35pm. They leave Hong Kong for Hǔmén at 9am, 1.45pm and 5.30pm.

SHĒNZHÈN 深圳
☎ 0755 / pop 10 million

Shēnzhèn, the Special Economic Zone (SEZ) straddling the Hong Kong border, went from a poor fishing village to China's richest city in just twenty years. The city draws a mix of businessmen, investors and illegal migrant workers to its golden gates, all of them trying to find a place in China's economic miracle. At least half of Shēnzhèn's population is illegal – the SEZ is a restricted zone and, in theory, Chinese nationals require a special pass even to enter it, much less live and work here. Though commercially successful, Shēnzhèn isn't a pleasant city and the extreme imbalance of wealth and poverty lends an air of desperation. The crime rate is high and visitors should be wary of walking alone after dark. Most travellers give the place a wide berth, but it is a useful transportation hub if you're coming from Hong Kong.

DIRTY FOREIGN MUD

Although trade in opium had been banned in China by imperial decree at the end of the 18th century, the *cohong* (local merchants' guild) in Guǎngzhōu helped ensure that the trade continued, and fortunes were amassed on both sides. When the British East India Company lost its monopoly on China trade in 1834, imports of the drug increased to 40,000 chests a year.

In 1839, the Qing government sent Imperial Commissioner Lin Zexu to stamp out the opium trade once and for all. Lin successfully blockaded the British in Guǎngzhōu and publicly burned almost half a tonne of the 'foreign mud' in Tàipíng. Furious, the British sent an expeditionary force of 4,000 men from the Royal Navy to exact reparations and secure favourable trade arrangements.

What would become known as the First Opium War began in June 1840 when British forces besieged Guǎngzhōu and forced the Chinese to cede five ports – Hong Kong, Guǎngzhōu, Xiàmén, Níngbō and Shànghǎi – to the British. With the strategic city of Nanking (Nánjīng) under immediate threat, the Chinese were forced to accept Britain's terms in the Treaty of Nanking.

The treaty abolished the monopoly system of trade, opened the 'treaty ports' to British residents and foreign trade, exempted British nationals from all Chinese laws and ceded the island of Hong Kong to the British 'in perpetuity'. The treaty, signed in August 1842, set the scope and character of the unequal relationship between China and the West for the next half-century.

SHĒNZHÈN 深圳市

INFORMATION	
Bank of China	
中国银行	**1** C2
China Travel Service Shenzhen	
深圳中国旅行社	**2** C2
HSBC 汇丰中国	**3** C2
Post Office	
邮局	**4** C1
Public Security Bureau	
市公安局	**5** B1
Tourist Information Centre	**6** C3

SIGHTS & ACTIVITIES	
Shenzhen Museum	
深圳博物馆	**7** A2

SLEEPING 🏠	
Century Plaza Hotel 新都酒店	**8** C2
Hailian Hotel & Unotel	
海联会馆，有一居	**9** C2
Shangri-La Hotel	
香格里拉大酒店	**10** C3

EATING 🍴	
Laurel 丹桂轩	(see 8)
Ocean King Restaurant	
海上皇酒家	**11** C2

DRINKING 🍷	
Bar Leo	(see 12)
Henry J Bean's Bar & Grill	(see 10)

SHOPPING 🛍	
Citic Plaza 中心城市广场	**12** B2
Dongmen Market	
东门市常	**13** D1
Luohu Commercial City	
罗湖商业城	(see 17)
MixC Shopping Mall	
万象成	**14** C2

TRANSPORT	
Bus 204 to Shékŏu	**15** C2
Hualian Hotel (Buses to Airport)	
华联大厦	**16** A2
Luohu Bus Station	
罗湖汽车站	**17** C3

At the time of research, visas for US citizens were *not* available at the Luóhú border crossing.

History

Shēnzhèn was no more than a backwater until it won the equivalent of the National Lottery and became a SEZ in 1980. Developers added a stock market, hotels and towering office blocks and the world as Shēnzhèn knew it came to an abrupt end.

Nowadays Shēnzhèn is a big shopping mall for Hong Kong residents, much to the chagrin of the Special Administrative Region's retailers. It's also a good place for cheap (legitimate and otherwise) massage and *yum cha*.

Orientation

The name Shēnzhèn refers to three areas: Shenzhen City (Shēnzhèn Shì), opposite the border crossing at Lóuhú; the Shenzhen SEZ; and Shenzhen County (Shēnzhèn Xiàn), which extends several kilometres north of the SEZ.

Information

SZ Party (www.shenzhenparty.com) For current events in Shēnzhèn.

MONEY
Bank of China (Zhōngguó Yínháng; 23 Jianshe Lu; ☉ 8.30am-5pm Mon-Fri, 9am-4pm Sat & Sun)
HSBC (Huìfēng Zhōngguó; Renmin Nanlu; ☉ 9am-5pm Mon-Fri) In the Century Plaza Hotel but on the east side.

POST
Post Office (yóujú; 3002 Jianshe Lu; ☉ 9am-8pm)

PUBLIC SECURITY BUREAU
PSB (Gōngānjú; ☎ 2446 3999; 4018 Jiefang Lu)

TOURIST INFORMATION & TRAVEL AGENCIES
China Travel Service Shenzhen (CTS; Zhōngguó Lǚxíngshè; ☎ 2519 2595; 3023 Renmin Nanlu; ☉ 9am-6pm)
Tourist Information Centre (Shēnzhèn Shì Yóukè Wènxùnchù; ☎ 8236 5043; ground fl, West Exit Hall, Luohu Train Station; ☉ 8am-6pm)

Sights

Shēnzhèn is known more for business than culture but there are a few interesting places to visit.

The **Shenzhen Museum** (Shēnzhèn Bówùguǎn; ☎ 8210 2993; Tongxin Lu; bus 3 & 12; admission Y10, Fri free; ☉ 9am-5pm Tue-Sun), in Lychee Park (Lìzhī Gōngyuán), contains some 20,000 jade, porcelain and bronze artefacts and has halls devoted to ancient Shenzhen, zoology and underwater life.

The **Shenzhen Art Gallery** (Shēnzhèn Měishùguǎn; ☎ 2540 9307; Aiguo Lu; admission Y5, Fri free; ☉ 9am-5pm Tue-Sun), within Donghu Park (Dōnghú Gōngyuán) to the northeast, holds decent exhibits of both traditional and contemporary Chinese art.

OCT Contemporary Art Terminal (Dāngdài Yìshù Zhōngxīn; ☎ 2691 1976; Enping Lu, Overseas Chinese Town; admission free; ☉ 10am-5.30pm Tue-Sun) Out in 'Overseas Chinese Town' (Huáqiáo Chéng) is this excellent museum with exhibits of international and local contemporary Chinese artists. Take metro line 1 to Qiáochéng Dōng station.

THEME PARKS
West of Shenzhen City and about halfway to Shékǒu are three theme parks. **Splendid China** (Jǐnxiù Zhōnghuá; ☎ 2660 0626; www.chinafcv.com; admis-

sion Y120; ☉ 9am-9.30pm) is a humdrum assembly of China's sights in miniature. Contiguous to Splendid China and included in the admission price, **China Folk Culture Villages** (Zhōngguó Mínzú Wénhuà Cūn) recreates two dozen ethnic minority villages and a number of dwellings. Famous monuments of the world are scrutinised at **Window of the World** (Shìjiè Zhīchuǎng; ☎ 2660 8000; www.szwwco.com; admission Y120; ☉ 9am-10.30pm). The parks can be reached by metro line 1 to 'Window of the World' station (Shìjiè Zhīchuāng Zhàn) or by catching bus 101 or minibus 423 from the centre. A taxi will cost about Y50.

Some 12km to the east of Shenzhen City is a 40,000-tonne decommissioned Soviet aircraft carrier called **Minsk World** (明思克航母世界; Míngsīkè Hángmǔ Shìjiè; ☎ 2525 1415; Shatoujiao, Dapeng Bay, Yantian District; admission Y110; ☉ 9.30am-6pm), complete with choppers and MiG fighter planes parked on the deck. Take bus 205 from the train station.

Sleeping

Hotels in Shēnzhèn commonly slash as much as 50% off the regular rack rates on weekdays, though you should ask for a discount at any time. This is also partially offset by the 10% or 15% tax/service charge levied by many hotels. All hotels have in-room broadband.

BUDGET & MIDRANGE
Happy Valley International Youth Hostel (Huānlè Gǔ Qīngnián Lǚguǎn; ☎ 8557 0315; Overseas Chinese Town, Nanshan District; 南山区华侨城欢乐谷内; dm Y55, d Y180; ☒ ☐) Located in a resort area only three minutes from Window of the World, this HI hostel has spotless rooms with internet access and bike hire. However, the location is isolated and a fair distance from town. Take bus 473 from the train station.

Hailian Hotel (Hǎilián Huìguǎn; ☎ 2518 0888; fax 2518 0218; 12 Yingchun Lu; 迎春路12号; d Y538-728; ☒ ☐) Centrally located, this friendly hotel has good-sized rooms, though slightly worn around the edges.

Unotel (Yōuyìjú; ☎ 2586 3300; 6th fl, Hailian Hotel; d Y600; ☒ ☐) Located on the sixth floor of the Hailian Hotel (see above), this small chain hotel is like a breath of fresh air with its large, contemporary style rooms, wood floors and attractive bathrooms.

TOP END
Century Plaza Hotel (Xīndù Jiǔdiàn; ☎ 8232 0888; 1 Chunfeng Lu 1; 春风路1号; s & d Y1024-1266, ste from

Y1900; 😊 🖥 🖳) This 401-room hotel offers a variety of high-standard rooms, though some are in better condition than others. It's a good idea to inspect before committing. There are discounts up to 50% and a choice of restaurants, including Laurel (see below).

Eating

Because of the influx of migrants and the proximity of Hong Kong, Shēnzhèn has a wide selection of restaurants representing various styles of Chinese and Western cuisines. The city is justly famous for its fresh seafood.

Laurel (Dānguìxuān; ☎ 8232 3888; 2nd fl, Century Plaza Hotel, 1 Chungfeng Lu; meals from Y150; ⏰ 7am-11pm) Considered one of the finest Chinese restaurants in town; expect to wait in line. *Yum cha* is served from opening till 3pm daily.

Ocean King Restaurant (Hǎishàng Huáng Jiǔjiā; ☎ 8223 9000; 1116 Jianshe Lu; meals from Y100; ⏰ 7am-midnight) This is one of Shēnzhèn's best seafood restaurants and is always full.

Muslim Hotel Restaurant (穆斯林宾馆大餐馆; Mùsīlín Bīnguǎn Dà Cānguǎn; ☎ 8225 9664; ground fl, Muslim Hotel, 2013 Wenjing Nanlu; dishes Y28-45; ⏰ 10am-11pm) If you fancy trying Huí (Chinese Muslim) food (eg various beef and mutton dishes, onion cakes) head for this hotel done up like a mock mosque. What's more, it's all halal.

Drinking

Most top-end hotels have international-style bars, including **Henry J Bean's Bar & Grill** (☎ 8233 0888, ext 8270; 2nd fl, Shangri-La Hotel, 1002 Jianshe Lu; ⏰ 5.00pm-2am) at the Shangri-La Hotel, which has occasional live music. In town there's also a bunch of places around Citic City Plaza (Zhōngxīn Chéngshì Guǎngchǎng), including **Bar Leo** (☎ 2598 9898; ground fl, shop A4, Citic City Plaza, 1093 Shennan Zhonglu, Futian District; ⏰ 11am-2am). Take the metro to Kēxué Guǎn.

Further afield, in the port of Shékǒu, are a number of bars, including **McCawley's Irish Bar & Restaurant** (☎ 2668 4496; shop 118, Sea World ⏰ 11.30am-2am), off Taizi Lu, with a great rooftop beer garden, and **Soho Restaurant & Night Club** (☎ 2669 2148; Taizi Lu, Shékǒu; ⏰ 11am-2am), a popular dance club with super, up-to-date décor.

You can reach Shékǒu from the city centre on bus 204 or 226.

Shopping

For many, Shēnzhèn is all about shopping Truth be told, most of the 'bargains' to be had can be found much cheaper in other mainland cities. The first port of call for most is overrated **Luohu Commercial City** (Luóhú Shāngyè Chéng), which greets visitors as they emerge from customs and immigration. Here you'll find five stories of shopping insanity, with corridor after corridor of stalls selling ceramics, curios, knockoff handbags, clothing, wigs, massages and pirated DVDs. This area is rife with pickpockets, drugs and prostitutes so keep your valuables hidden and stay safe. The quietest days to shop here are Wednesday and Thursday.

Another shopping area is at **Dōngmén**, a district full of department stores, stalls and boutiques. Here's where you can find shops selling a nice assortment of clothing, fashion copies, jewellery, bags, shoes, and even art and antiques. The main area is centred on Dongmen Zhonglu, with pedestrian streets running perpendicular to the main thoroughfare. By metro, get off at Lao Jie station and leave from exit 'A'. You can also take bus 102, 113 or 103.

MixC Shopping Mall (Wànxiàngchéng; ☎ 8266 8266; 1881 Bao'an Nanlu) is the largest shopping mall in Shēnzhèn and has a large selection of high-end clothing shops, a cinema, supermarket with imported items, as well as a collection of Western restaurants. There's even an Olympic-sized skating rink.

An invaluable book to guide you is *Shop in Shenzhen: An Insider's Guide* (HK$95/US$12) by Ellen McNally, available in bookshops throughout Hong Kong. You can also check the information out on the author's website at shopinshenzhen.com.

Getting There & Away

AIR

Shēnzhèn airport (Shēnzhèn Fēijīchǎng; ☎ 2777 6789; www.szairport.com) is now China's fourth busiest. There are flights to most major destinations around China.

BOAT

There are 13 jet-cat departures daily between **Shékǒu port** (☎ 2669 5600) and Hong Kong (day/night sailing Y108/125, 50 minutes) between 7.45am and 9.30pm. Seven of these go to the Macau ferry pier in Central, with the balance heading for the China ferry terminal in Kowloon. The same number of boats leave Hong Kong for Shékǒu from 7.45am to 9pm. Chikong Passenger Transport runs hourly ferries (Y238, 9am to 9.20pm, 2½ hours) from Shékǒu to Hong Kong International Airport.

TALLY, HO TAI TAI!

Mrs Ho is a *tai tai*. *Tai tai* simply means 'Mrs' and, strictly speaking, every married Chinese woman is a *tai tai*. But *tai tai* in southern China – and especially Hong Kong – has a somewhat different connotation. *Tai tais* are the well-to-do, leisured wives of successful businessmen. They lunch, take tea in the lobby of the Peninsula Hotel, gossip with their friends (mostly via mobile phone) and play mahjong. And they shop, especially in Shēnzhèn, because *tai tais* – however wealthy – are always in search of a bargain.

Mrs Ho took us to Shēnzhèn the first time we visited. No, that's not true in the strictest of senses. In fact, the incomparable *HK Magazine* had recently run a cover story about a *tai tai* named Ho who would board the KCR East Rail for Lóuhú in the morning at least once a week, spend the day shopping, nibbling and being pampered and return at the end of the day thoroughly relaxed, satiated and clothed – at half the price it would have cost her in Hong Kong.

Mrs Ho 'took' us for a tour of the Luohu Commercial City, then for lunch at the Laurel and to her favourite massage parlour (legitimate of course – after all, Mrs Ho is a married women with children!) for an hour's worth of foot rubbing after pounding the pavements of the SEZ all day. We did stop short of following Mrs Ho into the manicurist's where, 'feeling particularly whimsical', she had tiny flowers, butterflies and birds painted on each fingernail. That was, we thought, beyond the call of duty – for a guidebook writer.

Some people are snide about *tai tais*, dismissing them as lazy, self-indulgent creatures whose main concern is the quality of the oolong tea and the price of the knockoff Louis Vuitton bag. But we – and now you – know differently. *Tai tais* have got something to teach us all.

There are six departures daily to Kowloon's China ferry terminal from the **Fuyong ferry terminal** (Fúyǒng kèyùnzhàn; Shenzhen airport) and three to the Macau ferry pier in Central between 9am and 8.30pm (2nd/1st class Y171/271, one hour).

You can also reach Zhūhǎi (Y70, one hour) from Shékǒu every half-hour between 7.30am and 6.30pm.

Boats run between Hǎikǒu and Shékǒu (Y138 to Y450, 18 hours) every day except Saturday, leaving at 4pm.

BUS

Intercity buses leave from Luohu bus station (Luóhú qìchēzhàn) under the shopping centre. There are regular services to Cháozhōu (Y160, five hours), Guǎngzhōu (Y60, 1½ hours), Hǔmén (Y35, one hour), Shàntóu (Y150, four hours), Xiàmén (Y210, eight hours) and Zhōngshān (Y70, 1½ hours). For information on getting to/from Hong Kong, see p560.

TRAIN

There are frequent local trains (Y70, two hours) and high-speed trains (Y80, 55 minutes) between Guǎngzhōu and Shēnzhèn. The Kowloon-Canton Railway's East Rail offers the fastest and most convenient transport to Shēnzhèn from Hong Kong (see p561).

Getting Around

TO/FROM THE AIRPORT

Shēnzhèn's airport is 36km west of the city. Airport buses (Y20, 30 to 40 minutes) leave from the **Hualian Hotel** (Huálián Dàshà; Shennan Zhonglu), which can be reached on bus 101. A taxi to the airport will cost Y130 to Y150.

Many of the top-end hotels, including the New Times Hotel, run shuttles to/from Hong Kong International Airport (one way/return Y180/320).

BUS

Shēnzhèn has an efficient network of buses and minibuses (Y1 to Y3). From the train station, buses 12 and 101 head north and then east, passing Lychee Park. Bus 204 to Shékǒu leaves from a station north of the intersection of Jianshe Lu and Jiabin Lu.

METRO

Shēnzhèn's has two metro lines (tickets are between Y2 and Y5). Line 1, most useful for visitors, covers the stretch from the Luóhú border crossing to the Window of the World theme park (p613).

TAXI

The taxi flagfall is Y12.5 (Y16.10 from 11pm to 6am). It's then Y0.60 for every additional 250m travelled. Taxi drivers have a poor reputation in Shēnzhèn – make sure they turn on the meter. Women should avoid travelling solo in taxis at night.

SHÀNTÓU 汕头

☎ 0754 / pop 1.3 million

Shàntóu is one of China's five original SEZs. It's a port on the border with Fújiàn and seldom visited by travellers.

Language

The people who live here are largely Chiu Chow. They speak a dialect they call Taejiu (Chaoshan in Mandarin, a combination of Cháozhōu and Shàntóu, the two most important cities here), which is completely different from Cantonese. It is the language of many of the Chinese in Southeast Asia, especially those who emigrated to Thailand.

History

As early as the 18th century, when today's Shàntóu was just a fishing village, the East India Company had a station on an island outside the harbour. By the mid–19th century it had grown into an important trading port known to the outside world as Swatow.

The port was officially opened to foreign trade in 1860 under the Treaty of Tientsin, which ended the Second Opium War. By 1870 foreigners were living and trading in the town itself. A few of the old colonial buildings remain, but most are extremely dilapidated.

Orientation

Most of Shàntóu lies on a peninsula, bounded to the south by the South China Sea and separated from the mainland to the west and north by a river and canals. Most tourist amenities are in the southwestern corner of the peninsula.

Information

Bank of China (Zhōngguó Yínháng; 55 Changping Lu; ☎ 8.30am-noon & 2.30-5pm Mon-Sat, 8.30am-noon Sun)

China Travel Service (CTS; Zhōngguó Lǚxíngshè; ☎ 863 6332; 41 Shanzhang Lu; ☻ 8am-9.30pm) Bus and air tickets are sold at this office next to the Shantou Overseas Chinese Hotel.

Post Office (yóujú; Waima Lu; ☻ 8am-6pm)

Sights

If you're heading down memory lane, most of what remains of Shàntóu's **colonial buildings** can be seen in the area bounded by Waima Lu, Minzu Lu and Shengping Lu.

The centrepiece of **Stone Fort Park** (Shí Pàotái Gōngyuán; Haibin Lu; admission Y10; ☻ 7.30am-11pm), which faces the sea and the breezy **embankment** running above the shore, is a castle-like **battery** with solid walls and loopholes built in 1874. The fort is surrounded by a moat.

Sleeping

Shantou Overseas Chinese Hotel (Shàntóu Huáqiáo Dàshà; ☎ 862 9888; fax 825 2223; 41 Shanzhang Lu; 汕樟路41号; www.overseaschinese.com; d Y380-480, ste from Y580; ☒ ▣) This rambling, 300-room pile conveniently located south of the city bus station has a variety of rooms. It offers up to 40% discounts.

Swatow Peninsula Hotel (Tuódǎo Bīnguǎn; ☎ 831 6668; www.pihotel.com; 36 Jinsha Lu; 金沙路36号; s & d Y388-788, ste from Y988; ☒ ▣) The Thai- and Chinese-owned Swatow Pen offers smart upmarket rooms and huge discounts. You should be able to get a single or double for Y200.

Shantou Harbour View Hotel (Shàntóu Hǎijǐng Jiǔdiàn; ☎ 854 3838; fax 855 0280; sthvh@pub.shantou.gd.cn; 18 Haibin Zhonglu; 海滨中路18号; s & d Y668-788, ste from Y1400; ☒) This waterfront hotel offers wonderful views of the harbour and friendly service. Rooms are slightly worn around the edges but deep discounts of 50% make staying here a good deal.

Eating

Chiu Chow has a distinct cuisine that makes great use of seafood and accompanying sauces. A few specialities include: *chui jau lou sui ngoh* (Chiu Chow soy goose); *tim suen hung xiu ha/ha kau* (deep-fried shrimp/crab balls with honey sauce); and *chui jau yi min* (pan-fried egg noodles served over chives). And no meal here is complete without thimble-sized cups of strong and bitter *ti kwan yu*, a fermented oolong tea called 'Iron Buddha'.

Zhonglu Restaurant (Zhōnglù Jiǔjiā; ☎ 862 6207; 41 Shanzhang Lu; meals from Y25; ☻ 11.30am-4pm, 5.30-9pm) This friendly place in the courtyard between the Overseas Chinese Hotel and city bus station specialises in seafood.

Chaozhou Restaurant (Cháozhōu Càiguǎn; ☎ 854 6498; 2 Changping Lu; meals from Y35; ☻ 10.30am-4.30pm, 5.30-10.30pm) This is an excellent place to try Chiu Chow specialities such as prawn balls and crab noodles.

There's a positively frenetic **night market** (Fuping Lu) with an entire street of food stalls just west of Minzu Lu. If your Chinese isn't up to it, let your fingers do the talking.

SHÀNTÓU 汕头

INFORMATION
Bank of China (Main Branch)
中国银行 1 D1
China Travel Service
汕头中国旅行社 2 C1
Post Office 邮局 3 B2

SIGHTS & ACTIVITIES
Stone Fort Park
石炮台公园 4 C2

SLEEPING
Shantou Harbour View Hotel
汕头海景酒店 5 C2
Shantou Overseas Chinese Hotel
汕头华侨大厦 6 C1
Swatow Peninsula Hotel
鮀岛宾馆 7 C1

EATING
Chaozhou Restaurant 潮州菜馆 8 C2
Night Market................................. 9 A2
Zhonglu Restaurant 中旅酒家 10 C1

TRANSPORT
Long-Distance Bus Station
汽车客货运站 11 B1

The restaurant on the second floor of the Harbour View Hotel has a very good breakfast buffet for Y20 per person.

Getting There & Away

AIR

Shàntóu airport, 20km northeast of the centre, has flights to Bangkok and Hong Kong (Y1230, twice daily). Domestic destinations include Běijīng, Fúzhōu, Guǎngzhōu (Y610 to Y630), Guìlín, Hǎikǒu, Nánjīng and Shànghǎi. A taxi will cost about Y40 from the centre. You can also catch the airport shuttle (Y10) which runs between major hotels and the airport.

BUS

Buses arrive/depart from the **long-distance bus station** (Shàntóu shěng qìchēzhàn; Huoche Lu) and the more central city station behind CTS and the Overseas Chinese Hotel. Destinations include Fúzhōu (Y140, seven hours), Guǎngzhōu (Y130 to Y150, six hours), Hong Kong (Y180, five hours), Shēnzhèn (Y100, four hours) and Xiàmén (Y90, four hours). Buses to Hong Kong (Y210) leave from the

Shantou International Hotel. Minibuses to Cháozhōu (Y11, one hour) leave from a small office just south of the city station.

TRAIN

There are daily trains between Shàntóu and Guǎngzhōu (Y138, seven hours) and trains to Cháozhōu (Y20, 35 minutes). The station is 5km to the east of the centre.

Getting Around

Bus 2 links the centre with the train station via Jinsha Lu. Pedicabs and motorbikes are plentiful; flagfall is Y5.

CHÁOZHŌU 潮州

☎ 0768 / pop 1.24 million

A much prettier city than Shàntóu, Cháozhōu is an ancient commercial and trading city dating back some 1700 years. It is situated on the Han River (Hán Jiāng) and surrounded on three sides by the Jīn Shān (Golden Hills) and Húlú Shān (Calabash Hills). While travelling between the two cities you'll pass a number of fortified Hakka villages chock-a-block with traditional houses and ancient temples.

GUĂNGDŌNG

Sights

The most worthwhile area to explore is in the northern section of town, around Zhongshan Lu and Changli Lu. Here you'll find among the tightly winding lanes an eclectic mixture of neatly kept colonial and traditional Chinese architecture, with some buildings bearing stonework that dates back to the Ming dynasty. The former **Confucian Academy** (Hǎiyángxiàn Rúxuégōng; Changli Lu; admission Y4; ☉ 8am-5pm), now a museum with an interesting collection of old photos, is a good place to orientate yourself before you set out on your walk.

Cháozhōu's most famous attraction is **Kaiyuan Temple** (Kāiyuán Sì; admission Y5; ☉ 6am-5pm), built in AD 738 during the Tang dynasty to house Buddhist scriptures sent by Emperor

Qianlong. Recently renovated, the halls and pavilions contain some lovely figurative carvings and gardens. The first hall houses three Buddhas flanked by 18 gilded *arhats*. Kaiyuan is an active temple and most of it is off-limits to outsiders.

Cháozhōu's **old city wall** (gǔ chéng), the ramparts of which offer great views of the city, runs along the river for almost 2.5km and is interrupted by four ornate fortifications, including **Guangji Gate Tower** (Gǔangjīmén Lóu), which at the time of research was under renovation. From the wall look southeast to beyond the island and its modern **Phoenix Pavilion** (Fènghuáng Tái), to the much older **Phoenix Pagoda** (Fènghuáng Tǎ), a seven-story tower built in 1585. On the east bank of the Han and beyond **Guangji Bridge** (Gǔangjī Qiáo), first erected in the Song dynasty, is **Hanwen Temple** (Hánwén Gōngsì; admission Y5), which commemorates the Tang dynasty poet and philosopher Han Yu, who was banished to 'far-flung' Guǎngdōng for his outspoken views against Buddhism.

West Lake Park (Xīhú Gōngyuán; admission Y5; ☉ 5.30am-11.30pm), which extends up the hill beyond the eponymous lake, is a pleasant place to stroll, particularly in the early morning or evening.

Sleeping

Cháozhōu can be explored in a couple of hours and is best visited as a day trip from Shàntóu. However, there are some adequate hotels around the bus station if you want to stay overnight.

Yunhe Hotel (Yúnhé Dàjiǔdiàn; ☎ 213 6128; 26 Xihe Lu; 西河路26号; d Y110-180, tr Y150-220; ☒) This hotel offers non-fancy, run-of-the-mill rooms but remains a good budget option. The restaurant on the second floor serves excellent Cháozhōu-style food, with lobster as the house speciality.

Chaozhou Hotel (Cháozhōu Bīnguǎn; ☎ 233 3333; fax 238 2888; www.chaozhouhotel.com; cnr Chaofeng Lu & Yonghu Lu; 潮枫路与永护路交界; s/d Y488/538; ☒ 🖵) This large complex has a variety of elegantly decorated rooms to choose from, all recently renovated. Rooms are commonly discounted as much as 50% and contain in-room broadband.

Eating

Cháozhōu-style cuisine has a well-deserved reputation overseas and is now finally being appreciated in China. Cháozhōu has a collec-

SIGHTS & ACTIVITIES	
Confucian Academy 海阳县儒学宫	1 B1
Guangji Gate Tower 广济门楼	2 B2
Hanwen Temple 韩文公祠	3 B2
Kaiyuan Temple 开元寺	4 B2
Old City Wall 古城	5 B2
Phoenix Pavilion 凤凰台	6 B2
West Lake Park 西湖公园	7 A1

SLEEPING 🏠	
Chaozhou Hotel 潮州宾馆	8 A1
Yunhe Hotel 云和大酒店	9 A1

EATING 🍽	
Cíyuàn Jiǔjiā 瓷苑酒家	10 A1
Hú Róng Quán 胡荣泉	11 B1

TRANSPORT	
West Bus Station 西汽车站	12 A1

tion of restaurants where you can try some local dishes. One of the best places in town is **Cíyuàn Jiǔjiā** (☎ 225 3990; Huancheng Beilu; mains Y30-40; ☯ 11.30am-9.30pm) close to West Lake Park. Some superb dishes to try are the steamed crab and fish balls in soup. For snacks, make sure to head to the hole-in-the-wall **Hú Róng Quán** (Taiping Lu; ☯ 8am-late), a short walk north from Kaiyuan temple. Moon cakes and spring rolls are the top items here; those with a sweet tooth should try the gooey lotus paste buns.

Getting There & Away

Buses link Cháozhōu's west bus station with Shàntóu (Y11, one hour). Buses also depart from here for Guǎngzhōu (Y160, 5½ hours), Shēnzhèn (Y160, 4½ hours) and Xiàmén (Y80 to Y100, 3½ hours).

Cháozhōu's train station is 8km west of the centre; there are three trains a day to Guǎngzhōu (Y138, seven hours), leaving at 8.55am, 1.40pm and 2.04pm. A taxi to the station will cost Y15.

Hǎinán 海南

It's taken more than 2000 years, but the Chinese have finally started to see Hǎinán Dao (Hainan Island) as more than a 'gate of hell', a place to which recalcitrant officials were banished to a fate marginally better than death. Indeed, the rehabilitation of Hǎinán's reputation has been so fast and so complete that a visit to 'China's Hawaii' has become a status symbol in itself.

Feeding directly off China's booming economy, the country's smallest province now sees about 80% of its income washed ashore by tourism. But it's not just middle-class Chinese wearing Hawaiian-style shirt and shorts combos who are coming. London travel agencies are now offering Hǎinán packages alongside those to the Costa del Sol, and a growing number of independent travellers are finding that a side trip to China's best beaches is a wonderful way to punctuate a trip to this vast country.

Hǎinán is in many ways more like Indochina than the polluted skies, freezing winters and two billion elbows that are often hard to escape on the mainland. And as a traveller, it's hard not to appreciate that this is one of the few places where you can engage with Chinese unashamedly kicking back and having a good time.

Of course, it's not all falling coconuts and tanning oil, and the more adventurous will find their trip much enhanced by a little exploration into the central highlands, which have moderate temperatures, thick canopies of forest, and Li and Miao villages. Prices are generally higher in Hǎinán, but avoid the winter rush for some very attractive discounts on hotel accommodation.

HIGHLIGHTS

- Ride a wave on the long and virtually deserted beaches of **Shimei Bay** (p628)
- Enjoy delicious, cheap seafood and wonderful people-watching at **Sānyà's Number 1 Market** (p632)
- Soak up the sun, sand and cocktails in one of **Yalong Bay's** (p630) plush resorts
- Watch the Chinese having fun as they run, kick and dance their way around **Haikou Park** (p624)
- Explore the minority villages around **Wǔzhīshān** (p634)

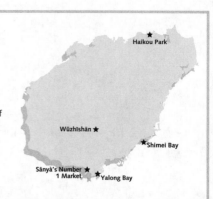

★ Haikou Park

Wǔzhīshān ★

★ Shimei Bay

Sānyà's Number ★
1 Market   ★ Yalong Bay

■ POPULATION: 8.2 MILLION

History

Until the economic boom of the last 20 years, Hǎinán had been a backwater of the Chinese empire since the first Han settlements appeared on the coast almost 2000 years ago. Largely ignored by a series of dynasties, Hǎinán was known as the 'tail of the dragon', a place at the furthest reaches of the empire that was best used as a repository for occasional high-profile exiles.

But while the island has played only the most peripheral part in Chinese history, it has been home to the ethnic Li for more than two millennia. Looked down upon by the Han, the Li lived a relatively primitive, subsistence existence and generally minded their own business. As long as the Han remained con-fined to their small communities on the coast it was a strategy that seemed to work. Indeed, groups of Li living as hunter-gatherers were found in the mountainous interior of Hǎinán as recently as the 1930s.

This lack of exploration comes as little surprise when you consider that Hǎinán was known mainly as a place of exile for most of the last 1000 years. When Li Deyu, a prime minister of the Tang dynasty, was exiled to Hǎinán he dubbed it 'the gate of hell'. So bad was the island's reputation that only 18 tour-ists are purported to have come to Hǎinán of their own volition during the entire Song, Yuan and Ming dynasties (almost 700 years)! That's about the rate per minute during winter nowadays.

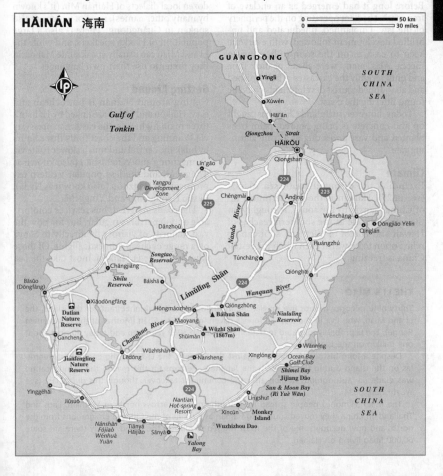

HĂINÁN 海南

Su Dongpo and Hai Rui are other notable exiles, both of whom have modest memorials in Hǎikǒu (opposite). More recently China's first communist cell was formed here in the 1920s, and the island was heavily bombarded and finally occupied by the Japanese during WWII. During the war Li and Han Chinese guerrillas waged an effective campaign to harass the Japanese forces. The Japanese retaliation, however, was brutal – they executed a third of the island's male population. And despite fighting alongside the communists the Li remain, together with a small population of Miao (H'mong), far the poorest people on Hǎinán.

In 1988 the entire island of Hǎinán was taken away from Guǎngdōng and established as a province and Special Economic Zone (SEZ). Before long it had emerged as an enclave of free-market bedlam operating on the periphery of the law. Unplanned, uneducated and unbridled development followed, with everyone keen to cash in on the soon-to-be tourism mecca. Alas, many were ahead of their time and until recently the carcasses of half-finished and abandoned tourist developments could be found littering the coast.

Today, however, mainland China has caught up and concrete is being poured, palm trees planted and vast pools dug at a truly alarming rate.

Climate

Excluding the disputed south sea islands (see p627), Hǎinán is the southernmost tip of China. Sānyà, in the south, is roughly on the same latitude as the southern reaches of Hawaii and Hanoi in Vietnam, so it can be relied upon to be warm even when the rest of China is freezing.

Weather is best from about November to early March, when average temperatures of 21°C (69.8°F) prevail; the yearly average is 25.4°C (77.7°F). Not surprisingly, this is also the busiest time. From March/April to October/November is not nearly as busy because it can be so diabolically hot and humid that you're liable to dissolve into a grease spot. The pay off is in heavily discounted hotel prices.

Hǎinán is hit by at least one typhoon a year, usually between May and October. And while it seldom gets the worst of the winds, even the edge of the typhoon can cripple transport and communication with the mainland.

Language

Hainanese is a broad term for the baker's dozen local dialects of Hǎinán Mǐn (it's known by many other names), most of which are also spoken in Guǎngdōng. There is also a large population of Hakka speakers, and while the Li and Miao can usually speak some Mandarin they prefer to use their own languages.

Getting Around

Getting around Hǎinán is both cheap and easy. Hǎikǒu and Sānyà are linked by Hǎinán's three main highways: the eastern expressway via Wànníng and the coast (only three hours by bus); the central and much slower route via Qióngzhōng and Wǔzhǐshān (also known as Tōngzhá); and the less popular western expressway via Dānzhōu (also known as Nàdà), Bāsuǒ (Dōngfāng) and Yīnggēhǎi.

The roads are great, bus services comfortable and departures regular, but for now the vast majority of visitors fly directly to Sānyà on a range of cheap domestic flights. Of those who do come via Hǎikǒu, most take the fast

---

THE LI & MIAO

Thirty-nine minority groups live on Hǎinán, including the original inhabitants of the island, the Li and Miao, who live in the tropical forests covering Límǔlǐng Shān (Mother of the Li Mountain Range). The Li probably migrated to Hǎinán from Fújiàn 3000 years ago and today number about one million on the island.

Despite a long history of rebellion against the Chinese, the Li aided the communist guerrillas on the island during the war with the Japanese. Perhaps for this reason the island's centre was made an 'autonomous' region after the communist takeover, though this didn't last (see Wǔzhǐshān, p634).

The Miao (H'mong) people spread from southern China across northern Vietnam, Laos and Thailand. In China they moved south into Hǎinán as a result of the Chinese emigrations from the north, and now occupy some of the most rugged terrain on the island. Today there are some 60,000 Miao living on Hǎinán.

but relatively boring eastern expressway to Sānyà. The central route is slower but much more interesting, passing through the central highlands and Li and Miao villages.

Buses come in two main classes: the larger, pink buses are air-conditioned, have almost business-class leg room and stop less frequently; green buses are window-conditioned and stop everywhere, but aren't much cheaper.

There are Japanese-era railways marked on the Hǎinán map and oft-talked-about plans to build a rail line right around the island, but as yet there are no useful train services on Hǎinán. There is, however, a train from Hǎikǒu to Guǎngzhōu (p626).

Few travellers hire cars on Hǎinán, but a growing number are choosing to take short trips out of Sānyà by motorbike. You can hire 125cc motorbikes for Y100 to Y250 per day.

HǍIKǑU 海口
☎ 0898 / pop 1.6 million
Hǎikǒu means 'Mouth of the Sea', but while sea trade remains relatively important, the buzzing provincial capital at the northern tip of Hǎinán is most notable for its boom-

ing economy. New and restarted construction projects are everywhere, and it's hard to avoid the conclusion that, ironically enough in 'communist China', capitalism is running almost out of control in Hǎikǒu. All of this commerce has attracted people from right around China and finding someone who was actually born on the island can be difficult.

While there really isn't much worth seeing, it's a pleasant enough place for a night or two. Sure, the traffic is as busy as any other medium-sized Chinese city, but the shade trees, the steamy tropical climes and surprisingly affable locals (is it the warm weather?) afford Hǎikǒu a wholly different feel. And the nights are best. As one guy we met told us: 'In the day, Hǎikǒu is very hot, but at night it is beautiful. You must come out at night.' We couldn't say it better ourselves.

Orientation
All your life support systems, including hotels, banks, food and travel agents, are found in the area of central Hǎikǒu around Haikou Park. The few historical sights are spread a little further afield, though it's easy enough to get to them by bus or taxi. To the northwest are the port area and the city's beach zone. The main bus station is southwest of town and the airport is about 25km to the east.

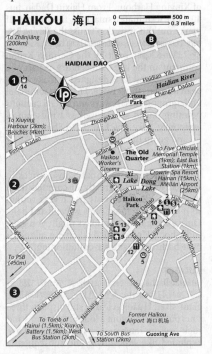

INFORMATION	
Bank of China 中国银行	**1** B2
Bank of China 中国银行	(see 6)
CTS 中国旅行社	**2** B2
Internet Café 网吧	**3** A2
Internet Café 网吧	(see 5)
Post & Telephone Centre 中国电信	**4** B2
Post & Telephone Office 邮局	**5** B3

SLEEPING 🏠	
Haikou International Financial Centre	
国际金融大厦	**6** B2
Huáqiáo Dàshà 华侨大厦	**7** B2
Hǎikǒu Bīnguǎn 海口宾馆	**8** B2
Hǎinán Mínháng Bīnguǎn 海南民航宾馆	**9** B2
Songtao Dàshà 松涛大厦	**10** B2

EATING 🍴	
Forever Café 天长地久	**11** B2
Gansu Restaurant & Other Street Food	**12** B3
Kuàihuólín 快活林	(see 10)
Western Restaurant	(see 8)
Yéfēngtáng 椰风堂	(see 8)

TRANSPORT	
China Southern Airlines 中国南方航空	**13** B2
Xīngǎng Passenger Ferry Terminal 海口新港 ..	**14** A1

MAPS
The annually published *Hainan Tourism Transportation Map* has a pretty good city map of Hăikŏu, a map of all of Hăinán, and another of Sānyà and Dàdōnghăi. Unfortunately, it's not entirely in English, but it's still worth buying (Y6) at the airport or from hotels.

Information

INTERNET ACCESS 网吧
Internet café (wăngbā; Nanbao Lu; per hr Y2; ⏰ 8am-11.30pm) Look for the 163 sign.

Internet café (wăngbā; 3rd fl, Jinzhou Hotel, 34 Jinlong Lu; per hr Y2; ⏰ 8am-midnight) There's no English sign.

MONEY
There are plenty of banks in Hăikŏu, dispensing cash through ATMs, including the following:
Bank of China (Zhōngguó Yínháng; 38 Datong Lu) Under the Haikou International Commercial Centre.
Bank of China (Zhōngguó Yínháng; cnr Haixiu Dadao & Haifu Dadao) Changes travellers cheques.

POST
Post & Telephone Centre (Yóudiàn Dàlóu; Jiefang Xilu)

TOURIST INFORMATION
Tourist information in English is hard to find in Hăikŏu.

The **China Travel Service** (CTS; Zhōngguó Lǚxíngshè; ☎ 6530 6003; cnr Haifu Dadao & Haixiu Dadao; ⏰ 8am-9pm) should be your first stop for travel info. The young, English-speaking staff can arrange plane, train and ferry tickets and tours around Hăinán and give you the lowdown on schedules. If they don't have it, they'll call. Ask them nicely and they might direct you to the latest nightspots, and maybe even take you. More formal, but with less English, is the **China Travel Service** (CTS; Zhōngguó Lǚxíngshè; ☎ 6675 7455; fax 6623 1585; 17 Datong Lu; ⏰ 8am-8pm) in the same building as Huáqiáo Dàshà.

Sights & Activities
Even when it's hotter than hell, strolling around Hăikŏu is the top 'thing to do'. The picturesque and partly restored **old quarter** along Xinhua Lu is nice enough, but our favourite activity here is an early morning or, even better, late afternoon wander through **Hăikŏu Park** (Hăikŏu Gōngyuán). The joggers, badminton players, tai chi artists, kung fu kickers, chess players and people-watchers are a wonder to behold. Even if you can't speak a word of Mandarin,

just bowl up and you'll soon be communicating with the locals. And don't miss the dancers; the 80-something geezer we saw could have cut a rug with Fred Astaire.

Five Officials Memorial Temple (五公祠; Wǔgōng Cí; 169 Haifu Dadao; admission Y15; ⏰ 8am-6pm) is an attractive Ming temple (restored during the Qing dynasty) dedicated to five officials who were banished to Hăinán in earlier times. The famous Song dynasty poet, Su Dongpo, was also banished to Hăinán and is commemorated here. Take bus 11 or 12 and get off one stop after the east bus station.

The more attractive **Tomb of Hairui** (海瑞墓; Hăiruì Mù; ☎ 6892 2060; Shugang Dadao; admission Y5; ⏰ 8am-6pm) was ravaged during the Cultural Revolution but has been restored in vibrant colour. Hairui was an incorruptible and popular Ming dynasty official who was eventually banished to the island after criticising the emperor. The tomb is in western Hăikŏu, off Haixiu Dadao; take bus 2 and tell the driver 'Hairui Mu!', or watch for a turn-off marked by a blue sign in English and Chinese. From there it's a 1km walk south.

Kilometres of smooth **sand beach** stretch west of Xiuying Harbour. From Haixiu Dadao, bus 40 (Y2) terminates smack in the middle. If you're out this way, don't miss the **Xiuying Battery** (Xiùyīng Gǔpàotái; off Jingmao Dong Lu; admission Y10; ⏰ 7.30am-6.30pm), built by the German Krupp company in the late 19th century as part of a series of coastal forts designed to make European invaders think twice. There are some cool underground passageways and several cannons pointing out to sea, as well as a museum of weaponry. Take bus 1 or 32 to Shimao Wan Lu and go up the hill.

Sleeping
Unlike the more seasonal Sānyà, prices in Hăikŏu tend to be greatly discounted from the published rates pretty much year-round, so it's the discounted rates we've listed here. Only during major holidays might you get a rude shock. Unless stated otherwise, all rooms have bathrooms and air-conditioning.

BUDGET
Huáqiáo Dàshà (Overseas Chinese Hotel; ☎ 6677 3288; fax 6677 2094; 17 Datong Lu; 大同路17号; s/d Y60/100) The giant-sized Huáqiáo Dàshà still displays three stars out the front, but a look at the rooms and rock-bottom rates suggests two of those have exploded like supernovae and subsequently

HĂINÁN

disappeared into the hotel-star black hole. That said, the cheery staff and central location make it a solid budget choice.

Songtao Dàshà (☎ 6672 9116; 5 Wuzhishan Lu; 五指山路5号; r Y80) Not far from Haikou Park, the Songtao is pretty basic but fair for the money. There's no English spoken and some rooms smell of smoke, but the staff were nice enough and it's hard to argue for this money.

Hăinán Mínháng Bīnguăn (Hainan Civil Aviation Hotel; ☎ 6650 6888; fax 6677 2610; 9 Haixiu Dadao; 海秀大道9号; r Y120-180) It's not setting any trends, but the location is unbeatable and the fading three-star rooms offer excellent value. As a bonus, the airport shuttle bus (Y15) starts and ends here.

MIDRANGE & TOP END

It's always worth inquiring about discounts (zhékòu) at Hăikŏu's midrange and top-end hotels. If you arrive in a peak period, expect to pay as much as double the rates we've listed here.

Hăikŏu Bīnguăn (☎ 6535 1234; www.haikouhotel.com; 4 Haifu Dadao; 海府大道4号; d/tw Y300-400, ste from Y600; ✗) Right in the middle of Hăikŏu, the Haikou Hotel offers slick service and attractive rooms at reasonable prices. Service is several cuts above most of its competitors, and the rooms are stylish and without the usual cheesy touches. The restaurant is excellent.

Haikou International Financial Hotel (Hăikŏu Guójì Shāngyè Dàshà; ☎ 6679 6999; www.hkjr-jasper.com.cn; 38 Datong Lu; 大同路38号; d/tw Y308-358; ✗ 🖳) This business hotel has a great location, but also a faded '80s feel. Although the rooms need a makeover, the service and facilities

(down to the bowling alley) outstrip many of its newer competitors.

Crowne Spa Resort Hainan (Huángguān Bīnhăi Wénquán Jiŭdiàn; ☎ 6596 6888; www.crownsparesorthainan.com; 1 Qiongshan Dadao; 琼山大道1号; r Y700-800, ste Y1600; ✗ 🖳 🕿) Formerly the Crowne Plaza, this city state–sized resort, 15km east of Hăikŏu and right on the beach, is a mix of luxury and gaudy kitsch. Done in a 17th-century French style, the hotel and hot-spring spa are very nice, if not quite as sharp as the competition in Yalong Bay. The spa's signature 'fish therapy' involves sitting in a pool while small fishes 'clean off the bacteria from your skin and improve your immunity and relax your soul and body by stimulating your nerve'. Do you have the nerve?

Eating & Drinking

A lot of evening eating is done in the refreshingly cool outdoors. In the city centre, Jiefang Lu, near the cinema, is good for cheap street food, while Daying Lu, between Wuzhishan Lu and Lantian Lu, has plenty of cheap but good Chinese cuisine, without English menus.

Gansu restaurant (cnr Daying Lu & Nanbao Lu; meals Y5-20) One of our favourites on Daying Lu is a nameless restaurant serving tasty Western Chinese dishes, including tŭdòu shāo niúròu (beef and potatoes), as well as its own noodles.

Kuàihuólín (1 Wuzhishan Lu; dishes Y10-30; 8am-9pm) Pick and choose your meal from dishes such as potstickers and green beans from the trolleys going around. There are also decent Western breakfasts (from Y14).

HĂINÁN FARE

There is a huge variety of Chinese cuisine available in Sānyà and Hăikŏu, but don't forget to try Hăinán's own famous four dishes. Even if you can't see them (or read them) on the menu, it's worth asking.

- **Dongshan mutton** (东山羊; dōngshānyáng) A black-woolled mountain goat fed camellias and orchids, and used in soups, stewed, roasted or cooked in coconut milk, or used in soups.
- **Hele crab** (和乐蟹; hélè xiè) Juicy crab, usually steamed but also roasted, from Hélè near Wànníng; it's best eaten in autumn.
- **Jiaji duck** (加积鸭; jiājī yā) To-die-for roast duck from Jiaji (Jiājī), near Qiónghăi.
- **Wenchang chicken** (文昌鸡; wénchāng jī) Most famous of all and originally cooked up in coastal Wénchāng, it's succulent chicken raised on a diet of rice and peanuts.

There are myriad other seafood dishes available, most of them using imported fish and crustaceans – Hăinán's fisheries having been largely fished out. When ordering, remember that prices are usually quoted in jin, which is 500g, not 1kg.

Yèfēngtáng (Cocowind Restaurant; ☎ 6535 1234; 4 Haixiu Dadao; dishes from Y25; ◷ 11am-2am) This place is a long-established restaurant in the Hǎikǒu Bīnguǎn (p625), with a phonebook-sized menu of delicious Chinese dishes.

Western Restaurant (☎ 6538 7528; 4 Haixiu Dadao; meals Y30-60; ◷ 7am-10pm) Behind the Hǎikǒu Bīnguǎn, unsurprisingly this place serves decent Western food, such as New Zealand mutton stew and the dangerous-sounding 'asbestos curry' (Y23)! It also does healthy breakfasts (Y12 to Y22).

Forever Café (☎ 6532 4658; 4 Jichang Donglu; ◷ 10am-midnight) One of several café-bars in this area, this one is particularly popular with a trendy young set.

Entertainment

Hǎikǒu has matured somewhat from the wild frontier town it was a few years ago. Prostitution is nowhere near as in-your-face as it used to be, and crime rates in general are down. Having said that, karaoke parlours remain popular and inside most of these you wouldn't need a compass to find a 'professional escort'.

Getting There & Away

AIR

Hǎikǒu's **Měilán airport** (www.mlairport.com) is well connected to most of China's major cities. For English-speaking advice, head to the **CTS office** (Zhōngguó Lǚxíngshè; ☎ 6530 6003; cnr Haifu Dadao & Haixiu Dadao). Alternatively, the **China Southern Airlines** (☎ 6666 8355; Haixiu Dadao) office on the ground floor of Hǎinán Mínháng Bīnguǎn can book flights on most airlines.

Low-season, one-way fares are cheap, and include Běijīng (Y1010), Guǎngzhōu (Y350), Kūnmíng (Y500), Nánníng (Y610), Shànghǎi (Y790) and Shēnzhèn (Y540). Prices to major cities can double in peak season.

There are also flights to Hong Kong, Bangkok, Kaohsiung (Taiwan), Singapore, Kuala Lumpur and Macau.

BOAT

Hǎikǒu has two harbours, but most departures are from **Xiùyíng Passenger Ferry Terminal** (☎ 6866 1943). Bus 3 goes to Xiuying Harbour. The other harbour is Xīngǎng, served by minibuses 212 and 218 (or buses 14 and 22) from the stop opposite Hǎikǒu Bīnguǎn. A taxi costs about Y20.

Ferries depart from Xiùyíng roughly every 1½ hours for Hǎi'ān (Y32, 1½ hours) on Léizhōu Peninsula, where there are bus connections to just about everywhere, including Zhànjiāng and Guǎngzhōu. Boats leave at 4pm Monday, Tuesday, Wednesday and Friday for Guǎngzhōu (Y110 to Y450, 20 to 25 hours).

There are daily overnight boats from Xīngǎng to Běihǎi in Guǎngxī, departing at 6pm. Tickets cost from Y90 (seat) to Y230 (cabin).

Tickets can be arranged and departure times checked at the ever-useful **CTS office** (Zhōngguó Lǚxíngshè; ☎ 6530 6003; cnr Haifu Dadao & Haixiu Dadao). If you've got time, a sense of adventure and a desire to travel like few others do, it's possible to take a boat from Hainan Dao to Vietnam. Boats are scheduled to leave Xiuying Port at 7pm on Mondays, Wednesdays and Fridays, but departures are actually less regular so check it with the CTS office in Haikou (see p624) when you get there. If the boat is running, it's supposed to take 13 hours and cost Y200/133 for a three/six-person cabin.

BUS

The new **south bus station** (汽车南站; ☎ 6680 3800; Nanhai Lu) is the one you're most likely to use. It's home to most of the combination ferry/sleeper buses going to Guǎngzhōu and other mainland destinations, though you can also take the ferry to Hǎi'ān and pick up a bus there. It is also the place for buses to Sānyà (with/without air-con Y79/49, three hours) and Wǔzhǐshān (with/without air-con Y66/46, four to five hours, 223km, five daily from 8.15am to 3.15pm) and pretty much everywhere else. The latter two go via the eastern expressway.

TRAIN

A relatively new and relatively comfortable train runs from Hǎikǒu to Guǎngzhōu (seat/hard sleeper Y138/265, 12 hours), via Sānshuǐ, Zhàoqìng, Màomíng and Zhànjiāng. For the trip across the Qiongzhou Strait to Hǎi'ān the whole train is bunted onto a ferry. It departs from Hǎikǒu daily at 6.48pm, and tickets can be bought at the train station, at the dedicated train counter in the **China Southern Airlines** (☎ 6666 8355; Haixiu Dadao) office, or most conveniently at (yes, you guessed it) the English-speaking **CTS office** (Zhōngguó Lǚxíngshè; ☎ 6530 6003; cnr Haifu Dadao & Haixiu Dadao).

Getting Around

Hǎikǒu's Měilán airport is 25km southeast of the city centre. An airport shuttle (Y15) runs every half-hour between the airport and Hǎinán Mínháng Bīnguǎn on Haixiu Dadao in the city centre. Taxi drivers will mob you as you leave the terminal and charge about Y40 or Y50 for the ride into the city, depending on your bargaining skills.

Hǎikǒu's city centre is easy to walk around, but there is also a workable bus system (Y1 to Y2). There are thousands of taxis and they're cheap, starting at Y10 for the first 3km.

WÉNCHĀNG 文昌
☎ 0898

Wénchāng is best known for its famous chicken dish (see the boxed text, p625) and as the birthplace of the Soong sisters, Meiling and Qingling, who later became the wives of Chiang Kaishek and Sun Yatsen. For the traveller, however, it's the **Dōngjiāo Yēlín** (东郊 椰林) coconut plantation, with cool, inviting pathways and glorious beaches, that makes Wénchāng attractive.

Dōngjiāo Yēlín has a wonderfully laid-back feel and, particularly in the low season when you'll have the beach virtually to yourself and room prices are low, it's an appealing alternative to Sānyà. There isn't the range of activities found further south, but just chilling out on the beach, wandering through the palms and sniffing out traditional meals in the nearby village should keep you from getting bored. Those with a nose for history might find the WWII-era concrete bunkers dotted along the beach interesting.

Accommodation is provided by a couple of resorts, the pick of which is the **Hainan Prima Resort** (海南百莱玛度假酒店; ☎ 6353 8222; hnprima@163.com; d & tw Y130-600), a wonderfully unpretentious place with one- and two-storey chalets priced by size and proximity to the beach. They are surprisingly stylish, comfortable and good value. There are two restaurants serving mainly Chinese cuisine, and cheaper food is available in the village. If the Prima isn't your bag, wander into the village where locals have been known to offer home stays.

Getting here is quite a trip. Frequent buses leave from Hǎikǒu (with/without air-con Y16/13, 1½ hours, 73km) between about 7am and 6pm. From Wénchāng's bus station, walk downhill and cross the canal, turn left and walk another five minutes or so to a newer bridge. From here, take a minibus to Qīnglán (about 20 minutes), from where regular ferries (Y2) or local boats (Y3) cross an inlet. Finally, take whatever transport is going through the plantation to the beach. Alternatively, a taxi from Hǎikǒu will cost about Y100, or from Wénchāng about Y75 – negotiate.

For Sānyà (Y50, four to five hours, 246km), buses leave Wénchāng five times daily between 7.40am and 1.40pm.

THE SPRATLY SPAT

Were it not such a contentious piece of real estate, few people would have heard of the Spratly Islands and the Paracel Islands. On a map, look for a parcel of dots far, far south of China in the South China Sea, hemmed in by Malaysia, Brunei, the Philippines and Vietnam. They, plus China, all claim the islands as their own.

Why the fuss over 53 specks of land, many of which are just reefs and shoals? The answer is oil, or at least the hope for oil.

China insists Han dynasty temples found on some islands validate its territorial rights. Vietnam has long disputed this claim and in 1933 its colonial French government annexed the islands, before losing them to Japan in 1939. Following Japan's WWII defeat, it was not until a Philippine claim in 1956 that the Taiwan-based Kuomintang government reasserted the traditional Chinese claim by occupying the largest of the islands, Taiping, where they remain. Vietnam thereafter hoisted a flag over the westernmost point of the islands. Things escalated in 1988 when the Chinese sank two Vietnamese patrol boats and forcibly occupied the islands. In 1995 the Philippine navy entered the fray at the appropriately named Mischief Reef, destroying a Chinese-built radar base there.

With several of the major players by now sporting bloodied noses, an agreement was reached to allow all nations access to the islands while individual disputes were settled. But it's unlikely that this fracas is finished for good. Given these countries' continuing military upgrades and China's desperation for fuel, the Spratly Islands remain one of the most potentially destabilising issues in Asia.

THE EAST COAST

Hăinán's east coast is a series of spectacular palm-lined beaches, long bays and headlands. The towns are not that exciting, but each of those mentioned here acts as a transport hub, meaning it's slow but simple enough to hop along the coast by local minibus.

About 60km south of Wénchāng, **Qiónghăi** (琼海) is famous as the place where China's first communist cell was formed in 1924. About 50km further south is unremarkable **Wànníng** (万宁), and it's another 23km of expressway to **Xínglóng** (兴隆), which is known as the home to more than 20,000 Chinese-Vietnamese and overseas Chinese refugees (mostly from Indonesia or Malaysia) who have settled at a cultural park known as the **Xinglong Overseas Chinese Farm** (兴隆华桥村; Xīnglóng Huáqiáo Cūn; ☎ 6225 1888, ext 8811; admission Y40; ⌚ 7.30am-6pm). Here Chinese returnees dress in Southeast Asian costumes and demonstrate a variety of tropical agriculture techniques, including making rubber and coffee; Xīnglóng coffee is famous throughout China. Xīnglóng is also famous as the transsexual capital of China and for its touristy hotspring hotels (nothing to rave about). From the bus stop to the hotels it costs Y3 by motorbike or Y5 by motor-tricycle.

Shimei Bay 石梅湾

Shimei Bay (Shímeí Wān) is a stunning stretch of coast that has, for now, avoided the mass commercialisation visited upon the Sānyà area. The wide, often palm-lined beaches are virtually deserted and, unlike their neighbours to the south, have real waves (see the boxed text, below).

For now, Shímeí remains blessedly undeveloped. This looks set to change in coming years, but there is still time to get here before the hordes. And it's worth it. Heading south from Wànníng get the minibus (Y5) to drop you at the Shímeí Wān turn-off. From here, motorbike taxis run down to the beach, where a couple of creaky old seafood restaurants compete for business.

Here you'll find the surprisingly classy, Hong Kong–owned Jiajing Café & Bar, which also arranges trips to and activities on nearby Jiajing Dao (Jiajing Island) through the attached **Wanning Shi Mei Wan Diving Co** (☎ 6252 5166).

Be sure to get your motorbike guy's mobile number and, when you're ready to move on, call him for the trip up to the **Ocean Bay Golf Club** (海滨高尔夫俱乐部; ☎ 6252 5999; baygolf@ 163.com; Nanyan Wan Beach; d Y550-750, with golf & full board Y900), at the far north end of the bay. This is a nice enough place to stay catering mainly to golfers, who play the wonderfully well-maintained course spread out below. But it's also the scene of the best surfing in China (see below) and a really beautiful piece of the world.

Located a few kilometres south of the Shímeí turnoff is **Sun and Moon Bay** (Rì Yuè Wān; 日月湾), where you will find more waves and more deserted beach. Get the minibus from either Shimei Bay or Língshuǐ to drop you on the expressway, from where it's a few hundred metres' walk.

If the minibus sounds too hard, a taxi from Sānyà costs about Y300, or about Y75 from Wànníng.

SURFING HĂINÁN

When young Chinese start taking to surfing in numbers, chances are Shimei Bay will be their ultimate domestic break. In the meantime anyone wanting to say they've surfed China should BYO board and get here first.

The place to come to is the headland jutting into the South China Sea beside the **Ocean Bay Golf Club**. Here 1m to 2m waves seem to roll in constantly on a 300m-long left-hand break. A few kilometres further south are several shorter beach breaks at **Sun and Moon Bay**, which are reported to be not quite as exhilarating but easier to get onto. Locals say the best waves are during the typhoon season, from May to November.

Occasional groups of local and expat surfers can be seen here, though unless things change fast, chances are the only people you'll see will be curious fishermen. That also means there is no gear for hire, so bring it all with you or, if you're desperate, ask around in Sānyà and you might get lucky. For more information on surfing in China, and to check when the next **720 China Surf competition** is due (usually late in the year at Shimei Bay), check out **Wannasurf** (www.wannasurf.com) or **China Seas** (www.chinaseas.com).

Língshuǐ & Monkey Island
陵水、南湾猴岛

Língshuǐ is one of the oldest settlements on Hǎinán, with archaeological evidence suggesting it has been a trading port since the Han dynasty. These days its few streets are interesting to wander around for an hour or two, with crumbling history the order of the day. However, the main reason for coming is to visit nearby Monkey Island, home to a population of Guǎngxī monkeys (*Macaca mulatta*).

About a thousand macaque monkeys live on this hilly peninsula. The **government research park** (Nánwān Hóudǎo; ☎ 6671 7080; admission Y88; ⌚ 8am-6.30pm) is a wildlife centre established to investigate the monkey business. It sounds tacky, but the preserve is peaceful if you avoid the tourist groups.

The animals are tame and anticipate tourist arrivals for snacks of peanuts. It's best not to touch them and to keep a tight grip on your camera – apparently some monkeys fancy themselves as photographers. Morning and evening are the best viewing times. During the mating season (February to May) males tend to be overly 'hospitable' and you might have to crowbar them off your leg.

To get there take an express bus from Sānyà's long-distance bus station to Língshuǐ (Y16, 1½ hours, 74km), then a minibus (Y3) to near to the harbour. It's then a 1km walk to the cable-car station, where you also buy your tickets. The admission price includes a return cable-car trip, making hiring a boat from Xīncūn to the island no longer really viable.

SĀNYÀ 三亚
☎ 0898 / pop 490,000

Of all the newly developed tourist meccas in China, Sānyà is arguably the most complete of the lot – it exists solely for tourism. Having stumbled over a few economic hurdles during the past 20 years it is absolutely booming now. The recent arrival of several international resorts has only confirmed that the Sānyà area has become a fully paid-up member of the international resort world.

While the full 40km or so of coastline dedicated to tourism is usually referred to as Sānyà, the region is actually made up of three distinctly different tourist zones. **Sanya Bay** (Sānyà Wān) is the least impressive beach, home to the bustling city centre and a long stretch of soulless new resorts aimed at mainland holidaymakers. More attractive **Dadonghai Bay** (Dàdōnghǎi Wān) is about 3km southeast, beyond the Luhuitou Peninsula, and is home to several budget and midrange hotels and two very good backpacker hostels. A further 15km east, exclusive **Yalong Bay** has the most stunning beach and – quite literally – wall-to-wall plush international resorts.

There is no denying that the Sānyà region is a modern construction in every way, with more than its fair share of cheesy attractions aimed at mainland tourists. Some would class the 2003, 2004 and 2005 Miss World pageants as pretty kitschy, too, but they certainly helped to put Sānyà on the map. Despite (or partly because of) all this, the region is quite a lot of fun. Sānyà is one of the few places where you can watch Chinese people (relatively) unselfconsciously having a good time, and it's hard not to get caught up in it when the air is clear, the sun is shining and everyone's enjoying themselves.

Of course, like any tourist haven, Sānyà does have its irritations. The stalking taxi drivers, relatively high prices and usual menu of low-level scams are the downsides.

Orientation

Sānyà city is oddly broken up. The bus station and a few tourist facilities are on the two main peninsulas protruding between Sanya Bay and Sanya River. Jiefang Lu runs north–south and is the main drag, where you'll find the long-distance bus station, banks, travel agencies, supermarkets and a few hotels. Most travellers, however, will pass straight through en route to either Dadonghai Bay or Yalong Bay.

Jiefang Lu is really the main road for the whole coast, branching into Gangmen Lu at its south end and then becoming Yuya Dadao as it heads southeast to Dàdōnghǎi Bay. This road eventually leads around to Yalong Bay and transport is fairly regular in both directions. Phoenix airport is about 20km northwest of Sānyà city. The *Sanya Hainan Island* map (Y6) is worth buying from hostels and hotels.

Information

There is the full gamut of internet cafés, banks and other life support systems in Sānyà city, though most places listed here are in Dàdōnghǎi because that's where most Western visitors stay.

HǍINÁN

INTERNET ACCESS 网吧

Most hotels and hostels are online and you can use their machines.

Ultra Speed Internet Café (wăngbā; Haiyun Lu; per hr Y2; ⏱ 8am-11.30pm) Next door to Chuānyà Bīnguăn.

MONEY

The following banks and many more have ATMs, as do the Yalong Bay resorts.

Bank of China (中国银行; Zhōngguó Yínháng; Yuya Dadao, Dàdōnghăi) Changes travellers cheques.

Bank of China (中国银行; Zhōngguó Yínháng; Jiefang Lu, Sānyà)

POST

Post & Telecommunications office (Jiefang Lu, Sānyà Yóujú) There is another office in Dàdōnghăi, at the eastern end of Yuya Dadao.

PUBLIC SECURITY BUREAU

PSB (公安局; Gōngānjú; ⏱ 8am-noon & 2.30-5.30pm Mon-Fri) It can renew visas.

TOURIST INFORMATION

Your best bet for tourist information is your hotel, though if they don't see many English speakers, even then might not be much help.

TRAVEL AGENCIES

For air tickets, we've heard good reports about the online consolidator **Travel China** (☎ 400 810 1119; www.elong.net), which delivered cheap domestic tickets to the hotel room door within 1½ hours of being called. Alternatively, the English-speaking staff at **Sanya Adventure Tour** (☎ 8821 0053; www.sanya-adv.com; Haiyun Lu; ⏱ 9am-8pm) can book tickets, hire bicycles (Y25/100 per hour/day) and motorbikes (Y250 per day), and arrange international calls for Y1 to Y2 per minute.

Sights & Activities

Unsurprisingly for a beach resort, the vast majority of things to see and do revolve around sand, sea and after-hours entertainment. The two main beaches are crescent-shaped **Dàdōnghăi** (大东海) and the superb 7km-long strip of white sand at **Yalong Bay** (亚龙湾; Yàlóng Wān; Asian Dragon Bay). Dàdōnghăi is convenient to the widest range of accommodation and eateries. It does get busy, however, and it's worth arriving reasonably early to secure one of those fixed umbrellas or risk being burned to a crisp – between March and November the sun can be blisteringly hot.

Yalong Bay is undoubtedly more attractive and less crowded, though with fewer shops and vendors budgeteers might want to bring their own food and water. Both beaches offer a wide range of activities, including jet-skiing, banana boats, snorkelling, diving and, at Dàdōnghăi, parasailing. China's beaches are theoretically open to everyone but at Yalong Bay there is a quasi-official Y50 fee if you're not staying at one of the beachfront resorts. To avoid this, walk through one of the hotels rather than entering the beach from the main square.

Particularly at Dàdōnghăi, one of the most entertaining activities is just to sit with a drink and people-watch. You will inevitably see that classic Sānyà sight – the couple or family of holidaying mainlanders dressed in identical, Hawaiian-style shirt and shorts combinations. Wonderful stuff! Generally speaking, first-time visitors to Hăinán wear these outfits, while more experienced travellers graduate to something more stylish.

Between Sānyà and Dàdōnghăi is the **Luhui-tou Peninsula** (鹿回头), from where sunset views are nice enough, but the statue of the deer turning its head is of limited interest. The beaches on the peninsula are poor, but they're uncrowded!

Two islands, **Xīmaò Zhōu** and **Dōngmào Zhōu**, are visible off Sānyà's coastline. Only Xīmaò Zhōu is open to visitors. At 2.6 sq km, it's fairly small, but you can hike around it or go snorkelling. Speak to Peter at Blue Sky International Youth Hostel (below) or Sanya Adventure Tour (left) to arrange a boat.

Sleeping

All options listed have air-conditioning, TV and hot-water bathrooms. For longer reviews, see the accommodation listings on the Lonely Planet website (www.lonelyplanet.com /accommodation).

BUDGET

Dàdōnghăi is the place to head for budget lodgings, with two excellent hostels and several cheap Chinese places in close proximity.

ourpick **Blue Sky International Youth Hostel** (Lántiān Guójì Qīngnián Lǚshè; ☎ 8818 2320, 133-2209 8659; sy.youthhostel@gmail.com; Haiyun Lu, Dàdōnghăi; 大东海海韵路夏日百货西侧; dm/s/tw/tr Y45/80/100/120; 🖳) When we stayed here we met people whose main reason for coming to Sānyà was to stay at Peter's place. That's a big call, but

SĀNYÀ 三亚

INFORMATION

Bank of China 中国银行	**1** B2
Bank of China 中国银行	**2** D4
Dàdōnghǎi Post & Telecommunications Office	**3** D4
Post & Telecommunications Office 邮电局	**4** B2
Sanya Adventure Tour	(see 11)
Ultra Speed Internet Café 网吧	**5** C4

SLEEPING

Blue Sky International Youth Hostel 蓝天国际青年旅舍	**6** D4
Chuānyà Bīnguǎn 川亚宾馆	**7** D4
Pearl River Garden Hotel 珠江花园酒店	**8** D4
Romantic Sea View Hotel 金岛嘉宁海景酒店	**9** C4
Sanya Eagle Backpacker Hostel 三亚老鹰背包客旅馆	**10** D4
Sanya Jinkai Holiday Resort 三亚金凯度假村	**11** D4
South China Hotel 南中国大酒店	**12** D4

EATING

Dōngběiwáng Jiǔdiàn 东北王酒店	**13** D4
Noodle Sellers	**14** B3
Number 1 Market 第一市场	**15** B2
Qidian Coffee House 启典咖啡厅	(see 16)
Roma 罗马比萨店	**16** C4

DRINKING

Rainbow American Café 云博美式西餐厅	**17** D4
Sky Bar	(see 16)

ENTERTAINMENT

Be There or Be Square 不见不散	**18** B3
Net Cat Nightclub 夜猫子迪斯科舞厅	**19** B3

TRANSPORT

Long-Distance Bus Station 长途汽车总站	**20** B2

it's hard to argue. The staff, the rooms, the chef and, most importantly, good-humoured and generous owner Peter give the Blue Sky a homey, welcoming and fun atmosphere. There are regular 'events', including a weekly DIY seafood barbeque (Y40) and free make-your-own dumpling sessions. There is also free wi-fi, limited free use of the fixed computers, and cheap motorbike hire, but only two double beds. It's in a lane running off Haiyun Lu – look for the blue HI sign. All up, highly recommended.

Sanya Eagle Backpackers Hostel (☎ 8821 1805, 139-7697 7924; bookhostel@163.com; 12th fl, Haitianhuiyuan Bldg, 96 Yuya Dadao, Dàdōnghǎi; 榆亚大道96号海天汇源大厦12楼; tw & tr per bed Y50; ▣) Sanya Backpackers is the perfect complement to the

more established Blue Sky. English-speaking manager Jane maintains a good vibe and 12 clean and comfortable rooms, including a triple that can act as a dorm. Jane organises diving trips and other tours. The entrance is around the back of the Kai Yuan Hotel.

Sanya Jinkai Holiday Resort (☎ 8821 0075; 71 Haiyun Lu; 海韵路71号; tw/f Y60/120) This place is far from a resort and the rooms are worn, but they're also spacious and offer good value. The management don't speak English, but the staff in Sanya Adventure across the lobby should be able to help.

Chuānyà Bīnguǎn (☎ 8822 7333; fax 8821 3568; Haiyun Lu; 海韵路; tw/tr/ste Y60/100/150) If the hostels are full, this standby has basic but clean rooms and friendly service.

MIDRANGE

Most hotels in Dàdōnghǎi are midrange. High-season rates start at Y350 for a double (more in winter). Outside peak periods 30% to 50% discounts are common.

South China Hotel (Nánzhōngguó Dàjiǔdiàn; ☎ 8821 9888; www.southchinahotel.com; Yuhai Lu, Dàdōnghǎi; 大东海榆海路; d Y880-1280; 🖳 💻) The South China is not as sharp as it was when Jiang Zemin stayed back in 1993, but it is in one of the best positions in Dàdōnghǎi and offers reasonable value in the low season. Internet access on the clunky old computers in each room costs Y5 an hour.

Romantic Sea View Hotel (Jǐn Dǎo Jiā Níng; ☎ 8821 6888; Haihua Lu, Dàdōnghǎi; 大东海海花路; r Y880-1480; 🖳) A reasonable midrange choice in a good location by the beach. Rooms are attractive, with soft beds, and prices usually start at Y240 during offpeak season, but in several windowless rooms there is no romantic view at all.

Pearl River Garden Hotel (Zhūjiāng Huāyuán Jiǔdiàn; ☎ 8821 1888; www.prgardenhotel.com.cn; Donghai Lu, Dàdōnghǎi; 大东海东海路; r Y980-2000; 💻) This fading, older hotel has a great seafront location, but the rooms are fading and many smell of smoke. Ask for a room on an upper floor for the best views. Prices are more than 50% less out of season.

TOP END

The top-end resorts are on the beach at beautiful Yalong Bay. The only problem is there is nothing more than resorts here, meaning you need to come into Dàdōnghǎi or Sānyà for local restaurants and shops. Big discounts are available from April to November. The region's true top-end resorts are all scattered along one nameless beachside street at beautiful Yalong Bay.

Sheraton Sanya Resort (喜来登度假酒店; ☎ 8855 8855; www.sheraton.com/sanya; r/ste from Y1500/2900; 🗙 🖳 💻) In its role as home to the Miss World contest from 2003 to 2005, this 511-room resort put Sānyà on the map for many people outside China. It has excellent kids facilities and generally high standards, but it's already starting to wear a little.

Mangrove Tree Resort (红树林度假酒店; ☎ 8855 8888; www.mangrovetreeresort.com; r/ste from Y1500/3800; 🗙 🖳 💻) This stylish five-star resort is visually stunning, with 502 spacious and chic rooms set around a deep-blue lagoon pool. Rooms without a sea view have a shower on the balcony as a consolation.

ourpick Hilton Sanya Resort & Spa (希尔顿温泉度假酒店; ☎ 8858 8888; www.sanya.hilton.com; r/ste from Y1580/3080; 🗙 🖳 💻) From the vast open lobby to the super-stylish rooms and restaurants, the brand-new Hilton manages to present modern beachside luxury without losing sight of the fact that you're in China. The rooms are great, some with huge circular love tubs, and all with subtly concealed Bose sound systems, internet connections and attractive décor. The best views are from buildings 4 and 8. Only the service was a little disappointing, though this should improve.

Eating

Sānyà is full of restaurants, most outdoor and boisterously casual; Shengli Lu has a good choice under the shade trees, and the south end of Jiefang Lu, just after the road splits, has plenty of noodle sellers. Dàdōnghǎi has a few international flavours to go with the Chinese places, while eating in Yalong Bay is limited to the hotel restaurants.

ourpick Number 1 Market (Dì yī shì chǎng; 第一市场; Jiefang Lu, Sānyà; 解放一路; ⏱ 7.30-11.30pm) The outdoor seafood restaurants either side of this night market are a great place to immerse yourself in the full Chinese experience. The atmosphere is palpably up, the seafood is excellent, and while you're waiting for the meal you can wander off to shop for cheap lingerie, floral shirt sets or myriad other items.

Dōngběiwáng Jiǔdiàn (东北王酒店; King of the Northeast Restaurant; ☎ 8821 2192; 135 Yuya Dadao, Dàdōnghǎi; mains Y8-40; ⏱ 11am-11pm) In this, one of Dàdōnghǎi's best restaurants (just see the parade of celebs on the wall as you go up the stairs), the food includes delicious northern Chinese dishes plus dumplings (Y20) and Wénchāng chicken (Y50). It's on the 1st floor of the Zhōng Yáng Hotel.

Roma (☎ 8867 7871; Haiyun Lu, Dàdōnghǎi; 大东海海韵路; meals Y60-70; ⏱ 12.30pm-1am) For something more European in a relatively refined atmosphere, try Roma's pasta and very tasty pizzas.

Qidian Coffee House (☎ 8867 7998; Haiyun Lu, Dàdōnghǎi; 大东海海韵路) For coffee, light meals and air-conditioning, this coffee house just next door to Roma is a safe option.

Drinking & Entertainment

Being a beachside resort, there is a reasonable range of after-hours entertainment. Most of the fun is in Sānyà city and Dàdōnghǎi, while the Yalong Bay hotels tend to have Filipino bands. The first two places listed here have a predominantly Western clientele, while the second two are mostly Chinese. Men can expect to be the subject of more attention than they might be used to – some of it from women looking for a paying gig. Remember, too, that bar and nightclub tastes change quickly, so ask around for what's hot when you're here.

Rainbow American Café (Yún Bó; Yuya Dadao, Dàdōnghǎi; ☺ 8pm-late) The most popular place among the backpacker crew when we passed, Rainbow has live music most nights, a pool table, dance floor and friendly staff. It also serves food.

Sky Bar (Haiyun Lu; ☺ 8pm-late) Loud but generally fun, Sky Bar tends to be the opening play of a night out in Dàdōnghǎi.

Be There or Be Square (Bu Jian Bu San; Gangmen Lu, Sānyà; ☺ 8pm-3am) Easy to find between the two bridges leading into Sānyà, this place has a good vibe and a decent range of music but no real dance floor, meaning the mostly Chinese patrons tend to dance at their tables. Admission is free and beers are about Y20.

Net Cat Nightclub (Yè Māo Zi; cnr Xinjan Lu & Shengli Lu, Sānyà; ☺ 8pm-2am) A younger crowd than Be Square, with mainly techno music and a dance floor. Admission is free but your first purchase needs to be a minimum of Y100, which conveniently buys a 10-bottle bucket of beer – take your friends. It's busiest from 9pm to 11pm.

Shopping

Southern Hǎinán is famous for its cultured pearls and infamous for the persistent saleswomen who flog them on Dàdōnghǎi beach, though in fairness they're not that bad. Most of the pearls are genuine, if not good enough to make the export market, and sell for just a few dollars. But there are some cases of people being duped into paying for fine-looking plastic. If in doubt, scratch away at the pearl – if it's plastic, it should flake or chip; a real pearl won't.

Getting There & Away

Phoenix airport has flights to a small number of international destinations and a stack of domestic destinations, including Shēnzhèn, Guǎngzhōu, Běijīng, Shànghǎi, Xī'ān and Kūnmíng. Prices vary greatly depending on the season, the airline and even the time of day, so it's worth shopping around. As a guide, a one-way flight to Shēnzhèn could cost as little as Y320 or as much as Y900. Check **Travel China** (☎ 400 810 1119; www.elong .net) for an idea of prices. Dàdōnghǎi is full of travel agencies, and the hostels and major hotels can also book plane tickets.

From Sānyà's **long-distance bus station** (☎ 8827 2440; Jiefang Lu) there are frequent buses and minibuses to most parts of Hǎinán, including many deluxe buses to Hǎikǒu (Y79, three to 3½ hours). Buses to Wǔzhǐshān Shi (slow/express Y17/20, 1½ to two hours) leave roughly every hour, and there are two departures daily for Qióngzhōng (about five hours) at 7.55am (Y35) and 8.40am (Y31).

Getting Around

Phoenix airport is 20km north of Sānyà city and 25km from Dàdōnghǎi. A shuttle bus runs from the airport to the Number 1 Market in Sānyà for Y10 but, for some weird reason, doesn't carry passengers back, so you'll need to take a taxi for about Y40/50/70 from Sānyà/Dàdōnghǎi/Yalong Bay.

There are several options for travelling along the coast. The cheapest is by minibus, with minibuses 102 and 202 running frequently between Sānyà and Dàdōnghǎi (Y1). Minibus 102 continues to Yalong Bay (Y3); the last minibus 102 departs from Yalong Bay just after 7pm. There is also a blue, double-decker tourist bus running between Underwater World in Yalong Bay and Tiānyá Hǎijiǎo every 30 minutes between about 7.40am and 6pm. It costs Y10 for the full trip, or Y5 between Sānyà and either end.

Motorcycle sidecars and plain old motorbike taxis cruise the streets and always ask more than the going rate, which is Y3 to Y5 to most places. A taxi from Dàdōnghǎi to Sānyà costs Y10, from Dàdōnghǎi to Yalong Bay is Y30 to Y40, and from Sānyà to Yalong Bay Y40.

It's possible to hire a minibus and driver from near the long-distance bus station for Y300 for a full day, depending on how far you go.

AROUND SĀNYÀ

You can take several half- and full-day trips from the Sānyà coast. Most are aimed squarely at the domestic tourism market and can be a bit too contrived for Western tastes. At these sights, and anything else calling itself a 'cultural village', be sure to ask clearly how much it will cost you before going to see that 'traditional wedding' or other event, as once the deed is done you'll likely be pressured to 'donate' a hefty 'bride price' to the smiling villagers.

Tiānyá Hăijiăo 天涯海角

Twenty-four kilometres northwest of Sānyà, **Tiānyá Hăijiăo** (admission Y50; ☉ 7am-7pm) literally means 'edge of the sky, rim of the sea', but seems to be universally known as the 'end of the earth' in English. The site is best known for the large rocks protruding from the surf just off the coast, which were until recently featured on the Y2 note. The area around has been landscaped into an attractive garden, but in truth this is a tourist trap and a must-see for Chinese tourists only. If you can't resist, take any minibus (Y3, 40 minutes) north along the main road or the blue, double-decker tourist bus (Y5, see p633).

Nánshān Fójiào Wénhuà Yuàn 南山佛教文化苑

About 20km west of Tiānyá Hăijiăo, **Nánshān Fójiào Wénhuà Yuàn** (Nanshan Buddhism Cultural Park; ☎ 8883 7888; admission adult/child 1.2-1.4m tall Y150/78, child shorter than 1.2m free; ☉ 8am-6pm) is another enormous tourist trap but at least there are some things worth seeing here. The most notable is the recently completed 108m-tall statue of A Ma, also known as Tin Hau (see the boxed text, p567), rising from the ocean at the end of a fancy causeway. That's 16m taller than the Statue of Liberty in New York, making it the tallest statue in the world. The rest of Nánshān is essentially a Buddhist theme park where you might find some spiritual enlightenment, but it might also lighten your wallet. Not a must-see, but definitely better than Tiānyá Hăijiăo – there's a lot of walking, so give yourself at least two hours.

Nantian Hot-spring Resort 南田温泉

About 50km northeast of Sānyà **Nantian Hot-spring Resort** (Nán Tiān Wēn Quán; ☎ 8881 1681; admission Y168; ☉ 3pm-midnight) is hugely popular with Chinese visitors and makes an entertaining evening (not morning) if you fancy soaking in one of the 40 pools of differing temperatures. It's quite an attractive site, with pools spread around landscaped gardens that also contain a couple of restaurants. Your money buys you use of the change rooms, towels and lockers.

The best way to get here is on the free shuttle bus that leaves from the Pearl River Garden Hotel (see p632) at 2pm, 4pm and 6pm, returning at 3pm, 5pm, 9pm and 11pm. Discounts of Y40 are available if you book through some hotels, including the Blue Sky International Youth Hostel (p630).

JIĀNFĒNGLÍNG NATURE RESERVE 尖峰岭自然保护区

Fifty years ago much of Hăinán was blanketed by tropical jungle. These days a lot of that has been cut down, but you can get an idea of how beautiful it once was at the **Jiānfēnglíng Nature Reserve** (Jiānfēnglíng Zìrán Băohùqū; ☎ 136-3762 5356; www.jianfengling.com; admission Y40). About 115km west of Sānyà, this lush area is high above the humidity of the coastal plain and is home to hundreds of species of plants and insects, including some 400 species of butterfly. The reserve was established in 1992, after the lower slopes had already been cleared, so the main forest is near the top of the Jiānfēng range, the highest peak of which rises to a chilly 1412m. To really get a feel for the place, stay overnight and spend the day walking in the reserve and the surrounding area.

There are several hotels spread around a lake below the main forested area, including the **Tiānchí Bìshǔ Shānzhuāng** (天池避暑山庄; ☎ 136-7645 9921; tw Y100).

To get here, take one of the regular buses from Sānyà's long-distance bus station towards Bāsuǒ (Y30, 1½ hours) and get off at the Jiānfēng exit. Walk 100m east and get either the infrequent minibus (Y1) or a motorbike (Y50/80 for one/two people) to take you the 27km to the reserve, stopping to buy your ticket in Jiānfēng village on the way. The last bus to Sānyà departs from the highway at about 5.30pm.

WǓZHǏSHĀN 五指山市 (TŌNGSHÍ 通什)
☎ 0898

Up in the hills in the centre of Hăinán, Wǔzhǐshān is one of the most interesting and genuine cities on the island. Wǔzhǐshān was until recently called Tōngzhá or Tōngshí, but its name was changed to that of a famous nearby mountain, Wǔzhǐ Shān. It is China's smallest city, being given such status when it became the capital of the Li and Miao Autonomous Prefecture back in the '80s. The idea was that the region would be self-

THE LOOP

So you've soaked up more sun than you need, drunk enough happy-hour beer and feel like you need to see more of Hǎinán than the Sānyà strip alone. Well, get on yer bike – literally. By hired motorbike or by bus (see p633), the following is an easy, entertaining and thoroughly off-the-beaten-track trip. We're describing it as a three- or four-day event, though you can cut or add corners to your heart's content.

Pack light and start early in **Dàdōnghǎi**, Sānyà (p629), heading north to **Wǔzhǐshān** (opposite) along the very smooth middle highway. It's an interesting drive that invites random stops in small villages. Plan to spend the night in Wǔzhǐshān and, if your Mandarin isn't up to exploring solo, you could wander up Qióngzhōu University to meet some English-speaking students. If (and only if) they are keen and won't be missing too much in the way of classes, they might be willing to tag along to act as a translator when you walk or take a motorbike to a nearby Li village. Back in town, soak up some beer, food and dancing at Jiā Jiā Shāo Kǎo Yuàn.

Once you've shaken off your hangover, you have a couple of options. You could head out to **Wǔzhǐ Shān** (p637), the mountain, for a look and a walk, or continue along Rte 224 to the town of **Qióngzhōng** (p637), from where the **Báihuā Shān waterfall** (p637) is an easy half-day trip. Stay the night in Qióngzhōng and enjoy the street-party atmosphere of the evenings, and head off early along the slow descent to the coast. It's a fun road, winding through terraced rice fields and tiny villages.

If you're on the bus, you're likely to go to Wànníng, but by bike it's better skipped. Either way, your destination is the beautiful and mostly deserted beaches of **Shimei Bay** (p628). Riding along the coast here is incredibly liberating, as you can stop at any one of dozens of places for a swim and just take your unhurried time.

You're on the home stretch now, with Dàdōnghǎi only a couple of hours away by road. Head straight through or stop at **Monkey Island** (p629) for a few hours. If you choose to stay another night, both **Xīnglóng** and **Língshuǐ** have hotels, or you might opt to stop into the hot-spring extravaganza at **Nantian Hot Spring Resort** (opposite) for an evening of soaking away the bumps of the road. Before you start be sure to pick up the *Sanya Hainan Island* map.

governing, giving the marginalised Li and Miao communities (see the boxed text, p622) an amount of control over themselves.

That situation, however, proved short-lived after newly empowered local politicians were done for corruption and money wasting on a scale remarkable even by Chinese standards. For evidence, look to the imposing and overly grand main building of **Qióngzhōu University**, overlooking the city, which was going to be the region's legislative assembly.

Bona fide sights are few. The **National Museum of Hainan** (Mínzú Bówùguǎn; ☎ 8862 2336; admission Y30; ◷ 8am-5.30pm), displaying a good range of Li and Miao artefacts plus the mandatory revolutionary propaganda, is the most notable, though the simple or nonexistent English labels can be frustrating.

But in many ways this lack of 'things to do' is central to Wǔzhǐshān's charm. It's the sort of laid-back place where you can happily spend a couple of days, getting to know some of the locals, drinking coffee and visiting surrounding villages (see the boxed text, p636).

If you don't speak Mandarin, you could consider employing an English student from the university. The English department is full of students keen to practice their English, and they might also be willing to guide you around the Wǔzhǐshān hotspots, including the lively **Jiā Jiā Shāo Kǎo Yuàn** area in the evenings, and the market and Jiefang Lu. It's best to arrange this the afternoon before you head out, and to clarify what if any payment will be involved - at the very least you should pay for their costs, such as transport, food and drink.

Orientation & Information

Wǔzhǐshān is built on either side of a horseshoe bend in the Nansheng River. The city's main road is Hǎiyu Lu, which leads from the coast into the city then north across a bridge before bending west past the bus station. Both the university and the museum are directly behind the bus station, up a steep hill.

There's no Bank of China but the **China Construction Bank** (中国建设银行; Jiànshè Yíng Háng; 五指山假日酒店对面), opposite Wuzhishan

---

VISITING MINORITY VILLAGES

There are dozens of Li and Miao villages scattered around Wǔzhǐshān, as close as a couple of kilometres down the road or far up into the hills along local trails. Apart from one depressing tourist trap, none of these villages is specifically kitted out for tourism and you'd be very lucky indeed to find any English speakers. However, the villagers we met told us they were happy to see travellers, especially if there is some means of communication.

So to avoid creating an unsustainable 'tourist trail' we are not listing any villages by name. Instead, we say take a student translator, if you don't speak Chinese, and go forth and discover. If yours is anything like our experience, you'll be invited to lunch and endless rounds of rice wine, discussing the war against the Japanese and the merits of toothlessness ('it's much easier eating with no teeth than it was when I only had two') with an ancient Li woman, all without being pestered to buy tacky souvenirs.

Good places to start hikes are heading in a northeasterly direction past Tōngzhá Lǚyóu Shān-zhuāng, at the head of Shānzhuāng Lu, or climbing into the hills behind the university.

Holiday Inn, has ATMs. There is no shortage of internet cafés, including one on the 1st floor of the **Jinyuan Dajiudian** (金源大酒店; ☎ 8662 2942; Hǎiyu Lu; per hr Y2; ☼ 8am-10pm).

Sleeping & Eating

Jinyuan Dajiudian (金源大酒店; ☎ 8662 2942; Hǎiyu Lu; 河北沿河西路; tw/tr Y100/120; ☐) This cheap and cheerful place is right opposite the bus station and very convenient. Rooms are bland but big and clean, and have squat toilets. Staff are happy to store luggage. Prices drop to Y70 out of season.

Wuzhishan Holiday Inn (☎ 8663 2777; yangzhouwzg@ yahoo.com.cn; 1 Shanzhuang Lu; 山庄路1号; s Y100, d & tw Y100-200, fm Y300, ste Y450) This stylish new hotel has nothing to do with the international chain, but does offer Wǔzhǐshān's best rooms at a budget price. It's right on the river and rooms have expansive views. The restaurant (meals about Y70, open 7am to 9.30pm) serves the famous Li dish *shuǐ mǎn yā* (boiled duck with rice and wine), plus a range of other Chinese cuisines. From the bus station, walk right and follow the road as it bends around to the left. The hotel is opposite the river.

Wuzhishan Resort Hotel (五指山旅游山庄; Wǔzhǐshān Luyou Shanzhuang; ☎ 8662 3188; www.wzs gov.cn/sz; 38 Shanzhuang Lu; 山庄路38号; r from Y200; ☐ ☎) In a quiet location on the edge of town this old government-run place is Chinese down to the faux tribal micro-mini skirts, karaoke and fishing pool (catch your dinner!). Take a motorbike taxi (Y1) or minivan taxi (Y5) from the bus station.

Jiā Jiā Shāo Kǎo Yuán (佳佳烧烤园; ☼ 6pm-late) It's at night that Wǔzhǐshān really comes alive and this place, hidden away behind a building about 100m east of and opposite the bus station, offers a delicious array of Xīnjiāng, Guìlín and other barbeque options, all eaten at outdoor tables and washed down with icy beer. After dinner follow your ears and the students upstairs to the rooftop dance floor.

Elsewhere, the area around the bus station has numerous small kerbside restaurants. The **Lù Dǎo Coffee Shop** (☎ 8663 9886; ☼ 8am-midnight), right next door to the Jinyuan Dajiudian, serves great Hainanese coffee.

Getting There & Away

Buses and minibuses depart every hour or so to and from Sānyà (slow/express Y17/Y20, 1½ to two hours, 88km), the last leaving Wǔzhǐshān at 5.30pm. Five express air-con buses travel to Hǎikǒu (Y67, 3½ hours, 223km), via the eastern expressway, with the last departing at 3.30pm. There are frequent slow buses north to Qióngzhōng (Y16, two hours), but only two going all the way to Hǎikǒu (Y46, 5½ hours), via the scenic middle highway, at 12.45pm and 4.30pm.

To head deep into the highlands, catch one of the three daily buses to Báishā (Y17, 2½ hours), 99km northwest of Wǔzhǐshān, with the last at 1.20pm.

For trips around Wǔzhǐshān it's easiest to just hire a motorbike taxi or minivan taxi (about Y100 to Y150 a day). Get the hotel staff to help negotiate and explain where you want to go.

AROUND WǓZHǏSHĀN

The mountain after which Wǔzhǐshān is named rises 1867m out of the centre of

Hǎinán island about 30km northeast of the city. **Wǔzhǐ Shān** (五指山; Five Fingers Mountain) is Hǎinán's highest, and perhaps because of this it is steeped in local lore, including that its five peaks represent the Lì people's five most powerful gods.

It's possible to climb the mountain in about three hours, though the peak is often clouded in so don't count on fantastic views at the top. There is, in theory, an entrance ticket for Y50, but there is rarely anyone to collect it. It's possible to stay at the bottom at **Wǔzhǐshān Bīnguǎn** (五指山宾馆), where basic rooms cost about Y80 to Y100 – take a bus from the city to Wuzhi Shan village, then whatever is going to the hotel. It's also possible to stay in Shǔimàn (水满), a dusty little village a bit further from the mountain, which has a couple of nicer places for similar prices.

There are two routes to the mountain. The first goes north along the highway and turns east off the highway just beyond Maoyang. The second and much preferable route heads south, turns east toward Nansheng, then runs north from there, via Shǔimàn. There is at least one minibus a day along the northern route to Wuzhi Shan village. To Shǔimàn you might need to take a couple of minibuses – ask at the bus station. Alternatively, hire a minivan or motorbike taxi.

QIÓNGZHŌNG 琼中

☎ 0898

The route between Wǔzhǐshān and Qióngzhōng passes through forested hills and small villages. It's certainly worth your while starting early in the day and getting off the bus at one of the villages, such as Hóngmáozhèn, taking a look around, then catching the next bus going through.

Qióngzhōng is a small, busy hill town that isn't much to look at but is surrounded by beautiful countryside. Like so many Chinese

towns, it's best in the evening when tables come out and the locals set about eating and socialising with quite some energy. Fortunately, much of the action is within crawling distance of the **bus station** (☎ 8622 2704) and hotels in the centre of town.

There are no real sights in Qióngzhōng, but the **waterfall** at **Báihuā Shān** (白花山), about 7km away, is quite beautiful as it drops more than 300m over three main cascades, the largest being about 75m high. Swimming is possible, if rather bracing much of the year. It's reachable by a bumpy motorcycle trip (Y50 return) in about 30 minutes; make sure your motorbike lady waits or it's a long walk back.

Most hotels are on Haiyi Lu, the main street, which is just below the bus station. The following two are both barely more than a minute from the bus station.

Jiāotōng Dàshà (交通大厦; Traffic Bldg; ☎ 8622 2615; 119 Haiyi Lu; 海怡路; r Y150) has basic but clean rooms for Y60 most of the year. Enter from the road sloping east from the bus station, about 100m along on the right.

The new, clean and smarter rooms at **Wàn Quán Bīnguǎn** (万泉宾馆; ☎ 3182 3777; Haiyi Lu; 海怡路; tw/d Y120/150), just west of the bus station, are good value, especially in the low season when rates drop to Y80. To find food, just wander the main street.

The middle highway links Qióngzhōng with Hǎikǒu (slow/express Y23/32, four hours, 137km) to the north, and Wǔzhǐshān (Y14, two hours) and Sānyà (Y30, four hours) to the south, though there are only two services direct to Sānyà, at 9.20am and 10.30am.

If you're on 'The Loop' (p635), you can take one of five daily buses on the scenic road to Wànníng (Y17, two hours, 93km), the last leaving mid-afternoon, and there are a couple of direct morning services to Wénchāng (Y30, four hours).

Guǎngxī 广西

The mysterious karst peaks of Guìlín and Yángshuò may lure most travellers to this province, but more and more, it's Guǎngxī's mosaic of nationalities that makes people linger.

While the limestone scenery, dotted with rice terraces, covered bridges and drum towers makes for a bewitching combination of sights and is one of the most photographed parts of China, those who head off to Guìzhōu or Guǎngdōng before dipping their toes further into the province are missing out on a great deal.

The less touristed south has China's best mainland beaches, the rock paintings on Left River (Zuǒ Jiāng), a border crossing with Vietnam and the binational Detian Waterfall. It's also where you'll hear Zhuang or Vietnamese spoken in the streets and see these languages sharing street signs with Chinese characters.

Nearly 75% of Guǎngxī is non-Han. Today the Zhuang are China's largest minority, with well over 15 million people concentrated in Guǎngxī. The Zhuang are virtually indistinguishable from the Han Chinese, and the province is often referred to as the Guǎngxī Zhuang Autonomous Region. The province is also home to smaller numbers of Dong, Maonan, Mulao, Jing (Vietnamese Gin) and Yi peoples.

Guǎngxī roughly translates as 'vast, boundless west', and for centuries its remoteness and challenging topography kept it poverty-stricken (a residual problem out of the main cities). Its area of 236,000 sq km ranks it ninth in size nationally; and with nearly 46 million habitants, it's the 11th most populated province in the country.

HIGHLIGHTS

- Take in China's legendary karst scenery as you cruise along the **Li River** (Lí Jiāng; p656) from Guìlín

- Pedal through the rice paddies and limestone peaks of **Yángshuò** (p656) in search of ancient villages

- Trek the **Dragon's Backbone Rice Terraces** (p663) near Lóngshèng and sleep in a Zhuang village

- Enter Guìzhōu province via the 'back door' of **Sānjiāng** (p665) – a lush, isolated region of lovely villages, river ferries and wooden bridges

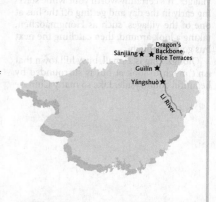

■ POPULATION: 45.9 MILLION   ■ www.gxi.gov.cn

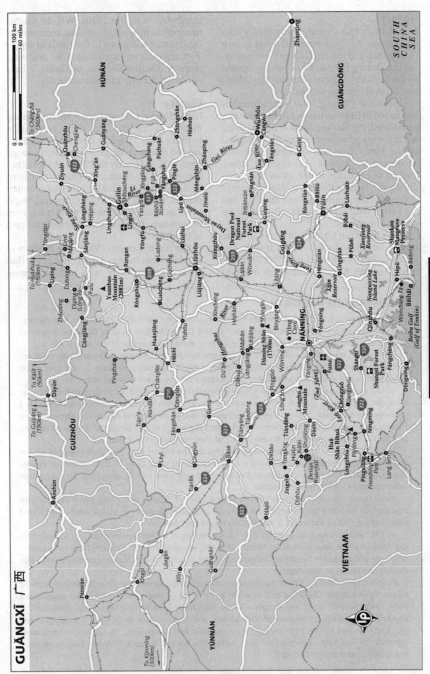

History

In 214 BC a Qin dynasty army finally conquered (on its third attempt) what is now Guăngdōng and eastern Guăngxī, overpowering the Zhuang people, who found sympathy in the northern regions with the Yao (Mien) and Miao (H'mong) people.

Unlike the Zhuang, who were ultimately immersed in Chinese customs and eventually assimilated, the Yao and Miao remained in the hill regions and were often cruelly oppressed by the Han. There was continuous conflict between the Chinese and the hill tribes, leading to uprisings in the 1830s and again during the Taiping Rebellion, which began in Guăngxī. Compounding these conflicts was the rough land and its great distance from central power.

The Qin built China's first canal (Ling Canal), but made little headway with it. The province was a backwater until the 20th century when anti-Kuomintang forces began to modernise it in the 1920s. WII devastated much of the progress. Herculean transport infrastructure laid down in the 1960s to supply Vietnam in its war against the US – and more recently, tourists flocking to Guìlín – have energised the province economically.

Climate

Latitudinally, Guăngxī approximates balmy Florida in the USA, but don't just pack a bathing suit. Tropical heat and humidity are the norm (average temperatures range from 13°C in January to 28°C in August), but a north/south distinction exists. Northern Guăngxī rises gradually into the Yúnnán plateau and, though still subtropical, highlands here are much more temperate, even in summer; frost and snow are not unheard of in winter.

Much of the annual 1500mm to 2000mm of rain falls from June to August; less heavy (but more constant) early rains in March bring

THE DRAGON TO THE NORTH

Uneasy neighbours, China and Vietnam have been at odds for more than 2100 years. Han dynasty armies conquered the first Vietnamese patriot, Tire Da, in the 2nd century BC. After dozens of attempts, Vietnam eventually threw off the yoke of imperialism in the 10th century AD.

After WWII, Western forces sent a 200,000-strong force of Chinese Nationalists to northern Vietnam to demobilise Japanese troops. The two nations have regularly been at war ever since, apart from when China supported Vietnam during the (American) Vietnam War.

In 1979, open war broke out. The Chinese incursion was impelled (according to the Chinese) after the Vietnamese signed a treaty with the Soviet Union – another border country with a Chinese love-hate relationship. Vietnam had also invaded Cambodia to topple the Khmer Rouge. Finally, and most importantly, Vietnam had seized the assets of and deported (or forced out) up to 250,000 huáqiáo (overseas Chinese), most of them to Yúnnán and Guăngxī.

The Chinese also claim Vietnamese forces crossed the border first. The Vietnamese of course deny this (most Western sources back the Vietnamese version). Over 16 days, scores of people were killed and five provincial border towns in Vietnam were heavily damaged. Bizarrely, both sides claimed to have won this battle.

Major battles erupted again in 1984 in several areas of Yúnnán and along much of Guăngxī's border. This time the Vietnamese used up to 10 expanded divisions to attack; while they didn't seize any land, they did inflict a humiliating lesson on China.

In 1997 Vietnam took its protests over China's selling of oil exploration rights in its waters to the Association of Southeast Asian Nations (ASEAN), which sided with Vietnam. Daily newspapers ran front-page banner headlines screaming about major Chinese border transgressions. This dispute continues to this day.

To everyone's surprise, China conceded on border issues, agreeing to clear landmines from 10 sq km. Cynics argue China did this as much to facilitate further trade – which had quadrupled from 1992 to 1997 along the border – as to encourage friendly relations. Soon after, Běijīng greeted a high-level contingent of Vietnamese, and historic sites in Dōngxīng (Guăngxī) dating Sino-Viet ties to the 19th century were restored and opened to the public. Perhaps most symbolic: in mid-1999, direct postal links, which had previously gone through Singapore, were finally restored through Guăngxī.

dismal, cold damp. Note that coastal regions can get hit by typhoons starting in summer. May, September and October are generally the best times to visit.

Language

Language geeks will have a blast in Guăngxī; you'll hear Cantonese along the Guăngdōng border; see bilingual Chinese-Vietnamese signs to the southern coast and western regions, and run into the Zhuang romanisation system (quite different from standard pinyin but still understandable) prominently displayed on Nanning's street signs. Numerous minority languages like Yi, Miao and even some Hakka round out the mix.

Getting There & Around

The Nankun rail line into Yúnnán boasts some of China's most modern trains and tracks; Guilín's airport is one of the nation's busiest and most efficient. Guăngxī also offers hydrophiles the chance to hop ferries to Hăinán.

An intraprovincial transport option is found in northern Guăngxī, where many minority villages are reached only by long-poled river ferries.

NÁNNÍNG 南宁

☎ 0771 / pop 1.3 million

Nánníng is a hard city to really love. It's got discouraging urban sprawl, no major sites and even worse, doesn't inspire the kind of enthusiasm among locals that sometimes win over visitors.

However, Nánníng has one of the friendliest populations of any city in the south and there's plenty to keep you busy whether you're just passing through or awaiting for a Vietnam visa.

Běijīng's thriving border trade and increasingly friendly ties with Hanoi makes Nánníng an ideal base to leave or enter Vietnam, and there are several places in town that can help with travel arrangements.

Orientation

In the north is the train station. Nánníng's main artery, Chaoyang Lu, runs roughly north–south towards Yong River (Yōng Jiāng), which bisects the city. Halfway down Chaoyang Lu is Chaoyang Garden.

MAPS

The *Nanning Street Map* (Y4) is sold at bookstores and kiosks around town.

Information

BOOKSHOPS

Foreign Languages Bookstore (Wàiwén Shūdiàn); Minzhu Lu) Packed with novels, dictionaries and phrase books in everything from English to Vietnamese.

Xinhua Bookshop (Xīnhuá Shūdiàn; Xinhua Lu) Has four levels jam-packed with books.

INTERNET ACCESS 网吧

Internet café (wǎngbā; per hr Y1.50) On Xinhua Lu, across the street from Xinhua Bookstore.

MONEY

Bank of China (Zhōngguó Yínháng; Minzhu Lu) This friendly and good-humoured branch gives credit-card advances and changes travellers cheques and cash. If asked to write down 'reasons for cashing cheques/exchanging money' resist the impulse to write 'sex, drugs and rock 'n' roll' or similar. Staff speak *very* good English here. An answer like 'shopping' or 'buying bus tickets' will suffice.

POST

Post office (yóujú; Minzhu Lu) The McDonald's of Nánníng post offices, this branch has you in and out in minutes and gives you service with a smile. Umpteen times more efficient and less bureaucratic than the city's bigger branches.

PUBLIC SECURITY BUREAU

PSB (Gōngānjú; ☎ 289 1260; Keyuan Dadao; ☉ 8am-4pm Mon-Fri) The Foreign Affairs office of the PSB is northwest of the city centre, north of the zoo.

TRAVEL AGENCIES

China International Travel Service (CITS; Zhōngguó Guójì Lǚxíngshè; ☎ 280 4960; 40 Xinmin Lu; ☉ 8.30am-5.30pm Mon-Fri) Only an OK place for independent travellers to get information. Also issues one-month Vietnamese visas (1-/2-/3-day processing Y650/550/450).

Guangxi Overseas Travel Service (Guăngxī Hǎiwài Lǚxíngshè; ☎ 261 2553) One building over from CITS. A one-month Vietnamese Visa (Y400) takes three days to process. Open Monday to Friday, though staff sometimes hang around on weekends too.

Sights & Activities

GUANGXI PROVINCIAL MUSEUM

广西省博物馆

This **museum** (Guăngxī Shěng Bówùguǎn; cnr Gucheng Lu & Minzu Dadao; admission Y8; ☉ 8.30-11.50am & 2.30-5.30pm Mon-Fri, 9am-5pm Sat & Sun) offers a browse through 50,000 years of Guăngxī history, the highlight being the world's largest bronze drum collection. In the tree-filled rear garden sit several

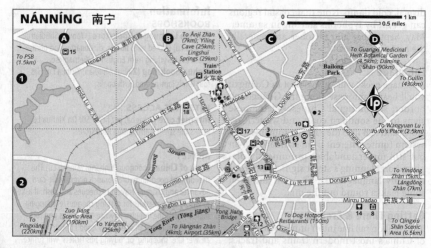

NÁNNÍNG 南宁

To Ānjí Zhàn (7km); Yíling Cave (25km); Língshuǐ Xuānqū (29km)

To PSB (1.5km)

To Guangxi Medicinal Herb Botanical Garden (4.5km); Dàmíng Shān (90km)

To Guìlín (430km)

Bàilóng Park

Train Station 火车站

To Wángyuán Lù / Jo Jo's Place (2.5km)

To Yíndōng Zhàn (5km); Lángdōng Zhàn (7km)

Zuo Jiang Scenic Area (190km)

To Píngxiáng (220km)

To Yángměi (25km)

Stream

Yong River (Yōng Jiāng)

Yong Jiang Bridge

To Jiāngnán Zhàn (4km); Airport (35km)

To Dog Hotpot Restaurants (150m)

Minzu Dadao 民族大道

To Qīngxiù Shān Scenic Area (6.5km)

full-size examples of Dong and Miao houses and a nail-less bridge.

The museum garden is a magnet for wedding photographers and also houses the giant drum restaurant. Catch bus 6 from the train station.

QINGXIU SHAN SCENIC AREA
青秀山风景区

A favourite summer retreat since the Sui and Tang dynasties, this **scenic area** (Qīngxiù Shān Fēngjǐngqū) offers verdant woods, springs, lakes and landscaped gardens. There are modest but scenic peaks of up to 180m that can easily be scaled for a more elevated perspective.

Local bus 10 heads to the park from the train station, but you still have a fair walk to the entrance. Tour buses to the park also depart from Chaoyang Garden.

GUANGXI MEDICINAL HERB BOTANICAL GARDEN 广西药用植物园

This fascinating **garden** (Guǎngxī Yàoyòng Zhíwùyuán; ☎ 561 7166; admission Y10; ☯ dawn to dusk) is the largest of its kind in China, with more than 2400 species of medicinal plants. The botanical gardens will be especially impressive if you are lucky enough to tag along with one of the centre's few English speakers. Stuck in an industrial wasteland northeast of the city, it takes about 30 minutes to get there on bus 101 or 102 from Chaoyang Garden. A taxi from town costs about Y25.

Tours

If you are in town during the summer months, take a wander along the pier off Linjiang Lu, south of the Yong Jiang bridge. Two-hour river tours often leave from here during high season.

Sleeping

Cháoyáng Fàndiàn (☎ 211 6388; www.cy-hotel.com; 86 Chaoyang Lu; 朝阳路86号; dm from Y18, s/d Y50-150, tr Y165-205, q Y155; ✳) Though it's kind of like staying in a giant state hospital, this place is nevertheless a rollicking good budget choice. It has a 24-hour store, several rooms with computers/internet, and the constant flood of humanity trundling in from the nearby train station is expertly handled with good humour by staff. One caution: hot water in dorms runs between 5pm and 1am only.

Xiángyún Dàjiǔdiàn (☎ 210 1999; xydjd@public.nn.gx.cn; 59 Xinmin Lu; 新民路59号; s/d/t Y320-460/380-430/520) This hotel is dark, severe and very 1970s but it still comes very much recommended. The discounts are substantial, internet in the business centre is only Y5 and the staff go out of their way for guests. Mouldy bathmats and dirty drain strings are the only let downs. Air-conditioning May to September only.

Yínhé Dàjiǔdiàn (Milky Way Hotel; ☎ 211 6688; www.yhhotel.com; 84 Chaoyang Lu; 朝阳路84号; s/d Y330-380/380; ✳) Also near the train station, the accommodation here is generically decorated but has newish wood furniture. Many rooms also have computers with internet. Unlike the Cháoyáng Fàndiàn, staff here don't cope well with the tour throngs and it can get quite chaotic.

Yōngjiāng Bīnguǎn (☎ 280 0888; fax 280 0535; 1 Linjiang Lu; 临江路1号; s & d from Y800; ✳) Deluxe rooms overlooking the Yong River are worth the splurge for the attention to detail; wash cloths are artistically folded, desks are outfitted with every conceivable office supply. Regular standard rooms are completely unremarkable and, even with discounts, aren't worth the price. Head to the Xiángyún Dàjiǔdiàn, where better quality standard rooms can be had for much less.

Eating

Nánníng is famous for its *gǒuròu huǒguō* (dog hotpot; 狗肉火锅). Zhongshan Lu, south of Qixing Lu, is where the locals go for this popular winter dish. There are tons of restaurants here. Just follow the crowds and take your pick.

The centrally located Gonghe Lu is another great place to look for sustenance. The southern end near Minsheng Lu is sprinkled with Chinese cafés and slick little Chinese fast-food joints. The road further north is packed with very friendly dumpling food stalls and point and choose places. **Wangyuan Lu** (望园路) is the place to head to if you want western fare or coffee.

Feeling 57 Bar (Fēilái 57 Jiŭba; 57 Minzu Lu; ✉ 8pm to late) For drinking and occasional live music, this bar near the Minority Museum is another popular watering-hole for expats. Many of them rave about the music and reasonably priced drinks.

Jo Jo's Place (Wangyuan Lu; ✉ 10am-late) This place, just south of Pinghu Lu, is popular with expats. There's a pool table, an extensive menu and a motley mix of foreigners that can include anyone from English teachers to Brazilian and Russian circus performers.

Pantry (Fúlín Zhīpī Shípīn; 34 Minzu Dadao) A great option for self-catering. It stocks hard to find cheeses and cold cuts. It's next to the Minority Museum on the left-hand side.

Getting There & Away

AIR

Domestic airlines fly everywhere, and there are multiple departures daily to almost all major cities, including Guăngzhōu (Y730), Shànghăi (Y1660), Shēnzhèn (Y890), Kūnmíng (Y630), Běijīng (Y2050), Guìyáng (Y650) and Hăikǒu (Y610).

Irregularly scheduled international flights leave throughout the week for Hong Kong and Hanoi (Hénèi).

Civil Aviation Administration of China (CAAC; Zhōngguó Mínháng; ☎ 243 1459; 82 Chaoyang Lu; ✉ 24hrs) is generally efficient, though travel agencies often have lower prices. From 8pm to 8am doors are barred shut and tickets are sold from the window round the side of the building.

BUS

Bus stations are sprinkled throughout Nánníng. You can buy tickets for most destinations from a window at the corner of Chaoyang Lu and Huadong Lu. This is a good idea as the city's stations can get chaotic.

The Lángdōng Zhàn bus station is east of town along the expressway. Frequent express buses depart to: Běihăi (Y55, 2½hrs), Guăngzhōu (Y180, 10 hours), Guìlín (Y80 to Y110, four to 4½ hours), Guìpíng (Y50 to Y63, three hours), Liŭzhōu (Y60, three hours) and Wúzhōu (Y90 to Y110, six hours). Bus 6 runs to the train station.

Northwest of the train station is the Běidà Kèyùn Zhōngxīn bus station; anything to the north departs from here, including buses to Dàxīn (Y30, 2½ hours) or Jìngxī (Y50, seven hours) and Băisè (Y50, three to four hours). Bus 52 links this station to the Yíndōng Zhàn via the train station.

For south-bound destinations, use the madhouse Jiāngnán Zhàn bus station, located south of Yong River. If the crowds toss you around too much, go to the information booth and look pathetic. Staff are usually too frazzled to be friendly but they do speak some English and will help foreigners buy tickets and walk them through the terminal to find their buses.

There's a daily Hanoi-bound bus (Y110, 8am, 10 hours). It will take you to Friendship Pass, after which you cross into Vietnam on foot and then board a Vietnamese bus the rest of the way to Hanoi. Bus 41 departs from Chaoyang Garden and runs along Chaoyang Lu to this station. Buses leave Ānjí Zhàn station every 15 minutes for Wǔmíng, useful for travellers heading to Yiling Cave.

TRAIN

To get to Píngxiáng and the Vietnam border, consider the convenient morning train (Y40 to Y55, 7.58am, 3½ hours).

Major direct rail links with Nánníng include Běijīng (T6, 9.50am, 29 hours), Chéngdū (K142, 5.51pm, 37 hours), Guǎngzhōu (K366, 11.55pm, 14 hours), Kūnmíng (K393, 6.10pm, 14 hours), Shànghǎi (K182, 9.26am, 30 hours), Xī'ān (K316, 10.47am, 36 hours) and Guìlín (N802, 8.25am, five hours).

The T6 for Běijīng also passes through Liǔzhōu (three hours), Guìlín (five hours), Wǔhàn (17 hours), Zhèngzhōu (22 hours) and Shíjiāzhuāng (26 hours). The K142 to Chéngdū passes through Guìyáng (19 hours) and Chóngqìng (29 hours).

The T905/M2 from Nánníng to Dong Dang (Tóngdēng) in Vietnam departs at 9.15pm, but think twice before hopping on. It takes forever with lengthy delays in Píngxiáng and at customs.

Getting next-day tickets at the train station doesn't seem to be too problematic. Foreigners can use any window, though window 15 is supposed to be 'the one'; window 16 is the place to go to change tickets.

Getting Around

TO/FROM THE AIRPORT

The most efficient way to reach the airport is by CAAC buses (Y15, 40 minutes), which depart regularly from the CAAC office on Chaoyang Lu (p643).

A taxi from downtown will cost Y80 to 100.

LOCAL TRANSPORT

There are abundant taxis and motorcycle taxis plying the streets. Taxi rides usually start at Y7; motorcycle taxis are around Y5.

Buses generally run from 6am to around 11pm and fares start at Y1.

AROUND NÁNNÍNG

Yángměi 扬美

This beautifully preserved 17th-century town on the Yong River (26km west of Nánníng, admission Y10) has become a popular day trip from Nánníng. Guides will offer their services upon arrival; some speak a little English.

The best way to get around the town is to hire an ox cart for the half-day (Y10).

Buses leave from a bus stop just north of Chaoyang Garden or from a stop two blocks west of the train station, but only in high season. A taxi to the village costs Y50 to Y60.

Yiling Cave 伊岭岩

Twenty-five kilometres north of Nánníng, **Yiling Cave** (Yílíng Yán; admission Y45; 🕐 8am-5pm daily) is a bit of a tourist trap, but fun all the same with its stalagmites and galactic lights. The surrounding countryside is also worth exploring.

Minibuses run from Chaoyang Garden on most weekends (especially during summer). Or, take bus 41 to the Ānjí Zhàn bus station where you can buy a ticket to Yiling Cave on a bus for Wǔmíng (武鸣; every 15 minutes, 6.15am to 10pm).

North of Yiling Cave is **Lingshui Springs** (灵水泉; Língshuǐ Quán), essentially a large outdoor mineral swimming pool. To reach the springs, continue on the bus past Yílíng to Wǔmíng, and catch a motorcycle taxi (Y3) the remaining few kilometres.

Dàmíng Shān 大明山

Some 90km northeast of Nánníng is **Dàmíng Shān** (admission Y20), an impressive mountain with an average elevation of over 1200m, and a maximum height of 1760m. With more than 1700 species of plants, the mountain is a provincially protected zone. The majority of the scenic spots are accessible within a day's hike, however, most visitors organise a guide to show them around because paths are poorly marked.

Most people spend the night in the small forestry village of **Dàmíngshān** at the base of the mountain. Try to make your sleeping arrangements beforehand. Accommodation here isn't necessarily staffed 24-hours outside of high season unless they are expecting someone. Try the **room reservation hotline** (☎ 9851122).

Hands way up for **Daming Shan Longteng Guesthouse** (大明山龙腾宾馆; Dàmíng Shān Lóngténg Bīnguǎn; ☎ 1397 815 3459; s/d/tr from Y150) if only because it is consistently staffed outside of high season. Rooms are average but service is helpful. Staff can help you arrange guides and transport to the mountain.

From Nánníng's Chaoyang Garden, there is one daily public bus (Y14, departing 3pm) that leaves on Renmin Lu. The bus terminates at Dàmíngshān where you'll find the ticket office, accommodation and a small shop. It is, however, another 27km from here to the top of the mountain and the bus will only continue up if there are enough paying passengers.

Consider hopping off the bus 5km earlier in **Léijiāng**, where you can find a room and arrange a motorbike (Y50) to take you up to the top early the next day. You can also reach Léijiāng on any buses bound for Dàhuà, Mǎshān or Liǎngjiāng from Wǔmíng or Nánníng.

A bus returns to Nánníng from Dàmíng Shān daily at 7.30am. There is sometimes a second bus on weekends.

ZUO JIANG SCENIC AREA
左江风景区

A boat trip down Left River (Zuǒ Jiāng) to the **Zuo Jiang Scenic Area** (Zuǒjiāng Fēngjǐngqū) around 190km southwest of Nánníng will take you through karst rock formations and offer glimpses of rock paintings.

The largest of 80 groups of paintings is in the area of **Huā Shān Bìhuà** (花山壁画; Flower Mountain; admission Y20), about three hours further south from the scenic area by boat. Here, a fresco 170m high and 90m across depicts some 2000 figures of hunters, farmers and animals. It is now believed that the Luoyue, ancestors of the Zhuang minority, painted these cliffs around 2000 years ago.

Halfway to the site is the cheerful village of **Pānlóng** (攀龙) and behind it, the rough, explorable **Longrui Nature Reserve** (陇瑞自然保护区; Lóngruì Zìrán Bǎohùqū; admission Y10). The reserve is the only known home of the rare

báitóu yèhóu (white leaf monkey). Hiking possibilities here are endless.

The low-key tourist resort of **Hua Shan Ethnic Culture Village** (花山民族山寨度假村; Huāshān Mínzú Shānzhài Dùjiàcūn; ☎ 862 8195; d 160-288, tr 160) is behind Pānlóng, and has decent rooms in Dong-style cabins. Guides can be arranged.

Catch a morning Píngxiáng train (or bus) from Nánníng as far as Níngmíng. Tour operators in Níngmíng are unmissable. They offer boat trips that vary from Y150 to Y200 depending on how many people they get. Expect to negotiate extra if you want to stop overnight in Pānlóng. A new road runs along the river from Níngmíng to Pānlóng; a ride in a taxi (Y30) takes about 20 minutes.

PÍNGXIÁNG 凭祥
☎ 0771 / pop 100,000

The staging post for onward travel to Vietnam, Píngxiáng is a trading town rife with markets and a sheen of sleaze but not much else. Some travellers, as they enter China, have had their Lonely Planet *China* guides confiscated by officials. We recommend you copy any essential details before crossing and put a cover on your guide.

Hotels around the bus and train stations have everything from battered doubles for Y50 to adequate midrange doubles for Y198, but there is no real need to stay. By early morning bus or train from Nánníng, you'll reach Píngxiáng by noon at the latest. Minibuses and private vehicles run to Friendship Pass (Yǒuyì Guān) from near the bus and train stations and costs Y5 to Y20, depending on the number of passengers. From Friendship Pass it's another 600m to the Vietnamese border post. Onward transport to Hanoi by train or bus is via the Vietnamese town of Lang Son (Liàngshān), 18km from the Friendship Pass. Note that Vietnam is one hour behind China; at the time of writing the border post was open till 7pm Vietnam time.

DETIAN WATERFALL 德天瀑布

Located at the 53rd boundary marker between China and Vietnam, most of the earth-shaking **Detian Waterfall** (Détiān Pùbù; admission Y30) is on the Chinese side. The cascade drops only 40m, but makes up for it by its more than modest breadth. It has a nice 'translational vibe' thanks to the tourists and the Vietnamese-Chinese hawkers camped out from dawn to dusk. July is the best time to visit, although water levels will be fairly high from May to late September. While wandering around, be particularly careful that you don't accidentally cross the border into Vietnam – it's no laughing matter for border officials.

Sleeping & Eating
There are a couple of **guesthouses** and a **restaurant** (☎ 377 3570) with a fantastic view. If you want to stay here, be sure to book with its Nánníng office for a discounted rate (☎ 362 7088). If you just turn up at the door, twins/quads cost Y450/680. If you get stuck in half-way-point Shuòlóng, there are a few grubby **guesthouses** at the main intersection.

Getting There & Away
From Nánníng one infrequent direct bus to the falls leaves at or around 8.30am (Y98, 4 hours), but generally only during high season. Otherwise, from Nánníng or Píngxiáng, you will need to first head to Dàxīn (Y40, 3 hours). From Dàxīn, hop on a bus heading to Xiàléi and get off in Shuòlóng (Y8, 1½ hours). In Shuòlóng, catch a rattletrap minibus or motorbike taxi through some lovely scenery for the final 14km (Y5). Leaving the falls, get back to Shuòlóng before late afternoon, as there isn't much movement on the main road in any direction after that. From Shuòlóng semiregular services run towards Dàxīn and Nánníng.

If you're heading for Jìngxī, either wait for a proper bus or leap-frog villages. First take a minibus (Y4) to Xiàléi, and then get another minibus (Y5) to Húrùn (pronounced Fúyuàn in these parts), from where you can get a 'proper' bus for the hour-long ride to Jìngxī. All up, the trip should take around two to three hours, and you may enjoy a fun ride with farmers and their pigs!

Jìngxī is a friendly town and home to the Jiuzhou Pagoda and some cheap places to stay. From Jìngxī, take one of many buses to Bǎisè, the largest city in northwest Guǎngxī. The interesting **Baise Uprising Museum** (粤东会馆; Yuèdōng Huìguǎn) traces every movement of Deng Xiaoping and the Seventh Red Army during the 1920s and 1930s. From Bǎisè it's easy to head into Guìzhōu or Yúnnán via Xīngyì.

BĚIHǍI 北海
☎ 0779 / pop 560,000
No time for the beaches of Hǎinán? Head directly here, your next-best alternative. This friendly, tree-lined port community, 229km

south of Nánníng, is the launching point for a ferry to Hǎinán but also has its own famed Silver Beach. More then 2000 years old, the city was once a major node on the ancient marine Silk Road – the harbour area retains lovely old buildings. Pearl production later cemented its reputation. Thousands of Chinese-Vietnamese refugees landed here after the 1979 Sino-Viet conflict – look for evidence of the Vietnamese community around the harbour.

Orientation & Information
The northern coast is home to the bus terminal, shops and most lodging options. The southern strip has the new International Ferry Terminal, hotels and that famous stretch of white sand.

Walking east from the main bus station along Beibuwan Lu, you'll pass by any number of **internet cafés** (网吧; wǎngbā; per hr Y2). The **Bank of China** (中国银行; Zhōngguó Yínháng; Beihai Dado; ☎ 8am-noon & 2.30-5.30pm Mon-Fri) lies between Guizhou Lu and Sichuan Lu; an ATM is here.

Activities
Silver Beach (Yíntān), a sleepy, 1.6km stretch of sparkling white sand, is the reason people come to Běihǎi. It has few crowds, a pleasant boardwalk and palms rustling in the breeze. It's not as exciting as Hǎinán but it's numbingly pleasant for sure.

The beach is about 10km southeast from downtown Běihǎi. To get here, walk west from the bus station, bear right at Woping Lu, which branches off behind the Běihǎi Yíngbīnguǎn, and catch bus 3 at the corner of Jiefang Lu (Y2, 20 minutes). A taxi costs Y20 to Y25.

There are showers and lockers available just off the boardwalk (Y10 each).

Sleeping
Tons of accommodation choices are available close to the beach. Budget offerings in this area are pretty bleak and often charge ludicrously high prices.

Táoyuán Dàjiǔdiàn (桃园大酒店; ☎ 202 0919; s/d Y180/200; 🕸) Squat toilets sit diagonally in the middle of bathrooms. Chinese wood carvings, imitation Greek sculptures and faux Van Gogh paintings pack the halls. This is budget kitsch at its best. Follow the signs down a lane across from the main bus station. Expect rooms to cost Y70/80 during off-peak season.

Liánggǎng Dàjiǔdiàn (良港大酒店; ☎ 208 6666; 10 Beibuwan Donglu; 北部湾东路10号; d from Y328; 🖳) The walls and halls look like they've taken a battering but the rooms are bright and clean, fixed up with blonde wood floors and yellow bedspreads. Outside the summer months you'll rarely pay more than Y190 for a standard room. Located about 500m east of the main bus station.

Beach Hotel (海滩大酒店; Hǎitān Dàjiǔdiàn; ☎ 388 8888; bhht@bh.gx.cninfo.net; Silver Beach Blvd; 银滩大道; s/d from Y580; 🖳) The beach's best option. Sea-view rooms are comfy, decorated in white and royal blue and have charming little balconies. Sea-view rooms start at Y580 and go up Y50 each floor. You should be able to nab good discounts here outside the summer months.

Shangri-la Hotel (香格里拉饭店; ☎ 206 2288; www.shangri-la.com; 33 Chating Lu; 茶亭路33号; d Y840–1050; 🖳 🖳) Bĕihǎi's most luxurious spot, this hotel is out of the way but has top-notch service and frequent discount rates including perks such as complimentary meals and 6pm checkout. The food here is spectacular and the harbour-view doubles are an absolute treat.

Eating

The place for fun, great photos ops as well as Bĕihǎi's most interesting food is **Wàishā Dǎo** (外沙岛), an islandesque spit of land filled with boisterous restaurants. You can gorge yourself on seafood for anywhere from Y10 to more than Y100 per person here.

Another place to check out sea critters is the nearby **seafood market** (shuǐchǎn shìchǎng; 水产市场). Take bus 2 or 8 here from the main bus station.

Getting There & Away

There is a helpful **ticket office** (☎ 202 8618; ⏲ 8am–10pm) on the ground floor of the Shangri-la Hotel selling boat, bus, train and plane tickets. There are also many other travel agencies around town.

AIR

Flights leave throughout the week between Bĕihǎi and Bĕijīng (Y1930), Guǎngzhōu (Y760) and Hǎikǒu (Y380).

BOAT

The **International Ferry Terminal** (Guójì Kèyùn Mǎtou) serves Hǎikǒu on Hǎinán and the nearby island of Wéizhōu. Boats for the 11-hour journey to Hǎikǒu leave once daily (6pm). Tickets cost from Y90 for a seat to Y230 for a cabin, and can be bought at the terminal or just north of Beibuwan Zhonglu on Sichuan Lu; buy your ticket and await your shuttle bus.

BUS

Express buses connect Bĕihǎi with Dōngxīng (Y45, three hours), Guǎngzhōu (Y180, 9½ hours), Guilín (Y160, seven hours), Liǔzhōu (Y115, five hours) and Nánníng (Y55 to Y73, 2½ hours). There's another bus terminal on Guangdong Lu, about 15 minutes by foot northeast of the main bus station, but it won't be of use to most travellers unless you can't find what you're looking for at the main station.

TRAIN

Train 820 departs Bĕihǎi at 8.46am for Nánníng (three hours), from where you can connect to points beyond.

Getting Around

TO/FROM THE AIRPORT

Comfortable buses meet planes at the airport, 21km north of town (Y10, 30 minutes). A taxi should cost about Y50.

BUS

Most of Bĕihǎi's buses congregate on Jiefang Lu, north of Zhongshan Park. Here you can catch bus 3 to Silver Beach and bus 2 west to the ferry docks and seafood market. Local buses cost Y2.

GUÌPÍNG 桂平

☎ 0775 / pop 151,341

This grey mess of a town is wildly friendly to the point of being surreal. (Where else in China do baton-swinging cops pepper visitors with 'Hello! How do you do? Welcome to Guìpíng!' before running off in giggles to their patrol cars?!) Perhaps there's something in the famous Xī Shān tea.

As for the town's more formal sights, Guìpíng is known for its gorgeous **Xi Shan Park** (西山公园; Xī Shān Gōngyuán; admission Y33; ⏲ dawn to dusk), with a modest mountain climb of 880m. To get there, walk 15 to 20 minutes west of the public square along Renmin Xilu. The mountain's Xī Shān tea is famous all over China and there are shops selling it everywhere.

Only 20km northwest of town is **Dragon Pool National Forest and Park** (龙潭国家森林公园; Lóngtán Guójiā Sēnlín Gōngyuán; admission Y50), which gives you the opportunity to delve into the rustic wilderness of Guăngxī's only remaining old-growth forest.

Direct transport to Dragon Pool Park doesn't exist. From Guìpíng, get the bus to Jīntiáncūn (Y2) and ask the driver to drop you off at the Dragon Pool Park access road (Longtan Lukou). Motorcycle taxis waiting at the intersection will take you to the park for about Y30. A two-day trip with the **Forestry Department** (☎ 338 0413) in Guìpíng, including guide, food, transport and accommodation, is about Y200.

Just 25km north of Guìpíng, **Jīntiáncūn** (金田村) is the birthplace of Hong Xiuquan, the schoolteacher who declared himself a brother of Jesus Christ and eventually led an army of more than a million followers against the Qing dynasty in what came to be known as the Taiping Rebellion – one of the bloodiest civil wars in human history. A museum, **Qǐyì Jìniànguǎn** (起义纪念馆; admission Y20) now stands at the site of Hong's home. For more information on Hong, see p45.

To reach Jīntiáncūn from Guìpíng, take a minibus from the main square at the corner of Guigui Lu and Renmin Lu (Y4 to Y5, 40 minutes). Backtrack 500m from the bus drop-off in Jīntiáncūn to the motorcycle taxis, from where the museum is a further 4km. The last bus back to Guìpíng departs Jīntiáncūn around 6pm.

Sleeping

Chángtài Bīnguǎn (长泰宾馆; ☎ 336 9988; fax 336 9000; Renmin Zhonglu; 人民中路; s/d Y198/298, family ste Y568; 🔊) Though some rooms have lovely views of the Yujiang River, the rest, with their sad-looking bathrooms, don't really warrant the going room rate. Make sure you negotiate a substantial discount. This hotel is very proud of its top-floor revolving restaurant, and all the employees will be reminding you about it every chance they get.

Guìpíng Fàndiàn (桂平饭店; ☎ 336 9292; fax 299 6338; 7 Renmin Zhonglu; 人民中路7号; s & d Y220; 🔊) This hotel is tidy, friendly and has green astro-turf carpeting. Showerheads perch over squat toilets despite bathrooms being squash-court-sized. Likely the best budget accommodation in town, and certainly the oddest. Discounts can bring the room rate down to Y100.

Getting There & Away

From Guìpíng, express buses leave for Nánníng every three hours (Y70, four hours). There are four express buses to Wúzhōu (Y30, three hours) and one daily to Guăngzhōu at 1pm (Y110, six hours). If you want to get to Guìlín or Liǔzhōu, head to Guìgăng (Y18) and change buses there.

WÚZHŌU 梧州

☎ 0774 / pop 330,000

Travellers will only hit Wúzhōu on the way to somewhere else, but it is still quite charming in its own right and it's worth an afternoon or day getting to know it.

In 1897, the British arrived at this busy trading town and set up steamer services to Guăngzhōu, Hong Kong and later Nánníng. European architecture left over from this period still looms over crowded back lanes making for some interesting walks around town.

Recently, big money has gone into developing the riverfronts, resulting in boardwalks, plaques and public art depicting everything from historical to space-age events.

Orientation

Situated at the confluence of Gui River (Guì Jiāng) and Xun River (Xún Jiāng), the city is effectively divided in two, with the modern and developed Héxī west of the river and the more interesting Dōnghé on the east bank.

Good maps of the city with bus routes (though not in English) are available at the shops inside both bus stations.

Information

Bank of China (Zhōngguó Yínháng) South of the park, on the corner of Zhongshan Lu.

Internet café (wǎngbā; Wenhua Lu; per hr Y1.80; ⏰ 24hrs) Located south of Zhongshan Park. The entrance is downstairs between the red Chinese lanterns.

Post & telephone office (Yóudiàn Dàlóu; Nanhuan Lu) East of Guìjiāng Yīqiáo.

Sights

SNAKE REPOSITORY 蛇园

Wúzhōu's **snake repository** (shé yuán) transports more than one million snakes to the kitchens of Hong Kong, Macau and other snake-devouring locales. At the time of research, the aging repository and the on-site snake restaurant were closed to the public for renovations, the schedule of which was still being hammered out. Before heading up,

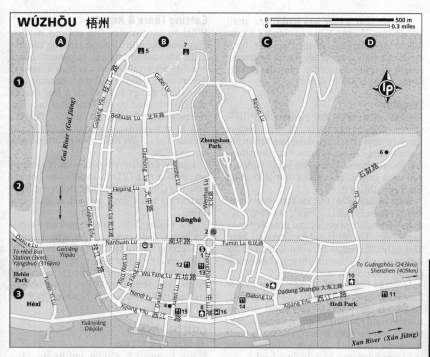

WÚZHŌU 梧州

check with your hotel to see if it has reopened. To get there walk along Shigu Lu for about 2km from the Wúzhōu Dàjiǔdiàn hotel.

WESTERN BAMBOO TEMPLE 西竹园
Bordering Zhongshan Park, **Western Bamboo Temple** (Xīzhú Yuán) overlooks the town and is home to around 40 Buddhist nuns. The temple's **vegetarian restaurant**, usually open for lunch on weekends, is highly recommended. The restaurant doesn't keep regular hours, but it seems the earlier you get there, the better. Entrance to the temple is free, but you should leave a donation of a few yuán after your visit.

To reach the temple from the city centre, continue straight up Wenhua Lu to the top end of Zhongshan Park. A pinyin sign will point you the rest of the way.

LÓNGMǓTÀI MIÀO 龙母太庙
Recently renovated, the multicoloured **Lóngmǔtài Miào** (Dragon Mother Temple; admission Y5; ⏰7.30am-5.30pm daily) was originally constructed during the Northern Song dynasty to honour the dragon mother of a mythical female

chieftain. A good time to visit is during the temple's main festival, held on the seventh and eighth days of the fifth lunar month and the 15th day of the eighth lunar month.

There's also a tiny **bird market** on Juren Lu between Xijiang Yilu and Nandi Lu (just follow the chirping). In nice weather, hundreds of bamboo cages filled with twittering songbirds spill out onto the sidewalks and the sound alone is just beautiful.

Sleeping

Jīnshān Jiŭdiàn (☎ 281 2080; Zhongshan Lu; 中山路; s/d from Y38/98, tr/q from Y88/138; 🛏) This budget stand-by opposite the Hedong bus station has a whole range of budget room combinations for you to choose from. Not spotless, but if you want convenience and a central location for cheap, this is it.

Wúzhōu Dàjiŭdiàn (☎ 204 8888; www.wzhotel .com.cn; 3 Xijiang Erlu; 西江二路3号; d Y230-430; 🛏) A very friendly option located near the Snake Repository. Go for the cheaper rooms here. The only differences between them and the deluxe rooms are that the cheapies have worse carpets and no teapot.

Lóngmén Jiŭdiàn (☎ 202 0066; fax 203 8880; 64 Dadongshang Lu; 大东上路64号; s/d Y280/318; 🛏) Low-midrange prices for way-above-average rooms could give the more expensive digs in town a run for their money. Old bedspreads and some mouldy bathroom fixtures are the only reminders you're in budget-land.

Eating & Drinking

Development has seen the north banks of the Xun River packed with restaurants and bars of all types. It hasn't quite taken off yet, and feels more Disneyland than Wúzhōu but there is plenty of delicious seafood on offer and it's worth a stroll to see what interesting places may have opened up. Head to the eastern end of Hedi Park.

For local flavours with a more laid-back atmosphere, try the small, popular **street restaurant** on the corner of Juren Lu and Xijiang Yilu.

For self-caterers, there are plenty of **fresh produce markets** along the backstreets.

This huge building may look unoccupied, but head to the 6th floor and you'll find a delightfully kitschy restaurant-like food court, **Jīchē Jīnlóng** (cnr Guo Zhongshan Lu & Wufang Lu; 🕙 11am-10pm), that serves up Chinese-Western dishes. The décor matches the menu. Wait staff dressed in minority costumes greet you when you come up the escalator and whisk you past Harley-Davidson memorabilia on the way to your table.

Getting There & Away

Wúzhōu has two new bus stations so slick they look like miniairports: Hédōng and the main bus station in Héxī. In general, buses heading for smaller and closer destinations depart from Hédōng and those heading further afield depart from Héxī. A free shuttle bus (for ticketed passengers) runs between the two stations every 40 minutes. Buses 2 and 12 also connect the stations (Y1.50, 20 minutes) or, if you're in a hurry, a taxi costs around Y20.

From Wúzhōu to Yángshuò expect a bumpy seven-hour ride (Y110), and it's another 1½ hours to Guìlín (Y110). Buses leave the Héxī station six times daily between 8.20am and 11pm.

For Guǎngzhōu, four expresses (Y105, 5½ hours) daily and more numerous slower buses cover the route (Y60 to Y70, six hours). There are also regular express bus connections throughout the day for Liǔzhōu (Y110, seven hours) and Shēnzhèn (Y160, seven hours), and every half-hour for Nánníng (Y90 to Y110, six hours).

GUÌLÍN 桂林

☎ 0773 / pop 670,000

When it comes to Guìlín and its stunning karst topography, there's good news and there's bad news.

The good news is the beauty of this scenic city, celebrated for generations by poets and painters, more than lives up to its reputation. If you can handle the hectic traffic, most of Guìlín's peaks and parks are a short bicycle ride away and Li River (Lí Jiāng) cruises take in some of the province's most breathtaking scenery.

The bad news is that rapid economic growth and a booming tourist trade have made it a challenge to enjoy Guìlín's charms.

Tourist sights levy heavy entry fees and many travellers tell of being grossly overcharged at restaurants. Touts (some persistent) appear at every turn, with many taxi drivers now aggressively in on the game (opposite). Humid days create an opaque haze, obscuring even the closer peaks.

Orientation

Most of Guìlín lies on the west bank of Li River. The main artery is Zhongshan Lu, which runs roughly parallel to the river, on its western side. At the southern end (Zhongshan Nanlu) is Guìlín's train station. Zhong-shan Zhonglu is a rapidly gentrifying stretch of tourist-class hotels, shops and expensive restaurants.

Closer to the centre of town, northeast of the lakes of Róng Hú and Shān Hú, is Guìlín's new Central Square (Zhōngxīn Guǎngchǎng) and the main shopping and eating district. Further along Zhongshan Beilu is the city's main commercial area.

Heading east on Jiefang Donglu and crossing over Liberation Bridge, will bring you to the large Qixing Park, one of the town's chief attractions.

MAPS

Several good maps are for sale around the city but these are in Chinese only. The *Tour & Communication Map of Guilin* (Y5) is decent and has some English.

Information

Bank of China (Zhōngguó Yínháng) Branches near the train station and on Yinding and Zhongshan Lu change money and travellers cheques, give credit-card advances and have ATMs.

CD Burning (Wángchéng Bǎihuò; Jiefang Donglu) Many of the computer kiosks on the 4th floor of this department store burn CDs for Y20 per disk.

CITS (Zhōngguó Guójì Lǚxíngshè; ☎ 286 1623; www .guilintrav.com; 41 Binjiang Lu) Reasonably helpful staff offer tours, including day-long city tours (Y400) and a full-day Li River tour (Y450).

Daofeng Bookshop (Dàofēng Shūdiàn; 18 Binjiang Lu; 9am-10.30pm) Books, movies and music are displayed alongside a small café in a store flooded with natural light. There are a few English titles and a good selection of maps in the travel section.

Internet cafés (wǎngbā; per hr Y2) There are dozens in the alleys near the Jīnfēng Bīnguǎn.

Post office (yóujú) On the north corner of the large square in front of the train station. Several smaller offices are north along Zhongshan Lu.

Public Security Bureau (PSB; Gōngānjú; ☎ 582 9930; 8.30am-noon & 3-6pm Mon-Fri) On the east side of Li River, south of Longyin Lu. Offers visa extensions.

Tourist booths dot the city but getting the staff off MSN messenger can be next to impossible at some. The city's website www.guilin.com.cn is outstanding for information.

Dangers & Annoyances

Taxi drivers can be among the most aggressive touts in the city. Travellers often arrive in Guìlín only to have the cabbie tell them there's a huge conference in town and the

hotel they're booked in or the sight they want to visit is full/bad/dangerous/too expensive. These drivers will get a big commission for taking you elsewhere and they can be relentless.

Don't accept any short detours 'just to look' or get drawn into conversations about your accommodation or visiting plans. Pretending you can't understand a word they're saying, getting out your map and looking like you mean business is usually the best strategy.

Several travellers wanting Li River cruises have reported feeling ripped off by guides using fake CITS business cards and trying to pass themselves (and their friends' creaky boats) off as the real thing. Ask at your accommodation or an official CITS office to make sure you're getting what you want.

Sights

SOLITARY BEAUTY PEAK 独秀峰
This 152m **pinnacle** (Dúxiù Fēng; admission Y15) is just north of the centre of town. The climb to the top is steep, but worth the effort for the splendid vistas.

At the foot of the peak is the 14th-century **Wáng Chéng**, a palace built by the nephew of a Ming emperor. The restored walls and gates of the palace surround the peak. You can reach the peak by bus 1 or 2 from Guìlín's train station.

FÚBŌ SHĀN 伏波山
Close to Solitary Beauty Peak, **Fúbō Shān** (Wave-Subduing Hill; admission Y15) offers equally good views.

On the hill's southern slope is **Returned Pearl Cave** (Huánzhū Dòng). A 1000-year-old Buddha image is etched into the cave wall, along with more than 200 other images of the Buddha, most dating from the Song and Tang dynasties. Somewhere, too, is a portrait and autograph by Mi Fu, a famous calligrapher of the Song dynasty.

Thousand Buddha Cave (Qiānfó Yán) is nearby. The name's an exaggeration – a couple of dozen statues at most date from the Tang and Song dynasties.

Bus 2 from the train station runs past the hill.

OTHER HILLS
North of Solitary Beauty Peak is **Diécǎi Shān** (Folded Brocade Hill; admission Y20). Climb the stone pathway that takes you through the

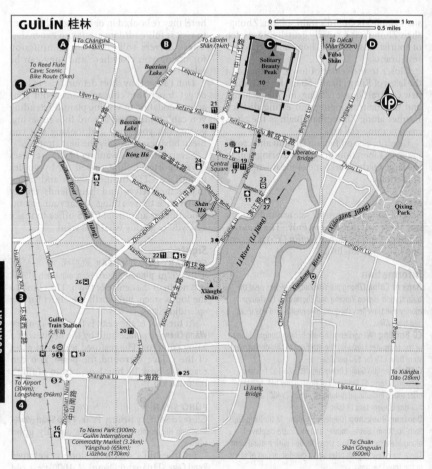

GUÌLÍN 桂林

GUÅNGXĪ

cooling relief of Wind Cave, with walls decked with inscriptions and Buddhist sculptures. The hill climb can be skirted by taking bus 1 or 2.

From Fúbō Shān there's a good view of **Lǎorén Shān** (Old Man Hill), a curiously shaped hill, from the centre of town 2km to the northwest. The best way to get there is by bicycle, as buses don't go past it. At the southern end of town, one of Guìlín's best-known sights is **Xiàngbí Shān** (Elephant Trunk Hill; admission Y25), which actually does resemble an elephant dipping its snout into Li River. The best way to see it is by bamboo raft (usually Y3 per person, 40 minutes) as the park itself is underwhelming. You can find the punters by Liberation Bridge.

QĪXĪNG GŌNGYUÁN 七星公园

If you only have the time (or the desire) to visit one thing in Guìlín, this is the best choice. One of China's most picturesque city parks, with wending trails and lovely picnicking, **Seven Star Park** (Qīxīng Gōngyuán; park/cave admission Y35/30; ☼ park 7am-10pm, cave 8am-5.30pm) is on the eastern side of Li River and covers 137 hectares (the seven peaks resemble the Big Dipper constellation). The park was one of the original tourist spots in southwest China, and first opened to sightseers during the Sui dynasty (AD 581–618). The park's two highlights are **Seven Star Cave** (Qīxīng Yán), a capacious chamber filled with bizarre stalactites and stalagmites coloured by floodlights, and **Dark Dragon Cave** (Lóngyīn Dòng), with inscribed stelae dating back more than 1500 years.

To reach the park, walk across Liberation Bridge or catch bus 10 or 11 (Y1 to Y2) from the train station. From the park, bus 13 (Y1 to Y2) runs across Liberation Bridge, past Fúbō Shān and across to Reed Flute Cave.

REED FLUTE CAVE 芦笛岩

Some of the most extraordinary scenery Guìlín has to offer – rock-concert lights blazing at stalactites – is underground at **Reed Flute Cave** (Lúdí Yán; admission Y60), 5km northwest of the city centre. At one time the entrance to the cave was distinguished by clumps of reeds used by the locals to make musical instruments, hence the name.

Inside, the Crystal Palace of the Dragon King alone can hold about 1000 people, although many more crammed in during WWII when the cave was used as an air-raid shelter. Despite the high entrance price, the cave is worth visiting.

Take bus 3 (Y1.50) from the train station or Zhongshan Zhonglu to the last stop. Otherwise, it's a pleasant bicycle ride. Follow Lijun Lu, which runs into Xishan Lu and then Taohua Jiang Lu. The latter parallels the small Taohua River (Táohuā Jiāng), and winds through fields and karst peaks. At Ludi Lu turn left and continue for another 1.2km back to Zhongshan Beilu.

RÓNG HÚ & SHĀN HÚ 榕湖, 衫湖

There are two lakes near the city centre, **Róng Hú** on the western side of Zhongshan Zhonglu and **Shān Hú** on the eastern side. Róng Hú is named after an 800-year-old banyan tree on its shore. The tree stands by the restored **South**

City Gate (Nán Mén) originally built during the Tang dynasty. It's gorgeous here at night and everything from the bridges to the trees is tastefully lit.

Tours

There's no shortage of tour operators offering half- or full-day tours of Guìlín's major sights usually outside the bus and train stations, and along Binjiang Lu. Be rigorous in asking questions about what you are getting.

Sleeping

BUDGET

Guilin Flowers Youth Hostel (Huāmén Lǒu; ☎ 383 9625; Block 2, 6 Shangzhi Lane, Zhongshan Nanlu; 中山南路, 尚智巷6号2栋; dm Y40, s/d without bathroom Y50/Y90; ⌘ 🖵) Some travellers find the steep prices a turn-off, but this is a lovely hostel with a bright, cosy common area and staff that go out of their way for guests. Facing the Plaza Hotel, go left and follow the hot pink 'Flowers' signs into the lanes. Locals often point confused-looking foreigners the rest of the way without even being asked.

Backstreet Youth Hostel (Hòujiē Qīngnián Lǚshè; ☎ 281 9936; 3 Renmin Lu; 人民路3号; dm Y40; ⌘ 🖵 🖵) This is another terrific, newly opened hostel in a fantastic central location. In general, rooms are bigger and fresher that what you'll find at Guilin Flowers Youth Hostel, though staff at Flowers are generally more helpful. There's also a good selection of hotel-quality singles and doubles.

Overseas Chinese Hotel (Huáqiáo Dàshà; ☎ 383 2055; fax 382 0290; 13 Zhongshan Nanlu; 中山南路13号; dm Y60, standard d Y280-350; ⌘) This hotel is a little inconveniently located, but its clean, unmemorable rooms are an old backpackers' stand-by and you should keep the address on hand in case Flowers Youth Hostel is full and you need accommodation near the buses and trains.

MIDRANGE

Meĭdōu Fàndiàn (☎ 283 8268; fax 288 6698; 17 Nanhuan Lu; 南环路17号; s/d/'spouse room' Y158/198/218; 🔲) Wooden floors and wall lights make the halls cosy and welcoming, though not much thought has gone into the rooms' wilted linens. But the riverside location and discounts of up to 66% make any room here a steal.

Jìnfēng Bīnguǎn (☎ 288 2793; lane off Yiren Lu; 依仁路近的; s/d Y388/488; 🔲) Down a bustling alley off Central Square; dark, dire halls hide enormous midrange rooms. You couldn't ask for a better location, and there's food stalls, cafés and restaurants right at your doorstep. Expect up to 60% discounts off the rack rates.

TOP END

Bravo Hotel (Guìlín Bīnguǎn; ☎ 282 3950; www.glbravo .com; 14 Ronghu Nanlu; 榕湖南路14号; r from Y918; ⊠ 🔲 🔲 🔲) Arguably one of Guìlín's best, this hotel has marble in the bathrooms and good food available in the hotel's Chinese, Japanese and Western restaurants. Check river-view rooms out before handing over your money, a few of them do face the Li River, but trees growing on the river's banks obstruct the view.

Eating

Guìlín is noted for its snake soup, wild cat or bamboo rat, washed down with snake-bile wine. You could be devouring some of these animals into extinction, and we don't recommend that you do. The pangolin (a sort of armadillo) is a protected species but still crops up on restaurant menus. Other protected species include the muntjac (Asian deer), horned pheasant, miniturtle, short-tailed monkey and gem-faced civet.

Mostly you'll find an infinite variety of *guìlín mǐfěn* (Guìlín rice noodles; 桂林米粉), generally eaten for breakfast and snacks. Strictly guarded recipes vary greatly from chef to chef; you'll find some not unlike Phad Thai, and others smacking of a horse-meat stew!

A Qing dynasty speciality, white fermented bean curd, is often used to make a dipping sauce for roast pork or chicken. Sanhua wine, actually more like mellow rice firewater, is a favourite local drink, as is local oil tea (though it's quite salty, with flecks of rice in it).

You'll find a good variety of eateries including buffet-style cafeterias, standard restaurants, trendy cafés and small hole-in-the-wall restaurants just north of Central Square along Yiren Lu.

Shíjì Mǐfěn (Jiefang Xilu; dishes from Y4) It sure doesn't look like much on the outside but locals flock here to scarf down the city's most famous dish for cheap. Staff are a bit brusque but they treat regulars the same way. You'll see two hole-in-the-wall stalls to the west of the China Telecom building. This restaurant is the one on the right.

Guìlín Rén (Yiren Lu; from Y5) Come here on a warm night and you'll hear the buzz from around the corner. A popular institution that's done up like a big, sleek fast-food operation, locals come here for all the usual Guìlín specialties as well as beef dishes like *gālí niúròu* (咖喱牛肉; curried beef).

Yíyuán Fàndiàn (Nanhuan Lu; dishes from Y18; 🕙 11.30am-2.30pm & 5.30-9.30pm) This outstanding Sichuanese restaurant is a longtime favourite with great food and great atmosphere (plants, dark wooden tables, friendly servers). There's an English menu. Try the stir-fried eel with dried chilli and Sichuan spices (Y22).

Shèngfā Fàndiàn (Zishan Lu) A very popular place with locals who come here to eat *píjiǔyú* (啤酒鱼; beer fish; Y18), which is wok-fried on your table and usually knocked down with the local Liqun Beer. Noodles are added at the end to mop up the sauce.

Rosemary Café (Yiren Lu; pizza Y25; 🕙 10am-midnight) The best western food in the city. The menu has all the usual suspects but there are some interesting flourishes such as the barbecued peanut pizza. On the cocktail front, Rosemary has nailed the hot chocolate and brandy combo like no other Western restaurant in Yángshuò.

There are a number of **supermarkets** around town, the most convenient of which is located in the Nikodo Plaza basement.

Drinking & Entertainment

Club 100% Bǎidú (Binjiang Lu; 🕙 8pm-late) Very hip, very loud. This is the most popular club in town and is a great place to meet locals.

Lìjiāng Theatre (Líjiāng Júchǎng; Binjiang Lu; admission Y120/160/180; 🕙 8pm) A show full of acrobats music, dance and lights. Not as popular as the big Yángshuò show, but travellers are enthusiastic about it nonetheless.

Shopping

For jewellery, clothing, souvenirs as well as pretty much anything else you can think of, check out Guìlín's **night market**. It sets up every night at around 7pm on Zhongshan Zhonglu between Ronghu Beilu and San-duo Lu.

Getting There & Away

AIR

CAAC (☎ 384 7252; ⏰ 7.30am-8.30pm) is at the cor-ner of Shanghai Lu and Minzhu Lu. You'll find **Dragonair** (☎ 282 5588, ext 8895) in the Bravo Hotel.

Guìlín is supremely well connected to the rest of China (and beyond) by air. Desti-nations include Běijīng (Y1920), Chéngdū (Y1100), Chóngqìng (Y860), Hǎikǒu (Y840), Guǎngzhōu (Y790), Guìyáng (Y710), Hong Kong (Y1895), Kūnmíng (Y970), Shànghǎi (Y1430) and Xī'ān (Y1220). Seats *may* be available for next-day purchase; shop around travel agents for discounted tickets.

International destinations include regu-lar flights to Seoul (Hànchéng) and Fukoka, Japan (Fúgāng). Less frequent flights also go to Bangkok, Singapore and Kuala Lumpur; more and more international flights are being added.

BUS

For short local runs such as Yángshuò (Y10, one hour) and Xīng'ān (Y8 to Y12, two hours), buses depart from in front of the train station as well as from the main bus station.

Guìlín's **bus station** (Zhongshan Nanlu) is north of the train station. Hourly buses run to Lóng-shèng (Y22, 1½ hours). There are several buses to Sānjiāng (Y39, five hours) between 6am and 7.30pm. Expresses to Quánzhōu leave every hour (Y10, one hour). Frequent buses also leave for Nánníng (Y80 to Y110, four to 4½ hours) every 15 minutes.

To Guǎngzhōu and Shēnzhèn, express and sleeper buses are available, however, the ex-presses are usually more reliable and smoother. Express buses head for Guǎngzhōu six times daily (Y100, nine hours) and to Shēnzhèn at 8pm and 9.30pm (Y220, 10 hours). Buses for Wúzhōu leave five times daily (Y110, eight hours).

TRAIN

Guìlín is not as convenient as Nánníng for train connections (not much starts here) and tickets are harder to come by. Outside national holidays, you might be lucky, but be prepared to wait an extra day or two for hard-sleeper tickets.

Direct train services include train T6 to Běijīng (3.06pm, hard sleeper Y449, 22 hours), K36/7 to Guǎngzhōu (6pm, Y229, 11 hours), K198 to Shànghǎi (2.08pm, Y400, 25 hours) and train K316 to Xī'ān (5.25pm, Y356, 25 hours). For Chóngqìng and Chéngdū, change trains at Guìyáng (or start in Nánníng).

To Kūnmíng, train 2055 departs at 8.52am and takes 22 hours (Y237); this is the only train that starts here, and the others can be tough to land tickets for. Consider a worth-while trip to Nánníng to hop on the direct Nánkūn line (15 hours).

Getting Around

TO/FROM THE AIRPORT

Guìlín's international airport is 30km west of the city. Buses run from **CAAC** (cnr Shanghai Lu & Minzhu Lu) to the airport for Y20, leaving half-hourly from 6.30am to 8.30pm. A taxi to the airport costs about Y90 (40 minutes).

BICYCLE

One of the best ways to get around Guìlín is by bicycle. There are plenty of bicycle-hire shops. You'll find some near the bus and train stations, and one next to the Overseas Chinese Hotel on Zhonghan Nanlu. Most charge Y10 to Y20 per day and require Y200 or your passport as security. Try to avoid handing over your passport.

BUS

Bus 58 is a tourist freebie (anything that be-gins with '5' should be free) that runs to many local sights, including Xiàngbí Shān, Qīxīng Gōngyuán and Reed Flute Cave.

Otherwise, most of the city buses that stop in front of Guìlín's bus and train stations will get you to the major sights, but a bicycle is definitely better, especially in the searing sum-mer heat. Bus 2 runs from the train station through town, passing Xiàngbí Shān, Libera-tion Bridge, Fúbō Shān and Diécǎi Shān. Bus 15 runs a circuit from the train station to the city's main tourist highlights. Local buses cost between Y1 and Y1.50.

TAXI

Flag falls start at Y7. Motorcycle taxis charge only Y5 per trip.

AROUND GUÌLÍN
Ling Canal 灵渠

Built from 219 to 214 BC to transport sup-plies to the armies of the first Qin emperor, **Ling Canal** (Líng Qú) is considered to be one of the three great feats of Chinese engineer-ing (the others being the Great Wall and the Du River irrigation system in Sìchuān). The 34km canal links Xiang River (Xiāng Hé), which flows into the Yangzi River (Cháng Jiāng), and Li River, which flows into the Zhu River (Zhū Jiāng), thus connecting two of China's major waterways.

Two branches of the canal flow through the market town of **Xīng'ān** (兴安), one at the northern end and one at the southern end.

The canal is in Xīng'ān County, about 70km north of Guìlín. From Guìlín, there are buses for Xīng'ān every half-hour until 6.30pm (Y8 to Y12, two hours) and hourly express buses to Quánzhōu (Y10, one hour).

Li River 漓江

Li River (Lí Jiāng) runs between Guìlín and Yángshuò; a phenomenally popular trip is the **boat ride** from Guìlín to Yángshuò. The price – which comes in at around Y500, includes lunch and the bus trip back to Guìlín from Yángshuò – does hurt. Joining a Chinese tour group lets you pay a nominal Y325 for the same service, though it's conducted *sans* English.

Boats (Y450) depart from Guìlín's tourist wharf opposite the Golden Elephant hotel (see Map p652) each morning at around 8am, although you have to take a shuttle bus to Zhújiāng or Mópánshān wharf downriver when the water level is low. The ticket office is nearby, or you can book through many hotels. The trip lasts all day.

YÁNGSHUÒ 阳朔
☎ 0773 / pop 300,000

Pedalling across the rice fields through Yángshuò's soaring limestone peaks is often the top experience of travellers in China. If you're like most, you'll come to Yángshuò for a couple of days after the Li River cruise but end up staying far longer.

Yángshuò is more of an international back-packing colony than a Chinese village but it's an ideal base from which to explore the coun-tryside. It certainly beats Guìlín for the unri-valled opportunity to soak up local flavours on the cheap. The activities and day trips from here could easily fill up a week or more.

Orientation

You'll probably only need to know two streets in Yángshuò. The first, Pantao Lu, forms the southwest perimeter of Yángshuò and is the main artery to and from Guìlín. The second, Xi Jie, is known as 'Foreigner Street'. It runs northeast to the Li River, and is lined with cafés, hotels and tourist shops. The further you go from Xi Jie or Pantao Lu at its intersection with Xi Jie, the closer you get to Chinese group-tour reality. Xi Jie itself has been turned into a pedes-trian mall (relatively) free from pesky wheels.

MAPS

Good English-language street maps of Yángshuò are available throughout town for Y3 to Y5. Maps of the surrounding villages and countryside are generally pretty poor and in some cases seem downright random. But no matter. Half the adventure is trying to find your own way through the rice paddies!

Information
CD BURNING
Kodak Express Shop (Xi Jie) Y15 per CD.

INTERNET ACCESS 网吧
One of the best internet cafés (*wǎngbā*) in town is on Chengzhong Lu near the corner of Xi Jie, Y5 per hour. It's open round the clock and even has a nonsmoking room.

MEDICAL SERVICES
There are a number of traditional medical clin-ics on the northern side of Pantao Lu offering therapeutic massage, acupuncture and tradi-tional medicine. It is even possible to enrol in brief courses at some of these centres.
People's Hospital (Rénmín Yīyuàn) North of the main tourist centre, not far from the PSB.

MONEY
Bank of China (Zhōngguó Yínháng; Binjiang Lu; ⏰ 9am-5pm) Will change cash and travellers cheques, give credit card advances and receive wire transfers, although the latter can take up to 15 days. Other banks on Xi Jie also cash travellers cheques.

POST & TELEPHONE
Post office (yóujú; Pantao Lu; ⏰ 8am-5pm) Has Eng-lish-speaking staff and long-distance phone services.

PUBLIC SECURITY BUREAU
PSB (Gōngānjú; Chengbei Lu; ⏰ 24hr) This PSB is well versed in dealing with travellers and has several fluent

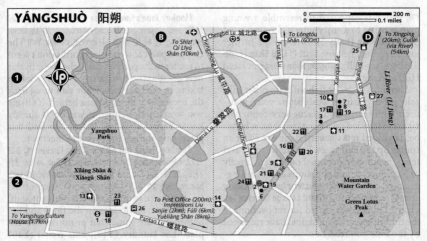

English speakers. That said, always be calm if complaining about a local business; losing your cool will get you nowhere. If you need a visa extension you'll have to head further afield as this office doesn't issue them.

TOURIST INFORMATION

This town is rife with travel agents. *Choose carefully.* Surfacing constantly are reports of aggressive agents not providing the service they sell. Flimsy bicycles for rent are the most chronic headache. Train tickets will never be easy unless you hike to Guìlín and do it yourself. Ask other travellers if anything dodgy has happened recently.

Dangers & Annoyances

While Yángshuò is relatively safe, it's important to keep your wits about you. Yuèliàng Shān (Moon Hill) has been particularly popular with muggers in recent years and some victims have been wounded with knifes.

The local PSB says all this is a thing of the past ('perfectly safe, even by yourself!') but it would still be wise not to stray off alone. Yángshuò is also the scene of many rip-offs, from hotel 'deposits' to dodgy tours.

Sights & Activities

People come to Yángshuò for the activities in the countryside but there's lots to keep you busy in town too. Established parks with trails dot the town.

In the southeastern corner of town is Yángshuò's main peak, **Green Lotus Peak** (Bìlián Fēng; admission Y30). It's also called Bronze Mirror Peak (Tóngjìng Fēng) because it has a flat northern face that is supposed to look like an ancient bronze mirror. The peak is next to Li River, in the **Mountain Water Garden** (Shān Shuǐ Yuán).

Yangshuo Park is in the western part of town, and here you'll find **Xīláng Shān** (Man Hill; admission

Y9), which is supposed to resemble a young man bowing to a shy young girl represented by **Xiǎogǔ Shān** (Lady Hill). There's a further jungle of hills nearby: **Shízǐ Qí Lǐyú Shān** (Lion Riding Carp Hill), **Lóngtóu Shān** (Dragon Head Hill) and the like.

Should you desire to hoof it up other hills solo, get advice from locals before you set off – there's no search and rescue service for foreigners stranded on a karst cliff face. A better bet is guided **rock climbing**; there are 75 or so routes up the cliff faces. For advice, gear and tours, neophyte climbers should head directly to Xianqian Jie and the shops and climbing-oriented cafés like **Karst Pizzeria** (www.karstclimber .com; 42 Xianqian Jie) and **Lizard Lounge** (Xianqian Jie). Lizard Lounge was closed for renovations at the time of research but should have reopened by the time you read this.

Cloud 9 Restaurant (cloud9restaurant03@yahoo.com; Chengzhong Lu) offers three-hour morning or afternoon cooking classes for Y80 a person. Each class starts off with a trip to the farmers' market for fresh ingredients.

A popular evening activity is to take part in one of the **cormorant fishing tours**. While it's entertaining, it's mainly a tourist attraction (the real thing lasts all night). However, in both cases, the river supports an ever-diminishing supply of fish. Tours begin around 7pm and last 40 minutes to one hour. Hotels and restaurants usually charge Y25 per person.

Sleeping

In peak periods, dirt-cheap beds along Xi Jie (or any bed for that matter) may be tough to find. However, new accommodation is opening all the time, so there's a good chance you'll be able to rustle up something in one of the back lanes or on less-touristed streets if you're in a pinch. Ask about weekly rates if you are planning to stay awhile. Credit cards are widely accepted, even at the cheapies.

BUDGET

On arrival you will no doubt be met by touts wielding business cards and photo albums of their abodes. Finding a clean dorm bed for Y10 or Y15 or a single/double with private bathroom for Y50 to Y100 is relatively easy outside summer weekends and holidays.

The most popular places to stay are on Xi Jie though with the late-night partying going on outside, rooms here can get noisy.

Monkey Jane's Guesthouse (Bēibāo Kèzhàn; ☎ 882 1603; monkeyjanesguesthouse@yahoo.com; 28 Lianfeng-zhongxiang; 连峰中巷28号; dm Y20, s/d from Y40) The chipped paint and cheerless dorms don't seem to matter to the party animals who swear by this new guesthouse. After a night on the rooftop taking in the river view while slamming back the brew's with Monkey Jane herself, it's likely you won't notice either. If you don't already know Yángshuò it will be hard to find this place, ring and ask the owner to meet you.

Bamboo House Inn & Café (Zhúlín Fàndiàn; ☎ 882 3222; bamboohouse23@hotmail.com; 23 Guihua Lu; 桂花路23号; dm Y20, s/d 50/60, with air-con Y60/70, with balcony Y80; ✿ 🖳) Down a small lane off Xi Jie, this place is quiet and has pleasant staff. Dorms have mattresses on the floor and the bathrooms are somewhat primitive but this place has laundry (Y12), bike rental (Y10) and free internet.

Yangshuo International Youth Hostel (Xījiē Guójì Qīngnián Lǚguǎn; ☎ 882 0933; hostel-ys@163.com; 102 Xi Jie; 西街102号; dm/tw/ste from Y25/80/200; ✿ 🖳) Very friendly and right in the thick of things, this YHA hostel gets great reviews from travellers for service, though earplugs are deemed essential given its location. The nine-bed dorms with desks and chairs are huge, as are the family suites. Check your room first, as some are quite musty. Bathrooms are clean, but be prepared for some monster rust caked on some of the drains and pipes.

Yangshuo Culture House (☎ 882 7750; www .yangshuo-study-travel.com; 110 Beisan Xiang, Chengxi Rd; 城西路北三巷110号; s & d Y60-80; ✿ 🖳) Run by Wei Xiao Geng and his family. A stay here could very well be one of the highlights of your trip. Rooms are bright and clean and three meals a day are included if you want them. Mr Wei can tell you absolutely anything about the region, and also offers taichi, calligraphy and Chinese lessons. It's located down a lane about 1.7km west of the bus station. You'll never find it on your own so call for a pick up. Reservations are recommended.

MIDRANGE

Most budget places also offer slightly cushier rooms for more money. A huge number of midrange places are located in town, most of them Chinese hotels found along Pantao Lu, west of Diecui Lu. All are decent, if unremarkable. The two mentioned here are very similar to each other but stand out from the rest of the crowd.

Morning Sun Hotel (Yángguāng Jiǔdiàn; ☎ 881 3899; www.morningsunhotel.com; 4 Chengzhong Lu; 城中路 4号; s/d/tr Y180/240/350, d with balcony Y280; ✷) Dark, hardwood flooring, well-chosen designs for amenities, and a relaxing atrium show that some thought went into the design of this place. Huge bathtubs in each room are what sets it apart from the Hotel Explorer.

Hotel Explorer (Wénhuà Fàndiàn; ☎ 882 8116; jimmyqin@hotmail.com; 40 Xianqian Lu; 县前路40号; s/d/tr with bathroom 368/418/548; ✷) Done up in ancient courtyard style with wood trims, sliding doors and indoor gardens, rooms here are spotless and have large modern bathrooms. Tucked down a side street, it's quiet despite being just seconds from Xi Jie. Outside holiday periods, expect discounts of around Y120.

TOP END

Paradise Yangshuo Resort Hotel (Yángshuò Bǎilèlái Dùjià Fàndiàn; ☎ 8222109; www.paradiseyangshuo.com; 116 Xi Jie; 西街116号; standard/deluxe d Y664/913; ✷ ✷) Standard rooms are immaculate, with wood floors and pristine furniture, but lack pizzazz. The deluxe rooms are another story with balconies, floor to ceiling windows, and if you nab a corner room, lots of light. The lobby is filled with pictures of US presidents to help the American tour groups feel at home. It's surrounded by lush green gardens.

New Century Hotel (Xīnshìjì Jiǔdiàn; ☎ 882 9819; fax 882 9809; beside Yangshuo Park; 阳朔公园旁; s/d Y680; ✷) Finally, some upscale rooms decorated with a little imagination. Rooms are done up in shades of plum, black and white and feature accents such as framed pictures and wooden elephant sculptures. Western buffet breakfast is available for Y35.

Eating & Drinking

Xi Jie is famous for its cafés offering Chinese-Western fusion cuisine as well as perennial travellers' favourites such as banana pancakes and pizza. Most cafés have mastered a couple of Western dishes but in general, the street's reputation for authentic fare far surpasses the often mediocre results. Many cafés also double as tourist information centres, show movies or host live music. However, Xi Jie is now so full of tour groups and pestering touts that the possibility of a quiet evening of dining alfresco is pretty much gone.

If you need a breather from Xi Jie, wander the labyrinth of back alleys and you'll discover many small markets and restaurants catering to locals and Chinese travellers.

Global Movie Café (cnr Xi Jie & Xianqian Jie; mains Y10-30; ☺ 9am-late) Films are shown every night at 7pm and 9pm on the 2nd floor. It's free as long as you buy a drink or snack. This is a great place to ask about Mandarin lessons or other interesting things that might be going on round town.

Dynasty of Dumplings (Xianqian Lu; 16 dumplings Y15; ☺ varies) Dumplings here range from veggie options to exotic lamb and melon combos. It also serves remarkable selection of local specialties like *píjiǔ yú* (beer fish; 啤酒 鱼) or *tiánwō jī* (hot snails in chicken soup; 田蜗鸡).

Meiyou Café (86 Xi Jie; mains Y10-40; ☺ 7.30am-1am) This café promises '*méi yǒu* bad service, *méi yǒu* warm beer' (*méi yǒu* means 'don't have'), and has delivered on this pledge seemingly forever.

Café Under the Moon (Yuèliàngxià Kāfēiguǎn; Xi Jie; mains Y15-30; ☺ 7am-1am) With blue and yellow linen, green plants and a cosy 2nd-floor balcony, this place has plenty of ambience. Service and food are only average but this place is usually packed nonetheless. The menu is good for entertainment value alone. Celery-apple-juice-chocolate-ice-cream milkshake, anyone?

Ming Yuan (Míng Yuàn Kāfēiguǎn; 50 Xi Jie; cappuccino Y20-37, sandwiches Y17; ☺ 9am-11pm) This tiny café serves the prettiest and most perfect coffee in town; rosettas top the cappuccinos, milk hearts deck out the lattes. With only a handful of tables, this is a quiet, calming place to while away the afternoon. Completely nonsmoking premises.

Le Vôtre Café (Lèdéfàshì Cāntīng; ☎ 882 8040; 79 Xi Jie; mains Y20-48; ☺ 9.30am-11pm) It doesn't always hit the mark with its French-inspired cuisine, but this place is worth a visit for the ginger tea and the huge, theatre-like dining room crammed with Buddha statues, Chinese wood carvings, Ming-style furniture and Mao portraits.

Farmers' Trading Market (Nóngmào Shìchǎng; Pan-tao Lu; ☺ 8am-8pm) Through an archway, this place is dark and atmospheric and is full of fishes, eels, chickens and rabbits. *Píjiǔyú* (啤 酒鱼; Y30 per kilogram) is Yángshuò's most famous dish and this may be the best and cheapest places to try it. Local Li River fish are cooked with chillies, spring onion, tomato, ginger and beer. A good winter alternative is *qīngshuǐyú huǒguō* (Li River catfish hotpot;

GUĂNGXĪ

清水鱼火锅). For the more adventurous, there is also *lǎoshǔgān* (fried dried rat with chillies and garlic; 老鼠干; Y20) or *sōngshǔgān* (fried squirrel; 松鼠干; Y20). Besides the food, this market is worth a visit for the people watching and photo opportunities alone.

A massive **night market** starts up after 6pm across from the bus station. The market has tents, tables and chairs, so you can settle in for a sampling of local delicacies like *tiánluóniàng* (stuffed field snails; 田螺酿) whatever the weather. Another smaller **night market** sets up on Chengzhong Lu.

Entertainment

The hot ticket in town is **Impressions Liu Sanjie** (Yínxiáng Liǔ Sānjiě; Y188-320; ☼ 8-9pm daily). Directed by movie maker Zhang Yimou, 600 performers, including local fishermen, take to the Li River (yes, that's right, they perform *on* the Li River). Twelve surrounding karst peaks are illuminated as part of the show Zhang describes as a 'folk musical'. Travellers give it rave reviews. Book through your accommodation and you can usually get tickets for Y150 to Y180. Middle seats are the best.

The show is tweaked every six months or so to keep it fresh.

Shopping

Yángshuò is a good place to do souvenir shopping. Good buys include silk jackets, scroll paintings and batiks (from Guìzhōu). Name chops (carved seals used for ink stamping) are available from between Y10 to Y60, but you are expected to bargain (hard) for everything. Don't forget that Yángshuò is not simply Xi Jie; for comparison shopping, take a wander around the backstreets, especially north around the **tourist market** (Lǚkè Shìchǎng; Binjiang Lu).

If you are in the market for a chop, bear in mind that it is not the size of the stone that is important in determining a price, but the quality of the stone itself.

Getting There & Away
AIR
The closest airport is in Guìlín; the numerous CITS outlets and many cafés dispense air tickets relatively cheaply. See p655 for details on available flights. Cafés and hotels can organise taxi rides from Yángshuò directly to the airport (Y150, one hour).

BUS
Most travellers arrive in Yángshuò via Guìlín, from where there are good connections to both domestic and international destinations.

Buses leave Guìlín for Yángshuò, every 20 minutes from 7am to 8pm from the main bus station and in front of the train station; express buses take one hour (Y13) regular buses take 1½ hours (Y10).

Moving on from Yángshuò other options include express buses to Guǎngzhōu (Y100, eight hours), Wúzhōu (Y110, seven hours) and Shēnzhèn (Y220, nine hours).

Cheaper ancient sleepers still ply many of these routes from the bus station; however, they're smoky, haphazard and excruciatingly slow.

TRAIN
The nearest train station is in Guìlín. Almost any café or travel outfit around Yángshuò will organise train tickets. Some offer hard sleepers for high-demand routes such as Guìlín to Kūnmíng for Y170 to Y270 (depending on the time of year) plus Y50 commission. To get any of these tickets you'll have to book at least two to three days in advance or further ahead during holidays.

Getting Around
Yángshuò itself is small enough to walk around, but hiring a bicycle is perhaps the local must-do. Average prices are Y10 per day. You'll see bikes for rent everywhere. Many places also charge a deposit. Thoroughly check gears, brakes, tyres, handle bars and cranks. The farmers' paths around Yángshuò put all bikes to the test and could leave you stranded miles away from your deposit. There have also been some ugly situations when travellers have been accused of returning bikes 'broken'; if this happens, don't expect the PSB to take your side.

Think twice if you're asked to fork over a Y400 deposit that's waived only if you agree to a 'private' bike tour costing anywhere from Y20 to Y60. Some travellers who've agreed say they've felt hijacked by the guides who were paid to take them to particular sights whether the travellers wanted to see them or not.

AROUND YÁNGSHUÒ
Exploring Yángshuò's countryside often makes travellers top 10 lists. The list below

is just to get you started. Whatever direction you head off in, you'll likely stumble across your own gems.

In Yángshuò, there are several locals offering guided tours of Yuèliàng Shān, the caves and other famous spots, as well as their home villages. Some now cook lunch or dinner as well. These minitours have garnered rave reviews from some travellers and they may be worth a try, although you may need to get at least three people and prices will vary wildly.

Yuèliàng Shān 月亮山

A limestone pinnacle with a moon-shaped hole, **Yuèliàng Shān** (Moon Hill; admission Y9) goes from full to crescent moon depending on your vantage point. The views from the top (some 1251 steps up, so reports one focused Frenchman) are incredible. You can espy Moon Hill Village and the 1500-year-old **Big Banyan Tree**. To reach Yuèliàng Shān by bicycle, take the main road south out of town towards the river and turn right on the road about 200m before the bridge. Cycle for about 8km – Yuèliàng Shān is on your right.

AROUND YÁNGSHUÒ
阳朔地区

Black Buddha Cave & Water Cave
黑佛洞, 水岩

These **caves** (Hēifó Dòng & Shuǐ Yán; Y128) have been opened up not far from Yuèliàng Shān. Both are worth a visit for their rock formations, mud baths and caverns. Water Cave is especially popular. It's easy to reach the caves by bike; if you head for Yuèliàng Shān, you will undoubtedly be intercepted by touts.

Keep in mind that official entrance fees and tours to these caves are just a guideline so bargain all you want. Talk to any traveller coming out of these caves and you might discover they've paid admission prices anywhere from Y50 to Y150!

Yulong River 遇龙河

The scenery along the Yulong River (Yùlóng Hé) rivals that of Li River, and it's an area that usually leaves the biggest impression on most visitors to Yángshuò – despite ongoing development.

It is possible to do a full-day tour of the river and neighbouring sights, including **Double Flow Crossing** (Shuāng Liǔ Dù), **Xiangui Bridge** (Xiānguì Qiáo), nearby **Xīniú Hú** (Rhinoceros Lake) and **Dragon Bridge** (Yùlóng Qiáo). This last bridge, built in 1412, is impressive; it's among Guǎngxī's biggest bridges at 59m long, 5m wide and 9m high.

From Yángshuò, head towards Yuèliàng Shān. Before crossing the bridge over Yulong River, turn right down the dirt trail. It's possible to continue along this path all the way to Dragon Bridge and the village of Báishā. Don't be tempted by the Báishā road as it is busy, noisy and dusty. A round trip to Dragon Bridge takes a full day, but it's worth it. Pack a lunch and plenty of water.

If you do this jaunt, make sure to stop in at **Jiùxián** (旧县) near the Xiangui Bridge, about 10km from Yángshuò. About 20 families live here. There is a Tang dynasty wall and the village is packed with Ming and Qing dynasty stone buildings that have interesting rooftop carvings and offbeat doors. There's a restaurant here that keeps irregular hours, and in the summer you can also rent bamboo rafts.

Shítóuchéng 石头城

If you want to get off the beaten track, this fascinating village is a brilliant day trip. Perched amongst karst peaks roughly 10km northeast-ish of Pútáo village (葡萄), the ancient gates and walls of Shítóuchéng's old town are mostly still intact, crowning a limestone peak. Depending on who you ask, the walls have housed notables from a renegade prince looking for a retreat from rivals, to Qing gangsters who made the walls a base from which to extort protection money from villages below.

Don't bother trying to find the ruins yourself. Ask one of the villagers to be your guide. (*Nǐ kěyǐ dài wǒ yóu gǔ chéng ma?;* 你可以带我游古城吗?; Can you show me around the old town?). At the time of research, Y30 to Y40 was considered a fair price for both you and them.

It's a steep 30 to 50 minute climb up the hill from the village's 'new town' to the 'old town' where the wall begins. Once at the top, it will take another four to five hours to walk around to all four gates.

If there's been any rain at all, you'll be (literally) up to your knees in mud and cow shit by the time you're done. Consider yourself warned.

Adventurous, independent travellers looking to get away from the crowds will get the most out of a trip here. The gates are small and not particularly impressive in and of themselves. The reward is the chance to stomp through the fields and see rural Chinese life up close. If you speak Mandarin or can bring someone to translate, getting to know your guide is worth the trip.

To get here, go to the Yángshuò bus station or stand on Chengxi Lu and flag down anything heading in the direction of Guìlín. Ask to get off at Pútáo (Y5). You should see a long dirt road heading east once you've stepped off the bus. A motorcycle (Y20) or tractor (Y30) will take you the rest of the way to Shítóuchéng. It's about a 30-minute ride along some very bumpy, windy, uphill dirt roads.

It's also possible to walk, but the way to Shítóuchéng is not marked and people and houses become scarce the further you go. If you reach a fork in the road, don't move until a farmer wanders by and you can ask for directions.

There are no stores or restaurants on your way here, so bring water and snacks.

Your guide or a villager should be able to arrange your motorcycle ride back to Pútáo; from there, you can flag down a south-bound bus back to Yángshuò.

River Excursions

Many villages along the Li River are worth checking out. **Yángdī** (杨堤) and **Xīngpíng** (兴坪) are two of the most picturesque.

Many cafés and travel agents organise boat trips to these villages, about three to four hours upstream from Yángshuò. The mountain scenery around Yángdī is breathtaking and around Xīngpíng you'll also spot many caves. Official prices for all boat trips run from Y100 to Y150 a ride, but the final price will depend on the number of people going on the tour and your bargaining skills. Local boats charge less than Y5 for the same trip, but are deemed dangerous and the owners are not allowed to take foreigners.

A good alternative is to ride your bike to Xīngpíng and then put your bike on the boat coming back. Any number of places in Yángshuò or Xīngpíng can organise boat tickets (Y30 to Y50 per person).

There's also a fantastic 24km hike between Yángdī and Xīngpíng going back and forth over the river. The entrance fee is Y16 and a moderately fit person can complete it in four to five hours. Though there are restaurants along the way, it's a good idea to take some water and snacks of your own. Outside of the high season many of the restaurants have irregular opening hours.

You can start the hike at either end, though most people start at Yángdī and end at Xīngpíng if only because there are more frequent buses leaving from the latter for Yángshuò.

Buses leave Yángshuò for Yángdī from 7am to 6pm (Y8, 80 minutes) from the main bus station roughly every 30 minutes. Buses for Xīngpíng (Y5.5, 45 minutes) supposedly leave every 20 to 30 minutes from 6.30am to 6pm daily but more often than not leave on the 'when full' principle, the last bus back is 6pm. In both cases buy your ticket on board.

Boat trips (Y30, 20 minutes) also depart from Xīngpíng to **Yúcūn** (渔村), a picturesque ancient village with wonderfully preserved architecture. The problem is that boats only depart with enough people – never a given in sleepy Xīngpíng.

Xīngpíng has some interesting lanes and streets to explore. Keep your eyes peeled for the restaurant with giant caged rats outside.

There are lots of guesthouses by the river if you need to stay the night, but it only takes the arrival of one or two tour buses to fill them up quickly. If this happens try the **Xingping Inn** (Xīngpíng Kèzhàn; ☎ 870 3089; s/d from Y50). It has small tidy rooms with squat toilets. It's not near the river but several of the rooms have balconies with limestone-peak views.

Right on the river, **Bamboo Café** is a good spot for a meal and refreshing drink. Just up from the Li River is the wonderful **One World Café**.

Another popular riverboat trip is to the village of **Fúlì** (福利). It's not quite as picturesque as it's made out to be but the trip there and the surrounding scenery are lovely. The village is known for its fans and you'll see them everywhere: on walls, in workshops, outside people's houses. A couple of boats a day putter to Fúlì from Yángshuò for around Y50, although most people tend to cycle here – it's a pleasant ride and takes around an hour. Head for Dutou village (渡头村) and take the boat across the river to Fúlì (Y3).

Several places also offer rafting trips, kayak hire and bamboo rafts, popular options in the warm summer months.

Markets

The villages in the vicinity of Yángshuò are best visited on market days, which operate *roughly* on a three-day, monthly cycle. Thus, markets take place every third day starting on the first of the month for Yángdī and Báishā, every third day starting on the second of the month for Fúlì and Pútáo, and every third day starting on the third of the month for Yángshuò and Xīngpíng. However, after the third market the next one is in four days, not three, but this doesn't happen in all towns (there are no markets on the 10th, 20th, 30th and 31st of the month). Confused? Definitely ask at your lodging or at cafés.

LÓNGSHÈNG 龙胜

☎ 0773 / pop 167,000

Close to the Guìzhōu border, this town and the surrounding area is home to a colourful mixture of Dong, Zhuang, Yao and Miao cultures. The Dragon's Backbone Rice Terraces and a *wēnquán* (hot spring) are also nearby.

Buses (Y5) to the hot spring pass through rolling hills sculptured with rice terraces and studded with Yao and Zhuang villages. It's possible to desert the bus around 6km from the hot spring and take off into the hills for some exploring. Other tourist sights around

Lóngshèng include forest reserves and unusual stone formations.

When you return from the day's outing, Lóngshèng offers cheap to midrange accommodation, and even cheaper food at its lively night market.

Information

Internet café (wǎngbā; per hr Y2; ☯ 8am-midnight daily) Walk behind Xinhua Bookstore. Go up the stairs on the right to 2nd floor.

Post & telephone office (Yóudiànjú; Gulong Lu)

Sleeping & Eating

Riverside Hotel (凯凯旅舍; Kǎikǎi Lǚshè; ☎ 758 8986; 5 Guilong Lu; 桂龙路5号; s without bathroom Y20, d with bathroom Y50) Down the road to Guìlín, this basic hotel is run by a sociable English teacher. The restaurant below takes valiant stabs at Western dishes and has an English menu.

Lóngshèng Dàjiǔdiàn (龙胜大酒店; ☎ 751 7718; Zhongxin Jie; 中心街; s/d Y200; ☒) A recent spruce-up has left rooms with new furniture and new carpets. Bathrooms didn't get the same attention and still look terribly battered.

Just past the bridge on Xinglong Xilu, **street stalls** start operating around 8pm, offering point-and-choose meals.

Getting There & Away

Buses leave the Lóngshèng bus station every 10 to 15 minutes for Guìlín (Y22, 1½ hours) and express buses depart every two hours (Y15, three hours). Buses depart Lóngshèng for Sānjiāng hourly (Y10, two to three hours).

AROUND LONGSHENG
Dragon's Backbone Rice Terraces
龙脊梯田

The **Dragon's Backbone Rice Terraces** (Lóngjǐ Tītián; admission Y50) is a feat of farm engineering that reaches all the way up a string of 800m peaks. A half-hour climb to the top delivers an amazing vista.

The 600-year-old Zhuang village of **Píng'ān** (平安) is on the main ridge of the backbone and has become a small travellers' centre and base camp for exploring the terraces.

Walking possibilities include the one-hour circuit walk from the village to the clearly marked Viewpoint 1 and Viewpoint 2; pricier accommodation (Y70 for a room with simple private bathroom) is at each spot and has sublime views. More extensive day walks are also possible along the Dragon's Backbone

GUĀNGXĪ

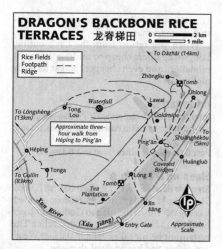

DRAGON'S BACKBONE RICE TERRACES 龙脊梯田

Rice Fields
Footpath
Ridge

To Dàzhài (14km)

Zhōngliú

Tomb

Ūhlong

Waterfall

Lawai

Tong
Lou

Goldmine

To Lóngshèng
(13km)

To
Shuānghékǒu
(5km)

Approximate three-
hour walk from
Héping to Píng'ān

Píng'ān

Héping

Tonga

Covered
Bridges

Huángluó

To Guìlín
(83km)

Tomb

Lóng Jí

Tea
Plantation

Jīn
Jiāng

Xùn River

(Xún Jiāng)

Entry Gate

Approximate
Scale

and down to Héping, or over the ridge and down into the valley behind. Some travellers insist that the three-hour trek to the Yao village of **Dàzhài** (大寨) is the only place to get away from the beaten path. Note that not all of these walks have established trails, so local guidance or advice is a good idea; it is not difficult to get lost.

Summer rains give the fields a sparkle, and they are stunningly golden in October; some travellers have remarked at the beauty of the terraces covered in snow. Winter and early spring bring heavy fog and mist that often shroud the terraces.

Most accommodation is found in Píng'ān. Other villages in the area also offer basic lodging in traditional wooden homes. A dorm bed costs between Y20 to Y30 in Píng'ān or at least Y20 elsewhere; most also have rooms with private, though spartan, bathrooms. **Countryside Café & Inn** (乡村旅馆; Xiāngcūn Lǚguǎn; liyue_lu@hotmail.com; ☎ 758 3020; d Y80) in Píng'ān is easy to access and has clean rooms and good food and service.

Buses to the terraces leave six times daily from 7.40am to 5pm (Y6.5) from Lóngshèng's bus station. Some buses will drop you off at the base of the terraces and continue on to Shuānghékǒu, so ask where you'll be deposited. The trip is only about 20km, however some buses stop midway at the town of Héping to try to pull in more passengers, dragging the trip out to 1½ hours. Returning to Lóngshèng, buses usually depart from the car park near the beautiful covered bridge at

the entrance to Píng'ān at 7.20am, 8.50am, 11am, 1pm, 3pm and 4.50pm.

The entrance fee is collected on the main road along the valley bottom.

SĀNJIĀNG 三江
☎ 0772 / pop 330,000

The reason for visiting the capital of the Sānjiāng Dong Minority Autonomous County (Sānjiāng Dòngzú Zìzhìxiàn) is to get out and explore the surroundings. It is also a worthy route into Guìzhōu. Approximately 20km to the north of town, Chengyang Wind & Rain Bridge and the wondrous patchwork of surrounding Dong villages are as peaceful and attractive as Sānjiāng is not.

Sights
CHENGYANG WIND & RAIN BRIDGE 程阳桥
Built in 1912, this 78m-long elegant **covered bridge** (Chéngyáng Qiáo; admission Y30) is considered by the Dong to be the finest of the 108 such structures in Sānjiāng County. It took villagers 12 years to build (theoretically achieved without the used of nails). Chéngyáng is a wonderful base to head off into the surrounding Dong villages in the countryside.

From the Sānjiāng bus station, you can catch hourly buses to Línxī (Y3), which go right past the bridge. Otherwise, catch one of the frequent minivan taxis (Y3) that congregate outside the bus station.

Sleeping
Chéngyáng is strewn with basic but comfy family-run hostels for about Y20 per bed.

Chengyang Bridge National Hostel (程阳桥招待所; Chéngyáng Qiáo Zhāodàisuǒ; ☎ 861 2444, 858 2568; fax 861 1716; dm/d with shared bathroom Y20/60) Just off to the left of the Chengyang bridge, on the far side of the river, this is easily the best abode in the area. The hotel is an all-wood, Dong-style building and the owners are friendly, informative and welcoming.

Chengyang Bridge Hotel (程阳桥宾馆; Chéngyáng Qiáo Bīnguǎn; d Y140; ❷) Expect to find OK accommodation down the street from the bus station. Despite the name, it is located in Sānjiāng.

Getting There & Away
Sānjiāng's bus station has several buses to Guìlín between 7.10am and 2.30pm (Y39, 5½ hours) and two daily to Wúzhōu at 3.10pm and 4.35pm (Y90, 9 to 10 hours). Buses to

Lóngshèng (Y10) leave every 40 to 50 minutes between 6.30am and 5.30pm.

SĀNJIĀNG TO KĂILĬ

If you have time on your hands, it's worth entering Guìzhōu province through the back door. From Sānjiāng's bus station parking lot, minibuses leave when full for Dìpíng (Lóng'é; Y14 to Y20), which is just across the Guìzhōu border. Though the journey is approximately three hours, delays may leave you stranded in Dìpíng for the night. There are frequent buses departing from Dìpíng for Lípíng (Y22, five hours).

The journey to Lípíng passes through some beautiful mountains, as well as the fabulous Dong village of Zhàoxīng (p684), the highlight of the trip and definitely worth a visit.

There are also frequent buses from Sānjiāng to Cóngjiāng in Guìzhōu. The road is new and improved but the route isn't as pretty. However, if you're in a hurry to reach Kăilĭ, there are numerous onward connections from Cóngjiāng.

Guìzhōu 贵州

Mention any of China's southwestern provinces and fellow travellers will pelt you with tips, advice or looks of envy. Tell them you're going to Guìzhōu, however, and you'll most likely receive a blank look and the question, 'Why?'

Despite blockbuster development and government efforts to turn the province into a kind of southwestern transport hub, complete with new expressways and airports, Guìzhōu can't shake its reputation as a backwater, and it remains one of the country's poorest provinces.

But there are several reasons why Guìzhōu should make it into your itinerary. The countryside is a mix of dense forests and cascading waterfalls, terraced hills and karst cave networks. There's a lively mix of people: almost 35% of Guìzhōu's population is made up of over 18 ethnic minorities, including the Miao and the Dong in the southeast and the Hui and the Yi in the west.

The Miao's traditional wooden homes dot the mountainous areas of the province, often perched at precarious angles overlooking sloping rivers. The Dong's wooden drum towers and intricate wind and rain bridges – constructed without a single nail or bolt – characterise the southeast region. Other minority groups include the Bouyi, Shui (Sui), Zhuang and Gejia. Together, they contribute to Guìzhōu's lively social calendar, which enjoys more folk festivals than any other province in China.

And for intrepid travellers looking to get off the beaten track, more often than not you'll have it all to yourself. Though getting to Guǎngxī via Guìzhōu's southeast villages is an increasingly popular trip, it's still possible to wander the rest of the province for days, and not see another foreigner.

HIGHLIGHTS

- Bob with black cranes on remote **Caohai Lake** (p679)
- Hop from village to village taking in the stunning scenery from **Kǎilǐ** (p683) into Guǎngxī
- Drop in on colourful Miao and Dong **festivals** and **country markets** (p682) in the villages around Kǎilǐ
- Explore the underground **Zhijin Cave** (p678), the largest cavern in China
- Get soaked behind the water curtain at **Huangguoshu Falls** (p678), China's premier cascade

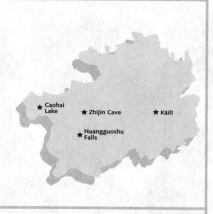

★ Caohai Lake ★ Zhijin Cave ★ Kǎilǐ

★ Huangguoshu Falls

■ POPULATION: 39.3 MILLION

History

Historically, no-one has wanted to have much to do with Guìzhōu. Chinese rulers set up an administration in the area as far back as the Han dynasty (206 BC–AD 220), but it was merely in an attempt to maintain some measure of control over Guìzhōu's non-Chinese tribes. Chinese settlement was confined to the northern and eastern parts of the province, and the western areas were not settled until the 16th century when rapid immigration forced the native minorities out of the most fertile areas.

It wasn't until the Sino-Japanese war, when the Kuomintang made Chóngqìng their wartime capital, that the development of Guìzhōu began: roads to neighbouring provinces were constructed, a rail link was built to Guǎngxī, and industries were established in Guìyáng and Zūnyì. Most of this activity ceased with the end of the war and it wasn't until the communists began construction of the railways that industrialisation of the area was revived.

Nevertheless, Chinese statistics continue to paint a grim picture of underdevelopment and poverty for Guìzhōu. GDP per capita in Shànghǎi is approximately 10 times higher than in Guìzhōu. The government is attempting to change all of this, mostly by constructing roads in every possible place to enable fast travel to tourist sights and also by promoting minority cultures as a local attraction.

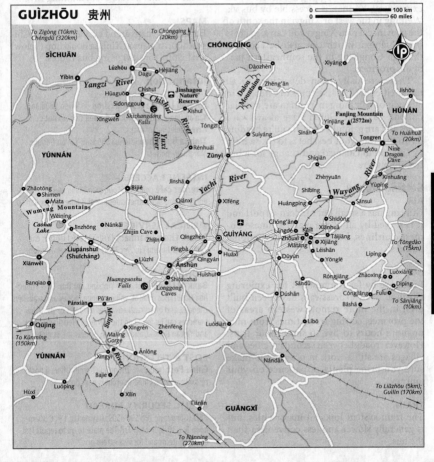

GUÌZHŌU 贵州

GUIZHOU

Climate

Guìzhōu has a temperate climate with an annual average temperature of 15°C. The coldest months are January and February when temperatures dip to around 1°C.

Language

Mandarin Chinese is spoken by the Han majority, Thai and Lao is spoken by some and Miao-Yao (Hmong-mien) dialects by the Miao and Yao.

Getting There & Away

You can fly to more than 40 destinations within China from Guìyáng's airport, including all major Chinese cities. International destinations include Bangkok.

Guìyáng and Chóngqìng are linked by an expressway. Yúnnán is accessible by bus via Wēiníng in the west or Xīngyì in the south of the province. From Xīngyì you can also cross into Guǎngxī, which can also be accessed through Cóngjiāng in the southeastern part of the province.

There are daily train departures to all major cities in China; sleepers to Chéngdū in Sìchuān or Kūnmíng in Yúnnán are popular options. Trains to Guìlín leave at awkward times and are painfully slow. If you're heading down this way, your best bet is to take a train to Liǔzhōu in Guǎngxī and change for a bus to Guìlín there.

Getting Around

AIR

Guìyáng has a small but modern airport and it is served by all of the major Chinese domestic airlines, but very few international airlines.

BUS

Buses are by far the best bet for exploring Guìzhōu. New expressways have been built even in the more remote western areas of the province, cutting travel times from nine or more hours to five to seven hour trips. However, roads between secondary cities and villages are still a work in progress so make sure you bring plenty of patience on your journey.

TRAIN

The train system links all major cities, but is generally slower and less convenient than the bus.

GUÌYÁNG 贵阳

☎ 0851 / pop 1.7 million / elevation 1070m

Guìyáng doesn't seem like much as you're rolling in on bus or train, but don't be discouraged. The riverside and Renmin Sq provide enjoyable areas to wander and relax, and elsewhere there's fantastic street food, lively markets and disorienting, maze-like shopping areas.

Orientation

Guìyáng is somewhat sprawling but it remains a manageable size and is easy enough to get around on foot or by public bus. The main commercial district is found along Zhonghua Zhonglu and Zhonghua Nanlu. If you continue south you'll reach Zunyi Lu and Renmin Sq. To the east of here is Jiaxiu Pavilion, a symbol of the city that hovers over Nanming River.

MAPS

English city maps aren't available but the Chinese tourist maps at Xinhua Bookshop (below) are helpful for navigating bus routes.

Information

BOOKSHOPS

Foreign Languages Bookshop (Wàiwén Shūdiàn; Yan'an Donglu) Isn't particularly well stocked but does have a selection of maps.

Xinhua Bookshop (Xīnhuá Shūdiàn; Yan'an Donglu) Marginally better.

INTERNET ACCESS 网吧

Internet café (wǎngbā; Longquan Xiang; per hr Y2) Literally dozens of internet cafés line this lane off Hequan Lu.

MEDICAL SERVICES

Ensure Chain Pharmacy (Yīshù Yàoyè Liáosuǒ; cnr Zunyi Lu & Jiefang Lu; ☼ 24hr) Near the train station.

MONEY

Bank of China (Zhōngguó Yínháng; cnr Dusi Lu & Zhonghua Nanlu) Has an ATM, will exchange money and travellers cheques, and offers cash advances on credit cards. Other branches can be found on the corner of Wenchang Beilu and Yan'an Donglu, and on Zunyi Lu near the station.

POST & TELEPHONE

China Post (yóujú; 46 Zhonghua Nanlu) Offers a poste restante service. China Telecom is next door.

PUBLIC SECURITY BUREAU

PSB (Gōngānjú; ☎ 590 4509; Daying Lu; ☼ 8.30am-noon & 2.30-5pm Mon-Fri) The place to go to report lost or stolen items and for visa extensions.

GUÌYÁNG 贵阳

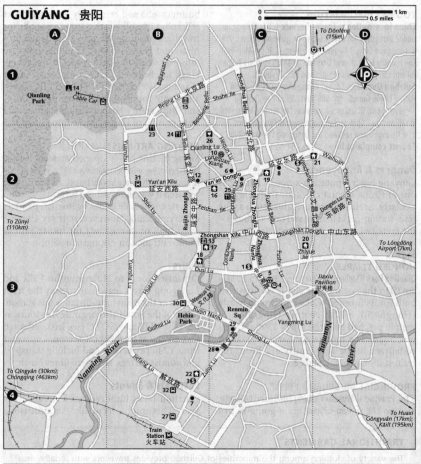

GUÌZHŌU

TOURIST INFORMATION

China International Travel Service (CITS; Zhōngguó Guójì Lǚxíngshè; ☎ 690 1660; www.guizhoutour.net; 7th fl, Longquan Bldg, 1 Hequn Lu; ⏰ 9am-5.30pm Mon-Fri) The friendly English- and German-speaking staff are helpful and can provide information on local festivals.

Guìzhōu Overseas Travel Company (GOTC; Guìzhōu Hǎiwài Lǚyóu Gōngsī; ☎ 586 4898; 28 Yan'an Zhonglu; ⏰ 9am-6pm) Offers similar services but is more interested in selling tours. Chinese-language tours to Qīngyán cost Y14; Huangguoshu Falls and the Longgong Caves is Y240.

Tourist complaint line (☎ 681 8436)

Dangers & Annoyances

Guìyáng has a reputation among Chinese as one of China's worst cities for theft. Be particularly careful in crowded areas such as the train station, night market and on local buses – the favoured haunts of pickpockets.

Sights

HONGFU TEMPLE 弘福寺

Qianling Park (Qiánlíng Gōng Yuán; ⏰ 6.30am-9pm; admission Y5) in the north of the city is worth a visit both for its forested walks and **Hongfu Temple** (Hóngfú Sì), a 17th-century Qing-dynasty temple perched near the top of 1300m Qiánlíng Shān. The monastery has a vegetarian restaurant in the rear courtyard. From the train station area take bus 2.

PROVINCIAL MUSEUM 省博物馆

The **Provincial Museum** (Shěng Bówùguǎn; Beijing Lu; admission Y10; ⏰ 9am-4.30pm) has a going-out-of business vibe and criminally lethargic ticket sellers but it's still worth a stop, especially for travellers pushing off to explore Guìzhōu's Miao and Dong villages. Exhibits showcase minority dress and customs from the Yelang kingdom, believed to have originated in the Warring States Period (475 BC–221 BC). Keep an eye out for displays concerning the 18th- and 19th-century Miao uprisings against rapid immigration of Han Chinese into Guìzhōu.

GUIYANG ART MUSEUM 贵阳美术馆

Swing by this newly opened **museum** (Guìyáng Měishùguǎn; Ruijin Zhonglu; admission Y15; ⏰ 10am-5pm) if you're in the neighbourhood. At the time of research it was showcasing a bizarre collection of male and female nudes by Russian painters of varying skills. However, staff say Chinese art is high on the agenda for future exhibitions. Entrance on Zhongshan Xilu.

Tours

Organised tours to Huangguoshu Falls and Longgong Caves leave daily from the train station or the main long-distance bus station. Many of the hotels also organise day tours, as does the CITS and GOTC (see left), although they are not as frequent off-season. Tours cost from Y240 per person and include transport and admission fees, and sometimes lunch.

Festivals & Events

Guìzhōu hosts hundreds of festivals every year. This might seem like an unfeasible

---

TRADITIONAL GARMENTS

The variety of clothing among the minorities of Guìzhōu provides travellers with a daily visual feast. Clothes are as much a social and ethnic denominator as pure decoration. They also show whether or not a woman is married and are a pointer to a woman's wealth and skills at weaving and embroidery.

Many women in remote areas still weave their own hemp and cotton cloth. Some families, especially in Dong areas, still ferment their own indigo paste as well, and you will also see this for sale in traditional markets. Many women will not attend festivals in the rain for fear that the dyes in their fabrics will run. Methods of producing indigo are greatly treasured and kept secret, but are increasingly threatened by the introduction of artificial chemical dyes.

Embroidery is central to minority costume and is a tradition passed down from mother to daughter. Designs include many important symbols and references to myths and history. Birds, fish and a variety of dragon motifs are popular. The highest quality work is often reserved for baby carriers, and many young girls work on these as they approach marrying age. Older women will often spend hundreds of hours embroidering their own funeral clothes.

Costumes move with the times. In larger towns, Miao women often substitute their embroidered smocks with a good woolly jumper (sweater) and their headdresses look suspiciously like mass-produced pink and yellow Chinese towels.

number of parties but the minority groups here, in particular the Miao and Dong, always seem to have something to celebrate. See the boxed text, p681.

Sleeping

BUDGET

Yóudiàn Bīnguǎn (Post Office Hotel; ☎ 558 5082; fax 558 5086; 166 Yan'an Donglu; 延安东路166号; 3-bed dm Y25, d Y168) It's got a great downtown location and some of the city's best food vendors right outside. Once renovations are done, this could be one of the better budget options in town.

Yidu Youth Hostel (Yídū Jiǔdiàn; ☎ 864 9777; fax 863 1799; 9 Zhiyue Jie; 指月街9号; 3-/4-/6-bed dm Y70/60/50, s/d from Y398) It's a bit removed from the action, but otherwise this is a terrific new hostel with modern rooms and wood floors. If you want dorms call ahead and reserve. This is the first port of call for Chinese tour/school groups and even in the off-season they can be booked solid.

Jīnlóng Dàjiǔdiàn (☎ 528 2321; 61 Yan'an Donglu; 延安中路61号; s Y109-139, d from Y179) Smack in the thick of things, including near city tourist offices, the rooms here are worn-down budget basic but tended to with pride. All's kept humming by an energetic, unilingual staff. Occasional blackouts mean you may be checking in by candlelight.

MIDRANGE

Yùjūnyuán Bīnguǎn (☎ 597 0701; 71 Zūnyì Lu; 遵义路 71号; s/d from Y158) A welcoming enough place where even the security guards give shy smiles and nods once they've gotten used to you. Staff do an admirable job of tending the rooms despite the obvious wear and tear. Closet-like bathrooms are made entirely of plastic.

Jīnqiáo Jiǔdiàn (Golden Bridge Hotel; ☎ 582 9958; 2 Rui jin Zhonglu; 瑞金中路6号; d from Y328) Tour groups and frazzled staff trample over ketchup- and mustard-coloured carpets. Red-nosed businessmen swarm in and out of 'superior' karaoke facilities 24 hours a day. It's a bit over the top but the weathered rooms are tidy and come with tiny balconies.

TOP END

Guìyáng's top-end rooms all look like they've been decorated by exactly the same person. The two below stand out from the crowd.

Nénghuī Jiǔdiàn (☎ 589 8888; fax 589 8622; 38 Ruijin Nanlu; 瑞金南路38号; d Y520-696; ❀ 🖳) Embroidered pillows and the odd splash of colour give some character to the rooms though bathrooms are a disappointment. Facilities include gym and sauna. The fabulous breakfast buffet is free the first night, Y25 afterwards.

Trade-Point Hotel (Bǎidún Jiǔdiàn; ☎ 582 7888; www .trade-pointhotel.com; 18 Yan'an Donglu; 延安东路18号; s/d Y800/900 plus 15% service charge; 🖳 ❀) Probably the slickest in town, this hotel has a central location, confident staff and a business centre to die for. If you need a splurge, do it here.

Eating

Some of the best food in Guìyáng can be found at the night markets. At dusk stalls spring up near the train station, all stacked with a huge choice of veggies, tofu and meat. Point at what you like, grab a beer and watch it be cooked. If you're feeling adventurous, tuck into some steamed pig snout and trotters, a popular local choice. If not, try the local varieties of *shāguō fěn*, a noodle and seafood, meat or vegetable combination put in a casserole pot and fired over a flame of rocket-launch proportions. The deep-fried skewered potatoes dusted in chilli powder are the best in the province.

Dongjia Family Restaurant (Dóngjiā Shífǔ; ☎ 650 7186; 42 Beijing Lu; dishes from Y10; ⏰ 9.30am-9pm) Specialising in minority cooking from all over Guìzhōu, every Guiyang-er knows this place. There's no English menu but the book-sized menu is filled with luscious pictures, from the chillies of Miao cuisine to the pickled vegetables of the Dong.

Yawen Restaurant (☎ 528 8811; Gongyuan Lu; dishes Y18-68; ⏰ lunch noon-2pm, dinner 6-10pm) This is popular with locals for its Sìchuān, Guìzhōu and Cantonese dishes. The food can get expensive but is first-rate. Only downsides are a stark white dining room and overly giggly staff.

New Zealand Western Restaurant (Niǔxílán Xīcāntīng; ☎ 651 2086; 157 Ruijin Beilu; lunch/dinner buffet Y48/58; ⏰ breakfast 6-9am, lunch noon-2.30pm, dinner 6-9.30pm) What this restaurant has to do with New Zealand is anyone's guess, but the lunch and dinner buffets are enormous.

Drinking

UBC Coffee (185 Ruijin Beilu; ⏰ 9am-2am) There's an extensive coffee and tea menu with the ever popular *zhēnzhū nǎichá* (pearl milk tea). It's a relaxed, friendly place with slightly tacky décor and a grand piano.

At the time of research, about a dozen bars, lounges and clubs were getting ready to open on Hequn Lu, north of Qianling Lu. Check them out when you're in town to see if they've taken off or not.

Getting There & Away

AIR

Airline offices in Guìyáng include the **Civil Aviation Administration of China** (CAAC; Zhōngguó Mínháng; ☎ 597 7777; 264 Zunyi Lu; ⏰ 8.30am-9pm), which has helpful English-speaking staff, and **China Southern Airlines** (☎ 582 8429; cnr Zunyi Lu & Ruijin Nanlu).

Destinations include Běijīng (Y1860), Shànghǎi (Y1730), Guǎngzhōu (Y990), Guìlín (Y710), Chéngdū (Y760), Xī'ān (Y900), Kūnmíng (Y570) and Chóngqìng (Y490). International destinations include Bangkok.

TRANSPORT

Guìyáng Buses

Buses from Guìyáng's Yan'an Xilu Bus Station include the following.

Destination	Price	Duration	Frequency	Departs
Ānshùn	Y25	1½hr	every 20min	7am-7pm
Chóngqìng	Y100	8hr	daily	1pm
Guǎngzhōu	Y230	17hr	2 daily	4.30pm & 6.30pm
Guìlín	Y108	10hr	2 daily	noon & 8pm
Wēiníng	Y70	7hr	daily	9am
Zūnyì	Y25-45	2½hr	half-hourly	7.30am-7.20pm

Buses from the Hebin Bus Depot:

Destination	Price	Duration	Frequency	Departs
Ānshùn	Y25	1½hr	every 20min	7am-7pm
Huangguoshu Falls	Y30-40	2½hr	every 40min	7.10am-noon
Kǎilǐ	Y50	2½hr	every 40min	7am-6pm
Xīngyì	Y60	6½hr	hourly	9am-6pm
Zūnyì	Y25-45	2½hr	half-hourly	7am-7pm

Buses from the Tiyu bus station on Jiefang Lu:

Destination	Price	Duration	Frequency	Departs
Chóngqìng	Y80	9hr	daily	1.30pm
Kǎilǐ	Y50	2½hr	every 20-30min	7.30am-7.30pm
Léishān	Y40	3hr	daily	3pm

Guìyáng Trains

Trains departing from Guìyáng:

Destination	Price	Duration	Frequency	Departs
Běijīng	Y490	29hr	daily	7.50am
Chéngdū	Y222	19hr	daily	3.38pm
Chóngqìng	Y135	10hr	daily	7pm
Guǎngzhōu	Y301	24hr	daily	12.15pm
Guìlín	Y200	17hr	2 daily	2.13am & 9.31am
Kǎilǐ	Y83	3hr	daily	8.10am
Kūnmíng	Y131	12hr	daily	7.30pm
Liùpánshuǐ	Y56-95	4hr	daily	10am
Shànghǎi	Y362	30hr	daily	11pm
Zūnyì	Y49	5hr	daily	5pm

BUS

There are three long-distance bus stations in Guìyáng. The main long-distance bus station (chángtú qìchē zǒngzhàn) is on Yan'an Xilu, quite a trek from the train station. The Hebin Bus Depot (Hébīn Qìchē Zhàn) is just south of main artery Dusi Lu. Another bus station, Tiyu Bus Station (Tǐyú Guǎng Chángtú Yuǎnzhàn), is further south on busy Jiefang Lu. They all have similar destinations at similar times and prices. See the boxed text, below, for timetables.

TRAIN

Guìyáng's gleaming train station has a modern, computerised ticket office, making it one of the more pleasant places in China to buy a train ticket. However, you'll probably find that it's easier (and quicker) to travel within Guìzhōu by bus. You can buy tickets four days in advance. Prices listed in the boxed text (p672) are for hard sleepers.

Getting Around

TO/FROM THE AIRPORT

Airport buses depart from the CAAC office every 30 minutes (Y10, 8.30am to 6.30pm). A taxi from the airport will cost around Y50.

BUS

Buses 1 and 2 do city tour loops from the train station, passing close to the main long-distance bus station. Bus 1 travels up Zhonghua Nanlu and heads westward along Beijing Lu. Buses cost Y1 and recorded announcements in Chinese and English let you know the name of the bus stops.

TAXI

Taxis charge a flat Y10 fare to anywhere in the city.

QĪNGYÁN 青岩

This ancient Ming town is packed with sights and makes a wonderful day trip from Guìyáng. The former military outpost was once a traffic hub between the southwest provinces, leaving the village with Taoist temples and Buddhist monasteries rubbing up against Christian churches and menacing watchtowers.

There's plenty to eat here and some of the most popular items are pig's feet, roasted sugar and tofu in every conceivable form, from baseball-sized spheres to oblong packages wrapped in leaves.

There's no entrance fee to the village, but most sights inside charge Y2 to Y10 to get in.

Be wary of groups of children pushing drawings or paper cranes in your hands. They're often trolling for money and have been known to stomp on visitors' feet or snatch money out of open wallets if they don't think you've been generous enough.

Getting There & Away

Only about 30km outside of Guìyáng, it takes about an hour to get here by bus. Buses leave regularly from the Hebin Bus Depot for Huaxi (Y3), from which a minibus will take you the rest of the way to Qīngyán (Y3). If you're dropped off in the new-town area (grey concrete buildings), just walk towards the walls with the large stone gate.

ZŪNYÌ 遵义

☎ 0852 / pop 484,980

If you're a modern-Chinese-history buff, this is the place for you. It was the location of the Zūnyì Conference, and the sights here will get you up close with Chinese Communist Party (CCP) history. If the CCP's 20th-century shenanigans aren't your thing, skip Zūnyì; it's neither picturesque nor particularly friendly.

History

On 16 October 1934, hemmed into the Jiāngxī soviet by Kuomintang forces, the communists set out on a Herculean, one-year, 9500km Long March from one end of China to the other. By mid-December they had reached Guìzhōu and marched on Zūnyì. Taking the town by surprise, the communists were able to stock up on supplies and take a breather.

From 15 to 18 January 1935, the top-level communist leaders took stock of the situation in the now-famous Zūnyì Conference. At the meeting the leaders reviewed their soviet-influenced strategies that had cost them their Jiāngxī base and caused them large military losses. Mao, who until this time had largely been overshadowed by his contemporaries, was highly critical of the communists' strategy thus far and the resolutions of the conference largely reflected his views. He was elected a full member of the ruling Standing Committee of the Politburo and Chief Assistant to Zhou Enlai in military planning. It would be another 10 years before Mao became the unrivalled leader of the Communist Party, but this event was a pivotal factor in his rise to power.

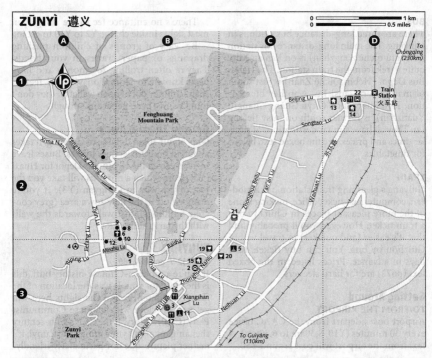

ZŪNYÌ 遵义

Information

Bank of China (Zhōngguó Yínháng; Minzhu Lu) Has an ATM, can change cash and travellers cheques, and offers cash advances on credit cards.

China Post (Zhonghua Nanlu; ⏰ 8am-8pm) Massive main post office. You can make long-distance calls here too.

Internet café (wǎngbā; Zhongshan Lu; per hr Y2; ⏰ 24hr) Look for a blue sign. The café is up a flight of dank stairs on the 2nd floor.

Public Security Bureau (PSB; Gōngānjú; Jinian Sq; ⏰ 8.30-11.30am & 2.30-5.30pm) Offers visa extensions.

Sights

COMMUNIST HISTORY SITES

The **Zūnyì Conference Site** (Zūnyì Huìyì Huìzhǐ; Ziyin Lu; admission Y40; ⏰ 8.30am-5pm) is hands down the most-visited communist-history attraction. Set in a colonial-style house, there are rooms filled with CCP memorabilia, as well as the meeting rooms and living quarters of the bigwigs. Outside, speakers blare revolutionary songs at raucous volumes for your listening pleasure.

Your ticket includes admission to umpteen related sites located nearby. The **Red Army**

General Political Department (Hóngjūn Zǒngzhèngzhìbù; lane off Ziyin Lu) has some of the more interesting photos and maps relating to the Long March and Zūnyì Conference. Exhibition halls share the grounds with a Catholic Church left behind by French missionaries.

Opposite is the **Residence of Bo Gu** (Bógǔ Jiújū), the general leader of the CCP Central Committee at the time of the Zūnyì Conference. Nearby, the **State Bank of the Red Army** (Huìyì Qījiàn) has some terrific money displays and decent English captions.

TEMPLES

Zūnyì has two active Buddhist temples. Built in the 1920s, **Xiangshan Temple** (Xiāngshān Sì) is situated on a small hill in a lively part of town. **Baiyun Temple** (Báiyún Sì) is more rundown but still quite charming.

Sleeping

There's some reasonable accommodation to be found in Zūnyì.

Zájì Bīnguǎn (☎ 822 3350; 89 Zhonghua Nanlu; 中华南路89号; d Y158-208) Disco or sleeping establishment? With the lobby's slick black stairs and multicoloured disco lighting, it is hard to tell what's supposed to be going on here. But whatever the case downstairs, upstairs rooms are generally terrific. Just look at several of them before paying anything. Two rooms may be identically priced with one sporting grubby bathrooms and potholed mattresses while another is gleaming and newly outfitted with extras such as comfy loveseats.

Shíshān Dàjiǔdiàn (☎ 882 2978; fax 882 5861; 108 Beijing Lu; 北京路108号; d with bathroom from Y168) Pleasant staff, retro-uniformed bellboys and weathered halls give this hotel a comfortable, old-fashioned feel. Rooms are well kept but decorated a toe-curling shade of lemon yellow.

Xībú Dàjiǔdiàn (☎ 319 1788; fax 319 1868; Waihuan Lu; 外环路; 汽车客远站旁; s/d Y110/188) Right around the corner from the bus station, most rooms here are basic affairs with cramped bathrooms and Chinese toilets. If you don't like what you see, ask for something on the 9th floor. Everything from rooms to halls are in better condition here.

Eating

Street food is your best bet in this town and there are some great hotpot, noodle and grill stalls to be found come dinner time. Some of the best places to look are the lively Xiangshan Lu or the alleys running southeast off Zhonghua Nanlu. Plentiful stands are also found around the main bus and train station.

Also be sure to check out the hotpot restaurants south of Xiangshan Temple.

Drinking

Zūnyì nightlife is generally shut up inside the giant KTV bars lining Zhonghua Beilu. So, if it's something other than karaoke you're looking for, you'll have to get out and hustle a bit. Clubs, pubs and discos open and close so fast even locals have trouble keeping track. Your best bet is to check out the cafés and tiny bars around **7:30 Bar** along Zhonghua Nanlu and see where the crowds are heading.

If searching out the new and the happening isn't your thing, **Dīngbùlā** (Zhonghua Nanlu) is a modern Taiwanese teahouse nearby that also serves beer and bar snacks, and attracts a young student crowd.

Getting There & Around

BUS

Useful local buses are buses 9 and 14 which run from the train station towards Minzhu Lu and the Bank of China.

For most destinations beyond Guízhōu you will have to head to Guìyáng and transfer.

GUIZHOU

ZŪNYÌ BUS TIMETABLES

Destination	Price	Duration	Frequency	Departs
Ānshùn	Y50	5½hr	3 daily	9am, 11am & 3pm
Chóngqìng	Y64	7½hr	daily	5pm
Guǎngzhōu	Y244	20hr	2 daily	1pm & 4pm
Guìyáng	Y20-40	2½hr	half-hourly	7am-7pm
Huángguǒshù	Y60	6½hr	2 daily	9am & 12.30pm

TRAIN

There are regular trains for Guìyáng (Y15 to Y26, three to five hours) but you're better off catching the bus. Other destinations include Chóngqìng (Y30 to Y44, six to nine hours, several per day) and Chéngdū (Y190, 15 hours, 7.37am, 2.40pm, 4.48pm and 6.31pm).

ĀNSHÙN 安顺

☎ 0853 / pop 217,000

Once a centre for tea and opium trading, Ānshùn remains the commercial hub of western Guìzhōu. Today, it's most famous as a producer of batiks, kitchen knives and the lethal Ānjiǔ brand of alcohol. The nearby aviation factory is also well known, and recently diversified production from fighter planes to hatchbacks.

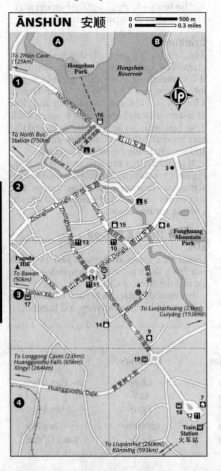

Most travellers come here for the easy access to Huangguoshu Falls and Longgong Caves.

Orientation

The long-distance bus and train stations are around 3km and 4km south of downtown, respectively. The main commercial and shopping area is found on Zhonghua Beilu and Zhonghua Nanlu.

Information

Bank of China (Zhōngguó Yínháng; cnr Tashan Xilu & Zhonghua Nanlu) Changes cash and travellers cheques, and offers cash advance on credit cards. ATM also.

China Post (Yóujú; cnr Zhonghua Nanlu & Tashan Nanlu) Look for it tucked next to the China Telecom building.

China Travel Service (CTS; Zhōngguó Lǚxíngshè; ☎ 323 4662, 323 4661; Tashan Donglu; ◷ 9am-5pm Mon-Fri) No English signs outside. Look for a blue sign with yellow Chinese characters.

Internet café (wǎngbā; Nanshui Lu; per hr Y2) East off Zhongnan Beilu.

Sights

Ānshùn doesn't have much in the way of sights, but there's interesting street life on weekends. Villagers come to sell their wares and **Gufu Jie**, a street of trendy clothing stores and bakeries, gets so packed it's hard to move.

For reprieve from the maddening crowds, check out the dilapidated but charming **Wén Miào** (admission Y5; 8am-5pm), a Confucian temple in the north of town. Weekends see the grounds scattered with locals who come here to drink tea, read and chat among the stunningly intricate carvings.

Southeast of here, **Donglin Temple** was built in AD 1405 (during the Ming dynasty) and restored in 1668. The resident Buddhist monks welcome visitors warmly.

Sleeping

Ānjú Bīnguǎn (220 1359; 火车站出站口对面; d Y100) Rooms are clean but ultra basic in this festively painted pink hotel. Closet-sized bathrooms have sinks and shower heads stacked over squat toilets. Contortions for bathing required.

Fēnghuángshān Dàjiǔdiàn (Golden Phoenix Mountain Hotel; 322 5663; 58 Tashan Donglu; 塔山东路58号; d Y218) With mounted, throne-like toilets and some serious red upholstery, rooms here certainly stand out. Pleasant staff make up for grotty bathrooms and the odd wall stain of perplexing origin. No English sign outside. Enter through the building done up like a Greek bank.

Xīxiùshān Bīnguǎn (221 1888; fax 221 1801; 63 Nanhua Lu; 南华路63号; s/d Y288/328) Conveniently located near bus and train stations, this hotel

has grounds in tip-top shape and is a favourite with tour groups. Reservations are a must even if arriving in the dead of winter.

Eating

Ānshùn is not bursting with culinary delights. Some buildings along Zhonghua Nanlu north of Tashan Donglu house restaurants on their 2nd floors but they seem all but deserted even at peak meal times.

Otherwise, there's an evening food market down an alley off Zhonghua Nanlu, just south of the Bank of China, and there are some great bakeries on Gufu Jie. A row of forgettable noodle stalls are located near the train station.

Be warned: dog is eaten in these parts – lots of dog. You'll see the skinned animals propped up outside restaurants as enticement.

Shopping

If you're looking for a Chinese market with everything from household wares to food to clothing, check out the market at the end of the long lane off Zhonghua Nanlu. For slicker stores, like Western-style clothing shops, check out Gufu Jie north of Tashan Donglu.

Getting There & Around
BUS

Minibus 1 is the most useful, zipping around town from the train station and up Tashan Donglu. Bus 2 travels between the train station and the north bus station. Buses costs Y1.

GUÌZHŌU

BUS TIMETABLES

Buses from Ānshùn Long-Distance Bus Station:

Destination	Price	Duration	Frequency	Departs
Guìyáng	Y15	2hr	every 20min	6.50am-7.10pm
Huángguǒshù	Y10	1hr	every 20min	7.30am-5pm
Kūnmíng	Y126	17hr	daily	1pm
Xīngyì	Y51	5hr	hourly	7am-3.30pm

Buses from Ānshùn Long-Distance Bus Station to the Southeast:

Destination	Price	Duration	Frequency	Departs
Fóshān	Y220	18hr	daily	noon
Fúzhōu	Y320	32hr	daily	noon
Guǎngzhōu	Y220	18hr	daily	noon
Shēnzhèn	Y220	18hr	daily	noon
Xiàmén	Y300	28hr	daily	noon

There are several bus stations in Ānshùn that are useful to travellers. The north bus station has buses to Zhījīn town (for Zhijin Cave) and the local bus station, located in the west of the city, is useful for travelling to Longgong Caves.

The long-distance station on the corner of Huangguoshu Dajie and Zhonghua Nanlu has a handful of handy destinations, and the long-distance bus station in front of the train station has buses for provinces in the southeastern part of China.

TRAIN
From Ānshùn, trains leave daily for Kūnmíng (Y130, 11 hours, 8.44am and 6.27pm) but it is virtually impossible to get sleeper reservations and you might well decide to head back to Guìyáng. To Chóngqìng two trains leave daily (Y68, 12 hours, 9.38pm and 11.42pm).

To Liùpánshuǐ (for Wēiníng) there are two trains daily at 10.52am and 11.34am (Y22, four hours). Four trains leave daily for Guìyáng (Y7 to Y12, two hours), although the bus is more convenient.

AROUND ĀNSHÙN
Longgong Caves 龙宫洞
The vast **Lónggōng** (Lónggōng Dòng; Dragon Palace; admission Y120; 8.30am-5.30pm) cave network snakes through 20 hills, but only a fraction is currently open to tourists. The recorded music and coloured spotlights can feel a bit over the top at times but most travellers enjoy drifting through the caves on rowboats with the low-key guides.

Guanyin Cave is a second, less impressive site about 4km before the main entrance.

Lónggōng is 23km south of Ānshùn and an easy day trip that can be combined with a visit to Huángguǒshù.

GETTING THERE & AWAY
Local buses depart every hour from Ānshùn's west bus station (Y10, 30 minutes). Returning, buses leave hourly until about 5pm.

Minibuses run between Lónggōng and Huángguǒshù (Y20, one hour).

Zhijin Cave 织金洞
As the largest cave in China, and one of the biggest in the entire world, a trip to **Zhijin Cave** (Zhījīn Dòng; admission Y120; 8.30am-5.30pm) is definitely worth the effort to come see for

yourself. Located at the edge of a small village some 15km outside Zhījīn, the cave is around 10km long and up to 150m high.

Calcium deposits create an abstract landscape of spectacular shapes and spirals, often reaching from the floor to the ceiling. As you move from the tiny passageways to cathedral-like main halls, it's hard not to be impressed.

Tickets to the site are steep but include a compulsory tour. Tours depart with a minimum of 10 people. Solo travellers visiting outside of peak summer months or Chinese holidays should be prepared for what can be a very, very long wait. While the tour itself is in Chinese only, you'll be glad to have someone around who knows the way back out of the maze of trails. Tours last from two to three hours.

GETTING THERE & AWAY
A trip to the cave can be made as a day trip from Ānshùn – just. Buses depart from Ānshùn's north bus station (Y18, three hours, every 25 minutes) for Zhījīn town. Once there, hop on a motorised rickshaw over to the town's second bus station and catch one of the local buses that leave regularly for the cave (Y3, one hour).

Returning from the caves, buses leave regularly. The last bus back to Ānshùn heads out of Zhījīn at 5.30pm.

Huangguoshu Falls 黄果树大瀑布
When these falls get going during the May to October rainy season, you can hear the thundering from kilometres away. Rainbows sprout from the **Rhinoceros Pool** below, while mist from the cascading waters carries all the way up to Huangguoshu Village nearby.

All this nabs busloads of tourists from all over China, eager to see the 81m-wide and 74m-tall **Huangguoshu Falls** (Huángguǒshù Dà Pùbù; Yellow Fruit Tree Falls; admission Y90; 8.30am-5.30pm), making it Guìzhōu's No 1 tourist attraction.

The cascades are actually part of a 450-sq-km cave and karst complex discovered when Chinese explored the area in the 1980s to gauge the region's hydroelectrical potential.

Entrance to the falls is just before Huangguoshu Village.

SLEEPING & EATING
You can do the falls in a day trip from Guìyáng at a push and it's an easy day trip

from Ānshùn. There are accommodation options everywhere in Huangguoshu Village but hotels are overpriced, grim and with a musty smell pervading most rooms.

Huángguǒshù Gōngsāng Zhāodàisuǒ (黄果树贡桑招待所; ☎ 359 2583; d/tr Y180/220) This police-run guesthouse is a little further up the road from Huángguǒshù Bīnguǎn; it has OK rooms. If they come with a discount then this is your best bet.

Huángguǒshù Bīnguǎn (黄果树宾馆; ☎ 359 2110; d Y380-480) Halfway between the bus stand and Huángguǒshù Village, this hotel has been redecorated but you still don't get much for your money. Rooms are somewhat musty and come with tiptoe views of the falls.

Along the main road in town are several restaurants with verandas at the back where you can eat and enjoy a great view of the falls.

GETTING THERE & AWAY

From Ānshùn, buses run every 20 minutes from the long-distance bus station (Y10, one hour, 7.30am to 5pm). Buses from Ānshùn to Xīngyì also pass by Huángguǒshù, leaving you about a 15-minute walk from the highway to the village.

Buses leave Guìyáng for Huángguǒshù every 40 minutes from the long-distance bus station (Y30 to Y40, 2½ hours, 7.10am to noon).

Heading out of Huángguǒshù, buses for Ānshùn and Guìyáng run regularly between 7am and 7pm. Buses for Xīngyì leave in the morning.

Minibuses run the route between Longgong Caves and Ānshùn (Y20 per person).

WESTERN GUÌZHŌU

Adventurers have always been drawn to Guìzhōu's wild west by its removed location, rough travel on rubble roads and remote natural sights. But these days, infrastructure money is leaving its mark. Western Guìzhōu is being developed as a kind of transportation hub, so you may find yourself sailing along smooth new expressways or flying into Xingyi's brand spanking new airport.

Improved transportation means tour groups, both Chinese and foreign, are increasingly making the trek to Weining's Nature Reserve at Caohai Lake or Xīngyì's Mǎlínghé Xiágǔ. But restless travellers shouldn't despair:

English around these parts is still nonexistent and independent travellers remain of novelty for most people in the region.

WĒINÍNG 威宁

☎ 0857

Wherever you've come from in China, you probably haven't seen a town like this. Men crack whips and scream as they race by on donkey-pulled chariots. Uighur music blasts out of Muslim kebab stands. Doors on the town's disintegrating taxi fleet flap open like bird wings whenever drivers take a corner.

And that's just at one intersection.

There's not much to do in Wēiníng, but it oozes character. There's a modern mosque serving the Hui minority in the northern part of town and a quiet market street in the old, eastern part of town. A larger market is held every three to four days.

The jewel-like **Caohai Lake** (草海湖; Cǎohǎi Hú; Grass Sea Lake) is the area's main draw and one of China's premier sites for seeing wintering migratory birds, especially the rare black-necked crane.

Sights & Activities
CAOHAI LAKE

The lake has a fragile history, having been drained during both the Great Leap Forward and the Cultural Revolution in hopes of producing farmland. It didn't work and the lake was refilled in 1980. Government tinkering with water levels in ensuing years impacted the local environment and villagers' livelihoods. The government has since enlisted locals in the lake's protection in an effort to remedy both problems. The 20-sq-km freshwater wetland has been a national nature reserve since 1992.

To get to the lake it's a 45-minute walk southwest of downtown Wēiníng or a five-minute taxi ride (Y3 to Y5).

Boaters and touts will mob you at the lakeside offering you a punt around the lake, a highlight for some travellers. The official price is Y60 per hour per boat though you'll have to bargain hard to get them down from starting prices of Y100 or more per person.

If you opt for a solo roam along the lakeside trails instead, be warned as the touts have a James Bond–like ability to show up wherever you are in Wēiníng to continue the haggle: your hotel in the morning, the kebab stand in the evening, the bus station as you're trying to leave town.

GUIZHOU

Sleeping & Eating

Cǎohǎi Bīnguǎn (草海宾馆; ☎ 622 1511; s/d/tr Y85/50/60) Right by the lake, rooms here are generally huge and comfortably furnished but can be damp and borderline glacial at night. The reception desk isn't always staffed so either make a lot of noise or be very patient when you arrive. The hotel's not easy to find so a taxi from the bus station is your best bet (Y3 to Y5).

Hēijīnghè Bīnguǎn (黑颈鹤宾馆; ☎ 622 9306; s/d with bathroom Y88/128) Despite damp, cold rooms and wall stains, this is the best accommodation in town. Central heating sputters to life with varying degrees of success between 9pm and 10pm. To get here, turn right out of the bus station and cross the intersection. Walk for about half a block and you'll see the hotel on your left.

Cǎohǎi Cāntíng (草海餐厅; dishes from Y5) About 200m east of Cǎohǎi Bīnguǎn, this is a cheap and friendly restaurant. There are a number of other good places to eat along this road.

South of Xinhua Bookshop on the main street are several point-and-choose restaurants, and you'll find a couple of Muslim restaurants near the mosque that serve tasty beef noodles.

Getting There & Away

The easiest way to reach Wēiníng is by bus from Guìyáng (Y70, seven hours, 9am daily).

Leaving Wēiníng you can backtrack to Guìyáng (8.30am daily) or take a bus south to Xiānwēi in Yúnnán (Y25, eight hours, 7.30am and 9am). If you catch the 7.30am bus to Xiānwēi you'll arrive just in time to catch the last bus to Kūnmíng (Y40, eight hours) at 3.30pm, although it's a lot of travelling to do in one day. From Wēiníng, there is also a sleeper bus to Kūnmíng (Y90, 16 hours, 5.30pm).

Alternatively, take the morning bus to Zhǎotōng (Y20, three hours; 7.20am and 8am), from where you can hop over to Xīchàng in southern Sìchuān and connect with the Kūnmíng–Chéngdū train line.

XĪNGYÌ 兴义

☎ 0859

Even with a new regional airport, construction sites galore and several new expressways, Xīngyì is still pretty unexciting. By 6pm people drain from town, and roaming the streets of this oversized concrete city is frankly a bit of a downer. But if you find yourself here on the way to Guìyáng, Nánníng or Kūnmíng, the surrounding countryside is definitely worth a visit if only for the beautiful karst scenery.

The main attraction in the area is the 15km-long **Maling Gorge** (马岭河峡谷; Mǎlínghé Xiágǔ; admission Y30). You can spend the better part of a day following the winding path into the lush gorge, across bridges and up to and behind high, cascading waterfalls. Bring waterproof gear, sturdy shoes and a torch (flashlight) to light your way through some of the caves. Minibuses to the gorge run every 20 minutes from Xīngyì's east bus station (Y2, 7am to 7pm) or you can grab a taxi (Y20).

Water levels permitting, it's also possible to do some rafting, although not in low season. Keep in mind that even when water levels are high, these aren't rapids and this is a slow descent. Speak to your accommodation providers or contact the **CITS** (☎ 690 1660; www.guizhoutour .net) in Guìyáng to arrange rafting trips.

Sleeping & Eating

Shuìwù Bīnguǎn (税务宾馆; ☎ 322 3927; Dongfeng Lu; dm Y15, d with bathroom Y98) South of the east bus station, this hotel is convenient if you happen to arrive in town late at night. There's a travel agency in front of the building that can be helpful in arranging guides or trips.

Pánjiāng Bīnguǎn (盘江宾馆; ☎ 322 3456, ext 8118; 4 Panjiang Xilu; dm Y48, dm/s/d/tr with bathroom Y50/280/380/380) This is the official tourist hotel, and is often full with groups. Don't even think of coming here without a reservation. Overworked staff have been known to shoo away visitors before they even reach the reception desk.

Aviation Hotel (Hángkōng Jiǔdiàn; 航空酒店; ☎ 312 6666; fax 312 6668; Ruijin Nanlu; 瑞金南路; d Y680; ✷) A huge hotel with fawning, five-star service but only so-so facilities. The bathrooms' intergalactic shower fixtures should come with an operations manual.

There's a serious lack of restaurants in Xīngyì; try your luck with some of the point-and-choose places near the east bus station.

Getting There & Away

There are two bus stations in Xīngyì. Buses to Guìyáng (Y93 to Y100, six to eight hours) leave every 40 minutes from the east bus station, stopping at Huangguoshu Falls (Y50) and Ānshùn (Y55) on the way.

GUÌZHŌU

From the west bus station there is a sleeper bus that leaves daily at 8pm for Kūnmíng (Y73, nine hours). There are also regular minibuses that go to Luópíng (Y20, two hours, every 30 minutes until 6pm), from where you can change for a bus to take you to Kūnmíng (Y35 to Y43, four hours, half-hourly until 5pm).

EASTERN GUÌZHŌU

Over 13 different minorities live in the forested hillsides and river valleys of this region, and it's worth making time in your trip to visit the extraordinary villages and surrounding countryside. Though some villages have started to be (overly) spruced up for tourism, many are still relatively untouched by China's modernising mania.

Booming country markets and festivals are held almost weekly, giving travellers a window into a completely unique way of life. China's largest Miao village, Xījiāng, with a colourful weekly market, and the remote Dong village of Zhàoxīng, in the southeast, are particularly recommended. If you have time, consider visiting them as part of the back-door route into Guǎngxī.

Outside Kǎilǐ there are no places to change money, so bring plenty of Renminbi with you.

KǍILǏ 凯里
☎ 0855 / pop 153,000
About 195km almost directly east of Guìyáng, Kǎilǐ is a compact, friendly town and a fantastic base for visiting minority villages or planning the back-door trip into Guǎngxī.

Information
Bank of China (Zhōngguó Yínháng; Shaoshan Nanlu) Changes cash and travellers cheques, and offers cash advance on credit cards. There is also an ATM here. A second branch on Beijing Donglu will also change cash.
China Post (yóuyú; cnr Shaoshan Beilu & Beijing Donglu) You can make international phone calls on the 2nd floor.
CITS (Zhōngguó Guójì Lǚxíngshè; ☎ 822 2506; 53 Yingpan Donglu; ⌚ 9am-5.30pm) If only every CITS in China was like this one! Staff here are universally helpful and there are fluent English, French and Japanese speakers. The place for information on minority villages, festivals, markets and organised tours.
Internet café (wǎngbā; Shaoshan Nanlu; per hr Y2, deposit Y10; ⌚ 24hr) Near the Kailai Hotel, with over 100 computers. If locals playing video games are camped out at all of them, try the internet café on Beijing Lu. Look for the 7Up sign. Computers are downstairs.
Public Security Bureau (PSB; Gōngānjú; ☎ 853 6113; 26 Yongle Lu; ⌚ 8.30-11.30am & 2.30-5.30pm Mon-Fri) Deals with all passport and visa inquiries.

Sights & Activities
There's not much to see or do in Kǎilǐ other than a visit to **Dage Park** (Big Pagoda Park) or **Jinquanhu Park**, which has a Dong-minority drum tower built in 1985. Also check out the **Minorities Museum** which should be reopened by the time you read this. At the time of research it was being moved from its former home above a furniture store into an enormous building that formerly housed the Wanbo bus station.

MARKETS
A huge number of markets are held in the villages surrounding Kǎilǐ. Xiānhuā has a huge market every six to seven days. Zhōuxī, Léishān and Táijiāng hold markets every six

---

FESTIVALS & MARKETS
Minority celebrations are lively events that can last for days at a time and often include singing, dancing, horse racing and buffalo fighting.

One of the biggest is the Lusheng Festival, held in either spring or autumn, depending on the village. The *lúshēng* is a reed instrument used by the Miao people. Other important festivals include the Dragon Boat Festival, Hill-leaping Festival and the Sharing the Sister's Meal Festival (equivalent to Valentines Day in the West). The Miao New Year is celebrated on the first four days of the 10th lunar month in Kǎilǐ, Guàdīng, Zhōuxī and other Miao areas. The Fertility Festival is only celebrated every 13 years.

All minority festivals follow the lunar calendar and so dates vary from year to year. They will also vary from village to village and shaman to shaman. The terrific CITS in Kǎilǐ (above) will provide you with a list of local festivals and markets. The CITS in Guìyáng (p670) is also helpful and has English- and German-speaking staff.

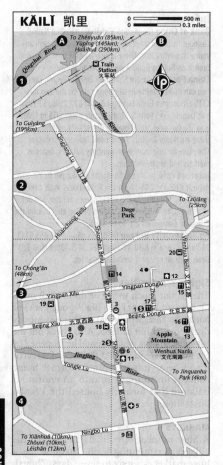

KĂILĬ 凯里

days. Dates and suggestions are available from the fabulous Kǎilǐ CITS (see p681).

Festivals & Events
Markets and festivals are one of Guìzhōu's major attractions, and the profusion of them around Kǎilǐ make this sleepy town the best place to base yourself for exploring them. For more details, see the boxed text, p681.

Sleeping
Shíyóu Bīnguǎn (☎ 823 4331; 44 Yingpan Donglu; 营盘东路44号; dm/s/d/tr Y26/80/120/120) This is a budget favourite despite the doorless shared bathrooms and some very draughty rooms. Consider reserving ahead, as dorms and singles fill up fast.

Guótài Dàjiǔdiàn (☎ 826 9888; fax 826 9818; 6 Beijing Donglu; 北京东路6; d Y258-288) Good discounts make these tidy, centrally located rooms great value. Probably the top midrange option in town, despite disappointing bathrooms and underwhelming service.

Kǎilái Jiǔdián (☎ 827 7888; fax 827 7666; 21 Shaoshan Nanlu; 韶山南路21号; s/d Y388/328) It's got spick and span rooms and staff who act like they've been waiting all year for your arrival. Cooks haven't quite mastered the supply and demand side of the free breakfast buffet and food runs out quickly. Replacement dishes can engender a mini stampede of sorts, so be prepared.

Eating
Kǎilǐ has some fantastic snack stalls lining its streets. Savoury crepes, potato patties, barbecues, tofu grills, noodles, hotpot, *shuǐjiǎo* (boiled dumplings) and wonton soup overflow for extremely reasonable prices. Check out the night market or the corner of Yingpan Donglu and Wenhua Beilu.

Also check out the little alcove located east of the Ludujia Ri Hotel on Beijing Donglu, where cafés and restaurants with names such as Bobo and Happy serve up Chinese and

Western-style food with varying degrees of success.

Lǐxiǎngmiàn Shídiàn (Wenhua Nanlu; dishes from Y5; ⏲ 7.30am-7.30pm) This modest eatery serves simple dishes such as wonton soup and noodles and is run by a very friendly family. Don't be surprised if they plop down at your table to ask you about your day. English menu available.

Getting There & Away
BUS
Kǎilǐ is served by two bus stations: the long-distance bus station on Wenhua Beilu has departures to most destinations, but if you can't find what you're looking for try the local bus station on Yingpan Xilu.

Destinations from the local bus station cover most surrounding villages, including Lángdé (Y9 to Y10), Chóng'ān (Y11, one hour), Májiāng (Y8 to Y10) and Huángpíng (Y13, 30 minutes). Check times when you arrive.

TRAIN
Kǎilǐ's train station is a couple of kilometres north of town but departures are infrequent and the train service slow; you're better off getting the bus. Trains leave round the clock for Guìyáng (Y16 to Y25), the majority between noon and midnight. These take three to five hours.

For longer distances, it's worth stopping in Guìyáng to secure a reservation. Six trains a day pass through Kǎilǐ on their way to Chóngqìng; three a day pass through on their way to Kūnmíng (1.51pm, 8.37pm and 8.50pm). You can't get a sleeper reservation in Kǎilǐ so you'll have to pray for intervention from a higher power (the conductor guard). The same advice is valid for east-bound services to Běijīng and Shànghǎi.

Getting Around
Bus fares cost Y0.5 in Kǎilǐ and almost all of the buses departing from the train station follow the same route: up Qingjiang Lu, past the long-distance bus station, along Beijing Donglu and down Shaoshan Nanlu to the Minorities Museum. For the train station take bus 2.

Taxis charge a flat rate of Y5 for anywhere in the city and Y10 to the train station.

AROUND KĂILĬ
It's easy to spend several weeks village-hopping around Guìzhōu's southeast. Base yourself at any of the following villages and go explore. If you are planning to village hop into Guǎngxī, plan on spending about a week. Make sure your itinerary is flexible, however, as bus schedules can be irregular in these parts.

Xījiāng 西江
Hidden in the folds of the Leigong Hills, Xījiāng is thought to be the largest Miao village and is well known for its embroidery and silver ornaments (the Miao believe that silver can dispel evil spirits). Set in a natural basin, it's bordered by paddy fields, with wooden houses rising up the hillside.

Dawn hikes through the paddies are spectacular and for those of you looking for more than an afternoon stroll, there's a three-day trek from here to Páiyáng (排羊), a Miao village north of Xījiāng. This trail winds its way through some remote minority villages and lush scenery.

You will probably find accommodation with locals en route but you shouldn't expect it so come prepared with sleeping bags, food and camping equipment.

Many families offer rooms with dinner for around Y40. Just go up the main street and ask around.

BUS TIMETABLES

Buses from the Kǎilǐ long-distance bus station:

Destination	Price	Duration	Frequency	Departs
Cóngjiāng	Y61	8hr	5 daily	7am-2pm
Guìyáng	Y45-51	2½hr	half-hourly	6am-7.15pm
Léishān	Y11	1hr	half-hourly	7am-7.30pm
Róngjiāng	Y45	6hr	every 40min	6.40am-4.40pm
Xījiāng	Y10-15	1½hr	2 daily	noon & 2pm

GUÌZHŌU

If everyone's full, try the **Yóudiàn Zhāodàisuǒ** (邮电招待所; ☎ 334 8688; dm Y15) near the bus drop-off. Guests say the kindness of the *fúwùyuán* (floor attendants) more than make up for the grubby facilities.

GETTING THERE & AWAY

From Kǎilǐ there are two buses a day to Xijiāng (Y10 to Y15, 1½ hours) at noon and 2pm. Returning to Kǎilǐ there are three to four morning buses a day. Alternatively, catch a bus to Léishān (Y8, 1½ hours, last bus 5pm) and from there head south towards Róngjiāng.

Lángdé 郎德

The terrific Miao architecture and cobbled pathways have turned this village into the first port of call for tour buses. Elaborate singing, dancing and reed flute performances are usually staged, after which the hard sell of local clothes and jewellery begins. But don't let the commercialisation put you off. The locals are friendly and there's a terrific 15km trail along the Bala River that will take you through several Miao villages.

GETTING THERE & AWAY

About 20km outside Kǎilǐ, buses pass by here on the way to Léishān (Y7 to Y8). The village is 2km from the main road. Getting away, get out on the street and flag down a bus back to Kǎilǐ.

Mátáng 麻塘

This village, 30km from Kǎilǐ, is home to the Gejia, a group that has been identified by the government as belonging to the Miao minority. The Gejia, who have different customs, dress and language, aren't particularly happy about this classification; nor for that matter are the Miao. The Gejia are renowned batik artisans and their traditional dress often features batik and embroidery. Their hats (which look a bit like heavily starched napkins) are also made out of batik. The village is incredibly friendly but be prepared for the army of women selling handicrafts who will pounce on you as soon as you arrive.

GETTING THERE & AWAY

The village is 2km from the main road and buses regularly run past the drop-off point in the direction of Chóng'ān (Y5) and Kǎilǐ (Y7). Just stand on the side of the road and flag down anything that comes your way.

Bāshā 岜沙

This fascinating Miao village up the hill from Cóngjiāng is famous for its men who still wear period clothes, carry swords and wear their long hair rolled up into topknots. Even young boys wear the topknot and carry daggers. Though most say these traditions date from the Ming dynasty, others believe they may date back to the Tang or Song era.

Neither Han culture nor modern technology has made serious inroads here (yet) and nobody, even the villagers themselves, seems sure why their ancient customs stay so well preserved.

The tricky part of a visit here is actually seeing the men, as during the day the majority are out hunting or farming. Try to time your visit with a festival for the chance to see the entire village.

Bāshā is increasingly showing up on travellers' itineraries as they village hop into Guǎngxī and the inhabitants are starting to respond. Chinese-English signs now point the way to various corners of this sprawling settlement and bilingual plaques explain the use of certain buildings.

There an irregularly collected Y15 entrance fee to Bāshā but if no-one's tracked you down for it by the time you're ready to leave, don't worry about it – it just means the Miao here have decided to give you a *laissez-passer*.

There are plenty of hotels and restaurants in Cóngjiāng if you want to spend the night.

GETTING THERE & AWAY

Bāshā is about 10km up the hill from Cóngjiāng. You can walk or take a taxi (around Y15), rickshaw or motorcycle (Y3 to Y5). Arrange a pick up for coming back or plan to walk back down to Cóngjiāng. Not much transportation hangs around the village.

Zhàoxīng 肇兴

This gorgeous Dong village is packed with traditional wooden structures, several wind and rain bridges and five remarkable drum towers. It's a lively place, with 700 households, and most villagers continue to wear traditional clothing and speak only their native Dong language.

Zhàoxīng is drawing an increasing number of foreign visitors and several guesthouses and eateries (some with English menus) have sprung up on the main street.

Be sure to check on the meat of the day, as rat meat (lǎoshǔ ròu) is common in this area. If you plan to do some day walks, it might be a good idea to bring some snacks along.

Wood Guesthouse (侗家木楼旅馆; Dòngjiā Mùlóu Lǚguǎn; r Y30; 🖳) has very basic wood rooms with hot showers down in the lobby. The most modern digs in the city can be found at **Zhàoxīng Bīnguǎn** (肇兴宾馆; d from Y120; 🗙). They're spotless, with tiny gleaming bathrooms.

GETTING THERE & AWAY

From Kǎilǐ you have to travel first to Cóngjiāng (Y61, eight hours) and change there for a bus to Zhàoxīng (Y15). Direct buses running from Cóngjiāng aren't frequent however, so consider getting on a Lípíng-bound bus and changing halfway (the bus driver will tell you) for a Dìpíng bus.

Alternatively, if you're looking to stretch your legs, take a Luòxiāng-bound bus from Cóngjiāng (Y15, two hours), and from Luòxiāng it's a lovely 1½-hour walk along a dirt road to Zhàoxīng, passing through a number of smaller villages en route.

From Zhàoxīng there is at least one Lípíng–Sānjiāng bus passing through each way. The trip to Sānjiāng, in Guǎngxī, takes about five hours. From there you can catch an onward bus to Guìlín (see p664).

GUÌZHŌU

Yúnnán 云南

Yúnnán has some of the most magical and diverse scenery in all of China. There are endless trekking opportunities in the south's tropical rainforests, and in the north, snow-capped Tibetan peaks hide dozens of tiny villages and temples rarely visited by tourists.

Yúnnán is also home to a third of all China's ethnic minorities (nearly 50% of the province is non-Han) and despite the best government efforts, numerous pockets of the province have successfully resisted Han influence and exhibit strong local identities.

Even Kūnmíng, the provincial capital, has a flavour that seems more than half a world away from Běijīng. Despite the rapid economic growth, Kūnmíng, 'Spring City,' retains an individuality that has earned it a reputation for being one of the more cosmopolitan and relaxed cities in the southwest.

Yúnnán is the sight of important archaeological discoveries, including sophisticated Bronze Age cultures around Diān Chí (Lake Dian) and the oldest human remains yet found in China (human teeth fragments dating from 1.75 million to 2.5 million years ago).

The province is also home to the nation's highest number of species of flora and fauna – including 2500 varieties of wild flower and plant – and is known for its mild climate year-round.

It's hard to comprehend all that Yúnnán has to offer until you get here. If you're a traveller planning to start your China journey in Yúnnán you should be warned, once you've come see it for yourself, you may never get further east than Kūnmíng.

HIGHLIGHTS

- Watch the sun rise and set on the magnificent **Yuányáng rice terraces** (p728)
- Escape the crowds and while away the days exploring low-key **Lúgū Hú** (p722)
- Soak up the Southeast Asian atmosphere in tropical **Xīshuāngbǎnnà** (p730)
- Get lost among the canals and cobbled lanes of **Lìjiāng's old town** (p711)
- Trek **Tiger Leaping Gorge** (p718), a breathtaking hike amid dramatic cliffs and waterfalls

- POPULATION: 42.1 MILLION
- www.yunnantourism.net

History

Yúnnán, China's sixth-largest province, has always been a bit of a renegade. Its remote location, harsh terrain and diverse ethnic make-up have made it a difficult province to govern, and for centuries it was considered a backward place inhabited by barbarians.

Qin Shi Huang and the Han emperors held tentative imperial power over the southwest and forged southern Silk Road trade routes to Burma, but by the 7th century the Bai people had established their own powerful kingdom, Nanzhao, south of Dàlǐ. Initially allied with the Chinese against the Tibetans, this kingdom extended its power until, in the middle of the 8th century, it was able to challenge and defeat the Tang armies. It took control of a large slice of the southwest and established itself as a fully independent entity, dominating the trade routes from China to India and Burma.

The Nanzhao kingdom fell in the 10th century and was replaced by the kingdom of Dàlǐ, an independent state that lasted until it was overrun by the Mongols in the mid-13th century. After 15 centuries of resistance to northern rule, this part of the southwest was finally integrated into the empire as the province of Yúnnán.

Even so, it remained an isolated frontier region, with scattered Chinese garrisons and settlements in the valleys and basins, a mixed aboriginal population in the highlands, and various Dai (Thai) and other minorities along the Mekong River (Láncāng Jiāng).

During the Republican period, Yúnnán continued to exercise a rebellious streak. When Yuan Shikai tried to abandon the republican government and install himself as emperor, military leaders in Yúnnán rebelled. One local military commander even renamed his troops the National Protection Army and marched them into Sìchuān, a stronghold for forces loyal to Yuan. Military forces elsewhere in China turned out in support and Yuan was forced to retreat.

Yúnnán, like the rest of the southwest, has a history of breaking ties with the northern government. During China's countless political purges, fallen officials often found themselves here, adding to the province's character.

Climate

Yúnnán has a climate as diverse as its terrain, with temperate, tropical and frigid zones; from the frozen northwestern region around Déqīn and Shangri-la (Zhōngdiàn) where winters (late November to February) reach chilling lows of −12°C and summer (June to August) temperatures peak at highs of 19°C, to the subtropical climate of Jǐnghóng where the summer months soar to 33°C. Dàlǐ has an ideal temperature year-round, with temperatures never dipping below 4°C in the winter months or above 25°C in summer.

Language

In addition to Mandarin, the other major languages spoken in Yúnnán province belong to the Tibeto-Burman family (eg the Naxi language), and the Sino-Tibetan family (eg the Lisu language).

Getting There & Around

AIR

Kūnmíng is served by all Chinese airlines and has daily flights to most cities. International destinations include Hong Kong, Hanoi, Bangkok, Rangoon and Seoul.

With domestic airports in almost all corners of Yúnnán province being served by daily flights from Kūnmíng and other major Chinese cities, travelling within Yúnnán has never been easier. The northwest is linked by Shangri-la, Dàlǐ and Lìjiāng. Mángshì provides Déhóng prefecture in the southwest with an air link and Jǐnghóng is Xīshuāngbǎnnà's air link.

Dàlǐ airport has flights to Kūnmíng and Guǎngzhōu. From Lìjiāng there are daily flights to Chéngdū, Shànghǎi, Shēnzhèn and Guǎngzhōu. From Shangri-la, Yunnan Airlines flies to Kūnmíng, Chéngdū, Lhasa, Guǎngzhōu, Shēnzhèn and Guìyáng.

Destinations from Jǐnghóng include Lìjiāng, Shànghǎi and Guǎngzhōu, as well as direct flights to Bangkok and Chiang Mai in Thailand. Mángshì currently only has flights to Kūnmíng.

BUS

A well-developed bus system covers the whole province and Yúnnán has seen a huge rise in the number of express highways in recent years. Expressways link Kūnmíng with Dàlǐ and Lìjiāng, and south to Bǎoshān and Jǐnghóng.

Road networks link Kūnmíng with Sìchuān, Guìzhōu and Guǎngxī and on to Myanmar, Laos, Vietnam and Thailand.

TRAIN

Most travellers arrive in Yúnnán by train to Kūnmíng. However within the province trains are less convenient, other than the popular overnight train from the capital to Dàlǐ. Development of the railways has been slower in Yúnnán than elsewhere; it was only in 1990 that the train line was extended out west to Dàlǐ. Railways link Yúnnán to Guìzhōu, Guǎngxī and Sìchuān.

CENTRAL YÚNNÁN

KŪNMÍNG 昆明

☎ 0871/pop 1,044,356

Kūnmíng has become a thoroughly modern Chinese city with wide, palm-lined roads and sky-scraping modern buildings. What was left of the quaint back alleyways and wooden buildings have been replaced by shopping malls and modern apartment blocks. However, as far as Chinese cities go, Kūnmíng is very laid-back and an enjoyable place to spend a few days.

At an elevation of 1890m, Kūnmíng has a milder climate than most other Chinese cities, and can be visited at any time of the year. Light clothes will usually be adequate, but it's wise to bring some woollies during the winter months when temperatures can suddenly drop. However, snow is still rare and afternoon daytime temperatures from December to January are often downright springlike. Winters are short, sunny and dry. In summer (June to August) Kūnmíng offers cool respite, though rain is more prevalent.

History

The region of Kūnmíng has been inhabited for 2000 years. Until the 8th century, the town was a remote Chinese outpost, but the kingdom of Nanzhao captured it and made it a secondary capital. In 1274 the Mongols came through, sweeping all and sundry before them.

In the 14th century the Ming set up shop in Yúnnánfǔ, as Kūnmíng was then known, building a walled town on the present site. From the 17th century onwards, the history of this city becomes rather grisly. The last Ming resistance to the invading Manchu took place in Yúnnán in the 1650s and was crushed by General Wu Sangui. Wu in turn rebelled against the king and held out until his death in 1678. His successor was overthrown by the Manchu emperor Kangxi and subsequently killed himself in Kūnmíng in 1681.

In the 19th century the city suffered several bloodbaths. The rebel Muslim leader Du Wenxiu, the sultan of Dàlǐ, attacked and besieged the city several times between 1858 and 1868; it was not until 1873 that the rebellion was finally and bloodily crushed.

The intrusion of the West into Kūnmíng began in the mid 19th century from British Burma and French Indochina. By 1900 Kūnmíng, Hékǒu, Sīmáo and Měngzì had been opened to foreign trade. The French were keen to exploit the region's copper, tin and timber resources, and in 1910 their Indochina train, started in 1898 at Hanoi, reached the city.

Kūnmíng's expansion began with WWII, when factories were established and refugees fleeing the Japanese poured in from eastern China. In a bid to keep China from falling to Japan, Anglo-American forces sent supplies to nationalist troops entrenched in Sìchuān and Yúnnán. Supplies came overland on a dirt road carved out of the mountains from 1937 to 1938 by 160,000 Chinese with virtually no equipment. This was the famous Burma Road, a 1000km haul from Lashio to Kūnmíng. Today, Renmin Xilu marks the tail end of the road.

In early 1942 the Japanese captured Lashio, cutting the supply line. Kūnmíng continued to handle most of the incoming aid from 1942 to 1945, when US planes flew the mission of crossing the 'Hump', the towering 5000m mountain ranges between India and Yúnnán. A black market sprang up and a fair proportion of the medicines, canned food, petrol and other goods intended for the military and relief agencies were siphoned off into other hands.

The face of Kūnmíng has been radically altered since then, with streets widened and office buildings and housing projects flung up. With the coming of the railway, industry has expanded rapidly, and a surprising range of goods and machinery available in China now bears the 'Made in Yúnnán' stamp. The city's produce includes steel, foodstuffs, trucks, machine tools, electrical equipment, textiles, chemicals, building materials and plastics.

Orientation

The jurisdiction of Kūnmíng covers 6200 sq km, encompassing four city districts and four rural counties. The centre of the city is the roundabout at the intersection of Zhengyi Lu and Dongfeng Xilu. East of the intersection is Kūnmíng's major north–south road, Beijing Lu. At the southern end is the main train station and the long-distance bus station.

MAPS

Several maps are available, some with a smattering of English names. The *Yunnan Communications and Tourist Map* (Y10) has good English labels on the provincial map, and on the Kunming city map on the flip side.

Information

BOOKSHOPS

Mandarin Books & CDs (West Gate, Yúnnán University) has guidebooks, novels, magazines and a selection of travel writing in English and other languages.

Xinhua Bookshop (Xīnhuá Shūdiàn; Nanping Jie) Dozens of regional and city maps are stuffed in a rack facing the cash register.

INTERNET ACCESS 网吧

Pretty well every hotel and café frequented by travellers offers email for Y5-10 per hour; try the Camellia Hotel (p693) and the Hump (p693).

MEDICAL SERVICES

Shuanghe Pharmacy (Shuānghè Dàyàofáng; Tuodong Lu; ☾ 24hr) Opposite Yúnnán Airlines.

Yanan Hospital (Yán'ān Yīyuàn; ☎ 317 7499, ext 311; 1st fl, block 6, Renmin Donglu) Has a foreigners' clinic.

MONEY

Bank of China (Zhōngguó Yínháng; 448 Renmin Donglu; ☾ 9am-noon & 2-5pm) Changes travellers cheques and foreign currency and offers cash advances on credit cards. There is an ATM here. There are branches at Dongfeng Xilu and Huancheng Nanlu.

POST & TELEPHONE

China Telecom (Zhōngguó Diànxìn; cnr Beijing Lu & Dongfeng Donglu) You can make international calls here.
International Post Office (Guójì Yóujú; 231 Beijing Lu); branch office (Dongfeng Donglu) The main office has a very efficient poste restante and parcel service (per letter Y3, ID required). It is also the city's Express Mail Service (EMS) and Western Union agent.

PUBLIC SECURITY BUREAU

PSB (☎ 571 7001; Jīnxīng Huáyuán, Jinxing Lu; ⏰ 9-5pm Mon-Fri) The Foreign Affairs Branch will issue visa extensions. The main entrance is off Erhuan Beilu. Take bus 3, 25 or 57.

TOURIST INFORMATION

Many of the popular backpacker hotels and some of the cafés can assist with travel queries.

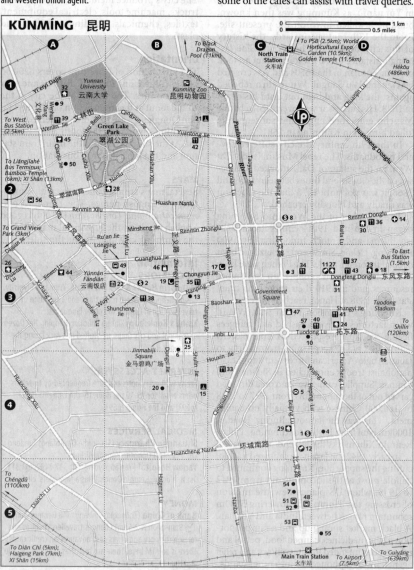

KŪNMÍNG 昆明

China International Travel Service (CITS; Zhōngguó Guójì Lǚxíngshè; ☎ 356 6730; 285 Huancheng Nanlu; ⏱ 9am-5.30pm) organizes tours. Also gives information to independent travellers, albeit reluctantly. English and French spoken.

Tourist Complaint & Consultative Telephone (☎ 316 4961) Where you can complain about or report dodgy tourist operations.

Dangers & Annoyances

Kūnmíng is one of the safest cities in China but take special precaution near the train and long-distance bus stations. The area can get seedy at night and there have been reports of travellers having their bags razored.

Sights & Activities

TANG DYNASTY PAGODAS

To the south of Jinbi Lu are two Tang pagodas. **West Pagoda** (Xìsì Tǎ; Dongsi Jie; admission Y2; ⏱ 9am-6pm) is the more interesting. Attached is a compound that is a popular spot for older people to get together, drink tea and play cards and mah jong.

East Pagoda (Dōngsì Tǎ; Shulin Jie) was, according to Chinese sources, destroyed by an earthquake; Western sources say it was destroyed by the Muslim revolt. It was rebuilt in the 19th century, but there's little to see.

YUANTONG TEMPLE 圆通寺

This **temple** (Yuántōng Sì; Yuantong Jie; admission Y4; ⏱ 8am-5pm) is the largest Buddhist complex in Kūnmíng and a draw for pilgrims. It's over 1000 years old, and has seen many renovations. To the rear a hall has been added, with a **statue of Sakyamuni**, a gift from Thailand's king. There's a great vegetarian restaurant (p694) across the main road from the temple entrance.

YÚNNÁN PROVINCIAL MUSEUM 云南省博物馆

Closed for renovations during research, this **museum** (Yúnnán Shěng Bówùguǎn; Wuyi Lu) covers the province's ancient bronze drums, Buddhist art and ethnic minorities. It's generally worth a visit and should be open again by the time you read this. Bus 5 goes here from the Camellia Hotel.

INFORMATION	
Bank of China 中国银行	1 C4
Bank of China 中国银行	2 B3
China Telecom 中国电信	3 C3
CITS 中国国际旅行社	4 D4
International Post Office 国际邮局	5 C4
Jinmabiji Sqaure 金马碧鸡广场	6 B3
King World Hotel 锦华大酒店	7 C5
Lao Consulate 老挝领事馆	(see 23)
Main Bank of China 中国银行	8 C2
Mandarin Books & CDs 五华书苑	9 A1
Myanmar Consulate 缅甸领事馆	(see 23)
Shuanghe Pharmacy 药店	10 C5
Thai Consulate 泰王国总领事馆	11 D3
Vietnamese Consulate 越南领事馆	12 C4
Xinhua Bookstore 新华书店	13 B3
Yanan Hospital 延安医院	14 D2

SIGHTS & ACTIVITIES	
East Pagoda 东寺塔	15 B4
Kunming City Museum 昆明市博物馆	16 D3
Mosque 清真寺	17 C3
Mr Chen Tours 陈先生旅游	18 D3
Nancheng Mosque 南城清真古寺	19 B3
West Pagoda 西寺塔	20 B4
Yuantong Temple 圆通寺	21 B1
Yunnan Provincial Museum 云南省博物馆	22 B3

SLEEPING	
Camellia Hotel 茶花宾馆	23 D3
Greenland Hotel 绿洲大酒店	24 D3
Hump 驼峰酒吧	25 B3
Kunming Cloudland International Youthhostel 昆明青年旅社	26 A3
Kunming Hotel 昆明饭店	27 D3
Kunming Youth Hostel 昆明国际青年旅社	28 B2
Kūnhú Fàndiàn 昆湖饭店	29 C4
Míngdū Dàjiǔdiàn 明都大酒店	30 D2
Sakura Kunming 昆明樱花酒店	31 D3
Yúndà Bīnguǎn 云大宾馆	32 A1

EATING	
1910 La Gare Du Sud 火车南站	33 C4
Brothers Jiang 江氏兄弟	34 C3
Carrefour Supermarket 家乐福超级市场	35 B3
Hotpot Restaurant 火锅	36 D2
Ma Ma Fu's 2 马马付	37 D3
Muslim Restaurants 清真饭店	38 B3
Salvador's	39 A1
Wei's Pizzeria 哈哈餐厅	40 D3
White Pagoda Dai Restaurant 白塔傣味厅	41 D3
Yuquanzhai Vegetarian Restaurant 玉泉斋	42 B2
Zhènxìng Fàndiàn 振兴饭店	43 D3

DRINKING	
Cafe de Camel 骆驼咖啡馆	(see 40)
Kundu Night Market 昆都夜市	44 A3
Speakeasy 说吧	45 A2

SHOPPING	
Flower & Bird Market 花鸟市场	46 B3
Tian Fu Famous Teas 天福茗茶	47 C3

TRANSPORT	
Bus Station 客运站	48 C5
Buses to Bamboo Temple 到筇竹寺的班车	(see 49)
Buses to Xī Shān 到西山的班车	49 B3
CAAC 中国民航	(see 57)
Dragonair 港龙航空	(see 12)
Fat Tyres Bike Shop	50 A2
Ko Wai Lin Travel 秣威霖旅游	(see 23)
Lao Aviation 老挝航空公司	(see 23)
Long-Distance Bus Station 长途汽车总站	51 C5
Malaysia Airlines 马来西亚航空公司	(see 31)
Sanye International Air Service 三叶国际航空服务有限公司	52 C5
Sleeper Bus Stand 铺汽车站	53 C5
Thai Airways 泰国航空公司	54 C5
Train Ticket Office 火车站售票处	55 D5
Xiǎoxīmén Bus Station 小西门汽车客运站	56 A2
Yunnan Airlines 南航公司	57 C3

YÚNNÁN

KUNMING CITY MUSEUM 昆明市博物馆
The left-hand hall of this **museum** (Kūnmíngshì Bówùguǎn; Tuodong Lu; admission Y5; ⊗ 10am-5pm Tue-Sun) is packed with swords, spears and surprises like mini bronze ox heads excavated in the Kunming area. The right-hand hall has an impressive 6.6m-pillar engraved with Buddhist scriptures from the Dali kingdom (937–1253). It's said Prime Minister Yuan Douguang of the Dali kingdom had it constructed for Kūnmíng's Military Administrator Gao Mingsheng. A middling dinosaur exhibit inhabits the second floor.

GREEN LAKE PARK 翠湖公园
Get to this **park** (Cuìhú Gōngyuán; Cuihu Nanlu; ⊗ 6am-10pm) early in the morning to watch taichi, browse the nearby shops or relax in one of the trendy or not-so-hip lakeside cafés.

MOSQUES 清真寺
The oldest of the lot, the 400-year-old **Nancheng Mosque** (Nánchéng Qīngzhēn Gǔsì; 51 Zhengyi Lu), was ripped down in 1997 in order to build a larger version. The new mosque looks vaguely like a bad Las Vegas casino. Not too far away is a lively strip of Muslim restaurants and shops selling skullcaps, Arabic calligraphy and pictures of Mecca. To get to the Mus-lim area from the Zhengyi Lu roundabout, walk west past Chūnchéng Jiǔlóu (Spring City Hotel) and then bear left a half-block to a small alley.

There's another **mosque** nearby, wedged between Huguo Lu and Chongyun Jie.

Tours
Several tour outfits cover Kūnmíng and its surrounding sights faster than public minibuses would, but be prepared to pay for them. They generally feature lots of sights most travellers find rather boring. Some tour operators refuse to take foreigners on their tours, claiming the language barrier causes too much trouble. More central sights like Yuantong Temple are just a short bicycle ride away – it hardly makes sense to join a tour to see them.

Mr Chen's Tour (☎ 318 8114; Room 3116, No 3 Bldg, Camellia Hotel, 154 Dongfeng Lu) can organise trips to almost anywhere you want to go, including flights and overland trips to Lhasa (see p696 for more details).

Sleeping
BUDGET
Kunming Cloudland Youth Hostel (昆明大脚氏请年旅舍; Kūnmíng Dàjiǎoshí Qīngnián Lǚshè; ☎ 410 3777; 23 Zhuantang Lu; 篆塘路23号; 4/6-bed dm Y30/20; ▢)

YÚNNÁN'S MUSLIMS

Yúnnán's sizeable Muslim population dates back to the 13th century, when Mongol forces swooped into the province to outflank the Song dynasty troops. Sayyid Ajall was named governor in 1274 and Yúnnán became the only part of China under a Muslim leader after Kublai Khan's forces arrived. Muslim traders, builders and craftsmen followed in the army's wake.

All over China mosques were simultaneously raised with the new Yuan dynasty banner. A Muslim was entrusted to build the first Mongol palace in Běijīng, where an observatory based on Persian models was also constructed. Dozens of Arabic texts were translated and consulted by Chinese scientists, influencing Chinese mathematics more than any other source. The most famous Yúnnán Muslim was Cheng Ho (Zheng He), a eunuch admiral who pushed Chinese seafaring as far away as the Middle East.

Ethnically indistinguishable from the Han Chinese, the Hui, as ethnic Chinese Muslims are known, have had an unfortunate history of repression and persecution, a recent low point being the years of the Cultural Revolution. Heavy land taxes and disputes between Muslims and Han Chinese over local gold and silver mines triggered a Muslim uprising in 1855, which lasted until 1873.

The Muslims chose Dàlǐ (Xiàguān) as their base and laid siege to Kūnmíng, overrunning the city briefly in 1863. Du Wenxiu, the Muslim leader, proclaimed his newly established kingdom of the Pacified South (Nánpíng Guó) and took the name Sultan Suleyman. But success was short-lived and in 1873 Dàlǐ was taken by Qing forces and Du Wenxiu was captured and executed. Up to a million people died in Yúnnán alone, the death toll rising to 18 million nationwide. The uprisings were quelled, but they also had the lasting effect of eliciting sympathy from Burma and fomenting a passion for indigenous culture among many of southwestern China's ethnic minorities, most of whom had supported the Hui.

This recently opened hostel is absolutely charming, with staff that makes a tremendous effort for guests. Dorms are bright, spotless and modern. To get here from the train or long-distance bus station, take city bus 64 and get off at the Yúnnán Daily News stop (云南日报社站).

Hump (Tuófēng Kèzhàn; ☎ 364 0359; Jinmabiji Square, Jinbi Lu; 金碧路, 金马碧鸡广场; 8-bed dm Y25) A magnificent budget option; dorms are enormous and come with individual lockers. There's a basketball court-sized common room and pool, and Ping-Pong tables on the terrace. Umpteen bars and discos are at your doorstep. What more do you need?

Kunming Youth Hostel (Kūnmíng Guójì Qīngnián Lüshè; ☎ 517 5395; youthhostel.km@sohu.com; 94 Cuihu Nanlu; 翠湖路94号; dm Y25, d from Y80) Tucked along a lane beside the Zhengxie Hotel, this hostel is basic but clean and quiet. Dorms are stark white and joltingly lit. However, the hostel is right by Green Lake Park and staff are laid-back and friendly.

Kūnhú Fàndiàn (☎ 314 3699; 202 Beijing Lu; 北京路202号; dm Y25, s & d with bathroom Y128) Near the train and bus stations, a good number of backpackers end up here. There's a travel service onsite, and clean, beaten up old dorms. Singles are big but furnished with doll-sized beds anyone over 160cm tall will have a struggle getting comfortable in. The hotel is two stops from the main train station on bus 2, 23 or 47, though it's easy enough to walk it.

Camellia Hotel (Cháhuā Bīnguǎn; ☎ 316 3000; fax 314 7033; 96 Dongfeng Donglu; 东风东96路; dm Y30, d Y188-288) In truth, this budget legend is getting a little rough around the edges with some downright grubby rooms on offer. But with travel services, bicycle hire, foreign-exchange, reasonably priced laundry services and a colossal breakfast buffet, the response of most backpackers is a resounding 'so what?' To get here from the main train station, take buses 2 or 23 to Dongfeng Donglu, then change to bus 5 heading east and get off at the second stop.

MIDRANGE

Yúndà Bīnguǎn (Yúnnán University Hotel; ☎ 503 3624; fax 5148513; Wenhua Xiang; 文化巷; d from Y160) If you want to stay in the university area then the standard doubles here are a good choice. It's next to the university's west gate. Incredibly friendly.

Míngdū Dàjiǔdiàn (☎ 624 0666; fax 624 0898; 206 Baita Lu; 白塔路206号; s/d Y388, ste 688) Breaking the beige conspiracy of most midrange Chinese hotels, rooms here are done up in a refreshing red-gold colour combo. Bathrooms are spacious and tidy.

TOP END

Kunming Hotel (Kūnmíng Fàndiàn; ☎ 316 2063; www .kunminghotel.com.cn; 52 Dongfeng Donglu; 东风东路52号; s & d Y780, ste Y1419; ⊠) With a bar, disco, karaoke hall, tennis court and even a bowling alley on-site you may never want to leave this place. There are also high-end restaurants, including Cháozhōu (featuring dishes from eastern Guǎngdōng: light, tasty cuisine with a liberal use of vegetables). Travellers who've made the splurge here give this hotel unreserved raves.

Sakura Kunming (Kūnmíng Yīnghuā Jiǔdiàn; ☎ 316 5888; 25 Dongfeng Donglu; 东风东路25号; d from Y800; ⊠) This super-luxury monster is opposite the Kunming Hotel. It has some excellent restaurants (Thai and southwestern American/Mexican, along with a popular breakfast/lunch buffet), a Western-style pub, a small health club, pool, and a disco.

Greenland Hotel (Lǜzhōu Dàjiǔdiàn; ☎ 318 9999; www.greenlandhotel.com.cn; 80 Tuodong Lu; 拓东路80号; s & d incl breakfast from Y945; ste from Y1527; ⊠) It's probably got the slickest service in the city. Rooms are nice and have a generous assortment of wine glasses, but lack the 'va-va voom' you'd expect after walking past the fish-filled fountain on the way to the lobby.

Eating

Kūnmíng has some great food, especially in the snack line. Regional specialities are qìguōjī (器锅鸡; herb-infused chicken cooked in an earthenware steam pot), guòqiáo mìxiàn (过桥米线; across-the-bridge noodles), rǔbǐng (乳饼; goats' cheese) and various Muslim beef and mutton dishes.

Roadside noodle shops will give you a bowl of rice noodles for around Y5 and a bewildering array of sauces with which to flavour the broth – most of them are hot and spicy. Go hunting for these near the long-distance bus station and the lanes running off Beijing Lu.

Another place to go snack hunting is Shuncheng Jie, an east–west street running south of Dongfeng Xilu. Here you'll find literally dozens of Muslim restaurants, kebab stalls and noodle stands. Try bānmiàn (扳面; a kind of spaghetti) or Uighur suoman (fried noodle squares with peppers, tomato and cumin).

Western-style cafés can be found near the Camellia Hotel and Kūnhú Fàndiàn, and the area surrounding Yúnnán University, in particular Wenlin Jie. These are also good areas to search out vegetarian fare.

Zhènxīng Fàndiàn (Yúnnán Typical Local Food Restaurant; cnr Baita Lu & Dongfeng Donglu; ☯ 24hr; dishes from Y5) You'll find a good range of dishes and snacks at this restaurant. The food gets decent reviews from both locals and foreigners, just don't come for the service.

Brothers Jiang (Jiāngshì Xiōngdì; Dongfeng Donglu; noodles Y10-60) This place has good across-the-bridge noodles that come with instructions on how to eat them. There are several branches situated throughout the city and they are easy to find: line-ups snake into the street during mealtimes. Pay upfront first at the cash register.

White Pagoda Dai Restaurant (Báitǎ Dǎi Wéitíng; ☎ 317 2932; 127 Shangyi Jie; dishes from Y10) All of Dai cuisine's greatest hits like pineapple sticky rice and spicy fish wrapped in bamboo shoots are found in this modest restaurant. It has also had a stab at creating some atmosphere, with a couple of thatched roofs over the tables and murals of 'Bǎnnà' on the walls.

Yuquanzhai Vegetarian Restaurant (Yùquánzhāi Cāntīng; Yuantong Jie; dishes from Y10) This outstanding vegetarian restaurant takes the practice of 'copying' meat-based dishes to a new level, with an encyclopaedic menu. The *tiěbǎn* (sizzling iron-pot) comes recommended. It's across the road from Yuantong Temple.

Salvador's (☎ 536-3525; Wenhua Xiang; dishes from Y15) Heaving with Chinese and foreign students from the nearby university, this café has superior coffee and hits like waffles and quesadillas. Though modern and on the slick side, Salvador's has the buzz of a student lounge and people here are generally relaxed and approachable.

Ma Ma Fu's 2 (Māmāfù Cāntīng; Baita Lu; dishes from Y15) This branch of the legendary Lìjiāng café is right around the corner west of the Camellia Hotel. Chinese dishes like the tongue-searing but outstanding spicy beef and rice (Y15) are by far the best, but most people order Western fare like pizza and apple pie.

1910 La Gare du Sud (Huǒchē Nánzhàn; ☎ 316 9486; dishes from Y20) This classy restaurant serving Yúnnán specialities in a pleasant neocolonial-style atmosphere gets terrific feedback from travellers. There's an English menu if you ask for it. It's hidden down an alley south of Jinbi Lu.

Wei's Pizzeria (☎ 316 6189; Tuodong Lu; pizzas from Y25, Chinese dishes from Y6) Most come here for wood-fired pizzas, others for cold beer served in frosted steins. But the menu is also loaded with regional specialities like the *taózá rǔbǐng* (fried goats' cheese and Yúnnán ham) that are definitely worth a try. The restaurant is down an alley off Tuodong Lu.

Hotpot Restaurant (Huǒguǒ; Renmin Donglu cnr Baita Lu; per stick from Y1) An absolute madhouse at peak mealtimes, this restaurant will take the very aggressive or the very brave to muscle their way though the throngs and eventually get fed. Nonetheless, with all the slick restaurant and eateries all over Kūnmíng these days, this is a breath of fresh air.

For self-catering try **Carrefour** (Jiālèfú; Nanping Jie), a branch of the popular French supermarket chain.

Drinking

You'll find plenty of places to drink in Kūnmíng no matter what your mood. For laid-back atmosphere, cold beers and music low enough you can still talk to your friends, prowl the cafés and bars around the university area. Wenhua Xiang is a good place to start. If you need strobe lights and dancing more

---

ACROSS-THE-BRIDGE NOODLES

Yúnnán's best-known dish is across-the-bridge noodles (过桥米线; *guòqiáo mǐxiàn*). You are provided with a bowl of very hot soup (stewed with chicken, duck and spare ribs) on which a thin layer of oil is floating, along with a side dish of raw pork slivers (in classier places this might be chicken or fish) and vegetables, and a bowl of rice noodles. Diners place all of the ingredients quickly into the soup bowl, where they are cooked by the steamy broth. They say the dish was created by a woman married to an imperial scholar. He decamped to an isolated island to study and she got creative with the hot meals she brought to him every day after crossing the bridge. This noodle dish was by far the most popular and christened 'Across-the-Bridge Noodles' in honour of her daily commute.

than conversation, there are dozens of super loud bars at **Jinmabiji Square**. And for hard-core techno, outrageous prices and all around silliness, the **Kundu Night Market** has dozens of discos frequented by the young, the rich and the (sometimes) weirdly dressed. Even more discos line Xinwen Jie nearby.

Other places to try include:

Speakeasy (Shuōbā; Dongfeng Xilu; ☼ 8pm-late) Part of the weekend pub crawl for most people between 20 and 40 years old. It doesn't get slagged like other places do for being either 'too foreign' or 'too Chinese' and there's always a great mix of expats and locals. It's down the stairs under the blue sign.

Café de Camel (Tuodong Lu; ☼ 9am-late) A popular place with locals and foreigners, this restaurant/coffee shop doubles as a drinking den on weekends when tables are moved to one side and a DJ plays tunes until dawn.

Shopping

You have to do a fair bit of digging to come up with inspiring purchases in Kūnmíng. Yúnnán specialities are marble and batik from Dàlǐ, jade from Ruìlì, minority embroidery, musical instruments and spotted-brass utensils.

Some functional items that make good souvenirs include large bamboo water pipes for smoking angel-haired Yúnnán tobacco; and local herbal medicines, such as Yúnnán Báiyào (Yúnnán White Medicine), which is a blend of over 100 herbs and is highly prized by Chinese throughout the world.

Yunnanese tea is an excellent buy and comes in several varieties, from bowl-shaped bricks of smoked green tea called *tuóchá*, which have been around since at least Marco Polo's time, to leafy black tea that rivals some of India's best.

One teashop worth checking out is **Tian Fu Famous Teas** (Tiānfú Míngchá; cnr Shangyi Jie & Beijing Lu).

The **Flower & Bird Market** (Huāniǎo Shìchǎng; Tongdao Jie) seems to sell everything except flowers and birds, instead you'll find old coins and wooden elephants, tacky wall murals and so-called 'antiques'.

For real antiques it's better to look among the privately run shops on Beijing Lu and Dongfeng Donglu.

Getting There & Away
AIR
Yunnan Airlines/CAAC (Zhōngguó Mínháng; ☎ 316 4270, 313 8562; Tuodong Lu; ☼ 24hr) issues tickets for any Chinese airline but the office only offers dis-

counts on Yunnan Airlines flights. From 8pm to 8am buy your tickets from the small ticket window on the left side of the building.

A good one-stop shop for booking flights is the **Sanye International Air Service** (Sānyè Guójì Hángkōng Fúwù Yǒuxiàn Gōngsī; ☎ 353 0773; fax 354 3370; 66-68 Beijing Lu), next door to the long-distance bus station. The office deals with more than 20 international carriers and all the national ones.

Flights are scheduled to depart daily from Kūnmíng for Běijīng (Y1940), Chéngdū (Y830), Chóngqìng (Y840), Guǎngzhōu (Y1290), Guìyáng (Y570), Nánjīng (Y1680), Nánníng (Y710), Shànghǎi (Y2030), Shēnzhèn (Y1370), Qīngdǎo (Y1730) and Xī'ān (Y1100).

There is now a weekly flight to Lhasa (Y1670).

Within Yúnnán province you can fly to Bǎoshān (Y640), Jǐnghóng (Y780), Lìjiāng (Y660), Mángshì/Déhóng (Y790), Xiàguān/Dàlǐ (Y520) and Shangri-la (Y770).

There are international flights to most major Asian cities including Hong Kong (Y2108, daily), Vientiane (Y985, Wed & Sun) and Kuala Lumpur (Y2256).

Foreign airline offices in Kūnmíng include the following:

Dragonair (☎ 356 1208, 356 1209; 2/F Kaīhuá Guǎngchǎng, 157 Beijing Lu)

Malaysia Airlines (☎ 316 5888; Sakura Kūnmíng, 25 Dongfeng Donglu) Office is outside, on your right-hand side approaching the hotel entrance.

Lao Aviation (☎ 312 5748; Camellia Hotel, 154 Dongfeng Donglu)

Thai Airways (☎ 351 1515; 68 Beijing Lu) Next to the King World Hotel.

BUS
There seem to be buses leaving from everywhere in Kūnmíng and bus transport can be a little confusing at first. However, the long-distance bus station on Beijing Lu is the best place to organise bus tickets to almost anywhere in Yúnnán or further afield. Exceptions to this are more local destinations like Diān Chí; see Around Kūnmíng p696 for more details on transport to individual attractions close to the city.

From the sleeper bus stand close to the main train station you can get sleeper buses to most of the same destinations. Buses here tend to be a bit older and so ticket prices are generally a bit cheaper.

For information on Shílín, see p700.

TRAIN

You can buy train tickets up to 10 days in advance, which is good news because at peak times, especially public holidays, tickets get sold out days ahead of departure.

At the time of writing, the train to Hekou in Vietnam had been suspended indefinitely, so you'll have to get the bus instead.

Rail options from Kūnmíng (all prices listed are for hard sleepers) include trains to Běijīng (Y578), Shànghǎi (Y519), Guìyáng (Y162), Guǎngzhōu (Y353), Xī'ān (Y258), Emei Town (Y209), Chéngdū (Y252) and Liùpánshuǐ (Y96). Several overnight trains run daily to Dàlǐ (Y95). Check at the train ticket office for times.

TO TIBET

It's now possible to fly to Lhasa from Kūnmíng. However, the situation is the same as in Chéngdū and you must have the requisite permit and travel as part of a group. Mr Chen's Tour (p692) can sort you out with the necessary permits and sign you onto a 'tour' with a bunch of people you'll never see again once you've landed in Lhasa. At the time of writing these packages cost around Y2750.

There are also flights from Shangri-la to Lhasa and it has recently become possible to travel overland from Shangri-la into Tibet (see p726). From Chéngdū Mr Chen can also organise overland travel to Tibet, although some travellers have reported his sales pitch to be better than his trips.

Getting Around

TO/FROM THE AIRPORT

Buses 52 and 67 run between the centre of town and the airport. A taxi will cost between Y15 and Y20.

BICYCLE

Many backpackers hotels and hostels also rent bikes for around Y15 per day.

Fat Tyres Bike Shop (☎ 530 1755; 61 Qianju Jie; per day Y20) has a large stock of bicycles including some very good mountain bikes. It also organises Sunday morning bike rides – you need to make reservations ahead of time.

BUS

Bus 63 runs from the east bus station to the Camellia Hotel and on to the main train station. Bus 23 runs from the north train station south down Beijing Lu to the main train station. Fares range from Y1 to Y4. The main city buses have no conductors and require exact change.

AROUND KŪNMÍNG

There are some fabulous sights within a 15km radius of Kūnmíng, but local transport hasn't quite caught up with people's interest in visiting them. What is available is time-consuming, awkward and very, very crowded. There are few crossovers for combined touring, so it would take something like five return trips, over three days or more, to see everything.

KŪNMÍNG BUS TIMETABLES				
Destination	**Price**	**Duration**	**Frequency**	**Departs**
Dàlǐ	Y116	5hr	frequent	7.30am–7.30pm
Dàlǐ (sleeper)	Y95	10hr	2 daily	9pm, 9.30pm
Lìjiāng	Y171	9hr	hourly	7.30–11.30am
Lìjiāng (sleeper)	Y139	10–12hr	2 daily	8pm, 8.30pm
Jǐnghóng	Y223	10hr	4 daily	9.30am, 6pm, 7.45pm, 8.30pm
Jǐnghóng (sleeper)	Y155	10hr	half-hourly	4–8pm
Shangri-la	Y142–161	13–15hr	1–3 daily	8am, 4.30pm, 6pm
Shangri-la (sleeper)	Y167	13–15hr	every 30min	4pm–8.30pm
Bǎoshān	Y171	7hr	4 daily	
Bǎoshān (sleeper)	Y142	12hr	2 daily	7.30pm, 8.30pm
Ruìlì	Y222	13hr	2 daily	10am, 6pm
Ruìlì (sleeper)	Y209	15hr	daily	8pm
Hékǒu	Y119	12hr	2 daily	9.45am, 1.30pm
Yuányáng	Y73–82	6–7hrs	3 daily	10.40am, 7.30pm, 8pm

prentices to fashion 500 *luóhàn* (arhats or noble ones). The figures are a sculptural *tour de force* – either very realistic or very surrealistic. Down one huge wall come some 70-odd incredible surfing Buddhas, riding the waves on a variety of mounts – blue dogs, giant crabs, shrimp, turtles and unicorns.

The statues have been constructed with the precision of a split-second photograph – a monk about to chomp into a large peach (the face contorted almost into a scream), a figure caught turning around to emphasise a discussion point, another about to clap two cymbals together, yet another cursing a pet monster. So lifelike are the sculptures that they were considered in bad taste by Li Guangxiu's contemporaries (some of whom no doubt appeared in caricature), and upon the project's completion he disappeared into thin air.

Unfortunately you have to make do with peering round the door as the hall has been closed to visitors to stop local tourists throwing coins at the statues – an act that is thought to bring them good luck (it obviously didn't work). If the temple is quiet when you visit, the friendly monks might be persuaded to let you in for a peek inside.

The temple is about 12km northwest of Kūnmíng. Minibuses (Y10, 30 minutes) leave when full from opposite Yúnnán Fàndiàn from 7am. Minibuses return regularly to Kūnmíng. A taxi to the temple will cost around Y45.

Golden Temple 金殿

Hidden amid a pine forest on Phoenix Song Mountain is **Golden Temple** (Jīn Diàn; admission Y20; 8.30am-5.30pm) a Taoist temple, and actually

Arranging a car and driver through your accommodation or seeing what tours CITS (p691) is offering are probably your best bets if you want to see everything fast.

If you don't have that much time, the Bamboo Temple (Qióngzhú Sì) and Xī Shān (Western Hills) are probably the most interesting. Both have decent transport connections. Diān Chí (Lake Dian) has terrific circular-tour possibilities of its own. If you have more time, get your hands on a good map, hire a good bicycle and tour the area on two wheels (although there are some steep hills lurking out there...).

Bamboo Temple 筇竹寺

Named for the bamboo groves that once surrounded it, this **temple** (Qióngzhú Sì; 8am-6pm; admission Y10) dates back to the Tang dynasty and is worth a visit for its tremendous life-sized clay sculptures.

The temple was burned down and rebuilt in the 15th century, then restored from 1883 to 1890 when the abbot employed master Sichuanese sculptor Li Guangxiu and his ap-

made of bronze, that was the brainchild of General Wu Sangui. Wu was dispatched by the Manchus in 1659 to quell uprisings in the region but instead turned on the Manchus and set himself up as a rebel warlord, with the Golden Temple as his summer residence. The current structure dates back to 1671; the original Ming temple stood in the same spot but was carted off to Dàlǐ. Out back, there's a 5m-high, 14-tonne bell.

Buses 10 or 71 run here from Kūnmíng's north train station or you can cycle. A cable car one-way/return Y15/25 runs from the temple to the World Horticultural Expo Garden.

World Horticultural Expo Garden
世界园艺博览园

This 218-hectare **garden complex** (Shìjiè Yuányì Bólǎnyuán; ☎ 501 2367; adult/student Y100/50; ☀ 8am-5pm, last entry at 4pm), about 10km northeast of Kūnmíng near the Golden Temple, was built in April 1999 for the World Horticultural Exposition. The gardens are a mix of pleasant Disney-style topiary work and strangely pointless exhibits left over from the expo; the place is worth a visit if you are interested in gardens and plants, otherwise give it a miss.

From Kunming's north train station take bus 10 to the terminal. A cable car (Y15) at the back of the gardens can take you to the Golden Temple.

Black Dragon Pool 黑龙潭

This is a rather mediocre **garden** (Hēilóng Tán; admission Y1; ☀ 9am-6pm), 11km north of Kūnmíng, with old cypresses, dull Taoist pavilions and no bubble in the springs. But the view of the surrounding mountains from the garden is inspiring. Within walking distance is the **Kunming Botanical Institute** (☀ 9am-5pm), where the flora collection might be of interest to specialists.

Take bus 9 from Kūnmíng's north train station.

DIĀN CHÍ 滇池

The shoreline of **Diān Chí** (Lake Dian), to the south of Kūnmíng, is dotted with settlements, farms and fishing enterprises; the western side is hilly, while the eastern side is flat country. The southern end of the lake, particularly the southeast, is industrial.

The lake is elongated – about 40km from north to south – and covers an area of 300 sq km. Plying the waters are *fānchuán* (pirate-

sized junks with bamboo-battened canvas sails). It's mainly for scenic touring and hiking, and there are some fabulous aerial views from the ridges at Dragon Gate in Xī Shān, below).

Grand View Park 大观公园

This **park** (Dàguān Gōngyuán; admission Y10) is at the northernmost tip of Diān Chí, 3km southwest of the city centre. It covers 60 hectares and includes a nursery, a children's playground, rowboats and pavilions. A Buddhist temple was originally constructed here in 1862. The **Grand View Tower** (Dàguān Lóu) provides good views. Its facades are inscribed with a 180-character poem by Qing poet Sun Ranweng, rapturously extolling the beauty of the lake.

Bus 4 runs to the park from Yuantong Temple via the city centre; bus 52 departs from near the Kunming Hotel. At the northeastern end of the park is a dock where you may be able to get a boat (Y5, 40 minutes) to **Longmen Village** (Lóngmén Cūn) and **Haigeng Park** (Hǎigěng Gōngyuán). From Longmen Village you can hike up the trail to Dragon Gate and Xī Shān, and catch a minibus back into town from near the summit at the Tomb of Nie Er. From Haigeng Park, take bus 44 to Kūnmíng's main train station.

Xī Shān 西山

Spread out across a long wedge of parkland on the western side of Diān Chí, **Xī Shān** (Western Hills) is full of walking trails (some very steep), and dotted with temples and other cultural relics, all just waiting to be explored. Its hills are also called the Sleeping Beauty Hills, a reference to the undulating contours, which are thought to resemble a reclining woman with tresses of hair flowing into the sea. The path up to the summit passes a series of famous temples – it's a steep approach from the north side. The hike from Gāoyáo bus station, at the foot of the hills, to Dragon Gate takes 2½ hours, though most people take a connecting bus from Gāoyáo to the top section, or take a minibus direct to the Tomb of Nie Er. Alternatively, it is also possible to cycle to the hills from the city centre in about an hour – to vary the trip, try doing the return route across the dikes of upper Diān Chí.

At the foot of the climb, about 15km from Kūnmíng, is **Huating Temple** (Huátíng Sì; admission Y4; ☀ 8am-6pm), a country temple of the Nanzhao kingdom believed to have been constructed in the 11th century, rebuilt in the 14th century, and extended in the Ming and Qing dynasties.

The road from Huating Temple winds 2km from here up to the Ming dynasty **Taihua Temple** (Tàihuá Sì; admission Y3; ⊙ 8am-6pm). The temple courtyard houses a fine collection of flowering trees, including magnolias and camellias.

Further along the road, near the minibus and cable car terminus, is the **Tomb of Nie Er** (Nièěr Zhīmù; admission Y1; ⊙ 8am-6pm). Nie Er (1912–36) was a talented Yúnnán musician who composed the national anthem of the People's Republic of China (PRC) before drowning in Japan en route for further training in the Soviet Union.

Sānqīng Gé, near the top of the mountain, was a country villa of a Yuan dynasty prince, and was later turned into a temple dedicated to the three main Taoist deities.

From the tomb you can catch a **chairlift** (one way/return Y15/30; ⊙ 8am-7pm) if you want to skip the fairly steep ascent to the summit. Alternatively a tourist tram takes passengers up to the Dragon Gate for Y2.

Further up, near the top of the mountain, is **Dragon Gate** (Lóng Mén; admission Y30; ⊙ 8am-6pm). This is a group of grottoes, sculptures, corridors and pavilions that were hacked from the cliff between 1781 and 1835 by a Taoist monk and co-workers, who must have been hanging up there by their fingertips. At least that's what the locals do when they visit, seeking out the most precarious perches for views of Diān Chí. The tunnel along the outer cliff edge is so narrow that only one or two people can squeeze by at a time, so avoid public holidays and weekends! Entrance to the Dragon Gate area includes Sānqīng Gé. It's possible to walk up to the Dragon Gate along the cliff path and return via the back routes.

GETTING THERE & AWAY

Minibuses (one way/return Y10/20, one hour, 7.30am to 2pm) leave when full from opposite Yúnnán Fàndiàn. The only trouble is you could be waiting for ages for the bus to fill up.

It's more reliable to use local buses: take bus 5 from the Kunming Hotel to the terminus at Liǎngjiāhé, and then change to bus 6, which will take you to Gāoyáo bus station at the foot of the hills. Minibuses (Y5) also leave from Liǎngjiāhé and drop passengers off at the Tomb of Nie Er.

To return to Kūnmíng take the bus or scramble down from the Dragon Gate area to the lakeside. Steps lead downhill a couple of hundred metres before Dragon Gate and the Sānqīng Gé area ticket office and end up in Longmen Village (Lóngmén Cūn), also known as Sānyì Cūn. When you reach the road, turn right and walk about 100m to a narrow spit of land leading across the lake. Continuing across the spit, you arrive at a narrow stretch of water and a small bridge. (You could also take the cable car across to Haigeng Park for Y30.)

Walk through Haigeng Park's far entrance and catch bus 44 to Kūnmíng's main train station. If you don't want to pay Y6 to cut through Haigeng Park, you'll have to walk 3km or so from the cable car to the entrance of the Yúnnán Nationalities Village or take a taxi (Y10).

Alternatively, bus 33 runs along the western lake shore through Longmen Village, or you can take a boat from Grand View Park.

Yúnnán Nationalities Museum
云南民族博物馆

On the northeast corner of the lake, the **Yúnnán Nationalities Museum** (Yúnnán Mínzú Bówùguǎn) is worth a visit if you have an interest in China's minority nationalities. Its halls display costumes, folk art, jewellery, handicrafts and musical instruments, as well as information concerning social structure and popular festivals on each of Yúnnán's 25 minority groups. Closed for renovations at the time of research, it will be reopened by the time you read this.

Chénggòng County 呈贡县

This county (Chénggòng Xiàn) is an orchard region on the eastern side of Diān Chí. Flowers bloom year-round, with the 'flower tide' in January, February and March. This is the best time to visit, especially the diminutive Dòunán village nearby. Once one of Yúnnán's poorest villages, it now sells more than 400,000 sprays of flowers each day. The village's per capita income went from US$13 to US$415 in four years.

Many Western varieties of camellia, azalea, orchid and magnolia derive from southwestern Chinese varieties. They were introduced to the West by adventuring botanists who carted off samples in the 19th and 20th centuries. Azaleas are native to China – of the 800 varieties in the world, 650 are found in Yúnnán.

During the **Spring Festival** (January/February) a profusion of blooms can be found at temple sites in and around Kūnmíng – notably the temples of Tàihuá, Huátíng, Yuántōng and the Golden Temple, as well as at Black Dragon Pool.

Take bus 5 heading east to the terminus at Júhuācūn, and change there for bus 12 to Chénggòng.

Zhenghe Park 郑和公园

At the southwest corner of Diān Chí, this **park** (Zhènghé Gōngyuán) commemorates the Ming dynasty navigator Zheng He (known as Admiral Cheng Ho outside China). A mausoleum here holds tablets with descriptions of his life and works. Zheng He, a Muslim, made seven voyages to more than 30 Asian and African countries in the 15th century in command of a huge imperial fleet (see the boxed text on p692).

From Xiǎoxīmén bus station take the bus to Jìnníng; the park is on a hill overlooking the town.

SHÍLÍN 石林
☎ 0871

This is one of those weird attractions that is equally the most visited and most derided (especially since the price hike) attractions in the Kūnmíng area. **Shílín** (Stone Forest; **☎** 771 0316; admission Y140) is a massive collection of grey limestone pillars located about 120km southeast of Kūnmíng. Split and eroded by wind and rain, the tallest reaches 30m high. Legend has it that the immortals smashed a mountain into a labyrinth for lovers seeking privacy.

Despite guides rather suddenly jumping out from behind pillars in minority dress (disturbing to say the least) and tour groups clogging the paths, there are ways to enjoy Shílín and make it worth the visit. Idyllic, secluded walks are within 2km of the centre and by sunset or moonlight the place becomes otherworldly.

Shílín can easily be done as a day trip from Kūnmíng. However if you decide to stay longer, then it's worth heading over to **Lùnán**, a small town that is about 10km north of Shílín. If you manage to time your visit with market day (Wednesday or Saturday), then you'll see Lùnán transform into a colossal jam of donkeys, horse carts and bikes. The streets are packed with produce, poultry and wares, and the Sani women are dressed in their finest.

Sleeping & Eating
Shílín doesn't have much in the way of accommodation and what it does offer is overpriced.

Stone Forest International Youth Hostel (Shílín Guójì Qīngnián Lüguǎn; **☎** 771 0768; 4-bed dm Y50, small s/d Y120, big s/d Y140) Directly opposite where the buses drop you off, this hostel offers the cleanest, best-value accommodation you will find in Shílín.

Shílín Bìshǔyuán Bīnguǎn (**☎** 771 1088; d/tr Y300/360, discounted Y240/288) If you're looking to splash out then the rooms here are quiet and have some good views over Shílín, but you still don't get a lot for your money.

Several restaurants next to the bus stop specialise in duck, roasted in extremely hot clay ovens with pine needles. A whole duck costs Y40 to Y50 and takes about 20 minutes to cook – have the restaurant staff put a beer in the freezer and it'll be just right when the duck comes out.

Near the main entrance is a cluster of restaurants and snack bars that are open from dawn to dusk. Check all prices before you order, as overcharging is not uncommon.

Entertainment
Sani song-and-dance evenings are organised when there are enough tourists. Shows normally start at around 8pm at a stage next to the minor stone forest but there are sometimes extra performances, so ask at the hotels; performances are free.

There are also Sani performances during the day between 2pm and 3pm. During the **Torch Festival** (July/August), wrestling, bullfighting, singing and dancing are held at a natural outdoor amphitheatre by Hidden Lake south of Shílín.

Getting There & Away
BUS
Buses to Shílín (Y30 to Y40, two hours, every 30 minutes, 8am to noon) leave from the **bus station** (Beijing Lu, Kūnmíng) that is opposite the long-distance bus station. Make sure you don't get dragged onto one of the tourist buses, unless of course you want to spend the entire morning stopping off at various temples (a national obsession) and market stalls en route.

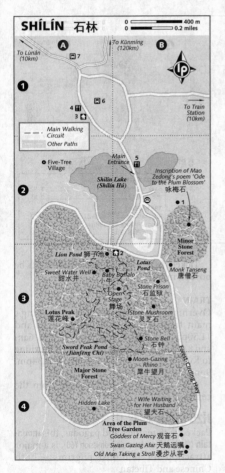

SHÍLÍN 石林

0 _____ 400 m
0 _____ 0.2 miles

To Lùnán (10km)

To Kūnmíng (120km)

To Train Station (10km)

Main Walking Circuit
Other Paths

Five-Tree Village
Main Entrance
Shilin Lake (Shílín Hú)
Inscription of Mao Zedong's poem 'Ode to the Plum Blossom' 咏梅石
Minor Stone Forest
Lion Pond 狮子池
Lotus Pond
Sweet Water Well 甜水井
Baby Buffalo 小牛
Stone Prison 石监狱
Monk Tanseng 唐僧石
Open Stage 舞场
Stone Mushroom 灵芝石
Lotus Peak 莲花峰
Stone Bell 石钟
Sword Peak Pond (Jiànfēng Chí)
Moon-Gazing Rhino 犀牛望月
Major Stone Forest
Forest Circling Hwy
Hidden Lake
Wife Waiting for Her Husband 望夫石
Area of the Plum Tree Garden
Goddess of Mercy 观音石
Swan Gazing Afar 天鹅远瞩
Old Man Taking a Stroll 漫步从容

SIGHTS & ACTIVITIES
Stage 舞台 **1** B2

SLEEPING
Shílín Bìshǔyuán Bīnguǎn 石林避暑园宾馆 **2** B3
Stone Forest International Youth
   Hostel 石林国际青年旅馆 **3** A1

EATING
Restaurants 餐厅饭店 **4** A1
Restaurants 餐厅饭店 **5** B2

TRANSPORT
Bus Stop 汽车出发处 **6** A1
Horse Carts 马车 ....(see **7**)
Minibuses to Lùnán 到路南的中巴车 **7** A1

Road and is still a key centre for transport in northwest Yúnnán. Xiàguān is the capital of Dàlǐ prefecture and is also referred to as Dali City (Dàlǐ Shì). This confuses some travellers, who think they are already in Dàlǐ, book into a hotel and head off in pursuit of a banana pancake only to discover they haven't arrived yet. There is no reason to stay in Xiàguān and you only need to come here in order to catch a bus or train.

To go straight to Dàlǐ, upon arriving in Xiàguān, turn left out of the long-distance bus station, and left again at the first intersection. Just up from the corner is the station for local bus 4, which runs to the real Dàlǐ (Y1.50, 30 minutes) until around 8pm. Bus 8 also runs from the centre of Xiàguān to Dàlǐ's west gate. If you want to be sure, ask for Dàlǐ Gǔchéng (Dali Old City).

Alternatively, minibuses run from a block east of the bus station (turn right out of the entrance) but you'll spend a lot of time waiting around for other passengers.

Information
Bank of China (Zhōngguó Yínháng; Jianshe Donglu) changes money and travellers cheques and has an ATM that accepts all major credit cards.
PSB (Gōng'ānjú; 21 Tianbao Jie; ⏰ 8-11am & 2-5pm Mon-Fri) handles all visa extensions for Xiàguān and Dàlǐ.

Getting There & Away
AIR
Xiàguān's airport is located 15km from the town centre. The Yunnan Airlines ticket office is inconveniently situated near the train station. There are no public buses to the airport; taxis will cost Y50 from Xiàguān or Y80 from Dàlǐ. There are three flights daily to Kūnmíng (Y430) and one to Guǎngzhōu (Y1540).

In the afternoon there are minibuses waiting at Shílín's car park, which leave when full (Y20).

Minibuses run between Lùnán and Shílín regularly (Y1, 10 minutes). At Shílín, they leave from a stand on the main road. Horse carts cost Y15. In Lùnán, flag down anything heading north of the main traffic circle. Minibuses to Kūnmíng (Y30, two hours) depart regularly from the western side of Lùnán's main roundabout until around 7pm.

XIÀGUĀN 下关
☎ 0872
Xiàguān lies at the southern tip of Ěrhǎi Hú, about 400km west of Kūnmíng. It was once an important staging post on the Burma

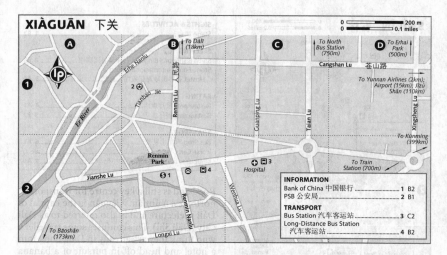

XIÀGUĀN 下关

BUS

Xiàguān has several bus stations, which throws some travellers. Luckily, the two main ones are both on the same side of the street, approximately two blocks apart. You might get dropped off at either one. Both have departures throughout the province, so if the long-distance bus station doesn't have a good departure time for you, wander over to the other one.

For Shangri-la (Y50-60, eight to nine hours, every 20 minutes from 6.20am to 8pm) and local destinations you need to catch your bus from the north bus station, a Y10 taxi ride away. Minibuses to Lijiang also run regularly from outside the long-distance bus staion and will cost Y20 to Y30 depending on the bus and your bargaining skills.

Tickets for nearly all destinations can be booked in Dàlǐ.

TRAIN

Overnight sleeper trains leave Kūnmíng's main train station at between 10pm and 11.30pm, arriving in Xiàguān between 6am and 8.05am. Hard sleepers are Y95. Returning to Kūnmíng, trains leave Xiàguān at 2.34pm, 9pm, 9.40pm, 10.02pm and 10.20pm.

Bus 1 goes to the train station from the centre of town.

JĪZÚ SHĀN 鸡足山

Packed with temples and pagodas, this **mountain** (Chicken-Foot Mountain; admission Y60), is a major attraction for Buddhist pilgrims – both Chinese and Tibetan.

XIÀGUĀN BUS TIMETABLES

Buses from Xiàguān's long-distance bus station:

Destination	Price	Duration	Frequency	Departs
Kūnmíng	Y90-126	7hr	every 40 min	7.50am-7pm
Lìjiāng	Y41-58	3hr	5 daily	8.30am, 10am, 2pm, 4pm, 7pm
Bǎoshān	Y48-58	2½hr	daily	10.30am
Jǐnghóng	Y170	17hr	3 daily	noon, 2pm, 7.30pm
Mángshì (Lùxī)	Y98	6-8hr	1 daily	6pm
Ruìlì	Y117-131	10-12hr	2 daily	8.30am, 8.20pm
Téngchōng	Y85	6hr	2 daily	10am, 1pm
Nínglàng	Y48	8hr	daily	8pm

At the time of the Qing dynasty there were approximately 100 temples on the mountain and somewhere in the vicinity of 5000 resident monks. The Cultural Revolution's anarchic assault on the traditional past did away with much that was of interest on the mountain, although renovation work on the temples has been going on since 1979.

Today, it's estimated more than 150,000 tourists and pilgrims clamber up the mountain every year to watch the sun rise. Jīndǐng, the Golden Summit, is at a cool 3240m so make sure to bring warm clothing.

Sights & Activities

Sights along the way include **Zhusheng Temple** (Zhùshèng Sì), the most important temple on the mountain, about an hour's walk up from the bus stop at Shāzhǐ.

Just before the last ascent is the **Magnificent Head Gate** (Huáshǒu Mén). At the summit is **Lengyan Pagoda** (Lèngyán Tǎ), a 13-tier Tang dynasty pagoda that was restored in 1927. There is basic accommodation at **Golden Summit Temple** (Jīndǐng Sì) next to the pagoda – a sleeping bag would be a good idea at this altitude.

A popular option for making the ascent is to hire a pony. Travellers who have done the trip claim it's a lot of fun. A cable car (Y30) to the summit is a good way to cheat, though the ride starts halfway up.

Sleeping & Eating

Accommodation is available at the base of the mountain, about halfway up and on the summit. Prices average Y20 to Y30 per bed. Food gets fairly expensive once you reach the summit so you may want to consider bringing some of your own.

Getting There & Away

From Xiàguān's north bus station take a bus to Bīnchuān (Y11, two hours), from where you'll have to change for a bus or minibus to Shāzhǐ at the foot of the mountain (Y10, one hour).

WĒISHĀN

Wēishān is famous for the Taoist temples on nearby **Wēibǎo Shān** (Weibao Mountain), about 7km south of town. There are reportedly some fine Taoist murals here. It's 61km due south of Xiàguān, so it could be done as a day trip. Buses leave regularly for Weishan

from the long-distance bus station (Y22, 1½ hours). At the Weishan main bus station, hop into a minibus for the 20- to 30-minute ride the rest of the way to the mountain (around Y8 to Y10).

DÀLĬ 大理

☎ 0872 / pop 110, 000

Dàlǐ or Lìjiāng? Travellers doing the northern Yúnnán backpacker circuit will find themselves having this conversation at least once as they bump into each other on buses, cobbled streets and guesthouses. In the balance, Dàlǐ's the one getting knocked these days. The beauty and character of Lìjiāng's old town seems to be able to win people over for the most part regardless of the suffocating crowds. Dàlǐ's historic area just doesn't muster up the same enthusiasm despite pizza and banana pancakes on (literally) every corner. Where Dàlǐ does come out ahead, however, is with its stunning location sandwiched between mountains and Erhai Lake (Ěrhǎi Hú). There's fascinating possibilities for exploring and getting to know the region's Bai culture. Just get your hands on a bike and get out of town.

History

Dàlǐ lies on the western edge of Ěrhǎi Hú at an altitude of 1900m, with a backdrop of the imposing 4000m-tall Cāng Shān (Jade Green Mountains). For much of the five centuries in which Yúnnán governed its own affairs, Dàlǐ was the centre of operations, and the old city retains a historical atmosphere that is hard to come by in other parts of China.

The main inhabitants of the region are the Bai, who number about 1.5 million. The Bai people have long-established roots in the Ěrhǎi Hú region, and are thought to have settled the area some 3000 years ago. In the early 8th century they grouped together and succeeded in defeating the Tang imperial army before establishing the Nanzhao kingdom.

The kingdom exerted considerable influence throughout southwest China and even, to a lesser degree, Southeast Asia, since it controlled upper Burma for much of the 9th century. This later established Dàlǐ as an end node on the famed Burma Road. In the mid-13th century it fell before the invincible Mongol hordes of Kublai Khan.

The influx of Chinese tour groups is changing Dàlǐ's character. The southern part of town has been radically renovated to create a new 'old Dàlǐ', complete with original gates and renovated city walls. Fuxing Lu is now lined with shops catering to Chinese tourists led around by guides dressed up in Bai costumes. The gentrification has been less successful than Lijiāng's, and some of the city's historical charm and authenticity has sadly been lost.

Orientation

Dàlǐ is a miniature city that has some pre-served cobbled streets and traditional stone architecture within its old walls and its easy enough to get your bearings by just taking a walk for an hour or so. It takes about half an hour to walk from the South Gate (Nán Mén) across town to the North Gate (Běi Mén). You can also get a good overview of the town and its surroundings by walking around the town walls (renovated in 1998).

Huguo Lu is the main strip for cafés – locals call it Yangren Jie (Foreigner's St) – and this is where to turn to for your café latte, burritos, ice-cold beer and other treats.

MAPS

Tourist maps of Dàlǐ and the Ěrhǎi Hú area are available at street stalls near the corner of Huguo Lu and Fuxing Lu. More useful ones can be picked up at **Mandarin Books & CDs** (Wǔhuá Shūyuàn; Fuxing Lu), along with a great selection of guidebooks and novels in Chinese, English and Dutch.

Information

INTERNET ACCESS 网吧

China Telecom (cnr Fuxing Lu & Huguo Lu; per hr Y2; ☯ 8am-10pm) Most hotels also offer free internet access for guests.

MONEY

Bank of China (Zhōngguó Yínháng; Fuxing Lu) Changes cash and travellers cheques. There is also an ATM here that accepts all major credit cards.

POST

China Post (Yóujú; cnr Fuxing Lu & Huguo Lu; ☯ 8am-8pm) The best place to make international calls as it has direct dial and doesn't levy a service charge.

PUBLIC SECURITY BUREAU

PSB (Gōngānjú; 21 Tianbao Jie, Xiàguān; ☯ 8am-11am & 2-5pm Mon-Fri) Visas cannot be renewed in Dàlǐ, so you'll have to journey to the office in Xiàguān. To get there, take bus 4 until just after it crosses the river in Xiàguān. The PSB office is a short walk south from here.

TOURIST INFORMATION & TRAVEL AGENCIES

All the hotels offer travel advice, and can arrange tours and book tickets for onward travel. There are also numerous travel agencies and cafés on Huguo Lu that offer all manner of tours, from half-day market trips to full-day trips to Ěrhǎi Hú. They can be expensive unless you can get a group together.

Jim's Tibetan Guesthouse & Peace Café (☎ 267 1822; www.china-travel.nl; 63 Boai Lu) Offers a long list of trips, including tours to Muslim markets and Yi minority markets, that come very highly rated by travellers. Jim and his wife Henriette also offer some more unusual trips including trekking in remote areas of Yúnnán and overland travel to Lhasa from Shangri-la (per person from Y5000).

Dangers & Annoyances

The hike up to Zhonghe Temple (Zhōnghé Sì) and along the mountain ridges is super, but there have been several reports of robbery of solo walkers. Try to find a partner.

Be careful on the overnight sleeper bus from Kūnmíng as someone often finds a bag pinched or razored. Chain them securely and try to cram them under the lower bunk as far back as possible.

Sights

THREE PAGODAS 三塔寺

Reproduced on thousands of postcards and calendars, these **three pagodas** (Sān Tǎ Sì; admission Y121, incl Chongsheng Temple; ☯ 8am-7pm) are among the oldest standing structures in southwestern China and a sort of symbol of Dali.

The tallest of the three, **Qianxun Pagoda**, has 16 tiers that reach a height of 70m. It was originally erected in the mid-9th century by engineers from Xī'ān. It is flanked by two smaller 10-tiered pagodas, each of which are 42m high.

Some travellers find the price steep given that you can't go inside the pagodas. However, the temple behind the pagodas, **Chongsheng Temple** (Chóngshèng Sì) almost makes up for it.

Laid out in the traditional Yunnanese style there are three layers of buildings lined up with a sacred peak in the background. The temple has been restored and converted into a museum chronicling the history, construction and renovation of the pagodas.

To get there, walk north along the Yúnnán–Tibet road. It's about 2km outside the old town walls.

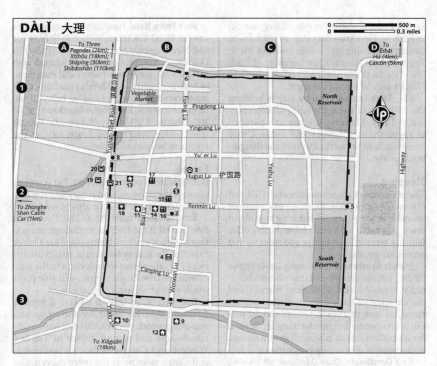

DÀLǏ MUSEUM 大理市博物馆

The **Dali Museum** (Dàlǐ Shì Bówùguǎn; Wenxian Lu; admission Y5; ⏰ 8.30am-6pm) houses a small collection of archaeological pieces relating to Bai history and has some moderately interesting exhibits on marble handicrafts. A number of marble stelae grace one wing.

Festivals & Events

If you don't mind crowds, the best time to be in Dàlǐ is probably during the **Third Moon Fair** (Sānyuè Jiē), which begins on the 15th day of the third lunar month (usually April) and ends on the 21st day. The origins of the fair lie in its commemoration of a fabled visit by Guanyin, the Buddhist Goddess of Mercy, to the Nanzhao kingdom. Today it's more like an extra-festive market, with people from all over Yúnnán arriving to buy, sell and make merry.

The **Three Temples Festival** (Ràosān Líng) is held between the 23rd and 25th days of the fourth lunar month (usually May). The first day involves a trip from Dàlǐ's South Gate to

YÚNNÁN

Sacred Fountainhead Temple (Shèngyuán Sì) in Xǐzhōu. Here travellers stay up until dawn, dancing and singing, before moving on to Jingui Temple (Jīnguì Sì) on the shore of Ěrhǎi Hú. The final day involves walking back to Dàlǐ by way of Majiuyi Temple.

The **Torch Festival** (Huǒbǎ Jié) is held on the 24th day of the sixth lunar month (normally July). Flaming torches are paraded at night through homes and fields. Other events include fireworks displays and dragon-boat racing.

Sleeping

There's heaps of accommodation in Dàlǐ, but places fill up quickly. During peak summer months, brace yourself for a long slog about town in search of a bed. Most hotels offer laundry service, bicycle hire and free internet access for guests.

Friends Guesthouse (Dàlǐ Gǔchéng Sānyǒu Kèzhàn; ☎ 266 2888; friendsinn@hotmail.com; 1 Wenxian Lu; 文献路1号; dm Y10, s & d Y50-80) Fun, friendly and the cheapest of the cheap, hard-core budget travellers love this place. Others should suss out a few rooms before checking in. Several house bathrooms of advanced grittiness and wall-stains of distracting proportions.

No 3 Guesthouse (Dìsān Zhāodàisuǒ; ☎ 266 4941; Huguo Lu; 护国路号; 6-bed dm Y20) A hugely kind staff helm some of the nicest budget accommodation in town. New wooden furniture fills the rooms with a pleasant pine-like smell and each bunk has individual lights and a bamboo curtain for privacy. Showers and Western-style toilets are immaculate.

MCA Guesthouse (☎ 267 3666; mcahouse@hotmail .com; Wenxian Lu; 文献路; dm Y20, s/d with bathroom Y100/120) Phenomenal value accommodation set around a garden filled with ponds and lush plants. Third floor singles are cute as a button with eccentric, slope-roofed bathrooms and stunning lake views. Dorms and doubles turn up surprises like wall art, hardwood floors or antique-style furniture. You can also book overland trips to Tibet leaving from Shangri-la here (see p726).

Tibetan Lodge (Dàlǐ Gǔchéng Qīngnián Lǚguǎn; ☎ 266 4177; tibetan_lodge@yahoo.com; 58 Renmin Lu; 人民路 58号; s/family ste, Y60/160) Set up on two floors around a courtyard, the lodge has cosy, comfy rooms, but the family suites are what sets it apart. Each one has ground floor twins for the kids and big comfy (very) private overhead lofts for the grownups.

Jim's Peace Hotel (Jímǔ Zángshí Jiǔdiàn; www.china -travel.nl; ☎ 267 7824; 13 Yuxiu Lu; 玉秀路中段13号; d Y200) Newly opened outside the city walls by this Dàlǐ longtimer, rooms here are heaped with antique Chinese-style furniture and manage to be both sleek and cosy. There's a garden, a rooftop terrace and restaurant and bar below. If you want the original, **Jim's Tibetan Guesthouse** (☎ 267 1822; 63 Boai Lu; 博爱路63号; s/d with breakfast Y140-200) is still going strong nearby. Travel services and tours can be booked at both.

Eating

Dàlǐ is overrun with restaurants. Eat your way through the streets to find something you like; new eateries seem to open almost weekly.

Bamboo Café (Zízhúwū; ☎ 267 1898; 71 Renmin Lu; dishes from Y8) If the Dàlǐ street throngs are getting to you, there's no better place for a break than this dark, cosy restaurant. Meals like bai fish (Y25) are a great introduction to the local cuisine and the English menu will give you a window to other local specialities.

Tibet Café (Xīzàng Kāfēi; ☎ 266 2391; 42 Huguo Lu; dishes from Y10) Richly decorated and set up with imposing wooden tables, this café has terrific atmosphere and a great choice of Tibetan, Western and Chinese dishes. It also consistently attracts some of the more experienced travellers in town, so is a good place to eavesdrop or just ask around about what's new.

Yúnnán Café and Bar (Yúnnán Kāfēiguǎn Jiǔbā; Huguo Lu; mains Y18-30) Run by a friendly couple, this not too big, not too small space is a great place to wind things down at night or start things up in the morning. The Western and Chinese stick-to-your ribs breakfasts are terrific. The Tibetan breakfasts (Y18) will have you set for the long bus rides to Kūnmíng and beyond.

Jim's Peace Café (☎ 267 1822; jimsguesthouse@hotmail .com; 63 Boai Lu; mains Y18-32) The Tibetan banquet (Y30, minimum 4 people) in this café is not to be missed. Jim's parade of dishes gets raves from travellers especially when washed down with his 'No 1 special'.

Drinking

The Western-style restaurants mentioned above double as bars. Also worth trying is the **Birdbar** (Niǎobā; ☎ 266 1843; 22 Renmin Lu), an off-the-main-drag watering hole with a pool table. There are no regular opening hours – you can come here pretty much anytime of the day or night and have a good chance of finding it open.

Shopping

Dàlǐ is famous for its marble, and while a slab of the stuff in your backpack might slow you down a bit, local entrepreneurs produce everything from ashtrays to model pagodas in small enough chunks to make it feasible to stow one or two away.

The city is also famous for its blue-and-white batik printed on cotton and silk. A lot of the batik is still made in Dàlǐ and hidden behind many of the shopfronts sit vast vats of blue dye – it's worth asking around at some of the shops to see if you can have a look at how the batik is made.

Huguo Lu has become a smaller version of Bangkok's Khao San Rd in its profusion of clothes shops. Most shopkeepers can also make clothes to your specifications – which will come as a relief when you see some of the items of ready-made clothing on offer.

Most of the 'silver' jewellery sold in Dàlǐ is really brass. Occasionally it is silver, although this will be reflected in the starting price. The only advice worth giving is to bargain hard. For those roving sales ladies badgering you incessantly, don't feel bad to pay one-fifth of their asking price – that's what locals advise. For marble from street sellers, 40% to 50% is fair. In shops, two-thirds of the price is average. And don't fall for any 'expert' opinions; go back later on your own and deal.

Getting There & Away

AIR

Xiàguān's new airport has brought Dàlǐ to within 45 minutes' flying time from Kūnmíng (see p714). A taxi from Dàlǐ to the airport will cost Y60 to Y80. Alternatively, you can take a bus to Xiàguān and pick up a taxi from there (Y50).

BUS

The golden rule about getting to Dàlǐ by bus is to find out in advance whether your bus is for Dàlǐ or Xiàguān. Many buses advertised to Dàlǐ actually only go as far as Xiàguān (p701). Coming from Lìjiāng, Xiàguān-bound buses stop at the eastern end of Dàlǐ to let passengers off before continuing on to their final destination. From here it's a 20-minute walk to the main guesthouses.

For information on getting to Dàlǐ from Kūnmíng, see p696. From the long-distance bus station near the west gate in Dàlǐ there are daily buses to Shangri-la (Y50, eight hours,

every 30 minutes from 7.30am to 11am & 7.20pm, 8pm, 8.30pm) and express buses to Kūnmíng (Y106, five hours, 9.30am, 10.30am and 4.30pm, 9pm). A slow bus for Kūnmíng also leaves daily at 8am (Y65). Buses to Lìjiāng (Y30 to Y50, three hours, every 30 minutes, 7.30am to 7.20pm) also leave from here.

Buses run regularly to Shāpíng, Xǐzhōu and other local destinations from opposite the long-distance bus station. A bus leaves for Shāpíng every Monday morning (Y5, one hour, 9.30am) for the market.

TRAIN

Probably the most popular means of getting to Dàlǐ is the overnight sleeper train from Kūnmíng (hard sleeper Y93). For more details see Train p696.

Getting Around

From Dàlǐ, a taxi to Xiàguān airport takes 45 minutes and cost around Y80; to Xiàguān's train station it costs Y30.

Bikes are the best way to get around (Y10 per day). Most of the guesthouses and several other places on Boai Lu rent bikes.

Bus 4 runs between Dàlǐ and central Xiàguān (Y1.50, 30 minutes) every 15 minutes from 6.30am, which means that unless your bus leaves Xiàguān earlier than 7.30am you won't have to stay the night there.

Bus 8 runs from Dàlǐ to Xiàguān's train station.

AROUND DÀLǏ
Markets

Usually markets follow the lunar calendar, but shrewd local operators have co-opted it into a regular scheme so that tourists have a market to go to nearly every day of the week. See p709 for information on the Monday Shāpíng market. Markets also take place in Shuānglǎng (Tuesday), Shābā (Wednesday), Yòusuǒ (Friday, the largest in Yúnnán) and Jiāngwěi (Saturday). Xǐzhōu and Zhōuchéng have daily morning and afternoon markets, respectively.

Wāsè also has a popular market every five days with trading from 9am to 4.30pm.

Most cafés and hotels in Dàlǐ offer tours or can arrange transportation to markets for around Y150 for a half day.

Ěrhǎi Hú 洱海湖

Exploring the areas around **Ěrhǎi Hú** (Ear-Shaped Lake) is one of the most fascinating

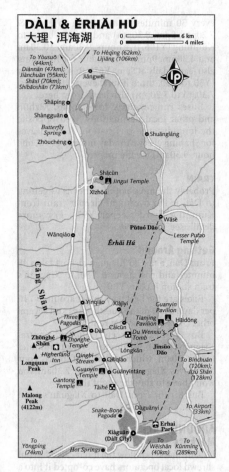

DÀLǏ & ĚRHǍI HÚ
大理、洱海湖

parts of a Dàlǐ visit. The seventh biggest freshwater lake in China, it sits at 1973m above sea level and covers 250 sq km. Ěrhǎi Hú is dotted with trails perfect for bike rides and villages to visit. It's a 50-minute walk from town or a 10-minute downhill zip on a bike.

The best way to explore is by either renting a bike or zipping across the water on the many ferries that crisscross the lake. A great bike trip that can be done in a day is from Dàlǐ to Shāpíng. Though the lakeside road may seem the most picturesque, it is too busy and congested to enjoy and you're better off on the secondary road, just to the west of the lakeside expressway. Travellers report stumbling across lovely temples and hill views just

by stopping in small villages along the way to buy food and water.

Ferries crisscross the lake at various points, so there could be some scope for extended touring. You could bus, walk or taxi to Cáicūn, a pleasant little village east of Dàlǐ (Y2 on minibus 2), then dart around the lake on ferries. There are regular ferries to Wāsè (Y3-5) on the eastern shore and plenty of locals take their bikes over.

Close to Wāsè are Pǔtuó Dǎo (Putuo Island; around Y1 on ferry) and Lesser Putuo Temple (Xiǎopǔtuó Sì), set on an extremely photogenic rocky outcrop. Other ferries run between Lóngkān and Hǎidōng, and between Xiàguān and Jīnsuō Dǎo (Jinsuo Island). Ferries leave early in the morning (for the market) and return around 4pm; timetables are flexible and departures are somewhat unreliable.

Roads now encircle the lake so it is possible to do a loop (or partial loop) of the lake by mountain bike. A few intrepid travellers have leapfrogged these villages, made for Shāpíng's market, then continued all the way around the lake stopping at other markets on the way before boating themselves and their bicycles back to Dàlǐ. From Dàlǐ to Wāsè it's around 58km by road.

Plenty of cafés in Dàlǐ can arrange a horse-and-carriage ride to the lake, then a boat ride to Tianjing Pavilion and Guanyin Pavilion, then Jīnsuō Dǎo or whatever else you dream up.

Zhonghe Temple 中和寺

This **temple** (Zhōnghé Sì; admission Y2) is a long, steep hike up the mountainside behind Dàlǐ. Some visitors find the temple itself underwhelming. So think of this trip more in terms of the journey and the views of Ěrhǎi Hú rather than the destination. To reach the top take the **chairlift** (one way/return Y30/50) up **Zhōnghé Shān** (Zhonge Mountain).

You can also hike up the hill, a sweaty two to three hours for those in moderately good shape (see Dangers & Annoyances p704). Walk about 200m north of the chairlift base to the riverbed, (often dry). Follow the left bank for about 50m and walk through the cemetery. Follow the path zigzagging under the chairlift. When you reach some stone steps you know you are near the top.

Branching out from either side of the temple is a trail that winds along the face of the mountains, taking you in and out of steep, lush valleys and past streams and waterfalls. From Zhōnghé it's an amazing 11km up-and-down hike south to **Gantong Temple** (Gǎntōng Sì) or **Qingbi Stream**, from where you can continue to the road and pick up a Dàlǐ-bound bus. There's also a new **cable car** (one way/return Y52/82) between the two temples.

Alternatively, you can spend more time here and stay the night at **Higherland Inn** (☎ 266 1599; www.higherland.com; dm Y25, s/d Y30/50), just above Zhonghe Temple at 2590m. If you want to get away from the crowds in Dàlǐ then this is the place to do it. The hostel has fabulous views, regular barbecues and bonfire parties and only a handful of rooms (seven) which means it's an incredibly relaxing place to stay.

Xīzhōu 喜洲
Among the 101 things to do while you're in Dàlǐ, try to fit in a trip to the old town of Xīzhōu for a look at its well-preserved Bai architecture. You can catch a local bus from the south gate in Dàlǐ (Y3) or take a taxi (Y30-35) to make the 18km trip, but a bicycle trip with an overnight stop in Xīzhōu (there's accommodation in town) is also a good idea. From here, the interesting town of **Zhōuchéng** is 7km further north; it too has basic accommodation.

Shāpíng Market 沙坪赶集
Every Monday at Shāpíng, about 30km north of Dàlǐ, there is a colourful Bai **market** (Shāpíng Gǎnjí). The market starts to rattle and hum at 10am and ends around 2.30pm. You can buy everything from tobacco, melon seeds and noodles to meat, jewellery and wardrobes. In the ethnic clothing line, you can look at shirts, headdresses, embroidered shoes and money belts, as well as local batik. Expect to be quoted ridiculously high prices on anything you set your eyes on, so get into a bargaining frame of mind before you go.

Getting to Shāpíng Market from Dàlǐ is fairly easy. Head out on the road to Lìjiāng and flag down anything heading north. Some of the hotels and cafés in town also run minibuses. By bike it will take about 2 hours at a good clip.

Guanyin Pavilion 观音堂
This **temple** (Guānyīn Táng; admission Y10; ☼ around 8am-6pm) is built over a large boulder that locals believe was placed there by Guanyin, the Buddhist Goddess of Mercy, disguised as an old woman in order to block the advance of an invading enemy. It is 5km south of Dàlǐ. If you follow the path uphill for 3km you will come across another temple, **Gantong Temple** (Gǎntōng Sì).

Shíbǎoshān 石宝山
About 110km northwest of Dàlǐ are the **Stone Treasure Mountain Grottoes** (Shíbǎoshān Shíkū). There are three temple groups: Stone Bell (Shízhōng), Lion Pass (Shīzī Guān) and Shadeng Village. They include some of the best Bai stone carvings in southern China and offer insights into life at the Nanzhao court of the 9th century.

To get to Shíbǎoshān, take a bus to Jiànchuān, 55km north of Dàlǐ on the old Dàlǐ–Lìjiāng road. Get off at the small village of Diànnán, about 8km south of Jiànchuān, where a narrow road branches southwest to the village of Shāxī, 23km away. You'll just have to wait for a bus for this leg. The grottoes are close to Shāxī.

NORTHWEST YÚNNÁN

LÌJIĀNG 丽江
new town ☎ 08891/**old town** ☎ 0888

Lìjiāng's maze of cobbled streets, rickety old wooden buildings and gushing canals makes it one of the most visited sites in northern Yúnnán. But its popularity has grown faster than its ability to absorb the microphone-toting tour groups. In peak visiting periods, frustrated locals share stories of 30-minute journeys just to move one kilometre through the shoulder-to-shoulder crowds.

While it's true many of the Naxi stalls have made way for the souvenir stands of Han entrepreneurs and that some of the old town's soul has gone with them, don't worry too much about the locals. Many are making a fortune leasing their highly coveted property in historic Lìjiāng and have happily decamped to slick, modern apartments in the new town.

But don't let the crowds – or any grumpy travellers you may meet on your way here – discourage a trip. Get up early and it will be just you, Lìjiāng and a handful of intrepid photographers. Just make sure you get the hell out of Dodge by 8.30am, when the tour group onslaught begins. There's a number of interesting sights around Lìjiāng, some of which can be reached by bicycle, offering a week or more's worth of excursions.

Apart from the writings of botanist-explorer Joseph Rock (p718), another venerable work on Lìjiāng that's worth reading if you can find it is the *Forgotten Kingdom* by Peter Goulart. Goulart was a White Russian who studied Naxi culture and lived in Lìjiāng from 1940 to 1949.

Beyond the Clouds is an excellent nine-hour documentary about Lìjiāng, made in 1994 by Britain's Channel 4, that is well worth seeking out.

Orientation

Lìjiāng is separated into old and new towns that are starkly different. The approximate line of division is Shīzī Shān (Lion Hill), the green hump in the middle of town that's topped by a radio mast and Looking at the Past Pavilion, a new pagoda. Everything west of the hill is the new town, and everything east is the old town. The whole of the old town is pedestrianised.

The easiest way into the old town is from the north, along Dong Dajie. This area was largely reconstructed following an earthquake in 1996. From the long-distance bus station head east one block and follow an alley lined with snack bars heading north. The old town is a maze of lanes that twist and turn so just accept you'll be lost for the most part.

Information

Lìjiāng's cafés and backpacker inns are your best source of information on the area. Most have noticeboards and travellers' books full of useful tips and advice from other travellers on surrounding sights, especially the Tiger Leaping Gorge trek.

BOOKSHOPS

Mandarin Book & CDs (Lìjiāng Wǔhuā Shūyuàn; Xin Dajie) Has a fantastic selection of English books and maps on Lìjiāng and the region.

CD BURNING

Kodak (Fuhui Lu) Y20 per CD.

INTERNET ACCESS 网吧

There are lots of places where you can go online in the old town.
Prague Café (p713; per hr Y5)

MONEY

Bank of China (Zhōngguó Yínháng; Dong Dajie) This branch is in the old town and has an ATM machine.

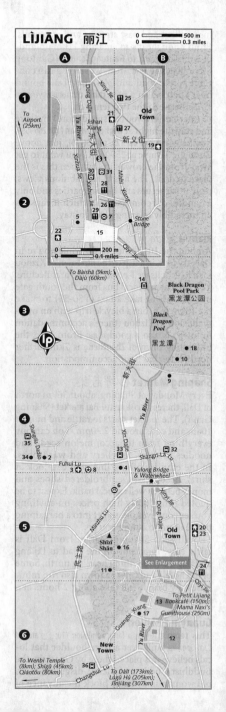

POST & TELEPHONE

Many of the backpacker cafés in the old town have IDD lines.

Post office (yóujú; Minzhu Lu; ⏲ 8am-8pm) Offers EMS (Express Mail Service), so your postcards might actually make it home before you do. Another post office is in the old town just north of the Old Market Sq.

China Telecom (Minzhu Lu), next door to China Post, is where you can make international calls.

PUBLIC SECURITY BUREAU

PSB (Gōngānjú; Fuhui Lu; ⏲ 8.30-11.30am & 2.30-5.30pm Mon-Fri) is reputedly very speedy with visa extensions.

TOURIST INFORMATION & TRAVEL AGENCIES

There's a slew of Travel Reception Centres all over the old town but they mostly arrange tours. The best place for info is at your accommodation.

CITS (Zhōngguó Guójì Lǚxíngshè; 3rd fl, Lifang Bldg, cnr Fuhui Lu & Shangrila Dadao) can arrange tours in and around Lìjiāng.

Eco-tours (☎ 131-7078 0719; www.ecotourchina.com) is run by Zhao Fan at the Café Buena Vista (p716). He can organise tours to nearly anywhere you want to go in northern Yúnnán, as well as trekking and camping trips in less well-known areas. Avid bike-riders should check out his free maps of Lìjiāng-area cycling trails.

Dangers & Annoyances

You'll need to be alert for pickpockets as you make your way through the old town's crowds. There's also been a handful of reports of solo women travellers being mugged when walking alone at night in isolated areas of his-toric Lìjiāng. Also take care if travelling alone to isolated sights like Xiàng Shān (Elephant Hill) in Black Dragon Pool Park (Hēilóngtán Gōngyuán) where you may be vulnerable to thieves.

Sights

OLD TOWN 古城

Crisscrossed by canals, bridges and a maze of narrow streets, the old town is the reason why people come to Lìjiāng. The town's web of artery-like canals once supplied the city's drinking water. There are several wells and pools still in use around town. You can see one of the original wells opposite the Well Bistro.

The focus of the old town is the **Old Market Sq** (Sìfāng Jiē). Once the haunt of Naxi traders, they've long since made way for tacky souvenir stalls. However, the view up the hill and the surrounding lanes are still extraordinary, just be prepared to share the experience with hundreds if not thousands of other people.

Above the old town is a beautiful **park** that can be reached on the path leading past the radio mast. Sit on the slope in the early morning and watch the mist clearing as the old town comes to life.

Now acting as sentinel of sorts for the town, the **Looking at the Past Pavilion** (Wànggǔ Lóu; admission Y15) was raised for tourists at a cost of over one million yuán. It's famed for a unique design using dozens of four-storey pillars – unfortunately these were culled from northern Yúnnán old-growth forests. A path (with English signs) leads from the Old Market Sq.

YÚNNÁN

MU FAMILY MANSION 木氏土司府
The former home of a Naxi chieftain, the **Mu Family Mansion** (Mùshì Tǔsīfǔ; admission Y35; ☻ 8.30am-5.30pm) was heavily renovated (more like built from scratch) after the 1996 earthquake. Mediocre captions do a poor job of introducing the Mu family but many travellers find the beautiful grounds reason enough to visit.

BLACK DRAGON POOL PARK 黑龙潭公园
On the northern edge of town is the **Black Dragon Pool Park** (Hēilóngtán Gōngyuán; Xin Dajie; admission Y30, free after 6pm; ☻ 7am-7pm). Apart from strolling around the pool – its view of Yùlóng Xuěshān (Jade Dragon Snow Mountain) is the most obligatory photo shoot in southwestern China – you can visit the **Dongba Research Institute** (Dōngbā Wénhuà Yánjiūshì; ☻ 8am-5pm Mon-Fri), which is part of a renovated complex on the hillside. Here

you can see Naxi cultural artefacts and scrolls featuring a unique pictograph script.

At the eastern side of the pool are buildings used for an art exhibition, a pavilion with its own bridge across the water and the Ming dynasty **Five Phoenix Hall** (Wǔfèng Lóu).

Trails lead up **Xiàng Shān** (Elephant Hill) to a dilapidated gazebo and then across a spiny ridge past a communications centre and back down the other side, making a nice morning hike. See also Dangers & Annoyances, p711.

The **Museum of Naxi Dongba Culture** (Nàxī Dōngbā Wénhuà Bówùguǎn; admission Y5; ☻ 8.30am-5.30pm) is at the park's northern entrance.

Festivals & Events
The 13th day of the third moon (late March or early April) is the traditional day to hold a **Fertility Festival**.

THE NAXI 纳西

Lìjiāng has been the base of the 286,000 strong Naxi (also spelt Nakhi and Nahi) minority for about the last 1400 years. The Naxi descend from ethnically Tibetan Qiang tribes and lived until recently in matrilineal families. Since local rulers were always male it wasn't truly matriarchal, but women still seem to run the show, certainly in the old part of Lìjiāng.

The Naxi matriarchs maintained their hold over the men with flexible arrangements for love affairs. The *azhu* (friend) system allowed a couple to become lovers without setting up joint residence. Both partners would continue to live in their respective homes; the boyfriend would spend the nights at his girlfriend's house but return to live and work at his mother's house during the day. Any children born to the couple belonged to the woman, who was responsible for bringing them up. The man provided support, but once the relationship was over, so was the support. Children lived with their mothers and no special effort was made to recognise paternity. Women inherited all property and disputes were adjudicated by female elders.

There are strong matriarchal influences in the Naxi language. Nouns enlarge their meaning when the word for 'female' is added; conversely, the addition of the word for 'male' will decrease the meaning. For example, 'stone' plus 'female' conveys the idea of a boulder; 'stone' plus 'male' conveys the idea of a pebble.

Naxi women wear blue blouses and trousers covered by a blue or black apron. The T-shaped traditional cape not only stops the basket worn on the back from chafing, but also symbolises the heavens. Day and night are represented by the light and dark halves of the cape; seven embroidered circles symbolise the stars. Two larger circles, one on each shoulder, are used to depict the eyes of a frog, which until the 15th century was an important god to the Naxi. With the decline of animist beliefs, the frog eyes fell out of fashion, but the Naxi still call the cape by its original name, 'frog-eye sheepskin'.

The Naxi created a written language over 1000 years ago using an extraordinary system of pictographs – the only hieroglyphic language still in use. The most famous Naxi text is the Dongba classic *Creation*, and ancient copies of it and other texts can still be found in Lìjiāng, as well as in the archives of some US universities. The Dongba were Naxi shamans who were caretakers of the written language and mediators between the Naxi and the spirit world. The Dongba religion, itself an offshoot of Tibet's pre-Buddhist Bon religion, eventually developed into an amalgam of Tibetan Buddhism, Islam and Taoism. The Tibetan origins of the Naxi are confirmed by references in Naxi literature to Lake Manasarovar and Mt Kailash, both in western Tibet.

Useful phrases in the Naxi language are '*nuar lala*' (hello) and '*jiu bai sai*' (thank you).

July brings the **Torch Festival** (Huǒbǎ Jié), also celebrated by the Bai in the Dàlǐ region and the Yi all over the southwest. The origin of this festival can be traced back to the intrigues of the Nanzhao kingdom, when the wife of a man burned to death by the king eluded the romantic entreaties of the monarch by leaping into a fire.

Sleeping

There is no shortage of charming Naxi guesthouses in the old town. The new town boasts lots of modern hotels, but staying there kind of defeats the purpose of visiting Lìjiāng.

Mama Naxi's Guesthouse (Gǔchéng Xiānggéyún Kèzhàn; ☎ 510 0700; 78 Wenhua Jie, Wuyi Jie; 五一街, 文化巷78号; dm Y15, s/d from Y50) There's nothing quite like arriving in Lìjiāng after a long sweaty bus ride, calling this hostel for directions. 'Directions? No worry, right *now* Mama come find *you!*' And that's just the beginning. Mama also cooks (Y2-10 per meal), make travel arrangements (including to Tiger Leaping Gorge) and distributes free tea and bananas to guests with wild abandon. Mama's team of four-legged friends also have their run of the place and have been known to leave their calling cards near the bedpost. Midnight curfew.

International Youth Hostel Lijiang (Lìjiāng Laǒxié Chēmǎdiàn; ☎ 511 6118; 25 Jishan Alley, Xinyi Jie; 新义街, 积善巷25号; dm Y20, s/d/tr Y40-120/100-140/150-180) A huge amount of effort has gone into this new hostel. There's an astounding choice of rooms with rate determined by size, bed width and attached amenities. Touches like flowers or patterned bedspreads sets it apart from the generic hostels in town. You can also rent bikes here for Y15 per day. Hot water from 6pm to 2am only.

Wang Gu Youth Inn (Wànggǔlóu Qīngnián Kèzhàn; ☎ 512 9778; 50 Huangshan Lane, Xinhua Jie; 新华街, 黄山下段50号; 4-bed dm Y20, d Y120) Perched on the hillside just off the path up to Looking at the Past Pavilion, dorms here are simple floor mattresses in bright, breezy rooms. It's all very simple, very clean and very tidy, but with views from the rooms and adjoining restaurant terrace that are spectacular, especially at night.

Moon Inn (Xīnyuégé Kèzhàn; ☎ 518 0520; mooninn@163.com; 34 Xingren Xiaduan, Wuyi Jie; 五一街, 兴仁下段34号; s & d Y200) This low-key inn is packed with charm. Bright and breezy rooms have wood furniture and brightly coloured striped bedspreads; and are set around a lovely courtyard. A bright common room has

TV and internet. Breakfast Y10, dinner Y20 per person.

Zen Garden Hotel (Ruíhé Yuán Jiǔdiàn; ☎ 518 9799; www.zengardenhotel.com; 36 Xingren Lane, Wuyi Jie; 五一街, 兴仁下段 36 号; d Y400, 'wedding rooms' Y1400) This museum-like hotel was opened by a Naxi teacher and decorated in conjunction with her artist brother. The results are sumptuous: the complimentary breakfasts of tiny cakes and hard-boiled eggs are ritually set up amid candles and a Chinese musician sets up in the courtyard twice week to play traditional music. Standard rooms are immaculate; 'wedding rooms' have Ming-style beds and silk sheets. Glittery night views of old Lìjiāng on the second floor.

Sānhé Jiǔdiàn (☎ 512 0891; 4 Jishan Xiang, Xinyi Jie; 新一街, 积善巷4号; s/d Y600/560) Everything here feels new and shiny. There's wood floors, blond wood furniture and sleek modern bathrooms. Staff are friendly and professional, but this is a bigger, slicker operation than most accommodation choices in the area so service is more impersonal than at other sleeping options listed here.

Eating

Like Dàlǐ, Lìjiāng has a legion of small, family-operated restaurants catering to travellers. The following run-down is by no means exhaustive, and almost every menu will have both Chinese and Western dishes.

Bābā is the Lìjiāng local speciality – thick flatbreads of wheat, served plain or stuffed with meats, vegetables or sweets. There are always several 'Naxi' items on the menu, including the famous 'Naxi omelette' and 'Naxi sandwich' (goats' cheese, tomato and fried egg between two pieces of local *bābā*). Try locally produced *yinjiu*, a lychee-based wine with a 500-year history – it tastes like a decent semi-sweet sherry.

Ma Ma Fu's (Māmāfù Cāntīng; Mishi Xiang; dishes from Y10) Walk the plank across the stream into one of Lìjiāng's stalwarts. While popular for its Western food, it rarely rises above mediocre; stick with the Chinese dishes which run from very good to outstanding.

Prague Café (18 Mishi Xiang; meals from Y15; ☘ from 7.30am) An old favourite, the Naxi breakfast (Y22) is a must; fried goats' cheese, ham and an obscenely large potato pancake are just some of the goodies heaped on your plate – you'll be set for the rest of the day. Great atmosphere with a loyal crowd, this café also has a book-exchange, magazines and internet (Y5 per hour).

Sakura Café (Xinhua Jie) This popular café serves up a belly-busting *bimbap* (rice, egg, meat and vegetables with hot sauce; Y23) set meal that should only be taken on by the masochistic. There are several other 'Sakura Cafés' along this lane; figuring out which is the original is part of the fun.

Petit Lijiang Bookcafé (☎ 511 1255; 50 Chongren Xiang, Qiyi Jie; dishes from Y15) Run by a travel-mad Chinese-Belgian couple, this café serves terrific Chinese and Western food along with surprises like fresh squeezed juice; in-season fruit pies and Australian Chardonnay. The book store has an outstanding collection of English and French language titles focusing on Yúnnán and elsewhere in China. You can also watch DVDs in the sitting room for free. Owners Mei and Olivier are also great sources of travel info and can suggest treks and off-the-beaten track trips around Lìjiāng.

Lamu's House of Tibet (Xìzàngwū Xīcāntīng; 56 Xinyi Jie; dishes from Y10) Away from the main drag, this place serves excellent food from a hugely varied menu. Try the *momo* (Tibetan dumplings) which come with a variety of fillings, but make sure you save room for the desserts – they're massive.

Blue Papaya (☎ 512 6635; Lán Mùguā; 70 Xinyi Jie; dishes from Y30) Serves terrific pasta and fish dishes by Chinese as well as any other benchmark. Service is outstanding and the menu has creative flourishes like pineapple or sweet potato ice cream. This is a perfect place to relax and linger over a first-rate meal.

Naku Café (☎ 510 5321; Ākú Kāfēi; 4 Jishan Xiang, Xinyi Jie; dishes from Y20) This is a low-key eatery run by some very shy but very friendly staff. The usual Chinese/Western/Japanese hybrid dishes litter the menu but the local dishes are most interesting. The Naxi claypot needs salt but is packed with tofu, potato, turnip, carrots, broccoli and cabbage. Free internet upstairs for diners.

Entertainment

One of the few things you can do in the evening in Lìjiāng is attend performances of the **Naxi Orchestra** (Nàxī Gǔyuè Huì; Naxi Music Academy; tickets Y100-140; ☺ performances 8pm) inside a beautiful building in the old town.

Not only are all 20 to 24 members Naxi, but they play a type of Taoist temple music (known as *dòngjīng*) that has been lost elsewhere in China. The pieces they perform are supposedly faithful renditions of music from the Han, Song and Tang dynasties, and are played on original instruments.

Xuan Ke usually speaks for the group at performances – speaks too much, some say – explaining each musical piece and describing the instruments. Taped recordings of the music are available; a set of two costs Y30. If you're interested, make sure you buy the tape at the show – tapes on sale at shops around town, and even in Kūnmíng, are often pirated copies.

The government-run **Dongba Palace** (Dong Dajie; tickets Y100-140; ☺ performances 8pm) has a less authentic song-and-dance show.

Getting There & Away

AIR

Lìjiāng's airport is 25km east of town. Tickets can be booked at the **CAAC** (Zhōngguó Mínháng; ☎ 516 1289; cnr Fuhui Lu & Shangrila Dadao; ☺ 8.30am-9pm). Most hotels in the old town also offer an air-ticket booking service.

From Lìjiāng there are oodles of daily flights to Kūnmíng (Y660), three flights daily to Chéngdū (Y1010) and Shànghǎi (Y2560) and two flights daily to Shēnzhèn (Y1760) and one daily to Guǎngzhōu (Y1790).

BUS

Lìjiāng has three bus stations: one is just north of the old town; the main long-distance bus station is in the south; and an express bus station to Kūnmíng and Xiàguān is in the north of town on Shangrila Dadao.

From the express bus station there are daily departures to Kūnmíng (Y171-193; 8am, 9am, 10am, 11am and 12.30pm). Two sleeper buses also leave daily for Kūnmíng at 8.30pm; one terminates at Kūnmíng's west station, the other at its south station. Buses also leave for the 160km trip to Xiàguān (Y41 to Y58, 3½ hours, 8am, 11.10am, noon, 2.10pm, 3.50pm and 6.10pm). Daily buses also leave for Shangri-la from here (Y45, five hours, 8.40am and 2.30pm).

Getting Around

Buses to the airport (Y15) leave from outside the CAAC office 90 minutes before flight departures.

Taxis start at Y6 in the new town and are not allowed into the old town. Bike hire is available at the International Youth Hostel Lijiang (Y15 per day).

LÌJIĀNG BUS TIMETABLES

Buses from the north bus station include the following:

Destination	Price	Duration	Frequency	Departs
Kūnmíng	Y119	8hr	daily	8pm
Xiàguān	Y35-37	3½hr	20 daily	7.30am-6pm
Shangri-la	Y39	5hr	2 daily	7.50am, 11am
Nínglàng	Y23	3-4hr	6 daily	8am, 9.30am, 10am, 12.30pm, 1.30pm, 2pm
Jīnjiāng	Y45-60	8hr	3 daily	7am, 8am, 11am

Buses from the long-distance bus station include:

Destination	Price	Duration	Frequency	Departs
Kūnmíng	Y151	12hr	hourly	8.30-11.30am & 1pm
Kūnmíng (sleeper)	Y119	8hr	11 daily	6.30-9pm
Xiàguān	Y35-50	3½hr	27 daily	7.10am-6.30pm
Shangri-la	Y39	5hr	15 daily	7.30am-5pm
Nínglàng	Y23	5hr	13 daily	8am-4.30pm
Qiáotóu	Y20	2hr	daily	1pm
Lúgū Hú	Y63	7-8hr	1 daily	9.30am

AROUND LÌJIĀNG

It is possible to see most of Lìjiāng's environs on your own, but a few agencies do offer half- or full-day tours, starting from Y150-200; it might be worth it if you take one that includes fees.

Monasteries

The monasteries around Lìjiāng are Tibetan in origin and belong to the Karmapa (Red Hat) sect. Most were extensively damaged during the Cultural Revolution and there's not much monastic activity nowadays. Nevertheless, it's worth hopping on a bicycle and heading out of town for a look.

PUJI MONASTERY 普济寺

This **monastery** (Pǔjì Sì) is around 5km northwest of Lìjiāng on a trail that passes the two ponds to the north of town. The few monks here are usually happy to show the occasional stray traveller around.

FUGUO MONASTERY 富国寺

West of Báishā lie the remains of this **temple** (Fùguó Sì), once the largest of Lìjiāng's monasteries. Much of it was destroyed during the Cultural Revolution. To get there head west from the main intersection in Báishā (p716) until you reach a small village. Turn right at the fork in the road and continue

for around 500m before taking the next left that you come to. Walk up the hill for about 30 minutes and you will come to the monastery ruins.

JADE PEAK MONASTERY 玉峰寺

This small **lamasery** (Yùfēng Sì) is on a hillside about 5km past Báishā. The last 3km of the track require a steep climb. If you decide to leave your bike at the foot of the hill, don't leave it too close to the village below – the local kids have been known to let the air out of the tyres (or worse)!

The monastery sits at the foot of Yùlóng Xuěshān (5500m) and was established in 1756. The monastery's main attraction nowadays is the **Camellia Tree of 10,000 Blossoms** (Wànduǒ Shānchá). Ten thousand might be something of an exaggeration, but locals claim that the tree produces at least 4000 blossoms between February and April. A monk on the grounds risked his life to keep the tree secretly watered during the Cultural Revolution.

WENBI MONASTERY 文笔寺

To get to this **monastery** (Wénbǐ Sì) requires a steep uphill ride 8km to the southwest of Lìjiāng. The monastery itself is not that interesting, but there are some good views and pleasant walks in the near vicinity.

AROUND LÌJIĀNG & SHANGRI-LA 丽江、香格里拉

Frescoes

Lìjiāng is famed for its temple frescoes. Most travellers probably won't want to spend a week or so traipsing around seeking them out, but it may be worth checking out one or two.

Most of the frescoes were painted during the 15th and 16th centuries by Tibetan, Naxi, Bai and Han artists. Many of them were restored during the later Qing dynasty. They depict various Taoist, Chinese and Tibetan Buddhist themes and can be found on the interior walls of temples in the area. However, the Red Guards came through here slashing and gouging during the Cultural Revolution, so there's not that much to see.

In Báishā (below) the best frescoes can be found in **Dabaoji Palace** (Dàbǎojī Gōng; admission Y15; 8.30am-5.30pm). Nearby, **Liuli Temple** (Liúlí Diàn) and **Dading Ge** also have some and in the neighbouring village of Lóngquán, frescoes can be found on the interior walls of **Dajue Palace** (Dàjué Gōng).

BÁISHĀ 白沙

Báishā is a small village on the plain north of Lìjiāng, near several old temples, and is one of

the best day trips out of Lìjiāng, especially if you have a bike. Before Kublai Khan made it part of his Yuan empire (1271–1368), Báishā was the capital of the Naxi kingdom. It's hardly changed since then and offers a close-up glimpse of Naxi culture for those willing to spend some time nosing around.

The star attraction of Báishā will probably hail you in the street. Dr Ho (or He) looks like the stereotype of a Taoist physician and has a sign outside his door: 'The Clinic of Chinese Herbs in Jade Dragon Mountains of Lìjiāng'. The travel writer Bruce Chatwin propelled the good doctor into the limelight when he mythologised Dr Ho as the 'Taoist physician in the Jade Dragon Mountains of Lìjiāng'. Chatwin did such a romantic job on Dr Ho that the doctor has subsequently appeared in every travel book (including this one) with an entry on Lìjiāng. Journalists and photographers from every corner of the world have since visited Báishā, and Dr Ho, previously an unknown doctor in an unknown town, has achieved worldwide renown.

Almost directly opposite Dr Ho's clinic is **Café Buena Vista** (Nànà Wéisītǎ Jùlèbù; ☎ 131-7078

THE CONDUCTOR *From* Songlines *(1987) by Bruce Chatwin*

The village schoolmaster was a chivalrous and energetic man with a shock of glinting blue-black hair, who lived with his childlike wife in a wooden house beside the Jade Stream.

A musicologist by training, he had climbed to distant mountain villages to record the folksongs of the Na-Khi tribe. He believed, like Vico, that the world's first languages were in song. Early man, he said, had learnt to speak by imitating the calls of animals and birds, and had lived in a musical harmony with the rest of Creation.

His room was crammed with bric-a-brac salvaged, heaven knows how, from the catastrophes of the Cultural Revolution. Perched on chairs of red lacquer, we nibbled melon seeds while he poured into thimbles of white porcelain a mountain tea known as 'Handful of Snow'.

He played us a tape of Na-Khi chant, sung antiphonally by men and women around the bier of a corpse: Wooo…Zeee! Wooo…Zeee! The purpose of the song was to drive away the Eater of the Dead, a fanged and malicious demon thought to feast upon the soul.

He surprised us by his ability to hum his way through the mazurkas of Chopin and an apparently endless repertoire of Beethoven. His father, a merchant in the Lhasa caravan trade, had sent him in the 1940s to study Western music at the Kunming Academy.

On the back wall, above a reproduction of Claude Lorrain's *L'Embarquement pour Cythère,* there were two framed photos of himself: one in white tie and tails behind a concert grand; the other, conducting an orchestra in a street of flag-waving crowds – a dashing and energetic figure, on tiptoe, his arms extended upwards and his baton down.

'In 1949,' he said. 'To welcome the Red Army into Kūnmíng.'

'What were you playing?'

'Schubert's *Marche Militaire*.'

For this – or rather, for his devotion to 'Western culture' – he got 21 years in jail.

He held up his hands, gazing at them sadly as though they were long-lost orphans. His fingers were crooked and his wrists were scarred: a reminder of the day when the Guards strung him up to the roof-beams – in the attitude of Christ on the Cross…or a man conducting an orchestra.

0719; info@ecotour.com) a lovely little café run by an artist, Zhao Fan, and his girlfriend. It also doubles up as an art gallery and is a good place to get travel information (see Eco-Tours p711).

There are a couple of frescoes worth seeing in town and surrounding the area; see opposite for details.

Báishā is an easy 20-30–minute bike ride from Lìjiāng. Otherwise take a minibus (Y15) from the corner of Minzu Lu and Fuhui Lu. From Báishā minibuses return to Lìjiāng regularly (Y20).

YÙLÓNG XUĚSHĀN 玉龙雪山

Also known as Mt Satseto, **Yùlóng Xuěshān** (Jade Dragon Snow Mountain; admission adult/student Y80/60, protection fee Y40) soars to some 5500m. Its peak was first climbed in 1963 by a research team from Běijīng and now, at some 35km from Lìjiāng, it is regularly mobbed by hordes of Chinese tour groups and travellers.

Dry Sea Meadow (甘海子; Gānhǎizi) is the first stop you come to if travelling by bus from Lìjiāng. A chairlift (Y160) ascends to a large meadow at 3050m which, according to geologists, was actually a lake 2000 years ago. It can often get freezing above even when warm down here; warm coats can be rented for Y30, deposit Y300, and oxygen tanks are Y40. (see p982)

Cloud Fir Meadow (云杉坪; Yúnshānpíng) is the second stop and a chairlift (Y40) takes you up to 4506m where walkways lead to awesome glacier views. Horses can be hired here for Y80.

Views from above are pretty impressive, but make sure you get here well before the first chair up at 8.30am. Unless you get a head start on the tour groups, prepare for up to an hour wait to get either up or down the mountain.

Around 60km from Lìjiāng, or a 30-minute drive from Dry Sea Meadow, is **Yak Meadow** (牦牛坪; Máoniúpíng) where yet another chairlift (Y60) pulls visitors up to an altitude of 3500m where there are ample hiking opportunities near Xuěhuā Hǎi (Snowflake Lake). Crowds and long waits are almost unheard of here.

JOSEPH ROCK

Yúnnán was a hunting ground for famous, foreign plant-hunters such as Kingdon Ward and Joseph Rock. Rock lived in Lìjiāng between 1922 and 1949, becoming the world's leading expert on Naxi culture and local botany. More than his academic pursuits, however, he will be remembered as one of the most enigmatic and eccentric characters to travel in western China.

Rock was born in Austria, the son of a domineering father who insisted he enter a seminary. A withdrawn child, he escaped into his imagination and atlases, discovering a passion for China. An astonishing autodidact – he taught himself eight languages, including Sanskrit – he began learning Chinese at 13 years of age. He somehow wound up in Hawaii, and in time became the foremost authority on Hawaiian flora.

Asia always beckoned and he convinced the US Department of Agriculture, and later Harvard University, to sponsor his trips to collect flora for medicinal research. He devoted much of his life to studying Naxi culture, which he feared was being extinguished by the dominant Han culture. He became *National Geographic* magazine's 'man in China' and it was his exploits in northwestern Yúnnán and Sìchuān for the magazine that made him famous.

He sent over 80,000 plant specimens from China – two were named after him – along with 1600 birds and 60 mammals. Amazingly, he was taking and developing the first colour photographic plates in his field in the 1920s! Tragically, container-loads of his collections were lost in 1945 in the Arabian Sea when the boat was torpedoed.

Rock's caravans stretched for half a mile, and included dozens of servants, including a cook trained in Austrian cuisine, trains of pack horses, and hundreds of mercenaries for protection against bandits, not to mention the gold dinner service and a collapsible bathtub.

Rock lived in Yùhú village (called Nguluko when he was there) outside Lìjiāng. Many of his possessions are now local family heirlooms.

The *Ancient Nakhi Kingdom of Southwest China* (1947) is Joseph Rock's definitive work. Immediately prior to his death, his Naxi dictionary was also finally prepared for publishing. For an insight into the man and his work, take a look at *In China's Border Provinces: The Turbulent Career of Joseph Rock, Botanist-Explorer* (1974) by JB Sutton, or Rock's many archived articles for *National Geographic*.

At the time of research, camping in the area was not prohibited but it's better to check when you get there as regulations have a tendency to change quicker than the cloud cover.

Bus 7 (Y15 to Y20) leaves for all three spots from the intersection of Minzu Lu and Fuhui Lu and passes by Báishā on the way. Returning to Lìjiāng, buses leave fairly regularly but check with your driver to find out what time the last bus will depart.

If you enter the region from the north (Tiger Leaping Gorge) there's no ticket gate.

TIGER LEAPING GORGE 虎跳峡
☎ 0887

A hike here has gone from obscure adventure to the 'can't miss' experience of northern Yúnnán and is well worth the hype. The gorge (Hǔtiào Xiá), one of the deepest in the world, measures 16km long and is a giddy 3900m from the waters of Jinsha River (Jīnshā Jiāng) to the snow-capped mountaintops of

Hābā Shān (Haba Mountain) to the west and Yùlóng Xuěshān to the east.

The best time to come is May and the start of June, when the hills are afire with plant and flower life.

Plan on three to four days away from Lìjiāng doing the hike though it can be done in two. Many travellers have lingered up to a week.

The first thing to do is to check with cafés in Lìjiāng for the latest gossip on the mini-trek, particularly the weather and its possibly lethal effects on the trail. Most cafés give away hand-drawn maps of the trek. They show paths, walking times and some places to stay, but remember that they aren't to scale.

Transport is easier than it once was. Finishing south in Qiáotóu allows for quicker transport back to Lìjiāng, but heading north towards Dàjù gives you the option of continuing on to Báishuǐtái (p727). Most people take a Shangri-la–bound bus early in the morning, hop off in Qiáotóu, and hike quickly to stay overnight in Walnut Garden.

Development is taking its toll on the gorge. After three years of Herculean blasting and building, a road now leads all the way through the gorge from Qiáotóu to Walnut Garden and a dirt track swings north to Báishuǐtái, joining the road to Shangri-la. Tour buses shuttle up and down the gorge and kitschy stop-off points are being constructed. This currently isn't too much of an annoyance for trekkers as the high path climbs way above all the activity.

This does mean that you can still see the gorge (if you don't want to trek) by taking a bus to Qiáotóu and then catching one of the ubiquitous microbuses that shuttle people to the main viewpoint 10km away. The cost will depend on your bargaining skills, but aim for as close to Y15 as you can. You could even take a taxi (Y50) the 23km from Qiáotóu to Walnut Garden and hitchhike back.

Admission to the gorge is Y50.

Dangers & Annoyances

The gorge trek is not to be taken lightly, particularly during the wet months of July and August – or any time it rains, really – when landslides and swollen waterfalls can block the paths, in particular on the low road. Half a dozen people – including a few foreign travellers – have died in the gorge. Most perished because they wandered off the trail, got lost and/or were unable to return to the trail, or fell. One hiker was buried while trying to scramble over a landslide and in 2004 a car was caught in a landslide on the low road and four people died. Two solo travellers have also reported being assaulted on the trail by locals, although this couldn't be officially confirmed.

Make sure you bring plenty of water on this hike, two to three litres is ideal, as well as plenty of sun screen and lip balm.

On a less severe note, several travellers have reported becoming ill after eating in Qiáotóu or from drinking water along the trek.

Activities

GORGE TREK

There are two trails – the higher (the older route, known as the 24-bend path, although it's more like 30), and the lower, new road, replete with fume-belching tour buses. Only the high trail is worth hiking. Arrows litter the high trail, pointing out the path and the way to guesthouses.

The following route starts at Qiáotóu.

To get to the high road, after crossing through the gate, cross a small stream and go 150m. Take a left fork, go through the school-yard's football pitch, and join the tractor road. Continue until the track ends and then follow the yellow arrows to the right. It's six hours to Běndiwān or a strenuous eight hours to Walnut Garden.

Guesthouses dot the trail which means you're usually never more than a few kilometres from a bed – good news for those not willing to start trekking at the crack of dawn. The following list is not exhaustive.

Naxi Family Guesthouse (Nàxī Kèzhàn; dm Y15) Eight kilometres into the trek, this place still gets rave reviews from travellers.

Halfway Lodge (Zhōngtú Kèzhàn, Běndiwān; dm Y15) This is an excellent, very popular place that's gone from a cosy little guesthouse to one of the bigger operations on the trek.

Five Fingers Guesthouse (Wǔzhǐ Kèzhàn; dm Y15) Run by a friendly, enthusiastic family, you can eat with them for Y10.

Tina's Guest House (Zhōngxiá Lǚdiàn; dm Y15) About 1½ hours from Běndiwān you descend to the road to this place – budget more time if you are ascending. Tina's is a friendly and convenient place to spend your first night from Dàjù. A good detour from here leads down 40 minutes to the middle rapids and Tiger Leaping Stone, where a tiger is once said to have leapt across the Yangzi, thus giving the gorge its name. The man who restored the path charges Y10 to take people down it (regardless of whether you want him to or not).

From Tina's to Walnut Garden it is a 40-minute walk along the road. A new alternative trail to Walnut Garden keeps high where the path descends to Tina's, crosses a stream and a 'bamboo forest' before descending into Walnut Garden.

Be aware that in peak times – particularly late summer – up to 100 people per day can make the trek, so bed space is short. Be prepared to sleep in a back room somewhere. Supplies of bottled water can be chancy; it's probably best to bring your own.

The second day's walk is slightly shorter, at four to six hours. There are two ferries and so two route options to get to Dàjù. After 45 minutes you'll see a red marker leading down to the new (winter) ferry (xīn dùkǒu; one way Y10); the descent includes one hairy section over planks with a sheer drop below.

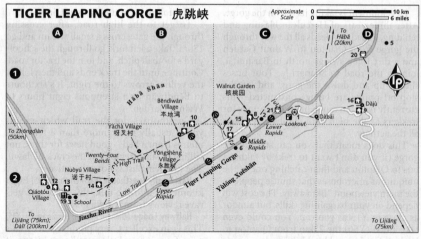

Many trekkers call it a day when they reach the bottom and flag down anything heading back Qiáotóu along the lower road. Or, you can try to arrange a car through your accommodation in Walnut Grove to meet you at the bottom and take you back to Qiáotóu.

The road to Dàjù and the village itself are pretty uninteresting so you won't be missing anything if you skip it.

If you do decide to head on to Dàjù, it's a hard climb to the car park where you should register with the Lìjiāng PSB (Gōngānjú). The PSB officer offers a car to take you into Dàjù for Y10, avoiding the dull 1½-hour's walk along the road.

The second, lesser-used option continues along the road from Walnut Garden until it reaches the permanent ferry crossing (Y10). From here paths lead to Dàjù.

If you're doing the walk the other way round and heading for Qiáotóu, walk north through Dàjù, aiming for the white pagoda at the foot of the mountains.

TIGER LEAPING GORGE TO BÁISHUĬTÁI

An adventurous add-on to the gorge trek is to continue north all the way to Hābā village and the limestone terraces of Báishuĭtái. This turns it into a four-day trek from Qiáotóu and from here you can travel on to Shangri-la. From Walnut Garden to Hābā, via Jiāngbiān, it is seven to eight hours. From here to the Yi village of Sānbà is about the same, following trails. You could just follow the road and hitch with the occasional truck or tractor but it's longer and less scenic. Some hardy mountain bikers have followed the trail but this is really only fun from north to south, elevations being what they are. The best way would be to hire a guide in Walnut Garden for Y50 to Y100 per day, depending on the number of people. For Y100 to Y120 per day you should be able to get a horse and guide. Eventually buses will make the trip, but that is still some time off.

In Hābā most people stay at the **Haba Snow Mountain Inn** (Hābā Xuěshān Kèzhàn; beds Y15) which has toilets and showers. In Sānbà, beds can also be found for around Y15. From Sānbà there is an 8am bus to Shangri-la (Y40, five hours), or you could get off at the turn-off to Bìtǎ Hǎi (Emerald Pagoda Lake) and hike there.

If you plan to try the route alone, assume you'll need all provisions and equipment for extremes of weather. Ask for local advice before setting out.

Sleeping & Eating

There are accommodation options at either end of the trek and all the way in between.

QIÁOTÓU

Jane's Guesthouse (☎ 880 6570; janetibetgh@hotmail .com; dm/s/d Y15/30/30; 🖳) Next to the school at the start of the trek, this is your best option in Qiáotóu. Jane is a character, massively helpful and can tell you everything there is to know about the gorge trek. There are left-luggage facilities and internet access here.

Travellers will be warmly welcomed at the **Youth Hostel** (dm/d Y15/50) on the village's main road but rooms don't look like they've ever been cleaned. There's a **hotel** (d Y280) next the Shangri-la–Qiáotóu bus drop-off that seems appealing but with the lack of phones, disappearing desk staff and oddities like broken, three-legged chairs it's horrific value for the money.

Gorged Tiger Café (☎ 880 6300) Run by an Australian woman, Margo, this is another place you should stop by before starting your trek to get up-to-date information on the trail. The food gets mixed reviews from travellers, but Margo herself gets raves.

DÀJÙ

Snowflake Hotel (Xuěhuā Fàndiàn) Gets most TLG trekkers but though it gets high marks for friendliness, some travellers have complained about dingy rooms. Staff can arrange for the 7.30am bus to Lìjiāng to pick you up at the hotel.

Daju Longhu Inn (Dàjù Lónghǔ Kèzhàn; standard/deluxe d Y20/50 without bathroom) If the Snowflake's owners are MIA (known to happen occasionally), climb the stone steps just opposite it and follow the road to the main street where this inn will be on your right. Communal showers and toilets are frankly monstrous, but rooms are quite nice. Standards are nondescript budget-basic, though the deluxe ones are quite impressively done up in gold decor.

THE END OF THE GORGE?

Tiger Leaping Gorge, one of the deepest canyons in the world and one of China's most spectacular natural attractions, could disappear in a matter of years if new plans to build eight dams along the upper reaches of the Yangzi River go ahead.

The proposed dams will stretch over 564km of river starting from Shígǔ near Lìjiāng and ending in Pānzhīhūa, Sìchuān. Once completed, the dams will flood more than 13,000 hectares of prime farmland, force over 100,000 people to relocate and wash away local culture, history, unique architecture and indigenous plant and animal life.

Officials say the dams are a necessity and that hydropower can solve China's energy shortage problems. While the country's economy races ahead, power supplies are struggling to keep up and many coastal manufacturing hubs experience regular blackouts. The proposed dams will also divert water towards Kūnmíng and help ease urban water shortages. One of the project's major backers is a power company headed by Li Xiaopeng, the son of Li Peng, the former prime minister who pushed through the controversial Three Gorges Dam project (p484). Local authorities are also said to be backing the scheme, which will produce an estimated US$50 million a year in tax revenue once power generation begins – double the current annual figure.

Although the central government has yet to grant final approval, Chinese media reports that preparatory work, including blasting, has already begun and proper construction on the dams is expected to begin by 2008. Local and international environmental groups are lobbying the government to halt plans, but others are also concerned. Locals are increasingly worried about their land and the impact that damning the gorge will have on the flow of tourist dollars to the region. However, with such a pro-development economic policy in full swing, it's hard to believe that those in charge will take much notice.

Sean's Spring Guesthouse (Shānquán Kèzhàn; ☎ 880 6300; www.tigerleapinggorge.com; dm Y15) This is one of the original guesthouses on the trail and still the spot for more lively evenings and socialising. Sean's has a free hot shower, electric blankets, mountain-bike hire (per hr Y10) and can organise camping, guides and horse trips.

Chateau de Woody (Shānbáiliǎn Lǚguǎn; dm Y15) Woody's is definitely one of the friendliest stops on the trek, though travellers say the food can be disappointing.

Getting There & Away

From Lìjiāng, Shangri-la–bound buses leave every hour or so from 7.30am to 5pm from the long-distance bus station and pass through Qiáotóu (Y20). The last bus to Shangri-la passes through at around 7pm.

From Dàjù to Lìjiāng buses (Y20) leave at 7.30am and 1.30pm.

Returning to Lìjiāng from Qiáotóu, buses start running through from Shangri-la around 9am. The last one rolls through around 7.40pm (Y20).

Eventually the new highway through the gorge will link Qiáotóu, Walnut Garden and the settlement across the river from Dàjù and then bend north to connect Báishuǐtái, allowing travellers to get to Shangri-la from here.

LÚGŪ HÚ 泸沽湖
☎ 0888

This stunning, forest-lined lake overlaps the remote Yúnnán–Sìchuān border and is home to several Tibetan, Yi and Mosu (a Naxi subgroup) villages. The Mosu are the last practising matriarchal society in the world (see the box, opposite) and many other Naxi customs lost in Lìjiāng are still in evidence here. The lake, formed by two sinking faults, is fairly high at 2685m and is usually snowbound over winter. Villages are scattered around the lake but Luòshuǐ (洛水) is heavily developed for tourism and is where your bus will drop you off.

Consider heading for Lǐgé (里格; opposite), a much smaller village on the northeastern shore of the lake.

The best times to visit the lake are April to May, and September to October, when the weather is dry and mild. Entrance to the lake is Y80.

Sights & Activities

From Luòshuǐ you can visit several islands on the lake by dugout canoe, which the Mosu call

'pig troughs' (zhūcáo). The canoes are rowed by Mosu who also serve as guides and usually take you out to Lǐwùbǐ Dǎo (里务比岛), the largest island. From here you can practically wade across to a spit of land in Sìchuān. The second largest island is Hēiwǎé Dǎo (黑瓦俄岛). Canoes leave from a beach area to the south of the hotel strip in Luòshuǐ. In Lǐgé any of the hostels can help arrange boat trips. The price will vary wildly, depending on exactly what you want to see and how many people are in your group. If you're in a group of six to eight people expect to pay around Y10 per person.

Near the bus stop in Luòshuǐ is the worthwhile **Mosu Folk Custom Museum** (摩俗民族博物馆; Mósú Mínsú Bówùguǎn; admission Y20; ☺ hit & miss). The museum is set within the traditional home of a wealthy Mosu family. Chinese-speaking guides will show you around and explain how the matriarchal society functions. There is also an interesting collection of photos taken by Joseph Rock in the 1920s.

In the outskirts of nearby Yǒngníng is **Zhamei Temple** (Zhāměi Sì), a Tibetan monastery with at least 20 lamas in residence. Admission is free, but a donation is expected. A private minivan costs Y15 per person for the half-hour ride. A bus passes through Luòshuǐ to Yǒngníng for Y5, or you could opt to walk the 20km or so through pleasant scenery.

Sleeping & Eating

Hotels and guesthouses line the lakeside in Luòshuǐ with doubles for from around Y50. Most have attached restaurants that serve traditional Mosu foods including preserved pig's fat and salted sour fish – the latter being somewhat tastier.

Husi Teahouse (湖思茶屋; Húsī Cháwū; ☎ 588 1170; dm Y15; 🖥) Run by Sichuaner Táng Bīn since 1998, this is one of the original and still the best backpacker hang-outs on the lake. Showers are a bit of a hike from the guesthouse, but there's a fleet of computers with internet, killer coffee, a terrific bar/café and travel info galore. If you're lucky, you'll be in one of four rooms with floor-to-ceiling windows overlooking the lake.

Mósuō Dàjiǔdiàn (摩梭大酒店; ☎ 588 1185; d/ cabins Y160/400) The nearby Mosu guesthouses will likely have better doubles, but there's a handful of cabins away from the main building worth looking at. They don't have lake views, but each includes a living room, bedroom and bathroom.

WALKING MARRIAGE

The Mosu are the last practising matriarchal society in the world. This system, whereby kinship and clan names, and social and political positions are passed on through the female line, has fascinated visitors since the area was developed for tourism in the early 1980s. What's proved to be the biggest draw, however, is the Mosu tradition of a 'walking marriage' (zǒu hūn).

Mosu women never marry nor cohabit; instead women are free to choose as many lovers as they like throughout their lives. Mosu women come of age when they reach 13, after which they no longer have to sleep in the communal living areas but are given their own bedroom. Her lover visits at night and returns to his mother's home in the morning, hence the expression 'walking marriage'.

This idea of such free and easy love has been heavily publicised. Traditionally referred to as Nǔ Guó (Woman's Kingdom), the area of Lúgū Hú was renamed Nǔ'ér Guó (Girl's Kingdom) in order to spice up the romantic and exotic image of the local women.

It's a strategy that's worked. Thousands of tourists have ventured up to this remote area, resulting in the Mosu becoming the richest ethnic minority group in Yúnnán. But it's also had some damaging effects on their culture. 'Walking marriage' has become synonymous with 'one night stand' and many men, in particular Han Chinese, visit the area in the hope of having a walking marriage themselves. This in turn has seen a rise in prostitution in the area and brothels disguised as karaoke bars now sit on the edge of Luòshuǐ town; the ultimate proof, if it was ever needed, that there's no such thing as free love.

Getting There & Away

Lìjiāng's long-distance bus station has one direct bus a day to the lake (Y63, seven to eight hours, 9.30am) but buy your ticket at least one day in advance as it's often fully booked. Alternately, you can go to Nínglàng (宁蒗) from Lìjiāng's north bus station (Y23, three to four hours, six buses daily from 8am to 2pm). From Nínglàng, there's a daily bus to the lake (Y20, three to four hours, 12.30pm).

For Lǐgé you will have to change for a minibus in Luòshuǐ (Y8 per person; if there are a lot of you they'll try to charge Y10 for the 20-25–minute ride).

Leaving Luòshuǐ, the direct bus to Lìjiāng leaves daily at 10am. Again, tickets should be bought at least a day in advance. There's also a daily bus to Nínglàng (Y20, check time when you arrive). From Nínglàng, there are 13 buses daily to Lijiāng (Y25, 7.30am to 4pm) and once a day, Xiàguān (Y48, 7.50am).

The daily bus to Xīchàng (Sìchuān) leaves at 8am (Y60, seven hours). There are also dozens of minibuses that prowl the villages around the lake on both the Sìchuān and Yúnnán sides if you want to do some exploring.

LǏGÉ 里格

With its velvet silence and vivid starry nights, arriving in this magical little village after Lìjiāng feels like arriving at the very tranquil end of the earth. Most travellers don't get past Luòshuǐ, so if you do make the effort to come here it will likely be just you, the Mosu and a handful of solo Chinese backpackers.

Set around a bay facing Lǐgé Dǎo (Lige Island), there's a day's worth of exploring to do either in the wilderness or on the lake, but a surprising number of travellers come and just chat, doodle and drink at one of the three waterside cafés.

But do get here as quick as you can. Construction plans are in the works and one part of the bay looks like it's being readied for the construction of at least a half-dozen two-storey guesthouses.

Sleeping & Eating

Yàsé Dàba Lǔxíngzhě Zhī Jiā (雅瑟达吧旅行堵之家; ☎ 588 1196; dm/d/tr Y20/40/60) Recently opened on the edge of the lake, this guest house has basic rooms with electric blankets, lovely owners and is just a spit away from the water. The cosy restaurant serves wonderful food (try Lugu Hu fish lúgū Hú Yú; 泸沽湖鱼) or sausage (xiāngcháng; 香肠) along with cold beer and an impressive choice of liqueurs (Bailey's anyone?). They can also suggest activities or arrange pretty much any excursion you want here. Bikes are Y20 per day, internet is Y5 per 30 minutes.

Right around the corner from here on the south side of this spit of land, is another terrific guesthouse (☎ 588 1015; d from Y30) Waves from the lake lick at the walls of this charming café it's so close to the water. It's all headed up by Susan, the fantastically friendly and relaxed owner.

SHANGRI-LA 香格里拉 (ZHŌNGDIÀN 中甸)

☎ 0887 / pop 125,000 / elevation 3200m

Shangri-la (also known as Zhōngdiàn) is home to remote temples, rugged scenery and the start of the Tibetan world. And while travellers have beat their way to northern Yúnnán's other ancient villages, this remote town hasn't shown up on many people's radars in the same way.

But seeing the town's potential to follow in the footsteps of Lìjiāng and Dàlǐ, Zhōngdiàn got the attention of the government in a big way.

Officials declared the town (and by extension the rest of the country) the location of British writer James Hilton's fictional Shangri-la, described in his novel *The Lost Horizon*. Poo-poo-ed as a cynical gimmick to drum up tourism, the thing is, it's actually worked and has got everyone from backpackers to tour groups interested in visiting.

Principally a Tibetan town (its Tibetan name is Gyeltang or Gyalthang) the main reason to come here is to visit the monastery and to get a taste of Tibet if you can't make it to the real thing.

Shangri-la is also the last stop in Yúnnán for more hardy travellers looking at a rough five- or six-day journey to Chéngdū via the Tibetan townships and rugged terrain of western Sìchuān.

Plan your visit to this neck of the woods between April and October. There is no point coming here during winter as the city is practically shut down and transportation is often halted completely by snow storms.

In mid-June Shangri-la plays host to a horseracing festival that sees several days of dancing, singing, eating and, of course, horseracing. Another new festival – usually in September – features minority artists of southwest China. Accommodation can be a bit tight around these times, so you may want to arrive a day or two early in order to secure a room.

Information

Agricultural Bank of China (Zhōngguó Nóngyè Yínháng; cnr Changzheng Lu & Xiangyang Lu; ☯ 8.30am-noon & 2.30-5.30pm Mon-Fri) Can change cash, travellers cheques and give cash advances on credit cards.

CD Burning (Noah's Café; Nuoya Kāfēi; Changzheng Lu) Y10 per CD.

China Telecom (Changzheng Lu) There are two telephone offices along this road that offer cheap international phone calls.

Khampa Caravan (☎ 828 8648; www.khampacaravan .com; Heping Lu) Organises some excellent adventures, from day treks in the surrounding countryside to week-long treks in the remote wilderness. It can also arrange overland travel into Tibet (see p726), as well as flights and permits from Shangri-la to Lhasa. The company also runs a lot of sustainable development programs within Tibetan communities. One of these projects, Trinyi Eco-lodge, is a couple of kilometres outside town and is easy to get to by bike.

PSB (Gōngānjú; Changzheng Lu; ☯ 8.30am-12.30pm & 2.30-5pm) Issues on-the-spot visa extensions.

Tibet Café (☎ 823 0282; www.tibetcafeinn.com; Changzheng Lu; internet access per hr Y12) Another great place to go for travel information; it also organises overland travel to Tibet. A particularly worthwhile trip is a visit to its eco-farm, Shangbala, 40km from Shangri-la, where you can spend the evening with a Tibetan family (per person Y20). All money goes directly to the Tibetan community.

Dangers & Annoyances

Altitude sickness is a real problem here and most travellers need at least a couple of days to acclimatize. Brutal winter weather can bring the town to a complete standstill so try to plan your visit between March and October.

Sights

About an hour's walk north of town is the **Ganden Sumtseling Gompa** (Sōngzànlín Sì; admission Y10; ☯ 7.30am-8pm), a 300-year-old Tibetan monastery complex with around 600 monks. The monastery is the most important in southwest China and is definitely worth the trip to Shangri-la. Bus 3 runs here from anywhere along Changzheng Lu (Y1). Be advised the government is planning to raise the admission price to around Y30.

The view of town from the top is gorgeous, and a sunset from here is particularly picturesque among the tinkling bells and the fluttering prayer flags.

Much closer to the centre of things, just south of town and overlooking the old town district, is another **monastery** with exceedingly friendly monks.

Hidden within the old town is the **Scripture Chamber** (Gǔchéng Cángjīngtáng), formerly a memorial hall to the Red Army's Long March.

Guishan Park (Guīshān Gōngyuán) is nearby and has a temple at the top with commanding views of the area.

Besides the sights listed below, Shangri-la is a wonderful place to get off the beaten track, with plenty of trekking and horseback riding opportunities, as well as little visited monasteries and villages. However, the remote sights are difficult to do independently given the lack of public transport. You'll need to arrange a guide, or car and driver through your accommodation.

Sleeping & Eating

There are always interesting guesthouses and hostels popping up near the old town and city outskirts. Be aware however that despite

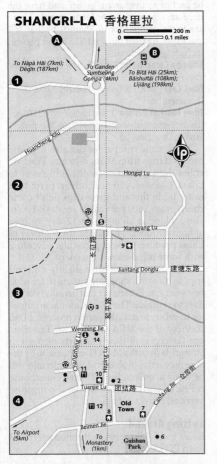

Shangri-la's often glacial night temperatures, many guesthouses are neither heated nor have 24-hour hot water.

Dragoncloud Guesthouse (Lóngxíng Kèzhàn; ☎ 688 7573; www.dragoncloud.cn; 94 Beimen Jie, Jiangtang Zhen; 建塘镇北门街94号; dm Y15-25, s/d with bathroom 80; 💻) The rooms here are in great condition with modern bathrooms. There's a great common area with fireplace, internet (Y4 per hour) and interesting comings and goings from the nearby old town. Bike rental for Y15 per day.

Shangri-La Traveller Club (Zàngdì Guójì Qīngnián Lǚshè; ☎ 822 8671; 98 Heping Lu; 和平路98号; dm/d Y20/50; 💻) If you want enthusiastic (or manic!) service this is a great, central place that attracts a real 'tumbleweed' type of traveller. Staff are also good setting up any kind of travel arrangements. You can rent bikes here (per day Y15) and go online (per hr Y6). The only downside is the cold, mad dash from the outdoor shower to the rooms.

International Youth Hostel (Guójì Qīngnián Lǚshè; ☎ 822 6948; Jiantang Lu; 建塘路; dm/d Y20/80) Spartan and on the chilly side at night, this hostel is in a quiet part of town and run by a lovely family who doesn't speak English but goes out of their way to help.

Noah Café (Nuoya Kāfēi; Changzheng Lu; dishes from Y10) You can walk the streets all day, never see another traveller, then walk in here and there's dozens. This café has become a real travellers hub with great Western food and friendly service. You can also burn CDs here for Y10.

Artist Space of the Sacred (Shèngdí Yíshú Kōngjiān; ☎ 823 1309; 16 Cangfang Jie; 仓房街16号; cocktails & beers Y10-Y30) A feast for the senses, set up by a local artist. Primarily a bar, the bar itself is all moody lighting and flimsy curtains, while outside there are tiered outdoor terraces with outrageous views. A Ming has a gallery full of paintings upstairs and will show you if you ask. It also has a 4-bed dorm with a Buddhist shrine, and a private room with one of the most romantic views in the city.

Have a look around the old town and on Tuanjie Lu for Tibetan and Western restaurants and cafés. Also look out for locally produced Shangri-la wine. French missionaries working in the Mekong area taught the Tibetans wine-producing techniques, a tradition which has fortunately carried on through to today – look for the bottle with a church on the label.

Getting There & Away
AIR
There are four flights daily to Kūnmíng (Y830), two a week to Guǎngzhōu (Y1880) and regular flights to Lhasa. Flights for other domestic destinations also leave from the airport but are completely irregular and destinations change from week to week. You can inquire about your destination or buy tickets at the **CAAC** (Zhōngguó Mínháng; ☎ 822 9901; Wenming Jie).

The airport is 5km from town and is sometimes referred to as Díqìng or Deqen – there is currently no airport at Déqīn. Don't expect to see any taxis here; they are rare around the airport. Shuttle buses (Y10) sometimes wait for incoming flights and will usually drop you right at your hotel. The drivers wear picture ID. If the shuttle bus isn't there you'll have to negotiate with the drivers of the black sedans in front of you or call your accommodation to try and arrange transport.

BUS
If you're up for the bus-hopping trek to Chéngdū, in Sìchuān, you're looking at a minimum of five to six days' travel at some very high altitudes – you'll need warm clothes. The first stage of the trip is Shangri-la to Xiāngchéng in Sìchuān. From Xiāngchéng, your next destination is Lǐtáng, though if roads are bad you may be forced to stay overnight in Dàochéng. From Lǐtáng, it's on to Kāngdìng from where you can make your way

west towards Chéngdū. For more details on these towns see Western Sìchuān & the Road to Tibet (p777).

Note that roads out of Shangri-la can be temporarily blocked by snow at any time from November to March. If you are travelling at this time bring lots of warm clothes and a flexible itinerary.

For Bēnzǐlán you can also catch the Déqīn bus which passes through Bēnzǐlán on the way. See also individual local destinations for transport details.

TO TIBET
There are now flights from Shangri-la to Lhasa, but the situation is much the same as in Kūnmíng and Chéngdū and travellers must be part of an organised 'group' and have the necessary permits in order to travel. There are three companies in Shangri-la that sell 'packages' to Tibet (around Y2570 per person, including air ticket):

Khampa Caravan (☎ 828 8648; www.khampacaravan .com; Heping Lu)

Tibet Café (☎ 823 0019; www.tibetcafeinn.com; Changzheng Lu)

Tibet Tourism Bureau (Xīzàng Lǚyóujù; ☎ 822 9028; yunnantibettour@yahoo.com.cn; room 2206, Shangbala Hotel, 36 Changzheng Lu)

These same companies can also organise overland trips from Shangri-la into Tibet via either the northern or southern highway to Lhasa. Likewise, you need official permits in order to do this and these trips don't come cheap (from Y800 per vehicle per day). You're also looking at an eight- to 12-day journey at high altitudes. That aside, the highway to Lhasa promises to be a spectacular adventure with some mind-blowing scenery.

The companies all offer slightly different trips so it's worth shopping around to see what best suits you. Remember that permits take five days to organise. The Tibet Café has arranged for travellers to start the permit process in Dàlǐ courtesy of the MCA Guesthouse. Travellers can fax copies of their passports through to Shangri-la from the MCA Guesthouse so by the time they arrive in Shangri-la their permits will be ready to collect. Jim's Tibetan Guesthouse & Peace Café (p704) in Dàlǐ can also organise overland travel to Lhasa.

Getting Around
Buses 1 and 3 zip between the monastery and town (Y1).

BUS TIMETABLES

Bus services from Shangri-la include the following:

Destination	Price	Duration	Frequency	Departs
Kūnmíng	Y167	15hr	7 daily	4-7.30pm
Lìjiāng	Y35	4½hr	13 daily	7.10am-5.40pm
Xiàguān	Y56	8hr	hourly	7am-12.30pm
Déqīn	Y38	6hr	4 daily	7.20-noon
Xiāngchéng	Y65	8-9hr	daily	7.30am
Dōngwàng	Y45	7-8hr	daily	7.30am
Báishuǐtái	Y23	4hr	2 daily	9.10am, 2.10pm
Bēnzǐlán	Y17	3hr	2 daily	1pm, 2pm

AROUND SHANGRI-LA

Some 7km northwest of Shangri-la you'll find the seasonal **Nàpà Hǎi** (Napa Lake; admission Y30), surrounded by a large grassy meadow. Between September and March there's a myriad of rare species, including the black-necked crane. Outside of these months, the lake dries up and there is little reason to visit.

Approximately 10km southeast of Shangri-la is the **Tiansheng Bridge** (Tiānshēng Qiáo; admission Y15; ☺ 9am-6pm Apr-Oct), a natural limestone formation, and further southeast, the subterranean **Xiagei hot springs** (admission Y15; ☺ 9am-late); for both places, ask at your accomodation for off-season hours. If you can arrange transport, en route is the **Great Treasure Temple** (Dàbǎo Sì), one of the earliest Buddhist temples in Yúnnán.

The above sites are wildly popular with Chinese tour groups, but many foreign travellers seem underwhelmed.

Emerald Pagoda Lake 碧塔

Some 25km east of Shangri-la, the bus to Sānbà (see Báishuǐtái, following) can drop you along the highway for **Bìtǎ Hǎi** (Emerald Pagoda Lake; admission Y60), which is 8km down a trail. There are lots of hiking options and ponies can be arranged at the lake. There is a second, southern entrance, from where it is 2km to the lake. It's possible to rent boats between the two ends of the lake.

A taxi will cost around Y300 for the return trip.

Báishuǐtái 白水台

Báishuǐtái is a limestone deposit plateau 108km southeast of Shangri-la with some breathtaking scenery and Tibetan villages en route. The **terraces** (admission Y30) are resplend-

ent in sunlight, but can be tough to access if rainfall has made trails slippery. There are normally horses for hire.

A couple of **guesthouses** at the nearby towns of Báidì and Sānbà have rooms with beds from Y25.

From Shangri-la there are two daily buses to Báishuǐtái at 9.10am and 2.10pm (Y23).

One option is to trek or hitch all the way from Báishuǐtái to Tiger Leaping Gorge; see p720 for information.

Bēnzǐlán 奔子栏

This laid-back Tibetan village makes an excellent base to explore the wonderful **Dhondrupling Gompa** (东竹林寺; Dōngzhúlín Sì), 22km from Bēnzǐlán, heading northwest along the main road.

Bēnzǐlán has plenty of restaurants and small hotels. All offer decent beds for Y25-30. **Duōwén Lǚguǎn** (bed Y25), around the bend in the northern end of town, is perhaps the best choice. This Tibetan-style place has a prayer wheel by the entrance and pleasant rooms.

To get to Bēnzǐlán take any bus between Shangri-la and Déqīn; buses pass through town between 11am and noon. There's two direct buses a day from Shangri-la (Y17, three hours, 1pm & 2pm). There are daily buses back to Shangri-la. Inquire about times when you arrive.

DÉQĪN 德钦

☎ 0887/elevation 3550m

Nestled in the wild west of Yúnnán, among ragged, snowy peaks Déqīn is the last outpost before Tibet. It's a terrific little rough-and-tumble town with plenty of atmosphere. Part of Díqìng Tibetan Autonomous Prefecture, the county is 80% Tibetan, though a dozen other minorities are found here, including one of the few settlements of non-Hui Muslims in China. For borderholics, east is Sìchuān, west is Tibet and Myanmar lies southwest. Déqīn County is also referred to as 'Shangri-la' in an effort to keep tourist dollars flowing up from the other Shangri-la (Zhōngdiàn).

Some 187km northwest of Shangri-la, the road crosses some serious ranges along this route and at any time from mid-October to late spring, heavy snows can close the road. Tibet beckons, to be sure, but the road is currently closed to individual travellers.

Sleeping & Eating

Deqin Tibet Hotel (Déqīn Lóu; 德钦楼; ☎ 841 2031; dm/d Y20/70) Still the most charming accommodation in town. There are bright murals on the walls and ceiling, some gorgeous views from the roof-top terrace rooms and a nice communal sitting area. You'll find this place 200m south of the bus station.

Deqin Dasheng Hotel (德钦大声大酒店; d Y468) Up the street on your right after leaving the bus station, this hotel offers huge discounts and is a good choice for those wanting something a bit slicker. Rooms have modern bathrooms and electric blankets – a god-send during the chilly nights. There's an **internet café** (per hr Y3) across the street that serves free, bottomless cups of green tea while you surf or email.

Wéixī Nóngjiā Fēngwèi (维西农家风味; dishes from Y5) Across from the Deqin Dansheng Hotel, this hole-in-the-wall eatery has the cheapest and some of the bets eats in town. It rarely sees tourists and gets a regular crowd of boisterous locals, particularly for the 7pm news.

Getting There & Away

From Shangri-la to Déqīn, buses leave four times daily between 7.20am and noon (Y38, five to six hours). The same number of buses return to Shangri-la from Déqīn on a similar schedule. For details on border crossings into Tibet, see p726.

AROUND DÉQĪN

Approximately 10km southwest of Déqīn is the small but interesting Tibetan **Feilai Temple** (Fēilái Sì).

A further 800m along the main road brings you to a row of **chörten** (stupas) and, weather permitting, breathtaking views of the Méilǐ

Xuěshān range, including the 6740m-high Kawa Karpo (also known as Méilǐ Xuěshān or Tàizǐ Shān). The more beautiful peak to the south is the 6054m-high Miacimu (Shénnǚ in Chinese). Locals come here to burn juniper incense.

There are no local buses here. To get here from Déqīn a taxi will cost you Y15-20, alternatively, get out on the road and flag down anything that moves.

Mingyong Glacier 明永冰川

Tumbling off the side of Kawa Karpo peak is the 12km-long **Mingyong Glacier** (Míngyǒng Bīngchuān; admission Y63, expect price spike if in high season). For millennia the mountain and glacier has been a pilgrimage site.

Trails to the glacier lead up from Míngyǒng's central square, marked by a new *chörten*. After 45 minutes a path splits off down to the scruffy toe of the glacier. Continuing on, after another 45 minutes you get to Tibetan **Tàizǐ Miào**, where there is a **guesthouse** (d Y100-120 low season; Y180 high season). A further 30 minutes along the trail is **Lotus Temple** (Liánhuā Miào), which offers fantastic views of the glacier framed by prayer flags and *chörten*. Horses can also be hired to go up to the glacier (Y150).

SLEEPING

Beds in all guesthouses are around Y25-30 and toilet facilities are basic. Electricity is iffy so bring a torch (flashlight) or some candles.

Up some steps from Míngyǒng's main square, where the bus drops you off, is **Míngyǒng Shānzhuāng**, a government-run place with decent dorm rooms.

Heading back along the road towards Déqīn are some friendly, family-run places where beds go for around Y20.

GETTING THERE & AWAY

From Déqīn, minibuses to Míngyǒng leave from the bridge near the market at the top end of town regularly (Y10 to Y30, one to two hours). You can also try to rent a car through your accommodation. Returning buses run fairly regularly.

YUÁNYÁNG RICE TERRACES
元阳梯田

Fashioned over hundreds of years by the Hani, these rice terraces cover roughly 12,500 hectares, and are one of Yúnnán's most spectacu-

YUÁNYÁNG RICE TERRACES 元阳梯田

Map Distances

Xīnjiē to Nánshā	30km
Xīnjiē to Lóngshùbà	4km
Xīnjiē to Qīngkǒu	6km
Xīnjiē to Lǎohǔzuǐ	18km
Xīnjiē to Bádá	16km
Xīnjiē to Duōyīshù	25km

lar sights. They can be done in two days from Kūnmíng, though a visit of three or more would be ideal.

Photographers and Chinese tourists flock here in droves to watch sunrises and sunsets turn the terraces into pools of gold, red and silver. Even in poor weather they can be breathtaking. Fog rolling into the terraced valleys leaves hill-top villages the only things visible, and the effect can be dramatic, like islands floating in the clouds.

Xīnjiē
☎ 0873

Yuányáng is actually split into two: Nánshā, the new town, and Xīnjiē, the old town, which is an hour's bus ride up a nearby hill. Either can be labelled Yuányáng, depending on what map you use. Xīnjiē is the one you want, so make sure you're getting off at the right one.

INFORMATION
Agricultural Bank of China (中国农业银行; Zhōngguó Nóngyè Yínháng) Gives cash advances on credit cards and changes money but will not cash travellers cheques.

Internet café (山城网吧; Shánchéng Wǎngbā; per hr Y2; ☼ 24hrs) There are plenty of internet places around Titian Square, but the fastest connections are at the ones down the stairs on your left facing the lookout.

Post office (yóujú) A bit hard to find. Go down the stone steps at the south end of Titian Square. Turn when you see the road fork behind you. The post office is halfway down on your left.

SIGHTS & ACTIVITIES
Dozens of villages spiral out from Xīnjiē. The terraces around each village have their own special characteristics which vary from season to season. Ask at your accommodation where the best place to start is, or just ask the photographers where they're going for the perfect shot.

Duōyīshù, about 25km from Xīnjiē, has the most spectacular sunrises and is the one you should not miss. For sunsets, **Bádá** and **Lǎohǔzuǐ** can be mesmerizing.

Maps are available at all accommodation in town and vary in quality from hand-drawn photocopies to slick brochures. Most are bilingual Chinese-English.

A fleet of minibuses leaves when full from Titian Square and whiz around the villages, but you are much better off arranging a car and driver through your accommodation. It's also easy just to hook up with other travellers and split the cost of chartering a minibus for the day (Y400-450).

There's also several **markets** worth checking out so check with your accommodation.

SLEEPING & EATING
Yuányáng Chénjiā Fángshé (元阳陈家放社; ☎ 562 2342; dm/s/tr Y10/40/60) This open and breezy guesthouse has spotless rooms with spectacular views of the rice terraces. It's all kept humming by four generations of the same family.

Government Guesthouse (元阳县山城大酒店; Yuányáng Xiancheng Dàjiǔdiàn; ☼ 564 2659; s/d Y150/180) Just off Titian Square, rooms here are grubby but the lobby has the best tourist information desk in the whole village.

Yúntī Dàjiǔdiàn (云梯大酒店; ☎ 562 4858; s/d Y328/258) These are the swankest digs in town with clean, modern rooms and a staff used to foreigners.

There are boisterous food stalls in town. **Lǎo Sìchuān Cāntīng Guǎn** (老四川餐厅官; ☼ 10am-around 11pm) is probably the most popular and has standing room only some nights. For a more tranquil atmosphere try **Liùjūn Fàndiàn** (六军饭店; ☼ 10am-9.30pm), the food is good and it's the cheapest in town.

GETTING THERE & AWAY
There are three buses daily from Kūnmíng to Yuányáng (Y90, 6½hrs, 10.40am, 7.30pm, 8pm). Other destinations include Hékǒu (Y37, four hours) and Gèjiú (Y22, one hour).

Buses from Xīnjiē back to Kūnmíng leave at 10.12am, 5pm and 9pm. Or, you can forge on to Xīshuāngbǎnnà. At the time of research, there were no direct buses to Jǐnghóng. To get there, take the 7.30am bus to Lǜchūn (Y25, four hours), there you'll have wait to get the Jiāngchéng bus at 4pm (Y31, five hours). By the time you arrive, there'll be now more buses but you can stay at the hotel attached to the bus station which has cheap **rooms** (dm/d Y10/60). Buses to Jǐnghóng (Y50, 8½ hours) start running at 6am.

This can be a gruelling route over bumpy dirt roads, but it will take you through some magnific scenery. Buses along this route are frequently stopped for routine police checks. It is likely that your passport will be collected and photocopied 'for your own protection.'

XĪSHUĀNGBĂNNÀ REGION 西双版纳

With its tropical forests, brilliant Dai cuisine and laid-back Southeast Asian feel, Xīshuāngbǎnnà (a Chinese approximation of the original Thai name, Sip Sawng Panna (12 Rice-Growing Districts) is one of the most exciting destinations in Yúnnán.

Just north of Myanmar and Laos, 'Bǎnnà' (as it is usually called) has become China's own mini-Thailand, attracting tourists looking for sunshine and water-splashing festivals, hikers readying for epic jungle treks and pissed-off expats fleeing the congestion and commercialization of Kūnmíng.

But despite Bǎnnà's popularity, it's still easy to get away from the crowds and explore the countryside and nearby villages while watching the weeks slip away.

Environment

Xīshuāngbǎnnà is home to many unique species of plant and animal life. Unfortunately, recent scientific studies have demonstrated the devastating effects of previous government policies on land use; the tropical rainforest areas of Bǎnnà are now as acutely endangered as similar rainforest areas elsewhere on the planet.

The jungle areas that remain contain dwindling numbers of wild tigers, leopards, elephants and golden-haired monkeys. To be fair, the number of elephants has doubled to 250, up 100% from the early 1980s; the government now offers compensation to villagers whose crops have been destroyed by elephants, or who assist in wildlife conservation. In 1998 the government banned the hunting or processing of animals, but poaching is notoriously hard to control.

People

About one-third of the 800,000-strong population of this region are Dai; another third or so are Han Chinese and the rest is made up of a conglomerate of minorities that include the Hani, Lisu and Yao, as well as lesser-known hill tribes such as the Aini (a subgroup of the Hani), Jinuo, Bulang, Lahu and Wa.

Xīshuāngbǎnnà Dai Autonomous Prefecture, as it is known officially, is subdivided into the three counties of Jǐnghóng, Měnghǎi and Měnglà.

Climate

The region has two seasons: wet and dry. The wet season is between June and August, when it rains ferociously almost every day. From September to February there is less rainfall, but thick fog descends during the late evening and doesn't lift until 10am or even later.

November to March sees temperatures average about 19°C. The hottest months of the year are from April to September, when you can expect an average of 25°C.

Festivals & Events

The **Water-Splashing Festival** is held in mid-April and washes away the dirt, sorrow and demons of the old year and brings in the happiness of the new. Jinhong usually celebrates it from the 13th to the 15th. Dates in the surrounding villages vary. In Jǐnghóng, the first day of the festival is devoted to a giant market. The second day features dragon-boat racing, swimming races and rocket launching. The third day features the water-splashing freakout. Foreigners get special attention so prepare to get drenched all day. Remember, the wetter you get, the more luck you'll receive.

During the **Tanpa Festival** in February, young boys are sent to the local temple for initiation as novice monks. At approximately the same time (between February and March), **Tan Jing Festival** participants honour Buddhist texts housed in local temples.

XĪSHUĀNGBĂNNÀ 西双版纳

0   50 km
0   30 miles

To Láncāng (24km); Měnglián (64km)

To Sīmáo (44km)

Mēngmǎn

Jǐngnè

Mekong River

Sanchahe Nature Reserve

Banna Wild Elephant Valley

LAOS

Nanjiao

Luosuo River

Mánna'nan

Mēngyǎng

Jǐnghóng

Jinuò

Měnglūn

Mēngzhē   Jīngzhēn

Mēnghǎi

Elephant-Shaped Banyan Tree

Xiding   Mànēn

Gāsà

Nanluoshan

Gēlǎnghé

Manfeilong Reservoir

Mānfēilong Jiāng

Mānfēilong (Lāncāng)

Mēnghǎn (Gānlǎnbà)

Jiāng

Mēngbàn

Dǎluò

Mēnghǔn

Manguo

Manbang Hot Spring

Mámùshù

Yáoqū

Xiāojiē

Bùlǎngshān   Dàmēnglóng

Mēnglà

Mangguanghan

Mēngpěng

MYANMAR (BURMA)

Mekong River

LAOS

Muang Sing

Shàngyǒng

Móhàn

Boten

The **Tan Ta Festival** is held during the last 10-day period of October or November, with temple ceremonies, rocket launches from special towers and hot-air balloons. The rockets, which often contain lucky amulets, blast off with a curious droning sound, like mini space shuttles, before exploding above; those who find the amulets are assured of good luck.

The farming season (from July to October) is the time for the **Closed-Door Festival**, when marriages or festivals are banned. Traditionally this is also the time of year that men aged 20 or older are ordained as monks for a period of time. The season ends with the **Open-Door Festival**, when everyone lets their hair down again to celebrate the harvest.

During festivals, booking same-day airline tickets to Jǐnghóng can be extremely difficult – even with 17 flights per day! You can try getting a flight into Sīmáo, 162km to the north, or take the bus. Hotels in Jǐnghóng town are booked solid and prices are usually tripled. Most people end up commuting from a nearby Dai village. Festivities take place all over Xīshuāngbǎnnà, so you might be lucky further away from Jǐnghóng.

JǏNGHÓNG 景洪

☎ 0691

Jǐnghóng is the capital of Xīshuāngbǎnnà prefecture, but with its palm-lined streets and relaxed ambience it can feel like a giant, over-populated village. With more and more multi-storey concrete buildings puncturing the skyline, Jǐnghóng is taking on some of the grey, concrete characteristics of typical Chinese provincial capitals.

Prepare yourself for searing late-day heat that can put the entire city into a kind of deep sleep or serious slow motion. Trying to rouse street vendors (or even bus drivers!) from their afternoon siestas can be near impossible.

Situated along the Mekong River, the town's name means 'City of Dawn' in Dai.

Information

The travellers' books at Mei Mei, Forest Café and the Mekong Café are by far the best source of travel tips and trek notes.

Bank of China (Zhōngguó Yínháng; Xuanwei Dadao); branch office (Ganlan Zhonglu) Changes travellers cheques and foreign currency, and has an ATM machine.

China Post & Telecom (Yóudiàn; cnr Mengle Dadao & Xuanwei Dadao; ☻ 8am-8.30pm) You can make international calls from here.

CITS (Zhōngguó Guójì Lüxíngshè; ☎ 663 8459; Jǐnghóng International Travel Bldg; Luandian Jie) can arrange all manner of one-day tours from Y200-300. However, you're better off going to the Mekong Café (opposite) and Mei Mei Café (opposite), which will help with trekking information and put you in touch with English-speaking guides.

Internet cafés (wǎngbā; Manting Lu; per hr Y2) There are literally dozens along this street.

Public Security Bureau (PSB; Gōngānjú; Jingde Lu; ☻ 8-11.30am & 3-5.30pm) Has a fairly speedy visa extension service.

Dangers & Annoyances

There have been two reports (unconfirmed) from travellers regarding drug-and-rob incidents (one successful, one not) on the Kūnmíng–Jǐnghóng bus trip. Like other countries in Southeast Asia, be careful who your friends are on buses, accept nothing, and leave nothing unattended when you hop off on breaks.

Sights

TROPICAL FLOWER & PLANTS GARDEN
热带花卉园

This terrific **botanic garden** (Rèdài Huāhuìyuán; ☎ 212 0493; 28 Jǐnghóng Xilu; admission Y40; ☻ 7am-6pm), west of the town centre, is one of Jǐnghóng's better attractions. Admission gets you into a series of gardens where you can view over 1000 different types of plant life. Take the path on the left-hand side as you enter the gardens to head towards the lovely tropical rainforest area. The gardens also house the **Zhou Enlai Memorial** (Zhōu Ēnlái Zǒnglǐ Jìniànbēi), a contemporary sculpture commemorating a 1961 visit by China's best-loved premier.

PEACOCK LAKE PARK 孔雀湖公园

This artificial lake in the centre of town isn't much, but the small **park** (Kǒngquè Hú Gōngyuán) next to it is pleasant. The English Language Corner takes place here every Sunday evening, so this is your chance to exchange views or to engage with the locals practising their English.

Activities

Jǐnghóng's oft-recommended **Blind Massage School** (Mángrén Ànmó; ☎ 212 5834; cnr Mengle Dadao & Jingde Lu; ☻ 9am-midnight) offers hour-long massages for Y30. Staff are extremely kind and

travellers give it terrific reports. Head down the lane off Mengle Dadao and climb the stairs on your left up to the second floor.

Nonguests can use the **swimming pool** at the Crown Hotel for Y5.

Sleeping

Banna College Hotel (Bǎnnà Xuéyuàn; ☎ 213 8365; Xuanwei Dadao; 宣慰大道; dm Y15, tw/d per person Y40/50; 🖳) This has the best-value rooms in town. Some of the staff speak English and are good for travel info. Bike rental for Y15 per day, Y150 deposit.

Dai Building Inn (Dǎijiā Huāyuán Xiǎolóu; ☎ 216 2592; 57 Manting Lu; 曼听路; dm Y25) People either love or hate this popular backpacker hang-out. All accommodation is in two- or four-bed bamboo bungalows on stilts. Some travellers have been less than impressed with the occasional rodent visitor and lack of privacy (the bamboo walls are definitely not soundproof!).

Wanli Dai Style Guesthouse (Wǎnlǐ Dàiwèi Cāntīng; ☎ 1357-811 2879; Manting Lu; 曼听路; dm Y30) With only a handful of simple rooms, this place is basic but comfortable, although the rooms can get very hot in the summer months. There is a nice garden here and a good restaurant.

Golden Banna Hotel (Jīn Bǎnnà Jiǔdiàn; ☎ 212 4901; Mengle Dadao; 猛渤大道; s/d Y380/580; 🖳) This hotel has a kind of industrial factory feel to it just because of the masses of people (and tour groups) that churn in and out. Though rooms are nondescript, staff are very efficient and offer great deals outside of festival times.

Tai Garden Hotel (Tàiyuán Jiǔdiàn; ☎ 212 3888; fax 212 6060; 8 Minghang Lu; 民航路8号; d Y640 plus 15% tax; 🖳 🖳) Quiet grounds replete with pool, sauna, gym and tennis court. It's full of the sophisticated and the moneyed, which makes the elegant morning buffet all the more entertaining when it inevitably disintegrates into a rough-and-tumble free-for-all.

Eating

Manting Lu is lined with restaurants serving Dai food, the majority of which dish up Dai dance performances along with their culinary specialities. Dai women thump drums at the entrance and the restaurants are filled nearly every night with tourists being festive.

Dai dishes include barbecued fish, eel or beef cooked with lemongrass or served with peanut-and-tomato sauce. Vegetarians can order roast bamboo shoot prepared in the same fashion. Other specialities include fried

THE DAI PEOPLE 傣族

The Dai are Hinayana Buddhists (as opposed to China's majority Mahayana Buddhists) who first appeared 2000 years ago in the Yangzi Valley and who were subsequently driven southwards by the Mongol invasion of the 13th century. The Dai state of Xīshuāngbǎnnà was annexed by the Mongols and then by the Chinese, and a Chinese governor was installed in the regional capital of Jinglan (present-day Jǐnghóng). Countless Buddhist temples were built in the early days of the Dai state and now lie in the jungles in ruins. During the Cultural Revolution, Xīshuāngbǎnnà's temples were desecrated and destroyed. Some were saved by serving as granaries, but many are now being rebuilt from scratch. Temples are also recovering their role as village schools where young children are accepted for religious training as monks.

The Dai live in spacious wooden houses, raised on stilts to keep themselves off the damp earth, with the pigs and chickens below. The most common Dai foods are sticky rice (*khao nio* in Dai) and fish. The common dress for Dai women is a straw hat or towel-wrap headdress, a tight, short blouse in a bright colour, and a printed sarong with a belt of silver links. Some Dai men tattoo their bodies with animal designs, and betel-nut chewing is popular. Many Dai youngsters get their teeth capped with gold, otherwise they are considered ugly.

Linguistically, the Dai are part of the very large Thai family that includes the Siamese, Lao, Shan, Thai Dam and Ahom peoples found scattered throughout the river valleys of Thailand, Myanmar, Laos, northern Vietnam and Assam. The Xīshuāngbǎnnà Dai are broken into four subgroups – the Shui (Water) Dai, Han (Land) Dai, Huayao (Floral Belt) Dai and Kemu Dai – each distinguished by variations in costume, lifestyle and location. All speak the Dai language, which is quite similar to Lao and northern Thai dialects. In fact, Thai is often as useful as Chinese once you get off the beaten track. The written language of the Dai employs a script that looks like a cross between Lao and Burmese.

In temple courtyards, look for a cement structure like a letterbox; this is an altar to local spirits, a combination of Buddhism and indigenous spirit worship. Some 32 separate spirits exist for humans.

Zhang khap is the name for a solo narrative opera, for which the Dai have a long tradition. Singers are trained from childhood to perform long songs accompanied by native flute and sometimes a long drum known as the elephant drum. Performances are given at monk initiations, when new houses are built, weddings and on the birthdays of important people; they often last all night. Even if you do understand Dai, the lyrics are complex – if not fully improvised. At the end, the audience shouts 'Shuay! Shuay!' which is close to 'Hip, hip, hooray!' Even courtship is done via this singing. Some Dai phrases include *doūzaŏ lǐ* (hello), *yíndií* (thank you) and *goīhán* (goodbye).

---

river moss (better than it sounds and excellent with beer), spicy bamboo-shoot soup and *shāokǎo* (skewers of meat wrapped in banana leaves and grilled over wood fires).

Mei Mei Café (Měiměi Kāfēitīng; ☎ 212 7324; Manting Lu roundabout; dishes from Y5) It's got cold beer, genius Dai chicken and some of the best travel information in Jǐnghóng (ask to see the travel binder). At the time of research, government officials were planning to boot Mei Mei's out of this location to make way for a multi-storey building. If it isn't here when you arrive, check out Manting Lu next to the Thai restaurant, where it was planned to relocate it.

Měngzì Guóqiáo Mǐxiàn (Jingde Lu; dishes Y5-20; ☯ 24hrs) This breezy, modest restaurant serves up round-the-clock noodles and rice dishes to

be washed down with beakers of quenching lemonade (Y4). English menu available.

Mekong Café (Méigōng Cānguǎn; ☎ 216 2395; 111 Manting Lu) The chicken in coconut (Y18) is an absolute must – you'll be served pieces of chicken and coconut flesh, bobbing in searing hot broth and served in a hollowed out coconut shell. The wait is worth it. The upstairs balcony is a pleasant place to sit with a beer in the winter and read about the sub-zero temperatures in Běijīng.

Thai Restaurant (Tàiguó Cāntīng; ☎ 216 1758; Manting Lu; mains Y8-15) Pounce the moment you spy a free seat at this popular Thai restaurant. Phad Thai devotees literally flock here and the crowds never really thin out. Wash the authentic Thai dishes down with snake whisky if you're feeling brave.

YÚNNÁN

There is a huge **night food market** by the new bridge over the Mekong where dozens of stalls serve up barbecued everything from sausages to snails. There are plenty of tables and chairs for those who want to linger.

Entertainment

Mengbala Naxi Arts Theatre (Měngbălá Nàxī Yíshùgōng; Ganlan Zhonglu; tickets Y160; ☻ 8.30pm) This theatre has daily song and dance shows.

YES Disco (Mengle Dadao; admission free; ☻ 9pm-late) Perch in any local café weekend mornings and you'll find at least one person nursing a killer hangover and recounting their antics at YES Disco the night before. YES remains the most popular nightspot in town.

Shopping

Market groupies have two terrific places to head for shopping, people-watching and at-

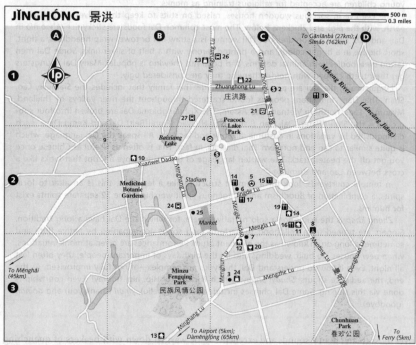

JĬNGHÓNG 景洪

0 500 m
0 0.3 miles

YÚNNÁN

mosphere. A fabulous fish and produce **market** is tucked behind some modern buildings across from the long-distance bus station. The **Jade Market**, nearby on Zhuanghong Lu, features lots of Burmese and other South Asians hawking their goods alongside locals.

Getting There & Away

AIR

There are several flights a day to Kūnmíng (Y730) but in April (when the Water-Splashing Festival is held) you'll need to book tickets several days in advance to get either in or out.

There's also two flights daily to Lìjiāng (Y840). You can also fly to Bangkok (Y1630) and Chiang Mai (Y1630) from here.

Tickets anywhere can be bought at the **CAAC booking office** (Zhōngguó Mínháng; ☎ 212 7040; Jingde Lu; ✆ 8am-9pm). Credit cards and travellers cheques are not accepted. Cash only.

BUS

The Jǐnghóng long-distance bus station (Minghang Lu) is the most useful for long-distance destinations. If you want to explore Xīshuāngbǎnnà, go to the No 2 bus station.

Getting Around

There's no shuttle bus or public transport to the airport 5km south of the city. A taxi will cost around Y20 but expect to be hit up for up to three times that during festivals.

Jǐnghóng is small enough that you can walk to most destinations, but a bike makes life easier and can be rented through most accommodation for Y15-25 a day.

A taxi anywhere in town costs Y5.

AROUND JǏNGHÓNG

While most travellers may base themselves in Jǐnghóng, it's the endless trekking possibilities and the minority villages that keeps them lingering weeks longer than they intended.

Some have cycled up to Měnghǎi and Měngzhē on mountain bikes (it's almost impossible on bikes without gears), and one French photographer hitched up with a local medicine man and spent seven days doing house calls in the jungle.

Obviously, it's the longer trips that allow you to escape the hordes of tourists and get a feel for what Xīshuāngbǎnnà is about. But even with limited time there are some interesting possibilities. Most destinations in Xīshuāngbǎnnà are only two or three hours

---

ETIQUETTE IN DAI TEMPLES

Around Dai temples the same rules apply as elsewhere: dress appropriately (no tank tops or shorts); take off shoes before entering; don't take photos of monks or the inside of temples without permission; leave a donation if you do take any shots and consider a token donation even if you don't – unlike in Thailand, these Buddhists receive no government assistance. It is polite to 'wai' the monks as a greeting and remember to never rub anyone's head, raise yourself higher than a Buddha figure or point your feet at anyone. (This last point applies to secular buildings too. If you stay the night in a Dai household it is good form to sleep with your feet pointing towards the door.)

---

away by bus, but generally they are not much in themselves – you need to get out and about. Note that to get to many villages, you'll often first have to take the bus to a primary village and stay overnight there, since only one bus per day – if that – travels to the tinier villages.

If you're a serious collector of local market experiences, there are plenty to be found in the region. Like anything else, markets are subjective things, but most people seem to prefer the Thursday market in Xīdìng, then Měnghùn, followed by Měnghǎi.

The best advice is to get yourself a bike or some sturdy hiking boots, pick up a map, put down this book and get out of town.

Villages

Before heading further afield, there are numerous villages in the vicinity of Jǐnghóng that can be reached by bicycle. Most of them you will happen upon by chance and it's difficult to make recommendations.

On the other side of the Mekong are some small villages, and a popular jaunt involves heading off down Manting Lu – if you go far enough (about 5km) you'll hit a ferry crossing point on the Mekong (Y1), beyond which there are plenty of Dai temples and villages to explore.

It can feel like every second village begins with the prefix 'Meng' and it's not unheard of to hear of travellers ending up at the wrong village because of communication problems. Have your destination written down in script

YÚNNÁN

before you head off. Even travellers who know Chinese have found themselves kilometres away from where they intended just because they've messed up one tone.

Sanchahe Nature Reserve
三岔河自然保护区

This **nature reserve** (Sānchàhé Zìrán Bǎohùqū), 48km north of Jǐnghóng, is one of five enormous forest reserves in southern Yúnnán. This one has an area of nearly 1.5 million hectares.

The part of the park that most tourists visit is **Banna Wild Elephant Valley** (Bǎnnà Yěxiànggǔ; admission Y25, with guide Y50), named after the 40 or so wild elephants that live in the valley; it's worth a visit if you want to see something of the local forest.

The reserve has two entrances. The main southern entrance has accommodation, displays on tropical birds and butterflies, and peacock shows. The other entrance has rather depressing 'wild' elephant performances for the throngs of shutterbug tourists. A 2km-**cable car** (one way/return Y40/60) runs over the treetops from the main entrance into the heart of the park. There is an elevated wooden

walkway running through the jungle canopy and a number of dirt paths that run between the two main gates.

If you want to stay by the park there's a generic **hotel** (d 200) at the main entrance, although it will seem pricy for what you get. Alternatively, you can stay in one of 22 Swiss Family Robinson-type **canopy treehouses** (d Y200) in the heart of the park. On the plus side, travellers who have stayed here have reported seeing elephants bathing in the stream beneath them at dawn. You might be able to get a discount.

Just about any bus travelling north from Jǐnghóng to Sīmáo will pass this reserve (Y12, one hour). Returning to Jǐnghóng there is a bus that leaves the north entrance daily at 2.30pm (Y10).

Měngyǎng 勐养

The much photographed **Elephant-Shaped Banyan Tree** (Xiàngxíng Róngshù) is why most people visit Měngyǎng. It's also a centre for the Hani, Floral-Belt Dai and Lahu, one of the poorest minorities in the region.

Měngyǎng is 34km northeast of Jǐnghóng on the road to Sīmáo.

BĀNNÀ BUS TIMETABLES

Buses from Bǎnnà long-distance bus station include the following:

Destination	Price	Duration	Frequency	Departs
Kūnmíng	Y156.50	9hr	2 daily	4pm, 7.30pm
Kūnmíng (sleeper)	Y145-169	9hr	20 daily	7.30am-7pm
Ruìlì	Y254	26hr	daily	9am
Bǎoshān	Y230	20hr	daily	noon
Xiàguān	Y152	18hr	daily	12.30pm

The following bus services leave from the No 2 bus station:

Destination	Price	Duration	Frequency	Departs
Sānchàhé	Y10-11.50	1½hr	every 20min	6.15am-6.30pm
Měngyǎng	Y7	40min	half-hourly	8am-6pm
Měnglún	Y14	2hr	every 20min	7am-6pm
Měnglà	Y33	4-5hr	every 20min	6.30am-6pm
Gǎnlǎnbà	Y7.50	40min	every 20min	7.15am-10pm
Dàměnglóng	Y15	3-4hr	every 20min	6.30am-6.30pm
Měnghǎi	Y11	45min	every 20min	7.30am-1.40pm & 2.20-7pm
Jǐngzhēn	Y11	2hr	every 20min	7am-6pm
Měnghùn	Y15	90min	every 20min	7am-6pm
Sīmáo	Y33	5hr	every 15min	6.15am-4pm & every 30min 4-6pm

From Měngyǎng it's another 19km southeast to **Jinuò**, which is home base for the Jinuo minority. Travellers have reported a cool reception here (some minorities dislike tourists), so if you want to overnight you'll probably have to stay in Měngyǎng.

Měnghǎn 勐罕 (Gǎnlǎnbà 橄榄坝)

Watching this town come alive in the evening after its long afternoon siesta is reason enough to visit. If you arrive mid-afternoon, Měnghǎn (or Gǎnlǎnbà as it's sometimes referred to), can seem almost deserted. Shop owners and hotel clerks fall into such deep sleeps, taps and calls barely get a response.

But once it cools down, it's as if someone flipped a switch on the place. The streets fill up with the smells of cooking, the sounds of gossip and wandering locals trying to escape the indoor heat.

It's worth coming by bike (or hiring one in Měnghǎn) as there's plenty of scope for exploration in the neighbourhood.

SIGHTS

The premier 'attraction' in Měnghǎn is the **Dai Minority Park** (傣族园; Dàizúyuán; ☎ 250 4099; Manting Lu; adult/student Y50/25; ⏲ 24hr), which is quite simply part of the town that has been cordoned off and had a ticket booth stuck at the entrance. Tourists can spend the night in villagers' homes and partake in water-splashing 'festivals' twice a day.

While the 'park' and Dai architecture are beautiful, spending the night here can feel a bit like you're spending the night in a zoo, albeit a minority one. Despite this, travellers who've come say it's been worth the trip and some have even stayed in touch with their host families.

If you do stay overnight in the park, your ticket is valid for the following day.

Travellers recommend heading to the south of town, crossing the Mekong by ferry (Y2 with a bike), and then heading left (east). The last ferry returns at 7pm. Check the visitors' book in the Sarlar Restaurant for further ideas.

SLEEPING & EATING

Beds in a Dai home within the park will cost around Y20 per person. Food is extra. Beds are traditional Dai mats and are usually very comfortable. Most homes will also have showers for you.

Yúnlì Bīnguǎn (运丽宾馆; ☎ 241 0204; Manting Lu; d/tr Y40/60) This is a modern hotel with spotless rooms that all come with private balconies.

Dai Family Restaurant (傣家餐厅; Manting Lu; mains around Y15-18) This place has an English menu on the wall and there are no prices listed, so check before you order as food is a little pricier than elsewhere.

You'll find a handful of Dai restaurants near the Dai Family Restaurant.

GETTING THERE & AWAY

Microbuses to Měnghǎn leave from Jǐnghóng's No 2 bus station (Y8, every 20 minutes, 7am to 6pm). Minibuses depart from Měnghǎn's bus station for destinations throughout the region including Jǐnghóng (Y8), Měnglún (Y10, one hour) and Měnglà (Y29, five hours).

It's possible to cycle from Jǐnghóng to Měnghǎn in a brisk two hours or a leisurely three hours, and it's a pleasant ride.

GETTING AROUND

You can rent a mountain bike (Y20 per day) at the entrance to the Dai Minority Park or from one of several bicycle shops (Y10 per day) along Manting Lu.

Měnglún 勐伦

Měnglún is the next major port of call east of Měnghǎn. The major attraction here is the **Tropical Plant Gardens** (热带植物园; Rèdài Zhíwùyuán; adult/student Y60/40; ⏲ 7am-midnight). The gardens are gorgeous and get high marks from visitors.

To get here, turn left out of the bus station and walk to the first corner. Walk one block and turn left again. You'll come to market hawkers, and a road leading downhill to the right side. Follow this until you reach a footbridge across the Mekong. The ticket booth is just in front of the bridge.

There's plenty of basic hotels in town and a couple near the park. Accommodation can get pretty run down, and some travellers have complained about the lack of basics like towels and promised hot water. It's worth taking a walk around when you arrive to see if anything new has opened up.

The **Bus Station Hotel** (车站招待所; Chēzhàn Zhāodàisuǒ; d Y30) is your best-value option. There's no aircon, but the shared bathrooms and showers are clean and there's a TV in each room.

THE JINUO PEOPLE 基诺族

The Jinuo, sometimes known as the Youle, were officially 'discovered' as a minority in 1979. The women wear a white cowl, a cotton tunic with bright horizontal stripes and a tubular black skirt. Earlobe decoration is an elaborate custom – the larger the hole and the more flowers it can contain the better. Teeth are sometimes painted black with the sap of the lacquer tree, which serves the dual dental purpose of beautifying the mouth and preventing tooth decay and halitosis.

Previously, the Jinuo lived in long houses with as many as 27 families occupying rooms on either side of the central corridor. Each family had its own hearth, but the oldest man owned the largest hearth, which was always the closest to the door. Long houses are rarely used now and the Jinuo seem to be quickly losing their distinctive way of life.

The **Friendship Restaurant** (友谊餐厅; Yǒuyì Cāntīng; Main Hwy) has lots of dishes made from strange vegetables, ferns and herbs only found locally.

From Jǐnghóng's No 2 bus station there are buses to Měnglún (Y14, two hours, every 20 minutes, 7am to 6pm). The buses pass through Měnghǎn. Some travellers have cycled here from Měnghǎn.

From Měnglún, there are buses to Měnglà (Y20-25, 2½ hours, 8.30am to 7.30pm) and Jǐnghóng every 30 minutes.

Měnglà 勐腊

Měnglà is a dire little town. The only reason you should find yourself here is if you're crossing into Laos at Móhān. As the bus journey from Jǐnghóng, or even Měnglún, will take the better part of a day, you'll probably be stuck here for the night.

There is a **Bank of China** (中国银行; Zhōngguó Yínháng; ☎ 8-11.30am & 3-6pm Mon-Fri) in the southern half of town that changes cash and travellers cheques but won't give cash advances on credit cards. To change Renminbi back into US dollars, you'll need your original exchange receipts.

Měnglà Bīnguǎn (勐腊宾馆; ☎ 812 2168; dm/d Y10/40) is set within a pretty shaded garden. The dorm beds are very basic but the doubles are clean and have their own balcony. It's near No 2 bus station; ask a local to point you in the right direction.

The **Jīnqiáo Dàjiǔdiàn** (金桥大酒店; ☎ 812 4946; d/tr Y50/60; ✘) is convenient for the north bus station just up the hill on the left, but don't expect much else.

There are loads of restaurants along Mengla Jie where you can get dishes for Y5.

Měnglà has two bus stations: the northern long-distance bus station which has buses to Kūnmíng (Y218, hourly, 8.30am-11.30am);

and No 2 bus station in the southern part of town. Buses from Měnglà's No 2 station are listed as follows:

Destination	Price	Frequency	Departures
Jǐnghóng	Y30-34	every 20min	6.20am-6pm
Měnglún	Y20-24	every 20min	6.20am-6pm
Yáoqū	Y12	4 daily	8.30am, 10.30am, 2.30pm, 4.30pm
Móhān	Y14	every 20min	8am-6pm

TO LAOS

The good news is that you can get an on-the-spot visa for Laos at the border. The price will depend on your nationality. From Měnglà there are buses to Móhān every 20 minutes or so from 8am. No matter what anyone says, there should be no 'charge' to cross. Once your passport is stamped (double-check all stamps) and you've waved goodbye to the border guards, you can jump on a tractor or truck to take you 3km into Laos for around Y5. Whatever you do, go early. Although the border doesn't officially close until 5.30pm Běijīng time (and don't forget that Laos is an hour ahead), things often wrap up earlier on the Lao side. There are guesthouses on both the Chinese and Lao sides; change money on the Lao side.

DÀMĚNGLÓNG 大勐龙

Dàměnglóng (written just 'Měnglóng' on buses) is one of those sleepy places to aim for when you want a respite from the beaten path and a base from which to do some aimless rambling. You won't find much to do in the village itself outside of visiting the Sunday market but the countryside is peppered with decaying stupas and little villages, and is worth a couple of days' exploration.

About 70km south of Jǐnghóng and a few kilometres from the Myanmar border,

Dàměnglóng is also a good base for hikes and bike rides through the surrounding hills. You can hire bicycles at Dàměnglóng Zhāodàisuǒ for Y15 per day.

The border crossing point (not open) with Myanmar (poetically named 2-4-0) has been designated as the entry point for a planned highway linking Thailand, Myanmar and China. If and when it does open, things should definitely pick up here.

Sights

WHITE BAMBOO SHOOT PAGODA 曼飞龙塔

This **pagoda** (Mànfēilóng Tǎ; admission Y5), built in 1204, is Dàměnglóng's premier attraction. According to legend, the temple was built on the spot of a hallowed footprint left by Sakyamuni Buddha, who is said to have visited Xīshuāngbǎnnà – if you're interested in ancient footprints you can look for it in a niche below one of the nine stupas. Unfortunately, in recent years a 'beautification' job has been done on the temple with a couple of cans of white paint.

If you're in the area late October or early November, check the precise dates of the Tan Ta Festival. At this time White Bamboo Shoot Pagoda is host to hundreds of locals whose celebrations include dancing, rocket launchings, paper balloons and so on.

The pagoda is easy to get to: just walk back along the main road towards Jǐnghóng for 2km until you reach a small village with a temple on your left. From here there's a path up the hill; it's about a 20-minute walk. There's an entry fee, but often there's no-one around anyway.

THE BULANG PEOPLE 布朗族

The Bulang live mainly in the Bulang Xīdìng and Bada mountains of Xīshuāngbǎnnà. They keep to the hills farming cotton, sugarcane and Pu'er tea, one of Yúnnán's most famous exports.

The men wear collarless jackets, loose black trousers and turbans of black or white cloth. They traditionally tattoo their arms, legs, chests and stomachs. The women wear simple, brightly coloured clothes and vibrant headdresses decorated with flowers. Avid betel-nut chewers, the women believe black teeth are beautiful.

BLACK PAGODA 黑塔

Just above the centre of town is a Dai monastery with a steep path beside it leading up to the **Black Pagoda** (Hēi Tǎ; admission free) – you'll notice it when entering Dàměnglóng. The pagoda itself is actually gold, not black. Take a stroll up, but bear in mind that the real reason for the climb is more for the views of Dàměnglóng and surrounding countryside then the temple itself.

Sleeping & Eating

Plenty of cheap options are available for foreigners.

Dàměnglóng Zhāodàisuǒ (大勐龙招待所; dm Y15) It's got basic beds and fragrant bathrooms but the main reason to take note of this hotel is for its bike rental (Y15 per day). To get here, walk uphill from the main highway to where the local government building sits. The hotel is in the grounds to the left, just past some ornamental frogs.

Lai Lai Hotel (来来宾馆; Láilái Bīnguǎn; d/tr Y20/30) Simple rooms and a lovely owner who is meticulous about cleanliness made this hotel the most popular accommodation choice with Dàměnglóng–Bùlǎngshān trekkers of yore. You'll see the English sign right next to the bus station.

There are a couple of decent restaurants down from the bus station, located near the steps leading up to the Black Pagoda; the Chinese signs proclaim them to be Dai restaurants.

Getting There & Away

Buses for the bumpy ride to Dàměnglóng (Y15, three to four hours, every 20 minutes, 6.30am to 6.30pm) leave from Jǐnghóng's No 2 bus station. Remember that the 'Da' character won't be painted on the bus window. Buses for the return trip run regularly between 6am and 6pm.

XIĂOJIĒ 小街

The village of Xiǎojiē, about 15km north of Dàměnglóng, is surrounded by Bulang, Lahu and Hani villages. Lahu women shave their heads; apparently the younger ones aren't happy about this any more and hide their heads beneath caps. The Bulang are possibly descended from the Yi of northern Yúnnán. The women wear black turbans with silver decorations; many of the designs are of shells, fish and marine life.

There's plenty of room for exploration in this area, although you're not allowed over the border.

MĚNGHĂI 勐海

This modern town is another popular base for exploring the countryside. Grab a bike and head north for the most interesting pagodas and villages.

If you're passing through Měnghǎi, it's worth visiting the huge daily **produce market** that attracts members of the hill tribes. The best way to find it is to follow the early morning crowds.

Buses run from Jǐnghóng's No 2 bus station to Měnghǎi (Y11, 45min, every 20 minutes 7.30am-1.40pm & 2.20-7pm). From Měnghǎi's flashy new bus station there are buses to Bùlǎngshān (Y18, 9am and 2pm), Xīdìng (Y11, 10.40am and 3.30pm), Měngmǎn (Y11, 7.30am, 8.30am, 9.30am and 5pm) and Kūnmíng (Y170-187, 2.30pm, 4.30pm, 5.30pm, 6.30pm) among other destinations. Buses return to Jǐnghóng every 20 minutes until 7pm.

AROUND MĚNGHĂI
Měnghùn 勐混

This quiet little village, about 26km southwest of Měnghǎi, has a colourful **Sunday market**. The town begins buzzing around 7am and the action lingers on through to noon. The swirl of hill tribespeople with the women sporting fancy leggings, headdresses, earrings and bracelets alone makes the trip worthwhile. Měnghùn is also a good place to buy local handicrafts for much cheaper prices than you would find in Kūnmíng (don't haggle too much, these women have yet to learn the idea of overcharging foreigners).

There are several guesthouses here, though none are remarkable. Y40 will get you a double with bathroom and TV but there's no air-conditioning.

Buses departing from Jǐnghóng for Měnghùn (Y15, 90 min, every 20 minutes, 7am to 6pm) run from Jǐnghóng's No 2 bus station.

From Měnghùn, minibuses run regularly to Měnghǎi (Y6), Xīdìng (Y11, 1½ hours, 7.10am and 4pm) and throughout the day to Jǐnghóng.

Unless you have a very good bike with gears, cycling to Měnghǎi and Měnghùn is not a real option. The road up to Měnghǎi is so steep that you'll end up pushing the bike most of the way. Cycling from Měnghùn back to Jǐnghóng on the other hand, is almost entirely downhill.

Xīdìng 西定

This sleepy hillside hamlet comes alive every Thursday for it's weekly **market**, reputedly one of the best in the region. At other times you'll find it almost deserted. If you want to see the market at its most interesting, you'll really have to get here the night before. The small guesthouse at the bus station has beds for Y20.

To get here by public transport you can either catch one of the two direct buses from Měnghǎi (Y11, 10.40am and 3.30pm) or travel via Měnghùn and change for a bus to Xīdìng. Buses from Xīdìng leave twice a day (Y11, 7.20am and 1pm) for Měnghùn. If you miss the bus you can always get a ride on a motorbike (Y30), a spectacular if hair-raising experience, from the only bike shop in town.

Jǐngzhēn 景真

In the village of Jǐngzhēn, about 14km west of Měnghǎi, is the **Octagonal Pavilion** (八角亭; Bājiǎo Tíng; admission Y10; ☺ 8am-6pm), first built in 1701. The original structure was severely damaged during the Cultural Revolution but renovated in 1978 and the ornate decoration is still impressive. The temple also operates as a monastic school. The paintings on the wall of the temple depict scenes from the *Jatatka*, the life history of Buddha.

Frequent minibuses from the minibus centre in Měnghǎi go via Jǐngzhēn (Y10 to Y15).

BĂOSHĀN REGION 保山

Other than English teachers or intrepid wanderers, the Bǎoshān area doesn't initially make it on many travellers itineraries. Say the word 'volcano' however, (the region has several of them) and it's enough to get most visitors off their Ruìlì-bound buses for a day or two exploring the dormant peaks and dipping in the hot springs.

Téngchōng in particular is worth a bit more time, with some interesting old quarters and many distinctive minority groups in the surrounding areas. Located on the other side of Gāolígòng Shān (Gaoligong Mountain)

TREKKING IN XĪSHUĀNGBĂNNÀ

Treks around Xīshuāngbănnà used to be among the best in China – you'd be invited into a local's home to eat, sleep, and drink *báijiŭ*. Increasing numbers of visitors have changed this in places. Don't automatically expect a welcome mat and a free lunch just because you're a foreigner, but don't go changing the local economy by throwing money around either.

If you do get invited into someone's home, try to establish whether payment is expected. If it's not, leave an offering (ask at the backpacker cafés what's considered appropriate) or leave modest gifts such as candles, matches, rice etc – even though the family may insist on nothing.

Also take care before heading off, it's a jungle out there, so go prepared, and make sure somebody knows where you are and when you should return. In the rainy season you'll need to be equipped with proper hiking shoes and waterproof gear. At any time you'll need water purification tablets, bottled water or a water bottle able to hold boiling water, as well as snacks and sunscreen.

The Dàmĕnglóng to Bùlăngshān trek was by far the most popular route and the 48km hike would take you through Dai, Hani, Bulang and Lahu villages. Unfortunately, a road built between the two villages has effectively killed the trek and backpacker cafés are no longer even producing maps of the route.

The good news is this has spread out people (and the money) a bit more. No one route dominates these days.

Check in with Mei Mei Café (p733) and Mekong Café (p733). Talk to their guides, browse their books and choose the best route for your experience and physical ability.

Forest Café (☎ 6918 985122; Galanba Nanlu), near Manting Lu, also has terrific trekking information and a fabulous website (www.forest-cafe.org/) where you can start your research.

Wherever you go, seriously consider taking a guide. You won't hear much Mandarin Chinese on the trail, let alone any English, so having a guide will allow you to communicate with villagers en route. Expect to pay around Y250 per day.

Try the Xishuangbanna Travel and Study Club (Xīshuāngbănnà Lŭxué Jùlèbù; Mengzhe Lu) for trekking equipment.

---

range, Téngchōng is also prime earthquake territory, having experienced 71 earthquakes measuring over five on the Richter scale since 1500.

As early as the 4th and 5th centuries BC (two centuries before the northern routes through central Asia were established), the Băoshān area was an important stop on the southern Silk Road – the Sìchuān–India route. The area did not come under Chinese control until the Han dynasty when, in AD 69, it was named the Yongchang Administrative District. In 1277 a huge battle was waged in the region between the 12,000 troops of Kublai Khan and 60,000 Burmese soldiers and their 2000 elephants. The Mongols won and went on to take Pagan.

TÉNGCHŌNG 腾冲
☎ 0875

With 20 volcanoes in the vicinity and lots of hot springs (p744) there's lots to explore should you find yourself in this neck of the woods.

The town itself is also worth a half-day ramble. For the most part it's a rather drab, grey provincial town, but bizarrely, in the midst of it all, some lanes are still packed with the traditional wooden architecture that used to be commonplace in many towns and cities in Yúnnán. Construction is encroaching on them quickly, however, so they're not as obvious as they once were. You'll need some patience while seeking them out.

Information
Bank of China (Zhōngguó Yínháng; cnr Fengshan Lu & Yingjiang Xilu) Will change cash and travellers cheques. There's also an ATM here.
China Post & Telecom (Yóudiàn; Fengshan Lu)
Internet café (wăngbā; Feicui Lu; per hr Y2)
PSB (Gōngānjú; Yingjiang Xilu; ⏰ 8.30-11.30am & 2.30-5.30pm Mon-Fri) Can help with visa extensions.

Sights & Activities
The best places for a random wander are the backstreets running off Yingjiang Xilu. There are a couple of small markets with plenty of

YÚNNÁN

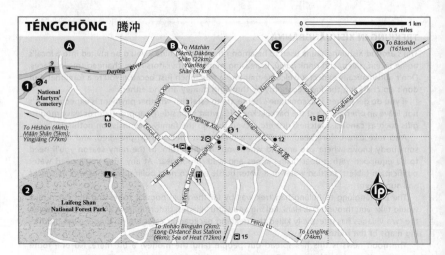

TÉNGCHŌNG 腾冲

colour and activity in the mornings. Walking along Fengshan Lu from Feicui Lu, the first side street on the left has a small **produce market**. Further down on the right is a large, covered **jade market** where you can sometimes see the carving process. Walk east along Yinjiang Xilu and you will come across a larger **produce market** on your right.

On the western edge of town is the **Laifeng Shan National Forest Park** (Láifēng Shān Guójiā Sēnlín Gōngyuán; admission Y10; ⏱ 8am-7pm). You can walk through lush pine forests to **Laifeng Temple** (Láifēng Sì) or make the sweaty hike up to the summit where a pagoda offers fine views. There are lots of further hiking possibilities.

In the western suburbs of town, **Xianle Temple** (Xiānlè Sì; admission Y5) is beside the small **Dieshui Waterfall**, which makes a good place for a picnic. The area makes a nice destination for a bike ride and you could easily combine it with a trip to **Héshùn** (opposite), a picturesque village 4km outside Téngchōng.

Sleeping & Eating

Téngchōng's accommodation options are fairly spread out. Rooms near the local bus station can get pretty decrepit. Check your bed sheets to avoid nasty surprises. Alternatively, try one of the new hotels along Rehai Lu north of the long-distance bus station. It's a less central location, but it's packed with new (clean!) hotels; some have doubles for as little as Y40 per night.

Jīnhào Bīnguǎn (Rehai Lu cnr Mashi Lu; s/d Y60, tr Y70) Possibly the biggest and brightest rooms on the entire street. If you're mid-slog through western Yúnnán, the pristine condition of bathrooms here will be cause for unbridled excitement if not full-on celebration. Head one block north from the long-distance bus station. The hotel is on the right side of the street. Discounted rooms usually go for Y30-40.

Xīnhuá Dàjiǔdiàn (☎ 513 2683; northeast of Laifang Shan National Forest Park; s/d Y220/380; ⏱) It's got cruddy halls with a 'going-out-of-business' vibe, but the rooms themselves are terrific – dark wood, handsome furniture, obscenely

YÚNNÁN

big bathrooms. Discounted doubles go for as little as Y120.

Your best option for lunch and dinner is the **food court** (cnr Feicui Lu & Laifeng Dadao; dishes Y5-10), where you'll find half a dozen restaurants serving up delicious food from morning to night. There's a huge choice of delicious dishes here including *shāokǎo*, grilled fish and chilli crabs.

Getting There & Away

There are two bus stations in Téngchōng: the shiny new long-distance bus station in the south of town and the old local bus station on Dongfang Lu. In general, for destinations north of Téngchōng, head to the long-distance bus station, and for all locations south of town head to the local bus station.

The local bus station has daily buses to Ruìlì (Y40, six hours, 7.40am, 8.30am, 10.40am and 11.40am) and Mángshì (Y22, 4½ hours, 7.30am, 10.20am and 1pm), and frequent departures to local destinations.

The long-distance bus station has sleeper buses to Kūnmíng (Y180, 12 hours, eight daily from 3.30pm to 8.10pm). An express bus also leaves for Kūnmíng at 8.30am (Y202, 11 hours). Buses to Bǎoshān (Y28 to Y35, five hours, 7.30am to 5.30pm) leave every 30 minutes. Xiàguān buses leave twice a day (Y87, 10.30am; Y93, 7.40pm).

Buses going to local destinations north of Téngchōng, such as Mǎzhàn, Gùdōng, Ruìdiǎn, Diàntān or Zìzhì either leave from, or pass through, Huoshan Lu in the northeast of town.

Getting Around

Téngchōng is small enough to walk around, but a bicycle is helpful for getting to some of the closer sights outside town – the surrounding scenery alone justifies a ride. You can hire a bike from a shop on Guanghua Lu (Y1 per hour).

Bus 2 runs from the town centre to the long-distance bus station.

AROUND TÉNGCHŌNG

There's a lot to see around Téngchōng but getting out to the sights is a bit tricky. Catching buses part of the way and hiking up to the sights is one possibility, while some of the closer attractions can be reached by bicycle.

Your other option is to hire a van, which may be affordable if there are several of you;

head down to the minibus stand just off the southern end of Huoshan Lu or to the minibus stand for the Sea of Heat in the south of town.

Some highlights of the region are the traditional villages that are scattered between Téngchōng and Yúnfēng Shān (Cloudy Peak Mountain). The relatively plentiful public transport along this route means that you can jump on and off minibuses to go exploring as the whim takes you.

Héshùn 和顺

Southwest of town is the village of Héshùn which is well worth a visit. It has been set aside as a retirement village for overseas Chinese, but it's of more interest as a quiet, traditional Chinese village with cobbled streets. There are some great old buildings in the village, providing lots of photo opportunities. The village also has a small **museum** (博物馆; *bówùguǎn*) and a famous old **library** (图书馆). Admission to the village is Y30, and it's open 8am to 7pm daily, however you may find modified hours from October to April outside of Chinese holidays.

Minibuses leave from the corner of Feicui Lu and Laifeng Xiang (Y1.50) in Téngchōng or you can hop on bus 3 that passes nearby. It's an easy bicycle ride out to the village but the ride back is an uphill slog.

Yúnfēng Shān 云蜂山

Yúnfēng Shān (Cloudy Peak Mountain; admission Y60), 47km north of Téngchōng, is a Taoist mountain dotted with 17th-century temples and monastic retreats. Most people take the **cable car** (one way/return Y30/50), from where it's a 20-minute walk to **Dàxióngbǎo Diàn** (大雄宝殿), a temple at the summit. **Lǚzǔ Diàn** (鲁祖殿), the temple second from the top, serves up great vegetarian food at lunchtime. It's a quick walk down but it can be hard on the knees.

To get to the mountain, go to Huoshan Lu where you can flag down a bus to Ruìdiǎn or Diàntān and get off at the turnoff to Yúnfēng (Y8). Alternatively, take a bus to Gùdōng (Y6) and then a microbus from here to the turn-off (Y2). From the turn-off you have to either hitch, or you can choose to take the lovely walk past the village of Heping to the pretty villages just before the mountain. Hiring a vehicle from Téngchōng to take you on a return trip will cost about Y300.

Volcanoes

Téngchōng County is renowned for its volcanoes, and although they have been behaving themselves for many centuries the seismic and geothermal activity in the area indicates that they won't always continue to do so. The closest one to town is **Mǎ'ān Shān** (马鞍山; Saddle Mountain), around 5km to the northwest. It's just south of the main road to Yíngjiāng.

Around 22km to the north of town, near the village of Mǎzhàn, is the most accessible cluster of **volcanoes** (admission Y20). The main central volcano is known as **Dàkòng Shān** (大空山; Big Empty Hill), which pretty much sums it up, and to the left of it is the black crater of **Hēikòng Shān** (黑空山; Black Empty Hill). You can haul yourself up the steps for views of the surrounding lava fields (long dormant).

Minibuses run frequently to Mǎzhàn (Y5) from along Huoshan Lu, or take a Gùdōng-bound minibus. From Mǎzhàn town it's a 10-minute walk or take a motor-tricycle (Y5) to the volcano area.

Sea of Heat 热海

This is a cluster of hot springs, geysers and streams about 12km southwest of Téngchōng. In addition to the usual indoor baths, the **Sea of Heat** (Rèhǎi; adult/student Y30/20, with pool access Y100; 7.30am-11pm) features a couple of outdoor hot springs and a nice warm-water swimming pool. If the steep entrance fee puts you off swimming then you can pay Y30 for a quick dip in the **Měinǚ Chí** (Beautiful Lady Pool) instead. Some of the springs here reach temperatures of 102˚C.

The site is a popular local resort and there are several hotels.

THE HANI (AKHA) PEOPLE 哈尼族

The Hani (also known in adjacent countries as the Akha) are of Tibetan origin and related to the Yi, but according to folklore they are descended from frogs' eyes. They stick to the hills, cultivating rice, corn and the occasional poppy and are famed for their intricate rice terraces.

Hani women (especially the Aini, who are a subgroup of the Hani) wear headdresses of beads, feathers, silver rings and coins, some of which are turn-of-the-century French (Vietnamese), Burmese and Indian coins.

Rehai Grand Hotel (热海大酒店; Rèhǎi Dàjiǔdiàn; 515 0366; d Y280) has two branches, one within the park and the other just outside the main entrance.

The basic rooms at **Rèhǎi Zhāodàisuǒ** (热海招待所; 515 0306; d & tr Y80) are a bit damp but come with free access to the hotel's very own bathing pool (not such a bonus once you've seen it). This place is to the left of the park entrance.

Microbuses leave for Sea of Heat (Y5) when full from the Dongfang Lu turn-off in the south of town.

DÉHÓNG PREFECTURE 德宏州

Déhóng Prefecture (Déhóng Lìsù) and Jingpo Autonomous Prefecture, like Xīshuāngbǎnnà, border Myanmar and is heavily populated by distinctive minority groups, but hasn't yet captured travellers' imaginations as Bǎnnà has. It's in the far west of Yúnnán and is definitely more off-the-beaten track than Xīshuāngbǎnnà.

Most Chinese tourists in Déhóng are here for the trade from Myanmar that comes through Ruìlì and Wǎndīng – Burmese jade is a popular commodity and countless other items are spirited over the border. The border with Myanmar is punctuated by many crossings, some of them almost imperceptible, so careful if you go wandering too close.

The most obvious minority groups in Déhóng are the Burmese (normally dressed in their traditional sarong-like *longyi*), Dai and Jingpo (known in Myanmar as the Kachin, a minority long engaged in armed struggle against the Myanmar government). For information on etiquette for visiting temples in the region see the boxed text, p735.

Around Déhóng are signs in Chinese, Burmese, Dai and English. This is a border region getting rich on trade – in the markets you can see Indian jewellery, tinned fruits from Thailand, Burmese papier-mâché furniture, young bloods with wads of foreign currency and Chinese plain-clothes police.

MÁNGSHÌ 芒市 (LÙXĪ) (潞西)

0692

Mángshì is Déhóng's air link with the outside world. It's a large, sprawling town and most travellers simply pass through on their way to Ruìlì. But if you're planning to fly out of Mángshì then you might have to stay overnight here, in which case there are enough things to keep you occupied for an afternoon or so. If you fly in from Kūnmíng there are minibuses running direct from the airport to Ruìlì and your best bet is to jump into one of these and head south.

Information
The **Bank of China** (Zhōngguó Yínháng; Dongfeng Lu) changes cash and travellers cheques and gives cash advances on credit cards. There is an ATM machine around the corner from the southern bus station on Weimin Lu.

Sights
Puti Temple (Pútí Sì), **Foguang Temple** (Fóguāng Sì) and **Five Clouds Temple** (Wǔyún Sì) dot the downtown area. The latter is heavily spruced up but still worth a visit, as much for the mischievous gang of oldsters that sets up in front of it, as for the temple itself.

Halfway along Youyi Lu, in a school playground, is the 200-year-old **Embracing Tree Pagoda** (Shùbāo Tǎ; admission Y5 when staffed), so named because over the years it has fused with the surrounding tree.

Sleeping & Eating
Chángjiāng Bīnguǎn (☎ 228 6055; 2 Weimin Lu; 为民路2号; s/d Y60/50, with bathroom Y100/80; ☒) This hotel is surprisingly clean and well kept up, however, do check the rooms before you hand over your cash as one or two smell a bit musty.

Xīngjiàn Jiǔdiàn (☎ 228 6788; Jianguo Lu; 建国路; s/d Y120) This is a newish, extremely welcoming hotel, in a good location down the street from the long-distance bus station. There's a gurgling fountain filled with gold fish in the lobby. Rooms are spotless with hard wood floors and clean bathrooms.

The best places to head for food in Mángshì are the point-and-choose places on Dongfeng Lu situated just west of the market or along Qingnian Lu. Otherwise try the extremely popular **noodle restaurant** (Tuanjie Dajie) near the southern bus station where you can get a big plate of fried noodles for Y5.

Fei Ma Movie and TV Bar (Fēi Mǎ Yíngxiáng Gōngzuò Shí; ☒ 10am-late; dishes Y15-18) serves coffee and valiant stabs at Western cuisine like pizza, serving it all up among the jungle-like decor.

Make sure you try a freshly squeezed lime juice (large/small Y3/2) from one of the numerous stands dotting the town.

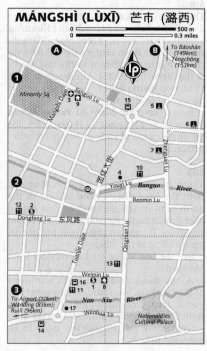

YÚNNÁN

MÁNGSHÌ BUS TIMETABLES

Bus services from Mángshì include the following:

Destination	Price	Duration	Frequency	Departs
Künmíng	Y160-180	10hr	3 daily	10.30am, 6.40pm, 9pm
Xiàguān	Y80-90	7hr	2 daily	11am, 8pm
Lìjiāng	Y133	14hr	daily	5pm
Jǐnghóng	Y239	24hr	daily	11.30am
Téngchōng	Y22	3½hr	8 daily	7.40am-4.20pm
Bǎoshān	Y35	4hr	11 daily	7.20am-3.30pm
Yinjiang	Y25	3hr	every 40min	7.30am-4.50pm

Getting There & Away

AIR

The airport is 10km from the city. There are daily flights between Mángshì and Künmíng (Y790). There are no buses from Mángshì airport to the town centre so you'll have no choice but to negotiate with the taxi sharks at the airport (Y20-25). Minibuses to Ruìlì (Y30, two hours) usually wait at the airport for incoming flights.

Buses leave the Mángshì **Yunnan Airlines** (Wenhua Lu; ✆ 8.30am-noon & 2.30-6pm) office for the airport around an hour before flight departures.

BUS

There are several bus stations in Mángshì. Both the long-distance bus station in the north of town and the southern bus station offer similar destinations at similar prices and schedules. If you don't find your bus at one, trudge along to the other.

See the box above for bus services from Mángshì.

A bus stand situated a block southwest of the southern bus stand has the most frequent departures to Wǎndīng (Y20) and Ruìlì (Y20, 7am to 8pm). Minibuses leave when they're full so you will need to be prepared to wait.

RUÌLÌ 瑞丽

☎ 0692

Ah, notorious Ruìlì. At one time, the town's reputation for wild nights, seedy casinos and bawdy karaoke bars drew everyone from the wild and adventurous to the shady and the crooked. Ruìlì was considered one of the 'it' places in Yúnnán, and young people with money would head here in droves, lured by the 'anything-goes' reputation and implicit prom-

ise that 'what-happens-in-Ruìlì-stays-in-Ruìlì' that the town's fringe location afforded.

Trade with Myanmar fuelled the boom. The border only opened for business in the 1990s but no sooner had it opened than Ruìlì became a hotbed of trade handling everything from raw goods to gems and arms. In return for the latter, China received huge quantities of heroin, which saw drug-taking and trafficking become part of everyday life.

The local government, with help from Běijīng, retaliated and drug dealers were hauled before sentencing panels and then executed.

These days Ruìlì can seem (dare we say it?) almost sterile. The dance halls and gambling dens are gone and shiny shopping malls and modern hotels stand in their place.

About the raciest thing the average traveller will encounter these days is the odd Burmese trader a little over-enthusiastically adjusting his sarong.

But despite the clean-up, Ruìlì has a great mix of Han Chinese, minorities and Burmese traders hawking jade, lively local markets and a laid-back Southeast Asian feel.

The minority villages nearby are also reason to come; the stupas are in much better condition than those in Xīshuāngbǎnnà, and it's worth getting a bicycle and heading out to explore.

Another draw for travellers is Myanmar, which lies only a few kilometres away from Ruìlì. Border-crossing restrictions are beginning to relax and although individual tourists are still not allowed to cross, organising permits to take you through the sensitive border area is becoming easier (see p748). New highways laid to facilitate border trade stretch all the way from the border to Mandalay, making what had been a horrible five-day journey much more sane. Foreign travellers may one day be able to recreate the 'Southern Silk Route', of which Ruìlì and Mandalay were a part.

Information

Bank of China (Zhōngguó Yínháng; Nanmao Jie) Provides all the usual services and will let you cash travellers cheques for US dollars in case you're headed to Myanmar.

China Post & Telecom (Yóudiàn; cnr Mengmao Lu & Renmin Lu) Despite (or perhaps because?) of its border location; sending any kind of package abroad from this branch is a full-on nightmare if not completely impossible. For anything more complicated than buying stamps or making international calls, wait until you've move on from Ruìlì.

Dielai Photograph Centre (Diélái Shéyíng Zhōngxīn; Nanmao Jie) Can burn CDs for Y10 each. Keep an eye out for the big yellow Kodak sign. **Internet café** (wǎngbā; Nanmao Jie, cnr Jiegang Lu; per hr Y2; ☺ 24hrs)

Public Security Bureau (PSB; Gōngānjú; Jianshe Jie; ☺ 8.30-11.30am & 2.30-5.30pm) Just up the road from Ruìlì Bīnguǎn.

Ruìlì Overseas Travel Company (Ruìlì Hǎiwài Lǚyóushí; ☎ 414 1880; 27 Jianshe Lu; ☺ 8-11.30am, 2.30-5.30pm & 7.30-10pm) If it happens to be staffed, you should be able to get information on the local area.

Xinhua Bookshop (Xīnhuá Shūdiàn; Renmin Lu) Sells the *Tourism and Traffic Map of Ruili,* which includes some English.

Dangers & Annoyances

Despite Ruìlì's new look, old problems die hard and prostitution remains an enormous industry in Ruìlì. You don't have to look very hard to see the evidence: brothels disguised as hairdressers fill the town.

Another major problem is of the poppy-derived variety, Ruìlì being an entry point for Burmese opium headed to Hong Kong. This has resulted in a serious IV drug-use problem in the Déhóng region and a spike in HIV. The province, with Běijīng's help, has poured millions of *yuán* into anti-drug efforts along the border with Myanmar.

All vehicles, including buses, leaving Ruìlì are searched. Authorities are usually more interested in locals and foreigners are often completely ignored and not even asked for ID. However some travellers have reported epic grillings bordering on the farcical.

Sights

A visit to Ruìlì is about atmosphere, people watching, markets and aimless wandering rather than formal sights. It's small enough that you can cover most of it in an hour or so. The huge **market** in the west of town is most colourful by day, especially in the morning, when the stalls are lined with Burmese smokes, tofu wrapped in banana leaves, snack stalls and charcoal sellers. There's also whir of people from nearby minority villages, Myanmar and far flung places like Pakistan.

At the other end of town, Ruìlì's **jade market** is a hoot and one of the best locations for people watching. Most of Ruìlì's sights are outside town, and you'll need a bicycle to get out and see them.

Sleeping

There are some good deals to be found in Ruìlì's hotels and all the accommodation is within easy walking distance of the long-distance bus station.

Límín Bīnguǎn (☎ 414 2249; Nanmao Jie; 南卯街; dm Y20, s & d Y40-80; ☒) The biggest and cheapest selection of rooms in town. There is little to distinguish the singles and doubles, so you might as well opt for the cheaper ones. Dorm rooms can get hot and stuffy, and the shared bathrooms can be noisy.

Ruby Hotel (☎ 419 9088; Nanmao Jie; 南卯街; s/d Y80/180) After the bright green exterior and halls bedecked with pebble-encrusted wall panels, the very plain rooms, while clean, are a minor let down. No matter, there's more than enough atmosphere at the terrace bar with its thatched huts and floor cushions.

Ruìlì Bīnguǎn (☎ 410 0555; Nanmao Jie; 南卯街; s&d Y200) Across the street from the Ruby Hotel, this place has no fireworks but is comfortingly average. Outside of holidays, rooms rarely go for more than Y100 though deft bargainers have gotten rooms for less.

New Kaitong International Hotel (Xīn Kǎitōng Guójì Dàjiǔdiàn; ☎ 415 777; fax 415 6190; 2 Biancheng Lu; 边城路2号; d Y360, discounted d Y180; ☒ ☒) This is the original luxury hotel in Ruìlì and offers good discounts which make it a worthwhile option. The outdoor swimming pool is perhaps the best feature and is open to non-residents for Y10.

Eating & Drinking

Reports concerning the existence of decent curries in Ruìlì are the result perhaps of wishful embellishment, but there is some good food available.

For good Burmese food, there are several restaurants in a small alley off Jiegang Lu. The one at the top of the northwestern corner is particularly good, and sees a lot of Burmese patrons. This is also the spot to go for Thai Mekong whisky, served Thai-style with soda water and ice. There are also lots of Cantonese restaurants here. At night a small but lively market sets up on Baijiang Xiang between Bianmao Jie and Biancheng Lu.

Huafeng Market (Huáfēng Shìchǎng; Jiegang Lu) Make sure you eat here at least once. It has an enormous outdoor food court with an incredible selection of food including Thai, Burmese, Chinese and even some Western dishes on offer. You can eat well here for Y8 to Y12.

Kūnmíng Guóqiáo Xíngxián (Mengmao Lu; dishes Y12) You may have had your fill of across-the-bridge noodles while in Kūnmíng, but this place is charming, with its dark wood furniture, blue-and-white checked table clothes. There's a little garden with outdoor seating in back.

Bobo's Cold Drinks Shop (Bùbù Lěngyǐndiàn; Baijiang Xiang; meals Y8) Serves excellent fresh fruit juices and small meals in a bright eating area buzzing with low-key commotion.

Getting There & Away

AIR
Ruìlì has daily flight connections to Kūnmíng via Mángshì p744, which is a two-hour drive away. You can buy tickets at **China Eastern Airlines** (☎ 411 1111; Renmin Lu; ☷ 8.30am-6pm). Shuttle buses leave daily from the office, three hours before scheduled flights (Y60). You can also use the ticket office to book and reconfirm return flights – do so early as this is an increasingly popular flight.

BUS
There are two bus stations in Ruìlì, the long-distance bus station in the centre of town and the north bus station at the top of Jiegang Lu. Head to the north bus station if you're trying to get to Mángshì (Y20, last bus 6pm, leaves when full) for everything else, you're better off going to the long-distance bus station.

For local destinations, minibuses and vans leave from the minibus stand near the jade market, or you can just flag one down in the street. Destinations include Wǎndīng (Y5), the border checkpoint at Jiěgào (Y5), and the village of Nóngdǎo (Y8). Buses to Zhāngfēng (Y10, one hour) leave from Xinjian Lu.

TO MYANMAR
To cross from China into Myanmar, travellers must have the correct visa, travel permits and be part of an official 'group'. The group, which might consist entirely of yourself and no-one else, will be escorted from Jiěgào in China to Hsipaw in Myanmar, an eight-hour drive from the border. Once you reach Hsipaw you can wave good bye to your guide and are

RUÌLÌ 瑞丽

0 ___ 500 m
0 ___ 0.3 miles

YÚNNÁN

RUÌLÌ BUS TIMETABLES

The following buses leave from Ruìlì long-distance bus station:

Destination	Price	Duration	Frequency	Departs
Téngchōng	Y25	6hr	every 40-50min	5.40-10.40am
Bǎoshān	Y45	6hr	every 30-40min	6am-2.30pm
Xiàguān	Y116	12hr	hourly	4-8pm
Kūnmíng	Y190	16hr	hourly	8am-8pm
Jǐnghóng	Y195	25hr	daily	8.30am

free to travel on your own further south to Mandalay, Rangoon and so on.

Ko Wai Lin Travel (☎ 0871-313 7555; myanmarwailin@yahoo.com; Room 221, Camellia Hotel, 154 Dongfeng Lu, Kūnmíng) in Kūnmíng (see Map p690) can arrange permit and group travel. Remember it's not possible to organise a visa for Myanmar in Ruìlì and you will have to do this in Kūnmíng at the Myanmar consulate (see p943).

Getting Around

Ruìlì is easily seen on foot, but all the most interesting day trips require a bicycle. Ask at your accommodation for the best place to rent one.

The flat rate for a taxi ride inside the city should be Y5, and up for negotiation from there. There are also cheaper motor and cycle rickshaws.

AROUND RUÌLÌ

Most of the sights around Ruìlì can be explored easily by bicycle. It's worth making frequent detours down the narrow paths leading off the main roads to visit minority villages. The people are friendly and there are lots of photo opportunities. The *Tourism and Traffic Map of Ruili* shows the major roads and villages.

The shortest ride is to turn left at the corner north of the post office and continue out of the town proper into the little village of Měngmǎo. There are half a dozen Shan temples scattered about; the fun is in finding them.

Golden Duck Pagoda 弄安金鸭塔
On the outskirts of town, on the main road, this **pagoda** (Nòng'ān Jīnyā Tǎ) is an attractive stupa set in a temple courtyard. It was established to mark the arrival of a pair of golden ducks that brought good fortune to what was previously an uninhabited marshy area.

Jiěgào Border Checkpoint 姐告边检点
There's not much here but border fanatics will find the trip satisfying if only to marvel at how everything seems so relaxed on both sides of the – quite literally – bamboo curtain.

On a thumb of land jutting into Myanmar, Jiěgào is the main checkpoint for a steady stream of cross-border traffic. As with Ruìlì this place has seen its popular casinos and other dens of iniquity replaced by lemonade stands and cheap electronic shops.

To get here, continue straight ahead from Golden Duck Pagoda, cross the Myanmar bridge over Ruìlì Jiāng and you will come to Jiěgào, about 7km from Ruìlì. (see opposite for more details).

Microbuses shuttle between the border and Ruìlì's long-distance bus station when full for Y5 or you can charter one for around Y25-30. Buses continue until late at night.

Wǎndīng Border Checkpoint 畹町边检站
West of Ruìlì lies Wǎndīng, a second checkpoint for crossing into Myanmar. It's not as busy here, nor is it as interesting as Jiěgào, but if you're a serious borderholic then it's worth making the 30-minute drive here just so you can take a photo and say you've been.

Minibuses for Wǎndīng (Y5) leave Ruìlì when full, and vice versa.

Temples
Just past Golden Duck Pagoda is a crossroad and a small wooden temple. The road to the right (west) leads to the villages of Jiěxiàng and Nóngdǎo, and on the way are a number of small temples, villages and stupas. None are spectacular but the village life is interesting and there are often small markets near the temples.

The first major Dai temple is **Hansha Zhuang Temple** (Hánshā Zhuāng Sì), a fine wooden

YÚNNÁN

structure that has a few resident monks. It's set a little off the road and a green tourism sign marks the turn-off. The surrounding Dai village is interesting.

Another 20 minutes or so further down the road, look out for a white stupa on the hillside to the right. This is **Léizhuāngxiāng**, Ruìlì's oldest stupa, dating back to the middle of the Tang dynasty. There's a nunnery in the grounds of the stupa as well as fantastic views of the Ruìlì area.

Once the stupa comes into view, take the next path to the right that cuts through the fields. You will see blue signs written in Chinese and Dai pointing the way through a couple of Dai villages. When you get to market crossroads at the centre of the main village, take the right path. You'll need to push your bicycle for the last ascent to the stupa. In all, it should take you about 50 minutes to cycle here from Golden Duck Pagoda.

About 2km past Jiéxiàng is **Denghannong Zhuang Temple** (Děnghánnóng Zhuāng Sì), a wooden Dai temple with pleasant surrounds.

It's possible to cycle all the way to Nóngdǎo, around 29km southwest of Ruìlì. There's a solitary hotel in town that has cheap doubles or you can return to Ruìlì on one of the frequent minibuses.

Golden Pagoda 姐勒金塔
A few kilometres to the east of Ruìlì on the road to Wǎndīng is the **Golden Pagoda** (Jiělè Jīntǎ), a fine structure that dates back 200 years.

Bàngmáhè 棒麻贺
Another possible cycling route takes you west of Ruìlì, past the old town of Měngmǎo, now a suburb of Ruìlì. After 4km, just past the village of Jiědōng, a turn-off north leads to Bàngmáhè village, a Jingpo settlement with a small waterfall nearby.

Sìchuān 四川

Interpret literally the five Chinese elements (water, earth, wood, metal, fire) and you may understand the attraction that Sìchuān has had for millennia. Sìchuān means 'Four Rivers' and the name pays tribute to that most essential element, water. Indeed, the 'four' are but the mightiest of the 1300-plus rivers roiling or sedately meandering across the southwest's most expansive province and long dominating the ethos.

Underappreciating the land ('earth') here defies possibility; one can't help but note the high quotient of set-in-Sìchuān poetry and *shānshuǐ huà* ('mountain water painting', a traditional Chinese form). Sìchuān is ensconced to the north, west, and south by sublime mountain ranges at once majestic and foreboding (and the reason why Sìchuān remained so isolated for so much of China's history). In the west, the sparsely populated Tibetan plateau, birthplace of many ribbony waterways, pushes skyward with each kilometre. The rivers spill eastward into the Chuānxī plain of the preternaturally fecund Sìchuān basin, which supports one of the densest (and most diverse) populations on the planet (and filling a billion other mouths).

With epic tracts of forest ('wood') and vast deposits of ore ('metal'), Sìchuān has become one of China's wealthiest provinces and in no small part is the engine of western China.

Ah, but fire may be the most esoteric. No volcanoes, but to toy with a metaphor, 'fire' here really means spice, as in *hot* (italics essential) peppers, the key 'element' of Sìchuān's renowned flamethrower cuisine. The preponderance of peppers isn't arbitrary; their spiciness is believed to help reduce a person's internal dampness caused by high humidity and rainy weather.

HIGHLIGHTS

- Wear out your legs, bribe some monkeys and hope for a blessed sunrise at the sacred mountaintop of **Éméi Shān** (p769)
- Feel your mortality (from the bottom up) on the **Sìchuān–Tibet Hwy** (p777) amid soaring snow-capped peaks, grasslands and Tibetan villages
- Indulge your inner cowpoke atop a (tame) pony through the magnificent splendour surrounding **Sōngpān** (p792)
- Coo baby talk to panda cubs at Chéngdū's **Giant Panda Breeding Research Base** (p757)
- Get some statuary exercise by scaling the Grand Buddha, the world's largest Buddha statue, in **Lèshān** (p774)
- Wander streets filled with funky traditional architecture and prepare for your Imperial examination in **Lǎngzhōng** (p768)

■ POPULATION: 84 MILLION

SÌCHUĀN 四川

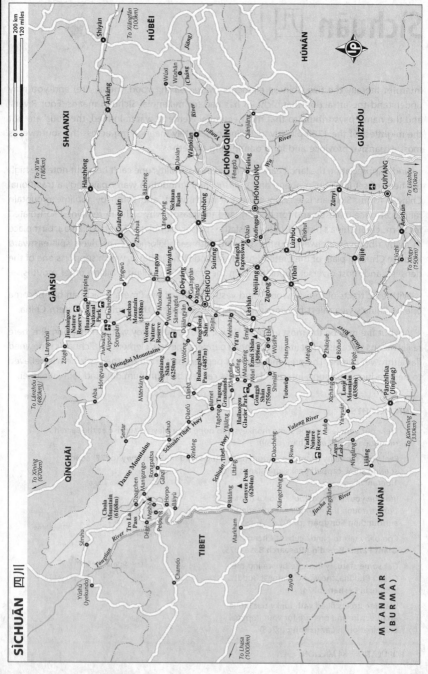

History

Not until 1986, with a major archaeological discovery of the late-Shang dynasty culture of Shu at Sānxīngduī, was the Sìchuān basin's importance to Chinese history fully realized. Never really a backwater as long assumed, the region's rough land (if not fiery food) perhaps giving rise to a rough character of people, it has been the site of various breakaway kingdoms, ever skirmishing with central authority. It was finally wrestled into control and established as the capital of the Qin empire in the 3rd century BC and it was here that the kingdom of Shu (a name by which the province is still known) ruled as an independent state during the Three Kingdoms Period (AD 220–80). The Kuomintang (p48) spent its last days in Sìchuān before being vanquished and fleeing to Taiwan; and most recently Chóngqìng split from Sìchuān when it was promoted to the status of Municipality in 1997.

During the Warring States period (475–221 BC) a famed engineer, Li Bing, managed to harness the Du River (Dū Hé) on the Chuānxī plain with his weir system, allowing Sìchuān some 2200 continuous years of irrigation and prosperity. No exaggeration – this bread-basket region in no small part helped unify (and feed) the nation. Sadly, the Great Leap Forward (p51) dealt Sìchuān an especially cruel blow: it's believed that one in 10 people starved.

In 1975 Zhao Ziyang, governor of Sìchuān and the province's first Communist Party secretary, became the driving force behind the agriculture and economic reforms that put Sìchuān back on the map (Zhao was also the CCP's national general secretary from 1987 to 1989 before he fell from grace and into lifelong house arrest for opposing the use of troops during the 1989 Tiananmen Square demonstrations). His system (the 'Responsibility System'), whereby plots of land were let out to individual farmers on the proviso that a portion of the crops be sold back to the government, was so successful that it became the national model and was later applied to the industrial sector. As of 2006, this fertile land of 'Heaven's Granary' was still producing over 10% of the nation's grain, soybeans, pork, and more.

Climate

Chéngdū and the east have a subtropical, humid monsoon climate with temperatures ranging from 3°C to 8°C in winter (Dec-Feb) and 25°C to 29°C in summer (Jun-Aug). The Qinghai-Tibet plateau in the west experiences intense sunlight and low temperatures most of the year with temperatures dropping to –9°C in winter and reaching highs of only 17°C in summer.

Language

In addition to Mandarin, which is spoken by the Han and the Hui, the other major languages in Sìchuān belong to the Tibeto-Burman family and are spoken by Tibetans and the Yi. Sichuanese is one of the 'Mandarin dialects', even though the pronunciation is different enough that it is often very difficult for those who speak standard Chinese to understand.

Getting There & Away

For more details about travelling between provinces see p966.

AIR

Chéngdū's Shangliu Airport is the largest international airport in southwest China. Air China and Sìchuān Airlines link Chéngdū with all major Chinese cities and fly direct to Lhasa in Tibet. Currently international flights serve Bangkok, Singapore, Hong Kong, Macau, Kuala Lumpur, Kathmandu, Japan, Vienna, Amsterdam and Seoul (more are always in the pipeline).

Jiuhuang Airport in northern Sìchuān closed in May 2006 for expansion to allow for flights from other major Chinese cities.

BUS

Sìchuān's provincial government has been throwing hundreds of billions into highway construction since the mid-1990s as part of China's 'Develop the West' migration plan. High-speed expressways link Chéngdū with Chóngqìng and Lèshān; and the construction of highways to link Chéngdū with Shànghǎi, Běihǎi in Guǎngxī province and Tibet are underway (to get to Tibet as yet requires superhuman endurance).

Travel to Gānsù is possible via Jiǔzhàigōu and Zōigê. To get to Yúnnán you can travel south via Lèshān, Éméi Shān and Pānzhīhuā on the border, or you can travel along the southern route of the Sìchuān-Tibet Hwy through Lǐtáng and Xiāngchéng to Shangri-la (Zhōngdiàn).

SÌCHUĀN

TRAIN

Chéngdū is an important railway hub in China's southwest. Direct trains run to cities such as Běijīng and Shànghǎi. Travel to Kūnmíng in Yúnnán and Xī'ān in Shaanxi tend to be the most popular options, although Chéngdū now has a direct train to Lhasa that is becoming wildly popular. To get to Gānsù you need to change in Hànzhōng, Shaanxi province.

Getting Around

Jiuhuang Airport connects Chéngdū with Sōngpān and Jiǔzhàigōu. New expressways connect Chéngdū with the eastern part of the province, including those from Chéngdū to Lèshān/Chóngqìng. The buses on this side of the province are generally modern and comfortable. Trains in the east have generally been slow and irregular, but in 2006 new high-speed lines to Miányáng, Lèshān, and Chóngqìng were being finalised.

Travel in the west of the province can only be done via bus (or hitching in logging trucks; see p971). But make sure you have enough time (and pain medication), the roads in this part of Sìchuān remain in buttbreakingly awful condition and the buses are, if possible, even worse.

CENTRAL SÌCHUĀN

CHÉNGDŪ 成都

☎ 028 / pop 4.1 million / elevation 500m

Judging by the laid-back attitude, admirable green space and pockets of, well, 'old' Chéngdū, you'd hardly know that the city is China's fifth-most populous city (the greater metropolitan area has just broached 13 million and is growing fast even by China's hyper standards). 'Charm' – not a word often used with Chinese supercities – is not altogether inappropriate. In 2006 Chéngdū was rated by several Chinese media as the nation's second-most liveable city.

Oh, true, the city is still in China. Traditional wooden architecture and tree-draped streets have been gradually giving way to neon-drenched malls, glassy high-rises, or resolutely practical new apartment complexes. That same survey above glumly noted that Chéngdū, while eminently liveable, is also choking on exhaust fumes, ranking third in cars per capita.

Yet bustling side streets chock-full of gingko trees and hibiscus flowers do exist, bicycles for the nonce almost equal cars and buses, and eating out with mates still trumps all else. You'll stumble upon markets, countless tiny restaurants specialising in Sìchuān snacks, and parks where old men walk their song birds or hunch over a game of chess (as auburn-haired seen-on-the-scene hipsters yapping on their mobile phones stroll nearby). A dash of old-time artisans – cobblers, weavers, itinerant dentists and the like – scattered throughout and you've got your lively-yet-relaxed Chéngdū.

History

'Chéngdū', or Perfect Metropolis, has seen the rise and fall of nearly a dozen independent kingdoms or dynasties since its founding in 316 BC; agricultural potential and strategic geography were key to its political power. Yet throughout history it has been equally well-known for culture; not by accident did the Tang dynasty poet Du Fu brush his strokes here. The city is also split by the Brocade River (Jǐn Jiāng), a reminder of the city's silk brocade industry which thrived during the Eastern Han dynasty (AD 25–220); from here the Southern Silk Road guided caravans to the known world. The city's name eventually shifted from Jǐnchéng (Brocade City) to 'Hibiscus City', still used today by locals. By the time of the Tang dynasty (AD 618–907) the city had become a cornerstone of Chinese society. Three hundred years later, during the Song dynasty, Chéngdū began to issue the world's first paper money.

It is also a survivor. Devastated first by the Mongols in retaliation for its fierce resistance, from 1644 to 1647 it was presided over by the rebel Zhang Xianzhong, who set up an independent state in Sìchuān and ruled by terror and mass executions. Three centuries later the city became one of the last strongholds of the Kuomintang.

Orientation

Ring roads circle the outer city: Yihuan Lu (First Ring Rd), Erhuan Lu (Second Ring Rd) and Sanhuan Lu (Third Ring Rd). These are divided into numbered segments (duàn). The main boulevard that sweeps through the centre of Chéngdū is Renmin Lu – in its north (běi), central (zhōng) and south (nán) manifestations.

STREET NAME HEADACHE

Chéngdū is a true Asian city in its noncha-
lant disregard of systematic street numbering and naming. It's not unusual, when
following street numbers in one direction,
to meet another set coming the other
way, leaving some places with five sets of
numbers on their doors. Street names, also,
seem to change every 100m or so – with
very little apparent logic involved. Try to
bear this in mind when you're looking for
somewhere in particular, and rely more on
nearby landmarks and relative locations on
maps than on street numbers and names.

The nucleus of the city is the square that
interrupts Renmin Lu, where you'll find the
Sìchuān Exhibition Centre, a sports stadium
and the colossal Mao statue. Just south is
Tianfu Sq, a pedestrianised neon extravaganza
and the main shopping district. Note that
a new subway system and ongoing plans to
relocate government offices and industries are
affecting the lay of the downtown land.

MAPS

Tourist maps of Chéngdū, including a handful
of English-language ones, abound at train and
bus stations, bookshops and newspaper kiosks.
City maps in Chinese can be useful for tracing
bus routes, though not even the best ones can
hope to capture the insanity that is Chéngdū's
street naming (see the box on above).

Information
BOOKSHOPS
South West Book Centre (Xīnán Shūchéng; Xiadong
Dajie) Has maps and a small selection of English titles.

INTERNET ACCESS 网吧
Well-located options include one on Chunxi
Lu, another above Xinnanmen bus station,
and one on Renmin Beilu south of the train
station. *All* guesthouses – but not all hotels –
have internet access (though few of these are
adept at CD burning and other higher-tech
endeavours, so do be patient with them). All
charge about Y3 per hour.

INTERNET RESOURCES
Chengdu (www.chengdu.gov.cn) This provincial government website has an OK English version with information
on the city and surrounding areas.

MEDICAL SERVICES
No 3 Hospital (Dongmen Jie) Helpful staff with a handful
of English speakers.
Global Doctor Chéngdū Clinic (☎ 8522 6058, 139-
8225 6966; ground fl, Kelan Bldg, Bangkok Garden Apts,
Section 4, 21 Renmin Nanlu; ⏰ 9-11am & 1.30-3.30pm
Mon-Fri) Has a 24-hour English-speaking helpline.

MONEY
Bank of China (Zhōngguó Yínháng; Renmin Nanlu;
⏰ 8.30am-6pm Mon-Fri, 8.30am-5pm Sat & Sun) Can
change money and travellers cheques and offer cash advances on credit cards. Other well-located branches include
those on Renmin Zhonglu and just north of Xinnanmen
bus station. All have ATMs.

POST & TELEPHONE
China Post (Yóujú; 71 Shawan Lu; ⏰ 8am-6pm) The
main international post office is west of the train station.
A smaller branch can be found on Dongchenggen Jie near
People's Park.

PUBLIC SECURITY BUREAU
PSB (Gōngānjú; ☎ 8640 7067; 136 Wenwu Lu; ⏰ 9am-
noon & 1-5pm Mon-Fri) The foreign affairs entrance is on
Tianzuo Jie; this is where you can get visa extensions. PSB
says it's a five-day wait. Period. Consider picking yours up
in Lèshān, Kāngdìng, or – best – Sōngpān.

TOURIST INFORMATION
The best source for up-to-the-minute restaurant, bar and entertainment listings is the free
monthly magazine *Go West* which you can
pick up at guesthouses and restaurants.
Tourist booth (⏰ 9am-9.30pm in summer) The city
maintains an information booth with English (well, some
anyway) speakers along Chunxi Lu.
Tourist hotline (☎ 8292 8555) Free hotline with
English-speaking operators.

TRAVEL AGENCIES
Every other building in the city seems to be
a travel agency; note that dissatisfaction with
private agencies is a none-too-rare thing, so
ask around first. Basically everywhere you
can lay your head has a travel agency of some
sort. The more useful travel agencies are at the
Dragon Town Youth Hostel, The Loft and
Sim's Cozy Guesthouse.

Tours offered differ at every place, but
many include those to Hǎiluógōu Glacier
Park, Wolong Nature Reserve, Jiǔzhàigōu,
Éméi Shān and Sōngpān. Also on offer are day
trips to the Giant Panda Breeding Research
Base and local Sìchuān opera performances.

SICHUĀN

CHÉNGDŪ 成都

To Giant Panda Breeding
Research Base (6km);
Xīndū (16km); Monastery
of Divine Light (18km);
Sānxīngduī (40km);
Guāngyuán (337km)

North Train
Station
北火车站

To Chadianzi Bus Station
(4km); Dūjiāngyán (60km);
Wòlóng (140km)

Bei Erhuan Lu

Bei Yihuan Lu

Shā River

To Qingchéng
Shān (65m);
Songxinqiao
Art City (250m);
Dù Fǔ's Cottage
(400m)

Culture
Park

Baihuatan
Park

Xizhu
Shijie
西珠市街

Cultural
Palace

People's
Park

Tianfu Sq

Chunxi
Lu

Renmin Donglu

Shanxi Jie

Shangdong
Dajie

Nanjiao
Park

Jīn Jiāng

Binjiang Lu

Binjiang Donglu

To Wuguiqiao
Bus Station (1km);
Lángzhōng (220km)

To Airport (18km);
Émei Shān (130km);
Lèshān (140km)

Nan Yihuan Lu

River Viewing
Pavilion Park

Nan Erhuan Lu

To South Train
Station (1.5km)

Prices depend upon the number of travellers but are generally good value.

Agencies can often arrange Yangzi River (Cháng Jiāng) cruise tickets, train and flight tickets and permits to Tibet.

China International Travel Service (CITS; Zhōngguó Guójì Lǚxíngshè; ☎ 8642 8212, 8666 4422; Renmin Nanlu) Arranges pricey tours including packages to Tibet, and offers train and airline ticket booking for a substantial fee.

Dangers & Annoyances

There have been several reports of foreigners becoming targets for rip-offs and theft in Chéngdū, though violent encounters are rare. Definitely lock your bicycle! Some travellers have reported having things stolen out of their bicycle basket while they're pedalling!

Sights

GIANT PANDA BREEDING RESEARCH BASE
大熊猫繁殖研究中心
About 10km north of Chéngdū at the **Giant Panda Breeding Research Base** (Dàxióngmāo Fánzhí Yánjiū Zhōngxīn; admission Y30; ☯ 8am-6pm) you can experience the *de rigueur* city activity: gushing over a panda.

The base holds nearly 50 giant and red pandas, although only a dozen are generally out and about. Breeding is the focus here (March to May is the 'falling in love period', wink wink) and if you visit in autumn, you may also have the opportunity to see tiny newborns in the 'nursery'. It costs Y50 to hold a baby red panda; Y400 to sit next to an adult panda; and a whopping Y1200 to hold a baby panda.

A museum has detailed exhibits on panda evolution, habits, habitats and conservation efforts, all with English captions.

Note that feeding takes place at around 9.30am and very soon thereafter the pandas return to their other favourite pastime – sleeping.

Getting to the base is tricky. Cycling is rough, as you run the risk of becoming road-kill on the congested streets. Bus 10 runs out to Qinglong, from where you'll have to change for bus 1 to the terminus. From here, hop on a motorised rickshaw to the breeding centre. A lot less hassle are the tours run by most guesthouses for Y50 including the entrance fee.

LIFE ON THE EDGE FOR THE GIANT PANDA *David Andrew*

The Giant Panda is one of the most instantly recognisable large mammals in the world, and in China you will see its moniker on everything from cigarette packs to souvenir tie pins. But although there are vague references to its existence in Chinese literature going back 3000 years, it was not until 1869 that a remarkable French curate-naturalist, Père Armand David, brought a pelt back to the West and formally described the Giant Panda to the scientific world. Endemic to China, it is now restricted to just five mountain ranges straddling the provinces of Sìchuān, Shaanxi and Gānsù, and is thought to number just 1000 or so individuals in the wild.

One Chinese name for the Giant Panda is *da xióngmāo* (big bear-cat), and it is so unlike other bears that scientists have long debated whether it in fact belongs to the raccoon family, or even whether it should be in a separate family of its own. Recent genetic evidence shows it to be a bear, and like other bears it has a carnivorous (meat-eating) ancestry. However, the similarities pretty well end there and almost every aspect of the Giant Panda's ecology and behaviour is adapted to a diet of bamboo. Bamboo is a poor food for a large, warm-blooded animal – it is low in protein and high in indigestible plant fibres, and barely provides enough nutrition to support the panda's metabolism. But it grows as a superabundant food resource in the damp, chilly mountains of southwest China, and through a suite of adaptations the Giant Panda has overcome the challenge of surviving on what is effectively woody grass.

Most famous of these adaptations is the 'panda's thumb' – not a real thumb, but a modified wrist bone that enables the Giant Panda to strip bamboo leaves from their branches, and to manipulate shoots and stems. Its rounded body shape (by bear standards, at least) and extremities conserve heat in winter, thus enabling the panda to feed year-round without hibernating. Its striking black-and-white coloration and prominent eye patches serve as a warning both to other pandas and to potential predators, since both social and threatening interactions would mean wasting precious energy.

However, the Giant Panda must still ingest an extraordinary amount of bamboo to extract its daily nutrition requirements. And just to make life interesting, every 25 or so years bamboos flower and die *en masse,* and the pandas must move to other feeding areas to survive. With the increased fragmentation of their natural forest habitat their choices for new feeding sites are limited, and in the mid-1970s more than 130 pandas starved to death when bamboos flowered and died in Mín Shān, Sìchuān.

With world attention focused on the panda's survival, the Chinese government has set up 11 panda reserves in the southwest and thrown itself behind a captive breeding program. Chinese laws now strictly forbid hunting or tree-felling in Giant Panda habitat. Peasants are offered rewards equivalent to double their annual salary if they save a starving panda, and life sentences or public executions are imposed on convicted poachers. Even though Giant Pandas are notoriously difficult to breed in captivity, Chéngdū's Giant Panda Breeding Research Base (p757) has recently had successes with the birth of a number of pandas. But sceptics would rather leave the pandas to their own devices and see more efforts made to preserve natural panda habitat; captive breeding has in only a very few cases been used successfully to save wild populations of large animals. And one cannot ignore the profit motive in China's burgeoning economy: Giant Pandas draw a crowd wherever they are displayed and nearly 200 are kept in China's zoos. Few, if any, captive-bred pandas have so far been released in the wild.

WENSHU TEMPLE 文殊院

This Tang dynasty monastery is Chéngdū's largest and best-preserved Buddhist temple. **Wenshu Temple** (Wénshū Yuàn; Renmin Zhonglu; admission Y5; 8am-5.30pm) epitomises a Buddhist temple – the air is redolent with incense, there's a low murmur of chanting, exquisite relief carvings, and best of all, there is a sense of serenity and solitude, despite the crowd of worshippers who flock to the temple. A vegetarian restaurant (p762) and two atmospheric teahouses (p762) are on the grounds.

The alleys surrounding the temple are their own curiosities, filled with joss-stick vendors, foot-callus removers, blind fortune-tellers with bamboo spills and, naturally, teahouses.

TOMB OF WANG JIAN 王建墓

In the northwest of town, the **Tomb of Wang Jian** (Wángjiàn Mù; Yongling Lu; admission Y40; 🕙 7am-7pm) was, until excavations undertaken in 1942, thought to be the pavilion in which Zhuge Liang (see Wuhou Temple, right) played his zither. Wang Jian (AD 847–918), a general who established the Former Shu kingdom after the collapse of the Tang in 907, ruled in a hands-off manner and during his reign agricultural output rose significantly.

The only mausoleum excavated in China so far that features above-ground tomb chambers, its main feature is a tomb surrounded by statues of 24 musicians all playing different instruments, considered to be the best surviving record of a Tang dynasty musical troupe.

ZHAOJUE TEMPLE 照觉寺

Zhaojue Temple (Zhàojué Sì; admission Y8; 🕙 7am-7pm) dates back to the 7th century although little remains of the original architecture. During the early Qing dynasty, it underwent extensive reconstruction under the supervision of Po Shan, a famous Buddhist monk who established waterways and groves around the temple. The temple has since served as a model for many Japanese and Southeast-Asian Buddhist temples.

The temple went through hard times during the Cultural Revolution and has only been restored during the last decade. There's a vegetarian restaurant on the grounds (p762) and a teahouse next door.

Zhaojue Temple is about 6km northeast of Chéngdū city centre. Loads of buses run to the nearby Zhaojue bus station (zhàojué chēzhàn) from around town. Cycling is possible though you risk asphyxiation from traffic fumes.

TEMPLE PARKS

West of the Mao statue is **Culture Park** (Wénhuà Gōngyuán; 🕙 7am-10pm), home to the **Green Ram Temple** (Qīngyáng Gōng; admission Y5; 🕙 7am-6.30pm), the oldest and most extensive Taoist temple in the Chéngdū area. What's with the name and the two bronze goats inside? Purportedly, Lao-tzu, the high priest of Taoism, was to meet a friend here. Arriving, the man saw only a boy leading two goats – and in an impressive leap of lateral thinking realised the boy was Lao-tzu. (The ungoat-like goat, by the way, combines features of all the Chinese zodiac animals. The other goat can vanquish life's troubles and pains if you stroke its flank.)

The highlight otherwise is an eight-sided pagoda – with no bolts or pegs used in construction – considered to be an architectural illustration of Taoist philosophy that 'the sky is round and the earth is square'.

The temple has excellent nightly performances of Sìchuān opera and theatrical performances.

It's well-nigh impossible not to find your muse at nearby **Du Fu's Cottage** (Dùfǔ Cǎotáng; 38 Qinghua Lu; admission Y60; 🕙 7am-7pm), former humble home of the revered Tang dynasty poet who has inspired countless generations of Chinese artists. Along with fellow Sìchuān poet Li Bai (Li Po), his work represents the zenith of Chinese poetry. Du Fu (AD 712–70) was born in Hénán but a young life of peregrination brought him to Chéngdū, where he lived for four years, penning more than 200 poems here on simple themes around the lives of the people who lived and worked nearby. Dance troupe performances are also given here regularly.

Next to **Nanjiao Park** (Nánjiāo Gōngyuán; admission Y2; 🕙 6am-10pm) is **Wuhou Temple** (Wǔhòu Sì; admission Y60; 🕙 6.30am-8pm), surrounded by picturesque gardens with mossy cypresses draped over walkways. Zhuge Liang was a legendary military strategist (known for his wisdom and culture) of the Three Kingdoms period (AD 220–80) and immortalised in one of the classics of Chinese literature, *The Romance of the Three Kingdoms*. The temple also features Sìchuān opera performances nightly. To the east of the temple is 'Jinli Lu', actually a gentrified (in the 'new-old' style of so many cities) historic district – during the Han Dynasty and Three Kingdom Period, this neighbourhood was filled with brocade workshops, and with alleys running north to the Jinjiang (the river) chock-full of shops, restaurants, pubs, teahouses and more.

In the southeast of town, near Sìchuān University, is **River Viewing Pavilion Park** (Wàngjiānglóu Gōngyuán; admission Y5; 🕙 6am-9pm). The impressive, restful, four-storey wooden Qing pavilion overlooking Brocade River was built in memory of Xue Tao, a female Tang dynasty poet with a great love for bamboo. Nearby is a well where Xue Tao is believed to have drawn water to dye her writing paper.

The park is justly celebrated for its bamboo and features over 150 varieties from China, Japan and Southeast Asia, ranging from bonsai-sized potted plants to towering giants.

PEOPLE'S PARK 人民公园

To the southwest of the city centre, **People's Park** (Rénmín Gōngyuán; admission Y2; ☯ 6am-8pm) is one Chinese park well worth visiting. The teahouse here draws most visitors (and locals after their taichi practice) for good reason (see p762).

Plopped in the middle of the park's bonsai and perennials is the **Monument to the Martyrs of the Railway Protection Movement** (1911). This obelisk memorializes an uprising of the people against corrupt officers who pocketed cash that was intended for railway construction. People's Park then was a private officer's garden, so it was a fitting place to erect the structure.

Across the lake from the teahouse is the entry to a one-of-a-kind underground **funhouse** (admission Y5). All aboard a ride on a rickety shuttle-train through a converted air-raid shelter (!), bypassing squeaky animatronic dioramas spanning the gamut: Wild West to Christmas via a horror movie and straight into the mouth of a shark. Tackily appealing.

SÌCHUĀN UNIVERSITY MUSEUM
四川大学博物馆

The **Sìchuān University Museum** (Sìchuān Dàxué Bówùguǎn) was one of the better museums in the southwest. The collection is particularly strong in the fields of ethnology, folklore and traditional art. Sadly, though, it's currently homeless, as the city's relocation of universities saw it bulldozed. It's tentatively slated to move to a location near Sòngxīnqiáo Art City (p763).

Sleeping
BUDGET

Chéngdū has a baker's dozen of backpacker-friendly places; nope, we do not have space for all!

Sim's Cozy Guesthouse (Guānhuá Qīngnián Lǚshè; ☎ 8691 4422; www.gogosc.com; 42 Xīzhù Shìjiè; 西珠市街42号; dm Y15-35, s/d without bathroom from Y50/70, with bathroom Y100/120; ✗ ✗ ⏸) A stone's throw from the serene Wenshu Temple, this rambling yet, well, cozy place in a century-old traditional building is run by a backpacker couple (he Singaporean, she Japanese) and the facilities, service and, true, warmth show they know the Road. Bottom line: it's that rare place where money doesn't seem to be the point. It's also got lovely minority-styled family rooms. Credit cards accepted.

Loft (Sìhào Gōngchǎng Lǚguǎn; ☎ 8626 5770; www.lofthostel.com; 4 Shangtongren Lu, Xiaotong Xiang; 同仁路4号小通巷; dm Y15-30, s/d without bathroom Y90/100, with bathroom Y140; ✗ ⏸) 'Chic hostel' is not oxymoronic here, a smart new place in an early 20th century printing factory. Billy, the friendly backpacker-owner and his team of artists painstakingly blended the original brick and wood work with new touches. A café serves Danish food, there's heat in winter and the relaxing top-floor loft has free internet.

Holly's Hostel (Jiǔlóngdǐng Qīngnián Kèzhàn; ☎ 8554 8131; Hollyhostelcn@yahoo.com; 246 Wuhouci Dajie; 武侯祠大街246号; dm Y20-30; ⏸) This boisterous place lies smack in the heart of the Tibetan quarter. Things are a tad cramped, but rooms are large and clean, and the staff are quite friendly.

Dragon Town Youth Hostel (Lóngtáng Kèzhàn; ☎ 8664 8408; www.dragontown.com.cn; 27 Kuan Xiangzi; 宽巷子27号; dm Y30, s/d without bathroom Y100, s/d with bathroom Y100/160; ✗ ⏸) Those wanting China-out-of-a-coffee table-book aesthetics need go no further. Tucked down a quiet back alley, this building – replete with courtyard – dates from the Qing dynasty. Rooms are clean and comfortable; staff are great. Honeymoon suites feature antique Chinese furniture.

MIDRANGE

There isn't much in the way of midrange options in Chéngdū, but fortunately all of the budget guesthouses have midrange value doubles for bargain prices.

Chéngdū Dàjiǔdiàn (☎ 8317 3888; 29 Renmin Beilu; 人民北路29号; d Y150-280; ✗) This place is a bit far north to be convenient for anything but the train station, but as the rooms are pretty much always on offer for a steep discount, it may be worth the trouble.

Jǐndì Fàndiàn (☎ 8691 5339; 8691 7778; 89 Xinhua Dadao; 新华大道89号; s/d Y220/280; ✗) Nicely located for sights and activities in the north of downtown (it's also off main drags and thus is a bit quieter), this place has always provided decent value for money.

Róngchéng Fàndiàn (☎ 8611 2933; 130 Shanxi Jie; 陕西街130号; d Y240; ✗) This place has cleaned up its act – that is, the rooms – quite a bit judging from a recent visit though the staff can be a bit flustered at times. Nice courtyard areas.

TOP END

With continuously growing competition, you may often get huge discounts (up to 40%) at top-end hotels during winter. A Shangri-la hotel (like a city-state) is in the works and if it matches the plans, it should be spectacular. The prices listed are what you can expect to pay during high season.

Tibet Hotel (Xīzàng Dàjiǔdiàn; ☎ 8318 3388; fax 8319 3838; 10 Renmin Beilu; 人民北路10号; s/d Y648/1330; ⊠ ⊠) The location is not the most convenient but the rooms here are beautifully decorated and the staff are lickety-split and solicitous. This hotel continually garners positive reviews from travellers.

Jǐnjiāng Bīnguǎn (☎ 8550 6666; www.jjhotel.com; 80, Section 2, Renmin Nanlu; 人民南路80号2段; d Y880-2200; ⊠ ⊠ 🖳) The first of the city's luxury hotels, this place has seen its ups and downs but of late has been upgrading with a bit of a verve to match – or exceed – any competition. The rooftop restaurant has superlative views.

Sheraton Chéngdū Lido Hotel (Tiānfú Lìdū Xīláidēng Fàndiàn; ☎ 8676 8999; www.sheraton.com/Chengdu; Section 1, 15 Renmin Zhonglu; 人民中路15号1段; d Y1310-2220; ⊠ ⊠ 🖳) Alternatively, one of the newer luxury – and that word is not misplaced here – hotels is this sybaritic place. Rooms aren't exactly spacious, but more than make up for it in careful appointment and décor.

Eating
CHINESE
Chinese people revere Sìchuān's hot and spicy cuisine (see boxed text, below). The most sali-

ent pepper flavour is *huājiāo* (*Xanthoxylon*, a wild pepper); some love it, some cringe at its over-the-top numbing effect (rural dentists purportedly use it as an anaesthetic) and say its aftertaste is a bit like a detergent.

You should also learn *xiǎo chī* (little eats); cheap, quick snacks are the way of life here. Popular with the on-the-fly lunchtime crowd is *shāokǎo*, Sichuanese barbecue. Skewers of meat, vegies and smoked tofu are brushed with oil and chilli and grilled.

Sadly, city officials have begun clearing many streets of itinerant roadside food stalls and instead of forming night markets for food, many have had to either close or move indoors. Yet prowling around you'll still find roadside stalls on back streets, many simply portable grills on bikes.

With more time you can savour *huǒguō* though it's becoming a bit of a yuppified sit-down affair. It's similar to fondue: dip skewered meat and vegies into big woks filled with hot, spiced oil and then into little dishes of peanut oil and garlic. Be forewarned – hotpot can be very hot; even many Sichuanese can't take it. To prevent the sweats, try asking for *báiwèi*, the hotpot for wimps. Peanut milk, sold in tins, can help arrest the dragonesque results.

Shìqiáo Shǒumiàn (Hongxing Lu; dishes Y2) This place serves up excellent bowls of filling noodles that you can watch being made fresh on

---

HOT & SPICY

The Chinese have a saying 'Shí zài Zhōngguó, wèi zài' Sìchuān' (China is the place for food but Sìchuān is the place for flavour). Flavour starts with mouth-singeing peppers. With such fiery food the Sichuanese themselves have a reputation for being a little hot-headed and the local women are even referred to as *là měizi* (spice girls). The province boasts a repertoire of over 5000 different dishes. This may be due to the province's history. 'Liáng Hú, Liáng Guǎng' translates as 'two Hus (Húběi and Húnán), two Guangs (Guǎngdōng and Guǎngxī)'. During an uprising, an enormous number of people in the province were slaughtered, and others from these provinces were forcibly relocated here by the emperor's troops, bringing their own cuisine with them. We'll just start with five of the most popular:

- *huíguō ròu* (boiled and stir-fried pork with salty and hot sauce; 回锅肉)
- *gōngbào jīdīng* (spicy chicken with peanuts; 宫保鸡丁)
- *shuǐzhǔ yú* (boiled fish in a fiery sauce; 水煮鱼)
- *gānbiān sìjìdòu* (dry-fried green beans; 干煸四季豆)
- *mápó dòufu* (pock-marked Mother Chen's bean curd; 麻婆豆腐)

The last two dishes can be made suitable for vegetarians, just ask them to leave out the meat 'bú fàng ròu' (不放肉).

the premises. The friendly staff are happy to cater to vegetarians.

Lóngchāoshǒu Cāntīng (cnr Chunxi Lu & Shandong Dajie; meals Y5-15) Run the whole gamut of the Chéngdū snack experience here at this long-time fave. The cheapest option gives you a range of sweet and savoury items, with each price bracket giving you the same deal on a grander and more filling scale. Unfortunately it hasn't much to offer vegetarians.

Chén Mápó Dòufu (Pockmarked Grandma Chen's Bean Curd; Jiefang Lu; dishes from Y5) *Mápó dòufu* is served here with a vengeance – soft, fresh bean curd with a fiery sauce of garlic, minced beef, salted soybean, chilli oil and fiery Sìchuān pepper. So popular is this place that a handful of franchise options are now found throughout town.

Bāguó Bùyī Fēngweijiǔlóu (4 Section, 20 Renmin Nanlu; dishes from Y10) This place is named after the traditional cotton clothing worn by peasants in an ancient state of eastern Sìchuān. Best described as country Sìchuān, the food here is superlative and the atmosphere (casually upscale) among the best in the province. An English menu helps, but it's more fun to wander and point.

VEGETARIAN

A special treat for vegetarians is to head out to the Wenshu Temple (p758) where there is an excellent vegetarian restaurant with an English menu (dishes Y6 to Y10).

Zhaojue Temple (p759) also serves up vegetarian dishes for lunch (from 11am to 3.30pm, dishes from Y8) and if you're really keen, you might ride out to Monastery of Divine Light (p765) in Xīndū, 18km north of Chéngdū, in time for lunch (11am to noon, dishes from Y7).

Most of the Western restaurants also feature vegetarian options on their menus.

WESTERN

The number of Western restaurants springing up in Chéngdū continues to grow and the following are just a few options.

Highfly Cafe (Gāofēi Kāfēi; ☎ 8544 2820; 18 Binjiang Zhonglu; dishes from Y12; ☼ 9am-late) The happy staff gets overwhelmed with hipster Chinese at times, but it's a relaxing place with great food; try the delicious calorie-laden fudge brownies. Free internet access.

Peter's Tex-Mex (Pídé Dézhōu Páfáng; ☎ 8522 7965; 117 Kehua Beilu; dishes from Y15; ☼ 7.30am-11pm) This place, with a jaw-dropping menu, gets a big-ol' cowboy *yee-haw* from carnivores and anyone who knows what it's like to be without refried beans and tortillas for too long. It's also – cool – wi-fi friendly.

Grandma's Kitchen & Deli (Zūmǔ Déchúfang; ☎ 8524 2835; 73/75 Kehua Beilu; mains from Y20) Burgers, steaks, salads and delicious desserts are great; a particular favourite are the shakes and smoothies. The deli here is also quite popular. A second branch, **Grandma's Kitchen** (☎ 8555 3856; 22 Renmin Nanlu) serves up similar dishes but has a more limited menu.

Drinking

TEAHOUSES

Positively nowhere in China more than Sìchuān better represents the culture of tea; hey, the 'art' of drinking tea dates back 3,000 years. Traditionally, the teahouse functioned as the centre of social life, a place where people had haircuts, watched opera performances, played cards, bantered over poetry, had their earwax removed (no kidding) and gossiped about their neighbours. A bit like going to the pub today, other than the earwax and opera.

Renmin Teahouse (Rénmín Cháguǎn; People's Park; tea Y5-20; ☼ 10am-6pm) This is one of Chéngdū's finest. A most pleasant afternoon can be spent here in relative anonymity over a bottomless cup of stone-flower tea.

Another charming family type teahouse is in Wenshu Temple (p758), with an amazingly crowded and steamy ambience. This is in addition to the huge tea garden outside – one of the largest and most lively in Chéngdū. If you want to join in, sit on the west side of the path, closest to the main temple, where tea costs Y2. The tea must be greener on the other side of the path where it costs Y10. Also, try the teahouse in **Temple of Mercy** (Dàcí Si; Dacisi Lu; admission Y1; ☼ 10am-6pm). The temple itself doesn't offer much to see, but the grounds, with tables piled high with mah jong pieces and teacups, are a perfect place for a lazy afternoon in the sun.

PUBS & BARS

Chinese media have finally begun to recognise Chéngdū as one of the country's most happening cities. Then again, like most Chinese cities, what is one week's hot spot is next week's ghost haunt with shuttered doors and a new Starbucks clone. Very problematic. Get hold of a copy of *Go West* (see p755) to keep up with the latest.

Shamrock Irish Bar & Restaurant (Sānyècǎo Àiěrlán Xīcān Jiǔbā; ☎ 8523 6158; 4 Section, 15 Renmin Nanlu; ☼ 10am-late) The name says it all – heavy on the Hibernian warmth and hospitality here. Great food during the day, then at night you'll hardly find a better spot for camaraderie and regular live music and/or dancing – you might find local rock acts, salsa, or even jazz.

Roo Bar (Dàdàishǔ Jiǔbā; ☎ 8540 1318; 6 Kehua Jie; ☼ 11.30am-2am) Equally boisterous – without as much live music – is this place, where in addition to your beer you can indulge in a burger with beetroot and egg, among other delicacies.

Entertainment

Chéngdū is the home of Sìchuān opera, which has a tradition dating back more than 250 years, and features slapstick, eyeglass-shattering songs, men dressed as women, gymnastics and even fire breathing. Several opera houses are scattered throughout the older sections of town, a couple of which are in temples listed above (the ones in the temples are pricey and filled with tourists). Many offer daily performances; some are weekends only. No matter where you go, it's a grand, fun-filled experience.

Try to go on the weekends when performances are often a combination of the highlights from a number of operas. Any of the guesthouses will be able to organise tours for a similar price; some even have local connections to possibly get you backstage.

Jinjiang Theatre (Jǐnjiāng Jùyuàn; Huaxingzheng Jie) This combination teahouse, opera theatre and cinema is one of the more centrally located. High-standard Sìchuān opera performances are given here every Saturday and/or Sunday afternoon (Y120 per person) though the teahouse itself often has performances for Y15!

Shopping

The main downtown shopping area extends from the eastern end of Renmin Donglu south to Shangdong Dajie, with trendy clothing shops and department stores. Glitzy department store complexes are pretty much ubiquitous now.

Qingshiqiao Market (Qīngshíqiáo Shìchǎng; Xinkai Jie) This large market is one of the most interesting and busiest places to wander in town. Shops and stalls sell brightly coloured seafood, flowers, cacti, birds, pets and a thousand dried foods.

South of the river, on a street across from the entrance of the Wuhou Temple, is a small Tibetan neighbourhood. While it's not evident in the architecture, it is in the prayer flags, colourful scarves, beads and brass goods for sale. You won't find the variety of things (nor the bargains) that you'll find in the northwest of Sìchuān, but it still makes for an interesting wander.

Sòngxīnqiáo Yìshùchéng (Songxinqiao Art City; Qinghua Jie) Not far from Du Fu's Cottage (p759), this large covered market features a selection of stalls selling art and antiques. It's not cheap but worth a browse.

Outdoor clothing and equipment are a big buy in the city (lots of folks headed into the western hills and Tibet, natch). **Mountain Dak Outdoor Sports Club** (Gāoshān Hùwài Lǚyóu Tànxiǎn Yòngpǐn) and **Airwolf** (Fēiláng Hùwài) are located near Highfly Café. Another half-dozen are to the south along Renmin Nanlu at the corner of Nan Yihuan Lu. Quality varies; experts don't call a lot of it 'North Fake' for nothing.

Tóng Rén Táng (Tong Ren Tang Pharmacy; 1 Zongfu Lu) Even if your knowledge of Chinese medicine is zilch, this traditional Chinese pharmacy, over 260 years old, is a superb place to just browse and gape at the enormity of knowledge accrued over four millennia.

Getting There & Away

AIR

Flights internally go everywhere, virtually all the time. Whatever you do, shop around; outside of highest periods posted rates should mean little. Internal destinations include Běijīng (Y1440, 2¼hr), Chóngqìng (Y440, 45 minutes), Dàlián (Y1810, 3½hr), Shànghǎi (Y1660, two hours and 20 minutes), Guǎngzhōu (Y1300, one hour and 50 minutes), Lìjiāng (Y880, one hour), Kūnmíng (Y700, one hour) and Xī'ān (Y630, one hour and 20 minutes).

Within Sìchuān there are four flights a day to Jiuhuang Airport (Y700, 40 minutes), the new air link for Jiǔzhàigōu and Sōngpān in northern Sìchuān.

International destinations include Hong Kong (Y2200, 2½hr), Tokyo (Y3000, 6½hr), Singapore (Y1900, four hours and 20 minutes), Seoul, and Bangkok (Y1700, two hours and 55 minutes). Flights should operate between Amsterdam, Vienna, and Macau by the time you read this.

CHÉNGDŪ BUS TIMETABLES

Buses from Xīnnánmén bus station:

Destination	Price	Duration	Frequency	Departs
Éméi	Y33	2hr	every 20min	6.40am-7pm
Dūjiāngyàn	Y17	1½hr	half-hourly	8-noon
Kāngdìng	Y98-122	6-8hr	hourly	7am-2pm
Lèshān	Y36	2hr	every 20min	7.30am-7.30pm
Jiǔzhàigōu	Y110	12-13hr		8am

For northern destinations you will need to trek over to the Chadianzi bus station in the northwest of the city.

Destination	Price	Duration	Frequency	Departs
Dūjiāngyàn	Y16	1½hr	every 40 minutes	7am-8pm
Jiǔzhàigōu	Y110	12-13hr	4 daily	7.20am, 8am, 8.40am, 4pm
Sōngpān	Y74	8hr	3 daily	6.30am, 7am, 7.30am
Wòlóng	Y24	4hr	daily	11.40am
Xiǎojīn	Y46	7hr	4 daily	6.30am, 7am, 7.30am, noon

For eastern and northeastern destinations your best bet is to try the north bus station, near the north train station. However, to get to Dazu, you'll most likely need to head to Wuguiqiao bus station outside the second ring road.

Destination	Price	Duration	Frequency	Departs
Éméi	Y33	2hr	half-hourly	6.30am-5.25pm
Chóngqìng	Y85-105	4-4½hr	hourly	7.30am-5pm
Dūjiāngyàn	Y16	1½hr	every 20 min	7am-6pm
Lèshān	Y36	2hr	every 40 min	6.40am-7pm
Lǎngzhōng	Y89	5hr	daily	8.30am

Airline offices in Chéngdū include:

Air China (Zhōngguó Mínháng; ☎ 8666 1100; 41, Section 2, Renmin Nanlu ☾ 8am-7.30pm).

Sìchuān Airlines (Sìchuān Hángkōng Gōngsī; ☎ 8665 7163, 8665 4858; 31, Section 2, Renmin Nanlu)

Dragon Air (Gǎnglóng Hángkōng Gōngsī; ☎ 8676 8828; Tiānfǔ Lìdū Xīláidēng Fàndiàn; Section 1, 15 Renmin Zhonglu). In the Sheraton Chéngdū Lido Hotel.

BUS

Connections in Chéngdū are more comprehensive than in other parts of the southwest. High-speed expressways from Chéngdū to Chóngqìng and Lèshān have greatly cut down travel time. More are under construction.

Xīnnánmén bus station in the southern part of town is the main bus station and has tickets to most places around Sìchuān.

See box above for bus times. Note that some destinations have departures from more than one station; not all can be listed so double-check with your guesthouse or hotel.

TRAIN

To repeat – *ad infinitum* – though train tickets are a lot easier to land these days, don't expect next-day middle-berth hard sleeper miracles for the most popular routes. Almost all the hostels can book tickets for trains (with a fee of around Y20) but read that note about miracles again. To wit: expect everyone and their dog to be trying to get on the Chéngdū–Lhasa train.

Daily departures include Kūnmíng (Y248, 18 hours), Éméi (Y22, two hours), Chóngqìng (Y91, 11 hours; express Y118, five hours), Běijīng (Y405, 26 hours) and Xī'ān (Y122, 18 hours). A high-speed train line has recently started between Chéngdū and Miányáng; another to Lèshān was close to finished at the time of writing. The express to Chóngqìng that started in 2006 is nearly as fast as the bus.

TO TIBET

OK, listen up, as this is topic *numero uno* in Chéngdū. As the Lhasa Express train opened service in October 2006 (see p924 for details), rumours abounded that the Chinese government would at some point ease the maddening, through-the-looking-glass regulations regarding travel to the Roof of the World.

That is, no, you still cannot fly solo and yes, you still must sign on for a 'tour' with a travel agency (in order to get the required Tibetan travel permit) – all guesthouses do this as necessary means of economic survival. You may have twenty people in your guesthouse's 'tour group' but you'll never see them again after you get off the plane. Yes, it's still an absurd shakedown. If the permits are canned and solo travellers are allowed in, outstanding; we'll believe it when we see it.

At the time of writing these packages were priced at about Y1900 including flights and were the most cost-effective way of getting into Tibet. CITS runs its own four to six day tours (Y2000 to Y4000).

If you can arrange for a permit from a travel agency (unlikely) you can try picking up a ticket from one of the airlines yourself; regulations change and travellers occasionally – no, rarely – get lucky. Just make sure you have the cash on hand to buy the ticket before they change their mind. Another trick is to ask for a 1st-class ticket.

Sìchuān's land borders into Tibet are still closed to foreigners. Some travellers attempt to sneak across but the majority are turned back and fined heavily. Don't believe anyone who says they can drive you to Lhasa; they can't. Stories of travellers being dumped off in the middle of nowhere once they've crossed the border into Tibet (minus their bags and money) are not uncommon. The US State Department in 2006 was reporting incidents of travellers being physically assaulted by authorities after they were caught.

Getting Around
TO/FROM THE AIRPORT
Shangliu Airport is 18km west of the city. Bus 303 (Y10) is actually an airport bus which leaves from outside the Air China office on Renmin Nanlu; *another* Bus 303 (Y1) is a local bus running to/from the north railway station, taking pretty much forever.

Sìchuān Airlines provides a free shuttle from your hotel to the airport if you purchase your ticket with them. A taxi will cost around Y70.

BICYCLE
Cycling is a great way to get around Chéngdū although the pollution (and traffic) can be terrible. Guesthouses rent bikes for about Y10 per day. The bikes are in fairly good condition but the usual rules apply: check your bike before you cycle off and make an effort to park it in a designated parking area. See Dangers & Annoyances p757).

BUS
The most useful bus is 16, which runs from Chéngdū's north train station to the south train station (*nán chēzhàn*) along Renmin Nanlu. Regular buses cost Y1, while the double-deckers cost Y2. Bus 81 runs from the Mao statue to Green Ram Temple and bus 12 circles the city along Yihuan Lu, starting and ending at the north train station. Bus 4 runs from the centre of town to Chadianzi bus station and Wuguiqiao bus station.

SUBWAY
In 2006 ground was broken (immediately snarling traffic) on the city's new subway, slated for a 2010 completion. When finished it will be one of the most extensive in China; expect traffic headaches till the day it's done.

TAXI
Taxis have a flag fall of Y5 (Y6 at night), plus Y1.4 per kilometre. Motorised rickshaws also scuttle around the city and are cheaper, but slower, than cabs.

AROUND CHÉNGDŪ
Monastery of Divine Light 宝光寺
In Xindu County, 18km north of Chéngdū, this is an active Buddhist temple complex founded in the 9th century (some parts date from the first century). The **Monastery of Divine Light** (Bǎoguāng Sì; admission Y5; ⏱ 8am-5.30pm) houses treasures including a white jade buddha from Myanmar (Burma), Ming and Qing paintings, calligraphy, a stone tablet engraved with 1000 Buddhist figures and ceremonial musical instruments. The 19th century **Arhat Hall** contains 500 2m-high clay figurines of Buddhist saints and disciples (and one of Boddhidarma).

Buses run to the monastery from a stop about 600m east of Chéngdū's north train station and north bus station from around 6am to 6pm. The trip takes just under an hour. On a Chinese bicycle, the round trip would be about 40km, or at least four hours cycling time.

SÌCHUĀN

Sānxīngduī 三星堆

Forty kilometres north of Chéngdū, west of Guǎnghàn, is a site some Chinese archaeologists regard as more important than the terracotta warriors of Xī'ān (gasp!). The smashing exhibits (with English captions) of **Sanxingdui Museum** (Sānxīngduī Bówùguǎn; ☎ 0838-550 0349; admission Y80; ☟ 8.30am-5pm; Y80) retell a gripping story: throughout the 20th century farmers continually unearth intriguing pottery shards and other dirt-encrusted detritus, but prevailing wisdom (and war and lack of funds) prevents anyone from taking it seriously. Until 1986, that is, when archaeologists finally launched a full-scale excavation. And – presto! – a major site of the kingdom of Shu was unearthed, a site considered the cradle of Chinese civilization in the upper reaches of the Yangzi River.

Buses run from Zhaojue (and possibly Xinnanmen) bus station to Guǎnghàn (Y10, two hours); from there you'll have to hop on bus 1 or 6 (Y2) for the remaining 10km to the site. You could also come here after a quick stop in Xindu and the Monastery of Divine Light.

Qīngchéng Shān 青城山

A holy Taoist mountain some 65km west of Chéngdū, with a summit of only 1600m, **Qīngchéng Shān** (Azure City Mountain; Y60) is an excellent day trip into the subtropics. It offers beautiful trails lined with gingko, plum and palm trees, boatloads of temples, picturesque vistas and plenty of atmospheric sights along its four-hour return route. The weather here is better than Éméi Shān, so the views are far less likely to be obscured by mist and cloud. It's also a far easier climb.

Note: the front of the mountain is chock-a-block with Chéngdū day-trippers clamouring for the Yuèchéng Hú (Yuecheng Lake) ferry (Y5) and then the cable car (one way/return Y30/50) to the near-summit.

Thus, the secret: head instead for **Qīngchéng Hòushān** (青城后山, Azure City Back Mountain) some 15km northwest of the base of Qīngchéng Shān proper. With over 20km of hiking trails, this mountain offers a more natural environment, with **Five Dragon Gorge** (Wǔlóng Gōu) offering dramatic vistas. Not a few travellers who come here spend several days. There is a cable car to help with part of the route, but climbing the mountain will still require an overnight stay; you won't want to rush the trip anyway.

SLEEPING & EATING

Besides pricey resort-style (and a few budget) hotels on the road leading up to Qīngchéng Shān's main gate, there are atmospheric temples on the mountain.

Shangqing Temple (Shàngqīng Gòng; dm Y36-60, d Y120) This charming wooden temple offers hotel-like facilities. Rooms are basic and clean and have common balconies that look out over the surrounding forests. The restaurant here serves up excellent food; its omelettes are especially good.

More restaurants, as well as snack stands and noodle stops, are scattered along Qīngchéng Shān's trails.

At Qīngchéng Hòushān there's accommodation in Great Peace Temple (Tài'ān Gé), at the mountain's base, or at Youyi Village (Yòuyī Cūn), about halfway up. Dorm beds at both are around Y15.

GETTING THERE & AWAY

To get to Qīngchéng Shān you generally must first travel to Dūjiāngyàn, 25km away. Buses run to Dūjiāngyàn (Y16, 1½ hours, 7am to 8pm) from Chéngdū's Chadianzi bus station,

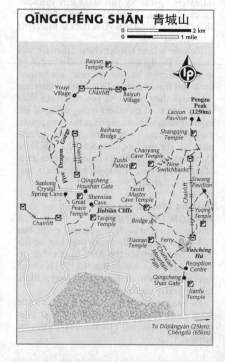

QĪNGCHÉNG SHĀN 青城山

0 —————— 2 km
0 —————— 1 mile

Baiyun Temple
Youyi Village
Chairlift
Baiyun Village
Pengzu Peak
Laojun Pavilion (1250m)
Shangqing Temple
Baihang Bridge
Five Dragon Gorge
Chairlift
Chaoyang Cave Temple
Nine Switchbacks
Zushi Palace
Taoist Master Cave Temple
Siwang Pavilion
Sanlong Crystal Spring Cave
Qingcheng Houshan Gate
Shenxian Cave
Chairlift
Yuqing Temple
Great Peace Temple
Jīnbiān Cliffs
Taiqing Temple
Bridge
Tianran Temple
Ferry
Yuèchéng Hú
Chunian Mountain Path
Reception Centre
Chairlift
Qingcheng Shan Gate
Jianfu Temple
To Dūjiāngyàn (25km); Chéngdū (65km)

departing when full. From Dūjiāngyàn frequent minibuses roll for the mountain, stopping at Qīngchéng Shān (Y4) and then Qīngchéng Hòushān (Y10). The last bus to Dūjiāngyàn leaves Qīngchéng Hòushān around 7pm. During the high season there are likely to be buses running directly between Chéngdū's bus stations and Qīngchéng Shān.

Dūjiāngyàn Irrigation Project
都江堰水利工程

Some 60km northwest of Chéngdū, the **Dūjiāngyàn Irrigation Project** (Dūjiāngyàn Shuĭlì Gōngchéng; admission Y60; ⊙ 6am-8pm) was undertaken in the 3rd century BC by prefect and engineer Li Bing to divert the fast-flowing Min River via weirs into irrigation canals (Chéngdū's riverside parks are an extension of the project). The Min River was subject to flooding at this point, yet when it subsided, droughts could ensue.

Li Bing's most brilliant idea was to devise an annual maintenance plan to remove silt build-up. Thus the mighty Mín was tamed and nary a flood has hit the Chéngdū plain since. Difficult enough today, positively Herculean then; the guy deserves every accolade.

The project is ongoing (and, naturally, modernising); it originally irrigated over a million hectares of land and since 1949 this has expanded to three million hectares. A good overall view of the outlay can be gained from **Èrwáng Miào** (Two Kings Temple), which commemorates Li Bing and his son, Er Lang.

While the whole idea of visiting a mocha-coloured, massive irrigation project may not be everyone's cup of tea, remember that were it not for Li Bing and his mountain-moving spirit, there would be no Sìchuān as we know it today.

GETTING THERE & AWAY

Buses run regularly to Dūjiāngyàn's bus station (in the south of town) from the Chadianzi bus station in Chéngdū (Y16, 1½ hours, 7am to 8pm). The last bus back to Chéngdū leaves around 8pm. There is also a direct bus from Dūjiāngyàn to Wòlóng (Y40.5, 2½ hours) at 8am and 2pm.

Bus 1 runs to the irrigation project from outside the bus station.

Wolong Nature Reserve
卧龙自然保护区

Wolong Nature Reserve (Wòlóng Zìrán Bǎohùqù; admission Y40) lies 140km northwest of Chéngdū, about four hours by bus (via Dūjiāngyàn). A UN-designated International Biosphere Reserve it's the largest (200,000 hectares) of the 16 panda conservation reserves (of these, 11 are in Sìchuān), and one which in 2005 and 2006 the Chinese government dropped more than a half-million US dollars to upgrade.

The **Giant Panda Breeding Station** (Dàxióngmāo Sìyǎng Chǎng; admission Y30; ⊙ 8am-noon & 1.30-5pm) is home to some 80 pandas that have been artificially bred in captivity. Techniques and facilities have improved so much that in 2005 11 females gave birth to 16 cubs; stunningly, and happily, all had survived through 2006. However, there is little chance of seeing a panda in the wild; the pandas have a hard enough time finding each other. In spring, the park is closed so that trekkers don't disturb the pandas' hunt for each other during their mating season.

The rainy season is a bad time to be here as leeches take over the park. Summer is the most popular time to visit. Doesn't much matter, as all year trekking here is fairly tough and the trails are faint. Other animals protected here are the golden monkey, takin, deer and snow leopard. The Park Administration Office in Wòlóng village (also called Shawan), at the centre of the reserve, can give information on hiking trails and researchers at the breeding station (some of whom speak English) are good sources of info on conditions. Be sure to bring your own supplies, including warm clothing.

And if you can't get here, you can check out the utterly cool 'Panda Cam' set up by the reserve on the internet (www.pandaclub.net).

At the breeding station, 6km from Wòlóng village, the **Panda Inn** (☎ 0837-624 3028; fax 0837-624 3014; d Y200) has clean, comfortable doubles with hot showers and heaters. There is also a restaurant in the hotel and barbecue stalls across the road.

Wòlóng village also has a so-so **museum** (☎ 624 6912; admission Y20; ⊙ 9am-noon & 1pm or 2-5pm), which is useful, however, for maps.

GETTING THERE & AWAY

One bus leaves daily from Chéngdū's Chadianzi bus station to Wòlóng village (Y24, four hours, 11.40am). If you miss that bus then head over to Dūjiāngyàn from where buses to Wòlóng run twice daily (Y12, 2½hr, 8am and 2pm). If you want to get dropped at the Conservation Centre, rather than Wòlóng village, be sure to tell the bus driver.

Onward buses continue on from Wòlóng village over the 4487m Bulangshan Pass to Rìlóng and Xiǎojīn, from where you can catch buses to Kāngdìng (p778). Schedules on these routes are irregular.

LǍNGZHŌNG 阆中
☎ 0817 / pop 112,000

Those decrying the demise of 'old' Chéngdū should immediately hop on a bus for this funky little town some 220km northeast of the capital. A significant chunk of it time has forgotten and tourists have overlooked, for the most part: photo-ops of endless black-tile roofs with swooping eaves overlooking the narrowest of alleys, flagstone streets and temples atop misty hills across a river. World Heritage site à la Píngyáo (Shānxī) or Lìjiāng (Yúnnán) it ain't – call it Lìjiāng Lite – but Lǎngzhōng has Sìchuān's largest grouping of extant traditional architecture and, in fact, was the capital for 17 years during the Qing dynasty. It has been the centre of provincial/regional/kingdom politics and economics for much of its 2300 years.

Orientation & Information

The town is sits on a peninsula surrounded by Jiālíng Hé and is laid out according to a traditional Tang dynasty plan. Zhangfei Lu is the main artery running roughly north–south through town. At the intersection with Xincun Lu as it heads west is a statue memorialising Zhang Fei; the old town is southwest of here.

No banks handle traveller's cheques or credit card issues.

An internet café (Y2 per hour) is not far from the corner of Dadong Jie and Neidong Jie in the old town.

Sights

Lǎngzhōng would require an entire book just to list the dozens of amazing sights, many of which showcase the town's rich history in advanced learning. Here astronomer Hong Luoxia developed the first complete written calendar and the world's first astronomical instrument (an achievement still feted by Unesco annually). Gòng Yuàn (Xuedao Jie; admission Y17; ☒ around 8am-5pm), a prime example, is the best-preserved imperial examination hall in China.

Most people will be happy just wandering the alleys and gaping at the eclectic architecture – a wondrous blend of North China quadrangle and South China garden styles. Most tourists head directly for **Zhang Fei Temple** (Zhāngfēi Miào; Xi Jie; admission Y30), the tomb of and shrine to local boy done good Zhang Fei, a respected general during the kingdom of Shu who administered the kingdom from here.

Across the river to the south and east you can have a grand time exploring. At the foot of Mt Daxiang sits the sedate-looking **Grand Buddha** (Dàfó Sì; 大佛), one of the largest buddha statues in Sìchuān. Nearby, among Buddhist statuary, grottoes, and caves littering the hillsides, is **No 1 Scholars Cave** (Zhuàngyuán Dòng; 状元洞), where two legendary court officials crammed for their examinations.

Sleeping & Eating

The modern town has loads of perfectly fine hotels, but a couple of options exist in the old town to let you really soak up the atmosphere.

Xīnyuè Kèzhàn (欣悦客栈; ☎ 801 9674; 100 Nanjie; 南街100号; s/d without bathroom Y100) Utterly unassuming as you walk past, this place is nonetheless a treat, with small and simple but spotless rooms (with clean facilities) and unvanquishably helpful owners – a real mom-and-pop kind of place.

Dùjiā Kèzhàn (杜家客栈; ☎ 622 4436; 63 Xiaxin Jie; 下新街63号; s/d from Y140/200; ☒) The finest option in Lǎngzhōng, this inn is housed in the largest – and one of the oldest – courtyard structure in town (seriously, leave a popcorn trail). Rooms run from basic but comfortable to sybaritically well-appointed. It's roaringly popular with tour groups who come for the tea, the food, and the legendary Lǎngzhōng leather puppet shows.

One thing you'll notice is the air redolent with essence of vinegar – indeed, everything is pickled here. Indeed, Lǎngzhōng has been one of China's four vinegar production centres for centuries; local recipes are guarded as seriously as those of Coke or any Scotch whisky distillery. You'll find infinite varieties of local soft drinks using this, er, unique brew. You'll also find – we kid you not – public vinegar bathhouses! Famed local fare otherwise includes *zhāngfēi niúròu* (local preserved beef) and myriad noodle soup variations – two faves being noodles cooked in goat entrails, or noodles in (naturally) pickled vegetables and bean curd.

Dàoxiāngcūn Jiǔjiā (稻香村酒家; ☎ 626 6333; Xincun Lu; 新村路; dishes from Y10) The old town has loads of great snacking joints, but this sit-down restaurant a bit outside the alleys hearkens back to the old days, with its rustic décor.

Getting There & Away
BUS
The town has two bus stations. The main one is north of the Zhang Fei statue, but you may be dropped off at the smaller one to the south. Buses to Chéngdū (Y89, five hours, 8am) are infrequent but this should change, as the province plans to upgrade highways in order to develop the town's tourism industry. Buses to Guǎngyuán (Y39, 5-6 hours) leave throughout the morning and wind their carsick-inducing way through the hills; from here you have train and bus options towards Xī'ān or west into the rough terrain of northern Sìchuān.

GUǍNGYUÁN
☎ 0839 / pop 213,200
This minor manufacturing centre roughly equidistant between Chéngdū and Xī'ān is the main hub to get to many of the sights in northeastern Sìchuān. The ancient Shǔdào, or the 'Way to Sìchuān' (which impelled Li Bai to brush his famous lines 'The way to Shu is harder than the way to heaven' – to translate it roughly) sliced right through what is the modern city. It's the site of China's largest nuclear weapons-grade plutonium production facility, so nobody really lingers here, but the locals sure are friendly.

Orientation
The city is separated into three chunks, split by Nán Hé and Jiālíng Hé. The train station and one of the two bus stations sits on the east side of a peninsula formed by the rivers' confluence. Another bus station is southwest, across a bridge over Nán Hé (any bus from the train station will go there). The main road is Shumen Lu, running through the heart of the city.

Sights
HUANGZE TEMPLE 皇泽寺
China's only female emperor (during the Tang dynasty), Wu Zetian, was born in Guǎngyuán, and she is feted among the temples, pavilions and 1000-odd statues lining the modest` cliffs at this **temple** (Huángzé Sì; admission Y15), on the west bank of the Jiālíng Hé.

Sleeping
Few cheap options (figure Y25 or so for a bed in a common room) exist, and these are all in the vicinity of the train station.

Bāshǔ Bīnguǎn (巴蜀宾馆; ☎ 288 7555; 46 Nanjie; 南街46号; s/d Y50-150) A block west of Shumen Lu, this is about the only cheap option downtown; luckily, it's decent. Every lodging option downtown is an overpriced two- or three-star option.

Getting There & Away
All trains running between Chéngdū and Xī'ān stop here and are your best option for the latter. To Chéngdū both bus stations have loads of buses, including expresses (Y80, three to four hours). From the bus station opposite the train station there are also buses to Jiǔzhàigōu (Y91, 10 to 12 hours).

ZHĀOHUÀ 昭化
Horses and carts clattering down slabstone streets, little old men shuffling along slurping their swamp-water tea or puffing on pipes, Ming and Qing architecture everywhere. By all appearances a Chinese movie set, but nope, tiny Zhāohuà is the real deal, another village that time forgot to take with it. The main – and pretty much only – street **Tài Shǒu Jiē** stretches between famed village gates, fragments of which (they claim) date from the Three Kingdoms era. There's but one tiny inn to stay in, but **Yí Xín Yua'n** (Y10-100) oozes history.

To get there buses (Y9, one hour) run from Guǎngyuán's southern bus station (not the one at the train station); they leave as they fill up, so you may have a wait. Don't start your trip here too late, as return buses taper off in the mid-afternoon.

ÉMÉI SHĀN 峨眉山
☎ 0833 / elevation 3099m
A cool, misty retreat from the Sìchuān basin's sweltering heat, Éméi Shān, 130km southwest of Chéngdū, is one of the Middle Kingdom's four famous Buddhist mountains (the others are Pǔtuóshān, Wǔtái Shān and Jiǔhuá Shān). Here you'll find lush mountain scenery, plantations of tea trees, scads of temples, macaques demanding tribute for safe passage, and the chance to see a sunrise so splendorous that you're considered blessed to see it. On the rare afternoon there is also a phenomenon known as Buddha's Aureole where rainbow rings,

produced by refraction of water particles, attach themselves to a person's shadow in a cloud bank below the summit. Devout Buddhists, thinking this was a call from yonder, used to jump off the Cliff of Self-Sacrifice in ecstasy.

Éméi Shān has little of its original temple-work left (from 100 odd temples dating from the advent of Buddhism in China). Glittering Jinding Temple (Jīndǐng Sì), with its brass tiling engraved with Tibetan script, was completely gutted by fire. Other temples suffered the same, and all were nicked to a various degree by war with the Japanese and Red Guard looting.

The waves of pilgrims, tourists and hawkers during peak season quickly eliminate solitude on the mountain but they do add to the atmosphere. The crowds hover largely around the monasteries; away from them, the path is not lined so much with stalls as with the fir, pine and cedar trees that clothe the slopes. Lofty crags, cloud-kissing precipices, butterflies and azaleas together form a nature reserve, and the mountain proudly joins Lèshān and Jiǔzhàigōu on Unesco's list of World Heritage sites.

Tickets
Tickets for Éméi Shān (Y120) include having your mug shot scanned onto the ticket which is then laminated – a ready-made souvenir. Entry to Declare Nation Temple and Crouching Tiger Monastery at the foot of the mountain do not require this ticket and have their own admission charge (see p772).

Internet Access 网吧
Two large internet cafés are a five-minute walk east of Declare Nation Temple (see p772); the Teddy Bear Hotel (see p773).

Climate
The best time to visit Éméi Shān is between May and October. Visiting in winter will present some trekking problems – iron soles with spikes can be hired to deal with encrusted ice and snow on the trails. Snowfall generally starts around November on the upper slopes. Try to avoid visiting during national holidays when the number of visitors to the mountain reaches epic proportions.

Temperate zones start at 1000m. Cloud cover and mist are prevalent all year round at Éméi Shān and generally interfere with views

of the sunrise. If you're very lucky, you'll be able to see Gònggā Shān (Gongga Mountain) to the west; if you're not so lucky, you'll have to settle for the less appealing Telecom tower and the meteorological station. Or, perhaps not even your hand in front of your face. Some average temperatures in degrees Celsius are:

Location	Jan	Apr	Jul	Oct
Éméi town	7	21	26	17
summit	6	3	12	-1

What to Bring
Definitely not your entire pack. Nevertheless, Éméi Shān is a tall *and steep* one at 3099m, so the weather is uncertain and it's best to prepare for sudden changes without weighing yourself down. The Teddy Bear Hotel (p773), stores bags for free (other places may levy a small charge).

Monasteries have no heating or insulation, but blankets are provided and some even have (godsend) electric blankets. You can also hire heavy overcoats at the top. Heavy rain can be a problem, as even a light mist can make the slate steps slippery and extremely treacherous. A good pair of rough-soled shoes or boots is a must. Flimsy plastic rainwear is sold on the mountain.

A fixed-length umbrella would be most useful – for the rain and as a walking stick and perhaps a warning to the brigand monkeys. The Teddy Bear Hotel (p773) lends walking sticks out for free. A torch (flashlight) is important if you're spending the night or planning to hike at dawn. Food stalls are ubiquitous; nevertheless, extra munchies wouldn't hurt. Finally, don't forget toilet paper.

Travellers have become sick from contaminated water supplies on the mountain; it's wise to drink only the bottled water available at stands along the way.

Routes
The most popular route up/down the mountain is to ascend via Long Life Monastery, Chu Temple (Chū Sì), Elephant Bathing Pool and on to the summit. On the way down, take the path off towards Magic Peak Monastery after you reach Elephant Bathing Pool. This path will also lead you past Venerable Trees Terrace (Hóngchūn Píng) and Pure Sound Pavilion. The majority of hikers agree that the descent is superior in sights and views.

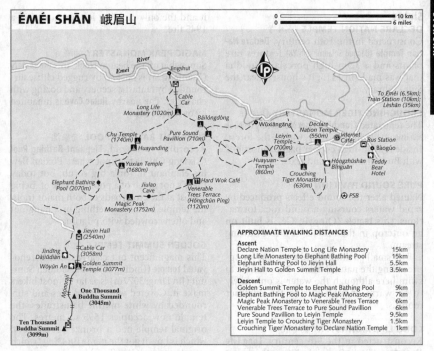

ÉMÉI SHĀN 峨眉山

APPROXIMATE WALKING DISTANCES

Ascent
Declare Nation Temple to Long Life Monastery	15km
Long Life Monastery to Elephant Bathing Pool	15km
Elephant Bathing Pool to Jieyin Hall	5.5km
Jieyin Hall to Golden Summit Temple	3.5km

Descent
Golden Summit Temple to Elephant Bathing Pool	9km
Elephant Bathing Pool to Magic Peak Monastery	7km
Magic Peak Monastery to Venerable Trees Terrace	6km
Venerable Trees Terrace to Pure Sound Pavillion	6km
Pure Sound Pavillion to Leiyin Temple	9.5km
Leiyin Temple to Crouching Tiger Monastery	1.5km
Crouching Tiger Monastery to Declare Nation Temple	1km

Buses go up the mountain from the bus station in Bàoguó village, near the Teddy Bear Hotel. Bus routes and prices are posted at the Bàoguó bus station and at the stops en route. A ride to the top costs Y30, to Wǔxiāngǎng costs Y10 and a return trip with a number of stops is Y60. Buses run half-hourly from approximately 6am to 5pm but you don't want to cut it too close on the way down – if you miss the last bus, it's a 15km walk down from Long Life Monastery.

One popular option is to take a bus to Wǔxiāngǎng and begin hiking from here. Alternatively stay on till Jìngshuǐ, from where you can get a cable car (up/down/return Y40/30/60, 6am to 6pm) up to Long Life Monastery. From the top of the cable car you can join the route to the summit. Buses run as far up the mountain as Jieyin Hall (Jiēyǐn Diàn; two hours) from where it's a steep two-hour hike or five-minute cable car ride (one way/return Y40/50) to the top.

For an epic one-day trek, most hotels can book you on a bus leaving at 3.30am (!), popular with Chinese tourists to 'cheat' and see the sunrise sweatlessly. BUT expect an immense traffic jam at the entrance gate followed by an enormous queue of tourists. Few actually make it in time.

These buses begin to head down from Jieyin Hall around mid-morning, stopping at various temples along the way and finally bringing you back to Bàoguó at around 5pm. The round trip costs about Y60 and will probably leave your head spinning.

Duration

Time? Well, you'll be told wildly different times by everyone you meet. While you don't require any particular hiking skills, it's a tough climb. It's possible to make it to the summit from Long Life Monastery and back down to Declare Nation Temple in two days but you must be willing to spend at least 10 hours hiking each day and hope for good weather. The altitude may play havoc with your breathing and ascending too quickly will only increase this. All up, it's wise to leave yourself three days for the trek.

The approximate distances on the map will give you an idea of what is involved; time yourself on the first kilometre or two and then average out your own probable duration.

Sights

DECLARE NATION TEMPLE 报国寺
Constructed in the 16th century, **Declare Nation Temple** (Bàoguó Sì; admission Y8) features rare plants and a 3.5m-high porcelain Buddha that was made in 1415; it's housed near the Sutra Library.

CROUCHING TIGER MONASTERY 伏虎寺
The renovated **Crouching Tiger Monastery** (Fúhǔ Sì; admission Y6) is hidden deep within the forest. Inside is a 7m-high copper pagoda inscribed with Buddhist images and texts.

PURE SOUND PAVILION 清音阁
Named after the sound effects produced by rapid waters coursing around rock formations, this **temple** (Qīngyīn Gé) is built on an outcrop in the middle of a fast-flowing stream.

The small pavilions here are great for appreciating the natural music. It's possible to swim here although the water is only likely to be warm enough during the summer months.

LONG LIFE MONASTERY 万年寺
Reconstructed in the 9th century, **Long Life Monastery** (Wànnián Sì; admission Y10) is the oldest surviving Éméi temple. It's dedicated to the man on the white elephant, the Bodhisattva Puxian, who is the protector of the mountain. This 8.5m-high **statue** is dated from AD 980, cast in copper and bronze and weighs an estimated 62,000kg. If you can manage to rub the elephant's hind leg, good luck will be cast upon you. The statue is housed in Brick Hall, a domed building with small stupas on

it and the only building left unharmed in a 1945 fire.

MAGIC PEAK MONASTERY 仙峰寺
Somewhat off the beaten track, this **monastery** (Xiānfēng Sì) is backed by rugged cliffs, surrounded by fantastic scenery and oozing with character. The nearby **Jiulao Cave** is inhabited by oversized bats.

ELEPHANT BATHING POOL 洗象池
According to legend, **Elephant Bathing Pool** (Xǐxiàng Chí) is the spot where Puxian flew his elephant in for a big scrub, but today there's not much of a pool to speak of. Being almost at the crossroads of both major trails, the temple here is something of a hang-out and often crowded with pilgrims.

GOLDEN SUMMIT TEMPLE 金顶寺
This magnificent but clearly recently renovated **temple** (Jīndǐng Sì) at the Golden Summit (Jīn Dǐng; 3077m) is as far as most hikers make it. Covered with glazed tiles and surrounded by white marble balustrades, the temple now occupies 1695 sq metres. The original temple had a bronze-coated roof, which is how it got the name Jīn Dǐng (which can also mean 'Gold Top').

It's constantly overrun with tourists, pilgrims and monks, and you will be continuously bumped and jostled. Sadly, the sun rarely forces its way through the mists up here.

From the Golden Summit it was once possible to hike to **Ten Thousand Buddha Summit** (Wànfó Dǐng), but pilgrims now take a monorail (a one-hour return ticket costs Y50).

MONKEY ETIQUETTE

The monkeys have got it all figured out. If you come across a monkey 'tollgate', the standard procedure is to thrust open palms towards the outlaw to show you have no food. The Chinese find the monkeys an integral part of the Éméi trip and many like to tease them.

The monkey forms an important part of Chinese mythology, and there is a saying in Chinese, 'With one monkey in the way, not even 10,000 men can pass' – which may be deeper than you think!

Some of these chimps are big, and staying cool when they look like they might make a leap at you is easier said than done. There is much debate as to whether it's better to give them something to eat or to fight them off.

One thing is certain, if you do throw them something, don't be too stingy. They get annoyed very quickly if they think they are being undersold. More than one traveller has told the tragic tale of having their Lonely Planet book being ripped to shreds in front of their eyes by an extortive simian.

Sleeping & Eating

ON THE MOUNTAIN

The old monasteries offer food, shelter, and sights all rolled into one. While some travellers complain about the spartan and somewhat damp conditions, others love what may be as many as a thousand years of character.

A few of the monasteries at key junctions have posted prices but at others you may well have to bargain with the monks. You can expect to pay between Y20 and Y40 for a bed in a dorm room (the cheapest beds are reserved for pilgrims), with plumbing and electricity provided in those at the higher end of the scale. The following should give you an idea as to where to head for the cheapest beds, but expect to pay more in the high season.

Venerable Trees Terrace (洪椿坪; Hóngchūn Píng; dm Y20-30, d Y160) is a good spot, with newer rooms, countless monkeys and fresh landscaping; Patrick Yang (☎ 137 0813 1210; patrickyanglong@yahoo.com.cn), a friendly and helpful local guide (he works with foreign adventure travel companies), acts as 'foreigner liaison' here (and at Declare Nation Temple). Other travellers like **Elephant Bathing Pool** (dm from Y20).

Declare Nation Temple (dm from Y20), **Pure Sound Pavilion** (dm Y15-20, d Y150), **Long Life Monastery** (dm Y10-40), **Crouching Tiger Monastery** (dm from Y50), **Golden Summit Temple** (dm Y15-40), Magic Peak Monastery (though some have found the monks unfriendly hosts) and Leiyin Temple (Léiyīn Sì) have monastery guesthouses. There's also a host of smaller lodgings at Chu Temple, Jieyin Hall, Yuxian Temple (Yùxiān Sì), Báilóngdòng (White Dragon Cave) and Huayuan Temple (Huáyuán Sì), among others. The smaller places will accept you if the main monasteries are full, often during peak season. Failing those, if night is descending, you can kip virtually anywhere – a teahouse, a restaurant. Be prepared to backtrack or advance under cover of darkness.

There are also guesthouses and hotels on Éméi Shān. Many close in the off season (and may give preference to locals over foreigners). On average you can expect to pay between Y150 and Y300 for a room. Most of these guesthouses are clumped behind Golden Summit Temple, to the west.

Jīndǐng Dàjiǔdiàn (☎ 509 8088, 509 8077; s/d/tr Y380/480/600) This three-star hotel is located at the base of the cable car and offers the ultimate luxury, 24-hour hot showers.

Vegetarian meals are included with the price of a bed at many of the monasteries.

Just up from Venerable Trees Terrace, **Hard Wok Café** is run by a friendly ex-army cook and his wife; find the best coffee on the mountain and fairly decent pancakes (wow!).

Small food stalls near the monastery grounds sell biscuits, instant noodles, peanuts and drinks – not to mention a wide variety of fungus. Be wary of teahouses or restaurants serving *shénshuǐ* (divine water), or any type of tea or food said to possess mystical healing qualities. Miracles are not guaranteed but the price of at least Y10 for the cup of water or tea is.

BÀOGÚO VILLAGE

Hotels are everywhere on the road leading to the mountain; most are nondescript and overpriced. Have a wander and check out a few options as prices and room conditions fluctuate.

Teddy Bear Hotel (☎ 559 0135, 138-9068 1961; www.teddybear.com.cn; dm Y20-30, s/d Y60-150) This 'backpacker central' kind of place has spotless rooms and sparkling shared bathrooms. Other perks include a free laundry, left-luggage service and a massage when you make it back down the mountain. The café inside is a great place to unwind and swap tall mountain tales.

Hóngzhūshān Bīnguǎn (☎ 552 5888; d Y350) You might want to splurge on a room here. Doubles in building No 7 are the best deal and, while they may not appear particularly special, the tranquil setting of lush forests and the view on the edge of a pond makes it feel like money well spent.

The street leading up to Declare Nation Temple is lined with restaurants including *huǒguō* and *shāokǎo* stalls which begin to appear as the evening approaches.

Getting There & Away

Éméi town lies 6.5km east of Éméi Shān and is the main transport hub for travel to and from the mountain. Buses from Chéngdū's Xinnanmen bus station run every 20 minutes to Éméi town (Y33, two hours, 6.40am to 7pm).

BUS

There is no direct public bus between Bàoguó village and Éméi town. If you don't want to catch a taxi (Y20) then take bus 1 bus from opposite the long-distance bus station (Y0.50).

Get off at the first stop, cross the road (past the statue) and catch bus 5 (Y1) to Bàoguó village.

Heading back to Éméi town, buses leave every 10 minutes from outside Bàoguó's long-distance bus station (Y1, 20 minutes, 7.30am to 7pm). You can also catch a direct bus to Chéngdū (Y36, two hours, hourly, 6.30am to 6pm), Lèshān (Y11, one hour, hourly, 6am to 5pm) and Chóngqìng (Y40, seven hours, 8.30am) from here.

TRAIN
Éméi train station is on the Chéngdū–Kūnmíng line and lies 3.5km from the centre of Éméi town. Bus 4 (Y0.50) runs between the train station and the long-distance bus station. Éméi town has trains to Chéngdū, Kūnmíng and Wūsīhé. A new high-speed train to Chéngdū should be running by the time you read this. The Teddy Bear Hotel can help you out with train times (they change frequently) and booking tickets.

LÈSHĀN 乐山
☎ 0833 / pop 155,930
The somnolent-looking but inspiring Grand Buddha, now the world's largest Buddha, with a fingernail taller than your average human. There's your main draw to this small riverside city of meandering, tree-draped alleys. Prospering from increasing droves of Chinese tourists (and Chéngdū commuters due to new expressways), Lèshān has revamped many of its old quarters, but it isn't all that apparent for most travellers. The town is relaxed and makes for a good day trip from the capital or a wind-down after tackling Éméi Shān.

Information
Bank of China (Zhōngguó Yínháng; Renmin Nanlu) Changes money and travellers cheques and offers cash advances on credit cards. There is also an ATM here.
China Post (Yóujú; Yutang Jie) Next door is China Telecom where you can make international phone calls.
Internet cafés (wǎngbā; Baita Jie; per hr Y2) These are scattered throughout the downtown (shown on the map).
Mr Yang (☎ 211 2046, 130-3645 6184; richardyangmin@yahoo.com.cn; Yang's Restaurant, 2F 128 Baita Jie) Has long been the guru of travel information in Lèshān and can organise almost anything (a visit to a local doctor, a local family, nearby villages, calligraphy lessons). One or two travellers have given lukewarm reviews, but the vast majority of feedback has been positive. (That said, the company he is affiliated with in Chóngqìng for Yangzi River

cruise tickets has not been so favourably reviewed.) So have a chat with this friendly and interesting character; if you're suspicious, do some homework and see.
People's Hospital (Rénmín Yīyuàn; ☎ 211 9310, out of hr emergencies ☎ 211 9328; 76 Baita Jie) Has a couple of English-speaking doctors.
PSB (Gōngānjú; 236 Chunhua Lu; ☑ 9am-noon & 2-6pm Mon-Fri) Two-day visa extensions are typical.

Sights
GRAND BUDDHA 大佛
Utter the words 'Dàfó' and locals beam and gesture animatedly. Yup, the serenely seated **Grand Buddha**, carved into a cliff face overlooking the confluence of Dadu River (Dàdù Hé) and Min River (Mín Hé), is the pride and joy of the city, a spiritual uncle. Qualifying as the largest Buddha in the world, here's the bottom line: he's 71m high, his ears are 7m long, his insteps 8.5m broad, and you could picnic on the nail of his big toe – the toe itself is 8.5m long. Holy smokes!

A Buddhist monk called Haitong started the whole thing in AD 713, hoping that the Buddha would calm the swift currents and protect boatmen from lethal currents in river hollows. Well, the big guy 'matured' slowly, and was finally completed 90 years after Haitong's death. Surplus rocks from the sculpting filled the river hollow and did the trick, but locals insist it's really the calming effect of the Buddha.

Inside the body, hidden from view, is a water-drainage system put into place to prevent weathering, although the stone statue has had its fair share of it. Soil erosion is an ongoing problem. A building once sheltered the giant statue, but it was destroyed during a Ming dynasty war. This idea has seen a resurgence; some scientists want to sheath it in a high-tech plastic bubble to protect it!

It's worth looking at the Grand Buddha from several angles and you need to get closer to him to really appreciate his magnitude. You can go to the top, opposite the head, and then descend a short stairway to the feet for a Lilliputian perspective.

THOUSAND BUDDHA CLIFFS 夹江千佛岩
About 30km north of Lèshān, 2.5km west of the train station at Jiājiāng, are the **Thousand Buddha Cliffs** (Jiājiāng Qiānfóyán; admission Y35; ☑ 8am-5pm). For once, the name is not an exaggeration: over 2400 Buddhas dot the cliffs, dating from as early as the Eastern Han dynasty.

The statues show a few signs of wear and tear but, considering their age, are in fairly good condition.

Set in a rather pretty location along a riverbank and on the edge of the countryside, this site takes something of an effort to reach. Catch one of the many buses from Lèshān's long-distance bus station down the bumpy road to Jiājiāng (Y5, one hour). From Jiājiāng bus station, take a pedicab (Y10) or taxi (Y15) to the site. The last bus returning to Lèshān leaves Jiājiāng at 6pm.

OTHER SIGHTS

The boardwalk along Binhe Lu follows Dadu River from its confluence with Min River up past Jiāzhōu Bīnguǎn. Popular for strolling in the evenings, if you follow it as far as Jiāzhōu Bīnguǎn, you'll see fan dancers, ballroom dancers and even tango lessons underway in a large square near the intersection with Baita Jie.

Travellers have recommended day trips to villages outside Lèshān, including **Luóchéng**, 50km southeast (famed for its old 'boathouse' architecture), and **Wǔtōngqiáo**, 25km south. Check with Mr Yang.

Tours

Tour boats pass by for panoramic views of the Grand Buddha (hovering in front for about 10 minutes), which reveal two guardians in the cliff side, not visible from land. You currently have a choice of three types of boat from the dockside along Binjiang Lu. Large tour boats (Y50, 7.30am to 7.30pm) and smaller speedboats (Y50, 7.30am to 7.30pm) leave regularly throughout the day from the dock near the central bus station.

The third option is to take the bargain Y3 ferry that leaves from a small dock not far

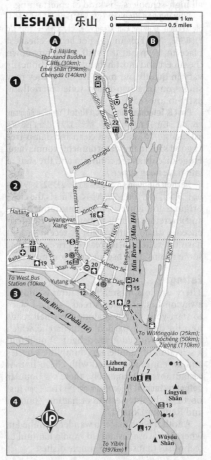

from the Táoyuán Bīnguǎn next to the Sleeping Buddha Tea Pavilion. This cheap option doesn't stop in front of the Buddha but you will still get a good view – you'll just have to be extra quick with your camera. The only drawback here is the infrequent departures (every 90 minutes 7am to 5.30pm April to September; every 90 minutes 8am to 5pm October to March).

A fun option is the local ferry (Y1) to Lizheng Island, in the middle of the two rivers' confluence. While this doesn't take you to the Buddha itself, it gives you unrivalled views. The ferry leaves regularly throughout the day from Lizheng Gate (look for a stone archway), not far from the Jiāzhōu Bīnguǎn.

The final destination for the boats leaving from the main docks is **Wuyou Temple** (Wǔyóu Sì; admission Y8; ☼ 8am-6pm). Like the Grand Buddha, this monastery dates from the Tang dynasty with Ming and Qing renovations. It commands panoramic views and is a museum piece containing calligraphy, painting and artefacts, many with English captions.

Wuyou Temple has a hall of 1000 terracotta *arhat* (Buddhist celestial beings, similar to angels) displaying an incredible variety of postures and facial expressions – no two are alike. The *arhat* are housed in the **Luohan Hall** which dates back to 1909. Inside is also a fantastic statue of **Avalokiteshvara**, the Sanskrit name of the Goddess of Mercy (Guanyin in Chinese).

If you get off the boat at Wuyou Temple, a visit through the temple will take you across Wǔyóu Shān and down to a small bridge which crosses over to **Língyún Shān** (Towering Cloud Hill). Here you can visit **Oriental Buddha Park** (Dōngfāng Fódū Gōngyuán; admission Y37), a newly assembled collection of 3000 Buddha statues and figurines from all around Asia. The park's centrepiece is a 170m-long reclining Buddha, said to be the world's longest. The park seems more of a hasty effort to cash in on Buddha-mania.

Next door is the **Mahaoya Tombs Museum** (Máhàoyámù Bówùguǎn; admission Y5), which has a modest collection of tombs and burial artefacts dating from the Eastern Han dynasty (AD 25–220).

Continuing past the museum and up Língyún Shān brings you to the entrance gate of **Dafo Temple** (Dàfó Sì; admission Y70). This is where you can get right up close to the Grand Buddha, with narrow staircases running head

to toe. Avoid visiting on public holidays or weekends, when traffic on the staircase comes to a complete standstill.

To return to Lèshān, you can either catch another boat from the ferry dock near the entrance to the Buddha or take bus 13, which leaves from the same place and will drop you back at Lèshān's dock.

This can take less than 1½ hours from the Lèshān dock, but that's pushing things a lot.

Sleeping

Táoyuán Bīnguǎn (☎ 210 1718; dm Y50, d Y198) It's in a perfect location almost directly opposite Lèshān's docks, but the rooms are approaching worn out. Still, the dorms are fine for a night and the staff – apparently consisting of all high-schoolers – is kind of entertaining.

Duìyángwān Bīnguǎn (☎ 501 0345, 336 7582; Middle Section, Duiyangwan Xiang; 兑阳湾巷中部; s/d Y100/168; 🖭) This might not be the cheapest place in town but the staff are hands-down the nicest and most helpful. Rooms honestly vary in quality but most are fine – they may stick you in a two-room suite for nothing extra in low season.

Post & Telecommunication Hotel (Yóudiàn Bīnguǎn; ☎ 213 5450; 32 Yutang Jie; 玉堂街32号; d/tr Y198/268 incl breakfast; 🖭) Basic but clean and damp-free (a good sign in this environment) rooms here. Huge discounts are common and the staff of late have been super.

Jiāzhōu Bīnguǎn (☎ 213 9888; fax 213 3233; 19 Baita Lu; 白塔街19号; s/d Y450/480; 🖭) This is the city's original foreigner-friendly midrange place and therefore your best bet for staff experienced with foreign guests. A recent facelift hasn't resulted in increased prices because some rooms didn't seem to be touched.

Eating

There are lots of small restaurants hidden away on Lèshān's side streets. A good place to start your search is along the small roads near the dock, in particular Xuedao Jie, which is buzzing with culinary delights. You'll find a selection of noodle and dumpling eateries and an entire alley lined with cheap hotpot restaurants. Alternatively, there's a popular **hotpot restaurant** (huǒguō cāntīng; ☼ 11am-9pm) just north of the intersection of Jiading Zhonglu and Renmin Donglu.

Another good place to wander is Binhe Lu, where there are restaurants and a handful of teahouses that serve up simple dishes.

Yang's Restaurant (Yàngjiā Cāntīng; 2F 128 Baita Jie; dishes Y15-25; 6-9pm) Run by Mr Yang the travel guru, this restaurant is in the living room of his home. His wife is the chef and serves good local food.

Getting There & Away
Expressways linking Lèshān to Chéngdū and Chóngqìng; another is being built to Yíbīn.

BUS
There are three bus stations in Lèshān. The main one for travellers is the Lèshān long-distance bus station, annoyingly located in the western reaches of the city though coming in you may be dropped at any of them. Another is in the northern reaches of town.

For Chéngdū, the third one, the bus station next to the Lèshān docks is the most convenient. Buses leave for Chéngdū's Xinnanmen bus station every hour (Y31, two hours, 7.30am to 6.30pm). There are also frequent departures to Éméi town from here (Y7, 7am to 6pm). For all other destinations you'll have to go to the long-distance bus stations.

See box below for bus info.

TRAIN
No matter that ticket sellers swear blind there is a station here, there simply is no train service to Lèshān. It still means Éméi Shān, or more likely Jiājiāng, both about an hour away by bus. (A new high-speed train is running from Chéngdū to Éméi Shān, but the bus is still faster.)

Getting Around
Bus 9 runs from the pier to the western bus station. Nos 1 and 8 run the length of Jiading Lu and connect the pier area with the northern long-distance bus station. Buses run from 6am to 6pm, at roughly 20-minute intervals. Bus 13 runs from Lèshān dock to Wuyou Temple.

Pedicab rides cost Y2 to Y5. Taxis start at a flat rate of Y3 for the first 3km.

Unfortunately there doesn't seem to be any bicycle hire in Lèshān – or many bicycles at all for that matter. But you probably wouldn't want to take them up and down the stairs at the Grand Buddha anyway.

WESTERN SÌCHUĀN & THE ROAD TO TIBET

To the north and west of Chéngdū is where green tea becomes butter tea, Confucianism yields to Buddhism and gumdrop hills leap into jagged snowy peaks. Much of the area kisses the sky at between 4000m and 5000m high.

To Tibetans and Tibetan-related peoples (Qiang), this area is part of the province of Kham which covers the eastern third of the Tibetan plateau. For travellers, it is Tibet sans the 'official' provincial border and all its hassles.

The Sìchuān–Tibet Hwy, begun in 1950 and finished in 1954, is one of the world's highest, roughest, most dangerous and most beautiful roads. It splits into northern and southern routes 70km west of Kāngdìng. As yet, there isn't much in the way of tourist facilities. For more information on Kham visit www.khamaid.org.

Dangers & Annoyances
Towns in these areas experience up to 200 freezing days per year; summers are blistering by day and the high altitude invites particularly bad sunburn. Lightning storms are frequent from May to October, when cloud cover can shroud the scenic peaks. Because of rapid weather changes, the tracks around Gònggā Shān can be treacherous.

LÈSHĀN BUS TIMETABLES
Buses from Lèshān's western (and some from the northern) long-distance bus station:

Destination	Price	Duration	Frequency	Departs
Chéngdū	Y33	2hr	every 20 min	7am-7.30pm
Chóngqìng	Y88	6hr	hourly	7am-5pm
Éméi	Y7	40min	every 15 min	7am-6pm
Kāngdìng	Y72-89	8hr	daily	9.30am
Yíbīn	Y49-52		5 daily	7am-3.10pm
Zìgòng	Y24-30		half-hourly	9am-5.10pm

If you're planning to attempt to cross into Tibet from Bātáng or Dégé, you may want to reconsider. The PSB keep a close eye on foreigners, and as truck drivers are severely punished for carrying foreigners across the border, they're unlikely to give you a lift. Some travellers have managed to bribe their way in but at costs that make flying from Chéngdū seem cheap. However, if you're arriving from Tibet into Sìchuān, nobody seems to give a damn.

The US State Department in 2006 was reporting incidents of travellers being physically assaulted by authorities after they were caught.

Be forewarned: at the time of writing it was not possible to change money or travellers cheques (except in Kāngdìng for these two) or to get advances on credit cards in Sìchuān's northwest. Bring your Renminbi with you.

KĀNGDÌNG (DARDO) 康定

☎ 0836 / pop 82,000 / elevation 2616m

Once a one-horse kind of town, Kāngdìng since the mid-1990s has become a bustling – for these parts – tourist town, though now more Chinese than Tibetan. Ensconced in a steep river valley at the confluence of the swift Zheduo and Yala Rivers (known as the Dar and Tse in Tibetan) and towered over by mighty Gònggā Shān (7556m), Kāngdìng is famous throughout China for a popular love song that the town's surrounding scenery inspired. If you're en route to western Sìchuān, chances are you'll end up overnighting here.

The town has long been a trade centre between Chinese and Tibetan cultures, with the exchange of wool, herbs and bricks of tea from Yǎ'ān wrapped in yak hide. It also served as an important staging post on the road to Lhasa, as indeed it does today. Kāngdìng was historically the capital of the local Tibetan kingdom of Chakla (or Chala) and later, from 1939 to 1951, the capital of the short-lived province of Xikang, when it was controlled by the opium-dealing warlord Liu Wenhui.

Information

Agricultural Bank of China (Zhōngguó Nóngyè Yínháng; Xi Dajie; ☉ 9am-5pm Mon-Fri) Can change US dollars and UK pounds. It has begun to change travellers cheques for some travellers – not all the time for some reason – but still does not offer cash advances on credit cards. There is no ATM in town.

Internet cafés (wǎngbā; per hr Y2-3; ☉ 8am-midnight) One is found one block east of Yanhe Donglu on Dongda Xiaojie, another along Guangming Lu. Still another is closer

to the bus station on Yanhe Xilu; you can get online at Sally's Knapsack Inn (see opposite).

PSB (Gōngānjú; ☎ 281 1415; Dongda Xiaojie; ☉ 8.30am-noon & 2.30-5.30pm) Three- to five-day service but if you sweet-talk politely, perhaps the same day.

Yala Snow Mountain Outdoor Shop (☎ 1333-079 5696, 1309-626 0537) Helpful Lin Yueh Luan speaks decent English and some Tibetan, and is knowledgeable about the area. He can arrange full-day tours (Y60) and horses (Y60 per day). North of the town square.

Sights

There are several lamaseries in and around Kāngdìng. Just behind Black Tent Guesthouse, **Anjue Temple** (Ānjué Sì; Ngachu Gompa in Tibetan) dates back to 1652 and was built under the direction of the fifth Dalai Lama. These days it's fairly quiet with several monks and a few old prayer wheels.

Nanwu Temple (Nánwù Sì) belongs to the Gelugpa (Yellow Hat) sect of Tibetan Buddhism and is the most active lamasery in the area with around 80 lamas in residence. Set not far south of the downtown area, it affords good views of Kāngdìng and the valley. Walk south along the main road, following its bend to the left for 2km. Cross the bridge at the southern end of town and continue on 300m. Next to a walled Han Chinese cemetery is a dirt path that follows a stream uphill to the lamasery.

You can also head up **Pǎomǎ Shān** for excellent views of Kāngdìng, the surrounding mountains and valleys and – if you're lucky – Gònggā Shān. The ascent takes you past oodles of prayer flags, several Buddhist temples and up to a white chörten (stupa). Take particular care when wandering around Pǎomǎ Shān and try to avoid hiking on your own. A British tourist was murdered here in the spring of 2000 and one or two muggings have been reported.

To reach the hill, bear left at the fork in the road just south of the bus station and walk about 10 minutes until you reach a lamasery on the left; a stairway leads up the hill from here. A second, more direct route, heads up the hill further south, beginning above the staircase on Dongda Xiaojie.

In the south of town is **Jingang Temple** (Jīngāng Sì), a 400-year-old monastery that was still under renovation but looking better. A taxi from the bus station will cost you Y5.

About 5km north of Kāngdìng are the **Erdao Bridge Hot Springs** (Èrdào Wēnquán; admission Y10), where you can have a half-hour bath in slightly egg-smelling, warm, sulphurous water. Take your own towel. You can reach the hot springs by taxi for about Y8.

In town, the **market** on Dongda Xiaojie is worth a look.

Festivals & Events

Kāngdìng's biggest annual festival, the **Walking Around the Mountain Festival** (Zhuànshānjié), takes place on Pǎomǎ Shān on the eighth day of the fourth lunar month to commemorate the birthday of the Historical Buddha, Sakyamuni. White-and-blue Tibetan tents cover the hillside and there's wrestling, horse racing and visitors from all over western Sìchuān. There's also a street fair that lasts for 10 days, making this a good time to visit Kāngdìng.

Sleeping

Kāngdìng has more than enough hotels and new ones are being built all the time; it's definitely a buyer's market.

Black Tent Guesthouse (Gōnggàshān Lǚshè; ☎ 886 2107; 28 Yanhe Xilu; 沿河西路28号; dm/d Y20/50) By far the most popular place, here atmospheric dorm rooms with wood floors are cosy; showers and toilets are clean but there's only one of each. A nice teahouse is great for relaxing, and the (shorthanded) staff is busy-busy but as helpful as possible.

Sally's Knapsack Inn (Bēibāo Kèzhàn; ☎ 283 8377, 130-6007 5296; dm Y20) Next to Jingang Temple is this laid-back hostel and café with colourful carved wooden beds. A taxi from the bus station will cost Y5. It was undergoing renovation at the time of writing so let us know how it goes.

Chángchéng Bīnguǎn (☎ 882 2956; Xinshi Qianjie; 新市前街; d Y50-120) Not far from the bus station, this hotel is one of a zillion offering decent cheap but good rooms. No frills to the n-th degree but OK.

Kǎlākǎ Dàjiǔdiàn (☎ 282 8688; fax 282 8777; 5 Yanhe Donglu; 沿河东路5号; d Y190) One of the more popular and better-run hotels, the rooms are basically furnished but clean and you're perfectly located. The hotel has connections with the Erdao Bridge Hot Springs (it can organise tours there for Y35). The café here has approximations of Western food.

Love Song Hotel (Qínggē Dàjiǔdiàn; ☎ 281 3333; fax 281 3111; 156 Dongda Xiaojie; 东大小街156号; d Y580) This flashy hotel seems out of place in Kāndìng; it even has a cinema attached to it. The rack rates are a bit much, though the rooms are fine, but a substantial discount would make the rooms/services worth it.

Eating

Hotpot is everywhere, as in most Sìchuān tourist towns.

Nine Bowls Vegetable of Country (Jiǔwǎn Nóngjiā Xiàng; ☎ 287 5199; Yanhe Xilu; dishes from Y5; ☷ 11am-9pm) You can't miss this cubbyhole place – the sign next door says 'Chongqing Strange Taste

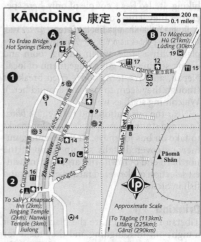

KĀNGDÌNG 康定

To Erdao Bridge Hot Springs (5km)
To Mùgécuò Hú (21km); Lúdìng (30km)
Yulai River
Dawa Dajie 大瓦大街
Xinshi Qianjie 新市前街
Yanhe Xilu 沿河西路
Guangming Lu 光明路
Zhedua River
Yanhe Donglu 沿河东路
Sichuan-Tibet Hwy 川藏路
Dongda Xiaojie 东大小街
Pǎomǎ Shān
To Sally's Knapsack Inn (2km); Jingang Temple (2km); Nanwu Temple (3km); Jiulong
To Tǎgōng (113km); Lǐtáng (225km); Gānzī (290km)
Approximate Scale
0   200 m
0   0.1 miles

Fish'! The exceedingly friendly staff is overseen by an equally hospitable manager who speaks decent English (it also has an English menu).

Try the whipped potatoes with pickled vegies (tǔdoùní); sounds gross but guaranteed you'll wolf down two bowls after a day of hiking. It also has a couple of only-here specialties they'll hip you to.

Droma Yudia-Khampa Tibetan Eatery (☎ 282 3463; Xinshi Qianjie; dishes from Y10; ☯ 9am-9pm) A newer place with a large, warm dining room and comfy seating, it's got a huge menu of local, Nepali, and Western food – even breakfast (though they seem to rise late around here). Welcoming staff, as well.

Near the bus station and market are bāozi (steamed stuffed buns) places, great for snacks to take on bus journeys. In the evening, numerous covered stalls set up camp at the northern end of town with arguably the widest selection of skewered meat, vegetables and fish in Sìchuān.

Drinking

Tibetan Dance Halls are the place to go for a night out in Kāngdìng and they make for a very entertaining evening. Traditional Tibetan and Chinese songs, including the famous Kāngdìng Love Song, are performed to ear-splitting techno beats and a very appreciative audience. Try the **Kangba Dancehall** (Kāngbā Dàwǔtái; ☎ 669 3255; Xidakai Lu; drinks from Y20), where you can get up and dance once the performances are finished.

Getting There & Away

An airport is being built on the way to Tǎgōng; it's slated for completion in 2009.

BUS

Improved roads have made Kāngdìng far more accessible. The completion of the Èrláng Shān tunnel has cut the ride to Chéngdū down to a comfortable eight hours. The bus station is in the northeast of town. See the Kāngdìng Bus Timetables box below.

TAXI

Taxis congregate on Xinshi Qianjie, not far from the Chángchéng Bīnguǎn. Trips to Lúdìng cost around Y20.

AROUND KĀNGDÌNG

There are several mountain lakes and hot springs in the vicinity of Kāngdìng. Lying 21km to the north of town up the Yala Valley, **Mùgécuò Hú** is one of the highest lakes in northwestern Sìchuān, at 3700m. Locals also boast that it's one of the most beautiful. Trails around the lake lead to other smaller lakes such as the **Red Sea** (Hóng Hǎi). Also worth checking out is **Seven Colour Lake** (Qīsè Hǎi), which lies a few kilometres before Mùgécuò. It's best not to wander around these parts alone or to stray too far off the path. The area of 'Wild Men's Lake', as Mùgécuò means in Tibetan, is home to wolves and other wild beasts.

There are no buses running to Mùgécuò but idle taxi drivers will be more than pleased to shuttle you there and back for Y150 to Y200 (1½ hours).

Mùgécuò Hú can quite easily be done as a day trip from Kāngdìng, but if you decide you want to stay out there, both **Qīsèhǎi Bīnguǎn** and **Mùgécuò Bīnguǎn** have beds that you might be able to sleep in for as little as Y30.

KĀNGDÌNG BUS TIMETABLES

Buses from Kāngdìng:

Destination	Price	Duration	Frequency	Departs
Bātáng	Y138	2 days	daily	6.45am
Chéngdū	Y101-122	8hr	hourly	6am-4pm
Dānbā	Y36	4hr	daily	8am
Dégé	Y166	24hr	daily	7.30am
Gānzī	Y106	12hr	daily	6.15am
Lèshān	Y72-89	8hr	daily	7am
Lǐtáng	Y80	8hr	daily	7am
Tǎgōng	Y33	4hr	daily	6am
Xiāngchéng	Y130	14hr	daily	7.15am

LÚDÌNG 泸定

☎ 0836 / elevation 1310m

Lúdìng is a small, bustling town about halfway between Kāngdìng and Móxī. As a minor connection point for buses between western Sìchuān and Chéngdū, Lèshān and Móxī, you may find yourself here.

Sights

Lúdìng is famous throughout China as the site of what is often regarded as the most glorious moment of the Long March. It took place on the **Lúdìng Bridge** (泸定桥; Lúdìng Qiáo; admission Y5), a 100m-long chain suspension bridge over Dadu River (Dàdù Hé). Then again, Jung Chang wrote that it never happened in her warts-and-all biography *Mao: The Unknown Story*.

In any case, it's a cool story. On 29 May 1935 the communist troops approached Lúdìng Bridge only to discover that Kuomintang troops had beaten them to it, removed the planks from the bridge and had it covered with firepower. In response, 20 communist troops crossed the bridge hand-over-hand armed with grenades and then proceeded to overcome the Kuomintang troops on the other side. This action allowed the Long March to continue before the main body of the Kuomintang forces could catch up with them.

The bridge is five minutes' walk from the bus station. Just follow the river into town and you'll find it. The original bridge was first constructed in 1705 and was an important link in the Sìchuān–Tibet road. Memorabilia – including artefacts left behind (or donated) by Long Marchers – are on display.

You can also get a gander at some of Mao's calligraphy on a shelter near the Buddhist Temple on the hillside above town.

Sleeping & Eating

The hotel situation in Lúdìng is good unless you're on a budget; for cheaper digs head for Móxī or Kāngdìng.

Chēzhàn Lüguǎn (车站旅馆; Bus Station Hostel; ☎ 139-9048 9606; dm Y20, d/tr Y30/60) It seems a redundancy in small town China – that is, the bus station has the best lodging – but once again this is your only cheap option; at least it's decent.

More upmarket accommodation options can be found in the new area of town across the river from the bus station. For a good bet try the **Lúdìng Qiáo Bīnguǎn** (泸定桥宾馆; ☎ 312 888; d Y480) where you can often get 50% discounts on rooms. It's the building with the large green dome on the roof.

Clustered around the bus station are a number of nondescript restaurants as well as a teahouse where you can while away your time until the next bus pulls into town.

Getting There & Away

From Lúdìng there are daily buses to Chéngdū (Y92-98, six hours, 6.30am, 10am and 1pm) and Shímián (Y20, three hours, 6am and noon). Minibuses run regularly to Kāndìng (Y20) and Móxī (Y20).

A second route between Éméi Shān and Lúdìng, without doubling back to Chéngdū, runs via Wūsíhé to the south. There is usually one morning bus at 6am from Lúdìng to Wūsíhé (Y20) but if it doesn't appear, jump on the bus to Shímián from where there is frequent onward transport. Once you reach Wūsíhé you'll need to hop on a train to Éméi town. The train departs Wūsíhé in the afternoon, meaning you shouldn't have to stay overnight here. If you're headed south to Pānzhīhuā or Kūnmíng, be advised that you can only buy hard-seat tickets in Wūsíhé and very few onward trains stop here.

MÓXĪ 磨西

☎ 0836

Nestled in the mountains around 50km southwest of Lúdìng, this peaceful village's main attraction is Hǎiluógōu Glacier Park (see p782). However, with lots of character, Móxī itself is a fun place to explore.

Sights

Móxī's older, traditional wooden buildings are at the bottom of the village. Also at this end is a multicoloured **Catholic church** (天主教堂; admission Y3) where Mao camped out during the Long March. It's open to the public and you will be given an obligatory tour by the old men that look after the place. From here, the village climbs its way up a hill. If you follow the dirt road up, about 200m past the main crossroads, on the right is **Guānyīnggǔ Gompa** (观音古寺), a 400-year-old Bön (Tibetan Buddhist sect) temple that is run by some delightful old women. In the courtyard is a mammoth, gnarled tree around which the temple has been built. Across the road from the temple is a small **pagoda** (塔) from where you can get a view of the surrounding scenery.

SICHUĀN

Sleeping & Eating

Móxī is loaded with good, cheap accommodation; this is but a thumbnail sketch.

Bīngchuān Fàndiàn (冰川饭店; dm Y20, d with bathroom Y50) Opposite the entrance to the church, this used to be one of those primitive-but-charming places you never forget. Renovations go on and on, but it's still cheap and great. And in front of the most amazing glacier vistas you'll see.

Hǎiluó Fàndiàn (海螺饭店; ☎ 326 6297; d Y60-80; 🖂) Up the road from the Bīngchuān Fàndiàn, this place has solid rooms for the price. Can't beat the magnificent views from the rooftop terrace.

There are a number of restaurants, barbeque stalls and hotpot places along the main road and the road leading to the glacier park entrance. Check prices before ordering.

Móxī's shops and fruit stands are well stocked if you need to buy some supplies for a trip to Hǎiluógōu.

Getting There & Away

Most visitors to Móxī arrive on a tour bus and the public transport system is erratic, if it runs at all. Most locals scoot around on motorbikes or catch a ride to Lúdìng (Y20) in one of the minibuses that ply between the two towns. These leave from the crossroads at the top end of town.

There is supposedly a 7am bus to Lúdìng (Y15, two hours) but don't count on it. Ditto Chéngdū (8.30am, eight hours, Y95). The owner of the Bīngchuān Fàndiàn will be able to help you out with transport. Change at Lúdìng for Chéngdū and Kāngdìng. If you're headed to Shímián, get off the bus at Māozǐpíng, on the other side of the bright-orange Rainbow Bridge. From here you can flag down a southbound bus.

To reach Móxī, get off your bus in Lúdìng from where you can grab a minibus to Móxī (Y20). Travelling from the south via Shímián, get off at Māozǐpíng and flag down a minicab to Móxī from there. If you're coming from Yǎ'ān, get the driver to let you off at Gāngǔdì (干谷地), from where you can get a taxi (Y20, one hour).

HǍILUÓGŌU GLACIER PARK
海螺沟冰川公园

Hǎiluógōu Glacier slides, literally, off the eastern slopes of Gònggā Shān to form the lowest glacier in Asia. **No 1 Glacier** (一号 冰川; Yīhào

Bīngchuān), the main glacier, is 14km long and covers an area of 16 sq km. It's relatively young as glaciers go: around 1600 years. The top of Hǎiluógōu can offer incredible vistas of Gònggā Shān and surrounding peaks, all above 6000m, but how much you actually see is entirely up to Mother Nature. Constantly framed with a backdrop of snowy peaks, the surrounding forests are also beautiful, with their ecosystems changing as you ascend the mountain.

The entrance to **Hǎiluógōu Glacier Park** (Hǎiluógōu Bīngchuān Gōngyuán; admission Y140) lies in Móxī and the park was once a popular choice for trekking and camping. It was once possible to ascend the mountain by foot or pony trek but these days there is not a neigh to be heard for miles. The road running from the park entrance to Camp No 3, via Camps No 1 and 2, has been paved over and most people travel to **Belvedere** (Guānjǐngtái; 观景台), 3km above Camp No 3, by minibus. From Belvedere the tour groups tend to continue their ascent to the base of No 1 Glacier via **cable car** (Y160; ⏰ 8.30am-4pm).

It is still possible to trek from Belvedere and it's a one- to two-hour walk up to No 1 Glacier. While not a tough climb, the walk is made more difficult as the path has been largely neglected and so at times is hard to follow. On a clear day, however, there are some beautiful views to be had and the trail passes through some lovely forest. En route to the base is the **Waterfall Viewing Platform** (冰川观景台; Bīngchuān Guānjǐngtái) at 3000m. From here you can see the main glacier tongue, plus **No 2 Glacier** (二号冰川; Èrhào Bīngchuān) and **Golden Peak** (金银峰; Jīnyínfēng) at 6368m.

The entrance fee to the park includes a guide, compulsory for all tourists going out on the glacier and handy for keeping you away from deep crevices and melting points. Guides meet you at the base of No 1 Glacier and take you on a 30-minute tour of the glacier after which you are free to go off and explore.

The park has become incredibly commercial. If you're looking for a real getaway into the wilderness, then sadly this is no longer it. But if your main interest is seeing and even walking across a glacier, then the park is still worth a visit. If you do plan to trek, come prepared with warm clothes and sunglasses. You'll also need to bring food and water, as you might not find much to buy en route until you reach Camp No 3 and its pricey restaurants. On maps of the park marked trails may be less than accurate and some may have disappeared.

The rainy season for this area spans July and August, although the locals say they get 200 days of rain a year. The best time to visit is between late September and November, when skies are generally clear. Autumn colours are particularly beautiful at this time, though it can be cold up at Camp No 3.

Sleeping & Eating

Accommodation options in the park tend to fall into one category: old and overpriced.

Camp No 1 (一号营地; Yīhào Yíngdì; dm Y150), at 1940m, still offers budget dorm beds but conditions are damp and dirty.

Camp No 2 (二号营地; Èrhào Yíngdì; dm Y150) sits at 2620m and has cramped, expensive dorm rooms although the price does include a dip into the hot springs.

Camp No 3 (三号营地; Sānhào Yíngdì) at 2940m is the highest camp and offers two resort-style hotels. The huge **Jīnshān Fàndiàn** (金山饭店; Golden Mountain Hotel; ☎ 326 6433; d Y150) and the new **Jīnshān Dàjiǔdiàn** (金山大酒店; Golden Mountain Grand Hotel; ☎ 326 6383; d Y480) sit side by side and offer the best – and most expensive – accommodation within the park.

The park authorities frown upon camping and in any case there isn't a great deal in the way of flat ground on the way up.

The camps sell some food and drinks although, out of season, you can only count on this at Camp No 3. Mineral water, soft drinks, beer and instant noodles are usually available at high prices.

Getting There & Away

The entrance to the park is in Móxī. Turn left at the main crossroads at the top of the hill and carry on to the ticket office, about 400m up the road. Móxī itself can be reached by minibus from Lúdìng (see opposite for details). Buses start running up the mountain from the park entrance gate at 7.30am and leave as soon as they have more than one passenger.

Minibuses (Y50 return, one hour) start running up the mountain from the park entrance gate at 7.30am and leave as soon as they have more than one passenger. The last bus leaves Belvedere around 7pm and stops at all three camps on the way down.

SÌCHUĀN–TIBET HWY (NORTHERN ROUTE)

This is the less heavily travelled route to Tibet for good reason. Some 300km longer than the southern route, it crosses Chola Mountain, the highest pass this side of Lhasa. If possible, the disrepair of roads here exceeds those on the southern route and offers a real test of the mettle of any mortal who dares set upon them.

The highlights are many, however. The highway also crosses through the increasingly popular and sublimely lovely Tǎgōng Grasslands (below). For a nice detour, head up to the splendid little town of Dānbā to check out its fabulous Qiang watchtowers.

This highway leads ultimately to the border town of Dégé, with its internationally revered printing lamasery. It also takes you to the north where it is possible to work your way up to Qīnghǎi province via Sêrshu.

Come prepared with warm clothing. Remember that bus services can be erratic – this is no place to be if you're in a hurry. It's also not possible to change money or travellers cheques so load up before you come.

Tǎgōng Grasslands 塔公草原

About 110km northwest of Kāngdìng lie the **Tǎgōng Grasslands** (Tǎgōng Cǎoyuán). The chocolate-drop–shaped hillocks dotting expanses of fields make for a challenging but relaxing few days of strike-off-on-your-own trekking. An annual horse-racing festival (sàimǎhuì) features thousands of local Tibetan herdsmen and Tibetan opera.

The small village of **Tǎgōng** offers a fantastic taste of Sìchuān's Tibetan Wild West. In the village, **Tǎgōng Temple** (Tǎgōng Sì; Y10) blends Han Chinese and Tibetan styles, and dates back to the Qing dynasty. Travellers have lined up horse treks with local guesthouses; most just hang out and wander the countryside longer than they'd planned.

The little town has 28 spartan guesthouses now! Top of the heap is the great **Snowland Guesthouse** (Xuěchéng Lǚshè; 雪城旅社; ☎ 286 6098; dm Y20) right next to Tǎgōng temple. It's got wooden everything and rigid but comfy beds; best are the thick blankets. The shower and facilities are clean.

Adjacent to this is the ineffable **Sally's Kham Restaurant** (☎ 139-9045 4672; tagongsally@yahoo.com). This place has Tibetan, Chinese and Western food (decently done), internet access, CD burning, bakery, travel information, bicycle and sleeping bag rental, and much more. Oh, and Sally, a most welcoming host.

One morning bus to Tǎgōng village (on its way to Dàofú) runs daily from Kāngdìng (Y23, four hours, 6am) and drops you outside the lamasery. More run this way but not for Tǎgōng-bound folks; you could also negotiate a share taxi fairly easily. During the horse festival buses are likely to be more frequent. If you're heading to Gānzī, you can pick up the same bus the next day at about 10am as it passes through town. To Dānbā you'll likely have to take a minivan to Bāměi (Y10, one hour), then another to Dānbā (Y25, two to three hours).

Returning to Kāngdìng, afternoon buses can be flagged down as they pass through Tǎgōng village. You can also catch a minibus on the main street that will take you to Yǎjiāng from where there are buses to Chéngdū or Lǐtáng.

Dānbā

☎ 0836 / pop 58,200 / elevation 1800m

Dānbā stretches almost impossibly along a valley of the Dadu River (Dàdù Hé), the town seemingly chiselled right into sheer riverine escarpments. The cliffs gradually back off and melt into imposing hills, and here you'll find a heavy Tibetan and Qiang populace in picturesque villages. Rising heavenward around the hamlets are the archaeological wonders of the area – dozens and dozens of ancient stone Qiang watchtowers gracefully aging as they still guard their locals, even after centuries. Not for nothing was this sublime little village rated in 2005 as the 'Best Village in China' by none other than Chinese *National Geographic*.

Technically not on the Sìchuān–Tibet Hwy, Dānbā is nonetheless a good place to take a brief detour. Inherent loveliness, sure, but the elevation is also much lower, so you can get a break from icy winds, intense sun and altitude giddiness.

ORIENTATION & INFORMATION

The narrow town meanders from east to west along the river; the only main road is Sanchahe Lu, paralleling the river. The bus station is in the far west end, and the recommended lodging in the far east end. Upward (literally) from here you'll find in the maze of alleys the **post office** (yóujú; 邮局) and **PSB** (Gōngānjú; 公安局).

Continuing on you'll eventually run into the town's sole 'sight', a pedestrian street of shops; follow this to the end and on the second floor of one of the last buildings on the left you'll find an **internet café** (wǎngbā; 网吧).

SIGHTS & ACTIVITIES

A half-dozen Tibetan villages dot the surrounding countryside. The best-known operate largely as touristy operations – though lovely and engaging – and actually charge an admission (Y30 or so generally). Most well-known are **Zhōng Lù Zàngzhài Diāoqún Gǔyízhǐ** (中路藏寨碉群古遗址), 6km east of town, and **Jiǎjū Zàngzhài** (甲居藏寨), 7km to the northwest. Transport is via taxis (whose drivers will find you) and – surprise, surprise – it's generally fairly cheap, depending on how many places you wish to visit.

Yet all one really has to do is trek out into the surrounding countryside, clamber up some hills and do some solo exploring. If you can arrange it, visit in autumn (September to November), when the scenery, a riot of colours, is downright inspirational.

A can't-miss good trip is to head east out of town along Sanchahe Lu. Approximately 5km away is a scattering of those legendary watchtowers at **Suōpō** (梭坡). A viewing platform is between kilometre markers 147 and 148. You can theoretically cross the river well before this and get an up close gander at them, but you'll be charged admission.

Easier and cheaper is to backtrack to kilometre marker 147 (almost exactly) and head up a dirt road to the top, passing more towers and lovely Tibetan villages (populated by wondrous folk). It's about 90 minutes if you don't poke about and are in good shape. *Do not shortcut*; one residual of the tower fortifications is ridiculously well-designed defensive stone walls full of flesh-ripping brambles.

SLEEPING & EATING

Any hotel near the bus station will be ecstatic to take you. Posted rates are laughably high.

Zháxī Zhuōkāng (扎西卓康; ☎ 352 1806; 35 Sanchahe Nanlu; 35 三岔河南路35号; s/d from Y50) The exceedingly friendly managers of this refurbished place have a hotel with a hostel complex, and that's a good thing. Spotless, airy rooms (all redone recently) should include dorm beds by the time you read this – they were literally pounding away to make them on the day of our visit. Zilch English but they communicate admirably nonetheless. It's on the eastern end of town, about a 15 minute hike from the bus station.

Curiously, the town has a dearth of eateries of any kind. The few restaurants that you find – strictly Sìchuān food – are at least cheap and good.

GETTING THERE & AWAY

Buses (but not that many) run to Kāngdìng (Y36 to Y42, four hours, 8.30am), Tǎgōng (Y30), Lúhuò, Gānzī, and, for northern Sìchuān or back to Chéngdū via Wòlóng, northeast to Mǎ'ěrkāng (Y40, four hours, 7am). Many times if passenger loads are low staff will pass you off to private minivan drivers, who may then troll maddeningly for more passengers. If you're heading for Kāngdìng you can negotiate with clusters of these drivers at the east end of town; to head towards Tǎgōng, go to the west end.

GĀNZĪ 甘孜

☎ 0836 / pop 61,400 / elevation 3394m

The lively market town of Gānzī sits in a valley at 3400m, surrounded by the sleeping giants of Chola Mountain. Some 385km northwest of Kāngdìng, Gānzī is the capital of the Gānzī (Garzê) Autonomous Prefecture and is mostly populated by Tibetans and Khambas.

Gānzī sees a growing number of foreigners sojourning here as an intermediate stop between Sêrshu and Kāngdìng or on their way west to Dégé. It is a friendly place and it's easy to spend several days here exploring the beautiful surrounding countryside, which is scattered with Tibetan villages and monasteries. Photo opportunities abound and it's impossible to take a bad picture here.

INFORMATION

Dorjee Tsewang (☎ 139-9049 6777) If you're looking for a local guide, Dorjee Tsewang in the neighbouring town of Rongpatse can arrange hiking and horse-riding treks (or anything else). He speaks fluent English.

SIGHTS & ACTIVITIES

Situated north of the town's Tibetan quarter, **Ganzi Temple** (甘孜寺; Gānzī Sì; Garzê Gompa in Tibetan; admission Y15) is a 540-year-old lamasery. Home to over 500 monks, this is the region's largest monastery and it glimmers with blinding quantities of gold. Encased on the walls of the main hall are hundreds of small golden

Sakyamunis. In a smaller hall just west of the main hall is an awe-inspiring statue of Jampa (Maitreya or Future Buddha), dressed in a giant silk robe. The monks are very friendly and will invite you in to look around.

To find the lamasery, take a left out of the bus station and head north for about 10 minutes until you reach the Tibetan neighbourhood. From there wind your way uphill, around the clay and wooden houses.

There are also a number of lamaseries in neighbouring towns that you might want to visit. **Beri Gompa** is about a half-hour drive west, on the road to Dégé. Also off this road, one hour from Gānzī, is **Dagei Gompa**. About 15km from here on a steep slope above the Yalong River sits **Hadhi Nunnery**, home to sixty or so nuns.

To reach Beri Gompa and Dagei Gompa, catch the morning bus to Dégé or one of the sporadic local buses heading west. A taxi costs around Y20.

Back in Gānzī, turn right out of the bus station and walk through the Tibetan housing until you reach a bridge festooned with prayer flags. There are endless possibilities for walks on the other side of the bridge.

SLEEPING & EATING

Most hotels and guesthouses in Gānzī seem to be accepting foreigners now. For dirt cheap guesthouses turn left out of the bus station, walk to the corner, turn left, and 50m ahead on the right side take your pick of two decent cheapies (Y15 beds).

Chéngxìn Bīnguǎn (城信宾馆; ☎ 752 5289; Dajin Jie; 打金街; s/d without bathroom Y60/80, with bathroom Y180) Opposite the bus station, this place has very clean rooms and great staff.

Jīnmáoníu Jiǔdiàn (金牦牛酒店; ☎ 752 2353; Dajin Jie; 打进街; dm Y30, d Y120-180) Attached to Gānzī's bus station, this is the most centrally located midrange option, with weary but OK rooms in an older building and smarter new doubles in the main complex.

The food in Gānzī is virtually all Sìchuān basics (but good). Around the bus station are several dumpling and bāozi stalls.

If you head west, up the hill at the main intersection you'll find eateries pumping out fresh Tibetan flatbread.

Gyalten Rinpoche Guesthouse (dm Y35) Several kilometres west of Dagei Gompa. Set against white-capped mountains with no neighbours to be seen for miles, this is a truly relaxing place to rest for a day or two, especially at nearby hot springs. Simple meals are available and you would be wise to bring a sleeping bag with you. To get there, you can ask a driver to let you off close enough to walk, or negotiate a ride from Dagei Gompa (if any drivers are around). From Dagei Gompa, just walk west along the road (less than 100m) and look for a pond; beyond this, a sign in English directs you up a dirt track a few kilometres to the guesthouse.

GETTING THERE & AWAY

Buses to Gānzī (Y106, 10 to 12 hours) leave Kāngdìng daily at 6.15am. A bus to Kāngdìng leaves Gānzī every morning at 6.30am. Buses to Dégé (Y60, eight to ten hours) run every two to three days if demand warrants it; it usually doesn't, so most of the time you hope for a seat on the daily bus which passes through from the south, usually at 8.30am or so.

Private minivans to Dégé are available for hire (Y450), not a bad deal if there's a group of you.

You can head north from Gānzī to Xīníng in Qīnghǎi province via Sêrshu (daily, Y94, nine hours). These buses come from Kāngdìng and stop in the morning around 8am; hope for a seat.

MANIGANGO 马尼干戈
☎ 0836

Manigango lies halfway between Gānzī and Dégé and is the jumping-off point for Dzogchen Gompa and Yihun Lhatso. Manigango itself is a dusty one-street town that looks unmistakably like the movie set for a Tibetan Western. It's a glorious multicoloured scene with Tibetans on horseback, monks in crimson robes on motorbikes and tractors piled precariously high with pilgrims rattling down the road. It's worth stopping off just for the atmosphere. A horse-racing festival is usually held here in the summer.

The town is known in Chinese as Yùlóng or Mǎnígāngē, but it's most commonly referred to by its Tibetan name Manigango.

Sights

DZOGCHEN GOMPA 竹庆佛学院

This important Nyingmapa **monastery** (Zhúqíng Fóxuéyuàn), 50km north of Manigango, has a stunning location at the foot of a glacial valley. The recently reconstructed monastery was founded in 1684 and is the home of the Dzogchen school, the most popular form of Tibetan Buddhism in the West. Several high Nyingmapa lamas, now exiled abroad, originate from nearby valleys.

The site includes the small town, 1.5km off the road, which has a few shops, *chörten* and a chapel with huge prayer wheels. Up the small gorge is the main monastery and 1km further is the *shedra* (monastic college).

Buses to Yùshù and Sêrshu run daily past Dzogchen but in practice it's easier to hitch. If you do plan to hitch make sure you set out in the morning, as there is little traffic on the roads come the afternoon. If you want to hire a car and driver then it will cost Y250 for the return journey. Getting here you have to cross over the Muri La Pass (4,633m) so make sure you have some warm clothes, especially if you're hitching in the back of a truck.

YIHUN LHATSO 新路海

Thirteen kilometres southwest of Manigango is **Yihun Lhatso** (Xīnlù Hǎi; admission Y20), a stunning holy alpine lake to rival any found in Jiǔzhàigōu. The lake is bordered by *chörten* and dozens of rock carvings, and the shoreline is sprinkled in places with pure white sand. It's possible to walk an hour or two up the left (east) side of the lakeshore for glacier views. The lake has many great places to camp though you need to guard against the mosquitoes. To get here you'll have to hitch on Dégé-bound traffic to the turn-off where there's a bridge and a 1km trail to the lake.

Activities

The countryside surrounding Manigango is crying out to be explored and one good way to do it is on horseback. The folks at the Mǎnígāngē Shísùdiàn (see next section) can help you organise a horse and guide for trekking in the neighbouring areas. Prices usually run at Y200 per day (for horse and guide) but you can probably negotiate. If you plan to go off camping for several days you will be expected to provide meals for your guide as well. Make sure you have all the equipment and food you need as there's hardly anything available to buy in Manigango let alone once you've left town.

Sleeping & Eating

Manigango seems to have the biggest population of mangy dogs in southwest China and they all come out to play at night. Manigango was also undergoing a construction boom last check, and upgrades were looming (hopefully not in prices!)

Mǎnígāngē Shísùdiàn (马尼干戈食宿店; dm Y10-20) This is where all the buses stop and has comfortable basic rooms. Ask for the toilets however and they'll point you half a mile up the road – make sure you bring a torch! The staff can help with travel information and bus timetables.

Yùlóng Shénhǎi Bīnguǎn (玉龙神海宾馆; dm Y15-30) Next door to the Mǎnígāngē Shísùdiàn, this hotel is more modern and has its own toilet – bonus! Look for the large red-and-white sign.

The restaurant at the Mǎnígāngē Shísùdiàn serves particularly tasty food and is very cheap. There is a good *niúròumiàn* (beef noodle) restaurant next door to the petrol station.

The college at Dzogchen Gompa offers beds for Y15 per night though you need a sleeping bag and your own food. There are a couple of well-stocked shops in the village below.

Getting There & Away

A daily bus passes through Manigango at 11am for Dégé (Y35, three to four hours). Coming from Dégé, a bus stops in Manigango at 11am and heads on to Gānzī (Y25, five to seven hours) and Lúhuò (Y50, five hours) where it overnights before heading on to Kāngdìng (Y130, overnight via Lúhuò) the following morning. A 9am bus leaves daily for Sêrshu (Y77).

DÉGÉ 德格

☎ 0836 / pop 58,520 / elevation 3270m

Resting in a valley with Chola Mountain to the east and the Tibetan border to the west, Dégé (Dêgê), home of the legendary Gesar, an altruistic king of Ling, is steeped in tradition and still sees little of the outside world. Things are naturally changing but it still remains timelocked for the most part. Dégé was renowned for its apothecary monks who developed traditional medicine, but now people come for its famed printing lamasery.

Getting to Dégé is a gruelling haul and it is not uncommon for buses to overturn on the icy, hairpin roads. Altitude sickness is also a very real possibility.

En route you'll see the towering snowy peaks of Chola Mountain stretching up 6168m, and the Xinhua Glacier which comes down almost to the road at 4100m. Chola

Mountain itself was first scaled in 1988 and you might begin to wonder if your bus driver is attempting the same, as the bus grumbles and inches its way uphill to the top of the peaks. At the Tro La (Chola) Pass of nearly 6000m, Tibetans on board will throw coloured prayer papers out the window and chant something that you can only hope will carry your bus to safety.

Sights

BAKONG SCRIPTURE PRINTING LAMASERY
德格印经院

At the heart of Dégé and perhaps the heart of the Tibetan world in many respects is this **lamasery** (Dégé Yìnjīngyuàn; admission Y25; ⏰ 8.30amnoon & 2-6.30pm), storehouse for Tibetan culture. Pilgrims circumambulate outside, performing many more than the 1000 circuits required in the process of cultural development.

The printing house has existed on this site for over 270 years and houses over 270,000 engraved blocks of Tibetan scriptures (and paintings) from the five Tibetan Buddhist sects, including Bön. Texts include ancient works on astronomy, geography, music, medicine and Buddhist classics. A history of Indian Buddhism, comprising 555 woodblock plates, is the only surviving copy in the world (written in Hindi, Sanskrit and Tibetan).

Built in the Qing dynasty by the 42nd prefect of Dégé, the lamasery is revered as one of the three most important Tibetan lamaseries (along with Sakya Monastery and Lhasa's Potala Palace) – not surprising since the material stored in Dégé makes up an estimated 70% of Tibet's literary heritage.

Within the lamasery hundreds of workers hand-produce over 2500 prints each day. Upstairs, an older crowd of printers produce larger prints of Tibetan gods on paper or coloured cloth that later find their way to hills and temples as prayer flags. If you catch them with a free moment, they'll print you one of your choice for Y10.

Storage chambers are lined floor to ceiling with bookshelves, a constant thwack emanates from paper-cutting and binding rooms. Protecting the monastery from fire and earthquake is a guardian goddess, a green Avalokiteshvara (Guanyin).

The entrance fee to the lamasery includes a tour guide who is excellent at communicating through pictures if your Chinese isn't up to scratch. The lamasery is closed holidays.

There are three other lamaseries in town, including a large one just behind the printing house, which is over 1000 years old.

To reach the printing house, turn left out of the bus station and right over the bridge. Continue up this road to the southeast of town and it will bring you to the lamasery's front door.

Sleeping

True or not, you will likely be told that the following place is your only option. That said, a few have had luck getting cheap beds in other hotels – just depends on the day and the mood of the PSB.

Dégé Bīnguǎn (德格宾馆; ☎ 822 2157; dm Y20; d Y180) Here's where you'll likely be told to go. The dorm rooms are worse than the roads coming in but the doubles are priced laughably high; worse, you may be directed across the street to the expensive wing (Y280).

One of those where you may have luck is **Wùzī Zhāodàisuǒ** (物资招待所; dm Y25). Located directly opposite the bus station, you'll recognise it from the multi-coloured bunting hanging outside.

Getting There & Away

Buses to Dégé (Y60, eight to ten hours) run from Gānzī every two to three days if you're lucky but most of the time you hope for a seat on the daily buses which pass through from the south, usually at 8.30am or so.

Private minivans to Gānzī and other places are available for hire (Y450).

Marginally more comfortable buses leave from Kāngdìng for Dégé daily at 7.15am (Y166, 24 hours), stopping overnight in Lúhuò. The return bus stops in Manigango (Y35, three to four hours), Gānzī (Y60, eight to 10 hours) and Lúhuò (Y86, 10 to 12 hours) on the way.

SÊRSHU 石渠

There are two places commonly called Sêrshu (or Sershul): the traditional monastery town to the west (Sêrshu Dzong) and the modern county town of Sêrshu (Shíqú Xiàn), 30km to the east, which has most of the hotels and transport connections.

While you'll probably stop in Shíqú Xiàn en route between Manigango and Yùshù in Qīnghǎi. The huge monastery of Sêrshu Dzong and its intensely Tibetan village, full of wild-haired nomads (there's not a Han

Chinese in sight here), is by far the more interesting place and well worth a stopover.

Sêrshu Gompa houses 1200 monks and has two assembly halls, a Maitreya chapel and several other modern chapels and a *shedra*, with a *kora* (circular pilgrimage trail) encircling the lot. The road westwards from here towards Qīnghǎi is classic yak and nomad country, passing several long *mani* (prayer) walls and dozens of black yak hair tents in summer.

Sleeping

In Sêrshu Dzong there's good accommodation at the **monastery guesthouse** (sèxū sì gāngjīng fàndiàn; 色须寺刚京饭店; dm Y10-20, tw Y40-50 per bed), though the restaurants in town offer better food.

In Shíqú Xiàn there are several decent places, including the **Zháxīkǎ Fàndiàn** (扎溪卡饭店; dm Y40, tw Y120) on the central crossroads and the monastery-run **Bumgon Choegyeling Monastery Guesthouse** (Mēngyí Sì Jiǔyù Guìfù Lǚdiàn; 蒙宜寺九欲归富旅店; dm Y20), down the town's main side street.

Getting There & Away

Shíqú Xiàn has a 7am bus to Gānzī (Y94, eight hours), via Manigango (Y77), from the bus station in the east of town. To get to Sêrshu Dzong take the 8am bus to Yùshù (Y30) from the bus stand in the far west of town.

From Sêrshu Dzong, you'll have to catch a through bus, passing through at 9am for Yùshù (Y20, four hours), or about 11am for Shíqú Xiàn (Y10, one hour). Coming from Yùshù, it's possible to get off the bus in Sêrshu Dzong, have a look around and then hitch or hire a minivan on to Shíqú Xiàn the same day.

SÌCHUĀN–TIBET HWY (SOUTHERN ROUTE)

A journey along this 2140km route takes you through vast, open landscapes with majestic peaks vaulting skyward. The plateau areas are dotted with castellated Tibetan homes and an infinite number of contentedly munching yaks.

With roads and transport improving (ha!) oh-so-gradually and restrictions for foreign visitors lifted, the Kāngdìng–Lǐtáng–Xiāngchéng–Shangri-la (Zhōngdiàn) route has become a popular back-door trail into Yúnnán.

As with the rest of northwest Sìchuān, warm clothing is a must. Some travellers experience difficulties with the high altitudes here; be on the lookout for side effects (see p982) and if you're feeling unwell, head to somewhere lower. There are no money-changing facilities here.

Lǐtáng 理塘

☎ 0836 / pop 51,300 / elevation 4014m

Lǐtáng is famed as the birthplace of the 7th and 10th Dalai Lamas and the area around the town has strong connections to the epic warrior Gesar of Ling.

However, you won't notice this at first. Lǐtáng lies at a wheeze-inducing altitude of 4014m, but the thin air isn't the only thing taking your breath away. Your rear is pounded mercilessly by the awful roads, yet you may not even notice, so intoxicated are you by the visual majesty – ice-capped peaks every which way and epic grasslands. On arrival, you'll know you're in Kham, China's 'Develop the West' campaign having hardly dented the Tibetan culture here. Yaks, sheep skins, yak-butter tea, nomads, khampas (people from Kham, in Tibet), all set in a town that time has for the nonce left unbothered.

Lǐtáng has a fantastically relaxed and friendly atmosphere. While there may not be much in the way of sights, you can easily fill your days hanging out with the local people under a blazing sun and starry night skies or exploring the spectacular walks into the surrounding hills. Advice on where to go (ie where isn't currently being used as grazing pastures or for sky burials; see Sky Burial, p790) should be sought from locals. Be sure to allow yourself time to acclimatise to the altitude before you set out.

If you do find yourself suffering from altitude sickness and can't get out of town, there is a local treatment consisting of medicated pills and re-hydration drinks. The woman running Crane Guesthouse (see right) may be able to help you out; however, this shouldn't be considered a remedy and you should still descend to a lower altitude as soon as possible.

INFORMATION

China Post (Yóujú; ⏰ 9am-11.30am & 2-5.30pm) On the main north–south street. Next door is a place to use internet phone (IP) cards.

Internet café (wǎngbā; per hr Y5) On the third floor in a building diagonally across from the High City Hotel.

Public showers (Yuánxǐyù Zhōngxīn; 园洗浴中心; Y8) Can be found south of the main crossroads.

SIGHTS & ACTIVITIES

At the northern end of town is the large **Lǐtáng Chöde Gompa** (理塘长青春科尔寺; Lǐtáng Chángqīng Chūnkē Ěrsì), a Tibetan lamasery, built for the third Dalai Lama. Inside is a statue of Sakyamuni that is believed to have been carried from Lhasa by foot. Tibetan homes lead up to the lamasery and you are likely to encounter friendly monks en route who may offer to give you a tour.

On the eastern edge of Lǐtáng is **Qūdēnggābù**, a newly erected *chörten* which active worshippers seem to be perpetually circling as they recite mantras and spin prayer wheels. Smaller *chörten* fill the courtyard, which itself is edged with a corridor of prayer wheels.

There are **hot springs** (温泉; wēnquán; admission Y6-7) at the western edge of town, 4km from the centre. A taxi costs Y7 one way.

FESTIVALS & EVENTS

The annual Lǐtáng Horse Festival is known as one of the biggest and most colourful in Tibet and every five years an even more spectacular event is staged. The festival usually starts on 1 August and lasts for 10 days, but it's worth checking at the hostels and travel agencies in Kāngdìng or Chéngdū before you head here. The festival includes horse racing, stunt demonstrations on horseback, dance competitions and an arts-and-crafts festival and trade fair.

SLEEPING & EATING

Lǐtáng has decent food and (now) tons of lodging, making it a fine place to stay for a day or more. Many hotels have no hot water and electricity everywhere can be unreliable. Cheapo hostels (Y10-15 per bed, no showers) are found around the bus station.

Crane Guesthouse (Xiānhé Bīnguǎn; 仙鹤宾馆; ☎ 532 3850; dm Y25) Cosy two- and three-bed dorms are a good deal here with electric blankets and heaters; a shower costs Y5. The two Tibetan sisters who run the place are quite helpful. Turn left out of the bus station and head about 350m east into town; it's on the right-hand side of the road.

Good Luck Guesthouse (Jíxiáng Bīnguǎn; 吉祥宾馆; ☎ 532 3688; d Y60, with toilet Y120) Another option with larger, clean rooms. The reception is accessed from the back.

High City Hotel (Gāochéng Bīnguǎn; 高城宾馆; d/tr Y100/120) The best you're gonna get is this government-run hotel; the spacious rooms come with a heater, TV, squat toilet and, they say,

SKY BURIAL

The white cloth is removed from the body while the *tomden* (a religious master of ceremonies) sharpens his large knife. He circles a small Buddhist monument, reciting mantras all the while, and slices into the body lying before him on the stone slab. The flesh is cut into large chunks and the bones and brain are smashed and mixed with barley flour.

The smell of flesh draws a large number of vultures that circle impatiently above. Eventually the Tomden steps away and the huge birds descend into a feeding frenzy, tearing at the body and carrying it in pieces up to the heavens.

This is sky burial (*tiānzàng*), an ancient Buddhist-Tibetan burial tradition that performs both a spiritual and practical function. According to Buddhist beliefs, the body is merely a vehicle to carry you through this life; once a body dies, the spirit leaves it and the body is no longer of use. Giving one's body as food for the vultures is a final act of generosity to the living world and provides a link in the cycle of life. Vultures themselves are revered and believed to be a manifestation of the flesh-eating God Dakinis.

Practically, this form of burial provides an ecologically sound way to dispose of bodies in a terrain where wood is scarce and the ground is often frozen solid.

The Chinese banned sky burials in the 1960s and '70s. It wasn't until the '80s, as Tibetans regained limited religious rights, that the practice was once again legalised. However, most Han Chinese still regard sky burials as a primitive practice. The fact that one Buddhist sect has been known to keep the tops of the skulls to use as enlarged sacred teacups has often been touted as proof of Tibetan savagery.

In Lhasa, tourists require official permission to attend a sky burial; in the more remote areas of Sìchuān, however, you may well be told where and when the burials are to take place. Nevertheless, local Tibetans have been unsurprisingly offended by travellers who have turned these funerals into tourist outings. Common decency applies – if you aren't invited, don't go, and whatever you do, do not attempt to capture the moment on camera.

hot water. The lobby has a killer karaoke unit, loaded and ready at all times.

Lǐtáng has countless small restaurants, the most popular of which can be found on the south side of the main road a couple of hundred metres west of the Crane Hotel. Of these, **Lianmeixian Restaurant** (廉美县 餐厅; Liánměixiàn Cāntīng; dishes Y8; ⏰ 10am-8pm) has an English speaker.

GETTING THERE & AWAY

Lǐtáng's bus station is chaotic and has unhelpful staff. At the time of writing daily buses were leaving Lǐtáng for Kāngdìng (Y80, eight hours, 6am or 7am) and Bātáng (Y59, six hours, 7.30am). One or two buses pass through Lǐtáng each day from Kāngdìng en route to Dàochéng and Xiāngchéng (Y60, five hours, 7am).

It looks easy to head north to Gānzī via Xīnlóng from here, but though roadwork continues, at the time of writing, it was still a no-go for public transport.

Lǐtáng to Shangri-la (Zhōngdiàn)

This is a back-door route to Yúnnán that takes you through 400km of spectacular scenery via Xiāngchéng to Shangri-la, (p726) also known as Zhōngdiàn.

Buses from Kāngdìng and Lǐtáng head for Xiāngchéng (see p780 and left respectively), where you'll have to spend the night. From Xiāngchéng you can catch a bus to Shangri-la in Yúnnán province between 7am and 8am. Going the other way, buses from Xiāngchéng head back to Lǐtáng at around the same time. Try to buy your onward ticket on arrival in Xiāngchéng as the ticket office is not always manned before the first buses leave in the morning. Be forewarned: the road between Xiāngchéng and Shangri-la is sometimes closed in the dead of winter (or even in spring and autumn) due to heavy snow. You'd be wise to check before heading out from Lǐtáng.

Xiāngchéng is a small border town that is quickly expanding with the usual tiled buildings and blaring horns. A hike up to the Tibetan temple (Y10) offers views over the valley and what's left of the town's traditional square stone houses. This lamasery itself is being completely rebuilt by hand and is worth a visit to watch carvers and painters at work.

The lamasery is at the opposite end of town from the bus station. To find it, follow the dirt track up on the left as you reach the edge of town.

Bamu Tibetan Guesthouse (☎ 582 6835; dm/d Y20-25/200) is your home for the night. Beds in clean, warm dorm rooms are a good deal. The ornate fronting of the hotel contrasts shockingly with the muddy bus station nearby.

More substantial hotels are being built in the newer part of town; just exit the bus station and walk towards the white tile.

Bātáng 八塘

☎ 0836 / elevation 2589m

Lying 32km from the Tibetan border and 5½ bumpy hours down a dirt track from Lǐtáng, low-lying Bātáng is the closest town to Tibet that is open to foreigners. An easy-going and friendly place with lots of streetside barbecue grills and outdoor seating, the town itself is quite modern but the surrounding suburbs of ochre Tibetan houses are lovely. Bātáng is much lower than surrounding areas; when it's still the end of winter in Lǐtáng it's already spring in Bātáng.

Many travellers try to sneak into Tibet from Bātáng, so, unsurprisingly, the local PSB is a little suspicious of foreigners.

SIGHTS

The Gelugpa sect **Chöde Gaden Pendeling Monastery** in the southwest of town is well worth a visit. The monks (over 500) are friendly and active (they had just finished building a sand mandala during our visit). There are three rooms behind the main hall: a protector chapel, giant statue of Jampa and a 10,000 Buddha room. Up some stairs via a separate entrance is a room for the Panchen Lama, lined with photos of exiled local lamas who now reside in India. Most images here are new but one upstairs statue of Sakyamuni is claimed to be 2000 years old. An old Chinese hospital is now used as monk accommodation. Stop in the kitchen for butter tea before leaving.

There are some fine walks around town. Head north to a lovely Tibetan hillside village and then west to a riverside *chörten* and a few inevitable pilgrims. Alternatively, head south from the town centre over a bridge and then east to a hilltop covered in prayer flags and offering views of the town.

SLEEPING & EATING

Jīnhuì Bīnguǎn (金汇宾馆; ☎ 562 2700; dm Y10-15, d Y70, tr without bathroom Y60) This is the old standby in Bātáng and though its plumbing can have its bad days, all in all it holds up OK, especially for the price. Rooms in the back are quieter and face a Tibetan village. From the bus station continue into town and take the first right after the hard-to-miss golden eagle; it's a block down on the left.

Bāwǔ Bīnguǎn (巴武宾馆; ☎ 562 2882; dm Y15-25, s/d without bathroom Y60/40, d with bathroom Y120) Some have written in that this hotel may have but a modicum of charm, yet its comfy doubles and clean(ish) hot showers are a good bet.

Government Hotel (迎宾楼; Yíngbīn Lóu; ☎ 562 1566; d Y266) Once the only 'top'-end place in town, this now has some rivals. Check out a few and bargain like mad (getting a comfy room for Y120 to Y160 is usually possible). This is still a good bet, and discounts down to Y180 are not unheard of.

There are plenty of Sichuanese restaurants around town. Local supermarkets stock everything from chocolate to French red wine.

GETTING THERE & AWAY

There are daily buses to Lǐtáng (Y59, six hours, 7am), Kāngdìng (Y138, two days via Lǐtáng) and Chéngdū (Y231, two days via Yǎjiāng). The road to Lǐtáng is under major construction until God knows when, so expect serious delays. The bus station is a 10-minute walk from the town centre.

Headed west, there are buses at 2pm (Y44, four hours) and afternoon microbuses (Y50) to Markham, 138km away inside Tibet. Foreigners will have problems buying tickets to Markham as the town is officially closed.

From Kāngdìng, a bus leaves for Bātáng (Y138) each morning at 6.45am, overnighting in Lǐtáng. Buses from Lǐtáng to Bātáng (Y59) leave daily at 7.30am.

NORTHERN SÌCHUĀN

Plopping aboard a pony for a trek around Sōngpān and hiking in the stunning – this is not hyperbole – nature preserve of Jiǔzhàigōu are how most travellers experience the carpets of alpine forest, swaths of grasslands, primevally icy lakes and breathtaking (literally and figuratively) mountains of Northern Sìchuān. None will ever forget it.

Northern Sìchuān is home to the Ābà, Tibetan and Qiāng Autonomous Prefectures. In the extreme northwest, the region around Zöigê and Lǎngmùsì is the territory of the Goloks, nomads who speak their own dialect of Tibetan, distinct from the local Amdo dialect. While these Tibetan destinations are less visited, you can incorporate them into an alternative route into Gānsù.

Most of northern Sìchuān is between 2000m and 4000m in altitude so make sure you take warm clothing. The grassland plateau in the northwest averages more than 4000m and even in summer, temperatures can dip to 15°C at night. The rainy season lasts from June to August.

Beyond the Sōngpān–Jiǔzhàigōu route, roads in the region aren't always in the best condition. (Buses aren't much better.) Roads are particularly hazardous in summer when heavy rains prompt frequent landslides. You might want to think about planning this trip for the spring or autumn, when the weather is likely to be better.

The beauty comes at a cost: one thing you are bound to see in the north are the countless logging trucks that shuttle up and down the Minjiang Valley (near Huánglóng), stripping the area of its forest. Some sources estimate that up to 40% of the region's forests have been logged in the last half decade, causing erosion, landslides and increased levels of silt heading downstream, eventually flowing into the Yangzi River (Cháng Jiāng).

One more time, bear in mind that there is nowhere to change money in this region, so bring sufficient Renminbi.

SŌNGPĀN 松潘
☎ 0837 / pop 71,650

This one-horse town actually has quite a few horses, as it draws loads of travellers coming for its horse treks and/or as a stopover point on the road to Jiǔzhàigōu. While the bustling downtown is filled with modern tourist shops selling Tibetan wares, old wooden buildings still line some of the side streets and residential areas. Tour groups eschew the place – their tour buses barrelling through on the way to Jiǔzhàigōu – so it is fairly relaxed.

On another note, be sure to bring a torch (flashlight) with you to Sōngpān, which is often plagued with faulty electricity. Infrastructure upgrades result in a lack of water from time to time as well.

Information

China Post (Yóujú; Shungjian Lu; ⏱ 9am-11.30am & 2-5.30pm) is on the main street about halfway between the north and south gates.

Along Shunjiang Lu, the Agricultural Bank of China has put in an ATM that is foreign-card friendly; others have had no problem but it didn't work for us. It cannot yet change travellers cheques, though you might, in a pinch, beg a cash exchange.

Not far from the Min River (Mín Hé) and teahouses are a couple of China Telecom shops where you can make cheap international calls with internet phone (IP) cards.

Emma's Kitchen (p794) has good internet access.

Quite literally the week we visited the Sōngpān PSB (Gōngānjú; Shunjiang Lu) had started renewing visas, often – gasp! – in a half-hour and – double gasp! – even on Saturday (if you're lucky). So be nice to them!

Sights

The ancient **gates** from Sōngpān's days as a walled city are still intact and a couple of old covered wooden bridges span the Min River. On the far western side of the river is **Guānyīn Gé**. Walking up to it will take you through a village-like setting and the small temple offers views over Sōngpān.

Activities

Several kilometres outside Sōngpān lie idyllic mountain forest and emerald-green lakes. One of the most popular ways to experience this is by joining up with a horse trek from Sōngpān. Guides can take you out through pristine, peaceful valleys and forests, all aboard a not-so-big, very tame horse. Many people rate this experience as one of the highlights of their travels in Sìchuān.

Treks are organised by **Shun Jiang Horse Treks** (Shùnjiāng Lǚyóu Mǎduì; ☎ 723 1201), located about 30m south of the bus station on your left. The guys here have been catering horse treks to backpackers for years. The vast majority of travellers are utterly happy, but now and again we get reports of lackadaisical if not disinterested (and occasionally gruff) guides. Check with travellers who have recently taken a trip; there will be loads of them. On offer are anything from one- to 12-day treks and trips can be tailored to suit you.

One of the most popular treks is the four-day trip to **Ice Mountain** (雪玉顶; Xuěyùdǐng)

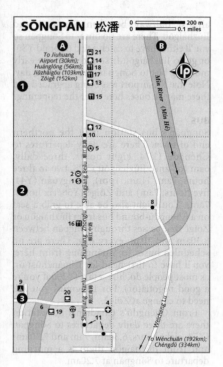

SŌNGPĀN 松潘

To Jiuhuang
Airport (30km);
Huánglóng (56km);
Jiǔzhàigōu (103km);
Zöigé (152km)

Min River (Mín Hé)

Shunjiang Beilu 顺江北路

Shunjiang Zhonglu 顺江中路

Shunjiang Nanlu 顺江南路

Weicheng Lu 卫城路

To Wénchuān (192km);
Chéngdū (334km)

INFORMATION
Agricultural Bank of China 中国农业银行 1 A2
China Post 邮局 2 A2
China Telecom 中国电信 3 A3
Hospital 医院 4 A3
PSB 公安局 5 A2

SIGHTS & ACTIVITIES
Covered Bridge 古松桥 6 A3
Covered Bridge 古松桥 7 A3
East Gate 东门 8 B2
Guānyīn Gé 观音阁 9 A3
North Gate 北门 10 A1
Shun Jiang Horse Treks 顺江旅游马队 ...... (see 13)
South Gate 南门 11 A3

SLEEPING
Ice Mountain Hostel 雪玉顶旅馆 12 A1
Shun Jiang Guesthouse 顺江自助旅馆 13 A1
Sōngzhōu Jiāotōng Bīnguǎn 松州交通宾馆 14 A1

EATING
Emma's Kitchen 小欧洲西餐厅 15 A1
Muslim Restaurant 穆斯林餐厅 16 A2
Song in the Mountain 17 A1
Yùlán Fànguǎn 玉兰饭馆 18 A1

DRINKING
Gǔchéng Cháyuán 古城茶园 19 A3
Teahouses 茶馆 20 A3

TRANSPORT
Bus Station 客运汽车站 21 A1

a spectacular trip through as yet unspoilt scenery.

If you're feeling particularly adventurous (and particularly flush) you can make the trip north to Zöigé on horseback, a trek that takes around 12 days. Bear in mind that you will have to cover the cost of the horses on their return journey to Sōngpān which can make it quite an expensive way to travel.

Rates are very reasonable (from Y100 per day per person); you get a horse, three meals a day, tents, bedding, warm jackets and raincoats. The guides take care of everything: you won't touch a tent pole or a cooking pot unless you want to. The only additional charge is entrance to the different sites (Y20 to Y110 each), but you'll be warned of these before you set out.

As food consists mainly of green vegetables, potatoes and bread, you may want to take along some extra snacks for variety.

Sleeping
Note that all the midrange hotels have boarded up here; if it's cosiness you want a couple of overpriced ones are fairly far south of town or, better, head north to Chuānzhǔsì,

launching point for Huánglóng Glacier. Dorm beds and cheap private rooms are no problem to find here. Figure Y50 for a comfortable double room with private bathroom in low season. Our favourite are those above the Yùlán Fànguǎn restaurant (seep794), which has Y50 doubles and, as a bonus, heat lamps in the clean bathrooms, a nice treat after a couple of days freezing in a tent.

Shun Jiang Guesthouse (Shùnjiāng Zìzhù Lǚguǎn; ☎ 723 1201, 723 1064; Shunjiang Beilu; 顺江北路; dm Y20) Run by the Shun Jiang Horse Trek company, this simple but clean guesthouse is right above their office, which means you can literally roll out of bed and into the saddle.

Ice Mountain Hostel (Xuěyùdǐng Lǚguǎn; ☎ 880 9609; Shunjiang Beilu; 顺江北路; dm Y20) Clean rooms and bathrooms and a nice owner at this new hostel (more like a homestay); the proprietress' son and playmates will undoubtedly introduce themselves to you!

Sōngzhōu Jiāotōng Bīnguǎn (☎ 723 1818, 723 1258; Shunjiang Beilu; 顺江北路; dm Y25-40, d/tr Y180/150) Attached to the bus station, this newish hotel has an enormous number of rooms to choose from. Most find it just fine, while others knock the reverberation from its cavernous interiors.

Truth be told, the rooms with private bathroom are a bit much for the rack rate, especially when staff insist on haggling (no one else in town does that much anymore).

Eating

Sōngpān has an excellent assortment of breads for sale, made and sold fresh all day at small stalls along Shunjiang Zhonglu – big crusty loaves, dumplings, Tibetan flatbread and sweet breads.

There are also a huge number of restaurants along Shunjiang Zhonglu including hotpot and noodle shops. Many have English signs and menus.

Yùlán Fànguǎn (Shunjiang Beilu; dishes from Y8; ☿ 8am-8pm) This is Sōngpān's original hangout for foreign travellers and remains popular today, with excellent food and good ambience. The friendly owners just put in some nice rooms upstairs.

Emma's Kitchen (Xiǎo Ōuzhōu Xīcāntīng; ☎ 880 2958; mains from Y10; ☿ 6.30am-late) Great food and atmosphere and some therapeutic sofas (which feel even more comfortable when you return from your horse trek) make this a popular place. Emma is *very* helpful – trust us, she'll find you – and can sort out almost anything from laundry to travel information.

Song in the Mountain (☎ 723 3916; mains from Y10; ☿ 7am-11.30pm) This small restaurant is run by the daughter of Fis Took Yang, 'the good guide with the bad eye' at the Shun Jiang Horse Trek. It's right next door to the office and serves up some decent food.

South of the intersection on Shunjiang Zhonglu is a recently refurbished **Muslim restaurant** (Mùsìlín Cāntīng; dishes from Y10) with fantastic food. Prices are a bit high and there's no English menu, but you can easily pick out what you want in the kitchen. The *yúxiāng qiézi* (fish-flavoured eggplant) is particularly good.

Drinking

Along the Min River, on the southern edge of town, are a number of teahouses where you can enjoy views of the covered wooden bridge, Guānyīn Gé and wooden houses. Try the **Gǔchéng Cháyuán** (Old Town Tea Garden; ☎ 723 3745), on the left before you cross over the bridge.

Getting There & Away
AIR

Jiuhuang Airport (九黄机场; Jiǔhuáng Jīchǎng) is near Chuānzhǔsì, a small town almost halfway between Sōngpān and Jiǔzhàigōu. There are no buses to Sōngpān so you'll either have to catch a taxi (around Y80) or go to Jiǔzhàigōu first and catch the early morning bus to Sōngpān the following day. Note that the airport was being upgraded and there may be buses here after the reopening.

BUS

Sōngpān's bus station is at the northern end of town. There are daily departures to Chéngdū (Y74, eight hours, three daily, 6am to 7am), Jiǔzhàigōu (Y28, two to three hours, 7am, 11am, 1pm), Hóngyuán (Y44, five hours, 7am) and Zöigê (Y56, six hours, 7am). You might also be able to grab a seat on a Chéngdū-bound bus from Jiǔzhàigōu or Zöigê that passes through Sōngpān between 8.30am and 10am every day. There are no scheduled buses to Huánglóng from here; you'll have to first head for Chuānzhǔsì or, as most people do, hire a taxi (Y200 if you're a good negotiator). For Lǎngmùsì you will need to change at Zöigê.

From Chéngdū's Chadianzi bus station there are three daily departures to Sōngpān (Y74, eight hours, 6.30am, 7am and 7.30am) and from Jiǔzhàigōu there is a morning departure to Sōngpān at 7.20am.

HUANGLONG NATIONAL PARK
黄龙景区

The name describes the tail of a yellow dragon slithering through a valley, helping the King of the Xia kingdom, Xiayu, create the Min River here at **Huánglóng** (Huánglóng Jǐngqù; Yellow Dragon Valley; www.huanglong.com; admission Y200; ☿ 7am-6pm). A national park, it is indeed laced with a golden-hued calcium carbonate which, in the right light, certainly could lead one to conjure an altruistic mythical beast.

All the colours of the rainbow are here, actually, the landscape studded with waterfalls and terraced, coloured limestone ponds of blue, yellow, white and green. Consequently, it has earned the nickname Wǔcǎichí (Five-coloured Pool). To see the pools in their full rainbow glory, the best time of year to visit is September and October.

The most spectacular ponds are behind **Huanglong Temple** (黄龙寺; Huánglóng Sì), deep in the valley and 7.5km from the road. (The temple was built to honour the dragon.) A round trip along a footpath takes about four hours, with the trail returning through dense (and dark) forest. While some people rave about the valley's beauty and love the peace and quiet here, others find it disappointing and prefer an extra day at Jiǔzhàigōu. If you do visit, there are no vendors, so bring some water and supplies.

A great time to visit is during the annual **Temple Fair** (庙会; Miào Huì). Held here around the middle of the sixth lunar month (usually July), it attracts large numbers of traders from the Qiang minority.

No lodging is allowed in the park anymore, and outside you've got one super-pricey option. Chuānzhǔsì has almost all places to stay.

Around 56km from Sōngpān, Huánglóng is almost always included on the itinerary of the seven-day Jiǔzhàigōu tours that run out of Chéngdū, as well as on the horse-trekking tours out of Sōngpān. Unfortunately, unless you've signed up on a tour, the valley can be difficult to reach. Currently, there is one bus a day from Jiǔzhàigōu (Y41, three hours, 7.10am) but this would leave you hung up, as the bus returns the next day with nary a cheap pillow for your head.

However, as Jiuhuang Airport has been expanded, more buses may at least operate between the airport and the national park (though you'd still have to shell out Y700 just to save money on a bus!).

JIUZHAIGOU NATURE RESERVE
九寨沟自然保护区
☎ 0837 / pop 62,000

Just inside Sìchuān's northern border lies **Jiuzhaigou Nature Reserve** (Jiǔzhàigōu Zìrán Bǎohùqū; Nine Village Gully; www.jiuzhaigouvalley.com; adult/student Y220/170; ☼ 7am-6pm), a national park and UN World Biosphere Reserve. To get things out of the way right away: you will hear grumping about the heart-locking ticket cost and tutting of the 'too-many-tourists' syndrome. True enough, but say, 'Pish!' and go anyway – it's a national treasure and you'll never forget a visit to this place.

Jiǔzhàigōu, meaning 'Nine Village Gully' refers to the nine Baima Tibetan villages that can be found in the valley. The area is lightly sprinkled with Bön prayer flags, *chörten* and prayer wheels that spin anticlockwise, powered by the current of the rivers. According to legend, Jiǔzhàigōu was created when a jealous devil caused the goddess Wunosemo to drop her magic mirror, a present from her lover the warlord God Dage. The mirror dropped to the

ground and shattered into 118 shimmering turquoise lakes.

Those pools of eye candy are what lie within your dreams after you leave, along with the snow-crusted mountain peaks, and forests and meadows, home to protected takins, golden monkeys and pandas.

The park is pristine, but resort-style hotels leading up to the park entrance have 20,000 beds; over 1.5 million people per year come here. (And both of these were true before the airport opened.) The original residents have been forced to move in order to 'protect' the park (those here actually work within the park's confines to keep up appearances). And as you're technically not allowed to strike off into the backcountry, it can be a bit disheartening as the efficient shuttle buses whiz by with an alarming regularity.

All true. Then again, considering all this, it's still a remarkable gem, and worth a splurge of yuán and time.

Orientation & Information
Buses from Chéngdū and Sōngpān will drop you outside the park reception centre and ticket office, just north of the park entrance. If you can produce something remotely resembling a student card you'll be given a discount. The price includes entrance to all areas of the park but does not include the bus (Y90) that ferries tourists around inside the park.

There is an ATM at the park entrance that accepts major credit cards.

Sights
The first official site inside the park is the Tibetan **Zaru Temple** (Zārú Sì; Zaru Gompa in Tibetan). The bus is unlikely to take you there, but it's only a short walk down the first fork off the main road.

If you continue on the main road, you'll follow **Zechawa River** (Zécháwá Hé) as it runs past **Heye Stockade** (Héyè Cūn) to **Huǒhuā Hú** (Sparkling Lake). This is the first in a series of lakes filled by the **Shuzheng Waterfall** (Shùzhēng Pùbù). Keep your eyes open for trees growing unexpectedly out of the middle of the river, lakes and waterfalls. This is caused by fertile pockets of calcium in the waterways which create impromptu flowerpots.

A walking trail begins north of Sparkling Lake and runs along the eastern edge of the river as far as **Shuzheng Stockade** (Shùzhēng Zhài). Here it crosses back over, leading you to a number of water-powered prayer wheels. The trail then continues up to the Shuzheng Waterfall.

South from here, just past **Promising Bright Bay Waterfall** (Nuòrilǎng Pùbù), the road branches in two, with the eastern road leading to **Long Lake** (Cháng Hǎi) and **Five-coloured Pool** and the western road to **Swan Lake** (Tiān è Hǎi). If you're looking to stretch your legs and clear your lungs, you'd be better off heading along the western route where there are a

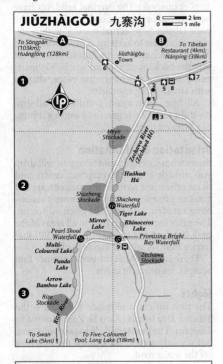

number of scattered sights and a quiet forest trail leading from **Mirror Lake** (Jìnghǎi) to **Panda Lake** (Xióngmāo Hǎi). Views from this trail are particularly good, especially of **Pearl Shoal Waterfall** (Zhēnzhūtán Pùbù). If you continue past Panda Lake, you will leave the majority of the traffic behind.

The eastern route is almost better done by bus as the narrow road sees a great deal of traffic from one end to the other. Nevertheless, the two lakes at the far end are both well worth a visit.

From the park entrance to Promising Bright Bay Waterfall is about 14km. It's a further 17.5km along the western road to the primary forest and 18km down the eastern road to Long Lake.

Tours

During summer, various companies in Chéngdū operate tours to Jiǔzhàigōu and the surrounding area. Most of the trips are advertised for a certain day, but the bus will only go if full. If you are unlucky you may have to spend days waiting, so don't pay first.

A standard tour includes Huánglóng and Jiǔzhàigōu, lasts seven days and starts from Y400 per person. Hotels, food and entry fees are not included in the price. Chéngdū travel agencies in the Dragon Town Youth Hostel and Jínjiāng Bīnguǎn (see p760 for these places) and CITS (p757) both offer tours.

A word of warning: several tour operators in Chéngdū have been blacklisted by travellers for lousy service and/or rudeness. Ask around among travellers to pinpoint a reliable agency.

Sleeping & Eating

Everywhere you look are upper-mid and top-end hotels but only a few budget ones. Expect a huge hike in prices during high season (July and August) and all national holidays. Rates quoted below are for the off season, at which time you can often still get great discounts. Staying inside the park is not allowed, but naturally some people manage to stay with locals anyway; if you don't expect them to feed or entertain you.

YouU Hostel (悠游度假连锁酒店; Yōuyóu Dùjià Liánsuǒ Jiǔdiàn; Kangba Noble Manor; 康巴林卡风情村; ☎ 776 3111; www.youuhotel.com; dm/d Y40/100; 🖳) Just prior to publication, a godsend: a new (read, untested) hostel opened near Jiuzhaigou's entrance. The YouU lies 2.5km north of the park entrance. Facing the park entrance, head right (uphill) till you see the English sign for the Kangba Noble Manor, cross the bridge and backtrack a bit, following the signs.

Jiǔtōng Bīnguǎn (☎ 773 9879; fax 773 9877; dm Y30, d Y100) Next to the bus station is the long-time standby, still going strong. Concrete floors and spartan, but just fine (staff know how to deal with you, too – they'll dash off to find an English speaker, most likely).

Lántiān Bīnguǎn (☎ 877 8888; d Y120-398, tr Y100-200) The haggling switches are always in the on position here, which is good. Above average detailing and appointments make it a good bet.

Héyè Yíngbīnguǎn (☎ 773 5555; fax 773 5688; d Y290) Just north of the park entrance, this hotel has lovely rooms with fancy marble bathrooms.

Sheraton Jiuzhaigou Resort (☎ 773 9988; fax 773 9666; www.sheraton.com/jiuzhaigou; d Y1200) One of the biggest hotels on the block and also one of the poshest. Rooms are elegant and the service is impeccable.

There isn't a huge choice of restaurants in Jiǔzhàigōu as most tourists tend to eat in their hotels. Several restaurants near the Lántiān Bīnguǎn serve up simple Chinese dishes.

Alternatively there is a good **Tibetan Restaurant** (阿布氇孜; Ābù Luzi; ☎ 889 7603, 844 8309; dishes from Y25; ☼ noon-9pm) that serves very good Chinese and Tibetan food. It's not cheap, but it's a nice place to treat yourself. The restaurant is not very conveniently located and you'll have to get a taxi here (Y10). It's next to Chángqīng Fàndiàn (长青饭店).

Inside the park eating options are even more limited (and expensive), especially if you visit during the off season.

Getting There & Away

AIR
Flights currently operate from Chéngdū (Y700, 40 minutes). A 2006 expansion will allow direct flights from Běijīng, Chóngqìng, Xī'ān, and one or two others.

Buses for Jiǔzhàigōu (Y45, 1½hr) wait at the airport for arrivals and leave when full. This means that you might have to wait around for a while, as most of your fellow passengers will be hopping off the plane and straight onto a tour bus.

Returning to the airport is much easier as a scheduled bus leaves from near the Lántiān Bīnguǎn.

Occasionally buses leave from the airport to Huánglóng (Y22, one hour) but only if there are enough people.

BUS
To Chéngdū can be done in 11 to 13 relatively painless hours. From Chéngdū's Chadianzi bus station there are four daily buses to Jiǔzhàigōu (Y92 to Y103, 7.20am, 8am, 8.40am and 2pm); Xinnanmen station also has one (Y92, 8am). If you're coming from Gānsù via Zöigê, you will have to go through Sōngpān. From Sōngpān to Jiǔzhàigōu (Y28, three hours, three times daily), the road goes up and over some gorgeous scenery.

From Jiǔzhàigōu to Sōngpān (Y28, two to three hours) there is a daily bus that leaves the park itself at 7.20am; otherwise, flag down buses which start from Nánpíng but don't stop at this station (bus station staff will let you know when!).

You could also take a leap over to Guǎngyuán (Y91, 10 to 12 hours), gateway to eastern Sìchuān and on the rail line to Xī'ān.

Between October and April, snow often cuts off access to Jiǔzhàigōu for weeks on end. Even at the best of times, transport is not plentiful. Hitching to Jiǔzhàigōu on tour buses has supposedly happened, but it's a rare occurrence indeed.

Getting Around
There is a bus service within the park that zips between the sights (Y90) stopping at Nuorilang bus station in the heart of the park. Unfortunately, these buses are often commandeered by tour groups who hop off at each sight, take their obligatory photos and hop back on 15 minutes later to race to the next. This can become rather tedious.

Buses run from about 7am until just before the park shuts at 6pm. If you're wandering around in the afternoon, it's best to make sure you're within an easy walking distance of your base as buses seem to travel more by the whim of their tour group than by any sort of schedule or route.

NORTHWEST ROUTE TO GĀNSÙ
This journey through the extreme northwest of Sìchuān has emerged as a popular backdoor route into Gānsù province for many travellers. Even if you're not headed north beyond the Sìchuān border, this area offers an opportunity to explore more remote Tibetan

towns and villages. At an average altitude of 3500m to 4000m, travel through this grassland bog is not recommended for those in a hurry – bus transport is slow and sporadic. If you plan to explore any of the towns or lamaseries on the way, you'll need a minimum of five days, more if you make a side trip to Jiǔzhàigōu.

In the winter months, roads often become impassable and temperatures plummet way past the tolerance levels of most mortals. While still cold, early autumn sees little rain and many clear and sunny skies. If you are travelling in the autumn or winter, it's best to buy your onward tickets as soon as possible as, during these colder months, the nomadic Goloks stay closer to main roads and towns and do much of their travel by bus.

The first leg of this route is from Chéngdū to Sōngpān (see p794 for more). Most travellers take a side trip from Sōngpān to Jiǔzhàigōu at this point. From Sōngpān you can travel 168km northwest to your next overnight stop in Zöigê, and from there it's worth heading to Lǎngmùsì, just inside the Sìchuān border, for a day or two before crossing into Gānsù.

Zöigê 若尔盖
☎ 0839 / pop 59,000

A dusty concrete town set amid the grasslands, Zöigê doesn't have much pull for travellers other than as a resting point en route to Lǎngmùsì and north to Gānsù province. It is easy enough to spend a day here sipping tea in the sun and at the northeastern edge of town is a gompa (寺院, sìyuàn) with pleasant, peaceful grounds. While the town's Chinese name is Ruòěrgài, it is most commonly referred to by its Tibetan name, Zöigê.

SLEEPING & EATING
Don't expect much in terms of washing facilities or hot water in Zöigê. The option here is the best for sleep. Others are a bit more grim.

Liángjù Bīnguǎn (量具宾馆; ☎ 229 8360; dm Y25) This is the best option in town. Beds are a bit more expensive but it's quiet, clean and cheerful. And the central heating works! Head right as you come out of the western bus station, take the first left onto the main street and then walk up about 15 minutes. This white-and-yellow hotel will be on your left-hand side.

Between Liángjù Bīnguǎn and the southwestern end of the main street are a number of small restaurants including hotpot and noodle shops.

Across from the ever-popular pool tables in the centre of town, Gābāfǎngzhào Cháguǎn (嘎巴仿照茶馆) is a teahouse where you can sit outside on the balcony, eat fresh bread and sip delicious eight-treasure tea.

There are also some small restaurants situated right next to the western bus station that sell fresh bread and dumplings in the mornings.

GETTING THERE & AWAY
Zöigê has two bus stations, one at the western edge of town and the other, on the same road, in the southeast. The western bus station has services to all destinations while the southeastern only has buses to Sōngpān. If you're heading to Sōngpān and can't get a ticket at the western station, it's worth trying at the southeastern one.

Buses run to Sōngpān (Y56, six hours, 6.30/6am summer/winter). Buses to Lǎngmùsì also run (Y25, 3½ hours, 2.30/2pm summer/winter); you could also await buses passing through from Hóngyuán. (A taxi to Langmusi costs approximately Y300.)

From Langmusi you can get to Hézuò in Gānsù province which is only a few hours from Xiàhé. From Xiàhé you have the option of travelling on to Lánzhōu or taking the more unusual option of heading to Xīníng in Qīnghǎi province, via Tóngrén.

Chóngqìng 重庆

After years as a kind of understudy to Sìchuān, Chóngqìng is getting its moment in China's spotlight.

While more or less ignored by the rest of the country since its glory days as the wartime capital, Chóngqìng's development is now seen by Běijīng as the key to getting China's interior up to speed with the east coast's economic success.

Chóngqìng is being showered with money in the hopes the boom will have a ripple effect, lifting the mega municipality's dozens of towns and hundreds of villages out of poverty.

It's a tall order for a city of five million and Chóngqìng is going through a fascinating awkward stage. Old stilted homes cling to hills in front of gleaming skyscrapers and massive architectural projects. Stick porters loaded with goods trot underneath the soaring new light-rail system.

For travellers, it makes Chóngqìng much more than just a place to kill time before your Three Gorges cruise.

Perched on the steep hills overlooking the confluence of the Yangzi River (Cháng Jiāng) and Jialing River (Jiālíng Jiāng), Chóngqìng spends most days blanketed by fog. By nighttime, however, the cloak is thrown off to reveal flashing neon and swooping spotlights.

A city ordinance against horns also means things are a lot quieter than in other Chinese cities. And with Chóngqìng's rolling hills you'll notice the absence of bicycles as motorbikes and cars fight for space on the city's crowded streets.

HIGHLIGHTS

- Explore Chóngqìng's ancient towns like **Shuāngjiāng** (p810) and **Láitān** (p810)
- Take on spicy hotpot, **Chóngqìng's** (p806) favourite and most famous dish
- Explore the exquisite Buddhist cave sculptures and grotto paintings in **Dàzú** (p809)

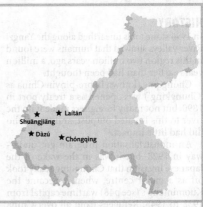

- AREA CODE: ☎ 023
- POPULATION: CITY 5 MILLION; MUNICIPALITY 31 MILLION

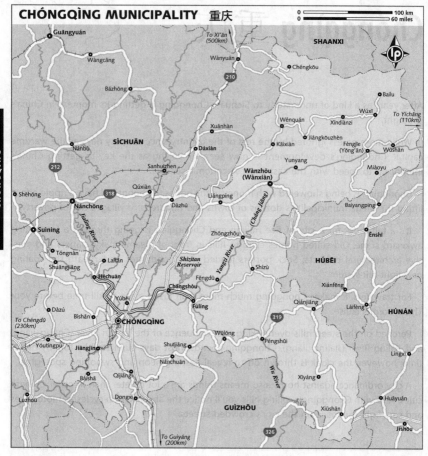

CHÓNGQÌNG MUNICIPALITY 重庆

HISTORY

In 1996 stone tools unearthed along the Yangzi River valleys showed that humans were found in this region two million years ago, a million years earlier than had been thought.

Chóngqìng (known in pre-pinyin China as 'Chungking') was opened as a treaty port in 1890, but not many foreigners made it up the river to this isolated outpost, and those who did had little impact.

An industrialisation program got underway in 1928, but it was in the wake of the Japanese invasion that Chóngqìng really took off as a major centre, when it became the Kuomintang's (see p48) wartime capital from 1938 to 1945. Refugees from all over China flooded in, swelling the population to over

two million. The bulk of Chóngqìng's sights are linked to this history.

In a city overpopulated and overstrained, with its bomb-shattered houses, these wartime residents must have found the name of their new home somewhat ironic: Chóngqìng means 'double happiness' or 'repeated good luck'. It was originally named Gongzhou but Emperor Zhaodun of the Song dynasty renamed it in 1190 when he ascended the throne. As he had previously been made the prince of the city, he called it Chóngqìng in celebration of these two happy events.

It was in Chóngqìng, under the shadow of Kuomintang military leaders, that representatives of the Chinese Communist Party (CCP), including Zhou Enlai, acted as 'liaisons' between the Kuomintang and the Communists' headquarters at Yán'ān, in Shaanxi province. Repeated efforts to bring the two sides together in a unified front against the Japanese largely failed due to mutual distrust and Chiang Kaishek's obsession with wiping out the Communists, even at the cost of yielding Chinese territory to an invading army.

For a long period the city lobbied for a special status akin to that of Shànghǎi. In 1997 what it got wasn't quite provincial status, but the three-county area separated from Sìchuān and became a 'special' municipality directly under central government control.

Billions of yuán have gone into its development and a major construction boom is on in full force. Just some of the ambitious projects that may be finished by the time you're reading this include a huge gleaming library in the Shāpíngbá district, a Science and Technology Exhibition Hall in Jiāngběi district and the 96,000-sq-metre Grand Theatre across from Chaotianmen Sq. The government hopes the theatre will become as much a symbol of Chóngqìng as the Opera House is of Sydney.

CLIMATE

Chóngqìng is known for two things throughout China: searingly hot summers and rain pretty much anytime else. Pack an umbrella and be prepared for the heat and humidity once July rolls around. Temperatures can exceed 40°C and this has earned the city a place among the country's 'three furnaces', along with Wǔhàn and Nánjīng.

ORIENTATION

The heart of Chóngqìng spreads across a hilly peninsula of land wedged between the Jialing River to the north and the Yangzi River to the south. The rivers meet at the tip of the peninsula at the eastern end of the city.

For most visitors, the central focus will be the Jiěfàngběi district, named for the Liberation Monument that stands in the middle of it. Originally a wooden structure built to commemorate Sun Yatsen's death, the monument was rebuilt in 1945 to celebrate the end of China's war with Japan.

This area is easy to explore on foot and has become very tourist-friendly thanks to the Chinese-English signs stuck on every street corner pointing the way to major sights and landmarks.

Maps

Good maps in Chinese and much less detailed ones in English are available on the first floor of the massive Xinhua Bookshop (see following) as well as from street vendors at Chaotianmen Sq.

INFORMATION
Bookshops

Xinhua Bookshop (Xīnhuá Shūdiàn; Zourong Lu; 9am-9pm) Foreign-language books (including bilingual English-Chinese novels) are on the 4th floor. Classics aside, there's a weird English collection favouring self-help books and National Hockey League (NHL) biographies.

Internet Access 网吧

Readers' Club Internet Café (Dúzhě 'Jùlèbù; 181 Minsheng Lu, 3rd fl; per hr Y8, deposit Y20; 24hr) Has a sea of computers. Probably the most comfortable option.

Media

Go West is a free, Sìchuān-based magazine that covers Chéngdū and Chóngqìng's bar, restaurant and entertainment scenes. Unfortunately, only a handful of copies (literally) of the bimonthly publication make their way to Chóngqìng. If you can't find any at the Marriott Hotel (across from the Flower & Bird Market), consider yourself out of luck.

Medical Services

There is a large pharmacy (yáofāng) next door to the Peace Hotel on Minzu Lu.
Global Doctor Chóngqìng Clinic (☎ 8903 8837; 7th fl, suite 701, Hilton Hotel, 139 Zhongshan Sanlu; 9am-5pm Mon-Fri, except holidays) For emergencies outside of regular hours, 24-hour on-call services are available by dialling the general clinic number.

Money

Bank of China (Zhōngguó Yínháng; 104 Minzu Lu; 9am-noon & 1.30-5pm Mon-Fri) Changes money and gives advances on credit cards. You'll need a good book and stiff whiskey if you want to change travellers cheques. Highlights may include, but are by no means limited to: a scolding for trying to cash more than US$100 at a time and being told your cheque is rejected because your signature is 'obviously not real English'. Thank goodness for their ATM.

Post

Post office (yóujú; Minquan Lu; 8.30am-9.00pm) Keep an eye out for the blue China Unicom sign. The post office is tucked way, way in the back. You can make international phone calls here too.

CHÓNGQÌNG

CHÓNGQÌNG CITY 重庆市

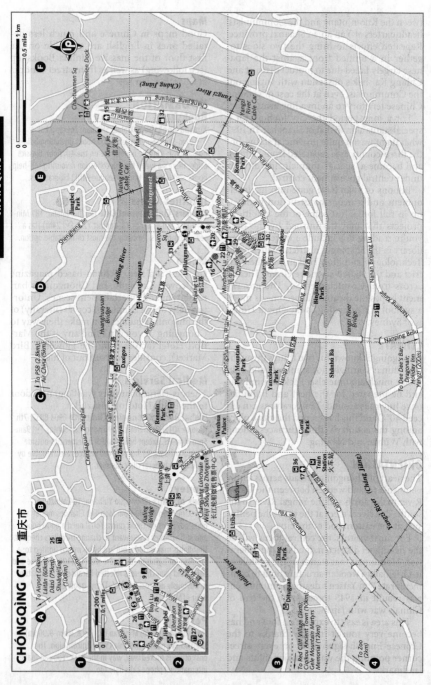

INFORMATION					
ATM 自动柜员机	1 A2	Báyī Bīnguǎn 八一宾馆	14 E3
Bank of China 中国银行	2 A1	Cháotiānmén Dàjiǔdiàn	
CITS 中国旅行社	3 D2	朝天门大酒店	15 F1
Global Doctor Chóngqìng		Chongqing Guesthouse	
Clinic	(see 4)	重庆宾馆	16 D2
Harbour Plaza Travel Centre		Fúyuán Bīnguǎn 富苑宾馆	17 B3
海逸旅游中心	(see 18)	Harbour Plaza	
Hilton Hotel 希尔顿酒店	4 C2	重庆海逸酒店	18 A2
Pharmacy 药方	5 A2	Huìxiānlóu Bīnguǎn	
Post Office 邮电局	6 A2	会仙楼宾馆	19 A2
Readers' Club Internet Café		Milky Way Hotel	
读者俱乐部网吧	7 D2	银河大酒馆	20 D2
Xinhua Bookshop 新华书店	8 E2	Square Hotel 赛格尔酒店	21 A2

SIGHTS & ACTIVITIES		EATING	
Arhat Temple 罗汉寺	9 A2	Hot Pot Restaurants 火锅	22 D2
Cháotiānmén Booking		Hot Pot Restaurants 火锅	23 D4
Hall朝天门码头售票处	10 E1	Hot Pot Restaurants 火锅	24 A2
Chongqing Planning Exhibition		Little Swan	
Gallery重庆市规划展览馆	11 F1	小天鹅火锅餐厅	25 B1
Stillwell Museum		Lǎo Sìchuān Dájiǔlóu	
史迪威将军旧居	12 B3	老四川大酒楼	26 A2
Three Gorges Museum		Pizza Almalfi 阿美菲比萨	27 A2
三峡博物馆	13 C2	Xiǎo Dóng Tiān 小洞天	28 A2

DRINKING	
Cotton Club 棉花Club	29 D3
Falling Disco	(see 26)
True Love	(see 26)

ENTERTAINMENT	
Díyí Shíjié 得意世界	30 D3

SHOPPING	
Carrefour 家乐福超级市场	31 A1
Chaotianmen Comprehensive	
Trade Market	
朝天门交易市场	32 F2
Flower & Bird Market	
花鸟市场	(see 29)

TRANSPORT	
Bus 104 to Red Cliff Village	
至红岩村汽车站	33 D2
Bus Service to Airport	
到机场的班车	34 D2
Buses to Martyrs Memorial	
Prisons 至中美合作所汽车站	35 B2
Long-Distance Bus Station	
长途汽车站	36 B3

Public Security Bureau

PSB (公安局; Gōngānjú; ☎ 6396 1996; 555 Huang-long Lu) The Entry-and-Exit Bureau issues visa extensions. To get there, take the 461 bus to the last stop.

Tourist Information

China International Travel Service (CITS; Zhōngguó Guójì Lǚxíngshè; ☎ 6903 7560; 8f, 151 Zourong Sq) Open daily; not much English is spoken at this office but it offers Chinese-only city tours (Y60) and day trips to Dàzú (Y220) that are generally cheaper than booking at your hotel. If you call ahead, the staff can try to find you an (expensive) English guide.

Harbour Plaza Travel Centre (Hǎiyì Lǚyóu Zhōngxīn; ☎ 6370 0888; 3rd fl, Harbour Plaza, Wuyi Lu; ☑ 7.50am-11pm) Staff here are used to dealing with expats and are near fluent in English. They're also better at ferreting out deals than other places in town. In addition, you can tap them for help with train tickets, Three Gorges tours or English guides.

DANGERS & ANNOYANCES

Chóngqìng is a relatively safe city, but pickpockets, especially children recruited from other provinces and supervised by nearby adults, are becoming a nuisance. Take care around the bus and train stations and around the dock area and crowded areas like department stores.

SIGHTS & ACTIVITIES

Chóngqìng's sights are scattered all over town. The best place to start is the downtown Jiěfàngbēi district. It has a gleaming new Planning Exhibition museum at its easternmost tip and the walk there will take you past interesting markets and street life. A few light-rail rides to the west of the centre is the sparkling new Three Gorges Museum as well as many of the most popular parks. The Shāpíngbà district, far west of downtown, is sprinkled with sights relating to Communist history and is worth visiting for Ciqikou Ancient Town.

Arhat Temple 罗汉寺

Built around 1000 years ago, this **temple** (Luóhàn Sì; admission Y5; ☑ 8am-5pm) has since been sandwiched between the skyscrapers and apartments of the city. At its peak, it was home to 70 monks; there are only around 18 in residence these days.

Luóhàn is the Chinese rendering of the Sanskrit *arhat*, which is a Buddhist term referring to people who have released themselves from the psychological bondage of greed, hate and delusion. Here, you'll find 500 terracotta *arhats* along with a large golden Buddha figure and an Indian-style *jataka* mural depicting Prince Siddhartha in the process of cutting his hair to renounce the world.

The temple's most remarkable feature is its long entrance flanked by rock carvings, many of which have survived the onslaught of time, the Cultural Revolution and the city's pollution amazingly well.

CHÓNGQÌNG

CHÓNGQÌNG

Chongqing Planning Exhibition Gallery 重庆市规划展览馆

Kudos to whoever conceived this fabulous **museum** (Chóngqìngshì Guīhuà Zhǎnlǎnguǎn; admission Y20; ☉ 9.30am-5.30pm Tue-Sun). It may not have the most balanced exhibits when it comes to presenting the Three Gorges Dam project but the rest of the exhibits devoted to Chóngqìng's history and future projects are flawless. Even those who find urban planning a bore will be won over by the models, lasers, lights and interactive consoles. Everything is well explained with expert English captions.

Downstairs, you'll find 40 rooms, each devoted to a different Chóngqìng county. As upstairs, the rooms and exhibits are beautifully done up, though the lack of English captions will make them impenetrable to most.

Ciqikou Ancient Town 磁器口古镇

Perched on a hill overlooking the Jialing River in the west of the city, Ciqikou Ancient Town (Cíqìkǒu Gǔzhèn) dates back to the late Ming dynasty. The buildings have been restored and preserved for tourists, and the main drag is lined with shops and restaurants; but there is still an air of authenticity about the place. Behind the shop fronts there's still a living, 'real' working village.

At one time there were five temples in town, but only **Bǎolún Sì** (admission Y5; ☉ 7am-6pm) remains today. The temple is in remarkable condition considering that it dates back to the Western Wei dynasty (AD 535–56), more than 1500 years ago.

Opposite the entrance to the temple is a small **museum** (admission Y2; ☉ 8am-6.30pm) dedicated to Chóngqìng's trackers, the coolies that used to haul ships up the Yangzi against the current. It's filled with wooden boat models with captions that are slowly being translated into English.

Bus 215 runs out here from Liberation Monument. The ride takes about an hour. A taxi takes 20 to 25 minutes and will cost Y30 to Y35.

Red Cliff Village 红岩村

During the Kuomintang-Communist alliance against the Japanese in WWII, this **village** (Hóngyán Cūn; admission Y18; ☉ 8.30am-5.15pm), outside Chóngqìng, was used as the offices and living quarters of the Communist representatives to the Kuomintang.

Among others, Ye Jianying, Zhou Enlai and Zhou's wife, Deng Yingchao, lived in Red Cliff Village. After the Japanese surrender in 1945, Mao Zedong also arrived in Chóngqìng – at the instigation of US ambassador Patrick Hurley – to join in the peace negotiations with the Kuomintang. The talks lasted 42 days and resulted in a formal agreement that Mao described as 'words on paper'.

One of China's better revolutionary history museums now stands at this site. There's a large collection of photos and though there are a few captions on the 3rd floor, the rest are in Chinese only.

To get to Red Cliff Village, take bus 104 from the bus stop on Beiqu Lu, just north of the Liberation Monument. The ride takes about an hour. A taxi from downtown will take about 20 minutes and will cost around Y20.

Gele Mountain Martyrs Memorial 歌乐山烈士陵园

In 1943 the USA and Chiang Kaishek signed a secret agreement to set up the Sino-American Cooperation Organisation (SACO), under which the USA helped to train and dispatch secret agents for the Kuomintang. The chief of SACO was Tai Li, the notorious head of the Kuomintang military secret service; its deputy chief was a US Navy officer, Commodore ME Miles.

Meanwhile, though the Kuomintang never recognised the Communist Party as a legal political entity, it in theory recognised the Red Army (which the Kuomintang called the 8th army) as allies in the struggle against the Japanese invaders. Despite this, civilian communists remained subject to repressive laws and hundreds were kept captive as political prisoners by the Kuomintang in SACO and other prisons. According to the communists, many were also executed.

Gele Mountain is now sprinkled with statues, plaques and three major **sites** (☉ 8.30am-7pm) relating to this period.

The Kuomintang once held hundreds of Communist Party members in **Zhāzǐ Dòng** (渣滓洞; admission Y10). Here, pictures and passable English captions line the former holding cells.

The **White House** (白公馆; admission Y10) is a 15- to 20-minute walk from the prison (just follow the signs). It's filled with more pictures and some gory Chinese films depicting the massacre of communist prisoners.

Further along down the road towards the bottom of the hill is the **Martyrs' Memorial** (烈士陵园; Liéshí Língyuán; admission Y5), towering over an enormous square and exhibition hall. The mega-slick hall is only mildly interesting, with still more photos referencing the war but no English captions.

Buses 210, 215 or 217 will get you to Gele Mountain. It's about a 45-minute ride from downtown. Make sure that the driver knows where you want to get off, as the place is not obvious.

Stillwell Museum 史迪威将军旧居

Undergoing renovations at the time of writing, this **museum** (Shǐdíwēi Jiāngjūn Jiùjū) is something of a novelty in China, as it sheds a relatively positive light on the US involvement in WWII. The museum is housed in the former VIP guesthouse of the Kuomintang and residence of General Stillwell, who was Commander of the US forces in the China-Burma-India Theatre and chief of staff to Chiang Kaishek in 1942. The museum should be reopened by the time you read this and may be of interest to American-history buffs. To get there take the light rail to the Liziba stop. The museum is a slow five-minute walk up the hill. You'll see it on your right.

Three Gorges Museum 三峡博物馆

Full of beautifully conceived displays, this recently opened **museum** (Sānxiá Bówùguǎn; adult/child Y40/20; ✆ 9.30am-5pm) definitely warrants setting aside a couple of hours to visit. Set in a gorgeous modern building, halls are devoted to telling the history of settlement in the Three Gorges and Chóngqìng region. There isn't much in the way of English captions but artefacts are so thoughtfully presented, it hardly matters. Keep an eye out for exhibits devoted to the ancient Ba kingdom and halls depicting street scenes from old 'Chungking'.

Parks

At 345m, **Pipa Mountain Park** (Pípá Shān Gōngyuán; admission Y5, plus temple Y3; ✆ 6am-10pm) marks the highest point on the Chóngqìng peninsula and is great for views of the city's night-time skyline.

Cable Car Trips

A ride on either of the city's two **cable cars** (Yangtze River Cable Car/Jialing River Cable Car Y2/1.5; ✆ 6.45am-9.45pm) spanning both the Jialing and Yangzi

Rivers will carry you over the precipitously stacked housing and polluting industrial estates for a bird's-eye view of the murky waters. Both cable cars are within walking distance of the Liberation Monument.

TOURS

Chóngqìng looks better by night when the grey of the city is replaced by the flash of neon. River cruises leave from Chaotianmen Dock, and are one of the best ways to enjoy the view. Most cruises sail around the peninsula and pass both the Jialing Bridge and the Yangzi River Bridge. Tickets can be bought from almost anywhere in town, including most hotels and the Cháotiānmén Booking Hall. Cruise times are: 11.30am to 1pm (Y35, with lunch); 3.30pm to 5pm (Y35, no meal); 7pm to 9pm (Y88 with dinner, Y68 no dinner); 9pm to 11pm (Y68, no dinner).

SLEEPING

If you're thinking of splurging, Chóngqìng is the place to do it. There's little in the way of budget accommodation. However, there are several good midrange options in town, most of which offer good discounts. There's no shortage of quality top-end hotels, and numerous five-star hotels are under construction.

Budget

Bāyī Bīnguǎn (☎ 6380 5400; fax 6383 4038; 250 Bayi Lu; 八一路250号; d from 150) Despite the run-down stairs, the peeling wallpaper and gritty-grotty bathrooms, rooms here are actually OK. The hotel is central and has a couple of cheerful English speakers on staff.

Fúyuán Bīnguǎn (☎ 6362 7333; 12 Caiyuan Lu; 菜袁路12号; s/d Y180-260, discounted Y120-148) Rooms here are delightful despite the battered bathrooms and musty halls, and this is the best budget option in town. Right by the bus and train station, it's got a great location for late arrivals/early departures but is out of the way for pretty much everything else. A huge internet café sits just off its lobby (Y2 per hour; Y10 deposit).

Midrange

Square Hotel (Saígéér Jiǔdiàn; ☎ 6373 3333; fax 6355 8222; 28 Wusi Lu; 五四路28号; d from Y258) Right smack downtown, this is a popular place for locals to send friends and business associates when they come to Chóngqìng. Rooms are weathered but many come with perks like microwaves and fridges and free buffet breakfast. Two horrendously slow elevators serve the entire building so prepare yourself for long waits. Check-in is on the 11th floor.

Chongqing Guesthouse (Chóngqìng Bīnguǎn; ☎ 6384 5888; www.cq-hotel.com/en/; 235 Minsheng Lu; 民生路 235号; old s/d Y228/260, VIP d Y435; 🖥) It's got bell-boys, a pool and amenities galore, making this midrange option feel more like a top-end choice. Just make sure you eyeball the room before handing over your deposit. Some rooms here, especially some of the business-floor suites, have strong musty smells.

Huìxiánlóu Bīnguǎn (☎ 6384 5101, ext 888; fax 6384 4234; 186 Minzu Lu; 民族路186号; s Y240, d Y260-320) There's an overpowering musty smell in the halls but even some of the basic single rooms are set up with TVs, couches and coffee tables. Dorm service occasionally offered during high-season summer months.

Cháotiānmén Dàjiǔdiàn (☎ 6310 0370; fax 6371 3035; 18 Xinyi Jie; 信义街18号; s/d/ste Y328/458/768) This 31-storey hotel towers near Chaotianmen Sq and has stunning night views of the river. Besides the odd wall and floor stain, rooms are well kept up. They don't get many foreigners here so prepare yourself for plenty of nervous giggles.

Milky Way Hotel (Yínhé Bīnguǎn; ☎ 6380 8585; fax 6381 2080; 49 Datong Lu; 大同路49号; d Y468) Recently renovated, rooms here are brighter and more comfortable than their counterparts at many of the city's five-star affairs. Bathrooms didn't get the same attention during the spruce up, but if you can nab a discount, this hotel is the best value in town.

Top End

Harbour Plaza (Chóngxìhǎiyì Jiǔdiàn; ☎ 6370 0888; www .harbour-plaza.com/hpcq; Wuyi Lu; 五一路; d Y1330; 🖥) Marshmallowlike duvets deck the beds and the hotel has amenities galore. The lobby is attached to the Metropolitan Plaza shopping mall so everything from shopping to video game arcades to bowling lanes are at your doorstep.

EATING
Street Food

The drag for a quick bite is Bayi Lu between Zourong Lu and Zhonghua Lu, a stretch known locally as 'tasty eating street'. There are numerous stalls selling all kinds of soups, barbeques and beasties on sticks. On week-ends, lines to buy them can run up to 25 people deep. If you want to sit down, check out **Xiǎo Dóng Tiān** (🕙 10am-10pm). Downstairs, just off Bayi Lu, this huge cafeteria has seating and is chock full of point-and-choose options and dumplings.

Hotpot

Chóngqìng's most famous dish has to be *huǒguō* (火锅; hotpot; see boxed text, opposite). While it's usually cheap, it's a good idea to check prices as you go along. Hotpot can be found wherever there are street vendors or small restaurants. Wuyi Lu has the greatest variety and is locally known as Huǒguō Jiē (Hotpot St). Another good place to look is Minsheng Lu, or if you're looking for somewhere a bit more lively then try any of the hotpot eateries along Nanan Binjiang Lu.

Little Swan (Xiǎotiān'é Huǒguō; ☎ 6785 5328; 78 Jianxin Lu; meals from Y100; 🕙 11am-2pm & 5-9pm) Up near the university district, this is reputedly Chóngqìng's best hotpot restaurant. It's usually one of the first hotpot restaurants that will be recommended to you by locals. It's self-service, which means it can get very expensive very quickly, but the hotpot is fantastic and more than lives up to its reputation. Take bus 411 or 902 from the Liberation Monument.

Restaurants

Undoubtedly the best place to look for restaurants is along Nanan Binjiang Lu on the other side of the Yangzi River. This restaurant strip is absolutely heaving with outdoor restaurants, from chaotic hotpot stalls to trendy restaurants where waitstaff serve meals wearing white gloves and surgical masks. It's worth going for the atmosphere alone and there's a boardwalk and some nice park space. On weekends, street musicians add to the carnival feel and you can happily spend several hours here enjoying your food and the crowds. To get there take the Yangzi River cable car (Chángjiāng Suǒdáo) to the south side of the river. From there, take a taxi (Y6 to Y8) or bus 338 or 373 (Y1) to the west and get off wherever it seems most interesting. Walking will take around 30 minutes.

There are also some great restaurants sprinkled around downtown.

Lǎo Sìchuān Dàjiǔlóu (Old Sichuan Restaurant; ☎ 6382 6644; Minzu Lu; dishes Y38; 🕙 11am-2pm & 5-9.30pm) This restaurant is where Chongqingers bring friends and family when they come to town.

HOT & VERY SPICY

Hotpot (*huǒguō;* literally 'fire pot') is Chóngqìng's favourite and most famous dish. It's eaten year-round, even in the summer months when the city itself resembles a furnace.

Born on the banks of the Yangzi River, hotpot was originally eaten by poor boatmen. Enterprising meat vendors would prepare a broth of chillies and Sìchuān pepper, and sell skewers of offal to cook in the spicy soup. Today, hotpot is no longer a poor man's dish and ingredients for dunking are not restricted to tripe. You can dip almost anything you like in your pot, from Chinese mushrooms and squid to tofu and lotus root.

Hotpot restaurants can be found all over Chóngqìng, not to mention all over China, but no one eats hotpot quite like a Chongqinger; the chillies they use are much, much hotter than the ones found in neighbouring Chéngdū.

If all this sounds like too much for your taste buds, ask for the *'yuānyāng'* version which is divided like a Yin and Yang symbol into a spicy side and a mild side (soup made of fish or chicken). Just tell the restaurateurs that you are *'pà là'* (scared of chilli spice). Don't be surprised if they laugh, however – you might as well be saying 'I'm a wimp'.

Even old standards like *málà dòufu* (麻辣豆腐; a spicy tofu dish) and crispy fish manage to stand out here. The décor is unremarkable bright red and gold but the atmosphere comes from the buzz. Order from the black-and-white English menu or the slick, colourful Chinese one loaded with pictures.

Pizza Almalfi (Āměifēi Bīsā; ☎ 6381 7868; Minzu Lu; pizza from Y45; ⏰ 9am-11pm) Pizzas here are missing the great slathering of tomato sauce that would make them slam-dunk authentic, but they have a good choice of toppings from the usual (sausages and olives) to the unique (chicken and cashews). It's a charmingly kitschy place decorated with happy faces and flickering heart lights and manned by an adorable waitstaff.

DRINKING

Chóngqìng nightlife revolves around flashy, high-tech karaoke bars, known as KTV bars, and strobe-lit discos that open and close so fast even locals have a hard time keeping track. Ask around when you arrive to see what's popular or (if you can find it) check out *Go West* magazine (see p801) for recommendations.

In the meantime, your first port of call should be **Díyí Shìjiè** (Jiǎochǎngkǒu), a massive KTV and bar complex right downtown with a huge choice of bars and discos. The truly eccentric **True Love** (Zhēn'ài Biǎoqíng; ⏰ 7pm-'never') is one of the best of the bunch. Theme nights here include anything from matchmaking (have your mini-bio read on stage along with your cell-phone number) to Arabian nights when staff dress up like sheiks while Chinese belly dancers shimmy next to curtain-draped tables. To find it, head down the stairs in the middle of the complex. When you hit the snobby but hugely popular **Falling Disco** (⏰ 8pm-8am) look around for the weird bear statue. True Love is just past it on your left.

Cotton Club (Mianhua Club; ⏰ 8pm-3am) You can also try this place across from the Marriott Hotel. Popular with expats, this bar has live bands playing Top 40 most weekends and one of the most welcoming staff in the city.

Dee Dee's Bar (酒吧; ☎ 6613 5941; 86 Nanping Beilu) Hands down the best choice for pints, pub grub and travel info. It's a hub for the city's tiny community of foreign workers and teachers. Watching grizzled expats hold court as newcomers hang on their every word is itself worth the trip. The bar is down some hard-to-find stone steps next to the Holiday Inn Yangzi.

SHOPPING

Carrefour (Jiālèfú Chāojíshìchǎng; Cangbai Lu, ⏰ 8:30am-10pm) Gleaming mega-markets are opening all over town these days but this branch of the French supermarket chain remains the old stalwart/gold standard. You want it they got it: cheese, envelopes, deck chairs, fine jewellery, pots and pans…

Flower & Bird Market (Huāniǎo Shíchǎng; ⏰ dawn to dusk) You can smell this fragrant lane from across the street. The flowers, herbs and bonsai trees lend a burst of colour to Chóngqìng's grey and foggy days. It's across from the Marriott Hotel.

Chaotianmen Comprehensive Trade Market (Cháotiānmén Jiāoyí Shíchǎng; Shaanxi Lu) Get here first thing in the morning when vendors clog the streets with motorcycles, trucks and rickshaws filled with foods, bolts of fabric and pretty much anything else you can think of. Come for the atmosphere, not for the goods.

GETTING THERE & AWAY
Air

Chóngqìng's Jiangbei airport (重庆江北飞机场) is 25km north of the city centre. You can purchase tickets at **Air China** (中国国际航空; ☎ 6787 8538; 30 Jianxin Beilu, Jiangbei) and **Dragonair** (港龙航空; ☎ 6372 9900; Room 2906, Metropolitan Plaza, 68 Zuorong Lu). You can book flights at most hotels and in the numerous ticket offices around Liberation Monument.

There are daily flights to nearly everywhere in China, including Chéngdū (Y460, 50 minutes), Kūnmíng (Y820, one hour), Guìyáng (Y470, 45 minutes), Guǎngzhōu (Y1290, 1½ hours), Wǔhàn (Y840, 1½ hours), Shànghǎi (Y1600; two hours), Běijīng (Y1670, two hours 10 minutes), Shēnzhèn (Y1390, two hours) and Hong Kong (Y2558, 2¼ hours).

Boat

Zillions of boats make the run from Chóngqìng down the Yangzi River to Yíchāng. The ride is a popular tourist trip and worth doing before the Chinese government finishes its massive dam project and floods the Three Gorges (see boxed text, p814). For details on Yangzi River trips, see p811.

Travelling upriver by boat from Chóngqìng hasn't been a viable option since the government pulled its money out of the ferry business and put it all behind the expressway. You may find private boats selling tickets for Yíbīn or Lèshān in the summer; however, it's considered by locals to be a risky ride.

Bus

Buses from Chóngqìng depart from the two-storey long-distance bus station next to the train station.

Train

Chóngqìng's enormous train station is inconveniently located southwest of the city.

GETTING AROUND
To/From the Airport

The Civil Aviation Administration of China (CAAC; Zhōngguó Mínháng) has a free bus service to and from the airport that runs from 6.30am to 5pm from the Shángqīngsí roundabout near the 401 bus stop. A taxi will cost around Y70 to Y100 depending on traffic, hitting umpteen toll booths along the way. No city buses go directly to the airport.

Bus

Buses in Chóngqìng can be painfully slow and, since there are no bicycles, they're even more

CHÓNGQÌNG TRAINS

Trains travel daily to the following destinations.

Destination	Price (Y)	Duration	Frequency	Departs
Běijīng	430	33hr	2 daily	12.26pm, 8.31pm
Chéngdū	118	4–5hr	daily	9.08pm
Guǎngzhōu	418	30hr	3 daily	7.35pm, 9pm, 10.33pm
Guìyáng	78	10hr	daily	10.55pm
Kūnmíng	227	22hr	2 daily	12.40pm, 2.42pm
Shànghǎi	490	33hr	2 daily	12pm, 8pm
Xī'ān	175	14hr	daily	9.48am

CHÓNGQÌNG BUSES

Buses from Chóngqìng go to the following places.

Destination	Price (Y)	Duration	Frequency	Departs
Chéngdū	112	6hr	every 20min	6.30am-8.30pm
Dàzú	45	3¼hr	every 30min	9.50am-5.50pm
Éméi	106	2hr	twice daily	9.30am, 11.30am
Lèshān	80	2½hr	hourly	7am-6pm

crowded than in other Chinese cities. Useful routes include: bus 401, which runs between the Chaotianmen Dock and the intersection of Renmin Lu and Zhongshan Sanlu; bus 405, running the length of Zhongshan Lu up to the Liberation Monument; and bus 102, which connects the train station and Chaotianmen Dock.

Light Rail

The city has a terrific new light-rail line open 7am to 10pm and costing Y2 to Y3 depending on how far you're travelling. There are announcements in English and Mandarin. Keep your ticket as you will need it to exit the stations.

Taxi

Taxi fares vary depending on the type of car, but most fares start at Y5, jumping to Y5.9 after 9pm. A plethora of one-way and 'no entrance' streets means drivers will be forced to do some circuitous driving on the way to your destination.

AROUND CHÓNGQÌNG

DAZU COUNTY 大足县

The grotto art of Dazu County, 160km northwest of Chóngqìng, is rated alongside China's other great Buddhist cave sculptures at Dūnhuáng, Luòyáng and Dàtóng.

Scattered over 40-odd places across the county, the cliff carvings and statues (with Buddhist, Taoist and Confucian influences) amount to thousands of pieces, large and small. The main groupings are at North Hill (Běi Shān) and the more interesting at Treasured Summit Hill (Bǎodǐng Shān). They date from the Tang dynasty (9th century) to the Song dynasty (13th century).

Sights

TREASURED SUMMIT HILL 宝顶山

The sculptures at this site (Bǎodǐng Shān; admission Y80; 8.30am-6pm) are definitely more interesting than those at North Hill. It is believed the sculptures were completed over 70 years, between 1179 and 1249.

The centrepiece is a 31m-long, 5m-high reclining Buddha depicted entering nirvana, with the torso sunk into the cliff face. Next to the Buddha, with a temple built around her for protection, is a mesmerising, gold Avalok-

iteshvara (or Guanyin, the Goddess of Mercy). Her 1007 individual arms fan out around her, entwined and reaching for the skies. Each hand has an eye, the symbol of wisdom.

Treasured Summit Hill differs from other grottoes in that it was based on a preconceived plan which incorporated some of the area's natural features – a sculpture next to the reclining Buddha, for example, makes use of an underground spring.

The site is about 15km northeast of Dàzú town. Minibuses (Y5, 45 minutes) travel there from 9am to 6pm, departing when full. A motorcycle taxi will take you there for Y20.

As you pass by on the bus, look out for solo sculptures on the cliff faces.

NORTH HILL 北山

According to inscriptions, this site (Běi Shān; admission Y60; 8.30am-5.30pm) was originally a military camp, with the earliest carvings commissioned by a general. The dark niches hold small statues, many in poor condition; only one or two really stand out. According to the locals it's travellers, and not the Cultural Revolution, that are responsible for the headless state of many statues.

North Hill is about a 30-minute hike from Dàzú town; aim straight for the pagoda visible from the bus station.

Sleeping & Eating

There are plenty of hotels in the area but none of them stand out. Check out your room for mustiness before checking in.

Dàzú Bīnguǎn (大足宾馆; ☎ 4372 1888; d from Y280) Your best bet in the region. Rooms are OK and comfortable, with good service. To find the hotel, turn left from the bus station, cross over the bridge and take the road branching to the right. It's a 30-minute walk from here to North Hill.

Finding a bite to eat in Dàzú is no problem. Shizi Jie (the first right after the roundabout) comes alive at night, with dozens of street stalls serving noodles, dumplings, hotpot and wok-fried dishes.

Getting There & Away
BUS

From Chóngqìng, buses make the two-hour trip to Dàzú (Y45) every half-hour from 6.30am to 8.30pm. Buses back to Chóngqìng follow roughly the same schedule. Buses also leave for Héchuān (Y24, two hours 20 minutes, depart

11.20am and 5.20pm), Tóngnán (Y16, one hour 40 minutes, roughly every hour from 7am to 3pm) and Chéngdū (Y88, four hours, depart 6.30am, 7.15am, 8.55am, 9.50am and 2pm).

TRAIN

Travelling to Dàzú by train is impractical and time-consuming. You're much better off taking a bus down the new expressways.

SHUĀNGJIĀNG 双江

An awesome day trip from Chóngqìng, this sprawling village is packed with terrific sights, but you'll need an adventurous spirit and plenty of patience to find them. No English is spoken here and even a Chinese tourist pulling out a camera can draw a crowd.

The old town's main drag has fascinating nooks and crannies including two **museums** and an old **teahouse**.

On the outskirts, an active **Catholic church** serves the friendly Christian community of about six. A travelling priest calls his congregation every several weeks to tell them when he'll be by for a service. To see inside, go to the mechanic's shop out back and ask for a key.

Further afield, there's an impressive Tang dynasty **Buddha**. Look for the nearby stone stairs, carved to imitate the Chinese tonal scale when stomped on. (Though centuries of pilgrims' footsteps have considerably muffled the effect.) They'll be some boulders to the left of them as you ascend. It's said if you blow on these, you'll hear your whistle inside the stone.

You'll need to negotiate transportation with a villager to get here.

Sleeping

Don't count on finding much in the way of accommodation in Shuāngjiāng. Head to Tóngnán (see right for directions) if you want to stay the night.

Tóngnán Dàjiǔdiàn (潼南大酒店; ☎ 4455 0988; fax 4456 0788; 38 Shiyuan Jie; 石院街38号; s/d 318/Y480)

It's worn around the edges but with discounts rooms go for Y150 to Y200.

Getting There & Away

Buses leave regularly between 7am and 5pm from Chóngqìng's long-distance bus station for Tóngnán (潼南; Y30, two hours). From there, get a minibus (Y2; 10 to 20 minutes) the rest of the way to Shuāngjiāng. Minibuses should run back to Tóngnán until around 5pm but confirm times with the driver on your way up to avoid getting stranded.

LÁITĀN 涞滩

This ancient village is known for its defensive walls and its 12.5m–Tang dynasty **Buddha** (二佛寺阁; Èrfó Sìgé; Y20) surrounded by 1700 mini statues. Most of them had their heads snapped off during the Cultural Revolution but, carved into a hillside cliff, this is still a lovely setting.

Keep and eye out for the small **Mófó** (摸佛) statue on the west side of the temple. It's said if you're unwell and touch him, you will then be cured.

The fortune tellers outside the temple also have a good reputation. Mr Liú Bánxiān (刘半仙) is particularly popular and some Chongqingers make the trip up here just to see him. (He charges Y40 and usually sits on the right-hand side of the road leading out of the temple.) He doesn't speak English so just give him your birth date and the time you were born, and record whatever he says in your MP3 player or iPod so someone can translate it for you later.

There are also a couple of stores to browse and several friendly restaurants that serve simple dishes as well as Láitān rice wine (mǐjiǔ; 米酒).

To reach Láitān take a bus from Chóngqìng's long-distance bus station to Héchuān (合川; Y12, one hour) and grab a minibus the rest of the way (Y10, about 30 minutes). Minibuses run back to Héchuān until around 6pm.

Cruising the Yangzi

THE THREE GORGES

China's mightiest – and the world's third-longest – river, the 6300km Yangzi (Cháng Jiāng), starts life as trickles of snow melt in the Tánggǔlǎ Shān of southwestern Qīnghǎi before spilling from Tibet, swelling through seven Chinese provinces, sucking in water from hundreds of tributaries and powerfully rolling into the East China Sea north of Shànghǎi.

Few riverine panoramas inspire such awe as the Three Gorges (Sānxiá). The vast chasms of rock, sculpted over aeons by the flowing mass of water, are the Yangzi River's most fabled piece of geology. Apocryphally the handiwork of the Great Yu (p327), a legendary architect of the river, the gorges – Qútáng, Wū and Xīlíng – commence just east of Fēngjié in Chóngqìng and level out west of Yíchāng in Húběi province, a journey of around 200km.

The imposing chasms span from 300m at their widest to less than 100m at their narrowest pinch. Their attraction is easily hyped, however, and some travellers register disappointment. The construction of the formidable Three Gorges Dam (see the boxed text, p814) has furthermore cloaked the gorges in as much uncertainty as their famous mists: will the gorges be humbled, vanishing forever beneath a huge lake, or will they shrug off the rising waters?

The truth lies somewhere in between. Experienced boat hands avow to a stunting of their magnificence, but first-timers – the majority of those

The Three Gorges Dam is designed to withstand an earthquake of 7 on the Richter Scale.

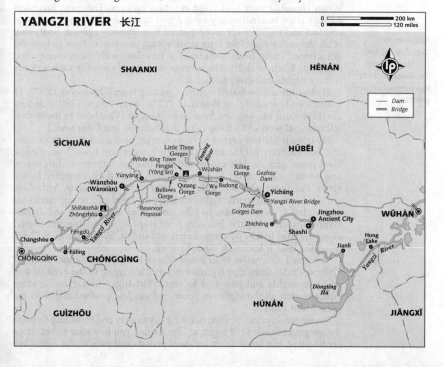

YANGZI RIVER 长江

on cruises – remain suitably awestruck. The waters have yet to rise to their full stature, but you can gauge the extent of the deluge from the riverside 175m markers, awaiting the water's highest reach. It's also worth noting that the gorges were clipped by 10m or so when the earlier Gezhou Dam in Yíchāng (Húběi province) went up, and seasonal variations in water level can be as much as 50m.

If a consensus emerges from travellers' reports, it is that the temples can be busy with jostling crowds (and overpriced) while the towns and settlements along the Yangzi River are quite modern-looking and uniform. It is the spectacular natural scenery that undoubtedly steals the show, although some find it possible to gorge oneself (excuse the pun) on the canyons. After the shock and awe of their first appearance, the cliffs can become repetitive, especially the overlong Xiling Gorge (Xīlíng Xiá). But if you don't expect to swoon at every bend in the river, the sheer pleasure of journeying downriver is a stimulating and relaxing adventure, not least because of the change of pace and perspective.

The principle route for those cruising the Yangzi River is between Chóngqìng and Yíchāng. The growth of speedier expressways sees fewer passenger boats nosing all the way down from Chóngqìng to Nánjīng or Shànghǎi, and most cruises focus on the Three Gorges themselves. High-season boats (April to May and October to November) can be a scrum; off-season, however, the trip is serene and a great opportunity to observe life on the river from a sedentary perspective – even better if you bring some binoculars with you.

BOATS & TICKETS

When choosing your boat you have three options. The most luxurious passage is on internationally owned tour cruise ships, where maximum comfort and visibility are accompanied by a leisurely agenda. Boats stop at all the major sights for long visits, giving passengers time to tour the attractions. These boats are ideal for travellers with time, money and negligible Chinese skills. The average number of days for such a cruise is three nights and three to four days.

Hydrofoils are the fastest option, speeding from Chóngqìng (Y370, 11 hours, four boats daily) or Wànzhōu (Y270, seven hours; Y390 including the three-hour bus journey from Chóngqìng to Wànzhōu) to the hydrofoil terminal west of Yíchāng (a further hour by bus from town).

Hydrofoils are not geared towards tourists so there's no outside seating, but visibility is OK, albeit through Perspex windows. Nonetheless, most passengers use hydrofoils solely for transportation, so while everyone is watching films on TV you can stand at the door, stupefied by the views. For those who find a day of gorge-viewing adequate, hydrofoils are ideal, although tourist sights are skipped. Food and refreshments are served, but it's a good idea to take along your own snacks and drinks. Hydrofoils make regular but very brief stops at towns (but not sights) along the river to take passengers on board and for disembarkation; check when the boat is leaving if disembarking.

The third alternative is to board one of the slow passenger boats or Chinese cruise ships that typically depart Chóngqìng in the evening and take two nights and two days to reach Yíchāng. Chinese cruise ships typically visit all the sights en route, but are less professional than the luxury tour cruises.

Passenger ships can be disappointing as you may end up sailing through the gorges in the dead of night, so check when you buy your ticket. Stops are frequent, but boats tie up for short periods and pass tourist sights by.

Plans for the Three Gorges Dam date from 1919 when Sun Yatsen (Sun Zhongshan) saw its huge potential for power generation.

Cramped and functional accommodation on passenger ships is as follows. First class (Y1525): two-bed cabins with shower room; second class (upper/lower bunk Y992/1060): two- to four-berth cabins with shower; third class (Y620/1060): six to 12 beds, depending on the boat; fourth class (Y530/553): eight to 12 (or even 24) beds; fifth class: a place (席; xí) on the floor. Shared toilets and showers can be grotty and meals on board are average, so take along your own food and drinks.

In theory, it's possible to buy your ticket on the day of travel, but it's probably worth booking one or two days in advance. Fares tend to be similar whether you buy them from an agency or direct from the ticket hall, but it's worth shopping around as there are often some good discounts available. If buying a ticket through an agent, ensure you know exactly what the price includes.

In Chóngqìng, buy tickets from the Chaotianmen Dock Ticket Office (朝天门码头售票处; Cháotiānmén Mǎtou Shòupiàochù) or the helpful **Chongqing Port International Travel Service** (重庆港国际旅行社; Chóngqìng Gǎng Guójì Lǚxíngshè; ☎ 6618 3683; www.cqpits.com.cn; 18 Xinyi Jie), where staff speak English. If you want a refund on your ticket, there is a cancellation fee of around 20%.

THE ROUTE

Most boats travel from Chóngqìng to Yíchāng or Wǔhàn. The Chóngqìng to Yíchāng route is by far the most travelled section of the Yangzi, threading through the Three Gorges and passing the namesake dam. The route can be travelled in either direction, but most passengers journey downstream from Chóngqìng to Yíchāng, a journey that can take anything from 11 hours (hydrofoil) to two nights and two days (passenger ships) or three nights and three days (cruise ships) to even longer tourist cruises. Some vessels soldier on beyond Yíchāng to Wǔhàn and on to Jiǔjiāng, Nánjīng and Shànghǎi, but boat numbers have dwindled in the face of alternative transport and the riverside scenery becomes distinctly ho-hum beyond Yíchāng.

Vessels stop at many of the towns between Chóngqìng and Yíchāng that can also be reached by road, so taking the bus can speed up your journey. If you buy your ticket from an agency, ensure you're not charged up front for the sights along the way as you may not want to visit them all and some of the entrance fees are steep. The only ticket really worth buying in advance is for the popular Little Three Gorges tour, which is often full (see the Wànzhōu to Yíchāng section, p815).

The Yangzi River will deposit over 500 million tons of silt every year into the reservoir behind the dam.

THE DAMNED YANGZI

The Three Gorges Dam is China's biggest engineering project since the construction of the Great Wall. Completed ahead of schedule in May 2006, it will eventually back the Yangzi River up for 550km, flood an area the size of Singapore and wash away the homes of up to two million people. It will rank as the world's largest dam – an epic show of communist might, evidence of man's dominance over capricious nature and the 21st-century symbol of a new superpower.

Located at Sandouping, 38km upstream from the existing Gezhou Dam, the Three Gorges Dam is a cornerstone of government efforts to channel economic growth from the dynamic coastal provinces into the more backward western regions, somehow transforming hinterland into heartland. Measuring 185m high and 2km wide, the dam will have a hydroelectric production capacity equivalent to 18 nuclear power plants.

The dam will improve navigation on the Yangzi River, which already transports 70% of the entire county's shipping, and will be instrumental in flood control, a problem that has claimed more than one million lives in the past 100 years alone.

However, the massive scale of the Three Gorges Dam project has caused disquiet among environmentalists, economists and human-rights activists, arousing some of the most outspoken criticism of government policy since the Tiananmen Square protests of 1989.

Construction of the dam was incredibly expensive, the initial estimates of US$20 to US$30 billion rising to an eventual US$75 billion. The social implications of the dam are enormous: an estimated 1.5 million people living in inundated areas will have been relocated and, more importantly, given a new livelihood. Environmentalists are perhaps the most vocal in their concerns, as it's thought that as the river slows, so will its ability to oxygenate. The untreated waste that pours into the river from over 40 towns and 400 factories, as well as the toxic materials and pollutants from industrial sites, could well create another world record for the dam: a 480km-long septic tank – the largest toilet in the world.

In addition, the dam will disrupt the environments of such endangered species as the Yangzi River dolphin and Chinese sturgeon. The rising waters will also cover countless cultural artefacts at more than 8000 important archaeological sites. Despite an ambitious plan of relocation and preservation, only one-tenth of all historic sites and relics will be saved.

In 1999, 100 cracks were discovered running the full height of the up-stream face of the dam. Yet despite this, in June 2003 the reservoir was filled to a depth of 127m. Chinese engineers say such problems are common in large dams and that the cracks have been repaired.

Fears about the project were further heightened when information was released about two dams that collapsed in Hénán province in 1975. After 20 years as a state secret, it is now apparent that as many as 230,000 people died when the Banqiao and Shimantan dams collapsed. If a similar accident was to happen on the Yangzi River, the entire population of nearby Yíchāng (480,000 souls) would be dead within an hour.

Planners insist that the Three Gorges Dam has been constructed according to safety regulations that would make such disasters impossible. Still, the collapse of the walls holding back the world's largest storage reservoir in one of the world's most densely populated pieces of real estate is a scenario that must keep even the most gung-ho supporters of the Three Gorges Dam project awake at night.

CHÓNGQÌNG TO WÀNZHŌU 重庆 – 万州

The initial stretch is slow-going and unremarkable, although the dismal view of factories gradually gives way to attractive terraced countryside and the occasional small town.

Passing Fúlíng, the next significant town and the first disembarkation point is **Fēngdū** (丰都), 170km from Chóngqìng. Nicknamed the City of Ghosts (Guǐchéng; 鬼城), the town faces inundation once all the sluice gates are shut on the Three Gorges Dam. This is the stepping-off point for crowds to belt up – or take the cable car up – **Míng Shān** (名山; admission Y60) and its theme-park crop of ghost-focused temples.

Drifting through the county of Zhōngzhōu, the boat takes around three hours to arrive at **Shíbǎozhài** (Stone Treasure Stockade; admission Y40; ⏱ 8am–4pm) on the northern bank of the river. A 12-storey, 56m-high wooden pagoda built on a huge rock bluff, the structure originally dates to the reign of Qing-dynasty emperor Kangxi (1662–1722). Your boat may stop for rapid expeditions up to the tower and for crowded climbs into its interior.

Most morning boats moor for the night at **Wànzhōu** (also called Wànx-iàn), a grimy town that rises in steep gradients above the river. Travellers aiming to get from A to B as fast as possible while taking in the gorges can skip the Chóngqìng to Wànzhōu section by hopping on a three-hour bus and then taking either the hydrofoil or a passenger ship from the Wànzhōu jetty.

WÀNZHŌU TO YÍCHĀNG 万州 – 宜昌

Boats departing Wànzhōu soon pass the **Zhang Fei Temple** (Zhāngfēi Miào; admission Y20), where short disembarkations may be made. Yúnyáng, a modern town strung out along the north bank of the river, is typical of many utilitarian settlements. Look out for abandoned fields, houses and factories, deserted in advance of the rising waters. Boats drift on past ragged islets, some carpeted with small patchworks of fields, and alongside riverbanks gorgeously striated with terraced slopes, rising like green ribbons up the inclines.

The ancient town of **Fēngjié** (奉节), capital of the state of Kui during the Spring and Autumn and Warring States, overlooks **Qutang Gorge** (瞿塘峡; Qútáng Xiá), first of the three gorges. The town – where most ships and hydrofoils berth – is also the entrance point to **White King Town** (Báidìchéng), where the King of Shu, Liu Bei, entrusted his son and kingdom to Zhu Geliang, as chronicled in the *Romance of the Three Kingdoms*.

Qutang Gorge – also known as Kui Gorge (夔峡; Kuí Xiá) – rises dramatically into view, towering into huge vertiginous slabs of rock, its cliffs jutting out in jagged and triangular chunks. The shortest of the three gorges, at 8km in length, Qutang Gorge is over almost as abruptly

The Yangzi River has caused hundreds of catastrophic floods, including the disastrous inundation of 1931, in which an estimated 145,000 died.

Pavilion above Wūshān (p816), overlooking the start of Wu Gorge
MARTIN MOOS

as it starts, but it is reckoned by many to be the most awe-inspiring. Also the narrowest of the three gorges, it constricts to a mere 100m or so at its narrowest point, where the waters flow at their fastest. The gorge offers a dizzying perspective onto huge strata and vast sheets of rock; the final rise of the water level will undoubtedly rob the gorge of some of its power, but for now the cliffs remain imposing. On the northern bank is **Bellows Gorge** (Fēngxiāng Xiá), where nine coffins were discovered, possibly placed here by an ancient tribe.

After Qutang Gorge the terrain folds into a 20km stretch of low-lying land before boats pull in at the riverside town of **Wūshān** (巫山), situated high above the river. Many boats stop at Wūshān for five to six hours so passengers can transfer to smaller tour boats for trips (Y150 to Y200) along the **Little Three Gorges** (小三峡; Xiǎo Sānxiá) on the Daning River (大宁河; Dàníng Hé). The landscape is gorgeous, and some travellers insist that the narrow gorges are more impressive than their larger namesakes.

Back on the Yangzi River, boats pull away from Wūshān to enter the penultimate **Wu Gorge** (巫峡; Wū Xiá), under a curiously bright red bridge that blots the landscape. Observe how some of the cultivated fields on the slopes overhanging the river reach almost illogical angles, and look out for the markers that signpost the water's highest reach.

Wu Gorge – the Gorge of Witches – is simply stunning, cloaked in green and carpeted in a profusion of shrubs, its cliffs frequently disappearing into ethereal layers of mist. About 40km in length, its cliffs rise to just over 900m, topped by sharp, jagged peaks on the northern bank. A total of 12 peaks cluster on either side, including **Goddess Peak** (Shénnǚ Fēng) and **Peak of the Immortals** (Jíxiān Fēng).

Boats continue floating eastwards out of Wu Gorge and into Húběi province, past the mouth of **Shennong Stream** (神农溪; Shénnóng Xī) and the town of Bādōng on the southern bank, along a 45km section before reaching the last of the Three Gorges.

At 80km, **Xiling Gorge** (Xīlíng Xiá) is the longest and perhaps least impressive of the gorges. Note the slow-moving cargo vessels on the river, including long freight ships loaded with mounds of coal ploughing downriver to Shànghǎi, their captains alerted to the shallows by beacons that glow from the bank at night. This gorge was traditionally the most hazardous, where hidden shoals and reefs routinely holed vessels, but it has long been tamed, even though river traffic slows when the fog reduces visibility.

The monumental **Three Gorges Dam** (Sānxiá Dàbà; admission Y240) looms up and boats stop so passengers can shuttle across to the dam's observation deck for a bird's-eye view of this mammoth project. Hydrofoils from Chóngqìng and Yíchāng pull in here for passengers to disembark. Boats continue and pass through the locks of the Gezhou Dam (Gézhōu Bà) before completing the journey 30km downstream to Yíchāng (p484).

Xīnjiāng 新疆

Xīnjiāng means 'New Frontier' and the province's far-flung geography has placed it in the bull's eye of competing powers for centuries. Fiercely independent, the people of the region have never really *been* independent. Today, Xīnjiāng 'belongs' to China, having been inextricably tethered to the Middle Kingdom for centuries in an endless push-pull relationship, one which China today maintains in strict form.

Xīnjiāng is like a whole other country enclosed within China's borders. Here the language is not just a different dialect, it's a completely different linguistic family; and it's no longer about whether you dip your dumplings in soy sauce or vinegar, it's how you want your mutton cooked.

What lies within such desolate lands that motivates faraway Běijīng? A thumbnail sketch: it's larger than Alaska (one-sixth of China's territory); hyper-rich with Silk Road history; populated by a mixed salad of nearly 50 ethnic minorities; geopolitically crucial, as it borders eight nations; and encompasses a geographical palette of shimmering desert aquarelles, taiga pastureland dotted with flocks of sheep and grand mountain ranges. Oh, and it sits atop 30% of China's oil reserves.

It's also woefully underappreciated by most of the tourists hopping off planes in the friendly invasion that is the modern Grand Tour of China. But this is quickly changing, as China ramps up the region's infrastructure and tourism PR. The ultimate goal, far down the line, for Běijīng, is to reestablish 'caravans' of travellers along the old Silk Road.

XĪNJIĀNG

HIGHLIGHTS

- Trade a camel for a bus (or donkey cart) and hit the **Silk Road** (p839) or the preternaturally lovely **Karakoram Hwy** (p838)

- Intoxicate yourself with alpine air and hunt for China's Nessie at **Kanas Lake** (p844)

- Haggle happily and munch kebabs in **Kashgar** (p836), one of Asia's greatest crossroads

- Sing campfire songs around a Kazakh yurt at **Tiān Chí** (p827)

- Sweat your soul out at the **Flaming Mountains** (p830) around Turpan; munch grapes afterwards

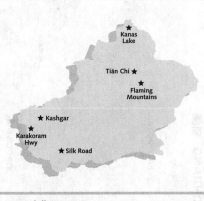

- ★ Kanas Lake
- ★ Tiān Chí
- ★ Flaming Mountains
- ★ Kashgar
- ★ Karakoram Hwy
- ★ Silk Road

■ POPULATION: 20.3 MILLION   ■ www.xinjiang.gov.cn

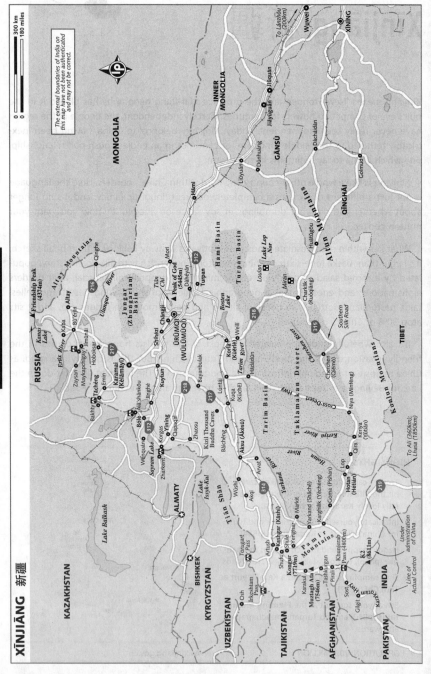

XĪNJIĀNG 新疆

History
NOMADS & OASIS DWELLERS
To grasp Xīnjiāng, begin with the region's two principal groups: the pastoral nomads, north of the Tiān Shān range, and the sedentary oasis dwellers, skirting the Tarim Basin. The original nomads were the Xiongnu, while the earliest known oasis dwellers were an Indo-European group generally referred to as the Tocharians. Over millennia, the ethnicities comprising these two groups have changed; however the groups themselves remained the basis of human civilisation in Xīnjiāng.

SILK & HORSES
Although evidence of Hotanese jade in China indicates that trade must have existed as far back as 7000 years ago, significant mention of the western regions doesn't appear in the Chinese annals until the Han dynasty.

In the 2nd century BC, in the hope of ending the devastating Xiongnu raids along their borders, the Chinese sought an alliance with the far off Yuezhi. Zhang Qian, the Chinese envoy charged with completing the mission, set out in 138 BC into the hitherto unexplored west. He was immediately taken prisoner and held for 10 years by the Xiongnu, but he did succeed in discovering the northern and southern routes around the Taklamakan Desert and into Central Asia, as well as the exceptional Ferghana horses.

While other goods were imported into China during this time, none took on the importance of the superior Central Asian steeds. By the end of the 2nd century BC, the Han had pushed their borders further west, military garrisons were established along the trade routes and silk flowed out of the empire in return for the 'Heavenly Horse'.

BUDDHISM
Along with goods from the west came ideas and languages, and by the 3rd century AD Buddhism had taken root throughout the Tarim Basin. A number of powerful Buddhist city-states arose, chiefly in Hotan, Kuqa and Turpan, leaving behind beautiful artwork that blended Kashmiri, Persian, Indian and even Greek styles.

In the 7th century, the Tang dynasty reasserted the imperial rule that had been lost following the collapse of the Han, and Chinese influence was once again felt in Xīnjiāng.

THE UIGHURS, ISLAM & THE MONGOLS
Records are scant but it's fairly certain that the sway of the Tang dynasty was never absolute. The Uighurs held quite a bit of control throughout the 8th century, and the An Lushan rebellion (AD 755–63) sapped the imperial strength even more.

It was during Kharakhanid rule in the 10th to 12th centuries that Islam took hold in western Xīnjiāng; the religion didn't penetrate the eastern areas until the 14th century.

Yīlí (Ili), Hotan and Kashgar fell to the Mongols in 1219 (whose rule was the only period when the Silk Roads were controlled by a single, albeit factious, power), and Timur, coming from the west, sacked Kashgar again in the late 14th century. The area was under the control of Timur's descendants or various Mongol tribes until the Manchu army marched into Kashgar in 1755.

THE STRUGGLE FOR TURKESTAN
During the 1860s and 1870s, a series of Muslim uprisings erupted across western China, and after Russian troops were withdrawn from a 10-year occupation of the Yīlí region in 1881, waves of Uighurs, Chinese Muslims (Dungans) and Kazakhs fled into Kazakhstan and Kyrgyzstan.

In 1865 a Kokandi officer named Yaqub Beg seized Kashgaria, proclaimed an independent Turkestan and made diplomatic contacts with Britain and Russia. A few years later, however, a Manchu army returned, Yaqub Beg committed suicide and Kashgaria was formally incorporated into China's newly created Xīnjiāng (New Frontier) province. With the fall of the Qing dynasty in 1911, Xīnjiāng came under the rule of a succession of warlords, over whom the Kuomintang (KMT; the Nationalist Party) had very little control.

The only real attempt to establish an independent state was in the 1940s, when a Kazakh named Osman led a rebellion of Uighurs, Kazakhs and Mongols. He took control of southwestern Xīnjiāng and established the Eastern Turkestan Republic in January 1945. The KMT, however, convinced the Muslims to abolish their new republic in return for a pledge of real autonomy.

Following the 1949 communist takeover, a Muslim league opposed to Chinese rule formed in Xīnjiāng, but, oddly, a number of its most prominent leaders subsequently died in a plane crash on their way to hold

THE BEGINNING OR THE END?

Uighurs have, with good reason, always viewed Han Chinese as invaders, and relations between the two nationalities have never been good. However, ties have become far more strained since the early 1950s, when communist China began bolstering the Xīnjiāng population with Han settlers.

Although China has invested a fair amount of money in developing Xīnjiāng's economy and infrastructure, Uighurs frequently argue that real opportunity – economic or otherwise – is reserved for Han Chinese. Little Han-Uighur interaction is apparent, although there is some in the capital, Ürümqi.

This long-simmering Uighur resentment saw several riots in the early 1990s; tensions boiled over in February 1997 when Muslim separatists in the northern city of Yíníng started serious riots that led to a swift crackdown by Chinese security forces. At least nine people died and nearly 200 were injured, making the protest the most violent to date, according to the Chinese media.

Hundreds of Muslim residents were arrested for their roles in the riots: three were executed on the day of their trial, the rest given life sentences. In response separatists blew up three buses in Ürümqi, killing at least nine passengers and wounding many others.

The violence returned to Yíníng in April 1997, when a mob attacked prison vehicles transporting some of the convicted February rioters. Again, several people were killed or wounded.

In 2001 Chinese secret police raided a number of Uighur underground mosques in Korla; one prominent leader and a handful of others were tried and executed.

And this was before 9/11. Běijīng took full advantage of the events following 9/11 to further crack down on Uighur nationalism by locking up or executing thousands of suspected 'Islamic terrorists' – with, ultimately, Washington's tacit approval (and the rest of the world's cacophonic silence).

Since 9/11 Běijīng has tightened its stranglehold on reporting of Uighur relations, no doubt due to its quixotic hope to develop Xīnjiāng into a Xī'ān-esque tourist hotspot and, more importantly, a world leader in oil production.

talks in Běijīng. Organised Muslim opposition to Chinese rule collapsed, although the Kazakh Osman continued to fight until he was captured and executed by the communists in early 1951.

Since 1949 China's main goal has been to keep a lid on ethnic separatism while flooding the region with Han settlers. The Uighurs once comprised 90% of the Xīnjiāng population; today that number has dropped below 50%. China's Develop the West campaign, launched in 2000, is ongoing. Han Chinese are being enticed to migrate to western provinces by social and economic incentives. Běijīng has funnelled nearly US$100 billion to build infrastructure (as much to exploit vast oil and natural gas reserves as anything) in Xīnjiāng.

Climate

Like its geography, Xīnjiāng's climate is one of extremes. Turpan is the hottest spot in the country (it gets up to 47°C from June to August), and the Tarim and Jungar Basins aren't much better at those times. As daunting as the heat may seem, spring (April and May) is not a particularly good time to visit, with frequent sandstorms and clouds obscuring the landscape and making travel difficult. Unless you're up in the mountains or in the far north, the one thing you won't have to worry about is rain. Winters (December to February) see the mercury plummet below zero throughout the province. Late May through June and September through mid-November (especially) are the best times to visit.

Language

Uighur, the traditional lingua franca of Xīnjiāng, is part of the Turkic language family and thus fairly similar to other regional languages you might come across such as Uzbek, Kazakh and Kyrgyz. The one exception is Tajik, which is related to Persian.

Notice the bilingual signs in Chinese and Arabic. In fact, the Arabic script (used phonetically – Uighur has no similarities to the Semitic languages) wasn't reinstituted until the era of Deng Xiaoping. From 1969 to 1983, Uighur was written with a Roman alphabet – phased out, it's said, because of the advantage this gave Uighurs in learning English. This may sound far fetched, until your neighbour on the bus leans over your shoulder and starts pronouncing the words in your book far more accurately than the average Chinese student.

Many Uighurs can't, or won't, speak Mandarin. Some ethnic rivalry, sure, but the main reason is that as of the early 21st century, more than 70% of Xīnjiāng's schools taught strictly in Uighur. Whether this was because of ethnic pride or because they simply couldn't find qualified teachers (arguably true, given that an elementary school teacher in rural Xīnjiāng earns less than a shepherd) remains debatable.

Learn a little bit of Uighur to travel more easily (and make dear friends for life). Lonely Planet's *Central Asia Phrasebook* is a good place to start.

Getting There & Away

Domestically, you can fly to Ürümqi from virtually everywhere.

New international flights are constantly being proposed (though not necessarily finalised). You can fly to Ürümqi from a number of Central Asian cities, including Almaty (Kazakhstan), Bishkek and Osh (Kyrgyzstan), Islamabad (Pakistan, via Kashgar), Novosibirsk (Russia), Moscow, Baku (Azerbaijan) and Tashkent (Uzbekistan). There's also continued talk of new flights to Lahore (Pakistan) and Punjab (India); seasonal flights go to Seoul. Linking Tashkent and Lahore with Kashgar has been debated forever.

There are overland border crossings with Pakistan (Khunjerab Pass), Kyrgyzstan (Irkeshtam and Torugart Passes) and Kazakhstan (Korgas, Ālāshānkǒu, Tǎchéng and Jímǔnǎi). Apart from Ālāshānkǒu, China's rail link with Kazakhstan, all of these borders crossings are by bus, though you can generally get a bike over.

Remember that borders open and close frequently due to changes in government policy; additionally, many are only open when the weather permits. It's always best to check with the Public Security Bureau (PSB; Gōngānjú) in Ürümqi for the official line, or Lonely Planet's Thorn Tree to see what other travellers are saying. A new crossing, the Kulma Pass to Tajikistan, may open to foreign travel in the coming years.

Heading back into China, the obvious route is the train running through Gānsù. More rugged approaches are along the southern Silk Road from Charklik to Qīnghǎi, and Karghilik to Ali (Tibet).

Getting Around

The railway coming from Gānsù splits in two near Turpan, with one branch heading west through Ürümqi to Kazakhstan, and the other going southwest along the Tarim Basin to Kashgar. More rail work includes a new rail line to Altay, which should be finished by 2008. Apart from this, travel around Xīnjiāng involves a *lot* of bus-sitting.

Bear in mind that although flying around the province may seem like a time-saver, flights are sometimes cancelled due to 'bad weather' (read: no passengers). This is decreasing, happily, but days-long sandstorms are also all too common.

CENTRAL XĪNJIĀNG

ÜRÜMQI 乌鲁木齐

☎ 0991 / pop 1.54 million

Ürümqi's Silk Road history does dominate the perceptions. Travellers disembark half-expecting oasis tents and hawkers bellowing their kebab quality. With all that cartographical earth-tone indicating desert nearby (trivia alert: it's the furthest place in the world from an ocean – 2250km), perhaps they also expect the odd camel or two chewing contentedly. Thus, many are not a little bit surprised when they find it a modern and relatively efficient city. With a few kebab sellers.

Its Mongolian name, Ürümqi (Wūlǔmùqí or Wūshì in Modern Standard Chinese), hints at a place of fertile pastureland. Those halcyon days have said bye-bye in this teeming city, jump-started in the late 1990s by the Chinese government's efforts to relocate skilled Han here to solidify it as a strategic and economic bulwark of China's west (read: oil exploration and extraction). Its skyscraper quotient may be modest compared to eastern megalopolises, but the city definitely has a hotwired economy fast becoming a Central Asian hotshot.

Apart from the provincial museum and nearby Tiān Chí, Ürümqi is basically a practical hub, from where you can make all the necessary preparations for various trips through Xīnjiāng, Central Asia or back into China.

XĪNJIĀNG

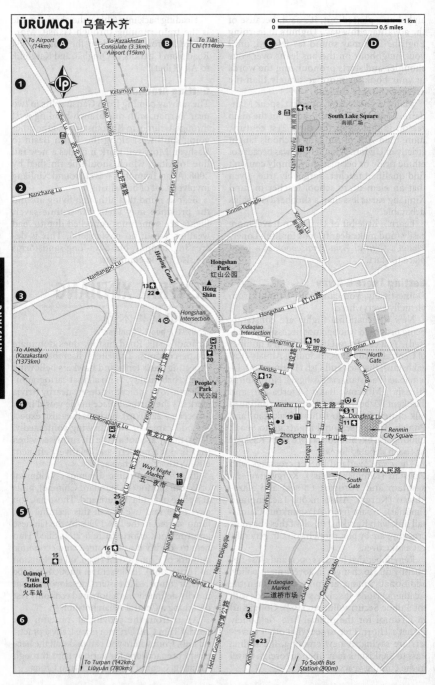

ÜRÜMQI 乌鲁木齐

INFORMATION	SLEEPING 🏠	EATING 🍴
Bank of China 中国银行............................1 D4	Bógédá Bīnguǎn	Carrefour 加乐福...........................17 C2
CITS 中国国际旅行社...............................2 C6	博格达宾馆..............................10 C3	Kraman 可拉曼餐厅........................18 B5
Ecol Travel 生态旅行社.....................(see 10)	Hǎidé Jiǔdiàn	Vine Coffeehouse 德曼咖啡屋 19 C4
Foreign Languages Bookshop	海德酒店..................................11 D4	
外文书店...3 C4	Jīngǔ Dàjiǔdiàn	DRINKING 🍷
Main Post Office 邮局..............................4 B3	金谷大酒店...............................12 C4	Fubar..20 B4
Post Office 邮局..5 C4	Kǒngquè Dàshà	
PSB 公安局..6 D4	孔雀大厦..................................13 B3	TRANSPORT
Tóngxīn Wǎngluò	Silver Birches International	Buses to Tiān Chí 去天池的汽车.....21 B3
同心网络...7 C4	Youth Hostel	China Southern Booking Office
	白桦林国际青年旅舍................14 C1	南方航空公司...........................22 B3
SIGHTS & ACTIVITIES	Xiāngyǒu Jiǔdiàn	Kazakh Train Booking Office ....(see 15)
Ürümqi City Museum	湘友酒店..................................15 A5	Kyrgyzstan Airlines/Huaqiao
乌鲁木齐市博物馆 8 C1	Xīnjiāng Fàndiàn	Bīnguan 华侨宾管 23 C6
Xinjiang Autonomous Region	新疆饭店..................................16 A5	North Bus Station 长途汽车站 24 A4
Museum 新疆自治区博物馆........9 A2		Siberian Airlines/Ramada Inn
		屯河华美大酒店........................25 B5

Orientation

Ürümqi is a sprawling metropolis and you'll need to take taxis or buses to get around. The city centre revolves around Minzhu Lu, Zhongshan Lu and Xinhua Beilu, where government offices, fancy hotels and department stores are located. Not far apart are the Xidaqiao and Hongshan intersections, both of which are transport hubs. The train and long-distance bus stations are in the southwest corner of the city.

Information

BOOKSHOPS

Foreign Languages Bookshop (Wàiwén Shūdiàn; 🕙 10.30am-8.30pm) On Xinhua Beilu, just south of Minzhu Lu.

INTERNET ACCESS 网吧

Tóngxīn Wǎngluò (Xinhua Beilu; per hr Y2) This is an enormous internet café directly to the right of the China Merchants Bank.

INTERNET RESOURCES

http://depts.washington.edu/uwch/silkroad One of the best online resources concerning the Silk Road. Of particular interest is the virtual art exhibit and related timeline.
www.silk-road.com Covers history, travel and culture along the Silk Road.
www.silkroadproject.org Focuses on the musical heritage of the Silk Road.
www.uygurworld.com Comprehensive introduction to the Uighur, with interesting links and an English–Uighur dictionary.

MONEY

Bank of China (Zhōngguó Yínháng; cnr Jiefang Beilu & Dongfeng Lu; 🕙 9.30am-7pm Mon-Fri, 11am-5pm Sat & Sun) Can handle most transactions and was planning a new ATM here (and at other branches) that, one hopes, should finally work. Other travellers have had success at the China Merchants Bank next to Tóngxīn Wǎngluò internet café, or China Construction Bank locations; not us.

POST

Main post office (yóujú; Hongshan intersection; 🕙 9.30am-8.30pm) The main branch handles all international parcels.

PUBLIC SECURITY BUREAU

PSB (Gōngānjú; ☎ 281 0452, ext 3456; Jiefang Beilu; 🕙 10am-1.30pm & 4-6pm Mon-Fri) Not much hassle renewing visas here.

TOURIST INFORMATION & TRAVEL AGENCIES

China International Travel Service (CITS; Zhōngguó Guójì Lǚxíngshè; ☎ 282 1428; www.xinjiangtour .com; 38 Xinhua Nanlu; 🕙 10am-1.30pm & 4-7.30pm Mon-Fri) Not far from Erdaoqiao Market and the Huáqiáo Bīnguǎn (Overseas Chinese Hotel), this office has information on Kazakhstan visas and other Central Asian issues.

Ecol Travel (☎ 886 1578; Bógédá Bīnguǎn gate) This agency has the best rates around for trips to Kanas Lake.

Dangers & Annoyances

In addition to petty theft around the bus and train stations, there have been reports of solo female travellers being sexually harassed in Ürümqi.

Sights

Apart from the major museum below, the city sports its own new museum – **Ürümqi City Museum** (Wūlǔmùqí Shì Bówùguǎn; Nanhu Nanlu) – at the time of writing not yet open to the public.

WHICH TIME IS IT?

Xīnjiāng is several time zones removed from Běijīng, which prefers to ignore the fact. While all of China officially runs on Běijīng time (Běijīng shíjiān), most of Xīnjiāng runs on an unofficial Xīnjiāng time (Xīnjiāng shíjiān), two hours behind Běijīng time. Thus 9am Běijīng time is 7am Xīnjiāng time. Almost all government-run services such as the bank, post office, bus station and airlines run on Běijīng time. To cater for the time difference, government offices (including the post office and CITS) generally operate from 10am to 1.30pm and from 4pm to 8pm. Unless otherwise stated, we use Běijīng time in this book. To be sure, though, if you arrange a time with someone make sure you know which, as well as what, time.

XINJIANG AUTONOMOUS REGION MUSEUM

The provincial **museum** (Xīnjiāng Zìzhìqū Bówùguǎn; ☎ 453 6436; 132 Xibei Lu; admission Y25; ⊗ 10am-1.30pm & 3.30-6.30pm) has finally finished a massive US$13 million renovation (ten spanking-new halls were built and English captions are being put up – hurrah!) and is a must for Silk Road aficionados. Desert-mummified bodies include the 'famous' old 'Loulan Beauty' of Indo-European ancestry, who became something of a Uighur independence symbol in the 1990s. The lost cities of Xīnjiāng – for example Niya, Loulan, Astana and Jiaohe – can basically only be studied here as they're now all either bare or off-limits (in particular Loulan, near one of China's nuclear test sites). New exhibitions include Buddhist frescoes from the Kizil Caves (p832) and an introduction to grasslands culture (indeed the museum does a much better job of representing all of the province's minorities now). From the Hongshan intersection, take bus 7 for four stops and ask to get off at the museum (bówùguǎn).

PEOPLE'S PARK & HONGSHAN PARK

There are two major parks in the city. **People's Park** (Rénmín Gōngyuán; admission Y5; ⊗ 7.30am-dusk) is the city's green oasis while **Hongshan Park** (Hóngshān Gōngyuán; admission Y10; ⊗ dawn-dusk) is more of an amusement park, though it does have better views. Both have north and south entrances.

ERDAOQIAO MARKET

This former Uighur market (Èrdàoqiáo Shìchǎng) is no better than a Chinese-run tourist trap these days, but the streets to the north are still the centre of Ürümqi's Uighur community.

Sleeping

BUDGET & MIDRANGE

Silver Birches International Youth Hostel (Báihuálín Guójì Qīngnián Lǚshè; ☎ 481 1428; syb-2000@sohu.com; 28 Nanhu Nanlu; 南湖南路28号; dm/tw Y35/100; 🖳) What the city really needed has finally arrived with this brand-new place, helmed by an exceedingly friendly and helpful staff (although only the manager speaks much English)! Rooms and facilities are clean and there's a good common area. Getting here is a pain, however: you have to make your way to the North Gate, from where you take bus 73 heading north and get off at South Lake Square (nánhú guǎngchǎng).

Xīnjiāng Fàndiàn (☎ 585 2511; 107 Changjiang Lu; 长江路107号; s/d without bathroom from Y60, with bathroom from Y80; 🖫) A ten-minute walk from the train station through a maze of cloverleafing roadways brings you to the best budget option in the south of town. The usual applies – the lobby looks better than the rooms and the desk staff (but not the floor staff!) can be grumpy, but overall it's a good option.

Kǒngquè Dàshà (Pea Fowl Mansion; ☎ 988 7777; 71 Youhao Nanlu; 友好南路71号; tw Y170-260, tr Y180-285; 🖫) This modern tower is a bit disconcerting at first – entering, it seems to be a modest office building. Not much in the way of services but rooms and (harried) staff are up to snuff.

Jīngǔ Dàjiǔdiàn (☎ 235 5336; fax 283 3613; 84 Xinhua Beilu; 新华北路84号; tw Y280-380; 🖫) This place has improved its attitude to match its well-kept rooms (and was planning some makeovers). At a recent check it was offering steeper discounts than most.

Xiāngyǒu Jiǔdiàn (☎ 585 6699; dm/tw from Y380; 🖫) This place attached to the train station complex used to be called the Yà'ōu Bīnguǎn and has recently renovated itself into midrange level accommodation; most everything works here! Twins are quite nice, but you simply must negotiate a discount.

Bógédá Bīnguǎn (☎ 886 3910; fax 886 5769; 10 Guangming Lu; 光明路10号; tw Y388; 🖫) The Bógédá has pleasant three-star twins that generally come with a 40% discount in the low season. The staff don't speak much English but are at least fairly used to foreigners. The travel agency here comes recommended.

TOP END

Hǎidé Jiǔdiàn (Hoi Tak Hotel; ☎ 232 2828; www.hoitak hotel.com; 1 Dongfeng Lu; 东风路1号; tw Y1200-4180; ☒) A crackerjack staff, splendidly detailed rooms and five-star facilities and services make this Hong Kong establishment *the* place to stay in Ürümqi. Winter rates drop as low as Y518.

Eating & Drinking

Ürümqi's dining is unpredictably cosmopolitan. Regional Chinese cuisine is good here; Jianshe Lu has the largest selection of restaurants, ranging from Uighur staples to affordable Cantonese. During July and August, markets are awash in fresh fruit.

Kraman (Kělāmàn; Huanghe Lu) This casual but spiffy (and spacious) place is among the top

choice for locals looking for that special night out. The speciality is *polo*, or rice pilaf (*zhuāfàn*), accompanied with pickled salad, yoghurt and fresh fruit. Two can eat well for Y30.

Vine Coffeehouse (Démàn Kāfēiwū; ☎ 230 4831; 65 Minzhu Lu; from Y18; ☽ 1.30-11.30pm, closed Mon) Run by a how-did-he-get-here head chef from Curaçao, this fine café brings you savoury West Indian cuisine in a Caribbean atmosphere. It's down a side street on the left. Wannabe English speakers come for the fun English corner.

Fubar (☎ 584 4498; 1 Gongyuan Beilu) This pub is the only foreigner-owned establishment in Xīnjiāng. Expect drinking, socialising and plenty of music (audiophiles will like the music collection) here, the expats' home away from home. Free wireless internet and a good source of travel information.

The animated night markets with shish kebabs and handmade noodles are also worth a gander. The most thriving by far is the **Wuyi night market**; bus 902 runs nearby between the

---

UIGHUR FOOD

Uighur cuisine includes all the trusty Central Asian standbys such as kebabs, *polo* (pilaf) and *chuchura* (dumplings), but has benefited from Chinese influence to make it the most enjoyable region of Central Asia in which to eat.

Uighurs boast endless varieties of *laghman* (pulled noodles; *lāmiàn* in Chinese), though the usual topping is a combination of mutton, peppers, tomatoes, eggplant and garlic shoots. *Suoman* are noodles fried with tomatoes, peppers, garlic and meat. *Suoman gush siz* are the vegetarian variety. *Suoman* can be quite spicy so ask for *laza siz* (without peppers) if you prefer a milder version.

Kebabs are another staple and are generally of a much better standard than the ropey *kawaps* of the Central Asian republics. *Jiger* (liver) kebabs are the low-fat variety. *Tonor* kebabs are larger and baked in an oven *tonor* – tandoori style.

Nan (breads) are a particular speciality, especially when straight out of the oven and sprinkled with poppy seeds, sesame seeds or fennel. They make a great plate for a round of kebabs. Uighur bakers also make wonderful *girde nan* (bagels).

Other snacks include *serik ash* (yellow, meatless noodles), *nokot* (chickpeas with carrot), *pintang* (meat and vegetable soup) and *gang pan* (rice with vegetables and meat). Most travellers understandably steer clear of *opke,* a broth of bobbing goat's heads and coiled, stuffed intestines.

Samsas (baked mutton dumplings) are available everywhere, but the meat-to-fat ratio varies wildly. Hotan and Kashgar offer huge meat pies called *daman* or *gosh girde*. You can even get *balyk* (fried fish).

For dessert try *maroji* (vanilla ice cream churned in iced wooden barrels), *matang* (walnut fruit loaf), *kharsen meghriz* (fried dough balls filled with sugar, raisins and walnuts) or *dogh* (sometimes known as *durap*), a delicious, though potentially deadly, mix of shaved ice, syrup, yoghurt and iced water. *Tangzaza* are triangles of glutinous rice wrapped in bamboo leaves covered in syrup.

Xīnjiāng is justly famous for its fruit, whether it be *uruk* (apricots), *uzum* (grapes), *tawuz* (watermelon), *khoghun* (sweet melon) or *yimish* (raisins). The best grapes come from Turpan; the sweetest melons from Hami.

Meals are washed down with *kok chai* (green tea), often laced with nutmeg or rose petals. Uighur restaurants usually provide a miniature rubbish bin on the table in which to dispose of the waste tea after rinsing out the bowl.

XĪNJIĀNG

train station and Xidaqiao intersection (tell the driver 'Wǔyī yèshì').

In Erdaoqiao Market and near Silver Birches International Youth Hostel are Carrefour centres – great for fresh fruit; both have cafeterias for tasty freshly-made (and cheap) food.

Getting There & Away
AIR
Ürümqi has international flights to neighbouring Central Asian countries. Destinations include: Almaty (Kazakhstan), Bishkek and Osh (Kyrgyzstan), Baku (Azerbaijan), Hong Kong, Islamabad (Pakistan), Novosibirsk (Russia), Moscow, Dushanbe (Tajikistan), and Tashkent (Uzbekistan). Some of these are seasonal and many are suspended for no real reason, especially in winter. Other flights are constantly being discussed; currently, it's a flight to Punjab (India).

There's also continued talk of new flights to Lahore (Pakistan) and Punjab (India); seasonal flights go to Seoul and possibly Istanbul. Linking Tashkent, Islamabad and Lahore with Kashgar (starting here) is debated incessantly.

Domestic flights connect Ürümqi with Běijīng (Y2330), Chéngdū (Y1370), Chóngqìng (Y1630), Lánzhōu (Y1190), Guǎngzhōu (Y2840), Shànghǎi (Y2800) and Xī'ān (Y1600), among others.

Destinations within Xīnjiāng include Altai (Ālètài), Hotan (Hétián), Kashgar (Kāshí), Kuqa (Kùchē), Tǎchéng and Yīníng. Kanas Lake will have an airport by 2008.

China Southern has a booking office next to the Kǒngquè Dàshà, but hotel travel agents will consistently get you better prices.

There are two primary international airline offices in town: **Siberian Airlines** (☎ 286 2326; Changjiang Lu) in the Ramada Inn, and **Kyrgyzstan Airlines** (☎ 231 6333; Xinhua Nanlu) in the Huáqiáo Bīnguǎn (Overseas Chinese Hotel).

BUS
Two long-distance bus stations in Ürümqi serve northern and southern destinations. The north bus station (chángtú qìchēzhàn) is on Heilongjiang Lu and has sleeper buses to Tǎchéng (Y112 to Y142, 11 to 12 hours), Yīníng (Y120 to Y150, 11 to 14 hours) and Bù'ěrjīn (Y127 to Y137, 13 hours). If you have a Kazakh visa, you can also go to Alamaty in Kazakhstan via a sleeper bus to Korgas (Y133, 14 hours). From Korgas it's another 12 hours

to Alamaty. A longer but more pleasant trip would be to travel to Alamaty via Yīníng. Bus 2 runs from the train station to Hongshan, passing Heilongjiang Lu on the way.

The south bus station (nánjiāo kèyùnzhàn) is south of the city and has frequent departures for Turpan (Y35, 2½ hours), Kuqa (Y106 to Y165, 10 to 17 hours), Kashgar (Y192 to Y212, 24 hours) and Hotan (Y220 to Y410, 19 to 26 hours), the latter crossing the Taklamakan Desert. Bus 1 runs between Xidaqiao and the south bus station, bus 109 will get you there from Hongshan intersection, and from the North Gate bus 104 will take you almost all the way (a ten-minute walk beyond the Xinjiang University stop).

TRAIN
The province is building several new rail lines, one of which is slated to serve Altay. Numerous trains serve Lánzhōu; the T296 (see table below) is the best choice. The schedule of direct daily departures from Ürümqi follows:

Destination	Train	Duration	Departs
Běijīng	T70	45hr	2.19pm
Chéngdū	1014	54hr	10.47pm
Kashgar	N946	23hr	3.49pm
Kuqa	N946	14hr	3.49pm
Lánzhōu	T296	25hr	6.47pm
Shànghǎi	T54	48hr	2.55pm
Xī'ān	1044	53hr	8.52pm

Trains depart Ürümqi twice a week for Alamaty, Kazakhstan, on Monday and Saturday at midnight. The journey takes a slow 32 hours, six of which is spent at both Chinese and Kazakh customs. Tickets start at around Y480 and can only be purchased in the lobby of the Xiāngyǒu Jiǔdiàn, at the **booking office** (⌚ 10am-1pm & 3.30-6pm Fri & Sat). You will need a visa for Kazakhstan.

Getting Around
TO/FROM THE AIRPORT
The airport is 16km from the Hongshan intersection; a taxi costs about Y40. An airport bus (Y10) runs straight south through town to the train station.

BUS
Useful bus (Y1) routes include 7, which runs up Xinhua Lu through the Xidaqiao and Hongshan intersections, linking the city

centre with the main post office; and 2, which runs from the train station through the Hongshan intersection and way up along Beijing Lu. Bus 1 goes from the south bus station through the city centre to Xidaqiao. Bus 8 runs from the train station along Heilongjiang Lu to the Minzhu Lu traffic circle.

TIĀN CHÍ 天池

Two thousand metres up in the Tiān Shān mountain range is **Tiān Chí** (Heaven Lake; admission Y90), a small but long, steely-blue lake plonked below the view-grabbing 5445m Peak of God (Bógédá Fēng). Scattered across the stunning spruce-covered slopes are Kazakh yurts and a heck of a lot of sheep. Tourists are multitudinous, yet there's plenty of backcountry out there. You can also take horse treks up to the snow line, although these get mixed reviews. While there, perhaps read Vikram Seth's wonderful China/Tibet travelogue *From Heaven Lake*.

In late May Kazakhs set up yurts around the lake for tourists (Y40 per person with three meals); Rashit is the best-known host. The yurts near the ticket office are authentic and take boarders (Y10); unfortunately you'll need to hitch a ride the rest of the way up. Alternatively, you can camp out.

Buses to the Tiān Chí car park leave Ürümqi from 9am to 9.30am from the north gate of People's Park and return between 5pm and 6pm. (In the low season they may not run at all.) The return fare is Y50 and the trip takes about 2½ hours. The drivers may annoyingly charge you Y50 even if you plan on spending the night.

From the car park, there's a chairlift (Y15 return) or bus (Y15 return) or you can hoof it an hour uphill. The path starts left of the chairlift.

Regardless of the temperature in Ürümqi, take warm clothes and rain gear, as the weather can be unpredictable.

DÀHÉYÁN 大河沿

Fifty-eight kilometres from the Turpan oasis is Dàhéyán (marked Tǔlǔfān on schedules), the nearest train station. Minibuses run from here to Turpan (Y8, one hour) once every 30 minutes throughout the day, starting at 6.30am. Shared taxis are Y10 per person or it's Y50 for the whole thing.

Most travellers need trains heading east or west, since people going to Ürümqi usually

take the infinitely faster bus. There are daily trains to Běijīng, Chéngdū, Lánzhōu (Y375, 22 hours), Xī'ān and Kashgar (Y360, 21 hours). Eastward trains pass through Dūnhuáng (eight hours) and Jiāyùguān (11 hours).

You can buy tickets at the station or through a travel agent in Turpan. Going east it can be difficult to get a hard sleeper.

TURPAN 吐鲁番
☎ 0995 / pop 57,100

In Ürümqi you'll likely grouse about the heat. Leaving, things are pleasant enough. Vast wind farms give way to salt lakes; the road knifes its way through cliffs. Then the wind stops dead as the descent into the Turpan Basin begins in earnest. The driver flicks

INFORMATION	
Bank of China 中国银行	1 A2
CITS 中国国际旅行社	(see 7)
Internet Café 网吧	2 A1
Main Post Office 邮局	3 A2
Post Office 邮局	4 A2
SIGHTS & ACTIVITIES	
Turpan Museum 吐鲁番博物馆	5 A1
SLEEPING	
Gāochāng Bīnguǎn 高昌宾馆	6 A1
Jiāotōng Bīnguǎn 交通宾馆	7 A2
Oasis Hotel 绿洲宾馆	8 B1
Tǔlǔfān Bīnguǎn 吐鲁番宾馆	9 B2
EATING	
John's Information Café	10 B2
TRANSPORT	
Long-Distance Bus Station 长途汽车站	11 A2

XĪNJIĀNG

on the air-con thereabouts for good reason: disembark from your bus and the heat will practically throw you to the ground.

Worry not. Turpan (Tǔlǔfān) is a legendary oasis; its various settlements have long been a stopover on the northern route of the Silk Road. At 154m below sea level, it's even better known as the second lowest depression in the world (after the Dead Sea) and the hottest spot in China – the highest recorded temperature here was 49.6°C! Today they're redirecting attention toward its delectable grapes.

Ah, those grapes. Some streets here are really pedestrian zones covered with grapevine trellis, a visual treat and a godsend in the fierce heat of summer. Given the oven-like temperatures, nobody really rushes around here. Good idea, because the sights are all out of town, in even hotter environs.

History
Settlements in the Turpan Basin predate the Han dynasty; the inhabitants have ranged from Indo-Europeans (possibly Tocharians related to the mummies in Ürümqi's museum) to the Chinese and Uighurs.

In the mid-9th century, the ancestors of the Uighurs were forced from their homeland in Mongolia, with one group eventually settling in Gaochang (Khocho). The city was the Uighur capital until 1250, and saw the Uighurs transform from nomads to farmers, and from Manicheans to Buddhists (they eventually converted to Islam in the 14th century).

Information
The **Bank of China** (Zhōngguó Yínháng; Laocheng Lu; �*9.30am-1pm & 4.30-8pm) can change cash and travellers cheques. West down the same street is the **main post office** (yóujú; �*10am-8pm). A couple of **internet bars** (per hr Y2) are just north of the main square on Gaochang Lu.

CITS (Zhōngguó Guójì Lǚxíngshè; ☎ 852 1352; �*8am-9pm) has a branch in the Jiāotōng Bīnguǎn and can help book train and plane tickets, as well as arrange tours.

The **Public Security Bureau** (PSB; Gōngānjú; Gaochang Lu) is north of downtown and will likely refer you to the capital.

Sights
EMIN MINARET 额敏塔
Emin Hoja, a Turpan general, founded this splendid Afghan-style mosque and **minaret**

(Émǐn Tǎ; admission Y23; ☀ dawn-dusk) in 1777. Also known as Sūgōng Tǎ (named after one of his sons), its 15 simple brick motifs including flowers and waves leap from the structure. The azure sky and lush green of the grape fields outside provide a wondrous photo backdrop. You can climb to the mosque's roof, but cannot enter the minaret.

Biking or strolling the 3km to get there is half the fun, the dusty, tree-lined streets an evocative – and fascinating – glimpse into 'old' Turpan.

CITY MOSQUE 清真寺
Several other mosques (Qīngzhēn Sì) are in town. The most active of them is on the western outskirts about 3km from the town centre.

TURPAN MUSEUM
Outside of a mummified Tang dynasty dumpling, there's not a whole lot in the local **museum** (Tǔlǔfān Bówùguǎn; Gaochang Lu; admission Y20; ☀ 9am-7.30pm) other than some small exhibits from Astana and Gaochang.

Sleeping
Tǔlǔfān Bīnguǎn (☎ 852 2301; lfhan-tl@mailxj.cninfo.net; 2 Qingnian Lu; 青年路2号; dm/tw Y40/380; 🖧 🖳) One of Turpan's original decent hotels, this place still holds up. Staff are friendly and helpful, and the doubles are good value, although it has bumped up dorm prices and cut back on bed space. Evening performances are popular here.

Jiāotōng Bīnguǎn (☎ 853 1320; 125 Laocheng Lu; 老城路125号; s/d Y50, tr Y100, standard tw Y160; 🖧) Despite its location near the noisy bus station, this spruced-up hotel is a good option, with solidly clean facilities and a travel service within.

Gāochāng Bīnguǎn (☎ 852 3229; 330 Gaochang Lu; 高昌路330号; tw Y180-388; 🖧) While not at the heart of the action, the Gaochang has seen an upgrade in quality (and price). Rooms aren't flash in the least but decent, though what it charges in high season is a bit much.

Oasis Hotel (Lǜzhōu Bīnguǎn; ☎ 852 2491; www.the-silk-road.com; 41 Qingnian Beilu; 青年北路41号; tw Y308-728; 🖧) The Oasis incorporates local aesthetics into its hotel design, including Uighur motifs on the wall trim and *khan* beds (padded brick beds – better than it sounds!). Service has always been good and rooms are approaching good value status (if a discount is factored in).

Eating

For Uighur cooking, nothing beats the food court at the **bazaar** (Shì Màoyì Shìchǎng), though finding the stalls – not the handful on the main alley – requires a bit of patience. The fresh 'pull noodles' (*sozoup laghman*) are excellent.

In addition to the lively market action surrounding the public square, dinner choices also include a string of hybrid Uighur-Chinese restaurants that set up tables under the trees on Qingnian Lu. *Laghman* and Chinese dishes run from Y5 to Y10.

John's Information Café (Qingnian Nanlu; dishes from Y10; ⏱ 7am-10pm) This place serves Western and Chinese meals in a shaded courtyard. The menu is in English, prices are fair and you can even get cold drinks with ice (much appreciated in Turpan's heat!).

Entertainment

A traditional Uighur music, song and dance show is staged at Tǔlǔfān Bīnguǎn in the courtyard nightly at 9pm in the high season (Y20). They're fun nights that usually end up with some of the audience being dragged out to dance with the performers.

Getting There & Away

The nearest train station is at Dàhéyán (p827), 58km north of Turpan. Minibuses to Dàhéyán (Y8, one hour) run approximately every 30 minutes between 7.30am and 8pm.

Buses to Ürümqi (Y33, 2½ hours) run every 20 minutes between 8am to 8pm. There is one daily bus at 10am to Kashgar (Y147, 26 hours) via Kuqa (Y69, 15 hours).

Getting Around

Public transport around Turpan is by taxi, minibus or bicycle. Bicycles (about Y25 per day), available from John's Information Café, are most convenient for the town itself. Or, John can line up a donkey cart for a local tour.

AROUND TURPAN

Some of Turpan's surrounding sights are fascinating and others are a waste of time. The only way to see them is on a tour – local drivers *will* find you and these generally work out best as you can choose what you want to see. For four people, figure on paying between Y50 and Y70 per person. The CITS minibus is a reliable Y60 for seven or eight sights, but you're locked into the standard programme.

You can bypass the **Astana Graves** (阿斯塔那古墓区; Āsītǎnà Gǔmùqū; admission Y20) and the **Bezeklik Caves** (柏孜克里克千佛洞; Bózīkèlǐkè Qiānfó Dòng; admission Y20), both essentially empty. The latter is infamous for having many of its distinctive murals cut out of the rock face by German archaeologists in 1905. Some buses may stop at **Grape Valley** (葡萄沟; Pútao Gōu; admission Y45) for lunch, but outside of the September harvest – when it's spectacular – it's underwhelming.

Two possible additions to tours include a **karez** (坎儿井; kǎněrjǐng; admission Y20) – though if you're travelling through Xīnjiāng, you'll have other opportunities to see less touristy ones – and **Aydingkul Lake** (艾丁湖; Àidīng Hú), the second lowest lake in the world. Be forewarned that it's more of a muddy, salt-encrusted flat than a lake.

You'll be gone for the day, so don't underestimate the desert sun. Hot – damn hot. Essential survival gear includes a water bottle, sunscreen, sunglasses and a hat.

Tuyoq 吐峪沟

Set in a green valley fringed by the Flaming Mountains, this tiny grape-producing **village** (Tǔyùgōu; admission Y30) is an excellent place to explore traditional Uighur life and architecture. Tuyoq has been a pilgrimage site for Muslims for centuries, and the devout claim that seven trips here equal one trip to Mecca. The *mazar*, or symbolic tomb of the first Uighur Muslim, is the object of pilgrimage, and is within the earthen walls on the hillside above the village.

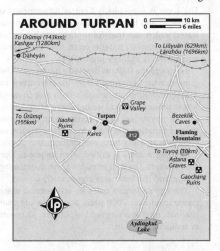

AROUND TURPAN 0   10 km / 0   6 miles

To Ürümqi (143km); Kashgar (1280km)
Dàhéyán
To Liùyuán (629km); Lánzhōu (1696km)
Grape Valley
To Ürümqi (155km)
Jiaohe Ruins
Turpan
Bezeklik Caves
Karez
Flaming Mountains
312
To Tuyoq (10km)
Astana Graves
Gaochang Ruins
Aydingkul Lake

XĪNJIĀNG

Up the gorge are a series of Buddhist caves dating back to the 3rd century AD.

Tuyoq is not yet on the standard tour, and private drivers may raise their prices slightly to include it.

Jiaohe Ruins 交河故城

During the Han dynasty, **Jiaohe** (Jiāohé Gùchéng; admission Y40) was established by the Chinese as a garrison town. Also called Yarkhoto, it's one of the world's largest (6500 residents lived here), oldest, and best-preserved ancient cities. If you only visit one desert city, make it this one: the buildings are more obvious than the ruins of Gaochang, and you can walk through the old streets and along the roads. A main road cuts through the city; at the end is a large monastery with Buddhist figures still visible.

The ruins are 7km or 8km west of Turpan and stand on a loess plateau bound by two small rivers. During the cooler months you can cycle out here.

Gaochang (Khocho) Ruins 高昌故城

Originally settled in the first century BC, **Gaochang** (Gāochāng Gùchéng; admission Y30) rose to power in the 7th century during the Tang dynasty. Also known as Khocho, or sometimes Kharakhoja, it became the Uighur capital in AD 850 and a major staging post on the Silk Road until it burned in the 14th century. Texts in classical Uighur, Sanskrit, Chinese and Tibetan have all been unearthed here, as well as evidence of a Nestorian church and a significant Manichean community – a dualistic Persian religion that borrowed figures from Christianity, Buddhism and Hinduism.

Today, though the earthen walls of the city (once 12m thick) are clearly visible, not much else is in good condition other than a large Buddhist monastery in the southwest. To the north, adjacent to an adobe pagoda is a two-storey structure (half-underground), purportedly the ancient palace.

Flaming Mountains 火焰山

Around Bezeklik and Tuyoq are the **Flaming Mountains** (Huǒyàn Shān), whose midday appearance is aptly compared to multicoloured tongues of fire. The Flaming Mountains were immortalised in the Chinese classic *Journey to the West* as a mountainous inferno that the monk Tripitaka had to pass through. Thankfully for Tripitaka, Sun Wukong (Monkey) managed to obtain a magic fan with which to extinguish the blaze. It's far removed from the actual life of the Tang pilgrim Xuan Zang, who journeyed some 5000km to India and back in search of Buddhist scriptures, but the legend's genesis isn't surprising.

Compare it to the Uighur version, in which a hero slays a child-eating dragon living within the mountains (its blood, hence, is the colour-

---

KAREZ

The *karez* is a peculiarly Central Asian means of irrigation that can be found in Xīnjiāng, Afghanistan and Iran. Like many dry, arid countries, Xīnjiāng has great underground reservoirs of water, which can transform otherwise barren stretches of land – if you can get the water up. This subterranean water is often so far underground that drilling or digging for it, with primitive equipment, is virtually impossible.

Long ago the Uighurs devised a better way. They dig a *karez*, known as the 'head well', on higher ground, where snowmelt from the mountains collects (in Turpan's case, the Bogda Mountains). A long underground tunnel is then dug to conduct this water down to the village farmland. A whole series of vertical wells, looking from above like giant anthills, are dug every 20m along the path of this tunnel to aid construction and provide access. The wells are fed entirely by gravity, thus eliminating the need for pumps. Furthermore, having the channels underground greatly reduces water loss from evaporation.

Digging a *karez* is skilled and dangerous work and the *karez-kans* are respected and highly paid workers. The cost of making and maintaining a *karez* was traditionally split between a whole village and the *karez* was communally owned.

The city of Turpan owes its existence to these vital wells and channels, some of which were constructed over 2000 years ago. There are over a thousand wells, and the total length of the channels runs to an incredible 5000km, all constructed by hand and without modern machinery or building materials.

ing) and slices it into eight pieces which each represent a valley here.

You can clamber around in places (steps now lead up), but only in the early morning – and don't forget your fan.

KUQA 库车
☎ 0997 / pop 69,200

Grimy strip-mall-modern meets traditional donkey carts amid dusty poverty in Kuqa (Kùchē), a former Buddhist city-state and oasis on the ancient Silk Road. Here Kumarajiva (AD 344?–413), the first great translator of Buddhist sutras from Sanskrit into Chinese, was born to an Indian father and Kuqean princess, before later being abducted to Dūnhuáng and then Cháng'ān to manage translations of the Buddhist canon. When the 7th-century monk Xuan Zang passed through, he recorded that two enormous 30m-high Buddha statues flanked Kuqa's western gate, and that the nearby monasteries held over 5000 monks.

Orientation & Information
The main thoroughfare that connects the new and old parts of town is Tianshan Lu/Renmin Lu (new town/old town). The bus station is east of town on Tianshui Lu, and the train station a further 5km southeast.

The **Bank of China** (中国银行; Zhōngguó Yínháng; ☺ 9.30am-8pm) is at 25 Tianshan Donglu. **Liántōng Wǎngbā** (Youyi Lu; internet per hour Y2) just south of Wenhua Lu has internet access on the second floor.

Sights
BAZAAR & MOSQUE 巴扎、清真寺
Every Friday a large **bazaar** (Lǎochéng Bāzā) is held about 2.5km west of town, next to a bridge on Renmin Lu. Nothing to rival Kashgar's, of course, but neither will you see a tour bus anywhere. About 150m further west from the bazaar is a small **mosque** (Qīngzhēn Sì) where large crowds of worshippers congregate on Friday afternoon. North of here through the old town is the Great Mosque (Qīngzhēn Dàsì), though it's less animated than its smaller counterpart.

To get here from the new town, take buses 1 or 3 from Tianshan Lu.

QIUCI ANCIENT CITY RUINS 龟兹故城
These **ruins** (Qiūcí Gùchéng) are all that is left of the capital of Qiūcí, one of several ancient feudal states. They are on the main road,

about a 20-minute walk northwest of the main intersection where Tianshan Lu forks in two. Expect, well, not much.

Sleeping & Eating
Jiāotōng Bīnguǎn (交通宾馆; ☎ 712 2682; 87 Tianshan Lu; s & tw Y50-120; 🖳) Overlook the grim concrete floors and you'll be fine. More expensive twins have air-con and hot water after 8pm.

Kùchē Bīnguǎn (库车宾馆; ☎ 712 2901; 76 Jiefang Lu; 解放路76号; tw Y240-388; 🖳) Kuqa's main hotel has airy, bright and fairly spacious rooms, and the grounds are the closest thing to leafy you'll get around here. It also has multi-person rooms, but probably not for you. The hotel is near the city centre and it easiest to catch a motorcab here.

The best place to get a bite to eat is under the shaded awnings at the **vegetable market** (菜市场; cài shìchǎng) south of the Youyi Lu and Tianshan Lu intersection. There are the usual kebabs, noodles and *samsas* (mutton dumplings) available for a few yuán.

Getting There & Away
AIR
The airport east of the city theoretically has daily flights to Ürümqi (Y590), but they rarely happen. A taxi there costs Y10.

BUS
The bus station has always been – and still is – an exercise in frustration. Expect some puzzled wandering to find a Samaritan helper. Heading east are a variety of sleepers to Ürümqi (Y106 to Y165, 10 to 17 hours) and five daily buses to Lúntái (Y13, 1½ hours), from where you can take the cross-desert highway to Hotan. For Kashgar (Y128, 16 hours) you have to wait for a sleeper from Ürümqi to pass and hope that it has berths.

Once the snow melts (mid-May), there is also a daily bus to Yīníng (Y148, 22 hours), a spectacular trip crossing the Tiān Shān range. You can try to get off at the Mongolian village of Bayanbulak, the mid-way point, but the area's PSB doesn't like foreigners nosing around.

TRAIN
Moving on to Ürümqi or Turpan (Y175, 14½ to 16 hours) is generally not a problem. If you're going west to Kashgar (slow/express train Y44/91, nine to 10 hours), however, sleeper tickets are not available – you'll need

to try your luck with an upgrade. Bus 2 runs
along Tianshan Lu to the train station.

Getting Around
Taxi rides are a standard Y5 per trip, while
motorcabs, tractors and donkey carts are generally Y1 to Y3, depending on the distance you
want to travel.

AROUND KUQA
Kizil Thousand Buddha Caves
克孜尔千佛洞
In the field of Central Asian studies, the **Kizil
caves** (Kèzǐěr Qiānfó Dòng; admission Y35; ☉ daylight hrs),
75km northwest of Kuqa, are an important
site, a wondrous hodgepodge of Central Asian
art and religion from six centuries. Begun in
the 3rd century, the patterns and motifs are
strikingly different to what you see in the
Mogao Caves at Dūnhuáng (see p866). They
also predate them by a century and contain
no Chinese influence whatsoever.

Unfortunately, of the more than 230 caves
here, only eight are open to the public, and
these are in pretty poor shape. One cave was
stripped by Western archaeologists and is entirely bare, while the others have been defaced
by both Muslims and Red Guards.

More interesting than the caves is the
hike through the desert canyon to the spring
Qiānlèi Quán. If you forgo the caves, admission is only Y5, but it's a long way to drive
just to go hiking. A roundtrip taxi will cost
around Y160 and takes 1½ hours.

Ancient City Ruins 苏巴什故城
There are several ruined cities in the Kuqa
region, but these consist of no more than a few
crumbling walls. The most famous is **Sūbāshí**
(temple admission Y15; city admission Y15; ☉ daylight hrs),
23km northeast of Kuqa, while 20km to the
south is Wushkat. A taxi to Sūbāshí and back
costs about Y40.

LÚNTÁI 轮台
Lúntái is a homonym for the word 'tyre', apt
indeed as the town stands amid oil fields near
the start of the Cross-Desert Hwy (p842) and
is the link between Kuqa and Hotan. To Kuqa
(Y12, 1½ hours) there are buses every half-
hour starting at 9.30am. If you're interested
in crossing the desert from the north, you'll
either need to hitch to the crossroads (40km
away) or take a share taxi for around Y10 per
person. Buses from Ürümqi pass by at night,

so you won't see too much of the desert. If
you get stuck here, the dependable Jiāotōng
Bīnguǎn next to the bus station has dorms
(Y15) and twins (Y100).

SOUTHWEST XĪNJIĀNG – KASHGARIA

Kashgaria, the rough-but-mellifluous sounding
historical name for the western Tarim Basin, is
the heartland of the Uighur. Although isolated
even today, Kashgaria was a major Silk Road
hub and has bristled with activity for over
2000 years. A ring of oases lined with poplar
trees and centred on weekly bazaars remains a
testament to the mercantile tradition.

KASHGAR 喀什
☎ 0998 / pop 340,000
Kashgar (Kāshí) is the end of China's New
Frontier, itself the end of China. The first
intrepid Chinese traders and emissaries must
have envisioned themselves at the end of the
earth as they approached this readymade oasis
for the first time, millennia ago. (Considering
it's 1000km through a desert furnace and its
varmint brigands from the site of modern
Ürümqi, they were some brave souls.) Its strategic crossroads location has seen it at the
epicentre of cultural conflict and cooperation
for over two millennia.

But modernity has swept in like a sand-
storm. A paved Silk Road preceded an airport
and in 1999 the Iron Rooster arrived, along
with a ton of Han Chinese. Donkeys have
mostly given way to taxis and motorbikes,
and sadly, much of the old architecture is
giving way to new.

Then again, Kashgar has seen it all before
and despite the tutting from some about the
'death' of 'traditional' Kashgar, in many ways
it is the same as it ever was. The great (times
five) grandsons of craftsmen and artisans still
hammer and chisel away in side alleys in the
old quarter; everything sellable is hawked and
haggled over boisterously; and the donkey
to taxi ratio is still equal parts furry in some
areas. And that Sunday market – now that's
a blast from the past, no matter how many
tour buses roll up.

Kashgar was globalised before globalised
was grammatical. A Babel of negotiation –
Kazakh, Urdu, Tajik and more mixed with

Uighur in a business stew – still goes on in shops and in hotel lobbies. Jets and buses have replaced camels (usually), but Kashgar is the nexus of a Central Asian high-tech Silk Road. Kashgar redux.

So soak it in for a few days, eat a few kebab, chat with a local medicine man in the back alley, and prepare your trip along the Southern Silk Road to Hotan, over the Torugart or Irkeshtam Passes to Kyrgyzstan or south up the stunning Karakoram Hwy to Pakistan.

Orientation

Official (Chinese) street names are given here. The town centre is a Tiānānmén-style square north of Renmin Park, dominated by a statue of Mao Zedong. The Uighur old town lies just north of here, bisected by Jiefang Beilu.

Information

INTERNET ACCESS 网吧
Internet bars (Y2 to Y4 per hour) are ubiquitous but the PSB mandates they register you. One is opposite the Chini Bagh Hotel.

LAUNDRY
There is a cheap laundry service (*gānxǐ diàn*) next to the Caravan Café.

MEDICAL SERVICES
Health Clinic (under the CITS bldg, Chini Bagh compound) Can administer first aid and medicines. Some staff speak English.
People's Hospital (Rénmín Yīyuàn; Jiefang Beilu) North of the river.

MONEY
The **Bank of China** (Zhōngguó Yínháng; main square; ☾ 9.30am-1.30pm & 4-7.30pm) can change travellers cheques and cash; ditto with the branch west at 239 Renmin Xilu. You can also sell yuán back into US dollars at the bank's foreign exchange desk if you have exchange receipts; this is a good idea if you are headed to Tashkurgan, where the bank hours are erratic. Staff also swear they're putting in a *working* ATM, but they've said this before. Some travellers have gotten money from a China Construction Bank ATM at the northwest corner of Jiefang Beilu and Renmin Xilu; we didn't.

POST
Post office (yóujú; 40 Renmin Xilu; ☾ 9.30am-8pm) The second floor handles all foreign letters and packages.

PUBLIC SECURITY BUREAU
PSB (Gōngānjú; 111 Youmulakexia Lu; ☾ 9.30am-1.30pm & 4-8pm) You can extend your visa here.

TOURIST INFORMATION & TRAVEL AGENCIES
The **Caravan Café** (p836) and **John's Cafe** (p836) both organise bookings, transport and excursions, and can link you up with other budget-minded travellers to help share costs.

Elvis (elvisablimit@yahoo.com), otherwise known as Ablimit Ghopor, is a local Uighur whose main business is buying and selling carpets (ask his advice if you're considering a purchase). He also takes tourists on offbeat tours of the old town and lines up desert treks. A proud connoisseur of *muqam* (Uighur traditional music), he can help you sample it. He operates out of the Old City Restaurant across from Sèmǎn Bīnguǎn (p835).

The main office of **CITS** (Zhōngguó Guójì Lǚxíngshè; ☎ 298 3156) is up one flight of stairs in a building just outside the Chini Bagh Hotel.

Dangers & Annoyances

Travellers have lost money or passports to pickpockets at the Sunday Market and even on local buses, so keep yours tucked away.

Some foreign women walking the streets alone have been sexually harassed. The Muslim Uighur women dress in long skirts and heavy stockings like the Uighur women in Ürümqi and Turpan, but here one sees more female faces hidden behind veils of brown gauze. It is wise for women travellers to dress as would be appropriate in any Muslim country, covering arms and legs.

Sights

SUNDAY MARKET & LIVESTOCK MARKET
星期天市场、动物市场
A Uighur primer: '*Boish-boish!*' means 'Coming through!' You'd best hip yourself to this phrase, or risk being ploughed over by a donkey cart or tuk-tuk at the **Sunday Market** (Yengi Bazaar; Xīngqītiān Shìchǎng). At sunrise, the otherwise somnolent town is invaded by about a bazillion bleating and whinnying animals, along with a 100,000-strong (so it is said) 'army' of friendly shepherds, traders, farmers, artisans, nomads and itinerants, as well as the curious, a pickpocket or two, and what seems like an equal number of tourists furiously clicking shutters, overwhelmed by the sheer lovely madness that is this market.

KASHGAR 喀什

XĪNJIĀNG

0 _____ 1 km
0 _____ 0.5 miles

INFORMATION
Bank of China 中国银行 **1** A4
China Construction Bank
　中国建设银行 **2** B3
CITS 中国国际旅行社 ....(see 4)
Former British Consulate
　英国领事馆 **3** B3
Health Clinic 诊所 **4** B3
Internet Café 网吧 **5** B3
Laundry 干洗店 ....(see 20)
Main Bank of China
　中国银行 **6** B4
Old City Restaurant
　喀什美协海尔依庄 **7** A3
Post Office 邮局 **8** B3
PSB 公安局 **9** A3

SIGHTS & ACTIVITIES
Id Kah Mosque
　艾提尕尔清真寺 **10** B3
Kashgar Regional Museum
　喀什地区博物馆 **11** D3
Mao Statue 毛泽东塑像 **12** B3
Old Town Admission Gate **13** C3
Old Town Walls **14** A3
Tomb of Yusup Has
　玉素甫哈斯哈吉甫陵墓 **15** B4

SLEEPING
Chini Bagh Hotel
　其尼瓦克宾馆 **16** B3
Kashi Gáěr Bīnguǎn
　喀什噶尔宾馆 **17** D3

Sèmǎn Bīnguǎn 色满宾馆 **18** A3
Tiānnán Fàndiàn 天南饭店 **19** C4

EATING
Caravan Café 凯瑞咖啡 **20** B3
Chinese Food Stalls 熟食街 **21** A4
Indy's Café 昆仑驿站 **22** B4
Intizar 银提扎尔餐厅 **23** A3
John's Cafe 约翰中西餐厅 ...(see 18)
Night Market 夜市 **24** B3
Uighur Teahouse 茶馆 **25** B3

SHOPPING
Uyghur Musical Instrument
　Factory **26** B3

TRANSPORT
CAAC Office
　中国民航公司 **27** B4
International Bus Station
　国际汽车站 **28** B2
Long-Distance Bus Station
　喀什站 **29** C4

To People's Hospital
(300m); Airport (12km);
Irkeshtam Pass (215km);
Tórugart Pass (312km);
Ürümqi (1180km)

Youmulakexia Lu
尤木拉克夏路

Seman Lu

色满路
Seman Lu

色满路

Seman Lu

Renmin Xilu

Renmin Xilu

人民西路

Old
Town

Old
Town

Jiefang Beilu

Square

Renmin Xilu

人民公园
Renmin
Park

Jiefang
Nanlu

Tian Nanlu
天南路

Tiyu Lu

Keziladwei Lu

Nanlu 新湖路

Payinapu Lu

红旗路

Dong Lake
东湖

Renmin Donglu

人民东路

Binhe Lu

滨河路

Aizirete Lu 艾孜热特路

Takwiluai Lu

缪伦路

Airslahan Lu

Sunday
Market

Tuman
River

To Abakh
Hoja Tomb
(1.5km);
Ha Noi Ruins
(35km)

To Train
Station
(10km)

To Livestock
Market

To Tashkurgan (240km);
Pakistani Border (1012km)

To Yarkand (175km);
Hotan (472km);
Tibet (600km)

The market is actually open daily and a little less crowded on weekdays. This is where you'll find carpets, clothing and boots, hats and Uighur knives (along with a ton of touristic junk).

Southeast of the city is the **Livestock Market** (Mal Bazaar; Dòngwù Shìchǎng), with an equal livestock-to-people ratio. (Here you may get ploughed over by a Uighur 'test driving' a horse!)

A taxi to the Sunday Market is Y5, and to the Livestock Market Y10. Otherwise, bus 16 runs to the Livestock Market from the main square.

Kashgar's Sunday Market can get fairly touristy, but don't be discouraged, there are plenty of other lesser-known markets to visit.

For starters, try the Sunday market at Hotan (p841), the Monday market in Upal (p838), the Tuesday market in Charbagh (p840) or the Friday market in Kuqa (p831).

OLD TOWN

Sprawling on both sides of Jiefang Lu are roads full of Uighur shops and narrow passages lined with adobe houses right out of an early–20th century picturebook. The old town is much smaller than it once was, but is still one of the most fascinating places in Xīnjiāng; better – tourism will likely preserve what's left.

Be warned that the residential area far to the east has been transformed into a moneymaker – you have to pay Y10 just to enter!

At the eastern end of Seman Lu stands a 10m-high section of the former town walls, which are at least 500 years old.

ID KAH MOSQUE 艾提尕尔清真寺

The yellow-tiled **Id Kah Mosque** (Ài Tígǎ'ér Qīngzhēn Sì; admission Y30), which dates from 1442, was once on the outskirts of town (atop a cemetery, it is said), but now is the heart of the city – and not just geographically. Enormous, its courtyard and gardens can hold 20,000 people during the annual Qurban Baiyram celebrations.

Non-Muslims may enter but Fridays are usually a no-go. Local women are rarely seen inside but Western women are usually ignored if they're modestly dressed (arms and legs covered and a scarf on the head); this goes for men as well (that is, no shorts and T-shirt). Take off your shoes if entering carpeted areas and be discreet when taking photos.

ABAKH HOJA TOMB 香妃墓

On the northeastern outskirts of town is the **Abakh Hoja Maziri** (Xiāngfēimù; admission Y40; ☼ daylight hrs), covered in splendidly mismatched glazed tile and best known among Uighurs as the resting place of Abakh Hoja, one of Kashgar's more popular rulers. Purportedly among others interred is Ikparhan, his granddaughter. Known as Xiang Fei ('Fragrant Concubine'), she led the Uighurs in revolt, was defeated and ended up Emperor Qianlong's concubine.

There are/were other tombs scattered throughout Kashgar, but many of these now sit under housing complexes. The only ones remaining, such as the **Tomb of Yusup Has**, are in a state of disrepair.

KASHGAR REGIONAL MUSEUM 喀什地区博物馆

This **museum** (Kāshí Dìqū Bówùguǎn; 19 Tawuguzi Lu; admission Y6; ☼ 7.30am-noon & 4-8pm) is on the eastern edge of Kashgar. Despite half-hearted attempts to liven up the exhibits here, most travellers come away underwhelmed.

HA NOI RUINS & MOR PAGODA 罕诺依古城、莫尔佛塔

At the end of a jarring 35km drive northeast of town are the ruins of **Ha Noi** (Hǎnnuòyī Gùchéng), a Tang-dynasty town built in the 7th century and abandoned in the 12th century. Little remains but a solid pyramid-like structure and the huge **Mor Pagoda** (Mù'ěr Fótǎ).

CITS will take you to Ha Noi for Y200 per 4WD or you can hire a car from the CITS for Y70 per person. John Hu, at John's Cafe (see p836), charges Y350 per car.

Tours

Both the Caravan Café and John's Cafe organise multiday trips. Some of the more popular destinations for trekking around Kashgar include the K2 base camp, Muztagh Ata and camel tours through the Taklamakan Desert. If you're looking for a challenge, you can also consider biking the Karakoram Hwy.

Sleeping

Accommodation can be tighter on the days preceding the Sunday Market than afterward. In low season you should be able to coax out some discounts.

Tiānnán Fàndiàn (☎ 282 4023; 27 Renmin Donglu; 人民东路27号; dm Y20, tw Y238) Across from the long-distance bus station, the multi-building Tiannan is a convenient place to lay your head if you've just jumped off an interminable, dusty bus ride. Virtually all the dorm rooms have been renovated into standard doubles, but for the nonce some cheap beds exist. It doesn't see many foreigners and this actually kinda tickles 'em.

Sèmǎn Bīnguǎn (☎ 258 2129; fax 258 2861; 337 Seman Lu; 色满路337号; dm Y20-30, tw Y60-680; ☐) A labyrinthine complex with a variety of rooms and quality. Dorms are decent, but the toilets/showers apparently haven't been cleaned since the Tang dynasty. Around the back is the former Russian consulate, with seven (somewhat gaudy) rooms for the well-heeled Great Game aficionado.

Chini Bagh Hotel (Qínìwàkè Bīnguǎn; ☎ 298 2103; fax 298 2299; 93 Seman Lu; 色满路93号; dm Y35-40, tw Y180-380; ✂ ☐) The Chini Bagh, situated on the grounds of the former British consulate (now a restaurant), remains the best all-around choice. Dorms are clean and they have private bathrooms. The three-star International Building is, yuán for yuán, the best value in town.

Kāshí Gáěr Bīnguǎn (☎ 265 2367; fax 265 4679; 57 Tawuguzi Lu; 塔吾古孜路57号; tw/ste Y288/888; ✂) If you're looking for a quiet place to stay, this is it. Set in spacious gardens 3km east of the centre, the rooms here were renovated in 2004 and are the most comfortable in Kashgar. A taxi to the main square is Y5.

Eating

UIGHUR

Intizar (Yíntízǎěr; Renmin Xilu) A jam-packed Kashgar favourite, the classic dish here is *tohu gangpan* (*jīròu mǐfàn*), spicy chicken and potatoes with rice (Y5).

Another good spot to sample Uighur cooking is at the food stalls at the night market opposite the Id Kah Mosque (and other individual stalls in the vicinity). Vendors sell noodles, chickpeas, poached eggs, kebabs, breads and boiled goat heads; bring your own fork. For dessert there is watermelon by the slice, *tangzaza, kharsen meghriz* or simply a glass of hot milk and a pastry. In restaurants, *suoman, suoman gush siz* and *polo* are all recommended. See the boxed text on p825 for more about Uighur food.

For good views of the old town street life, make sure you pay a visit to the rickety second-floor teahouse *(chai hanna)*, north of the music shop.

CHINESE

Chinese fast-food stalls serve oily but cheap lunches in an alley off Renmin Xilu, behind the Bank of China. This is a good option for vegetarians. Just point and pay; a tray of ready-cooked food costs about Y5. Go at noon when the food is hot.

WESTERN

Indy's Café (Kūnlún Yìzhàn; ☎ 283 8989; Paheta Baza Nanlu; coffee Y15) South a block or so off Renmin Xilu, this is a real haven for genuine coffee and tea with tastefully appointed interiors. Internet access is available.

Caravan Café (☎ 298 1864; www.caravancafe.com; 120 Seman Lu; mains from Y15; ◷ 9am-9.30pm Apr-Oct) Next to the Chini Bagh Hotel, it serves scrumptious light Western food and is extraordinarily clean, and these days is just as popular for its travel services.

John's Cafe (☎ 258 1186; www.johncafe.net; mains from Y10) In Sèmǎn Bīnguǎn courtyard, this is another popular hang-out, offering both (pricey) Western and (cheaper) Chinese dishes.

Shopping

SOUVENIRS

The citizens of Kashgar have been selling things for 2000 years, so be ready to bargain. For serious shopping go to the old town; but beware, Sunday Market prices tend to be higher. Hats, teapot sets, copper and brass ware and Uighur knives are among the souvenirs you'll find around town.

CARPETS

Most carpet dealers display their wares at the Sunday Market pavilion. The rugs here are made out of everything from silk to synthetics, so do your homework if you plan on buying. The brightly coloured felt *shyrdakhs* from Kyrgyzstan are a good buy – don't pay more than Y350 for a large one. The best regional carpets were once made in Hotan; however, the quality of a Hotanese rug today is dubious.

MUSICAL INSTRUMENTS

The family-run **Uighur Musical Instrument Factory** is on the street north of the post office. Here you'll find long-necked stringed instruments running the gamut from souvenirs to collectors' items. If any traditional performances are on, Mohammed (the owner) will know where to find them.

Getting There & Away

It's imperative when you buy tickets in Kashgar to verify what 'time' the person who's selling the tickets has set their watch to. Officially it's Běijīng time, but unsurprisingly, this isn't always the case.

AIR

There are three daily flights to Ürümqi (Y1230), which are sometimes cancelled due to poor turnout or sandstorms. It's possible to fly to Islamabad (Pakistan); another route to Lahore (Pakistan) hasn't yet started (and possibly never will). The **Civil Aviation Administration of China office** (CAAC; Zhōngguó Mínháng; ☎ 282 2113; 95 Jiefang Nanlu; ◷ 10am-1pm & 4.30-8pm) will have more information.

BUS

To Kyrgyzstan

There are two passes into Kyrgyzstan: the Torugart, which leads to Bishkek, and the Irkeshtam, which goes to Osh. Getting to Osh (US$50, two days) is straightforward, with a bus leaving the **international bus station** (guójì qìchēzhàn; Jiefang Beilu) on Monday (and perhaps Thursday if demand warrants it) at 10am. Another option is to hire a taxi up to the border, which should work out to be a similar price. Crossing the Torugart Pass, however, is a different matter (see opposite). For the record, a Chinese bus runs twice weekly

---

OVER THE TORUGART PASS

Officially the Torugart Pass is a 'second grade' pass and therefore for local not international traffic. Except, of course, that it is. What you require on the Chinese side is a *xǔkězhèng* permit from the PSB entry-exit section in Ürümqi. Most agents in Kashgar can get this (CITS claim in three working days), though no one will arrange a permit without transport. The most popular option now is with the Caravan Café's travel service (www.caravancafe.com) in Kashgar (see below for prices).

The hitch is getting into Kyrgyzstan without booking Kyrgyz transport. Officially the Chinese won't let you leave the arch without onward transport into Kyrgyzstan and Chinese travel agencies are reluctant to take you without booking onward transport. But it looks likely that the Chinese guards will let you cross if you can find a lift from the border gateway to the Kyrgyz border post. If you do manage to get to the Kyrgyz border post you will need to find onward transport to Naryn or Bishkek – though be forewarned, you could be in for a long wait. In the event there are taxi sharks at the crossing, they may open the bidding at US$200 or more to Bishkek (and may lead you to think that's for the vehicle, then later tell you it's per person), though US$50 for the car is a more realistic amount.

There are public buses to Kyrgyzstan over the Torugart Pass, but at the time of writing foreigners were *still* not allowed to take these services. Without a permit, you'll most likely be thrown off the bus at the customs post. You must already have a Kyrgyzstan visa.

---

from the international bus station to Naryn (US$25) and Bishkek (US$50).

To Pakistan

Buses to/from Sost (Y270 plus Y2 per bag, two days) in Pakistan leave the international bus station daily at 10am. The 500km trip stops overnight at Tashkurgan. Bring water, snacks and warm clothes as nights can be cold all year. Sit on the left for the best views.

Customs procedures are conducted at Tashkurgan.

If buses have stopped for the season but you're desperate to cross the border, Pakistani traders may have space in a truck or chartered bus. You can also hire a taxi or a 4WD from one of the tour outfits.

Other Destinations

Other buses use the **long-distance bus station** (kāshí zhàn; Tian Nanlu). There have been instances of theft at the bus station, especially in the early morning crush.

Making the 1480km trip to Ürümqi are nonstop coaches, soft-seat or sleeper (Y192 to Y212), that take about 24 hours. They leave frequently between 7.30am and 7.30pm.

Local buses to Tashkurgan leave daily at 10.30am (Y44, six hours) and charge the full fare to drop you off in Karakul.

There are seven buses for Hotan (Y65 to Y85, seven to 10 hours) between 9am and 9pm, but it is more enjoyable to stop off in Yengisar (Y7, 1½ hours), Yarkand (Y22, three

hours) or Karghilik (Y29, four hours). Buses to these last three towns run hourly.

For information on buses to Tajikistan see p963.

CAR

You can hire 4WDs (four to six passengers) and minibuses (eight to 12 passengers) from the Caravan Café, John's Cafe, or CITS. At the time of research, rates for a 4WD to meet/drop you off at Torugart averaged around Y1000, plus Y200 per person to arrange the requisite permits (minimum two-day wait though three is more likely). Food and lodging are extra, and the driver pays for his own.

HITCHING

You might be able to hitch a lift to Tashkurgan, but from there to Pakistan you'll probably have to wait for an empty seat on the bus. There are plenty of trucks crossing the Torugart Pass to Kyrgyzstan but you'll likely have problems getting past the customs post.

TRAIN

Daily trains to Ürümqi depart at 9.30am and 2.50pm and take 30 and 23 hours, respectively. Middle-berth sleeper tickets on the faster train are Y360.

Getting Around

TO/FROM THE AIRPORT

The airport is 12km northeast of the town centre. A bus (Y5) leaves from the CAAC ticket office 2½ hours before all departures, and one bus meets all incoming flights. A taxi there should cost the same price.

BICYCLE

A bike is the cheapest and most versatile way to get around Kashgar. One-gear clunkers can be hired by the hour or the day (Y20) at John's Cafe.

BUS

Useful bus routes are buses 2 (Jiefang Lu to the airport), 10 (Renmin Lu to the Kashgar Hotel and Abakh Hoja Tomb), 9 (international bus station to the Chini Bagh and Sèmǎn Bīnguǎn), 16 (main square to the Livestock Market) and 28 (main square to the train station). The fare is Y1.

TAXI

Taxis seem to breed here and were set to be metered at the time of research.

KARAKORAM HWY 中巴公路

The **Karakoram Hwy** (Zhōngbā Gōnglù) over the Khunjerab Pass (4800m) is the gateway to Pakistan. For centuries this route was used by caravans plodding down the Silk Road. Khunjerab means 'valley of blood', a reference to local bandits, who took advantage of the terrain to plunder caravans and slaughter the merchants.

It took nearly 20 years to plan, push, blast and level the present road between Islamabad and Kashgar, and more than 400 road-builders died in the process. Facilities en route are being steadily improved, but take warm clothing, food and drink on board with you – once stowed on the bus roof it's unavailable.

Even if you don't go to Pakistan, the trip up to Tashkurgan is worthwhile. From Kashgar, you first cross the Pamir Plateau (3000m), passing the foothills of 7719m-high Kongur Mountain (Gōnggé'ér Shān) and nearby Muztagh Ata Mountain (Mùshìtǎgé Shān; 7546m).

The journey continues through stunning scenery – high mountain pastures with grazing camels and yaks tended by yurt-dwelling Tajiks. The last major town on the Chinese side is Tashkurgan at 3600m.

Officially, the border opens on 15 April and closes on 31 October. However, the border can open late or close early depending on conditions at Khunjerab Pass. Travel for-

malities are performed at Sost, on the Pakistan border; the Chinese border post is located at Tashkurgan.

You'll need to get your papers in order ahead of time, as China doesn't let anyone out of the country if they don't have an onward visa, and you can't get one in Kashgar. If you're coming in from Pakistan, make sure you have enough cash on hand – the bank in Tashkurgan doesn't change travellers cheques.

Kashgar to Karakul Lake

If you'd like to see the Karakoram Hwy, Karakul Lake, a glittering mirror of glacial peaks, makes for a good destination. Like Tiān Chí, it can get crowded here during the day, but evenings and mornings you'll have the place to yourself, and you can hike up into the hills or circumnavigate the lake. Most settlements as far as Karakul are Kyrgyz.

An hour from Kashgar is **Upal** (Wùpàěr in Chinese), where the Kashgar–Sost bus normally stops for lunch. There's a great weekly market here every Monday.

Two hours from Kashgar you enter the canyon of the Ghez River (Ghez Darya in Uighur), with wine-red sandstone walls at its lower end. Ghez itself is just a checkpost; photographing soldiers or buildings here can result in confiscated film. Upstream, the road is cut into sheer walls or inches across huge boulder fields. At the top of the canyon, 3½ hours above the plain, is a huge wet plateau ringed with sand dunes, aptly called Kumtagh (Sand Mountain) by locals.

The bus will drop you off after five or six hours next to the lake, ringed by magnificent ice mountains. One hotel has yurts (Y40) and rooms (and a restaurant). Camping is possible but not recommended; travellers have warned of strong-arm tactics from local leaders who 'control' the area (they also don't like foreigners staying with locals in yurts though some do anyway). There is now an entrance fee of Y50.

One bus daily leaves the long-distance bus station at 10am, takes five to six hours and costs Y45. The bus to Sost from the international bus station also stops off here. It's supposed to leave at 10am but noon isn't unheard of! Day-trippers can rent a taxi for as little as Y400 (return). The official price is double this, but someone is always ready to bargain.

SOUTHERN SILK ROAD

The Silk Road east of Kashgar splits into two threads in the face of the huge Taklamakan Desert. The northern thread follows the course of the modern road and railway to Kuqa and Turpan. The southern road charts a more remote course between desert sands and the huge Pamir and Kunlun ranges. The ancient route is marked by a ring of abandoned cities deserted by retreating rivers and encroaching sands. Some cities, like Niya, Miran and Yotkan, remain covered by sand; others, like Yarkand and Hotan, remain important Uighur centres.

While there are no spectacular sights, the journey takes you about as far into Uighur heartland as you can get. It's possible to visit the southern towns as a multiday trip from Kashgar before crossing the Taklamakan Desert to Ürümqi, or as part of a rugged backdoor route into Tibet or Qīnghǎi.

YENGISAR 英吉沙

The tiny town of Yengisar (Yīngjíshā), 58km south of Kashgar, is synonymous with knife production. There are dozens of knife shops here (though prices are not much better than in Kashgar) and it's sometimes possible to visit the knife factory (小刀厂; *xiǎodāochǎng* in Chinese; *pichak chilik karakhana* in Uighur) in the centre of town to see the knives being made. Each worker makes the blade, handle and inlays himself, using only the most basic of tools. From the main highway walk east past Yīngjíshā Bīnguǎn (英吉沙宾馆) then turn left to the bazaar. The factory is just west of the bazaar. Try not to visit between the noon to 4pm lunchbreak.

Getting There & Away

Buses pass through the town regularly en route to Yarkand (Y13, 1½ hours) and Kashgar (Y7.5, 1½ hours). There's no bus station per se; ask a motorcab to take you to the drop off point (Y2).

YARKAND 莎车

Yarkand (Shāchē), Samarkand, Kashgar – put this town on the list of those beckoning to bygone Silk Road days. At the end of a major trade route from British India, over the Karakoram Pass from Leh, Yarkand was for centuries an important caravan town and centre for

Hindu tradesmen and moneylenders. Today it's important because a branch road leads north to Aksu.

The town is known for the dead. Tombs honouring royalty are the primary draw; the most famous of which is the tomb of Ammanisahan, a Uighur queen and musician famed for her work collecting the Uighur *muqam*.

Sights otherwise really means the alleys of the intriguing old quarter, where craftsmen still work their wares – noisily and sweatily – with ball-peen hammers and grindstones.

Orientation

Modern Yarkand is split into a Chinese new town and an Uighur old town. Heading right out of the bus station will bring you to the main avenue. Take a right here, and flag down any public bus (Y0.50), which will take you past the Shāchē Bīnguǎn, the Altyn Mosque and the old town.

Sights

Getting to the old town is slightly tricky – the best way to find it is to use the **Altyn Mosque complex** (阿勒电清真寺; Āqíndiàn Qīngzhēn Sì; admission Y10) as a landmark. The complex is on a smaller street off the main avenue. To get to the old town, take a left off the main avenue as if heading to the mosque, then take the first right down a dirt lane and keep going. To visit the town's sprawling, overgrown cemetery and *mazar* (pilgrimage site), take a left off this lane after five minutes. There is no charge to enter the complex.

Other **tombs**, most for Altun kings, located out of town include Hajiman Deng Mazar, Sud Pasha Mazar and Hayzi Terper Mazar. There is plenty of scope here to take many interesting walks around the surrounding countryside.

Yarkand also has a **Sunday Market**, untouristed but smaller than the markets at Kashgar (p833) or Hotan (p841). The market is held a block north of the Altyn Mosque.

Sleeping & Eating

Finding a place to stay can be a problem in Yarkand.

Shāchē Bīnguǎn (莎车宾馆; ☎ 851 2365; 4 Xincheng Lu; 新城路4号; tw/tr Y280/240) You will be led to this blah place because the PSB won't let others accept you (though what the heck – give the bus station cheapies a shot).

The old town has tempting noodle shops with patrons sitting on *kangs* instead of chairs.

Getting There & Around

Buses leave half-hourly for Kashgar (Y22, three hours), Yengisar (Y14, 1½ hours) and Karghilik (Y6, one hour). There are two daily buses at 11am and noon to Hotan (Y29, six hours), and five daily to Ürümqi (Y170 to Y190, 24 hours).

From the bus station it's about 1.5km to Shāchē Bīnguǎn and the same again to the start of the old town.

KARGHILIK 叶城

Karghilik (Yèchéng) is a convenient place to break the long trip to Hotan. There are decent places to stay and you could enjoyably spend some time exploring the old town. Karghilik is also of importance to travellers as the springboard of legendary highway 219, the Xīnjiāng–Tibet highway that helped 'open' Tibet. Considering the long overland trip to Ali in Tibet? Be sure you understand the dangers to you and any drivers who take you (see right).

The main attraction to take in here is the 15th-century **Friday Mosque** (Jama Masjid) and covered bazaar out front. The traditional adobe-walled backstreets of the old town spread south behind the mosque.

The town of **Charbagh**, located 10 minutes' drive towards Yarkand, has a large market on Tuesday.

Sleeping & Eating

Jiāotōng Bīnguǎn (交通宾馆; ☎ 728 5540; 1 Jiaotong Lu; 交通路1号; dm Y40, tw Y80-100) Right by the bus station, you may be pressured to stay here (the PSB again, hoping to corral foreigners, all of whom they assume are sneaking into Tibet), but that's OK as it's the best place anyway.

There are busy Uighur eateries outside the Friday Mosque and 24-hour food stalls across from the bus station.

Getting There & Away

There are buses to Yarkand (Y6) and Kashgar (Y25, four hours) every half hour until 8.30pm and six buses to Hotan (Y24, five hours) between 10.30am and 8.30pm. There are also five daily sleeper buses to Ürümqi (Y173 to Y182, 25 hours).

TO TIBET

The 1100km-long road to Ali, in western Tibet, branches off from the main Kashgar–Hotan road 6km east of Karghilik. Tibetan Antelope buses make the trip, but were only running thrice monthly at the time of writing, so you may have to hitch a ride with a truck. Ticket prices fluctuate wildly according to the severity of recent PSB crackdowns; count on paying anywhere between Y400 and Y1000, for either the bus or a truck. This is a very tough road with some passes over 5400m, and several foreigners have died, either from exposure or in traffic accidents. You should come equipped with warm clothes, enough food for a week (even if the trip to Ali can take as little as three days) and as a safety precaution, something to fend off nomads' dogs. Although this road is officially closed to foreigners, a number of travellers have been making it around the checkpoints in recent years – but not everyone. You may be fined upon arrival in Ali (Y300), or you may be booted out entirely, and will need to pick up a Y50 permit. See Lonely Planet's *Tibet* guide for more details.

HOTAN 和田

☎ 0903 / pop 104,900

You can call it a real 'Jade Gate'. Archaeologists have locally unearthed jade artefacts from around 5000 BC, proving that Hotan (Hétián; also known as Khotan) and its jewel trading preceded by a large chunk of time the horse-trading that later spurred Chinese trade routes westward.

Hotanese also uncovered the secret of Chinese silk by the 5th century AD – thus the famed road names hereabouts – and later established themselves as the region's foremost carpet weavers.

But Hotan today is certainly no Kashgar and the silk, carpets, and jade exist, but mostly in highly touristic fashion. Visits to carpet and silk factories are interesting for some, but what may make the 500km-long slog from Kashgar worthwhile is the fantastic Sunday Market, the largest and least visited in Xīnjiāng.

For those setting off on the infrequently explored southern Silk Road, via Keriya (Yútián), Cherchen (Qiěmò), Charklik (Ruòqiāng) and on to Golmud, this is the last place to take care of important errands like changing money, stocking up on supplies or extending your visa.

Orientation

Beijing Xilu is the main east–west axis running past the enormous main square (Tuánjié Guǎngchǎng). The bank and PSB are to the southwest of the square, while the hotels and bus stations are north from here. The Jade Dragon Kashgar River runs several kilometres east of town.

Information

The **Bank of China** (中国银行; Zhōngguó Yínháng; 9.30am-1.30pm & 4-8pm Mon-Fri) at the corner of Urumqi Nanlu and Beijing Xilu cashes travellers cheques.

Situated cross the street is the **PSB** (Gōngānjú; 22 Beijing Xilu; 9.30am-1.30pm & 4-7.30pm Mon-Fri), which will (if they like you) process visas in one day.

There's an internet café a few minutes north of the Hétián Yíngbīnguǎn.

CITS (Zhōngguó Guójì Lǚxíngshè; ☎ 202 6090; 23 Tamubake Xilu, 3f), located to the south off Wulumuqi Nanlu, can arrange tours of the silk factory as well as expensive excursions with a car and guide to the ruins at Yotkan and Melikawat.

Sights

You can check out the local selection of jade, supposedly pulled from the muddy Jade Dragon Kashgar River, at the rows of stores and stalls along Beijing Lu.

SUNDAY MARKET 星期天市场

Hotan's most popular attraction is its traditional weekly **market** (sometimes on Friday as well), which rivals Kashgar's in both size and interest. The colourful market swamps the northeast part of town and reaches fever pitch between noon and 2pm Xīnjiāng time. The most interesting parts to head for are the *gillam* (carpet) bazaar, which also has a selection of atlas silks, the *doppi* (skullcap) bazaar and the livestock bazaar.

CARPET & SILK FACTORIES 地毯厂、丝绸厂

On the eastern bank of the Jade Dragon Kashgar River is a small **carpet factory** (*gillam karakhana* in Uighur). Even with up to 10 people working on the large looms, one square metre in a wool carpet takes 20 days to complete. The tour is interesting, although Kashgar is a far better place to shop. To get here, take

XĪNJIĀNG

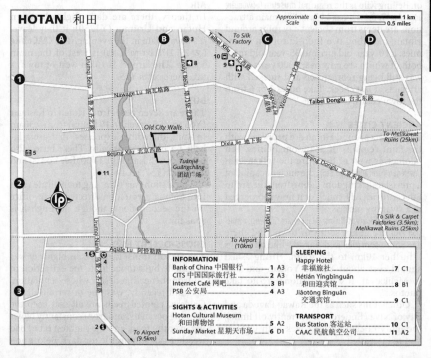

HOTAN 和田

Approximate Scale   0 — 1 km   0 — 0.5 miles

To Silk Factory

Nàwàge Lu 纳瓦格路

Old City Walls

Beijing Xilu 北京西路

Dixia Jie 地下街

Taibei Donglu 台北东路

To Melikawat Ruins (25km)

Beijing Donglu 北京东路

Tuánjié Guǎngchǎng 团结广场

To Silk & Carpet Factories (3.5km); Melikawat Ruins (25km)

Aqiàle Lu 阿恰勒路

To Airport (10km)

To Airport (9.5km)

INFORMATION	
Bank of China 中国银行	1 A3
CITS 中国国际旅行社	2 A3
Internet Café 网吧	3 B1
PSB 公安局	4 A3

SIGHTS & ACTIVITIES	
Hotan Cultural Museum 和田博物馆	5 A2
Sunday Market 星期天市场	6 D1

SLEEPING	
Happy Hotel 幸福旅社	7 C1
Hétián Yíngbīnguǎn 和田迎宾馆	8 B1
Jiāotōng Bīnguǎn 交通宾馆	9 C1

TRANSPORT	
Bus Station 客运站	10 C1
CAAC 民航航空公司	11 A2

minibus 2 heading east, which leaves from the main crossroads downtown, and then change to minibus 3 or walk 20 minutes over the bridge.

Past the carpet factory is the small town of Jíyǎxiāng, a traditional centre for atlas silk production. You can look around the fascinating **workshop** (atlas karakhana in Uighur; admission Y10) to see how the silk is spun, dyed and woven using traditional methods. A round trip in a taxi to the carpet and atlas factories costs Y30.

Hotan Silk Factory (Hétián Sīchóu Chǎng; ☺ 9am-1.30pm & 3.30-7.30pm Mon-Fri) uses a less traditional form of silk production, employing over 2000 workers. Staff at the office will give you a tour of the plant to see the boiling of cocoons and spinning, weaving, dyeing and printing of silk. If you don't speak at least some Chinese, you are better off arranging a visit through CITS. No photos are allowed in the factory. To get there, take minibus 1 from outside the bus station to the end of the line and then walk back 150m.

HOTAN CULTURAL MUSEUM 和田博物馆
In new digs but quite a hike to the west of town on Beijing Xilu is the regional **museum** (bówùguǎn; admission Y7; ☺ 9am-2pm & 4-7pm). The main attractions are items from ancient city ruins around Hotan, including two Indo-European mummies, a 10-year-old girl and 35-year-old man, both of whom are now over 1500 years old. It was still being reorganised and stocked with artefacts at last check. Take buses 2 or 6 from the town centre to get here.

ANCIENT CITIES 故城
The deserts around Hotan are peppered with the faint remains of abandoned cities. Ten kilometres west of town are the **Yotkan Ruins** (Yuètègān Yízhǐ; admission Y15), the ancient capital of a pre-Islamic kingdom dating from the 3rd to 8th centuries AD, much of it now submerged in a swampy morass.

The **Melikawat Ruins** (Mǎlìkèwǎtè Gùchéng; admission Y10) are 25km south of town, and there are some temples and pagoda-like buildings a further 10km to the south. Hiring a taxi should cost about Y30 to Yotkan and Y75 to Melikawat. It's an additional Y5 to take photos.

Other ruins such as the Rawaq Pagoda and city of Niya (Endere) are currently off limits; though you can always check with CITS if you're interested.

Sleeping & Eating
Happy Hotel (Xìngfú Lüshè; ☎ 202 4804; Taibei Xilu; 台北西路; bed Y30) The name of this basic-but-clean Uighur-style alternative certainly befits the owners, a wondrous Ma and Pa Uighur couple who are pleased as punch to have foreign guests.

Jiāotōng Bīnguǎn (☎ 203 2700; Taibei Xilu; 台北西路; tw Y80-180; ⚇) Next to the bus station, the Jiaotong has somewhat tired rooms, although they're still worth the lower end of the price range. There are cheaper rooms, but you'll need all your bargaining skills to get in.

Hétián Yíngbīnguǎn (☎ 202 2824; fax 202 3688; 4 Tanaiyi Beilu; 塔乃依北路4号; dm Y20, tw Y90-180; ⚇) The main building here is likely the nicest place to stay in Hotan, and the cheaper rooms in the old wing aren't bad either (though they may not let you in those). To get here, take a taxi (Y5) from the bus station.

Uighur staples are found throughout the town but otherwise Hotan is throwing up fast food places faster than you can blink.

Getting There & Away
AIR
In theory, there are daily flights between Hotan and Ürümqi (Y1250); if they leave, it's always late in the evening. The **CAAC office** (☎ 251 2178; Urumqi Nanlu) is west of the main square. The airport is 10km west of town; a taxi there costs Y15.

BUS
There are seven buses from Hotan to Kashgar (Y65 to Y85, seven to 10 hours) from 9.30am to 4pm, including 'expresses' that are a labelled a bit optimistically. These buses also pass through Karghilik (Y30, five hours) and Yarkand (Y37, six hours).

The station was planning to institute rides into Sìchuān; you'll be directed to an office on the second floor, though no English is spoken.

CROSS-DESERT HWY
The 500km trans-Taklamakan highway was originally built to facilitate the extraction of oil from beneath a desert whose reputation, up until recently, was one of certain death. Grids of planted reeds are all that keep the rippling ocean of sand from constantly blowing over the road, and the slightest bit of bad weather can stop traffic for days. Before you

even reach the desert, you'll see dust devils erupting in the distance like yellow geysers, and the snowy Kunlun Mountains towering forebodingly over the gravelly plain.

Sound good? The earliest bus to Ürümqi leaves at 11am (Y220, 25 hours) or the express at 1pm (Y330, 20 hours) to make the most of it. There are six other buses throughout the day, which cross the desert at night. If you're interested in going to Kuqa, you can get off near Lúntái (Y130, 15 hours); buses also pass through Korla. Drivers work in shifts, so it's not a bad idea to reiterate your destination. Bring plenty of water and food in case of breakdowns or storms.

Getting Around

Bus 10 runs from the bus station past the bazaar to the east bus station. Taxis in town cost a flat Y5; cycle rickshaws are Y2.

HOTAN TO GOLMUD 和田至格尔木

To continue east along the southern Silk Road, you'll need to catch the 8.30am bus to Cherchen (且末; Qiěmò), 580km away. The one-*very*-long-day trip costs Y78 and goes via the Uighur towns of Keriya (于田; Yútián) and Niya (民丰; Mínfēng); obviously, this often stretches into two days. Buses leave from the east bus station (东站; *dōng zhàn*) in Hotan; bus 10 runs here from the main bus station. Cherchen/Qiěmò has cheap hostels (Y10) and a small erstwhile manor-cum-museum.

From Cherchen/Qiěmò, three buses a week continue another 320km east to Charklik (若羌; Ruòqiāng); a nice hotel (Y50 double) is next to the bus station. The trip takes anywhere from 13 to 16 hours under good conditions, and tickets are Y60. From Charklik you may be able to get a bus to Golmud, though it's more likely you'll have to resort to a combination of private jeep and minibus services to get you the nine hours to Huātǔgōu (花土沟; from Y150 to Y200). From here you can reportedly catch a public bus to Golmud (Y140, 17 hours) or, usually, Xīníng (Y198, 24 to 28 hours).

This route requires a few overnight stops, and roads in this area are plagued by washouts and landslides, so don't go this way if you're in a hurry.

The completion of the railway to Lhasa would also theoretically allow one to hop aboard that train in Golmud – presuming,

naturally, that foreigners are allowed to do so at that time.

NORTHERN XĪNJIĀNG

Until the 1990s, this region of thick evergreen forests, rushing rivers and isolated mountain ranges was a quiet backwater, closed off to foreigners due to the proximity of the Russian, Mongolian and Kazakhstan borders. The highlight of the area is beautiful Kanas Lake (Hānàsī Hú) and the surrounding valleys.

BÙ'ĚRJĪN 布尔津

☎ 0906 / pop 60,000

Bù'ěrjīn, meaning 'dark green water' in Mongolian, is named after the nearby Bu'erjin River, which is a tributary of the Ertix River, the only river in China to flow into the Arctic Ocean. Bù'ěrjīn, 620km north of Ürümqi, marks the end of the desert and the beginning of the grasslands and mountains to the north. The town's population is mainly Kazakh (57%), but there are also Han, Uighurs, Tuva Mongolians and Russians.

There isn't much to see in Bù'ěrjīn, but you may need to stay here if you're headed to Kanas Lake.

Orientation

Bù'ěrjīn's main street is Xingfu Lu, bisected by Wenming Lu. One block to the west of Wenming Lu is Xiangyang Lu, with the PSB, and further south, the night market.

Information

You can't change travellers cheques in Bù'ěrjīn, but the local Industrial & Commercial Bank (ICBC) can change major currencies. Should you need a permit for a closed area, the PSB is on the corner of Xiangyang Lu and Xingfu Lu.

Sleeping & Eating

Jiāotōng Bīnguǎn (交通宾馆; ☎ 652 2643; Wenming Lu; 文明路; dm/tw Y10/90) It's at the old cheap and convenient bus station, and there is often no hot water, but the staff are helpful (though English is nonexistent).

Jiākèsī Jiǔdiàn (嘉客思酒店; ☎ 652 1716; Huancheng Nanlu; 环城南路; tw Y120-280) This place has nice rooms right by the night market (at the corner with Xiangyang Lu), with hot water in the evening. Friendly staff, if a bit inept.

XINJIANG

For a hearty bowl of beef noodle soup, make a beeline for the **Yínchuān Huímín Fàndiàn** (银川回民饭店; Wenming Lu). It's at the corner on the end of Wenming Lu. Opposite Jiākèsī Jiǔdiàn is a tiny night market specialising in grilled fish and fresh yoghurt.

Getting There & Away

There are two buses to Ürümqi (Y120 to Y137, 13 hours) at 11am and 8pm, and Jímǔnǎi (Y12, two hours) at 11am and 6pm.

You could also take a bus to Altai (Ālètài, Y15, 1½ hours) and try from there. Altai also has an airport with daily flights to/from Ürümqi (Y450). At the time of writing a new rail line was also being constructed from the capital to Altai. Buses run to/from the city hourly (Y15, 1½ hours) between 9am and 7pm.

KANAS LAKE NATURE RESERVE
哈纳斯湖自然保护区

Travellers rave about the splendid alpine scenery at R&R-perfect Kanas Lake, a long finger of a lake found in the southernmost reaches of the Siberian taiga ecosystem. The forests, dominated by spruce, birch, elm and Siberian larch, are spectacular in autumn; semi-nomadic Kazakhs love to meet travellers.

Many come hoping to see a cameo by the Kanas Lake Monster (it deserves a more poetic moniker), a mythical beast – yes, yes, China's Nessie – that has long figured in stories around yurt campfires to scare the little 'uns. Apparently he/she reappeared in 2005 and again in 2006, bringing tons of journalists and conspiracy hounds (puzzled Chinese scientists insist it's just a big school of salmon-like fish).

Big changes are coming. The government is simultaneously trying to draw oodles more tourists here – it's swarming already in summer – and do it with less of a footprint. All lodging and restaurants are slated to be removed from the area and rebuilt elsewhere, probably at Tuva, 18km away.

A great day-hike is to the lookout point, Guanyu Pavilion (观鱼亭; Guānyú Tíng; 2030m). It's a long, ambling walk from the village (tons of steps); from the top are superb panoramas of the lake, Friendship Peak and the nearby grasslands. It's possible to return to the village via a circuitous scenic route down the eastern slope by following the dirt road, a loop that takes a lazy five hours. If you're short on time, a bus (Y30 return) drives to

the Guanyu Pavilion steps from outside the village.

There are similar landscapes in the neighbouring valley of Hemu Kanas (Hémù Hānàsī) and the Bai Kaba (Báihābā) village. You may be able to hire a taxi from Kanas Lake to the village (Y150) or if hiring a taxi from Bù'ěrjīn to Kanas Lake, you may be able to negotiate a detour on the way.

Eighteen kilometres past the entrance to the **reserve** (Hānàsī Hú Zìrán Bǎohùqū; admission Y100) is a Tuva village, which now serves as the tourist centre. The area is only accessible from mid-May to mid-October, with ice and snow making transport difficult the rest of the year.

Sleeping & Eating

Remember that bit above about closing all facilities at the lake.

Officially, the only options for accommodation are the log cabins and wooden yurts around the village school (学校; xuéxiào). The going rates per bed are: yurts Y30, dorms Y60 and twins Y80. During the peak summer months, there are nightly barbecues accompanied by Kazakh and Mongolian dancing and a roaring bonfire.

While camping is off-limits, it's unlikely that anyone will come out looking for you – just remember the area is still unspoiled, so stay low impact. No matter where you sleep, food is extremely expensive and monotonous. Bring your own supplies.

Getting There & Away

This is the hard part. During July and August there should be tourist buses (Y50) that head to the lake from Bù'ěrjīn's bus station. Unfortunately, it's impossible to count on them, because most tourists come up here with a tour group from Ürümqi. Your best bet is to hire a taxi to make the four-hour, 170km trip. The bidding starts at Y400, with Y250 being a reasonable target (one way).

You might also consider doing a tour. The four-day trip out of Ürümqi with Ecol Travel (p823) in the Bógédá Bīnguǎn is an excellent deal. For Y580 you get an air-con minibus (only 10 hours to Bù'ěrjīn), two nights in Bù'ěrjīn, a park entrance ticket, one night's lodging at the lake and a visit to the strange rock formations at Wuerhe Ghost Town, where the movie *Warriors of Heaven and Earth* was filmed. It's cheaper, easier and will give you the chance to make friends with Chinese tourists.

FRIENDSHIP PEAK 友谊峰

Standing on the glacier-covered summit of Friendship Peak (Yǒuyì Fēng; 4374m) allows you to be in three nations at once. Presumably you won't need a visa for each one, but you will need a climbing permit, guide, ice axe, crampons and other appropriate mountaineering paraphernalia.

JÍMǓNǍI 吉木乃

The only reason to visit this town is if you're going to Kazakhstan. The border here is generally open, but come armed with a plan B in case you don't get through; check with Bù'ěrjīn PSB to make sure it's still OK to do this. The first major town in Kazakhstan is Maykapchigay, from where you can catch a taxi to Zaysan and then a bus to Semey (12 hours).

A couple of buses depart from the bus station and the main intersection for Ürümqi between 4pm and 5pm daily. The trip takes 14 hours and costs Y130 for a sleeper or a seat, although prices are negotiable with the private operators. There are two daily buses that make the dusty trip to Bù'ěrjīn (Y15, two hours).

There is no reliable public transport to the border, but a taxi will make the 30km trip for Y25. Coming the other way, you can share a taxi to Jímǔnǎi for Y5.

TǍCHÉNG 塔城

In a lonely corner of northwestern Xīnjiāng, Tǎchéng is a relatively obscure border crossing into neighbouring Kazakhstan. Now and then the gates are closed; if you do make it here and can't get through, don't despair. Tǎchéng is a pleasant enough place to relax before catching a bus south to Ālāshānkǒu or north to Jímǔnǎi.

Information

The post and telephone office (邮电大楼; Yóudiàn Dàlóu) is in the centre of town, on the corner of Xinhua Lu and Ta'er Bahetai Lu. The PSB is on Jianshe Jie. The Bank of China is south of here on Guangming Lu and can handle cash and travellers cheques.

Sleeping

Tǎchéng Bīnguǎn (塔城宾馆; ☎ 622 2093; Youhao Jie; 友好街; dm Y35, tw Y100-140) This hotel, tucked away in the northwest of town, has beds in a Russian-style building. The twins are reasonable and there's 24-hour hot water.

Getting There & Around
AIR

Daily flights operate between Ürümqi and Tǎchéng; you can purchase your tickets (Y390) from **CAAC** (中国民航; Zhōngguó Mínháng; ☎ 622 3428).

BUS

There are two daily buses to Tǎchéng (Y132 to Y142, 12 hours) from Ürümqi, departing at 11am and 7pm. From Tǎchéng to Ürümqi the time and price are similar.

TAXI

Tǎchéng is small enough to get around on foot. If you're coming from Kazakhstan, take a shared taxi for Y5 into town.

YĪNÍNG 伊宁
☎ 0999 / pop 240,000

Also known as Gulja, leafy and friendly Yīníng lies about 390km west of Ürümqi. The centre of the Ili Kazak Autonomous Prefecture, Yīníng is of primary interest as a stopover on the way to Kazakhstan.

Looking at the city today, you'd hardly know it was the scene of violent separatist riots in 1997. Yīníng has since gone the Sinicised way of most frontier towns in Xīnjiāng, and many of the original Kazakh and Uighur inhabitants seem to have been swallowed up without a trace.

Even though the Chinese appear to currently dominate the border regions, there is no doubt that the easily accessible Ili Valley causes them concern. Yīníng itself was occupied by Russian troops between 1872 and 1881, and as recently as 1962 there were major Sino-Soviet clashes along the Ili River (Yīlí Hé).

Běijīng's major fear now is that separatist elements from the neighbouring Central Asian republics will continue to provide fuel to an ever-restless 'Uighurstan'.

Information

The **Bank of China** (中国银行; Zhōngguó Yínháng; Jiefang Lu; 🕙 10am-8pm Mon-Fri, 11am-4.30pm Sat & Sun), situated east of the bus station, changes cash and travellers cheques. The post office is located opposite; internet access (per hour Y2) is available on the 3rd floor. The **Public Security Bureau** (公安局; Gōngānjú; Stalin Jie) is opposite Yīlítè Dàjiǔdiàn (Yilite Grand Hotel).

XĪNJIĀNG

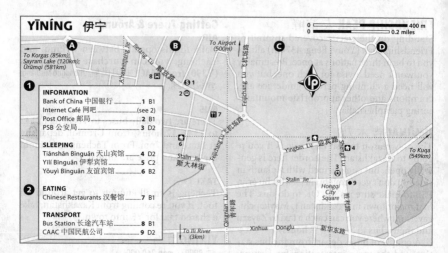

Sights

Just to the south of town is a long line of **open-air restaurants** and **teahouses** where you can sit and watch the Ili River slide by. To get there, hop on bus 2 and get off at the last stop, just before the bridge over the river. They're only open when the weather is nice.

Sleeping & Eating

A taxi to any of the hotels below shouldn't cost more than Y5.

Tiānshān Bīnguǎn (☎ 802 2304; Shengli Lu; 胜利路; dm Y20, tw Y70) This small place is in exceptional condition and is the only budget accommodation that accepts foreigners.

Yílí Bīnguǎn (☎ 802 3799; fax 802 4964; 8 Yingbin Lu; 迎宾路8; tw Y140-400) Its rooms aren't always the fanciest, but the Yili certainly has character. Old Soviet buildings lost in a quasi-forest full of chirping birds, dance performances and puttering-about-but-friendly staff make this hotel the top choice.

Yǒuyì Bīnguǎn (☎ 782 3111; fax 782 3222; 7 Stalin Jie, 3 Xiang; 斯大林街7, 巷3; tw Y218) A comfortable hotel with international standards, it holds up against more expensive competition.

THE GREAT ENERGY GAME

China may be pledging to cut back on coal consumption, but there can be little doubt that raw energy is something the country will need increasingly more of, not less. Xīnjiāng already sits atop 30% of China's oil and natural gas reserves and Běijīng in 2006 announced some extraordinarily ambitious plans to turn the province into a 21st-century Texas, and then some. Unsurprisingly, the vast oil and gas reserves in the rest of Central Asia are also one of PetroChina's principle targets.

In 2004 China and Kazakhstan finalised a deal to build a 3000km pipeline stretching from the Caspian Sea all the way through Ālāshānkǒu into Xīnjiāng. China's heavy investment in the Central Asian republics is generally regarded as an economic carrot, ensuring security both in and around the country's most unstable province. With the encroaching interests of neighbours Russia, India and Pakistan in the area, and military presence in Afghanistan, there can be little doubt that China is seen scrambling to establish itself as the big kid on the block.

And if you've begun to think Xīnjiāng is culturally and geographically more similar to a Central Asian state than China, you're not alone. Not only does Běijīng want to tie up the natural resources of its relatively new trading partners, it also wants promises from its neighbours to weed out Uighur separatist groups taking refuge beyond Chinese soil. The area's porous borders have previously seen large-scale migrations, and continuous persecution of the Uighurs has, at the very minimum, engendered little love for the PRC among your average Uzbek, Kyrgyz and Kazakh.

YĪNÍNG BUS TIMETABLES

Destinations from Yīníng include the following:

Destination	Price	Duration	Frequency	Departs
Almaty	US$30	10hr	4 weekly	8am
Bólè	Y39	4hr	3 daily	10.30am, 11.30am, 12.45pm
Kuqa	Y140	24hr	3 daily	noon, 3pm, 6pm
Ürümqi	Y120-150	11-14hr	8 daily	9am-9pm

There are plenty of street markets that set up stalls in the evenings around town. The first street west of the main traffic circle is home to the city's expanding collection of Chinese restaurants.

Getting There & Away

AIR

There are daily (evening) flights between Ürümqi and Yīníng for Y740. The **CAAC office** (Zhōngguó Mínháng; ☎ 804 4328) is inside the Yīlítè Dàjiǔdiàn, opposite Hongqi City Sq (Hóngqí Guǎngchǎng). A taxi to/from the airport is Y20.

BUS

See the table, above, for bus times.

Buses leave Yīníng on Monday, Wednesday, Thursday and Saturday for Almaty in Kazakhstan (this may change); visas are not available here. To Ürümqi, there are three choices: soft seat, regular sleeper or express. The first leaves in the morning, the latter two in the afternoon. Although numerous buses pass by Sayram Lake (three hours), they all charge full price; the best deal is the bus to Bólè.

The spectacular bus ride to Kuqa (May to October) passes over Tiān Shān and through the small Mongolian village of Bayanbulak. This would be a good place to break the journey, but at last check the area was closed to foreigners. Amazingly, three daily buses also leave for Kashgar (Y246).

AROUND YĪNÍNG

Ili Valley 伊犁谷

The farmland of the Ili Valley (Yīlí Gǔ) is home to some 20,000 Xibe (Xībózú), who were dispatched by the Qing government to safeguard and colonise the region during the 18th century. This is the only place in China where you'll find a population capable of reading and writing Manchurian, which otherwise died out when the Manchus were assimilated into Chinese culture.

As intriguing as the Xibe sound, there's actually very little to see here. The Lamaist temple **Jingyuán Sì** (靖远寺; admission Y10), outside nondescript Qapaqal (Chábùchá'ěr), is hardly worth the admission fee, and generally speaking, the Xibe resemble the Han. If you're interested nonetheless, you can catch a minibus to Qapaqal (Y3, 30 minutes) outside the Yīníng bus station.

Sayram Lake 塞里木湖

The vast Sayram Lake (Sàilǐmù Hú), 120km north of Yīníng, is an excellent spot to explore the Tiān Shān range. The lake is especially colourful during June and July, when alpine flowers blanket the ground.

It's not hard to access the more pristine mountainous areas, and you could conceivably stop here for a day hike. However, if you want to spend significant time exploring, it's best to bring a tent. While there is some food around, the selection is limited and prices expensive, so take what you need. In the height of summer, there are also Kazakh yurts (about Y30 per night, with meals) scattered around the lake willing to take boarders, although the PSB has been cracking down on unauthorised homestays.

Buses from Yīníng to Sàilǐmù Hú take about three hours, and drop passengers off at the 'yurt village' (consisting of fake yurts) along the main road. All buses between Ürümqi and Yīníng pass by the lake, so just stand by the road and wave one down.

Gānsù 甘肃

For over a millennium Silk Road camel caravans wound their way through the mountain and desert corridor of Gānsù, transferring goods and ideas between China and Central Asia along the world's first information superhighway. Travellers, pilgrims, artists and merchants entered the Middle Kingdom using a string of oasis towns as stepping stones. The Buddhist art, military garrisons, beacon towers and tombs they left behind form one of the Silk Road's richest treasure troves.

While Gānsù is most known for its Silk Road legacy – the series of ancient Buddhist grottoes stretching from the eastern edge to western tip – what makes the province truly spectacular is the unexpected variety of landscapes and peoples within its elongated borders.

Despite its rich history, an unforgiving arid climate has made life hard here. Outside of the oases, most of the land west of the capital is barely habitable, and up until recently Běijīng did little to relieve the area of its isolation. Even with the completion of the vital Lánzhōu–Ürümqi railway line in 1963 and the subsequent development of mining and industry, Gānsù remains one of China's five poorest provinces.

Nevertheless, for travellers Gānsù is a highlight of the northwest. The province contains an unimaginable trove of Buddhist paintings and sculptures, a fascinating glimpse of the vibrant Tibetan culture of Amdo and the idyllic, little-visited rural scenery in the southeastern corner. Some of the diverse people you might meet on your way include the Hui, Tibetans, Mongols, Salar, Dongxiang and Kazakhs.

GĀNSÙ

HIGHLIGHTS

- Step back into the origins of Chinese Buddhist art at the **Mogao Caves** (p866)
- Stock up on good karma at Xiàhé's Tibetan **Labrang Monastery** (p856), with its traveller cafés and pilgrim shops
- Explore forgotten Silk Road remains around **Tiānshuǐ** (p869) and **Luòmén** (p871)
- Hike through hazy **Moon Canyon** (p872) or up the ridges of the **Qílián Shān range** (p860)
- Take the yak-inhabited back roads to Sìchuān via **Lángmùsì** (p859)

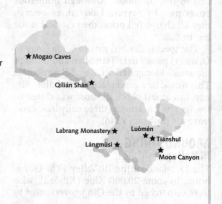

★ Mogao Caves

Qílián Shān ★

Labrang Monastery ★   Luòmén ★ ★ Tiānshuǐ

Lángmùsì ★

Moon Canyon ★

- POPULATION: 26.4 MILLION
- www.gansu.gov.cn/en

Climate

Gānsù can be roughly divided into three climatic regions: the low-altitude green belt south of Tiānshuǐ; the arid Hexi Corridor extending from Lánzhōu to Dūnhuáng; and the alpine grasslands rising up along the borders of Qīnghǎi and Sìchuān. Since the province rarely sees rain, dust storms are not uncommon, particularly in the spring. Winters get nippy from November to March. May, June, September and October are probably the best months to visit; June to September is the 'high season'.

Language

Gānsù has its own group of regional Chinese dialects, loosely known as Gansuhua (part of the northwestern Lanyin Mandarin family). On the borders of Qīnghǎi and Sìchuān is a significant Tibetan population speaking the Tibetan Amdo dialect.

Getting There & Around

Lánzhōu has flights around the country; other airports such as Dūnhuáng and Jiāyùguān only have a handful of flights to major cities, with fewer flights in the winter.

Train is the best way to connect the province's Silk Road sights and continue along the popular rail routes to Xīnjiāng or Xī'ān.

A major highway construction programme will soon shave off bus times to southern sights around Xiàhé and Lángmùsì. A new train station at Dūnhuáng and upgraded airport at Jiāyùguān will further aid access.

LÁNZHŌU & SOUTHERN GĀNSÙ

Most travellers end up passing through Lánzhōu but the real gems lie further south in the Muslim- and Tibetan-flavoured grasslands around Xiàhé, Hézuò and the roads south to Sìchuān.

LÁNZHŌU 兰州

☎ 0931 / pop 2,804,600

The first major city along the Yellow River (Huáng Hé), Gānsù's capital has been an important garrison town since ancient times. Following the communist victory and the

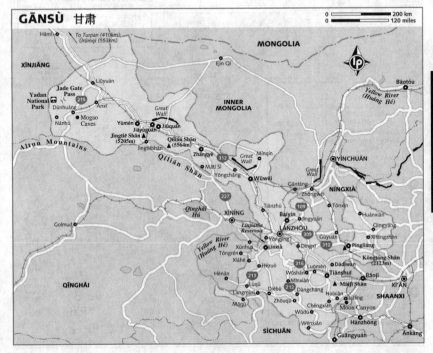

GĀNSÙ 甘肃

city's integration into the expanding rail network, Lánzhōu developed quickly, perhaps too quickly – for a time in the late 1990s it was considered the world's most polluted city.

Lánzhōu is a major transport hub, and the beginning of some epic overland journeys into Xīnjiāng, Sìchuān and Tibet. While there are a number of great destinations surrounding the capital, there's little reason to linger here any longer than it takes to extend your visa or book your train ticket.

Orientation

Geography has conspired to make Lánzhōu a city of awkward design. At 1600m above sea level, it's crammed into a narrow valley walled in by steep mountains, forcing it to develop

westwards in a long, urban corridor that extends for more than 20km along the southern banks of the Yellow River. The most practical area to base yourself is in the east.

Information

Bank of China (Zhōngguó Yínháng; Tianshui Lu; ⊗ 8.30am-noon & 2.30-6pm Mon-Fri) You can change travellers cheques (counter 10 or 11) and use the ATM here.

Chāofán Guódù (Tianshui Lu; per hr Y2; ⊗ 24hr) Internet access.

China International Travel Service (CITS; Zhōngguó Guójì Lüxíngshè; ☎ 883 5566; www.citsgs.com; 11th fl, Tourism Bldg, Nongmin Xiang) Located on the street running behind the hotel Lánzhōu Fàndiàn.

Foreign Languages Bookshop (Wàiwén Shūdiàn; 35 Zhangye Lu; ⊗ 8.30am-6.30pm)

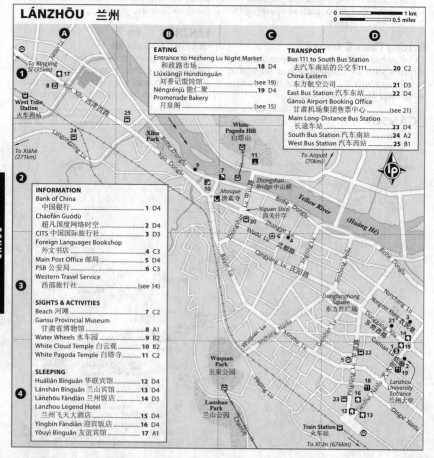

LÁNZHŌU 兰州

EATING
Entrance to Hezheng Lu Night Market	
和政路市场	**18** D4
Liúxiāngjì Húndùnguǎn	
刘香记馄饨馆	(see 19)
Néngrénjù 能仁聚	**19** D4
Promenade Bakery	
月泉阁	(see 15)

TRANSPORT
Bus 111 to South Bus Station	
去汽车南站的公交车111	**20** C2
China Eastern	
东方航空公司	**21** D3
East Bus Station 汽车东站	**22** D4
Gānsù Airport Booking Office	
甘肃机场集团售票中心	(see 21)
Main Long-Distance Bus Station	
长途车站	**23** D4
South Bus Station 汽车南站	**24** A2
West Bus Station 汽车西站	**25** B1

INFORMATION
Bank of China	
中国银行	**1** D4
Chāofán Guódù	
超凡国度网络时空	**2** D4
CITS 中国国际旅行社	**3** D3
Foreign Languages Bookshop	
外文书店	**4** C3
Main Post Office 邮局	**5** D4
PSB 公安局	**6** C3
Western Travel Service	
西部旅行社	(see 14)

SIGHTS & ACTIVITIES
Beach 河滩	**7** C2
Gansu Provincial Museum	
甘肃省博物馆	**8** A1
Water Wheels 水车园	**9** B2
White Cloud Temple 白云观	**10** B2
White Pagoda Temple 白塔寺	**11** C2

SLEEPING
Huálián Bīnguǎn 华联宾馆	**12** D4
Lánshān Bīnguǎn 兰山宾馆	**13** D4
Lánzhōu Fàndiàn 兰州饭店	**14** D3
Lanzhou Legend Hotel	
兰州飞天大酒店	**15** D4
Yíngbīn Fàndiàn 迎宾饭店	**16** D4
Yǒuyì Bīnguǎn 友谊宾馆	**17** A1

GĀNSÙ

Main Post Office (yóujú; cnr Minzhu Lu & Pingliang Lu; ⏰ 8am-7pm)

PSB (Gōngānjú; 482 Wudu Lu; ⏰ 8.30-11.30am & 2.30-5.30pm Mon-Fri) The foreign-affairs branch is located on the ground floor, next to a giant Orwellian tower. Visa extensions are generally granted on the same day. One photo required.

Western Travel Service (Xībù Lǚxíngshè; ☎ 885 0529; 486 Donggang Xilu) Located on the 2nd floor of the west wing of Lánzhōu Fàndiàn. It has English-speaking staff, and offers competitive-priced tours and ticket bookings.

Sights

GANSU PROVINCIAL MUSEUM 甘肃省博物馆

Gānsù's **museum** (Gānsù Shěng Bówùguǎn; Xijin Xilu; admission Y30; ⏰ 9am-5pm Tue-Sun) is the one sight definitely worth visiting in Lánzhōu. Major renovations finally came to a close in late 2006. Significant exhibits include 10,000-year-old painted pottery taken from Dàdìwān, 300km southeast of Gānsù.

Other displays dating from the Han dynasty (206 BC–AD 220) include inscribed wooden tablets used to relay messages along the Silk Road, and a graceful bronze horse galloping upon the back of a swallow. The latter, known as the 'Flying Horse of Wuwei', has become a popular symbol throughout northwestern China since its discovery in 1969. One piece that may set your mind pondering is a 2nd-century BC silver plate depicting Bacchus, the Greco-Roman God of Wine – it was unearthed 120km northeast of Lánzhōu.

WHITE CLOUD TEMPLE 白云观

This renovated Qing-dynasty **Taoist temple** (Báiyún Guàn; Binhe Zhonglu; ⏰ 7am-5.30pm) comes complete with a former opera stage, fortune-telling monks and kite-eating trees. Overlooking the Yellow River, it's one of the city's few links to the past. A short stroll from here are two huge **water wheels** (admission Y2), copies of irrigation devices that once lined the Yellow River. East of here is a **beach** area, bursting on weekends with volleyball games, kites, speedboats and coracle raft trips across the chocolate-coloured river (Y30).

LANSHAN PARK 兰山公园

Rising steeply to the south of the city is the Lánshān mountain range, whose **park** (admission Y6; ⏰ 8am-8pm) offers fine views and a cool repose in the summer heat. The quickest and easiest way up is by the **chairlift** (lǎnchē; one way/

return Y20/25; ⏰ 8am-8pm May-Oct), accessible from behind **Wuquan Park** (Wǔquán Gōngyuán; admission Y6; ⏰ 6am-6pm).

From the train station take bus 31 or 34 five stops, get off and continue walking until you reach Jinchang Nanlu. Turn left here and walk about 500m to the Wuquan Park ticket office. The cable car is a five-minute walk down a side alley – ask the way often. As the ticket office says, 'the joy will be boundless'.

WHITE PAGODA HILL 白塔山

This **park** (Báitǎ Shān; admission Y5; ⏰ 6.30am-8.30pm summer) is on the northern bank of the Yellow River. At its zenith is **White Pagoda Temple** (Báitǎ Sì), originally built during the Yuan dynasty (AD 1206–1368), from where there are good views across the city. There's a **chairlift** (one way/return Y15/20) spanning the river; the terminal is just to the west of Zhongshan Bridge. Bus 34 comes here from in front of the train station on Tianshui Nanlu.

Sleeping

It's always worth asking for a discount in Lánzhōu. Note that most budget hostels in the vicinity of the train station won't accept foreigners.

Lánshān Bīnguǎn (☎ 861 7211; 6 Tianshui Nanlu; 天水南路6号; s/tw/tr with bathroom Y98/138/168, without bathroom Y46/56/60) This old dinosaur is not yet extinct, but only those looking for bargain-basement beds will want to consider it. Hot water is available from 8pm to 11pm.

Huálián Bīnguǎn (☎ 499 2000; 7-9 Tianshui Nanlu; 天水南路7-9号; d without bathroom Y58, s Y98, tr Y138-278) Directly across from the train station, the Hualian has excellent-value rooms and good discounts of 20% to 40%. The only drawbacks are the traffic noise and the slow lifts. Hot water is available mornings and evenings.

Yǒuyì Bīnguǎn (Friendship Hotel; ☎ 233 3051; 16 Xijin Xilu; 西津西路16号; tw old wing Y60, tw with bathroom Y108-198, new wing Y380; 🖳) This long-standing hotel is on the western side of the city, handy for the museum and south or west bus stations. The old-fashioned cheapo rooms feel like a boarding school but are decent, with shared bathrooms. The architecture is best described as 'Great Wall of Kitsch'.

Yíngbīn Fàndiàn (☎ 888 6552; 37 Tianshui Nanlu; 天水南路37号; tw with bathroom Y80-158; 🖳) Unfortunately, the dimly lit rooms aren't quite as nice as the lobby; the cheaper en suite rooms don't have a window. The cheapest

GĀNSÙ

rooms with shared bathrooms are off-limits to foreigners.

Lánzhōu Fàndiàn (☎ 841 6321; fax 841 8608; 434 Donggang Xilu; 东岗西路434号; tw Y360-800; ⚙) This large, constantly renovated Sino-Stalinist edifice has cosy four-star rooms (50% discounts) and nonsmoking floors; the cheaper rooms aren't up to much.

Lanzhou Legend Hotel (Lánzhōu Fēitiān Dàjiǔdiàn; ☎ 853 2888; www.lanzhoulegendhotel.com; 529 Tianshui Nanlu; 天水南路529号; r Y920; ⚙) This four-star joint-venture hotel is well run and very comfortable, with good restaurants, English-speaking staff and money-changing facilities. Discounts drop the price by up to 50% and credit cards are accepted.

Eating

Lánzhōu's big highlight is eating out. The Hezheng Lu night market, extending from Tianshui Lu to Pingliang Lu, is one of the best places to savour the flavours of the northwest. The mix of Hui, Han and Uighur stalls offers everything from goat's head soup to steamed snails, as well as *ròujiābǐng* (肉夹饼) – mutton served inside a 'pocket' of flat bread.

Lánzhōu is also known for its *niúròumiàn* (牛肉面), beef noodle soup that's spicy enough to make you sweat, even in winter. Two handy phrases are *'jiā ròu'* (with beef; 加肉) and *'búyào làjiāo'* (without chillies; 不要辣椒).

Néngrénjù (Tianshui Lu; hotpot for 2 people Y50) Try this eatery, south of the university, which serves mutton hotpot accompanied by a delicious peanut sauce. Recognise it by the façade of Beijing opera masks.

Liúxiāngjì Húndūnguǎn (204 Tianshui Lu) Next door to Néngrénjù, this place serves some of the city's best *bāozi* (steamed savoury buns with tasty meat filling; 包子; Y4).

Promenade Bakery (Tianshui Nanlu) Just next to Lanzhou Legend Hotel, this bakery makes brick-sized banana bread (Y12) – great for day hikes.

Getting There & Away

AIR

Lanzhou has daily flights to Běijīng (Y1340), Chéngdū (Y940), Guǎngzhōu (Y1890), Ürümqi (Y1600) and Xī'ān (Y600). Other weekly destinations include Jiāyùguān (Y910) and Dūnhuáng (Y1030). Discounts can bring fares down by 40%. Thrice-weekly flights to Lhasa are in the pipeline.

China Eastern (Zhōngguó Dōngháng; ☎ 882 1964; Donggang Xilu; ⏰ 8.30am-9pm)

Gānsù Airport Booking Office (Gānsù Jīchǎng Jítuán Shòupiào Zhōngxīn; ☎ 888 9666; 520 Donggang Xilu; ⏰ 8.30am-9pm) Next to China Eastern (not at the airport), this office can book all airlines at discounted prices.

BUS

Lánzhōu has at least four bus stations. The **main long-distance bus station** (chángtú chēzhàn; Pingliang Lu) and the **south bus station** (qìchē nánzhàn; Langongping Lu) are the most useful (see the table, opposite). Touts can be very pushy at the south bus station. All stations have departures for Xīníng.

The **west bus station** (qìchē xīzhàn; Xijin Xilu) handles departures to Liújiāxiá (Y12, two hours); for Bǐnglíng Sì, see opposite.

The **east bus station** (qìchē dōngzhàn; Pingliang Lu) has a few additional departures to such eastern destinations as Gùyuán (Y44, eight hours, 6.30am).

TRAIN

Lánzhōu is the major rail link between eastern and western China and trains run to every corner of China. Heading west, there are overnight trains to Jiāyùguān (10 hours), Dūnhuáng (12 hours) and Turpan (22 hours). The most popular route west is to Ürümqi (24 hours) on train T295 (hard sleeper Y365) and east is to Xī'ān on train K120 (hard sleeper Y175). In summer buy your onward tickets a couple of days in advance to guarantee a sleeper berth.

A soft seat in one of the double-decker express trains is by far the most civilised way to get to Xīníng (hard/soft seat Y33/50, 3½ hours). Trains depart at 8.25am and 3.43pm.

For details on trains to Lhasa, see p924.

Getting Around

The airport is 70km north of the city. **Airport buses** (☎ 896 8555) leave from beside the China Eastern office three hours before scheduled flight departures (Y30, one hour). A speedier taxi costs around Y120, or Y30 per seat.

The most useful bus routes are buses 1, 31 and 137 running from the train station to the west bus station and Yǒuyì Bīnguǎn via Xiguan Shizi. Bus 111 runs from Zhongshan Lu (at the Xiguan Shizi stop) to the south bus station. Buses 7 and 10 run from the train station up the length of Tianshui Nanlu before heading west and east, respectively. Public buses cost Y1; flagfall for taxis is Y7 (for the first 3km).

GĀNSÙ

LÁNZHŌU BUS TIMETABLES

The following services depart from the south bus station:

Destination	Price (Y)	Duration	Frequency	Departs
Hézuò	44	6hr	half-hourly	7.30am-4pm
Lángmùsì	71	10hr	1 daily	8.30am
Línxià	27-29	3hr	half-hourly	7am-5pm
Xiàhé	45	6hr	3 daily	7.30am, 8.30am, 2pm
Zhāngyè	98	12hr	1 daily	6pm

The following services depart from the main long-distance bus station:

Destination	Price (Y)	Duration	Frequency	Departs
Píngliáng	76	5hr	5 daily	7.30am-4pm
Tiānshuǐ	60	4hr	half-hourly	7.30am-5pm
Yínchuān	96	6hr	two hourly	7.30am-5pm
Xīníng	53	2½hr	90min	8am-5pm
Zhāngyè	79	8hr	hourly	8am-2pm

BǏNGLÍNG SÌ 炳灵寺

Due to its relative inaccessibility, **Bǐnglíng Sì**
(adult/student Y50/25) is one of the few Buddhist
grottoes in China to survive the tumultuous 20th century unscathed. Over a period
spanning 1600 years, sculptors dangling from
ropes carved 183 niches and sculptures into
the porous rock along the dramatic canyon
walls. Today the cliffs are isolated by the
waters of the Liujiaxia Reservoir (Liújiāxiá
Shuǐkù) on the Yellow River. All considered,
come here for a nice day out rather than for
the cave art alone, which doesn't compare to
somewhere like Dūnhuáng.

Like other Silk Road grottoes, wealthy
patrons, often traders along the route west,
sponsored the development of Bǐnglíng Sì,
which reached its height during the prosperous Tang dynasty. The star of the caves is the
27m-high seated statue of Maitreya, the future
Buddha, but some of the smaller, sway-hipped
bodhisattvas and guardians, bearing an obvious Indian influence, are equally exquisite.
Photos are allowed. Across the canyon is a
large 1500-year-old sleeping Buddha, his heart
ripped out by treasure seekers. Art buffs can
climb the staircase to Tang-dynasty caves 169
and 172 for an extra fee of Y300.

If you've hired your own boat, and thus
have more time at the site, you can take a jeep
(Y40) or hike 2.5km further up the impressive
canyon to a small Tibetan monastery.

Note that from November to March water
levels may be too low to visit the caves, so
check before setting off.

Tours

Western Travel Service (Xībù Lǚxíngshè; ☎ 0931-885
0529; 486 Donggang Xilu) in Lanzhou can organise
a visit to the caves for two people for Y340
per person.

Getting There & Away

You can visit Bǐnglíng Sì as a day trip from
Lánzhōu or en route to Línxià.

Frequent buses from Lánzhōu's west bus
station (Y12, two hours) run past the Liujiaxia
Reservoir, and will drop you 500m from the
boat ticket office. Ironically this bus is the
only route left in Gānsù where you might be
pestered for local insurance.

Going rates for a covered speedboat (seating up to eight people) are Y400 for the one-
hour trip. The boat ticket office is good at
hooking up independent travellers with small
groups, which will make the price around Y65
to Y80 per person. For this you'll get about 1½
hours at the site, which is really a minimum.
Private operators near the dam will pester you
with similar rates, and perhaps cheaper speedboats (Y200). For those with time, the ferry
(May to October) is just Y30 return, but it's a
pretty dreary seven-hours return trip! Bring
snacks, sunscreen and cold drinks.

GĀNSÙ

If you're heading to Línxià after the caves, you can arrange for a speedboat to drop you off at Liánhuātái (莲花台) on the way back. From there, minibuses will taxi you on to Línxià (Y10, one hour).

LÍNXIÀ 临夏
☎ 0930 / pop 203,200

Línxià was once an important terminus on the Silk Road. Since then it's become a major centre for Hui Muslims, as reflected by the large number of skullcaps, wispy beards and onion-domed mosques in town. Línxià maintains a market crossroads atmosphere, and shops sell a variety of products from carved gourds, daggers, saddlery, carpets and oversized brown spectacles to Muslim and Buddhist religious paraphernalia.

Surrounding Línxià are pockets of the Dongxiang people, who speak an Altaic language and are believed to be descendants of 13th-century immigrants from Central Asia, moved forcibly to China after Kublai Khan's Middle East conquest.

Information
Bank of China (中国银行; Zhōngguó Yínháng; Jiefang Lu; ☼ 8.30am-noon & 2.30-6pm Mon-Fri) Changes travellers cheques and cash, five minutes' walk north of the hotel Shuǐquán Bīnguǎn.

Sights
WANSHOU TEMPLE 万寿观
If you have a bit of time to kill, this cedar-scented **Taoist complex** (Wànshòu Guàn; admission Y10; ☼ 7am-8pm) extends seven levels up the hillside at the northwest fringe of Línxià. Along the cliffs you can visit other surrounding temples overlooking the city. Take bus 6 to the west bus station and head for the nine-storey pagoda on the ridge that is located opposite.

Sleeping & Eating
Shuǐquán Bīnguǎn (水泉宾馆; ☎ 631 4715; Sandaoqiao Guangchang; 三道桥广场; s/d/tr Y20/36/45, tw with bathroom Y56-88) At the intersection 200m to the right as you leave the south bus station, this lively hotel attracts an array of mountain characters. Some mattresses are better than others.

Hehai Mansion (Héhǎi Dàshà; 河海大厦; ☎ 623 5455; 50 Hongyuan Lu; 红园路50号; tw Y102-142; ✉) Near Línxià Fàndiàn, this is a solid two-star option, with decent rooms.

Línxià Fàndiàn (临夏饭店; ☎ 623 2100; 9 Hongyuan Lu; 红园路9号; tw from Y120; ✉) The new block here boasts the freshest rooms in Línxià, although it's not in the most exciting part of town.

Línxià is not a great place for eating, so don't knock yourself out looking for food. The open-air Muslim restaurants by the Shuǐquán Bīnguǎn are a good bet.

Getting There & Away
There are two long-distance bus stations in Línxià, the south (*nán zhàn*) and the west (*xī zhàn*). There's little reason to go to the west bus station, though you may be dropped off there. Bus 6 runs between the two bus stations, or take a taxi for Y4. For bus details, see the table (below).

One interesting route is to Xúnhuà (Y20, three hours) in Qīnghǎi, for the Mengda Nature Reserve (p906). Buses leave every hour or two from a courtyard behind the Liángyóu Fàndiàn (粮油饭店), five minutes' walk east of Shuǐquán Bīnguǎn.

XIÀHÉ 夏河
☎ 0941

Set in a beautiful mountain valley, Xiàhé is most definitely worth a visit, especially if you can't get to Tibet. It's the leading Tibetan

LÍNXIÀ BUS TIMETABLES
The following services depart from the south bus station:

Destination	Price (Y)	Duration	Frequency	Departs
Hézuò	13	2½hr	half-hourly	6am-5pm
Lánzhōu	27	3hr	half-hourly	5.30am-4pm
Xiàhé	13.5	3hr	half-hourly	7am-4.30pm
Xīníng	45	9hr	1 daily	6am

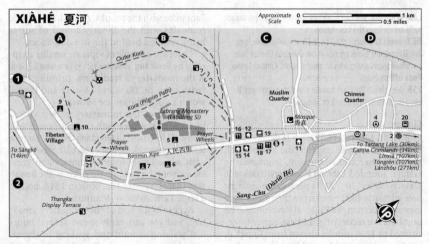

XIÀHÉ 夏河

INFORMATION		
Agricultural Bank		
中国农业银行		1 C2
Lèlè Wǎngbā 乐乐网吧		2 D2
OT Travels & Tours		(see 14)
Post Office 邮局		3 D2
PSB 公安局		4 D1
SIGHTS & ACTIVITIES		
Barkhang		5 B2
Dewatsang Chapel		6 B2
Gongtang Chörten 贡唐宝塔		7 B2
Monastery Ticket Office		
售票处		8 B1

Ngakpa Gompa 红教寺		9 A1
Nunnery 尼姑庵		10 A1
SLEEPING		
Gāngjiàn Lóngzhū Bīnguǎn		
刚坚龙珠宾馆		11 C2
Labrang Baoma Hotel		
拉卜楞宝马宾馆		12 C2
Lābǔléng Bīnguǎn		
拉卜楞宾馆		13 A1
Overseas Tibetan Hotel		
华侨饭店		14 C2
Tara Guesthouse		
卓玛旅社		15 C2

EATING		
Everest Café		(see 14)
Nomad Restaurant		
牧民齐全饭庄		16 C2
PS Café		17 C2
Tsewong's Café		18 C2
DRINKING		
Teahouses 茶馆		19 C2
TRANSPORT		
Bus Station 汽车站		20 D1
Buses to Dájiǔtàn		
到达久滩的中巴车		21 A2

monastery town outside of Lhasa and many Tibetans come here on pilgrimage dressed in their finest, most colourful clothing. Walking through the warrens and alleys of the huge Labrang Monastery (Lābǔléng Sì), side by side with the prostrating pilgrims and monks in fuchsia-coloured robes, feels like you've entered another world, which in many ways you have. The surroundings were long part of the Tibetan region of Amdo.

The religious focal point is Labrang Monastery, one of the six major Tibetan monasteries of the Gelugpa order (Yellow Hat sect of Tibetan Buddhism). The others are Ganden, Sera and Drepung Monasteries near Lhasa; Tashilhunpo Monastery in Shigatse; and Kumbum (Tǎ'ěr Sì) near Xīníng, Qīnghǎi (see p903).

Labrang is the seat of the Jamyang, a line of reincarnated rinpoches (Living Buddhas) that rank third in importance after the Dalai and Panchen Lamas. The current Jamyang works for the government in Lanzhou.

Xiàhé is a microcosm of southwestern Gānsù, with the area's three principal ethnic groups represented. In rough terms, Xiàhé's population is 50% Tibetan, 40% Han and 10% Hui.

Orientation

At 2920m above sea level, the Sang-Chu (Dàxià Hé) river flows through the town. Labrang Monastery is roughly halfway along, and marks the division between Xiàhé's mainly Han and Hui Chinese eastern quarter and the Tibetan village to the west. Note that street names haven't been provided for listings in this section as they are all on Xiàhé's only street, Renmin Xijie.

Information

Agricultural Bank (Zhōngguó Nóngyè Yínháng) Changes cash US dollars and euros, and should have an ATM by the time you read this book. Change travellers cheques before you arrive.

GĀNSÙ

Lèlè Wǎngbā (per hr Y2; ⏱ 24hr) Internet access diagonally across from the bus station.

OT Travels & Tours (☎ 712 2642; othotel@public.lz.gs .cn) This reliable travel agency at the Overseas Tibetan Hotel can arrange cars and guides to nearby sights. Contact Losang.

Post office (yóujú; ⏱ 8am-6pm)

PSB (Gōngānjú) Does not handle visa extensions; you'll need to go to Hézuò, Línxià or Sōngpān.

Sights

LABRANG MONASTERY 拉卜楞寺

Ngagong Tsunde (E'angzongzhe in Chinese), the first-generation Jamyang, from nearby Gānjiā, founded **Labrang Monastery** (Lābùléng Sì; admission Y40) in 1709. At its peak the monastery housed nearly 4000 monks, but their ranks were greatly reduced in the Cultural Revolution. The numbers are recovering, and are currently restricted to 1200 monks, drawn from Qīnghǎi, Gānsù, Sìchuān and Inner Mongolia.

In addition to the numerous chapels, residences and living quarters for the monks, Labrang is also home to six *tratsang* (monastic colleges or institutes), covering Esoteric Buddhism, Theology, Medicine, Astrology and Law.

The only way to visit the interior of these buildings is with a tour, which generally includes the Institute of Medicine (currently under renovation), the Manjushri Temple, the Serkung (Golden Temple) and the main Prayer Hall (Grand Sutra Hall), plus a museum of relics and yak-butter sculptures. English tours of the monastery leave the ticket office around 10.15am and 3.15pm; take the morning tour if you can as there's more to see. An alternative is to latch on to a Chinese tour. Even better is to show up at around 6am or

7am to be with the monks. At dusk the hillside resonates with the throaty sound of sutras being chanted behind the wooden doors.

There are a couple of separate smaller chapels. The **Barkhang** (admission Y5; ⏱ 9am-noon & 2-5pm) is the monastery's traditional printing press (with over 20,000 wood blocks) and is well worth a visit. Photos are allowed.

The rest of the monastery is best visited by walking the kora path (see the boxed text, below). The 31m-tall **Gongtang Chörten** (Gòngtáng Bǎotǎ; admission Y10) is a spectacular new stupa with some lovely interior murals and great views from the roof. If you're keen, the **Dewatsang Chapel** (admission Y10), built in 1814, houses a large 12m-statue of Manjushri.

Access to the rest of the monastery area is free, and you can easily spend several hours just walking around and soaking in the atmosphere. Try to make friends with a monk or two: they'll probably be happy to invite you into their living quarters, which always makes for an interesting house call. The Tibetan greeting, in the local Amdo dialect, is 'Cho day mo' (How do you do?) – a great icebreaker.

The best morning views of the monastery come from the Thangka Display Terrace, a popular picnic spot, or the forested hills south of the main town.

OTHER SIGHTS

Xiàhé also has a welcoming **nunnery** (*ani gompa* in Tibetan, *nígūsi* in Chinese) on the hill above the Tibetan part of town.

Next door is the **Ngakpa Gompa** (Hóngjiào Sì; admission Y5), a small Nyingmapa (Red Hat) school monastery, whose lay monks wear striking red and white robes and long braided hair.

WALK LIKE A TIBETAN

The best way to get a feel for Labrang Monastery is to take the 3km **kora** (pilgrim path) past rows of prayer wheels (1174 of them!), *chörtens* (Tibetan stupas) and chapels that encircles the monastery. Late afternoon is a particularly good time to join in. En route you can pop into the Gangtong Chörten and Dewatsang Chapel (see above). Look also for the tiny meditation cells on the northern hillside.

If you're up for a short hike, the more strenuous **outer kora** path takes about an hour and climbs high above the monastery. From the nunnery in the west of town make your way up the ridge behind and to the left, winding steeply uphill to a bunch of prayer flags and the ruins of a hermitage. The views of the monastery open up as you go along. At the end of the ridge there's a steep descent into town; alternatively descend into the small valley to the side, passing a sky burial site en route.

If you're interested in multiday treks around Labrang, check out Gary McCue's *Trekking in Tibet*, which has details of the **five-day trek** from Labrang to Repkong (Tóngrén).

Festivals & Events

Festivals are important not only for the monks, but also for the nomads who stream into town in multicoloured splendour from the grasslands. Since the Tibetans use a lunar calendar, dates for individual festivals vary from year to year.

The **Monlam (Great Prayer) Festival** starts three days after the Tibetan New Year, which is usually in February or early March. On the morning of the 13th more than 100 monks carry a huge *thangka* (sacred painting on cloth) of the Buddha, measuring more than 30m by 20m, and unfurl it on the hill facing the monastery. This is accompanied by spectacular processions and prayer assemblies.

On the 14th there is an all-day session of Cham dances performed by 35 masked dancers, with Yama, the lord of death, playing the leading role. On the 15th there is an evening display of butter lanterns and sculptures. On the 16th the Maitreya statue is paraded around the monastery.

During the second month (usually starting in March or early April) there are several interesting festivals, with a procession of monastery relics on the seventh day.

Sleeping

Tara Guesthouse (Zhuōmǎ Lǚshè; ☎ 712 1274; tsering tara@aol.com; dm Y15-25, tw Y60-70) This hotel is the best budget choice, but the bathrooms are pretty basic. Rooms are small but fairly comfortable – the nicest digs (including *kang*-style twins; ie with a traditional Chinese raised sleeping platform) are on the top floor. There's a nice sitting area, and a rooftop terrace with fantastic views over the monastery. Hot water is available from 6.30pm to 10pm. Access is through the back of the shop.

Overseas Tibetan Hotel (Huáqiáo Fàndiàn; ☎ 712 2642; othotel@public.lz.gs.cn; dm/tw Y20/80, d with bathroom Y200; 🖳) A well-run and bustling place focusing on budget tour groups, but with cheaper twins and dorm beds out the back. The comfortable en suite rooms are decorated with Tibetan paintings. There's a popular café, bike hire and travel agency, and the friendly owner does a great job.

Labrang Baoma Hotel (Lābǔléng Bǎomǎ Bīnguǎn; ☎ 712 1078; www.labranghotel.com; dm Y25, tw Y150-180; 🖳) Friendly Tibetan place with a nice interior courtyard and comfortable en suite rooms. Bike hire and laundry are available.

Lābǔléng Bīnguǎn (☎ 712 1849; dm Y30-40, tw Y120-260) The location by the river outside of town is serene and some rooms are in the former summer palace of the Jamyang (known as the Tashi Rabten), but the rooms are showing serious wear. The kitschy concrete tents have to be seen to be believed. A minivan here costs about Y5.

There are lots more Chinese-style hotels in town, including the **Gāngjiān Lóngzhū Bīnguǎn** (☎ 712 3600; tw Y100-160), which has the cheapest en suite rooms in town.

Eating

Popular Tibetan dishes that you'll find in Xiàhé are *momo* (boiled dumplings) and *tsampa*, a porridge of roasted barley flour.

Nomad Restaurant (Mùmín Qíquán Fànzhuāng; dishes Y5-25) Not only does it have a great location and a sunny terrace, but it also offers the best Tibetan cooking around. *Jaathik* (noodle soup) and boiled yak meat (better than it sounds) are two local dishes to try here. It's on the 3rd floor just before the monastery walls.

Everest Cafe (dishes Y10-30) Part of the Overseas Tibetan Hotel, the Everest has the best breakfasts in town (Y15), and also offers delicious Nepali-style curries (Y20), sizzlers (Nepali-style dish that comes on a heated iron plate) and masala tea.

PS Café (dishes Y4-8) A couple of doors down from Tsewong's Cafe, this cheap local place serves much-praised *shakshuka* (Israeli vegetable dish).

Tsewong's Cafe (☎ 712 5842; tsewong@yahoo.com; dishes Y20-30) A switched-on travellers café with great pizzas and kebabs (more like a Turkish Iskender kebab, with tomatoes, yoghurt and bread), plus internet access.

For Chinese or Hui food, try the restaurants around the bus station.

The string of upper-storey teahouses across the road are a great place to take in some sun and write a postcard.

Shopping

Xiàhé is one of the best places to pick up Tibetan handicrafts, including cowboy hats, *chubas* (Tibetan cloaks), juniper incense, furry yellow monks' hats, prayer flags, brocaded silks (around Y40 per metre), Tibetan cloth and even Tibetan-style tents. You can pick up a pair of authentic monks' boots for Y120.

XIÀHÉ BUS TIMETABLES

The following services depart from Xiàhé.

Destination	Price (Y)	Duration	Frequency	Departs
Hézuò	9	2hr	half-hourly	6am–5pm
Lángmùsì	41	6½hr	1 daily	7.30am
Lánzhōu	44	5–6hr	3 daily	6.30am, 7.30am, 2.30pm
Línxià	13	2½–3hr	half-hourly	6am–5.30pm
Tóngrén	21	5hr	1 daily	7.30am
Xīníng	46	7hr	1 daily	6am

Getting There & Away

There are continual rumours of an airport being built at Sāngkē, but for the time being Xiàhé is accessible only by bus. Most travellers head on to either Lánzhōu or Sìchuān; the road less travelled takes you over the mountains to Tóngrén. See the table (above) for details.

If you can't get a direct ticket to/from Lánzhōu, take a bus to Línxià and change there (see p854 for details).

Getting Around

Most hotels and restaurants hire bikes for Y10 to Y15 per day. Minivans cost Y1 per seat for a short trip around town, including to the bus station or monastery.

AROUND XIÀHÉ

Sangke Grasslands 桑科草原

Around and beyond the village of Sāngkē, 14km up the valley from Xiàhé, are large expanses of open grassland, where the Tibetans graze their yak herds. In summer these rolling pastures are at their greenest and abound with wildflowers. Unfortunately, development is rapidly turning the grasslands cheesy, with touristy horse rides and fake tourist yurts.

You can cycle up in about one hour. The twice daily bus to Dájiǔtān (达久滩; Y8) passes by Sāngkē but timings mean you have to hitch back. A minivan costs about Y25 return.

Ganjia Grasslands 甘加草原

If you're willing to spend a little more, the Ganjia Grasslands (Gānjiā Cǎoyuán), 34km from Xiàhé, are much less developed and offer a great day trip from Xiàhé.

The bumpy road crosses the Naren-Ka pass and quickly descends into the wide grasslands. Past Gānjiā Xiàn village a side road climbs

12km to **Trakkar Gompa** (白石崖寺; Báishíyá Sì; admission Y5), a monastery of 90 monks set against a backdrop of vertical rock formations. A 10-minute walk behind the monastery is the **Nekhang** (白石崖溶洞; admission Y20), an awesome cave complex where pilgrims lower themselves down ropes and ladders into two sacred underground chambers. A Dutch traveller fell to his death here in 2006, so you'll have to see if it's closed to tourists. It's incredibly slippery so take extreme care. A reliable torch is essential.

From Takkar it's a short drive to the impressive 2000-year-old Han-dynasty city of **Bājiǎo** (八角; Karnang in Tibetan), whose remarkable 12-sided walls now shelter a small village. From here, it's a short 5km diversion to the newly renovated **Tseway Gompa** (佐海寺; Zuóhǎi Sì; admission Y10), one of the few Bön monasteries in Gānsù. There are great views of Bājiǎo from the ridge behind the monastery.

OT Travels & Tours (see p856) and Tsewong's Café (p857), both in Xiàhé, can arrange a car for four people and an English-speaking guide for Y200 to Y300 for the day.

Tarzang Lake 达尔宗湖

Around 30km from Xiàhé towards Lánzhōu is this small sacred Tibetan lake (Dáěrzōng Hú; admission Y5). It's a lovely spot but has recently been given the Chinese tourism kiss of death – car parks, techno music and entry tickets. You can bicycle here or take a Hézuò- or Línxià-bound bus, get off when you see a white-on-blue sign by the road and hike an hour uphill to the lake.

HÉZUÒ 合作

☎ 0941

The booming regional capital of Gānnán prefecture, Hézuò is a transit point for travellers plying the excellent overland route between Gānsù and Sìchuān provinces.

To extend visas, walk 500m to your right (south) as you exit the main bus station to the **PSB** (公安局; Gōngānjú; ☎ 821 2812; Tengzhi Jie). The **China Construction Bank** (中国建议银行; Zhōngguó Jiànyì Yínháng), across from the bus station, changes money.

About 2km from the bus station along the main road towards Xiàhé is the towering **Milarepa Palace** (Sekhar Gutok; Jiǔcéng Fógé; 九层佛阁; admission Y20; ☼ 8am-6pm), whose nine-storey interior is a head-spinning blur of colourful murals and Tantric deities. The tower design is almost unique in the Tibetan world. There's also a sacred meteorite inside. The town's main monastery, **Tso Gompa**, is a short walk from here. Bus 1 runs here from the centre of town.

If headed north, you won't have to spend the night here. If headed south, there are some cheap homestays 100m south of the south bus station, including the **Línmào Lǔshè** (临茂旅舍; ☎ 330 2495; dm Y15). Alternatively, there's the **Jīndù Bīnguǎn** (金都宾馆; ☎ 821 1135; 60 Tengzhi Jie; 腾志街60号; dm/tw Y30/90), to the left (north) as you exit the main bus station, or the better **Gānnán Fàndiàn** (甘南饭店; ☎ 821 2611; Maqu Lu; 玛曲路; dm Y30, tw Y100-200) in the southwest corner of the central square.

Getting There & Away

Hézuò is where buses from Zöigê (Ruòěrgài), in Sìchuān, and Xiàhé meet. The central main bus station has frequent buses to Xiàhé (Y9, 1½ to two hours), Línxià (Y12.5, two to 2½ hours) and Lánzhōu (Y44, five to six hours) from 6.30am to 4pm.

Going south is a different story. There is only one bus daily to Zöigê, leaving at 7.30am (Y50, five hours), and two daily to Lángmùsì (Y28, three hours), leaving at 7am and 12.20am. Both of these depart from the south bus station.

A taxi between the two bus stations costs Y2 per person.

LÁNGMÙSÌ 郎木寺
☎ 0941

Straddling the border between Sìchuān and Gānsù is Lángmùsì (Taktsang Lhamo in Tibetan), a rural Tibetan village nestled among steep grassy meadows, evergreen forests and snow-clad peaks. An enchanting place, surrounded by countless red and white monastery buildings and with numerous possibilities for hikes and horse treks, it's easy to spend a few relaxing days here.

The government allegedly has plans to 'renovate' the entire town in 2007 and 2008, which has us wincing, so you should expect some disturbance.

Note that street names haven't been provided for listings in this section as they are all on Lángmùsì's only street.

Information

Note there's nowhere to change money in Lángmùsì.

Internet access (wǎngbā; per hr Y3; ☼ 1.30am-11pm) Available on the 2nd floor of the building opposite the Lángmùsì Bīnguǎn.

Sights & Activities

The White Dragon River (Báilóng Jiāng) divides the town in two. On the Sìchuān side is **Kerti Gompa** (Nàmó Sì; 纳摩寺; admission Y15), built in 1413 and home to around 700 monks. Behind the monastery is a gorge, which has several sacred grottoes, one dedicated to the Tibetan goddess Palden Lhamo, the other known as the Tiger's Cave, which gives the town its Tibetan name. There's good hiking here.

On the Gānsù side, higher up on the hills, is the smaller and less impressive **Sertri Gompa** (Sàichì Sì; 赛赤寺; admission Y16), dating from 1748. Unfortunately buying an entry ticket here doesn't guarantee that any of the chapels will be open! On the hill above the monastery is a sky burial site (see p790). Both monasteries are best visited in the morning (7am to 8am and 10.30am to 1pm) and late afternoon (6pm to 8pm).

Langmusi Tibetan Horse Trekking (☎ 667 1504; www .langmusi.net), across from the Lángmùsì Bīnguǎn, runs good horse treks from one to four days, overnighting at nomads' tents en route, with the option of climbing nearby Huāgài Shān. Prices are Y120 to Y150 per day.

Kelsang at the Lángmùsì Bīnguǎn can arrange guides (Y150 per day) for hikes up the gorge behind Kerti Gompa and transport (Y80 to Y120) for a trip to some hot springs outside town.

Sleeping & Eating

Lángmùsì Bīnguǎn (郎木寺宾馆; ☎ 667 1086; dm Y10-30, tw with bathroom Y60-90) The English-speaking staff are very friendly and the rooms with bathrooms are comfortable, making this the obvious choice. Staff can do laundry, and hot water is available evenings only.

Lhamo Monastery Hotel (郎木寺院宾馆; Lángmù Sìyuàn Bīnguǎn; dm Y15-20, s/tw with bathroom Y60/70) Across the road, this modern monastery-owned block has good-value rooms, but morose staff.

Two quiet and clean budget places include the tiny **Xiùfēng Bīnguǎn** (秀峰宾馆; ☎ 667 1020; dm Y20), run by a friendly Hui family, and **Sànà Bīnguǎn** (萨娜宾馆; ☎ 667 1062; dm/d Y20/50), accessed through the back of a shop. Both are on the main street, and have common toilets and hot-water showers.

Lesha's Restaurant (丽沙咖啡馆; Lìshā Kāfēiguǎn; ☎ 667 1179) This wonderful place is along the main road. Lesha whips up fresh apple pie, Yunnanese coffee, 'yak attack' burgers and even burritos. Be warned – the servings are humungous!

Getting There & Away

There's one daily bus to Zöigê (Ruòěrgài; Y20, three hours) at 7am and two daily buses to Hézuò (Y28, three hours), departing at 7am and noon. For Sōngpān you have to overnight in Zöigê, hitch or hire a car (Y700).

If you don't take a direct bus to Lángmùsì, you'll have to get off at the intersection 4km from the town, from where minivans ferry passengers into town for Y2.

HEXI CORRIDOR

Bound by the Qílián Shān range to the south and the Mǎzōng (Horse's Mane) and Lóngshǒu (Dragon's Head) ranges to the north, this narrow strip of land, around which the province is formed, was once the sole western passage in and out of the Middle Kingdom.

ZHĀNGYÈ 张掖

☎ 0936 / pop 98,000

Zhāngyè is a pleasant, if slightly bland, town. The main reason to stop here is to visit China's largest sleeping Buddha and do some hiking in the Qílián Shān range around Mǎtí Sì.

The **Great Buddha Temple** (Dàfó Sì; 大佛寺; ☎ 821 9671; adult/student Y41/21; ⏰ 7.30am-6.30pm) originally dates to 1098 (Western Xia dynasty) and contains a 35m-long sleeping Buddha surrounded by deteriorating clay arhats and Qing-dynasty murals. Take a good look at the main hall – it's one of the few wooden structures from this era still standing in China. Out the back is an impressive white stupa (tǔ tǎ).

One block north, in the main square, you'll find the **mù tǎ** (wooden pagoda; 木塔; admission Y5; ⏰ 7.30am-6.30pm) a brick and wooden structure that was first built in AD 528.

For orientation, the drum tower (鼓楼; gǔlóu) stands in the centre of town; the Great Buddha Temple complex is on a Qing-style pedestrian street two blocks south and one block west of here.

The **Bank of China** (中国银行; Zhōngguó Yínháng; Dong Jie) by the Liángmào Bīnguǎn has an ATM and changes travellers cheques.

Sleeping & Eating

Liángmào Bīnguǎn (粮贸宾馆; ☎ 825 2398; Dong Jie Shizi; 东街什字; dm Y18, tw Y60-120) Five minutes' walk east of the drum tower is this seven-storey hotel with a wide range of clean, airy rooms.

Xīnyuán Bīnguǎn (馨园宾馆; ☎ 825 1766; Oushi Jie Shizi; 欧式街什字; tr without bathroom Y120, tw with bathroom Y168; 🖭) This place has the best-value midrange rooms, offering discounts of 40%, in the western half of town near the Marco Polo statue and the west bus station.

To eat, head 300m west of the drum tower and look for Mingqing Jie (明清街), an alley of faux-Qing architecture that is lined with dozens of clean, friendly restaurants.

Getting There & Away

The town has three bus stations, in the south, east and west. The south bus station (nán zhàn), near the Great Buddha Temple, is the most convenient, but the modern new west bus station (xī zhàn) has the most frequent departures (see the table, opposite).

While arriving by train is no problem, departures are limited. The train ticket office can book sleepers on the T295 to Dūnhuáng (Y125 hard sleeper, 6¼ hours, 11.45pm) and train 908 to Lánzhōu (Y94 hard sleeper, 11 hours, 8pm). A taxi to/from the train station is Y10 or take bus 1 (Y1).

MǍTÍ SÌ 马蹄寺

In the foothills of the icy Qílián Shān range lie the former Tibetan and Chinese Buddhist grottoes of **Mǎtí Sì** (Horse Hoof Monastery; admission Y45). While the area isn't a national park, it very well could be, with kilometres of trails rising up along the high ridges overlooking the Hexi Corridor. There are several good day hikes, including the five-hour loop through pine forest and talus fields to the Linsong

ZHĀNGYÈ BUS TIMETABLES

The following services depart from the west bus station:

Destination	Price (Y)	Duration	Frequency	Departs
Dūnhuáng	100-135	12hr	3 daily	7.50am, 5pm & 6.30pm (sleepers after 5pm)
Jiāyùguān	32-45	4-5hr	8 daily	9.30am-5pm
Lánzhōu	70-76	9hr	hourly	7am-9pm (sleepers after 5pm)
Xīníng	71	10hr	2 daily	7am & 6pm

Waterfall (临松瀑布; Línsōng Pùbù) and back down past 'Sword Split Stone' (剑劈石; Jiànpīshí). For unrivalled panoramas, take the elevator-like ascent of the ridge behind the white *chörten* at Sānshísāntiān Shíkū (三十三天石窟). Unfortunately the temples here, built miraculously into the sandstone cliff, have mostly been destroyed inside.

The **Wòlóng Shānzhuāng** (卧龙山庄; dm/tw Y20/100) at Mǎtí Sì is a good place to stay. If you're adequately prepared for camping, some overnight trips are also possible.

GETTING THERE & AWAY

Buses leave every 30 minutes from Zhāngyè's south bus station for the crossroads village of Mǎtí Hé (Y7.5, 1½ hours), from where you can catch a minibus or taxi (Y15) for the final 7km or so. Direct buses to Mǎtí Sí depart at 3.40pm and you might find a direct bus on weekend mornings. The last bus back from Mǎtí Hé leaves at 4pm.

JIĀYÙGUĀN 嘉峪关

☎ 0937 / pop 130,900

Jiāyùguān marks one of the defining points of the Silk Road. Following the construction of the Ming-dynasty fort here in 1372, Jiāyùguān came to be known colloquially as the 'mouth' of China, while the narrow Hexi Corridor, leading back towards the *nèidì* (inner lands), was dubbed the 'throat'.

Even today the metaphor remains lodged in the Chinese psyche, and Jiāyùguān continues to mark the symbolic end of the Great Wall, the western gateway of China proper and, for imperial Chinese, the beginning of nowhere.

A mandatory stop for tour groups, the city and its surrounding sights aren't unmissable but are well worth a stop if you have an interest in Silk Road history.

Information

Bank of China (Zhōngguó Yínháng; Xinhua Zhonglu; ☼ 9.30am-5.30pm Mon-Fri, 10am-4pm Sat & Sun) Changes cash and travellers cheques. Other branches change cash only.

China Telecom Internet Café (cnr Xinhua Zhonglu & Xiongguan Donglu; per hr Y2; ☼ 10am-10pm) Next to the post office. There are plenty of other internet places along Xinhua Zhonglu.

Jùdiǎn Wǎngbā (Lanxin Xilu; per hr Y2; ☼ 8am-midnight) Internet café next to the bus station.

Post office (yóujú; cnr Xinhua Zhonglu & Xiongguan Donglu; ☼ 8.30am-7pm Mon-Fri, 10am-6pm Sat & Sun) At the traffic circle in the centre of town.

PSB (Gōngānjú; ☎ 631 6927, ext 2039; 312 Guodao; ☼ 8.30am-noon & 2.30-6pm Mon-Fri) At the southern edge of town, diagonally opposite the stadium. Visa extensions available.

Sleeping

Wùmào Bīnguǎn (☎ 628 0855; 8 Shengli Nanlu; 胜利南路8号; dm from Y30, tw Y60-180) Just west of the bus station, this is a slightly run-down budget option.

Jīnyè Bīnguǎn (☎ 620 1333; 12 Lanxin Xilu; 兰新西路12号; d without bathroom Y60, tw Y160-280; ✲) Discounts of 40% are standard here, making the en suite rooms particularly good value. It's clean and quiet, with a useful location by the bus station.

Tàihé Shānzhuāng (泰和山庄; ☎ 639 6622; Jiayuguan Fort; 嘉峪关城楼; d Y80-120) This peaceful hotel has been designed to look like a Qing-era courtyard house. It's located at Jiayuguan Fort, next to the museum, 5km from town; take the back entrance to the fort.

Eating

Restaurants are few and far between in Jiāyùguān. If in doubt, head for the food stalls at the Fuqiang Market (Fùqiáng Shìchǎng), north of the traffic circle.

GĀNSŪ

Liuyuan Restaurant (Yuànzhōngyuàn Jiǔdiàn; Lanxin Xilu; dishes from Y15) Directly across from the bus station is this classy Sìchuān restaurant. The cooking and ambience is a notch above your standard fare, and there's an English menu.

Getting There & Away

AIR

Jiāyùguān's newly renovated airport offers flights to Lánzhōu (Y1140), Xī'ān (Y1790), Běijīng (Y1880) and Ürümqi (Y790).

Book tickets at **Air China** (Guójì Mínháng; ☎ 623 6778; ⏰ 8am-10pm), at the front gate of the Jiāyùguān Bīnguǎn.

BUS

Jiāyùguān's bus station is by a busy six-way junction on Lanxin Xilu, next to the main budget hotels. See the table (opposite) for travel details.

TRAIN

Jiāyùguān lies on the Lánzhōu–Ürümqi railway line. From Jiāyùguān it's four hours to Liǔyuán (for Dūnhuáng) and three hours to Zhāngyè. Sleeper tickets to Lánzhōu (nine hours) and to Xī'ān (20 hours) are generally available, but the only sleepers to Ürümqi (15 hours) have an inconvenient 3am departure.

You can purchase tickets at the **train booking office** (huǒchē zhàn shòupiào chù; Xinhua Zhonglu; ⏰ 9.30am-5.30pm), to the right of the huge China Construction Bank, for a commission of Y5.

Jiāyùguān's Luhua train station is 5km south of the town centre. Bus 1 runs here from Xinhua Zhonglu (Y1). A taxi costs Y10.

Getting Around

TO/FROM THE AIRPORT

The airport is 13km northeast of the city. A taxi costs Y30.

BICYCLE

Bikes are excellent for getting to some of the surrounding attractions. The gatekeeper at the Jiǔgāng Bīnguǎn hires them for Y6 per day (with a Y300 deposit).

TAXI

A taxi to the Wei Jin Tombs, Jiayuguan Fort and the Overhanging Great Wall in half a day should cost you no more than Y100; if you just go to the fort and Overhanging Wall, figure on Y50. A one-way trip to the fort costs about Y10.

AROUND JIĀYÙGUĀN

Jiayuguan Fort 嘉峪关城楼

One of the classic images of western China, the **Jiayuguan Fort** (Jiāyùguān Chénglóu; Y61/31; ⏰ 8.30am-7.30pm) guards the pass that lies between the snow-capped Qílián Shān peaks and Hēi Shān (Black Mountains) of the Mǎzōng Shān range.

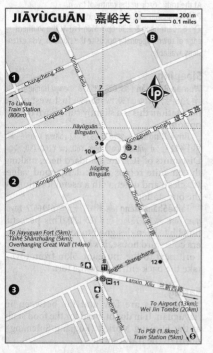

GĀNSÙ

JIĀYÙGUĀN BUS TIMETABLE
The following services depart from Jiāyùguān:

Destination	Price (Y)	Duration	Frequency	Departs
Dūnhuáng	66.5	7hr	3 daily	9am, 10.30am, 11.30am
Lánzhōu	150	12hr	3 daily	2.30pm, 4.30pm, 6.30pm (all sleepers)
Zhāngyè	30-44	4-5hr	half-hourly	9am-3pm

Built in 1372, the fort was christened the 'Impregnable Defile Under Heaven'. Although the Chinese often controlled territory far beyond the Jiāyùguān area, this was the last major stronghold of imperial China – the end of the 'civilised world', beyond which lay only desert demons and the barbarian armies of Central Asia.

At the eastern end of the fort is the Gate of Enlightenment (Guānghuà Mén) and in the west is the Gate of Conciliation (Róuyuǎn Mén), from where exiled poets, ministers, criminals and soldiers would have ridden off into the oblivion. Each gate has 17m-high towers with upturned flying eaves and double gates that would have been used to trap invading armies. On the inside are horse lanes leading up to the top of the inner wall.

Admission also includes an excellent Great Wall museum, with photos, artefacts, maps and Silk Road exhibits.

Only 5km west of town, it's possible to cycle here in about half an hour.

Overhanging Great Wall 悬壁长城

Running north from Jiāyùguān, this Ming-dynasty section of **wall** (Xuánbì Chángchéng; adult/student Y21/11; ☉ 8.30am-dusk) is believed to have been first constructed in 1539, though this reconstruction dates from 1987.

A nearby second section of **wall** (Shíguānxiá Xuánbì Chángchéng; 石关峡; admission Y10; ☉ 8.30am-5.30pm) was restored in 2001 by a private individual and offers perhaps a more authentic experience, as not all of the wall has been restored. From the upper tower high on a ridge you get a sweeping view of the desert and the glittering snow-capped peaks in the distance. Both sections of wall are 9km from the fort.

Wei Jin Tombs 新城魏晋墓

These **tombs** (Xīnchéng Wèijìnmù; admission Y31; ☉ sunrise-sunset) date from approximately AD 220–420 (the Wei and Western Jin periods) and contain extraordinarily fresh brick wall paintings depicting scenes from everyday life, from making tea to picking mulberries for silk production. There are literally thousands of tombs in the desert 20km east of Jiāyùguān, but only one is currently open to visitors, that of a husband and wife. The small museum is also worth a look. You can preview some of the painted bricks at the Jiayuguan Fort museum.

July 1st Glacier 七一冰川

The **July 1st Glacier** (Qīyī Bīngchuān; admission Y51) sits high in the Qílián Shān range at 4300m. It is about 90km southwest of Jiāyùguān and is reached via the train (Y4.5) to the iron-ore town of Jìngtiěshān, which departs from Jiāyùguān's Luhua train station at 8.10am. It's a scenic three-hour train trip to Jìngtiěshān, where you can hire a taxi to the glacier (Y120 return, 20km). Hikers can walk a 5km trail alongside the glacier. It's not possible to visit between November and March; in fact at this elevation it gets cold even in summer, so come prepared.

You could theoretically do this in one day, but it's better to stay the night in Jìngtiěshān. This leaves you with enough time the next morning to hire a taxi (Y50 return) up to Tiān'é Hú and the Tibetan village of Qíqīng. Return trains depart around 1.40pm. There is a cheap and basic hostel (zhāodàisuǒ) in town. A return taxi here from Jiāyùguān costs around Y400.

LIǓYUÁN 柳园

☎ 0937

Liǔyuán, a forlorn little town on the Lánzhōu–Ürümqi railway line, is the jumping-off point for Dūnhuáng, 130km to the south. The **Liǔtiě Fàndiàn** (柳铁饭店; ☎ 557 2102; dm Y30, tw with bathroom Y100-120) is to the right of the train station, but unless you're catching an early morning train, there should be no need to stay here.

GĀNSÙ

There are six trains daily in each direction. Going west, the T197 is a good option to Turpan (eight hours) and Ürümqi (10 hours), departing at 11.16pm. The overnight T194/1 is a good option eastbound to Lánzhōu (12½ hours) or Xī'ān (23 hours), departing at 11.37pm. Trains 1046 and 1084 leave in the morning for Jiāyùguān (four hours).

Tickets can be purchased up to three days in advance, here or at the booking office in Dūnhuáng (p866). There are also daily departures to Běijīng, Chéngdū, Shànghǎi and Xī'ān.

Minibuses for Dūnhuáng (Y15, two hours) depart from in front of the train station when trains arrive. A shared taxi generally costs around Y30 per person.

DŪNHUÁNG 敦煌

☎ 0937

After travelling for hours towards Dūnhuáng (Blazing Beacon), the monotonous desert landscape suddenly gives way to lush, green cultivated fields with mountainous rolling sand dunes as a backdrop. The area has a certain haunting beauty, especially at night under a star-studded sky. It's not so much the desert dunes and romantic nights that attract so many tourists to Dūnhuáng, but the superb Buddhist art at the nearby Mogao Caves.

Information

Bank of China (Zhōngguó Yínháng; Yangguan Zhonglu; ☽ 8am-noon & 3-6.30pm) Change travellers cheques or use the ATM here.

Feitian Travel Service (☎ 882 2726, ext 8619; Fēitiān Bīnguǎn, 22 Mingshan Lu) Can arrange buses to Mogao, local tours and car hire.

Laundry (Gānxǐdiàn; Huancheng Nanlu; per piece Y2; ☽ 8am-9pm) Attached to the Yǒuhǎo Bīnguǎn.

Post office (yóujú; cnr Yangguan Zhonglu & Shazhou Beilu; ☽ 8am-7pm) Located in the China Telecom building on the main traffic circle.

PSB (Gōngānjú; Yangguan Zhonglu; ☎ 886 2071; ☽ 8am-noon & 3-6.30pm Mon-Fri) Same-day visa extensions.

Shíkōng Wǎngbā (Mingshan Lu; per hr Y2; ☽ 8am-midnight) Internet access.

Sights

DUNHUANG MUSEUM 敦煌博物馆

This local **museum** (Dūnhuáng Bówùguǎn; ☎ 882 2981; Yangguan Donglu; admission Y15; ☽ 8am-6pm) is really a disappointment. There's not much here that you can't see at the Mogao Caves (p866) or the museum at the Jade Gate Pass (p868).

Sleeping

Competition among Dūnhuáng's hotels is fierce, and you should get significant discounts outside of summer.

Fēitiān Bīnguǎn (☎ 882 2337; 22 Mingshan Lu; 鸣山路22号; dm Y20-30, tw Y160-360; ✷) This long-standing two-star hotel is in a good location. Dorms are clean and spacious, with communal hot showers, and the air-conditioned twins (50% discount available) are comfortable.

Yǒuhǎo Bīnguǎn (☎ 882 2678; 25 Mingshan Lu; 鸣山路25号; tw with bathroom Y80-160, tr Y180) These are the cheapest en suite twins in town. The air-conditioning doesn't really work, but each room gets a fan.

Jiàrì Dàjiǔdiàn (☎ /fax 882 5258; 18 Mingshan Lu; 鸣山路18号; s/tw Y180/380; 🔀) Opened in 2004, the 'Holiday' is bright, clean and offers discounts of up to 60% most of the time.

Grand Sun Hotel (Tàiyáng Dàjiǔdiàn; ☎ 882 9998; www.dhsuntravel.com; 5 Shazhou Beilu; 沙洲北路5号; tw Y488-688; 🔀) The Tàiyáng is a reliable mid-range place, with some Japanese touches and spacious rooms.

Silk Road Dunhuang Hotel (敦煌山庄; Dūnhuáng Shānzhuāng; ☎ 888 2088; www.the-silk-road.com; Dunyue Lu; 敦月路; tw US$100-150, ste US$250-1200; 🔀) If you're going to splurge on one hotel in northwest China, this would be a good choice. About 2km from the Míngshā Shān sand dunes, the rooms match the desert landscape perfectly. Imagine Central Asian rugs, a cool stone floor and tasteful Chinese antiques. It's worth coming for a sunset beer (Y10 to Y20) from the rooftop. A taxi from town costs Y10 or take minibus 3.

Eating

There are three Western travellers cafés in town, all with similar food and prices (dishes Y10 to Y20): **Charley Johng's Cafe** (☎ 388 2411; 21 Mingshan Lu), **Shirley's Cafe** (Mingshan Lu) and **John's Information Café** (☎ 882 7000; Fēitiān Bīnguǎn courtyard, 22 Mingshan Lu). In addition to providing internet access and bike hire, these are good spots to exchange information with other travellers along Mingshan Lu. There are loads of other local restaurants along Mingshan Lu.

Dūnhuáng's night market is an extremely lively scene and worth a visit. Spilling out of a large courtyard off Yangguan Donglu, it houses scores of restaurants and kebab stands.

Gastronomes can try the town's dubious speciality, *lǘròu huáng miàn* (驴肉黄面; noodles with donkey meat).

A popular Central Asian dish is *dàpánjī* (大盘鸡), a whole chicken cut up and stir-fried with noodles, onions and peppers, then drowned in a pool of chilli sauce. For an authentic meal, the raucous restaurant **Lǎozìhào Jìngyuán Yánggāoròu** (Huancheng Nanlu) around the corner from the Yǒuhǎo Bīnguǎn is a sure bet. One serving will feed three people (Y45). For noodles and dumplings at Chinese prices, try the stalls along Shichang Xiang.

Getting There & Away
AIR

There are regular flights to Lánzhōu (Y1140), Xī'ān (Y1790) and Běijīng (Y1990), Ürümqi (Y820) and Chéngdū (Y2190), although flights are less frequent from November to March. Seats can be booked at **CAAC** (Zhōngguó Mínháng; ☎ 882 2389; 12 Yangguan Donglu; 🕐 8am-noon & 2-8pm) or at the **air ticket office** (míngshān hángkòng shòupiào chù; ☎ 882 3619; 6 Mingshan Lu) in the Míngshān Bīnguǎn.

BUS

Dūnhuáng's long-distance bus station is located in the heart of the action on Mingshan Lu. Arriving in Dūnhuáng you may be dropped off at a station just south of Yǒuhǎo Bīnguǎn. See the table (below) for details.

The regular bus to Golmud leaves at 8am, and takes a rugged but scenic route that crosses the Altun Mountains. There's also a sleeper bus in the evening (take warm clothes). To get to Turpan by bus, you'll need to change buses in Hāmì.

Buses leave hourly for the train station at Liǔyuán (Y20, two hours), or you can get a seat in a faster taxi for Y30. If there's a sand storm blowing, the trip can take up to four hours.

DŪNHUÁNG BUS TIMETABLES

The following services travel direct to/from Dūnhuáng:

Destination	Price (Y)	Duration	Frequency	Departs
Golmud	89-98	9hr	2 daily	9am & 7.30pm (sleeper)
Hāmì	70	7hr	2 daily	8.30am & 5pm
Jiāyùguān	67-79	7hr	hourly	7am-10.30pm
Lánzhōu	227	17hr	2 daily	8.30am & 10.30am (both sleepers)
Ürümqi	180	14 hr	1 daily	6pm (sleeper)

GĀNSŪ

TRAIN

By the time you read this Dūnhuáng's new train station should have direct services to/ from Lánzhōu and Ürümqi, and maybe other destinations. Other trains will continue to go only to Liǔyuán (p863), even though they may be marked 'Dūnhuáng' on timetables. In short, check exactly where your train is going when shelling out for a ticket.

You can purchase tickets at the **train booking office** (tiělù shòupiàochù; Yangguan Donglu; ☼ 8am-noon & 3-6pm), to the right of a small Bank of China branch, for a commission of Y5.

Getting Around

You can hire bikes from the travellers cafés for Y1 per hour. Getting to some of the outlying sights by bike is possible, but hard work at the height of summer.

To charter a ride for the sights around town, the minibuses across from the Jiàrì Dàjiǔdiàn on Mingshan Lu is one place to start negotiations.

Dūnhuáng's airport is 13km east of town. A taxi costs Y20.

AROUND DŪNHUÁNG

Most people visit the Mogao Caves in the morning, followed by the Míngshā Shān sand dunes in the late afternoon.

Mogao Caves 莫高窟

The Mogao Caves (Mògāo Kū) are, simply put, one of the greatest repositories of Buddhist art in the world. At its peak, the site housed 18 monasteries, over 1400 monks and nuns, and countless artists, translators and calligraphers. Wealthy traders and important officials were the primary donors responsible for creating new caves, as caravans made the long detour past Mogao to pray or give thanks for a safe journey through the treacherous wastelands to the west. The traditional date ascribed to the founding of the first cave is AD 366.

Following the collapse of trade along the Silk Road after the Yuan dynasty, this vast series of grottoes – stretching 1700m along a canyon wall and containing over a millennium of art – lay forgotten for centuries amid the encroaching sands of the Gobi. Only in the early 20th century was this treasure house of art 'rediscovered' by a string of foreign explorers (see Foreign Devils on the Silk Road, opposite).

NORTHERN WEI, WESTERN WEI & NORTHERN ZHOU CAVES

The earliest caves are distinctly Indian in style and iconography. All contain a central pillar, representing a stupa (symbolically containing the ashes of the Buddha), which the devout would circle in prayer. Paint was derived from malachite (green), cinnabar (red) and lapis lazuli (blue), expensive minerals imported from Central Asia.

The art of this period is characterised by its attempt to depict the spirituality of those who had transcended the material world through their asceticism. The Wei statues are slim, ethereal figures with finely chiselled features and comparatively large heads. The Northern Zhou figures have ghostly white eyes. Don't be fooled by the thick, black modernist strokes – it's the oxidisation of lead in the paint, not some forerunner of Picasso.

SUI CAVES

The Sui dynasty (AD 581–618) began when a general of Chinese or mixed Chinese-Tuoba origin usurped the throne of the Northern Zhou dynasty and reunited northern and southern China for the first time in 360 years.

The Sui dynasty was short-lived, and very much a transition between the Wei and Tang periods. This can be seen in the Sui caves: the graceful Indian curves in the Buddha and Bodhisattva figures start to give way to the more rigid style of Chinese sculpture.

TANG CAVES

During the Tang dynasty (AD 618–907), China pushed its borders westward as far as Lake Balkash in today's Kazakhstan. Trade expanded and foreign merchants and people of diverse religions streamed into the Tang capital of Chang'an.

This was the high point of the cave art at Mogao. Painting and sculpture techniques became much more refined, and some important aesthetic developments, notably the sex change (from male to female) of Guanyin and the flying *apsaras*, took place. The beautiful murals depicting the Buddhist Western Paradise offer rare insights into the court life, music, dress and architecture of Tang China.

Some 230 caves were carved during the Tang dynasty, including two impressive grottoes containing enormous, seated Buddha figures. By this time space in the caves was at a premium and many murals were painted over existing images. The statue residing in cave 96 (believed to represent Empress Wu Zetian, who used Buddhism to consolidate her power) is a towering 34.5m tall, making it the world's third-largest Buddha. The Buddhas were carved from the top down using scaffolding, whose anchor holes are still visible.

POST-TANG CAVES

Following the Tang dynasty, the economy around Dūnhuáng went into decline, and the luxury and vigour typical of Tang painting began to be replaced by simpler drawing techniques and flatter figures. The mysterious Western Xia kingdom, who controlled most of Gānsù from 983 to 1227, made a number of additions to the caves at Mogao and began to introduce Tibetan influences.

ADMISSION

Entrance to the **caves** (☎ 886 9071; admission Y100; ⏱ 8.30am-6pm Apr-Oct, 9am-5.30pm Nov-Mar) is strictly controlled – it's impossible to visit them on your own. The general admission ticket grants you a two-hour tour of 10 caves, including the infamous Library Cave (No 17 – see Foreign Devils on the Silk Road, below) and a related exhibit containing rare fragments of manuscripts in classical Uighur and Manichean. Excellent English-speaking guides are always available (costing Y20), and you can generally arrange tours in many other languages.

The 20 'open' caves are rotated fairly regularly, making recommendations useless, but tours always include the two big buddhas, 34.5m and 26m tall respectively. It's also possible to visit 12 of the more unusual caves for an additional fee. Prices are from Y100 (No 217, early Tang) to Y500 (No 465, Tantric art).

Most caves are lit only by indirect sunlight from outside, making a torch (flashlight) imperative. Your guide will have one, but bring your own if possible. Photography is strictly prohibited everywhere within the fenced-off caves area, and cameras and bags must be deposited at an office near the entrance gate. Note that if it's raining, snowing or sandstorming, the caves will be closed.

Despite the high admission and the rigidity of the guide system, don't be discouraged – entering your first cave will make it all seem worthwhile.

After the tour it's well worth visiting the Dunhuang Research Centre, where eight more caves, each representative of a different period, have been flawlessly reproduced, along with selected murals.

If you have a special interest in the site, check out the **International Dunhuang Project** (http://idp.bl.uk), an online database of digitalised manuscripts from the Library Cave at Mogao.

FOREIGN DEVILS ON THE SILK ROAD

Few things raise the ire of a Chinese intellectual faster than the subject of cultural relics destroyed or carted off by marauding Western imperialists. Near the top of the list of crimes is Dūnhuáng's Library Cave (No 17), where in 1900 the self-appointed guardian, Wang Yuanlu, discovered a hidden library filled with tens of thousands of immaculately preserved manuscripts and paintings, dating as far back as AD 406. It's hard to describe the exact magnitude of the discovery, but stuffed into the tiny room were texts in rare Central Asian languages, military reports, music scores, medical prescriptions, Confucian and Taoist classics, and Buddhist sutras copied by some of the greatest names in Chinese calligraphy – not to mention the world's oldest printed book, the *Diamond Sutra* (AD 868). In short, it was an incalculable amount of original source material regarding Chinese, Central Asian and Buddhist history. Exactly to whom this information should belong, however, went on to become something of a thorny issue.

Seven years after the discovery rival archaeologists Aurel Stein and Paul Pelliot – only two of the numerous European adventurers hauling away Central Asian Buddhist art from the old Silk Roads – together managed to get their hands on close to 20,000 of the cave's priceless manuscripts, smuggling them to museums in England and France respectively. Today defenders of the pair point to the widespread destruction that took place during the Cultural Revolution, and the defacing of Buddhist artwork by Muslim iconoclasts. But what really provokes the wrath of the Chinese is the amount the two 'donated' to Wang Yuanlu for their haul: in total, the paltry sum of UK£220.

GETTING THERE & AWAY

The Mogao Caves are 25km (30 minutes) from Dūnhuáng. A bus leaves at 8.30am from in front of Fēitiān Bīnguǎn (each way Y10), returning at noon, which isn't really enough time at the site. A return taxi costs from Y60 to Y80 for the half day.

Some people ride out to the caves on a bicycle, but be warned that half the ride is through total desert – hot work in summer.

Western Thousand Buddha Caves
西千佛洞

These little-visited **caves** (Xī Qiānfó Dòng; adult/student Y30/20; ☉ 7am-5.30pm), 35km west of Dūnhuáng, stand in stark contrast to the intense tourist conveyer belt at Mogao.

There are 16 caves hidden in the cliff face of the Dǎng Hé gorge, of which six are open to the public. The caves range from the Northern Wei to the Tang dynasties. While the art doesn't compare to Mogao, the lack of crowds make it much more conducive for appreciating the artwork. You can even wander off on a walk through the desert canyon.

The caves are best reached by taxi (Y60 return) or minibus. Alternatively catch a bus to Nánhú (南湖) from the intersection of Heshui Lu and Yangguan Zhonglu in Dūnhuáng and ask the driver to drop you off at the turn-off to the caves, from where it's a 10-minute walk across the desert.

Crescent Moon Lake 月牙泉

Six kilometres south of Dūnhuáng at **Míngshā Shān** (Singing Sands Mountain; admission Y80; ☉ 6am-10pm), the desert meets the oasis in a most dramatic fashion. From here it's easy to see how Dūnhuáng gained its moniker Shāzhōu (Town of Sand). At the base of the colossal mega dunes, whose highest peak stands at 1715m, lies a miraculous pond, known as **Crescent Moon Lake** (Yuèyáquán). The climb to the top of the dunes is sweaty work, but the view across the undulating desert sands and green poplar trees below makes it a spectacular sight.

In recent years the dunes have turned into a no-holds-barred tourist playpen, with the mayhem including camel rides (Y60), dune buggies, 'dune surfing' (sand sliding, Y10), paragliding (jumping off the dunes with a chute on your back, Y60) and even microlighting. If your sole interest is in appreciating the dunes in peace, you'll do better to

hire a bike and find your own stretch of sand elsewhere.

You can ride a bike to the dunes in around 20 minutes. Minibus 3 (Y1) shuttles between Dūnhuáng and the dunes from 8am to 9.30pm. A taxi costs Y10 one way. Most people head out here at about 6pm when the weather starts to cool down.

Western cafés like Charley Johng's offer overnight camel trips to the dunes (Y300 per person), as well as five- to eight-day expeditions out to the Jade Gate Pass and even as far as Lop Nor in the deserts of Xīnjiāng.

Yadan National Park & Jade Gate Pass
雅丹国家地质公园, 玉门关

The weird eroded desert landscape of **Yadan National Park** (Yǎdān Guójiā Dìzhì Gōngyuán; admission Y60 incl tour) is 180km northwest of Dūnhuáng, in the middle of the awesome nothingness of the Gobi Desert. A former lake bed that eroded in spectacular fashion some 12,000 years ago, the weird rock formations provided the backdrop to the last scenes of the Zhang Yimou's film *Hero*. The desert landscape is dramatic, but you can only tour the site on the group minibus, so there's little scope to explore on your own.

To get to Yadan you have to pass by (and buy a ticket to) the **Jade Gate Pass** (Yùmén Guān; admission Y30), 102km from Dūnhuáng. Both this and the South Pass (Yáng Guān; 阳关), 78km west of Dūnhuáng, were originally military stations, part of the Han-dynasty series of beacon towers that extended to the garrison town of Loulan in Xīnjiāng. For caravans travelling westwards, the Jade Gate marked the beginning of the northern route to Turpan, while the South Pass was the start of the southern route through Miran. The Jade Gate derived its name from the important traffic in Khotanese jade.

The entry fee includes a small but interesting museum (with scraps of real Silk Road silk); a nearby section of Han-dynasty Great Wall, built in 101 BC and impressive for its antiquity and refreshing lack of restoration; and the ruined city walls of Hécāng Chéng, 15km away on a side road.

The only way to get out here is to hire a car for a long day trip to take in Yadan, the Jade Gate and the Western Thousand Buddha Caves. The Feitian Travel Service (see p864) organises air-conditioned cars for about Y450; you might get a minivan for around Y350.

EASTERN GĀNSÙ

The southeast of Gānsù holds some of the prettiest country in northwest China. Tamped earthen houses and terraced wheat and corn fields are interspersed with lush, forested hills, and the Silk Road remnants at Tiānshuǐ and Luòmén are in relatively good condition compared with much of what you'll see to the west.

TIĀNSHUǏ 天水

☎ 0938 / pop 400,000

Located near one of the legendary cradles of Chinese civilisation, Tiānshuǐ is famous for the nearby Buddhist caves at Màijī Shān and the less interesting Fu Xi Temple in Qínchéng. Booming Tiānshuǐ is the second-largest municipality in Gānsù, but it's not too overwhelming and is a pleasant first stop for those following the Silk Road west. Of note are the ancient cypress trees, some more than 1000 years old, growing in the temples of Qínchéng.

Orientation

Tiānshuǐ is in fact two separate towns connected by a long freeway – the gritty railhead sprawl, known as Běidào, and the central commercial area to the west, known as Qínchéng. While Běidào is ultimately more convenient, Qínchéng is marginally the nicer place to stay. Màijī Shān is 35km south of Běidào.

Information

In Běidào you can change cash and use the ATM at the **Bank of China** (Zhōngguó Yínháng; ◷ 8.30am-noon & 2.30-5.30pm) opposite the train station. For travellers cheques go to the branch on Weihe Nanlu, 600m south of here, or the main branch on Minzhu Donglu in Qínchéng.

The **post office** (yóujú; Ziyou Lu; ◷ 8am-6pm) is in Qínchéng, with a branch on Yima Lu in Běidào.

There is a **CITS** (Zhōngguó Guójì Lǚxíngshè; ☎ 821 3621; 8 Minzhu Donglu) office in Qínchéng, 200m east of the Bank of China.

In Qínchéng there are a few internet cafés in the Wénmiào Shāngchǎng pedestrian area. In Běidào there are two internet cafés by the Diànxìn Zhāodàisuǒ. Access at all costs Y2 per hour.

Sights

The grottoes at Màijī Shān are the main reason to come to Tiānshuǐ, but if you have time to kill you could explore the other sights.

The Ming-dynasty **Fu Xi Temple** (Fú Xī Miào; admission Y30; ◷ 8am-6pm) was begun in 1483. The main hall is one of the most elaborate structures in Gānsù, with intricate wooden door panels and original paintings of the sixty-four hexagrams (varying combinations of the eight trigrams used in the I Ching) on the ceiling.

One of the mythic progenitors of the Chinese people, leaf-clad Fú Xī was reputedly a Chenji local (present-day Tiānshuǐ) who introduced the domestication of animals, hunting and the eight trigrams (used for divination) to early Chinese civilisation.

Situated on the hillside above Qínchéng is the rambling Taoist **Yuquan (Jade Spring) Temple** (Yùquán Guàn; adult/student Y20/10; ◷ 7.30am-6.30pm). Although the 'vicissitudes of life' have taken their toll, it's still a pleasant place to wander.

Sleeping & Eating

Tiānshuǐ has plenty of accommodation, so discounts of up to 40% are pretty standard.

Diànxìn Zhāodàisuǒ (☎ 261 4938; Yima Lu; 一马路; rm Y30-50) A clean and friendly cheapie near the train station. The Y50 doubles are surprisingly stylish, if you don't use the bathroom.

Tiělù Zhāodàisuǒ (☎ 493 9660; 26 Yima Lu; 一马路 26号; d/tr without bathroom Y50/60, tw with bathroom Y100) A convenient place near the train station for simple but cheap rooms. Turn right as you leave the square in front of the train station and continue for about 50m.

Tiānshuǐ Dàjiǔdiàn (☎ 828 9999; 1 Dazhong Lu; 秦成大众南路1号; d Y50-90, tw with bathroom Y90-192) The *pǔtōng* (economy) rooms with shared bathroom are perhaps the best budget bet in this part of town, with hot showers down the hall and a very central location.

Dōngān Fàndiàn (☎ 261 3333; Yima Lu; 一马路; s/d/tw Y180/268/280) A comfortable and double-glazed three-star option 50m east of the train station. Discounts of 40% make it great value.

In Qínchéng, there are scores of good restaurants and snack stalls down Xiaochi Jie (Snack St) and Guangming Xiang, to the east and south of the Tiānshuǐ Dàjiǔdiàn.

There's more great snack food in Běidào down Erma Lu, the pedestrian alley just south of the train station. Best of these is

Lǔjì' Tiěbǎnshāo, which offers you excellent teppanyaki-style sizzling dishes for pennies.

Getting There & Away

BUS

See the table (opposite) for travel details.

Buses to Lánzhōu also depart throughout the day from the forecourt of the train station in Běidào. There are also two morning departures a day from here to Huīxiàn.

TRAIN

Tiānshuǐ is on the Xī'ān–Lánzhōu railway line; there are dozens of daily trains in either direction. If you arrive early, you can visit Màijī Shān as a day trip, avoiding the need to stay overnight in Tiānshuǐ.

From Tiānshuǐ it's four to six hours to either Lánzhōu (Y52 hard seat) or Xī'ān (Y51).

Getting Around

Taxis shuttle passengers between Qínchéng (from the Tiānshuǐ Dàjiǔdiàn and long-distance bus station) and the train station in Běidào for Y5. Alternatively take the much slower bus 1 or 6 (Y2.2, 40 minutes) from Dazhong Lu.

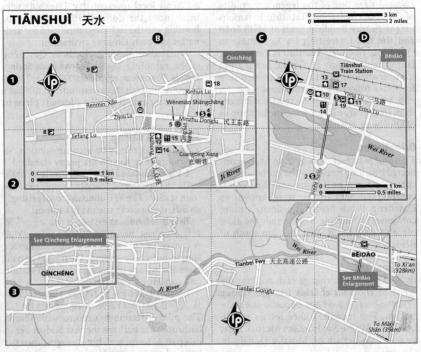

INFORMATION		SIGHTS & ACTIVITIES		EATING	
Bank of China		Fu Xi Temple 伏羲庙 8 A2		Lǔjì' Tiěbǎnshāo 吕记铁板烧............14 D1	
中国银行 1 B1		Yuquan Temple 玉泉观 9 A1		Snack St 小吃街 15 B2	
Bank of China					
中国银行 2 C2		SLEEPING		TRANSPORT	
Bank of China		Diànxìn Zhāodàisuǒ		Buses 1 & 6 Terminus	
中国银行 3 D1		电信招待所 10 D1		一路车和六路车终点 16 B2	
CITS 中国国际旅行社 4 B1		Dōngān Fàndiàn		Buses to Lánzhōu and Huīxiàn	
Internet Cafés 网吧 5 B1		东安饭店 11 D1		往兰州和徽县的汽车 17 D1	
Internet Cafés 网吧 ....(see 10)		Tiānshuǐ Dàjiǔdiàn		Long-Distance Bus Station	
Post Office 邮局 6 B1		天水大酒店 12 B2		长途汽车站 18 B1	
Post Office 邮局 7 C1		Tiělù Zhāodàisuǒ		Minibus 34 to Màijī Shān	
		铁路招待所 13 D1		往麦积山的34路车站 19 D1	

TIĀNSHUĬ BUS TIMETABLES

The following services depart from the depart from the long-distance bus station in Qínchéng:

Destination	Price (Y)	Duration	Frequency	Departs
Huìxiàn	30	3hr	hourly	6.30am-6pm
Gùyuán	42	7hr	1 daily	7am
Lánzhōu	49-57	4hr	hourly	7am-6pm
Línxià	47	8hr	1 daily	6.30am
Luòmén	15	3hr	1 daily	6.30am
Píngliáng	45	5-6hr	7 daily	7am-3pm
Yínchuān	80	12hr	2 daily	12.30pm & 4.30pm

AROUND TIĀNSHUĬ
Màijī Shān 麦积山

These **grottoes** (Haystack Mountain; adult/student Y70/35; ☉ 8am-6pm) are one of China's four largest temple groups; the others are at Dàtóng, Luòyáng and Dūnhuáng. The solitary rock formation, sticking up out of the verdant, rolling landscape like a giant haystack (kind of, anyway), is riddled with niches and statues carved principally during the Northern Wei and Zhou dynasties (AD 386–581), though new grottoes were added continuously over the following fifteen centuries. Catwalks and steep spiral stairways have been built around the cliff face, so while the art is not as amazing as at Dūnhuáng, getting to it is more fun, and you have more freedom to venture at your own pace.

Besides the hard-to-miss Sui-dynasty trinity of Buddha and Bodhisattvas (No 13), the most impressive sculptures are along the upper walkways, especially at the marvellous seven niches of Cave 4, with their powerful protector statues. It's not certain just how the artists managed to clamber so high; one theory is that they created piles from blocks of wood reaching to the top of the mountain before moving down, gradually removing them as they descended. Stone was evidently brought in from elsewhere, since the local rock is too soft for carving, as at Dūnhuáng.

An English-speaking guide charges Y150 for the day. It's possible to view a selection of normally closed caves for an extra fee of Y500 per group. The admission ticket includes entry to a small **botanical garden** (zhíwùyuán).

Minibus 34 leaves every seven minutes from in front of the Tiānshuǐ train station (Y4, 40 minutes). It may drop you at the crossroads, 5km before the site, from where a minivan or

tractor costs Y2 per seat. The ticket office is 1.5km before the site. A taxi from Tiānshuǐ costs around Y100 return.

Luòmén 洛门

A trip to the **Water Curtain Caves** (Shuǐlián Dòng; 水帘洞; admission Y11; ☉ 7am-7pm), 17km from Luòmén, is like visiting the China of your dreams. Eroding sandstone domes rise above lush canyon walls, and Taoist and Buddhist temples lie hidden in the cliffs, seemingly transported from a Song-dynasty landscape painting. OK, it's not that good…but it's close.

The main sight is Lāshāo Sì, an overhanging cliff sheltering an amazingly vibrant 31m-high painted figure of Sakyamuni (the historical Buddha) seated cross-legged upon a throne of lotus petals, lions, deer and elephants. The bas-relief carving and accompanying mint-green and salmon coloured frescoes were completed in the Northern Wei dynasty (AD 386–534).

The secondary sights here are the eponymous Taoist temple of Shuǐlián Dòng, a short walk uphill, and the faded remnants of the

---

SHÍKŪ: GROTTO

The top of the character shí (stone, rock) is like the corner of a rock or a cliff, whereas the bottom half is a cake of rock. The top of kū means a cave or an earth room. The bottom half sees someone bending to carry something into or out of the cave or room, which would usually have a very low ceiling.

GĀNSÙ

Thousand Buddha Cave (Qiānfó Dòng), a 10-minute walk up a side valley. Minibuses in Luòmén will take you to the Water Curtain Caves for Y60 return; a motor tricycle is cheaper at around Y35.

Luòmén is on the Lánzhōu–Xī'ān rail line, but only a couple of trains per day stop here. The best option is the 7.38am train from Tiānshuǐ (train 347; Y12, 70 minutes). One direct bus daily leaves from Tiānshuǐ's long-distance bus station (in Qínchéng; three hours, Y15) at 6.30am; otherwise change buses in Gāngǔ (甘谷). From Luòmén it's a 20-minute minibus ride (Y2) on to Wǔshān (武山) and then a short bus ride to Lóngxī (陇西), from where there are frequent trains to/from Lánzhōu.

The only place to stay is the decent **Luòmén Bīnguǎn** (洛门宾馆; ☎ 322 7668; tw with/without bathroom Y60/30).

MOON CANYON 月亮峡

Tucked in a hidden corner of southeastern Gānsù, the rushing rivers and towering rock walls of **Moon Canyon** (Yuèliàng Xiá; admission Y20) and the surrounding Three Beaches National Park (Sāntān Zìrán Bǎohùqū) is a rare corner of the Middle Kingdom that still has some pristine wilderness. The bad news is that the tranquillity of the valley is under threat from clumsy tourism development, so get here soon.

At the entrance to the valley is **Moon Canyon Retreat** (月亮峡度假村; Yuèliàng Xiá Dùjiàcūn; ☎ 755 7888; www.threebeaches.com; dm/tents/cabins Y50/100/120, tw with bathroom Y220; Apr–Oct), where the four spartan but low-impact lodges will soon be dwarfed by an ill-conceived 100-bed hotel and swimming pool.

Perhaps a better place to stay is two hours' hike away, up to the village of Yánpíng (严

坪), where there are half a dozen **homestays** (nóngjiālè; 农家乐; dm Y10), marked by tourism signs. Accommodation is basic but friendly, and local dishes are available. It's a great base for hikes around the valley. There is one shop in the village, so bring some snacks.

For those with camping equipment, it's a five-hour hike up to the Sān Tān (Three Beaches); one possible three-day trek is to the purported old growth forest (原始森林; yuánshǐ sēnlín) upstream. Jeeps ferry Chinese tourists up to the first pool (Y250 return) but not beyond.

Getting There & Away

Moon Canyon is on the Chéngdū–Xī'ān rail line near the village of Jiālíng (嘉陵). There is only one stop per day in either direction (both at around 1pm) – the closest major rail links are Guǎngyuán (Sìchuān) and Bǎojī (Shaanxi). Frequent buses run between Tiānshuǐ and Huīxiàn (徽县; Y25 to Y30, three hours), from where you can hire a minivan (Y60) for the final 26km. Alternatively take a minibus on to Jiālíng and then hire a minivan (Y20) or walk (6km) from there.

PÍNGLIÁNG 平凉

☎ 0933 / pop 106,800

Píngliáng is a quintessentially booming Chinese mid-size town. The busy shop-lined streets hardly seem like the sort of place a Taoist immortal would want to hang around, and, in fact, all of these folks have wisely retired to Kōngtóng Shān – the main reason for visiting the area.

Orientation & Information

The train station is in the northeastern part of town and the main bus station in the far western part. They are connected by Dajie,

PÍNGLIÁNG BUS TIMETABLES

The following services depart from Píngliáng's main bus station, in the western part of town:

Destination	Price (Y)	Duration	Frequency	Departs
Gùyuán	15	1½hr	hourly	8.30am–5pm
Lánzhōu	62–80	5hr	hourly	7am–4.30pm
Tiānshuǐ	42	7hr	2 daily	6.40am & 8.50am
Xī'ān	50	6hr	5 daily	9am–3pm
Yán'ān	82	9hr	1 daily	6am

home to the town's major hotels, restaurants and shops.

The **Bank of China** (中国银行; Zhōngguó Yínháng; 17 Xi Dajie; ☯ 8.30am-noon & 2.30-5.30pm Mon-Fri) and the **post office** (邮局; yóujú; 91 Dong Dajie; ☯ 8am-7pm) flank the main intersection, 200m apart. Internet cafés are in the Sizhong Alley market (see below).

Sleeping & Eating

Qīnghuá Bīnguǎn (清华宾馆; ☎ 823 4241; 90 Xi Dajie; 西大街90号; dm Y25-35, d with bathroom Y90) A friendly budget place next door to the Píngliáng Bīnguǎn.

Píngliáng Bīnguǎn (平凉宾馆; ☎ 825 3361; 86 Xi Dajie; 西大街86号; tw Y160-228) Centrally located old-school place, with slightly smoky rooms but friendly staff.

If you plan to arrive or leave town at an unsociable hour, there are a couple of decent budget places by both the train station and west bus station.

About 200m west of the Píngliáng Bīnguǎn is the Sizhong Alley market (sìzhōng xiàng shìchǎng), with numerous restaurants and stalls.

Getting There & Away

BUS

See the table (opposite) for travel details. For Tiānshuǐ there are more frequent departures from the east bus station (qìchē dōngzhàn).

TRAIN

Getting to Píngliáng is easiest by train. There are overnight trains to Lánzhōu (train N905; Y86, 11 hours), Xī'ān (Y98, seven hours) and Yínchuān (train K361; 8½ hours).

Getting Around

Bus 1 runs from the train station to the main bus station along Dajie. A taxi to town is Y5.

AROUND PÍNGLIÁNG
Kōngtóng Shān 崆峒山

On the border of Níngxià in the Liùpán Shān range, **Kōngtóng Shān** (admission Y60; ☯ 8am-6.30pm) is an important peak in the Taoist universe. It was first mentioned by the philosopher Zhuangzi (399–295 BC) and illustrious visitors have included none other than the Yellow Emperor. Numerous paths lead over the hilltop past dozens of picturesque temples to the summit at over 2100m.

The main entrance is on the north side of the mountain. You can make a nice loop trip by descending the mountain via the steps on the south side and taking a taxi from the base. If you'd rather not walk, a vertigo-inducing cable car (suǒdào; Y30 return) spans the reservoir on the south side of the mountain to the top of the cliffs.

There is accommodation and food on the mountain at the **Kōngtóng Shānzhuāng** (崆峒山庄; dm Y40-60, tw Y240; ☯ closed Nov-Apr).

GETTING THERE & AWAY

Kōngtóng Shān is 11km west of Píngliáng. You might find a minibus from the opposite side of the park across from the main bus station (Y5), or hire a minivan for Y20/40 one way/return. Both will drop you near the ticket office, where you need to pay for a separate vehicle to take you the 3.5km up to the mountain (per person/car Y10/50). Hourly buses also pass the park's main entrance on the way to Jīngyuán in Níngxià.

GĀNSÙ

Níngxià 宁夏

Níngxià resembles a leftover puzzle piece that doesn't quite fit between its neighbouring deserts and mountain ranges. Hanging precariously to the Yellow River (Huáng Hé) that runs along its northern border, the region was never solid ground for the Chinese, who began building earthen fortifications in the Liùpán Shān as early as the Warring States period (475–221 BC). Níngxià's brightest moment in history came under the Western Xia (Xīxià; AD 1038–1227), a powerful kingdom that rose up around Xìngqìng (Yínchuān) and controlled an enormous swath of today's northwest.

In terms of age and size, the province is no more than a mere babe, belatedly formed as an autonomous region for the Hui in 1958. The Hui, Muslim descendants of Arab and Persian traders who began settling in China during the Tang dynasty, comprise one third of the population and live primarily in the poorer south.

Day-to-day existence here is anything but a bed of roses. Beyond the Yellow River and the ancient irrigation channels that run off it, the land is parched – bad news for a population that consists mainly of farmers. Poor land reform, little social aid and recurrent droughts have turned many of the inhabitants into migrant workers, forced to venture out to big cities such as Lánzhōu and Hohhot in order to support their families.

Entirely off the beaten track, this small province remains a place of specific interests: the beautiful but harsh desert, remnants of the enigmatic Western Xia and a look at how Islam functions in a largely forgotten corner of China.

HIGHLIGHTS

- Explore the mysterious pyramid tombs of the Western Xia outside Níngxià's capital, **Yínchuān** (p879)
- Raft down the Yellow River past the sand dunes of the **Tengger Desert** (p882)
- Seek out the isolated Buddhist grottoes at **Xūmí Shān** (p882)

★ Yínchuān

★ Tengger Desert

Xūmí Shān ★

■ POPULATION: 5.9 MILLION

NÍNGXIÀ

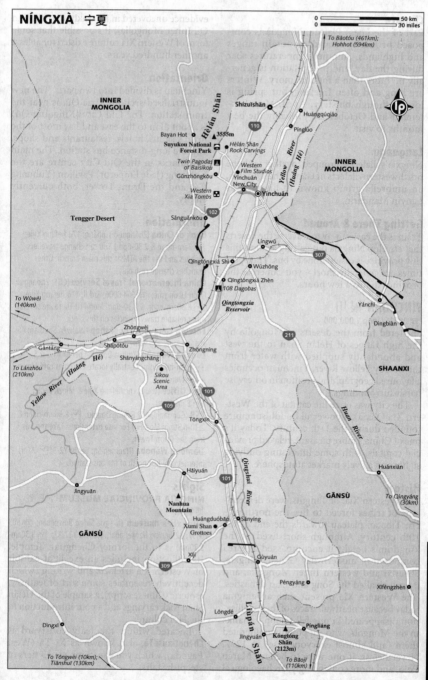

NÍNGXIÀ 宁夏

| 0 | 50 km |
| 0 | 30 miles |

INNER MONGOLIA

Hèlán Shān

Shízuǐshān

To Bǎotóu (461km);
Hohhot (594km)

Huángqúqiáo

110

Pínglúo

Bayan Hot

3555m

Suyukou National
Forest Park

*Hèlán Shān
Rock Carvings*

Twin Pagodas
of Baisikou

*Yellow
River
(Huáng Hé)*

INNER
MONGOLIA

Gúnzhōngkǒu

Western
Film Studios

Western
Xia Tombs

Yinchuan
New City

◉ **Yínchuān**

Sānguānkǒu

102

Tengger Desert

Língwǔ

Qīngtóngxiá Shì

Wúzhōng

307

To Wǔwēi
(140km)

Qīngtóngxiá Zhèn

108 Dagobas

*Qingtongxia
Reservoir*

Yánchí

Dīngbiān

Zhōngwèi

211

Gāntáng

Shāpótóu

Zhōngníng

Yellow River (Huáng Hé)

Shānyángchǎng

SHAANXI

To Lánzhōu
(210km)

Sikou
Scenic
Area

Huan River

109

101

Tóngxīn

Hǎiyuán

Huánxiàn

Jingyuán

101

Qingshui River

GĀNSÙ

To Qìngyáng
(30km)

**Nanhua
Mountain**

Huángduóbǎo

Sānyíng

GĀNSÙ

Xumi Shan
Grottoes

Xījí

Gùyuán

309

Péngyáng

Xīfēngzhèn

Lóngdé

Jingyuán

**Kōngtóng
Shān**
(2123m)

Pīngliáng

Dīngxī

To Tǒngwèi (10km);
Tiānshuǐ (130km)

Liùpán Shān

To Bǎojī
(110km)

NÍNGXIÀ

Climate

Part of the Loess Plateau, Níngxià is composed primarily of arid mountain ranges and highlands. Summer temperatures soar during the day, and precipitation is generally no more than a fond memory. Winters are long and often freezing, but spring is lovely, though blustery. April, May, September and October are probably the best months to visit.

Language

Níngxià's dialect is grouped together with the northwestern dialects of Gānsù and Qīnghǎi, an umbrella group known to linguists as Lanyin Mandarin.

Getting There & Around

Train is the easiest way to traverse the deserts that envelop Níngxià but getting around this tiny province is easiest done by bus. Transport times are generally short – you can cross the province in just a few hours.

YÍNCHUĀN 银川

☎ 0951 / pop 1,000,000

Sheltered from the deserts of Mongolia by the high ranges of Hèlán Shān to the west and abundantly supplied with water from the nearby Yellow River, Yínchuān occupies a favoured geographical position in otherwise harsh surroundings.

The city was once the capital of the Western Xia (Xīxià), a powerful Buddhist empire founded during the 11th century. Today it's one of China's more pleasant, relaxed provincial capitals, with some interesting outlying sights and a lively market atmosphere.

History

The Western Xia, or Tanguts, were descendants of tribes forced to flee the northeastern Tibetan plateau towards the end of the 10th century. Although short-lived, at the kingdom's height it encompassed an area composed of modern-day Gānsù, Níngxià, Shaanxi and western Inner Mongolia, and it even rivalled the Song and Liao dynasties. The Western Xia present such an enigma today because nearly all traces of their civilisation disappeared in one fell swoop – thanks to the Mongols, who supposedly obliterated them (and almost everyone else) in 1227. Nevertheless, if one were to believe Marco Polo, and more convincingly, archaeological

evidence uncovered in Kharakhoto (near Ejin Qi, Inner Mongolia), it's possible that some form of Western Xia culture existed for at least another hundred years.

Orientation

Yínchuān is divided into two parts. The new industrialised section, Xīxià Qū, is near the train station. The Old City (Xìngqìng Qū) is about 8km to the east and has most of the town's sights, hotels, restaurants and shops, and the long-distance bus station. The main landmarks in the Old City centre are the Yuhuang (Jade Emperor) Pavilion (Yùhuáng Gé) and the Drum Tower, both currently empty.

Information

Bank of China (Zhōngguó Yínháng; 170 Jiefang Xijie; ☯ 8am-noon & 2.30-6pm) You can change travellers cheques and use the ATM at this main branch. Other branches change cash only.

China International Travel Service (CITS; Zhōngguó Guójì Lǚxíngshè; ☎ 504 8006; 3rd fl, 116 Jiefang Xijie; ☯ 8.30am-noon & 2.30-6pm Mon-Fri) There are several other reliable travel agencies on this block.

Foreign Languages Bookshop (Wàiwén Shūdiàn; 46 Jiefang Xijie; ☯ 9am-7pm daily)

Lóngbā Wǎngbā (Xinhua Dongjie; per hr Y1.5-2.5; ☯ 8am-midnight) Centrally located internet café, down a courtyard.

Post Office (yóujú; cnr Jiefang Xijie & Minzu Beijie; ☯ 8am-6pm)

PSB (Gōngānjú; 472 Beijing Donglu; ☯ 8.30am-noon & 2.30-6.30pm Mon-Fri) For visa extensions. Take the bus 3 from the Drum Tower.

Tiānlóng Wǎngbā (Nanmen Sq; per hr Y2-3; ☯ 24hr) Internet café just north of the bus station.

Sights

NINGXIA PROVINCIAL MUSEUM 宁夏省博物馆

Níngxià's **museum** (Níngxià Shěng Bówùguǎn; ☎ 503 6497; 32 Jinning Nanjie; adult/student Y22/12; ☯ 8.30am-5.30pm) is in the former Chengtian Temple. Its collection includes an excellent exhibit of Western Xia artefacts and writing (which deceptively resembles some sort of feathery, esoteric Chinese script), a sample of the Hèlán Shān rock carvings and a poor introduction to the Hui culture.

Located within the leafy courtyard is **Chéngtiānsì Tǎ**, also known as Xī Tǎ (West Pagoda), which you can climb via 13 tiers of steepish stairs.

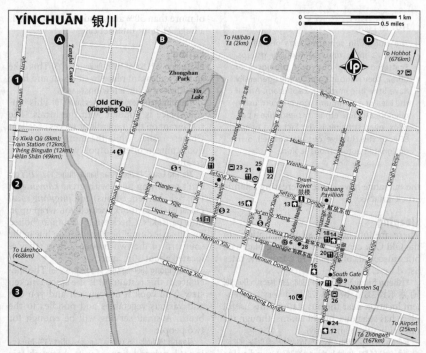

YÍNCHUĀN 银川

To Hǎibāo Tǎ (2km)

To Hohhot (676km)

Zhongshan Park

Yín Lake

Old City (Xìngqìng Qū)

To Xīxià Qū (8km); Train Station (12km); Yíhéng Bīnguǎn (12km); Hèlán Shān (49km);

To Lánzhōu (468km)

To Airport (25km)

To Zhōngwèi (167km)

HĂIBĂO TĂ 海宝塔

Also known as Běi Tǎ (North Pagoda), this fifth-century **pagoda** (admission Y10; ☉ 9am-5pm) was toppled by an earthquake in 1739 and rebuilt in 1771 in the original style. You can climb up the nine storeys for views out over the Hèlán Shān to the west and the Yellow River to the east. Check out the *Alice in Wonderland*–style 2m-tall incense sticks.

Take minibus 20 north on Jinning Beijie for five stops to the 'Běitǎ Lùkǒu' (北塔路

口) and then walk north for 15 minutes, or take a taxi (Y5).

NANGUAN MOSQUE 南关清真寺

Yínchuān's main **mosque** (Nánguān Qīngzhēnsì; Yuhuangge Nanjie; admission Y10; ☉ 8am-6pm) is a modern Middle Eastern–style structure that was originally constructed in the Ming dynasty, razed in the Cultural Revolution and rebuilt in 1981. There's little here to justify the entry fee but the shops beside

NÍNGXIÀ

> **HUÍ** 回
>
> The Huí are in some respects one of the country's more unusual minority groups. Scattered throughout most provinces of China, their various communities generally have little in common except Islam. And if the idea of a communist government using religion to define ethnicity seems like a paradox, even stranger is the fact that nearly 80% of the Huí live outside of their own designated autonomous region.

the entrance have some interesting Islamic knick-knacks.

Sleeping

There are lots of good sleeping options in the Old City centre. The following places all offer discounts of 20% to 30% from the rates listed here.

Yìshèng Bīnguǎn (☎ 604 1888; 235 Nanxun Donglu; 南薰东路235号; tw Y118-128) In a very convenient location near the bus station, this useful place has spacious, bright rooms, though it's not brilliantly maintained.

É'ěrduōsī Dàjiǔdiàn (☎ 409 1612; Shengli Beijie; 胜利北街; d/tr Y55/90, d with bathroom Y138) A good-value and welcoming place, both for budget rooms and spacious en suite rooms, with 24-hour hot water.

Gǔlóu Fàndiàn (☎ 602 8784; fax 602 2573; 26 Jiefang Dongjie; 解放东街26号; s/d Y138-198, with shared bathroom Y60/76) The Gulou is right in the heart of the action and, though slightly knackered, tries hard, with the odd Chinese huāniǎo (bird and flower) painting and some rooms overlooking the Drum Tower.

Xīnhuá Fàndiàn (☎ 603 1353; 203 Xinhua Dongjie; 新华东街203号; r Y186-238; 🖳) A good option, this place is super clean, with some surprising flashes of style and classy wooden floors.

Yuánhēng Dàjiǔdiàn (☎ 602 9998; 58 Zhongxin Xiang; 中心巷58号; tw Y208-338) This place is an excellent lower midrange option, with a good location, modern rooms and good-value discounts. There are lots of small restaurants nearby.

Yíhéng Bīnguǎn (☎ 396 5366; Xingzhou Beijie; 兴洲北街; tw Y278-398; 🖳) Way out in the New City and just 500m south of the train station, this midrange hotel is handy if you're leaving by train at some odd hour of the night. Discounts

of more than 50% are standard. Next door is a huge 24-hour internet café.

Eating

Ālǐ Dàngāo (Ali Cake; 55 Minzu Beijie; coffee Y3) This cake shop is a pleasant place to sit down and have breakfast or write a few postcards.

Yíngbīnlóu (Jiefang Xijie; dishes from Y10) This raucous place is popular with the locals. The restaurant on the upper floor serves excellent Chinese dishes, while the muttony ground-floor canteen offers hotpot, yoghurt and ice cream.

Xiānhè Lóu (118 Zhongshan Nanjie; dishes Y12-22) You can't go wrong here, with great kǎoyángpái (烤羊排; barbequed ribs) and jīngjiāng ròusī (京酱肉丝; soy pork), which you wrap up in little pancakes. Check out the shuǐjiǎo (boiled ravioli-style dumplings) production line in the southern of the two branches here (they're located about 30m apart).

Shāojīgōng (Jiefang Xijie; small dishes Y36) The speciality of this restaurant is the spicy chicken stew. You cook it up yourself and you can add various vegetables and noodles to the broth. A small serving will be enough for two people.

Napoli (Nàbōlǐ; 195 Xinhua Dongjie; buffet Y39) Heaving at lunch and dinner for its chopstick-free buffet of pizza, fruit and salad.

For self-caterers, the **Hualian Supermarket** (Huálián Cháoshì; Nanmen Sq), underneath Nanmen Sq, stocks everything from roast chicken to deodorant.

Getting There & Away
AIR

Yínchuān's main ticket office of the **Civil Aviation Administration of China** (CAAC; Zhōngguó Mínháng; ☎ 691 3456; 540 Changcheng Donglu; ⏰ 8am-6pm) is located south of the bus station. You can also buy tickets from **China Air Express** (Mínháng Kuàidì; ☎ 401 3333; 36 Minzu Beijie), across from Ālǐ Dàngāo.

Plane flights connect Yínchuān with Běijīng (Y1080) and Chéngdū (Y1110), Guǎngzhōu (Y1890), Shànghǎi (Y1500), Ürümqi (Y1350, three weekly) and Xī'ān (Y600), among other destinations.

BUS

The long-distance bus station is in the southeastern part of town on Nanmen Sq near the South Gate (Nán Mén). For some northern destinations you may be referred to the north-

YÍNCHUĀN BUS TIMETABLES

Destinations from the long-distance bus station include the following:

Destination	Price	Duration	Frequency	Departs
Gùyuán	Y46-71	4-6hr	half-hourly	8am-8.50pm
Lánzhōu	Y96	6hr	hourly	8am-4pm
Xī'ān	Y128-138	11-14hr	6 daily	7.40am-4.30pm
Yán'ān	Y67-98	8-12hr	4 daily	7.15am, 8.40am, 9.10am, 5.30pm (sleeper)
Zhōngwèi	Y24-37	2-3hr	hourly	8am-5.45pm

ern bus station *(běimén zhàn)*; to get there from the long-distance bus station hop on bus 4(Y1).

The frequent *kuàikè* (express buses) to Zhōngwèi and Gùyuán are definitely worth the added expense.

TRAIN

Yínchuān is on the Lánzhōu–Běijīng railway line, which runs via Hohhot (11 hours) and Dàtóng (13 hours) before reaching Běijīng (19 hours). If you're heading for Lánzhōu (8½ hours, Y97 hard sleeper), the handy overnight train N901 leaves at 10.05pm. For Xī'ān (14 hours), try train 2587 (Y122 hard sleeper), leaving at 4.16pm, or train K359, leaving at 8.38pm. The train station is in the New City, about 12km west of the Old City centre.

There's a **train booking office** (huǒchē shòupiàochù; 140 Xinhua Dongjie; commission Y5; 8am-7pm) in the Old City, in the ICBC Bank (Gōngshāng Yínháng), next to Dico's Burgers. Buy tickets at counter No 1.

Getting Around

The airport is 25km from the Old City centre; buses (Y15) leave from in front of the CAAC office. Coming from the airport you can ask to be dropped off at the Yùhuáng Gé. A taxi to/from the airport costs around Y40.

Bus 1 (Y1) runs from the long-distance bus station in the Old City, along Jiefang Jie and then on to the train station in the New City, between 6am and 11.30pm. Minibus 1 (Y2) covers the same route faster. Count on a minimum 30-minute trip.

Taxis cost Y5 for the first 3km. A taxi between the train station and the Old City costs around Y15.

AROUND YÍNCHUĀN
Western Xia Tombs 西夏王陵

About 33km west of Yínchuān, these remarkable pyramid-shaped **tombs** (Xīxià Wánglíng; adult/student Y40/20; 8am-7pm) are easily Níngxià's most famous sight. The series of tombs was started a millennium ago by the Western Xia's first ruler, Li Yuanhao. There are nine imperial tombs, plus 200 lesser tombs, in an area of 50 sq km.

Leading up to the main tomb is a processional way, flanked by carved stellae bases, a sacrificial platform and watchtowers. The 23m-tall main tomb was originally built as an octagonal seven-storey wooden pagoda, similar to the Genghis Khan mausoleum near Dōngshèng (see p894), but all that remains is the large earthen core.

The examples of Buddhist art in the good site **museum** offer a rare glimpse into the ephemeral Western Xia culture, and point to clear artistic influences from neighbouring Tibet and Central Asia.

If you have time, the best way to get a feel for the site is to hike out to some of the remoter tombs, the most impressive of which are the photogenic 'twin tombs', 5km to the south, or Tomb No 5, 5km to the west. During summer you can take an electric car out to the former for Y10 per person. Dozens of smaller tombs litter the plains to the north. You can't enter any of the tombs (which are actually underground), so it's more of a visual experience.

A return taxi to the tombs costs around Y90. You could take bus 2 to its terminus in Xīxià Qū and then take a cheaper taxi (Y15 each way) from there. In summer you might just find a direct bus from Yínchuān's long-distance bus station.

Hèlán Shān 贺兰山

The razorback ridges of the Helan Mountains are clearly visible from Yínchuān. The range forms an important natural barrier against desert winds and invaders alike, and the foothills are peppered with graves taking advantage of the range's excellent feng shui.

About 54km northwest of Yínchuān's New City is the historic pass village of **Gǔnzhōngkǒu** (滚钟口; admission Y20, car Y10), with walking trails leading up past pagodas and temples into the surrounding hills.

Another 9km north of Gǔnzhōngkǒu are the **Twin Pagodas of Baisikou** (拜寺口双塔; Bàisìkǒu Shuāngtǎ; admission Y10), which are 13 and 14 storeys high and decorated with Buddha statuettes.

A further 6km on is **Suyukou National Forest Park** (苏峪口国家森林公园; Sūyùkǒu Guójiā Sēnlín Gōngyuán; admission Y40, car Y5, museum Y20), which offers some good hiking if you have time for more than a passing visit. A cable car (Y25 up, Y45 return) whisks you up to cool pine-covered hills.

Another 5km past the junction is a boulder-strewn gorge filled with **rock carvings** (贺兰山岩画; Hèlánshān Yánhuà; admission Y25) thought to date back 10,000 years. There are over 2000 pictographs, depicting animals, hunting scenes and faces, including one (so local guides like to claim) of an alien. Most of the carvings are by the valley mouth, on the north side. Don't miss the images of the Rastafarian-like sun god (climb the side steps up the hill) or the tiger (continue along the main trail to the reservoir). The pictographs are the only remnants of early nomadic tribes who lived in the steppes north of China.

On the way back to Yínchuān, fans of the Zhang Yimou film *Red Sorghum* can stop at the **Western Film Studios** (镇北堡西部影城; Zhènběibǎo Xībù Yǐngchéng; admission Y40; ☻ 8am-6pm), where the film was shot. The fortress and old city movie sets are phoney but fun.

Public transport is almost nonexistent here. A taxi for the day (130km) should cost about Y200, and you can generally throw in the Western Xia tombs for the same price. **CITS** (Zhōngguó Guójì Lǚxíngshè; ☎ 504 8006; 3rd fl, 116 Jiefang Xijie, Yínchuān; ☻ 8.30am-noon & 2.30-6pm Mon-Fri) asks double this price, but includes an English-speaking guide. Tourist buses head out to Suyukou National Forest Park (Y30 return) from Yínchuān's north bus station between May and October if there are enough people.

108 Dagobas 108 塔

These unusual Tibetan-style **Buddhist dagobas** (Yìbǎilíngbā Tǎ; admission Y20; ☻ 8am-7pm), or stupas, are 83km south of Yínchuān, near the town of Qīngtóngxiá Zhèn. The 12 rows of white, vaselike structures date from the Yuan dynasty and are arranged in a large triangular constellation on the banks of the Yellow River. Be warned – the stupas were heavily renovated.

To get here, jump on one of the frequent buses (Y11, 2½ hours) from Yínchuān's long-distance bus station to Qīngtóngxiá Zhèn (you may have to change at the larger town of Qīngtóngxiá Shì). Once you arrive, walk 15 minutes south to the dam, up the steps and down the eastern river bank to the dock, where you can take a boat to the far bank (Y15 return).

Bayan Hot 阿拉山左旗

Bayan Hot (Ālāshān Zuǒqí) is a town just across the border in Inner Mongolia, some 105km from Yínchuān, and a worthy day trip. It lies surrounded by desert and has an outpost feel to it. In town is the **Yánfú Sì** (延福寺; admission Y10), a small Mongolian temple that dates back more than 300 years; once populated by 200 lamas, it now houses around 30.

Halfway to Bayan Hot ('Rich City') the road broaches crumbling, yet still mighty, remains of the Great Wall at **Sānguānkǒu** (三关口).

Frequent buses depart from Yínchuān's long-distance bus station for Bayan Hot (Y25, 2½ hours). The return buses peter out after about 5pm.

ZHŌNGWÈI 中卫
☎ 0953

Zhōngwèi lies 167km southwest of Yínchuān on the Lánzhōu–Bāotóu railway, between the sand dunes of the Tengger Desert (Ténggélǐ Shāmò) to the north and the Yellow River to the south. In addition to its unusual setting, Zhōngwèi has a fairly relaxed pace – a nice change from the rush of most Chinese cities.

Information

Bank of China (Zhōngguó Yínháng; cnr Gulou Beijie & Gulou Dongjie; ☻ 9am-5pm) Has an ATM.

Desert Travel Service (Shāpōtóu Lǚxíngshè; ☎ 703 3415; shamo@ypall.com; Gulou Beijie) Pricey but professional outfit for camel and rafting trips (see p882), in the Zhōngwèi Dàjiǔdiàn.

Fēitiān Wǎngbā (Gulou Xijie; per hr Y2; ☻ 24hr) Next to the Gulou Department Store, on the 4th floor inside a

ZHŌNGWÈI 中卫

courtyard, is this internet café. There are also internet cafés on the east side of Renmin (People's) Square.

Peace Travel (Hépíng Lǚxíngshè; ☎ 701 4880; Gulou Xijie) English-speaking travel agency at the entrance to the Zhōngwèi Dàjiǔdiàn (for tours, see p882).

Post office (yóujú; Gulou Xijie)

PSB (Gōngānjú; Renmin Sq)

Sights

GĀO TEMPLE 高庙

The main attraction in town is the **Gāo Temple** (Miào; Gulou Beijie; admission Y20; ⏰ 7am-6.30pm), an eclectic, multipurpose temple that at one time

catered to the needs of Buddhism, Confucianism and Taoism. It's still a hodgepodge of architectural styles, but the revitalised Buddhist deities have muscled out the original Taoists and Confucians.

The real oddity is the former bomb shelter, built beneath the temple during the Cultural Revolution and later converted into a Buddhist hell/haunted house. The eerie, dimly lit tunnels echo with the haunting screams of the damned. Try not to get too freaked out.

Sleeping & Eating

A nice alternative to staying in town is the desert guesthouse at Shāpōtóu (see p882).

Xīngxiáng Bīnguǎn (☎ 701 9970; 61 Changcheng Donglu; 长城东路61号; dm Y20-30, tw Y80-180) The rock-hard dorm beds here are offset by heat lamps in the common showers.

Zhang's Hotel (Zhāngshì Jítuán Hòulóu Bīnguǎn; ☎ 701 0808; 61 Changcheng Donglu; 长城东路61号; dm Y25, tw 80-166; 🖥) For slightly nicer twins, ask the Chóngqìng Restaurant (below) about this hotel, located just behind Xīngxiáng Bīnguǎn.

Yìxīng Dàjiǔdiàn (☎ 701 7666; 2 Gulou Beijie; 鼓楼北街2号; tw Y150-368; 🖥) This is the most upmarket place in town, overlooking the Drum Tower. Discounts of 30% are common.

Zhōngwèi Dàjiǔdiàn (☎ 701 2219; 53 Gulou Beijie; 鼓楼北街53号; tw Y290-318; 🖥) Check if this place is still discounting its plush and spacious midrange doubles to as low as Y120; if so, it's the best deal in town.

Night Market (Yèshì; Zhongshan Jie) The best place to eat is this happening spot with lots of cheap eats. Two favourites are *ròujiāmó* (肉夹馍; fried pork or beef stuffed in pita bread, sometimes with green peppers and cumin) and *shāguō* (沙锅; minihotpot).

Chóngqìng Restaurant (Changcheng Donglu; 长城东路; dishes from Y7) This friendly home-style restaurant is excellent; staff are often willing to prepare smaller, cheaper versions of dishes for solo travellers.

Getting There & Away

BUS

The **long-distance bus station** (*chángtú qìchēzhàn*) is 1km east of the Drum Tower, on the southern side of Dong Dajie. A taxi here is Y3. Frequent buses to Yínchuān (Y24, three hours) leave every half hour from 6.30am to 6pm; express buses (Y34, two hours) make the trip six times daily. To get to Gùyuán, you'll need to first get to Zhōngníng (Y9, one hour) or Tōngxīn (Y17, two hours) and change there.

TRAIN
From Zhōngwèi you can catch trains heading to the north, south and southeast. By express train it will take you 2½ hours to reach Yínchuān, six hours to Lánzhōu (train K43; 9.20am) and 12 hours to Xī'ān (train 2586; 7.08pm). For Gùyuán (3½ hours) take the Xī'ān train.

AROUND ZHŌNGWÈI
Shāpōtóu 沙坡头
The desert playground of **Shāpōtóu** (admission Y65; ◯ 7am-5.30pm), 10km west of Zhōngwèi, lies on the fringes of the Tengger Desert, at the dramatic convergence of desert dunes, the Yellow River and lush farmlands. It's based around the Shapotou Desert Research Centre, which was founded in 1956 to battle the ever-increasing problem of desertification in China's northwest.

Shāpōtóu has become something of a desert amusement park, with camel rides, speed boats, zip lines (Y60), bungy jumps (Y120), sand sleds (Y20) and a climbing wall (Y30). The scenery is impressive, but it's heavily commercialised. There are two entrances to the area: the main one at the guesthouse and the other at the top of the sand dunes, from where you can access the main desert (a camel ride here costs Y60).

A traditional mode of transport on the Yellow River for centuries was the *yángpí fázi* (leather raft) made from sheep or cattle skins soaked in oil and brine and then inflated. An average of 14 hides are tied together under a wooden framework, making a strong raft capable of carrying four people. Touts at Shāpōtóu offer boat rides up to Shuāngshīshān (双狮山) for Y60 per person, from where you can raft back downstream.

A day trip up the river to a working water wheel at Běichángtān (北长滩), some 70km west from Zhōngwèi, costs Y320.

TOURS
Both **Peace Travel** (Hépíng Lǚxíngshè; ☎ 0953-701 4880; Gulou Xijie, Zhōngwèi) and **Desert Travel Service** (Shāpōtóu Lǚxíngshè; ☎ 0953-703 3415; shamo@ypall.com; Gulou Xijie, Zhōngwèi) in Zhōngwèi offer several enticing river and desert trips. A three-day camel trek through the Tengger Desert with a visit to the Great Wall and camping in the dunes costs around Y300 per person per day for transport, guide and accommodation (minimum three people).

Another option is a one-day leather raft trip down the Yellow River, starting at the water wheel at Běichángtān and ending at Mèngjiāwān. This costs Y250 per person, including transport to and from Zhōngwèi, or you can add it on to a camel trip for Y100.

SLEEPING
Shāpō Shānzhuāng (沙坡山庄; ☎ 768 9073; tr/tw per bed Y40/50; ◯ Apr-Oct) It's nice to be out of the town on the Yellow River by the sand dunes but the accommodation itself is uninspiring. With its choice location at a bend in the Yellow River, is a decent choice if you want to sleep near the dunes, though the surroundings are more inspiring than the rooms. There's a small restaurant on the premises.

GETTING THERE & AWAY
There are frequent public minibuses between Zhōngwèi and the main entrance of Shāpōtóu (Y4, 45 minutes), petering out around 6.30pm. They leave from inside a courtyard opposite the long-distance bus station, stopping briefly at the Gulou Beijie and Changcheng Xilu intersection in Zhōngwèi. A taxi costs Y30/50 one way/return.

Sikou Scenic Area 寺口风景区
One new place worth exploring is the **Sikou Scenic Area** (Sǐkǒu Fēngjǐngqū; admission Y60), a dramatic sandstone area of gorges, temples and caves, 56km southeast of Zhōngwèi. South of Shānyángchǎng the road branches at a pagoda, leading to the two halves of the scenic area. The western section boasts a suspension bridge over the dramatic gorge, while the eastern section features the Sikou gorge, caves, walkways and plenty of scrambling. The cliffs offer some of northwest China's best rock climbing. The only way to get here is to hire a taxi for the day (from Y200 to Y300).

GÙYUÁN 固原
☎ 0954
Gùyuán on the border of southern Níngxià is of little interest, except perhaps for its **museum** (固原博物馆; gùyuán bówùguǎn; Xicheng Lu; admission Y20; ◯ 8am-noon & 2-6pm Tue-Fri, 9am-4pm Sat & Sun), currently under renovation. Fifty kilometres northwest of Gùyuán, however, are the little-visited Buddhist grottoes of **Xūmí**

THE WORLD ACCORDING TO MA YAN

Gender inequality and rural poverty are hardly breaking news in China, but rarely does one have the chance to view them first-hand through the eyes of a young girl. In 2001, 14-year-old Ma Yan found herself face-to-face with a future not uncommon to Chinese women: unable to pay the tuition fees for three children, Ma Yan's parents decided to pull her out of school, for the sake of her brothers' education.

Ma Yan's school diaries were later thrust upon a French journalist, at the time a last-ditch cry for help from a desperate mother, herself deprived of an education and married at 16. Reading them can be an unsettling experience – some days she has no more than a bowl of rice to eat, other days even less. But no other book will bring you closer to understanding just how hard it is to make ends meet in Níngxià, or the extremity with which the Communist Party has turned its back on its original *raison d'être*.

The subsequent translation and publication of extracts from the diary not only introduced the world to the people of Níngxià, it also changed the fates of hundreds of families. Readers sent in personal donations to keep Ma Yan in school, and continuing interest sparked the publication of the entirety of Ma Yan's diaries in book form. Royalties from sales and reader donations were put into a grass-roots fund to help provide tuition fees for children throughout the province. Ma Yan herself is still in high school. Her plans? To enrol in Běijīng's Qinghua University to study journalism.

The Diary of Ma Yan has since been translated into 17 languages, and the organisation **Enfants du Ningxia** (www.enfantsduningxia.org) has helped ensure the right to an education for several hundred children in southern Níngxià – no small accomplishment for the diary of a teenage girl.

Shān (须弥山; admission Y30). Xūmí is the Chinese transliteration of the Sanskrit word *sumeru*, a Buddhist paradise.

Cut into the five adjacent sandstone hills are 132 caves housing more than 300 Buddhist statues dating back 1400 years, from the Northern Wei to the Sui and Tang dynasties. Cave 5 contains Xūmí Shān's largest statue: a colossal Maitreya (future Buddha), standing 20.6m high. It remains remarkably well preserved, even though the protective tower has long since collapsed and left it exposed to the elements. Around the corner in cave 1 is a smaller standing Buddha. Further uphill, the best statues are protected by the Yuanguan (caves 45 and 46; 6th century) and Xiangguo (cave 51; 7th century) Temples, where you can walk around the interior and examine the artwork up close – amazingly, the paint on several of the statues has yet to wear away.

There's one direct bus a day to the caves (Y8, 1½ hours), leaving Gùyuán at around 2.30pm and returning the next morning at 8am, so you'd have to overnight at the site **guesthouse** (dm Y30), which isn't a bad idea at all. Otherwise, catch a bus from Gùyuán to Sānyíng (三营; Y6, one hour), on the main road 40km north of Gùyuán near the Xūmí Shān turn-off. From Sānyíng you can hop on a minibus to Huángduóbǎo (Y2 when full) and then find a tractor or hire a minivan for the 9km to the caves. A minibus from Sānyíng to Xūmí Shān is the best bet at Y50 return.

Sleeping

Tiědào Bīnguǎn (铁道宾馆; train station; 火车站; s/d Y40/80) If you arrive late at night, this place has excellent-value rooms.

Gùyuán Bīnguǎn (固原宾馆; ☎ 203 2479; Zhengfu Jie; 政府街; tw Y140-180, without bathroom Y60-100) Gùyuán's government hotel is fresh and clean, with a wide range of rooms. A taxi from the bus station costs Y3.

Liùpánshān Bīnguǎn (六盘山宾馆; ☎ 202 3339; 77 Zhongshan Jie; 中山街77号; tw Y80) Five minutes' walk to the right as you exit the bus station is this hotel's main building; from here you'll be directed to the dependable twins in the foreign-approved wing.

Xīnshìjì Bīnguǎn (新世纪宾馆; Wenhua Jie; 文化街; tw without/with bathroom Y80/50) Just outside the bus station, to the right, this clean and good-value place is the most convenient option.

There are lots of good restaurants on Zhengfu Xiang, such as the Níngfēng Shífǔ (宁丰食府). Take a left out of the bus station, then another left to the alley. The Gùyuán Bīnguǎn has a good buffet (Y18), if you can't face grappling with another Chinese menu.

NÍNGXIÀ

Getting There & Away

Gùyuán is on the Zhōngwèi–Bǎojī railway line, with trains to Xī'ān (eight hours), Yínchuān (six hours) and Lánzhōu (10 hours), but sleeper tickets are near impossible to get, and the majority of trains depart in the middle of the night. Useful local trains include the 11.14am (train 8782) to Zhōngwèi (five hours); 8.22am (train 1014) and 4.37pm (train 8781) to Píngliáng (2½ hours); and 9.32pm overnight to Lánzhōu (train N905). To get to the train station you'll need to take bus 1 or a taxi (Y5).

Gùyuán is one of the last places in the country to try to charge foreigners double fare. Buses to Yínchuān (Y37 to Y60, 4½ hours) leave every half-hour between 8am and 5.30pm from the long-distance bus station.

There are buses running once daily to Lánzhōu (Y51, nine hours) and Tiānshuǐ (Y42, seven hours) at 6am, and three morning buses to Xī'ān (Y57, seven hours). There are also frequent buses to Píngliáng (Y15, 1½ hours) and Jīngyuán (Y20, two hours).

Inner Mongolia
内蒙古

Inner Mongolia (Nèi Měnggǔ) covers an enormous expanse of land, its intriguing and often desolate landscapes stretching some 2150km, as the hawk flies, from the Gobi Desert in the west to the Argun River (É'ěrgǔnà Hé) along the Russian border in the northeast.

For most people, Inner Mongolia's big attractions are the rolling steppes and the chance to glimpse the Mongolian way of life, where herders traditionally moved with the seasons in search of pastures for their animals, living in transportable circular tents known as yurts. Some travellers are disappointed that 'Mongolian life' here has been packaged for tourists, with visits to 'yurt camps' and folkloric dance shows, rather than encounters with genuine nomads on the grasslands. Still, it's possible to learn something of Mongolian ways, particularly for adventurous travellers who seek out more authentic experiences. And the wide open spaces of Inner Mongolia's 'big sky country' are a welcome relief from China's urban centres.

In Inner Mongolia's far north, the culture is influenced by the proximity of Russia, as Russian traders cross the border to wheel and deal in towns such as Mǎnzhōulǐ. Minority peoples, including the Ewenki and the Daur, still live in remote northern territories as well.

The region is also home to the mausoleum of the legendary Genghis Khan, the controversial conqueror who led the Mongols to build a vast empire that stretched from Asia into Europe. And not far from the mausoleum, you can begin exploring the region's expansive deserts.

HIGHLIGHTS

- Sleep in a yurt and explore Mongolian culture on the grasslands near **Hǎilāěr** (p896)
- Hang out with Russian traders or sample Russian food in the border town of **Mǎnzhōulǐ** (p897)
- Gallop across the **grasslands** (p891) at Xilamuren, Gegentala or Huitengxile
- Watch the Naadam festivities – horse racing, archery and wrestling – in **Hohhot** (p890)
- Take a quick trip to the desert at **Resonant Sand Gorge** (p894)

■ POPULATION: 24.5 MILLION   ■ www.nmgnews.com.cn

History

The nomadic tribes of the northern steppes have always been at odds with the agrarian Chinese. Seeking a solution to the constant skirmishes with the numerous Xiongnu clans, the first emperor of the Qin dynasty (221–207 BC), Qin Shi Huang, began building the Great Wall to keep them out. It was only under the Qing dynasty (1644–1911) that much of the Mongolian homeland came under Chinese rule for good, divided into the 'Inner' and 'Outer' regions.

THE MONGOL EMPIRE

United by Genghis Khan and later led by his grandson Kublai Khan, the Mongols went on to conquer not only China but most of the Eurasian continent, founding an empire that stretched from Vietnam to Hungary. Begun in 1211, it was a conquest won on horseback: the entire Mongol army was cavalry, allowing rapid movement and deployment of the armies.

Even after Genghis Khan's death in 1227, successful campaigns thundered across Central Asia, Tibet, Persia and Russia, eventually reaching Europe's threshold. The subjugation of the West was only called off when Genghis Khan's successor, Ogadai, died in 1241.

The Mongols eventually moved their capital from Karakoram in Mongolia to Běijīng, and after conquering southern China in 1279, Kublai Khan became the first emperor of the Yuan dynasty. His empire was the largest nation the world has ever known. The Mongols improved the road system linking China with Russia, promoted trade throughout the empire and with Europe, instituted a famine relief scheme and expanded the canal system, which brought food from the countryside to the cities.

By the end of the 14th century, however, a series of incompetent rulers led to the disintegration of the Mongol Empire. The Mongols again become a collection of disorganised roaming tribes, warring among themselves and occasionally raiding China, until the Qing emperors finally gained control in the 18th century.

RELIGION

Early Mongols based their religion on the forces of nature, revering the moon, sun, stars and rivers. Mongol shamans could speak to the gods and communicate their orders to the tribal chief, the khan.

With the establishment of the Yuan dynasty, the Mongols, particularly Kublai, began to express a growing interest in Tibetan Buddhism. It wasn't until after the collapse of the empire, though, that the doctrine of the Gelugpa (Yellow Hat) school would radically alter Mongolian culture.

Critical in the conversion of his people was Altan Khan, who invited the Gelugpa Lama, Sonam Gyatso, to Qīnghǎi Hú (Lake Kokonor) in 1578. Altan conferred upon the Tibetan leader the new title of 'Dalai Lama' (*dalai* being the Mongolian translation of *gyatso*, or ocean), rekindling a powerful relationship between the two cultures. Lamaism swept Mongolia, influencing all aspects of society – up to 40% of the male population would enter the monastic life.

INNER MONGOLIA TODAY

The Chinese government established the Inner Mongolia Autonomous Region in 1947 and has tried hard to assimilate the Mongolians, who make up about 15% of Inner Mongolia's total population. (Most of the other 85% are Han Chinese with a smattering of Hui, Manchu, Daur and Ewenki.) The traditional nomadic lifestyle is fading fast, as is the practice of Tibetan Buddhism. The population is concentrated in the heavily industrial southern part of the province, in cities such as Hohhot and Bāotóu.

Climate

Siberian blizzards and cold air currents rake the Mongolian plains from December to March; in winter you'll even witness snow on desert sand dunes. June to August brings pleasant temperatures, but in the west it gets scorchingly hot during the day. Pack warm clothing for spring (March to May) and autumn (September to November).

The best time to visit is between June and September, particularly to see the grasslands,

---

A YURT BY ANY OTHER NAME...

'Yurt,' the common name for traditional Mongolian tents, is a Russian word. The Mongolian word is *ger*, and the Chinese call them '*Měnggǔ bāo*,' – literally 'Mongolian buns' – perhaps because the white structures with their conical tops resemble puffy steamed breads.

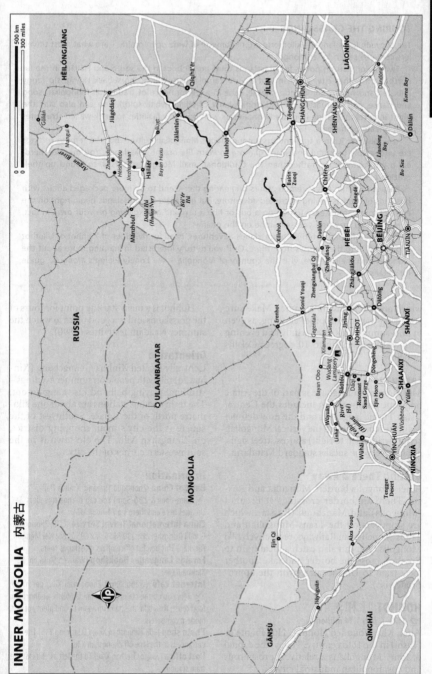

INNER MONGOLIA 内蒙古

TOURING THE GRASSLANDS

The cǎoyuán (grasslands) – kilometre after kilometre of wide open prairie – are what most travellers come to see in Inner Mongolia.

Two major starting points for grasslands tours are Hohhot in the south and Hǎilāĕr in the far north. From either city, you can visit a yurt 'camp' where you go horseback riding, sip tangy milk tea and nibble homemade cheese, take in a performance of traditional Mongolian song and dance, sup on roast lamb and drink plenty of báijiǔ (white spirit). You can also stay the night in yurts that range from traditional tents with primitive facilities to brick-walled structures with private bathrooms.

You may not learn a tremendous amount about Mongolian culture, but the remote settings are undeniably beautiful and you'll glimpse modern life on the grasslands. You may see herders using motorcycles, rather than the traditional small Mongolian horses, to round up their grazing herds!

Because Hohhot is less remote, tours originating there tend to be more packaged affairs with busloads of tourists having a scripted adventure. But in Hǎilāĕr the grasslands begin right on the edge of town, so it's easy to hop on a bus or hire a taxi and go exploring on your own. In fact, in Hǎilāĕr you may find yourself alone on the prairies.

For more off-the-beaten-path grasslands adventures, head for the cities of Xilinhot or Ulanhot and set off onto the steppes from there. Or if you're truly interested in learning more about the Mongols and their culture, visit the country of Mongolia – see Lonely Planet's Mongolia guide for details.

which are green only in summer. Make sure you bring warm, windproof clothing, as even in mid-summer, it's often windy and evening temperatures can dip to 10 degrees Celsius or below.

Language

The Mongolian language is part of the Altaic linguistic family, which includes the Central Asian Turkic languages and the now defunct Manchurian. Although the vertical Mongolian script (written left to right) adorns street signs, almost everyone speaks standard Mandarin.

Getting There & Away

Inner Mongolia borders Mongolia and Russia. There are border crossings at Erenhot (Mongolia) and Mǎnzhōulǐ (Russia), which are stopovers on the Trans-Mongolian and Trans-Manchurian Railways, respectively. To Mongolia, you can also catch a local train to Erenhot, cross the border and take another local train to Ulaanbaatar (with the appropriate visa).

HOHHOT 呼和浩特

☎ 0471 / pop 1.14 million

Altan Khan founded Hohhot (Hūhéhàotè or Hūshì) in the 16th century. Today, the capital of Inner Mongolia is a relatively prosperous and cosmopolitan industrial city.

Hohhot is a main starting point for tours of the grasslands and is a good place to watch the summer Naadam festivities (p890).

Orientation

Centrally located Xinhua Guangchang (Xinhua Sq) fills with people on summer evenings – strolling, playing ball and just hanging out. The train and bus stations are about one kilometre north of the square. Southwest of the square is the city's main shopping district, on Zhongshan Xilu. The old town is in the southwestern corner of the city.

Information

Bank of China (Zhōngguó Yínháng; Xinhua Dajie; ☯ 8am–noon & 2.30-5pm) You can change travellers cheques here and there's a 24-hour ATM.

China International Travel Service (CITS; Zhōngguó Guójì Lǚxíngshè; ☎ 230 8056; fax 695 2288; Nèi Měnggǔ Fàndiàn) This helpful office offers grasslands tours.

Foreign Languages Bookshop (Wàiwén Shūdiàn; 58 Xinhua Dajie)

Internet café (wǎngbā; off Zhongshan Xilu; per hr Y3; ☯ 24hr) Go up the stairs to the Mǎndá Měishí Guǎngchǎng food court, then take the stairs up again to find plenty of fast, modern computers.

Photo shop (108 Zhongshan Xilu; CD burning Y15) The entrance is in the lane off Zhongshan Xilu.

Post office (yóujú; Chezhan Xijie) To the left as you exit the train station.

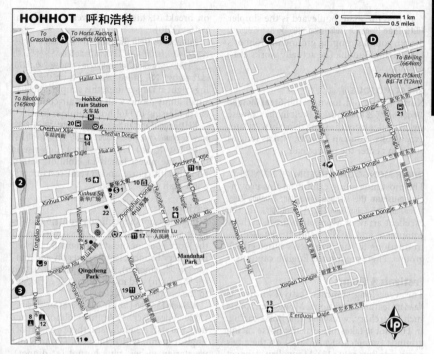

HOHHOT 呼和浩特

Public Security Bureau (PSB; Gōngānjú; 30 Zhongshan Xilu; 8.30am-noon & 2.30-5pm Mon-Fri) For visa extensions and other inquiries, the foreign affairs bureau is to the left of the main building, outside the gated compound.

Sights
WUTA PAGODA 五塔寺
This striking Indian-influenced five-tiered **pagoda** (Wǔtǎ Sì; Wutasi Houjie; admission Y15; 8am-6pm) was completed in 1732. Its main claim to fame is the Mongolian star chart around the back,

though the engraving of the Diamond Sutra, in Sanskrit, Tibetan and Mongolian, extending around the entire base of the structure, has weathered the years in much better condition. Bus 1 runs by the pagoda.

DÀ ZHÀO & XÍLÌTÚ ZHÀO 大召 · 席力图召
Dà Zhào (Danan Jie; admission Y20; 8am-6.30pm) is a large, well-maintained lamasery that is still used as a temple. In the sacred main prayer hall, you may come upon groups of monks chanting and praying.

Across the main boulevard is the simpler **Xílìtú Zhào** (Danan Jie; admission Y10; ☻ 8am-6.30pm), the purported stomping ground of Hohhot's 11th Living Buddha (he actually works elsewhere).

GREAT MOSQUE 清真大寺
North of the old town is the **Great Mosque** (Qīngzhēn Dàsì; 28 Tongdao Beilu). Built in the Chinese style, it dates from the Qing dynasty with later expansions. You can look around as long as you don't enter the prayer hall.

INNER MONGOLIA MUSEUM 内蒙古博物馆
The most interesting exhibits at this provincial **museum** (Nèi Měnggǔ Bówùguǎn; 2 Xinhua Dajie, at Hulunbei'er Lu; admission Y10; ☻ 9am-5pm) are the excellent array of Mongolian dress, archery equipment and saddles, and the detailed introductions to the province's other ethnic groups. There are limited English captions.

Festivals & Events
The week-long summer festival known as **Naadam** features traditional Mongolian sports such as archery, wrestling and horse racing. In Hohhot it takes place at the horse racing grounds (sàimǎchǎng; 赛马场) on the city's north side (bus route 13). Mongolian clans get to the fair on any form of transport they can muster and create an impromptu yurt city.

The exact date of Naadam varies in China but is usually between mid-July and mid-August.

Sleeping
Běiyuán Fàndiàn (☎ 226 4222; fax 696 4629; 28 Chezhan Xijie; 车站西街28号; dm Y20-40, d without/with bathroom Y75-100/120-160) Opposite the bus and train stations, this basic budget hotel has decent if aging dorms and doubles. Some of the rooms without bathrooms are dreary, so be sure to look first.

Binyue International Hostel (Bīnyuè Guójì Qīngnián Lǚshè; ☎ 660 5666; fax 431 0808; 52 Zhaowu Dalu; 昭乌达路52号; dm/d Y50/180; 🖳 🖳) Perhaps because Hohhot's Hostelling International affiliate is run by the posh Binyue International Hotel, it feels more deluxe than a typical hostel. The small doubles seem pricey, but the four-bed dorms are good value. From the train station, take bus 34 southeast to Normal University (师范大学; Shīfàn Dàxué); the hotel tower is a half-block further south. The hostel is behind the main hotel. If you want to splurge

on breakfast, the hotel serves a wonderful buffet (Y30).

Hūhéhàotè Tiělù Bīnguǎn (Hohhot Railway Hotel; ☎ 225 4001; fax 695 4746; 131 Xilin Guole Beilu; 锡林郭勒北路131号; d without/with bathroom Y100/198-240, tr 270, incl breakfast; 🖳) More peaceful than the lodgings right at the stations, this simple hotel has small sunny rooms with Arctic air-conditioners (a blessing in Hohhot's summer heat).

Nèi Měnggǔ Fàndiàn (Inner Mongolia Hotel; ☎ 693 8888; www.nmghotel.com; Wulanchabu Xilu; 乌兰察布西路; d Y660-960; 🖳 🖳) This 14-storey high-rise is one of the nicest hotels in Hohhot, with a pool, health centre and several restaurants. Some staff speak English.

Eating
Mongolia's notable culinary contribution is huǒguō (火锅; hotpot), a refined version, so the story goes, of the stew originally cooked in soldiers' helmets. People generally add mutton (羊肉; yángròu), noodles (面; miàn), tofu (豆腐; dòufu) and mushrooms (蘑菇; mógu) to the bubbling cauldron.

Mǎlàqín Fàndiàn (☎ 691 7738; Julong Changjie; dishes Y10-30; ☻ lunch & dinner) At this Hohhot institution, the staff is helpful and there's a (sort of) English menu, which includes Chinese and vegetarian dishes, plus hotpot (at dinner). Cool off with refreshing buckwheat noodles topped with pickled radishes or with a plate of cold greens.

Xiǎoféiyáng Huǒguōchéng (Little Fat Sheep Hotpot City; ☎ 668 7799; Xilin Guole Lu; for 2 people from Y40; ☻ lunch & dinner) Part of a large chain based in Inner Mongolia, this sophisticated hotpot restaurant makes some of the best – with a rich garlicky broth, high-quality lamb and other fresh ingredients.

Renmin Lu, south of Xinhua Sq, is lined with local restaurants, including **Bātáijiào Jiāchángcài** (☎ 692 2233; dishes from Y8), which serves tasty Mongolian-Chinese fare. Wenhuagong Jie, between Guangming Dajie and Xinhua Dajie south of the train station, is a market street and cheap-eats district. Tempting street stalls are located around the Great Mosque and at the horse racing grounds.

Getting There & Away

AIR
The **Civil Aviation Administration of China** (CAAC; Zhōngguó Mínháng; ☎ 696 4103; Xilin Guole Beilu) office is on the south side of Xinhua Sq. There are daily flights to Běijīng (Y500, one hour),

ON TO MONGOLIA

Hohhot is a reasonable departure point for trips northward into Mongolia. Two direct trains a week run between Hohhot and Ulaanbaatar, the Mongolian capital. There is also a daily train to Erenhot (二连浩特; Èrliánhàotè; seat/sleeper Y36/80, nine hours) at the Mongolian border, leaving at 10.30pm. Erenhot is listed on Chinese train timetables as Èrlián (二连).

Aero Mongolian Airlines (☎ 687 4770; www.aeromongolia.mn; 5 Dongying Nanjie) flies to Ulaanbaatar (Y1440/Y2235 one way/return, 2¾ hours) on Monday and Thursday. Its office is in the same building as the **Mongolian consulate** (Měnggǔ Lǐngshìguǎn; ☎ 430 3254; 8.30am-12.30pm Mon, Tue & Thu), where you can arrange for a Mongolian visa.

Xī'ān (Y830, 1½ hours), Hǎilāěr (Y1310, 2½ hours) and Xilinhot (Y560, 1¼ hours), as well as several flights a week to Guǎngzhōu (Y1880, three hours) and Shànghǎi (Y1350, 2½ hours). Service to several of these cities is reduced in winter.

BUS
See the box below for bus details.

TRAIN
From Hohhot, express trains go to Běijīng (seat/sleeper Y92/170, 10 hours), Dàtóng (Y44, four hours), Bāotóu (Y25, two hours) and Yínchuān (seat/sleeper Y95/175, nine hours).

Sleeper tickets, especially to Běijīng, can be hard to come by in July and August; CITS or hotel travel desks can book sleepers for a Y30 commission.

Getting Around
Useful bus routes include bus 1, which runs from the train station to the old part of the city, via Zhongshan Xilu; bus 33, which runs east on Xinhua Dajie from the train station; bus 5, which plies the length of Xilin Guole Lu; and bus 13 to the horse racing grounds. Tickets for local buses are Y1.

Hohhot's airport is located 15km east of the city. The airport bus (Y5) leaves from the CAAC office; a taxi (flag fall Y6) will cost about Y25.

AROUND HOHHOT
In the middle of the fields just past the airport, about 18km east of Hohhot, is **Bái Tǎ** (白塔; White Pagoda; admission Y35), a striking seven-storey octagonal tower built during the Liao dynasty. After a steep climb to the top, you're rewarded with views of the countryside. The easiest way to get here is by taxi (Y60 to Y70 return); have the driver wait as not many cabs cruise the area. Alternatively, minibuses to 'Hexi' (Y5, about 40 minutes), which depart regularly from a parking lot on Xinhua Dajie one block east of Zhanlanguan Donglu, will drop you in front of the pagoda. Buses 2, 3 or 33 travel from the train station to the stop for the Hexi buses.

THE GRASSLANDS 草原
Tours
Organized tours to the grasslands (cǎoyuán) from Hohhot generally go to three areas: Xilamuren (1½ to two hours from Hohhot), Gegentala and Huitengxile (both two to 2½ hours from Hohhot). Xilamuren, the closest one, is predictably the most developed. If you want to spend the night, aim for one of the latter two. The area around Huitengxile is lined with wind-power generators, scattered across the grasslands like oversized pinwheels, but they are surprisingly quiet.

Travel agents lie in wait at the Hohhot train station, bus station and hotel lobbies, and depending on where you stay, they may be

HOHHOT BUS TIMETABLES

Destination	Price	Duration	Frequency	Departs
Bāotóu	Y20-30	2hr	half-hourly	6.40am-7.30pm
Běijīng	Y100	7-10hr	10 daily	7.30am-7.30pm
Dàtóng	Y40	4hr	hourly	7.20am-5.40pm
Dōngshèng	Y56	3hr	every 30min	7.20am-6pm

FIDDLER ON THE GRASSLANDS

With horses such an important part of traditional Mongolian life, it's no surprise that a classic Mongolian instrument takes its inspiration from the noble steed. It's a two-stringed instrument called the *mǎtóuqín* or horsehead fiddle. Played with a bow, the *mǎtóuqín*'s music can be slow and haunting or exuberant and lively.

According to legend, a dead horse came to its former owner in a dream and implored him to make an instrument with his body. That way, the animal's spirit could accompany its owner across the grasslands. Early instruments were made from horse's hide and bones, but today, only the strings are made from horsehair. The top of the instrument is carved in the shape of a horse's head, in honour of Mongolians' essential animal companion.

calling your room before the massage girls even know you've checked in. While annoying, this abundance of tour options puts you in a stronger bargaining position. A day trip to Xilamuren will cost around Y150 to Y180 (after bargaining), including transport and lunch; horse riding is an extra Y50 to Y60 per hour. Be clear about what your tour includes; if possible, get it in writing before you leave.

CITS in Hohhot runs tours that are a bit more expensive, but they've gotten good reviews from travellers. Xilamuren day tours cost about Y180, and overnights start at Y230; trips to Gegentala and Huitengxile are about Y200 (a day trip) or Y260 (overnight). If you have a small group, CITS can put together a private tour for only slightly more than the large-group rates. A group of four can go to Huitengxile by van, take in an evening music and dance show, stay the night at a basic family-run yurt camp and return to Hohhot the following day for about Y320 per person. Three meals (lunch, dinner and breakfast) are included, but horseback riding is extra. If your party includes vegetarians who don't fancy a lamb banquet, CITS may be able to arrange for meat-free dishes.

To get to Xilamuren independently, take a morning bus to Zhàohé (召河; Y15, two hours). From here you can arrange tours including lunch and horseback riding for a good deal cheaper than in Hohhot.

Another alternative is to negotiate with a taxi driver around the stations for a self-styled grassland tour. The starting price is Y300 (extra if you stay overnight), but again, exert your bargaining skills to the utmost. Be aware that these unofficial tours get mixed reviews. Also, sanitation in the hinterlands is not a strong point, so watch what you eat and drink.

BĀOTÓU 包头

☎ 0472 / pop 2.08 million

The largest city in Inner Mongolia, Bāotóu is a rather grim industrial centre. The only reason to stop here is for its convenience as a transit point.

Orientation

Sprawling across roughly 20km, Bāotóu is divided into eastern and western sections. Most travellers stay in the eastern district (Dōnghé), because it's a useful transit hub, although the western districts (Kūndūlún and Qīngshān) have more services.

The train station in the western area is Bāotóu Zhàn; in the eastern area it's Bāotóu Dōngzhàn.

Information

Bank of China (Zhōngguó Yínháng; Nanmenwai Dajie; ☼ 8am-5.30pm) This branch near the East Bāotóu train station has a 24-hour ATM.

CITS (Zhōngguó Guójì Lǚxíngshè; ☎ 511 6824; cnr Shaoxian Lu & Shifu Donglu, West Bāotóu; ☼ 8.30-11.30am & 2.30-5pm Mon-Fri)

Internet Plaza (Liántōng Wǎngyuàn; cnr Gangtie Dajie & Minzu Xilu, West Bāotóu; per hr Y2; ☼ 8am-midnight)

Post office (yóujú; off Nanmenwai Dajie near the East Bāotóu station; ☼ 8am-5.30pm)

Public Security Bureau (PSB; Gōngānjú; Gangtie Dajie; ☼ 8.30-11.30am & 2.30-5pm Mon-Fri) In a futuristic tower east of the Bank of China in West Bāotóu.

Sleeping

Xīhú Fàndiàn (West Lake Hotel; ☎ 418 7101; 10 Nanmenwai Dajie; 南门外大街 10 号; dm Y31, d Y158-188, ste Y418 incl breakfast; ✷) A five-minute walk from the East Bāotóu bus and train stations, this convenient hotel has a range of choices, from three-bed dorms, to standard doubles, to more upmarket suites.

Bīnlì Jiǔdiàn (☎ 696 0000; 19 Nanmenwai Dajie; 南门外大街 19 号; d Y150-200 incl breakfast; ✷) This newish hotel in a funky mirrored building may be East Bāotóu's most stylish lodging. The great-value rooms are done in chrome,

EAST BĀOTÓU (DŌNGHÉ)
包头东河区

0 — 500 m
0 — 0.3 miles

INFORMATION	
Bank of China 中国银行	.... 1 A2
Post Office 邮局	.... 2 A2

SLEEPING	
Bīnlì Jiǔdiàn 宾利酒店	...................3 A1
Xīhú Fàndiàn 西湖饭店	...................4 A2

EATING	
Hóngfǔdà Fàndiàn 宏府大饭店	......5 A1
Tiěxì Páigǔguǎn 鐵西排骨館	..........6 A2

TRANSPORT	
Long-Distance Bus Station	
汽车站	....7 A2

glass and warm woods; the beds are comfy; and the affable staff may even welcome you with a fruit plate.

Eating

Tiěxì Páigǔguǎn (☎ 416 7001; 8 Nanmenwai Dajie; dishes Y6-20; ☯ lunch & dinner) Indulge your inner Fred Flintstone with mastodon-sized ribs of meltingly tender beef at this cacophonous East Bāotóu eatery. Do as the locals do, and order noodle soup, too; the noodles are handmade, and you can dip your meat into the rich gravy-like broth.

Hóngfǔdà Fàndiàn (☎ 414 4157; 19 Nanmenwai Dajie; dishes Y16-32; ☯ 24 hr) The best deal among the tasty Chinese dishes on offer at this restaurant

next to Bīnlì Jiǔdiàn may be the hearty bowl of noodle soup brimming with veggies, pork and shrimp (Y15). Other yummy choices include stir-fried cabbage or crisp salty green beans with dried shrimp. The photo-filled menu makes ordering simple.

Getting There & Away
AIR
The **CAAC** (Zhōngguó Mínháng; ☎ 513 0941; 26 Gangtie Dajie) ticket office is next to the Bank of China in West Bāotóu. There are flights connecting Bāotóu with Běijīng (Y590, one hour) and Shànghǎi (Y1350, 2¼ hours).

BUS
See the box below for bus times.

The latter two destinations are in Shaanxi province. From West Bāotóu, buses leave from the intersection of Tuanjie Dajie and Baiyun E'bo Lu.

TRAIN
Frequent trains between Hohhot and Bāotóu stop at both the east and west stations (Y25, two hours). There are also trains running to Běijīng (seat/sleeper Y106/197, 13 hours), Yínchuān (seat/sleeper Y70/133, seven hours), Tàiyuán (seat/sleeper Y53/117, 14 hours) and Lánzhōu (seat/sleeper Y121/223, 15 hours).

Getting Around
TO/FROM THE AIRPORT
The airport is 2km south of the East Bāotóu train station. In spite of the short distance, taxis will ask around Y30 for the one-way journey.

BUS
Bus 5 (Y2) takes 45 minutes to shuttle between Bāotóu's two districts. In East Bāotóu, you can catch this bus on Nanmenwai Dajie near the train station. Some bus 5 services run express between the east and west sides in 30 to 35 minutes; board these at regular bus stops.

EAST BĀOTÓU BUS TIMETABLES

Destination	Price	Duration	Frequency	Departs
Hohhot	Y20-30	2-3hr	every 20-30 min	6.30am-7.30pm
Dōngshèng	Y25	1½hr	every 20-30 min	7.30am-6pm
Yúlín	Y40	5hr	3 daily	6.30am, 8.40am, 1pm
Yán'ān	Y100	12hr	1 daily	4pm

Bus 101 runs between the bus station and main (west) train station.

A taxi between the east and west districts costs Y30 to Y40 and isn't much faster than the express buses.

AROUND BĀOTÓU

Resonant Sand Gorge 响沙湾

Imagine a slice of the Sahara dropped into the Inner Mongolian grasslands. That's the setting for this dramatic **gorge** (Xiǎngshāwān; ☎ 0477-396 3366; admission Y60), a section of the Kubuqi desert with sand dunes up to 110m high. The gorge itself, 60km south of Bāotóu en route to Dōngshèng, has a carnival atmosphere, with camel rides (Y40 for 30 minutes) and a don't-miss sand slide (Y10), but you can hike away from the crowds and simply enjoy the desert. The admission price includes a ride on Inner Mongolia's oldest cable car to and from the entrance.

Bring plenty of water, and slather on the sunscreen. You can rent brightly coloured booties (Y10) to protect your feet and legs from the hot sand – worth it for the fashion statement alone!

Buses from East Bāotóu's long-distance bus station leave about every 20 minutes for Dáqí (达旗,Y9, one hour, 8am to 5.30pm), the town nearest to the gorge. From there, you'll have to take a taxi (Y40 to Y50, 20 to 30 minutes). Alternatively, you can hire a taxi for the day from Bāotóu (about Y300 return). Some travellers have reported that the Bāotóu–Dōngshèng buses will drop you at the road to the gorge, but from there, it's a dusty walk of several kilometres to the entrance, unless you can flag down a passing vehicle.

CITS in Hohhot runs two-day tours that include an overnight at the Xilamuren grasslands paired with a visit to the desert; prices start at Y230 per person.

Wudang Lamasery 五当召

Built in 1749, this was once one of the largest **lamaseries** (Wǔdāng Zhào; admission Y30; ⏱ 8am-6.30pm) in Inner Mongolia, housing 1200 monks belonging to the Gelugpa sect of Tibetan Buddhism. Today, it's a bit forlorn, but its attractions are the beautiful Qing murals in the main prayer hall and the unusual arid landscape.

The monastery is 67km northeast of Bāotóu. A direct air-con bus (Y10, 1½ hours) departs from in front of East Bāotóu's long-distance bus station around 9.30am and leaves the

monastery around 1pm. Other direct buses leave the East Bāotóu depot throughout the morning, whenever they are full, returning in the early afternoon.

Alternatively, bus 7 (Y5, one hour) from the East Bāotóu station parking lot goes to Shíguǎi (石拐), 40km from Bāotóu. From Shíguǎi you can hire a taxi to the monastery (Y50 return).

DŌNGSHÈNG 东胜

☎ 0477 / pop 102,000

The main reason to come to Dōngshèng, south of Bāotóu, is to reach Genghis Khan's Mausoleum further south. If you get an early start, it's possible to come here from Hohhot or Bāotóu, visit the mausoleum and then move on that afternoon. The bus station is on Hangjin Beilu; you can choose from several inexpensive hotels nearby if you do decide to stay overnight.

Hóngyè Bīnguǎn (宏业宾馆; ☎ 834 1518; 6 Hangjin Beilu; 杭锦北路6号; s Y80, d Y218-248) If you're looking for a place to lay your head for the night, this basic hotel will fit the bill. Turn right as you exit the bus station and walk south for about five minutes.

Dōngshèng Dàjiǔdiàn (东胜大酒店; ☎ 399 6688; fax 399 6111; 1 Hangjin Beilu; 杭锦北路1号; s Y350, d Y298-580, tr Y380 incl breakfast; 🖵) The rooms may not be as lavish as the chandelier-bedecked lobby at this midrange tower, but they're a great deal. After bargaining, standard doubles go for Y170 to Y180, and more deluxe 'A' building rooms cost Y270 to Y280. It's a 10-minute walk south of the bus station.

Restaurants are clustered near the intersection of Hangjin Beilu and Yijinhuoluo Jie. Try **Liúshì Měishí Dàtuányuán** (刘氏美食大团圆; ☎ 832 8858; Yijinhuoluo Dongjie; hotpot for 2 people from Y25; ⏱ lunch & dinner), a sociable spot serving flavourful hotpot; it's one block east of Hangjin Beilu.

AROUND DŌNGSHÈNG

Genghis Khan's Mausoleum 成吉思汗陵园

The tribute to the Mongol Empire's greatest leader is a bus ride from Dōngshèng, in the middle of nowhere. Unless you have a special predilection for Genghis Khan, however, consider that a visit to this **mausoleum** (Chéngjí Sīhán Língyuán; admission Y80; ⏱ 7am-7pm) is a long way to come to see very little.

The reason why this site is believed to be the final resting place of the Great Khan is unclear,

DŌNGSHÈNG BUS TIMETABLES

Destination	Price	Duration	Frequency	Departs
Bāotóu	Y25	1½hr	every 20-30 min	6.20am-8pm
Hohhot	Y56	3hr	every 30 min	7.10am-5pm
Xī'ān	Y130	18hr	1 daily	2.20pm
Yúlín	Y36-40	3-4hr	hourly	6.30am-4pm

as it contains no actual remains. Although there is little inside – a few historical artefacts and some weaponry – the mausoleum is an important sacred place for Mongolians. Ceremonies are held several times a year to honour Genghis Khan's memory. Butter lamps are lit, *khata* (ritual scarves) presented and roast sheep are piled high before the Khan's stone statue, while chanting is performed by Mongolian monks and specially chosen Daur elders.

GETTING THERE & AWAY

Buses (Y25, one to 1½ hours, hourly) from Dōngshèng to Wūshěnqí (乌审旗) drop you at a rather forlorn tourist village just off the highway about 5km from the mausoleum. Buses heading to Yúlín (榆林; p438) in Shaanxi province may also let you off; in the Dōngshèng depot, ask for buses to Chénglíng (成陵) to confirm which bus will take you. From the tourist village, you'll need to take a taxi (Y10) to the mausoleum entrance. To return, take a cab back to the main highway and flag down any Dōngshèng-bound bus. Buses should pass by regularly till about 5pm, but don't linger here too late into the afternoon.

HǍILĀĚR 海拉尔
☎ 0470 / pop 216,000

The northernmost major town in Inner Mongolia, Hǎilāěr is a base for visiting the surrounding Hulunbei'er Grasslands, a vast expanse of prairie that begins just outside the city.

In the grasslands around Hǎilāěr are several tourist 'yurt camps' where you can eat, listen to traditional music and sometimes stay the night. Although they're not places where Mongolians actually live, you can still learn a bit about Mongolian culture, and the settings on the wide-open prairies are striking. More authentic (if more rustic), you can stay with local families in the grasslands, although this is easiest to organise if you speak a bit of Mandarin (or Mongolian).

Orientation & Information

The main square is on Zhongyang Dajie, near Xingan Lu. Hotels and services are conveniently located near the main square, but sights are scattered around town and beyond.

Bank of China (Zhōngguó Yínháng; Xingan Donglu at Zhongyang Dajie; ⏰ 8am-5.30pm summer, 8.30am-5pm winter) Next door to Bèiěr Dàjiǔdiàn in the centre of town, this office has a 24-hour ATM.

CITS (Zhōngguó Guójì Lǚxíngshè; ☎ 822 4017; fax 822 1728; 22 Alihe Lu) In Hédōng ('east of the river'), on the 2nd floor of Běiyuán Bīnguǎn.

Internet café (wǎngbā; cnr Zhongyang Dajie & Xingan Xilu, lower level; per hr Y2) Opposite Bèiěr Dàjiǔdiàn.

Post & Telephone Office (Yóudiàn Dàlóu; Zhongyang Dajie at Yueju Xilu; ⏰ 8.30am-5.30pm)

Public Security Bureau (PSB; Gōngānjú; Alihe Lu) Opposite CITS in Hédōng.

Sights

EWENKI MUSEUM 鄂温克博物馆

Roughly 20,000 Ewenki people live in northern Inner Mongolia, most in the Hulunbei'er grasslands surrounding Hǎilāěr. At this modern **museum** (Èwēnkè Bówùguǎn; ☎ 881 7866; admission Y10; ⏰ 8.30am-noon & 2.30-5.30pm), you can glimpse their history and culture. The Ewenki have traditionally been herders, hunters and farmers; they're one of the few peoples in China to raise reindeer. The museum has Ewenki household artefacts, clothing and artwork, as well as photos of present-day Ewenki life. Although captions are only in Chinese and

BLOWIN' IN THE WIND

The Ewenki people of northern Inner Mongolia traditionally practised 'wind burials.' Rather than burying their dead in the ground, they would hang the body in a cradle between two trees and let the remains dry in the breeze. They believed that the spirit would reach heaven more quickly this way, carried by the wind.

Mongolian, you can easily spend an hour looking around.

The museum is on the southeastern edge of town. Bus 3 runs here from the main square; a taxi will cost Y25 to Y30 (return).

UNDERGROUND FORTRESS 海拉尔要塞遗址

In the mid-1930s, during the Japanese occupation of Manchuria, this **network of tunnels** (Hǎilāěr Yàosài Yízhǐ; admission Y20) was constructed in the grasslands north of Hǎilāěr. Today you can wander underground and peek into 'rooms' where soldiers bunked. The grasslands setting is pretty, too.

A taxi between the tunnels and the town centre costs about Y30 (return). The tunnels are on the road to Jinzhanghan (right), so you might negotiate a stop here en route.

Sleeping & Eating

Bèiěr Dàjiǔdiàn (Bei'er Hotel; ☎ 835 8388; fax 833 4960; 36 Zhongyang Dajie; 中央大街36号; d without bathroom Y80, s/d with bath Y480, incl breakfast;) The enthusiastic staff at this central, midrange hotel even push the elevator call button for you when they see you coming. Except during Hǎilāěr's summer Naadam festival, standard doubles go for Y200 or less.

Guófǔ Shāngwù Jiǔdiàn (Guofu Business Hotel; ☎ 835 9999; fax 835 9900; 35 Zhongyang Dajie; 中央大街35号; s/d/tr Y580/560/680 incl breakfast;) With bright, cheery rooms and high-speed internet access, this 10-storey tower is slightly spiffier (and a bit more expensive) than Bèiěr Dàjiǔdiàn across the street. Upper-floor rooms look out over the city.

Xiǎoféiyáng Huǒguōchéng (Little Fat Sheep Hotpot City; Xingan Xilu; hotpot for 2 from Y40; lunch & dinner) This branch of the Inner Mongolia-based hotpot chain is one block west of Bèiěr Dàjiǔdiàn.

On Xinfengbuxing Jie, a pedestrian street off Zhongyang Dajie, a **food market** houses vendors selling dumplings, fruit and other snacks.

Getting There & Away

CAAC (Zhōngguó Mínháng; ☎ 833 7490; Dong Dajie, off Qiaotou Dajie; 8am-5pm) is near the bridge. There are direct daily flights from Hǎilāěr to Běijīng (Y1150, two hours) and Hohhot (Y1310, 2¼ hours). CITS and hotel ticket agencies also book flights.

From the **long-distance bus station** (Chángtú Qìchēzhàn; Jinxinzi Lu, off Chezhan Jie), there are regu-

lar buses to Mǎnzhōulǐ (Y31). At the time of writing, however, the road between Hǎilāěr and Mǎnzhōulǐ was being rebuilt, making the trip a bone-jarring five-and-a-half-hour slog. When construction is completed, the ride should take about three hours; until then, the train is the faster, more comfortable option to take.

Several daily trains go to Mǎnzhōulǐ (Y22 to Y29, three to 3½ hours). There are also daily trains between Hǎilāěr and Hāěrbīn (seat/sleeper 93/191, 11 hours), Qíqíhāěr (seat/sleeper Y72/141, eight to nine hours) and Běijīng (seat/sleeper Y181/317, 28 hours).

The train station is in the northwestern part of town. If you arrive by train, cross the tracks using the footbridge to the left of the station as you exit and get a bus or taxi from there. Taxi fare from this side of the tracks to the city centre hotels is Y5.

Getting Around

The airport bus (Y3) leaves from the CAAC office. A taxi costs about Y20.

Bus 1 runs from Hédōng to the train station. Taxi fares start at Y5.

AROUND HǍILĀĚR

Jinzhanghan Grasslands 金帐汗草原

Set along a winding river about 40km north of Hǎilāěr, this **grasslands camp** (Jīnzhànghán; ☎ 133 2700 0919; admission Y20; Jun-early Oct) may be designed for tourists, but it still has a spectacular setting. You can occupy an hour or so looking around and sipping milk tea, spend the day horseback riding or hiking, or come for an evening of dinner, singing and dancing.

If you want to stay the night, you can sleep in one of the yurts (Y60 per person), though they're made of brick (not the traditional portable variety). There's no indoor plumbing but there is a toilet hut.

To get here, you'll have to hire a taxi from Hǎilāěr (about Y120 return, 40 minutes).

Bayan Huxu Grasslands 白音呼硕草原

On these grasslands (Báiyīn Hūshuò Cǎoyuán) 40km southeast of Hǎilāěr, there's a more 'upscale' **yurt camp** (per person Y300, meals about Y25; late Jun-early Oct). The two-person yurts have twin beds and even attached bathrooms. There's a restaurant onsite with evening entertainment. The setting isn't quite as gorgeous as Jinzhanghan, but it's still remote and attractive.

In the village along the Bayan Huxu road, a local family houses guests in their **yurts** (☎ 131-3497 7479; per person Y50-60); rates include meals. The yurts are cosy, although there are no washroom facilities.

Buses to Bayan Huxu leave hourly from Hǎilǎěr's long-distance bus station (Y10, one hour). The bus drops you at the Bayan Huxu road, about a 2km walk from the yurt camp. The last bus back to Hǎilǎěr stops at the Bayan Huxu road at 5.30pm.

Hēishāntóu 黑山头

This outpost on the Russian border, 150km northwest of Hǎilǎěr, was the site of a fortress built during the Liao dynasty. Although all that remains of the fortress are grass-covered mounds out in the steppes, an excursion here provides an excuse for a day-trip across the grasslands.

The actual border crossing is south of the fortress site. You can pull up to the gate, but the guards aren't enthusiastic about foreigners wandering around and the crossing isn't open to foreigners.

To get to Hēishāntóu, take a bus from Hǎilǎěr's long-distance bus station to the town of Zhabudalin (拉布达林; Lābùdálín; Y23, two hours); buses leave every 40 minutes from 7.30am to 5pm. If you have time, it's worth going for a wander around Zhabudalin; the village has a small Russian population, visible in the Cyrillic signs and in the hearty breads for sale in the public market near the bus station.

From Zhabudalin, the only way to Hēishāntóu is by taxi (Y90 to Y120 return, one hour). The last bus back to Hǎilǎěr leaves Zhabudalin at 5.25pm.

MǍNZHŌULǏ 满洲里
☎ 0470 / pop 55,400

This laissez-faire border town, where the Trans-Siberian Railway crosses from China to Russia, feels far more Russian than Chinese. A steady stream of Russians crosses the border from Siberia to purchase Chinese goods in Mǎnzhōulǐ's many markets, and Russian-built log houses still dot the town. Unless you look Asian, expect shopkeepers to greet you in Russian.

Orientation & Information
Mǎnzhōulǐ is small enough to get around on foot. The town centre sits between the train station in the south and Beihu Park in the north.

Bank of China (中国银行; Zhōngguó Yínháng; ☎ 622 3707; cnr Sandao Jie & Xinhua Lu; ⏰ 8am-noon & 2.30-5.30pm summer, 8am-noon & 2-5pm winter)
CITS (中国国际旅行社; Zhōngguó Guójì Lǚxíngshè; ☎ 622 4241; 35 Erdao Jie; ⏰ 8.30am-noon & 2.30-5pm Mon-Fri) On the 1st floor of Guójì Fàndiàn (International Hotel). Sells tickets for the Trans-Siberian Railway.
Internet café (网吧; wǎngbā; 2nd fl, Xinhua Lu, btwn Erdao Jie & Sandao Jie; per hr Y3; ⏰ 24hr)
Post & Telephone Office (邮电大楼; Yóudiàn Dàlóu; cnr Haiguan Jie & Sidao Jie)
Public Security Bureau (公安局; PSB; Gōngānjú; cnr Sandao Jie & Shulin Lu) East of the centre.
Xinhua Bookshop (新华书店; Xīnhuá Shūdiàn; cnr Sidao Jie & Xinhua Lu) Sells maps of Mǎnzhōulǐ (Y4).

Sights
DÁLÀI HÚ 达赉湖
Besides the Russian traders, Mǎnzhōulǐ's main attraction is **Dálài Hú** (admission per person/vehicle Y7/10), one of the largest lakes in China. Called Hulun Nur in Mongolian, it unexpectedly pops out of the grasslands like an enormous inland sea. You can go fishing here or simply stroll along the rocky lakeshore.

The easiest way to get to Dálài Hú, 39km southeast of Mǎnzhōulǐ, is to hire a taxi (about Y150 return).

Sleeping & Eating
At the time of writing, the top-end Shangri-La chain was building a hotel in the centre of town (scheduled to open in 2008).

Diànlì Shāngwù Dàjiǔdiàn (电力商务大酒店; ☎ 398 8888; 1 Sandao Jie; 三道街1号; d Y100 incl breakfast) At this decent-value place east of the centre, the rooms have high ceilings, but some have peeling paint and weary bathrooms, so look at more than one.

Míngzhū Fàndiàn (明珠饭店; ☎ 624 8977; fax 622 3261; 4 Xinhua Lu; 新华路4号; s/d/tr Y498/428/468 incl breakfast) Many Russians stay at this lively hotel at the corner of Yidao Jie.

Yǒuyì Bīnguǎn (友谊宾馆; Friendship Hotel; ☎ 624 8881; fax 622 3828; 26 Yidao Jie; 一道街26号; s/d/tr Y468/458/428 incl breakfast) Also popular with Russian visitors, these comfortable rooms with fridges usually go for Y200 or less. The rooms facing the rear of the building are sunny, but they get noise from the nearby rail yards.

Míngdiǎn Měishí (名点美食; ☎ 622 8885; cnr Sidao Jie & Shizheng Lu; dishes Y8-20; ⏰ lunch & dinner) Unwind in a wicker swing by the window

INNER MONGOLIA

at this laid-back café, where the speciality is handmade noodles.

Russian restaurants (dishes Y10-30) line Erdao Jie, near Xinhua Lu and Zhongsu Lu. A Chinese **bakery-café** (cnr Sidao Lu & Xinhua Lu; dishes Y8-15) serves bowls of tasty noodles, rice plates and gooey desserts; order at the counter before you sit down.

Getting There & Away

Mǎnzhōulǐ has a small airport on the edge of town; a taxi to the airport will take about 15 minutes. There are flights to Běijīng (Y1410, 2¼ hours) Monday, Wednesday, Friday and Sunday, and in summer to Hohhot (Y1310, 2½ hours) daily.

You can reach Mǎnzhōulǐ by train from Hǎilāěr (Y22 to Y29, three to 3½ hours), Hāěrbīn (seat/sleeper Y92/181, 13 hours) or Qíqíhā'ěr (seat/sleeper Y61/125, 11 hours).

From the train station to the town centre, it's a 10- to 15-minute walk. Turn right immediately as you exit the station, then right

again to cross the footbridge. You'll come off the bridge near the corner of Yidao Jie and Zhongsu Lu, a block west of Míngzhū Fàndiàn and Yǒuyì Bīnguǎn.

Taxis charge Y15 from the station to the centre. Otherwise, most trips around town are Y7.

Many Russians drive over the border (9km from town) in private vehicles, and you might be able to organise a lift across. A taxi to the checkpoint costs Y20. Naturally, you'll need a Russian visa.

The Trans-Siberian to Moscow from Běijīng passes through town early Monday morning. CITS sells tickets for Moscow; if you want to stopover here, confirm it when you buy your ticket in Běijīng.

Buses leave all day for Hǎilāěr (Y31, 3½ hours) from the long-distance bus station on Yidao Jie, west of Míngzhū Fàndiàn. Check the status of the Hǎilāěr–Mǎnzhōulǐ road, since major construction work was causing significant delays at the time of research.

Qīnghǎi 青海

Lying on the northeastern border of Tibet, Qīnghǎi is one of the great cartographic constructions of our time. For centuries the area was part of Amdo in the Tibetan world; these days it's separated from the Tibetan Autonomous Region by little more than the colours on a Chinese-made map.

A relatively unknown province, nicknamed 'China's Siberia' for its gulags and nuclear dumping grounds, Qīnghǎi may not immediately strike you as an ideal travel destination. Think again: this vast area is also home to dozens of Tibetan monasteries, epic grasslands, one of Tibet's holiest mountains (Amnye Machen) and the headwaters of three of Asia's greatest rivers – the Yellow (Huáng Hé), Yangzi (Cháng Jiāng) and Mekong (Láncāng Jiāng).

Add to this a mix of ethnic groups, including Tibetans, Goloks, Tu, Mongols, Salar and Hui, and a vibrant religious life. The current Dalai Lama, the 10th Panchen Lama and Tsongkhapa, founder of the Gelugpa sect of Tibetan Buddhism, were all born in present-day Qīnghǎi.

For the traveller, Qīnghǎi forms the launching pad for some of China's wildest journeys: the new train link to Lhasa; overland to Yùshù (Jyekundo) and on into the wilds of western Sìchuān; through the back door to Gānsù and the Labrang Monastery; or west from Golmud, following the deserts of the southern Silk Road into Xīnjiāng.

China's economic miracle has been slow to come to Qīnghǎi; it's the country's fourth-largest province but its third poorest. Travel can be a little rough here and few travellers make it further than Xīníng. Those visitors that do explore the region keep their secrets well; Qīnghǎi is one of the frontiers of adventure travel in China.

HIGHLIGHTS

- Drop in on a local artist in **Tóngrén** (p905) and buy a *thangka* (Buddhist painting) direct from the source
- Take the train overland to Lhasa traversing the **Tibetan Plateau** (p924) via Golmud
- Visit Qīnghǎi's namesake, the bird-watcher's delight of **Qīnghǎi Hú** (p904)
- Make the overland journey across the grasslands to the Tibetan monastery town of **Yùshù (Jyekundo)** (p908) and on into western Sìchuān, crossing from Amdo into Kham province

- POPULATION: 5.3 MILLION

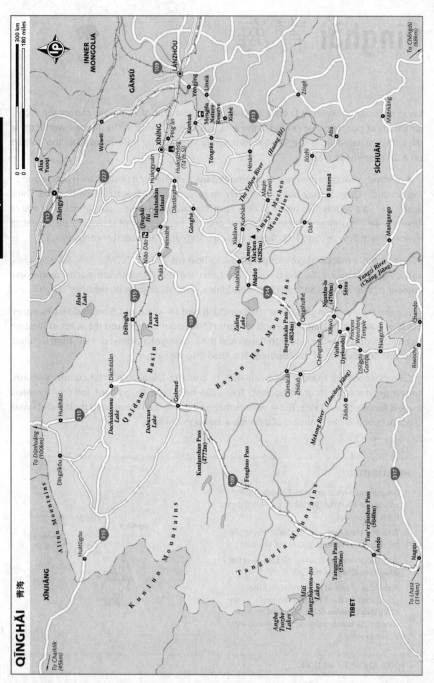

QĪNGHǍI

QĪNGHǍI 青海

Climate

Qīnghǎi's climate is determined by the high altitude – wherever you go, it's likely to be cold and arid, though during the day the sun can get pretty intense. Summer (June to September) is the best time to visit.

The east and south are high, grassy plateaus, with elevations varying from 2500m to 5000m. Both the Tanggula Range along the border of Tibet and the Amnye Machen Mountains in the east have peaks at more than 6000m.

Northwestern Qīnghǎi is a large basin consisting mainly of barren desert, salt marshes and saline lakes. The Kunlun Mountains along the border with Xīnjiāng have summits that top out at a dizzying 6860m.

Language

Most of the population in Qīnghǎi speaks a northwestern Chinese dialect similar to Gānsùhuà (part of the Lanyin Mandarin family). Tibetans speak the Amdo or Kham dialects of Tibetan.

Getting There & Around

Most people train it into the province, either via nearby Lánzhōu or along the controversial new line to/from Tibet (see p924). Distances are huge in Qīnghǎi and you'll probably need a combination of overnight trains or sleeper buses to cover much ground. Out in the remote southeast corner, bus is the only option.

XĪNÍNG 西宁
☎ 0971 / pop 770,000

Xīníng is the only large city in Qīnghǎi and is the capital of the province. Long established as a Han Chinese outpost, it's been a military garrison and trading centre since the 16th century.

Perched on the edge of the Tibetan plateau, the booming city is not the most aesthetic, but it's more manageable in size than its big brother Lánzhōu (in Gānsù). The food and lodging is good and it's a perfect springboard from which to dive into the surrounding sights.

Information
INTERNET ACCESS 网吧

Tiāntáng Niǎo (per hr Y2-5; 🕑 24hr) Down the alley, just to the east of Da Shizi, with sofas and cold drinks.

Xiàdū Wǎngjīng (Huzhu Lu; per hr Y2; 24hr)

LAUNDRY

Laundry (Gānxǐdiàn; Huzhu Lu) An inexpensive place next door to the Post Hotel.

MONEY

Bank of China (Zhōngguó Yínháng; 🕑 8.30am-5.30pm Mon-Fri, 9.30am-4.30pm Sat & Sun) main branch (Dongguan Dajie); smaller branch (Dong Dajie) The two banks change cash and travellers cheques.

POST

Post office (yóujú; Da Shizi, cnr Xi Dajie & Nan Dajie; 🕑 8.30am-6pm)

PUBLIC SECURITY BUREAU

PSB (Gōngānjú; 35 Bei Dajie; 🕑 8.30-11.30am, 2.30pm-5.30pm Mon-Fri) Extends visas in three days. Take bus 14 from Dongguan Dajie or 24 from Bei Dajie.

TOURIST INFORMATION & TRAVEL AGENCIES

China International Travel Service (CITS; Zhōngguó Guójì Lǚxíngshè; ☎ 613 3844; 156 Huanghe Lu) Open weekends from May to October only.

China Travel Service (CTS; Zhōngguó Lǚxíngshè; ☎ 823 4935; 3rd fl, 124 Changjiang Lu)

Qinghai Tibet Adventures (Sānjiāngyuán Tànxiǎn Lǚxíngshè; www.cqta.com; ☎ 824 5548; Rm 301, 13 Bei Dajie) Trekking and mountaineering.

Wind Horse Adventure Tours (Xīhǎi Gōngmín Chūrùjìng Fúwùzhōngxīn; www.windhorseadventuretours.com; ☎ 824 4629; Nan Dajie) Trekking and cultural excursions.

Sights
QINGHAI PROVINCIAL MUSEUM
青海省博物馆

This good **museum** (Qīnghǎi Shěng Bówùguǎn; 58 Xiguan Dajie; admission Y15; 🕑 9.30am-4pm Tue-Sun) has a Tibetan focus, with a real sand mandala and great festival masks. It also has a few Silk Road exhibits and some amazing Stone Age jade ritual implements. The entrance is on the west side. To get there, take bus 9, 16 or 104 from near the train station, or bus 25 from Dongguan Dajie.

BĚISHĀN SÌ 北山寺

A 15-minute jaunt up the barren mountainside northwest of the city brings you to **Běishān Sì** (North Mountain Temple; admission Y5). The hike and views are pleasant, though the dramatic 1700-year-old cliff-face temples are mostly closed. Bus 107 runs near here from the train station.

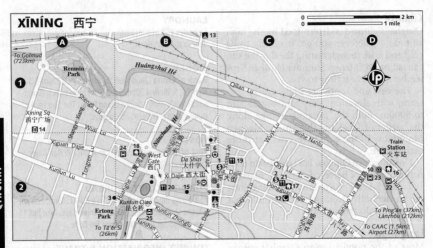

INFORMATION
Bank of China 中国银行 **1** C2
Bank of China 中国银行 **2** C2
CITS 中国国际旅行社 **3** A2
CTS 中国旅行社 **4** B2
Laundry
　干洗店 .... (see 16)
Post Office 邮局 **5** B2
PSB 公安局 **6** B2
Qinghai Tibet Adventures
　三源探险旅行社 **7** B2
Tiāntáng Niǎo
　天堂鸟网吧 **8** B2
Wind Horse Adventure Tours
　西海公民出入境服务中心 **9** B2
Xiàdū Wǎngjǐng
　夏都网景 **10** D2

SIGHTS & ACTIVITIES
Jīntǎ Sì　金塔寺 **11** B2
Mosque 清真大寺 **12** C2
North Mountain Temple
　北山寺 **13** B1
Qinghai Provincial Museum
　青海省博物馆 **14** A1
Shuijing Xiang Market
　水井巷商场 **15** B2

SLEEPING
Post Hotel
　邮政宾馆 **16** D2
Yǎháo Huāyuán Bīnguǎn
　雅豪花园宾馆 **17** C2
Yínlóng Dàjiǔdiàn
　银龙大酒店 **18** B2

EATING
Daxin Jie Night Market
　大新街夜市 **19** C2
Mǎlínhàn 马林汉古城第一烤 **20** B2
Xiǎoyuánmén Měishígōng
　小圆门美食宫 **21** C2
Yínlóng Dàjiǔdiàn 银龙大酒店 ...... (see 18)

TRANSPORT
Buses to Airport
　(Mínzhǔ Bīnguǎn) **22** D2
Long-Distance Bus Station
　长途汽车站 **23** D2
Minibuses to Huángzhōng & Tǎ'ěr Sì
　去湟中、塔尔寺的汽车 **24** B2
Taxis to Tǎ'ěr Sì
　去塔尔寺的出租车 **25** B2

SHUIJING XIANG MARKET 水井巷商场
Xīníng's largest market (Shuǐjǐng Xiàng
Shāngchǎng) occupies several streets and is
an enjoyable place to browse and watch the
crowds watch you. There is a good supply of
snacks at the west end if you need to stock
up. It extends east from the West Gate (Xī
Mén).

OTHER SIGHTS
The city's main mosque (Qīngzhēn Dàsì; 30 Dongguan
Dajie; admission Y10; ⏱ 8am-noon, 2-5pm) is one of
the largest in China's northwest, and worshippers still spill out into the surrounding
streets during Friday lunch-time prayers. The
architecture is more Běijīng than Baghdad.
You can't enter the main building, but you
can stroll around the grounds. It was built
during the late 14th century and has since
been restored.

Also worth a quick visit is the **Jīntǎ Sì** (19
Hongjuesi Jie), a small but lovely Tibetan-style
temple named after a long-destroyed golden
chörten (Tibetan stupa).

Sleeping
Post Hotel (Yóuzhèng Bīnguǎn; ☎ 813 3133; 138 Huzhu
Lu; 互助路138号; dm Y10-14, d without bathroom Y36-
45, r with bathroom Y55-65) This long-time budget
choice is still as reliable as ever. You'll need
some training in the hot-water contraption
in the rooms with showers.

Yǎháo Huāyuán Bīnguǎn (☎ 814 8377; fax 817 1900;
150 Dongguan Dajie; 东关大街150号; tw Y160-180; ❄)
Rooms here are a bit snug, but they're much
nicer than any other midrange option and discounts of up to 40% make it a great deal. Take
bus 1 four stops from the train station.

Yínlóng Dàjiǔdiàn (☎ 616 6666; www.ylhotel.net; 36
Huanghe Lu; 黄河路36号; tw Y980; ❄ ❚ 💻) This

21-storey tower is surprisingly stylish, glamorous even, and easily the top place in town. Discounts of 30% are common.

Eating

Mǎlínhàn (Shuijing Xiang Market; dishes from Y5) If you're tired of the same old kebabs, Mr Ma and his family also skewer vegetables smothered in a special sauce. Take the western side of the market alley south from Xi Dajie for about 500m.

Daxin Jie night market (Daxin Jie; dishes from Y4) This is the best place for dinner. You can dine for pennies on grilled squid kebabs, fried potato slices and punnets of strawberries.

Xiǎoyuánmén Měishígōng (126 Dongguan Dajie; dishes Y18-24) This upmarket Muslim restaurant has a good reputation among locals. Look for the hanging red lanterns.

Yínlóng Dàjiǔdiàn (☎ 616 6666; 36 Huanghe Lu; dishes Y68; ◷ 6-9pm) This place has a blowout buffet that offers excellent value. The spread includes sushi and seafood, plus free beer!

Getting There & Away

AIR

There are flights available from Xīníng to Běijīng (Y1450), Chéngdū (Y990), Guǎngzhōu (Y1650), Shànghǎi (Y1850), Golmud (Y840, twice weekly) and Xī'ān (Y650, thrice weekly). There is also a twice-weekly flight to Lhasa (Y1720); at the time of research you still had to go through the CITS (p901) in order to purchase your ticket, but this should change in the future.

The **Civil Aviation Administration of China** (CAAC; Zhōngguó Mínháng; ☎ 818 9056; 32 Bayi Xilu; ◷ 8.30am-6.30pm) has a booking office on the eastern edge of town. To get there, take the eastbound bus 25 to Bayi Lu, or bus 28 from the train station.

BUS

The **long-distance bus station** (Jianguo Lu), near the train station, serves all destinations except Tǎ'ěr Sì. Foreigners are not allowed on the buses to Lhasa (Y355, 30 hours) but bus drivers will likely proposition you anyway.

For the overland route to Sêrshu in Sìchuān, head first for Yùshù and continue on from there via Xiêwú.

TRAIN

Xīníng has two express trains to Lánzhōu (hard/soft seat Y33/50, 2¾ hours) leaving at 12.12pm and 7.23pm, plus many more long-distance trains. There are three evening sleeper trains to Golmud (hard/soft sleepers Y131/202, 16 hours).

For information on trains from Lánzhōu to Lhasa, see p924.

You can buy tickets at the train station or **city train ticket office** (◷ 8.30am-noon, 1.30pm-5.30pm; 2nd fl, Post Office, Da Shizi; commission Y5).

Getting Around

The airport is 27km east of the city. A shuttle bus (Y16) leave two hours before flights from the Mínzhǔ Bīnguǎn on Huzhu Lu.

Bus 1 (Y1) runs from the train station along Dongguan Dajie to Da Shizi and the West Gate. Taxi flagfall is Y6, which covers the first 3km.

AROUND XĪNÍNG
Tǎ'ěr Sì 塔尔寺

One of the six great monasteries of the Yellow Hat sect of Tibetan Buddhism, **Tǎ'ěr Sì** (admission Y80; ◷ 8.30am-6pm), or Kumbum in Tibetan, is in the town of Huángzhōng, 26km south of Xīníng. It was built in 1577 on hallowed ground – the birthplace of Tsongkhapa, founder of the Yellow Hat sect.

BUSES FROM XĪNÍNG

Buses leaving from the long-distance bus station include the following:

Destination	Price	Duration	Frequency	Departs
Hēimǎhé	Y25.30	4hr	7 daily	7.30am-2pm
Lánzhōu	Y53	3hr	hourly	7.50am-6pm
Tóngrén	Y30	4hr	half-hourly	7.30am-5pm
Xúnhuà	Y26	5hr	half-hourly	7.20am-4.30pm
Yùshù	Y154	20hr	4 daily	12.30pm, 3.30pm, 4.30pm
Zhāngyè	Y69	9hr	3 daily	7.30am, 5.30pm, 6.30pm

While of enormous historic significance, Tǎ'ěr Sì today seems to have been relegated to museum status by Běijīng. The artwork and architecture are redeeming, yet the atmosphere and scenery pale in comparison with other monasteries in Amdo. If the thought of being led around a Tibetan monastery by a Chinese tour guide dressed in fake Tibetan clothes makes you wince, then spend your time at Labrang Monastery instead (see p856).

Nine temples are open, the most important being the Grand Hall of Golden Tiles, where a 11m-high *chörten* marks the spot of Tsongkhapa's birth. The monastery is also famous for its sculptures of human figures, animals and landscapes carved out of yak butter.

Admission tickets are sold at the building diagonally opposite the row of stupas. Photography is prohibited inside the temples.

SLEEPING
Kumbun Motel (Chányuè Zhàn; 禅越栈; dm Y20, tw with bathroom Y160) If for some reason you want to spend the night, this motel is situated in the old monks' quarters.

GETTING THERE & AWAY
The best bet is to take one of the shared taxis (Y6 per seat) that queue up at the Kunlun Bridge traffic circle south of the West Gate (Xī Mén). Bus 3 runs here from the train station.

If you take a minibus (Y4) back to Xīníng, you may be dropped at the private **bus station** (26 Xiguan Dajie), from where buses 22 or 29 will take you into the centre of town.

Píng'ān
About 30km southeast of Píng'ān, in the sleepy village of Taktser (Hóngyá; 红崖) is the **birthplace of the Dalai Lama** (dìshísì dálài gùjū; 第十四达赖故居). The building, a former school, is (perhaps surprisingly) open to visitors and you can visit the room where his Holiness was born (marked by a golden *chörten*), as well as a restored chapel that has his former bed and throne. A side room displays some old family photos, including those of the Dalai Lama's parents, sister and brothers.

The Dalai Lama last visited here in 1955 en route to Beijing to meet with Chairman Mao. The previous (13th) Dalai Lama paused here en route to Labrang just long enough predict his own next reincarnation. Spot the building by its large wooden gate tied with *katags* (white ceremonial scarves).

Minibuses shuttle frequently from Xīníng to Píng'ān (40 minutes), from where you can hire a minivan for around Y80 for the half day. The route takes you through Sānhé and Shíhuīyáo villages, before the final 6km climb to Taktser village. Alternatively, minivans run when full to Shíhuīyáo (石灰窑), from where it's a tough hour's walk.

On the way back, just 2km from Píng'ān, you could visit **Báimǎ Sì** (白马寺), a dramatic cliff-front temple that looks better the further you are from it.

QĪNGHǍI HÚ 青海湖
☎ 0970
Qīnghǎi Hú (Lake Kokonor) is a somewhat surreal-looking saline lake west of Xīníng. The huge lake (more like an inland sea) has often served as the symbolic midway point between Tibet and Mongolia. It was here in 1578 that the Mongolian leader Altan Khan conferred upon Sonam Gyatso (then head of the Gelugpa sect) the title of Dalai Lama, *dalai* being the Mongolian translation of *gyatso*, or ocean.

The main attraction is **Niǎo Dǎo** (鸟岛; Bird Island; admission Y58), located on the western side of the lake, and about 300km from Xīníng. It's a breeding ground for thousands of wild geese, gulls, cormorants, sandpipers, extremely rare black-necked cranes and other bird species. Perhaps the most interesting are the bar-headed geese. These hardy birds migrate over the Himalayas to spend winter on the Indian plains and have been spotted flying at altitudes of 10,000m. You will only see great numbers of birds during the breeding season between March and early June. Niǎo Dǎo is no longer an island, although it used to be before the lake receded and made it part of the mainland.

Be aware that tourism here is depleting the native fish population, which the birds depend upon for survival. Stating that you don't eat fish (wǒ bù chī yú; 我不吃鱼) well in advance of any meals is highly encouraged.

Qīnghǎi Hú is also ground zero in China's struggle against avian flu. If there has been an outbreak recently, you may find the lake is off limits to visitors.

Tours
Between May and early October, tour buses run daily to Niǎo Dǎo (four hours). CTS in Xīníng (p901) charges Y150, transport only,

for a long day trip (8am to 5pm). Most day trips visit the closer, uninteresting Jiāngxīgōu harbour – if you want any amount of time at Niǎo Dǎo, you are better off with a two-day trip.

Tours generally include a brief stop at the twin pagodas of Sun Moon Pass (Rìyuè Shānkǒu; admission Y25), where Princess Wencheng stopped in the year 641 en route to Tibet (p910).

Sleeping & Eating

Niǎo Dǎo Bīnguǎn (鸟岛宾馆; ☎ 865 2447; dm/tw Y20/160) If you're not content with a day trip, you can stay here overnight. It's north of Hēimǎhé on the west side of the lake, and has a restaurant on the premises.

Getting There & Away

Unfortunately there are no public buses to Niǎo Dǎo. The closest you can get is to the small settlement of Hēimǎhé, 50km away, from where a taxi will cost Y50. From Xīníng there are six departures to Hēimǎhé (Y33, four hours) between 7.45am and 3.30pm; the return schedule is similar.

TÓNGRÉN (REPKONG) 同仁

☎ 0973

Tóngrén (Repkong in Tibetan) is an amiable midsized monastery town of Tibetan monks and Hui shop owners, both of whom cater to the valley's many monasteries. For several centuries now, the villages outside town have been famous for producing some of the Tibetan world's best *thangkas* and painted statues, so much so that an entire school of Tibetan art is named after the town.

Visiting the monastery Wútún Sì (right) not only gives you a chance to meet the artists, but also to purchase a painting or two, fresh off the easel. You can't change money here, so have a little extra Renminbi on hand, in case something strikes your fancy.

The villages surrounding the monasteries are a mixture of Tibetans and Tu, distant cousins of the Mongols.

Sights

RONGWO GONCHEN GOMPA 隆务寺

Tóngrén's main **monastery** (Lóngwù Sì; admission Y18) is a huge and rambling maze of renovated chapels and monks' residences, dating from 1301. It's well worth a wander, especially in the morning, though what you actually get

to see depends on which chapels are open. The road leading to the monastery is lined with shops selling everything a Tibetan Buddhist could want, from monk's cloaks to yak butter.

WÚTÚN SÌ 吾屯寺

Sengeshong village, 6km from Tóngrén, is the place to head if you're interested in Tibetan art. There are two monasteries, divided into an **Upper (Yango) Monastery** (上寺; Shàng Sì; admission Y10), closest to town, and a **Lower (Mango) Monastery** (下寺; Xià Sì; admission Y10). The monks will show you around whatever chapels happen to be open and then take you to a showroom or workshop. These are no amateur artists – commissions for their work come in all the way from Lhasa, and prices aren't cheap. Consider that even a small *thangka* takes a minimum of one month to paint. Note that no-one speaks English.

The Lower Monastery is easily recognisable by its eight large *chörten* out front. The 100-year-old Jampa Lhakhang and the new chapels dedicated to Chenresig and Tsongkhapa are worth a look.

The Upper Monastery has the better art school. Worth visiting here is the old *dukhang* (assembly hall) and the new chapel dedicated to Maitreya (Shampa in Amdo dialect). The murals here are superb.

To get here, take a minivan (Y2 per seat) from Tóngrén. Visit in the mornings for the best chance of finding the chapels open.

GOMAR GOMPA 郭麻日寺

A pleasant hike across the valley from Wútún Sì is the mysterious 400-year-old **Gomar Gompa** (Guōmárì Sì; admission Y10), which resembles a medieval walled village. There are supposedly 130 monks in residence but the place always seems to be deserted. Next to the entrance is an enormous modern *chörten*.

From here you could walk back to Tóngrén in an hour along the west edge of the river, passing **Nyentok Gompa** (Niándōuhū Sì; 年都乎寺) en route.

Further up the valley is **Gasar Gompa**, marked by its distinctive eight *chörtens*.

Festivals & Events

Besides the **Monlam Festival** (see Xiàhé, p857) at the beginning of the Tibetan New Year, Tóngrén is particularly famous for its five-day body-piercing **Lurol (Shaman) Festival**, beginning

BUSES FROM TÓNGRÉN

Destination	Price	Duration	Frequency	Departs
Línxià	Y34	3hr	1 daily	8am
Xiàhé	Y21	3hr	1 daily	8am
Xīníng	Y30	4hr	hourly	7.20am-4pm
Xúnhuà	Y14	2½hr	5 daily	8am-3pm

on the 21st day of the sixth lunar month (July or August). Also called the 'shaman' festival, the event has its roots in the pre-Buddhist Bön religion and takes place in four different villages on different days.

Sleeping & Eating

Sānxin Bīnguǎn (三鑫宾馆; ☎ 872 5776; 80 Zhongshan Lu; 中山路80号; dm Y15, s/d with bathroom Y60/70) An excellent-value place next to the market, with hot water available only in the en suite rooms.

Huángnán Bīnguǎn (黄南宾馆; ☎ 872 2293; 18 Zhongshan Lu; 中山路18号; dm Y15, tw Y70-288) This foreigner-friendly place has a wide range of rooms, the best of which are set back off the road. Rooms are dark but clean.

Homeland of Rebkong Arts Restaurant (Règòng Yìréngé; 热贡艺人阁; Zhongshan Lu; dishes from Y5) A cosy Tibetan-style restaurant run by the Huángnán Bīnguǎn serving Chinese and some Tibetan dishes. There's an English menu.

Getting There & Away

The road to/from Xiàhé is particularly scenic, passing some dramatic red rock scenery and the impressive Gartse Gompa, where local Tibetan herders board the bus to sell fresh yoghurt.

MENGDA NATURE RESERVE
孟达天池

This pleasant **reserve** (Mèngdá Tiān Chí; admission Y25) is located in the mountains above the Yellow River, 190km southeast of Xīníng. The focus of the reserve is Heaven Lake (Tiān Chí), which is a sacred lake for both the local Salar Muslims and Tibetan Buddhists. The Salar have their origins in Samarkand and speak an isolated Turkic language, giving the nearby crossroad town of Jiēzǐ a Central Asian feel.

Mengda is a spectacular one-hour bus ride from Xúnhuà, and the roadside scenery is every bit as beautiful as the reserve itself. The road is cut into arid cliffs, following the coppery-green Yellow River as it snakes its way along below.

You need to hire a minivan (Y60) to get off the main road to the reserve car park, from where it's a stiff 40-minute hike up to the lake. You can walk around the lake in half an hour. You could take a minivan (from outside Xúnhuà bus station) bound for Dàhéjiā (Y8) to the turn-off and then hitch or take a motorbike taxi the remaining 6km up to the car park.

From May to October it's possible to stay at the lakeshore **Báiyún Shānzhuāng Bīnguǎn** (白云山庄宾馆; tw Y120-180) or you can stay in the nearby town of Xúnhuà (循化) at the **Jiāotōng Bīnguǎn** (交通宾馆; dm Y13-30, tw Y70-90), next door to the bus station.

From Xúnhuà there are six daily buses to Línxià (Y19, three hours); four daily buses to Tóngrén (Y14, 2½ hours); and hourly buses to Xīníng (Y25, five hours).

GOLMUD 格尔木
☎ 0979 / pop 200,000

Unless you are an engineer or an escaped convict on the run, the only reason to visit this strange outpost in the oblivion end of China is to continue overland into Tibet. While it isn't a terrible place, you probably would not want to stay around Golmud (Géěrmù) more than a day, and few visitors do. The booming town owes its existence to mining and oil drilling and, most recently, to the construction of the train line to Lhasa, for which it is a logistical base.

Information

Bank of China (Zhōngguó Yínháng; cnr Kunlun & Chaidamu Lu; ☐ 8.30am-6.30pm Mon-Fri, 10am-4pm Sat & Sun) You can change travellers cheques and cash here.

CITS (Zhōngguó Guójì Lǚxíngshè; ☎ 841 2764; ☐ 8.30am-noon & 2.30-6pm Mon-Fri) CITS has offices on the 2nd floor of the Golmud Hotel and, less reliably, at the Tibet bus station. If the office is closed the hotel reception can call and someone will come. If you're planning to go to Lhasa legally, this is your first stop (see opposite).

Internet Plaza (Liántōng Wǎngyuàn; China Unicom Bldg, cnr Zhongshan Lu & Bayi Lu; per hr Y2; ☐ 24hr)

GOLMUD 格尔木

INFORMATION

Bank of China 中国银行	**1** A2
CITS 中国国际旅行社	(see 6)
CITS 中国国际旅行社	(see 13)
Internet Plaza 联他网苑	**2** A1
Post Office 邮局	**3** B2
Post Office 邮局	(see 6)
PSB 公安局	**4** B2
Rùnzéyuán Wǎngbā 润泽源网吧	**5** A2

SLEEPING

Golmud Hotel 格尔木宾馆	**6** A2
Golmud Mansions 格尔木大厦	**7** B2

EATING

Jiale Supermarket 家乐超市	**8** A1
Xī āngsìhǎi Xiǎochǎo 香四海小炒	**9** A1
Ā lán Cāntīng 阿兰餐厅	**10** A1

TRANSPORT

CAAC 机场售票处	**11** B2
Golmud Bus Station 长途汽车站	**12** B2
Tibet Bus Station 西藏汽车站	**13** A1

Post office (yóujú; Chaidamu Lu) There's a branch office in front of the Golmud Hotel.

PSB (Gōngānjú; Chaidamu Lu; 8am-noon & 2.30-5pm Mon-Fri) Bus 2 comes here from the train station.

Rùnzéyuán Wǎngbā (56-14 Kunlun Lu; per hr Y2; 24hr) Internet access.

Sleeping & Eating

Golmud Mansions (Gēěrmù Dàshà; ☎ 845 2208; 33 Yingbin Lu; 迎宾路33号) dm Y30, tw Y120-238) This good option is conveniently located next to the bus and train stations, with good triple-bed dorms but no common showers.

Golmud Hotel (Gēěrmù Bīnguǎn; ☎ 842 4288; 219 Kunlun Zhonglu; 昆仑中路219号; r without bathroom Y40, tw with

bathroom Y100-258) There are two buildings – the *bīnguǎn* (upmarket hotel) and the *zhāodàisuǒ* (hostel). Get the rooms with a bathroom (Y120) in the hostel wing for best value. Hot water in the common showers can be temperamental.

Xiāngsìhǎi Xiǎochǎo (Kunlun Lu; dishes Y5-20) Just across from the main gate of the Golmud Hotel, this is a great Sichuanese restaurant. The *guōbā ròupiàn* (pork with rice crisps) is enough for two.

Ālán Cāntīng (48-1 Bayi Lu; dishes from Y6) is a good Muslim restaurant that serves great *gànbàn miàn* (spaghetti-style noodles with meat sauce; 干扳面).

Jiale Supermarket (Jiālè Chāoshì; cnr Kunlun & Bayi Lu) Located underground, this is a good place to stock up on food for the bus ride.

Getting There & Away

AIR

Nobody actually flies to Golmud, but if you want to buck the trend, the city has four weekly flights to Xīníng (Y920) and Chéngdū (Y1350). Airport buses (Y10) depart from **CAAC** (☎ 842 3333; Chaidamu Lu), or take a taxi (Y30).

BUS

The Golmud bus station is opposite the train station. The 524km trip from Golmud to Dūnhuáng departs twice daily, at 8am (Y88, eight hours) and 6pm (Y95 to Y100, 12 hours); the latter is a sleeper. It's a scenic trip through the desert and mountains, but take a jacket as it can get cold at night. You may need to pick up an annoying permit *(lǚxíng zhèng)* at the PSB (Y50) before you buy your ticket – remember it's closed weekends.

Buses to Lhasa depart from the **Tibet Bus Station** (Xīzàng Chēzhàn; Xizang Lu) at 3pm and take anywhere from 20 to 25 hours; see p915.

If you're planning on taking the southern Silk Road to Kashgar, kick things off with the 3pm sleeper bus to Huātǔgōu (Y175; 14 hours), from where there are morning buses to Charklik (Ruòqiāng) in Xīnjiāng.

TRAIN

Express trains depart in the evening for Xīníng (train 5702, 14 hours) and Lánzhōu (train N904, 18 hours). A hard sleeper berth to Xīníng costs Y131 to Y156. Avoid the slower local train (8760).

Transport to Tibet was all up in the air at the time of research. Practical details for the Lhasa train were sketchy at time of writing. No

QĪNGHǍI

trains actually start in Golmud but you should be able to buy tickets on a through train, of which there are four or five a day. A hard seat on the morning train costs Y143 but at the time of writing you couldn't buy a ticket at the train station without first shelling out Y1440 to CITS for a tour/permit. This may change. Bear in mind that long-distance trains often arrive a few hours late. The 1140km trip takes around 15 hours. See p924 for more.

Getting Around

Bus 1 (Y1) runs from the train station to the Golmud Hotel. Taxis in town cost Y5.

MT AMNYE MACHEN 阿尼玛卿山

The 6282m peak of Machen Kangri, or Mt Amnye Machen, is Amdo's most sacred mountain – it's eastern Tibet's equivalent to Mt Kailash in western Tibet. Tibetan pilgrims travel for weeks to circumambulate the peak, believing it to be home to the protector deity Machen Pomra. The circuit's sacred geography and wild mountain scenery make it a fantastic, though adventurous, trekking destination.

The full circuit takes seven to nine days, or five on a horse, though many foreigners limit themselves to a half circuit. Several monasteries lie alongside the route, including Guri Gompa near Xiàdàwǔ and Chörten Kharpo (White Stupa) at Chuwarna. Some nearby spots are linked to the Tibetan hero Gesar of Ling.

Independent trekkers can hire pack horses and Tibetan- and Chinese-speaking guides (Y50 per day for a horse) from Xuěshān and Xiàdàwǔ, the two main starting points for the trek, but beyond that you need to be totally self-sufficient. Organised trips are possible but not cheap. Travel agencies such as **Qinghai Tibet Adventures** (Map p902; Sānjiāngyuán Tànxiǎn Lǚxíngshè; ☎ 824 5548; www.cqta.com; Rm 301, 13 Bei Dajie) and **Wind Horse Adventure Tours** (Xīhǎi Gōngmín Chūrùjìng Fúwùzhōngxīn; www.windhorseadventuretours.com; ☎ 824 4629; Nan Dajie) arrange all-inclusive trips for around US$80 to US$110 per day. At the mountain you may find yourself asked for an admission fee of Y100, as well as an 'environmental fee' of Y30 per day.

With almost all of the route above 4000m, and the highest pass hitting 4600m, it's essential to acclimatise before setting off, preferably by spending a night or two at nearby Mǎqìn (3760m). You can make a good excursion

70km north of town to **Rabgya Gompa** (Lājiā Sì; 拉加寺), an important branch of Tibet's Sera Monastery. The best months to trek are May, June and September.

Getting There & Away

You can approach the mountain from two directions. It's possible to take the bus to Mǎqìn (Tawo) and then hitch or hire a minivan out to Xuěshān (Chuwarna), the traditional starting point of the kora (pilgram path). Buses to Mǎqìn (nine hours) depart Xīníng at 8.45am (Y62) and 9.30am (Y77) and there are also evening sleepers (Y82).

From the west, first get yourself to Mǎduō or Huāshíxiá, and then find a jeep to Xiàdàwǔ. From Xīníng, buses to Mǎduō (Y83, 10 hours) leave daily at 8am.

YÙSHÙ (JYEKUNDO) 玉树
☎ 0976

Yùshù (Jyekundo) is one of the remotest corners of one of the remotest provinces of China. Straddling the grasslands of Amdo to the north and the deep forested valleys of Kham to the south, the prefecture is overwhelmingly (97%) Tibetan and dotted with dozens of impressive monasteries.

Long an important caravan town along the trade routes to Tibet, Yùshù bursts at the seams during its three-day horse festival (from 25 July), when tens of thousands of Tibetans swagger into town. At any time of year, you'll see crowds of Tibetans hunkered down in the central square selling yartse gompa, a highly valued medicinal caterpillar fungus collected from the surrounding grasslands.

The few foreigners who make it out here are mostly headed along the wonderful overland route to western Sìchuān, though it is theoretically possible to continue south to Nangchen and on to remotest eastern Tibet.

Note that there's nowhere to change money in Yùshù.

Information

Etóng Tiānxià Wǎngbā (7-7 Minzhu Lu; per hr Y3) Internet access, down a side alley.

Post office (yóujú; Shengli Lu; ⏰ 9.30am-5.30pm)

PSB (Gōngānjú; ☎ 882 8915; 144 Minzhu Lu; ⏰ 9am-noon, 3-6pm Mon-Fri) Can extend visas.

Yángguāng Wǎngbā (Shengli Lu; per hr Y3; ⏰ 24hr) Internet access.

YÙSHÙ (JYEKUNDO) 玉树

warrior-god whose epic deeds are remembered in the world's longest epic poem of the same name.

At dusk join local pilgrims on a walk around the white **Namgyal Chörten** in the west of town.

Sights

The **Jyekundo Dondrubling Monastery** (Jiégǔ Sì) has a dramatic location in a natural bowl overlooking the town. First built in 1398, the rebuilt main assembly hall is very atmospheric, with a fantastic inner sanctum of towering Buddhas. The monks here are friendly and you'll probably get invited in for a cup of butter tea. A *kora* leads up the hill behind the monastery for great views of the town. The best way to get here is to go on foot through the old town via the atmospheric *mani lhakhang* (chapel containing a large prayer wheel). Alternatively get a taxi for Y10.

One sight you shouldn't miss is the **Sengze Gyanak Mani** (Mání Shíchéng; 嘛尼石城), which is one of the largest *mani* walls in Tibet, founded in 1715 and consisting of an estimated two billion mantras that are carved in stone. Pilgrims circumambulate the wall continuously, tuning rows of prayer wheels, some of which are over 10m tall. The wall is 3km east of town in Xīnzhài (新寨) village. Minibuses 1 and 2 run here from town (Y1).

The town's dramatic central statue is of King Gesar of Ling, a revered Tibetan

Sleeping & Eating

Wàimào Bīnguǎn (Shengli Lu; 胜利路; tw without bathroom Y60-80, tw with bathroom Y80-120) This is a good bet, just five minutes from the bus station. The friendly floor ladies do their best to keep the bathroom odours under control and the helpful manager can arrange a laundry service. Rooms have a kettle and basin for washing clothes.

Yùshù Bīnguǎn (☎ 882 2999; 12 Minzhu Lu; 民主路 12号; tw Y80, tw with bathroom Y140; 🛜) This place is located in a new block and will offer the best rooms in town when finished in 2007.

Labu Monastery Hotel (Lābùsì Bīnguǎn; ☎ 882 7369; Shengli Lu; 胜利路; tw Y80, tw with bathroom Y140-160) It's less about yak butter and more about en suite bathrooms at this other monastery-run place. The rooms are clean and the dorms have common showers in the courtyard.

Jiégǔ Sì Bīnguǎn (☎ 882 8018; 67 Hongwei Lu; 红卫 路67号; dm Y10-20, d Y60, tw Y150) This monastery guesthouse, 250m from the central crossroads, offers good value dorms and the monks add plenty of local flavour.

Shengli Lu is lined with tiny Muslim and *shāguō* (mini-hotpot) restaurants. For a more Tibetan atmosphere try the upstairs booths of the **Snowlands Namtso Restaurant** (Xuěyù Nàmùcuò Hú Fànguǎn; teas Y5-8, dishes Y10-30) on Hongwei Lu.

Getting There & Away
AIR
Yùshù's new airport, 25km south of town at the old military airfield in Batang, hadn't opened at the time of research but you can expect weekly flights to Xīníng and maybe even Lhasa.

BUS
Yùshù is an intimidating 20-hour, 820km-long sleeper bus ride across the grasslands from Xīníng. The trip isn't as bad as it sounds but be prepared for an altitude headache (much of the route is above 4200m) and get a window berth so you can at least suck in a modicum of fresh air to dilute all the cigarette smoke. Buy your ticket the day before to guarantee a good berth. Formal toilet stops are few and far between.

Sleepers leave Yùshù's main bus station at noon and 1pm for Xīníng (Y154). Nonsleepers leave at 8.30am and 9am (Y115) and pass through Mǎduō (Y47) around 3pm.

For Sìchuān there is a daily bus to Sêrshu (Shíqú) at 7.30am (Y30, five hours) from Hongwei Lu, which runs via Xiēwú (Y8) and the 4700m Nganba-la pass.

The separate prefectural bus station (*zhōu kèyùnzhàn*) runs a daily buses to Gānzī (Y134) at 8am, though you'd be nuts to take the direct sleeper bus to Chéngdū (Y280, 30 hours, every other day).

Other destinations are more hit and miss. You should be able to track down daily buses to Záduō (Y40) and Chēngduō (Y20) at 8am. Cramped minivans depart when full from the main square for Zhìduō (Y40 per person) and Qūmácài (Y50).

AROUND YÙSHÙ
There are lots of monasteries around Yùshù and you could spend a couple of great days exploring the surrounding valleys.

Princess Wencheng Temple
文成公主庙
Hidden down a side valley, 20km south of Yùshù, this famous **temple** (Wénchéng Gōngzhǔ Miào; admission Y10) marks the spot where Chinese Princess Wencheng paused for a month en route to marry (and eventually convert to Buddhism) King Songtsen Gampo of Tibet. The inner chapel has a rock carving of the Tibetan god Vairocana (Nampa Namse in Tibetan) that allegedly dates from the 8th century.

It's well worth joining the pilgrims on the 40-minute *kora* above the temple. The trail ascends from the end of a row of eight *chörtens*, just past an ancient rock inscription in Tibetan, and climbs through webs of prayer flags to great views of the gorge.

From the temple you can make a 30-minute detour on foot back towards the main road and then south to **Zhira Gompa** (Jírán Sì; 吉然寺). The small monastery backs onto a cliff riddled with holy caves, and has a meditation retreat and *kora*. At the far end of the *kora*, continue south for 15 minutes to the impressive Chörten Kharpo (White Stupa) sky burial site.

On the way back to Yùshù you can stop off at sprawling **Trangu Gompa** (Chángǔ Sì; 禅古寺), which has some fine modern Repkong-style murals in its twin assembly halls.

A monastery minibus runs to the temple from Yùshù at 10am (Y4), passing Trangu Gompa (Y2) en route, and returning around 1pm. Hitching back shouldn't be a problem. A return minivan costs around Y50.

Yùshù to Xiēwú
Just 11km north of Yùshù is the large **Domkar Gompa** (Dāngkǎ Sì; 当卡寺), a steep 20-minute hike (or short drive) up the hillside. Home to 200 monks, most of the chapels here have been newly renovated. From the southern chapels it's a five-minute walk to a sky-burial spot, from where you can hike down to Die-ger (Dōngfēng) village and catch a lift back to Yùshù.

Further on the road crosses the Tōngtiān Hé over a new bridge. A side road branches off to the right for 6km (1½ hours' walk) to **Sebda Gompa** (Sāibā Sì; 赛巴寺), an excellent potential day trip from Yùshù. The turn-off is just north of the checkpost and marked by a 'Welcome to Sebda' sign. After 20 minutes of walking, branch off up the side valley (don't cross the bridge). The main assembly hall is impressive but most surprising is the new chapel featuring a huge 18m statue of Guru Rinpoche. The adjacent **ethnographic museum** (admission Y5) has some offbeat gems and good English captions. A huge 38m rock carving of the Chenresig (the Bodhisattva of Compassion) is being built on the cliff next door. If you have more time you can explore the ruins of the old monastery on the ridge behind the *gompa* or do some great hiking in the opposite valley.

Finally, at Xiēwú village, by the turn-off to Sêrshu, is the Sakyapa-school **Drogon Gompa** (Xiēwú Sì; 歇武寺), on a fine hillside location. Atop the hill is the scary *gönkhang* (protector chapel), adorned with snarling stuffed wolves and Tantric masks. Only men may enter this chapel.

Minivans buzz up and down this road (Y10), or you can take the 8am Sêrshu bus to Xiēwú and then work your way back. Hiring a minivan for the day is the safest bet.

Nangchen 囊谦

Perhaps the most ambitious route is south to the former Tibetan kingdom of Nangchen, and then on to Riwoche and Chamdo in eastern Tibet. The paved road to Nangchen goes over three passes and via Lungshi Gompa (Lóngxī Sì; 龙西寺) en route.

Minivans and the odd Land Cruiser leave for Nangchen (Nángqiān; Y40 per seat, three hours) from Yùshù's main bus station when full, sometime around 8am. Stay overnight at the **Nángqiān Bīnguǎn** (囊谦宾馆; dm Y30, tw Y150), before taking another minivan for the rough 245km route to Riwoche (Y100 per person). You'll have to bluff your way past the checkpoint at the Tibetan border and bear in mind that without a permit you may well get sent back.

Tibet 西藏

In China, hyperbole and metaphorical association rule – everything is described as 'the (blank) of (blank)'. How remarkable is Tibet (Xīzàng, or the 'Western Treasure House' in Chinese), then, that its most famed moniker – 'the Rooftop of the World' – is an understatement? Saying Tibet is atop a vast plateau that is 4000m to 5000m high hardly begins to describe things.

Say 'Tibet'. Imagine the highest of azure skies; serene *drokpas* (nomads) atop their horses; city-state temples; rivers of orange-clad monks and flapping prayer flags. It is one-eighth of China's area (three Texases!) but home to a mere 2.7 million people. Its forbiddenness and isolation has helped seal the mesmerising grip Tibet has long held on the western mind.

Of course, there's that one thorny modern issue. There simply seems no middle ground on the dilemma of China and Tibet – one must either believe that the opportunistic Han are 'ruin- ing' Shangri-la, or that they wrested literally millions of slaves from feudal serfdom. The truth, as always, lies somewhere in between. Loathe it, love it, or remain uncomfortably ambivalent about it, Chinese rule is likely (and Chinese cultural influence *definitely*) here to stay.

In the end, simply remember this as you travel around: living in the harshest of environments and under endless cultural strain, Tibetans have never had it easy. Remarkably resilient, they have managed to maintain not only their culture and religion, but also their joyful outlook.

The verdant Yarlung Tsangpo (Brahmaputra) valley is the soul of Tibet. Western Tibet is higher still, and its spiritual and geographical focal point is sacred Mt Kailash (Kang Rinpoche), in whose vicinity rise the sources of the Indus, Sutlej and Brahmaputra Rivers.

HIGHLIGHTS

- Make a personal pilgrimage and be awed by the Potala Palace, Jokhang Temple and Barkhor circuit in the holy city of **Lhasa** (p917)

- Wind your way up Gyantse's **Kumbum Chörten** (p929), Tibet's architectural master- piece

- Breathe heavily and marvel at the indescrib- able colours at **Nam-tso Lake** (p927)

- Feel your soul change as you gaze at a Mt Everest sunrise from **Rongphu Monastery** (p932)

- 'Enjoy' the teeth-rattling trip on the Friendship Hwy from **Lhasa to Kathmandu** (p915) over the plateau's high passes and down into the subcontinent, before this bad boy gets paved

- Scrape the sky as you traverse the wilds of Tibet (and Qīnghǎi) on the **Qinghai–Tibet railway** (p924), the world's highest and a monumental feat of engineering

▪ POPULATION: 2.7 MILLION   ▪ www.tibet.com

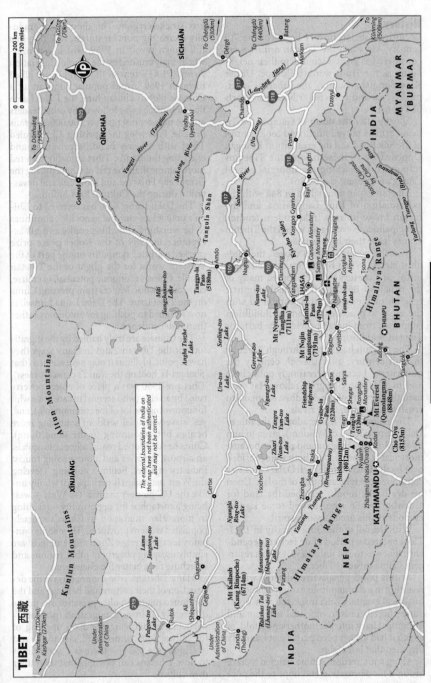

TIBET 西藏

0 — 200 km
0 — 120 miles

The external boundaries of India on this map have not been authenticated and may not be correct.

History

Recorded Tibetan history began in the 7th century AD when the Tibetan armies were considered as great a scourge to their neighbours as the Huns were to Europe. Under King Songtsen Gampo, the Tibetans occupied Nepal and collected tribute from parts of Yúnnán.

Shortly after the death of Gampo, the Tibetan armies moved north and took control of the Silk Road and the great city of Kashgar. Opposed by Chinese troops, the Tibetans responded by sacking the imperial city of Chang'an (present-day Xī'ān).

Tibetan expansion halted in 842 with the assassination of King Langdarma, and the region broke up into independent feuding principalities. Never again would the Tibetan armies leave their high plateau.

Into the power vacuum moved the Buddhist clergy. When Buddhism reached Tibet in the 3rd century AD, it adopted many of the rituals of Bön, the traditional animistic religion of the region; this, combined with the esoteric practices of Tantric Buddhism (imported from India), provided the basis for Tibetan Buddhism.

The religion had spread through Tibet by the 7th century; after the 9th century the monasteries became increasingly politicised; and in 1641 the Gelugpa (Yellow Hat sect) used the support of the Buddhist Mongols to crush the Sakyapa, their rivals.

The Yellow Hats' leader adopted the title of Dalai Lama (Ocean of Wisdom), given to him by the Mongols; religion and politics became inextricably entwined and both were presided over by the Dalai Lama. Each Dalai Lama was considered the reincarnation of the last. Upon his death, the monks searched the land for a newborn child who showed some sign of embodying his predecessor's spirit.

With the fall of the Qing dynasty in 1911, Tibet entered a period of de facto independence that was to last until 1950, when a resurgent China invaded Tibet.

At this point perspectives diverge wildly, resulting in a *Rashomon*-like interpretation of historical events. China insisted it was 'liberating' the Tibetans from feudal serfdom and bringing it back into the motherland's fold, of which it had always been part. Tibet naturally disputed that last claim.

Along with freedom, China claimed to have brought modernisation and hope to the poverty-stricken region. This didn't stem gradually increasing popular unrest, resulting in a full-blown revolt in 1959, which was overwhelmingly crushed by the People's Liberation Army (PLA) – tens of thousands were killed through 1960. Amid popular rumours of a Chinese plot to kidnap him, the Dalai Lama fled to India; he was followed by other leaders and he now represents over 100,000 Tibetans in exile. Following the uprising, China ruled Tibet with a heavy hand, imprisoning and executing thousands. Tibet arguably suffered more famine than the rest of China during the Great Leap Forward and more cultural devastation during the Cultural Revolution.

The Dalai Lama, who has referred to China's policies as 'cultural genocide', continues to be worshipped by his people, and his acceptance in 1989 of the Nobel peace prize marked a greater sympathy on the part of the Western world for the plight of the Tibetan people. China's economic potential, of course, cows many world leaders from pressing China on the Tibet issue. The Dalai Lama himself is now resigned to pushing for autonomy rather than independence.

The Chinese are truly baffled by the ingratitude of the Tibetans, and in many ways they have a point. Idyllic as it may have seemed (that 'Shangri-la' hold on the world's consciousness), Tibet pre-1950 was a place of abject poverty ruled by an elite (who seemed to care not a whit for improving the lot of the common folk), and, yes, slavery (feudal serfdom sounding more benign but amounting to the same thing). China has developed roads, schools, hospitals, an airport, factories and a burgeoning tourist industry in Tibet. Beijing's ongoing 'Develop the West' campaign is perhaps not wholly unlike the US' pioneer mantra 'Go West' – west being a metaphor for opportunity – resulting in more Han migration to China's sparsely populated western provinces. (Have some sympathy for the Average Zhou migrant; most are simply escaping poverty in other regions and searching for a better life elsewhere.)

Many Tibetans, who cannot forgive the destruction of their culture and heritage and the continued military/police presence, see things differently. If inward migration increases – particularly following the 2006 opening of the railway line connecting Lhasa to the rest of China (see p924) – there is a question as to how Tibetans can possibly maintain their own culture.

For help with Tibetan language, see the Language chapter, p985.

Climate

Most of Tibet is a high-altitude desert plateau at more than 4000m and many passes exceed 5000m. Days in summer (June to September) are warm, sunny and dry, and you can expect some rainfall in southern Tibet in the evenings, but temperatures drop quickly when it gets dark. The best time to visit depends on what part of Tibet you're heading to, but for most places pick May, June or October.

You can now buy low-grade trekking gear in Lhasa, but it is advisable to bring sunscreen, lip balm, deodorant, a water purification system and any medication you might need from home. Travellers will need to be particularly aware of acute mountain sickness (AMS); for a full discussion of prevention and treatment, see p982.

Getting There & Away

Although there are five major road routes to Lhasa, foreigners are officially allowed to use the Nepal and Qīnghǎi routes only. For more information on the new rail line, see p916 and p924.

NEPAL ROUTE

The 920km road connecting Lhasa with Kathmandu is known as the Friendship Hwy. It's a spectacular trip over high passes and across the Tibetan plateau, the highest point being Gyatso-la pass (5220m) outside Lhatse. The rough terrain truly taxes the body and spirit (though paving has already started).

By far the most popular option for the trip is renting a Land Cruiser and driver through a travel agency in Lhasa (p924). A five-day Land Cruiser trip from Lhasa to the Nepalese border, via Shigatse, Everest Base Camp (EBC) and Tingri costs about Y1400 per person. It's also possible to bus and hitchhike along the Friendship Hwy. Public transport runs as far as Shegar (sometimes called New Tingri) and the occasional bus runs all the way from Shigatse to Zhāngmù.

When travelling from Nepal to Lhasa, foreigners must arrange transport and permits through travel agencies in Kathmandu (see Travel Restrictions, p916). Be very careful with whom you organise your trip – the vast majority of complaints about Tibet have been about travel agencies in Kathmandu.

Whatever you do, when coming from Nepal do *not* underestimate the sudden rise in elevation; altitude sickness is all too common.

At the time of writing, travel agencies in Kathmandu were offering budget tours to Lhasa from US$130 to US$150 for a five-day overland bus/jeep trip. Seven-day trips via EBC cost roughly US$400 per person. For a flight to Lhasa you need to buy a three-day tour for US$360. This includes the flight ticket (US$273), airport transfers in Kathmandu and Lhasa, Tibetan Tourism Bureau (TTB) permits and dormitory accommodation for three nights in Lhasa.

QĪNGHǍI ROUTE

A rail network connecting Lhasa to Qīnghǎi is up and running and offers a modern alternative to buses. For more information see p924.

The monotonous 1754km road that connects Xīníng with Lhasa via Golmud crosses the desolate, barren and virtually uninhabited northern Tibetan plateau. The highest point is the Tanggu-la pass (5180m).

The Xīníng bus station staff won't deal with walk-in tourists. Most travellers must first head to Golmud, where China International Travel Services (CITS; p906) has an iron grip on foreign bus tickets from Golmud to Lhasa – all travellers must buy their tickets through the travel agency, and they pay dearly for it. The trip costs more than Y1700 (which doesn't include entrance fees into Lhasa).

Buses depart from the **Tibet Bus Station** (Xizang Lu) at 3pm and take anywhere from 20 to 25 hours (though 30 isn't unheard of), assuming the weather, traffic and bus engine cooperate. The other option is to hang around the regular bus station and make a deal with one of the drivers. They ask for about Y600 (bus) or Y800 (jeep), which includes a bribe for the Public Security Bureau (PSB). There's definitely a risk involved, and there's no way to guarantee that you won't be fined and sent back – or worse. Ideally the bulk of the payment should be made only once you've arrived.

Take supplies and warm clothing. It can easily get down to -10°C or lower in those mountain passes at night; although the buses are heated, you could be in serious trouble if you are ill equipped and there is a breakdown. Keep an eye on your possessions. Some travellers buy oxygen canisters (Y30) from the CITS office. Diamox is a better bet.

TIBET

In Lhasa you are free to purchase a ticket to Golmud or Xīníng without the need for any travel permits.

Things do change, right? The **Lonely Planet Thorn Tree** (http://thorntree.lonelyplanet.com) online forum is a good way to stay up to date.

OTHER ROUTES

Between Lhasa and Sìchuān, Yúnnán or Xīnjiāng provinces are some of the wildest, highest and most dangerous routes in the world. They are also still very closed to foreigners.

The lack of public transport on these routes makes it necessary to hitchhike, but that is also officially prohibited. The authorities sometimes come down very heavily on truck drivers giving lifts to foreigners, particularly on the Yúnnán and Sìchuān routes in or out of Tibet, so don't expect to find a ride easily. More importantly, be aware that if you ask a truck driver for a lift, you are putting him at risk of being fined and losing his licence. In 2006 the US embassy was warning that more than one traveller had been physically assaulted by authorities for attempting to cross into Tibet from Sìchuān.

A few travel companies in Yúnnán have started to run overland trips from Kūnmíng (p696) or from Zhōngdiàn (p726) to Lhasa, but prices are stratospheric.

TRAVEL RESTRICTIONS

Current regulations (which could change tomorrow) state that all foreigners wanting to visit Tibet must be part of a group (though a 'group' can be only one person!). Then you must obtain the TTB permit required to buy an air ticket into Tibet. In the high season (July to September) you may also need a return ticket to either Kathmandu, Chéngdū or Golmud, and perhaps a few nights' accommodation. Check at guesthouses listed in this guide, online at Lonely Planet's Thorn Tree, and with other travellers to find out current restrictions.

The reality is that most travellers buy a package through a budget travel agency. The cheapest way into Tibet is an air 'package' to Lhasa from Chéngdū for around Y1900, which includes the flight (Y1250), the semimythical TTB permit (which you'll never see) and, usually, transfer to Chéngdū airport. On arrival in Lhasa these temporary 'groups' disband. It's now also possible to fly to Lhasa from Zhōngdiàn in Yúnnán by first arranging the ticket and permits through a travel agency in Kūnmíng. See p696 and p755 for more info.

From Kathmandu, you will have to sign up for a tour to Tibet (p915) to get the TTB permit that will allow you to cross the border at Zhāngmù. Moreover, it's currently impossible to enter Tibet from Nepal on an independent visa, even if you have one in your passport. Travellers will have their Chinese visa cancelled and be put on a group visa, which comes as a separate piece of paper rather than a stamp in your passport. It is possible to get your own personal group visa, which is well worth asking for as you are then free to travel independently after the tour ends for the duration of your group visa without the considerable hassle of having to split from a group visa. It is possible to extend a group visa, and some have tried changing a group visa to an individual visa. However, you cannot do this in Tibet. For this you need to go to Chéngdū or Xīníng and possibly Kūnmíng, and even that might not work. Ah, the Chinese catch-22!

Once in Tibet, entry to anywhere outside the Lhasa prefecture and the cities of Shigatse and Tsetang (ie to places such as EBC, Samye, Sakya and Mt Kailash) requires you to procure a travel permit. To get a permit you again have to be a member of a tour group arranged through an authorised travel agency. At the time of research, Shigatse's PSB was *sometimes* issuing travel permits (Y50) to individual travellers for independent travel along the Friendship Hwy to Nepal, but generally only if travellers fibbed a bit.

THE IMPERMANENCE OF TRAVEL

In 2006 the hottest rumour around was the possible scrapping of the asinine travel-permit system (TTB), mostly due to the effect of the Qinghai–Tibet Railway. We'll believe it when we see it – there's too much money to lose by eliminating this cash cow!

More likely is a relaxing of the system – perhaps a permit will still be necessary to get in and another to travel around Tibet but permits will (finally) be easier to obtain for independent travellers, who can then use public transport.

Getting Around

Transport can cause a headache if you want to explore the backwaters.

Minibuses run around Lhasa prefecture, from Lhasa to the main towns of Shigatse, Tsetang and Ali, and along the Friendship Hwy as far as Shegar. Beyond this, Land Cruisers are the most common form of transport. It's pricey, but not impossible for a nonbudget traveller group splitting costs.

In 2006 the government was beaverishly upgrading the entire Friendship Hwy and linking roads. There were constant closures and bottlenecks yet nothing really seems to be paved!

As for cycling – it's possible, but not without its hazards. Aside from hassles with the PSB, cyclists in Tibet have died from road accidents, hypothermia and pneumonia. Tibet is not the place to learn the ins and outs of long-distance cycling – do your training elsewhere. For experienced cyclists, the Lhasa–Kathmandu trip is one of the world's great rides. Check out *Tibet Overland: A Route and Planning Guide for Mountain Bikers and Other Overlanders*, by Kym McConnell, and www.tibetoverland.com.

LHASA 拉萨

☎ 0891 / pop 120,940 / elev 3700m

Lhasa. It's the sacred city and spiritual centre of the Tibetan world – perhaps even the real 'Forbidden City'. In 1950, when the PLA came marching in, the city dropped from world view. Still, a mystical Shangri-la can't be held down forever. Beginning in the 1980s the Chinese government, likely tired of foreigners banging on the door (or sneaking in the symbolic window), finally 'opened' Tibet to outside travellers.

In they trickled – paying dutiful tithings to the Chinese government for the privilege – to discover that this utopia had developed a Han complex. A modern city had swallowed the old: karaoke bars and brothels sat side by side with temples; rice had replaced *tsampa* (roasted barley meal), runway-esque thoroughfares ploughed alongside holy sites; and taxi drivers didn't speak Tibetan.

That was just the beginning for Lhasa. With the arrival of the Qinghai–Tibet Railway, Lhasa will experience what the rest of China

INFORMATION	
Bank of China 中国银行	**1** B1
China Post 中国邮局	**2** C2
China Unicom 中国联通	**3** C2
Nepalese Consulate 尼泊尔领使馆	**4** A2
PSB (Travel Permits) 公安局	**5** D2
PSB (Visa Extensions) 公安局外事科	**6** C1
Wind Horse Travel	**7** B1

SIGHTS & ACTIVITIES	
Norbulingka 罗布林卡	**8** A2
Potala Palace 布达拉宫	**9** B1
Zoo 动物园	**10** A2

SLEEPING	
Lhasa Hotel 拉萨饭店	**11** A1
Tibet Hotel 西藏宾馆	**12** A1

TRANSPORT	
Airport Bus Departures 机场班车发车处	**13** C1
CAAC 中国民航	(see 13)
Long-Distance Bus Station 汽车站	**14** A2

TIBET

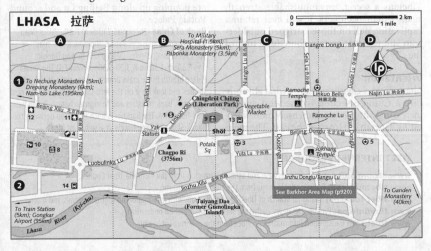

A TIBETAN GAZETTEER

Most travellers have little trouble making themselves understood when wandering about. If not, show this to your driver!

Lhasa	ལྷ་ས
Drepung Monastery	འབྲས་སྤུངས
Sera Monastery	སེ་ར་དགོན་པ
Ganden Monastery	དགའ་ལྡན
Nam-tso Lake	གནམ་མཚོ
Yarlung Valley	ཡར་ཀླུང་གཞུང
Samye Monastery	བསམ་ཡས་དགོན་པ
Tsetang	རྩེད་ཐང
Yumbulagang	ཡུམ་བུ་བླ་སྒང
Yamdrok-tso Lake	ཡར་འབྲོག་མཚོ
Gyantse	རྒྱལ་རྩེ
Shigatse	གཞིས་ཀ་རྩེ
Sakya	ས་སྐྱ
Rongphu Monastery	རོང་ཕུ་ཆེ་དགོན་པ
Everest Base Camp	ཇོ་མོ་གླང་མའི་ག་ཞས་འོག
Tingri	དིང་རི
Zhāngmù (Dram)	འགྲམ

has: tens of years of development compressed into a few heart-stopping calendar turns. This city at the centre of a land known for its isolation will have to deal with the coming touristic free-for-all.

The devastation to Tibetan culture is tragic, yet Lhasa will forever be a city of wonders. No ugly office tower could ever overcome the powerful vista of the Potala Palace, a vast white and ochre fortress soaring over one of the world's highest cities. This will always give Tibetans a secret, unvanquishable strength against their occupiers; it will ever retain a captivating pull on those intrigued outsiders who still feel that certain something toward the city.

Orientation

Lhasa divides clearly and somewhat abruptly into a Chinese section in the west and an increasingly fragile but immensely more interesting Tibetan old town in the east. The main

east–west artery is Beijing Lu, with Potala Palace Sq smack in the middle. To the west is Chinatown. To the east, the colourful Tibetan part of town, the Barkhor area, envelops the Jokhang Temple and is home to the best hotels and restaurants.

Information

The best place for the latest on individual travel in Tibet these days is in the courtyards of the popular hotels, where you'll see travellers gazing at notice boards, taking down numbers or putting up signs for shared rides.

INTERNET ACCESS 网吧
Internet access is available around the place for Y3 to Y5 per hour.
Summit Fine Art Café (Dǐngfēng Měiyìshù Kāfēidiàn; Map p920; ☎ 691 3884; Danjielin Lu; per hr Y3-5) This great café has wireless internet access.

LAUNDRY
The Kirey and Banak Shöl Hotels offer free laundry for guests.
Snowlands Laundry (Map p920; Xuěyù Xǐyīdiàn; Mentsikhang/Zangyi Lu) Next to Snowlands Hotel, this laundry charges Y3 per piece and it ain't quick.

MEDICAL SERVICES
Military Hospital (Xīzàng Jūnqū Zhōngyīyuàn; ☎ 625 3120; Nangre Beilu) Near the Sera Monastery, this is the best option (if you have one).

MONEY
In addition to the bank ATMs here, others are popping up along Beijing Lu and around Potala Palace.
Bank of China (Zhōngguó Yínháng) Potala Palace (Map p917; Lingkuo Xilu; ⏰ 9am-6.30pm Mon-Fri, 10am-3pm Sat & Sun); Barkhor (Map p920; Beijing Donglu; ⏰ 8.30am-1.30pm & 3.30-5.30pm Mon-Fri) The Potala Palace branch is the main branch – turn right at the yak statues and look for it on the left. Come here for credit-card advances, bank transfers and foreign exchange. It also has a 24-hour ATM. The Barkhor branch is located between the Banak Shöl and Kirey hotels. It also has an ATM.

TIBET INTERNET RESOURCES

VISITING MONASTERIES & TEMPLES

Most monasteries and temples extend a warm welcome to foreign guests, and in remote areas will often offer a place to stay for the night. Please maintain this good faith by observing the following courtesies:

■ Always circumambulate monasteries, chapels and other religious objects clockwise, thus keeping shrines and *chörten* (Tibetan stupa) to your right.

■ Don't touch or remove anything on an altar and don't take prayer flags or *mani* (prayer) stones.

■ Don't take photos during a prayer meeting. At other times always ask permission to take a photo, especially when using a flash. The larger monasteries charge photography fees, though some monks will allow you to take a quick photo for free. If they won't, there's no point getting angry, as you don't know what pressures they may be under.

■ Don't wear shorts or short skirts in a monastery, and take your hat off when you go into a chapel.

■ Don't smoke in a monastery.

■ If you have a guide, try to ensure that he or she is Tibetan, as Chinese guides invariably know little about Tibetan Buddhism or monastery history.

POST
China Post (Zhōngguó Yóujú; Map p917; Beijing Donglu; ☯ 9am-8pm Mon-Sat, 10am-6pm Sun) East of the Potala Palace. Buy stamps from the counter in the far left corner as you walk through the main door. Staff wince when they see parcels.

PUBLIC SECURITY BUREAU
Neither of the **Public Security Bureau** (PSB; Gōngānjú) offices in Lhasa really wants to see you or, thus, is worth your time. The office (Map p917) at the eastern end of Beijing Donglu issues travel permits, but not to you; you will instead be referred to a travel agency.

The office (Map p917) on Linkuo Beilu occasionally grants visa extensions of up to seven days in an emergency (then only maybe). If you require a longer extension contact one of the travel agencies.

TELEPHONE
China Unicom (Zhōngguó Liántōng; Map p917; Beijing Donglu; ☯ 9am-8pm) Offers the cheapest long-distance rates.

Telecom Booths (Map p920; ☯ 10am-11pm) Several private phone booths near the Kirey and Banak Shöl Hotels offer cheap international calls.

TRAVEL AGENCIES
To trek or visit remote areas, you need to visit a travel agency to secure a permit, transport and (possibly) a guide. Previously, solo travellers were required to do this through Foreign & Independent Travellers (FIT) agencies.

However, at our last visit, things had been reversed, with every private agency clamouring for business. In case Big Brother reverts to old habits, the FIT agencies below are longstanding (we've had a couple of complaints about the Kirey Hotel's FIT branch).

China Workers International Travel Service (CWTS; Zhígōng Guójì Lǚxíng Shè; ☎ 632 0833; 83 Beijing Zhong Lu) The super friendly Tibetan staff here have competitive prices and they gave us a great trip.

FIT Snowlands Hotel (Map p920; ☎ 634 9239; Danjielin Lu); Banak Shöl Hotel (Map p920; ☎ 634 4397; Beijing Donglu) The two branches operate independently and offer different prices.

Sights
In addition to the main sights listed here, numerous modest temples (there's even a Muslim neighbourhood with a mosque) lie within the maze of Lhasa's back streets and alleys.

BARKHOR 八廓
One cannot help but be swept up in the wondrous swell of humanity that is the **Barkhor** (Bākuò; Map p920), not a sight per se but a *kora* (pilgrim circuit) that proceeds clockwise around the periphery of the Jokhang Temple. You'll swear it possesses some mystical spiritual gravity, as every time you approach within 50m, you somehow get sucked right in and gladly wind up making the whole circuit again! Spiritual wares and tourist baubles are hawked

TIBET

along every centimetre: prayer flags, block prints of scriptures, turquoise jewellery, Tibetan boots, Nepalese biscuits, yak butter and juniper incense plus a lot of *Yak, Yak, Yak, Yak – Tibet!* T-shirts. Start your haggling engines.

The Tibetan travellers here – indeed, most are actually pilgrims – are captivating. Braided-haired Khambas from eastern Tibet stride around with ornate swords or daggers; and Goloks (Tibetan nomads) from the northeast wear ragged sheepskins or, for women, incredibly ornate braids and coral headpieces.

JOKHANG TEMPLE 大昭寺

The 1300-year-old **Jokhang Temple** (Dàzhāo Sì; Map p920; admission Y70; ☸ inner chapels 8am-noon &

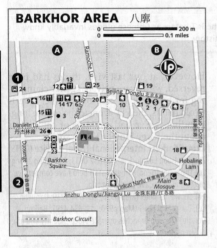

sometimes 3-5.30pm) is the spiritual centre of Tibet. The waves of awestruck pilgrims prostrating themselves outside and the distinctive golden dome are mesmerising – planes could use the dome for navigation.

Commemorating the marriage of the Tang princess Wencheng to King Songtsen Gampo, the temple was built atop a pool that the princess thought was a witch's heart. The temple houses a pure gold statue of the Buddha Sakyamuni brought to Tibet by the princess, along with extraordinary Tibetan religious art treasures (though some are duplicates).

The Jokhang Temple is best visited early in the morning; during the afternoon you'll have to enter via the side door to the right of the main entrance, and interior chapels may be shut. There are often prayers led by monks on the roof at about 6.30pm. The outer halls and the roof are open from sunrise to sunset.

POTALA PALACE 布达拉宫

What can one say about the magnificent and justifiably world-famous **Potala Palace** (Bùdálā Gōng; Map p917; admission Y100; ☎ 9.30am-3pm before 1 May, 9am-3.30pm after 1 May, interior chapels close 4.30pm), once the seat of the Tibetan government and the winter residence of the Dalai Lamas? You can't miss it – it's the one touching the sky.

An architectural wonder even by modern standards, the palace rises 13 storeys from 130m-high Marpo Ri (Red Hill) and contains more than a thousand rooms. Pilgrims murmuring prayers shuffle through the rooms to make offerings of *khatak* (ceremonial scarves) and liquid yak butter.

The first recorded use of the site dates from the 7th century AD, when King Songtsen Gampo built a palace here. Construction of the present structure began during the reign of the fifth Dalai Lama in 1645 and took divisions of labourers and artisans more than 50 years to complete. It is impressive enough to have caused Zhou Enlai to send his own troops to protect it from the Red Guards during the Cultural Revolution.

The layout of the Potala Palace includes the White Palace (the eastern part of the building), used for the living quarters of the Dalai Lama, and the Red Palace (the central building rising above), used for religious functions. The most stunning chapels of the Red Palace house the jewel-bedecked *chörten* tombs of previous Dalai Lamas. The apartments of the 13th and 14th Dalai Lamas, in the White Palace, offer a more personal insight into life in the palace. The roof – off-limits for reconstruction at the time of writing – proffers commanding views of Lhasa.

Grand aesthetics and history aside, one can't help noticing that today it is essentially an empty shell, a cavernous memorial to what once was.

At research time foreigners had to enter via the northwest entrance, accessible by road, and exit via the southern settlement of Shöl. Pilgrims visit in the other direction, and are most numerous on Monday, Wednesday and Friday when they're admitted free of charge. Photography isn't allowed inside the chapels.

Tickets are limited. You must line up *around 5pm the previous day* with your passport (one person can take several) to register. Get a receipt, then go back the next morning. Alternatively try sweet-talking the gatekeeper! Note that ticket prices look set to rise to Y300.

NORBULINGKA 罗布林卡

About 3km west of the Potala Palace is the **Norbulingka** (Luóbùlínkǎ; Jewel Park; Map p917; admission Y60; 9am-1pm & 2.30-6pm), the former summer residence of the Dalai Lama. The pleasant park contains several palaces and chapels, the highlight of which is the **New Summer Palace** (Takten Migyü Potrang), but it's hard to justify the high Norbulingka entry fee.

Festivals & Events

Tibetan festivals are held according to the Tibetan lunar calendar, which usually lags at least a month behind the West's Gregorian calendar. Following is a brief selection of Lhasa's major festivals:

Losar Festival (New Year Festival) Taking place in the first week of the first lunar month, there are performances of Tibetan drama, pilgrims make incense offerings and the streets are thronged with Tibetans dressed in their finest. The next dates for this festival are 18 February 2007, 8 February 2008 and 25 February 2009.

Lantern Festival Held on the 15th day of the first lunar month, huge yak-butter sculptures are placed around Lhasa's Barkhor circuit. The next dates for this festival are 3 March 2007, 21 February 2008 and 11 March 2009.

Mönlam (Great Prayer Festival) This is held midway through the first lunar month (officially culminating on the 25th). An image of Maitreya from Lhasa's Jokhang Temple is borne around the Barkhor circuit. Start dates for Mönlam are 14 March 2007, 2 March 2008 and 21 March 2009.

Saga Dawa (Sakyamuni's Enlightenment) The 15th day of the fourth lunar month (full moon) is an occasion for outdoor operas, and also sees large numbers of pilgrims at the Jokhang Temple, on the Barkhor circuit and climbing Gephel Ri, the peak behind Drepung Monastery. The next dates for this festival are 31 May 2007, 19 May 2008 and 7 June 2009.

Worship of the Buddha During the second week of the fifth lunar month, the parks of Lhasa, in particular the Norbulingka, are crowded with picnickers. The festival will be held late June 2007, mid-June 2008 and late June 2009.

Shötun Festival (Yoghurt Festival) This is held in the first week of the seventh lunar month. It starts at Drepung Monastery and moves down to the Norbulingka. Operas and masked dances are held. The next dates for this festival are mid-August 2007, early August 2008 and late August 2009.

Palden Lhamo The 15th day of the 10th lunar month has a procession around the Barkhor circuit bearing Palden Lhamo, protective deity of the Jokhang Temple. The next dates for this festival are 24 November 2007, 12 December 2008 and 2 December 2009.

Sleeping

Backpacker hotels we mention here have (lower-end) midrange rooms that are decent for a small budget-traveller splurge.

BUDGET

Banak Shöl Hotel (Bālángxué Lǚguǎn; Map p920; 632 3829; 8 Beijing Donglu; 北京东路8号; dm Y25, s/d Y60/80, d with bathroom Y100-160) This stand-by sees droves of travellers but the staff keep the place up pretty well; bonuses include a free laundry service (no socks or undies please!) and a superb rooftop restaurant. Rooms vary, so take a look; the midrange doubles remain the best value in Lhasa.

Kirey Hotel (Jírì Lǚguǎn; Map p920; ☎ 632 3462; 105 Beijing Donglu; 北京东路105号; dm Y25, d with/without bathroom Y120/60; ☐) Pretty much always near capacity is this buzzing hotel, also with a harried but up-to-snuff staff. The Y60 doubles offer the best value; those with bathroom are a bit aged but sport fresh paint replete with lovely Tibet motifs. It has reliable hot showers and a free laundry service. Travellers will also find the consistently good Tashi II (opposite) restaurant/hang-out and a reliable internet café here.

Yak Hotel (Yàkè Bīnguǎn; Map p920; ☎ 632 3496; 100 Beijing Donglu; 北京东路100号; dm/d/tr Y30/100/150, s/d with bathroom Y280-380; ☐) The granddaddy of Lhasa's budget hotels remains loyal to budget travellers even after a face-lift. Spartan but well-kept dorms are popular, and there's a laundry list of rooms thereafter, all the way to excellent twins with Tibetan-style décor. A new rooftop patio has commanding views of Potala. Internet access is good.

Dongcuo International Youth Hostel (Dōngcuò Guójì Qīngnián Lǚguǎn; Map p920; ☎ 627 3388; tibetyouth hostel@163.com; 10 Beijing Donglu; 北京东路10号; dm Y30, s/d without bathroom Y60/80, with bathroom Y160; ☐) This newish hostel has worked out the kinks and is a decent place to stay, overall. Staff are friendly and rooms are smallish but well maintained. Korean-style rooms are a nice option.

MIDRANGE

Hotel Kyichu (Lāsà Jìqǔ Fàndiàn; Map p920; ☎ 633 1541; fax 632 0234; 18 Beijing Zhonglu; 北京中路18号; s/d Y200/280, deluxe d Y320, all with bathroom; ☐) This hotel tops the list for many repeat travellers to Lhasa – crackerjack management really keeps things ship shape. Rooms are spotless, and the nice garden restaurant is a tranquil spot to dine.

Flora Hotel (Hādáhuāshén Lǚguǎn; Map p920; ☎ 632 4491; florahtl@hotmail.com; Hobaling Lam; dm Y35, d/tr with bathroom Y188/228) Drifting off to sleep to the haunting sounds of evening prayers isn't what you'd associate with Lhasa, yet this friendly and extremely well-run (rooms are kept up fabulously) Nepalese-operated place sits smack in the middle of the quiet Muslim quarter. Decent three-bed dorms out the back offer a quiet alternative to Lhasa's backpacker hotels.

Dhood Gu Hotel (Dùngù Bīnguǎn; Map p920; ☎ 632 2555; dhoodgu@public.ls.xz.cn; 19 Shasarsu Lu; 敦固宾馆; s/d with bathroom Y320/480; ☐) At this Nepalese-run hotel the buzzing crowds in the alley below are as much a sight as that of the Potala from the rooftop patio. Rooms – many sporting Tibetan décor – come with modern bathrooms, though the singles are cramped.

Tibet Gorkha Hotel (Xīzàng Guòěrkà Fàndiàn; Map p920; ☎ 627 1992; tibetgorkha7@hotmail.com; 45 Linkuo Nanlu; 林廓南路45号; s/d Y388, tr Y280; ☐) Rave reviews – with good reason – come in for this place, in a quiet location south of Barkhor Sq. Staff are solicitous, rooms are exceedingly well appointed, and the central garden courtyard may be Lhasa's best sanctuary from the crowds.

TOP END

Lhasa Hotel (Lāsà Fàndiàn; Map p917; ☎ 683 2221; fax 683 5796; 1 Minzu Lu; 民族路1号; tr Y980, d Y1020-1328, Tibetan ste Y1555; ☐) Standards have dropped considerably since the Holiday Inn – its erstwhile owner – pulled out in 1997, but it's still a group-tour (and cadre) favourite. A discount of 30% is standard.

Tibet Hotel (Xīzàng Bīnguǎn; Map p917; ☎ 683 9999; fax 683 6787; 64 Beijing Xilu; 北京路64号; old block d/tr Y880/980, discounted to Y580/680; ☐) Ask for the four-star rooms in the old block which are well worth the extra Y100. The location is fairly inconvenient though.

Eating

The staple diet in Tibet is *tsampa* and *bö cha* (yak-butter tea). Tibetans mix the two in their hands to create doughlike balls. *Momo* (dumplings that are filled with vegetables or yak meat) and *thukpa* (noodles with meat) are also local comfort food. Variations include *thanthuk* (fried noodle squares) as well as *shemre* (rice, yoghurt and yak-meat curry).

Tibetans consume large quantities of *chang* (a tangy alcoholic drink derived from fermented barley). The other major beverage is *cha ngamo* (sweet milky tea).

Summit Fine Art Café (Dǐngfēng Měiyìshù Kāfēidiàn; Map p920; ☎ 691 3884; Danjielin Lu; coffee Y15) Cosy sofas and easy chairs, soft music, wireless internet, melt-in-mouth desserts, killer coffee and smoothies. 'Nuff said.

Tashi I Restaurant (Map p920; cnr Danjielin Lu & Beijing Donglu; dishes Y8-15) Ah, it's so good to see this tireless budget haunt still whipping out its famed *bobi* (chapatti-like unleavened bread), which comes with seasoned cream cheese and fried vegetables or meat.

Tashi II (Map p920; ☎ 632 3462; 105 Beijing Donglu; dishes Y8-15) Located in the Kirey Hotel, this has the same menu and food as Tashi I, but friendlier service.

Nam-tso Restaurant (Map p920; ☎ 632 1895; 8 Beijing Donglu; mains Y20, set breakfast Y20) Found on the rooftop of the Banak Shöl Hotel, prices here are a little higher than at other budget eateries, but the chicken sizzler (Y20) is the linchpin of a splendid menu.

Dunya Restaurant (Map p920; ☎ 633 3374; www .dunyarestaurant.com; 100 Beijing Donglu; dishes Y25-40) With sophisticated décor, excellent, wide-ranging food and interesting specials, this foreign-run eatery is pricey, but it's popular with travellers who aren't on a shoestring. The homemade bread and soups, daily buffet breakfast and Saturday brunch (Y25), served 11am to 2pm, are popular.

Potala Traditional Snack Bar (Bùdálā Fēngqíng cānbā; Map p920; ☎ 633 6664; 127 Beijing Donglu; dishes Y8-50). A modest new little eatery, this friendly place's name says it all. A telephone-directory-sized menu features real-deal Tibetan and Nepalese (and a smattering of great Western) dishes – yak tongue anyone?

Drinking

Dunya (100 Beijing Donglu; bottled beer Y12) At Dunya Restaurant (Map p920), the upstairs bar is popular with local expats and tour groups. The happy hour offers a Y2 discount between 7pm and 9.30pm.

Ganglamedo (Gānglà Méiduŏ; Map p920; 127 Beijing Donglu; beer Y10) This lovely café-bar has great décor, atmosphere and music. It sports one of the Barkhor area's best selections of imported beers and spirits. The walls are a gallery show-casing local artists.

Shopping

Whether it's prayer wheels, *thangkas*, sun hats or muesli, you shouldn't have a problem finding it in Lhasa. The Barkhor circuit is especially good for buying souvenirs. Most of this stuff is mass-produced in Nepal. Haggle, haggle, haggle.

Dropenling (Map p920; ☎ 633 0898; www.tibetcraft .com; 11 Chaktsal Ganglu; ⏱ 10am-7pm) Wander through the Tibetan old town to this excellent new initiative established by the Tibet Artisans' Fund to support local handicrafts. Quality and prices are top end, and well worth a look because you can watch local craftspeople at work on site.

Dozens of shops in Lhasa sell Chinese-made Gore-Tex jackets, fleeces, sleeping bags, stoves, tents, mats and so on. **Outlook Outdoor Equipment** (Kàn Fēngyún Biànhuàn Yuǎnjìng; Map p920; ☎ 634 5589; 11 Beijing Donglu) is probably the best and most convenient place, and it also rents out equipment.

Getting There & Away
AIR

Lhasa has flights departing for Kathmandu (Y2511, two or three times weekly); Chéngdū (Y1590, three times daily); for Xī'ān (Y1740, four times weekly); Zhōngdiàn (Y1450, twice weekly); Kūnmíng (Y2120, twice weekly); Chóngqìng (Y1450, weekly); and also for Xīníng (Y1450, four times weekly). Flight connections continue to Běijīng (Y2520), Shànghǎi (Y2880) and Guǎngzhōu (Y2500). These tickets are often discounted by up to 20%. More direct flights are always being instituted, so check before you purchase tickets.

No matter where you fly in from, all tickets to Lhasa have to be purchased through a travel agency, which will arrange your TTB permit (see p916). Air China won't sell you a ticket without a permit.

Leaving Lhasa is a lot simpler, as tickets can be purchased (and changed) without hassle from the **Civil Aviation Administration of China** (CAAC; Zhōngguó Mínháng; Map p917; ☎ 633 3446; 88 Niangre Lu; ⏱ 9.30am-8pm).

BUS

Tickets for buses from Lhasa to Golmud (Y200 sleeper bus, 24 to 30 hours) can be bought at the long-distance bus station in the southwest of town, near the Norbulingka. There are also sleeper buses that continue all the way to Xīníng (Y340, two to three days), the capital of Qīnghǎi. Hard-core masochists might be attracted by the epic nonstop 3287km sleeper bus to Chéngdū (Y500, three days and four nights), via Golmud, and Xī'ān (Y480, three-plus days), though most sane people will take the plane.

One bus every Friday runs to Kathmandu (Y580, three days). Foreigners are able to go; you need your passport to get a ticket.

Destinations around Tibet are a little trick-ier, as the long-distance bus station ticket sellers vary on whether they'll sell tickets to foreigners. There are minibuses every 30 min-utes to Tsetang (Y22 to Y40, three or more hours) and Shigatse (Y55 to Y100, six to seven hours), and daily departures to Nagqu (Y63 to Y100, six to seven hours). You can often buy tickets direct from drivers.

Private minibuses to Shigatse (Y50, seven hours) and Nagqu sometimes depart from the junction of Ramoche Lu and Beijing Donglu at around 7am (often earlier), though some travellers have been refused tickets because these buses are not officially allowed to take foreigners. There is also a bus at 8.30am from the lot next to the Gang Gyen Hotel on Beijing Donglu; drivers seemed willing to take anyone. The easiest way to get to Gyantse is to change buses in Shigatse; there is very little public transport via Yamdrok-tso Lake.

Buses leave around 6.30am for Ganden Monastery (Y20 return, 1½ hours), 7am for Samye (桑耶; Y40, 3½ hours) and 7.30am for Tsetang (advertised as Shannan, 山南, the Chinese name of the county; Y30, three hours) from the west side of Barkhor Sq. Buy tickets on the south side of Jokhang Temple in a little kiosk.

CAR HIRE

The most popular way around Tibet in recent years is with a hired car. One of the best routes is a leisurely and slightly circuitous journey down to Zhāngmù on the Tibetan–Nepalese border, taking in Yamdrok-tso Lake, Gyantse, Shigatse, Sakya, Tingri and EBC on the way. A six- to seven-day trip of this sort in a Land Cruiser costs around Y6000, including all necessary permits, driver, guide and car, and can be divided between four (five at a pinch) passengers. Look for trips advertised on the notice boards at the main backpacker hotels.

Other popular trips include Mt Kailash (17 to 21 days), Nam-tso Lake (three days) and various options in eastern Tibet.

For trips around Lhasa prefecture (which require no permits) there is nothing to stop you talking directly to a driver or any travel agency.

TRAIN

The Lhasa Express (our moniker, official name be damned) is up and running. The train station, 5km southwest of the city, is noted for its energy-saving construction and for its design, which limits the amount of walking passengers must do in the thin air. Its architecture, emulating the Potala Palace, is sacrilege to some. (The new bridge lead-

ing to it represents a Tibetan prayer scarf.) Another station on the city side of the river is purportedly in the works.

At the time of writing, foreigners still needed a Tibet travel permit in order to buy a train ticket, though this could well change soon. You also have to fill out a health card. All passengers have access to piped-in oxygen through a special socket beside each seat or berth. The train is completely nonsmoking between Golmud and Lhasa. It's nonsmoking within the carriages throughout the journey, but, from Běijīng to Golmud, you can smoke at the ends of carriages. Soft-sleeper berths come with individual TVs.

Getting Around
TO/FROM THE AIRPORT

Gongkar airport is 65km from Lhasa. Airport buses (Y25, 90 minutes) leave at 6.30 or 7am (depends on the day), and at several other times of day, from the courtyard in front of the CAAC building. Tickets are sold on the bus, so show up early to guarantee a seat. Buses greet all incoming flights.

If you need to get to or from the airport more quickly, taxis cost around Y200 (the driver may ask you for Y350), but you might find a shared taxi for Y25 per seat.

BICYCLE

The best option is to hire a bike. Bikes can be hired from the Banak Shöl and the Snowlands Hotel for Y2 to Y3 per hour (Y20 per day) and a couple of other places around Barkhor Sq.

MINIBUS

Privately run minibuses travel frequently on and around Beijing Lu. There is a flat Y2 charge. Minibuses 402, 200 and 204 run to the Norbulingka and the long-distance bus station. Minibuses 301 to 303 run to Drepung Monastery from Beijing Donglu (there are also, at peak periods, monastery minibuses from the west side of Barkhor Sq), and minibuses 503 and 502 run to Sera Monastery from the junction of Duosenge Lu and Beijing Donglu.

TAXI

These charge a standard fare of Y10 to anywhere within the city. Few Chinese drivers know the Tibetan names for even the major sites. Bicycle rickshaws – the ones that nearly

TRAINS TO TIBET

Train number	From	To	Departure time	Duration
T27	Běijīng West	Lhasa	daily 9.30pm	47½ hrs
T22/23	Chéngdū	Lhasa	daily 6.18pm	48 hrs
T222/3	Chóngqìng	Lhasa	daily 7.20pm	47 hrs
T264/5	Guǎngzhōu	Lhasa	daily 10.29am	57½ hrs
K917	Lánzhōu	Lhasa	daily 4.45pm	30½ hrs
T164/5	Shànghǎi	Lhasa	daily 4.11pm	51½ hrs

Fares

Route	Distance	Hard seat/Hard sleeper/Soft sleeper
Běijīng to Lhasa	4064km	Y389/813/1262
Chéngdū to Lhasa	3360km	Y331/712/1104
Chóngqìng to Lhasa	3654km	Y355/754/1168
Guǎngzhōu to Lhasa	4980km (approx)	Y451/896/1434
Lánzhōu to Lhasa	2188km	Y242/552/854
Shànghǎi to Lhasa	4373km	Y406/821/1314

Train Titbits

- Laptops and MP3 players can malfunction on the trip due to the altitude.
- 120km of bridges were built over the permafrost and sections of cooling pipes were inserted to keep the boggy ground frozen.
- The highest point of the trip is 5072m – the highest point you can reach by train.
- A luxury joint-venture train, the Tangula Express, is due to start in 2007 complete with glass observation cars and luxury cabins – see www.tgzpartners/projects.
- By 2009 the line will extend a further 270km to Shigatse, just a few hundred kilometres from the Indian border.

TIBET

run you down all day – start at Y5 around the Barkhor Sq area.

AROUND LHASA
Drepung Monastery 哲蚌寺

A preternaturally spiritual 1½-hour-long *kora* around this 15th-century **monastery** (Zhébàng Sì; admission adult/student Y55/45; 9am-5pm), 7km west of Lhasa, is among the highlights of a trip to Tibet. Along with Sera and Ganden Monasteries, Drepung functioned as one of the three 'pillars of the Tibetan state' and this one was purportedly the largest monastery in the world (around 7000 monks once resided here).

Kings of the Tsang and the Mongols savaged the place regularly, destroying some 40% of the structures; oddly, the Red Guards pretty much left it alone during the Cultural Revolution. With concerted rebuilding, this village – its name means 'rice heap' due to the white build-

ings dotting the hillside – once again resembles its proud former self. Around 700 monks reside here and in nearby **Nechung Monastery** (admission Y5; 9am-4pm), a 10-minute walk downhill. Try to catch the lunch break when the monks feast on *tsampa* and yak-butter tea. In the afternoons you can often see them debating in Tibetan. Some hardy souls have hiked into surrounding hillsides and slept in hermitages (bring food and prepare for cold).

Drepung Monastery is easily reached by bike, although most people take minibuses 301 to 303 (Y2, around 20 minutes) from Beijing Donglu, or the monastery minibuses from the west side of Barkhor Sq. There is a Y20 charge per chapel for photography.

Sera Monastery 色拉寺

About 5km north of Lhasa, this **monastery** (Sèlā Sì; admission adult/student Y55/35; 9am-5pm) was

HEAD IN THE CLOUDS – PRIDE & PROPAGANDA *Calum Macleod*

The Kunlun Mountains: backbone of Asia. Yuzhu Peak: where China's climbing team train. Tuotuohe: source of the Yellow River. 'Quick, quick, the Tuotuohe tape!' shouts broadcaster Wang Lirui to her colleague in the propaganda cabin, as Tuotuohe station flashes by. 'We've only done this once,' Wang apologises, watching the sparse scenery to guess when to play her 19 introductions to natural highlights between Golmud and Lhasa.

Wang need not panic. The record-shattering, yak-scaring Qinghai–Tibet Railway (QTR) may be the world's highest, but there is no single must-see sight en route. You are already so high that the snowy mountains glimpsed at the edge of the plateau rarely look like world-beaters. And with four trains a day headed for Lhasa since July 2006, Wang and her fellow Han Chinese train attendants, plus thousands of tourists and job-seekers, will soon get used to visiting a once forbidden land.

Some journeys shouldn't be too easy. Flying into Lhasa always felt like cheating – as well as robbing the visitor of time to acclimatise. The hazardous roads dug by Chairman Mao's army in the 1950s remain hazardous. Now a third option awaits. With a little paperwork, and a pioneering spirit, you can traverse miles of permafrost, over towering mountain passes, right to the heart of this beautiful, tragic region.

The train itself is an upmarket, oxygen-pumping version of the new carriages rattling China's rails nationwide. Just US$50 will buy you a hard seat all the way from Beijing to Lhasa, plus change for a bottle of warm Bud in the restaurant car. This is a political project, resigned to operate at a loss for years to come. Buy a bed instead (US$100 to US$158). There are 48 hours and 2500 miles (4000 kilometres) to go. And alcohol won't help your head come day three.

While away the hours chatting to other passengers and you'll hear the mixed emotions this engineering marvel has inspired. 'The Chinese people are truly incredible,' says Buddhist and Communist Party member Chang Qiming, leaning against a framed propaganda poster by Hu Jintao, China's president. 'This train is like a dragon, climbing up the slope and bending this way and that.' Fellow soft-sleeper Ge Honggui, a martial arts master, declares 'only the Chinese people would dare to do what others don't even dare think of!'

Down in the hard-seat section, Tibetan students pass the time watching DVDs on laptops. 'It used to take me seven days to get home from Beijing; now it's only two and a half,' says Puchong, 23. The railway is so revolutionary that in June 2006 authorities issued a list of 28 new and standardised Tibetan terms for train-related words like 'platform', 'tickets' and 'soft sleeper'. But progress exacts its price. 'I worry many Chinese workers will come to Lhasa on the train,' says Puchong. 'I know that has happened in [Muslim] Xīnjiāng. And there must be environmental damage too.'

Some 33 passageways have been built under and over the railway to allow animals to follow annual migration routes – or end up as rail-kill. The train's windows are sealed to prevent littering of Tibet's fragile ecosystem. But there is no defence against the wave of Han Chinese–led commerce and migration that has provoked the Dalai Lama to warn of 'cultural genocide' following the first mass-transit link between his mountainous homeland of 2.8 million people and China's seething 1.3 billion.

founded in 1419 by a disciple of Tsongkhapa and was, along with Drepung Monastery, one of Lhasa's two great Gelugpa monasteries.

About 600 monks are now in residence, well down from an original population of around 5000 monks. Debating (in Tibetan) takes place from 3.30pm to 5pm in a garden next to the assembly hall in the centre of the monastery. Like Drepung, there's a fine *kora* path around the monastery. Note that women may be refused entry to certain chapels.

Minibuses 502 and 503 run to Sera for Y2, or it's approximately a 30-minute bicycle ride from central Lhasa. There is a Y30 fee per chapel for photography, and it's Y850 for video.

From Sera Monastery it's possible to walk northwest for another hour to **Pabonka Monastery**. Built in the 7th century by King Songtsen Gampo, this is one of the most ancient Buddhist sites in the Lhasa region and is well worth the walk.

Ganden Monastery 甘丹寺

About 40km east of Lhasa, this **monastery** (Gāndān Si; admission Y45; ☉ dawn-dusk), founded in 1417 by Tsongkhapa, was the first Gelugpa monastery. Still the heart and soul of this sect, it's the one out-of-Lhasa sight to choose if your time is limited. Two *kora* are spread through the splendid 4500m-high Kyi-chu Valley (it's all visual eye candy) and you'll likely meet more pilgrims here than anywhere else.

Some 400 monks have returned and extensive reconstruction has been underway for some time now. There is a Y20 fee per chapel for photography, and it costs Y1500 for video.

Pilgrim buses leave for Ganden Monastery (Y20 return) at 6.30am (and often at 7am) from the west side of Barkhor Sq. They return around 2pm. Buy tickets a day ahead if possible from a ticket kiosk on the south side of Jokhang Temple.

NAM-TSO LAKE 纳木错

The water of sacred **Nam-tso** (Nàmùcuò; Y40), 195km north of Lhasa is of a turquoise-ish blue so transcendent, shimmering in the rarefied air of 4500m, as to defy an artist's colour charts. Geographically part of the Changtang Plateau, bordered to the north by the Tangula Shan range and to the southeast by 7111m Nyenchen Tanglha peak, the scenery around it is equally breathtaking.

But the view is not as breathtaking as the altitude. Nam-tso is 1100m higher than Lhasa so do *not* rush here. Count on a week in Lhasa at the minimum to avoid AMS; see p982.

Tashi Dor Monastery (elevation 4718m), which is on the edge of the lake, is one of your basic lodging options or you can camp nearby. Two **guesthouses** (dm Y25-50, tents Y100-160) are replete with karaoke machines but no toilets

so bury your waste and burn all your toilet paper after use.

The closest public transport to Nam-tso Lake takes you to Damxung (Dāngxióng), a small town with a couple of guesthouses and Sichuanese restaurants, but the lake is still another 40km or more. Some hotel travel agencies do arrange two-day trips (Y200 to Y300) to the lake, but these depend on gathering enough travellers. The quickest – and most popular – option would be to organise a Land Cruiser in Lhasa, which should cost Y1200 to Y1600 for a two- or three-day trip.

Permits and guides are not necessary for the area.

YARLUNG VALLEY 雅鲁流域

About 170km southeast of Lhasa, the Yarlung Valley (Yǎlǔ Liúyù) is considered to be the birthplace of Tibetan culture. Getting around is a pain in the rear.

A new tourist bus has recently started a peak-season daily service from Barkhor Sq to the following three sights listed as well as a couple of others during a 13-hour odyssey. Again, if your driver suspects or cares that you don't have a permit, you might not get on, but drivers were perfectly happy selling us a ticket at last check. The whole trip costs Y80 (excluding admission tickets); you can buy tickets from a small kiosk on the west side of Barkhor Sq.

Samye Monastery 桑耶寺

About 30km west of Tsetang, on the opposite bank of the Yarlung Tsangpo (Brahmaputra) River, this **monastery** (Sāngyē Si; Y40) was founded in AD 775 by King Trisong Detsen as the first monastery in Tibet. Famed for its mandala design, its main hall represents Mt Meru, the centre of the universe, and many of the

---

GANDEN TO SAMYE TREK

The most popular – but not the easiest – trek in Tibet is the four- to five-day hike from Ganden Monastery to Samye Monastery, an 80km spiritual cleansing connecting two of Tibet's most important monasteries. It begins less than 50km from Lhasa and takes you over Shuga-la pass (5250m) and Chitu-la pass (5100). Along the way are myriad vistas of lakes, alpine forests and meadows but also quite a bit of strenuous (medium to difficult) exertion, so it shouldn't be underestimated.

Obviously, know before you go. This means the land and the capabilities of mind and body. And, of course, Big Brother – the big issue is getting a permit, which is not easy for individual travellers. Eminently helpful is **Wind Horse Travel** (☎ 683 3009; jampa_w@hotmail.com; 48 West Lingkhor Xilu, Lhasa; per day $120), one of the best agencies in Lhasa.

buildings are designed to represent Tibetan cosmology. It's difficult to get there, but you cannot beat the solitude, beauty and history and many travellers have stayed longer than they planned.

Buses from Barkhor Sq leave at 7am, cost Y40 and drop you at the Samye ferry crossing; other buses have begun to run directly, using a bridge east of Tsetang. Some travellers have been refused tickets (but not of late). Police sniffing about at the ferry crossing for permit-lacking travellers isn't unknown, though these have become rarer and rarer.

Obviously, before you leave Lhasa, ask around about the current situation. Even the FIT agencies' advice is to just go and if stopped or fined (upwards of – ouch – Y500) sheep-ishly and obsequiously plead ignorance.

The ferry leaves when full. The crossing costs Y3 but foreigners are often charged Y10. From the far shore, a bumpy lift in the back of a truck or tractor (Y3) will carry you the 9km to Samye Monastery.

Simple accommodation is available at the **Monastery Guesthouse** (dm Y30-40, d/tr Y100/150) or the **East Friendship Hotel** (d Y40), a cosy and basic family guesthouse outside Samye's east gate. The monastery restaurant serves cheap dumplings and noodles, but a better option is the **Friendship Snowland Restaurant** (meals Y8-18), also outside the east gate, which serves Chinese dishes, banana pancakes and mugs of milky tea.

Tsetang 泽当
☎ 0893 / elev 3550m

Ho-hum Tsetang (Zédāng), about 180km from Lhasa, is a mostly Chinese town used as a jumping-off point for exploration of the Yarlung Valley area. You don't need a permit for the town itself but you do to venture into the surrounding area, which can only be done by arranging a Land Cruiser and guide. The omniscient Tsetang PSB are notoriously ill-humoured; perhaps out of sheer boredom, they seem to enjoy harassing foreigners. Keep a low profile if you don't have a permit.

Accommodation for foreigners is restricted to *way*-overpriced hotels.

SLEEPING
Postal House Hotel (邮电公寓; Yóudiàn Gōngyù; ☎ 782 1888; Naidong Lu; 乃东路; d Y188-318, ste Y666, extra bed Y88) Dingy and a bit embarrassing considering the price, but the cheaper doubles are

probably the best deal you'll get in Tsetang (foreigners pay a 50% surcharge). At least if you choose a Tibet-style room, you get free yak-butter tea.

Tsetang Hotel (泽当饭店; Zédāng Fàndiàn; ☎ 682 9364; fax 683 2604; 21 Naidong Lu; 乃东路21号; s/d/tr/ste Y888/1680/1320/Y2200, extra bed Y300) This is the town's premier lodging. For the price you get – and you should get – a laundry list of extras such as a tea house, bowling alley, billiards room and nice, if small, gardens.

GETTING THERE & AWAY
Buses for Tsetang leave Lhasa at 7.30am from Barkhor Sq and every 30 minutes from Lhasa's long-distance bus station. Buses and minibuses heading back to Lhasa (Y22 to Y40, three to four hours) depart from the bus station every hour from 8.30am (the 8.30am bus travels nonstop) until about 5pm.

Yumbulagang 雍布拉康
About 12km southwest of Tsetang on a dirt road, **Yumbulagang** (Yōngbùlākāng; admission Y15) is the legendary first building in Tibet. At first glance, it underwhelms, yet climb around and you'll soon realise it soars in splendour and offers commanding valley views.

On your way to Yumbulagang it's well worth stopping at **Trandruk Monastery** (昌珠寺; Chāngzhū Sì; admission Y30), 7km from Tsetang and 6km from Yumbulagang, one of Tibet's oldest Buddhist monasteries and a popular destination for pilgrims.

Bus 2 runs from the Tsetang roundabout to Yumbulagang and Tranduk; or some people hike and hitch a ride on a tractor.

YAMDROK-TSO LAKE 羊卓雍错
On the old road between Gyantse and Lhasa, dazzling Yamdrok-tso Lake (4488m) can be seen from the summit of the Kamba-la pass (4794m). The lake lies several hundred metres below the road, and in clear weather is a fabulous shade of deep turquoise. Far in the northwest distance is the huge massif of Mt Nojin Kangtsang (7191m).

Nangartse is a small town along the way that has some basic accommodation and a couple of restaurants. No public transport, though, runs to the lake from the town.

A 20-minute drive or a two-hour walk from Nangartse brings you to **Samding Monastery** (admission Y10), a charming place with scenic views of the surrounding area and lake.

GYANTSE 江孜

☎ 0892 / elev 3950m

Gyantse (Jiāngzī) is one of the least Chinese-influenced towns – more of a village – in Tibet and is worth a visit for this reason alone. Historically, it was noted for its wood and wool production, especially the latter, from which it made legendary carpets.

Most people visit Gyantse as part of an organised tour down to the Nepalese border, but it's also possible to visit independently. Permits are normally available from Shigatse's PSB (right) for Y50, but many travellers risk going without one.

Sights

The **Pelkhor Chöde Monastery** (admission Y40; ⏱ 8.30am-7pm), founded in 1418, is notable for its superb **Kumbum Chörten** (10,000 Images Stupa), the largest *chörten* in Tibet, which has nine tiers and, according to the Buddhist tradition, 108 chapels. Take a torch (flashlight) to see the excellent murals.

Dzong (Old Fort; admission Y30; ⏱ 8.30am-8.30pm) towers above Gyantse, and has amazing views of the neighbouring sights and surrounding valley. Entry is via the large gate at the main intersection.

In the middle of the fourth lunar month (mid-July), the town hosts a great **horse-racing & archery festival**.

Sleeping & Eating

Jianzang Hotel (建藏饭店; Jiànzàng Fàndiàn; Yingxiong Nanlu; 英雄南路; ☎ 817 3720; d Y180-200, tr with/without bathroom Y150/120) Operated by an English-speaking Tibetan doctor, this hotel gets our vote as the best in town. The balcony is particularly cosy. Staff are friendly (they'll do laundry for Y3 per piece).

Wutse Hotel (乌孜饭店; Wūzī Fàndiàn; ☎ 817 2909; fax 817 2880; Yingxiong Nanlu; 英雄南路; dm Y40, s/d/tr with bathroom Y220/286/320) This is a popular place set around a courtyard. Dorms are in musty quads and shared toilets are a bit rough, but there are clean showers and a decent restaurant. Midrange doubles are better; discounts of 20% are available.

Zongshan Hotel (宗山饭店; Zōngshān Fàndiàn; ☎ 817 5555; 10 Weiguo Lu; 卫国路10号; s/d Y150/288) This place is the newest in town and hasn't degraded yet! The clean, carpeted rooms have 24-hour hot water and there are some unadvertised cheaper rooms without bathrooms, so ask. Discounts of 20% (or more) are standard.

Restaurant of Zhuang Yuan (庄园餐厅; Zhuāngyuán Cāntīng; Yingxiong Nanlu; dishes Y15-35) Not the cheapest place in town, it nonetheless has cheery proprietors. Prices are flexible and portions are large. The sweet and sour chicken (Y35) is legendary; make sure you are in the kitchen to see the pyrotechnics.

Getting There & Away

The easiest way to Gyantse is via Shigatse, which gives you the chance – emphasise chance – to get a travel permit first. A minibus leaves every 30 minutes or so from in front of Shigatse's bus station (Y28, 1½ hours). Minibuses circle the main intersection in Gyantse looking for passengers.

SHIGATSE 日喀则

☎ 0892 / elev 3900m

Shigatse (Rìkāzé) is the second-largest city in Tibet. The vast majority of residents are Tibetan, unlike in Lhasa, and there's a palpably unhurried pace of life here. As the traditional capital of the central Tsang region, it has long been a rival with Lhasa for political control of the country. The Tsang kings and later governors exercised their power from the once imposing heights of the Shigatse Fortress – the present ruins only hint at its former glory. Since the Mongol sponsorship of the Gelugpa order, Shigatse has been the seat of the Panchen Lama, who is traditionally based in Tashilhunpo Monastery, Shigatse's foremost attraction.

Information

INTERNET ACCESS 网吧
China Telecom Internet Bar (Zhōngguó Diànxìn Wǎngbā; Shandong Lu; per hr Y4; ⏱ 24hr) A handful of others are located on both sides of Shandong Lu downtown.

MONEY
Bank of China (Zhōngguó Yínháng; Shanghai Zhonglu; ⏱ 9am-1pm & 3.30-6.30pm Mon-Fri, 10am-5pm Sat & Sun, until 5pm in winter) A bit south of the Shigatse Hotel, changes travellers cheques and cash and supposedly gives credit-card advances. There's a 24-hour ATM outside.

POST
China Post (Zhōngguó Yóujú; cnr Shandong Lu & Zhufeng Lu; ⏱ 9am-noon & 4-7pm) This building was slated for renovation and may temporarily be closed or relocated.

PUBLIC SECURITY BUREAU
Shigatse itself is an open town, so a permit is not required to visit. If you want to travel in the

TIBET

closed areas of Tsang without the cost of a tour and Land Cruiser, you can ask for a permit at the Shigatse **PSB** (Gōngānjú; Qingdao Lu, signposted West Qingdao Lu; 9.30am-12.30pm & 3.30-6.30pm Mon-Fri). If you're lucky you might catch it open on the weekend also. It does not normally extend visas but may do so in an emergency.

Previously it had been issuing 10- to 15-day permits for all towns along the Friendship Hwy to the border (including EBC), and for Gyantse and Shalu Monastery. However, a steady stream of solo travellers has made the PSB waver of late. Rates vary – some travellers have been charged Y50, some Y100; others have been denied. Still others have gotten them only through a bit of, er, verbal subterfuge.

TELEPHONE
The cheapest places to make calls are the many private telephone booths around town.

China Telecom (Zhōngguó Diànxìn; Zhufeng Lu; 9am-6.30pm) You can send faxes and make international phone calls here.

Sights
Tashilhunpo Monastery (Zhāshílúnbù Sì; admission Y55; 9am-noon & 3.30-6.30pm) is the seat of the Panchen Lama and one of Tibetan culture's six great Gelugpa institutions (along with Drepung, Sera and Ganden in Lhasa and Kumbum and Labrang in Amdo – modern Gansu and Qinghai provinces). Built in 1447 by a nephew of Tsongkhapa, the monastery once housed over 4000 monks, but there are now only 600.

Apart from a giant statue of Jampa (Maitreya) Buddha (nearly 27m high) in the Temple of the Maitreya, the monastery is also famed for its Grand Hall, which houses the opulent tomb (containing 85kg of gold and masses of jewels) of the fourth Panchen Lama. Photography inside the monastic buildings costs a whopping Y75 *per chapel*.

Little remains of the skyline-obscuring **Shigatse Fortress**. In 2006, though, the hillsides were sheathed in bamboo rigging to start a mammoth reconstruction effort. Expect ersatz antiquity and a hefty admission fee when work is done. The best way to see it is to follow the *kora* around the monastery (clockwise) and then continue to the *dzong* (fortress) for good views of the town.

Sleeping
Shambhala Hotel (Xióngbālā Fàndiàn; 882 7666; cnr Qingdao Lu & Shanghai Zhonglu; 青岛路和上中海路口; dm Y25, d with/without bathroom Y120/Y60) The friendly staff dither and the place is a bit chaotic but it's a good back-up lodging option to the excellent Tenzin Hotel. The dorms are clean and spacious (the 4th floor is quietest) with communal squat toilets and sinks; hot showers cost Y5.

Tenzin Hotel (Tiānxīn Lǚguǎn; 882 2018; fax 883 8080; 10 Pangchel Gong; dm/tr Y35/40 per bed, s without bathroom Y100, d with/without bathroom Y200/120, deluxe Y260) The budget traveller's dream spot,

SHIGATSE 日喀则

0 ——— 500 m
0 ——— 0.3 miles

with spotless dorms and clean facilities (the top-floor triples are quieter for almost the same price). The comfortable doubles with bathroom are often discounted to Y160. The shared bathrooms are excellent and usually have 24-hour hot water. The restaurant is pricey, but is a good place to hang out.

Qomolongma Friendship Hotel (Zhūfēng Yǒuyì Bīnguǎn; ☎ 882 1929; 14 Dechen Podrang Lu; dm Y35, d Y200-258, tr Y288) This place is often used by budget tour companies from Nepal, so it's best used as a last resort. (That said, the hotel often gives a 50% discount, which makes the doubles pretty much worth it. And the restaurant is decent.) The dorm block at the back is basic, with pit toilets. Public showers (Y5) are just outside the hotel's front door, to the left.

Manasarovar Hotel (Shénhú Jiǔdiàn; ☎ 883 9999; www.hotelmanasarovartibet.com; 20 Qingdao Lu; 青岛路 20号; ordinary/superior d Y280/480, tr Y320) This relatively new three-star option is the best mid-range place in town. Rooms are spacious and spotless, with nice Tibetan detailing, and the services offered are actually available! Discounts of up to 50% are on offer.

Shigatse Hotel (Rìkāzé Fàndiàn; ☎ 882 2525; fax 882 1900; 13 Shanghai Zhonglu; 上海中路13号; d/tr Y500/600) This is a three-star tour-group palace in the south of town. The Tibetan-style rooms are cosy, though the bathrooms are decidedly average. Doubles are often discounted to Y240.

Eating

Galgye Tibetan Restaurant (Xueqiang Lu; dishes Y10-15) A decent Tibetan restaurant serving dishes such as Tibetan noodles, curry potatoes and Lhasa beer (Y6).

Kailash (☎ 899 5923; Zhufeng Lu; mains Y15-35) Great ambience and food. Another Nepali-run place, this friendly operation has spacious interiors with comfy tables and a lengthy list of Nepalese, Tibetan and Western dishes. Eat your yak while gazing at Tashilhunpo Monastery!

Hole-in-the-wall Chinese eateries with foreign menus sit on Xueqiang Lu around the corner from the Tenzin Hotel. Names and owners change regularly, but the menus don't. The English-version menus in these restaurants are 25% more expensive. Places include **Tianfu Restaurant** and the **Yuanfu Restaurant**. Further down is the **Zhengxin Restaurant**, which is good and has some breakfast foods, such as pancakes and banana yoghurt.

Getting There & Away

BUS

Private buses to Lhasa (Y50, six to seven hours) leave from around 8am from a dusty parking area on Qingdao Lu on the eastern side of Shigatse. The bus station on Zhufeng Lu has a similar service as well as express buses (Y65, five to six hours). Taxis do the trip for around Y70 per person.

Minibuses to Gyantse (Y28, 1½ hours) run when full from outside the bus station from 10am until 8pm daily, but drivers can be reluctant to take foreigners. Taxis also run when full for Y20 per seat or Y80 for the taxi; taxi drivers love to take you (even when the PSB is standing right there hassling them about it!) but will likely start negotiations at Y35 per seat.

There are daily west-bound morning minibuses to Lhatse (Y38, five hours) and Tingri (Y69) and occasional buses to Zhāngmù. Those aiming for the Nepalese border may be better off inquiring at the Tenzin Hotel about minibuses or Land Cruisers heading out to the border to pick up tour groups (around Y250 per person). Otherwise, some people hitch from Lhatse or Tingri.

CAR HIRE

Next to the carpet factory, the FIT (☎ 883 8068, 899 0505; Zhufeng Lu) branch office can arrange Land Cruiser hire along the Friendship Hwy (only). Sample prices are Y3400 per vehicle for a three-day return trip to Rongphu Monastery, or Y3300 for a three- to four-day trip to the Nepalese border.

You could also try to hire a Land Cruiser unofficially by talking to the drivers who park outside the Tenzin Hotel. Renting vehicles in Shigatse is more difficult than in Lhasa. Expect to pay Y2500 to Y3000 for a vehicle to Rongphu Monastery and the Nepalese border, but you'll have to arrange your own permits with the PSB.

SAKYA 萨迦
☎ 0892 / elev 4280m

The monastic town of Sakya (Sàjiā) is one of Tsang's most important historical sights. Even more than Gyantse, Sakya is very Tibetan in character, making it an interesting place to spend a day or so. (Note the distinctive local colouring of buildings – ash grey with red and white vertical stripes, symbolising both the Rigsum Gonpo, the trinity of Bodhisattvas,

TIBET

and Sakya authority.) You need a permit, but the formerly strict PSB hasn't been hassling travellers much of late.

Sakya's principal attractions are its northern and southern monasteries on either side of the Trum-chu (Trum River). The imposing southern **monastery** (gompa; admission Y50; ⏰ 9.30am-1pm, 4pm onwards) is of interest. The original, northern monastery has been mostly reduced to picturesque ruins, though restoration work is ongoing.

Sleeping & Eating

Sakya Guesthouse (萨迦招待所; Sàjiā Zhāodàisuǒ; ☎ 824 2233; dm Y15-20) The rooms are more bearable if you have a sleeping bag (hold your nose in the common toilets), and there's a certain timeless feel about the place. Look for the English sign saying 'Hotel'.

Manasarovar Sakya Hotel (神湖萨迦宾馆; Shénhú Sàjiā Bīnguǎn; ☎ 824 2555; 1 Kaisang Xilu; dm Y30-40, d Y280, tr Y220-280) Rooms range from basic but clean to mostly comfy. One of the dorms comes with toilet and shower; the others have no access to a shower. Rooms are clean and there are superb views from the roof. Discounts of 33% are available. Its restaurant (mains Y15 to Y25) is the best place for Western dishes.

Sakya Monastery Restaurant (☎ 824 2267; dishes Y7-12) This restaurant belongs to the southern monastery and serves cheap Tibetan-style dishes.

Getting There & Away

There are daily minibuses departing from Shigatse's bus station to Sakya (Y36 to Y43, four to six hours) at around 8am and possibly at 3.30pm. Minibuses return from the Sakya Guesthouse at around 11am. Another option is to take a Lhatse-bound bus to the Sakya turn-off and then hitch the remaining 25km. You'll most likely have to pay the full fare to Lhatse, though.

Most people arrange to see Sakya as an overnight stop when hiring a Land Cruiser to the border or to the EBC.

RONGPHU MONASTERY & EVEREST BASE CAMP 绒布寺、珠峰

Before heading to the border, many travellers doing the Lhasa–Kodari trip take in Rongphu Monastery and Everest Base Camp (EBC; also known as Mt Qomolangma, or Chomolungma Base Camp; 5200m), where the vistas are far superior to those in Nepal.

You'll freeze your buns off and be slap-happy giddy from the heights. Yaks take up residence in the putrid, overflowing latrines. Too cold to sleep? It doesn't matter because the Tibetans in surrounding tents will be singing all night.

But sunrise at Everest makes it all worth the trouble.

Before you set off you'll need to stop in Shegar (or Tingri if coming from Nepal) to pay the Qomolangma National Park entrance fee of Y405 per vehicle, plus Y65 per passenger.

Later, as vehicle traffic to Rongphu Monastery and environs is now strictly limited, you must stop off at a new 'entrance' and fork over yet another Y80 for an 'eco-bus' – ironically, a pollution-spewing Dodge Ram – for the last two hours or so to Rongphu Monastery.

The walk from Rongphu Monastery to EBC takes about two hours, or it's 45 minutes in a horse cart (Y60). The route is obvious, going past a glacial moraine and across a sandy plain. In May there are usually dozens of tents belonging to various expeditions. The China Post kiosk here is the world's highest post box.

There is a **guesthouse** (dm Y25) next to Rongphu Monastery. It has a restaurant that also sells simple supplies. A new two-star hotel nearby is laughably expensive. It's possible to stay in **tent guesthouses** (dm Y20-25) at EBC; you'll find loads of blankets, but very basic food.

TINGRI 定日

☎ 8054 / elev 4390m

Tingri (Dìngrì) is a huddle of Tibetan homes that overlooks a sweeping plain bordered by the towering Himalayan peaks of Mt Everest (8848m) and Cho Oyu (8153m). It's where many travellers spend their first or last night in Tibet en route to/from Nepal.

Ruins on the hill overlooking Tingri are all that remain of the **Tingri Fortress**. This fort was destroyed in a late 18th-century Nepalese invasion. Many more ruins on the plains between Shegar and Tingri shared the same history.

All the budget hotels have the same layout – a quad of rooms set around a dusty courtyard. Of these, the **Amdo Hotel** (Y25 per bed) is popular with budget Land Cruiser trips and has a hot shower.

The all-brick rooms at the **Snow Leopard Guest House** (☎ 826 2711; d Y80-160) are the most comfortable in town. Its solar shower block (hot water 7pm to midnight) is spotless.

There's also a cosy restaurant (dishes Y25) and a sitting area/reception. It's about 400m east of the other hotels.

From Tingri it's four or five spectacular hours to the Nepalese border – up, up and up to the views from Tong-la pass (5120m) and then down, down, down via the town of Nyalam to Zhāngmù.

ZHĀNGMÙ 樟木

☎ 0892 / elev 2300m

Zhāngmù (Khasa in Nepalese, Dram in Tibetan) is a remarkable town – everything is incredibly green and luxuriant, the smells of curry and incense in the air are from the subcontinent; and the babbling sound of fast-flowing streams that cut through the town is music to the ears.

The **Bank of China** (Zhōngguó Yínháng; ✍ 9.30am-1.30pm & 3.30-6.30pm Mon-Fri, 11am-2pm Sat & Sun) will change cash and travellers cheques into yuán, and also yuán into US dollars, euros or UK pounds if you have an exchange receipt (ie the receipt you get when you change foreign currency into yuán). (Note: rupees are not accepted.)

Moneychangers change every combination of US dollars, yuán and Nepalese rupees.

The **Gang Gyen Hotel** (轻工宾馆; ☎ 874 2188; dm Y40-50, d Y150) is just up the street from Chinese immigration. Not precisely Shangri-la here, but the dorms are at least a bit spacious. Communal bathrooms are about as good as they get in town. The rooftop shower is decent and has hot water 24 hours. The restaurant adjacent is pricey but its food is recommended.

Just five minutes uphill from the Gang Gyen Hotel is the dirt cheap but good value **Zhangmu Hongqiao Hotel** (樟木红桥宾馆; Zhāngmù Hóngqiáo Bīnguǎn; ☎ 874 2261; dm Y20-25, d Y100-120). Not much English is spoken here but the rooms and shared facilities are decent.

ZHĀNGMÙ TO KODARI

After you pass through **Chinese immigration** (✍ 9.30am-6.30pm, sometimes closed 1.30-3.30pm), access to Nepal is via the Friendship Bridge and Kodari, around 8km below Zhāngmù. It's generally no problem to get a lift across this stretch of no-man's-land (Y10). Occasional landslides mean that travellers may find themselves scrambling over debris in the places where vehicles can't pass.

It is possible to get a Nepalese visa at the border for the same price as in Lhasa (US$30 cash, plus one passport photo), though it would be sensible to get one beforehand in Lhasa just in case. There are a few hotels that offer rooms on the Nepalese side. For those planning to continue straight on to Kathmandu, there are a couple of buses a day from Kodari that leave when full. If you can't find a direct bus, you'll have to change halfway at Barabise. The other option is to hire a vehicle from near Nepalese immigration. A ride to Kathmandu (four to five hours) costs Rs 1500 to Rs 2000 per car, or around Rs 500 per person. There are currently around a dozen military checkpoints along the road. Bus passengers have to disembark at many of these, causing the trip to last around seven hours.

Nepal is 2¼ hours behind Chinese time.

Directory

CONTENTS

ACCOMMODATION

Overall, accommodation in China is no cause for great excitement, although it is gradually improving. Beyond Hong Kong and Macau, you won't find a classic hotel of real stature and pedigree like the Raffles Hotel in Singapore. Few historic hotels of character exist outside Hong Kong, Macau, Běijīng and Shànghǎi (and at a stretch Tiānjīn).

Be warned that the star rating at China's hotels can be misleading. Hotels are often awarded four or five stars, when they are patently a star lower in ranking. This might not be immediately obvious to guests approaching

---

BOOK ACCOMMODATION ONLINE

For more accommodation reviews and recommendations by Lonely Planet authors, check out the online booking service at www.lonelyplanet.com. You'll find the true, insider lowdown on the best places to stay. Reviews are thorough and independent. Best of all, you can book online.

---

the reception desk (总台; *zǒngtái*) with high expectations, so take time to wander round and make a quick inspection of the overall quality or stick to chain hotels with recognisable names.

Hotels in this book are divided into three categories: budget, midrange and top end. The majority of rooms in China are 'twins', which means two single beds placed in one room. Single rooms (one bed per room; 单间; *dānjiān*) are quite rare. Double rooms (双人房; *shuāng rén fáng*; also called 标准间; *biāozhǔn jiān*) will often be a twin, with two beds. Suites (套房; *tàofáng*) are available at most midrange and top-end hotels. For most accommodation listed in this guide, addresses are provided in Chinese. If you're having difficulty finding your hotel, show the address to a Chinese speaker.

The Chinese method of designating floors is the same as that used in the USA, but different from, say, Australia's. What would be the ground floor in Australia is the 1st floor in China, the 1st is the 2nd, and so on.

The policy at almost every hotel in China is that you check out by noon. If you check out between noon and 6pm there is a charge of 50% of the room price – after 6pm you have to pay for another full night.

Almost every hotel has a left-luggage room (*jìcún chù* or *xínglǐ bǎoguān*), and in many hotels there is one on every floor. If you are a guest in the hotel, use of the left-luggage room should be free.

Male guests regularly receive phone calls from prostitutes, who ask whether *ànmó* (massage) or *xiǎojie* (a young lady) is required; if you don't want their services, unplug your phone, as they can be persistent.

Budget

Budget rooms can be found in hotels rated two stars or less. Outside of the belatedly growing band of fresh youth hostels (www .hostelchina.cn), expect basic facilities, grimy bathrooms, dirty carpets, flickering TVs, noisy neighbours, very basic or nonexistent English-language skills and a simple restaurant or none at all. Virtually all budget hotel rooms should come with air-conditioning and TV, but not all rooms have telephones (at youth hostels, for example), so ask beforehand.

Foreign travellers have traditionally been steered away from ultra-cheap Chinese guesthouse accommodation towards lodgings approved by the Public Security Bureau (PSB), which were invariably more expensive. This is beginning to change, but many cheaper guesthouses still refuse foreigners. In far-flung villages, families open their houses to guests, generally for a pittance; such accommodation options are called *nóngjiā* (农家).

In some cities and towns it is worth going with touts who collect at the train and bus stations, as they can introduce you to cheap accommodation, but only if they can offer a good price.

In all cases, ask to see a room before taking it and check for smoke alarms. Hotel fires are quite common in China, and fires can get the upper hand because of the lack of smoke alarms and locked fire exits (check the exits on your floor and complain if they are locked).

The pinyin and Chinese characters for guesthouses:

zhāodàisuǒ	招待所
lǚdiàn	旅店
lǚguǎn	旅馆

Certain temples and monasteries (especially on China's sacred mountains) can provide accommodation. They can be very cheap, but extremely ascetic, with no running water or electricity.

Staying in a university dorm is sometimes one of your cheapest options. Many universities will rent out vacant dorm rooms in the foreign student dormitory. Universities also sometimes have actual hotels, although the prices are usually on a par with regular budget hotels.

Midrange

Midrange hotels (three to four stars) offer comfort and a measure of style, but are often

---

PRACTICALITIES

- There are four types of plugs in China: three-pronged angled pins (as in Australia), three-pronged round pins (as in Hong Kong), two flat pins (US style but without the ground wire) or two narrow round pins (European style). Electricity is 220 volts, 50 cycles AC.

- The standard locally published English-language newspaper is the *China Daily* (www.china daily.com.cn). China's largest circulation Chinese-language daily is the *People's Daily* (*Rénmín Rìbào*). It has an English-language edition at www.english.peopledaily.com.cn. Imported English-language newspapers such as the *Times*, the *International Herald Tribune*, the *Asian Wall Street Journal*, the *Financial Times* and the *South China Morning Post* can be bought from five-star hotel bookshops, as can imported English-language international magazines such as *Time, Newsweek, Far Eastern Economic Review* and the *Economist*. Look out for expat English-language magazines with local bar, restaurant and events listings in town. Magazines include *That's Beijing, That's Shanghai* and *That's Guangzhou*.

- Listen to the BBC World Service (www.bbc.co.uk/worldservice/tuning/) or Voice of America (www.voa.gov), although these websites are quite often jammed. China Radio International (CRI) is China's overseas radio service and broadcasts in about 40 foreign languages. The national TV outfit, Chinese Central TV (CCTV), has an English-language channel – CCTV9; CCTV4 also has some English programs. Your hotel may have ESPN, Star Sports, CNN or BBC News 24.

- China officially subscribes to the international metric system, but you are also likely to encounter the ancient Chinese weights and measures system that features the *liǎng* (tael, 37.5g) and the *jīn* (catty, 0.6kg), which are both commonly used. There are 10 *liǎng* to the *jīn*.

bland and unimaginative, and housed in recently built and sterile exteriors. You should find someone who can speak English, but language skills are rarely good and often problematic even at reception. When making a choice, opt for Sino-foreign joint-venture hotels over the Chinese-owned hotels, wherever possible. Furthermore, try to opt for the newer establishments as midrange hotels rapidly get set in their ways and quickly lose their freshness. Several new chains such as **Home Inn** (www.homeinns.com) and **Motel 168** (www.motel168 .com) are expanding across China, offering lower midrange comfort and convenience; these are often superior to the more established midrange options. Chinese midrange hotels should, but may not, have a Western restaurant and a bar.

Rooms will all come with a bath/shower room, air-con and telephone; they may have satellite TV, cable TV or an in-house movie channel; they should also come with a kettle (and coffee sachets), water cooler, safe and minibar; and there could be broadband internet connection. You may receive a free newspaper, but at best only the *China Daily*.

Top End

Hotels in the top-end range can cost anything up to US$300 – prices in this category vary considerably – and they are typically four to five stars.

As China, outside of Hong Kong, has few independent hotels of real distinction, it's advisable to select chain hotels that offer a proven standard of excellence and quality across the board when opting for top-drawer accommodation. Shangri-La, Marriott, Holiday Inn, Hilton, St Regis, Marco Polo and Grand Hyatt all have a presence in China and can generally be relied upon for high standards of service and comfort.

Some Chinese-owned hotels display five stars, when they are clearly four stars, so be warned. Five-star hotels should be equipped with top-quality sport (including swimming pool and tennis courts), recreational and shopping facilities, and there should be a wide selection of dining options and ATMs that take international cards. Five-star hotel rooms should have a kettle (and coffee sachets), safe, minibar, satellite or cable TV, broadband internet connection, free newspaper (typically the *International Herald Tribune*) and nightly turn-down service. Superior comfort should

also be available on executive floors, which typically provide free drinks upon arrival and in the afternoon, complimentary breakfast and business facilities. Service should be top-notch. Most top-end hotels list their room rates in US dollars, but you will have to pay in local currency. Practically all hotels will change money for guests and most midrange and top-end hotels accept credit cards. All hotel rooms are subject to a 10% or 15% service charge.

Discounts & Reservations

It is always important to bargain for a room, as discounts (*dǎzhékòu*) are generally in force in all but the cheapest accommodation options (see the boxed text, p23). It is best to do this in person at reception; if you book ahead, you can end up paying well over the odds. Apart from during the busy holiday periods (the first week of May and October, and Chinese New Year), rooms should be well below the rack rate and rarely booked out. At reception, you should be able to get a discount of 10% to 50% off the tariff rate, and 30% is typical. Booking online is an excellent way to secure a good price on a room, and should be the first place you look. Often you actually get a discount by booking through an agency – and these can be substantial, up to 40% to 50% off the walk-in rate (although don't use Chinese online agencies, which simply offer rates you can get from the hotels themselves). Accommodation websites that could be useful for travellers booking accommodation include www.redflag.info, www.asia-hotels.com, www.sinohotel.com and www.china-hotel guide.com. Airports at major cities often have hotel-booking counters that offer discounted rates. Once in China, you can always contact **Ctrip** (☎ 800 820 6666; www.english.ctrip.com) to book a discounted room in many cities across China.

At check-in, you will need your passport and a registration form will ask what type of visa you have. For most travellers, your visa will be 'L'; for a full list of visa categories, see the table under Visas, p953. A deposit (*yājīn*) is required at most hotels; this will be either a cash deposit or your credit card details will be taken. If your deposit is paid in cash, you will be given a receipt which you should hold on to for later reimbursement. Credit cards can usually be used for payment at three-star hotels and up, but always check beforehand.

ACTIVITIES

A whiff of the tourist dollar has sent Chinese entrepreneurs scrambling up the rock face of the adventure-sport economy. Even in and around Běijīng the choice of activities is mushrooming, including paragliding, hang-gliding, rock climbing, diving with sharks, skiing, bungee jumping, horse riding and more. Glance at expat magazines in Běijīng, Guǎngzhōu and Shànghǎi for information on other activities such as running, mountain biking, football, cricket, swimming, ice skating, skateboarding and water-skiing.

Outfits in China itself, such as **Wildchina** (www.wildchina.com), offer a host of dramatic treks in remote parts of China.

Golf

Golf is an increasingly popular sport in China, with courses springing up everywhere. Běijīng has more than a dozen golf courses and others can be found throughout China, from Guǎngzhōu to Shànghǎi. For details of well-known golf courses, check www.worldgolf.com/courses.

Horse Riding

Horse-riding expeditions aimed at tourists can be found in Xīnjiāng, Gānsù, Inner Mongolia, Sìchuān and beyond. Lángmùsì in Gānsù offers good horse-trekking opportunities, and horse riding around both Gānzī and Sōngpān in Sìchuān are popular.

In the big cities, a growing number of equestrian clubs can be found: check the classified pages of expat mags for details.

Skiing

It is not worth going to China for a skiing holiday, but if you are in China during the winter months you can visit northeast China, which is the venue for downhill skiing (see p395 and p380). In the vicinity of Běijīng there are several ski resorts, such as the Nanshan and Saibei ski resorts.

ADMISSION COSTS

At some sights, such as temples and palaces, after you have bought an entrance ticket (门票, *ménpiào*), you can be hit with further charges for drawcard halls or sights within the complex. A more expensive through ticket (套票, *tàopiào*; also referred to as *tōngpiào*, 通票) can be bought at the entrance that will grant you access to all sights.

Tickets must be purchased for virtually every museum, temple, park or sight in China and you will find there is precious little you can do for free. Furthermore, ticket prices for many temples and historical monuments are increasing way ahead of inflation, which raises concerns about regulation. At the time of writing, entry to Huáng Shān was Y200 (in 2001 it was Y82), while entry to Wǔtái Shān was Y90, up from Y48 in 2001. At certain sights that carry heavy ticket prices, there is little attempt at either conservation or restoration, which makes you wonder where all the money goes.

BUSINESS HOURS

China officially has a five-day working week. Banks, offices and government departments are usually open Monday to Friday, roughly from around 9am (some closing for two hours in the middle of the day) until 5pm or 6pm. Saturday and Sunday are both public holidays, but most museums stay open on weekends and sometimes make up for this by closing for one day during the week. Museums tend to stop selling tickets half an hour before they close. Travel agencies and foreign-exchange counters in tourist hotels have similar opening hours, but generally do not close for lunch and are usually open on Saturday and Sunday (at least in the morning). Department stores and shops are generally open from 10am to 10pm, seven days a week. Note that businesses in China close for three week-long holidays (p945). Many parks, zoos and monuments have similar opening hours; they're also open on weekends and often at night. Internet café opening hours vary; they typically open at 8am and close at midnight, but many are increasingly open 24 hours.

Chinese restaurants are generally open from around 10.30am to 11pm or midnight, but some shut at around 2pm and reopen at 5pm or 6pm. The Chinese are accustomed to eating much earlier than Westerners, lunching at around midday and having dinner in the region of 6pm.

CHILDREN

Children will feel more at home in the large cities of Hong Kong, Běijīng, Shànghǎi and Guǎngzhōu, but may feel out of place in smaller towns and in the wilds. Don't be surprised if a complete stranger picks up your child or takes them from your arms:

Chinese people openly display their affection for children. If taking a buggy (stroller) with you, prepare for much inconvenience as pavements are often uneven (the Chinese rarely use buggies) and escalators at metro stations are often up only.

Practicalities

Baby food and milk powder is widely available in supermarkets, as are basics like nappies, baby wipes, bottles, medicine, dummies (pacifiers) and other paraphernalia. Practically no cheap restaurants have baby chairs and finding baby-changing rooms is next to impossible. Ask a doctor specialised in travel medicine for information on recommended immunisations for your child.

Bear in mind that the simple convenience of family car travel is almost out of the question in China, even in large cities (see p970), so be prepared for long train and bus rides or plane journeys and the difficulties associated with them. Protesting infants on a long-haul train trip can make travel very stressful.

Many sights and museums have children's admission prices, which usually apply to children under 1.1m to 1.3m in height. Infants under the age of two fly for 10% of the full airfare, while children between the ages of two and 11 pay half the full price for domestic flights and 75% of the adult price for international flights.

Always ensure that your child carries a form of ID and a hotel card, in case they get lost.

For more information on travelling with children, turn to the following:

- *Travel with Children* (Maureen Wheeler, Cathy Lanigan; Lonely Planet)
- *Travelling Abroad with Children* (Samantha Gore-Lyons; Arrow)
- *Take the Kids Travelling* (Helen Truszkowski; Take the Kids series)
- *Backpacking with Babies and Small Children* (Goldie Silverman; Wilderness Press)
- *Adventuring with Children* (Nan Jeffrey; Avalon House Travel Series)

CLIMATE

Spread over such a vast area, China is subject to the worst extremes in weather, from bitter cold to unbearable heat. The land can be roughly divided into the following climatic regions: north and northeast, northwest, cen-

tral, south and Tibet. See p22 for advice on the best times to visit China's various regions; climatic information is also included in each destination chapter.

The best time to visit China is generally either spring (March to May) or autumn (September to early November). Winters in China's north and northeast fall between November/December and March/April, and are very cold. North of the Great Wall and into Inner Mongolia and Hēilóngjiāng, temperatures can drop to -40°C. Summer is hot and dry, and falls roughly between May and August.

In central China – in the Yangzi River (Cháng Jiāng) valley area, including Shànghǎi – the summers are typically uncomfortable, long, hot and humid. The three cities of Wǔhàn, Chóngqìng and Nánjīng are called the 'three furnaces', sweltering between April and October. Winters are short, wet and cold, and the weather can be miserable.

Hǎinán, Hong Kong and Guǎngdōng province in the south of the country are hot (temperatures can reach 38°C) and humid from April to September. This is also the rainy season, with typhoons liable to hit the southeast coast between July and September. Winters are short, between January and March; it's not nearly as cold as in the north (Hǎinán is warm and, apart from the north of the province, Yúnnán is pleasant), but you will still need warm clothes as far south as Hong Kong.

China's northwest is very hot and dry in summer, while in winter this region is as formidably cold as the rest of northern China. In Ürümqi, the average temperature in January is around -10°C, with minimums down to almost -30°C.

In Tibet you can easily get the impression that all four seasons have been compressed into one day. Temperatures can be below zero during the evening and early morning, and can soar to a sizzling 38°C at midday, but it always feels remarkably cool in the shade. Winter brings intense cold and fierce winds. Tibet is arid, with rainfall scarcest in the north and west. Kūnmíng in Yúnnán is famed for its clement weather.

COURSES

An abundance of courses can be found in China, whether you want to learn Mandarin (or any other dialect), Chinese cookery (see

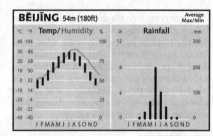

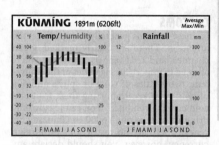

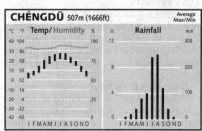

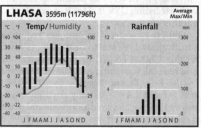

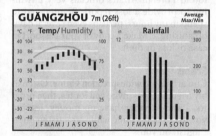

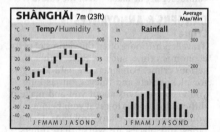

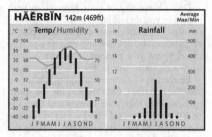

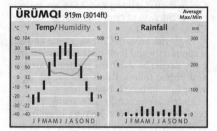

p105), Chinese martial arts, Chinese medicine, qìgōng, paper-cutting, feng shui, calligraphy, Chinese painting or how to play a traditional Chinese musical instrument. One popular organisation is the enterprising Běijīng-based **Chinese Culture Club** (☎ 010-6432 9341; www.chinesecultureclub.org), which offers a range of events and courses from taichi to Beijing Opera face-painting as well as regular Chinese culture–related seminars and tours around China. When searching for Chinese language schools, weigh up the fees and syllabus carefully as many outfits charge expensive fees while using non-international teaching methods that may not suit Westerners. A good place to start looking for a course is in expat magazines such as *That's Beijing*, *That's Shanghai* and *That's Guangzhou*.

DIRECTORY

CUSTOMS

Chinese customs generally pay tourists little attention. There are clearly marked 'green channels' and 'red channels'. Duty-free, you're allowed to import 400 cigarettes or the equivalent, two bottles of wine or spirits and 50g of gold or silver. Importing fresh fruit and cold cuts is prohibited. You can legally only bring in or take out Y6000 in Chinese currency. There are no restrictions on foreign currency; however, you should declare any cash exceeding US$5000 (or its equivalent in another currency).

Objects considered as antiques require a certificate and red seal to clear customs when leaving China. To get the proper certificate and red seal, your antiques must be inspected by the **Relics Bureau** (Wénwù Jiàndìng; ☎ 010-6401 4608, no English spoken). Basically anything made before 1949 is considered an antique and needs a certificate, and if it was made before 1795 it cannot legally be taken out of the country.

DANGERS & ANNOYANCES
Crime

Travellers are more often the victims of petty economic crime, such as theft, rather than serious crime. Foreigners are natural targets for pickpockets and thieves, but as long as you keep your wits about you and make it difficult for thieves to get at your belongings, you shouldn't have any problems. Certain cities and places are worse than others – Guǎngzhōu, Guìyáng and Xī'ān are notorious. Incidences of crime increase around the Chinese New Year.

High-risk areas in China are train and bus stations, city and long-distance buses (especially sleeper buses), hard-seat train carriages and public toilets. Don't leave anything of value in your bicycle basket.

Hotels are generally safe; many have attendants on each floor, keeping an eye on the rooms and safeguarding the keys. Dormitories obviously require more care. Don't be overly trusting of your fellow travellers – many of them are considerably less than honest. All hotels have safes and storage areas for valuables – use them. Don't leave anything you can't do without (passport, travellers cheques, money, air tickets etc) lying around in dorms.

Carry just as much cash as you need and keep the rest in travellers cheques. Always take a money belt for larger sums of cash, along with your passport and credit cards.

A worrying trend is the increasing number of reports of foreigners attacked or even killed for their valuables, especially in more rural locations (a Western tourist was killed on Moon Hill in Yángshuò and another was killed camping out on the Great Wall), so be vigilant at all times. Travelling solo carries obvious risks; it's advisable to travel with someone else or in a small group.

LOSS REPORTS

If something of yours is stolen, report it immediately to the nearest Foreign Affairs Branch of the PSB. Staff will ask you to fill in a loss report before investigating the case and sometimes even recovering the stolen goods.

If you have travel insurance (highly recommended; see p946), it is essential to obtain a loss report so you can claim compensation. Be warned, however: many travellers have found Foreign Affairs officials very unwilling to provide a loss report. Be prepared to spend many hours, perhaps even several days, organising it. Make a copy of your passport in case of loss or theft.

Scams

Con artists are widespread in China. Ostensibly friendly types invite you for tea, then order food and say they have no money, leaving you to foot the bill, while practising their English on you.

Don't leave any of your belongings with someone you do not know well. The opening economy in China has also spawned a plague of dishonest businesses and enterprises. The travel agent you phoned may just operate from a cigarette-smoke-filled hotel room.

Be alert at all times if changing money on the black market. One trick is for the moneychanger to take your money and then say he has made a mistake and wants to recount the money he has just given you. Taking the money back as if to recount it, the last you see of him and your cash is his heels moving at velocity down the road.

Lǎowài!

You will often hear calls or muttered whispers of 'lǎowài' when walking down the street. An excruciating 'Hellooooo', with ensuing hoots of laughter, often follows. Lǎowài means 'foreigner' and is used by one Chinese person to indicate to others the presence of someone non-Chinese. *Lǎowài* is used in conversation by all Chinese to refer to foreigners.

Some travellers find it annoying to hear the word uttered by onlookers wherever they go. It is hardly ever said with anything but surprise and curiosity, however. Despite decades of foreign TV and films, and ever increasing droves of Western travellers, the Chinese still find novelty in the sudden appearance of foreigners. Calls of *lǎowài* are far more common and more vocal in smaller towns than in the big cities. More neutral terms for foreigners are *wàiguórén* (foreigner) and *wàibīn* (foreign guest).

Pollution & Noise

Pollution (see p113) is a serious problem in China and can make travel unpleasant for everyone, but especially if you have allergies, skin conditions or chest, eye, nose and throat problems. According to the World Bank, China has 16 of the world's 20 most polluted cities, and by some counts Běijīng is the world's most polluted city. The pollution in the capital and Shànghǎi can be astonishing, and with some estimates predicting that China's air pollution could quadruple over the next 15 years, an environmental disaster could be in the making.

In recent years the Chinese government has launched an anti-noise-pollution campaign. The government is on a loser with this one, but a number of cities have banned the use of car horns within the city. The Chinese are generally much more tolerant of noise than most foreigners. If it's peace and quiet you want, head for a remote part of China – try the desert in Xīnjiāng, or a mountain top in Tibet.

Spitting

When China first opened to foreign tourism, many foreign travellers were shocked by the spitting, which was conducted noisily by everyone everywhere. Campaigns to stamp out the practice have been partially successful in the major urban centres – there is less public spitting in Guǎngzhōu, Shànghǎi and Běijīng these days (some areas impose a Y50 fine), but in the country, the phlegm still flows.

Queues

In China a large number of people with a common goal (a bus seat, a train ticket, purchasing a mobile phone, ordering a Big Mac etc) generally form a surging mass, although elements of queuing are appearing (see p277). It is one of the more exhausting parts of China travel, and sometimes it is worth paying extra in order to be able to avoid train and bus stations.

DISABLED TRAVELLERS

China has few facilities geared for disabled travellers, but that doesn't necessarily put it out of bounds for those with a physical disability (and a sense of adventure). Most hotels have lifts, so booking ground-floor hotel rooms is not essential, unless you are staying in very budget accommodation. Some hotels at the four- and five-star level have specially designed rooms for people with physical disabilities.

The roads and pavements make things very difficult for the wheelchair-bound or those with a walking disability. Pavements can often be crowded, in an appalling and dangerous condition and with high kerbs. People whose sight, hearing or walking ability is impaired must be extremely cautious of the traffic, which almost never yields to pedestrians. Escalators leading from subways in large cities like Běijīng frequently go up only. Travelling by car or taxi is probably the safest transport option.

Hong Kong is more user-friendly to the disabled than the rest of China, but it presents substantial obstacles of its own, such as the stairs at the subway stations, numerous overhead walkways and steep hills.

Get in touch with your national support organisation before leaving home. They often have travel literature for holiday planning and can put you in touch with travel agents who specialise in tours for the disabled.

In the USA, contact the **Society for Accessible Travel & Hospitality** (SATH; ☎ 212-447 7284; www.sath .org; Suite 601, 347 Fifth Ave, New York, NY).

In the UK, the **Royal Association for Disability & Rehabilitation** (RADAR; ☎ 020-7250 3222; www.radar.org .uk; 12 City Forum, 250 City Rd, London) produces three holiday fact packs for disabled travellers.

In France, try the **Comité National Français de Liaison pour la Réadaption des Handicapés** (CNFLRH; ☎ 01 53 80 66 66; 236 bis rue de Tolbiac, Paris).

You will find loads of information that is useful for wheelchair-bound travellers – including recommended travel agents geared towards disabled travellers – online at www .disabilitytravel.com.

DIRECTORY

EMBASSIES & CONSULATES
Chinese Embassies & Consulates
To obtain a complete list of Chinese diplomatic representation around the world, go to the Ministry of Foreign affairs website at www.fmprc.gov.cn/eng and click on Missions Overseas.

Australia Canberra (☎ 02-6273 4783, 6273 7443; http://au.china-embassy.org; 15 Coronation Dr, Yarralumla, ACT 2600); Sydney consulate (☎ 02-8595 8000; http://sydney.chineseconsulate.org/eng); Melbourne consulate (☎ 03-9822 0604; http://melbourne.china-consulate.org/eng); Perth consulate (☎ 08-9222 0302)

Canada Ottawa (☎ 613-789 3434; www.chinaembassycanada.org/eng; 515 St Patrick St, Ottawa, Ontario K1N 5H3); Toronto consulate (☎ 416-964 7260); Vancouver consulate (☎ 604-736 3910); Calgary consulate (☎ 403-264 3322)

Denmark Copenhagen (☎ 039-460 889; www.chinaembassy.dk; Oeregarrds Alle 25, 2900 Hellerup, Copenhagen)

France Paris (☎ 01-47 36 77 90; www.amb-chine.fr; 20 rue Washington, 75008 Paris)

Japan Tokyo (☎ 03-3403 3389, 3403 3065; www.china-embassy.or.jp; 3-4-33 Moto-Azabu, Minato-ku, Tokyo) Consulates in Fukuoka, Osaka and Sapporo.

Malaysia Kuala Lumpur (☎ 03-242 8495; 229 Jln Ampang, Kuala Lumpur) Consulate in Kuching.

Netherlands The Hague (☎ 070-355 1515; Adriaan Goekooplaan 7, The Hague)

New Zealand Wellington (☎ 04-472 1382; www.chinaembassy.org.nz; 2-6 Glenmore St, Wellington) Consulate in Auckland.

Singapore (☎ 65-734 3361; 70 Dalvey Rd)

Thailand Bangkok (☎ 02-245 7032/49; 57 Th Ratchadaphisek, Bangkok)

UK London (☎ 020-7299 4049, 24hr visa information 0891-880 808, visa section 020-7631 1430; www.chinese-embassy.org.uk; 31 Portland Pl, London; ⏰ visa section open 2-4pm); Manchester consulate (☎ 0161-224 7478); Edinburgh consulate (☎ 0131-337 3220)

USA Washington (☎ 202-338 6688; www.china-embassy.org; Room 110, 2201 Wisconsin Ave NW, Washington DC); Chicago consulate (☎ 312-803 0098); Houston consulate (☎ 713-524 4311); Los Angeles consulate (☎ 213-380 2508); New York consulate (☎ 212-330 7410); San Francisco consulate (☎ 415-563 9232)

Embassies & Consulates in China
EMBASSIES
There are two main embassy compounds in Běijīng – Jianguomenwai and Sanlitun. Embassies are open from 9am to noon and 1.30pm to 4pm Monday to Friday, but visa departments are often only open in the morning.

The following embassies are in the Jianguomenwai area:

India (Map pp118-19; ☎ 010-6532 1908; fax 6532 4684; 1 Ritan Donglu)

Ireland (Map pp118-19; ☎ 010-6532 2691; fax 6532 2168; 3 Ritan Donglu)

Japan (Map pp118-19; ☎ 010-6532 2361; fax 6532 2139; 7 Ritan Lu)

Mongolia (Map pp118-19; ☎ 010-6532 1203; fax 6532 5045; 2 Xiushui Beijie)

New Zealand (Map pp118-19; ☎ 010-6532 2731; fax 6532 4317; 1 Ritan Dong Erjie)

North Korea (Map pp118-19; ☎ 010-6532 5018; fax 6532 6056; Ritan Beilu)

Philippines (Map pp118-19; ☎ 010-6532 1872; fax 6532 3761; 23 Xiushui Beijie)

Singapore (Map pp118-19; ☎ 010-6532 3926; fax 6532 2215; 1 Xiushui Beijie)

Thailand (Map pp118-19; ☎ 010-6532 1903; fax 6532 1748; 40 Guanghua Lu)

UK (Map pp118-19; ☎ 010-5192 4000; fax 6532 1937; 11 Guanghua Lu)

USA (Map pp118-19; ☎ 010-6532 3831; fax 6532 3431; 3 Xiushui Beijie)

Vietnam (Map pp118-19; ☎ 010-6532 1155; fax 6532 5720; 32 Guanghua Lu)

The Sanlitun compound is home to the following embassies:

Australia (Map pp118-19; ☎ 010-5140 4111; fax 6532 6957; 21 Dongzhimenwai Dajie)

Cambodia (Map pp118-19; ☎ 010-6532 2790; fax 6532 3507; 9 Dongzhimenwai Dajie)

Canada (Map pp118-19; ☎ 010-6532 3536; fax 6532 4072; 19 Dongzhimenwai Dajie)

France (Map pp118-19; ☎ 010-6532 1331; fax 6532 4757; 3 Sanlitun Dong Sanjie)

Germany (Map pp118-19; ☎ 010-6532 2161; fax 6532 5336; 17 Dongzhimenwai Dajie)

Italy (Map pp118-19; ☎ 010-6532 2131; fax 6532 4676; 2 Sanlitun Dong Erjie)

Kazakhstan (Map pp118-19; ☎ 010-6532 6182; fax 6532 6183; 9 Sanlitun Dong Liujie)

Laos (Map pp118-19; ☎ 010-6532 1224; 11 Sanlitun Dong Sijie)

Malaysia (Map pp118-19; ☎ 010-6532 2531; fax 6532 5032; 13 Dongzhimenwai Dajie)

Myanmar (Map pp118-19; ☎ 010-6532 1425; fax 6532 1344; 6 Dongzhimenwai Dajie)

Nepal (Map pp118-19; ☎ 010-6532 1795; fax 6532 3251; 1 Sanlitun Xi Liujie)

Netherlands (Map pp118-19; ☎ 010-6532 1131; fax 6532 4689; 4 Liangmahe Nanlu)

Pakistan (Map pp118-19; ☎ 010-6532 2504/2558; 1 Dongzhimenwai Dajie)

Russia (Map pp118-19; ☎ 010-6532 1381; fax 6532 4853; 4 Dongzhimen Beizhongjie) West of the Sanlitun Compound in a separate compound.

South Korea (Map pp118-19; ☎ 010-6505 2608; fax 6505 3067; 3rd & 4th fl, China World Trade Center, 1 Jianguomenwai Dajie)

Spain (Map pp118-19; ☎ 010-6532 1986; fax 6532 3401; 9 Sanlitun Lu)

Sweden (Map pp118-19; ☎ 010-6532 5003; fax 6532 5008; 3 Dongzhimenwai Dajie)

CONSULATES
Chóngqìng

Canada (Map p802; ☎ 023-6373 8007; 17th fl, Metropolitan Tower, Zourong Lu)

Denmark (Map p802; ☎ 023-6373 6008; 31st fl, Metropolitan Tower, Zourong Lu)

Japan (Map p802; ☎ 023 6373 3585; 14th fl, Commercial Wing, Chongqing Hotel, 283 Minsheng Lu)

UK (Map p802; ☎ 023-6369 1500; 28th fl, Metropolitan Tower, Zourong Lu)

Guǎngzhōu

Australia (Map pp590-1; ☎ 020-8335 5911; fax 8335 0718; Room 1509, 15th fl, Main Tower, Guangdong International Hotel, 339 Huanshi Donglu)

Canada (Map pp590-1; ☎ 020-8666 0569; fax 8667 2401; Room 801, Wing C, China Hotel, Liuhua Lu)

France (Map pp590-1; ☎ 020-8330 3405; fax 8330 3437; Room 803, 8th fl, Main Tower, Guangdong International Hotel, 339 Huanshi Donglu)

Germany (Map pp590-1; ☎ 020-8330 6533; fax 8331 7033; 19th fl, Main Tower, Guangdong International Hotel, 339 Huanshi Donglu)

Japan (Map pp590-1; ☎ 020-8333 8999, ext 197; fax 8387 8835; 2nd fl, East Tower, Garden Hotel, 368 Huanshi Donglu)

Netherlands (Map pp590-1; ☎ 020-8330 2067; fax 8330 3601; Room 905, 9th fl, Main Tower, Guangdong International Hotel, 339 Huanshi Donglu)

Thailand (Map pp590-1; ☎ 020-8188 6968, ext 310; Room 310, White Swan Hotel, 1 Shamian Nanjie)

UK (Map pp590-1; ☎ 020-8335 1354; fax 8332 7509; 2nd fl, Main Tower, Guangdong International Hotel, 339 Huanshi Donglu)

USA (Map pp590-1; ☎ 020-8121 8000; fax 8121 8428; 1 Shamian Nanjie, Shamian Dao)

Hohhot

Mongolia (蒙古领事馆; Ménggǔ Lǐngshìguǎn; Map p889; ☎ 680 3540; 5 Dongying Nanjie; ⏱ 8.30am-12.30pm Mon, Tue & Thu) It's possible to get a one-month visa for Mongolia here. Visas take a week to be issued (Y236) or there's an express 24-hour service for Y446; you'll need a letter of invitation from a travel agency to get one. US citizens do not need a visa to visit Mongolia.

Hong Kong

Australia (Map pp530-1; ☎ 0852-2827 8881; 23rd fl, Harbour Centre, 25 Harbour Rd, Wan Chai)

Canada (Map pp526-7; ☎ 0852-2810 4321; 11th-14th fl, Tower I, Exchange Sq, 8 Connaught Pl, Central)

France (Map pp526-7; ☎ 0852-3196 6100; 26th fl, Tower II, Admiralty Centre, 18 Harcourt Rd, Exchange Sq, Admiralty)

Germany (Map pp526-7; ☎ 0852-2105 8788; 21st fl, United Centre, 95 Queensway, Admiralty)

Japan (Map pp526-7; ☎ 0852-2522 1184; 46th & 47th fl, Tower I, Exchange Sq, 8 Connaught Pl, Central)

Laos (Map pp526-7; ☎ 0852 2544 1186; 14th fl, Arion Commercial Centre, 2-12 Queen's Rd West, Sheung Wan)

Netherlands (Map pp526-7; ☎ 0852-2522 5127; Room 5702, 57th fl, Cheung Kong Centre, 2 Queen's Rd, Central)

New Zealand (Map pp530-1; ☎ 0852-2877 4488, 2525 5044; Room 6508, 65th fl, Central Plaza, 18 Harbour Rd, Wan Chai)

South Africa (Map pp530-1; ☎ 0852-2577 3279; Room 2706-2710, 27th fl, Great Eagle Centre, 23 Harbour Rd, Wan Chai)

UK (Map pp526-7; ☎ 0852-2901 3000; 1 Supreme Court Rd, Admiralty)

USA (Map pp526-7; ☎ 0852-2523 9011; 26 Garden Rd, Central)

Vietnam (Map pp530-1; ☎ 0852 2591 4510; vnconsul@netvigator.com; 15th fl, Great Smart Tower, 230 Wan Chai Rd, Wan Chai)

Kūnmíng

Laos (Map p690; ☎ 0871-317 6624; Room N120, ground fl, Camellia Hotel, 96 Dongfeng Donglu; ⏱ 8.30am-noon & 1.30-4.30pm Mon-Fri)

Myanmar (Map p690; ☎ 0871-360 3477; fax 360 2468; www.mcg-kunming.com; B503, Longyuan Haozhai, 166 Weiyuan Jie; ⏱ 8.30am-noon & 1-4.30pm Mon-Fri)

Thailand (Map p690; ☎ 0871-314 9296; fax 316 6891; Ground fl, South Wing, Kunming Hotel, 52 Dongfeng Donglu; ⏱ 9-11.30am Mon-Fri)

Vietnam (Map p690; ☎ 0871-352 2669; 2nd fl, Kaihua Plaza, 157 Beijing Lu; ⏱ 8am-noon & 2-5.30pm Mon-Fri)

Lhasa

Nepal (Map p917; ☎ 0891-682 2881; fax 683 6890; ⏱ 10am-12.30pm Mon-Fri for visa applications) On a side street between the Lhasa Hotel and Norbulingka. Visas are issued in 24 hours. The current fee for a 30-day visa is Y255. Bring a visa photo. It's also possible to obtain visas for the same cost at Kodari, the Nepalese border town, although you'd be wise to do this in an emergency only.

Qīngdǎo

South Korea (Map pp226-7; ☎ 0532-8897 6001; fax 8897 6005; 101 Xianggang Donglu; ☒ 9am-noon & 1.30-5.30pm Mon-Fri)

Shànghǎi

Australia (Map pp244-5; ☎ 021-5292 5500; www .shanghai.china.embassy.gov.au; 22nd fl, CITIC Square, 1168 West Nanjing Rd)

Canada (Map pp244-5; ☎ 021-6279 8400; www .shanghai.gc.ca; Suite 604, West Tower, Shanghai Centre, 1376 West Nanjing Rd)

France (Map pp248-9; ☎ 021-6289 7414; www.consul france-shanghai.org; Room 1204, United Plaza, 1468 West Nanjing Rd)

Germany (Map pp244-5; ☎ 021-3401 0106; www .shanghai.diplo.de; 181 Yongfu Rd)

Italy (Map pp248-9; ☎ 021-6471 6980; 12th fl, Qihua Tower, 1375 Central Huaihai Rd)

Japan (Map pp242-3; ☎ 021-5257 4766; www.shanghai .cn.emb-japan.go.jp; 8 Wanshan Rd, Hongqiao)

Netherlands (☎ 021-6209 9076; 4th fl, East Wing, Taiyang Plaza, 88 Xianxia Rd)

New Zealand (Map pp248-9; ☎ 021-6471 1108; www .nzembassy.com; 15A, Qihua Tower, 1375 Central Huaihai Rd)

Russia (Map pp244-5; ☎ 021-6324 2682; fax 6306 9982; 20 Huangpu Rd)

South Korea (Map pp242-3; ☎ 021-6219 6417; fax 6219 6918; 4th fl, International Trade Centre, 2200 West Yan'an Rd)

Thailand (Map pp244-5; ☎ 021-3313-0365; fax 6323-4140; www.thaishanghai.com; 7 East Zhongshan No 1 Rd)

UK (Map pp244-5; ☎ 021-6279 7650; www.uk.cn/bj; 3rd fl, Room 301, Shanghai Centre, 1376 West Nanjing Rd)

USA (Map pp248-9; ☎ 021-6433 6880; http://shanghai .usembassy-china.org.cn; 1469 Central Huaihai Rd) Entrance on Wulumuqi Rd. Another branch is in the Westgate Tower (Map pp244-5; ☎ 021-3217 4650, after-hr emergency number for US citizens 021-6433 3936; 8th fl, Westgate Tower, 1038 West Nanjing Rd).

Shěnyáng

Japan (Map p360; ☎ 024-2322 7530; fax 2322 7490; 50 Shisi Wei Lu)

North Korea (Map p360; ☎ 024-8690 3451; fax 8690 3482; 37 Beiling Dajie) Visas for North Korea are more likely to be obtained at the North Korean embassy in Běijīng.

Russia (Map p360; ☎ 024-2322 3927; fax 2322 3907; 31 Nanshisan Wei Lu)

South Korea (Map p360; ☎ 024-2385 7845; 14th fl, Mingzhe Dasha, 51 Shisi Wei Lu)

USA (Map p360; ☎ 024-2322 1198; fax 2323 1465; 52 Shisi Wei Lu; ☒ 1.30-4.30pm Mon-Wed & Fri)

Ürümqi

Kazakhstan (Hāsàkèsītǎn Lǐngshìguǎn; Map p822; ☎ 0991-383 2324; 31 Kunming Lu; ☒ 10am-1.30pm Mon-Thu) At the time of writing you could get a three-week visitor visa here for US$30 to US$50 (price depends on nationality), plus a Y45 handling fee. A letter of invitation was not obligatory, but if one is required, CITS (p823) can help. The visa takes three days to be issued, but a week isn't unheard of. Show up early and don't expect calls to be taken. A taxi here will cost about Y30. If you take bus 2 to Xiǎo Xī Gōu, turn right at the first intersection and then again five minutes later; this will put you on Kunming Lu. From there it's a five-minute walk. The Kazakhs are notorious for changing their visa requirements – check the Lonely Planet website for the latest.

FESTIVALS & EVENTS

January/February

Chinese New Year/Spring Festival (Chūn Jié)

This starts on the first day of the first month in the lunar calendar. Many people take a week off work. Be warned: this is China's biggest holiday and all transport and hotels are booked solid. Demand for accommodation skyrockets and prices rise steeply. If you can't avoid being in China at this time, then book your room in advance and sit tight until the chaos is over. The Chinese New Year will fall on 7 February 2008 and 26 January 2009.

Lantern Festival (Yuánxiāo Jié)

It's not a public holiday, but it is very colourful. Children make (or buy) paper lanterns and walk around the streets in the evening holding them. It falls on the 15th day of the first moon, and will be celebrated on 22 February 2008 and 9 February 2009.

March

Guanyin's Birthday (Guānshìyīn Dàchén Shēngrì)

The birthday of Guanyin (see p196), the Goddess of Mercy, is a fine time to visit Buddhist temples, many of which have halls dedicated to the divinity. Guanyin's birthday is the 19th day of the second moon and falls on 26 March 2008 and 15 March 2009.

April

Tomb Sweeping Day (Qīng Míng Jié)

A day for worshipping ancestors, when people visit and clean the graves of their departed relatives. They often place flowers on the tomb and burn ghost money for the departed. The festival generally falls close to Easter, on 5 April in most years, or 4 April in leap years.

Water-Splashing Festival (Pō Shuǐ Jié)

Held in the Xīshuāngbǎnnà region in Yúnnán, this event is held in mid-April (usually 13 to 15 April). The purpose is to wash away the dirt, sorrow and demons of the old year and bring the happiness of the new. The event is staged virtually daily for tourists.

April/May

Mazu's Birthday (Māzǔ Dàchén Shēngrì) Mazu, Goddess of the Sea, is the friend of all fishing crews. She's called Mazu in Fújiàn province and Taiwan. She is also called Tianhou (pronounced 'Tin Hau' in Hong Kong) and Niangniang. Her birthday is widely celebrated at Taoist temples in coastal regions as far south as Vietnam. Mazu's birthday is on the 23rd day of the third moon; 9 May 2007, 28 April 2008 and 18 April 2009.

June

Dragon Boat Festival (Duānwǔ Jié) This is the time to see dragon boat races and eat *zòngzi* (triangular glutinous rice dumplings wrapped in reed leaves). It's a fun holiday despite the fact that it commemorates the sad tale of Qu Yuan, a 3rd-century BC poet-statesman who hurled himself into the mythological Mi Lo river in Húnán to protest against the corrupt government. This holiday falls on the fifth day of the fifth lunar month; 19 June 2007, 8 June 2008 and 28 May 2009.

August

Ghost Month (Guǐ Yuè) The devout believe that during this time the ghosts from hell walk the earth and it is a dangerous time to travel, go swimming, get married or move house. If someone dies during this month, the body will be preserved and the funeral and burial will be performed the following month. The Chinese government officially denounces Ghost Month as a lot of superstitious nonsense. Ghost Month is the seventh lunar month, or really just the first 15 days (usually from early August).

September

Birthday of Confucius (Kǒngzi Dàchén Shēngrì) The great sage has his birthday on 28 September. This is an interesting time to visit Qūfù in Shāndōng, the birthplace of Confucius, although getting a hotel room may be tricky. A ceremony is held at the Confucius Temple (p220) starting around 4am, and other similar temples around China observe the event.

September/October

Mid-Autumn Festival (Zhōngqiū Jié) This is also known as the Moon Festival, and is the time to gaze at the moon and eat tasty *yuè bǐng* (moon cakes); it's also a traditional holiday for lovers. The festival takes place on the 15th day of the eighth moon, and will be celebrated on the following dates: 25 September 2007, 14 September 2008 and 3 October 2009.

FOOD

Don't settle for that sweet Chinatown schlock any more, China is where it's at (see p96) and food should be one of the main reasons you come to China in the first place. Although it depends where in China you travel, a meal for one at budget eateries should cost under Y30, midrange dining options will cost between Y30 and Y100, and top-end choices can cost up to Y800 or more.

GAY & LESBIAN TRAVELLERS

The Chinese Psychiatric Association no longer classifies homosexuality as a mental disorder. Greater tolerance exists in the big cities than in the more conservative countryside. However, even in urban China it is not recommended that gays and lesbians be too open about their sexual orientation in public, even though you will see Chinese same-sex friends holding hands or putting their arms around each other. The situation is changing slowly as an increasing number of gay singers and actors in China are 'outed', but the police periodically crack down on gay meeting places.

On the other hand, there are many recognised gay discos, bars and pubs in the big cities that appear to function without official harassment, although they tend to keep a fairly low profile (see individual city entries for listings of these venues). Venues are listed for cities where gay and lesbian bars exist.

Check out www.utopia-asia.com/tipschin.htm for loads of tips on travelling in China and a complete listing of gay bars nationwide. Other links with useful information and pointers for gay travellers include www.mygayweb.com, www.gayguide.net, www.outandabout.com and www.gaytimes.co.uk. You can also contact the **International Gay and Lesbian Travel Association** (☎ +1-954-776 2626; fax 776 3303; www.iglta.com) in the USA.

Useful publications include the *Spartacus International Gay Guide* (Bruno Gmunder Verlag), a best-selling travel guide for gay travellers, currently in its 35th edition.

HOLIDAYS

The People's Republic of China has nine national holidays, as follows (Hong Kong and Macau have different holidays):

New Year's Day 1 January
Chinese New Year (Spring Festival) Falls on 18 February in 2007, 7 February in 2008, 26 January in 2009 and 14 February in 2010
International Women's Day 8 March
International Labour Day 1 May
Youth Day 4 May
International Children's Day 1 June

DIRECTORY

Birthday of the Chinese Communist Party 1 July
**Anniversary of the Founding of the People's
Liberation Army** 1 August
National Day 1 October

Many of the above are nominal holidays that
do not result in leave. The 1 May holiday
is a week-long holiday, as is National Day
on 1 October, and the Chinese New Year is
also a week-long holiday for many. It's not a
great idea to arrive in China or go travelling
during these holidays as things tend to grind
to a halt. Hotel prices all over China rapidly
shoot up during the May and October holiday
periods.

INSURANCE

A travel insurance policy to cover theft, loss,
trip cancellation and medical problems is a
good idea. Travel agents can sort this out for
you, although it is often cheaper to find good
deals with an insurer online or from a broker.
Some policies offer lower and higher medical
expense options; the higher ones are chiefly
for countries such as the USA, which have
extremely high medical costs.

Some policies specifically exclude 'dangerous activities' such as scuba diving, skiing and
even trekking. A locally acquired motorcycle
licence is not valid under some policies. Check
that the policy covers ambulances or an emergency flight home. You may prefer a policy
which pays doctors or hospitals directly rather
than you having to pay on the spot and claim
later. If you have to claim later, make sure you
keep all documentation. Some policies ask
you to call back (reverse charges) to a centre
in your home country where an immediate
assessment of your problem is made. See the
Health chapter (p977) for further information
on health insurance.

Note that there is a choice of private medical care in large cities and booming towns
such as Běijīng, Shànghǎi, Guǎngzhōu and
Qīngdǎo, but in smaller towns and backwaters, facilities can be basic.

A few insurance brokers in Běijīng and
Shànghǎi (eg Pacific Prime) offer international medical and travel insurance.

INTERNET ACCESS

Chinese may be lined up to be the world's
largest online language by 2007, but the authorities closed scores of internet cafés (网
吧; wǎngbā) after a fire in a Běijīng internet

café in 2002 killed 25 people. Internet café
numbers in some large cities such as Běijīng
are way down after authorities were startled to
find online consoles appearing in hairdressers
and even butchers. Cafés that are allowed to
operate have to use filters to strain out irregular content. In large cities, the area around the
train station is generally a good place to find
internet cafés.

Rates at China's internet cafés should be
around Y1.5 to Y3 per hour for a standard,
no-frills outlet, but comfier and smarter options naturally charge more (up to Y20 per
hour), sometimes with a coffee thrown in.
Deposits of Y10 are sometimes required or
you may be asked for ID.

Agonisingly slow connections are frequent,
especially on congested sites. Up to 10% of
websites are inaccessible in China due to a
policy of censorship. This does not seem to
upset the Chinese very much, but it can be
very inconvenient for foreign travellers wanting to access, for example, the BBC.

Most travellers make constant use of internet cafés and free web-based email such
as **Yahoo** (www.yahoo.com), **Hotmail** (www.hotmail.com)
or **Gmail** (www.gmail.com). For information on
websites with China content, see p25.

If your laptop has a wireless modem, many
café chains and tourist hotels now have broadband wi-fi access. If you're travelling with an
old notebook or hand-held computer, your
modem may not work once you leave your
home country. For more information on travelling with a portable computer, see www
.teleadapt.com.

Most hotels in big cities have in-room
broadband connections. To access the internet using a laptop from your hotel room (if it
has no broadband internet connection), free
dial-up access can be achieved by hooking up
through the phone line and using the local
dial-up number (usually ☎ 163 or 169, but
ask your hotel what the local number is). Use
the same number as the account name and
password, and you can get online. Throughout this book the internet icon ⌨ is used in
hotel reviews to indicate the presence of an
internet café or a terminal where you can
get online.

LEGAL MATTERS

Anyone under the age of 18 is considered a
minor, and the minimum age at which you
can drive is also 18. The age of consent for

marriage is 22 for men and 20 for women. There is no minimum age that restricts the consumption of alcohol or use of cigarettes. China's laws against the use of illegal drugs are harsh, and foreign nationals have been executed for drug offences (trafficking in more than 50g of heroin can result in the death penalty). The Chinese criminal justice system does not ensure a fair trial and defendants are not presumed innocent until proven guilty. Note that China conducts more judicial executions than the rest of the world put together, up to 10,000 (27 per day) according to some reports. If arrested, most foreign citizens have the right to contact their embassy.

MAPS

Top-quality maps of almost every Chinese city and many small towns are readily available in China. Many are detailed, illustrating bus routes (including names of bus stops) and the locations of hotels, shops and so on, and cost around Y2 to Y4. Unfortunately, most maps are only in Chinese. They can be purchased from bookstalls or street vendors around train and bus stations, from branches of the Xinhua Bookshop or from hotel front desks. City and town road atlases can also be purchased from the same places, but again, they are largely in Chinese.

Tourist centres, hotel gift shops, Friendship Stores (Yǒuyì Shāngdiàn) and from time to time foreign-language bookshops in large cities stock English versions. Here you may also find Chinese- and English-language atlases of China. Also ask at the concierge desk as it could well have a map of town in English.

Some of the most detailed maps of China available in the West are the aerial survey 'Operational Navigation Charts' (Series ONC). These are prepared and published by the Defense Mapping Agency Aerospace Center, St Louis Air Force Station, Missouri, USA. Cyclists and mountaineers have recommended these highly. In the UK you can obtain these maps from **Stanfords Map Centre** (☎ 020-7836 1321; www.stanfords.co.uk; 12-14 Long Acre, London) or the **Map Shop** (☎ 0800 085 4080; www.themapshop.co.uk; 15 High St, Upton upon Severn, Worcestershire).

Australians can contact **Mapland** (☎ 03-9670 4383; www.mapland.com.au; 372 Little Bourke St, Melbourne) or the **Travel Bookshop** (☎ 02-9241 3554; 20 Bridge St, Sydney). In New Zealand try **MapWorld** (☎ 0800 627967; www.mapworld.co.nz; 173 Gloucester St, Christchurch).

In France see **Ulysse** (☎ 01 43 25 17 35; 26 rue Saint Louis en l'Île) or **IGN** (☎ 01 43 98 80 00; 107 rue de la Boetie) in Paris.

In the United States, contact **Map Link** (☎ 1-800 962 1394; www.maplink.com; Unit 5, 30 S La Patera Lane, Santa Barbara, CA).

GeoCenter publishes an excellent map of China. Lonely Planet publishes *Beijing* and *Hong Kong* city maps. The *Hong Kong Guidebook* by Universal is a first-rate colour map of the city that is regularly updated. Nelles publishes good detailed regional maps of China, and Berndtson has an excellent detailed *Beijing* map.

MONEY

Consult the Quick Reference on the inside front cover for a table of exchange rates and refer to p23 for information on costs.

ATMs

ATMs (Automated Teller Machines) advertising international bank settlement systems such as GlobalAccess, Cirrus, Maestro Plus and others are common in Hong Kong and Macau. On the mainland, ATMs that take international cards include branches of the Bank of China and the Industrial and Commercial Bank of China, where you can use Visa, MasterCard, Cirrus, Maestro, Plus and American Express (AmEx) to withdraw cash. The network largely applies to sizable towns and cities. Large airports such as Beijing Capital Airport, five-star hotels and some department stores have ATMs. Most other ATMs in China can only be used for withdrawing Renminbi in domestic accounts. The exchange rate on ATM withdrawals is similar to credit cards but there is a maximum daily withdrawal amount. If you plan on staying in China for a long period, it is advisable to open an account at a bank like the Bank of China with a nationwide network of ATMs.

For your nearest ATM, consult the ATM locator on www.international.visa.com/ps or on www.mastercard.com/cardholderser vices/atm; both have comprehensive listings. For those without an ATM card or credit card, a PIN-activated **Visa TravelMoney card** (☎ US 1-877-394 2247) will give you access to predeposited cash through the ATM network. ATMs are listed in the Information sections (under Money) in destinations throughout this book.

DIRECTORY

Counterfeit Bills

Counterfeit notes are a problem in China. Very few Chinese will accept a Y50 or Y100 note without first checking to see if it's a fake. Old, tattered or torn notes are also sometimes hard to spend. You can exchange old notes for new ones at the Bank of China – counterfeits, however, will be confiscated. Examine large denomination notes if given to you as change by street vendors; they could well be dumping a forged banknote on you.

Forgeries vary in quality from poor to good: inspect the watermark (not distinct on fake notes), the metal thread (which should again be distinct), the colour of the bill, the paper quality and its feel. Use a genuine note, eg a Y100 note given to you by the bank, as a reference.

Credit Cards

Credit is not big in China. The Chinese don't like to be in debt, however short-term that debt may be. Increasing numbers of young people are using credit cards, but numbers remain low compared to the West. Foreign plastic is therefore of limited use, but cards that can be used include Visa, MasterCard, AmEx and JCB. Don't expect to be able to use them everywhere, and always carry enough cash. You should be able to use credit cards at upmarket hotels and restaurants, supermarkets and department stores. Where they are accepted, credit cards often deliver a slightly better exchange rate than in banks. Money can also be withdrawn at certain ATMs in large cities (see p947) on credit cards such as Visa, MasterCard and Amex. Credit cards can still not be used to buy train tickets, but Civil Aviation Administration of China (CAAC) offices readily accept international Visa cards for buying air tickets. Certain cards offer insurance and other benefits.

Credit card cash advances have become fairly routine at head branches of the Bank of China, even in places as remote as Lhasa. Bear in mind, however, that a 4% commission is generally deducted. The Bank of China does not charge commission on AmEx cash withdrawals.

Currency

The Chinese currency is the Renminbi (RMB), or 'People's Money'. Formally the basic unit of RMB is the yuán, which is divided into 10 jiǎo, which is again divided into 10 fēn. Colloquially, the yuán is referred to as kuài and jiǎo as máo. The fēn has so little value these days that it is rarely used.

The Bank of China issues RMB bills in denominations of one, two, five, 10, 20, 50 and 100 yuán. Coins come in denominations of one yuán, five jiǎo, one jiǎo and five fēn. Paper versions of the coins remain in circulation.

Hong Kong's currency is the Hong Kong dollar and Macau's is the pataca.

Exchanging Money

Renminbi is not readily convertible in many countries outside China, so you will probably have to wait till you reach China to exchange money. Those travelling to Hong Kong and most Southeast Asian countries can get Renminbi there. Foreign currency and travellers cheques can be changed at border crossings, international airports, branches of the Bank of China, tourist hotels and some large department stores; hours of operation for foreign-exchange counters are 8am to 7pm (later at hotels). Top-end hotels will generally change money for hotel guests only. The official rate is given almost everywhere and the exchange charge is standardised, so there is little need to shop around for the best deal. See the exchange rate table on the inside front cover and consult a newspaper for the current rate of exchange.

Australian, Canadian, US, UK, Hong Kong and Japanese currencies and the euro can be changed in China. In some backwaters, it may be hard to change lesser-known currencies – US dollars are still the easiest to change.

Keep at least a few of your exchange receipts. You will need them if you want to exchange any remaining RMB you have at the end of your trip.

Tipping

In China (including Hong Kong and Macau) almost no-one asks for tips. Tipping used to be refused in restaurants, but nowadays many midrange and top-end eateries include their own (often massive) service charge; cheap restaurants do not expect a tip. Taxi drivers throughout China do not ask for or expect tips.

Travellers Cheques

These are worth taking with you if you are principally travelling in large cities and tourist areas. Not only will they protect your money against theft or loss, but the exchange rate for travellers cheques is higher than for cash (around 2% higher). You can make a large saving, especially if you have paid no commission for your travellers cheques in the first place. They cannot be used everywhere, however. You should have no problem cashing them at tourist hotels in China, but they are of little use in budget hotels and restaurants. As with credit cards, ensure that you always carry enough ready cash on you. If cashing them at banks, aim for the larger banks such as the Bank of China or the CITIC Industrial Bank. Bear in mind that most hotels will only cash the cheques of guests. It's a good idea to change your money at the airport when you arrive as the rate there is roughly the same as everywhere else. Keep your exchange receipts so you can change your money back to its original currency when you leave. Cheques from most of the world's leading banks and issuing agencies are now acceptable in China – stick to the major companies such as Thomas Cook, AmEx and Visa. In big cities they are accepted in almost any currency, but in smaller destinations it's best to stick to big currencies such as US dollars or UK pounds. Some banks won't change travellers cheques at the weekend.

PASSPORTS

You must have a passport with you at all times; it is the most basic travel document (all hotels will insist on seeing it). The Chinese government requires that your passport be valid for at least six months after the expiry date of your visa. You'll need at least one entire blank page in your passport for the visa.

Have an ID card with your photo in case you lose your passport; even better, make photocopies of your passport – your embassy may need these before issuing a new one (a process that can take weeks). Also report the loss to the local PSB (公安局; Gōng'ānjú). Long-stay visitors should register their passport with their embassy. Be careful who you pass your passport to (eg dodgy bike-rental operators as a deposit), as you may never see it again.

PHOTOGRAPHY

In large towns and cities, good photographic outlets where you can find colour slide film, a range of batteries and you can have digital images downloaded to CD are reasonably easy to find. Kodak is the main player in the market, with branches everywhere. If your camera uses nonrechargeable batteries, it's a good idea to stock up in town before heading to far-flung sights, as batteries sold by hawkers are astronomically expensive. Stick to Duracell (jīnbàwáng) and avoid cheap local Chinese batteries such as Nanfu and White Elephant, which don't last long.

POST
Sending Mail

The international postal service is efficient, and airmail letters and postcards will probably take around five to 10 days to reach their destinations. Domestic post is swift – perhaps one or two days from Guǎngzhōu to Běijīng. Intracity it may be delivered the same day it's sent.

Postage is no longer cheap. Postcards to overseas destinations cost Y4.50. Airmail letters up to 20g cost Y5 to Y7 to all countries except Taiwan and Hong Kong and Macau (Y1.50). Domestic letters cost Y0.80 and postcards Y0.50. Like elsewhere, China charges extra for registered mail, but offers cheaper postal rates for printed matter, small packets, parcels, bulk mailings and so on.

China Post operates an Express Mail Service (EMS) which is fast, reliable and ensures that the package is sent by registered post. Parcels sent to domestic destinations by EMS cost Y20 (up to 200g; Y5 for each additional 200g). International EMS charges vary according to country and sample minimum rates (parcels up to 500g) include Australia (Y164), USA (Y184) and UK (Y224). Not all branches of China Post have EMS, so try larger branches.

Apart from local post offices, branch post offices can be found in major tourist hotels where you can send letters, packets and parcels, but you may only be able to post printed matter. Other parcels may require a customs form attached at the town's main post office and a contents check. Even at cheap hotels you can usually post letters from the front desk – reliability varies, but in general it's fine.

If you are sending items abroad, take them unpacked with you to the post office to be inspected and an appropriate box or envelope will be found for you. Most post offices offer materials (for which you'll be charged) for packaging, including padded envelopes, boxes and heavy brown paper. Don't take your own packaging as it will probably be refused.

DIRECTORY

If you have a receipt for the goods, put it in the box when you're mailing it, since it may be opened again by customs further down the line.

In major cities private carriers such as United Parcel Service, DHL, Federal Express and TNT Skypak have a pick-up service as well as drop-off centres, so call their offices for the latest details.

Receiving Mail

There are fairly reliable *poste restante (cúnjú hòulǐng)* services in just about every city and town, usually in the main post office. The collection system is not uniform, but the charge should be Y1 to Y2.30 for each item of *poste restante* mail you collect. Take your passport along for retrieving letters or parcels. Some larger tourist hotels will hold mail for their guests.

SHOPPING
Bargaining

Since foreigners are often overcharged in China, bargaining is essential. You can bargain *(jiǎngjià)* in shops, markets and hotels, but not everywhere. In large shops and department stores where prices are clearly marked, there is usually no latitude for bargaining (although if you ask, the staff sometimes can give you a 10% discount). In small shops and street stalls, bargaining is expected, but there is one important rule to follow – be polite. Keep in mind that entrepreneurs are in business to make money – they aren't going to sell anything at a loss. Your goal should be to pay the Chinese price, as opposed to the foreigners' price – if you can do that, you've done well.

Where to Shop

The place to go to really roll up your sleeves and get to grips with local rock-bottom prices is the local markets. Blankets spread on the pavement and pushcarts in the alleys – this is where you find the lowest prices. In street markets, all sales are final; forget about warranties and, no, they don't take AmEx. Nevertheless, the markets are interesting, but be prepared to bargain hard.

The Friendship Stores you will encounter in China's larger cities are an anachronistic echo from an earlier epoch when imported luxury goods were hoarded under one roof for the privileged few.

Hotel gift shops should be avoided, except for newspapers, magazines or books. Don't ever buy paintings or antiques from such shops – visit local markets, otherwise you'll be hit with a vastly inflated price.

The explosion of shopping malls and department stores, feeding the consumer revolution in China, has been a slap in the face to communist-era service standards. Market forces have jolted sleeping sales staff awake, but you may still meet a defiant clique of the old guard: slumped comatose on the counter or yacking to each other, oblivious to customers shrieking at them.

While journeying the land, don't get too weighed down with souvenirs and trinkets – there's nothing worse than buying a replica Buddha statue in Dūnhuáng, only to spot exactly the same one in a Běijīng market the day before you fly home.

It's sensible to save your shopping for imported electronic consumer items for Hong Kong and Macau – import duties are still too high in the rest of China.

Some shopping tips: make sure you keep receipts and try to hang on to the bag from the shop where you bought each item in case you need to return it. When returning something, try to return to the same store where you bought it; be as firm as possible, as perseverance often pays off. If returning clothes, the sales tags should still be on them and there should be no signs that you have worn the item. Exchanging items is easier than getting a refund. Find out what the time limit is for returning goods bought at the store. Some stores, such as the clothing outlet Esprit, have a no-quibble refund policy; others won't refund or exchange goods.

Antiques

There are very few antiques of real worth left in China, apart from those that remain sealed in tombs, temples, in private hands or museums – basically beyond reach. Most of the antiques you'll find in markets and shops are replicas or ersatz. The quality of replication technology can be quite dazzling, but that monochrome Qing Guangxu imperial yellow bowl in your hands is far more likely to be a Hu Jintao–era imitation. It's worth bearing in mind that even auction houses get caught out quite regularly, and experts assume that a considerable percentage of material that passes under the gavel is of dubious authenticity.

MORE THAN MEETS THE EYE...

Once upon a time in China you got what you paid for. If the sales clerk said it was top-quality jade, then it was top-quality jade. Times have changed, and cheap forgeries and imitations flood the market, from Tibetan jewellery to Qing coins, guidebooks and pirate DVDs to bogus Nike, Burberry, Gucci, train tickets and beyond. The reason why Chinese TV is stuck showing US and German films from the 1970s and '80s is probably because the pirate DVD market brings you the very latest, without the adverts in between.

Despite all the government's bluster and periodic CCTV footage of steamrollers grinding fake Rolexes and CDs, the pirating industry is in fine fettle. Fake goods just reappear in force after hitting the deck for a while. Wherever you voyage in China, you'll be cursing the number of forgeries, then snapping them up when you glance at the price tag. Just make sure your change doesn't include a counterfeit note. And if you are after genuine antiques, try to get an official certificate of verification – and make sure the ink is dry.

Street markets are the best places to try your luck at antique shopping. Professional antique hunters will need to have a real nose for the business – you need to know the culture intimately. For your average traveller, take everything with a pile of salt.

Only antiques that have been cleared for sale to foreigners are permitted to be taken out of the country. When you buy an item over 100 years old it will come with an official red wax seal attached. However, bear in mind that this seal does not necessarily indicate that the item is an antique. You'll get a receipt of sale, and you have to show this to customs when you leave the country; otherwise customs will confiscate the antique.

Paintings & Scrolls

Watercolours, oils, woodblock prints, calligraphy – there is a lot of art for sale in China. Tourist centres like Guìlín, Sūzhōu, Běijīng and Shànghǎi are good places to look out for paintings. Convincing imitation oils of Níngbō-born artist Chen Yifei (who died in 2005) can be found everywhere, along with copies of other contemporary artists. Don't buy these from hotel shops, however, as you will be massively ripped off.

Much calligraphy is very so-so and some is downright bad; you will have to know your subject, and don't take anybody's word for the quality of the brushwork.

Stamps & Coins

China issues quite an array of beautiful stamps that are generally sold at post offices in the hotels. Outside many of the post offices, you'll find amateur philatelists with books full of stamps for sale; it can be extraordinarily hard

bargaining with these enthusiasts. Stamps issued during the Cultural Revolution make interesting souvenirs, but these rare items are no longer cheap. Check out www.cpi.com .cn/cpi-e, a website on Chinese philately. Old coins are often sold at major tourist sites, but many are forgeries.

TELEPHONE

Both international and domestic calls can be easily made from your hotel room or from public telephones on the street. Local calls from hotel-room phones are generally cheap (and sometimes free), although international phone calls are expensive and it is best to buy a phonecard (see p952) if calling abroad. Public telephones are plentiful, although finding one that works can be a hassle. The majority of public telephones take IC cards (p952) and only a few take coins. If making a domestic call, look out for public phones at newspaper stands (报刊亭; bàokāntíng) and hole-in-the-wall shops (小卖部; xiǎomàibù); you make your call and then pay the owner (local calls are typically around Y1. Domestic and international long-distance phone calls can also be made from main telecommunications offices and 'phone bars' (话吧; huàbā).

Domestic long-distance rates in China vary according to distance, but are cheap. Cardless international calls are expensive (Y8.2 per minute or Y2.2 for calls to Hong Kong and Macau), but calls made between midnight and 7am are 40% cheaper; it's far cheaper to use an IP card.

If you are expecting to receive a call to your hotel room, try to advise the caller beforehand of your room number as hotel operators and staff at reception frequently have trouble

DIRECTORY

ESSENTIAL NUMBERS

There are several telephone numbers that are the same for all major cities. However, only international assistance is likely to have English-speaking operators:

- International assistance ☎ 115
- Local directory assistance ☎ 114
- Long-distance assistance ☎ 113/173
- Police ☎ 110
- Fire ☎ 119
- Ambulance ☎ 120

with foreign names. Otherwise, inform the receptionist that you are expecting a call and write down your name and room number for them.

The country code to use to access China is 86; the code for Hong Kong is 852 and Macau is 853. To call a number in Běijīng, for example, dial the international access code (00 in the UK, 011 in the USA), dial the country code (86) and then the area code for Beijing (010), dropping the first zero, and then dial the local number. When calling China from Hong Kong or Macau, you also use the country code 86. For telephone calls within the same city, drop the international and area code (qūhào). If calling internationally from China, drop the first zero of the area or city code after dialling the international access code, and then dial the number you wish to call.

Area codes for all cities, towns and destinations appear in the relevant chapters.

Mobile Phones

Mobile-phone shops (手机店; shǒujīdiàn) can sell you a SIM card, which will cost from Y60 to Y100 depending on the phone number (Chinese avoid the number four as it sounds like the word for death) and will include Y50 of credit. When this runs out, you can top up the number by buying a credit-charging card (chōngzhí kǎ) for Y50 or Y100 worth of credits. The local per-minute, nonroaming city call charge for China Mobile is seven jiǎo if calling a landline and 1.50 jiǎo if calling another mobile phone. Receiving calls on your mobile is free from mobile phones and costs seven jiǎo from landline phones. Intraprovincial calls are Y1.40 per minute. Roaming charges cost an additional two jiǎo per minute, but

the call receiving charge is the same. Overseas calls can be made for Y4.80 per minute plus the local charge per minute by dialling ☎ 17951, followed by 00, the country code, then the number you want to call. Otherwise you will be charged the IDD call charge plus seven jiǎo per minute.

Phonecards

A wide range of local and international phonecards exists in Běijīng.

Integrated Circuit (IC) cards (IC 卡; IC kǎ), available from kiosks, hole-in-the-wall shops, internet cafés and from any China Telecom office, are prepaid cards that can be used in most public telephones, in Telecom offices and in most hotels. IC cards come in denominations of Y20, Y50, Y100 and Y200, and appear in several varieties. Some cards can only be used in Běijīng (or locally, depending on where the card is purchased), while other cards can be used throughout China. If you want to call abroad, make sure the IC card can make international calls (dǎ guójì diànhuà), although international calls using IC cards are much more expensive than using Internet Phone (IP) cards. Purchasing the correct card can be confusing, as the instructions for use on the reverse of the card are usually only in Chinese.

If you wish to make international calls, it is much cheaper to use an IP card. International calls on IP cards (IP 卡; IP kǎ) are Y1.80 per minute to the USA or Canada, Y1.50 per minute to Hong Kong, Macau and Taiwan, and Y3.20 to all other countries; domestic long-distance calls are Y0.30 per minute. You dial a local number, then punch in your account number, followed by a pin number and finally the number you wish to call. English-language service is usually available. IP cards come in denominations of Y50, Y100, Y200 and Y500, and substantial discounts are offered, so bargain (you should be able to buy a Y100 card for around Y35). Extra credits are also regularly included on IP cards. IP cards can be found at the same places as IC cards (although in some cities they can be impossible to find), and placards for vendors of both IC and IP cards are commonplace. Again, some IP cards can only be used locally, while others can be used nationwide, so it is important to buy the right card (and check the expiry date). If you want to use an IP card from a public telephone, you will need an IC card for the local call (you may find that the public telephone will not connect you, so you will have to use your hotel phone).

TIME

The Chinese live by both the Gregorian and the lunar calendar. Time throughout China is set to Běijīng time (see the boxed text, p824), which is eight hours ahead of GMT/UTC. When it's noon in Běijīng it's also noon in far-off Lhasa, Ürümqi and all other parts of the country. Since the sun doesn't cooperate with Běijīng's whims, people in China's far west follow a later work schedule so they don't have to commute two hours before dawn. There is no daylight saving time in China.

When it's noon in Běijīng the time is 2pm in Sydney, 4am in London, 11pm in New York (previous day) and 8pm in Los Angeles (previous day).

TOILETS

Travellers on the road relate Chinese toilet tales to each other like comparing old war wounds. Despite proud claims to have invented the first flushing toilet, China really does have some wicked loos. Large cities and towns have made a start on making their public toilets less of an assault course of foul smells and primitive appliances, but many are still pungent and sordid. Steer towards fast-food outlets, hotels or department stores for cleaner alternatives. Toilet paper is rarely provided – always keep a stash with you. In some places the sewage system can't handle paper. In general, if you see a wastebasket next to the toilet, that's where you should throw the toilet paper. Some public loos levy a small fee (around five máo) which you pay as you enter. Squat loos are ubiquitous, so be prepared.

Rural toilets are ghastly – just a hole in the ground or a ditch over which you squat, and many cannot be flushed at all. Hyperventilate before tackling toilets on the older trains, or go in with a strong cigarette (eg Temple of Heaven brand).

Remember:

men	男
women	女

TOURIST INFORMATION

Outside Hong Kong (Hong Kong Tourism Board; www.discoverhongkong.com) and Macau (Macau Government Tourist Office; www.macautourism.gov.mo), tourist information facilities in China are rudimentary

and of little use. Western travellers, used to relying on nationwide chains of helpful tourist information centres for free maps and useful info, will be disappointed. In the absence of a national tourism board, individual provinces, cities, towns and regions promote tourism independently. Large cities such as Běijīng and Shànghǎi have relatively better tourist information infrastructure, but even in Shànghǎi, tourist information facilities are primitive. Elsewhere, you may have to fall back on the China International Travel Service (CITS; 中国国际旅行社; Zhōngguó Guójì Lǚxíngshè). Most towns and cities have a branch of CITS, and addresses and contact details of offices are listed throughout this book. There is usually a member of staff who can speak English who may be able to answer questions and offer some travel advice, but the main purpose of CITS is to get you onto a tour.

VISAS

A visa is required for the PRC, but at the time of writing visas were not required for most Western nationals to visit Hong Kong (see p522) or Macau (p569). Be aware that if you visit Hong Kong or Macau from China, you will need to have a multiple-entry visa to re-enter China or else get a new visa.

For most travellers, the type of visa issued is an L, from the Chinese word for travel (lǚyóu). This letter is stamped right on the visa. The L visa can be either a multiple- or single-entry visa.

Visas are readily available from Chinese embassies and consulates in most Western and many other countries. A standard 30-day, single-entry visa from most Chinese embassies abroad can be issued in three to five working days. Prices for visas have risen steadily over recent years, and express visas cost twice the usual fee. At the time of writing, prices for a standard 30-day visa are US$50 for US citizens and US$30 for citizens of other nations. For double-entry visas, it's US$75 for US citizens and US$45 for all other nationals. For multiple entry visas (for six months) it's US$100 for US citizens and US$60 for all other nationals.

You normally pay up front for the visa, rather than on collection. You can get an application form in person at the embassy or consulate, or obtain one online from a consular website (try www.fmprc.gov.cn/eng – click on About China, then Travel to China

DIRECTORY

and then Visa Information). A visa mailed to you will take up to three weeks. Rather than going through an embassy or consulate, you can also make arrangements at certain travel agencies. Visa applications require at least one photo (normally 51mm x 51mm).

When asked on the application form, try to list standard tourist destinations such as Běijīng and Chéngdé; if you are toying with the idea of going to Tibet or western Xīnjiāng, just leave it off the form as it may raise eyebrows; the list you give is not binding in any way.

Three-day visas are available at the Macau–Zhūhǎi border (see p608 for details).

A 30-day visa is activated on the date you enter China, and must be used within three months of the date of issue. Sixty-day and 90-day travel visas are no longer issued outside China. You need to extend your visa in China if you want to stay longer.

A Chinese visa covers virtually the whole of China, although some restricted areas (eg Yìxiàn, p443) still exist that will require an additional permit from the PSB, at a cost. In addition to a visa, permits are also required for travel to Tibet (p916).

At the time of writing, Chinese embassies in the US were no longer accepting mailed visa applications, so this may mean that you will have to send your passport in the mail to a visa service agency, which will then deal with it.

Many people use the **China Visa Service Center** (1-800 799 6560; www.mychinavisa.com), which offers impeccable and prompt service. The procedure takes around 10 to 14 days.

Be aware that political events can suddenly make visas more difficult to procure.

When you check into a hotel, there is a question on the registration form asking what type of visa you hold. The letter specifying what type of visa you have is usually stamped on the visa itself. There are eight categories of visas, as follows:

Type	Description	Chinese name
L	travel	lǚxíng
F	business or student	fǎngwèn
D	resident	dìngjū
G	transit	guòjìng
X	long-term student	liúxué
Z	working	rènzhí
J	journalist	jìzhě
C	flight attendant	chéngwù

Getting a China Visa in Hong Kong

Hong Kong is still the best place to pick up a visa for China. China Travel Service (CTS) and any of the other companies listed under Travel Agencies (p522) will be able to obtain one for you or you can apply directly to the **Visa Office of the People's Republic of China** (Map pp530-1; ☎ 3413 2300; 7th fl, Lower Block, China Resources Centre, 26 Harbour Rd, Wan Chai; ◷ 9am-noon & 2-5pm Mon-Fri). Visas processed here in one/two/three days cost HK$400/300/150. Double/six-month multiple/one-year multiple visas are HK$220/400/600 (plus HK$150/250 for express/urgent service). Be aware that American and UK passport holders must pay considerably more for their visas. You must supply two photos, which can be taken at photo booths in the MTR and at the visa office for HK$35.

Getting Other Types of Visas
LAOS

It is now possible to get a visa for Laos at the border (p738). Alternatively, you can visit the Laos consulate (p943) in Kūnmíng for a 15-day tourist visa. For those from Western Europe, Australia and New Zealand, visas cost Y270 and for American, Japanese and German nationals the cost is Y320. You must bring one passport photo with your application. Visas take three working days to process or you can pay a surcharge for next-day service.

MYANMAR

Travel to Myanmar is slowly getting easier. For a start, you no longer have to change US$200 prior to entering the country. The Myanmar consulate (p943) in Kūnmíng can issue a 28-day tourist visa (Y185). Visas take three working days to process or you can pay a Y100 surcharge for same-day processing and Y50 for next-day processing. Overland travel into Myanmar is possible, although you must be part of a tour (p748).

THAILAND

Travellers from most countries won't need a Thai visa unless they're planning on staying in the country longer than 30 days. The Thai consulate (p943) in Kūnmíng can issue a 60-day tourist visa for Y200. Visas take two days to process.

VIETNAM

Kūnmíng has a Vietnam consulate (p943) where you can pick up a 30-day tourist visa

(Y400). Visas take three working days to process or you can pay an extra Y200 for the express service. You must bring along a passport photo with your application.

Residence Permit

The 'green card' is a residence permit, issued to English teachers, foreign expats and long-term students who live in China. Green cards are issued for a period of six months to one year and must be renewed annually. Besides needing all the right paperwork, you (and your spouse) must also pass a health exam (for which there is a charge). Families are automatically included once the permit is issued, but there is a fee for each family member. If you lose your card, you'll pay a hefty fee to have it replaced.

Visa Extensions

The Foreign Affairs Branch of the local PSB (公安局; Gōngānjú) – the police force – deals with visa extensions.

First-time extensions of 30 days are easy to obtain on single-entry tourist visas, but further extensions are harder to get and may only give you another week. Offices of the PSB outside of Běijīng may be more lenient and more willing to offer further extensions, but don't bank on it.

Extensions to single-entry visas vary in price, depending on your nationality. American travellers pay Y185, Canadians Y165, UK citizens Y160 and Australians Y100; prices can go up or down. Expect to wait up to five days for your visa extension to be processed.

The period of extension can differ from city to town. Travellers report generous extensions being decided on the spot in provincial towns and backwaters. If you have used up all your options, popping into Hong Kong to apply for a new tourist visa is a reliable option.

The penalty for overstaying your visa in China is up to Y500 per day. Some travellers have reported having trouble with officials who read the 'valid until' date on their visa incorrectly. For a one-month tourist (L) visa, the 'valid until' date is the date by which you must enter the country (within three months of the date the visa was issued), not the date upon which your visa expires. Your visa expires the number of days that your visa is valid for after the date of entry into China.

WOMEN TRAVELLERS

Principles of decorum and respect for women are deeply ingrained in Chinese culture. Despite the Confucianist sense of superiority accorded to men, women often call the shots and wield considerable clout (especially within marriage). Chinese males are not macho, and there is a strong sense of balance between the sexes. Nonetheless, in its institutions, China is a patriarchal and highly conservative country where virtually all positions of political and state authority are occupied by (old) men.

In general, foreign women are unlikely to suffer serious sexual harassment in China, but there have been reports of problems in Xīnjiāng. Wherever you are, it's worth noticing what local women are wearing and how they are behaving, and making a bit of an effort to fit in, as you would in any other foreign country. Try to stick to hotels in the centre, rather than the fringes of town. Taking a whistle or alarm with you would offer a measure of defence in any unpleasant encounter. As with anywhere else, you will be taking a risk if you travel alone. If you have to travel alone, consider arming yourself with some self-defence techniques.

Tampons (卫生棉条; wèishēng miántiáo) can be found almost everywhere, especially in big supermarkets. It's best to take plentiful supplies of the pill (避孕药; bìyùnyào) unless you are travelling to the big cities where brands like Marvelon are available from local pharmacies, as are morning-after pills (紧急避孕药; jǐnjí bìyùnyào). Condoms (避孕套; bì'yùntào) are widely available.

WORK

Go East, young man. With its booming economy, China offers considerable scope for travellers looking for work. Teaching English can be particularly lucrative, and there are opportunities for acting, modelling work, editing, proofreading, freelance writing and IT work. Large numbers of Westerners work in China through international development charities such as VSO (www.vso.org.uk), which can provide you with useful experience and the chance to learn Chinese. Although finding employment is easier in Hong Kong than on the mainland, those with Chinese-language skills will find it much easier to source work. Useful places to start looking for positions include Chinajob .com (www.chinajob.com) and Chinaonline (www.chinaonline.cn.com). To legally work in China, you will require a work permit (left).

TRANSPORT

Transport

CONTENTS

GETTING THERE & AWAY

ENTERING THE COUNTRY

There are no particular difficulties for travellers entering China. The main requirement is a passport (valid for travel for six months after the expiry date of your visa; see p949) and a visa (see p953). As a general rule, visas cannot be obtained at the border. At the time of writing visas were not required for most Western nationals to visit Hong Kong or Macau and some visa-free transits exist. For travel to Tibet, see p916. Chinese Immigration officers are scrupulous and, by definition, highly bureaucratic, but not difficult or overly officious. Travellers arriving in China will be given a health declaration form and an arrivals form to complete.

AIR
Airports & Airlines

Hong Kong, Běijīng and Shànghǎi are China's main international air gateways. **Hong Kong International Airport** (HKG; ☎ 0852-2181 0000; www.hkairport.com) is located at Chek Lap Kok on Lantau Island in the west of the territory. Běijīng's **Capital airport** (PEK; ☎ arrivals & departures 010-6454 1100) has benefited from considerable investment and a new terminal. An even newer terminal – due to be the world's larg-

est – was under construction at the time of writing. Shànghǎi has two airports: **Hongqiao airport** (SHA; ☎ 021-6268 8899/3659) in the west of the city and **Pudong airport** (PVG; ☎ 021-6834 1000, flight information 021-6834 6912) in the east.

The best direct ticket deals are available from China's international carriers, such as China Eastern. Air China, China's national flag carrier, has a good safety record, and to date it has only had one fatal crash (in 2002). Air China should not be confused with China Airlines, the crash-prone Taiwan carrier.

Airlines flying to and from China:
Aeroflot Russian Airlines (SU; www.aeroflot.org) Běijīng (☎ 010-6500 2412); Shànghǎi (☎ 021-6279 8033)
Air Canada (AC; www.aircanada.ca) Běijīng (☎ 010-6468 2001); Shànghǎi (☎ 021-6279 2999)
Air China (CA; www.airchina.com.cn) Běijīng (☎ 800 810 1111); Shànghǎi (☎ 021-5239 7227)
Air France (AF; www.airfrance.com) Běijīng (☎ 4008 808 808); Shànghǎi (☎ 4008 808 808)
Air Macau (NX; www.airmacau.com.mo) Běijīng (☎ 010-6515 8988); Shànghǎi (☎ 021-6248 1110)
Air New Zealand (NZ; www.airnz.com) Hong Kong (☎ 852-2862 8988)
All Nippon Airways (NH, ANA; www.ana.co.jp) Běijīng (☎ 800 820 1122); Shànghǎi (☎ 021-5696 2525)
Asiana Airlines (OZ; www.us.flyasiana.com) Běijīng (☎ 010-6468 4000); Shànghǎi (☎ 021-6219 4000)
Austrian Airlines (OS; www.aua.com) Běijīng (☎ 010-6462 2161); Shànghǎi (☎ 021-6340 3411)
British Airways (BA; www.british-airways.com) Běijīng (☎ 010-8511 5599); Shànghǎi (☎ 021-6375 8866)
China Eastern Airlines (MU; www.ce-air.com) Běijīng (☎ 010-6464 1166); Shànghǎi (☎ 021-95108)

China Southern Airlines (CZ; www.cs-air.com) Běijīng (☎ 010-950 333); Shànghǎi (☎ 021-950 333); Guǎngzhōu (☎ 020-950333)

Dragonair (KA; www.dragonair.com) Běijīng (☎ 010-6518 2533); Shànghǎi (☎ 021-6375 6375)

El Al Israel Airlines (LY; www.elal.co.il) Běijīng (☎ 010-6597 4512)

Garuda Indonesia (GA; www.garuda-indonesia.com) Běijīng (☎ 010-6505 2901)

Iran Air (IR; www.iranair.com) Běijīng (☎ 010-6512 4945)

Japan Airlines (JL, JAL; www.jal.com) Běijīng (☎ 010-6513 0888); Shànghǎi (☎ 4008 880 808)

KLM (KL; www.klm.nl) Běijīng (☎ 010-6505 3505); Shànghǎi (☎ 021-6884 6884)

Korean Air (KE; ☎ 4006 588 888; www.koreanair.com) Běijīng (☎ 010-8453 8137); Shànghǎi (☎ 021-6275 2000)

Koryo Air Běijīng (JS; ☎ 010-6501 1557)

Laos Airlines (QV; ground fl, Camellia Hotel, 154 Dongfeng Lu, Kūnmíng)

Lufthansa Airlines (LH; www.lufthansa.com) Běijīng (☎ 010-6468 8838); Shànghǎi (☎ 021-5352 4999)

Malaysia Airlines (MH; www.malaysia-airlines.com.my) Běijīng (☎ 010-6505 2681); Shànghǎi (☎ 021-6279 8607)

MIAT Mongolian Airlines (OM; www.miat.com) Běijīng (☎ 010-6507 9297)

Northwest Airlines (NW; www.nwa.com) Běijīng (☎ 010-6505 3505); Shànghǎi (☎ 021-6884 6884)

Pakistan International Airlines (PK, PIA; www.piac .com.pk) Běijīng (☎ 010-6505 1681)

Qantas Airways (QF; www.qantas.com.au) Běijīng (☎ 010-6567 9006); Shànghǎi (☎ 021-6145 0188)

Royal Nepal Airlines (TG; www.royalnepal.com) Běijīng (☎ 010-6505 5071); Shànghǎi (☎ 021-6270 8352)

Scandinavian Airlines (SK, SAS; www.sas.dk) Běijīng (☎ 010-8527 6100); Shànghǎi (☎ 021-5228 5001)

Singapore Airlines (SQ; www.singaporeair.com) Běijīng (☎ 010-6505 2233); Shànghǎi (☎ 021-6289 1000)

Thai Airways International (TG; www.thaiairways .com) Běijīng (☎ 010-6460 8899); Shànghǎi (☎ 021-5298 5555); Kūnmíng (☎ 0871-351 1515)

United Airlines (UA; www.ual.com) Běijīng (☎ 010-6463 1111); Shànghǎi (☎ 021-3311 4567)

Uzbekistan Airways (HY; www.uzbekistan-airways .com) Běijīng (☎ 010-6500 6442); Shànghǎi (☎ 021-6307 1896)

Virgin Atlantic (VS; www.virgin-atlantic.com) Shànghǎi (☎ 021-5353 4600)

Tickets

The cheapest tickets to Hong Kong and China can often be found either online or in discount agencies in Chinatowns around the world. Other budget and student travel agents offer cheap tickets, but the real bargains are with agents that deal with the Chinese who regularly return home (travelling at festival times such as the Chinese New Year will be more expensive). Firms such as **STA Travel** (www .statravel.com) with offices worldwide also offer competitive prices to most destinations. The cheapest flights to China are with airlines requiring a stopover at the home airport, such as with Air France to Běijīng via Paris or Malaysian Airlines to Běijīng via Kuala Lumpur. Air fares to China peak between June and September.

An increasing number of airlines fly to China, with Air China and China Eastern offering some of the cheapest fares. The cheapest available airline ticket is called an APEX (Advance Purchase Excursion) ticket, although this type of ticket includes expensive penalties for cancellation and changing dates of travel. Tickets listed in this section are quoted by airline offices and you will be able to find cheaper rates through travel agencies.

For browsing and buying tickets on the internet, try these online booking services:

Cheapflights.com (www.cheapflights.com) No-frills website offering flights to numerous destinations.

Expedia (www.expedia.com) Offers discounted tickets.

Lonely Planet (www.lonelyplanet.com) Use Travel Services to book multistop trips.

One Travel.com (www.onetravel.com) Offers some good deals.

Travel.com.au (www.travel.com.au) A New Zealand version also exists (www.travel.co.nz).

Travelbag (www.travelbag.co.uk) Good for holiday bargains and speciality travel.

To bid for last-minute tickets online, try **Skyauction** (www.skyauction.com). **Priceline** (www.priceline .com) aims to match the ticket price to your budget.

Discounted air-courier tickets are a cheap possibility, but they carry restrictions. As a courier, you transport documents or freight internationally and see it through customs. You usually have to sacrifice your baggage and take carry-on luggage. Generally trips are on fixed, round-trip tickets and offer an inflexible period in the destination country. For more information, check out organisations such as the **Courier Association** (www.aircourier.org) or the **International Association of Air Travel Couriers** (IAATC; www.courier.org).

Australia

STA Travel (☎ 1300 733 035; www.statravel.com.au) has offices in all major cities and on many

TRANSPORT

university campuses. **Flight Centre** (☎ 133 133; www.flightcentre.com.au) has offices throughout Australia.

From Australia, Hong Kong is a popular destination and is also the closest entry point into China. Although it's a shorter flight, fares from Australia to Hong Kong are generally not that much cheaper than fares to Běijīng or Shànghǎi. Low-season return fares to Shànghǎi or Běijīng from the east coast of Australia start at around A$1000, with fares to Hong Kong starting from A$910.

Cambodia

China Southern Airlines has a daily flight from Phnom Penh to Guǎngzhōu (one way/ return US$280/400). Shanghai Airlines flies three times weekly to Phnom Penh (one way/ return US$290/390).

Canada

Canadian discount air ticket sellers are also known as consolidators and their air fares tend to be about 10% higher than those sold in the USA. Check out travel agents in your local Chinatown for some real deals and browse agency ads in the *Globe & Mail*, the *Toronto Star*, the *Montreal Gazette* and the *Vancouver Sun*. **Travel CUTS** (☎ 1866 246 9762; www.travelcuts.com) is Canada's national student travel agency and

has offices in all major cities. For online bookings try **Expedia** (www.expedia.ca) and **Travelocity** (www.travelocity.ca).

From Canada, fares to Hong Kong are often higher than those to Běijīng. Air Canada has daily flights to Běijīng and Shànghǎi from Vancouver. Air Canada, Air China and China Eastern Airlines sometimes run super cheap fares. Return low-season fares between Vancouver and Běijīng start at around US$700.

Continental Europe

Generally there is not much variation in air fare prices from the main European cities. The major airlines and travel agents usually have a number of deals on offer, so shop around. **STA Travel** (www.statravel.com) and **Nouvelles Frontières** (www.nouvelles-frontieres.fr) have branches throughout Europe.

Return fares to Běijīng from major Western European cities start at around €900 with Lufthansa, Air France and KLM. Flights to Hong Kong are slightly more expensive, with return fares starting from around €1000 to €1100.

FRANCE

France has a network of student travel agencies that can supply discount tickets to travellers of all ages.

CLIMATE CHANGE & TRAVEL

Climate change is a serious threat to the ecosystems that humans rely upon, and air travel is the fastest-growing contributor to the problem. Lonely Planet regards travel, overall, as a global benefit, but believes we all have a responsibility to limit our personal impact on global warming.

Flying & Climate Change

Pretty much every form of motor transport generates CO_2 (the main cause of human-induced climate change) but planes are far and away the worst offenders, not just because of the sheer distances they allow us to travel, but because they release greenhouse gases high into the atmosphere. The statistics are frightening: two people taking a return flight between Europe and the US will contribute as much to climate change as an average household's gas and electricity consumption over a whole year.

Carbon Offset Schemes

Climatecare.org and other websites use 'carbon calculators' that allow travellers to offset the greenhouse gases they are responsible for with contributions to energy-saving projects and other climate-friendly initiatives in the developing world – including projects in India, Honduras, Kazakhstan and Uganda.

Lonely Planet, together with Rough Guides and other concerned partners in the travel industry, supports the carbon offset scheme run by climatecare.org. Lonely Planet offsets all of its staff and author travel.

For more information check out our website: www.lonelyplanet.com.

Recommended agencies:
Anyway (☎ 0892 302 301; www.anyway.fr)
Lastminute (☎ 0899 785 000; www.fr.lastminute.com)
Nouvelles Frontières (☎ 0825 000 747; www.nouvelles-frontieres.fr)
OTU Voyages (☎ 0155 823 232; www.otu.fr) This agency specialises in student and youth travellers.
Voyageurs du Monde (☎ 01 40 15 11 15; www.vdm.com)

GERMANY
Recommended agencies:
Expedia (www.expedia.de)
Just Travel (☎ 089-747 3330; www.justtravel.de) An English-language travel agency.
Lastminute (☎ 01805-284 366; www.lastminute.de)
STA Travel (☎ 0697-4303 292; www.statravel.de) For travellers under the age of 26; branches in major cities.

ITALY
A good agent, specialising in student and youth travel, is **CTS Viaggi** (☎ 06-462 0431; www.cts.it).

NETHERLANDS
A recommended agency is **Airfair** (☎ 0900-7717 717; www.airfair.nl).

SPAIN
Recommended agencies include **Barcelo Viajes** (☎ 902 200 400; www.barceloviajes.com) and **Nouvelles Frontières** (☎ 902 124 212).

Hong Kong
Dragonair has 11 flights daily from Běijīng to Hong Kong (one way Y2530) and 15 flights from Hong Kong to Shànghǎi (one way Y1780). It's cheaper to fly to Guǎngzhōu or Shēnzhèn and then take the train or bus to Hong Kong.

Iran
Iran Air has twice-weekly flights from Tehran to Běijīng (one way/return US$620/900).

Israel
El Al Israel Airlines has twice-weekly flights between Běijīng and Tel Aviv (one way US$630).

Japan
There are daily flights operating between Tokyo and Běijīng, with one-way fares starting at around US$775. There are also regular flights between Osaka and Běijīng, with one-way fares at around US$600. Daily flights link Shànghǎi to Tokyo and Osaka, and there are

also flights from Japan to other major cities in China, including Dàlián and Qīngdǎo.
Reliable travel agencies used to dealing with foreigners:
No1 Travel (03-3205 6073; www.no1-travel.com)
STA Travel (www.statravel.co.jp) Tokyo (☎ 03-5391 2922); Osaka (☎ 06-262 7066)

Kazakhstan
China Southern Airlines has four flights weekly between Ürümqi and Almaty (one way US$290). There are three flights weekly between Běijīng and Almaty with Kazakhstan Airlines (one way US$390).

Kyrgyzstan
There are flights from Ürümqi to Bishkek and Osh.

Laos
Laos Airlines has two flights weekly from Vientiane to Kūnmíng. China Eastern Airlines has three flights weekly between the two cities (one way/return US$140/260)

Macau
Air Macau has daily flights between Běijīng and Macau (return US$510) and several flights daily between Shànghǎi and Macau (return US$360).

Malaysia
Malaysia Airlines operates four flights weekly between Běijīng and Kuala Lumpur (return US$630) and two flights daily between Shànghǎi and Kuala Lumpur (return US$480).

Mongolia
MIAT Mongolian Airlines has five flights weekly between Běijīng and Ulaanbaatar (return US$410). Air China also flies between Běijīng and Ulaanbaatar. It can sometimes take a week to get a ticket and schedules are reduced in winter.

Myanmar (Burma)
Air China has two flights weekly from Yangon to Běijīng, with a stopover in Kūnmíng (one way US$694). There are two flights weekly from Kūnmíng to Yangon (Y1630, Wednesday and Sunday) and three flights from Kūnmíng to Mandalay (Y1450, Monday, Wednesday and Friday). Air tickets and visas are available from the Myanmar consulate (p943) in Kūnmíng.

TRANSPORT

Nepal

Royal Nepal Airlines operates two flights weekly between Kathmandu and Shànghǎi (one way/return US$200/400) and three flights weekly between Hong Kong (one way/return US$200/400) and Kathmandu. There are also two or three flights weekly from Lhasa to Kathmandu (Y2511). See the Tibet chapter (p912) for advice on travel to Tibet.

New Zealand

Both **Flight Centre** (☎ 0800 243 544; www.flightcentre .co.nz) and **STA Travel** (☎ 0508 782 872; www.statravel .co.nz) have branches throughout the country.

International airlines such as Malaysia Airlines, Thai Airways International and Air New Zealand have return fares from Auckland to Shànghǎi for around NZ$1380 during the low season. Return low-season fares to Běijīng start at around NZ$1560.

North Korea

There are four flights weekly between Běijīng and Pyongyang with Koryo Air and China Northern Airlines (one way/return US$160/300).

Pakistan

Pakistan International Airlines operates two flights weekly from Karachi to Běijīng (one way/return US$510/950). Air China has a weekly flight to Karachi from Běijīng. There is one weekly flight between Ürümqi and Islamabad on Xinjiang Airlines (one way US$280). A flight to Lahore from Ürümqi is a possible new route in the future.

Russia

Aeroflot has daily direct flights connecting Běijīng and Moscow (one way US$510), and China Eastern Airlines has three flights weekly between Shànghǎi and Moscow (one way US$560). Moscow and Novosibirsk are also connected to Ürümqi by air.

Singapore

STA Travel (☎ head office 6737 7188; www.statravel.com .sg) has three offices in Singapore. Singapore, like Bangkok, has hundreds of travel agents offering competitive discount fares for Asian destinations and beyond. Chinatown Point Shopping Centre on New Bridge Rd has a good selection of travel agents.

Fares to Běijīng are about US$550 return, while fares to Hong Kong start at US$350 return; there are also daily flights to Shànghǎi for US$500 return.

South Korea

Discount travel agencies in Seoul include **Xanadu Travel** (☎ 02-795 7771; fax 797 7667; www.xanadu .co.kr).

Air China, Asiana Airlines and Korean Air have daily flights between Běijīng and Seoul (return US$510). Flights to Shànghǎi with China Eastern Airlines and Asiana Airlines are similar (return US$490). Seoul is also connected by air to Hong Kong, Tiānjīn, Shěnyáng, Qīngdǎo and Guǎngzhōu.

Thailand

Khao San Rd in Bangkok is the budget travellers headquarters. Bangkok has a number of excellent travel agents but there are also some suspect ones; ask the advice of other travellers before handing over your cash. **STA Travel** (☎ 02-236 0262; www.statravel.co.th; Room 1406, 14th fl, Wall Street Tower, 33/70 Surawong Rd) is a good and reliable place to start.

One-way fares from Bangkok to Běijīng with Thai Airways or Air China are around US$300 or US$470 return. Other one-way fares from Bangkok include Hong Kong for around US$200, Chéngdū for US$230, Kūnmíng for US$190 and Shànghǎi for US$300. There are two flights weekly between Kūnmíng and Chiang Mai (Y1344, Thursday and Sunday).

UK & Ireland

Discount air travel is big business in London. Advertisements for many travel agencies appear in the travel pages of the weekend broadsheet newspapers, in *Time Out*, the *Evening Standard* and in the free magazine *TNT*.

Travel agents in London's Chinatown that deal with flights to China include **Jade Travel** (☎ 0870-898 8928; www.jadetravel.co.uk; 5 Newport Place, London), **Sagitta Travel Agency** (☎ 0870-077 8888; fax 075 2888; www.sagitta-tvl.com; 9 Little Newport St, London) and **Reliance Tours Ltd** (☎ 0800-018 0503; www.reliance -tours.co.uk; 12-13 Little Newport St, London).

For further agents, look at **Chinatown Online** (www.chinatown-online.co.uk), which also includes a list of travel agents outside London that specialise in tickets to China.

From the UK, the cheapest low-season return fares to Běijīng start at around UK£350 with British Airways; flights to Hong Kong are a little bit pricier.

Recommended travel agencies:

Flightbookers (☎ 0870-814 4001; www.ebookers.com)

Flight Centre (☎ 0870-499 0040; www.flightcentre.co.uk)

North-South Travel (☎ 01245-608 291; www.north southtravel.co.uk) Donates part of its profit to projects in the developing world.

Omega Travel (☎ 0870-027 8668; www.omegatravel .ltd.uk)

Quest Travel (☎ 0871-423 0135; www.questtravel.co.uk)

STA Travel (☎ 0870-163 0026; www.statravel.co.uk) For travellers under 26 years.

Trailfinders (☎ 0845-058 5858; www.trailfinders.co.uk)

Travel Bag (☎ 0800-082 5000; www.travelbag.co.uk)

USA

Discount travel agents in the USA are known as consolidators. San Francisco is the ticket-consolidator capital of America, although some good deals can also be found in Los Angeles, New York and other big cities. Consolidators can be found through the *Yellow Pages* or the travel sections of major daily newspapers.

From the US west coast, low-season return fares to Hong Kong or Běijīng start at around US$850. Fares increase dramatically during summer and the Chinese New Year. From New York to Běijīng or Hong Kong, low-season return fares start at around US$890.

STA Travel (☎ 800-781-4040; www.sta-travel.com) has offices in most major US cities.

The following agencies and websites are recommended for online bookings:

- www.cheaptickets.com
- www.expedia.com
- www.flychina.com
- www.itn.net
- www.lowestfare.com
- www.orbitz.com
- www.sta.com
- www.travelocity.com

Uzbekistan

From Běijīng there are thrice-weekly flights to Tashkent with Uzbekistan Airways (one way/return US$450/600), and there are also flights between Ürümqi and Tashkent.

Vietnam

Air China and Vietnam Airlines fly between Ho Chi Minh City and Běijīng (return US$410). China Southern Airlines flights are via Guǎngzhōu. From Běijīng to Hanoi there are two flights weekly with either China Southern Airlines or Vietnam Airlines (one way/return US$180/350). Shanghai Airlines

has five flights weekly to Ho Chi Minh City (return US$420) from Shànghǎi.

LAND

If you're starting in Europe or Asia, it's possible to travel all the way to China by land. Numerous routes include the Trans-Mongolian and Trans-Manchurian Railway trek from Europe or the border crossings of China–Vietnam, Tibet–Nepal, Xīnjiāng–Pakistan, Xīnjiāng–Kyrgyzstan and Xīnjiāng–Kazakhstan.

Border Crossings

China shares borders with Afghanistan, Bhutan, India, Kazakhstan, Kyrgyzstan, Laos, Mongolia, Myanmar, Nepal, North Korea, Pakistan, Russia, Tajikistan and Vietnam. China also has official border crossings between its special administrative regions, Hong Kong and Macau. The borders with Afghanistan, Bhutan and India are closed. If planning an extensive trip to China overland, make sure you enter China within the given time after your visa is issued (see p953). Note that some travellers, as they enter China, have had their Lonely Planet *China* guides confiscated by officials, primarily at the Vietnam–China border. We recommend you copy any essential details before you cross and put a cover on your guide.

HONG KONG

Hong Kong is an excellent place to enter China and there is a range of options for crossing over the border by land. See p561 for details on how to enter China from Hong Kong overland.

KAZAKHSTAN

There are border crossings from Ürümqi to Kazakhstan via the border post at Korgas, Ālāshānkǒu, Tǎchéng and Jímǔnǎi (see p826); crossing the border shouldn't really be a problem as long as you have a valid Kazakhstan (obtainable in Běijīng) or China visa. Apart from Ālāshānkǒu, China's rail link with Kazakhstan, all of these borders crossings are by bus, though you can generally get a bike over. Remember that borders open and close frequently due to changes in government policy; additionally, many are only open when the weather permits. It's always best to check with the Public Security Bureau (PSB; Gōngānjú) in Ürümqi for the official line, or Lonely Planet's Thorn Tree to see what other travellers are saying.

Two trains weekly also run between Ürümqi and Almaty (see p826 for details).

TRANSPORT

TRANSPORT

KYRGYZSTAN

There is a weekly bus from Kashgar via Irkesh-tam to Osh (see p836 for details). Ensure you have a valid Kyrgyzstan visa (available from Běijīng or Hong Kong). From June to September it's theoretically possible to cross the dramatic 3752m Torugart Pass (p837) on a rough road from Kashgar to Bishkek.

LAOS

From the Měnglà district in China's southern Yúnnán province it's legal to enter Laos via Boten in Luang Nam Tha province if you possess a valid Lao visa. The good news is that you can now get an on-the-spot visa for Laos at the border, the price of which depends on your nationality (but you cannot get a China visa here). From Měnglà there are buses to Móhān every 20 minutes or so from 8am. Although the border doesn't officially close until 5.30pm Běijīng time (and don't forget that Laos is an hour ahead), things often wrap up earlier on the Lao side. The majority of travellers from Kūnmíng go via Jǐnghóng to Měnglà and then on to the border at Mohan (which shuts at 5.30pm). As the bus journey from Jǐnghóng will take the better part of the day, you will probably have to stay overnight at Měnglà. See p738 for more information.

Lao visas can be obtained in Běijīng (p942); alternatively, the Lao consulate in Kūnmíng (p943) issues 15-day tourist visas (valid for two months from date of issue; visa extensions in Laos are possible). See p954 for more information on visas.

MACAU

See p583 for details on entering China by bus from Macau to Zhūhǎi.

MONGOLIA

As well as Trans-Mongolian Railway trains that run from Běijīng to Ulaanbaatar via Dàtóng (see p964), the K23 departs from Beijing Train Station at 7.40am every Tuesday, reaching Ulaanbaatar at 1.20pm the next day. In the other direction, the K24 departs from Ulaanbaatar every Thursday at 8.05am, reaching Běijīng the following day at 2.31pm. Two trains weekly also run between Hohhot and Ulaanbaatar.

MYANMAR (BURMA)

The famous Burma Road, originally built to supply the forces of Chiang Kaishek in his struggle against the Japanese, runs from Kūnmíng, in China's Yúnnán province, to the city of Lashio. Today the road is open to travellers carrying permits for the region north of Lashio, although you can legally cross the border in only one direction – from the Chinese side (Ruìlì) into Myanmar via Muse in the northern Shan State. Land crossings from China are only possible if you join an organised tour group from a Chinese travel agency (eg Ko Wai Lin Travel in Kūnmíng or Way Thar Li Tour & Travel Company Ltd in Ruìlì), who can arrange visas and permits. See p748 for more details on journeying to Myanmar.

A second route, a little further northwest, from Lwaigyai to Bhamo, is also open in the same direction. You cannot legally leave Myanmar by either route.

NEPAL

The 920km road connecting Lhasa with Kathmandu is known as the Friendship Hwy. It's a spectacular trip across the Tibetan plateau, the highest point being Gyatso-la Pass (5220m). By far the most popular option for the trip is hiring a 4WD through a hotel or travel agency and then organising a private itinerary with a driver (see p924).

Visas for Nepal can be obtained in Lhasa (p943), or even at the Nepalese border (see p933). When travelling from Nepal to Lhasa, foreigners still have to arrange transport through tour agencies in Kathmandu.

If you already have a Chinese visa, you could try turning up at the border and organising a permit in Zhāngmù (p933), but transport out will be a problem and rules and regulations regularly change – it's far better to join an economy tour to Lhasa in Kathmandu. See p933 for further information, including transport from Kodari to Kathmandu.

In 2005 Nepal's state bus company Sahja Yatayat started a weekly direct bus service between Kathmandu and Lhasa. The service costs US$70 per person, plus US$60 for three nights' accommodation and a service fee. Foreigners currently aren't allowed to take the bus due to Chinese visa and permit hassles but this could change.

The following agencies in Kathmandu operate trips to Tibet. Most agencies advertising in Thamel are agents only; they don't actually run the trips.

Ecotrek (☎ 442 4112; www.ecotrek.com.np, www.kailash tour.com; Thamel)

Explore Nepal Richa Tours & Travel (☎ 442 3064; www.explorenepalricha.com; 2nd fl, Namche Bazaar Bldg, Tri Devi Marg, Thamel)

Green Hill Tours (☎ 470 0968; www.greenhilltours.com .np; Thamel)

Royal Mount Trekking (☎ 424 1452; www.royal-mt -trekking.com, www.royaltibet.com; Durbar Marg)

Tashi Delek Nepal Treks & Expeditions (☎ 441 0746; www.tashidelektreks.com; Thamel)

NORTH KOREA

Visas are difficult to arrange to North Korea, and at the time of writing it was impossible for US and South Korean citizens. Those interested in travelling to North Korea from Běijīng should get in touch with Nicholas Bonner or Simon Cockerell at **Koryo Tours** (☎ 010-6416 7544; www.koryogroup.com; Red House, 10 Chunxiu Lu, Chaoyang), who can get you there (and back).

There are five weekly flights and four international express trains (K27 and K28) between Běijīng and Pyongyang.

PAKISTAN

The exciting trip on the Karakoram Hwy, over the 4800m Khunjerab Pass and what is said to be the world's highest public international highway, is an excellent way to get to or from Chinese Central Asia. There are daily buses (10am) from Kashgar for the two-day trip to Sost when the pass is open, with customs procedures conducted at Tashkurgan. See p837 for more information.

RUSSIA

A twice-weekly train (N23 and N24, Wednesday and Saturday) connects Haerbin East train station with Vladivostok. Also see Trans-Siberian Railway (p964) for information on trains to Moscow from Běijīng. The Russian border 9km from Mǎnzhōulǐ is quite busy and reliable. Officially, the only public transport that crosses the border is the Trans-Manchurian, but there are also ample opportunities for picking up a lift in Mǎnzhōulǐ or at the border.

TAJIKISTAN

The Kulma Pass (4362m), linking Kashgar with Murghob (via Tashkurgan), opened in 2004, with three monthly buses making the trip. At the time of writing the pass was not open to foreign travellers: go to **Travel Tajikistan** (www.traveltajikistan.com/roadrail/road.html) for the latest updates.

VIETNAM

Travellers can enter Vietnam overland from China and exit Vietnam to China on a standard visa. You cannot obtain visas at the border, but Vietnam visas can be acquired in Běijīng (p942) or Kūnmíng (p943). Chinese visas can be obtained in Hanoi. The Vietnam–China border crossing is open from 7am to 4pm, Vietnam time, or 8am to 5pm, China time. Set your watch when you cross the border – the time in China is one hour later than in Vietnam. There are currently two border checkpoints (see below and p964) where foreigners are permitted to cross between Vietnam and China.

There are two weekly trains from Běijīng to Hanoi. Trains leave Beijing West Train Station at 4.16pm on Monday and Friday, arriving in Hanoi at 6.50am on Wednesday and Sunday. Trains depart from Hanoi at 6.50pm on Tuesday and Friday and arrive in Běijīng at 1.38pm on Thursday and Sunday. The train stops at Shíjiāzhuāng, Zhèngzhōu, Hànkǒu (in Wǔhàn), Wǔchāng (Wǔhàn), Chángshā, Héngyáng, Yǒngzhōu, Guìlín North, Guìlín, Liǔzhōu, Nánníng and Píngxiáng.

Friendship Pass

The busiest border crossing is at the Vietnamese town of Dong Dang, an obscure town (nearest city is Lang Son 18km to the south) 164km northeast of Hanoi. The closest Chinese town to the border is Píngxiáng in Guǎngxī province, but it's about 10km north of the actual border gate. The only place in Guǎngxī where foreigners can cross is Friendship Pass, known as Huu Nghi Quan in Vietnamese or Yǒuyì Guān in Chinese. Buses and minibuses on the Hanoi–Lang Son route are frequent. For details on reaching Friendship Pass from Píngxiáng, see p645.

Píngxiáng is connected by train to Nánníng, capital of China's Guǎngxī province, 220km away. Train 5518 to Nánníng departs from Píngxiáng at 2.40pm, arriving in Nánníng at 6.36pm. In the other direction, train 5517 departs from Nánníng at 7.58am, arriving in Píngxiáng at 11.40am. There are more frequent buses (once every 30 minutes), which take four hours to make the journey and cost US$4.

A word of caution – because train tickets to China are expensive in Hanoi, some travellers buy a ticket to Dong Dang, walk across the border and then buy a train ticket on the Chinese side. This isn't the best way because it's several kilometres from Dong Dang to Friendship Pass, and you'll have to hire someone to take you by motorbike. If you're going by train, it's best to buy a ticket from Hanoi to Píngxiáng, and then in Píngxiáng buy a ticket to Nánníng or beyond.

From Nánníng, there's a daily Hanoi-bound bus (Y110, 10 hours, 8am) that runs to the Friendship Pass, after which you can cross into Vietnam on foot and board a Vietnamese bus to Hanoi.

Lao Cai–Hékǒu
A 762km metre-gauge railway, inaugurated in 1910, links Hanoi with Kūnmíng, although at the time of writing the twice-weekly international train service had been suspended due to floods and landslide damage. The border town on the Vietnamese side is Lao Cai, 294km from Hanoi. On the Chinese side, the border town is Hékǒu, 468km from Kūnmíng.

When operational, domestic trains run daily on both sides of the border. On the Chinese side, Kūnmíng–Hékǒu takes about 16 hours.

Mong Cai–Dōngxīng
Vietnam's third, but little known, border crossing is at Mong Cai in the northeast corner of the country, just opposite the Chinese city of Dōngxīng.

Train
TRANS-SIBERIAN RAILWAY
The Trans-Siberian Railway and connecting routes comprise one of the most famous, romantic and potentially enjoyable of the world's great train journeys. Rolling out of Europe and into Asia, through eight time zones and over 9289km of taiga, steppe and desert, the Trans-Siberian makes all other train rides seem like once around the block with Thomas the Tank Engine.

There is some confusion here as there are, in fact, three railways. The 'true' Trans-Siberian line runs from Moscow to Vladivostok. But the routes traditionally referred to as the Trans-Siberian Railway are the two branches that veer off the main line in eastern Siberia to make a beeline for Běijīng.

Since the first option excludes China, most readers of this book will be making the decision between the Trans-Manchurian and the Trans-Mongolian; however, it makes little difference. The Trans-Mongolian (Běijīng to Moscow, 7865km) is faster, but requires you to purchase an additional visa and endure another border crossing, although you do at least get to see the Mongolian countryside roll past your window. The Trans-Manchurian is longer (Běijīng to Moscow, 9025km). A useful source of information on the Trans-Siberian Railway can be found at www.seat61.com /Trans-Siberian.htm.

Trans-Mongolian Railway
Train K3 leaves Běijīng on its five-day journey at 7.40am every Wednesday (arriving in Moscow on the following Monday at 2.19pm), passes through Dàtóng and travels to the Mongolian border at Erenhot, 842km from Běijīng. The train continues to Ulaanbaatar before reaching the last stop in Mongolia, Sukhe Bator. From Moscow, train K4 leaves at 10.03pm on Tuesdays, arriving in Běijīng on the following Monday at 2.31pm. Departure and arrival times may fluctuate slightly.

The train offers deluxe two-berth compartments (with shared shower), 1st-class four-berth compartments and 2nd-class four-berth compartments. Fares start at around US$253 one way in 2nd class or US$418 in 1st class.

Trans-Manchurian Railway
Departing from Běijīng at 10.56pm Saturday (arriving in Moscow the following Friday at 5.55pm), train K19 travels through Tiānjīn, Shānhǎiguān, Shěnyáng, Chángchūn and Hāěrbīn before arriving at the border post Mǎnzhōulǐ, 2347km from Běijīng. Zabaykal'sk is the Russian border post and the train continues from here to Tarskaya, where it connects with the Trans-Siberian line. Train K20 leaves Moscow at 11.58pm every Friday, arriving in Běijīng on the following Friday at 5.20am. Note that departure and arrival times may fluctuate slightly.

Trains have 1st-class two-berth compartments and 2nd-class four-berth compartments, with prices similar to the Trans-Mongolian Railway.

Visas
Travellers will need Russian and Mongolian visas if they take the Trans-Mongolian Rail-

way, as well as a Chinese visa. These can often be arranged along with your ticket by travel agents such as China International Travel Service (CITS, Zhōngguó Guójì Lǚxíngshè). Mongolian visas come as two-day transit visas (three-day process US$30, express process US$60) or 90-day tourist visas (three-day process US$40, express process US$60). A transit visa is easy enough to get (just present a through ticket and a visa for your onward destination). The situation regarding visas changes regularly, so check with a Mongolian embassy (p942) or consulate. All Mongolian embassies shut down for the week of National Day (Naadam), which officially falls around 11 to 13 July.

Russian transit visas (one-week process US$50, three-day process US$80, one-day process US$120; see p942) are valid for 10 days if you take the train, and will only give you three or four days in Moscow at the end of your journey. You will need one photo, your passport and the exact amount in US dollars. For a transit visa, you will also need a valid entry visa for a third country plus a through ticket from Russia to the third country.

Tickets
In Běijīng, tickets can be conveniently purchased from **CITS** (Zhōngguó Guójì Lǚxíngshè; ☎ 010-6512 0507) in the **Beijing International Hotel** (Běijīng Guójì Fàndiàn; 9 Jianguomen Neidajie). Abroad, tickets can be arranged through one of the following agencies.

Intourist Travel (www.intourist.com) has branches in the UK, USA, Canada, Finland and Poland, and offers a range of Trans-Manchurian and Trans-Mongolian tours and packages, including flights to and from Moscow, 2nd-class travel, and accommodation in Moscow, Běijīng and Irkutsk.

White Nights (☎ /fax 1800 490 5008; www.wnights .com; 610 Sierra Dr, Sacramento, CA) in the USA offers a range of trips, including Trans-Manchurian tickets for US$460 (2nd class) or US$710 (1st class) and Trans-Mongolian tickets for US$400 (2nd class) or US$710 (1st class). The company also offers visa support, and has contact addresses in Russia, Germany, Switzerland and the Netherlands.

Intours Canada (☎ 416-766 4720; fax 766 8507; www.tourussia.com; Ste 308, 2150 Bloor St West, Toronto, ON) in Canada offers tours and packages on the Trans-Siberian and Trans-Mongolian. A typical 13-day Moscow–Beijing Trans-Mongolian

tour costs C$2195/C$2825 (2nd/1st class), including hotel accommodation.

The Russia Experience (☎ 020-8566 8846; www .trans-siberian.co.uk; Research House, Fraser Rd, Perivale, Middlesex) in the UK has a great choice of tickets and is in the know (it's also the company to get in touch with for trips to Mongolia and Russia). Get full details and prices from its downloadable website brochure.

Gateway Travel (☎ 02-9745 3333; www.russian -gateway.com.au; 48 The Boulevarde, Strathfield, NSW) in Australia can arrange tickets and tours.

Travel Service Asia (☎ 07351-373 210; www.tsareisen .de, in German; Schmelzweg 10, Biberach/Riß) in Germany offers package tours and tickets on Trans-Mongolian and Trans-Manchurian routes.

Moonsky Star Ltd (Map p532; ☎ 2723 1376; www .monkeyshrine.com; Flat 6, 4th fl, E block, Chungking Mansions, Nathan Rd) in Hong Kong arranges trips on the Trans-Siberian and has an informative website with a downloadable brochure. It has an info centre in Běijīng called **Monkey Business** (Map pp118-19; ☎ 010-6591 6519; www.monkeyshrine.com; Room 35, Red House, 10 Chunxiu Lu, Chaoyang).

SEA
Hong Kong
Some ships still ply the waters between Hong Kong and the mainland, but numbers and destinations have been cut back and largely travel to destinations in Guǎngdōng. See p560 for details.

Japan
There are weekly ferries between Osaka and Shànghǎi (roughly 44 hours) and twice-monthly services between Kōbe and Shànghǎi (roughly 44 hours). Ticket prices to both destinations range from Y1300 to Y6500. Boats depart from Shànghǎi at 1pm on Saturday and arrive in Kōbe at 9.30am on Monday. Boats leaves Kōbe on Tuesday at noon and arrive in Shànghǎi at 9.30am on Thursday. Ticket prices start at Y1300. See p274 for more details.

From Tiānjīn (Tánggū), there is a weekly ferry to Kōbe in Japan (p184; Y1540 to Y5250, 51 hours). Check in two hours before departure for international sailings. The **Tianjin Jinshen Ferry Company** (☎ 022-2420 5777; www.tifeco .com.cn/jinshen) operates a boat that departs from Tiānjīn at 11am on Monday and arrives in Kōbe at 2pm on Wednesday. From Kōbe, it departs at noon on Friday and arrives in Tiānjīn at 2pm on Sunday.

There are also boats from Qīngdǎo to Shimonoseki (Y1200) every two weeks; see p230 for details.

Korea

Travelling from Korea, international ferries connect the South Korean port of Incheon with Wēihǎi, Qīngdǎo, Tiānjīn (Tánggū), Dàlián and Dāndōng.

The **Weidong Ferry Company** (☎ 822-3271 6710; www.weidong.com; 10th fl, 1005 Sungji Bldg, 585 Dohwadong, Mapo-gu, Seoul) runs boats on the routes to Wēihǎi (Y750 to Y1370, three weekly in each direction) and Qīngdǎo (Y750 to Y1370, three weekly in each direction) in Shāndōng province. It can also be contacted at the **International Passenger Terminal** Incheon (☎ 8232-777 0490; 71-2 Hangdong); Wēihǎi (☎ 0631-522 6173; 48 Haibin Beilu); Qīngdǎo (☎ 0532-8280 3574; 4 Xinjiang Lu). Check its website for the latest timetables and prices. Children under two years are free; children between two and 12 years get 30% discounts, while seniors over 65 years garner discounts of 20%.

In Seoul, tickets for any boats to China can be bought from the **International Union Travel Agency** (☎ 822-777 6722; Room 707, 7th fl, Daehan Ilbo Bldg, 340 Taepyonglo 2-ga, Chung-gu). Prices cost US$88 to US$300, and depending on the destination, boats leave anytime from once to three times weekly.

For the Tiānjīn ferry you can also get tickets in Seoul from **Taeya Travel** (☎ 822-514 6226), in Kangnam-gu by the Shinsa subway station. In China, tickets can be bought cheaply at the pier, or from CITS – for a very steep premium. The cheapest price is Y888 for a dorm bed.

To reach the International Passenger Terminal from Seoul, take the Seoul–Incheon commuter train (subway line 1 from the city centre) and get off at the Dongincheon station. The train journey takes 50 minutes. From Dongincheon station it's either a 45-minute walk or five-minute taxi ride to the ferry terminal.

INCHEON TO WĒIHǍI

There are three boat services a week between Incheon and Wēihǎi (2nd/1st class Y750/1370, 15 hours, departs Tuesday, Thursday and Sunday at 7pm from Wēihǎi). See p236 for more details, and **Weidong Ferry** (www.weidong .com) for an updated schedule.

INCHEON TO QĪNGDǍO

There are three boats a week between Qīngdǎo and Incheon (Y750 to Y1370, 15 hours, departs Monday, Wednesday and Friday). Phone or consult the website of **Weidong Ferry** (☎ 0532-8280 3574; www.weidong.com; 4 Xinjiang Lu) in Qīngdǎo to confirm days.

INCHEON TO TIĀNJĪN

There are two boats a week between Tiānjīn and Incheon (from Y1000, 25 hours). Boats from Incheon depart at 1pm and 9pm on Tuesday, and boats leave Tiānjīn at 11am on Thursday and Sunday. As with boats from Japan, the boat does not dock at Tiānjīn proper, but rather at the nearby port of Tánggū, where there are buses to speed you to either Tiānjīn or Běijīng. Boats to Tiānjīn are run by the **Jinchon Ferry Company** Seoul (☎ 822-517 8671); Incheon (☎ 8232-777 8260); Tiānjīn (☎ 022-2331 1657). See p184 for more details.

INCHEON TO DÀLIÁN

A boat leaves for Incheon in South Korea at 3.30pm on Monday, Wednesday and Friday (Y850 to Y1469, 18 hours) from Dàlián; tickets can be bought at the ferry terminal. Boats leave Incheon for Dàlián at 4.30pm on Tuesday, Thursday and Saturday. Contact **Da-In Ferry** Seoul (☎ 822-3218 6551); Incheon (☎ 8232-891 7100); Dàlián (☎ 0411-8270 5082).

INCHEON TO DĀNDŌNG

Three boats a week run between Dāndōng and Incheon in South Korea. Boats leave for Incheon at 3pm on Tuesday, Thursday and Saturday (Y1000 to Y1900, 15 hours). Boats leave Incheon for Dāndōng at 5pm on Monday, Wednesday and Friday. Contact **Dandong Ferry** Incheon (☎ 8232-891 3322); Dāndōng (☎ 0415-317 0081).

GETTING AROUND

AIR

While trundling around China in buses or chugging across the land by train is great on occasion, China is a country of vast distances. If you don't have the time or inclination for a drawn-out land campaign, take to the air.

China's air network is extensive and the country's rapid economic development means that its civil aviation fleet is expected to triple in size over the next two decades, with up to 2000 more airliners being added to the existing fleet by 2022. With predictions that China could become the world's most visited tourist destination by 2020, the nation is shaping up for a further upsurge in domestic air travel. Airports are being built and upgraded all over the land, making air transport increasingly appealing, with new airports including Shànghǎi's Pudong airport, Běijīng's new Capital airport terminal (and a new terminal currently under construction), Hong Kong's spiffing Chek Lap Kok airport and Guǎngdōng's Baiyun International Airport. China is running out of pilots to fly its growing fleet and foreign pilots have reportedly been hired.

The Civil Aviation Administration of China (CAAC; Zhōngguó Mínháng) is the civil aviation authority for numerous airlines, which include the following:

Air China (☎ in Běijīng 010-6601 7755; www.airchina .com.cn) Largely flies economically priced international routes.

China Eastern Airlines (☎ in Shànghǎi 021-6268 6268; www.ce-air.com) Range of international destinations, including London and Los Angeles, with flights out of Běijīng and Shànghǎi.

China Southern Airlines (☎ 020-8668 2000; www .cs-air.com) Guǎngzhōu-based airline serving a number of international routes as well as a nationwide web of air routes, including Běijīng, Shànghǎi, Xī'ān and Tiānjīn.

China Southwest Airlines (☎ in Chéngdū 028-666 8080; www.cswa.com) Chéngdū-based airline serving a number of international routes as well as domestic cities.

Chunqiu Airlines (☎ 021-6252 0000; www.china-sss .com) Shànghǎi-based budget airline, with connections between Shànghǎi and tourist destinations, including Qīngdǎo, Guìlín, Xiàmén and Sānyà. No food or drink served on board.

Some of the above airlines also have subsidiary airlines; for example, subsidiaries of China Southern Airlines include Xiamen Airlines and Guangxi Airlines. Note that not all Chinese airline websites have English-language capability. Airline schedules and airfares are listed within the relevant chapters.

CAAC publishes a combined international and domestic timetable in both English and Chinese in April and November each year. This timetable can be bought at some airports and CAAC offices in China. Individual airlines also publish timetables. You can buy these from ticket offices throughout China.

Shuttle buses often run from CAAC offices in towns and cities through China to the airport.

TRANSPORT

DOMESTIC AIRFARES

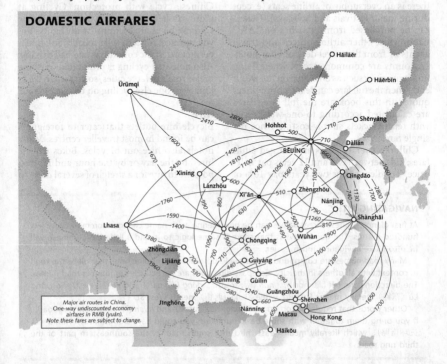

Major air routes in China.
One-way undiscounted economy
airfares in RMB (yuán).
Note these fares are subject to change.

TRANSPORT

On domestic and international flights the free baggage allowance for an adult passenger is 20kg in economy class and 30kg in 1st class. You are also allowed 5kg of hand luggage, though this is rarely weighed. The charge for excess baggage is 1% of the full fare for each kilogram. Baggage reclamation facilities are rudimentary at the older airports and waits can be long; lost baggage compensation is Y40 per kilogram. Remember to keep your baggage receipt label on your ticket as you will need to show it when you collect your luggage.

Planes vary in style and comfort. The more regularly travelled routes between cities employ Boeing or Airbus, more far-flung regions still depend on Soviet-built passenger jets. You may get a hot meal, or just a small piece of cake and an airline souvenir. On-board announcements are delivered in Chinese and English.

International and domestic departure tax is included in the price of the ticket.

Tickets

Tickets are easy to purchase as at most times there is an oversupply of airline seats (except during major festivals and holidays). Tickets can be purchased from branches of CAAC nationwide, other airline offices and travel agents or from the travel desk of your hotel. Discounts are common, except when flying into large cities such as Shànghǎi on the weekend, when the full fare can be the norm; prices quoted in this book are the full fare. Fares are calculated according to one-way travel, with return tickets simply costing twice the single fare.

Children over 12 years are charged adult fares; kids between two and 12 years pay half-price. Toddlers under two years pay 10% of the full fare. You can use credit cards at most CAAC offices and travel agents.

Cancellation fees depend on how long before departure you cancel. On domestic flights, if you cancel 24 to 48 hours before departure you lose 10% of the fare; if you cancel between two and 24 hours before the flight you lose 20%; and if you cancel less than two hours before the flight you lose 30%. If you don't show up for a domestic flight, you are entitled to a refund of 50%.

When purchasing a ticket, you may be asked to buy insurance (Y20). It's not compulsory and the amount you can claim is very low.

BICYCLE

Bicycles (*zìxíngchē*) are an excellent method for getting around China's cities or patrolling tourist sights.

Outdoor bicycle-repair stalls are found on every other corner in larger cities, and repairs are very cheap.

Despite the convenience of cycling, take care when you're on your bike. Helmets can be difficult to find in China as virtually no Chinese cycle with protection. Cycling at night can be hazardous, mainly because few Chinese bikes are equipped with lights. But your greatest concern will probably be China's pernicious traffic conditions and bad driving. Also note that cycling is prohibited on some major roads in large cities, so you will have to join everyone else cycling on the pavement.

Hire

Bicycle hire outlets that cater to foreigners can be found in most traveller centres. Many hotels also hire out bicycles. Bikes can be hired by the day or by the hour and it's also possible to hire for a stretch of several days, so

---

NAVIGATING CITIES

At first glance, Chinese street names can be bewildering, with name changes common every few hundred metres. The good news is that there is some logic to it, and a little basic Chinese will help to make navigating much easier.

Many road names are compound words made up of a series of directions that place the road in context with all others in the city. Compass directions are particularly common in road names. The directions are: *běi* (北; north), *nán* (南; south), *dōng* (东; east) and *xī* (西; west). So Dōng Lù (东路) literally means East Rd, while Xī Jiē (西街) means West St.

Other words that regularly crop up are *zhōng* (中; central) and *huan* (环; ring, as in ring road). If you bring them together with some basic numerals, you could have Dēngsānhuán Nánlù (东三环南路), which literally means 'east third ring south road' or the southeastern part of the third ring road.

touring is possible. Rates for Westerners are typically Y5 per hour or Y20 to Y40 per day but you could pay as much as Y20 per hour at some tourist sights. Note that big hotels typically charge ridiculous rates, so it's worth looking around.

Most hire outlets will ask you for a deposit of anything up to Y500 (get a receipt) and to leave some sort of ID. Sometimes the staff will ask for your passport. Give them some other ID instead, like a student card or a drivers' licence. In most large towns and cities bicycles should be parked for a small fee at designated places on the pavement (typically Y0.50 to Y1).

Purchase

If you're planning to stay in one place for any length of time, it may be worth buying your own bike and then selling it later. Bike shops are plentiful and prices should be clearly marked. The very cheapest mountain bikes start in the region of Y250, but single-speed bikes are even cheaper. A good local brand is Giant. It's important to buy a decent cable or U-lock as theft is common. If you want to sell your bike, advertising it on local university notice boards is a good idea, or in expat magazines like *That's Beijing* or *That's Shanghai* (which often means you can advertise online – an ideal place also to look for secondhand bikes).

Touring

Touring China by bike can be immensely rewarding, although there are problems with 'open' and 'closed' areas. It's illegal for foreigners to visit closed areas (eg Yīxiàn, p443) without a permit (permits can be obtained from the PSB). Foreigners can transit a closed area – that is, you can travel by train or bus through a closed area as long as you don't exit the vehicle in this 'forbidden zone'. The question is: Should riding a bicycle through a closed area be classified as 'transiting' or 'visiting' it?

Chinese law is as clear as mud on this issue. Most of the time, the police won't bother you.

If you get caught in a closed area, it's unlikely to be while you are on the road. The law keeps firm tabs on transients via hotels. If you're staying overnight in an open place, but you are suspected of having passed through a closed area, the police may pull a raid on your hotel. You can be hauled down to the police station where you will have to submit to a lengthy interrogation, sign a confession and pay a fine. Fines vary from Y50 to whatever they think you can afford. There is some latitude for bargaining in these situations, and you should request a receipt (*shōujù*). Don't expect police to give you any tips on which areas are closed and which are open – they seldom know themselves – although such areas are usually near international borders or zones of a sensitive military nature, as well as much of Tibet.

BOAT

Boat services within China are limited. In coastal areas, you are most likely to use a boat to reach offshore islands like Pǔtuóshān or Hǎinán. The Yāntái–Dàlián ferry will likely survive because it saves hundreds of kilometres of overland travel, despite the loss of more than 200 lives when a ferry on this route sank in heavy seas in 1999. Elsewhere the outlook for coastal passenger ships is not too good.

There are also several inland shipping routes worth considering, but these are also vanishing. For details of each trip see the appropriate sections in this book.

The best-known river trip is the three-day boat ride along Yangzi River (Cháng Jiāng) from Chóngqìng to Yíchāng or Wǔhàn (p811). The Li River (Lí Jiāng) boat trip from Guìlín to Yángshuò is a popular tourist ride. You can also travel the Grand Canal from Hángzhōu to Sūzhōu on a tourist boat.

Hong Kong employs a veritable navy of vessels that connect with the territory's myriad islands, and a number of popular boats run between the territory and other parts of China (principally Guǎngdōng province), including Macau, Zhūhǎi, Shékǒu (for Shēnzhèn) and Zhōngshān. See p560 for details.

Boat tickets can be purchased from passenger ferry terminals or through travel agents, such as CITS.

BUS

Long-distance buses (长途公共汽车; *chángtú gōnggòng qìchē*) are one of the best means of getting around. Services are extensive, main roads are rapidly improving and with the increasing number of intercity highways, bus journeys are getting quicker (often quicker than train travel). Another plus is that it's easier to secure bus tickets than train tickets and they are often cheaper. Buses also stop every so often in small towns and villages, so you get to see parts of the countryside you wouldn't see if you travelled by train, although breakdowns can be a problem.

On the down side, some rural roads and provincial routes (especially in the southwest, Tibet and the northwest) remain in shocking condition, dangerously traversed by bone-rattling hulks that shatter the nerves. Precipitous drops, pot holes, dangerous road surfaces and reckless drivers mean that accidents in black-spot areas, such as parts of Sìchuān, remain common. Long-distance bus journeys can also be cramped and noisy, with Hong Kong films looped on overhead TVs and 3-D sound. Drivers lean on the horn at the slightest detection of a vehicle in front.

Routes between large cities sport larger, cleaner and more comfortable fleets of private buses (many equipped with toilets and you could get a free bottle of mineral water), such as comfy Volvos; shorter and more far-flung routes still rely on rattling minibuses into which the driver crams as many fares as is possible and waits to fill up before departing.

On popular long-haul routes, sleeper buses (卧铺客车; *wòpù kèchē*) may cost around double the price of a normal bus service, but many travellers swear by them, although bunks can be short. Watch out for your belongings on them, however.

It's safe to estimate times for bus journeys on nonhighway routes by calculating the distance against a speed of 25km/h. Also factor in driving techniques – drivers are loathe to change gears and appear to prefer to almost stop on a slope rather than change from third into second. Coasting in neutral downhill is common.

If taking buses to high-altitude destinations in winter, make sure you take plenty of warm clothes. A breakdown in frozen conditions can prove lethal for those unprepared.

Bus journey times given throughout this book should be used as a rough guide only and do not factor in variables, such as weather, breakdowns or bad traffic conditions.

Bus Stations & Ticketing
All cities and most towns across China have one or more long-distance bus station (长途汽车站; *chángtú qìchēzhàn*). Tickets are easy to purchase, and it's usually just a case of turning up at the bus station and buying your ticket

there and then, rather than booking them in advance. Wherever you're going, weigh up the options: besides that bone-rattling tin creature that you're being shoved onto by ticket operators, a plush, air-conditioned (albeit slightly more expensive) coach could well be heading to the same destination. Bus drivers and ticket sellers at bus stations can press gang you aboard their vehicles; try to resist until you know what other choices exist.

In many cities in China, the train station forecourt doubles as a bus station.

CAR & MOTORCYCLE
For those who'd like to tour China by car or motorbike, the news is bleak. It's not like India, where you can simply buy a motorbike and head off. The authorities remain anxious about foreigners driving at whim around China, so don't plan on hiring a car and driving off wherever you want.

Driving Licence
To drive in Hong Kong and Macau, you will need an International Driving Permit. To drive in China, you will need a residency permit and you will need to apply for a Chinese driving licence. You also have to perform a health examination and perform a written test. Foreigners can drive motorcycles if they are residents in China and have a Chinese motorcycle licence.

Hire
Cars can be hired in Hong Kong and Macau, but at the time of writing you needed a residency permit and a Chinese driving license to hire a car elsewhere (eg in Běijīng or Shànghǎi), effectively barring tourists from the roads.

If you want to use a car, it's easy enough to book a car with a driver. Basically, this is just a standard long-distance taxi. Travel agencies like CITS or even hotel booking desks can make the arrangements. They generally ask excessive fees – the name of the game is to negotiate. If you can communicate in Chinese or find someone to translate, it's not particularly difficult to find a private taxi driver to take you wherever you like for less than half the CITS rates.

Road Rules
Cars in China drive on the right-hand side of the road. You're more likely to get fined for

illegal parking than speeding. Indeed, with China's gridlock traffic, opportunities for speeding are vanishing, except on the highways. Even skilled drivers will be unprepared for the performance on China's roads; cars lunge from all angles and chaos abounds. You see cars driving from minor onto major roads, their drivers totally ignoring oncoming vehicles. The figures make for grim reading: China tops the highway mortality charts with 450 people losing their lives daily on China's roads (a figure that is growing by 10% yearly), despite there being fewer vehicles per head than in Western countries.

HITCHING

Hitching is never entirely safe in any country in the world, and we don't recommend it. People who do choose to hitch will be safer if they travel in pairs and let someone know where they are planning to go.

Many people have hitchhiked in China, and some have been amazingly successful. It's not officially sanctioned and the same dangers that apply elsewhere in the world also apply in China. Exercise caution, and if you're in any doubt as to the intentions of your prospective driver, say no.

Hitching in China is rarely free, and passengers are expected to offer at least a tip. Some drivers might even ask for an unreasonable amount of money, so try to establish a figure early to avoid problems later.

The main reason to do it is to get to isolated outposts where public transport is poor. There is, of course, some joy in meeting the locals this way, but communicating is certain to be a problem if you don't speak Chinese. There is no Chinese signal for hitching, so just try waving down a truck.

LOCAL TRANSPORT

Long-distance transport in China is not really a problem – the dilemma occurs when you finally make it to your destination. While China boasts a huge and often inventive choice of local transport, vehicles can be slow and overburdened, and the transport network very confusing for visitors. Hiring a car in China is largely impractical or impossible for tourists, and hiring a bike may be inadequate. Unless the town is small, walking is not usually recommended, since Chinese cities tend to be very spread out. On the plus side, local transport is cheap.

Bus

Apart from bikes, buses are the most common means of getting around in the cities. Services are fairly extensive, buses go to most places and fares are inexpensive. The problem is that they are almost always packed. If an empty bus pulls in at a stop, a battle for seats ensues. Even more aggravating is the slowness of the traffic. You just have to be patient, never expect anything to move rapidly and allow lots of time to get to the train station to catch your train.

Improvements in bus quality have been matched by a steady increase in congestion on the roads. Bus routes at bus stops are generally listed in Chinese only, without Pinyin, so navigation can be difficult. In larger towns and cities, more expensive private minibus operations follow the same routes as the larger public buses.

Good maps of Chinese cities and bus routes are readily available and are often sold by hawkers outside the train stations. When you get on a bus, point to where you want to go on the map and the conductor (who is seated near the door) will sell you the right ticket. They usually tell you where to get off, provided they remember, but the bus stop may be quite a distance from your destination.

Metro & Light Rail

Going underground is highly preferable to taking the bus, as there are no traffic jams, but this transport option is only possible in a handful of cities: Hong Kong, Běijīng, Shànghǎi, Guǎngzhōu, Tiānjīn, Nánjīng and Shēnzhèn. Wǔhàn has a limited light rail system in Hànkǒu, as does Tiānjīn (linking it to Tánggū), while Chóngqìng now benefits from a monorail.

By far the best and most comprehensive is Hong Kong's funky system; Běijīng's network is limited but is being expanded in preparation for the 2008 Olympics. The Shànghǎi metro system is also being massively extended.

Taxi

Many large Chinese cities endlessly sprawl and taxis (出租汽车; chūzū qìchē) are the best way to get around for first-time visitors. Taxis are cheap and plentiful and always on the lookout for customers, so finding one is rarely difficult. In fact, the ceaseless honking at or sidling alongside foreign travellers can be wearing. If you can't find a taxi, likely congregation points include the train and

TRANSPORT

long-distance bus stations. Some large cities also have taxi pickup points.

Taxi drivers speak little, if any, English. If you don't speak Chinese, bring a map or have your destination written down in characters. It helps if you know the way to your destination; sit in the front with a map.

If you encounter a taxi driver you trust or who speaks a smattering of English, ask for his card (名片; *míngpiàn*). You can hire a taxi driver for a single trip or on a daily basis – the latter is worth considering if there's a group of people who can split the cost.

Taxi rates per kilometre are clearly marked on a sticker on the rear side window of the taxi; flag fall rates vary from city to city and also depend upon the size and quality of the vehicle.

While most taxis have meters, they are often only switched on in larger towns and cities. If the meter is not used (on an excursion out of town, for example), a price should be negotiated before you get into the taxi and bargaining employed. Write the price down if you have to and secure an agreement, so that the price is not suddenly upped when you arrive. If you want the meter to be used, ask for *dǎbiǎo* (打表). Try to remember to ask for a receipt (发票; *fāpiào*); if you leave something behind in the taxi, the taxi number is printed on the receipt so it can be tracked down.

Chinese cities impose limitations on the number of passengers a taxi can carry. The limit is usually four – though minibuses can take more – and drivers are usually unwilling to break the rules and risk trouble with the police.

It's hard to find rear seat belts in China's older taxis, and front passenger seat belts are so rarely used they are often grimy or locked solid. Even so, take the front seat if you are travelling alone and ignore inane protestations from taxi drivers that you don't need to wear a seat belt. Be prepared for bad driving. If sitting in the rear, try to position yourself so you don't lose an eye on one of the sharp corners and edges of the security cage the driver sits in if he suddenly halts (or crashes). Watch out for tired drivers – they work long and punishing shifts.

Useful phrases for solo travellers include *pīnchē* (拼车) – to share a car or minibus, ie to pay per seat, rather than pay for your own car (包车; *bāochē*).

Other Local Transport

An often bewildering variety of ramshackle transport options can be found throughout China, providing employment for legions of elderly Chinese. The motor tricycle (三轮摩托车; *sānlún mótuōchē*) – for want of a better name – is an enclosed three-wheeled vehicle with a driver at the front, a small motorbike engine below and seats for two passengers behind. They tend to congregate outside the train and bus stations in larger towns and cities.

The pedicab (三轮车; *sānlúnchē*) is a pedal-powered tricycle with a seat to carry passengers. Chinese pedicabs have the driver at the front and passenger seats at the back. Pedicabs congregate outside train and bus stations or hotels in parts of China. In a few places, pedicabs cruise the streets in large numbers (Lhasa, for example); Qūfù (p218) has pedicabs in pestilential proportions.

In some towns you can get a ride on the back of someone's motorcycle for about half the price of what a regular four-wheeled taxi would charge. If you turn a blind eye to the hazards, this is a quick and cheap way of getting around. You must wear a helmet – the driver will provide one. Obviously, there is no meter, so fares must be agreed upon in advance.

Prices of all of the above can compare with taxis; however, check beforehand and bargain. Also note that none of the above offer decent protection in a crash, so taking a taxi is often the more sensible option (unless the seatbelts don't work…).

TRAIN

Although crowded, trains are the best way to get around in reasonable speed and comfort. The network covers every province, except Hǎinán, and the link to Lhasa was completed in 2006 (p924). At any given time it is estimated that over 10 million Chinese are travelling on a train in China, except during Chinese New Year when most of China seems to be on the railway.

Travelling by train is an adventurous, fun and efficient way of getting around China and meeting the local people. A variety of classes means you can navigate as you wish: if you can endure a hard seat, getting from A to B is very cheap. Opting for a soft sleeper means things can get pricey.

The safety record of the train system is also good (despite the grim and graphic photographs displayed in train stations warning of the perils of transporting fireworks and explosives), but keep an eye on your belongings (see p940).

The new fleet of trains that run intercity routes is a vast improvement on the old models – they are much cleaner and equipped with air-conditioning. The new 'Z' class express trains (eg between Běijīng and Shànghǎi) are very plush, with meals thrown in on some routes, mobile-phone charging points and well-designed bunks. The ultrafast maglev train that connects Pudong airport to the Shànghǎi metro system is perhaps a sign of things to come. Trains nationwide are very punctual and leave on the dot.

Most trains have dining cars where you can find passable food. Railway staff also regularly walk by with pushcarts offering *miàn* (instant noodles), *miànbāo* (bread), *héfàn* (boxed rice lunches), *huǒtuǐ* (ham), *píjiǔ* (beer), *kuàng quán shuǐ* (mineral water) and *qìshuǐ* (soft drinks).

Many train stations require that luggage be X-rayed before entering the waiting area.

Virtually all train stations have left-luggage rooms (寄存处; *jìcún chù*) where you can safely dump your bags for about Y5 to Y10 (per day per item).

An excellent online source of information on China's rail network is www.seat61.com /China.htm. For bundles of info on China's railways and trains, consult the tremendous **Railways of China** (www.railwaysofchina.com).

Classes

Train tickets are calculated simply according to the kilometre distance travelled and, on longer routes, the class of travel.

Hard seat (硬座; *yìng zuò*) is actually generally padded, but the hard-seat section can be hard on your sanity – it can be very dirty and noisy, and painful on the long haul. Hard seat on tourist trains, express trains or newer trains is more pleasant, less crowded and air-conditioned.

Since hard seat is the only class most locals can afford, it's packed to the gills. You should get a ticket with an assigned seat number, but if seats have sold out, ask for a standing ticket (无座; *wúzuò*; or 站票; *zhànpiào*), which at least gets you on the train where you may find a seat or you can upgrade. Because hard-seat tickets are relatively easy to obtain, you may have to travel hard seat even if you're willing to pay for a higher class.

On short express journeys (such as Běijīng to Tiānjīn) some trains have soft-seat (软座; *ruǎn zuò*) carriages. These trains have comfortable seats arranged two abreast and overcrowding is not permitted. Soft seats cost about the same as hard sleeper and carriages are often double-decker.

Hard-sleeper (硬卧; *yìng wò*) carriages are made up of doorless compartments with half a dozen bunks in three tiers, and sheets, pillows and blankets are provided. It does very nicely as an overnight hotel. There is a small price difference between berths, with the lowest bunk (下铺; *xiàpù*) the most expensive and the top-most bunk (上铺; *shàngpù*) the cheapest. You may wish to take the middle bunk (中铺; *zhōngpù*) as all and sundry invade the lower berth to use it as a seat during the day, while the top one has little headroom and puts you near the speakers. As with all other classes, smoking is prohibited in hard sleeper. Lights and speakers go out at around 10pm. Each compartment is equipped with its own hot-water flask (热水瓶; *rèshuǐpíng*), which is filled by an attendant. Hard-sleeper tickets are the most difficult of all to buy; you almost always need to buy these a few days in advance.

Soft sleeper (软卧; *ruǎn wò*) is very comfortable, with four comfortable bunks in a closed compartment, with lace curtains, teacups, clean washrooms, carpets and air-conditioning. Soft sleeper costs twice as much as hard sleeper (the upper berth is slightly cheaper than the lower berth), so it is usually easier to purchase soft rather than hard-sleeper tickets; however, more and more Chinese are travelling this way.

If you get on the train with an unreserved seating ticket, you can find the conductor and upgrade (补票; *bǔpiào*) yourself to a hard sleeper, soft seat or soft sleeper if there are any available.

Reservations & Tickets

The vast majority of tickets are one way (单程; *dānchéng*) only. Buying hard-seat tickets at short notice is usually no hassle, but you will not always be successful in getting a reserved seat. Tickets can only be purchased with cash.

Tickets for hard sleepers can usually be obtained in major cities, but with more difficulty in quiet backwaters. Don't expect to obtain a hard-sleeper ticket on the day of travel. Plan ahead and buy your ticket two or three days

TRANSPORT

RAIL DISTANCE CHART (KM) & SEA ROUTES

	Beijing 北京	Chángchūn 长春	Chángshā 长沙	Chéngdū 成都	Chóngqìng 重庆	Dàlián 大连	Dāndōng 丹东	Erenhot 二连	Fúzhōu 福州	Guǎngzhōu 广州	Guìyáng 贵阳	Hángzhōu 杭州	Hā'ěrbīn 哈尔滨	Héféi 合肥	Hohhot 呼和浩特	Jílín 吉林	Jǐ'nán 济南	Jǐnzhōu 锦州	Kūnmíng 昆明
Beijing 北京	---																		
Chángchūn 长春	1006	---																	
Chángshā 长沙	1587	2729	---																
Chéngdū 成都	2042	3048	1672	---															
Chóngqìng 重庆	2087	3092	1595	504	---														
Dàlián 大连	937	702	2524	2979	3024	---													
Dāndōng 丹东	1103	582	2714	3149	3194	674	---												
Erenhot 二连	842	1848	2429	2807	1812	1779	1949	---											
Fúzhōu 福州	2334	3229	985	2525	2246	3125	3201	3176	---										
Guǎngzhōu 广州	2294	3436	707	2461	1897	3231	3284	3136	1514	---									
Guìyáng 贵阳	2544	3550	957	901	463	3481	3647	3275	1838	1434	---								
Hángzhōu 杭州	1664	2670	1006	2760	2322	2380	2431	2506	828	1609	1859	---							
Hā'ěrbīn 哈尔滨	1248	242	2971	3285	3329	944	824	2085	3471	3588	3787	2726	---						
Héféi 合肥	1110	2082	881	1955	1778	1901	2217	1952	2217	1410	1734	445	2247	---					
Hohhot 呼和浩特	659	1650	2246	2316	2637	1596	1766	491	2897	2594	2544	2309	1887	1735	---				
Jílín 吉林	1134	128	2721	3176	3221	843	710	1976	3370	3428	3678	2700	303	2146	1604	---			
Jǐ'nán 济南	497	1392	1294	2287	1967	1288	1364	1321	1837	2001	2251	1092	1634	761	1142	1533	---		
Jǐnzhōu 锦州	499	547	2182	2637	2585	443	494	1336	2551	2889	3048	1937	789	1458	1352	688	845	---	
Kūnmíng 昆明	3138	4189	1596	1100	1102	4120	4286	3804	2477	1637	639	2719	4426	2373	3233	4317	2890	3737	---
Lánzhōu 兰州	1803	2809	2085	1172	1466	2740	2910	1635	2650	2792	1929	2234	3046	1789	1144	2937	2069	2297	2272
Liǔzhōu 柳州	2321	3327	734	1577	1073	3258	3428	3163	1615	824	610	1636	3569	1511	2976	3455	2028	2916	1544
Mǎnzhōulǐ 满洲里	2346	1177	3776	4361	4433	1830	1759	3188	4680	4483	4483	3559	935	3422	2661	1238	2392	1724	5529
Mǔdānjiāng 牡丹江	1603	597	3190	3645	3690	1157	1037	2445	3826	3897	4147	3081	355	355	2262	649	1989	1144	4786
Nánchāng 南昌	1449	2455	419	1766	1624	2372	2423	2291	622	956	1272	643	2678	462	2108	2583	1134	1929	1911
Nánjīng 南京	1160	2055	1119	2048	1996	1951	2002	1984	2002	1804	2487	429	2297	266	1805	2196	663	1508	3126
Nánníng 南宁	2566	3582	989	1832	1328	3503	3673	3418	1870	809	865	1891	3819	1766	3235	3700	2283	3171	828
Píngxiáng 凭祥	2796	3802	1209	1612	1108	3733	3893	3198	2090	1029	645	2111	4039	1986	3015	3930	2503	3391	608
Qīngdǎo 青岛	890	1896	1687	2680	2360	1681	1757	1732	2344	2467	2823	1485	2027	761	1549	1926	393	1238	3512
Qíqíhā'ěr 齐齐哈尔	1343	481	2930	3385	3430	1157	1037	2143	3582	3637	3887	3559	288	2358	1968	1238	1745	900	4526
Shànghǎi 上海	1463	2358	1207	2351	2523	2254	2305	2282	2305	1810	2060	201	2600	615	2103	2494	966	1811	2699
Shěnyáng 沈阳	703	305	2424	2879	2788	397	278	1543	2847	3131	3245	2233	547	1754	1648	431	1087	242	3884
Shíjiāzhuāng 石家庄	277	1379	1310	1765	1810	1315	1366	1111	1921	2017	2267	1371	1621	926	936	1411	301	872	2906
Tàiyuán 太原	508	1514	1722	1493	1441	1445	1615	815	2146	2437	1904	1596	1735	640	1642	532	1062		2543
Tiānjīn 天津	137	1032	1697	2152	2091	928	966	979	2197	2404	2563	1452	1274	973	796	1173	360	485	3252
Ürümqi 乌鲁木齐	3768	4774	3826	3026	3358	4705	4875	4610	4542	4533	3821	4126	5011	3681	2684	4902	3745	4363	4126
Wǔchāng 武昌	1225	2367	362	1375	1233	6162	2215	2068	1013	1069	1319	1034	2609	585	1348	2359	932	1820	1958
Xī'ān 西安	1200	2302	1409	842	790	2137	2280	1466	1974	2116	1253	1558	2443	1113	1291	2334	1853	1795	1942
Xīníng 西宁	2092	3089	2301	1388	1682	3029	3199	2934	3000	3008	2145	2450	3335	2005	1360	3226	2069	2687	2488
Xúzhōu 徐州	814	1709	949	1702	1650	1605	1656	1638	1656	1839	2089	775	1951	296	1459	1850	317	1162	2728
Yínchuān 银川	1335	2341	2255	1640	1636	2272	2442	1167	2954	2962	2099	2944	2578	1959	676	2469	1822	1829	2740
Zhèngzhōu 郑州	689	1791	898	1353	1301	1727	1778	1523	1597	1069	1855	1047	2033	602	1348	1823	550	1526	2494
Zhūzhōu 株州	1639	2781	52	1806	1368	2576	2710	2481	933	655	905	954	2887	829	2298	2773	1346	2476	1544

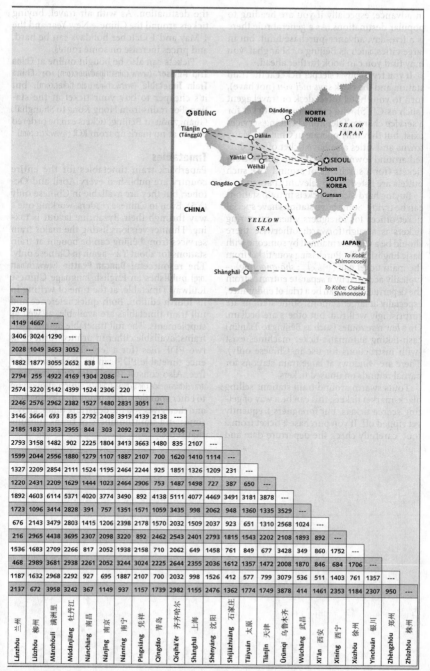

	Lánzhōu 兰州	Liǔzhōu 柳州	Mǎnzhōulǐ 满洲里	Mǔdānjiāng 牡丹江	Nánchāng 南昌	Nánjīng 南京	Nánníng 南宁	Píngxiáng 凭祥	Qīngdǎo 青岛	Qíqíhā'ěr 齐齐哈尔	Shànghǎi 上海	Shěnyáng 沈阳	Shíjiāzhuāng 石家庄	Tàiyuán 太原	Tiānjīn 天津	Ūrümqi 乌鲁木齐	Wǔchāng 武昌	Xī'ān 西安	Xīníng 西宁	Xúzhōu 徐州	Yínchuān 银川	Zhèngzhōu 郑州	Zhūzhōu 株洲
Lánzhōu 兰州	---																						
Liǔzhōu 柳州	2749	---																					
Mǎnzhōulǐ 满洲里	4149	4667	---																				
Mǔdānjiāng 牡丹江	3406	3024	1290	---																			
Nánchāng 南昌	2028	1049	3653	3052	---																		
Nánjīng 南京	1882	1877	3055	2652	838	---																	
Nánníng 南宁	2794	255	4922	4169	1304	2086	---																
Píngxiáng 凭祥	2574	3220	5142	4399	1524	2306	220	---															
Qīngdǎo 青岛	2246	2576	2962	2382	1527	1480	2831	3051	---														
Qíqíhā'ěr 齐齐哈尔	3146	3664	693	835	2792	2408	3919	4139	2138	---													
Shànghǎi 上海	2185	1837	3353	2955	844	303	2092	2312	1359	2706	---												
Shěnyáng 沈阳	2793	3158	1482	902	2225	1804	3413	3663	1480	835	2107	---											
Shíjiāzhuāng 石家庄	1599	2044	2556	1880	1279	1107	1887	2107	700	1620	1410	1114	---										
Tàiyuán 太原	1327	2209	2854	2111	1524	1195	2464	2244	925	1851	1326	1209	231	---									
Tiānjīn 天津	1220	2431	2209	1629	1444	1023	2464	2906	753	1487	1498	727	387	650	---								
Ūrümqi 乌鲁木齐	1892	4603	6114	5371	4020	3774	3490	892	4138	5111	4077	4469	3491	3181	3878	---							
Wǔchāng 武昌	1723	1096	3414	2828	391	757	1351	1571	1059	3435	998	2062	948	1360	1335	3529	---						
Xī'ān 西安	676	2143	3479	2803	1415	1206	2398	2178	1570	2032	1509	2037	923	651	1310	2568	1024	---					
Xīníng 西宁	216	2965	4438	3695	2307	2098	3220	892	2462	2543	2401	2793	1815	1543	2202	2108	1893	892	---				
Xúzhōu 徐州	1536	1683	2709	2266	817	2052	1938	2158	710	2062	649	1458	761	849	677	3428	349	860	1752	---			
Yínchuān 银川	468	2989	3681	2938	2261	2052	3244	3024	2225	2644	2355	2036	1612	1357	1472	2008	1870	846	684	1706	---		
Zhèngzhōu 郑州	1187	1632	2968	2292	927	695	1887	2107	700	2032	998	1526	412	577	799	3079	536	511	1403	761	1357	---	
Zhūzhōu 株洲	2137	672	3958	3242	367	1149	937	1157	1739	2982	1155	2476	1362	1774	1749	3878	414	1461	2353	1184	2307	950	---

in advance, especially if you are heading to popular destinations. As a general rule there is a five-day, advance-purchase limit, but in large cities, such as Běijīng or Shànghǎi, you may find you can book further ahead.

If you try to buy a sleeper ticket at the train station and the clerk says *méi yǒu* (not have), turn to your hotel travel desk or travel agent (such as CITS) who can sell you a ticket for a service charge. Telephone booking services exist, but they only operate in Chinese. Many towns and cities also have ticket offices dotted around town where you can obtain train tickets (for a surcharge of around Y5); such outlets are listed in the relevant chapters.

Buying hard-sleeper tickets in train stations can be trying. Some large stations have special ticket offices for foreigners where procuring tickets is straightforward; otherwise there should be a window manned by someone with basic English skills. Purchasing your ticket from the main ticket hall (售票厅; *shòupiàotīng*) – typically accessed by a separate entrance from the departure hall – can be a trial of endurance, especially at larger stations. Some stations are surprisingly well run, but others are bedlam. On a few rare routes (such as Běijīng to Tiānjīn) cash-taking automatic ticket machines exist (with instructions for use in Chinese only). There are windows at large train stations for partial refunds on unused tickets.

Touts swarm around train stations selling black-market tickets; this can be a way of getting scarce tickets, but foreigners frequently get ripped off. If you purchase a ticket from a tout, carefully check the departure date and the destination. As with air travel, buying tickets around the Chinese New Year and the 1 May and 1 October holidays can be hard, and prices increase on some routes.

Tickets can also be bought online at **China Trip Advisor** (www.chinatripadvisor.com) or **China Train Timetable** (www.china-train-ticket.com), but it's cheaper to buy your ticket at the station. For trains from Hong Kong to Shànghǎi, Guǎngzhōu or Běijīng, tickets can be ordered online at no mark up from **KCR** (www.kcrc.com).

Timetables

Paperback train timetables for the entire country are published every April and October, but they are available in Chinese only (Y5). Even to Chinese readers, working one's way through their Byzantine layout is taxing. Thinner versions listing the major train services from Běijīng can be bought at train stations for about Y2 – again in Chinese only. The resourceful **Duncan Peattie** (www.chinatt.org) publishes an English-language Chinese Railway Timetable, at the time of writing in its fourth edition. Both quick reference and full train timetables are available, as well as supplements. The full timetable details 2400 trains, available either in printed form or as two PDF files (for a fee). The quick reference timetable PDF can be downloaded for free. Also consult **Travel China Guide.com** (www.travelchinaguide.com/china-trains/), which allows you to enter your departure point and destination, and then gives you the departure times, arrival times and train numbers of trains running that route.

Health Dr Trish Batchelor

CONTENTS

Overall China is a reasonably healthy country to travel in, but there are a number of health issues worthy of your attention. Pre-existing medical conditions, such as heart disease, and accidental injury (especially traffic accidents), account for most life-threatening problems. However, becoming ill in some way is not unusual. Outside of the major cities medical care is often inadequate and food and waterborne diseases are common. Malaria is still present in some parts of the country and high-altitude sickness can be a problem, particularly in Tibet.

In case of accident or illness it's best just to get a taxi and go to hospital directly – try to avoid dealing with the authorities if possible.

The following advice is a general guide only and does not replace the advice of a doctor trained in travel medicine.

BEFORE YOU GO

Pack medications in their original, clearly labelled, containers. A signed and dated letter from your physician describing your medical conditions and medications (using generic names) is also a good idea. If carrying syringes or needles, be sure to have a physician's letter documenting their medi-

cal necessity. If you have a heart condition, bring a copy of your ECG taken just prior to travelling.

If you take any regular medication bring double your needs in case of loss or theft. In China you can buy many medications over the counter without a doctor's prescription, but it can be difficult to find some of the newer drugs, particularly the latest antidepressant drugs, blood pressure medications and contraceptive methods. In general it is not advised to buy medications locally without a doctor's advice.

Make sure you get your teeth checked before you travel, and if you wear glasses take a spare pair and your prescription.

INSURANCE

Even if you are fit and healthy, don't travel without health insurance – accidents do happen. Declare any existing medical conditions you have – the insurance company *will* check if your problem is pre-existing and will not cover you if it is undeclared. You may require extra cover for adventure activities such as rock climbing. If you're uninsured, emergency evacuation is expensive (bills of over US$100,000 are not uncommon).

Make sure you keep all documentation related to any medical expenses you incur.

RECOMMENDED VACCINATIONS

Specialised travel-medicine clinics are your best source of information; they stock all available vaccines and can give specific recommendations for you and your trip. The doctors will take into account factors such as past vaccination history, the length of your trip, activities you may be undertaking and underlying medical conditions, such as pregnancy.

Most vaccines don't produce immunity until at least two weeks after they're given, so visit a doctor six to eight weeks before departure. Ask your doctor for an International Certificate of Vaccination (otherwise known as the yellow booklet), which will list all the vaccinations you've received.

The only vaccine required by international regulations is yellow fever. Proof of vaccination will only be required if you have visited a country in the yellow fever zone within the six days prior to entering China. If you are travelling to China directly from South America or Africa, check with a travel clinic as to whether you need yellow fever vaccination.

MEDICAL CHECKLIST

Recommended items for a personal medical kit:

- Antibacterial cream, eg Muciprocin
- Antibiotics for skin infections, eg Amoxicillin/Clavulanate or Cephalexin
- Antibiotics for diarrhoea, including Norfloxacin, Ciprofloxacin, or Azithromycin for bacterial diarrhoea; or Tinidazole for giardia or amoebic dysentery.
- Antifungal cream, eg Clotrimazole
- Antihistamine – there are many options, eg Cetrizine for daytime and Promethazine for night-time
- Antiseptic, eg Betadine
- Anti-spasmodic for stomach cramps, eg Buscopan
- Decongestant, eg Pseudoephedrine
- DEET-based insect repellent
- Diamox if going to high altitudes
- An oral rehydration solution (eg Gastrolyte) for diarrhoea, diarrhoea 'stopper' (eg Loperamide) and anti-nausea medication (eg Prochlorperazine)
- Elastoplasts, bandages, gauze, thermometer (but not mercury), sterile needles and syringes, safety pins and tweezers
- Ibuprofen or another anti-inflammatory

RECOMMENDED VACCINATIONS

The World Health Organization (WHO) recommends the following vaccinations for travellers to China:

Adult diphtheria and tetanus Single booster recommended if none in the previous 10 years. Side effects include sore arm and fever. A new ADT vaccine containing pertussis is also available and may be recommended by your doctor.

Hepatitis A Provides almost 100% protection for up to a year; a booster after 12 months provides at least another 20 years protection. Mild side effects such as headache and sore arm occur in 5% to 10% of people.

Hepatitis B Now considered routine for most travellers. Given as three shots over six months. A rapid schedule is also available, as is a combined vaccination with Hepatitis A. Side effects are mild and uncommon, usually headache and sore arm. In 95% of people lifetime protection results.

Measles, mumps and rubella Two doses of MMR recommended unless you have had the diseases. Occasionally a rash and flu-like illness can develop a week after receiving the vaccine. Many adults under 40 require a booster.

Typhoid Recommended unless your trip is less than a week. The vaccine offers around 70% protection, lasts for two to three years and comes as a single shot. Tablets are also available; however, the injection is usually recommended as it has fewer side effects. Sore arm and fever may occur. A vaccine combining Hepatitis A and typhoid in a single shot is now available.

Varicella If you haven't had chickenpox discuss this vaccination with your doctor.

The following immunisations are recommended for long-term travellers (more than one month) or those at special risk:

Influenza A single shot lasts one year and is recommended for those over 65 years of age or with underlying medical conditions such as heart or lung disease.

Japanese B encephalitis A series of three injections with a booster after two years. Recommended if spending more than one month in rural areas in the summer months, or more than 3 months in the country.

Pneumonia A single injection with a booster after five years is recommended for all travellers over 65 years of age or with underlying medical conditions that compromise immunity such as heart or lung disease, cancer or HIV.

Rabies Three injections in all. A booster after one year will then provide 10 years' protection. Side effects are rare – occasionally headache and sore arm.

Tuberculosis A complex issue. High-risk adult long-term travellers are usually recommended to have a TB skin test before and after travel, rather than vaccination. Only one vaccine is given in a lifetime. Children under five spending more than three months in China should be vaccinated.

Pregnant women and children should receive advice from a doctor who specialises in travel medicine.

- Indigestion tablets, such as Quick Eze or Mylanta
- Iodine tablets (unless you are pregnant or have a thyroid problem) to purify water
- Laxative, eg Coloxyl
- Paracetamol
- Permethrin to impregnate clothing and mosquito nets
- Steroid cream for allergic/itchy rashes, eg 1% to 2% hydrocortisone
- Sunscreen and hat
- Thrush (vaginal yeast infection) treatment, eg Clotrimazole pessaries or Diflucan tablet
- Ural or equivalent if prone to urinary infections

HEALTH ADVISORIES

It's usually a good idea to consult your government's travel-health website before departure, if one is available:
Australia (www.dfat.gov.au/travel/)
Canada (www.travelhealth.gc.ca)
New Zealand (www.mfat.govt.nz/travel)
UK (www.dh.gov.uk) Search for travel in the site index.
US (www.cdc.gov/travel/)

INTERNET RESOURCES
There is a wealth of travel health advice on the internet. For further information, **Lonely Planet** (www.lonelyplanet.com) is a good place to start. The **World Health Organization** (WHO; www.who.int/ith/) publishes a superb book called *International Travel & Health*, which is revised annually and is available online at no cost. Another website of general interest is **MD Travel Health** (www.mdtravelhealth.com), which provides complete travel-health recommendations for every country and is updated daily. The **Centers for Disease Control & Prevention** (CDC; www.cdc.gov) website also has good general information.

FURTHER READING
Lonely Planet's *Healthy Travel – Asia & India* is a handy pocket size and packed with useful information including pretrip planning, emergency first aid, immunisation, and information on diseases and what to do if you get sick on the road. Other recommended references include *Traveller's Health* by Dr

Richard Dawood and *Travelling Well* by Dr Deborah Mills – check out the website (www.travellingwell.com.au).

IN TRANSIT

DEEP VEIN THROMBOSIS (DVT)
Deep vein thrombosis occurs when blood clots form in the legs during flights, chiefly because of prolonged immobility. Though most blood clots are reabsorbed uneventfully, some may break off and travel through the blood vessels to the lungs, where they may cause life-threatening complications.

The chief symptom of DVT is swelling or pain of the foot, ankle or calf, usually but not always on just one side. When a blood clot travels to the lungs, it may cause chest pain and difficulty in breathing. Travellers with any of these symptoms should immediately seek medical attention.

To prevent the development of DVT on long flights you should walk about the cabin, perform isometric compressions of the leg muscles (ie contract the leg muscles while sitting), drink plenty of fluids, and avoid alcohol and tobacco. Those at increased risk should wear compression socks.

JET LAG & MOTION SICKNESS
Jet lag is common when crossing more than five time zones; it results in insomnia, fatigue, malaise or nausea. To avoid jet lag try drinking plenty of fluids (nonalcoholic) and eating light meals. Upon arrival, seek exposure to natural sunlight and readjust your schedule (for meals, sleep etc) as soon as possible.

Antihistamines such as dimenhydrinate (Dramamine), promethazine (Phenergan) and meclizine (Antivert, Bonine) are usually the first choice for treating motion sickness. Their main side effect is drowsiness. An herbal alternative is ginger, which works like a charm for some people.

IN CHINA

AVAILABILITY OF HEALTH CARE
There are now a number of good clinics in major cities catering to travellers. Although they are usually more expensive than local facilities, you may feel more comfortable dealing with a Western-trained doctor who speaks

HEALTH

your language. These clinics usually have a good understanding of the best local hospital facilities and close contacts with insurance companies should you need evacuation.

Self-treatment may be appropriate if your problem is minor (eg traveller's diarrhoea), you are carrying the relevant medication and you cannot attend a clinic. If you think you may have a serious disease, especially malaria, do not waste time – travel to the nearest quality facility to receive attention.

Buying medication over the counter in China is not recommended, as fake medications and poorly stored or out-of-date drugs are common.

To find the nearest reliable medical facility, contact your insurance company or your embassy.

INFECTIOUS DISEASES
Avian Influenza (Bird Flu)

'Bird flu' or Influenza A (H5N1) is a subtype of the type A influenza virus. This virus typically infects birds and not humans; however, in 1997 the first documented case of bird-to-human transmission was recorded in Hong Kong. As of July 2006 there have been 19 confirmed human cases in China, of whom 12 have died. Currently very close contact with dead or sick birds is the principal source of infection and bird to human transmission does not easily occur.

Symptoms include high fever and typical influenza-like symptoms with rapid deterioration leading to respiratory failure and death in many cases. The early administration of antiviral drugs such as Tamiflu is recommended to improve the chances of survival. At this time it is not routinely recommended for travellers to carry Tamiflu with them – rather immediate medical care should be sought if bird flu is suspected. At the time of writing there have been no recorded cases in travellers or expatriates.

There is currently no vaccine available to prevent bird flu. For up to date information check these two websites:

- www.who.int/en/
- www.avianinfluenza.com.au

Dengue

This mosquito-borne disease occurs in some parts of southern China. It can only be prevented by avoiding mosquito bites – there is no vaccine. The mosquito that carries dengue bites day and night, so use insect avoidance measures at all times. Symptoms include high fever, severe headache and body ache (previously dengue was known as 'break bone fever'). Some people develop a rash and diarrhoea. There is no specific treatment – just rest and paracetamol. Do not take aspirin. See a doctor to be diagnosed and monitored.

Hepatitis A

A problem throughout China, this food- and waterborne virus infects the liver, causing jaundice (yellow skin and eyes), nausea and lethargy. There is no specific treatment for hepatitis A, you just need to allow time for the liver to heal. All travellers to China should be vaccinated.

Hepatitis B

The only sexually transmitted disease that can be prevented by vaccination, hepatitis B is spread by contact with infected body fluids, including via sexual contact. The long-term consequences can include liver cancer and cirrhosis. All travellers to China should be vaccinated.

HIV

HIV is transmitted via contaminated body fluids. Avoid unsafe sex, blood transfusions and injections (unless you can see a clean needle being used) in China. Always use condoms if you have sex with a new partner and never share needles.

Influenza

Present particularly in the winter months, symptoms of the flu include high fever, runny nose, muscle aches, cough and sore throat. It can be very severe in people over the age of 65 or in those with underlying medical conditions such as heart disease or diabetes – vaccination is recommended for these individuals. There is no specific treatment, just rest and painkillers.

Japanese B Encephalitis

This is a rare disease in travellers; however, vaccination is recommended if spending more than a month in rural areas during the summer months, or more than three months in the country. There is no treatment available and one-third of infected people will die, while another third suffer permanent brain damage.

Malaria

For such a serious and potentially deadly disease, there is an enormous amount of misinformation concerning malaria. Before you travel, be sure to seek medical advice to see if your trip warrants taking antimalaria medication and if it does, to ensure that you receive the right medication and dosage for you.

Malaria has been nearly eradicated in China and is not generally a risk for visitors to the cities and most tourist areas. It is found mainly in rural areas in the southwestern region – principally Hǎinán, Yúnnán and Guǎngxī bordering onto Myanmar, Laos and Vietnam. There is more limited risk in remote rural areas of Fújiàn, Guǎngdōng, Guǎngxī, Guìzhōu, and Sìchuān. Generally medication is only advised if you are visiting rural Hǎinán or Yúnnán.

Malaria is caused by a parasite transmitted by the bite of an infected mosquito. The most important symptom of malaria is fever, but general symptoms such as headache, diarrhoea, cough or chills may also occur. Diagnosis can only be made by taking a blood sample.

Two strategies should be combined to prevent malaria – mosquito avoidance and antimalaria medications. Most people who catch malaria are taking inadequate or no antimalarial medication.

You should always take general insect avoidance measures in order to help prevent all insect-borne diseases, not just malaria. Travellers are advised to prevent mosquito bites by taking these steps:

- Use a DEET-containing insect repellent on exposed skin. Wash this off at night, as long as you are sleeping under a mosquito net. Natural repellents such as Citronella can be effective, but must be applied more frequently than products containing DEET.
- Sleep under a mosquito net impregnated with permethrin.
- Choose accommodation with screens and fans (if not air-conditioned).
- Impregnate clothing with permethrin in high-risk areas.
- Wear long sleeves and trousers in light colours.
- Use mosquito coils.
- Spray your room with insect repellent before going out for your evening meal.

Rabies

This is an increasingly common problem in China. This fatal disease is spread by the bite or lick of an infected animal – most commonly a dog. Seek medical advice immediately after any animal bite and commence post-exposure treatment. Having pretravel vaccination means the post-bite treatment is greatly simplified. If an animal bites you, gently wash the wound with soap and water, and apply an iodine-based antiseptic. If you are not prevaccinated you will need to receive rabies immunoglobulin as soon as possible, followed by a series of five vaccines over the next month. Those prevaccinated require only two shots of vaccine after a bite.

Contact your insurance company to find the nearest clinic that stocks rabies immunoglobulin and vaccine. It's common that immunoglobulin is unavailable outside of major centres – it's crucial that you get to a clinic that has immunoglobulin as soon as possible if you have had a bite that has broken the skin.

Schistosomiasis

Also known as bilharzia, this disease is found in the central Yangzi River (Cháng Jiāng) basin. It is carried in water by minute worms which infect certain varieties of freshwater snail found in rivers, streams, lakes and particularly behind dams. The worm enters through the skin and attaches itself to your intestines or bladder. The infection often causes no symptoms until the disease is well established (several months to years after exposure) and damage to internal organs irreversible.

Avoiding swimming or bathing in fresh water where bilharzia is present is the main method of prevention. A blood test is the most reliable way to diagnose the disease, but the test will not show positive until weeks after exposure. Effective treatment is available. There is no way of knowing if water is infected.

STDs

Sexually transmitted diseases most common in China include herpes, warts, syphilis, gonorrhoea and chlamydia. People carrying these diseases often have no signs of infection. Condoms will prevent gonorrhoea and chlamydia but not warts or herpes. If after a sexual encounter you develop any rash, lumps, discharge or pain when passing urine seek immediate medical attention. If you have been sexually active during your travels have an STD check on your return home.

HEALTH

Tuberculosis (TB)

Medical and aid workers, and long-term travellers who have significant contact with the local population, should take precautions against TB. Vaccination is usually only given to children under the age of five, but adults at risk are recommended to have pre- and post-travel TB testing. The main symptoms are fever, cough, weight loss, night sweats and tiredness.

Typhoid

This serious bacterial infection is spread via food and water. Symptoms are headache and a high and slowly progressive fever, which may be accompanied by a dry cough and stomach pain. Be aware that vaccination is not 100% effective so you must still be careful with what you eat and drink. All travellers spending more than a week in China should be vaccinated.

TRAVELLER'S DIARRHOEA

Traveller's diarrhoea is by far the most common problem affecting travellers – between 30% to 50% of people will suffer from it within two weeks of starting their trip. In most cases, traveller's diarrhoea is caused by a bacteria (there are numerous potential culprits), and therefore responds promptly to treatment with antibiotics. Treatment with antibiotics will depend on your situation – how sick you are, how quickly you need to get better, where you are etc.

Traveller's diarrhoea is defined as the passage of more than three watery bowel actions within 24 hours, plus at least one other symptom such as fever, cramps, nausea, vomiting or feeling generally unwell.

Treatment consists of staying well hydrated; rehydration solutions like Gastrolyte are the best for this. Antibiotics such as Norfloxacin, Ciprofloxacin or Azithromycin will kill the bacteria quickly.

Loperamide is just a 'stopper' and doesn't get to the cause of the problem. It can be helpful, for example if you have to go on a long bus ride. Don't take Loperamide if you have a fever, or blood in your stools. Seek medical attention quickly if you do not respond to an appropriate antibiotic.

Amoebic Dysentery

Amoebic dysentery is actually rare in travellers and is overdiagnosed. Symptoms are similar to bacterial diarrhoea, ie fever, bloody diarrhoea and generally feeling unwell. You should always seek reliable medical care if you have blood in your diarrhoea. Treatment involves two drugs: Tinidazole or Metronidazole to kill the parasite in your gut, and then a second drug to kill the cysts. If left untreated complications such as liver or gut abscesses can occur.

Giardiasis

Giardia is a parasite that is relatively common in travellers. Symptoms include nausea, bloating, excess gas, fatigue and intermittent diarrhoea. 'Eggy' burps are often attributed solely to giardia, but work in Nepal has shown that they are not specific to giardia. The parasite will eventually go away if left untreated but this can take months. The treatment of choice is Tinidazole, with Metronidazole being a second option.

Intestinal Worms

These parasites are most common in rural, tropical areas. Some may be ingested in food such as undercooked meat (eg tapeworms) and some enter through your skin (eg hookworms). Infestations may not show up for some time, and although they are generally not serious, if left untreated some can cause severe health problems later. Consider having a stool test when you return home to check for these and to determine the appropriate treatment.

ENVIRONMENTAL HAZARDS
Air Pollution

Air pollution is becoming a significant problem in many Chinese cities due to increasing industrialisation. People with underlying respiratory conditions should seek advice from their doctor prior to travel to ensure they have adequate medications in case their condition worsens. It is very common for healthy people to develop irritating coughs, runny noses etc while in urban Chinese centres as a result of the pollution. It is a good idea to carry symptomatic treatments such as throat lozenges, and cough and cold tablets.

Altitude Sickness

There are bus journeys in Tibet, Qīnghǎi and Xīnjiāng where the road goes over 5000m. Acclimatising to such extreme elevations takes several weeks at least, but most travellers come up from sea level very fast – a bad move! Acute mountain sickness (AMS) results from a rapid ascent to altitudes above 2700m. It usually commences within 24 to 48 hours of arriving at altitude and symptoms include headache, nausea, fatigue and loss of appetite (it very much feels like a hangover). If you have altitude sickness the cardinal rule is that you must not go higher as you are sure to get sicker and could develop one of the more severe and potentially deadly forms of the disease. These are high altitude pulmonary oedema (HAPE) and high altitude cerebral oedema (HACE). Both of these forms of altitude sickness are medical emergencies and there are no rescue facilities similar to those in the Nepal Himalaya here, so prevention is the best policy. AMS can be prevented by 'graded ascent' – it is recommended that once you are above 3000m you ascend a maximum of 300m daily and have an extra rest day every 1000m. You can also use a medication called Diamox as a prevention or treatment for AMS after discussion with a doctor experienced in altitude medicine. Diamox should not be taken by people with a sulphur drug allergy.

If you have altitude sickness you should rest where you are for a day or two until your symptoms resolve. You can then carry on, but ensure you follow the graded ascent guidelines. If symptoms are getting worse you must descend immediately before you are faced with a life-threatening situation. There is no way of predicting who will suffer from AMS but certain factors predispose you to it – rapid ascent; carrying a heavy load and working hard; and having a seemingly minor illness such as a chest infection or diarrhoea. Make sure you drink at least 3L of noncaffeinated drinks daily to stay well hydrated. The sun is intense at altitude so take care with sun protection and ensure you have adequate clothing to avoid hypothermia – temperatures drop rapidly once the sun goes down and winds can be intense.

Food

Eating in restaurants is the biggest risk factor for contracting traveller's diarrhoea. Ways to avoid it include eating only freshly cooked food, and avoiding food that has been sitting around in buffets. Peel all fruit, cook vegetables and soak salads in iodine water for at least 20 minutes. Eat in busy restaurants with a high turnover of customers.

DRINKING WATER
- Never drink tap water.
- Bottled water is generally safe – check the seal is intact at purchase.
- Avoid ice.
- Avoid fresh juices – they may have been watered down.
- Boiling water is the most efficient method of purifying it.
- The best chemical purifier is iodine. It should not be used by pregnant women or those with thyroid problems.
- Water filters should also filter out viruses. Ensure your filter has a chemical barrier such as iodine and a small pore size, eg less than four microns.

Heat Exhaustion

Dehydration or salt deficiency can cause heat exhaustion. Take time to acclimatise to high temperatures, drink sufficient liquids and do not do anything too physically demanding.

Salt deficiency is characterised by fatigue, lethargy, headaches, giddiness and muscle cramps; salt tablets may help, but adding extra salt to your food is better.

Hypothermia

Too much cold can be just as dangerous as too much heat. If you are trekking at high altitudes or simply taking a long bus trip over mountains, particularly at night, be aware. In Tibet it can go from being mildly warm to blisteringly cold in a matter of minutes – blizzards have a way of just coming out of nowhere. If you're out walking, cycling or hitching, this can be dangerous.

It is surprisingly easy to progress from very cold to dangerously cold due to a combination of wind, wet clothing, fatigue and hunger, even if the air temperature is above freezing. It is best to dress in layers; silk, wool and some of the new artificial fibres are all good insulating materials. A hat is important, as a lot of heat is lost through the head. A strong, waterproof outer layer (and a space blanket for emergencies) is essential. Carry basic supplies, including food containing simple sugars to generate heat quickly, and fluid to drink.

Symptoms of hypothermia are exhaustion, numb skin (particularly the toes and fingers), shivering, slurred speech, irrational or violent behaviour, lethargy, stumbling, dizzy spells, muscle cramps and violent bursts of energy.

To treat mild hypothermia, first get the person out of the wind and/or rain, remove their clothing if it's wet and replace it with dry, warm clothing. Give them hot liquids – not alcohol – and some high-calorie, easily digestible food. The early recognition and treatment of mild hypothermia is the only way to prevent severe hypothermia, which is a critical condition and requires medical attention.

Insect Bites & Stings
Bedbugs don't carry disease but their bites are very itchy. They live in the cracks of furniture and walls and then migrate to the bed at night to feed on you. You can treat the itch with an antihistamine.

Lice inhabit various parts of the human body but most commonly the head and pubic areas. Transmission is via close contact with an affected person. Lice can be difficult to treat and you may need numerous applications of an antilice shampoo such as Permethrin. Pubic lice (crab lice) are usually contracted from sexual contact.

Ticks are contracted after walking in rural areas. Ticks are commonly found behind the ears, on the belly and in armpits. If you have had a tick bite and experience symptoms such as a rash at the site of the bite or elsewhere, fever or muscle aches you should see a doctor. Doxycycline prevents some tick-borne diseases.

WOMEN'S HEALTH
Pregnant women should receive specialised advice before travelling. The ideal time to travel is in the second trimester (between 14 and 28 weeks), when the risk of pregnancy-related problems is at its lowest and pregnant women generally feel at their best. During the first trimester there is a risk of miscarriage and in the third trimester complications such as premature labour and high blood pressure are possible. It's wise to travel with a companion. Always carry a list of quality medical facilities available at your destination and ensure you continue your standard antenatal care at these facilities. Avoid rural travel in areas with poor transportation and medical facilities. Most of all, ensure travel insurance covers

all pregnancy-related possibilities, including premature labour.

Malaria is a high-risk disease in pregnancy. WHO recommends that pregnant women do *not* travel to areas with Chloroquine-resistant malaria.

Traveller's diarrhoea can quickly lead to dehydration and result in inadequate blood flow to the placenta. Many of the drugs used to treat various diarrhoea bugs are not recommended in pregnancy. Azithromycin is considered safe.

Supplies of sanitary products may not be readily available in rural areas. Birth control options may be limited so bring adequate supplies of your own form of contraception. Heat, humidity and antibiotics can all contribute to thrush. Treatment is with antifungal creams and pessaries such as Clotrimazole. A practical alternative is a single tablet of Fluconazole (Diflucan). Urinary tract infections can be precipitated by dehydration or long bus journeys without toilet stops; bring suitable antibiotics.

TRADITIONAL MEDICINE
Traditional Chinese medicine (TCM) views the human body as an energy system in which the basic substances of *qì* (vital energy), *jīng* (essence), *xuè* (blood, the body's nourishing fluids) and *tǐyè* (body fluids; blood and other organic fluids) function. The concept of Yin and Yang is fundamental to the system. Disharmony between Yin and Yang or within the basic substances may be a result of internal causes (emotions), external causes (climatic conditions) or miscellaneous causes (work, exercise, sex etc). Treatment modalities include acupuncture, massage, herbs, diet and *qìgōng*, and aim to bring these elements back into balance. These therapies are particularly useful for treating chronic diseases and are gaining interest and respect in the Western medical system. Conditions that can be particularly suitable for traditional methods include chronic fatigue, arthritis, irritable bowel syndrome and some chronic skin conditions.

Be aware that 'natural' doesn't always mean 'safe', and there can be drug interactions between herbal medicines and Western medicines. If you are utilising both systems ensure you inform both practitioners what the other has prescribed.

Language

CONTENTS

CHINESE

The official language of the PRC is the dialect spoken in Běijīng. It is usually referred to in the west as 'Mandarin', but the Chinese call it Putonghua – common speech. Putonghua is variously referred to as *hànyǔ* (the Han language), *guóyǔ* (the national language) or *zhōngwén* or *zhōngguóhuà* (simply 'Chinese').

THE SPOKEN LANGUAGE
Dialects

Discounting its ethnic minority languages, China has eight major dialect groups: Putonghua (Mandarin), Yue (Cantonese), Wu (Shanghainese), Minbei (Fuzhou), Minnan (Hokkien-Taiwanese), Xiang, Gan and Hakka. These dialects also divide into many more sub-dialects.

With the exception of the western and southernmost provinces, most of the population speaks Mandarin, although regional accents can make comprehension difficult.

THE WRITTEN LANGUAGE

Chinese is often referred to as a language of pictographs. Many of the basic Chinese characters are in fact highly stylised pictures of what they represent, but most (around 90%) are compounds of a 'meaning' element and a 'sound' element.

So just how many Chinese characters are there? It's possible to verify the existence of some 56,000 characters, but the vast majority of these are archaic. It is commonly felt that a well-educated, contemporary Chinese person might know and use between 6000 and 8000 characters. To read a Chinese newspaper you will need to know 2000 to 3000 characters, but 1200 to 1500 would be enough to get the gist.

Writing systems usually alter people's perception of a language, and this is certainly true of Chinese. Each Chinese character represents a spoken syllable, leading many people to declare that Chinese is a 'monosyllabic language.' Actually, it's more a case of having a monosyllabic writing system. While the building block of the Chinese language is indeed the monosyllabic Chinese character, Chinese words are usually a combination of two or more characters. You could think of Chinese words as being compounds. The Chinese word for 'east' is composed of a single character (*dōng*), but must be combined with the character for 'west' (*xī*) to form the word for 'thing' (*dōngxī*). English has many compound words too, examples being 'whitewash' and 'backslide'.

Theoretically, all Chinese dialects share the same written system. In practice, Cantonese adds about 3000 specialised characters of its own and many of the dialects don't have a written form at all.

Simplification

In the interests of promoting universal literacy, the Committee for Reforming the Chinese Language was set up by the Běijīng government in 1954. Around 2200 Chinese characters were simplified. Chinese communities outside China (notably Taiwan and Hong Kong), however, continue to use the traditional, full-form characters.

Over the past few years – probably as a result of large-scale investment by overseas Chinese and tourism – full-form or 'complex' characters have returned to China. These are mainly seen in advertising (where the traditional characters are considered more attractive) and on restaurant, hotel and shop signs.

GRAMMAR

Chinese grammar is much simpler than that of European languages. There are no articles (a/the), no tenses and no plurals. The basic point to bear in mind is that, like English, Chinese word order is subject-verb-object. In other words, a basic English sentence like 'I (subject) love (verb) you (object)' is constructed in exactly the same way in Chinese. The catch is mastering the tones.

MANDARIN

PINYIN

In 1958 the Chinese adopted a system of writing their language using the Roman alphabet. It's known as *pīnyīn*. The original idea was to eventually do away with characters. However, tradition dies hard, and the idea has been abandoned.

Pinyin is often used on shop fronts, street signs and advertising billboards. Don't expect Chinese people to be able to use Pinyin, however. There are indications that the use of the Pinyin system is diminishing.

In the countryside and the smaller towns you may not see a single Pinyin sign anywhere, so unless you speak Chinese you'll need a phrasebook with Chinese characters.

Since 1979 all translated texts of Chinese diplomatic documents, as well as Chinese magazines published in foreign languages, have used the Pinyin system for spelling names and places. Pinyin replaces the old Wade-Giles and Lessing systems of Romanising Chinese script. Thus under Pinyin, 'Mao Tse-tung' becomes Mao Zedong; 'Chou En-lai' becomes Zhou Enlai; and 'Peking' becomes Běijīng. The name of the country remains as it has been written most often: 'China' in English and German, and 'Chine' in French. In Pinyin it's correctly written as Zhōngguó.

Now that Hong Kong (a Romanisation of the Cantonese for 'fragrant harbour') has gone over to China, many think it will only be a matter of time before it gets renamed Xiānggǎng.

PRONUNCIATION
Vowels

a	as in 'father'
ai	as in 'aisle'
ao	as the 'ow' in 'cow'
e	as in 'her', with no 'r' sound
ei	as in 'weigh'
i	as the 'ee' in 'meet' (or like the 'oo' in 'book' after c, ch, r, s, sh, z or zh)
ian	as the word 'yen'
ie	as the English word 'yeah'
o	as in 'or', with no 'r' sound
ou	as the 'oa' in 'boat'
u	as in 'flute'
ui	as the word 'way'
uo	like a 'w' followed by 'o'
yu/ü	like 'ee' with lips pursed

Consonants

c	as the 'ts' in 'bits'
ch	as in 'chop', but with the tongue curled up and back
h	as in 'hay', but articulated from farther back in the throat
q	as the 'ch' in 'cheese'
r	as the 's' in 'pleasure'
sh	as in 'ship', but with the tongue curled up and back
x	as in 'ship'
z	as the 'dz' in 'suds'
zh	as the 'j' in 'judge' but with the tongue curled up and back

The only consonants that occur at the end of a syllable are **n**, **ng** and **r**.

PINYIN *Charles Qin*

While there are many dialects across China, the one thing all Chinese speakers have in common is their written language. Efforts have been made over the last 100 years to reform the written language, and a system called Pinyin (literally meaning 'spell sound') was invented last century as the standard for spelling Chinese characters. While Pinyin started life as a communist ploy to unite the peoples and popularise Mandarin within China, in its short life it has become the United Nations standard for 'spelling' Chinese characters, and for transliterating the names of people, places and scientific terms. Taiwan initially promulgated a different system of Romanisation, but recently announced that it was switching to the communist-designed Pinyin system, falling into line with the rest of the world.

Pinyin was not the first foray into spelling out Chinese characters. As early as the 17th century, foreign missionaries sought effective ways to spread the word and various spelling systems arose; even the Bible was reproduced in such scripts. In the late 19th century the Chinese themselves started to explore the issue of phonetic spelling systems. In 1933 the communists worked with a Russian and designed what they called Latinised New Script. This was based on Mandarin pronunciation and in 1958 the communist government implemented this as the official system, coinciding with its decision to adopt Mandarin as the official language of China. This new script came to be known as Pinyin. The government's prime purpose for adopting a Roman alphabet spelling of Chinese characters was to promote Mandarin throughout the nation. Although Mandarin was the the language of government, it had previously only enjoyed the same status as numerous other dialects spoken in China. A secondary purpose was to enable non-Chinese ethnic groups in China to create or reform their languages with a common base.

Another, less important, aim of Pinyin was to assist foreigners to learn Chinese. As foreign language learners will tell you, Pinyin is a fantastic tool, particularly at the beginning of a quest on the road to fluency. Unlike English, once you learn the Pinyin pronunciation system it is completely consistent. However, once the pronunciation system is learnt, problems start to arise: for one, Pinyin does not itself indicate tones (Mandarin has four tones) and there may be dozens of characters represented by one Pinyin word: for example there are about 80 dictionary entries for the word pronounced and written *yi*. Luckily, context and grammatical structure, as well as the formation of compound words when *yi* combines with other sounds, usually give a few clues as to which of the 80 possibilities is meant. To assist travellers, this book has used tones throughout for towns, cities, sights, hotels, restaurants and entertainment venues.

Pinyin has permeated some groups in Chinese society, but most ordinary Chinese cannot use it very effectively, and some people argue that Pinyin is for foreigners. For those travelling in China using either this book or the Lonely Planet *Mandarin Phrasebook*, the ability to use Pinyin and the government's regulation that all signs be in Pinyin and characters will be a blessing.

In Pinyin, apostrophes are occasionally used to separate syllables in order to prevent ambiguity, eg the word *píng'ān* can be written with an apostrophe after the 'g' to prevent it being pronounced as *pín'gān*.

Tones

Chinese is a language with a large number of words with the same pronunciation but a different meaning; what distinguishes these 'homophones' is their 'tonal' quality – the raising and lowering of pitch on certain syllables. Mandarin has four tones – high, rising, falling-rising and falling, plus a fifth 'neutral' tone which you can all but ignore. To illustrate the importance of getting tones right, look at the word *ma*, which has four different meanings according to tone:

high tone	*mā* (mother)
rising tone	*má* (hemp, numb)
falling-rising tone	*mǎ* (horse)
falling tone	*mà* (scold, swear)

Mastering tones is tricky for newcomers to Mandarin, but with a little practice it can be done.

GESTURES

Hand signs are frequently used in China. The 'thumbs-up' sign has a long tradition as an indication of excellence. Another way to indicate excellence is to gently pull

CHINESE SAYINGS

Chinese is an extremely rich idiomatic language. Many sayings are four-character phrases that combine a great balance of rhythm and tone with a clever play on the multiple meanings of similar-sounding characters. Perhaps most interesting is how many phrases have direct English equivalents.

缘木求鱼 (yuánmù qiúyú)
Like climbing a tree to catch fish (a waste of time)

问道于盲 (wèndào yú máng)
Like asking a blind man for directions (another waste of time)

新瓶装旧酒 (xīnpíng zhuāng jiùjiǔ)
A new bottle filled with old wine (a superficial change)

坐井观天 (zuòjǐng guāntiān)
Like looking at the sky from the bottom of a well (not seeing the whole picture)

水落石出 (shuǐluò shíchū)
When the tide goes out the rocks are revealed (the truth will out)

守株待兔 (shǒuzhū dàitù)
Like a hunter waiting for a rabbit to kill itself by running into a tree (trusting to dumb luck)

临阵磨枪 (línjūn móqiāng)
To not sharpen your weapons until the battle is upon you (to do things at the last minute)

热锅上的蚂蚁 (règuōshàng demǎyǐ)
Like ants on top of a hot stove (full of worries)

殊途同归 (shūtú tóngguī)
Different roads all reach the same end

同床异梦 (tóngchuáng yìmèng)
To sleep in the same bed but have different dreams (different strokes for different folks)

削足适履 (xiāozú shìlǚ)
Like trimming the foot to fit the shoe

种瓜得瓜 (zhòngguā déguā)
If a man plants melons, so will he reap melons

酒肉朋友 (jiǔròu péngyou)
An eating and drinking friend (fair-weather friend)

晴天霹雳 (qíngtiān pīlì)
Like thunder from a blue sky (a bolt from the blue)

沐猴而冠 (mù hóu ér guàn)
A monkey dressed in a tall hat (a petty official)

燃眉之急 (ránméi zhījí)
A fire that is burning one's eyebrows (extremely urgent)

your earlobe between your thumb and index finger.

PHRASEBOOKS

Phrasebooks are invaluable, but sometimes seeking help by showing a phrase to someone can result in them wanting to read every page! Reading place names or street signs isn't difficult, since the Chinese name is usually accompanied by the Pinyin form; if not, you'll soon learn lots of characters just by repeated exposure. A small dictionary with English, Pinyin and Chinese characters is also useful for learning a few words.

Lonely Planet's *Mandarin Phrasebook* has script throughout and loads of useful phrases – it's also a very useful learning tool.

ACCOMMODATION

I'm looking for a ...
Wǒ yào zhǎo ...   我要找 . . .
  camping ground
  lùyíngdì   露营地
  guesthouse
  bīnguǎn   宾馆

hotel
lǚguǎn   旅馆
tourist hotel
bīnguǎn/fàndiàn/jiǔdiàn   宾馆/饭店/酒店
hostel
zhāodàisuǒ/lǚshè   招待所/旅社
youth hostel
qīngnián lǚshè   青年旅舍

Where is a cheap hotel?
Nǎr yǒu piányí de lǚguǎn?
哪儿有便宜的旅馆?
What is the address?
Dìzhǐ zài nǎr?
地址在哪儿?
Could you write the address, please?
Néngbunéng qǐng nǐ bǎ dìzhǐ xiě xiàlái?
能不能请你把地址写下来?
Do you have a room available?
Nǐmen yǒu fángjiān ma?
你们有房间吗?

I'd like (a) ...
Wǒ xiǎng yào ...   我想要 . . .
  bed
  yí ge chuángwèi   一个床位

single room
yìjiān dānrénfáng　　　一间单人房
double room
yìjiān shuāngrénfáng　　一间双人房
bed for two
shuāngrén chuáng　　　双人床
room with two beds
shuāngrénfáng　　　　　双人房
economy room (no bath)
pǔtōngfáng (méiyǒu yùshì) 普通房 (没有浴室)
room with a bathroom
yǒu yùshìde fángjiān　　有浴室的房间
standard room
biāozhǔn fángjiān　　　标准房间
deluxe suite
háohuá tàofáng　　　　豪华套房
to share a dorm
zhù sùshè　　　　　　住宿舍

How much is it ...?
... duōshǎo qián?　　　. . . 多少钱?
per night
měitiān wǎnshàng　　　每天晚上
per person
měigerén　　　　　　　每个人

May I see the room?
Wǒ néng kànkan fángjiān ma?
我能看看房间吗?
Where is the bathroom?
Yùshì zài nǎr?
浴室在哪儿?
Where is the toilet?
Cèsuǒ zài nǎr?
厕所在哪儿?
I don't like this room.
Wǒ bù xǐhuān zhèijiān fángjiān.
我不喜欢这间房间
Are there any messages for me?
Yǒu méiyǒu rén gěi wǒ liú huà?
有没有人给我留话?
May I have a hotel namecard?
Yǒu méiyǒu lǚguǎn de míngpiàn?
有没有旅馆的名片?
Could I have these clothes washed, please?
Qǐng bǎ zhè xiē yīfu xǐ gānjìng, hǎo ma?
请把这些衣服洗干净, 好吗?
I'm/We're leaving today.
Wǒ/Wǒmen jīntiān líkāi.
我/我们今天离开

CONVERSATION & ESSENTIALS

Hello.　　　*Nǐ hǎo.*　　　　你好
　　　　　　　Nín hǎo. (pol)　您好
Goodbye.　*Zàijiàn.*　　　　再见
Please.　　*Qǐng.*　　　　　请

CHINGLISH

Help!

Initially you might be puzzled by a sign in the bathroom that reads 'Please don't take the odds and ends put into the nightstool'. In fact this is a warning to resist sudden impulses to empty the contents of your pockets or backpack into the toilet. An apparently ambiguous sign with anarchic implications like the one in the Lhasa Bank of China, 'Question Authority', is really just an economical way of saying 'Please address your questions to one of the clerks'.

On the other hand, just to confuse things, a company name like the 'Risky Investment Co' means just what it says. An English-Chinese dictionary proudly proclaims in the preface that it is 'very useful for the using'. And a beloved sign in the Liangmao Hotel in Tài'ān proclaims:

Safety Needing Attention!
Be care of depending fire
Sweep away six injurious insect
Pay attention to civilisation

If this all sounds confusing, don't worry. It won't be long before you have a small armoury of Chinglish phrases of your own. Before you know it, you'll know without even thinking that 'Be careful not to be stolen' is a warning against thieves; that 'Shoplifters will be fined 10 times' means that shoplifting is not a good idea in China; that 'Do not stroke the works' (generally found in museums) means 'No touching'; and 'very liking' something means liking it very much.

The best advice for travellers in China grappling with the complexities of a new language is not to set your sights too high. Bear in mind that it takes a minimum of 15 years of schooling in the Chinese language and a crash course in English to be able to write Chinglish with any fluency.

Thank you.	*Xièxie.*	谢谢
Many thanks.	*Duōxiè.*	多谢
You're welcome.	*Búkèqi.*	不客气
Excuse me, ...	*Qǐng wèn, ...*	请问, . . .

(When asking a question it is polite to start with the phrase *qǐng wèn* – literally, 'may I ask?' – this expression is only used at the beginning of a sentence, never at the end.)

I'm sorry.
Duìbùqǐ. 对不起
May I ask your name?
Nín guìxìng? 您贵姓?
My (sur)name is ...
Wǒ xìng ... 我姓...

Where are you from?
Nǐ shì cóng nǎr lái de? 你是从哪儿来的?
I'm from ...
Wǒ shì cóng ... lái de. 我是从...来的
I like ...
Wǒ xǐhuān ... 我喜欢...
I don't like ...
Wǒ bù xǐhuān ... 我不喜欢...
Wait a moment.
Děng yíxià. 等一下

Yes & No

There are no specific words in Mandarin that specifically mean 'yes' and 'no' when used in isolation. When a question is asked, the verb is repeated to indicate the affirmative. A response in the negative is formed by using the word 不 *bù* (meaning 'no') before the verb. When *bù* (falling tone) occurs before another word with a falling tone, it becomes *bú* (ie with a rising tone).

Are you going to Shanghai?
Nǐ qù shànghǎi ma? 你去上海吗?
Yes.
Qù. ('go') 去
No.
Bú qù. ('no go') 不去
No.
Méi yǒu. ('not have') 没有
No.
Búshì. ('not so') 不是

DIRECTIONS

Where is (the) ...?
... zài nǎr? ...在哪儿?
Go straight ahead.
Yìzhí zǒu. 一直走
Turn left.
Zuǒ zhuǎn. 左转
Turn right.
Yòu zhuǎn. 右转
at the next corner
zài xià yíge guǎijiǎo 在下一个拐角
at the traffic lights
zài hónglùdēng 在红绿灯
map
dìtú 地图

Could you show me (on the map)?
Nǐ néng bunéng (zài dìtú shang) zhǐ gěi wǒ kàn?
你能不能(在地图上)指给我看?

behind	*hòubianr*	后边儿
in front of	*qiánbianr*	前边儿
near	*jìn*	近
far	*yuǎn*	远
opposite	*duìmiànr*	对面儿
beach	*hǎitān*	海滩
bridge	*qiáoliáng*	桥梁
island	*dǎoyǔ*	岛屿
main square	*guǎngchǎng*	广场
market	*shìchǎng*	市场
old city	*lǎochéng*	老城
palace	*gōngdiàn*	宫殿
sea	*hǎiyáng*	海洋

HEALTH

I'm sick.
Wǒ bìngle. 我病了
It hurts here.
Zhèr téng. 这儿疼
I need a doctor.
Wǒ děi kàn yīshēng. 我得看医生
Is there a doctor here who speaks English?
Zhèr yǒu huì jiǎng 这儿有会讲
yīngyǔ de dàifu ma? 英语的大夫吗?

I'm ...
Wǒ yǒu ... 我有...
  asthmatic
  xiàochuǎnbìng 哮喘病
  diabetic
  tángniàobìng 糖尿病
  epileptic
  diānxiánbìng 癫痫病

EMERGENCIES

Help!
Jiùmìng a! 救命啊！
emergency
jǐnjí qíngkuàng 紧急情况
There's been an accident!
Chūshìle! 出事了！
I'm lost.
Wǒ mílùle. 我迷路了
Go away!
Zǒu kāi! 走开！
Leave me alone!
Bié fán wǒ! 别烦我！
Could you help me please?
Nǐ néng bunéng bāng 你能不能帮
wǒ ge máng? 我个忙？

Call ...!
Qǐng jiào ...! 请叫...！
　a doctor
　yīshēng 医生
　the police
　jǐngchá 警察

I'm allergic to ...
Wǒ duì ... guòmǐn. 我对...过敏
　antibiotics
　kàngjūnsù 抗菌素
　aspirin
　āsīpǐlín 阿司匹林
　bee stings
　mìfēng zhēcì 蜜蜂蜇刺
　nuts
　guǒrén 果仁
　penicillin
　qīngméisù 青霉素

antidiarrhoea medicine
zhǐxièyào 止泻药
antiseptic cream
xiāodúgāo 消毒膏
condoms
bìyùn tào 避孕套
contraceptive
bìyùnyào 避孕药
diarrhoea
lā dùzi 拉肚子
headache
tóuténg 头疼
medicine
yào 药
sanitary napkins (Kotex)
fùnǚ wèishēngjīn 妇女卫生巾

sunscreen (UV) lotion
fángshàiyóu 防晒油
tampons
yuèjīng miánsāi 月经棉塞

LANGUAGE DIFFICULTIES

Do you speak English?
Nǐ huì shuō yīngyǔ ma?
你会说英语吗？
Does anyone here speak English?
Zhèr yǒu rén huì shuō yīngyǔ ma?
这儿有人会说英语吗？
How do you say ... in Mandarin?
... zhōngwén zěnme shuō?
...中文怎么说？
What does ... mean?
... shì shénme yìsi?
...是什么意思？
I understand.
Wǒ tīngdedǒng.
我听得懂
I don't understand.
Wǒ tīngbudǒng.
我听不懂
Please write it down.
Qǐng xiěxiàlai.
请写下来

NUMBERS

0	líng	零
1	yī, yāo	一，幺
2	èr, liǎng	二，两
3	sān	三
4	sì	四
5	wǔ	五
6	liù	六
7	qī	七
8	bā	八
9	jiǔ	九
10	shí	十
11	shíyī	十一
12	shí'èr	十二
20	èrshí	二十
21	èrshíyī	二十一
22	èrshí'èr	二十二
30	sānshí	三十
40	sìshí	四十
50	wǔshí	五十
60	liùshí	六十
70	qīshí	七十
80	bāshí	八十
90	jiǔshí	九十
100	yìbǎi	一百
1000	yìqiān	一千
2000	liǎngqiān	两千

LANGUAGE

PAPERWORK

name	xìngmíng	姓名
nationality	guójí	国籍
date of birth	chūshēng rìqī	出生日期
place of birth	chūshēng dìdiǎn	出生地点
sex (gender)	xìngbié	性别
passport	hùzhào	护照
passport number	hùzhào hàomǎ	护照号码
visa	qiānzhèng	签证
extension	yáncháng	延长

Public Security Bureau (PSB)
gōng'ānjú 公安局
Foreign Affairs Branch
wàishìkē 外事科

QUESTION WORDS

Who?	Shuí?	谁?
What?	Shénme?	什么?
What is it?	Shì shénme?	是什么?
When?	Shénme shíhou?	什么时候?
Where?	Zài nǎr?	在哪儿?
Which?	Něige?	哪个?
Why?	Wèishénme?	为什么?
How?	Zěnme?	怎么?

SHOPPING & SERVICES

I'd like to buy ...
Wǒ xiǎng mǎi ... 我想买...
I'm just looking.
Wǒ zhǐshì kànkan. 我只是看看
How much is it?
Duōshǎo qián? 多少钱?
I don't like it.
Wǒ bù xǐhuan. 我不喜欢
Can I see it?
Néng kànkan ma? 能看看吗?
I'll take it.
Wǒ jiù mǎi zhèige. 我就买这个
It's cheap.
Zhè búguì. 这不贵
That's too expensive.
Tài guìle. 太贵了
Is there anything cheaper?
Yǒu piányi yìdiǎn 有便宜一点
de ma? 的吗?
Can I pay by travellers cheque?
kěyǐ fù lǚxíng 可以付旅行支票吗?
zhīpiào ma?

Do you accept ...?
... shōu bushōu? ...收不收?
  credit cards
  xìnyòngkǎ 信用卡

travellers cheques
lǚxíng zhīpiào 旅行支票

more	duō	多
less	shǎo	少
smaller	gèng xiǎo	更小
bigger	gèng dà	更大
too much/many	tài duō	太多

Excuse me, where's the nearest ...?
Qǐng wèn, zuìjìnde ... zài nǎr?
请问, 最近的... 在哪儿?
I'm looking for a/the ...
Wǒ zài zhǎo ... 我在找...
  automatic teller machine
  zìdòng guìyuánjī 自动柜员机
  bank
  yínháng 银行
  Bank of China
  zhōngguó yínháng 中国银行
  chemist/pharmacy
  yàodiàn 药店
  city centre
  shìzhōngxīn 市中心
  ... embassy
  ... dàshǐguǎn ...大使馆
  foreign affairs police
  wàishì jǐngchá 外事警察
  foreign exchange office/currency exchange
  wàihuì duìhuànchù 外汇兑换处
  hospital
  yīyuàn 医院
  hotel
  bīnguǎn/ 宾馆/
  fàndiàn/ 饭店/
  lǚguǎn 旅馆
  market
  shìchǎng 市场
  museum
  bówùguǎn 博物馆
  police
  jǐngchá 警察
  post office
  yóujú 邮局
  public toilet
  gōnggòng cèsuǒ 公共厕所
  telephone
  diànhuà 电话
  telephone office
  diànxùn dàlóu 电讯大楼
  the tourist office
  lǚyóujú 旅游局

change money
huàn qián 换钱

telephone card
diànhuà kǎ　　　　电话卡
international call
guójì diànhuà　　　国际电话
collect call
duìfāng fùfèi diànhuà　对方付费电话
direct-dial call
zhíbō diànhuà　　　直拨电话
fax
chuánzhēn　　　　　传真
computer
diànǎo　　　　　　电脑
email (often called 'email')
diànziyóujiàn　　　电子邮件
internet
yīntèwǎng　　　　　因特网
(more formal name)
(hùliánwǎng)　　　 (互联网)
online
shàngwǎng　　　　　上网

Where can I get online?
Wǒ zài nǎr kěyǐ shàngwǎng?
我在哪儿可以上网?
Can I check my email account?
Wǒ chá yīxià zìjǐ de email hù, hǎo ma?
我查一下自己的email户, 好吗?

TIME & DATES
What's the time?
Jǐ diǎn?　　　　　　几点?
... hour ... minute
... diǎn ... fēn　　　...点...分
3.05
sān diǎn líng wǔ fēn　三点零五分
When?
Shénme shíhòu?　　　什么时候?

now　　　　*xiànzài*　　　现在
today　　　*jīntiān*　　　今天
tomorrow　　*míngtiān*　　明天
yesterday　　*zuótiān*　　　昨天
in the morning　*zǎoshang*　　早上
in the afternoon　*xiàwǔ*　　　下午
in the evening　*wǎnshang*　　晚上
weekend　　*zhōumò*　　　周末

Monday　　　*xīngqīyī*　　星期一
Tuesday　　　*xīngqī'èr*　　星期二
Wednesday　　*xīngqīsān*　　星期三
Thursday　　*xīngqīsì*　　　星期四
Friday　　　*xīngqīwǔ*　　星期五
Saturday　　*xīngqīliù*　　星期六
Sunday　　　*xīngqītiān*　　星期天

January　　*yīyuè*　　　一月
February　　*èryuè*　　　二月
March　　　*sānyuè*　　三月
April　　　*sìyuè*　　　四月
May　　　　*wǔyuè*　　　五月
June　　　*liùyuè*　　　六月
July　　　*qīyuè*　　　七月
August　　*bāyuè*　　　八月
September　　*jiǔyuè*　　　九月
October　　*shíyuè*　　　十月
November　　*shíyīyuè*　　十一月
December　　*shíèryuè*　　十二月

TRANSPORT
Public Transport
airport
fēijīchǎng　　　　飞机场
long-distance bus station
chángtú qìchē zhàn　长途汽车站
subway (underground)
dìtiě　　　　　　地铁
subway station
dìtiě zhàn　　　　地铁站
train station
huǒchē zhàn　　　火车站

What time does ... leave/arrive?
... jǐdiǎn kāi/dào?　　...几点开/到?
boat
chuán　　　　　　船
intercity bus; coach
chángtú qìchē　　　长途汽车
local/city bus
gōnggòng qìchē　　公共汽车
minibus
xiǎo gōnggòng qìchē　小公共汽车
microbus taxi
miànbāochē, miàndī　面包车, 面的
plane
fēijī　　　　　　　飞机
train
huǒchē　　　　　火车

I'd like a ...
Wǒ yào yīge ...
我要一个...
one way ticket　*dānchéng piào*　单程票
return ticket　*láihuí piào*　来回票
platform ticket　*zhàntái piào*　站台票
1st class ticket　*tóuděngcāng*　头等舱
2nd class ticket　*èrděngcāng*　二等舱
hard-seat　　*yìngxí/yìngzuò*　硬席/硬座
soft-seat　　*ruǎnxí/ruǎnzuò*　软席/软座
hard-sleeper　*yìngwò*　　硬卧
soft-sleeper　*ruǎnwò*　　软卧

When's the ... bus?
... bānchē shénme shíhou lái?
... 班车什么时候来?

first	*tóu*	头
last	*mò*	末
next	*xià*	下

I want to go to ...
Wǒ yào qù ...
我要去...

The train has been cancelled/delayed.
Huǒchē tuīchí le/qǔxiāo le.
火车推迟了/取消了

CAAC ticket office
zhōngguó mínháng shòupiào chù
中国民航售票处

boarding pass	*dēngjī kǎ*	登机卡
left-luggage room	*jìcún chù*	寄存处
platform number	*zhàntái hào*	站台号
ticket office	*shòupiào chù*	售票处
timetable	*shíkèbiǎo*	时刻表

Private Transport

I'd like to hire a ...
Wǒ yào zū yíliàng ...
我要租一辆...

car	*qìchē*	汽车
4WD	*sìlún qūdòng*	4轮驱动
motorbike	*mótuōchē*	摩托车
bicycle	*zìxíngchē*	自行车

How much is it per day?
yìtiān duōshǎo qián? 一天多少钱?
How much is it per hour?
yíge xiǎo shí duōshǎo qián? 一个小时多少钱?
How much is the deposit?
yājīn duōshǎo qián? 押金多少钱?
Does this road lead to ...?
Zhè tiáo lù dào ...? 这条路到...?

road	*lù*	路
section	*duàn*	段
street	*jiē/dàjiē*	街/大街
No 21	*21 hào*	21号

Where's the next service station?
xià yíge jiāyóuzhàn zài nǎr?
下一个加油站在哪儿?
Please fill it up.
Qǐng jiāmǎn yóuxiāng.
请加满油箱
I'd like ... litres.
Wǒ yào ... gōngshēng.
我要...公升

ROAD SIGNS

减速让行	*Jiǎnsù Mànxíng*	Give Way
绕行	*Ràoxíng*	Detour
不得入内	*Bùdé Rùnèi*	No Entry
不得超车	*Bùdé Chāochē*	No Overtaking
不得停车	*Bùdé Tíngchē*	No Parking
入口	*Rùkǒu*	Entrance
保持畅通	*Bǎochí Chàngtōng*	Keep Clear
收费	*Shōufèi*	Toll
危险	*Wēixiǎn*	Danger
减速慢行	*Jiǎnsù Mànxíng*	Slow Down
单行道	*Dānxíngdào*	One Way
出口	*Chūkǒu*	Exit

diesel	*cháiyóu*	柴油
leaded petrol	*hánqiān qìyóu*	含铅汽油
unleaded petrol	*wúqiān qìyóu*	无铅汽油

How long can I park here?
Zhèr kěyi tíng duōjiǔ? 这儿可以停多久?
Can I park here?
Zhèr kěyi tíngchē ma? 这儿可以停车吗?
Where do I pay?
Zài nǎr fùkuǎn? 在哪儿付款?
I need a mechanic.
Wǒ xūyào jīxiūgōng. 我需要机修工
We need a mechanic.
Wǒmen xūyào jīxiūgōng. 我们需要机修工
The car has broken down (at ...)
Qìchē shì (zài ...) huài de. 汽车是(在...)坏的
The car won't start.
Qìchē fādòng bùqǐlái. 汽车发动不起来
I have a flat tyre.
Lúntāi biě le. 轮胎瘪了
I've run out of petrol.
Méiyǒu qìyóu le. 没有汽油了
I had an accident.
Wǒ chū shìgù le. 我出事故了

TRAVEL WITH CHILDREN

Is there a/an ...?
Yǒu ... ma? 有...吗?
I need a/an ...
Wǒ xūyào ... 我需要...

baby change room
yīng'ér huànxǐshì 婴儿换洗室
baby food
yīngér shípǐn 婴儿食品
baby formula (milk)
pèifāngnǎi 配方奶
baby's bottle
nǎipíng 奶瓶

child-minding service
tuōér fúwù 托儿服务
chidren's menu
értóng càidān 儿童菜单
(disposable) nappies/diapers
(yícìxìng) niàopiàn (一次性)尿片
(English-speaking) babysitter
(huì shuō yīngwén de) (会说英文的)
yīng'ér bǎomǔ 婴儿保姆
highchair
yīng'ér gāojiǎoyǐ 婴儿高脚椅
potty
yīng'ér biànpén 婴儿便盆
pusher/stroller
yīng'ér tuīchē 婴儿推车

Do you mind if I breastfeed here?
Wǒ kěyǐ zài zhèr wèi nǎi ma?
我可以在这儿喂奶吗?
Are children allowed?
Yǔnxǔ értóng ma?
允许儿童吗?

CANTONESE

What a difference a border makes. Cantonese is still the most popular dialect in Hong Kong, Guǎngzhōu and the surrounding area. It differs from Mandarin as much as French differs from Spanish. Speakers of both dialects can read Chinese characters, but a Cantonese speaker will pronounce many of the characters differently from a Mandarin speaker. For example, when Mr Ng from Hong Kong goes to Běijīng the Mandarin-speakers will call him Mr Wu. If Mr Wong goes from Hong Kong to Fújiàn the character for his name will be read as Mr Wee, and in Běijīng he is Mr Huang.

For a more detailed guide to Cantonese, with script throughout, loads of phrases, and information on grammar and pronunciation, get a copy of Lonely Planet's *Cantonese Phrasebook*.

ROMANISATION & PRONUNCIATION

Unfortunately, several competing systems of Romanisation of Cantonese script exist and no single one has emerged as an official standard. A number have come and gone, but at least three have survived and are currently in use in Hong Kong: Meyer-Wempe, Sidney Lau and Yale. In this language guide we use the Yale system. It's the

most phonetically accurate and the one generally preferred by foreign students.

Vowels

Note that the examples given below for the pronunciation of vowels reflect British pronunciation.

a	as in 'father'
ai	as the 'i' in 'find', but shorter
au	as the 'ow' in 'cow'
e	as in 'let'
ei	as the 'a' in 'say', but without the 'y' sound
eu	similar to the 'ur' in 'urn' with lips pursed, but without the 'r' sound
i	as in 'marine'
iu	similar to the word 'you'
o	as in 'not'; as in 'no' when at the end of a word
oi	as the 'oy' in 'boy'
oo	as in 'soon'
ou	as the word 'owe'
u	as in 'put'
ue	as the 'u-e' in 'suet'
ui	as 'oo-ee'

Consonants

In general, consonants are pronounced as in English. Three that may give you a little trouble are:

g	as in 'go'
j	as the 'ds' in 'suds'
ng	as in 'sing'

Tones

Cantonese has seven tones (although you can easily get by with six). In the Yale system used in this language guide, six basic tones are represented: three 'level' tones, which do not noticeably rise or fall in pitch (high, middle and low), and three 'moving' tones, which either rise or fall in pitch (high rising, low rising and low falling).

Remember that it doesn't matter whether you have a high or low voice when speaking Cantonese as long as your intonation reflects relative changes in pitch. The following examples show the six basic tones. Note how important they can be to your intended meaning:

high tone: represented by a macron above a vowel, as in *fōo* (husband)

middle tone: represented by an unaccented vowel, as in *foo* (wealthy)

low tone: represented by the letter 'h' after a vowel, as in *fooh* (owe); note that 'h' is only pronounced if it occurs at the start of a word; elsewhere it signifies a low tone

middle tone rising: represented by an acute accent, as in *fóo* (tiger)

low falling tone: represented by a grave accent followed by the low tone letter 'h', as in *fòoh* (to lean)

low rising tone: represented by an acute accent and the low tone letter 'h', as in *fóoh* (woman)

ACCOMMODATION & SHOPPING

Do you have any rooms available?
yáhùh mó fóng a?
有冇房呀？

I'd like a (single/double) room.
ngóh séuhng yiùh yāt gāahn (dāahn yàhn/séuhng yàhn) fóng
我想要一間(單人/雙人)房？

How much per night?
gèih dōh chín yāt máhàhn a?
幾多錢一晚呀？

How much is this?
nī goh gèih dōh chín a?
呢個幾多錢呀？

That's very expensive.
hó gwaih
好貴

Can you reduce the price?
pèhng dī dāk m dāk a?
平啲得唔得呀？

I'm just looking.
ngóh sīn tàih yāt táih
我先睇一睇

CONVERSATION & ESSENTIALS

Hello, how are you?
néhìh hó ma?
你好嗎？

Fine, and you?
gèih hó, néhìh nē?
幾好，你呢？

Good morning.
jó sàhn
早晨

Goodbye.
bāahìh baahìh/joih gin
拜拜/再見

Thank you very much.
dōh jē saàhih/
m gòih saàhìh
多謝晒/唔該晒

Thanks. (for a gift or special favour)
dōh jē
多謝

Thanks. (making a request or purchase)
m gòih
唔該

You're welcome.
m sàih haàhk hèih
唔使客氣

Excuse me. (calling someone's attention)
m gòih
唔該

I'm sorry.
m hó yi si
唔好意思

What is your surname? (polite)
chéng mahn gwaìh sing?
請問貴姓？

My surname is ...
siùh sing ...
小姓 . . .

Is it OK to take a photo?
hóh m hóh yíh yíng
séùhng a?
可唔可以影相呀？

Do you speak English?
néhìh sìk m sìk góng
yìng mán a?
你識唔識講英文呀？

I don't understand.
ngóh m mìhng
我唔明

Pronouns

I	ngóh	我
you	néhìh	你
he/she/it	kúhìh	佢
we/us	ngóh dēih	我哋
you (plural)	néhìh dēih	你哋
they/them	kúhìh dēih	佢哋

NUMBERS

0	lìhng	零
1	yāt	一
2	yìh (léhùhng)	二(兩)
3	sāahm	三
4	sēih	四
5	ng	五
6	luhk	六
7	chāt	七
8	baàht	八
9	gáùh	九
10	sahp	十
11	sahp yāt	十一
12	sahp yìh	十二
20	yìh sahp	二十
21	yìh sahp yāt	二十一
100	yāt baàhk	一百
101	yāt baàhk lìhng yāt	一百零一
110	yāt baàhk yāt sahp	一百一十
120	yāt baàhk yìh sahp	一百二十
200	yìh baàhk	二百
1000	yāt chīn	一千
10,000	yāt máhàhn	一萬
100,000	sahp máhàhn	十萬

TRANSPORT

airport	gèih chèhùhng	機場
bus stop	bā sí jahàhm	巴士站
pier	máh tàhùh	碼頭

USEFUL PORTUGUESE

A few words in Portuguese will come in handy when travelling in Macau. Portuguese is still common on signs (along with Cantonese script) and where opening and closing times are written.

Monday	segunda-feira	22	vint e dois
Tuesday	terça-feira	30	trinta
Wednesday	quarta-feira	40	quarenta
Thursday	quinta-feira	50	cinquenta
Friday	sexta-feira	60	sessenta
Saturday	sábado	70	setenta
Sunday	domingo	80	oitenta
		90	noventa
1	um/uma	100	cem
2	dois/duas	1000	mil
3	três		
4	quatro		
5	cinco	Entrance	Entrada
6	seis	Exit	Saída
7	sete	Open	Aberto
8	oito	Closed	Encerrado
9	nove	No Smoking	Não Fumadores
10	dez	Prohibited	Proíbido
11	onze	Toilets	Lavabos/WC
20	vint	Men	Homens (H)
21	vint e um	Women	Senhoras (S)

subway station	dèih tit jahàhm	地鐵站
north	bāk	北
south	nàhàhm	南
east	dūng	東
west	sāih	西

I'd like to go to ...
ngóh séuhng huìh ...   我想去 . . .
Where is the ...?
... hàih bìn doh a?   . . .喺邊度呀?
Does this (bus, train etc) go to ...?
huìh m huìh ... a?   去邊去 . . .呀?
How much is the fare?
gêih dōh chín a?   幾多錢呀?
Please write down the address for me.
m gòih sé goh dèih jí   唔該寫個地址俾我
béih ngóh

TIBETAN

PRONUNCIATION

Tibetan has its fair share of tricky pronunciations. There are quite a few consonant clusters, and Tibetan makes an important distinction between aspirated and unaspirated consonants.

Lonely Planet's *Tibetan Phrasebook* has script throughout and is an excellent tool for those wishing to learn the language in greater depth.

Vowels

The following pronunciation guide reflects standard British pronunciation.

a	as in 'father'
ay	as in 'play'
e	as in 'met'
ee	as in 'meet'
i	as in 'big'
o	as in 'go'
oo	as in 'soon'
ö	as the 'u' in 'fur', with no 'r' sound
ü	as in 'flute'

Consonants

With the exception of those listed below, Tibetan consonants should be pronounced as in English. Where consonants are followed by an 'h', it means that the consonant is aspirated (ie accompanied by an audible puff of air). An English example might be 'kettle', where the 'k' is aspirated and the 'tt' is unaspirated. The distinction is fairly important, but in simple Tibetan the context should make it clear what you're talking about even if you get the sounds muddled up a bit.

ky	as the 'kie' in 'Kiev'
ng	as the 'ng' in 'sing'
r	produced with a slight trill
ts	as the 'ts' in 'bits'

ACCOMMODATION

guesthouse	dhön-khang
hotel	drü-khang/fan-dian
Do you have a room?	kang mi yöpe?
How much is it for one night?	tsen chik la katsö ray?
I'd like to stay with a Tibetan family.	nga phöbe mitsang nyemdo dendö yö

CONVERSATION & ESSENTIALS

Hello.	tashi dele
Goodbye. (to person leaving)	kale phe
Goodbye. (by person leaving)	kale shoo
Thank you.	thoo jaychay
Yes, OK.	la ong
I'm sorry.	gonda
I want ...	nga la ... go
Do you speak English?	injeeke shing gi yö pe?
Do you understand?	ha ko song-ngey?
I understand.	ha ko song
I don't understand.	ha ko ma song
How much?	ka tsö ray?
It's expensive.	gong chenpo ray
What's your name?	kerang gi ming lakary zer gi yö?
My name is ...	ngai ... ming la
... and you?	... a ni kerang zer gi yö?
Where are you from?	kerang lungba ka-nay yin?
I'm from ...	nga ...-nay yin

I	nga
you	kerang
he/she	khong
we	nga-tso
you all	kerang-tso
they	khong-tso

HEALTH

I'm sick.	nga bedo mindu
Please call a doctor.	amchi ke tongda
altitude sickness	lādu na
diarrhoea	troko she
fever	tsawa
hospital	menkang

TIME & NUMBERS

What's the time?	chutsö katsö ray?
hour/minute	chutsö/karma
When?	kadü?
now	thanda
today	thiring
tomorrow	sangnyi
yesterday	kesa
morning	shogay
afternoon	nying gung gyab la
evening/night	gonta

Note: to form compound numbers, add the appropriate number for one to nine after the word in brackets, eg 21 is *nyi shu tsa chig*, 32 is *sum shu so nyi*.

1	chig
2	nyi
3	sum
4	shi
5	nga
6	troo
7	dün
8	gye
9	gu
10	chu
11	chu chig
20	nyi shu (tsa ...)
30	sum shu (so ...)
40	shi chu (shay ...)
50	nga chu (ngay ...)
60	doog chu (ray ...)
70	dun chu (don ...)
80	gye chu (gya ...)
90	gu chu (go ...)
100	chig gya
1000	chig tong

OUT & ABOUT

I want to go to ...	nga ... la drondö yö
I'll get off here.	nga phap gi yin
What time do we leave?	ngatso chutsö katsö la dro gi yin?
What time do we arrive?	ngatso chutsö katsö la lep gi yin?
Where can I rent a bicycle?	kanggari kaba ragi ray?
How much per day?	nyima chik laja katsö ray?
Where is the ...?	... kaba yo ray?
I'm lost.	nga lam khag lag song
airport	namdrutang
bicycle	kanggari
bus	lamkhor

right	yeba
left	yönba
straight ahead	shar gya
north	chang
south	lo
east	shar
west	noop
porter	dopo khur khen
pack animal	skel semchen

Geographical Terms

cave	trapoo
hot spring	chuzay
lake	tso
mountain	ree
river	tsangpo
road/trail	lam
valley	loong shon
waterfall	papchu

LANGUAGE

Glossary

(C) Cantonese; (M) Inner Mongolian; (T) Tibetan; (U) Uighur

A
adetki mashina (U) – ordinary bus
ali mashina (U) – soft-seat coach
amah – a servant who cleans houses and looks after the children
apsaras – Buddhist celestial beings, similar to angels
aptoos biket (U) – long-distance bus station
arhat – Buddhist, especially a monk who has achieved enlightenment and passes to nirvana at death

B
báifàn – rice
báijiǔ – literally 'white alcohol', a type of face-numbing rice wine served at banquets and get-togethers
bāozi – steamed savoury buns with tasty meat filling
běi – north; the other points of the compass are *nán* (south), *dōng* (east) and *xī* (west)
biānjiè – border
biéshù – villa
bīnguǎn – tourist hotel
bìxì – mythical, tortoise-like dragon
Bodhisattva – one worthy of nirvana but who remains on earth to help others attain enlightenment
Bön – the pre-Buddhist indigenous faith of Tibet, pockets of which survive in western Sìchuān
bówùguǎn – museum

C
CAAC – Civil Aviation Administration of China
cadre – Chinese government bureaucrat
cāntīng – restaurant
cǎoyuán – grasslands
catty – unit of weight; one catty *(jīn)* equals 0.6kg
CCP – Chinese Communist Party, founded in Shànghǎi in 1921
chang (T) – a Tibetan brew made from fermented barley
Chángchéng – the Great Wall
chau (C) – land mass, such as an island
cheongsam (C) – originating in Shànghǎi, a fashionable tight-fitting Chinese dress with a slit up the side
chí – lake, pool
chim (C) – sticks used to divine the future. They're shaken out of a box onto the ground and then 'read'
chop – see *name chop*
chörten – Tibetan stupa, see *stupa*
chūzūqìchē – taxi
CITS – China International Travel Service; deals with China's foreign tourists

cohong – a local merchants' guild
CTS – China Travel Service; originally set up to handle tourists from Hong Kong, Macau and Taiwan and overseas Chinese
cūn – village

D
dàdào – boulevard
dàfàndiàn – large hotel
dàjiē – avenue
dàjiǔdiàn – large hotel
dānwèi – work unit, the cornerstone of China's social structure
dǎo – island
dàpùbù – large waterfall
dàqiáo – large bridge
dàshà – hotel, building
dàshèngtǎ – pagoda
dàxué – university
déhuà – a type of white-glazed porcelain
dìtiě – subway
dōng – east; the other points of the compass are *běi* (north), *nán* (south) and *xī* (west)
dòng – cave
dòngwùyuán – zoo
dòufu – tofu

E
értóng – children

F
fàndiàn – a hotel or restaurant
fēng – peak
fēngjǐngqū – scenic area
fēng shuǐ – geomancy, literally 'wind and water'; the art of using ancient principles to maximise the flow of *qì*, or universal energy
fó – a Buddha

G
gǎng – harbour
gé – pavilion, temple
ger (M) – the Mongolian word for a circular tent made with animal skin or felt; see *yurt*
godown (C) – a warehouse, usually located on or near the waterfront
gompa (T) – monastery
gōng – palace
gōngyuán – park
gōu – gorge, valley

gǔ – valley
guān – pass
guānxì – advantageous social or business connections
gùjū – house, home, residence
gwailo (C) – a foreigner; literally meaning 'ghost person' and interpreted as 'foreign devil'

H
hǎi – sea
hǎitān – beach
Hakka – a Chinese ethnic group
Han – China's main ethnic group
hé – river
hong (C) – a company, usually engaged in trade; often refers to Hong Kong's original trading houses, such as Jardine Matheson or Swire
hú – lake
huáqiáo – overseas Chinese
Hui – ethnic Chinese Muslims
húndùn (C) – wontons
huǒchēzhàn – train station
huǒguō – hotpot
huǒshān – volcano
hútòng – a narrow alleyway

I
IC kǎ – IC card
IP kǎ – IP card (phone card)

J
jiāng – river
jiǎo – see *máo*
jiàotáng – church
jiǎozi – stuffed dumpling
jīchǎng – airport
jiē – street
jié – festival
jīn – see *catty*
jǐngchá – policeman
jīngjù – Beijing opera
jìniànbēi – memorial
jìniànguǎn – memorial hall
jìniàntǎ – monument
jīpiào – air ticket
jiǔdiàn – hotel
jū – residence, home
junk – originally referred to Chinese fishing and war vessels with square sails; now applies to various types of boating craft

K
kadimi shahr (U) – the old part of town; see also *yangi shahr*
kaido (C) – a small- to medium-sized ferry that makes short runs on the open sea; usually used for nonscheduled service between small islands and fishing villages

kǎoyādiàn – roast duck restaurant
kapala – a kind of skull cup, generally from Tibet
karakhana (U) – workshop, factory
karst – denotes the characteristically eroded landscape of limestone regions, such as the whimsical scenery of Guìlín and Yángshuò
KCR – Kowloon-Canton Railway
Kham – traditional name for eastern Tibet, encompassing western Sichuān
KMB – Kowloon Motor Bus
kora (T) – pilgrim circuit
kuài – colloquial term for the currency, *yuán*
kuàizi – chopsticks
kūnjù – a regional form of classical opera developed in the cities of Sūzhōu, Hángzhōu and Nánjīng
Kuomintang – Chiang Kaishek's Nationalist Party, now one of Taiwan's major political parties

L
lama – a Buddhist priest of the Tantric or Lamaist school; a title bestowed on monks of particularly high spiritual attainment
lǎobǎixìng – common people, the masses
lǎochéngqū – the old part of town
lǎowài – foreigners
liǎng – see *tael*
lín – forest
líng – tomb
lìshǐ – history
lóu – tower
LRT – Light Rail Transit, in Hong Kong
lù – road
lǚguǎn – hotel
lúnchuán mǎtou – passenger ferry terminal
luóhàn – Buddhist, especially a monk who has achieved enlightenment and passes to nirvana at death; see also *arhat*
lúshēng – a reed pipe that features in many festivals in Guìzhōu

M
mah jong – popular Chinese card game for four people, played with engraved tiles
Mandate of Heaven – a political concept where heaven gives wise leaders a mandate to rule and removes power from those who are evil or corrupt
máo – colloquial term for *jiǎo*, 10 of which equal one *kuài*
mǎtou – dock
mén – gate
ménpiào – entrance ticket
Miao – ethnic group living in Guìzhōu
miào – temple
motor tricycle – an enclosed three-wheeled vehicle with a small motorbike engine, a driver at the front and seats for two passengers in the back

MTR – Mass Transit Railway, in Hong Kong
mù – tomb

N
name chop – a carved name seal that acts as a signature
nán – south; the other points of the compass are *běi* (north), *dōng* (east) and *xī* (west)

O
obo (M) – a pile of stones with a hollow space for offerings; a kind of shaman shrine
oolong (C) – high-grade Chinese tea, partially fermented

P
páilou – decorative archway
pedicab – pedal-powered tricycle with a seat to carry passengers
piāolǚ – rafting trip
Pinyin – the official system for transliterating Chinese script into roman characters
pípá – a plucked string instrument
PLA – People's Liberation Army
Politburo – the 25-member supreme policy-making authority of the CCP
PRC – People's Republic of China
PSB – Public Security Bureau/Police; the arm of the police force set up to deal with foreigners
pùbù – waterfall
púsa – Bodhisattva
Putonghua – the standard form of the Chinese language used since the beginning of this century, based on the dialect of Běijīng

Q
qarvatlik mashina (U) – sleeper coach
qì – vital energy (life force) or cosmic currents manipulated in acupuncture and massage
qiáo – bridge
qìchēzhàn – bus station
qìgōng – exercise that channels *qì*
qīngzhēnsì – mosque

R
rénmín – people, people's
Renminbi – literally 'people's money', the formal name for the currency of China; shortened to RMB
ROC – Republic of China, also known as Taiwan
ruǎnwò – soft sleeper (train ticket)
ruǎnzuò – soft seat

S
sampan (C) – a small motorised launch, too small for the open sea
sānlún mótuōchē – motor tricycle
sānlúnchē – pedal-powered tricycle

SAR – Special Administrative Region
savdo dukoni (U) – commercial shops
sēnlín – forest
shān – mountain
shāngdiàn – shop, store
shāokǎo – barbecue
shěng – province, provincial
shì – city
shí – rock
shìchǎng – market
shìjiè – world
shíkū – grotto
shòupiàochù – ticket office
shuǐkù – reservoir
sì – temple, monastery
sìhéyuàn – traditional courtyard house
special municipality – the name given to centrally administered regions such as Běijīng, Tiānjīn, Chóngqìng and Shànghǎi
stele (stelae) – a stone slab or column decorated with figures or inscriptions
stupa – usually used as reliquaries for the cremated remains of important *lamas*

T
tǎ – pagoda
tael – unit of weight; one tael *(liǎng)* equals 37.5g; there are 16 tael to the *catty*
taichi – the graceful, flowing exercise that has its roots in China's martial arts; also known as *tàijíquán*
taipan (C) – boss of a large company
tán – pool
Tanka – a Chinese ethnic group who traditionally live on boats
thangka – Tibetan sacred art
tíng – pavilion
triads – secret societies; originally founded to protect Chinese culture from the influence of usurping Manchurians, their modern-day members are little more than gangsters
tripitaka – Buddhist scriptures

W
walla walla – a motorised launch used as a water taxi and capable of short runs on the open sea
wān – bay
wǎngbā – internet café
wēnquán – hot springs

X
xī – west; the other points of the compass are *běi* (north), *nán* (south) and *dōng* (east)
xī – small stream or brook
xiá – gorge
xiàn – county

xiàng – statue
xuěshān – snow mountain

Y

yá – cliff
yán – rock or crag
yangi shahr (U) – the new part of town, usually Han-dominated; see also *kadimi shahr*
yìngwò – hard sleeper
yìngzuò – hard seat
yóujú – post office
yuán – the Chinese unit of currency; also referred to as Renminbi or RMB
yuán – garden

yurt (M) – the Russian word for a circular tent made with animal skin or felt; see *ger*

Z

zhào – lamasery
zhāodàisuǒ – basic lodgings, a hotel or guesthouse
zhāpí – a pint (of beer)
zhékòu – discount, eg off room price
zheng – a 13- or 14-stringed harp
zhíwùyuán – botanic gardens
zhōng – middle
Zhōngguó – China
zìrán bǎohùqū – nature reserve
zǔjū – ancestral home

Behind the Scenes

THIS BOOK

This 10th edition of *China* was written by a team of authors led by Damian Harper. The team consisted of Andrew Burke, Julie Grundvig, Carolyn Heller, Thomas Huhti, Bradley Mayhew, Min Dai, Christopher Pitts and Eilís Quinn. Damian also coordinated the 8th and 9th editions. David Andrew wrote the Environment chapter, and both Damian Harper and Korina Miller wrote the History chapter. Julie Grundvig wrote the Culture and Food & Drink chapters. Dr Trish Batchelor wrote the Health chapter. Lin Gu wrote the boxed text 'Coming Home' in the History chapter and Calum MacLeod wrote the 'Head in the Clouds – Pride & Propaganda' boxed text in the Tibet chapter.

This guidebook was commissioned in Lonely Planet's Melbourne office, and produced by the following:

Commissioning Editors Rebecca Chau & Errol Hunt
Coordinating Editor Carolyn Boicos
Coordinating Cartographer Malisa Plesa
Coordinating Layout Designer Jacqueline McLeod
Managing Editor Suzannah Shwer
Managing Cartographers Owen Eszeki & Julie Sheridan
Assisting Editors David Andrew, Janet Austin, Michelle Bennett, Kate Cody, Michael Day, Laura Gibb, Evan Jones, Shawn Low, Anne Mulvaney, Kristin Odijk, Charlotte Orr, Dianne Schallmeiner, Jeanette Wall & Kate Whitfield
Assisting Cartographers James Bird, Ross Butler, David Connelly, Matthew Kelly, Sophie Richards, Helen Rowley, Amanda Sierp & Jody Whiteoak
Assisting Layout Designers Jim Hsu, Indra Kilfoyle & Cara Smith

Cover Designer Rebecca Dandens
Project Manager Fabrice Rocher
Language Content Coordinator Quentin Frayne

Thanks to Jessa Boanas-Dewes, David Burnett, Sally Darmody, Mark Germanchis, Geoff Howard, Nancy Ianni, Rebecca Lalor, Lushan Charles Qin, Colin Mackerras, Wayne Murphy, Averil Robertson, LPI, Lyahna Spencer, Nick Stebbing, Glenn van der Knijff, Corinne Waddell & Celia Wood

THANKS
DAMIAN HARPER

Big thanks as ever to Daisy, Timothy and Emma for all of their help, support and encouragement. Gratitude also to Dai Lu for everything she has helped with – much appreciated. Liu Meina again deserves special thanks for helping to look after the little ones and also for her generosity and constant helpfulness; thanks to Dai Ruibin for the same reasons. In Jiāngxī, Zhang Guorong was a source of much advice, as was Wang Hejian in Húnán. A nod of appreciation to Piers Pickard for his companionship in southern Ānhuī and thanks also to all the travellers who wrote in with tips and advice. Cheers also to the staff at LP for helping to put this book together and a big thumbs up to the *laobaixing* of China who make a trip to their land such a fun and fascinating experience.

ANDREW BURKE

Researching Hong Kong, Macau and Hǎinán would not have been nearly as successful, not to mention fun, without the assistance of a host of friends,

---

THE LONELY PLANET STORY

The story begins with a classic travel adventure: Tony and Maureen Wheeler's 1972 journey across Europe and Asia to Australia. There was no useful information about the overland trail then, so Tony and Maureen published the first Lonely Planet guidebook to meet a growing need.

From a kitchen table, Lonely Planet has grown to become the largest independent travel publisher in the world, with offices in Melbourne (Australia), Oakland (USA) and London (UK). Today Lonely Planet guidebooks cover the globe. There is an ever-growing list of books and information in a variety of media. Some things haven't changed. The main aim is still to make it possible for adventurous travellers to get out there – to explore and better understand the world.

At Lonely Planet we believe travellers can make a positive contribution to the countries they visit – if they respect their host communities and spend their money wisely. Every year 5% of company profit is donated to charities around the world.

old and new. In Hong Kong, Troy Dunkley, Terry Pontikos, Emma Phillips and Mikey were generous hosts and are great friends – thanks. Other friends whose company was much appreciated include Damien Haarsma, Penny Hunter, John Church, Bridget and Erik Uebel, Ben O'Neill and Suzy, and Niall Fraser.

In Macau, the eternally enthusiastic Teresa Costa-Gomez was a great help, as was Ludovic Bodin. In Hǎinán, a huge thanks to May Xiao, who was both eager and indefatigable as a guide and translator, and Peter Liu, who unselfishly shared his vast local knowledge and translation skills. Thanks also to Pete Karnas and Ross McKinnon in Wǔzhǐshān. Last but not least, thanks again to my wife Anne Hyland, who is always there when I get home, and to my ever-supportive family.

JULIE GRUNDVIG

A heartfelt thanks to my husband Yipeng for all his encouragement and help while on the road. Special thanks also to Lu Tengsheng and Li Ren for the crash course in Cantonese cuisine and for letting me stay in their house for several weeks. Their patience in answering all of my countless questions was truly amazing. A big hug goes to Liangming Hao, who was a terrific tour guide in Kāipíng and to my sister-in-law Lu Wenhua for all the extra assistance. I'm also eternally grateful to Feng Liang for taking care of Mulan. Gratitude also to Rebecca Chau, Damian Harper and all the Lonely Planet staff and authors who worked so hard on this book.

CAROLYN B HELLER

A big xièxiè to travel companions Lynn Bryant (for staying cheerful despite magic-fingers buses, fugawi days, and the mushroom-soup incident) and Lucy Albert (aka 'Let's Go Lucy'). My gratitude to Lin Bin for his generosity in Jí'ān; Michael and Joy Abboud for chūnbǐng and advice in Hāěrbīn, and Larry Laberge for introducing us; Ma Xiao Dan (Joy) for assistance in Hǎilāěr; Wang Xiao Tong and friends for companionship at Chángbái Shān; 'Ice' in Jí'ān for barbecue and conversation; Song Liqiang (Mǔdānjiāng), Liu Kai (Hǎilāěr) and Wu Yu Wei (Hohhot); and countless others who offered information and smiles.

Special thanks to Michael Zheng of Access China Tours for letting me pepper him with questions and to Seoul Train codirector Jim Butterworth. For Mandarin lessons and extra help, thank you Shou-Fang Hu-Moore, Daisy Ching, Elisabeth Lokke Owre, Mark Matsuno and my Langara classmates. And cheers to LP colleagues Rebecca Chau, Damian Harper, Corinne Waddell and Chris Pitts.

I'm extremely grateful to Audrey Heller, Ken Heller and Richard Manning for their help at home; to Michaela and Talia, two of the best travelling buddies a mom could have; and to Alan for, well, everything.

THOMAS HUHTI

Thanks as always to the extraordinary people of China. Your curiosity, friendliness and generosity are unparalleled and make what can be a tough slog ultimately so unbelievably rewarding. Karma for special help and/or being eminently cool travel mates to Xi Nan, Wang Wenkun, Billy Zhao, José Sotomayor, Jens Veltmann, Bertrand Sinechal, He Bing, Miao Yuyuan, Dr Xavier Coll, Ali, Levi Tillemann-Dick, and Sim/Maki/Lancey/Chelsea and the gang, and all the others whose names I've so shamefully misplaced. Thanks for friendship (and sofa space, rides and music) to Kevin Caldwell, Sau Ching, Melissa, and Tiger in Hong Kong. Kudos to mom and dad for Bighead-sitting and to my second home at WESLI for letting me get away with it all. An appreciative nod to the Ownby household – Meredith, Gabby, Leo, Eva (and Lucy) – for their friendship. A final thanks to all the travellers who take the time to communicate with us and, thus, other travellers – this is global cooperation of the best kind.

BRADLEY MAYHEW

Cheers to Calum for putting me up in Běijīng and for his boxed text on riding the rails to Lhasa. See you soon, buddy. Special thanks to Tshering Losang in Xiàhé and greetings to Kalsang in Lángmùsì. Thanks also to Rebecca Chau for giving me the extra words to go exploring in Jyekundo.

MIN DAI

This project would have been impossible without the help and support of Rebecca Chau, Cath Lanigan, Dai Lu and, last but not least, my husband; thanks so much. Many thanks also to all the helpful travellers and personalities who thronged the route, including Meng Hong, Tao Liming and Xu Jie, all of whom provided entertaining and practical advice. Kisses and hugs to both of my patient children, Timothy and Emma, as ever.

CHRISTOPHER PITTS

Much thanks to Xue Manlin in Běijīng for keeping her myriad fingers on China's whirling vortex of a pulse; the Pavillards for endless and critical family support; Rebecca for providing lots of flexibility; Fayette for great, last-minute comments; Munson

Wu for the phone call; and Perrine, Elliot and Céleste for keeping me awake at night and young at heart.

EILÍS QUINN
Huge thanks are due to all the travellers who were so generous in sharing their time, travel journals and experiences, especially Mary in Běijīng, Francine and Jean-Pierre from Belgium and Catherine, Jacques and Olivier from France. *Merci beaucoup* also to André, Michel and Vincent for popping up all over Yúnnán with fabulous tips, contacts and hilarious travel stories. This trip wouldn't have been the same without the gang in Chóngqìng: Dorothy, Liu Yonghong, Shen Hongli, David, Allen, Philippe and 'Number One Handsome Man' Li Lian. Thank you all for getting everything off to such a rollicking (and rice-wine fuelled) start!

OUR READERS
Many thanks to the travellers who used the last edition and wrote to us with helpful hints, useful advice and interesting anecdotes:

A Helen Abbott, Maya Alexandri, Kirsten Allen, Lior Almaro, Eric Amanto, Gilead Amir, Raymond Ang, James Angel, Darren Armstrong, Bruce Arnold, Jackie Arnold, Adele Arthur, Dean Atkinson, Forest Atkinson, Lyn Avery, Michelle Ayers **B** Rupert Bacon, Symon Bacon, Marcel Baer, Rocky Balsom, Moumita Banerjee, Michelle Barlow, Ian Barry, Penny Barten, Melvin Bashner, Michael Bauer-Kwan, Olwyn Beatty, Niels Becker, Nigel Bellamy, Vanessa Bellett, Nat Bem, Karl Benson, Tori Bentley, Nicoletta Berardi, Mika Berger, Pamela Berghegen, Julie Bert, Daniel Bester, Jan-Willem Beuker, Philippe Bierny, Charlotte Bigg, Janet Birchnall, Hezy Biron, Adriana Bishop, Ben Blight, Jennifer Bluston, Patrick Boeert, Wim Boerefijn, Bram Bos, Max Branner, Erin Kendall Braun, Dafna Breket, Beau Briese, Leesa Bridson, Catherine Brinkley, Graeme Brock, Daniel Brown, Tia Brown, Rolf Bueschi, Lars Buesing, Lesley Burch, Camila Burda, Andre Burdet, Arjen & Volker Buschmann, Emma Butterworth **C** Nicola Calabrese, Greg Cameron, Laura Caniglia, Sam Carpenter, Larry Castle, Ken Chapman, Kathy Charmley, Christine Chen, Ben Cheng, Cynthia Chewter, Rodrigo Chia, Jeff Childers, Chen Chong, Nettekoven Christof, Tom Clark, Maggie Coaton, Chris Coggins, Michael Cohen, Alastor Coleby, Garry Coombe, Pam Coulson, Raimund Crone, Anthony Cross, Ian Cruickshank, John Curington **D** Erik Dam, Terry Danne, Alex Daue, William Davis, Jenni Day, David Dayton, David A Dayton, Charles de la Quintana, Andrea Dealey, Harm Demon, Stef Derluyn, Christopher Doetzel, Ken Dolen, Matt Donnelly, Stephan Dorrenberg, Rachel Dorsey, Sheridan Draper, Lenny Dunmark, Tyler Durden **E** Catherine Eagles, James Elliott, Steve Emms, Eric Engdahl, Pascal Enz, Kirk Evans, Stephen Evans, Ty Evans, James Evelyn **F** Orr Fabian, Christopher Feierabend, Ana Ferreira, Blaise Fiedler, Willie Fields, Barbara Filippi, Del Ford, Bernard Forest, Kolleen Forstinger **G** Lee Gellatly, Jim Gennrich, Chris Goddard, Bob Goldfarb, Sue Goodwin, Robert Gottschewski,

Fredrik Graffner, Victoria Grierson, Charles Griffith, Neil Griffith, Fabian Gumucio, Anders Gustafsson, Tenzing Gyatotsang **H** Erik Hakansson, Anette Hansen, Kelly Hardwick, Wolf Harlfinger, Carey Harmer, Anne Harper, Lynda & Antony Harrington, Sybil Harrison, Peter Harvey, Joji Hattori, Erik Havekes, Alberta Heagney, John Healam, Pieter & Emily Heesterbeek, Jess Hemmings, Mary Higonnet, John Hogan, Vincent Hogenboom, Henric Höglind, Amir Horowitz, Nigel Hoult, Francis Hsueh, Angela Huang, Isabelle Huchett, John Humphreys, Dominique Sandra Hunziker, Sally Huskinson **I** Goran Iremalm **J** Larry Jackson, Ralpha Jacobson, Caroline Jaggard, Andrew Janowczyk, Bert Jansen, Nicolai Jensen, Wei Ji Ma, Greg Jockerst, Barry Johnston, David Jones, Rowan & Anna Jones, Jostein Juriks **K** Slobodan Kadic, Lynne Kahsnitz, Uri Kammay, Andrea Kelleher, Jan Kellerhoff, Elizabeth Keppel, David Kerkhoff, Jamie Kern, Tania Kettell, Kelly Kilarciyan, Eugene Kim, Hyungtae Kim, Sunny Kim, Diana Kincaid, Audun Kjorstad, Kathy Koch, Annemarie Koelliker, Edwin Koh, Roy Korn Jr, Marie Kuge, Elina Kyllönen **L** Adam Lacey, Leo Lacey, Zenobia Lagerweij, Alasha Lantinga, Fredrik Larsen, Ian Larsen, Madeline Lasko, Andrew Lawwer, Alex Lee, Eugene Lee, Shay Lelegren, Genevieve Lemire, Laura Leroy, Emlyn Lewis-Jones, Jiwei Li, Yuan Liang, Jack Lilley, Keri Lim, Mary Grace Lin, Jutta Lorenzen, Billy Lucius, Frank Lukasseck, Deborah Luke **M** Ally Macdonald, Zoe Macfarlane, Colin Macintyre, John Maclachlan, Trever Madsen, Rodney Mantle, Andrew Marcus, Ato Mariano, Mela Marks, Adam Mayo, Sarah McArdle, Bob McAteer, Bixler McClure, Steve McFarlane, Angela McFeeters, Kevin McGrath, Ryan McLaughlin, Alan Mead, Hai Mei, Guido Mellicovsky, Mohit Melwani, Anze Mihelic, Dennis Mogerman, Kathryn Mohrman, K Edward Moore, Rebecca Morgan, Pete Moss, Stephen Murray **N** Masaki Nagai, Junko Nakai, Shawn Nance, David Nataf, Shara Neidell, Alexander Nicolas, Marion Nielsen, Toffler Niemuth, Pal-Andrej Nitsche, Andreas Nix, Dave Noble, Wil Nuijen, Craig Nunn **O** Michaela & Aviv Ofir, Karin Ohlin, Stefan Ohlson, Andrew O'Keeffe, Daniel O'Kelly, Gloria Orozco, Brent Owen, Paul Ozorak **P** Stella Pafford, Simon Parker-Shames, Elisa Parmigiani, Cheryl & Kai Parsons-Galka, Darren Pearce, Jan Pennington, Karene Perkins, Inge Peters, Amanda Peterson, Matt Peterson, John Pierce, Andre Pires, Ishay Pomerantz, Aviv Ponger, Anne Preston, Alice Princess, Rosalyn Pursley **Q** Patrick Quinn **R** Nick Racanelli, Jedrzej Radzikowski, Billy Red, Anika Redhed, Robbie Reeves, Manfred Reimert, Henk-Jelle Reitsman, Maurer Richard, Che Richards, Ning Rita, Brad Roberts, Kevin Rose, Theran Ross, Anne Rota, Boaz Rottem, Eric Rottenberg, Joost Ruitenberg, Charli Rumsey, Patti Ryan **S** Aurelie Salvaire, Samara Sanchez, Jennifer Sandblom, Julie Santens, Marcus Schmid, Robert Schönfeld, Bonny Schoonakker, Linda Schueler, Stacy Seeland, Philip Sen, Phyllis B Shafer, Neil Silver, Gordon Simpson, Sancha Simpson-Davis, Tony Sinclair, Hima Singh, Paul Skeet, Matt Slade, Kevin Smith, Sarah Smith, Thomas Speirs, Van Steenbergenweg, Ariel Steiner, Rob Street, Barb Strother, Ed Styles, Hamish Symington **T** Carme Tapias, Mihai Nicolae Teognoste, Jennifer Thome, Bruce Thomson, Rob Tidd, James Timmis, Sean Tm, Christina To-Atkins, Joshua Tokita, Catherine Tollerton, Alice Tomkinson, Sven Erik Topp, Karen Tripp, Gönül Türkdogan, Richard Turney, Scott Tuurie **V** Annemieke van den Dool, Erwin van Engelen, Janet van Ham, Gabrielle van Hooser, Randy van Mingeroet,

Johannes van Staden, Rick Vaughn, Matt Veld, Albert Verleg, Katleen Verloo, Alessandro Vernet, Aranka Vos **W** Rebecca Wall, Rebekah Watts, Melba Waugh, Tim Weeple, Mijia Wei, Mike Weigh, Linda White, Augustinus Wibowo, Quirien Wijnberg, Alex Wilkinson, Ellen Willard, Paul Wills, Suzanne Wilson, Doug Witt, Jessica Woan, Martin Wong, Anthony Wreford **Y** Alice Yang, Louise Yang, Andrew Young **Z** Jige Zhang, Zhengqiang Zhu, Rolf Zinniker

ACKNOWLEDGMENTS

Many thanks to the following for the use of their content: Hong Kong MTR System Map (c) 2006 MTR Corporation. Extract from *Songlines* by Bruce Chatwin published by Jonathan Cape. Used with permission of The Random House Group Limited and Gillon Aitken Associates Limited.

SEND US YOUR FEEDBACK

We love to hear from travellers – your comments keep us on our toes and help make our books better. Our well-travelled team reads every word on what you loved or loathed about this book. Although we cannot reply individually to postal submissions, we always guarantee that your feedback goes straight to the appropriate authors, in time for the next edition. Each person who sends us information is thanked in the next edition – and the most useful submissions are rewarded with a free book.

To send us your updates – and find out about Lonely Planet events, newsletters and travel news – visit our award-winning website: **www.lonelyplanet.com/contact**.

Note: we may edit, reproduce and incorporate your comments in Lonely Planet products such as guidebooks, websites and digital products, so let us know if you don't want your comments reproduced or your name acknowledged. For a copy of our privacy policy visit www.lonelyplanet.com/privacy.

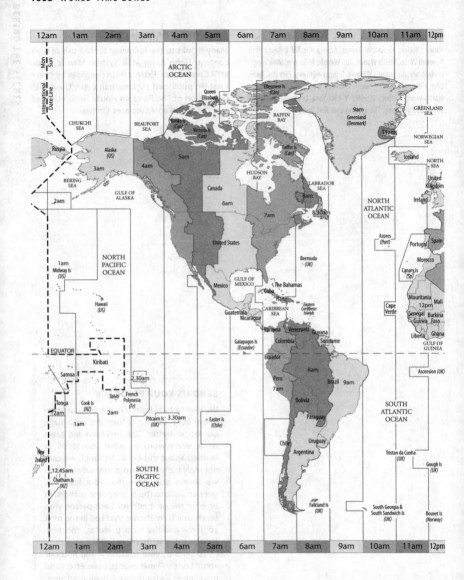

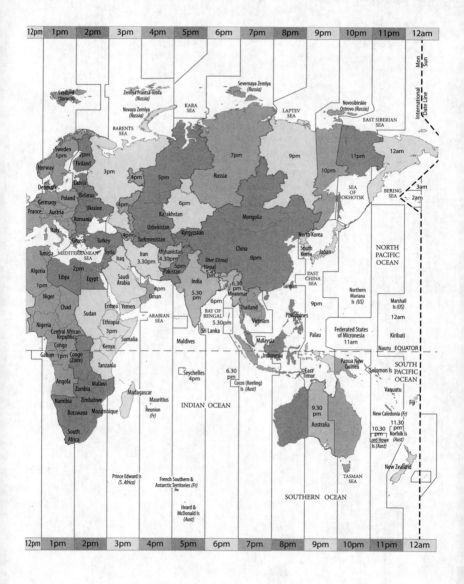

Index

INDEX

INDEX

INDEX

000 Map pages
000 Photograph pages

INDEX

INDEX

INDEX

INDEX

MAP LEGEND

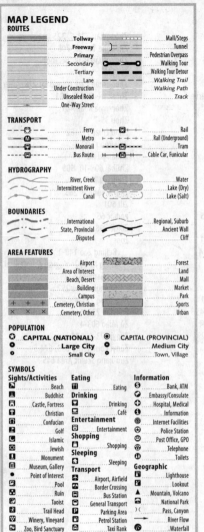

ROUTES

Tollway	Mall/Steps
Freeway	Tunnel
Primary	Pedestrian Overpass
Secondary	Walking Tour
Tertiary	Walking Tour Detour
Lane	Walking Trail
Under Construction	Walking Path
Unsealed Road	Track
One-Way Street	

TRANSPORT

Ferry	Rail
Metro	Rail (Underground)
Monorail	Tram
Bus Route	Cable Car, Funicular

HYDROGRAPHY

River, Creek	Water
Intermittent River	Lake (Dry)
Canal	Lake (Salt)

BOUNDARIES

International	Regional, Suburb
State, Provincial	Ancient Wall
Disputed	Cliff

AREA FEATURES

Airport	Forest
Area of Interest	Land
Beach, Desert	Mall
Building	Market
Campus	Park
Cemetery, Christian	Sports
Cemetery, Other	Urban

POPULATION

○ CAPITAL (NATIONAL)	◉ CAPITAL (PROVINCIAL)
● Large City	● Medium City
○ Small City	○ Town, Village

SYMBOLS

Sights/Activities	Eating	Information
Beach	Eating	Bank, ATM
Buddhist	**Drinking**	Embassy/Consulate
Castle, Fortress	Drinking	Hospital, Medical
Christian	Café	Information
Confucian	**Entertainment**	Internet Facilities
Golf	Entertainment	Police Station
Islamic	**Shopping**	Post Office, GPO
Jewish	Shopping	Telephone
Monument	**Sleeping**	Toilets
Museum, Gallery	Sleeping	**Geographic**
Point of Interest	**Transport**	Lighthouse
Pool	Airport, Airfield	Lookout
Ruin	Border Crossing	Mountain, Volcano
Taoist	Bus Station	National Park
Trail Head	General Transport	Pass, Canyon
Winery, Vineyard	Parking Area	River Flow
Zoo, Bird Sanctuary	Petrol Station	Waterfall
	Taxi Rank	

LONELY PLANET OFFICES

Australia
Head Office
Locked Bag 1, Footscray, Victoria 3011
☎ 03 8379 8000, fax 03 8379 8111
talk2us@lonelyplanet.com.au

USA
150 Linden St, Oakland, CA 94607
☎ 510 893 8555, toll free 800 275 8555
fax 510 893 8572
info@lonelyplanet.com

UK
72–82 Rosebery Ave,
Clerkenwell, London EC1R 4RW
☎ 020 7841 9000, fax 020 7841 9001
go@lonelyplanet.co.uk

Published by Lonely Planet Publications Pty Ltd
ABN 36 005 607 983

© Lonely Planet Publications Pty Ltd 2007

© photographers as indicated 2007

Cover photograph: Boys waving the Chinese national flag, Tiananmen Square, Běijīng, China/Getty Images. Many of the images in this guide are available for licensing from Lonely Planet Images: www.lonelyplanetimages.com.

Printed by SNP Security Printing Pte Ltd, Singapore